eum	ΑΥΤΟΝ
adpropinquare	ΕΓΓΙΖΕΙΝ
damasco	ΤΗΔΑΜΑϹΚΩ
etrepente	ΚΑΙΕΞΕΦΝΗϹ
circumfulsit	ΠΕΡΙΗϹΤΡΑΨΕΝ
eum	ΑΥΤΟΝ
lux	ΦΩϹ
decaelo	ΑΠΟΤΟΥΟΥΝΟΥ
etprocedens	ΚΑΙΠΕϹΩΝ
interram	ΕΠΙΤΗΝΓΗΝ
audiuit	ΗΚΟΥϹΕΝ
uocem	ΦΩΝΗΝ
dicentem	ΛΕΓΟΥϹΑΝ
sibi	ΑΥΤΩ
saule	ϹΑΟΥΛΕ
saule	ϹΑΟΥΛΕ
quidme	ΤΙΜΕ
persequeris	ΔΙΩΚΕΙϹ
durumtibiest	ϹΚΛΗΡΟΝϹΟΙ
contrastimulum	ΠΡΟϹΚΕΝΤΡΑ
calcitare	ΛΑΚΤΙΖΙΝ
dixitautem	ΕΙΠΕΝΔΕ
quis	ΤΙϹ
es	ΕΙ
domine	ΚΥΡΙΕ
dominusautem	ΟΔΕΚ̄Ϲ̄

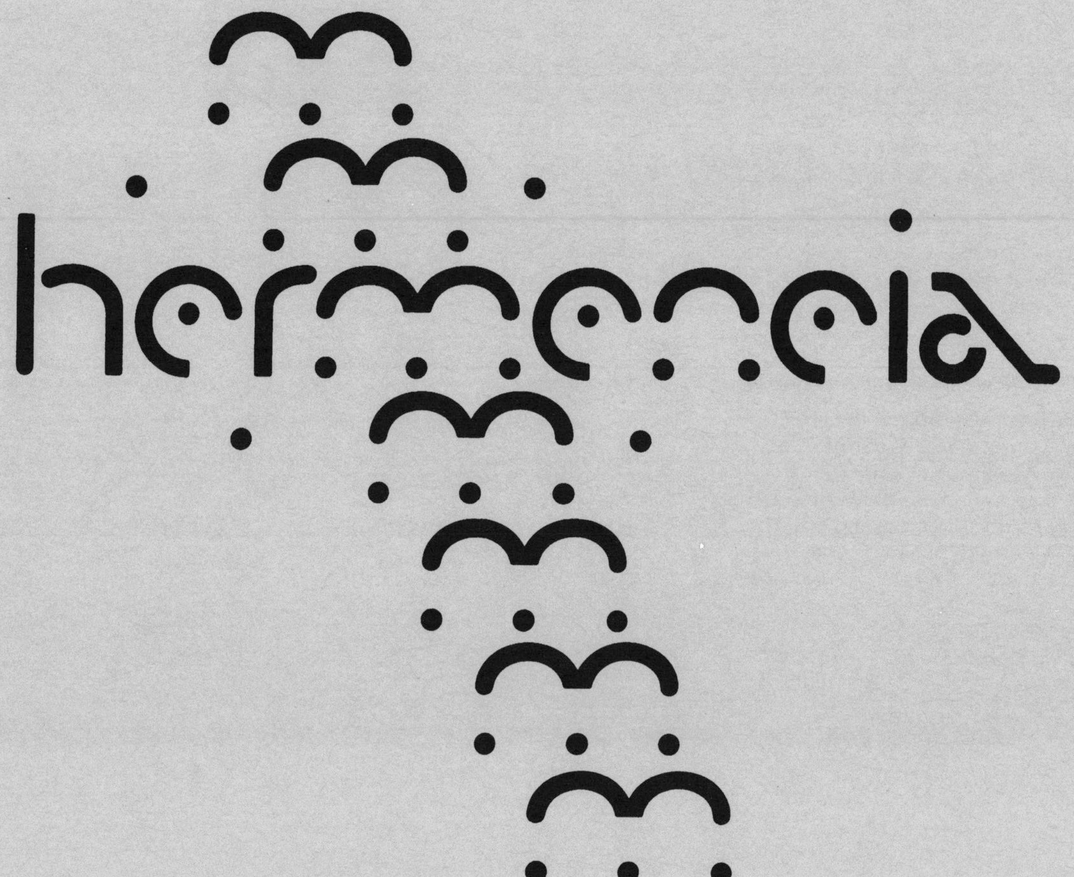
hermeneia

Hermeneia —A Critical and Historical Commentary on the Bible

Acts

A Commentary

by Richard I. Pervo

Edited by
Harold W. Attridge

Fortress
Press

Minneapolis

Acts
A Commentary

The Hebraica, Payne, and Semitica fonts used to print this work are available from Linguist's Software, Inc., PO Box 580, Edmonds, WA 98020-0580 USA. Tel. 425-775-1130. www.linguistsoftware.com.

Cover and interior design by Kenneth Hiebert
Typesetting and page composition by
The HK Scriptorium

Library of Congress Cataloging-in-Publication Data

Pervo, Richard I.
Acts : a commentary / by Richard I. Pervo ; edited by Harold W. Attridge.
p. cm. — (Hermeneia)
Includes bibliographical references and index.
ISBN-13: 978-0-8006-6045-1 (alk. paper)
1. Bible. N.T. Acts—Commentaries. I. Attridge, Harold W. II. Title.
BS2625.53.P42 2008
226.6'077—dc22

2008003463

The paper used in this publication meets the minimum requirements of American National Standard for Information Sciences—Permanence of paper for Printed Library Materials, ANSI Z329.48–1984.

Manufactured in the U.S.A.

13 12 11 10 09 1 2 3 4 5 6 7 8 9 10

■ *This book is for Karen*

The Author

Richard I. Pervo, born 1942 in Lakewood, Ohio, received his B.A. from Concordia College, Fort Wayne, Indiana; his B.D. from the Episcopal Theological School, Cambridge, Massachusetts; and his Th.D. from Harvard University. He taught at Seabury-Western Theological Seminary, Evanston, Illinois, from 1975 to 1999, and at the University of Minnesota from 1999 to 2001. His specialization has been the interaction of early Jewish and Christian writings with ancient fiction. Previous books on Acts include Profit with Delight: The Literary Genre of the Acts of the Apostles (Fortress, 1987), Luke's Story of Paul (Fortress, 1990), (with Mikeal Parsons) Rethinking the Unity of Luke and Acts (Fortress, 1993 [reissued 2007]), and Dating Acts: Between the Evangelists and the Apologists (Polebridge, 2006).

Contents
Acts

Back Matter

The name *Hermeneia,* Greek ἑρμηνεία, has been chosen as the title of the commentary series to which this volume belongs. The word *Hermeneia* has a rich background in the history of biblical interpretation as a term used in the ancient Greek-speaking world for the detailed, systematic exposition of a scriptural work. It is hoped that the series, like its name, will carry forward this old and venerable tradition. A second, entirely practical reason for selecting the name lies in the desire to avoid a long descriptive title and its inevitable acronym, or worse, an unpronounceable abbreviation.

The series is designed to be a critical and historical commentary to the Bible without arbitrary limits in size or scope. It will utilize the full range of philological and historical tools, including textual criticism (often slighted in modern commentaries), the methods of the history of tradition (including genre and prosodic analysis), and the history of religion.

Hermeneia is designed for the serious student of the Bible. It will make full use of ancient Semitic and classical languages; at the same time, English translations of all comparative materials—Greek, Latin, Canaanite, or Akkadian—will be supplied alongside the citation of the source in its original language. Insofar as possible, the aim is to provide the student or scholar with full critical discussion of each problem of interpretation and with the primary data upon which the discussion is based.

Hermeneia is designed to be international and interconfessional in the selection of authors; its editorial boards were formed with this end in view. Occasionally the series will offer translations of distinguished commentaries which originally appeared in languages other than English. Published volumes of the series will be revised continually, and eventually, new commentaries will replace older works in order to preserve the currency of the series. Commentaries are also being assigned for important literary works in the categories of apocryphal and pseudepigraphical works relating to the Old and New Testaments, including some of Essene or Gnostic authorship.

The editors of *Hermeneia* impose no systematic-theological perspective upon the series (directly, or indirectly by selection of authors). It is expected that authors will struggle to lay bare the ancient meaning of a biblical work or pericope. In this way the text's human relevance should become transparent, as is always the case in competent historical discourse. However, the series eschews for itself homiletical translation of the Bible.

The editors are heavily indebted to Fortress Press for its energy and courage in taking up an expensive, long-term project, the rewards of which will accrue chiefly to the field of biblical scholarship.

The editor responsible for this volume is Harold W. Attridge, Lillian Claus Professor of New Testament and Dean at the Yale Divinity School.

Peter Machinist	*Helmut Koester*
For the Old Testament Editorial Board	For the New Testament Editorial Board

Editor's Note

The commentary by Richard Pervo contains a fresh translation of the text of the Book of Acts. Translations from the rest of the New and Old Testament are usually from the *NRSV*. Quotations of Latin and Greek authors, except where noted, follow the texts and translations of the Loeb Classical Library, as indicated.

The front endsheets show Acts 9:3-5, and the back endsheets show Acts 28:31, in Manuscript E (Number 08, "Laudianus"), a sixth-century Latin and Greek bilingual manuscript at the Bodleian Library, Oxford (MS. Laud Gr. 35). Photo courtesy Bodleian Library, University of Oxford.

Preface

Ernst Haenchen began his work on Acts while reading the Greek text on a train ride to Switzerland in 1944 (*The Acts of the Apostles* [trans. and ed. B. Noble et al.; Philadelphia: Westminster, 1971], vii). My own interest was aroused while reading Acts in Greek on an airplane flight to St. Louis in 1971. Two years later I read Haenchen's commentary in preparation for exams while also working up the ancient novels. This led to a dissertation and a career-long preoccupation with both Acts and ancient "popular" literature.

Commentators cannot answer every question about their subjects, but those writing a Hermeneia commentary must seek to address most of them. Commentaries on ancient books must deal with the question of the best recoverable text. Biblical commentaries require attention to theology. Analyses of a narrative have to attend to the story and how it is presented. These matters I have attempted to address. This commentary is the first in recent times to be based on the hypotheses that Acts was written c. 110–120 CE and that the author made use of Pauline epistles and the writings of Josephus. In addition, it constantly examines Acts as a "popular" book that seeks to engage its readers' interest while purveying its various messages.

No list of thanksgivings could be complete. Three of my revered teachers, George MacRae, Dieter Georgi, and John Strugnell, have departed this life. Helmut Koester inspired me to undertake advanced study in the field of Christian origins. Others, from Irenaeus of Lyons to those with fresh doctorates, have generated most of the ideas advanced in the following pages. Specific thanks are owed to Matt Skinner, Timothy B. Sailors, François Bovon, Dennis R. MacDonald, and the Trial Balloon Society of St. Paul, Minnesota. Paula Harbage, David Gillingham, Harold and Janis Attridge have been treasured friends for a generation. For editorial aid I thank Harold Attridge once more, as well as the staff of Fortress Press and the HK Scriptorium.

Splendor paternae gloriae,
De luce lucem proferens,
Lux lucis et fons luminis,
Diem dies illuminans

Ambrose, Bishop of Milan

Reference Codes

1. Sources and Abbreviations

AB	Anchor Bible
ABD	*The Anchor Bible Dictionary* (ed. David Noel Freedman; 6 vols.; New York: Doublday, 1992).
ABRL	The Anchor Bible Reference Library
Achilles Tatius	
Leuc. Clit.	*Leucippe et Clitophon*
ACNT	Augsburg Commentary on the New Testament
Act. Andr.	*Acts of Andrew*
Act. Barn.	*Acts of Barnabas*
Act. John	*Acts of John*
Act. Paul	*Acts of Paul*
Act. Pet.	*Acts of Peter*
Act. Phil.	*Acts of Philip*
Act. Thom.	*Acts of Thomas*
ACW	Ancient Christian Writers
Aelian	
Nat. an.	*De natura animalium*
Var. hist.	*Varia historia*
Aeschines	
Ctes.	*In Ctesiphonem*
AGJU	Arbeiten zur Geschichte des antiken Judentums und des Urchristentums
AJA	*American Journal of Archaeology*
AJP	*American Journal of Philology*
alt.	altered
AnBib	Analecta Biblica
ANRW	*Aufstieg und Niedergang der römischen Welt* (ed. Hildegard Temporini and Wolfgang Haase; Berlin/New York: de Gruyter, 1972–).
ANTC	Abingdon New Testament Commentary
Anth. Pal.	*Anthologia Palatina*
Ap. Const.	*Apostolic Constitutions*
Apoc. Abr.	*Apocalypse of Abraham*
Apoc. Paul	*Apocalypse of Paul*
Apoc. Pet.	*Apocalypse of Peter*
Apoc. Zeph.	*Apocalypse of Zephaniah*
Apollonius Rhodius	
Argon.	*Argonautica*
Appian	
Bell. civ.	*Bella civilia*
Apuleius	
Met.	*Metamorphoses*
Aratus	
Phaen.	*Phaenomena*
Aristides	
Apol.	*Apology*
Aristotle	
Ath. pol.	*Athenain politeia*
Nic. Eth.	*Nicomachean Ethics*
Top.	*Topica*
Arrian	
Anab.	*Anabasis*
Artemidorus	
Onir.	*Onirocritica*
ARW	*Archiv für Religionswissenschaft*
Asc. Isa.	*Ascension of Isaiah*
As. Mos.	*Assumption of Moses*
ASNU	Acta Seminarii Neotestamentici Upsaliensis
AsSeign	*Assemblées du Seigneur*
Athanasius	
Vit. Ant.	*Vita Antonii*
AThANT	Abhandlungen zur Theologie des Alten und Neuen Testaments
Athenaeus	
Deipn.	*Deipnosophistae*
Athenagoras	
Leg.	*Legatio pro Christianis*
ATLA Bib Ser	American Theological Library Association Bibliography Series
ATR	*Anglican Theological Review*
Augustine	
Adim.	*Contra Adimantum*
Enarr. in Ps.	*Enarrationes in Psalmos*
Ep.	*Epistulae*
Serm.	*Sermones*
Serm. Dom.	*De sermone Domini en monte*
Util. cred.	*De utilitate credendi*
Aulus Gellius	
Noct. att.	*Noctes atticae*
BA	*Biblical Archaeologist*
BAR	*Biblical Archaeology Review*
Barn.	*Epistle of Barnabas*
BCH	*Bulletin de correspondence hellénique*
BDAG	Walter Bauer, *A Greek-English Lexicon of the New Testament and Other Early Christian Literature* (ed. William F. Arndt, F. Wilbur Gingrich; 3rd ed. rev. by Frederick W. Danker; Chicago: University of Chicago Press, 2000).
BDF	F. Blass and A. Debrunner, *A Greek Grammar of the New Testament and Other Early Christian Literature* (ed. Robert W. Funk; Chicago: University of Chicago Press, 1961).
BECNT	Baker Exegetical Commentary on the New Testament
BeO	*Bibbia e oriente*
BEThL	*Bibliotheca Ephemeridum Theologicarum Lovaniensium*

BGBE	Beiträge zur Geschichte der biblischen Exegese
BGU	*Berlinischer griechische Urkunden*
BHT	Beiträge zur historischen Theologie
Bib	*Biblica*
BibInt	*Biblical Interpretation*
BibNotiz	*Biblische Notizen*
BibRev	*Bible Review*
BIFCS	Book of Acts in Its First Century Setting
BIS	Biblical Interpretation Series
BJRL	*Bulletin of the John Rylands Library*
BJS	Brown Judaic Studies
BK	Bibel und Kirche
BR	*Biblical Research*
BTB	*Biblical Theology Bulletin*
BT	*The Bible Translator*
BWANT	Beiträge zur Wissenschaft vom Alten und Neuen Testament
BZ	*Biblische Zeitschrift*
BZNW	Beihefte zur *Zeitschrift für die neutestamentliche Wissenschaft*
c.	circa, approximately
CahRB	Cahiers de la Revue biblique
CBQ	*Catholic Biblical Quarterly*
CBR	*Currents in Biblical Research*
CCSA	Corpus Christianorum, Series Apocryphorum
CCSL	Corpus Christianorum, Series latina
CD	*See under* Qumran writings
CE	Common Era
chap.	chapter
Chariton	
Chaer.	*De Chaerea et Callirhoe*
CHJ	*Cambridge History of Judaism* (ed. W. D. Davies et al.; 4 vols.; Cambridge: Cambridge University Press, 1984–2006).
Chrysostom	
Hom.	*Homilies*
Sac.	*De Sacerdotio*
Cicero	
Ad Fam.	*Epistulae ad familiares*
Amic.	*De amicitia*
De or.	*De oratore*
Div.	*De divinatione*
Inv.	*De inventione rhetorica*
Leg.	*De legibus*
Nat. Deor.	*De natura deorum*
Off.	*De officiis*
Phil.	*Orationes philippicae*
Pis.	*In Pisonem*
Resp.	*De republica*
Tusc. disp.	*Tusculanae disputationes*
CIG	*Corpus Inscriptionum Graecarum* (ed. A. Boeckh; 4 vols.; Berlin: Ex oficina academica, 1828–77).
CIJ	*Corpus Inscriptionum Judaicarum* (ed. Jean-Baptiste Frey; 2 vols.; Rome: Pontificio istituto di archeologia cristiana, 1936–52).
ClassPhil	*Classical Philology*
1, 2 Clem.	*First, Second Epistle of Clement*
Clement of Alexandria	
Paed.	*Paedagogus*
Protrep.	*Protrepticus*
Strom.	*Stromateis*
ConBNT	Coniectanea Biblica, New Testament Series
Corp. Herm.	*Corpus Hermeticum*
CPJ	*Corpus papyrorum Judaicarum* (ed. Victor A. Tcherikover, A. Fuks, and M. Stern; 3 vols.; Cambridge, Mass.: Harvard University Press, 1957–64).
CRINT	Compendia rerum iudaicarum ad Novum Testamentum
CSEL	Corpus scriptorum ecclesiastorum latinorum
CurrTheolMiss	*Currents in Theology and Mission*
Cyril of Jerusalem	
Myst. cat.	*Mystagogical Catecheses*
DAC	*Dictionary of the Apostolic Church* (ed. James Hastings; 2 vols.; Edinburgh: T&T Clark, 1915–18).
DACL	*Dictionnaire d'archéologie chrétienne et de liturgie* (ed. F. Cabrol; 15 vols.; Paris, 1907–53).
DBI	*Dictionary of Biblical Imagery* (ed. Leland Ryken et al.; Downers Grove, Ill.: InterVarsity, 1998).
DDD	*Dictionary of Deities and Demons in the Bible*, ed. Karel van der Toorn et al.; 2nd rev. ed.; Leiden: Brill; Grand Rapids: Eerdmans, 1999.
Demosthenes	
Philip.	*Philippica*
Did.	*Didache*
Dio of Prusa	
Or.	*Oration*
Diogn.	*Epistle to Diognetus*
Dionysius of Halicarnassus	
Ant. Rom.	*Antiquitates romanae*
Rhet.	*Ars rhetorica*
Thuc.	*De Thucydide*
DSS	Dead Sea Scrolls
EB	Études bibliques
ed(s).	editor, edition, or edited by
EDNT	*Exegetical Dictionary of the New Testament* (ed. Horst Balz and Gerhard Schneider; 3 vols.; Grand Rapids: Eerdmans, 1990–93).
EHPR	Études d'histoire et de philosophie religieuses

EKK	Evangelisch-Katholischer Kommentar zum Neuen Testament
Ep.	*Epistle*
Ep. Apos.	*Epistle to the Apostles*
Epictetus	
Diss.	*Discourses*
Epiphanius	
Pan.	*Panarion. Medicine Chest against the Heresies*
EPRO	Etudes préliminaires aux religions orientales dans l'empire romain
ERE	*Encyclopaedia of Religion and Ethics* (ed. James Hastings; 13 vols.; Edinburgh: T&T Clark; New York: Charles Scribner's Sons, 1908–27).
esp.	especially
EstBíb	*Estudios Bíblicos*
ET	English translation
et al.	et alii, and others
EThL	*Ephemerides theologicae Lovanienses*
EThR	*Études théologiques et religieuses*
Euripides	
Andr.	*Andromache*
Bacch.	*Bacchae*
Iph. Aul.	*Iphigenia aulidensis*
Iph. taur.	*Iphigenia taurica*
Orest.	*Orestes*
Eusebius	
Dem. ev.	*Demonstratio evangelica*
H.E.	*Historia ecclesiastica*
Praep. ev.	*Praeparatio evangelica*
Vit. Const.	*Vita Constantini*
EvTh	*Evangelische Theologie*
Exp.	*Expositor*
ExpT	*Expository Times*
FD	Fouilles de Delphes III, 1929
FGH	*Die Fragmente der griechischen Historiker* (ed. F. Jacoby; 3 vols.; Berlin: Weidmann; Leiden: Brill, 1923–69).
FilolNT	*Filologia Neotestamentaria*
FoiVie	*Foi et Vie*
frg(s).	fragment(s)
FRLANT	Forschungen zur Religion und Literatur des Alten und Neuen Testaments
FzB	Forschung zur Bible
GBS	Guides to Biblical Scholarship
GNS	Good News Studies
GNT	*Greek New Testament* (United Bible Societies)
Gos. Heb.	*Gospel of the Hebrews*
Gos. Jas.	*Gospel of James*
Gos. Pet.	*Gospel of Peter*
Gregory Nazianzos	
Orat.	*Oratio*
Gregory the Great	
Hom. in Ezech.	*Homily on Ezekiel*
Regula Past.	*Regula Pastoralis*
HDR	Harvard Dissertations in Religion
Heliodorus	
Aeth	*Aethiopica (Ethiopian Story)*
(Ps.) Heraclitus	
Ep.	*Epistle*
Hermas	*The Shepherd of Hermas*
Man.	*Mandates*
Sim.	*Similitudes*
Vis.	*Visions*
Herodotus	
Hist.	*Historiae*
Hesiod	
Op.	*Opera et dies*
Theog.	*Theogonia*
Hippolytus	
Ref.	*Refutatio omnium haeresium*
HNT	Handbuch zum Neuen Testament
HNTC	Harper's New Testament Commentaries
Homer	
Il.	*Iliad*
Od.	*Odyssey*
Horace	
Epod.	*Epodes*
HSCP	*Harvard Studies in Classical Philology*
HThK	Herders Theologischer Kommentar zum Neuen Testament
HTR	*Harvard Theological Review*
HTS	Harvard Theological Studies
HUTh	Hermeneutische Untersuchungen zur Theologie
I. Caria	*La Carie: histoire et géographie historique avec le recueil des inscriptions antiques* (Paris: Adrien-Maisonneuve, 1954–).
I. Didyma	Albert Rehm, *Didyma, II. Die Inschriften* (Berlin 1958).
I. Eph.	*Die Inschriften von Ephesos* (ed. H. Wankel, R. Merkelbach, et al.; Bonn, 1979–84).
I. Magn.	*Die Inschriften von Magnesia am Maeander* (ed. Otto Kern; Berlin, 1900).
Iamblichus	
De Vit. Pythag.	*On the Life of Pythagoras*
Myst.	*De mysteriis*
IB	*Interpreters Bible*
ibid.	ibidem, in the same place
ICC	International Critical Commentary
IDB	*The Interpreter's Dictionary of the Bible* (ed. G. A. Buttrick; 4 vols.; Nashville: Abingdon, 1962).

idem, eadem	the same, the same as previously mentioned
IEJ	*Israel Exploration Journal*
IG	*Inscriptiones Graecae* (editio minor; Berlin, 1924–).
Ignatius	
Eph.	*Letter to the Ephesians*
Magn.	*Letter to the Magnesians*
Phld.	*Letter to the Philadelphians*
Polyc.	*Letter to Polycarp*
Rom.	*Letter to the Romans*
Smyrn.	*Letter to the Smyrneans*
Trall.	*Letter to the Trallians*
IGR	*Inscriptiones Graecae ad res Romanas pertinentes* (ed. R. Cagnat et al.; 4 vols.; Chicago: Ares, 1975).
IK	Inschriften griechischer Städte aus Kleinasien (1972–).
ILS	*Inscriptiones latinae selectae* (ed. Hermann Dessau; 3 vols.; Berlin: Weidmann, 1954–55).
Int	*Interpretation*
Irenaeus	
A.H.	*Adversus haereses*
IRT	Issues in Religion and Theology
Isocrates	
Areop.	*Areopagiticus*
JAAR	*Journal of the American Academy of Religion*
JAC	*Jahrbuch für Antike und Christentum*
JBL	*Journal of Biblical Literature*
JECS	*Journal of Early Christian Studies*
JEH	*Journal of Ecclesiastical History*
Jerome	
Comm. in Isaiam	*Commentary on Isaiah*
Comm. in Titum	*Commentary on Titus*
De vir. ill.	*De viris illustribus*
Ep.	*Epistulae*
JFSR	*Journal of Feminist Studies in Religion*
JHC	*Journal of Higher Criticism*
JHS	*Journal of Hellenic Studies*
JJS	*Journal of Jewish Studies*
Jos. Asen.	*Joseph and Aseneth*
Josephus	
Ant.	*Antiquities of the Jews*
Ap.	*Against Apion*
Bell.	*The Jewish War*
Vit.	*Life*
JQR	*Jewish Quarterly Review*
JRS	*Journal of Roman Studies*
JRT	*Journal of Religious Thought*
JSJ	*Journal for the Study of Judaism*
JSNT	*Journal for the Study of the New Testament*
JSNTS	Journal for the Study of the New Testament Supplement Series
JTS	*Journal of Theological Studies*
Julian	
Or.	*Orations*
Justin Martyr	
1, 2 Apol.	*First, Second Apology*
Dial.	*Dialogue with Trypho*
Epit.	*Epitome of Trogus*
Juvenal	
Sat.	*Satires*
KEK	Kritisch-exegetische Kommentar über das Neue Testament
Lampe	*A Patristic Greek Lexicon* (ed. G. W. H. Lampe; Oxford: Clarendon, 1961).
LCC	Library of Christian Classics
LCL	Loeb Classical Library
LD	Lectio divina
LEC	Library of Early Christianity
lit.	literally
LNTS	Library of New Testament Studies
Longus	
Daphn.	*Daphnis and Chloe*
LSJ	Henry George Liddell, Robert Scott, and Henry Stuart Jones, *A Greek-English Lexicon* (9th ed.; Oxford: Clarendon, 1940; reprinted, 1966).
Lucian	
Abdic.	*Abdicatus*
Alex.	*Alexander*
Bis acc.	*Bis accusatus*
Demon.	*Demonax*
Deor. conc.	*Deorum Concilium*
Eunuch.	*Eunuchus*
Fug.	*Fugitivi*
Hermot.	*Hermotimus*
Icar.	*Icaromenippus*
Imag.	*Imagines*
Jupp. conf.	*Juppiter confutatus*
Jupp. trag.	*Juppiter tragoedus*
Lex.	*Lexiphanes*
Men.	*Menippus*
Merc. cond.	*De mercede conductis*
Nav.	*Navigium*
Nigr.	*Nigrinus*
Peregr.	*De morte Peregrini*
Philops.	*Philopseudes*
Sacr.	*De sacrificiis*
Salt.	*De saltatione*
Syr. d.	*De syria dea*
Tox.	*Toxaris*
Ver. hist.	*Vera historia*
Vit. auct.	*Vitarum auctio*
LXX	Septuagint; all citations are from Alfred Rahlfs, *Septuaginta* (2 vols.; Stuttgart: Württembergische Bibelanstalt, 1965).

m.	Mishnah tractate
MAMA	*Monumenta Asiae Minoris Antiqua* (Manchester, 1928–).
Mart.	*Martyrdom of*
Mart. Perp.	*Martyrdom of Perpetua*
Mart. Pol.	*Martyrdom of Polycarp*
Maximus of Tyre	
Or.	*Orations*
Melito	
Apol.	*Apology*
Minucius Felix	
Oct.	*Octavius*
M-M	J. H. Moulton and G. Milligan, *The Vocabulary of the Greek Testament* (London, 1930; reprinted, Peabody, Mass.: Hendrickson, 1997).
MT	Masoretic Text
MThS	Münchener theologische Studien
N-A	Nestle-Aland, *Novum Testamentum graece*
NAB	*New American Bible*
NAC	New American Commentary
Nag Hammadi writings	
Dial. Sav.	*Dialogue of the Savior*
NCB	New Century Bible
NEB	*New English Bible*
NewDocs	*New Documents Illustrating Early Christianity* (ed. G. H. R. Horsley and S. Llewelyn; North Ryde, N.S.W.: Ancient History Documentary Research Centre, Macquarie University, 1981–).
NF	Neue Folge
NGG PH	Nachrichten der K. Gesellschaft der Wissenschaften zu Göttingen. Philologisch-historische Klasse
NHC	Nag Hammadi Codex
Nicephorus Callistus	
H.E.	*Ecclesiastical History*
NICNT	New International Commentary on the New Testament
NIGTC	New International Greek Testament Commentary
NIV	*New International Version*
NovT	*Novum Testamentum*
NovTSup	Novum Testamentum Supplements
NPF	Nicene and Post-Nicene Fathers
NRSV	*New Revised Standard Version*
NRT	*Nouvelle Revue de Theologie*
n.s.	new series
NTApoc	Edgar Hennecke, *New Testament Apocrypha* (ed. Wilhelm Schneemelcher; ET ed. R. McL. Wilson; 2 vols.; rev. ed.; Cambridge: James Clarke; Louisville: Westminster John Knox, 1991, 1992.
NTAbh	Neutestamentliche Abhandlungen
NTC	New Testament Commentary
NTD	Das Neue Testament Deutsch
NTDH	Neukirchener Theologische Dissertationen und Habilitationen
NTM	New Testament Message
NTMon	New Testament Monographs
NTOA	Novum Testamentum et Orbis Antiquus
NTS	*New Testament Studies*
NTTS	New Testament Tools and Studies
OBO	Orbis Biblicus et Orientalis
OBT	Overtures to Biblical Theology
OCD	*Oxford Classical Dictionary*
Odes Sol.	*Odes of Solomon*
OGIS	*Orientis graeci inscriptiones selectae* (ed. W. Dittenberger; 2 vols.; Leipzig, 1903–5).
ÖKTNT	Ökumenischer Taschenbuch-kommentar zum Neuen Testament
OLZ	*Orientalistiche Literaturzeitung*
Origen	
Adnot. Exod.	*Adnotationes in Exodum*
Cels.	*Contra Celsum*
De Orat..	*De oratione*
Fr. Jer.	*Fragmenta in Jeremiam*
Philoc.	*Philocalia*
OTP	James H. Charlesworth, ed., *Old Testament Pseudepigrapha* (2 vols.; Garden City, N.Y.: Doubleday, 1983, 1985).
Ovid	
Am.	*Amores*
Fast.	*Fasti*
Metam.	*Metamorphoses*
Papyri	
P. Coll. Youtie	*Collectanea Papyrologica: Texts Published in Honor of H. C. Youtie* (ed. Ann Ellis; Bonn: Habelt, 1976).
P. Lond.	*Greek Papyri in the British Museum* (London, 1893–74).
P. Oxy.	*Oxyrhynchus Papyri* (ed. B. Grenfell, A. Hunt, et al.; Oxford, 1898–).
P. Tebt.	*The Tebtunis Papyri* (Oxford: Egypt Exploration Fund, 1902–76).
par(r).	parallel(s)
PerspRelStud	*Perspectives in Religious Studies*
PG	*Patrologiae cursus completus: Series graeca* (ed. J.-P. Migne; 162 vols.; Paris, 1857–86).
PGM	*Papyri Graecae Magicae*, the Greek Magical Papyri; all refer-

	ences to this collection refer to the edition by Karl Preisendanz and Albert Henrichs (rev. ed.; Stuttgart: Teubner, 1973–74).
Philo	
Abr.	*De Abrahamo*
Cher.	*De cherubim*
Conf. ling.	*De confusione linguarum*
Dec.	*De decalogo*
Deus	*Quot Deus sit immutabilis*
Flacc.	*In Flaccum*
Hypoth.	*Hypothetica*
Jos.	*De Iosepho*
Leg. all.	*Legum allegoriae*
Leg. Gaj.	*Legatio ad Gaium*
Migr. Abr.	*De migratione Abrahami*
Mut. nom.	*De mutatione nominum*
Omn. prob. lib.	*Quod omnis probus liber sit*
Op. mun.	*De opificio mundi*
Praem. poen.	*De praemiis et poenis*
Prov.	*De providentia*
Q. Exod.	*Quaestiones et solutiones in Exodum*
Som.	*De somniis*
Spec. leg.	*On the Special Laws*
Virt.	*De virtutibus*
Vit. cont.	*De vita contemplativa*
Vit. Mos.	*De vita Mosis*
Philostratus	
Vit. Apoll.	*Vita Apollonii*
Vit. Soph.	*Vita sophistarum*
Pindar	
Ol.	*Olympionikai*
Pyth.	*Pythionikai*
PL	*Patrologiae cursus completus: Series Latina* (ed. J.-P. Migne; 217 volumes; Paris, 1844–64).
Plato	
Apol.	*Apologia*
Gorg.	*Gorgias*
Lach.	*Laches*
Leg.	*Leges*
Phaedr.	*Phaedrus*
Prot.	*Protagoras*
Resp.	*Respublica*
Soph.	*Sophista*
Tim.	*Timaeus*
Plautus	
Amph.	*Amphitryo*
Pliny the Elder	
Hist. nat.	*Naturalis historia*
Pliny the Younger	
Ep.	*Epistulae*
Pan.	*Panegyricus*
Plutarch	
Aem.	*Aemilius Paullus*
Alc.	*Alcibiades*
Alex.	*Alexander*
Alex. fort.	*De Alexandri magni fortuna aut virtute*
Amat.	*Amatorius*
Ant.	*Antonius*
Caes.	*Caesar*
Cat. Min.	*Cato Minor*
Cons. Apoll.	*Consolatio ad Apollonium*
Conviv. Septem	*Septem sapientium convivium*
Cor.	*Marcius Coriolanus*
Def. orac.	*De defectu oraculorum*
Dem.	*Demetrius*
E Delph.	*De E apud Delphos*
Fac.	*De facie in orbe lunae*
Frat. amor.	*De fraterno amore*
Galb.	*Galba*
Is. Os.	*De Iside et Osiride*
Lib. ed.	*De liberis educandis*
Luc.	*Lucullus*
Per.	*Pericles*
Praec. ger. rei publ.	*Praecepta gerendae rei publicae*
Pyth. orac.	*De Pythiae oraculis*
Quaest. conv.	*Quaestionum convivialum libri IX*
Stoic. rep.	*De Stoicorum repugnantis*
Tranq. an.	*De tranquillitate animi*
Tu. sen.	*De tuenda sanitate praecepta*
PNF	*Post-Nicene Fathers*
Polycarp	
Phil.	*Letter to the Philadelphians*
Porphyry	
Christ.	*Contra Christianos*
Ps.-Clem.	Pseudo-Clementine
De Virg.	*De Virginitate*
Hom	*Homilies*
Rec.	*Recognitions*
PTMS	Pittsburgh Theological Monograph Series
PW	*Paulys Realencyclopädie der classischen Altertumswissenschaft*
PWSup	Supplement to PW
QD	Quaestiones disputatae
Qumran writings	
CD	Cairo (Genizah) text of the *Damascus Document*
1QH	*Hodayoth* (*Thanksgiving Hymns*) from Cave 1
1QS	*Community Rule* from Cave 1
RAC	*Reallexikon für Antike und Christentum*
RB	*Revue Biblique*
REJ	*Revue des études juives*
RGG	*Religion in Geschichte und Gegenwart* (ed. K. Galling; 7 vols.; Tübingen, 1957–65).
RHPhR	*Revue d'histoire et de philosophie religieuses*
RHR	*Revue de l'histoire des religions*
RivB	*Rivista Biblica*
RivBSup	Rivista Biblica Supplements
RNT	Regensburger Neues Testament
RQ	*Römische Quartalschrift für christliche Altertumskunde und Kirchengeschichte*

RSPhTh	*Revue des sciences philosophiques et théologiques*
RSR	*Religious Studies Review*
RThPh	*Revue de théologie et philosophie*
SacPag	Sacra Pagina
Sallust	
Bell. Cat.	*Bellum catalinae*
Bell. Jug.	*Bellum jugurthinum*
SANT	Studien zum Alten und Neuen Testament
Sb.	*Sammelbuch griechischer Urkunden aus Aegypten* (ed. F. Preisigke et al.; Strasburg: Tribner, 1915–77).
SBL	Society of Biblical Literature
SBLDS	SBL Dissertation Series
SBLEJL	SBL Early Judaism and Its Literature
SBLMS	SBL Monograph Series
SBLRBS	SBL Resources for Biblical Study
SBLSBS	SBL Sources for Biblical Study
SBLSP	*SBL Seminar Papers*
SBLSS	SBL Semeia Studies
SBLSymS	SBL Symposium Series
SBLT-CS	SBL Text-Critical Studies
SBLTT	SBL Texts and Translations
SBLWGRW	SBL Writings from the Greco-Roman World
SBS	Stuttgarter Bibelstudien
SBT	Studies in Biblical Theology
SCHNT	Studia ad Corpus Hellenisticum Novi Testamenti
SciEsp	*Science et Esprit*
SEÅ	*Svensk exegetisk årsbok*
SecCent	*Second Century*
SEG	*Supplementum epigraphicum graecum*
Sem	*Semeia*
Seneca	
Ben.	*De beneficiis*
Ep. mor.	*Epistulae morales*
Ira	*De Ira*
Nat.	*Naturales quaestiones*
Sib. Or.	*Sibylline Oracles*
SIG	*Sylloge inscriptionum graecarum* (ed. Wilhelm Dittenberger; 4 vols.; 3rd ed.; Leipzig, 1915–24).
SNTSMS	Studiorum Novi Testamenti Societas Monograph Series
Socrates	
H.E.	*Ecclesiastical History*
Sophocles	
Ant.	*Antigone*
El.	*Elektra*
Oed. col.	*Oedipus coloneus*
Oed. tyr.	*Oedipus tyrannus*
Phil.	*Philoctetes*
ST	*Studia Theologica*
STDJ	Studies on the Texts of the Desert of Judah
StudDoc	Studies and Documents
StNT	Studien zum Neuen Testament
Stobaeus	
Ecl	*Eclogae*
StudNTUmwelt	*Studien zum Neuen Testament und seiner Umwelt*
Suetonius	
Aug.	*Divus Augustus*
Claud.	*Divus Claudius*
Dom.	*Domitianus*
Jul.	*Divus Julius*
Tib.	*Tiberius*
Tit.	*Divus Titus*
Vesp.	*Vespasianus*
Sulpicius Severus	
Ep.	*Epistulae*
SUNT	Studien zur Umwelt des Neuen Testaments
s.v.	*sub verbum*
Synesius	
Ep.	*Epistulae*
T. Jac.	*Testament of Jacob*
T. Job	*Testament of Job*
T. Jos.	*Testament of Joseph*
T. Jud.	*Testament of Judah*
T. Naph.	*Testament of Naphthali*
Tacitus	
Ann.	*Annales*
Hist.	*Historiae*
TAM	Titulae Asiae Minoris, 1923–
TAPA	*Transactions of the American Philological Association*
TDNT	*Theological Dictionary of the New Testament* (ed. G. Kittel and G. Friedrich; trans. and ed. Geoffrey W. Bromiley; 10 vols.; Grand Rapids: Eerdmans, 1964–76).
Terence	
Ad.	*Adelphi*
Tertullian	
Apol.	*Apologeticus*
Bapt.	*De baptismo*
Idol.	*De idololatria*
Mon.	*De monogamia*
Nat.	*Ad nationes*
Prax.	*Adversus Praxean*
Pud.	*De pudicitia*
Res.	*De resurrectione carnis*
TextsS	Texts and Studies
Theocritus	
Id.	*Idylls*
Theophilus	
Autolyc.	*To Autolycus*
ThLZ	*Theologische Literaturzeitung*
ThQ	*Theologische Quartalschrift*
ThRu	*Theologische Rundschau*
trans.	translator, translation, translated by
ThHKNT	Theologische Handkommentar zum Neuen Testament
ThZ	*Theologische Zeitschrift*

TRE	*Theologische Realenzyklopädie* (ed. G. Krause and G. Müller; Berlin, 1977–).
TRev	*Theologische Revue*
TSAJ	Texte und Studien zum antiken Judentum/Texts and Studies in Ancient Judaism
TThZ	*Trierer theologische Zeitschrift*
TU	Texte und Untersuchungen zur Geschichte der altchristlichen Literatur
TynBul	*Tyndale Bulletin*
Virgil	
Aen.	*Aeneid*
v.l.	*varia lectio,* variant reading
VT	*Vetus Testamentum*
WBC	Word Bible Commentary
WMANT	Wissenschaftliche Monographien zum Alten und Neuen Testament
WUNT	Wissenschaftliche Untersuchungen zum Neuen Testament
Xenophon	
Anab.	*Anabasis*
Cyr.	*Cyropaedia*
Mem.	*Memorabilia*
ZKG	*Zeitschrift für Kirchengeschichte*
ZKTh	*Zetischrift für katholische Theologie*
ZNW	*Zeitschrift für die neutestamentliche Wissenschaft*
ZPE	*Zetischrift für Papyrologie und Epigraphik*
ZThK	*Zeitschrift für Theologie und Kirche*
ZWTh	*Zeitschrift für Wissenschaftliche Theologie*

2. Short Titles of Commentaries, Studies, and Articles Often Cited

Aejmelaeus, *Rezeption*
Lars Aejmelaeus, *Die Rezeption der Paulusbriefe in der Miletrede* (Helsinki: Suomalienen Tiedeakatemia, 1987).

Alexander, *Literary Context*
Loveday C. A. Alexander, *Acts in Its Ancient Literary Context: A Classicist Looks at the Acts of the Apostles* (LNTS 298; London: T&T Clark, 2005).

Alexander, *Preface*
Loveday C. A. Alexander, *The Preface to Luke's Gospel: Literary Convention and Social Context in Luke 1.1-4 and Acts 1.1* (SNTSMS 78; Cambridge: Cambridge University Press, 1993).

Alexander, "The Preface to Acts"
Loveday C. A. Alexander, "The Preface to Acts and the Historians," in Ben Witherington, *History,* 73–103.

Allen, *Death*
O. Wesley Allen Jr., *The Death of Herod: The Narrative and Theological Functions of Retribution in Luke-Acts* (SBLDS 158; Atlanta: Scholars Press, 1997).

Aune, *Prophecy*
David E. Aune, *Prophecy in Early Christianity* (Grand Rapids: Eerdmans, 1983).

Balch, "Areopagus Speech"
David L. Balch, "The Areopagus Speech: An Appeal to the Stoic Historian Posidonius against Later Stoics and the Epicureans," in idem et al., eds., *Greeks, Romans, and Christians: Essays in Honor of Abraham J. Malherbe* (Minneapolis: Fortress Press, 1990), 52–79.

Balch, "*ΜΕΤΑΒΟΛΗ ΠΟΛΙΤΕΙΩΝ*"
David L. Balch, "*ΜΕΤΑΒΟΛΗ ΠΟΛΙΤΕΙΩΝ*: Jesus as Founder of the Church in Luke-Acts: Form and Function," in Penner, *Contextualizing,* 139–88.

Barclay, *Jews*
John M. G. Barclay, *Jews in the Mediterranean Diaspora from Alexander to Trajan (323 BCE–117 CE)* (Berkeley: University of California Press, 1996).

Barrett
Charles Kingsley Barrett, *A Critical and Exegetical Commentary on the Acts of the Apostles* (2 vols.; ICC; Edinburgh: T&T Clark, 1994, 1998).

Barrett, "Paul Shipwrecked"
Charles Kingsley Barrett, "Paul Shipwrecked," in Barry Thompson, ed., *Scripture: Meaning and Method: Essays Presented to Anthony Tyrrell Hanson* (Hull: Hull University Press, 1987) 51–64.

Bauckham, "James and the Gentiles"
Richard Bauckham, "James and the Gentiles (Acts 15.13-21)," in Witherington, *History,* 154–84.

Bauckham, *Palestinian Setting*
Richard Bauckham, ed., *The Book of Acts in Its Palestinian Setting* (BIFCS 4; Grand Rapids: Eerdmans, 1995).

Bede
Bede, *Expositio Actuum Apostolorum* (ed. Max L. W. Laistner; CCSL 121; Brepols: Turnholt, 1983).

Berger, *Formgeschichte*
Klaus Berger, *Formgeschichte des Neuen Testaments* (Heidelberg: Quelle & Meyer, 1984).

Betz, *Lukian*
Hans Dieter Betz, *Lukian von Samosata und das Neue Testament* (TU 76; Berlin: Akademie, 1961).

Bieler, ΘΕΙΟΣ ΑΝΗΡ
Ludwig Bieler, ΘΕΙΟΣ ΑΝΗΡ*: Das Bild des "Göttlichen Menschen" in Spätantike und Frühchristentum* (2 vols.; 1935–36; reprinted, Darmstadt: Wissenschaftliche Buchgesellschaft, 1967).

Black, "John Mark"
C. Clifton Black, "John Mark in the Acts of the Apostles," in Thompson, *Literary Studies,* 101–20.

Boismard, *Texte*
Marie-Émile Boismard and Arnaud Lamouille, *Le texte occidental des Actes des Apôtres: Reconstitution et réhabilitation* (2 vols.; Paris: Editions Recherche sur les civilizations, 1984).

Borgen, *Philo*
Peder Borgen, *Philo, John and Paul: New Perspectives on Judaism and Early Christianity* (BJS 131; Atlanta: Scholars Press, 1987).

Bornkamm, *Tradition*
Günther Bornkamm, *Tradition and Interpretation in Matthew* (trans. P. Scott; Philadelphia: Westminster, 1963).

Bousset, *Kyrios Christos*
Wilhelm Bousset, *Kyrios Christos: A History of the Belief in Christ from the Beginnings of Christianity to Irenaeus* (trans. J. Steely; Nashville: Abingdon, 1970).

Bovon, *Actes apocryphes*
François Bovon et al., eds., *Les Actes apocryphes des apôtres: Christianisme et monde paien* (Geneva: Labor et Fides, 1981).

Bovon, *Luke the Theologian*
François Bovon, *Luke the Theologian: Fifty-five Years of Research (1950–2005)* (2nd ed.; Waco: Baylor University Press, 2006).

Bovon, "Saint-Esprit"
François Bovon, "Le Saint-Esprit, l'Église et les relations humaines selon Actes 20,36–21,16," in Kremer, *Actes,* 339–58.

Bovon, "Tradition et redaction"
François Bovon, "Tradition et redaction et Actes 10,1–11,18," *TZ* 26 (1970) 22–45.

Breytenbach, *Apostelgeschichte*
Ciliers Breytenbach et al., eds., *Apostelgeschichte und die hellenistische Geschichtsschreibung: Festschrift für Eckhard Plümacher zu seinem 65. Geburtstag* (AGJU 57; Leiden/Boston: Brill, 2004).

Breytenbach, *Paulus & Barnabas*
Ciliers Breytenbach, *Paulus & Barnabas in der Provinz Galatien: Studien zu Apostelgeschichte 13f; 16,16; 18,23 & den Adressaten des Galaterbriefes* (AGJU 38; Leiden: Brill, 1996).

Brosend, "Means"
William F. Brosend II, "The Means of Absent Ends," in Witherington, *History,* 348–62.

Brown, *Apostasy*
Schuyler Brown, *Apostasy and Perseverance in the Theology of Luke* (AnBib 36; Rome: Pontifical Biblical Institute, 1969).

Brown and Meier, *Antioch*
Raymond E. Brown and John P. Meier, *Antioch and Rome: New Testament Cradles of Catholic Christianity* (Ramsey, N.J.: Paulist, 1983).

Bruce
Frederick F. Bruce, *The Acts of the Apostles* (3rd ed.; Grand Rapids: Eerdmans, 1990).

Bultmann, *History*
Rudolf Bultmann, *The History of the Synoptic Tradition* (trans. John Marsh; 2nd ed.; New York: Harper & Row, 1968).

Bultmann, *Theology*
Rudolf Bultmann, *Theology of the New Testament* (2 vols.; trans. Kendrick Grobel; New York: Charles Scribner's Sons, 1951–55).

Burchard, *Dreizehnte Zeuge*
Christoph Burchard, *Der dreizehnte Zeuge* (FRLANT 103; Göttingen: Vandenhoeck & Ruprecht, 1970).

Cadbury, *Book*
Henry J. Cadbury, *The Book of Acts in History* (New York: Harper & Bros., 1955).

Cadbury, "Commentary"
Henry J. Cadbury, "Commentary on the Preface of Luke," in Foakes Jackson and Lake, *Prolegomena II,* 489–510.

Cadbury, "Dust and Garments"
Henry J. Cadbury, "Dust and Garments," in Lake and Cadbury, *Additional Notes,* 269–77.

Cadbury, *Making*
Henry J. Cadbury, *The Making of Luke-Acts* (1927; reprinted, London: SPCK, 1958).

Cadbury, "Names"
Henry J. Cadbury, "Names for Christians and Christianity in Acts," in Lake and Cadbury, *Additional Notes,* 375–92.

Cadbury and Lake
Henry Cadbury and Kirsopp Lake, *Commentary on Acts,* vol. 4 of Foakes Jackson and Lake, *Beg.* (New York: Macmillan, 1920–33; reprinted, Grand Rapids: Baker, 1979).

Calvin
Jean Calvin, *The Acts of the Apostles* (trans. J. W. Fraser and W. J. G. McDonald. *Calvin's Commentaries,* vols. 6–7; Grand Rapids: Eerdmans, 1995).

Campbell, "Who Are We?"
William S. Campbell, "Who Are We in Acts? The First-Person Plural Character in the Acts of the Apostles" (Diss., Princeton Theological Seminary, 2000).

Carroll, *Response*
John T. Carroll, *Response to the End of History: Eschatology and Situation in Luke-Acts* (SBLDS 92; Atlanta: Scholars Press, 1988).

Casey, "Simon Magus"
Robert P. Casey, "Simon Magus," in Lake and Cadbury, *Additional Notes,* 151–63.

Cassidy, *Society*
Richard J. Cassidy, *Society and Politics in the Acts of the Apostles* (Maryknoll, N.Y.: Orbis Books, 1987).

Clark
Albert C. Clark, *The Acts of the Apostles: A Critical Edition with Introduction and Notes on Selected Passages* (Oxford: Oxford University Press, 1933).

Clark, *Parallel Lives*
Andrew C. Clark, *Parallel Lives: The Relation of Paul to the Apostles in the Lucan Perspective* (Carlisle, U.K./Waynesboro, Ga.: Paternoster, 2001).

Clarke, "Use of the Septuagint"
William Kemp L. Clarke, "The Use of the Septuagint in Acts," in Foakes Jackson and Lake, *Prolegomena II,* 66–105.

Cohoon, *Dio Chrysostom*
J. W. Cohoon, trans., *Dio Chrysostom* (5 vols.; LCL;

Cambridge, Mass.: Harvard University Press, 1932–51).

Conzelmann
Hans Conzelmann, *Acts of the Apostles: A Commentary on the Acts of the Apostles* (trans. James Limburg, A. Thomas Kraabel, and Donald H. Juel; ed. Eldon J. Epp with Christopher Matthews; Hermeneia; Philadelphia: Fortress Press, 1987).

Conzelmann, *Theology*
Hans Conzelmann, *The Theology of St. Luke* (trans. G. Buswell; New York: Harper & Row, 1960).

Courtney, *Juvenal*
Edward Courtney, *A Commentary on the Satires of Juvenal* (London: Athlone, 1980).

Crossan, *Who Killed Jesus*
John Dominic Crossan, *Who Killed Jesus? Exposing the Roots of Anti-Semitism in the Gospel Story of the Death of Jesus* (San Francisco: HarperSanFrancisco, 1995).

Cunningham, *Tribulations*
Scott Cunningham, *Through Many Tribulations: The Theology of Persecution in Luke-Acts* (JSNTS 142; Sheffield: Sheffield Academic Press, 1997).

Czachesz, "Commission Narratives"
István Czachesz, "Apostolic Commission Narratives in the Canonical and Apocryphal Acts of the Apostles" (Diss., Groningen, 2002).

Dahl, "Abraham"
Nils A. Dahl, "The Story of Abraham in Luke-Acts," in Keck and Martyn, *Studies*, 139–58.

Danker, *Benefactor*
Frederick W. Danker, *Benefactor: Epigraphic Study of a Graeco-Roman and New Testament Semantic Field* (St. Louis: Clayton, 1982).

Deissmann, *Bible Studies*
Adolf Deissmann, *Bible Studies* (trans. A. Grieve; Edinburgh: T&T Clark, 1901).

Deissmann, *Light*
Adolf Deissmann, *Light from the Ancient East* (trans. Lionel Strachan; New York: Harper & Bros., 1927).

Delebecque, *Les Deux Actes*
Édouard Delebecque, *Les Deux Actes des Apôtres* (EB n.s. 6; Paris: Gabalda, 1986).

Dibelius, *Studies*
Martin Dibelius, *Studies in the Acts of the Apostles* (trans. Mary Ling and Paul Schubert; ed. Heinrich Greeven; New York: Charles Scribner's Sons, 1956).

Dibelius and Conzelmann, *Pastoral Epistles*
Martin Dibelius and Hans Conzelmann, *The Pastoral Epistles* (trans. and ed. Helmut Koester; Hermeneia; Philadelphia: Fortress Press, 1972).

Doody, *True Story*
Margaret Anne Doody, *The True Story of the Novel* (New Brunswick: Rutgers University Press, 1996).

Dupont, "Conclusion"
Jacques Dupont, "La conclusion des Actes et son rapport à l'ensemble de l'ouvrage de Luc," in Kremer, *Actes*, 359–404.

Dupont, *Le discours de Milet*
Jacques Dupont, *Le discours de Milet: Testament pastoral de Saint Paul (Actes 20,18-36)* (Paris: Cerf, 1962).

Dupont, *Nouvelles études*
Jacques Dupont, *Nouvelles études sur les Actes des apôtres* (LD 118; Paris: Cerf, 1984).

Edwards, *Religion and Power*
Douglas Edwards, *Religion and Power: Pagans, Jews, and Christians in the Greek East* (New York: Oxford University Press, 1996).

Egger, "Women in the Greek Novel"
Brigitte M. Egger, "Women in the Greek Novel: Constructing the Feminine" (Diss., University of California, Irvine, 1990).

Ehrman, *Apostolic Fathers*
Bart D. Ehrman, *The Apostolic Fathers* (2 vols.; LCL; Cambridge, Mass.: Harvard University Press, 2003).

Elliott, *Apocryphal New Testament*
James Keith Elliott, *The Apocryphal New Testament* (Oxford: Clarendon, 1993).

Engelmann, *Delian Aretalogy*
Helmut Engelmann, *The Delian Aretalogy of Sarapis* (EPRO 44; trans. Ewald Osers; Leiden: Brill, 1975).

Epp, "Anti-Judaic Tendencies"
Eldon Jay Epp, "Anti-Judaic Tendencies in the D-Text of Acts: Forty Years of Conversation," in Tobias Nicklas and Michael Tilly, eds., *The Book of Acts as Church History: Textual Traditions and Ancient Interpretations* (BZNW 120; Berlin: de Gruyter, 2003) 111–46.

Epp, "Ascension"
Eldon Jay Epp, "The Ascension in the Textual Tradition of Luke-Acts," in idem and Gordon D. Fee, eds., *New Testament Textual Criticism: Its Significance for Exegesis; Essays in Honour of Bruce M. Metzger* (Oxford: Clarendon, 1981) 131–45.

Epp, *Tendency*
Eldon Jay Epp, *The Theological Tendency of Codex Bezae Cantabrigiensis in Acts* (SNTSMS 3; Cambridge: Cambridge University Press, 1966).

Epp and Fee, *Textual Criticism*
Eldon Jay Epp and Gordon D. Fee, eds., *New Testament Textual Criticism: Its Significance for Exegesis; Essays in Honour of Bruce M. Metzger* (Oxford: Clarendon, 1981).

Esler, *Community*
Philip F. Esler, *Community and Gospel in Luke-Acts: The Social and Political Motivations of Lucan Theology* (SNTSMS 57; Cambridge: Cambridge University Press, 1987).

Feldman, *Jew and Gentile*
Louis H. Feldman, *Jew and Gentile in the Ancient World* (Princeton: Princeton University Press, 1993).

Finger, *Of Widows and Meals*
Reta Halteman Finger, *Of Widows and Meals: Communal Meals in the Book of Acts* (Grand Rapids: Eerdmans, 2007).

Fitzmyer
Joseph A. Fitzmyer, *The Acts of the Apostles* (AB 31; New York: Doubleday, 1998).

Fitzmyer, *Luke I–IX*
Joseph A. Fitzmyer, *The Gospel according to Luke* (2 vols.; AB 28/28A; Garden City, N.Y.: Doubleday, 1981, 1985).

Foakes Jackson
Frederick J. Foakes Jackson, *The Acts of the Apostles* (New York: Harper, 1931).

Foakes Jackson and Lake, *Beg.*
Frederick J. Foakes Jackson and Kirsopp Lake, eds., *The Beginnings of Christianity* (5 vols.; New York: Macmillan, 1920–33; reprinted, Grand Rapids: Baker, 1979).

Foakes Jackson and Lake, *Prolegomena II*
Frederick J. Foakes Jackson and Kirsopp Lake, *Prolegomena II*, vol. 2 of Foakes Jackson and Lake, *Beg.*

Fox, *Pagans and Christians*
Robin Lane Fox, *Pagans and Christians* (New York: Knopf, 1989).

Franklin, *Christ the Lord*
Eric Franklin, *Christ the Lord: A Study in the Purpose and Theology of Luke-Acts* (Philadelphia: Westminster, 1975).

Funk, *Narrative Poetics*
Robert W. Funk, *The Poetics of Biblical Narrative* (Sonoma, Calif.: Polebridge, 1988).

Gager, *Curse Tablets*
John G. Gager, ed., *Curse Tablets and Binding Spells from the Ancient World* (New York: Oxford University Press, 1992).

Gamble, *Books and Readers*
Harry Y. Gamble, *Books and Readers in the Early Church: A History of Early Christian Texts* (New Haven: Yale University Press, 1995).

Garrett, *Demise*
Susan R. Garrett, *The Demise of the Devil: Magic and the Demonic in Luke-Acts* (Minneapolis: Fortress Press, 1989).

Gärtner, *Areopagus Speech*
Bertil Gärtner, *The Areopagus Speech and Natural Revelation* (ASNU 21; Uppsala: Gleerup, 1955).

Gaventa, *Darkness*
Beverly Roberts Gaventa, *From Darkness to Light: Aspects of Conversion in the New Testament* (OBT; Philadelphia: Fortress Press, 1986).

Georgi, *Opponents*
Dieter Georgi, *The Opponents of Paul in Second Corinthians* (Philadelphia: Fortress Press, 1985).

Georgi, *Remembering*
Dieter Georgi, *Remembering the Poor: The History of Paul's Collection for Jerusalem* (Nashville: Abingdon, 1992).

Gilbert, "Roman Propaganda"
Gary Gilbert, "Roman Propaganda and Christian Identity in the Worldview of Luke-Acts," in Penner, *Contextualizing*, 233–56.

Gill and Gempf, *Setting*
David W. J. Gill and Conrad Gempf, eds., *The Book of Acts in Its Graeco-Roman Setting* (BIFCS 2; Grand Rapids: Eerdmans, 1994).

Goold, *Callirhoe*
G. P. Goold, ed. and trans., *Chariton, Callirhoe* (LCL; Cambridge, Mass.: Harvard University Press, 1995).

Goulder, *Type*
Michael Goulder, *Type and History in Acts* (London: SPCK, 1964).

Grant, *Miracle*
Robert M. Grant, *Miracle and Natural Law in Greco-Roman and Early Christian Thought* (Amsterdam: North-Holland, 1952).

Hadas, *Aristeas*
Moses Hadas, *Aristeas to Philocrates: Letter of Aristeas* (New York: Harper, 1951).

Haenchen
Ernst Haenchen, *The Acts of the Apostles* (trans. and ed. Bernard Noble et al.; translation revised and brought up to date by R. McL. Wilson; Philadelphia: Westminster, 1971).

Haenchen, "We"
Ernst Haenchen, "'We' in Acts and the Itinerary," *The Bultmann School of Biblical Interpretation: New Directions? Journal for Theology and Church* 1 (1965) 65–99.

Haenchen, "Schriftzitate"
Ernst Haenchen, "Schriftzitate und Textüberlieferung in der Apostelgeschichte," *ZThK* 51 (1954) 153–67.

Hanson, *Apuleius*
J. Arthur Hanson, *Apuleius Metamorphoses* (2 vols.; LCL; Cambridge, Mass.: Harvard University Press, 1989).

Harmon, *Lucian*
A. M. Harmon, *Lucian* (8 vols.; LCL; Cambridge, Mass.: Harvard University Press, 1913–67).

Harnack
Adolf von Harnack, *The Acts of the Apostles* (trans. J. R. Wilkinson; London: Williams & Norgate; New York: Putnam, 1909).

Harnack, *Mission*
Adolf von Harnack, *The Mission and Expansion of Christianity in the First Three Centuries* (trans. J. Moffatt; 2 vols.; New York: Putnam, 1908).

Havelaar, "Hellenistic Parallels"
Henriette Havelaar, "Hellenistic Parallels to Acts 5,1-11 and the Problem of Conflicting Interpretations," *JSNT* 67 (1997) 63–82.

Head, "Problem"
Peter Head, "Acts and the Problem of Its Texts," in Winter and Clarke, *Setting*, 1:415–44.

Hedrick, "Paul's Conversion/Call"
Charles W. Hedrick, "Paul's Conversion/Call: A Comparative Analysis of the Three Reports in Acts," *JBL* 100 (1981) 415–32.

Hemer, *Book*
Colin J. Hemer, *The Book of Acts in the Setting of Hellenistic History* (ed. Conrad J. Gempf; Winona Lake, Ind.: Eisenbrauns, 1990).

Hengel, *Acts and the History*
Martin Hengel, *Acts and the History of Earliest Christianity* (trans. John Bowden; Philadelphia: Fortress Press, 1979).
Hengel, *Between*
Martin Hengel, *Between Jesus and Paul: Studies in the History of Earliest Christianity* (trans. J. Bowden; Philadelphia: Fortress Press, 1983).
Hengel and Schwemer, *Paul*
Martin Hengel and Anna Maria Schwemer, *Paul between Damascus and Antioch: The Unknown Years* (London: SCM, 1997).
Hilgert, *Ship*
Earle Hilgert, *The Ship and Related Symbols in the New Testament* (Assen: Van Gorcum, 1962).
Hill, *Hellenists*
Craig C. Hill, *Hellenists and Hebrews: Reappraising Division with the Earliest Church* (Minneapolis: Fortress Press, 1992).
Hills, "Acts"
Julian Hills, "The Acts of the Apostles in the *Acts of Paul*," in Eugene Lovering, ed., *SBLSP 1994* (Atlanta: Scholars Press, 1994) 24–54.
Hock, *Social Context*
Ronald F. Hock, *The Social Context of Paul's Ministry* (Philadelphia: Fortress Press, 1980).
Hoffmann, *Porphyry*
R. Joseph Hoffmann, *Porphyry's Against the Christians: The Literary Remains* (Amherst, N.Y.: Prometheus Books, 1994).
Holladay, "Acts and the Fragments"
Carl Holladay, "Acts and the Fragments of Hellenistic Jewish Historians," in Moessner, *Heritage,* 171–98.
Holladay, *Fragments*
Carl Holladay, *Fragments from Hellenistic Jewish Authors* (5 vols.; Chico, Calif.: Scholars Press, 1983).
Horsley, "Inscriptions"
Gregory H. R. Horsley, "The Inscriptions of Ephesos and the New Testament," *NovT* 34 (1992) 105–67.
Horst, "Acts 3 and 4"
Pieter W. van der Horst, "Hellenistic Parallels to Acts Chapters 3 and 4," *JSNT* 35 (1989) 37–46.
Jacobson, "Paul"
Glenn R. Jacobson, "Paul in Luke-Acts: The Savior Who Is Present," in Kent H. Richards, ed., *SBLSP 1983* (Chico, Calif.: Scholars Press, 1983) 131–46.
Jacquier
Eugène Jacquier, *Les Actes des apôtres* (2nd ed.; EB; Paris: Gabalda, 1926).
Jervell
Jacob Jervell, *Die Apostelgeschichte: Übersetzt und erklärt* (KEK 17; Göttingen: Vandenhoeck & Ruprecht, 1998).
Johnson
Luke Timothy Johnson, *The Acts of the Apostles* (SacPag 5; Collegeville, Minn.: Liturgical Press, 1992).
Johnson, *Literary Function*
Luke Timothy Johnson, *The Literary Function of Possessions in Luke-Acts* (The Père Marquette Lecture in Theology, 2002; Milwaukee: Marquette University Press, 2002).
Jones, "A Jewish Christian"
F. Stanley Jones, "A Jewish Christian Reads Luke's Acts of the Apostles: The Use of the Canonical Acts in the Ancient Jewish Christian Source behind Pseudo-Clementine *Recognitions,* 1.27–71," *SBLSP 1995* (Atlanta: Scholars Press, 1995) 617–35.
Käsemann, "Disciples"
Ernst Käsemann, "The Disciples of John the Baptist in Ephesus," in *Essays on New Testament Themes* (trans. W. J. Montague; SBT 41; London: SCM, 1964) 136–49.
Kauppi, *Foreign*
Lynn A. Kauppi, *Foreign but Familiar Gods: Greco-Romans Read Religion in Acts* (LNTS 277; London: T&T Clark, 2006).
Keck and Martyn, *Studies*
Leander Keck and J. Louis Martyn, eds., *Studies in Luke-Acts: Essays Presented in Honor of Paul Schubert* (Nashville: Abingdon, 1966).
Kennedy, *Rhetorical Criticism*
George A. Kennedy, *New Testament Interpretation through Rhetorical Criticism* (Chapel Hill: University of North Carolina Press, 1984).
Kerényi, *Romanliteratur*
Karl Kerényi, *Der antike Roman* (Darmstadt: Wissenschaftliche Buchgesellschaft, 1971).
Klauck, *Ancient Letters*
Hans-Josef Klauck, with D. R. Bailey, *Ancient Letters and the New Testament* (Waco: Baylor University Press, 2006).
Klauck, *Magic*
Hans-Josef Klauck, *Magic and Paganism in Early Christianity: The World of the Acts of the Apostles* (trans. Brian McNeil; Edinburgh: T&T Clark, 2000).
Klein, *Zwölf*
Günter Klein, *Die zwölf Apostel: Ursprung und Gehalt einer Idee* (FRLANT 77; Göttingen: Vandenhoeck & Ruprecht, 1961).
Klutz, *Exorcism Stories*
Todd E. Klutz, *The Exorcism Stories in Luke-Acts: A Sociostylistic Reading* (SNTSMS 129; Cambridge: Cambridge University Press, 2004).
Knibbe, "Via Sacra"
Dieter Knibbe, "Via Sacra Ephesiaca: New Aspects of the Cult of Artemis Ephesia," in Koester, *Ephesos,* 141–55.
Knox
Wilfred L. Knox, *The Acts of the Apostles* (Cambridge: Cambridge University Press, 1948).
Knox, *Hellenistic Elements*
Wilfred L. Knox, *Some Hellenistic Elements in Primitive Christianity* (1942 Schweich Lectures; London: British Academy, 1944).
Knox, *St Paul*
Wilfred L. Knox, *St Paul and the Church of the*

Gentiles (Cambridge: Cambridge University Press, 1939).

Koch, "Kollektenbericht"
Dietrich-Alex Koch, "Kollektenbericht, 'Wir'-Bericht und Itinerar: Neue Überlegungen zu einem alten Problem," *NTS* 45 (1999) 367–90.

Koester, *Ephesos*
Helmut Koester, ed., *Ephesos: Metropolis of Asia* (HTS 41; Valley Forge, Pa.: Trinity Press International, 1995).

Kratz, *Rettungswunder*
Reinhard Kratz, *Rettungswunder: Motiv-, traditions- und formkritische Aufarbeitung einer biblischen Gattung* (Frankfurt: Peter Lang, 1979).

Kremer, *Actes*
Jacob Kremer, ed., *Les Actes des Apôtres: Traditions, redaction, théologie* (BEThL 48; Leuven: Leuven University Press, 1979).

Krodel
Gerhard A. Krodel, *Acts* (ACNT; Minneapolis: Augsburg, 1986).

Kurz, *Reading*
William Kurz, *Reading Luke-Acts: Dynamics of Biblical Narrative* (Louisville: Westminster John Knox, 1993).

Labahn and Peerbolte, *Wonders*
Michael Labahn and Bert L. Peerbolte, eds., *Wonders Never Cease: The Purpose of Narrating Miracle Stories in the New Testament and Its Religious Environment* (LNTS 288; London: T&T Clark, 2006).

Lake, "Communism"
Kirsopp Lake, "The Communism of Acts II. and IV.–VI. and the Appointment of the Seven," in Lake and Cadbury, *Additional Notes,* 140–51.

Lake, "Gift"
Kirsopp Lake, "The Gift of the Spirit on the Day of Pentecost," in Lake and Cadbury, *Additional Notes,* 111–21.

Lake and Cadbury, *Additional Notes*
Kirsopp Lake and Henry J. Cadbury, eds., *Additional Notes to the Commentary,* vol. 5 of Foakes Jackson and Lake, *Beg.*

Lambrecht, "Farewell"
Jan Lambrecht, "Paul's Farewell-Address at Miletus, Acts 20, 17-38," in Kremer, *Actes,* 307–37.

Lampe, "Acta 19"
Geoffrey W. H. Lampe, "Acta 19 im Spiegel der ephesischen Inschriften," *BZ* 36 (1992) 59–77.

Lampe, "Miracles"
Geoffrey W. H. Lampe, "Miracles in the Acts of the Apostles," in Moule, *Miracles,* 163–78.

Lampe, *Paul to Valentinus*
Geoffrey W. H. Lampe, *From Paul to Valentinus: Christians at Rome in the First Two Centuries* (trans. Michael Steinhauser; ed. Marshall D. Johnson; Minneapolis: Fortress Press, 2003).

Lausberg, *Handbook*
Heinrich Lausberg, *Handbook of Literary Rhetoric* (trans. Matthew T. Bliss et al.; ed. David Orton and R. Dean Anderson; Leiden: Brill, 1998).

Lentz, *Luke's Portrait*
John Clayton Lentz, Jr., *Luke's Portrait of Paul* (SNTSMS 77; Cambridge: Cambridge University Press, 1993).

Leppä, *Critical Use*
Heikki Leppä, *Luke's Critical Use of Galatians* (Vantaa, Finland: Dark Oy, 2002).

Levick, *Government*
Barbara Levick, *The Government of the Roman Empire: A Sourcebook* (Totowa, N.J.: Barnes & Noble, 1985).

Levine, *Feminist Companion*
Amy-Jill Levine, ed., *A Feminist Companion to the Acts of the Apostles* (Cleveland: Pilgrim, 2004).

Levinskaya, *Diaspora Setting*
Irina Levinskaya, *The Book of Acts in Its Diaspora Setting* (BIFCS 5; Grand Rapids: Eerdmans, 1996).

Lifshitz, *Donateurs*
Baruch Lifshitz, *Donateurs et fondateurs dans les synagogues juives* (CahRB 7; Paris: Gabalda, 1967).

Lightfoot, *Apostolic Fathers*
J. B. Lightfoot, *The Apostolic Fathers* (London/New York: Macmillan, 1891).

Lindars, *Apologetic*
Barnabas Lindars, *New Testament Apologetic: The Doctrinal Significance of the Old Testament Quotations* (London: SCM, 1961).

Lindemann, "Der 'Äthiopische Eunuch'"
Andreas Lindemann, "Der 'Äthiopische Eunuch' und die Anfänge der Mission unter den Völkern nach Apg 8–11," in Breytenbach, *Apostelgeschichte,* 109–33.

Lipsius-Bonnet, *Acta*
Richard A. Lipsius and Maximilian Bonnet, *Acta Apostolorum Apocrypha* (2 vols.; Leipzig: Hermann Mendelssohn, 1891–1903).

Lohfink, *Conversion*
Gerhard Lohfink, *The Conversion of St. Paul: Narrative and History in Acts* (trans. Bruce J. Malina; Chicago: Franciscan Herald, 1976).

Loisy
Alfred Loisy, *Les Actes des Apôtres* (Frankfurt am Main: Minerva, 1973).

Long, "Paulusbild"
William R. Long, "The Paulusbild in the Trial of Paul in Acts," in Kent H. Richards, ed., *SBLSP 1983* (Chico, Calif.: Scholars Press, 1983) 87–105.

Löning, "Circle of Stephen"
Karl Löning, "The Circle of Stephen and Its Mission," in Jürgen Becker, ed., *Christian Beginnings: Word and Community from Jesus to Post-Apostolic Times* (trans. A. S. Kidder and R. Krauss; Louisville: Westminster John Knox, 1993) 103–31.

Löning, *Saulustradition*
Karl Löning, *Die Saulustradition in der Apostelgeschichte* (NTAbh 9; Münster: Aschendorff, 1973).

Lüdemann
Gerd Lüdemann, *Early Christianity according to the Traditions in Acts* (trans. John Bowden; Philadelphia: Fortress Press, 1989).

Lüdemann, *Acts*
Gerd Lüdemann, *The Acts of the Apostles: What Really Happened in the Earliest Days of the Church* (Amherst, N.Y.: Prometheus Books, 2005).

Lüdemann, *Opposition*
Gerd Lüdemann, *Opposition to Paul in Jewish Christianity* (trans. M. Eugene Boring; Minneapolis: Fortress Press, 1989).

MacDonald, *Imitate Homer*
Dennis R. MacDonald, *Does the New Testament Imitate Homer? Four Cases from the Acts of the Apostles* (New Haven: Yale University Press, 2003).

MacDonald, "Shipwrecks"
Dennis R. MacDonald, "The Shipwrecks of Odysseus and Paul," *NTS* 45 (1999) 88–107.

Mack, *Rhetoric*
Burton L. Mack, *Rhetoric and the New Testament* (GBS; Minneapolis: Fortress Press, 1990).

MacMullen, *Enemies*
Ramsay MacMullen, *Enemies of the Roman Order: Treason, Unrest, and Alienation in the Empire* (Cambridge, Mass.: Harvard University Press, 1966).

MacMullen, *Paganism*
Ramsay MacMullen, *Paganism in the Roman Empire* (New Haven: Yale University Press, 1981).

Magie, *Roman Rule*
David Magie, *Roman Rule in Asia Minor to the End of the Third Century after Christ* (2 vols.; Princeton: Princeton University Press, 1950).

Malherbe, "Corner"
Abraham Malherbe, "'Not in a Corner'": Early Christian Apologetic in Acts 26:26," *SecCent* 5 (1985–86) 193–210.

Malherbe, *Paul*
Abraham J. Malherbe, *Paul and the Popular Philosophers* (Minneapolis: Fortress Press, 1989).

Malherbe, *Thessalonians*
Abraham J. Malherbe, *The Letters to the Thessalonians* (AB 32B; New York: Doubleday, 2000).

Malina and Neyrey, *Portraits*
Bruce J. Malina and Jerome H. Neyrey, *Portraits of Paul: An Archaeology of Ancient Personality* (Louisville: Westminster John Knox, 1996).

Marguerat, *Historian*
Daniel Marguerat, *The First Christian Historian: Writing the "Acts of the Apostles"* (trans. Ken McKinney et al.; SNTSMS 121; Cambridge: Cambridge University Press, 2002).

Matson, *Household Conversion*
David L. Matson, *Household Conversion Narratives in Acts: Pattern and Interpretation* (JSNTS 123; Sheffield: Sheffield Academic Press, 1996).

Matthews, *First Converts*
Shelly Matthews, *First Converts: Rich Pagan Women and the Rhetoric of Mission in Early Judaism and Christianity* (Stanford: Stanford University Press, 2001).

Mealand, "Close"
David L. Mealand, "The Close of Acts and Its Hellenistic Greek Vocabulary," *NTS* 36 (1990) 583–97.

Metzger, *Textual Commentary*
Bruce Metzger, ed., *A Textual Commentary on the Greek New Testament* (2nd ed.; New York: American Bible Society, 1994).

Meyers, *Women*
Carol Meyers et al., eds., *Women in Scripture* (New York: Houghton Mifflin, 2000).

Millar, *Emperor*
Fergus Millar, *The Emperor in the Roman World* (Ithaca: Cornell University Press, 1977).

Millar, *Near East*
Fergus Millar, *The Roman Near East: 31 BC–AD 337* (Cambridge, Mass.: Harvard University Press, 1993).

Miller, *Convinced*
John B. F. Miller, *Convinced That God Had Called Us: Dreams, Visions, and the Perception of God's Will in Luke-Acts* (BIS 85; Leiden: Brill, 2007).

Moessner, *Heritage*
David P. Moessner, ed., *Jesus and the Heritage of Israel: Luke's Narrative Claim upon Israel's Legacy* (Harrisburg, Pa.: Trinity Press International, 1999).

Moule, *Idiom Book*
Charles F. D. Moule, *An Idiom Book of New Testament Greek* (2nd ed.; Cambridge: Cambridge University Press, 1963).

Moule, *Miracles*
Charles F. D. Moule, ed., *Miracles: Cambridge Studies in Their Philosophy and History* (London: Mowbray, 1965).

Moulton, *Grammar*
James H. Moulton, *A Grammar of New Testament Greek* (3rd ed.; 4 vols.; Edinburgh: T&T Clark, 1908–76).

Murphy-O'Connor, *Saint Paul's Corinth*
Jerome Murphy-O'Connor, *Saint Paul's Corinth* (GNS 6; Wilmington, Del.: Glazier, 1983).

Musurillo, *Christian*
Herbert Musurillo, *The Acts of the Christian Martyrs* (Oxford: Clarendon, 1972).

Musurillo, *Pagan*
Herbert Musurillo, *The Acts of the Pagan Martyrs* (Oxford: Clarendon, 1954).

Myllykoski, "Being There"
Matti Myllykoski, "Being There: The Function of the Supernatural in Acts 1–12," in Labahn and Peerbolte, *Wonders*, 146–79.

Neyrey, "Acts 17"
Jerome H. Neyrey, "Acts 17, Epicureans and Theodicy: A Study in Stereotypes," in David Balch et al., eds., *Greeks, Romans, and Christians: Essays in Honor of Abraham J. Malherbe* (Minneapolis: Fortress Press, 1990) 118–34.

Neyrey, "Forensic Defense Speech"
Jerome H. Neyrey, "The Forensic Defense Speech and Paul's Trial Speeches in Acts 22–26," in Talbert, *Luke-Acts,* 210–24.

Neyrey, *Social World*
Jerome H. Neyrey, ed., *The Social World of Luke-Acts: Models for Interpretation* (Peabody, Mass.: Hendrickson, 1991).

Neyrey, "Symbolic Universe"
Jerome H. Neyrey, "The Symbolic Universe of Luke-Acts: 'They Turn the World Upside Down,'" in Neyrey, *Social World,* 271–304.

Nicklas and Tilly, *Book of Acts*
Tobias Nicklas and Michael Tilly, eds., *The Book of Acts as Church History: Textual Traditions and Ancient Interpretations* (BZNW 120; Berlin: de Gruyter, 2003).

Nickle, *The Collection*
Keith F. Nickle, *The Collection: A Study in Paul's Strategy* (SBT 48; Naperville, Ill.: Allenson, 1966).

Nippel, *Public Order*
Wilfried Nippel, *Public Order in Ancient Rome* (Key Themes in Ancient History; Cambridge: Cambridge University Press, 1995).

Nock, *Conversion*
Arthur Darby Nock, *Conversion: The Old and the New in Religion from Alexander the Great to Augustine of Hippo* (London/New York: Oxford University Press, 1961).

Nock, *Essays*
Arthur Darby Nock, *Essays on Religion and the Ancient World* (ed. Zeph Stewart; 2 vols.; Cambridge, Mass.: Harvard University Press, 1972).

Nock, "Paul and the Magus"
Arthur Darby Nock, "Paul and the Magus," in Lake and Cadbury, *Additional Notes,* 164–88 (= *Essays,* 1:308–30).

Norden, *Agnostos Theos*
Eduard Norden, *Agnostos Theos: Untersuchungen zur Formengeschichte Religiöser Rede* (1913; reprinted, Darmstadt: Wissenschaftliche Buchgesellschaft, 1974).

O'Collins and Marconi, *Luke and Acts*
Gerald O'Collins and Gilberto Marconi, eds., *Luke and Acts* (Festschrift Emilio Rasco; trans. Matthew J. O'Connell; New York: Paulist, 1993).

Ollrog, *Paulus*
Wolf-Henning Ollrog, *Paulus und seine Mitarbeiter* (WMANT 50; Neukirchen-Vluyn: Neukirchener Verlag, 1979).

Omerzu, *Prozess*
Heike Omerzu, *Der Prozess des Paulus: Eine exegetische und rechtshistorische Untersuchung der Apostelgeschichte* (BZNW 115; Berlin: de Gruyter, 2002).

O'Toole, *Unity*
Robert F. O'Toole, *The Unity of Luke's Theology: An Analysis of Luke-Acts* (GNS 9; Wilmington, Del.: Michael Glazier, 1984).

Painter, *Just James*
John Painter, *Just James: The Brother of Jesus in History and Tradition* (Columbia: University of South Carolina Press, 1997).

Parsons, *Body and Character*
Mikeal C. Parsons, *Body and Character in Luke and Acts: The Subversion of Physiognomy in Early Christianity* (Grand Rapids: Baker Academic, 2006).

Parsons, *Departure*
Mikeal C. Parsons, *The Departure of Jesus in Luke-Acts: The Ascension Narratives in Context* (JSNTS 21; Sheffield: Sheffield Academic Press, 1987).

Parsons and Pervo, *Rethinking*
Mikeal C. Parsons and Richard I. Pervo, *Rethinking the Unity of Luke and Acts* (Minneapolis: Fortress Press, 1993).

Pattengale, "Berea"
Jerry A. Pattengale, "Berea," *ABD* 1:675.

Pease, *Natura*
Arthur Stanley Pease, ed., *M. Tulli Ciceronis De Natura Deorum* (2 vols.; Cambridge, Mass.: Harvard University Press, 1958).

Penner, *Contextualizing*
Todd Penner and Caroline Vander Stichele, *Contextualizing Acts: Lukan Narrative and Greco-Roman Discourse* (SBLSS 20; Boston/Leiden: Brill; Atlanta: SBL, 2004).

Penner, "Madness"
Todd Penner, "Madness in the Method? The Acts of the Apostles in Current Study," *CBR* 2 (2004) 223–93.

Penner, *Praise*
Todd Penner, *In Praise of Christian Origins: Stephen and the Hellenists in Lukan Apologetic Historiography* (Emory Studies in Early Christianity 10; New York: T&T Clark, 2004).

Pervo, *Dating*
Richard Pervo, *Dating Acts: Between the Evangelists and the Apologists* (Santa Rosa, Calif.: Polebridge, 2006).

Pervo, "Happy Home"
Richard Pervo, "My Happy Home: The Role of Jerusalem in Acts 1–7," *Forum* n.s. 3.1 (2000) 31–55.

Pervo, "Hard Act"
Richard Pervo, "A Hard Act to Follow: *The Acts of Paul* and the Canonical Acts," *JHC* 2 (1995) 3–32.

Pervo, *Luke's Story*
Richard Pervo, *Luke's Story of Paul* (Minneapolis: Fortress Press, 1990).
Pervo, "Meet Right"
Richard Pervo, "Meet Right–and Our Bounden Duty," *Forum* n.s. 4.1 (Spring 2000) 45–62.
Pervo, "ΠΑΝΤΑ ΚΟΙΝΑ"
Richard Pervo, "ΠΑΝΤΑ ΚΟΙΝΑ: The Feeding Stories in the Light of Economic Data and Social Practice," in Lukas Bormann et al., eds., *Religious Propaganda and Missionary Competition in the New Testament World: Essays Honoring Dieter Georgi* (NovTSup 74; Leiden: Brill, 1994) 164–94.
Pervo, *Profit*
Richard Pervo, *Profit with Delight: The Literary Genre of the Acts of the Apostles* (Philadelphia: Fortress Press, 1987).
Pervo, "Social Aspects"
Richard Pervo, "Social and Religious Aspects of the Western Text," in Dennis Groh and Robert Jewett, eds., *The Living Text: Essays in Honor of Ernest W. Saunders* (Lanham, Md.: University Press of America, 1985) 229–41.
Pervo, "Wisdom and Power"
Richard Pervo, "Wisdom and Power: Petronius' *Satyricon* and the Social World of Early Christianity," *ATR* 67 (1985) 307–25.
Peterson, ΕΙΣ ΘΕΟΣ
Erik Peterson, ΕΙΣ ΘΕΟΣ: *Epigraphische, formgeschichtliche und religionsgeschichtliche Untersuchungen* (FRLANT 41; Göttingen: Vandenhoeck & Ruprecht, 1926).
Phillips, *Acts and Ethics*
Thomas E. Phillips, ed., *Acts and Ethics* (NTMon 9; Sheffield: Sheffield Phoenix, 2005).
Plümacher, *Lukas*
Eckhard Plümacher, *Lukas als hellenistischer Schriftsteller: Studien zur Apostelgeschichte* (SUNT 9; Göttingen: Vandenhoeck & Ruprecht, 1972).
Polhill
John B. Polhill, *Acts* (NAC 26; Nashville: Broadman, 1992).
Porter, *Paul of Acts*
Stanley E. Porter, *The Paul of Acts* (WUNT 115; Tübingen: Mohr Siebeck, 1999).
Porton, "Sadducees"
Gary G. Porton, "Sadducees," *ABD* 5:892–95.
Praeder, "Acts 27"
Susan Marie Praeder, "Acts 27:1–28:16: Sea Voyages in Ancient Literature and the Theology of Luke-Acts," *CBQ* 46 (1984) 683–706.
Praeder, "Parallelisms"
Susan Marie Praeder, "Jesus-Paul, Peter-Paul, and Jesus-Peter Parallelisms in Luke-Acts: A History of Reader Response," in *SBLSP 1984* (Chico, Calif.: Scholars Press, 1984) 23–39.
Praeder, "Problem"
Susan Marie Praeder, "The Problem of First Person Narration in Acts," *NovT* 39 (1987) 193–218.
Preuschen
Erwin Preuschen, *Die Apostelgeschichte* (HNT; Tübingen: Mohr Siebeck, 1912).
Price, *Widow Traditions*
Robert M. Price, *The Widow Traditions in Luke-Acts: A Feminist-Critical Scrutiny* (SBLDS 155; Atlanta: Scholars Press, 1997).
Rackham
Richard B. Rackham, *The Acts of the Apostles* (2nd ed.; London: Methuen, 1904).
Radl, "Befreiung"
Walter Radl, "Befreiung aus dem Gefängnis: Die Darstellung eines biblischen Grundthemas in Apg 12," *BZ* 27 (1983) 81–96.
Radl, *Paulus*
Walter Radl, *Paulus und Jesus im lukanischen Doppelwerk: Untersuchungen zu Parallelmotiven im Lukasevangelium und in der Apostelgeschichte* (Europäische Hochschulschriften 23/49; Frankfurt: Peter Lang, 1975).
Ramsay, *Church*
William M. Ramsay, *The Church in the Roman Empire* (London: Hodder & Stoughton, 1897).
Ramsay, *Cities*
William M. Ramsay, *The Cities of St. Paul: Their Influence on His Life and Thought* (London: Hodder & Stoughton, 1907).
Ramsay, *St. Paul the Traveller*
William M. Ramsay, *St. Paul the Traveller and the Roman Citizen* (London: Hodder & Stoughton, 1897).
Rapske, *Roman Custody*
Brian Rapske, *The Book of Acts and Paul in Roman Custody* (BIFCS 3; Grand Rapids: Eerdmans, 1994).
Rapske, "Travel"
Brian Rapske, "Acts, Travel and Shipwreck," in Gill and Gempf, *Setting*, 1–47.
Reardon, *Novels*
Brian P. Reardon, *Collected Ancient Greek Novels* (Berkeley: University of California Press, 1989).
Reimer, "Virtual Prison Breaks"
Andy M. Reimer, "Virtual Prison Breaks: Non-Escape Narratives and the Definition of 'Magic,'" in Todd E. Klutz, ed., *Magic in the Biblical World: From the Rod of Aaron to the Ring of Solomon* (JSNTS 245; London: T&T Clark, 2003) 125–39.
Reitzenstein, *Hellenistische Wundererzählungen*
Richard Reitzenstein, *Hellenistische Wundererzählungen* (Leipzig: Teubner, 1906).
Reynolds and Tannenbaum, *Jews and Godfearers*
Joyce Reynolds and Robert Tannenbaum, *Jews and Godfearers at Aphrodisias* (Cambridge Philological Society Supp. 12; Cambridge: Cambridge University Press, 1987).
Richard, *Acts 6*
Earl Richard, *Acts 6:1–8:4: The Author's Method of Composition* (SBLDS 41; Missoula, Mont.: Scholars Press, 1978).

Richard, "Polemical Character"
Earl Richard, "The Polemical Character of the Joseph Episode in Acts 7," *JBL* 98 (1979) 255–67.

Richter Reimer, *Women*
Ivoni Richter Reimer, *Women in the Acts of the Apostles: A Feminist Liberation Perspective* (trans. Linda M. Maloney; Minneapolis: Fortress Press, 1995).

Robbins, "Social Location"
Vernon K. Robbins, "The Social Location of the Implied Author of Luke-Acts," in Neyrey, *Social World,* 305–32.

Robinson and Koester, *Trajectories*
James M. Robinson and Helmut Koester, *Trajectories through Early Christianity* (Philadelphia: Fortress Press, 1971).

Rohde, *Psyche*
Erwin Rohde, *Psyche: The Cult of Souls and Belief in Immortality among the Greeks* (trans. W. B. Hillis; London: Routledge & Kegan Paul, 1925).

Roloff
Jürgen Roloff, *Die Apostelgeschichte* (NTD 5; Göttingen: Vandenhoeck & Ruprecht, 1981).

Romm, *Edges of the Earth*
James S. Romm, *The Edges of the Earth in Ancient Thought* (Princeton: Princeton University Press, 1992).

Ropes, *Text*
James Hardy Ropes, *The Text of Acts,* vol. 3 of Foakes Jackson and Lake, *Beg.*

Rothschild, *Rhetoric*
Clare K. Rothschild, *Luke-Acts and the Rhetoric of History: An Investigation of Early Christian Historiography* (WUNT 2.175; Tübingen: Mohr Siebeck, 2004).

Rudolph, *Gnosis*
Kurt Rudolph, *Gnosis: The Nature and History of Gnosticism* (trans. and ed. R. McL. Wilson; San Francisco: Harper & Row, 1983).

Sabbe, "Son of Man"
M. Sabbe, "The Son of Man Saying in Acts 7,56," in Kremer, *Actes,* 241–76.

Saddington, "Roman Military"
Dennis Bain Saddington, "Roman Military and Administrative Personnel in the New Testament," *ANRW* 2.26.3 (1996) 2409–35.

Sanders, *Jews*
Jack T. Sanders, *The Jews in Luke-Acts* (Philadelphia: Fortress Press, 1987).

Schenke, *Apostelgeschichte 1,1–15,3*
Hans-Martin Schenke, *Apostelgeschichte 1,1–15,3 im mittelägyptischen Dialekt des koptischen (Codex Glazier)* (TU 137; Berlin: Akademie, 1991).

Schnackenburg, *Ephesians*
Rudolf Schnackenburg, *Ephesians: A Commentary* (trans. H. Heron; Edinburgh: T&T Clark, 1991).

Schneider
Gerhard Schneider, *Die Apostelgeschichte* (2 vols.; HThK 5; Freiburg: Herder & Herder, 1980, 1982).

Schoedel, *Ignatius*
William R. Schoedel, *Ignatius of Antioch* (Hermeneia; Philadelphia: Fortress Press, 1985).

Schürer, *History*
Emil Schürer, *History of the Jewish People in the Age of Jesus Christ (175 B.C.–A.D. 135)* (rev. and ed. Geza Vermes and Fergus Millar; 2 vols.; Edinburgh: T&T Clark, 1973–87).

Schüssler Fiorenza, *Aspects*
Elisabeth Schüssler Fiorenza, ed., *Aspects of Religious Propaganda in Judaism and Early Christianity* (Notre Dame, Ind.: University of Notre Dame Press, 1976).

Schüssler Fiorenza, *Memory*
Elisabeth Schüssler Fiorenza, *In Memory of Her: A Feminist Theological Reconstruction of Christian Origins* (New York: Crossroad, 1983).

Schüssler Fiorenza, "Miracles, Mission"
Elisabeth Schüssler Fiorenza, "Miracles, Mission, and Apologetics: An Introduction," in Schüssler Fiorenza, *Aspects,* 1–25.

Schwartz, *Agrippa I*
Daniel R. Schwartz, *Agrippa I: The Last King of Judaea* (TSAJ 23; Tübingen: Mohr Siebeck, 1990).

Schwartz, "Trial Scene"
Saundra Schwartz, "The Trial Scene in the Greek Novels and in Acts," in Penner, *Contextualizing,* 105–37.

Scott, "Geographical Horizon"
James M. Scott, "Luke's Geographical Horizon," in Gill and Gempf, *Setting,* 483–544.

Seim, *Double Message*
Turid Karlsen Seim, *The Double Message: Patterns of Gender in Luke and Acts* (Nashville: Abingdon, 1994).

Selinger, "Demetriosunruhen"
R. Selinger, "Die Demetriosunruhen (Apg 19,23-40): Eine Fallstudie aus rechtshistorischer Perspektive," *ZNW* 88 (1997) 242–59.

Shauf, *Theology*
Scott Shauf, *Theology as History, History as Theology: Paul in Ephesus in Acts 19* (BZNW 133; Berlin: de Gruyter, 2005).

Sherwin-White, *Roman Society*
Adrian N. Sherwin-White, *Roman Society and Roman Law in the New Testament* (Oxford: Clarendon, 1963).

Skinner, *Locating*
Matthew L. Skinner, *Locating Paul: Places of Custody as Narrative Settings in Acts 21–28* (SBL Academia Biblica 13; Atlanta: SBL, 2003).

Slingerland, "Acts 18:1–18"
Dixon Slingerland, "Acts 18:1-18, the Gallio Inscription, and Absolute Pauline Chronology," *JBL* 110 (1991) 439–49.

Smallwood, *The Jews*
E. Mary Smallwood, *The Jews under Roman Rule: From Pompey to Diocletian* (SJLA 20; Leiden: Brill, 1976).

Smith, *Voyage*
James Smith, *The Voyage and Shipwreck of St. Paul* (4th ed.; London: Longmans, Green, 1880).
Smyth, *Greek Grammar*
Herbert Weir Smyth, *Greek Grammar* (rev. G. M. Messing; Cambridge, Mass.: Harvard University Press, 1956).
Soards, *Speeches*
Marion L. Soards, *The Speeches in Acts: Their Content, Context, and Concerns* (Louisville: Westminster John Knox, 1994).
Söder, *Apokryphen Apostelgeschichten*
Rosa Söder, *Die apokryphen Apostelgeschichten und die romanhafte Literatur der Antike* (Stuttgart: Kohlhammer, 1932).
Spencer, *Portrait*
F. Scott Spencer, *The Portrait of Philip in Acts* (JSNTS 67; Sheffield: JSOT Press, 1992).
Spencer, "Wise Up"
F. Scott Spencer, "Wise Up, Young Man: The Moral Vision of Saul and Other νεανίσκοι in Acts," in Phillips, *Acts and Ethics*, 34–48.
Spencer, "Women"
F. Scott Spencer, "Women of 'the Cloth' in Acts: Sewing the Word," in Levine, *Feminist Companion*, 134–54.
Spicq, *Lexicon*
Ceslas Spicq, *Theological Lexicon of the New Testament* (3 vols.; trans. and ed. J. D. Ernest; Peabody, Mass.: Hendrickson, 1994).
Squires, *Plan*
John T. Squires, *The Plan of God in Luke-Acts* (SNTSMS 76; Cambridge/New York: Cambridge University Press, 1993).
Stegemann, "Bürger"
Wolfgang Stegemann, "War der Apostel Paulus ein römischer Bürger?" *ZNW* 78 (1987) 200–29.
Stenschke, *Gentiles*
Christoph W. Stenschke, *Luke's Portrait of Gentiles Prior to Their Coming to Faith* (WUNT 108; Tübingen: Mohr Siebeck, 1999).
Stephens and Winkler, *Greek Novels*
Susan A. Stephens and John J. Winkler, eds., *Ancient Greek Novels: The Fragments* (Princeton: Princeton University Press, 1995).
Sterling, *Apologetic Historiography*
Gregory Sterling, *Historiography and Self-Definition: Josephos, Luke-Acts and Apologetic Historiography* (NovTSup 64; Leiden: Brill, 1992).
Sterling, "Athletes of Virtue"
Gregory E. Sterling, "'Athletes of Virtue': An Analysis of the Summaries in Acts (2:41-47; 4:32-34; 5:12-16)," *JBL* 113 (1994) 679–96.
Stern, *Authors*
Menahem Stern, *Greek and Latin Authors on Jews and Judaism* (3 vols.; Jerusalem: Israel Academy of Sciences, 1974–84).
Stoops, "Riot"
Robert F. Stoops Jr., "Riot and Assembly: The Social Context of Acts 19:23-41," *JBL* 108 (1989) 73–91.
Strange, *Problem*
William A. Strange, *The Problem of the Text of Acts* (SNTSMS 71; Cambridge: Cambridge University Press, 1992).
Swanson, *Manuscripts*
Reuben Swanson, ed., *New Testament Greek Manuscripts: The Acts of the Apostles* (Sheffield: Sheffield Academic Press, 1998).
Tajra, *Martyrdom*
Harry W. Tajra, *The Martyrdom of St. Paul: Historical and Judicial Context, Traditions, and Legends* (WUNT 2.67; Tübingen: Mohr Siebeck, 1994).
Tajra, *Trial*
Harry W. Tajra, *The Trial of St. Paul: A Juridical Exegesis of the Second Half of the Acts of the Apostles* (WUNT 35; Tübingen: Mohr Siebeck, 1989).
Talbert
Charles H. Talbert, *Reading Acts: A Literary and Theological Commentary on the Acts of the Apostles* (Reading the New Testament; New York: Crossroad, 1997).
Talbert, *Literary Patterns*
Charles H. Talbert, *Literary Patterns, Theological Themes, and the Genre of Luke-Acts* (SBLMS 20; Missoula, Mont.: Scholars Press, 1974).
Talbert, *Luke-Acts*
Charles H. Talbert, ed., *Luke-Acts* (New York: Crossroad, 1984).
Talbert, *Perspectives*
Charles H. Talbert, ed., *Perspectives on Luke-Acts* (Danville, Va.: National Association of Baptist Professors of Religion, 1978).
Talbert and Hayes, "A Theology"
Charles H. Talbert and John H. Hayes, "A Theology of Sea Storms in Luke-Acts," *SBLSP 1995* (Atlanta: Scholars Press, 1995) 321–36.
Tannehill, *Narrative Unity*
Robert C. Tannehill, *The Narrative Unity of Luke-Acts: A Literary Interpretation* (2 vols.; Philadelphia/Minneapolis: Fortress Press, 1986, 1990).
Taylor, "St Paul"
Justin Taylor, "St Paul and the Roman Empire: Acts of the Apostles 13–14," *ANRW* 2.26.2 (1995) 1190–1231.
Theissen, *Miracle Stories*
Gerd Theissen, *Miracle Stories of the Early Christian Tradition* (trans. Francis McDonagh; ed. John Riches; Edinburgh: T&T Clark, 1983).
Thomas, "At Home"
Christine M. Thomas, "At Home in the City of Artemis: Religion in Ephesos in the Literary Imagination of the Roman Period," in Koester, *Ephesos*, 81–117.
Thompson, *Literary Studies*
Richard Thompson, ed., *Literary Studies in Luke-Acts: Essays in Honor of Joseph B. Tyson* (Macon, Ga.: Mercer University Press, 1998).

Thornton, *Der Zeuge*
C.-J. Thornton, *Der Zeuge des Zeugen: Lukas als Historiker der Paulusreisen* (WUNT 56; Tübingen: Mohr Siebeck, 1991).

Trebilco, "Asia"
Paul R. Trebilco, "Asia," Gill and Gempf, *Setting*, 291–362.

Trebilco, *Early Christians*
Paul R. Trebilco, *The Early Christians in Ephesus from Paul to Ignatius* (WUNT 166; Tübingen: Mohr Siebeck, 2004).

Trebilco, *Jewish Communities*
Paul R. Trebilco, *Jewish Communities in Asia Minor* (SNTSMS 60; Cambridge: Cambridge University Press, 1991).

Trocmé, *Actes et l'histoire*
Étienne Trocmé, *Le livre des Actes et l'histoire* (EHPR 45; Paris: Presses Universitaires de France, 1957).

Turner, *Power*
Max Turner, *Power from on High: The Spirit in Israel's Restoration and Witness in Luke Acts* (Journal of Pentecostal Theology Supplement Series 9; Sheffield: Sheffield Academic Press, 1996).

Turner, *Style*
Nigel Turner, *Style*, vol. 4 of James H. Moulton, *A Grammar of New Testament Greek* (3rd ed.; 4 vols.; Edinburgh: T&T Clark, 1908–76).

Tyson, *Images*
Joseph B. Tyson, *Images of Judaism in Luke-Acts* (Columbia: University of South Carolina Press, 1992).

Tyson, "The Problem of Food"
Joseph B. Tyson, "The Problem of Food in Acts: A Study of Literary Patterns with Particular Reference to Acts 6:1-7," in *SBLSP 1979* (Missoula, Mont.: Scholars Press, 1979) 69–85.

Verheyden, *Unity*
Jozef Verheyden, ed., *The Unity of Luke-Acts* (BEThL 92; Leuven: Leuven University Press, 1999).

Vielhauer, "Paulinism"
Philipp Vielhauer, "On the 'Paulinism' of Acts," in Keck and Martyn, *Studies*, 33–51.

Wall, "Successors"
Robert W. Wall, "Successors to 'the Twelve' according to Acts 12:1-17," *CBQ* 53 (1991) 628–43.

Walton, *Leadership*
Steve Walton, *Leadership and Lifestyle: The Portrait of Paul in the Miletus Speech and I Thessalonians* (SNTSMS 108; Cambridge: Cambridge University Press, 2000).

Weaver, *Plots*
John B. Weaver, *Plots of Epiphany: Prison Escape in Acts of the Apostles* (BZNW 131; Berlin: de Gruyter, 2004).

Wedderburn, "Dilemma"
Alexander J. M. Wedderburn, "The 'We'-Passages in Acts: On the Horns of a Dilemma," *ZNW* 93 (2002) 78–98.

Wehnert, *Die Wir-Passagen*
Jürgen Wehnert, *Die Wir-Passagen der Apostelgeschichte: Ein lukanisches Stilmittel aus jüdischer Tradition* (Göttingen: Vandenhoeck & Ruprecht, 1989).

Weiser
Alfons Weiser, *Die Apostelgeschichte* (2 vols.; ÖKTNT 5.1/2; Gütersloh: Mohn, 1981, 1985).

Wellhausen, *Kritische Analyse*
Julius Wellhausen, *Kritische Analyse der Apostelgeschichte* (Abhandlungen der Königlichen Gesellschaft der Wissenschaften zu Göttingen, Phil.-Hist. Klasse, NF 15.2; Berlin: Töpelmann, 1914).

Wendt
Hans H. Wendt, *Die Apostelgeschichte* (9th ed.; KEK; Göttingen: Vandenhoeck & Ruprecht, 1913).

Wikenhauser, *Geschichtswert*
Alfred Wikenhauser, *Die Apostelgeschichte und ihr Geschichtswert* (NTAbh; Münster: Aschendorff, 1921).

Wilckens, *Missionsreden*
Ulrich Wilckens, *Die Missionsreden der Apostelgeschichte: Form- und Traditionsgeschichtliche Untersuchungen* (WMANT 5; 2nd ed.; Neukirchen-Vluyn: Neukirchener Verlag, 1963).

Williams, "Personal Names"
Margaret H. Williams, "Palestinian Jewish Personal Names in Acts," in Bauckham, *Palestinian Setting*, 79–113.

Wills, *Jewish Novel*
Lawrence M. Wills, *The Jewish Novel in the Ancient World* (Ithaca: Cornell University Press, 1995).

Wilson, *Law*
Stephen G. Wilson, *Luke and the Law* (SNTSMS 50; Cambridge: Cambridge University Press, 1983).

Wilson, *Luke and the Pastoral Epistles*
Stephen G. Wilson, *Luke and the Pastoral Epistles* (London: SPCK, 1979).

Winter, "Food Shortages"
Bruce W. Winter, "Acts and Food Shortages," in Gill and Gempf, *Setting*, 59–78.

Winter, "Official Proceedings"
Bruce W. Winter, "Official Proceedings and the Forensic Speeches in Acts 24–26," in Winter and Clarke, *Setting*, 305–36.

Winter and Clarke, *Setting*
Bruce W. Winter and Andrew D. Clarke, eds., *The Book of Acts in Its Ancient Literary Setting* (BIFCS 1; Grand Rapids: Eerdmans, 1993).

Witherington
Ben Witherington, *The Acts of the Apostles: A Socio-Rhetorical Commentary* (Grand Rapids: Eerdmans, 1998).

Witherington, *History*
Ben Witherington, ed., *History, Literature and Society in the Book of Acts* (Cambridge: Cambridge University Press, 1996).

Wordelman, "Cultural Divides"
Amy L. Wordelman, "Cultural Divides and Dual Realities: A Greco-Roman Context for Acts 14," in Penner, *Contextualizing*, 205–32.

Zehnle, *Discourse*
Richard F. Zehnle, *Peter's Pentecost Discourse: Tradition and Lukan Reinterpretation in Peter's Speeches of Acts 2 and 3* (SBLMS 15; Nashville: Abingdon, 1971).

1. The Earliest Witnesses to Acts and Its Canonical History

The earliest explicit references to Acts appear in the *Adversus Haereses* of Irenaeus (c. 180), who cites the book and regards it as an authoritative composition by the author of the Gospel of Luke.[1] The *Acts of Paul* and the *Didascalia Apostolorum* quite probably knew and drew upon Acts, without attribution. The dates of these works are uncertain, but they indicate that the work existed in the middle of the second century. Polycarp of Smyrna may cite Acts (*Phil.* 1:2). This would bring the date of indirect attestation down to c. 130. It is possible that the author of the Pastoral Epistles was familiar with Acts. This book was therefore known in Asia Minor during the second quarter of the second century but did not have a strong impact in circles associated with emergent "orthodoxy" until Irenaeus seized upon its value as a weapon in the struggle against Marcion and various "Gnostic" writers and systems. This utility was not entirely accidental.

Acts played a vital role in the formation of a collection of "apostolic" writings.[2] One could argue that, for Irenaeus, Acts was the horse that drove the cart of Luke, for this book served to show the unity of the apostolic witness under the guidance of the Spirit (Irenaeus, *A.H.* esp. book 3). Although first found in the manuscript tradition as the narrative complement to the four Gospels ($\mathfrak{p}^{53}$), Acts was later associated with the letters, placed either before the Catholic Epistles or the Pauline corpus in NT MSS. All three locations testify to its role in promoting apostolicity. From the time of Irenaeus (*A.H.* 3.13.3) Acts served not only as the background to the epistles, but also, to a large degree, as a criterion for their exegesis.[3] – Placement to promote Pauline apostolicity

2. The Text

Martin Dibelius concluded his 1941 essay on the text of Acts with these comments:

> The chief purpose of this brief sketch was simply to show (1) that the textual criticism of Acts must not be restricted to the question of the evaluation of the Western text; (2) that the exegetes of Acts, instead of aiming at an explanation of many impossible readings, should rather attempt conjectural improvements of such readings; and (3) that the history of Acts before its acceptance into the New Testament entitles us to resort to such conjectures.[4]

1 The data have been thoroughly canvassed. See Andrew Gregory, *The Reception of Luke and Acts in the Period before Irenaeus* (WUNT 169; Tübingen: Mohr Siebeck, 2003). The fullest survey of data up to Irenaeus is Henry J. Cadbury, "The Tradition," in Frederick J. Foakes Jackson and Kirsopp Lake, eds., *The Beginnings of Christianity* (5 vols.; New York: Macmillan, 1920–33; reprinted Grand Rapids: Baker, 1979) 2:209–64. Charles Kingsley Barrett (*A Critical and Exegetical Commentary on the Acts of the Apostles* [2 vols.; ICC; Edinburgh: T&T Clark, 1994, 1998] 1:30–48, with further judgments in 2:42) is acute. See also Hans Conzelmann, *Acts of the Apostles: A Commentary on the Acts of the Apostles* (trans. James Limburg, A. Thomas Kraabel, and Donald H. Juel; ed. Eldon Jay Epp with Christopher R. Matthews; Hermeneia; Philadelphia: Fortress Press, 1987) xxvii–xxxii, and Ernst Haenchen, *The Acts of the Apostles: A Commentary* (trans. and ed. Bernard Noble et al.; Philadelphia: Westminster, 1971) 3–14, both with judicious comments. Gerhard Schneider (*Die Apostelgeschichte* [HThKNT 5; 2 vols.; Freiburg: Herder & Herder, 1980–82] 1:169–76) has a full set of references, without original texts.

2 See David W. Kuck, "The Use and Canonization of Acts in the Early Church," (S.T.M. thesis, Yale University, 1975); Jens Schröter, "Die Apostelgeschichte und die Entstehung des neutestamentlichen Kanons: Beobachtungen zur Kanonisierung der Apostelgeschichte und ihrer Bedeutung als kanonischer Schrift," in J.-M. Auwers and H. J. de Jonge, eds., *The Biblical Canons* (BETHL 163; Leuven: Leuven University Press, 2003) 395–429; and David E. Smith, *The Canonical Function of Acts: A Comparative Analysis* (Collegeville, Minn.: Liturgical Press, 2002).

3 On the ancient reception of Acts, see François Bovon, "The Reception of the Book of Acts in Antiquity" (forthcoming in *Contemporary Studies in Acts* [ed. Thomas E. Phillips; Macon, GA: Mercer University Press, 2009]). For a concise review of reception up to the Enlightenment, see Schneider, 1:176–82.

4 Martin Dibelius, *Studies in the Acts of the Apostles* (trans. Mary Ling and Paul Schubert; ed. Heinrich Greeven; New York: Charles Scribner's Sons, 1956) 92.

The passage of two generations has not rendered his judgments obsolete. The translator of Acts soon discovers that the conventional text (N-A[27]/UBS[4]) represents what its editors view as the earliest recoverable text, based on that reading which best explains the origin of the others, rather than a fully intelligible Greek composition. This is a worthy objective, but it does not provide the translator with a finished product. In part because of the abundance of Greek evidence,[5] these editors are extremely loath to engage in conjectural emendation.[6] They also assign quite limited value to patristic and versional evidence. With both of these views this commentary disagrees.[7] Caution, unfortunately, has become a prominent characteristic of the standard editions in recent decades.[8]

The abundance of data from Greek MSS. does not exclude primitive corruption, since the base was quite slender until c. 250, a period in which many copies were lost or destroyed as a result of persecutions.[9] A full textual base derived from complete MSS. does not emerge until the fourth century CE, at which point editorial activity can be conjectured or identified.[10] Despite its patent difficulties, patristic evidence can be useful because the date, provenance, and tendencies of its sources are relatively identifiable.[11] Versions can preserve old readings eliminated from the Greek tradition by standardization. When translations representing widely separated geographic areas, such as those in Latin and Syriac, agree, the probability that they reflect a similar Greek prototype rises.

The text of Acts is less secure than that of Luke, for example. At a number of points it appears to be corrupt. Possibilities include 1:2; 2:43; 3:16; 4:25; 5:13; 6:9; 7:46; 9:25; 10:11, 30, 36; 12:25; 13:27-29, 32, 34, 43; 14:8; 15:21; 16:12, 13; 19:13-14, 25, 40; 20:6, 24, 28; 21:15-16; 22:30; 24:19; 25:13; 26:16; and 26:20. These require either conjectural emendation, resignation, or strained efforts to support unlikely readings. Explanations for the difficulties vary.[12] In the end it makes little differ-

5 James K. Elliott ("The Greek Manuscript Heritage of the Book of Acts," *FilolNT* 9 [1996] 37–50) identified 612: 13 papyri, 32 uncials, and 567 cursive MSS. His basis was Kurt Aland, ed., *Text und Textwert der griechischen Handschriften des Neuen Testaments,* vol. 3: *Die Apostelgeschichte* (Berlin: de Gruyter, 1993). Others continue to appear, such as p[112]. Barrett (1:2–15) has a useful annotated discussion of witnesses.

6 Acts 16:12 counts as a partial exception to this rule, as there is Latin support for the reading chosen. Historical considerations may have motivated this decision.

7 In light of this disagreement it would be churlish of the author to overlook the contributions of Bruce M. Metzger (who died while this section was being drafted, in February 2007), from whose textbook (*The Text of the New Testament: Its Transmission, Corruption, and Restoration* [3rd ed.; New York: Oxford University Press, 1992] he first learned to appreciate textual criticism over four decades ago, and from whose *Textual Commentary on the Greek New Testament* (2nd ed.; New York: American Bible Society, 1994) he has greatly profited. All who work with the Greek NT are deeply indebted to the vast labors of Kurt and Barbara Aland and their predecessors.

8 See Eldon Jay Epp, "The Twentieth Century Interlude in New Testament Textual Criticism," *JBL* 93 (1974) 386–414 (= idem and Gordon D. Fee, eds., *Studies in the Theory and Method of New Testament Textual Criticism* [StudDoc 45; Grand Rapids: Eerdmans, 1993] 83–108), which brought the wrath of the Alands down upon his head (Kurt Aland, "The Twentieth Century Interlude in New Testament Textual Criticism," in Ernest Best and Robert McL. Wilson, eds., *Text and Interpretation: Studies in the New Testament Presented to Matthew Black* [Cambridge: Cambridge University Press, 1979]), evoking a sequel by Epp: "A Continuing Interlude in New Testament Textual Criticism," in Epp and Fee, *Studies*, 109–23.

9 The only substantial third-century MS. witness for Acts, p[45], contains c. 261 verses from fourteen chapters, about one-quarter of the text.

10 "Alexandrian" editing, often resulting in improved Greek, is the most obvious and undisputed element of such activity.

11 Difficulties include uncertainty about whether the author erred in the citation, which may have come from memory, and the need to recognize that patristic texts have their own manuscript history.

12 One popular notion is that the author left the text unfinished, a suggestion as least as old as Adolf von Harnack, *The Acts of the Apostles* (trans J. R. Wilkinson; New York: G. P. Putnam's Sons, 1909) 48. Johannes de Zwaan developed the argument at length: "Was the Book of Acts a Posthumous Edition?" *HTR* 17 (1924) 95–153. He proposed that the writing was based on incomplete work by the writer of the Third Gospel and therefore that the final editor of Acts was not the author of Luke.

ence whether the critic determines what the author should have written or what he originally wrote.[13]

The chief textual difficulty is the existence of different editions. One hundred and fifty years of arduous labor and vigorous discussion have not resolved the questions of the so-called Western Text (hereafter D-Text),[14] a phenomenon that, although not limited to Acts, is particularly acute for this book. The prevalent view is that the D-Text of Acts is *generally* secondary. There is sufficient material with consistent qualities to label the D-Text of Acts as an "edition." The task has long been to provide explanations for (1) the origin of this edition, (2) its date and provenance, and (3) its purpose or tendency/ies.

Those who work through the most recent edition of the D-Text prepared by Marie-Émile Boismard[15] will come to doubt that the D-Text represents a single tradition or type, but one can identify enough features to postulate a profile that probably derives from a person or circle active in the mid-second century, probably in Asia Minor. That conclusion derives from the examples of D-Text readings in the *Acts of Paul* and a heightened interest in the role of the Spirit.[16] The D-Text represents, in several ways, a transition between the mentality (and theology) of the canonical Acts and its apocryphal successors.[17] From

13 NT scholars, who work with popular texts, are taught to venerate the *lectio difficilior.* Those who edit classical texts presume that their subjects were competent and seek readings that reflect literary skill. Luke is, at best, midway between a writer with a limited education and a learned author.

14 Metzger has a succinct survey of research in his *Textual Commentary*, 222–36. See also William A. Strange, *The Problem of the Text of Acts* (SNTSMS 71; Cambridge: Cambridge University Press, 1992) 1–34; and the perceptive analysis of Peter Head, "Acts and the Problem of Its Texts," in Bruce W. Winter and Andrew D. Clarke, eds., *The Book of Acts in Its Ancient Literary Setting* (BIFCS 1; Grand Rapids: Eerdmans, 1993) 415–44, esp. 415–28; Joël Delobel, "The Text of Luke-Acts: A Confrontation of Recent Theories," in Jozef Verheyden, ed., *The Unity of Luke-Acts* (BEThL 92; Leuven: Leuven University Press, 1999) 83–107; and Eldon Jay Epp, "Western Text," *ABD* 6:909–12. Almost every contribution to Tobias Nicklas and Michael Tilly, eds., *The Book of Acts as Church History: Textual Traditions and Ancient Interpretations* (BZNW 120; Berlin: de Gruyter, 2003) deals with the D-Text. See esp. Eldon Jay Epp, "Anti-Judaic Tendencies in the D-Text of Acts: Forty Years of Conversation," in Nicklas and Tilly, *Book of Acts*, 111–46, which provides a useful survey of research.

15 *Le texte occidental des actes des apôtres* (EB 40; Paris: Gabalda, 2000). The project of Marie-Émile Boismard, begun in conjunction with Arnaud Lamouille (see their *Le texte occidental des Actes des Apôtres: Reconstitution et réhabilitation* [2 vols.; Paris: Editions Recherche sur les civilizations, 1984]), is quite controversial. This work involved a complex theory dealing with the composition and editing of Luke and Acts. They have at least produced a collection of deviant readings deserving attention and have exercised, despite claims to the contrary, methodological consistency. Boismard's *Texte* claims to be fully revised and to have a more modest goal: the establishment of the precanonical text of Acts (*Texte*, 11). The revised volume prints both "Alexandrian" and "Western" texts together with a critical apparatus and offers justifications on a passage-by-passage basis, effectively shifting toward a cumulative rather than a chiefly theoretical argument. This text is translated as the D-Text throughout the commentary because it represents the most complete database for the D-Text tradition. Reservations, as the notes often indicate, may be appropriate.

16 On the Spirit in the D-Text, see, e.g., Head, "Problem," 434–35. On Asia Minor as a likely provenance of the D-Text, see Colin J. Hemer, *The Book of Acts in the Setting of Hellenistic History* (ed. Conrad J. Gempf; Winona Lake, Ind.: Eisenbrauns, 1990) 200. Barbara Aland attempted to deny that a text of this type existed in the second century: "Entstehung, Charakter und Herkunft des sog. westlichen Textes untersucht an der Apostelgeschichte," *EThL* 62 (1986) 5–65. Her case has not been sustained. Some edition(s) of the D-Text existed in the second century. It stands behind the Old Latin version and is found in Irenaeus. For evidence, see Christopher Tuckett, "How Early is the 'Western' Text of Acts?" in Nicklas and Tilly, *Book of Acts*, 69–86.

17 See Charles K. Barrett, "Is There a Theological Tendency in Codex Bezae?" in Ernest Best and Robert McL. Wilson, eds., *Text and Interpretation: Studies in the New Testament Presented to Matthew Black* (Cambridge: Cambridge University Press, 1979) 15–27, esp. 27; Dennis R. MacDonald, "Apocryphal and Canonical Narratives about Paul," in William S. Babcock, ed., *Paul and the Legacies of Paul* (Dallas: Southern Methodist University Press, 1990) 25–45;

theological[18] and ecclesiastical[19] perspectives, the D-Text keeps Acts up-to-date. This is a manifestation of the "contemporization" that was responsible for the production of Deutero-Pauline letters and editorial changes in the Pauline corpus. These indications of a date c. 150 raise nearly insuperable difficulties for hypotheses that the author is, in one way or another, responsible for both editions.[20]

Other notable and extensive qualities of this tradition are attempts to remove blemishes and to connect all the dots.[21] The basis of that activity was an early text that almost certainly retained some important readings. Eclectic textual criticism is justified in pruning away apparent additions while giving serious attention to those that do not seem to represent a deviant tendency.[22] One may anachronistically compare the production of the D-Text with that of a pedantic copy editor, in this case a careful reader (or a series of readers) mindful of error and inconsistency and eager to correct it.[23] Authors appreciate corrections of this nature, but are often less open to pedantic additions. Indeed, one of the leading merits of the D-Text is to illustrate, via contrast, the ability of Luke, who realized that authors can suggest a complete picture with a few well-chosen details, whereas excess of detail may dampen a narrative's impact.[24]

Although the D-Text is usually described as longer, largely on the basis of Codex Bezae, which in its extant sections is c. 8.5 percent longer than the conventional text, Boismard indicates a number of points at which

---

Carlo M. Martini, "La tradition textuelle des Actes des Apôtres et les tendances de l'Église ancienne," in Jacob Kremer, ed., *Les Actes des Apôtres: Traditions, redaction, théologie* (BEThL 48; Leuven: Leuven University Press, 1979) 21–35; James K. Elliott, "An Eclectic Textual Study of the Book of Acts," in Nicklas and Tilly, *Book of Acts*, 9–30, esp. 10; and István Czachesz, "The Acts of Paul and the Western Text of Luke's Acts: Paul between Canon and Apocrypha," in Jan N. Bremmer, ed., *The Apocryphal Acts of Paul and Thecla* (Kampen: Kok Pharos, 1996) 107–25. Note also Head, "Problem," 437–38.

18 Head ("Problem," 429–34) finds the christological titles of the D-Text appropriate to the mid second century. See also Bart D. Ehrman, *The Orthodox Corruption of Scripture: The Effect of Early Christological Controversies on the Text of the New Testament* (New York: Oxford University Press, 1993) 150–65.

19 Examples include 8:37 (baptismal confession) and the later forms of the "Apostolic Decree" (15:23-29). In his "Anti-Judaic Tendencies," Epp presents reasons for attributing this emphasis to the second century. Günther Zuntz ("On the Western Text of the Acts of the Apostles," in *Opuscula Selecta: Classica, Hellenistica, Christiana* [Manchester: Manchester University Press, 1972] 189–215) aptly characterizes the paradigmatic quality of many D-Text alterations. See also Richard Pervo, "Social and Religious Aspects of the Western Text," in Dennis E. Groh and Robert Jewett, eds., *The Living Text: Essays in Honor of Ernest W. Saunders* (Lanham, Md.: University Press of America, 1985) 229–41.

20 For literature on second editions in ancient literature, see Marco Frenschkowski, "Der Text der Apostelgeschichte und die Realien antiker Buchproduktion," in Nicklas and Tilly, *Book of Acts*, 87–107. Head ("Problem," 420–44) offers a review of scholarship with a penetrating critique of these theories. The notion goes back to Jean Leclerc (1685), who was also the first person to repudiate the theory. Friedrich Blass (*Acta apostolorum sive Lucae ad Theophilum liber alter: Editio philologica apparatu critico, commentario perpetuo, indice verborum illustrata* [Göttingen: Vandenhoeck & Ruprecht, 1895] 24–38) developed the idea in detail, theorizing that the D-Text was the first draft and the "Alexandrian" text a revision. He preferred a number of D-Text readings. Although initially well received (most notably by Theodor Zahn), this argument met strong criticism and fell out of favor. The Oxford thesis of Strange (*Problem*) inverted Blass: Luke marked one copy of Acts with a number of marginal notes and the like. The editions arose from copies of these autographs.

21 Examples of pedantic editing include the D-Text of 2:41-47; 3:1-9; 5:17-26; 11:20; and 12:1-3. For a general description see James Hardy Ropes, *The Text of Acts* (vol. 3 of Foakes Jackson and Lake, *Beg.*) ccxxxi–xxxii.

22 Biblical citations in the D-Text traditions, for example, are often more deviant from the LXX than are those in the conventional text and are possibly more original. Note, e.g., 2:17-21 and the citations in Stephen's speech (chap. 7).

23 On the role of the reader in manuscript alteration, see Michael W. Holmes, "Codex Bezae as a Recension of the Gospels," in D. C. Parker and C.-B. Amphoux, eds., *Codex Bezae: Studies from the Lunel Colloquium June 1994* (NTTS 22; Leiden: Brill, 1996) 123–60, esp. 145–50, and Epp, "Anti-Judaic Tendencies," 136–38.

24 If one were to take up the thesis that both texts derive from the author (see above) through a liter-

the D-Text is shorter. In most cases this is due to intentional abbreviation[25] of passages deemed unduly wordy. It is possible that the same reader/editor who expanded portions of the text abbreviated others; it is no less possible that these represent the work of different persons. At the very least it is apparent that the text of Acts could still be treated with considerable freedom in Egypt in the fifth and later centuries and that Latin texts of the D-type were sufficiently common to be used for medieval European versions.

3. The Date and Place of Composition; the Author

Acts was written c. 115 by an anonymous author whose perspective was that of Ephesus or its general environs. This date[26] is close to the end of the second generation of Deutero-Pauline activity, the era of the Apostolic Fathers and the Pastoral Epistles, when the focus was on the protection of established communities from external and internal threats.[27] The standing of believers, who may be called "Christians," in the larger society became a leading concern, for both missionary and political reasons. Rival interpretations of the Christian message constituted serious problems.

The question of provenance has become complicated.[28] The notion that one can extract from a narrative data that will indicate where it was written now seems old-fashioned, for research must deal with the concepts of an implied author and a principal narrator.[29] Sources further complicate the question, since an author who lived in Antioch, the traditional home of the author of Acts,[30] might possess a relative wealth of material about the Aegean region. If, moreover, the actual author was a companion of Paul, he lived in several places, ranging from Caesarea in Palestine to Rome in Italy, and could have done some composition or note taking in each. The proposed date rules out this last option. The actual author was not a companion of Paul.

A question that can be addressed is the geographical perspective and focus of the implied author. Ephesus suits the former and is almost certain for the latter. The Aegean region is the center of interest. There "we" (outside of 27:1–28:16) appear.[31] Whereas Cyprus and the south coast and center of Asia Minor are little more than place-names, concrete information emerges about the missions, together with dashes of local color, for Philippi, Thessalonica, Athens, Corinth, and, above all, Ephesus. Many of these data are arguably due to use of Paul's letters, but the fact of selectivity is not without force. The narrator exhibits limited knowledge about

ary lens, the D-Text would look like the first draft, skillfully cut in a subsequent revision.

25 In 27:1–28:16 the conventional text is 26.6 percent longer than Boismard's D-Text. His reconstruction of this section is subject to debate, however.

26 The argument for the period c. 110–120 is developed in Richard Pervo, *Dating Acts: Between the Evangelists and the Apologists* (Santa Rosa, CA: Polebridge, 2006). For an update, see idem, "Acts in the Suburbs of the Apologists" (forthcoming in *Contemporary Studies in Acts* [ed. Thomas E. Phillips; Macon, GA: Mercer University Press, 2009]).

27 This statement generally follows the typology presented by Margaret Y. MacDonald, *The Pauline Churches* (SNTSMS 60; Cambridge: Cambridge University Press, 1988). The projects of building, stabilizing, and protecting communities cannot be divided into impermeable categories. They serve to identify the most prominent goal. The first Deutero-Pauline generation extended from c. 65–c. 90. Ephesians stands on the border between stabilization and protection. In this period the Jesus-movement was becoming a "religion" distinct from Judaism, which was also engaged in a process of (re-)self-definition.

28 Modern commentators often ignore provenance or give it the scantiest attention (e.g., Jacob Jervell, *Die Apostelgeschichte: Übersetzt und erklärt* (KEK 17; Göttingen: Vandenhoeck & Ruprecht, 1998) 86.

29 For example, the narrator of James Joyce's *Ulysses* is located in Dublin, and readers will also place the implied author there. The actual author lived in several continental cities while writing the novel (although he had spent his first twenty-two years in Dublin and remained in contact with it).

30 The old Gospel Prologue (Kurt Aland, ed., *Synopsis Quattuor Evangeliorum* [Stuttgart: Württembergische Bibelanstalt, 1964] 532–33) characterizes the author as one Luke, an Antiochene, physician by trade, a pupil of the apostles who remained with Paul until his martyrdom and died in Boetia at age eighty-four, unmarried and childless. The Gospel was written in Greece. Acts followed. This prologue is not a unified piece and is not earlier than c. 200.

31 See the excursus "'We' in Acts," pp. 392–96.

the geography of Palestine and the interior of Asia Minor, but details about travel time in the Aegean are reasonable. Acts 19:1 speaks of "upper regions." This is the "hinterland from perspective of Ephesus."[32] Peder Borgen concludes, "The horizon of Luke-Acts may be defined as the geographical perspective of the world as seen from the standpoint of pagans, Jews, and Christians in Ephesus."[33]

Data about Ephesus not derived from the epistles include Paul's use of the "Hall of Tyrannus" (19:9), a civic assembly that meets in a theater (19:29), the cult of Artemis, whose image is of divine origin, the title "Neocoros," the "Executive Secretary" (19:35), and an organization of silversmiths (19:25). Everyone, as it were, knew about Artemis of Ephesus, but the details in Acts reflect intimate local knowledge and a desire to exploit it.

If detail suggests focus, volume goes a long way toward confirming it. Seventy verses, c. 7 percent of the text, take place in or are related to the Asian metropolis (18:19–19:40 [less 18:22-23, 28]; 20:16-38).[34] Only one site (Pisidian Antioch) receives a third as much space, and about that site the reader learns no more than that it contained a synagogue. Ephesus was the center of Paul's lengthiest mission (19:10). Ephesus also has tentacles, for Jewish pilgrims from that city incite the riot that brings about Paul's final arrest (21:27-29). More important are the tentacles trailed by Paul: Ephesus is the depository of the Pauline legacy and the center of the battleground over that inheritance (20:17-38). Paul's address to the Ephesian presbyters is a paradigm for all believers everywhere. Ephesus is the navel of the Deutero-Pauline universe, the site from which the departed Paul remains a living voice.

The actual author was likely to have lived for a considerable time in Ephesus. There one could find the *corpus Paulinum*, possibly including letters not preserved for posterity. In Ephesus one could garner oral traditions about the apostle, and somewhere in that region one could gain access to copies of Josephus's works and the sources of the Synoptic tradition. Ephesus suits the geographical perspective of Acts, is almost undoubtedly its focus, and is the most likely site of its actual provenance. The author exudes a cosmopolitan viewpoint, suitable for a major Mediterranean city.[35] Ephesus has greater probability than Antioch,[36] while Alexandria seems to be out of the question, since the author says nothing about Christian origins there. The speech in 20:17-35 indicates that Ephesus was also the primary, but not exclusive, destination of this book.

The author adopts anonymity neither out of modesty nor even in conformity with Mark, but because the name of an actual human author would seriously compromise the technique of narrative omniscience. Papias, who probably wrote closer to c. 130 than to

32 Henry J. Cadbury and Kirsopp Lake, Commentary on Acts (vol. 4 of Foakes Jackson and Lake, *Beg.*) 236.

33 Peder Borgen, *Philo, John and Paul: New Perspectives on Judaism and Early Christianity* (BJS 131; Atlanta: Scholars Press, 1987) 282; note pp. 273–85. Borgen says that Ephesus played a role for Luke similar to Alexandria for Philo. See also Karl Löning, "Paulinismus in der Apostelgeschichte," in Karl Kertelge, ed., *Paulus in den neutestamentlichen Spätschriften: Zur Paulusrezeption im Neuen Testament* (QD 89; Freiburg: Herder, 1981) 202–34, esp. 205–9.

34 Jan Lambrecht ("Paul's Farewell-Address at Miletus, Acts 20, 17–38," in Kremer, *Actes*, 307–37) says, "There can be no doubt that, in Luke's view, Ephesus dominates the whole third missionary journey of Paul" (p. 330).

35 Vernon K. Robbins, "The Social Location of the Implied Author of Luke-Acts," in Jerome H. Neyrey, ed., *The Social World of Luke-Acts: Models for Interpretation* (Peabody, MA: Hendrickson, 1991) 305–32, esp. 318.

36 Frederick F. Bruce (*The Acts of the Apostles* [3rd ed.; Grand Rapids: Eerdmans, 1990] 8–9) discusses the traditions about Antioch. Schneider (1:121) favors Antioch because of the availability of Mark. Mark was, however, also known to Papias. Arguments based on knowledge of the Christian community at Antioch can be found in August Strobel, "Lukas der Antiochener (Bemerkungen zu Act 11,28D)," *ZNW* 49 (1958) 131–34, and R. Glover, "'Luke the Antiochene' and Acts," *NTS* 11 (1964) 97–106. Because these data are sometimes in conflict with Lucan views, they are likely to stem from a source. On Antioch, see also Joseph A. Fitzmyer, *The Gospel according to Luke I–IX.* (AB 28; Garden City, N.Y.: Doubleday, 1981) 41–47.

c. 110, discussed the Gospel of Mark and, perhaps, that of Matthew (Frg. 3).[37] No information about Luke is recorded. Papias was concerned about the authenticity of the tradition. Justin was content to leave the Gospels in comfortable anonymity (*1 Apol.* 66.3). Irenaeus was not, notably in the case of Luke, whom he identified as the author of Luke and Acts and as an "inseparable companion" of Paul (*A.H.* 3.14.1).

An early researcher who presumed that the use of "we" in Acts established the author as a companion of Paul, and that this companion was probably of gentile background, could have taken note of the greetings in the imprisonment epistles. In Phlm 24 Luke is one of four. These names reappear, with expansions, in Col 4:10-14. 2 Tim 4:11 reports that "Luke alone is with me" and therefore the most likely nominee for author.[38] Two questions arise: Could this tradition be correct, and, is the tradition itself the result of deduction from these texts? With regard to the former, it is highly improbable that the author of Acts was a companion of Paul, and the textual basis is questionable, for only Philemon is undisputedly genuine. That letter (apparently) and Colossians were directed to the Lykos valley, a missionary region not discussed in Acts.

In support of the second possibility is Irenaeus, who appeals to Col 4:14 and 2 Tim 4:11 to make his case for Lucan authorship (*A.H.* 3.14.1). The earliest argument for Luke the physician and companion of Paul as the writer of Luke and Acts is based on deductions from these post-Pauline epistles. No independent or external tradition was evidently available to Irenaeus, who may have been the originator of the claim. The authorship of Luke and Acts is an element of the early orthodox synthesis. For Irenaeus, Acts, written by Luke, was crucial, for, if the author of Acts also wrote the Gospel, Marcion's understanding of Luke could not stand. Those who affirm the traditional ascription of Acts to Luke, a companion of Paul, must ask how much has been saved by retaining a Luke who was a companion of Paul but who did not trouble himself to learn about the major struggles in which Paul was engaged.[39]

Other data about the author—in fact the implied author—are inferred from his work. Limited understanding of Judaism and strong familiarity with the LXX suggest a gentile who had thoroughly immersed himself in Greek Scripture, perhaps a believer of long or even lifelong standing. Familiarity with rhetorical technique and contact with such authors as Homer and Euripides suggest an education that had progressed beyond the elementary level, but his stylistic limitations indicate that he did not reach the advanced stages. Luke, as he is conveniently denominated, had at least occasional access to a wide range of Hellenistic Jewish literature. His cosmopolitan outlook strongly suggests an urban background.

4. Language and Style

The author of Luke and Acts could write in middlebrow *Koine* Greek.[40] His greatest facility is an ability to "write like the Bible," that is, to imitate the language of the

37 For the fragments of Papias, see Bart D. Ehrman, *The Apostolic Fathers* (2 vols.; LCL; Cambridge, Mass.: Harvard University Press, 2003) 2:85–118, esp. 96–105.

38 Reference to Aristarchus in 27:2 also points investigators toward the epistles. His name is on the greeting list in Phlm 24 (and Col 4:10).

39 In the *Acts of Paul* Luke is a character in the martyrdom (11/14.1, 5, 7). In chap. 1 Luke, who had come from Gaul (or Galatia), met Paul upon the latter's arrival in Rome. He was also a witness at Paul's tomb (5–7). His role there does not support the view that he wrote the canonical book. For ancient or medieval conjectures that Clement of Rome or Barnabas wrote Acts, see Theodor Zahn, *Introduction to the New Testament* (trans. and ed. M. W. Jacobus; 3 vols.; Edinburgh: T&T Clark, 1909) 3:3 n. 1.

40 For bibliography, see Jervell, 72–76. See, in addition to the major commentaries (the fullest treatment of which is Eugène Jacquier, *Les Actes des apôtres* [2nd ed.; EB; Paris: Gabalda, 1926] clxiv–cc); Eduard Norden, *Die antike Kunstprosa* (2 vols.; 1915; reprinted Stuttgart: Teubner, 1995) 2:479–92; Henry J. Cadbury, *The Style and Literary Method of Luke* (HTS 6; Cambridge, Mass.: Harvard University Press, 1920); idem, *The Making of Luke-Acts* (1927; reprinted London: SPCK, 1958) 213–38; idem, "Four Features of Lucan Style," in Leander Keck and J. Louis Martyn, eds., *Studies in Luke-Acts: Essays Presented in Honor of Paul Schubert* (Nashville: Abingdon, 1966) 87–102; Wilfred L. Knox, *Some Hellenistic Elements in Primitive Christianity* (1942 Schweich Lectures; London: British Academy, 1944) 8–12; Loveday C. A. Alexander,

LXX, most notably in Luke 1–2.[41] He can suit style to matter. As Acts moves into the Greek world, in its second half, the quality of its Greek improves. When Paul faces a learned or elite audience, as in chaps. 17 and 26, his Greek reaches its highest point. These examples also show that, although he can deploy a few optatives and Attic idioms, Luke had difficulty when attempting to write good Greek periods. His literary ambition exceeded his ability.[42]

A parallel from prose nonfiction is the Latin biographer Cornelius Nepos, whose style and content are uneven.[43] His attempts at periodic style were generally unsuccessful, and the *Lives* are replete with historical errors and exaggerations.[44] Nepos, who can be characterized as a "popular" writer, wrote interesting stories in an easy, lucid style. From the realm of Greek prose fiction *Callirhoe* and *An Ephesian Tale* provide many interesting formal, thematic, and stylistic analogies to Acts. One candidate from the Jewish sphere is the *Biblical Antiquities* known as "Pseudo-Philo," which employs similar narrative techniques.[45] These data suggest an audience uninterested in, possibly unable to appreciate, sophisticated thought and style, or at least an audience that did not always demand such material.[46]

Among early Christian writers, Luke may be compared to the author of *1 Clement*. His literary background included a strong immersion in Greek Jewish literature, including but not limited to the LXX (which, it should be noted, displays a broad linguistic range). Receipt of a basic education is confirmed by his ability to compose speeches and letters and his familiarity with the techniques covered in those ancient rhetorical handbooks, entitled *Progymnasmata*. By one means or another, Luke learned how to organize relatively large literary projects. Negative reflection on style obscures a far from inconsiderable narrative gift. Luke is an accomplished storyteller who has learned many narrative techniques and how to deploy them with impressive skill. Although famed for notable stories, he is also able to forge these into a single, coherent narrative and thereby create (rather than simply report) a sense of historical movement.[47]

Skills include the ability to build suspense through various means, to tell the same story *n* times without apparent repetition, to evoke atmosphere with a single

Acts in Its Ancient Literary Context: A Classicist Looks at the Acts of the Apostles (LNTS 298; London: T&T Clark, 2005) 231–52. Note also James H. Moulton, *A Grammar of New Testament Greek* (3rd ed.; 4 vols.; Edinburgh: T&T Clark, 1908–76) vol. 4: *Style* (by Nigel Turner) 45–63; and Gerard Mussies, "Variation in the Book of Acts," *FilolNT* 4 (1991) 165–82; and idem, "Variation in the Book of Acts (Part II)," *FilolNT* 8 (1995) 23–61.

41 The classic study of Lucan imitation of the LXX, which can be related to the culture of *mimesis* (imitation), is Eckhard Plümacher, *Lukas als hellenistischer Schriftsteller: Studien zur Apostelgeschichte* (SUNT 9; Göttingen: Vandenhoeck & Ruprecht, 1972) 38–72. See also Cadbury, *Making,* 219–24; W. K. L. Clarke, "The Use of the Septuagint in Acts," in Foakes Jackson and Lake, *Beg.* 2:66–105; Turner, *Style,* 56–57; Haenchen, 73–81; and Fitzmyer, *Luke I–IX*, 107–25.

42 BDF §485: "Acts is indeed excellent in structure and arrangement, but in presentation strongly 'amateurish' (ἰδιωτικὴ φράσις in contrast to τεχνική)." One example of this overreaching is the use of relative clauses as main clauses. Haenchen (139 n. 7) lists these examples: 1:3, 11; 2:24; 3:2, 3, 21; 5:36; 6:6; 7:20, 39, 45, 46; 8:15; 9:39; 10:38, 40; 11:6, 23, 30; 12:4, 31, 43; 14:9, 16; 16:2, 14, 24; 17:10; 18:27; 19:25; 21:4, 32; 22:4, 5; 23:14, 29, 23; 24:18, 19; 25:16, 18, 26; 26:7, 10, 12, 19; 27:17; 28:8, 10, 14, 18, 23.

43 For the following, see Edna Jenkinson, "Nepos—An Introduction to Latin Biography," in Thomas A. Dorey, ed., *Latin Biography* (New York: Basic Books, 1967) 1–15.

44 *Lives* 25.16.4 reports that Cicero was a true prophet of future events.

45 See Eckart Reinmuth, *Pseudo-Philo und Lukas: Studien zum Liber Antiquitatum Biblicarum* (Tübingen: Mohr Siebeck, 1994). Parallels may also be found in various Lives of the Prophets. See Anna Maria Schwemer, *Studien zu den frühjüdischen Prophetenlegenden Vitae Prophetarum* (2 vols.; TSAJ 49; Tübingen: Mohr Siebeck, 1996).

46 Even today, it is rumored, the highly educated may, from time to time, dip into a light mystery. They are unlikely to claim that Agatha Christie is great literature, whereas a person of more limited schooling might feel proud of such accomplishments.

47 See Luke T. Johnson, "Luke-Acts, Book of," *ABD* 4:403–20.

deft stroke, and to vary narrative, alternating scene with summary or speech with story. Luke knows how to make the improbable look probable. He can so bedazzle his audience that the critic must patiently point out how the components do not cohere, engaging reluctantly in the technique of slicing up a great painting in pursuit of what often seem tawdry goals. The metaphor is not accidental. That tradition that made Luke an artist recognized that he is a painter rather than a photographer. Historians prefer photographs. Luke gives them paintings.[48]

Three related features of Lucan technique important to the understanding and evaluation of the narrative are parallelism, repetition, and the use of stereotyped patterns and scenes. Parallelism has generated the most discussion.[49] Comparison (σύγκρισις) was a component of basic rhetorical education.[50] Ancient instruction concentrated on the comparison of unequals, for the purpose of assigning praise or blame.[51] In this sense σύγκρισις applies only to the presentations of Jesus and the Baptizer in Luke 1–2 and Philip and Simon (Acts 8:5-13) but comparison could also be used to demonstrate equality: "Syncrisis is parallel scrutiny of goods or evils or persons or things, by which we try to show that the subjects under discussion are both equal to each other or that one is greater than the other."[52]

Most of the less disputable parallels in Luke and Acts are biographical, and all are implicit. Luke does not say that Jesus could do what Moses, Elijah, and Elisha did, for example. He depicts Jesus doing what these ancient Israelite heroes did (and Peter and Paul doing what these worthies and Jesus did, etc.). Luke narrates more through showing than through telling. The obvious comparison, roughly contemporary to Luke and Acts, is the famous *Parallel Lives* of Plutarch, eighteen of twenty-two of which include explicit comparison. This corpus

48 The same may be said of every ancient author.

49 Important monographs and commentaries exploring these parallelisms include Mathias Schneckenberger, *Über den Zweck der Apostelgeschichte* (Bern: Fisher, 1841); Richard B. Rackham, *The Acts of the Apostles* (2nd ed.; London: Methuen, 1904); Robert Morgenthaler, *Die Lukanische Geschichtsschreibung als Zeugnis* (2 vols.; AThANT 14, 15; Zurich: Zwingli, 1949); Michael Goulder, *Type and History in Acts* (London: SPCK, 1964); Charles Talbert, *Literary Patterns, Theological Themes, and the Genre of Luke-Acts* (SBLMS 20; Missoula, Mont.: Scholars, 1974); Walter Radl, *Paulus und Jesus im lukanischen Doppelwerk: Untersuchungen zu Parallelmotiven im Lukasevangelium und in der Apostelgeschichte* (Europäische Hochschulschriften 23/49; Frankfurt: Peter Lang, 1975); Gudrun Muhlack, *Die Parallelen von Lukas-Evangelium und Apostelgeschichte* (Theologie und Wirklichkeit 8; Frankfurt: Peter Lang, 1979); Jean Noël Aletti, *Quand Luc raconte: Le récit comme théologie* (Lire la Bible 115; Paris: Cerf, 1998) esp. 69–112; and Andrew C. Clark, *Parallel Lives: The Relation of Paul to the Apostles in the Lucan Perspective* (Carlisle, U.K./Waynesboro, Ga.: Paternoster, 2001). Noteworthy articles include Andrew J. Mattill Jr., "The Jesus-Paul Parallels and the Purpose of Luke-Acts: H.H. Evans Reconsidered," *NovT* (1975) 15–47; Robert F. O'Toole, "Parallels between Jesus and His Disciples in Luke-Acts: A Further Study," *BZ* 27 (1983) 195–212; the important methodological study of Susan M. Praeder, "Jesus-Paul, Peter-Paul, and Jesus-Peter Parallelisms in Luke-Acts: A History of Reader Response," in *SBLSP 1984* (Chico, Calif.: Scholars Press, 1984) 23–39; eadem, "Miracle Worker and Missionary: Paul in the Acts of the Apostles," *SBLSP 1983* (Chico, Calif.: Scholars Press, 1981) 107–29; David Moessner, "'The Christ Must Suffer': New Light on the Jesus—Peter, Stephen, Paul Parallels in Luke-Acts," *NovT* 28 (1986) 221–27; and Marilyn McCord Adams, "The Role of Miracles in the Structure of Luke-Acts," in Eleonore Stump and Thomas P. Flint, eds., *Hermes and Athena: Biblical Exegesis and Philosophical Theology* (Notre Dame: University of Notre Dame Press, 1993) 235–65. On the parallels between Jesus and Stephen, note Robert F. O'Toole, *The Unity of Luke's Theology: An Analysis of Luke-Acts* (Wilmington, Del.: Michael Glazier, 1984) 63–73. For a survey of research see Radl, *Paulus*, 44–59, and Clark, *Parallel Lives*, 63–73.

50 The subject is treated, usually following encomium and invective, in the *Progymnasmata*: Theon 10, Hermogenes 8, Aphthonius 10, Nicolaus 9, and John of Sardis 10.

51 An example (that may represent a reworked school exercise) of the practice is Plutarch's essay on whether Alexander's accomplishments were due to skill or luck (*Mor.* 326D–345B).

52 Nicolaus *Progymnasmata* 9, trans. George A. Kennedy, *Progymnasmata: Greek Textbooks of Prose Composition and Rhetoric* (SBLWGRW 10; Atlanta: Society of Biblical Literature; Leiden/Boston: Brill,

provides a useful external control.[53] With regard to Plutarch, two basic interpretations are possible: from these lives Greeks could learn that the Romans also produced great men; Romans, for their part, could be reminded that there had been many illustrious Hellenes.

No one reasonably debates the existence of biographical parallels in Luke and Acts. Discussion revolves about their extent and purposes. Their chief purpose is the demonstration of continuity in salvation history. This continuity extends from Abraham to Paul, which is to say that it legitimates the Jesus movement by demonstrating the continuity between "Moses" and "Jesus," so to speak, and the legitimacy of Pauline gentile Christianity by showing the continuity between Peter and the apostles (and their predecessors, especially Jesus) and Paul. This broad statement meets widespread approval. Disagreement about other purposes is to be expected, for, as the example from Plutarch indicates, comparisons of this sort are amenable to a number of interpretations.[54] Competing interpretations do not invalidate arguments for parallels.

Identification involves four major features: form (e.g., healing stories), vocabulary, narrative details (e.g., healing of a cripple outside a temple), and placement in the narrative (e.g., the beginning of one's active ministry).[55] The occurrence of two or more constitutes good evidence for parallelism. Against a mechanical approach stands the author's skill at variation. Peter's healing shadow (5:14-15) and Paul's therapeutic cloths (19:11-12) are among the most patent parallels in Acts, but fail to meet most of these criteria. Reflection suggests that each of these summaries marks a high point of their respective ministries, Peter's in metropolitan Jerusalem, Paul's in Asia.

The larger question is whether Luke and Acts, individually and as a pair, are to be viewed as parallel compositions, reflecting a pleasing and significant symmetry. The danger, apparent from Charles Talbert's proposal,[56] is that proponents of the approach will identify dubious parallels for the sake of the scheme. This objection does not invalidate the hypothesis that there are numerous parallels within and between Luke and Acts. Pursuit of these has led to many interesting observations and useful discoveries about the author's message. A more controversial proposal pursued in this commentary is that the climactic stories about Peter and Paul (Acts 12; 27–28) represent parallels to Jesus in that they serve as "passion narratives."

The parallels conform to Lucan notions about Christology and anthropology. If Peter and Paul can appear as potent as Jesus, this is because they are, in part. Jesus was a prophet exalted by God. In their earthly roles Peter and others are also powerful speakers and workers of wonders. One important difference is that they are empowered by the Spirit poured out because of the messianic exaltation of Jesus. It must, however, be conceded that Paul is also a savior figure. If the departure of Jesus was a great boon, the absence of Paul is not a bane, for his influence endures. This is a common thread in the trends that make up "Deutero-Paulinism."

Little controversy attaches to Luke's use of repetition. Prominent among repeated stories are three accounts of the conversions of Cornelius (10:1-48; 11:1-18; 15:7-9) and Paul (9:1-19a; 22:3-21; 26:2-18), and three statements that Paul is turning to the gentiles (13:46-48; 18:6; 28:28).[57] The most obvious function of repetition is to underline importance. Repetitions also hold together the various sections of Acts. Luke uses them for narrative effect. All involve end-stress—the third occurrence is the most important—and, most obviously in the story of Paul's change of view, successive retellings allow the author to shape the story as he wishes it to be understood.

2003) 162. (This attestation is indirect; see the note of Kennedy.) On the comparison of equals, see also Hermogenes 8.

53 See Clark, *Parallel Lives*, 84–88.

54 See Praeder, "Parallelisms," 38.

55 On the identification of criteria for internal controls, see Clark, *Parallel Lives*, 73–80.

56 Talbert, *Literary Patterns;* see also Thomas Bergholz, *Der Aufbau des lukanischen Doppelwerkes: Untersuchungen zum formalliterarischen Charakter von Lukas-Evangelium und Apostelgeschichte* (Europäische Hochschulschriften, Reihe 23, Theologie 545; Frankfurt: Lang, 1995).

57 Other examples are the three prison deliveries in chaps. 5; 12; and 16, and three statements of the "Apostolic Decree" (15:20, 28-29; 21:25), although the second of these is in such close proximity to the first that its status as a triplet is questionable.

Narrative patterns, such as that found in chaps. 3–7,[58] can conform to conventional schemes, such as models used to relate the foundation of a cult.[59] Like the parallels, they also demonstrate the pattern of salvation history: the people of God and/or their leaders resist the messengers sent them by God, but these efforts are doomed to failure. The pattern of Paul's missionary work in Acts 13–19 shows little variation. He begins with efforts to win Jews, meets resistance from at least some of them, and leaves town because of civic or legal pressures. Nowhere is Luke's availability to produce interesting variations upon a simple theme more apparent than in this part of his story. The preceding comment reveals skepticism about whether this pattern always or often reflects reality. Luke uses persecution as the engine that drives his plot. When to this proclivity for stereotyped description one adds the narrator's propensity for relating what he has to say about one particular site in the context of a single (usually the first) visit, the corrosive effect on history is intensified. This use of narrative molds into which to fit his stories is, rather than invention of episodes or poor data, the principal reason for the difficulties of treating Acts as simple history. Historians, modern no less than ancient, are likely to look for patterns and primary causes and may be charged with ignoring data that do not fit their theses, but Luke's narrative is so lacking in subtlety and nuance that penetrating skepticism is quite justified. In sum, the author of Acts is a skilled narrator who can produce a variety of styles. His proclivity for patterns enhances the appeal and impact of his work, while detracting from the factual value of his narrative.

Like most good writers, Luke has a number of key tropes, themes that are usually both real and symbolic. An outstanding example is money, the right use of which is crucial, but money also functions as a revealer of people's hearts, minds, and souls. "Magic" represents vulgar religion, with particular reference to the use of religious rites or activities as a source of income. In Acts, magic belongs to, and is a trope for, the realm of Satan. To defeat magic is to trounce the devil. The rule of thumb for identifying magic is the association of religious activities with money. These key tropes thus interlock.

Confinement, including arrest, incarceration, and bondage, is a literal feature in more than one-third of Acts (4:3-31; 5:17-41; 6:12–7:60; 8:3; 9:2; 12:1-17; 16:22-40; 17:6-9, 19-33; 18:12-17; 21:30–28:31). Prison is also a symbol of the powers of death, Satan, and his earthly minions (cf. Luke 13:16). Freedom from bondage is the essential result of the exodus, a dominant biblical theme in Lucan thought. Darkness is another symbol for death or alienation from God. The passage from darkness to light characterizes conversion, for light is a general symbol of salvation. The blind cannot see this light; like others, Luke uses blindness to portray a spiritual condition. More specifically Lucan is the theme of "light for the nations," a phrase borrowed from Luke's "favorite book of the Bible," Deutero-Isaiah (49:6). The vehicle for spreading light is travel. Mission requires going from place to place. The journeys of Jesus, Paul, and others also symbolize the life of faith, which for Luke is a journey. His preferred name for "Christianity," "the movement" (ἡ ὁδός), epitomizes this key symbol.

As a competent writer, Luke knew how to create verisimilitude. The plausibility of a narrative does not establish its historicity, nor do minor details, such as the age of a patient or the duration of an illness, prove that a miraculous cure actually happened. Verisimilitude is more important for writers of fiction than for recorders of history. Literatures of differing eras and cultures exhibit varying conventions of "realism." The description of the disturbance at Ephesus (Acts 19:23-40) may strike modern readers as highly realistic, at least in part, but it does not conform to the general tenor of ancient historians' descriptions of such events.[60]

Realistic touches, like bits of local color, help the reader to enter the story world. They can also be features of pure fantasy. The navigational details and temporal markers that recur throughout Lucian's *True History* are quite like those found in Acts 27:1–28:16.[61]

58 See p. 97.

59 See pp. 389–90.

60 This issue propelled Erich Auerbach's *Mimesis: The Representation of Reality in Western Literature* (trans. Wilfred R. Trask; Garden City, N.Y.: Doubleday, 1957); for his comments on ancient texts, see 1–66.

61 Formally these items belong to the category of *Beglaubigungsapparat*, techniques enhancing credibility. In ancient literature these techniques might

Acts is not fantasy, but the issue remains: verisimilitude does not establish historicity.[62] A less realistic Lucan proclivity is failure to bow down before the idol of consistency. A lack of theological consistency reveals that Luke was not a systematic theologian (below); narrative inconsistency is best attributed to his popular style. Characters may change without warning, and events may display an unlikely sequence. Efforts to defend or rationalize inconsistencies are not unjustified, but they can degenerate into apologetic. Luke was not a modern, highbrow author.[63]

5. Sources[64]

Extant sources[65] used by the author include the LXX,[66] the Gospel of Mark, a collection of Paul's letters, and some of the writings of Josephus.[67] The hypotheses that Luke used Paul and Josephus are not new but have long been out of favor. With regard to Paul's letters the burden lies on those who contend that Luke did not use them. It is almost impossible to claim that the author of Acts had not heard of the epistles, and it is difficult to propose circumstances in which he had not come into contact with them. The choices are either that Luke knew of the letters but declined to consult them or that he made such use of them as suited his needs and purposes. *Tertium non datur.* Use did not entail acknowledgement. Although Luke is aware of the use of letters in church life (15:23-29; 18:27), he does not associate Paul with this form. This fact reflects not simply the reluctance of ancient authors to list their sources but more specifically the controversial status of the epistles when Luke wrote. If one of his intentions was to provide a framework for understanding the epistles, he was very successful.

Postulating that Luke utilized Josephus also answers more questions than it raises. Many of the details in Acts about events in Judea in the period from c. 1 to c. 60 CE are most logically and economically explained as derived from this Jewish historian, particularly because Luke shares some of Josephus's understandings and interests. One could attribute the names of such figures as Felix and Festus to information derived from Paul or his circle, for example, but this explanation will not account for the census of c. 6 CE (Luke 2:1-7; Acts 5:37).[68]

---

involve the discovery of long-lost manuscripts, as in Antonius Diogenes' *Marvels beyond Thule*, and the works attributed to Dictys and Dares about the Trojan War. Modern police procedural may include police reports and other documents. (The first person is also a means for making narrative appear authentic.)

62 On verisimilitude, see John R. Morgan, "Make-Believe and Make Believe: The Fictionality of the Greek Novels," in Christopher Gill and Thomas P. Wiseman, eds., *Lies and Fiction in the Ancient World* (Austin: University of Texas Press, 1993) 175–229; David Konstan, "The Invention of Fiction," in Ronald F. Hock et al., eds., *Ancient Fiction and Early Christian Narrative* (SBLSymS 6; Atlanta: Scholars Press, 1998) 3–17; and Todd Penner, "Madness in the Method? The Acts of the Apostles in Current Study," *CBR* 2 (2004) 223–93, here 252.

63 Barrett, discussing 23:13-35, states the matter in these words: "Luke's strength as a writer lies in the presentation of a single event, not in the linking of a sequence of events" (2:1071).

64 For a representative survey of proposals and positions since Jacques Dupont, *The Sources of Acts* (trans. K. Pond; New York: Herder & Herder, 1964), see Pervo, *Dating*, Appendix 1, 347–58.

65 For arguments about these sources, see idem, 21–199.

66 On the use of LXX passages as the model for and inspiration of various episodes in Acts, see under "Style," above.

67 Possible literary sources include some of the Jewish historians whose work survives in fragments, such as Artapanus and Eupolemus. On these possibilities, see Carl Holladay, "Acts and the Fragments of Hellenistic Jewish Historians," in David P. Moessner, ed., *Jesus and the Heritage of Israel: Luke's Narrative Claim upon Israel's Legacy* (Harrisburg, Pa.: Trinity Press International, 1999) 171–98. Classical sources include Homer and Euripides. Dennis R. MacDonald (*Does the New Testament Imitate Homer? Four Cases from the Acts of the Apostles* [New Haven: Yale University Press, 2003]) contends that Homer was a major source. Some, at least, of his arguments (as in the case of chap. 27) are worthy of consideration. An epic model is also proposed by Marianne P. Bonz, *The Past as Legacy: Luke-Acts and Ancient Epic* (Minneapolis: Fortress Press, 2000), who favors Virgil's *Aeneid*. One conventional definition of the novel is "a popular epic in prose." See, e.g., Jaroslav Ludvíkovsky, *Recky Roman Dobrodruzny–Le roman grec d'aventures* (Prague: Filosofika Fakulta University Karlova, 1925).

68 On the census, see Pervo, *Dating*, 152–60.

These sources were not used in large chunks, as were Mark and Q in Luke. Two continuous sources are proposed. One, the "gentile mission source" provided the major documentary basis for chaps. 1–15.[69] This hypothetical text is a reenvisioned form of the "Antioch Source" first postulated by Harnack.[70] As here construed, this document did not relate the origins of the Christian community in Antioch but served as a description and justification of the gentile mission. The gentile movement traced its origins back, via the Seven, to Jerusalem, viewed charismatic phenomena as legitimizing, and regarded Peter as its apostolic hero. The source was not anti-Pauline in the sense of the Pseudo-Clementines (or even of Matthew), but it took care to note that Paul began as a subordinate of Barnabas and Antioch, and that Barnabas took the side of Peter in a conflict at Antioch. Stephen evidently did not seek to convert gentiles, but his successors did so. Since missionary work by members of the Seven and the Spirit-guided decision of the Antiochene community to launch a mission without guidance from the apostles in Jerusalem conflict with Luke's own portrait, these themes are best attributed to a source. Traces of this source may be detected in 2:1-13; 4:36-37; 6:1-6; 6:8–7:60 (minus 7:1-53/54); 8:1-13; 10:10-16; 11:19-26; 12:12-17; chaps. 13–14, *partim;* and 15:19-21. This source provided Luke with more than data. In several important ways it constituted a model for the composition of Acts: charismatically endowed missionaries guided by the Spirit reach out to gentiles despite persecution, which serves only to help the mission expand. Apart from material from this hypothetical text, very little in chaps. 2–7 can be confidently assigned to a source.[71]

Although 15:36–19:40 represents the center and culmination of Paul's missionary career—his work, in the scholarly consensus, as an independent missionary—no sustained source can be detected for this material. Luke did not possess an "itinerary" for this stage of Paul's career, although the use of some independent traditions and data is probable. (The term *tradition* is often used quite loosely in the study of Acts. Properly understood, *tradition* presupposes a social context, including both reasons for gathering and sharing material and the desire to do so. Bits of data may be available and utilized, but these are not identical with tradition in the technical sense.[72]) Much of 20:1–21:19 and possibly some elements from the subsequent chapters appear to derive from a source. This hypothetical source dealt with the results of the collection for the church in Jerusalem, climaxing with the failure of that project and Paul's arrest, in the form of a letter written by Paul's colleagues and circulated to the communities that participated in the collection.[73] The fragment preserved in 2 Corinthians 8 indicates that an accounting would have been highly desirable, if not necessary. This hypothesis cannot be demonstrated and is therefore not a basis for further speculation. Its advantages are the use of a known form (the letter), a probable setting, and a clear purpose. The "itinerary" is also an attested form, but none of its proponents have been able to make a strong case for the preparation and preservation of such a document.[74]

69 For discussion see Richard Pervo, "'Antioch, farewell! For wisdom sees . . . ': Traces of a Source about the Early Gentile Mission in Acts 1-15," *Forum* (forthcoming).

70 For a concise summary of Harnack's source theories, see Matti Myllykoski, "Being There: The Function of the Supernatural in Acts 1-12," in Michael Labahn and Bert Jan L. Peerbolte, eds., *Wonders Never Cease: The Purpose of Narrating Miracle Stories in the New Testament and Its Religious Environment* (LNTS 288; London: T&T Clark, 2006) 146–79, esp. 151–53.

71 See Richard Pervo, "My Happy Home: The Role of Jerusalem in Acts 1-7," *Forum* n.s. 3.1 (2000) 31–55.

72 For example, one might have been able to hear, in Ephesus c. 115, stories about Prisca and Aquila. These would be "traditions." If the "Hall of Tyrannus" were pointed out as a place where Paul once taught, that would be a datum, although both were preserved by similar means.

73 Only after formulating this hypothesis (Pervo, *Dating*, 358) did I discover that Dietrich-Alex Koch had reached similar conclusions: "Kollektenbericht, 'Wir'-Bericht und Itinerar: Neue Überlegungen zu einem alten Problem," *NTS* 45 (1999) 367–90.

74 See Gottfried Schille, "Die Fragwürdigkeit eines Itinerars der Paulusreisen," *ThLZ* 89 (1959) 165–74.

The first person plural would have been appropriate for this hypothetical letter. Its disappearance should occasion no surprise, for the motivation to preserve the story of a failure would have been relatively low.[75] Remains of this hypothetical source can be identified in 20:1b-6, 13-16; 21:1-19. Subsequent traces cannot be detected, but this does not prove that the source ended with Paul's arrest. Acts 21:20–26:32 is almost entirely Lucan composition. It is possible that some items in this section derived from one or more other lost letters of Paul.[76]

Tensions between chap. 27 and its context indicate that some historical source material may be embedded in the account. Verse 1 is a harsh and somewhat dissonant transition from the foregoing. Paul is but one of a number of prisoners who, one might deduce from v. 42, are condemned criminals. The presence of Aristarchus (v. 2) is mysterious. The first plural returns, but it is not unified (i.e., there is more than one "we" narrator).[77] Whatever traditions were used have been inundated by other sources and editorial contributions. Acts 28:17-31 is entirely Lucan composition.

The speeches (and letters) in Acts do not derive from sources. Ancient writers were expected to compose their own speeches, and the author of Acts is no exception. As the commentary indicates, aspects and sections of these addresses can be related to Greco-Roman rhetorical practices, but they are often too brief to yield to conventional rhetorical analysis. Authorial responsibility for their content does not exclude the use of traditional materials, especially creedal formulae, but it is preferable not to take them as examples of preaching in the author's own time (c. 110–120), since none of the more substantial addresses is a sermon directed to an assembly of "ordinary" believers.

In Acts, the author is, more than in the Gospel, the master of his sources. Attempts to identify the sources of this book have two principal values. One is the secondary project of utilizing Acts to uncover early Christian history. The other is negative, for it reveals how much of this book is the creation of the author and how freely he used the sources at his disposal.

6. Genre

Genre is one of the most hotly contested topics in the study of Acts.[78] Two issues drive this controversy. One is formal. Unlike the Gospel, which can be compared to and contrasted with other Christian Gospels and with a variety of biographical texts, Acts is without peers in the NT. The quest for form involves the identification of comparable texts. Genre involves expectations and standards. This generates the second issue. Defense of the historical accuracy of Acts long propelled the desire to classify it as historiography.[79] This circular argument has been pierced. Although some still associate the author of Acts with Thucydides and Polybius[80] and claim a high level of accuracy for the book, NT scholarship

75 Cf. the edition of Romans that concluded with chap. 14. Romans 15 discussed two unsuccessful projects: delivery of the collection and a proposed mission to Spain.

76 The Pauline corpus is a collection, the result of a process including selection of some items, rejection of others, and at least some editorial activity. Paul probably wrote a number of short letters other than Philemon and the fragments preserved in 2 Corinthians 8–9 and Phil 4:10-20. Copies of at least a number of these may have been available in Ephesus.

77 See the comments on 27:1–28:16.

78 See the following surveys: Richard Pervo, "Must Luke and Acts Belong to the Same Genre?" in David J. Lull, ed., *SBLSP 1989* (Atlanta: Scholars Press, 1989) 309-16; Mikeal C. Parsons and Richard I. Pervo, *Rethinking the Unity of Luke and Acts* (Minneapolis: Fortress Press, 1993) 20–44; Alexander J. M. Wedderburn, "Zur Frage der Gattung der Apostelgeschichte," in Hubert Cancik, Hermann Lichtenberger, and Peter Schäfer, eds., *Geschichte–Tradition–Reflexion: Festschrift für Martin Hengel zum 70. Geburtstag*, vol. 3, *Frühes Christentum* (Tübingen: Mohr Siebeck, 1996) 303–22; and Thomas E. Phillips, "The Genre of Acts: Moving Toward a Consensus?" *CBR* 4 (2006) 365–96. Note also Alexander, *Literary Context*, 133–63, and Penner, "Madness," 223–93.

79 See the valuable bibliographical survey of Joel B. Green and Michael C. McKeever, *Luke-Acts and New Testament Historiography* (Grand Rapids: Baker, 1994); and Clare K. Rothschild, *Luke-Acts and the Rhetoric of History: An Investigation of Early Christian Historiography* (WUNT 2.175; Tübingen: Mohr Siebeck, 2004) 32–59.

80 For example, Hemer, *Book;* and Ben Witherington, *The Acts of the Apostles: A Socio-Rhetorical Commentary* (Grand Rapids: Eerdmans, 1998).

Ancient Romance that creates history.

in general has taken at least a step or two back from that position, while the objectivity of ancient historians has been subject to sharp qualification, to which injury postmodern thought has added the insult of narrowing the gap between history and fiction. It has even become possible to say that, because Acts is a representative of historiography, one should not expect it to be factual.[81] The question of accuracy cannot be resolved by appeal to genre, nor does the identification of genre resolve the debate about accuracy.

Acts is a history. The author has produced a coherent story in conformity with a plan, and his subject includes historical persons, places, and events. These facts do not establish the genre or the reliability of the work; the same statement would apply to *Aseneth* and the *Alexander-Romance*. Judgments about the historical accuracy of particular passages and statements depend on the results of historical criticism, which can often do no more, when external confirmation or disproof is lacking, than identify varying degrees of probability. This is a cumulative enterprise. Findings of more or less credibility incline critics to evaluate individual statements in the light of the preponderance of their findings. Conclusions vary. Two common principles are methodologically questionable. One is the historical equivalent of "innocent until proven guilty," the assumption that every statement should be regarded as true until proven otherwise. The other is the assumption that authors usually deemed reliable should be given the benefit of the doubt when they make unsupported claims. Historical criticism requires that every putative fact or claim be treated without prejudice.

Acts gains from comparison with "biblical historiography."[82] This phrase refers not to a genre but to ways of narrating history found in the LXX. Luke has a "Deuteronomic" viewpoint. From the biblical tradition comes the technique of omniscient narration and its companion, anonymous authorship. Luke's style can be biblical, and his technique of presenting history through the lives of a succession of great leaders can be referred to biblical models. The cycles centered on Elijah and Elisha served as a fertile source of inspiration. The books of the Maccabees were important structural and stylistic resources. With 2 (and 3) Maccabees the stream of biblical historiography has begun to flow into the river of Hellenism.

In the Hellenistic and subsequent eras, rhetoric exercised an oft-lamented influence on historiography. This is not surprising, since rhetoric constituted the basis of education. On the positive side, rhetorical education taught how to construct a persuasive argument based on a thesis. Rhetoric did not, however, privilege objectivity, nor did it award a premium to truth. Its goal was the best case, and its methods included beguiling, diverting, distracting, and, when necessary, hoodwinking the audience. Rhetoric allowed historians to make blatant and sometimes gratuitous appeals to their readers' emotions. In such an environment, Lucian's shrill and conventional insistence on the priority of truth is intelligible (*Quomodo historia* 9).

The two most vital proposals for affiliation under the banner of historiography are the monograph and "apologetic historiography." The former has been advanced by Hans Conzelmann and his students, especially Eckhard Plümacher,[83] the latter by Gregory Sterling.[84] Monographs had a specific focus and could overlap with both biography[85] and fiction.[86] Comparison with the monograph is appropriate, as monographs tended to

81 Todd Penner, *In Praise of Christian Origins: Stephen and the Hellenists in Lukan Apologetic Historiography* (Emory Studies in Early Christianity 10; New York: T&T Clark, 2004) 366. (Penner is speaking of the pervasive influence of rhetoric on historiography.)

82 For discussion, see Parsons and Pervo, *Rethinking*, 33–35; and B. Rosner, "Acts and Biblical History," in Winter and Clarke, *Setting*, 65–82.

83 Recently, Eckhard Plümacher, "Cicero und Lukas: Bemerkungen zu Stil und Zweck der historischen Monographie," in Verheyden, *Unity*, 759–75. See also idem, "Die Apostelgeschichte als historische Monographie," in Kremer, *Actes*, 457–66; Darryl W. Palmer, "Acts and the Ancient Historical Monograph," in Winter and Clarke, *Setting*, 1–29; Charles H. Talbert, "The Acts of the Apostles: Monograph or *Bios*?" in Ben Witherington, ed., *History, Literature and Society in the Book of Acts* (Cambridge: Cambridge University Press, 1996) 58–72; and Alexander, *Literary Context*, 37–40.

84 Gregory Sterling, *Historiography and Self-Definition: Josephos, Luke-Acts and Apologetic Historiography* (NovTSup 64; Leiden: Brill, 1992).

85 Arnaldo Momigliano, *The Development of Greek Biography* (Cambridge, Mass.: Harvard University Press, 1971) 83.

86 Parsons and Pervo, *Rethinking*, 26–27.

display artistic unity and did not need to shy away from apologetic purposes. The weaknesses of this categorization include the fluidity of the genre, which can embrace fiction, and the relative paucity of the database.

Sterling's copious argument for apologetic historiography approaches the question from a different angle. Rather than show how Acts conforms to classical models, he takes up the ethnographic tradition, represented in part by Herodotus but also through insider and outsider descriptions of non-Hellenic nations and cultures. Apologetic historiography—a genre that Sterling christened—has links with methods ranging from ancient science to ancient fiction. Sterling's major model was Josephus, but some of the texts he surveys were of a decidedly popular character, directed to audiences that did not require elegant Greek and sophisticated explication of incident. This hypothesis identifies Luke's most important Hellenistic Jewish antecedents and inspiration. Those who hold that Luke knew some of Josephus's work may wish to simplify the argument: Luke took that Jewish historian as a model.[87] There were other models, including Artapanus, whose similarities to Acts Sterling explores.[88] Artapanus brings apologetic historiography into the orbit of the historical novel.[89]

Others seek to affiliate Luke and Acts with a single genre. In general these efforts proceed from the presumption that the unity of Luke and Acts requires generic unity. The two books could belong to the same genre, but this is not a necessary presupposition.[90] David Aune and David Balch have advocated types of "General" or "Universal" history.[91] The latter long focused on the "Antiquities" type produced by Dionysius of Halicarnassus and his evident imitator, Josephus. One advantage of this orientation is the light it sheds upon Luke's "political" understanding of the church and his transformation of traditional political history.[92] Difficulties are also apparent: one of the two books amounts to a biography, while the other relates the spread of a cult, largely by focusing upon prominent missionaries.[93]

Charles Talbert has sought to address these difficulties by appeal to intellectual history, specifically the succession narratives of the philosophical tradition, traces of which can be seen in Diogenes Laertius's *Lives of the Philosophers*.[94] This proposal deals with the major problem of Aune's classification, for it recognizes the Gospel as a biography. It also recognizes Luke's focus on continuity in salvation history. Despite these merits, Talbert's hypothesis has not gained general acceptance, for the contents of Diogenes Laertius's work do not conform to the pattern stipulated by Talbert, and Luke does not treat succession in the formal way found in later succession lists.[95] Hubert Cancik has made an interesting comparison of Acts to the manner of narrating the history of an institution. This proposal, which does not

87 Sterling ventured no stronger statement than "[I]t is impossible to establish the dependence of Luke-Acts on the *Antiquitates*" (*Apologetic Historiography,* 366).

88 Sterling, *Apologetic Historiography*, 167–87, 268–83, 363–65; see also Richard Pervo, *Profit with Delight: The Literary Genre of the Acts of the Apostles* (Philadelphia: Fortress Press, 1987) 117–19.

89 Sterling rejects the usual definition of Artapanus as a "romance" on the grounds that it is not a love story (*Apologetic Historiography,* 184–86). These criteria are inappropriate; his own definition, "romantic national history," is acceptable.

90 See Richard Pervo, "Must Luke and Acts Belong to the Same Genre?" in David J. Lull, ed., *SBLSP 1989* (Atlanta: Scholars Press, 1989).

91 David Balch has shifted toward a biographical understanding of Luke and Acts. See "*ΜΕΤΑΒΟΛΗ ΠΟΛΙΤΕΙΩΝ*: Jesus as Founder of the Church in Luke-Acts: Form and Function," in Todd C. Penner and Caroline Vander Stichele, *Contextualizing Acts: Lukan Narrative and Greco-Roman Discourse* (SBLSS 20; Boston/Leiden: Brill; Atlanta: Society of Biblical Literature, 2004) 139–88.

92 See also Todd C. Penner, "Civilizing Discourse," in Penner, *Contextualizing*, 65–104; and, in the same volume, Gary Gilbert, "Roman Propaganda and Christian Identity in the Worldview of Luke-Acts," 233–56.

93 Rothschild (*Rhetoric*) relates the Gospel to antiquarian historiography and Acts to political history.

94 The thesis was first advanced in Talbert, *Literary Patterns,* and has been refined in subsequent works, including idem, *What Is A Gospel?* (Philadelphia: Fortress Press, 1977) and "Biographies of Philosophers and Rulers as Instruments of Religious Propaganda in Mediterranean Antiquity," *ANRW* 2.16.2 (1978) 1619–51.

95 For a sympathetic critique of Talbert's classification see Alexander, *Literary Context*, 43–68. On succession, see Parsons and Pervo, *Rethinking*, 36.

focus upon biography, introduces the realm of technical, "scientific" prose.[96]

Although each of the attempts to associate Acts with a particular type of Greco-Roman historiography has made, and will continue to make, valuable contributions to its understanding, serious impediments to the enterprise exist. Among these are (1) the preface(s) to (Luke and) Acts do not conform to those found in ancient historiography.[97] (2) The subject (rise and expansion of a cult) is not a suitable theme for ancient historiography.[98] (3) The speeches, often held to align Acts with historiography, are not consonant with the orations found in histories. Those tend to comment on or explain decisions, but the speeches in Acts are very often part of the narrative, provoking action or advancing the plot. Insofar as they do comment, they tend to be repetitious. (4) The quantity of direct speech, around 51 percent of the book, has no parallel in history or biography.[99] (5) Narration is consistently omniscient. The narrator knows what characters think and can report private conversations and the like in direct speech. (6) The nature, quantity, and perspective of "supernatural" activity, miracles, visions, and divine guidance differ from presentations found in ancient historians, who were likely to place some distance ("it is said") between themselves and the prodigies.[100] (7) The narrator of Acts makes no claims to objectivity. The author writes as a believer who does not seek to represent opposing views with any degree of fairness. (8) The book is devoid of a chronological framework.[101] (9) The style does not achieve the standards expected of historians. Josephus is an example. He writes away from the LXX, improving its style, whereas Luke writes toward it, viewing the LXX as a worthy object of imitation (rather than Thucydides or Dionysius of Halicarnassus, for example).[102] Luke often improves Mark's Greek (as does Matthew), but he does not transform it into good biographical or historical prose.[103] Acts is more nearly an example of the sorts of historical writings Lucian despised than a model of what he recommended.[104]

(10) A number of the narrator's techniques have more in common with ancient fiction than with historiography. These include the following: (a) the mode(s) of characterization. In Acts the leading characters are endowed with extraordinary powers and insight. Peter, Stephen, and Paul are "supermen" with more or

96 Hubert Cancik, "The History of Culture, Religion, and Institutions in Ancient Historiography: Philological Observations concerning Luke's History," *JBL* 116 (1997) 681–703. For a critique of his proposal, see Mark Reasoner, "The Theme of Acts: Institutional History or Divine Necessity in History?" *JBL* 118 (1999) 635–59; and Christoph Heil, "Arius Didymus and Luke-Acts," *NovT* 42 (2000) 358–93.

97 See the excursus "The Prefaces to Luke and Acts" in the commentary on Acts 1.

98 Willem C. van Unnik, "Luke's Second Book and the Rules of Hellenistic Historiography," in Kremer, *Actes*, 37–60, here 39.

99 See the excursus "Direct Speech in Acts" in the commentary on Acts 1.

100 Against Eckhard Plümacher, "*TEPATEIA*": Fiktion und Wunder in der hellenistisch-römischen Geschichtsschreibung und in der Apostelgeschichte," *ZNW* 89 (1998) 66–90.

101 On chronology, see Pervo, *Profit*, 5 and 144 n. 1. One must distinguish between chronological information supplied by the narrator and inferences made from data in the text that can be used to construct a chronological framework. The one clear datum supplied is "under Claudius" (11:28). This is not very specific. From the names of officials that can be dated, a framework of around thirty years can be postulated (Pilate to Festus). For results based on these data, see, e.g., Schneider, 1:129–33; and Witherington, 77–78. In addition are references to passage of time: one year (11:25), eighteen months (18:11), two years (19:10; 28:30), two years, possibly (24:27), and indications of some or many days, a fortnight, and so on (e.g., 1:3; 9:18, 23; 10:30; 18:18; 25:6), and indications of time on journeys (e.g., chaps. 20–21; 27:1–28:16). Chapter 12 is an instructive example. The critic must first determine that "King Herod" is Agrippa I (41–44 CE) and then date the material to his last year. No reader would imagine that around fourteen years have elapsed since the beginning of the story.

102 See also Pervo, *Profit*, 3–8.

103 On Luke's modifications of Mark, see Wilfred L. Knox, *The Acts of the Apostles* (Cambridge: Cambridge University Press, 1948), 6.

104 Lucian *Quomodo historia*. For a Latin example of the kind of target Lucian had in mind, see Fronto *Ad Verum Imp.* 2.3. Lucius Verus wanted Fronto to compose an encomiastic history of his Parthian campaign. He, like Cicero (*Ad fam.* 5.12), would supply the raw data, which Fronto was to put into proper form. Only the lengthy and highly artificial preface survives.

less identical qualities. (b) Plot devices. Persecution is the chief motive of the plot. Although belief is both a genuine and an ostensible factor, the actual reason for persecution is *jealousy* based on *success*. The overarching plan of God that drives the narrative can be compared with historiography, but the specifics belong to the realm of novelistic narrative. The story is told in the form of adventurous episodes. The mode of narration is that of popular narrative. Parallels from histories certainly exist, but what amount to occasional instances and asides, digressions and anecdotes in Tacitus or even Josephus are the staple of Acts. (c) Too many episodes are, from the perspective of historiography, fictions concocted in conformity with the values of the narrator and framed in accordance with popular taste. Examples of episodes invented by historians can certainly be adduced; quantity is the determining factor.

Acts is a "popular" work. Unrestrained by the conventions governing elite literature, popular writers were able to blend genres and create new ones. This freedom from formal restraints, conventions not expected by their consumers that may often have passed unappreciated when they were followed, was not always advantageous to ancient popular writers. There is a difference between discarding conventions one has thoroughly learned in favor of the fresh and failure to observe conventions that one has failed to grasp. Ancient popular writers tended to fall closer to the latter side of this scale. In any case they broke the rules by utilizing prose for purposes that tradition generally assigned to poetry.[105] Out of these efforts the novel came to birth. Popular history did not rob the realm of poetry, but its proponents offered limited homage to Clio, at most. The outcome may look very much the same. C. K. Barrett puts it this way: "The form of the romance is popular history, and that is the kind of history that Acts is."[106]

Luke's achievement as a historian lies more in his success at creating history than in recording it. With his considerable skills this author fashioned what became and has remained the normative story of Christian origins.[107] This is epitomized in his contribution to the two components of the Christian year: the solar cycle based on Christmas, which determines the dates of the Annunciation and Candlemas (March 25 and February 2, both deduced from the later selection of December 25 for the Nativity), as well as the lunisolar cycle from Easter to Pentecost. All of these events except Easter derive exclusively from Luke and Acts.[108] Daniel Marguerat, in a useful investigation, calls this "poetic" or "epic" history.[109] Rigorous historians of today will object to the use of "history" in terms that evoke myth and poetry, whereas the ancient predecessors would have said that stories of this nature should have been cast in poetic form, but the result speaks for itself. The major impetus—which is not to be confused with genre—for Acts and its apocryphal successors was not history, but the content of the canonical Gospels.[110] When he turned to writing Acts, Luke did not discard the hat of an evangelist.

7. The Unity/ies of Luke and Acts

Studies of Luke and Acts face two challenges: to account for the similarities of the two works, including interrelationships, and to explain the differences.[111] The former

105 James M. Dawsey ("Characteristics of Folk-Epic in Acts," in David Lull, ed., *SBLSB* 1989 [Atlanta: Scholars Press, 1989] 317–25) discusses a number of features in Acts that are typical of popular storytelling.

106 C. K. Barrett, "The First New Testament?" *NovT* 38 (1996) 94–104, esp. 98.

107 Luke T. Johnson: "So successful was Luke that his narrative has become the etiological or foundational myth of gentile Christianity" (*The Writings of the New Testament* [Philadelphia: Fortress Press, 1986] 204).

108 Matthew contributes an Epiphany story (2:1-12) but does not describe the birth of Jesus.

109 Daniel Marguerat, *The First Christian Historian: Writing the "Acts of the Apostles"* (trans. Ken McKinney et al.; SNTSMS 121; Cambridge: Cambridge University Press, 2002) 20–22. These terms are quite appropriate, but they also apply to the works of Homer and Virgil, which became myths of origins.

110 See François Bovon, "The Synoptic Gospels and the Non-Canonical Acts of the Apostles," *HTR* 81 (1988) 19–36.

111 The earliest known explanation for the separation of Luke and Acts is that of Chrysostom: "And why did he not make one book of it? . . . For clearness, and to give the brother [Theophilus] a pause for rest. Besides, the two treatises are distinct in their subject matter" (*Hom.* 1, in J. Walker et al., *Saint*

has been dominant for the past eighty years.[112] The same person wrote canonical Luke and the Acts. Knowledge of one is enriched by knowledge of the other, particularly when one sees how Acts develops, fulfills, and plays on themes and so on found in the Gospel. Luke does not require Acts. Its story is complete even for those not familiar with Matthew, Mark, or John. The uninformed (a group not envisioned by the narrator) who took up Acts would be able to learn the basic elements of the gospel story—the creed, in effect—and would learn that the earthly Jesus was a beneficent Galilean healer who succeeded John the Baptizer. Acts could stand independently. Even the preface to Acts does not resolve this question.[113]

Although the second volume continues the first, it tells a different story with different methods and some different themes. The last is apparent in the altered role assigned to Jesus. In the formulation articulated by Rudolf Bultmann, the Jesus of Luke is the proclaimer of God's reign. In Acts, he is the proclaimed,[114] the object of the message rather than its source.[115] In this sense Acts is more like Paul and his theology than like Luke. Two principal themes of Jesus' message, eschatology and ethics, receive limited coverage in Acts, which focuses on the means of salvation, an assumed need not related to an imminent end. Both Luke and Acts present their heroes as itinerant teachers who may be compared to philosophers. In Luke, there is minimal information about the course of the journeys and incidents therein. Travel, especially Jesus' journey to Jerusalem (9:51—19:27), is a platform for teaching; in Acts, however, details about stations are numerous and missionary adventures dominate the content. The ethical focus of Acts is on the use of money. This subject emerges through inference and example rather than by exhortation. In short, much of Luke teaches by telling, whereas Acts generally communicates by showing.

Another clear formal difference is the presence in Acts of a number of speeches composed by the author. The Gospel also inclines toward longer speeches than, for example, Mark, but the components of these addresses can often be identified as traditional items transferred into a new context and provided with some rhetorical organization (see Luke 12). In Acts, the writer used his sources with more freedom than in the Gospel. Even the most ardent proponent of the unity of the two books must grant that the Christology of Acts differs considerably from that of Luke.[116] In the former, Jesus is a traveling teacher and sage, executed, raised, and taken into heaven. In the latter, he is a heavenly being who bestows the Spirit and appears in visions to counsel and exhort.

The unities of Luke and Acts are questions to be pursued rather than presuppositions to be exploited.[117]

Chrysostom: Homilies on the Acts of the Apostles and the Epistle to the Romans [NPF 11; 1889; reprinted Grand Rapids: Eerdmans, 1979] 4).

112 See, e.g., Parsons and Pervo, *Rethinking*; Marguerat, *Historian*, 43–64; some of the essays in Verheyden, *Unity*; C. Kavin Rowe, "History, Hermeneutics and the Unity of Luke-Acts," *JSNT* 28 (2005) 131–57; Markus Bockmuehl, "Why Not Let Acts Be Acts? In Conversation with C. Kavin Rowe," *JSNT* 28 (2005) 163–66; Luke T. Johnson, "Literary Criticism of Luke-Acts: Is Reception-History Pertinent?" *JSNT* 28 (2005) 159–62; Michael F. Bird, "The Unity of Luke-Acts in Recent Discussion," *JSNT* 29 (2007) 425–48; C. Kavin Rowe, "Literary Unity and Reception History: Reading Luke-Acts as Luke and Acts," *JSNT* 29 (2007) 449–58; Andrew Gregory, "The Reception of Luke and Acts and the Unity of Luke-Acts," *JSNT* 29 (2007) 459–72; and Patrick E. Spencer, "The Unity of Luke-Acts: A Four-Bolted Hermeneutical Hinge," *CBR* 5 (2007) 341–66.

113 With regard to the preface, Alexander says: "Acts may be read either as 'Volume II' of a unified composition, or as an independent monograph which simply reminds the reader that its narrative is a sequel to the earlier work" (*Literary Context*, 27).

114 Rudolf Bultmann, *Theology of the New Testament* (2 vols.; trans. Kendrick Grobel; New York: Charles Scribner's Sons, 1951, 1955) 1:33–37.

115 Luke solves Bultmann's problem by having Jesus announce this shift in his farewell messages (Luke 24:44-49; Acts 1:8). The risen one teaches his followers to understand his status and proclaim it as his witnesses.

116 The Christology of Acts is based on the resurrection, without reference to the events and empowerment of Luke 1–2.

117 Henry J. Cadbury, the first vigorous proponent of unity, revealed his prejudice with this comment: "Fortunately our author had the judgment or foresight to make each of his two volumes somewhat self-sufficient, though in doing so he has perhaps prevented some modern readers from recognizing their fundamental unity" (*The Book of Acts in History* [New York: Harper & Bros., 1955] 139).

Pursuit is most fruitful in the area of themes, as Robert Tannehill's work has richly demonstrated.[118] The continuity of salvation history is a governing theme that integrates the two volumes. This commentary does not presume that the author planned and executed his books in advance. Acts is best understood as a sequel to Luke.[119] If canonical Luke represents the original form of that Gospel, Acts could have been composed as much as a decade later.[120]

8. Structure

Acts exhibits careful attention to structure at several levels. The work begins where its author chose to start and ends where he wished to close.[121] Structural organization is apparent also in units of different sizes, such as the cycles of persecution in chaps. 3–7, and individual units such as 19:1-7.[122] Ring composition (chiasmus) and inclusion are means for presenting rounded sections.[123] Chapters 13–14, for example, are framed by a complex inclusion. When travel is involved, the pattern follows the time-honored "there and back" formula, as in Jerusalem–Samaria–Jerusalem (8:14-25). This pattern continues with Paul, who repeatedly returns to Jerusalem, but is broken decisively in chaps. 27–28. The story ends in Rome. Although this presumably reflects history, it shows that Jerusalem has ceased to play a central role. Conflicts also exhibit a "there and back" pattern: All is well, then a problem appears. The issue is resolved, and all is once more well (e.g., 6:1-7; 4:32–5:11; 5:12-42; 8:6-13, 14-25; 11:1-18; 15). This accords with the technique of popular literature, in which tension alternates with relaxation. Chapters 27–28 both continue and deviate from this pattern. Paul is arrested and remains in custody, but the story concludes in an atmosphere devoid of tension.

The variety of plans presented for Acts in the various commentaries indicates not only the use of different models (thematic,[124] geographical,[125] literary[126]) but also Luke's propensity toward a fluid, overlapping

118 Robert C. Tannehill, *The Narrative Unity of Luke-Acts: A Literary Interpretation* (2 vols.; Philadelphia/Minneapolis: Fortress Press, 1986, 1990).

119 "Sequel" is at least apt insofar as the Apocryphal Acts viewed the book as separable and a suitable object for imitation. For arguments that the canonical Acts served as their model, see Gonzalo del Cerro, "Los hechos apócrifos de los Apósteles: Su género literario," *EstBíb* 51 (1993) 207–32. Jervell (57 n. 23) puts it thus: Luke and Acts are two works by the same author, not one book in two parts.

120 The question of whether canonical Luke is the earliest edition of that Gospel continues to arise. Joseph Tyson has recently restated the hypothesis that canonical Luke is subsequent to the edition known to, for example, Marcion (*Marcion and Luke-Acts: A Defining Struggle* [Columbia: University of South Carolina Press, 2006]). If this hypothesis is correct, the author who produced canonical Luke wrote Acts as a companion piece. The hypothesis cannot be demonstrated (saving the discovery of a MS.), but it is not easily refuted. The question of the unity of Luke and Acts as discussed here relates to the canonical edition of the Gospel.

121 Contrast with the canonical Gospels illustrates this relative freedom.

122 Careful attention to the structure of both small and large units is a feature of Charles Talbert's compact commentary, *Reading Acts: A Literary and Theological Commentary on the Acts of the Apostles* (Reading the New Testament; New York: Crossroad, 1997). Jacques Dupont provides detailed analyses of the structure of many episodes; see *Études sur les Actes de apôtres* (LD 45; Paris: Cerf, 1967) and *Nouvelles études sur les Actes des apôtres* (LD 118; Paris: Cerf, 1984). See also G. Leonardi, *Atti degli apostoli, traduzione strutturata, analisi narrativa e retorica* (2 vols.; Sussidi Biblici 61–61b; Reggio Emilia: San Lorenzo, 1998).

123 Mary Douglas argues that ring composition is an important clue to understanding many traditional works, esp. those of non-Western origin (*Thinking in Circles: An Essay on Ring Composition* [New Haven: Yale University Press, 2007]).

124 Rebecca I. Denova (*The Things Accomplished among Us: Prophetic Tradition in the Structural Pattern of Luke-Acts* [Sheffield: Sheffield Academic Press, 1997]) bases her structural analysis on prophetic patterns, coordinating structure with typology and source criticism (e.g., the Elijah-Elisha cycle).

125 These range from outlines based on the geographical locations of the action (e.g., Jürgen Roloff, *Die Apostelgeschichte* [NTD 5; Göttingen: Vandenhoeck & Ruprecht, 1981] 13–14) to the sophisticated approach of James M. Scott, "Luke's Geographical Horizon," in David W. J. Gill and Conrad Gempf, eds., *The Book of Acts in Its Graeco-Roman Setting* (BIFCS 2; Grand Rapids: Eerdmans, 1994) 483–544.

126 Witherington (p. 74), for example, utilizes the

technique.[127] Units, notably but far from exclusively the summaries,[128] function as bridges, concluding one section and introducing the next. A leading question is whether chap. 15 is to be regarded as the pivotal point dividing Acts into two major sections. Although that division was once common,[129] modern commentators tend to divide Acts into three or more major sections.[130] One may ask whether focus on chap. 15 is not due at least as much to an understanding of church history as to the author's plan. The Pauline mission that embraces gentiles continues after chap. 15 in the same fashion exhibited in chaps. 13–14. The old plan (which goes back to Arator's *De actibus apostolorum*) that places the decisive division after chap. 12 is arguably more reflective of Acts' internal parallelisms.[131] Chapter 13 inaugurates the Diaspora mission that quickly brings Paul to the leadership. This division is not merely biographical, although Peter and Paul symbolize the Jerusalem mission that began converting gentiles and the mission "to the ends of the earth," respectively.

9. General Purpose

Acts (and Luke) can blandly but accurately be characterized as "legitimating narrative." "Narrative" is the function: making a case by telling a story (or stories), rather than by means of a treatise or a dialogue. "Legitimating" serves to express the object of the work, whether this is construed more narrowly as the legitimacy of Pauline Christianity (possibly in rivalry to other interpretations) or generally as the claim of the Jesus-movement to possess the Israelite heritage.[132] Since Aristotle, a major reason for composing a history of a subject has been the bestowal of legitimacy upon it.[133] Luke's project has many companions. The adjective also locates Acts on a continuum between an evangelist such as Mark and an apologist such as Justin.[134] Median points are likely to be ambiguous, and that is the case with Acts, which seeks to gather many chicks under its wings. It is not, therefore, surprising that scholars can find evidence to support opposing positions regarding Lucan views.

The ostensible addressees of formal apologies are "outsiders." Luke and Acts speak to insiders,[135] believers in Jesus, rather than to polytheists or to Jews who did not accept Christian claims. Arguments for legitimacy intimate accusations of illegitimacy. What and whom do Luke and Acts seek to legitimate, and how? Against what and whom are these claims made, and how? Acts certainly seeks to legitimate a social body comprising

growth statements of 6:7; 9:31; 12:24; 16:5; 19:20, to identify the structure. Bruce W. Longenecker ("Lukan Aversion to Humps & Hollows: The Case of Acts 11:27–12:25," *NTS* 50 [2004] 185–204) posits these divisions: 1:1–8:3; 8:4–12:25; 13:1–19:41; 20:1–28:31. His basis is rhetorical means of organization.

127 On the overlapping nature of Acts' structure, see G. Betori, "La strutturazione del libro degli Atti: un proposta," *RivB* 42 (1994) 3–34. Betori sees five interlocking parts, with an introduction and a conclusion.

128 See the excursus "The Summaries in Acts" in the commentary on Acts 2.

129 An example Conzelmann, *Acts of the Apostles*, xlii–xliii.

130 E.g., Alfons Weiser, *Die Apostelgeschichte* (2 vols.; ÖKTNT 5.1/2; Gütersloh: Mohn, 1981, 1985) 1:27–28 (three); Schneider, 1:68 (three); Jervell, 52–54, (four); Joseph A. Fitzmyer, *The Acts of the Apostles* (AB 31; New York: Doubleday: 1998) 119–23 (seven sections, with good summary of various plans and bibliography on the subject).

131 Talbert, *Reading Acts*, 93–94. On this scheme, note also Rackham, xlviii; and Philippe H. Menoud, *Jesus Christ and the Faith: A Collection of Studies* (trans. E. M. Paul; PTMS 18; Pittsburgh: Pickwick, 1978) 131 n. 2.

132 "Legitimating" is not a synonym for "apologetic." It derives from the sociology of knowledge set forth in Peter L. Berger and Thomas Luckmann, *The Social Construction of Reality* (Garden City, N.Y.: Doubleday, 1967) and is intimately related to the notion of a "symbolic universe." The seminal application of this concept to Lucan studies was Philip F. Esler's *Community and Gospel in Luke-Acts: The Social and Political Motivations of Lucan Theology* (SNTSMS 57; Cambridge: Cambridge University Press, 1987); see esp. 16–23, and 45.

133 See R. French's general introduction to Tamsyn Barton, *Ancient Astrology* (London: Routledge, 1994) xvi–xvii.

134 "Legitimating" is, from the social-scientific perspective, a proper task of the second and later generations of a movement, although it may well begin at the time of origin.

135 One may contrast Epaphroditus, the patron and dedicatee of several of Josephus's works, who

both "Jews" and gentiles, and to do so by the erection and maintenance of a symbolic universe that includes theological views, notably a Christology. The purpose is to explain and defend a body that has existed for some time and whose identity has been challenged rather than, for example, to nurture a young and fragile body grappling to discover its identity.[136]

10. Theology

At one time it was presumed that the theology of Acts was to be discovered in its speeches.[137] This view is out of favor: Acts is a narrative, and its theology must be recovered from the narrative rather than from the embedded speeches.[138] If, however, the claim is made that the narrative is a triumphal story built on the words and deeds of Spirit-endowed leaders, objections will arise, many based on various items from the speeches. Although the privilege given to the narrative strikes closer to Luke's heart, many of the themes and concepts of the speeches remain important. One could not construct a valid summary of Lucan theology by attending to the narrative alone, for the speeches explain why and how the story happened. The speeches are also components of the narrative.

Sixty years ago Lucan theology did not exist as a distinct subject (which is not to say that it was never the object of reflection). Since then, it has occasioned considerable debate.[139] The subject first flourished in the springtime of redaction criticism, the primary motive of which was to profile the theology of the Synoptic evangelists. Hans Conzelmann took up the discussion by asking what problem Luke was addressing.[140] His answer, "the delay of the parousia," focused on one dimension of a larger issue: the nature and identity of the church as it became an enduring body in a larger society. Conzelmann also addressed Luke as a theologian of salvation history. In circles influenced by Bultmann, "salvation history" amounted to betrayal. Conzelmann sought, not without reservations, to place this orientation in a more positive light. He thus identified what is more or less universally accepted: Luke's principal theme is the continuity of salvation history.[141] He engaged this issue in the context of Deutero-Pauline conflicts with particular attention to both those who argued that God's send-

will receive desired information, with the at least somewhat "informed" Theophilus of Luke 1:4. For a pointed discussion of the role of "apologetic" in Luke and Acts, see Esler, *Community*, 205–19.

136 Michael Wolter, "Das lukanische Doppelwerk als Epochengeschichte," in Ciliers Breytenbach et al., ed., *Apostelgeschichte und die hellenistische Geschichtsschreibung: Festschrift für Eckhard Plümacher zu seinem 65. Geburtstag* (AGJU 57; Leiden/Boston: Brill, 2004) 253–84, focuses on the issue of identity, arguing, against Conzelmann, that the formation of Christianity constitutes a single epoch of Israelite history.

137 See, e.g., Charles F. D. Moule, "The Christology of Acts," in Keck and Martyn, *Studies*, 159–85. (Moule holds that the Christology of Acts differs from that of Luke and that it is not consistent.)

138 E.g., Beverly Roberts Gaventa, "Toward a Theology of Acts: Reading and Rereading," *Int* 42 (1988) 146–57. A leading pioneer of this approach is David Moessner, whose *Lord of the Banquet: The Literary and Theological Significance of the Lukan Travel Narrative* (Minneapolis: Augsburg Fortress, 1989), although devoted to Luke, demonstrates the merits of basing theological analysis on literary rather than redaction criticism.

139 See the comprehensive review by François Bovon, *Luke the Theologian: Thirty-three Years of Research (1950–1983)* (trans K. McKinney; Allison Park, Pa.: Pickwick, 1987), now revised in a second edition, *Luke the Theologian: Fifty-five Years of Research (1950–2005)* (Waco: Baylor University Press, 2006). Studies of the theology of Acts include J. C. O'Neill, *The Theology of Acts in Its Historical Setting* (London: SPCK, 1961); Jacob Jervell, *The Theology of Acts* (New Testament Theology; Cambridge: Cambridge University Press, 1996); Petr Pokorny, *Theologie der lukanischen Schriften* (FRLANT 174; Göttingen: Vandenhoeck & Ruprecht, 1998); and I. Howard Marshall and David Peterson, eds., *Witness to the Gospel: The Theology of Acts* (Grand Rapids: Eerdmans, 1998).

140 Hans Conzelmann, *The Theology of St. Luke* (trans. G. Buswell; New York: Harper & Row, 1960).

141 Conzelmann's attempt to show that Luke set forth epochs of salvation history is out of favor at present, but it has some merit, even if the precise delineations are debatable. For an illuminating discussion of the Lucan situation, see Walther Schmithals, "Identitätskrise bei Lukas und Anderswo?" in Breytenbach, *Apostelgeschichte*, 223–51.

ing of Jesus had utterly inverted and disrupted salvation history and those who viewed Paul as a saboteur of saving history.

Luke appropriated more than a little from Paul. He views Torah observance as an inadequate means for salvation. The Law is, for him, soteriologically irrelevant. He speaks of justification by faith (13:38-39) as the result of grace (15:11), but, because the choice between two competing soteriological systems—one based on Torah, the other on faith—was no longer relevant, the Pauline opposition of faith to works appeared antinomian, and Luke prefers to view δικαιοσύνη as "just behavior" rather than "justification."[142] Demands that believers keep Torah (e.g., 15:1) are just that. They are not linked to the Abrahamic covenant.[143]

Related to this stance is Luke's view of the crucifixion, which is not an ultimate and paradoxical apocalyptic act of God but a tragic and revelatory act reversed by the resurrection. Insofar as there is a Lucan "theology of the cross," it is expressed through continuities: the continued rejection of God's prophets by God's people, and Jesus' continuation of his ministry to seek and save the lost (Luke 23:39-43). For Luke Paul's breathtaking interpretation of the crucifixion was unduly conducive to dualism and actively promoted the discontinuity Luke wished to rebut.[144]

In a manner similar to, but not identical with, that of Paul, Luke viewed the resurrection as the defeat of Satan. Like Paul (and, perhaps, others), he viewed the Holy Spirit as a "replacement" for the "kingdom of God." Acts 1:6-8 makes this explicit.[145] Jesus was a human being, a prophet, exalted by God to the divine realm, an action that made the universal gift of the Spirit possible (Acts 2:33). One result of this is a potential confusion between Jesus and the Spirit. Luke was not a systematic theologian, and he did not prize consistency.[146] The strains evident are due in part to his efforts to preserve a theocentric perspective and in part to his imperfect efforts to incorporate elements of different systems. Lucan consistency emerges in his firm commitment to monotheism and his attempt to portray the continuity of salvation history. Consistency notwithstanding, the Spirit, with its various roles and functions, is a vital element of the theology of Acts.[147] The importance of the Spirit in Acts is a pervasive and palpable testimony to the presence of the Pauline legacy. The gift of the Spirit serves both as a means for portraying continuity, signaled by the quotation from Joel in Peter's Pentecost sermon, and as an (unwelcome) indicator of discontinuity.

Appeal to the Spirit as the principal mode of legitimation is essentially charismatic. This view was shared by both Paul and those who produced the gentile missionary source. Acts does not seek to justify the

142 Pervo, *Dating*, 266–68.

143 "Covenant" (διαθήκη) appears but twice in Acts. In the Petrine speech in 3:25 it is related to the promise of universal beatitude, that is, an intimation of the gentile mission. Stephen's reference to the "covenant of circumcision" (7:8) is fuel for his accusations in 7:51-53.

144 This subject generates considerable controversy. Some arguments for a Lucan "theology of the cross" involve harmonization with Pauline thought and the presumed consensus of nascent Christianity. An example of this approach is H. Douglas Buckwalter, *The Character and Purpose of Luke's Christology* (SNTSMS 89; Cambridge: Cambridge University Press, 1996). More sophisticated efforts seek to profile the place of suffering in Lucan thought, e.g., David Moessner, "The 'Script' of the Scriptures in Acts: Suffering as God's 'Plan' (βουλή) for the World for the 'Release of Sins,'" in Witherington, *History*, 218–50. See also Scott Cunningham, *Through Many Tribulations: The Theology of Persecution in Luke-Acts* (JSNTS 142; Sheffield: Sheffield Academic Press, 1997).

145 Note also Luke 17:20-21: the kingdom is "within you."

146 For examples of inconsistency, see David Seeley, *Deconstructing the New Testament* (BIS 5; Leiden: Brill, 1994) 81–102.

147 Note the important study of Max Turner, *Power from on High: The Spirit in Israel's Restoration and Witness in Luke Acts* (Journal of Pentecostal Theology Supplement Series 9; Sheffield: Sheffield Academic Press, 1996). The Spirit can be studied as a character within the narrative, as by William H. Shepherd (*The Narrative Function of the Holy Spirit as a Character in Luke-Acts* [SBLDS 147; Atlanta: Scholars Press, 1994]), and made the object of literary inquiry (Ju Hur, *A Dynamic Reading of the Holy Spirit in Luke-Acts* [JSNTS 211; Sheffield: Sheffield Academic Press, 2001]).

acceptance of gentiles by appeal to Scripture or other formal norms. The Spirit validated acceptance of gentiles (10:1–11:18).[148] Charismatic legitimation typically emerges from dissident circles. Luke finessed this potential contradiction with two moves. Scripture, properly understood, foretells the christological facts, which thus belong to the sacred story from the beginning. This depends on an entirely Christian view of Israelite Scripture, in which prophecy has priority over regulations for community life. Prophecy can be found where it is sought; that is, Luke does not, as it were, list the promises and then look for their realization in "the events that have been fulfilled among us" (Luke 1:1). He argues from fulfillment to promise: since, in effect, this is how God did it, the prophets must have spoken about it. The Bible may include the same texts, but Christian use of these texts—although not without Jewish parallels[149]—shows that two religions are in view. The other move is to integrate the Spirit into salvation history by depicting Israelite leaders as powerful speakers and miracle workers who were rejected by the people and thus resisted repeated manifestations of God's Spirit (7:51). Lucan "parallelism" is one of the more important instruments of his narrative theological repertory. Miracles introduce the controversial theme of Luke's alleged "theology of glory."

Ernst Haenchen found little to admire in Acts' focus on miraculous delivery and the busy hand of providence in its plot.[150] This theology is not, by contemporary standards, particularly mature. When it appeared, the Christian movement was far from mature, and its world was neither cozy nor comfortable. Transference of this perspective into the lives of upper-middle-class residents of the United States in the form of a Gospel promising money, power, and success was an abuse that brought a backlash against Lucan theology.[151] It is no less abusive to apply Lucan triumphalism to a national situation. *Abusus non tollit usum.* In the original setting, these disputed components of Lucan thought had value, as they may in kindred situations.[152] Something positive may also be said about miracles. The individual miracles in Acts are symbols. The text does not claim that all who suffer from misfortune are entitled to immediate relief.[153] For Luke, the theology of glory was a tool rather than a program, a means rather than an end.

Providence is active at both the individual and corporate levels. The latter coordinates with the concept of salvation history and may be compared with philosophies of history.[154] Luke probably picked up this theme from Josephus and others whom he had read, but he is no philosophical theologian and he does not reflect on issues related to the success and failure of nations and movements over time. God supports those who have the right understanding (5:35-39). In the most vulgar sense, God is on the side of the winners. This empirical dimension was doubtless stimulated by Luke's aversion to dualistic understandings of the message and is properly introduced when the church becomes invisible to the extent of nonexistence. This was an important contribution to the catholic understanding of Christianity, which holds the church to account for failures no less than successes throughout its history. Belief in providence serves to sustain hope. Because God is God, no situation is totally devoid of the possibility for redemption.

These issues bring in their wake the θεῖος ἀνήρ ("divine man") debate. In the Roman era, this expression was always complimentary and applied to a range of figures,[155] among whom miracle working was not the most prominent quality.[156] The Christian leaders in Luke and Acts, including Jesus, Peter, and Paul, are

148 In 15:13-18, James adduces arguments for the gentile mission from Scripture, exemplifying the method of arguing from fulfillment to promise.
149 Cf. the prophetic function of Scripture at Qumran.
150 Like many Germans who lived in the first half of the twentieth century, Haenchen (who suffered throughout his life from wounds received in WWI) was allergic to promises of miraculous deliverance, as the Nazi regime had continually proclaimed that marvelous weapons (*Wunderwaffen*) would deliver them from the Allied and Soviet forces.
151 The author's *Profit with Delight* was composed in the heyday of the money, power, success gospel.
152 See p. 149.
153 See the excursus "Power in Luke and Acts" pp. 42–43.
154 See John T. Squires, *The Plan of God in Luke-Acts* (SNTSMS 76; Cambridge/New York: Cambridge University Press, 1993).
155 Ludwig Bieler's survey, *ΘΕΙΟΣ ΑΝΗΡ*: *Das Bild des "Göttlichen Menschen" in Spätantike und Frühchristentum* (2 vols.; 1935–36; reprinted Darmstadt: Wissenschaftliche Buchgesellschaft, 1967) might better have been titled *Bilder*, or "images," rather than "the image."
156 David L. Tiede, *The Charismatic Figure as Miracle*

charismatically endowed individuals whose powers are not always attributed to the authorities they invoke. Whatever the formula or circumstance, however, God is always the ultimate source of these spiritual graces. A subordinationist Christology devoid of preexistence was no embarrassment to an uncompromising monotheist.[157] "Divine man" has been used to characterize one of the Christologies that stands behind the canonical Gospels, elements of which were opposed by Mark, John, and Paul. Of all canonical authors, Luke is the least critical of this tendency, which accords with his anthropology.[158] One result is a reduction of the gap between Jesus and the subsequent leaders. They are not, however, identified. The right hand of God is in no danger of becoming overcrowded. What this does mean is a continuation of the work of Christ through the Spirit in the church. In all probability, various charismata were known to the churches with which Luke was familiar.

Lucan ecclesiology is a difficult subject, for it is all but submerged in his missiology. The growth of the church is his constant focus; it is, by definition, a missionary institution.[159] The concept of the church as a cosmic body (e.g., Colossians and Ephesians; cf. Ignatius of Antioch) is implicitly rejected. The Spirit rules the church; the church does not control the Spirit. Nonetheless, charismatic phenomena occur in ecclesiastical settings and involve the presence of leaders.[160] Luke is familiar with the emerging catholic orders of bishop, presbyter, and deacon. He prefers government by a body, be they called "presbyters" or "bishops." Succession is not presented in a formal manner. From the ecclesiological perspective, Luke is a collaborator with "early catholicism" rather than a vigorous proponent of it.[161] The church represents the reformed, authentic Israelite tradition. This reformation, like later reform movements, claimed to have recovered the original purposes of God, revealed in prophetic Scripture. Reform is not simply institutional; it is manifested in personal behavior, notably in the use of resources, and is a model for the reform of society.[162]

Eschatology, long a burning issue in the study of the Gospel, is not a prominent topic in Acts.[163] Judgment and parousia remain on the calendar, without an explicit assertion of imminence or concern about the subject. Hints of the tendency to individualize eschatology, one mark of the absence of imminence, are present.[164] Acts' refusal to consider the question of "when" gives prominence to Luke's primary understanding. For the Paul of Acts, resurrection is the hope of Israel (26:6-7; 28:20). Resurrection is therefore the essence of eschatology. The parousia and judgment are components of resurrection rather than events subsequent to it.

11. Bibliography and History of Research

The bibliography in this volume concentrates on works consulted. Printed bibliographies include the valuable contribution of Andrew J. Mattill and Mary B. Mattill, *A Classified Bibliography of Literature on the Acts of the Apostles* (NTTS 7; Leiden: Brill, 1966), which treats works published through 1961. Watson E. Mills, *The Acts of the*

Worker (SBLDS 1; Missoula, Mont.: Scholars Press, 1972).

157 The existence of early and/or proto-Marcionite theologies and the forms of incipient Gnosis provided no encouragement to the formulation or support of higher Christologies by Luke.

158 See Parsons and Pervo, *Rethinking*, 84–114.

159 See, e.g., Francis Pereira, *Ephesus: Climax of Universalism in Luke-Acts–A Redaction-Critical Study of Paul's Ephesian Ministry (Acts 18:23–20:1)* (Jesuit Theological Forum Studies 10.1; Anand, India: Gujarat Sahitya Prakash, 1983).

160 The exception is Ananias's healing of Paul (9:17-18), which probably derives from a source and fades out of the subsequent accounts.

161 See Pervo, *Dating*, 203–18. Vittorio Fusco has a recent survey of the question: "La discussione sul protocattolicesimo nel Nuovo Testamento: Un capitolo di storia dell'esegesi," *ANRW* 2.26.2 (1995) 1645–91.

162 On the church as a reform movement, see Jerome Neyrey, "The Symbolic Universe of Luke-Acts: 'They Turn the World Upside Down,'" in Neyrey, *Social World*, 271–304.

163 John T. Carroll's study, *Response to the End of History: Eschatolgy and Situation in Luke-Acts* (SBLDS 92; Atlanta: Scholars Press, 1988) 121–64, examines the eschatology of Acts, concentrating on four passages (1:3-11; 2:17-21; 3:19-26; 28:17-31).

164 Carroll (*Response*, 60–71) argues against individualization. Even if his conclusions are accepted, it is noteworthy that the question must be addressed.

Apostles(Lewiston, N.Y.: Mellen, 1996), includes material through 1994. Günter Wagner, *An Exegetical Bibiliography of the New Testament: Luke and Acts* (Macon, Ga.: Mercer University Press, 1985) 331–550, is organized by verses and passages and extends into 1981. The recent commentaries of Joseph A. Fitzmyer and Jacob Jervell include substantial bibliography for each unit.

The second volume of *The Beginnings of Christianity* included chapters on British and German scholarship on Acts (pp. 363–433). Haenchen offered a penetrating analysis of research in his commentary (pp. 14–50, 116–32). This was continued in the last German edition by Erich Grässer, whose several contributions were gathered up in *Forschungen zur Apostelgeschichte* (WUNT 2.137; Tübingen: Mohr Siebeck, 2001).[165] Eckhard Plümacher contributed articles on "Acta-Forschung 1974–82" in *ThRu* 48 (1983) 1–56; 49 (1984) 104–69; Jens Schröter continues with "Acta Forschung seit 1982. I Formgeschichte und Kommentare, *ThR* 72 (2007) 179–203. Todd Penner, "Madness in the Method? The Acts of the Apostles in Current Study," *CBR* 2 (2004) 223–93, surveys the period from c. 1985 to c. 2003. The most valuable resource is François Bovon's revised *Luke the Theologian: Fifty-five Years of Research (1950–2005)* (2nd ed.; Waco: Baylor University Press, 2006), which includes, in its supplementary essays (pp. 463–564), comments about literary and other matters.

165 See also Gerhard Schneider, "Literatur zum lukanischen Doppelwerk. Neuerscheinungen, 1990–91," *TRev* 88 (1992) 1–18; and José Antonio Jáuregui, "Panorama de la evolución de los estudios lucanos," *EstBib* 61 (2003) 351–98.

Commentary

Acts of the Apostles

The best-attested title[1] for this book is πράξεις ἀποστόλων ("Acts of the Apostles"). ℵ 1175 *pc* have πράξεις ("acts," "accomplishments") alone, but this must be an abbreviation, since this noun requires a genitive or the equivalent. In due course, this title became more elaborate, for example, "The Acts of the Holy Apostles, composed by St. Luke the Apostle and Evangelist.[2] "Acts of the Apostles" could not have been the original title, since the major figure of the book, Paul, is not, by the author's definition (1:21-22), an apostle. The only use of the word "acts" in the text is an unmodified reference to the practice of "magic" (19:19).[3] The book is anonymous and would not have needed a title.[4]

Titles, however, provide useful information about the reception of the book. They indicate how readers of the middle and late second century, when titles are first attested, would have understood the contents and purpose of Acts.[5] The earliest witnesses to the familiar, though not yet fixed, title are Irenaeus (*A.H.* 3.13.3) and Clement of Alexandria (*Strom.* 5.82). Irenaeus also refers to Acts as *Lucae de apostolis testificatio* ("Luke's Testimony about the Apostles" [*A.H.* 3.13.3; cf. 3.15.1]), as well as to material that is *ex sermonibus et actibus apostolorum* ("from the words and deeds of the apostles" [*A.H.* 3.12.1]). Tertullian employs *Commentarius Lucae* ("Luke's Memoirs" [*De ieiunio* 10]), as well as *Acta Apostolorum*, a usage followed by Cyprian.[6] The phrase is somewhat analogous to Justin's τὰ ἀπομνημονεύματα τῶν ἀποστόλων ("The Memoirs of the Apostles" [*1 Apol.* 67.3]), used to define the in-house word "Gospels" (ibid. 66.3). Acts, therefore, unlike the Gospels, did not acquire a lasting "Christian" designation.[7]

In historical writings, πράξεις was used as a title for accounts of political and military careers that were not full biographies and did not evaluate character,[8] as in the translation of Latin *Res Gestae* in the *Res Gestae Divi*

1 On the title, note Theodore Zahn, *Introduction to the New Testament* (trans. and ed. Christopher S. Thayer; 3 vols.; Edinburgh: T&T Clark, 1909) 3:59, 87; Alfred Wikenhauser, *Die Apostelgeschichte und ihr Geschichtswert* (NTAbh; Münster: Aschendorff, 1921) 95–107 (with a valuable discussion of πράξεις literature); Cadbury and Lake, 4:1–2; Christian Maurer, "πρᾶξις," *TDNT* 6:642–44; Eckhard Plümacher, "Apostelgeschichte," *TRE* 3:483–528, esp. 483; Schneider, 1:74–75; Sterling, *Apologetic Historiography*, 314–15; Raoul Mortley, "The Title of the Acts of the Apostles," in *Lectures anciennes de la Bible* (Cahiers de Biblia Patristica 1; Strasbourg: Centre d'analyse et de documentation patristiques, 1987) 105–12; David E. Aune, *The New Testament in Its Literary Environment* (LEC; Philadelphia: Westminster, 1987) 78; Gonzalo del Cerro, "Los Hechos apócrifos de los Apósteles: Su género literario," *EstBíb* 51 (1993) 207–32, esp. 215–16; John Economou, *The Problem of the Title "Acts of the Apostles"* [in Greek] (Thessaloniki, 1995) and Christopher Mount, *Pauline Christianity: Luke-Acts and the Legacy of Paul* (NovTSup 104; Leiden: Brill, 2002) 40–43. Sterling (*Apologetic Historiography*, 315) rightly observes that the title is inappropriate but that it reveals that the early church viewed Acts as a historical work. The same observation may be made about the Apocryphal Acts. Finally, Haenchen (146–47), after observing the extent to which the title is not appropriate, concedes that "the book's title is not wholly a misnomer," since the apostles are the heads of the early church and Paul is a kind of "suffragan apostle."

2 For various forms of the title, see N-A[27], 735; and Constantinus von Tischendorf, *Novum Testamentum Graece: Editio Octava Critica Maior* (Leipzig: Hinrichs, 1869) 2:1.

3 Christian Mauer ("πρᾶξις," *TDNT* 6:644) states that most of the NT uses of the word have a derogatory nuance. This is quite true of the three instances of the plural: Acts 19:18; Rom 8:13; Col 3:9.

4 Conzelmann, 3.

5 See the extensive comments of Harry Gamble, *Books and Readers in the Early Church: A History of Early Christian Texts* (New Haven: Yale University Press, 1995) 37–38.

6 Later Latin tradition preferred the fourth declension *actus* to the second declension *acta*. The latter is a more accurate rendition of πράξεις ("acts").

7 Irenaeus's "Testimony about the Apostles" could have been a candidate for a specialized title, but it did not endure and it is not clear whether it was ever intended to be a kind of title or was used by others.

8 Examples include the πράξεις Ἀλεξάνδρου ("Accomplishments of Alexander") by Callisthenes (c. 330 BCE; *FGH* 124 F 14, and, following this, in MSS. of the *Alexander Romance* (with or without βίος ["life"], quite possibly dependent on Callisthenes, as in the novel circulated under his name); Sosylus's Ἀννίβου πράξεις (c. 200, *FGH* 176 F 1), in MSS.).

Augusti ("Accomplishments of the Deified Augustus"), and not infrequently in the bodies of historical works.[9] In this sense, it occurs in the later historical books of the LXX.[10] Because of the association of *πράξεις* with mighty accomplishments, the term could be understood as "miracles," raising modern questions about its suitability, though educated readers of the second century would have been more likely to understand the title (*πράξεις*) to refer to a historical work focused on the career of an individual.[11]

The tradition of associating the noun "acts" with a single name (such as Alexander, Hannibal, Pompey, or Augustus) raises the possibility that the title passed to the canonical work from the *Acts of Paul*.[12] The eventual title "Acts of the Apostles" could serve as a counter to works focused on particular missionaries. This sentiment reaches its most hopeful form in the claim of the Muratorian Fragment that Luke wrote "the acts of all the apostles" (*acta omnium apostolorum* [line 34]). The notion that the apostles as a body formed a unified front against all practices and teachings viewed as aberrant is certainly congenial to Acts (e.g., 15:22-29) and is manifest in titles such as *The Teaching of the Twelve Apostles*, *The Apostolic Tradition*, and, in due course, "The Apostles' Creed."[13]

Πράξεις thus suggests that the material it characterizes will be an account of the accomplishments of an important person. The received title, "Accomplishments of the Apostles," accepts this characterization—rather than, for example, a label indicating a narrative about the growth of the Christian mission or the dissemination of the word of God—but applies it to a body, the apostles, instead of to an individual. "Acts" implies that this volume was viewed as more or less biographical, while the subjective genitive "apostles" stresses the unity of the tradition, possibly in opposition to those who appealed to a particular apostle, such as Paul (e.g., Marcion), Peter (e.g., the Pseudo-Clementines), Thomas (e.g., the *Gospel of Thomas*), and so on.

9 See, e.g., Xenophon *Cyr.* 1.2.16 (Cyrus); Josephus *Ant.* 14.68 (Pompey); and Cassius Dio 62.29 ("All the deeds of the Romans").

10 2 Chr 12:15; 13:22; 27:7; 28:26. Cf. 1 Macc 16:23, of the sayings and actions of monarchs. See also the subscript to 2 Maccabees in MSS. Alexandrinus and Venetus, which read *Ἰοῦδα τοῦ Μακκ(αβ)αίου πράξεων ἐπιστολή/ἐπιτομή* ("A letter/epitome of the accomplishments of Judas Maccabeus"), respectively.

11 Cf. Anton Fridrichsen, *The Problem of Miracle in Primitive Christianity* (trans. Roy A. Harrisville and John S. Hanson; Minneapolis: Augsburg, 1972) 163 n. 9. Writing in 1925, Fridrichsen noted that the famous historian E. Meyer protested against the title, so understood, whereas the great philologist Ulrich von Wilamowitz-Möllendorff found it "perfectly suited" to Acts. Richard Reitzenstein and Paul Wendland shared that opinion, but Harnack strongly disagreed, as did Wikenhauser and, for that matter, Fridrichsen.

12 Cadbury (*Book* 157–58) allows this possibility.

13 See Manfred Hornschuh, "The Apostles as Bearers of the Tradition," in Edgar Hennecke, *New Testament Apocrypha* (ed. Wilhelm Schneemelcher; ET ed. Robert McL. Wilson; 2 vols.; Philadelphia: Westminster, 1965) 2:74–87, esp. 74–79; and Wolfgang A. Bienert, "The Picture of the Apostle in early Christian Tradition," in *NTApoc*, 2:5–27.

1

1:1-5 Preface

1/ **In the previous book, Theophilus,
I dealt with all that Jesus did
and taught from the beginning
2/ until that day when he was
taken up after instructing the
apostles whom he had been
inspired to choose.[a] 3/ For forty
days after his passion he gave
them numerous proofs[b] that he
was alive. He appeared to them[c]
and spoke[d] about God's reign.
4/ During a meal, he directed
them not to leave Jerusalem.[e]
"Wait here," he said, "to receive
what the Father has promised,
about which I have told you.
5/ John baptized with water.
Before many days have passed[f]
you will be baptized with Holy
Spirit."**

a The translation of these two verses is quite disputed. Alternatives for v. 1 include "all that Jesus *began* to do and teach," "all that Jesus did and taught *from the beginning*," or "all that Jesus did and taught." In v. 2 it is not certain whether "inspired" (lit. "through Holy Spirit") refers to his instruction or to the choice of the apostles. John J. Kilgallen argues for translating διά as "because of" (a meaning normally found with the accusative) ("'The Apostles Whom He Chose because of the Holy Spirit': A Suggestion Regarding Acts 1,2," *Bib* 81 [2000] 414–17).

b David Mealand concluded that the phrase is "normal in Hellenistic Greek" ("The Phrase 'Many Proofs' in Acts 1,3 and in Hellenistic Writers," *ZNW* 80 [1989] 134–35, here 135). Witherington (108) erroneously states that it is "very rare in Greek literature *except* in Greek historiographical works."

c The form ὀπτάμενος is a deponent that means "to make an appearance." See Cadbury and Lake, 4. Haenchen (140 n. 5) observes that Luke does not wish the appearances to be viewed as visions. This changes after the ascension. Paul summarizes this special era in 13:31.

d In place of "speak," the participle in some D-Texts is διδάσκων ("teaching"), which aptly reinforces the *inclusio* with 28:31.

e In the NT, "Jerusalem" may be either a transliterated indeclinable noun (as in v. 12) or a hellenized neuter plural, as here. Efforts to find a distinction between them as a basis for detecting sources have not been successful. As Acts moves into the Hellenic world the neuter plural becomes prevalent.

f Lit. "Not after many these days." The phrase (which includes an improper demonstrative) is an odd way to say "within a few days." This may be the first instance of the figure of litotes, of which Luke is quite fond. The same phrase, including the misplaced demonstrative, appears in the *Act. Paul* 11/14.6 (4). This is a strong example of the knowledge and use of Acts by the *Acts of Paul.* See Julian Hills, "The Acts of the Apostles in the *Acts of Paul,*" in Eugene Lovering, ed., *SBLSP 1994* (Atlanta: Scholars Press, 1994) 24–54, esp. 49. On the syntax, see, e.g., Charles F. D. Moule, *An Idiom Book of New Testament Greek* (2nd ed.; Cambridge: Cambridge University Press, 1963) 61–62. Before οὐ μετὰ πολλὰς ταύτας ἡμέρας, a number of D-Texts (D* it; Aug[pt]) add ὅ καὶ μέλλετε λαμβάνειν ("which you also will receive"). At the close, D* sa mae aug[pt] add "until Pentecost," a typically anticlimactic and pedantic expansion, which does, however, prepare the way for the abrupt beginning of 2:1. On this, see Strange, *Problem*, 113–15.

Analysis

Acts 1–7 moves the narrative firmly but without haste toward the gentile mission, the legitimacy of which is the governing theme of the book. The pace is deliberate insofar as the narrator wishes to show that Christianity is the divinely directed final manifestation of Israelite faith.[1] Although the resurrection demonstrates that Jesus is the Messiah foretold in the Scriptures, the Jewish leaders reject their evidence and attempt to stifle the rapidly growing movement, which they perceive as a threat. Success among those of Greek-speaking Diaspora background raises questions about loyalty to Torah and temple. The general public then shifts from strong support to fervent opposition.

Acts begins like Luke's Gospel. The first two chapters present an ideal situation marked by loyalty to Israelite tradition and the absence of conflict.[2] Both narratives are set in Jerusalem[3] and open in an atmosphere brimming with epiphanies (e.g., Luke 2:8-14; Acts 1:9-11; 2:1-12), most of which include angelic announcements or messages (Luke 1:11-20, 26-38; 2:10-12; Acts 1:11). There are also differences. Formally, for example, the first two chapters of Luke are notable for their canticles composed in the style of the LXX and in the manner of Hebrew poetry (Luke 1:13-17, 46-45; etc.). Acts 1–2, by contrast, lacks such poetry. Instead, there are speeches of Peter (1:16-22; 2:14-41, which cite the LXX.[4] In retrospect this marks a characteristic difference between the two books. Luke 1–2 uses biblical forms of discourse, while Acts 1–2 uses set-piece speeches. This distinction hints at the different milieux of the books; the second volume will engage the wider, specifically Greek-speaking, world.

If the parallels between Acts 1–2 and Luke 1–2 are formal and modal, the links between the close of Luke (24:36-53) and the beginning of Acts (1:1-14) are specific and thematic. Both contain a postresurrection appearance in which Jesus promises the disciples forthcoming endowment with heavenly power, commissions them as "witnesses,"[5] and directs them to remain in Jerusalem (Luke 24:36-49; Acts 1:3-8). Both report an ascension outside of Jerusalem and the subsequent return of the disciples to the city (Luke 24:50-52; Acts 1:9-12).[6] These similarities contribute to the leading problem of the structure of Acts 1: where does the introduction or prologue end?

The preface, which lacks a clear ending, complicates resolution of this question. Moreover, the syntactical nature of v. 3 is disputed, and the summary—if that is what it is—shifts from indirect to direct speech in the course of v .4. One may also ask whether v. 6 introduces a distinct scene. Since this preface appears to be the type that offers a recapitulation of the previous book without a preview of this one, it is reasonable, but not necessary, to hypothesize that the prologue will end at the point where new information appears.

Excursus: The Prefaces to Luke and Acts

Scholarship has long held that by the inclusion of prefaces Luke and Acts make a bid to be considered as literature and that the two books are to be considered historiography. The scrupulous research of Loveday Alexander has challenged these assumptions.[7] She has shown that these prefaces do not conform to the conventions and style of historical writings (which in Greco-Roman antiquity belonged to the realm of *belles lettres*) but are most similar to those used by authors of "scientific," technical

1 "Christianity" is not an anachronism in reference to Acts; see on 11:26.

2 One may attribute this to authorial plan, but it is also possible that this is how Luke preferred to begin books.

3 On the role of Jerusalem in Luke and Acts, see Mikeal Parsons, "The Place of Jerusalem on the Lukan Landscape: An Exercise in Symbolic Cartography," in Richard Thompson, ed., *Literary Studies in Luke-Acts: Essays in Honor of Joseph B. Tyson* (Macon, Ga.: Mercer University Press, 1998) 155–71.

4 On the use of the LXX in Acts, see, in general, Pervo, *Dating*, 29–35. For bibliography, see Luke Timothy Johnson, *Septuagintal Midrash in the Speeches of Acts* (The Père Marquette Lecture in Theology, 2002; Milwaukee: Marquette University Press, 2002) 58 n. 42 and 60 n. 53, to which add Dietrich Rusam, *Das Alte Testament bei Lukas* (BZNW 112; Berlin: de Gruyter, 2003).

5 A biblical basis for Luke's understanding of "witness" is Isa 43:8-13. For a concise summary of the theme in Luke and Acts, see Weiser, 1:72–75.

6 See Goulder, *Type*, 16–17, who lists nine parallels.

7 Loveday C. A. Alexander, *The Preface to Luke's Gospel: Literary Convention and Social Context in*

books.[8] Neither preface invites the informed reader to expect that the contents will belong to the sphere of historiography (which does not, of course, mean that they are not historical or history).

Acts has a secondary preface. Such prefaces, used intermittently in multivolume productions, delineate both a break and a link: this new volume/roll bears some relation to another or to others. The most common feature of secondary prefaces is a recapitulation (*anakephalaiōsis*) of the preceding work.[9] This may also include a preview (*proekthesis*) of the current volume. The μέν of v. 1 (this is a Greek particle that plays various syntactical roles) leads one to expect that a preview of the second volume will follow, but it does not, even if v. 8 fulfills some of that function. This omission has some bearing on the relation between Luke and Acts, since such statements may indicate a change of subject, as in Philo *Vit. Mos.* 2.1, or a continuation of the previous, as in Josephus *Ap.* 2.2.[10] The preface permits one to read Acts either as "volume 2" or as a separate writing.[11] This means that the preface to Acts does not illuminate the question of whether the preface to Luke applies to both volumes or to the Gospel alone. Those who stress the unity of Luke and Acts are likely to hold that the Gospel prologue applies also to Acts; those who see the relation as somewhat looser tend toward the opposite understanding.[12] Both views are possible and neither is demonstrable, although general limitation of Luke 1:1-4 to the Gospel is somewhat more likely.[13]

Joseph Fitzmyer would conclude the prologue with v. 2, on the grounds that vv. 1-2 "combine different literary forms and use some pre-Lucan tradition."[14] This reasoning is cloudy. Verse 3 is a relative clause modifying "apostles."[15] I. Howard Marshall is an example of those who define vv. 1-5 as the prologue, which summarizes

Luke 1.1-4 and Acts 1.1 (SNTSMS 78; Cambridge: Cambridge University Press, 1993); eadem, "The Preface to Acts and the Historians," in Witherington, *History*, 73–103; and eadem, "Formal Elements and Genre: Which Greco-Roman Prologues Most Closely Parallel the Lukan Prologues?" in Moessner, *Heritage*, 9–26. See also Joseph B. Tyson, *Marcion and Luke-Acts: A Defining Struggle* (Columbia: University of South Carolina Press, 2006) 109–16.

8 An example from symposium literature is Plutarch's preface to his fictional account of a banquet of the seven sages; see David E. Aune, "Septem Sapientium Convivium (Moralia 146B–164D)," in Hans Dieter Betz, ed., *Plutarch's Ethical Writings and Early Christian Literature* (SCHNT 4; Leiden: Brill, 1978) 51–105. He comments on the similarities to Acts and returns to the same text in "Luke 1.1-4: Historical or Scientific *Prooimion*?" in Alf Christophersen et al., eds., *Paul, Luke, and the Graeco-Roman World: Essays in Honour of Alexander J. M. Wedderburn* (JSNTS 217; London: Sheffield Academic Press, 2002) 138–48, to argue that strict divisions among types of prefaces are undesirable. (Christian examples of such improbable prefaces include those to the *Acts of Barnabas* and the *Lausiac History*.)

9 Recapitulations were more of an exception than a rule in ancient historiography; see Alexander, "Preface to Acts," 89–90.

10 These examples are apt because each comes from the second book of a two-volume work. Although Josephus's preface to *Contra Apionem* is frequently cited as a parallel to Acts 1:1-3 (e.g., Sterling, *Apologetic Historiography*, 368–69), Josephus's work is not historiography. See also David Moessner, "The Lukan Prologues in the Light of Ancient Narrative Hermeneutics: παρηκολουθηκότι and the Credentialed Author," in Verheyden, *Unity*, 399–417.

11 Alexander, "The Preface to Acts," 82; eadem, *Context*, 210.

12 Cadbury ("Commentary on the Preface of Luke," in Cadbury and Lake, 2:489–510, esp. 489–90) maintains that the preface to Luke applies to both books. He is followed by, for example, Fitzmyer, *Luke I–IX*, 287–302; and I. Howard Marshall, "Acts and the 'Former Treatise,'" in Winter and Clarke, *Setting*, 163–82, esp. 172–74. Tannehill (*Narrative Unity*, 1:9–12) evidently assumes this view, since all of his references to the terms of the prologue to Luke are from Acts. Opposed are, for example, Haenchen (136 n. 3), who says that the preface to Luke applies only to the Gospel, as well as those who view Acts as a historical monograph.

13 On the subject, see the balanced observations of Alexander, "The Preface to Acts," 76–82; she finds attempts to apply Luke 1:1-4 to Acts problematic (77 n. 11).

14 Fitzmyer, 191–98, here 191.

15 One element of Lucan style, to be sure, is the use of relative clauses as somewhat independent sentences, but that is not fully true of v. 3. Stephen G. Wilson suggests that it may be a parenthesis (*The Gentiles and the Gentile Mission in Luke-Acts* [SNTSMS 23; Cambridge: Cambridge University Press, 1973] 101). It is barely possible to take v. 4 as a sequence to v. 3.

the Gospel. At v. 6 fresh material appears.[16] Yet there is fresh material in v. 5 (baptism with the Spirit is but a few days away), and not all that follows is new. Luke T. Johnson views vv. 1-11 as a recapitulation of the Gospel and thus the prologue.[17] Acts 1:12, however, repeats Luke 24:52, while the list of v. 13 is essentially that of Luke 6:12-16, and v. 14 is parallel to Luke 24:53. Genuinely new material begins in v. 15. It is therefore preferable to regard all of Acts 1:1-14 as the prologue.[18] Verse 14a, which reads like a brief example of the summaries in Acts, supports this division.[19]

The implication of these observations is that the author evidently envisioned the possibility of reading Acts independently of Luke. That book related "all that Jesus did and said," but those words and deeds do not play a major role in Acts—notably in the sphere of ethics.[20] The one saying of Jesus that is cited outside of the prologue is not found in the Gospel (20:35).

The difficulties of the relationship between Luke 24 and Acts 1, which include both similarities and differences—most notably the disparate accounts of the ascension—have prompted proposals that the present opening of Acts is the secondary result of the division of the work into two books for the purposes of canonization.[21] "Canonization," however, is an anachronism when applied to second-century Christian activity. Gospel collections and harmonies did appear in that era, but the evidence for the independent existence of Acts is, if anything, earlier than clear evidence for a formal Gospel collection.[22] In addition, proponents of this editorial process must explain why the redactor introduced divergent information about the ascension. The hypothesis seeks to explain an assumption—that Luke and Acts were once a single book—for which there is no evidence.[23]

Structural divisions within vv. 1-14 are problematic. *μὲν οὖν* (a particle)[24] in v. 6 may mark a transition, and it transpires that vv. 6-11 are a scene. The author, not a later editor, is responsible for these difficulties. Verse 3 is particularly difficult, a relative clause modifying the "apostles" of v. 2, followed in v. 4 by a return to "Jesus" as subject. If v. 3 is taken as a parenthesis, vv. 1-5 recapitulate, with additions, the ending of Luke.[25] The focus is on the apostles, who were chosen by Jesus as recipients of convincing proofs of his resurrection and of a forthcoming gift of the Spirit. This gift prepares and equips them for their role as inspired witnesses to Jesus.

Comment

■ **1** The opening *μέν solitarium* is not untoward (cf. 3:13, 21; 21:39; 27:21; 28:22), but, as noted, it does lead readers to expect a balancing *δέ* clause ("book 1 told the story of

16 I. Howard Marshall, *The Acts of the Apostles: An Introduction and Commentary* (Tyndale Commentary; Grand Rapids: Eerdmans, 1980) 55.

17 Luke Timothy Johnson, *The Acts of the Apostles* (SacPag 5; Collegeville, Minn.: Liturgical Press, 1992) 23–32. Haenchen (135–47) treats 1:1-8 as the prologue, but he does not justify this decision.

18 So also, e.g., Talbert, *Reading Acts,* 19; Barrett, 1:61; and Weiser, 1:46–47.

19 Linguistic evidence includes the periphrastic form of *προσκαρτερεῖν* ("devote oneself to"; 1:14; 2:42; cf. 2:46) and the adverb *ὁμοθυμαδόν* (2:46; 5:12). On the summaries see pp. 88–89.

20 See Parsons and Pervo, *Rethinking*, 38–40.

21 On these proposals, see Haenchen, 145.

22 Irenaeus is the earliest witness to a formal collection of Gospels, the plurality of which he is obliged to defend (*A.H.* 3.1.11). Marcion and Justin are important here, as both utilize an edition of the Gospel of Luke but not Acts. The division hypothesis would have either to claim that Marcion excised all of Luke's work that is now found in Acts or to attribute the separation to a predecessor of his. That action would have to be assigned to the early first quarter of the second century, much earlier than the practice of Gospel collections. The imitation of Acts in the *Acts of Paul* and the *Acts of Peter* supports the view that Acts had an independent existence by the middle of the second century. On the evidence for a four-Gospel collection, see Helmut Koester, *Ancient Christian Gospels: Their History and Development* (Philadelphia: Trinity Press International, 1990) 242–44. On early witnesses for Acts, see the introduction, p. 1.

23 Mikeal Parsons addresses literary and textual issues of Luke 24 and Acts 1 in *The Departure of Jesus in Luke-Acts: The Ascension Narratives in Context* (JSNTS 21; Sheffield: Sheffield Academic Press, 1987).

24 On this phrase in Acts, see Moule, *Idiom Book*, 162–63. BDF §251 states that it is ambiguous here.

25 Alexander ("The Preface to Acts") finds the lack of

Jesus; book 2 will tell about . . .").[26] "Volume" (λόγος) is a vague term that sheds no light on genre or content.[27] "Theophilus" is the same dedicatee as in Luke 1:3. Dedication was not customary in historiography.[28] Critical opinion holds that Theophilus, whose name was common among Jews,[29] was a real person. The basis for this is the use of the epithet "most excellent" in Luke 1:3.[30] In any case, the name readily yields to a symbolic interpretation.[31] The characterization of Theophilus in Luke 1:1-4 functions also to define the implied reader.[32] In the latter sense, at least, few commentators on Acts have improved upon Bede: "Theophilus means 'lover of God' or 'loved by God.' All lovers of God may therefore believe that [Acts] was written to them, because Luke the Physician wrote so that they might find health for the soul here."[33]

No convincing inference can be made about the social status of author or dedicatee. Dedicatees are normally of higher standing than dedicators, but the status of the latter here is unknown. The relation between dedication and patronage is too complicated to allow firm conclusions,[34] and a connection between Acts and a Christian community (or communities) would make any relationship atypical.[35]

"All that Jesus did and taught from the beginning": writers of prefaces like to include the word "all"; for Luke it also anticipates any appeal to secret teachings of Jesus (or Paul: 20:20, 27).[36] The translation "from the beginning" would evoke the sense of "beginning" (ἀρχή) found in Luke 1:2 (cf. Mark 1:1; John 1:1) that could underlie the verb ἤρξατο, which may, however,

---

a transition from recapitulation to new narration unparalleled. If Luke was attempting to write in a literary style, he was not successful.

26 πρῶτος is inelegant. Cadbury and Lake (2) give preferable Greek expressions. Luke also uses this word to mean "the former of two" in 7:12.

27 Barrett, 1:64.

28 Alexander, "The Preface to Acts," 85. Josephus is the earliest example. Alexander (89) warns against the common practice of using Josephus as a model in assessing the prefaces. Insofar as Josephus is not typical, this is an important caution. If, however, Luke made use of Josephus (see p. 12), his prefaces may have been direct models. It is interesting that Luke and Josephus share a number of atypical elements in the matter of composing prefaces. The "most excellent Diognetus" (κράτιστε Διόγνητε) of *Diognetus* 1 could be a real person or a literary fiction, precisely like Theophilus, as Andreas Lindemann observes in *Paulus im Ältesten Christentum* (BHT 58; Tübingen: Mohr Siebeck, 1979) 344. On this, see Giovanni Menestrina, "L'incipit dell'epistola 'ad Diognetum', Luca 1,1-4 e Atti 1,1-2," *BeO* 19 (1977) 215–18; and Ehrman, *Apostolic Fathers*, 2:126. The Philocrates to whom *Aristeas* is addressed (1, 120, 171, 295, 322) is almost certainly fictional. Aristides, Justin (*1 Apol.*), and Athenagoras address their apologies to the emperors. The Autolycus to whom the three books of Theophilus are addressed (2.1; 3.1) is unknown and could be imaginary. In short, when the dedicatees are known, it is almost certain that they did not read the work and certain that they did not request it. As for the others, it makes little difference whether they are real or imaginary.

29 Louis H. Feldman goes so far as to call it "distinctly Jewish" (*Jew and Gentile in the Ancient World* [Princeton: Princeton University Press, 1993] 58).

30 For various understandings of the dedicatee, see Robert F. O'Toole, "Theophilus," *ABD* 6:511–12. On the social role of dedication, note Alexander, *Preface*, 187–200; and Robbins, "Social Location," 320–23.

31 Symbolic elucidations of the name are attested since Origen (e.g., *Hom. in Lucam* 1.10-11), who has no difficulty including "most excellent" in his interpretation. See also the citation from Bede in the text. The proposal that "Theophilus" is a pseudonym for a highly placed person whose Christian sympathies Luke would not dare expose (e.g., Jacquier, 3) unintentionally opens a can of worms: how could such an individual perform many of the traditional duties of literary patronage without undesirable publicity?

32 See William S. Kurz, "Narrative Approaches to Luke-Acts," *Bib* 68 (1987) 195–220, esp. 208–12. For further observations on the implied reader, see idem, *Reading Luke-Acts: Dynamics of Biblical Narrative* (Louisville: Westminster John Knox, 1993) 12–16. Theophilus is the "overt narratee," the person to whom the story is ostensibly told.

33 Bede, *Expositio Actuum Apostolorum* (ed. Max L. W. Laistner; CCSL 121; Brepols: Turnholt, 1983) 6 (author's trans.).

34 See Alexander, *Literary Context*, 30 n. 35.

35 See Richard P. Saller, *Personal Patronage under the Early Empire* (Cambridge: Cambridge University Press, 1982) 123. Gamble, *Books and Readers*, 102.

36 Alexander, *Preface*, 130.

be no more than the equivalent of a weak auxiliary (cf. Luke 4:21; 9:12).[37] Some view it as emphatic: Jesus continues to work through the Holy Spirit.[38] Since Luke often refers to the beginning of Jesus' ministry (Luke 3:23; 23:5; Acts 1:22; 10:37), some emphasis seems appropriate.[39] The verbs "did and taught" go a fair way toward defining Luke as a biography. The philosophical tradition in particular stressed the necessity of concord between words and deeds as the test of the validity of an intellectual system.[40]

■ **2** The text and translation of this verse present major problems that are difficult to compartmentalize.[41] The text of N-A[27], *ἄχρι ἧς ἡμέρας ἐντειλάμενος τοῖς ἀποστόλοις διὰ πνεύματος ἁγίου οὓς ἐξελέξατο ἀνελήμφθη* (lit. "until the day in which, after giving orders to the apostles through the Holy Spirit whom [masculine plural] he had chosen he was received up"[42]) has overwhelming support in MSS., versions, and citations. The problem is its awkwardness: does "through [the] Holy Spirit" modify "ordered" or the choice of the apostles? One solution is to delete *διὰ πνεύματος ἁγίου*.[43] This phrase may be a reading of the D-type that became general in the tradition.[44] Against this solution is the objection that an interpolator would have chosen a better place to make this insertion, but such appeals reveal little more than what critics would have done had they made the interpolation, and it is difficult to dispute that the phrase makes no apparent contribution. The text may be corrupt. This corruption would have occurred quite early, for the various alternatives—there are at least

37 See Cadbury and Lake, 3; Conzelmann, 3.

38 This is the view of Barrett, 1:66–67. cf. also Bruce, 98.

39 Conzelmann, 3.

40 This view was part of the philosophical tradition from Plato *Lach.* 188C-E onward. It was emphasized by the Stoics (e.g., Diogenes Laertius 7.40) despite the contrary claims of Plutarch *Stoic. rep.* 1 (*Mor.* 1033A-B). See the notes in Harold Cherniss, *Plutarch's Moralia* XIII, part II (LCL; Cambridge, Mass.: Harvard University Press, 1976) 412–13. Note also Luke 6:47, 49. A similar phrase about Jesus appears in Papias (Eusebius *H.E.* 3.39.5). "Teach" is effectively an *inclusio*: Acts 1:1 (of Jesus), 28:31 (of Paul).

41 Metzger has a lucid discussion of the issues (*Textual Commentary*, 236–41). Note also Ropes, *Text*, 256–61; Kirsopp Lake, "The Preface to Acts and the Composition of Acts," in idem and Henry J. Cadbury, eds., *Additional Notes to the Commentary* (vol. 5 of Foakes Jackson and Lake, *Beg.*) 1–7, esp. 1–4; John M. Creed, "The Text and interpretation of Acts i.1-2," *JTS* 35 (1934) 176–82; Eldon Jay Epp, "The Ascension in the Textual Tradition of Luke-Acts," in idem and Gordon D. Fee, eds., *New Testament Textual Criticism, Its Significance for Exegesis: Essays in Honour of Bruce M. Metzger* (Oxford: Clarendon, 1981) 131–45; and Parsons, *Departure*, 117–35. Arie W. Zwiep argues that the D-Text removes the suggestion of a physical ascension and is thus related to theological controversies of the second and third centuries ("The Text of the Ascension Narratives [Luke 24.50-53; Acts 1.1-2. 9-11]," *NTS* 42 [1996] 219–44). See also Gijs Bouman, "Der Angang der Apostelgeschichte und der 'westliche' Text," in Tjitze Baarda et al., eds., *Text and Testimony: Essays on the New Testament and Apocryphal Literature in Honour of A. F. J. Klijn* (Kampen: Kok, 1988) 46–55, who argues that the D-Text had no ascension narrative.

42 On the meaning of *ἀνελήμφθη* in v. 2, see Pieter A. Stempvoort, "The Interpretation of the Ascension in Luke and Acts," *NTS* 5 (1959) 32–33; and Parsons, *Departure*, 128–33.

43 The phrase is Pauline and Deutero-Pauline: Rom 5:5; 2 Tim 1:14; and *1 Clem.* 8:1. For arguments against its originality, see Dibelius, *Studies*, 90.

44 J. Rendell Harris associated the D-Text with Montanism in his *Codex Bezae: A Study of the So-Called Western Text of the New Testament* (TextsS 2.1; Cambridge: Cambridge University Press, 1891) 148–53, 228–34. It is probably more prudent to observe that the second century witnessed a number of spiritual revivals, discernible in works as distinct as the *Shepherd of Hermas* and the *Acts of Paul*, and that the D-Text bears imprints of this interest. For early refutations of Harris's specific theory, see the references in Eldon Jay Epp, *The Theological Tendency of Codex Bezae Cantabrigiensis in Acts* (SNTSMS 3; Cambridge: Cambridge University Press, 1966) 2 n. 2. D-Text interest in the role of the Spirit is indisputable. See the variants in 6:10; 11:17; 15:7, 29, 32; 19:1; 20:3, discussed by, among others, Epp, *Tendency*, 7, 103–4, 116–18, 153–54; and Head, "Problem," 415–4, esp. 434–35. A different view is taken by Matthew Black, "The Holy Spirit in the Western Text of Acts," in Epp and Fee, *Textual Criticism*, 159–70. Luke 6:13, where the apostles were chosen, does not refer to the Spirit, nor does Luke 24.

five—to the text of N-A[27] all seem to be efforts to improve on that text.

One of these is Codex Bezae, which reads ἄχρι ἧς ἡμέρας ἀνελήμφθη ἐντειλάμενος τοῖς ἀποστόλοις διὰ πνεύματος ἁγίου οὓς ἐξελέξατο καὶ ἐκέλευσε κηρύσσειν τὸ εὐαγγέλιον ("Until the day when he was taken up . . . **and instructed them to proclaim the gospel**"), shifting "he was taken up" toward the beginning and filling in the contents of Jesus' instruction with typical (and conventional) material.[45] Efforts to establish the true D-Text have yielded: ἐν ᾗ ἡμέρᾳ τοὺς ἀποστόλους ἐξελέξατο διὰ πνεύματος ἁγίου καὶ ἐκέλευσεν/ἐνετείλατο κηρύσσειν τὸ εὐαγγέλιον ("**on the** day when **he chose the apostles through the Holy Spirit and instructed them to proclaim the gospel**").[46] This proposal, which deletes the reference to the ascension, resolves some of the syntactical problems, but it is unlikely to be original.[47]

■ **3** Following the evident summary, Luke adds the information that the period of apostolic instruction lasted for forty days. This dissonance between Luke and Acts allows the risen Christ time to provide detailed explication of the Scriptures that foretold his fate (Luke 24:44-48a) and to mark an interim between the ministry of the earthly Jesus and that of his followers. The passage thus functions in a way analogous to the temptation story of Luke 4:1-13.[48] Another divergence between the Gospel and Acts is that, whereas the risen Jesus appears to members of the general community in Luke,

45 Cf. Mark 1:14; 13:10; 14:9; Pseudo-Mark 16:15 may be the immediate source. Note *Barn.* 5:9. Epp (*Tendency*, 64–65) relates the phrase "preach the gospel" to the gentile mission, by way of Luke 24:47.

46 This is the proposal of Boismard, *Texte*, 48–49. Others have contributed to the task, including Friedrich Blass, James Hardy Ropes, and Albert Curtis Clark. See Metzger, *Textual Commentary*, 236–41.

47 According to the Gospel, Jesus chose the apostles in Luke 6:13. Alteration of the opening relative expression is unlikely to have been original, since there is no good rationale for changing "on" to "until." The epexegetic infinitive phrase is certainly secondary. On the probability that the reference to the ascension is primary, see Epp, "Ascension"; and Parsons, *Departure*, 117–35.

48 "Forty" is, of course, a good biblical number, too good for those who wish to pin down a particular symbol for or antitype to Acts. See Talbert, *Reading Acts*, 23, for a list. The reference to "commands" in v. 2 evokes Moses' time on Sinai (Exod 24:18). This parallel would evoke a period of preparation and instruction. See Philippe Menoud, "'Pendant quarante jours' (Actes i 3)," in *Neotestamentica et patristica: Eine Freundesgabe, Herrn Professor Dr. Oscar Cullmann zu seinem 60. Geburtstag überreicht* (NovTSup 6; Leiden: Brill, 1962) 148–56, whose views promote the parallelisms between Luke and Acts. Conzelmann (*Theology*, 203) is content to refer to "a sacred period between the times." Talbert (*Reading Acts*, 23) notes that *2 Bar.* 76:1-5 is similar: Baruch teaches the people for forty days before being taken to heaven. Luke does not appear to be attempting to place the Ascension within a specific time frame. Not until the fourth century does the liturgical season of Easter take its present shape. Tertullian says, "With certain disciples he spent forty days in Galilee, a region of Judaea, teaching them what they should teach. Then he appointed them to the duty of preaching throughout the world, and, with a cloud cast about him, he was caught up to heaven—far more truly than any Romulus of yours in the tale of Proculus" (*Apol.* 21.23; [trans. Terrot R. Glover; LCL; Cambridge, Mass.: Harvard University Press, 1931] 113). Note that Tertullian places this instruction in Galilee and that he does not dispute the aptness of a "pagan parallel" to the ascension of Jesus, but only its veracity. (Proculus served as the witness to the deification of Romulus [Livy 1.16]). The time of the ascension (when distinguished from the resurrection) varies from Easter day to twelve years later (Kirsopp Lake, "The Ascension," in Lake and Cadbury, *Additional Notes*, 16–22). Luke probably did not take the figure of forty days from tradition but devised it to accord with his own views and plan. See Gerd Lüdemann, *Early Christianity according to the Traditions in Acts* (trans. John Bowden; Philadelphia: Fortress Press, 1989) 28. It is possible that Luke introduced the interval to combat other accounts of postresurrection appearances to the apostles.

appearances in Acts are restricted to the apostles.[49] They are the focus of chap. 1.

"Passion" is a later technical term that suits here, for, as the adjective "living" (Luke 24:5) indicates, it includes death.[50] The Lucan tendency to submerge the passion in the resurrection is quite apparent.[51] To speak about the reign of God (Luke 31 times; Acts 6 times) amounts to "proclaiming the gospel" (cf. Acts 8:12; 14:22 is different). It summarizes the message of and about Jesus. Both "teach" (v. 1) and "reign of God" appear at 28:31, forming an *inclusio* that is not simply a circle but an indication of a major thematic element: what Jesus does in Jerusalem Paul does in Rome. In vv. 4-5, the instructions shift from general to particular and the discourse from indirect to direct. The word συναλιζόμενος (v. 4) is uncertain on both text-critical and lexicographical grounds. The choice is between understanding συναλιζόμενος in the rare sense of "eat with" (supported by many versions, but lacking Greek evidence for c. 100 and earlier), or as a misspelling of συναυλιζόμενος ("stay with").[52] "Eat with" follows Lucan convention. In particular, the combination of a meal scene with a farewell address echoes Luke 22. Moreover, since the text claims that Jesus made appearances to the apostles, "stay with" seems inappropriate.[53]

■ **4** The verse begins with a paraphrase of Luke 24:49. Acts 2:33 will reiterate and expound the sentiment. The abrupt shift from indirect to direct speech provides one more bit of confusion, but with it the narrator directly engages the reader with a grasp that will never be relaxed.[54] The phrase "what the Father has promised" is a not-especially-elegant effort to clarify that they are going to get not a promise for the future but fulfillment of a promise past. This is the Lucan antithesis of the Synoptic commands to go to Galilee.[55] The allusion in v. 5 to John's saying in v. 5 ("I baptize you with water; but one who is more powerful than I is coming; I am not worthy to untie the thong of his sandals. He will baptize you with the Holy Spirit and fire" [Luke 3:16])[56] is another evocation of the "beginning." One might expect the risen one to say, "*I* shall baptize you with the Holy Spirit *and fire*," but the passive here suggests that God is the agent. Omission of "fire" (cf. 2:3) places all of the emphasis on the gift of the Spirit.[57] "Before many days have passed" is an intentionally vague means of raising suspense.

Excursus: Direct Speech in Acts

Although the use of set-piece speeches in Acts—which distinguishes this book from the Gospel—has long invited comparisons with historiography, Acts has proportionately more speeches than do various types of historiography (particular histories, universal histories, and historical monographs), as well as biography. Moreover, and more importantly,

49 John Dominic Crossan, *Who Killed Jesus? Exposing the Roots of Anti-Semitism in the Gospel Story of the Death of Jesus* (San Francisco: HarperSanFrancisco, 1995) 205–6.

50 Cf. Luke 22:15; 24:26, 46; Acts 3:18; 17:3; 26:23; and Haenchen, 140 n. 4.

51 See Conzelmann, *Theology,* 202-6; and Eric Franklin, *Christ the Lord: A Study in the Purpose and Theology of Luke-Acts* (Philadelphia: Westminster, 1975) 29–41.

52 See the lengthy discussion in Cadbury and Lake, 4–6; Bruce, 101, who cites a number of translations; BDAG, *s.v.* συναλίζω; and Metzger, *Textual Commentary*, 241–42.

53 So also Barrett, 1:71–72.

54 The practice of moving from indirect to direct speech, or vice versa, appears from Homer onward. See BDF §470 (2); and Marius Reiser, "Der Alexanderroman und das Markusevangelium," in Hubert Cancik, ed., *Markus-Philologie* (WUNT 33; Tübingen: Mohr Siebeck, 1984) 131–63, 148 and n. 50. Examples include Luke 5:14; Acts 14:22; 23:23-24 (reverse) and 25:4-5. The D-Text improves the shift to direct discourse by reading, instead of ἠκούσατέ μου ("You have heard me"), ἠκούσατε, φησιν, δια τοῦ στόματος μου ("You have heard," he said, "through my mouth").

55 Cf. also Luke 24:6, the Lucan revision of Mark 16:7.

56 By 11:16 the transformation is complete: the saying is ascribed to Jesus rather than to John.

57 Most of the textual variants in v. 5 involve conformity to the Synoptic tradition. See Metzger, *Textual Commentary*, 243. Ropes (*Text*, 2–4) suspects, from Augustine (*Ep.* 265.3), a Greek text Ἰωάννης μὲν ἐβάπτισεν ὕδατι, ὑμεῖς δὲ ἐν πνεύματι ἁγίῳ ("John baptized with water, you with Holy Spirit") and asks whether this might be the source of the different readings. It is probably a secondary solution to a problem. When Peter commands that his hearers be baptized (2:37), he is introducing a novelty, for Jesus had not so ordained. (Ropes [*Text,*

Acts as Pop Lit

about 51 percent of the verses in Acts contain some direct speech.

This volume is unprecedented for either history or biography. For comparable percentages of direct speech one must turn to works that modern criticism classifies as fiction.[58] Those data and this fact do not in and of themselves catapult Acts into the realm of fiction. They do, however, quite strongly suggest that Acts is a representative of "popular literature."[59] Such a profile is one of the obstacles to the classification of Acts, for popular writers were often indifferent to the elite social conventions that governed various literary genres.[60] The sudden eruption of direct speech in Acts 1:4 is therefore stylistically appropriate; it indicates the author's desire for immediate and vivid communication.

4] eventually comes to this position also.) At Pentecost, the apostles were not "baptized" in the formal sense. This nice antithesis, "John baptized with water, but you will baptize with [the] Holy Spirit," describes their role as it was later understood and authorizes the same.

58 For data, see Richard Pervo, "Direct Speech in Acts and the Question of Genre," *JSNT* 28 (2006) 285–307.

59 For a definition of "popular" literature in the ancient Greek world, see William Hansen's introduction to his *Anthology of Ancient Greek Popular Literature* (Bloomington: Indiana University Press, 1998) xi–xxiii; and the conference essays edited by Oronzo Pecere and Antonio Stramaglia, *La letteratura di consumo nel mondo greco-latino* (Cassino: Università degli studi di Cassino, 1996), and Pecere's comments, 5–7.

60 See p. 17.

1

1:6-14 The Ascension

6/ On one of these occasions the
apostles asked Jesus: "Lord,
are you going to reestablish the
kingdom of Israel now?"[a]
7/ "The choice of times and occa-
sions is up to God, not you," he
replied.[b] 8/ "You will receive
power after the Holy Spirit has
come upon you[c] and you will
be my witnesses in Jerusalem
and in[d] the rest of Judea, in
Samaria, and to the ends of the
earth."
9/ Then, as they watched, he was
taken up, hidden from their
sight by a cloud.[e] 10/ As he
went, they continued to stare[f]
into the sky, when two men
in white suddenly appeared
right next to them, and said:
11/ "Why are you standing here
looking into the sky,[g] Galileans?
Jesus has been taken up from
your midst into the sky, from
which he will return in the same
way that you saw him leave."
12/ They then headed back to Jeru-
salem from Mount Olive Grove,
which is about half a Sabbath's
journey from the city. 13/ They
went up to the second floor
room in which they had been
staying. These people were
Peter and John, James and
Andrew, Philip and Thomas,
Bartholomew and Matthew,
James the son of Alphaeus and
Simon "the zealot," and Judas,
son of James. 14/ All these
men, as well as the women dis-
ciples[h] and Mary the mother of
Jesus and his siblings, devoted
themselves to a common life of
prayer.[i]

a According to Boismard (*Texte*, 52), the D-Text reads: *οἱ μὲν οὖν συνελθόντες ἐπηρώτων αὐτὸν λέγοντες κύριε, εἰ ἐν τῷ χρόνῳ τούτῳ ἀποκατασταθήσῃ καὶ πότε ἡ βασιλεία τοῦ Ἰσραήλ;* ("Lord, will you be reinstated at this time, and when will there be the kingdom of Israel?"). This moves the question in the direction of Luke 17:20.

b This construes *τίθημι* as "placed within God's power" rather than "appointed." See Barrett, 1:78. Witnesses vary on the introduction to the answer. There is slender support (Cyprian, Augustine) for reading "no one can know the time." This assimilates to Mark 13:32.

c The same verb (*ἐπέρχομαι*) is used of the conception of Jesus in Luke 1:35 (where *δύναμις* ("power") is also found. Note Isa 32:15.

d A C* D 81 323 *pc* omit *ἐν* ("in") before "the rest of Judea." If included, it strengthens the distinction between "Jerusalem" and other parts of Judea. (D-texts have "me" in the dative and omit "and" before "ends of the earth.")

e Ropes (*Text*, 5, followed by Boismard, *Texte*, 54) proposed this D-Text: *καὶ ταῦτα εἰπόντος αὐτοῦ νεφέλη ὑπέλαβεν αὐτὸν καὶ ἐπήρθη ἀπ' αὐτῶν* (Aug, sah) ("After he had said this a cloud covered him and removed him from them"). He concludes that *βλεπόντων αὐτῶν* is secondary, as it "badly overloads the sentence." That it may, but Luke wishes to stress that the disciples witnessed the event (see below). The D-Text is probably an assimilation to Luke 9:34 (the transfiguration).

f On this verb (*ἀτενίζω*), see Rick Strelan, "Strange Stares: *Atenizein* in Acts," *NovT* 41 (1999) 235–55.

g A number of D-Text witnesses (D 33c 242 326* and some Old Latin) omit the third of the monotonous repetitions of "into the sky." Haenchen (150 n. 8) says that Luke wished to emphasize this absence with a fourfold repetition. He is probably correct.

h The Byzantine tradition adds *καὶ δεήσει*, "prayer and supplication"; cf. Phil 4:6. D (and other D-Texts [Barrett, 1:89]) reads *σὺν γυναιξὶν καὶ τέκνοις*, thus "their wives and children." See Pervo, "Social Aspects," 236–37; and Metzger, *Textual Commentary*, 246. Barrett (1:59) renders "their wives." Luke is not in favor of matrimony and has no married missionaries. The expression is usually articular and may be anarthrous here because the proper names are anarthrous. At the close, a group of witnesses (B C[3] E Ψ 𝔐) adds a second *σύν* before *τοῖς ἀδελφοῖς*. This separates the women from the "brothers" and may also reflect a mariological interest, as Metzger observes (*Textual Commentary*, 246–47).

i The term *ὁμοθυμαδόν* cannot mean "of one mind" in every case. The sense is that of the LXX, "together." One could read the articular noun as "place of prayer," that is, "synagogue," but this is unlikely. See Cadbury and Lake, 10–11.

Analysis

The first episode in Acts is narrated from the viewpoint of the apostles.[1] Readers are not immediately aware that these verses constitute a distinct episode, and its location is revealed only at its close (v. 12). The "Mount of Olives," as it is usually called in English ("Olive Grove Hill" is more accurate[2]), had served as Jesus' base while he was teaching in Jerusalem (Luke 19:29, 37; 21:37; 22:39) and was a common locale for appearances of the Savior.[3] Its significance here derives from an occasion on which Luke did not mention this hill: Mark 13:3, the eschatological address, from which Luke will now take a leaf.[4] A single verse will do for the ascension; the emphasis lies on the spoken words that envelop it. These announcements affirm and establish the political and eschatological outlooks of Acts.

Viewed structurally, vv. 6-11 contain three units, of which the ascension (v. 9) is the center. Surrounding it are words or actions of the apostles that receive correction:

A. V. 7. Question of apostles about "the kingdom"
B. V. 8. Implicit rebuke by Jesus, followed by a promise
C. V. 9. Jesus taken up into heaven
A'. V. 10a. Apostles' attention fixed on the sky
B'. Vv. 10b-11. Messengers rebuke behavior, followed by a promise.

This apophthegmatic "sandwich" establishes the meaning of the ascension and sets out the future program, which rejects both political messianism and imminent expectation in favor of vigorous mission.

Comment

■ **6** The vocative marks a change. For the first time Jesus is addressed as "Lord."[5] As a climax to forty days of instruction on the reign of God, however, the question is excruciatingly inept. Literary tradition permitted pupils to ask dull or inappropriate questions so that teachers could promulgate the correct view. This question is delicately posed. The apostles do not ask if Jesus will now ascend the throne.[6] Jesus does not say no. The response, based on Mark 13:32,[7] removes calculation about the time of the end from the human sphere.[8] In place of an answer, the apostles receive a promise that functions as the indicative and imperative. The indicative resides in the promise of power, which will enable the hearers to fulfill the implicit imperative of world mission. The ends of the earth rather than the end of the world will be the subject of this book.[9] The promise of power is another evocation of the beginning and close of Luke (1:35; 24:39) and a component of both accounts of the ascension. The fulfillment of that

1 It is technically possible to render the opening words as "now they who had come together," and thus treat v. 6 as continuing the previous verse, but this would be quite awkward and seems unlikely.

2 Acts 1:12 is clear. In other cases one cannot tell whether ἐλαιων is the nominative singular of that word or the genitive plural of "olives." See Bruce, 104–5.

3 Of revelation Gospels, Helmut Koester says, "The scene is usually on a mountain, preferably the Mount of Olives," in Helmut Koester and James M. Robinson, *Trajectories through Early Christianity* (Philadelphia: Fortress Press, 1971) 194. Examples are *Ep. Pet. Phil.* NHC 8,2, 132.12; The *Coptic Psalm Book* 2.187.27–29 (Allberry); The *Questions of Bartholomew* 3.1–4.12; *Apoc. Pet.* (Ethiopic) 1; *Apoc. Paul* 51; *Ap. John*, NHC 2,1, 1.19–20, and the opening of the *Pistis Sophia*. It is unlikely that all of these usages derive directly or indirectly from Acts.

4 The eschatological significance of this locale first appears in the oracles added to Zechariah (14:4-5). For mountains as sacred sites, see Leland Ryken et al., eds., *Dictionary of Biblical Imagery* (Downers Grove, Ill.: InterVarsity, 1998) 573–74.

5 As Moule ("The Christology of Acts," in Keck and Martyn, *Studies*, 159–85, esp. 160) notes, "Lord" is used by the narrator in Luke but not by the disciples.

6 Augustine (*Sermon* 265) understood v. 6 as asking whether Jesus, who had hitherto not been visible to ordinary eyes, would now "go public" in proof of his vindication. This interpretation shows the difficulty of a concrete understanding.

7 Pervo, *Dating*, 35–36.

8 The phrase "times and seasons" (χρόνοι καὶ καιροί) belongs to the vocabulary of early Christian edification. See Schneider, 1:202.

9 For Haenchen (143) the response is decisive, for it sets discipleship on the path followed ever since: the task of finding a new relationship to the world.

promise in the subsequent narrative has generated a bitter debate about Lucan theology.

Excursus: Power in Luke and Acts

"Power" is a key word in Lucan theology, an indicator of its consistency and transparency no less than of its difficulties.[10] In the simplest of both social-scientific and theological formulation, power is what people want and what God can give them. The Hellenistic and early Roman eras intensified questions about the nature of power, questions that religion and tradition, custom and convention had tended to obscure. Frequent and rapid changes of sovereignty and regime, culture and society, coupled with striking vicissitudes in the fortunes of individuals, contributed to the development of learned and popular cosmologies brimming with friendly and hostile forces.[11] For the religion of Israel these interests and events stimulated the development of angelology and demonology, conveniences that threatened the unity of God and the concept of divine rule. They also led to a logical and concomitant emphasis on the eschatological manifestation of the power of God.[12]

It would not be erroneous to say that for Luke the essence of power is the miraculous, so long as one understands that every manifestation of divine power is a miracle, and that such epiphanies include judicial acquittals no less than wondrous deliverances from incarceration.[13] Power is an attribute (e.g., Luke 1:35; 5:17; 24:49; Acts 1:8), even a name (Luke 21:27; 22:69), of God, but Satan is not without power (Luke 10:19). Considered as a philosophical historian, Luke stands with those who, like Josephus, view history as governed by providence, rather than as a canvas illustrated by the caprices of fate, of whom Polybius is an example.[14] Luke was not, however, a philosophical theologian. As the narrative episodes of Acts indicate, his battle takes place in the trenches of popular religion against "magic" and its practitioners, in opposition to demons, and in the aid of their victims. Through the beneficence of God, the powers of Satan can be defeated.[15]

Because Luke is a popular writer, the explicit manifestations of divine power in Acts tend to be thaumaturgic and charismatic. The author wishes to produce a vivid and accessible narrative that focuses on concrete, empirical evidence. Unlike Mark, John, and Paul, Luke does not engage in what theologians since the Reformation era would regard as critical reflection on the potential abuse of miracle stories. For him, the abusers are "magicians" (Acts 8:9-24; 13:6-12; 19:17-20) and those who exploit supernatural power for financial gain or other unworthy motives (Acts 16:16-19; 19:13-17). His understanding of power is not, for that reason, to be dismissed as entirely unreflective.[16]

Luke regards miracle as a mode of authorization.[17] This understanding was not a given in the Greco-Roman world; it rather constitutes a fundamental difference between Lucan and Pauline thought. In Acts 3–5, for instance, miracles lie at the nexus of a debate between the apostles and the "authorities." Readers are to assume that these healings (Acts 3:1-10; 5:12-16) legitimate the apostles and their message, while disqualifying the authority of their opponents. The proper inference is that the torch has been passed on. Those who do not accept the assumption that miracles and numerical growth establish legitimacy in a situation of social conflict will find much of Acts unpersuasive.[18] Luke does not dispute the possibility of marvels performed by nonbelievers. He rather assures the reader that the deeds of Christian missionaries are qualitatively and

10 For the general background, see Walter Grundmann, "δύναμαι," *TDNT* 2:284–317.

11 "Gnostic" systems and Neo-Platonism were among eventual results of this process.

12 Both developments can be seen in the distinctive (sectarian) texts from Qumran.

13 See Parsons and Pervo, *Rethinking*, 92–96.

14 See Squires, *Plan*.

15 See, in particular, Susan R. Garrett, *The Demise of the Devil: Magic and the Demonic in Luke-Acts* (Minneapolis: Fortress, 1989) 65–66. On the phenomena, see Hans-Josef Klauck, *Magic and Paganism in Early Christianity: The World of the Acts of the Apostles* (trans. Brian McNeil; Edinburgh: T&T Clark, 2000).

16 On the role of power in popular religion, see Arthur Darby Nock, *Essays on Religion and the Ancient World* (2 vols.; ed. Zeph Stewart; Cambridge, Mass.: Harvard University Press, 1972) 1:34–45; and Martin P. Nilsson, *Greek Piety* (trans. Herbert Jennings Rose; New York: Norton, 1969) 103–10. Douglas Edwards provides many valuable insights on the subject, with particular attention to Luke and Acts (*Religion and Power: Pagans, Jews, and Christians in the Greek East* [New York: Oxford University Press, 1996]).

17 Power is the capacity to achieve one's will. Authority is power that is bestowed or recognized by society. In Lucan thought, authority (ἐξουσία) is both potential power and a character bestowed or revealed by δύναμις. See Luke 4:32, 36; 5:24; 10:19; Acts 8:19.

18 Origen may have been the first Christian author to affirm that miracles in and of themselves prove

quantitatively superior (Acts 8:9-13). Since the narrator takes no great pains to establish this understanding of power and miracle, it is apparent that the implied reader of Acts embraces Luke's views. One element of Lucan theological integration is the association of power with Spirit. Power is a medium through which the Spirit is active in the life of Jesus and the activity of early missionaries and the church.  Power is therefore not a phenomenon more or less restricted to the end times.[19]

■ **8** Verses 3-8 contain two references each to the "kingdom" (vv. 3, 6) and the Spirit (vv. 5, 8). The narrative invites the readers, like the apostles, to look for the coming of the Spirit rather than for the advent of God's rule. The Spirit is "an essential and characteristic feature" of Acts.[20] One of the important contributions of literary analyses of Luke and Acts has been to indicate that the author communicates theological views by showing rather than telling, through story rather than through exposition. So it is here: the narrator does not say, or have Jesus say, "For a number of reasons it is preferable to replace incendiary and misleading talk about 'the kingdom of God' with discourse about the gift of the Spirit, language that is comprehensive of both erudite philosophical reflection and unbridled charismatic enthusiasm." Instead his narrative approach makes Lucan theology more accessible to the unreflective and more obscure to the analytical.

Verse 8b raises two questions. Is this verse intended to be an outline of the book? What is the meaning of "to the ends of the earth"? As an outline the promise is inadequate. It carries the reader no further than chap. 8. A related approach is to take 1:8 as indicating that geography determines the structure of Acts.[21] Geographical outlines have their uses, but they do not necessarily expose penetrating insights into the structure of a work. A preferable understanding is that this is a "programmatic statement."[22] "Jerusalem" reflects the understanding of this city as the "navel" of the Israelite earth,[23] but the preposition "from" is significant. The story moves away from this ambiguous capital. Judea refers to the Jewish mission, Samaria to the transitional phase, which includes "God-Fearers" (8:26-39), followed by the gentile world. The outline is salvation-historical rather than geographical. The literary function of 1:8b is like that of the "introductory oracle" found in some ancient narratives. These prophecies or predictions usually seek to engage the reader by revealing the plot in an indirect or opaque manner.[24]

---

nothing (*Cels.* 3.51). This is not the same as criticizing a faith that demands miracle.

19 See Conzelmann, *Theology*, 181–83.

20 Barrett, 1:63.

21 See Werner Georg Kümmel, *Introduction to the New Testament* (trans. Howard Clark Kee; Nashville: Abingdon, 1975) 155.

22 This is what Marshall (61) appears to mean: "[I]n a broad sense the programme outlined here corresponds to the structure of Acts as a whole." Cf. also Haenchen, 144.

23 See Bruce J. Malina and Jerome H. Neyrey, *Portraits of Paul: An Archaeology of Ancient Personality* (Louisville: Westminster John Knox, 1996) 120–25; and Mikeal Parsons, "The Place of Jerusalem on the Lukan Landscape: An Exercise in Symbolic Cartography," in Richard Thompson, ed., *Literary Studies in Luke-Acts: Essays in Honor of Joseph B. Tyson* (Macon, Ga.: Mercer University Press, 1998) 155–71.

24 A relevant example of the "introductory oracle" is Addition A to Greek Esther, in the form of a dream. The interpretation of this in Addition F frames the book. Other examples or similarities include Jonah 1:1, Xenophon of Ephesus *An Ephesian Tale* 1.6.2; Achilles Tatius *Leuc. Cit.* 1.3; Philostratus *Vit. Apoll.* 1.4-5; Longus *Daphn.* 1.7-8; Heliodorus *Aeth.* 1.18, 2.35; *Parthenope* (in Susan A. Stephens and John J. Winkler, eds., *Ancient Greek Novels: The Fragments* (Princeton: Princeton University Press, 1995) 78; Antonius Diogenes *Wonders beyond Thule*; Photius *Library* 110a 16; Petronius *Satyrica*, frg. 44; Pseudo-Clementine *Hom.* 12.8.4; and Apuleius *Metam.* 2.12 (a parody). See also Rosa Söder, *Die apokryphen Apostelgeschichten und die romanhafte Literatur der Antike* (Stuttgart: Kohlhammer, 1932) 44–46, 171, 180; John R. Morgan, "Heliodoros," in Gareth Schmeling, ed., *The Novel in the Ancient World* (rev. ed.; Leiden: Brill, 2003) 444–45; and "On the Fringes of the Canon: Work on the Fragments of Ancient Greek Fiction 1936–1994," *ANRW* 2.34.4. (1998) 3293–3390, here 3345. See also J. Bradley Chance, "Divine Prognostications and the Movement of Story: An Intertextual Exploration of Xenophon's *Ephesian Tale* and the Acts of the Apostles," in Ronald F. Hock, J. Bradley Chance, and Judith Perkins, eds., *Ancient Fiction and Early Christian Narrative* (SBLSS 6; Atlanta: Scholars Press, 1998) 219–34.

The intriguing element here is the phrase "to the ends of the earth." As a geographical expression, the location of this limit depends on the extent of geographical knowledge and the orientation of the speaker or narrator.[25] The latter contributes to the metaphorical sense of "far, far away." The range of geographical options is wide.[26] The two locations most applicable to Acts are Ethiopia[27] and Rome,[28] the former because of the symbolism of 8:26-39, the latter because it is the geographical destination of the book. It is unlikely that Luke means the phrase in a particularly literal sense. When Christ wishes to tell Paul that he is destined for Rome, he does so (23:11). The phrase had an exotic allure for ancients, somewhat comparable to the appeal of planetary exploration today.[29]

The phrase "the ends of the earth" regularly appears in accounts of world "missions." Heracles, one learns from Dio of Prusa's first oration *On Kingship*, "held empire over every land from the rising of the sun to the setting thereof" (*Oration 1* 60).[30] Alexander is a less mythical figure (in fact, if not in story): "He advanced to the ends of the earth (ἕως ἄκρων τῆς γῆς), and plundered many nations" (1 Macc 1:3; cf. 3:9).[31] Dio applied the phrase to his own career. Perplexed about his future, he decided to consult the Delphic oracle:

> And then when I consulted him [Apollo], he gave me a strange sort of reply and one not easy to interpret. For he bade me to keep on doing with all zeal the very thing wherein I am engaged, as being a most honourable and useful activity, "until you come," he said, "to the uttermost parts of the earth" (ἐπὶ τὸ ἔσχατον . . . τῆς γῆς). (Dio of Prusa *Oration 13* 9)[32]

Dio, whose career as an itinerant teacher provides a number of illustrations for the Lucan depictions of Jesus and Paul, received an oracle commissioning him as a universal missionary. The activity of such individuals as Heracles and Alexander rapidly acquired the patina of a *mission civilisatrice*, a goal that was equally congenial to Luke.[33] "The ends of the earth" could thus be a symbol of universality. For Luke, universality meant first and foremost universalism. He applies the phrase to the gentile mission. The "mystery" is resolved in 13:47b: "'I have made you a light for the gentiles and a means of salvation to the ends of the earth'" (ἕως ἐσχάτου τῆς γῆς).[34] The sun of salvation will soon shine upon everyone.[35] The church is a missionary institution.[36]

25 For various ancient views, see James S. Romm, *The Edges of the Earth in Ancient Thought* (Princeton: Princeton University Press, 1992). On the importance of orientation, see L. Völkl, "'Orientierung' im Weltbild der ersten christlichen Jahrhunderte," *Rivista di archeologia cristiana* 25 (1949) 55–70. James M. Scott discusses the geographical orientation of Acts in "Luke's Geographical Horizon," in Gill and Gempf, *Setting*, 483–544, esp. 526–27.

26 For a survey, see E. Earle Ellis, "The End of the Earth (Acts 1:8)," *Bulletin for Biblical Research* 1 (1991) 123–32. Ellis views the term as strictly geographical and identifies Spain as the most logical location.

27 In Homer, the Ethiopians are "the most distant peoples" (ἔσχατοι ἀνδρῶν; e.g., *Od.* 1.23). See Romm, *Edges of the Earth*, 49–60; cf. Luke 11:31.

28 *Ps. Sol.* 18:15 may refer to Rome. More timely and certain is Ignatius (*Rom.* 2:2), who views himself as on a journey from the far east to the far west.

29 Cf. Pervo, *Profit*, 70–72.

30 In James W. Cohoon, trans., *Dio Chrysostom I* (LCL; Cambridge, Mass.: Harvard University Press, 1932) 33. Ragnar Höistad analyzes the image of Heracles in Cynic thought of the imperial era in his *Cynic Hero and Cynic King* (Uppsala: n.p., 1948) 50–73. For a discussion of Dio's views of kingship, see 150–223.

31 Alexander was believed to have reached the ends of the earth in his own lifetime (Aeschines *Ctes.* 165). His postmortem travels, recounted in various versions of the *Alexander Romance*, do not detract from that picture. See Richard Stoneman, *The Greek Alexander Romance* (London: Penguin, 1991) 25 n. 35.

32 In James W. Cohoon, trans., *Dio Chrysostom II* (LCL; Cambridge, Mass.: Harvard University Press, 1939) 97 alt. The context is worth consulting.

33 See below on Acts 14:8-18.

34 This precise phrase occurs nowhere except in these places and writers who quote them. The parallel in Luke 24:47-48 is confirmatory: καὶ κηρυχθῆναι ἐπὶ τῷ ὀνόματι αὐτοῦ μετάνοιαν εἰς ἄφεσιν ἁμαρτιῶν εἰς πάντα τὰ ἔθνη. ἀρξάμενοι ἀπὸ Ἰερουσαλὴμ 48 ὑμεῖς μάρτυρες τούτων ("and that repentance and forgiveness of sins are to be proclaimed in his name to all nations, beginning from

■ **9-12** There are, according to the prevailing text-critical arguments, two accounts of the ascension in Luke and Acts.[37] This is, for those who wish to maintain the seamless unity of the narrative, one in excess of the maximum. For Luke the ascension of the risen Christ is both ending and beginning.[38] This insight and understanding may be no less sophisticated than that which tabulates the number of ascensions. The meaning is clear: the ascension is the postlude to the career of Jesus on earth and the prelude to the advent of the Spirit. Because Jesus has been "exalted to the right hand of God" (2:33), he can pour out the Spirit upon "all flesh." The scheme involves some theological shortcuts, since Luke does not expound a doctrine of Christ's exaltation, but it reflects the eventual creedal understanding of resurrection, ascension, and exaltation as distinct "events."[39]

It is entirely characteristic of Lucan theology that the physical body of the risen Christ departs into the divine realm. This body was not, to be sure, subject to ordinary limitations. It could assume different forms (Luke 24:15-16) and appear or disappear at will (24:31, 36), but it was capable of being touched and of taking nourishment (Luke 24:36-43; cf. Acts 1:4). Placing to one side the confusing mixture of religio-historical and traditional conceptions, it would have been quite possible for Jesus simply to vanish after 1:8. Luke, however, elected to use the vehicle, as it were, of an ascension, for which event there were varied traditional warrants.[40]

Ascensions are parallel to birth narratives in that they are suitable means by which "heroes" might make their departure. The range of circumstances, themes, and motifs indicate that those who wished to recount an ascension had a substantial repertory from which to select details.[41] These stories illuminate the world of the first readers of Acts.

For Luke, the most cogent parallel or model was the story of Elijah's ascension in 2 Kgs 2:1-14, for this story, which also appears near the beginning of a book,[42] deals with *succession*. The ascension of Elijah leads to the endowment of his successor Elisha with *Spirit*. Details support this allusion, which the implied reader may well have been expected to recognize.[43] Since the Elijah-Elisha cycle served as a source for the Jesus tradition in general

Jerusalem. You are witnesses of these things"). Origen (*Comm. Matt.* 10.18) already associated "all the gentiles" of Matt 28:19 with Acts 1:8.

35 Insofar as Rome is a trope for the whole world, the identification is valid. Cf. Barrett, 1:80. Ethiopia (8:26-39) has anticipatory value, but it does not signal the fulfillment of 1:8. See Bertram L. Melbourne, "Acts 1:8 Re-examined: Is Acts 8 Its Fulfillment?" *JRT* 58 (2005) 1–18.

36 In reflecting on the alleged deficiencies of the preface, Haenchen (145–46) remarks: "Luke has in fact described the contents of Acts through the words of Jesus in verse 8. He has done so, moreover, in a manner incomparably superior to the classical scheme, for now the whole action of Acts becomes the fulfillment of Jesus' word, and this is much more than a mere table of contents: it is a promise!"

37 See p. 36 n. 41. Weiser (1:60–62) discusses the question of underlying traditions.

38 For a detailed study, see Arie W. Zwiep, *The Ascension of the Messiah in Lukan Christology* (NovTSup 87; Leiden: Brill, 1997); and idem, "*Assumptus est in caelum:* Rapture and Heavenly Exaltation in Early Judaism and Luke-Acts," in Friedrich Avemarie and Hermann Lichtenberger, eds., *Auferstehung–Resurrection* (WUNT 135; Tübingen: Mohr Siebeck, 2001) 323–49.

39 Luke evidently appropriated his understanding of the meaning of Christ's exaltation from Deutero-Pauline sources. See Pervo, *Dating*, 263.

40 Lüdemann (29) says, "Underlying this is a tradition the form of which can no longer be recognized," and he points to Luke 24:50-53 as "a doublet of this tradition which has been worked over even more intensively by Luke." This claim does not assert a great deal and is of limited use in the analysis of the text.

41 Talbert (*Reading Acts,* 20–22) succinctly surveys varieties of ascension stories and their functions. For more detailed analysis and a very full discussion, see Gerd Lohfink, *Die Himmelfahrt Jesu: Untersuchungen zu den Himmelfahrts- und Erhöhungstexten bei Lukas* (Munich: Kösel, 1971) and Zwiep (n. 38). Clouds, for example, were media for the rescue and rapture of heroes in Greco-Roman literature. See Homer, *Il.* 3.381; 20.444; 3.381; Virgil *Aen.* 1.411; Horace *Odes* 2.7.14. On the cloud, see Bruce, 104. It is used in the description of the parousia in Mark 13:46 parr. and plays a role in the transfiguration (Luke 9:34-35). Note, in addition, Albrecht Oepke, "νεφέλη," *TDNT* 4:902–10.

42 Luke presumably did not know 2 Kings as the second of two books and thus like Acts, but as Fourth Kingdoms.

43 Note the use of ἀναλαμβάνω in 2 Kgs 2:9, 10 and

and especially for Luke, this explanation is inherently probable.[44] It also points to contrasts. Whereas the other followers of Elijah were distraught about the news and instituted a search for their leader (2 Kgs 2:15-18), Jesus' followers exhibit neither doubt nor grief.

Their demeanor also contrasts with that initially presented in the resurrection stories (24:11, 36-43), but Luke takes care to portray the ascension, which is, strictly speaking, an "assumption" here, as an "Easter event" and thereby preserves the unity of the resurrection story. He achieves this unity by assigning the role of interpretation to "two men" in striking dress,[45] as at the tomb. Here, also, they have a rebuke that begins with "why?" (24:4-5). Jesus is to be seen neither at the grave nor in the sky. Verse 11 confirms that Jesus is now in the divine realm, from which he will return.[46] This confirms Luke 21:27. The parousia is in view,[47] not some future postresurrection appearance, but the answers to two pressing questions are neglected: *when* Jesus will return, and *why*? Passive gazing into heaven is *Luke*'s rebuke of that approach to imminent expectation which advocates passivity and withdrawal.[48] Not until later (2:33; cf. 7:56) will the reader learn that in his ascension Jesus took a place of power at the right hand of God. This status differentiates his experience from that of Jewish heroes and is somewhat comparable with descriptions of apotheoses, including those of Roman emperors.[49]

As often, the transitional v. 12 can be taken either as the conclusion to the prior section or as the beginning of a new unit.[50] Lucan style is often fluid and is thus resistant to rigid divisions. Equally characteristic of Luke is the withholding of an important detail until the end. The potent eschatological symbol of the Mount of Olives comes as if it were an afterthought. To this, Luke appends an item that bathes the episode in verisimilitude and quotidian homeliness. With this one stroke, the permissible distance for a Sabbath day's walk,[51] characters and narrative are firmly located in a world of Torah observance.

■ **13-14** The entire group can lodge in a second-floor room. The word ὑπερῷον evidently reveals the normal meeting places of the community or communities familiar to the author: the second floor of a house or apartment.[52] At this juncture, the reader is treated to a fresh list of the apostles. The only substantive difference from the list in Luke 6:12-16 is the relocation of John, who will be paired with Peter in the subsequent narrative (chaps. 3–4, and 8:14-25).[53] Lists in Acts signal an important transition in the narrative (6:5; 13:1; 20:4). If Luke and Acts form a seamless narrative, this repetition of an earlier list is difficult to explain. With these "key players," Luke associates two other groups: "the women," female disciples who had been with Jesus in Galilee and Jerusalem, and the family of Jesus. These

Power & Body

Acts 1:2, 11, 22 (but not in Luke 24:51); the phrase εἰς τὸν οὐρανόν in 2 Kgs 2:1, 10, four (possibly three) times in Acts 1:10-11; and the specific reference to the follower/s as watching the ascension in 2 Kgs 2:10, 12; Acts 1:9-10. There are also differences. Elijah was assumed in a whirlwind, and Elisha saw a vision.

44 See Pervo, *Dating*, 23–35, for examples and references. Note also Zwiep, "*Assumptus est*."

45 "Two men": see 2 Macc 3:26-33.

46 Acts 3:20-21 fleshes out details of this interval and return.

47 The cloud evokes the parousia. Cf. Luke 21:27 (and its basis in Dan 7:13).

48 Identification of the audience as "Galileans" evokes the passion (e.g., Luke 22:56), prepares the way for 2:7, and underlines the geographical scope of Luke and Acts: from provincial Galilee to "the ends of the earth."

49 See Gary Gilbert, "The List of Nations in Acts 2: Roman Propaganda and the Lukan Response," *JBL* 121 (2002) 497–529; and David Balch, "*ΜΕΤΑΒΟΛΗ ΠΟΛΙΤΕΙΩΝ*: Jesus as Founder of the Church in Luke-Acts: Form and Function," in Penner, *Contextualizing*, 139–88, esp. 162 n. 72. For a parody of such apotheoses, see Lucian *Peregr.* 40.

50 Cf. Haenchen, 154.

51 For details about the limits imposed on Sabbath travel, see Barrett, 1:85–86. This is merely a rough measure of distance, not an indication that the incident occurred on a Saturday.

52 Cf. Acts 9:37, 39; 20:8. In Dan 6:11, this area serves, as evidently here, as a place of prayer. Note also *Mart. Pol.* 7:1. The term is not identical with the locale of the Last Supper (Luke 22:12; ἀνάγαιον). These references, together with the "house churches" of 12:12 and elsewhere, place a control on the claims of "thousands" or "myriads" of believers (2:41; 4:4; 21:20).

53 On these names, see Margaret H. Williams, "Palestinian Jewish Personal Names in Acts," in Richard Bauckham, ed., *The Book of Acts in Its Palestinian Setting* (BIFCS 4; Grand Rapids: Eerdmans, 1995) 79–113, esp. 84–99. The basic source is Mark

women and Mary make their first and only appearance in Acts.[54]

Identification of Jesus' mother and siblings is a surprise, because the last reference to them was in Luke 8:19-21. Luke does not portray the family of Jesus as hostile to his mission; he idealizes them.[55] Two reasons stand out for their prominence in the original group (which numbered 120, according to v. 15). One is continuity with the past. The mother of Jesus, who played a prominent role in Luke 1, reappears in Acts 1.[56] A second reason, probably, is that among the "siblings" is James, who will appear without other advertisement in a prominent role in 12:17 and will eventually lead the Jerusalem community.[57] Acts 1:13-14 was probably composed with Gal 2:9 in mind, which names Peter, James, and John as the "three pillars." What is indisputable is that Luke has suppressed any data he possessed about a Galilean movement, including resurrection appearances there.[58]

Although the apostles are the ostensible subjects and audience of 1:1-14, the true audience is the readers of the book, who here learn answers to some fundamental questions about the meaning of Jesus' resurrection/departure and the relation of these events to God's final vindicating action. Rather than participate in a worldwide empire, believers are to engage in a universal mission. In place of the eschaton will come the eschatological gift of the Spirit. "When" is the wrong question, and waiting for the end is the wrong behavior. As for life, it seems much like before. After the ascension, the apostles walk back to their lodgings—on feet, not clouds—there to engage in worship and prayer. The difference is that believers now walk in hope.

3:13-19, paralleled in Matt 10:1-4 and Luke 6:12-16. Other lists are John 21:1-2, which notes the presence of seven, the *Gospel of the Ebionites* (according to Epiphanius *Pan.* 30.13, 2-3), the *Act. Thom.* 1; the *Ep. Apos.* 2; Papias (Eusebius *H.E.* 3.39.4), who names seven, followed by the equivalent of "et cetera," and the *First Book of Jeu* 3, which speaks of "all the apostles" but names only five.

54 Luke 8:2-3; 23:49–24:10. On women in (Luke and) Acts, see, among others, Turid Karlsen Seim, *The Double Message: Patterns of Gender in Luke and Acts* (Nashville: Abingdon, 1994); Ivoni Richter Reimer, *Women in the Acts of the Apostles: A Feminist Liberation Perspective* (trans. Linda M. Maloney; Minneapolis: Fortress Press, 1995); Helga Melzer-Keller, "Frauen in der Apostelgeschichte," *BK* 55 (2000) 87–91; and the essays in Amy-Jill Levine, ed., *A Feminist Companion to The Acts of the Apostles* (Cleveland: Pilgrim, 2004). On the text, see p. 40 n. *h* above. Acts is less positive in its portrayal of women than Luke: the "double message" is becoming singular.

55 John Painter provides a good analysis of the Gospel materials pertinent to Jesus' family in *Just James: The Brother of Jesus in History and Tradition* (Columbia: University of South Carolina Press, 1997) 11–41. The notion that the family of Jesus were unbelievers until converted by the resurrection, endorsed by Haenchen (155), is an invention based on the view that the antipathy displayed in Mark is historical. Neither 1 Cor 15:7 nor the *Gospel of the Hebrews* (Jerome *De vir. ill.* 2), cited by Haenchen, supports this interpretation.

56 On Mary in Luke and Acts, see Raymond E. Brown et al., eds., *Mary in the New Testament* (Philadelphia: Fortress Press, 1978) 105–77. The additional σύν ("with," B et al.) prefixed to "Mary" may indicate a mariological interest. Arator (*Historia Apostolica* [ed. A. P. Orbán; CCSL 130–130a; Turnholt: Brepols, 2006]) takes the opportunity here to put in a few good words for the female sex (1.57-68).

57 Luke (like Paul) nowhere identifies James as the brother of Jesus.

58 Acts 9:31 speaks of believers in Galilee, without indicating how the movement arose.

1:15-26 Replenishing the Apostolic College

**15/ A few days later Peter arose to
address the assembled believers, who then numbered about
120.[a] 16/ "My fellow believers,
the scripture about Judas, a
prediction of the Holy Spirit
through David, had to be
fulfilled.[b] Judas showed those
who arrested Jesus where to
find him. 17/ Judas belonged to
our company and had a share
in this ministry. 18/ While on
the farm he had obtained with
his ill-gotten gains, he fell flat
on his face. His stomach burst
open, and all of his insides
poured out. 19/ Everybody in
Jerusalem learned about this,
and so they called the place
"Blood Farm"—"Akeldama" in
their language. 20/ Scripture
says, in the Book of Psalms:
'His homestead is to become a
deserted place where no one
will live,' as well as, 'Someone
else is to assume his responsibilities.' 21/ For that we must
have one of the men who have
been with us from the Lord
Jesus' arrival to his departure,
22/ that is, from his baptism by
John until he was taken up from
us. This person must, like us, be
a witness of his resurrection."**

**23/ Two names were presented: that
Joseph known as "Barsabbas,"[c]
also known as "Justus," and
Matthias. 24/ After offering
this prayer: "Lord, to whom all
hearts are open, show[d] which
of these two you have chosen
25/ to assume this place of
apostolic ministry[e] that Judas
abandoned to go to his rightful
place, 26/ they cast lots." The
lot indicated that Matthias was
chosen to join the other eleven
apostles.[f]**

a In place of ἀδελφῶν ("siblings," often "believers," an expression of "fictive kinship") are the variants μαθητῶν ("disciples") in D and ἀποστόλων ("apostles") in $\mathfrak{P}^{74}$, both evidently attempts to avoid confusion with the family (ἀδελφοῖς) of Jesus in v. 14.

b The D-Text reads δεῖ. This present tense ("must") may come from the view that the fulfillment is not complete until someone else has taken the position. The widely attested variant "this scripture," which points ahead to the psalm verse, is clearly secondary. On the singular "scripture," see Barrett, 1:96.

c "Sabbath's child."

d Cf. Luke 10:1, where the same verb (ἀναδείκνυμι) is used of the appointment of the seventy/seventy-two.

e The terminology is rather bureaucratic. The translation takes διακονίας ταύτης καὶ ἀποστολῆς (lit. "this ministry and apostleship") as a hendiadys, an understanding supported by the following relative, which is singular.

f Not understanding the idiom, or wishing to avoid confusion, some representatives of the D-tradition read "twelve."

Analysis

Verses 15-26 propel the reader *medias in res*. The believers have assembled, evidently in conformity with v. 14. The narrative seems straightforward enough: following the departure of their Lord, the community, led by Peter, attends to its first order of business: the selection of a replacement for Judas. As is his wont, the narrator moves so briskly and persuasively that one does not pause to ask questions. Among these are: Why is Peter the leader, why is a twelfth apostle needed, what is the apostolic role, and why did not Jesus select a twelfth prior to the ascension? Most briefly and comprehensively, why tell this story describing a method not employed thereafter to select a person who has no role in the narrative? The key must be, as Étienne Trocmé states, the nature and function of apostleship in vv. 21-22.[1] Apostleship centers upon, but cannot be mechanically reduced to, witness to the resurrection.[2] Luke seeks to supply a historical and institutional basis for the witness of the Spirit, thereby to block unbridled "enthusiasm."[3] The association of the Spirit with God's will (δεῖ) in this passage is a vital link in the authentication of the Lucan theological program.[4]

Had Luke simply concocted the whole thing, Jesus no doubt would have chosen a successor for Judas.[5] Elements of the selection of Matthias certainly derive from tradition, as, presumably, does the notion of "the Twelve," an expression found seven times in the Gospel (Luke 8:1; 9:1, 12; 18:31; 22:3, 30, 47) but only once in Acts (6:2).[6] It is difficult to find an important role for "the Twelve" *qua* twelve in Acts.[7] After devoting twelve verses to the choice of the twelfth, the narrator restores Matthias to that oblivion from which he had so briefly emerged.[8]

The functions of the apostles must be deduced from the narrative. "Witness" is a primary, albeit not exclusive, function.[9] Apostles exercise, in a manner not described, leadership over the community (e.g., 6:1-6) and receive funds (4:35). Direction of missionary enterprise is apparent in 8:14, but they play no decision-making role in 11:1-18 and silently share that responsibility with (James and) the presbyters in chap. 15. Jerusalem, with varying leaders, is in charge of "foreign missions." For Luke, the time of the apostles lies in the distant, vague, and idealized past. After chap. 15 the views of the apostles are to be found in their epistle

1 Étienne Trocmé, *Le livre des Actes et l'histoire* (EHPR 45; Paris: Presses Universitaires de France, 1957) 199.

2 Paul could assert, presumably as generally understood, a vision of the risen Lord as qualification for apostleship (1 Cor 9:1; cf. 15:8-9).

3 In some senses it is appropriate to say that for Luke the Spirit is a substitute for the parousia/kingdom. This view should be placed not only in the context of those who looked for an imminent end or were dismayed by the continuation of history, but also of those for whom the Spirit *was* the parousia. Luke, like Paul, stood between those who claimed nothing for the present but the certainty of final vindication and those who believed that believers possess the fullness of eschatological life in the present.

4 See Erich Fascher, "Theologische Beobachtungen zu *Dei*," in *Neutestamentliche Studien für Rudolf Bultmann: zu seinem 70. Geburtstag am 20. August 1954* (ed. Walther Eltester; BZNW 21; Berlin: A. Töpelmann, 1954) 228–54, here 246.

5 Dennis R. MacDonald argues that Luke concocted the story, noting its similarities to ancient epic, specifically *Il.* 7.123-82 (*Does the New Testament Imitate Homer? Four Cases from the Acts of the Apostles* [New Haven: Yale University Press, 2003] 105–19).

6 Lüdemann (33–35), who is alert to possible tradition, is quite modest about its extent in 1:15-26. There is general agreement about the presence of tradition as well as doubts about its recoverability in detail. Roloff (29–34) says that Luke has created the scene (and speech) from some probably oral traditions about Judas and the Twelve. Rudolph Pesch (*Die Apostelgeschichte* [EKK; 2 vols.; Zurich: Benziger, 1986] 1:82–92) envisions a pre-Lucan legend of the death of Judas and material about the replenishment of the apostolic circle, and sees the form of the speech as Lucan. Weiser (1:64–68) has a judicious analysis. See also Talbert, *Reading Acts,* 36–37.

7 Luke 12:29-30 ("and I confer on you, just as my Father has conferred on me, a kingdom, so that you may eat and drink at my table in my kingdom, and you will sit on thrones judging the twelve tribes of Israel") is doubtless relevant, as Talbert (*Reading Acts*, 35–37), for example, maintains, but Matthias was not among those addressed, whereas Judas was (Luke 21:22). The Matthean parallel does speak of twelve thrones, ignoring the presence of Judas (19:28). Luke 22:30 derives from Q, according to James M. Robinson et al., eds., *The Critical Edition of Q* (Hermeneia; Minneapolis: Fortress Press, 2000) 560–61.

8 Later writers filled in this gap. See Walter Bauer, "Accounts," in *NTApoc.* 2:35–74, here 65–66.

9 Apostles as witnesses: 1:8, 22; 2:32; 3:15; 5:32; 10:39, 41; 13:31. Paul appeals to this authority in 13:28-31 and bears the title "witness" in 22:15; 26:16. See Talbert, *Reading Acts*, 37. The basis for the theme of witness appears in Luke 23:49. The next scene (Acts 2) shows the apostles as witnesses to Israel (Tannehill, *Narrative Unity*, 2:22). "Witness" is also found in philosophical contexts: Epictetus *Diss.* 1.29.45; 3.24.11; Seneca *Ep.* 20.9; see Arthur Darby Nock, *Conversion: The Old and the New in Religion from Alexander the Great to Augustine of Hippo* (London/New York: Oxford University Press, 1961), 195–96. See also the comments on Acts 26:16.

(16:4). Peter assumes leadership, without a hint of authorization from above or from below.[10] It is reasonable to suppose that the implied reader of Acts was familiar with the concepts of twelve apostles and the presidency of Peter.

The lesson and thrust of the narrative are obvious. Judas was inconstant, abandoned his office, misused money for personal purposes, and died horribly. Jesus rose while Judas fell flat on his face. That had to be. There also has to be a new member of the Twelve, one who was a constant companion of Jesus and who will fulfill apostolic ministry by proclamation of life. Pastorally, 1:15-26 demonstrates that betrayal cannot impede the growth of the community.[11]

The general structure of vv. 15-26 is clear, as is the purpose. After a brief introduction[12] Peter makes a speech recommending the selection of a replacement for Judas, with qualifications for the candidates. Two are proposed, one of whom is selected by lot. The apostolic college has been replenished.[13] An implicit method also appears: Scripture, when searched, forecasts events that might otherwise appear to be great misfortunes, and,

since it is reliable in prediction, one must also trust its solutions. This method also appears to justify the action taken. The replacement of Judas is mandated by Ps 109:8. Less transparent is the passage that forecasts his betrayal: "His homestead is to become a deserted place where no one will live" (Ps 69:26). In order to establish the relevance of those words, Peter had to relate the otherwise somewhat extraneous story of the last days of Judas, who must acquire a farm in order to be eligible for the psalmist's judgment. This exegesis—if that is the proper word for the procedure—is a forcible reminder that there are some vast chasms separating the world of the modern reader from that of Acts.[14]

This first formal speech in Acts also reveals, quite unblushingly, that speeches are addressed to the readers of the book, since vv. 17-19, as commentators since Calvin have recognized, are inappropriate for the dramatic audience.[15] A rhetorical approach yields the following scheme:

I. Vv. 16-17. Address and exordium
II. Vv. 18-19. Narration
III. V. 20. Proofs (inartistic)
IV. Vv. 21-22. Thesis and peroration

This is a useful outline, for negative reasons. It shows that this speech, like many of those in the book, is far too brief to be analyzed in rhetorical categories. Moreover, it is not a sound example of deliberative rhetoric. Peter does not urge the desirability of nominating a successor to Judas. That would require more justification. He rather asserts the necessity of finding a successor

10 Luke 22:32, "but I have prayed for you that your own faith may not fail; and you, when once you have turned back, strengthen your brothers," suggests a role, but, in the balance of the Gospel Peter's faith does appear to fail (22:54-62), and he neither formally repents nor "strengthens" the others (24:12, 34).

11 Cf. Barrett, 1:94. Leadership failures, such as apostasy and financial misconduct, were not just theoretical possibilities to Luke's readers. On the subject of Judas's apostasy, see the detailed analysis of Schuyler Brown, *Apostasy and Perseverance in the Theology of Luke* (AnBib 36; Rome: Pontifical Biblical Institute, 1969) 53–57, 82–97.

12 Acts 1:15 was inspired by Num 1:18. See Haenchen, 159.

13 Inspiration from the LXX is evident: when new leadership is required, qualifications are identified and suitable candidates duly set apart. Cf. Exod 18:14-25; Num 27:12-33. This imitation suggests that Luke composed the incident (or so thoroughly revised the source) that underlying tradition cannot be isolated.

14 Cf. Haenchen, 161 n. 5.

15 Calvin's approach was redactional: "I think it probable that this account of the death of Judas was inserted by Luke, and I therefore set it within a parenthesis to distinguish it from the address of Peter. For what object was there in recounting what the disciples well knew? Further it would have been absurd to declare before them that the field bought with the proceeds of the betrayal was called by the Jews in their own tongue, Aceldama. . . . Besides, how could the word Jerusalem be suitably used, when Peter was delivering his sermon in that place? Why should he interpret in Greek among Jews a word of their own mother-tongue? Therefore Luke himself inserts this sentence, in case readers ignorant of the events should find Peter's words obscure" (Jean Calvin, *The Acts of the Apostles* [trans. James W. Fraser and William J. G. McDonald; *Calvin's Commentaries* vols. 6–7; Grand Rapids:

and what the requirements are. Finally, the narrative is, as noted, not relevant to the specific subject. A formal and thematic outline is more revelatory:

(V. 16a: address)

I. Vv. 16-20a. The Fate of Judas Was Necessary and Foretold in Scripture
   A. Vv. 16b-17. Scripture said that betrayal had to occur. Judas fulfilled that role
   B. Vv. 18-19. The Story of Judas's End
   C. V. 20a. Scriptural Proof

II. Vv. 20b-22. The Traitor Must be Replaced by a Witness of Jesus' Entire Earthly Ministry
   A. V. 20b. Scriptural Proof
   B. V. 21a. The Necessity of Replacement
   C. Vv. 21b-22. The Qualifications for a Successor: companion and witness

This plan indicates that the two LXX citations form the pivot of the short address, each part of which has a form of δεῖ ("must").[16] It is not accidental that this initial speech exhibits Luke's understanding of Scripture as well as the related themes of salvation history and providence.[17] The two parts have corresponding references to the companions of Jesus (vv. 16, 21) and to ministry (vv. 17, 20b), and a fundamental contrast between Judas the betrayer and the true office of resurrection witness (vv. 17, 22).[18]

Comment

■ **15** The temporal phrase in v. 15 (lit. "And in these days") marks an important break (cf. 6:1; 11:27[19]). "In the midst of" is a common marker for the beginning of a speech in Acts (1:15; 2:22; 17:22; 27:21). "[He] said" is followed by an arcane parenthesis that evidently intends to be archaic.[20] One hundred twenty is a number of appropriate size and symbolism for an occasion of this magnitude. Attempts to find a basis for this statistic in accurate tradition overlook the ancient approach to such matters.

■ **16** The address ἄνδρες ἀδελφοί ("gentlemen and brethren") is modeled on the opening of Attic orations, "Gentlemen of Athens" (as in Acts 17:22). "Gentlemen and brethren" appears fourteen times in Acts, four altogether in *1 Clement*, and elsewhere only in works dependent on Acts.[21] The vital words "it was necessary," "fulfill," "Scripture," "the Spirit foretold,"[22] are packed into the opening.

■ **16-18** Luke's account of the demise of Judas introduces to Acts a fresh mechanism: the punitive miracle or action. The operative principle is that the punishment should suit—and thus verify—the crime. Monarchs who perished through an infestation of worms, for

Eerdmans, 1995] 6:41). Similarly, Cadbury and Lake (11–15) incline to view vv. 18-19 as an addition to the source, as well as the first quotation, in v. 20. Bruce (109) agrees. Haenchen (163) demolishes the idea that the speech contains an insertion.

16 Paired quotations function similarly in the kerygmatic speeches of chap. 2 (vv. 25-28, 34-35) and chap. 3 (vv. 22-23).

17 On these themes see p. 22. Note that there is no difference in the use of Scripture in this speech from that in chap. 2; that is, Peter could make similar arguments before the gift of the Spirit. This is another indication that the author has composed the address.

18 On the careful structure of this speech, see Jacques Dupont, "La destinée de Judas prophétisée par David," *CBQ* 23 (1961) 41–51. Verses 17, 18-19, 20a, and 20b, for example, have an A B B A pattern (ministry, parcel of land, habitation, office).

19 This phrase is not especially common. Luke is fond of it. In addition to the three examples from Acts, see Luke 1:39; 6:12; cf. 24:18. Uses in the LXX (Jdt 14:8; Zech 8:9, 15) are different in nature. Other examples are Dionysius of Halicarnassus *Ant. Rom.* 7.71.3; Cassius Dio 73.16.2.

20 ὄχλος ὀνομάτων ἐπὶ τὸ αὐτό (lit. "there was a crowd of names together") uses two Septuagintalisms: "name" as a metonymy for "person" (cf. Num 1:18, 20, 22; etc., and, in general, Barrett, 1:96) and ἐπὶ τὸ αὐτό, a LXX idiom that comes to mean something like "in plenary session" in early Christian literature. See Bruce, 108. Cadbury and Lake (12) view it as the equivalent of "amounting to." The τε here is not grammatically sound; see BDF §443 (1).

21 *1 Clem.* 14:1; 37:1; 43:4; and 62:1. In addition, the phrase occurs four times in the *Acts of Paul*, which is dependent on Acts, and once in the *Acts of John*, which takes it from Acts or the *Acts of Paul*. (If there is an intertextual relationship between Acts and *1 Clement*, it is more probable that the former used the latter.) Chrysostom (*Hom.* 3) noted that ἄνδρες (lit. "men") was inclusive.

22 Use of verbs with the prefix προ-, such as προεῖπεν ("predict") in v. 16, is not found in the LXX, but is

example, established themselves as tyrants.[23] In the case of Judas, there are three accounts: Acts 1; Matt 27:3-10; and Papias, frg. 3/4.[24] Attempts at discovery of an historical basis are ill-advised.[25]

Excursus: Punitive Miracles

In his reflections on Lactantius's treatise *De mortibus persecutorum,* Pierre de Labriolle observed, "The idea that Providence manifests in the world below the effects of its rigour by the chastisement whereby it strikes the impious in their bodies and in their life had for long brought to the Christians (as to the Jews . . .) its avenging consolations."[26]

Behind this arch observation stands the longing for justice. For those who believe themselves dreadfully oppressed, the concept of vengeance nurtures hope. Light fiction's fondness for the equitable assignment of rewards and punishments shows that this hope is general.[27] Framing Acts are two stories about punitive miracles, one (the fate of Judas) that occurred before the story opened, and another (28:1-6) that did not meet popular expectations. Others include the deaths of Ananias and Sapphira (5:1-11), the death of Herod (12:20-23), the blindings of Paul (9:1-19a) and Elymas (13:6-12), and the punishment of Sceva's heirs (19:13-17). The most important punitive action in the book is implicit: the destruction of Judea for its rejection of Jesus.

Punitive miracles are thus synecdoches for the righteous providence of God. Gerd Theissen classifies them among "rule miracles," for they maintain sacred boundaries.[28] Unlike healings or exorcisms, they need not be "miraculous." People do die from dreadful illnesses, and vipers can be deadly. These stories clearly demonstrate that "miracle" is a matter of interpretation. The popular quality of individual punishments is apparent in their fondness for the *lex talionis.* Such judgments may also serve to reform miscreants, such as Paul (and, possibly, Elymas), for whom the punishment is then reversed or withdrawn.[29]

Punishment miracles, which are absent from the canonical Gospels but found in the various Acts,[30] grate against modern Western sensibilities. Their frank endorsement of injury and violence portrays

common in Josephus (Squires, *Plan,* 130–31), from whom Luke may have derived the practice. Note Acts 2:23; 3:18, 20; 4:28; 7:52; 10:41, 42; 17:26, 31; 22:14; 26:16. This prefix does not always carry temporal significance, however.

23 See below on Acts 12:20-23.

24 This is frg. 3 in the edition of Funk-Bihlmeyer *Die Apostolischen Väter* (rev. ed.; ed. Andreas Lindemann and Henning Paulsen; Tübingen: Mohr Siebeck, 1992) 294–306, and frg. 4 in the edition of Ehrman, *Apostolic Fathers,* 2:105–6. For other traditions about Judas in early Christianity, see William Klassen, "Judas Iscariot," *ABD* 3:1091–96. See also Hans-Josef Klauck, "Judas der 'Verräter'? Eine exegetische und wirkungsgeschichtliche Studie," *ANRW* 2.26.1 (1992) 717–40. Both Klauck (*Judas, Ein Jünger des Herrn* [QD 111; Freiburg: Herder, 1987]) and Klassen (*Judas: Betrayer or Friend of Jesus?* [Minneapolis: Augsburg Fortress, 1996]) have sought to rehabilitate the historical Judas, a project anticipated in the recently published *Gospel of Judas,* for which see Rodolphe Kasser, Marvin Meyer, and Gregor Wurst, *The Gospel of Judas* (Washington, D.C.: National Geographic, 2006). See also Arie Zwiep, *Judas and the Choice of Matthias: A Story of Context and Concern of Acts 1:15-26* (WUNT 187; Tübingen: Mohr Siebeck, 2004).

25 Pierre Benoit, "La mort de Judas," in *Synoptische Studien: Alfred Wikenhauser zum siebzigsten Geburtstag am 22. Februar 1953, dargebracht von Freunden, Kollegen, und Schülern* (Münster: Aschendorff, 1954) 1–19. Kirsopp Lake ("The Death of Judas," in Lake and Cadbury, *Additional Notes,* 22–30) demonstrated the futility of harmonization. See also Raymond E. Brown, *The Death of the Messiah: From Gethsemane to the Grave; A Commentary on the Passion Narratives in the Four Gospels* (ABRL; 2 vols.; New York: Doubleday, 1994) 1:636–60; and Crossan, *Who Killed Jesus?* 71–75.

26 Pierre Champagne de Labriolle, *History and Literature of Christianity from Tertullian to Boethius* (trans. Herbert Wilson; New York: Knopf, 1925) 74.

27 Agamemnon says: "It is the common wish of each person privately and each city that the bad should get bad treatment while the good enjoy good fortune" (Euripides *Hecuba* 902-4 [trans. David Kovacs, *Euripides II* (LCL; Cambridge, Mass.: Harvard University Press, 1995) 381]).

28 Gerd Theissen, *Miracle Stories of the Early Christian Tradition* (trans. Francis McDonagh; ed. John Riches; Edinburgh: T&T Clark, 1983) 106–12. He provides a range of examples, with discussion.

29 Theissen finds such "educative miracles" more common in the Greek tradition. He does not take into account descriptions of those struck down by gods for some violation.

30 Examples from the Apocryphal Acts: *Act. Pet.* frg. (*NTApoc.* 2:286); 2; 15 (Verc.); *Act. John* 41–42, 86; *Act. Thom.* 6; *Act. Andr. Narr.* 36 (*Epit. Gr.* 15). Condign punishment is common in popular fiction, e.g., Heliodorus *Aeth.* 4.19, where Charikles, who had sinned with his eyes, claimed to be punished

a deity of the sort journalists refer to as an "Old Testament God." One purpose they serve is to give the lie to such characterizations. The Hebrew Bible has no monopoly on divine violence. Punitive stories embrace and nurture the temptation to characterize misfortune as divine judgment.[31] This is a theological danger of which Luke is aware (Luke 13:1-9),[32] and, for those with ears to hear, 28:1-6 could also be taken as a bit of a cautionary tale. Few would have done so. In Acts, the death of Judas and the deliverance of Paul are contrasting episodes. At the macro level, providence is manifested in the unfolding of God's plan. At the micro level, providence is manifested in a judicious distribution of rewards and punishments.[33]

■ **19-20** In Acts, Judas illustrates his betrayal of Jesus by using his reward money to purchase a field, the precise opposite of the action of loyal believers, who sell their fields and donate the proceeds to the community (2:45; 4:34-37). His loyalty to self is the opposite of true loyalty, and so Judas literally turns inside out.[34] His property, like his office, become vacant. Such is the "reward of iniquity" (v. 18), which becomes a double entendre.[35] πρηνὴς γενόμενος (v. 18) evidently means "becoming prone," that is, "falling down." This could be less awkwardly phrased, leading to efforts from antiquity onward to associate the adjective with πρήθω ("swell up") or πίμπρημι ("burn"). Attempts to harmonize Acts with Matthew (and Papias) confound the lexical and text-critical questions.[36] The proper setting for the death of Judas is the passion narrative. This is apparent not only on intrinsic grounds,[37] but also in the scriptural source and warrant for the account of Judas's death.

■ **20** The citation is from Psalm 69 (68), while general inspiration appears to have come from the reflections in Wis 4:17-20 on the fates of the righteous and the unrighteous.[38] Psalm 69 is a primary source for understanding the passion of Jesus,[39] while stories about the suffering righteous served as a basis for its narrative development.[40] Luke has evidently placed a tradition about Judas's death in the present context and given it a new focus: the vacancy of his office.[41]

Each of the quotations unveils another element about the early Christian use of Scripture. Not only are "events" conformed (or concocted) to the biblical

by losing sight of the one he loved. For a catalogue of such punishments, see Weiser, 1:139-42.

31 Labriolle's sarcasm is once again equal to the challenge: "Lactantius is indiscreet in the zeal which he displays in endeavouring to unravel God's designs with the intrepid certitude which he reveals in all their details, as if these had been confided to him from above" (216).

32 On Luke 13:1-9, see p. 216 n. 30.

33 See also Lorenzo Tosco, *Pietro e Paolo ministri del giudizio di Dio: Studio del genere letterario e della funzione di At 5,1-11 e 13,4-12* (RivBSup 19; Bologna: Edizioni Dehoniane, 1989).

34 See the analysis of Robert L. Brawley, *Text to Text Pours Forth Speech: Voices of Scripture in Luke-Acts* (Bloomington: Indiana University Press, 1995) 61–75.

35 This genitive (τῆς ἀδικίας) is probably objective (i.e., they rewarded his unrighteousness.). On the phrase, note 2 Pet 2:13, 15.

36 See the lucid discussion by Lake, "The Death of Judas," in Lake and Cadbury, *Additional Notes*, 22–30; as well as Metzger, *Textual Commentary*, 247–48.

37 See Brawley, *Text to Text*, 65.

38 Wis 4:19, "because he will dash them speechless to the ground (ῥήξει αὐτοὺς ἀφώνους πρηνεῖς), and shake them from the foundations; they will be left utterly dry and barren, and they will suffer anguish, and the memory of them will perish.

39 Barnabas Lindars, *New Testament Apologetic: The Doctrinal Significance of the Old Testament Quotations* (London: SCM, 1961) 99–108. He discusses Acts 1:20 on 102–3.

40 George W. E. Nickelsburg, "The Genre and Function of the Markan Passion Narrative," *HTR* 73 (1980) 153–84.

41 Comparison of Acts 1:16-20 to Matt 27:3-10 indicates that the common element is the purchase of land and its designation as a "Field of Blood," a known location. Behind this view of Judas's death as the antitype of Jesus' is an understanding of Jesus' death as an atoning sacrifice. Since this is not the Lucan understanding, he is unlikely to have concocted this tradition independently. Haenchen (159 n. 9) says that the two verses are treated as one quotation; but Johnson (35) would, without support from the text, restrict the formula to the first quotation.

models that they fulfill; the text of Scripture itself can be adjusted to highlight this fulfillment:

Ps 68:26 LXX	Acts 1:20b-c
γενηθήτω ἡ ἔπαυλις αὐτῶν ἠρημωμένη, καὶ ἐν τοῖς σκηνώμασιν αὐτῶν μὴ ἔστω ὁ κατοικῶν.	γενηθήτω ἡ ἔπαυλις αὐτοῦ ἔρημος καὶ μὴ ἔστω ὁ κατοικῶν ἐν αὐτῇ.
Let their homestead become abandoned and let there be no dweller in their tents.	Let *his* homestead become *an empty place* and let there be no dweller in *it*.

Ps 108:8b LXX	Acts 1:20d
καὶ τὴν ἐπισκοπὴν αὐτοῦ λάβοι ἕτερος.	τὴν ἐπισκοπὴν αὐτοῦ λαβέτω ἕτερος.
May someone else take his position.	*Let* someone else take his position.

Acts alters the subject of the citation from Psalm 69 from plural to singular, by adjusting a pronoun and removing a clause.[42] Otherwise it could scarcely be applied to Judas. The verb in Ps 109 (108):8 has been changed from optative, which may denote a mere wish, to imperative, thus coordinating the two verbs (γενηθήτω/λαβέτω) and necessitating action.[43]

The address is, as noted, impossible in the dramatic setting. It displays considerable chronological and linguistic distance from a Jerusalem community around six weeks after the first Easter. The concept of a college of twelve apostles is also a good deal later.[44] The oration positively reeks of technical terms pertinent to Christian "ministry" that are familiar from the late first century onward, such as κλῆρος, τόπος, ἐπισκοπή, and ἀποστολή.[45] The exegesis depends on the LXX, rather than the MT, and thus derives from Greek-speaking Christianity.[46]

■ **21-22** The concluding sentence, which states how the imperative of the psalm is to be fulfilled, is awkward even if the sense is clear.[47] The one who replaces Judas must be a male who was associated with Jesus continually "from the beginning." "From the baptism of John" probably refers to John's baptism of Jesus, despite Luke 3:21-22. The phrase reflects a tradition that the Jesus movement began with John the Baptizer and, possibly, that Jesus' disciples came from that circle. This idea is not integrated into the picture developed in the Gospel.[48] The speech views the beginning and the end of Jesus' earthly ministry as events equally remote in time. Luke certainly did not invent the qualifications for apostleship, since they exclude Paul. The "office" of witness is definitely vital to Luke, and this will include Paul.[49]

■ **23** Peter does not indicate the procedure by which "one of these" will be chosen. The verse may well reflect the abrupt introduction of another piece of tradition.

42 "In it" (ἐν αὐτῇ) refers to the "homestead" (ἔπαυλις), rather than to "their tents."

43 The two citations constitute an ABA triplet of imperatives in -τω with a rhyme at the close of the first and third line (ἔρημος . . . ἕτερος)

44 See, in general, Günter Klein, *Die zwölf Apostel: Ursprung und Gehalt einer Idee* (FRLANT 77; Göttingen: Vandenhoeck & Ruprecht, 1961). Klein's claim that Luke invented the identification of "the Twelve" with "the apostles" is an exaggeration, since Matt 10:2 refers to "the twelve apostles." Notable studies include Lucien Cerfaux, "Pour l'histoire du titre ἀπόστολος dans le Nouveau Testament," *RSR* 48 (1960) 76–92; Eduard Lohse, "Ursprung und Prägung des christlichen Apostolates," *TZ* 9 (1953) 259–76; P.-H. Menoud, "Les additions au groupe des Douze Apôtres d'après le Livre des Actes," *RHPR* 37 (1957) 71–80; Beda Rigaux, "Die 'Zwölf' in Geschichte und Kerygma," in Helmut Ristow and Karl Matthiae, eds., *Der historische Jesus und der kerygmatische Christus* (Berlin: Evangelische Verlagsanstalt, 1961) 468–86, and Hans von Campenhausen, "Der urchristliche Apostelbegriff," *ST* 1 (1948) 96–130.

45 For details on these terms, see Pervo, *Dating*, 269, 272, and 289.

46 So Haenchen, 163.

47 The subject of the initial δεῖ ("must") in v. 21 does not come until the close of v. 22. The verb lacks a complement. The phrase εἰσῆλθεν καὶ ἐξῆλθεν ἐφ᾽ ἡμᾶς ὁ κύριος Ἰησοῦς is elliptical (BDF §479 [2])—it lacks "from us." ἀρξάμενος ("beginning") in v. 22 is best seen as a "frozen nominative" effectively equivalent to an adverb (or a preposition). Cf. 10:37; 11:4; Luke 23:5; 24:27, 47 (and Matt 20:8; John 8:9).

48 Theologically, vv. 21-22 conflict with the birth narratives in Luke 1–2. In narrative terms they conflict with Luke 3–5, which places the call of the first disciples (5:1-11) at some distance from the activity of John.

49 This function of "witness" in Acts is well evoked by Christoph Burchard, *Der dreizehnte Zeuge* (FRLANT

Ms. E smooths the transition with an initial *καὶ τούτων λεχθέντων* ("After these statements . . ."). Other D-Text witnesses read the verb here, and the initial participle in v. 24, as singular.[50] Peter, like a later *monepiskopos*, promulgated the criteria and nominated the candidates.[51] The implication of the preferred text is that the community as a whole proposes (by a means not described and from a pool of unstated size) the two candidates.[52] Identification of the first of these takes seven words;[53] Matthias, who will be chosen, merits but one.

■ **24** The prayer has formal elements that would become standard in the liturgical "collect": address, ascription, and petition.[54] The petition is grounded in the attribute "knowledge of human hearts."[55] Does "Lord" here refer to God, as in 15:8, or to Jesus, as in v. 2? The former appears more probable.[56]

■ **25** The verse rounds off the account by summarizing vv. 16-20. The prayer is the first instance of unison speech,[57] a device with several ramifications, the most obvious of which is the demonstration of divine guidance. In this sense, it is not unlike the double dream.[58] Thematically, like unison property, unison speech manifests the marvelous unity of the community.[59] As a religio-historical phenomenon, unison speech may be related to acclamation. Although sustained unison public chants, such as the invocation of Artemis in Acts 19:28, 34, may seem little more than the eager cheers of devoted fans, ancients were willing to view them as no less inspired than inspiring.[60] In the NT, public acclamation is a common element at the conclusion of miracle stories.[61] These "choral endings" point to the literary function of unison speech. Like dramatic choruses, they comment on the action; choral speech also allows the reader to participate in—better, to identify with—the action as a part of the anonymous "crowd."[62]

■ **26** The narrator once more (cf. v. 12) withholds vital information until the end: the decision was reached by casting lots.[63] For Luke, the principal value of what was

---

103; Göttingen: Vandenhoeck & Ruprecht, 1970). The meaning of Acts 1:21-22 is clarified in 10:39.

50 See Boismard, *Texte*, 58–59.

51 See Pervo, "Social Aspects," 229–41, esp. 232–35.

52 It would be unwise to assume that Luke viewed James (v. 14) as ineligible. The use of different traditions probably accounts for the absence of his name.

53 "Justus" is probably the Greco-Roman form of "Joseph." Williams ("Personal Names," 101–2) states that "Barsabbas" is probably a nickname. Apart from here and 15:22, it is unattested in Palestine. A character named Barsabbas appears in the *Act. Paul* Martyrdom 2 and 6. See also Papias (in Eusebius *H.E.* 3.39.9-10). Orthography varies. A D-Text alternative for "Joseph" is "Joses." This name is attested also in 4:36, the meaning of which becomes apparent in the variant "Barnabas" (D 6[s] *pc* it vg[mss]) for "Barsabbas." This elevates the status of Barnabas and integrates him into the apostolic circle.

54 Unlike the standard collect, this prayer lacks the purpose clause. For a brief description of the form and history of these prayers, see Marion J. Hatchett, *Commentary on the American Prayer Book* (New York: Seabury, 1981) 163–64.

55 The noun *καρδιογνώστης* ("knower of the heart") is attested only in Christian literature: Acts 15:8; *Hermas* 31 (*Man.* 4.3.4); *Act. Paul* 3.24; *Act. Pet.* 2; Clement of Alexandria *Strom.* 4.14, 16; *Ap. Const.* 2.24.6; 3.7.8; 4.6.8; etc. All refer this quality to God. See the comments of Hills, "Acts," 24–54, here 45. The concept is, of course, biblical (Barrett, 1:103).

56 So, e.g., Conzelmann, 25; and Jervell, 128; although Barrett (1:102) argues for Jesus on the grounds that the selection of apostles is his prerogative.

57 Cf. also 4:23-31 (community prayer), 5:29-32 and 6:2-4 (the apostles), 14:14-17 (Paul and Barnabas), and 21:20-25 (James and the presbyters).

58 See p. 58 n. 1.

59 So Haenchen, 162.

60 See Cassius Dio's comments on acclamation in the hippodrome, 75.4, 5-6.

61 Examples include Luke 7:16; Acts 8:10; 14:11-12. On the subject, see Rudolf Bultmann, *The History of the Synoptic Tradition* (trans. John Marsh; 2nd ed.; New York: Harper & Row, 1968) 225–26, 427; in greater detail, Theodor Klauser, "Akklamation," *RAC* 1 (1950) 216–33; Theissen, *Miracle Stories*, 152–72; and Klaus Berger, *Formgeschichte des Neuen Testaments* (Heidelberg: Quelle & Meyer, 1984) 231–39.

62 See p. 119 n. 48.

63 One would expect *ἔβαλον κλήρους* ("they cast lots") rather than *ἔδωκαν* (lit. "they gave"). Cadbury and Lake (15) argue for "gave" with the possible connotation of "casting votes," but says that it is not a Hebraism. Barrett (1:104–5) argues otherwise. Luke wishes to evoke the atmosphere of classical government, but he wishes even more

evidently a tradition[64] was to provide a contrast between the pre- and post-Pentecost periods. Thereafter, the community will trust in or listen to the Spirit. Through this practice of choosing officers by lot from among qualified candidates Luke can portray the community as an ideal political body, like, for example, Athens of old.[65] The verb συγκατεψηφίσθη intimates the atmosphere of an election, without the fact thereof.[66]

Excursus: The Beginning of Acts

An alternative approach to the "acts of the Apostles" holds a prominent place in early Christian literatrue. *1 Clem.* 42.3-4 reports:

> When, therefore, the apostles received his commands and were fully convinced through the resurrection of our Lord Jesus Christ and persuaded by the word of God, they went forth proclaiming the good news that the kingdom of God was about to come, brimming with confidence through the Holy Spirit. And as they preached throughout the countryside and in the cities, they appointed the first fruits of their ministries as bishops and deacons of those who were about to believe, testing them by the Spirit.[67]

This summary, probably written c. 100, is quite independent of Acts, which does not proclaim the imminence of divine rule (1:6-7). Justin, some years later than Acts, has a similar picture: "For a band of twelve men went forth from Jerusalem, and they were common men, not trained in speaking, but by the power of God they testified to every race of humankind" (*1 Apol.* 39.3).[68] Justin thus also deviates here from the picture of Acts.[69] Eusebius (*H.E.* 3.1) asserts that "the holy Apostles and disciples" dispersed over the entire world, referring to a lottery.[70] Just such a method of determining particular

strongly to indicate that God made the decision. The narrator leaves the method of casting lots to the imagination of the reader.

64 Luke may have been aware of other explanations of Judas's death, but he does not appear to be engaging in correction of them. This story may be his own invention. Josep Rius-Camps and Jenny Read-Heimerdinger argue that Luke (i.e., the D-Text) does not approve of adding an apostle; "After the Death of Judas: A Reconsideration of the Status of the Twelve Apostles," *Revista Catalana de Teología* 29 (2004) 305–34. If that were the case, he could have omitted the episode.

65 Lots were in widespread use in political and religious contexts, including the practice of the Jerusalem temple (Cadbury and Lake, 15; Barrett, 1:104; cf. Luke 1:9—another parallel between the openings of the two books), and the Roman Senate (Livy 23.2), as well as classical Athenian democracy (Aristotle, *Ath. pol.* 8). Pindar (*Ol.* 7.54-63) reports that the gods, anticipating the apostles, cast lots to see which land would belong to each. See also the excursus on "the List of Nations," pp. 66–68. On the practice, note Nock, *Essays,* 1:255; Todd Penner, in "Civilizing Discourse," in idem, *Contextualizing,* 65–104, esp. 96 n. 94; and Conzelmann (25), who shows that 1QS 8.1 is not a valid parallel. Use of the term "lot" in the Qumran texts is important for the understanding of κλῆρος, here and elsewhere in the NT, but not for the selection of officers. See also Lynn A. Kauppi, *Foreign but Familiar Gods: Greco-Romans Read Religion in Acts* (LNTS 277; London: T&T Clark, 2006) 19–26.

66 Pervo, *Profit,* 39–40. The verb is of uncertain meaning. Luke may be using an overly elaborate term. Georg Braumann ("ψῆφος," *TDNT* 9:604–7, esp. 607, with nn. 27-30) says that, if καταψηφίζομαι is the basis, it means that Matthias was given an official place along with the eleven. "If, however, we take συμψηφίζω as the basis . . . the meaning is that he was counted with the eleven" (n. 30). The *v.l.* αὐτῶν ("their," D* E ψ m it vg[mss] sy[h]) reflects the difficulty of interpretation. See Metzger, *Textual Commentary,* 250. Luke nowhere intimates that officials are elected. The community chooses the seven (6:1-6), by a means not identified, but these are not officials and have no place with the "apostles and presybters" in, for example, chap. 15.

67 Trans. Ehrman, *Apostolic Fathers,* 1:109–11.

68 Trans. Edward R. Hardy (alt.) in Cyril C. Richardson, ed., *Early Christian Fathers* (LCC 1; New York: Macmillan, 1970) 266.

69 For varying accounts and perceptions, see Walter Bauer, "Accounts," in *NTApoc.* 2:35–74, 43–44. Bauer (44 n. 2) cites, in addition to biblical references, the *Kerygma Petrou* frg. 4, the *Ep. Apost.* 30 (41), the *Diatessaron,* Aristides, Irenaeus, the *Ascension of Isaiah,* the *Apostolic Church Order,* and the *Pistis Sophia.*

70 Eusebius appeals to book 3 of Origen's commentary on Genesis, but the scope of this reference is not clear.

mission fields is depicted in the openings of the *Acts of Thomas*, the *Martyrium Andreae Prius,* and the *Acts of Andrew and Matthias*.[71] These two elements, a catalogue of the nations and a lottery, may be creative developments from Acts 1–2, but the legend of the division of the world into territories for each apostle may antedate Luke and Acts. It is in any case noteworthy that early Christianity in general preferred this alternate picture to that of Acts.

71 The loss of the openings of all but the *Acts of Thomas* makes it impossible to determine how general the "apostolic lottery" was, although it is unlikely to have been a component of the *Acts of Paul* and quite probably did not feature in the *Acts of Peter.*

2

2:1-13 The Descent of the Spirit at Pentecost

1/ **On the day of Pentecost the entire group was together. 2/ A sudden noise from above, like the roar of a strong rushing wind, filled the house in which they were sitting.[a] 3/ Phenomena resembling jagged fiery tongues appeared.[b] One of these settled upon each person. 4/ All were filled with Holy Spirit[c] and, all, directed by the Spirit to give utterance, began to speak in foreign tongues.**

5/ **Among the residents of Jerusalem were devout persons from every country under the sun. 6/ In response to the noise a crowd flocked together, for each and every one of them heard these people speaking in their native languages. 7/ In absolute bewilderment they exclaimed: "Aren't all these people who are speaking Galileans? 8/ How can it be that each of us is hearing[d] our original language? 9/ There are Parthians, Medes, Elamites, residents of Mesopotamia, [___],[e] Cappadocia, Pontus, Asia, 10/ Phrygia and Pamphylia, Egypt, residents of Cyrenean Libya, visiting Roman citizens, 11/ Jews by birth and Jews by choice, Cretans and Arabs. Yet we are hearing these Galileans glorifying God in *our own* languages! 12/ All were bewildered and perplexed, constantly asking one another, "What is going on?" 13/ although there were some who made fun of the whole business by announcing, "They're full of cheap wine."**

a Boismard (*Texte*, 60) omits "filled . . . sitting." See below.

b Boismard (*Texte*, 60) reads καὶ ὤφθη αὐτοῖς ὡσεὶ πῦρ ("There appeared something like fire . . ."), eliminating the "(divided) tongues."

c Boismard (*Texte*, 62) omits "all . . . Spirit."

d The tense and number of the verb "hear" vary in the textual tradition.

e See the discussion of the text.

Analysis

Acts 2 follows a general pattern that is dominant in the first half of Acts, Apocryphal Acts, and what may be called "narrative of religious propaganda" in general: a miracle draws a crowd which is rewarded with a sermon, leading to an accession of devotees, followed often enough by persecution.[1] The essence is that miracles bring converts. Acts 2 introduces a novelty in NT narrative: a chapter-long episode including an incident, an explanatory address, and an appropriate reaction by the hearers, followed by a summary.[2] The style of the Gospel is being set aside.

1 Examples include Acts 3:1-26; 9:32-35 (in telescoped form); 14:8-18; *Act. And.* Epit. 6; *Act. Pet. and And.* 13–23; *Act. John* 37–45; *Act. Paul* 5/6; *Act. Pet.* (Verc.) 10–13; 25–29; *Act. Thom.* 30–38. On the role of crowds in Acts, see Richard S. Ascough, "Narrative Technique and Generic Designation: Crowd Scenes in Luke-Acts and in Chariton," *CBQ* 58 (1996) 69–82.

2 Cf. Conzelmann, 13.

Verses 1-4 constitute a single sentence framed by statements about "all": all were gathered (v. 1); all were filled with the Holy Spirit (v. 4). The intervening vv. 2-3 exhibit a parallel structure, the first part of which introduces a noun qualified by a simile, followed by a clause with a predicate:

- A. V. 2. *Sound* like
- B. V. 2. *Sound* filled (cf. also v. 4)
- A^1. V. 3. *Tongues* like
- B^2. V. 3. *Tongues* sat

This relatively tight structure encases events of the most extraordinary and irregular nature. The next paragraph, vv. 5-13, consists of

- A. V. 5. Parenthetical introduction: Jerusalem had a diverse population.
- B. V. 6. Summary: The noise attracted them. Confusion resulted.
- C. Vv. 7-12. Development of summary[3]
  - a^1. V. 7a. Astonishment
  - b^1. Vv. 7b-8. Paradox: Galileans speaking languages of the whole world
  - c. Vv. 9-11a. List of groups and types
  - b^2. V. 11b. Native languages (inclusion with v. 8)
  - a^2. V. 12a. Astonishment
  - d. V. 12b. Conclusion: Confusion (cf. B, v. 6)
- D. V. 13. A contrary interpretation

This outline indicates that the paragraph is carefully organized but not well balanced. Confusion prevailed. And so it does. Pentecost may be the most exciting and the least comprehensible episode in Acts.[4] The story collapses at the slightest breeze. It begins with a group gathered in a house, perhaps for devotion (cf. 1:13-14).[5] These (12? 120?) persons experience a complicated epiphany that issues in inspired speech, possibly glossolalia (vv. 1-4). Somehow this noise within a house becomes loud enough to attract a crowd evidently composed entirely of non-native residents who somehow perceive that the speakers are from Galilee, although they hear neither ecstatic speech nor Palestinian Aramaic (which may have betrayed a Galilean origin to the experienced ear), but, to their utter amazement, a religious message in their respective native tongues (vv. 5-12).[6]

In a logical narrative, each would have heard (a group?) speaking Latin, Egyptian, or the like, leading to a conversation in which one participant says to another, "Do you know what that language is? It's Phrygian," to which the companion replies, "Oh no. That's the indigenous language of rural Cyrene," and so forth. The narrative telescopes such conversation, reporting that all spoke these words in unison, somehow grasping the precise distribution of ethnic origins among them. Some could not determine what all this meant, but others were clear: "they're drunk" (v. 13). That charge *would* fit glossolalia, and Peter assumes that it is the opinion held by the entire audience (vv. 14-15). Most amazingly—and quite revelatory from the narrative perspective—nothing specific is said about the *content* of the message they heard.

This is a confusion worthy of Babel. A redactional solution almost leaps from the page: Luke had a story

3 The technique of an initial summary followed by a more detailed description (rather than vice versa) is not unusual in ancient popular narrative. See, e.g., *Ephesian Tale* 1.8.1-3 (κατέκλινον . . . κατέκλιναν) and 1.14.1-3 (κατεφλέχθησαν . . . κατεφλέγοντο), treating the escort of the couple to the bridal chamber and the destruction of their ship, respectively.

4 For a review of scholarship on the Pentecost story, see François Bovon, *Luke the Theologian: Thirty-three Years of Research (1950–1983)* (trans., Ken McKinney; Allison Park, Pa.: Pickwick, 1987) 229–38. See also Jacob Kremer, *Pfingstbericht und Pfingstgeschehen: Eine Exegetische Untersuchung zu Apg 2,1-13* (SBS 63/64; Stuttgart: Katholisches Bibelwerk, 1973).

5 One hundred twenty is a large number for a house.

6 The *Letter of Peter to Philip* (NHC VIII,2) presents an alternative "Pentecost." The work, which has several reminiscences of Acts (e.g., the heavenly Christ's statement that the apostles are "witnesses" [135, 5-6]), records a general bestowal of the Spirit in a Christophany, followed by each apostle's healing and preaching (140, 7-15) and their subsequent departure on a world mission. Although Peter is the undisputed leader, all share in the gifts of the Spirit and subsequent ministry. See Klaus Koschorke, "Eine gnostische Pfingstpredigt: Zur Auseinandersetzung zwischen gnostischem und kirchlichem Christentum am Beispiel der 'Epistula Petri ad Philippum' (NHC VIII, 2)," *ZThK* 74 (1977) 324–43.

about ecstatic speech that he transformed, either out of distaste for glossolalia or to expound universalism, or both, into a linguistic miracle focusing on what was heard. This remedy recognizes the presence of conflicting elements and posits a likely source, but it is more of a description of the problem than an unraveling of it.[7]

Comment

■ **1** The verse is difficult to translate because the present infinitive *συμπληροῦσθαι* should mean something like "was being completed" or possibly "was approaching," whereas the sense seems to demand "had arrived." The best solution may be to posit that Luke was more interested in producing a sonorous Septuagintal phrase[8] that intimated the fulfillment of prophecy while evoking a parallel with Luke 9:51 that retains the theological unity of the saving events (passion, resurrection, ascension, gift of the Spirit[9]) and therefore to conclude that it means no more than "on Pentecost."[10] The D-Text is an evident improvement.[11] "All the apostles" (326 [614], 1505 *al* p* t) resolves the problem of who received the gift.[12]

"Pentecost" is the Greek form (Josephus *Ant.* 3.252; *Bell.* 1.253; Tob 2:1; 2 Macc 12:31-32) of the HB "Festival of Weeks."[13] Like other festivals, Weeks was rooted in the annual cycle of nature. Like other festivals, Weeks was ultimately linked to salvation history, specifically, the Sinai covenant, but the date of this association is difficult to establish. It would be easier to understand the association of Weeks with the Pentecost episode if the former feast were associated with a revelatory event.[14] Despite the failure of both Philo and Josephus to link Weeks to sacred history, it is possible that such associations may have been customary in some circles, although "unofficial" before 70 CE and eventually regularized in rabbinic Judaism.[15]

---

7 Kirsopp Lake explored this hypothesis in "The Gift of the Spirit on the Day of Pentecost," in Lake and Cadbury, *Additional* Notes, 111–21, esp. 117–20. Lüdemann (40–42) develops the ramifications of the assumption that the primary source was an ecstatic event. For Conzelmann (15), however, "the original substratum is precisely the miraculous speech in many languages." He refers to Otto Bauernfeind and Eduard Schweizer in support of this view. On this issue, see also Schneider, 1:243–47; Roloff, 37–40; Weiser, 1:78–81; Barrett 1:109–10 (who has a good summary of the discussion); and Alexander J. M. Wedderburn, "Traditions and Redaction in Acts 2.1-13," *JSNT* 55 (1994) 27–54.

8 Although literate Greek makes use of the articular infinitive, the expression ἐν τῷ + inf. as the equivalent of a temporal clause reflects a Hebrew idiom, literally rendered.

9 Luke 9:51: *Ἐγένετο δὲ ἐν τῷ συμπληροῦσθαι τὰς ἡμέρας τῆς ἀναλήμψεως αὐτοῦ καὶ αὐτὸς τὸ πρόσωπον ἐστήρισεν τοῦ πορεύεσθαι εἰς Ἰερουσαλήμ* ("When the days drew near for him to be taken up, he set his face to go to Jerusalem"). This key verse introduces the central section of the Gospel: Jesus' journey to Jerusalem.

10 On the problems of translation and various attempts, see Ropes, *Text*, 16 (who prefers "toward the completion of the weeks," a version that requires thinking across two languages); Moule, *Idiom Book*, 129; Bruce, 113; and Barrett, 1:110–11.

11 *καὶ ἐγένετο ἐν ταῖς ἡμέραις ἐκείναις τοῦ συνπληροῦσθαι τὰς ἡμέρας τῆς πεντηκόστης ὄντων αὐτῶν πάντων ἐπὶ τὸ αὐτό.* (2) *καὶ ἰδοὺ ἐγένετο* . . . (When the **days** of Pentecost were concluding, **as all of them were** together . . . ," Boismard, *Texte*, 60). This notes a major transition and makes it more OT-like (and less Lucan, as Luke 9:51 indicates). Boismard allows that "in those days" may come from liturgical usage (the introduction of a reading).

12 ℵ* and E delete "all." This may have a similar effect, suggesting that the subject is the Twelve of 1:26. Instead of ὁμοῦ C³ E Ψ 33 *et al.* read ὁμοθυμαδόν. If this is different, it refers to their spiritual state ("of one mind" rather than "together"). Since the following prepositional phrase makes ὁμοῦ seem redundant, it is an intelligent correction and thus presumed secondary.

13 See James C. VanderKam, "Weeks, Festival of," *ABD* 6:895–97.

14 It is not likely that Luke's tradition included the date of Pentecost.

15 Barrett (1:111–12) has a concise discussion of the evidence and comes to the minimal conclusion that Pentecost was the next pilgrim feast after Passover. Jervell (132–33 and 137–39, with numerous references) argues for the Sinai tradition as the background; cf. also Haenchen, 174; and Schneider, 1:246. Good evidence for pre-rabbinic, "unofficial" interpretations of Weeks comes from *Jubilees* and Qumran. The *Temple Scroll* (11QT and frgs.) envisions several "Pentecosts," while *Jubilees* associates

■ **2** The signs accompanying the revelation are those of the classic HB epiphany: wind, fire, and noise, of which the Sinai theophany (Exod 19:16-19) is a prime example.[16] There are many others, but Sinai deserves priority because it is a foundational epiphany. The readers of Acts need not have known this specific intertextual link nor the proposed liturgical connection. They are windows into the author's mind, as it were, bridges that could be burned after crossing. Philo's reflections on this theophany (*De Decalogo*) are also illustrative:

> The philosophical exegete proceeds from the miraculous generation of an "invisible sound" (ἦχος) that is transmuted into "flaming fire (πῦρ φλογοειδές), sounded forth like the breath (πνεῦμα) through a trumpet an articulate voice (φωνήν). . . . Then from the midst of the *fire* that streamed from heaven there sounded forth to their utter amazement a *voice*, for the flame became articulate speech in the language (διάλεκτον) familiar to the audience" (*Dec.* 33, 46).[17]

Philo's wrestling with these images indicates that the learned were not bound to view such items as an unrelated sequence of remarkable phenomena, but as marvelous demonstrations of the deity's ability to manipulate and transmute the elements, that is, that such wonders could be understood "scientifically." Although Luke had no overt interests in developing theories like that of Philo, he envisioned no conflict between "miracle" and "science."[18]

Not unrelated to this theme is the most obvious intertextual connection to Pentecost: the story of Babel (Gen 11:1-9).[19] By reversing linguistic disunity, the experience is revealed as both an eschatological event of new creation[20] and a utopian restoration of the unity of the

a number of covenants with this time of year. On the Qumran material, see Fitzmyer, 233–35. VanderKam ("Weeks") discusses the relevant passages from *Jubilees*. One may hypothesize that the agricultural basis was quite suitable for the temple but that synagogues (and probably Qumran) would have been motivated to find another basis for this popular celebration. In the post-temple period, one of these bases became normative. (A Christian analogy is January 6, on which various places and communities have commemorated different epiphanies.) In the Christian tradition, the first solid evidence for the observance of Pentecost as a distinct festival comes from the fourth-century diary of Egeria (*Peregrinatio* 43.1-3). As early as the third century (Tertullian *Bapt.* 19; Origen *Cels.* 8.22; cf. *Act. Paul* 7/9), the term was used for the "Great Fifty Days" of Easter. Weiser (1:78) offers support for the Sinai tradition as part of the exegetical background. Stefan Schreiber proposes another theme: the work of God in the present for the people ("Aktualisierung göttlichen Handelns am Pfingsttag: Das frühjüdische Fest in Apg 2,1," *ZNW* 93 [2002] 58–77). Heinz Giesen also focuses on the calendar ("Gott steht zu seinen Verheissungen: Eine exegetische und theologische Auslegung des Pfingstgeschehens [Apg 2, 1-13] *StudNTUmwelt* 28 [2003] 83–126).

16 The history-of-religions background is the epiphany of a storm god on a mountain. Note also 1 Kgs 19:11; Isa 66:15; *4 Ezra* 13:10.

17 Francis Henry Colson, trans., *Philo VII* (LCL; Cambridge, Mass.: Harvard University Press, 1937) 23, 29 (emphasis added). In the present context, *Spec. leg.* 2.189 is worthy of note. There Philo speaks of the trumpet of Exod 16:19 as a sound that penetrated to the ends of the earth.

18 Philo justifies "visible sounds" from the LXX of Exod 20:18 (ἑώρα τὴν φωνήν, lit. "[all the people] saw the voice"). Cf. also *Migr. Abr.* 47; *Vit. Mos.* 2.213. Visible sounds occur in the *Act. And.* Epit 33 (healing of a leper), on which see Dennis R. MacDonald, *Christianizing Homer: The* Odyssey, *Plato, and The Acts of Andrew* (New York: Oxford University Press, 1994) 200, 215 n.145.

19 According to a tradition found in *Jub.* 10:26 and *Sib. Or.* 3:97-109, the tower of Babel was cast down by a violent wind. The oracle was cited by Josephus *Ant.* 1.118. Theophilus of Antioch (*Autolyc.* 2.31) also cites this passage, adding *Sib. Or.* 8:4-5, which concludes, . . . γλῶσσαι τ' ἀνθρώπων / εἰς πολλὰς ἐμερίσθησαν διαλέκτους. Cf. διαμεριζόμεναι in Acts 2:3. The most interesting verbal parallel (other than references to languages) is the verb συγχέω ("confuse"; Gen 11:7, 9; Acts 2:6). This supports the interpretation that the author wished to evoke the story of Babel.

20 Barrett (1:113) notes a parallel with the "wind" of Gen 1:2, although he does not find much value in it. A possible intertextual connection that has an eschatological cast is Isa 66:15, 18: "For the Lord will come in fire (ὡς πῦρ [Acts 2:3]), and his chariots like the whirlwind . . . and his rebuke in flames of fire (ἐν φλογὶ πυρός). . . . For I know their works and their thoughts, and I am coming to gather all nations and tongues (ἔρχομαι συναγαγεῖν πάντα τὰ ἔθνη καὶ τὰς γλώσσας); and they shall come and shall see my glory."

human race.[21] In this thrilling narrative Luke expresses fundamental theological principles: the gift of the Spirit is the present eschatological benefit, and this gift is for the entire human race.[22] Pentecost reaffirms and explicates Acts 1:6-8. Bede's crisp Latin grasps the point and more: *Vnitatem linguarum quam superbia Babylonis disperserat humilitas ecclesiae recolligit, spiritaliter autem varietas linguarum dona variarum significant gratiarum.*[23]

■ **2-4** The next two verses describe (unlike Philo, *supra*) a series of events, first the windlike sound, followed by the firelike tongues.[24] The narrator does not state that the sound ceased before the tongues appeared. The primary referents are in the similes: wind and fire.[25] This pair was a biblical symbol of theophany and judgment.[26] "Wind/spirit" (in Greek the word πνεῦμα can mean either) evokes the prophecy of John (Luke 3:16), echoed in Acts 1:5.[27] "Phenomena resembling jagged fiery tongues" may refer to the jagged edges of flames, an image found in Enoch's vision of heaven,[28] but the suitability of the metaphor cannot be ignored.[29] "Fire" alone is a frequent sign of epiphanies. The participle διαμεριζόμεναι could be read as circumstantial, yielding the meaning "tongues that looked like fire appeared, and after distributing themselves among the group, one tongue rested upon each person," but "divided" is adequate.[30] Evidently the reader is to envision a single (object shaped like a) tongue resting on each person. This establishes a parallel between "baptism with the Holy Spirit" and the baptism of Jesus.[31] "Filled with/full of the Holy Spirit"

21 On miracle and science in the Greco-Roman world, see Parsons and Pervo, *Rethinking*, 94–96, followed by observations on the unity of the human race, 96–101. According to *Jub.* 3:28 and Josephus *Ant.* 1.41, all creatures spoke the same language in Eden. In the end-time there will once more be γλῶσσα μία ("one language"); *T. Jud.* 25:3. Plutarch says that Zoroastrian eschatology envisions a new world in which there will be "one manner of life and one form of government for a blessed people who shall all speak one tongue" (*Is. Os.* 47 [*Mor.* 370B], in Frank Cole Babbitt, trans., *Plutarch's Moralia V* [LCL; Cambridge, Mass.: Harvard University Press, 1936] 115).

22 In his treatise on Babel, Philo views a single human language as the source of more good than harm (*Conf. Ling.* 12–13) and thus takes pains to supersede a literal interpretation of the event (190–92).

23 "The church in its humility recovers the unity of languages that Babylon in its arrogance had dispersed. At the spiritual level the variety of languages points to the gifts of different forms of grace." Bede, 16 (author's trans.).

24 Boismard, as noted above,

25 This is apparent in the subsequent verbs. The subject of "filled" in v. 2 could be either (properly) "sound" or "wind," while "sat" (v. 3) is singular, suggesting that "fire" is the envisioned subject into which it has been attracted.

26 The biblical references are numerous. Note, in addition to n. 19 above, Isa 29:6; 30:27-28; 40:24; 41:16; Ezek 1:4; Joel 2:28-30.

27 See on Acts 1:5.

28 Greco-Roman examples of fire associated with the head include the striking passage in Virgil *Aen.* 2.682–84, characterized as a portent (*monstrum*): *ecce levis summo de vertice visus Iuli fundere lumen apex, tactuque innoxia mollis lambere flamma comas et circum tempora pasci* ("Lo! From above the head of Iülus a light tongue of flame seemed to shed a gleam and, harmless in its touch, lick his soft locks and pasture round his temples"). In Henry Rushton Fairclough, trans., *Virgil I* (LCL; Cambridge, Mass.: Harvard University Press, 1974) 341; see also *Il.* 18.214; Euripides *Bacch.* 348–49; Ovid *Fast.* 6.635; Josephus *Bell.* 7.43; and Iamblichus *Myst.* 3.4. For other instances of fire on the head as a portent or mark of inspiration, see Pieter W. van der Horst, "Hellenistic Parallels to the Acts of the Apostles (2.1-47)," *JSNT* 25 (1985) 49–60. The Dionysiac epiphany in Longus *Daphn.* 2.25.3 begins with a sudden light, followed by fire and a loud noise. The baptism of Jesus in the Jordan included an epiphany of fire, according to Justin *Dial.* 88. Irenaeus (*A.H.* 1.20.4) and Hippolytus (*Ref.* 7.32) allege that the Carpocratians made use of fire in the baptismal ceremony. These references suggest that a Greek audience would grasp the meaning of the phenomenon, but the immediate background is arguably Semitic. See Glen Menzies, "Pre-Lukan Occurrences of the Phrase 'Tongue of Fire,'" *Pneuma: Journal of the Society for Pentecostal Studies* 22 (2000) 27–60. He examines *1 Enoch* 14:8-25; 71:5-8; 1Q22; 1Q29; and 4Q375-76 and concludes that the image refers to an epiphany.

29 In Greek, as in many languages, "tongue" can be a metonym for "language."

30 Cf. BDAG, *s.v.* διαμερίζω. For "distributed" see Barrett, 1:114. This distributive sense helps account for the singular "sat." (The plural is a secondary *v.l.*)

31 Luke 3:21 reports that the Spirit in a visible form

is a common Lucan expression.[32] The result of this gift is solemn[33] speech in "other languages," which is the most likely translation.[34]

Boismard's D-Text of vv. 2-4 is shorter and less complicated. The "windlike sound" is not said to fill the entire house (v. 2). It is difficult to imagine how such a loud sound would not fill a house. The somewhat confusing image of "divided tongues" in v. 3 is also omitted. Most remarkably, v. 4a, "All were filled with the Holy Spirit," does not appear. This could be viewed as redundant, since v. 4b refers to the Spirit. These readings apparently derive from an edition (or editions) that abbreviated and simplified the text by reducing the (intentionally) confusing and overloaded imagery of the conventional text.[35]

Excursus: Glossolalia and Prophecy in Acts

The quotation from Joel in Acts 2:17-21 directs the reader to understand the phenomenon described in 2:1-13 as prophecy. This leads Hans Conzelmann to say, "It should be noted that Luke himself no longer has any exact conception of the original glossolalia. He identifies it with prophecy (10:46; 19:6)."[36] The second observation is correct.[37] Luke *does* wish to identify "speaking in tongues" with prophecy. The opinion that Luke did not comprehend the nature of ecstatic speech is quite unlikely, for, as Conzelmann elsewhere observed, this is a widespread phenomenon.[38] A more probable explanation is that Luke chose to view the phenomenon as intelligible prophecy out of a desire to dissociate the Christian movement from hostile criticism (and, possibly, to discourage Christians from venerating unintelligible

descended upon Jesus. Note also φωνή ("voice," "sound") in Luke 3:22 and Acts 2:6.

32 Luke 1:15 (John), 41 (Elizabeth), 67 (Zechariah). The phrase is used before speeches, as in Acts 4:8 (Peter), or miracles, as in 13:9 (Paul). It is a component of the baptismal gift (9:17, Paul) and is unambiguously bestowed on the entire community (4:31). Luke therefore uses the term variously and not consistently.

33 "Solemn" seems appropriate for ἀποφθέγγεσθαι, which essentially refers to loud, clear, and emphatic speech and can refer to oracles, including ecstatic prophecy (cf. Mic 5:11 (5:12 MT), where it means "soothsayers"; Plutarch *Pyth. orac.* 23 (*Mor.* 405E) of the Pythian oracles; and *T. Job* 48:3; 50:1, where Job's daughters declaim verses in the angelic language (on which note 1 Cor 13:1). For other references, see Johannes Behm, "ἀποφθέγγομαι," *TDNT* 1:447. In Acts, the verb is used of the rational proclamation of the message (2:14, immediately following, and 26:25, where it is opposed to "madness"). Otherwise, the verb refers to weighty utterances (whence "apophthegm").

34 Cf. the prologue to Greek Sirach v. 22, and, in detail, Christian Wolff, "λαλεῖν γλώσσαις in the Acts of the Apostles," in Alf Christophersen et al., eds., *Paul, Luke, and the Graeco-Roman World: Essays in Honour of Alexander J. M. Wedderburn* (JSNTS 217; London: Sheffield Academic Press, 2002) 189–99.

35 Boismard's evidence is almost entirely patristic and of varied provenance. See the comments in *Texte*, 60, 62. He contends with justification that these are not unrelated errors but the result of editorial activity.

36 Conzelmann, 15. His view is far from isolated. See, e.g., Lüdemann, 41.

37 Acts 10:46 (Cornelius) says that Peter and company heard the gentiles "speaking in tongues and glorifying God" (λαλούντων γλώσσαις καὶ μεγαλυνόντων τὸν θεόν). Acts 19:6 reports that the twelve former disciples of John "began to speak in tongues and prophesied" (ἐλάλουν τε γλώσσαις καὶ ἐπροφήτευον). Acts 10:46 uses a phrase evocative of 2:11 and thus of what Peter's speech identified as "prophecy." In both cases it might be argued that the καί ("and") is sequential (". . . and then to praise God/prophesy"), but this is unlikely. The conjunction either records simultaneous activity or is explanatory.

38 See Hans Conzelmann, *First Corinthians* (trans. James W. Leitch; Hermeneia; Philadelphia: Fortress Press, 1975), 205–6, and the references in nn. 12–13. In the Greek orbit, "enthusiasm" was well known (and often related to oracular prophecy) from the time of Plato (*Phaedr.* 244A-B; *Tim.* 71E-72B) onward. From the first century BCE, note Cicero *Div.* 1, 32, 70-71. Plutarch, roughly contemporaneous with Acts, discusses ecstatic possession in *Def. orac.* 14 (*Mor.* 417C) and *E Delph.* 6-24 (*Mor.* 387B-406F). For data from the later second century, see Apuleius *Metam.* 8.27 and Lucian *Jupp. trag.* 30. Jewish and Christian evidence includes *T. Job* 48-52 and Tertullian *Nat.* 2.7. Glossolalia is a widely attested phenomenon. See Felicitas D. Goodman, *Speaking in Tongues: A Cross-Cultural Study of Glossolalia* (Chicago: University of Chicago Press, 1972). For examples from antiquity, see Johannes Behm, "γλῶσσα," *TDNT* 1:719–27, esp. 722–24. Its appeal may be seen in the ubiquitous "*voces magicae*" in the magical papyri, on which see John Gager, ed., *Curse Tablets and Binding Spells from the Ancient World* (New York: Oxford

ecstasy). Acts 2:1-4, 13 reads like a narrative presentation of the hypothetical situation set out in 1 Cor 14:23: "If, therefore, the whole church comes together (ἐπὶ τὸ αὐτό, cf. Acts 2:1) and all speak in tongues (πάντες λαλῶσιν γλώσσαις; cf. Acts 2:4), and outsiders or unbelievers enter (cf. Acts 2:5-6), will they not say that you are out of your mind"? (cf. Acts 2:13)[39]

In this instance, the entire community had come together, all spoke in tongues, outsiders overheard, and some of them concluded that the speakers were deranged, albeit with drink.[40] Scholarship has seen the relevance of 1 Cor 14:23 (and 1 Corinthians 12–14 in general) for Acts 2:1-13 and has tended to focus on the differences between Luke and Paul.[41] Luke was evidently familiar with the text of 1 Corinthians,[42] but that assumption is not necessary to understand that Luke has reservations about unintelligible ecstasy. Rather than make an uninformed and highly inaccurate guess about "speaking in tongues," the author of Acts has altered a tradition that he well understands.[43] In this matter, as in others, Luke followed Paul's inclination without refinement or qualification.[44]

The primary difficulty for those who claim that this account describes either glossolalia proper or xenoglossia/xenologia is the text, which speaks neither of unintelligible, ecstatic speech (glossolalia) nor of speech in foreign languages unknown to the speaker (one type of xenoglossia),[45] but describes what the audience *heard*.[46] By any reasonable criterion the primary recipients of the Spirit are the hearers.[47] That is an observation that will receive attention later. For the present, it is sufficient to say that the situation is anomalous and that the simplest explanation of the anomaly is to attribute it to the

University Press, 1992) 5–12. Widespread occurrence does not mean that glossolalia is not a valid religious experience; prayer is also widespread. See also Luke T. Johnson, "Tongues, Gift of," *ABD* 6:596–600.

39 Luke's lack of interest in exploiting the phenomenon is confirmed by the subsequent sermon, which refers only to prophetic activity.

40 In Acts 26:24-25 Luke will refute the charge of madness.

41 Kirsopp Lake ("The Gift of the Spirit on the Day of Pentecost," in Lake and Cadbury, *Additional Notes*, 111–21) intelligently remarks (118), "Even if—as is probable—he had never read 1 Corinthians, he can hardly have been ignorant of Paul's teaching." Others are likely to assume Luke's ignorance of Paul's thought. See, e.g., Haenchen, 172; Lüdemann, 41; Johnson, 42; Barrett, 1:115.

42 See Pervo, *Dating*, 51–147, with the summary on 139.

43 The issue is not that Luke regards ecstasy as a form of prophecy. Paul's careful separation of the two may be his own contribution, since the history-of-religions tradition (n. 38) is familiar with ecstatic prophecy; it is that he identifies "speaking in tongues" with lucid proclamation of the gospel. It may also be noted that Luke never portrays a series of spontaneous prophecies (and/or other spiritual gifts) along the line of the "orderly" situation proposed by Paul in 1 Cor 14:26-33. At Pentecost all proclaim an identical message in unison.

44 Other examples are the consumption of food offered to idols (15:20; cf. 1 Corinthians 8; 10:14—11:1), the leadership of women, which Luke does not highlight, and marriage, which he does not recommend.

45 Representatives of the Greek patristic tradition (e.g., Gregory Nazianzos [*PG* 36:443], Cyril of Jerusalem *Myst. cat.* 17 [*PG* 93:388]) judged that those inspired spoke in foreign tongues. See also the excursus of Jacquier (787–95), who discusses patristic and later judgments.

46 See the summary of Fitzmyer (239), who lists proponents of both views. An example of the former is Turner, *Power.* In this useful study of Luke and Acts from a Pentecostal viewpoint, Turner (441) states that Acts 2:4 is an example of "the distinctively new Christian phenomenon of invasive glossolalia." On the phenomenon, see Hans-Josef Klauck, "Von Kassandra bis zur Gnosis: Zum Umfeld der frühchristlichen Glossolalie," *ThQ* 179 (1999) 289–312. Christopher Forbes seeks to discredit the evidence for ancient parallels to glossolalia (*Prophecy and Inspired Speech in Early Christianity and Its Hellenistic Environment* [WUNT 75; Tübingen: Mohr, 1995]). Since little is known about either the phenomenon or many of the proposed parallels, he can make a case, but Paul does state that the phenomenon would resemble "madness" (1 Cor 14:23), and Luke deals with the claim of exuberant inebriation, both good grounds for presuming an ecstatic state. On that subject, see David E. Aune, *Prophecy in Early Christianity* (Grand Rapids: Eerdmans, 1983) 19–21. The phenomenon that we label "glossolalia" has occurred in a number of contexts, not all of them religious, and can be characterized in physiological terms. See the study by Goodman (*Speaking in Tongues* [n. 38 above]), who provides a social and psychological analysis of xenoglossia on 149–51. Her findings correlate with the "apologetic" explanation of Luke's presentation of speaking in tongues.

author, who has concocted a story that does not fit into the categories of religious experience.

■ **5-13** The scene shifts, without formal notice, from indoors to outdoors, where an excited crowd, drawn by the noise, gathers.[48] Verses 5-6 propel the narrative in a new and surprising direction, but the opening has no hint of the unusual or the novel. Bruce Metzger asks why Luke should think it worth noting that Jews lived in Jerusalem.[49] Early editors and copyists shared his concern. ℵ * and MSS. of the Vulgate omit the word, and its place in other MSS. varies considerably. "Devout" is absent from some Old Latin texts. "Such confused evidence raises a strong suspicion that κατοικοῦντες and Ἰουδαῖοι ['residents' and 'Jews'] may be additions to the text, derived probably from . . . ii.14. . . ."[50] In 2:14, the opening phrase might be rendered "Judeans and residents of Jerusalem."[51] Lake concludes that "Jews" is a gloss. He further proposes that Luke wished to suggest that the audience at Pentecost included gentiles. That inference is less likely,[52] but it is probable that "Jews" is a pedantic D-Text gloss that has entered the broader tradition.[53] "From every country under the sun" supplies the requisite intimation of that universality that will rise from firmly Jewish foundations.[54]

■ **5-6** Verse 6 is quite intelligible without v. 5, if not more so.[55] Verse 5 gives profile to the "crowd" or "multitude" that assembles.[56] The hearers were not an idle mob loitering at street-corners but, one might reasonably infer, observant Jews whose piety had led

47 The contention that because the hearers say, "we hear *them speaking* in our languages" the speakers rather than the hearers are inspired (e.g., Barrett, 1:124; and, in more detail, Witherington, 134–35) is inadequate. If each speaker used one language, the result would be babble. Bede attempted explanations of the situation based on the presumption that only one person could speak at a time, recognizing that this might yield the view that the miracle resided "more in the hearing than the speaking" (*ad* 2:6, p. 17). This got him in hot water. In his *Retractatio* (*ad* 2:6, pp. 110–11) Bede defended himself by saying that he had cribbed his exegesis from Gregory Nazianzos, as indeed he had, from *Orat.* 4.15, in Rufinus's translation, followed by an even more elaborate explanation.

48 The effect of Luke's technique—whatever its causes—is rather more vivid than a narrative comment to the effect that, "meanwhile, outdoors a large crowd. . . ." There is a similar sudden transition to the streets in Apuleius *Metam.* 11.7. Greek mime could also shift from indoors. The examples are connected with religious festivals: Sophron wrote a mime about women viewing the Isthmian festival, evidently imitated by Theocritus *Id.* 15.

49 Metzger, *Textual Commentary*, 251. He also observes that it is odd to speak of "Jews from every ἔθνος" ("nation, people"), since the Jews were a people.

50 Lake, "Gift," 111–21, citing 113.

51 A further problem is that "residents" is repeated in v. 9, with reference to those who live in Mesopotamia and other places. On "both Jews and proselytes, Cretans and Arabs" of v. 11, see below.

52 See, however, the comments at the end of this section.

53 See also Ropes, *Text*, 112–13; and Barrett, 1:117–18. Metzger (*Textual Commentary*, 251) supports its originality on the grounds that so difficult a word would not have been added; that is, it is the *lectio difficilior*. Such glosses often cause more problems than they solve. In this instance, the motive for the addition is clear: to prevent the inference that the group included "heathens." Acts uses "devout" (εὐλαβής) only of Jews and elsewhere also with ἀνήρ ("male"): 8:2; 22:12 (cf. Luke 2:25).

54 The hyperbolic "every nation under heaven" is characteristic of Deutero-Pauline emphasis on the universal proclamation of the message. See, e.g., Col 1:23. In *Vit. Mos.* 2.20, Philo contrasts the universal openness of Judaism to gentile xenophobia: "[our institutions] attract and win the attention of all, of barbarians, of Greeks, of dwellers on the mainland and islands, of nations of the east and the west, of Europe and Asia, of the whole inhabited world from end (ἀπὸ περάτων ἐπὶ πέρατα)" (trans. Frank Henry Colson, *Philo VI* [LCL; Cambridge, Mass.: Harvard University Press, 1935] 459). Note the allusion to the "ends of the earth" (Acts 1:8).

55 D-Texts tend to prefer καί ("and") to ὅτι ("because"). This makes the narrative a bit less abrupt but does not explain why they gathered.

56 πλῆθος has a range of meanings in Acts, most often referring to the civic (e.g., 14:4) or religious (e.g., 15:12) body, but it can also be applied to a crowd (e.g., 28:3) or a large number (e.g., 17:4). The most common sense is "the general public."

them to spend the remainder of their natural lives in Jerusalem.[57] The "noise" (φωνή) that attracted them is ambiguous for the sake of suspense, but v. 6b immediately clarifies the situation, in a sense, for, although it is not difficult to imagine outsiders hearing the mighty noise of v. 2, it is less easy to understand why hearing a

person or persons speaking one's native language would generate confusion.[58]

■ **7-11** These verses simultaneously rationalize their reaction and underline the wondrous character of the event, both with a considerable want of realism, for they can discern that the speakers have Galilean accents, while their speech indicates facility in an exotic language.[59] Narrative compression eliminates the process by which the miracle was detected (above).[60] The story symbolizes both the universality of the message ("every nation") and the capacity of the gospel to address all sorts and conditions of people in their own terms.

Excursus: The List of Nations

In vv. 9-11 the crowd of foreign-born residents recites a catalogue of nations.[61] Such lists are very widely attested.[62] The purpose of this catalogue is patent: to symbolize—in fact, to achieve—the universal mission of the church.[63] It is equally clear that Luke did not invent this list, an insight that has launched a quest for its source and origin while also proffering solutions for some of the conflicts in the text. The catalogue does not have a consistent form. It begins with the enumeration of three ethnic groups, "Parthians, Medes, and Elamites," then shifts to a series of nouns that are objects of the attributive participial phrase "those who inhabit." That participle, *κατοικοῦντες*, apparently conflicts with v. 5, where it characterizes the audience. This group (if "Judea" is deleted) has two subsections, each with a pair joined by "both and" (τε καί), followed by two others lined by "and." At v. 10b there is another shift: "visiting Roman citizens!"[64] That is a suitable climax, followed in v. 11a by the inclusive reference to "Jews by birth and Jews by choice." Unfortunately, however, the list continues by reverting to ethnic groups: "Cretans and Arabs."[65] Any underlying source has been edited. As a catalogue of the nations of the Mediterranean *oikoumenē*, it is deficient. The most astonishing omission, from the perspective of Acts, is the entire Greek peninsula (Macedonia and Achaea). The most astonishing inclusion, from the perspective of Acts, is the initial "Parthians, Medes, and Elamites," an obscure and archaic trio not otherwise encountered. The text is problematic.

57 See Schneider, 1:251.

58 For this meaning of συνεχύθη, see Haenchen, 169 n. 1.

59 The word διάλεκτος does not have the modern sense of "dialect." See Barrett, 1:119. It is reasonable to ask, with Haenchen (169 n. 2), how many Diaspora Jews, most of whom lived in Greek-speaking cities, would have known the local languages, but this is beside the point.

60 Among Luke's inconsistencies is that the miracle appears to be in the hearing. Alternatives such as having each of twelve apostles speak one language would have recreated Babel rather than reverse it. That may be the viewpoint of the D-Texts (D syr$^{p. hmg}$ mae Aug) that read λαλοῦντας ταῖς γλώσσαις αὐτῶν or ταῖς γλώσσαις αὐτῶν λαλούντων αὐτῶν ("[they heard] them speaking in their tongues"). Cf. Ropes, *Text*, 13. Strictly speaking, the Spirit should have fallen upon the audience. Moreover, Peter is able to address the entire audience in a language that they understand. Those who pursue consistency or concrete reality in this story are barking up the wrong tree.

61 Witherington (136 n. 27) says that the list is a parenthetical insertion by the author, an irrational claim in defense of the rationality of the text.

62 Many examples are provided in Scott, "Geographical Horizon," 483–544. This thorough review includes a survey of research and a wealth of bibliographical data. See also Gilbert, "Roman Propaganda," 233–56, esp. 249–50 and n. 58.

63 This function can be seen not only in Jewish lists, such as that in Philo *Leg. all.* 281-82, but also in the Isis cult, as in the list of cult names in *P. Oxy.* 1380, 1-136 and in Apuleius *Metam.* 11.5. See the comments of Nock, *Conversion*, 150–53, as well as Borgen, *Philo*, 273–85, who discusses the geographical orientation of Philo and the significance of his various lists.

64 In Acts, Ῥωμαῖοι means "Roman citizens"; see Cadbury and Lake, 20. The word ἐπιδημοῦντες appears to mean "visiting" in 17:21 and 18:27, but the distinction should not be pressed.

65 The expression "residents of" seems more suitable in a catalogue of Diaspora Jews than do ethnic adjectives, but 11:20, "some men from Cyprus and Cyrene," suggests caution.

"Judea" (v. 9) is questionable, since one would not expect to find the homeland in a catalogue of the Diaspora and because native Judeans would experience no surprise at hearing their native language. One answer to the first objection is that Acts is listing "every nation under heaven" rather than Diaspora locations.[66] This does not resolve the second problem. The probability that Luke based his list on an existing catalogue opens the possibility that he overlooked the inept presence of "Judea." Against this appeal to carelessness are the anarthrous form (as an adjective "Judea" should have the article[67]) and, more cogently, that it is out of place. Judea does not lie between Mesopotamia and Cappadocia.[68] Without it, the list would progress counterclockwise from Mesopotamia. "Armenia" would fit nicely, as the African Latin tradition (Tertullian, Augustine [once]) recognized. Other options exist.[69] Many of the numerous catalogues introduced for comparison lack "Judea." The best option may be to omit the word as a later addition to the text. The structure of vv. 9-10b (above) supports deletion. Another possibility is to mark the spot with a blank space, indicating that the original cannot be identified with reasonable certainty. Of the conjectural alternatives "Armenia" is the strongest.[70]

James M. Scott has offered a contribution to the questions of both form and source.[71] He traces the developments of the "Table of Nations" in Genesis 10 through its various ramifications in subsequent Israelite writings. Among the features of this tradition are the convention of *pars pro toto,* that is, lack of completeness; examples of "a more random structure," that is, lack of orderly progression; and vacillation "between names of peoples and names of lands."[72] These lists normally viewed Jerusalem as "the navel of the universe."[73] That is one possible geographical framework for Acts 2:5-11; it is not Luke's own geographical horizon.[74] Scott's model is generic; it does not identify a specific source against

66 At its face value the catalogue is a list of Diaspora locations. Hemer (*Book,* 217) presumes this view; see his evidence on 222–23.

67 See BDF §261 n. 4 (although Luke's use of the article with place-names is irregular).

68 Martin Hengel proposes that "Judea" could include Syria ("Ἰουδαῖα in der geographischen Liste Apg 2,9-11 und Syrien als 'Grossjudäa,'" *RHPhR* 80 [2000] 83–86).

69 See Ropes, *Text,* 14–15; Metzger, *Textual Commentary,* 253–54; and Boismard, *Texte,* 65. Jerome speaks of those who dwell in Syria (an apparent generalization); Chrysostom read "India" (not likely in this place). According to Metzger (*Textual Commentary,* 254), Burkitt, with reference to some Arabic MSS., proposed "Gordyaia," while Dibelius (*Studies,* 91) inclines toward "Galatia" or "Gallai."

70 The construction τε καί supports the hypothesis that another name once filled the place. One might also propose that τε comes from the interpolator. D* it vg[cl] omit the particle or its equivalent. On this construction, see Knox, 11. Haenchen (170 n. 2) lists those who view "Judea" as an error, including Harnack, Preuschen, Wellhausen, Wendt, and Loisy. Conzelmann (14) is uncertain. Barrett (1:121) is ultimately willing to delete the word. Metzger (*Textual Commentary,* 253–54) clings unhappily to "Judea." Boismard (*Texte,* 65) proposes for the D-Text a shorter catalogue that does not include "Judea": "Parthians, Medes, Elamites, [in asyndetic style] and those who inhabit Mesopotamia, Armenia, and Pontus, Asia, Phrygia, and Pamphylia."

71 Scott, "Geographical Horizon," esp. 527–30.

72 Ibid., 529.

73 Alexander (*Context,* 79–80) reports the view of Richard Bauckham, expressed in a paper, that the list views the world from Jerusalem. This may reflect how the author wished it to be understood, although it was probably not the view of his source.

74 The long-standing argument over a "Jewish" or an "astrological" background is misplaced. In 1948, Stefan Weinstock proposed that the list in Acts 2 corresponded to an ancient geographical scheme ("The Geographical Catalogue in Acts 2, 9-11," *JRS* 38 [1948] 43–46). Cf. also John A. Brinkman, "The Literary Background of the 'Catalogue of the Nations' (Acts 2, 9-11)," *CBQ* 25 (1963) 418–27. In 1970, Metzger wrote a detailed critique of this hypothesis: "Ancient Astrological Geography and Acts 2:9-11," now collected in his *New Testament Studies: Philological, Versional and Patristic* (NTTS 10; Leiden: Brill, 1980) 46–56. Scott's claim ("Geographical Horizon," 528 n. 171) that Weinstock's position represents "the usual view" is erroneous. The idea that each people had its tutelary divine being was widespread. (This was one matter on which the views of Celsus and Origen converged [Origen *Cels.* 1.24; 5.25].) This could be correlated with the view that each people had its own star (Manilius *Astronomica* 4.696-700). See Ramsay MacMullen, *Paganism in the Roman Empire* (New Haven: Yale University Press, 1981) 82 and 185 n. 31; and Franz Cumont, "La plus ancienne géographie astrologique," *Klio* 9 (1909) 263–73. A "deep" astrological background for any scheme of twelve nations is far from unreasonable, and the polemic against it overlooks the use of astrological

which it will be possible to determine Luke's editorial activity, nor would the identification of a precise source be likely to shed any new light on interpretation.[75] Problems nonetheless remain. "Twelve" would seem to be the right number of nations, and this is the figure that results from the deletion of Judea and inclusion of "Romans."[76] "Cretans and Arabs" must then be left dangling, but they are difficult to fit in by any measure.[77] All in all, it is difficult to dispute Howard Marshall's conclusion: "It is an odd list."[78] One feature of its oddity is that it is fearfully old-fashioned.[79] If the catalogue is of Jewish origin,[80] it evidently reflects the period and perspective of the Seleucid era (312/311–63 BCE).[81] This perspective points to Antioch and to a possible Antiochene source.[82] Whatever the source, the event is a bit of fiction, a list derived from literature recited by a crowd in unison via an omniscient narrator who can report that crowd's reaction from its own point of view. The same narrator prevents them from spoiling the plot by reducing their report of what they heard to "praising God."[83]

■ **12-13** Recognition of the artificial nature of vv. 6b-11 stimulates the hypothesis that Luke has transformed an account of unintelligible glossolalia into intelligible speech, yet vv. 12-13 are, in their present form, no less an authorial composition than what precedes. Some of the gapers drawn by the phenomenon concluded that the speakers had taken a drop or two more than the situation strictly required. This judgment would apply to ecstatic speech but makes little sense as a reaction to hearing Arabic or Persian and is illogical. Its elements

symbolism in various contexts, notably apocalyptic. A list of twelve nations/regions that corresponded to the zodiac would be an excellent representation of universality and was so used in, for example, the mosaics of synagogues in the Holy Land, as late as the sixth century CE (Beth Alpha). According to Scott ("Geographical Horizon," 516), Josephus adjusted the Table of Nations to correspond to Daniel's picture of a succession of world empires, a scheme influenced by astrological symbolism. Tamsyn Barton (*Ancient Astrology* [London: Routledge, 1994] 180–82) says that Manilius's assignment of zodiac signs to geographical zones is the oldest extant list, but no version established itself, as the several lists in plate 12, p. 182, demonstrate. Carl Holladay recognizes the possible relevance of an astrological background ("Acts and the Fragments," 171–98, esp. 194–95). Malina and Neyrey (*Portraits,* 120–25) note the highly geocentric quality of ancient cultures. All regarded their native place as the center of the universe.

75 Barrett (1:121–24) comes to a similar conclusion.

76 See the insightful and charming, if romantic, comments of Harnack, 65–71.

77 From the perspective of Jerusalem, these peoples may represent the west and the east, respectively; so Fitzmyer, 243. Haenchen (171 n. 1) traces this view to Eissfeldt and finds it "a mere stopgap." Scott ("Geographical Horizon," 529–30) attempts to rationalize the list in terms of the old Table of Nations. For other guesses, see his n. 179 on p. 529. Knox (82 n. 2) proposed that they were "added by Luke himself or by a very early copyist, in deference to Paul's visit to Arabia and Titus's real or supposed mission to Crete (Titus 1. 5)." Haenchen (171) agrees that it is a later addition.

78 Marshall, 71. Relations to the contents of Acts are thin: Pontus is the home of Aquila and Priscilla (18:2); Phrygia and Pamphylia are prominent in chaps. 13–14. Cyrene brings to mind 11:20 and 13:3, and Egypt is the home of Apollos (18:24).

79 Note those "Medes" and "Elamites," who were no longer in the picture. An equally old-fashioned list can be found in Q. Curtius Rufus's *History of Alexander* (probably mid-first century CE). See Conzelmann (14–15), who notes that this list, which includes the Medes, also mixes territorial and ethnic names.

80 Scott's valuable analysis notwithstanding, those in quest of the closest specific parallel to Acts 2:5-11 will have difficulty choosing between the catalogue found in Philo *Leg. Gaj.* 281-82 and that of Curtius Rufus (see previous note).

81 If the list were based on Seleucid claims of conquest and dominance, Syria could have been omitted as the "homeland," while Greece and the west would be absent because they were outside the Seleucid sphere. J. Taylor ("The List of Nations in Acts 2:9-11," *RB* 106 [1999] 408–20) traces the list back to the Achaemenid period.

82 See Klauck, *Magic,* 10–11, who suggests an Antiochene origin and aptly identifies a proleptic function: the old list of military conquests now serves to forecast the conquest of the world by the gospel. On this, see Gary Gilbert, "The List of Nations in Acts 2: Roman Propaganda and the Lukan Response," *JBL* 121 (2002) 497–529, and idem, "Roman Propaganda," 233–56, esp. 247–53, as well as Edwards, *Religion and Power,* 88.

83 τὰ μεγαλεῖα τοῦ θεου ("God's great deeds" = μεγαλύνειν τ. θεόν ["praise God"]): Luke 1:46 (the Magnificat), 58; Acts 5:13; 10:46; and 19:17

are Lucan: διαπορέω ("to be at a loss") appears only in Luke (once) and Acts (thrice) in the NT. The hearers' question is that of the Athenians (17:18-20) as is the mockery by some (17:32).[84] Whatever his hypothetical source may have contained, Luke has constructed 2:12-13 to show what Jerusalem had in common with Athens.[85] The price of this parallelism is a painful contradiction[86] that v. 15 will intensify. Barrett regards this as "simply a matter of careless writing" rather than a clash of sources.[87] It rather seems to be a typical Lucan contradiction that has things both ways: all testify to the miracle, which is thus validated, but an alternative must be refuted. In this very clumsy manner Luke acknowledges the ambiguity of wonders. To proclaim an event as a miracle is to embrace an interpretation of the event. Other views are possible.[88] The objection is quite opportune, for it is both a social slur that the subsequent eloquence of Peter will utterly quash[89] and an allusion to the familiar association between drunkenness and inspiration.[90] Readers may detect an irony. Although certain

(of Jesus' name). The adjective is found in the LXX (e.g., Deut 11:2; Ps 70:19) and often in Sirach (e.g., 36:7). In the D-Text (Boismard, *Texte,* 65), "hear" in v. 11 is in the third person and thus is a comment by the omniscient narrator.

84 The simple and complex verbs (δια)χλευάζω are *hapax legomena* in the NT.

85 Crowd divisions are another Lucan motif (Acts 14:4; 23:7), frequently found in popular narrative, for example, Chariton *Chaer.* 5.4.1; Heliodorus *Aeth.* 1.13; the *Tobiad Romance* (Josephus *Ant.* 11.230); and *Act. Paul* 3.24.

86 The D-Text of vv. 12-13 is, according to Boismard (*Texte,* 66), "So they were bewildered and perplexed **at what had happened** (ἐπὶ τῷ γεγονότι), constantly asking one another 'What is *this business about*?' 13 There were some who made fun of the whole business by announcing: '**all** these characters are **carrying a heavy load** of cheap wine'" (διεχλεύαζον λέγοντες οὗτοι γλεύκει πάντες βεβαρημένοι εἰσίν). "At what had happened" is a painfully pedantic addition. The transfer of "all" from v. 12 to v. 13 seeks to alleviate the contradiction. The participle (lit. "weighed down") suggests slurred rather than excited speech and is thus not appropriate to the situation.

87 Barrett, 1:125.

88 In a work with a viewpoint, such as Acts, the interpretation is usually made or assumed by the narrator. For modernity, the event is a problem: "things like this do not happen." In the world of Acts, the possibility of a marvelous healing is accepted. Controversy is likely to arise over the means utilized. Cf. the healing of a cripple in Acts 4:7 and 14:11. In the first case, the religious authorities are concerned about the authority behind the healing, while in the second, the populace concludes that Zeus and Hermes are paying a visit.

89 The charge of intoxication with new wine suggests a cheap drunk. The problem of the availability of new wine this early in the year has given rise to solutions involving chemical means (Cadbury and Lake, 20; Bruce, 119). Fitzmyer (235) notes a "Feast of New Wine" as one of the "pentecosts" stipulated in the *Temple Scroll* (19:11-14). Why attempts should be made to defend these mistaken and hostile critics is not clear. Another social dimension emerges in v. 15: it is but 9:00 A.M. Imbibing before the sun was barely above the yardarm was a mark of the most degenerate types, including Mark Antony, whose drinking behavior Cicero excoriates (*Phil.* 2.41, 104; see also Terence *Ad.* 955). Readers may here detect an ironic allusion to the new wine of the Christian message (Luke 5:37—although this evangelist agrees with the objectors about the superiority of less recent vintages [v. 39]).

90 Philo's treatise on "high sobriety," *De ebrietate,* contains a famous passage that speaks of the ecstasy of inspiration: "Now when grace fills the soul, that soul thereby rejoices and smiles and dances, for it is possessed and inspired (βεβάκχευται), so that to many of the unenlightened it may seem to be drunken, crazy and beside itself" (146; trans. Frank Henry Colson and George Herbert Whitaker, *Philo III* [LCL; New York: G. P. Putnam's Sons, 1930] 395). See the entire passage, 146–48. The text to which Philo refers is 1 Sam 1:11-15, the alleged drunkenness of Hannah. See, in addition, *Som.* 2.248-49. The latter begins, "And, when the happy soul holds out the sacred goblet of its own reason, who is it that pours into it the holy cupfuls of true gladness, but the Word (λόγος), the Cup-bearer of God and Master of the feast (οἰνοχόος τοῦ θεοῦ καὶ συμποσίαρχος), who is also none other than the draught which he pours" (trans Frank Henry Colson and George Herbert Whitaker, *Philo V* [LCL; Cambridge, Mass.: Harvard University Press, 1935] 555). Note also Plutarch *Def. orac.* 50 (*Mor.* 437D-E), in which the inspiration of the Pythia is compared with intoxication from alcohol, and Lucian *Nigr.* 5 (enthusiasm for philosophy leaves Nigrinus giddy). In the NT, see Eph 5:18, "Do not get drunk with wine, for that is debauchery; but be

people claim that they are filled (μεμεστωμένοι) with wine, the speakers have in reality been filled (ἐπλήσθησαν) with Holy Spirit.[91]

Within the Christian tradition, the events of Pentecost, Acts 2:1-41, are viewed as the birth of the church. This view is correct in that it relates the shift from Jesus as a *subject* who gathers followers by proclaiming the presence of God's reign and demonstrating that advent through healings, exorcisms, and acceptance of all at table, to Jesus as the *object* of proclamation by disciples who now recruit followers. Pentecost, to state the matter in terms of the issue identified by Rudolf Bultmann, tells how—or at least when—the Proclaimer (the earthly Jesus) became the Proclaimed (the heavenly Lord).[92] In achieving this, Luke does not, like John 20:19-23, combine bestowal of the Spirit with explicit authority over subsequent followers, nor does he report an appearance at which the risen one orders his followers to recruit and baptize disciples, as in Matt 28:16-20.[93] In Luke 24 and Acts 1, the appearances include instruction in scriptural interpretation, theology, and the promise of the coming gift of the Spirit. None apart from God possesses the authority to forgive sins, and baptism is a matter of course.[94] These differences do not obviate similarities. In Acts, the authority of the apostles over other believers is assumed. John 20 and Acts 1–2 share a common theme: the ascended Christ empowered the church through the gift of the Spirit. Eph 4:7-8 reflects the same understanding. It is probable that Luke acquired his understanding in a Deutero-Pauline environment, but John 20:19-23 shows that the concept was shared in other circles toward the close of the first century.[95]

Acts 2:1-4 relates the spiritual empowerment of the disciples, but the following paragraph focuses on the endowment of their audience, while Peter's sermon climaxes with the promise that through baptism all believers will receive the Spirit (2:38). For Luke, this gift is essential and, in a number of instances, is attended with visible effects (2:1-4; 8:17-18; 10:44-46; 19:6). With the evident exception of the initial endowment, all of these cases involve believers who possess less than impeccable credentials: Samaritans, gentile "God-Fearers," and adherents of John the Baptizer. The most unambiguous of these episodes is that about the gentile Cornelius and his entourage (chap. 10), the diction of which evokes Pentecost.[96] Peter will use that experience as justification for the baptism of gentiles both on the spot (10:47) and subsequently in Jerusalem, where it is accepted (11:15-18). Luke did not invent the contention that the manifestation of spiritual gifts demonstrated the acceptability of gentile converts. Paul utilizes it in Gal 4:6: "And because you are children, God has sent the Spirit of his Son into our hearts, crying, 'Abba! Father!'"[97]

filled with the Spirit," and the comments on this in Pervo, *Dating*, 295–96, as well as Herbert Preisker, "μέθη," *TDNT* 4:545–47; and David E. Aune, "Septem Sapientium Convivium (Moralia 146B-164D)," in Hans Dieter Betz, ed., *Plutarch's Ethical Writings and Early Christian Literature* (SCHNT 4; Leiden: Brill, 1978) 51–105, esp. 92–94.

91 Arator (1:150–55) relates this to new wine in new bottles.

92 Bultmann, *Theology*, 1:33–37.

93 Cf. also the comments of Barrett, 1:108.

94 On the theology and practice of baptism in Acts, see Friedrich Avemarie, *Die Tauferzählungen der Apostelgeschichte: Theologie und Geschichte* (WUNT 139; Tübingen: Mohr Siebeck, 2002).

95 Both Acts 2:38 and Eph 4:7 speak of a gift (δωρεά); John does not use this noun (or a synonym) in connection with the Spirit, but cf. John 16:7, which also views Jesus as the source of the Spirit/Paraclete. On the subject, see Lindars, *Apologetic*, 51–59.

96 Acts 10:46a: ἤκουον γὰρ αὐτῶν λαλούντων γλώσσαις καὶ μεγαλυνόντων τὸν θεόν (lit. "For they heard them speaking in tongues and extolling God's greatness"); 2:11b: ἀκούομεν λαλούντων αὐτῶν ταῖς ἡμετέραις γλώσσαις τὰ μεγαλεῖα τοῦ θεου (lit. "We hear them speaking in our tongues the great deeds of God"). See Earl Richard, "Pentecost as a Recurrent Theme in Luke-Acts," in idem, ed., *New Views on Luke and Acts* (Collegeville, Minn.: Liturgical Press, 1990) 133–49.

97 For details, see Hans Dieter Betz, *Galatians: A Commentary on Paul's Letter to the Churches in Galatia* (Hermeneia; Philadelphia: Fortress Press, 1979) 209–11. This is one of a series of proofs of the validity of the Galatian believers' credentials.

The roots of the Pentecost story may be in the Diaspora missionary experience; that is, the "original source" of the story may have been a justification of the gentile mission, not unlike Acts 10:44-47 in content. This proposal is highly speculative, but it does account for Luke's emphases upon the experience of the hearers and the suitability of the catalogue of nations to evoke the gentile world.[98] If behind the Pentecost pericope lay a story of the reception of the Spirit by interested gentiles, a number of its difficulties would be alleviated. Antioch would be a reasonable source for this putative story, and the catalogue of nations (which is suitable to the environs of Antioch[99]) may have been associated with it. Driving this hypothesis is a skeptical attitude toward a coherent "Jerusalem source," an attitude widely supported by the scholarly tradition,[100] and the well-established view that the leading purpose of (Luke and) Acts is to demonstrate the legitimacy of the gentile mission. Its heuristic value derives from its inversion of the conventional assumptions that Luke has given his portrait of Pentecost a broad splash of universalistic color and that the story of Cornelius in Acts 10 imitates Acts 2. Neither set of assumptions has a preponderant weight of probability; each derives from a particular understanding of Luke's sources.

The achievement of 2:1-13 is considerable. With splendid vividness, Luke has been able to intimate the coming gentile mission without prematurely inaugurating it. Jews are the missionary target, but without limit on place or language—and, it should be added, without the inconvenience of discontinuity. The occasion is an Israelite festival, and the events fulfill earlier promises. On Pentecost, the firstfruits of the ecumenical harvest are taken in. The wind that erupts on this day will not abate until its stormy gusts have propelled Paul to Rome.

98 Cf. the proposal of Lake, "Gift," 111–21, esp. 114, noted above.

99 See the excursus on the list of nations, above.

100 See pp. 12–14.

2:14-41 Peter's Speech at Pentecost

**14/ At that Peter took his place with
the other eleven apostles and
addressed the crowd in a strong
and solemn tone: "Judeans, and
all residents of Jerusalem: there
is something that you need to
know, so please pay attention.
15/ Now these people are not,
as you suppose, drunk. It's only
900! 16/ No; this is what the
prophet[a] spoke of: 17/ 'After
this it shall come to pass'—God
is speaking—'that I shall pour
out some of my spirit upon the
whole human race. Then your
sons and daughters will prophesy. Your young people will
become visionaries and your
elderly will become dreamers.
18/ Yes; in those days I shall
pour out some of my spirit upon
the men and women who serve
me. 19/ I shall provide portents
in the sky above and signs on
the earth below: blood, fire, and
misty vapor. 20/ The sun will be
darkened and the moon take on
a bloody hue before the arrival
of the Day of the Lord, that
great and glorious day. 21/ It
shall come to pass that anyone
who calls upon the name of the
Lord will be saved.**

**22/ "My fellow Israelites, listen to
what I have to say. There was
Jesus the Nazorean, a man
whom God brought to your[b]
attention by performing mighty
deeds, wonders, and signs
through him in your very midst.
Of these things you are well
aware. 23/ You had Jesus killed,
nailed up by wicked hands. He
was betrayed—but this was in
accordance with God's prior
knowledge and fixed plan!
24/ God cut loose Hades' dreadful cords and brought Jesus
back to life, because death
could not maintain its grip
on him. 25/ With reference to
Jesus, David says: 'I foresaw
that the Lord was always with
me; because he is at my right
side I shall not be perturbed.
26/ Therefore my heart has
been happy and my tongue full
of joy. Indeed, my flesh will live
in hope, 27/ for you will not let
my soul languish in Hades, nor
will you allow your sacred one
to experience decay. 28/ You**

a The name "Joel" should probably be omitted, as D-Text witnesses indicate. Luke does not normally name "minor prophets" (7:42-43; 13:40-41; 15:16-17) and probably viewed the "Book of the Twelve" as a single work. Moreover, his normal procedure is to say "PN the prophet" rather than "the prophet PN." See, e.g., Ropes, *Text*, 16; Barrett, 1:135.

b D* *et al.* read ἡμᾶς ("us"). This reading may be anti-Jewish, but there is the ever-present *caveat* that the forms of "you" plural and "us" were identical in sound.

c The grammar of vv. 32-33 is difficult. Formally, the apostles are witnesses of Jesus, although one expects them to be witnesses of the resurrection (1:22). Bruce (126), proposes reading the relative οὗ as neuter, "of which fact." This is possible but not likely. The logical subject of v. 33 is "God," but the nominative participles clearly refer to Jesus. It is tempting to read τῇ δεξιᾷ ("to the right [hand]") as instrumental and render "by divine power" (cf. Ps 117:6; *Odes Sol.* 25:9), but the context suggests that the dative is locative, according to BDF §199. The second main clause is awkward: "Having received . . . he poured this which you see. . . ." The textual variants (e.g., "this gift") are improvements and thus suspicious. See Metzger, *Textual Commentary*, 260. "The father" (one could render, "his father") implies that Jesus is the Son of God. See Roloff, 59. Luke would certainly agree (Luke 3:22; etc.), albeit not in Nicene terms.

d An alternative rendition for ἐν τῇ ἡμέρᾳ ἐκείνῃ might be "during that period," or the like (cf. BDF, §438 4), but this proposal looks like a rationalization. It is more likely that that Luke wishes to report a big day in immediate response to the sermon.

have shown me the paths of
life; your presence will fill me
with gladness.'
29/ "Brothers and sisters, if I may
be candid with you about the
patriarch David, he is dead
and buried. His tomb remains
in our midst today. 30/ Since,
then, he was a prophet and
knew that God had solemnly
'vowed to him' that 'one of his
descendants would sit upon
his throne,' 31/ David spoke
with foreknowledge about the
resurrection of the Messiah
when he said, 'He was neither
left to languish in Hades, nor'
did his flesh 'face destruction.'
32/ Accordingly, God brought
this Jesus back to life. To that
fact we can testify. 33/ Therefore, after he had been exalted
to God's right hand and had
received from the father the
promised Holy Spirit, he
poured it out in your sight and
hearing.[c] 34/ David did not
ascend into the heavens, but he
does say, 'The Lord said to my
Lord, "Take a seat at my right
35/ until I make your enemies
a resting place for your feet."'
36/ The entire nation of Israel
must recognize beyond any
doubt that God has made him
both sovereign and Messiah,
this Jesus whom you people
crucified."
37/ These words stung the con-
sciences of the audience, and
so they said to Peter and the
other apostles: "What shall we
do, brothers?" 38/ Peter replied,
"Change your ways. All of you
must be baptized in the name
of Jesus [the Messiah] for the
forgiveness of your sins. You
will then receive the gift of the
Holy Spirit. 39/ The promise
is for you, for you and your
children and all those far away,
whomever the Lord our God
might invite." 40/ Peter pressed
his argument for some time,
continually urging them: "Save
yourselves from this unscrupulous generation." 41/ Those
who accepted Peter's message
were therefore baptized. On
that day[d] God brought three
thousand persons into the
community.

Analysis

For this premier missionary address and fundamental exposition of the Christian message, the narrator makes no attempt to provide a detailed description of the setting or make any concessions to the conventions of realism. Peter is, to be sure, readily imagined as standing before the eleven others—but where? Is one to envision them on a balcony? At a street-corner? The residential section of Jerusalem would not have contained a suitable space for a crowd of at least three thousand people. All in all, it is not advisable to imagine how baptisms (by immersion) took place. If an actual event in Jerusalem were the basis of the Pentecost story in 2:1-13, it would not have been a likely occasion for a public speech.

The theological ground of the speech is the theme of promise and fulfillment.[1] The remarkable events are to be understood as the specific fulfillment of a general promise: the future outpouring of the Spirit (vv. 16-21). On that basis, Peter argues that the experiences of Jesus are specific fulfillments of "messianic prophecies" taken from the Psalms (vv. 22-35), concluding the claim that Jesus is the Messiah (v. 36). The actual audience in mind is not the crowd of the narrative but the readers of the book.

The alibi for sobriety advanced in v. 15 is rather thin, since the early hour does not prove that people were not drinking, only that they should not have been so occupied.[2] The internal narrator, Peter, detaches himself from the situation, for one would expect him to say, "*We* are not drunk." The voice is that of a distant—and omniscient—narrator commenting on the situation. The subsequent evidence about the miracles of Jesus and the resurrection is asserted rather than argued, and the basis of these assertions is the LXX rather than the HB or an Aramaic text familiar to the dramatic audience.[3]

"Acts 2 comes to us as the most finished and polished specimen of the apostolic preaching, placed as it were in the shop window of the Jerusalem church and of Luke's Narrative."[4] The speech is, for all that, mixed in type. Its ultimate thrust is symbouleutic, as vv. 37-41 demonstrate, but vv. 14-21 refute an opposing view, while vv. 22-36 climax with an indictment. These last two are features of forensic rhetoric.[5] The net result is not unique in the history of Christian preaching. The hearers have done something wrong, that is, sinned, and should do something about it, that is, repent, but the mixed type reveals that Luke has two goals: the narrative object of gaining adherents and the theological object of vindicating Jesus from false charges. Although one is tempted to see the increasingly intimate vocatives in vv. 14, 22, and 29 as structural markers, a better understanding emerges when vv. 22-36 (III, below) are

1 On links between this speech and Luke 1–2, see Tannehill, *Narrative Unity,* 2:29–31.

2 See n. 89.

3 One decisive example can be seen in v. 25a: προορώμην τὸν κύριον ἐνώπιόν μου διὰ παντός ("I foresaw that the Lord was always with me"). Semitic versions could use the equivalent of "Lord" for the tetragrammaton, but the MT here uses a verb meaning "set" (שִׁוִּיתִי) rather than "see," and Hebrew and Aramaic did not possess compound verbs like that rendered "foresaw" (προορώμην). That verb, in turn, provides, as it were, the theological justification for the passage, since it is taken to refer to divine foresight, that is, providence (cf. the Vg rendition: *providebam*). The verb reappears in v. 31.

4 John A. T. Robinson, "The Most Primitive Christology of All?" in idem, *Twelve New Testament Studies* (SBT 34; London: SCM, 1962) 139–53, here 149 (=JTS n.s. 7 [1956] 177–89). The speeches in Acts 2 and 3 should be studied in tandem, as by Robinson. Note Richard F. Zehnle, *Peter's Pentecost Discourse: Tradition and Lukan Reinterpretation in Peter's Speeches of Acts 2 and 3* (SBLMS 15; Nashville: Abingdon, 1971); Ulrich Wilckens, *Die Missionsreden der Apostelgeschichte: Form- und traditionsgeschichtliche Untersuchungen* (WMANT 5; 2nd ed.; Neukirchen-Vluyn: Neukirchener Verlag, 1963) 32–44 (on the structure); and Marion L. Soards, *The Speeches in Acts: Their Content, Context, and Concerns* (Louisville: Westminster John Knox, 1994) 31–44. Note also the short and sharp analysis of Burton L. Mack, *Rhetoric and the New Testament* (GBS; Minneapolis: Fortress Press, 1990) 88–92.

5 See George A. Kennedy, *New Testament Interpretation through Rhetorical Criticism* (Chapel Hill: University of North Carolina Press, 1984) 117. The evident admixture of types is not surprising because, as Mack (*Rhetoric*, 35) observes, "Most attempts to define precisely the issue of an early Christian argument fail, however, simply because the social circumstances of the early Christian movements did not correspond to the traditional occasions for each type of speech." This should be taken not as a warrant for dispensing with analysis but as a warn-

taken as a tightly knit chiastic unit.[6] This is a core statement of Lucan Christology, similar to that in the speech of chap. 3.[7] Framing this are the assertion that what has happened fulfills prophecy about the general gift of the Spirit (vv. 14-21, II), which is a logical beginning that has no intrinsic connection to section III, and the closing reaction, exhortation, and result (vv. 37-41, IV).

The logic of the sermon is implicit, but clear to the Christian reader. The Holy Spirit has been granted to these people, who believe that Jesus is God's Messiah, as his deeds and final triumph prove. The gift of the Spirit demonstrates that their beliefs are correct. Those who wish to participate in the promised fulfillment will consequently adopt the same belief. Although Peter presents two presumably Davidic texts (and allusions to others) to show that Jesus is the Messiah, in actual fact both (II C[1] and [2], vv. 29-31, 34a) prove no more than that David was not speaking about himself. These proofs are signs for believers rather than for unbelievers. They argue from fulfillment to prophecy.[8] Although the ostensible audience is world Jewry, represented by the cosmopolitan crowd, only Christian readers would find the arguments persuasive. Despite the appearance of pastiche, sections I and III complement each other. The quotation from Joel ends with a promise of salvation for "any who call upon the name of the Lord" (v. 21), echoed in vv. 38-39, which speak of "the name of Jesus Christ" and a universal promise.

Outline[9]

(Vv. 1-13: Narrative Introduction)

I. Vv. 14-21. What is taking place/has happened.
  A. V. 14. Introduction
  B. V. 15. One hypothesis rejected
  C. Vv. 16-21. Events fulfill prophecy
    1. V. 16. Claim of fulfillment
    2. Vv. 17-21. Proof from Scripture

II. Vv. 22-36. Proof that Jesus is God's promised Messiah
  A[1]. Vv. 22-24. Thesis: Jesus the Nazorene, a man attested by God, you crucified, but God raised
    B[1]. Vv. 25-28. Scriptural proof (David)
      C[1]. Vv. 29-31. Interpretation of Scripture
        D[1]. V. 32. Resurrection; apostles as witnesses
        D[2]. V. 33. Exaltation; consequent gift of Spirit; audience as witnesses
      C[2]. V. 34a. Interpretation of Scripture
    B[2]. Vv. 34b-35. Scriptural proof (David)
  A[2]. V. 36. Thesis: Jesus, whom you crucified, but made Lord and Messiah by God

III. Consequences: vv. 37-41
  A. V. 37. Hearers moved and seek advice
  B. Vv. 38-39. Proposition
    1. V. 38a. Repent and be baptized in name of Jesus the Messiah (cf. vv. 22-36)
    2. V. 38b. You will receive the gift of spirit (cf. vv. 1-13, 36)
    3. V. 39. Promise is for you and many (cf. vv. 17-21)
    4. V. 40. Summary: Save yourselves (cf. v. 21)
  (C. Vv. 41 [42]. Narrative Conclusion)

Comment

■ **14-16** (I)[10] The introduction is solemn. Peter stands rather like an Ignatian bishop with his crescent of attendant presbyters.[11] The appearance of the Twelve suggests that Luke understood the "all" of v. 4 to refer

ing that it may not yield precise results. On the same page Mack states, "In general, early Christian rhetoric was deliberative."

6 See Gerhard A. Krodel, *Acts* (ACNT; Minneapolis: Augsburg, 1986) 83, as well as Schneider, 1:264.

7 The distinctiveness of 2:22-36 leads Barrett (1:132–33), to ruminate about possible sources. This is valid to the extent that Luke did not invent the theology/ies contained therein.

8 From the perspective of formal rhetoric, Scripture quotations should be "inartistic," self-validating appeals to fundamental principles, but these citations must be treated as "artistic" or technical in that they require elaborate interpretation.

9 For other detailed outlines, see Mack, *Rhetoric*, 89–91; and Soards, *Speeches*, 32.

10 Misunderstanding is also the point of departure for speeches in 3:12 and 14:15.

11 Ignatius usually speaks of presbyters as a college, comparable to the apostles (*Magn.* 6:1; *Trall.* 2:2; 3:1; *Phld.* 5:1; *Smyrn.* 8:1). James takes a similar place with the presbyters. See the comments on 21:18. Orators stand (whereas teachers sit). Cf. also 5:20; 11:13; 17:22; 25:18; 27:21. D cop[mae] sy[p] preface the verse with τότε, an adverb of which the D-Text is quite fond. The word provides clear transitions where Luke does not. Some D-Texts insert πρῶτος ("first") before "raised." This evidently means

to the apostles of 1:26.[12] Repetition of ἀποφθέγγομαι ("declaim") and φωνή ("sound" here) establishes a link with v. 4—and gives additional disclaimer to the notion that the preceding speech was mere jabber.[13] The general concept of v. 4 acquires particularity. The address[14] expands the audience to include "Judeans"—unless one is to think of the residents as gentiles, which is unlikely.[15] ἐνωτίσασθε lends an air of solemnity.[16] γνωστὸν ἔστω (lit. "let this be known") forms an *inclusio* with γινωσκέτω (lit. "let [the entire house of Israel] know") of v. 36.[17] Through the awkward insertion of the mockery, the narrator provides a platform that does not deal with the language miracle.[18] The narrator takes no pains to establish theological realism: Peter propounds early Christian doctrine.[19]

Excursus: The Text of Acts 2:17-21

The text of this citation from Joel is difficult to establish.[20] Manuscript data provide no warrant for appeal to alternate forms of Joel here,[21] and hypotheses about *florilegia*, collections of "testimonies," deal with christological texts rather than quotations about spiritual gifts and are not applicable. The variants therefore belong to the textual history of Acts. The dominant alternatives are an "Alexandrian" and a "Western" text.[22] N-A[27] amounts to a compromise between these two traditions.[23] I believe that both of these are subsequent editions and that the most likely text of Acts is closer to that of the LXX. The translation is based on the following text, set out for comparative purposes against the texts of Boismard[24] and N-A[27].

"Peter as the leader." See Pervo, "Social Aspects," 232–35.

12 D, supported by an Ethiopic MS., reads "with the ten," a reading accepted by Boismard, *Texte,* 67.

13 The D-Text simplifies this to "said" (εἶπεν), missing the connection. On the verb see Cadbury and Lake, 21. "Raised his voice" (lit.) appears in Judg 9:7 and *Act. Paul* 3/4.29, the latter probably imitating Acts.

14 This is the first occurrence of an address beginning with ἄνδρες ("gentlemen"), an evocation of classical oratorical practice, in which one was addressing an all-male jury or assembly. It received a wide extension. In *An Ethiopian Story* 1.19.3 the chief of a robber-band addresses his colleagues as ἄνδρες συστρατιῶται ("Fellow soldiers").

15 The double address is parallel to that of Paul's inaugural sermon in 13:16, where "Israelites" and "God-Fearers" constitute the two groups.

16 This verb is not infrequent in the LXX, but occurs only here in the NT.

17 The phrase (1:19; 4:10, 16; 9:42; 13:38; 19:17; 28:22; Ezra 4:12, 13; 5:8; 1 Esdr 2:14) forms a kind of inclusion.

18 See Haenchen, 185.

19 One might ask, for example, how Peter knew that Jesus had been exalted to the right hand of God (v. 33). This was not part of the angelic message of 1:11. Richard Bauckham ("Kerygmatic Summaries in the Speeches of Acts," in Witherington, *History,* 216) says, "Luke's kerygmatic summaries are not, as such, summaries of his own Gospel. They are attempts to represent what the apostles preached." This recognizes the lack of theological unity between Luke and Acts.

20 This particular passage has been the basis of a dialogue between George Kilpatrick and Albertus F. J. Klijn. Kilpatrick's proposals in "An Eclectic Study of the Text of Acts," in J. Neville Birdsall and Robert W. Thomson, eds., *Biblical and Patristic Studies in Memory of Robert Pierce Casey* (Freiburg: Herder, 1963) 64–77, prompted Klijn's "In Search of the Original Text of Acts," in Keck and Martin, *Studies,* 103–10, leading to Kilpatrick's "Some Quotations in Acts," in Kremer, *Actes,* 81–97, esp. 81–83, 94–97. See also Ernst Haenchen, "Schriftzitate und Textüberlieferung in der Apostelgeschichte," *ZThK* 51 (1954) 153–67, esp. 162 (= *Gott und Mensch: Gesammelte Aufsätze* [Tübingen: Mohr Siebeck, 1965] 157–71, esp. 165–66. See also Epp, *Tendency,* 66–72; and Josep Rius-Camps, "La Utilización del Libro de Joel (JL 2,28-32a LXX) en el Discurso de Pedro (Hch 2,14-21)," in David G. K. Taylor, ed., *Studies in the Early Text of the Gospels and Acts* (SBLT-CS 1; Atlanta: Society of Biblical Literature, 1999) 245–70.

21 The text of the LXX (= MT 2:28-32) is relatively secure. Nearly all of the variants noted by Joseph Ziegler in his Göttingen edition (*Duodecim prophetae* [2nd ed.; Göttingen: Vandenhoeck & Ruprecht, 1967] 235–36) are traceable to the influence of MT or to the reverse influence of Acts. See also Zehnle, *Discourse,* 28–35. The agreement of Qumran texts with the later MT provides no other opening for an appeal to a divergent Hebrew textual base (Martin Abegg, Peter Flint, and Eugene Ulrich, *The Dead Sea Scrolls Bible* [San Francisco: HarperSanFrancisco, 1999] 430–41).

22 Discussion reasonably begins with Ropes (*Text,* 16–18) although he was not the first to identify the different types.

23 Metzger (*Textual Commentary,* 255–58) summarizes the issues and the conclusions reached by the editors.

This Edition	Boismard	N-A[27]
17 καὶ ἔσται μετὰ ταῦτα,	[ ] ἔσται ἐν ταῖς ἐσχάταις ἡμέραις,	17 καὶ ἔσται ἐν ταῖς ἐσχάταις ἡμέραις,
λέγει ὁ θεὸς	λέγει ὁ κύριος,	λέγει ὁ θεός,
ἐκχεῶ ἀπὸ τοῦ πνεύματός μου ἐπὶ πᾶσαν σάρκα, καὶ προφητεύσουσιν οἱ υἱοὶ ὑμῶν καὶ αἱ θυγατέρες ὑμῶν,	ἐκχεῶ [ ] τὸ πνεῦμά μου ἐπὶ πᾶσαν σάρκα, καὶ προφητεύσουσιν οἱ υἱοὶ καὶ αἱ θυγατέρες αὐτῶν	ἐκχεῶ ἀπὸ τοῦ πνεύματος μου ἐπὶ πᾶσαν σάρκα, καὶ προφητεύσουσιν οἱ υἱοὶ ὑμῶν καὶ αἱ θυγατέρες ὑμῶν
καὶ οἱ πρεσβύτεροι ὑμῶν ἐνύπνια ἐνυπνιασθήσονται, καὶ οἱ νεανίσκοι ὑμῶν ὁράσεις ὄψονται,	καὶ οἱ νεανίσκοι [ ] ὁράσεις ὄψονται καὶ οἱ πρεσβύτεροι [ ] ἐνυπνίοις ἐνυπνιασθήσονται	καὶ οἱ νεανίσκοι ὑμῶν ὁράσεις ὄψονται καὶ οἱ πρεσβύτεροι ὑμῶν ἐνυπνίοις ἐνυπνιασθήσονται·
18 καὶ ἐπὶ τοὺς δούλους μου καὶ ἐπὶ τὰς δούλας μου	καί γε ἐπὶ τοὺς δούλους μου καὶ ἐπὶ τὰς δούλας μου [ ]	18 καί γε ἐπὶ τοὺς δούλους μου καὶ ἐπὶ τὰς δούλας μου
ἐν ταῖς ἡμέραις ἐκείναις ἐκχεῶ ἀπὸ τοῦ πνεύματός μου. 19 καὶ δώσω τέρατα ἐν τῷ οὐρανῷ [ἄνω] καὶ σημεῖα ἐπὶ τῆς γῆς [κάτω],	ἐκχεῶ τὸ πνευμά μου, καὶ προφητεύσουσιν. καὶ δώσω τέρατα ἐν τῷ οὐρανῷ ἄνω καὶ σημεῖα ἐπὶ τῆς γῆς κάτω,	ἐν ταῖς ἡμέραις ἐκείναις ἐκχεῶ ἀπὸ τοῦ πνεύματος μου, καὶ προφητεύσουσιν. 19 καὶ δώσω τέρατα ἐν τῷ οὐρανῷ ἄνω καὶ σημεῖα ἐπὶ τῆς γῆς κάτω,
αἷμα καὶ πῦρ καὶ ἀτμίδα καπνοῦ,		αἷμα καὶ πῦρ καὶ ἀτμίδα καπνοῦ.
20 ὁ ἥλιος μεταστραφήσεται εἰς σκότος καὶ ἡ σελήνη εἰς αἷμα	ὁ ἥλιος μεταστραφήσεται εἰς σκότος καὶ ἡ σελήνη εἰς αἷμα, [.]	20 ὁ ἥλιος μεταστραφήσεται εἰς σκότος καὶ ἡ σελήνη εἰς αἷμα,
πρὶν ἐλθεῖν ἡμέραν κυρίου τὴν μεγάλην καὶ ἐπιφανῆ. 21 καὶ ἔσται πᾶς, ὃς ἂν ἐπικαλέσηται τὸ ὄνομα κυρίου, σωθήσεται.	πρὶν ἢ ἐλθεῖν ἡμέραν κυρίου τὴν μεγάλην [ ]. και [ ] πᾶς ὃς ἂν ἐπικαλέσηται τὸ ὄνομα τοῦ κυρίου σωθήσεται.	πρὶν ἐλθεῖν ἡμέραν κυρίου τὴν μεγάλην καὶ ἐπιφανῆ. 21 καὶ ἔσται πᾶς ὃς ἂν ἐπικαλέσηται τὸ ὄνομα κυρίου σωθήσεται.

Although the editorial interests of the D-Text have been carefully scrutinized, it is also possible to identify "Alexandrian" features. Since Luke tends to handle quotation from the LXX conservatively, readings that conform to the Septuagint should enjoy a certain preponderance of probability.[25] Against this probability stands the critical tendency to honor deviations from the LXX on the grounds that ancient editors were more likely to correct toward the LXX than to deviate from it. Some alterations of the biblical text here were required.

The least debatable of these was clarification of the speaker: God,[26] rather than the prophet. Context also encouraged the deletion of the second half of Joel 3:5 (on which see below). The dangling prepositional phrase in v. 17, μετὰ ταῦτα (lit. "after these things") is awkward without context. The term σημεῖα ("signs" [v. 19]) also relates to the context, since it permits the familiar "signs and wonders" that will be introduced as evidence in v. 22.[27] Other deviations from the LXX are stylistic and structural.

24 Boismard, *Texte*, 68–69. His text differs slightly from that of Alfred C. Clark, *The Acts of the Apostles: A Critical Edition with Introduction and Notes on Selected Passages* (Oxford: Oxford University Press, 1933) 10.

25 Examples of Lucan fidelity to the text of the LXX include, to go no further than this very sermon, Acts 2:25-28//Ps 15:8-11 and 2:34-35//Ps 109:1. The classic study of Luke's use of the LXX is Clarke, "Use of the Septuagint," 66–105. Max Wilcox attempted to overturn the consensus in "The Old Testament in Acts 1–15," *Australian Biblical Review* 5 (1956) 1–41, but Earl Richard has refuted his claims in "The Old Testament in Acts: Wilcox's Semitisms in Retrospect," *CBQ* 42 (1980) 330–41. In general, see Craig A. Evans and James A. Sanders, *Luke and Scripture: The Function of Sacred Tradition in Acts* (Minneapolis: Fortress Press, 1993), esp. Evans, 171–224. Fitzmyer (90–95) has a good summary of the issues. Metzger (*Textual Commentary*, 255) affirms that "Acts displays a remarkable degree of faithfulness to the text of the Septuagint."

26 The *v.l.* "Lord" is less likely, since it is more conventional.

27 Note the order in v. 22: δυνάμεσι καὶ τέρασι καὶ σημείοις (lit. "miracles and portents and signs"), rather than the normal "signs and wonders." The order conforms to the citation.

Most of the alleged theological changes appear in the D-Text.[28] The vast majority of modern editors and commentators prefer the D-Text ἐν ταῖς ἐσχάταις ἡμέραις ("in the last days") to the LXX "after this."[29] (μετὰ ταῦτα: B 076 cops Cyril of Jerusalem). Haenchen is an exception.[30]

Haenchen considered the reading ἐν ταῖς ἐσχάταις ἡμέραις secondary because it did not conform to Lucan theology. "The text of B, μετὰ ταῦτα, is the original: in Lucan theology the last days do not begin as soon as the Spirit has been outpoured!"[31] Many have disagreed.[32] Even the apostle of the "delay of the parousia," Hans Conzelmann, accepted "in the last days" as a mere "stereotyped expression."[33] If Lucan theology is the guiding criterion, the longer phrase is the more difficult choice. The understanding of ecstatic prophecy as an eschatological event is congenial with the emphasis on the Spirit and other features of the D-Text that are sometimes labeled "Proto-Montanist."[34] Spiritual enthusiasm is characteristic of much early African Latin Christianity.[35] Internal grounds for assigning this phrase to the D-Text are the omission of ἐν ταῖς ἡμέραις ἐκείναις ("in those days") from v. 18 in the D-Text tradition. The introductory "in the last days"

28 An exception is "my" with men and women "slaves" in v. 18. The Christian form derives from the use of δοῦλος ("slave") as a trope for those who belong to God. On this, see Karl H. Rengstorf, "δοῦλος," *TDNT* 2:261–80, esp. 267–69, 273–77. Epp (*Tendency*, 68–70) proposes a rationale for the D-Text differences: the "intention of the D-Text . . . [is] . . . both to by-pass Judaism and to emphasize universalism." This conforms to features of the D-Text in general and Bezae in particular that can be observed elsewhere. Kilpatrick rejects the view that the D-Text is anti-Jewish ("Some Quotations in Acts," in Kremer, *Actes*, 82–83, 96).

29 Metzger (*Textual Commentary*, 256) views this "as the work of an Alexandrian corrector who brought the quotation in Acts into strict conformity with the prevailing text of the Septuagint."

30 Haenchen, "Schriftzitate," 161–62, which was a response to Lucien Cerfaux, "Citations scripturaires et tradition textuelle dans le Livre des Actes," first published in *Aux sources de la tradition chrétienne: Mélanges offerts à M. Maurice Goguel à l'occasion de son soixante-dixième anniversaire* (Bibliothèque théologique; Neuchâtel: Delachaux et Niestlé, 1950) and later collected in *Recueil Lucien Cerfaux: Études d'exégèse et d'histoire religieuse de Monseigneur Cerfaux* (3 vols.; BEThL 6–7, 18; Gembloux: Duculot, 1954–62) 2:93–103. Note also Cadbury and Lake, 21.

31 Haenchen, 179, with reference to his article. Traugott Holtz took a similar position: *Untersuchungen über die alttestamentlichen Zitate bei Lukas* (TU 104; Berlin: Akademie-Verlag, 1968) 7. See also Martin Rese, *Altestamentliche Motive in der Christologie des Lukas* (StNT 1; Gütersloh: Mohn, 1969) 51–52.

32 For example, Franz Mußner, "'In den letzten Tagen' (Apg. 2,17a)," *BZ* 5 (1961) 263–65. Jervell (142), who regards μετὰ ταῦτα as "clearly secondary," views "in the last days" as a temporal marker. (His n. 207 is a compact history of recent scholarship on the question.) Barrett (1:136) resolves the question in favor of "in the last days" by reference to Christian theology in general.

33 Conzelmann (19) with reference to 1 Tim 4:1; 2 Tim 3:1. For his understanding of the phrase "last days" see idem, *Theology*, 95. In the third edition (*Die Mitte der Zeit: Studien zur Theologie des Lukas* [Tübingen: Mohr Siebeck, 1960] 87), Conzelmann conceded that Haenchen may have been correct. Equivocation is also apparent in Lüdemann (44), who understands the time in question as that of the church, whatever the reading. Elsewhere these precise words occur only in Isa 2:2.

34 See p. 36 n. 44.

35 Note the preface to the *Acts of Perpetua and Felicity* 1.3-4, which cites Acts 2 in support of the *exuperationem gratiae in ultima saeculi spatia decretam* ("the extraordinary graces promised for the last stage of time"; trans. Herbert Musurillo, *Acts of the Christian Martyrs* [Oxford: Clarendon, 1972] 107, whose Latin edition is cited here). The text reads *In novissimis enim diebus, dicit dominus, effundam de Spiritu meo super omnem carnem, et prophetabunt fillii filiaeque eorum; et super servos et ancillas meas de meo Spiritu effundam, et iuvenes visiones videbunt, et senes somnia somniabunt*" ("For in the last days, God declares, I will pour out my Spirit upon all flesh and their sons and daughters shall prophesy and on my manservants and my maidservants I will pour my Spirit, and the young men shall see visions and the old men shall dream dreams" [trans. Musurillo, 107]). This may be a "pure" form of the D-Text of the opening verses of the passage in question. Boismard (*Texte*, 68), says that the "old African" text is embodied in the Pseudo-Cyprianic treatise *De Rebaptismate*. In this passage *De Rebaptismate* consistently supports Boismard's witnesses TO. Finally, D alone reads the verb

rendered the second temporal phrase superfluous.[36] Luke does not employ "last" in conjunction with "day," while words to this effect appear elsewhere in connection with the appearance of false teaching.[37] Luke uses the phrase as a connective.[38] Readers of Acts might well have construed it to mean "following the passion, death, resurrection and ascension of Jesus." On both textual and theological grounds it is reasonable to posit "in the last days" as part of a D-Text revision of Acts 2:17-21.

The adverbs "above" and "below" in v. 19 are additions to the text of Joel found throughout the textual tradition of Acts. They are nonetheless somewhat surprising, for the contrasted pairs ἄνω/οὐρανός ("above/heaven") and κάτω/γῆ ("below/earth") are at home in the philosophical tradition, particularly Platonism, as in Philo, Clement of Alexandria, Origen, and others.[39] Luke was no dualist. He may have introduced these adverbs to provide each of the two clauses with an end rhyme.

The conclusion is that neither the so-called "B Text" nor the D-Text of Acts 2:17-21 is a pure representative of a single text type and that comparison of the two yields three or four changes that quite probably go back to Luke: the almost necessary "God says" in v. 17, together with the following "and" (καί); the metaphorical understanding of "slaves" in v. 18; and, in all likelihood, the addition of "signs" in v. 19. There are no convincing arguments for attributing other changes to Lucan redaction. The chief rationale behind the text proposed here is that Acts is generally faithful to the LXX.

■ **17-21** (I.C.2) This quotation from Joel 3:1-5 (LXX = MT 2:28-32) resembles what has become known as *pesher* exegesis from the numerous examples found in the Dead Sea Scrolls.[40] It illustrates some of the qualities attending "proofs from prophecy." The original context, which spoke of deliverance for returning Israelites, restricts itself to Jerusalem, and proceeds to denounce gentiles, is not helpful.[41] The citation therefore omits the last part of v. 5. Moreover, as the interpolation of "signs" in v. 19 shows, prophecy can be revised in the interest of history.[42] The exhilarating promises of vv. 17b-18 find limited fulfillment in the subsequent narrative. Dreams and visions are restricted to important male characters (Peter, Ananias, Cornelius, and Paul), and any prophesying by daughters takes place offstage.

By adding the pronoun "my" to "slaves" in v. 19 Luke has shifted the emphasis from broad inclusion (male/female, old/young, slave/free) to an emphasis on the "servants of God," that is, believers (see above). The general purpose of vv. 19-20 is to give a clear frame for Christian existence (cf. 1:6-8), which takes place between (and is determined by) Pentecost and parousia. In that epoch believers will be sustained by the gift of the Spirit. The details are more vague, not least because Luke has inserted "signs" to make v. 19b a distinct clause that refers to the time of Jesus and the life of the

"change" in v. 20 as a present passive rather than as a future: "The sun is giving way to/being altered to darkness." This is arguably an intentional change to exhibit an eschatology that is in the process of realization.

36 So Ropes, *Text*, 16: "The 'Western' substitute in vs. 17 was thus widely adopted in non-western texts, but the corresponding 'Western' omission in vs. 18 scarcely at all."

37 See, e.g., 1 Tim 4:1; 2 Tim 3:1; 1 John 2:18; Jude 18//2 Pet 3:3. Compare the beginning of *Did.* 16:3, ἐν γὰρ ταῖς ἐσχάταις ἡμέραις with the verbally similar warnings about false prophets in Mark 7:15 and Matt 24:11-12, which lack this temporal specification.

38 See Luke 5:27 (of activity of Jesus); 12:4 and 17:8 (general); Acts 7:7 (citation); 13:20 (in survey of salvation history); 15:16 (citation); and 18:1 (of activity of Paul). The phrase occurs twenty-five times in the NT and frequently elsewhere.

39 This combination appears in Philo *Leg. all.* 3.4, 82; *Migr. Abr.* 182; Clement of Alexandria *Protrep.* 4.62; and Origen *De Orat.* 23.4; *Philoc.* 1.23, *Adnot. Exod.* 17.16; and *Fr. Jer.* 1.1. See also Plutarch *Fac.* 936D and Theophilus *Autolyc.* 3.9. A and 69 omit ἄνω. Since they include κάτω, this is presumably an error.

40 More precisely, Acts 2:17-21 is a kind of inverted *pesher* exegesis, since it begins with events and explains them by reference to the prophetic text. On the subject, see Devorah Dimant, "Pesharim, Qumran," *ABD* 5:244–51.

41 See Klauck, *Magic*, 11–12.

42 The variant opening "in the last days" is a similar adjustment.

church (see above). In any event, the reader of Acts is invited to admire "signs on earth" but is not encouraged to investigate cosmological phenomena.[43] Verse 21 hints at the universalism that the allusion to Isa 57:19 (2:39) will bring into the full light of day. Although the language miracle drew the crowd to the scene, Luke effectively ignores the phenomenon by subsuming it under the rubric of prophecy.[44]

■ **22-24** (II.A[1]) Following the citation, the oration proper begins with a display of Luke's attempt to compose rhetorical prose. The address begins with a series of smooth initial vowels, then six uses of the vowel *-ou-*. Alliteration (e.g., *ἄνδρα ἀποδεδειγμένον ἀπὸ*[45]) and assonance (e.g., *σημείοις οἷς ἐποίησεν . . . μέσῳ ὑμῶν καθὼς αὐτοὶ οἴδατε*) abound. The first sentence begins with the object, the subject of which comes at the close of v. 23, followed by an astrigent antithesis, itself alliterative (*ἀνείλατε . . . ἀνέστησεν*), then by the mellifluous *λύσας τὰς ὠδῖνας*. Note also the beginning of v. 23: *τοῦτον τῇ ὡρισμένῃ βουλῇ καὶ προγνώσει τοῦ θεοῦ ἔκδοτον,* in which the adjectives frame the euphonious adverbial dative phrase. Verses 22-24 do not constitute a true period, but such jingly and vigorous prose probably represents popular style.[46] In addition are some choice terms: *ἀποδεδειγμένον* ("shown," "appointed"), *ἔκδοτον* ("betrayed"), and *προσπήξαντες* ("nailed to"). No reader would be surprised had Luke used "handed over" (*παραδοθέντα*; cf. Luke 24:7; Acts 3:13) and "crucified" (*σταυρωθέντα*; cf. Luke 24:7; Acts 2:36), and *συσταθέντα* or *μεμαρτυρημένον* (cf. Acts 6:3) would have done for the first.[47]

The Christology is, by later standards, "adoptionistic," but the label is an anachronism if viewed as pejorative. "Jesus the Nazorean"[48] is a male human being

43 The omission of *καὶ ἐπιφανῆ* (and glorious) by a and ℵ and a number of D-Texts is difficult to explain. Metzger (*Textual Commentary*, 258) proposes visual errors. To Luke's readers, this adjective might call to mind the understanding of the parousia as an epiphany: 2 Thess 2:8; 1 Tim 6:14; 2 Tim 4:1, 8; *2 Clem.* 12:1; 17:4, on which see Martin Dibelius and Hans Conzelmann, *The Pastoral Epistles* (trans. and ed. Helmut Koester; Hermeneia; Philadelphia: Fortress Press, 1972) 104.

44 See pp. 63–65.

45 The preposition appears to have been selected to complement the verb (in place of the standard *ὑπό* ["by"]).

46 For example, the hexametric oracle of Apis in *An Ephesian Tale* 5.4.11: *Ἀνθία Ἀβροκόμην ταχὺ λήψεται ἄνδρα τὸν αὐτῆς* ("Anthia will soon have Habrocomes, her very own husband"), and lines 21–25 of a second-century BCE popular mime: *οὐκ ἤνεγκε νῦν τὴν τυχοῦσαν ἀδικίην. μέλλω μαίνεσθαι, ζῆλος μ᾽ ἔχει, καὶ κατακαίομαι καταλελειμήνη* ("[the one who] has not now borne the present hurt. I am about to go mad; for jealousy holds me, and I am burning at being deserted"; trans. I. C. Cunningham in Jeffrey Rusten and I. C. Cunningham, *Theophrastus, Characters*; *Herodas, Mimes*; *Sophron and Other Mime Fragments* [LCL; Cambridge, Mass.: Harvard University Press, 2002] 364–65. The early Sophists utilized jingly prose of this nature, and examples appear in classical poetry, for example, Euripides *Supplices* 161: *εὐψυχίαν ἔσπευσας ἀντ᾽ εὐβουλίας* ("It was bravery rather than prudence that you pursued"; trans. David Kovacs, *Euripides III* [LCL; Cambridge, Mass.: Harvard University Press, 1998] 31).

47 Ignatius uses the adjective *ἀποδεδειγμένοι* of deacons ("appointed with the consent of Jesus" in *Phld.* inscr. On the meaning, see Cadbury and Lake (22), who translate the term as "appointed" and note the absence of a title (such as "messiah"). The word is used of those designated for an office, but can be used after the term has begun. One may compare Latin *consul designatus*, "consul elect" (e.g., *OGIS* 379.5), which brings 3:20 (*προκεχειρισμένον*, "appointed" or "destined" messiah) to mind. The text is interesting. Boismard (*Texte*, 70) reads the shorter *ἄνδρα ἀποδεδειγμένον σημεῖοις καὶ τέρασιν* ("a man accredited by signs and portents"). He does not even refer to the text of Dd. The former reads *ἄνδρα ἀπὸ τοῦ θεοῦ -----ασμένον*. . . . Note that the prepositional phrase ("by God") precedes the participle, which is generally restored to *δεδοκιμασμένον,* per the Latin of d: *virum a deo probatum*, but *approbatum* would better render the Greek restoration. Tertullian (*Pud.* 21; cf. *Res.* 15) reads *destinatum.* It is tempting to ask whether *ἀποδεδειγμένον* might be an "orthodox" correction, but the difference seems minor, and no adjective would diminish the adoptionistic character of "man."

48 This term is difficult to explain because of the long *ō*, but it is quite likely that for Luke this was synonymous with "Nazarene" (*Ναζαρηνός*). Both appear in the Gospels: "Nazarene" (e.g., Mark 1:24||Luke 4:34; Luke 24:19), "Nazorean" (Matt 2:23; 26:71; John 18:5, 7; 19:19, and seven times in Acts [where "Nazarene" does not occur]). See Hans

(ἀνήρ), a status that still applies to Jesus as eschatological judge (Acts 17:31).[49] Jesus is a prophet elevated by God, but this was not a promotion based on merit; Jesus' role was determined by God prior to his conception (Luke 1:31-35), ratified at his baptism (Luke 3:22), and subsequently confirmed (Luke 9:35; etc.). In theological language, all that happened regarding Jesus took place in accordance with "God's prior knowledge[50] and fixed plan" (v. 23).[51] That compressed expression of Luke's view of divine providence is invoked to account for the gruesome death of Jesus. The claim that for Luke there is no "scandal of the cross" is an overstatement, but Luke is more interested in relieving the offense than in glorying in it. No appeal to providence is required for the miracles of Jesus, which are assumed to be probative.[52] Examples need not be adduced, as these deeds were familiar to the audience. That knowledge intensifies their guilt, although their responsibility is qualified: wicked people were the agents of betrayal.[53]

Mellifluous as it is, λύσας τὰς ὠδῖνας τοῦ θανάτου is vexing.[54] The text is not certain. Although "pangs of death" enjoys wide support, the D-Text alternative "pangs of Hades" (τὰς ὠδῖνας τοῦ ᾅδου) has good early attestation.[55] Another group of witnesses[56] invert the order: τοῦ θανάτου τὰς ὠδῖνας, suggesting disturbance at some point in the transmission. Metzger is certain that "Hades arose out of assimilation to the same word in vv. 27 and 31."[57] The argument is quite reversible: "death" is an assimilation to the (slightly) more common LXX locution,[58] as Barrett notes, adding the comment "or thinking of the victory of Christ over the powers of the underworld (cf. Matt 16:18)," before noting the possibility of internal assimilation.[59] If Polycarp *Phil* 1:2 is based on Acts, which seems quite possible,[60] and if Acts is dated in the second decade of the second century, the probability that Polycarp attests the original text is rather high. The difference is admittedly minor, but Luke may have preferred reference to a place, rather than to a concept.[61]

Literally, the phrase means "having eased the pangs of death/hell," an odd characterization of resurrection. Appeal to a Semitic background offers a way out, for the different vocalizations of חבל yield either "pang" or "cord." The LXX could confuse the two.[62] "Bonds of death" would fit the context: "because death could not maintain its grip upon him."[63] Research is best advised

H. Schraeder, "Ναζαρηνός, Ναζοραῖος," *TDNT* 4:874–79.

49 Acts 17:31 uses the verb ὁρίζω ("determine," "appoint") found in participial form in 2:23.

50 Divine foreknowledge: 1 Pet 1:20. For similar conceptions, see Luke 22:22; 24:26, 46; Acts 3:18; 4:28; 17:3; 26:23; cf. Acts 10:42. Compare also Rom 1:4 (in some sense a probable source) and Heb 4:7.

51 For the links between this understanding of Jesus' death and the Lucan passion story, see Schneider, 1:272.

52 A more developed exposition of these themes can be seen in the Ps.-Clem. *Rec.* 1.41.1–2, which, according to F. Stanley Jones, is dependent on Acts here ("A Jewish Christian Reads Luke's Acts of the Apostles: The Use of the Canonical Acts in the Ancient Jewish Christian Source behind Pseudo-Clementine *Recognitions,* 1.27-71," *SBLSP 1995* [Atlanta: Scholars Press, 1995] 617–35, esp. 626).

53 The expression διὰ χειρός ("by the hand of") is a common synecdoche, found thirty-three times in the LXX. Cf. also Acts 17:25; 19:11; 21:11; and 28:17. ἄνομοι is of uncertain meaning. It could refer to gentiles (Wis 17:12), in the sense of "those who are outside Israelite legal tradition . . . and act contrary to its moral standards" (BDAG 86, *s.v.*), as in the *Act. Paul* 10/13. Haenchen (180 n. 11) notes its application to the Romans "in Jewish writings." Walter Gutbrot ("ἄνομος," *TDNT* 4:1086–87) says that it is "a common term for the Gentiles" (1087). Luke, who does not exaggerate the role of the Romans in the death of Jesus, may here acknowledge that they were agents of the Jewish authorities.

54 See Pervo, *Dating*, 17–20.

55 D [itar, c, d, dem, e, gig, p ph, r, rot, w] vg syr[p] cop[bo, mae] Polycarp Ir[lat] Epiphanius Augustine Cassiodorus.

56 syr[h, pal] cops arm eth geo slav Eusebius Athanasius Ps-Athanasius Greg Nyssa Chrysostom Cyril Theodotus of Ancyra; Greek MSS.[acc to Bede].

57 Metzger, *Textual Commentary*, 259.

58 See n. 62.

59 Barrett, 1:143.

60 See p. 1.

61 "Hades" is a place in Luke 10:15; (Q); 16:23, as well as in Acts 2:27 (cit.) and 31 following.

62 2 Kgdms 22:6; Ps 17:5-6; and Ps 114:3 have "pangs of death" (ὠδῖνες θανάτου) where "bonds" is the proper word.

63 Thus Charles Cutler Torrey, *The Composition and Date of Acts* (HTS 1; Cambridge, Mass.: Harvard University Press, 1916) 28–29, who says "Luke had

to focus on the Greek text rather than point the finger at an incompetent translator.[64] Birth pangs (a common application of ὠδῖνες) are associated with the pangs of hell in 1QH xi.8-10:

> For the children have come to the throes of death, and she labours in her pains who bears a man for amid the throes of Death (שברי מות) she shall bring forth a man-child, and amid the pains of Hell (בהבלי שול) there shall spring from her child-bearing crucible a Marvellous Mighty Counsellor; and a man shall be delivered from out of the throes[65]

The phrase λύειν ὠδῖνας can refer to relieving labor pains,[66] and Georg Bertram argues for this view.[67] Barrett considers another proposal, that the resurrection of Jesus terminated the messianic woes. This reading views Death as the personified bearer of children (the dead).[68] In such an exegetical thicket, one can see why many find it desirable to prefer the LXX.[69] This trope views death as a power.[70] Since Lucan theology follows other paths, it is likely that Luke took the phrase from the tradition, possibly liturgical,[71] esteeming it a suitable introduction to v. 24b, which, in turn, lays the ground for (and interprets) the citation from Ps 15:10 LXX in v. 27.[72]

■ **25-31** (II.B[1]-C[1]) Ps 15:8-11 is quoted without deviation from the LXX, omitting the final clause.[73] The interpretation in v. 29, which begins with an apt rhetorical understatement, proceeds from the principle that often justifies figurative exegesis. Scripture is true. Since the words do not apply to David,[74] the presumed author, they must apply to someone else.[75] Luke does not, however, exploit this incongruity to uncover spiritual meaning; the citation shows that David was a "prophet,"

before him the words שׁרא חבליא די מיתא, 'loosing the bands of death.'" Cadbury and Lake (23) and Haenchen (180 n. 14) reject this proposal. This image is found elsewhere, for example, "snares of death" (*mortis laqueis*) in Horace *Odes* 3.24.8.

64 A second objection is that Acts 2:24b is almost certainly Lucan. The notion of "impossibility" implies "necessity," resonating with the theme of a divine plan introduced in v. 23. Furthermore, v. 24b prepares for the subsequent citation. See below and Zehnle, *Discourse*, 34.

65 Trans. Geza Vermes, *The Complete Dead Sea Scrolls in English* (New York: Penguin, 1997) 259. (In earlier editions, col. XI was col. III.)

66 BDAG 607 4, *s.v.* λύω. Note Job 39:1-3 and Aelian *Nat. an.* 12.5. See also the references in Lampe, *s.vv.* λύω, 817 B3e, and ὠδίν, 1555 1B. In these later writers the phrase is a metonym for "be born," "give birth." "Jervell (146) is also hesitant to declare "pangs" an error.

67 Georg Bertram, ὠδίν," *TDNT* 9:667–74, esp. 673. He is followed by Walter Radl, "ὠδίν," *EDNT* 3:506.

68 Barrett, 1:143–44. The reading "Hades," viewed as a place, is less amenable to this interpretation.

69 So Cadbury and Lake, 23; Haenchen, 180–81; and Barrett, 1:143–44, among others.

70 See Jervell, 146.

71 So Haenchen, 6; and Plümacher, *Lukas, 42;* but evidence for this attractive proposal is lacking.

72 The Latin translations of Irenaeus, Augustine (in part), and some Coptic witnesses read "by them," evidently referring to "the pangs of hell." Boismard (*Texte*, 70) takes this as the D-Text. The plural would eminently suit the interpretation "bonds of death."

73 In the light of v. 33 (exaltation to God's right hand), it seems odd that the quotation did not include the closing τερπνότητες ἐν τῇ δεξιᾷ εἰς τέλος ("joys at your right hand forever"). Franklin (*Christ the Lord,* 33) has an answer. Luke wishes to differentiate between resurrection and ascension and uses a different proof for each. By omitting the end of Psalm 15 LXX, he leaves room for Psalm 110 to be fulfilled by the ascension. One may ask, with Bruce (125), why Luke did not end the citation with v. 27. This ignores the metaphorical understanding of resurrection as "paths to life" (ὁδοὺς ζωῆς) that produce the joy of divine presence in v. 28. "Way" (ὁδός) is Luke's image of choice for the Christian "movement." This phrase and the fortuitous "tongue" of v. 26 provide both literary enhancement and support for the interpretation. Barrett (1:144–46) supplies ample details on the quotation. Both passage and interpretation are borrowed in *Act. Phil.* 6, 14 (François Bovon et al., eds., *Les Actes apocryphes des apôtres* [Geneva: Labor et Fides, 1981] 204).

74 David's tomb: Neh 3:16; Josephus *Bell.* 1.61; *Ant.* 7.393; 13.249; 16.179-83. On the site, see Fitzmyer, 257. The phrase is evocative of the creed in 1 Cor 15:3-4. The implied contrast between David, who died and was buried, and Jesus, who died, was buried, and was raised, is independent of the claim that Jesus also had a tomb. "Patriarch," an LXX coinage, is otherwise restricted in the NT to Abraham, Isaac, Jacob, and his sons. See Bruce, 126.

75 For a similar style of argumentation, also utilizing David, see Heb 4:6-11.

inspired to speak about future events.[76] Similar arguments appear in Paul's initial sermon (13:16-47), establishing both the similarity between the two missionaries and the uniformity of the messianic message.[77] Supporting this prophetic gift was David's knowledge of the promise (v. 30).[78] The participle προϊδών ("foreseeing") in v. 31 establishes the meaning of the verb in v. 25 (see above).[79] The exegesis presumes resurrection of the flesh and is therefore not a residue of the primitive Christian message.[80]

■ **32-36** (II.D^1-A^2) Verses 32-33 show the development of the Christian creed. Resurrection, exaltation/ascension, session at God's right hand,[81] and the gift of the Spirit are distinct theologoumena, sequential events, in Luke's thought. These elements are more or less accumulated, but not without some integration. The fundamental assumption is that Jesus had to be exalted, with or without a specific resurrection and/or ascension, as the ground for bestowal of the Spirit. This view is not unique to Luke, and he does not need to justify or expound it. For Acts, Jesus is the source of the Spirit received by believers. The father had promised the Spirit to him. The result of this is the phenomenon seen and heard by the audience, thus cementing the claim of vv. 16-21.[82] Verses 34-35 continue to build the verbal sandwich, with interpretation preceding proof. The citation of Ps 109:1 LXX shows that Luke equates ascension with exaltation, that is, empowerment.[83] The benefits of this citation are well summarized by Barrett.[84] It links Jesus to David while proclaiming his superiority and explains that his departure meant reception into heaven in a privileged position. As a celestial messiah, Jesus can be called κύριος ("Lord," "sovereign"), justifying the attribution of other biblical uses of that title to him, rather than to God.

■ **36** The verse structurally completes the elaborate ring constituting the core of the speech (vv. 22-36). Rhetorically, it is the peroration—a concluding summary of the

76 The HB does not classify David as a prophet, but he is so denoted in 11QPs 27:2-11 and by Josephus *Ant.* 6.166. See Fitzmyer, 258.

77 Acts 13:22-23 identifies Jesus as David's promised heir, as does 2:30; Acts 13:34-37 follows the argument of 2:25-31, also citing Psalm 15 LXX. For other parallels, see the comments on that speech.

78 Verse 30 exhibits semiticizing, "biblical" language. "Heart" (καρδίας) may be a euphemistic correction by D*. "Belly" (κοιλίας), found in many D-Text witnesses, assimilates to the text of the underlying psalm: 131:11 LXX. The direct object is the prepositional phrase (lit. "from fruit of his loins"). This stimulated a number of variants that supply the expected infinitive after "swear." These include the wordplay "the messiah would arise" (ἀναστῆσαι [-σειν] τὸν χριστον). Many D-Texts add "in the flesh" (κατὰ σάρκα). That phrase, which may be anti-Gnostic (but note "flesh" in v. 31), entered the Textus Receptus. On the throne of David, see Luke 1:32. The expression "fruit of his loins" is borrowed in *Act. Paul* 10/13. See Hills, "Acts," 24-54, here 48.

79 The *v.l.* προειδώς ("knowing in advance") evidently picks up from the "knowing" of v. 30.

80 Outside of the Lucan writings, the earliest insistence on the resurrection of Jesus in the flesh is found in Ignatius, notably *Smyrn.* 3:2-3. cf. *Eph.* 7:2; *Magn.* 1:2; and *Smyrn.* 12:2.

81 The session of Christ at God's right hand (Psalm 110 is in the background; cf. also 1 Kgs 2:19) appears in Rom 8:34, in the sequence died, rose, is seated. Note Acts 7:55-56; Col 3:1; Heb 1:3; 8:1; 10:12. On the concept of the *sessio ad dextram* (seating at right hand of God), see Franklin, *Christ the Lord,* 29–41; and Robert F. O'Toole, "Luke's Understanding of Jesus' Resurrection-Ascension-Exaltation," *BTB* 9 (1979) 106–14.

82 "See" is a bit surprising, since the earlier focus was on hearing (2:6, 8, 11). Although it may be claimed that the audience would grasp the notion of a promised gift of the Spirit, full understanding is available only to the readers (1:4-5).

83 Verse 34a may be an echo of Ps 68:19. See Lindars, *Apologetic,* 43–55. Fitzmyer lists those who support this proposal, which he views with strong skepticism. Eph 4:7-16 may be a more fruitful area for investigating intertextuality, since Acts and Ephesians appear to reflect similar views (here and elsewhere, on which see Pervo, *Dating,* 293–99).

84 Barrett, 1:150–51. See also David P. Moessner, "*Two* Lords 'at the Right Hand'? The Psalms and an Intertextual Reading of Peter's Pentecost Speech (Acts 2:14-36)," in Thompson, *Literary Studies,* 215–32. Moessner elucidates the connections among the citations from Joel and Psalms 15 and 109 LXX. He shows that in the LXX Psalm 15 is a psalm of the suffering righteous and thus relates the experiences of David to those of Jesus and serves as a hinge between the citations of Joel and Psalm 109. On Psalm 109, see also David M. Hay, *Glory at the Right Hand: Psalm 110 in Early*

argument. The initial ἀσφαλῶς ("beyond any doubt") emphasizes the quality of the argument.[85] "House of Israel" is a suitably biblical phrase[86] stressing corporate responsibility. Said responsibility rapidly transpires in a crisp, closing antithesis to this well-packaged argument: God has made the one whom "you" killed both sovereign and messiah. Psalm 110 established the former; Psalm 16 the latter.[87]

■ **37-40** (41) (III) The response is all that could be hoped for.[88] The narrator states that the primary reaction was not joy that God had given Israel a sovereign messiah but remorse for the contribution to the execution of Jesus.[89] The hearers ask[90] the essential question posed by all seekers of salvation: "What shall I/we do?"[91] In response, Peter issues[92] two commands ("repent," "be baptized") with two promises, one implicit (forgiveness of sins,[93]), the other the gift of the Holy Spirit, followed by a reassuring rationale: the promise is universal. The language does not permit attributing forgiveness to repentance and the gift to baptism. The scenario appears to be based on Luke 3 (Q): an exhortation to be baptized for remission of sins reinforced by citations of prophetic Scripture. In any case, it fulfills the promise of John about a coming baptism with the Spirit (Luke 3:16; Acts 1:5).

This is the first reference to baptism in the name of Jesus.[94] The narrative assumes that its readers are aware of Christian baptism and that it is too firmly fixed in the life of the community to require specific dominical warrant. Verse 38 states the fundamental principle that

Christianity (SBLMS 18; Nashville: Abingdon, 1973); and Donald Juel, *Messianic Exegesis: Christological Interpretation of the Old Testament in Early Christianity* (Philadelphia: Fortress Press, 1988), esp. 146–47.

85 Luke 1:4 also uses a form of the verb "know" (ἐπιγινώσκω) with the noun ἀσφάλεια (rendered "truth" by *NRSV*). This suggests that "knowledge of the truth" is the result of rhetorical persuasion rather than the mere acknowledgment of data. See Ceslas Spicq, *Theological Lexicon of the New Testament* (3 vols.; trans. and ed. J. D. Ernest; Peabody, Mass.: Hendrickson, 1994) 1:219.

86 πᾶς οἶκος Ἰσραήλ occurs nine times in the LXX (often with the article, on which see Moule, *Idiom Book*, 95).

87 Taken strictly, the verse suggests that Jesus became Lord and Messiah following his exaltation. The designation "man" in v. 22 does not discourage this understanding, but this is not Luke's meaning. See Conzelmann, 21. Lucan theology is robustly subordinationist. Verse 36 was troublesome to anti-Arian theologians because of the verb "make" (ποιέω). C. Kavin Rowe ("Acts 2.36 and the Continuity of Lukan Christology," *NTS* 53 [2007] 37–56) argues that it is not temporal but stated from the viewpoint of the hearer. This is valid, but it is also correct to observe that the implied Christology of Luke 1–2 is overlooked in Acts, which takes its departure from the resurrection rather than from the birth of Jesus.

88 Termination of speeches by interruption is a common device in ancient literature. Other examples from Acts include 5:32-33; 7:53-54; 10:43-44; 17:23; 22:21-22; 26:23. Interruptions do not occur before the narrator has made his point.

89 The D-Text is interesting. Boismard (*Texte*, 73) reconstructs the following: *τότε πάντες οἱ συνελθόντες καὶ ἀκούσαντες κατενύγησαν τῇ καρδίᾳ καί τινες ἐξ αὐτῶν εἶπον πρὸς Πέτρον καὶ τοὺς ἀποστόλους τί οὖν ποιήσομεν ἄνδρες ἀδελφοί; ὑποδείξατε ἡμῖν* ("Then all who had gathered and heard were conscience-stricken, and some of them . . . show us"). Apart from stylistic changes, this makes a less abrupt transition and, although stressing that *all* were moved, assigns the question to only some of the auditors. The change illustrates the narrator's indifference to realistic description and the desire of some editors to correct this. See also Epp, *Tendency*, 73–74. ("Show us" [ὑποδείξατε ἡμῖν] may derive from Luke 3:7, suggesting that the editor of this text recognized the parallel between the close of Peter's address and the message of John the Baptist, on which see below.)

90 The D-Text omits "other" (λοιπούς), which is amenable to the interpretation that Peter enjoys a higher status. Metzger (*Textual Commentary*, 260) views the omission as "accidental."

91 Luke 3:12, 14; Mark 10:17 parr.; Acts 16:30; 22:10. Their use of the vocative employed by Peter in v. 29, ἄνδρες ἀδελφοί (lit. "brothers") indicates that they accept his message.

92 Metzger (*Textual Commentary*, 261) makes a good case for viewing φησίν as secondary. The varying forms and placement of "he said" suggest that the earliest text lacked this verb.

93 The omission of "your" with "sins" (found in some D-texts but not admitted into Boismard's edition [*Texte*, 75]) could, as Epp (*Tendency*, 72) suggests, give the text a more universalistic application. Ropes (*Text*, 22), however, viewed this as a second-

baptism conveys the primary gift of the Spirit. Variations on this order are likely to be ad hoc requirements of the narrative rather than the result of conflicting views or a confused narrator.[95] The theology of Acts cannot be separated from its narrative context, which is to say that efforts to extract it from that setting and present it in systematized form are precarious, albeit sometimes necessary, enterprises.

■ **39-40** The first verse is a parenetic reinforcement of the preceding verse, with a specific reference to "the promise," evoking 1:4 in general and 2:30 in particular. Added to this are a strong hint of universalism[96] and a reference to the close of the quotation from Joel in v. 21, neatly rounding off the entire speech. The language evokes Third Isaiah, which rivals Second Isaiah as Luke's "favorite book of the Bible."[97] This allusion to Isa 57:19 comes from the (Deutero-) Pauline workshop (cf. Luke 2:14; Eph 2:13, 17). Verse 40 reinforces the parallel with the Baptizer's call for repentance by way of a vague summary[98] illustrated with a vivid exhortation of apocalyptic tenor.[99] The exhortation to be saved also conforms to the promise found in the last word of the quotation from Joel in v. 21.[100]

Within the symmetries of Luke and Acts, this speech fills several niches. It is an inaugural address like that of Jesus in Luke 4:16-27.[101] Both include a public announcement of salvation, via Deutero-Isaiah. In both structural position and specific content, the Pentecost address displays many affinities to Paul's address in Antioch (13:16-47).[102] The narrative conclusion, with its question from the hearers, exhortation to repentance, (implicit) threat of judgment, and mass baptism recalls the ministry of the Baptizer, Luke 3:2b-18 (21). Peter will be a forerunner of Paul. In the immediate context, the speech fulfills the command that the apostles be witnesses to Jesus in Jerusalem after they have received the gift of the Spirit.

■ **41** The place of v. 41[103] in the structure is unclear. The particle *μὲν οὖν* often marks major decisions, and the *δέ* in v. 42 links that verse to v. 41. The syntax thus encourages assignment of v. 41 to a new paragraph,[104] but narrative logic pulls in the other direction: v. 41 concludes the entire section; *μὲν οὖν* can be emphatic, as in 1:6. The majority of critics therefore include v. 41 with the paragraph beginning at v. 37. The same question may be raised about the summary v. 42. This

ary conformation to the Gospel tradition, followed by Metzger, *Textual Commentary*, 261–62.

94 The addition of "Lord" by a range of witnesses is clearly secondary. Boismard (*Texte*, 74), supported by logic and some evidence, omits "Messiah." This may be the earliest reading.

95 This is not to imply that Luke would subordinate the Spirit to the authority of an institution, nor that the exceptions can be swept under the rug. See the comments on 8:14-17; 10:44-48.

96 The D-Text typically shifts the pronouns to the first person: "*us* and *our* children." This is a move in the direction of the removal of the Jews from salvation history (Epp, *Tendency*, 70–72).

97 N-A[27] (pp. 792–93) lists twenty-eight allusions to Isaiah 55–66 in Luke and Acts.

98 Compare Luke 3:18, *πολλὰ μὲν οὖν καὶ ἕτερα παρακαλῶν εὐηγγελίζετο τὸν λαόν* ("So, with many other exhortations, he proclaimed the good news to the people"), to Acts 2:40a. For similar phrases, see Sallust *Bell. Jug.* 32.1; Xenophon *Hell.* 2.4, 42; Polybius *Histories* 3.111; 11; and Tacitus *Ann.* 14.1, 3; cf. Pseudo Lucian *Onos* 24.2.

99 "Unscrupulous generation": note Deut 32:5; Ps 77:8 LXX; and Luke 9:41; 11:29. Compare John's "generation of vipers" (a different, albeit related, word) in Luke 3:7-9.

100 For Chrysostom, the invitation of God is the greatest of all miracles (*Hom.* 5).

101 On the links between these two speeches, see, e.g., Tannehill, *Narrative Unity*, 2:29.

102 See above and the commentary on that speech.

103 Some D-Texts indicate that they received the message "gladly" (*ἀσμένως*; cf. 21:17). D reads *οἱ μὲν οὖν πιστεύσαντες τὸν λόγον αὐτοῦ ἐβαπτίσθησαν* ("Those who believed his message were baptized"). Boismard (*Texte*, 75) prints *οἱ δὲ ἀσμένως ἀποδεξάμενοι τὸν λόγον ἐπίστευσαν καὶ ἐβαπτίσθησαν* ("Those who gladly accepted the message believed and were baptized"). Both of these constructions emphasize that not all accepted the message and that their baptism was based on (a confession of) faith. The question of faith motivated the addition of 8:37. D-Texts also omit "about" (*ὡσεί*) before "three thousand."

104 So, e.g., Cadbury and Lake, 27; and Barrett, 1:159. (Barrett connects this decision to the use of sources, which is unlikely here.)

is very similar to 1:14, which is viewed as the conclusion of a unit, and the inclusion of this summary with vv. 43-47 involves an awkward repetition of "devoted" (προσκαρτεροῦντες) in v. 46.[105] These questions reveal the character of Lucan structure, which is both tightly woven and fluid.[106] A strong reason for grouping v. 42 with vv. 43-47 is that all are imperfect (or the equivalent) and thus relate repeated, habitual action, the proper form for narrative summary. Talbert, however, proposes an A B C B' A' arrangement encompassing vv. 41-47 (v. 41 growth; v. 42, community life; v. 43 miracles; vv. 44-47a community life; and v. 47b growth[107]). The weakness of this is that B' (vv. 44-47a) is out of balance. It seems preferable to view vv. 41 and 47 as concluding their respective units and v. 42 as the general introduction to the summary, followed by details in vv. 43-47.[108]

Excursus: The Size of the Early Jerusalem Church

Acts 1:15 reports that the community had about 120 members, that around three thousand received baptism on Pentecost, and that, by the time of 4:4, there were five thousand adult males, permitting readers to envision a total of about twenty thousand believers. It therefore comes as no surprise when James later observes that there are "myriads" of observant believers (21:20). Although Luke frequently notes quantitative growth,[109] specific data are provided only for Jerusalem in the early days of the post-Easter movement. This generates several intertwined questions: Are these approximate numbers likely to be accurate? Do they derive from a source? And why are they restricted to this time and place? Regarding the Pentecost report there is also the question whether three thousand could be converted and baptized on a single occasion.

Although those of even moderately critical inclination might be expected to doubt the reliability of these data, commentators tend to pass over the numbers in silence.[110] The data are not without defenders. Marshall says that there is "nothing incredible" about the number.[111] The Romans would not have worried about so peaceable an assembly. Witherington does not require accuracy of the number: "[I]t could just mean that Luke is indicating a surprisingly large number of the crowd responded positively,"[112] but he maintains, "On the other hand, the number itself is not out of the realm of possibility." Festival pilgrims would swell the population to as much as two hundred thousand, and there was plenty of water for baptisms. Both the assumption of Roman indifference and the appeal to pilgrim multitudes contradict the views of the narrator, for whom opposition comes from Jewish authorities and according to whom the converts were not Pentecost visitors but permanent residents from the Diaspora. Pilgrim crowds will not readily account for the five thousand males of 4:4.[113]

Wolfgang Reinhardt seeks to refute negative opinions with critical research.[114] He rejects the standard population figure of thirty thousand for Jerusalem at this time as too low, preferring a range of sixty thousand to one hundred twenty thousand. His detailed argument on this point merits recognition. To this theoretical populace Reinhardt adds a large number of pilgrims.[115] He concludes, "Since there is also no convincing theological interpretation of the figures 'about 3,000' and (about) 5,000, one will instead have to accept that Luke was dependent

105 UBS[4] marks vv. 37-42 as a single paragraph (p. 415). For various divisions in various editions and versions, see the segmentation apparatus on that page.

106 On this fluidity, see Henry J Cadbury, "The Summaries in Acts," in Lake and Cadbury, *Additional Notes*, 395 and n. 3.

107 Talbert, *Reading Acts*, 50. Gregory E. Sterling takes vv. 41 and 47 as forming an *inclusio*, viewing this as decisive ("'Athletes of Virtue': An Analysis of the Summaries in Acts [2:41-47; 4:32-34; 5:12-16]," *JBL* 113 [1994] 679–96, esp. 680 n. 7). The distinction between literary inclusion and parallel endings probably cannot be resolved.

108 Arguments similar to those given above are advanced by Maria Anicia Co, "The Major Summaries in Acts (Acts 2,42-47; 4,32-35; 5,12-16," *EThL* 68 (1992) 49–85, esp. 58–61.

109 See 5:14; 6:1, 7; 9:31; 11:21, 24; 12:24; 14:1; and 19:20.

110 One exception is Roloff (63), who regards the number as "unreal."

111 Marshall, 82; see also his article "The Significance of Pentecost," *SJT* 30 (1977) 347–69.

112 Witherington, 156; he offers no proof or parallels to the use of three thousand to indicate a surprisingly large number. This is just another way of calling the figure a Lucan fiction.

113 Among those who note the swollen population at Pentecost are Pesch (1:126) and Reinhardt (see the following notes).

114 Wolfgang Reinhardt, "The Population Size of Jerusalem and the Numerical Growth of the Jerusalem Church," in Bauckham, *Palestinian Setting*, 237–65.

115 Ibid., 259–63. Reinhardt staves off the problem of 2:5-11 by arguing that the language (specifically,

on a reliable transmission of these figures."[116] Other possibilities are excluded.[117]

Population estimates cannot vault these statistics into the orbit of probability. One objection comes from the calculations of Rodney Stark, who has produced the most sophisticated estimate of the numerical growth of Christianity. He uses a base of one thousand for the year 40.[118] If one used the "Lucan base" of twenty thousand in 30, the numbers would be around 210,827 by the year 100 and 1,133,878 by 150. That is far too large.[119] More specific grounds for comparison come from movements discussed by Josephus, who claims that there were six thousand male Pharisees late in the reign of Herod (i.e., near the turn of the eras [*Ant.* 17.42]) and about four thousand Essenes in the late first century (*Ant.* 18.20). Had the Christian movement been of comparable size in the mid-first century, the historian would have been likely to contribute more than the thirteen words devoted to the subject in *Ant.* 18.64 (presuming that these are relatively genuine).[120] Christians can be dismissed as a "tribe" that has not yet vanished. Since the figures in Acts are beyond the realm of reasonable probability, and since they do not fit into the propensities of any source theories, they are most likely Lucan inventions.[121]

A "theological" or "symbolic" interpretation is not, in fact, difficult to postulate. Form criticism indicates that large round numbers are appropriate at the close of mass miracles, notably the feeding of the five thousand (Mark 6:44 parr.).[122] By including the numeric data in 2:41 and 4:4, Luke affirms that the advent of the gospel message caused an explosion of new life.[123] Those who prefer parables to miracles may wish to think of the hundredfold harvest gathered from the good soil (Luke 8:8), but Luke wished to depict a miracle. The statistics given in the early chapters of Acts are congruent with his overall portrait of the early Jerusalem community as an ideal body. The miraculous numerical explosion of new life at Pentecost will be followed by a summary of the miraculous quality of that life.[124]

κατοικέω) can be taken to refer to pilgrims as well as residents and that many of these remained for a few days, thus accounting for the figure of 4:4. Since Luke provides no chronological data, the amount of time deemed to have past between 2:41 and 4:4 is a construction of the reader and cannot form the grounds of a reasonable argument. Peter's speech does not take pilgrim hearers into account, for it accuses the dramatic audience of killing Jesus (vv. 23, 36). Reinhardt and others are compelled to overlook or override the plain meaning of the text at several points in order to preserve the historical value of the statistics. This is not simply perverse; it shows that their approach misunderstands Acts. Reta Halteman Finger (*Of Widows and Meals: Communal Meals in the Book of Acts* [Grand Rapids: Eerdmans, 2007] 21) doubts that sufficient food and water for a million pilgrims could be supplied.

116 Note that Reinhardt supplies "about," which is not found in the text of 4:4. The quotation is from p. 265.

117 Cf. Pesch (1:126), who rejects both Lucan invention and symbolic interpretations, leaving no option but data from a source. This viewpoint goes back to Wikenhauser, *Geschichtswert,* 119–22.

118 Rodney Stark, *The Rise of Christianity: A Sociologist Reconsiders History* (Princeton: Princeton University Press, 1996) 7–13 (see table 1.1, p. 7). Stark bases his calculations on an average growth rate of 40 percent per decade. This derives from recent movements, to be sure, but he finds corroboration from both archaeological and literary data. See also the review of these calculations by Keith Hopkins, "Christian Number and Its Implications," *JECS* 6 (1998) 185–226.

119 According to Stark's model, Christianity reached this size in c. 250, giving rise to the first empire-wide persecutions. In 150, the church did not yet present so great a threat to the Roman Empire.

120 Josephus's account of the death of James (*Ant.* 20.200) does not indicate that he was the leader of a movement of myriads.

121 Wolfgang Reinhardt does not take up the claim that the three thousand converts immediately constituted themselves as a well-organized community with a vibrant worship program and a full-fledged charitable system ("The Population Size of Jerusalem and the Numerical Growth of the Jerusalem Church," in Bauckham, *Palestinian Setting,* 237–65).

122 Cf. also Mark 6:9 (feeding of the four thousand) and John 20:30-31. Mark 6:44, followed by Luke 9:14, speaks of "adult males," permitting the same extrapolation as in Acts 4:4.

123 Three thousand is a multiple of twelve, while the value of five thousand is established by the feeding story, but precise identification of a "mystical" referent would miss the point. (Bede, 22, *ad* 2:41, for example, links the three thousand to the Trinity).

124 For further comments on the function of these "notes on growth," see the comments on the structure of chaps. 3-7, pp. 96–98 below. For other creative uses of the numbers associated with miracle stories, see the comments on 4:22 and 27: 37.

2

2:42-47 A Summary

42/ The believers devoted themselves to the apostles' teaching, cultivation of unity, their meal, and their prayers. 43/ Awe overtook everyone. The apostles became the agents of numerous portents and miracles. 44/ All the believers remained together and shared everything. 45/ They would sell their goods and property and distribute the proceeds to everyone on the basis of need. 46/ Every day they met together in the temple and ate in homes, taking their food with happy and sincere[a] hearts 47/ that were filled with praise to God. Everyone approved of them, and the Lord increased daily the number of those who were being saved together.

a The meaning of ἀφελότητι is debatable. Cadbury and Lake (29–30) incline toward "generosity." Barrett (1:171) favors "simplicity."

Analysis

As after the ascension (Acts 1:13-14), summary follows an exciting account. Narrative is well served by interludes between dramatic high points. Such pauses allow readers to digest the story and prevent them from becoming jaded. Summaries, in sum, give readers a rest.[1] The specific purpose of this summary is to offer a glimpse at the community that erupted into life at Pentecost and its nature prior to the rise of conflict. The similarity to succeeding summaries (4:4, 32-35; 5:12-16) is no flaw. Conflict had no negative effect on the community's life or growth.

Excursus: The Summaries in Acts

In a 1923 essay that may be said to have inaugurated most, if not all, of the more productive contemporary approaches to the study of Acts, Martin Dibelius identified the narrative purpose of the detailed summaries in the early part of the book (2:41/42-47; 4:32-35; 5:12-16)[2] and their inspiration.[3] These summaries produce the appearance of a connected narrative by linking otherwise isolated episodes. Luke may well have learned from Mark the value of using summaries to transform isolated reports of Jesus' deeds into examples of his typical behavior.[4] A decade later Cadbury provided the details to support Dibelius's proposal.[5] In *The Making of Luke-Acts,* Cadbury had laid out the major functions of these summaries, "to divide and to connect . . . [to] indicate that the material is typical, that the action was continued, that the effect was general."[6]

Both were building on an important insight offered by Eduard Schwartz in a footnote.[7] Schwartz observed that the relationship between incident and generalizing summary in Acts 4:32-35 minimized the

1 Cf. Roloff, 65.

2 There are brief summaries at 1:14; 6:7; 9:31; 12:24; 16:5; 19:20; 28:30-31; and statements about growth at 2:41; 4:4; 5:14; 6:1, 7; 9:31; 11:21, 24; 12:24; 14:1; 19:20

3 Dibelius, *Studies,* 9 ("Style Criticism of the Book of Acts").

4 The process is apparent in Mark 1: 21-34. Verses 23-28 relate an exorcism, followed by a healing in vv. 29-31. There follows in vv. 32-34 a general report of healings and exorcisms on that same day. To narrate each of these incidents in detail would be unnecessarily boring. Cf. also Mark 3:10-12 and 6:53-56. Although Luke may have learned this technique from other sources, his use of the summary from Mark 6 in Acts is demonstrable (see Pervo, *Dating,* 36–38).

5 Henry J. Cadbury, "The Summaries in Acts," in Lake and Cadbury, *Additional Notes,* 392–402.

6 Cadbury, *Making,* 58.

contribution of Barnabas, who became one of many rather than an example of outstanding generosity. An implication of Schwartz's observation is that the summaries do not simply "pad" the narrative; they may contradict it. This particular contradiction calls into question the historical value of Luke's portrait of the early community.[8] Although there have been some dissenters, the mainstream of research upon the summaries has followed the trail blazed by Dibelius.[9] As the author of these summaries, Luke has therefore created a portrait of the early Jerusalem community, the only church for which he attempts such a description. Since this uniqueness is not due to the possession of source material about the Jerusalem church that was lacking in other cases, a purpose is to be sought.

That purpose is basic to Luke's theological goals and reveals his method and stance. The description has an apologetic thrust;[10] the method is narrative fiction. More recent insights into the function of summaries have come from the realm of literary criticism. Summary in one form or another dominates narrative. Few authors could keep the attention of an audience if they constantly spelled out all of the details of "I then went home and went to bed." When such matters constitute a scene, they make contributions to character or plot. For a cogent example from Acts, contrast the summary account of travel in 13:25-26a with that of chap. 27. Just as scene can illuminate summary, so summary can highlight scene.[11]

7 Eduard Schwartz, "Zur Chronologie des Paulus," in *Nachrichten von der königlichen Gesellschaft der Wissenschaften zu Göttingen, Philologisch-historische Klasse* (Berlin:Weidmann, 1907) 263–99, esp. 282 n. 1.

8 Brian Capper defends the historical accuracy of the record ("The Palestinian Cultural Context of Earliest Christian Community of Goods," in Bauckham, *Palestinian Setting*, 323–56). He establishes this cultural context from 1QS and descriptions of Essene life by Philo and Josephus. Aware that the Essene community was of a different nature from the early Christian movement, Capper posits, on the basis of Acts 5:4, the existence of an "inner group" (337). Luke knows of no such divisions. In discussing the action of Barnabas, Capper (340) does not deal with its relation to the summary. Although his thesis is weak, Capper has assembled and discussed a wealth of valuable data. See also his "Community of Goods in the Early Jerusalem Church," *ANRW* 2.26.3 (1996) 1730–74. S. Scott Bartchy ("Community of Goods in Acts: Idealization or Social Reality?" in Birger Pearson, ed., *The Future of Early Christianity: Essays in Honor of Helmut Koester* [Minneapolis: Fortress Press, 1991] 309–18) presents a somewhat different defense. Using ancient conventions about friendship and modern social-scientific analysis, Bartchy claims that the early community lived as a fictive kin group, that is, as a family that pooled its resources. The issue is not whether the account, granting a bit of hyperbole and "Hellenic" coloring (as Bartchy does), is plausible, nor what actually happened. The latter cannot be determined from Acts. The only identifiable potential sources (Barnabas, Ananias [and Sapphira], 4:36-37; 5:1-5 [11]) do not support the claims of the summaries for universal sharing. Finger (*Of Widows and Meals*) develops Capper's and Bartchy's arguments in considerable detail

9 See Haenchen, 190–96, 230–35, and 242–46. For other views, see Sterling, "Athletes of Virtue," 680. Note also the contribution of Maria Anicia Co, "The Major Summaries," and Ulrich Wendel, *Gemeinde in Kraft: Das Gemeindeverständnis in den Summarien der Apostelgeschichte* (NTDH 20; Neukirchen-Vluyn: Neukirchener Verlag, 1998); Andreas Lindemann, "The Beginnings of Christian Life in Jerusalem according to the Summaries in the Acts of the Apostles (Acts 2.42-47; 4.32-35; 5.12-16)," in Julian V. Hills et al., eds., *Common Life in the Early Church: Essays Honoring Graydon F. Snyder* (Harrisburg, Pa.: Trinity Press International, 1998) 202–18; and idem, "The Community of Goods among the First Christians and among the Essenes," in David Goodblatt et al., eds., *Historical Perspectives: From the Hasmoneans to Bar Kokhba in Light of the Dead Sea Scrolls; Proceedings of the Fourth International Symposium of the Orion Center for the Study of the Dead Sea Scrolls and Associated Literature, 27–31 January 1999* (STDJ 37; Leiden: Brill, 1999) 147–61. Earlier contributions include Lucien Cerfaux, "La composition de la première partie du Livre des Actes," *EThL* 13 (1936) 667–91; idem, "La première communauté chrétienne à Jérusalem (Act., II, 41–V, 42)," *EThL* 16 (1939) 5–31; Heinrich Zimmerman, "Die Sammelberichte der Apostelgeschichte," *BZ* 5 (1961) 71–82; Jacques Dupont, "Community of Goods in the Early Church," in idem, *The Salvation of the Gentiles: Studies in the Acts of the Apostles* (New York/Ramsey, N.J./Toronto: Paulist, 1979) 85–102.

10 See Sterling, "Athletes of Virtue."

11 Sijbolt J. Noorda, "Scene and Summary: A Proposal for Reading Acts 4:32–5:16," in Kremer, *Actes*, 475–83, is a pioneering probe of the literary functions of summaries. See also Tannehill, *Narrative Unity*, 2:43–44.

Luke is a writer of narrative. Acts resembles the "evangelists" in that he presents his message in and as a story, while his viewpoint has much in common with the later Christian apologists,[12] but the lack of a fully coherent viewpoint indicates that the author was either not seeking to present an integrated philosophical picture or did not perceive its inconsistency. The summaries in Acts 2 and 4 showcase the early Jesus movement in Jerusalem as a utopian community in which an entire society operates like a band of friends (or an extended family)[13] by eliminating the barriers imposed by the unequal distribution of wealth.

Similarities in theme and diction between these passages and Greco-Roman utopian thought are widely recognized.[14] Evaluations of the connections differ.[15] Descriptions of utopias and utopian programs appear in a great variety of ancient genres from many cultures.[16] Although stories about utopia can be quite entertaining,[17] these accounts usually serve political, philosophical, or religious purposes. Utopias set in the distant past or future tend to be critiques of things as they are. Plato's influence is pervasive. The ideal state of the *Republic* rejects "private property."[18] Bowing to the power of myth, Plato also portrays primitive Athens as a time when all was held in common.[19] The "myth" in view is the portrait of the "golden age," when the gods had direct charge of things and such iniquities as individual ownership of real property were unthinkable.[20]

Utopias set in the (dramatic or actual) present time, on the other hand, often serve to enhance a particular group or system. Relevant examples include the portraits of the Essenes offered by Philo and Josephus.[21] These, like Acts, describe the life of particular bodies within a larger society with the object of extolling that society. Just before observing that the Essenes hold their possessions in common, Josephus praises them for maintaining their way of life without interruption over a long period.[22] That comment reveals an apologetic aim: the Jews have philosophical sects that are superior to any of the Greeks, since their virtues are both lofty and enduring. Proper apologetic might have used the present tense and/or affirmed that these practices continue. The absence of such claims in Acts has led to the (often convenient) conclusion that Luke described a "communistic experiment" that failed.[23] "Propaganda" may be somewhat more apt than "apologetic," so long as it is

12 Pervo (*Dating*) develops this thesis in detail.
13 On the friendship tradition, see n. 25.
14 For example, Conzelmann, 24; Plümacher, *Lukas*, 16–18; David L. Mealand, "Community of Goods and Utopian Allusions in Acts 2–4," *JTS* 28 (1977) 96–99; and Johnson, 62.
15 David P. Seccombe (*Possessions and the Poor in Luke-Acts* [SNTU 6; Linz: F. Plochl, 1982]) 200) regards the allusions as unintentional, since Luke would abhor associations with polytheist mythology.
16 See Pervo, *Profit*, 69–70, 163. A more recent general study is Doyne Dawson, *Cities of the Gods: Communist Utopias in Greek Thought* (New York: Oxford University Press, 1992).
17 On utopian novels, see Niklas Holzberg, "Utopias and Fantastic Travel: Euhemerus, Iambulus," in Gareth Schmeling, ed., *The Novel in the Ancient World* (rev. ed.; Leiden: Brill, 2003) 621–28. Sterling ("Athletes of Virtue," 687) wishes to exclude these from comparison to Acts on the grounds of fictionality. This criterion is not very helpful. Philo's Therapeutae (*Vit. cont.*) are not historically well attested, and Sterling draws upon Philostratus's historically dubious accounts of Indian and Egyptian sages (*Vit. Apoll.* 3.10-51; 6.6).
18 Plato *Resp.* 424A, 449C, 416D, 464D, 543B; cf. also the later *Leg.* 679B-C; 684C-D; 744B-746C; 757A.
19 Plato *Critias* 110C-D; cf. also *Tim.* 18B.
20 For the extent of this conception, see Arthur O. Lovejoy and George Boas, *Primitivism and Related Ideas in Antiquity* (2 vols.; Baltimore: Johns Hopkins University Press, 1935).
21 Philo *Omn. prob. lib.* 75-91; *Hypoth.* 8.11.1-18; Josephus *Bell.* 2.120-61; *Ant.* 18.18-22. Parallels with the communal life of the Qumran community are of general interest but fail to take important differences into account. Haenchen is quite trenchant, noting that the Qumran community was scrupulously observant and demanded a long period of probation: "One should therefore refrain from matching isolated details of primitive Christian life with similar features of Qumran, but rather take into account the whole circumstantial context. Only so can one learn what the primitive Church on the one hand had in common with contemporaneous phenomena, and what particularly marked it out on the other" (165).
22 Josephus *Ant.* 18.20. (Both text and translation are uncertain.)
23 "But after a short time the 'communistic' experiment broke down for two reasons." Kirsopp Lake, "The Communism of Acts II. and IV.-VI. and the Appointment and the Seven," in Lake and Cadbury, 140–51, esp. 141. Lake's reasons were not,

understood that the message, unlike formal apologetic, is not even ostensibly addressed to outsiders.[24] Iamblicus's *De Vita Pythagorica* (*On the Pythagorean Way of Life*) is a useful parallel to Acts for more than linguistic reasons.[25] Luke has commingled a portrait of the ideal "golden age" with the apologetic picture of a specific group (or subgroup). To state that the church once realized the social ideals of the ancient world is not quite the same as maintaining that this fulfillment is part of its enduring life.[26] It may well suggest that, when maintained, these principles will yield admirable results.[27]

Luke can be labeled an apologist manqué and capable of invention, but the question of the proper use of possessions was not for him a matter of minor

however, economic, and he understood that "communism" is not a suitable description, since it has come to refer to common ownership of the means of production. For the view that it was impractical, see Rackham, 42. Alphons Steinmann (*Die Apostelgeschichte* [4th ed.; Bonn: Peter Hanstein, 1934] 43) is representative of an era when it was important to stress that the early Christians had nothing to do with socialism. Wikenhauser (69) observes that Communism is an economic system, but he does consider Ernst Troeltsch's "religious communism motivated by love" (*religiösen Liebeskommunismus*) as a possible characterization. Troeltsch had, in fact, strongly insisted that early Christians maintained the right to private property (*The Social Teaching of the Christian Churches* (2 vols.; 1911; trans. O. Wyon; New York: Harper & Brothers, 1960) 1:115–18. Bruce (74) says that difficulties arose when the original enthusiasm began to wane. This is a religio-historical judgment that would have horrified Luke. For references to the discussion of this practice in political thought, see Conzelmann, 24 n. 10; and Wolf-Dieter Hauschild, "'Christentum und Eigentum': Zum Problem eines altkirchlichen 'Sozialismus,'" *Zeitschrift für evangelische Ethik* 16 (1972) 34–49. The major theologians of the Protestant Reformation took issue with the literal interpretation of Acts 2:42-47; 4:32-35 for two major reasons: the monastic tradition viewed itself as meeting these ideals (cf. Jerome's [fictitious] *Life of Malchus* 7; and Augustine *Ep.* 211, used as a basis of their rule by the Augustinian Canons [eleventh century]) and radical reformers advocated this "communism" as the basis of Christian social life. Calvin attacks both, but his ire is chiefly directed at the Anabaptists (1:87-88 *ad* 2:44; 1:128-30 *ad* 4:32-35). See also Finger's review of research, *Of Widows and Meals*, 18–47.

24 Sterling ("Athletes of Virtue," 691 n. 42) recognizes this distinction, which places a qualification on his thorough and useful profile of (Luke and) Acts as "apologetic historiography."

25 Iamblichus *De Vit. Pythag.* 167-68: . . . *μιᾶς ψυχῆς* . . . *κοινὰ γὰρ πᾶσι πάντα καὶ ταῦτα ἦν, ἴδιον δὲ οὐδεὶς οὐδὲν ἐκέκτητο* ("one soul . . . for all was common and the same for all, and no one possessed anything as his or her own") is often cited in discussion of these summaries (e.g., Bruce, 132; and Conzelmann, 24). Although the dramatic date of the work is in the distant past, it is intended as a text for students of Platonism c. 300 CE, not as a historical record but as "a dramatized study of a way of life" characterized by John Dillon and Jackson Hershbell as a "gospel," *Iamblichus On the Pythagorean Way of Life* (SBLTT 29; Atlanta: Scholars Press, 1991) 25. Iamblichus wished to show that Plato was quite dependent upon Pythagoras—community of property (*De Vit. Pythag.* 167-68) is one example of this dependence—just as Luke strove to show that Paul proclaimed the message of the Jerusalem apostles. Iamblichus's account of the daily life of the Pythagoreans reads very much like what Philo and Josephus say about the Essenes. This work also shows the overlap between theories about friendship and descriptions of communal life, since Iamblichus presents friendship as the keystone of Pythagoras's philosophy (*De Vit. Pythag.* 229-33). This helps to explain why Alan C. Mitchell ("The Social Function of Friendship in Acts 2:44-47 and 4:32-37," *JBL* 111 [1992] 255–72) and Bartchy ("Community of Goods") utilize the same evidence. The notion that friends share everything was common in the Greek world: see, e.g., Plato *Resp.* 4, 424A; 5, 449C; Aristotle *Nic. Eth.* 8.9, 1159 b31; Philo *Migr. Abr.* 235; Cicero *Off.* 1.16.51; Ps. Clem. *Rec.* 10.5; and Lucian *Peregr.* 13.

26 Louis William Countryman reviews the data on commonality of property from Acts onward, indicating that it is in the foothills of the apologists (*The Rich Christian in the Church of the Early Empire: Contradictions and Accommodations* [New York: Edwin Mellen, 1980] 76–80). He also observes that the claims of various authors that believers have all in common gain no support from their writings in general. There is no good evidence for commonality of property until the rise of coenobitic monasticism. Statements such as those of Justin *1 Apol.* 14 refer to almsgiving.

27 Josephus (*Ap.* 2.146) says that the Mosaic "constitution" is "excellently designed to promote piety (*εὐσέβεια*), friendly relations (*κοινωνία*) with each other, and humanity (*φιλανθρωπία*) toward

concern. As Luke T. Johnson has shown, money was both a fundamental symbol and a pressing reality for this author, a very concrete means of communicating his ethical message.[28] Historical accuracy has no monopoly upon truth.

Comment

■ **42** The nouns, all datives associated with the verb προσκαρτερέω ("devote oneself to"), can be variously understood. The conventional text[29] makes "breaking bread" appear to be an appositive to κοινωνία ("fellowship," "sharing").[30] Some D-Texts (d vg syr^{p} cop$^{s\ bo}$) confirm the relationship by placing "breaking" in the genitive, permitting κοινωνία to mean "(sacramental) communion."[31] That is anachronistic.[32] The phrase τῇ διδαχῇ τῶν ἀποστόλων might refer to the *content* of apostolic teaching (cf. the *Didache*) or to the *activity* of teaching.[33] It is the earliest assertion that valid Christian doctrine derives from what the apostles taught. Barrett argues that there are four items arranged in two pairs: teaching and fellowship, breaking of bread and prayers.[34] This construction would be more likely if there were an intermediate element distinguishing the two pairs. The chief difficulty is the meaning of κοινωνία here. "Communal lifestyle" is one strong possibility, supported by both the Greco-Roman philosophical tradition in general and data about the Essenes in particular.[35] This interpretation understands vv. 44-45 as an explication of the term κοινωνία. Verses 46-47 would likewise explicate "the breaking of bread" (and "the prayers"?).

Yet the older argument of Heinrich Seesemann that the term refers to "spiritual" togetherness has the merit of identifying four different qualities or marks of the "primitive church": attention to apostolic teaching, spiritual fellowship, the communal meal, and a life of prayer.[36] This would give the use of possessions a

---

the world at large, besides justice (δικαιοσύνη), hardihood, and contempt of life" (trans. Henry St. J. Thackeray, *Josephus I* [LCL; Cambridge, Mass.: Harvard University Press, 1926] 351).

28 Luke T. Johnson, *The Literary Function of Possessions in Luke-Acts* (SBLDS 39; Missoula, Mont.: Scholars Press, 1977). Note also Richard Pervo, "PANTA KOINA: The Feeding Stories in the Light of Economic Data and Social Practice," in Lukas Bormann et al., eds., *Religious Propaganda and Missionary Competition in the New Testament World: Essays Honoring Dieter Georgi* (NovTSup 74; Leiden: Brill, 1994) 164–94; and Gerd Theissen, "Urchristlicher Liebeskommunismus: Zum 'Sitz im Leben' des Topos *hapanta koina* in Apg 2,44 und 4,32," in Tord Fornberg and David Hellholm eds., *Text and Contexts: Biblical Texts in Their Textual and Situational Contexts: Essays in Honor of Lars Hartman* (Oslo: Scandinavian University Press, 1995) 689–712.

29 א^{2} E Ψ 33 1739 m sy insert καί before τῇ κλάσει. This would distinguish "fellowship" from "breaking bread."

30 Cadbury and Lake (27–28) propose an appositional relation.

31 Boismard (*Texte*, 76) does not admit this reading into his text. Another secondary *v.l.* is the insertion of "in Jerusalem" after "apostles" or "prayer."

32 Lampe (*s.v.* κοινωνία, C, 763) provides no authorities for this understanding before the fourth century.

33 Attempts to establish a strong contrast between *kerygma* (proclamation of the message) and *didachē* (instruction, e.g., of a moral nature) can be misleading when applied to Acts. Cf. 5:28; 13:12; 17:19, all of which refer to public proclamation. For another view, see Fitzmyer, 270.

34 Barrett, 1:162.

35 On the Qumran/Essene parallels, see Moshe Weinfeld, *The Organizational Pattern and the Penal Code of the Qumran Sect: A Comparison with Guilds and Religious Associations of the Hellenistic-Roman Period* (NTOA; Göttingen: Vandenhoeck & Ruprecht, 1986) 13–14, who argues that the use of יחד has only this sense in the DSS (13 n. 29; cf. 1QS 5:1-2). Weinfeld believes that this is due to the influence of the Greek terms and κοινόν and κοινωνία. Philo (*Omn. prob. lib.* 84, 91) and Josephus (*Bell.* 2.122-23) use this stem in their descriptions of Essene life. Weinfeld does observe that the LXX renders this Hebrew word as ἐπὶ τὸ αὐτό, a phrase found in Acts 1:15; 2:1, 44, 47; 4:26. Fitzmyer (270) discusses the Qumran data. He regards borrowing from the Essenes as possible, although he stresses the difference in organization.

36 Heinrich Seesemann, *Der Begriff ΚΟΙΝΩΝΙΑ im Neuen Testament* (BZNW 74; Giessen: Töpelmann, 1933) 87–92. Cf. also Friedrich Hauck, "κοινός," *TDNT* 3:789–809, esp. 809 ("an abstract and spiritual term for the fellowship of brotherly concord established and expressed in the life of the community").

religious ground. "Worship" and "service" were not separate realms.[37] Apostolic instruction produced unity of purpose and will, expressed both in prayer (cf. 4:24-31) and in the communal meal, made possible by the generosity aroused by unity.[38] Apostolic authority is central to this life. This role and its abstraction to "instruction" show that for the author the apostles belonged to a distant (as well as idealized) past.[39]

There is no dispute that the Lucan portrait is idealized.[40] Frederick J. Foakes Jackson aptly observes its most remarkable feature: "The believers are supposed instantly to have formed a society, characterized by submission to apostolic authority, unanimity, and devotion."[41] The narrator is not merely idealistic; he is attempting to portray the immediate crystallization of a large and smoothly functioning community.

■ **43** The N-A[27] text of this verse is chiastic: "There happened to every person fear, and many miracles through the apostles happened." Did the author intend this rather lame repetition of ἐγίνετο, possibly considering it artistic? Boismard thinks not. The text is possibly corrupt and definitely uncertain.[42] The apparently pedantic and labile "in Jerusalem" also pops up here at two places in the tradition.[43] Although its varied placements in vv. 42-43 are arguments in favor of its secondary character, the irregularity also points to confusion in the history of the transmission. The D-Text is attractive: ἐγίνετο σημεῖα καὶ τέρατα διὰ τῶν ἀποστόλων ἐν Ἰερουσαλήμ, ἐγίνετο δὲ φόβος μέγας ἐπὶ πᾶσαν ψυχὴν ("The apostles became the agents of portents and miracles *in Jerusalem. Enormous* awe overtook everyone"). This arrangement places awe in its normal position as a response to the supernatural.[44] This order, as Ropes perceived, is probably closer to the original text than is that of B et al. (N-A[27]).[45] The text of ℵ A C, which has both the initial reference to "awe" and the statement that "Enormous awe overtook everyone" at the close of the verse,[46] is likely to be a conflation of the two forms.[47] "Jerusalem" may not be so otiose as it seems, since the summary in 5:16 speaks of appeal to adjacent regions. This picture of the expanding circles of the mission, from Jerusalem to other parts of Judea (1:8), is characteristically Lucan and is less likely to have occurred to a subsequent editor. The expression "signs and portents" is a characteristic element of summaries. It appears eight times in Acts 1–15.[48]

---

37 It is unlikely that a formal distinction between "Eucharist" and "*agapē*" was made in Luke's time, or, in any case, that Luke wished to show the "primitive church" as celebrating symbolic (as opposed to nourishing) meals. Conzelmann (23) intelligently observes that Luke views the unity of Eucharist and meal as one indicator of the ideal nature of the early church. "Breaking of bread" is not a normal term for a meal. In Hebrew and Aramaic, it refers to the beginning of a repast. In early Christian literature, however, it serves as synecdoche for the eucharistic meal. Cf. the "institution narratives" in 1 Cor 11:24 par., as well as Luke 24:35; Acts 2:46; 20:7, 11; 27:35; *Act. John* 110; *Act. Paul* 3.5; *Did.* 14:1.

38 Jean-Marc Prieur ("Actes 2, 42 et le culte réformé," *FoiVie* 94 [1995] 61–72) understands the four items as central components of worship, although without a fixed order.

39 See Jude 17||2 Pet 3:2. The apostles received their message from Christ: *1 Clem.* 42:1-2; Ignatius *Magn.* 7:1; 13:1; Polycarp *Phil.* 6:3.

40 See Bruce, 135. Ferdinand W. Horn ("Die Gütergemeinschaft der Urgemeinde," *EvTh* 58 [1998] 370–83) takes up the historical question and concludes that these descriptions of communalism had no historical basis.

41 Frederick J. Foakes Jackson, *The Acts of the Apostles* (New York: Harper, 1931) 20.

42 Boismard, *Texte*, 76. Metzger (*Textual Commentary*, 262) defines the problem as "exceedingly difficult."

43 After the second ἐγίνετο in E 33 104 *pc* sy[p], placed after "apostles" by cop[mae] and accepted by Boismard, *Texte*, 76.

44 See (for the noun φόβος) Luke 5:26; 7:16; Acts 5:5, 11; 9:17. The verb φοβέομαι ("to be afraid," "in awe") is similarly used in the Gospel: 1:13, 30; etc. An editor may have rearranged Acts 2:43 to agree with 5:12, where "awe" precedes the summary of miracles, although it is the formal conclusion to the story of Ananias and Sapphira.

45 Ropes, 24.

46 ℵ 88 have a second ἐγίνετο, which the others lack.

47 Haenchen (192 n. 3) says that it may be an attempt to smooth the transition to v. 44. This would rationalize a conflation rather than exclude it.

48 The order "portents and signs" is found in 2:19, 43; 6:8; and 7:36; "signs and portents" appears in 4:30; 5:12; 14:3; and 15:12.

■ **44-45**[49] "Shared everything" is ambiguous, but from 4:32–5:10 it seems most likely that the narrator envisions the liquidation of property followed by presentation of the proceeds to the community–*κτήματα* and *ὑπάρξεις* are evidently equivalent to "real and personal property."[50] Verses 46-47 comprise two sentences. Verse 47c is short and simple. The first is rather complex, involving four circumstantial participles related to the phrase "they would take nourishment" (*μετελάμβανον τροφῆς*). This is not good hypotactic prose.[51] The temple appears for the first time. Luke does not state explicitly that the believers worshiped there. The only follower of Jesus who indubitably participates in the cult is Paul.[52] For the apostles, the temple is a place for teaching.[53] Luke here quietly introduces a basic inversion of apocalyptic proportions: the house(hold) will become the locus of God's saving message and actions, while the temple constitutes the center of resistance to grace.[54] The temporal focus is on the present.[55]

■ **47** "Praise of God" is both the appropriate response to grace and a characteristic of all that the believers did. "Everyone approved of them" (*ἔχοντες χάριν πρὸς ὅλον τὸν λαόν*) evidently intends to associate a horizontal plane to the vertical.[56] If this is accepted–more on logical grounds than linguistic–the question remains whether this refers to favor extended toward others[57] or admiration from them. The context supports the latter: charity is directed toward insiders only, while popular admiration remains strong until the advent

49 The witnesses divide over whether to read the participle "believers" as present (A C D E P most) or as aorist (ℵ B 0142 it^{p} Origen *Speculum* Salvian *et al.*). Logic seems to favor the present–active believers–whereas the aorist could refer to converts. Since v. 47 speaks of additional converts, the present looks preferable, but Barrett (1:167) is hesitant, with good reason.

50 Note the iterative use of *ἄν* (without the optative), reinforcing the notion of continual action. See §BDF 367.

51 The D-Text, according to Boismard (*Texte*, 77) recasts vv. 45-46: *καὶ ὅσοι κτήματα εἶχον ἢ ὑπάρξεις ἐπίπρασκον καὶ διεμέριζον τὰς τίμας αὐτῶν τοῖς χρείαν ἔχουσιν. καθ᾽ ἡμέραν τε προσκαρτέρουν ἐν τῷ ἱερῷ καὶ ἦσαν ἐπὶ τὸ αὐτὸ κλῶντες ἄρτον, μετελαμβάνοντες τροφῆς* ("All who had real or personal property liquidated it and distributed their proceeds to those in need. They participated in the temple on a daily basis and broke bread together [in the same place?], taking their nourishment"). D and sy^{p} place "daily" here. This is secondary, placing the responsibility for liquidation and distribution in the hands of those with property, who were limited in number. This edition improves the syntax of v. 46, making *προσκαρτερέω* ("participate assiduously") the finite verb. By eliminating *κατ᾽ οἶκον* ("in houses"), this text implies that they celebrated the meal in the temple. (This is not the reading of D, which Boismard [78], with good reason, finds incoherent.) Some representatives of the Latin D-Text tradition (perp gig r–the latter reading *orationi instantes* ["constant in prayer"]) omit "in the temple," possibly from hostility toward Judaism. There is no firm D-Text for this verse. Ropes (*Text*, 25) sees D as emphasizing the eucharistic overtones. Metzger (*Textual Commentary*, 264), on the other hand, finds them mysterious.

52 Paul in the temple: Acts 21:26-30; 22:17.

53 Teaching in the temple: Acts 3:12-26; 5:20-25, 42. It may be inferred that Peter and John visited in 3:1 with the intent of worship, but they do not do so.

54 See the convincing analysis of John H. Elliott, "Temple versus Household in Luke-Acts: A Contrast in Social Institutions," in Neyrey, *Social World*, 211–40. Elliott finds the contrast to be pervasive (note the summary on 229–30). He observes that the contrast is implicit in the (Pauline-influenced) parable of the Pharisee and the tax collector (Luke 18:9-14), in which the latter goes to his *house* "justified," whereas the Pharisee is left in the temple, presumably not justified (Elliott, 213–14). In contrast to the oft-noted use of the temple as an inclusion in Luke (1:5-23; 24:49-53), Acts begins and ends in a house (1:6, apparently; 1:12; 28:30-31) (Elliott, 215). On house churches, see the comprehensive survey by Bradley Blue, "Acts and the House Church," in Gill and Gempf, *Setting*, 2:119–222. The theme is developed by David L. Matson, *Household Conversion Narratives in Acts: Pattern and Interpretation* (JSNTS 123; Sheffield: Sheffield Academic Press, 1996).

55 "Daily": Acts 2:46-47; 3:2; 16:5; 17:11; 19:9. The theological significance of the term is apparent in Luke 9:23 (bearing the cross) and 11:3 ("daily bread").

56 See Fitzmyer, 272–73.

57 So T. D. Andersen ("The Meaning of *ΕΧΟΝΤΕΣ ΧΑΡΙΝ ΠΡΟΣ* in Acts 2.47," *NTS* 34 [1988] 604–10), who makes a strong linguistic argument for this sense of the phrase.

of Stephen in chap. 6 (note 5:26).[58] The closing verse[59] brings to mind the Gospel summaries about the growth and development of Jesus: Luke 1:80; 2:52. Converts are characterized as "those (being) saved." Salvation is a present experience in Luke and Acts.[60] The final ἐπὶ τὸ αὐτό is quite difficult in this position, stimulating textual emendation. The D-Text substitutes "in the church," an excellent guess.[61] E Ψ 33 m sy shifted δέ (a particle that is often the signal of a new sentence) to stand before "Peter," thus placing ἐπὶ τὸ αὐτό in the next sentence (3:1). This is very likely a secondary improvement.[62]

If chap. 1 moved in a matter-of-fact manner, chap. 2 breaks barriers of sound and shock. The narrator seizes his audience's attention with a breathless series of arresting images. The outpoured Spirit floods through the city, gathering a crowd in its tow. They were not disappointed by Peter's address, which was an immense missionary success. By the end of that day the community had grown by a factor of twenty-five, and the machinery of a smoothly functioning social and religious organization, characterized by marvelous unity and long-sought justice, sprang into existence. The birth of the church was like the advent of Athena. It required no maturation. Through this depiction, Luke not only foreshadowed the glorious future but also depicted the formation of Christian community as an eschatological event, a miracle.

58 For the vertical and horizontal in a different sense (apparently), note Luke 2:13-14.

59 Acts 2:47 is evoked four times in the *Act. Pet.* chaps. 9, 31, 33, and 41.

60 The participle "being saved" appears in *1 Clem.* 58:2, and in the perfect in Eph 2:5; Polycarp *Phil.* 1:3.

61 Codex Bezae is fond of the phrase, which it adds three times in 2:44-47. See Metzger, *Textual Commentary*, 263.

62 See Barrett, 1:172–73, for a discussion of the issues.

3

3:1-10 Peter and John Heal a Paralytic

**1/ While Peter and John were on
their way to the temple precincts at the time of the 1500
service, 2/ a man who had been
crippled from birth was being
carried in—his people would
place him at the gate called
"Beautiful" every day to solicit
alms from those entering the
sanctuary. 3/ When he realized
that Peter and John were on
their way in, he began to beg
alms from them. 4/ Peter, along
with John, fixed his gaze upon
the man and said: "Look at us."
5/ That he did, expecting to get
something from them, 6/ but
Peter said, "I have no money,
but what I do have I shall give
you. In the name of Jesus Christ
the Nazorean get up and walk!"
7/ He then grabbed him by the
right hand and raised him up.
Strength immediately came
to his feet and ankles. 8/ He
sprang to his feet and began
to walk about. Then he went
into the sanctuary with them,
leaping and walking and praising God. 9/ When everyone
saw him doing these things,
10/ they recognized him as the
fellow who had sat begging
at the Beautiful Gate of the
temple and were overcome with
amazement at what had happened to him.**

Analysis

The first two chapters portray the origin and growth of the community in an atmosphere devoid of conflict. In chaps. 3–7, opposition erupts. Henceforth, persecution will drive the plot of Acts.[1] Rather than narrow the outlook of the movement or quash its development, hostility leads to ever-increasing numbers and widening boundaries. The narrative follows a stereotyped pattern, elaborated with highly skillful variation.[2] The plot is like that of the Gospels in that the public will long serve as a blocking character that inhibits the officials from achieving their ends.[3] Two particular differences stand out: reversal of public opinion is restricted to

1 See the analysis of Norman R. Petersen, *Literary Criticism for New Testament Critics* (Philadelphia: Fortress Press, 1978) 83–92.

2 Talbert (*Reading Acts*, 50–51) shows the numerous parallels among the various episodes.

3 Another model that may also have influenced the Gospel tradition is Jer 26:1—29:32, which contains three episodes of conflict between Jeremiah and the authorities. Note, in particular, Jeremiah 26, his sermon in the temple and subsequent trial.

Greek-speaking Jews affiliated with certain synagogues (Acts 6:8-12), and the Roman government has gone on a convenient holiday from Jerusalem, not to return until the need arises to rescue Paul from a similar mob making similar accusations with the identical objective (21:27-36). The story unfolds with increasing intensity and an expanding horizon that will, in due and providential course, take the mission beyond the heart of Judea and, step by step, to gentiles. The general scheme reflects a widely attested pattern of cult foundation, framed by Luke around these narrative elements:[4]

A. A miracle draws attention and followers.
B. Teaching is addressed to those attracted by the wonder.
C. Concerned and jealous Jewish officials arrest the missionary/ies.
D. Legal action ensues.
E. The eventual result is miraculous vindication of the mission.

Luke deploys this pattern three times in Acts 3–7, with important "interludes," including summaries, narratives about community life, and a number of notes on numerical (and spiritual) growth. The variations on a theme develop a crescendo: threat of punishment, whipping, execution. The first and third cycles adhere to the pattern closely; the middle episode displays greater elaboration. The interludes (here denoted with *X* for comments about growth and *Y* for summary or narrative about community life) serve both to show that growth goes on despite opposition and to introduce variety into an otherwise repetitious account.

(Y_1. 2:42-46)
(X_1. 2:47)
I. Peter and John
   A. 3:1-11. Peter and John heal a cripple at the temple gate. A crowd gathers.
   B. 3:12-26. Peter delivers a missionary address.
   C. 4:1-3. The chief of the temple police and the Sadducees interrupt the speech to arrest the alleged miscreants.
   (X_2. 4:4)
   D. 4:5-22. At a subsequent trial the apostles are accused of practicing magic, to which they respond in the manner of philosophers confronting tyrants.
   E. 4:23-31. The council releases the pair with a warning. An epiphanic earthquake affirms their cause.
   (Y_2. 4:32–5:11)
II. All the apostles
   A. 5:12-16. Miracles reported in summary form.
   B_1. 5:12b. The apostles teach in the temple, like (Jesus and various) philosophers.
   (X_3. 5:13-14)
   C_1. 5:17-18. The high priest and the Sadducees arrest them.
   E_1. 5:19-20. An angel engineers a miraculous release.
   B_2. 5:21a. The apostles continue to teach.
   D_1. 5:21-25. Meanwhile, back in the courtroom, the trial aborts for lack of accused.
   C_2. 5:26-27a. The accused are returned to custody.
   D_2. 5:27b-39. The trial may therefore resume. Gamaliel forestalls an imminent threat of death.
   E_2. 5:40-42. The Twelve are whipped, then released. They return to their teaching mission.
III. Stephen
   (Y_3. 6:1-6)
   (X_4. 6:7)
   A. 6:8. Stephen works miracles (summary).
   B. 6:9-10. He teaches (summary).[5]
   C. 6:11-12. As a consequence, Stephen is arrested and arraigned before the Sanhedrin.
   D. 6:13–7:57. A full-length report of the trial is given.
   E. 6:15; 7:55-56, 59-60. Stephen is murdered. Signs of divine approval mark his vindication.

Although Luke inserted a few slices of evident tradition, such as the death of Stephen, into this artfully constructed narrative, he was not attempting to tease a feasible historical reconstruction from surviving pieces of the past. Acts 3–7 is the literary creation of the author. Further insight into the author's literary method derives from the recognition that this section reflects the early ministry of Jesus in Luke, perhaps most notably the

4 The following comes from Pervo, *Profit*, 19–21. For examples of the general pattern, see 146 n. 11. John B. Weaver develops a sophisticated analysis of this scheme in *Plots of Epiphany: Prison Escape in Acts of the Apostles* (BZNW 131; Berlin: de Gruyter, 2004) 19–91.

5 A lengthy sample of Stephen's teaching is provided in 7:2-53.

healing of a cripple in 5:17-26, which goaded scribes and Pharisees to opposition.[6]

Narrative analyses tend to embrace chaps. 3–5 under a single head.[7] Without prejudice to these valuable contributions, from the perspective of the general plot and structure of Acts, there is merit in viewing chaps. 3–7 as a related sequence, within which other sequences can be identified. Luke is the master of his scheme, not its servant. Following the "revolutionary" approach of chap. 2, the narrator presents in section I an even more complex literary unit, framed by summaries.[8] The action unfolds in four scenes (3:1-10; 3:11–4:4; 4:5-22; 4:23-31). This is one of the longer narrative sequences in Acts.[9]

Comment

■ **1-10** (Scene 1).[10] This unit gives body to the summary report of miracles in 2:43 and the statement about visiting the temple in v. 46. Acts 3:1-10 is a healing story of a traditional type, about which there are two widespread assumptions: that the account comes from tradition[11] and that it is quite similar to Jesus' healing of a cripple in Luke 5:17-26 and Paul's similar action at Lystra in Acts 14:8-11. It would thus constitute one of the Jesus-Peter-Paul parallels in Luke and Acts.[12] The two assumptions are not complementary, for parallel accounts raise the suspicion of composition. In this instance that suspicion is likely to fall on 14:8-11.[13] In support of deriving this story from tradition are its abrupt beginning,[14] the reference to the mysterious "Beautiful Gate" in v. 2, and the awkward transition to the speech in vv. 11-12 (on which see below). The most apparent Lucan additions to the putative tradition are John, whose presence contributes little beyond the unrelieved awkwardness of v. 4 (lit. "Peter, gazing intently at him—along with John—said . . ."); the reference to money in v. 6a; and v. 8b, which overloads the narrative and provides a transition to the next section.[15] In addition is the apparent transposition to 4:22 of the patient's age, a motif that indicates the duration of the suffering from which he has been relieved. This effectively incorporates all of the intervening material into the story.

Formally, the story is a novella, developed with detail and a subsidiary theme, which is then expanded into a lengthier story. In Acts, Luke was moving in a direction similar to that of the Fourth Evangelist. Miracle stories form the core of narrative elaboration.[16] The clumsy repetition visible in v. 9 marks it as the basis of this subsequent elaboration. Verse 46 has prepared the way for the apostles' action, quite unlike such introductions as Mark 3:1. As the story opens, the main characters (who will remain on stage through 4:22[17]) enter: Peter and John motivated (presumably) by piety, the cripple by poverty. Verse 2 evokes an abundance of pathos in

6 On these parallels, see, e.g., Talbert, *Literary Patterns*, 16; and Tannehill, *Narrative Unity*, 2:50–51.

7 See Robert C. Tannehill, "The Composition of Acts 3–5: Narrative Development and Echo Effect," in idem, *The Shape of Luke's Story: Essays on Luke-Acts* (Eugene, Ore.: Wipf & Stock, 2005) 185–219; and Robert W. Funk, *The Poetics of Biblical Narrative* (Sonoma, Calif.: Polebridge, 1988) 75–97.

8 The scenic division is that of Funk, *Narrative Poetics*, 73–91.

9 Acts 3:1–4:31 contains fifty-seven verses. Other lengthy units include the story of Stephen (sixty-nine verses), the conversion of Cornelius (sixty-six verses), and the voyage to Rome (sixty verses).

10 On this passage, see P. Walaskay, "Acts 3:1-10," *Int* 42 (1988) 171–75; Danielle Ellud, "Actes 3:1-11," *EThR* 64 (1989) 95–99; Gilberto Marconi, "History as a Hermeneutical Interpretaion of the Difference between Acts 3:1-10 and 4:8-12," in Gerald O'Collins and Gilberto Marconi, eds., *Luke and Acts* (trans. Matthew J. O'Connell; Festschrift Emilio Rasco; New York: Paulist, 1993) 167–80; M. Dennis Hamm, "Acts 3:1-10: The Healing of the Temple Beggar as Lucan Theology," *Bib* 67 (1986) 305–19; and Mikeal Parsons, *Body and Character in Luke and Acts: The Subversion of Physiognomy in Early Christianity* (Grand Rapids: Baker Academic, 2006) 109–22.

11 So, for a telling instance, Haenchen, 201. See also Lüdemann, 53.

12 Luke 5:17-26 is followed by a symposium with dialogue in 5:27-39; Peter and Paul preach in response to the healing (Acts 3:11-26; 14:14-18).

13 See Lüdemann (159–60), who traces this hypothesis back to Bruno Bauer. (Luke 5:17-26 is based on Mark 2:1-12.)

14 Haenchen, 197. The textual tradition signals this awkwardness through both the placement of the particle δέ before "Peter" (above) and in the D-Text introduction "in those days."

15 Cf. Weiser, 1:108.

16 Note John 5; 9; and 11. Such activity was in

a few words. He is so helpless that he must be carried, an arduous task possibly performed twice per day, day after day, year after year. Peter and John are his first opportunities on this afternoon. Their response to his petition raises his hopes, which are promptly dashed. The comment about money is the first half of a memorable antithesis foreshadowing those of the subsequent address. "In the name of Jesus the Nazorean" the cripple is ordered to walk. Without hesitation he begins—for the first time in his life—not only to walk but to leap for joy. The "name" is the leitmotif of this section of Acts.[18] His transformation draws an excited crowd, whose recognition rounds off the action by underlying the contrast between motionless beggar and bounding beneficiary (v. 10). Wonderful as all this is, it is only the prelude to the full story, as it sets the stage for a confrontation with the authorities.

■ **1-2** These verses introduce the novella.[19] The imperfect tense shows the principal actors converging from different points. This is the first time in Acts where Peter is paired with John, who never takes an independent part in the action.[20] The "hour of prayer" is that of the evening sacrifice.[21] Simultaneously, a lifelong[22] cripple[23] was approaching his conventional pitch.[24] The adverbial "daily" (omitted by the D-Text) shows the contrast between the life of the believers (2:46) and the miserable existence of this unfortunate fellow[25] whose productivity was limited to begging at the "Beautiful Gate."[26]

■ **3-7** These verses comprise the core of the healing. The D-Text of vv. 3-4 is quite different. As proposed by Boismard, it reads *οὗτος ἀτενίσας τοῖς ὀφθαλμοῖς αὐτοῦ καὶ ἰδὼν Πέτρον καὶ Ἰωάννην εἰσίοντας εἰς τὸ ἱερὸν ἠρώτα αὐτοὺς ἐλεημοσύνην. (4) ἐμβλέψας δὲ ὁ Πέτρος εἰς αὐτὸ ἔστη καὶ εἶπεν ἀτένισον εἰς ἐμέ.* ("*The cripple*, **gazing intently with his eyes and** seeing Peter and John **entering** the temple began to ask **them** for alms. **Catching sight** of him Peter **stopped and** said:

accordance with basic rhetorical education, which taught students to produce narrative elaborations of anecdotes and so on.

17 It is characteristic of miracle stories that nothing more is said about the recipient, not even that he became a believer.

18 Acts 2:21, 38; 3:6, 16; 4:7, 10, 12, 17, 18, 30. See Tannehill, *Narrative Unity*, 1:48.

19 The D-Text provides a proper transition with an initial "in those days," and transforms the bald opening *καί* ("and") of v. 2 into the biblical *καὶ ἰδού* ("and lo and behold").

20 See Cadbury and Lake, 31. John is probably selected on the basis of Gal 2:9, which places him on an approximate par with Peter. Note, however, Luke 22:8||Mark 14:13, where these two are given responsibility to prepare for Passover.

21 See the rubrics in Exod 29:38-42; Num 28:1-8. Note also Josephus *Ant.* 14.66. The hours of the daily sacrifices evidently became times of prayer. Cf. Dan 6:10; 9:21 (and *m. Tamid* 5.1; 6.4). Ancients divided the day into twelve hours that varied in length in accordance with the time of year. "The ninth hour" is around 1500, or three o'clock in the afternoon. The D-Text (Boismard, *Texte*, 78) reads "evening" instead of "the ninth hour." This may attempt to improve the unusual word order, in which the adjective "ninth" is a second attributive following the genitive "of prayer."

22 Lit. "from his mother's belly." This trope comes from the LXX: Cadbury and Lake, 31. Only here and in 14:8 does it appear in miracle stories. Cf. also Matt 19:12; Luke 1:15; John 3:4; and Gal 1:15. This characterization succinctly depicts the duration of the illness, the contrast between parental hopes for an unborn child and dour reality, and staves off any counterclaims that the disability was temporary.

23 "Lame" is not an appropriate translation of *χωλός*, since it suggests that the individual could more or less walk. See Pieter W. van der Horst, "Hellenistic Parallels to Acts Chapters 3 and 4," *JSNT* 35 (1989) 37–46, here 37; and Parsons, *Body and Character*, 110–16. D-Texts omit the apparently superfluous *ὑπάρχων* ("being") and thus miss the wordplay in v. 6.

24 Temples were ideal locations for begging, both because of the presence of large numbers of people and the religious duty of almsgiving (on which, see Johnson, 65). According to Dio of Prusa (*Or.* 32.9), Cynics begged at temple gates.

25 The healing of "cripples" (*χωλοί*) is a feature of salvation announced by Jesus (Luke 7:22). They will be invited to the banquet (Luke 14:13, 21). On their status as "outcasts," see Johnson (65), who cites HB and Qumran texts.

26 The nickname is otherwise unattested. For attempts to identify it, see Barrett, 1:179–80. In the face of such useless pedantry, it is tempting to admire Bede's *porta templi speciosa dominus est* ("The beautiful gate of the temple is the Lord") (23 *ad* 3:2, evidently with Luke 13:24; John 10:7 in

'Gaze at me'").[27] In v. 5 this edition reads ἠτένισεν ("gazed") rather than the ἐπεῖχεν ("was attentive to"). Apart from stylistic revision and simplification,[28] the D-Text deletes the awkward role of John. As often, its variants serve to confirm what is almost certainly an earlier text. One source of the awkwardness is that Peter (and John) must take the initiative. This is, in general, viewed as a feature of later stories,[29] but in this instance it is required, for Peter has no reputation as a healer. In its present shape, this appears to be an account of Peter's first miracle. That may derive from tradition, be fortuitous, or be the result of editorial activity.[30] In any case, the account develops slowly, generating suspense.

■ **6** The elegant dative of possession in v. 6a is a Lucan addition serving more than literary purposes. It assures readers that the apostles do not have community funds at their personal disposal, dissociating them from the stereotype of greedy, exploitative religious quacks,[31] even from mendicant missionaries. They carry no money (Luke 9:3). Peter's sentiment is suitable for a philosopher.[32] Utopian communities do without currency.[33] Thus far the story has exposed two poles, each marked by the verb ὑπάρχω ("be"): the man is crippled and must beg; Peter is penniless.

■ **6b-7** These verses collapse that gap with a full and elaborate account of the healing, which involves both command and touch. Peter wisely chooses the appropriate formula: "In the name of Jesus Christ[34] the Nazorean. . . ." This, unlike the formula used in 9:34, for example, introduces the theme of "the name," which will figure in the subsequent debate.[35] The evidence for omission of "get up and" before "walk" is strong (א B D cop[sa]), but form-critical considerations indicate that these two words were omitted because Peter raised the man. Formally, the command is conventional (Matt 9:5; Mark 2:9; Luke 5:23; John 5:8). There are no examples of healings with the bare imperative "walk."[36] The Name works *ex opere operato*. There is no statement about the patient's confidence in Peter's skill or a confession by the patient of his faith in Jesus.[37] The effect is instantaneous, just as it should be. Rather than simply state that he rose, the narrator allows the reader to envision wholeness returning to his feet and legs (and life).[38]

■ **8-10** These verses conclude the story, albeit not in a typical way, for patient and healer(s) do not take separate paths. The D-Text is different: (7b) "He **stood up** (ἐστάθη) immediately, and strength came to his feet and ankles. 8 He began to walk about, rejoicing and leaping. Then he went into the sanctuary with them [omit *walking and leaping and*] praising God."[39] Conzelmann rightly observes that the conventional text, with its repetition of "walking" and "leaping," seems overloaded. He attributes this to redactional preparation for v. 11.[40] That is intelligent, preferable to Barrett's appeal

mind), for he at least understands that identification of a physical site would contribute nothing to interpretation. C. J. Cowton ("The Alms Trader: A Note on Identifying the Beautiful Gate of Acts 3.2," *NTS* 42 [1996] 475–76) notes that any gate used by visitors would do for a beggar.

27 Boismard, *Texte*, 80.

28 The verb ἐπέχω could have been understood as "holding on to." Cadbury and Lake (33) say that there is an implied "mind" or "eyes," with reference to 2 Macc 9:35 et al. See also Barrett, 1:181. For examples of ἐρωτάω with the infinitive (rather than double accusative), see BDF §392 (1), and §409 (5).

29 Bultmann, *History*, 66.

30 Thereafter, initiative comes from others (5:15). The same sequence appears in 9:32-35, where Peter heals Aeneas on his own initiative, after which he is sought (9:38).

31 Famous examples of such scandals include Josephus *Ant.* 18.65-80 (missionaries of Isis), 81-84 (Jewish missionaries), and Ps.-Lucian *Onos* 36–41, developed with greater detail by Apuleius *Metam* 8.24-31.

32 Cf. Lucian *Fug.* 20, where personified Philosophy says, "As to gold or silver, Heracles! I do not want even to own it" (trans. A. M. Harmon, *Lucian V* [LCL; Cambridge, Mass.: Harvard University Press, 1936] 77).

33 So primitive Athens: Plato *Critias* 112B (on which see the excursus "The Summaries of Acts" in the commentary on Acts 2:42-47). Pliny the Elder says that the Essenes have no money (*Hist. nat.* 7.53). The internal Pauline parallel is Acts 20:33.

34 "Christ" is preferable to "messiah" here, as it seems to be a proper name; see Fitzmyer, 28.

35 See above, n. 18.

36 Barrett (1:183) argues for the shorter text.

37 Verse 16 will correct this (see below).

38 See Cadbury and Lake, 33–34, for the physiological details.

39 Boismard, *Texte*, 82–83. Other variants do not affect the meaning.

40 Conzelmann, 23; Barrett, 1:184.

to the lack of final revision. It seems more likely that a later editor simplified the text than that subsequent revision introduced the repetitions. The redundancy effectively underlines the ebullience of the former cripple. Its formal function is to demonstrate the effectiveness of the cure, doing so in language evocative of Isa 35:6 (and Luke 7:22).[41] Verses 9-10 contain another typical confirmatory factor, public acclamation. The crowd's reference to the "Beautiful Gate" produces an *inclusio* with v. 2 (cf. John 9:8-9). The focus remains on the former cripple through v. 11.

■ **8** The verse says that the man accompanied Peter and John into (or toward) the temple, without mention of their progress. The two principal editions of Acts exhibit different understandings of this movement. According to the conventional text, Peter and John heal the man at the gate and then enter "the sanctuary" (*τὸ ἱερόν*). They draw a crowd in the Portico of Solomon, evidently viewed as part of the temple precincts. The D-Text (according to Boismard, *Texte*, 84–85) has a different notion. The apostles exit from the "temple" with the healed person, while the people stand in awe in the Portico of Solomon. This edition evidently takes *τὸ ἱερόν* as "temple building" and views the Portico of Solomon as outside of the "temple." The D-Text is topographically more correct. Dibelius's literary explanation is preferable: the D-Text is later. Those inclined toward historical solutions are likely to prefer the D-Text.[42] The allusion to Isa 35:6 in v. 8, coupled with the reference to more than forty years of disability (4:22), invites a particular symbolic understanding: this healing represents an opportunity for the restoration (cf. 3:21) of Israel.[43] The initial response suggests that this restoration will occur, but this hope will be dashed.

41 On Luke 7:22, see n. 25. *Leucippe* 7.15.3 is a good formal parallel.

42 Literary: Dibelius, *Studies*, 85. Historical: Kirsopp Lake, "Localities in and near Jerusalem Mentioned in Acts," in Lake and Cadbury, *Additional Notes*, 5:474–86, esp. 479–86. Strange believes that Bezae represents the introduction of marginal notes into the text, smoothed out by later editors (*Problem*, 115–19). For a general review, see Cadbury and Lake, 32; and Metzger, *Textual Commentary*, 267–69. Josephus describes this colonnade as a component of Solomon's original construction (*Bell.* 5.184; *Ant.* 8.98). On the basis of John 10:23, it seems likely that there was a tradition associating the Portico of Solomon with the followers of Jesus.

43 Cf. also Parsons, *Body and Character*, 118–19.

3:11—4:4 Peter Addresses the Crowd

**11/ The man who had been healed
would not let go of Peter and
John. Meanwhile the people,
filled with astonishment,
flocked toward them in Solomon's colonnade. 12/ Peter
addressed the gathered crowd:
"My fellow Israelites, Why do
you find this so remarkable?[a]
Why are you staring at us as if
we, by our personal power or
piety, have made him able to
walk? 13/ The God of Abraham,
the God of Isaac, the God of
Jacob, the God of our forebears[b]
has honored his son[c] Jesus.
You people handed him over
and disowned him to Pilate's
face, after he had decided to let
Jesus go. 14/ You, yes you, disowned the Holy and Just One,
demanding the pardoning of
a murderer 15/ and murdering
him who opens the way to life.
But God raised him from the
dead. We are witnesses of him.[d]
16/ God has made this person
you see here, one well known to
you, strong because of confidence in the name of Jesus. The
confidence that comes through
Jesus has given him full health,
and that right before your eyes.[e]**

**17/ "I am certain, sisters and broth-
ers, that you acted in ignorance,
as did your rulers, 18/ but God,
who had predicted through all
the prophets that the Messiah
would suffer, fulfilled those
predictions in the manner
described. 19/ Therefore, you
must change your hearts and
orient yourselves to God. Get
the slates of your sins wiped
clean, 20/ so that God may
provide relief from the pressures of this age and send
Jesus, designated to be your
Messiah. 21/ He has to remain
in heaven until the time for
universal restoration arrives.
Through the holy prophets God
has spoken of that restoration
from the beginning. 22/ Moses
said, 'Your sovereign God will
raise up a prophet from your
midst, just as he raised up me.
Attend to whatever he tells
you.[f] 23/ Anyone who does not
attend to that prophet will be
rooted out from the people.'**

a *Or*: "Why are you surprised by this person?"

b There is a textual question as to whether the term "God" is to be placed before each proper name. Since it cannot be attributed to assimilation to the LXX of Exod 3:6 or to the Gospels (Luke 20:37||Mark 12:26), the longer form may be preferable (but see Acts 7:32).

c *Or*: "servant."

d *Or*: "of this."

e An alternative version that does not emend the text: "and of the surety of his name. The name of Jesus, as well as the confidence that it brings, has restored this person you see here, one who is well-known to you."

f The D-Text reads "Moses said *to our ancestors*. . . ." As often, the MSS fluctuate between "your" and "our."

24/ Every articulate prophet from Samuel on announced the coming of these days. 25/ You are the heirs of the prophets and the covenant that God fashioned with your forebears when he told Abraham, 'Every family on earth will be blessed through your descendant.' 26/ God raised up his son[g] for you first of all and sent him to give each and all of you the opportunity to abandon your wicked ways."

4:1/ While Peter and John were addressing the crowd, the priests, the chief of the temple police, and the Sadducees burst onto the scene. 2/ These people were fed up with the apostles for teaching in public, specifically for arguing the case of Jesus as proof of the resurrection of the dead,[h] 3/ so they apprehended them and, as it was by now evening, had them put into custody until the next day. 4/ Many who had heard the message became believers. The number of men alone had risen to about five thousand.

g *Or*: "servant."

h *Or*: "For saying that Jesus was the means of resurrection. . . ."

Analysis

(Scene 2: I.B-C) The balance of chap. 3 conforms its structure to that of chap. 2: a miracle that draws a crowd, which is rewarded with an oration. The sermon of Acts 2 ended with a successful call for repentance. Repentance is also the closing note of 3:12-26, but the aftermath is arrest by angry officials. The general contents of this sermon closely resemble those of its predecessor, but Luke avoids vain repetition. The style is different, attempting Greek antithesis,[1] and the christological images also vary.

Chapter 2 presented a "Son of David" Christology, while this speech seems to evoke the servant model, refers also to the "Prophet like Moses," and employs other concepts or titles: "holy and righteous one,"[2] "author of life, "the Messiah who suffered and is appointed to return at a later time, and "the descendant of Abraham." Luke has packed a great variety of christological imagery into these initial addresses.[3] This profusion alone rebuts any contention that the speech preserves "primitive" traditions traceable to an actual Petrine sermon.[4] Remarkably, there is no reference to baptism or to the gift of the Spirit. This speech is no less artificial than the Pentecost address, for here, as in 2:15, Peter attributes a viewpoint to the audience. Here

1 See Haenchen, 210.

2 Verse 14 links "holy" and "righteous" with a single article. They are not presented as distinct titles. Luke may have taken the combination from Mark 6:20, where it is used of John the Baptist. These adjectives frame the Lucan characterization of Jesus: Luke 1:35 (holy; cf. also 4:34) and 23:47 (righteous; cf. also 7:52; 22:14).

3 See the discussion of these titles in Wilckens, *Missionsreden*, 156–78; Zehnle, *Discourse*, 47–53; and Weiser, 1:113–15, who has many references to secondary discussions.

4 For refutation of the claim that some of the christological titles in Acts 3 are primitive, see Pervo, *Dating*, 335–36. On the difficulty of identifying "primitive theology" in this speech in general, see Soards, *Speeches*, 40 n. 84.

he takes the position that the audience believes that the healing derives from the apostles' personal powers. Although this belief may have been typical of the Greco-Roman environment—Luke can come rather close to it himself—it is not the conventional Jewish view, in which the primary question is the basis of authority (cf. Mark 3:22-30). That is the very question posed by the officials who examine Peter and John in 4:7. The argument boils down to the claim that the healing proves Jesus to have been holy and innocent and, as a matter of fact, the predicted Messiah, obliging the hearers to repent of their assent to his execution. The logic of this rhetoric is accessible only to Christians who believe that Jesus is the Messiah and that the miracle substantiates that claim.

Because vv. 12-16 take the miracle as a point of departure, it may appear that this sermon is apposite to its circumstances, but the connection is no less superficial than it was in the Pentecost address. Peter does not say, "Give God, rather than us, the glory for this healing," but "God glorified his servant Jesus, whom you killed." The convoluted v. 16 introduces the theme of πίστις ("faith," "trust," "confidence"), a fine subject but not one that is relevant to this story. Such confidence is a component of the parallel in 14:9, but it is absent here and cannot be supplied by implication.[5] If Luke were following the practice recommended for ancient historians, which was to compose speeches portraying what might well have been said upon a particular occasion, he was not especially successful. These negative judgments are not apt, for, as more or less always, the speeches are addressed to the reader rather than to the dramatic setting. The structure of this deliberative speech[6] is rather clear, but its style is not: "The construction of almost every sentence in this speech is obscure, and some of it is scarcely translatable, but the general meaning is plain."[7]

Although there is general agreement that this sermon has two major parts, disagreement arises about the point of division: at v. 17 or at v. 19.[8] The καὶ νῦν ("and now") and the vocative "brothers and sisters" of v. 17 are important clues,[9] and the content also favors this division. Krodel identifies a ring composition in each segment:[10]

- I. The Healing (and the "Problem") 3:12-16.
  - A. V. 12. The healing was not wrought by human power.
    - B. V. 13a. God glorified his servant,
      - C. V. 13b. Whom you betrayed and denied.
      - C'. Vv. 14a-15a. You denied and killed the source of life.
    - B'. V. 15b. God raised him.
  - A'. V. 16. The healing came about by faith in the power of the name.
- II. The Solution (and the Healing of All) 3:17-26.
  - A. Vv. 17-18 The evil (but ignorant, despite the prophets) ways of Jerusalem.
    - B. V. 19. Repent and be forgiven,
      - C. Vv. 20-21a. So that you may be fit to receive the Messiah.
        - D. Vv. 21b-23. Function of Scripture and citation
          - E. V. 24. All the prophets have proclaimed this message.
          - E'. V. 25a. You are heirs of the prophets.
        - D'. V. 25b. Scripture citation.
      - C'. V. 26a. God sent the son
    - B'. V. 26b. so that you might turn
  - A'. V. 26c. from your evil ways.

The two parts are joined by the use of παῖς ("child," "servant,") in vv. 13 and 26. This outline confirms that

5 In miracle stories, the fundamental meaning of πίστις is confidence on the part of the patient or others in the possibility of the miracle. The patient here was looking for money.

6 George Kennedy (*Rhetorical Criticism*, 118–19) identifies vv. 12-18 as judicial rhetoric. Luke would not have been the only author to commingle the rhetorical species. As Kennedy observes, the "judicial" portion is the presupposition to the deliberative argument. The speaker must convince the hearers that they have done something that demands repentance.

7 Cadbury and Lake, 34–35.

8 For different approaches to the structure, see Soards, *Speeches*, 39.

9 Note the use of a similar formula in Paul's speech at Miletus (20:22, 25, 32).

10 Krodel, 18–19, 99–108. (Part II of this outline does not follow Krodel.) For a similar outline, see Talbert, *Reading Acts*, 55.

the deliberative speech was fortunately completed. The officials did not interrupt before Peter could finish his plea.[11] Had 4:4, which provides the sermon with a suitable conclusion quite like that of 2:41, followed directly on 3:26, nothing would seem amiss. Verse 11 awkwardly serves to get the crowd (which one may imagine as quite numerous) into a suitable place. The narrator touchingly depicts the former cripple as unwilling to let go of his benefactors.

Comment

■ **12-16** (I) The grounds for Peter's objection are difficult to fathom, since the onlookers know that the former cripple is praising God (v. 9). Apart from providing grounds for a strong antithesis, this question prepares the way for 4:7. Verse 13 dramatically introduces a new subject: the God of Israel. The speech presumes that Jesus was familiar to the audience. In fact, 3:13 depends on 2:22. The kerygmatic summary[12] of vv. 13-15 denounces the hearers for their role in the condemnation of Jesus.[13] Antithesis, alliteration, and assonance abound. Although Pilate[14] acquitted Jesus,[15] the public preferred a murderer. The viewpoint is that of the Lucan passion narrative.[16] The learned tradition strongly supports viewing παῖς in v. 13 in terms of the suffering servant of Isa 52:13,[17] but, as Soards observes, Greek readers innocent of the Semitic background might well understand it to mean "son."[18] Suffering receives no more emphasis here than elsewhere. Conzelmann renders as "servant," but attributes the epithet to the liturgical tradition, where it is an "honorific title."[19] The word ἀρχηγός ("the one who opens the way to life") comes from the world of Hellenism, which had a great interest in founders, inventors, discoverers, and origins of all sorts. Luke does not wish to ascribe to Jesus the "invention" of (genuine) life. For him, the meaning may be that Jesus is leader by virtue of his standing as the first to rise from the dead.[20] The final relative, rendered "We are witnesses of him," exhibits

11 "Not until all has been said that needs to be said is the speech interrupted" (Talbert, *Reading Acts*, 56).

12 On the use of the "relative connective," see BDF §458. Eduard Norden identified the importance of participial and relative clauses for the recognition of creedal material (*Agnostos Theos: Untersuchungen zur Formengeschichte religiöser Rede* [1913; reprinted, Darmstadt: Wissenschaftliche Buchgesellschaft, 1974] 380–87.

13 The text is emphatic: ὑμεῖς μέν ("*YOU*"). There is no true balancing of δέ to make a comparison or contrast. D 6 *pc* omit the particle. The repeated references to denial in vv. 13 and 14 do not suit the character of the speaker, Peter. Contrast *Act. Pet.* 7, in which the apostle freely admits his failure in denying Christ.

14 Pilate would still have been in office, by any reconstruction of the dramatic date. The text inclines readers to view him as a figure of the past rather than the current governor.

15 The D-Text corrects this remarkable claim to "wished to release him," conforming the text to Luke 23:20. Other D-Text readings in vv. 13-15 intensify the condemnation. After "handed over" in v. 13 the D-Text adds a clarifying "to condemnation" (εἰς κρίσιν). In v. 14, D reads ἐβαρύνατε ("oppressed") instead of ἠρνήσασθε and underscores the antithesis by supplementing "murderer" with the infinitive "to live and . . . ." Verse 15 notes that the killing took place by crucifixion. Epp (*Tendency*, 56) argues that these changes are more than the usual pedantic expansions.

16 On the relation of vv. 13-15 to the Lucan passion narrative, see Wilckens, *Missionsreden*, 127–31.

17 In Isa 52:13, the noun παῖς is associated with the verb δοξάζω, as in Acts 3:13.

18 Soards, *Speeches*, 40–41, with n. 84.

19 Conzelmann, 28. He notes *1 Clem.* 59:2-4; *Did.* 9:2-3; *Barn.* 6:1; 9:2; *Mart. Pol.* 14:1; 20:2. On "servant," see Wilckens, *Missionsreden*, 163–68.

20 Cf. 1 Cor 15:20 and Acts 26:23. On the term in this context, see Cadbury and Lake, 36; Wilckens, *Missionsreden*, 175–76; Barrett 1:197–98; and, in general, Knox, *Hellenistic Elements*, 26–27. For the broader context, see Gerhard Delling, "ἄρχω," *TDNT* 1:478–89, esp. 487–88. Religious use focuses on founders of communities, often a "hero" (on this, see Erwin Rohde, *Psyche: The Cult of Souls and Belief in Immortality among the Greeks* [trans. W. B. Hillis; London: Routledge & Kegan Paul, 1925] 527–28, 146 n. 51; 147 n. 56; 149 n. 75). Those who look for a specific Christian context postulate an exodus (Mosaic) or Davidic typology, both of which could be arguable here. On the former, see Leopold Sabourin, *Priesthood: A Comparative Study* (Studies in the History of Religions; Numen Supp. 25; Leiden: Brill, 1973) 210; advocates of the latter include Paul-Gerhard Müller, *ΧΡΙΣΤΟΣ ΑΡΧΗΓΟΣ: Der Religionsgeschichtliche und theologische Hintergrund einer*

the same difficulty as 2:32 (*q.v.*). This phrase, "we are witnesses to him [= Jesus]," apparently functions apart from grammatical context. The antithetic style of vv. 13-15 foreshadows the full-blown "Asianism" of Melito.[21]

■ **16** The verse appears impossible.[22] Acts evidently wishes to say that invocation of Jesus' name has healing power, but/and that faith in Jesus is a factor, that is, that the name does not work "magically."[23] Shifting the initial phrase, καὶ ἐπὶ τῇ πίστει τοῦ ὀνόματος αὐτοῦ, in effect, "We are witness of him and to (the power of) faith in his name," is unlikely;[24] the text is probably corrupt. One approach to emendation is to postulate καὶ ἐπὶ τῇ πίστει τοῦ ὀνόματος αὐτοῦ as a gloss that has entered the text.[25] That gloss would presumably have been designed to clarify the meaning of the pronoun "his" in καὶ ἡ πίστις ἡ δι᾽ αὐτοῦ (lit. "and the faith through him"). The selected alternative takes τὸ ὄνομα αὐτοῦ ("his name") as a gloss on the same prepositional phrase, yielding καὶ ἐπὶ τῇ πίστει τοῦ ὀνόματος αὐτοῦ τοῦτον ὃν θεωρεῖτε καὶ οἴδατε, ἐστερέωσεν, καὶ ἡ πίστις ἡ δι᾽ αὐτοῦ ἔδωκεν αὐτῷ τὴν ὁλοκληρίαν ταύτην ἀπέναντι πάντων ὑμῶν, a *parallelismus membrorum* evidently fashioned for rhetorical purposes.[26] The miracle, of which the hearers are witnesses, shows that Jesus was wrongly executed, and the apostles can verify that he returned from the dead.

■ **17-26** (II)[27] The mode of proof shifts from eyewitness to scriptural testimony. With a new, warmer form of address, Peter mollifies his accusation. Those who killed Jesus acted in ignorance. "Ignorance" of the truth is an

---

neutestamentlichen Christsuprädikation (Europäische Hochschulschriften Reihe 23, vol. 28; Frankfurt: Peter Lang, 1973); and George Johnston, "Christ as Archegos," *NTS* 27 (1981) 381–85. Müller, who also contributed the *EDNT* article on ἀρχηγός (1:163–64), argues for "leader" as the proper translation. Weaver (*Plots,* 124 n. 119) prefers "founder." It is doubtful that the author of Acts reflected on the religio-historical background of this fine-sounding title.

21 The homily of Melito of Sardis *On the Pascha*, which is usually dated c. 160–170, exemplifies both the liturgical features first analyzed by Norden (n. 12) and the florid rhetorical style known as "Asianic." See Stuart G. Hall, *Melito of Sardis On Pascha and Fragments* (Oxford Early Christian Texts; London: Clarendon, 1979). For a brief review of the florid type of "Asianic" rhetoric, see George Kennedy, *The Art of Rhetoric in the Roman World* (Princeton: Princeton University Press, 1972) 97–100.

22 The *NRSV* renders: "And by faith in his name, his name itself has made this man strong, whom you see and know; and the faith that is through Jesus has given him this perfect health in the presence of all of you." This is not English.

23 The text combines two theological views of the healing: (1) "The name caused the healing" is susceptible to a magical understanding. (2) "Faith caused the healing" allows for two different views of faith: confidence in the power of Jesus' name (a common use of πίστις in healing stories), and "faith deriving from Jesus" or the Name. In the adjectival prepositional phrase ἡ πίστις ἡ δι᾽ αὐτοῦ, the pronoun can be construed either as neuter, referring to the name, or as masculine, referring to either Jesus or to the patient. Metzger (*Textual Commentary,* 270–72), has a full discussion of the issues. Luke has introduced the element of faith to ward off the charge of magical practice. On "magic," see pp. 207–9.

24 This idea was supported by F. C. Burkitt in 1919, according to Frederick J. Foakes Jackson and Kirsopp Lake, "The Internal Evidence of Acts," in eidem, *Prolegomena II* (vol. 2 of *The Beginnings of Christianity* [5 vols.; New York: Macmillan, 1920–33] 121–204, esp. 142). A difficulty is that μάρτυς is not elsewhere used with the dative. See the discussion of Metzger, *Textual Commentary*, 270–72.

25 According to Bruce (142), Barrett proposed in 1984 that the author added this phrase to his source.

26 According to Boismard (*Texte*, 88), the Peshitta and an old French version omit τὸ ὄνομα αὐτοῦ. If correct, this may reflect either an early correction or, possibly, an earlier text. The Old Latin h omits the prepositional phrase ἡ δι᾽ αὐτοῦ, which improves the text. Bezae (Greek only) reads καὶ ἐπὶ τῇ πίστει τοῦ ὀνόματος αὐτοῦ τοῦτον θεωρεῖτε καὶ οἴδατε, ὅτι ἐστερέωσεν ("And in faith in his name you see this person and know that he has been made strong"). This offers some relief. Boismard views the omission of the relative as the result of haplography. Finally, it is possible that ἡ πίστις ἡ δι᾽ αὐτοῦ refers to *fides quae* (cf. Moule, *Idiom Book*, 58).

27 See the detailed analysis of 3:19-26 in Carroll, *Response,* 137–54.

important theme in Jewish and Christian missionary and apologetic literature.[28] The past behavior of (repentant) polytheists may be overlooked. For Luke, "ignorance" levels the playing field for both Jews (here) and gentiles (17:23, 30).[29] The Jews did not know that "they" killed God's son; gentiles were not aware of the true God. The obvious preparation for this is Luke 23:34 ("Father, forgive them; for they do not know what they are doing."), a verse excluded from the text by N-A[27].[30]

■ **18** The verse states a dogmatic early Christian presupposition to biblical exegesis:[31] the prophetic tradition in its entirety had announced that the Messiah would suffer. Those who examine the surface meaning of the HB will have to agree with Cadbury and Lake: "None of the prophets, rather than all of them, made this prophecy."[32] At this juncture, the dramatic audience would have decided that Peter was drunk, crazy, or abominably ignorant, but for the actual audience—Christian readers of Acts—the claim requires no justification. The logical consequences of this action, execution of the Messiah, follow. The audience is summoned to a change of view.

■ **19-21** These verses constitute a single sentence, containing a twofold call to repentance linked to two promises, the second of which has two parts. *Μετανοέω* is an intellectual image ("change one's mind"), while *ἐπιστρέφω* is concrete ("turn around"). The verbs are also combined in 26:20.[33] Conzelmann says that this views conversion as including changes both of mind and conduct.[34] The relation between the two purpose clauses is not certain.[35] Barrett says that the first "introduces the immediate personal consequence of repentance," and the second "the wider cosmic-historical consequence."[36] Both are corporate, however. The second includes the arrival of both (lit. "times of refreshment";[37] *καιροὶ ἀναψύξεως*) and the dispatch of the Messiah.[38] It is difficult to establish sequential and consequential relations. General repentance/conversion as a prelude to the parousia is a reasonable postulate,[39] but one might expect the arrival of the Messiah to precede rather than follow relief. An additional question is the relation between the "times of refreshment" and the era of universal restoration (*χρόνων ἀποκαταστάσεως πάντων*). Are these essentially synonymous? Luke has almost certainly made use of some traditional material here—witness the atypical words and concepts. Questions include his source(s) and the implications of them,

---

28 In the NT, note Eph 4:18; 1 Pet 1:14; 1 Tim 1:13; and 2 Pet 2:12. Other references include Ignatius *Eph.* 19:3; *Preaching of Peter*, frg. 4. For a somewhat casuistic approach, see *Hermas Man.* 29; *Sim.* 60. Examples from the Acts include *Act. John* 107.14-15 and *Act. Pet.* 2.21-25.There are many examples in apologetic literature, e.g., Justin *1 Apol.* 7.5; 12.11(*bis*); 61.10; *2 Apol.* 14.1; Athenagoras *Leg.* 2.6; 28.4; and Melito *Apol.* Frg. 1.3. Christian writers took up the theme from Hellenistic Judaism, e.g., *3 Macc.* 5:27; *Jos. Asen.* 13:11-13; and *T. Jud.* 19:3. On the subject, see Rudolf Bultmann, "ἀγνοέω," *TDNT* 1:116–21, esp. 116–19

29 Ignorance does not convey absolution in Acts, but it does leave open the possibility of forgiveness and thus hope. For other uses of this theme, note Wis 14:22; Rom 1:18-32 (ignorance is no excuse); and Acts 13:27, where it is also less than complimentary.

30 On Luke 23:34, see the comments on Acts 7:60. The D-Text of Acts 3:17 reads "*Gentlemen* (ἄνδρες ἀδελφοί), *we* know that <u>*you*</u>, *for your part*, did *an evil deed*, in ignorance. . . ." The first two changes accommodate to the context or convention. Addition of the emphatic pronoun (ὑμεῖς), "for your part" (μέν), and the object "evil deed" make the clause polemical. They may have been ignorant, but what the Jews did was wrong and quite against the will of God.

31 This view is as old as the conviction that Jesus is the Messiah. It is present in the pre-Pauline creed stated in 1 Cor 15:3.

32 Cadbury and Lake, 37.

33 The verb ἐπιστρέφω appears nine other times in Acts (seven in Luke), while μετανοέω is found in three additional places in Acts (nine in Luke),

34 Conzelmann, 29; for details, see idem, *Theology*, 99–101.

35 The formal variation (one uses preposition with infinitive, the other ὅπως ἄν with the subjunctive) is not significant.

36 Barrett, 1:203.

37 The phrase "times of refreshment" evokes, without description, the leisure and abundance of the eschatological era. On this, see Pervo, "PANTA KOINA," 187–92.

38 The phrase ἀπὸ προσώπου τοῦ κυρίου (v. 20) is difficult. "From the presence of the Lord" would translate the idiom (BDAG, 888 *s.v.* προσώπου), but in English this suggests that God is present. It seems preferable to view the idiom as indicating the source of refreshment.

39 Cf. 2 Pet 3:12, which moralizes the theme.

that is, whether this is "the most primitive Christology of all,"[40] and whether it might reflect the views of Peter and/or the first believers in Jerusalem.

In the parallel verse of the Pentecost address (2:38) Peter also summons the audience to repent and receive forgiveness of sins, but the means thereof is baptism and the result, the gift of the Holy Spirit. That is without doubt Luke's primary theological understanding. If this is taken as a base, the "periods of refreshment" would be the present eschatological blessings enjoyed by the baptized, followed—at some unspecified point—by the parousia. Acts 3:19-21 coordinates the Christology of the speech in Acts 2, which states that because Jesus has gone to the realm of God[41] he can bestow the Spirit. A somewhat different, and probably preferable, interpretation follows the rhetorical doubling and regards "periods of refreshment" and "times of restoration" as synonymous.[42] In any case Conzelmann is, at least in part, correct.[43] This passage asserts that there is to be an interval between the two appearances of the Messiah and that the contribution of the Jews to his death was not an unpardonable sin. Just how Luke came upon the atypical expressions in these verses is a matter for (not necessarily fruitless) conjecture.[44] Elements of Lucan style are readily identifiable.[45] In conclusion: although the author may have utilized some traditional material, it has been integrated into Lucan thought and shaped by the context.[46] The lack of reference to baptism and the Spirit is a further indication that the speech addresses its readers rather than the dramatic audience.

■ **21b-25** This portion of the speech supports the claim that all has happened in accordance with God's plan by appeal to prophetic tradition,[47] not, however, by citing an apocalyptic text, but through asserting that Jesus is the "prophet like Moses" predicted in Deut 18:15.[48] The focus of this speech is on the "first" sending (v. 26), rather than the "second" (v. 20). Although a good deal of material from disparate sources suggests

40 This is the thesis of John A. T. Robinson, in an essay of that title, first published in 1956 (= "The Most Primitive Christology of All," in idem, *Twelve New Testament Studies* [SBT 34; London: SCM, 1962] 139–53).

41 The term δέξασθαι ("receive") is based on a common Greek petition or declaration that the gods welcome or provide suitable hospitality for the deserving (BDAG, 221, *s.v.* δέχομαι, 3). "Must" affirms the view that the absence of Jesus is in accordance with the will and plan of God.

42 So John B. Polhill, *Acts* (NAC 26; Nashville: Broadman, 1992) 134; Jervell, 166–68; and Eduard Schweizer, "ἀνάψυξις," *TDNT* 9:664–65. Carroll (*Response*, 137–48) argues that both nouns apply to the present of Acts, since the mission is the restoration of Israel. See also Turner, *Power*, 309.

43 Conzelmann, 29.

44 The verb ἐξαλείφω is not "primitive." Col 2:14 suggests that it is at home in the Deutero-Pauline world. Note also *1 Clem.* 18:2, 9 (cit.) and *2 Clem.* 13:1. Phrases like "from the face of" (ἀπὸ προσώπου) and "through the mouth of" (διὰ στόματος) are Septuagintalisms. Verse 20 is related to Isa 32:15, notably in the (presumably much later) version of Symmachus: ἕως ἂν ἐπέλθῃ ἐφ᾽ ὑμᾶς ἀνάψυξις ἐξ ὕψους. (In place of ἀνάψυξις LXX reads πνεῦμα!) The D-Text adds ὑμῖν, evidently conforming the text to Isaiah. The term "restoration" has prompted proposals to link the theology of vv. 19-21 with the circle of John the Baptist. See Otto Bauernfeind, "Tradition und Komposition in dem Apokatastasisspruch Apostelgeschichte 3,20f," in Otto Betz, Martin Hengel and Peter Schmidt, eds., *Abraham unser Vater: Juden und Christen im Gespräch über die Bibel: Festschrift für Otto Michel zum 60. Geburtstag* (Leiden: Brill, 1963) 13–23; cf. also Stephen G. Wilson, *Luke and the Pastoral Epistles* (London: SPCK, 1979) 79; and Plümacher, *Lukas*, 92. This is unlikely, for there is no reference to judgment, a leading theme of the Baptizer's message. See also Roloff (72–73), who refers to Romans 9–11, esp. 11:25-36, for the missionary context.

45 The verb προχειρίζω ("arrange in advance" [v. 20]) is an important Lucan concept. See also its use in the speeches of 22:14; 26:16. Both the verbal form of "restoration" and the nouns "times and seasons" appear in 1:6-7, indicating that the statements are parallel. Note also Luke 21:24 (the "times [καιροί] of the gentiles").

46 This is the judgment of Polhill, 134–35.

47 Verse 21b is a Lucan formulation (Luke 1:70). Carroll (*Response*, 140 n. 82) notes a number of correspondences between Luke 1:70-75 (the Benedictus) and Acts 3:19-26. The D-Text omits "from the beginning" (ἀπ᾽ αἰῶνος), perhaps on the pedantic grounds that there were no human prophets in the beginning. For similar hyperbole, see Acts 15:7, 18. The expression "all the prophets" is Lucan (Luke 11:50; 13:28; 24:27; Acts 3:18, 24; 10:43).

48 Deut 18:15-20 was a key text in early Christianity (Mark 9:7 parr.; John 1:21; 5:46; Luke 7:39; 24:25;

the development of a prophet with messianic features, Luke's "prophetic Christology" follows a different path.[49] For Luke, (the earthly) Jesus is more a prophet like Moses (and Elijah, etc.) than a messiah endowed with prophetic qualities.[50]

Judgment appears in the threat cited, with modifications,[51] from Lev 23:29: those who do not listen to Jesus and heed the call to repent will be expelled from the people of God.[52] This warning is a mirror of the promise in 2:39. Luke is foreshadowing the emergence of conflict associated with the rejection of the message by "the Jews." Verse 24 postulates, with a maximum of solemnity and a minimum of clarity, the uniformity of the prophetic tradition on this matter.[53] The speech is moving rapidly toward its climax and close. As heirs of the prophets, the auditors enjoy a privileged status that they must use or lose. They are also heirs of the abruptly introduced Abrahamic covenant,[54] a status that permits a hint of the universal mission. Verses 25-26 reveal Luke's appropriation of Pauline theology. Gentiles can also be heirs of Abraham and thus of the covenant,[55] but the announcement is made to Jews first.[56] The repeated second person, while rhetorically appropriate, reveals a difference between Paul and Luke. It is no longer "we" who are Jews but "you people."[57] The Jews have become the other. Repeatedly, they had the first chance, and repeatedly they rejected the offer, as Acts will demonstrate. Fulfillment of the promise to Abraham began with Jesus' call to repentance. Once more, Luke abolishes a potential gap between "the earthly Jesus" and "the heavenly Christ."[58] The gap between gentiles and Jews also has narrowed: Jews wishing to share in the promise to Abraham must repent.[59]

Richard Zehnle's study of the speeches in Acts 2 and 3 concluded that Acts 2 is a summary of Lucan theology, whereas Acts 3 attempts to depict a specific appeal to Jews. He inclines to attribute Acts 3:12-26 to sources, but allows for the possibility that the author is responsible for the "archaizing,"[60] a view that Conzelmann endorses with complete confidence.[61] Zehnle's final comment on this speech is: "However, if it is decided that the material is *not* in itself primitive, then it must be conceded that Luke intended it to be so." His own notes and citations go a long way toward proving the thesis that Acts 3 is not "primitive." Luke's sources, of whatever sort,

---

as well as Acts 7:37). Zehnle (*Discourse*, 75–89) traces the various aspects of the Moses typology and their relevance for Acts. Acts 3:22 is directly imitated in Ps. Clem. *Rec.* 1.36.2, as shared deviations from the LXX and inclusion of a paraphrase of Lev 23:29 prove. On the text of the citation, see Barrett, 1:208–9.

49 Barrett (1:207–8) gives a short and sharp review of the texts and hypotheses about a "prophetic messiah."

50 It is possible to trace a line, through Theophilus of Antioch, from Luke to the "Word/person" Christology associated with Antioch. See Pervo, *Dating*, 327.

51 The LXX of Lev 23:29 says that "all who do not humble themselves on that day" (ἥτις μὴ ταπεινωθήσεται ἐν αὐτῇ τῇ ἡμέρᾳ ταύτῃ) will be excluded. This is an example of the Christian corruption/modification of Scripture. See Barrett, 1:209–10.

52 Haenchen (209) says, "The idea that the Christians are the true Israel is here brought into sharp relief."

53 Verse 24 is not a true sentence, as it lacks a verb. The syntax confounds two ways of saying "starting with Samuel and continuing thereafter." See Haenchen, 209; and Barrett, 1:210–11.

54 Note, however, that v. 13 introduced the name of Abraham, thus laying the groundwork for this theme.

55 Verse 25b is not a direct citation of a particular verse but a conflation of Gen 12:3; 18:18; and 22:18. Gal 3:16 may have influenced Luke's argument here.

56 Abraham: Gal 3:6-18; Jews first: Rom 1:16, etc. On these dependencies (and the use of πατριαί), see Pervo, *Dating*, 77, 104–5, 297.

57 The choice between "your" and "our" "ancestors" in v. 25 is a text-critical dilemma. "Your" corresponds to the subject of the sentence ("you") and is preferable.

58 Note also the use of "raise" in v. 25, where ἀναστήσας ὁ θεὸς τὸν παῖδα (lit. "God, raising his son/servant") could, at first glance, appear to refer to the resurrection, but means instead the "raising up" of a prophet.

59 In theory ἐν τῷ ἀποστρέφειν ἕκαστον could be transitive, "by causing each of you to turn away from your sins," but the meaning is almost certainly intransitive, "If each of you turns."

60 See the conclusions of Zehnle, *Discourse*, 75.

61 Conzelmann, 29.

probably came from contemporary Jewish-Christian thought.[62]

Haenchen tended to regard the quest for the sources of Acts as a red herring.[63] Acts 3 is—to shift metaphors—one of the sharpest arrows in his quiver, for the miracle story in 3:1-10, although based on tradition, does no more to put scholars in touch with the earliest days of the movement than does the Coptic *Act of Peter*, while the speech of vv. 12-26 is, in its present form, Lucan.[64] This address also illustrates the contribution of intertextual studies, a discipline that assumes that every text is a web of allusions, known and unknown. The difficulty of identifying the specific contours of a possible source is not limited to vv. 19-21; none of the scriptural citations in vv. 22-23, 25 is an exact quotation. Luke did not work with scissors and paste. Although it would be lazy to attribute all of the differences between the speeches of Acts 2 and 3 to the desire for rhetorical variation, that well-known Lucan proclivity is a partial answer to the alleged difficulties of comparison.[65]

Haenchen's occasionally exaggerated disdain for sources allowed him to ask the important question: Why has Luke given what amounts to a repeat of the sermon in Acts 2?[66] Despite some theological variation, theology does not provide an answer. Literary criticism does. The speech provides a basis for the advancement of the plot. Opposition now erupts, not from the people but from officials and Sadducees. One ostensible warrant for their action is that Peter is teaching in the temple precincts.[67] The contrast between the promise of 2:39 and the threat of 3:23 will be, in retrospect, a foreshadowing of the ultimate Jewish reaction to the message. Acts 3 illuminates chap. 2 by contrast. The events of Pentecost indicate the course events would have followed had the officials left the movement alone. The ultimate irony is that growth will be unhindered by opposition.

Various functionaries arrest Peter and John. Readers of the Gospel know what to expect: some sort of rigged trial by the Sanhedrin, for the Sanhedrin[68] of Acts can and will administer capital punishment. Despite its power and solemnity, the authorities do not have an easy day. Nonplussed by the courage and skill with which the apostles rebuke their tyrannous behavior and the charge of practicing magic, the body must also deal with its ineptness at including the former cripple in their

62 Zehnle was still influenced by the logical assumption that "Jewish" means "early." The opposite is more nearly true. As Jervell understood, there was a strong resurgence of "Jewish Christianity" *after* 70 CE. Ephesians and *1 Clement* are two quite different examples of this phenomenon, which is germane to Acts.

63 See his preface (vii) and, on this passage, 203–12.

64 See, in addition to the foregoing comments and references, William S. Kurz, "Acts 3:19-26 as a Test of the Role of Eschatology in Lukan Christology," *SBLSP 1977* (Missoula, Mont.: Scholars Press, 1977) 309–23; Schneider, 1:315, 323–27; Roloff (70–79), who analyzes the details with considerable care and regards this, along with Stephen's speech in Acts 7, as "archaizing," still holds that it is a Lucan composition. Barrett (1:186–214) holds to the view that much of the speech is based on "an independent piece of tradition which Luke inserted at this point . . ." (189).

65 On Luke's penchant for "elegant variation," see Cadbury, "Four Features," 87–102.

66 Haenchen, 211.

67 Jesus also taught in the temple (Luke 19:47; 21:37).

68 The text does not identify this assembly as "the Sanhedrin." When the word appears in v. 15, it may well refer to a place. Jack T. Sanders (*The Jews in Luke-Acts* [Philadelphia: Fortress Press, 1987] 4–5) argues that this is the normal (but not exclusive) meaning of the word in Acts. It is no longer possible to assume that there was a standing governing body called "the Sanhedrin," roughly equivalent to the Roman Senate, that sat in Jerusalem. "Sanhedrins" were, in effect, meetings of advisors to the high priest. See, e.g., Martin Goodman, *The Ruling Class of Judaea: The Origins of the Jewish Revolt against Rome A.D. 66–70* (Cambridge: Cambridge University Press, 1987) 112–16; E. P. Sanders, *Judaism: Practice and Belief 63 BCE–66 CE* (Philadelphia: Trinity Press International, 1992) 472–84; and Fergus Millar, *The Roman Near East: 31 BC–AD 337* (Cambridge, Mass.: Harvard University Press, 1993) 360–61. Luke does assume that there was an authoritative body with police powers and the authority to execute capital punishment. As Steve Mason shows, Luke's picture is quite similar to that of Josephus ("Chief Priests, Sadducees, Pharisees and Sanhedrin in Acts," in Bauckham, *Palestinian Setting*, 115–77, esp. 175–76.

proceedings. He will not be a useful witness for them. An executive session elicits no better plan than a gag order that the apostles defy with impunity. The narrative closes with an eloquent prayer offered by the entire community, followed by a powerful epiphany.[69]

■ **4:1-4** These verses are both the formal conclusion to the speech and the introduction to the subsequent trial. The statistics in v. 4 are an exact parallel to those of 2:41 and demonstrate that Peter's appeal was, once again, remarkably effective.[70] This summary "punctuation" also serves the retardation introduced by v. 3. Because it was evening, the action will be delayed until the next day. For those unfamiliar with the passion narrative (Mark 14:43[71]), the arresting force[72] that bursts upon the scene[73] is an odd body: the clergy, the chief of the temple police (probably[74]), and the members of a political party.[75] This is the ancient equivalent of a "celebrity arrest" that draws a gallery of luminaries, albeit not to bask in the attendant publicity but to represent the forces of evil. Talk of arrest is anticipatory; for all the reader knows, these worthies have come to catch the remainder of the sermon. Verse 2 makes immediately clear that their visit is not friendly. The authorities are doubly aggrieved—because the apostles are *teaching*, which is a usurpation of their own responsibility, and because of *what* they are teaching (evidently the resurrection), which agitates the Sadducees, as well as their use of the name of Jesus.[76] Luke's compression is vivid but inept.[77]

69 On the historical basis for this, see Lüdemann (60), who can finally say no more than that the actions of the authorities would occasion no surprise.

70 This is the last time that Acts supplies even approximate data on the number of converts. See the excursus "The Size of the Jerusalem Church," pp. 86–87.

71 Luke 22:47 abbreviates Mark 14:43. Both use a genitive absolute to indicate that Jesus was interrupted while speaking. On the "improper" genitive absolute of Acts 4:1, an imitation of the arrest of Jesus, see BDF §423.

72 The D-Text pedantically provides an object for the participle "speaking," overlooking the parallel with the passion story, and omits "the chief of the temple police. B C read οἱ ἀρχιερεῖς ("the leading priests"). There are thus three different constructions of the arresting group. "High priests" is an obviously secondary improvement (Metzger, *Textual Commentary*, 275). D-Texts may have omitted reference to the "chief" because it belonged either at the beginning or at the end of the series.

73 For a similar, aggressive, use of ἐφίστημι, see Luke 20:1, where "high priests, scribes, and elders" burst in to question Jesus. The participle λαλούντων ("as they were speaking") intimates that both Peter and John were preaching (Acts 3:12). This will justify the arrest of both apostles.

74 The στρατηγὸς τοῦ ἱεροῦ (= *sāgān* in Hebrew) may have been an official with police powers. See Cadbury and Lake, 40; Barrett, 1:218–19; Martin Hengel, *Judaism and Hellenism: Studies in Their Encounter in Palestine during the Early Hellenistic Period* (trans. John Bowden; 2 vols; Philadelphia: Fortress Press, 1974) 1:25; and Emil Schürer, *History of the Jewish People in the Age of Jesus Christ (175 B.C.–A.D. 135)* (rev. and ed. Geza Vermes and Fergus Millar; 2 vols.; Edinburgh: T&T Clark, 1973–87) 2:277–78. Josephus uses the simple ὁ στρατηγός, "the officer in charge (*Bell.* 6.294; *Ant.* 20.131). In any event this person ranked second to the high priest.

75 Fitzmyer (298) observes, "In Luke's view the Sadducees are the archenemies of Christianity." That is the most salient datum. This party included most of the aristocracy, lay and priestly. They were conservative defenders of the status quo, who would have been unlikely to support dissident movements. See Schürer, *History*, 2:404–14; and Gary G. Porton, "Sadducees," *ABD* 5:892–95.

76 Foakes Jackson (32) observes that modern readers understand the message of resurrection to be an affirmation that there is a future life, but that "[t]o the Jews at this time it meant imminent world-catastrophe, in which the powers on earth would be destroyed and a new order miraculously set up." He is correct about the apocalyptic background and its threat of revolution, but already for Luke resurrection means continuing existence after death rather than political upheaval.

77 Both verbs, "teach" and "proclaim," are infinitive objects of the preposition διά ("because of"), joined with one article. The chief difficulty is the phrase ἐν τῷ Ἰησοῦ. The preposition ἐν is the "maid of all work," with an even wider range of meanings than its English (etc.) cognate "in." The leading options are instrumental (Jesus is the means of resurrection; so Moule, *Idiom Book*, 77), and referential ("in the case of Jesus"). Barrett (1:219) observes that if the phrase were omitted the text would be clear. This is one basis for a solution. Luke has compressed two charges. Cf. 17:18. See Barrett, 1:220; Haenchen, 214 n. 5; Conzelmann,

Only after expending thirty-five words does the narrator reveal the goal of these visitors: arrest.[78] Depiction of the officials as the arresting officers indicates the enormity of their rage: in most cases agents would perform this task. The D-Text of this verse represents a propensity toward paraphrase for its own sake: "so they **seized** them and **handed** them **over** into custody until the morrow; **now** it was already evening." At this dire moment the narrator closes the unit by reporting the results. About[79] five thousand males had become adherents. The number evokes the feeding stories (Mark 6:32-44 parr.) and intimates a much larger total.[80] This is the last time Luke provides specific numbers, possibly intimating the end of an era.

32, who points to 26:23; and Bruce, 148. The D-Text (in addition to its charming replacement of *διαπονούμενοι* with *καταπονούμενοι* ["they were fed up with"]), apparently solves the problem by inverting the order: *ἀναγγέλειν τὸν Ἰησοῦν ἐν τῇ ἀναστάσει τῶν νεκρῶν* ("they are proclaiming Jesus by speaking of the resurrection of the dead"), although Metzger, (*Textual Commentary*, 274) finds it "curious, to say the least."

78 Haenchen (215) observes that the idiom *ἐπιβάλλειν τὰς χεῖρας* will take its place in the technical terminology of hagiography. See BDAG 367, *s.v.* *ἐπιβάλλω*, 1b.

79 The word *ὡς* or the equivalent is textually uncertain. Luke likes to qualify statistics, but $\mathfrak{p}^{74}$ ℵ A 81 1175 *pc* vg omit it, suggesting the possibility that it was added to harmonize with 2:41. Metzger (*Textual Commentary*, 275) finds the decision difficult. The D-Text omits "message" and paraphrases the awkward statement of number (Boismard, *Texte*, 93).

80 Bede (25) already evoked the feeding stories. The figure is imitated in Ps. Clem. *Rec.* 1.71.2, on which see Jones, "A Jewish Christian," 626–27.

4

4:5-22 Peter and John before the High Priests

5/ The next day there was an
assembly of their leaders,
including the elders, the local
legal experts, 6/ and, notably,
the high priest Annas, as well
as Caiphas, Jonathan,[a] Alexander, and the whole high-priestly
clan. 7/ They had Peter and
John brought before them and
asked, "By what power or with
what name have you people
done this?" 8/ Directed by the
Holy Spirit, Peter answered:
"Leaders of the people, elders.
9/ If we are being examined
today regarding a good deed for
a disabled person, that is, how
he was healed, 10/ all of you—
and all the people of Israel—
need to know that he stands
before you in good health by
virtue of the name of Jesus
Christ the Nazorean, whom you
people crucified but whom God
raised from the dead. 11/ This
Jesus is the stone that, scorned
by you, the builders, has
become the keystone. 12/ There
is no salvation by anyone else.[b]
There is no other name provided to mortals in the whole
world through which salvation
can be gained."

4:13-17: Conventional Text

13/ The Council began to wonder
when they saw the assur-
ance with which Peter and
John—mere amateurs[c] in their
view—spoke. They also realized that these men had been
companions of Jesus. 14/ Since,
however, the man who had
been healed was standing with
the apostles in plain sight,
they could offer no refutation.
15/ After directing them to
leave the chamber, the members of the council began to
deliberate.
16/ "What shall we do about these
people? The miracle they
performed has become public
knowledge in Jerusalem.[d] It is
as clear as day, and we cannot deny it. 17/ But, to quash
further dissemination, let us
enjoin them to make no mention of This Name to anyone."

4:13-17: D-Text[e]

13/ *All* the members of the council
marveled when they *heard* the
assurance with which Peter and
John spoke, [ ] because they
were *convinced* that they were
mere uneducated amateurs. [ ]
14/ Since, however, the *afflicted*
man who had been healed was
standing with the apostles in
plain sight, they could *do* nothing, *but some of them* began to
recognize that they had *associated* with Jesus. [ ] 15/ They
then *engaged in conversation,
asking* one another, 16/ "What
shall we do with these people?
It has become public knowledge
in Jerusalem that a miracle *took
place* through them. This is *all
too* clear, and we cannot deny
it. 17/ But, to prevent further
dissemination *of these matters* among the public, *we shall*
enjoin them to make no mention of This Name to anyone."

18/ **They recalled the two and charged them absolutely not to engage in proclamation or to give instruction in the name of Jesus.[f] 19/ Peter and John replied, "It's up to you to determine whether it is right in God's sight to listen to you or to God. 20/ For our part, we cannot desist from speaking about what we have seen and heard."**

21/ **They then let them go, after piling on additional admonitions, since public pressure prevented them from finding a pretext for punishment. Everyone was praising God because of what had taken place, 22/ for the man who had been wondrously healed was over forty years old.**

a *Or:* "John."

b *Or:* "by any other means."

c On the meaning of these words, see Pieter W. van der Horst, "Hellenistic Parallels to Acts Chapters 3 and 4," *JSNT* 35 (1989) 37–46, here 42; Gamble, *Books and Readers*, 9 n. 30, and Thomas J. Kraus, "'Uneducated,' 'Ignorant,' or even 'Illiterate'? Aspects and Background for an Understanding of *ΑΓΡΑΜΜΑΤΟΙ* (and *ΙΔΙΩΤΑΙ*) in Acts 4.13," *NTS* 45 (1999) 434–49. For ancient views about the academic credentials of the apostles, see Walter Bauer, "The Picture of the Apostle in Early Christian Tradition: 1. Accounts," in *NTApoc*, 2:35–74, esp. 39–40. On the term ἰδιώτης, note Hippolytus on Zephryinus, whom he calls ἄνδρα ἰδιώτην καὶ ἀγράμματον καὶ ἄπειρον τῶν ἐκκλησιάστικων ὅρων (*Ref.* 9.11.1). The antonym of ἰδιώτης is πεπαιδεύμενος ("educated"). Note also Tertullian *Prax.* 3: *simplices, imprudentes, idiotae*. References from apologists include Irenaeus *A.H.* 2.26.1; Athenagoras *Leg.* 15; Minucius Felix 2.4.31; and Tertullian *Apol.* 49.4. See, in addition, Eusebius *Praep. ev.* 132b; *Dem. ev.* 3.7; and *H.E.* 2.20.5; 3.24.3. This was a sensitive issue. Celsus uses the term to describe the vulgar and illiterate Christians (Origen *Cels.* 1.27). Lucian employs ἰδιώτης in his religious and philosophical polemic: *Alex.* 30, *Hermot.* 1; *Syr. d.* 8, 11, 28; *Fug.* 21; *Vit. auct.* 11; *Men.*; and *Peregr.* 13, 18.

d *Or:* "that a striking miracle has been performed by them has become public knowledge in Jerusalem and we can't deny it."

e The basis is Boismard, *Texte*, 96–102. For a slightly different reconstruction, based on h and cop[mae], see Metzger, *Textual Commentary*, 277. Bezae is, as often, a conflation/compromise of and between text types. In v. 13, D omits καὶ ἰδιῶται. This may be due to reverence, but it is not clear why "uneducated" is acceptable and "nonprofessional" is not. Epp (*Tendency*, 122–23) concludes that the omission meant that, although untrained, they were not ineloquent. In v. 13 a number of witnesses read δέ instead of τε. This allows an adversative force and is probably secondary, as Luke seems quite fond of τε. See BDF §447 (7). In v. 15, Bezae has them dragged out (ἀπαχθῆναι) rather than excused. This intensifies the tyrannical character of the judges. In Semitic style Ψ 33 m sy[h] preface the verb with ἀπειλῆ, which permits the court to speak in proper biblical style. This may be inspired by 5:28.

f The D-Text opens v. 18 with, "After they had come to an agreement on the matter, they summoned them. . . ."

Comment

■ **5-7** (I. D; Scene 3). The arrival of day brings the trial. The initial verses constitute a single sentence (of sorts) intended to convey the solemnity of the occasion, to underscore the formidable character of the opposition, and, no doubt, to effect additional retardation. The style is Septuagintal (ἐγένετο + infinitive). "Leaders" (evidently the high priests), "elders," and "legal experts" ("scribes") are components of a quite variable formula that occurs in the Gospels and Acts.[1] The scene evokes the arraignment of Jesus.[2] These are "their" authorities. Jewish officialdom belongs to the realm of the other.[3] "In Jerusalem" adds a note of formality and possible irony.[4] The grammar is botched: v. 6 places additional subjects of the infinitive in the nominative case.[5] There are also problems with the data. Annas was not the high priest at the time of Jesus' crucifixion. This is evidently a Lucan error, rather than a mistake taken from a source.[6] Whereas Caiaphas requires no introduction,[7] Alexander cannot be identified.[8] The expression γένος ἀρχιερατικόν ("high-priestly family") is a stock phrase.[9] Luke may have derived these names from a source or tradition (not necessarily connected to the arrest of an apostle) other than Josephus. In short, like the synchronism of Luke 3:1-2, this is a mixed bag of known and obscure data.

The officials, who, like the apostles, can be portrayed as speaking in unison, do not initially address either of the charges mentioned in v. 2. They rather take up, in language intelligible only to the reader, the healing of 3:1-10. With words derived from the challenge to Jesus in Mark 11:28,[10] they ask by what means the undisputed healing was achieved.[11] The implicit accusation is that these two yokels (v. 13) have been dabbling in magic. That concern motivates the issue of the name invoked.[12] Peter knows how to handle the opening provided.[13] His speech (vv. 8-12) is extremely brief, but it contains

1 For data on the various officers, with parallels from Josephus, see, in general, Schürer, *History*, 2:212–13. For Luke and Acts (and a comparison with Josephus) note Steve Mason, "Chief Priests, Sadducees, Pharisees and Sanhedrin in Acts," in Bauckham, *Palestinian Setting*, 115–77.

2 Note, in particular, Luke 22:66: "*When day came,* the assembly of the elders of the people (τὸ πρεσβυτέριον), both chief priests and scribes (γραμματεῖς), gathered together (συνήχθη), and they brought him to their council."

3 The omission of "their" in the D-tradition (below) may be due to the grammatical principle that would have αὐτῶν apply to the converts of v. 4.

4 Rackham (57) points to the contrast with "Nazareth" in v. 10.

5 The variants are almost certainly revisions. In Boismard, *Texte*, 94, the edition of the D-Text uses a finite verb with a string of nominatives. See also Metzger, *Textual Commentary*, 275–76.

6 Cf. Luke 3:2, where the reference to Caiaphas (ἐπὶ ἀρχιερέως Ἄννα καὶ Καϊάφα) is a patent interpolation.

7 Caiaphas is a derogatory nickname ("monkey"?), perhaps taken as family name. See Williams, "Personal Names," 102.

8 D and some other "Western" texts (gig h p* mss of the Vulgate) read the equivalent of "Jonathan," which permits identification with a son of Annas (according to Josephus *Ant.* 18.123). Ropes (*Text*, 34–35) views this as preferable and notes that Jerome included "Jonathan" in a list of names to be found in Acts. He doubts that the D-reviser had resort to Josephus here. "John" would therefore be the substitution of a familiar name for one less familiar. "Jonathan" seems slightly preferable. See also Barrett, 2:225; and Bruce, 150–51.

9 Josephus *Ant.* 15.40 uses the same expression. See also *CIG* 4363.

10 καὶ ἔλεγον αὐτῷ· ἐν ποίᾳ ἐξουσίᾳ ταῦτα ποιεῖς; ("By what authority are you doing these things?"). This question is raised by "the *high priests*," "the *scribes*," and "the *elders*" to Jesus in response to his action in the temple (Mark 11:15-17).

11 Boismard (*Texte*, 94), based solely on h, reads ἐποίησαν ("they did"), thus making this a discussion among the authorities, into which Peter injects his response. The final, emphatic "you" of v. 7 is probably derogatory.

12 Cf. Luke 11:14 (Beelzebul).

13 "Filled with the Holy Spirit" is a stereotyped description of characters in the first half of Acts: 5:32; 6:3; 7:55; 11:24; 13:9. Cf. the promise in Luke 12:21. The same quality was attributed to Jesus (Luke 4:14).

the essential features of the sermons in chaps. 2 and 3: address, scriptural allusion,[14] christological kerygma, and two references to the leaders' actions in killing Jesus. These matters can be presented in summary fashion because they are familiar to the readers. For suitability to the context, this orationette must receive high marks. It almost qualifies as dialogue, albeit rhetorically shaped. As such it is not unique in Acts.[15] The grammar presents some difficulties,[16] and the text is not stable.[17]

■ **8-12** Peter immediately turns the challenge against the accusers: are they on trial for performing a *benefaction*? Neither such courage,[18] nor such language, nor such activity[19] was deemed suitable for Galilean fisherfolk. From this moral high ground the apostle explains

14 The citation of Psalm 118 (117):22 here is distinct from that in the Synoptics (Mark 14:10 parr) and 1 Pet 2:4, 7, which follow the LXX. On "head," see Col 1:18; 2:10, 19; Eph 1:22; 4:15. This important term will become a title, but it is not one here. Note that in Luke 20:17 (vs. Mark) the second part of the citation is omitted.

15 Cf. Acts 5:29-32; 23:1-9. Soards (*Speeches*, 44–47) recognizes this dimension by including 4:19-20 in his analysis.

16 In particular, the gender of ἐν τίνι (v. 9) and ἐν τούτῳ (v. 10) is unclear. These pronouns could refer to name (neuter) or Jesus (masculine). Verse 11 is an awkward intrusion. See Cadbury and Lake, 43. On the strange attributive participle τὸ δεδόμενον ("given") in v. 12, see Moule, *Idiom Book*, 103. The syntax of v. 12 is difficult if the text of N-A[27] is accepted. (See the following note.)

17 The *v.l.* "elders of Israel" in v. 8 is probably secondary, to balance "leaders of the people." "Elders of Israel" does not occur elsewhere in the NT or elsewhere in Greek literature in the period 200 BCE–200 CE. In v. 9, the D-Text adds a typically pedantic "by you" after "examined." Verses 10 and 12 present an interesting textual problem. In v. 10 a number of D-Text witnesses read at the close: ἐνώπιον ὑμῶν σήμερον ὑγιής καὶ ἐν ἄλλῳ οὐδενί (adding "and by no other [means/person]"). In v. 12 the opening clause, καὶ οὐκ ἔστιν ἐν ἄλλῳ οὐδενὶ ἡ σωτηρία ("There is no salvation by anyone else") is omitted by some Old Latin witnesses (h, Irenaeus, *Rebaptism,* Cyprian, Priscillian, Augustine, and some versions made from the Old Latin [Boismard, *Texte,* 95]). D and p omit ἡ σωτηρία ("salvation"). Briefly stated, the argument is either that "in no one else" was interpolated into v. 10 from v. 12 (so Metzger, *Textual Commentary,* 276) and the opening clause of v. 12 was then dropped as redundant (replacing οὐδέ with οὐκ, not indicated in the editions), or that the omission of καὶ ἐν ἄλλῳ οὐδενί was accidental and that the first clause of v. 12 replaced it, with the later addition of ἡ σωτηρία. The latter is the argument of George Kilpatrick, building on Clark (Clark, *Acts,* 340; Metzger [*Textual Commentary*, 256–57] summarizes Kilpatrick's argument). Although the steps of the reconstruction are debatable, Kilpatrick has a strong argument. Verse 12 is cumbersome. The D-Text of v. 12 reads "for there is no other name under heaven given to humans by which . . ."), omitting the first clause, reading a simple οὐκ ("not") instead of οὐδὲ γάρ (lit. "for nor"), and dropping the preposition ἐν, making the meaning "to" plain. With it, the phrase could be taken as "among humans." On the whole passage, see also Epp, *Tendency*, 120–26.

18 παρρησία ("boldness") has two anchors in early Christian thought. One derives from the realm of politics and philosophy, the other from apocalyptic. The latter usage stresses the *confidence* of the wise/righteous in the face of judgment. This quality derives from its political origin in the world of Greek democracy, meaning something like our "freedom of speech," the characteristic of those who "tell it like it is." Boldness is a common virtue of the missionaries in Acts: 4:29; 13:46; 18:26; 19:8; 26:26; and 28:31. See Heinrich Schlier, "παρρησία," *TDNT* 5:871–86, esp. 882–86, who concludes that in Acts the word refers to rhetorical ability. Note also Spicq, *Lexicon*, 3:56–62; Stanley B. Marrow, "*Parrhêsia* and the New Testament," *CBQ* 44 (1982) 431–46; and Penner, *Praise,* 166–67 and his references.

19 Verses 9-12 abound with alliteration and assonance. The reference to the "despised" stone is, in the dramatic context, an elegant allusion, although readers would be inclined to view it as a christological proof text. Verse 10b-e is syntactically chiastic, two prepositional phrases with ἐν ("in") framing relative clauses beginning with ὅν ("whom"). The noun εὐεργεσία ("benefaction") occurs elsewhere in the NT only in 1 Tim 6:2. The verb is used of Jesus' healing activity in another Petrine speech before a distinguished audience in Acts 10:38.

the incident. The effective power was the name of Jesus, and the healing was a synecdoche, as we should say, of that name as the sole basis of salvation.[20] The hearers had crucified Jesus, but God had the last word. The accused has become the accuser.

■ **13-17** Reporting the response requires more words than the speech itself. Since they had not expected that these rude and barbarous creatures could manifest such eloquence and temerity, the court is taken aback. The convenient presence of the healed man made things even worse. Sensing the need to regroup, they go into executive session.

The D-Text has a number of improvements that Luke might well wish that he had thought of. Details aside, it is more lucid and exhibits superior dramatic development. The narrator reports the prior conviction of the apostles' "ignorance," better justifying and emphasizing their subsequent surprise. Next comes the realization that the presence of the patient makes effective rejoinder impossible. Only then does recognition begin to dawn. (Verse 13b has been transferred into v. 14.)[21] In addition to exhibiting better narrative logic, the D-Text is historically more plausible. First, the recognition that this pair had been associates of Jesus is stated more clearly in the judges' own terms rather than in the language of Christian discipleship, and this recognition is not universal but, as is probable, limited to "some." The conventional text reports recognition in conjunction with the officials' surprise at the apostles' assurance. In the D-Text, recognition dawns at the sight of the former cripple and the realization that they are outgunned. Second, this edition eliminates the exclusion of the pair from the hearing, eliminating also the need for an embarrassingly omniscient narrator to report what was said. In sum, this edition has both greater literary and greater historical plausibility. It is nonetheless patently secondary, for it exceeds the bounds of probability to imagine that someone would revise this rather well-crafted and logical paragraph into what is found in the conventional text. Early readers of Acts already perceived that omniscient narration could be a problem.

No reader of the preceding speech would consider Peter an "uneducated amateur."[22] This observation in v. 13 (made by a mind-reading narrator) proves just how adept the little rejoinder was. In fulfillment of Luke 21:12-15,[23] the followers of Jesus have all the eloquence they may require.[24] It is hard to square this surprising discovery of their connection to Jesus with the grounds for arrest in v. 2.[25] Be that as it may, the presence of the former cripple, who for some unexplained reason is on the scene,[26] is said to make any rebuttal impossible. Why this is so is not immediately apparent, for the judges did

20 The speech plays on the various meanings of the stem σω-, which include "health," "safety," "rescue," and "salvation" in the religious sense. Tannehill (*Narrative Unity*, 2:61 n. 6) comments on the problematic δεῖ here, which can be taken as tying God's hands, so to speak. For Luke, the verb refers to the divine plan of salvation for all. The intention of this phrase is more clearly expressed in another Petrine speech in 15:12.

21 Note also that v. 17 has been supplied with a subject.

22 John is, as so often in Acts, awkwardly included. Cf. 16:37, where Silas must also hold Roman citizenship. The episode is given an expanded interpretation in Ps. Clem. *Rec.* 1.62. Note 1.62.2, "Then he [Caiaphas] further accused me of audacity because though I was an unlearned fisher and a boor, I was so bold as to assume the office of a teacher" (trans. of the Latin by F. Stanley Jones, *An Ancient Jewish Christian Source on the History of Christianity: Pseudo-Clementine Recognitions 1.21–27* [SBLTT 37; Atlanta: Scholars Press, 1995] 96).

23 Luke 21:12-15: "But before all this occurs, they will arrest you (ἐπιβαλοῦσιν ἐφ᾽ ὑμᾶς τὰς χεῖρας αὐτῶν) and persecute you; they will hand you over to synagogues and prisons (φυλακάς), and you will be brought before kings and governors because of my name (ὀνόματός μου). 13 This will give you an opportunity to testify. 14 So make up your minds not to prepare your defense in advance; 15 for I will give you words and a wisdom that none of your opponents will be able to withstand or contradict."

24 The narrator possesses an eloquence of his own. Verse 13 offers two possibilities: to read αὐτούς ("them") as the object of the first verb and the ὅτι clause as the object of the second, in which case there is *prolepsis*, or, more likely if less elegantly, to construe both as objects of the second verb (ἐπεγίνωσκον). Cf. BDF §408 and the longer discussion of Barrett, 1:233–34.

25 In the D-Text, this dissonance is even greater. See Cadbury and Lake, 44.

26 Perhaps readers will think that he has been arrested with the apostles, to whom he was last seen clinging (v. 11). He seems to have been forgotten in vv. 15-21, for, if among the "them" (αὐτούς) excluded in v. 15,

not claim that the healing was fraudulent.[27] Disarray calls for an executive session.[28]

■ **15b-17** These verses function as a summary of the debate, but the form is direct speech.[29] This is a quality of popular narration. The absence of the concerned parties does nothing to alleviate their situation. Everyone, they reveal, knows about the miracle.[30] They cannot even articulate what they are talking about.[31] Lest bad lead to worse, they will promulgate a gag order: "speaking in this name" is forbidden.[32] This tyrannical demand, which possesses not even a shred of legal justification, they promptly proceed to issue,[33] with a solemn and ominous injunction[34] that finally brings together the two points of v. 2: teaching and Jesus.[35] No sanctions are mentioned. No sanction would have impeded the apostles,[36] who, after teaching in the portico of a temple, like philosophers (3:11), now—and not for the last time—wrap themselves in the mantle of Socrates[37] and anticipate the stand of Martin Luther.[38] They can do nothing else. This places them in the role of genuine philosophers who boldly rebuke tyrants and let the chips fall where they may.

Excursus: Confronting Tyrants

"Tyranny" in the sense of arbitrary one-person rule was contrary to Greco-Roman ideals of good government. One of the actions of a tyrant was suppression of free speech (παρρησία; cf. Acts). Conversely, tackling an alleged tyrant was one means of acquiring philosophical credentials. The themes of the debate were established in Plato's *Gorgias* and changed little thereafter.[39] Excesses ensued. Dio of Prusa noted the propensity of some first-century Cynics (and others) to test the limits of free speech (*Or.* 32.11; 77/78.37, 45). Lucian's *Peregrinus*, a parody of the true philosopher, went over the top to achieve expulsion by a benevolent emperor (18).

The range of resisters was quite broad, including prophets of ancient Israel who stood up to monarchs, victims of hostility to Judaism, anti-Semites, holy men and women of various creeds and convictions, and political opponents of Nero (and

he would be included in those (αὐτούς) summoned in v. 18 and admonished in v. 21.

27 The actual function of v. 14 is to prepare for vv. 16 and 21.

28 The same tactic will be used in 5:33.

29 Acts 2:37 makes the rhetorical question "what shall we do?" ironic.

30 Formally, it is dissemination of the "sign" that they lament, but the meaning must be "news about this sign."

31 Verse 17 lacks a stated subject. One may infer a delicate "it." Haenchen (219 n. 4) asks whether ἐπὶ πλεῖον ("further") is spatial (outside of Jerusalem) or temporal (keep on spreading). He prefers the latter, with a glance at 24:4. Conzelmann (33) agrees.

32 The first use of the phrase (v. 17) is ambiguous. It could refer to healing formulas.

33 The D-Text provides a different introduction to v. 18, required by its context: "*Since they had agreed upon a plan*, they ordered them . . ."

34 Should the article be taken with the adverb or with the infinitive? The latter is slightly preferable. See Barrett, 1:236. ℵ* B solve the problem by omitting it. The present tense of the infinitives implies that they should cease what they are doing.

35 Acts 5:28 clarifies the official understanding of this injunction.

36 A number of D-Text witnesses utilize a singular participle but do not otherwise alter the construction. This would follow the tendency of enhancing Peter's status. See Pervo, "Social Aspects," 232–35.

37 On this phrase, see the comments on 5:29. This is the stance of Jewish heroes, including Sus 23; 2 Macc 7:2; 4 Macc 5:16-20; Dan 3:16-18; Josephus *Ant.* 17.159; 18.268. For parallels from early Christian literature, note Luke 20:25; 1 *Clem.* 14:1; and 2 *Clem.* 4:4.

38 On μᾶλλον ἤ ("rather than") see BDF 245a (1, 3) and Barrett, 1:237. D* omits the final μή. Boismard (*Texte*, 101) resolves the problem by preferring the verb "deny."

39 Plato *Gorgias* 469. On philosophical resistance in the Roman Empire, see Ramsay MacMullen, *Enemies of the Roman Order: Treason, Unrest, and Alienation in the Empire* (Cambridge, Mass.: Harvard University Press, 1966) 46–94, 305–16; Erkki Koskienniemi, *Der philostrateische Apollonios* (Commentationes humanarum litterarum 94; Helsinki: Societas Scientiarum Fennica, 1991) 31–44; Jaap-Jan Flinterman, *Power, Paideia, and Pythagoreanism: Greek Identity, Conceptions of the Relationship between Philosophers and Monarchs and Political Ideas in Philostratus' Life of Apollonius* (Dutch Monographs on Ancient History and Archaeology 13; Amsterdam: Gieben, 1995) 165–69; and Alexander, *Literary Context*, 65–66, 196 n. 39.

others, especially Domitian), as well as the merely young and attractive.[40] These scenes possessed an obvious and excellent quality of timeless drama: the desperate circumstances of life and death situations. They allowed the accused to display all of their gifts and virtues. The theme became a standard feature of ancient rhetorical training[41] and played a role in historical[42] and romantic[43] fiction, as well as in the martyrological and hagiographic tradition.[44]

Several elements of this theme are important for Acts. One is the tendency for stories about prophets and religious martyrs to assimilate to the philosophical tradition. With this comes the influence of the figure of Socrates.[45] A third is that, by invoking this theme, authors of popular writings raise the status of both their characters and their texts.

■ **18-22** The apostles' insulting refusal assumes that the views of this supreme religious body are at variance with those of God. For the narrator—and the readers—the miracle establishes the validity of this thesis. Because the general public holds the same view, the hands of the authorities are tied. They can do no more than lock the barn doors after the horse has fled. After piling on some threats, they discharge the accused.[46] Reference to the healing permits mention of the patient's age, and thus the duration of his illness. That feature is an appropriate characteristic of a healing story.[47] Another typical feature is public acclamation at the wonder, reported here by the judicial body.[48] By transferring these features to this point, Luke integrates the narrative: all of 4:1-22 is a miracle story.[49] The lack of specific resolution and the presence of threats provide suspense and leave space for plot development. The authorities have not given up on the apostles, but thirty-one verses will intervene before there is another arrest. For the present, the hapless leaders can do no more than utter shrill threats, since public opinion inhibits them from anything more drastic. The formerly wavering apostles now imitate their master in stirring sermons and mighty deeds, receiving, like Jesus, popular acclaim and official scorn.

40 John Darr presents a useful and insightful survey of the theme in general (*Herod the Fox: Audience Criticism and Lukan Characterization* [JSNTS 163; Sheffield: Sheffield Academic Press, 1998] 92–136).

41 Stanley Frederick Bonner, *Roman Declamation in the Late Republic and Early Empire* (Liverpool: University of Liverpool Press, 1949) 34–43.

42 See, e.g., *Chion of Heraclea* and the *Acta Alexandrinorum*.

43 See Pervo, *Profit*, 47, 155.

44 See Herbert Musurillo, *The Acts of the Pagan Martyrs* (Oxford: Clarendon, 1954) 236–46.

45 On the influence of the image of Socrates, see Moses Hadas and Morton Smith, eds., *Heroes and Gods: Spiritual Biographies in Antiquity* (New York: Harper & Row, 1965) 115–18; and Alessandro Ronconi, "Exitus illustrium virorum," *RAC* 6:1258–68. For its influence on Acts, see Cadbury and Lake, 212; Plümacher, *Lukas*, 19, 97–98; and Abraham Malherbe, "'Not in a Corner'": Early Christian Apologetic in Acts 26:26," *SecCent* 5 (1985–86) 193–210, esp. 198 n. 26. (Socrates' condemnation by a democratic jury does not seem to have retarded his absorption into the tradition of the antityrannical philosopher.)

46 On the syntax of v. 21b (μηδέν is an accusative of respect, while τό substantivizes the indirect question), see Barrett, 1:238. The D-Text has the simpler μὴ εὑρισκοντες αἰτίαν. Epp (*Tendency*, 126) notes that this strengthens the parallel with Jesus (Acts 13:28).

47 Bultmann, *History*, 221.

48 The last clause of v. 21 is a natural sequel to 3:8-10: the crowd first expresses awe and then praises the responsible deity, as does the former patient. The phenomenon of acclamation is treated with considerable depth by Theissen, *Miracle Stories*, 71–72, 152–53. See also Erik Peterson, *ΕΙΣ ΘΕΟΣ: Epigraphische, formgeschichtliche und religionsgeschichtliche Untersuchungen* (FRLANT 41; Göttingen: Vandenhoeck & Ruprecht, 1926); and Theodor Klauser, "Akklamation," *RAC* 1:216–33. The phenomenon is found also in popular literature, e.g., *Ephesian Tale* 5.13.3–5; Longus *Daph.* 2.29.2; Achilles Tatius *Leuc. Clit.* 7.16.1; *Apollonius of Tyre* 50. This is one means by which the crowd (and the readers) participate in the story.

49 The genitive beginning with ἐτῶν ("years") is evidently adjectival. The D-Text ἐγεγόνει τὸ σημεῖον τῆς ἰάσεως, which omits the demonstrative, is considered to be possibly original by Ropes, *Text*, 40.

4

4:23-31 Prayerful Celebration

23/ Once released the apostles went to their people and reported everything that the chief priests and the elders had said. 24/ Whereupon they raised a unison prayer to God:

"Master, maker of heaven, earth, sea, and all that is in them; 25/ you said to our ancestors, through your servant David:[a]

Why did gentiles rage,
And peoples plot in vain?
26/ The monarchs of the earth got ready for combat,
And the rulers came together,
Against the Lord and against the Lord's Messiah.

27/ "In fact Herod and Pontius Pilate, with gentiles and Israelites, did come together in this city against your holy servant Jesus, whom you anointed. 28/ They accomplished what your power and plan had previously determined would take place. 29/ Take notice of their threats now, O Lord, and grant that your slaves may proclaim your message with complete boldness, 30/ while you stretch forth your healing hand and bring about portents and wonders through the name of your holy servant Jesus."

31/ After their prayer was finished, the place in which they were gathered shook. All were filled with the Holy Spirit and continued to speak God's message boldly.

a *Or:* "you said through your servant David."

Analysis

(I.E; Scene 4) This unit describes the pair's return to the community (?). Those assembled offer a prayer for courageous proclamation and accompanying wonders. A quake affirms that their petitions have been heard. Courageous proclamation follows. The prayer echoes a number of themes from the immediate context: threats (v. 21), bold proclamation (v. 13), healing (3:1-10), the name of Jesus (v. 10, etc.), who is characterized as the "servant/son" (παῖς) of God (3:13). The thematic unity suggests that the scene is a Lucan composition. This is the consensus of the commentators. The exegetical portion of the prayer (vv. 25-27) raises questions, since Luke does not agree with its thesis that the death of Jesus took place through a collaboration between Herod and Pilate.[1] Consistency was not a Lucan virtue, however, and the Gospel of Luke includes an encounter with Herod evidently developed on the basis of Psalm 2 (Luke 23:6-12).[2] This exegesis of the *pesher* type[3] was

1 Cf. Conzelmann, 35.

2 Cf. also the *Gos. Pet.* 1.1–2. See Crossan, *Who Killed Jesus?* 82–88. Dibelius argued that Luke 23:6-12 was based on Psalm 2 (*Botschaft und Geschichte: Gesammelte Aufsätze* [2 vols.; Tübingen: Mohr Siebeck, 1953–56] 1.289–92). On the suitability of the title "king" for Herod, see Loisy, 254.

3 4QFlor (174) 1:18–19 interprets these verses of

clearly useful to the author of Acts.[4] It sheds light on the history of composition, since Acts, although composed after Luke,[5] reveals the source of a passage from the Gospel.[6]

Prayers may be compared with speeches. By and large, they are deliberative rhetoric addressed to the deity. This prayer contains an address, an ascription that is parallel to a *captatio benevolentiae,* a citation from Scripture, a *narratio*, and a peroration in the form of a petition.[7] The "collect" form represented here is based on Hellenistic Jewish prayers[8] and is representative of Christian liturgical language around 100 and later. The vocative δέσποτα ("Master") is typical of that era, as is the identification of God as creator.[9] The structure reveals the concinnity between prayer and sermon.[10]

I. Vv. 24b-25a Exordium
  A. V. 24b Address
  B. Vv. 24b-25a Ascriptions: Creator and Inspirer
II. Vv. 25b-26 Citation
III. Vv. 27-28 Narration: application of Scripture
IV. Vv. 29-30 Petition/peroration[11]

The closest intrabiblical parallel is the prayer of Hezekiah (*in re:* Sennacherib), Isa 37:16-20, which invokes God as ruler and creator of heaven and earth, begs the deity to *look* upon the threatening situation brought about by *kings*, includes the phrase "in truth" (ἐπ' ἀληθείας),[12] and culminates with a miracle (vv. 36-38). The differences are also illuminating. The enemies are foreign polytheists, the essence of the petition is a prayer for deliverance, and the miracle consists of punishment.[13]

■ **23** The expressions πρὸς τοὺς ἰδίους (lit. "to their own people"),[14] and "place" (τόπος) in v. 31 leave the setting quite vague. One possibility is to take ἰδίους to mean "the other apostles." Supporting this are the

Psalm 2 eschatologically. There is a messianic interpretation of Ps 2:9 in *Ps. Sol.* 17:23-24; cf. Rev 19:19.

4 Lüdemann (58–59) ultimately assigns the exegesis to tradition.

5 See Pervo, *Dating*, 48.

6 Weiser (1:131) points to difficulties in assigning the use of Psalm 2 to tradition here.

7 The D-Text of v. 24 supplies a reaction to the report, reading, instead of (lit.) "hearing," "**perceived the working of God**" and interpolates "God" after "you." Luke does not otherwise use ἐνέργεια ("working"), which is found (with δεσπότης, "Master") in similar contexts in 2 Macc 3:29; *3 Macc.* 4:21. Although Luke is fond of the Maccabean literature, it is unlikely that he would have offered such a banality at this point and thus disrupted the unity of the passage (cf. Epp, *Tendency*, 127, and 149 n. 2, where he notes a similar summary in the D-Text of Acts 16:40). "God" is a secondary, liturgical and reverential addition.

8 See p. 56 n. 54 (on 1:24ff.) There are also numerous allusions to Scripture, including Isa 37:16-20 (below), Pss 23:1; 145:6 (which is essentially cited in v. 24), and 2 Kgs 19:19.

9 "Master": see Pervo, *Dating*, 265–66. The invocation of God as creator became a standard feature of Jewish prayers ("Blessed are you, Lord our God, king of the universe . . ."). Earlier examples are Jdt 9:12 and *3 Macc.* 2:2. Formal parallels include Jdt 5:20 and 2 Macc 14:36; 15:22-36. Close early Christian parallels include *Did.* 10:3; *1 Clem.* 8:2; 20:11; 33:2; 52:1. Note also *Diogn.* 3:2; 8:7. For a general parallel in structure and content that is probably more indicative of the actual length of such prayers, note *1 Clem.* 59:3–61:3. Although the appeal to God as maker of all derives from Judaism, emphasis on this role in early Christianity may have been stimulated by tendencies to devalue creation. Cf. also Acts 14:15; 17:24. The passage is evidently imitated in *Act. Paul* 3.24: "[Thecla] cried out: 'Father, who *made heaven and earth*, the Father of the beloved *servant and son*, Jesus Christ.'" There opposition to Marcionite and Gnostic theology is quite probable.

10 Cf. Latin *oratio/oro*, which became standard designations for prayer.

11 Another indication of (probably Lucan) compositional care is the imperfect chiasm apparent in vv. 25b-27. "Nations" and "people(s)" constitute the frame. Between them are "kings," "rulers," "the Lord and his Messiah," in the center, followed by "Herod" (a king), and "Pilate" (a ruler).

12 This phrase appears three times in Luke and twice in Acts (4:27; 10:34) of seven times in the NT.

13 See Witherington, 203.

14 Cadbury and Lake (45) translate the word as "friends," leaving open the possibility of a particular group that is not necessarily identical to the apostles and definitely less extensive than the entire community.

references to preaching in vv. 29, 31, and 33 (the last of which has the apostles as its subject). Although proclamation is not limited to apostles (Stephen, Paul!),[15] it is an activity of leaders in Acts. Nonetheless, Luke never reports a meeting of apostles alone,[16] and the parallel situation in 12:12 envisions the entire community gathered in prayer—without James (and other leaders?)—in a house.[17]

■ **25** The text of v. 25a printed in N-A[27] appears to be corrupt.[18] The difficulties are grammatical, theological, and stylistic. The genitives "of our father . . . David your servant" are widely separated. God does not elsewhere speak "through the Holy Spirit."[19] David is overburdened with two roles: father and servant. Luke does not otherwise characterize David as "our ancestor." The syntactic/semantic issues focus on intermediate agency, often expressed in Greek via *διά* with the genitive. "God spoke through David" is the evident meaning. Competing with this is the problematic reference to the Holy Spirit, another redundancy possibly added in an era of more developed notions of inspiration and/or emergent trinitarian theology.[20] It should be deleted. B. F. Westcott proposed *τοῖς πατράσιν* ("to our ancestors") in place of the gentive "of our father."[21] This phrase appears in Acts 7:44 and is suitable for liturgical language (Heb 1:1). It would, as in 3:13, 25, stress the venerable antiquity of this "prophecy."[22] The proposed text, inspired by Westcott and Dibelius,[23] is *ὁ τοῖς πατράσιν ἡμῶν διὰ στόματος Δαυὶδ παιδός σου εἰπών*. The alternative is to follow the Byzantine/majority tradition and delete both "father" and "Holy Spirit," which is the path also followed by the D-Text, as reconstructed by Boismard.[24]

■ **26-28** For the purposes of exegesis "peoples" and "kings" were evidently construed as "poetic plurals."[25] The interpretation presumes that the conspiracy of Psalm 2 forecasts the fate of Jesus.[26] The implied understanding is that the encounter of Peter and John with

15 Cf. also Philip (8:5), Barnabas (11:26), and Apollos (18:11), as well as anonymous missionaries (8:4; 11:19).

16 Acts 21:19 does speak of a meeting of Paul with James and the presbyters. On the question, see Urban C. von Wahlde, "Acts 4,24-31: The Prayer of the Apostles in Response to the Persecution of Peter and John—and Its Consequences," *Bib* 77 (1996) 237–44.

17 The issue of size—a facility that could contain five thousand males (4:4)—is not truly relevant to the problem, for, whatever he says about numbers, Luke always envisions a group that can meet within a house, doubtless in accord with his own experience. See Haenchen, 226; and the less certain ruminations of Barrett, 1:243.

18 Cadbury and Lake (46–47) describe the text as "an incoherent jumble of words." Metzger (*Textual Commentary*, 279–81) admits that it is unsatisfactory, but will not emend it.

19 The metonymy "through the mouth of" is common in Luke and Acts for human agents: Luke 1:70 (prophets); Acts 1:16 (David); 3:18, 21, (prophets).

20 Note that the Spirit is "community property" in v. 31. This may have motivated the addition in v. 25: if believers spoke in the Spirit, should this be overlooked in the case of biblical writers?

21 Westcott's conjecture was gleaned from Metzger, *Textual Commentary*, 281.

22 This would also conform to Conzelmann's temporal model: "Fathers" = Law and Prophets (vv. 25-26); fulfillment in time of Jesus (vv. 27-28), and time of church ("now," vv. 29-30). See his commentary (p. 104 *ad* 13:25 and the reference to Wilckens). Note also Weiser, 332–33.

23 Dibelius (*Studies*, 90) agrees that, by expunging "Holy Spirit . . . and perhaps also *τοῦ πατρὸς ἡμῶν*, a good sense results." Haenchen (226) is forthright and deletes both. See also idem, "Schriftzitate," 156–57.

24 Boismard, *Texte*, 102–3. Dibelius (*Studies*, 90) also noted, in reference to 4:25, the problematic mention of the Spirit in 1:2. He concluded that these "may have been influenced by a view which might be called a theology of the Holy Spirit." Long before Dibelius, scholars had proposed that one feature of some D-Texts could be labeled "proto-Montanist." See p. 36 n. 44. It is not certain that the mention of the "Spirit" here comes from the general D-Text tradition, for Boismard, as noted, excludes it as contamination from the "Alexandrian Text," and he may be right, but Dibelius did well to consider the passages together.

25 For various uses of the plural in a singular sense, see Herbert Weir Smyth, *Greek Grammar* (rev. G. M. Messing; Cambridge, Mass.: Harvard University Press, 1956) §§1000–1012. More concretely, E 3 326 Hilary Aug Theophylact read "peoples" in v. 27 as a singular.

26 On the promise/fulfillment theme here, see Ulrich Borse, "Die geschichtliche Absicherung (Luke 23,5-16) des christologischen Psalmwortes (Ps 2,1s/

the authorities is like the experience of Jesus, who is an example for those arraigned before courts.[27] As often in the early chapters of Acts, there is no sense that the subject is "current events." "Herod" is viewed as a monarch here, as in Mark, but not Luke, another indicator of pre-Lucan tradition. They have Jewish and gentile (cf. 2:23) allies.[28] Verse 28 affirms the belief of those praying that these events conform to God's foreordained plan.[29] Therein resides the fundamental irony of the execution of Jesus, variously developed by early Christian theologians.[30]

■ **29-30** The petition[31] seeks not deliverance[32] but courageous proclamation, accompanied by confirmatory wonders.[33] Gratification will not be long delayed. After the confirming quake comes bold public preaching;[34] healings follow in 5:12-16. Appeal to the name—the last time that *leitmotif* sounds in this section—of God's "holy servant Jesus" cannot be related to a "suffering servant" Christology, not simply because of the absence of any reference to suffering, but primarily because of the parallel with God's servant David in v. 25, supported by the earlier reference to his regal status.[35]

■ **31** "At the appearance of the gods temples shake," comments Servius, laconically.[36] He knew whereof he spoke. When earth tremors of all sorts are added to the inventory, the number of parallels might register 5.5 on the history-of-religions' Richter scale. One may safely assume that Luke's readers could grasp the significance of this quake.[37] Servius's comment highlights the transition of the divine presence from temple to house. The

LXX) und seiner Auslegung (Apg 4,25-28)," *StudNTUmwelt* 26 (2001) 129–38.

27 Schmithals (52) says that Luke's exemplaristic Christology is a response to a "hyperpauline theology of the cross." This may explain part of its function, but not its origin, which is deeply rooted in Lucan theology and ethics.

28 A number of witnesses, including the Textus Receptus, strike out "in this city." Metzger (*Textual Commentary*, 281) attributes this to its absence from Psalm 2. Boismard (*Texte*, 103), in his edition of the D-Text, reads "all" instead of "in truth" and omits the name "Jesus," as well as "Pontius."

29 The verb (προώρισεν) is singular. Are χείρ and βουλή ("hand and plan") a kind of hendiadys? The situation is complicated by the textual uncertainty of "your" here and in v. 30. If only one pronoun is to be read ("your hand"), the case for hendiadys is stronger. Cf. BDAG, 1083, *s.v.* χεῖρ, which says that the combination "almost = will." On the textual problems, see Metzger, *Textual Commentary*, 282. "Hand," an anthropomorphic synecdoche best viewed as a metaphor, is a common trope: 4:30; 11:21; 13:11. Cf. the appearance of a hand in the synagogue paintings at Dura Europos to indicate divine intervention. The verse is quite similar to 2:23 (which also refers to Jesus' death at the hands of the "lawless").

30 Because Luke is more of a "romantic" than an "ironic" theologian, he concentrates more on the fact and fulfillment of God's plan than on what it reveals about the human situation, the tragic nature of existence, or the contrast between appearance and reality.

31 The shift is marked by καὶ νῦν ("and now"), on which see Barrett, 1:248.

32 Insofar as Acts has an external apologetic goal, it seeks to halt official (and other) attacks upon Christians. At the same time, its thesis, amply illustrated throughout the book, is that persecution promotes growth. These contradictory claims are of the very essence of early Christian apologetic, most famously summarized by Tertullian *Apol.* 50.13: *Plures efficimus quoties metimur a vobis, semen est sanguis Christianorum* ("The more you mow us down, the more we grow; the blood of Christians is seed"), although his objective was to protest persecution. Cf. also *Diogn.* 6:9; 7:8; and Justin *Dial.* 110.

33 The infinitive with ἐν τῷ in v. 30 is instrumental. BDF §404 (3) and Moule (*Idiom Book*, 57) justify the rendition "through."

34 Internal "testimony" is not meant, since the subject is defiance of the court order. See Haenchen, 228; Schneider, 1:361; and the remarks below. This is the understanding of the D-Text, which adds, at the conclusion of v. 31, πάντι τῷ θέλοντι πιστεύειν ("to everyone who desired to believe"). For an argument that the apostles alone are in view, see Johnson, 90 (who therefore translates ἰδίους as "associates").

35 Jesus is characterized as God's "holy servant" in both v. 27 and v. 30. For Luke, the "anointing" (ἔχρισας) of Jesus is symbolic, but it is difficult to determine from Acts precisely when this took place.

36 *Adventu deorum moveri templa*, Servius *Commentary on Vergil, ad.* Aen. 3.89–92.

37 In addition to the commentaries, note Arthur Stanley Pease, ed., *M. Tulli Ciceronis De Natura Deorum* (2 vols.; Cambridge, Mass.: Harvard University Press, 1958) 2:583; van der Horst, "Acts 3 and 4,"

internal parallel is to Acts 16:25-26. Although that experience opens a prison, both are epiphanies that follow prayer, and both are, in the end, signs for the believers. The occurrence of an epiphany together with the gift of the Spirit issuing in speech suggests a parallel with Pentecost. In the heyday of source criticism, this episode lay under the suspicion of being a doublet of 2:1-12.[38] Conzelmann has an intelligent approach: "Luke is indicating how Pentecost became a present reality."[39] It is preferable to say that this episode assures the reader that the gifts of Pentecost endured and, should the question arise, shows what side God has taken in the conflict.[40]

Verse 31c is imperfect ("they began to speak and continued to do so") and is thus a mini-summary, complementary to that which follows. Readers are to envision what 5:21 makes clear: the apostles returned to their preaching duties in the temple precincts. This, with the healings reported in 5:12-16, will form the basis for the next arrest (5:17-18). Both petitions of 4:29-30 will be granted.[41] While the leaders are thus engaged, Luke will pause to give some glimpses of community life (4:32—5:16).

44–45; and Hans Dieter Betz, *Lukian von Samosata und das Neue Testament* (TU 76; Berlin: Akademie, 1961) 165. Examples include LXX Ps 17:7-8; Vergil *Aen.* 3.88–92; Ovid *Met.* 15.671–772; Plautus *Amph.* 1062–96 (in which the quakes are in response to prayer). In the background is the epiphany of a sky or storm god, as can be seen in such references to Zeus/Jupiter, as Homer *Il.* 1.528–30; Vergil *Aen.* 9.106; Catullus 64.205–7. Some other Jewish examples are *T. Levi* 3:9, Ps.-Philo *Liber Antiquitatum Biblicarum* 9.5; Josephus *Ant.* 7.76–77. One of Poseidon's epithets was "earth-shaker" (Homer *Il.* 13.43, etc.), and many gods got into the act, including Diana (Statius *Thebaid*, 4.331–32), Isis (Ovid *Met.* 9.782–84), and, notably, Dionysius, as in Aeschylus frg. 58 ἐνθουσιᾷ δὴ δῶμα βακχεύει στέγη ("The home writhes in ecstasy; the house dances in bacchic frenzy"). Finally, and not unimportantly, charismatic persons could bring about earth tremors, as in Lucian *Men.* 9–10 (cf. *Philops.* 22).

38 See Harnack, 175–86.

39 Conzelmann, 34–35. For a different approach, see Witherington, 200.

40 Barrett (1:249) observes that the quake added another traditional epiphanic sign to those enumerated in 2:2-3. He had been anticipated by Richard Pervo, *Luke's Story of Paul* (Minneapolis: Fortress, 1990) 18 (who also noted the cloud in 1:9). Both had overlooked Rackham (61), who had the epiphany to Elijah (1 Kgs 19:11-12) in mind. Barrett's conclusion that 2:1—4:31 constitute part of a major structural unit is debatable. See also Weaver, *Plots*, 125–26; and Myllykoski, "Being There," 167–68.

41 Apart from the addition discussed in n. 28 above, in 4:31 the D-Text omits "all," thus encouraging the restriction of the activity to the apostles, and "holy" before "Spirit," according to Boismard, *Texte*, 104–5.

4

4:32—5:16 Community Life and Outreach

32/ The body of believers was one in
heart and soul. Not even one of
them would say, "That's mine,"
about any of their possessions,
but they held all in common.
33/ The apostles continued to
give very powerful testimony[a]
to the resurrection of the Lord
Jesus, and all enjoyed an abundance of divine favor. 34/ None
of them was in need, for all
who owned land or houses sold
those objects and placed the
35/ proceeds at the disposal of
the apostles; they were distributed in accordance with
need. 36/ Joseph, a Levite from
Cyprus, whom the apostles
nicknamed "Barnabas"[b]
("preacher"), 37/ had a piece of
property. He sold it and gave
the money to the apostles.
5:1/ Now a man named Ananias
(whose wife was Sapphira) sold
a piece of property. 2/ With
the connivance of his wife, he
withheld some of the proceeds
and placed the balance at
the disposal of the apostles.
3/ Peter said, "Ananias, why did
you let Satan move you to lie
to the Holy Spirit and withhold
some of the proceeds from your
land? 4/ Wasn't that property
yours to keep? Once you sold
it, wasn't the money at your
disposal? What gave you the
idea to do this? You have not
lied to mortals but to God."
5/ When Ananias heard this, he
dropped dead. Terror struck all
who witnessed this exchange.
6/ The young people then covered him and took the body out
for burial.
7/ Three hours later his wife, who
was unaware of what had happened, showed up. 8/ Peter
asked her, "Tell me, did you sell
the field for *X* amount?"
"Yes, for *X*."
9/ "Why did you two agree to challenge the Spirit of the Lord?
Look, those who buried your
husband are at the door. They
will be carrying you out, too."
10/ She dropped dead at his
feet. The young people came
back and, finding her dead as
well, removed her for burial
next to her husband. 11/ Dread

a *Or:* "testimony supported by remarkable miracles."

b *Or:* "Joseph surnamed 'Barnabas of the apostles.'"

terror struck the entire community and everyone who learned what had happened.
12/ The apostles worked numerous miracles and portents among the people. They now frequented the Portico of Solomon in a body, 13/ and no outsiders ventured to get too close to them,[c] while the general public sang their praises. 14/ Indeed, men and women alike joined the community in droves. 15/ The crowds were so large that people would actually put their sick out on the street in beds and stretchers, so that Peter's shadow might fall upon one or another of them as he was passing by. 16/ The populace of those towns near Jerusalem flocked in, bringing the ill and those tormented by impure spirits, all of whom[d] were made well.

c "No outsiders . . ." This clause is very obscure; the text may be corrupt.

d Like some other postclassical writers, Luke uses forms of the complex relative pronoun, such as *οἵτινες* here, as equivalents of the simple relative where the latter could be confused with the article.

Analysis

The structure of 4:32–5:16 (Y_2–II.A) is quite uncomplicated. Following the summary of vv. 32-35 are two examples, one of which is positive: the generosity of Barnabas. The other, which narrates the grim fate of Ananias and Sapphira, is negative. Critical commentators find tension between summary and specific instance—and not without reason, since summaries often generalize single reports, but the narrator has no such worries.[1] Moreover, in this section the interests of redaction criticism and literary criticism can be in conflict, as separate analysis of the summaries in 4:32-35; 5:12-14, 15-16 tends toward the understanding that the material is composed of a few episodes, probably derived from sources, that have been generalized by means of the summaries. Acts 4:32 is a brief note about community life, followed in v. 33 by another summarizing apostolic activity, after which come detailed reports on community life in vv. 34-35 (general) and 4:36–5:11 (particular). These are followed by a general summary of apostolic miracles (5:12), comments on the popularity and growth of the movement (vv. 13-14), and the climactic report about Peter's healings (vv. 15-16).[2] The narrative alternates reports about community life and the apostolic mission. While providing relaxation from the tension aroused by 4:1-22, as well as suspense—since few will imagine that the authorities have thrown in the towel—Luke is preparing the ground for 6:1-7, where continued expansion will place pressure on existing arrangements.

The summary in vv. 32-35 should be compared to that in 2:42-47. The subjects are similar, but the emphases differ. There is little in ch. 4 about community worship, while the means of sharing, together with its basis and effect, receives a richer description. Both summaries begin with a general note about community life (2:42; 4:32), paired with a summary of apostolic activity (2:43; 4:33). The central figures are the apostles, who engage in preaching and function as the recipients of contributions. Substantial growth has not generated the development of a more complex and hierarchical structure. The wording of v. 32 is somewhat unusual,

1 See the excursus "The Summaries in Acts" pp. 88–89.

2 This is the view also of Sijbolt J. Noorda, "Scene and Summary: A Proposal for Reading Acts 4,32–5:16," in Kremer, *Actes*, 475–83.

as it begins with the genitive qualifier of the compound subject.[3] "Heart and soul" is a kind of hendiadys.[4] As an expression of universalism, Luke combines both Jewish and Hellenic values. "Heart" in the senses of "disposition" and "morality" is at home in the Hebrew world;[5] v. 34 is a near citation of the Hebrew ideal expressed in Deut 15:4.[6] "One soul"[7] and "all in common"[8] are Greek proverbs relating to friendship.[9] Verse 33 is equally unusual, leading to what are evidently textual improvements.[10] It is not intrusive. Grace empowered this generosity.[11] Verse 34 is more picturesque than 2:45, shifting from the ideal ("all in common") to the reality: the needy received support from contributions of those with more means,[12] who liquidated their holdings and presented them to the apostles for distribution.[13] This conveyance is not intended to enhance the status of the apostles but to show how early Christians prevented the more wealthy members of the community from acquiring power by making "clients" of others.[14]

The dissonance that modern readers discover between the summary of 4:34-35 and the subsequent examples is based on sound logic, but Luke was not

3 On the meaning of πλῆθος ("body"), see the admirable note in Cadbury and Lake, 47–48. Since "heart and soul" is the subject, the variants that mark these nouns with the article are grammatically correct—and therefore probable corrections. The text of vv. 32-35 is rather unstable, but the meaning is clear.

4 The verb is singular.

5 Cf. BDAG, 509, *s.v.*, καρδία 1 b η; and Friedrich Baumgärtel and Johannes Behm, "καρδία," *TDNT* 3:605–13. Parallelism between "heart" (καρδία) and "soul" (ψυχή) occurs frequently in Deuteronomy, such as the "summary of the law" (6:5).

6 The sentiment is not limited to Torah: similar notions are found in Thucydides 7.82.2; Isocrates *Areop.* 83; and Seneca *Ep.* 90.38.

7 According to Diogenes Laertius, Aristotle defined friendship as "one soul inhabiting two bodies" (*Lives* 5.20). Among other examples are Euripides *Andr.* 376–77, *Orest.* 1046; Plutarch *Amores* 21.9 (*Mor.* 967e); Cicero *Amic.* 25.92; *Off.* 1.56.

8 Diogenes Laertius cites Timaeus as an authority for Pythagoras as originator of this proverb (*Lives* 8.10). See also above on Acts 2:44. Euripides *Andr.* 376–77 indicates that it could be used for cynical manipulation. Aristotle unites these two proverbs in *Nic. Eth.* 9.8, 1168b.5. Note the similar language of *Did.* 8:4: "Do not shun a person in need, but share all things with your brother and do not say that anything is your own. For if you are partners in what is immortal, how much more in what is mortal?" (Ehrman, *Apostolic Fathers*, 1:425). *Barn.* 19:8 belongs to the same tradition. Cf. also the *Sentences of Sextus* 227. The idea was familiar to Lucian, who mocks it: "They [the Christians] despise all things (ἁπάντων) indiscriminately and consider them common property (κοινά)" (*Peregr.* 13, trans. Austin Morris Harmon, *Lucian V* [LCL; Cambridge, Mass.: Harvard University Press, 1936] 15). Acts 4:32 reflects common early Christian ethics.

9 The D-Text (Boismard, *Texte*, 105) recasts the sentence. Among the differences are the placement of πλῆθος ("body") in the nominative, putting "soul and heart" (in that order) in the dative and adding, after "one," καὶ οὐκ ἦν διάκρισις ἐν αὐτοῖς οὐδεμία ("there were no disagreements among them"). The additional sentence looks like an idealizing addition—although one could argue on the grounds of 6:1, with which it disagrees, that it was original and later deleted. If original, it might well have meant "discrimination," à la 1 Cor 12:10.

10 On the order and variants, see BDF §473.2; Ropes, *Text*, 33; and Metzger, *Textual Commentary*, 283–84. Haenchen (231 n. 3) notes, with reference to one variant, that Luke never uses "the apostles" as a title with the genitive. (Other variants are the addition of "Christ" and "our Lord.") Ropes utilizes these variants to postulate two basic stemmata. On the translation of "power" as "miracle," see Barrett, 1:254; and Schneider, 1:365. χάρις is better rendered "favor" than "grace. See Barrett, 1:254. Acts 2:47 is different, while Luke 2:40 is parallel.

11 Johnson (86 and 91) notes that Luke correlates authority with his leading symbol of power: the use of possessions. Cf. also Rackham, 63.

12 For Luke a "rich" person is someone with real property, including owners of small farms.

13 The frequentative imperfects of vv. 34-35 indicate that the activity was normal and continual. The use of the (singular!) passive διεδίδετο ("was distributed") avoids stating that the apostles themselves undertook the distribution. On the expression "at the feet," see Haenchen, 231 n. 5.

14 Chrysostom (*Hom.* 11) presumes that no slaves were included, as the believers would have manumitted them.

a logician.[15] The narrative does not suggest that the contributions were involuntary or that Barnabas's action was quite unusual or that no one retained their property.[16] The "everyone who" (ὅσοι) of v. 34 is a hyperbole, but even writers far more scrupulous than this one descend to an occasional hyperbole. Before recounting the example of a couple who fell short of the ideal, it was desirable to present someone who did the right thing, and no harm could come from allowing an eventually important figure in the narrative to play this role. The hypothesis that the stories about Barnabas and Ananias inspired the summary of vv. 34-35 is scarcely stronger than the proposition that Luke invented "the donation of Barnabas."

With this relatively elaborate introduction[17] of (Joseph)[18] Barnabas, Acts brings onto the stage the character who will serve as the link between the immediate followers of Jesus and the gentile mission eventually led by Paul.[19] Is this correct? One would not gather from the undisputed Pauline letters that Barnabas was from Jerusalem,[20] but it is arguable that Paul may not have wished to stress that connection when he wrote Galatians. The strongest argument for this pivotal role is that Luke's source on the origins of the gentile mission[21] may have placed Barnabas in Jerusalem, and done so correctly, although this hypothesis is open to challenge, given Luke's proclivity to link all missionaries to Jerusalem.[22] The traceable lines of that source associate the mission at Antioch with "the Hellenists," less tendentiously with those who left Jerusalem after the death of Stephen (8:4; 11:19-22). Acts does not associate Barnabas with those affiliated to Mary, the mother of John Mark (12:12), or with "the Hellenists," although these people also spoke Greek and engaged in the gentile mission. The practice of liquidating property, of which Barnabas is the sole positive example, was not, according to Acts, transferred with Barnabas to Antioch[23] or promulgated in the missions established by (Barnabas and) Paul. Much must remain unknown, including the connection between Barnabas and Jerusalem. Whatever the historical background, the narrator has ably brought Barnabas into the story. He debuts as an example of one with the proper attitude toward wealth. Of preaching and the like, nothing is said at present, as it would not fit the picture Luke has painted.

15 See the pithy analysis of Haenchen, 232–33.

16 That is, the home of Mary in 12:12 is not a formal contradiction of the narrative. The voluntary nature of these contributions invalidates comparison with Qumran or other societies in which renunciation of property was a condition for full membership. Luke claims that people donated their resources because they had become members of the community, not vice versa. For a detailed evaluation of the relation between Acts and the Qumran community, see Marcello Del Verme, *Comunione e condivisione dei beni: Chiesa primitiva e giudaismo esseno-qumranico a confronto* (Brescia: Morcelliana, 1977).

17 Contrast the introduction of Paul in 7:58. (The introductions are similar in that the character first appears in a relatively minor role.) *An Ephesian Tale* 2.2.3 introduces an important character in a similar manner.

18 Acts is the only source for the notion that "Barnabas" was not a given name. Luke suggests that this man, like Peter (and, in a sense, Paul), earned a new cognomen. (The latter, however, is rather more easily explained than is "Barnabas.")

19 Aspects of the textual tradition actively resisted this distinction of Barnabas from Jesus' disciples. D-Texts (Boismard, *Texte*, 107) read "Joses," which, although it could be taken as the Greek form of this name (Metzger, *Textual Commentary*, 284), allows identification with the person or persons named in Mark 6:3 (a brother of Jesus) and 15:47. Mss 181 pc (w) propose "Barsabbas" as the surname, identifying the individual as the unsuccessful candidate for apostleship in 1:23 (where some D-Texts identified this person as "Barnabas").

20 The statement in Col 4:10 that Barnabas was the cousin of Mark may be incorrect. In any case, identification of this person with the "John Mark" of Acts 12:12, who lived in Jerusalem, is uncertain.

21 See pp. 12–14.

22 One certainly incorrect example is Paul. Others open to question are (John) Mark (12:12, 25) and Silas (15:22).

23 When that church wishes to aid the needy, it takes up an offering (11:30). Lüdemann (63) does not doubt the gift, but says that the time cannot be determined. It could have been made after the conference, when it was decided to raise money for Jerusalem.

This is in some tension with the name "Barnabas," which, according to Luke, was a nickname supplied by the apostles.[24] Semitic languages use such "patronymics" to denote status or quality.[25] The interpretation appears to be an example of folk etymology.[26] It does fit the character, since the verb παρακαλεῖν is associated with Barnabas in 11:23 and 14:22. The expression λόγος παρακλήσεως ("consoling message") is one formal description of a sermon.[27] Barnabas is identified as a "Levite"[28] from Cyprus,[29] combining excellent Jewish credentials with a Diaspora background. Paul will share these qualifications.[30] Acts works to make Barnabas a sidekick of Paul, despite visible evidence to the contrary.[31]

Acts 5:1-11 concludes the unit begun in 4:32.[32] Ananias and Sapphira are the subject of the second example, which begins well enough. A single clause distinguishes their action from that of Barnabas (v. 2a). They wished to enjoy the renown of perfect generosity while retaining something for a rainy day. The narrative assumes that the practice would have been acceptable. What was not acceptable was their deceit. Spiritual power is not limited to healing cripples or opening ears. In this instance, the Spirit serves as both financial auditor and executioner, through the mind and voice of Peter. The identical fate of Sapphira does much to enhance the quality of the narrative. At the theological level, her demise eliminates any possibility that Ananias's expiration was a piece of particularly bad luck. The couple who falsely claimed that they had deposited all at Peter's feet were presently deposited six feet under. The coincidence of the "young men's" return with Sapphira's departure is both dramatically effective and theologically apt. The Spirit of God is directing this scene. The author of the deception is, of course, Satan. The pair's fate is an apposite reminder that Satan can find other agents than wicked officials and evil priests. Some of them are close to home. Among the refinements in the

24 The rather barbarous ἀπό as a mark of agency (ὑπό, a *v.l.*, is proper) might be rendered "Barnabas from/of the apostles," but that does not fit easily with the proposed translation.

25 Cf. "son of peace" (lit.), in Luke 10:6. The idiom is found also in Greek. See I. Howard Marshall, *Commentary on Luke* (NIGTC; Grand Rapids: Eerdmans, 1978) 419–20.

26 Barrett (1:258–59) has not given up the search for a Semitic antecedent, but see Fitzmyer (320–21), whose knowledge of Semitic philology is substantial. For one explanation of how false etymology might have arisen, see Sebastian Brock, "βαρναβᾶς υἱὸς παρακλήσεως," *JTS* 25 (1974) 93–98. According to Williams ("Personal Names," 101), "Barnabas" is quite rare in the Jewish world (she found only one example), but not uncommon among other Semites. One hypothesis is that Barnabas was nicknamed "the preacher" and that the alleged etymology is secondary. Eduard Schwartz ("Zur Chronologie des Paulus," in *Nachrichten von der königlichen Gesellschaft der Wissenschaften zu Göttingen. Philologisch-historische Klasse* [Berlin: Weidmann, 1907] 263–99, esp. 282 n. 1) proposed that the information about Barnabas came from the source of 13:1-3. He suggested that the title "son of consolation" was originally applied to Manaen (whose name means "consoler") and was somehow transferred to Barnabas.

27 Acts 13:15, where Barnabas is present and Heb 13:22; cf. Acts 15:32 and the proposal of Eduard Schwartz in the previous note.

28 D-Texts omit "Levite" (Boismard, *Texte*, 107), possibly on anti-Jewish grounds.

29 Strictly, τῷ γένει means "in nationality," which would suggest gentile origin, but the noun is used loosely here.

30 Another quality that Paul and Barnabas share is wealth. Barnabas is a model whom those with means should emulate.

31 See Bernd Kollmann, *Joseph Barnabas: Leben und Wirkungsgeschichte* (SBS 175; Stuttgart: Katholisches Bibelwerk, 1998); Wolfgang Reinbold, *Propaganda und Mission im ältesten Christentum: Eine Untersuchung zu den Modalitäten der Ausbreitung der frühen Kirche* (FRLANT 188; Göttingen: Vandenhoeck & Ruprecht, 2000) 84–106; and Markus Öhler, *Barnabas: Die historische Person und ihre Rezeption in der Apostelgeschichte* (WUNT 156; Tübingen: Mohr Siebeck, 2003). Note also Clark, *Parallel Lives*, 294–319.

32 For a survey of research on this passage see Marguerat, *Historian*, 155–57. He identifies five distinct exegetical solutions. On p. 158, he shows how the author has shaped the sequence. Other recent studies include V. K. Ntumba, "Ac 5,1-11: Ananie et Saphire; Lecture exégetique et réflexions théologiques," *Hekima Review* 34 (1995) 43–55; Henriette Havelaar, "Hellenistic Parallels to Acts 5,1-11 and the Problem of Conflicting Interpretations," *JSNT* 67 (1997) 63–82; Robert F. O'Toole,

tale are many cross-references, including the ubiquitous and ironic "feet," the contrast between God and mortals (5:4), which binds this with the previous (4:19) and subsequent (5:29) trials and parallels with the story of Judas (Luke 22:1-6; Acts 1:15-26).[33] From the narrative perspective, two miracles have been reported: the generosity of Barnabas and the "executions" of the deceiving couple. Vividness does not require realism. As is usually the case, the narrative evidently presumes that the community is assembled for some purpose and that they remain so for some hours (cf. 4:23; 12:12). The timely arrival of Ananias's burial party is the sort of coincidence that most often requires a friendly narrator—or the hand of Providence.

The story of Susanna (Daniel 13 LXX) presents a number of points for comparison. It is a literary example of how the deceiving couple could be presented as a short novella. An introduction of the wealthy couple (cf. Sus 1-4) would be followed by a detailed description of their plans for a gift, climaxing with their discovery of shared greed and the conspiracy (cf. Sus 7-14). The donation scene would receive due elaboration, after which the plot would take a sudden turn with Peter's separate prosecutions of Ananias (cf. Sus 52-55) and, upon her return, Sapphira (cf. Sus 56-59) and the communal response (cf. Sus 60-62). Shared themes and motifs include a "deadly sin" (lust, greed), separation of the offending pair, and exposure by questioning.[34] God is responsible for the deaths in both stories.[35] Luke could have presented this episode as a lengthy story, just as he could have summarized the speech of Stephen in a few verses or recounted Paul's journey to Rome in a short paragraph or two. Brevity and length lie within the purview of the narrator. One should not simply presume that Luke said to himself, as it were, "I have so much to recount that I shall have to be concise here." Nor does brevity always mean diminished importance. Subsequent comments will attempt to show that the very compressed nature of the account enhances its power.

The structure is transparent: two scenes (vv. 1-6, 7-11), each of which includes a response (vv. 5, 11). Daniel Marguerat analyzes the piece as a "diptych," noting these correspondences: vv. 2/8, vv. 3/9a, vv. 5a/10a, and vv. 5b/11.[36] The parallelism enhances the drama of the narrative. As step replicates step, the readers wonder whether death will follow death. This punitive activity involves a "rule miracle."[37] In this instance the ruling is underscored by doubling, producing an effect not unlike that of the "double dream" in which two persons receive identical or complementary revelations.[38] Luke is responsible for producing the diptych and for a good bit of the wording of vv. 1-6.[39] A generally recognized verbal source is the story of Achan (Josh 7:1, 6-26). The verb ἐνοσφίσατο ("withheld") is a strong

"'You Did Not Lie to Us but to God' (Acts 5,4c)," *Bib* 76 (1995) 182–209; and Julian Hills, "Equal Justice under the (New) Law: The Story of Ananias and Sapphira in Acts 5," *Forum* n.s. 3 (2000) 105–25.

33 Brown (*Apostasy*, 98–113) notes five links between this story and that of Judas: (1) Satan is the cause (Luke 22:3; Acts 5:3); (2) money is the basis (Luke 22:5-6; Acts 1:18; 5:3); (3) the deed is intentional (Luke 22:6; Acts 5:4); (4) real estate is involved (Acts 1:18; 5:11), and (5) the result is sudden death.

34 Note the use of "lie" as the cause of death in Sus 55, 59.

35 Daniel announces that the "angel of God" will administer justice to the wicked elders (vv. 55, 59). The human agents of these executions are the members of the community (vv. 61-62). Although readers of today might view Susanna as more realistic, the ancient authors would have found these differences relatively unimportant.

36 Marguerat, *Historian*, 158.

37 See the excursus "Punitive miracles" in the commentary on 1:15-26. Havelaar, "Hellenistic Parallels," 63–82, analyzes a number of themes and discusses ancient parallels. In addition to the oft-cited Healing no. 36 from Epidauros (*IG* IV² 1, 122 = Emma J. Edelstein and Ludwig Edelstein, *Asclepius: A Collection and Interpretation of the Testimonies* [2 vols.; Baltimore: Johns Hopkins University Press, 1945] 1:228, no. 423) and Lucian *Philops.* 20, Havelaar points to a roughly contemporary (118/119 CE) dedication to the god Men (Eugene N. Lane, *Corpus Monumentorum Religionis Dei Meni* [4 vols.; Leiden: Brill, 1971–78] 1:51), which deals with the punishment by death of one Apollonius because he had refused to fulfill a financial obligation taken under oath.

38 On "double-dreams" see on 9:1-19a below.

39 See Theissen (*Miracle Stories*, 63–64), who notes ἀνὴρ δέ τις Ἀνανίας ὀνόματι ("a man by the name of"), ἐπώλησεν κτῆμα ("sold a piece of property"), used in 4:37; "at the apostles' feet," used in 4:35, 37, and the contrast between human and divine plans, which appears in 5:29, 38-39.

signal.[40] The questions put by Peter to each partner in turn resemble Josh 7:25: "Why did you bring trouble on us? The LORD is bringing trouble on you today." Death is the immediate sequel in all three instances.[41] In the search for a suitable context, exegetes have long called attention to 1 Cor 5:1-5 (cf. v. 13).[42] Another possibility is that 1 Corinthians constituted a major source of Acts 5:1-10. This economical solution to the question of source illuminates the development of early Christian thought and literature.[43] Even without consideration of 1 Corinthians, critical scrutiny leaves very little material for source criticism. It is quite possible that there was an early believer, somewhere, who violated a major community rule, suffered a formal curse and ban, and died shortly thereafter. Such things happened (and happen).[44] The putative underlying story need not have been related to financial misconduct, since money is an important Lucan symbol,[45] while sex is excluded from his repertory.

The story must be ranked among the most difficult for modern readers of Acts. It portrays Peter as a man of supernatural insight who is able to pronounce effective curses upon sinners, just like Paul in 13:8-11. The story appears to present the working of the Spirit in almost magical fashion. Neither Ananias nor Sapphira is apparently offered any chance of repentance, and the way in which the former was buried without his wife's knowledge sounds heartless, to say nothing of being improbable.[46]

I. Howard Marshall well summarizes some of the questions this episode raises. Theological objections to this story did not have to wait patiently for the incursion of modernity. On the basis of 5:1-11, the Manicheans rejected Acts for broadcasting actions unworthy of God.[47] Porphyry added his own scathing criticism.[48] Interpreters from Chrysostom to Calvin and beyond stressed the exemplary effect of the tale, often noting that the death of this pair could save the lives/souls of many.[49] More recent commentators of an apologetic orientation are likely to claim that this unpleasant episode shows that Luke did not simply idealize the life

Theissen also suspects that the emphasis on the Holy Spirit may be Lucan, since this is a leading theme of that author. In addition, 5:4 is reminiscent of Luke 22:3 (Judas). The secondary nature of Sapphira is evident not only from the almost identical language of the two episodes (Theissen) but also by the syntax of vv. 1-2. The main verbs there are singular and refer to the husband. Sapphira enters the story in two awkward phrases that, if omitted, would improve the narrative flow. Luke is fond of pairs, especially male-female pairs. See p. 252. For discussion of whether both partners were part of the tradition see Marguerat, *Historian*, 158.

40 Biblical usage is limited to 7:1; 2 Macc 4:32 (which depends on Joshua), and Titus 2:10. See Spicq, *Lexicon*, 2:546–47; and the note in Cadbury and Lake, 50 (a "rather obscure word").

41 Joshua does not include burial of the victim. Josephus *Ant.* 5:44 mentions the burial of Achan, but this conclusion is probably coincidental.

42 Havelaar ("Hellenistic Parallels") emphasizes the theme of excommunication, which accords with 1 Corinthians 5.

43 See Pervo, *Dating*, 70–73, which examines this passage in the light of Joshua 7, 1 Corinthians 5, and 1 Timothy 1:20.

44 Harold Remus points to anthropological and laboratory data on the possible effects of "excommunication" (*Pagan-Christian Conflict over Miracle in the Second Century* [Patristic Monograph Series 10; Cambridge, Mass.: Philadelphia Patristic Foundation, 1983] 92–93, 256 n. 27).

45 See p. 11.

46 Marshall, 110. In his comments (110–13) he attempts to ameliorate some of these objections.

47 Augustine countered by pointing out punitive miracles in the Apocryphal Acts, of which the Manicheans did approve (*Adim.* 17), with evident reference to the tale preserved in the Coptic *Act of Peter*.

48 See R. Joseph Hoffmann, *Porphyry's Against the Christians: The Literary Remains* (Amherst, N.Y.: Prometheus Books, 1994) 54–55. The material comes from Macarius Magnes's *Apocriticus* 3.20. Porphyry says that Peter put the couple to death for withholding "a little for their own use." ("A little" is P.'s own contribution). Even if this act were wrong, there is the demand of Jesus to forgive up to 490 sins. Moreover, Peter should have recalled his own false statement that he did not know Jesus.

49 Origen (*Comm. on Matthew* 15.15) discussed this passage in detail in commenting on Matt 10:21 ("if you wish to be perfect . . ."). Arator (1:431-32) saw the story as admonitory. For the exemplary view, see also Chrysostom *Hom.* 12. Bede (30) is quite

of the early church,[50] to rationalize it,[51] or to ignore its theological ramifications.[52] In this milieu, John Polhill is refreshing: "When all is said and done, there is no 'comfortable' solution to the passage."[53] The last thing that should be said about this story is that it demonstrates the absence of an idealizing tendency. Nothing is more idealized than the picture of a world in which vice is promptly punished and virtue properly rewarded. Acts 5:1-11 is a stumbling block for those of a modern Western orientation both because it seems to depict the deity as executing a cheating couple *pour encourager les autres* and because, like 1 Cor 5:1-5, it focuses on the welfare of the community rather than on the correction of an errant pair.[54] The story is not an account of conflict; no principles or issues are contested, nor do parties with different views emerge. Finally, as Haenchen shows, the narrative is consistent neither in itself or in its context.[55]

Comment

■ **1-6** At the outset, the narrative appears to be recounting a parallel to the deed of Barnabas.[56] Ananias and Sapphira[57] (the first married couple identified among believers in Acts) sold a piece of property.[58] Verse 2 blocks a positive interpretation of the act: they "withheld," "embezzled" as it were,[59] some of the proceeds. In this compressed manner, the narrator indicates that Ananias represented the proffered sum as his total receipts. There is no indication of what benefits the couple[60] hoped to reap from their deception, and

laconic: *ceteris exemplum* ("an example for others"). Jerome's *Life of Hilarion* (which has much of Jerome and little of Hilarion) says that the aspiring ascetic divided his deceased parents' property among his siblings and the poor because of fear that by retaining any for himself he might share the fate of Ananias and Sapphira (3). On patristic approaches, see also Marguerat, *Historian*, 172 n. 44. Calvin (1:134–38) endorses the exemplary interpretation: "[T]he punishment of one was a warning for all" (138). He also views the deaths as a prod to liberality in almsgiving and is aware that many find it incredible that a multitude of other deceivers are allowed to prosper. To that, he offers the view that miracles were a particular feature of the early church intended to serve as enduring signs. Rackham (64) finds a different lesson. This episode shows that all attempts—from Novatian to the Puritans and beyond—to maintain a pure and perfect community are misguided. These sentiments are commendable, but they are not germane.

50 An example is Tannehill, *Narrative Unity*, 2:79.

51 So Marshall (112), who states that the death of Ananias was "probably a case of heart-failure due to shock." On the next page, moving toward a social-scientific orientation, he speaks of the effects of a curse in "primitive societies."

52 Witherington devotes six pages (214–20) to the passage without reflecting on the underlying theology, as is apparent in his critique of Philippe Henri Menoud's proposal that the original motivation was the death of believers before the parousia ("La mort d'Annanias et de Saphira [Actes 5, 1-11]," in *Aux sources de la tradition chrétienne: Mélanges offerts à M. Maurice Goguel à l'occasion de son soixante-dixième anniversaire* [Neuchâtel: Delachaux et Niestlé, 1950] 146–54): "One must ask of this theory why Luke, in an apologetic document keen on evangelism, would expand or report the expanded story in this way. Surely, this story would scare more off than it would attract! It is much more likely that he had hard evidence that this story had a strong basis in fact, and he felt he must include at least some traditions that showed that the earliest church was not perfect" (Witherington, 216 n. 82).

53 Polhill, 161.

54 Weiser (1:138–48) attends to theology in his analysis of this passage.

55 Haenchen (239–41) does his usual job of deconstructing the rationalizers while using their proposals to expose the holes in the narrative.

56 For the phrase ἀνὴρ δέ τις ὀνόματι ("a certain man named"), see 8:9 (Simon "the magician"); 10:1 (Cornelius). The δέ is not adversative (i.e., "in contrast to Barnabas"); see Cadbury and Lake, 49.

57 On the name "Ananias," see Williams, "Personal Names," 85. On "Sapphira," see Richard Pervo, "Sapphira," in Carol Meyers et al., eds., *Women in Scripture* (New York: Houghton Mifflin, 2000) 149–50. The detailed study of Richter Reimer (*Women*, 1–29) has many valuable data and observations. Her perspective is historicizing and rationalizing.

58 As noted above, the verbs in vv. 1-2 are singular; "Ananias" is the subject. "Sapphira" is limited to a prepositional phrase. Cf. the introduction of Aquila and Priscilla in 18:2.

59 Haenchen (237 n. 4) defines ἐνοσφίσατο in a concise note.

60 According to Jewish legal traditions, Sapphira

speculation about the matter will not enhance the credibility of the story.[61] By omitting all but the essential details, the narrator focuses on the central issue. Peter, who, like Jesus, can read minds (see Luke 5:22; 6:8; 9:46-47), challenges the donor. The crabbed syntax of vv. 3-4 results from dramatic elaboration.[62] Ananias lied about what he received, and this lie was against the Holy Spirit. This charge is contained in four sections, framed by questions using the words "heart"[63] and "lie." This is not a fact-seeking interrogation. Peter gives no opportunity for response.[64] Ananias answers by dying.[65] He (with his wife) has committed "the sin against the Holy Spirit" (Luke 12:10).[66] Luke is prepared to classify financial misrepresentation as the most grievous of all sins, more or less equating it with ϑεομαχία ("opposition to God").[67] Ananias's death confirms the truth of Peter's words and the gravity of the offense. The response is appropriate for a miracle and indicates that the message was received.[68] Without prompting, "the young"[69] gather up the corpse[70] and cart it off for burial.

---

had to know what was happening if she were to be found guilty. See the regulations in Lev. 5:1; CD 14.20–21; 1QS 6.24–25.

61 If such contributions were truly voluntary, any amount would have been appreciated. Otherwise, one must assume a particular status for those who had sold all and given it to the poor (Luke 18:22) and that Luke has evidently concealed this two-tiered approach to community members. Cf. Brown, *Apostasy*, 99. On p. 106, Brown states that the verb "withhold" indicates that Ananias regarded the property as "his own" and that he should have contributed all of the proceeds. Haenchen says that v. 4 conflicts with 4:32, 34. These are two interpretations of the same dissonance. I think it unlikely that Luke would have been bound to the literal interpretation of his own idealistic summary, but Brown may see the essence of the issue.

62 Haenchen (237) notes that Luke often compresses two ideas into a question; cf. 1:4. Here the underlying question is "Why have you done this?" The answer ("Satan has filled your heart") is subsumed within the question. The verb ψεύσασϑαι ("lie" or "falsify") is evidently a final infinitive, paralleled by νοσφίσασϑαι ("mulct," "withhold"); that is, the second infinitive is the result of the first (§BDF 391 [4]). Verse 4a is odd, lit. "Didn't it remain yours while it remained?" The second clause in v. 4 may be declarative, with little difference in meaning.

63 "Heart"; cf. 4:32. The idea that Satan (etc.) enters or controls the heart is at home in apocalyptic; cf. the *Asc. Isa.* 3.11. The anthropology is elaborated in 1QS 3.13—4.25. Use of "fill" in this context is a Septuagintalism. See Metzger, *Textual Commentary*, 285–86.

64 𝔓[74] and witnesses of the D-tradition improve or clarify the language of v. 4b. The variations suggest that the text has become confused.

65 The D-Text adds παραχρῆμα ("immediately"), a word of which it is fond and one quite suitable to miracle stories (e.g., Luke 4:39; 5:25; 8:44; Acts 3:7, etc.). Luke reserved this for v. 10. E includes it in v. 6. Witherington (216 and n. 81) wishes to stress the medical usage of ἐκψύχω. Since it is found in Acts only in 5:5, 10 and 12:23, it is preferable to say that Luke utilizes it for divine executions.

66 See Brown (*Apostasy*, 107–9), who shows that Luke places this saying about the sin against the Spirit in the era of the church. Goulder (*Type*, 91) came to the same conclusion.

67 Cf. the speech of Gamaliel in 5:35–39.

68 "Awe" (φόβος) is one way of characterizing the confirmatory crowd response to a miracle (*Wunderglaube*), as in Luke 5:26; See Knox, 22. It is the proper response to the presence of the numinous (cf. Luke 1:12) and can have the sense of fear that motivates corrective action, as in Acts 19:17. Verse 5 does not specify that those "who heard" were present at the event. It probably includes both those and others to whom they conveyed the news.

69 The indifferent use of νεώτεροι in v. 6 and of νεανίσκοι in v. 10, typical Lucan "elegant variation," speaks against the notion that there was an organized "order" of youth. See Pervo, *Dating*, 220. The presence of these persons does seem to indicate that Luke envisions an assembly of the community. See also F. Scott Spencer, "Wise Up, Young Man: The Moral Vision of Saul and Other νεανίσκοι in Acts," in Thomas E. Phillips, ed., *Acts and Ethics* (NTMon 9; Sheffield: Sheffield Phoenix, 2005) 34–48, esp. 40–41.

70 The verb συστέλλω means, "cover," "wrap up," probably not with reference to a winding sheet (BDAG, 978, *s.v.* 3). Cadbury and Lake (51) say that the meaning of this word is not very clear. A bland rendition is thus preferable.

■ **7-11** An interval[71] of about three hours ensues.[72] Sapphira, who has not been told of her loss,[73] arrives for some unspecified reason. Without consolation upon her bereavement or further ado, Peter launches his interrogation.[74] All details that do not focus upon the crime are ignored. The proposal that by his questioning Peter offers Sapphira a way out is misplaced.[75] Trick questions are not an acceptable means of eliciting repentance. A two-sentence exchange is sufficient to entrap the freshly minted widow. Verse 9 brings a query like that of v. 3.[76] Both questions are accusations. Sapphira then learns that she has become a widow but that her tenure in that status will not be lengthy. Some nice touches accompany this stunning coincidence.[77] The feet[78] of those who buried Ananias are at the door.[79] "Feet" is also the place where gifts, including that of Ananias and Sapphira (v. 2), are offered. At his feet, she will also die.[80] With this well-shod piece of poetic justice, the lesson is complete and she goes to join her husband.[81] Peter kills the pair with words just as he heals others with words. God is the ultimate cause; Peter is God's human agent. Comparison of his role with that of the *mĕbaqqēr* of the Qumran community is erroneous.[82] Verse 11, the parallel to v. 6, introduces two groups: "the community," and "everyone else who heard about it." This is the first use of ἐκκλησία in Acts.[83] The intention of this bifurcation may be to lay the ground for v. 13, but it also shows that the passage is ecclesiological, illustrating the nature of the Christian community.[84]

---

71 The syntax of v. 7 is difficult. BDF §144 finds two constructions: ἐγένετο . . . καί and an asyndetically prefixed nominative absolute of time. See also Cadbury and Lake, 52. Barrett (1:269) disagrees.

72 Readers may imagine how this time passed. Marshall (113 n. 1) says, "Haenchen's picture of the apostle still sitting on his chair without intermission three hours after Ananias's death with the money lying at his feet is pure fantasy." So it would be, had Haenchen said it. He takes the τοσούτου in v. 8 to mean that the money "still lies at the Apostles' feet" (Haenchen, 239).

73 The participles συνειδυίης (v. 2) and μὴ εἰδυῖα (v. 7) nicely characterize Sapphira.

74 The verb ἀποκρίνομαι can mean "speak up" (BDAG, 114 *s.v.* 2). There are variations to the question, including the D-Text's more refined ἐπηρωτήσω σε εἰ ἄρα ("Let me ask you whether . . ."). This seems to heighten the sarcasm. It probably imitates Luke 20:3, but see Metzger, *Textual Commentary*, 286. Cop^Mae is more blunt: "Peter said to her, I asked you about the sale. Did you sell the garden for this money?"

75 The view that Peter was giving Sapphira an opportunity to confess is at least as old as Chrysostom. Modern exponents of the view include Marshall (113) and Witherington (217).

76 The wording συνεφωνήθη ὑμῖν is unique. See §BDF 202. Luke is striving for elegance. For Luke, "Spirit of the Lord" and "Holy Spirit" are interchangeable. The *v.l.* "Holy Spirit" is clearly secondary. It is not clear, however, whether the phrase means "the Spirit of God" or "the Spirit of Christ."

77 For reassurance that Ananias could have been buried within three hours, see Witherington, 219 n. 95. Rackham (67) was less confident: "The rapidity of the burials and the apparent absence of enquiry suggest difficulties to our minds."

78 "Feet" is, in this instance, a synecdoche; cf. Isa 52:7.

79 𝔓[74] A 1175 bo read "at the door<u>s</u>," which transforms the setting into a large building, like the churches of post-Constantinian times.

80 Marguerat (*Historian*, 155) views v. 9b as a bit of grim humor.

81 Complementing the use of "feet" is the preposition πρός, used both of the spot where she died and her final resting place. The D-Texts (D [sy^p]) that pedantically have her prepared for burial unintentionally illustrate the economy of the narrative.

82 On this comparison, see Joseph A. Fitzmyer, "Jewish Christianity in Acts in Light of the Qumran Scrolls," in Keck and Martyn, *Studies*, 233–57, esp. 247–48; Haenchen, 240–41; and Hans-Josef Klauck, "Gütergemeinschaft in der klassischen Antike, in Qumran und im neuen Testament," *Revue de Qumran* 11 (1982) 47–79. The grounds for such a comparison require the assumption that the story is a legend, the "historical kernel" of which is that Peter administered discipline and is therefore a kind of "bishop." Although Acts shows Peter as the leader of the Jerusalem community at this point, it gives him no special title and portrays no authorization. According to 1QS 6:24-25, intentional lies about property carried a penalty of one year's exclusion from the community meal and a reduction of rations.

83 On the term, see Barrett, 1:271; Fitzmyer, 325. It is anachronistic.

84 See Marguerat (*Historian*, 164–65), who stresses the ecclesiological nature of the passage.

Since greed holds pride of place among sins in Acts, it is appropriate that malefactors suffer considerable discomfort,[85] but these two believers who lie about money drop dead. Acts happily represents the view that the "ban" demanded by Paul for a man living in an unlawful relationship be applied—with no doubts about its efficacy—to a pair that misrepresented their generous contribution. This is the world of the Pastorals (1 Tim 1:20),[86] representative of an era and a milieu in which the church was determined to uphold its morality in the face of criticism by outsiders. For Luke, this episode contained not the least hint of embarrassment; fear is an appropriate motive for Christian behavior. Marguerat aptly compares their deed to the sin of the first couple.[87] The "primitive church" had utopian qualities, but sinlessness was not among them.[88]

■ **12-16** The summary in vv. 12-16 is, like many of the summaries in Acts, a hinge, closing one section and inaugurating another. It takes up the petitions of 4:23-31, both of which are (further) fulfilled, resulting in additional growth. Verses 15-16, like 4:36-37, provide specification by reporting the healing career of Peter, who has so many patients that he is enabled to bestow mercy without even the need to pause and wave a beneficent hand. For the first time, the movement attracts people from outside of Jerusalem. This much is clear, but the meaning of v. 13a is not, and the transitions are far from smooth. Considerable exegetical ingenuity is required to absolve vv. 12-14 of contradiction, since vv. 12-13 suggest that awe motivated outsiders to keep their distance from the believers, whereas v. 14 has them joining in droves. Appeals to a blend of tradition and redaction flourish in such an atmosphere,[89] but they do not explain the author's apparently loose grip on his material.

If διά ("through") in v. 12 has the sense of intermediate agency, the first sentence would mean "God worked many miracles[90] through the apostles,"[91] but it is probably instrumental.[92] The phrase ἐν τῷ λαῷ seems quite otiose. The translation presumes that it anticipates the contrast between "the people" and "the outsiders" of v. 13. "Solomon's Portico," although evidently linked with tradition,[93] advances Luke's portrait of Christianity as a philosophical school[94] associated (like Cynics, Platonists, Stoics, Aristotelians, and Epicureans) with a particular meeting place.[95] Verse 13 is exceptionally

85 Examples: Simon (8:18-24, dire threat), Elymas (presumably threatened with loss of his vision and position, 13:8-11), the owners of the slave at Philippi (16:19-20), the sons of Sceva at Ephesus (19:13-17), and the artisans energized by Demetrius (19:24-27) in the same city all face loss of revenue.

86 Note also 1 Tim 6:10: "the love of money is a root of all kinds of evil."

87 Marguerat, *Historian*, 172–78, the conclusion of his valuable study. Rackham (xxxiv) anticipated this view, with many examples. Comparison (via contrast) to the temptation of Jesus (Luke 4:1-13), as proposed by, e.g., Weiser (1:146) and Pesch (1:204), is less germane. Cf. also Thomas E. Phillips, "Creation, Sin and Its Curse, and the People of God: An Intertextual reading of Genesis 1–12 and Acts 1–7," *Horizons in Biblical Theology* 25 (2003) 146–60.

88 The situation remains utopian in that justice is directly administered by God rather than through the often corrupt and frequently biased media of human judges. See Saundra C. Schwartz, "The Trial Scene in the Greek Novels and in Acts," in Penner, *Contextualizing*, 105–37, esp. 120.

89 For a survey of proposed solutions, see Myllykoski, "Being There," 168 n. 66. Barrett (1:273) would like to attribute the various linguistic difficulties to the inept merger of traditions about Peter with the authorial summary. This is a reasonable approach, but the evidence for "traditions" about Peter comes to his shadow. This is an insufficient basis. Haenchen (244–46) exposes the weaknesses of various interpolation hypotheses.

90 The phrase "signs and wonders" evokes the world of the Hebrew Bible (see Acts 2:43; 4:16, 22, 30; 5:12; 6:8; 8:6, 13; 14:3; 15:12). It is essentially limited to the first half of Acts.

91 The "all" of v. 12 evidently designates the entire body of the apostles (cf. v. 18), as does "to them" in v. 13, but these may intend to refer to the community of believers.

92 Moule, *Idiom Book*, 57.

93 See on 3:11.

94 See Pervo, *Dating*, 177–78.

95 Cf. Haenchen, 245: "Each might now summon up a vision of a colonnaded hall in which the apostles were teaching like the ancient philosophers." A specific example is Diogenes Laertius *Lives* 7.5. D-Texts preface "in the sanctuary" to "in the Portico of Solomon," although D-Texts in chap. 3 tended to place this portico outside of the sanctuary. E reads ἐν τῷ ναῷ συνηγμένοι ("having assembled in the temple"), intimating that they met in a building.

difficult. The chief difficulty is the meaning of οἱ λοιποί ("outsiders" [?]), but κολλᾶσθαι (rendered "get too close to") is also unclear.[96] If the "all" of v. 12 refers to the apostles, οἱ λοιποί might be applied to the other believers. This is not very likely. The internal contrast is between οἱ λοιποί and "the people," suggesting the leadership and generating a number of conjectural emendations, none of which has been well received.[97] Haenchen observed that Luke 8:10 replaces the οἱ ἔξω ("the outsiders") of Mark 4:11 with οἱ λοιποί.[98] If so construed, the verse would mean that nonbelievers (evidently mindful of what befell Ananias and Sapphira) kept a respectful distance, which should not be taken to imply that the reputation of the apostles had declined.[99] In short, exegetes must attempt to say what they think Luke meant. The text is quite possibly corrupt beyond repair.[100] Verse 14 does nothing to ameliorate the situation, since it is difficult to fit into the sequence.[101]

■ **15-16** Luke composed vv. 15-16 on the basis of Mark, especially Mark 6:55-56.[102] Verse 15 is grammatically rugged.[103] Barrett exclaims: "No more astounding piece of miracle-working is described in the NT; Peter does not need to speak, to touch, or, it seems, to give any attention to the sick person."[104] In the background is the notion that the shadow is an extension of one's person or personality.[105] This is the basis for Haenchen's strictures about the account.[106] Individual miracles can be viewed as symbols of God's inbreaking rule of love and related to individual faith and response. Acts 5:15 merely requires that one be in the right place at the right time. For Luke, Acts 5:15—and 19:11-12—communicate at a different "symbolic" level from stories about individuals.[107] The internal parallel with Paul in chap. 19 indicates that the purpose of vv. 15-16 is to show that this is the climax of Peter's career in Jerusalem. Word

96 See the discussion of Witherington, 225, and the succinct summary of Haenchen, 242 n. 5.

97 See Metzger, *Textual Commentary*, 287.

98 Haenchen, 242.

99 So Barrett, 1:274–75, following Conzelmann, 39. Note also Bruce, 167. To add to the difficulties, Luke does not otherwise (Luke 1:46, 58; Acts 10:46; 19:17) make human beings the object of μεγαλύνω ("glorify").

100 The D-Text smooths the opening of v. 13: καὶ οὐδεὶς τῶν λοιπῶν ("and/but none of the others").

101 BDF §465 (1) classifies this as a parenthesis, a polite way of saying that it does not fit.

102 See Pervo, *Dating*, 36–38.

103 On ὥστε καί ("actually") indicating result (of what?), see Bruce, 168. Note Mark 3:10-11, which is similar. The infinitives have no stated subject. If v. 14 is taken as a parenthesis, that subject will be the public of v. 13. See Haenchen, 243. The phrase ἐρχομένου Πέτρου could be taken as an improper genitive absolute, with little difference in meaning. See Cadbury and Lake, 55. Despite the ἄν, B 33 614 1241 1505 *al* place ἐπισκιάσῃ in the future indicative.

104 Barrett, 1:276.

105 On the subject, see Erwin Preuschen, *Die Apostelgeschichte* (HNT; Tübingen: Mohr Siebeck, 1912) 30; Betz, *Lukian*, 151 n. 7; and Pieter van der Horst, "Peter's Shadow: The Religio-Historical Background of Acts V.15," *NTS* 23 (1976–77) 204–12. Key parallel passages are quoted by Barrett, 1:276–77. That the mere sight of a charismatically endowed individual may convey healing is stated by Pliny the Younger (*Pan.* 22.3), who says that the sick dragged themselves to places where they could see Trajan at his arrival. See Geoffrey W. H. Lampe ("Miracles in the Acts of the Apostles," in C. F. D. Moule, ed., *Miracles: Cambridge Studies in Their Philosophy and History* [London: Mowbray, 1965] 163–78, esp. 175), who points to the use of "overshadow" in Luke 1:35; 9:34. This may point to Luke's symbolic understanding of the concept. See n. 107.

106 Haenchen, 246. Barrett (1:276–77) follows Schneider (1:382 n. 33) in affirming that Haenchen's criticism does not recognize that God is the source of all miraculous power. This jejune observation is not relevant.

107 The kind of reservation raised by Polhill (164), for example, that the text does not make the fact of healings explicit, was anticipated by D-Text expansions: unwilling to leave it at "the shadow knows," the rough transition at the close is eased by D-Text expansions: ἀπηλλάσσοντο γὰρ ἀπὸ πάσης ἀσθενείας ὡς εἶχεν ἕκαστος αὐτῶν ("For each was relieved from every infirmity from which he or she suffered") D (p cop^{mae}); καὶ ῥυσθῶσιν ἀπὸ πάσης ἀσθενείας ἧς εἶχον. διὸ συνήρχετο ("And they were delivered from every infirmity that they had. [] Therefore . . .") E gig vg^{cl} Lcf. Inspiration for this supplement came from 19:12b. See Epp, *Tendency*, 156–57. It is not likely that the narrator wished to imply that the hopes of these superstitious fools were dashed. For the author's understanding of this verb, see Luke 1:35: "The Holy Spirit will come upon you, and the power of

of this therapeutic power spread, resulting in an influx from the surrounding settlements.[108]

Acts 4:32—5:16 is an interlude between formal persecutions. Official opposition had no chilling effect on evangelism. All of the apostles conspicuously defied the official admonition given to Peter and John. The band of believers continued its rapid increase. The community exhibited remarkable unity and charity. The slightest hint of corruption brought decisive divine intervention, while healings conveyed relief to an ever-growing number of the afflicted. Peter became a veritable healing cornucopia, overflowing with heaven-sent beneficence. Three believers from "the rank and file" receive particular attention. Two of these are Ananias and Sapphira, who promptly depart in death and disgrace. The other is one Barnabas, a generous Levite from the Diaspora. In the light of this activity, renewed interest from the authorities will occasion no surprise.

---

the Most High will overshadow (ἐπισκιάσει) you." In Luke 9:34 (the transfiguration, from Mark 9:7), the verb is concrete but illustrates an element of the background: overshadowing by a cloud as a symbol of divine presence. This, despite Barrett, 1:277, is not what Luke means. *Act. Thom.* 59 imitates this passage. Sick persons were placed on the route by which Thomas was traveling, as in Acts, but he healed each in the name of the Lord, after which those who had received succor gave praise to Jesus, who had healed them through Thomas. Intertextuality here provides interesting commentary. The author of the *Acts of Thomas* has stripped the canonical account of its "questionable" details and produced a much more "orthodox" summary. Not all reservations about the character of Acts 5:15 are of recent vintage. Bede (30) deals with the passage by a series of ingenious wordplays to show that Peter is a trope for the church.

108 The translation assumes that Luke uses "cities" (πόλεις) casually. (There were no cities in the vicinity of Jerusalem.) The usage supports his picture of Christianity as an urban movement. A variety of witnesses have the crowds come "*to* Jerusalem." This apparently treats πέριξ as an adverb, which is how BDAG 802 takes it. Note Josephus *Bell.* 4.241: ἐν ταῖς πέριξ κώμαις τε καὶ πόλεσι ("In both the neighboring villages and cities" [of Jerusalem]). Instead of the (typically Lucan) semi-independent relative clause, D-Texts tend to say "and all were healed" (ἰῶντο). Cf. the summary of Philip's mission to Samaria in 8:7.

5

5:17-42 The Apostles in Prison and on Trial

17/ As a result, the high priest and
his colleagues, that is, the Sadducees, turned green with envy.
18/ They seized the apostles
and had them held in official
custody. 19/ An angel[a] of the
Lord opened the prison doors
at night and escorted them out,
saying, 20/ "Go take your place
in the sanctuary and proclaim
to the public everything about
this way of life." 21/ In response
they went to the sanctuary at
dawn and began to teach.
When the high priest and his
colleagues arrived, they
convoked the council, that is,
the entire Israelite Senate,[b]
and then sent instructions to
the jail for the prisoners to be
conveyed to court. 22/ The
agents dispatched for this task
did not find them in the prison
and returned with this report:
23/ "We found the prison-house
locked and well secured, with
guards at the doors, but, when
we opened the doors, we didn't
find anyone inside!" 24/ When
they heard this information,
the chief of the temple police
and the leading priests couldn't
figure out what was going on.
25/ At that moment someone
came in and announced, "Listen! Those people whom you
had put in prison are standing in the temple teaching the
populace!" 26/ Thereupon the
police chief and his men set out
to bring them back, with a minimum of force, since they were
afraid that the populace would
stone them.

5:27-39: Conventional Text

27/ The authorities arraigned the
apostles before the council[c] for
examination by the high priest:
28/ "We strictly enjoined you[d]
not to teach in 'this name,' but
look at what you've gone and
done: *filled* Jerusalem with this
teaching! In addition, you are
trying to make *us* responsible
for this fellow's death!"
29/ "We must obey God rather than
mortals," replied Peter and the
other apostles. 30/ "Our ances-

5:27-39: D-Text

27/ Now when they brought the
apostles *before* the Sanhedrin,
the high priest *began to speak*
to them: 28/ "Did we not
strictly enjoin you not to teach
in 'this name'? Look at what
you've gone and done: *filled*
Jerusalem with this teaching!
In addition, you are trying to
make *us* responsible for the
death of *that* fellow!"
29/ *"Whom must we obey? God or*
mortals?" replied Peter. *He said,*

tral God raised Jesus, whom
you took and hung upon a
cross. 31/ Divine power exalted
him to become Leader and
Savior, in order to give Israel
opportunity to change its heart
and find forgiveness for sins.
32/ As for us, we are witnesses
of these matters, as is the Holy
Spirit that God gives to those
who *are* obedient."

33/ Cut to the quick, the audience
was eager to kill them. 34/ At
that point a learned and universally revered Pharisee named
Gamaliel took the floor. After
directing that the defendants
be removed for a while, 35/ he
spoke:
"My fellow Israelites, think carefully about what you propose
to do to these people. 36/ Some
time ago Theudas rose up in
rebellion, claiming that he was
someone special. He gained
about four hundred adherents,
but, after he had been eliminated, all of his followers were
dispersed, and the movement
evaporated. 37/ Subsequently,
at the time of the census, Judas
of Galilee also rose up and gathered a pack of rebels. He also
perished, and all of his followers were put to flight. 38/ My
advice in this matter is that you
keep your distance from these
people. Let them go, for, if this
scheme or enterprise happens
to be of human origin, it will
be thwarted, 39/ but, if it is of
divine origin, you will not be
able to thwart them. Be careful
to avoid conflict with God!"
They found his argument persuasive. 40/ The officials then
recalled the apostles and, after
beating them, released them
with the command to cease
speaking in the name of Jesus.

41/ The apostles left the Sanhedrin
rejoicing that they had been
deemed worthy to suffer abuse
for the sake of the Name.
42/ They continued to teach
and to proclaim that Jesus is
the Messiah, day after day, both
in the temple and in houses.

"God." Peter said to him,
30/ . . .

31/ God exalted him *in glory* to
become . . . sins *in him*.

32/ As for us, we are witnesses of *all*
these matters. . . ."

33/ Cut to the quick, the hearers
were at the point of resolving
to kill them. 34/ At that . . .
and *member* of the Sanhedrin
named Gamaliel took the floor.
After directing that the *apostles*
be removed for a while, 35/ he
said to [*the leaders and*] *the*
entire Sanhedrin: "Gentlemen of Israel, beware *of* these
people and what you propose to
do to them. 36/ *For* before *this*
time one Theudas rose up in
rebellion, claiming that he was
a *great* leader. About four hundred followed him, but, after
he had committed suicide,[e] all
of his followers evaporated.
37/ After *him*, at the time of the
census, Judas of Galilee then
rose up and raised a *large* body
of rebels. He also perished,
and his followers were put to
flight. 38/ *Now then, broth-*
ers, I advise you to keep your
distance from these people and
let them alone, without defiling
your hands. For, if *this authority*
happens to be of human *inten-*
tion, its power will disappear,
39/ but, if this authority is of
divine intention, you will not be
able to thwart them—*neither*
you, nor monarchs, nor tyrants.
40/ Therefore, keep away from
them, lest you also be in conflict with God!" They found his
argument persuasive.

a *Or:* "the angel."

b *Or:* "the council, together with the entire Israelite Senate."

c *Or:* "in the council chamber." In place of ἀκούσαντες δὲ E Cop[mae] sy[p] arm begin ἐξελθόντες δὲ ἐκ τῆς φυλακῆς . . . ("leaving the prison").

d *Or:* "Did we not strictly enjoin . . . ?"

e The phrase ὅς διελύθη δι᾽ αὐτοῦ ("who perished at his own hand"), D (cf. Cop[mae]) may be due to the substitution of διελύθη for the more probable ἀνῃρέθη.

Analysis

The episode (II. C_1–E_2 in the organization suggested above) reports the second collision between the new movement and the religious authorities. The episode follows, in general, the path of 4:1-22, but the development is complicated by two unexpected twists, and both the number of the accused and the danger facing them are greater. After a thrilling ride on this narrative roller coaster, the story ends where it had commenced—with the apostles teaching in the temple. The story contains four principal sections:[1]

1. 5:17-21a: Arrest and Release. The high priest—with the Sadducees—apprehends and incarcerates the apostles. Evidently, it is too late for a trial on that day, as in 4:3b.[2] That night, an angel opens the prison doors and directs them to resume their evangelistic ministry. This they do, early the next day. Matters remain as they were before the arrest. Tension has not abated, but readers are reassured about the power and commitment of God.

2. 5:21b-26: Assembly and Re-arrest. The Sanhedrin and Senate solemnly assemble to try the prisoners. A humorous scene recounts their dismay at the discovery that the prisoners are not available. The pitiable Sanhedrin is all dressed up with nowhere to go, for the prisoners have escaped. At that moment a messenger arrives to announce that the apostles are up to their old tricks. When the prisoners are, with prudent caution, extracted from the admiring throng, proceedings may resume. This is a brief and welcome bit of comic relief, but the trial still looms.[3]

3. 5:27-40: The Trial. (A) Peter responds to the accusations of the high priest with the same defense that was offered at 4:19, some accusations of his own, and a summary of the kerygma. As a defense speech, it was not successful. The omniscient narrator informs the readers that the jurors were determined to execute the lot.[4] (B) Executions would have promptly followed, had not Gamaliel come to the rescue with a sparkling little speech in another (cf. 4:15) executive session, again thoughtfully contributed by the omniscient narrator. Although he is said to have convinced the body to leave the matter in God's hands, they nonetheless have the apostles flogged and repeat their prohibition.

4. 5:41-42: The Result. Honored to be abused for their views—rather than shamed (or disabled) by the beating—the apostles resume the mission. The court cannot bully them into silence. Although this lengthy account has made no particular contribution to history—nothing would be lost had it been omitted—Luke has written a thrilling and entertaining episode that shows the Sanhedrin to be no less inept than it is unethical. If the group trusted Gamaliel's plea to let God decide, they would have said, in effect, "Go ahead and try your luck. God will decide." Luke portrays the apostles as fearless philosophers whom neither a tyrannical court nor the effects of the whip can quell.

Comment

■ **17-21a** (1. Arrest and Release) No setting is provided, but v. 28 permits the assumption that the arrest takes place in Solomon's Portico.[5] The arresting agents are now the high priest and his political allies, the

1 "Scenes" is not quite appropriate, as some of the sections unfold in more than one place.

2 The unstated rationale is evidently that the officials wait for evening when the crowds have diminished or left before apprehending the apostles.

3 Marguerat (*Historian*, 160) calls the recapture of apostles a "grotesque interval."

4 There is a textual variant. See below.

5 The participle ἀναστάς ("rising") appears twenty-eight times in Luke and Acts. Elsewhere, there is some context or qualification. Boismard (*Texte*, 111)

Sadducean party.[6] Their motive is specific and ignoble: jealousy. The Greek word ζῆλος has a variety of meanings ("ardor," "zeal," "rivalry," "envy"[7]). In the Greek intellectual tradition (of which Philo is a good representative in this instance[8]), the term is largely positive, relating to an ethic grounded in competition, but there also a negative side appears: mere resentment of what another has accomplished has no relation to the pursuit of excellence. Paul uses the concept both positively (e.g., Rom 10:2; 2 Cor 9:2; Phil 3:6) and negatively (e.g., Rom 13:13; 1 Cor 3:3; Gal 5:20). In Acts 5:17; 13:45 (noun); 7:9; 17:5 (verb), the term accounts for the persecution of such characters as Joseph, the apostles, and Paul. Representatives of the good are persecuted because their success arouses envy. This simplification is a perennial theme of popular narrative.[9] "Zeal for Torah" (Acts 21:20; 22:3), which can justify murder (Num 25:11, 13 LXX; 1 Macc 2:24), is not utterly irrelevant, but it does not address the literary function of jealousy (which is not restricted to Jews) in Acts. The presence of the high priest and the Sadducees does nothing to shade the black-and-white characterization; it also serves to symbolize the narrator's understanding of the conflict: the Sadducees, who killed Jesus and do not believe in resurrection, wish to suppress information about their double condemnation: God raised Jesus from the dead.[10]

---

prefers the versional "Annas" (which must derive from a Greek source). E provides some context: ταῦτα βλέπων ("When he observed these occurrences . . ."). Both are probably secondary. See Metzger, *Textual Commentary*, 288. A bland introduction was necessary, since the immediate context speaks of miracles, whereas the formal basis for the arrest (v. 28) is public teaching.

6 Both here and in v. 21, the singular participle violates grammatical concord. The effect of this "error" is to make "those with" the high priests a mere parenthesis. The apparently otiose attributive participle οὖσα (from "be") is vexatious. See the long note in Cadbury and Lake, 56–57, who after much data and discussion approve "local," as does Barrett, 1:282–83. Haenchen (248 n. 2), however, omits it as jargon. Conzelmann (41) holds a similar view. For yet other ideas, new and old, see Bruce, 169–70. "Local" will work elsewhere, but not in this instance. The term δημοσίᾳ is an adverb elsewhere in Acts (16:37; 18:28; 20:20). Lake and Cadbury (*Additional Notes*, 57) favor that interpretation. BDAG, 222 *s.v.* δημόσιος, disagrees, with reason. Within a few verses, the authorities will be apprehensive about making a public arrest. The D-Text reassures readers that the arresting party retired for the evening after apprehending their quarry. The wording is evidently derived from (Ps.-)John 7:53 (but note Acts 21:6).

7 For references to the theme of jealousy in Greco-Roman narrative, see Johnson, 96 and 98. See also Pervo, *Dating*, 270. Josephus (*Ap.* 1.224) says that two basic motives for anti-Judaism are hatred and envy. See Feldman, *Jew and Gentile*, 266–67.

8 Cf. the examples from Philo and others in Albrecht Stumpff, "ζῆλος," *TDNT* 2:877–88.

9 Often enough, the motive may be assumed, as in the plot of the envious son of Pharaoh against Aseneth, in which he enlists the aid of four of Joseph's brothers, whose jealousy was well established (*Jos. Asen.* 24). Other examples from the realm of Jewish fiction include the *Tobiad Romance* (Josephus *Ant.* 12.154–234, esp. 174), the tale of the royal family of Adiabene (Josephus *Ant.* 20.17–96, esp. 21, 20) and Artapanus, frg. 3.7 (432D). In romantic novels, the jealousy of rival suitors and lovers is a standard propellant of the plot, for example, *Ninus* (frg. B); Chariton *Chaer.* 5.9.4; 6.6–7 (among many); *Ephesian Tale* 2.7.4; Achilles Tatius *Leuc. Clit.* 5.5.6; 7.3.7; et al.; Heliodorus *Aeth.* 1.11.5; 7.2.4; 8.62; et al. The jealousy of Chaireas launches the adventures in *De Chaerea et Callirhoe* (1.2.5–6; 5.1), while the jealous of the heroine Sinonis adds a great deal to the plot complication of *A Babylonian Tale*—not to mention the monarch's jealousy of the hero's success. Jealousy is crucial to the tale of Cupid and Psyche in Apuleius *Metam.*, e.g., 4.34). For secondary literature, see Martin Braun, *Griechischer Roman und hellenistische Geschichtsschreibung* (Frankfurter Studien zur Religion und Kultur der Antike; Frankfurt: Klostermann, 1934) 19; and Brigitte Egger, "Women in the Greek Novel: Constructing the Feminine" (Diss., University of California, Irvine, 1990) 97–98, 342. For the use of jealousy as a theme in ethical exhortation, see *1 Clem.* 4:1–6:4, which offers a number of examples.

10 Johnson (96) points to the Greco-Roman proclivity for identifying envy as the basis of a desire to kill (cf. v. 33), citing Plato *Leg.* 869E–870A and Plutarch *Frat. amor.* 17 (*Mor.* 487F). He also notes its appearance in Hellenistic Judaism: Wis 2:24; Philo

The term αἵρεσις ("party," "sect," "school," "faction") is deployed by Luke in two ways.[11] It facilitates his view of the Jesus movement as a philosophy, "a school." At the same time, it permits a critique of Judaism, which, unlike Christianity, is rent by sects or factions, a state of affairs that is not compatible with authentic religious belief and practice.[12] The positive sense Luke evidently appropriated from Josephus,[13] whereas the negative understanding derives from Paul and the post-Pauline world (1 Cor 11:19; Gal 5:20).[14]

■ **18-20** As v. 18 ends, matters are just as they were in 4:3, except that all twelve are now under arrest. Verse 19 brings an astonishing development: an angel of the Lord[15] liberates the Twelve.[16] This is the first of three prison (or door) miracles in Acts.[17] Like that in 12:6-10, which liberates Peter, and that in 16:25-34, which affects Paul, these wonders receive no public recognition or acclamation. Comparison with similar scenes in the Dionysiac tradition and the Apocryphal Acts illuminates the "apologetic" orientation of Luke, who will make no propaganda about disruptions of official authority, even when the disrupter is God.[18] After extracting the apostles from prison, the angel directs them not to go into hiding but to resume their proclamation of "everything about this way of life." That such activity may—and will—lead to loss of life gives the phrase a Johannine ring (cf. John 6:63, 68). Luke is not fond of such paradoxical irony, but the term is scarcely accidental.[19] They have been liberated not so that they may gain security but for the furtherance of their mission.[20]

Jos. 12; *T. Jos.* 1:3; *T. Gad* 4:5–6; *T. Benj.* 7:1–2; *T. Sim.* 2:7, 11.

11 The word appears in 5:17; 15:5; 24:5, 14; 26:5; 28:22.

12 Emergent rabbinic Judaism shared this negative view of sects. See Shaye J. D. Cohen, *From the Maccabees to the Mishnah* (LEC 7; Philadelphia: Westminster, 1987) 224–31. Luke was probably aware of this principle.

13 See Pervo, *Dating*, 168–69.

14 On the Lucan understanding, which is moving toward the notion of "heresy," see Pervo (previous note).

15 "Of the Lord" prevents the word from being construed as "a messenger." The anarthrous expression ἄγγελος κυρίου ("angel of the Lord") is an LXX form expressing divine epiphanies and is often a circumlocution for "God." See Fitzmyer, 335. An angel appears also in Luke 1:11, 26; 2:9, 13; 22:43 (possibly secondary); 24:23; Acts 7:30-38; 8:26; 10:3, 7, 22; 11:13; 12:7-15, 23; 27:23.

16 The D-Text prefaces the verse with that τότε of which it is so fond and reads—with much of the tradition—"open" as an indicative.

17 For a general overview of this phenomenon, see Pervo, *Profit*, 21–24, 147; Reinhard Kratz, *Rettungswunder: Motiv-, traditions- und formkritische Aufarbeitung einer biblischen Gattung* (Frankfurt: Peter Lang, 1979); and, in particular, Weaver, *Plots*.

18 The symbolic nature of release from bonds is important in the Dionysiac tradition, where it illustrates the god's gift of liberation. Among the Christian works, *Act. Thom.* 107–22 is illustrative. Although this material in *Acts of Thomas* is clearly based on Acts 5 and 16, viewing liberation as either symbolic (108–13) or for the purpose of convenience, followed by a return to prison (119–22), there is not a hint of respect for lawful authority. *Act. Paul* 7/9 is similar, and related to, *Act. Thom.* 119–22. John was delivered from imprisonment by some unknown means in a lost episode that fell between chaps. 36 and 87 of the *Acts of John* as now arranged. See also the *Acts of Andrew and Matthias* 21–22, 29–30. Deliverance is never the path to easy street. The case of Peter (Acts 12:1-17) may seem to be an exception, but his exit from prison is also his departure from the narrative (apart from his brief speech in chap. 15). Luke may have received some inspiration from Artapanus frg. 3 (b), 22–24. Cf. also *History of the Rechabites* 10.4–6, which may be early. This includes a bright light (cf. Acts 12:7), angels, and deliverance to a protected place.

19 Barrett (1:284) thinks that "it is the new life offered by Jesus as the ἀρχηγὸς τῆς ζωῆς (3:15, rendered as '[the one] who opens the way to life')." An advantage of "way of life" is that 3:15 views that life as a journey. For Haenchen (249 n. 3), "life" = "salvation" (picking up on Cadbury and Lake [57], who took it as a Semiticism).

20 Cyprian cites this passage in *On the Unity of the Catholic Church* 12. God was with the apostles because they were "guileless and of one mind" (*quia simplices* [cf. 4:13] *quia unanimes erant*). 𝔓[74] reads ἐν τῷ λαῷ, omitting the temple. This may be due to the understanding that the Portico of Solomon was outside the temple, or it may be anti-Jewish. Varied placement of the phrase shows that it was absent from more than one MS and may have been an interpolation.

Brief as this report is, it makes an important contribution to the symbolic thrust of Acts.[21] By using themes of the exodus tradition it relates the liberation of the apostles to the liberation of the people of God. "The angel of the Lord" is a common element in HB epiphanies, notably those of liberation.[22] The verb ἐξάγω (lit. "lead out" [v. 19]), which is prominent in accounts of the exodus (e.g., Exod 16:6; cf. Acts 7:36, 40; 13:17), appears in all three accounts of prison escapes in Acts (12:17; 16:39). "House of bondage" is a common trope for Israel's condition in Egypt.[23] "Prison," in turn, is a common symbol of death.[24] The narrator is readying the soil for Peter's experiences in chap. 12. This account is less interested in the escape as a symbolic resurrection, for the apostles had not been formally condemned, than in exhibiting the power of resurrection, viz., empowerment for mission.[25] The noun "life" (ζωή), used to summarize the apostolic proclamation in v. 20, focuses on resurrection.[26]

■ **21b-26** (2. Assembly and Re-arrest) The next day, presumably,[27] those who had made the arrest[28] returned to their posts and convoked the court.[29] Haenchen understands the language: "The grandiose enumeration of the antagonists in v. 21 stands in intentional contrast to the pitiful fiasco in store for them."[30] Lackeys dispatched to escort the prisoners to the bar of justice discover a glitch: the cell is empty. Their report provides the readers with details not revealed in v. 19. Those familiar with prison-escape stories will probably infer that the guards had been put to sleep or otherwise bewitched by the angel.[31] Those reading Acts for the second time will appreciate another irony: the Sadducees have been thwarted by the action of a being in which they do not believe (23:8). Luke's dramatic vividness is illustrated by his editors: the D-Text reports[32] that the servants opened the prison doors and found no one there before continuing the account, pedantically filling in the narrative at the expense of its effect.

This information reduced the court to hapless perplexity[33] from which they were delivered by the fortunate advent[34] of a messenger, a medium richly developed in ancient drama.[35] The apostles are back in business! This news allows the narrator to omit any reflections about how the alleged miscreants escaped custody or to waste any space about deliberations issuing in the obvious. The action alone is described. No

21 See the valuable analysis of Weaver, *Plots*, 93–117.

22 Ibid., 96–101.

23 E.g., Exod 13:3; 20:2; Jdg 6:8; 2 Esdr 1:6.

24 See p. 309 n. 92. Conversely, deliverance from prison symbolizes rescue from oppression: Ps 107:10-14; Isa 24:22; 43:7; *3 Macc.* 6:2-29; Bel 31-39. See Weaver, *Plots*, 102–3.

25 "Open door" is a common trope for missionary opportunity; see Acts 14:27; 1 Cor 16:9; 2 Cor 2:12; Col 4:3; Rev 3:8, 20, as Weaver (*Plots*, 113 n. 68) observes. That opening is the greatest of the door miracles in Acts, of which the prison escapes are a symbol.

26 Weaver, *Plots*, 112–14.

27 The D-Text, having sent them home the night before, helpfully indicates that those who made the arrest arose at the crack of dawn (i.e., when the apostles returned to their preaching). See Boismard, *Texte*, 112.

28 Verse 21b returns the characters of v. 17a to the stage.

29 Since this is the first occasion on which Luke uses συνέδριον to mean a body (rather than a place), it is probable that the καί is explanatory rather than conjunctive. For this view, see Haenchen, 249; Bruce, 170; and Fitzmyer, 335. Schneider (1:390) and Weiser (1:136) regard the phrase as referring to two different bodies. For the equivalence of συνέδριον and γερουσία, see Dionysius of Halicarnassus *Ant. Rom.* 2.12. *IGR* IV.836.8 refers to "the most august Council of the Gerousia" (συνέδριον γερουσίας) at Hierapolis. Cf. also David Magie, *Roman Rule in Asia Minor to the End of the Third Century after Christ* (2 vols.; Princeton: Princeton University Press, 1950), who records that συνέδριον was in use in Ephesus (2:858–59). Note also the use of γερουσία in *Gos. Jas.* 4:6. Sources for the specific phrase include Exod 12:21; 1 Macc 12:6; 2 Macc 1:10.

30 Haenchen, 250. On the scene, see Pervo, *Profit*, 61–62.

31 Those not familiar will discover how the escape was engineered when they read 12:6-10.

32 Boismard, *Texte*, 113.

33 The textual tradition of v. 24 includes a number of variations, none of which alters the basic sense. E (sy^p) report that they found the information surprising as well as confusing.

34 The narrator makes characters appear (and disappear) at will. Note the use of παραγίνομαι in vv. 21, 22, and 25. (This is a Lucan word; of thirty-six uses in the NT, eight are in Luke and twenty in Acts.)

35 Dramatic messengers make varied contributions,

one ever had to exhort Luke to "cut to the chase scene." On this occasion the captain of the temple constabulary[36] will give the matter personal attention. The situation is delicate, requiring a decorous[37] arrest to prevent inflaming the enthusiastic masses. Like Jesus (Luke 22:2), the apostles enjoy popular favor. This estimate will not permanently endure.[38] The stage is now ready for the action envisioned by the arrest in vv. 17-18. The intervening "parenthesis" has not, however, been fruitless. The angelic deliverance shows where the Almighty stands on the question, the officials have been made to look ridiculous, and the court has to reckon with the fact that the word of God cannot be locked in chains and that their animosity toward the apostles is at variance with popular sentiment.

■ **27-33** In these verses (3a. The Trial), Peter (and the others)[39] appears, as will Paul (22:30), before the high court. Dispensing with any questions about how the apostles got out of custody, the high priest accuses them of ignoring the earlier (4:18) injunction and complains that they are blaming their leaders for the death of Jesus. To this, the entire body affirms the earlier position of Peter and John. This collision of irresistible force and immovable object can have but one result: a mass execution. The high priest's accusation is stated in solemn Septuagintal form.[40] Emphasis lies on the second half: "You not only ignored our injunction, but even tried to place this fellow's death upon our shoulders."[41]

The structure of this unison speech, which lacks either address or conclusion, is an uncomplicated chiasmus:

A. V. 29. Thesis: It is preferable to *obey God*.
  B. V. 30. Narrative: God raised, you killed, an antithesis (Christology).
  B'. V. 31. Narrative: God exalted Jesus to provide repentance (Christology; soteriology).
A'. V. 32. Proof: Witnesses include the speakers and the Spirit given to those who *obey God*.

This defense falls into the category of *qualitas absoluta* (ἀντίληψις), essentially an appeal to a higher law.[42] The defendants affirm the charge but deny that it is blameworthy. The outline form is permissible for this skeleton of a speech because the readers know the details from the speeches of chaps. 2 and 3 (as does the dramatic audience). The D-Text follows a different path. Peter is the sole speaker, probably to enhance his role,[43] possibly also because of distaste for unison speech.[44] In the D-Text this encounter takes the form of an apophthegm, not unlike Mark 12:13-17 (paying tribute): question, counterquestion, answer, pronouncement.[45] The contrast between divine and human will

including the narration of events that could not be portrayed on stage. Revelation is their principal function. In *Oedipus Tyrannus*, the messenger from Corinth engages in a lengthy dialogue that leads to the disclosure of Oedipus's identity (924–1185). The second messenger, who enters at 1222, describes the suicide of Jocasta and Oedipus's self-mutilation. For another use of a technique from the drama, see below on 12:13-16. The D-Text, possibly concerned about the mysterious appearance of the messenger, eliminated him (and supplied pedantic expansions); Boismard, *Texte*, 114.

36 On στρατηγός see 4:21.

37 The omission of the negative by D* ("with force") is probably not, *pace* Bruce (171), a scribal mistake.

38 The shift comes in 6:12, where the people join their leaders in apprehending Stephen. In 21:30-36 the people employ violence against Paul.

39 As elsewhere, one should add "other" (BDF §306 [5]).

40 παραγγελίᾳ παρηγγείλαμεν reflects the Hebrew infinitive absolute rather than an underlying Aramaic idiom. See BDF §198 (6); Moule, *Idiom Book*, 177–78; and Fitzmyer, 336. For an LXX prototype, see Gen 43:3.

41 The D-Text substantially revises the introduction. Because this edition has no interrogative verb, the initial οὐ of v. 28 marks it as a question. That marker has entered other layers of the textual tradition, but should be viewed as secondary. See Metzger, *Textual Commentary*, 289. Instead of τούτου ("this"), the D-Text aptly reads ἐκείνου ("*that* fellow," a pejorative circumlocution that is a common mode of referring to Jesus among Jews.

42 Cf. Cicero *Inv.* 1.11; 2.71.

43 See Richard I. Pervo "Social and Religious Aspects of the Western Text." In *The Living Text: Essays in Honor of Ernest W. Saunders* (ed. Dennis Groh and Robert Jewett; Lanham, Md.: University Press of America, 1985) 229–41.

44 On unison speech, see p. 542 n. 6. Haenchen (251) recognizes that unison speech is proof of inspiration. It also serves a dramatic purpose, since it justifies action against all of the apostles.

45 Clark (*Acts*, 341–42) prefers the longer text. His arguments serve to support the contrary position.

unites this and the following speech (vv. 38-39). In v. 29 the parallel with Socrates is more direct than in 4:19.[46] The apostles teach like philosophers and, like Socrates (and others), are prepared to suffer for the truth.[47] Verse 30 describes, for the first time,[48] crucifixion with the LXX phrase[49] "hanging upon a tree." Luke may have taken the expression from Gal 3:13, but he uses it in a different way from Paul's paradoxical critique of a covenantal theology.[50] Here the OT allusion seeks to shame the hearers.[51] Verse 31 moves from resurrection to exaltation.[52] Although the titles "leader" and "savior" may seem to be a result of the exaltation, Luke does not construe christological categories in a chronological fashion (cf. 3:20). Jesus was Messiah and savior at birth (Luke 2:11), and the earthly Jesus summoned people to repent (Luke 5:32). Through the resurrection and exaltation, his benefits became available to all. Universalism is so central to the gentile Christianity known to Luke that he can write as if Jesus became the Messiah at the resurrection, while his drive for continuity presses him in the opposite direction: to extend the attributes of the heavenly Christ into the life of the earthly Jesus.[53]

The word ἀρχηγός has a somewhat different meaning here from that in 3:15. Paired with "savior" (see *2 Clem.* 20:5; cf. Heb 2:10), it approaches the significance of titles given to rulers.[54] The noun "savior" is at home in the post-Pauline world;[55] δεξιᾷ ("right [hand]") is probably instrumental, a synecdoche.[56] Verse 31b means "to provide the opportunity for repentance and the consequent forgiveness of sins."[57] As proof of "these matters,"[58] the apostles add to their own testimony the manifestation of the Spirit, not Scripture here but a present gift, one example of which is their eloquent speech delivered in concert (cf. Luke 12:11-12).[59] The contrast between "we" (v. 32) and "you" (v. 30) underlines the contention that the judges have not benefited from the gift of the Spirit. The reaction (v. 33) indicates that the apostles' fate is sealed.[60] These

46 In the Greek tradition, Plato *Apol.* 29D is the primary reference, but the idea is central to the *Antigone* of Sophocles (note 453–56). See also Plutarch *Conviv. Septem* 7 (*Mor.* 152C); Epictetus *Diss.* 1.30.1; and Livy 39.37. For Jewish and early Christian parallels, see on 4:19. Note also Plümacher, *Lukas*, 18–19. Pesch (1:222–24) reviews the use of this maxim within the Christian tradition. See also Squires, *Plan*, 175 n. 104, for many references.

47 Socrates. See p. 119 n. 45.

48 The phrase is used again in 10:39 (Peter); see also 13:29 (Paul). Other references include 1 Pet 2:24; *Barn.* 5:13; 8:1; 12:1, 7; Justin *Dial.* 86.6.

49 Examples include Deut 21:22-23; 26:26; Gen 40:19; Josh 10:26; Esth 5:14. For extrabiblical parallels, see *T. Benj.* 9:3; *Sib. Or.* 5:257; 6:26. On the citation, see Max Wilcox, "Upon the Tree—Deut. 21:22-23 in the New Testament," *JBL* 96 (1977) 85–99.

50 Other sources are possible, but "passion apologetic" would not readily use a phrase that characterizes criminals cursed by God.

51 The later association, by metonymy, of the cross with the tree of Eden inspired patristic preachers and gave birth to some splendid Latin poetry, of which the *Pange lingua* of Venantius Fortunatus is the most famous example.

52 See p. 45.

53 Luke must deal with tensions between the heavenly lord and the terrestrial preacher; like Paul, he begins with the former.

54 See Dibelius and Conzelmann, *Pastoral Epistles*, 102–3, 144–47. Note also Savior (v. 31). See Gilbert, "Roman Propaganda," 237–42.

55 Cf. Pervo, *Dating*, 287–88.

56 BDF §199 says that the phrase is local, "to God's right hand" rather than "by God's right hand." The same problem applies to the D-Text alternative, δόξῃ, which is less "crude" and therefore secondary. See Metzger, *Textual Commentary*, 290. In Heb 12:2 ἀρχηγός is linked to the exaltation.

57 So Barrett, 1:291; and Conzelmann, 42, who refers to the different view of Jacques Dupont. On the theme of repentance in Luke and Acts, see Pervo, *Dating*, 273–78. The D-Text adds "in him" to the end of v. 31 to clarify the Christology.

58 *Or:* "for these claims"; cf. 10:37. Bruce (173) views this usage of ῥήματα as a Septuagintalism.

59 The text of v. 32 exhibits considerable variation. Metzger (*Textual Commentary*, 290) attributes this to the association of "his" with "witnesses," in conformity to 1:8. The omission of the relative ("We are witnesses, and God gave . . .") in B *pc* Cyril of Jerusalem may be due to fourth-century arguments about the Trinity or simply to a desire not to "equate" the apostles with the Spirit. Use of the masculine pronoun in D* E may be due to the influence of Latin (in which "spirit" is masculine in gender).

60 The verb διαπρίω occurs also in 7:54, where it leads to the death of Stephen.

people wish to kill them,[61] and they have the power to do so.[62] The message of opportunity to repent and be forgiven has not been well received.

■ **34-39** Deliverance comes from an unexpected quarter:[63] a Pharisee[64] named Gamaliel.[65] He was a historical figure about whom little is known. Confusion with Gamaliel II (a contemporary of Luke) further contaminates the data. The entire scene is a Lucan composition based upon a topos[66] and is designed to showcase Lucan apologetic theology on the lips of an outsider. The source of the name "Gamaliel" is unknown. Luke characterizes him as a popular "law-teacher" (lit.).[67] Such esteem made him a formidable figure (cf. v. 26). Luke may well have taken this idea of Pharisaic popularity from Josephus (e.g., *Ant.* 18.17) and particularized it in his portrait of Gamaliel.[68]

The speech is deliberative, making use of historical *exempla*, in the approved manner.[69] Gamaliel argues that the court should leave the matter in God's hands, as the consequences of action could be dire. The conclusion follows two parallel sections, each based on a warning:

- I. Vv. 35-37
  - A. V. 35. Address, Admonition
  - B. V. 36-37. Examples
    - 1. V. 36. Theudas
    - 2. V. 37. Judas
- II. Vv. 38-39c
  - A. V. 38a-b. Admonition
  - B. Vv. 38c-39. Possible outcomes
    - 1. V. 38c. If human, it will fail.
    - 2. V. 39a. If divine, it cannot be destroyed.
- III. V. 39b. Conclusion: consequence of ignoring this admonition.

The construction is tight. The conclusion is a clause expressing apprehension, which completes and frames the warnings.[70] Retardation also marks the examples, the purpose of which is not initially clear. The logical order is this: movements of human origin fail, as the following examples demonstrate. Movements backed by divine power cannot be repressed, and those who attempt to do so range themselves against God. Therefore, the court will be well advised to let this movement take its course. The actual arrangement raises the suspense and thus makes the climax more dramatically effective. The impact also gains from the parallel

61 The *v.l.* ἐβουλεύοντο ("they planned," rather than the common Lucan ἐβούλοντο, "wished") has broad support. It carries a suggestion of formal deliberation. Metzger (*Textual Commentary*, 291) rejects it as a blunder: "[T]he members of the Sanhedrin, being enraged, were scarcely in a mood quietly to take counsel." Conzelmann (42) supports this with a triplet from Achilles Tatius *Leuc. Clit.* 7.1.1: ἤχθετο, ὠργίζετο, ἐβουλεύετο ("He became vexed, got angry, and engaged in further reflection"). Note, in addition, the parallel with v. 28.

62 It is preferable to view v. 33 as the conclusion to the first part of the section, rather than the beginning of the next.

63 An illustrative literary parallel occurs in Apuleius *Metam.* 10.8: As a verdict of guilt was about to be finalized, "one of the councillors, a physician whose known honesty and outstanding authority excelled that of the rest, covered the mouth of the urn with his hand to prevent anyone idly dropping in his pebble. Then he addressed these words to the council" (trans. Patrick G. Walsh, *Apuleius the Golden Ass. The World's Classics* [Oxford: Oxford University Press, 1995] 197).

64 This is the first of nine occurrences of "Pharisee" in Acts. Six fall in 23:6-9, five of which are in the plural. Two refer to Paul (23:6; 26:5). Acts 15:5 speaks of believers in Jesus. Gamaliel is the only Jewish Pharisee specifically identified in Acts. For a discussion, see Sanders, *Jews*, 84–131. On this person, see Bruce Chilton, "Gamaliel (2)," *ABD* 2:903–6.

65 Haenchen (252) says, "It is enough for this universally revered jurist to rise to his feet for all the storming councilors to be brought to their senses."

66 See Squires, *Plan*, 176 and n. 109.

67 The word νομοδιδάσκαλος is attested only in Christian literature.

68 The notion of Pharisees' popularity is characteristic of Josephus's portrait of them in his *Antiquities* and differs from that in the earlier *War.* It is arguable that Josephus invented this idea to promote the Pharisaic program in the light of the postwar situation. Jacob Neusner gives a succinct summary of this argument in *From Politics to Piety: The Emergence of Pharisaic Judaism* (Englewood Cliffs, N.J.: Prentice-Hall, 1973) 45–66.

69 On historical examples in speeches, see Conzelmann, 42.

70 Cadbury and Lake (62) say μήποτε probably introduces not a dependent purpose clause but an independent sentence of warning. Barrett (1:297) allows for both interpretations. The translation

constructions used for both examples (vv. 36-37) and both outcomes (vv. 38c-39a). An additional nice touch appears in the general condition employed to describe human efforts ("if this plan and activity happen to be of human origin") and the particular condition that characterizes divinely endorsed enterprises. This contrast is a subtle statement of Gamaliel's view of the matter.[71] The speech also exhibits features of popular rhetoric.[72] This is among the best of Luke's miniature addresses.

Many of the variants in the D-tradition are typical clarifications, simplifications, or harmonizations. Among the more interesting expansions are the additions of "power" terms (ἐξουσία, δύναμις) in vv. 38-39 and the reference to "monarchs" and "tyrants" in v. 39. The latter addresses a difficulty in Gamaliel's examples, neither of which dealt with the procedures of Israelite justice, but rather with rebellions suppressed by Roman soldiers, which could have been deemed irrelevant. They also encompass persecution of Christians beyond the limits of this court and the boundaries of Judea.[73] "Power" and "authority" could be an intelligent effort to bring about a closure to the argument that began in 3:11, but this appears to be internal to the D-tradition.[74] Moreover, ἡ βουλή in v. 38 is rather vague to those who are not sympathetic readers of Acts and therefore realize that the "plan of God" is the subject.[75] Especially gratuitous is the added "without defiling your hands" in v. 38, which distinguishes Gamaliel from his colleagues ("your hands") and concedes the point of responsibility for the death of Jesus—and its impropriety.[76]

■ **36** Gamaliel's examples present the most egregious anachronism in Acts.[77] Theudas is his first case.[78] Theudas led a rebellion in c. 44 CE, well over a decade later than the dramatic date of the speech, while the revolt associated with Judas took place in 6 CE.[79] The most probable explanation of this error is that Luke took the examples from Josephus (*Ant.* 20.97-102), who once referred to these persons in inverse chronological

treats the clause as independent, but its function is to complete the admonition(s).

71 The second "if" approximates "since." See Conzelmann, 43; and Bruce, 178.

72 Note the use of assonance and alliteration and of repetition with variation, for example, the parallel endings to vv. 36 and 37: (36) ἀνῃρέθη, καὶ πάντες ὅσοι ἐπείθοντο αὐτῷ διελύθησαν (37) ἀπώλετο καὶ πάντες ὅσοι ἐπείθοντο αὐτῷ διεσκορπίσθησαν. The use of two differing types of conditional sentences in vv. 38 and 39 is also to be considered a bit of Lucan elegance.

73 See Epp, *Theological Tendency*, 131–32; and Metzger, *Textual Commentary*, 293, who identifies the source of this expansion: Wis 12:13-14. Note also Haenchen, 253 n. 3.

74 Acts 3:12 (cf. 4:7) uses δύναμις and εὐσέβεια; ἐξουσία is a D-Text variant, prompting the conclusion that 5:39 reflects the same editorial viewpoint.

75 The phrase ἡ βουλὴ αὕτη ἢ τὸ ἔργον τοῦτο (translated "this scheme or enterprise") refers, in a legal sense, to both intention and action, but there are clearer ways to say this. Note Luke 23:51, which says that Joseph of Arimathea "had not agreed to their plan and action" (τῇ βουλῇ καὶ τῇ πράξει αὐτῶν). For the sentiment (with reference to councils rather than sects), see *Pirqe ʾAbot* 4.14: "R[abbi] Jochanan the sandalmaker said: Every assembly which is for the sake of Heaven will in the end be established, and *every assembly* which is not for the sake of Heaven will in the end not be established" (trans. R. Travers Herford, *Pirke Aboth: The Ethics of the Talmud: Sayings of the Fathers* [1925; New York: Schocken, 1962] 109). The Jewish author of *3 Maccabees* assigns a similar view to an enlightened polytheist (7:9). Note that, according to Luke 7:30, the Pharisees rejected the "plan (βουλή) of God."

76 So Epp, *Theological Tendency*, 130–31, who also views the phrase as enhancing the status of the apostles. Even for Luke, this phrase would have been too much.

77 See Pervo, *Dating*, 152–58. Only Clark (liv–lv) takes the view that the textual tradition has inverted the order of the rebels and thus corrects it by transposition. Calvin (153) is quite willing to consider the possibility that Gamaliel changed the historical order, but prefers the view that the examples are not presented in chronological order.

78 The initial phrase πρὸ γὰρ τούτων τῶν ἡμερῶν ("some time ago") appears also in 21:38, in a similar context ("the Egyptian"), where it must refer to the recent past. It cannot mean "more than twenty-five years ago."

79 Luke 2:1 erroneously places this activity in the reign of Herod the Great (d. 4 BCE). Use of the definite article here ("the census") is a major blow to the old theory that there were two censuses. On the subject, see Schürer, *History*, 1:399–427; and Pervo, *Dating*, 158–60. Among the early commentators, Ephrem Syrus (cited from the Latin translation from the Armenian of F. C. Conybeare, in Ropes, *Text*, 402) takes the narrative chronology

order. Other explanations involve elaborate hypotheses, unlikely coincidences, and dubious assumptions. This is, moreover, but one of a number of instances in which Luke's use of Josephus is quite probable.[80] If Luke erred in reading his source here, he would not be the only writer who has been guilty of such a mistake.

■ **38** The learned Pharisee suggests leaving the matter in God's hands. This was scarcely responsible advice, for it urges the council to abrogate the duties for which they have been appointed, and, as noted, his examples were not truly relevant. The narrator must find some way to get out of the corner into which he has painted himself—it will not do to send the apostles on their way with a blessing if they are doing God's will or a curse if they are not.[81] The means is effective limitation of Gamaliel's persuasiveness in dropping the death penalty. The narrator cannot call attention to this finesse, as it amounts to a contradiction.[82] The actual result is that the previous injunction remains in place, reinforced with a judicial whipping. In this way, Luke demonstrates the obstinacy, brutality, and futility of the court. They can do no more than reiterate a command that they can have no hope of seeing obeyed, and they discharge their pique by means of the lash. The readers know that the members of the court are what Gamaliel warned them against becoming—"opponents of God."[83]

■ **39-40** Although Gamaliel speaks as an influential member of the Sanhedrin, he is distinguished from it. His colleagues are always addressed as "you" (vv. 35, 38, 39). The final "you" of v. 39 becomes the following "they," which extends through v. 40 and cannot be associated with him. Gamaliel should have objected to this injunction and punishment, but his part in the drama is finished. In both speech and action, Gamaliel is as much an outsider as is Peter.[84] Finally, the two speeches effectively comprise a single unit bounded by an *inclusio*: The contrast between divine and human that opens the apostolic oration returns as the climax to Gamaliel's words in vv. 38-39.[85] Both speeches express the same Lucan theme. That observation dismisses the quest for useful sources here.[86] For Luke, any questions about the merits of a pudding can be resolved by a taste test. He is cheating in so far as time had shown that the Jesus movement had not been quickly extinguished but had continued to grow for decades, to be sure, yet the tender of Gamaliel conforms to essential Lucan values. Theology should

---

at face value: Theudas is described as a magician (*unctus magia*, lit. "anointed with magic") who rebelled at the time of the nativity (about which he had learned from Satan). His source is unknown. Bede, however, refers to Josephus and summarizes his account (which he obtained from Rufinus's translation of Eusebius's *Historia ecclesiastica*).

80 See p. 12.

81 The inconsistency between agreement with Gamaliel's views and the subsequent punishment has been used to posit a basis for the story in a tradition, or traditions. See Roloff, 100; Pesch, 1:213; Fitzmyer, 332–33; and Jervell, 213. The literary explanation is sufficient and raises fewer questions. One possible source—or inspiration—is the speech of Achior in Judith 5, esp. vv. 20-21.

82 Haenchen (258) recognizes the difficulty but does not seek to explain it.

83 The dire fate in store for those who "fight against the gods" is well attested in Greek mythology. Cf., e.g., Homer *Il.* 6.128–43. θεομάχος and θεομαχέω play a noteworthy role in Euripides *Bacchae* 45, 325, and 1255; cf. also 625. Note also his *Iph. Aul.* 1408. Closer to Luke's world is 2 Macc 7:19. The context of Josephus *Ap.* 1.246, 263 is different, but it is possible that Luke took his inspiration from Euripides, indirectly if not directly. See Otto Bauernfeind, "μάχομαι," *TDNT* 4:527–28, esp. 528, and the thorough study by Weaver, *Plots*, 43–44, 132–48.

84 John Darr ("Irenic or Ironic? Another Look at Gamaliel before the Sanhedrin [Acts 5:33-42]," in Thompson, *Literary Studies*, 121–39) rebuffs the notion that Gamaliel is pro-Christian. This is certainly correct. His position is pragmatic.

85 The Pseudo-Clementine *Recognitions* revises this episode. The preaching of Peter brings objections from the high priest Caiaphas in 1.62. Peter goes on to forecast destruction of the temple and a mission to the gentiles (64). All walked out but Gamaliel, the national leader and a secret believer, who urges that they still their anger, as the movement will come to an end if it is not from God, but if it is of divine origin, opposition would be sin. Note that the text has, *inter alia*, corrected the name of the high priest and dropped the examples. Gamaliel promises a public debate on the next day, at which he will refute Peter and company (65). The faithful pray all night. On the next day (67–68) Gamaliel makes a peaceful speech inviting James to speak. This he did, dealing with such issues as the proper use of the scriptural prophecy about Jesus (1 Samuel—2 Kings), the necessity for baptism, the Trinity, and sexuality in

be concrete rather than esoteric. Christianity is certainly not just one more boutique in the free market of religious enterprises, but it is willing to compete by the standards of the marketplace. The leading indicators of that willingness are the emphases on statistics, rhetoric, and miracles.[87] The distinction from Paul could scarcely be greater, and one would be hard put to find a similar position advanced by any other NT writer. This empirical orientation is one dimension of the "apologetic" quality of Luke's thought. He represents a movement with a vigorous confidence in its program for the future and can, to use his own words, speak boldly.[88]

Haenchen sharply exposed the dangers and weaknesses of Lucan theology in his famous commentary and has called forth waves of reaction against his hyperbole and sarcasm. A more fruitful approach is to build on the positive features of Luke's particular understanding and to recognize that his theology is not without its uses. Whenever the church is in danger of becoming genuinely invisible and/or indifferent to the world and its needs, this theology will assist calls to return to its vision and mission. Inability to forgive Luke for not being Paul is, in the end, no more useful than refusing to forgive Paul for not being Luke. Critical scholarship has performed the useful service of distinguishing the two to the potential advantage of each. Noncritical scholarship faces the danger of weakening each to the advantage of neither.

■ **41-42** The final section (4. The Result) is brief. The whipping adds to the crescendo of violence, but it is utterly without effect. The apostles suffer the punishment that Pilate had proposed for Jesus.[89] These heroes could shrug off a beating that would have confined most to a period of recuperation and killed some.[90] This poetic license allows Luke to set forth the apocalyptic inversion of values that is central to the Gospel. Shame suffered "for the Name's sake" is honor.[91] "The name" is that of Jesus, as variants seek to make clear,[92] but the term here does not mean "for Jesus' sake" so much as "for the movement that bears the name of Jesus"; that is, by metonymy "name" approximates "church" or "Christianity."[93] Verse 42 is a closing summary affirming the apostles' disdain for the commands of the court. The language evokes 2:46. Nothing has changed. House and temple remain the centers of the apostles' daily activity.[94] For the first time, the verb εὐαγγελίζομαι

---

the divine. This address on the temple steps was disrupted by a certain opponent of the movement (who is, in fact, Paul). On this adaptation, see Jones, "A Jewish Christian," 623–24. Bede (31) refers to this passage (*ut Clemens indicat* ["as Clement notes"]) for the characterization of Gamaliel. With the *Recognitions* one may compare Hemer (*Book*, 342 n. 72), who also introduces Paul into this story: Paul probably got an account from Gamaliel "at a time when his mind was much exercised over the new teaching." Acts 5:34-39 "might be Paul's first latent imprint on the narrative."

86 Those who believe that Acts 5:35-39 includes a historical report of Gamaliel's words and beliefs must explain why he did not raise the same objection some months earlier, at the trial of Jesus (Luke 22:66-71).

87 Another indicator is the ideal nature of community life, including not only its achievement of utopian goals but also its ability to manage conflict and difficulty smoothly and rapidly.

88 Examples from the context are 4:13, 29, and 31. This terminology brackets the missionary endeavors of Paul (9:27, 28; 13:46; 14:3; 19:8) and serves to summarize his career and the entire book (28:31).

89 Luke 23:22: "[Pilate said] . . . I will therefore have him flogged and then release (ἀπολύσω) him."

90 Even if the beating did not consist of thirty-nine lashes, as readers of 2 Cor 11:24 are likely to assume, it would have been "a cruel punishment" (Polhill, 174). For the heroic characterization, see Pervo, *Profit*, 41. See also 14:19-20.

91 Cf. Luke 6:22-23. The idea can also be found in philosophical contexts: Epictetus *Diss.* 1.29.49; 2.1.38–39. The latter reads "[D]o you practise how to die, how to be enchained, how to be racked, how to be exiled. Do all these things with confidence, with trust in Him who has called you to face them and deemed you worthy (ἄξιον) of this position" (trans. William Abbot Oldfather, *Epictetus I* [LCL; Cambridge, Mass.: Harvard University Press, 1925] 225).

92 See Metzger, *Textual Commentary*, 294.

93 See Pervo, *Dating*, 281.

94 It is preferable not to link "teaching" to one place (temple, house) and "preaching" to another.

("proclaim the message," "evangelize") appears. It often marks transitions in the story.[95] This is indeed the final word for many chapters (21:20) about the mission to the native (i.e., Aramaic-speaking) inhabitants of Jerusalem. Resemblance to 8:39-40 (Philip) and to 28:31 is not accidental.[96]

These twenty-six verses amount to a repeat of chap. 4, where there was also an arrest, a hearing, a robust declaration that divine authority outranks human, and an eventual release. With his accustomed skill, Luke has avoided monotony. This achievement included not only heightened drama, a spectacular rescue, a comic moment, and elevated suspense, but also doubling many of the components.[97] There are two arrests, two rescues, and two speeches. The speeches are finely crafted. One rescue comes from an angel of God, the other from an angel of mercy. The arrests show that the common people loved the followers of Jesus, whereas the Sadducees hated them. On the one side stand God, the followers of Jesus, and, to a degree, the most prominent Pharisee of his time. The high priestly leadership and their supporters constitute the opposition. These allegiances will not remain permanently undisturbed. The advent of missionaries who speak Greek will create the conditions that make execution a live option for the authorities.

95 Cf. 8:4, 12, 25, 40; 11:20; 13:32; 14:7; 15:35. The verb *εὐαγγελίζομαι* occurs fifty-four times in the NT, ten of these in Luke, fifteen in Acts. Pauline influence is probable, for Paul uses it nineteen times (and Ephesians, twice).

96 See Barrett, 1:229.

97 Tannehill (*Narrative Unity*, 2:74–76) has a number of apposite observations on the value of repetition in narrative.

6

6:1-7 The Appointment of Seven Assistants

**1/ Around that time, as the number
of followers continued to grow,
those who spoke Greek charged
those who spoke Aramaic[a] with
unfair treatment of Greek-
speaking widows in the daily
ministry. 2/ The Twelve convened a community meeting,
at which they announced: "It
is undesirable for us to neglect
proclamation of God's message
in order to administer charity.
3/ Please choose for yourselves,
sisters and brothers, seven men
of your number who are well
recommended and notable for
their spiritual and intellectual
capacity. We shall place them
in charge of this function,
4/ while we shall continue to
devote ourselves to prayer and
to the ministry of proclamation." 5/ The entire community
approved of this solution.
They chose Stephen, who was
notable for his strong spiritual
convictions and gifts, Philip,
Prochorus, Nicanor, Timon,
Parmenas, and Nicholas from
Antioch, a convert to Judaism.
6/ They presented these seven
to the apostles for prayer and
the laying-on of hands. 7/ Proclamation of God's message
expanded; the number of followers in Jerusalem increased
substantially, including priests,
a large number of whom began
to embrace the faith.**

a The meaning of "Hellenists" and "Hebrews" is disputed. See the comments.

Analysis

(III in the outline in 3:1—4:31) For the historian of nascent Christianity, the story of the "Hellenists" introduced in chap. 6 testifies to a crucial link between Jesus and Paul.[1] The chief difficulty for investigators since Ferdinand Christian Baur is that Luke does not attempt to make this link transparent. The result is that every researcher must attempt to discover what the narrator has chosen not to reveal before engaging in a reconstruction. The contemporary commentator on Acts will do more to illuminate the difficulties of such reconstructions than to facilitate them.[2] The critical question for the historian is whether 6:1-7 conceals something, viz., a doctrinal conflict. The subsequent attack on Stephen strongly suggests that it does, but this cannot be established beyond doubt.[3]

1 Martin Hengel is an example of such historians. Much of his research on the NT has been devoted to the project of the background of Paul and his theology.

2 Todd Penner (*Praise*) ably illuminates these matters.

3 See the detailed arguments of Craig C. Hill, *Hellenists and Hebrews: Reappraising Division with the Earliest Church* (Minneapolis: Fortress Press, 1992) and n. 17.

In the broad outline of Acts 1–7 chap. 6 launches the third and climactic cycle of the pattern that shapes chaps. 3–7, the story of Stephen. The narrative marks a fresh beginning. The similarities to 1:15-26, both verbal and thematic, underline both the importance and the nature of the transition.[4] Verses 1-7 comprise a unit bracketed by references to growth. Its structure contains a number of additional internal echoes, including "ministry" (vv. 1, 2, 4), "community" (vv. 2, 5), and "what is desirable" (vv. 2, 5). This may not constitute a chiasmus, but it is a tightly constructed passage.[5]

The shape of the narrative follows a pattern for the provision of subordinate leaders that is found in the Pentateuch (Exod 18:14-25; Num 11:16-30; 27:12-23; Deut 1:6-18).[6] By utilizing this pattern, which also conforms to a common Lucan narrative shape,[7] the narrator suggests that the early history of the church is like that of Israel and of comparable import. The contents are clear: the alleged neglect of widows belonging to a certain group presents a problem. The proposed solution is the selection of seven men to take charge of charitable distribution. Growth continued. The sort of glitch that rapid expansion is likely to produce was rapidly and effectively ameliorated by the appointment of a number of qualified specialists. Clarity is otherwise a scarce commodity.

Areas of uncertainty include the nature and composition of the groups involved, the meaning of "daily ministry," just what "unfair treatment" means, and what the solution to the problem was. Given the size of the unit, this is not a particularly short list of quandaries. The story is problematic not because it is unlikely that the distribution of food would be a source of friction but because "[i]t is not clear how the choice of seven members of one party would satisfactorily provide for the poor widows of both parties, nor why men chosen to allow the Twelve to preach rather than to 'serve tables' appear later only as preachers and evangelists."[8] In contemporary terms, Acts 6 almost immediately deconstructs.

The broader context shows that 6:1-7 begins the transition toward the gentile mission. Stephen, one of the Seven, preaches in Greek-speaking synagogues and is murdered for his pains (6:8—8:2). His colleague Philip initiates a mission to Samaria, converts a court official from Ethiopia, and then engages in evangelism in the Greek-speaking coastal border (8:4-40). After the conversion of Paul and his subsequent mission among Greek-speaking Jews, Peter, in the course of a mission in the same region, converts an indisputable gentile (chaps. 9–10). This context is the most important key for attempts to unravel 6:1-7.

The most glaring inconsistency is the difference between the stated duties of the Seven and their reported activities. The narrator never depicts them engaged in oversight over the distribution of food. Stephen and Philip are missionaries. Of the rest nothing is said. The most probable conclusion is that Luke's source(s) depicted the Seven as missionaries, since it is unlikely that he would have concocted nonapostolic evangelists at this point in the narrative. The consequence of this highly probable hypothesis is that the business of food distribution was Luke's own contribution, possibly adapted from divergent tradition, but not from any source treating the work of the Seven.

Other reasons support this conclusion. The pericope conforms to a typical Lucan narrative pattern in which threats to the stability of the community are resolved

4 Verbal parallels include the phrase "in those days," last used in 1:15, the list of names, another omen of change (on which see the comments on 1:13), the initial use of the words μαθητής ("disciple"), found twenty-eight times between 6:1 and 21:16, πληθύνω ("increase in number," "multiply"), which appears also in 6:7; 7:17; 9:31; and 12:24. Note also "ministry" (διακονία), used in 1:17, 25 of the apostles; cf. 20:24; 21:19, of Paul. In 11:29 and 12:25 the meaning is like that here. On the term, note Hans Dieter Betz, *2 Corinthians 8 and 9: A Commentary on Two Administrative Letters of the Apostle Paul* (Hermeneia; Philadelphia: Fortress Press, 1985) 46.

5 On the structure, see Penner, *Praise*, 64, who argues for chiasmus.

6 See David Daube, "A Reform in Acts and Its Models," in Robert Hamerton-Kelly and Robin Scroggs, eds., *Jews, Greeks, and Christians: Religious Cultures in Late Antiquity; Essays in Honor of William David Davies* (SJLA 21; Leiden: Brill, 1976) 151–63; and Talbert, 73.

7 See n. 9 below

8 Henry Joel Cadbury, "The Hellenists," in Lake and Cadbury, *Additional Notes*, 59–74, esp. 62.

by appropriate action.[9] The situation is anachronistic. It envisions a community that has an identifiable body of widows and subordinate ministers who function like deacons, although Luke does not use the title. The world of Acts 6 is like that of the Pastorals and Polycarp, a realm in which organized bodies of widows seek to keep the male leadership on its toes. If the instructions given the apostles by Jesus in Luke 17:7-10 mean that community leaders are to perform all functions, the apostles cancel those directions in Acts 6.[10] Moreover, meals are an important theme and symbol in Acts.[11] For example, the charge laid against Peter in 11:3 is not that he baptized Cornelius, but that he associated and *ate with* uncircumcised men. That charge evokes Gal 2:12 and disputes about *kashrut* (dietary regulations) in mixed communities.[12] A passage often associated with the proposed Antiochene source has intimations of a conflict known to have taken place in Antioch at a later date. That observation should play a role in any solution to the problems of 6:1-7.

In addition to the abrupt introduction of different issues, indicators of a source include the list of names, the unexplained labels "Hebrews," "Hellenists," and "the Twelve," used only here of the apostles in Acts.[13] The noun "wisdom" (σοφία) may also be related to a source or tradition, since Luke is not a proponent of the speculative "wisdom theology" that is prominent in the Pauline and Deutero-Pauline tradition.[14] There are also editorial indications of the modification of a source. Acts 7:55 appears to resume 6:15: Stephen's face is transfigured in 6:14 because it reflects the "glory" (δόξα) of God. Acts 8:1b reports a persecution that "put to flight" (διασπείρω) all but the apostles. The implication is that those put to flight were allied to the Seven, since Philip (8:4-40) is the specific example. Acts 11:19 resumes this narrative thread, linking the story of the

9 On this pattern, see Joseph B. Tyson, "The Problem of Food in Acts: A Study of Literary Patterns with Particular Reference to Acts 6:1-7," in *SBLSP 1979* (Missoula, Mont.: Scholars Press, 1979) 69–85, esp. 69–75. More generally, this pulse of tension and relaxation is generally characteristic of popular narrative, which tends to occupy a midpoint between oral stories, which feature instant gratification, as in miracle stories, and the more elegant products of cultured literacy, which cultivate lengthy, overarching plots. See Lawrence M. Wills, *The Jewish Novel in the Ancient World* (Ithaca: Cornell University Press, 1995) 1–39.

10 See Paul S. Minear, "A Note on Luke 17:7-10," *JBL* 93 (1974) 82–87. This similitude assumes that a farmer with a single slave will expect that person to perform both field and domestic tasks. The verbs ἀροτριάω ("plow") and ποιμαίνω ("tend sheep") in v. 7 and διακονέω ("serve," "wait at table") in v. 8 are metaphors related to church leadership: *payment of leaders* (1 Cor 10:9); pastoral care (John 21:16; Acts 20:28; 1 Pet 5:2; cf. 1 Cor 9:7); and διακονέω and related words (Luke 22:27, Acts 6:2; 2 Cor 3:6; 1 Tim 3:8; etc.). Since "planting" is a common image for missionary activity (Mark 4; 1 Cor 3:6), "plowing" in Luke 17:7 would relate to evangelism, "tending sheep" to pastoral leadership and care, and "serving" to the provision of concrete assistance. (As Acts 6:4 and 2 Cor 3:6 indicate, διακονία is the most comprehensive of these terms.) The spirit of this passage is far removed from that of Luke 22:24-27.

11 See Tyson, "The Problem of Food"; and Esler, *Community*, 71–109.

12 The verb συνεσθίω ("eat with") is not particularly common. It appears four times in the LXX, but never with reference to dietary laws (Gen 43:32 is closest: Egyptians consider it an abomination to eat with Hebrews!) In Mark 2:13-17, Jesus is criticized for table fellowship with sinners, but only in Luke 15:2 does the verb appear, in association with διαγογγύζω ("grumble," "complain"; cf. 19:7 and γογγυσμός in Acts 6:1). *Jos. Asen.* 7:1 uses the term in the sense of *kashrut*.

13 See nn. 6–7 on Acts 1:15-26.

14 Apart from 6:3, where it is paired with "Spirit" in a possible hendiadys, and 6:10, where it is applied to Stephen (although Luke 21:15 may be the source), this noun is used elsewhere only of Moses (in Stephen's speech [7:10, 22]). On the subject, see Hans Conzelmann, "Die Schule des Paulus," in *Theologia Crucis: Festschrift für Erich Dinkler zum 70. Geburtstag* (ed. Carl Andresen and Günter Klein; Tübingen: Mohr Siebeck, 1979) 85–96; Hans-Martin Schenke, "Das Weiterwirken des Paulus und die Pflege seines Erbs durch die Paulusschule," *NTS* 21 (1975) 505–18; and, for a broad and general background, Dieter Georgi, *The Opponents of Paul in Second Corinthians* (Philadelphia: Fortress Press, 1985) 83–151, 422–34. On its use here, see Martin Hengel, *Between Jesus and Paul: Studies in the History of Earliest Christianity* (trans. J. Bowden; Philadelphia: Fortress Press, 1983) 18–19.

"Hellenists" to the origins of the mission at Antioch. Contained—"buried" might be a better word—within Acts 6 are elements of the "gentile mission source."[15]

Among the many unknowns is whether "Hellenists" and "Hebrews" were terms used in that source. The failure of the narrator to explain them does not guarantee that they should have been familiar to the implied reader.[16] The context and linguistic logic determine that Ἑλληνιστής here should mean "Jews who spoke Greek as their native language";[17] 9:29 supports this.[18] The chief difficulty with this understanding is that Ἑβραῖοι is not normally a linguistic term.[19] In the NT era, "Hebrews" normally refers to Israelites of ancient ("biblical") times. As such, it could be a proud self-designation. Paul applies it in this sense to rivals and to himself, both Greek-speaking (2 Cor 11:22; Phil 3:5).[20] It is possible that the native Palestinian speakers of Aramaic defined themselves as "Hebrews" and used the term "Hellenists" in a somewhat disparaging way, but the safest path lies in modesty: "Hebrews" were Jews whose primary language was Aramaic[21] and who used that language in worship, whereas "Hellenists" spoke Greek and did not find Aramaic a suitable language for worship.

If one envisions a historical setting for these groups, the "Hellenists" would have been Diaspora Jews who settled in "the Holy City." Such persons were intrinsically unlikely to have been predisposed to take a relaxed approach to Torah-observance. If the "Theodotus inscription" is properly dated to the period before 70 CE, it constitutes extrinsic evidence of a synagogue for "Hellenists."[22] The text refers to a building constructed by one Theodotus, who bears a typical Jewish Greek name.

15 On this putative source see pp. 13–14.

16 It is not even clear that Luke understood what "Hellenist" meant in his source—presuming that the source contained the term.

17 Henry J. Cadbury ("The Hellenists," in Lake and Cadbury, *Additional Notes*, 59–74) argues that the word means "gentile," but few have followed him. One who does is Tyson, "Problem of Food," 78–80. The word is quite rare, not found, apart from comments on Acts, before the second half of the fourth century (Julian *Letter* 84.35). See Hengel, *Between*, 6–11. The linguistic understanding is the consensus of the commentators, e.g., Barrett, 1:308–9. See also Wolfgang Reinbold ("Die 'Hellenisten': Kritische Anmerkungen zu einem Fachbegriff der Neutestamentlichen Wissenschaft," *BZ* 42 [1998] 96–102), who maintains that it means "spoke Greek." Other contributions come from Walter Grundmann, "Das Problem des hellenistischen Christentums innerhalb der Jerusalemer Urgemeinde," *ZNW* 38 (1939) 45–73; Hengel, *Between*, 1–29; Nikolaos Walter, "Apostelgeschichte 6.1 und die Anfänge der Urgemeinde in Jerusalem," *NTS* 29 (1983) 370–93; Hill, *Hellenists*; Heikki Räisänen, "Die 'Hellenisten' der Urgemeinde," *ANRW* 2.26.2 (1995) 1468–514; idem, "The 'Hellenists': A Bridge between Jesus and Paul?" in *Jesus, Paul, and Torah: Collected Essays* (trans. David E. Orton; JSNTS 43; Sheffield: Sheffield Academic Press, 1992) 149–202; Thomas W. Martin, "Hellenists," *ABD* 3:135–36; Stephen R. Wiest, "The Story of Stephen in Acts 6:1–8:4: History Typologized or Typology Historicized?" *Forum* n.s. 3 (2000) 121–53; Torrey Seland, "Once More—The Hellenists, Hebrews, and Stephen: Conflict and Conflict-Management in Acts 6–7," in Peder Borgen et al., eds., *Recruitment, Conquest, and Conflict: Strategies in Judaism, Early Christianity, and the Greco-Roman World* (Emory Studies in Early Christianity 6; Atlanta: Scholars Press, 1998) 169–207; Witherington, 240–43; and Penner, *Praise*, 1–103. The source, which was focused on gentiles, may have used "Hellenist" with intentional ambiguity. Other views exist. Martin Bodinger ("Les 'Hébreux' et les 'Hellénistes' dans le livre des *Actes des Apôtres*," *Henoch* 19 [1997] 39–58) argues that language is not the basis for understanding these terms, which are an invention aimed at the broader issues of Jewish and gentile participation in the Jesus movement.

18 On the text of 9:29 and 11:20, where the witnesses include both Ἑλληνιστάς ("Hellenists") and Ἕλληνας ("Greeks") see the comments on those passages.

19 Note, however, Philo *Conf. ling.* 129, which contrasts "Hebrews" with Greek-speakers ("us"). Luke otherwise uses the stem only in a linguistic sense (Acts 21:40; 22:2; 26:14).

20 On "Hebrews," see Georgi, *Opponents*, 41–46; Hengel, *Between*, 9–11; J. Wanke, *EDNT* 1:369–70; and K. G. Kuhn, "Ἰσραήλ, κ.τ.λ.," *TDNT* 3:359–69, esp. 367–69.

21 For evidence that "Hebrew" usually means "Aramaic" in the NT, see Hengel, *Between*, 9–10.

22 *CIJ* 2, no. 1404. For recent discussion of this inscription, see Rainer Riesner, "Synagogues in Jerusalem," in Bauckham, *Palestinian Setting*, 179–211, esp. 192 and 200; and Donald D. Binder, *Into the Temple Courts: The Place of the Synagogues in the Second Temple Period* (SBLDS 169; Atlanta: Society of Biblical Literature, 1999) 104–9. The

He states that he is a priest and a third-generation synagogue leader (ἀρχισυνάγωγος).[23] The purpose of the synagogue is εἰς ἀν[άγ]νωσ[ιν] νόμου καὶ εἰς [δ]ιδαχὴν ἐντολῶν ("for the reading of the law and for the teaching of the commandments" [lines 4–5]). This program would, as Martin Hengel says, be congenial to the Pharisees.[24] Representatives of this or a similar synagogue might well have taken issue with Stephen *if he were in opposition to such a program* (cf. vv. 13-14).

Since the narrator of Acts is so vague about the complaint[25] and never troubles to portray the seven appointees engaged in relief work, critical readers investigate, or speculate about, their actual role. All have Greek names, none either typically Jewish or evocative of polytheism. Since one is identified as a "proselyte," all are Jews. Their names suggest a Diaspora milieu.[26] The sole exception to this is "Philip," a name "well-established" in Palestine.[27] "Stephen" was common enough among Greeks, but rare in Palestine and not attested for Palestinian Jews.[28] The name "Prochorus" is otherwise unattested.[29] "Nicanor" is more likely to reflect the Diaspora than the homeland.[30] There are no (other) Jewish examples of the common Greek name "Timon"[31] and none for the less common "Parmenas." "Nicholas" is a name attested for Jews, but this person is identified as a convert. "That he was a proselyte and from Antioch are additions to this name that excite our curiosity."[32] The order of the names may be construed as hierarchical, beginning with the two most prominent and concluding with a convert. This order could therefore be pre-Lucan. It is like lists of the Twelve (e.g., Acts 1:13).[33] This order also foreshadows the plot of this part of Acts, from Stephen's mission to Greek-speaking Jews to the evangelization of gentiles at Antioch.

---

principal criterion for dating this inscription to the period before the destruction of the temple is the archaeological context. This is not absolute, but it is reasonably probable.

23 From line 8 it appears that his father and grandfather were leaders of this community; that is, that it existed from around the beginning of the first century CE.

24 Hengel, *Between*, 18. "Facilities for water" (lines 6–7, χρησ[τ]ήρια τῶν ὑδάτων) may refer to a ritual bath.

25 As in the case of Ananias and Sapphira (see on 5:1-11), claims that this conflict shows Luke's lack of idealization (e.g., Tannehill, *Narrative Unity*, 2:79–81; and Witherington, 247–48) are ill-advised. An account narrating the immediate resolution of a difficult issue without a whisper of dissent, objection, or even the need for discussion is quite idealistic. Strictly speaking, Acts does not relate a conflict, which requires two sides, but the resolution of a grievance. Contrast with the debate about circumcision (chap. 16) is telling.

26 The following data are based on Hengel, *Between*, 144 n. 89; and Williams, "Personal Names," 110–12. See also Schneider, 1:428.

27 Williams, "Personal Names," 112. Hengel (*Between*, 144 n. 89) lists eight occurrences: four in Josephus and two each from Egypt and Europe. Some of this popularity may have been due to its appearance in the Herodian family (as in Philip the Tetrarch). Philip is also the only nominal overlap with the list of apostles (1:13). It is possible, as Hengel holds (*Between*, 14), that this is the same person and that he changed "affiliation." The *Acts of Philip* assume this identification, which most view as a harmonization: Frédéric Amsler, *Acta Philippi* (CCSA 11–12; vol. 11, ed. François Bovon, Bertrand Bouvier, Frédéric Amsler; vol. 12, ed. Frédéric Amsler; Turnhout: Brepols, 1999) 12:441–68. Christopher R. Matthews argues for the identity of the two: *Philip: Apostle and Evangelist* (NovTSup 105; Leiden: Brill, 2002.)

28 There is one certain reference to Stephen in a third-century Roman Jewish catacomb and another possible in an adjacent setting.

29 Prochorus was to enjoy a pseudonymous literary career as the author of a relatively orthodox edition of the *Acts of John*. (The name means "leader of the dance," but the famous dance (*Act. John* 94–97) is not found in this work, on which see Eric Junod and Jean-Daniel Kaestli. *Acta Iohannis* [2 vols.; CCSA 1–2; Turnhout: Brepols, 1983] 2:718–49).

30 Williams, "Personal Names," 110. A Nicanor of Alexandria built a gate for the temple (the "Beautiful Gate"?), *CIJ* 2, no. 1256.

31 Latin *h* reads *Simonem*, an example of the substitution of the familiar for the rare.

32 Cadbury and Lake, 65. The "Nicolaitans" of Rev 2:6 may have claimed him as their founder in order to acquire a link with early tradition, but any historical association is unlikely, according to Schneider 1:428 n. 66, but Nikolaos Walter ("Proselyt aus Antiochen, und die Nikolaiten in Ephesos und Pergamon: Ein Beitrag auch zum Thema: Paulus und Ephesos," *ZNW* 93 [2002] 200–206) is willing to consider the possibility of a connection.

33 On the function of lists in Acts, see on 1:13.

Luke does not call these persons "Hellenists" here, nor does he refer to them as "the seven." Acts 21:8, however, characterizes Philip as "the evangelist" and as one of "the seven," resident in the Greek city of Caesarea. This strongly suggests that there was a body known as "the Seven," a title exactly parallel to "the Twelve," with functions not limited to relief assistance in Jerusalem—unless Philip had abandoned his responsibilities. Seven, a number of vast and ecumenical symbolic potency,[34] was a common symbol for completeness, leading to such groupings as the Seven Sages and the Seven Wonders of the World.[35] The number served as a title for groups, such as the Roman priestly college called the *Septemviri*,[36] and, most relevantly, for the number of leaders of Jewish communities in the first century.[37] "The Seven" were leaders of an organized group—or groups[38]—of Greek-speaking followers of Jesus.[39] Their roots were in the Diaspora.

Almost every other datum about this proposed group—their origin, location, and ideology, for example—is a matter for speculation. In Acts, they spring forth like Athena. The Gospels, written in Greek, do not describe the mission that evidently gave them birth.[40] These seven were evidently foundational figures for the Diaspora mission, linked in Acts to the later work of Barnabas and Paul, but the independent Paul did not refer to them. One can understand why Hengel is led to conclude: "Luke is even more a master of limitation and omission than he is of the art of elaboration."[41] The missionary careers of Stephen and Philip raise profound doubts about the actual function of these seven and therefore about the nature of the incident that Luke describes. Luke's repeated stress on unity and harmony[42] makes it unlikely that he invented a disagreement where none existed.

Even those who would prefer to take the text at face value have to confront the difficulty that Luke is vague about both the issue and its resolution.[43] The

34 See Karl Heinrich Rengstorf, "ἑπτά," *TDNT* 2:627–35.

35 The names and constituents of these groups varied (as do those of the Twelve). The concept of seven, rather than its components, was normative.

36 The *Septemviri* were originally in charge of a religious banquet. Their number varied, although the title endured. Cf. Cicero *De or.* 3.73; Livy 33.42.1 (on the origins); and Tacitus *Ann.* 3.64. There is a Greek parallel: *SIG* 1.495.2.

37 While in command of Galilee, Josephus appointed seven leaders for each municipality (*Bell.* 2.571). Note *Ant.* 4.214, where he introduced the number seven into the order to appoint judges for each community in his paraphrase of Deut 16:18. For talmudic references, see Hengel, *Between*, 147 n. 104. The *Acta Hermaisci* (*P. Oxy.* 1242) lines 13–16 lists seven names as members of a delegation elected (χειροτονοῦνται, line 13) by "the Jews" of Alexandria: "Simon, Glaucon, Theudes, Onias, Colon, Jacob, with Sopatros of Antioch as their advocate" (trans. Musurillo, *Pagan*, 47). Although these envoys come from the capital of "Jewish Hellenism," three (Theudes, Onias, Jacob) have Semitic names, while "Simon" is, to all intents and purposes, interchangeable. (That the last person comes from Antioch is no more than an interesting coincidence.) Apollonius of Tyana had seven disciples (1.18). Finally, the list of Paul's companions in Acts 20:4—originally a group representing gentile communities who sent funds to Jerusalem—also includes seven names.

38 It is a reasonable assumption that the Hellenists were based on house churches in various communities. The only house-based body located in Jerusalem identified in Acts is owned by a woman with a Greek name (Mary), who has a slave with a Greek name (Rhoda) and a double-named son (John Mark—Mark is Latin) (12:12-17).

39 Although the notion, promoted by Walter Schmithals (*Paul and the Gnostics* [trans. John E. Steely; Nashville: Abingdon, 1972] 261 n. 62), that the number seven is a symbol for the gentile mission lacks scholarly support, it is interesting that Mark associates this number with Jesus' activities on the eastern side of the Lake of Galilee, largely gentile territory (Mark 8:5, 8, 19-20 vs. 6:43). Werner Kelber understands this activity as a symbol of the inclusive mission (*The Kingdom in Mark: A New Place and a New Time* [Philadelphia: Fortress Press, 1974] 57–62).

40 John 12:20-26 locates a mission to Greeks after the death of Jesus.

41 Hengel, *Between*, 2.

42 Cf. the use of ὁμοθυμαδόν ("with one mind") in 1:14; 2:46; 4:24; 5:12, and ἐπὶ τὸ αὐτό ("together") in 1:15; 2:1, 44, 47; 4:26.

43 Barrett represents those determined to beat back the claim that there were two parties. He supports this with the claim that "Luke had no precise understanding of a party of 'Hellenists' in the primitive church" (1:309). This seems a bit moot. If Luke viewed these groups as parties, the tradition would have accepted his claim. The issue is

"Hellenists" complain to the "Hebrews" that "their widows" were receiving unfair treatment "in the daily ministry." The view reflects an androcentrism that would have pleased the author of the Pastoral Epistles ("the Pastor") and his ilk. Rather than raise their own complaints, the widows report them to their group.[44] The text does not, in fact, state that "the Hebrews" were slighting "Hellenist widows." This is a reasonable inference, but no more than an inference.[45] Verse 2 apparently indicates that the ministry in question was a meal, no doubt a nourishing meal, but all meals had a religious character, so that it is also reasonable to conclude that the meal in view was the Christian Eucharist (or its prototype). Joseph Tyson therefore concludes that the "Hellenist" widows (whom he regards as gentiles) "were habitually being excluded from the daily meal."[46] Feminist criticism also brings insights to bear on this problem.[47]

These interpretations shed light on later conflicts (commensality, as in the mixed community at Antioch; church organization and office; the gradual elimination of women from leadership positions) and make valid observations about Lucan thought, but they underline the anachronism of the account. The grievance of the widows is no more than a temporary structure to explain the relation of the Twelve to the Seven.[48] Luke's readers evidently understood "Hebrews" and "Hellenists" as interest groups, parties, factions, or coalitions related in some fashion to matters touching on the place of Torah observance in missionary policy and activity. Meals, not least in Luke and Acts, highlight the problems of inclusiveness and disunity, specifically factionalism.[49] Most readers viewed the account as the "foundation legend" of the diaconate, an order of ministry devoted to service. The references to groups denominated "Hellenists" and "Hebrews" in the context of a meal suggest that Luke is willing to permit the inference that the events in question are related to conflicts that later emerged over the gentile mission.

Ferdinand Christian Baur was quite prepared to accept this inference, which he made the starting point for his understanding of early church history.[50] Baur's picture of nascent Christianity in terms of a conflict between "Judaizers" and proponents of gentile Christianity has proved to be too clear-cut; he did, however, grasp that Acts had conciliatory and reconciling aims and could not be taken at face value. Scholarly consensus holds that Baur was, in a general sense, correct: behind Acts 6 lies a conflict about Torah observance (including temple worship). A number of data in the text support this understanding: (1) the Hellenist–Hebrew conflict, (2) the list of the Seven, (3) the charges laid against Stephen (6:13-14), (4) his subsequent speech (chap. 7), (5) Philip's work among Samaritans and his conversion of an Ethiopian official (chap. 8), and (6)

whether those who attempt to look behind Luke for the existence of parties (the existence of which he would strongly deny) have any justification. See also Strange, *Text*, 122–26.

44 Cf. 1 Cor 14:35, which is probably an interpolation based on 1 Timothy. The text also resembles the apologetic perspective of the Pastorals in that the only group described as living at community expense is the widows, a group that *prima facie* excluded the lazy and the "spongers." The perspective is that of the donors. Luke does not touch on such issues as the use of community resources to free slaves (on which see James Albert Harrill, *The Manumission of Slaves in Early Christianity* [HUTh 32; Tübingen: Mohr Siebeck, 1995]) or for other purposes.

45 Bede (32) provides one of the earliest interpretations: the Hebrews preferred their own widows because they were *eruditiores*, "better educated." Chrysostom says that the Hebrew widows were "more important" (αἰδεσιμώτεροι; *Hom.* 14, 129E), although later in the same sermon he attributes this to general carelessness rather than to malice (132E).

46 Tyson, "The Problem of Food," 80.

47 See below.

48 Barrett aptly concludes his discussion: "If we now forget the widows we are in good company, for so does Luke . . ." ("Acts and Christian Consensus," in Peter Wilhelm Bøckman and Ronald E. Kristiansen, eds., *Context: Festskrift til Peter Johan Borgan/Essays in Honour of Peder Johan Borgen* (Trondheim: Tapir, 1987) 19–33, esp. 21.

49 See 1 Corinthians 14 and the discussions of Richard Pervo, "Wisdom and Power: Petronius' *Satyricon* and the Social World of Early Christianity," *ATR* 67 (1985) 307–25, and "PANTA KOINA." See also p. 350 n. 16.

50 For a thorough review of research on this matter up to the date of publication, see Heinz-Werner Neudorfer, *Der Stephanuskreis in der Forschungsgeschichte seit F. C. Baur* (Monographien und Studienbücher 309; Giessen: Brunnen, 1983). Hill (*Hellenists*, 5–17) gives a more concise review.

the links between associates of the Seven and a gentile mission that did not explicitly demand observance (11:19-20). In addition is the inference from 8:1 that the persecution described there did not affect those associated with the Twelve. These data are of varied origin and quality. (1) and (4) are in essence Lucan, as is the linkage between persecution and mission. It is precarious to mine Stephen's speech for his own views or to discover "the theology of the Hellenists." The accusations (3) are based in part on Mark and are similar to those made against Paul (21:28; cf. 25:8). The residue is that tradition reported that Stephen (the leader of the Hellenists?) had been attacked by other Hellenophone Jews. The hypothesis that the Greek-speaking followers of Jesus held some opposing views about the place of temple and Torah is reasonable—although not certain—but the correlative hypothesis that the historical "Hebrews" were zealots for the law of Moses is far from certain and is unlikely as a blanket description of those who had followed Jesus in and from Galilee.[51]

Insofar as a trajectory of the Jerusalem community can be traced, it appears that the more observant gained power in the 40s, resulting in the dominance of James, a trend reflected in Acts (12:17; 15; 21:18-25).[52] The available data indicate that the gentile missions(s) precipitated factions in the Jerusalem community rather than that the mission owed its existence to one or more extant factions.[53] This perception may be incorrect, but Acts 6–7 does not supply sound evidence for an alternative reconstruction. Luke takes some pains to establish links between the two "groups," but all of these are likely to be redactional.[54] The gentile mission source was apologetic—legitimating—and, although probably not strongly anti-Pauline, it promoted Peter as its hero. If this source were "anti-Hebrew," and set forth a rivalry between "the Twelve" and "The Seven," that view may have been anachronistic, but it seems more probable that the source held that the original mission of the Seven was supported by the Twelve, led by Peter. In conclusion: "The Hebrews" of Acts 6:1 may be a foreshadowing of later opposition to the gentile mission, but they do not establish an early conflict *among followers of Jesus*. That there was a conflict is not improbable, as different stances toward Torah are likely to have existed from the beginning. The data of Acts are not sufficient to establish this understanding. The most prudent view is that the "Hellenists" conducted an independent mission that provoked opposition from other Greek-speaking Jews.[55]

Comment

■ **1** The initial γογγυσμός[56] ("murmuring") is, like the narrative form,[57] evocative of the wilderness epoch, but not flattering to its subject. The D-Text ("In **those** days, as the **body** of followers continued to grow in number, there was a complaint that the widows of those who spoke Greek were treated unfairly in the daily distribution of assistance **by the servants of** those who spoke Aramaic") offers a solution to this problem: the "murmuring" lacks attribution,[58] so that the Hellenists cannot be blamed, and responsibility for the neglect is assigned to the Hebrews.[59] The verb παρεθεωροῦντο

51 A *caveat*: the canonical traditions about Jesus were transmitted in Greek and are therefore open to the charge that they represent "Hellenist" bias. If this hypothesis were to be accepted, it would concede a particular "Hellenist" theological tendency—better, some tendencies.

52 For a review of these changing relationships, see Bengt Holmberg, *Paul and Power: The Structure of Authority in the Primitive Church as Reflected in the Pauline Epistles* (Philadelphia: Fortress Press, 1980) 1–80.

53 This statement presumes that "factions" enjoy some degree of organization and that they may be distinguished from "tendencies" and the like. John Painter identifies, largely on the basis of inferences from the epistles, no fewer than six different factions representing different views about the relation of Torah to mission (*Just James*, 73–78).

54 Acts 6:1-7 presupposes a single community; in 8:14-25 the Jerusalem apostles support (and "complete") the Samaritan mission of Philip. Acts 11:23 states that Barnabas went to Antioch as an authorized agent of the Jerusalem church.

55 Hill (*Hellenists*) exposes many of the weaknesses of Baur's hypothesis in its varied ramifications, but Hill does a better job of exposing the difficulties of Acts 6:1–8:4 than of proving Baur wrong. See the review by Philip Esler, *BibInt* 3 (1995) 119–23, and Penner, *Praise*, 41.

56 Cf. Exod 16:8-12; Num 17:5, 10. NT references are John 7:12; Phil 2:14; 1 Pet 4:9.

57 See above.

58 This depends on thin evidence (Boismard, *Texte*, 123–24), but is not improbable.

59 The agents of this neglect are the "deacons"

(lit. "overlook," a *hapax legomenon*) is a frequentative imperfect, indicating that the problem did not arise from a single incident. "Daily ministry" (διακονία καθημερινή) probably does not reflect a change in community life and practice.[60] This is the "breaking of bread" mentioned in the summary of 2:46,[61] the common sacred meal.[62]

■ **2** The apostles promptly respond[63] by convoking a community meeting,[64] which they open with a rather formal unison declaration that is no less oblique than v. 1: the subject of their displeasure is unstated; that is, they do indicate that God[65] would take exception to their "waiting on tables" (the literal translation).[66] The implication of this statement, supported by v. 4, is that the apostles have not been directly engaged in overseeing the distribution of food for the community meal. Were they to assume this responsibility, equity would doubtless result, but that would be an inappropriate use of their time, as it would detract from missionary and pastoral activity.[67] Luke was familiar with what would eventually be called different "orders of ministry." As the use of biblical sources indicates, he does not ground these in divine ordinance, but portrays them as a human and practical response to friction caused by growth. His accomplishment is manifold: with this single shaft he dispatches the notion of tension between "the Twelve" and "the Seven" while suggesting that, although the Diaconate is not a necessary order, the apostles did, in fact, "ordain" its progenitors.

(διάκονοι) of the Hebrews (cop^{mae}, h). The text presumes that the various orders existed from the beginning. The solution to the problem was therefore to appoint a number of Hellenist deacons to take care of their own people. These variants, which both content and placement show to be secondary, are adduced by Epp (*Tendency*, 95) as evidence of the anti-Judaic character of the D-Text. For another view, see Strange, *Text*, 122–26, who argues, against the canons of textual criticism, that the D-Text may better represent the original. The other D-Text variants are stylistic.

60 Kirsopp Lake ("The Communism of Acts II. and IV.–VI. and the Appointment of the Seven," in Lake and Cadbury, *Additional Notes*, 140–51) asserts that "the 'communistic' experiment broke down . . ." (141). This is a rationalistic judgment that well reflects the history of many communal experiments but has no basis in the text. Since the "communalism" of Acts is, in essence, a Lucan creation, it could not have failed. His data on Jewish charitable practice (148–49) are valuable for comparative purposes but provide no historical model, since the evidence is from a much later period. In any case, one need not find models for a daily "soup kitchen," as such programs are logical and have appeared in many times and places.

61 The adjective καθημερινή is a *hapax legomenon*, but it is equivalent to the important prepositional phrase καθ' ἡμέραν ("daily," "day by day"), found, for example, in the Lucan form of the Our Father (Luke 11:3) and in the command to bear one's cross (Luke 9:23) and eleven times altogether in Luke and Acts. "Ministry" is useful because it can refer both to charitable activities, as in 11:29, and to the function of church leaders, as in 1:17.

62 See above.

63 The narrator emphasizes their promptness by omitting intermediate steps, for example, "In due course word of this complaint reached the apostles, who took counsel and . . ."

64 On these assemblies, see Richard Pervo, "Meet Right—and Our Bounden Duty," *Forum* n.s. 4.1 (Spring 2000) 45–62. The word πλῆθος has varying meanings, including "the general public," "the common people," and "the popular assembly." Josephus uses the phrase προσκαλεσάμενος τὸ πλῆθος twice in the first meaning (*Bell.* 2.172 with Pilate as subject and with Agrippa II in *Bell.* 2.344). The third meaning is applicable here. One parallel is *1 Clem.* 53:5, on which see Barbara Bowe, *A Church in Crisis* (HDR 23; Minneapolis: Fortress Press, 1988) 95. See also Cadbury and Lake, 47–48; and Barrett, 1:311.

65 Haenchen (259), in fact, places "to God" in parentheses in his version. Werner Foerster agrees ("ἀρέσκω," *TDNT* 1:455–57, esp. 456). He cites a Pythagorean aphorism found in Stobaeus *Ecl.* IV, p. 277, to show the antiquity of "pleasing to God" in the intellectual tradition.

66 The D-Text resolves this problem by reading "It is not *fair* . . ." (δίκαιον). Other variations (such as "the *entire* community," derived from v. 5) are pedantic. διακονίζειν τραπέζαις could mean, in effect, "take over the finances," since "table" is the metonymic source of the word "bank" in many languages, including English (cf. Mark 11:15 and parallels). Bruce (182) thinks that this interpretation may be correct. Haenchen (262 n. 2) rejects it, and rightly. For argument that the phrase refers to a meal, see Tyson, "The Problem of Food," 77–78.

67 The model remains valid. Rather than focus on

Excursus: Luke's View of Ecclesiastical Office

Luke was familiar with the concepts of "supervision," "seniority," and "ministry," the first and third of which are present as abstract nouns.[68] He uses the terms "presbyters" (πρεσβύτεροι) and "bishops" (ἐπίσκοποι) but not "deacons" (διάκονοι). Luke does not regard διάκονος as a prestigious title, as it was in Paul's time.[69] The sole occurrence of ἐπίσκοποι in Acts (20:28) applies to those also called "presbyters" (20:17). The lack of a clear distinction between these two "titles" is also found in *1 Clement* and in the Pastoral Epistles.[70] The matter is quite complex, but it may be said that these texts say, in effect, "It makes no great difference whether these leaders are known as "presbyters" or "*episkopoi*."[71] In both Acts and the Pastoral Epistles, these leaders are to stave off false teaching and to lead by moral example.[72] *1 Clement* shares with Acts the use of the term ἐπισκοπή ("oversight"). In 44:1, 3 the term refers to a title and function that relate to the Corinthian *presbyters*. In sum: (Luke and) Acts reflects both emerging church order and debates about it. This is the world of *1 Clement*, Ignatius, Polycarp, and the Pastoral Epistles, the milieu of the "Apostolic Fathers." The texts relate to debates over the nature and function of church offices. The author is sufficiently aware of "bishops" of the Ignatian type to have reservations about them. The author of Acts prefers to describe "ministry" in abstract terms, emphasizing the functions to be performed.[73] His preference is for leadership by (one or more) presbyters. Like the author of the Pastorals, he anachronistically presents Paul as ordaining presbyters, indicating thereby his preference.

■ **3-4** In v. 3[74] the apostles direct[75] the community[76] to identify seven men with appropriate qualifications.[77] The process follows the conventions of civic life: the leaders (or a "constitution") determine the number of officials and the criteria for the position. The "commons" nominate an appropriate number of qualified persons, after which, when all is functioning smoothly, the leaders accept these nominations and induct the candidates into office.[78] The scene depicts the church

assigning blame, they seek to solve the problem (which is assumed to be valid).

68 For more references and details, see Pervo, *Dating*, 203–29. Note also the survey of Burton Scott Easton, *Early Christianity: The Purpose of Acts and Other Papers* (ed. F. C. Grant; Greenwich, Conn.: Seabury, 1954) 67–79.

69 See Georgi, *Opponents*, 27–32.

70 In the Pastorals, it is noteworthy that *episkopos* ("bishop") is always singular. The earlier "Bishop-Deacon" scheme is apparent also in that "deacons" are associated with "bishops" but not with presbyters.

71 Hans von Campenhausen says that the object is "to fuse the two traditions," *Ecclesiastical Authority and Spiritual Power* (trans J. A. Baker; Stanford: Stanford University Press, 1969) 81. Although dated (the German edition appeared in 1953), Campenhausen's essay "The System of Elders and the Beginnings of Official Authority" (76–123) remains important.

72 Wilson (*Luke and the Pastoral Epistles*, 53–68) points to the similarities between the two on the matter of "Church and Ministry." Note his impressive summary (68). He does not, however, take account of the differences, for he views the Pastorals as a development by the same author of the ideas he had expressed in Acts.

73 The noun διακονία ("ministry") occurs once in Luke and eight times in Acts. The verb διακονέω appears eight times in Luke and twice in Acts. The word διάκονος ("minister") is absent from both; ἐπικσκοπή is found in Acts 1:20 (Luke 19:44 is different). There are no verbal or abstract forms for "presbyter," which appears more than twenty times in a variety of meanings (ten in reference to Christian leaders), always in the plural. In Acts 15–16, πρεσβύτεροι ("elders," "presbyters") and "apostles" are paired six times. Luke implies that the presbyters are "successors" of the apostles, as the contrast between 15:2, etc., and 21:18 indicates. *1 Clement* is more explicit about succession (chaps. 44 and 46).

74 The D-Text eases the abruptness of the narrative with an introductory τί οὖν ἐστιν; ("Well, then, what's it going to be?"). This phrase was imported from 21:22. See Metzger, *Textual Commentary*, 294. Boismard (*Texte*, 125) does not take this as a question. Ms. A achieves a similar effect by reading δή, a stronger particle than δέ. For other variants, see Metzger, *Textual Commentary*, 295.

75 B alone reads a hortatory subjunctive ("let us scrutinize"). Ropes attributed this variant to a possible desire to include the apostles in the selection, but notes that it is in conflict with v. 6. Cadbury and Lake (65) nonetheless accept the first plural.

76 If one takes the five thousand males of 4:4 and the notes of large accessions in 5:14 and 6:1, the facility would need to accommodate around twenty thousand persons. This is one more indication that Luke pays no heed to his own statistics.

taking action as a totality[79] and exhibits an ecclesial orientation. Rather than ask what Jesus might do in such a situation, for example, the leaders make rules for community life confident in their guidance by the Spirit.

■ **5-6** The first verse echoes the ἀρεστόν of v. 2. This is not a formal *placet* (approval),[80] but the function is similar.[81] In a typical bit of Lucan foreshadowing, the list comes to a pregnant ending: Nicholas is a former gentile from Antioch.[82] The failure to mark a change of subject in v. 6 is due to compressed style.[83] The verb καταστήσομεν ("we shall place them in charge" [v. 3]) establishes the subject. The people presented the candidates to the apostles, who then prayed and laid hands on the Seven. Prayer and the imposition of hands are principal features of an ordination,[84] and καθίστημι is regularly used of the action.[85] Since Irenaeus (*A.H.* 1.26.3; 3.12.10; 4.15.1), followed by most of the tradition,[86] this passage has been understood as the foundation of the diaconate.[87] The presumed source certainly did not view the Seven as a body instituted by—and therefore subordinate to—the apostles, and even more certainly did not see them as "table-servants." Luke is therefore responsible for the ordination terminology. He describes an ordination not to explain the origin of the diaconal order but to subordinate the Seven to the Twelve and let the chips fall where they may.

The issue Luke constructed to motivate the institution of the seven "assistants" was a recurrent problem: the equitable distribution of limited resources. Theologically, this is framed as the priority of the "ministry of the word" over the "ministry of service." That priority reflects the viewpoint of those with more money and education. If the very poor had a voice, it would almost certainly cry that the primary duty of community leaders was to see to the distribution of the loaves and fishes[88] and let the faithful be able to concentrate on hearing the word without the interference of growling stomachs. Luke's contrary view is apparent both in the

77 Verse 3 is based on Deut 1:13. "Spirit and wisdom" may be a hendiadys: "spiritual discernment." A range of witnesses, moved at least in part by v. 8, preface "Holy" to "spirit." Qualifications for office are prominent in the Pastorals (e.g., 1 Tim 3:1-13) and Polycarp (5:1–6:1), on which see Dibelius and Conzelmann, *Pastoral Epistles,* 50–51, Appendices 3–4, 158–60, and, with many data, Ceslas Spicq, *Les épitres pastorales* (2 vols.; EB; 4th ed.; Paris: Gabalda, 1969) 1:426–63; 2:627–34. A literary example may be found in *Aristeas* 39. King Ptolemy directs the high priest to choose six elders from each tribe. Before the necessary qualities of legal experience (ἐμπειρίαν . . . τοῦ νόμου) and translation skills (δυνατοὺς ἑρμηνεῦσαι), the monarch stipulates proven good character (καλῶς βεβιωκότας). In his reply, Eleazar characterizes them as "perfect gentlemen" (καλοὺς καὶ ἀγαθούς, a Greek cliché). (Verses 47–50 list their names.) Qualifications in Acts 6:3 include recommendations (μαρτυρομένους).

78 The word χρεία means "office" or "duty" here: BDAG, 1088, *s.v.*

79 Cf. 15:22, 30—and note the differences. Unlike 1 Cor 4:3; 5:3-4; 2 Cor 2:6, Acts presumes different roles and responsibilities for different "orders" in decision making.

80 Haenchen, 257.

81 For the wording, see 2 Kgdms 3:36; 1 Macc 8:21. The D-Text pedantically adds τῶν μαθητῶν from v. 1. Rules notwithstanding, πᾶς means "entire" (Moule, *Idiom Book*, 94).

82 Stephen alone receives qualifying epithets (lit. "full of faith and Holy Spirit"). The variation from v. 3 (lit. "full of spirit and wisdom") is stylistic. In v. 8 he is "full of grace and power," while "wisdom" appears in v. 10, with "spirit."

83 D p syr^p clarify this ambiguity.

84 Cf. Acts 13:3; 1 Tim 4:14; 2 Tim 1:6. Note also 1 Tim 5:22.

85 On the political use of this word, see Albrecht Oepke, "καθίστημι," *TDNT* 3:444–47, esp. 444. For ecclesiastical usage, see Titus 1:5; *1 Clem.* 42:15; 43:1; 44:2, 3; 54:2, which refer to presbyters, and so on. For other uses of this term in reference to the appointment/ordination of leaders, see Lampe, 690 1, *s.v.*

86 Chrysostom was an exception. Although he viewed the action as an ordination (*Hom.* 14, 133E), he stated that the Seven were not deacons but holders of a unique office, like the seventy(-two) of Luke 10:1-12 (133A). (His views were approved by the Trullan Council in 692, canon 16.)

87 For a review of research, see Joseph Coppens, "L'imposition des mains dans les Actes des Apôtres," in Kremer, *Actes*, 405–38, esp. 415–23, and, for a detailed study of evidence from the second and third centuries CE, Robert Cabié, "Quand les 'Sept' deviennent des diacres," *BullLittEccl* 97 (1996) 219–26. Note also Pesch, 1:232; Roloff, 109–10.

88 Pervo ("PANTA KOINA") argues that the Gospel feeding stories (Mark 6:30-44 parr.) reflect the

Gospel (Luke 10:38-42) and here. It is not accidental that women are prominent in both places. In part, this may be due to the tendency of male authors to tell stories about women to illustrate male problems, but, as critics have proposed, genuine issues may be involved. The preparation and serving of food (not to mention washing up) were traditional female responsibilities.[89] Elisabeth Schüssler Fiorenza, attentive to the normal meaning of διακονία, considers the possibility "that the conflict between the Hellenists and the Hebrews involved the role and participation of women at the eucharistic meal."[90] It is, however, arguable that Luke identified widows as the subject because his readers would find them a likely source of grievances.[91]

■ **7** While accomplishing the main goal of relating the Seven to the internal life of the Jerusalem community, Luke also manages to show how unity was (and can be) achieved, with particular reference to matters of commensality involving different "ethnic groups," and suggests that leaders not be held responsible for conflicts about the distribution of resources, which should be resolved by a division of labor rather than by assigning the ministry of service a higher priority than mission and instruction.[92] At this point, Luke is happy to drop the entire discussion. With a truly audacious gap, the narrator forgoes any reference to the subsequent fate of the "daily ministry." Rather than speak of contented widows, v. 7 reports the result: unshackled by

viewpoint of the poor. Dispute about the two types of ministry appears to have been general in the third Christian generation. See 1 Pet 4:10-11, and the comments of Leonhard Goppelt, *A Commentary on 1 Peter* (ed. F. Hahn; trans. John E. Alsup; Grand Rapids: Eerdmans, 1993) 302–7.

89 Presidency at meal ceremonies (toasts, prayers, libations, etc.) fell within the male sphere, however. Respectable women were not present at Greek symposia.

90 Elisabeth Schüssler Fiorenza, *In Memory of Her: A Feminist Theological Reconstruction of Christian Origins* (New York: Crossroad, 1983) 166; see 164–66, where she observes a parallel division between preaching and serving like that in 1 Tim 5:17 and 3:8-13. If a historical background to the complaint is to be sought, this is a good probability. Note also Richter Reimer, *Women*, 234–37; Seim, *Double Message*, 108–12; and Robert M. Price, *The Widow Traditions in Luke-Acts: A Feminist-Critical Scrutiny* (SBLDS 155; Atlanta: Scholars Press, 1997) 210–16. These studies draw attention to the similarities between this passage and Luke 10:38-42 (Mary and Martha). Barbara E. Reid ("The Power of the Widows and How to Suppress It [Acts 6.1-7]," in Amy-Jill Levine, *Feminist Companion*, 71–88, esp. 83–84) notes that διακονεῖν does not appear in feeding stories and thus sees a conflict about "ministry" or finances as the probable background.

91 1 Timothy devotes more space to the qualities of widows (1 Tim 5:3-16) than to either bishops (3:1-7) or deacons (3:8-13). Polycarp's thoughts about widows are remarkably similar: *Phil.* 4:3; cf. also Acts 9:36-41. In his *Homily* 14 (134C) on Acts, Chrysostom remarks that the management of widows requires a great deal of "philosophy." He was not thinking about their skill in debates over epistemology. Bonnie Bowman Thurston offers a sympathetic portrait of widows with a discussion of many relevant texts in *The Widows: A Women's Ministry in the Early Church* (Minneapolis: Fortress Press, 1989). See also Richard Pervo, "Aseneth and Her Sisters: Women in Jewish Narrative and in the Greek Novels," in Amy-Jill Levine, ed., *"Women like This." New Perspectives on Jewish Women in the Greco-Roman World* (SBLEJ 1; Atlanta: Scholars Press, 1991) 145–60, esp. 155–59; and Pervo, *Dating*, 216–17, 219–20. On the provisions taken for care of widows in the patristic era, see *NewDocs* 2 (1982) no. 108, pp. 192–93, and 8 (1998) no. 7, pp. 106–16 (by J. R. Harrison). Episodes involving widows are frequent in the Apocryphal Acts, e.g., *Act. John* 30, 32, 37; *Act. Pet.* 8, 17, 19–20; 28–29; *Act. Paul* 4; and *Act. Thom.* 59. On these, see Price, *Widow Traditions*, 204–8. On this passage, see also Clarice Martin, "The Acts of the Apostles," in Elisabeth Schüssler Fiorenza, ed., *Searching the Scriptures: A Feminist Commentary* (2 vols.; New York: Crossroad, 1994) 2:780–82; and F. Scott Spencer, "Neglected Widows in Acts 6.1-7," *CBQ* 56 (1994) 715–33.

92 Karl Löning says that Acts 6:1-7 provides details not about the conflict between Hellenists and Hebrews, "but its resolution" ("The Circle of Stephen and Its Mission," in Jürgen Becker, ed., *Christian Beginnings: Word and Community from Jesus to Post-Apostolic Times* [trans. Annemarie S. Kidder and Reinhard Krauss; Louisville: Westminster John Knox, 1993] 103–31, esp. 105). He improves this claim two sentences later by asserting that "Luke is less interested in the solution's result—that is, the settling of a conflict of days past—than the solution's method, the differentiation of church tasks." This is the crucial point. Acts is interested in neither the underlying historical problem nor in the outcome, but only in the means of resolution.

"waiting on tables," "proclamation[93] of God's message[94] expanded." By appending the note that priests[95] joined the church[96] in large numbers, Luke assures readers that the appeal to native Israelites, including those of high status,[97] remained undiminished. This is the final comment about the expansion of the Jerusalem community.[98] Without further ado the narrative takes a momentous leap, narrating the tempestuous career of Stephen.

93 How can ὁ λόγος τοῦ θεοῦ (lit. "the message/word of/about God") be the subject of a verb meaning "grow"? "Word" seems to be a kind of personification, a "hypostasis," but is better viewed as a kind of metonymy, in which the attribute or cause stands for the effect. It derives from the Pauline view of the church as a creation of the word (Rom 9:8-9). See Daniel Marguerat, *La première histoire du christianisme: les actes des apôtres* (LD 180; Paris: Cerf, 1999) 57–58, and his references. Barrett (1:316) agrees that it "is an odd expression" but goes on to observe, "Luke evidently liked it (12:24; 19:20)." These summaries in several sections of Acts suggest that "word" is a kind of agent. The phrase describes the conquest of the world by the Gospel. Insofar as the proclamation is official, it also has an ecclesial function, on which see Jerome Kodell, "The Word of God Grew: The Ecclesial Tendency of λόγος in Acts 6,7; 12,24; 19,20," *Bib* 55 (1974) 505–19. For background, note Isa 2:3; 55:1-11 and the redactional modification in Luke 8:11, where the term is nominative. A probable inspiration is Col 1:6, which speaks of the "gospel message" (λόγος τοῦ εὐαγγελίου) "growing" (αὐξανόμενον). The concept of "growth" (and "multiplication," as in 12:24) echoes that of the growth of the Israelites, as in Exod 1:7, 20 (to which compare also Acts 19:20).

94 The text displays the customary variant κυρίου ("the message about/of the Lord") in the D-Text and other witnesses. Acts uses both. Verse 2 suggests that "God" is preferable here. See Metzger, *Textual Commentary*, 296.

95 ℵ* pc syᵖ read "Jews" instead of "priests." This shows the skepticism with which the claim was met, but does not seem to realize that "Jews" is, at this point in Acts, otiose. The D-Text (Boismard, *Texte*, 126) revises the sentence in a different direction: "a large crowd *heard about* the faith *in the temple*." Metzger (*Textual Commentary*, 296) views this as the result of corruption, but it appears to be intentional revision harmonizing with 5:21, 42. Goulder (*Type*, 21) says that these defections foreshadow the coming denunciation and supersession of the temple. The plural verb ὑπήκουον (lit. "were becoming obedient to") is a *constructio ad sensum* (BDF §134 [1c]).

96 Lit. "the faith," which here has the sense of *fides quae* (faith as creed) and thus is "almost synonymous with 'the Church'"; Cadbury and Lake (66) trace the development of this notion from Paul to the Pastorals. See Pervo, *Dating*, 285–86.

97 In the Greco-Roman world, priests were drawn from established and wealthy families. The Jewish priesthood embraced a wide socioeconomic spectrum.

98 James claims that "myriads" were added subsequently (21:20).

6

6:8-15 Stephen's Ministry

8/ Endowed with power and favor,[a]
Stephen began to perform
remarkable[b] miracles among
the people. 9/ Opposition
arose from some who belonged
to the Synagogue of Former
Slaves, whose members came
from Cyrene and Alexandria.
People from Cilicia and Asia[c]
also engaged in debate with
Stephen, 10/ but were help-
less against the wisdom and
vigor of his message. 11/ These
people thereupon prompted
some to allege: "We have heard
this fellow uttering blasphe-
mies against Moses and God!"
12/ Their allegations agitated
not only the general public but
also the elders and the legal
experts, who ambushed and
kidnapped Stephen, then took
him to the council. 13/ There
they produced lying witnesses,
who said, "This character
incessantly denounces the holy
place and the Torah. 14/ We
have heard him claim that this
fellow Jesus the Nazorean will
destroy this place and alter the
practices that Moses gave us."
15/ When all those who were
seated in the council chamber
glared at Stephen, they saw
that his face was as radiant as
an angel's.

a *Or:* "attractive power."
b "Remarkable" may be secondary.
c The text and meaning of v. 9 are uncertain.

Analysis

Stephen's story (6:8–8:1a, 2) is a fine example of artful narration. Although nearly seventy verses in length,[1] three-fourths of which are devoted to his speech, the reader gains a vivid impression of a meteoric career, a mission that immediately detonated an explosion. The historical Stephen—presuming that the person existed—may, in fact, have engaged in patient labor for a year or more until one fine day, as it were, he was killed. Acts 6:8-10 succinctly narrates activity nearly identical to that of the apostles: miracles spark opposition, which provokes irrefutable rhetoric. The difference is that opposition comes not from the priestly authorities but from the synagogue. This should be a surprise, for references to synagogues have hitherto been lacking. If one or more synagogues constituted the basis of opposition to Stephen, it is logical to presume that he must have been active in them. This dissonance is additional evidence for the presence of a source. Verses 11-14 reveal that the proper model is not Peter but Jesus, as the account rapidly dons the vestments of the passion narrative.[2]

While insisting on Stephen's verbal and spiritual prowess (vv. 5, 8, 10), the narrator does not cite a word of his until 7:2. Verses 11-14 are largely the reported words of his opponents. When Stephen does begin to speak, he does so at considerable length, and his enemies are not allowed to say so much as "he blasphemes!" The high court, like the Greek-speaking synagogue(s), could not refute him. After that rapid opening, the narrator

1 This is slightly longer than the story of Cornelius (10:1–11:18).
2 See below.

introduces a lengthy retardation. Arrested within five verses of the outset, sixty verses intervene before the assault. The story of Stephen encases the sturdy meat of his address within two very thin slices of bread. All of this, it need not be said, is due to authorial design. The structure is unpretentious. Verse 8 serves as a (discontinuous!) summary introduction. Five verses of narrative follow, generated by opposition to the mission. The failure of refutation (v. 10) leads to foul means that will become familiar as Acts proceeds: slanderous accusations agitate the people; the authorities initiate legal action, at which slander takes the form of perjury (vv. 11-14). Verse 15 frames the unit by recalling Stephen's supernatural endowment (v. 7).

The major exegetical questions are the elucidation of the synagogue or synagogues mentioned in v. 9 and the matter of sources. The core comes from the gentile mission source, which apparently related the martyrdom of Stephen not simply to glorify a hero but to explain its subsequent history. Although the outlines of this source are apparent (see above), it also follows a basic Lucan pattern: persecution leads to new mission. One possibility is that the source presented this view and that Luke took it over—indeed, he may have found therein the germ of his thesis. Another is that he manipulated the source to make it conform to his scheme. It is difficult to decide between these alternatives. The former is somewhat more likely. The most concrete datum from this source is v. 9. The source also reported Stephen's death, apparently at the hands of a mob.[3] For the rest, Luke has so shaped the tradition to conform to the experiences of Jesus and Paul that it is probably fruitless to seek more traces of his model. The major and least disputable source is the gospel tradition, which accounts, at least in large part, for vv. 10-12 and 14. Luke 21:15 is the literary source for v. 10; Mark 14:55-60, 63-64 for vv. 11-14 and 7:1.[4] Intertextuality and "Lucan parallelism" have rendered the task of excavating the specific words of the source all but impossible. One word that probably belonged to the source is σοφία ("wisdom," on which see above). "Spirit" (πνεῦμα) is probably another, although it is anything but alien to Luke.[5] The source evidently portrayed Stephen (and Philip, 8:5-7) as missionaries of great spiritual power.[6] This may well have a historical basis, but such credentials would have been useful for those who lacked direct links to Jesus and his earthly followers. This dimension of the "Theology of the Seven" is indirectly represented both in the theology of Luke, who may have received it at some greater or lesser remove from that circle and from the theology of some of Paul's opponents.[7]

Comment

■ **8** The imperfect in v. 8 is evidently inceptive: after his "installation" by the apostles, Stephen "began to work" impressive miracles.[8] The awkward[9] "full of grace and power"[10] (lit.) creates continuity with vv. 3 and 5. The

3 The sequel to this was the work of Philip in Samaria (and along the coast).

4 For details, see Pervo, *Dating*, 38–40. On this matter, there is agreement that Luke used Mark, but alleged disagreement between vv. 11 and 12-13 has been advanced as the basis for detecting source material in the latter case. For this view, see Lüdemann, 79–84, with numerous references to earlier work. This is more probably an example of literary technique. The terse accusations of v. 11 receive elaboration in the trial. The difficulty for readers is that the accusations are said to be false but yet seem to be in some degree true.

5 See also Lüdemann, 80; and Hengel, *Between*, 18–19.

6 Abraham Smith discusses Luke's characterization of Stephen in terms of ancient philosophical values ("'Full of Spirit and Wisdom': Luke's Portrait of Stephen (Acts 6:1–8:1a) as a Man of Self-Mastery," in Leif Eric Vaage and Vincent L. Wimbush, eds., *Asceticism and the New Testament* (London: Routledge, 1999) 97–114. His qualities anticipate those of the postconversion Paul.

7 The background of these claims is set out in Georgi, *Opponents*. It is also apparent in the cycles of miracle stories that form major sources of Mark and John.

8 Boismard (*Texte*, 126) rejects, with slender but diverse support, μεγάλα ("remarkable" [miracles]). Since this is just the kind of decoration one might expect from the D-Text, it may be original, but editors may have eliminated it because it made Stephen look superior to the apostles (e.g., 5:12).

9 On the syntax, see BDF §418 (6).

10 As the translation indicates, χάρις καὶ δύναμις is probably tautological. His power was of divine origin. On the meaning of χάρις here, see Conzelmann in Hans Conzelmann and Walter Zimmerli,

closing "among the people" establishes an ironic contrast in v. 12, where "the people" are manipulated into opposition.[11] Verse 9 introduces the conflict with the synagogue and the Jewish people that will overshadow the balance of the book. The apostles enjoyed popular approval and support; opposition came from the high priestly authorities. This position is historically dubious.

Hypothetical historical reconstruction logically posits a difference between conflict with the temple leadership and quarrels with synagogue organizations. The ruling class was sensitive to threats to the established order, while the latter could have been more concerned about deviation in the matter of observance.[12] Luke portrays believers in Jesus as observant, and he places the climax of this episode in a Sanhedrin trial where, like the apostles, Stephen attacks members of the governing council for killing Jesus. None of the stories about the persecution of the apostles by the high priests in Acts 3–5 has much claim to historical reliability. Although such persecutions would not have been improbable, the evidence is lacking. Claims that Jesus is the Messiah constituted a direct challenge to the ruling class, but it is not clear how and why such views provoked opposition from synagogues. Galatians 1 supports this understanding, although it also presumes that believers were not factions within synagogues but distinct bodies (Gal 1:13, 22). The evidence is insufficient to provide certainty, but the traditions about Stephen and the animus of a Pharisee like Paul suggest that belief in Jesus was coupled with deviant attitudes toward Torah (and temple). The Synoptic tradition, transmitted in Greek through the agency of "Hellenists" of some sort, presents Jesus as an opponent of the extant temple system who also took issue with aspects of Torah.[13] The evidence from Josephus indicates that the Romans took vigorous action to suppress political threats.

■ **9** The difficulty is to determine the number of synagogues in question and whether "groups" are included as well as organized bodies among the "some" of v. 9[14] The text may be corrupt, and the grammar allows more than one interpretation. Semantics is also involved. "Former slaves, Cyrenians, and Alexandrians" do not seem to make a logical grouping. Since Theodore Beza (1556), scholars have been tempted to emend *libertini* to "Libyans," which makes a geographical trio.[15] This emendation has lost impetus, not only because "libertines" is the more difficult reading, but also because former slaves were quite likely to form their own associations.[16] There may be one, two, or as many as five synagogues. The syntax runs *τινες τῶν . . . καὶ . . . καὶ τῶν ἀπὸ. . . .* This suggests a division of two parts. The singular "synagogue" (without *καὶ τῆς*) makes it somewhat likely that only one organization is in view. The attributive participle *τῆς λεγομένης* supports this

"*χάρις κτλ*," *TDNT* 9:372–402, esp. 392. Variants include "faith" instead of "grace" (𝔐 sy[h] GrNy); E has "grace and faith"; *Ψ* "faith, grace, and spirit." These enhance continuity with the previous verses and make understanding easier.

11 The D-Text adds "in the name of Jesus Christ," strengthening the parallel with the apostles.

12 Cf. the "Theodotus inscription," n. 22.

13 Since the Pharisaic understanding of Torah was a minority position, deviations by Jesus-people would have to have been substantial.

14 The word *τινες* is a conventional means for identifying adversaries; see also 2 Cor 2:5-11; Gal 1:7; and Acts 15:1. Ignatius defines this policy in *Smyrn.* 5:3: "Their names, which are faithless, it did not seem right to me to record; indeed, I would rather not even remember them until they repent in regard to the passion, which is our resurrection" (trans. William R. Schoedel, *Ignatius of Antioch* [Hermeneia; Philadelphia: Fortress Press, 1985] 230). See also 235 n. 28 and, in general, the Roman penchant for *damnatio memoriae* (literally "condemnation of his/her memory," in effect becoming what George Orwell called an "unperson."). (One may compare the old political tradition of referring to "my opponent" or to the long-dominant advertising "rule" against naming competitors.)

15 Dibelius (*Studies*, 91) approved this in a different form. On the subject, see Metzger (*Textual Commentary*, 296–97), who notes that "Libyans" is read in the Armenian tradition, while one Arabic version has "Corinthians." Ropes (*Text*, 58) suspects that the Armenian tradition is an interpretation (i.e., a conjectural emendation) rather than a true variant.

16 On this subject, see Harrill, *The Manumission of Slaves in Early Christianity* (HUTh 32; Tübingen: Mohr Siebeck, 1995) 56–66, on Jewish ex-slaves, and, on this synagogue, 61 n. 214, with much data and numerous references. In 1932, Jean-Baptiste Frey proposed that Pompeii may have had a synagogue with a similar name ("Les Juifs à Pompei," *RB* 42 [1933] 370–72).

(but major Alexandrian witnesses read the phrase in the plural![17]), and the participle may be Luke's customary means of identifying foreign words rather than the mark of a proper name.[18]

A reasonable solution benefits from redaction criticism. The source spoke of one synagogue established by ex-slaves from North Africa (Cyrenians and Alexandrians). The final pair, which is different in form,[19] identifies two groups by their province of origin: "(some) people from Cilicia[20] and Asia."[21] They are not identified as a part of this or another synagogue. Luke is likely to have made this addition. Africa does not fall within his story of the mission (although he mentions persons from those places),[22] whereas Cilicia is Paul's province and Jews from Asia will bring about his ultimate arrest (21:27). Through this addition, the narrator introduces a hint of Paul's presence into the story and identifies the enemies of Stephen with those of his hero,[23] as well as portraying Stephen as victorious over a wide range of enemies.[24] These anonymous persons remain the grammatical subject through v. 12a, where they are evidently replaced by others equally anonymous.

■ **10** Readers will presume that the ground of opposition to Stephen is jealousy aroused by his miracles, which attract attention to and confirm his message (cf. 5:17). Coupled with the Lucan nature of v. 8, this exposes v. 9 as an isolated fragment of the source, since the compressed narrative is not intelligible apart from both the context of Acts 1–5 and its narrative logic. Verse 10 is also Lucan, combining the promise of assistance from the Spirit in Luke 12:12 with Jesus' promise of irresistible speech and wisdom in Luke 21:15. Fulfillment of prophecy places Stephen among the disciples, to whom Luke 21:15 was addressed. In this way, Luke establishes Stephen's legitimacy and the continuity of the message.[25] Fair means having failed, the opponents

17 These include ℵ A 0175 and 33, as well as the D-Text gig. (Some omit it, perhaps in error.)

18 *Libertini* is a Latin word and intimates an Italian provenance for the founders of this community. Fitzmyer (354) suggests that the participle marks a nickname. (A contemporary analogy would be "the American Cathedral in Paris.") German translations, such as Haenchen, 222 (plural); Roloff, 111; Pesch, 1:234; Schneider, 1:431; and Jervell, 223, adopt this view in their translations: "aus der sogenannten Synagoge . . ."

19 This construction uses "from" (ἀπό) with the name of the province. See also 15:38; 18:2, 5; 21:10, 27; and 24:19 (Asia); 23:34 (Cilicia); 27:21; 28:21.

20 Cilicia was not reconstituted as a separate province until 72 CE, but Luke does not seem to have been aware of this (23:34).

21 A D* and one lectionary omit "and Asia." This is accidental, according to Metzger, *Textual Commentary*, 297.

22 These are Lucius of Cyrene (13:1; cf. 11:20) and Apollos of Alexandria (18:24).

23 For a similar view, see Haenchen, 271; Schneider, 1:435; Johnson, 104, 106; Talbert, 76; and Jervell, 225. This was the view of the Old Latin codex h, which reads *libertinorum et alii Cyrenaei et ab Alexan[dria e]t Cilicia et Asia*. Cadbury and Lake (66), Conzelmann (47), Barrett (1:323–25), Bruce (187), and Fitzmyer (358) incline toward one synagogue, shared by all the groups. Roloff (113) says that the tradition identified five separate synagogues. Pesch (1:236) suspects that two synagogues are in view. On the question, see also Penner, *Praise*, 79 n. 62. The text would seem to imply that, if more than one synagogue was involved, their members were able to unite for the purpose of quashing Stephen.

24 Haenchen, 271.

25 The expansions of the D-Text in vv. 10-11 (Boismard, *Texte*, 127–28) attempt to relieve the compressed narrative style: *οἵτινες οὐκ ἴσχυον ἀντιστῆναι τῇ σοφίᾳ τῇ οὔσῃ ἐν αὐτῷ καὶ τῷ πνεύματι τῷ ἁγίῳ ᾧ ἐλάλει, διὰ τὸ ἐλέγχεσθαι ὑπ᾽ αὐτοῦ μετὰ πάσης παρρησίας. τότε οὖν μὴ δυνάμενοι ἀντοφθαλμεῖν τῇ ἀληθείᾳ*. Lit. "who [= these people] could not withstand the wisdom *that was in him* and the *Holy* Spirit with which he spoke, *because they were refuted by him with all boldness. Therefore, since they were unable to confront the truth* . . . ." See Metzger, *Textual Commentary*, 297–98, for another reconstruction. Metzger refers to Rendell Harris's association of this with a Montanist interest (see p. 36 n. 44) and points also to Wis 12:14 as a possible source. Epp (*Tendency*, 116–18) attributes the focus on the Holy Spirit in the D-Text as one element of an interest in the newness of Christianity over against its Israelite parent. On 132–33 he states that the D-Text makes Stephen look better and the Jews worse. Stephen is not merely spirited but inspired. (This merely anticipates what v. 15 shows and is thus jejune.) Epp further observes (133) that διὰ τὸ ἐλέγχεσθαι ὑπ᾽ αὐτοῦ ("because they were refuted by him") derives from Luke 3:19, John's reproof of Herod. If this is an intentional parallel to the Baptizer, as Epp suggests, it may seek to evoke Stephen as a forerunner

roll out men[26] inspired[27] to charge Stephen with blasphemy.[28] These sensational allegations, which will presently become more specific, are all the more vivid because they occur in direct speech. Under those conditions the accusers have no difficulty motivating both citizens and officials to apprehend[29] Stephen and haul him off to court.[30]

■ **11-14** These verses constitute a single rapid sentence that propels Stephen from the receipt of criticism by members of a synagogue to the object of the gravest charges before the highest court in the land.[31] Stephen, it suddenly transpires, will follow the footsteps of Jesus.

Table 1. Parallel Passions: Stephen and Jesus[32]

Action	Mark	Luke	Acts
1. Refutation impossible	12:34	yes	6:10
2. Seizure by officials	14:43, 46	yes	6:12[33]
3. Trial by Sanhedrin	14:53	yes	6:12; 7:1
4. False Witness	14:56-57	no	6:13
5. Will destroy temple	14:58	no	6:14
6. Temple = artifact	14:58	no	7:48
7. Son of Man saying	14:62	yes	7:56[34]
8. Blasphemy	14:64	no	6:11
9. Question of high priest	14:61	no	7:1
10. "Commit my spirit"	–	yes	7:59
11. Loud cry	15:34	yes	7:60
[12. Prayer for enemies	–	23:34	7:60][35]

of Paul, but it is possible that this addition simply reflects the editor's thorough familiarity with the text of Luke and Acts.

26 Women were not viewed as legitimate witnesses in such cases.

27 For ὑποβάλλω in the sense of "prompt," cf. *Mart. Pol.* 17:2.

28 "Blasphemy" is used in the Greek sense of abusive speech. Technically, blasphemy (the remedy for which was stoning) is defamation of God. Later tradition defined it narrowly, requiring use of the divine name (*m. Sanh.* 7.5). "Moses" is a metonym for Torah; the temple is God's dwelling place (vv. 13-14). Craig C. Hill ("Acts 6.1—8.4: Division or Diversity?" in Witherington, *History*, 129–53, esp. 140–52) shows that the charges are typical of Luke and therefore not readily attributable to the source.

29 For συναρπάζω, see also Luke 8:29; Acts 19:29; 2 Macc 4:41; *4 Macc.* 5:4.

30 The word συνέδριον may have different meanings in vv. 12 and 15. In the former "council," that is, the body of the court, is probable, whereas "council chamber" suits v. 15.

31 Although N-A[27] prints a full stop at the end of v. 11, *GNT*[4] and Bruce (188), for example, use a raised stop. The particle τε ("and," etc.) can, on occasion, connect entire sentences, but a full stop suggests that v. 12 introduces a new subject. The rapid and paratactic style makes the sorting out of subjects difficult. Grammatically, the subjects who apprehended Stephen are those of v. 9, but logic prefers that these be the people and officials. See Fitzmyer, 359. For Luke it made little difference.

32 For other attempts to list and describe these similarities, recognized already by Ephrem (407), see Rackham, 91; Goulder, *Type*, 41–42; Earl Richard, *Acts 6:1–8:4: The Author's Method of Composition* (SBLDS 41; Missoula, Mont.: Scholars Press, 1978) 281; Schneider, 1:433; and Hill, *Hellenists*, 59–61 (with discussion of details).

33 Mark 14:43 reports that "high priests, scribes, and elders" arrived and "laid hands on him and arrested him" (v. 46). Luke does not mention the composition of the group that apprehended Jesus until 22:52 ("the chief priests, the officers of the temple police, and the elders"). Acts 22:54 uses a milder term for the actual arrest (συλλαμβάνω,

The inventory (**Table 1**) demonstrates that the passion of Stephen has the same general structure as that of Jesus and succinctly illustrates the extent to which Luke drew on material from Mark that was omitted from the Gospel. Verses 13-14 elucidate the contents of v. 11 in appropriate legal jargon. The accusers introduce[36] their agents as "witnesses," whom the narrator has characterized as perjurers.[37] This is necessary because the readers have not heard a sample of Stephen's preaching, but it produces some discomfort for many modern critical readers, who, in the light of the subsequent speech, are likely to find these accusations not wholly without substance.[38] Craig Hill takes issue with this understanding.[39] He is correct in that Stephen does not make explicit claims to this effect in his speech, but he has nothing very positive to say about the sanctuary and accuses his readers of not observing the law. The readers of the book, to whom these words are directed, well knew that the temple *had* been destroyed and believed that the Torah was an impossible burden (15:10). Luke was no more interested in achieving consistency between the charges and Stephen's words than he was in presenting a proper rhetorical defense against these charges, the substance of which would have boiled down, according to v. 13, to "I did not say what they allege and therefore deny any blasphemy."

■ **13** This clause states the general categories: repeated critique of temple and Torah, each of which receives specification in the following verse.[40] Stephen's message was christological. Jesus will destroy the temple and alter the Torah.[41] The readers were well aware that the Romans destroyed the temple in putting down a rebellion, and they saw this as appropriate punishment for rejecting Jesus, who, in that sense, was responsible. The second charge—"[Jesus[42] will] alter the practices that Moses gave us"—may not appear to be an attack on the law, but rather promote an alteration of "customs" (Pharisaic traditions?).[43] For Luke, however, ἔθη ("practices," "customs") is more or less interchangeable with "law,"[44] and the verb "alter" (ἀλλάξει) evokes the "reform" of Antiochus Epiphanes.[45] The attackers conjure up the most horrific moment in previous Israelite

lit. "take with"). Acts 6:10 speaks of "the people, the elders, and the scribes." The tenor of Acts 6 is closer to that of Mark than to Luke.

34 On the text of 7:56, see below.

35 On Luke 23:34, see below on 7:60.

36 Lit. "stand" (cf. 4:7). Use of the same verb (ἔστησαν) in vv. 6 and 13 underlines the contrast between the church and the Sanhedrin. The subject is presumably the τινες ("certain individuals") of v. 9. The D-Text begins with καί instead of δέ (both meaning "and," etc.). This makes it easier to posit the members of the council as the subject.

37 With its inimitable pedantry, the D-Text supplies "against him."

38 Calvin (1:166–67, citing 167), who accepts that the witnesses were false, says, "[Stephen] never spoke about Moses or the temple except with respect," and continues, "And yet this charge was not brought against him for nothing; for he had taught the abrogation of the Law."

39 Hill, *Hellenists*, 56–58.

40 The expression οὐ παύεται ("incessantly denounces") indicates that Stephen is incorrigible. The variant "blasphemous (words)" is unnecessary, probably imported from v. 11. "This" may have been added to "place" in v. 13 on the basis of v. 14. See Metzger, *Textual Commentary*, 298.

41 One may ask how Jesus of Nazareth will do these things. In his role as future Messiah (cf. 3:20)? The charges presume that Stephen approved of these prospective actions. It would be futile to attempt to make theological sense of these claims: they are lies. Mark 14:58 is the source of the temple claim. Cf. also John 2:19 and, on the theme, John 4:21 and *Gos. Thom.* 71.

42 The demonstrate οὗτος is derogatory and distances the speakers from acknowledgment of his authority. Its omission from D-Texts (Boismard, *Texte*, 129) supports this interpretation.

43 So Hengel (*Between*, 22), who speaks of legal reform.

44 Stephen G. Wilson (*Luke and the Law* [SNTSMS 50; Cambridge: Cambridge University Press, 1983] 1-11) demonstrates that Luke uses "custom" (ἔθος) more or less interchangeably with "law" (νόμος). A cogent example is 21:21 (charges that Paul teaches nonobservance of Torah). He notes that this usage is like that of Jewish apologetics, in particular Josephus. All nations have their customs, including the Jews. Cf. Josephus *Ant.* 16.35–36. The advantage of this posture to Luke is that the Torah can be viewed as the particular customs of an ethnic group, appropriate for Jews but not to be imposed on gentile believers.

45 1 Macc 1:41-50 summarizes letters sent by Antiochus to all the component peoples of his empire requiring them, for the sake of unity, to abandon their particular practices. Verses 44-49 deal with

history, the Seleucid emperor's desecration of the temple and cancellation of Torah, and represent the Jesus whom Stephen proclaims as an Antiochus *redivivus*.[46] Attention is naturally drawn to the accused, but those who gaze upon him are not rewarded by an appearance brimming with guilt.[47]

■ **15** The transfiguration[48] of Stephen probably stems from the source.[49] The chief characteristic of an angelic countenance is not a particular beauty but a brightness, a reflection of the glory of God.[50] Acts 7:55 establishes this. The proper reaction to such an epiphany is reverential fear (Greek Esth 15:13). This audience ignores it. For the philosophically inclined, Stephen's vision of God established him as an "athlete of virtue" who has mastered all the passions and ingested every facet of wisdom.[51] For preachers, transfiguration was a sign of the authenticity and spiritual power of their message. This dimension of popular religion was likely to have been familiar to Luke and to his readers.[52] It illuminates the summary expression "wisdom and spirit" of v. 10. This characterization informs readers that they are to understand the subsequent address as an inspired piece of exposition that holds its hearers spellbound—up to the climactic point.

Judea. The last verse states the purpose: "so that they would forget the law and change all the ordinances (ὥστε ἐπιλαθέσθαι τοῦ νόμου καὶ ἀλλάξαι πάντα τὰ δικαιώματα). A polytheistic example can be found in Diodorus Siculus 1.73.3. Changing or abolishing customs was a serious offense in Greco-Roman antiquity. Cf. Dionysius of Halicarnassus *Rom. Ant.* 8.34.3; 8.80.2. For discussion, see Squires, *Plan*, 43.

46 The D-Text (according to Boismard, *Texte*, 129) reads "will destroy this *temple* and *has altered the practice* that Moses . . ." Singular ἔθος here might well be translated "lifestyle." This is a "historical" correction: the historical Jesus changed Torah; the heavenly Christ will destroy the temple. At this point the reviser might well have deleted "false" in v. 13.

47 The D-Text paraphrases v. 15. After "angel," D-witnesses add "of God, standing in their midst" (Boismard, *Texte*, 129–30). This may derive from Luke 1:11, in which case it misunderstands the text.

48 Transfiguration of leading characters is common in popular narrative. Note Dan 3:92; *Jos. Asen.* 18:7–9; *Mart. Pol.* 12–14, esp. 12:1 (also in a martyrological context); *Act. Paul* 3.1 (the famous description of Paul); 7/9.1–3; *Act. Thom.* 8; *Act. Andr.* (Epitome of Gregory 11); Eusebius *H.E.* 5.1.35; and Sulpicius Severus *Ep.* 3.17–18. A rabbinic example can be found in *Qohelet Rabbah* 8.1. See also *Ethiopian Story* 8.9.13 and the comments of Schwartz, "Trial Scene," 122.

49 If Luke were to "invent" transfigurations, he would have been likely to supply them for Peter and Paul also. (D-Text traditions supply this deficit. See on 24:10.)

50 Ezekiel's vision is a leading source; see Ezek 1:27. Traditions based on Ezekiel's description of the glory of God can be seen, for example, in Dan 10:5-6; 2 Macc 3:25-26; *Jos. Asen.* 14:9; *2 En.* 1:3–5; *Apoc. Abr.* 11:1–3; *Apoc. Zeph.* 6:11–15.

51 On the relevance of the theme of "athletes of virtue," see Sterling, "Athletes of Virtue." Philo's principal example was none other than Moses: *Vit. Mos.* 1.158 (cf. 289). On the subject, see Wayne A. Meeks, "The Divine Agent and His Counterfeit," in Elisabeth Schüssler Fiorenza, ed., *Aspects of Religious Propaganda in Judaism and Early Christianity* (Notre Dame, Ind.: University of Notre Dame Press, 1976) 43–67, esp. 50.

52 One understanding of the notoriously difficult 2 Cor 3:7-18 is that it refutes the claim that "truly spiritual" preachers can make their faces glow with heavenly light while expounding a heavenly message. (At the concrete level, this phenomenon presumably referred to apparently glowing eyes.) The phenomenon also appeared in rabbinic Judaism: "Then Eliezer sat down and *expounded*. His face shone like the light of the sun and his radiance beamed like that of Moses, so that no one knew whether it was day or night" (*Pirqe Rabbi Eliezer*, chap. 2; trans. G. Friedlander, cited in Jacob Neusner, *First Century Judaism in Crisis: Yohanan ben Zakkai and the Renaissance of Torah* [Nashville: Abingdon, 1975] 109 [emphasis added]).

7

7:1-53 Stephen's Speech

1/ The high priest asked,[a] "Are
these charges true?"
2/ "Fathers and brothers, please lis-
ten," he replied. "Our glorious
God appeared to our ancestor
Abraham while he was in Meso-
potamia, before he settled in
Haran: 3/ 'Leave your land and
your relatives and go[b] to the
land that I shall show you,' God
said.
4/ "So Abraham[c] left the land of
the Chaldeans and settled in
Haran, from which, following
the death of his father, God had
him relocate in this land that
you now inhabit. 5/ God did
not, however, provide him with
even so much as a square meter
of it, but did promise to award
it to him and to his descendants
thereafter, although Abraham
was then childless. 6/ God said,
in effect, that 'his descendants
would be aliens in a foreign
land, whose inhabitants would
enslave and abuse them for four
hundred years. 7/ I shall con-
demn the nation that enslaves
them, and they shall thereafter
leave it and serve me in this
place.' 8/ God then made a cov-
enant ratified by circumcision
with Abraham. Therefore, when
Isaac was born he circumcised
him on the eighth day, as did
Isaac for his son Jacob, who did
likewise for the twelve patri-
archs whom he sired.
9/ "The patriarchs, however,
became jealous of Joseph
and sold him into slavery in
Egypt, but God was on his
side, 10/ rescuing him from all
his afflictions and bestowing
upon him wisdom and charm
that won the favor of Pharaoh,
the king of Egypt. God made
him the governor of Egypt and
put him in charge of Pharaoh's
household.[d] 11/ Then all of
Egypt and Canaan experi-
enced a famine, which brought
terrible affliction. Our ances-
tors could find no provisions.
12/ When Jacob heard that
there was grain in Egypt he sent
our ancestors to Egypt for the
first time. 13/ On their second
visit Joseph revealed himself to
his brothers, and thus Pharaoh

a D-Texts add "asked *Stephen*." There are other minor variants that reinforce the interrogative character of the utterance.

b This phrase (καὶ δεῦρο) appears only in "Lucianic" MSS. of the LXX. This exemplifies the problem of contamination. It is possible that Acts 7:3 is the source of that reading.

c The proper name is found in some D-Texts. It is secondary, included here for clarity.

d It is not clear whether "in charge of" (ἐπί) applies to both Egypt and the royal household. An almost equal number of witnesses either repeat the preposition or take it as one phrase.

e Variants include ὡμολόγησεν, "avowed" ($\mathfrak{p}^{74}$ ℵ A B C *et al* vg sy^{hmg} sa), ἐπηγγείλατο, "promised" ($\mathfrak{p}^{45}$ D E p vg^{mss} mae), and ὤμοσεν, "swore" (Ψ 1739 m gig sy^{p} bo). Metzger (*Textual Commentary*, 302) argues that ὡμολόγησεν was vulnerable because of its technical use for confessing the faith and that ἐπηγγείλατο is a kind of secondary septuagintalism. Cadbury and Lake (74) note a similar fluctuation between Mark 6:23 and Matt 14:7.

f The form ᾔδει ("knew") is the wording of Exod 1:8 LXX. The D-Text ἐμνήσθη ("remembered") (D E gig p Chrysostom) may well be more original. The D-Text also omits the superfluous "over Egypt" (Boismard, *Texte*, 133). For a different view, see Metzger, *Textual Commentary*, 303.

g D sy^{p} reads καί instead of the demonstrative; d has neither. The result is a single sentence with the previous. The possessive ἡμῶν ("our") is another difficult choice, probably secondary. To "infants," E gig add "male." The placement shows that this is secondary.

h The D-Text adds, pedantically, "into the river" (Boismard, *Texte*, 134).

i For this meaning, see BDAG 64, *s.v.* ἀναιρέω, 3, which finds "adopted" (Cadbury and Lake, 75) "too loose."

j The D-Text accusative of respect (Boismard, *Texte*, 134) is probably based on an adverbial dative, indicating that the preposition ἐν is secondary, since an alteration of the prepositional phrase would have been much less likely.

k *Or:* "Moses, who could not stop marveling, went closer to investigate. . . ."

l The variants that supply some form of "over us" after "ruler and judge" are secondary harmonizations with v. 27.

m The καί that would make the predicate objectives "both . . . and" is absent from $\mathfrak{p}^{45.74}$ ℵ* A C. It may well be a scribal addition. See Metzger, *Textual Commentary*, 306.

n D-Text and other witnesses add "Listen to him." This is a secondary harmonization with Deut 18:15 and other NT citations (n. 132).

learned about Joseph's family. 14/ Joseph then sent for his father Jacob and his entire family, seventy-five persons altogether. 15/ So Jacob went to Egypt, where he himself died, as did the patriarchs. 16/ Their bodies were transported to Shechem and placed there in the tomb that Abraham had acquired for a sum from the offspring of Hamor.

17/ "When the time for fulfillment of the promise God made[e] to Abraham was drawing near, the Israelites in Egypt spread and increased, 18/ until there came a king who did not recall Joseph.[f] 19/ He exploited our race and oppressed our ancestors, compelling them to expose their infants so that they would not survive.[g] 20/ At that time Moses was born. This divinely beautiful child was nurtured in his father's home for three months, 21/ but after he had been exposed,[h] Pharaoh's daughter claimed him[i] and reared him as her own son. 22/ Moses learned all that Egyptian wisdom had to offer[j] and became persuasive in speech and effective in action.

23/ "When he had attained the age of forty, Moses decided to pay a visit to his kindred, the Israelites. 24/ While so doing he found one of them being abused. Moses came to his aid and gave his Egyptian oppressor what he deserved: death. 25/ He presumed that his kindred understood that God was using him to rescue them, but they did not. 26/ On the very next day, he came upon some Israelites fighting and sought to settle the dispute without violence. 'You belong to the same people,' he said. 'Why are you harming each other?' 27/ The aggressor rebuffed him. 'Who appointed *you* as our ruler and judge? 28/ Are you going to kill me, just as you killed that Egyptian yesterday?' 29/ At that Moses fled and took up residence as an alien in Midian, where he fathered two sons.

30/ "Forty years after he had left

o The variant "your god" is probably conformation to the LXX. B D 36 453 *pc* gig sy[p] sa ir[lat] Or omit it.

p *Or*: "God of Jacob."

q D-Texts (Boismard, *Texte*, 140) read a simple "The most high does not live in artifacts." This may be related to the position of the negative, which is not really ambiguous (BDF §433 [1]). 𝔓[74] has "But it is not the case that . . ."

r In place of "your forebears" D-Texts read "those people" (ἐκεῖνοι) (Boismard, *Texte*, 142).

s Boismard's D-Text omits "now," probably because it could be, or was, misconstrued.

Egypt, while he was in the
desolate region around Mount
Sinai, an angel appeared to
Moses in the flame of a fiery
bush. 31/ Taken aback by the
sight,[k] he drew close to investigate, when the voice of the
Lord erupted: 32/ 'I am the God
of your ancestors, the God of
Abraham, Isaac, and Jacob.'
Moses became too frightened
to investigate further. 33/ The
Lord said: 'Remove your sandals, for the place where you
are standing is holy ground.
34/ I have fully observed the
misery of my people in Egypt,
and have heard their groans;
I have come down to deliver
them. So now I am sending you
to Egypt.'
35/ "Moses was the one whom
they repudiated by saying,
'Who appointed *you* as ruler
and judge?'[l] Moses was the
one whom God sent with the
assistance of the angel who
appeared to him in the bush to
be both[m] ruler and redeemer.
36/ Moses led them out after
he had worked portents and
miracles in Egypt and at the
Red Sea and, for forty years,
in the wild. 37/ Moses it was
who told the Israelites 'God will
raise up a prophet like me for
you from among your number.'[n]
38/ Moses was the one who
was with an angel that spoke to
him on Mount Sinai during the
wilderness assembly and there
received vital precepts. 39/ Our
ancestors, who also were with
him, did not choose to be obedient to Moses, but rebuffed him
and turned their hearts toward
Egypt. They said to Aaron:
40/ 'Manufacture some gods to
carry in front of us, for we do
not know what has happened
to this Moses who led us out
of the land of Egypt.' 41/ They
then concocted a calf, made
offerings to this idol and took
pleasure in their handiwork.
42/ So God turned away and
abandoned them to their worship of heavenly bodies. As the
book of the Prophets says: 'Did
you bring me animal and other
sacrifices during those forty

years in the wilderness, house
of Israel? 43/ No, but you did
take the tent of Moloch and the
star of the[o] god Rompha, those
images that you fabricated in
order to worship them. I am
going to remove you to some
place east of Babylon.'
44/ "While they were out in the wild,
our forebears had the tent of
testimony, fashioned by Moses
in compliance with the instructions given by the one who had
spoken with him and in accordance with the design that
he had been shown. 45/ Our
forebears carried this tent with
them while later, under Joshua,
they dispossessed the gentiles whom God expelled, and
they retained it until the time
of David. 46/ God approved of
David, who asked to provide an
abode for the house of Jacob,[p]
47/ yet it was Solomon who
actually built a temple for God.
48/ Nonetheless, the Most
High does not inhabit abodes
of human manufacture.[q] This
is how the prophet puts it:
49/ 'The sky is my throne and
earth my footstool. What kind
of a dwelling could you fashion
for me,' says the Lord, 'or where
shall I take my rest? 50/ Did not
I create all these things?'
51/ "You obdurate creatures, cut
off from the covenant in heart
and hearing! You, like those
who went before you, always
line up against the Holy Spirit.
52/ Which of the prophets did
your forebears[r] neglect to persecute? They murdered those
who foretold the coming of the
righteous one! Now that he has
come,[s] you betrayed and murdered him. 53/ You received the
Torah through angelic agency,
but you have not observed it."

Analysis

Following a lengthy speech that questions the need for a temple and hurls the charge of lawbreaking at the Sanhedrin (7:48, 53),[1] Stephen meets a violent death. This speech, the longest in Acts,[2] has generated immense discussion. At first sight this is surprising, since it contains little more than an indubitably partisan review of biblical history up to the construction of the first temple, followed by a brief but sharp attack on the auditors. The initial impression is that much of this speech is not relevant to its immediate context, the charges made against Stephen in 6:11-14.[3] If Luke is responsible, to a large degree, for both the specific accusations and for the speech, the two should cohere, but Stephen does not take up the charges directly and refute them. Martyrs—when given free rein in literature—are more likely to defend what they represent than to weave a detailed legal fabric; they prefer death to dishonor, as the saying goes, and freely boast of their beliefs.[4] Stephen says nothing about his own conduct, statements, or beliefs, although his views can often be inferred from his judgments.[5] With a similar lack of directness, vv. 45-53 take up the accusations about the temple and the Torah, while also defending Jesus, whom the witnesses had disparaged.

The chief interpretive task raised by these perceived anomalies is to account for the origin of the speech without overlooking its role in the narrative of Acts.[6] In this sense, Stephen's speech is peculiar, since one expects authors to compose speeches, and Acts otherwise meets that expectation.[7] The major options are (1) to maintain that this is a report of the speech Stephen made before his judges, (2) to ignore the question of origins and focus upon the contents of the speech, (3) to assume that it is a Lucan composition, (4) to posit a Hellenistic Jewish source, or (5) to hold that it stems from a source that represents a non-Pauline type of Greek-speaking Christianity that may (or may not) represent the views of the "Hellenists."[8] These approaches are not mutually exclusive.

Option 1 is not possible, since a Greek speech based on the LXX with this content is wholly unsuitable for the context, a blasphemy trial before the high court of the Jewish people.[9] Robert Tannehill is representative of option 2, in accordance with that literary-critical approach which leaves source issues aside.[10] In essence, the exegetical result of the following approach will resemble that of option 3, a recent and able representative of which is Luke T. Johnson.[11]

1 Both of these anticipate later developments. In 15:10 Peter proclaims the yoke of Torah unbearable. Acts 17:24 (Areopagus sermon) asserts that God does not abide in artifacts of human design.

2 Roloff (117) observes that the speech comprises around 5 percent of the book.

3 Dibelius (*Studies*, 167) identified this as "the real problem of exegesis."

4 Death to dishonor: e.g., 2 Macc 7:2; *4 Macc.* 5:36-38. This idea is implicit in the apostolic rejection of human authority (4:19; 5:29). "I am a Christian": *Mart. Pol.* 10.9; *Mart. Carpus* et al. 5; *Mart. Ptolemaeus and Lucius* 11; *Mart. Justin and Companions* 3.4; *Martyrs of Lyon* 10, etc.

5 Paul's more conventional defense speeches in 24:10-11 and 26:1-29 begin with a *captatio benevolentiae* and proceed to deny the charges, offering explanations of his actions. Luke cannot be accused of not knowing what form an apologetic address should take.

6 Delbert L. Wiens indicates the extent to which the speech reflects major themes of Luke and Acts (*Stephen's Sermon and the Structure of Luke-Acts* [North Richland Hills, Tex.: Bibal, 1995]).

7 See p. 14.

8 The list excludes the proposal that Samaritan thought influenced the speech, on which see Abram Spiro, "Stephen's Samaritan Background," Appendix 5 in Johannes Munck, *The Acts of the Apostles: Introduction, Translation, and Notes* (AB 31; Garden City, N.Y.: Doubleday, 1967) 285–300; and Martin Scharlemann, *Stephen: A Singular Saint* (AnBib 34; Rome: Pontifical Biblical Institute, 1968), or that it derives from Qumran, as once suggested by A. F. J. Klijn, "Stephen's Speech—Acts VII, 2–53," *NTS* 4 (1957) 25–31. Neither of these views has gained credence. For reviews of scholarship, see, in addition to the commentaries and those monographs devoted to the speech, the succinct summary of Earl Richard, "The Polemical Character of the Joseph Episode in Acts 7," *JBL* 98 (1979) 255–57.

9 Witherington (261) admits that the speech "originated in Greek," but maintains that it is a précis of the actual speech, possibly derived from Paul, although Luke has provided the structure and that "[i]t suits well his perspectives on salvation history." Fitzmyer (365) views the speech as a Lucan composition in its present form but regards it as "an inherited form of Stephen's speech" that may derive from Antioch.

10 Tannehill, *Narrative Unity*, 2:94–97. He does, however, place it after the destruction of the temple (95) and thus implies that it is not historical.

11 Johnson, 119. For a detailed argument, see Johannes Bihler, *Die Stephanusgeschichte im Zusammenhang der Apostelgeschichte* (MThS 16; Munich: Max Hüber, 1961); Richard, *Acts 6*; and John J. Kilgallen, *The Stephen Speech: A Literary and Redactional Study of Acts 7,2-53* (AnBib 67; Rome: Biblical Institute, 1976), all of whom are supported by Hill, *Hellenists*, 80–92.

Even those who are generally skeptical about identifying sources for Acts—especially for the speeches—incline toward the presence of source material in Acts 7.[12] The bases for this view are, in addition to the allegedly irrelevant historical review, the presence of some distinctive theologumena, the absence of typical Lucan christological formulations (the "kerygmatic" formulae found in the speeches of chaps. 2–4), and, it might be added, the lack of the rather tight structure that marks other speeches.[13]

Dibelius, a proponent of option 4, already inferred that the speech breathes the atmosphere of the Diaspora synagogue.[14] This was a cogent suggestion. A résumé of salvation history would be far more suitable in a homiletic context than in a speech to leading priests and legal experts.[15] The argument depends on the LXX, not least at a point where it deviates strongly from the MT (v. 43), and a number of the stylistic features are characteristic of religious rhetoric.[16] These factors led Hartwig Thyen to include Acts 7 in his database for the study of Hellenistic Jewish preaching.[17] If the synagogue sermon is a suggestive formal parallel, one may posit that such a piece was the ultimate *source* of Stephen's speech.[18] Supporting this view are the contents: vv. 2-50 focus on epiphanies and revelations that took place outside of the Holy Land.[19] A good half of this material (vv. 9-34) is set in Egypt, where the Israelites had their ups and downs but remained faithful. Slightly more space is devoted to Joseph (vv. 9-16) than to Abraham (vv. 2b-8). It is therefore a reasonable conjecture that at some remove behind Acts 7 stood a piece of Alexandrian homiletic. Although similar contents could be found elsewhere,[20] the style favors an oratorical rather than a narrative prose model. Reasonable conjectures do not constitute bases for deductive arguments. This particular conjecture is chiefly valuable for the light it sheds on a *Sitz im Leben* for the address.[21]

Jürgen Roloff advocates option 5.[22] Here the normal practice of fitting speech to occasion is wanting. Conceding that individual themes and motifs are from Hellenistic Judaism, the polemical thrust of the speech as a whole militates against the view that a Jewish source was lightly revised. The source is Christian, built on the typological relationship of Jesus to Moses, and views obedience to God's messengers as the true mode of service. Instead of the Pauline view of Christ as "the end of the law" (Rom 10:4) is a radicalized notion of the law like that found in Matthew. Like others, Roloff notes similarities to Hebrews.[23] Marcel Simon and others have developed this argument in detail, with attention to *Barnabas* also.[24] Simon thinks that this distinctive theology may reflect Stephen and his circle. Conzelmann is not willing to leap from these data to the historical Stephen, but he agrees that "[h]ere we come to know

12 Eduard Norden saw some admirable features in the speeches of Acts and did not believe that Luke could have written this speech, since the author had no feel for the Greek language (*Die antike Kunstprosa* (2 vols.; 1915; reprinted, Stuttgart: Teubner, 1995) 2:448. For Norden, imitation of the LXX was simply unacceptable for a writer with even a vestige of Hellenic sensibility.

13 Divergences from the LXX (many of which are noted in the detailed commentary) likewise speak for an extrabiblical source (or sources).

14 Dibelius, *Studies*, 169.

15 Roloff (117) says that a disinterested reader would have difficulty understanding why the judges do not interrupt and urge Stephen to get to the point. This is a modern viewpoint, but it does identify a problem.

16 See below.

17 Hartwig Thyen, *Der Stil der jüdisch-hellenistischen Homilie* (FRLANT 65; Göttingen: Vandenhoeck & Ruprecht, 1955) 19–20.

18 Luke would presumably have acquired this source secondhand, for example, embedded in some literary source.

19 Verse 2 (Mesopotamia); vv. 30-34 (Sinai).

20 E.g., Philo: *Jos.* and *Vit. Mos.*; *T. Jos.*, and Artapanus. Also worthy of comparison are *Jubilees*, the various *Lives of the Prophets* (on which see Cadbury and Lake, 82; Anna Maria Schwemer, *Studien zu den frühjüdischen Prophetenlegenden Vitae Prophetarum* [2 vols.; TSAJ 49; Tübingen: Mohr Siebeck, 1996)]); and the *Liber Antiquitatum Biblicarum* (on which, see Frederick J. Murphy, *Pseudo-Philo: Rewriting the Bible* [New York: Oxford University Press, 1993]). Popular narratives like the prophetic Lives, Artapanus, and Ps.-Philo are close to the "spirit" of Acts. Johnson compares Acts verse by verse with a number of Jewish writings.

21 This social context is explicit in Acts 13:14b-41, Paul's synagogue sermon at Antioch in Pisidia.

22 Roloff, 117–19.

23 His examples are the prominence of the Moses/Christ typology (Heb 3:1-6), Jesus as helper and deliverer to his kindred (Heb 2:14-18), a didactic

how a Hellenistic Jewish-Christianity of a non-Pauline type views the Bible and history."[25] The effort to sift this speech for data that assist in the construction of a history of early Christian theology is important, but it is interpretation *based on* Acts rather than interpretation *of* Acts. The benefit of this proposal is that it envisions a unified source.

Disadvantages include making one of two tacit assumptions: Luke either had at his disposal a lengthy account of Stephen's last words, or he, somewhat in the manner of a modern historian, wished to give the first martyr a distinctive message to illuminate the differences between the Twelve and the Seven and between the Seven and Paul. The former implicitly postulates a source that includes at least one lengthy oration and thus something approximating a finished historical treatise.[26] This is not impossible, but it conflicts with every reconstruction of the gentile mission ("Antiochene") source and is intrinsically unlikely. The latter must presume that just here, at a vital point in the narrative, the author decided to illuminate the theological variety of the early church rather than maintain the portrait of theological unity that pervades the rest of Luke and Acts. That is incredible. If Luke did use such a source it was not because he was eager to grasp an opportunity to showcase the distinctive aspects of Hellenist theology but because he did not concern himself with any apparent inconsistencies between the source and the views that he wished to promulgate. Finally—and all but definitively—the speech has the appearance of an insertion between 6:14 and 7:55, and the source appears to have reported a lynching rather than a trial.[27] The trial is an insertion into a source, and the speech did not derive from that source. Any attempts to extract the theology of Stephen from Acts 7 must posit another Stephen source that contained speeches. If such an unlikely source existed, the speech (or speeches) would have been authorial compositions rather than the words of its subject.[28]

Those who assume a source (option 4) tend to take a redactional approach based on the identification of discontinuous elements that give the address a negative "spin." Haenchen views vv. 25, 35, 37, 39-43, and 48-53 as insertions into a sermon surveying sacred history.[29] Lüdemann takes a more drastic and less clear approach.[30] These (and other[31]) authors call attention to the existence of such historical reviews as Deut 6:20-34; 26:5-9; Josh 24:2-13; Ezekiel 20; Neh 9:6-31; Judg 5:6-18; 1 Macc 2:52-60; Psalms 78; 105; and 136; Wisdom 10; Sirach 44–50; *3 Macc.* 2:2-12; *4 Ezra* 3:4-36; Josephus *Bell.* 5.377–400; and Ps.-Clem. *Rec.* 1.27–38.[32] These examples show that surveys of the past were traditional

view of words and wonders (Heb 2:3-4), and, especially, the view of Jesus in relation to the temple and the end of cult (Hebrews 10).

24 Marcel Simon, *St. Stephen and the Hellenists in the Primitive Church* (New York: Longmans, Green, 1958). After a review of the arguments about the affinities between Acts 7 and *Barnabas*, James Carlton Paget concludes that *Barnabas* is related to a tradition that goes back to the "Hellenists" (*The Epistle of Barnabas* [WUNT 64; Tübingen: Mohr Siebeck, 1994] 200–207).

25 Conzelmann, 57.

26 The data imply that speeches were often introduced in the final stage of composition. This can be inferred for Thucydides, whose unfinished final book lacks speeches. Lucian places his comments on the making of speeches at the end of his treatise on history (*Quomodo Historia* 58).

27 See above on 6:15 and below. The absence of formal condemnation or of any legal procedure marks the event as a lynching. Contrast the lengthy directions about legal stoning in *m. Sanh.* 6.1–4. (This is not to suggest that the Mishnah represents procedures in use during the first century, but it does indicate what a proper legal process would include.) Deut 19:16-21 includes provisions for detailed examination, a process that Daniel demands be followed in the case of Susanna (Sus).

28 The gospel tradition demonstrates this. Lengthy discourses, whether the Sermon on the Mount (Matthew 5–7) or the Johannine discourses, are the products of editorial assembly and/or authorial composition.

29 Haenchen, 288–89. Conzelmann (57) is similar. Barrett (1:334–40) agrees on the use of such a source, but is much more vague about the author's alterations.

30 Lüdemann, 86–89. He allows the possibility that vv. 2-38 are a historical review, but also proposes a number of minor changes and the assignment of vv. 17-38 to Luke.

31 Note, in particular, Weiser, 1:180–82.

32 For a discussion of these surveys, see Traugott Holtz, *Untersuchungen über die alttestamentlichen Zitate bei Lukas* (TU 104; Berlin: Akademie, 1968) 100–109.

and that they were restricted to no one form, purpose, or setting.[33] They do not account for the origin of this sermon and cannot provide sufficient basis for a hypothetical "neutral source." Luke may have availed himself of a source here, but its limits cannot be securely identified and thus used as an aid to understanding the passage.[34] If he has not completely assimilated his source, Luke has shaped it to meet his goals.[35] In sum, the quest to explain this speech by identifying its origin is, for the purpose of interpreting Acts, a blind alley. The most prudent solution is to posit the use of a *model*, derived not simply from biblical sources but, as Gregory Sterling has argued, through the medium of Hellenistic Jewish tradition.[36]

Luke has supplied earlier examples of stout testimony before the high priests, whose homicidal proclivities have been apparent since 5:33. The narrator's eyes are turned toward the future. Stephen's speech defends not his doomed self but Luke's understanding of history and of the gentile mission that lies ahead.[37] Reflections on its form support this judgment. If encountered as an isolated discourse, the text would be classified as epideictic rhetoric accusing the Jewish people of disobedience and resistance to the beneficent will of God.[38] Although it is replete with historical examples and contains a retrospective narrative that is typical of forensic rhetoric, the focus is on the present: "God does not dwell in artifacts" (v. 48); "you have not kept the law" (v. 53).[39] In its dramatic setting, the speech is prophetic in content, but it contains no summons to change, no threat of punishment if disobedience continues, no promise in response to repentance; nor, finally, is there an announcement of judgment.[40] Readers know that "the Jews" did not repent of killing Jesus and that judgment has already taken place.[41] Like nearly every speech in the book, Acts 7 is appropriate when it is understood as addressed to the audience of the book.[42] This sermon on Israelite history endows their beliefs with legitimacy. Rejection of

33 Barrett (1:336) has apposite comments on the disparity of these surveys. Johnson (120) finds historical reminiscences typical of speeches in Greek historiography, as they are, but none of his examples relates to the trial of an individual.

34 So also Jervell, 249, with a summary of views in nn. 744–45. The number of details that deviate from a straightforward reading of the LXX and the recurrence of just these deviations and legendary embellishments establish the high probability that one or more extrabiblical summaries were used. Cadbury (*Book*, 102–4) lists most of these items and posits familiarity with Jewish traditions.

35 Kilgallen (*Stephen Speech*, 121) and Richard (*Acts 6*, 252–84) arrive at a similar conclusion. Richard ("Polemical Character," 264) says it well: "He treats Hebrew history with both reverence and bitterness."

36 Gregory Sterling, "'Opening the Scriptures': The Legitimation of the Jewish Diaspora and the Early Christian Mission," in Moessner, *Heritage*, 199–225. As his subtitle indicates, a major function of this tradition was to justify the Diaspora as a valid locus for Jewish existence. See also Nils A. Dahl, "The Story of Abraham in Luke-Acts," in Keck and Martyn, *Studies*, 139–58, who includes many useful theological observations.

37 See Conzelmann, 57, who follows Dibelius, *Studies*, 169.

38 Penner (*Praise*, 303–27) has developed this classification with emphasis on the implicit positive elements of the speech.

39 Kennedy (*Rhetorical Criticism*, 121–22) proposes that this stasis is "counter-accusation," which amounts to a stasis of jurisdiction: the tribunal has no right to charge him. Counter-accusation is reserved to the end, while the notion of jurisdiction is, at best, implicit. Witherington also claims that the speech is forensic (relying on Jacques Dupont, "La structure oratoire du discours d'Étienne [Actes 7]," *Bib* 66 [1985] 153–67). He states that the technique is *insinuatio*. *Insinuatio* proper is a technique for winning the sympathy of the audience (Lausberg, *Handbook* §§280–81, pp. 132–33). Despite his classification, Witherington (259) defines the speech as a criticism of disobedient Jews. Defense of historicity is the primary motive behind the desire to discover judicial rhetoric here.

40 Tannehill (*Narrative Unity*, 2:94–95) agrees, with references to the Deuteronomic view of salvation history, that such judgment is in view, while contending that the implied author has not given up hope for the Jewish people. This is an excellent sentiment, but it is not Luke's sentiment.

41 Luke 19:44 links the destruction of Jerusalem to rejection of Jesus.

42 Dibelius, *Studies*, 169: "It needs to be appreciated, not within the setting of the martyrdom but of the book as a whole. It inaugurates that section of Acts (6–12) which portrays the progress of the gospel to the Gentile world."

God-sent leaders and confidence in cultic performance are so typical of Israelites that the rejection of Jesus is an argument in favor of his status.

Dupont proposed the following rhetorical outline: v. 2a, *exordium*; vv. 2b-34, *narratio*; v. 35 *propositio*; vv. 36-50, *argumentatio*; vv. 51-53, *peroratio*.[43] This is not very convincing. Verse 35 is more an illustration of a thesis made more explicit in v. 52 than the thesis of the entire speech, and vv. 36-50 contain more narrative as well as argumentation. It does possess the merit of showing that argumentation becomes more overt from v. 35 onward. George A. Kennedy assigns vv. 2b-48 to the narration and locates the thesis in v. 51, viewing the indictment as gradual. Rhetorical analysis has limited value when the material is as formally defective as Acts 7. Kennedy included vv. 54-56 as a narrative epilogue, followed by Marion L. Soards, who extended this to v. 60. The speech is not free-standing but has been integrated into the narrative. Most analysts rely on content rather than form to expose the structure.[44] Content reveals a biographical focus that extends through v. 43, at which point the locus of worship becomes the theme. Abraham (vv. 2b-8) represents an ideal time of promise.[45] With Joseph (vv. 9-16) resistance in the form of jealousy emerges.[46] The story of Moses (vv. 17-43) is climactic and elaborate, with three sections that portray Moses in a fashion scarcely imaginable in a Jewish encomiastic work. Verses 17-22 are a biographical introduction, followed by two missions to his people, each marked by a reference to "forty years" (vv. 23, 30). His first "visitation"[47] included the rescue of a countryman and an effort to bring "salvation" (σωτηρία [v. 25]) via reconciliation. This ended in rejection and flight (vv. 23-29). In his second mission, Moses, empowered by God, delivers the people, only to be rejected once more, as they prefer idolatry (vv. 30-43). Manufactured images (v. 40[48]) provide a means of transition to the later project of building a temple, the theme of the penultimate section. God gave up on those who had twice rejected Moses (v. 42). The parallels with Jesus are patent. In the case of both Joseph and Moses the second "appearance" was decisive. So, by implication, will be that of Jesus. Luke is clearly responsible for this long central section of the speech, as it fits hand in glove with his Christology. Since the biographical organization of this address is also characteristic of Luke, it is abundantly clear that the author of Acts is responsible for the overall content and shape of this speech.

The relationship between the speech and the charges of 6:11-14 is Lucan and shrewd. Although the charges are labeled as false, Stephen does attend to each in due course. In so far as "Moses" is a metonym for Torah, the hearers would do well to attend to their lack of obedience. Those in search of "blasphemies against Moses" may begin with what their own forebears said about him and their response to the divine oracles he promulgated. As for the temple, it was not part of the original scheme and, all in all, not a good idea. Luke thus relativizes both temple and Torah without directly attacking either.[49] He has fashioned a velvet glove for the fist of Paul. The argument that Stephen does not criticize temple or Torah is refuted by the sequence. Philip undertakes a mission to the Samaritans, who worship in a different place. Jerusalem approves. Philip then baptizes a eunuch, a person disqualified by Torah from membership in the people of God. Following the conversion of Paul, Peter converts uncircumcised gentiles. After reporting the acceptance of this action in Jerusalem, the narrative turns to a gentile mission outside of the Holy Land. Acts 8–11 make sense only if chap. 7

43 Jacques Dupont, "La structure oratoire du discours d'Étienne (Actes 7)," *Bib* 66 (1985) 153–67.

44 So Soards (*Speeches*, 58–59), who includes a number of other plans in n. 138. Others include Weiser, 1:178–80; Krodel, 139; and Fitzmyer, 365.

45 Penner (*Praise* 306–8) also focuses on context and content, taking 7:2-8 as the basis of his analysis.

46 On jealousy, see p. 141.

47 Note other uses of the verb ἐπισκέπτομαι in Luke 1:66, 78, and the corresponding noun in Luke 19:44.

48 The verb ποίησον ("make") in v. 40 provides a link to χειροποιήτοις (lit. "handmade"). Cf. also "handiwork" (ἔργοις τῶν χειρῶν) in v. 41. Marcel Simon comments, "[T]he building of the Temple by Solomon seems to stand on the same plane as the making of the golden calf" ("St. Stephen and the Jerusalem Temple," *JEH* 2 [1951] 127–42, esp. 127).

49 Josephus uses the same apologetic argument in precisely the opposite sense: the temple was erected in accordance with God's providential plan (see *Ant.* 8.109). On Josephus's use of Greek philosophical theology in connection with the temple,

had undermined the twin pillars of temple and Torah. From the stones cast at Stephen, God will raise up new children for Abraham (Luke 3:8).

In addition to a number of direct citations of the LXX,[50] allusions abound.[51] The citations account for most of the text-critical problems. Ropes noted around thirty instances in which the "Alexandrian" text diverges from that of Bezae.[52] Bezae tends to conform to the LXX.[53] As a general principle, agreement with the LXX is a sign of secondary status, but this principle cannot serve as a rule.[54]

Comment

■ **1-8** The high priest asks for an answer yes or no. With the briefest of honorifics[55] and a blunt demand for attention, Stephen launches into his survey. The first section appears to be a bland sketch of the life of Abraham. The patriarch possesses no heroic qualities, unlike Joseph and Moses. He is held throughout in the leading strings of God, who propels him hither and thither.[56] This is Luke's means of showing providential governance, while the shape of the story establishes the overarching theme of promise and fulfillment. Agents of the promise are a succession of righteous, suffering, or persecuted prophets,[57] against whom runs the counterpoint of resistance by the expected beneficiaries of the promise.[58] As usual,[59] the first part of the story lacks conflict.

■ **3** For readers of the Gospel, Abraham's call (v. 3) presages that of Jesus' disciples, who also left family[60] and surroundings for an itinerant life. Neither God nor the people of God have a permanent residence.[61] Similarities to Hebrews are obvious, but Luke has no interest in developing the theme of God's wandering people. It is adequate to suggest that the people of God are "*in via*," on a journey through history, of which physical travel is but a symbol.[62] Pursuant to these goals, the narrator states, against Genesis 12, that this revelation preceded Abraham's residence in Haran.[63] All of Abraham's travels took place after the initial revelation. The verb ὤφθη ("appeared") treats the biblical oracle

see Louis Feldman, "Josephus as an Apologist to the Greco-Roman World: His Portrait of Solomon," in Schüssler Fiorenza, *Aspects*, 69–98.

50 For details on the LXX citations, see Barrett, 1:341–78, who cites the relevant texts in full.

51 Richard (*Acts 6*, 33–155) offers a detailed study of the relation of the speech to the LXX.

52 Ropes, *Text*, 60–61. See also Metzger, *Textual Commentary*, 299–300.

53 The most important exception is in v. 18.

54 A complicating factor is that fourth-century MSS. of the Greek OT are also subject to being conformed to NT quotations. Contamination was a two-way street.

55 Paul uses the same formula, "fathers and brothers," in Acts 22:1.

56 On the relation of this narrative technique to popular writing and Lucan theology, see Pervo, *Profit*, 74.

57 The motif of refusal to heed prophets and that of their persecution are common. For references, see Talbert, 78.

58 On this passage, see Dahl, "Abraham," esp. 142–48.

59 Cf. Luke 1–3; Acts 1–3.

60 On συγγενεία ("relations"), see Spicq, *Lexicon*, 3:301–7.

61 The stem *oik-* ("dwell[ing]") works like a leitmotif in this speech, appearing about sixteen times: vv. 2, 4 (three times), 6, 10, 20, 29, 42, 43, 46, 47 (twice), 48, and 49 (twice). (There is a textual dispute about v. 46.) These are concentrated at the beginning, five instances in vv. 2-6, and eight in vv. 42-49. Included in this stem is "temple" (οἶκος, lit. "house"). The verb μετοικίζω ("relocate") reappears in v. 43, with considerable irony. (Acts 7:4, 43 are the only uses of this verb in the NT.)

62 Conzelmann (57) properly observes that this theme receives no consistent exposition, but he does not connect it with the theme of "the way."

63 This deviation probably explains some textual variants. Some Old Latin MSS. shift "After his father's death" to the beginning of v. 3. On this, see Metzger, *Textual Commentary*, 300. Boismard (*Texte*, 131) begins v. 4 with "*and* relocated . . . ," omitting "So Abraham . . . father." This abridgment may be due to secondary summaries of Acts (so Ropes, *Text*, 62). Gen 15:7, where the narrative begins, could be grounds for claiming that Abraham received his call in Ur. Cf. also Neh 9:7. Philo *Abr.* 71–72 presents a similar plot, and he also locates his father's death in Haran (*Abr.* 177). (Haran is placed in Mesopotamia in, e.g., Jdt 5:7; Josephus *Ant* 1.152.) For an explanation of how one could arrive at the conclusion that Abraham left Haran after his father's death, see Dahl, "Abraham," 143 and 153 n. 25.

of Gen 12:1-3 as an epiphany,[64] corresponding to that at the burning bush (v. 30). Both occur outside of the holy land; no theophanies are associated with the temple.[65]

■ **4-5** These verses stress that, when in the promised land, Abraham was an alien without property.[66] The next two verses assert that his descendants will continue to be sojourners until God chooses to rescue them so that they may worship "in this place."[67] The balance of the speech will report the fulfillment of this prophecy.[68] That prediction is made possible by dropping the conclusion of Gen 15:14 (which refers to booty) and replacing it with a modification of Exod 3:12, "you shall worship God on this mountain." By changing "mountain" to "place," the "Scripture" creates a link to v. 33 and to the citation in v. 49.[69] Any place, including wilderness tents, Phrygian synagogues, and house churches in Jerusalem and Ephesus, is suitable for the service of God, the purest form of which is not conquest or loot but worship.[70]

■ **8** At the opening of *Homily* 16 *on Acts*, Chrysostom exclaims that years have passed since the promise "and nowhere sacrifice, nowhere circumcision." He was doubtless inspired by Paul, but Luke may have had the same motivation (cf. Rom 4:1-17). For Luke, circumcision is no longer controversial, although believers of Jewish background are not prohibited from continuing the practice.[71] Verse 8 establishes the succession through the patriarchs.[72] Stephen omits all of Isaac's life beyond his birth in his haste to reach his account about Joseph.

■ **9-16** Verbal markers link these verses to the preceding and subsequent sections.[73] As in the case of Abraham, this is, at first glance, a good summary of Joseph's life, but Luke uses this prototype of the "righteous sufferer"[74] to suggest that the story of Joseph foreshadows (and thus prophesies) the story of Jesus. Joseph's own people rejected him, but God reversed this misfortune and exalted Joseph as ruler, in which role he was a benefactor to those who had rejected him. As in the case of Moses, there are two "parousias." Here also the parallel with Jesus is patent.

Nearly every phrase of this passage has been taken from Genesis 37–50,[75] yet the summary has an edge. The

64 The verb does not appear in Genesis 12 until v. 7. "God of glory" (lit.) is found elsewhere in Ps 28:3 LXX (cf. Eph 1:17). This makes an inclusion of sorts with v. 55.

65 Chrysostom sees polemic already in v. 2: "[He shows] . . . that the temple is nothing, that the customs are nothing either, without their suspecting his drift" (*Hom.* 15, trans. J. Walker, 95).

66 The D-Text (Boismard, *Texte*, 132) makes the adversative sense explicit: "but . . ." (ἀλλ᾽).

67 In v. 4, Stephen appears to break character and speak with the voice of the narrator: "this land that you now inhabit." Major D-Text witnesses add "your/our forebears" in some form or another, softening this dissonance.

68 Note the repetition of κατάσχεσις ("possession" [v. 5]) in v. 45.

69 Penner (*Praise*, 308–10) traces the meaning of "place" in chaps. 6–7. The term applies to the temple (6:13-14) and, by way of 7:7, to the land in 7:4-5. The result is that the promise to Abraham is fulfilled when the people enter the land (7:45).

70 Similarly Dahl, "Abraham," 145. Cf. the Benedictus, esp. Luke 1:73-75, where the first part climaxes with an interpretation of the promise to Abraham as freedom to worship "in holiness and righteousness" (also noted by Dahl, 147). Cf. also Löning, "Circle of Stephen," 111.

71 Gentile male believers need not be circumcised (11:1-18; 15), but it is expected of those of Jewish parentage (16:1-3; 21:21). Verse 8c may well imply both verbs: "beget" and "circumcise." Löning ("Circle of Stephen," 110) states the matter concisely: "For Luke, the argument over the 'law' is a dispute over the obligatory nature of Jewish culture."

72 The term "patriarch" (πατριάρχης) is evidently a creation of Hellenistic Judaism and reflects Hellenistic concerns with origins and founders. Also nonbiblical are "our father Abraham" and "covenant of circumcision," although the last is semiticizing Greek.

73 The last noun of v. 8, "patriarchs," is the first of v. 9. "Egypt" (vv. 15, 17) is the link between the stories of Joseph and Moses, while reference to "Abraham" in vv. 16 and 17 joins all three of the first parts of the speech.

74 George W. Nickelsburg investigated the history of this theme in various literary and theological ramifications; see *Resurrection, Immortality, and Eternal Life in Intertestamental Judaism* (HTS 26; Cambridge, Mass.: Harvard University Press, 1972). Note also his "The Genre and Function of the Markan Passion Narrative," *HTR* 73 (1980): 153–84. See also Pesch, 1:250.

75 See the chart in Richard, "Polemical Character," 266–67, and the detailed observations in his *Acts 6*, 60–76.

narrator wishes to demonstrate that "family fights," the most recent of which pits the followers of Jesus against the Jewish leaders, are characteristic of Israelite history. For base and vile motives, as well as simple infidelity, large numbers of the descendants of Abraham have rejected the righteous. The experience of Stephen is but one more squalid chapter in a dismal history. "The patriarchs" (not "the *eleven other* patriarchs")[76] sold Joseph into slavery, out of jealousy. Their motive was thus identical to that which led the chief priests to assault the apostles in 5:17. Genesis 37 does not report that Joseph's brothers sold him.[77] The complex story, with its progress from robes to rags and back again, from prisoner to prime minister, is reduced to a single sentence describing Joseph's betrayal by all his brothers and his subsequent exaltation over Egypt. The result is a formula: humiliation followed by exaltation. Through its abbreviations, the narrative highlights Joseph's role as a leader not only in Egypt but also of his people.

■ **10** "But God was on his side, rescuing him . . ."[78] The word θλίψεις ("afflictions") does not come from Genesis. The phrase "wisdom and charm" (χάρις καὶ σοφία [v. 10b]) in the immediate context encompasses the qualities of attractiveness and acumen needed to gain official recognition. In the wider context, these qualities unite the various figures. Stephen has the same two characteristics (6:3, 8, 10), while David enjoyed χάρις from God (v. 46) and Moses was renowned for wisdom (v. 22), as was Jesus (Luke 2:52).[79] The verb "made" ("appointed," καθίστημι) was applied to Stephen in 6:3 and will be used of Moses in vv. 27 and 35. Stephen is the most recent link in a very ancient chain.[80]

■ **11** The verse introduces a new subject: famine,[81] characterized as a disaster of apocalyptic quality.[82] The noun permits a contrast with the "terrible affliction" of v. 11. Since "our ancestors" had to turn to unbelievers for assistance, readers may infer that God was not on their side.[83]

■ **12-15** These verses resolve the problem of famine while laying the groundwork for the story of Moses. The subject is Jacob, who sends "our ancestors" in search of grain. It is reasonable to ask whether the implied reader is familiar with the story, since it appears to make limited sense,[84] but those unfamiliar with Genesis could conclude that more than one expedition occurred and that only on the second did Joseph discover the purchasers. In any case, the narrator places the weight on the two "comings" and the recognition.[85] Moses will also come twice to his people. In both cases, the second "advent" manifests power. The pertinent analogy is Jesus, whose return/second coming also involved recognition scenes (Luke 24:25, 36-42). The narrative has been stripped of all that lacks typological significance. Verses 14-16 bring Jacob and the patriarchs to Egypt

76 That is, the narrative distinguishes the official leaders and pillars from the "good guy." In the same manner, "the Jews" will be used to characterize the opponents of the movement.

77 This charge comes from Joseph's accusation in Gen 45:4.

78 The conjunction καί (v. 9b) is certainly adversative. "God was (lit.) with him." The same phrase is applied to Jesus in 10:38; cf. also Deut 20:1. On the LXX use of this phrase, see Johnson, *Literary Function,* 62 n. 2. The verb for "rescue" is ἐξείλατο, used of delivery from Pharaoh (Exod 18:8) and of Peter from "Herod" (Acts 12:11).

79 Acts adds χάρις (often rendered "grace") to Gen 39:21 and eliminates the prison superintendent.

80 The grammar of v. 10d is difficult, since "God" is the subject of all four clauses, which means that the final αὐτοῦ ("his") is logically "God's house." The sense is clear, however (cf. Gen 45:8). On the article, see Barrett, 1:347.

81 In 11:27-30, sufferers from a famine will also benefit from the generosity of others. The article is rarely used with "Egypt." See BDF §101 (7).

82 For the phrase θλῖψις μεγάλη ("terrible affliction"), see Neh 9:37; 1 Macc 9:27; Matt 24:21; Rev 2:22. The noun is found in Gen 42:21, although in a different sense.

83 Richard ("Polemical Character," 260–62) supports this interpretation by appeal to Deut 31:17 and 2 Chr 20:6-17. He notes Ps 36:18-19, which uses χορτασθῆναι ("be satiated") as an explanation of the unusual noun for food in v. 11 (χορτάσματα). The last may be elegant variation with σιτία (itself a rare word, altered in some MSS.) in v. 12, for, although the noun means "fodder" in the LXX, it can be used for "sustenance" (M-M 690, *s.v.*). The form ηὕρισκον is a conative impf.: "tried to find (without success)."

84 Cf. Conzelmann, 52: "The purpose is not to report the events, but to interpret them."

85 In v. 13, A B it^{p} vg read the simple ἐγνωρίσθη ("was made known," "identified himself"). This

so that they may die in that foreign land and be buried thereafter in Shechem. The size of the community is reminiscent of 1:14.[86] Oaks begin as acorns.

■ **16** Insofar as readers would identify "Shechem" as a place in Samaria, v. 16 foreshadows the Samaritan mission of the following chapter. It is not likely, however, that the implied reader would make this connection, and chap. 8 avoids the name "Shechem."[87] The text is unclear. Variants attest and contribute to these difficulties. The claim that Jacob and all the patriarchs were buried at Shechem is not found elsewhere. Luke has either confused or telescoped a number of traditions.[88] The object is clear: so far from possessing the land by nationality or birth, Abraham had to purchase a burial plot. His living descendants are now domiciled in Egypt, where the next chapter of their story will unfold.

■ **17-44** Momentum builds. The parallel between Moses and Jesus is detailed and undeniable, while the people's failures extend beyond rejecting their God-sent leader to apostasy from the God who sent Moses. The rhetorical technique here stresses a three-fold crescendo (Abraham, Joseph, Moses) that echoes the pattern underlying Acts 3–7.

■ **17-22** A Mosaic "infancy narrative" opens with a solemn, salvation-historical statement reminiscent of, and possibly inspired by, Gal 4:4. "Promise" is not a concept of the MT. The Christian understanding of Israelite Scripture as "promise," central to Paul and Luke, among others, is what makes those scriptures the "Old Testament."[89] The statement on growth comes from Exod 1:7 ("people" is Luke's term). It provides a parallel with the statements on growth in Acts (6:1, 7; 9:31; 12:24; 19:20), of which it is a probable source. Following Exodus, the account reports the advent of a wicked Pharaoh who seeks to exterminate the people by requiring the exposure of infants.[90] Omission of other incidents allows the narrator to highlight the attempted genocide.

■ **20-22** At this dire moment, the style of Luke's Greek improves. Moses deserves one of his better efforts. The passage is built on the conventional biographical pattern ("born, reared, educated") found also in 22:3.[91] This parallel heightens the probability that Luke is responsible for the material. The word καιρός ("occasion") has salvation-historical significance. The predicate ἀστεῖος τῷ θεῷ (v. 20) does not mean that God found him attractive (despite what humans might have thought), since the idea is that Pharaoh's daughter found this baby so cute that she simply had to have him.[92] It is

may be a correction based on the interpretation of ἀναγνωρίζω as "identify himself again," according to Metzger, *Textual Commentary*, 301. LXX MSS. have both verbs. On the article with "Joseph," see Metzger, *Textual Commentary*, 301. For the dative of agent, see BDF §191 (2).

86 On the difference between "seventy" (MT) and "seventy-five" (LXX) see Cadbury and Lake, 73. The preposition ἐν here is the rough equivalent of an accusative of respect. See BDF §220 (2). Moule (*Idiom Book*, 79) calls this use of the preposition "descriptive."

87 Foreshadowing: Richard, "Polemical Character," 259.

88 *Jub.* 45:16; 46:9-10 and Josephus *Ant.* 2.199–200 all report that they were buried at Hebron. The biblical texts are not consistent. See Johnson, 118–19; and, in particular, Barrett, 1:350–51. The αὐτός of v. 15 logically refers to Jacob, but some readers may have applied it to the principal subject, Joseph. The D-Text has no conjunction at the beginning of v. 15. According to Ropes (*Text*, 65), this links his journey to his death. Options are καί and δέ. The former fits the biblical style of the passage. D-Texts (Boismard, *Texte*, 132) place the first two verbs of v. 16 in the singular. This makes the burial apply to Jacob alone and is an obvious correction. There are three options before "Shechem": "in," "of," and "of in." The genitive τοῦ could make Shechem a person, although Boismard, who reads this in his D-Text (*Texte*, 133), treats it as a place.

89 "Promise" emerges in early Judaism, although not in so sweeping a sense as in early Christianity. See Julius Schniewind and G. Friedrich, "ἐπαγγέλω," *TDNT* 2:576–86, esp. 579–81.

90 The articular infinitive τοῦ ποῖεν ("by making" = "compelling") is, in effect, epexegetic. See BDF §400 (8).

91 On this pattern, see below on 22:3. Luke may have drawn it from a source, as traces of the same pattern are visible in Ezekiel the Tragedian, Philo, and Josephus. (See n. 97.)

92 On Moses' beauty, see Pompeius Trogus *Historiae Philippicae* 36; Justin *Epit.* 2.11; Philo *Vit. Mos.* 1.9; Josephus *Ant.* 2.224, 231–32. Philo describes him as "more than just good-looking" (ἢ κατ' ἰδιώτην). This may tone down a phrase like that of Acts. Josephus states that the child's appearance attracted Pharaoh's daughter (§224). In §232 he speaks of "divine" good looks (μορφῇ θεῖον), another possible intimation of a source. For a good brief discussion of the theme in general and

evidently a dative of standard of judgment, that is, a kind of comparison.[93] Not even the achievements of the Greeks dimmed the luster that attached to Egyptian erudition throughout antiquity—and beyond.[94] Its scope ranged from philosophy to magic.[95] This is not the most extravagant statement made about Moses and Egyptian culture.[96] The education of Moses was an important topic for Hellenistic Jewish authors.[97] The intra-Lucan parallels are Jesus (Luke 2:40, 52) and Paul (Acts 22:3). The second half of v. 22[98] amounts to a statement of Luke's thesis: Moses and Jesus were prophets no less potent in word[99] than in deed.[100] At the popular level, this means that both were rousing orators and miracle workers. From the learned perspective, it validated their views, as the essential test for an intellectual system in the Greco-Roman world was congruence between word and deed.[101]

■ **23-29** Moses' early adult career is the subject of the next section. Upon the attainment of maturity, he takes up the role of protector and conflict manager, but is so thoroughly rebuffed that he must flee for his life and become a resident alien, the status of his forebears.[102] This is his "first" visit. Chronological markers delineate the sections beginning in vv. 20, 23, and 30. They are bells tolling the course of redemptive history. Luke apportions the life of Moses into three periods of forty

---

Moses in particular, see Feldman, *Jew and Gentile*, 249–51.

93 The adjective alone is used in Exod 2:2. On this construction, see BDAG, 145, *s.v.* ἀστεῖος; Smyth, *Greek Grammar*, §1512; BDF §192 (a Hebraism, as "possibly," Moule, *Idiom Book*, 46 and 189); Cadbury and Lake, 75; and Barrett, 1:354. Comparison of human beings with gods is a cliché in Greek literature, e.g., Chariton *Chaer.* 1.1.1 "[Callirhoe's] beauty was not so much human as divine" (trans. G. P. Gould, *Chariton Callirhoe* [LCL; Cambridge, Mass.: Harvard University Press, 1995] 29).

94 "Greeks find all Egyptian lore and legend irresistibly attractive," according to the Egyptian Kalasiris (*Ethiopian Story*, 2.27, trans. J. R. Morgan in Brian P. Reardon, *Collected Ancient Greek Novels* [Berkeley: University of California Press, 1989] 401). Cf. also 2.34; 3.12 (Homer was educated in Egyptian wisdom), and 3.16. Note Lucian *Philops.* 34: *μεμφίτης ἀνὴρ τῶν ἱερῶν γραμματέων, θαυμάσιος τὴν σοφίαν καὶ τὴν παιδείαν πᾶσαν εἰδὼς τὴν Αἰγύπτιον* ("a man from Memphis, one of the scribes of the temple, wonderfully learned, familiar with all the culture of the Egyptians," trans. A. M. Harmon, *Lucian III* [LCL; Cambridge, Mass.: Harvard University Press, 1919] 371–73). Eusebius uses Acts 7:22 to compare Constantine to Moses (*Vit. Const.* 1.12). In 1.96.2, Diodorus Siculus enumerates some who have benefited from Egyptian wisdom, including Orpheus, Daedalus, Homer, Lycurgus, Solon, Plato, Pythagoras, Democritus, and Eudoxus.

95 As late as the fifth century, the alleged translations of Horapollon showed continuing fascination with hieroglyphics. For philosophy, note Plutarch *De Iside et Osiride* and Apuleius *Metamorphoses*. The *Corpus Hermeticum* exemplifies the appeal of Egyptiana in more popular philosophy and religion, while the Greek magical papyri illustrate a wide intellectual range. (Magic is the theme in Lucian's *Philops.* 34 [see preceding note]). On the negative side, Hippolytus (*Ref.* 7.27.13) writes of the heresies Basilides imbibed with his immersion in Egyptian wisdom.

96 Authors such as Eupolemus (frg. 1) and Artapanus (frg. 3) credit him with the invention of much of it. On parallels with Stephen's speech in Artapanus, see Sterling, *Apologetic Historiography*, 363–65.

97 According to Philo *Vit. Mos.* 21–24, Moses had teachers from many realms, including Greece, although he quickly surpassed them all. Ezekiel the Tragedian is more general (frg. 1; 2 lines 8–10), as is Josephus *Ant.* 2.236. Luke is less sophisticated in that he is content merely to equip Moses with Egyptian wisdom from top to bottom.

98 The D-Text (Boismard, *Texte*, 134) reads τε δυνατός instead of δέ. The former clearly presents two coordinate clauses; the latter could be read as viewing the second as the result of first: because of his wisdom Moses was powerful. Luke is fond of τε, but in this case it may well be a correction intended to prevent presumed misinterpretation.

99 Just as this is in conflict with Exod 4:10 on Moses' ability as a speaker, so Acts disagrees with Paul's own evaluation of his rhetorical abilities (2 Cor 10:10).

100 Luke 24:19: ἀνὴρ προφήτης δυνατὸς ἐν ἔργῳ καὶ λόγῳ (Jesus was "a man powerful in word and deed"); Acts 7:22: ἦν δὲ δυνατὸς ἐν λόγοις καὶ ἔργοις αὐτοῦ (Moses "was powerful in his words and deeds").

101 See under 1:1.

102 The word πάροικος appears in vv. 6 and 29.

years. The fortieth year was the traditional time of maturity.[103] Moses resolves[104] to "visit" his people. The verb ἐπισκέψασθαι could be neutral, but for Luke it refers to redemptive action.[105] This solemn opening creates an atmosphere quite different from that of Exod 2:11-15. Abbreviation once more serves to highlight the hero's mission.[106] Verse 25 is the narrator's explanation of the motive for this murder. It was not an impulsive intervention but a symbol of the role God had in store for Moses. Because their hearts and minds were not open, the Israelites failed to understand.[107] By this interpretation, Luke transforms Moses into a prototype of Jesus.[108]

■ **26-27** Moses next attempts to serve as a reconciler. Verse 26 strongly deviates from Exod 2:13, which speaks of accusation rather than reconciliation.[109] Reconciliation is part of the mission of the genuine sage and leader.[110] This is yet another parallel with Jesus—better, with Christology, since the Jesus tradition is not rich in examples.[111] Reconciliation is an important role of the cosmic Christ in the Deutero-Pauline world, from which Luke took it up and retrojected it to both the earthly Jesus and Moses (cf. Col 1:20; Eph 2:17).[112] The author regards reconciliation as one of his own most vital tasks. Luke and Acts were composed, in large part, as an attempt to bring peace to warring "brothers." The words assigned to Moses in v. 26 were invented to replace the accusation of Exod 2:13. "Them" (αὐτοῖς) in v. 26 has no antecedent beyond the general "kindred" of v. 25, but v. 27 assumes a quarrel between two persons. One must ask how intelligible the narrative would be to those unfamiliar with the story.[113] The effort backfires (v. 27) when the wrongful party (of whom the reader first learns) rebukes (an addition to the tradition) Moses, by asking who put him in charge and whether he will resolve this matter by murder also.[114] At this point, v. 25 becomes a problem, since readers might expect Moses to say "God," but the narrative ignores this and treats the question as unanswerable. The effect is

103 Horst Balz, "τέσσαρες," *TDNT* 8:127–39, esp. 135–36. Forty was the minimum age for many offices. Cf. the practice of assuming that people achieved prominence at age forty and thus estimating time of birth as forty years prior (*floruit*).

104 Although BDF §3 n. 4 classifies ἀνέβη ἐπὶ τὴν καρδίαν αὐτου (lit. "ascended into his heart") as "spoken Jewish Greek," it is septuagintal. Cf. 4 Kgdms 12:5; Jer 3:16; 28:50; Isa 65:16; see also Moule, *Idiom Book*, 183; and Bruce, 198, who lists other examples.

105 Luke 1:68; 7:16; 19:44; and Acts 15:14. Cf. Gen 21:1; 50:24-25; Exod 3:16; 4:31; 13:19.

106 Acts omits Moses' attempts to avoid detection (Exod 2:12), his subsequent fear, and Pharaoh's attempt to kill him (vv. 14-15). Stephen's Moses is bold and fearless. Not perceiving this, D-Texts (Boismard, *Texte*, 134–35) add, after ἀδικούμενον, ἐκ τοῦ γένους αὐτοῦ. ("One *of his own people* being abused"). At the close, D (w) add καὶ ἔκρυψεν αὐτὸν ἐν τῇ ἄμμῳ ("and hid him in the sand" [Exod 2:12]). "The Egyptian" (v. 24) would be mysterious to those unfamiliar with Exodus.

107 Cf. Mark 6:52; Luke 24:16, 45.

108 On Moses typology in the NT, see Ferdinand Hahn, *The Titles of Jesus in Christology: Their History in Early Christianity* (trans. Harold Knight and G. Ogg; Cleveland: World, 1969) 372–88. On Acts in particular, see Leonhard Goppelt, *Typos: The Typological Interpretaion of the Old Testament in the New* (trans. D. H. Madvig; Grand Rapids: Eerdmans, 1982) 121–24.

109 The verb συνήλλασσεν is a conative imperfect: "He undertook to reconcile them." A E Ψ 33 m read συνήλασε, from συνελαύνω ("compelled them to comply"). This is either an error or an infelicitous correction.

110 On the role, see Lucian *Demon.* 9; Philostratus *Vit. Apoll.* 1.15. An example is Dio of Prusa *Or.* 38. Note Plutarch's characterization of Alexander as a "heaven-sent governor and reconciler of the whole world (θεόθεν ἁρμοστὴς καὶ διαλλακτὴς τῶν ὅλων) (*Alex. fort.* 1.6 [*Mor.* 329C]).

111 "Peace" as a theme is associated with the ministry of Jesus (Luke 1:79; 2:14, 29; Acts 10:36), but Jesus refuses the role of reconciler in Luke 12:14 and claims to be an agent of division rather than peace in 12:51.

112 The inspiration is Pauline, e.g., 2 Cor 5:16-21.

113 The D-Text attempts to correct this oversight by reading, after "the next day," "He *saw* (εἶδεν instead of ὤφθη) *some people mistreating one another*" and omits ἐστε, so that ἄνδρες ἀδελφοί becomes the typical vocative (Boismard, *Texte*, 135). (Bezae is conflate here.)

114 "Ruler and judge" (v. 27 = Exod 2:14) could be hendiadys: "ruler with juridical authority." The D-Text "ruler *or* judge" has some claim to originality in that it differs from the LXX.

that the people, in this representative,[115] reject their God-chosen leader and that, because of them, rather than through fear of Pharaoh, Moses must become a refugee in a land hateful to Israelites.[116]

■ **30-35** This section of the speech relates the call of Moses. As in the case of Abraham, the epiphany (ὤφθη [vv. 2, 30]) is in a foreign land.[117] This account eliminates Exod 2:16-31a, which narrate Moses' marriage to the daughter of a local priest and his career as a shepherd. Neither was especially flattering. Luke supplies the psychological details of wonder and fear (vv. 31-32).[118] Information about emotional reactions is expected in Greco-Roman writings. It also expresses the proper response to the presence of the divine. Acts reverses the order to remove his sandals[119] and God's self-introduction. This summary also omits the revelation of God's proper name. This may be because of the belief that God had no proper name (such as "Zeus" or "Demeter"). What is disclosed is the continuity of revelation and of salvation history.[120] "Place" is crucial (v. 33; note vv. 7 and 49). Neither Abraham, the progenitor of the people, nor Moses, its teacher, needed a particular location. Where there is a vision of God, there is holy ground. The climax is the commission in v. 34. God sent Moses to the people, as Jesus (3:26) and Paul (22:21; 26:19) will be sent.

The text of these verses is too chaotic to permit confidence about the original, although few of the variants greatly affect the interpretation.[121] Mae greatly expands vv. 31-34 with material from Exodus and elsewhere:[122]

115 In v. 39, this rejection becomes general (ἀπώσαντο).

116 "Flight" is Luke's substitute for the more discreet "withdrew" of the LXX. The D-Text οὕτως καὶ Μωυσῆς ἐφυγάδευσεν ("*As a result* Moses *took flight*") may be more original. See Metzger, *Textual Commentary*, 304. E treats the rare verb φυγαδεύω as transitive. That may be the "original" D-Text, with the sense that the wrongful party caused Moses to run away. "Two sons"—only one is mentioned in Exod 2:22 (Gershom); Eliezer appears in 18:3-4.

117 Verse 30 prefers the familiar "Sinai" to "Horeb" (a name found in the E and D traditions) of Exod 3:1.

118 The expression of numinous fear (ἔντρομος γενόμενος) in v. 32 is found again in 16:29 (the Philippian jailer).

119 The requirement for bare feet in holy places springs from two religio-historical principles. One is the concept that divine force must be unobstructed. This is related to cultic nudity (so Cadbury and Lake, 77). That which seems operative in the Semitic world is related to purity codes: shoes bear impurity, as in *m. Ber.* 9.5. See Lorenz Dürr, "Zur religionsgeschichtlichen Begründung der Vorschrift des Schuhausziehens an heiliger Stätte," *OLZ* 41 (1938) 410–12.

120 Haenchen, 282.

121 In v. 30, the D-Text begins "*After this*, when forty years had been completed for him . . ." A range of witnesses notes that it was an angel "of the Lord." This is an obvious addition. Alexandrian and some other texts ($\mathfrak{P}^{74}$ A C E 36 *al*) read πυρὶ φλογός, rather than φλογὶ πυρὸς ("flaming fire" rather than "fiery flame"). This is probably a correction, but deviation from the LXX gives it some weight. (Note also 2 Thess 1:8; see BDF §165; and Bruce, 199.) The expression derives from the epiphany of a storm god (Ps 29:7) and is an attribute of deity (Rev 1:14; 2:18; 19:12) and a symbol for punishment of the wicked (Isa 66:15; Joel 2:5; Sir 21:9). In v. 31, A B C ψ 33 1175 pc prefer the aorist of θαυμάζω ("taken aback"). A alone omits τὸ ὅραμα ("the sight"), which appears to be an accusative of respect. Instead of the dramatic and difficult ἐγένετο φωνὴ κυρίου ("There came a voice of the Lord"), D-Texts offer the more conventional "The Lord spoke to him, saying . . ." In v. 33, however, the situation is reversed. This is an intelligent improvement, since it makes the usage more understandable and also clarifies the object to which the voice was directed. As often, witnesses disagree over whether "God" should be placed before the name of each patriarch. (See comments on 3:13.) Regarding v. 34, the D-Text (Boismard, *Texte*, 137) replaces the imitation of the Hebrew infinitive absolute with καὶ ἰδὼν γὰρ ("For, having also seen"). D 1175 *pc* read "heard" in the perfect, an improvement; αὐτῶν ("their") is the more likely origin of the variants, since it is less correct. The future is read instead of the evidently hortatory subjunctive ἀποστείλω ("send") by Ψ 33 m, perhaps to prevent it from being viewed as a rhetorical question. See Moule, *Idiom Book*, 22; and Bruce, 200.

122 N-A[27] fails to note this text; Boismard (*Texte*, 138) merely observes that cop[mae] cites Exod 3:7-10 in full. It is included as an example of editorial freedom that cannot be attributed to scribal carelessness. The editor evidently found Acts defective here.

And[123] when **more than** forty years had been completed, there appeared to him the angel **of the Lord** in the wilderness at Mount Sinai in a flame of fire **from the** thornbush. 31. But Moses, when he saw [it], marveled at the sight. When he was of a mind to draw closer so that he might inspect [it], **the Lord spoke with him in a voice, in which he said**: 33.[124] **"Moses, Moses." He then said, "Who is it, Lord."**[125] **He said to him, "Do not come nearer to this place! Remove the sandals that are on your feet! For the place on which you stand is a holy ground." He said to him**, 32. **"I am the one who is the God of your father, the God of Abraham, the God of Isaac, and the God of Jacob." Moses then turned away his face, for he was afraid to gaze directly in the presence of God**. 34. **God said to Moses**, "I have certainly seen the mistreatment of my people who are in Egypt and I have heard their cry **about their overseers; for I know their unhappiness**. I have come here in order to deliver them **from the hand of the Egyptians**. Come now, I am sending you to Egypt, **so that you might lead them out of that land and bring them to the land that is good and large, a land that abounds in milk and honey, in the region of the Canaanites, Hittites, Amorites, the Perizzites, the Hivites, and the Jebusites. Look, the cry of the children of Israel has constrained me and I have seen the sufferings that the Egyptians have imposed upon them. Come now, so that I may send you to Pharaoh the King of Egypt and that you may lead my people, the children of Israel, out of the land of Egypt."**

■ **35-43** In v. 35, the speech erupts into an encomium of Moses. The style, marked by the use of anaphora (initial *τοῦτον* twice, followed by three initial uses of *οὗτος* [demonstrative pronouns rendered as "he"], vv. 35-38) and relative clauses or equivalent participial phrases (vv. 35, 37, 38 [three times]), is not unfamiliar to readers of Acts. The same "creedal style"[126] is found in the kerygmatic portions of other speeches, most notably 3:13-15, with which there are also specific parallels, most notably application of the verb "repudiate" (*ἀρνέομαι* [3:14; 7:35]) and the antithetical structure ("You denied, but God . . ."). Authenticating miracles (v. 36) are found also in the kerygmatic summary of 2:22-24 (v. 22, of Jesus; cf. Stephen in 6:8).

■ **35** The verse generalizes the rebuke of Moses by one person (v. 27; Exod 2:14) into a universal denial of his mission by the people and overlooks the chronology, for Moses had not yet been given his commission. This is a rather vicious bit of polemic. God sent[127] Moses to be a ruler and a redeemer. The first title is applied to many leaders in the LXX. The second is rare and used only of God.[128] The concluding prepositional phrase affirms that these titles characterize God's purpose in the undefined commission of v. 34. The angel, a normal substitute for God in postexilic Judaism,[129] provides continuity.[130]

■ **36-38** Shifting to the nominative *οὗτος* ("he"), vv. 36-38 summarize three key features of Moses' career: over forty years (cf. vv. 23, 30; 13:21) he exercised his leadership through working miracles, foretold the coming of a prophet like himself, and received the revelation at Sinai. The first two establish him as a prototype of

123 This version generally follows Hans-Martin Schenke, *Apostelgeschichte 1,1–15,3 im mittelägyptischen Dialekt des koptischen (Codex Glazier)* (TU 137; Berlin: Akademie, 1991) 138–40. Cf. also the rendition of Theodore C. Petersen, provided in Metzger, *Textual Commentary*, 304–5.

124 Schenke (*Apostelgeschichte 1,1–15,3*, 139n) observes that this text practically replaces Acts 7:32-34 with Exod 3:4b-10.

125 Schenke (*Apostelgeschichte 1,1–15,3*) renders "What is it, Lord?" This is possible. "Who" is preferable if Acts 9:5 is the inspiration.

126 On the third-person anaphoric style, see Norden, *Agnostos Theos*, 163–66. He offers examples from the "prose hymns" of Aristides (XLIII, XLV) and theoretical comments from Menander Rhetor. Other examples include Philo *Leg. Gaj.* 145–48 (Augustus), and Melito *On Pacha* 68–71; 83–86. One example still in use is the prose hymn *Exultet* from the Western Easter Vigil, with its repeated *haec est nox*, "This is the night." Norden discusses the participial style on pp. 166–68 and devotes pp. 168–76 to the use of relative clauses.

127 The perfect tense of *ἀπέσταλκεν* is surprising. Moule (*Idiom Book*, 14–15) calls it a "perfect of allegory," used when expounding a sacred text or event.

128 Pss 18:15; 77:35. The verb is used of the expected mission of Jesus in Luke 24:21. Luke 1:68 uses the noun "redemption" with the verb "visit" (cf. Acts 7:23, of Moses).

129 For examples of this substitution, see Cadbury and Lake, 78.

130 That phrase, *σὺν χειρὶ ἀγγέλου* (lit. "with hand

Jesus, while the third disposes of the charge that Stephen reviled Moses and the Torah (6:11, 13) and lays the ground for his explicit attack: those who received the law have not observed it. Verse 36 is notable for ascribing both leadership and the performance of miracles to Moses.[131] Deuteronomy 18:15 (v. 37) was a key passage in early Christian scriptural apologetic.[132] The verb "raise up" (ἀνίστημι) allows the passage to serve as a prophecy of the resurrection. For Luke, it is no embarrassment that Jesus is a "prophet like Moses." This suits his Christology.[133] Verse 38 pulls together several assertions. If the order is rearranged,[134] this asserts that Moses was in the desert "assembly"[135] with "our ancestors" as well as in regular communication with the angel on Mount Sinai, where he received "vital oracles."[136] Lake and Cadbury made the tentative suggestion that μετά in v. 38 might mean "between" and might thus depict Moses as a mediator between God and the Israelites, but this proposal has received limited support.[137] Verse 38 is probably careless writing rather than a corrupted text. Luke was not troubled about theological consistency here, and, in any case, he viewed "messianic prophecy" as the essence of Torah, as the citation in v. 37 indicates.[138]

■ **39-43** The pivot of these verses involves two uses of the verb "turn," a Hebrew idiom for change of will or intent. In v. 39 the people "turned" their minds back to Egypt. As a result God "turned" (v. 42). At the beginning of v. 39 the relative style still prevails—disobedience was directed toward Moses rather than God—but he ceases to be the primary subject thereafter. "Our ancestors"[139] willfully—rather than through ignorance—disobeyed Moses. In heart and mind, they returned to Egypt, a symbol of moral and religious depravity. In the absence of Moses—yet again one must ask what sense the narrative would make to readers unfamiliar with the story—they petition Aaron to construct some idols, to which entities they offer solemn worship. The irony is devastating, no less so because the narrative omits any reference to the subsequent punishment and return to obedience (Exod 32:7–34:28). Verse 39 cements the link with the earlier rejection (v. 27) by repeating the same verb (ἀπωθέω, "rebuff").[140] Verse 40 picks up, with slight modification, a rhetorically effective anacoluthon from Exod 32:2, which includes an ironic (in this context) οὗτος ("this fellow"). At this point (v. 41) the speaker

of an angel"), is simply embarrassing, since this preposition is used for accompaniment rather than instrument. BDAG, 1083, *s.v.* χείρ 2 b δ, suggests "with the help of an angel." See also BDF §217 (2), and, on the anarthrous "angel," §270 (3).

131 Compare and contrast *As. Mos.* 3:11. "Moyses . . . qui multa passus est in Aegypto et in mari rubro et in heremo annis xl" ("Moses . . . who suffered many things in Egypt and in the Red Sea and in the desert over forty years").

132 Mark 9:4, 7 parr. (the transfiguration); Luke 7:39; 24:25; John 1:21; 5:46. Most cogently, it is central to the speech of Acts 3 and cited in 3:22.

133 Johnson (135) finds this theme to be a key feature of Lucan theology.

134 So Fitzmyer, 380.

135 Christian believers would understand this word (ἐκκλησία) as a prototype of their assemblies (although it is common in the LXX).

136 Translation of λόγια ζῶντα is difficult. One regrets that the "lively oracles" of the Authorized Version will no longer suffice. On the noun, see Rudolf Kittel, "λόγιον," *TDNT* 4:137–41. The participle may mean "oral," in the sense of the "living voice" of oral tradition, which ancients tended to prefer to written texts (from Plato *Phaedr.* 276a-c onward; cf. Philo *Spec. leg.* 4.149 and Papias [Eusebius *H.E.* 3.39.4], in reference to his exposition of "the Oracles [λογία] of the Lord"). Another possibility is that these oracles convey "life" to those who obey them. The word could also mean "of enduring effect," on which note Sophocles *Oed. tyr.* 841–42 (μαντεῖα . . . ζῶντα).

137 Cadbury and Lake (78) base this suggestion on Hebrew idiom, of which there are no examples in translation. Bruce (202) and Barrett (1:365–66) reject this possibility. Conzelmann (54) rejects the Hebrew idiom, but states that Moses is viewed as a mediator. Luke may have so understood this, via Gal 3:19-20. See Pervo, *Dating*, 77–78.

138 The evidence between "to us" and "to you" is divided. Metzger (*Textual Commentary*, 306) says that "you" is an Alexandrian change. The first person is slightly preferable.

139 There is the usual MS. fluctuation between "our" and "your," with some probability for the former. D alone has ὅτι ("because") instead of the relative "to whom." This is an infelicitous change, possibly an accidental error. The other D-Text differences in v. 39 (Boismard, *Texte*, 139) are stylistic improvements.

140 Paul will have the same experience. Acts 13:46 uses

abandons citation of Exodus for a brief summary.[141] "Rejoiced in their handiwork": "hand" and "make" reverberate throughout.[142] By inference, innuendo, and insinuation, the temple of Solomon (and its successors) is drawn into the belly of the golden calf.[143]

■ **42** The verse leaps into prophetic condemnation of idolatry.[144] The citation from Amos[145] is a comment on the idolatry described in vv. 39-42b; similarly, the citation from Isaiah in vv. 49-50 comments on vv. 44-47. Because the people had turned their backs on the true worship of God (v. 39), God turned away from them[146] and delivered them[147] to veneration of heavenly bodies.[148] The pattern is like that of the critiques of *gentiles* in Wis 14:21-31 and Rom 1:18-28,[149] withholding the consequence until v. 51: Abandonment of the true God leads to idolatry, which leads, in turn, to immorality.[150] Amos 5:25 disagrees with the pentateuchal tradition about sacrifices during the wilderness period. In this context the meaning is that the people sacrificed to other gods. The citation generally follows the LXX.[151] In place of "Damascus," Acts has "Babylon."[152] To rub in the polemic, the text glosses the purposes for which the images were made: worship. The vital words for the author are *τύπους*, which means "images" in the citation but can also mean "model" and "tent." These two terms will provide the links to the subsequent section.

■ **44-50** Equipped with the proper tent ("the wilderness tabernacle"), fashioned (*ποιέω*) in accordance with the model (*τύπος*) supplied by God, the people went from triumph to triumph, until David, who, like Joseph

this verb of the rejection of Paul's message by Jews in Pisidian Antioch, followed by "turn," as in 7:39.

141 On the anacoluthon, see BDF §466 (1). D-texts and others (D E Ψ m; Cyr) read "happened" in the perfect (*γέγονεν*). Since this deviates from the LXX, it is quite possibly more original than the aorist *ἐγένετο*. "They made a calf" (*ἐμοσχοποίησαν*), a NT *hapax legomenon*, illustrates the present limits of knowledge about Hellenistic Judaism, in which environment the word was almost certainly coined, for it appears four times in Justin *Dial.* (e.g., 19.5) and the related noun is used by Clement, Origen, and later writers (Lampe, 886, *s.vv.*), but there are no attestations of Jewish (or other) usage.

142 "Hand": the hand of Moses, v. 25, and the hand of an angel, v. 35, contrast with the idolatrous hands of v. 41. The "hand of God" made (*ποιέω*) all (v. 50), contrasting with the manufacture (*μοσχοποιέω*; cf. v. 40: *ποίησον ἡμῖν θεούς*) of the calf in v. 41, the manufactured images of v. 43, and the view that God inhabits artifacts (*χειροποιήτοις*), v. 48.

143 Similarly, Marcel Simon, "Saint Stephen and the Jerusalem Temple," *JEH* 2 (1951) 127–42, esp. 127.

144 The opening of v. 42 may reflect Rom 1:24, 26, 28.

145 Cop[mae] reads "Amos the prophet." Instead of "the Book of the Prophets." See the comments on 2:16.

146 "Turned" (*ἔστρεψεν* [v. 42]) could be transitive ("cause to turn") or intransitive ("changed," "turned away"). Barrett (1:368) says that the transitive usage is more common, but he prefers the intransitive. Because of the parallel with v. 39 the intransitive seems preferable. See Haenchen, 283; and Bruce, 203. The D-Text makes this verb definitely transitive by adding the object "them" (Boismard, *Texte*, 139).

147 The same verb (*παραδίδωμι*) is used for the "betrayal" of Jesus and his delivery to the authorities (Mark 3:19; 9:31; etc.)

148 The "heavenly army" (*στρατιὰ τοῦ οὐρανοῦ*) refers to the actual planets and stars and, by metonymy, to the supernatural powers that govern them. Cf. 3 Kgdms 22:19; Jer 7:18; 19:13; Neh 9:6 (LXX).

149 On Romans 1, see n. 144 above. Luke regards ignorance as an excuse for gentiles (17:22-31). He can use the condemnatory approach here because the Israelites could not appeal to ignorance.

150 Those familiar with Exodus (e.g., 32:6) would know that immorality had gone hand in hand with idolatry in the wilderness, but Luke does not make that point here.

151 For details, see Barrett, 1:368–71. The major difference from the MT is due to different pointing of "Sakkuth your king" (5:25), interpreted as "the tent of Moloch." (*CD* 7.15 also construes סכות as "tent.") The spelling of "Rompha" varies greatly. See Ropes, *Text*, 70. (On this god, see Marten Stol, "Kaiwan," *DDD*, 478.) On the origin of the obscure "Rompha," see H. Klein, "Wie wird aus Kaiwan ein Romfan? Eine textkritische Miszelle zu Apg 7,42f.," *ZNW* 97 (2006) 139–40.

152 Richard (*Acts 6*, 126) reports that "most commentators" view this as "a post-exilic correction." See also his n. 233. Rather than postexilic, it is more likely to reflect the post-70 situation. After the fall of Jerusalem, "Babylon" became a code word for Rome: 1 Pet 5:13; Rev 14:8; 16:19; 17:5; 18:2, 10, 21; *2 Bar.* 11:1; 67:7; *4 Ezra* 3:1; 28:31; *Sib. Or.* 5:143–59. The narrator implies a parallel between the Babylonian captivity and the more recent Roman destruction of Jerusalem.

(v. 10) found "favor" (χάρις) with God.[153] With carefully chosen words the narrator tiptoes around the biblical account of David's unworthiness to build the temple. Solomon did the building, and it was not a completely salutary act, as the prophet had warned.[154] The implication is that, if a tent were good enough for God and Moses, it should have been good enough for Solomon.[155] Put more sharply, the speech suggests a parallel between the rejection of Moses that led to idolatry in the wilderness and the replacement of the wilderness worship facility with a permanent building. There is no room here for such subtleties as denouncing as an abuse the claim that God "dwells" in the temple; this does not abrogate the use. The argument attributed to Stephen would have offended Jews.[156]

■ **44-46** These verses resume (and complete) the historical summary in one long, awkward sentence. One source of awkwardness is the desire to place "tent of testimony"[157] first.[158] That tent served during the wilderness period and while the people were gaining control of the land. It was certainly good enough for Moses, for its designer was God, who communicated its structure and appointments in a vision (cf. vv. 2 and 30).[159] Verse 44 suggests that the author (or his source) was familiar with the Hellenistic Jewish world of thought developed by Philo and in Hebrews.[160] From this, Luke appropriated only the view that the wilderness tabernacle was of heavenly origin. Verse 45 affirms, laboriously enough, that this state of affairs lasted through the time of David.[161] "God liked David,[162] and . . ." The nature of

153 "Tent": note 15:16 (James's citation of Amos's reference to the "fallen tent of David").

154 A number of philosophers opposed the idea of buildings for a deity. Examples include the Stoic Zeno; Diogenes Laertius 7.33; Plutarch *Stoic. rep.* 6 (*Mor.* 1034b); Clement of Alexandria *Strom.* 5.11; and Origen *Cels.* 1.5. Plato had reservations: Plato *Leg.* 955E–956B; Cicero *Leg.* 2.18.45, Clement (as previous), and Eusebius *Praep. ev.* 3.18. See also Squires, *Plan*, 67 n. 156.

155 See Huub Van de Sandt, "The Presence and Transcendence of God: An Investigation of Acts 7,44-50 in Light of the LXX," *EThL* 80 (2004) 30–59.

156 Those who argue that the speech does not criticize the temple (such as Hill, *Hellenists*, 79–80; Tannehill, *Narrative Unity*, 2:92–93; and Witherington, 261–64) supply material the text lacks. Hill states: "the tabernacle was also handmade" (79). This is correct, but Acts does not make that point. On the next page he observes: "David, whose idea it was to construct the temple, is treated favorably and is not chastised for his wish" (80). Acts 7:46 does not, however, report these events. Tannehill says: "Stephen warns against any implied restriction of God to the temple" (93). If this were true the speech would say something like, "Do not imagine that God is limited to the temple." Appeal to the positive view of the temple in Luke 1–2 (e.g., Witherington, 262) neglects Luke's view of the unfolding course of salvation history. Finally, this interpretation makes it difficult to understand why Stephen was killed.

157 The expression σκηνὴ τοῦ μαρτυρίου is a LXX phrase used for two Hebrew expressions, meaning "tent for meeting" and "tent for testimony" (e.g., Exod 29:10; Num 1:50. 𝔓[74] 33 326 *pc* omit "our." This is probably secondary (see v. 45, where there is no variant).

158 Readers who viewed vv. 42-43 as historical summary might imagine that there were two tents in the wilderness, that of Moloch and the tent of testimony, but the narrator probably wishes to stress the antithesis between the two.

159 Boismard (*Texte*, 140) prefers the perfect ἑώρακεν to the pluperfect. The important fact is that the verb comes from the perfect system, indicating an enduring effect.

160 It is possible, although not demonstrable, that the author of Acts knew Hebrews. Heb 8:5 cites Exod 25:40, to which v. 44 clearly alludes. Philo *Vit. Mos.* 2.74, 76 says that Moses "saw with the soul's eye (ἰδέας τῇ ψυχῇ θεωρῶν) the immaterial forms of the material objects. . . . So the shape of the model (τύπος τοῦ παραδείγματος) was stamped upon the mind of the prophet, a secretly painted or moulded prototype, produced by immaterial and invisible forms" (trans. F. H. Colson, *Philo VI* [LCL; Cambridge, Mass.: Harvard University Press, 1935] 485–87). The word παράδειγμα ("example") comes from Exod 25:9; τύπος ("model") from 25:40. ("Seeing with the eye of the soul" is Platonic.) On the subject, see Harold W. Attridge, *The Epistle to the Hebrews: A Commentary on the Epistle to the Hebrews* (Hermeneia; Philadelphia: Fortress, 1989) 219–20, on Heb 8:5, as well as his excursus on the heavenly temple (222–24).

161 Cadbury and Lake (80) say that the thesis resides in the participle διαδεξάμενοι ("in succession"), but this may have no more than adverbial force (Barrett, 1:371). For the LXX texts on which this is based, see Richard, *Acts 6*, 189, but he is more impressed with internal correspondences within

this καί is uncertain. It may be a bland connective, as usual, or it could have the nuance of result ("and so . . ."). The inspiration for the second half of v. 46 is the synonymous parallelism of Ps 131:5: ἕως οὗ εὕρω τόπον τῷ κυρίῳ, σκήνωμα τῷ θεῷ Ιακωβ ("until I *find* a place for the Lord, a *habitation* for the God *of Jacob*."). The benefits of this text for Luke were the ambiguous words "find"[163] and "habitation" (σκήνωμα), the importance of which emerges in the unambiguous "built a house" of the next verse. Despite the general meaning of σκήνωμα, it resembles "tent" (σκηνή). The speech avoids saying tout court that David's plan to build a temple was thwarted. Interpretation bears on—and is strongly influenced by—the text of the final two words.

■ **46** The options are "house of Jacob" and "God of Jacob." "House" has better MS. support (𝔭[74], ℵ*, B, D, H, 049, *pc* sa[ms]), a wide range of strong witnesses. "House" is also stronger on the grounds that "God" assimilates to the LXX. "House" is a leitmotif of this speech and is therefore a likely Lucan contribution.[164] The strongest support for "God" is the pronoun αὐτῷ ("for him") in v. 47. The logical antecedent—almost the only possible antecedent—for this is "God": Solomon built a house for God. This argument is reversible: "house" is the more difficult reading, altered to conform to v. 47. It is easier to conceive how scribes might alter "house" to "God" than vice versa.[165] In a case so strongly approaching *non liquet*, it is unwise to use a text-critical decision as the basis for interpretation.

■ **47-50** The verse is slightly adversative: "Now Solomon went ahead and did it." On the bases of vv. 48-50, Solomon's action must be judged a mistake. Learned Jews, at least, would have viewed the contention that God inhabits the temple as blasphemous. Stephen attacks a creature of straw, but the obvious thrust of vv. 48-50 is against the temple itself. The speech is doubtless informed by "enlightened" tendencies to spiritualize worship, but the driving force here is, as Conzelmann says, not Greek rationalism but the application of Israelite critiques of polytheism and its practices to the Jews.[166] *Sib. Or.* 4:8-11 says much the same as Acts 7:48, but it is a critique of polytheism.[167] Paul delivers the same message in Athens (17:24).[168] Jews and gentiles occupy a level playing field. Both must be instructed on the futility of erecting houses for God. This message is for the reader of the book and fits Luke's general program, but Luke has evidently utilized early Christian apologetic tradition, for *Barnabas* makes the same argument, supported by the same citation, with a shared variant:

> I will also speak to you about the Temple, since those wretches were misguided in hoping in the building rather than in their God who made them, as if the Temple were actually the house of God (οἶκον θεοῦ). 2 For they consecrated him in the Temple almost like [*sic*] the Gentiles do. But consider what the Lord says

the speech. The clearest of these is κατάσχεσις ([dis]possession), found in v. 5. The pledge to Abraham was fulfilled.

162 Lit. "[David] found favor in God's sight." On this LXX phrase, see Richard, *Acts 6*, 131 n. 245. "Favor" (χάρις) echoes v. 10 (Joseph).

163 On the phrase "asked to find" (lit.), see BDF §409 (5).

164 See p. 180 n. 61.

165 In support of "house," see Metzger, *Textual Commentary*, 308–9, with extensive discussion; Cadbury and Lake, 81; Schneider, 1:466; Barrett, 1:372; and Jervell, 344. The majority prefer "God": Ropes, *Text*, 72 (with caution); Bruce, 206, with numerous references; Haenchen, 285; Conzelmann, 56; Kilgallen, *Stephen Speech*, 29–30; Richard, *Acts 6*, 131–32, with numerous references; and Fitzmyer, 383. Boismard (*Texte*, 140) takes "house" as the "Alexandrian" form and "God" as the D-Text.

166 Conzelmann, 56. Third Isaiah, cited here (vv. 49-50 = Isa 66:1-2) expresses sentiments not unlike those of the Greek philosophers and intellectuals.

167 "[*I am not a false seer but a prophet*] . . . of the great God, whom no hands of men (χερὶ θνητῇ) fashioned / in the likeness of speechless idols of polished stone. / For he does not have a house (οἶκον), a stone set up as a temple" (trans. John J. Collins, *OTP* 1:384).

168 ὁ θεὸς ὁ ποιήσας τὸν κόσμον καὶ πάντα τὰ ἐν αὐτῷ, οὗτος οὐρανοῦ καὶ γῆς ὑπάρχων κύριος οὐκ <u>ἐν χειροποιήτοις ναοῖς κατοικεῖ</u> ("The God who fashioned the universe and all that is does not, as sovereign over heaven and earth, dwell in temples of human manufacture"). The underlined words are also found in 7:48-50.

in order to invalidate it: [A citation of Isa 40:12 is followed by Isa 66:1] (*Barn.* 16:1-2)[169]

The citation[170] speaks for itself while resonating with earlier passages. "Footstool" evokes v. 5, intimating that the circle is approaching completion. Note also the occurrence in this citation of the resonant terms "house," "place," and "hand." Verse 50 asserts one ground of the Christian apologetic argument: creation requires universalism. Once again similarity to the Areopagus address (17:22-31) is apparent. The speech does not make this point, but it is essential to the underlying argument and would be cogent only for those who had swallowed the doctrine of universalism whole.[171]

■ **51-53** The attack here becomes direct, with a new posture and a different subject. The speaker distinguishes himself from the Jewish people and presents a new theme. The Israelites have always done away with prophets.[172] Although opposition to God's elect leaders was apparent in the story of Joseph (vv. 9-16) and manifest in the career of Moses (vv. 17-43), the subject of murder emerges for the first time. This permits a reference to the death of Jesus, an act that demonstrates the tribunal's solidarity with its predecessors. On those grounds, Stephen can now take up the question of Torah directly. His judges have not kept it.[173]

This peroration begins with epithets derived from the wilderness tradition.[174] The harsh style is appropriate when addressing the intractable.[175] "Uncircumcised" (v. 51) recalls v. 8 (covenant of circumcision), and v. 57 will give "ears" a certain piquancy. After v. 51a the speech abandons close links to the LXX.[176] Resistance to the Holy Spirit has specific reference to the prophetic spirit, as v. 52 indicates. The notion that the Israelites persecuted the prophets has its roots in the Deuteronomic tradition. In early Judaism, it gained momentum and literary support.[177] The theme is prominent in the Q-tradition (see Luke 6:23b; 11:47-50). To this tradition, Luke adds in v. 52b a specifically Christian apologetic notion: the prophets were killed to suppress their predictions of the advent of the Messiah.[178] Since murder is a clear violation of the God-given Decalogue,[179] Stephen has an egregious example of nonobservance[180] with which to flail his hearers. Their response to Jesus was entirely predictable and utterly characteristic. Little

169 Trans. Ehrmann, *Apostolic Fathers*, 2:71. Both Acts and *Barnabas* read ἤ τίς τόπος instead of καὶ ποῖος τόπος (both meaning "what [sort of] place"). An intertextual explanation is unlikely. See James Carleton Paget, *The Epistle of Barnabas: Outlook and Background* (WUNT 2.64; Tübingen: Mohr Siebeck, 1994) 172 n. 334.

170 Cop[mae] identifies the author as "Isaiah," in line with its proclivity. There are some minor variants, most of which are harmonizations with the LXX. Boismard (*Texte*, 141) includes a few harmonizations in his D-Text, but also some differences, which, although minor, would command attention were it not for *Barn.* 16:2.

171 On the subject, see Parsons and Pervo, *Rethinking*, 96–98, and the comments on 17:22-31 below.

172 Note Luke 13:34-35, which associates stoning the prophets with the loss of the temple.

173 Knox (*Hellenistic Elements*, 15) tabulates the quantity of "harsh consonants" (unvoiced stops and *X*) based on the rhetorical tradition.

174 Examples include Exod 33:3, 5; 34:9; Lev 26:41 (uncircumcised heart); Deut 9:6, 13, etc. Cadbury and Lake (82) note the combination of circumcision and hardheartedness in Deut 10:16. For "uncircumcised ears," see Jer 6:10. Richard (*Acts 6*, 137–38) provides details. Presumably the qualifiers (hearts and ears) apply to both. The absence of an article with "hearts" is unusual. Secondary traditions correct this perceived deficit.

175 Conzelmann (56) notes that martyrs may attack their persecutors, citing 2 Macc 7:14-19; *4 Macc.* 5–12.

176 Isa 63:10 is not the source of v. 51b.

177 On the lives of the prophets, see n. 20 and Odil Hannes Steck, *Israel und das gewaltsame Geschick der Propheten: Untersuchungen zur Überlieferung des deuteronomistischen Geschichtsbildes im Alten Testament, Spätjudentum und Urchristentum* (WMANT 23; Neukirchen-Vluyn: Neukirchener Verlag, 1967).

178 E.g., Cadbury and Lake, 83; Schneider, 1:469. The language reflects early-second-century usages: "coming" (ἔλευσις): *1 Clem.* 17:1; Polycarp *Phil.* 6:3. On "the Just one" as a christological title, see on 3:14.

179 Unlike Paul, from whom Luke has taken this phrase (Pervo, *Dating*, 77–78), the text assumes that angelic agency enhances the gift of the Torah. See Jer 9:25 LXX; Rom 2:27-29; Heb 2:2; as well as the discussion in Bruce, 209; and Barrett, 1:378. BDF §206 (1) classifies the surprising εἰς διαταγάς as the equivalent of instrumental ἐν (whence

doubt can remain about their disposition of the present case.

Those who hold that Stephen's speech is critical of temple and Torah have a better argument than do their adversaries, but that argument is largely extraneous to the author's project.[181] The very existence of this argument and the data that can be mustered on either side are due to the complexity of the bridge that Luke is constructing to span the vast chasm between Israelite religion and gentile Christianity. His Stephen is certainly no Marcion, nor is he a James. Indeed, he is not even a Paul. He is, as represented in this speech, entirely a creature of his maker, Luke. Precisely because he does not represent the apostles, James, or Paul, Stephen can give voice to views about which Acts is elsewhere silent. The temple is long gone and this is no tragedy, for it belonged to an earlier era. The world is God's temple.[182] Although he does not say it in so many words, the Decalogue ("moral law") remains valid, while "ceremonial law," much of it related to the temple cult, is not binding on Christians.[183] The same judgment applies to male circumcision, about which Luke is slightly more explicit.[184] Despite its circumcision, Israel is uncircumcised in heart and ears; Israelites always resist the Holy Spirit. If resisting the Spirit implies that circumcision has become uncircumcision, receiving the Spirit can imply that the uncircumcised can participate in the promises (Acts 10:45; 11:2-3). The implicit theological assumption is that charismatic phenomena bestow legitimacy. The Jesus movement is valid because God has bestowed on it the Spirit. Most Jews, certainly those of the dramatic audience, would not agree that spiritual gifts can nullify Torah. Acts 7:2-53 is, in short, not an effort to deal with issues between Christians and Jews. It justifies the separation of the two bodies in the light of subsequent intra-Christian debate.

Excursus: Popular Justice in the Ancient Mediterranean World

Lynching, which is far from extinct and has left an indelible stain on the American conscience, held an established place in the ancient Mediterranean world. Reasons for this standing include the general absence of a criminal justice system, including police and prosecutors,[185] a prevailing sense of purity, which required the community to act in concert to remove defilement;[186] and the related notion that

the translation "through angelic agency"). On the translation, see also Fitzmyer, 386.

180 φυλάσσω refers to Torah observance in Luke 11:28; 18:21; Acts 16:4; 21:24. The noun "angel" neatly rounds off a series of references in vv. 6:15; 7:30, 35, 38. Stephen is the one who looks like an angel at present. The claim that Jews do not keep the law derives from Paul (Gal 6:13).

181 Esteemed representatives of each view produced successive editions of commentaries in the KEK series: Haenchen (289–90) stresses the polemic against Judaism, and Jervell (249–50) rejected that interpretation.

182 Emergent rabbinic Judaism accepted the same principle, as it were, and applied the purity codes of temple worship to all of daily life everywhere. In neo-orthodox terms, God is free to do with or without a temple. Cf. Tannehill, *Narrative Unity*, 2:93. For ancient views of the universe as a temple, see n. 160; cf. Ps.- Heraclitus *Ep.* 7.

183 Compare Justin, who divides the precepts of the law into three parts: those about the worship of God and virtuous living, those pertaining to the "mystery of Christ," and those imposed because of the Jews' hardness of heart (*Dial.* 44; cf. 45). The *Letter of Ptolemy to Flora* also sets forth a tripartite definition of the law, further subdivided. The Decalogue is God's pure law (Epiphanius *Pan.* 33.4–5). Cf. also the Pseudo-Clementine understanding of true and false (male/female) prophecy and of interpolations in the Torah (e.g., *Hom.* 2.38; 3.47). These are varying refractions of an early Christian apologetic principle. Marcel Simon comes to a similar conclusion, although he may draw more from the speech than is there (*St. Stephen and the Hellenists in the Primitive Church* [New York: Longmans, Green, 1958] 48–51). What he attributes to the historical Stephen, as it were, I regard as due to Lucan theological assumptions (albeit not without influence from earlier constructions).

184 See pp. 164–84.

185 The "lawless" American West of the nineteenth century provides an apposite analogy to this situation. For evidence and discussion, see Wilfried Nippel, *Public Order in Ancient Rome* (Key Themes in Ancient History; Cambridge: Cambridge University Press, 1995).

186 The concept was not that one bad apple could spoil a bushel through gradually spreading corruption but that the entire bushel was contaminated because of the presence of a single bad apple. It is well illustrated by Heb 12:20, which summa-

manifest crime should be punished immediately by collective action.

Jews under Roman rule (and perhaps under the preceding Hellenistic monarchies) lacked capital jurisdiction. Torrey Seland has argued that Philo's discussions of Torah passages on vigilantism are not simply hypothetical but relate to actual practice.[187] People might "take the law into their own hands" because law was lacking and/or because they viewed this as a religious and civic duty.[188] In the Greek and Jewish worlds stoning was a hallowed form of vigilantism, as it provided for universal participation and left a useful monument of misdeed and requital.[189] The Mishnah includes detailed instructions for death by stoning following a proper trial (*m. Sanh.* 6).[190] Not every reference to stoning or other forms of vigilantism would have been viewed as the unlawful actions of a misguided mob, although those with apologetic interests may have preferred to portray them as such.[191]

If the (presumably) historical Stephen died by stoning, his executioners would have maintained that they were carrying out a lawful act against a grievous sinner regardless of any shortcomings in judicial procedure. The same is patently true of that mob which sought to lynch Paul in the temple (21:27-36).

---

rizes the command of Exod 19:12-13 to stone any creature that approaches the mountain. Cf. also Apuleius *Metam.* 1.10.1 (stoning of a witch) and Philostratus *Vit. Apoll.* 4.10 (stoning of a demon in the theater).

187 Torrey Seland, *Establishment Violence in Philo and Luke: A Study of Non-Conformity to the Torah and Jewish Vigilante Reactions* (BIS 15; Leiden: Brill, 1995).

188 Cf. Apuleius *Metam.* 10.6.3, in which a father so inflames the civic assembly by (false) reports of his son's adultery with his stepmother and fratricide that the people demand waiver of a trial and cry "in unison that this curse on the people should be punished by the people, crushed under a rain of stones" (trans. J. Arthur Hanson, Apuleius, *Metamorphoses* [LCL; Cambridge, Mass.: Harvard University Press, 1989] 2:227).

189 As a formal ritual, stoning engaged the entire community in a rite of removing the source of impurity. See Walter Burkert, *Homo Necans: The Anthropology of Ancient Greek Sacrificial Ritual and Myth* (trans. Peter Bing; Berkeley: University of California Press, 1983) 5, 55, and 183; Gregory Nagy, *The Best of the Achaeans* (Baltimore: Johns Hopkins University Press, 1979) 280–90, esp. 280; Richard Pervo, "A Nihilist Fabula: Introducing the *Life of Aesop*," in Ronald F. Hock, J. Bradley Chance, and Judith Perkins, eds., *Ancient Fiction and Early Christian Narrative* (SBLSS 6; Atlanta: Scholars Press, 1998) 77–120, esp. 115–18; and Arthur Stanley Pease, "Notes on Stoning among the Greeks and Romans," *TAPA* 38 (1907) 5–18. Nippel (*Public Order*, 43 n. 389) observes that the preferred Roman technique, at least in military situations, involved tearing the condemned to pieces by hand. Stoning was often a spontaneous form of lynching (John 10:31-33; 11:8; Acts 5:26; 14:19). Any who threatened the community were liable to such assault. See Ramsay MacMullen, *Roman Social Relations: 50 B.C. to A.D. 284* (New Haven: Yale University Press, 1974) 66 and his nn. 30–31, 171. Other examples are Josh 7:25 (Achan; cf. the discussion of Acts 5:1-11); 1 Kgs 21:8-14; Josephus *Ant.* 14.22–25 (the godly Onias, stoned by a mob during a siege of the temple, c. 65 BCE); Chariton *Chaer.* 1.5.4; 8.14.4; Apuleius *Metam.* 1.10; 2.28; 4.6; 10.6; Lucian *Peregr.* 15; 19; *Alex.* 45; *Apollonius of Tyre* 50; Philostratus *Vit Apoll.* 1.16; 4.8; *Act. Paul* 2; *Act. Phil.* 6.9–10; *Ethiopian Story* 1.13.4, and the Hero of Temesa, a sailor of Odysseus who was stoned to death for sexual misconduct and later heroized (Pausanius 6.6.7–11; Strabo 6.1.5; Aelian *Var. hist.* 8.18). Note also W. Michaelis, "λιθάζω," *TDNT* 4:267–68.

190 Other such constitutions existed. Euripides' *Orestes*, for example, envisions that the civic assembly at Argos might order that Orestes and Electra be killed by stoning.

191 Acts 5:26 and 14:5 envision mob actions, and 14:19-20 probably fit this category. See also 2 Cor 11:25; Matt 21:35; Luke 13:34 (Q); John 10:31-33; 11:4; Heb 11:37; Ps.-John 8:5.

7

7:54–8:3 Stephen's Martyrdom

54/ The audience gnashed their teeth in rage at his slashing words. 55/ Stephen, on the other hand, was brimming with inspiration. He gazed upward and saw the nimbus of divinity and Jesus standing to God's right.[a]
56/ "I see heaven revealed,"[b] he proclaimed. "The Son of Man[c] is standing at the right side of God."
57/ At this his hearers shrieked, stopped their ears, and rushed at him en masse. 58/ They thrust Stephen outside of the city limits and proceeded to stone him. The witnesses left their coats in the care of a young man named Saul.[d] 59/ As he was being pelted with stones, Stephen invoked the Lord, saying, "Lord Jesus, accept my spirit." 60/ He then knelt and, after crying out in a loud voice, "Lord, do not hold this sin against them," Stephen died.
8:1/ Saul was in favor of this murder. That same day[e] saw the beginning of a virulent persecution of the church in Jerusalem. All but the apostles fled into the countryside[f] of Judea and Samaria. 2/ Some devout men buried Stephen[g] and raised a loud lament over his body. 3/ Saul began to wreak havoc against the church. He entered one house after another to drag out both men and women and toss them into jail.

a D-Texts read "the Lord Jesus" and place the participle "standing" at the end (Boismard, *Texte*, 142).

b 𝔓[74] D (*) E Ψ 33 m read the more conventional ἀνεῳγμένους (cf. 10:11, e.g.).

c George Kilpatrick contended over many years (e.g., "Acts VII, 56: Son of Man?" *ThZ* 21 [1965] 209; idem, "Again Acts VII,56," *ThZ* 34 [1978] 232) and orally to those who met him that "Son of God" (p[74] 614 cop[mss] geo) was probably original, but it seems quite unlikely that editors would replace the mysterious "Son of Man" formula with the clear "Son of God" title. (Ancient critics might have observed that nowhere else does "Son of Man" occur on the lips of anyone but Jesus, but this is more likely to be the result of more recent scholarship.)

d The D-Text revises the last clause, without alteration of meaning (Boismard, *Texte*, 143). (Many authorities of the D-tradition (D gig p [t vg[mss]] sy[p]) read "a *certain* young man," which is better Greek.

e Possibly "At that time there was . . ." Verse 2 suggests prompt burial, however.

f "Countryside." So Cadbury and Lake, 87. "Regions" is also possible.

g Although the basic meaning of συγκομίζω is "bring in," it is a euphemism for burial; see BDAG, 952 *s.v.*, 2; and Barrett, 1:392. One might say, "[they] brought in Stephen's body and buried it." The D-Text simply says "buried" (ἔθαψαν; Boismard, *Texte*, 145).

Analysis

Stephen's prophetic denunciation of the Jewish people for killing prophets is verified by the audience reaction. They kill him. The martyrdom of Stephen has been shaped to conform to the passion of Jesus.[1] In addition to previously noted material from Mark utilized in 6:12-14, there are (1) the absence of a formal sentence (Luke 22:71 vs. Mark 14:64); (2) a climactic Son of Man saying (Luke 23:69; Acts 7:56); (3) a reference to garments (Luke 23:54; Acts 7:58); (4) the final words in a loud voice and a prayer (Luke 23:46; Acts 7:60); (5) the prayer for forgiveness of enemies (Luke 23:34; Acts 7:60), if the Lucan passage be admitted;[2] and (6) burial by "devout" person(s) (Luke 23:50-53; Acts 8:2). That this parallelism is due to Luke rather than to a source is highly likely, given the prevalence of Lucan vocabulary,[3] the absence of a judgment (1), and the similarity

1 Thomas L. Brodie has identified another possible source for this account: "The Accusing and Stoning of Naboth (1 Kgs 21:8-13) as One Component of the Stephen Text (Acts 6:9-14; 7:58a)," *CBQ* 45 (1983) 417–32.

2 See p. 107 n. 199.

3 For a detailed analysis of the Lucan nature of the vocabulary of this episode, see M. Sabbe, "The Son of Man Saying in Acts 7,56," in Kremer, *Actes*, 241–79.

between Luke 4:28-29 and Acts 7:54, 58. Luke 4:16-30 is an essentially Lucan composition foreshadowing the fate of Jesus and his followers, as well as the gentile mission. Like Stephen, Jesus so enrages a Jewish audience with his words (Luke 4:28; Acts 7:54) that they evict him from the city limits and attempt to administer popular justice.[4]

There is scant room remaining for external source material. Apart from 7:55, which, although its language is thoroughly Lucan, appears to link up with 6:15, there is ἐλιθοβόλουν ("They began to stone [him]," v. 58).[5] Although the repetition of the word in v. 59 could be a typical editorial device to resume the narrative after an insertion, other explanations are possible. There is little dispute that Acts 7:58b is Lucan.[6] It disrupts the context, as the repeated verb in v. 59 indicates. Acts 8:1a, "Saul approved of this murder," is likewise quite possibly Lucan. The verb συνευδοκέω appears five times in the New Testament: three in Luke/Acts and twice in Paul.

The literary technique becomes clear when one notes that vv. 53, 57, and 59 yield a smooth sequence. The narrator interrupts this flow twice, first to provide the report of Stephen's vision (vv. 55-56, with v. 54 as a prelude) and next to report the presence of Saul (v. 58b). Into this thin porridge of visible data about Stephen's end, Luke has stirred two ingredients, one encapsulating the story of Jesus, another introducing what will be his major character. The repetitions permit two literary touches: the "hearts and ears" of v. 51 are echoed in v. 54 ("hearts") and 57 ("ears"). The response confirms the reproach. The old theory that Luke blended two accounts, one describing a lynching, the other condemnation by the Sanhedrin,[7] is left without a basis. The alternatives are these: a formal trial that led to the execution of Stephen by the approved penalty of stoning[8] or a lynching that Luke transformed into a Sanhedrin trial, with the motives of constructing a martyrdom like that of Jesus, reviling the high court, and providing opportunity for a suitable oration. The latter solution best fits the data, scanty as they are.[9] Tradition evidently viewed Stephen as the victim of a mob of Greek-speaking Jews. For the author of Acts, his enemies had to be the same as those who had handed Jesus over to death and nearly executed the apostles.

---

4 Luke 4:28: ἀκούοντες ταῦτα; Acts 7:54: ἀκούοντες δὲ ταῦτα (lit. "after hearing these words"); Luke 4:29: ἐξέβαλον αὐτὸν ἔξω τῆς πόλεως; Acts 7:58: ἐκβαλόντες ἔξω τῆς πόλεως (lit. "They drove/driving [him] outside of the city"). Other similarities could be noted, including the presence of the Spirit (Luke 4:18; Acts 7:55) and "grace" (Luke 4:22; Acts 6:8). Execution by being thrown from a cliff was considered appropriate for those guilty of sacrilege and other heinous crimes. The Tarpeian Rock was used for this purpose in Rome, as was the *barathron* (a gully near the Acropolis) in Athens. Aesop was so executed at Delphi, according to the *Life of Aesop* 132, as a blasphemer. See also n. 7.

5 Lüdemann provides the evidence for viewing most of 7:54-60 as Lucan in theme and style.

6 The conclusion of Lüdemann (91) is typical.

7 Cadbury and Lake (84) consider a two-source hypothesis and Barrett (1:382–84) accepts it. It is possible that Luke was also inspired by Josephus's account of the death of James (*Ant.* 20:200–201). The common elements are convocation of an assembly of judges (συνέδριον κριτῶν), death by stoning, and disapproval by some of the observers (cf. Acts 8:2). All of these elements, except stoning, are part of the Jesus tradition, making use of Josephus unlikely. Eusebius states that Clement reported that James was thrown from the pinnacle of the temple and clubbed to death (*H.E.* 2.1.4). His later account, allegedly derived from Hegesippus, includes an affirmation (in a loud voice) that the Son of Man is seated in heaven on the right hand of the great power (= God) and will come again. The source of this is Mark 14:62, but influence from Acts seems likely. Eusebius has probably expanded the material from Hegesippus. See also the story of James's death in Ps.-Clem. *Rec.* 1.64–70, where influence from Acts is probable. The temple pinnacle probably derives from the temptation of Jesus (Luke 4:9||Matthew 4:5; cf. also Luke 4:28-29).

8 Torrey Seland (*Establishment Violence in Philo and Luke: A Study of Non-Conformity to the Torah and Jewish Vigilante Reactions* [BIS 15; Leiden: Brill, 1995]) defends the position that Stephen was legally executed. See the review by Richard Pervo, *The Studia Philonica Annual* 8 (1996) 208–10. Löning ("Circle of Stephen," 113–14) proposes that such a legal execution could have taken place in 36, under Marcellus, sent by A. Vitellius, governor of Syria, as a replacement for Pilate, whom he had removed. Little is known about this person, who, even if

Comment

■ **54-56** The initial verse repeats the same body's reaction to a speech of the apostles (διαπρίοντο, "they were infuriated").[10] On this occasion, Gamaliel will not intervene. Oblivious to their discontent, Stephen is inspired to receive a vision,[11] narrated indirectly in v. 55 and directly in v. 56.[12] Repetition is one form of emphasis; here it allows both the reliable narrator's view and Stephen's actual words to emerge. Stephen is well endowed with that which his hearers always resist (v. 51). In a moment they will confirm that resistance. He sees the "glory of God," a nice inclusion with the first words of his address (7:2, lit. "God of glory").[13] The saying derives from Luke 22:69[14] and is therefore not an independently transmitted tradition. It functions here both to confirm that Jesus is the heavenly Son of Man and that Stephen is about to be received into glory. The vision and saying vindicate both Jesus and Stephen against their critics, at least for the readers. The vision raises two questions. One asks why the usually seated Son of Man (as in Luke 22:69) is depicted as *standing*. The second is whether this vision portrays an individualizing eschatology. Little can be made of the former, although scholars have made many proposals about its meaning.[15] Verse 59 shows that an individualistic approach to eschatology is in view. From both "parables" (Luke 12:16-20; 16:9) and narrative (e.g., Luke 23:43), it appears that Luke views judgment as an individual postmortem experience.[16] He, like many Christians since, does not seek to integrate this belief with the notion of a final judgment.[17]

The Martyrdom of Polycarp explains that martyrs endure their torments with great nobility because the Lord stands by (παρεστώς) to comfort them (2:2). A vision warned Polycarp of his coming trial (5:2). Consoling visions would become a standard element of martyrological accounts.[18] Such reassurance distinguishes

temporary, was not lacking in authority. Schürer (*History*, 1:383) thinks that Marcellus may be the same person as Marullus, who was prefect of Judea until c. 41. E. Mary Smallwood views Marcellus as a temporary appointee (*The Jews under Roman Rule: From Pompey to Diocletian* [SJLA 20; Leiden: Brill, 1976], 171–72). Barrett (1:382) is properly dubious. The time frame is quite narrow and the date (late 36, possibly early 37) seems too late. On his death, see also Klaus Haacker, "Die Stellung des Stephanus in der Geschichte des Urchristentums," *ANRW* 2.26.2 (1995) 1415–53.

9 See Pervo, *Profit*, 44, 154; and idem, "My Happy Home: The Role of Jerusalem in Acts 1–7," *Forum* n.s. 3.1 (2000) 31–55, esp. 52–53, for data.

10 "Gnashing teeth" is a metonym for rage, often, in the LXX, for the fury of the unjust, e.g., Job 16:9; Ps 34:16; 36:12; 111:10; Lam 2:16.

11 The D-Text (Boismard, *Texte*, 142) begins ὁ δὲ ὑπάρχων ἐν πνεύματι ἁγίῳ ("but he, being in the Holy Spirit"). The first is an improvement over the conventional text, in which ὑπάρχων is technically circumstantial. "To be in the Holy Spirit" is not conventional. It is therefore tempting to view the weakly attested D-Text as original, but note Luke 4:1 (Jesus). See Ropes, *Text*, 74; and Cadbury and Lake, 83–84.

12 According to Aune (*Prophecy*, 270) this is a prophetic announcement of judgment.

13 Vision of God's glory (δόξα) is a form of authorization; see Isa 6:1, and note Acts 22:11. "Open heaven(s)" are the prelude to an epiphany (e.g., the baptism of Jesus in Luke 3:21) or other revelation (e.g., Acts 10:11).

14 See Sabbe, "Son of Man," 241–79. (Luke omits the Marcan reference to "coming with power.") Cf. also Luke 12:8-9.

15 See, e.g., Winter and Clarke, *Setting*, 84; Bruce, 210; Haenchen, 292 n. 4; Conzelmann, 59–60; Fitzmyer, 392–93; Johnson, 139; Barrett, 1:384–85; Talbert, 79; and, above all, Sabbe, "Son of Man," 267–75, with their references. Aune (*Prophecy*, 270) also notes the omission of "coming." He concludes that "standing" is a Lucan alteration of tradition. It is far from certain that this posture was important to Luke. It is appropriate for Jesus, as God's vindicated righteous one, to stand (Wis 5:1), and is also suitable for welcoming Stephen. Bede (38), citing Gregory the Great, related standing to the posture of assistance. Arator (1:610–12) stated that Jesus rose to greet the martyr. Subsequent exegetes have increased the options but not improved on the interpretation. Chrysostom (*Hom.* 18, 150) says that Stephen spoke of Jesus as standing because the idea of his session at God's right hand was offensive to Jews.

16 See p. 25.

17 Luke appears to regard humans as possessing an immortal element (the πνεῦμα ["spirit"] according to Luke 23:46; Acts 7:59). See Parsons and Pervo, *Rethinking*, 101.

18 *Asc. Isa.* 5.7 (which may be pre-Christian); *Act.*

the death of Christian martyrs from that of Jesus. Although some of the features of Stephen's execution were typical—tradition influenced accounts of the death of Jesus, after all—it is difficult to differentiate between such elements and the literary influence of this story on the Christian tradition.[19]

■ **57-58** Stephen's report propelled the audience into action. If he had more to say, the authorities did not permit him to continue. Emitting a loud cry, the judges blocked their ears, presumably to protect them from blasphemy. Those ears were, however, uncircumcised (v. 51). What they will not hear is the truth (as the narrator views it). In v. 60, Stephen will also cry loudly.[20] What the judges cried is unknown. Stephen's shout was a prayer for their forgiveness. A further irony is adverbial: they[21] charge upon him en masse (*ὁμοθυμαδόν*), a word often used to illustrate the unity of the community.[22] Without further ado, Stephen was hauled beyond the city limits and stoned. After an agonizing delay, the story has resumed a rapid pace. At this point, the narrator introduces a new character, "a young man named Saul."[23] As in the case of Barnabas (4:36-37), one who is to play a major role makes an unobtrusive entry onto the narrative stage.[24] Would a first reader—would the implied reader—know that Saul was also called "Paul"? Since Acts is the only source for the name "Saul,"[25] the more likely answer may be no. Youth suggests innocence, or at least inexperience, intimating that the story will tell of his learning and growth, his passage to experience. That expectation will be met in surprising ways.

"The witnesses" (v. 58)[26] placed their coats in Saul's care.[27] One would expect the victim's clothes to be removed. Perhaps the narrator envisions them removing their outer garments to gain ease of movement.[28]

■ **59-60** In typical martyrological style, Stephen appears unfazed by this brutal assault.[29] He has "two last words." The first is a prayer[30] that Jesus "receive his spirit." This is quite parallel to Luke 23:46, but the Lord Jesus takes

---

Paul 3.21; *Acta Carpi et al.* 4; *Acta Perpetuae et al.* 4. Prospective martyrs often look, like Stephen, upward toward heaven, e.g., *Acta Cononis* 5 (and Apollonius: Philostratus *Vit. Apoll.* 8.4). For other examples, see Cadbury and Luke, 84; Betz, *Lukian*, 132 n. 6; and Conzelmann, 51.

19 On the story of Stephen as a typical martyrdom story, see Pervo, *Profit*, 28–29, 149. For subsequent development of the story, see François Bovon, "Beyond the Book of Acts: Stephen, the First Christian Martyr, in Traditions outside the New Testament Canon of Scripture," *PerspRelStud* 32 (2005) 93–107.

20 Verses 57 and 60 use the same construction: *κράζω φωνῇ μεγάλῃ* (lit. "shout in a loud voice").

21 The D-Text begins *τότε ὁ λαὸς ἔκραξεν* ("*Then the people* cried out") and states that "*all* rushed" (Boismard, *Texte*, 143). This makes the Jewish public in general responsible for the lynching. See Epp, *Tendency*, 133–34.

22 Acts 1:14; 2:46; 4:24; 5:12. Its use in this context is not unusual. See Job 16:10 LXX; and Haenchen, 292 n. 7.

23 A *νεανίας* was a man between youth and maturity (c. twenty-four to fifty), but the other uses in Acts (Eutychus [20:9]; Paul's nephew [23:17]) lead modern readers, at any rate, to imagine someone closer to what we call late adolescence.

24 "The great example of S. Luke's dramatic sense is the first introduction of the chief actor as *a young man named Saul*" (Rackham, xxxiii).

25 The grecized form of "Saul," *Σαῦλος*, had the connotation of an exaggerated form of walking, particularly of males who wiggled their hips in an "effeminate" manner: Anacreon frg. 66b; 113; Aristophanes *Wasps* 1173; Lucian *Lex.* 10; and Clement *Paed.* 3.11.69. Josephus does not use this spelling for King Saul. It appears once in *Bell.* 2.418 for a member of the Herodian family. Since that same person's name is spelled *Σαοῦλος* in §556 (like the king), the earlier use may be a scribal error.

26 This term suggests a juridical execution, but one word will not establish the existence of a separate source. The narrator has the "false witnesses" of 6:13 in mind. The problem is solved by gig perp Ephr, which read "false witnesses" in v. 58 (Ropes, *Text*, 407).

27 This is another irony, as *παρὰ τοὺς πόδας* ("at the feet") was used for the gifts placed at the apostles' feet (4:35, 37; 5:2).

28 B *pc* read the emphatic "*their* garments." Ψ m gig have no modifier, possibly permitting the reader to think that Stephen's clothes were removed (but Greek does not require a possessive in such constructions).

29 Compare Jesus' behavior on the cross in Luke 23:27-35 (and John 19:16-30, both in contrast to Mark 15:20-37). Cf. *4 Macc.* 9–12; *Martyrs of Lyons* 16–20. *Mart. Pol.* 2:2 (cited above) provides a rationale.

30 The present participles *ἐπικαλούμενον καὶ λέγοντα* allow the possibility that this petition

the place of God. This prayer helps to interpret his vision (vv. 55-56). Prayers for reception are common at moments of death.[31] Piously kneeling,[32] in full control of body and mind, he begs God to forgive[33] his murderers and expires.[34] The "loud voice" echoes v. 57 ironically, and Luke 23:46 devoutly. The prayer for forgiveness corresponds to Luke 23:34 ("Then Jesus said, 'Father, forgive them; for they do not know what they are doing'"). The strong and widespread evidence against this verse leads N-A[27] to reject this verse in Luke, but not to exclude it. Metzger states that it cannot be "a deliberate excision" but that it "bears self-evident tokens of its dominical origin."[35] If it is judged not to be part of the Gospel, the verse should be relegated to a collection of noncanonical sayings of Jesus. Behind Metzger's view is the dogma, inherited from F. J. A. Hort, that there are no dogmatic alterations in the major MSS. of the NT. Epp rejects this dogma, with the support of Rendel Harris and Adolph Harnack.[36] It is far from improbable that scribes would delete Luke 23:34 on the grounds of anti-Jewish sentiment, specifically the belief that the Jewish people had not been forgiven for their responsibility in Jesus' death.[37] These two verses should be taken in tandem. One must either suppose that an editor took note of Acts 7:60, decided that what was appropriate for Stephen was at least as appropriate for Jesus, and then composed Luke 23:34 on its basis, transforming Stephen's prayer into more conventional language and, for good measure, adding the ignorance motif from Acts 3:17,[38] or one must suspect that Luke 23:34 was deleted because of the authority behind it (Jesus) and because it was absent from the other Gospels. Stephen's petition that his enemies not be held responsible for his death is another parallel with the passion of Jesus. Within the narrative it helps to till the ground for the conversion of Saul,[39] implying that "holding this sin against them" has the connotation of hardening their hearts against the truth.[40]

■ **8:1-3** Scholarship rejects the medieval division that begins a new chapter at 8:1a,[41] but that apparent infelicity stemmed from the realization that this section is one of Luke's hinges. Persecution is and will long remain the catapult that launches new missions.[42] In these verses, he weaves together Stephen's death, Paul's activity as a persecutor, and the beginning of the Diaspora mission. An orderly sequence would report that Stephen died and was buried. A general persecution then erupted, causing the believers to scatter, although the apostles did not flee. Paul followed up his role in the execution of Stephen by arresting believers. Problems arise from the abundance of narrative claims. Despite the "great persecution," right-thinking Jews did not approve of Stephen's execution. All but the apostles fled, but Paul can still find believers to incarcerate. Questions include: How could approximately twenty thousand refugees

was repeated during the stoning, but this is unlikely. The absolute use of ἐπικαλούμενον ("calling upon") is unusual. Perhaps the content of the prayer made it unnecessary to state the object.

31 One example is Lucian *Peregr.* 36. *Mart. Pionius* 21 imitates Acts.

32 Moule (*Idiom Book*, 192) classifies "kneel" as a latinism: *genua ponere* (lit. "place the knees").

33 On the meaning of μὴ στήσῃς, see Cadbury and Lake (86), who say that it is equivalent to ἄφες ("forgive"); BDAG §482, *s.v.*, 3 prefers "establish" (presumably in the sense of "place on their account").

34 The verb κοιμάω ("fall asleep") is a common euphemism for death (BDAG, 551, *s.v.*).

35 Metzger, *Textual Commentary*, 154.

36 Epp, *Tendency*, 45–46.

37 Although it is true that Luke 23:34b does not follow v. 34a smoothly, the same may be said of its relation to v. 33.

38 N-A[27] marks this passage with *p*), suggesting harmonization. Only Acts 7:60 so qualifies.

39 Kurz, *Reading*, 84.

40 That connotation may illuminate the use of μὴ στήσῃς ("do not hold against") rather than the direct "forgive."

41 This is a reversion to the older division of *kephalaia*, which mark a new section at 8:1b. For various modern divisions, see the segmentation apparatus in *GNT*[4], p. 435. Commentators vary. Cadbury and Lake (88), Haenchen (300), Johnson (144), Schneider (1:481), Pesch (1:268), Witherington (279), Talbert (82), and Jervell (257) have no break until 8:4. Bruce (40, 214) has a partial break at 8:1a and a full break at v. 1b. Roloff (128, 130) has these divisions: 8:1b; 8:4-25. Conzelmann (59) breaks at 8:4. Fitzmyer (396) treats 8:1b-4 as a unit.

42 See pp. 96–98.

find sanctuary in "Judea and Samaria"? Why did the persecutors neglect to attack the apostles, who were well known from their earlier encounters with the authorities (chaps. 3–5)? And how was Paul transformed from "hat-check boy" to a prime agent of persecution within a few days?

A prominent critical solution has been to posit a persecution of the "Hellenists."[43] This explains why the apostles did not seek asylum. They (as leaders of the "Hebrews") were not affected by it. Craig Hill has exposed the weaknesses of this position, which evaluates Acts 6:1—8:3 on the grounds of a division between two groups of believers,[44] a view not derived from the text (although it may be valid[45]). Those who assume this division do not take up the difficulty that no source was likely to have supported it and that the traditions Luke is alleged to have covered up probably did not exist. Even Paul, who was not reluctant to discuss intra-Christian arguments, takes pains to date conflict to a later period, following the Jerusalem conference (Gal 2:11-14). The gentile mission source was not likely to have claimed that the Seven carried out their work in the face of opposition from the apostles.

That source reported that the turmoil attending the death of Stephen led to a dispersal of those engaged in the mission to Greek-speaking Jews (11:19).[46] It may be permissible to describe this θλῖψις as a "persecution," but the term could just as well mean that Stephen's associates decided to leave Jerusalem rather than experience a similar fate. The "great persecution" of 8:1b is probably a Lucan creation. The only concrete evidence for it is Acts 8:3 (cf. also 26:10-11), and that datum conflicts with Paul's own statements.[47] The source apparently proceeded to a brief summary of Phillip's activity in Samaria and his subsequent move to Caesarea.

■ **8:1** The first part of the verse serves to keep Paul in view and to clarify his stance. He supported the execution of Stephen.[48] This is slight preparation for the role he will presently assume. "In Jerusalem" appears gratuitous, but it sets the stage for the subsequent expansion.[49] Luke wishes to keep the apostles in town because of v. 14. This requirement mitigates the view that the statement derives from a source. By positing a general and vigorous persecution, the author implicitly refutes the idea that Stephen's speech contained any views that distinguished him from the others. The apostles' avoidance of flight has the additional advantage of displaying their heroic fearlessness.[50]

■ **2** This is a Lucan composition creating a parallel to the burial of Jesus (Luke 23:39-45).[51] The narrator does

---

43 See, e.g., Haenchen, 297–98; and Hengel, *Between*, 25.

44 Hill, *Hellenists*, 32–40. See also pp. 152–56.

45 Hill's specific object was not to prove that there were no divisions but to challenge the constructs that oppose "conservative," observant Jewish Christianity to "liberal" Hellenistic Christianity.

46 The verb διασπείρω, which appears only in Acts 8:1, 4; and 11:19 in the NT, may derive from the source.

47 See below.

48 Cf. 22:10, which combines 7:58 and 8:1a, and Luke 11:48, a woe against the lawyers: "So you are *witnesses* and approve of [συνευδοκεῖτε, the same verb as in Acts 8:1] the deeds of your ancestors; for they killed them, and you build their tombs." The periphrastic ἦν συνευδοκῶν stresses an abiding conviction.

49 "Enormous persecution" (διωγμὸς μέγας) occurs only here in the NT. D-Texts (Bosimard, *Texte*, 144) begin "and in those days." This conforms to convention and disposes of questions about what "that day" means. D (h sa[mss] mae) read καὶ θλῖψις after "persecution." (h and cop[sa] place "affliction and" before.) This is a clever coordination with 11:19, but probably not original. (Mark 4:17, which is not in Luke, combines θλῖψις with διωγμός.) D-Texts also read "villages" (κώμας instead of χώρας, "countryside"). At the close 1175 adds μόνοι ("[apostles] only"). D* 1175 it sa[mss] cop[mae] pedantically add οἱ ἔμειναν ἐν Ἰερουσαλημ ("[apostles] who remained in Jerusalem"). These variants reveal the difficulties early readers found in v. 1.

50 The question of whether it was acceptable to go into hiding in times of persecution was hotly debated, especially in Africa. For Tertullian in his Montanist phase, it was unthinkable (*On Flight in Time of Persecution*). Cyprian exercised a pastoral judiciousness. (The story of Polycarp reveals no embarrassment on the subject [*Mart. Pol.* 4–7].) Apollonius declined to withdraw when persecution threatened (Philostratus *Vit. Apoll.* 4.37).

51 Their "lamentation" (κοπετός) is parallel to that made over Jesus in Luke 23:27; cf. 23:48.

not identify these "devout men"[52] as believers or worry about how they could have conducted these obsequies in the midst of a terrible persecution.[53]

■ **3** Ancient readers may have been less perplexed by Paul's rapid advancement than are contemporaries.[54] Consistency of character was not a value highly honored by popular authors, and, even for elite writers, character was a quality more often revealed than attained.[55] A different source may be involved, but source theories alone cannot justify the transition.[56] In due course, the narrative will disclose that this "young" Paul was a member of the Sanhedrin who had no qualms about executing believers (26:10). The sentence is well designed, ABBA in structure, with two finite verbs in the frequentative imperfect and two durative participles showing that the action continued for an indefinite period. The harsh verbs (*λυμαίνω*, "wreak havoc," "attempt to obliterate,"[57] and *σύρω*, "drag"[58]), topped off by his willingness to arrest women as well as men attest to Saul's extreme ferocity. Luke has derived at least part of his portrait of Paul the persecutor from Paul's letters, although the epistles deny that his "persecutions" took place in Jerusalem.[59]

The death of Stephen concludes the cycle that began at 3:1. It is a story of the rapid and enormous growth of an ideal community that persecution cannot eliminate or even check. Into the furrows of this carefully crafted dramatic narrative, with its alternation of tension and relaxation amidst an increasing crescendo of violence, the narrator has cast the seeds of the future Diaspora and gentile missions. The presence of source material does not obviate the Lucan character of this story. It is an authorial creation that retails few bare facts but admirably explains how the followers of Jesus set out on the road to a gentile mission in the Mediterranean region.

52 The word *εὐλαβής* elsewhere refers to ethnic Jews: Luke 2:25 (Simeon); Acts 2:5 (those at Pentecost); 22:12 (Ananias). Barrett (1:392) says that they are "good Jews" who, if not converts, are amenable to the Christian position.

53 If they are viewed as non-Christians, 2 Macc 4:49 is a relevant parallel.

54 Cf. Burchard, *Dreizehnte Zeuge*, 42: "Damit wäre der Kleiderwächter noch am gleichen Tag zum Kommissar geworden" ("With this stroke the guardian of coats is transformed into a Commissar on the very same day.")

55 See Mary Ann Tolbert's succinct description of "illustrative" and "representative" characters (*Sowing the Gospel: Mark's World in Literary-Historical Perspective* [Minneapolis: Fortress, 1989] 76–77). Ancient characterization generally focuses on illustration, often of virtue or vice. Plutarch's biographies can be disappointing to those in search of character development and/or demonstration that character determines the fate of individuals. See his comments at the beginning of his *Alexander* (1.2–3). One motive for "infancy stories" (e.g., ibid. 4.8–5.6) is the view that character is inherent and can be revealed at an early age. Postmodern literary criticism has demonstrated the weaknesses of dogmas about literary characterization inherited from the nineteenth century.

56 A source (cf. 9:1-2) may have introduced Paul as a vicious persecutor without further ado. The language is, however, quite Lucan, so that neither the length nor the specific content of the source may be identified. Karl Löning relates Acts 8:3 to the beginning of the pre-Lucan novella (*Die Saulustradition in der Apostelgeschichte* [NTAbh 9; Münster: Aschendorff, 1973] 93). See the comments on 9:1-2.

57 Cf. Euripides *Bacch.* 632–33; Philo *Leg. Gaj.* 134 (anti-Jewish outrages at Alexandria), *P. Lond.* 1912, 85–86 (= A. S. Hunt and C. C. Edgar, eds., *Select Papyri* [3 vols.; LCL; Cambridge, Mass.: Harvard University Press, 1929–] 2:212 = *CPJ* 2.153, the Letter of Claudius to Alexandria). Cadbury and Lake (88) have a good note.

58 Cf. Acts 14:19; 17:6; *Act. Paul* 7/9.

59 Texts: Gal 1:13, 22-23; 1 Cor 15:9; Phil 3:6; 1 Tim 1:13. See Pervo, *Dating*, 74–75, on the sources.

8

8:4-13 Simon of Samaria

Acts 8:4-8: Conventional Text

4/ Meanwhile, those who had fled
proclaimed the message in the
course of their travels. 5/ Philip,
for example, went to the[a] city
of Samaria and began to tell
the people about the messiah.
6/ Large crowds hung on his
every word, for they not only
heard his message but could
also see the miracles that he
performed. 7/ Impure spirits
departed with loud shrieks from
many who were possessed,
while many of the infirm and
disabled were healed. 8/ There
was loud rejoicing in that city.

9/ Prior to all this an individual
named Simon had practiced
magic in the city. The populace
of Samaria held him in awe. He
claimed to be a great person.[d]
10/ All classes of people, from
top to bottom, now became
devoted to him and exclaimed,
"He is the Power of God called
'Great.'"[e] 11/ The cause of this
devotion was the awe evoked
by Simon's long-standing[f] feats
of wizardry. 12/ Yet, when they
came to believe Philip's mes-
sage about God's reign and the
name of Jesus Christ, they, men
and women alike, began to have
themselves baptized. 13/ Even
Simon came to believe and,
after his baptism, became a
firm adherent of Philip; when he
saw miracles and other power-
ful deeds occurring, he was
astonished.

Acts 8:4-8: D-Text[b]

4/ Therefore, those who had been
scattered preach*ed* the word[c]
in the course of their travels
through cities and villages.
5/ And Philip went down to *a*
city of Samaria and *began* pro-
claiming *Jesus* to them. 6/ *Now*
when* the multitudes *heard,
***they were persuaded* by what**
was said by Philip, *for they saw*
the *many* signs that *were being*
***performed through him,* 7/ for**
many who had unclean spirits
were healed,
8/ and there was *great* rejoicing in
that city.

---

a *Or:* "a city."

b Boismard, *Texte*, 145–48. This involves the conjectural deletion of "crying out with a loud voice." Metzger (*Textual Commentary*, 312) condemns the D-Text expansions as "jejune superfluity" and goes on to speak of "the still more turgid reading of syr[p] ("and when the men who were there had heard his preaching, they gave heed to him and acquiesced to all that he had said"). Boismard apparently agrees. His reconstruction of the underlying D-Text is susceptible to criticism.

c D-Texts (primarily) add "of God."

d Three participles are associated with v. 9. Two, μαγεύων and ἐξιστάνων ("practicing magic," "astonishing") may be taken as either circumstantial or supplementary—the former according to §BDF 414 (1), the latter in the view of Conzelmann (63 n. 3) and Barrett (1:406). If circumstantial, one might render "astonished the populace by practicing magic." The third, λέγων ("claiming"), is definitely circumstantial. Some D-Texts (not mentioned by Boismard) invert the relationship, placing "astonish" in the indicative, a secondary improvement that reveals the awkward syntax.

e *Or:* "They acclaimed him as the so-called Great Power of God."

f The phrase ἱκανῷ χρόνῳ (the acc. would be preferable) testifies to the declining significance of the cases in Greek.

Analysis

In contrast with chaps. 3–7, Acts 8:4—11:18 does not display a tight organization. The cloud of persecution that hung so low in the previous section has vanished and will not return until chap. 12. The dominant and unifying theme of 8:4—11:18 is conversion. The crescendo moves from Samaritans—evidently "irregular" Jews—to the foreign official to an actual gentile household. Enmeshed in these accessions are one unsuccessful conversion (Simon), the conversion of Saul from persecutor to proponent, and the conversion of Peter to accept gentiles. These incidents invite readers to reflect on the meaning of "conversion," individual and communal. The geographical horizon expands to Samaria and "all Judea" and beyond into Syria. The promise of 1:8 is being fulfilled.

The source apparently included a brief summary of Philip's activity in Samaria and his subsequent move to Caesarea.[1] Although 8:5-8 may contain vestiges of the source, vv. 9-25 do not appear to derive from it.[2] If the source reported the conversion of an Ethiopian official (vv. 26-39), traces of non-Lucan material are not readily detectable; as it stands, this episode is the creation of the author.[3] An alternative approach, advocated by C. K. Barrett, for example, doubts that the source described any mission of Philip to Samaria. "[I]t seems clear that Luke knew little more than that Philip was one of the Hellenist Seven and that whereas the main Hellenist group founded the church at Antioch Philip was to be connected with Caesarea."[4] This is possible. Luke may have had information about work in Samaria conducted by anonymous missionaries and attributed this to Philip. He would then have created, in effect, "the Acts of Philip" in chap. 8. In support of this view is the anonymous character of those who began the gentile mission in Antioch (11:19-21).[5]

On the other side, it is difficult to imagine that Luke attributed the mission to Philip on his own initiative, since it does not fit with his overall picture[6] and because he must introduce apostles to "regularize" the activity. Moreover, if the source dealt with the origins of the gentile mission from an Antiochene perspective, work in Samaria would not be anomalous. It is preferable to assign Philip's activity to the source. The history of traditions associates Simon with Peter, making it more likely that the encounter between Philip and Simon did not derive from a source. The tradition of a mission to Samaria has a historical basis otherwise reflected in John 4.[7] In the Gospel, the Samaritans represent "the other."[8] In Acts, Samaria is a place adjacent to Judea. If the narrator wishes Samaritans to be viewed as Jews, albeit deviant, he does not say so. Samaria is simply a place, with a city and villages. The message they receive is summarized with the same words ("messiah," "reign of God," "the Name of Jesus Christ" [vv. 5, 12]) used to summarize the evangelization of Jews and gentiles.

Philip provides the focus for 8:4-40. His missionary activity includes Samaria and the coastal region (8:4, 40). In each case, Peter follows in Philip's footsteps (8:14; 9:32).[9] This is the result of Luke's intention to

1 For a recent history of research on 8:4-25 (including Simon), see V. J. Samkutty, *The Samaritan Mission in Acts* (LNTS 328; Edinburgh: T&T Clark, 2006) 18–53.

2 For attempts to identify underlying source material here, see Weiser, 1:199–201; and Lüdemann, 98–100. Both find tradition behind vv. 9-13 (Weiser subtracts v. 12). Whereas Weiser argues for tradition behind vv. 18-24, Lüdemann views this passage as Lucan composition, although he allows for tradition in v. 21.

3 The proposed tentative reconstruction indicates that the gentile mission source did not narrate the conversion of individuals. See pp. 12–14.

4 Charles Kingsley Barrett, "Light on the Holy Spirit from Simon Magus (Acts 8, 4-25)," in Kremer, *Actes*, 281–95, citing 285.

5 On the anonymity of the missionaries to Antioch, see below on 11:18-25.

6 Weiser, 1:199.

7 Oscar Cullmann used these data to hypothesize a relation between the "Hellenists" and the Samaritans (*The Johannine Circle* [trans. J. Bowden, Philadelphia: Westminster, 1976] 42–49). Gerhard Schneider strongly criticizes this hypothesis ("Stephanus, die Hellenisten und Samaria," in Kremer, *Actes*, 215–40).

8 Individual Samaritans are examples of "the other" who does the right thing (Luke 10:33-35; 17:12-19). As a body, they are hostile (Luke 9:52-56).

9 On the role of Peter, see Ernst Haenchen, "Simon Magus in der Apostelgeschichte," in K. W. Tröger, ed., *Gnosis und Neues Testament: Studien aus Religionswissenschaft und Theologie* (Gütersloh: Mohn,

show that all legitimate missionary activity received approval from the Jerusalem apostles (note also 11:22 and cf. 9:27-30). Luke portrays, via the Samaritan mission, the distinction between belief in Jesus and vulgar "magic." Verses 4-25 constitute a distinct narrative section, marked by an inclusion in vv. 4 and 25 and a single subject: the mission to Samaria. The structure of this section is clear: there are two large units, vv. 4-13 and vv. 14-25. Most of the material in vv. 4-13 is narrative summary. Although there is no formal pattern for the conversion of an opponent or rival (v. 13), vv. 18-24 do represent a pattern: the story of Ananias and Sapphira (5:1-11). Both are stories that feature converts for whom money was more important than their membership in the community and who were denounced by Peter.

The structure is as follows:

I. Vv. 4-13
   A. V. 4. Introduction
   B. Vv. 5-8. Philip's mission in Samaria
   C. Vv. 9-11. Simon's earlier mission in Samaria
   D. Vv. 12-13. Philip and Simon
II. Vv. 14-25
   A. Vv. 14-17 The visit of the apostles Peter and John to Samaria
   B. Vv. 18-24. The encounter between Peter and Simon
   C. V. 25. Closing summary

Clarity of structure does not automatically entail linear sequence. Susan Garrett offers this summary: "The story starts in the middle, proceeds to the beginning, takes unexpected turns, and comes to two apparent closes (vv. 8, 13) before it finally skids to the actual close."[10] These bumps and loops are due to the "parallel lives" of Philip and Simon (I. B-D):

Table 2. Philip and Simon

Philip	Simon
1. V. 5. **City**: Philip arrives.	1. V. 9. **City**: Simon is there.
2. Vv. 5, 12. **Message**: Christ and reign of God.	2. V. 9: **Message:** Claims to be "great."
3. Vv. 6-7, 13. **Activity**: Signs and *"great acts of power"* (δυνάμεις μεγάλας).	3. Vv. 9-11. **Activity**: "Magical" deeds; "astounds" (ἐξιστάνων) the populace; hailed as "great power (δύναμις μεγάλη) of God."
4. Vv. 6, 8, 12. **Response**: All "follow" (προσεῖχον); considerable joy.	4. V. 11: **Response**: All "follow" (προσεῖχον).
5. V. 12 **Result**: Populace comes to faith and is baptized.	5. V. 13. **Result**: Simon comes to faith and is baptized, "astonished" (ἐξίστατο) "inseparable from Philip."

Section I of the outline above is an implied comparison and contrast between Philip and Simon.[11] The author achieves this through the awkward insertion of a flashback about his rival (vv. 9-11). That unit has an A B A B configuration: (ἐξιστάνων, "astonish") (προσεῖχον, "follow") (ἐξεστακέναι, "astonish") (προσεῖχον, "follow"). The flashback technique was required because the narrator wished to get Philip to Samaria before introducing Simon. Rather than say, "Philip fled to Samaria and found that a certain Simon had seduced the entire populace with magic," the narrator prefers to open with an account of missionary success. The result is the cumbrous resumption of v. 12, which prepares the ground for the conversion of Simon in the subsequent

1973) 267–79. The Pseudo-Clementines appear to capitalize on this theme: Simon Magus establishes communities in the coastal cities from Caesarea to Antioch with his preaching and miracles, but Peter follows in his path and persuades these foundations to accept his own position.

10 Garrett, *Demise*, 62.

11 This outline is adapted from Karlmann Beyschlag, *Simon Magus und die christliche Gnosis* (WUNT 16; Tübingen: Mohr Siebeck, 1974) 101. On the figure of σύγκρισις (comparison), see Berger, *Formgeschichte*, 222–23, and the introduction, pp. 9–10. Note also the remarks of Klauck, *Magic*, 18–19.

verse. Luke's goals also require that the narrative come to a sudden end after v. 13, abandoning Philip until v. 26.[12] Philip does not depart in defeat. He has not just gained many converts and vanquished a formidable rival; he has even drawn the rival's retinue into the fold. To this story of almost unparalleled success Jerusalem reacts by sending two apostles to tidy up the little matter of the gift of the Spirit.

Comment

■ **4** (Section I in the outline) The verse[13] implies that all of the refugees became evangelists.[14] This generalization exposes the Lucan view of persecution as the motor that drives mission.

■ **5** The article in v. 5 is a problem. If read, it implies that Samaria had but one city, perhaps called Samaria.[15] This is the evident meaning of perp: *Samaria in civitate.* ℵ* alone has "Caesarea," a correction based on tradition.[16] External support for the article is strong: 𝔓[74] ℵ A B 1175 *pc*. Metzger says that "internal evidence" led to the placement of brackets around the article.[17] "Internal evidence" boils down to the desire to eliminate a mistake from the text. It certainly does no homage to the principle of *lectio difficilior*. The more probable text implies that Samaria had but one city. This is wrong, but Luke may have thought otherwise.[18] Acts 8:25, which speaks of "Samaritan villages" (rather than "cities and villages"), supports this understanding. In any case, mission is always centered on a city, and Samaria is "a welcome transition zone, geographically and religiously speaking, from Judaism to paganism."[19] Samaritans represent people, Jews or gentiles, whom the Christian mission can deliver from exploitation by magicians. In Lucan language: Samaria stands between "Judea and the ends of the earth" (1:8).

■ **5-7** These verses narrate the mission in summary form. The subject, Philip, is not identified, but he is presumably the second of the Seven enumerated in 6:5-6, as the apostles, including Philip, remained in Jerusalem (8:1). Acts 8:40 locates him in Caesarea, where he is found in 21:8 with the label "the evangelist." Later tradition confounded him with the apostle of 1:13 (and other lists).[20] The evangelist Philip alone has something like a historical profile, although the other Philip—presuming that there were two—plays a minor role in the Gospel according to John (1:43-51; 6:1-15; 12:20-26), which does not provide a list of the Twelve. Judging from the references to him (and to his daughters), Philip was an important figure in early Christianity, as the relative prominence he receives in Acts attests.[21] Philip, like Jesus, the apostles, and Stephen, evangelized[22] in word and deed. The miracles (σημεῖα) were both a part of his

---

12 Cf. Haenchen, 303.

13 Verses 4 and 25 begin οἱ μὲν οὖν (and include the verb "evangelize"). In the former instance, this may be adversative (Moule, *Idiom Book*, 162), but that cannot be said of the latter.

14 Note that Barnabas was still in Jerusalem when Paul arrived there (9:27). This indicates the artificiality of Luke's scheme, as well as its flexibility.

15 The old city Samaria was renamed Sebaste when refounded by Herod c. 27 BCE. Hemer (*Book*, 225–26) suggests that the old name may have persisted in popular use, citing several passages from Josephus, such as *Ant.* 15.246 (ἐν Σαμαρείᾳ τῇ κληθείσῃ Σεβάστῃ, "Samaria called Sebaste"), which refers to Herod. On the history of the city, see Schürer, *History*, 2:160–64. This city was later superseded in importance by Neapolis (the native city of Justin), founded by Vespasian, on which see Millar, *Near East*, 368.

16 Ropes, *Text*, 76.

17 Metzger, *Textual Commentary*, 311.

18 For this view, see Cadbury and Lake, 89; Barrett, 1:402; and Conzelmann, 62.

19 Klauck, *Magic*, 14.

20 Bede (39) distinguishes him from the apostle on the intelligent grounds that the apostle Philip would have been able to lay hands on them so that they would receive the Spirit. See p. 213 n. 1.

21 See Frédéric Amsler, *Acta Philippi* (CCSA 12; Turnhout: Brepols, 1999) 441–68. Christopher Matthews challenges the idea that there were two persons with this name in early Christianity, viewing the distinction as a Lucan invention (*Philip: Apostle and Evangelist* [NovTSup 105; Leiden: Brill, 2002]).

22 The verb κηρύσσω has its first appearance in v. 5 (of sixty in the NT, there are nine in Luke and eight in Acts).

message and a confirmation of its validity. Philip proclaimed Christ, whereas Simon proclaimed . . . Simon.

■ **6-8** The first verse aptly telescopes the narrative, beginning not with deeds that drew crowds, but with the crowds already formed, as it were. This [description] resembles, and prepares the ground for, the flashback technique used in vv. 9-12. The verb προσεῖχον ("cling to") provides comparison with Simon, to whom it also applies (vv. 10-11).[23] The word ὁμοθυμαδόν ("with one accord," often difficult to translate) brings these converts into the realm of the Jerusalem church (e.g., 1:14). Verse 7, with exorcisms and healings of the infirm as well as the disabled, resembles the summaries of Jesus' therapeutic activity (esp. Luke 4:40-41). As a healer, Philip has nothing to concede to Peter.[24] The first half of v. 6 is impossible. It begins, like the second half, with "many" + some kind of affliction but ends with a verb that should have "spirits" as its subject, although a singular verb would be preferable for the neuter πνεύματα ("spirits"). The numerous MS. variants are secondary attempts at improvement.[25] This may represent an authorial error. The translation corrects the sense without proposing an emended text. Verse 8 provides a closing summary. The "joy" finds its counterpoint in v. 39 and reveals the awkwardness of the flashback in the following unit.[26]

Excursus: Simon of Samaria

The tradition that attributes to Simon the foundation of a religious movement in Samaria and traces his influence to Rome (Acts 8; Justin *1 Apol.* 26.1–3) may be historically valid.[27] Everything else is open to dispute. The Simon of the Acts literature (Acts, *Acts of Peter*) is a magician worsted by Peter in Jerusalem, Samaria, and the ends (or at least the center) of the earth. The heresiological tradition regards Simon as a strong rival to the orthodox faith and, with a nice inversion of "Gnostic" claims to possess apostolic tradition, as the source of all heresies (Irenaeus *A.H.* 1.23–27; preface to book 3). Attempts to construct a

23 Cf. also 16:14 (Lydia, to Paul) and the comments in Cadbury and Lake, 89.

24 Acts 8:7 is the only use of "infirm" (παραλελυμένοι) in the plural. Jesus (Luke 5:17-26 parr.) and Peter (Acts 9:32-35) heal individual paralytics. For "lame" in the plural, see Luke 7:22.

25 See Metzger (*Textual Commentary,* 312–13), who also lists a number of proposed conjectural improvements. The most tempting of these is by A. Hilgenfeld, who proposed πνεύματα ἀκάθαρτα ἃ . . . , taking the initial πολλοί ("many") with the final verb "healed." Note the comments in Cadbury and Lake, 90, which points to a similar omission by A in the preceding verse.

26 The D-Text reconstructed by Boismard (n. *b*) is briefer and smoothes over the difficulties of the conventional text: It is clearly secondary.

27 The literature on this subject is vast. Robert Pierce Casey's survey of the heresiological data ("Simon Magus," in Lake and Cadbury, *Additional Notes,* 5:151–63) remains useful. Robert F. Stoops's "Simon 13," *ABD* 6:29–31, presents a good summary of data and views. For earlier literature, see Haenchen, 302 n. 7. The impasse in research is apparent in two reviews: Wayne A. Meeks, "Simon Magus in Recent Research," *RSR* 3 (1977) 137–42; and Kurt Rudolph, "Simon-Magus oder Gnosticus? Zum Stand der Debatte," *ThR* 42 (1977) 279–359. Note also Robert McL. Wilson, "Simon and Gnostic Origins," in Kremer, *Actes,* 485–91. Rudolph has a brief review of the Gnostic Simon in his *Gnosis: The Nature and History of Gnosticism* (trans. and ed. R. McL. Wilson; San Francisco: Harper & Row, 1983) 294–98. On the Gnostic question, see also Stephen Haar, *Simon Magus: The First Gnostic?* (BZNW 119; Berlin: de Gruyter, 2003). Note, in addition, the brief and illuminating observations of Klauck, *Magic,* 14–17. Klaus Berger suggests that Simon represented an independent group of Jesus followers in Samaria, treated in typical fashion by Luke ("Propaganda und Gegenpropaganda im frühen Christentum: Simon Magus als Gestalt des Samaritanischen Cristentums," in Lukas Bormann et al., eds., *Religious Propaganda and Missionary Competition in the New Testament World: Essays Honoring Dieter Georgi* (NovTSup 74; Leiden: Brill, 1994) 313–17. This proposal is less speculative than others but remains no more than an interesting hypothesis. Florent Heintz (*Simon 'le Magicien': Actes 8 5-25 et l'accusation de magie contre les Prophètes thaumaturges dan l'antiquité* [CahRB 39; Paris: Gabalda, 1997]) also seeks to uncover the history behind the text. For the later history of the figure of Simon, see Albert Ferreiro *Simon Magus in Patristic, Medieval, and Early Modern Traditions* (Studies in the History of Christian Traditions 125; Leiden: Brill, 2005). (See also n. 31.)

viable bridge between these two Simons, as it were, have not succeeded.[28] The social type portrayed in the Acts literature resembles Lucian's hostile portrait of Alexander of Abounoteichus—and, to a degree, his Peregrinus—or an Apollonius of Tyana. The prophets ridiculed by Celsus (Origen *Cels.* 7.8–9[29]) could be viewed like the foregoing, but they also resemble "Gnostic" proclaimers.[30] The Simonian tradition, as described by Christian heresiologists, represents their eponymous founder as a prophetic revealer, descended from heaven.[31]

When the issue is framed as the choice between downgrading a prophet into a magician and promoting a religious leader to the status of celestial revealer by later seekers of a foundational figure, the former looks less probable. Simon had a strong impact, and the efforts to degrade him indicate that he was a formidable rival of the early Christian movement. The acclamation cited in v. 8, "great power of God,"[32] which is not characteristic of either magicians in general or of those described as charlatans in Acts (13:6-12; 19:13-17), supports the suspicion that Luke knew of Simon as a theologian, whose views he ridiculed by characterizing them as "magic" and thus of diabolical origin.[33] The nature and specific theological characteristics of Simon's original movement or of his followers in Luke's own time cannot be determined from the data in Acts, and this passage cannot be used as evidence for a variety of pre-Christian Gnosticism, as Haenchen once argued,[34] but the weakness of his case does not prove the opposite. It is important to distinguish between the dramatic date and the date of composition. When Luke wrote, around eighty years later, there may well have been a Simonian Gnosis.[35]

Although the narrator reports that Simon had a tremendous impact on the Samaritan people, he is presented as a rather labile and weak character, overwhelmed by Philip and demolished by Peter. As far as the reader knows, he could have come from anywhere. For the author of Acts, Simon serves, as Susan Garrett has shown, as a useful example of the distinction between the power and effect of "true religion" and nefarious "magic."[36]

Excursus: "Magi," "Magic," and "Magicians"

In Greek "magus" bore different meanings: (1) the member of an Iranian priestly caste, (2) one who had and utilized knowledge of the transcendent, (3) a practitioner of "magic," and, metaphorically, (4) "a deceiver" or "seducer."[37] Matthew 2 uses the term in the second sense; Acts 13, in the third. Simon is not called a "magus" in Acts. He is characterized as "practicing magic" (μαγεύων [8:9]) and amazing people with "magical deeds" (μαγείαι [8:11]).[38]

"Magic" is a difficult term, better seen as a component of various religions in the Greco-Roman period than as an entity distinct from, or an antithesis to, "religion."[39] The claim that religion venerates the supernatural while magic seeks to manipulate it is not tenable. The label "magic" could be applied, with or without prejudice, to nearly any unofficial

28 Despite his alleged Samaritan origins, Simon is not reputed to have been involved with Jews of any sort. His appeal was to gentiles only.

29 On this description ("I am God [or a Son of God, or a divine spirit"]), see Norden, *Agnostos Theos*, 188–201; and Henry Chadwick's notes in *Origen, Contra Celsum* (Cambridge: Cambridge University Press, 1953) 402 (from which the translated words of 7.9 are taken).

30 Ps.-Clem. *Rec.* 2.37.6–7, and the comments of Rudolph, *Gnosis*, 297.

31 See David R. Cartlidge, "The Fall and Rise of Simon Magus," *BibRev* 21 (2005) 24–36, who discusses traditions about Simon through the Middle Ages.

32 On this see Klaus Berger, "Propaganda und Gegenpropaganda im frühen Christentum," 313–17, esp. 314 n. 1.

33 Cf. chaps. 19–20, in which opposed teachings (19:1-7; 20:29-31 appear in a context marked by the defeat of magic (19:13-19). On the subject, see Garrett, *Demise*.

34 Ernst Haenchen, "Gab es eine vorchristliche Gnosis?" *ZThK* 49 (1952) 316–49 (= *Gott und Mensch: Gesammelte Aufsätze* [Tübingen: Mohr Siebeck, 1965] 265–98).

35 So, e.g., Burton Scott Easton, *Early Christianity: The Purpose of Acts and Other Papers* (ed. F. C. Grant; Greenwich, CT.: Seabury, 1954) 66. See below, on v. 23, for Lüdemann's proposal.

36 Garrett, *Demise*, 63–78.

37 Gerhard Delling, "μάγος," *TDNT* 4:356–59, esp. 356–57.

38 In v. 9, Irenaeus reads *magicam exercens, et seducens gentem Samaritanorum*, "practicing magic and leading the Samaritan people astray," assuming that (3) implies (4).

39 A recent general study of this difficult field is Fritz Graf, *Magic in the Ancient World* (trans. Franklin Philip; Revealing Antiquity 10; Cambridge, Mass.: Harvard University Press, 1997). Georg Luck takes a somewhat different approach in *Arcana Mundi: Magic and the Occult in the Greek and Roman Worlds: A Collection of Ancient Texts*

religious activity (as well as to some official activities). The distinction between "good" and "bad" magic endured.[40] In commenting on the commandment prohibiting murder Philo says:

> Now the true magic, the scientific vision by which the facts of nature are presented in a clearer light, is felt to be a fit object for reverence and ambition and is carefully studied not only by ordinary persons but by kings and the greatest kings, and particularly those of the Persians, so much so that it is said that no one in that country is promoted to the throne unless he has first been admitted into the caste of the Magi. But there is a counterfeit (παράκομμα) of this, most properly called a perversion of art, pursued by charlatan mendicants (μηναγύρται) and parasites (βωμολόχοι) and the basest of the women and slave population, who make it their profession to deal in purifications and disenchantments and promise with some sort of charms and incantations to turn love into deadly enmity and their hatred intro profound affection. The simplest and most innocent natures are deceived by the bait till at last the worst misfortunes come upon them and thereby the wide membership which unites great companies of friends and relatives falls gradually into decay and is rapidly and silently destroyed. (*Spec. leg.* 3.100–101)[41]

The social distinction is clear: "good magic" is the province of scholars/philosophers and monarchs, while women, slaves, and unprincipled hustlers engage in "bad magic," which has a deleterious effect on social life. These magicians appear as private practitioners engaged in problem-solving and/or self-serving activities. Surviving texts attest to Philo's complaints.[42] Many magical formulas and recipes could be, and were, used by individuals in pursuit of particular goals. In this sense, magic represents a principle celebrated in the Protestant Reformation: anyone could have, through magic, access to the divine without benefit of clergy. Although most early Christians fell into Philo's category of "the simple and innocent," Luke assumes, for apologetic and other purposes, the same social disdain. Christianity despises magic and can serve the public good by motivating people to renounce this threat to organized religion and the social order.[43] Simon is a typical charlatan, whose poor dupes have been liberated from superstition and exploitation through the good offices of Philip. "Magician" was often a pejorative label applied to opponents in religious and philosophical competition: "Our" heroes and leaders

(Baltimore: Johns Hopkins University Press, 1985) 3–60. See also Christopher A. Faraone and Dirk Obbink, eds., *Magika Hiera: Ancient Greek Magic and Religion* (New York: Oxford University Press, 1991); and Marvin Meyer and Paul Mirecki, eds., *Ancient Magic and Ritual Power* (Religions in the Graeco-Roman World 129; Leiden: Brill, 1995). See also the several introductions to the collections of primary texts in n. 42. Note also the astute observations of Garrett, *Demise*, index *s.v.* "Magic," 178; the brief and relevant discussion by Klauck, *Magic*, 14–16; Johnson, 146–47; Delling, "μάγος," *TDNT* 4:356–59, as well as the important essay of Arthur Darby Nock, "Paul and the Magus," in Lake and Cadbury, *Additional Notes*, 164–88. More recent surveys include David Aune, "Magic in Early Christianity," *ANRW* 2.23.2 (1980) 1507–57; Alan F. Segal, "Hellenistic Magic: Some Questions of Definition," in Roelof van den Broek and Maarten J. Vermaseren, eds., *Studies in Gnosticism and Hellenistic Religions* (EPRO 91; Leiden: Brill, 1981) 349–75; Todd E. Klutz in idem, ed., *Magic in the Biblical World: From the Rod of Aaron to the Ring of Solomon* (JSNTS 245; London: T&T Clark, 2003) 1–9; Andy M. Reimer, *Miracle and Magic: A Study in the Acts of the Apostles and the Life of Apollonius of Tyana* (JSNTS 235; London: Sheffield Academic Press, 2002), and the articles by various authors in *RGG*[4] 5:661–79. Scott Shauf (*Theology as History, History as Theology: Paul in Ephesus in Acts 19* [BZNW 133; Berlin: de Gruyter, 2005] 178–218) has a valuable and relevant review of the issues.

40 With Neo-Platonic theurgy, magic in the positive sense achieved its apotheosis. The distinction remained—witness the contrast between "white" and "black" magic that is familiar to nearly everyone in the Western world.

41 Trans. Francis H. Colson, *Philo VII* (LCL; Cambridge, Mass.: Harvard University Press, 1937) 539–41, *alt.* Cf. *Omn. prob. lib.* 74.

42 Collections of texts include Karl Preisendanz, ed. and trans., *Papyri Graecae Magicae* (2 vols.; 2nd ed., ed. Albert Henrichs; Stuttgart: Teubner, 1973–74); Hans Dieter Betz, ed., *The Greek Magical Papyri in Translation*, vol. 1: *Texts* (Chicago: University of Chicago Press, 1986); John G. Gager, ed., *Curse Tablets and Binding Spells from the Ancient World* (New York: Oxford University Press, 1992); and Marvin Meyer and Richard Smith, eds., *Ancient Christian Magic: Coptic Texts of Ritual Power* (San Francisco: HarperSanFrancisco, 1994).

43 See the comments on Acts 19:18-20, below.

are "divine persons," "servants of God," etc., while "theirs" are "magicians," "deceivers," "charlatans," etc.[44] So it is in Acts, where Luke is able, in apologetic fashion, to exploit the resemblance between the deeds of his protagonists and the magic tricks of his opponents. Magic is thus both a reality of the religious competition in which Luke is engaged and a symbol of the false and satanic.[45] Equally useful to the Lucan project is the association between magicians and/or false prophets and money. One can practically distinguish between the true prophet or the genuine healer and the false prophet or magician on the grounds of any interest in remuneration.[46]

■ **9-10** It transpires that Philip had had competition from one Simon,[47] who had astonished the populace[48] with his magical prowess (vv. 9, 11). The narrator does not characterize Simon as a false prophet or a blasphemer, nor does the text suggest that he is making a good living from his practice. His claim (lit. "claiming himself to be someone great") is scarcely less awkward in Greek than in English, tempting editors either to delete it, à la 5:36,[49] or emend *μέγαν* ("great") to *μάγον* ("magus"),[50] but the infelicity is probably due to Luke's polemic.[51] The verb in the relative clause of v. 10, "become devoted to" (*προσεῖχον*), establishes a precise comparison between Simon and Philip.[52] Both had attracted large numbers.[53] Verse 10b ends, like v. 9, with a participial phrase introduced by "saying." The narrator does not state that Simon called himself "Great Power (of God)". This acclamation[54] came from his admirers.

Questions about that acclamation include its text, translation, meaning, place in the history of religions, and origin. At the narrative level, none of these questions seems pertinent. Far from being a "great power" (*δύναμις μεγάλη*), Simon was awestruck by the "great powers/miracles" (*δυνάμεις μεγάλας*) performed by Philip and ends his appearance in Acts groveling before Peter. The phrase is so opportune that one is tempted to label it a Lucan invention, but opportunities can be found no less than created.

The participle *καλουμένη* ("called") is quite awkward in a quotation but intelligible in the sense, "there are numerous powers, but this is the *Great* Power." The qualifier prevents confusion with the "great powers/miracles" of v. 13 and thus looks authorial. The textual variants may have arisen from a failure to recognize this function.[55] Another candidate for authorial intervention is the adnomial genitive "of God" after "Power," since that word is a circumlocution for "God," as in Mark 14:62, where Luke 22:69 adds a confusing "of God."[56] Documentary evidence indicates, however, that "Great Power of God" is possible.

44 See Richard Reitzenstein, *Hellenistische Wundererzählungen* (Leipzig: Teubner, 1906) 37.

45 See Garrett, *Demise*, 77.

46 See p. 216 n. 29 below.

47 Georgi (*Opponents*, 83–228) provides a broad profile of the missionary model envisioned in this passage with specific discussion of Philip and Simon (see esp. 168–69).

48 In a strict sense *τὸ ἔθνος τῶν Σαμαρίτων* ("the nation of the Samaritans"), as in "the nation of the Jews" (10:22; cf. Josephus *Ant.* 18.85), would be preferable, but it would be imprudent to build a case on this phrase.

49 Blass, BDF §301 (1), would delete the adjective and view *τινα* as emphatic ("a real somebody").

50 Cadbury and Lake, 90.

51 Cf. Metzger, *Textual Commentary*, 313.

52 Note *Ephesian Tale* 1.1.3, of the hero: *προσεῖχον δὲ ὡς θεῷ τῷ μειρακίῳ καί εἰσιν ἤδη τινὲς οἳ καὶ προσεκύνησαν ἰδόντες καὶ προσηύξαντο* . . . ("They treated the boy like a god, and some even prostrated themselves and prayed at the sight of him"; trans. G. Anderson, in Reardon, *Novels*, 128). Irenaeus says that Marcus was able to persuade many to join themselves to him (*προσέχειν αὐτῷ*) by his magical tricks (*A.H.* 1.13.1, on which see also n. 61).

53 "From insignificant to great" is a common LXX phrase, according to Cadbury and Lake, 90; cf. 26:22.

54 See p. 55.

55 MSS. 614 *pc* have *λεγομένη*, which could be understood as pedantic—the "so-called power," while Ψ m sy^p sa cop^mae omit. One question is whether this is a correction of *καλουμένη* or an interpolation. See Metzger, *Textual Commentary*, 313. Boismard (*Texte*, 149) omits it from the D-Text.

56 Eusebius (*H.E.* 2.23.13), who claims to be following Hegesippus, reports James as saying that the "Son of Man . . . is sitting in heaven on the right hand of the great power" (*ἐκ δεξιῶν τῆς μεγάλης δυνάμεως*). Cf. Mark 14:62; Acts 7:56.

An undated altar from Saittai in Lydia bears the dedication: εἷς θεὸς ἐν οὐρανοῖς, μέγας Μὴν Οὐράνιος, μεγάλη δύναμις τοῦ ἀθανάτου θεοῦ ("[There is] one god in heaven, the great Heavenly Men, great power of the immortal god").[57] This "monotheizing" formula is not typical of the god Men. The epithet "great" is very common, but "great power" with a genitive "of god" is not. A painted inscription from Sebaste, c. 300 CE, probably associated with a statue of Kore, reads: εἷς θεὸς ὁ πάντων δεσπότης μεγάλη κόρη ἡ ἀνείκητος ("[There is] one god, the ruler of all, the great Maiden [Kore], the invincible one").[58] If this refers to but one deity,[59] it assigns her an epithet otherwise proper to the Sun (*Sol Invictus*). Note also PGM 4.1275–76: ἐπικαλοῦμαί σε τὴν μεγίστην δύναμιν τὴν ἐν τῷ οὐρανῷ ("I invoke you, the greatest power in heaven," a spell that calls on the constellation of the Bear).[60] Possibility does not establish probability, let alone certainty. Luke could be reporting a tradition about Simon (although the language of vv. 9-12 is generally Lucan), or he could be using standard language about teachers he viewed as rivals. Calling one's opponents "magicians" was a widespread practice (above) and claims to possess "great power" were associated with more than one "Gnostic" theologian.[61]

■ **11-13** "Power" is one of the most important tools in Luke's theological tool chest,[62] and those who allow themselves to be acclaimed the "Great Power (of God)" are not likely to flourish. So it is here. Simon, who had been winning devotees in large numbers by his magical prowess, is soon reduced to the status of a convert awed by the great wonders of another. Verse 12 prepares for this with the flashback to the work of Philip, whose message led Samaritans[63] to faith, followed by baptism.[64] Of these evidently numerous converts, there is one specific example: Simon.[65] Readers informed by Simon's subsequent failure may presume that there was something inadequate in his faith, since it was based solely on his admiration for Philip's miracles. The narrative has described an implicit

On this periphrasis, see Cadbury and Lake, 9; Casey, "Simon Magus," 153; and Barrett, 1:407 (but δύναμις in *Gos. Pet.* 19 almost certainly does mean "God"). Haenchen (303) and Schneider (1:489), for example, view "of God" as a Lucan gloss. For Luke "power" is not acceptable as a divine periphrasis because power is what God employs and bestows rather than what God is.

57 My translation; see *NewDocs* 3 (1978) no. 7, pp. 31–32, with a valuable commentary.

58 My translation; see *NewDocs* 1 (1976) nos. 67–68, pp. 105–7, with detailed remarks.

59 For a goddess, one would expect δεσποίνα, δεσπότειρα, or δεσπότις. Cf. FD III.II.35 (Delphi, of Artemis); TAM V.9 (of the maiden [κόρα] Athena, with whom the Simonians identified Helena, according to Irenaeus *A.H.* 1.16.3, etc.), and IK Knidos B 9 (Demeter).

60 See Hans-Dieter Betz, ed., *The Greek Magical Papyri in Translation*, vol. 1: *Texts* (Chicago: University of Chicago Press, 1986) 62.

61 On the style, see Lüdemann, 94–95. Irenaeus states that Simon viewed the highest god as the *sublimissimam virtutem*, which could render δύναμις μεγίστη ("greatest power"), and Hippolytus (*Ref.* 6.9.4) refers to a Simonian source entitled Ἡ Μεγάλη Ἀπόφασις ("The Great Assertion," [?] usually transliterated), which speaks of the first principle, fire, as sometimes called the "unbounded power" (ἀπέραντος δύναμις). Yet Irenaeus uses similar language about Marcus, who had received the "highest power" (δύναμις μεγίστη) and practiced magic (*A.H.* 1.13.1).

62 See the excursus "Power in Luke and Acts" pp. 42–43.

63 The emphatic "both men and women" may stress quantity, as in 5:14. It is possible that the narrator wishes to stress the conversion of men, as magicians were often said to seduce women, who were viewed as ignorant and labile.

64 The combination of "God's reign and the name of Jesus Christ" as the object of εὐαγγελιζομένῳ ("evangelizing," "proclaiming the official message") is interesting. "God's reign" ("the kingdom of God" in conventional language) evidently serves as a summary for the Christian life and message (cf. 28:23), whereas "the Name" embraces the manifestation of God's power. In short, the "name" makes the "kingdom" present and effective. For more detail, see Barrett, 1:408–9. Verse 12 does not, therefore, distinguish between proclamation of the creed and the deeds that confirm its validity.

65 Some D-Texts (mae 945, and a medieval version) omit the reference to Simon's baptism, the reading followed by Boismard, *Texte*, 149. This is clearly the result of theological concerns.

competition in which the public tested the words of two teachers by their respective deeds.[66] So convincing was Philip's victory that he even brought his rival, who might be expected to appreciate a good miracle when he saw one, into his camp and entourage. Simon did not even attempt to compete.[67] The sophisticated modern reader may well prefer the subtlety of Luke's account to the detailed narration of the contest between Peter and Simon in Rome (*Actus Vercellenses* 11–32[68]), but ancient popular taste did not concur with this view.[69] One major purpose of the Apocryphal Acts and related literature was to give continuing and overwhelming proof that Christian leaders were better miracle workers than their Jewish and polytheist rivals.[70] Thus ends the first of two curious episodes about Simon. One might gather that the narrator was reporting the winning of a noteworthy convert rather than a victory over a formidable rival.[71]

66 Ramsay MacMullen argues that miraculous demonstrations alone produced converts in *Paganism*, 96, with references on 191 n. 1. He overstates the case, but rightly notes that Nock (*Conversion*) gave undue emphasis to the intellectual tradition.

67 Rackham (113) noted that Simon's lack of opposition is surprising, but had no answer. Chrysostom (*Hom.* 18) answers the question of why Simon was baptized by referring to Jesus' selection of Judas.

68 Cf. also Eusebius *H.E.* 2.13–15; Hippolytus *Ref.* 6.20.2–3.

69 Exodus 7–12, a contest between the power of God and Egyptian "magic," provides important background for the theme of religious competition here.

70 So Elisabeth Schüssler Fiorenza, "Miracles, Mission, and Apologetics: An Introduction," in eadem, *Aspects*, 1–25, esp. 7.

71 Cadbury and Lake, 94.

8

8:14-25 The Spirit, Peter, and Simon

14/ When the apostles at Jerusalem learned that Samaria had accepted God's message, they sent Peter and John to visit them. 15/ After the two had arrived, they prayed that the converts might receive the Holy Spirit, 16/ for the Spirit had not yet fallen upon any of them. They had merely been baptized in the name of the Lord Jesus. 17/ After praying, the apostles laid their hands upon them,[a] and the converts started receiving the Holy Spirit. 18/ When Simon observed that the Spirit[b] was conveyed through the imposition of apostolic hands, he offered them money, 19/ saying, "Bestow upon me this power, so that anyone upon whom I lay my hands may receive Holy Spirit."

20/ Peter replied, "The hell with you and your money, for you have decided that you can acquire with cash that which God supplies gratis. 21/ There is no place or role for you in this enterprise, for your heart is not right with God. 22/ Abandon this wickedness and beg the Lord in the hope that he will perhaps forgive your wicked intention, 23/ for I am aware[c] that you have been snared and poisoned by evil." 24/ "Will all of you please intercede with the Lord for me," Simon answered, "entreating that none of these things you have mentioned will happen to me."

25/ After speaking about what they had seen and heard[d] and proclaiming the message, Peter and John set out for Jerusalem. On their return journey, they preached the gospel in a number of Samaritan villages.

a $\mathfrak{P}^{45}$ D* E Ψ m Ir read the imperfect, evidently to coordinate with the tense of ἐλάμβανον ("started receiving").

b Most witnesses add "Holy" before "Spirit." This is secondary.

c D-Texts (D E 614 *pc* Boismard, *Texte*, 151) read θεωρῶ, "I perceive."

d Lit. "witnessing." The function of apostolic witness was testimony to the resurrection of Jesus.

Analysis

A surprising aftermath follows the report of Philip's mission. The apostles send two of their company to bestow the Spirit on the Samaritan converts. This leads to a confrontation between Peter and Simon, who made Peter an offer that had to be refused. After a vigorous denunciation of both the offer and its proponent, Simon does not drop dead, as had Ananias and Sapphira earlier (5:1-11). One reason for the failure of Peter's curse is that Simon had not expired at that moment, and that fact was well known. Approval by Jerusalem was a requirement, and an apostolic visitation seems highly appropriate. The announced purpose, that these new believers should receive the Holy Spirit, comes as a shock. The preceding narrative has given no hint that the baptisms were defective. Logic would call for Philip to report to Jerusalem that he had baptized many, but that no one had received the gift of the Spirit. As the text stands, readers are free to infer that this charism required the imposition of apostolic hands, and many have so inferred, but the preceding narrative has not hinted that water baptism must be supplemented by apostolic prayer and the imposition of hands.[1] The objection that no such mention has been required, since all baptisms could have been administered by apostles, falls before the evidence that the initial gift of the Spirit may come without reference to baptism, as in 2:1-4 or, prior to it, as in 10:44-46, while no questions about the Spirit arise when Philip baptizes an Ethiopian official in the very next episode (vv. 26-39). The patent fact is that the Spirit comes at the opportune moment. Behind this literary device is a theological conviction: the wind blows where it wills. No institution or person can manipulate the Spirit of God, a point doubly made in this passage.[2]

The structure is straightforward. Verses 14-17 constitute a unity in summary form. A problem is announced and resolved. The next section is a specific scene, formally similar to an apophthegm. The only action is Simon's tender of cash, by which he reveals that he has a "problem," for which Peter proposes a solution.[3] Verse 25 does triple duty, transforming this visit into a general mission, completing the action begun in v. 14, and, finally, rounding off the entire description of the evangelism of Samaria.

Comment

■ **14-16** The initial verse depicts the apostles "receiving," like a political body,[4] a report, the origin of which is not stated. "Samaria" is a common synecdoche.[5] As in 3:1–4:22 John accompanies Peter.[6] From vv. 15-16, one might deduce that only after arriving did these apostles discover that the converts had not received the Spirit but had only been baptized in the name of Jesus![7] The (remedial?) action includes prayer and the imposition of hands. All was then well. Samaria had a "Pentecost" of its own, and the unity of the community with that in Jerusalem, as well as the authenticity of the conversions, is established beyond doubt.[8]

■ **17-19** Simon, who had not thought to attempt to purchase from Philip the ability to work miracles and

1 On postbaptismal imposition of hands, see Joseph Coppens, "L'imposition des mains dans les Actes des Apôtres," in Kremer, *Actes*, 405–38, esp. 423–32.

2 It must be admitted, however, that the Spirit is at the beck and call of the narrator.

3 Verses 15 and 24 frame the episode within purpose (ὅπως) clauses. The phrase "receive the Spirit" is a leitmotif, occurring at the end of vv. 15, 17, and 19. On the anarthrous use of "Holy Spirit" see BDF §257 (2). The question is whether this should be seen as a personification or as a kind of metonymy, that is, the result of the descent of the Spirit, spiritual gifts.

4 "Received" (δέδεκται); cf. *I. Magn.* 13.1.1; 1.1.97 (a cultic ordinance). A similar phrase, in the aorist tense, appears in Acts 11:1, 22.

5 On this use of the capital for the entire region, see Conzelmann, 65. Paul may be the source of this usage (Rom 15:26; 2 Cor 9:2).

6 When last in the vicinity of Samaria, John had wanted to call down fire on its inhabitants (Luke 9:54). Now he will bring down the "fire" (cf. 2:1-4) of the Spirit. See also V. J. Samkutty, *The Samaritan Mission in Acts* (LNTS 328; Edinburgh: T&T Clark, 2006) 136–40.

7 Cf. 19:1-7, where Paul asks some "disciples" whether they had received the Spirit at baptism. Learning that this was not so, they were baptized "in the name of the Lord Jesus," and this was followed by imposition of hands and the receipt of the Spirit.

8 Klauck (*Magic*, 19–20) comments intelligently about the issues. The various gifts of baptism were "naturally" marked with particular ritual actions, which could, in turn, be given symbolic interpretations (such as undressing) and, for varying reasons in different circumstances, be distinguished as separate ceremonies. The imposition of hands bears a primary sense of the transfer or bestowal of power. For a full discussion of the various controverted theological issues involved, see Turner, *Power*, 360–75; see also John C. O'Neill, "The Connection between Baptism and the Gift of the Spirit in Acts," *JSNT* 63 (1996) 87–103.

perform exorcisms, does just that very thing in this instance (vv. 18-19).[9] The implication is that the gift of the Spirit produced a perceptible result, such as prophesying and/or glossolalia, some sort of ecstatic behavior.[10] The difficulty is to imagine a type of ecstatic behavior that would arouse Simon's envy and greed—presuming that he was not simply interested in the capacity to bestow this gift.[11] The reader must assume the desirability of the gift. Were people really more likely to desire ecstasy than relief from major disabilities? With this insight, the narrative loses verisimilitude and credibility from the religio-historical perspective, while the idea of the gift acquires enhanced mystery from the literary angle: it must be quite fabulous if Simon simply had to have it.[12] The amount proffered is not specified.[13] It is irrelevant, for a farthing would have been iniquitous. His request is reminiscent, not by chance, of the tempter's offer in Luke 4:6.[14] Through this offer he reveals that he remains, at heart, a magician.[15] His willingness to regard Peter and John as professional colleagues is not very logical, but it allows the narrator to illustrate the difference between Christian thaumaturges and magicians: followers of Jesus not only do not take money, but they take offense at the very idea.[16] This is Luke's chief goal: to show that Christianity has nothing in common with magic.[17]

■ **20-23** Peter's response is quite vigorous and somewhat eloquent.[18] Simon, whose crime may seem more abominable than that of Ananias and Sapphira, is,

9 The hypothesis that this episode reflects—and deflects—criticism of Paul is an inference based on an inference. That Paul was accused of trying to purchase the legitimacy of his apostleship through the Collection is a very reasonable inference, but it lacks direct evidence. Luke's putative attribution of this attempt to Simon would be a nice reversal of the technique utilized in the Pseudo-Clementines, where Paul's theology is attributed to Simon, but it is difficult to see how this episode would be an effective refutation of any charge against Paul, since his enemies could have added this example to their accusation: Paul tried to do what Simon had attempted.

10 For one example, see Gal 4:6.

11 One possibility is a vision. The magical papyri contain numerous recipes for dreams and visions, e.g, PGM 5.54–69; 7.222–49, 250–54, 319–34. In the Nag Hammadi tractate III,5, *Dial. Sav.* 36 (135,1–16), the Savior lays a hand upon the disciples, and Judas has a vision. Although Acts reports visions, as in 10:9-16 (cf. also the citation from Joel 3 in Acts 2:17), visions are not associated with the initial gifts of the Spirit, which relate to speech and hearing.

12 Casey ("Simon Magus," 151) says, "Simon's professional instinct appears to have been reawakened." The question is, Why? The request, "[that] . . . anyone upon whom I lay my hands may receive Holy Spirit," does not suggest that faith or prior baptism was in prospect.

13 D-Texts (Boismard, *Texte*, 150) intensify the request by having Simon beg (παρακαλῶν) the apostles and by making his "I" emphatic.

14 His "simony" is an attempt to purchase the capacity (ἐξουσία) to bestow the Spirit. When ordination came to be regarded as conveying power to effect sacramental actions rather than authorization to administer sacraments, "simony" acquired its present meaning: bribery to obtain office.

15 See Garrett, *Demise*, 70, 145 n. 39; and Charles Kingsley Barrett, "Light on the Holy Spirit from Simon Magus (Acts 8, 4-25)," in Kremer, *Actes*, 287–88.

16 Cf. 3:6; 16:16-23; 19:19; 20:33-35. See Mark 6:6b-13; *Did.* 11:6, 9, 12; Hermas *Man.* 11:12. In *Act. Thom.* 20 the informants of King Gundaphorus advise him that Thomas's deeds indicate that he is a magician, but his refusal to take money and his ascetic lifestyle convince them that he is a righteous person. Note Plato *Leg.* 909A-B; cf. 933A; Juvenal *Sat.* 6.546; Lucian *Philops.* 15–17; Philostratus *Vit. Apoll.* 8.7.3; Origen *Cels.* 1.68.

17 Accusations of magical practice are made only indirectly in Acts, notably in 4:7. For an understanding of the environment, it is useful to consider the Apocryphal Acts. See the survey of Gérard Poupon, "L'accusation de magie dans les Actes apocryphes," in Bovon, *Actes Apocryphes*, 71–94.

18 Both sentences (vv. 20b-21 and 22-23) posit the subject at the end. The address opens with a curse. BDF §384 states that this is "the single example of the present optative in a wish" in the NT. The translation is idiomatic English, but ἀπώλεια ("destruction," on which see Dan 2:5; 3:30, 96 Theod; PGM 4.1247–48 is euphemistic). The recommended purpose of Simon's petition is delicately phrased: εἰ ἄρα ἀφεθήσεται (rendered "in the hope that he will perhaps forgive"). On the use of εἰ in expressions of hope, etc., see BDF §375 and Moule, *Idiom Book*, 158 n. 1. Each of the sentences

unlike them, offered a chance for repentance.[19] The text does not specify whether Simon had himself received the Spirit but there is no reason to exclude him from the general bestowal reported in v. 17. The motive for the curse[20] is compressed, as if Simon were seeking to purchase the free gift of God[21] rather than the power to convey it. Verse 21 states the consequence and its motive: v. 21a looks final—Simon is separated from the community.[22] He lacks the proper disposition.[23] Verse 22 speaks of this again: *ἡ ἐπίνοια τῆς καρδίας σου* ("intent of your heart" [NRSV]). Lüdemann detects in this *hapax legomenon* a reference to the use of *ennoia/epinoia* as a technical term in Simonian theology. He may be right.[24]

■ **24** Rather than beg God for forgiveness on the spot, Simon requests the prayers of Peter and John that he may elude the sentence pronounced on him.[25] Since few, least of all magicians familiar with such actions, wish to experience the effects of a curse, his disposition remains unclear.[26] On that uncertain note, the episode ends. Not all of Luke's editors were fond of such endings.[27] The D-Text of v. 24 reads: "Simon replied **to them**, 'Will all of you **please** intercede with **God** [. . .] that none **of these evil** things you have mentioned will happen **to me**.' **He continued to weep ardently**."[28] The editor did not concoct this conclusion out of whole cloth. The evident source is another Simon: Peter (Matt 26:75). The D-Text wishes to emphasize Simon's dejection, possibly his remorse. Although this conclusion is technically "open," readers were unlikely to conclude that Simon

---

contains the key word "heart." The *χολὴν πικρίας καὶ σύνδεσμον ἀδικίας* (lit. "gall of bitterness and bond of injustice") of v. 23 is a pleasant bit of LXX pleonastic style (Prov 5:4; Deut 29:17; Isa 58:6—the last an important verse for Luke, who interpolated it into his citation from Isaiah 61 in Jesus' speech at Nazareth [Luke 4:18]), whereas *οὐκ . . . μερὶς οὐδὲ κλῆρος* (lit. "neither portion nor lot") resembles the pleonastic style of Deutero-Pauline rhetoric (2 Cor 6:15; Col 1:12). See also n. 22.

19 "Seem" is important, for it is likely that Luke viewed the crime of Ananias and Sapphira as more heinous, "the sin against the Holy Spirit." Even a proposal so devoid of understanding as Simon's was not an unforgivable sin. This would place Luke on the more "lenient" side of the debate about repentance that would trouble the Christian church for more than a century. Cf. Klauck, *Magic*, 100.

20 This is understood as a curse in *Act. Pet.* (*Verc.* 23), where it is located in Jerusalem. See the detailed commentary of Garrett, *Demise*, 70–72.

21 The noun *δωρεά* ("gift") is associated with the Spirit in Acts 2:38 (Pentecost); 10:45; 11:16 (conversion of gentiles).

22 The terms *μερίς* and *κλῆρος* (rendered "allotment or inheritance" in NRSV) are used of Levites and others, including orphans and widows, who are to be invited to feasts, etc., in Deut 12:12; 14:27-29. Note 1:17, where *κλῆρος* (in the sense of "allotted office") is used of the place of Judas. See Garrett, *Demise*, 146 n. 50. The influence of Col 1:12 on v. 21 is also probable.

23 The adjective *εὐθύς* ("straight," "proper") appears also in Paul's confrontation with a magus (13:10) where the allusion to Isa 40:3 (cf. Luke 3:4) is apparent. It is associated with "heart" in Ps 77:37 LXX. The translation of *λόγος* is difficult. "Matter" is safe but too narrow in English. "Enterprise" is a business metaphor, appropriate with the word. This is evidently how the D-Text paraphrase *τῇ πίστει ταύτῃ* ("in this 'religion'") understood it (Boismard, *Texte*, 151).

24 Lüdemann, 100. Barrett (1:416) agrees that this is not a coincidence, although he is prepared to consider another explanation of the relationship.

25 The prayers of great prophets and wonder-workers are potent, for example, Alexander of Abonouteichos, according to Lucian *Alex.* 22.

26 See Talbert (87), who states that Simon wishes to evade the curse of a magician more potent than he.

27 The catena provides another ending, by way of information to the reader: Simon fled to Rome, thinking the apostles would not arrive there. See Ropes, *Text*, 409.

28 Boismard, *Texte*, 152: *ἀποκριθεὶς δὲ ὁ Σίμων εἶπεν πρὸς αὐτούς παρακαλῶ δεήθητε ὑμεῖς πρὸς τὸν θεὸν ὅπως μηδὲν ἐπέλθῃ μοι τούτων τῶν κακῶν ὧν εἰρήκατε. πολλὰ κλαίων οὐ διελίμπανεν.* (Bezae takes the final sentence as a relative clause. Mae and sy[hmg] do not follow this aberration.) This text was known to the Pseudo-Clementines (*Hom.* 20.21; *Rec.* 10.63), which transform it into tears of anger. The only other NT use of *διαλιμπάνω* ("weep") is in Bezae (17:13).

soon returned to the fold. This observation bears upon other "open endings," particularly the close of the book. If Acts ends on a tragic note, the story of Simon may also be viewed as tragic.[29] Theologically, open or unfinished endings affirm that the future belongs to God. Literarily, such endings are often far more effective than conclusions that connect every dot. They also involve a risk, which is that those so inclined will view them as tragedy or comedy, alternatively as grounds for confidence or as invitations to complacency.[30] From time to time this was a risk that Luke was willing to take. In this instance the risk was minimal. Simon does not demonstrably change.[31]

The narrative has taught a number of lessons: Christian leaders are not magicians and are not interested in acquiring money, inappropriate desire for which has led to the downfall of Judas (1:16-20), Ananias and Sapphira (5:1-11), and now Simon.[32] Miracle, magic, and money are elements of power. The episode is thus a lesson in the proper use of power. It also affirms that baptism does not preclude apostasy or other failure.[33] Having accomplished all of this, the narrator sends the apostles on their way.[34]

29 See the excursus "The Ending of Acts" in the commentary on chap. 28.

30 Luke 13:1-9 seeks to frustrate interpretations of this type. The examples in vv. 1-5 warn against cheap shots: these persons died to exhibit divine justice. The subsequent parable (vv. 6-9) warns against cheap grace: the assumption that continued survival is a sign of divine approval. That parable is left with a genuinely open ending. Choice is in the reader's hands. The conclusion to the parable of the Prodigal Son (Luke 15:11-32) is also "open," but it is most unlikely that the older brother will "repent."

31 Garrett, *Demise*, 72: "But if anything, the magician resembles a cornered criminal, frightened at the prospect of punishment although not obviously remorseful over his crimes."

32 Klauck (*Magic,* 21) points to the interpretation of the parable of the sower in Luke 8:14: the seed among thorns represents those "choked by the cares and riches and pleasures of life." See Pervo, *Dating,* 218–29.

33 Acts 8:14-24 expresses in a narrative the specific theme of 1 Corinthians 10. Here, as in 5:1-11, there is a cautionary purpose. Eusebius (*H.E.* 2.1.11) prefers to assert that Simon's faith was feigned.

34 The *μὲν οὖν* is, as often, problematic. Here it appears to mark a transition (cf. v. 4). Philip is probably not included in the "they" (*οἱ*), as the δέ ("but") in v. 26 indicates. For differing interpretations, see Cadbury and Lake, 95; Barrett, 1:418.

8

8:26-40 Philip Converts an Ethiopian Official

26/ **A messenger of the Lord said to
Philip: "Travel[a] at noon[b] along
the desert road that leads from
Jerusalem to Gaza."[c] 27/ So
Philip set out. Just then a
eunuch from Ethiopia, an official in charge of the treasury of
Candace, their queen,[d] was on
his way home from a pilgrimage
to Jerusalem. 28/ He[e] was reading the prophet Isaiah while
seated in his chariot.[f] 29/ The
Spirit said to Philip: "Go up
and get close to his chariot."
30/ When Philip caught up with
him,[g] he heard him reading
Isaiah. "Do you really perceive
what you are perusing?" he
asked.[h]**
31/ **"How could I possibly understand without someone to
guide me?" he replied, and
then invited Philip to come up
and sit with him. (32/ This was
the passage he was reading:
"As is a sheep, he was led to
slaughter, and, as a lamb taken
to the shearer is mute, so he
did not open his mouth. 33/ In
his humiliation the judgment
against him was lifted.[i] Who
will tell the story of his times,
because his life has been
removed from the earth?")**
34/ **The eunuch said, "Please tell me,
about whom does the prophet
make this statement,[j] himself
or someone else?" 35/ Using
this passage as a starting point,
Philip opened his mouth and
told him the message about
Jesus.[k] 36/ In the course of their
journey they came upon some
water.[l] The eunuch exclaimed:
"Look, water! Is there any
reason why I cannot be
baptized?"[m] 38/ He ordered that
the chariot be halted. Philip
and he both descended into the
water, where Philip baptized
him. 39/ When they arose from
the water, a[n] spirit of the Lord
removed Philip from the scene.
The eunuch did not see him
again, but he resumed his journey filled with joy. 40/ As for
Philip, he appeared at Azotus,[o]
from which point he began to
travel along the coast, preaching the gospel in all the cities as
far north as Caesarea.[p]**

a The form and tense of this command vary in the MS. tradition.

b *Or:* "southwards."

c *Or:* "to Gaza in the desert."

d Boismard (*Texte*, 153) omits "official" (δυνάστης). D* (t) have "a certain queen." Boismard speculates that this might derive from a text that omitted the name. 1739 m read the article before "queen," suggesting a proper name ("Queen Candace").

e As often, there is fluctuation between τε and δέ (read by B C 614 *pc* e p sy^{h}). Boismard reads all three verb forms as asyndetic participles (ὑποστρέφων . . . καθήμενος . . . ἀναγινώσκων). This grammatically difficult construction appears to be a revision of Luke's LXX style.

f Bezae lacks 8:29–10:14 (d has 10:4-14).

g $\mathfrak{p}^{50}$ *pc* read προσελθών ("going toward"), conforming the participle to the preceding imperative.

h Some D-Texts have "said *to the eunuch*" (Boismard, *Texte*, 154).

i *Or:* "He was humiliated by the denial of justice."

j B* *pc*; Cyr omit the pronoun: "About whom does the prophet speak?"

k Various D-Texts (Boismard, *Texte*, 156) have the imperfect, "He set out to tell the message." Boismard also supports deletion of the pronoun "him," which he finds uncharacteristic of Luke with this verb (εὐαγγελίζομαι).

l $\mathfrak{p}^{74}$ 326 *pc* read "the water" rather than "some." Perhaps the Mediterranean is in mind.

m Erasmus included what would become v. 37 in his edition of the Greek NT, whence, because it was also included in the Clementine edition of the Vulgate, it entered into the major European translations. This verse elicits a christological confession prior to baptism. Since it is difficult to imagine grounds for omission, this (mainly) D-Text reading is obviously secondary. Strange (*Problem*, 69–77) has attempted to rehabilitate it, arguing that the *disciplina arcani* led to its deletion. The practice of withholding the Creed from the unbaptized will not account for deliberate omission. Friedrich W. Horn ("Apg 8,37, der Westliche Text und die frühchristliche Tauftheologie," in Nicklas and Tilly, *Book of Acts*, 211–39) argues that v. 37 is not an early baptismal formula. This is a second argument against Strange.) Note 16:31 (a probable basis for the interpolation) and 19:1-7. Boismard (*Texte*, 157) includes it in his D-Text (without rationale). The addition is pedantic. The narrator assumes that Philip's message met with a positive response and that the request for baptism was based on proper faith. This addition should not be separated from the gift of the Spirit in v. 39; the D-Text fills in missing details of normal baptismal practice. See below on expansions to v. 35, and, in general, Metzger, *Textual Commentary*, 315–16. Bede (43), who had access to E e, opined that the verses fell out because of scribal error (*scriptorum vitio*). (Note that no confession of faith is required from Cornelius.)

n *Or:* "The spirit . . ."

o That is, Ashdod.

p Boismard (*Texte*, 158) proposes the following D-Text: "But Philip was found *to be present* at Azotus: and *returning from there*, he preached the gospel *city by city*, till he came to Caesarea." This is essentially a paraphrastic revision (although "returning" is difficult and has some claims for attention). See the full citation of mae below.

Analysis

If Luke had a source for this splendid episode,[1] it has been concealed with such success that proposals of its extent involve little more than that Philip was said to have converted someone (perhaps a person of importance?) somewhere at some time. Lüdemann extracts these elements: (1) "An Ethiopian, a eunuch" (v. 27b), (2) who descended with Philip into the water for baptism (v. 38), and (3) v. 39. These items suffice, in his view, to identify the passage as a "conversion story."[2] These data are rather sparse. The chief criterion appears to be plausibility, with the important exception of (3), which has nothing to do with "conversion stories." Verse 39 is a proper conclusion to an epiphany, which may begin conversion stories (as in chaps. 9 and 10, variously), but is not a conventional means for ending them.

A formal parallel is the conversion of King Izates of Adiabene (Josephus *Ant.* 20.44–46). Izates was a "God-Fearer" in that he remained uncircumcised (for political rather than personal reasons, upon the advice of a religious mentor). Eleazar, a Galilean Jew noted for his strict (ἀκριβής) approach to traditional observances (τὰ πάτρια), arrived to find the good monarch reading the Law of Moses. Eleazar chastised Izates: one should not simply read Torah but obey it. His auditor found this argument persuasive, and the initiatory rite followed immediately.[3] Both stories involve the initiation of a prominent figure encountered while reading Scripture. The differences are also illuminating. Izates

1 Important studies of this passage include Franklin Scott Spencer, *The Portrait of Philip in Acts* (JSNTS 67; Sheffield: JSOT Press, 1992) 128–87; Beverly Roberts Gaventa, *From Darkness to Light: Aspects of Conversion in the New Testament* (OBT; Philadelphia: Fortress Press, 1986) 98–107; Erich Dinkler, "Philippus und der *ΑΝΗΡ ΑΙΘΙΟΨ* (Apg 8.26-40): Historische und geographische Bemerkungen zum Missionsablauf nach Lukas," in E. Earle Ellis and Erich Grässer, eds., *Jesus und Paulus: Festschrift für Werner Georg Kümmel zum 70. Geburtstag* (Göttingen: Vandenhoeck & Ruprecht, 1975) 85–95; Willem C. van Unnik, "Der Befehl an Philippus," in idem, *Sparsa Collecta* (3 vols.; NovTSup 29–31; Leiden: Brill, 1973, 1980, 1983) 1:328–39; James Millard Gibbs, "Luke 24:13-33 and Acts 8:26-39: The Emmaus Incident and the Eunuch's Baptism as Parallel Stories," *Bangalore Theological Forum* 7 (1975) 17–30; Clarice J. Martin, "A Chamberlain's Journey and the Challenge of Interpretation for Liberation," *Sem* 47 (1989) 105–35; Abraham Smith, "A Second Step in African Biblical Interpretation: A Generic Reading Analysis of Acts 8:26-40," in Fernando F. Segovia and Mary A. Tolbert, eds., *Reading from This Place: Social Location and Biblical Interpretation in the United States* (2 vols.; Minneapolis: Fortress Press, 1995) 1:213–28; Stefan Schreiber, "'Verstehst du denn, was du liest?' Beobachtungen zur Begegnung von Philippus und dem äthiopischen Eunuchen (Apg 8,26-40)," *StudNTUmwelt* 21 (1996) 42–72; Andreas Lindemann, "Der 'Äthiopische Eunuch' und die Anfänge der Mission unter den Völkern nach Apg 8–11," in Breytenbach, *Apostelgeschichte*, 109–33; and Parsons, *Body and Character*, 123–41.

2 Lüdemann, 104–5. See also the comments on 9:1-19a. Weiser (1:208–11) holds that the story was told about Philip but that the source has been submerged in Lucan composition. Franklin Scott Spencer ("A Waiter, a Magician, a Fisherman, and a Eunuch: The Pieces and Puzzles of Acts 8," *Forum* n.s. 3 [2000] 165–78) agrees that some traditions were available but that the story as it stands is Lucan composition.

3 On this story, see Wills, *Jewish Novel*, 208–9. It is possible that Acts 8:26-39 was influenced by Josephus (Pervo, *Dating*, 185–86).

had avoided circumcision on the grounds of expediency; the Ethiopian official was technically ineligible for full membership in the Jewish community—a point that Luke leaves to the reader's knowledge. For Izates, the driving issue was obedience to Torah; Christology dominated the Ethiopian's mind. What they were reading was equally crucial and indicative of a major difference between the respective faiths. Had Izates been pondering Isaiah and the Ethiopian studying Leviticus, their respective instructors would have been required to take a different course of action.[4] There is another important difference: whereas the story of Izates takes the form of history—presumably historical fiction—the story of the official is highly legendary,[5] with more proximity to the world of myth than to the everyday.[6]

Haenchen states that the story of the Ethiopian official was the "Hellenist" parallel to the conversion of Cornelius.[7] He does not integrate this proposal into his source theory. Haenchen himself offered strong arguments against the derivation of the two stories about Philip from a single source. The stories are quite unlike, not least in their characterization of Philip.[8] The gentile missionary source did not contain this story, since it identified Antioch as the location of the first gentile mission (11:19-21). Source theories are thus left up in the air. What is much closer to earth is the abundance of Lucan vocabulary, themes, motifs, and interests.[9] The close parallel between this episode and another famous Lucan pericope—the road to Emmaus (Luke 24:13-35)—is striking.[10]

Table 3. Emmaus and the Road to Gaza

Incident	Luke 24	Acts 8
1. Traveler meets traveler(s)	24:15	8:30
2. Question answered with question	24:17-18	8:30-31
3. Subject of conversation is the death and the resurrection of Jesus, demonstrated by scriptural interpretation	24:26-27	8:32-35
4. Invitation/request	24:29	8:36
5. Ritual action	24:30-31	8:38
6. Disappearance of teacher	24:31	8:39
7. Emotional Reaction of pupil(s)	24:32	8:39

The stories share the same narrative skeleton: an outline that is not a development of a conventional form (such as an apophthegm or an exorcism). This pattern exhibits Lucan theology in a nutshell expressed in Lucan fashion: faith kindled in a conversation that includes "word and sacrament" and is developed in the course of a journey. Luke 24:13-35 would stand close to the top of any list of probable authorial creations in Luke and Acts.[11] Just above it would stand Acts 8:26-39.

4 Encounter in the very act of reading and the convenience of the subject matter are indicators of the legendary nature of both stories.

5 Dibelius, *Studies*, 15.

6 For a literary study of the passage with comparison to ancient fiction, see Abraham Smith, "Do You Understand What You Are Reading? A Literary Critical Reading of the Ethiopian (Kushite) Episode (Acts 8:26-40)," *Journal of the Interdenominational Theological Center* 22 (1994) 48–70.

7 Haenchen, 315.

8 Haenchen, 316.

9 Weiser (1:208–11) identifies twelve redactional features.

10 Spencer (*Portrait*, 141–44) discusses this parallelism in detail. He observes that the subsequent appearance in Luke 24:36-49 justifies the gentile mission. Note also James M. Gibbs, "Luke 24:13-33 and Acts 8:26-39: The Emmaus Incident and the Eunuch's Baptism as Parallel Stories," *Bangalore Theological Forum* 7 (1975) 17–30; Joseph A. Grassi, "Emmaus Revisited (Luke 24:13-35 and Acts 8:26-40)," *CBQ* 26 (1964) 463–67; and Robert F. O'Toole, "Philip and the Ethiopian Eunuch (Acts viii, 25-40)," *JSNT* 17 (1983) 25–34. See also Pervo, *Dating*, 30–35.

11 Composition does not preclude the use of sources. Behind Luke 24:13-35 and John 21:1-14 may be a story about eucharistic recognition. (Note that Luke uses the theme of the miraculous catch in 5:1-11—although John 21 may have been written with Luke in mind.) See Richard J. Dillon, *From Eyewitnesses to Ministers of the Word: Tradition and Composition in Luke 24* (AnBib 82; Rome: Pontifical Biblical Institute, 1978) 69–155; Hans Dieter Betz, "The Origin and Nature of Christian Faith according to the Emmaus Legend (Luke 24:13-32)," *Int* 23 (1969) 32–46; Arthur A. Just, *The Ongoing Feast: Table Fellowship and Eschatology at Emmaus* (Collegeville, Minn.: Liturgical Press, 1993); and Geoffrey F. Nuttall, *Moment of Recognition: Luke as Story-Teller* (London: Athlone, 1978).

An equally Lucan contribution is the scriptural passage in view: Isa 53:7-8.[12] The quest for tangible sources leads to the LXX.

Connections with the Elijah/Elisha tradition are quite dense. This imitation is another indicator of Luke's hand. Etienne Trocmé pointed to 1 Kings 18.[13] In 2 Kings 2 there is also a "rapture" of the prophet, followed by the statement that the other no longer saw Elijah (2 Kgs 2:11). Thomas Brodie argues for the pervasive use of 2 Kings 5, which also features a prominent non-Israelite official equipped with a chariot, washing in a body of water, and substantial providential direction.[14] However tenuous some of the proposals may appear, it is reasonably certain that allusions to the Elijah/Elisha cycle provide many of the details for this episode.[15] More than eight decades ago, William K. L. Clarke speculated that this passage had been "built up out of hints contained in Zephaniah and other parts of the Old Testament."[16]

The initial impression is that Clarke's suggestion is rather far-fetched, based on no more than several names in common—Gaza, Ashdod/Azotus, and Ethiopia—

Table 4. Acts 8 and Zephaniah 2–3

Acts 8	Zephaniah
26 *Ἄγγελος δὲ κυρίου ἐλάλησεν πρὸς* **Φίλιππον** *λέγων· ἀνάστηθι καὶ πορεύου κατὰ* **μεσημβρίαν** *ἐπὶ τὴν ὁδὸν τὴν καταβαίνουσαν ἀπὸ Ἰερουσαλὴμ εἰς* **Γάζαν** Get up and go toward the **south** to the road that goes down from Jerusalem to **Gaza** 27 *καὶ ἀναστὰς ἐπορεύθη.* So he got up and went. *καὶ ἰδοὺ ἀνὴρ* **Αἰθίοψ** *εὐνοῦχος δυνάστης Κανδάκης βασιλίσσης Αἰθιόπων, ὃς ἦν ἐπὶ πάσης τῆς* **γάζης** *αὐτῆς, ὃς ἐληλύθει* **προσκυνήσων** *εἰς Ἰερουσαλήμ* Now there was an **Ethiopian** eunuch, a court official of the Candace, queen of the Ethiopians, in charge of her entire **treasury**. He had come to Jerusalem to worship. 40 **Φίλιππος** *δὲ εὑρέθη εἰς* **Ἄζωτον**· But Philip found himself at **Azotus**	2:4 *Διότι* **Γάζα** *διηρπασμένη ἔσται . . . καὶ* **Ἄζωτος μεσημβρίας** *ἐκριφήσεται* For Gaza shall be deserted . . . Ashdod's people shall be driven out at *noon*, 2:11-12 . . . *καὶ* **προσκυνήσουσιν** *αὐτῷ ἕκαστος ἐκ τοῦ τόπου αὐτοῦ, πᾶσαι αἱ νῆσοι τῶν ἐθνῶν.* and to him shall bow down, each in its place, all the coasts and islands of the nations. 12 *Καὶ ὑμεῖς,* **Αἰθίοπες**, *τραυματίαι ῥομφαίας μού ἐστε.* You also, O Ethiopians, shall be killed by my sword. 3:10 *ἐκ περάτων ποταμῶν* **Αἰθιοπίας** *οἴσουσιν θυσίας μοι.* From beyond the rivers of Ethiopia my suppliants, my scattered ones, shall bring my offering.

12 Note also the absence of "spiritual gifts" from a baptism administered by Philip.

13 Trocmé, *Actes et l'histoire*, 180. His correspondences included (1) the initial divine command (1 Kgs 18:1; Acts 8:26); (2) the desert locale (1 Kgs 18:2, 5; Acts 8:26); (3) meeting with royal official (1 Kgs 18:3-4, 7; Acts 8:27-28); (4) religious figure runs to chariot (1 Kgs 18:46; Acts 8:30); (5) pair converse (1 Kgs 18:7-15; Acts 8:30-35); (6) ritual act is climax (1 Kgs 18:20-40; Acts 8:32-35); (7) needed water provided (1 Kgs 18:41-45; Acts 8:36); (8) both religious figures removed by "rapture" (1 Kgs 18:12, 46; Acts 8:39). Cf. also Jean-Daniel Dubois, "La figure d'Elie dans la perspective lucanienne," *RHPhR* 53 (1973) 155–76; Craig A. Evans, "Luke's Use of the Elijah/Elisha Narratives and the Ethic of Election," *JBL* 106 (1987) 75–83; and Spencer, *Portrait*, 135–36.

14 Thomas L. Brodie, "Towards Unraveling the Rhetorical Imitation of Sources in Acts: 2 Kings 5 as One Component of Acts 8, 9-40," *Bib* 67 (1986) 41–67.

15 See the summary and evaluation of Spencer, *Portrait*, 135–41.

16 Clarke, "Use of the Septuagint," 101–2. (I have omitted Clarke's comparison of Acts 8:39 to Zeph 3:4.)

as well as a few concepts: noon/south (μεσημβρία), desert, and foreigners bowing down before the God of Israel. More concretely, there is the Greek pun on γάζα, meaning both a place, Gaza, and "treasure," a wordplay exploited, evidently, in both the LXX and Acts. Zephaniah certainly did not provide the narrative framework for this passage. Yet these items do not occur elsewhere in such close proximity. Zephaniah proclaims the joy of Zion at God's universal reign of justice, a universalistic message well suited to Acts 8:26-39. There is room to doubt that Luke extracted chariots, officials, divine guidance and other motifs from the story of Elijah, seasoned them with elements from Zephaniah, and then poured the mixture into the mold provided by Emmaus, but claims that these resemblances are merely fortuitous are even less probable. The style and contents speak against viewing this as either a touched-up historical reminiscence or as a foundational conversion story. It has no tangible impact upon the rest of Acts.[17] Rather than establish a precedent, as did the conversion of Cornelius (10:1–11:18; 15:7), this narrative trails off into the happy and almost literally wild blue yonder. It has a fairy-tale quality. Philip is in an unusual place, at an unusual time, heading in a strange direction, and happens to meet a most unusual person who has been engaged in a highly atypical pilgrimage.[18] The story takes place in the symbolic land of the desert, the region in which Israel experienced direct contact with the divine and the beneficence of nurture provided from on high, gained without toil. It involves a representative of another never-never land: Ethiopia.

Excursus: Ethiopia and Ethiopians

The Ethiopia in view in Acts 8:26-39 is not the actual ancient kingdom of Meroe[19] so much as the legendary land of romance,[20] an exotic region[21] whose inhabitants enjoyed that utopian[22] existence available to those noted for their exemplary piety.[23] "This story . . . has a romantic character that neither the author nor his first readers would have missed."[24] This understanding endured throughout antiquity, from Homer (e.g., *Il.* 1.424–25) to Heliodorus, whose fourth-century CE novel *An Ethiopian Story* depends on the venerable stereotype.[25] These characteristics were derived not from archaeological research or authentic ethnographical study but from the location of Ethiopia: the ends of the earth. That view is reflected in classical,[26] biblical (e.g., Isa 18:1-7; Luke 11:31), and patristic[27] sources. It is the key to

17 By the late second century, Irenaeus could report that the official became a missionary (*A.H.* 3.12.8). Cf. also Eusebius *H.E.* 2.2.13–14; Jerome *Comm. in Isaiam* 14, *ad* Isa 53:7 (*PL* 24:508–9). Foakes Jackson (75) observes that this conversion "is an incident separated from the rest of the narrative and completely isolated from the rest of the history."

18 Barrett (1:426) is straightforward: "One must ask whether a man could be found of whom all these predicates are true: he was an Ethiopian; he was a eunuch; he belonged to the ruling class of his people; he read the Bible; he went on pilgrimage to Jerusalem. He was certainly a rare bird."

19 Cadbury (*Book*, 17–18) details the major historical problems in this story. The Romans launched a military expedition to Ethiopia in 23 BCE (Cassius Dio 54.5; Pliny *Hist. Nat.* 6.35), followed by a "scientific" probe in 62 CE (Seneca *Nat.* 6.8.3), on which see Plümacher, *Lukas*, 13.

20 On romantic and mythical views of Ethiopia, see Albin Lesky, "Aithiopika," *Hermes* 87 (1957) 27–38; Frank Snowden, *Blacks in Antiquity* (Cambridge, Mass.: Harvard University Press, 1970) 100–120, 144–55; and Romm, *Edges of the Earth*, 49–60.

21 On Luke's interest in the exotic, see Cadbury, *Book*, 15–17; and Pervo, *Profit*, 70, 163. For the religious appeal of the exotic, see Nock, *Conversion*, 106.

22 On utopian societies and literature, see pp. 90–91. Two differing perspectives on the ideal character of the Ethiopian state appear in Philostratus *Vit. Apoll.* 6.1–27, and Heliodorus's novel.

23 On Ethiopian piety, see Diodorus Siculus 3.2.2–4; Nicholas of Damascus frg. 142 (*FGH* 2:385); Pausanias 1.33.4; Philostratus, *Vit. Apoll.* 6.2, 4. This is a dimension of the topos on the piety of "barbarians," on which see Erwin Rohde, *Der griechische Roman und seine Vorlaüfer* (3rd ed.; Darmstadt: Wissenschaftliche Buchgesellschaft, 1974) 210–24. On Ethiopian piety, see Knox, *Hellenistic Elements*, 16 n. 3.

24 Cadbury, *Book*, 15.

25 See Talbert, 88.

26 E.g., Homer *Od.* 1.23 (ἔσχατοι ἀνδρῶν, "the furthest of humans"); Herodotus 3.115; Strabo 17.2.1–3; Heliodorus 1.6.15; 10.16.6.

27 E.g., Athanasius *Expositiones in Psalmos* (*PG* 27:303), who says that the official came from τὰ πέρατα τῆς γῆς ("the boundaries of the earth").

understanding why the person whom Philip baptizes is an Ethiopian.

A list of those who visited Ethiopia, for one purpose or another, often encountering the Candace, reads like a catalogue of legendary heroes, including such subjects of romance as Semiramis, Sesoosis/Seostris,[28] Moses (Artapanus frg. 3.7–8),[29] Cambyses (Herodotus 3.25), Alexander the Great (*Alexander Romance* 3.18–24 [encounter with Candace]), and Apollonius of Tyana (6.1–27). "After Sesostris the conquest of Ethiopia becomes a commonplace of the hero romance."[30] Philip too becomes a sort of "conqueror" of Ethiopia.[31]

Angelic direction leads the herald to a most unlikely encounter: few Ethiopian officials were to be found traveling from Jerusalem to his home south of Egypt.[32] Just as Philip arrives, the chamberlain was reading (in Greek) a key passage for early Christian theology. Just when it was needed, water appeared, in the desert. A story that opened with direction from "an angel of the Lord" closed with an intervention by "(the/a) Spirit of the Lord." Only one other passage in the NT contains as much explicit supernatural guidance as this: the conversion of Cornelius in Acts 10:1—11:18.[33] This supernatural tissue is thoroughly Lucan, a demonstration of the firm hand of providence. The fairy-tale atmosphere may be a deficit for those seeking concrete history, but for the author it brings numerous advantages. Precisely because this story belongs to the world of myth, it bears an explicitly paradigmatic and universal significance. Here is the story of Acts in a pericope, which, like Luke 24:13-35 is also the story of every believer. The world of 8:26-39 is thus nowhere and everywhere. Philip, who evangelized Samaria, now symbolically sends the message to "the ends of the earth."[34] The project of 1:8 has reached a kind of fruition. This interpretation induces the thoughtful reader to raise a pertinent question. If this passage fulfills, in some fashion, the mission announced in 1:8 and if it closely corresponds in shape to Luke 24:13-35, why does the author not place it at the close of his work? Leaving to one side the awkwardness of introducing Philip in chap. 28 or having Paul encounter an Ethiopian official in Rome, the answer is that this episode immediately precedes the conversion of Paul, who will reveal the actual significance of that phrase, "to the ends of the earth," which is more than geographic. The universalism expressed in this phrase is to be realized in the gentile mission (13:47). This convert is a great catch, socially and symbolically.[35] He is a male member of the ruling class and, at the same time, a marginal figure (inasmuch as actual eunuchs were theoretically excluded from the people of God).[36] This acquisition fulfills the promise of Isa 56:3-7. It is a mark of Lucan talent that 8:26-40 is, despite its intertextual

28 On Semiramis and Seostris as conquerors of Ethiopia, see Sterling, *Apologetic Historiography*, 180.

29 See Carl Holladay, *Fragments from Hellenistic Jewish Authors* (5 vols.; Chico, Calif.: Scholars Press, 1983) 1:235 n. 56; and Sterling, *Apologetic Historiography*, 180.

30 Martin Braun, *History and Romance in Greco-Oriental Literature* (Oxford: Basil Blackwell, 1938) 18.

31 The psalmist summoned God to conquer Ethiopia: "Let bronze be brought from Egypt; let Ethiopia hasten to stretch out its hands to God" (Ps 68:31, applied to this passage by Bede, 40). Luke and his readers doubtless viewed the latter as conversion.

32 Verse 38 indicates that the official was accompanied by a driver. The narrative otherwise ignores this person.

33 Haenchen, 315. Tannehill (*Narrative Unity*, 2:110–11) notes other parallels with the story of Cornelius. Spencer (*Portrait*, 154–58) discusses the element of supernatural guidance in detail.

34 Goulder (*Type*, 196) and Gaventa (*Darkness*, 106) also identify this episode as symbolic.

35 Spencer (*Portrait*, 158–65) discusses the full range of religious and status issues.

36 Josephus *Ant.* 4.290–91 expands the prohibition against males with defective genitals (e.g., Deut 23:1) by adding moral warrants. He reflects ancient prejudices against eunuchs: they are effeminate and lack respect for life. Philo repeats these prejudices and rationales in *Spec. leg.* 1.324–25. Some Jewish writers dissented. In addition to the hope offered by Isa 56:3-7, Wis 3:14 protests against the assumption that eunuchs are cursed. On distaste for eunuchs, see Ovid *Am.* 2.3; Philo *Leg. all.* 3.8; Dio Chrysostom 79.11; Martial *Epigrams* 3.91; 6.2; 11.75; Epictetus *Diss.* 2.20.17–20; Lucian *Eunuchus*, esp. 6. Literature: Betz, *Lukian*, 78; and John P. Sullivan, *Martial: The Unexpected Classic* (Cambridge: Cambridge University Press, 1991) 189–90. In religious circles, eunuchs functioned as chaste persons. See Arthur Darby Nock, "Eunuchs in Ancient Religion," in idem, *Essays*, 1:7–15. Critics stated that they had made themselves women. Domitian banned the practice of castration: Suetonius *Dom.*

weight and symbolic freight, a story that is so enchanting that detailed reflection is required to expose its oddities, and that, when critical dissection has done its utmost, its force and charm remain unsullied.

Franklin Scott Spencer has argued for an elaborate nineteen-part chiastic structure for vv. 25-40. This is based on linguistic data.[37] Krodel proposes a thematic ring-composition scheme.[38] Both of these plans are flawed,[39] but they do suggest a balanced opening and closing, with the dialogue (vv. 30-35) as the central section. Each character receives an "introduction" (vv. 26-28); the Spirit brings the two together (v. 29), followed by the exchange of questions (vv. 30-31a), the invitation to Philip (v. 31b), the citation (vv. 32-34), and the official's second question (v. 34), which leads to the summary of Philip's exposition (v. 35). The official's third question prompts his baptism (vv. 36, 38), after which the two go their separate ways (vv. 39-40). The opening and closing units mirror each other: the two meet through the agency of the Spirit and separate because of the Spirit's intervention.[40] The central section (vv. 30-35) is framed by Philip's speech, but the narrative propellant comes from the three questions of the official. This reveals that he is, as Gaventa says, "the real protagonist of the story."[41] The well-written[42] account of Philip's conversion of this exotic official is less a conversion story than a story of "conversion," a foreshadowing of the gentile mission.[43]

Comment

■ **26** Providence brings the two characters together in vv. 26-28.[44] For Luke, an "angel" and "the Spirit" can sometimes be interchangeable.[45] It therefore seems unwise to distinguish between the agents of vv. 26 and 29. Logically, *μεσημβρία* would mean "south" here, but "noon" is the proper time for revelation in Acts (10:9; 22:6), as well as for Elijah's experience on

7; Martial 6.2 (Romans associated circumcision with castration, i.e., as a form of genital mutilation.) See Spencer, *Portrait*, 166–72; Louis H. Gray, "Eunuch," *ERE* 5:575–79; J. Schneider, "*εὐνοῦχος*," *TDNT* 2:765–68; Gerd Petzke, "*εὐνοῦχος*," *TDNT* 2:80–81; and Lindemann, "'Der Äthiopische Eunuch,'" 121–23. Finally, the Ethiopian Eunuch of Zedekiah, Ebed-Melech, rescued Jeremiah (Jer 38:7-13). Parsons (*Body and Character*, 123–41) illustrates Greco-Roman prejudice against eunuchs. Even those unfamiliar with the restrictions of the Torah would be likely to view eunuchs as undesirable. Note, however, that, although Martial and Statius praised Domitian for outlawing castration, both also praised Earinus, the emperor's eunuch lover. See Anthony R. Birley, *Hadrian: The Restless Emperor* (London: Routledge, 1997) 28.

37 Spencer, *Portrait*, 131–34.

38 Krodel, 167.

39 Spencer shifts bases. The most egregious example is D/D´(132), which is based upon "Philip" as object in v. 26 and "Philip" as subject in v. 40, while it ignores the subject of v. 26, "the Spirit." Krodel's arrangement is broader, with eleven components. His A includes three verses (vv. 26-28), balanced by v. 40, and his C components are Philip's question in v. 30 and the baptism (v. 38), on the grounds that the official now understands what he has been reading. This "parallel" comes from inference and interpretation—the official never says that he understands what he has been reading. Spencer does attempt to relate his structural analysis to interpretation. Talbert's identification of two "balanced panels" in vv. 26-28 and 29-30, each of which contains verbs of speaking, motion, and sense perception, indicates why the efforts to discover a chiastic structure run into difficulty.

40 Cf. Roloff, 139.

41 Gaventa, *Darkness*, 102.

42 On the quality of the Greek, see Haenchen, 311; Schneider, 1:198–99; and Barrett, 1:428, with the references of each.

43 Tannehill, *Narrative Unity*, 2:108.

44 $\mathfrak{P}^{50}$, a curious piece of uncertain date (c. 300–400), contains Acts 8:26-32; 10:26-31 in one sheet folded to make four 13.8 cm x 17.7 cm pages. The thematic connection between the two incomplete selections is clear, but the purpose of the document is not. See Philip W. Comfort, and David P. Barrett, eds., *The Complete Text of the Earliest New Testament Manuscripts* (Grand Rapids: Baker, 1999) 352–54, who propose that it "may have been designed to promote evangelism to Gentiles" (352). By any estimate of the date, no such encouragement was needed. One wonders if it served as a kind of amulet. Johnson (159–60) suggests that it may have been "used as an *aide-mémoire* in preaching, perhaps even on the occasion of a baptism." The text is conflate, with D-Text elements (despite Comfort and Barrett, 352).

45 Cf. 23:8 and the comments in Cadbury and Lake, 95; and Kirsopp Lake, "The Holy Spirit," in Lake and Cadbury, *Additional Notes*, 96–111, esp. 109.

Mount Carmel (1 Kgs 18:26-29), so that a temporal reference is slightly more probable.[46] The phrase *αὕτη ἐστιν ἔρημος* (lit. "which is devoid of habitation") is also ambiguous. It is likely that this should be viewed as a narrative intrusion rather than as part of the angel's direction, and that the author wished to stress the symbolic locality rather than to stress that it was a "desert road" or, as the grammar implies, that Gaza was deserted.[47] The narrator intimates that the angel sent Philip forth onto an empty road at an unlikely time of day.

■ **27** As Philip was engaged in obeying this direction, there appeared[48] an individual identified by nationality, physical condition, and position. "Eunuch" can refer to a courtier, regardless of position,[49] but the accompanying *δυνάστης* indicates that the term refers to his physical state. Readers would expect that the officials of "oriental despots" were eunuchs—another reason for decrying oriental despotism. "Candace" was evidently a title often misconstrued as a proper name.[50] The omniscient narrator supplies this information, adding that he was the queen's treasurer.[51] That datum allows Luke to indulge in the pun on the word *γάζα* ("Gaza" and "treasure"),[52] and, by implication, to show that Philip, unlike Simon, had no interest in money. A second relative clause awkwardly follows this notice:[53] the official had gone to Jerusalem for the purpose of worship. The narrator does not say that this project had been accomplished,[54] nor does he identify this person as a Jew or as a convert to Judaism or as a gentile "God-Fearer." Readers who attempt to fill in this gap are missing the point, which is that the official is moving away from the temple and toward the prophets (cf. Jerome *Ep.* 55.3). For Jews no less than gentiles this is (in Lucan terms) progress.

■ **28** The syntax of v. 28 is difficult, the D-Text alternative only slightly less so. *ἅρμα* is best rendered "chariot," which exhibits the parallels with the Elijah/Elisha tradition and the exotic character of the passage.[55]

■ **29-31** In these verses the narrator, through the agency of the Spirit, brings the two characters together.[56] The scene will not benefit from a realistic reconstruction, in which a hard-breathing Philip will gasp out a request that the chariot halt, followed by proper introductions. Philip recognizes the text being read[57] and poses what might in some circumstances be construed as an impolite question. The form of the question presumes that

46 See Gaventa, *Darkness*, 101–2; Spenser, *Portrait*, 156. A southerly direction is contained in the phrase "from Jerusalem to Gaza."

47 See Cadbury and Lake, 95; Barrett, 1:423–24; and Schürer, *History*, 2:98–102, esp. 102 n. 77, which cites a geographical fragment (from an edition of 1717) that speaks of "New Gaza," then *ἡ ἔρημος Γάζα*, then Ascalon. BDF §289 (1) observes that it would be unusual to refer to a road as "uninhabited territory."

48 The words *καὶ ἰδού* must have the weight of "there appeared" in this instance.

49 The term means "chamberlain" (*εὐνὴν ἔχων* "holding [the] bed") and comes from the practice of placing castrated males in charge of the women's quarters. (The LXX uses both *εὐνοῦχος* and *δυνάστης* to render Hebrew סריס [Barrett, 1:424]. Eunuchs were valued not just for putative celibacy but because they would not conspire to place their children upon the throne.

50 On Candace, see Alfred Wikenhauser, *Die Apostelgeschichte und ihr Geschichtswert* (NTAbh; Münster: Aschendorff, 1921) 361–62; and Erich Dinkler, "Philippus und der *ΑΝΗΡ ΑΙΘΙΟΨ* (Agp. 8.26–40): Historische und geographische Bemerkungen zum Missionsablauf nach Lukas," in E. Earle Ellis and Erich Grässer, eds., *Jesus und Paulus: Festschrift für Werner Georg Kümmel zum 70. Geburtstag* (Göttingen: Vandenhoeck & Ruprecht, 1975) 92–94. Texts include Strabo 17.1.54; Cassius Dio 54.5.4–5; and Pliny *Hist. Nat.* 6.186. Bion of Soli (*Aethiopica* 1) says that this title was given to the queen mother, who was the real head of government. For the notion that "Candace" was a proper name, see *Alexander Romance* 3.18–24. In the patristic period (e.g., Bede, 41), this monarch was identified with the queen of Sheba (cf. Luke 11:31).

51 For a eunuch placed in charge of a royal treasury, see Plutarch *Dem.* 25.5.

52 See above for the same pun in Zephaniah.

53 Boismard (*Texte*, 153) omits the second relative. This is almost certainly a secondary improvement. Ropes (*Text*, 81) says, "The relative was omitted because the full sentence-building virtue of *ἰδού* was not felt."

54 Josephus (*Ant.* 3.318–19) speaks of "some persons from beyond the Euphrates" who had come to the temple for the purpose of offering sacrifice but did not complete the rites because they were not (observant) Jews.

55 Note, however, Gen 41:43; 46:29, and, for realistic possibilities, Bruce, 227.

the individual mounted on the chariot is a gentleman, for it is relatively elegant.[58] Philip uses an apt pun.[59] The answer confirms his wisdom, for it is even more eloquent: a potential optative as the apodosis of a general condition.[60] The official asks for a "guide" (lit. "one to lead the *way*" [ὁδός]). This verb encapsulates much of the meaning of this passage: life is a journey that requires a guide. The official's question, which is also a plea for direction, assumes Luke's conviction that Scripture is not self-interpreting.[61] Followers of Jesus do not reject Jewish Scripture; they reinterpret it with a new key, the basis of which is what Jesus did (and said). Luke can therefore claim that Christianity is a reform movement within Israelite religion.[62] The Ethiopian assumes that Philip can provide the required guidance.

■ **32-35** The passage[63] (Isa 53:7-8a LXX[64]) is a narrative aside that could not have been more suitable had Luke himself selected it.[65] Isa 53:4-6, 8b, which immediately precede and follow the selection, are highly suitable, when applied to Jesus, as an interpretation of his death as a saving event.[66] Luke did not stress this conception of the atonement. To understand v. 33 requires attention to the possible meanings of the Greek text rather than evaluation of it as a version of the MT. Interpretation depends on the verb *αἴρω,* which can refer to exaltation or to removal. If the former is preferred, the contrast is between humiliation (the passion) and the reversal of this verdict through the resurrection.[67] The latter would imply that justice was denied and that he accepted this humiliation with silence.[68] Both views are arguably

56 The chariot had a driver (v. 38), but the narrator exhibits no interest in this person, an example of Acts' characteristic social snobbery.

57 Reading aloud was the normal practice in antiquity. See, e.g., Cadbury, *Book*, 16. Exceptions (Talbert, 89) do not disprove the rule. (*Scriptio continua*, writing in upper-case letters without punctuation or word division, all but requires this.)

58 Although this is formally an open question, the particle γε may convey some doubt, whence "really." See Moule, *Idiom Book*, 158, and, with more discussion and less certainty, Barrett, 1:428.

59 BDF §488 (1b). 2 Cor 3:2 utilizes the same wordplay and may have inspired Luke.

60 A range of witnesses ($\mathfrak{p}^{74}$ A B[2] Ψ 1739 m) have the correct subjunctive. Given the literary quality of the verse and the use of *μή,* it is tempting to believe this more likely to be original, although the principles of textual criticism speak against it. Cf. Barrett, 1:428. Boismard (*Texte*, 154–55) in his D-Text presents a nice problem. It is much less elegant: εἰ γινώσκεις ἃ ἀναγινωσκεις . . . πῶς δύναμαι γινώσκειν ἐὰν μή τις διδάξει με ("Know what you are reading?" . . . "How can I know unless someone will teach me?"). In comparison the conventional text looks like an Alexandrian improvement, but the context speaks in favor of the "better Greek," ὁδηγέω is an apt Lucan metaphor, and much of Boismard's evidence is from versions and thus less secure for such fine points.

61 Jervell (272–73) stresses that Luke does not view Scripture as mysterious or as the repository of deep secrets. This is correct, but clarity does not mean that every plowboy at his plough, to paraphrase William Tyndale, could read Israelite Scripture and discover its christological meaning. So Irenaeus, in speaking of this passage, says that study of the prophets had acquainted the Ethiopian with the creator God and the rules for proper living. He lacked but one thing: knowledge of the appearance of the Son of God (*A.H.* 4.23.2). As a defense of the OT, this argument has its value, but the incarnation is no minor fact.

62 See Neyrey, "Symbolic Universe" 295. Talbert (90–91) provides an outline of the principal features of this model.

63 On the fine points of the antecedent of ἥν ("which,") in v. 32, see Barrett, 1:429.

64 There are two differences: The participle of "shear" (v. 32) is present in the LXX, aorist in the preferred text, since the present *v.l.* is conformation to Isaiah. The addition of αὐτοῦ after "humiliation" in v. 33 is more difficult. It is not in the LXX and is omitted by a range of important witnesses. See Metzger, *Textual Commentary*, 315. I think that it is probably a christological addition that makes the application to the passion of Jesus explicit, which was deleted to make the text conform. In v. 33b a range of witnesses ($\mathfrak{p}^{74}$ E [Ψ] 33. 1739 m it vg[mss]; Ir[lat]) insert the conjunction δέ. This has strong claims to originality. See Barrett, 1:430.

65 This appears to be a common "messianic" proof text. Examples are *1 Clem.* 16:7-8; Justin *Dial.* 72.3; Melito *On Pascha* 64. See also *Act. Phil.* 78.

66 Cf. Rom 4:25–5:1 (possibly); 1 Cor 15:3; 1 Pet 2:24-25. For discussions of this careful excision, see the references in Spencer, *Portrait*, 175 n. 6.

67 Spencer (*Portrait*, 177–78) discusses the use of the humiliation/exaltation pattern in Luke and Acts.

68 For this understanding, see Fitzmyer, 411.

compatible with Lucan theology. The former is preferable because it includes the element of vindication. The word γενεά (lit. "generation" [v. 33]) is another difficulty. It probably applies to the "life of Jesus," as well as to "the (depraved) era in which Jesus lived,"[69] an interpretation supported by the verb διηγέομαι.[70] Another possibility is to relate it to the uncountable number of believers in Jesus.[71]

■ **34** About this passage the official has but one question:[72] Who is its subject? The alternative seems inept. This is evidently an ancient way of raising the question of whether prophetic texts apply primarily to their own times or to later eras. Historical criticism assumes the former, Luke the latter. The suffering servant about whom Isaiah wrote is Jesus. Philip's response to this question picks up the citation from v. 32 ("open . . . his mouth") and uses this passage as the starting point of his christological proclamation.[73]

■ **35-38** In due course water appeared (in the desert),[74] leading to the third, climactic question.[75] Although the language of inhibition may reflect technical terminology (*κωλύειν*, "prevent"),[76] the negative form underlines his status and thus the meaning of the story. One possible response—presuming that the theme of accepting males with defective sexual organs is a Lucan concern here—was, "This is not possible because you are a eunuch," with a citation of a relevant prohibition. Luke's narrative ability is patent in the subsequent silence. Philip does not say, "Nothing" or "good idea," or mouth some platitudes about inclusiveness. Actions will speak louder than words.[77] The baptism includes—for the first and only time—the usual "descend/ascend" terminology[78] but says nothing about the ritual, with which the implied reader of Acts is familiar.

■ **39-40** The surprise comes (in the conventional text) at the close. The Spirit[79] does not fall on the newly baptized official, but instead removes Philip from the scene. This "rapture" bears marks of an ἀφανισμός (disappearance).[80] Rapture (of the living) is appropriate to prophets and other religious figures.[81] Here it echoes traditions about Elijah and Elisha.[82] The term ἀφανισμός indicates a quality of supernatural beings, the status of whom can be demonstrated by their disappearance.[83] In Acts 8:39(-40), it demonstrates the relation of this episode to Luke 24:13-35.[84] A feature of both is the statement that the one taken could no longer be seen

69 Cf. Luke 1:43-50; 7:31; 9:41; 11:29-32, 50-52; 16:8; 17:25-26; Acts 13:36; 14:16; 15:21; and V. Hasler, "γενεαλογία," *EDNT* 1:42. Justin *Dial.* 76 cites Isa 53:8 to prove that the origin of Christ is indescribable (evidently equating the word with γένεσις). So, evidently, Irenaeus *A.H.* 3.12.8, who renders the word as "nativity" (*nativitas*).

70 Luke wrote a διήγησις ("narrative") of the γενεά ("genealogy," "era") of Jesus.

71 Haenchen, 312; Barrett, 1:431; and Klauck, *Magic*, 28.

72 The initial ἀποκριθείς (lit. "answering") amounts to no more than the advance warning of a direct quotation, but it also marks the citation as a parenthesis.

73 For ἀρξάμενος, cf. Luke 24:27.

74 The theme of water in the desert may intend to evoke Exod 17:1-7; Num 20:2-13.

75 From the ensuing it is apparent that Luke presumes that summaries of the gospel (εὐαγγελίζεσθαι) include discussion of baptism (cf. 2:38).

76 Cf. Mark 10:14||Luke 18:16, which may refer to initiation. The same verb occurs in Acts 10:47, with reference to the baptism of Cornelius. In Ps.-Clem. *Hom.* 13.5.1, a woman asks: "What then prevents me from being baptized this day?" (This may, of course, be dependent on Acts.) The final comment on this theme is the final word of Acts: ἀκωλύτως ("unhindered").

77 One of the infelicities of the addition of v. 37 is the failure to recognize this literary technique.

78 Cf. Mark 1:10 (with "descend" implied); *Barn.* 11:11; Hermas *Sim.* 9.16.4 (93).

79 The text literally reads "Spirit of Lord" (πνεῦμα κυρίου). Ammonius's Canon indicates that "the spirit of the Lord" is an acceptable rendition. Note Isa 61:1 LXX, cited in Luke 4:18.

80 On this phenomenon in the NT, see Theissen, *Miracle Stories*, 95, 97, and 186.

81 Gods may "snatch up" a mortal for protection or other purposes, as when Zeus "raptures" Ganymede (*Homeric Hymn* 5.202–3 [ἥρπασεν]; cf. *Od.* 15.250) or when Aphrodite rescues Paris from an impending defeat (*Il.* 3.380–82), or when Apollo snatches up Hector (ἐξήρπαξεν) to save him from Achilles (*Il.* 20.441–44; cf. 21.597). Ezekiel was also transported by the Spirit (11:24; cf. 3:12; 8:3; 11:1; 11:24). In the famous saying of *Gospel of the Hebrews* 2, Jesus was carried by the Holy Spirit to Mount Tabor. Bel 36 (Daniel) may have inspired this; cf. also John 6:15. The Spirit carried away Hermas

(8:39).[85] The divine agency that had brought the pair together now propels them on their separate paths,[86] the official toward his destination and Philip back into itinerant missionary work. Luke has not provided this remarkable conclusion solely to underline his source(s). The close of this episode stresses its "magical," symbolic character. "Real" time and life are restored. Verse 40 rounds off the entire account from 8:4 and complements v. 25. This is also a typical Lucan summary that serves to expand the range of the mission. In this instance it also explains why Peter can find believers in Lydda and Joppa (which lie between Azotus and Caesarea). Azotus (Ashdod)[87] is a logical starting point, given its proximity to Gaza, but his ultimate destination, Caesarea, may derive from the gentile mission source.[88]

The structural problem of this story is that it appears, without making the matter explicit, to narrate the conversion of a gentile "God-Fearer" prior to Peter's visit to Cornelius and his family. Attempts to posit different sources[89] do not resolve the issue. Just as the story takes place in a "magical" world, so it stands outside the sequential development of the gentile mission. Here all of the focus falls on an individual who symbolizes not only "the ends of the earth"—universalism—but also the nature of individual faith. This paradigmatic account becomes the presupposition to and model for other conversions, few of which take up personal belief.[90] This is, as Andreas Lindemann contends, the reason for its apparently awkward place in the narrative.[91]

while he was traveling in the country (Hermas *Vis.* 1.1.3 [1]). Eusebius (*H.E.* 5.16.14) places a negative spin on claims that the Montanist prophet Theodotus was taken up to heaven on various occasions. Mani enjoyed similar experiences; see the *Cologne Mani Codex*, e.g., 51, 6–12; 52, 2–7; 55, 16–19; 57, 16–19. Anthony was miraculously transported across a river to preserve his modesty (Athanasius *Vit. Ant.* 60). Apollonius was transported miraculously from Rome to Dicaearchia (Philostratus *Vit. Apoll.* 8.10). Paul uses the verb for those taken up temporarily (2 Cor 12:2, 4) or permanently (1 Thess 4:17) into the celestial regions.

82 Note 2 Kgs 2:11-12: a *chariot* takes Elijah to heaven, after which Elishah can no longer see him. Note also the speculation in v. 16: the Spirit may have transported Elijah elsewhere (as in 1 Kgs 18:7-16).

83 See Jane L. Lightfoot, *Parthenius of Nicea* (Oxford: Clarendon, 1999) 478, commenting on Parthenius 15.4, in which Leucippus κατὰ θεῶν βούλησιν ἀφανὴς γίγνεται ("became invisible [= disappeared] in accordance with the will of the gods").

84 Note also εὑρέθη ("was/ was found"), which occurs in Luke 9:36 (the transfiguration) and in Acts 8:40. Cf. 1 Kgs 18:12, 46; and *1 Clem.* 9:3 (of Enoch).

85 Cf. Mark 9:8, where the awkward construction points to an underlying statement that they saw no one; and 2 Kgs 2:12 (above). Lollianos's novel *Phoinikika* contains a "ghost" scene in which ὁ νεάνισκος ἠφανίσθη ("the youth disappeared"), after which Glauketes turns to determine whether he could see him, but could not (*P. Oxy.* 1368 II.11–15).

86 The expression τὴν ὁδόν ("path," "journey") in v. 39 is best viewed as an adverbial accusative. Luke uses χαίρων ("rejoicing") as the final word in Luke 15:5; 19:6. Here it also echoes the final noun (χαρά, "joy") in v. 8, the close of Philip's Samaritan mission. The same participle closes the *Act. John* 115 (death of the apostle). Another noteworthy parallel is the final words of Apuleius *Metam.*, *gaudens obibam* ("I went about rejoicing"). See the excursus "The Ending of Acts" in the commentary on chap. 28. The expression is attested elsewhere, e.g., Euripides *Medea* 756 (χαίρων πορεύου, "depart in joy").

87 On this city, see Paul L. Redditt, "Azotus," *ABD* 1:541–42. As noted above, this may have been based on Zeph 2:4-5. Martin Hengel suggests that Philip's presence there reverses the ancient curse against that place; *Acts and the History of Earliest Christianity* (trans. John Bowden; Philadelphia: Fortress Press; London: SCM, 1980) 79.

88 Caesarea, once named Strato's Tower, was built by Herod the Great as a Greco-Roman city. It became and remained the Roman provincial capital. For a survey of its history and excavation, see Kenneth G. Holum et al., *King Herod's Dream: Caesarea on the Sea* (New York: Norton, 1988).

89 E.g., Haenchen, 305–8.

90 The exception is the Philippian jailer (16:27-34); this episode also involves a household.

91 Lindemann, "Der Äthiopische Eunuch," 132–33.

Some elements of the tradition, in particular the D-Text (A^c 36 323 453 945 1739 1891 *pc* l [p w sy^{h**}] mae),[92] strongly dissented from this conclusion, stating instead that the *Holy* Spirit fell upon the official, while an *angel* of the Lord snatched Philip away. Efforts to view this as the original cannot explain why an editor would introduce the unusual features of the conventional text.[93] The tendency of the D-Text throughout this passage may be best preserved by cop^{mae}:[94]

> 30 **"But he** [Philip] **was not in the least perplexed** . . . said **to the eunuch** . . . (31) . . . guide me **into the very same scriptures and instruct me about them . . . urgently** invited . . . 32 **He** [Philip] **opened the book and found the passage . . .** 35 **Then Philip took the initiative from this very passage and was ignited in the Spirit. And he began to interpret the scripture to him, in the course of which** he proclaimed **the Lord Jesus Christ to him.** 36 **In the course of their journey, as they conversed with one another, they came upon a pool of** water. The eunuch said **to Philip**: "Look, water! **Who** is there that would prevent me from being baptized?" 37 **Philip answered and said to him, "If you believe with your whole heart, it is possible." The eunuch answered and said, "I believe in Jesus Christ, that he is the Son of God."** 38 **Philip said** that the chariot should be halted. Both descended into the water, and **Philip** baptized **the eunuch**. 39 When they arose from the water, **the Holy** Spirit **descended upon the eunuch; but the angel** of the Lord removed Philip from the scene. The eunuch did not see him again, but resumed his journey filled with joy, **exulting in the view that he was (still) seated beside him.**

In addition to a form of v. 37, the reception of the Spirit by the newly baptized, and other D-Text features and pedantries (such as the constant provision of proper names), this text notes that Philip accepted the Spirit's direction without demur, makes the official's request text-specific, and removes the awkward narrative parenthesis by having Philip locate and read the passage. Verse 35 adds a reference to the Spirit, and v. 39 evidently explains how the official could go on his way rejoicing: by imagining that Philip was still with him.[95] Behind this evidently lies the view that baptism was all well and good but that separation from a person of (more or less) apostolic quality removed any occasion for joy. By describing the gift of the Spirit to the official, this edition dealt with any doubts about the completeness of the baptism (while raising questions about why the Spirit appeared here but not in Samaria). The most important observation is that the D-Text fails to understand (or agree with) Luke's purposes in this passage. It introduces a rational element, odd as this may sound in the present context.

Although Luke's ostensible solution to the "problem" of traditions about the Seven and the Twelve was to portray the Seven as administrative assistants, his actual solution was to present them as "forerunners" of both Peter and Paul. An obvious model was the Synoptic characterization of John the Baptizer as forerunner of the Messiah, a move that evidently found favor in Luke's sight, as he developed and expanded it.[96] Luke's depiction of continuity through parallelism also involves subordination. By portraying Philip as Peter's forerunner Luke can uphold not only the continuity of redemptive history but also the unity of the community.[97] This

92 See Boismard (*Texte*, 158), who prints this as his D-Text, with substantial data.

93 One example of an attempt to defend the D-Text as original is Strange, *Problem*, 67. All that he (and others) can show is that the conventional text is atypical. For arguments for the superiority of the conventional text, see Metzger, *Textual Commentary*, 316.

94 Schenke, *Apostelgeschichte 1,1–15,3*, 150–52.

95 This text also permits the view that the official was alone by removing the intimation of a driver from v. 38.

96 For details and discussion of Luke's use of John as a forerunner, see Spencer, *Portrait*, 220–32. Spencer makes the interesting suggestion that, as "forerunner," Philip, like John, does not impart the Spirit. He also describes (234–40) a similar relation between the ministries of Apollos and Paul in Ephesus.

97 A similar scheme is apparent—insofar as the fragments permit conclusions—in Artapanus, whose depictions of both Abraham and Joseph focused on their work in Egypt and thus as predecessors of Moses. Stephen's speech (Acts 7:2-53) takes a comparable approach by focusing on a series of rejected leaders culminating in Jesus.

larger narrative and theological goal permits the very different characterization of Philip in the two stories.[98] The activities of proclamation (which effectively equals scriptural interpretation) and miracle-working, which highlight the careers of Peter (chaps. 2–5) and Stephen (6:8-10), are divided, as it were, into two separate episodes in the case of Philip.

98 Clarice Martin ("A Chamberlain's Journey and the Challenge of Interpretation for Liberation," *Sem* 47 [1989] 105–35) stresses the difference in characterization (and genre) between the two stories about Philip.

9

9:1-19a The Call of Saul

**9:1/ Now Saul, who still fulminated
murderous threats against
the disciples of the Lord,
approached the high priest 2/ to
request that he issue letters to
the synagogues in Damascus
authorizing him to take back to
Jerusalem in chains any adherents of the Movement[a] he might
find there, women no less than
men.**
**3/ As he was nearing Damascus in
the course of his journey, a light
from above suddenly engulfed
him. 4/ He fell on the ground
and heard a voice saying to him,
"Saul, Saul, why are you persecuting me?"**
**5/ "Who are you, Lord?"
"I am Jesus, whom you are
persecuting.[b] 6/ Now get up and
enter the city. You will be told
what you must do."[c] 7/ Those
traveling with Saul were standing there speechless, for they
heard the voice but saw no one.
8/ After Saul had been picked
up from the ground and opened
his eyes, he could not see,[d] so
they took him by the hand and
led him into Damascus. 9/ For
three days he remained blind
and neither ate nor drank.**
**10/ In Damascus there was a disciple
named Ananias, whom the Lord
addressed in a vision:
"Ananias!"
"Yes, Lord."**
**11/ "Go[e] to Straight Street and
inquire at the house of Judas
for a man from Tarsus named
Saul. He is at prayer 12/ and has
seen [in a vision][f] a man named
Ananias enter and place a hand[g]
upon him to restore his sight."**
**13/ "Lord, many people have told
me[h] about this character and
all of the horrible things that
he has done to your people[i] in
Jerusalem. 14/ Now he is here
with authority from the high
priests to arrest everyone who
calls upon your name."**
**15/ "Get going, because this man
is the medium I have selected
to carry my name to gentiles,[j]
monarchs, and Israelites. 16/ I
shall show him how much he
will have to suffer for the sake
of my name."[k] 17/ Ananias
went to the house and laid his**

a The awkward expression τῆς ὁδοῦ ὄντας (lit. "those being of the way") has yielded six readings, most of which are demonstrable attempts at improvement. See Metzger, *Textual Commentary*, 316–17. The D-Text prefers "this movement."

b Variants include addition of "the Nazorean" (from 22:8) and "Christ," a typical later expansion.

c The Textus Receptus includes the proverb "Don't kick . . ." here, followed by (6) τρέμων τε καὶ θαμβῶν εἶπε, Κύριε, τί με θέλεις ποιῆσαι; καὶ ὁ κύριος πρὸς αὐτόν (In both fear and astonishment he said, "Lord, what do you want me to do?" The Lord replied . . .). This belongs to the D-Text tradition, introduced into the Greek NT by Erasmus from the Vulgate.

d 𝔓^{74} ℵ A* B e vg syr p h sah cop^{mae} read "no one." This conforms to the transfiguration but does not make for blindness. See Metzger, *Textual Commentary*, 318.

e B *pc* have an imperative: ἀνάστα ("get up!").

f "In a vision" is difficult. Its placement varies, raising the suspicion that it is secondary. The internal arguments that it could have been omitted as pedantic (Paul was blind; how else could he see?) are of slightly less weight than those that it was added as a pedantic supplement. On the other hand, the variation in word order could be an attempt at improvement of the construction, which is Lucan. Haenchen (324 n. 2) points to a similar order in 14:8. See Metzger, *Textual Commentary*, 319–20. Cadbury and Lake (103) say that, if a gloss, "it is a correct explanation."

g The text is difficult. 𝔓^{74vid} ℵ* A C 81 *et al* omit the article; Ψ 33. m it vg^{mss} sy read (anarthrous) "hand" in the singular. The normal word with "lay upon" (ἐπιτίθημι) is "the hands," as in v. 17. "Hand" may well be original, and "the hands" conformity to convention and v. 17.

h The variant in the perfect tense is probably a secondary improvement.

i Lit. "holy persons" (ἅγιοι), a Pauline term used first here, elsewhere in vv. 32, 41, and 26:10. The word helps to link the various sections of chap. 9 (and the Christian mission) together. This Pauline term may derive from the source used by Luke. It appears only in conversion accounts (26:10) outside of this chapter. See Barrett, 1:455.

j B C* *pc* include an article with ἐθνῶν ("gentiles," "nations"). This destroys the symmetry of the phrase. See also Barrett, 1:456.

k On the pronoun and conjunction, see Barrett, 1:457.

l A number of witnesses omit "Jesus." This may derive from v. 5, but support is diverse and strong. See Metzger, *Textual Commentary*, 320.

m The D-Text adds, quite typically and gratuitously, that his sight returned "immediately" (Boismard, *Texte*, 164).

hands upon him, with these words: "Brother Saul, the Lord has dispatched me—Jesus,[l] who appeared to you on the way here—so that you might see again and be filled with the Holy Spirit." 18/ At that moment a flaky substance fell from his eyes, and his sight returned.[m] Saul got up and was baptized. 19/ After he had taken some nourishment[n] his strength revived.

n A variant ($\mathfrak{p}^{45}$ B C* 323, 945, 1175, 1739 *pc*) places this in the passive voice, probably to coordinate with "was baptized."

Analysis

Acts 9 is embedded in a series of remarkable conversions, the most important of which is the conversion of Christian leaders to the acceptance of gentiles. Saul's experience follows the paradigmatic baptism of an Ethiopian official (8:26-39). The narrator then turns to reports that Peter continued the work of Philip (8:40) along the coast of Palestine (9:32-43). After the conversion of a full-fledged gentile by Peter, and its subsequent approval at Jerusalem (10:1–11:18), attention returns to the "Hellenist" missionaries, whose work with gentiles in Antioch motivates Jerusalem to send Barnabas. He, in turn, sends for Saul (11:19-26), bringing to a close the story of the "Hellenists," which the narrator had entwined with that of Saul from the beginning (7:58). The story of Stephen, itself the climax to a cycle, became the starting point for a new sequence and epoch. After an interlude that will provide a fitting climax to the story of Peter, the way is open for the extended story of Paul and his mission (chaps. 13–28).

Appreciation of the conversion story also requires attention to 7:58; 8:1a, 3, which introduced Saul the persecutor. Acts 9:1-30, which resumes his story, has eight sections: (1) Introduction (vv. 1-2); (2) Vision on way to Damascus (vv. 3-9); (3) Vision of Ananias (vv. 10-16); (4) Healing and initiation of Saul (vv. 17-19a); (5) Saul's ministry in Damascus (vv. 19b-22); (6) Saul's escape from Damascus (vv. 23-25); (7) Saul's acceptance and ministry in Jerusalem (vv. 26-28), and (8) Saul's escape from Jerusalem (vv. 29-30). The account opens with Saul as a persecutor of the Jesus movement accredited by the Jewish leaders in Jerusalem and closes with Saul as a persecuted missionary for the Jesus movement accepted by the leaders of that community in Jerusalem.[1] This movement from persecutor to persecuted intimates a concentric, or ring, composition, but 9:1-30 does not have an apparent overall artistic structure. There are two parallel units in vv. 1-19a, followed by two parallel episodes in vv. 19b-25 and 26-30,[2] dealing with Saul's conversion and initiation/commission and his initial ministry in Damascus and Jerusalem, two localities in which he was associated with persecution of believers.

Luke evidently possessed, in addition to the Pauline corpus, a written account of Paul's conversion from an enemy of God to a missionary of the new faith. That source narrated Paul's activity as a persecutor (without which 9:4, which is surely derived from a source, would be meaningless) and his punishment, repentance, baptism, and commission. The introduction of Saul into the story of Stephen's death is a Lucan contribution, and the summary in 8:3 is probably an abbreviation of a somewhat longer description, while 9:1-3a has been altered to conform to another Lucan invention: Jerusalem as Saul's base of operations. Other authorial elements include the association of Saul with the high

1 For a comparison of the three accounts, see the excursus "Three Accounts of Paul's Conversion/Call" in the commentary on chap. 26. The outline of Galatians 1–2 is similar, with the important differences that Paul claims to have no contact with the Jerusalem leaders following his change of allegiance, nor does he present himself as the target of persecution.

2 Two differing examples of these divisions are Talbert, 100, and Krodel, 173–74.

priestly leadership and use of "the Movement" (ἡ ὁδός) for those who followed Jesus. From the source quite possibly derive the "murderous threats against" believers and some data about Damascus as the target. The source may have depicted Tarsus as the point of origin for this journey.[3]

This leads to the question: Why Damascus?[4] On both narrative and historical grounds, Damascus was not a logical target. Logically, Luke would narrate a course of persecution extending to the environs of Jerusalem (cf. 5:16), then to Samaria, then to the area along the coast (chap. 8)—that is, persecution would follow mission. Saul plans instead to vault to the relatively distant city of Damascus. The resolution to this alleged dilemma is clear: Luke had no data about general and systematic opposition to the Jesus movement in Judea apart from Jerusalem (and precious little—e.g., the death of Stephen—about persecution *within* Jerusalem). Damascus is the next site because tradition associated Paul with that city.[5] He proceeds thither from Jerusalem because Luke wishes, against Gal 1:22, to portray Paul as a longtime resident of the holy city. Moreover, from Gal 1:17 it seems probable that Paul had carried out his opposition to the Jesus movement *in* Damascus. Acts, however, restricts persecution in Damascus to an intent that was thwarted by divine intervention.

Although Acts 9 seems to be a tightly fashioned narrative, it readily deconstructs.[6] Acts 9:4 states that Saul heard a voice. Those traveling with him also heard the voice, but "saw no one" (v. 7). Nor was Saul said to have seen anyone or anything, but in v. 17 Ananias refers to "Jesus, who appeared to you on the way here." Saul's companions escort him to Damascus and then vanish from a narrative into which they had suddenly intruded in v. 7. In v. 6, Saul receives instructions to enter the city, instructions that he will not be able to follow, since he cannot see. According to 9:9, Saul spends three days blind, without food or drink. As far as the reader knows, he could have been in the streets, with other blind beggars. Verse 11 reveals that he is at the house of one Judas on Straight Street. It does not say how he got there or anything about this particular Judas. It would seem unlikely that he was a believer, but that is mere logic.[7]

Ananias *was* a believer, and he received a vital vision. Jesus had said no more to Saul than to reveal his identity and tell him to "enter the city" and await further instructions. This raises suspense at the expense of probability, as subsequent reports (chaps. 22 and 26) will demonstrate. While responding to Ananias's objections "the Lord" tells him what Saul's task will be (v. 15). This is, in fact, the missionary commission. The Lord further advises Ananias that Saul is experiencing a vision in which Ananias comes to heal him. Readers now know what to expect. Ananias will come to Saul, introduce himself, refer to the vision, heal him, and share the commission. Yet Ananias does not mention Saul's vision but refers instead to the appearance of Jesus, which is not narrated. Furthermore, he says nothing about Saul's future career! Instead, he baptizes Saul, an act not mandated by the heavenly vision.

Ananias thereupon exits the narrative, without introducing Saul to any believers. Readers learn only

3 "Tarsian" in v. 11 is definitely not Lucan, for Luke would have said "Jerusalemite." Tarsus is given as the point of departure in the *Epistle of the Apostles* 33, which may depend on the *Acts of Paul* here.

4 Damascus is, because of its water supply, fertile soil, and proximity to trade routes, one of the oldest continually inhabited cities in the Mediterranean region. See John McRay, "Damascus: The Greco-Roman Period," *ABD* 2:7–8; and Millar, *Near East*, 310–17. The city evidently had a large Jewish population in the first century CE (Josephus *Bell.* 2.559–61).

5 Galatians was not the only basis for associating Paul with Damascus. It would seem that Paul presumed that his hearers knew of his connection with (residence in?) that city (Gal 1:17). Stories about Paul's conversion were, as Galatians indicates, a topic of some interest, as well as a subject for malicious gossip. See Olof Linton, "The Third Aspect: A Neglected Point of View; A Study in Gal. i–ii and Acts IX and XV," *ST* 3 (1951) 79–95.

6 On the following, see also István Czachesz, "Apostolic Commission Narratives in the Canonical and Apocryphal Acts of the Apostles" (Diss., Groningen, 2002) 63–64.

7 This problem is solved by the *Act. Paul* 7/9, which identifies Judas with the brother of Jesus.

that Saul spent some time with "the disciples," of whom nothing more will be heard. Verse 20 reports that he took up his (undelivered) missionary commission by preaching in the synagogues. Where, one wonders, had Saul learned that the one whom he had persecuted was "the Son of God" (v. 20). Readers may assume that Ananias had filled in such details, but the text makes no mention of it. It presently transpires that the message was not so objectionable as the messenger, evidently because of his success. Those who had been members of the movement before Saul arrived—the very people whom he had come to arrest—play no role in the story. When he needs assistants (v. 25), they will be "his disciples" rather than believers in general.

"The Jews" decided to kill Saul when he attempted to leave Damascus, the gates of which they patrolled. As a means of halting his mission, this plot was singularly inept.[8] When it was uncovered, Saul made a surreptitious exit. The refugee from a Jewish plot elected to go to Jerusalem, only to find himself unwelcome. Barnabas (who, according to 8:1, ought to have been elsewhere) came to Saul's aid, introducing him to the apostles and relating that Saul had seen Jesus (again, an incident not specified) and describing the mission in Damascus. How, one may ask, had Barnabas learned these interesting facts? From Saul? In that case, Saul could have spoken for himself. When hostility to his message breaks out in Jerusalem, the leadership dispatches Saul to Tarsus. No reason is given for this destination, and, as far as Acts is concerned, Saul simply rested there until Barnabas once more came into the picture (11:25-26). It is difficult to understand why Barnabas and the apostles could live in Jerusalem in peace while Saul could not. Readers will probably infer that those who engaged in theological disputes with the "Hellenists" did so at the risk of their lives (Stephen, 6:9; Saul, 9:29). Just why this mission was so lethal is a matter about which readers must speculate.

Readers will be unlikely to note these difficulties, in part because of the narrator's skill, and perhaps also because implied readers knew more about "Saul" than the text states. In large part, however, it is because the focus of the narrator is on the reader of the book. Ananias does not need to report the missionary commission to Saul because readers already know of it. All the characters share in the narrator's omniscience: they are aware of everything that has taken place in the story. They thus know what readers know, as if they had been reading along. These factors mitigate, but do not obviate, the difficulties raised by Acts 9. Every subsequent report of this event, including Acts 22 and 26, the D-Text tradition, the *Acts of Paul*, and others,[9] attempted to remedy some of the gaps and glitches in this story. Chief among these are (1) it is everywhere assumed that Paul had a vision of the risen Jesus, but Acts 9:3-8 does not narrate that vision;[10] and (2) it is not stated when and how (by instruction or revelation) Saul learned the "gospel" that he began to proclaim in 9:20.

The primary causes of these difficulties are the abbreviation and modification of a hypothetical source behind Acts 9:1-19a. This account differed from Galatians 1, the essential features of which Luke, far from wishing to ignore or to suppress, interjected into his narrative source. The collision between these two accounts explains the chief difficulties identified in the previous paragraph, since Galatians reports Paul's vision and insists that he did not learn the Christian message at second hand (Gal 1:12-17). Efforts to delineate Luke's use of this source require some reflection on its form.

"Conversion story" is appropriate, but not sufficient, since there were many types of conversion stories.[11] The most relevant examples of reflective conversion stories derive, as Arthur Nock pointed out seventy years ago,

8 See Pervo, *Dating*, 60–63.

9 Czachesz ("Commission Narratives") takes up all of these texts.

10 Acts 9:8 would lead one to infer that Saul had kept his eyes shut, presumably in response to the intolerably bright light.

11 Talbert (96) lists a number of examples of various types from a broad range of literature. In "Conversion in the Acts of the Apostles: Ancient Auditors' Perceptions," in Thompson, *Literary Studies*, 141–53, Talbert introduced a new classification, dividing conversion stories into "moral" and "cognitive" types. Philosophical conversions usually involve a shift from vice to virtue, as in the tale of Polemon. Cognitive conversions include a new orientation to life and truth, a paradigm shift. Many

from the philosophical tradition.[12] In contrast to the "s/he saw and believed" conversion in response to a miracle (e.g., Acts 8:4-13; 9:32-35; 13:6-12), the "philosophical" accounts either relate a lengthy quest for truth, culminating in discovery of the correct school or system, of which Justin is an example (*Dial.* 3–8), or describe a reprobate induced to undergo a complete change of life, as in the story of Polemo (Lucian *Bis acc.* 17; Diogenes Laertius 4.3.16).[13] Acts 9 has no more in common with the "quest for truth" model than does Galatians 1.[14] It belongs to the second general category, for it relates the conversion of an opponent of God's will.[15]

Other features have been proposed as the formal basis of Acts 9:1-19a.[16] Hans Windisch, for example, postulated the story of Heliodorus (2 Maccabees 3) as the model, if not the actual source.[17] This approach is, for determination of the form of the entire passage, a blind alley.[18] Charles Hedrick, following Étienne Trocmé, proposed that a healing story lay behind the account expanded by Luke.[19] This proposal has merit, but it fragments the story by giving priority to one feature of the narrative. Christoph Burchard has shown that the most cogent parallels to the entire passage come from religious fiction, in particular *Jos. Asen.* 1–21, and Apuleius *Metam.* 11.1–30.[20] He finds these two accounts so similar that Aseneth is like a "sister of Lucius" (the hero of Apuleius's novel).[21] Saul and Aseneth have many sterling qualities and virtues, but each lacks proper religious understanding and each has one serious flaw: Aseneth "regularly despised and spurned every man and was always boastful and arrogant" (2:1),[22] while Saul was, as noted, out of control.[23] Mighty Saul loses the ability to control his own movements and must be led by the hand. Aseneth loses her beauty (while Lucius loses his entire human appearance). These disabilities are not enduring punishments. They, like the respective fasting and self-abasement, are part of the process of (initiation and) change. The promises or affirmations made to or about them are not to be confused with commissions.[24] The following table is an English version of Burchard's Greek synopsis.[25]

---

stories are mixed. Luke's source emphasized moral elements, as well as cognitive change. Paul's own view of his conversion was cognitive. The desire for edification spurred the introduction of moral elements into essentially cognitive accounts.

12 Nock, *Conversion*, 164–86 *et passim*.

13 See Appendix 1.

14 Length may vary considerably, as in the two accounts of Polemon's conversion (previous note). The same basic outline can appear in a brief apophthegm (or the like) or as a developed novella. Cf. the two accounts of the call of Peter: Mark 1:16-17; Luke 5:1-11. Talbert (97) refers to "stable components" of conversion stories, including (a) the context, (b) catalysts motivating change, (c) obstacles, (d) the conversion proper, and (e) confirmation of its genuine character. These amount to little more than the essential features of such stories.

15 The stories about the Ethiopian official (8:26-39) and Cornelius (10:1-48) are different, and essentially Lucan. They concern persons who could not, or would not, become proper Jewish proselytes.

16 For a concise review, see Jervell, 291 n. 60. For more detail and bibliography, see John Townsend, "Acts 9:1-29 and Early Church Tradition," in Thompson, *Literary Studies*, 87–98.

17 Hans Windisch, "Die Christusepiphanie vor Damaskus (Act 9,22 und 26) und ihre religionsgeschichtlichen Parallelen," *ZNW* 31 (1932) 1–23. Note also *4 Macc.* 3:19—4:14, which imitates 2 Maccabees.

18 See Burchard, *Dreizehnte Zeuge*, 55–59; and Löning, *Saulustradition*, 66–70.

19 Charles W. Hedrick, "Paul's Conversion/Call: A Comparative Analysis of the Three Reports in Acts," *JBL* 100 (1981) 415–32, esp. 422–23. See Trocmé, *Actes et l'histoire*, 176–77. Hedrick observes that the *Coptic Act of Peter* (Berlin Gnostic Papyrus 8502, 135–38) contains a story with similar features. This may, however, be dependent on Acts 9. Another example of this type is the *Genesis Apocryphon 20.*

20 See Burchard, *Dreizehnte Zeuge*, 59–88, which includes a detailed synopsis with texts and summaries from *Joseph and Aseneth*, the *Metamorphoses*, and *An Ephesian Tale*.

21 Burchard (*Dreizehnte Zeuge*, 90–1) places these passages in parallel columns. The citation is from p. 83.

22 The English translation is Burchard, "Joseph and Aseneth," in 2:177–247, esp. 224–25, *alt*. His notes list a number of important parallels to the text.

23 John Clayton Lentz, Jr. (*Luke's Portrait of Paul* [SNTSMS 77; Cambridge: Cambridge University Press, 1993] 84–87) demonstrates that the preconversion Paul's moral failing was a lack of self-control, manifest in his rage. The strengths and growing edges of these characters are appropriate

Table 5. *Aseneth* 14:1-9 and Acts 9:3-8

***Joseph and Aseneth* 14**	**Acts 9**
When Aseneth had ceased making confession to the Lord, behold the morning star rose out of heaven in the east. Aseneth saw it and rejoiced and said, "So the Lord God listened to my prayer, because this star rose as a messenger and herald of the light of the great day. 2 She kept looking, and behold, close to the morning star, the heaven was torn apart and	3 As he was nearing Damascus in the course of his journey
great and unutterable **light** appeared. 3 Aseneth saw (it) and **fell** on (her) face on the ashes. A man came to her from heaven and stood by Aseneth's head. 4 He called her and said, "**Aseneth, Aseneth**." 5 She said, "Who is he that calls me, because the door of my chamber is closed and the tower is high, and how then did he come into my chamber?" 6 The man called her a second time, "Aseneth, Aseneth." 7 She	a **light** from above suddenly engulfed him. 4 He **fell** on the ground and heard a voice saying to him, "**Saul, Saul**, why are you persecuting me?"
said, "Behold, (here) I (am) **Lord. Who are you,** tell me." 8 He said, "**I am** the chief of the house of the Lord and commander of the whole host of the Most High. **Rise** and stand on your feet, **and I will tell you** what I have to say." 9 Aseneth raised her head and *saw* . . .	5 "**Who are you**, Lord?" "**I am** Jesus, whom you are persecuting. 6 Now **get up** and enter the city. **You will be told** what you must do." 7 Those traveling with Saul were standing there speechless, for they heard the voice but saw no one. 8 When Saul **arose** and opened his eyes, he could not **see** . . .

Differences between *Jos. Asen.* 14 and Acts 9 are apparent. Aseneth's actions relate to a god for whom she is an enemy alien. The (implicit and attenuated) element of repentance in Acts follows the epiphany. Aseneth's story is longer and exhibits more dramatic suspense.[26] Common elements are eight in number: a manifestation of supernatural light; the subject falling prostrate; an address with double vocative; the question: "Who are you?" with the response: "I am . . ." (identification formula); the command to rise; a promise that subject will be told something; and the statement that the subject stood.

The underlying form of Acts 9 is therefore appropriate to the conversion of an "enemy alien" of God,[27]

to the themes: Aseneth's misandry is suitable for a love story, as is Habrocomes' rejection of romance in an *Ephesian Tale*. Lucius dabbles in matters that do not befit mortals (magic) and engages in sexual misconduct (Apuleius *Metam.* 11.15).

24 The statements made to Ananias in Acts 9:15-16 are like the promises delivered to Zechariah about John and to Mary about Jesus (Luke 1:14-17, 32-33); that is, they would be suitable for an annunciation. Rather than commission Saul, they describe his future career. For the promises made to Aseneth, see *Jos. Asen.* 15:2-7. Isis's promises to Lucius occur in Apuleius *Metam.* 11.6.

25 Burchard, *Dreizehnte Zeuge*, 90–91.

26 Luke's source may have been equally long. See below.

27 The *Testament of Job* 3 (also a work of fiction) exhibits another close formal parallel. Job had, not unlike Aseneth, come to question whether the local idol was indeed the creator god. Gerhard Lohfink (*The Conversion of St. Paul: Narrative and History in Acts* [trans. Bruce J. Malina; Chicago: Franciscan Herald, 1976] 61–69) shows that the "appearance dialogue" in 9:4-6 conforms to epiphanies in the Hebrew Bible. This is useful and valid, but it does not define the form of the episode as a whole. On the form, see also Weiser, 1:217–19.

rather than to an expanded punishment miracle, healing story, or call story.[28] This striking story almost certainly arose in a gentile milieu, since it represents Saul as more or less a polytheist. Acts 9:5 has the remarkable phrase: "Who are you, Lord?" Such a question is at home in a polytheistic environment, where one needs to know which particular god one has offended and the reason for the epiphany, and is quite suitable for "conversion stories," but scarcely here.[29] The Saul of Acts had no doubts about whom he was persecuting or about how many beings merited the title "Lord." The persecutor on view in Acts 9 is a typical θεόμαχος: a gentile enemy of the people of God.[30]

Nothing could be further from the mind of Luke, who will provide Paul with Jewish credentials superior to those he actually possessed and prefers a call story—which is what this story will become by Acts 26. In addition, neither form (conversion story like that of Aseneth) nor content (Paul as "pagan") is in line with Lucan interests and emphases relative to Paul. It is reasonable to conclude that Acts 9:1-19a derives from a source.[31] Both comparative study and internal analysis lead to the suspicion that Luke has edited the first part of his source (8:3; 9:1-9) more through abbreviation than through supplementation.[32] Karl Löning proposes a somewhat complex pre-Lucan history, in which a novella about the miraculous punishment of an opponent has been transformed into a legend about God's surprising choice of a "chosen vessel."[33] That novella would have been a cautionary tale about what God may do to opponents of the divine will. Löning's proposal provides an explanation for the absence of an appearance of the risen Christ in this scene, as well as the lack of some sort of commission. Acts 9:3-9 supports this argument: the persecutor is put out of business, not converted or turned into a missionary.

This can be illustrated from a tradition late enough to have worked out most of the problems. In the *Martyrium Petri et Pauli* 39//*Acta Petri et Pauli* 60,[34] Peter explains to Nero that Paul was a one-time opponent of the faith not because of jealousy (φθόνος) but because of ignorance (ἀγνοία). Paul had to contend with numerous false prophets and messiahs (of whom Simon is a relevant example) and thus defended truth and persecuted error in these unbiblical manifestations. The Truth therefore addressed him from heaven, "I am

28 Talbert (*Reading Acts*, 95–103) provides three views of the material: conversion, punishment, and call. In effect, these represent different reading strategies, and he rightly notes the tendency of Lucan redaction to focus on call or commission. The underlying form is, nonetheless, a conversion story. Walther Zimmerli first proposed that the account was based on the narratives of prophetic calls. Odil Hannes Steck engaged this critically in "Formgeschichtliche Bemerkungen zur Darstellung des Damaskusgeschehens in der Apostelgeschichte," *ZNW* 67 (1976) 20–28. Subsequently, "commission story" has gained currency. See Czachesz, "Commission Narratives." On the assimilation to biblical call stories, see the comments on chaps. 22 and 26. A recent general study is B. Kowalski, "Widerstände, Visionen und Geistführung bei Paulus," *ZKTh* 125 (2003) 387–410.

29 Cf. *Homeric Hymn 7: To Dionysus*, lines 17–21. *Corp. Herm.* 1.2 φημὶ ἐγώ, Σὺ γὰρ τίς εἶ Ἐγὼ μέν, φησίν, εἰμι ὁ Ποιμάνδρης, ὁ τῆς αὐθεντίας νοῦς ("Who are you?" I asked. "I am Poimandres," he said, "mind of sovereignty"), trans. Brian P. Copenhaver, *Hermetica* (Cambridge: Cambridge University Press, 1992) 1. Cf. also *Hermas Vis.* 25:3. A formal parallel to the question is Homer *Il.* 22.8–9.

30 On the term, see on 5:39. For similar portraits of Paul as a wretched sinner, essentially a gentile, see, e.g., Eph 3:8 and 1 Tim 1:12-17, cited below.

31 Lohfink (*Conversion*, 86–87) argues that use of the LXX form of "Appearance Dialogue" indicates that Luke essentially composed this episode, although he recognizes the existence of source material, possibly a narrative. His strongest point is the similarity of this story to the narrative of the conversion of Cornelius in chap. 10, but Luke could have used his source in chap. 9 as partial inspiration for the Cornelius story, and the presence of themes uncongenial to Luke is quite persuasive.

32 There are a number of "true" imperfects in this chapter, iterative or conative in meaning. These may come from a source, but it is at least equally possible that some of them represent Lucan abbreviation of a source.

33 Löning, *Saulustradition*, 78–99.

34 Richard A. Lipsius and Mazimilian Bonnet, *Acta Apostolorum Apocrypha* (2 vols.; Leipzig: Mendelssohn, 1891–1903) 1:152 and 205, respectively. On these texts, which belong, in their present form, to the sixth century CE, see A. de Santos Otero, "Later Acts of the Apostles," *NTApoc* 2:426–82, esp. 440–42.

Jesus, whom you persecute. Now stop persecuting me, because I am the truth." Thereupon Paul became an advocate of the truth. This expanded form of the saying eliminates the embarrassing question, "Who are you?" and, like Acts 26, any reference to blinding. It adds the command to desist from persecution and a motive: Jesus is "the Truth." The epiphany corrects Paul's understanding of the facts and presumes that he will cease persecuting believers of his own volition now that he knows said truth. It makes more sense of the subsequent story of Paul in Acts than does 9:1-5.

The shift begins ever so much earlier than these apocrypha, however. Verse 6 does not fit the narrative. It is an awkward, near non sequitur introduced with a strong conjunction (ἀλλά, "but"),[35] something on the order of "I am Jesus whom you persecute. Nonetheless, get up and go into the city." This could be an (presumably pre-Lucan) insertion that transformed a punishment miracle into a conversion story. Without it, vv. 10-19a would be difficult to imagine. Because of it, readers will view Saul's fast of v. 9 as repentance rather than, for example, the result of shock or suicidal dejection.

In v. 3, light inundates Saul. One expects this to presage the appearance of a heavenly being, often an angel.[36] That may have been the case here, or the source may have envisioned the glorified Christ as a being of light. Luke, for whom the risen Jesus would retain his earthly form even in heaven (cf. Acts 1:11), rejected that view, which would eventually become heretical. The source appears to view the church as the body of Christ ("persecute *me*"), as does Paul, but not Luke. If this verse were Lucan composition, the voice would be likely to say: "I am Jesus, the followers of whose way you are persecuting."[37] For all of the characters thereafter, it is axiomatic that Saul saw Jesus (9:17, 27).[38] Verse 7 intimates that the source presented the glorified being as the heavenly Christ, since it says that Saul's companions saw "*no one*" (μηδένα).[39] That verse is unlikely to be editorial, for Luke prefers epiphanies to be concrete and public, not the "internal" experience of one member of a crowd.[40] Luke also omitted information about Saul's companions from the beginning of the story and quite probably various details that elevated the pathos and drama of the scene, an absence noted by later editors, at least some of whose additions appear in the D-Text variants. It is a reasonable conjecture that the source also narrated Paul's eventual destination, for example, "His companions led him by the hand to Damascus, where they found lodging for him in the home of a certain Judas." In summary: behind Acts 8:3; 9:1-9 evidently stood a tale about the thrilling and exemplary punishment[41] of an enemy of God, transformed into a conversion story.

With regard to the second major unit (vv. 10-19a), the figure of Ananias derives from a source. Luke would scarcely invent this character, not only because the name otherwise belongs to wicked persons,[42] but more importantly because Luke reduces his role in Acts 22 and eliminates him in Acts 26. The source may have reported parallel visions to Ananias and to Paul. Although the use of dreams, visions, apparitions,

35 The word is, in effect, an elliptical adversative, opposing an unstated alternative. See Moulton, 3:330, and, in particular, Barrett, 1:451.

36 Cf. Luke 2:9; *Jos. Asen.* 14:2, but note *T. Job* 3:1, in which the light speaks. For the verb περιαστράπτω ("shine") see 4 Macc 4:10 (in a similar context).

37 Bede (44) understood "me" to refer to the church as the body of Christ. His comment was evidently based on Augustine *Ennarationes in Psalmos* 30.2.3 (CSL 38:192). Fitzmyer (425) is an example of those who reject this interpretation because it is non-Lucan. That judgment presumes that Luke composed the passage.

38 Lohfink (*Conversion*, 26) is probably correct in saying that this epiphany is not an "Easter appearance" and that is why Paul sees only "the light." Paul would, of course, disagree (1 Cor 15:3-8). This speaks in favor of Löning's hypothesis.

39 It would have been simple to state that they saw "nothing" (μηδέν).

40 Contrast Mark 1:10 (baptism of Jesus), where Jesus sees the Spirit, with Luke 3:22, which relates a public epiphany.

41 With this transformation, the blinding becomes less a punishment and more a reduction of the persecutor to helplessness. Cf. Conzelmann, 72.

42 For characters named Ananias, see 5:1-11; 23:2. See Lüdemann, 113.

and angelic direction helps to unite the stories of the Ethiopian official, Saul, and Cornelius (8:26–11:18), this is the only true "double dream" in Acts.[43] That phenomenon is characteristic of religious fiction.[44] The earliest source evidently represented Ananias as healer of the blind Saul. Luke is responsible for "and be filled with the Holy Spirit" in v. 17, suggesting that v. 12, which speaks only of healing, derives from said source. Verse 13 probably comes from Luke, for it represents an objection very much like that of Peter in Acts 10:14. On stylistic grounds, vv. 14-16 are to be attributed to Luke.[45] In Luke's immediate source—following the hypothesis of Löning—there may have been a prediction about Paul's subsequent career, with emphasis on his suffering. Statements about the future are appropriate in conversion stories (above), and Luke does not cherish the view of Paul as a "suffering apostle."[46] That image is Pauline, intensified in some parts of the Deutero-Pauline tradition (e.g., Col 1:24). Luke's source probably contained some statement about suffering in the conversion story.[47] Since initiation is a common element in tales of conversion, Paul's baptism was quite likely introduced into the conversion source (which would account for its absence from the Lord's directions to Ananias).

Whereas abbreviation seems quite probable for the first half of the story, some expansion is more likely for the second. The earliest source appears to have reported the healing of the wretched Paul by Ananias, who did so only at divine direction, his pathway smoothed by a corresponding vision for the patient. The obvious question is: what, if anything, followed in the source available to Luke, for it is clear that Paul has not become a missionary, even if his fate has been intimated. The safest answer is "nothing," that this story stood on its own. If, however, the story was something like "the opening chapter in a novel about Paul," as Burchard suggests, further revelation or instruction would have been in order.[48]

43 John B. F. Miller has recently published a detailed study of revelatory devices in Acts: *Convinced That God Had Called Us: Dreams, Visions, and the Perception of God's Will in Luke-Acts* (BIS 85; Leiden: Brill, 2007). This includes a thorough review of research and religio-historical background material. See also the reference to John Hanson's article in the next note.

44 A "Double-Dream" in the strict sense is a dream/vision experienced by two different persons. A related phenomenon is the occurrence of complementary dreams to different individuals. This is an example of "rationalization" or "secularization" of a religious phenomenon, wherein identical dreams eliminate any possibility of chance. Yet another type involves two dreams with a similar meaning, as in Genesis 41. Examples of the proper type from fiction with a religious element include Chariton *Chaer.* 12.2.1; 3.7.4; *Jos. Asen.* 15:9; 19:6; Longus *Daph.* 1.7–8; 2.11; Apuleius *Metam.* 8.9; 11.1–3, 6, 21–22, 26–27; Achilles Tatius *Leuc. Clit.* 4.1.4–8; *Ethiopian Story* 3.11–12; 18.4; 12:9.25, and 10.3 (with 3.1), and *Act. John* 18 (probably imitating Acts), for example. The study of Alfred Wikenhauser, "Doppelträume," *Bib* 29 (1948) 100–111, amounts to a catalogue of examples. See also John S. Hanson, "Dreams and Visions in the Greco-Roman World and Early Christianity," *ANRW* 2.23.2 (1980) 1395–1427, esp. 1414–21. There are also examples in prose nonfiction: e.g., Livy 8.6.8–16; Dionysius of Halicarnassus *Ant. Rom.* 1.55–59; Strabo 4.1.4. Josephus (*Ant.* 11.327, 334 [Alexander and the high priest]) illustrates the historical value of these accounts. Hagiography continues the phenomenon. See, e.g., Gregory the Great's *Life of Benedict* 22.2; 37.3. Note also A. Stramaglia, "Innamoramento in sogno o storia di fantasmi? PMich Inv 5 = PGM 2 XXXIV (Pack2 2636) + PpalauRib Inv. 152," *ZPE* 88 (1991) 73–86, esp. 80 n. 36; and Karl Kerenyi, *Die griechisch-orientalische Romanliteratur* [1927; reprinted, Darmstadt: Wissenschaftliche Buchgesellschaft, 1962) 165–70, esp. 166–67, who includes other examples from the religious world. See also the discussion in Lohfink, *Conversion*, 73–77. He logically attributes this element to the author.

45 For details, see Lüdemann, 111–12; and Hedrick, "Paul's Conversion/Call," 419–21.

46 Barrett (1:457) correctly identifies the ambivalence of Luke, who wishes to show both that Paul is ready to suffer and that God will deliver him from his trials.

47 Haenchen (325) points out that this is the inverse of Ananias's own words.

48 Burchard, *Dreizehnte Zeuge*, 127.

Excursus: Source Hypotheses for Acts 7:58; 8:1, 3; 9:1-19

The following is a reconstruction of the sources underlying the material in the story of Saul's call. The reconstruction uses these sigla:

Plain text = hypothetical source[1] (Tale of Paul's miraculous punishment and healing)
Italics = hypothetical source[2] (Revision of source[1] into tale of Paul's conversion)
Underline = uncertain material//Lucan revision/abbreviation of source
Bold = Lucan editorial additions
[ ] = Possible contents of source[1], omitted in source[2]
[. . .] = Probable Lucan omissions from source
[?] = Possible Lucan omissions from source
[Bracketed material in the **sans serif** font suggests the type of material omitted by subsequent revisers, not actual proposed wording. This is *exempli gratia.*]

7:58 . . . **and the witnesses laid aside their robes at the feet of a young man named Saul. 8:1 And Saul was in hearty agreement with putting him to death. [There once was a man named Paul, who]** 3. But **Saul** began ravaging the church, entering house after house; and dragging off men and women, he would put them in prison. 9:1 Now **Saul, still** breathing threats and murder against the disciples of the Lord, **went to the high priest,** 2 **and asked for letters from him to the synagogues at Damascus, so that if he found any belonging to the way, both men and women, he might bring them bound to Jerusalem.** 3 **And it came about that as he journeyed, he was** [. . .] approaching Damascus, and suddenly a light from heaven flashed around him; 4 and he fell to the ground, and heard a voice saying to him, "Saul, Saul, why are you persecuting Me?" 5 And he said, "Who are you, Lord?" **[Jesus appeared to him]** And He said, "I am Jesus whom you are persecuting, [?] 6 *but rise, and enter the city, and it shall be told you what you must do.*" 7 And the men who traveled with him stood speechless, hearing the voice, but seeing no one. 8 And Saul got up from the ground, and though his eyes were open, he could see nothing; leading him by the hand, they brought him into Damascus. [. . .] 9 And he was three days without sight, and neither ate nor drank.

10 Now there was a certain disciple at Damascus, named Ananias; and the Lord said to him in a vision, "Ananias." And he said, "Behold, here am I, Lord." 11 And the Lord said to him, "Arise and go to the street called Straight, and inquire at the house of Judas for a man from Tarsus named Saul, *for behold, he is praying,* 12 *and he has seen in a vision a man named Ananias come in and lay his hands on him, so that he might regain his sight.*" 13 **But Ananias answered, "Lord, I have heard from many about this man, how much harm he did to your saints at Jerusalem;** 14 **and here he has authority from the chief priests to bind all who call upon your name."** 15 But the Lord said to him, "Go **[lay hands on him so that he may regain his sight],** for he is a chosen instrument of mine, **to bear my name before the gentiles and kings and the sons of Israel;** 16 **for** *I will show him how much he must suffer* **for my name's sake.**" 17 And Ananias **departed and entered [went to]** the house **[of Judas],** and after laying his hands on him said, "Brother **Saul**, the Lord Jesus, who appeared to you **on the road by which you were coming,** has sent me so that you may regain your sight, **and be filled with the Holy Spirit.**" 18 And immediately there fell from his eyes something like scales, and he regained his sight, *and he arose and was baptized;* 19 and he took food and was strengthened.

In summary, Acts 9:1-19a is the third stage of a tradition. The earliest apparent stage (source[1]) was an edifying novella about the punishment and subsequent healing of a notorious enemy of God. Subsequently this story was transformed into a narrative about the conversion of Paul (source[2]). That account was taken up by Luke, modified, and integrated into his overall literary plan. Although this partial reconstruction may seem unduly speculative and overly complex, appeal to hypothetical "pieces of tradition" involves more speculation than does an attempt to identify a known form and setting. Least likely is the attribution of the entire narrative to the author of Acts for the clear and simple reason that Luke was interested in neither a story about punishment and healing nor in a tale of conversion, as becomes apparent from the subsequent retellings of the story. Acts 9 is the least congenial to Lucan themes and emphases of the three accounts. This is not to overlook its great dramatic value and its useful moral: persecution does not pay. It fits quite aptly into the context of chaps. 8–10, as advocates of Lucan composition are not hesitant to point out.[49]

49 This argument, which follows those of Burchard and Löning (cf. also Weiser, 1:219–22), is quite different from the conclusion of Lüdemann (115–16) and Lohfink (*Conversion*), who believes that Luke is

The portrait of Paul presented in Luke's immediate source possessed enduring vitality. Its exemplary merit can be seen in the autobiographical 1 Tim 1:12-17, which presents Paul as a great sinner and, essentially, as a "pagan" unbeliever, ignorant, like other gentiles, of the true God. Note also Eph 3:8, where Paul is "the most insignificant of saints,"[50] and 2:3, "*All* of us once lived among them in the passions of our flesh, following the desires of flesh and senses, and *we* were by nature children of wrath, like everyone else" (emphasis added), which indicates that this understanding had taken hold by the close of the first century.[51] These parallels show how the story of Paul's conversion has been adopted to serve as a model for gentile converts.

This comparative material suggests a tentative date of c. 85–90 for Luke's immediate source in Acts 9:1-19a. The story comes from an environment like that of Ephesians: gentile Christianity strongly influenced by the language, literature, and thought of Judaism. The story could have been told in Ephesus and received with appreciation in that milieu, where conversion was viewed as the passage from darkness to light (Eph 5:8). Luke takes up, probably in dependence upon Ephesians, the same image in Acts 26:18.[52] Equally congenial to Ephesians is the understanding of the church as Christ's body (Eph 1:22-23; 4:15-16).

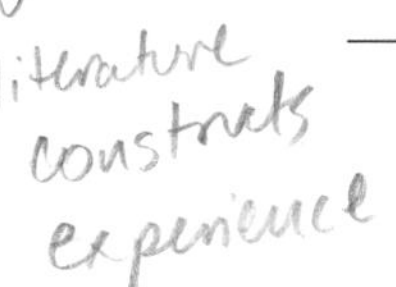

Comment

■ **3** The story picks up from 8:3. Saul continues (ἔτι, "still") his unbridled[53] assault on believers.[54] Insane rage was a common attribute of the persecutor,[55] for failure to check one's temper was, especially in the Greek world, a serious character flaw.[56] The narrative assumes that Saul has ready access to the chief priest and that this official can issue warrants authorizing the apprehension of persons in Damascus and their extradition to Jerusalem. Both are Lucan fictions (cf. Luke 2:1).[57] The

responsible for altering his source into a conversion story to conform with the contiguous conversions of 8:26-39 and 10:1-48. These similarities may, as noted, account for Luke's willingness to utilize this source, but it receives limited support from formal analysis and is, for this and other reasons, less persuasive.

50 The author gilds the lily by adding a comparative suffix to the superlative ἐλάχιστος, that is, "least-est" of all.

51 Cf. also Eph 4:17-18, which views gentile unbelievers as ignorant.

52 In the speculative context from which Ephesians derives, the concept of the heavenly Lord as a being of pure light (Acts 9:3-4) would have been highly congenial. "Light/enlightenment" occurs five times in Eph (1:18; 3:9; 5:8-9, 13-14) and is obviously a key symbol in this Deutero-Pauline letter.

53 The translation takes ἐμπνέων ἀπειλῆ καὶ φόνου (lit. "breathing threat and murder") as a hendyadis, against Cadbury and Lake, 99, which has a good comment on the link between anger and breath in "Semitic physiology." They cite Ps 17:16 LXX. See also Barrett, 1:445. The verb ἐμπνέω means something like "fume," or "pant."

54 Only here in Acts is the word "disciples" modified by "of the Lord."

55 For example, the characterization of Pentheus in Euripides' *Bacchae* (θυμὸν ἐκπνέων [620]) and the tyrants in 2–4 Maccabees (2 Macc 3:1-40; *3 Macc.* 1:8–2:24; *4 Macc.* 4:1-14). "Curse" (ἀπειλή), for example, is found in *3 Macc.* 2:24; *4 Macc.* 4:8. An indication of Saul's severity is the shackling of women, also a continuation of 8:3.

56 Uncontrolled rage was the opposite of σωφροσύνη ("self-control," "moderation"), which is opposed to "madness" (μανία) in 26:24. See Lentz, *Luke's Portrait*, 83–91.

57 The proposed action is like that of the royal letter in *3 Macc.* 3:25. 1 Macc 15:16-21 may have provided inspiration. Bruce (233) views that passage and Josephus *Ant.* 14.192–95 as confirmation of the right, but the decree of Julius Caesar that Josephus cites is both vague and without reference to any rights to remand Jews from other jurisdictions. Conzelmann (71) gives a summary dismissal to the problems of using these texts to rationalize 9:1-2. Witherington (316) correctly observes that there is no discussion of a "legal right" here. Authority is assumed rather than asserted. His claim that "the impression left is that the high priest was providing letters *requesting permission* for such actions by Saul" is groundless. The text also assumes that the letters were issued. For a formal parallel about an Egyptian official with letters of authorization (συστατικάς [i.e., ἐπιστολάς]) to send alleged miscreants to a high priest under guard see *P. Tebt.* 315.29–32 (= Arthur S. Hunt, *Select Papyri* [3 vols.; LCL; London: Heinemann, 1932–34] 1:330, no. 127). Hanson ("Dreams," 113) rationalizes by claiming that the authorization is permission to conduct a covert operation and kidnap the believers.

letters sought are to be addressed to "the synagogues" in Damascus,[58] viewed as legal bodies without whose consent the arrests could not be carried out. For the first time in Acts, the Jesus movement is identified as a specific sect.[59]

The text of vv. 3-9 exhibits a great deal of contamination from the parallel accounts in chaps. 22 and 26.[60] The opening of the verse, 9:3a, is Lucan in style[61] and probably abbreviates a source that narrated, in more or less detail, the assembly and journey of the caravan. As is dramatically appropriate, "disaster" struck when the journey was almost over. A heavenly light[62] engulfed *Saul.* The focus is upon him. He fell to the ground out of reverence (cf. *1 Enoch* 14:15), not because he was "knocked off his horse" by God, as popular lore has it.[63] A voice addressed him in the LXX form[64] of his name with the double vocative that is characteristic of epiphanies.[65] The narrator does not identify the author of the voice. The question makes this clear. Jesus asks why Saul is persecuting *him.* The word "persecute" represents a point of view. The Israelites have persecuted all of the prophets (cf. 7:52), but this declaration is appropriate to a supernatural being.[66]

■ **5-7** Even less Lucan is Saul's question. When confronted by an epiphany, Jews typically say, "Here I am lord," or the equivalent, as will Ananias in v. 10.[67] What appears to be the opening of a dialogue is abruptly terminated with vague and mysterious instructions.[68] The literary function of v. 6 is to raise suspense.[69] Again, one expects a statement by Saul and/or a description of the departure of the light. Instead, v. 7 reports the experience of Saul's companions,[70] whose existence is first acknowledged. A typical feature of epiphanies is that others do not see the divine being.[71] Only after he has

58 The easiest solution is to construe εἰς Δαμασκόν as equivalent to "in Damascus." The general condition is legal jargon. Saul does not seek to visit Damascus on the odd chance that he might find some believers there. Johnson (162) observes that failure to describe the expansion of Christianity to Damascus is "stunning evidence of Luke's selectivity." The Pseudo-Clementines deal with the improbability: According to *Rec.* 1.65, 67, "the enemy [Paul] received a commission from Caiaphas to go to Damascus in pursuit of believers because he believed that Peter had fled there. Cf. also 1.71.3–4; and Jones, "A Jewish Christian," 624–25.

59 The noun ὁδός appears six times in Acts, always in connection with Paul. A similar term was the self-designation of the Qumran sect: 1QS 9:18; 10:21; CD 1:13; 2:6; 20:18. See Eero Repo, *Der "Weg" als Selbstbezeichnung des Urchristentums: Eine traditionsgeschichtliche und semasiologische Untersuchung* (Annales Academia Scientiarum Fennicae B.132/2; Helsinki: Suomalainen Tiedeakatemia, 1964); and Fitzmyer, 432–24. Cf. Isa 40:3, cited in the Gospel tradition, e.g., Luke 1:76; 3:3-5.

60 See Metzger, *Textual Commentary*, 317.

61 On "drawing near to *X*," see Luke 18:35; 19:29; Acts 10:9.

62 On "light," see above. Its sudden arrival is an indicator of supernatural origin (cf. Luke 2:13).

63 Verse 7 reports that his companions were standing; that is, the journey was made on foot. Corina Combet-Galland ("Paul l'apôtre: un voyage contrarié pour baggage," *EThR* 80 [2005] 361–74) discusses the theme of interrupted Pauline journeys.

64 The name Σαούλ appears 381 times in the LXX.

65 Double vocative: Gen 22:11; 46:2; Exod 3:4; 1 Sam 3:4; Exod 3:4; *Jub.* 44:5; and many examples from Greek literature, such as *Jos. Asen.* 14:4. (The last is cited in **Table 5** above.)

66 So in the *Bacchae* those who attack the follower attack the leader (Dionysios, a god). Luke may have understood this along the lines of Luke 10:16 ("Whoever rejects you rejects me"), which views Jesus as Wisdom. Barrett (1:449) seeks to evade this identification by appealing to Luke's lack of theological depth.

67 For examples, see Burchard, *Dreizehnte Zeuge*, 88 n. 115. Note the emphatic pronouns: "*I* am Jesus, whom *you* persecute."

68 The verb ἀνάστηθι is appropriate in this context, as Saul is on the ground, but it often introduces commissions and the like: Gen 21:18; 31:13; 1 Kgs 17:9; Jonah 1:2. The passive voice (λαληθήσεται, "it will be said") introduces a note of mystery and is not simply a reverential periphrasis, but the use of δεῖ suggests divine purpose.

69 For a hypothesis about the source issues see above.

70 For such companions, see Achilles Tatius *Leuc. Clit.* 7.3.7 and Lucian *Peregr.* 24. The verb is a *hapax legomenon* in the NT. Although the companions are not specifically identified as engaged in the same mission as Saul, it is reasonable to suppose that the narrative envisions colleagues or assistants of some sort. Saul already has an entourage.

71 Euripides *Bacchae* 500–503 states the point clearly: the godless do not see the god. Note also 1086, where others do not hear the voice. In *Il.* 1.198, only Achilles saw Athena when she appeared to him. Other examples include *Od.* 16.154–63

arisen[72] and opened his eyes (closed against the glare of the light?) does Saul discover that he is blind. The punishment[73] comes as a surprise, understated and without announcement.[74] Readers may reasonably presume that Saul's companions took him to Damascus,[75] on the strength of the voice that they had heard.

■ **8-9** The contrast between the one who would lead (ἀγάγῃ [v. 2]) alleged miscreants in chains from Damascus to Jerusalem and the one led by the hand (χειραγωγοῦντες [v. 8]) is manifest: "Such is the pitiful state in which the terror of the Christians makes his entry."[76] A gap follows v. 8. This may come from the abbreviation of the source, but it further raises suspense: How did his companions dispose of Saul? Did they take him to the addressees of the letters he was carrying or simply abandon him to walk about in the streets as a blind beggar?[77] Verse 11 does not answer these questions. The purpose of his subsequent fast is unstated.[78]

■ **10-19a** These verses include two scenes: vv. 10-16 and 17-19a. The narrator[79] shifts from fasting Saul to

(Odysseus); Apollonius Rhodius *Argon.* 4.850–55 (Thetis to Peleus); OT texts include Deut 4:12 (Sinai; the emphasis is that God lacks a form); Wis 18:1 (the exodus); Dan 10:7 (vision). The same motif, possibly by imitation, appears in *Mart. Pol.* 9.1 and in *Act. Thom.* 27. Conzelmann (71) cites Maximus of Tyre 9 (Dübner 15) 7d-f, concerning an epiphany in which some heard, others saw, and still others experienced both. Acts 9:7b is chiastic.

72 The verb ἠγέρθη could be taken as the equivalent of the middle. The passive translation contrasts with v. 18, in which Saul raises himself.

73 Blinding was the most common type of punishment miracle (Otto Weinreich, *Antike Heilungswunder* [Giessen: Töpelmann, 1909] 189–94). There are many examples involving Isis. See Juvenal *Sat.* 13.93–94 and the note of Edward Courtney, *A Commentary on the Satires of Juvenal* (London: Athlone, 1980) 548. Other examples are *Il.* 6.130–40 (Lycurgus), (Coptic) *Act of Peter* a (James Keith Elliott, *The Apocryphal New Testament* [Oxford: Clarendon Press, 1993] 398); *Infancy Gospel of Thomas* 5.1; *Ethiopian Story* 4.19. Martial (*Epig.* 4.30) reports the blinding of a man for fishing illegally in a pool belonging to Domitian. On the theme of blinding as punishment and recovery of sight for repentance, see Herodotus *Hist.* 2.111 (Pheron, king of Egypt; cf. also Diodorus of Sicily *Library* 1.59); Healing tablets at Epidauros A 11 B2 (22) (*IG* iv 952) (peeping into forbidden place, neglecting to make offering for cure); Plato *Phaedr.* 243a (the poet Stesichorus, blinded for criticism of Helen, wrote a recantation and recovered sight); *Historia Augusta, Hadrian* 25.1–3 (an old woman who disobeyed a command); Theodectes the Tragedian, who got cataracts when he was going to include a biblical theme in a play but was healed when he retracted the idea (*Aristeas* 316). Ovid (*Tristia ex Ponto* 1.1.51–58) can use blindness as an image and example in his discussion of repentance. Artificial blinding is a common feature of initiation rituals, on which see G. Rachel Levy, *Religious Conceptions of the Stone Age and Their Influence upon European Thought* (= *The Gate of Horn*, 1948) (New York: Harper & Row, 1963) 290. Epiphanies can lead to permanent blindness, as in the case of Homer, according to the *Vita Romana* 5. Homer prayed at the tomb of Achilles to see the hero in his replacement armor. When he appeared, Homer was blinded by its brightness. Cf. Ps.-Plutarch *Greek and Roman Parallel Stories* 1, 305c. Blindness is used as a metaphor for "ignorance" prior to conversion to a philosophical way of life in Lucian *Nigr.* 3–5. On this see Nock, *Conversion*, 80.

74 Contrast Zechariah (Luke 1:20) and Elymas (Acts 13:11).

75 The necessity of being led by the hand (χειραγωγέω) proves that Saul is blind. Note 13:11 (Elymas) and cf. Tobit 11:16 (א) and Spicq, *Lexicon*, 3:507.

76 Haenchen, 323.

77 The gradual changes in the behavior and experience of Saul's companions in 22:9 and 26:14 are due to Luke's efforts to transform them from contrasting figures to witnesses of the epiphany, as Gaventa (*Darkness*, 59) observes. The D-Text h smoothes over the problem by reading *sic mansit* ("Thus he stayed/remained").

78 "Three days" suggests a prebaptismal period of fasting (cf. *Did.* 7:4; Justin *1 Apol.* 61.1 and the later "Ember Days," three days of seasonal fasting after which ordinations were frequently held). This practice may have been familiar in Luke's environment. Fasting often marks a period of preparation (cf. Lent): Dan 4:33a-b LXX; *Prayer of Nabonidus* 1.3; see Johnson 164. For fasting or abstinence as a prerequisite of initiation, see *Jos. Asen.* 10:17 (20); Apuleius *Metam.* 11.23.1; 28; 30.1.

79 Verse 10 is awkward, beginning with the reasonably "correct" Greek ἦν δέ τις ("Now there was a . . ."), then shifting, after "Ananias," to the more "biblical" "and God said to him. . . ." Cf. the similar language in 16:1.

believing Ananias,[80] one of Saul's targets (a fact of which he was well aware, although he was not aware of Saul's misfortune), who receives a vision[81] of the Lord (Jesus). With regard to content, this is a dialogue of the prophetic sort, with an objection overruled by the visitor. That "visitor" issues one direct order: proceed to the house of Judas[82] and inquire for a Tarsian named Saul. What he might do for or with that person emerges not in a direct order but rather in a vision within a vision. This Chinese-box technique is novelistic[83] and derives from the source: the Lord reports, within a vision, another vision that serves to advise the recipient of the primary vision. Fasting Saul is at prayer and thus in the proper state for a vision.[84] The secondary vision also says, by implication, that Saul is blind. Ananias will heal him.[85] That is another indication of a source, since Luke and Acts otherwise restrict healings to religious leaders. Judas's guest is identified, rather gratuitously, as a resident of Tarsus. No reader of Acts would expect this information. Saul is from Jerusalem. It evidently derives from the source, which may not have envisioned strong ties between Paul and Jerusalem. Luke will subsequently use Tarsus as a place in which to "park" his hero between 9:30 and 11:25 and as the source of his Hellenic credentials (21:39).

■ **13-16** To this mandate Ananias vigorously objects. Saul's reputation has preceded him.[86] The pattern will be replicated in chap. 10, where fasting Peter will also voice a perfectly valid objection to a divine direction. Verses 13-16 contain a number of complementary terms: to the ὅσα κακά ("all the horrible things") of v. 13, the Lord rejoins with "how much (ὅσα) he will have to suffer" in v. 16. "Name" likewise appears in vv. 14-16.[87] The next verses, 15-16, are a kind of "introductory oracle" for the ministry of Saul.[88] The language is reminiscent of Paul's self-descriptions in both genuine and Deutero-Pauline letters. The image is rather blunt: the missionary is a casket,[89] as it were, for presentation of the name of Christ. Not that any container would do: he is a chosen vessel.[90] The order of those to whom Saul will "bear the Lord's name"[91] is odd: gentiles, monarchs, Israelites. This statement, if understood as a description

80 The only information given about Ananias is that he is a "disciple." Cadbury and Lake (102–3) offer detailed observations.

81 Apart from Matt 17:9 (the transfiguration), this word, which may refer to experiences received either while awake or asleep, occurs only in Acts (eleven times; it is found five times in *Hermas*). See Wilhelm Michaelis, "ὅραμα," *TDNT* 5:371–72; and Alfred Wikenhauser, "Die Traumgeschichte des Neuen Testaments in religionsgeschichtlicher Sicht," in *Piscisculi: Festschrift für F. J. Dölger* (2 vols.; Münster: Aschendorff, 1939) 1:320–33, esp. 320–21.

82 The inclusion of "Straight Street" is no doubt necessary, but also provides an element of verisimilitude to the story. Cf. 9:43.

83 An elaborate use of stories enclosed within stories (within a story) in ancient narrative is found in Heliodorus's *Ethiopian Story*. Antonius Diogenes' *Marvels beyond Thule* is another example, according to Photius's summary of its plot.

84 Cf., e.g., Dan 10:3; 2 Esdr 5:13; *2 Bar.* 5:7–8; *Asc. Isa.* 2:7.

85 Either a vision including a voice announcing that one Ananias would come to cure him or a vision in which Saul saw *someone* come and cure him would be logical. The narrative states that Saul *saw* a person named Ananias, as if he were wearing a nametag. The text is compressed, further indication of a source that has been modified.

86 Verse 14 confirms that Saul received the authority requested in v. 2. "High priest" is singular in v. 1, plural in vv. 14 and 21. Luke tends to use the plural, unless he is referring to a specific person (e.g., 4:1 vs. 4:6), but this is insufficient to establish a different source for v. 1.

87 On the term "name," see Pervo, *Dating*, 281. "Those who call upon the/this name" is a Deutero-Pauline expression, found also in v. 21 and, with reference to Paul's baptism, 22:16; cf. 15:17. (In 1 Cor 1:2 the phrase is part of an interpolation that makes the address universal.)

88 On "Introductory oracles," see the comments at 1:8. For a prediction of suffering, note Xenophon's oracle in *Ephesian Tale* 1.6.2.

89 The noun σκεῦος ("vessel," "instrument") is often an unflattering word; cf. 2 Cor 4:7 (treasure in earthen vessels).

90 The verbal reflex of this noun appears in 1:2, 24 (of apostles) and 6:5 (the Seven). Luke 9:35 (the transfiguration) establishes a parallel between Jesus and Paul: "This is my Son, my Chosen" (ἐκλελεγμένος). Note also Rom 9:23; 2 Tim 2:21. Barrett (1:456) agrees that this is intentional use of Pauline language. The Pseudo-Clementines pick up the phrase; *Rec.* 3.49 characterizes Simon as a "choice vessel for the wicked one," *vas electionis maligno*.

91 The meaning of the image "bear the name" (βαστάζειν τὸ ὄνομα) is not clear. In the

of Saul's missionary career, is the clearest hint yet in Acts of a gentile mission. The passage harks back to Luke 21:12-13, which forecasts witness before "monarchs and rulers."[92] One would expect Luke to list Israelites first. The prediction of suffering in v. 16 is a common feature. In short, if you want to be a narrative hero, be prepared to suffer.[93]

■ **17-19a** The second scene moves rapidly: Ananias goes to Saul and does what the vision commanded. The single word, "brother," indicates that he embraces Saul as a member of the community. There are two additions: his comment indicates that Saul has experienced an appearance[94] and that Jesus has directed that Saul be filled with (the) Holy Spirit. This "apostolic ordination" places Saul in the ranks of the Baptizer and Jesus.[95] The healing, performed with touch only, contains a novelistic detail: a flaky substance falls from Saul's eyes (cf. Tob 3:17; 11:12).[96] After his sight returns, he is baptized. Light comes to one who sat in darkness (cf. Luke 1:79).[97] Saul's ability to get up and feed himself serves both symbol and reality. The dejected condition of v. 9 has been fully reversed.

Similitudes of Hermas it means "to be/act like a Christian" 76.3 (8.10.3); 91.6 (9.14.6) 105.5 (9.28.5). cf. Polycarp *Phil.* 6.3 (φέρω). The language is more appropriate to a conversion than to a call. See Conzelmann, 72. The philosopher can also be characterized as a "witness" (μάρτυς) (Epictetus *Diss.* 3.24, 112).

92 Cf. *1 Clem.* 5:7, which speaks of Paul's testimony before rulers. This had already become part of the tradition in Mark (13:9-10), as had the gentile mission (eliminated by Luke 21:12-13).

93 A dramatic example that summarizes the standard picture can be read in the speech of Heracles, who makes an appearance from his heavenly home to announce "the plans of Zeus." Heracles tells of his many (ὅσους) labors to win glory and predicts fame for Philoctetes after his many sufferings (Sophocles *Phil.* 1409–44).

94 The participle ὀφθείς characterizes the event as a resurrection appearance, in both Pauline (1 Cor 15:5-8) and Lucan (Luke 24:34) language.

95 John the Baptist (Luke 1:15); Jesus (Luke 4:1, 14). See Turner, *Power*, 377–78. This is not the baptismal gift of the Spirit.

96 For refutation of any notion that this is a medically informed comment, see Cadbury and Lake,104. Johnson (165) says that ὡς ("like") indicates that the phrase is metaphoric. It is not, but it is symbolic. Cf. Chrysostom *Hom.* 20, 175d: "a double blindness is removed."

97 Luke exploits this symbolism in 26:18. The author probably intended the symbolic possibilities: initiation is the passage from darkness to light. The ritual actions—fasting, immersion, rising, eating—correspond to rising to new life and participation in the meal of the redeemed.

9

9:19b-31 Saul in Damascus and Jerusalem

19b/ Saul spent some time[a] with the disciples in Damascus, 20/ where he set right out to preach about Jesus in the synagogues, proclaiming, "He is the Son of God."[b] 21/ This bewildered his hearers,[c] who wondered, "Isn't this the fellow who wreaked havoc on those who call upon the name of Jesus in Jerusalem? Hadn't he come here so that he might take those of this ilk back to the high priests in chains?" 22/ Yet Saul worked even harder. He dismayed the Jews of Damascus by proving that Jesus is the Messiah. 23/ After this had gone on for some time, the Jews concocted a plot to kill him. 24/ Saul caught wind of it: They were keeping a twenty-four-hour watch at the city gates[d] so that they might apprehend and slay him, 25/ but his disciples took him by night and let him down by lowering him in a hamper from an aperture in the wall.

26/ Upon his arrival in Jerusalem, Saul attempted[e] to associate with the disciples, but they were all afraid of him because they were unwilling to believe that he was one of them. 27/ Then Barnabas took charge of Saul and conducted him to the apostles. He related how Saul had seen the Lord on his expedition and what Jesus had said to him. He further reported how vigorously Saul had preached in the name of Jesus at Damascus. 28/ Saul thereupon became part of their company in and around Jerusalem.[f] He preached vigorously in the name of Jesus[g] and 29/ engaged in contentious debate with the Hellenists,[h] who launched an effort to kill him. 30/ The believers discovered this, so they escorted him to Caesarea[i] and sent him to Tarsus.

31/ The church[j] throughout all Judea, Galilee, and Samaria then began to enjoy a time of peace. It grew in quantity and quality, living in reverence for the Lord and with the support of the Holy Spirit.

a The thinly attested "many days" ($\mathfrak{p}^{45}$ h) is probably due to the influence of v. 23 or to general verisimilitude. Luke does not always draw a sharp distinction between "some" and "many."

b This could be taken as indirect discourse. (The choice is between *ὅτι* as a conjunction introducing a noun clause and *ὅτι recitativum*.) A noun clause would yield a smoother translation.

c The omission of *οἱ ἀκούοντες* ($\mathfrak{p}^{45vid. 74}$ Ψ* *pc*) is, according to Barrett (1:464), without reason. Nonetheless, it conforms to Lucan style: Luke 1:66; 2:18, 47.

d The translation does not take *δὲ καί* as adverbial. See Cadbury and Lake, 105.

e The variant *ἐπειρᾶτο* (E L *et al.*), which clearly means "attempted," seeks to remove any ambiguity attaching to *ἐπείραζεν*.

f The literal wording, "and he was with them, entering and leaving into/at Jerusalem," is difficult. $\mathfrak{P}^{74}$ and m omit "and leaving," which might intend to say that Saul did not enter Jerusalem proper until introduced to the apostles. On the preposition, see 12:24.

g Variants include "the Lord," "the Lord Jesus," and "Jesus Christ," all of which miss the significance of "the name of Jesus."

h As usual, "Hellenes" ("Greeks," possibly meaning "polytheists") is a variant. Cf. also 11:20.

i The D-Text reports that the trip to Caesarea was made "by night," as in v. 25. This novelistic detail is uninformed, since Paul had an escort and Caesarea could not be reached in a single night.

j D and other texts pluralize the sentence ("churches/communities"), probably to conform with the more general usage of Acts. See also Barrett, 1:475.

Analysis

The section describes how Saul took up the mantle of Stephen. In contrast with Galatians 1, a gentile mission is not in prospect.[1] There are two parallel units. Verses 19b-25 summarize Saul's successful work in Damascus, leading to the brief description of his successful escape from the resultant plot. Verses 26-30, in turn, summarize his work in Jerusalem, culminating in another plot and his withdrawal. In the course of that enterprise Paul finds an ally in Barnabas and subsequently friendship with the apostles. Verses 19b-25 set the pattern for almost all the rest of the book: Saul/Paul will elude successive Jewish intrigues. Both of these episodes are Lucan compositions.

The second unit (vv. 26-30) is patterned after the ministry of Stephen (6:8-11), while the model for vv. 19b-25 is the beginning of Jesus' public ministry in Luke 4:16-30: proclamation of a message of salvation in the synagogue, to which the audiences react with amazement, illustrated by a question about the speaker's background, and escape from an attempt to take his life.[2] This parallelism is not just a literary device.[3] Other sources for vv. 19b-25 include Paul's letters, notably Galatians 1 and 2 Cor 11:32-33. Although these two units are not improperly classified as episodes, vv. 19b-23 and 28-30 are written in summary style, in the imperfect tense, indicating a ministry of some duration in each place.

Comment

■ **19b-22** The first paragraph is framed by the creedal expression "He is" (οὗτός ἐστιν). Together they identify Jesus as both "Son of God"[4] and "Messiah." Luke thereby characterizes the content of Saul's preaching.[5] Those wishing to discover how Saul learned these beliefs may take refuge in v. 19b, but Luke, as noted, is loyal to Galatians in avoiding any reference to human teachers of Paul. Not in the least embarrassed by the evidently skeptical astonishment of the public, which echoes the words of Ananias (vv. 14, 21), Saul redoubled his efforts. His arguments, like those of Stephen, could not be refuted (6:10).[6] Violence may resolve what logic cannot.

■ **23-25** The little episode of these verses demonstrates that Luke could handle his sources for Acts with at least as much freedom as that used in the Gospel. Paul, who claimed that he evaded the magistrate of Aretas,[7] told this story on himself, a mock-heroic account that parodies the military exploit of being the first soldier to scale a fortified wall. Luke has made two substantial alterations to the story, transforming the adventure into a daring escape[8] and changing Saul's adversaries into "the

1 For details, see Barrett, 1:460–61.

2 See Esler, *Community*, 39.

3 It is probable that πάντες οἱ ἀκούοντες (lit. "all who heard") is original, since it is exactly parallel to Luke 2:47 (Jesus in the temple). Omission of this participial phrase (p[45vid] p[74] Ψ* *pc*) makes the astonishment general and more like a miracle story.

4 Acts 9:20 is the only definite use of the title "Son of God" in proclamation in Acts. It probably derives from Gal 1:16 and thus conforms to Paul's account of his call. See Pervo, *Dating*, 76–77. The verb "ravage" (πορθέω) appears only in Acts 9:21 and Gal 1:13, 23 in early Christian literature.

5 So Wilhelm Bousset, *Kyrios Christos: A History of the Belief in Christ from the Beginnings of Christianity to Irenaeus* (trans. John Steely; Nashville: Abingdon, 1970) 96.

6 Evidently not appreciating the rhetorical force of συμβιβάζω (e.g., Aristotle *Top.* 7, 5p. 150a, 36), C E *pc* h 1 p (mae) insert (ἐν) τῷ λόγῳ ("in rhetorical acumen").

7 Aretas (c. 9/8 BCE–c. 40/41 CE) was the most famous member of a royal Nabatean family whose fortunes were not unlike those of the Herodian dynasty. See David F. Graf "Aretas. (4)?" ABD on CD-ROM Version 2.0c, 1995, 1996. Glen W. Bowersock, *Roman Arabia* (Cambridge, Mass.: Harvard University Press, 1983) 51–69; and Martin Hengel and Anna Maria Schwemer, *Paul between Damascus and Antioch: The Unknown Years* (London: SCM, 1997) 106–32. The only reasonable interpretation of 2 Cor 11:32-33 is that Damascus was a part of the Nabatean realm at the time of Paul's difficulties (perhaps during the reign of Gaius); so Bowersock, 68. See also Victor Paul Furnish, *II Corinthians: Translated with Introduction, Notes, and Commentary* (AB 32A; Garden City, N.Y.: Doubleday, 1984) 540–42.

8 For Chrysostom, 176e, this escape demonstrated Paul's ἀρετή (sagacious courage). See Josh 2:15 LXX (which may also have influenced 2 Cor 11:33). Popular stories are familiar with the use of

Jews"[9] of Damascus. Other manufactured details include the theme of a conspiracy, exposed by some unrevealed means, and the unremitting nature of the vigilance. Attempts to harmonize the two accounts are doomed to failure[10] and there is no defensible basis for an alternate source.[11] Acts 9:23-25 is Lucan in style and characteristics.[12] It also—and this is not highly unusual—makes no sense, since it is not likely that the ruling powers would allow potential assassins to mount a permanent guard at the city gates and even less likely that the plotters would allow the mission to continue unhindered until Saul decided to make his departure rather than find a much less public place[13] in which to remove this odious opponent from the scene.

■ **26-30** In Jerusalem, whither the courageous Saul had fled from a Jewish plot, he found no welcome from the believers, who refused to accept his change of allegiance. Their attitude, which resembles the disciples' reactions to reports of the resurrection (Luke 24:11, 41), reinforces the miraculous character of his conversion and also the unprincipled ferocity of his former role as a persecutor. To the rescue comes Barnabas, who has somehow learned Saul's story,[14] and through whose auspices Saul is introduced to the apostles, with whom he functions on a collegial basis, engaging in wide-ranging missionary labor. When, however, he follows the path of the fallen Stephen by debating with "the Hellenists," they attempt to murder him, also. This irony pointedly illustrates the full circle Saul has traversed, from an ally of Stephen's opponents to the top of their "most wanted dead or alive" list.

This paragraph, a virtual doublet of vv. 19b-25,[15] is

baskets to introduce or extract people into or out of dangerous situations, such as a lover's quarters. See Sophie Trenkner, *The Greek Novella in the Classical Period* (Cambridge: Cambridge University Press, 1958) 129 n. 3. For a realistic report of such an escape, see Plutarch *Aem.* 26.2 and Athenaeus *Deipnosophistae* 5.52 (from Posidonius?). Helen claimed that she had repeatedly attempted to descend the walls of Troy by climbing down ropes: Euripides *Trojan Women* 955–58, a more athletic endeavor than that attributed to Paul.

9 For the first time, Ἰουδαῖοι is used to denote Israelites who did not accept Christian claims and therefore a distinct social group different from one's own. It is not accidental that this occurs in connection with the work of Paul. See Richard Pervo, "Israel's Heritage and Claims upon the Genre(s) of Luke and Acts: The Problems of a History," in Moessner, *Heritage*, 127–43, esp. 137–38.

10 See the study of Mark Harding, "On the Historicity of Acts: Comparing Acts 9.23-5 with 2 Corinthians 11.32-3," *NTS* 39 (1993) 518–38. Fitzmyer (433–34) does not really harmonize the two accounts; he seeks rather to defend Luke, while Hemer (*Book*, 182) appeals to the possibility of two opponents—Jews and magistrates—working together, a methodologically dubious ploy.

11 See Pervo, *Dating*, 60–62.

12 Although N-A[27] prints *οἱ μαθηταὶ αὐτοῦ* ("his disciples") in v. 25, Metzger (*Textual Commentary*, 321–22; cf. Haenchen, 332 n. 3) prefers *αὐτόν* ("the disciples took him") on the grounds that, "it is scarcely conceivable that Jewish converts to Christianity in Damascus would be called 'Paul's disciples'" (Metzger, 321). This is a historicizing assumption. Metzger's further claim, "the variant reading in 14.20 D E *κυκλωσάντων δὲ τῶν μαθητῶν αὐτοῦ* ['When his disciples had gathered around him'] provides no real explanation for the present verse" (322 n. 7), is incomprehensible. The genitive in 9:25 is supported by 𝔓[74] ℵ A B C 81* vg *al*, a formidable body of witnesses. It is easier to explain why "his" would be adjusted to "him" than vice versa. Recognizing this, Metzger (*Textual Commentary*, 322) proposes the "conjecture" that the "oldest text" is corrupt.

13 In v. 24, A *pc* read *πιάσωσιν* ("seize," taken from 2 Cor 11:32) and place "night and day" at the end, that is, "so that they might seize him in daylight or dark." This text is more reasonable, since it envisions apprehending Saul at the gates and, presumably, taking him elsewhere for the murder.

14 Note that v. 27 once more (cf. vv. 7, 17) speaks of an appearance of Christ, although 9:3-6 does not describe one. It would defy the conventions of grammar to assume an unannounced subject change in mid-verse, that is, that Barnabas took him to the apostles, after which *Saul* told (see Barrett, 1:469; Fitzmyer, 439). If one follows Bruce (243) and reads *ὅ τι* rather than *ὅτι*, the sequence becomes, in effect "how . . . what . . . how," rather than "how . . . that . . . how." Cf. v. 6.

15 In addition to the shape—preaching, plot, escape—there are the skeptical reaction (vv. 21, 26) and the words "kill" (*ἀναιρέω*) and "discover" (*γινώσκω*), in vv. 23-24, 29, and 24, 30, respectively.

almost certainly a Lucan composition in its entirety.[16] It serves a number of purposes. The prophecy of v. 16 has already been twice fulfilled: Saul is on no easy path. The ministry of Stephen was not quashed by his death. Those who traduced Stephen will learn that they have made a bad trade. More importantly, this passage introduces the warm association between Saul and Barnabas, who first met not in Antioch but in Jerusalem, where both enjoyed the equally warm association with and support of the apostles[17] and, indeed, of the Jerusalem community, which takes steps to protect Saul by escorting him to safety and (evidently) paying his travel expenses. All of this lays groundwork for chap. 15,[18] but it is remarkable that the crucial link between Barnabas and Saul is related in words so casual and unemphatic.[19] The narrator uses the technique for Saul that was used for Philip, depositing him in a place where he will remain until next required (Philip: 8:40; 21:8; Saul: 9:30; 11:25).[20]

■ **31** The verse is a summary framed in solemn and mellifluous language.[21] From the author's perspective, this summary concludes the section begun in 8:1b, as well as providing a transition to the following material.[22] The persecution led by Saul has given way to peace for the whole church. The term ἐκκλησία appears twenty-three times in Acts[23] between chap. 5 and chap. 20; twenty of the occurrences refer to Christians.[24] Lucan usage is similar to Paul's. The most common application is for local communities,[25] but the word may refer to an assembly,[26] and some instances are ambiguous (e.g., 8:3; 18:22). In two cases, 9:31 and 20:28,[27] Luke reveals an awareness of the Deutero-Pauline and later view of *the* church as an institution that transcends local communities and can be treated as a hypostasis.[28] Acts 9:31 is not far from Ignatius's distinction between the local community and "the catholic church" (*Smyrn.* 8:2).[29] There is one rather startling bit of information in this fulsome sentence: Christian communities have been founded (or exist) in Galilee.[30] Luke evidently slips this in for the sake of completeness. It is idle to speculate how much he might have known about Galilean Christianity.

---

16 Lüdemann, 117–18. Bede (45) inspired by Jerome's *Commentary on Galatians* (*PL* 26:328a-b) flatly rejected the statement that Paul went to Jerusalem shortly after his baptism.

17 The awkward language of v. 28a (see n. *f* above) is evocative of the ministry of Jesus (1:21). Cf. also 1 Sam 18:16 and John 10:9.

18 Chaps. 21–26 will present a different picture, marked by the absence of support from the Jerusalem community.

19 See the comments of Painter, *Just James*, 46–48.

20 Acts 9:30 is probably indebted to Gal 1:21.

21 It is not clear how the nouns "reverence" (φόβος) and "support" (παράκλησις) are to be correlated with the two participles οἰκοδουμένη and πορευομένη (lit. "being built up" and "journeying"). The simplest assumption is that both nouns relate to both participles. "Reverence" is the proper response to the divine, not scrupulous anxiety about possible misdeeds, and so on. Cf. the roughly contemporary 2 Cor 7:1 (which is non-Pauline) and Eph 5:21.

22 See Barrett, 1:472–73. The particle μὲν οὖν last appeared in 8:4 and will recur at 11:19.

23 See Karl Ludwig Schmidt, "ἐκκλησία," *TDNT* 3:501–36, esp. 504–5.

24 Acts 7:38 refers to the Israelite community; 19:32, 29, 41 to a civic assembly.

25 E.g., Acts 8:1; 11:22; 13:1; 14:23; 15:41; 16:5; 20:17.

26 So 5:11 (probably); 11:26 (possibly); 14:27; 15:3, 4, 22, although disagreements are possible.

27 Acts 20:28 uses the Pauline expression "church of God" (Schmidt, "ἐκκλησία," 506–7). See also K. N. Giles, "Luke's Use of the Term *'ekklesia'* with Special Reference to Acts 20.28 and 9.31," *NTS* 31 (1985) 135–42.

28 See Schmidt, "ἐκκλησία," 509–13. Hubert Cancik makes a number of interesting observations on the term in "The History of Culture, Religion, and Institutions in Ancient Historiography: Philological Observations concerning Luke's History," *JBL* 116 (1997) 681–703, esp. 673–80.

29 Luke would not for a moment accept Ignatius's view of the bond between bishop and church, of course. On Ignatius's use of ἡ καθολικὴ ἐκκλησία ("the entire church"), see Schoedel, *Ignatius*, 243–44.

30 On what little can be said about the early church in Galilee, see Adolph von Harnack, *The Mission and Expansion of Christianity in the First Three Centuries* (2 vols.; trans. J. Moffatt; New York: G. P. Putnam's Sons, 1908) 2:97–120, 330.

9

The D-Text of Acts 9:3-22

9:3/ **As he was nearing Damascus in the course of his journey a light from above suddenly engulfed him. 4/ He fell on the ground *in great confusion*[a] and heard a voice saying to him, "Saul, Saul, why are you persecuting me? *It is hard to kick against the goads.*[b] "Who are you, Lord?" 5/ "I am Jesus, whom you are persecuting." *Overcome with fear at what had happened to him, he said, "Lord, what do you wish me to do?"*[c] 6/ *The Lord replied,*[d] "Get up and enter the city, and *there* you will be *shown*[e] what you must do." 7/ Those traveling with Saul were standing there speechless, for they heard the voice but saw no one *speaking. 8/ He said to them, "Lift me up from the ground." When they raised him* and (he) had opened his eyes, he could not see,[f] so they took him by the hand and led him into Damascus. 9/ *He remained thus* for three days, seeing *nothing* and neither ate nor drank.[g] 10/ In Damascus there was a disciple named Ananias, whom the Lord addressed in a vision: "Ananias!" *He answered, "Certainly,* Lord"[h] 11/ "Go to Straight Street and inquire at the house of Judas for a *person of* Tarsian origin[i] named Saul. *He* is at prayer." *[Omit v.12]* 13/ "Lord, I have heard about this character *[ ]*[j] and all of the horrible things that he has done to your people in Jerusalem. 14/ *Look,*[k] he has authority from the high priests to arrest everyone who calls upon your name." 15/ "Get going, because this *person* is the medium I have selected to carry my name to gentiles, monarchs, and the Israelites. 16/ I shall show him how much he will have to suffer for the sake of my name." 17/ Ananias *then arose,*[l] went to the house and laid *a hand in the name of Jesus Christ.*[m] He said, "Brother Saul, the Lord has dispatched me—Jesus, who appeared to you on the way here—so that you might see again and be filled with Holy**

- a This phrase provides Paul with a suitable emotion.
- b This proverb is proper to 26:14, introduced here in many MSS. to harmonize the accounts.
- c The phrase "what do you want me to do" comes from 22:10.
- d The phrase is a pedantic addition.
- e Lit. "and there it will be shown" (ὑποδείξεται). This might "correct" the text to conform to the vision of v. 12, which some D witnesses omit.
- f The D-Text inverts the word order "saw nothing" preceding "open his eyes."
- g The variants are stylistic revisions.
- h The D-Text replaces the Semitic idiom ἰδοὺ ἐγώ (lit. "behold I") with conventional Greek.
- i Here and in v. 15 Saul is identified as a "person" (ἄνθρωπος). One Sahidic MS. does not have "by the name of Saul." Some use the conventional (Act 4:36; 18:2; 18:24). "A native of Tarsus" (τῷ γένει).
- j Omit "from many." Some D-Text witnesses also omit "that he has done to your people."
- k Instead of "here" (ὧδε) some D-Text witnesses read ἰδού, conforming to a common expression (omitted in v. 10!).
- l "Then." Bezae is fond of τότε. "Arose" (ἐγερθείς) is pedantic (cf. v. 11).
- m Cf. 6:8; 9:40; 14:10; 18:4, 8. Addition of the formula makes the healing more conventional.
- n "Many" days (cf. v. 23) is a rationalization. Damascus is pedantically glossed as a "city." The Greek is improved by using διῆγεν instead of ἐγένετο.
- o The sentence is rewritten to state that Saul entered the Jewish synagogues, conforming his behavior to that of Jesus (Mark 2:1) and Paul elsewhere (Acts 18:19; 19:8). The phrase "with all boldness" is added, perhaps from 19:28, but it is a nice touch, since it places a bracket around Paul's Christian ministry (cf. 28:31). It is clearly secondary, since no motive exists for eliminating it.
- p "All" is a fine example of D-Text pedantry.
- q The addition of "in rhetorical acumen" (ἐν τῷ λόγῳ) prevents readers from concluding that Paul gained strength of a physical sort.
- r This expansion (gig h p mae) may be a gloss based on Matt 3:17||Luke 3:22. Irenaeus read "He is the Son of God, the Messiah," which combines the titles found in vv. 20 and 22 of the conventional text. Behind that could stand "This is the Messiah, the Son of God in whom he is well pleased," altered by Irenaeus for theological reasons. On the grounds of its unusual character, this reading has some claims to preference (Cadbury and Lake, 105). Luke does not despise adoptionist Christology, but the reading is so inept (could there be a Messiah/Son with whom God is *not* pleased?) that it is probably secondary.

Spirit." 18/ At that moment a flaky substance fell from his eyes, and his sight returned *at that instant*. Saul got up and was baptized. 19/ After he had taken some nourishment, his strength revived. Saul *passed many days* with the disciples in *the city of* Damascus.[n] 20/ He *entered the Jewish synagogues and* preached *without inhibition* about *the Lord* Jesus, proclaiming, "He is the Son of God."[o] 21/ This bewildered his hearers, who wondered, "Isn't he the fellow who wreaked havoc on *all*[p] those who call upon the name of Jesus in Jerusalem? Didn't he come here so that he might take those of this ilk back to the high priests in chains?" 22/ Yet Saul grew stronger *in rhetorical acumen*,[q] confounding the Jews of Damascus by proving that Jesus is the Messiah, *in whom God is well pleased*.[r]

Most of these changes are of the type one would expect in secondary D-Text readings: pedantic glosses and edifying expansions. They indicate that such items as the addition of "then" and "immediately" are not limited to Codex Bezae (which is lacking here). Some expose difficulties in the conventional text, such as the addition to vv. 5-6a, 8, and the omission of v. 12. On purely literary grounds, these would be considered better readings. The expansions of the encounter near Damascus indicate a different interpretation of the event, one that stressed Paul's remorse and repentance, his willingness to be punished for his sins, and the claim that he had acted in ignorance, another customary theme in descriptions of conversion.[1] The D-Text has reinforced the understanding of this passage as a story of the conversion of a notorious sinner.

Galatians 1–2 vigorously defends the independence of Paul from any institutional or ecclesiastical context and recounts how he became a missionary to gentiles. Acts 9 tells a story that is essentially the diametrical opposite. Saul is a missionary to Jews only and will remain such until invited by Barnabas, the authorized delegate of Jerusalem, to work in Antioch (11:19-26). Although Saul is the only active missionary in both Damascus and Jerusalem, he is well integrated into both communities, as the work of István Czachesz has shown.[2] Luke portrays Saul's relationship with a community, including its leaders, in Jerusalem alone. This emphasis is Lucan, for, apart from Ananias, who could otherwise be taken as a resident charismatic healer,[3] all of the data come from vv. 19b-30, which are Lucan composition. In fewer than a dozen verses Luke depicts his hero's transformation from a fully accredited representative of the persecutors to a fully accredited representative of the persecuted and sets the standard pattern of his missionary career.

1 Ignorance. Note Acts 3:17 (Jews); 17:30 (gentiles); *Jos. Asen.* 6:4; 13:11-13; *T. Jud.* 19:3; Wis 14:22; Eph 4:18; and 1 Pet 1:14. See also the *Hermas Sim.* 5.7.3-4 and numerous references in the apologists, e.g., Aristides *Apol.* 17.4; Justin *1 Apol.* 61.10 and four other times in his two apologies. It appears six times in writings wrongly attributed to Justin, and in Athenagoras *Leg.* 21.6 and 28.7, as well as in frg. 1 of Melito's *Apology*. In addition, note Ignatius *Eph.* 19:3; the *Preaching of Peter*, frg. 4; *Hermas Man.* 4.1.5.

2 Czachesz, "Commission Narratives," 61–65.

3 For Ephrem Ananias functioned only as a healer, *curator* (Ropes, *Text*, 412).

9:32-43 Peter Launches a Mission along the Coast

32/ While visiting all of the commu-
nities[a] Peter came in due course
to the people of God dwelling
at Lydda. 33/ There he discov-
ered a man named Aeneas, who
had been confined to his cot by
disability for about eight years.[b]
34/ "Aeneas," he said,[c] "Jesus
Christ[d] has made you well.
Rise and tend to your bed."
Aeneas got right up. 35/ When
all the dwellers in Lydda and
the coastal plain saw him, they
converted.
36/ In Joppa lived a disciple
named Tabitha (which means
"gazelle"[e]). She abounded in
good works and charitable
acts. 37/ While Peter was in the
vicinity, she fell ill and died.
They washed her corpse and
laid her out in an[f] upper room.
38/ When the disciples learned
that Peter was in Lydda, which
is not far from Joppa, they sent
two men[g] who importuned him,
"Please come to us as soon as
possible." 39/ Peter went with
them. When he got there all
the widows presented them-
selves, weeping as they showed
him the clothes and coats that
Dorcas had made while she was
with them. 40/ Peter had all of
them leave the room, then knelt
down in prayer. Addressing his
attention to the corpse, he said,
"Tabitha, get up." She opened
her eyes, saw Peter, and sat up.
41/ After helping her up[h] with a
hand, he summoned all of God's
people, including the widows,
and presented her alive and
well. 42/ The news spread all
over town,[i] and many came to
believe in the Lord. 43/ Peter
stayed in Joppa for some time,[j]
lodging with a tanner named
Simon.

a *Or:* "While traveling through the entire region."

b Less likely: "Since he was eight." The phrase ἐξ ἐτῶν ὀκτώ is ambiguous. If the narrator had wished to say "since the age of eight," he would probably have given the current age. In either case, the point is to demonstrate that the disability was genuine.

c Boismard's D-Text (*Texte,* 167) reads "gazing intensely at him, Peter said . . ." This is a secondary assimilation to 3:4; 14:9.

d The formula varies in the MS. tradition. See Metzger, *Textual Commentary*, 323.

e "Dorkas" in Greek, which has become the English name "Dorcas."

f The *v.l.* "the" (= "her/of her house") has good support, but is probably secondary.

g 𝔐 *et al.* omit "two men," eliminating a parallel with the story of Cornelius (10:7). Metzger (*Textual Commentary,* 324) attributes this to the problems raised by 10:19. Two messengers conform to standard practice: Joachim Jeremias, "Paarweise Sendung im Neuen Testament," in *New Testament Essays: Studies in Memory of Thomas Walter Manson* (ed. Angus John Brockhurst Higgins; Manchester: Manchester University Press, 1959) 136–43.

h The *v.l.* τε, instead of δέ, ($\mathfrak{p}^{74}$ A *pc* it) is quite difficult and may be original. The intended meaning will not change.

i On the question of the article before "Joppa" ("town" here), see Metzger, *Textual Commentary*, 324. Luke tends to use the article in such combinations.

j The construction is improved by the *v.l.* αὐτόν, which is therefore suspect (Metzger, *Textual Commentary*, 325).

Analysis

If the summary form of v. 31 is given its weight, 9:32–11:18 constitutes a unit.[1] The pattern is similar to that of 13:1–15:29: missionary work in several communities includes the conversion of gentiles, resulting in a conference in Jerusalem. At the simplest level, the two acts of Peter in 9:32-43 bring him into proximity to

1 See Rackham, 104; and Talbert, 103.

Caesarea.[2] It is equally apparent that Peter (now without John) once more follows up on the work of Philip.[3] Although the initial miracle stories may appear to be no more than traditions woven by Luke into his account because he knew them, they are dense with references to the stories of Elijah/Elisha (1 Kgs 17:17-24; 2 Kgs 4:32-37 [Acts 9:36-42]),[4] Jesus (Luke 5:18-26; [7:11-17]; 8:40-56), and Paul (14:8-12; 20:7-13). They exhibit the continuity of salvation history. The first gentile with whom Peter will interact will be a centurion, as was also true of Jesus (Luke 7:2-10).[5] The sequence exhibits dramatic intensification: the restoration of a cripple followed by a resurrection (cf. Mark 5:21-43).

Although it is reasonable to attribute both miracle stories to tradition, Lucan composition is also a possibility.[6] The argument that the stories were linked prior to Acts is difficult to sustain because most of the data that hold them together are Lucan.[7] The missionary setting is secondary in both cases, for in each an editorial statement that the miracles brought about numerous conversions replaces the conventional audience reaction.[8] The author has made the shift that will govern the description and function of miracles in subsequent Acts: miracles yield conversions. Luke is also fond of pairing stories about a male and a female, respectively.[9] The stories probably derive from some tradition, but few details can be identified with any security. In terms of language and function, they may be viewed as Lucan compositions.[10]

Comment

■ **32** The verb διέρχομαι (lit. "go through" [v. 32]) may refer to missionary travel, but here the visits are of a pastoral nature.[11] Readers may conclude that the "peace" of 9:31 made such travel feasible. "People of God" unites

2 The Pseudo-Clementines utilize this theme by placing Peter's evangelism and confrontations with Simon in the same geographical arena.

3 As Roloff (158–59) emphasizes, the narrative does not present Peter as bringing these communities under Jerusalem's wing. He would attribute this to the source, but it is more probable that the scheme of 8:14-25 was ad hoc.

4 2 Kings 5, which tells of the conversion of a foreign military officer, has a general parallel in Acts 10. Weiser (1:238) lists all of the corresponding features.

5 All of these interconnections were identified by Rackham, 144.

6 For an attempt to identify pre-Lucan elements, see Weiser, 1:239–41. The presence of a translation for the name Tabitha is a strong intimation of tradition.

7 Schneider (2:49) provides reasons for viewing the pairing as pre-Lucan, but see Lüdemann (120–22), who shows the redactional nature of the links.

8 Cf. on 3:10.

9 Parables: Luke 13:18-21 (mustard seed, leaven); 15:1-10 (lost sheep, lost coin); Miracles: Luke 7:1-17 (centurion, widow of Nain). See Tannehill, *Narrative Unity*, 1:132–35.

10 Roloff (159) envisions a cycle of "Jerusalem Peter legends," including also 3:1-11; 10:1-48; and 12:1-17. Such a collection is not a priori unlikely—cf. the *Act. Pet.*—but these items lack coherence in their present state and are not associated with Jerusalem. Roloff's further suggestion that 9:32-42 derives from local foundation stories is at such variance with the text that accepting it would concede that Luke has altered his sources beyond recognition. Haenchen (341) and Weiser (1:237) speak of "local tradition." Although the city, renamed Diospolis, later had a vigorous Christian community (and eventually became renowned as the site of St. George's martyrdom), it was burned early in the First Revolt and resettled within a few years under Roman auspices (Josephus *Bell.* 2.155; 4.445). An even worse fate befell Joppa, which was sacked and burned by Cestius, occupied by pirates, and again destroyed by Vespasian, who had it burned to the ground (ibid. 2.507–8; 3.417–27. It is not likely that local Christian traditions from these two cities survived these devastations. If a source existed, it would most probably have been a collection (?) of stories about Peter. See pp. 12–14.

11 The chief difficulty is διὰ πάντων. If it were feminine, one could supply "cities," "villages," or "regions" without difficulty. Because it is masc./neut., the best solution is to supply τόπων ("places"; cf. Luke 11:24). See Barrett, 1:479. The D-Text "through cities and regions" (διὰ πολέων καὶ χώρων) (Boismard, *Texte*, 167) is a secondary improvement. A lesser problem is the adverbial καί ("also," "even"), rendered "in due course" here.

these two stories (vv. 32, 41) and the chapter (v. 13).[12] The Lucan phrase "dwellers at" (οἱ κατοικοῦντες)[13] frames the brief healing story. In Acts, unlike in the Synoptics, the healer regularly takes the initiative.

■ **33** At Lydda,[14] Peter encounters[15] one Aeneas,[16] who suffered from a long-standing disability and lay, like other cripples, on a pallet. The influence of Mark 2:1-12 is evident.[17] This is not due to intra-Luke and Acts parallelism, since Luke 5:17-26 accounts for that phenomenon. The author evidently drew directly on Mark for this episode, as he will for the next. The healing formula, however, is atypical,[18] framed as an indicative[19] with an imperative, rather than as a simple command.

■ **34** The phrase στρῶσον σεαυτῷ is of uncertain meaning. One must supply an object. From the perspective of form criticism "make your bed" is preferable, as a kind of pregnant means of saying "pick up your bed and walk," thus calling for a demonstration that the healing is genuine.[20] In the event, the text simply reports that Aeneas stood up "immediately," as is proper for those healed. Peter's order to "get up" (ἀνάστηθι) links the two stories (vv. 34, 40) and emphasizes the essential identity of all wonders performed for individuals: they symbolize rising to new life.[21] Nothing more is said of Aeneas. It is utterly irrelevant to the story whether he was a believer. The healed man was a poster of such potency that the entire region converted.[22]

■ **36-43** Following the terse healing of Aeneas, the narrator recounts a novella.[23] Tradition alone—least of all in this case—will not explain this difference in type. Revivifications are never short, but authors could choose to expand or contract the episodes. The story of Aeneas could have been told at some length, and that of Tabitha more briefly. The contrast here prevents monotony, but more importantly, it develops a crescendo: each of the three stories is longer than its predecessor. The story

12 Whether this is due to an authorial inclination to repetition (on which see Cadbury, "Four Features," 97–101) is not material.

13 Acts 1:19, 20; 2:5, 9, 14; 4:16; 9:22; 11:29; 13:27; 19:10, 17; 22:12.

14 On the site (Hebrew "Lod") see Melvin Hunt, "Lod," *ABD* 4:346–47.

15 The initial "find" is Lucan: Acts 13:6; 18:2; 19:1.

16 Names are usually secondary details. "Aeneas" is attested for Palestinian Jews from the second century BCE to the fourth century CE (Williams, "Personal Names," 110).

17 Both κατάκειμαι ("lie") and κράβαττος ("pallet") are found in Mark 2:4 and not elsewhere within a sentence. Luke avoids the latter word (which is vulgar) in the Gospel (5:17-26), but uses it in Acts. (See on 5:15). The word παραλελυμένος, on the other hand, is Lucan (Luke 5:18, 24; Acts 8:7). Mark prefers παραλυτικός (five times in 2:1-12; the text of Luke 5:24 is uncertain.)

18 Weiser (1:239) marshals a number of arguments in support of the view that the formula is Lucan. This formula does not diminish the role of Peter as healing agent. Not just anyone could announce that Christ had made a sick person well.

19 The verb ἴαται ("heal") is probably perfect rather than present, since that is more suitable to the form. Cf. the use of σέσωκεν (Luke 7:50; 17:19; 18:42). See Cadbury, "A Possible Perfect in Acts 9:34," *JTS* 49 (1948) 57–58.

20 The alternative, "arrange a meal" (Cadbury and Lake, 109), would be like Mark 1:29-31 (Peter's mother-in-law), but leads nowhere. BDAG, 949a, *s.v.* στρώννυμι, says "make your own bed." See Johnson, 177; and Barrett, 1:481.

21 For Bede (47), the directive to make one's bed refers to the energy with which those who have embraced belief will address themselves to good works. For an application of the symbolism of being raised to new life, see Eph 2:4-7.

22 The relative οἵτινες (which Luke often uses as an equivalent of the "simple relative," to avoid confusion with the article) "introduces a subsequent act" (Cadbury and Lake, 109). The D-Text improves the grammar by transforming εἶδαν ("they saw") and deleting the relative pronoun (Boismard, *Texte*, 168).

23 Richter Reimer (*Women*, 31–69) has studied this passage in substantial detail. Note also the review of research, with attention to feminist interpretations, by Janice Capel Anderson, "Reading Tabitha: A Feminist Reception History," in Levine, *Feminist Companion*, 22–48; and F. Erichson-Wendt, "Tabitha—Leben an der Grenze: Ein Beitrag zum Verständnis von Apg 9, 36-43," *BibNotiz* 127 (2005) 67–87. The last draws attention to the interaction of boundaries and transitions represented here, most notably life and death.

of Tabitha is a hinge between the healing of Aeneas, which shows that Peter exercised a similar ministry both within and beyond Jerusalem (3:1-10), and the elaborately narrated conversion of Cornelius. Both Tabitha and Cornelius were benefactors.[24] She was a (presumably pious) believer, he a pious gentile (9:36; 10:2). By 10:48, both will be pious (and presumably generous) believers—she by restoration to life, he by the gift of new life.[25] This arrangement comes from the author rather than his putative source(s). Whatever source Luke had for the story of Tabitha did not derive from an earlier period, for it presumes communities that have bodies of widows. The story belongs to the world of the Apostolic Fathers and the Pastorals and would be at home in the Apocryphal Acts.[26] It is difficult to imagine a date much earlier than 100 CE for 9:36-42 in its present shape.[27]

In Luke 8:51, 54, the author omitted the phrase "expelling everyone" (ἐκβαλὼν πάντας) from his source, Mark 5:37-40, 41. It appears, however, in Acts 9:40.[28] The motif of privacy is congruent with the "messianic secret" theme of Mark. Barrett views the interesting similarity between Mark's "Talitha" and the "Tabitha" of Acts as most probably "pure coincidence."[29] The case for coincidence here is weakened by the variant "Tabitha," rather than "Talitha" in Mark 5:41.[30] Even if this is attributed to contamination from Acts, it indicates that early Christian editors and scribes saw a link between the two passages.[31] The resemblances of this story to those of Elijah and Elisha in 1 Kgs 17:17-24 and 2 Kgs 4:32-37, respectively, include both general pattern[32] and specific details.[33] Beyond the name "Tabitha," little of the putative source remains.

Formally, this is a revivification story. Theissen rightly classifies accounts of the raising of the dead with "healings," for they are not resurrections like that of Jesus—let alone the resurrection of the "last day"—but, like healings, restoration of persons to their former life.[34] All wonders have an eschatological dimension, as signs, synecdoches, foretastes, and so forth, of God's promises, but this dimension applies differently to the stories about Aeneas and Tabitha. The difference is not

24 Both engaged in charitable activities (ποιεῖν ἐλεημοσυνάς; 9:36; 10:2).

25 Both stories also involve the dispatch of two messengers (9:38; 10:7).

26 For examples of parallels from Christian apocrypha and many interesting comments on 9:36-42 see Price, *Widow Traditions*, 85–100.

27 Barrett (1:478; cf. 1:484) says that these widows are not an order, as they do not perform service. This would be a valid objection if explicitly stated. He further observes, "Their existence suggests a community not of recent origin." These objections all but prove the opposite. Verses 39 and 41 speak of "*the* widows," in the latter case distinguished from οἱ ἅγιοι (lit. "the saints").

28 This phrase does not appear elsewhere in early Christian literature. On the use of Mark here, see Pervo, *Dating*, 41–42.

29 Barrett, 1:485, with a review of opinions.

30 W a r[1]: Ταβιθα; D: Θαβιτα e: *tabea*. Both Matt 5:25 and Luke 8:54 eliminated the Aramaic formula, Matthew probably because of its magical character; Luke, who translated it, because it is a foreign language.

31 Eduard Zeller observed that Mark was the source of this passage (*The Contents and Origin of the Acts of the Apostles, Critically Investigated* [2 vols.; trans. J. Dare; London: Williams & Norgate, 1875–76] 1:271; 2:310–11).

32 See the table of Weiser, 1:238.

33 So, for example, the healer is summoned in all three cases, enters the house (an "upper room" [ὑπερῷον] in 1 Kgs 17:19; Acts 9:37); the public is excluded; prayer is a part of the ritual; all of the dead are "returned" to family or friends. In 2 Kgs 4:35 and Acts 9:40, the first sign of revivification is the opening of the eyes (ἤνοιξεν τοὺς ὀφθαλμούς). For more details, see Tannehill, *Narrative Unity*, 2:126–27.

34 Theissen, *Miracle Stories*, 90 n. 25. Cultures draw the boundaries between "life" and "death" differently. The definition of death is subject to debate. Even today, mistakes may be made about persons presumed to be dead. The theme of "apparent death" (p. 360), to which Theissen refers, owes part of its popularity in ancient popular literature to its credibility. Ancient Hebrews made free and vigorous use of "death" as a metaphor; see Jonah 2:2-6. For references and discussion, see "Death," *DBI*, 198–99, and, for philosophical and theological reflections, Rudolf Bultmann, "θάνατος," *TDNT* 3:7–25. It is no more possible to understand "death" in NT stories on the basis of current cultural assumptions than it is to make modern medical definitions of biblical "demon possession" or "leprosy."

qualitative but quantitative.[35] The revival of Tabitha foreshadows the extension of Christ's defeat of sin and death to the gentiles. With the story of Cornelius, it shares a social dimension. Of Aeneas's friends, relatives, and religious preference, the reader learns nothing. Tabitha is restored for and to a community. So also for Cornelius the result will not be a boon to an individual, but the potential inclusion of a numberless host within the people of God.[36]

■ **36** The narrator shifts attention away from Peter. Joppa is an apt location.[37] From there Jonah reportedly set out to avoid his mission to summon gentiles to repent (Jonah 1:2). Joppa contained a believer[38] named Tabitha,[39] evidently a woman of some means. There is no information about her status (virgin, divorcée, widow, wife).[40] Her name is suggestive of servile background.[41] The focus is on her benefactions.[42]

■ **37** The verse laconically reports her death. The ubiquitous "they" (presumably women, whose duty this normally was) wash the body. The detail verifies the actuality of the death.[43]

■ **38** The verse is the thread that joins, somewhat awkwardly,[44] and quite coyly, the two stories. Some link may have been present in a source, but for the dramatic arrangement here—rather than have the believers say, "Peter is not far away and could get here quickly. Let us send for him to come and raise Tabitha"—proximity is the primary factor, while the only request conveyed by the two emissaries is for haste.[45] Peter alone is unaware of what has happened. Nonetheless, he goes with them,

35 The essential similarity between healings and revivifications is well illustrated by one of the sources: in Mark 5:21-43||Luke 8:40-56 two persons, the afflicted woman and the synagogue official's daughter, are restored to life.

36 Richter Reimer (*Women*, 53–61) is attentive to the social and economic implications of the story.

37 This city (modern Jaffa) became the port of Judea from its capture in 143 BCE until the First Revolt (n. 10). See Jacob Kaplan and Haya R. Kaplan, "Joppa," *ABD* 4:946–49.

38 The term *μαθητρία* appears elsewhere in early Christian literature only of Mary Magdalene (*Gos. Pet.* 12.50) and of Eubula, a follower of Paul (*Act. Paul* 7/9 [a partial but probable restoration]).

39 This name, with its probable translation almost certainly comes from tradition and thus indicates the use of a source. Note that only here is *ἤ* a relative in Acts and that Luke uses *μεθερμηνεύομαι* elsewhere (Acts 4:36; 13:8) for the meaning of names. For the possible meaning, *tabta*, "good, precious," see Lucinda A. Brown, "Tabitha," in Carol Meyers, ed., *Women in Scripture* (New York: Houghton Mifflin, 2000) 161–62.

40 Franklin Scott Spencer ("Women of 'the Cloth' in Acts: Sewing the Word," in Levine, *Feminist Companion*, 134–54) notes that three Jewish-Christian women in Acts, Tabitha, Lydia, and Priscilla, are associated with fabric. In all three cases, the activity is income-producing.

41 Williams, "Personal Names," 96. Specific Jewish examples are lacking, but Williams notes that this (and its masculine equivalent) was a generic slave name at a later period. The Greek equivalent, Dorcas, is not well attested for Jews (Williams, "Personal Names," 103).

42 Richter Reimer (*Women*, 36–41) has a full study of the meaning of the language about Tabitha's benefactions. "Good works" (*ἔργα ἀγαθά*) is a Pauline and Deutero-Pauline term (Rom 2:7; 13:3; 2 Cor 9:8; Eph 2:10; Phil 1:6; Col 1:10; 1 Tim 2:10; 5:10; 2 Tim 2:21; 3:17; Titus 1:16; 3:1). Only four of the twelve uses derive from the undisputed epistles.

43 Although Richter Reimer (*Women*, 42) stresses the washing of the body as Jewish, it is probably universal, dictated by the physiology of death. For Roman practice, see Jocelyn M. C. Toynbee, *Death and Burial in the Roman World* (Aspects of Greek and Roman Life; Ithaca: Cornell University Press, 1971) 44; and for Greek usage, see Rohde, *Psyche*, 163; and Robert Garland, *The Greek Way of Death* (Ithaca: Cornell University Press, 1985) 23. Bodies were also anointed (Mark 15:46 parr.) and dressed.

44 The D-Text (Boismard, *Texte*, 168) presents this in indirect speech. The expansion of cop[mae], "For the city was not distant. When the men arrived there, they importuned him to come with them without delay," suggests, because of its redundancy, that it conflates two traditions, in one of which (possibly the "true" D-Text) information about the proximity of the two places came at the end. This revision reveals the awkwardness of the conventional text.

45 The phrase *μὴ ὀκνήσῃς* ("please don't hesitate") is part of the polite language of epistolography (M-M, 444, *s.v.* *ὀκνέω*). Literary use emerges in the second century: Erotian frg. 60.14; Lucian *Jupp. conf.* 6; *Imag.* 3; Pseudo-Clementine *Letter of Clement to James* 19.3; Theophilus *Autolyc.* 3.1; cf. Dio of Prusa 1.56; Achilles Tatius *Leuc. Clit.* 1.2.2. It can also be construed as septuagintal: Num 22:16.

no questions asked. A few words bring him to the upper room and the revelation of the problem.

■ **39** With typical succinctness, the last half of the verse exposes the depth of the problem: this was not the unfortunate end of a single life, but a disaster for "the widows," introduced here. This is a moment of pathos—distraught widows[46] exhibiting[47] the fruit[48] of Dorcas's (the Greek name appears here) labors.[49]

■ **40** Without a word, Peter performs three actions: he empties the room[50] (save for the omniscient narrator), kneels in prayer,[51] and (after rising, presumably) turns toward[52] the corpse. Then he speaks his only two words in the entire episode: "Tabitha, get up."[53] The critics who stressed how v. 34 showed that Jesus Christ, rather than Peter, was responsible for the healing of Aeneas must remain silent here.[54] Editors of the D-Text hastened to add "in the name of [our Lord] Jesus Christ."[55] Peter's command was sufficient. Tabitha opened her eyes and sat up.[56]

■ **41-42** Once she is on her feet the apostle summons both the faithful[57] and "the widows"[58] to present[59] the revived Tabitha.[60] The community envisioned could fit within a single room (cf. 1:13; 20:8). As in v. 35, a report of conversions replaces the acclamation.[61] Just as the episode took place in the city from which Jonah attempted

46 "All the widows" heightens the pathos and indicates a substantial number of women. The text does not identify them as "believers" or the like because it assumes that they were an organized group. The D-Text says that the widows "surrounded" (*περιέστησαν αὐτόν*) him (Boismard, *Texte*, 168). This is a good touch, but it misses the nice contrast with the repeated *παρίστημι* ("present") in v. 41.

47 The middle participle *ἐπιδεικνύμεναι* could mean "modeling," but "exhibiting" is more likely.

48 Comparison of the relatives with *ποιέω* in vv. 36 and 39 shows that *ὅσα* in the latter is the equivalent to the simple relative. See also the data in Cadbury and Lake, 111.

49 On the pathos, see Pervo, *Profit*, 67. The text may allow for the possibility that Tabitha employed indigent widows in a house-based clothing factory, but the more likely meaning is that she had produced all of these garments and, one is evidently to assume, gave them to widows. The D-Text (Boismard, *Texte*, 168) clarifies the problem: "that Dorcas made for them." For details on the clothing, see Richter Reimer, *Women*, 42–43.

50 Healers, magicians, and the like, often work in secret (a motif used by Mark to expand his theme of "messianic secrecy"). One example is the sham healing in *Ethiopian Story* 4.5.3.

51 His prayer is a reflection of the Elijah/Elisha tradition, e.g., 2 Kgs 4:33.

52 This is the same verb (*ἐπιστρέφω*) that is used for "converted" in v. 35.

53 "Get up" (*ἀνάστηθι*) appeared also in v. 34.

54 E.g., Witherington (332), who stresses the source of the healing in v. 34 (330), but remains silent regarding v. 40. The apologetic argument is otiose: God is always the primary agent of miracles, regardless of the formula (against Paul Achtemeier, "Jesus and the Disciples as Miracle Workers in the Apocryphal New Testament," in Schüssler Fiorenza, *Aspects*, 149–86).

55 Boismard, *Texte*, 169. (The formula varies, and a number of D-Text witnesses include their always-popular "immediately" before "she opened her eyes." See Metzger, *Textual Commentary*, 324.)

56 The opened eyes are an echo of the Elijah/Elisha tradition (e.g., 2 Kgs 4:35). The verb sat up (*ἀνεκάθισεν*) occurs but twice in the entire Greek Bible: here and in the related story of the raising of the widow of Nain's son (Luke 7:15).

57 The term "God's people" (*ἅγιοι*) helps unite the two episodes (v. 32; cf. also 9:13).

58 On this combination, see above. Note the use of both *ἅγιοι* ("God's people") and "widows" in 1 Tim 5:10, which also—and quite specifically—distinguishes the widows from the other believers.

59 See n. 46.

60 The linguistic parallel between 1:3 (Jesus) and 9:41 points to the effects of the resurrection. Jesus "presented him*self* alive."

61 That the healing of disabled Aeneas resulted in the conversion of everyone while the resuscitation of Tabitha yielded "many" indicates that such expressions are very general. Cop[mae] may represent the "D-Text" in expanding this verse: "**Now people in all Joppa kept on talking about what had happened to her**; many came to believe **and turned to God**," followed by the expansion discussed in the following note.

to avoid his mission to the gentiles, so it closes with the note that Peter remained there, for reasons not given,[62] at the home of a tanner. This lodging will provide a strong contrast with that of his next host: a centurion.[63]

62 The D-Text gives a reason: Peter was constrained to remain in Joppa (Boismard, *Texte*, 169). This addition also improves the syntax.

63 The datum in v. 43 is most likely traditional, for Luke would not have invented it. Tanners practiced an unenviable craft, as Joachim Jeremias indicates (*Jerusalem in the Time of Jesus* [trans. F. H. and C. H. Cave; Philadelphia: Fortress Press, 1975] 303–12, esp. 310), but Jeremias (whose evidence is centuries later than the time of Jesus) does not speak of ritual impurity in connection with tanning. Were Peter lodging with someone the reader considered ritually impure, the vision of chap. 10 would lose its force, as commentators observe (e.g., Weiser, 1:245). Still, the occupation was despised. Artemidorus 1.51 says that dreaming of tanning hides "is ill-omened for all. For the tanner handles dead bodies and lives outside the city" (trans. R. White, *The Interpretation of Dreams: The Oneirocritica of Artemidorus* [Park Ridge, N.J.: Noyes, 1975] 43). Loisy (431–32) records some speculation on this host.

10

10:1–11:18 The Conversions of Peter and Cornelius

1/ There lived in Caesarea a centurion of the Italian Cohort named
Cornelius. 2/ He was a pious
and God-fearing individual,
as was his entire household.
Cornelius gave generously to
the people of Israel and was
constant in prayer to God.[a]
3/ One day at about[b] 1500 hours
he had a vision in which he
distinctly saw an angel of God,[c]
who came in and said, "Cornelius!" 4/ Gazing at him in awe,
the centurion said, "What may I
do for you, lord?"[d]
"God is mindful of your devotions
and charitable acts. 5/ Therefore, please send some men[e] to
Joppa to invite one[f] Simon, surnamed Peter, 6/ who[g] is staying
with Simon, a tanner, whose
house is on the seashore."[h]

7/ When the angel who addressed
him had left, Cornelius summoned two of his household
slaves and a pious soldier from
his staff. 8/ After explaining the
entire matter to them,[i] he sent
them off to Joppa.

9/ The next day, around 1200 hours,
as their[j] journey was bringing
them close to Caesarea, Peter
went up to the roof to pray.
10/ He began to feel hungry and
decided to have a meal. While
this was being prepared, he
fell into a trance. 11/ He had a
vision of an object like a large
cloth suspended by its four
corners that descended from
the opened sky to the ground.[k]
12/ In it were all the four-legged
animals and reptiles of earth
and all the birds of the sky.
13/ A voice said: "Go kill and
eat *these creatures*."[l]

14/ "Certainly not, sir," he answered.
"I have never tasted anything
that was unclean and impure."[m]
15/ The voice from above
spoke again: "Stop designating
'unclean' what God has made
pure." 16/ This was repeated
twice more, after which the
whole apparatus was hauled[n]
back up into the sky.

17/ While Peter was struggling to
make sense of the vision that
he had seen,[o] the men[p] who
had been sent by Cornelius had
obtained directions to Simon's

house and arrived at the door.
18/ They called out, "Is Simon
surnamed Peter a guest here?"[q]
19/ As Peter continued to try to
figure out the vision, the Spirit
said:[r] "Listen! Two[s] men are
here, looking for you.[t] 20/ So
go downstairs and accompany
them, no questions asked, for
I have sent them. 21/ So Peter
went down and said to the
men, "I'm the person you're
looking for. What has brought
you here?"

22/ "Centurion Cornelius[u] has sent
us. He is an upright and rever-
ent person, well recommended
by all Jewry. He has been
directed by a holy angel of God
to invite you to his home so
that he may hear what you have
to say." 23/ Peter then invited
them to come in and receive
some hospitality.

10:23b-27: Conventional Text	10:23b-27: D-Text[v]
The next day Peter set out with them, accompanied by some of the believers from Joppa, 24/ and on the following day he reached Caesarea. In expectation of their arrival Cornelius had invited his relatives and close friends. 25/ As Peter was about to enter, Cornelius came to meet him, falling to his knees in homage. 26/ At this Peter pulled him up, saying, "Please stay on your feet; I too am a mortal." 27/ Peter continued to converse with him as he entered the house, where he found a sizable gathering.	. . . 24/ "Now Cornelius *made preparations to receive* them. He invited his relatives and close friends and then proceeded to wait. (25)/ As Peter was drawing near to Caesarea, one of the servants ran ahead and announced that he had arrived. Cornelius thereupon jumped up and met him,[w] and falling down at[x] his feet reverenced him. Peter [ ] said, "What are you doing?[y] [ ][z] I too am a mortal just like you."[aa] And, after entering, he found a sizeable gathering.

28/ "All of you are aware,"[bb] he said,
"that it is taboo[cc] for Jews to
associate intimately with or to
visit those of another race,[dd]
but[ee] God has shown me that
no person is unclean or impure.
29/ I therefore came when summoned. Please explain why you
have asked me to be here."

30/ "Three days ago,"[ff] replied
Cornelius, "I was at home
praying at 1500 hours,[gg] when
an elegantly dressed man
appeared before me and said:

"Cornelius, God has heard your
prayers and is mindful of your
charitable acts. 32/ Therefore
send to Joppa and invite Simon
surnamed Peter who is staying with Simon a tanner by the
seashore."[hh] 33/ That I promptly
did, and you have been so kind
as to come. We are now gathered, in the sight of God,[ii] to
hear what the Lord has directed
you to say."
34/ "I am beginning to grasp,"
replied Peter, "that God really
is non-discriminatory 35/ and
accepts all who revere him and
conduct themselves properly,
regardless of national or ethnic
background. 36/ God issued the
message of peace to the Israelites through Jesus Christ (he
is the sovereign of all people).
37/ You are familiar with what
happened[jj] throughout Judea. It
began in Galilee, following the
baptism that John proclaimed.
38/ You know about Jesus of
Nazareth, who, when[kk] God had
invested him with the power
of the Holy Spirit,[ll] went about
doing good and healing all who
were oppressed by the devil,[mm]
because God was with him.
39/ We can attest to all[nn] that
Jesus did in Jewish territory
and at[oo] Jerusalem. There they
actually put him to death by
hanging him on a tree, 40/ but
God raised him two days later[pp]
and arranged for him to be
seen—41/ not by everyone but
by us, witnesses selected by
God in advance. We regularly
ate and drank with him after
God raised him from the dead.[qq]
42/ He charged[rr] us to proclaim
to the people and to testify that
he is God's appointed judge
of the living and of the dead.
43/ The prophets are in full
agreement that all who believe
in him will obtain release from
sins through his name."
44/ While Peter was still speaking,
the Holy Spirit fell upon all who
were listening to his sermon.
45/ All the Jewish believers
who had accompanied Peter
were amazed that the gift of the
Holy Spirit had been bestowed
even upon the gentiles, 46/ for

they heard the audience speaking in tongues[ss] and praising
God. Peter said,[tt] 47/ "There is
no reason why these people,
who have received the Holy
Spirit just as we did, cannot be
baptized with water, is there?"
48/ He thereupon directed that
they be baptized in the name of
Jesus.[uu] After this they invited
Peter to stay for several days.

11:1-2: Conventional Text

News that gentiles had also welcomed God's message came to
the apostles and other believers
in Judea.
2/ When Peter
got back to Jerusalem,

11:1-2: D-Text[vv]

It became known to the apostles
and the other believers in Judea
that gentiles had also welcomed God's message, *and they*
blessed God. 2/ Now Peter had
for some time wanted to go to
Jerusalem.[ww] *After summoning*
the believers for a strengthen-
ing message, he left. In the
course of his journey through
the region he engaged in a
good deal of teaching.[xx] When
he arrived at Jerusalem *he*
reported about God's grace.

The circumcised took issue with
him: 3/ "Why[yy] did you enter
the home of uncircumcised men
and eat with them?"[zz]
4/ Peter undertook a point by point
explanation. 5/ "I was in Joppa,
saying my prayers, when a
trance came upon me. I had a
vision of an object like a large
cloth that descended from
the sky, suspended by all four
corners. It came right down
in front of me. 6/ As I carefully scrutinized it, attempting
to figure out what it meant, I
saw tame and wild animals,
reptiles, and birds. 7/ A voice
told me: 'Peter, go kill and eat
these creatures.' 8/ 'Certainly
not, sir,' I answered. 'I have
never tasted anything that was
unclean or impure.' 9/ The voice
from the sky spoke again: 'Stop
designating "unclean" what
God has made pure.' 10/ This
was repeated two more times,
and then the whole apparatus
was hauled back up into the
sky. 11/ At that very moment
three men appeared at the
house where I was staying.
Cornelius had sent them to find

me. 12/ The spirit told me[a‡] to
go with them, avoiding distinc-
tions. Together with these six
believers we went there and
entered the man's house. 13/ He
then told us[b‡] how the angel
had appeared in his home and
said, 'Send to Joppa and sum-
mon Simon Peter. 14/ He will
tell you how you can be saved—
you and your household.'
15/ Shortly after I began to
speak, the Holy Spirit fell upon
them—just as upon us in the
beginning. 16/ I remembered
the Lord's words: 'Now John
baptized by means of water,
but you will be baptized with
Holy Spirit.' 17/ Since, therefore
God had bestowed upon them a
gift identical to that which we
received when we came to faith
in the Lord Jesus Christ, could I
try to block God's path?"

18/ These words stilled their objections and brought forth praise: "Look at that! God has also offered the gentiles conversion to new life!"

---

a Boismard (*Texte*, 170) omits "to God" from his D-text. It is somewhat superfluous but probably included to emphasize the object of his piety.

b 𝔐 and the Latin tradition omit the preposition here. Greek does not require a preposition and can use the accusative to indicate time when. See Cadbury and Lake, 113; and Barrett, 1:502.

c *Or*: "a messenger of God." The D-Text (Boismard, *Texte*, 170) omits "of God."

d Lit. "What is it?" In English, this phrase suggests a superior addressing an inferior. The vocative κύριε could be rendered "sir," but Cornelius is aware that his visitor is from the divine realm. In Boismard (*Texte*, 170), the D-Text uses the phrase of Saul (9:6): "Who are you, sir?" This is secondary, since it requires a response with "I am . . ."

e The D-Text (Boismard, *Texte*, 170) omits "men."

f ℵ E ψ 33 𝔪 it syh sa mae Ir[lat] omit τινα. Metzger (*Textual Commentary*, 325) speculates that this equivalent for the indefinite article may have been regarded as demeaning to Peter. From the perspective of Cornelius it is quite appropriate.

g 69[mg] *pc* p[c] vg[cl] add οὗτος λαλήσει σοι τι σε δεῖ ποιεῖν ("He will tell you what you must do.") This is indebted to 9:6. An alternative, weakly supported (436 *pc* [bo[mss]]) variant simply includes here the words of 11:14. Haenchen (347) notes that this addition eliminates the "blind obedience" of both Cornelius and Peter, who respond without gaining a promise.

h The D-Text (Boismard, *Texte*, 171) paraphrases this.

i D-Texts may have read ὅραμα ("vision") instead of ἅπαντα ("the entire matter"). See Cadbury and Lake, 114; and Boismard, *Texte*, 171.

j The choices are either ἐκείνων or αὐτῶν, the former a distant reference ("those people"), the latter more neutral ("they"). It is difficult to decide between them on external evidence. Since the subject promptly changes to Peter, the demonstrative is better Greek. At the close, a number of witnesses (A gig 1 vg[mss]) add, somewhat pedantically, "of the day."

k On the text of v. 11, see Preuschen (65), who makes a case that the *Didascalia* ("an object let down by its four corners descending to the ground") is more original.

l *"These creatures"* is added for clarification. *Or:* "Peter, go . . ." Various witnesses omit "Peter." Barrett (1:507) asks why any would delete it and is thus inclined to omit it as secondary. This is a good point. Formally, however, a vocative is conventional in these settings (cf. v. 3, Cornelius). Boismard

(*Texte*, 173) omits the vocative and reads "Get up [impv.], *and* kill and eat."

m The D-Text (Boismard, *Texte*, 173) omits the strong "certainly not" and has "unclean *or* impure." On the importance of καί, see Mikeal C. Parsons, "'Nothing Defiled AND Unclean': The Conjunction's Function in Acts 10:14," *PerspRelStud* 27 (2000) 263–74.

n *Or:* "quickly hauled." The omission of εὐθύς ("quickly") in the D-Text is telling, as it often adds this or similar words. An alternative is πάλιν ("again"), on which see Boismard, *Texte*, 173. It is probably an assimilation from 11:10. The earliest text probably lacked any adverb. The word εὐθύς does not otherwise occur in Acts, and a number of witnesses (including 𝔭[45]) lack an adverb. Word order also differs. See Metzger, *Textual Commentary*, 327.

o D p add ἐγένετο after the prepositional phrase. This makes the phrase a clause meaning "when he came to himself."

p καὶ ἰδού ("and lo"), rather than plain ἰδού, is read by C D E Ψ 𝔪 p sy[h]. Ropes (*Text*, 94) prefers this as more difficult. Metzger (*Textual Commentary*, 327) agrees. It is a septuagintalism.

q Cadbury and Lake (116) take the question as direct, with references to 4:7; 23:19; 1:6; 19:2. In addition, ἐνθαδε means "here." If the text read ἐκεῖ ("there"), it would be indirect. Luke prefers direct speech. See also Moule, *Idiom Book*, 154; Conzelmann, 82; and Barrett, 1:510.

r B reads an anarthrous πνεῦμα ("[a?] spirit"). The pronoun αὐτῷ ("to him") appears in different places and may be an addition. See Metzger, *Textual Commentary*, 327–28.

s *Or:* "three men," or "some men." D-Text and 𝔪 omit any number. This makes for a rough subject: ἄνδρες ("men"), but cf. v. 5. B has "two," which seems an evident error, but Ropes (*Text*, 94) says that it assumes that only the two slaves are "responsible messengers, the soldier merely serving as a guard." Although slaves, these two would have some of the authority of their master and would thus "outrank" a mere enlisted person. He says that this judgment would be that not of a scribe but of the author. The alternatives are improvements. Haenchen (349 n. 1) prefers "two." Bruce (256–57), who does not, nonetheless cites *Od.* 9.90 and 10.102 in its favor. Metzger (*Textual Commentary*, 328) promotes the copyist to the rank of "a discriminating scribe" (and thus a corrector).

t Many witnesses present "seek" as a finite verb. Metzger (*Textual Commentary*, 328) observes that it is difficult to imagine why anyone would transform a finite verb into a participle. ἰδού can function as a kind of copula. (cf. French *voici*). BDF §128 (7) says the copula is to be supplied.

u D sy[p] add τις ("One Cornelius, a centurion"). This is a sharp emendation, fashioning a precise parallel with "one Peter" in v. 5. (See n. *f*.)

v Cf. Boismard, *Texte*, 178–79. As often, this text is unlikely to be original because of the lack of a good explanation for how the conventional text could have arisen from this alternative.

w As Epp notes (*Tendency*, 161), Cornelius's reverence would take place in public, enhancing its dramatic quality.

x Bezae uses the conventional πρός rather than ἐπί.

y This enhances the parallel with—or is borrowed from—14:15.

z The problem here is like that of 3:6. Editors may have eliminated the command (lit. "Stand up") as redundant. Boismard (*Texte*, 178) omits it, but he cites no witnesses that remove both the narrative and the command. (See, however, Boismard's note on 178–79.) Some Latin texts include or conclude with *deum adora* ("worship God"). This may derive from Rev 19:10.

aa The D-Text of v. 27 may be irrecoverable. See below.

bb Before ἐπίστασθε D mae insert βέλτιον, "As you well know." This is a nice touch and is difficult to see as other than an addition. Compare the D-Text elative in 4:16.

cc "Taboo": Bruce, 259.

dd 𝔓[50] D sy[p] add ἀνδρί (lit. "a foreign man").

ee This καί is adversative.

ff *Or:* "Four days have passed"

gg See the discussion of the text.

hh C D E Ψ 1739 𝔪 it sy (sa cop[mae]) add at the close ὅς παραγενόμενος λαλήσει σοι ("who will speak to you when he gets there."). This addition is probably based on 11:14, which it seeks to justify. The interpolator failed to observe that the grammatical antecedent is Simon the Tanner. See Metzger, *Textual Commentary*, 331–32.

ii *Or:* "We are here with you."

jj Use of ῥῆμα to mean "event" is septuagintal, the result of Hebrew influence. This would constitute a difficulty for the dramatic audience.

kk D* it sy cop[mae] read the relative ("whom") and delete "him." This is a secondary improvement.

ll The translation takes the phrase "holy Spirit and power" as hendiadys, a view Barrett (1:524) finds "not wrong." Boismard (*Texte*, 183) omits "holy" (= "with spiritual power"). This may be preferable as less likely.

mm E reads "Satan" instead of "the devil." On the constative aorist ("always went about"), see BDF §332 (1).

nn The D-Text (Boismard, *Texte*, 184) reads, "We are *his* witnesses of what he did in Jewish territory, whom *the Jews rebuffed* and killed. . . ." "His" is harmonizing: 2:32; 3:15 (but cf. 5:32).

oo As elsewhere, witnesses divide rather evenly on whether "Jerusalem" should be marked with a (second) preposition. This applies to whether "Judea" and "Jerusalem" are effectively two places, and possibly to the use of τε (on the latter, see BDF §444 [5]).

pp Witnesses vary on the form of this expression. See Metzger, *Textual Commentary*, 334.

qq Conzelmann (84) prefers to render the infinitive ἀποστῆναι as transitive ("God raised"), arguing that the intransitive second aorist derives from tradition, but that Luke's perspective (cf. v. 40) prefers the transitive.

rr The D-Text (Boismard, *Texte*, 185) reads ἐνετείλατο. Cf. 1:2. This does not change the meaning.

ss Possibly "in foreign tongues."

tt The D-Text reads "and said" (Boismard, *Texte*, 185). Luke uses ἀποκρίνομαι (lit. "answer") to introduce speech, especially in response to action (e.g., 3:11).

uu "Jesus" is the D-Text reading proposed by Boismard, *Texte*, 187. "Lord" or "Lord Jesus" is also possible. "Jesus Christ" is well supported (Metzger, *Textual Commentary*, 336) and conforms to v. 36, but the simple "Jesus" best accounts for the variety of readings.

vv Boismard, *Texte*, 187–89.

ww Note the D-Text of 21:17.

xx *Or:* "As he traveled through the country he taught, giving a full account." See Strange, *Problem*, 82.

yy The ὅτι is ambiguous. If the second person is read, it is *recitativum*, a quotation mark. With the third person, which has strong MS. support ($\mathfrak{p}^{45}$ B *et al.*), it could function as the introduction to a noun clause or indirect discourse, or it can be subordinate: "objected because he . . ." Most presume that it = τί ὅτι (BDAG 2b, 732). Lucan preference for direct speech gives weight to the second person readings and "why," presuming that this was misunderstood or corrected. See BDF §300 (2); Cadbury and Lake, 124; Moule, *Idiom Book*, 159. Haenchen (354) understands it as *recitativum*.

zz *Or:* "The circumcised complained that he had entered the home of uncircumcised men and eaten with them."

a‡ Word order varies in the textual witnesses.

b‡ $\mathfrak{P}^{74}$ places the verb in the passive voice.

Analysis

The Conversion of Cornelius is the longest story in Acts, rivaled only by Paul's journey to Rome.[1] Length is one criterion of importance. Others include the careful scenic structure, the use of repetition, and the dense supernatural apparatus of vision and epiphany. The first conversion of an identified gentile was in no sense due to individual whimsy, but came about through the Spirit's express direction in the face of substantial pious resistance. Moreover, this first gentile convert was not some anonymous member of the urban or rural workforce but a prominent soldier and citizen, and the agent of his conversion was no "Hellenist" or radical but the very leader of the apostles. The issues generated by this chapter will not meet their final resolution until chap. 15, but the controversy surrounding Paul's fulfillment of them will remain unresolved at the end of the book. The fundamental problem of Acts is the validity of the gentile mission. Everything else is prelude and excursus, sideshow and background. Luke has so successfully integrated his leading theme into the other material that all major structural divisions are arguable. Johnson well explicates the source of dramatic tension: the gulf between divine intention and human understanding.[2] Literary irony derives from the reader's knowledge, which, thanks to the omniscient narrator, is superior to that of any of the human characters. Readers can enjoy the ignorance of Cornelius and the perplexity of Peter without worry. The suspense and mystery of this story

1 Sixty-six verses are devoted to Cornelius. The trip to Rome (27:1–28:16) contains sixty verses. A recent literary analysis is Edith M. Humphrey, "Collision of Modes?—Vision and Determining Argument in Acts 10:1–11:18," *Semeia* 71 (1995) 65–84. Dennis MacDonald (*Imitate Homer*, 19–65) points to concinnities with Homer.

2 Johnson (186–88) presents an excellent literary perspective on 10:1–11:18.

are not of the sort that grip readers with doubt. The implied reader of Acts, a Christian of gentile background, knows that a gentile mission will take place. One of the literary pleasures of Acts is learning how this project came about.[3]

Although length is a more or less universal means for emphasis, nearly all of the other features are Lucan and raise the question of sources.[4] As Lüdemann observes, nearly every verse has Lucan features,[5] but he participates in the consensus that the story rests on tradition. As always, the important question is not whether there was a source, but the extent, form,[6] setting, and function of the sources. From the perspective of this commentary, the question is whether a Cornelius story was a part of the gentile mission source. With this goes the question of its linkage to the two miracles related in 9:32-43. Difficulties in the narrative—a number of which were recognized by ancient editors—provide a foothold for exploration of these questions. Peter's vision (10:9-16) is gratuitous. The instruction of the Spirit (v. 20) suffices to send him to the home of Cornelius. Granting this "insertion,"[7] vv. 28-29a should also be set aside, and, since vv. 30-33 are a repetition of the Lucan words of vv. 1-8, vv. 28-33 should be assigned to the author. Verses 25-27 also raise difficulties that would be alleviated if Peter were simply to enter the centurion's domicile without an initial encounter.[8] The climax (vv. 44-48) is not wholly suitable in the present context. Since Peter had already become convinced, on the basis of his own experience, direction from the Spirit, and Cornelius's account of the angelophany, that gentiles could be acceptable and had undertaken to proclaim the gospel message to them, he would presumably have been prepared to authorize their subsequent baptism. Verse 47 presumes, in some tension with the prior narrative, that there were doubts about the acceptability of gentiles.[9]

One motive for including the vision of Peter was to provide a parallel with the twin visions of 9:10-16. As such, it merits comparison with "double dreams,"[10] but this is only a corresponding vision. If both visions had been components of the source, the correspondence would have been much closer, as in chap. 9. The paired visions are more than a literary link; they constitute part of the redundant apparatus of divine direction verifying God's approval of the gentile mission. The detailed exegesis will argue that the angelophany to Cornelius is so thoroughly Lucan in form, style, and purpose that no trace of an underlying basis can be discovered. Luke most probably contributed this entire scene, including the status and piety of Cornelius, who is a successor to the centurion of Luke 7:1-10. One can no longer determine whether the hypothetical source opened with an

3 In comparison, one of the "theological pleasures," as it were, of the book is reinforcement of the view that God directed the gentile mission.

4 On the question of tradition and redaction in Acts 10:1—11:18 note Dibelius, *Studies,* 109–22; Lüdemann, 124–33; Haenchen, 355–63 (with a review of earlier research); Weiser, 1:353–62; Barrett, 1:491–98; Bovon, "Tradition et redaction," 22–45; Karl Löning, "Die Korneliustradition," *BZ* 18 (1974) 1–19; Klaus Haacker, "Dibelius und Cornelius: Ein Beispiel formgeschichtlicher Überlieferungskritik," *BZ* 24 (1980) 234–51; Joseph Tyson, "Themes at the Crossroads: Acts 15 in Its Lukan Setting," *Forum* n.s. 4 (2001) 105–24; and the detailed study of Josef Zmijewski, "Die Stellung des Stephanus in der Geschichte des Urchristentums," *ANRW* 2.26.2 (1995) 1415–53. Turner (*Power,* 378–97) devotes an excursus to the question.

5 Lüdemann, 130.

6 Analysts presume that a legend forms the core of tradition here. In its present form, the narrative lacks the unities of time and place that normally characterize popular tradition. See Knox, 31.

7 The subsequent exegesis will show that Luke was not likely to have concocted the vision.

8 See below.

9 François Bovon's detailed analysis ("Tradition et redaction en Actes 10,1–11,18," *TZ* 26 [1970] 22–45) yields these results: an account of conversion of the pious centurion with initial vision (vv. 1-8); the Spirit's command to Peter (vv. 19b-20); Peter's arrival (vv. 24-33, less 27-29a); and the eruption of the Spirit, followed by admission to baptism without further condition. The other source was the etiological story encompassed within Peter's vision. This analysis is as sound as any, but, with regard to vv. 1-8, one can recover little underlying material—except to say that the story had to begin somewhere. The hypothesis that the source reported the Spirit's intervention before Peter could speak is possible, but the interruption of speeches is common in Acts.

10 See p. 238 n. 44.

invitation from Cornelius (if that was his name) and/or with a direction from the Spirit to Peter.[11]

Three elements support the view that the source, in whole or part, derives from the story of the gentile mission. One is the name and prominence of Peter, who was the apostle of choice for the Antiochene community.[12] Another is the vision recorded in 10:9-16, which appears to be independent of/prior to Mark (7:1-23).[13] This revelation was not, in all probability, part of the conversion story, in which it plays a subsidiary role.[14] It would have found a welcome home in Antioch, for it justifies Peter's approach to dietary laws in Antioch.[15] It may well have belonged to the source, from which Luke inserted it into the story about Cornelius. This, like the gifts of the Spirit, constituted charismatic legitimation of Christian practice.

The third item is the gift of the Spirit (vv. 44-47a). Although the language of these verses is Lucan, it represents, as proposed above,[16] a fundamental justification for the gentile mission. Among the difficulties are the questions of place and personality. Chapter 10 continues the practice, begun in chap. 8 (Samaria), of having Peter follow in the traces of Philip, who reached Caesarea in 8:40. This scheme is generally viewed, with good reason, as Lucan. Was this story originally located in Caesarea and its subject Peter, or are one or both of these due to the author of Acts? One hypothesis is that Philip was the "original" agent of this conversion story and that Luke "replaced" him with Peter and created the incident of the Ethiopian official for Philip. An advantage of this proposal is the location of Philip in Caesarea. In its present form, the Cornelius story does not reflect the Antiochene viewpoint, for that community viewed Peter not as the founder of a gentile mission but as the close follower of Jesus who strongly supported a mixed Jewish-gentile community.[17] The simplest proposal is that this story was not a component of the gentile mission source but possibly was from a cycle of "Acts of Peter" that climaxed with his escape from death in Acts 12,[18] although the evidence for that source is not particularly compelling.

The passage falls into a number of scenes, although the points of division are a matter of disagreement. The principle of scenic duality is generally operative.[19]

11 The Ps.-Clem. *Rec.* 1.72 states that James sent Peter to Caesarea to confront Simon and that he required regular reports.

12 See p. 13.

13 This vision does not conflict with Gal 2:11-14, which reports, on the authority of Paul, that Peter did not insist on *kashrut*, nor (against, e.g., Barrett, 1:493) is it in conflict with Acts 15:20, which does not identify any foods as unclean. Clinton Wahlen, "Peter's Vision and Conflicting Definitions of Purity," *NTS* 51 [2005] 505–18, argues that the purity code is not abolished, since the mixture of clean and unclean creatures makes all unclean. This is ingenious, but the text does not support it. J. Duncan M. Derrett ("Clean and Unclean Animals [Acts 10:15; 11:9]: Peter's Pronouncing Power Observed," *Heythrop Journal* 29 [1988] 205–21) illuminates the role of the vision in questions of authority about dietary regulations, strengthening the view that it relates to conflicts over food. He also proposes links to the "Apostolic Decree" of 15:20. Weiser (1:255–56) lists reasons for viewing this as pre-Lucan but not part of the basic source: it is not well integrated into the story; Peter's new insight, that salvation does not depend on membership in an ethnic group (vv. 34-35), does not come from the vision; it is not a proper double dream; and the story would not change if it were deleted.

14 Acts 10:20 suffices to justify Peter's visit. The vision plays an important role in chap. 11.

15 So also Klauck, *Magic*, 33–34.

16 See on 2:1-12.

17 The view of Peter as chief disciple from the time of Jesus is probably from the same Antiochene tradition and sources that inform the Gospels. It is not supported by Gal 1:18–2:10, which, while concentrating on Paul's relations with Peter, envisions three "pillars." (This is not to deny that James may have gained in influence vis-à-vis Peter during the years after Paul's conversion.)

18 As Lüdemann (131) sees, the story does not appear to be a Caesarean foundation legend. Conzelmann's concise excursus presumes "a conversion legend in edifying style" (80). On this ground, he proposes that "all passages in this chapter which elevate the singular story into one of principle may be assigned to Luke," on the grounds that the gentile mission did not come about through a single act. This is valid, but its assumption that Luke transformed a conversion story into a principle is open to challenge.

19 In scenes 1–2 the other "character" is a medium of revelation.

(9:43: Peter a guest at home of Simon)
Scene 1. (10:1-8) Cornelius. (revelation)
Scene 2. (10:9-16) Peter. (revelation)
Scene 3. (10:17-23a) Peter meets the envoys of Cornelius.
Interlude (10:23b-27) Journey of Peter (and entourage); meeting of Peter and Cornelius.
Scene 4. (10:28-48) Peter and Cornelius in the latter's home in Caesarea.
- a. (vv. 28-33) Peter and Cornelius converse.
- b. (vv. 34-43) Peter's address to Cornelius and his entourage.
- c. (vv. 44-46a) The Spirit falls upon the auditors. (revelation)
- d. (vv. 46b-48a) Peter directs that they be baptized.

(10:48b: Peter a guest at home of Cornelius.)
Scene 5. (11:1-18) Peter explains his actions to the community in Jerusalem.

The narrative technique involves the interlacement of a series of parallel events.[20] There are two visions, two journeys, two speeches, and two confirmations of the result.[21] This detailed literary structure eliminates any doubts that the story as it exists is a Lucan construct.

Comment

■ **1-8** (Scene 1) The narrator turns (cf. 9:10) to a different character, one Cornelius, a centurion of the Italic Cohort, evidently stationed in Caesarea, where he has a home large enough to accommodate his relations and the friends he has acquired during his term of service, quarters that include slaves as well as military subordinates. His rank and unit,[22] if not his name, are probably Lucan contributions to the narrative, for centurions are important persons in Luke and Acts.[23] This person appears to be modeled in part on the centurion of Luke 7:2-10,[24] and the unit to which he is said to belong was, to the best of available knowledge, not stationed in Judea prior to the First Revolt.[25] His name evokes one of the most distinguished and venerable of Roman patrician clans.[26] Status was not Cornelius's only virtue. He was pious and generous. His generosity resembles that of Tabitha (9:36), while the description of his piety is reminiscent of the values ascribed to the characters in Luke 1–2.[27] This, as the angelophany indicates, was far from fortuitous. Just as the angelophany experienced by Zechariah (Luke 1:11-20) set in motion the groundwork for a new era in salvation history, so the angelic visit to Cornelius will inaugurate the fulfillment of Simeon's prophecy (Luke 2:32). The story is beginning anew. Cornelius appears to have nothing in common with Elizabeth and Zechariah. They are an elderly, childless couple from backward Galilee, while he is a privileged representative of the ruling power. The implied reader must assume that Cornelius has gone as far as possible on his "spiritual journey" toward membership in the people of God,

20 On these techniques, see Pervo, *Profit*, 133–34.

21 On the parallelism, see Gaventa, *Darkness*, 111–12. Her discussion of the several scenes includes many useful literary insights.

22 A legend would have been likely to have an anonymous centurion. See the following note.

23 Luke 7:2, 6; 23:47; Acts 10:1, 22; 21:32; 22:25, 26; 23:17, 23; 24:23, 27 (five times). Their prominence is a clue to the narrator's social orientation. Centurions were among the most mobile persons in the Roman Empire, capable of rising from the ranks to, in a few instances, the equivalent of a decurion. See Peter Garnsey and Richard Saller, *The Roman Empire: Economy, Society and Culture* (Berkeley: University of California Press, 1987) 124, and the references in Hengel, *Between*, 203–4 n. 111. In Acts they enjoy a rather high status.

24 Lüdemann, 125–26.

25 See T. R. S. Broughton, "The Roman Army," in Lake and Cadbury, *Additional Notes*, 427–45, esp. 441–43; Schürer, *History*, 1:365; Hengel, *Between*, 203–4 n. 111; Dennis Bain Saddington, "Roman Military and Administrative Personnel in the New Testament," *ANRW* 2.26.3 (1996) 2409–35; and Hemer, *Book*, 164 and n. 9. Saddington thinks that the unit in view was the *Cohors II Italica Civium Romanorum*.

26 *Kleine Pauly* discusses sixty of the hundreds of Cornelii known to history (1:1307–1320). The Scipios and Sulla are among the more famous bearers of this name. From the emancipations of the latter in particular, the name proliferated among freed slaves and their descendants.

27 Zechariah and Elizabeth (Luke 1:5); Simeon (Luke 2:25); Anna (Luke 1:36-37).

a point that the narrator senses no obligation to address (beyond the vague reference to his "prayers" [v. 4]). He is at the "dead end" of "God-fearing" piety, unable to take the final step of full conversion, which would presumably require abandonment of his office.[28] Cornelius is thus the first and representative "God-Fearer" of Acts[29] and a person who has more in common with Elizabeth and Zechariah than first appears. After bestowing suitable and well-earned compliments, the angel does no more than direct the attention of Cornelius to Peter. This is even more mysterious—for Cornelius, if not for all but the most unimaginative reader—than was 9:6. If this is baffling to the centurion, he does not pause to share any feelings, but, as one who knows to take orders (cf. Luke 7:8), he dispatches some emissaries forthwith.[30]

■ **1-3** These verses constitute a single Greek sentence,[31] lending an appropriate solemnity to the beginning of the story, which opens in Lucan fashion.[32] From the Lucan perspective, Caesarea is "midway between Jerusalem and Antioch."[33] Thirty-four words introduce and characterize Cornelius. After recounting his rank and unit, the narrator reports that he is "pious."[34] This quality is developed in three participial phrases: his piety is directed toward the God of Israel and includes generosity and regular prayer.[35] The acquiescence of his entire household to his religious convictions indicates that it is a proper and well-managed domestic establishment, without the slightest whiff of sentiments like those of Luke 12:49-53; 14:26.[36] At around 1500 hours[37] on an unspecified day, an angel appeared to him in a vision. The form is conventional: the being appears; is seen; and addresses the subject, who reacts with fear; is told that God is pleased, and receives a command, which he obeys (cf. Josh 5:13-15).

■ **4b-6** The angelic announcement consists of an indicative and an imperative. Tobit 12:12 may have served as a direct source of v. 4b.[38] Cornelius's prayers and alms (the nature of which is unspecified) have found favor with God. The phrase *ἀνέβησαν εἰς μνημόσυνον* is a cultic metaphor[39] that assumes the legitimacy of "spiritual sacrifices," a concept known to the Greco-Roman world,[40] the Hebrew Bible,[41] sectarian Judaism,[42] nascent Christianity,[43] and rabbinic Judaism.[44] Religious activity of any kind became the equivalent of the sacrificial cult. The narrative assumes this concept and uses it to bridge the gap between Jews and gentiles. The subsequent

28 It is equally true that baptism would appear to prevent one from participation in the religious life of the Roman army.

29 See the excursus "'God-fearers' in Acts" in the commentary on 13:13-52.

30 The angel reinforces the social propriety that "superiors" send for, rather than visit, their inferiors. Luke has more in mind, however, than the preservation of social conventions.

31 𝔐 gig vg sy simplify the construction by introducing the verb *ἦν*. This would make the first sentence end with v. 2 and leave v. 3 without a stated subject.

32 Cf. 5:1 (Ananias) and 8:9 (Simon of Samaria).

33 Conzelmann, 81.

34 Luke uses *εὐσεβής* of the gentiles here and in v. 7. For Jews he prefers *εὐλαβής* ("devout") (Luke 2:25; Acts 2:5; 8:2; 22:12). See Pervo, *Dating*, 236–37.

35 Prayer and almsgiving often occur together: Tob 12:8; Matt 6:2-6; 1 Pet 4:7-8; *Did.* 15:4; *2 Clem.* 16:4. Constant (lit. "perpetual," *διὰ πάντος*) prayer is another (and obvious) characteristic of the highly devout life. Note Luke 24:53 and Heb 13:15 (where it is viewed as a form of "sacrifice").

36 On religion in the household, see David Balch, *Let Wives Be Submissive: The Domestic Code in 1 Peter* (SBLMS 26; Chico, Calif.: Scholars Press, 1981).

37 The temporal marker lends verisimilitude to the account and provides a bit of symmetry with the similar reference in v. 9.

38 In Tob 12:12, the archangel Raphael says, *καὶ νῦν ὅτε προσηύξω σὺ καὶ ἡ νύμφη σου Σαρρα, ἐγὼ προσήγαγον τὸ μνημόσυνον τῆς προσευχῆς ὑμῶν ἐνώπιον τοῦ ἁγίου* ("So now when you and Sarah prayed, it was I who brought and read the record of your prayer before the glory of the Lord . . . [NRSV renders ℵ]). Note the initial *καὶ νῦν*, which introduces Acts 10:5.

39 The underlying concept is that of an offering of cereal or incense that attracts a deity with its fragrance. Cf. Lev 6:15; Isa 66:3; Sir 38:11; 45:16. "Memorial Offering" (*μνημόσυνον*) was used also for righteous persons (Ps 111:6 LXX). Sir 35:1-13 urges and expounds upon the offerings of the righteous. See Johnson, 183; Spicq, *Lexicon*, 2:500–501, and Otto Michel, "*μνημονεύω*," *TDNT* 4:682–83.

40 E.g., *Sentences of Sextus* 47; Persius *Satires* 2.73–75; *Corp. Herm.* 13.18; 19; and 21.

41 E.g., Ps 51:17 (often cited or alluded to in early Christian literature, e.g., *1 Clem.* 18:16-17; 52:4; *Barn.* 2:10).

42 E.g., 1QS 8:1–9; 4QFlor 1:1–6.

43 E.g., from the NT: Rom 12:1-2; Phil 4:18; Heb 13:15-16; 1 Pet 2:5. For early Christian literature,

vision of Peter will eliminate another obstacle separating the two groups.[45] The surprising use of "Simon"[46] probably comes not from a source but from the impropriety of a nickname: "Send for Rocky." The order is socially appropriate. Superiors do not rush off to visit their inferiors, not least at the home of a tanner, but Peter's visit will result in the conversion of an entire household. The brisk and mysterious conclusion was more than some ancient readers could tolerate—and conflicted with 11:14, which was levied to yield a suitable conclusion.

■ **9-16** (Scene 2) The narrator, without losing track of the delegation, returns attention to Peter, who has, almost a full day later, piously gone up to the roof for prayer. In due course, he became hungry.[47] The informed reader may suspect that his prayer was preceded by fasting. Visions may come to those who fast.[48] Not all revelations convey good news. Jesus' hunger from fasting preceded a visit from Satan (Luke 4:2). Falling into a trance, Peter has a fascinating vision: spread about on something like a linen sheet are the various animals of the earth. A "voice" directs him to prepare and consume these creatures. Like Ananias (9:13), Peter objects, reminding the heavens of his piety. The voice contrasts Peter's views with those of God, who counts all clean. Three times the command comes forth; three times does Peter demur. The possible allusion to Jesus' wilderness temptation may be a hint that Peter, like his master, has thrice said no to Satan. Another possibility is that his threefold denial of Jesus (Luke 22:54-61) has just been repeated. As in the first scene, the narrator has introduced an element of mystery.[49]

Mystery does not obviate questions. The meaning of the vision-*cum*-voice seems quite clear to readers: a major component of the purity code has been abolished. One may seek to justify Peter's confusion by noting that Mark 7:1-23 is not included in Luke. The Gospel is, however, familiar with the slogan πάντα καθαρά ("all things are pure"); see Luke 11:41: "So give for alms (δότε ἐλεημοσύνην) those things that are within; and see, everything will be clean (πάντα καθαρά) for you," where the slogan is relativized with a moral element, almsgiving, found also in Acts 10.[50] When the missionary instruction of Luke 10:8, "Eat what is set before you," is taken into consideration, it is apparent that one can rationalize Peter's attitude only by assuming a dissonance between Luke and Acts. The ground of this dissonance, as Mark Plunkett has clearly stated, is that Peter's confusion is a Lucan device to shift the subject from questions of *kashrut* to the issue of gentile inclusion.[51] Although this revelation to Peter presumably derives from tradition, in its present form it shows the influence of Rom 14:14-20.[52] The evocation of Gen 1:24-25 (cf. also Gen 6:20; 7:14) shows that the background is that gentile

see Johannes Behm, "θύω," *TDNT* 3:180–90, esp. 190. The Eucharist was viewed as a sacrifice at least as early as *Did.* 14:2. Irenaeus (*A.H.* 4.17–18) promotes this concept in contradistinction to the sacrificial cult of the Hebrew Bible.

44 For examples, see Johannes Behm, "θύω," *TDNT* 3:180–90, esp. 187.

45 Calvin (6:288) complains that "the papists abuse" v. 4 by suggesting that Cornelius received grace through merit, which abuse requires two pages of refutation. "Papa Gregorius," as Bede calls Gregory the Great, insisted that Cornelius did not arrive at faith by works but that faith led him to works (*non operibus ad fidem sed fide venit ad opera*). His good deeds pleased God, who bestowed upon him the gospel message and baptism (*Hom. in Ezech.* 2.7–8 [CCSL 142:322–23]). Gregory's interpretation shows a better grasp of the text than Calvin's. Luke certainly assumes that Cornelius's actions found favor in God's sight, un-Pauline as that sentiment may seem.

46 Only in this story (10:5, 32; 11:13—but note "Simeon" in 15:14) is the proper name found.

47 Midday meals were not a normal part of the daily routine in the Roman world. The willingness of Peter's hosts to prepare him food is an indication of his high standing.

48 Cf. Dan 10:2-9. On the relation of ascetic behavior to ecstasy, see Franz Pfister, "Ekstase," *RAC* 4:944–87, esp. 970; and Rudolph Arbesmann, "Fasten," *RAC* 7:447–94, esp. 462–63.

49 Gaventa (*Darkness*, 110–11) emphasizes that these mysterious features contribute to the drama of the story, and she notes that dreams in literature often lack meaning prior to interpretation.

50 For a similar moralization, see *Sentences of Sextus* 102 and 110. Cornelius is not asked and does not volunteer to renounce all of his property.

51 Mark A. Plunkett, "Ethnocentricity and Salvation History in the Cornelius Episode," *SBLSP 1985* (Atlanta: Scholars Press, 1985) 465–79. Plunkett believes that Luke was indifferent to circumcision, dietary regulations, and other requirements.

52 Pervo, *Dating*, 247–49.

Christian apologetic (inspired by Diaspora Jewish thought[53]) which argued against Mosaic legislation by appeal to the original intent of the creator, in this instance, the goodness of creation.[54] Luke is familiar with such theological speculation but does not wish to invoke it. The Genesis allusion therefore probably comes from the source.

■ **9-11** The next day, at high noon,[55] as the delegation is providentially drawing near,[56] Peter ascends to the roof[57] to pray, like Jesus (e.g., Luke 9:28). The time and fasting state intimate the experience of Paul.[58] These are minor Peter–Paul parallels that also show the nature of the events: climactic change is in the offing. The narration begins with a mixture of biblical style (repeated ἐγένετο ["was," "happened"] in vv. 10a, b, and 13),[59] genitive absolutes (vv. 9-10), and a rare historical present (ϑεωρεῖ ["sees"]) in v. 11.[60] Peter's trance precedes a vision[61] of the "opened heaven," a sign of revelation.[62] If what the vision represents in general is apparent, the language is obscure. The alternate texts all fall under the suspicion of secondary revision, but the text may be corrupt.[63] The text of v. 12

53 E.g., *Aristeas* 120–69; §129 states the challenge: if creation is unitary, why did the creator fashion some unclean creatures?

54 Note Gen 1:26, 31. Mark 10:1-12 is an example of this approach. Verses 3-8 have been inserted into the apophthegm to provide a ground in creation that stems from a Hellenistic Christian environment that is reflected also in Eph 5:22-33. In 1 Cor 10:26 Paul cites Scripture in support of the intrinsic goodness of created objects. Already by Luke's time the argument was acquiring a new basis in the conflict with those who viewed creation or parts thereof as suspect. Cf. the Pastorals, specifically 1 Tim 1:5; 3:9; 2 Tim 1:3; 2:22; Titus 1:5; 2:14. Similar impetuses stimulated early Christian theologians toward merging the realms of creation and redemption, interpreting such passages as Romans 8 in the light of a framework of realized eschatology.

55 $\aleph^2$ 36 *pc* make it the "ninth hour," to coordinate with the time of Cornelius's vision. For noontime theophanies in Greco-Roman literature, see Henry J. Cadbury, "Some Lukan Expressions of Time," *JBL* 82 (1963) 272–78.

56 The distance of around fifty kilometers is rather long for a day's journey on foot. See Cadbury and Lake, 114. On the D-Text emendation of this itinerary, see on v. 30.

57 For the roof as a place for prayer, see Jdt 8:5-6. Cadbury and Lake (114) refer to Origen's *Hom. in Jer.* 19:13 for a detailed discussion of the custom. The Latin d (and other D-Texts—D is lacking) has Peter go to an "upper room" (*cenaculum*) to pray. This appears to be a harmonization with 1:13; 9:37, 39; 20:8. The Greek may have been δωμάτιον, which is a diminutive of δῶμα.

58 Noon only in 26:22; fasting: 9:19. At a distance is the "drawing near" (ἐγγίζω) in 9:3; 10:9.

59 Options for the colorless second ἐγένετο include ἐπέπεσεν (ἐπέσπεσεν) and ἦλϑεν. These appear to be secondary improvements. See Metzger, *Textual Commentary*, 326. Boismard (*Texte*, 171) prefers a form of "fell." This is not mere "elegant variation," since it strengthens the allusion to Gen 15:11 (Abraham). The term ἔκστασις is used only in this episode and in 22:17 (Paul) of individuals in Luke and Acts. On the subject, see A. Oepke, "ἔκστασις," *TDNT* 2:449–460; and M. Lattke, "ἔκστασις," *EDNT* 1:421–22. See also n. 48.

60 The historical present may derive from the source. Luke is not fond of this style. See John C. Hawkins, *Horae Synopticae* (Grand Rapids: Baker, 1968) 143–49, 213–14, for statistics.

61 Despite the reference to hunger, the narrator has no interest in proposing that the vision was the result of suggestion due to deprivation, as Polhill (254) intimates.

62 See on 7:56. Note in particular Luke 3:21-22 (the baptism of Jesus, also accompanied by a voice and the language of descending . . . ascending).

63 Metzger (*Textual Commentary*, 326) says, "apparently the Western text lacked καταβαῖνον ["descending"] . . . and described the vessel as "tied (δεδέμενον) at (the) four corners." "Old uncials" speak of the object "being lowered by/at four corners." Boismard (*Texte*, 172) prints καὶ ϑεωρεῖ τὸν οὐρανὸν ἀνεῳγμένον καὶ τέσσαρσιν ἀρχαῖς δεδέμενον σκεῦος καϑιέμενον ἐπὶ τῆς γῆς ("and he sees the heaven opened and an object tied by its four corners being let down to the ground"). The difficulty is to imagine how one would transform this text into that of the conventional text, or why one would wish to do so. To Haenchen (347 n. 6) the D-Text is a rationalization of obscure language. That is a strong point against originality. One possibility, not mentioned by Metzger, is that the conventional text of chap. 10 has been harmonized with that of chap. 11, where the text-types do not differ. (Harmonization is also at issue in v. 12.)

also exhibits variants, evidently due to internal and external harmonization.[64]

■ **12-13** Whatever the specific words, heaven has provided Peter with a complete display of earthly fauna.[65] A voice[66] directs him to satisfy his hunger with these creatures.[67] His refusal is emphatic,[68] coupled with a declaration that unclean food has never passed his lips. This assertion represents the classical Jewish rejection of forbidden food in the face of pressure.[69] The equally emphatic[70] voice demands that Peter retract this view.[71] The theological basis is not clear. Does the imperative depend on God's initial creation, all of which was "good," or on redemption, an act of purification? Acts 15:9, which speaks of God's "cleansing the hearts" of gentiles "by faith," supports the latter, but that is based on the figurative interpretation of this passage.[72] In either case (creation or redemption), the action is viewed as accomplished. Two additional repetitions of this exchange eliminate any uncertainty.[73] The vision evidently closes with the return of the display to heaven, whence it came (v. 11).[74]

■ **17-23a** (Scene 3) As in the story of Saul and Ananias (chap. 9), two persons have received divine visitations. The narrative is lively, pivoting back and forth between the visitors and Peter. Direct speech predominates. In chap. 9 matters were clear; in this instance the connection is less direct. As Peter wrestled with his perplexity, the emissaries from Cornelius opportunely arrive. The Spirit notifies Peter of their arrival and instructs him to accompany them, adding an ambiguous phrase. The

---

64 There are two grounds of harmonization: Gen 1:24-25 (etc.) and 11:6 (which also exhibits textual variants. The biblical phrase includes both domestic and wild animals. In an urban environment, wild game may have been omitted as irrelevant. See Metzger, *Textual Commentary*, 326. Boismard (*Texte*, 172) omits the verb (which Greek does not require) and the prepositional phrase "of the earth." This is the least harmonistic reading and thus possibly more original.

65 Bede (50), in dependence on Augustine (*Serm.* 149, 5–6) and Arator (904–6), views the "four corners" as representing the four points of the compass and thus universalism. Luke would not have objected to this interpretation.

66 "Voice" is another word that occurs in chaps. 9 (vv. 4, 7) and 10 (vv. 13, 15). The combination of φωνὴ with ἐγένετο occurs at important moments: Mark 1:11 (baptism of Jesus; cf. Luke 3:22); Luke 9:35 (transfiguration); Acts 7:31 (burning bush); cf. *Mart. Pol.* 9.1.

67 Although the earlier sense of θύω referred to cultic sacrifice, "kill" is the more common meaning. The phrase occurs only in this passage and citations of it.

68 μηδαμῶς appears only in this episode (twice) in the NT and but a few other times in early Christian literature, notably *1 Clem.* 33:1; 45:7; 53:4. Ezek 4:14 uses the same adverb in a similar setting: "Then I said, 'Ah (μηδαμῶς) Lord God! I have never defiled myself; from my youth up until now I have never eaten . . .'" (οὐδεποτε . . . πᾶν). The use of a negative with "all" to mean "none" and the like, rather than the "not every" that Greek and English would imply, is Semitic, here based on Ezek 4:14 LXX. See BDF 302 (1), although Barrett (1:508) holds that it is not entirely foreign to Greek use.

69 Cf. 1 Macc 1:62: But many in Israel stood firm and were resolved in their hearts not to eat unclean food (τοῦ μὴ φαγεῖν κοινὰ). Acts glosses this with "unclean," as this is a specialized (for the NT, note Rom 14:14; Heb 10:29; Rev 21:27) use of κοινός, which has hitherto meant "common" in a positive sense. See *Aristeas* 315, where κοινός has the sense of "the vulgar masses" (i.e., gentiles); and, in general, Friedrich Hauck, "κοινός," *TDNT* 3:789–809, esp. 790–91.

70 The translation of v. 15 reflects the "strong" sense of the present imperative ("stop doing . . ."), justified here because Peter *has* been calling these things unclean. Cf. Bruce, 256.

71 BDAG, 488, *s.v.* καθαρίζω.

72 See n. 13. Bovon ("Tradition et redaction," 34) assigns a literal sense to the source, and the figurative meaning to Luke. This is quite probable.

73 Johnson (185) observes that the direction is resisted three times: by Peter here, then in Jerusalem in 11:1-18, and finally by some Pharisees (chap. 15). Marguerat (*Historian*, 100–101) shows that this series of interpretations is progressive.

74 The language of v. 16 is precisely parallel to that used for the ascension of Jesus (1:9-11).

advice seems appropriate in the light of Peter's strong reluctance. So he meets the messengers, hears their report, and offers them lodgings (in someone else's home). Hospitality implies the acceptance of a social bond.[75] The chief critical difficulty for the modern reader is that Peter's vision does not seem the least bit enigmatic.[76]

■ **17-18** There are a number of textual questions in the central section of this chapter. Boismard proposes this D-Text for v.17: Ὡς δὲ διηπόρει ὁ Πέτρος τί ἂν εἴη τὸ ὅραμα ὃ εἶδεν, καὶ ἰδοὺ οἱ ἄνδρες οἱ ἀπεσταλμένοι ὑπὸ τοῦ Κορνηλίου ἐπέστησαν ἐπὶ τὸν πυλῶνα ("Now while Peter was much perplexed in himself what the vision which he had seen might mean, and behold, the men that were sent by Cornelius stood before the gate, 18 **inquiring** whether Peter were lodging there").[77] This is an intelligent abbreviation, if such it is, but much of it depends on versions that may have had difficulty with how to render, if not simply how to understand, the participial phrase.

■ **19-20** The elaborate detail of vv. 17-18 draws out the narrative, generating suspense.[78] Verse 19 stitches the two perspectives together, emphasizing the simultaneity, which points to the directing hand of providence. It also reflects the tension between the vision of Peter and the underlying narrative line, for the Spirit's command (v. 20)[79] does not refer to the visit.[80] The participial phrase μηδὲν διακρινόμενος is multivalent. It may mean "without doubt," "without hesitation," "without reservations," "without distinctions," or "without discrimination."[81] The narrative will capitalize on these possibilities. The warrant is quite unusual: "I have sent them." ἀποστέλλω in the first singular is otherwise used by God[82] or Jesus,[83] but not by the Spirit. This is another example of the "interchangeability" of Jesus and the Spirit in Acts.[84]

■ **21-23a** Variants in vv. 21-23 show the merits of Luke's economical style. The D-Text of v. 21 introduces this encounter with the "then" of which it is so fond (cf. also v. 23); a number of witnesses note that the men were "those dispatched to him by Cornelius."[85] D-Texts double Peter's question, inserting "What do you want?"[86] before "What has brought you here?"[87] Their report shows a slightly different, more gentile viewpoint than that of vv. 1-8. In place of εὐσεβής ("pious"), Cornelius is characterized as "upright" (δίκαιος). This summarizes in a single word his charitable activity.[88] They note that he comes highly recommended by "the Jewish nation."[89] This is indebted to a report about another

75 See Andrew E. Arterbury, "The Ancient Custom of Hospitality, the Greek Novels, and Acts 10:1–11:18," *PerspRelStud* 29 (2002) 53–72.

76 See above, where it is postulated that one must assume that Peter regarded *kashrut* as a fundamental and inviolable commandment.

77 Boismard, *Texte*, 174.

78 With v. 17 compare *Jos. Asen.* 18:1: "while Aseneth was still saying these things to herself, a young man . . . rushed in." This follows an angelophany.

79 On ἀλλά, see on 9:6.

80 With v. 17 compare Luke 1:29 (Mary, following the annunciation).

81 The pronoun μηδὲν can be taken as object or as an accusative of respect. Rom 14:23 probably provided inspiration. See Pervo, *Dating*, 106–7. On the verb, see Friedrich Büchsel, "διακρίνω," *TDNT* 3:946–49; and Gerhard Dautzenberg, "διακρίνω," *EDNT* 1:305–6.

82 E.g., Exod 23:20 (cited in Mark 1:2 parr.); Mal 3:22.

83 E.g., Matt 23:34; Luke 10:3; 22:34; 24:49; John 4:38; 17:8; Acts 26:17. In Luke 11:49, Wisdom is the subject. (The first person singular of πέμπω is used by Jesus in John 20:21; Rev 21:16).

84 Note that in vv. 5-6 an angel issued the command. At some level, however casual the expression, God is the author of these orders.

85 This fact was stated in v. 17.

86 Boismard (*Texte*, 176) omits "or."

87 Barrett (1:512) refers to this as "[a] characteristic Western reading, adding liveliness but no substance." For Haenchen (349 n. 3), it means that "[w]e can see what the second century considered edifying." They show the hand of a pedantic stylist, who could be caricatured by fabricating such questions as "Will someone suspect that Peter waited several hours before responding to the Spirit's command?" or "Might these have been some other men?" In v. 23, D p sy^{p} τότε εἰσαγαγὼν ὁ Πέτρος ("Then, after he had brought them in, Peter . . ."). Barrett (1:512) attributes this to the rarity of the verb εἰσκαλέομαι, a NT *hapax legomenon.*

88 Barrett (1:512) and Fitzmyer (457) construe δίκαιος as "observant." The latter refers to 10:35, but that verse does not speak of observance and tends rather to disprove the claim. Luke tends to stress the "ethical" rather than the "ritual."

89 Verse 10 speaks of "the people" (ὁ λαός), a Jewish

centurion (Luke 7:5).[90] The most noteworthy difference is that the angelic message now includes a purpose for the invitation: to hear what Peter has to say. There is no suspicion that the purpose of Peter's visit was to admire the needlework of the women in Cornelius's household. The information here is for Peter's benefit. He learns, at second hand, that an angel has advised Cornelius that he will address his household. The addition justifies the sermon of vv. 34-43. The apostle's subsequent hospitality is a silent demonstration of his acceptance of the Spirit's direction.[91]

■ **23b-27** (Interlude) At v. 23b the narrator temporarily abandons the scenic division.[92] Verses 23b-24 are summary, and vv. 25-26 (27) are too brief to constitute a scene. This material is therefore designated as an "interlude."[93] The summary depicts the actions of the two bodies, while the brief narrative highlights the initial meeting of the two leading characters.[94] Much of the narrative awkwardness, with its clumsy repetition of εἰσέρχομαι ("enter") in vv. 24, 25, and 27, may be due to the insertion of this encounter into a source that said, in effect, "When Peter arrived at Caesarea, he entered the home and found . . ."[95] Discovery of these difficulties is not recent, for they evidently motivated the substantive revision apparent in the D-Text. This narrative disruption portrays an even more disruptive social inversion. As Peter crossed the barrier that separated gentile from Jew, the Roman officer prostrated himself. The faith is turning the world upside down.

When Peter set out on the following day, he was accompanied by some local believers. Apart from providing a suitable entourage, the purpose of their accompaniment is not clear. They will serve as witnesses (11:12, which gives their number as six).[96] The D-Text here offers one of its most successful revisions, smoothing out a syntactic difficulty, resolving a narrative anomaly, and presenting a continuous narrative. The first is the genitive articular infinitive construed with ὡς at the beginning of v. 25. Parallels are not wanting,[97] but the difficulty remains. Verse 24 does not explain how Cornelius knew, even roughly, when the guests would arrive. Peter's response to Cornelius's veneration seems abrupt.

Luke uses action rather than words to portray the meeting. Cornelius prostrates himself before Peter. This posture amounts to reverence for the divine and was an "oriental" practice long odious to Western sensibilities, as it was associated with the ruler cult.[98] Refusal to accept such veneration was a mark of the true ruler. At the same time, the gesture—or its equivalent—served to show how ordinary people regarded outstanding persons.[99] As with Paul (14:8-18; 28:1-6), Luke uses this episode to show how the apostles were perceived, but at the

---

self-designation, whereas the ἔθνος ("nation," "ethnic body") of v. 22 represents a gentile perspective. With "recommend" (μαρτυρέω) compare 16:2 (Timothy).

90 The adjective "holy" would be superfluous with ἄγγελος in a Jewish context, where the word usually means "angel."

91 As v. 10 intimated, Peter, although technically a guest, is effectively master of Simon's home.

92 This presumes that a scenic division requires a change of location, character(s), or time, and that it includes some development.

93 One difficulty with this division is that vv. 27-29 are a full sentence in N-A[27]. Luke's use of τε is not always in conformity with "the rules," however, and the sequence καὶ . . . καὶ . . . τε is unconventional. A raised stop at the close of v. 27 would be appropriate.

94 For a close parallel to the narrative of their encounter, see *Jos. Asen.* 5:3–7 (cf. 22:5).

95 The theme and language of v. 24 are Lucan: Luke 1:58; 14:12; 15:6, 9.

96 The main verb of v. 24 is pluralized in a number of witnesses (𝔭[74] [א C] A E 33. 1739 𝔐 gig sy[hmg]). The singular is likely to be original, as the focus is on Peter throughout. See also Barrett, 1:513.

97 Note Luke 17:1; Acts 27:1; *Act. Barn.* 7. Moule (*Idiom Book*, 129) calls this an "appositional use." Cf. also BDF §400 (7), who regards this as a pleonasm.

98 The classic case was that of Alexander: Plutarch *Alex.* 45.1; 51.5; 54.3. From Diocletian (284–305) onward, such obeisance became standard, as can be seen in Gregory's *Pastoral Rule* 2.6. He deems Cornelius to have acted appropriately. On the concept and views about it, see Heinrich Greeven, "προσκυνέω," *TDNT* 6:758–66.

99 Numerous examples are found in ancient novels, including Chariton *Chaer.* 3.14; *Ephesian Tale* 1.1, 3; 2.2, 7; 1.12, 1; *Daphnis and Chloe* 4.33,4; *Ethiopian Story* 1.2, 5; 2.2, 1-2. For discussion, see Kenneth Scott, "Ruler Cult and Related Problems in the Greek Romances," *ClassPhil* 33 (1938) 380–89; and Parsons and Pervo, *Rethinking*, 90–94, with the

same time he spurns such "deification."[100] Josephus used a similar technique in his depiction of Moses.[101] In this instance, the narrative must be sparse, since Cornelius, unlike the "rude barbarians" whom Paul encountered, is a "God-Fearer" who must be presumed to have abjured polytheism in general and the deification of human beings in particular.[102] The association was immediately transformed into intimate conversation.[103] The participle *συνομιλῶν* depicts Peter's newfound openness to gentiles.[104] Peter's command is, in Greek, identical to the directions to disabled Aeneas and dead Tabitha (9:36, 40) and thus bears symbolic weight: Cornelius, too, is on the path toward new life.

■ **28-33** (Scene 4a) This section lays the groundwork for Peter's missionary address. He first notes the prohibition against association with gentiles.[105] (There was no specific commandment against intercourse[106] with gentiles. Observance of purity codes prevented the strictly observant from such activities as eating in gentile homes.[107]) The apostle then reports the revelation that he has received. Although he does not say so, this revelation is an interpretation of the vision.[108] That interpretation is the moment of decision. This is also the moment of his own "conversion," which the narrator presents not as the result of a direct command but as the result of reflection.[109] This phenomenon is, whatever explanations might be offered, quite remarkable. Despite all the apparatus of divine control, Peter is no puppet here.[110] Acts sets forth the understanding that the impetus for the gentile mission resulted from

references there. For a Jewish context, see *Jos. Asen.* 5–6. Other examples include *Act. John* 26–29; *Act. Pet.* (Verc.) 3; 5; 10. For yet others, see Rosa Söder, *Die apokryphen Apostelgeschichten und die romanhafte Literatur der Antike* (Stuttgart: Kohlhammer, 1932) 95–101 (who also includes many references from Greek literature.) Note also Ludwig Bieler, *ΘΕΙΟΣ ΑΝΗΡ*: *Das Bild des "Göttlichen Menschen" in Spätantike und Frühchristentum* (2 vols.; 1935–36; reprinted, Darmstadt: Wissenschaftliche Buchgesellschaft, 1967) 1:134–40.

100 Among those who spurned such honors was Apollonius of Tyana (Philostratus *Vit. Apoll.* 4.31).

101 See Louis H. Feldman, *Jew and Gentile in the Ancient World* (Princeton: Princeton University Press, 1993) 258–59. Although Josephus takes care to present Moses as other than divine, he awards him an ascension scene, which Feldman compares to the death of Oedipus in Sophocles' *Oedipus at Colonus*.

102 This qualification does not justify Fitzmyer's claim (461) that the action "shows his esteem for the heavenly authority attached to Peter's visit and mission." No motive is supplied.

103 Conzelmann (82) notes the artificiality of this transformation, while Haenchen (350 n. 2) correctly observes that realism is not the narrator's goal here.

104 D omits the opening participial phrase, *συνομιλῶν αὐτῷ* ("Peter continued to converse with him"). Metzger (*Textual Commentary*, 330) suggests that it may have seemed superfluous. Whoever thought so missed its significance. Barrett (1:514) points out that the resultant *καὶ εἰσελθών τε καὶ εὗρεν* ("both entering and he found") is impossible Greek, and he wisely observes that this may be due to the conflation of the conventional text with the D-Text revision.

105 On the term *ἀλλόφιλος* ("of another race") in v. 28, see David Balch, "*ἀκριβῶς . . . γράψαι* (Luke 1:3): To Write the *Full* History of God's Receiving All Nations," in Moessner, *Heritage*, 229–50, esp. 245.

106 The verbs *κολλάω* and *προσέρχομαι* ("associate intimately with" and "visit") are those used, in the opposite order, in 8:29 (direction for Philip to approach official).

107 Cf. Dan 1:8-16; Tob 1:10-13; Jdt 10:5; 12:1-20; Esth 14:17 LXX. See also Philo *Vit. Mos.* 1.278. Aristeas (139, 142) views the food laws as barriers to prevent (immoral) mingling—although the largest portion of the book involves a mixed banquet in the Egyptian palace in which the food was prepared by gentile cooks. See also n. 53.

108 For narrative comparison, *Ethiopian Story* offers a most instructive parallel. Thyamis had a perplexing dream, the meaning of which he struggled to understand (1.18). In 1.30 he came to a different understanding of what he had seen. On the function, compare the dream in 2 Macc 15:12-16, which is interpreted as authorizing warfare on the Sabbath. (On this, see Wills, *Jewish Novel*, 201.)

109 So Krodel, 193.

110 See p. 392.

the decision that a revelation was to be interpreted in a symbolic manner. Behind this conclusion stands the early Christian method of interpreting the LXX. Peter's "heart has been opened" (cf. Luke 24, esp. vv. 32 and 45). He follows the acknowledgement of his change with a polite question about the nature of their request. Cornelius responds by recounting the angelic message. The experiences of the two major characters have now been shared and made public.[111]

■ **28-29** The style of these verses is above average for Luke, suitable for an audience including many of above-average education.[112] Peter attributes his visit solely to his (interpretation of the) vision, omitting any reference to the direction of the Spirit (vv. 19-20). Mention of the Spirit would anticipate v. 44. Since that vision was not a part of the hypothetical source, this entire section must be attributed to the author.

■ **30** Nothing laudatory may be said of the style of v. 30. It is evidently corrupt, possibly owing to an authorial error.[113] The narrator evidently wishes to represent Cornelius as saying that, as he was engaged in prayer three/four days earlier, he saw. . . . The N-A^{27} text is not properly translatable; the D-Text (insofar as it can be recovered[114]) preserves one major difficulty while clearly revising another, as well as adding an edifying note, and the Textus Receptus is only superficially readable.

The opening phrase ἀπὸ τετάρτης ἡμέρας is not a conventional means for saying "three/four days ago,"[115] but it seems possible.[116] This colloquialism (if it is such) was not recognized by or deemed acceptable to scribes, who introduced a conventional correlative, μέχρι ("from . . . until/to").[117] Emendations that eliminate both ἀπό and μέχρι[118] cannot explain why the preposition was introduced. This is the proposed provisional text: ἀπὸ τετάρτης ἡμέρας ὥραν ἐνάτην ἤμην προσευχόμενος ("three days ago I was praying at 1500 hours"). The vulgar opening phrase, coupled with a (presumably) unmarked accusative meaning "time when,"[119] set off a chain of attempted corrections. Both the D-text and Textus Receptus state that Cornelius said he was fasting. One could argue that this is due to the frequent combination of the two[120] and is thus secondary. It is, however, also possible that this contradicts vv. 1-4 and was therefore deleted at this point.[121] Since 10:1-4 does not mention prayer, it is probable that this is a D-Text addition.

111 Although Cornelius had communicated his experience to his envoys (v. 8), the narrator does not state that Peter had informed them or his colleagues about the vision.

112 On "You know" (with ἐπίσταμαι), see n. 129; ὡς in the sense of ὅτι ("that") is rare in the NT. Note also the impersonal (ἀθέμιτον) with the dative. (On this, note 2 Macc 6:5; 7:1, which refer to unlawful sacrifice and the consumption of pork; and Pervo, *Dating*, 261; as well as Cadbury and Lake, 117; and Barrett, 1:515.) Verse 29 has the rare and euphonious adverb ἀναντιρρήτως ("without objection") and a causal dative: τίνι λόγῳ (in effect, "why").

113 See Cadbury and Lake, 118 ("The phrase does not read like ordinary Greek"); Barrett, 1:517 (who comes down on the side of authorial error); and Conzelmann, 82 ("The wording here is impossible because two statements have been combined in a confusing manner"). Ropes (96), however, defends the conventional text as "vulgar Greek or Semitic." Semitic influence presumes an unlikely Aramaic background. Metzger states that the editorial committee decided "it is just possible that the Greek may be explained as colloquial koine or as Semitized Greek" (*Textual Commentary*, 331).

114 See Boismard, *Texte*, 181. Cop^{mae} appears to preserve the most independent form of the D-Text: "Four days ago at this time I was fasting. And while I was praying in my house at the ninth hour of the day . . ." This is a conflation.

115 The translation "three days ago" presumes inclusive reckoning (e.g., "Jesus rose after three days," although we say "two days later"). D, however, reads "third," evidently based on the "next day" in vv. 9, 23, and 24. See Bruce, 259.

116 BDAG, 105, *s.v.*, accepts "since" for ἀπό (but not "four days ago" for this passage, presuming the μέχρι), and one can note 2 Cor 8:10; 9:2, where ἀπὸ πέρυσι must mean "a year ago."

117 Haenchen (350) takes the view that μέχρι is an insertion, "possibly under the influence of the idea of the constantly praying Cornelius" from v. 2.

118 Metzger (*Textual Commentary*, 331) notes those of Blass and Schmiedel.

119 On this use of the temporal accusative, see Moule, *Idiom Book*, 34. In v. 3 a similar usage was evidently corrected by adding περί.

120 See n. 48.

121 See Metzger, *Textual Commentary*, 331.

While adding this reference to his prayer, Cornelius omitted reference to the visionary nature of this experience, transforming it into a direct epiphany.[122] He also characterizes the angel by appearance ("an elegantly dressed man").[123] These variations present the experience from Cornelius's perspective: the omniscient narrator did not mention prayer, and Cornelius did not know that he was seeing a vision, while (as a "God-Fearer"!) he knew nothing of angels.

■ **33** The D-Text of v. 33 reads (with variations),[124] "That I promptly did, **beseeching that you come to us**, and you have been so kind as to do so **rapidly**. *So*, we are now before **you, wishing** to hear **from you** what **God** has directed you to say."[125] Most of this is edifying expansion.[126] The final phrase generates suspense, for the reader knows that Peter has received no particular instructions.

■ **34-43** (Scene 4b) One might expect that Peter would speak of his own vision and remark on the startling coincidence, but this is not how the narrator treats "double dreams." It suffices for the reader to appreciate what has happened.[127] Instead, he delivers his single sermon to gentiles,[128] a brief and symmetrical speech of a catechetical rather than missionary type. The outline is that of Luke's Gospel, and its content amounts to a résumé of the Christian message.[129] The biographical summary is reminiscent of Stephen's portrayals of Joseph and Moses (chap. 7). The content is that of the creed. The cultural model is that of the "benefactor," an important social type at all levels of Greco-Roman society. This is the first reported instance of the "cultural adaptation" of the Christian message to particular circumstances.[130] The speech includes traditional elements, such as the use of phrases beginning with *οὗτός ἐστιν* ("He is"), relative clauses, and participial phrases,[131] but such typical features do not serve as grounds for positing a specific source.[132]

---

122 The verb *ἔστη* ("stood") is typical of such reports.

123 Cf. Luke 24:4 ("gleaming"); Acts 1:10 ("white"). The adjective used here suggests upper-class clothing (cf. Luke 23:11; Jas 2:2-3 [and the dress of the heavenly bride: Rev 19:10]).

124 Boismard, *Texte*, 182.

125 *ἐξαυτῆς οὖν ἔπεμψα πρὸς σέ, παρακαλῶν ἐλθεῖν σε πρὸς ἡμᾶς σύ τε καλῶς ἐποίησας παραγενόμενος ἐν τάχει. νῦν ἰδοὺ πάντες ἡμεῖς ἐνώπιον σοῦ βουλόμενοι παρὰ σοῦ ἀκοῦσαι πάντα τὰ προστεταγμένα σοι ἀπὸ τοῦ θεοῦ.*

126 On the use of "you" (Peter) rather than "God" as the object of the preposition, Ropes (98) finds it less religious and possibly preferable. Epp (*Tendency*, 160–62) says that many of the D-readings here subordinate Cornelius to Peter. The potential convert, despite his high status, is more than deferent to the great apostle. He views "you" as a magnification of the apostle. "God" is, however, the more difficult reading, as its meaning is unclear.

127 Cf. 9:17-18, where neither Ananias nor Saul reports his visions to the other.

128 See also Wilckens, *Missionsreden*, 63–70; and David L. Balch, "ἀκριβῶς . . . γράψαι (Luke 1:3): To Write the *Full* History of God's Receiving All Nations," in Moessner, *Heritage*, 241–42.

129 Note the use of "you know," in v. 37, reminiscent of Paul's "memory" formulas (on which see the comments on 20:18). Tannehill (*Narrative Unity*, 2:140–42) indicates the extent to which the speech presents, or alludes to, the career of Jesus in chronological order. He concludes this discussion with the apt comment: "Nor is the story replaced by a series of christological propositions. The story is full of interpretation and will give rise to much further interpretation, but it retains its integrity as a story, capable of inspiring different and complex human responses" (142).

130 Rackham (164), writing just over a century ago, lamented the difficulty of achieving racial equality in church missions: "It is hard to believe that the principle that God is no respecter of persons has been fully realized as yet." (He belonged to the religious order [Community of the Resurrection] that nurtured Desmond Tutu.)

131 See p. 105 n. 12.

132 Schneider (2:62-64) refers to Klaus Haacker, "Dibelius und Cornelius: Ein Beispiel formgeschichtlicher Überlieferungskritik," *BZ* 24 (1980) 234–51, in support of a pre-Lucan missionary speech in the source. Pesch (1:333) says that the gift of the Spirit and baptism require a sermon in the source. He notes Lucan contributions on 348–49. Bruce (251; cf. 261–64) indicates that the speech goes back to tradition, at the very least. Barrett (1:488–98, 519–28) is willing to entertain the possibility that the source of the Cornelius story contained a sermon, to which the author has contributed. Witherington (355–59) views this as a summary of the message delivered on the occasion. Fitzmyer (459–66) says that this sermon shows more signs of source material than do the

The strongest candidates for known, rather than hypothetical, sources are the inaugural sermon of Jesus, Luke 4:14-30,[133] and the Pauline corpus. The adjective δεκτός, a key term in that sermon (4:19, 24), occurs elsewhere in the Lucan writings only in this address (v. 35) and may signal this connection. In both passages it relates to the inclusion of gentiles. The same may be suggested of "Nazareth" (10:38), elsewhere used in Luke 1–2 and 4:16 (although with an orthographic difference). Verse 36 echoes Luke 4:18 (cf. also Ps 106.20 LXX), (Jesus as "sent" by God), the verb εὐαγγελίζεσθαι ("proclaim 'good news'" [Luke 4:18; Acts 10:36; cf. also Isa 52:7; 61:1]),[134] the association of "Spirit" and "power" (δύναμις) in Luke 4:14 and Acts 10:38, and, most substantially, the reference to anointing by the Spirit in Luke 4:18 and Acts 10:38. None of these echoes would convey much meaning to gentiles other than the Lucan "God-Fearer," who is thoroughly familiar with Deutero-Isaiah. Verse 36 also echoes the angelic annunciation in Luke 2:9-14, which also uses the verb εὐαγγελίζεσθαι and announces "peace . . . among those whom [God] favors."[135] That sentiment resembles Acts 10:34-35. In that context (Luke 2:15, 17), the somewhat elusive word ῥῆμα ("thing," "matter," "word") appears, as in 10:37.[136] The thematic importance of these allusions, which require a most attentive reader, is that they reinforce the suggestion clearly made in the opening scene: the story is beginning anew. The gentile mission forecast in both the infancy stories and in the inaugural synagogue sermon of Jesus has now become a reality.[137] The gentile context gains reinforcement from a number of allusions to Paul's letters, notably the concept of divine impartiality (Rom 2:11; Gal 2:6; cf. Col 3:25; Eph 6:9). Verse 36 reflects Eph 2:17, and v. 43 is also Pauline (cf. Rom 3:22).[138] Peter becomes an apostle to the gentiles by borrowing from his colleague.

Marion L. Soards shows that this address is highly compressed in that he notes seven sections (and six subsections).[139] Rhetorically analyzed, vv. 34-35 are a proposition, vv. 36-42 narrative, and v. 43 proof.[140] This reveals that the speech is scarcely more than an outline and that the *narratio* does not support the *propositio*. A content-based approach regards vv. 37-41 as (typical) christological kerygma, surrounded by an introduction and a conclusion.[141] A mixed analysis, based on theme and content, is preferable. The distinctive theme is "universalism."[142] The structure is symmetrical.[143]

- I. Vv. 34b-36. The universal God.
  - A. Vv. 34b-35. God discriminates on the basis of conduct, not ethnicity.
  - B. V. 36a. The message came to Israel first, through Jesus.
  - C. V. 36b. Christ is Lord of All.
- II. Vv. 37-40. The mission of Jesus.
- III. Vv. 41-42a. The apostolic mission.
- IV. Vv. 42b-43. The universal judge.
  - C'. V. 42b. God has made Christ judge of all.
  - B'. V. 43a. So say the prophets.
  - A'. V. 43b. Faith in Christ is the criterion.

The speech shows Luke grappling with the problem of linking the proclaimer to the proclaimed: Jesus did

other speeches in Acts. These views do not provide adequate distinction between traditions utilized and an actual speech contained in the source. The brevity of the sermon makes these traditional elements, which can be found in all of the sermons, more prominent.

133 See Turner, *Power*, 261–62, and his references.

134 The latter is evoked in both Luke 4:18 and Acts 10:38.

135 Tannehill, *Narrative Unity*, 2:138–39. The different social orientation of Acts is apparent in the change from proclamation of "good news to the poor," etc., in Luke 4:18 to the proclamation of "peace" in Acts 10:36.

136 See Christoph Burchard, "A Note on ῬΗΜΑ in JosAs 17:1f.; Luke 2:15, 17; Acts 10:37," *NovT* 27 (1985) 281–95.

137 There are also points of contact with Paul's inaugural sermon (the audience of which also includes "God-Fearers") in 13:16-41. As Haenchen (351–52) notes, 13:26 illuminates 10:36.

138 See Pervo, *Dating*, 108–9.

139 Soards *Speeches*, 70–77. Soards includes vv. 28-29, 34-43, and 47 in his analysis.

140 Cf. Witherington (355), who regards the speech as apologetic. A difficulty with this is that no charges have been lodged or implied. He is reacting against Kennedy (*Rhetorical Criticism*, 122–23), who classifies the speech as epideictic.

141 E.g., Fitzmyer, 460.

142 Talbert (109) proposes the same theme.

143 Krodel (195) has a similar outline.

not, especially in Luke, announce salvation by faith to Jews and gentiles alike. The tenuous thread is that Jesus offered his services to "all."[144] He labored only in "Judea," but did not discriminate. From this summary one would not perceive that Jesus did not minister only to the "righteous." Here appears a keystone of what would become "normative Christianity." The church worships Jesus as universal savior, but sets aside his "ethics" in favor of conventional, "bourgeois morality" derived from Paul (and, presumably, others) but hardened into firm rules in the post-Pauline world. There is no better summary of Luke's Paulinism than this passage, which preaches both *iustificatio piorum* (v. 35)[145] and salvation by faith (v. 43).[146] For Luke, righteousness is primarily what one does, not a state declared by God.[147]

This sermon is improbable if read as an account of how to evangelize an upper-class (from the narrator's social perspective) "God-Fearer." As a bridge between the mission of Peter and the work of Paul, between the mission to the Jews and proclamation to gentiles, on the other hand, it is quite effective, summarizing much of Luke and Acts and postulating the (Hellenistic-Jewish formulation of the) principle that gentiles can be righteous.[148] It is addressed to the readers. Only with some difficulty can one construct circumstances in which Cornelius and others "knew" that Jesus was executed for his benefactions to the downtrodden and sick.[149] The more or less dangling "he is sovereign of all" is a summary of the creed of "early Hellenistic Christianity" in that it views "Christ" as a proper name and hails him as universal lord. This does not rest easily with the imagery of "anointing" in v. 38, which is a trope derived from Hebrew practice. Then there is the difficulty of that "high Christology" of v. 35 ("universal sovereign"), followed by the "low Christology" two verses later: "God was with him." The speech is difficult because the author attempts to compress too much thought derived from different sources into a brief space. It abbreviates themes developed in earlier speeches and is scarcely intelligible to others than readers of the book, who, as the following detailed exegesis indicates, will fill in many gaps.

■ **34-35** The author might well disagree with the foregoing judgment about his Paulinism and argue that vv. 34-35 are based on Rom 2:10-11 (above). That is correct, but Paul was not speaking about soteriology there. The concept of "divine impartiality" is difficult because it often occurs in contexts that seem to assert partiality.[150] In the Jewish background is the ideal of an incorruptible and absolutely unbiased judge[151] who may therefore find in favor of justice. In this instance the meaning is that God is not prejudiced in favor of a "chosen people."[152] Although Luke took up the term from Paul, he applied it in the light of Greco-Roman views about the unity of the human race.[153] Verses 34-35 show that Luke was interested not in *kashrut* but in barriers based on ethnocentricity.[154]

144 The word πᾶς ("all," "everyone") appears four times (vv. 36, 38, and 43 [*bis*]).

145 Cf. Rom 4:5. "Justification of the *un*godly" (*impiorum*) was a fundamental component of Martin Luther's interpretation of Paul's theology.

146 On the Deutero-Pauline motif of "near and far" (Acts 2:39), see Pervo, *Dating*, 294.

147 See Pervo, *Dating*, 266–68.

148 Parallels with the speeches of chaps. 2–3 (e.g., v. 39) and with that of 13 (esp. v. 36) and 17 (esp. v. 42) establish this link.

149 See Dibelius, *Studies,* 111 n. 5.

150 *T. Job* 4:8; Rom 2:11; Gal 2:6; Col 3:25||Eph 6:9; 1 Pet 1:17; Jas 2:1, 9; *1 Clem.* 1:3; *Barn.* 4:12; Polycarp *Phil.* 6:1.

151 E.g., Deut 10:17; Wis 6:7 is important here because it associates God's impartiality with lordship of all (ὁ πάντων δεσπότης) and universal providence (προνοεῖ περὶ πάντων). The concept of impartiality is expressed with a Hebrew idiom, rendered as (lit.) "take face": πρόσωπον λαμβάνω. See Eduard Lohse, "πρόσωπον," *TDNT* 6:768–80, esp. 779–80, and, for the Semitic background of the expression, Fitzmyer, 462–63. On impartiality in general, see Jouette M. Bassler, *Divine Impartiality: Paul and a Theological Axiom* (SBLDS 59; Chico, Calif.: Scholars Press, 1979).

152 The term ἔθνος is difficult to render. BDAG, 276, *s.v.*: "a body of persons united by kinship, culture, and common traditions, *nation, people*" is comprehensive, but does not resolve the problem that neither "nation" nor even "people" is a proper English equivalent here.

153 Bassler took up this subject in "Luke and Paul on Impartiality," *Bib* 66 (1985) 546–52.

154 See Plunkett (n. 51). This is further evidence that the author did not compose vv. 9-16, for visions in Acts are not ambiguous.

■ **36-38** The editors of N-A[27] are not certain about the text of v. 36, as the bracketed relative pronoun ὅν indicates.[155] Neither text is particularly translatable, a judgment that also applies to vv. 37-38.[156] One must presume either that the text is corrupt and emend it or that the author made a mistake and translate what one believes he wished to write. The latter is a covert form of emendation. Harald Riesenfeld and Christoph Burchard have put forth grammatical hypotheses. Riesenfeld accepts the relative and takes v. 36 in apposition to vv. 34-35.[157] This is barely possible from a grammatical viewpoint, but is not possible in terms of content, for if God had sent Jesus to preach the acceptability of gentiles, then the gentile mission would have met no objections and Peter's vision would have been utterly otiose. Burchard suggests that the τὸν λόγον introducing v. 36 is an accusative of respect.[158] Again, this is possible, but the result ("With regard to the message that God sent . . . through Jesus Christ, he [Christ] is sovereign of all") is unsuccessful.[159]

If one attempts to construe vv. 36-38 as a loose period, the Pauline "memory" formula ὑμεῖς οἴδατε ("you know") of v. 37[160] is the logical subject.[161] One problem raised by this unusual syntax is the determination of its object. Accusatives include λόγον ("message" [v. 36]), ῥῆμα ("what happened"), and "Jesus" (v. 38). This last may be taken as an appositive with ῥῆμα, but the result is not satisfactory. The apparent logic of the text—not its syntactical logic—is based on the assertions that, although God does not discriminate against gentiles, the saving message was sent first to the Jews, through Jesus, who—although universal sovereign—labored and died in Judea. The phrase "he is the sovereign of all people," looks like a gloss but is so central to the argument that it is best to regard it as an unfortunate parenthesis.[162] One other difficulty may be traced to the author. The expression "following the baptism that John proclaimed" in v. 37 is compatible with Luke's avoidance of such statements as "after John baptized Jesus he was anointed by the Holy Spirit."[163] The tentative conclusion is that the syntactical difficulties of vv. 36-38 stem from the author's inept effort to compress the message.[164] This leads to taking v. 36 as a sentence and construing the "you know" of v. 37 with v. 38 also. The only point where textual corruption appears reasonable is at the opening of v. 36.[165] Emendation requires rewriting all three verses,[166] and the variants are best explained as corrections of the conventional text.[167]

155 See Metzger, *Textual Commentary*, 333–34.

156 Barrett, 1:521.

157 Harald Riesenfeld, "The Text of Acts 10:36," in Ernest Best and Robert McL. Wilson, eds., *Text and Interpretation: Studies in the New Testament Presented to Matthew Black* (Cambridge: Cambridge University Press, 1979) 191–94. Jervell (300) evidently follows this proposal in his translation; cf. also Schneider, 2:76.

158 Christoph Burchard, "A Note on ῬΗΜΑ in JosAs 17:1f.; Luke 2:15, 17; Acts 10:37," *NovT* 27 (1985) 293.

159 Rom 8:3 is not a good parallel, for there the accusative of respect permits an intelligible reading.

160 See n. 129.

161 This is the solution followed by a number of English versions, including *NRSV*, *NAB*, and *NIV*.

162 In an oral context, such ejaculations (e.g., "the Holy One—Blessed be His Name") are—and probably were—common, but such realism seems unlikely here, to say the least. Cadbury and Lake (120) describe it as an "ejaculatory parenthesis."

163 Cf. Luke 3:19-22. The emendation proposed in Cadbury and Lake (119–20) recognizes this but does not take Luke's aversion into account.

164 Barrett (1:524) finally comes down on the side of poor writing.

165 Repeated accusative-case terminations in -ον could explain both the addition and the removal of the relative ὅν.

166 Dibelius (*Studies*, 91) well states the problem: v. 36 is "enigmatic in its lack of connection with vv. 35 and 37. It is best understood as a doublet to v. 37 (but in that case we must read τὸν λόγον ὅν)." Elimination of v. 36 would produce a smooth text, but that verse is fundamental to Luke's argument.

167 The D-Text (Boismard, *Texte*, 183), which freely alters and introduces relatives and conjunctions, is most likely secondary on the grounds that omission of its improvements is inexplicable, while those improvements are not sufficient to make a construable sentence out of the jumble. In v. 37, Bezae omits ῥῆμα ("what happened"), which accomplishes no more than deliver it from an unusual meaning. See Ropes, 98. The hanging nominative ἀρξάμενος ("beginning") is especially awkward here, but probably not impossible. Metzger (*Textual Commentary*, 334) has a good note. See also BDF §137 (3) and Moule, *Idiom Book*, 181.

In discussing v. 36, Rackham observed that Eph 2:11-22 is the best commentary.[168] Another way to state this is that v. 36 represents Deutero-Pauline theology, with direct influence from Ephesians a distinct possibility, for "peace" there is understood as the reconciliation of Jews and gentiles and the subject of Jesus' proclamation.[169] Verse 38 exhibits the typical Lucan adoptionist approach to Christology.[170] The summary utilizes the Greco-Roman theme of benefaction.[171] The text does not speak of Jesus as an itinerant philosopher and teacher of morality, as he is portrayed in Luke (especially chaps. 9–19). Peter summarizes Jesus' powerful deeds. The source of this power is restated in a paraphrase: "God was with him." Conzelmann justifiably describes this as *θεῖος ἀνήρ* ("divine man") language,[172] for it was also used of Joseph in Stephen's speech (7:9).[173] His benefactions are nonetheless portrayed in language more at home in apocalyptic: Jesus was at war with the devil.[174]

■ **39-43** "We" in v. 39 is evidently a careless repeat of 2:32, etc. Peter is not surrounded by apostles here.[175] The description of Jesus' execution is borrowed from 5:30, but the agents are anonymous. This omission may be politic, but the compressed summary would be difficult for the dramatic audience, which might have difficulty with "God raised him" without the qualifier "from the dead," which will not appear until the close of v. 41, as well as *καὶ ἔδωκεν αὐτὸν ἐμφανῆ γενέσθαι* (lit. "and granted that he become visible"), a kind of Greek that requires familiarity with the LXX.[176] Verse

168 Rackham, 157 n. 4.

169 Note Eph 2:17: *καὶ ἐλθὼν εὐηγγελίσατο εἰρήνην ὑμῖν τοῖς μακρὰν καὶ εἰρήνην τοῖς ἐγγύς* ("So he came and proclaimed peace to you who were far off and peace to those who were near"). Although "Lord of all" (which refers to persons here) does not appear in Ephesians, the adjective *πᾶς* ("all") is found fifty times. Conzelmann (83) states that this phrase, for which he offers a number of religious and political parallels, is "not yet cosmologically oriented." It correctly summarizes Lucan thought, but both Luke and Ephesians are attempting, in different ways, to deflect focus from the cosmological. Note also Cadbury, "The Titles of Jesus in Acts," in Lake and Cadbury, *Additional Notes*, 361–62.

170 Luke 1–2 promotes the idea that Jesus was the Messiah from conception/birth. This does not exclude the evidence for adoptionism, which is equally clear. From the perspective of composition, it is another indication that the infancy material was written last. Theologically, it is another indication of Luke's lack of consistency. The speeches in Acts 2–3 present a third view: that Jesus became the Messiah at his exaltation into heaven.

171 Frederick Danker has emphasized the importance of this theme in his research: see his *Benefactor: Epigraphic Study of A Graeco-Roman and New Testament Semantic Field* (St. Louis: Clayton, 1982), and his commentary *Jesus and the New Age* (2nd ed.; Philadelphia: Fortress Press, 1988). Luke's use of the term to summarize his own Gospel is strong support for Danker's proposal. A standard study of the theme is Paul Veyne, *Le pain et le cirque: sociologie historique d'un pluralisme politique* (Paris: Seuil, 1976). "Benefactor" was often paired with "Savior" in the ruler cult and related phenomena. On that, see Arthur Darby Nock, "*Soter* and *Euergetes*," *Essays*, 2:720–35. Plutarch's *De Iside et Osiride* 12 (*Moralia* 355E) says that, at the birth of Osiris a "voice" (*φωνή*) proclaimed him lord of all (*ὁ πάντων κύριος*). An alternative has the voice announce the birth of "great king and benefactor" (*μέγας βασιλεὺς εὐεργέτης*). On this theme, see also Anton Fridrichsen, *The Problem of Miracle in Primitive Christianity* (trans. Roy A. Harrisville and John S. Hanson; Minneapolis: Augsburg, 1972) 65–67.

172 Conzelmann, 82. For a comparable summary see *Act. Paul* 10/13. Apollonius was described as a benefactor (Philostratus *Vit. Apoll.* 8.7).

173 That phrase comes from the LXX (Gen 39:21), but this source does not define its range of meaning. For Luke this was a characteristic of the divinely endowed benefactor. Cf. also "the hand of God was with them," as in 11:21. Other characters of whom this is said are Mary (Luke 1:66) and John the Baptizer (Luke 1:66). Also in the background is Ps 106:20 (LXX): "[God] sent out his word and healed them (*ἀπέστειλεν τὸν λόγον αὐτοῦ καὶ ἰάσατο αὐτούς*), and delivered them from destruction." That psalm serves as a structural model for the cycles of miracles in Mark 4:35—8:26.

174 Susan Garrett explicates this theme in *Demise*. Luke does not "replace" apocalyptic concepts—in this case—with Hellenic categories. He rather presents them in terms that Greeks can comprehend.

175 An editorial "we" is excluded by the singular in v. 34. See n. *nn*.

176 See Cadbury and Lake, 121.

41 returns to the theme of witness. An apologetic note is creeping in.

The risen Jesus did not appear in public but only to certain witnesses, who were chosen in advance rather than being random observers. Peter continues to speak as if accompanied by other apostles. Verses 41 and 43 briefly propose two types of proof: eyewitness testimony to the fact that Jesus returned to life after the crucifixion and the inartistic witness of Scripture to his status as judge. Each of these proofs is supported by a claim of divine determination.[177] Luke integrates his proof with assertions about the divine plan; that is, this is an implied enthymeme, arguing from the events to God's intention. The language of "eating and drinking"[178] conforms to Luke's unabashedly materialistic view of the resurrection,[179] but its major function here may be to stress the intimacy and extent of the apostles' relationship with the risen Jesus.[180] The summary of Jesus' message is in creedal form:[181] he is judge of the living and the dead. Only here and in the Areopagus address (17:31) is this role explicitly attributed to Jesus. The phrase "living and dead" extends the concept of "universal sovereign" (v. 36) throughout time.[182] The reader will probably presume that this activity is an eschatological event, but the text does not make such qualifications. After the implicit threat of v. 42 comes the promise of v. 43:[183] all the prophets (cf. 3:24) testify that *everyone* who believes will be forgiven by means of the name of Jesus.[184] Although this assertion appears to repeat what has been said earlier (e.g., 2:38-39), it means that the prophetic texts apply also to gentiles. Unlike the earlier speeches (2:38; 3:19), however, Peter does not demand that his auditors repent.[185] The wisdom of his position will presently become clear. He closes with a dramatic statement of its central theme, which is also an *inclusio*.[186] The speech is complete.

■ **44-48** (Scene 4c-d) The Spirit replicates the experience of Pentecost. Baptism inevitably followed, after which Peter accepted Cornelius's hospitality, ratifying his unqualified acceptance of these new converts (and setting up the objections raised in 11:1-3). Although ecstatic, the situation is somewhat artificial. Only Cornelius and company receive the gift of the Spirit, permitting Peter and company to serve as objective witnesses to the phenomenon. It could be argued that, for Luke, the manifestation of the Spirit was a one-time occurrence linked with initiation. The difficulty of disproving this notion underlines the schematic nature of the narrative and reinforces the implication of 2:1-11: the author had a certain reserve about ecstatic phenomena. Although few occasions of worship are described, it would have been possible to report glossolalia at some of these.[187]

177 The witnesses were προκεχειροτονημένοις ("selected in advance"); Jesus was ὡρισμένος ("determined"). The subject of both was God (vv. 41-42).

178 This may clarify the participle συναλιζόμενος in 1:4.

179 (Luke and) Acts appear to be aware of docetic Christologies and to refute them with highly realistic language.

180 The D-Text of v. 41b (Boismard, *Texte*, 184) reinforces this understanding: "ate and drank with **and accompanied** him after he . . . **for forty days**." See Metzger, *Textual Commentary*, 335.

181 The D-Text (Boismard, *Texte*, 185) overlooked the form and changed οὗτος to the simple pronoun "he."

182 "Judge of living and dead": Rom 14:9; 1 Thess 5:9-10; 2 Tim 4:1; 1 Pet 4:5; *Barn.* 7:2; Polycarp *Phil.* 2:1; *2 Clem* 1:1; Justin *Dial.* 118.1, and thence into the "Apostles' Creed." See Cadbury and Lake, 122.

183 The initial τούτῳ of v. 43 could be masculine (referring to Jesus) or neuter (referring to this pronouncement). Barrett (1:528) prefers the neuter: the prophets speak about facts, not a person. The "creedal style" suggests masculine, as Conzelmann (80), for example, translates. The actual name (Jesus) has not been mentioned since v. 38, compounding the difficulty of parsing the pronouns.

184 Mss. 36. 453 read "blood" rather than "name." This is a dogmatic correction, based on a non-Lucan theology of the atonement.

185 As Cadbury and Lake (122) indicate, v. 43 does not depend on a doctrine of "original sin." The parallel, Luke 24:46, speaks of proclaiming repentance that will bring forgiveness. Tannehill (*Narrative Unity*, 2:141–42) sees this as a modification of Luke 24:47-48. The apostles will not necessarily conduct the gentile mission.

186 See the outline above.

187 Examples are 13:1-2; 20:7-12, and, for that matter, chap. 15. Turner (*Power*, 407–18) is obliged to

Luke is fond of interrupting speeches, but these disruptions do not prevent speakers from saying all that they desire or need to communicate.[188] Resemblances to Pentecost (2:1-13) are abundant, not only in form but also in vocabulary.[189] No reader will miss the connection. By the logic of the narrative this demonstration was not necessary, since Peter had become convinced that gentiles could be worthy and deigned to preach the message. "Jewish believers" (v. 45, literally "the believers of the circumcision") prepares the reader for 11:2.[190] It is more reasonable here, as gentiles are present. Since the descent of the Spirit took them by surprise, one might surmise that they did not find Peter's words convincing, but this is one more indicator of the artificiality of the narrative. What is the reader to understand the phenomenon to be? The preferred text has the simple γλώσσαις, which is rendered by convention "in tongues," rather than the "other tongues" (ἑτέραις γλώσσαις) of 2:4, which, as the context shows, means "foreign languages." Variants exist.[191] In any case the response is unusual, presumably ecstatic,[192] but of sufficient intelligibility to indicate that God was being praised.[193]

The omniscient narrator reports the conclusion of these witnesses.[194] Peter alone speaks, evoking 2:38 and 8:36.[195] The phrase ὡς καὶ ἡμεῖς ("just as we did") is less clear than it appears.[196] Peter may yet be speaking as if among fellow apostles.[197] His order, which presumes that others will administer the baptisms,[198] may reflect the view that apostles do not baptize (cf. 8:14, 17).[199] The

---

explain the absence of overt references by arguing that such expressions as "exhort/console" (παρακαλέω, παράκλησις) refer to charismatic phenomena and, finally, to say that the reader is to fill in the gaps.

188 Mark 14:43 is one possible inspiration for the practice. See Dibelius, *Studies*, 160; and Conzelmann, xliv. Other examples from Acts include 4:1; 7:54; 17:32; 19:28; 22:22; and 26:24. See Pervo, *Profit*, 166 n. 108.

189 E.g., ἐξίστημι (2:7, 12; 10:45); "hear them speaking in tongues" (2:11; 10:46); τὰ μεγάλεια/μεγαλούντων (2:11; 10:46), and the "gift of the Holy Spirit": (2:38; 10:45). See Turner, *Power*, 380–81; and Earl Richard, "Pentecost as a Recurrent Theme in Luke-Acts," in idem, ed., *New Views on Luke and Acts* (Collegeville, Minn.: Liturgical Press) 133–49, esp. 137–39.

190 In both 10:45 and 11:2, Peter is not included as one of "those belonging to the circumcision."

191 There is an erasure in D: λαλούντων γλώσσαις καὶ μεγαλυνόντων ("speaking ~~in tongues and praising~~"). The Latin d has *praevaricatis linguis et magnificantes* ("In diverse/new/other tongues"). This adjective could represent ποικίλαις, καιναῖς, or ἑτέραις ("diverse," "new," "other"). One MS. of the Vulgate reads *linguis variis* ("in diverse tongues"), and there is Coptic support for "other tongues." The *Treatise on Rebaptism* has *linguis suis* ("in their languages"). See Ropes, *Text*, 100; and Metzger, *Textual Commentary*, 336. The question is whether what seems to have been the D-Text was a harmonization with the "other tongues" of 2:4 (ἑτέραις γλώσσαις) or an alternative to it. Since it would not be in character for the D-Text to eliminate glossolalia, the original may have said "other tongues." BDF §480 (3) regards γλώσσαις λαλεῖν as an ellipsis for "in other tongues."

192 Haenchen (354) is emphatically certain that "tongues" means "ecstatic utterance."

193 This combination makes sense within a charismatic perspective, where glossolalia is presumed to be doxological; that is, v. 46 implies, for whatever reason, such a context.

194 As Conzelmann (84) claims, the phrase "the gentiles" is deliberately general.

195 The negative with verbs of hindering and denying is redundant and may have caused problems for ancient translators. See BDF §400 (4) and Moule, *Idiom Book*, 157. The complex relative may have its full meaning here (Moule, 124). The order of the opening words varies. Boismard (*Texte*, 186) prints: μή τις τὸ ὕδωρ κωλῦσαι δύναται αὐτούς, οἵτινες τὸ πνεῦμα τὸ ἅγιον ἔλαβον ὡς καὶ ἡμεῖς ("Can anyone refuse water to those who have received the Holy Spirit . . . ?"). This reading is so much better than that of the conventional text that it is difficult to construct a situation in which the former would be derived from this. It is more likely that Luke wrote a clumsy—not impossible—sentence.

196 Chrysostom (*Hom.* 24) observes that one might almost say that Peter is there to be taught.

197 Note 11:15, where the first plural is appropriate.

198 Cf. the *v.l.* αὐτοῖς ("issued orders to them" [i.e., his companions]), a "learned correction" that misses the grammatical function of the pronoun (Metzger, *Textual Commentary*, 336).

199 1 Cor 1:17 may be in mind.

narrative is quite terse. Readers are to presume that this order was carried out and that Peter accepts the offer of hospitality.[200] Social intercourse has theological significance.[201] The essence of Christian community is that all believers are acceptable.[202] In this, as the following chapter indicates, Luke is firmly allied to the position of Paul.[203] Peter's vision removed any barriers to a gentile mission. From the Lucan perspective, that barrier was not just "uncleanness" but the wall that prevented social relations.[204] The implication of this is that, for Luke, observance is little more than an old-fashioned superstition to be tolerated only insofar as it is not an obstacle to life together. Peter's sojourn *chez* Cornelius serves the plot by allowing time for word of these events to make its way to Jerusalem.

This is the first report of a household conversion in Acts—and appropriately the longest, providing details that the reader may assign to the others.[205] In his study of these accounts David L. Matson shows that they are anticipated and justified by Luke 10:1-16 (esp. vv. 5-7), and that they support the theme of universalism, signified by the shift from temple to home as the focus of Christian life and worship.[206]

■ **11:1-18** (Scene 5) The general structure of this episode is straightforward: (1) critique of Peter's actions (vv. 1-3), (2) his defense (vv. 4-17), and (3) the result (v. 18). When, in due course, Peter returned to Jerusalem, he was taken to task by "those of Jewish birth." The scene intimates Peter's declining authority: he is called on the carpet, as it were, by the entire community. This loss of prestige is associated with the gentile mission. This may have been accidental, an ad hoc requirement of the narrative, but it is possible that Luke was aware of more than he divulged.

These objectors took issue not with the baptism of gentiles but with Peter's willingness to associate with them.[207] In the course of the narrative, it transpires that the setting is some kind of community assembly. By eschewing any reference to a formal convocation or resolution, Luke will have his cake and eat it too. On the one hand, there is resounding public approval of conversion without circumcision prior to the gentile mission of Paul. On the other, an official decision by "the apostles and believers" would either obviate the need for a later discussion or endorse the Pauline claim that the Antiochene dissidents had acted in bad faith.

Peter's defense is a detailed summary of chap. 10. Repetition again serves the object of emphasis. This account, which could have been corroborated by the six witnesses from Joppa whom Peter had the foresight to bring with him, stifled all objections.[208] Admission of gentiles produces yet one more cause for gratitude to God. Peter, then, not Philip or Paul, was the human agent of the gentile mission, but the actual initiative was not of human origin. Peter's speech trumps rather than refutes the charges. Taking a leaf from the brief of Gamaliel (5:34-39), he questions the wisdom of resisting the divine (11:17). This stifles the opposition, which drops all reference to circumcision and praises the God who offers salvation to gentiles. In this path-breaking act, his ministry in Acts has come to an effective end. From the perspective of the principle

200 The candidates receive no attention. They are not asked if they wish to be baptized or to make a confession of faith. Cf. the secondary 8:37.

201 Cf. Gaventa, *Darkness*, 109.

202 Cf. 16:14, to which the D-Text (Boismard, *Texte*, 187) conforms 10:48; cf. John 4:40. See also John J. Kilgallen ("Clean, Acceptable, Saved: Acts 10," *ExpT* 109 [1998] 301–2), who presses for distinctions among these categories.

203 A difference is that in Galatians 2 Paul confronts Peter, whereas in Acts Peter comes under the fire of believers in Jerusalem.

204 Note once more Eph 2:11-22, esp. v. 14, with its reference to peace achieved by shattering the dividing wall, on which see Rudolf Schnackenburg, *Ephesians: A Commentary* (trans. H. Heron; Edinburgh: T&T Clark, 1991) 112–14.

205 Others are Lydia (16:11-15), the Philippian jailer (16:25-34), and Crispus (18:1-11).

206 On Cornelius, see David Matson, *Household Conversion Narratives in Acts: Pattern and Interpretation* (Sheffield: Sheffield Academic Press, 1996) 86–134.

207 No complaints were raised about the behavior of his companions. Peter is the only person whose behavior is important.

208 The presence of these six is awkward, since it presumes that they must have remained with Peter until he decided to return to Jerusalem. It further presumes that Peter was aware of the forthcoming complaints.

established, this non-meeting is the most important meeting in Acts.

As in 8:14 (Samaria) and 11:22 (Antioch), Jerusalem (which supervises all missionary activity) "hears" about a new missionary endeavor. Although such centralization is unlikely and was certainly not accepted by Paul, its primary function in Acts is not to promote hierarchy but to show that the leaders in Jerusalem endorsed the gentile mission. In the cases mentioned, supervisory personnel were dispatched to the site. The subject here is broader than "the apostles" of 8:14, and with reason. The addition of "believers" gives scope for objectors who are not apostles. The phrase "those from/of/belonging to the circumcision" encompasses every male believer in Jerusalem.[209] This anachronism reveals that Galatians 1–2 is the external source of this passage. Luke's desire to have Peter deal with the conflict about gentile believers has led to the fabrication of this episode,[210] including the introduction of a "circumcision party" before the fact.[211] Such a faction could have existed only if there were a "circumcision-free party." The objection is phrased in a verb (διακρίνομαι, "take issue" [v. 2]) that readers will find ironic, for the Spirit used this word while instructing Peter to visit gentiles (10:20). Even more telling, for those familiar with the Gospel tradition, is the similarity of these charges to objections raised by Jesus' opponents to his behavior (see Luke 5:30; 15:2; 19:7). The first complaint implies potential ritual impurity, for which there were ceremonial remedies.[212]

How the accusers knew that Peter had eaten with gentiles is not clear.[213] Eating with gentiles was not formally prohibited.[214] A more precise charge would state that Peter had eaten non-kosher food and/or food prepared by (unclean) gentiles. The objection fits, from a strictly observant position, gentile polytheists.[215] It is not quite so likely to have been applicable to a "God-Fearer" like Cornelius.[216] These are additional data in support of the

209 Every other NT use of *οἱ ἐκ τῆς περιτομῆς* (Acts 10:45; Rom 4:12; Gal 2:12; Col 4:11; Titus 1:10) refers to circumcised persons, that is, Jews (and "Jewish-Christians"). For Witherington (362), they constitute "apparently a particularly vocal smaller group within the Jerusalem church."

210 *Didascalia* 6.12 is of interest here (chap. 24 in the edition of R. Hugh Connolly [Oxford: Clarendon, 1929] 204–8, commingles Acts 11 and Acts 15): "The believers at Antioch, who taught, '*Except ye be circumcised and conduct yourselves according to the law of Moses,*' and keep yourselves clean from meats, and all the rest, '*ye cannot be saved* . . .' they sent to us certain men (that were) believers and had knowledge of the Scriptures . . ." [not mentioning Paul and Barnabas, although the names appear later] (206, Connolly's trans., with italics for overlap with Acts). Peter (speaking in the first singular) begins, citing Acts 15:7, which is expanded by way of chap. 10, and esp. chap. 11. After the object was taken back up to heaven (p. 107), "Thereupon I bethought me, and understood the word of the Lord, how that he had said, [11:16] "Rejoice, ye gentiles, with the people" [Deut. 33:43||Rom 15:10] and that everywhere he had spoken of the calling of the gentiles; and I rose up and went my way. And when I was entered into his house and had begun to speak the word of the Lord, the Holy Spirit lighted down upon him and upon all the gentiles that were there present." The text then reverts to Acts 15:8-11, with appended citations from Matthew 11:28-30 and a conclusion, followed by the speech of James from Acts 15:13-29 (in the first singular). Ropes (*Text*, cxci–cxcviii) argued that the original *Didascalia*, a major source of *Apostolic Constitutions* 1–6, exhibited a "Western Text." This section is an interesting item in the history of the reception of Acts and suggests that the author/compiler of the *Didascalia,* who had at least a mixed text, located Acts 11 in Jerusalem and deemed it best to combine this with chap. 15 and thereby eliminate troublesome questions.

211 Barrett (1:536–37) struggles to fashion a kind of proto-faction from the phrase, but without adequate grounds. This would mean that the phrase bears different meanings in 10:45 and 11:2, which would impose an unacceptable burden upon the reader.

212 Cf. Luke 5:30; 19:7; 15:2.

349 The verb "enter" (*εἰσέρχομαι*) is shorthand for "visited the home of." *ἀκροβυστίαν ἔχοντας* (lit. "men having a foreskin") is rather crude.

213 Acts 10:48 says nothing about commensality.

214 No doubt the easiest solution for the observant was to avoid eating with gentiles. Esler (*Community*, 73–84) speaks of "Jewish antipathy to dining with gentiles." See also Menachem Stern, *Greek and Latin Authors on Jews and Judaism* (3 vols.; Jerusalem: Israel Academy of Sciences and Humanities, 1974–84) 2:39, who says, "During the first century C.E., the separation of Jews from gentiles in dietary matters became more marked." Apart from chronological and partisan issues—many of the texts are either

view that the charge is a general and hypothetical objection to associating with gentiles.

■ **1-2** The D-Text of vv. 1-2 (which is evidently contaminated and difficult to recover) is probably a more elegant[217] and circumstantial revision[218] that fails to perceive that Peter's accusers damaged themselves and removed the need for additional defense. This recension enhances internal parallels[219] and, most notably, makes it quite clear that Peter did not choose, or have, to hasten back from Caesarea to give an account of his activity.[220] As a bonus, he engages in pastoral care and additional missionary work.[221]

The speech (vv. 4-17) has features of forensic rhetoric.[222] There is no address[223] or proem, and the peroration consists of a single rhetorical question. In effect, it is all *narratio*, with potential artistic proof from the witnesses (v. 12)—although no testimony is taken—and the inartistic vision and command of the Spirit (as well as the saying of Jesus, v. 16). Formally, this type of defense is called μετάστασις, which "consists in the defendant's acknowledging the deed as wrong . . . but shifting the blame for it onto someone else, whom he describes as the (generally intentional) perpetrator of exactly this deed and hence as the guilty party."[224] One does not, however, need to turn to Cicero or Quintilian to find out what is going on here. Peter replies to the charge by reporting his revelation, which is sufficient. "Divine law possessed the greatest degree of force and self-evidence."[225] There are four instances of divine initiative (vv. 5-9, 12, 13, and 15). The evidence is valid for those

second century or later or sectarian—the issue is not *eating with* gentiles, but the *nature* of the food consumed. See p. 274 n. 107. Judith, for example, ate with Holofernes, although from her own provisions (12:19).

215 See, e.g., Johnson, 197.

216 Barrett (1:538) recognizes this. Cf. Juvenal's "Judaizing" family: the father observes Sabbath and abstains from pork; the son accepts circumcision (*Sat.* 14.96–99, cited below in the excursus "Syrian Antioch" in the commentary on 11:20).

217 The opening ἀκουστὸν δὲ ἐγένετο ("It became known") is familiar from the LXX (Gen 45:2; Isa 23:5; 48:3, 20) and elsewhere (Josephus *Ant.* 4.40; Justin *Dial.* 26.3). "They praised God" at the close of v. 1 establishes an inclusio with v. 18 and sharpens the distinction between "the community" and the objectors.

218 Strange (*Problem*, 77–87) has, following Boismard and Lamouille, put forth an interesting argument in favor of the longer text. He rightly contends that the language of the longer text is, by and large, Lucan. The core of his argument is that the longer text does not speak of a meeting in Jerusalem—a name he believes to be absent from the original D-Text—but of repeated (with an eye to the imperfects in vv. 2 and 4) encounters in *Judea*. Objections to his hypothesis include the following: (1) Acts does not envision the apostles as scattered about Judea. They remain at headquarters. (2) Acts 11:18 refers to a *single* reaction to a *single* narration. Strange does not discuss (2). With regard to (1) he argues that apostles were not a part of these debates. Luke does not place them among the opponents, nor would he. Strange cannot explain why "Jerusalem" enters into the discussion at all if it is not in view. For Luke, Jerusalem is the head of the movement and the place where problems are resolved. Strange does not offer adequate motive for a later editor to make a Jerusalem meeting out of a series of meetings in the Judean countryside. The appeal to 15:3-4 rather damages the case than supports it, for in those verses Luke shows that he can describe such a trip with clarity. Finally, in 15:7-9 Peter can refer to these events in language borrowed from chap. 11 as familiar to the Jerusalem community.

219 Acts 8:25 and 15:3 are probable sources of the longer text.

220 On the ideological implications of the D-Text, see Cadbury and Lake, 124; Epp, *Tendency*, 105–7; and Metzger, *Textual Commentary*, 337–38.

221 Cf. 8:25; 15:3. The atmosphere reminds one of the Pseudo-Clementines, one mark of how the D-Text often stands as a kind of stage between the canonical Acts and the Christian Apocrypha.

222 Johnson, 200; Soards, *Speeches*, 77; Witherington, 363.

223 By avoiding an address, the speaker refrains from stating that the objectors were members of the community. Only in v. 18 does it become apparent that they evidently were believers.

224 Heinrich Lausberg, *Handbook of Literary Rhetoric* (trans. Matthew T. Bliss et al.; ed. David E. Orton and R. Dean Anderson; Leiden: Brill, 1998) §183 (p. 77). See Quintilian 7.4.14. *Ad Herennium* 1.25 is more appropriate: one can admit an act but claim that s/he was driven to do it by the crimes of others. Cf. also 2.22 and Cicero *Inv.* 2.78–82. A classic case was that of Orestes.

225 Lausberg, *Handbook* §176, p. 74, which cites Plato *Apol.* 29D and Acts 5:29.

who endorse Christian presuppositions. Jewish teachers within what became the normative tradition would not—and did not—accept the view that a vision (let alone the report of a vision by an uneducated Galilean fisherman) could cancel provisions of the Torah.[226] This, the most important action in Acts, is accepted without any proof from Scripture or appeal to tradition. Continuity is certainly important for Luke, who grounds his argument on it, but at this point a link in the chain is absent.[227] When he comes to the inauguration of the gentile mission, the narrator ignores scriptural argument in favor of a dense concentration of supernatural interventions.

■ **3** The opening accusation and the juridical elements show that this is, in effect, a "trial" of Peter.[228] The narrator has so arranged matters that Peter can make a persuasive defense of his actions without having to undergo the embarrassment of a formal hearing. The speech permits Peter to frame the story as *argument* and to present it from his own viewpoint.[229] The external frame is the objection of v. 3 and its withdrawal in v. 18, both in direct speech:

I. Vv. 5-10. Peter's vision at Joppa. (Embedded proofs include the ecstatic vision.)
II. Vv. 11-12. Arrival of envoys and travel of delegations to Caesarea. (Embedded proofs include the exhortation of the Spirit and the presence of witnesses. The Spirit's message is at the center of the narration and contains an implicit thesis.)
III. Vv. 13-14. Account of "the Man." (Embedded proof is the angelophany.)
IV. Vv. 15-16. Event and interpretation. (Embedded proofs are ecstasy and exegesis.)
   A. V. 15. Gift of the Spirit to hearers (not qualified or described.)
   B. V. 16. Peter's inspired recollection of a saying of Jesus.
V. V. 17. Conclusion (framed as rhetorical question).

The actual audience is, as usual, the reader. Those unfamiliar with the preceding chapter would have considerable difficulty in understanding the summary of vv. 13-14, which does not even name Cornelius.[230] Within Acts, this speech shares some characteristics of Paul's address in chap. 20. Each is addressed to believers, defends the speaker against charges, and includes a saying of Jesus at its close. The introduction is unusual in that it characterizes the speech as a *seriatim* exposition.[231] Debates about the meaning of καθεξῆς in Luke 1:3 gain some clarification from v. 4.[232] The speech follows the sequence of chap. 10, but is neither a complete summary nor in full agreement with that narrative.[233]

■ **5-6** Peter omits references to hunger and food while piling up references to sight. Acts 10:11 used θεωρέω; 11:6 contributes ἀτενίζω, κατανοέω, and ὁράω, adding

226 Jacob Neusner sketches the declining role of the Holy Spirit in Early Judaism; *From Politics to Piety: The Emergence of Pharisaic Judaism* (Englewood Cliffs, N.J.: Prentice-Hall, 1973) 129–36.

227 See Joseph B. Tyson, *Images of Judaism in Luke-Acts* (Columbia: University of South Carolina Press, 1992) 119–25. (In 15:15-18 scriptural evidence will be presented.)

228 Johnson (199) says: "Luke therefore constructs the sort of 'trial scene' that is so frequently found in Hellenistic novels to summarize, articulate, or advance the significance of the events related by the narrative."

229 Tannehill (*Narrative Unity*, 2:143–45) shows how this focus strengthens the argument.

230 Bruce (268) sees this and must propose that the dramatic audience knew the story, but were "now for the first time hearing a full and trustworthy account."

231 The oft-troubling participle ἀρξάμενος ("beginning") is evidently pleonastic, although it bears some relation to καθεξῆς ("in order"). See Barrett (1:538–39), who shows that the usage is proper Greek.

232 See Alexander, *Preface*, 131–32.

233 There are additions: the number of witnesses is specified as "six" (*v.l.* "some" in 10:23). This number is quite large. The most surprising expansion is the attribution to the angel that Peter will deliver a saving message (v. 14), which numerous textual witnesses correct. Peter also reports in Jerusalem that he recalled Jesus' contrast of the baptism of John with that of the Spirit (v. 16; cf. 1:5). The comparison with Pentecost is explicit (v. 15). Details about Peter's vision differ. He does not mention his initial perplexity. The middle participle of 10:20 is active in 11:12. His entertainment of the visitors is not mentioned. The chronological framework is absent. For other examples, see the following exegesis, as well as Cadbury and Lake, 123–24; and Schneider, 2:83. Haenchen (355) rightly observed that such differences are due to Lucan stylistic

that the object came close to him. The contents of the sheet are described in language closer to Genesis 1.[234] Like the story of Saul's conversion/call, this account includes a heavenly voice, specific directions, and numerous references to seeing. These are typical elements of conversion stories.

■ **11-12** Metzger says that "I was" in v. 11 is apparently irrelevant.[235] Its purpose is to claim that the half-dozen believers from Joppa who accompanied him were already lodging in the house of Simon and thus were witnesses from start to finish. The text of v. 12 raises questions. 𝔐 assimilates to 10:20: *διακρινόμενον* ("no questions asked") and is clearly secondary. 𝔓[74] reads *ἀνακρίναντα,* of similar meaning. Most strongly supported is *διακρίναντα,* aorist active in form, without important difference in nuance. The D-Text (in part supported by 𝔭[45]) omits the words. This omission would contribute to the drama of the summary, but the narrative is not interested in drama here, and support of this omission would generate the following development: interpolation of the phrase from 10:20, followed by modification of tense, voice, and (in one case) word. That is unlikely, and it is even more unlikely that Luke would eliminate what he regarded as a key concept.[236] By shifting the voice of the participle from middle to active in v. 12a Peter indicates that he has come to understand the Spirit's message as eliminating discrimination against gentiles. Verse 12b effectively summarizes 10:21-29.

■ **13** The article with "angel" in v. 13 is, if original,[237] an authorial slip that betrays the actual audience. This speech passes over the unnamed Cornelius's status as a "God-Fearer," his piety (which might well include sensitivity to the purity code), and its reward. The effect of this climactic repetition is to treat all gentiles as worthy, not just high-status admirers of Judaism such as the estimable Cornelius. This prepares the way for Peter's final words on the subject in 15:7-11.

■ **14** The initially astounding v. 14, which adds a promise to the angelic message, does not come out of the blue. The three subsequent recountings of the vision (10:22, 30-32; 11:14) include references to Peter's message. "Like a precious stone, the vision is turned this way and that, to discover new facets and refractions in the light."[238] This is an inference, as it were, from Peter's activity—proclamation of the gospel—and a summary of his speech, which he may thus claim had barely begun before the Spirit took action.[239]

■ **15-16** The verse explicitly equates the experience with that of Pentecost. "In the beginning" (*ἐν ἀρχῇ*) is a technical term,[240] variously applied, including creation (John 1:1), the annunciation of the Baptizer's birth (Luke 1:2), and here, the beginning of the post-resurrection community. This use tends to separate Acts from Luke.[241] Pentecost was a "new beginning." That separation is made explicit by formal[242] citation of Acts 1:5.[243] The "you" of that promise includes all believers, not just the apostles.

---

variation. Recognition of that license requires reservation about all of the circumstantial details in Acts.

234 The verb for the withdrawal of the object, *ἀνασπάω*, differs from 10:16.

235 Metzger, *Textual Commentary*, 339. The D-Text *et al.* read "I was," apparently assimilating to v. 5.

236 See Ropes, *Text*, 104; Cadbury and Lake, 125–26 (who are more open to the possibility of a "Western non-interpolation"); Barrett, 1:540; and Metzger, *Textual Commentary*, 339. Note also the use of *διακρίνω* in 11:2.

237 Omission is supported by the interesting combination of 𝔭[45] D Ψ, but omission is more easily explained than addition.

238 Klauck, *Magic*, 33.

239 On the aorist infinitive, see BDF §404 (2). Bruce (269) takes the infinitive expression as a semiticizing auxiliary (and thus not literal). Note Barrett's sharp comment (1:541); and John J. Kilgallen, "Did Peter Actually Fail to Get a Word In? (Acts 11,15)," *Bib* 71 (1990) 405–10.

240 Hans Conzelmann, "'Was von Anfang war,'" in Walther Eltester, ed., *Neutestamentliche Studien für Rudolf Bultmann zu seinem 70. Geburtstag am 20. August 1954* (BZNW 21; Berlin: Töpelmann, 1954) 194–201, esp. 196 nn. 10–11.

241 Note, however, the participle "beginning" (*ἀρξάμενος*) in 1:22; 10:37. The term also suggests that the ascension belongs in the relatively distant past, although the narrative could easily fit into a few months.

242 On the quotation formula, see Helmut Koester, in James M. Robinson and Helmut Koester, *Trajectories through Early Christianity* (Philadelphia: Fortress, 1971) 87–98.

243 "Water" is an instrumental dative, while the multipurpose preposition *ἐν* delimits "Spirit." This may

■ **17-18** The import of the verse is clear, although the grammar is rather fuzzy.[244] Those familiar with 10:44-48 will grasp the meaning: "Since God[245] sent the Spirit, I authorized baptism." One difficulty is that Peter could have refused baptism, but he could not have inhibited God. The perceived need to repeat the identity of the experience ("us") adds to the difficulty.[246] Finally, the nice touch of repeating "able to prohibit" (δύναμαι κωλύειν) from 10:47[247] generates further difficulty, as textual variation demonstrates.[248] Peter's explanation satisfied the objectors, who (like Cornelius and company [10:46]), burst into praise. This is the appropriate response to a miracle.[249] The gift[250] of life has burst the fence of Torah and the boundaries of Israelite observance.[251] This fine ending does not lead the reader to ask what decisions were taken. The issue of circumcision, mentioned here only in the context of the purity regulations, will appear in chap. 15.

be traditional. See Moule, *Idiom Book*, 77. Cadbury and Lake (126) note that Lucan usage with both nouns is consistent and "stylistic." Barrett (1:542) is less certain.

244 For example, the interrogative is a predicate nominative; BDF §298 (5).

245 A number of D-Text witnesses (Boismard, *Texte*, 192) omit "God." Ropes (*Text*, 104–5) attributes this to the view that Christ bestows the Spirit.

246 Note that only here (v. 17) does the text speak of belief on the part of Peter's auditors.

247 On the possible technical use of "prohibit" (κωλύειν), see the comments on 8:36.

248 The D-Text (Boismard, *Texte*, 192) omits δυνατός ("capable," meaning "be able" with a form of "be") and concludes with (prohibit God) "from giving them Holy Spirit," with such expansions (rejected by Boismard) as "to those who believe in him/the Lord Jesus Christ. . . ." The former is an improvement that is difficult to explain as an "Alexandrian" deletion, while the latter is typical D-Text pedantry.

249 Cadbury and Lake (127) note the equivalence.

250 Both "equal" (ἴση) and "gift" (δωρεά) are important. The Spirit arrived as a gift, not as an achievement, and its nature was the same in both cases.

251 On the translation of μετάνοια as "conversion," see Pervo, *Dating*, 273–78. "Repentance" would be inept here, as chap. 10 made no appeal for acknowledgment of sins. "Life" (ζωή) has a "Johannine" sense here, as in 3:15, and requires some modifier.

11

11:19-30 The Church Spreads to Antioch

19/ Now those who had fled as a
result of the oppression that
broke out because of Stephen
traveled through Phoenicia,
then Cyprus, until they came
to Antioch. They proclaimed
the message to Jews only.
20/ Among them were some
Cypriotes and Cyreneans who,
when they reached Antioch,
began to proclaim the message about the Lord Jesus to
all who spoke Greek. 21/ The
Lord was on their side,[a] so that
a large number turned to him
in faith.[b] 22/ When this news
came to the attention of the
church in Jerusalem, they sent
Barnabas to Antioch.[c] 23/ After
he had arrived and seen the
very grace of God at work, he
was overjoyed and set out to
urge that all remain true to the
Lord with heartfelt resolve.
24/ Now Barnabas was a fine
man, notable for his spiritual
gifts and conviction. His work
resulted in a huge increase of
believers.[d] 25/ Barnabas then
went to Tarsus to seek out
Saul, 26/ whom he located and
brought back to Antioch, where
they worked together in the
community[e] for an entire year
and instructed a huge number.
Indeed, it was in Antioch that
the followers of Jesus were first
labeled "Christians."

27/ Around that time some prophets
came to Antioch from Jerusalem. 28/ One of them, Agabus,
made an inspired indication
that a dreadful famine would
fall upon the entire civilized
world. (This famine occurred
during the reign of Claudius.[f])
29/ The followers of Jesus
arranged to send support to the
believers in Judea, all con-
tributing in accordance with
their resources. 30/ They sent
Barnabas and Saul to deliver
this offering to the elders.

a *Or:* "God . . . turned to Jesus."

b The article with πιστεύσας ("having come to faith") is an atypical attributive: BDF §412 (4). Its omission in D E Ψ 33 1739 𝔪 is probably secondary.

c Two textual problems vex v. 22. The otiose participle "local" (lit. "being," οὔσης) does not appear in A D H L P and 𝔪. It is more likely that scribes would omit this word, which appears in 13:1; 28:17, than interpolate it. Luke may have borrowed this expression from Paul (e.g., 1 Cor 1:2) and utilized it in his own manner. Omission of the infinitive διελθεῖν ("travel to"), which is characteristically Lucan (Luke 2:15; Acts 9:38; 11:19), is difficult to explain. The omission has strong support: 𝔭[74] ℵ A B 81 *et al.* In balance, it seems best explained as a pedantic D-Text addition. Boismard (*Texte*, 193) omits the participle and includes the infinitive. On this problem, see Metzger, *Textual Commentary*, 343.

d Lit. "to the Lord," taken here as a kind of metonymy. Somewhat less likely is the view that "Lord" is the agent (i.e., "God added"). See Fitzmyer, 477.

e *Or:* "joined forces together for an entire year in the community."

f The D-Text reads "Claudius *Caesar*."

Analysis

Although not an integrated unit, Acts 11:19–12:25 constitutes a distinct section. Acts 12:25, which completes 11:30, establishes these bounds. Luke's model was Mark 6, in which the account of the mission of the disciples (6:7-13, 30) is interrupted by the story of the Baptizer's death (6:14-29). Into its account of the gentile mission, Acts inserts 12:1-24, stories about the persecutions by and fitting end of a wicked Herod.[1] Heretofore the narrative has moved around the axis of Jerusalem, including more or less adjacent regions. In 11:19–15:35 the axes will be Antioch and Jerusalem. Thereafter, Jerusalem will retain its symbolic role, but the mission will shift from a particular center to "the ends of the earth." One result of these overlapping spheres is ambiguity about the major division within Acts (or whether there should be such a division). Peter's labors end, effectively, in the climactic deliverance of chap. 12. Thereafter Paul (whose actual and familiar name first appears in chap. 13) becomes the central character. The issue of the gentile mission is not ultimately resolved until chap. 15, after which Paul moves into new fields. Luke prefers a fluid, overlapping structure to firmly delineated sections. On literary grounds, the major sections of Acts are chaps. 1–12 and 13–28. Theologically, there is a strong case for viewing chap. 15 as the watershed.

Verses 19-30 contain two reports. The first, vv. 19-26, summarizes events ranging widely over time and space, including a mission of one year's duration, a length hitherto unheard of in Acts. Verses 27-30 treat in detail a specific incident, the prediction of a famine and action to provide relief. The first is noteworthy for its lack of detail and absence of connection to the foregoing.[2] Logic leads one to expect that the Jerusalem community would inaugurate missions to the gentiles. Instead, the narrator leaps, without preparation or transition, backward in time to events following the persecution consequent upon Stephen's martyrdom.[3] Anonymous itinerant missionaries traveled from Phoenicia (the region of Tyre and Sidon[4]) to Cyprus and Antioch, movement along normal sea routes. This endeavor, the narrator notes, was limited to Jews. In Antioch, however, for reasons that receive no explanation and are reported with all of the enthusiasm attending the announcement of a one-degree decline in temperature, the target changed. The more likely reading, "Hellenists"—that is, Greek-speaking persons—is difficult to comprehend, since it is most likely that their previous work had involved the use of Greek. This mission was a great success and, in accordance with previous experience (8:14; 11:1), came to the attention of Jerusalem, which sent Barnabas (rather than Peter and John, for example) to Antioch, for reasons unspecified. Success continued, motivating Barnabas to travel to Tarsus in search of Saul, who became his colleague in Antioch, where growth abounded.

The account is hard to swallow. Few doubt that gentile converts are in view, leaving readers to wonder why the policy changed in Antioch and how Saul accepted this momentous shift without objection. Nothing is said about Torah—whether male converts had to be circumcised and all had to observe *kashrut*. The historical Barnabas was a, if not the, founder of the Antiochene community, but he was not an official envoy from Jerusalem, nor is it likely that he hit upon the idea of recruiting Paul and made a personal journey to do so. What this account does achieve is to relieve Paul from responsibility for innovation.[5] The second unit (vv. 27-30) also relates to Pauline controversies, for it is based upon Paul's Collection for Jerusalem.

Comment

■ **19-26** The author returns to the gentile missionary source, as the resumption of the account broken off at 8:4 indicates. The absence of proper names is probably due to Luke. Verse 20 labels "some" of them as "Cypriotes and Cyrenians." This suggests that the identities of at least two can be found in 13:1, which includes Barnabas (a Cypriote, according to 4:36[6]) and Lucius, from Cyrene.[7] Another may have been Nicholas, a convert from Antioch (6:5). They are anonymous here because the narrator chose to have Barnabas sent from Jerusalem. The source probably assumed that these persons sought gentile converts from the beginning.[8] One can

1 Similarly Schneider, 2:101–2; and Talbert, 113.

2 Lüdemann, 136: "Not a single story is told, but a relatively large number of facts is set side by side."

3 Acts 9:31 reported the restoration of peace, followed by Peter's coastal journey; 11:1 takes note of believers other than apostles in Jerusalem.

4 Mark 3:8 suggests early Christian missionary work in this region. Note also Acts 12:20.

5 Löning, "Circle of Stephen," 117–18.

6 Note also the mission to Cyprus in 13:4-12; cf. 15:39.

7 Acts 2:10 includes "Libyans" at Pentecost. Cyrenians oppose Stephen in 6:9.

8 To reiterate the hypothesis: the source validated the gentile mission by reference to a "pentecostal event," which was transferred by the author of Acts

only speculate about the original length of this material, but it is probable that, except for a story of the irruption of the Spirit, no more than summaries were provided before Antioch, where the mission experienced considerable success (and where the source was composed).[9] Other traces of source material are difficult to isolate. Verse 20a, which is against the grain of Luke's view of the origins of the gentile mission, has a traditional basis, as does the data about the work of Barnabas and Paul in Antioch, although much of this has been recast in Lucan language.[10]

Prominent authorial features can be identified in v. 20b, which follows the Lucan formula of "Jews first,"[11] and the dispatch of Barnabas from Jerusalem, which also fits Luke's pattern, but is effectively contradicted by the sequel, which describes his active participation in the mission without any notion of reporting to Jerusalem or returning there. This characterization of Barnabas, who combines the qualities of Joseph of Arimathea, Cornelius, and the Seven,[12] is due to Luke. In Acts, Barnabas is not a pioneer missionary and sometime colleague of Paul. His role is to serve as the intermediary between Jerusalem/the apostles and Paul.[13] Once he has accomplished that task and Paul is recognized by Jerusalem as a missionary to the gentiles, the narrator discards him (15:39).

■ **20** The verse presents a textual conundrum.[14] Verses 19 and 20 contain parallel constructions, stylistically varied: "speak the *message to x*." Since the *x* in v. 19 is (exclusively) "Jews,"[15] the parallel evidently must include "non-Jews," that is, gentiles. That word, which came so happily to the lips of the Jerusalem community two verses earlier, does not appear. The viable choices[16] are Ἑλληνιστάς and Ἕλληνας ("Hellenists" and "Hellenes," "Greeks"). The latter word could mean "polytheists," that is, "gentiles." In 6:1 "Hellenists" probably means "Greek-speaking Jews," yet that term has very strong internal and external support in 11:20.[17] One must ask what would motivate the change from "Hellenists" to "Hellenes." A number of critics therefore read or render "Greeks," on the grounds of sense.[18] The author evidently used the term "Hellenists" in line with the apparent desire to introduce the gentile mission in Antioch with a minimum of fanfare, trusting that readers (for whom the word may have been as obscure as it is for modern scholars) would get the point.[19]

Excursus: Syrian Antioch[20]

The most famous of foundations named "Antioch" by Seleucid rulers, Syrian Antioch (established c. 300 BCE) served as the capital of the Seleucid empire and was, after Rome absorbed the remains of that dominion, the third most important city in the early empire. Antioch, situated at the juncture of Syria and Asia Minor, was the site of substantial economic and cultural interaction. Its large Jewish community

to Jerusalem and the "beginning" of the postresurrection movement.

9 Lüdemann (136) does not believe that the passage comes from the source, appealing to Trocmé, *Actes et l'histoire*, 166–67. The argument is essentially literary: the choppiness of the account speaks against a source. The alternative, supported here, is that the style is due to abbreviation, as well as to substantial editing.

10 On the use of sources in 11:19-26, see Weiser, 1:274–75; and Lüdemann, 136–37.

11 See p. 109 n. 50.

12 Cf. Luke 1:6; 23:50; Acts 6:3; 9:36; 10:2, 22, as noted by Lüdemann, 134.

13 This role is explicit in 9:27, implicit in 11:19-30; 12:25.

14 See Metzger, *Textual Commentary*, 340–2.

15 "Judeans" is not possible here.

16 The εὐαγγελιστάς ("evangelists") of ℵ* is an impossibility that must derive from Ἑλληνιστάς. (ℵ[2] reads "Greeks.")

17 Only two first hands, 𝔭[74] and A, support "Greeks."

18 Examples include Haenchen, 365 n. 5; Conzelmann, 87; Fitzmyer, 476; Bruce, 272; Hengel, *Between*, 8; Weiser, 1:271; Lüdemann, 134; Johnson, 203; and Jervell, 320. Boismard (*Texte*, 193) reads "Greeks." It is often noted (e.g., Metzger, *Textual Commentary*, 341) that the versional evidence is worthless, as the term "Hellenists" is lacking in other languages. This is not completely correct, since translators could have engaged in paraphrase.

19 See the comments in Ropes, *Text*, 128.

20 For a survey see Frederick W. Norris, "Antioch of Syria," *ABD* 1:265–69. A general history is Glanville Downey, *History of Antioch in Syria from Seleucus to the Arab Conquest* (Princeton: Princeton University Press, 1961). On the Jews of Antioch, see Carl H. Kraeling, "The Jewish Community at Antioch," *JBL* 51 (1932) 130–60; and Irina Levinskaya, *Diaspora Setting* (BIFCS 5; Grand Rapids: Eerdmans, 1996) 127–35. On Jewish–Christian

survived the difficulties engendered by the First Revolt (66–73/74) and was still competitive with Christianity in the fourth century. Antioch was the first metropolis to house a Christian community,[21] establishing the urban character that the movement had until the early Middle Ages.

Since Antioch was, as both Acts and Galatians indicate, the effective cradle of early gentile Christianity,[22] it was there that much of the pre- and non-Pauline remains of early gentile Christianity emerged. Antioch's hero was not Paul, however, but Peter. The mediating, tolerant posture of flexibility that he adopted at Antioch (Gal 2:11-14) prevailed there and may be at least partly responsible for Peter's prominent place in the gospel tradition. That prominence can also be seen in the use of Peter's name as patron of the intensely anti-Pauline Christianity that can be seen in the Pseudo-Clementines and related literature.

Paul was not permanently rejected by all Antiochene believers—witness the thoroughly Pauline Ignatius, who may already have been bishop there when Acts was written.[23] If Barnabas was responsible for the growth, if not the foundation, of the Christian church at Antioch, he may well have been the principal developer of the "community-organizer" model of urban mission that Paul took up with considerable success.[24] The issue of ecclesiastical organization illustrates the complexity of the situation, for between c. 90 and c. 130 Antioch and environs exhibit (1) Matthew's substantial reservations about any officers other than teachers and, perhaps, prophets (whatever the actual situation was); (2) Ignatius's arguments for a strong bishop, assisted by deacons and accompanied by presbyters; and (3) the *Didache*'s testimony to an enduring conflict between itinerant charismatic prophets and the resident bishops and deacons.[25] In his account of Antioch, Luke makes his first references to Christian prophets and elders (the latter at Jerusalem), while 13:1 takes note of prophets and teachers. Because of Paul's failure to prevail in his dispute at Antioch and Luke's desire to attribute the gentile mission to the Jerusalem leaders, much about this crucial center and era is lost in the mist.

The author says absolutely nothing about what motivated the extension of proselytizing to gentiles, but the message is clear: The missionaries proclaimed that Jesus is Lord. This formula, anticipated in the awkward clause of 10:36, encapsulates a basic shift. The Jesus worshiped by these mixed Jewish-gentile urban communities was a powerful heavenly being, not a Galilean prophet vindicated by resurrection, nor simply a future apocalyptic judge.[26] Attempts to elucidate that shift drove the research of the *religionsgeschichtliche Schule* and much thereafter, but it remains easier to describe its function and to speak of meeting the needs of various social groups, and the like, than to trace the development of this idea.[27] Luke assumes that "the Christ-cult"

interaction, see Wayne A. Meeks and Robert L. Wilken, *Jews and Christians in Antioch in the First Four Centuries of the Common Era* (SBLSBS 13; Missoula, Mont.: Scholars Press, 1978). John P. Meier reviews the Christian community there in Raymond E. Brown and John P. Meier, *Antioch and Rome: New Testament Cradles of Catholic Christianity* (Ramsey, N.J.: Paulist, 1983) 12–86. Note also Walter Bauer, *Orthodoxy and Heresy in Earliest Christianity* (trans. and ed. Robert Kraft and Gerhard Krodel; Philadelphia: Fortress Press, 1971) index 308 *s.v.* "Antioch"; and Helmut Koester, in Robinson and Koester, *Trajectories*, 121–26. Rodney Stark's vivid and gritty portrait of nonaristocratic life there is unforgettable (*The Rise of Christianity: A Sociologist Reconsiders History* [Princeton: Princeton University Press, 1996] 147–62).

21 Hengel and Schwemer, *Paul*, 196.

22 Acts 19:26d (the name "Christian") is Luke's apparent homage to the place of Antioch in early Christianity.

23 Ignatius probably died in the first half of Hadrian's reign (117–138) rather than c. 115. See Pervo, *Dating*, 366.

24 See Gerd Theissen, *The Social Setting of Pauline Christianity: Essays on Corinth* (trans. and ed. with an introduction by J. Schütz; Philadelphia: Fortress Press, 1982) 35–54.

25 Matthew is most often assigned to Antioch (see Meier in n. 20). The same region is most suitable for the *Didache*. See, e.g., Kurt Niederwimmer, *The Didache* (trans. Linda M. Maloney; Hermeneia; Minneapolis: Fortress Press, 1998) 53–54. The data permit no firm conclusions, but Antioch best fits the circumstances of these texts.

26 The same phrase is used to describe Philip's proclamation to the Ethiopian official, 8:35.

27 Bousset's *Kyrios Christos* manifests all of the flaws of his era and orientation, but it did recognize the problem with admirable clarity. See the sketch by Burton L. Mack, *A Myth of Innocence: Mark and Christian Origins* (Philadelphia: Fortress Press,

existed from the beginning, and Paul is, in this case, a witness to the general accuracy of his assumption. In short, those missionaries probably did what Luke says they did.[28]

■ **21-24** Luke describes the missionaries in traditional language. Growth shows which side God favored, as Gamaliel had earlier indicated (5:34-39).[29] The second half of v. 21 is difficult. "Lord" (κύριος) appears three times in vv. 20-21. The first refers to Jesus, the second presumably to "the Lord God." The third is uncertain.[30] As in the parallels (8:14; 11:1), v. 22 utilizes indefinite language.[31] One effect of this technique is to intimate success. The conversions are so numerous that they become newsworthy. The first-time reader may expect that, as in 8:14, apostles will be sent to lay hands upon these converts. Peter would be the logical candidate, since he performed this role in Samaria and has had experience with gentile believers. Strangely enough, the representative chosen is Barnabas, who has hitherto played no administrative or missionary role. The critical solution is that v. 22 is a Lucan invention and that the narrator will have no need of demonstrable spiritual gifts at conversion for some time (cf. 19:1-6). Verse 23, a relative clause that amounts to an independent sentence, livens things up with some rhetorical flourishes.[32] Barnabas's qualifications, summarized in v. 24, help to explain his success.[33] Thus far, the mission to Antioch has enjoyed success like that of Jerusalem in the early days.

■ **25-26** The D-Text of vv. 25-26 is not certain.[34] Metzger proposes *ἀκούσας δὲ ὅτι Σαῦλός ἐστιν εἰς Θάρσον ἐξῆλθεν ἀναζητῶν αὐτὸν καὶ ὡς* (-D²) *συντυχὼν παρεκάλεσεν* (*αὐτὸν* D² Sy^hmg) *ἐλθεῖν εἰς Ἀντιόχειαν. Οἵτινες παραγενόμενοι ἐνιαυτὸν ὅλον συνεχύθησαν ὄχλον ἱκανόν, καὶ τότε πρῶτον ἐχρημάτισαν ἐν Ἀντιοχείᾳ οἱ μαθηταὶ χρειστιανοί* and translates: "and **having heard that Saul was at Tarsus**, he went to seek him; and **when he had met him, he entreated him to come** to Antioch. **When they had come**, for a whole year a large company of people **were stirred up**, and **then** for the first time the disciples in Antioch were called 'Christians.'" This rendition treats *συνεχύθησαν* as a passive, which would require a nominative plural subject, rather than the accusative singular *ὄχλον ἱκανόν* ("large crowd"). Boismard therefore prefers *συνήχθησαν τῇ ἐκκλησίᾳ καὶ ἐδίδασκον ὄχλον ἱκανόν* ("they were assembled with the church and taught a large crowd"). Ropes, however, saw support for *συνεχύθησαν* in versions and viewed it as an explanation for the absence of *ἐν* ("in") before "the church" in some witnesses. The verb *συγχέω* appears about a half-dozen times in Acts and may be used in the passive

1988) 98–124, and the provocative synthesis of John Dominic Crossan, *The Birth of Christianity: Discovering What Happened in the Years Immediately after the Execution of Jesus* (New York: HarperSanFrancisco, 1998).

28 For an attempt at reconstructing the history of this mission, its theology and techniques, see Hengel and Schwermer, *Paul*, 196–221.

29 Lit. "the hand of the Lord," used in Luke 1:66; Acts 4:28; 13:11. The image is discussed under "Hand," *DBI*, 360–62. On "with them," see the comment on 10:38. "Number" appears in a similar summary at 6:5; cf. 16:5.

30 People usually "turn to" (ἐπιστρέφω) God, as in Luke 1:16; Acts 14:15; 15:19; 26:20. Acts 9:35 is ambiguous and may refer to Jesus. Cadbury and Lake (129) take this view, as does Weiser, 1:277.

31 Verse 22 has a biblical flavor. The opening words echo Isa 5:9 LXX. Cf. Luke 1:44.

32 These include assonance: five sounds in *-ar-*, paronomasia (χάριν, ἐχάρη, play on name of Barnabas [υἱὸς παρακλήσεως]), rhyme (?) (ἐχάρη καὶ παρεκάλει), and alliteration (four *p*-sounds in the second line). The phrase τῇ προθέσει τῆς καρδίας ("with heartfelt resolve") is odd. See Cadbury and Lake, 129. The second attributive article provides emphasis. It does not seem to be a good case for a "pedantic insertion made by Alexandrian scribes," which is Metzger's proposal (*Textual Commentary*, 343). The insertion of ἐν before τῷ κυρίῳ, B Ψ 181 *al* looks secondary. Metzger (*Textual Commentary*, 343) attributes it to imitation of Paul.

33 Barnabas alone in Acts is called "an excellent man." The only other example in the NT is Joseph of Aramathea in Luke 23:50. The phrase ἀνὴρ ἀγαθός (nominative singular, in this order) is common in ethical (e.g., Aristotle *Nic. Eth.* 1130b.27) and biographical (twenty times in Plutarch) writings. A third Joseph deemed worthy is the son of Hyrcanus, Josephus *Ant.* 12.224.

34 On this text, see Ropes, *Text*, 108; Metzger, *Textual Commentary*, 333–34; Strange, *Problem*, 46 (with

in an active or intransitive sense.[35] Although probably not original, this verb may have entered the D-Text to correct the difficult συναχθῆναι.[36]

The D-Text thus began with the statement that Barnabas learned that Saul was (still) at Tarsus and thus why he should have gone there in quest of him.[37] Rather than say "found and took" as if Saul were a passive object, this edition describes an encounter in which Barnabas "begged" Saul to come to Antioch, promoting the image of Paul as fully independent and not subordinate to Barnabas. If some form of συγχέω were part of the D-Text, it transferred to Syrian Antioch what readers learn about this person elsewhere: wherever he went, there was a stir.[38] The "shortcomings" corrected by the D-Text may point to the source, which, although it probably did not have Barnabas fetch Saul from Tarsus,[39] would be expected to note Paul's originally subordinate status.[40] The meaning of συναχθῆναι ("to be gathered") in v. 26b is troublesome.[41] The narrator may be attempting to indicate, without undue emphasis, the collaboration of the two in mission[42] rather than record their reception by the community.[43] The close of Acts 11:26 implies that the missionary labors of Barnabas and Paul in Antioch were so successful that the movement gained public recognition. The word "Christians" supplies an impressive close to this terse narrative.[44]

Excursus: The Name "Christian"

The advent of the adjective "Christian" (v. 26d)[45] marks the followers of Jesus as a body recognized by outsiders as distinct from Judaism.[46] "Christian"

detailed listing of evidence); and Boismard, *Texte*, 194–95.

35 BDAG, 953, *s.v.*

36 See below.

37 One may ask if Barnabas had forgotten 9:30, where Saul was sent to Tarsus. In response, Acts does not include Barnabas among those who dispatched Saul, and a reader might not believe that a dynamo like Saul would sit quietly at ease in Tarsus until the omniscient narrator decided to put him back into play.

38 Hengel and Schwermer (*Paul*, 409 n. 774) characterize the style of the D-Text as similar to that of the Apocryphal Acts.

39 Tarsus, an ancient settlement in the Plain of Cilicia, was already somewhat hellenized prior to the Seleucid era. According to 2 Macc 4:30-31, Antiochus IV (175–164 BCE) established a Jewish colony there. When, in 64 BCE, Cilicia became a Roman province, Tarsus was its capital. See W. Ward Gasque, "Tarsus," *ABD* 6:333–34. Pre-Lucan tradition (see on Acts 9:11) identified Tarsus as Paul's hometown. There is no independent verification of this tradition, but it may be correct. The idea that Paul was a citizen of Tarsus is a Lucan invention (see on 21:39). Efforts to account for Paul's theology and career on the grounds of his Tarsian birth are, at best, tenuous and could be made for a number of cities. See Hengel and Schwermer, *Paul*, 158–77.

40 Löning ("Circle of Stephen," 117) says of Barnabas's mission to fetch Paul: "This personal drama is certainly a Lukan fiction."

41 On the use of ἐγένετο ("be," "become") with the dative, see BDF §409 (4).

42 The omission of the adverbial καί by mainly later witnesses is due to its unusual character. I suspect it marks the unprecedented length of the mission in Acts.

43 Cf. Haenchen (367), who speaks of "joining forces." The verb συνάγω may imply that their activity took place in worship, rather than, for example, in street-preaching. Cf. Hengel and Schwermer, *Paul*, 221–24.

44 Foakes Jackson, 101: "Henceforward the records of the brotherhood of believers in Jesus become the history of Christianity."

45 Bibliography includes Henry J. Cadbury, "Names for Christians and Christianity in Acts," in Lake and Cadbury, *Additional Notes,* 375–92, esp. 383–85; Elias J. Bickerman, "The Name of Christians," *HTR* 42 (1949) 109–24; Harold B. Mattingly, "The Origin of the Name *Christiani,*" *JTS* 9 (1958) 26–37; Erik Peterson, "Christianus," *Frühkirche, Judentum und Gnosis: Studien und Untersuchungen* (Freiburg: Herder, 1959) 64–87; Ceslas Spicq, "Ce que signifie le titre de chrétien," *ST* 15 (1961) 68–78; Paul Zingg, *Das Wachsen der Kirche: Beiträge zur Frage der lukanischen Redaktion und Theologie* (OBO 3; Freiburg: Herder, 1974) 217–22; Edwin A. Judge, "Judaism and the Rise of Christianity: A Roman Perspective," *TynBull* 45 (1994) 355–68; Hengel and Schwemer, *Paul*, 222–30, with copious notes; Paul Trebilco, *The Early Christians in Ephesus from Paul to Ignatius* (WUNT 166; Tübingen: Mohr Siebeck, 2004) 554–60.

46 Since the author is familiar with, if not fond of, the term, it is not anachronistic to use "Christian" in commenting on Acts.

is a Greek word of Latin form and Semitic background and thus, like the inscription on the cross (John 19:19-20), encapsulates the cosmopolitan background of emergent Christianity.[47] Adjectives of this sort were commonly applied to adherents of a person, such as Julius Caesar or Herod (see Mark 3:6; 12:13).[48] Outsiders are more likely than insiders to coin such nicknames.[49] E. A. Judge says that such adjectives were not applied to followers of a god. This form "classifies people as partners of a political or military leader, and is mildly contemptuous."[50] The earliest occurrences of "Christian" are attributed to outsiders (Acts 11:26; 26:28; 1 Pet 4:16)[51] or are applied by outsiders (Josephus *Ant.* 18.64; Tacitus *Annals* 15.44; Pliny *Letters* 10.96–97). As a self-designation, the name first emerges in Ignatius (e.g., *Eph.* 11:2) and *Did.* 12:4.

The evidence indicates that the designation "Christian" probably had its origin in popular usage and became the official legal designation sometime before 110 CE, quite possibly a good decade earlier. Since neither Paul nor any other writer of the first two generations uses this term, it is rather unlikely that this label first emerged in Antioch during the 30s and 40s CE. The terms "Christian"/"Christianity" erupted in the 90s and later in writings linked in one way or another to Rome, Antioch, or Asia Minor. On linguistic grounds, Rome may be the most likely place of origin, but Antioch is possible. This boast could come from the gentile missionary source, which would therefore be dated c. 90–100 in the form available to Luke.

■ **27-30** The narrator gets down to specifics that reveal the strong connections between Antioch and Jerusalem, the presence of prophetic inspiration in the church and charitable activity that shows the bonds between two leading communities, one of which is the mother church of the gentile mission, the other the mother of the entire church. Edifying as this brief story is, one does not know what to make of it. Agabus's prophecy brings to mind the woes of the end-time, yet, rather than proclaim an imminent end of the world, the believers turn to practical action. In the face of an ecumenical threat, the Antiochene faithful take no reported action in their own behalf but think only of the needs of those at Jerusalem.

Source theories help to unravel some of the dilemmas. The raising of funds for Jerusalem is based on Paul's controversial collection.[52] One possible source for the account of famine relief is Josephus *Ant.* 20.51–53, 101, which praises Queen Helena of Adiabene for her efforts to provide *famine relief* during the reign of *Claudius*.[53] The figure of Agabus raises questions. His name is not otherwise attested.[54] The prophet appears here and in 21:10-11, in both cases as a visitor from Jerusalem/Judea to a mixed or gentile community. One possibility is that Agabus appeared in two sources: the account of the gentile mission and the report on the delivery of the collection.[55] Another is that his role in

47 The stem *christ-* translates Hebrew משיח ("anointed," "messiah"); *-ian-* is a Latin adjectival suffix. Most known examples of Greek words in *-ian-* are translations of Latin words.

48 For other examples, see Hengel and Schwermer, *Paul*, 228–29.

49 Bickermann, Spicq, and Zingg (n. 44) argue that believers coined the name. The non-Christian evidence is, as Lüdemann says, decisive.

50 E. A. Judge, "Judaism and the Rise of Christianity: A Roman Perspective," *TynBul* 45 (1994) 355–68, esp. 363.

51 Both uses in Acts are linked to Paul. 1 Pet 4:16 probably, but not certainly, refers to outsider language.

52 See below.

53 The accounts share the terms "great famine" (note also Luke 4:25, which derives from 2 Kgs 6:25) and the preposition ἐπί ("under," "during the reign of"). Moreover, Acts 11:29 reads "Judea," the same geographical term that occurs in Josephus, although one would expect "Jerusalem," as in 12:25. See Pervo, *Dating*, 193–94.

54 Its meaning is unclear. Williams, among others, says ("Personal Names," 84) that it comes from Hebrew חגב ("grasshopper"), but Fitzmyer (481) finds this improbable. One might as well conjecture an Iranian background (cf. Aeschylus *Persae* 690–91). Mss. of Josephus *Ant.* 13.424 refer to a Palestinian place-name "Agaba," but this may well be an error. See the note of Ralph Marcus in *Josephus VII* (LCL; Cambridge, Mass.: Harvard University Press, 1943) 441.

55 See pp. 12–14.

Antioch (from the mission source) inspired the episode of Acts 21. If the prophecy is regarded as a floating bit of tradition, critics must explain why and how it was preserved and then assume that Luke stripped the oracle of its eschatological framework.[56] Unsuccessful predictions of the end did not enjoy a perfect survival rate. The greatest probability, therefore, is that Luke borrowed Agabus from the collection source and introduced him into this episode, which also deals with fund-raising[57] and developed the oracle from Mark 13:8.[58] If the argument that Luke has created 11:27-30 from disparate sources, has validity, it is likely that he has also invented the participation of Agabus here.

The introduction to v. 27 has no temporal value. As in 6:1—which also dealt with the sharing and distribution of resources—it marks a narrative shift. The reference to prophets prepares readers for 13:1.[59] As usual, the narrator introduces an office (or function) without warning or preparation.[60] The narrative was much too abrupt for the D-Text, which reads, after "Antioch": **There was abundant joy, and when we were gathered together** . . . (28).[61] Insertion of "we" reflects a second-century preference for eyewitness accounts.[62] This use of the first plural either reflects or helps to create the association of the author of Acts with Antioch.[63]

Agabus was inspired to deliver an oracle[64] predicting a universal famine.[65] Famine is an enduring human problem.[66] A worldwide famine would be a disaster of apocalyptic proportions. Prophetic oracles are fond of *οἰκουμένη* ("worldwide"),[67] and prophecies of widespread famine are typical items in lists of the afflictions that will signal the end.[68] The obvious difficulty in this passage is that Agabus predicts universal famine while the response appears to address a *local* famine in Palestine. There is ample evidence for local famines in the eastern Mediterranean in the late 40s (during the reign of Claudius).[69] Those seeking a historical basis will refer to this data, downgrade "famine" to "food shortage,"

56 Aune (*Prophecy*, 264–65) concludes that there was an oracle and that Luke has deleted its eschatological features.

57 So also Lüdemann, 197.

58 Mark 13:8; Matt 24:7; Luke 21:11; and Acts 11:28 all contain the word "famine" (*λιμός*) and the future of the verb "to be." (In Mark 13 and parr., "famine" is plural.

59 On prophets in Acts, see Aune, *Prophecy*, 191, 263–66. He states that Acts mentions twelve Christian prophets and that the existence of others may be inferred.

60 The exception is 6:1-7, in which those chosen are given no title, while neither of those whose activity is described performs the designated function.

61 Boismard, *Texte*, 195–96. The D-Text includes several other revisions.

62 "We" does not otherwise occur after the arrival of new characters in Acts.

63 Haenchen (374 n. 7) argues on the basis of Ephrem's commentary (Ropes, *Text*, 416, 442) that the author was identified with Lucius of Cyrene (Acts 13:1). This is likely. See also Barrett, 1:564.

64 On the use of *σημαίνω* ("signify") in oracular communication, see Cadbury and Lake, 131; and Johnson, 205.

65 A varied range of witnesses omits the apparently redundant *μέλλειν* (which would not be redundant in direct speech). This verb is common in oracles. Cf. Mark 13:4.

66 On famine in the ancient world, see MacMullen, *Enemies*, 249–54; Peter Garnsey, *Famine and Food Supply in the Graeco-Roman World: Responses to Risk and Crisis* (Cambridge: Cambridge University Press, 1988) 3–33; and Bruce W. Winter, "Acts and Food Shortages," in Gill and Gempf, *Setting*, 59–78. Winter's study supersedes that of Kenneth S. Gapp, "The Universal Famine under Claudius," *HTR* 28 (1935) 258–65. Other specific studies are Jacques Dupont, "La famine sous Claude, Actes 11.28," *RB* 62 (1955) 52–55; and Robert W. Funk, "The Enigma of the Famine Visit," *JBL* 75 (1956) 130–36.

67 Translated as "civilized world," as the term is limited in application. Indeed, for Luke it may amount to the Roman Empire (Luke 2:1; Acts 17:6; 19:27; 24:5. Prophetic uses include Isa 10:14, 23; 13:5, 9, 11; 14:17, 26; 37:18.

68 Prophetic examples include Isa 8:21; 14:30; Jer 15:2; Ezek 5:17; 14:13. Predictions of famine from Jewish apocalyptic are *1 Enoch* 80:2; *2 Bar.* 27:6; 70:8; *4 Ezra* 6:22; *Jub.* 23:18; *Sib. Or.* 3:540–42. Early Christian examples of this theme include Mark 13:8||Matt 27:7||Luke 21:11; Rev 6:8; 18:8.

69 For data, see Schürer, *History*, 1:457; Bruce, 276; Barrett, 1:562–64; Winter, "Food Shortages," 63–64, and their references.

and discard the "hyperbole" of v. 28.[70] Data could probably be found for most regions in one period or another, and one must, in any case, ask what useful information has been preserved when these deductions have been made.[71] Bruce Winter concludes: "And, as he reflected on the duration and intensity of local shortages in the Claudian principate known to him, the author of Acts concluded that it was a fulfillment of the prophetic word to which Christians in Antioch responded appropriately."[72] Those who cannot read Luke's mind may doubt this conclusion. The conviction that the author of Acts knew of local shortages during the reign of Claudius is particularly questionable, for the comment that the famine took place "under Claudius" suggests a considerable distance from his reign.[73]

The chronological reference injects uncertainty. Are readers to presume that the money was collected (and sent) in advance of the famine, or does v. 29 jump forward to that period, indicating that, when the misfortune struck, those in Antioch raised money? All of this vagueness, together with the absence of any shortage in Antioch, strengthens the hypothesis that the Pauline collection is in mind. Verse 29 attempts a bit of elegance.[74] Economic arrangements in Antioch are vastly different from those in Jerusalem, where the term διακονία ("ministry," here rendered "support") appeared (6:1). The text assumes that some members of the community are prospering (εὐπορέω),[75] and that their resources are entirely at their own disposal. Offerings for the needy effectively replace the communalism of the early chapters.[76] This is a typical Lucan finesse, showing change without discussion or explanation. By acting to relieve hunger, the early Christians of Antioch showed themselves as benefactors performing a valuable service in support of order, since famine was a major source of social discontent and riot.[77]

As stated above, the model for this activity is the collection. Evidence for this includes use of διακονία ("support") in the Pauline sense,[78] limitation of the project to believers in Judea, the apparent use of 1 Cor 16:2 as the basis for v. 29a, and dependence on Gal 2:10 in v. 30.[79] Luke did not take up these Pauline allusions simply as convenient analogies. His intention was to diffuse the controversy surrounding the collection project by making it a voluntary effort of the Antiochene church carried out on its own initiative rather than in fulfillment of a contract made by Paul with leaders in Jerusalem. The inclusion of Barnabas, inspired by Gal 2:1-10, also helps to shift onus from Paul.[80] The act was entirely

---

70 This is the tactic of Hemer, *Book*, 165, for example.

71 Winter ("Food Shortages," 69) concludes that available evidence points to "a shortage of an uneven intensity spread over a number of years."

72 Ibid., 78.

73 The phrase "under Claudius" (ἐπὶ [τοῦ] Κλαυδίου) is found in the *Acts of the Alexandrian Martyrs* 8.70 (after 115), Justin *1 Apol.* 26.2 (c. 160, *re:* Simon Magus) Cassius Dio 59.15.5 (third century CE), and in Dictys Cretensis (a fictional account of the Trojan War) *Test.* 1a 49 T.26. See Pervo, *Dating*, 313–14.

74 Haenchen, 275. On the use of "each" (ἕκαστος) with a plural verb, see 2:6. The D-Text simplifies the construction (Boismard, *Texte*, 197).

75 See Spicq, *Lexicon*, 2:134–35.

76 Note the parallel language of 4:35 and 11:29, the former referring to the need of each person, the latter to the resources of each. K. Mineshige (*Besitzverzicht und Almosen bei Lukas: Wesen und Forderung des Lukanischen Vermögensethos* [WUNT 163; Tübingen: Mohr Siebeck, 2003]) concludes that almsgiving and renunciation of property are distinct activities in Luke and Acts and cannot be correlated.

77 Cf. the references in n. 66. One example is a riot caused by a food shortage in Rome during the reign of Claudius (Tacitus *Annals* 12.43.2; Suetonius *Claudius* 18.2).

78 This word is a Pauline trope for the collection (1 Cor 16:15; 2 Cor 8:4; 9:1-13; Rom 15:31).

79 For evidence and argument, see Pervo, *Dating*, 79. It is possible that one basis for this was the gentile mission source. The initial plan for a collection came from an agreement made by Paul and Barnabas as representatives of the Antiochene community (Gal 2:10). Paul's project was carried out independently. The believers at Antioch may have raised and delivered an offering on their own. See Friedrich W. Horn, "Die Kollektenthematik in der Apostelgeschichte," in Breytenbach, *Apostelgeschichte*, 135–56.

80 If the "famine visit" is a Lucan creation, there is no need to reconcile it with Galatians 2 and Acts 15. Jervell (326–29) allows that money may have been sent, but not through the agency of Paul at a time prior to or during the reign of Agrippa I (41–44 CE). This would conform to its presence in the gentile mission source. Barrett (1:558–60) contends

voluntary, without the least hint of manipulation or compulsion. Just as v. 27 speaks of hitherto unknown "prophets" in Jerusalem, v. 30 refers to "presbyters" as the official recipients of the offering.[81] With the onset of a gentile-inclusive urban mission outside of Jerusalem, Luke begins to slip subsequent arrangements into the story. He intends to intimate continuity by positing overlap rather than, for example, by describing, as does *1 Clement* (42; 44:1-4), presbyters as the successors of apostles.

that this is the same historical visit that is narrated in Acts 15 and Gal 2:1-10. See also Haenchen, 375–79. Identification of Acts 11:27-30 with Gal 2:1-10 is advocated by some who believe that Acts 15 deals with a later meeting. For this position, see William Ramsay, *St. Paul the Traveller and the Roman Citizen* (London: Hodder & Staughton, 1897) 46–47; and Hemer, *Book*, 266–67. Bruce (278) rejects the view that Acts 11 is a doublet of the visit reported in chap. 15.

81 On presbyters, see Pervo, *Dating*, 114. The introduction of presbyters is so abrupt that Conzelmann (91) suspects the presence of a source.

12

12:1-23 Persecution by Herod and Peter's Miraculous Escape

12:1/ **At that time King Herod began to attack some members of the church.[a] 2/ He had John's brother James put to the sword. 3/ When he observed that the Jews approved of this,[b] he proceeded to arrest Peter also, whom[c] he seized during the Days of Unleavened Bread 4/ and placed in custody, setting a guard of four squads of four soldiers each.[d] Herod intended to bring Peter to public justice once the feast was over. 5/ Peter therefore remained in custody[e] while the church prayed fervently to God in his behalf.**

6/ **On the night before Herod was going to bring him to justice, Peter was sleeping, cuffed with two chains between two guards while two others kept watch outside the door. 7/ Suddenly an angel of the Lord appeared and a light shone in the facility. The angel aroused Peter with a blow in the side and said, "Get up quickly!" The shackles fell from his hands.[f] 8/ The angel then said: "Belt up your robe and put on your sandals." Peter complied. "Put on your coat and follow me," the angel continued. 9/ Peter followed him out, not knowing that the angel had actually done all this, for he imagined that it was a vision. 10/ They passed by the first guard station, then the second, coming finally to the iron gate that leads to the city. This opened to them on its own accord. They went out and traveled a block,[g] at which point the angel suddenly left him.**

11/ **At that Peter came to his senses[h] and exclaimed: "Now I know that the Lord[i] really did send an angel and that he has delivered me from Herod and all the expectations of the Jewish people!" 12/ Once he had realized this, he proceeded to the house of Mary, who was the mother of John surnamed Mark, where a large group had gathered for prayer.[j] 13/ A maid named Rose came in response to his knock on the courtyard gate.[k] 14/ When she recognized**

a D-Texts add "in Judea." This pedantic supplement provides a link to 11:29. See Cadbury and Lake, 132–33.

b D-Texts (Boismard, *Texte*, 198) specify just what was pleasing: ἡ ἐπιχείρησις αὐτοῦ ἐπὶ τοὺς πιστοὺς [(καὶ) ἁγίους], "when he realized that **his assault upon the believers (and/or saints)** . . ." This is little more than pedantic expansion. Cop^{mae} expands the verse even more, and more pedantically.

c D-Texts (Boismard, *Texte*, 199) prefer the demonstrative τοῦτον ("him") and omit "and."

d $\mathfrak{P}^{74}$ *pc* omit the last two words, "to guard him." They are redundant. 0244 omits the unnecessary word "soldiers." Cop^{mae} "did the math" and reports that Peter was supervised by sixteen guards.

e $\mathfrak{P}$* vg^{ms} sy^{h**} (mae) read *a cohorte regis* ("by the royal battalion"). Cop^{mae} adds, unnecessarily, that the custody was "secure." See Metzger, *Textual Commentary*, 346.

f Boismard (*Texte*, 200) prefers ἐλύθησαν ("were loosed") to ἐξέπεσαν ("fell off") for the chains and ascertains that the hands were "his."

g *Or:* "along a street." Several versions omit "leading to the city" after "iron gate." $\mathfrak{P}^{74vid}$ A read ἀπῆλθεν instead of ἀπέστη. This simplification overlooks the frame in vv. 7 and 10 (below).

h The phrase is acceptable if it is not taken to mean "came out of a trance." Cf. v. 9: he realized that he was *not* dreaming. Cf. Luke 15:17, where the prodigal realizes his situation. On this Greek idiom, see *Ephesian Tale* 3.12.6 and the *Onos* 13.

i The D-Text includes one of its frequent additions of τότε, "then" (Boismard, *Texte*, 201). There is the usual variation between "God" and "Lord" (as well as the harmonizing "Lord God"), with weak support for the former. Boismard (*Texte*, 201) omits "the people," on slender grounds.

j On whether the article should be read before "Mary," see Barrett, 1:583. Some Latin and other versions speak of assembled "brothers and sisters," adopted by Boismard (*Texte*, 202) into his D-Text.

k Boismard (*Texte*, 202) reads the simple "door." There is D-Text support for "came outdoors" rather than "to the gate." Bezae has been erased. The Latin side d has *foris* ("outside"). See Ropes, *Text*, 112. This would make Mary's home less ostentatious and thus demonstrates the relative luxury of her living arrangements.

l E reads αὐτῷ τὴν θύραν, "(did not open) the door for him." This is related to the notion of a simpler house discussed in the previous note.

m The D-Text makes this imperfect: "They **kept saying to her** . . ." (Boismard, *Texte*, 203).

n D-Texts (Boismard, *Texte*, 203) soften to "**Perhaps** it is his guardian angel."

Peter's voice, she became so excited from joy that she did not open the gate,[l] but dashed back in to announce that Peter was standing outside. 15/ "You're crazy!" was their answer,[m] but she was so persistent in her claim that they began to say, "It's his guardian angel."[n] 16/ Meanwhile, Peter continued knocking, so they opened the gate and, upon seeing him, were astonished. 17/ Peter gestured that they should be quiet and then related[o] how the Lord had led him out of prison. "Tell James and the believers about this," he said, before leaving them and going elsewhere.

18/ **The following day the soldiers were confused[p] about what had become of Peter.[q] 19/ After Herod had looked for him without success, he interrogated the guards, disposed of them, then left Judea to pass some time in Caesarea.[r]**

20/ **Herod was furious with the people of Tyre and Sidon. They approached him jointly, because their region depended upon Herod's realm for its food supply. After securing the support of Herod's chamberlain, Blastus, they petitioned for an amicable resolution of the conflict. 21/ On the day fixed for the formalities, Herod took his place on the throne, vested in his royal garb,[s] to deliver a public address. 22[t]/ The populace kept chanting: "This is a god's voice, no mere mortal's!" 23/ An angel of the Lord immediately struck Herod with a blow, because he had not given proper honor to God.[u] He died from an infestation of worms.[v]**

o There is an almost even division of witnesses as to the presence of αὐτοῖς ("to them") here. Since it is difficult to explain its deletion, probability favors the view that it is an addition to the text.

p *Or:* "were considerably confused." A literal translation of the conventional text is "no little disturbance" (τάραχος οὐκ ὀλίγος). Litotes is a common Lucan figure (Acts 14:28; 15:2; 17:4, 12; 19:23, 24; 27:20). The same phrase appears in 19:23. D-Texts read either "a great disturbance" or, as Boismard (*Texte*, 204) prefers, "a disturbance." The history appears to be "no little disturbance" → "great disturbance" → "disturbance," but it is possible that the litotes is an assimilation. See Ropes, *Text*, 113. (Witherington's [389 n. 106] claim that litotes is also characteristic of Thucydides is erroneous.)

q The D-Text adds "or how he had got out." In his comments, Boismard (*Texte*, 204–5) indicates that this edition might have omitted the first clause and said simply, "the soldiers were confused about how Peter got out." The translation takes the pronoun "what" as the predicate: BDF §299 (2).

r The D-Text (Boismard, *Texte*, 205–6) states frankly that Herod executed the soldiers and simplifies the close to "he went . . . to Caesarea." The elimination of διέτριβεν (lit. "he spent time") makes way for the alterations in the next verse, where the D-Text (Boismard, *Texte*, 206) offers several improvements: "**for** Herod was furious with the people of Tyre and Sidon. Now a united delegation **from both cities** approached **the king**, because their region*s* depended upon **his** for its food supply." The postpositive γάρ ("for") links to v. 19. The quarrel is why Herod went to Caesarea. The rest are pedantic clarifications of the obvious.

s In Greek, both "vested" and "seated" are circumstantial participles. The evidence and argument for whether they should be linked with "and" (καί) are evenly divided. It is omitted here.

t The D-Text (Boismard, *Texte*, 206) inserts "after he had been reconciled with them . . ." This presumes that the king was sitting in judgment and that the quarrel was not resolved until after he had spoken. It appears to miss the point that the crucial act was the "persuasion" of Blastus.

u The D-Text (Boismard, *Texte*, 206) omits the article, allowing the possibility that it takes the phrase as in John 9:24, and elsewhere, where it means "tell the truth."

v The D-Text (Boismard, *Texte*, 207) states, "after he had descended from his throne, he was infested by worms while still alive and thus perished." See Metzger, *Textual Commentary*, 350; and Epp, *Tendency*, 145–46.

Analysis

Chapter 12 consists of two linked stories (vv. 1-17; 18-23), a conventional note on growth (v. 24), and a brief report (v. 25).[1] The last item completes 11:27-30 and encloses the narrative of chap. 12 within a frame. That framework exhibits two contrasting approaches to food shortages. The two stories share a principal character: "King Herod." These observations invite the critic to view the entire unit as an integrated whole. Acts 12:1-23 is, in fact, a well-crafted novella containing different forms drawn from several sources. Questions of source, form, editing, and historical tradition are not insignificant, but they ought not detract from recognition of the overall literary achievement.[2] The complexity of the tradition indicates the presence of an authorial hand. Popular (oral) tradition may recount one legend about Peter's escape and another about the death of a persecutor. The manner in which they are introduced and connected to one another to form a narrative of some complexity all but excludes the possibility that Luke simply assembled disparate traditions.

Some tradition evidently stands behind the execution of James (vv. 1-2). The story of Peter's deliverance contains two episodes: vv. 7-10 and 12-17, the former of which *might* derive from tradition, while the latter is very probably a Lucan composition. The account of "Herod's" death may be based on Josephus.[3] Each has, in effect, three sections. Verses 1-5 introduce the story of Peter; vv. 6-11 describe his rescue; and vv. 12-17 recount his recognition and departure. Verses 18-19 introduce the tale of Herod's demise, v. 20 his conflict with two cities, and vv. 21-23 his departure. The unit is, broadly speaking, chiastic, for it begins with Herod the persecutor (A), relates two linked incidents about Peter (B, B'), and closes with the punishment of Herod (A').

Acts 12:7-10 is a miraculous deliverance that includes two motifs: the breaking of bonds and a door miracle.[4] The three prison-escape stories in Acts (5:17-26; 16:19-40) occur at important points in the narrative and appear, in retrospect, to presage important changes. Following the trial in chap. 5 (which reveals the murderous intent of the Sanhedrin) comes the appearance of the Hellenists. Peter's escape marks the end of his mission. Chapter 16 follows the "Apostolic Council" and highlights the beginning of Paul's labors in the Aegean region. The liberation stories are, in a general sense, associated with breakthroughs of the message. The threefold occurrence of escape stories decreases, rather than increases, the probability of individual sources, since the hypothesis that circumstances had kindly supplied Luke with stories of this nature about both Peter and Paul is improbable.

One possibility of a source for this episode in Acts 12 is an episode from the extant fragments of Artapanus.[5] In response to Moses' statement that God had sent him to liberate the Jews, Pharaoh imprisoned him. At night, the prison doors opened of their own accord (αὐτομάτως; cf. Acts 12:10).[6] The guards either die or sleep. Moving from prison to palace, Moses aroused the king (cf. Acts 12:7). When he learned from Moses the name of the God who had sent him, the monarch collapsed, but was revived by Moses. Common elements include the exodus context, an imprisoned hero, nocturnal release by miracle, and the "death" of a wicked ruler. Luke may well have known Artapanus,[7] and the modifications made would accord with his observable use of sources. If one could presume that this story

1 For full surveys, see Kratz, *Rettungswunder,* 351–451; Yvan Mathieu, *La figure de Pierre dans l'oeuvre de Luc* (EB 52; Paris: Gabalda, 2004) 287–308; and Weaver, *Plots*, 149–217.

2 The analysis by Lüdemann (139–46) of Acts 12, for example, does little to illuminate this passage. See also Weiser, 1:286–88.

3 See below.

4 Kratz (*Rettungswunder,* 441) states that miracles of delivery function as propaganda to support new religious cults by encouraging their members.

5 Artapanus frgs. 3 and 3b; Eusebius *Praep. ev.* 9.27.23–25; Clement of Alexandria *Strom.* 1.23.154.2–3 (Holladay, *Fragments*, 1:218).

6 Clement rationalizes this by attributing the action to God's will (βούλησις).

7 See pp. 12–14. (Luke would have presumably had access to the full text of Artapanus's work, which survives only in summarizing fragments.) Carl Holladay ("Acts and the Fragments," 171–98, esp. 181) notes these correspondences: the hero opposes a wicked monarch, nocturnal imprisonment, and doors that open of their own accord. Swords fall apart in Artapanus; chains fall off in Acts. In both,

about Moses was generally familiar,[8] this "exodus" from captivity would constitute an additional parallel between Moses and Peter.[9] The epic tradition also influenced stories of this nature.[10]

Verses 18-23 include many of the typical features of the death of a tyrant. The two episodes are complementary.[11] In the case of Peter, God intervenes to rescue; God puts Herod to death. Like all miracles, these stories raise moral questions for modern readers. Why does God allow James to be put to death but not Peter? Is retribution against individuals appropriately ascribed to God? If so, why have so many wicked wretches *not* been devoured by worms? Miracle stories are best not viewed against the backdrop of universal justice. They are *stories*, understood from very early times as symbols of what God means and wills rather than as norms for daily life.

Howard Marshall frames and answers the historical question: "At first sight the story is unnecessary to the developing theme of the expansion of the church; had it been omitted, we should not have noticed the loss."[12] The literary response is that we should have been poorer without this passage. As Marshall subsequently acknowledges, the unit does answer historical questions. It points to "the end of the apostolic age" and the succession of Peter by James.[13] Since, however, these answers are apparent only to those who already know them, the quest for "objective" historical intention encounters severe difficulties.

This commentary argues that the narrative is a symbolic portrayal of Peter's "passion," "resurrection," and vindication that, through initiatory language, makes it a paradigm of Christian experience.[14] "Symbolic" does not mean "allegorical."[15] Luke shows his literary skill in that symbolism never engulfs the narrative, the surface structure of which is a vivid story complete with adventure, suspense, humor, and a worthy end to a dastardly villain. Peter's deliverance also provides a parallel with and a contrast to Paul's deliverance in 16:25-40. While the evil intent of a wicked ruler requires detailed divine intervention to extricate Peter, the Roman judicial process will eventually vindicate Paul.

Comment

■ **12:1** The story begins in a formal[16] and general manner. "King Herod" launched an attack[17] on the church, specifically on its leaders. The "peace" achieved in 9:31 has been shattered. On the grounds of the similarity of his death to that of Agrippa I ([37] 41–44),[18] historians identify the two, but Luke is not writing history here. "King Herod" is a folkloristic wicked tyrant, comparable to the baby-killing Herod the Great (Matt 2:16-18) or, more relevantly, to his prototype, the Pharaoh of

the monarch dishonors God. "Death" and revival feature in each. Weaver (*Plots,* 201–3) reviews the data and decides against intertextuality.

8 Louis Ginzberg (*The Legends of the Jews* [7 vols.; Philadelphia: Jewish Publication Society, 1909–38] 6:424 n. 155) gives no other sources for this story.

9 In the scheme of Artapanus, this episode creates a parallel between Joseph and Moses.

10 See MacDonald, *Imitate Homer,* 123–45, for a number of interesting parallels.

11 Kratz (*Rettungswunder,* 442, 445, 473) notes that release miracles are often associated with the punishment of those responsible for incarcerating those favored by the god.

12 Marshall, 206.

13 Robert W. Wall ("Successors to 'the Twelve' according to Acts 12:1-17," *CBQ* 53 [1991] 628–43) argues that chap. 12 is shaped to show continuity of leadership.

14 A similar interpretation will be offered for Paul's experience in 27:1–28:10.

15 For allegorical approaches to this story, see Arator 1:1007–76.

16 "At that time" is used by historians, especially Josephus (twenty-seven times) and others (notably Galen). The phrase may represent a vague synchronism, but can also be used when the author seems to have no notion of the date, according to Cadbury and Lake, 132. Note also 2 Macc 3:5.

17 The phrase is awkward and would improve if κακῶσαι were not present (and the preposition were ἐκ instead of ἀπό [both meaning "from"]. "Lay hands upon" is conventional in persecutions. Cf. Luke 21:12; Acts 4:3; 5:18. One may take κακῶσαι as a superfluous infinitive of purpose, "seized with the intent of doing injury." The phrase is used with an infinitive in *1 Esdr* 9:20. See, e.g., Barrett, 1:574.

18 See below.

Exodus, or to the prophet-beheading "King Herod" of Mark 6:14-29 (who was not a king),[19] whose story has helped to inspire this passage. The appellation "Herod" will do for any Jewish ruler, particularly for those who are bad.[20] There is no evidence that Agrippa I ever bore the nickname "Herod."[21]

■ **2-6** No motive is provided for the persecution. By this point, none may be required. Verse 3 will suffice for that. Herod executed James. Traditions about the martyrdom of the sons of Zebedee are relatively early, but James otherwise has no individual role.[22] The action evokes the execution of the Baptizer by another Herod (above). Herod discovered that the execution had enhanced his popularity, pursuit of which will not always work to his advantage (vv. 21-23). Since the death of Stephen, it has been assumed that "the Jews" hated followers of Jesus—and the ruler decided to continue his course.[23] The seven words allotted by the narrator for recounting the fate of James make it quite clear that Herod does not make empty threats. Peter was his next victim.[24] The king is attacking the church from the top down. But, as a parenthesis reveals,[25] Passover[26] is at hand, so Peter will have to wait. The parallel with Jesus' passion is clear, as is the irony: Peter will pass the feast of liberation in bondage. Security is exceptionally tight (v. 4), a necessary precaution, given the experience of 5:21b-26. No ruler has ever been able to design an angel-proof jail, but this possibility does not rise to the surface. Suspense does rise, however. Within a week, the tyrant will bring his prisoner to justice.[27] With Peter swaddled in guards,[28] the situation looks hopeless. Verse 5 extends the retardation with a summary: Peter pines; the people pray.[29] Cf. v. 12.[30] Two vigils are under way: the watch of the guards who hover over the manacled

---

19 Nebuchadnezzar is another example of the type, on which see Morton Enslin, *The Book of Judith* (Leiden: Brill, 1972) 58–59. Tannehill (*Narrative Unity*, 2:152) acknowledges that readers might confuse this figure with the Herod who killed John.

20 Justin *1 Apol.* 31 identifies "King Herod" as the recipient of the request from King Ptolemy for translators of the Hebrew Bible. In the *Gospel of Peter*, "King Herod" is in charge of the crucifixion (1.1–2). Similarly, the "Herod" of the *Protevangelium of James* cannot be identified as Herod the Great with complete certainty. Luke and Acts refer to "Herod king of Judea" (Luke 1:5), Herod the Tetrarch ("ruler" [= Antipas]; Luke 3:1, 19; 9:7 [which may be a secondary correction of the text]; Acts 13:1; and "Herod" [Luke 8:3; 13:31; 23:7-15; Acts 4:27]). It is not certain that otherwise uninformed readers would keep all of these figures distinct. Rulers of the Herodian family persecute some figures (John the Baptizer, James, Peter) but acquit the leading character (Jesus, Paul) in each book. See Sanders, *Jews*, 20–22; Klauck, *Magic*, 39–40; and Weaver, *Plots*, 209–10.

21 Daniel R. Schwartz (*Agrippa I: The Last King of Judaea* [TSAJ 23; Tübingen: Mohr Siebeck, 1990]) refutes the notion that there is any numismatic evidence for applying the name "Herod" to Agrippa (120 n. 50). For Eusebius the name "Herod" for Agrippa was a problem (*H.E.* 2.10.10).

22 Martyrdom: Mark 10:35-40. On these, see Cadbury and Lake, 133; and Bruce, 280–81. James is included in the central group of disciples (with Peter, John, and Andrew), but does not appear with John among the "pillars" of Gal 2:9 (cf. Acts 3:1; 8:14, where John is Peter's companion). This absence has fueled speculation about the date of James's death. Boismard (*Texte*, 198) proposes for his edition of the D-Text "**And** he killed **John** the brother of **James**. . . ." His evidence is slender, and this inversion is, in any case, secondary.

23 Luke 20:19, where fear of the people holds back plans to execute Jesus, is a telling contrast. That verse also includes "lay hands upon" (ἐπιβάλλειν τὰς χεῖρας), found in 12:1.

24 According to BDF §435 (a) προσέθετο συλλαβεῖν (lit. "added to arrest") is an example of a verb expressing an adverbial sense that amounts to a Hebraism. Cadbury and Lake (134) are less certain. Cf. Luke 22:33: *Peter* said to *Jesus*, "Lord, I am ready to go (πορεύεσθαι [cf. v. 17]) with you to prison (φυλακήν) and to death!" Contrast Mark 14:29.

25 On the parenthesis between vv. 3 and 4, see BDF §465 (1).

26 Luke treats "Days of Unleavened Bread" and "Passover" as synonyms. Cf. Luke 22:1; Acts 20:6. The usage was familiar to Josephus *Ant.* 14.21.

27 On the use of ἀνάγω ("bring before") as a juridical term, see Cadbury and Lake, 134; and BDAG, 612, *s.v.* As Barrett (1:577) notes, the sense here is not of a formal trial but of a public execution.

28 Cadbury and Lake (134) cite Vegetius *De re militari* 3.8 to explain the arrangements. Roman guards stood three-hour watches.

29 Chaps. 22–28 will record no such prayers (or any other assistance) for the imprisoned Paul.

30 The wording is somewhat awkward, perhaps to achieve a somewhat chiastic structure. The D-Text

apostle and the novena of the faithful.[31] The ponderous and repetitious language plods along like a death march.[32] Action seems to resume in v. 6. On the very night[33] before the execution,[34] Peter lay asleep. Since he was evidently shackled to two guards, this repose indicates no fear of death.[35] Action has, however, not resumed. That state of affairs is about to change.

■ **7-8** The arrival and departure of an angel (ἄγγελος κυρίου ἐπέστη . . . ἀπέστη ὁ ἄγγελος) frame vv. 7-10. Readers know what to expect: the angel will escort Peter out of prison and give him instructions. The first of these expectations will be fulfilled, with excruciating detail that produces nail-biting suspense, savored with amusement.[36] As for what Peter is to do after his escape, the angel is silent. With the angel comes light. Illumination could be useful, but it might also draw the attention of the guards.[37] Neither angel nor light disturbs the sound apostolic slumber. Deliverance begins with a kick[38] in the ribs and a command to get up. At this moment, his chains fall off. The fracture of shackles is a key feature of the miraculous prison-break.[39] Getting the chains off is no problem. Getting Peter dressed is. A maddening dialogue ensues, as the angel supervises every detail of Peter's toilet (v. 8). Worried readers will not understand why these niceties cannot wait. When his wardrobe finally meets the standards of this celestial valet, Peter is told to follow. The story is back on track.[40] As in 8:26-39, the human characters are puppets maneuvered from on high.

■ **9-10** Peter is not on track. As far as he is concerned, he was having a dream.[41] This resonates ironically with

(Boismard, *Texte*, 199) shifts "in his behalf" and prefers "much" to "fervently." A number of witnesses read "fervent." On this language, cf. Jdt 4:9; Luke 22:44; Acts 26:7; *1 Clem.* 34:7. For comment, see Metzger, *Textual Commentary*, 346.

31 The initial μὲν οὖν may be resumptive or may represent two different particles. It is preferable to take this as a μέν . . . δέ ("on the one hand . . . on the other") construction. Haenchen (382) views it as transitional: "Now begins . . . the real story of Peter." Barrett (1:578) sees it as "summing up the position so far reached." See also Moule, *Idiom Book*, 162. For translators and editors, the question is where to mark a new paragraph.

32 The omissions of some words by various witnesses (n. *e*) testify to redundancy. Notice also the repetition of τηρέω ("watch," "guard"). Indeed, all of v. 6 is essentially repetitious.

33 On the suspense here, cf. 21:27 (Paul).

34 Both verb and tense are textually uncertain. The aorist of προάγω is preferable. See BDAG, 864, *s.v.*; and Metzger, *Textual Commentary*, 346. Acts 16:20 indicates a different meaning for προσάγω.

35 So slept Socrates before his death: Plato *Crito* 43b.

36 On the humor, see Pervo, *Profit*, 62–63.

37 This light is not itself an epiphany, as in 9:3. Luke 2:9 is a better comparison. The D-Text (D it syr[h*] cop[mae] [Boismard, *Texte*, 200]) states that the angel appeared to Peter, implying that the others did not see it. This is a rationalization. Some D-Text versions (syr[hmg] g p r Lcf) state that light shone *from* the angel. This is, in terms of angelology, also a rationalization. On light in epiphanies, see Weaver, *Plots*, 165 and n. 49.

38 A number of D-Texts (Boismard, *Texte*, 200) have the angel "nudge" (νύξας) Peter rather than kick him. This variant achieves two results: it enhances the parallelism between Jesus and Peter (John 19:34) and obviates the parallelism between Peter and Herod in vv. 7 (πατάξας) and 23 (ἐπάταξεν).

39 This item is common in the Dionysiac tradition, for example, Euripides *Bacch.* 447–48; Ovid *Metam.* 3.699–700. For a broad survey of themes and motifs in prison-escape stories, see Richard Pervo, "The Literary Genre of the Acts of the Apostles" (Diss., Harvard University, 1979) 54–90.

40 Cop[mae] reads, "But he [the angel] grabbed him [Peter], went ahead of him, and took him out, and Peter followed. . . ." This emphasizes Peter's helplessness, perhaps on the grounds that he did not know what was happening. Boismard (*Texte*, 200) accepts this reading, finding some support from Ephrem. Note that this text omits the command to follow. In the final clause, B reads γάρ rather than δέ. "For" is smoother than "and." Another textual improvement in v. 9 is ὑπό ("by") rather than διά ("through") governing "the angel."

41 Verse 9b is awkwardly stated. The initial καί must be adversative ("but"). For a dream of prison escape, see *Ephesian Tale* 2.8.2, the Greek of which well illustrates the form: The hero, Habrocomes, in a private prison, dreamt that his father came, freed him, and led him out of custody: ἔδοξεν ἰδεῖν . . . [his father] ἐπιστάντα δὲ τῷ δεσμωτηρίῳ λῦσαί τε αὐτον καὶ ἀφιέναι ἐκ τοῦ οἰκήματος, "He dreamt he saw [his father] arriving at the prison to free him and take him out of the place." Underlined words appear in Acts 12.

the vision of 10:17. Acts 12:15 will compound the irony. The pair must negotiate their way through a maze of guards posted at stations[42] to foil any shenanigans.[43] The final barrier is an iron gate, the most awesome and impenetrable of all. Without further ado, this swings open magically, and the city lies before them. Door miracles are another leading element of divinely engineered prison-breaks. Peter has been delivered from a formidable combination of human and material forces. To this point, the story is more or less a repeat of 5:19: Peter has been jailed by the authorities and delivered by an angel.[44] Alas, he is not yet out of the woods. After escorting him for a block, his rescuer departs without a word. This is not a common feature of escape stories or of any other type of legend. The narrative has moved from legend to literature. Peter has another adventure to undergo.

■ **11-12** When Peter grasps what has happened, he offers an interpretation. His words echo the "did not know" of v. 9 (*οὐκ ᾔδει ὅτι ἀληθές . . . οἶδα ἀληθῶς*). He has passed from ignorance to truth. The quotation in v. 11, which evokes the LXX,[45] represents the views of the narrator.[46] The somewhat redundant opening of v. 12 underlines its formal character.[47] His destination is the house of one Mary, who is identified neither by the name of her father nor that of husband, as was conventional for women, nor even by her place of origin (such as Mary of Magdala), but through her son. The tradition behind this (if such there were) belongs to the subsequent generation.[48] The situation depicted here is unusual in Acts: a house church under the patronage of a woman.[49] Mary was evidently a widow (or divorcée) of means, quite unlike the widows of 6:1 or 9:39, since her home was large enough to have an entrance gate and her household included slaves.[50] Since the only identified slave has a Greek name and her son is known by the

42 Verse 10 shows Luke's use of *πρῶτος* ("first") when there are but two items, a change that was general in Hellenistic Greek (BDF §62). The question is germane to the issue of whether "first volume" (*πρῶτος λόγος*) in 1:1 necessarily contemplates a third. The word *φυλακή* here has a different meaning. "Guard station" gives a good sense. Fitzmyer (488) prefers "sentinel."

43 The D-Text evidently considered the wording of v. 10 too abrupt and added, "They descended the steps." D is the most exuberant of these variants: *et cum exissent descenderunt septem grados et processerunt gradum unum et continuo discessit angelus ab eo* ("After they went out the iron gate, **they descended the seven steps and went on one step**"). The translator must have misunderstood *ῥύμην* ("block," a length of street before an intersection; see Barrett, 1:582). This circumstantial detail, especially the "seven steps" of Bezae, was once given considerable credence. Clark (348) says that John Mark got the detail from Peter and took it to Antioch, where "we" could be found (11:27, D-Text). Bruce (284) says that it "might well be taken for a genuine . . . ," while Hemer (*Book*, 56) rejects it as "gratuitous." The fantasy was effectively killed by Cadbury and Lake (136). See also Metzger, *Textual Commentary*, 347–48. Boismard notes that the seductive "seven" belongs only to D d and attributes it to an error in the archetype of Bezae.

44 Schwartz ("Trial Scene," 123) characterizes Acts 12 as poetic justice. In n. 65 she notes "precise parallels" with the preliminaries of trial in Achilles Tatius *Leuc. Clit.* 7.7–16.

45 Especially Exod 18:4, on which see below. Note also Dan 3:95; 6:23 Theod.

46 One could scarcely imagine that the historical Peter would distinguish himself from "the Jews." "Expectations" (*προσδοκία*) encapsulate the reversal of popular opinion. Luke implies that they have exchanged messianic hopes (*προσδοκοῦντος* [Luke 3:15]) for the reward of seeing the Messiah's followers executed.

47 "Once he had realized" is a sound translation of *συνιδών*. The perceived difficulty (Metzger, *Textual Commentary*, 348; Barrett, 2:583) arises from its similarity to the opening words of v. 11. The narrator might have written, "When Peter realized that the angel had rescued him, he set out for. . . ." Boismard (*Texte*, 202) omits the first two words, following several versions.

48 Cf. Mark 15:21. The unknown Mary is identified by the known John Mark.

49 Lydia (chap. 16) also appears to have had a house-based community, but the text is not explicit.

50 Jerome Murphy-O'Connor depicts a house church of this type in *Saint Paul's Corinth* (GNS 6; Wilmington, Del.: Michael Glazier, 1983) 153–59. For some of the social implications of such communities see Richard Pervo, "Wisdom and Power: Petronius' *Satyricon* and the Social World of Early Christianity," *ATR* 67 (1985) 307–25, and idem, "PANTA KOINA."

Greco-Roman "Mark,"[51] the household has a cosmopolitan cachet. Indeed, it would seem to be a suitable gathering place for the "Hellenists."[52] Why would Peter select this place for refuge? One may conjecture that it was the closest available, but the narrator offers no explanation. It is possible that this community was located in Antioch and was associated with Peter in the gentile mission source.[53] Mark is linked to both Antioch and Barnabas in Acts (12:25; 13:5; 15:39), and (as "Mark," without "John") to Barnabas in Col 4:10, as well as to Peter (1 Pet 5:13; Eusebius *H.E.* 3.39.16).[54] Like many characters in Acts, Mark is introduced without fanfare.[55] It so happened that a body of the faithful had assembled at Mary's to pray for Peter, an activity noted in v. 5b.

■ **13-14** This is all quite interesting, but the narrator seems to have forgotten that Peter is in considerable danger, an escaped convict under the sentence of death who must find somewhere to hide from the authorities, who will soon raise an alarm. The thirty-two words of vv. 11-12 produce almost unbearable suspense. One door yet separates Peter from (relative) freedom. Upon this door he will have to knock[56] and thus expose himself to the attention of any curious and hostile neighbors. No angel will get Peter through this gate. An old debt has come due. Rose ("Rhoda"),[57] the portress,[58] comes to his summons.[59] This flighty servant recognizes him and is so excited that she imprudently leaves the all-too-recognizable apostle out in the dangerous cold and rushes back with the good news. Rather than a realistic character whose presence supports the veracity of the narrative, Rhoda is, as J. Albert Harrill has shown,[60] a figure out of New Comedy, the *servus currens* ("running slave"), who provides irony and comic relief just when things look hopeless.[61] Such slaves are prone to instruct their betters and discover imaginary people at the door.[62]

■ **15-16** Rose dashes in to share the good news, only to find her claims dismissed.[63] It is, her betters assure her,

51 On the name, see Williams ("Personal Names," 105), who says that it is not otherwise known among Palestinian Jews. In the Diaspora, it appears only as the praenomen of Jews with (Roman) citizenship.

52 See Schüssler Fiorenza, *Memory*, 166.

53 The house of Mary would have been an appropriate place to house Saul and Barnabas, who were in Jerusalem at this time, given the house's size, "Hellenistic" character, and the subsequent association of Mark with Barnabas, but the narrator draws no such links.

54 See Clayton N. Jefford, "Mark, John," *ABD* 4:557–58, who summarizes some of the later legendary material; and Clifton C. Black, "John Mark in the Acts of the Apostles," in Thompson, *Literary Studies*, 101–20.

55 Cf. Barnabas: Acts 4:36-37.

56 It may be appropriate to recall the sayings about knocking on doors: Luke 11:9-10 (Q); 12:36 (notable because of the context, on which see below); 13:25; cf. Rev 3:20.

57 Rhoda, which means "rose" in Greek, was a typical slave name; see Williams, "Personal Names," 111. Anthia, the heroine of *Ephesian Tale*, has a slave with this name. In Horace *Odes* 3.19.27, Rhoda is the name of a (servile) mistress.

58 Maids had the responsibility of tending the door. Cf. Chariton *Chaer.* 1.3.4 and Apuleius *Metam.* 1.22. The latter suggests that such servants could be arrogant.

59 𝔓[74] has ὑπαντῆσαι ("met," often of formal receptions). This is suitable to the status of Peter, but neglects her ignorance of who was at the gate.

60 J. Albert Harrill, "The Dramatic Function of the Running Slave Rhoda (Acts 12.13-16): A Piece of Greco-Roman Comedy," *NTS* 46 (2000) 150–57. For an episode involving knocking on a door, see his citation (p. 154) of Plautus *Stichus* 300–314. Cadbury and Lake (138) represent the position that the encounter with the slave is "convincing," while conceding that questions may be raised about the escape story. Verisimilitude is not verity.

61 The running slave appears in two catalogues of stock comedic characters: Terence *Heauton timorumenos* 31–32; 37; *Eunuchus* 36–38. On the comic elements here, see also Kathy Chambers, "'Knock, Knock—Who's There?' Acts 12:6-17 as a Comedy of Errors," in Levine, *Feminist Companion*, 89–97.

62 Rhoda is not, unfortunately, an example of a slave whose faith has made her an equal, as Richter Reimer (*Women*, 242) would have it, but a stereotype of the stupid slave, as Harrill ("Running Slave Rhoda," 157) concludes.

63 For the motif, see Sophocles *El.* 879–883. Electra dismisses the news that Orestes is alive as madness.

Peter's guardian angel.[64] What has looked like a happy ending has become an impending disaster. Ironies are piling up. Those who know about guardian angels will do well to leave room for liberating angels (5:19). If women are prone to hysteria, slave girls are off the scale, but, as an opponent will one day point out—not for the first time, no doubt—belief in the resurrection of Jesus owes much to reports of women.[65] Despite their fervent prayers (vv. 5, 12), the believers seem to lack any hope; they believe that Peter has been killed. Such evident irony—most of the contrasts appear within a dozen verses—is quite atypical of Luke and requires critics to admit that he could, at times, be more complex than is often conceded. Luke seizes upon this episode as an opportunity to chide believers for lack of faith (cf. Luke 7:1-17). These fine points of angelology amount to fiddling while Rome burns, as Peter once more finds himself in dire straits (cf. v. 5), knocking loudly in the increasingly ominous outdoors. He has no alternative to pounding loudly away until someone comes up with a brilliant idea: let's see who is at the door. This plan, in due course, they execute.

Peter had an earlier encounter with a female slave outside a house. In a similar setting, he had denied Jesus (Luke 22:54-61 [62]). The author draws attention to the painful parallel by means of the verb διϊσχυρίζετο ("be persistent"), found only in Luke 22:59 and 12:15.[66] The *Acts of Peter* evidently saw the connection and provided an additional parallel.[67] As that imitation indicates, such literary play is characteristic of developing Christian literature, the narrative equivalent to the search for typologies and correspondences. Rose is "a perfect flower of poetic justice."[68] Peter's dose of poetic retribution adds suspense to the narrative. When Herod's turn to experience poetic justice comes, as it presently will, the consequences will be somewhat graver.

■ **17** If those at Mary's were astonished to learn that it really was Peter (v. 16b), readers will find that the sequence is even more surprising. The narrator does not even report Peter's entry.[69] One might expect his reception and a general celebration (cf. 4:23-31). Instead, he silences them with an oratorical gesture,[70] delivers a report and directs that the message be conveyed to James and others, then leaves for an undisclosed location.[71] Questions are numerous. Among them are: Who is James and why does he have priority? Why are "the believers" (lit. "the sisters and brothers") distinguished from this gathering? And, most pressingly, to what "other place" did Peter go?[72] Another major character (James; cf. John Mark, v. 12) has been introduced *en passant*. The college of apostles has effectively disappeared.[73] When Peter has "gone to another place," James

---

64 Chrysostom (*Hom.* 26) says that everyone has an angel. Bede (59) already referred to *Hermas Man.* 6.2.2–3. See also Gen 48:16; Tobit 5:4-16, 22 [LXX]; Jdt 13:20; Ps.-Philo 59.4; *T. Jac.* 1.10; (Latin) *Apoc. Pl.* 49; and Martin Dibelius, *Der Hirt des Hermas* (HNT; Apostolischen Väter 4; Tübingen: Mohr Siebeck, 1923) 494–95. Greeks (including Socrates) might speak of a personal δαίμων ("divine being," used in many senses), which might be malevolent ("my evil angel"), as in *Ethiopian Story* 1.26.4.

65 The critic was Celsus: Origen *Cels.* 2.55; cf. 2.59. On the subject, see Margaret Y. MacDonald, *Early Christian Women and Pagan Women: The Power of the Hysterical Woman* (Cambridge: Cambridge University Press, 1996).

66 The participle appears in Bezae at Acts 15:2. "Slave girl" appears in Luke and Acts only in these episodes and 16:16-18.

67 *Act. Pet.* 9 (Verc.): Peter arrives at the door of Marcellus, where Simon Magus was residing. "When he came to the door he summoned the keeper and said to him, 'Go and tell Simon, "Peter, on whose account you left Judaea, awaits you at the door!"' The door-keeper answered and said to Peter, 'I do not know, sir if you are Peter'" (trans. Elliott, *Apocryphal New Testament*, 406). This episode also plays with the denial: "I do not know" of Luke 22:57, 59.

68 Richard Pervo, "Rhoda," in Meyers, *Women*, 145.

69 This omission is repaired by the D-Text (Boismard, *Texte*, 204). As Haenchen (385 n. 6) observes, this means that the participle ἐξελθὼν ("going away") in v. 17 refers to leaving the house rather than, for example, Jerusalem.

70 The word κατασείσας is a formal sign that a speech is in the offing. Cf. the comments on 13:16.

71 The ἐξήγαγεν (lit. "lead out," on which see n. 105) rounds off the ἀναγαγεῖν (lit. "lead to") of v. 4.

72 It is arguable that Luke did not wish to say explicitly that Peter fled Jerusalem, as this would conflict with 8:1. Ephrem states that Peter went off to engage in evangelism (416).

73 That the narrator brings the entire cast—apostles,

will lead.[74] Luke learned that James was the leader of the Jerusalem community when the collection was presented.[75] He knew or inferred that Peter was no longer in Jerusalem. This brief reference prepares for that change without offering any explanation of it. Hereafter James will be the leader in Jerusalem.[76]

The expression "going elsewhere," literally "go to a place" (πορεύεσθαι εἰς τόπον), is ominous. It was last used by Peter himself in regard to the fate of Judas (1:25) and is used of Peter's own end (*1 Clem.* 5:4).[77] This has led to the speculation that Acts 12 reports (while covering up) the martyrdom of Peter in Jerusalem.[78] Except to remind everyone of the conversion of Cornelius in 15:7-11, Peter's part in Acts is over. His career effectively ends at 11:18. With these apparently unnecessarily mysterious words, the story closes. Other difficulties can be identified, the most glaring of which are connected to the appearance of the angel (vv. 7-8). The blow in v. 7c has already received an explanation: it corresponds to v. 23, creating a link between the stories of Peter and "Herod." The angelic instructions do not serve this purpose. They raise suspense and are quite humorous. This angel could be the patron of nannies. One is relieved when Peter is not admonished to wash his hands. These are not the only functions of these instructions, and other means of raising suspense and generating humor were available. These details relate to the most patent imagery of the story: Passover, with much that the theme implies.

The action takes place during Passover (v. 3), which provided the temporal setting for Jesus' death.[79] The meaning is clear: Peter will follow the path of his master.[80] The shackles of v. 6 are a synecdoche for captivity, the opposite of freedom, the dominant example of which was Israel's bondage in Egypt.[81] Verse 10 contains a transparent paschal reference: Exod 18:4, "The God of my father was my helper and has rescued me from the hands (καὶ ἐξείλατό με ἐκ χειρός)[82] of Pharaoh." This allusion portrays "Herod" as a wicked butcher of the people of God and offers Peter as an example of one liberated from death during the feast of liberation. The angel's instructions are based on the rubrics for the paschal feast,[83] eaten at night (Acts 12:6), in haste (12:7), with girded loins and shod feet. Peter steps out of prison to the tune of a paschal march. In this context, the door miracle and the passage out of prison evoke the transit

James, presbyters (the Seven excepted)—back onto the stage in chap. 15, where Peter makes a speech and James determines what is to be done, only illustrates the artificiality of that assembly.

74 The implied reader of Acts evidently knows who James is. He is not a character who requires introduction or explanation—with respect to his leadership of the community. When James appears in person (chaps. 15 and 21) the "decree" is in view.

75 The hypothetical collection source would have provided this information.

76 On 12:17, see Painter, *Just James*, 42–43.

77 The image (or euphemism) is widespread. Plutarch (*Cons. Apoll.* 13) speaks of the possibility that death conveys one to another place (μετάγειν εἰς ἕτερον τόπον [*Mor.* 108D]).

78 Priority for this argument belongs to Carl Erbes, "Petrus nicht in Rom, sondern in Jerusalem gestorben," *ZKG* 22 (1901) 1–47, 161–224. Fitzmyer (489–90) lists a number of proposals and references.

79 O. Wesley Allen details a large number of allusions to Exodus in Acts 12: *The Death of Herod: The Narrative and Theological Functions of Retribution in Luke-Acts* (SBLDS 158; Atlanta: Scholars Press, 1997) 98–107. Note also August Strobel, "Passa-Symbolik und Passa-Wunder in Act XII. 3ff.," *NTS* 4 (1957–58) 210–15; Jacques Dupont, "Pierre delivré de prison (ac 12,1-11)," *AsSeign* 1/84 (1967) 14–26 (= *Nouvelles études*, 329–42); Walter Radl, "Befreiung aus dem Gefängnis: Die Darstellung eines biblischen Grundthemas in Apg 12," *BZ* 27 (1983) 81–96; Susan R. Garrett, "Exodus from Bondage: Luke 9:31 and Acts 12:1-24," *CBQ* 52 (1990) 656–89; Wall, "Successors," 628–43; and David T. N. Parry, "Release of the Captives: Reflections on Acts 12," in Christopher M. Tuckett, ed., *Luke's Literary Achievement: Collected Essays* (JSNTS 116; Sheffield: Sheffield Academic Press, 1995) 156–64. Note also Marie-Émile Boismard and A. Lamouille, *Les Actes des deux Apôtres* (3 vols.; EB 13; Paris: Gabalda, 1990) 2:70; and Tannehill, *Narrative Unity*, 2:151–58.

80 The role of "the people" evokes Luke 23:13-23.

81 Cf. Ps. 107:10-14; Isa. 52:2 and 61:1-2. The last is cited in Luke 4:18.

82 Note the contrasting use of helping "hand" in 11:30. On the verb ἐξείλατο ("delivered"), see, in addition to its uses in Exodus 18, the Song of the Three (*Benedicite*) 65 and cf. Dan 3:28; 6:28 Theod.

83 Exod 12:11-12: "This is how you shall eat it: your loins girded (περιεζωσμέναι), your sandals (ὑποδήματα) on your feet, and your staff in your hand;

of the Red Sea. Peter has undergone a sort of personal passover. The summary in v. 17, "how the Lord had led him out of prison," corresponds to a basic creedal formula.[84] Why should this be? One aspect of the answer is that Peter's march followed the steps of Jesus. The association of Jesus' death with Passover is quite early, as 1 Cor 5:7 indicates. Christians were not slow to exploit the fortuitous resemblance of πάσχα, a Greek transliteration of the Aramaic word for Hebrew "Passover," to πάσχω, "suffer," applied to the "passion" of Jesus.[85]

A possible allusion to a corporate "Gethsemane" (Luke does not name the place) may be seen in v. 4.[86] Rather more apparent are motifs in vv. 12-16 that resonate with Luke 24. Rose, another echo of the passion narrative, responds to Peter's return from the "dead" with joy, as did the disciples upon seeing Jesus (Luke 24:41).[87] She, in turn, is greeted with disbelief, another "payback," for the apostles had not believed the message of the women (Luke 24:11).[88] Those who claimed that she had seen a ghost were astonished[89] at the sight of Peter in the flesh, a clear allusion to Luke 24:36-49, where Jesus also appears to an assembled group. "Resurrection" language first appears in the angelic command of v. 7: "Get up" (ἀνάστα), which, although quite realistic here, is used for raising the dead (e.g., Tabitha [9:40]). The return of Peter from the realm of the "dead" is a "resurrection" story, following his passion.[90] Like the vindicated Jesus, the vindicated Peter has a message. The former delivered instruction (Acts 1:1-8); the apostle intimates who will succeed him. These data raise questions of purpose.

In addition to the specific biblical themes of exodus and resurrection enumerated above is the very widespread ancient use of chains and prison as symbols of death and the corresponding view of release from prison as resurrection. An example of the trope of prison = death that is not distant from the time and place of Acts is Chariton *Chaer.* 3.7.4–5: When Callirhoe dreamed that her husband was in chains, she concluded that he was dead. Relevant instances from the biblical world are Isa 24:22; Jonah 2:6; and Ps 107:10-14. Christ's descent into the realm of the departed is described as "preaching to the spirits in prison"[91] (1 Pet 3:19).[92] Conversely, deliverance from prison could be viewed as a kind of resurrection and new birth, e.g., Plutarch *Luc.* 18.1 (ἀναβίωσιν καὶ δευτέραν τινὰ γέννησιν). These symbolic associations were neither esoteric nor obscure.[93]

Why does Acts not relate the actual death of Peter? Although it probably took place in Rome, it was an event unlikely to have eluded the author's notice. The same question is frequently raised, with equal justice, about the death of Paul. The narrator leaves both leading characters dangling. Luke's decision to terminate the

---

and you shall eat it hurriedly. It is the passover of the Lord. For I will pass through the land of Egypt that night, and I will strike down (πατάξω) every firstborn in the land of Egypt. . . ." The verb πατάσσω ("strike," "smite"), used in vv. 7 and 23 also appears in Exod 12:29, where the angel of the Lord strikes down the firstborn of Egypt, and in reference to the preceding plagues. See Heinrich Seesemann, "πατάσσω," *TDNT* 5:939–40, esp. 940.

84 Exod 32:1; Deut 5:6; Lev 23:43, on which see Radl, "Befreiung," 89–91.

85 On the term, see Joachim Jeremias, "πάσχα," *TDNT* 5:896–904.

86 Cf. v. 12. Luke 22:44 is the only other use of the adverb ἐκτενῶς (in the comparative degree), and v. 43 describes the appearance of an angel (cf. Acts 12:7), but the text is doubtful. (Peter, one might note, is once again asleep, albeit positively).

87 On χαρά ("joy"), see also Luke 1:14; 2:10; 8:13; 10:17; 15:7, 10; 24:52; Acts 8:8; 13:52; 15:3. The same expression, ἀπὸ τῆς χαρᾶς, is used of the good news that Leucippe is not, as thought, dead (Achilles Tatius *Leuc. Clit.* 7.15.3).

88 Cf. Bede, 59.

89 Luke 24:41 and Acts 12:16 use different but synonymous verbs for amazement (θαυμάζω, ἐξίστημι).

90 Allen (*Death*, 138–40) provides a copious list of correspondences between the passion/resurrection/ascension of Jesus and the experiences of Peter. See also Radl, "Befreiung," 92–95; and Wall, "Successors," 639–41. Weaver (*Plots*, 172–77) characterizes this scene as an epiphany.

91 614 *pc* Ambst read "Hades," confirming the trope.

92 "Chains or fetters are common symbols of death or any misfortune leading to or similar to death" (H. S. Versnel, *Ter Unus: Isis, Dionysus, Hermes: Three Studies in Henotheism* [Inconsistencies in Greek and Roman Religion 1; Leiden: Brill, 1990] 84). See also Weaver, *Plots*, 113. Prison was often enough the last stop on the path to death, as in Luke 22:31; Acts 22:4.

93 The use of Jonah as a prefiguration of the

career of Peter before fully launching that of Paul is the result of a literary (and theological) plan that lies at a considerable remove from the truth, for the facts overlooked are both unpleasant and important.[94] The narrator wishes to remove Peter from the stage once he has completed his primary task: inauguration of the gentile mission, but he will not send him into the wings without a thrilling and memorable exit.

That memorable exit includes more than a hagiographical interest in glorifying the prince of the apostles. This is a paradigmatic story, a model for Christian life grounded in the power of baptism. The light that shines in darkness (v. 7) is a typical motif of conversion imagery.[95] The metaphor of transferal from darkness (ignorance, sin) to light (knowledge, salvation) has a long history in descriptions of "conversion" to philosophy and of religious transformation. In Christian texts, the image characterizes the transformation wrought by baptism.[96] The best commentary on the word "rise" (*ἀνάστα*) in v. 8 in this context is Eph 5:14: "Sleeper, awake! Rise from the dead (*ἀνάστα ἐκ τῶν νεκρῶν*), and Christ will shine on you," which is evidently a fragment from a baptismal hymn exhibiting many parallels in the history of religions.[97] "Sleep" is a common metaphor for death, spiritual or actual.[98] "Prison" is, as noted, another. Deutero-Isaiah developed the image of breaking open prison doors as a symbol of "conversion," mission, and liberation (Isa 42:6-7; 45:1-2). The narrator paints Peter's deliverance from prison as an "exodus," a passage from death to life.[99] The preferred time for administration of initiation is night.[100]

Just as the Deutero-Pauline tradition described conversion as a passage from darkness to light, so it portrayed baptism as resurrection—and used this as the basis for exhortation (cf., e.g., Col 3:1-3). One point of departure for this was the need for the newly baptized to get dressed. That activity also enjoys a rich symbolic history.[101] Relevant here are the Deutero-Pauline developments of the baptismal formula in Gal 3:27. Whereas Paul wrote of believers having "put on Christ," the writer of Colossians exhorts his hearers: "seeing that you have stripped off the old self with its practices and have clothed yourselves with the new self" (Col 3:9-10).[102] The portrayal of Peter as a newborn babe who must be told by his nurse or mother how to dress himself is yet another initiatory reference. A well-known

resurrection of Jesus goes back to the last decade of first century CE, at the latest. Cf. Matt 12:38-42 (vs. Q: Luke 11:29-32).

94 The most important of these relate to the conflict between Peter and Paul at Antioch and Peter's loss of power at Jerusalem.

95 See Hans Conzelmann, "*φῶς*," *TDNT* 9:310–58, with large bibliography. Note also Spicq, *Lexicon*, 3:470–91. For philosophical and patristic examples, see Graeme W. Clarke, trans. and ed., *The Octavius of Minucius Felix* (New York: Newman Press, 1974) 167–68 n. 8. See also "Darkness," *DBI*, 191–93, and "Light," *DBI*, 509–12.

96 See the literary study by Guy D. Nave Jr., *The Role and Function of Repentance in Luke-Acts* (Academica Biblica 4; Atlanta: Society of Biblical Literature, 2002). Examples of the theme of "darkness to light" include Isa 42:16; Acts 26:19; Eph 1:18; 5:8; 1 Pet 2:9 (cf. Heb 6:4; 10:32); Philo *Virt.* 179; *Jos. As.* 8:10; *1 Clem.* 59:2–3; *Odes Sol.* 14:18–19; Minucius Felix *Oct.* 1:4; Melito *On Passover* 69; Apuleius *Metam.* 11:25; Lucian *Nigr.* 4; *Aesop* 5. Jaroslav Pelikan surveys usage in *The Light of the World: A Basic Image in Early Christian Thought* (New York: Harper, 1962).

97 See Rudolf Schnackenburg, *Ephesians: A Commentary* (trans. H. Heron. Edinburgh: T&T Clark, 1991) 228–29.

98 The corresponding parenesis thus calls for vigilance, "staying awake," as in Luke 21:34-36.

99 David W. Pao argues that the Exodus as portrayed in Deutero-Isaiah is a governing theme of Acts; *Acts and the Isaianic New Exodus* (WUNT 130; Tübingen: Mohr Siebeck, 2000).

100 Cf., e.g., *Apostolic Tradition* 20.9–10. Night was also the time at which Lucius received initiation into the mysteries of Isis: Apuleius *Metam.* 11.23. Initiation at Eleusis took place at night: Walter Burkert, *Greek Religion* (trans. J. Raffan; Cambridge, Mass.: Harvard University Press, 1985) 285–90.

101 An example is the "Hymn of the Pearl," *Act. Thom.* 111–12, lines 72–78 (associated with the symbol of awakening). For the symbol of clothing in mystery religions, see Kerenyi, *Romanliteratur*, 144.

102 Note in addition Rom 12:13-14. On the image in Colossians, see Eduard Schweizer, *The Letter to the Colossians* (trans. A. Chester; Minneapolis: Augsburg, 1982) 195–96.

evocation of this imagery of the neophyte is 1 Pet 2:1-2: "Rid yourselves,[103] therefore, of all malice, and all guile, insincerity, envy, and all slander. Like newborn infants, long for the pure, spiritual milk, so that by it you may grow into salvation." The use of paschal imagery in 1 Peter is an appropriate example of the theme of this unit, which is the life open to those who have been regenerated (in baptism [1:3, 23]). Metaphorical and literal uses of the expression "dressed for action" are common, with or without paschal symbolism.[104] Inspired by the prison-release imagery of such passages as Isa 42:6-7 and 45:1-2,[105] second-century writers developed complex baptismal typologies that in turn influenced ceremonies. The same material was applied to the doctrine of Christ's "Harrowing of Hell."[106]

The indicative arising from baptismal empowerment is encapsulated in two words: "follow me" (v. 8). Logical enough in the context, they also constitute the invitation to discipleship (Luke 5:27; 9:59; 18:22). Like every other believer, Peter has been delivered from the power of darkness to find himself not on easy street but in the danger-filled nocturnal streets of urban life. This is to say that Peter's experience is intended as a paradigm of Christian existence. Through these series of allusions to baptism as resurrection—deliverance from death and the power of Satan—Luke makes the story of Peter applicable to all believers. The concept of a "Christian Passover" and its association with initiation does not suit the milieu of c. 65–85 CE. This complex is at home in the baptismal thought and scriptural typology of the early second century.[107] The text is not only about the experience of individuals. It is also ecclesiological, signaling the formation of a new religious body. Verse 1 uses the term "church" (ἐκκλησία), while "people" (λαός) in v. 11 is qualified with "the Jews."[108] Just as the exodus formed the Israelites, so the "exodus" of Jesus (Luke 9:31) forms the true people of God.[109]

Luke may not have wholly embraced the theology

---

103 This term, ἀποθέμενοι, is similar in meaning to "put/take off" in Colossians and Ephesians.

104 Examples include Luke 12:35 (which cites Exod 12:11, an allusion noted by Bede, 58); Eph 6:14; Polycarp *Phil.* 2:1; cf. John 21:18. Acts 12 and 1 Peter are similar in that exhortations to be sober, alert, and ready for action have an eschatological orientation, as in Luke 12:42-46, and there have been proposals to link 1 Pet 1:13 to Luke 12:35-48 (esp. vv. 42-46) intertextually. Paul Achtemeier (*1 Peter* [Hermeneia; Minneapolis: Fortress Press, 1996] 118) is skeptical about these, and not without reason. For a discussion of the take off/put on imagery, see Edward Gordon Selwyn, *The First Epistle of St Peter* (2nd ed.; London: Macmillan, 1947) 393–400.

105 Isa 42:6-7: "I am the LORD . . . I have given you as a covenant to the people, a *light* to the nations, 7 to open the eyes that are blind, to *bring out the prisoners from the dungeon, from the prison those who sit in darkness*" (ἐξαγαγεῖν ἐκ δεσμῶν δεδεμένους καὶ ἐξ οἴκου φυλακῆς καθημένους ἐν σκότει). The words ἐξάγειν ἐκ φυλακῆς recur in Acts 12:17. Isa 45:1-2: "Thus says the LORD to his anointed (χριστῷ), to Cyrus, whose right hand I have grasped to subdue nations before him and strip kings of their robes, *to open doors* before him—and the gates shall not be closed: 2 I will go before you and level the mountains, I will break in pieces the *doors* of bronze and cut through the *bars of iron*."

106 Note the application of Isa 45:2-3 to baptism in *Barn.* 11:4 and the citation of Isa 42:6-7; 49:6-7; 61:1-2 in 11:7-8 and the exegesis of "milk and honey" in 6:7-19. These images are important in the *Odes of Solomon*, for example, 24; 17:10-12; and 42:10-20. The relation of these texts to baptism has generated considerable discussion. For the various views, see the commentary of James H. Charlesworth, *The Odes of Solomon* (SBLTT; Missoula, Mont.: Scholars Press, 1977). On the development of the doctrine of the "descent into hell" and its place in the creed, see John N. D. Kelly, *Early Christian Creeds* (3rd ed.; London: Longman, 1972) 378–83.

107 The Quartodecimans celebrated "Easter" on 14 Nissan. Cf. *Epistula Apostolorum* 15, which places Peter (anonymously) in prison while the community observes the night-long paschal vigil. On the theology of baptism in the second century, see André Benoit, *Le baptême chrétien au second siècle* (Paris: Presses universitaires de France, 1953).

108 Note 12:4, where λαός does not include followers of Jesus. Contrast 2:47; 3:9, 11, etc., through 10:2 (and note 10:42).

109 This is well presented by Radl, "Befreiung." Garrett (*Demise*, 157) views Luke 9:31 as the nexus of the histories of Jesus and Israel.

of these traditions, but he was evidently familiar with developments like those found in *Barnabas* and, quite possibly, to have expected his implied readers to know them also, for they, like him, probably learned such expositions in the homiletic and catechetical activity of the church. Objections can be raised against interpretations of this nature. The advantage of this exposition is that it is supported by a wealth of verbal and thematic data, builds on explicit (Passover) imagery in the text,[110] is based on contemporary theological methods and themes, and, perhaps most important, accounts for some of the oddities of what is, in fact, a highly unusual narrative.

■ **18-19** The next section evens up two scores. In v. 18, the narrator returns to the prison. Daylight brings some understandable confusion.[111] After conducting his own investigation, Herod has the responsible guards executed—someone has to die[112]—and leaves Judea for Caesarea.[113] Readers will note the irony that Peter had brought new life to a soldier in Caesarea. Herod is, as the next verses will continue to reveal, the mirror opposite of his enemy. The tyrant picks another quarrel, with the citizens of the biblically notorious Sidon and Tyre.[114] Mindful of Herod's ability to starve them out, they sue for peace. To enhance their case, they make application to Blastus, the royal chamberlain.[115] Ancient readers would probably assume that a little money has changed hands.[116] Benefactors deserve praise—even when their benefactions amount to no more than not turning up the heat—so a convocation is held, at which Herod dons his regal vestments[117] and offers a few suitable words. The crowd responds in accord with the conventions of the ruler cult: beneficent monarchs are divine.[118] God takes exception and arranges for a death through an infestation of worms, no less pleasant than revelatory, for that is just how tyrants should die.

Excursus: The Source of 12:20-23

Luke may have drawn this story from Josephus's accounts of the death of Agrippa I (*Ant.* 19.343–50).[119] The stories follow a similar outline,[120] and the motive of self-deification as the "cause" of death is common to both, although Acts points the reader toward the conclusion that Herod dies as punishment for his persecution of the church, a theme that has also yielded rich literary fruit.[121] The Israelite tradition contains a number of examples of

110 With this one may contrast C. S. C. Williams's proposal (*The Acts of the Apostles* [HNTC; New York: Harper & Bros., 1957] 152–53) that Acts 10–12 is based on the story of Jonah. This typology overlooks many contrasts between the two and depends on vague similarities. His point of departure is the reluctance of Peter to visit Cornelius and that of Jonah to go to Ninevah. The typological horse drags the cart, for Acts says nothing about reluctance to visit Cornelius. The name "Simon bar-Jonah" is an import from Matt 16:17.

111 The reader will conclude that the guards were prevented from perceiving Peter's exit.

112 An early example of carping criticism can be seen in Porphyry's statement that Peter caused the death of the guards. See R. Joseph Hoffmann, *Porphyry's Against the Christians: The Literary Remains* (Amherst, N.Y.: Prometheus, 1994) 55. Punishment of guards is a standard feature of prison-rescue miracles (Kratz, *Rettungswunder,* 445). Chariton *Chaer.* 3.4.18 suggests that such punishments were unremarkable.

113 The narrator appears to equate "Judea" with "Jerusalem," a kind of synecdoche.

114 Mark R. Strom ("An Old Testament Background to Acts 12.20-23," *NTS* 32 [1986] 289–92) seeks to show that Acts 12:20-23 is dependent on Ezekiel 28. This is far less probable than other hypotheses, but does show the associations evoked by the names. For their reputation in the biblical tradition, see Luke 10:13-14. Note also Susan R. Garrett, "Exodus from Bondage: Luke 9:31 and Acts 12:1-4," *CBQ* 52 (1990) 656–89, esp. 675–77; and Allen, *Death,* 97–98.

115 On this office, see *OGIS* 256, 5, and *SIG* no. 7.

116 Rackham, 181: "In plain words, they had bribed him."

117 On the clothing of monarchs, see Weaver, *Plots,* 179 n. 85

118 On the links between 12:20-23 and the ruler cult, see Kauppi, *Foreign,* 42–60.

119 The evidence for this is examined in Pervo, *Dating,* 170–78. Some details may have been gleaned from the accounts of the death of Herod the Great (Josephus *Ant.* 17.146–99; cf. *Bell.* 1.647–56). Chrysostom (*Hom.* 27) introduces Josephus's account into his discussion.

120 See Allen, *Death,* 7; and Klauck, *Magic,* 41–43.

121 Wilhelm Nestle ("Legenden vom Tod der Gotteverächter," *ARW* 33 [1936] 246–69) collected a large inventory of examples, with a synoptic chart

the dire fate of rulers who deify themselves.[122] This generated the hypothesis of a legend from which, in some form, both Josephus and Luke drew. The difficulty in both cases is v. 20, for Josephus says nothing about this conflict, on the one hand, while, on the other, it is difficult to attribute such apparently historical data to a "naïve" legend that Luke might have found lying about somewhere.[123] If Luke took vv. 20-23 from a written source, it would have been a hypothetical work of history.[124] The best candidate for that position is the romantic biography of Agrippa proposed by Daniel Schwartz.[125] Since Josephus is the source from which this "Life of Agrippa" is extracted, since reasons for thinking that it contained the conflict with Tyre and Sidon are lacking, and since evidence of Luke's use of Josephus elsewhere exists,[126] this hypothesis is unnecessary.

One would therefore have to posit yet a third historical source that associated the climactic scene with the conflict between Agrippa and the cities.[127] In the face of such desperation, it is reasonable to explore the possibility that Luke concocted the argument. Undesirable as this may seem, it cannot be denied that the only clear "fact" in v. 20 relates to food supply, a theme that provides a nice contrast to the Christian approach to such matters.[128] Believers raise funds for the needy; polytheists use their resources to suborn officials. Luke could have learned from Josephus, if not elsewhere (including general knowledge), that Tyre and Sidon, especially the former, depended on the adjacent regions for food.[129] Josephus *Ant.* 18.153 speaks of a boundary conflict between Sidon and Damascus that involved the promise of a large bribe by the Damascenes to Agrippa in turn for his support. Luke is willing to invent characters and events, as the episode of Demetrius and the silversmiths, in which the evidence for Lucan creation is quite strong, attests (19:23-40). In favor of dependence on Josephus are availability (which, to be sure, depends in good part on the hypothesis that Luke utilized Josephus elsewhere), the theme of deification, which is somewhat extraneous to the implicit thesis of Acts, the ease with which details in Josephus's account fill gaps in the compressed narrative of Acts,[130] and the crucial place of a "messenger" (ἄγγελος) in both stories (*Ant.* 19.346||Acts 12:23), although they have different roles. In Josephus, the messenger is part of a literary scheme that frames the story of Agrippa and is not likely to have appeared in an independent legend.[131] In sum, the hypothesis that Luke used Josephus is at least as strong as the alternatives.

■ **20-23** This paragraph is not particularly coherent. The basis of the king's anger is not provided. Where was the assembly held? Who were "the people" of v. 22, the residents of Caesarea or those of Tyre and Sidon?[132]

of motifs. His subject was Lactantius's tract *De Morte Persecutorum*.

122 For examples see Talbert, 122–23.

123 This is the solution preferred by Dibelius (*Studies*, 19–20), who finds Luke's account more primitive than that of Josephus.

124 Witherington (389) refers vv. 20-23 to Luke's Herodian source. On p. 169 he states that Joanna could have provided "stories about the Herods." According to Luke 8:3, Joanna was the wife of one of Herod's [Antipas?] managers. In 24:10 she is among the resurrection witnesses. Witherington evidently assumes that she remained in the Jesus community and was available to provide material to the author of Acts a few decades later (while Luke was in Caesarea). One difficulty is that Joanna had left the court to follow Jesus before 30 and would have been unlikely to possess later inside information about the Herodian family.

125 Schwartz, *Agrippa I*, 31–37. This would be comparable to the hypothetical *Tobiad Romance* and *Royal Family of Adiabene* analyzed by Wills, *Jewish Novel*, 185–93, esp. 206–11, a rags-to-riches-to-ruin story with a tragic or melodramatic orientation.

126 See Pervo, *Datiing*, 149–99.

127 Cf. Knox, 38 n. 2: "A good historian might of course have recorded the death of Herod as a punishment for ὕβρις and Luke might have carried over the irrelevant detail, but it is hard to conjecture who this historian can have been."

128 Cf. Allen (*Death*, 72), who notes that the only function of Blastus was to show the reader that Tyre and Sidon are amenable to offering bribes.

129 See Gerd Theissen, *The Gospels in Context: Social and Political History in the Synoptic Tradition* (trans. Linda M. Maloney; Minneapolis: Fortress Press, 1991) 73–74.

130 See Klauck, *Magic*, 42. (Klauck does not think that Acts used Josephus here.)

131 See *Ant.* 18.195, 200. The alternative explanation, that Josephus transformed an angel of the Lord into a portent—his messenger is an owl—and then introduced it into the beginning of the story, is most improbable.

132 On this question, see Allen, *Death*, 71. He is probably correct in assuming that the δῆμος is a collective character representing the populace of the two cities. The rational approach (e.g., Bruce, 288) rejects this interpretation.

What was the purpose of the meeting? Did it seek to resolve the issue and achieve the desired reconciliation, or was it a celebration of that accomplishment?[133] How much time elapsed between Herod's buffet by an angel and his death? A number of these problems were noted and addressed by the D-Text.[134] The narrator's interests are to characterize Herod and illuminate the contrast between his fate and that of Peter. Verse 20 makes a further contribution to the portrait of Herod the tyrant. If his actions toward Peter bespeak calculation, his relations with Tyre and Sidon exhibit unbridled rage.[135] The "peace" to be achieved will amount to little more than submission to the royal wrath, submission that must be purchased. Both events took place at a particular time (vv. 6, 21). Both protagonists got dressed (vv. 8, 21). Herod's interest in popular approval inspired his planned execution of Peter (v. 3). His failure to reject popular acclaim led to his downfall (v. 23).[136] Rose recognized the "voice" of Peter (φωνή [v. 14]); an adoring populace recognize the divine voice (φωνή) of Herod in v. 22. Both delivered speeches (vv. 17, 21).[137] The decisive contrast is the angelic buffet (πατάσσω) that propels Peter to life and Herod to death (vv. 7, 23).[138] The confusing "immediately" (παράχρημα) in v. 23 marks the event as a miraculous punishment,[139] while the mode of death verifies that he was a tyrant.[140] The lives of Peter and Herod unfold in inverse order. Peter moves from death to life, helplessness to freedom; Herod from apparently absolute mastery over life and death to a painful and ignominious end.[141]

■ **23** According to v. 23, the punishment was for failure to honor God, whose angel[142] acted before Herod had opportunity to reject this adulation (as had Peter in 10:25-26) or (as in Josephus *Ant.* 19.246) to tolerate it. This may well be another example of excessive compression, but it permits the conclusion that the cultivation of divine honors is but one more proof that Herod is a ϑεομάχος, an enemy of God. With this vague and

133 The atmosphere of the scene is well illuminated by *Ethiopian Story* 7.3: "Arsake gave orders for a pavilion to be erected beneath a canopy of purple embroidered with gold. Then, exquisitely arrayed, she took her seat on an elevated throne, encircled by her bodyguard in their gilded armor. Holding aloft a herald's staff to signify that she wished to negotiate peace" (trans. J. R. Morgan, in Reardon, *Novels,* 489).

134 See the notes to the translation.

135 The verb ϑυμομαχεῖν (v. 20) is usually associated with physical violence, a notion enhanced here by the noun εἰρήνη ("peace"). It is unlikely that Acts implies actual war, but it does seek to show violent rage, an emotion quite disapproved by the philosophical tradition, most particularly for rulers. Seneca wrote a three-volume treatise on the subject, which he called "the most morbid and uncontrolled emotion of all" (*affectum . . . maxime ex omnibus taetrum ac rabidum*) (*De Ira* 1.1.1).

136 Contrast Peter's rejection of prostration at 10:25.

137 On δημηγορέω ("deliver a public address"), see *4 Macc.* 5:15.

138 Herodotus's story (*Hist.* 3.27–64) of the fate of Cambyses is an illuminating parallel. He strikes the bull representing Apis in the thigh, a wound that became mortal through neglect. Cambyses met his fate when he accidentally injured himself while mounting his horse. His sword entered his thigh, in the very spot where he had injured the bull (64).

139 The adverb enhances miracles in Luke 1:64; 4:39; 5:25; 8:44, 47, 55; 13:11; 18:43; Acts 3:7; 13:11. Most notably, it is found in Acts 5:10 (death of Sapphira), associated with the only other NT use of ἐξέψυξεν ("expired").

140 Death by worms: note 2 Macc 9:5; cf. Jdt 16:17. Wikenhauser, *Geschichtswert,* 398–401, collected a large number of examples. See also Hans-Josef Klauck's essay, "Das Ende des Gottlosen: Variationen eines Themas," in *Judas, ein Jünger des Herrn* (QD 111; Freiburg: Herder, 1987) 116–21. Allen (*Death,* 14–21) has a good survey and analysis. As his work implies, it is undesirable to argue from ancient descriptions of symptoms to classification of a disease in modern medical terms. Ancients were also interested in symptoms, but might use them for different purposes. Infestation by worms more or less "proved" that the victim was a wicked tyrant.

141 Cf. 2 Macc 9:10 (Antiochus IV): "Because of his intolerable stench no one was able to carry the man who a little while before had thought that he could touch the stars of heaven." In v. 12 the king concludes that he had overreached the limits imposed on mortals.

142 On such avenging angels see, e.g., Sus 55, 59.

general language, the narrator permits the interpretation that Herod perished for his persecuting activity.

Acts 12:1-23 is a literary triumph. In this, the final "Peter/Jesus parallel" in Acts, the narrator concludes the story of Peter with a sort of passion and resurrection that correspond to the fate of the founder. Peter did follow Jesus, to the brink of the grave and to new life. Luke knew, from Galatians, that Peter had been to Antioch, and he very probably had heard that the apostle had gone to Rome and actually died there, but he chose to conclude the story of Peter on this climactic, and symbolic, note. Peter must "go to his place," so that Paul may rise to prominence.

12

12:24-25 A Summary

24/	**Proclamation of God's[a] message expanded and abounded. 25 Barnabas and Saul returned to Antioch from Jerusalem after completing their mission of relief. They took with them John surnamed Mark.[b]**	a	B and Vg read "Lord" rather than "God," possibly under the influence of v. 23. See Metzger, *Textual Commentary*, 350, although Barrett (1:594) is less certain. On the translation of λόγος ("word"), see the note on 6:7. On the figure, see on 19:20.
		b	Ephrem's commentary (Ropes, *Text*, 416) includes "Lucius of Cyrene" with "Mark." This reflects the same (D-Text?) tradition as the "we" in 11:28. This Lucius was presumed to be the author of Acts, who had been in Jerusalem until this point, at which juncture he began to associate with Paul.

Comment

■ **24-25** The brief summary of v. 24[1] affirms that persecution cannot slow the progress of the mission.[2] Verse 25 does not suggest that the demise of Herod made it possible for believers to appear in public. Its structural function is to mark the unit begun at 11:19. Repetition of διακονία ("mission of relief") from 11:29 also places a bracket around the intervening tales. More importantly, it stresses the contrast between the beneficent expedition from Antioch and the manufactured benefaction of the late Herod.

Without context, one would render the text of v. 25a in N-A[27] (*Βαρναβᾶς δὲ καὶ Σαῦλος ὑπέστρεψαν εἰς Ἰερουσαλὴμ πληρώσαντες τὴν διακονίαν*) as: "After finishing their charitable mission Barnabas and Saul returned to Jerusalem." The difficulty is that the pair was *in* Jerusalem (11:30) and returned to *Antioch*, where the next verse (13:1) locates them. The preposition εἰς does not go unchallenged.[3] Since the D-Text, which provides support for "*from* Jerusalem," includes witnesses that gloss "Saul" with "who was surnamed Paul," "from" may suffer from the company it keeps.[4] Metzger argues that the evidence for "from" is a house divided against itself, as there are two prepositions (ἀπό and ἐκ). He goes on to state that "from" "is also discredited by the fact that it is not the common usage of Acts to specify the place *whence* return is made," noting 1:12 as the single exception.[5]

One may look at various statistics in other ways. Acts uses ἐκ with "Jerusalem" twice; ἀπό three times.[6] Luke and Acts exhibit twenty-seven uses of εἰς with Jerusalem. In twenty-one of these it is "proper," that is, "to Jerusalem," while six mean "at" (= ἐν). Luke and Acts use ὑποστρέφω thirty-three times. Sixteen of these are intransitive (e.g., "Jesus returned"). The other seventeen employ εἰς, seven times with "Jerusalem" as its object. The verb never appears with εἰς in the sense of "in," "at," "to," or "for." This case would be unique. Construing εἰς as "at" does violence to the

1 On this summary, see Weaver, *Plots*, 211–13.

2 Note that the verbs "expanded and abounded" in v. 24 describe the growth of the people in Egypt: Acts 7:17 (Exod 1:7).

3 𝔭[74] A 33. 945. 1739 *al* read ἐξ, while D E Y 36. 323. 453. 614. 1175 *al* offer ἀπό. Furthermore, after "Jerusalem" E 104. 323. 945. 1175. 1739 *pc* p w sy[p] sa add εἰς Ἀντιόχειαν or the equivalent. The text is supported by ℵ B 𝔐 sa[ms] sy[hmg].

4 See Boismard, *Texte*, 207. Some D-Texts read "returned" in the singular, apparently focusing on Paul and presuming the gloss.

5 Boismard, *Textual Commentary*, 351. For other discussions, note Cadbury and Lake, 141; Fitzmyer, 493, with his references; Witherington, 374–75; and Barrett, 1:595–96. Note 13:13, which also includes a participle and ὑποστρέφω + εἰς, with no doubt about the meaning.

6 Both uses of ἐκ are in speeches of Paul: 22:18 ἐξ Ἰερουσαλήμ (to Jews in Jerusalem) and 28:17 ἐξ Ἱεροσολύμων (to Jews in Rome). The preposition ἀπό appears in 1:4 and 25:7 (declined) and 8:26 (undeclined—to my knowledge no one has been able to provide a convincing explanation for the spelling variants).

word order, and sense expects that, after the passage of around twenty-five verses, the destination be given. The solution adopted here is to emend the text to read εἰς Ἀντιόχειαν ἀπὸ Ἰερουσαλήμ.[7] John Mark appears here as a thread linking Peter, Barnabas, and Paul.

7 If the error is to be attributed to the author, the likely cause is due to Gal 2:1: *Ἔπειτα διὰ δεκατεσσάρων ἐτῶν πάλιν ἀνέβην εἰς Ἰεροσόλυμα μετὰ Βαρναβᾶ συμπαραλαβὼν καὶ Τίτον*. In that case the commentator should read εἰς and label it an error. Acts is quite possibly dependent on Galatians here (Pervo, *Dating*, 79–86). Knox (37 n. 1) noted this connection and attributed the change of preposition to "a stupid copyist who was trying to harmonise Acts with Galatians."

13

13:1-12 Paul and Barnabas in Cyprus

1/ The community at Antioch
included[a] prophetic teachers:[b]
Barnabas, Simeon, known as
"Blacky (Niger)," Lucius from
Cyrene, Manachen, a child-
hood companion of Herod the
Tetrarch, and Saul. 2/ Once,
while they were engaged in
worshiping the Lord and fast-
ing, the [Holy][c] Spirit said: "Be
so good as to reserve Barnabas
and Saul for the task to which I
have called them." 3/ Therefore,
after fasting and prayer, they
laid hands upon the two and
sent them on their way.

4/ Thus dispatched by the Holy
Spirit,[d] the two[e] proceeded[f] to
Seleucia, where they caught a
ship to Cyprus. 5/ When they
arrived in Salamis they began
to proclaim the message of
God[g] in the Jewish synagogues.
John was with them as an
assistant.[h] 6/ After crossing[i]
the entire island they reached
Paphos, where they came upon
one Bar-Jesus,[j] a Jewish practi-
tioner of sorcery and prophetic
quackery.[k] 7/ He was in the reti-
nue of the proconsul, Sergius
Paulus, a cultured man. Sergius
sent for Barnabas and Saul,
whom he asked to expound
to him the message of God.
8/ Elymas the magician (for
that is what his name means)
argued with them in an effort to
deflect the proconsul from the
faith. 9/ In response Saul, also
known as Paul, was motivated
by the Holy Spirit to fix his eye
upon Elymas and 10/ say: "You
satanic creature, master of
every foul trick and unscrupu-
lous technique,[l] you enemy of
anything that is upright, must
you always attempt to turn the
straight ways of the Lord[m] into
crooked paths? 11/ Look, you
have got the Lord's attention.
For some time you will be blind,
deprived of the light of day." At
that moment mist and gloom
overtook him. Elymas began
to grope about in search of a
guide. 12/ When the proconsul
saw what had happened, he
was utterly astonished at the
teaching about the Lord and
became a believer.

a Two variants suggest that these names were selected from a larger number. E Ψ 𝔪 sy^{h} read τινες ("some," which also helps smooth the syntax). The D-Text reads, after "teachers," "among whom. . . ." See Metzger, *Textual Commentary*, 353.

b *Or:* "prophets who also taught," or, less likely, "prophets and teachers" construed as two different groups.

c Omission of "holy" in D-Text witnesses (Boismard, *Texte*, 208) has some claim to originality.

d D-Text versions (Boismard, *Texte*, 209) read "by the saints." This avoids a repetition of "Holy Spirit" and conforms to the usual notion of a "bon voyage" escort (21:4-5).

e Variants to αὐτοί ("they") include "these persons" (οὗτοι) and the simple article. The last is taken as the D-Text by Boismard (*Texte*, 209).

f The D-Texts D (gig; Lcf) read a participle: κατα-βάντες δέ. This is rejected by Boismard (*Texte*, 209) as incoherent. It may conceal a greater D-Text variation, somewhat conflated by Bezae.

g The D-Text (Boismard, *Texte*, 210) reads "of the Lord." Metzger (*Textual Commentary*, 353–54) says that this is dogmatic, "Christianization of the tradition." He provides statistics of the usage.

h D 614. 845. 1175. 1739 *et al.* lat sy^{h} read: ὑπηρετοῦντα αὐτοῖς ("providing assistance to them"). E vg read εἰς διακονίαν ("for service"). Metzger (*Textual Commentary*, 353) rejects the view of Weiss that these imply subordination, but Barrett (1:612), with ref to 2 Tim 4:11, says that the prepositional phrase strengthens this interpretation. Metzger is incorrect in invoking Luke 1:2. Also on meaning of ὑπηρέτης, see Black ("John Mark," 105–7), who concludes that the term is vague.

i The D-Text (Boismard, *Texte*, 210) reads καὶ περι-ελθόντων αὐτῶν. This "improper" genitive absolute could be rendered "going around." Haenchen (397 n. 2) says that this means that they sailed around the island and thus explains the absence of other stops.

j The witnesses include several variations of this name. Boismard (*Texte*, 210) prefers "Bar-Iesoua" (Βαριησοῦα) for the D-Text. Most of these are probably attempts to avoid use of the name "Jesus," which was not uncommon at the time and thereafter for Jews. See Moshe Schwabe and Baruch Lifshitz, *Beth She'arim*, vol. 2: *The Greek Inscriptions* (New Brunswick, N.J.: Rutgers University Press, 1974) 32.

k *Or:* "a magician and Jewish false prophet."

l The D-Text (Boismard, *Texte*, 212) omits "every" before ῥᾳδιουργίας ("unscrupulous technique").

m The D-Text (Boismard, *Texte*, 212) reads "ways . . . that are (οὔσας) straight." This is apparently pedantic.

Analysis

One plan of the structure of Acts places the major division after chap. 12.[1] Content supports this orientation: Jerusalem and Peter are central in chaps. 1–12; Paul and the Diaspora in chaps. 13–28. Although chaps. 13–14 form a distinct unit (below), chaps. 13–19 relate the Pauline mission, and chap. 19 has echoes of chaps. 13–14.[2] One may also identify similarities between 8:4—11:18 and 13:1—15:35. Both involve missionary enterprises that include gentile converts and result in a decision in Jerusalem. Just as Peter's conversion of Cornelius required ratification in Jerusalem in the face of challenges, so must that of Paul and Barnabas. The question for the reader is why this problem, evidently resolved in 11:1-18, must be taken up again. The formal difference is that Acts 15 addresses a different issue: how mixed communities including believers of both Jewish and gentile background are to manage their common life and worship.[3] The narrator never says this; it is an inference from the text. One must ask why Acts is not explicit about this important question. The immediate result of this second resolution of the question, a resolution that is not simply theoretical but includes concrete regulations, is the Aegean mission, which is, in several senses, the center of Acts. Luke's proclivity for overlapping units is more than artistic: it permits him to indicate how things changed while remaining the same.

The popular notion that Acts describes three missionary journeys of Paul derives from the nineteenth-century Protestant overseas missions. Acts 13:4—14:28 is, nonetheless, a "missionary journey," a rounded unit based on a new axis: Antioch.[4] The account of this journey raises two questions: (1) is it historical—did Paul at this time, prior to the meeting in Jerusalem described in Galatians 2, engage in evangelism in Cyprus and southern Asia Minor, and (2) what sources did the author utilize?[5] As presented, the account does not read like a historical report of a particular missionary foray.[6]

The major reasons for this view are: the difficulty of the itinerary presented, the scarcity of concrete information (including geographical data), and Paul's statements in Galatians 1. Gal 1:13-21 reports that, after his "conversion," Paul returned to Damascus, visited Jerusalem three years later, and then "went into the regions of Syria and Cilicia" (v. 21). The phrase may be seen as a rhetorical abbreviation of broader travels,[7] but since Paul's apparent goal was to put as much distance as possible between himself and Jerusalem during this period, it is legitimate to ask why, for rhetorical purposes, he did not include other provinces. The counterargument that Paul did not wish to emphasize the magnitude of his work as an agent of Antioch associated with Barnabas is not without force. In short, Acts 13–14 reports activity that Paul did not choose to mention and that can be inserted into his biography only by inference.[8]

In contrast to the narrative of chaps. 16–19, these chapters are noteworthy for the absence of specifics.[9] The only named convert is the Roman governor of Cyprus, Sergius Paulus. There is a single touch of local color: the temple of Zeus Before the City in Lystra, the existence of which is quite possible but has not been

1 See pp. 20–21.

2 See pp. 325–26.

3 Acts 11:2 anticipates this: the charge against Peter is not that he baptized gentiles but that he associated with them.

4 See Marshall, 214. Note the inclusio of 13:3; 14:23. A literary study of this material is Szu-Chuan Lin, *Wundertaten und Mission: Dramatische Episoden in Apg. 13-14* (Europäische Hochschulschriften, Reihe 23, Theologie 163; Berlin: Lang, 1998).

5 Weiser (2:308) adds chronology, which raises the historical question.

6 Ciliers Breytenbach offers a concise summary of research on the question (*Paulus & Barnabas in der Provinz Galatien: Studien zu Apostelgeschichte 13f; 16,16; 18,23 & den Adressaten des Galaterbriefes* [AGJU 38; Leiden: Brill, 1996] 16–20).

7 So, e.g., Fitzmyer, 136–38.

8 An alternative that respects Gal 1:21 locates these missionary activities *after* the agreement made in Jerusalem (Gal 2:1-10). For a concise summary and evaluation of the arguments, see Haenchen, 400–401, 438–39. The data do not permit a secure conclusion. On the grounds of 15:23, one could propose that Luke envisioned that the mission of chaps. 13–14 took place in Cilicia.

9 This is one reason for rejecting the fruitful hypothesis of Dibelius (*Studies*, 197–201 and index, 228, under "The Itinerary") that chaps. 13–21 were based upon an itinerary of mission stations.

verified. The narrator does not note that both Antioch and Lystra were Roman colonies, for example, and no local, provincial, or imperial officials appear. Insofar as one can tell, the cities of southern Asia Minor are governed by mobs. Geography is elusive, at best. In 14:6 the missionaries fled from Iconium to "Lystra and Derbe." Derbe is almost twice the distance from Lystra that Lystra is from Iconium. The route taken by Barnabas and Paul is difficult to comprehend.

The normal way for those who set out from Syria to visit Derbe, etc., would be overland from Antioch, as the terrain presented a formidable barrier to penetration from the south.[10] Pisidian Antioch would be an unlikely first stop after Perge,[11] as would Iconium following Antioch. Iconium, Lystra, and Derbe form a rough isosceles triangle, with Derbe as the point. All lay within Lycaonia. From Derbe, the pair reverses course back to the point of origin (omitting Cyprus). If the geography is difficult, the narrative is even more challenging, especially their adventures on Cyprus.

After preaching in synagogues across the island, the missionaries "found" a magician in Paphos. The nature of this contact and its location went unrecorded. No success is reported until they encounter the governor, who had evidently retained the magician as his spiritual director. Paul, as he is now known, cursed the magus and, by the way, converted the governor. Rather than exploit the obvious advantages of such an adherent, they turned their backs upon Cyprus and sailed off to penetrate Lycaonia from the south. Thus the beginning. The closure is scarcely less odd. After having been driven successively out of Antioch, Iconium, and Lystra, Paul and Barnabas went back over that circuit in 14:21-23, visiting each community in turn without the slightest indication of any opposition. The narrator has a reservoir of persecution that can be turned on and off at will. The stereotyped nature of these episodes is noteworthy, even for Acts. The conclusion that this journey is an authorial construction is difficult to avoid.[12] This does not mean that Luke concocted all of the material. Traditions are at least arguable.

2 Tim 3:11 ("my persecutions, and my suffering the things that happened to me in Antioch, Iconium, and Lystra. What persecutions I endured! Yet the Lord rescued me from all of them.") and *Act. Paul* 3/4 (Paul and Thecla) reflect tradition. The Pastorals may be

10 See Pervo, *Profit*, 55, with his notes; Roloff, 192; and Kirsopp Lake, "Paul's Route in Asia Minor," in Lake and Cadbury, *Additional Notes*, 224–40. William Ramsay (*The Church in the Roman Empire* [London: Hodder & Stoughton, 1897] 61–64), who knew the territory before the rise of such amenities as modern medicine and transportation, offers a vivid description. The circumstances are well described by Foakes Jackson, 114: "Paul and Barnabas decided upon what seems to us to have been a desperate enterprise. Abandoning the settled districts they embarked on a journey across a barren and dangerous country, subject to floods from the mountain watercourses, with a bad reputation owing to the prevalence of banditry."

11 Witherington (403–4) cites Robin Lane Fox, *Pagans and Christians* (New York: Knopf, 1989) 293–94 (whose authority was Stephen Mitchell ["Population and Land in Roman Galatia," *ANRW* 2.7.2 (1980) 1053–81, esp. 1073–74]) in support of an argument that goes back to W. M. Ramsay. The object of this theory (based on the later-attested Sergii Pauli in Antioch) is to explain the textual leap from Cyprus to Pisidian Antioch and the difficult route taken. Breytenbach (*Paulus & Barnabas*, 38–45) also follows this argument. One shortcoming of the hypothesis is that Acts does not narrate a visit to members of the upper class of this Roman colony, but an appearance in the synagogue. When the upper classes do emerge (v. 50), they have Paul and Barnabas expelled. The narrative does not seem, therefore, to provide firm grounds for believing that Paul made the arduous journey to Pisidian Antioch because he had in hand a letter of recommendation to the local aristocracy. The surviving vestiges of Ramsay's reconstruction are put to rest by M. Christol and T. Drew-Bear, "Les Sergii Pauli et Antioche," in *Actes du Ier congrès international sur Antioche de Piside* (ed. Thomas Drew-Bear, Mehmet Taşhalan, and Christine M. Thomas; Collection Archeologie et Histoire de l'antiquité, Université Lumière-Lyon 2, vol. 5; Paris: Boccard, 2002) 177–92. See also Justin Taylor, "St Paul and the Roman Empire: Acts of the Apostles 13–14," *ANRW* 2.26.2 (1995) 1190–1231, esp. 1205–7.

12 Conzelmann (98–99), taking a cue from Philippe-Henri Menoud ("The Plan of Acts," in idem, *Jesus Christ and the Faith: A Collection of Studies* [PTMS 18; Pittsburgh: Pickwick: 1978] 121–32, esp. 125) characterizes this as a "prototype" that sets the pattern for later activity and develops the problem that chap. 15 will solve. See the analysis of

independent of Acts and yet list the stations in the same order, beginning with Iconium. The *Acts of Paul* is not independent of Acts.[13] The opening of that section, "As Paul was going to Iconium after his flight from Antioch," presumes Acts 14:6,[14] but the legends about Thecla are independent and local[15] stories that strongly conflict with the ideology of 1 Timothy.[16] These data are probably—perhaps only in oral form—as old as Acts.[17] The journey to Cyprus (13:4-12) is a Lucan contribution, albeit inspired by the association of Barnabas with Cyprus (4:36; 15:39).

Acts 13:1-3, which authorizes and launches the journey, derives from tradition.[18] There Barnabas is mentioned first, as he is in 13:7 and 14:14. In addition, the noun "apostles" in 14:4, 14 is properly ascribed to tradition. It is arguable, but not certain, that 14:7 is a seam, continued in v. 21. If this be true, it is reasonable to suspect that Luke has reworked a report of this journey.[19] Finally, the stoning of Paul in 14:19-20a can be referred to 2 Cor 11:25 in support of the general historicity of the material.[20] Since, however, Luke had access to at least the fragment found in 2 Corinthians 10–13,[21] that could have been the source of this episode, which is, in any case, usually viewed as an insertion into the source.

Since it is highly unlikely that Luke would simply have drawn from a hat the names of such sites as Pisidian Antioch and Iconium, about which he knew precious little, it is probable that the gentile mission source stands behind Acts 13–14. Insofar as one can tell, the source indicated little, if any, more than that Barnabas and Paul had labored in southern Asia Minor as accredited representatives (ἀπόστολοι) of the Antiochene community.[22] Reasons for including these data in the gentile mission source may have included the desire to demonstrate the independence of the mission and the subordinate role of Paul within it. This account would have helped to justify the Antiochene community's position in the light of Paul's break with and departure from it, as well as its independence.[23]

Comment

■ **1** In sequence to 12:25, the narrator returns to Antioch, the locality of 11:19-30. The list suggests a written source. Three of those named appear only here, and in this passage alone is there reference to "prophets and teachers" as local officials. Acts 11:27 reported the visit of prophets from Jerusalem;[24] 13:1 mentions local prophets, who were evidently also teachers, although the functions were often differentiated.[25] The list, like others (1:13; 6:5; 20:3-4), signals a transition. The names "Barnabas" and "Saul" frame the list, not accidentally. The group is cosmopolitan. It includes a Cypriote of

Haenchen, "'We' in Acts and the Itinerary," *Journal for Theology and Church* 1 (1965) 65–99, esp. 74–80.

13 This conclusion is reached, on different grounds, by Julian Hills, "Acts," 24–54; Richard Bauckham, "The Acts of Paul as a Sequel to Acts," in Winter and Clarke, *Setting*, 105–52; Richard Pervo, "A Hard Act to Follow: *The Acts of Paul* and the Canonical Acts," *JHC* 2 (1995) 3–32; and Daniel Marguerat, *La première histoire du christianisme: les actes des apôtres* (LD 180; Paris: Cerf, 1999) 369–91.

14 Trans. Elliott, *Apocryphal New Testament*, 364. (The section pertaining to Antioch is highly fragmentary.)

15 In its present state, the *Acts of Paul* do not distinguish sharply between Syrian and Pisidian Antioch.

16 K sy^{hmg} 181 gloss "in Iconium"with *τουτέστιν ἅ διὰ τὴν Θέκλαν ἔπαθεν* ("i.e., what he experienced because of Thecla"). This gloss indicates that the *Acts of Paul* could be more memorable than Acts 14:1-5.

17 Dennis R. MacDonald, *The Legend and the Apostle: The Battle for Paul in Story and Canon* (Philadelphia: Westminster, 1983).

18 E.g., Lüdemann, 146–48.

19 E.g., Weiser, 2:309.

20 E.g., Weiser, 2:309–10.

21 See pp. 246–47.

22 Cf. Roloff, 194–95.

23 This is more or less the conclusion of Barrett (1:664, cf. also 599–601, 622–23), who does not speculate about the motive for preserving this material.

24 On the unusual expression *τὴν οὖσαν ἐκκλησίαν* (lit. "the being church") cf. on 5:17. The adjective evidently means "local." The D-Text, according to Boismard (*Texte*, 208) omits "Antioch" and reads simply "in the church."

25 Aune (*Prophecy*, 265) states that these titles were probably not distinct, 1 Cor 12:28-29 ("apostles, prophets, teachers"); Eph 2:20; 3:5; 4:11 ("prophets); Eph 4:11; 1 Tim 1:11; 4:3 ("teachers"). *Did.*

Levitic background, a Cyrenian,[26] a former associate of the Tetrarch Herod,[27] and a man from Tarsus.[28] This group is quite different from the Seven (6:5) and reflects different circumstances. Without resort to Jerusalem, guided by the Spirit, the evident leaders of Antiochene believers decide to launch a mission.[29] That perspective would have been quite appropriate to the source, but it does not fit Luke's scheme.

■ **2-3** In the context of worship[30] an oracle[31] emerges, presumably through the mouth of one of those not named.[32] Aune defines this as a "prescriptive oracle."[33] Whereas the oracle in 11:28 was summarized in indirect speech, 13:2 is direct. The language of the oracle is evocative of both Paul and Luke.[34] The Spirit knows how to generate suspense, for the oracle gives no hint about the nature of the work in question. The repetition of "fasting" in v. 3 suggests that the actual ceremony took place at a later time.[35] For the readers of the book, the attendant ceremony looked like an ordination: fasting, prayer, and imposition of hands.[36] The prophetic element included both prayer for the gift of the Spirit and some sense of revealed approval. Note the roughly

---

15:2 urges its audience to choose (χειροτονήσατε) "bishops and deacons" who will also perform the service (λειτουργοῦσι, cf. Acts 13:2) of "prophets and teachers." That "service" is common to both. (The *Didache* is often placed in W. Syria.) See Karl H. Rengstorf, "διδάσκω," *TDNT* 2:135–65, esp. 158–59. (The varied conjunctions do not distinguish two groups here: BDF §444 [4].) The association of prophets with local communities rather than the church in general is Pauline. See Heinrich Greeven, "Propheten, Lehrer, Vorsteher bei Paulus: Zur Frage der 'Ämter' im Urchristentum," *ZNW* 44 (1952–53) 1–43.

26 Cf. 11:20. On this person and speculation about his possible relation to the author of Acts see Henry J. Cadbury, "Lucius of Cyrene," in Foakes Jackson and Lake, *Beg.* 5:489–95.

27 The epithet applied to Manachen, σύντροφος ("brought up together with") does not necessarily mean a social peer. In the *Ephesian Tale*, for example, it is applied to Rhode, the slave of the heroine, Anthia, e.g., 2.1.4; 2.3.3; 2.3.7; 2.4.1; 5.6.3. See also Jerome H. Neyrey, "Luke's Social Location of Paul: Cultural Anthropology and the Status of Paul in Acts," in Witherington, *History*, 251–79, 263. On the proper name see Williams, "Personal Names," 92, who says that it is not common and that this spelling is unique.

28 The Latin name of Simeon, *Niger*, means "black" (often "swarthy") but offers no clue to his ethnic background. Cf. *CPJ* 162, 164.

29 Concretely interpreted, the mission is entirely the work of the Spirit, to whom alone the agents would be accountable, as Adoph v. Harnack notes (*Mission*, 1:335), but this ignores the role of the community in "commissioning" Barnabas and Saul.

30 The text does not say that the entire community was involved. See *Act. Paul* 9/12, where the community is assembled in a house. When the time came for Paul to depart, he offered some inspired parenesis. Cleobius then prophesied Paul's death. After objections, Myrta was inspired to foretell great success for Paul at Rome. When the Spirit had resided within her, the community celebrated the eucharist and sang psalms and hymns. Although dependent upon Acts 20–21 (and 1 Corinthians 14), this scene reflects the sort of milieu that readers of a generation or two after Acts would have presumed for Acts 13:1-3, and it is likely to have been generally valid for the time of composition. On λειτουργέω ("worship"), a term of secular origin that developed religious connotations in appropriate contexts and was used for cultic activity in the translation of the Torah and subsequently included other forms of worship, see Rudolf Meyer and Hermann Strathmann, "λειτουργέω," *TDNT* 4:215–31, and Spicq, *Lexicon*, 2:378–84.

31 On oracles as the basis for missions see pp. 404–6.

32 Aune (*Prophecy*, 265) views this as imitation of a technique from the Hebrew Bible.

33 Aune, *Prophecy*, 265–66. On p. 321 he defines this form as "a type of prophetic speech in which the supernatural speaker enjoins a particular type of action or behavior." Most of these deal with behavior. Both of the exceptions noted on 321–22 come from Acts: 13:2 and 21:4.

34 "Separate . . . from" (ἀφορίζω εἰς): Rom 1:1. The other NT use of προσκαλέω in the sense of "call for a special task" is Acts 16:10 (also perfect). The relative pronoun is taken as an accusative of respect, but one may also construe it with the preposition.

35 The D-Text, according to Boismard (*Texte*, 208), omits the first reference to fasting.

36 Burton Scott Easton, *Early Christianity: The Purpose of Acts and Other Papers* (ed. F. C. Grant; Greenwich, Conn.: Seabury, 1954) 53. Efforts to discover what these actions might have meant in the source—if it contained them—are probably vain. Similarly, Weiser, 2:307. See also Fitzmyer, 497. D adds "all" here, a practice suitable to baptisms and

contemporary 1 Tim 1:18; 4:14; 2 Tim 1:6, as well as Acts 20:28, which assumes that the Ephesian presbyters have been authorized by the Holy Spirit.[37]

■ **4-12** These verses present an odd narrative. After a summary of the voyage to Cyprus,[38] the text summarizes evangelistic activity in the "Jewish synagogues" of Salamis.[39] Verse 5 reports neither success nor failure, indicating at this point that John was the missionaries' assistant. Verse 6 whisks them across the island to Paphos, where they encounter a magus,[40] described in terms of his relation to the proconsul. The latter subsequently invites Barnabas and Saul to preach, to the considerable disappointment of the magus, who evidently—one could argue for two different persons—has two names. Saul, now Paul, blinds him, which leads to the conversion of the proconsul, followed by the prompt departure of the missionaries.

If it is conceded that there is no visible traditional basis for a mission of Paul and Barnabas to Cyprus, it follows that the entire episode is, as it stands, unhistorical. Redaction criticism establishes the Lucan character of vv. 4-6a,[41] which sets out, in Lucan language, the Lucan principle of "Jews first," although the community in Antioch was said to have been reaching out to gentiles for more than a year (11:20).[42] This leaves the concrete episode of vv. 6b-12 hanging. This punitive miracle[43] does not follow the normal path of such stories. Apart from the narrative twists and turns that confound the exposition, the concluding belief of Sergius Paulus is a quite atypical "audience reaction." The conventional reaction to a punitive miracle is religious awe (5:5, 11; 19:17). The narrative logic—as opposed to the narrative sequence—would be at home in the *Acts of Peter*, for example: a magician in danger of losing his patron attempts to refute an apostle, is properly humiliated for his efforts, and the patron goes over to the apostle (*Act. Pet.* [Verc.] 8-15). One possibility is that Luke has compressed a source to the point of near incomprehension, perhaps relying on the reader's familiarity with such episodes.[44] If, however, this mission is a Lucan contribution to the source, where is the underlying story to be situated?

This is the chief conundrum for those seeking to identify sources. Granting that Luke might have come up with the name of Sergius Paulus—a concession that few would make—it is most unlikely that he would have concocted the name "Bar-Jesus" for a magician. The latter name almost certainly comes from tradition.[45] The story in its present shape closely resembles Josephus's account of the wooing of Drusilla by Felix (*Ant.* 20.141-43). Both involve a Roman governor (Felix in Josephus) and a Jewish magician from Cyprus who is an agent of the governor (Atomos in Josephus). The variant

ordinations. It also omits the finite verb in v. 3, evidently by accident. E lat sy; Lcf add the object "them." On the combination of prayer with fasting, often linked to revelation, see Johnson, 221.

37 Chrysostom *Hom.* 28 (241) assumes that Paul was ordained here and that his name was changed at the same time. Cf. also the comments of Ephrem: ". . . They laid hands upon them either so that they would receive the priesthood or that from the action they might receive tongues and works" (Ropes, *Text*, 416). This action Ephrem coordinates with Gal 2:9 (!).

38 Cyprus: Terence B. Mitford, "Roman Cyprus," *ANRW* 2.7.2 (1995) 1286-1384; and Alana Nobbs, "Roman Cyprus," in Gill and Gempf, *Setting*, 279-89. Nothing is said of the earlier mission to Cyprus (11:19).

39 On Salamis see Conrad Gempf, "Salamis," *ABD* 5:904-5. Josephus speaks of Jews in Cyprus c. 100 BCE in his account of Hyrcanus (*Ant.* 13.284-87). See also 1 Macc 15:23; Philo *Leg. all.* 282.

40 On the term, see pp. 207-9.

41 Cf. Ludemann, 148-51; Weiser, 2:312-14.

42 Talbert (126) outlines the alternation of "Jews and gentiles" throughout chaps. 13-14.

43 See the analysis of Weiser, 2:310-11. On the miracle, see the excursus "Punitive Miracles," pp. 52-53.

44 See Nock, "Paul and the Magus," 187-88: "The conclusion to which one is driven is that Luke has some definite tradition which he has incorporated *tant bien que mal*." See also John J. Kilgallen, "Acts 13:4-12: The role of the '*magos*,'" *EstBib* 55 (1997) 223-37.

45 The governor is correctly placed in (New) Paphos. On attempts to identify this individual, see Kirsopp Lake, "The Chronology of Acts," in Lake and Cadbury, *Additional Notes*, 445-74, esp. 455-59; Hemer, *Book*, 166; and Rainer Riesner, *Paul's Early Period: Chronology, Mission Strategy, Theology* (trans. D. Stott; Grand Rapids: Eerdmans, 1998) 137-43. Although it is quite reasonable that a person named

name "Simon" in Josephus[46] may be attributed to Christian scribes who wished to identify him with "Simon Magus," but the variant "Etoimas" in Acts 13:8 cannot be dismissed with such ease.[47] If "Etoimas" represents a corruption of "Atomos" introduced by a scribe who identified the two magicians, said scribe evidently recognized the parallel and made the alteration, but, given the generally "amateurish" character of the D-Text, this is no more than one possibility.[48] The jumble of names has evoked some heroic scholarly efforts.[49] If Luke were inspired by Josephus,[50] some of the confusion would be explained, but no more than some. A reasonable hypothesis is that a story about Barnabas has been transferred to Paul, with substantial alterations. In short, the story must be taken as it stands, for its purposes are as clear as its sources are opaque. This episode fits the Lucan pattern in that encounters with authorities usually come at the end of the report (e.g., Gallio in 18:12-17). This provides some support for the hypothesis that Luke knew of a story about a triangular encounter involving a missionary, a magician, and the proconsul (of Cyprus?) and that he devised 13:4-12 to utilize this tale for strategic reasons. The slightly less likely alternative is that he composed the encounter with the aid of Josephus.

Paul, as the character named "Saul" (who has appeared at several points beginning with the death of Stephen [7:58]) is now revealed to be, makes a splendid début, crushing a minion of Satan and converting a senatorial magistrate. Peter had also cursed a practitioner of magic (8:20-24)[51] and worked a punitive miracle (5:1-11). Paul's first gentile convert was, like Peter's, a Roman of high status—the highest, in fact, save the emperor. These were no accidents.[52] If readers are disposed to compare Peter to Paul, the latter has taken the greater prize.[53] For these parallels and the symbolic impact of these opening moments, Luke was willing to forfeit some literary logic.

■ **6** The narrator—to shift the analytic perspective—simply cannot wait to get to Paphos,[54] not for a synagogue mission but for a significant meeting. The trio happens upon[55] one Bar-Jesus, characterized as a Jewish false prophet and magician, who was associated with the proconsul, Sergius Paulus, described as "discerning." This produces dissonance, for the reader may properly ask what an intelligent governor is doing with a creature

Sergius Paulus was Proconsul of Cyprus, there is no definite evidence. Breytenbach (*Paulus & Barnabas*, 38 n. 52) recognizes that the name "Sergius Paulus" in *IGR* III.395 (= SEG XX.302) is a restoration (only $\Sigma\epsilon\rho$ is clear, and the γ is uncertain), but he treats it as established fact thereafter. See Alanna Nobbs, "Cyprus in the Book of Acts," in Gill and Gempf, *Setting*, 279–89, esp. 283–84. Douglas A. Campbell, "Possible Inscriptional Attestation to Sergius Paul[l]us (Acts 13:6-12) and the Implications for Pauline Chronology," *JTS* 56 (2005) 1–29; Taylor, "St Paul," 1192–94. Since the restoration is derived from Acts, it cannot be used as evidence for Acts.

46 See Louis Feldman, *Josephus IX* (LCL; Cambridge, Mass.: Harvard University Press, 1965) 464 n.*e*; and Heinz Schreckenberg, "Flavius Josephus und die Lucanischen Schriften," in Wilfrid Haubeck and Michael Bachmann, eds., *Wort in der Zeit: Neutestamentliche Studien: Festgabe für Karl Heinrich Rengstorf zum 75. Geburtstag* (Leiden: Brill, 1980) 179–209, esp. 198–99.

47 This appears in v. 6 as "Paratus" (= ἑτοῖμος) in gig w; Lcf; in v. 8 as Ετοιμας in D*; etoemas in d and Lcf. Boismard reads it in his D-Text (*Texte*, 211) in 13:8. See Haenchen's long note (398 n. 2). Support for this reading was damaged by the excesses of T. Zahn's identification of the two persons, on which see Klauck, *Magic*, 50.

48 See the note of Metzger, *Textual Commentary*, 355–56. (The view that it is more likely that the obscure "Elymas" was altered to the more intelligible "Etoimas" derives from modern struggles to elucidate "Elymas." For ancient scribes, the names were equally rare and obscure.)

49 Still useful is the discussion of Wikenhauser, 396–98. See also Barrett, 1:615–16.

50 See Pervo, *Dating*, 186–87. The case for dependence receives some support from Luke's apparent use of Josephus for his portrayal of Drusilla in 24:24-26.

51 Rackham, 198: "Saul emerges as Paul, and as a second Peter binds a second Simon Magus." See also Nock, "Paul and the Magus," 330.

52 Cf. Schüssler Fiorenza, "Miracles, Mission," 16.

53 Luke 1–2 provide a number of comparisons between John the Baptizer and Jesus in which the latter always emerges as the greater.

54 The "new" city of Paphos was, as the following verses confirm, the administrative capital of the province. See Conrad Gempf, "Paphos," *ABD* 5:139–40.

55 The same wooden expression appears in 19:1,

of this ilk in his entourage. The narrator is in a cruel bind, for he must explain what motivates the governor to wish to hear the message while making the magus the link. For that reason, the nature of the relationship is unstated and the transition obscure. Readers—not least modern scholars—will fill in the details by reference to known social types. The "prophecy" of Bar-Jesus is not like that of Barnabas, Simeon, et al. (13:1).[56] He is a fortune-teller who serves the public by providing desired information. Bar-Jesus has struck it rich. Rather than peddle data for pennies and hope for an encounter with a wealthy Roman, like the Jewish "high priestess" of Juvenal,[57] he has gained access to the proconsul, for whom he might perform such services as dream interpretation, astrological forecasts, various other divinations, and, perhaps, an occasional curse upon some impediment to the governor's work. A well-known comparison is Rutilianus, a Roman senator of consular rank who became quite close to Alexander of Abonoteichus, designated a "false prophet" in the title of Lucian's biographical sketch.[58] The number of his counterparts is almost legion.[59] One member of that company was Josephus, whose gift of prophecy rescued an apparently moribund career.[60]

Luke has no greater admiration for Bar-Jesus than Lucian had for Alexander. Perhaps the sagacious Sergius Paulus will recognize something better when opportunity arises. When the governor issues a summons to Barnabas and Saul for the purpose of hearing their message, it appears that he is to be viewed as a "God-Fearer" like Cornelius, and that his interest in Bar-Jesus was more grounded in his relation to the faith of Israel than to his divinatory acumen. The D-Text fills this gap by concluding v. 8 with the statement that Sergius Paulus liked what he heard,[61] but this is obviously secondary. The text gives no explanation for the governor's invitation and does not even state that Barnabas and Saul had an opportunity to preach. His subsequent belief is based on the cursing of the magus, which he could quite easily understand as an effective magical spell. The attentive reader of Acts is pressed again to ask why Luke included this confused story.[62]

The answer is that this episode is a kind of trope for the Pauline mission and "Lucan apologetic" (which are often one and the same). The Jesus movement can appeal to the empire and serve it by extirpating crude religious phenomena, "*barbara superstitio*" ("un-roman religion"). *Paul* is the primary agent of this *mission civilisatrice*, Sergius Paulus the exemplary gentile believer, while the magus takes the role of "everything that Luke did not like":[63] Jews, magic, and misuse of or misunderstanding of prophecy. At the end of Paul's Aegean activity, the same trio of vulgar Judaism (the sons of Sceva [19:13-17]), defeat of magic (19:19-20), and

where Paul discovers some followers of John the Baptizer.

56 Bruce, 296.

57 Juvenal *Sat.* 5.542–47, on whom see Georgi, *Opponents*, 88–111, with many comments and references; and Courtney, *Juvenal*, 332–33. This character appears in a satire, and the description of her status and activities cannot be taken at face value, but the satire depends on known social types for its effect.

58 *Alexander or the False Prophet* (ψευδομάντις).

59 Examples of court diviners from Suetonius's *Lives* include Tiberius (*Tiberius* 14.4; cf. Juvenal *Sat.* 10.93–94); Nero (36.1); Otho (4.1; 6.1); Vespasian (25); Domitian (15.3). Even Marcus Aurelius enjoyed the services of Arnuphis, an Egyptian magician (Cassius Dio 71.8.4). See also Nock, "Paul and the Magus," 183–84; and, with a full study and analysis of context, David S. Potter, *Prophets and Emperors: Human and Divine Authority from Augustus to Theodosius* (Cambridge, Mass.: Harvard University Press, 1994).

60 Josephus *Bell.* 3.399–408. His experience was very similar to that of Thrasyllus, the astrologer who predicted the ascension of Tiberius and enjoyed his support thereafter (Tacitus *Ann.* 6.20.2–21; cf. Suetonius *Tib.* 14.4).

61 ἥδιστα ἤκουεν αὐτῶν ("He heard them with considerable pleasure" [Boismard, *Texte*, 211]). This phrase, which also motivates the magician's hostility, may be influenced by Mark 6:20 (Herod's appreciation of John the Baptizer). Note also *Act. Paul* 3.20, where the governor listens appreciatively to Paul (ἡδέως ἤκουεν). This indicates that the *Acts of Paul* as extant may have known Acts in a D-Text edition. The combination appears elsewhere, e.g., Plutarch *Dem.* 25.7; Cassius Dio 69.11, but is relatively rare.

62 For its imitation in *Act. Pet.* 15, see Robert F. Stoops, "Departing to Another Place: The *Acts of Peter* and the Canonical Acts of the Apostles," *SBLSP 1994* (Atlanta: Scholars Press, 1994) 390–404, esp. 402.

63 Barrett, 1:613.

approval by citizens of very high standing (the Asiarchs [19:31]) appears, forming a parenthesis around the mission of Paul. One can evaluate the movement by taking account of both its enemies and its friends.

■ **8** As Susan Garrett shows, Paul and Bar-Jesus "represent superhuman figures."[64] In literary terms, their function is symbolic. The magus, now identified as "Elymas," with the incomprehensible explanation that renders this name or title,[65] took exception to the pair. The setting is utterly vague. Is the reader to envision an interview in the gubernatorial palace, with Sergius seated while Saul and Barnabas address him (in turn?), and the magus in his normal place, or a less formal conversation in private rooms? If the pair had no opportunity to speak, what was the ground of Bar-Jesus's objection (and v. 12b)? A discussion on a street-corner seems quite unlikely. There is no background; all is foreground, the confrontation, marked by "seek" (*ζητέω* [vv. 7, 8, 11]), "proconsul," "faith"/"believe" (*πίστις, πιστεύω* [vv. 7, 8, 12]). Between these two pillars, Bar-Jesus is crushed. His attempt to dissuade results in persuasion. The favored magus becomes a blind beggar.[66] The "change of names" evidently serves the same end. The good Jew Saul is also the good Roman Paul,[67] while the barbarous appellation "Bar-Jesus" belongs to Elymas (or Hetoimas, etc.), who is better titled "Bar-Satan" (v. 10).[68]

■ **9-11** Paul, filled with the power of the Spirit,[69] like Jesus at the beginning of his career (Luke 4:14), pronounces a most formidable and potent curse. The language of this Lucan composition is septuagintal[70] and invigorated with the rhetorical flourishes of which he is fond, as well as ominously sonorous cadences and clever repetitions.[71] This is an oracle of judgment[72] delivered by an inspired speaker consisting of an accusation in the

64 Garrett, *Demise*, 79–87, citing 80.

65 Luke otherwise uses such expressions to provide Greek equivalents of foreign words. Haenchen (398 n. 2), for example, assumes that "magus" interprets "Elymas." He has normal word order on his side; the difficulty is the abrupt introduction of "Elymas." Jervell (346 n. 424) says that it may represent Aramaic *haloma* ("magician"), but this does not convince Fitzmyer (502): "No one knows what it means."

66 Nock ("Paul and the Magus," 185) says: "There may be in it some suggestion of the outdoing of the magician at his own game: blinding is one of the things which his type claimed to be able to do." For examples from Cyprus, see Gager, *Curse Tablets,* nos. 45–46, pp. 132–37.

67 Gustave A. Harrer ("Saul Who Is Also Called Paul," *HTR* 33 [1940] 19–34) provides a good deal of information, but argues from Roman citizenship to the conclusion that "Paul" was the *cognomen*, assuming a hypothesis. Note also Cadbury and Lake, 105. On Roman names and their adoption by others, see also John P. V. D. Balsdon, *Romans and Aliens* (Chapel Hill: University of North Carolina Press, 1979) 146–55. For recent speculation on the change, see Sean M. McDonough, "Small Change: Saul to Paul, Again," *JBL* 125 (2006) 390–91.

68 This presumes that the implied reader would recognize the Aramaic *bar-* as a patronymic and thus see the contrast between "Bar-Jesus" in v. 6 and *υἱὲ διαβόλου* in v. 10. Acts 4:36 suggests that such knowledge is probable.

69 Note also the phrase *ἄχρι καιροῦ,* found only in Luke 4:13 and Acts 13:11.

70 See Plümacher, *Lukas*, 47 n. 58; and, in particular, Garrett (*Demise*, 82–83), who refers to Deut 28:29 and the curse material in Deuteronomy 28–29, with a note to an allusion to Deut 29:19-20 (LXX) in the parallel Acts 8:20-23 (curse against Simon), and the use of light/darkness imagery in the Qumran exposition of the critique of idolatry (1QS 2:11–19), as well as material from early Christian literature. Verse 11 is the equivalent of a paraphrase of Luke 1:20 *καὶ ἰδοὺ ἔσῃ σιωπῶν καὶ μὴ δυνάμενος λαλῆσαι ἄχρι ἧς ἡμέρας γένηται ταῦτα, ἀνθ᾽ ὧν οὐκ ἐπίστευσας τοῖς λόγοις μου, οἵτινες πληρωθήσονται εἰς τὸν καιρὸν αὐτῶν* ("But now, because you did not believe my words, which will be fulfilled in their time, you will become mute, unable to speak, until the day these things occur"). Note the use of a periphrastic future in each case, as well as "until . . . time" (*ἄχρι . . . καιρός*).

71 Note the alliteration of plosive *p*- sounds (eight in vv. 9-10), the abundance of long *e*- sounds (eight also). Eleven words and an ejaculation (on "O," see BDF §146 1b) precede the formulation of the accusation in v. 10. In addition to "seek" and "(have) faith" (above), *διαστρέφω* ("divert") occurs in vv. 8 and 10.

72 Note *καὶ νῦν* ("and now"), one way of introducing an oracle of judgment, in v. 11. See Claus Westermann, *Basic Forms of Prophetic Speech* (trans. Hugh C. White; Philadelphia: Westminster, 1967) 155.

form of a question (v. 10, as in 5:3), a threat (v. 11a), and the immediate fulfillment of the prophecy (v. 11b).[73] In another reminiscence of the story of Jesus, the magus is accused of trying to make God's straight paths crooked (v. 10b). This is a patent allusion to the activity of the Baptizer (Luke 3:4, citing Isa 40:3; cf. Luke 1:76, 79) that justifies the epithet "false prophet" of v. 6. His punishment, in a nice turnabout, echoes that of Paul.[74] The one who had sought to dissuade the proconsul from accepting the message is reduced to stumbling about crookedly seeking guides.[75] Blinding is a typical punishment, to be sure,[76] but also yields the precise symbolic opposite of Paul's mission: to bring people from darkness (the realm of the devil [Luke 22:53]) to light.[77] This imagery brackets Paul's career. In the very last scene of Acts, he denounces the "blindness" of his Jewish hearers (28:6-7).[78]

■ **12** The result is all that could be asked—and a great deal less. Nock (writing in nonegalitarian times) observed: "The proconsul's conversion, which would have been an event of the first importance, is just stated as though it were that of a washer-woman. And it has no consequences."[79] Further, in what looks like a last-minute effort to give some credit to the message, the narrative perplexingly reports his astonishment at the message.[80] The close of v. 12 corresponds to Luke 4:32 (following Mark 1:22), adding one more parallel to the respective inaugurations of the ministries of Jesus and Paul.[81]

The outset of this new venture is thus marked by a victory over Satan and the conversion of a member of the small senatorial class that rested atop a vast social pyramid. Since senators were not noted for affiliating with revolutionary sects or lower-class cults, hearers may conclude that this movement deserved respect. At this time, Paul, as he will be henceforward, emerges as the leader. The narrator achieves this not with a bald statement of fact but through showing the missionary vanquishing a fraud and garnering a prime convert. Verse 13 will make his new standing perfectly clear.

73 See Aune (*Prophecy*, 269–70), who attributes the assignment of the oracle to an inspired person (rather than to a messenger) to Greco-Roman influence.

74 Bar-Jesus (like Simon of Samaria) remained unrepentant and continued to obstruct the mission, according to the *Act. Barn.* 19, in which he is an anti-Christian Jewish agitator rather than a magician. Bede (61) says, somewhat rationalistically, that Paul remembered his own experience, which showed that physical blindness could restore light to the mind. One who attempted to take away the mental eyes of others did not deserve physical eyes.

75 Compare the blinded Saul's need for guides (χειραγωγοῦντες [9:8]) with the plight of the magus, who must find guides (χειραγωγούς [13:11]). This is fine irony, the magician punished by "the hand of the Lord" (lit., v. 11: χεὶρ κυρίου) must seek people to lead him by the hand. On the parallels and differences between the respective careers of Paul and the magus, see Garrett, *Demise*, 84.

76 See above on 9:1-19a. For blinding as the result of a curse, see Apuleius *Metam.* 8.25.

77 See Garrett, *Demise*, 83–84, with many references. Cf. also Geoffrey W. H. Lampe ("Miracles in the Acts of the Apostles," in Moule, *Miracles*, 177), who says that this incident is like the reverse of a conversion story.

78 Blindness is also a common symbol for various mental and spiritual defects, for example, Philo *Deus* 130 (on the symbolic meaning of a form of leprosy): "and thus, as people in a mist and profound darkness [ἐν ἀχλύι καὶ σκότῳ; two words used in combination in Acts 13:11], it sees nothing of what it should do, but like a blind man tripping over every obstacle" (trans. Francis H. Colson and George H. Whitaker, *Philo III* [LCL; New York: G. P. Putnam's Sons, 1930] 75, alt.).

79 Nock, "Paul and the Magus," 329. Acts 17:34 shows that "believe" (πιστεύω) alone can be used for proper conversions.

80 If taken as a subjective genitive, this could be understood as saying that the "teaching" (διδαχή) took place in the miracle, that is, that from it the governor learned of the power of God. This would reduce the tension. On the grammatical issues, see Barrett, 1:618.

81 The D-Text (Boismard, *Texte*, 212) missed this allusion and revised the sentence to read, "When the proconsul saw what had happened, he was **amazed and** believed in **God**" (ἰδὼν δὲ ὁ ἀνθύπατος τὸ γεγονὸς ἐθαύμασεν καὶ ἐπίστευσεν τῷ θεῷ).

13

13:13-52 Paul Preaches in Antioch of Pisidia

13/ **Paul and his companions sailed**
from Paphos to Perga in
Pamphylia. John, however,
left them and went back to
Jerusalem. 14/ Meanwhile, the
others left Perga and traveled
on to Antioch of Pisidia,[a] where
they went to the synagogue on
the Sabbath and took a seat.
15/ Following the readings from
the Torah and the Prophets, the
synagogue officials extended
this invitation, "Brothers, if
you have a sermon, please
deliver it."
16/ **In response Paul stood up and**
indicated[b] that he would speak.
"My fellow Israelites and you
that revere God, please listen.
17/ The God of this people Israel
chose our ancestors.[c] During
their stay in Egypt[d] he fashioned
them into a great nation and
subsequently brought them out
of that country with a substan-
tial display of force.[e] 18/ Over
some[f] forty years he cared
for them[g] in the wilderness.
19/ After eradicating seven
nations in the land of Canaan, he
conferred it upon the Israelites.[h]
20/ Roughly 450 years later God
appointed judges, who served
until the time of the prophet
Samuel.[i] 21/ At that point the
people demanded a king, so
God appointed Saul, son of
Kish, from the tribe of Benja-
min, who ruled for forty years
22/ until God removed him and
elevated David to the throne,
with this recommendation:
'I have found David, the son
of Jesse, a man after my own
heart. He will do everything
that I want.'[j] 23/ As promised,
God has produced a savior for
Israel from David's descendants:
Jesus.[k] 24/ John spoke of Jesus
before his appearance, while he
was proclaiming baptism and a
change of heart to all the people
of Israel. 25/ As his mission was
drawing to a close he used to
say, 'What do you imagine that
I am? I am *not* "the one,"[l] but
after me will come one whose
sandal straps I am not fit to
untie.'
26/ **"My fellow believers and heirs**
of Abraham's line, as well as

a This follows the D-Text (Boismard, *Texte*, 214) and some other witnesses, as opposed to "Pisidian Antioch" (Ἀντιόχειαν τὴν Πισιδίαν), read by a number of Alexandrian authorities. Ropes (*Text*, 119) thinks that the genitive may be due to boundary shifts over time. The site was called "Antioch near Pisidia" (Strabo 12.6.4).

b The D-Text (Boismard, *Texte*, 215) adds "that they should be quiet." This is a thoughtless addition from 12:17, where people were speaking excitedly.

c Boismard (*Texte*, 215) prefers the variant διὰ τὸν λαόν ("because of the people"). This leaves ὕψωσεν without an object.

d The septuagintal ἐν γῇ Αἰγύπτου is bad Greek (BDF §261 [7]). D-Text and other witnesses improve it (Boismard, *Texte*, 215).

e In Greek this is a common LXX trope. Johnson (231) lists a number of examples. The instrumental use of μετά ("with") is poor Greek.

f The D-Text (Boismard, *Texte*, 216) omits the characteristic Lucan ὡς, probably because the number is not approximate, and reads simply "for forty years" (ἔτη τεσσεράκοντα). Another question arises from omission of the initial καί ("and," B *et al.*). This evidently takes the ὡς of v. 18 as a temporal conjunction. The question is, as Ropes observes (*Text*, 121), whether this conventional use should or would be applied to a number so common as forty. See Metzger, *Textual Commentary*, 357–58.

g *Or:* "put up with them." See below.

h The *v.l.* κατεκληροδότησεν, "parcel out by lot" (323. 440. 945. 1243. 1505. 1739 has merit, since the stem κληρονομ- ("inherit-") is more common, but it may have been introduced because the ergative sense of κατακληρονομέω ("cause to inherit") was not understood.

i *Or:* "God then appointed judges during the next 450 years, until the prophet Samuel." The article before "Samuel" is uncertain and is probably a later addition.

j The various hands of E omit some or all from μαρτυρήσας to ποιήσει, ". . . recommendation . . . he will carry out. . . ."

k The D-Text (Boismard, *Texte*, 217) revises ἤγαγεν ("produced") to the more conventional "raised up" (ἤγειρεν, cf. v. 22) and alters the close to "salvation for Israel," omitting "Jesus" and changing the noun. This makes much of the following incomprehensible, as Jesus is not mentioned again until v. 33. Metzger (*Textual Commentary*, 359) explains the error as due to misreading abbreviations of *nomina sacra*.

l *Or:* "I am not what you think I am."

m By omitting καί ("and") $\mathfrak{P}^{45}$ B eliminate the "God-Fearers." This may be because the address can be read as calling them "sisters and brothers."

those of you that revere God,[m]
this message of salvation was
directed to *us*.[n] 27/ For the resi-
dents of Jerusalem, together
with their[o] leaders, failed to
recognize Jesus. In condemning
him they brought to fulfillment
the declarations of the proph-
ets, which they also failed to
perceive, although these are
heard every single Sabbath.
28/ These people demanded[p]
to Pilate that he be executed,
failure to find him guilty of any
capital crime notwithstanding.
29/ When they had brought to
pass all that had been written
about him, they removed him
from the cross[q] and placed him
in a tomb. 30/ Yet God raised
him from the dead. 31/ Over
the course of many days he
appeared to those who had
traveled with him from Galilee
to Jerusalem. They are his wit-
nesses to the public,[r] 32/ while
we are here to announce the
achievement of the promise
made to the[s] ancestors. 33/ God
has fulfilled it for us their
heirs[t] by raising Jesus,[u] as the
first[v] Psalm says, 'You are my
son; today I have become your
father.' 34/ To indicate that[w] the
one raised will never return to
the decay of death, God says,
'To you I shall offer the Davidic
promises, which are sacred and
inviolable.' 35/ In support of
this God says in another place,[x]
'You will not allow your sacred
one to experience decay.'
36/ Now David served God's
purpose in his own generation,[y]
after which he died, was buried
with his ancestors, and *did*
experience decay, 37/ but the
one whom God raised did *not*
experience decay.
38/ **"There is something you need**
to know, my fellow believers:
through this person comes to
you a message of forgiveness
of sins. 39/ Through Jesus all
who have trust are acquitted of
everything for which the law of
Moses has no remedy. 40/ Be
careful, therefore, that you do
not experience[z] the judgment
announced by the prophets:[aa]
41/ 'Take a look, you scoffers,

n The variant "to you" is a common error, due to the similarity of the pronouns, which did not differ in pronunciation.

o D-Texts (Boismard, *Texte*, 219) read "its leaders."

p Use of the same verb for demanding the execution of Jesus and the request for a monarch (ᾐτήσαντο [vv. 21, 28]) may throw a negative light on the term, but the speech does not condemn the monarchy (without which David would not have appeared).

q Lit. "wood." See p. 145 n. 49.

r The D-Text (Boismard, *Texte*, 221) shifts "many days" to follow "Jerusalem," and says that they are "*at present* his witnesses."

s The D-Text (Boismard, *Texte*, 222) makes "*our* ancestors" explicit.

t The earliest text ($\mathfrak{p}^{74}$ ℵ A b C* D lat, etc.) reads "our children." Aland's text, τοῖς τέκνοις [αὐτῶν] ἡμῖν ("for their children," probably taking "for us" with the following participle, "raising"), is only defensible as a correction. The translation reads, in effect: τοῖς τέκνοις ἡμῖν. Cf. Haenchen, 411; Conzelmann, 105; and Barrett 1:645.

u A number of D-Texts (D [614 sy^{h**} cop^{mae}]) expand the name into a title: "the Lord Jesus Christ."

v Enumeration of the Psalter varied, where it existed at all. Patristic evidence supports "second," while the earliest Greek MS., $\mathfrak{p}^{45}$, reads ἐν τοῖς ψαλμοῖς ("in the psalter"), which is almost certainly a harmonization (cf. Mark 1:2). Note also the singular in v. 35, which probably refers to a psalm. It is more likely that "second psalm" and "the psalter" are subsequent corrections of what would become the standard enumeration than that "first" was a correction based on another system. See Ropes, *Text*, 263–65; Clark, 356; and Metzger, *Textual Commentary*, 363–65.

w The D-Text reads "but when" (ὅτε). This is a bit easier to comprehend, but ὅτι resumes the declaration of v. 33. See Metzger, *Textual Commentary*, 365.

x The D-Text (Boismard, *Texte*, 223) omits διότι ("in support of," lit. "wherefore"). Other textual traditions have the simple διό (therefore). Omission makes a straight sequence of quotations without causal relationship.

y For other ways of construing this sentence, see Barrett, 1:648.

z The well-attested variant "come *upon you*" (ἐπέλθῃ ἐφ᾽ ὑμᾶς) is an obvious improvement the removal of which would be inexplicable.

aa Cop^{mae} adds, as usual, the name of the prophet (Habakkuk). See on 2:16.

bb Omission of the rhetorically effective and theologically central repetition of "deed" (ἔργον [D-Text, 𝔪]) serves to conform the text to the LXX.

cc *Or:* "As Paul and Barnabas were leaving."

dd The term συναγωγή in v. 43 means "assembly." (Its

be astonished, and then drop dead! I am going to do something in your lifetime, an act[bb] that you will not believe even if you are told about it.'"

42/ As they were leaving,[cc] Paul and Barnabas were urged to say more about their message on the following Sabbath. 43/ After the service[dd] many Jews and observant converts congregated about the two, who exhorted them to hold fast to God's grace.

44/ When[ee] that Sabbath arrived, almost the entire city had gathered to hear the Lord's message.[ff] 45/ When the Jews saw the size of the crowd, they were filled with jealousy and attempted to refute Paul's arguments with slanderous claims. 46/ Undaunted, Paul and Barnabas said,[gg] "We were obliged to preach God's message to you first. Since you reject it and show that you are unworthy of eternal life, we are therefore going to turn to the gentiles. 47/ That is what the Lord has directed us to do:

'I have made you a light for the gentiles and a means of salvation to the ends of the earth.'"

48 When the gentiles heard this, they were overjoyed and praised[hh] the Lord for the message they had received. All who were destined for everlasting life became believers. 49/ The message about the Lord[ii] was disseminated throughout[jj] the entire region. 50/ In response, the Jews aroused their influential women sympathizers and the leaders of the city and inaugurated a persecution of Paul and Barnabas,[kk] whom they drove out of their jurisdiction. 51/ So the two shook the dust from their feet in judgment against them and moved on[ll] to Iconium. 52/ Their followers, however,[mm] continued to abound in joy with the presence of the Holy Spirit.

history is precisely parallel to the ἐκκλησία, which means "assembly" and then, by metonymy, the place where the assembly meets.)

ee B E 𝔪 sy[h] read τε ("and"), rather than δέ (which can amount to a punctuation mark). This would unite vv. 43 and 44. Luke's use of τε can be idiosyncratic, but the vv. should be construed as separate.

ff The MSS. show the usual variation of "Lord" and "God."

gg On the tense of the verb and the participle (both aor.), see BDF §420 (3), which says that this is the result of assimilation to one another.

hh The D-Text (Boismard, *Texte*, 220) reads "received" (ἐδέξαντο), as in Luke 8:13. This is probably due to the unique expression of praise for the word, rather than God, but corruption is possible. "Praised God" is another variant, and some witnesses harmonize. For details, see Metzger, *Textual Commentary*, 369–70.

ii 𝔓[45] and some other witnesses omit the prepositional phrase. The omission makes for a smoother reading and is more likely to be secondary.

jj There is good support for the preposition καθ', which is adopted here in accordance with Lucan idiom (BDAG, 511, *s.v.* κατά).

kk D reports "a major harassment and persecution" (θλῖψιν μεγάλην καὶ διωγμόν). This is clearly a conflation: "major" comes from 8:1, where a number of D-Texts also add "harassment." The preposition ἐπί ("upon," "against") suggests that διωγμός ("persecution") is more original. Boismard (*Texte*, 230) prefers "harassment."

ll D reads κατήντησαν ("arrived"). This is much less probable and would command respect if supported by other D-Texts. Boismard (*Texte*, 230) adopts it as the D-Text.

mm As often, there is strong support for δέ instead of τε. The latter indicates a strong link. Luke uses the particle τε casually. Although it is probably more original, the translation treats it as equivalent to an adversative δέ here.

Analysis

The narrative leaps more than 375 kilometers (as the crow flies), to Pisidian Antioch. In Cyprus, Paul demonstrated his miraculous power; the power of his rhetoric will be on display in Pisidia. Within a space of about eight days, Paul preaches a long sermon (vv. 16-41) that wins many adherents from among the Jews and their friends, but, when a subsequent sermon attracts many gentiles, the Jews turn against Paul and chase him out of the city (vv. 42-52).

Since it was evidently not possible to sail[1] to Perga, while 14:25 mentions the port of Attalia, the narrator may have abbreviated an already terse account.[2] The narrator is in a great hurry to get to Antioch, a remote but important Roman colony.[3] "Paul and his companions" is Lucan, for it asserts, presumably against the source, that Paul is now the leader.[4] In any case, the only information about Perga is the departure of John. No reason is given for his return. It is quite possible that his inclusion with and departure from the mission is a Lucan invention designed to explain the eventual separation of Paul and Barnabas (15:37-39, where he is called "Mark").

Within two verses after converting Sergius Paulus, Paul and Barnabas are seated in a synagogue on the Sabbath.[5] Details about the reading of the Law[6] and the Prophets slow the narrative, providing verisimilitude and evoking the dramatic passage that opened the inaugural sermon of Jesus (Luke 4:16-20a). Paul follows up his defeat of Satan with a synagogue sermon, as had Jesus (Luke 4:1-13).[7] Although both met with some success (Luke 4:22; Acts 13:42), both were ultimately chased out of town (Luke 4:23-30; Acts 13:44-50).[8] Verisimilitude wanes in the second half of v. 15, when the officials[9] invite the two visitors to preach.[10] Responsible leaders were unlikely to issue such invitations to perfect strangers, the dangers of which are aptly illustrated by

1 The introductory participle is probably a nautical term (cf. 16:11; 18:21; 20:3, 13; 21:1, 2; 27:2, 4, 12, 21; 28:10, 11).

2 David H. French ("Acts and the Roman Roads of Asia Minor," in Gill and Gempf, *Setting*, 49–58, esp. 50–53) reconstructs these stations: Attalia, Perge, then the *Via Sebaste* through Comama to Antioch.

3 See Stephen Mitchell, "Antioch of Pisidia," *ABD* 1:264–65. William Ramsay's description in *The Cities of St. Paul: Their Influence on His Life and Thought* (London: Hodder & Stoughton, 1907) 247–314, is dated but contains much valuable detail. See Taylor, "St Paul," 1200–1205; and Robert L. Mowery, "Paul and Caristianus at Pisidian Antioch," *Bib* 87 (2006) 223–42, for information on the city in first century. There is no definite evidence for the presence of Jews in first-century Pisidian Antioch. On a later Jewish inscription that probably does not refer to Pisidian Antioch, see Irina Levinskaya, *Diaspora Setting* (BIFCS 5; Grand Rapids: Eerdmans, 1996) 150, on Jewish communities in Asia Minor. See Paul Trebilco, *Jewish Communities in Asia Minor* (SNTSMS 60; Cambridge: Cambridge University Press, 1991), supplemented by his "The Jews in Asia Minor, 66–c. 235 CE," *CHJ* 4:85–92.

4 BDF §228 says that this phrase, *οἱ περὶ Παῦλον*, is a literary idiom. The roughly contemporary *Ephesian Tale* uses the equivalent at 1.5.8; 1.3.4; 2.2.1; and 2.3.1.

5 On the nature and contents of the synagogue service at this time, see Schürer, *History*, 2:447–63; and, with detailed critical analysis, Stefan C. Reif, "The Early Liturgy of the Synagogue," *CHJ* 3:326–57. There was no fixed form.

6 The Theodotus inscription (pp. 154–55) states that one purpose of the synagogue that he built was as a place for "reading the Law" (*ἀνάγνωσιν νόμου* [lines 4–5]).

7 Julius Wellhausen (*Kritische Analyse der Apostelgeschichte* [Abhandlungen der Königlichen Gesellschaft der Wissenschaften zu Göttingen, Phil.-Hist. Klasse, n.F. 15.2; Berlin: Topelmann, 1914] 25–26) already noted the parallels, which were evoked in considerable detail by Radl, *Paulus*, 82–102. Klauck (*Magic*, 54) sees a relation to temptations in Luke 4. See also Johnson, 227; and Tannehill, *Narrative Unity*, 2:163 n. 15.

8 Cf. Johnson, 237.

9 One would expect the singular ἀρχισυνάγωγος. As Cadbury and Lake (148–49) observe, one Lucan idiosyncrasy is the use of the plural where one expects the singular for such words as "high priest," "Asiarch," and "proconsul."

10 The phrase λόγος παρακλήσεως (lit. "message of exortation") is the equivalent of what we should call a sermon. Note especially Heb 13:22. Boismard (*Texte*, 214–15) reads λόγος σοφίας (lit. "message of wisdom") as the D-Text, but speculates that the archetype included both genitives. "Wisdom" is more likely a secondary change.

the current example.[11] A sermon is what they asked for, and a sermon is what they will get. Up to this point Paul, the principal character of Acts, has been given but two verses of direct speech (13:10-11, and three words at 9:5). His hour has finally come.

Excursus: "God-Fearers" in Acts

Acts has sparked a vigorous debate about the general existence of gentiles who frequented synagogues and found much that appealed in the religion of Israel but did not always become converts.[12] Acts does speak of such people, with two different participles: *φοβούμενοι*, a general term frequently used in the LXX and elsewhere, often of proper followers of the God of Israel (13:17, 26), and *σεβόμενοι* (13:43; 13:50 [of "proselytes"]; 16:14; 17:4, 17; 18:7). The terminology is inconsistent and confusing, by no means technical.[13] Two points are beyond dispute: (1) Luke makes his understanding of the concept quite clear in his description of Cornelius (10:2; cf. 10:22, 35). God-Fearers are devout and charitable gentiles, familiar with Scripture and obedient to the "ethical commandments." (2) Such persons did exist. If no other evidence for them existed, Juvenal would suffice:

> Those whose lot it was that their fathers worshipped the Sabbath
> Pray to nothing now but the clouds and a spirit in Heaven;
> Since their fathers abstained from pork, they'd be cannibals sooner
> Than violate that taboo. Circumcised, not as the Gentiles,

11 Witherington (406) deals with this problem by using the plural "officials" to conjure up a scene in which the congregants of several local synagogues assemble to hear these itinerant Jewish preachers. Because Luke's account is "elliptical," previous contact with the officials must be assumed. The account is therefore quite probable. This fine little fiction misses Luke's point: behind the invitation lay the hand of Providence.

12 Modern discussion of the question begins with Kirsopp Lake's still-useful note, "Proselytes and God-Fearers," in Lake and Cadbury, *Additional Notes*, 74–96. See also Louis H. Feldman, "Jewish 'Sympathizers' in Classical Literature and Inscriptions," *TAPA* 81 (1950) 200–208; Baruch Lifshitz, "Du nouveau sur les 'Sympathisants,'" *JSJ* 1 (1970) 77–84; Folker Siegert, "Die 'Gottesfürchtige' und Sympathisanten," *JSJ* 4 (1973) 109–64. Discussion was rekindled by A. Thomas Kraabel's "The Disappearance of the God-Fearers," *Numen* 28 (1981) 113–26. See also his "The Roman Diaspora: Six Questionable Assumptions," *JJS* 33 (1982) 445–64; and idem, "Greeks, Jews, and Lutherans in the Middle Half of Acts," in George W. E. Nickelsburg and George W. MacRae, eds., *Christians among Jews and Gentiles: Essays in Honor of Krister Stendahl* (Philadelphia: Fortress Press, 1986) 157–67, followed by Max Wilcox, "The 'God-fearers' in Acts: A Reconsideration," *JSNT* 13 (1981) 102–22; Thomas Finn, "The God-Fearers Reconsidered," *CBQ* 47 (1985) 75–84; John G. Gager, "Jews, Gentiles, and Synagogues," in *Christians among Jews and Gentiles* (above), 91–99; Robert S. MacLennon and A. Thomas Kraabel, "The God-Fearers—A Literary and Theological Invention," *BAR* 12 (1986) 46–53; Robert F. Tannenbaum, "Jews and God-Fearers in the Holy City of Aphrodite," *BAR* 12 (1986) 54–57; Louis H. Feldman, "The Omnipresence of the God-Fearers," *BAR* 12 (1986) 58–63; J. Andrew Overman, "The God-Fearers: Some Neglected Features," *JSNT* 32 (1988) 17–26; Jacob Jervell, "The Church of Jews and Godfearers," in Joseph Tyson, ed., *Luke-Acts and the Jewish People: Eight Critical Perspectives* (Minneapolis: Augsburg, 1988) 11–20; Louis H. Feldman, "Proselytes and 'Sympathizers' in the Light of the New Inscriptions from Aphrodisias," *REJ* 148 (1989) 265–305; idem, *Jew and Gentile*, 342–82; Trebilco, *Jewish Communities*, 58–60; Levinskaya, *Diaspora Setting*, 51–126; Jerome Murphy-O'Connor, "Lots of God-Fearers? *Theosebeis* in the Aphrodisias Inscription," *RB* 99 (1992) 418–24; Hans-Josef Klauck, "Gottesfürchtige im Magnificat?" *NTS* 43 (1997) 134–39; Bernd Wander, *Gottesfürchtige und Sympathisanten* (WUNT 104; Tübingen: Mohr Siebeck, 1998); John J. Collins, *Between Athens and Jerusalem* (2nd ed.; Grand Rapids: Eerdmans, 2000) 264–70; and Dietrich-Alex Koch, "Proselyten und Gottesfürchtige als Hörer der Reden von Apostelgeschichte 2,14-39 und 13,16-41," in Breytenbach, *Apostelgeschichte*, 83–107; Koch, "The God-Fearers between Facts and Fiction: Two Theosebeis Inscriptions from Aphrodisias and Their Bearing for the New Testament," *ST* 60 (2006) 62–90. For additional bibliography, see Heikki Solin, "Juden und Syrer im westlichen Teil der römischen Welt," *ANRW* 2.29.2 (1997) 587–789, 1222–49, esp. 618–21; and Fitzmyer, 450.

13 In inscriptions, the word *θεοσεβής* is the preferred term for "God-Fearers," although definite instances are rare.

They despise Roman law, but learn and observe and revere
Israel's code, and all from the sacred volume of Moses
Where the way is not shown to any but true believers,
Where the uncircumcised are never led to the fountain.
Remember the Sabbath Day, to keep it lazy. The father,
Setting this day apart from life, is the cause and the culprit. (*Sat.* 14.96–106)[14]

Juvenal appears to assume that his readers will be familiar enough with males who revere the God of Israel,[15] observe the Sabbath, and follow other Jewish practices to find this a cogent vignette. Additional evidence does exist.[16] Conflict surrounds the depiction of the God-Fearers in Acts. A. T. Kraabel has exposed two weaknesses in the conventional view.[17] The first is the claim that the term has a single, religious meaning. This view derives from the second, that the role and description of God-Fearers in Acts is simple fact.

The label "God-Fearer" could be applied to any whom Jews viewed as supportive, whether for political, humanitarian, religious, or other motives. According to Josephus *Ant.* 20.195, Poppaea Sabina, the wife of Nero, was a ϑεοσεβής. The least likely explanation of this epithet is that she was a near-convert. Poppaea most probably earned the label because she had Jewish favorites and was open to their requests.[18] The limitations of the conventional view became manifest when a long list of "God-Fearers" (ϑεοσεβεῖς) at Aphrodisias were assumed to be inclined toward Jewish religiosity although the data suggest that they supported a Jewish or charitable enterprise.[19] Luke 7:1-10 describes a centurion recommended to Jesus by local elders, "for he loves our people, and it is he who built our synagogue for us" (v. 5). Admiration for an ethnic group and the performance of benefactions for it do not require religious interest. Polytheists also built synagogues.[20] Shaye Cohen has ably tabulated the wide range of types of interest in Judaism and the multiple meanings of "God-Fearer."[21] It is appropriate to view the God-Fearers of Acts as clones of Cornelius, but this religious interpretation does not apply to all God-Fearers everywhere. The importance of this understanding becomes clear in the thesis of Joyce Reynolds and Robert Tannenbaum: "It is with the God-fearers that Paul has many of his best results, in terms of conversion; this is why it is so important to the history of Christianity to understand who they are."[22]

14 Trans. R. Humphries, *The Satires of Juvenal* (Bloomington: Indiana University Press, 1958) 164.

15 *Metuentem sabbata* (line 96; cf. also *metuunt ius*, line 101) raise the question of a technical term, but *metuens* has its own history and is not a simple translation of one or all of the Greek expressions. See Trebilco, *Jewish Communities*, 248 n. 20. On this passage, see also Menachem Stern's commentary, *Authors*, no. 301, 2:102–7; John Ferguson, *Juvenal, The Satires* (New York: St. Martin's, 1979) 308; and Courtney, *Juvenal*, 571–72.

16 See the full range of data in Feldman, *Jew and Gentile* (n. 12).

17 See the references in n. 12.

18 Smallwood, *The Jews*, 281 n. 284.

19 The inscription was published by Joyce Reynolds and Robert Tannenbaum in *Jews and Godfearers at Aphrodisias* (Cambridge Philological Society Supp. 12; Cambridge: Cambridge University Press, 1987). See D.-A. Koch, "The God-Fearers between Facts and Fiction: Two Theosebeis Inscriptions from Aphrodisias and Their Bearing for the New Testament," *ST* 60 (2006) 62–90. He represents a growing consensus that these inscriptions date from 4–5 CE and divides the prize: one list is more social in character, the other more religious.

20 Cf. *CIJ* 1443 (= Baruch Lifshitz, *Donateurs et fondateurs dans les synagogues juives* [CahRB 7; Paris: Gabalda, 1967] 95 (p. 79) and *OGIS* 96). An example of a polytheist synagogue builder closer to the home and date of this part of Acts is Julia Severa, of Akmonia in Phrygia, a woman with consular connections. See Lifshitz, *Donateurs* 33 (= *MAMA* 6:264, *CIJ*, 766). For a resumé of her career and connections, see Trebilco, *Jewish Communities*, 58–60.

21 Shaye J. D. Cohen, *The Beginnings of Jewishness: Boundaries, Varieties, Uncertainties* (Berkeley: University of California Press, 1999) 146–48, 168–74.

22 Reynolds and Tannenbaum, *Jews and Godfearers*, 52. The evidence they adduce, Acts 13:43 (cf. 48); 14:1-2; 17:4, 12; and 18:47 (73 n. 203), does not, in fact, support this conclusion.

There were indeed some gentile admirers of Judaism, and some of them became Christians. But the "God-Fearers" serve Luke as a literary device.[23] They are low-hanging fruit whose openness to the Christian message is a foil to the general obstinacy of "the Jews." One might gather from the central chapters of Acts that Paul practically picks the synagogues clean of their gentile sympathizers. An issue that the receptivity of the God-Fearers tacitly and implicitly exposes is the place of Torah observance. The implied reader is evidently one who believes that gentiles are eager to participate in the divine promises but find observance an obstacle.[24] God-Fearers long for the sausage promised by the prophets without the harsh casing of Torah. This thesis would have come as a surprise to the author of Galatians.[25]

The speech[26] (vv. 16-41) fully exposes the unhistorical character of the missionary speeches in Acts. Although it purports to be a speech of Paul in a Diaspora synagogue,[27] even a superficial reading indicates that the sermon is directed to the readers of the book rather than to the dramatic audience, which would have found much of it confusing and/or unintelligible.[28] It is not likely that these persons would have been familiar with the stories of the Baptizer and Jesus or would have known about Pilate.[29] Second, this address accords with other speeches in (Luke and) Acts. The parallels between this sermon and the initial sermons of Jesus in Luke, Peter's sermons in Acts 2; 3; and 10, Stephen's address in Acts 7,[30] and Paul's sermons elsewhere,[31] demonstrate the unity of the Christian message and its messengers. This is not to suggest that readers sense another repetition of the same old sermon. The setting is ably evoked with a few words, while v. 42 communicates the enthusiasm of a crowd that has heard something fresh and exciting.[32]

The general structure also follows the pattern of Acts 2–5. Paul, like Peter, preaches one sermon in a conflict-free setting. Peter's sermon in Acts 3 was interrupted by the police (4:1). Paul's second performance also met

23 Cf. Michael J. Cook, "The Mission to the Jews in Acts: Unraveling Luke's 'Myth of the "Myriads,"'" in Joseph Tyson, ed., *Luke-Acts and the Jewish People: Eight Critical Perspectives* (Minneapolis: Augsburg, 1988) 102–23, esp. 120; and Shelly Matthews, *First Converts: Rich Pagan Women and the Rhetoric of Mission in Early Judaism and Christianity* (Stanford: Stanford University Press, 2001) 66–68.

24 The idea that Torah observance could be an obstacle to participation in the covenant rather than the medium for participation is a gentile perspective. The leading candidate for the role of implied reader is the dedicatee of Luke and Acts, Theophilus. Joseph Tyson has a detailed study of the implied reader's knowledge and interests (*Images*, 19–41).

25 Although the "South Galatian" (province) hypothesis owes its very existence to Acts, it is difficult to reconstruct a situation that would have made Paul's gentile (including "God-fearing") converts receptive to Jewish practice in the light of the narrative, which presents "the Jews" as implacable opponents and Torah observance as an obstacle.

26 On the history of the discussion about the origins of this speech, see Schneider 2:129–30. The proposal of John W. Bowker ("Speeches in Acts: A Study in Proem and Yelammedenu Form," *NTS* 14 [1967–68] 96–104) that this represents a form of synagogue homily runs into the specific difficulty that one must posit the lessons read in order to support the theory. For the difficulties in attempting to defend this as (the summary of) an actual sermon preached on the occasion, see Hemer, *Book*, 420–24. See also the detailed study of Matthäus F. J. Buss, *Die Missionspredigt des Apostels Paulus im Pisidischen Antiochien* (FzB 38; Stuttgart: Katholisches Bibelwerk, 1980).

27 Conzelmann, 103: "The content of the speech is a fundamental encounter between church and synagogue, based upon salvation history."

28 Conzelmann (105) notes the obscurity of the citation of Isa 55:3 in vv. 34-35, explained by way of 2:27. Johnson, 238: "The argument would obviously not be convincing for anyone who was not already committed to its governing premise."

29 Cf. Cadbury and Lake, 152.

30 Haenchen, 415: "As far as possible, Luke avoids repeating anything already said in Stephen's speech. Hence the Patriarchs and Moses are not mentioned. The *reader* already knows their significance." Krodel (232) and Johnson (238) have concise summaries of the parallels with Peter's first sermons. Note also Tyson, *Images*, 135–37. On Acts 10, see, e.g., Bruce, 306. Johnson (237) sums it up: "Paul's speech looks in equal parts like the discourses of Peter and the speech of Stephen."

31 On the relations among Paul's sermons in Acts 13, 17, and 20, see M. Quesnell, "Paul prédicateur dans les Actes des Apôtres," *NTS* 47 (2001) 469–81.

32 See Rackham, *xxx*.

resistance (13:44-52). In both cases persecution leads to greater success (4:4; 13:49). The speech is delineated by an inclusion of sorts: the leaders asked Paul and Barnabas for some exhortation (παράκλησις [v. 15]). At the end, the hearers beg (παρεκάλουν [v. 42]) for more. Its rhetorical function is symboleutic.[33] The author indicates the structure by the repeated address: vv. 16b, 26, and 38.[34] (I) Verses 16b-25 are a review of salvation history through David, leading to the thesis of v. 23: Jesus is the savior. (II) Verses 26-37 set forth the message of salvation, with a reiteration of the thesis in v. 32. (III) Verses 38-41 are a sort of peroration, with a promise and threat that resemble the *Krisenspruch* (declaration of judgment) found in prophetic and sapiential speeches. Although the speech is steeped in scriptural allusion and citation, it is Christian in character. The survey of salvation history ignores both covenant and Torah.[35] The latter appears in a negative reference toward the close. The influence of Galatians is patent in vv. 38-39[36] and quite possibly in v. 23 (where the use of Romans may also be detected,[37] but disputes about covenant and Torah are no longer vital. Promise and fulfillment[38] are the keys; forgiveness of sins (v. 38), the goal.

This sermon elucidates two general understandings of the speeches in Acts. One is what Soards calls their unifying effect.[39] They hold the narrative together in other ways than by demonstrating the consistency of the messages of the various preachers. Unlike the speeches found, for example, in historians, they cannot usually be removed without reducing the narrative to incomprehensibility. The second is that much of the content of this sermon is difficult for those not familiar with chaps. 2–10. A number of the textual expansions seek to alleviate these difficulties. Comparison of the two addresses to gentiles (chaps. 14 and 17) leads to a similar conclusion regarding those speeches.[40]

Comment

■ **16-20** Insofar as the narrative indicates, Paul spoke from where he had been sitting. Although the invitation was addressed to both visitors, Paul alone responds. He is *the* speaker (cf. 13:13; 14:12). The address includes "God-Fearers," who, in typical fashion, are not introduced or explained. The implied reader will evidently think of Cornelius. The opening words nonetheless assume that the hearers are Jews ("our ancestors"). This may be due to careless use of typical material or, if intention is bestowed on the narrator, it may be seen as revealing the isolation of the God-Fearers. The historical review[41] begins with the sojourn in Egypt[42] (rather than with Abraham or Moses) and moves expeditiously to the point where Stephen began to abbreviate his survey (cf. 7:45). The impetus is election theology, which, as it emphasizes divine free choice, will open the way for a crucified savior of both Jews and gentiles. Verse 18 presents a difficult textual choice between two similar verbs, ἐτροποφόρησεν and ἐτροφοφόρησεν, with quite different meanings. The former would mean "endured," the latter, "nourished." Grassmann's Law could make them formally identical.[43] The choice lies between the slightly hostile "put up with" and the more

33 Witherington (407) provides this rhetorical analysis: v. 16, *exordium*; vv. 17-25, *narratio*; v. 26, *propositio*; vv. 27-37, *probatio*; vv. 38-41, *peroratio*. It is unlikely that v. 26 is the thesis, and proof is scattered throughout, but this attempt shows the general conformity to rhetorical organization. Kennedy (*Rhetorical Criticism*, 124–25) is his source, but Kennedy views the speech as epideictic, since it seeks faith, rather than action. This is based on the presumption of historicity.

34 For discussions of structure, see, for example, Wilckens, *Missionsreden*, 50–54; Soards, *Speeches*, 79–80; Barrett, 1:623; and Fitzmyer, 507–8. The last three summarize the conclusions of other scholars.

35 Cf. Rackham, 212.

36 See below.

37 For the descendants (σπέρμα) of David and Abraham, see Rom 1:3; 4:13, 16, etc.; Gal 3:16, 19, 29.

38 Promise: vv. 23, 32; fulfillment: vv. 27, 32, 40 (potential).

39 Soards, *Speeches*, 182–83.

40 This view derives from Dibelius, *Studies*, 138–85. Cf. also Schneider, 1:97 n. 80.

41 2 Sam 7 appears to be a major immediate or proximate source. See Soards, *Speeches*, 82.

42 Sojourn (παροικία): cf. Wis 19:10, and the adjective in Acts 7:6, 29.

43 Grassmann's Law deals with the dissimilation of aspirates, as in τίθημι, rather than *θιθημι (cf. δίδωμι). (On this principle and its difficulties, see Neville E. Collinge, *The Laws of Indo-European*

neutral "cared for." The subtle hostility that creeps into Stephen's speech supports the former, but the emphasis of this section on God's graciousness inclines toward "nurtured."[44] "God" is the subject of every clause in vv. 17-23.[45] The function of the chronology[46] is mainly rhetorical, infusing the survey with the glow of objectivity,[47] but it has yielded textual problems.[48] Probability suggests that Luke (or his source) took a casual approach to the "450 years"[49] and that subsequent editors attempted to correct this or to remove misunderstanding. It is easier to understand the text printed by N-A[27] as liable to correction than as a corruption.[50] The 450 years of v. 20 and the forty assigned to Saul total 490, which may reflect an underlying apocalyptic scheme.[51]

■ **21-25** By the end of v. 20, the survey has already reached Samuel. In this speech, the prophetic era extends from Samuel to the Baptizer.[52] With Samuel comes kingship. After forty years of Saul[53] come David and the promise, the object of the entire sketch.[54] The citation in v. 22 derives from several texts: Ps 88:21 LXX; 1 Kgdms 13:14; and Isa 44:28. The first two

[Amsterdam: John Benjamins, 1985] 47–61.) Application of this principle would lead to "correcting" ἐτροφοφορ- by ἐτροποφορ-.

44 Not only are the NT witnesses almost evenly divided, but the LXX prototype in Deut 1:31 exhibits the same variants with adequate support for each. Translation variants are unlikely here, since these usually differ by more than a single word, although correction is a slight possibility. Metzger (*Textual Commentary*, 357) prefers "endured" on the grounds of nonconformity with the LXX. Fitzmyer (510) takes a similar view. Haenchen (408) prefers "nurture," with a list of earlier scholars in agreement. Barrett (1:632) agrees "with anything but complete confidence." Jervell (355) accepts "put up with," but denies that it has a negative nuance. Johnson (231) prefers "nurture" because of the emphasis on God's gracious actions. Clarification was wanted; witness the (apparently) secondary addition of αὐτοῖς by a range of witnesses (A C D[2] E 1739 𝔪 lat sy[p]). Note also the D-Text reading (Boismard, *Texte*, 216), "the land of foreigners" (ἀλλοφύλων) rather than "their" (αὐτῶν), which evidently overlooks the role of "the land" in Israelite tradition.

45 Verses 2 and 21 use the verb "gave" (ἔδωκεν).

46 Use of a temporal dative to express duration of time in v. 20 looks barbarous, but it was common in postclassical Greek (BDF §201). (Contrast v. 36, which exhibits conventional practice.)

47 Cf. Johnson (231), who compares the use of chronology in Stephen's speech: 7:6, 23, 30, 36, 42.

48 It is less likely that the chronology indicates periodization, since the eras differ greatly in length. Periods are marked by the proper names: Samuel, John the Baptizer, and so on.

49 Bede (*Retractatio* 146) allows the possibility that this information is based on "a popular report" (*nisi forte vulgarem in loquendo famam secutus est*).

50 There is no firm evidentiary base: Josephus (*Ant.* 8.61) and 1 Kgs 6:1 differ, and the MT and the LXX of the latter differ. Calculation was, in any case, difficult, and numbers in Greek MSS. are notoriously subject to corruption. Josephus was not consistent, as *Ant.* 11.112 and 20.230 indicate. See Bede (62), who worked out a solution that he later withdrew (146); Clark, 354–56; Cadbury and Lake, 150–51; Metzger, *Textual Commentary*, 357–58; Barrett, 1:633; and Fitzmyer, 551. The D-Text (Boismard, *Texte*, 216) states, unambiguously, that the period of the judges lasted 450 years.

51 Seven "weeks" of seventy years each would locate David at the beginning of the eighth "week," the time of fulfillment. A similar scheme, based on seventy-seven, may stand behind the Lucan genealogy (Luke 3:23-38). See Raymond E. Brown, *The Birth of the Messiah* (ABRL; rev. ed.; New York: Doubleday, 1993) 93; and Cadbury and Lake, 151. The forty-year reign conforms to Josephus *Ant.* 6.378, but the text there may have been adjusted to agree with Acts. See the note of Ralph Marcus in *Josephus V* (LCL; Cambridge, Mass.: Harvard University Press, 1934) 357.

52 Cf. Conzelmann, *Theology*, 22–27. Although his exegesis of Luke 16:16-18 is strongly disputed, Acts 13 supports the division. John the Baptizer is a hinge figure who points both ways, but he belongs to the time of promise, which is the sphere of the Law and the Prophets. For a different interpretation, see Weiser, 1:333. Acts 3:24 begins the "prophetic era" with Samuel.

53 Hemer (*Book* 183) finds an "undesigned coincidence" between v. 21 and Phil 3:5. This presumes that the reference to Paul's tribe is autobiographical. The insertion of such a reference into an extremely short survey of Israelite history would not flatter Paul, since the subsequent sentence describes Saul's deposition.

54 A sermon that focused on God-Fearers might be expected to discuss the universal promise to Abraham. That promise was the subject of 7:5.

appear also in *1 Clem.* 18:1, from which Luke may have drawn the combination.[55] The implication is clear: those who do not follow God's will are likely to be set aside, like Saul. The promise to David,[56] the centerpiece of this part of the argument, is not cited. Hearers would have to be familiar with a text like 2 Sam 7:12, another indication that the speech is intelligible only to the readers of the book. Rather than the monarch or messiah suggested by that passage, however, fulfillment is a "savior" (σωτήρ) Jesus, otherwise unidentified. This title, used in the present sense (as opposed to a future savior), is a relatively late development. Here one can see language common in the ruler cult replacing such explicitly Jewish concepts as "messiah" or the dangerous and confusing term "king."[57] The second half of the sentence (v. 24) reverses course, with its reference to one John, who, prior to the arrival of Jesus, preached repentance associated with the idea of a baptism of all Israelites. The odd language is due to the passage's evocation of Mal 3:1-2.[58] Those who grasp this allusion will understand John's role as forerunner. The summons to repentance summarizes his activity. Verse 25 reveals his role as herald. Although he repeats the affirmation that John's activity stands at the beginning of Jesus' mission,[59] Luke is not able or prepared to integrate the mission of the historical Baptizer with his Christian function.[60] Instead, he places them in sequence. As John's activity was drawing to a close,[61] he denied that he was "it." Again, it is difficult to imagine that this statement would make much sense to those unfamiliar with the gospel tradition.[62]

■ **26-37** The next section sets forth the message of salvation intimated in the first. The parallels to Peter's speeches in Acts 2 and 3 are patent.[63] This is not simply because "the kerygma" followed fixed patterns. Luke wishes to show the commonality of the "gospel" of Peter and Paul. Both preach the same message, in Jerusalem and in the Diaspora. The text of vv. 27-29 is either careless or corrupt.[64] In the end, it makes little difference, for conjectural emendations amount to composition rather than correction, and the D-Text alternative is both difficult to reconstruct and arguably corrective of a text more or less identical to that of N-A[27].[65] That text is intelligible to readers who will resolve the difficulties by reference to Peter's speech in 3:12-26. Although the pronoun τοῦτον in v. 27 is ambiguous, since the logic of grammar applies it to the nearest appropriate proper

---

55 These two share the use of μαρτυρέω ("witness," "testify") and ἄνδρα ("man") instead of the LXX ἄνθρωπον ("person"), making it somewhat less likely that a collection of "testimonies" stands behind each. For such a collection, which utilizes texts about David in 2 Samuel, see 4Q174, 8–13. See Pervo, *Dating*, 301–2.

56 Verse 23 reflects the "creedal" style, placing the demonstrative τούτου ("he," emphatic) in first position. The D-Text either misses or disapproves of this and revises the word order (Boismard, *Texte*, 217).

57 On "savior," see Pervo, *Dating*, 287–88.

58 The difficult πρὸ προσώπου (lit. "before his face"), as, in effect, a preposition, stems from Mal 3:1 (Luke 1:17; 7:22; Rev 22:16), while εἴσοδος appears in Mal 3:2. On this term, the antonym of *exodus* (Luke 9:31), see Wilhelm Michaelis, "εἴσοδος, ἔξοδος," *TDNT* 5:103–8. It refers to the beginning of Jesus' public ministry, not to his birth.

59 See the comments on 1:22.

60 The historical Paul never mentions John the Baptizer.

61 "Course" is a somewhat faded athletic metaphor that has become part of the language of Deutero-Pauline parenesis. Cf. Haenchen, 409. Note Acts 20:24; 2 Tim 4:7. On the image, see Otto Bauernfeind, "τρέχω," *TDNT* 8:226–35. One example is Euripides *Electra* 953–56.

62 Cf. the questions about John in Luke 7:24-27 (Q) and John 1:19-27. The variant τίνα ("whom?") is a secondary improvement. The alternative translation (n. *l*) is based on construing the phrase as declarative and τί as equivalent to a relative ("what" = "that which"). See BDF §298 (4); and Moule, *Idiom Book*, 124.

63 The following are some of the parallels and correspondences between speeches of Acts 2 and 13: 2:22||13:27; 2:23||13:28; 2:24||13:30; 2:25||13:35; 2:27||13:35; 2:29||13:36; 2:20 (cf. 13:23; 2:31||13:37. See also Krodel, 232.

64 Cadbury and Lake (153) view the text as "extraordinarily corrupt."

65 For reconstructions of the D-Text, see Ropes, *Text*, 261–63 (with many valuable comments); Clark, 356; and Boismard, *Texte*, 219–21.

noun, "the message of salvation" in v. 26, the author has "Jesus" (v. 24) in mind. The participle ἀγνοήσαντες ("being ignorant," one of four participles in the verse), may have two objects, the pronoun and τὰς φωνὰς ("declarations"), or the latter may be the object of ἐπλήρωσαν ("brought to fulfillment").[66] Finally, κρίναντες ("condemning") simply dangles,[67] and with it εὑρόντες ("finding") in v. 28. Epp correctly points to 3:17 as the basis for comprehension.[68]

D-Texts revise ἀγνοήσαντες ("being ignorant") to μὴ συνίεντες ("not understanding"). Although this is often viewed as anti-Jewish,[69] it is a sensible correction, since the same verse speaks of the weekly reading of the prophets. Failure to understand was a quality shared by the disciples of Jesus (Luke 24:45).[70] In v. 28, the D-Text reads εὑρόντες ἐν αὐτῷ, "finding no capital guilt in him."[71] The most important change is an addition at the beginning of v. 29: "After he had been crucified they asked Pilate to take him off the cross. With his consent they did so and placed [him] in a tomb."[72] This replaces "When they had brought to pass all that had been written about him" (omitted by sy^{hmg} and cop^{mae}). That phrase had become gratuitous.[73] These modifications reflect the demands of clarity and realism. The summary of the passion was too concise and crabbed for those unfamiliar with the message. So short is this summary that a reader might conclude that Jesus was buried by his enemies![74]

■ **30-33** For the dramatic audience (as envisioned by the reader), vv. 30-31 would have been no less a shock than the admission that the savior had been crucified.[75] Verse 31[76] summarizes the message of Acts 1:1-22 and the role of the apostles (not so designated) in 2:32; 3:15; 5:32.[77] Paul's proper role is set forth in v. 32: to "evangelize."[78] At this point he shifts toward proof of the resurrection, introduced by reference to the promise made to David in v. 23. For this purpose, the writings of David will aptly serve. The citation of Ps 2:7 in this context

66 Dibelius (*Studies*, 91) resolves the problem by deleting τοῦτον.

67 Friedrich Blass (*Acta apostolorum sive Lucae ad Theophilum liber alter. Editio philologica* [Göttingen: Vandenhoeck & Ruprecht, 1895], 151) proposed emending this to μὴ ἀνακρίναντες ("without a proper judicial inquiry"), 151. This presumes corruption. It is unlikely that the author of Luke 22:66-71 would have written this, but, in favor of this hypothesis, it is also possible that someone familiar with the passion narrative would have corrected it, but both this emendation and κρίναντες conflict with the following statement. Ropes deletes it from the D-Text here as a contamination and transfers it, with a pronoun ("condemning him") to v. 28.

68 Epp, *Tendency*, 46–48.

69 E.g., ibid., 46.

70 This argument, regardless of the participle used, belongs to the sphere of early Christian apologetics: the Jews did not understand their own Scriptures. Examples are *Barn.* 10:2–9; Justin *1 Apol.* 31.

71 Conzelmann (105) asks whether the phrase might mean "*because* they found no guilt." On the accusatives with the verb and infinitive in v. 28, see BDF §409 (5).

72 μετὰ τὸ σταυρωθῆναι αὐτὸν ἠτήσαντο Πιλᾶτον ἀπὸ τοῦ ξύλου καταιρεῖν αὐτόν. Και ἐπιτυχόντες καθελόντες αὐτὸν ἔθηκαν εἰς μνημεῖον. This is the text of Boismard, *Texte*, 220. Clark (356) accepts the μὲν σταυρῶσαι of D and supplements it with a conjecture of Bornemann: "They kept on demanding (ᾐτοῦντο, impf. instead of aor.) of Pilate that he crucify [Jesus] but release Barabbas" (τὸν δε Βαραββᾶν ἀπολῦσαι). Ropes (*Text*, 262) suspects that the particle μέν derives from the preposition μετά.

73 It may also have seemed incorrect, in that it omits the resurrection from the prophecies. The basis is Luke 18:31. On the verb τελέω ("bring to pass") in reference to the fulfillment of prophecies, see Squires, *Plan*, 124 n. 21.

74 On this, see Conzelmann, 105.

75 The D-Text (Bosimard, *Texte*, 221) begins v. 30 with the relative ὅν ("whom") and omits δέ, as well as αὐτόν (followed by the demonstrative οὗτος instead of the relative in v. 31 ("this one" instead of "who"). "From the dead" is also omitted. The result is certainly more dramatic.

76 The word οἵτινες is a relative connective, not very acceptable in Greek (BDF §458).

77 The word νῦν ("at present") is an acute problem. Does this seek to distinguish Paul's statement from other references to witnesses, or was it removed because it was not in those references? Various placements and modifications suggest that it was unstable, but it may be original. Notice also the apparent compromise of Ψ: "they are fellow witnesses" (σύνεισιν). Perhaps it was omitted because it suggests that the apostolic witness is not abiding. See Metzger, *Textual Commentary*, 361. Paul does

is compatible with the view that Jesus was made the Messiah at his resurrection.[79] The D-Text expands the quotation to include v. 8: "Ask of me, and I will make the nations your heritage, and the ends of the earth your possession." This lamely anticipates v. 47.[80]

■ **34-35** At first glance, it appears that v. 34b is superfluous and confusing. The citation from Isaiah buttresses the assertion in v. 34a, and perhaps, since it is plural, generalizes it: all will receive the gifts. "Confusing" aptly characterizes the citation (with a different verb) of Isa 55:3: δώσω ὑμῖν τὰ ὅσια Δαυὶδ τὰ πιστά (lit. "I shall give you the holy things [of] David the things that are trustworthy"). Translations are tempted to reach back to the underlying Hebrew (e.g., *NRSV*), but this is not legitimate. Problems include the meaning of the neuter, the nature of the construction, and the case of the anarthrous "David." The last is almost certainly a genitive, and "promises" appears to suit the context.[81] Cop[mae] expands the verse: "He has raised him up from the dead **in such a way as** never again to return to decay, **that all the people may know** (it) **and repent**. **For thus it is written in the prophet Isaiah**, 'I will make **with you an everlasting covenant**, the holy things of David.'"[82] This amounts to an early conjectural emendation The argument has thus circled back to vv. 22-23. The promise to David will now receive elaboration and explanation.

■ **36-37** These verses reiterate the argument of 2:27-31.[83] The christological argument is that Jesus was unjustly killed and buried, as prophesied, but raised by God and thus authenticated as the one of whom David spoke. The presumably pre-Lucan medley of texts (Ps 2:7; Isa 55:3; Ps 16:10), which seeks to explicate words ("give" [δίδωμι] and "holy" [ὅσιος] here[84]) by associating their appearance in different contexts (called *gezerah shewa* by the rabbis) views the resurrection as the enthronement of Jesus to the post of messianic ruler (cf. Rom 1:4). The background is thus an exaltation Christology (cf. Hebrews) that is not based on the resurrection proper. Luke nonetheless unabashedly asserts the return to physical life of the undecayed flesh-and-blood body of Jesus. In comparison with the discretion of Paul, this seems crude. It is reasonable to suspect that Luke was aware of docetic notions and wished to rebut them.[85]

■ **38-41** The peroration, consisting of an elaboration of the promise followed by a threat extracted from the prophets, begins with a Lucan formula[86] and an address

not here include himself among the witnesses of the resurrection (cf. 1 Cor 9:1; 15:8).

78 The construction of vv. 32-33a is unusual. The subject of proclamation is that God has fulfilled for their descendants the promise made to the ancestors, but the arrangement makes both promise and fulfillment objects of the verb.

79 Cf. Luke 3:22, which applies this text (according to a variant with a strong claim to be original) to the baptism.

80 See Epp, *Tendency*, 79–81. Clark (357) finds it "necessary to the sense," one thing that it is not. Boismard (*Texte*, 222) excludes it from his edition.

81 On the problems and possible solutions, see Cadbury and Lake, 155–56; Bruce, 310 (who concentrates on the meaning of the LXX); Barrett, 1:647–48; and Fitzmyer, 517. All solutions involve elements of conjecture and desperation. Conzelmann sees that πιστά here does not mean "worthy of credence" but matters incapable of nonfulfillment.

82 Schenke, *Apostelgeschichte*, 190–91.

83 It is not clear whether "in his own generation" belongs to David or to the participle, i.e., as indirect object. See the alternatives in Haenchen, 412 and n. 3. (The point is that the promise cannot refer to David himself.) Note also Barrett, 1:648–49. "Foreseeing" (προιδών) in 2:31 corresponds to "the plan of God" (βουλή, "purpose")

84 For this reason, the vague ἐν ἑτέρῳ (lit. "in another") probably does not mean "in another Psalm" but, "in another passage." The D-Text (Boismard, *Texte*, 223) compromises with ἑτέρως ("otherwise"). In the LXX, the verb is διαθήσομαι (with object). This suggests that the two citations were combined in pre-Lucan tradition, as Lüdemann (157), among others, proposes. For discussion, see also Gert J. Steyn, *Septuagint Quotations in the Context of the Petrine and Pauline Speeches of the Acta Apostolorum* (Contributions to Biblical Exegesis and Theology 12; Kampen: Kok Pharos, 1995) 182.

85 Charles Talbert, *Luke and the Gnostics* (New York: Abingdon, 1966) 46–48. Luke may not have reflected on the background of the textual medley that he took up, but it is also possible that he wished to blunt it by combination with the theme of resurrection of the flesh.

86 The formula γνωστὸν ἔστω (lit. "let it be known") is used by Peter in 2:14; 4:10, and by Paul in 28:28. It thus introduces the close of Paul's initial and final addresses.

that makes no distinction between Israelites proper and gentile listeners. This is appropriate, for the speaker is about to set forth the Pauline doctrine of justification by faith.[87] The equation of justification with forgiveness of sins shows that his understanding is Deutero-Pauline.[88] Luke does not quite describe Jesus as the means of forgiveness: through him forgiveness is announced. How and why "forgiveness of sins" became a major concern in post-Pauline gentile Christianity is not clear. Forgiveness evidently derived from the need to convince gentiles of the reality of sin as a major disruption of the relationship between humans and God.[89] The forgiveness announced by Paul achieves "justification" not available in the law of Moses. For the reader, this shorthand is pure Paulinism, but for the dramatic audience it would have made little sense. Insofar as "justification" was concerned, Torah was quite sufficient. This is not, then, a dialogue with Jewish theology proper, but a somewhat etiolated reflection of Paul's arguments with "Judaizing" Christians.[90] The limits of the coordination attempted appear in two prepositional phrases: διὰ τούτου and ἐν τούτῳ. In both cases, the demonstrative is best understood as personal: "him" = "Jesus." The former is probably instrumental,[91] as is the latter, which is due to the introduction of Pauline language.[92]

The D-Text revises this statement "forgiveness of sins is proclaimed, and **repentance** from all from which you could not be justified by the law of Moses. By this one, **therefore**, all believers are justified **before God**."[93] This changes the construction by linking vv. 38 and 39. The addition of repentance also clarifies that forgiveness is not handed out gratuitously but as the result of change. The addition of οὖν ("therefore") makes v. 39 a clearly independent statement.[94] The addition of "repentance" is an attempt to be "Lucan," but Luke does not coordinate repentance and forgiveness. The former brings the latter.[95] Verse 41[96] establishes that the promise is not unalloyed good news. Those who reject the message

87 There is almost universal consensus that vv. 38-39 indicate Luke's familiarity with Pauline thought (e.g., Witherington, 414). Pervo (*Dating*, 58–59) proposes that Gal 3:11; 5:4 may be in mind. Phillip Vielhauer ("On the 'Paulinism' of Acts," in Keck and Martyn, *Studies*, 33–51, esp. 42) says: "Luke did know that Paul proclaimed justification by faith, but he did not know its central significance and absolute importance; he thought it was valid primarily for the Gentiles." It is more likely that Luke *did* know its significance but attempted to blunt its edges. Luke will not say that Torah is of no value to Jews. For a detailed study, see Josef Pichler, *Paulusrezeption in der Apostelgeschichte: Untersuchungen zur Rede im pisidischen Antiochien* (Innsbruck: Tyrolia, 1997).

88 Paul does not use the term ἄφεσις ("forgiveness"), although the similar πάρεσις appears at Rom 3:25 (with ἁμαρτήματα, "sins"). This is a basis of post-Pauline development. "Forgiveness of sins" (ἄφεσις τῶν ἁμαρτιῶν), the phrase used here, is found in Col 1:14||Eph 1:7, where it is equated with "redemption" (ἀπολύτρωσις). Cf. Fitzmyer, 507.

89 This is implied by Rudolf Bultmann, "ἀφίημι," *TDNT* 1:509–12. For Luke, the concept creates continuity between the message of John (e.g., Luke 3:3; cf. Acts 13:24). John's program was different: an alternative to the requisite sacrifices.

90 On the differences between Paul's views of "justification" and Jewish understandings, see E. P. Sanders, *Paul and Palestinian Judaism: A Comparison of Patterns of Religion* (Philadelphia: Fortress Press, 1977), e.g., 505–6. For a comparison of the Lucan and Pauline views on justification, see Adolf von Harnack, *Neue Untersuchungen zur Apostelgeschichte* (Leipzig: Hinrichs, 1911) 48.

91 Note also the variant ($\mathfrak{p}^{74}$ B* 36 [1175 *al*]) διὰ τοῦτο ("therefore"), which may attempt improvement. Metzger (*Textual Commentary*, 366) regards it as probably accidental.

92 This is apparent in the contrast between ἐν νόμῳ and ἐν τούτῳ ("by the law . . . by him"). The καί ("and") after "announced" (καταγγέλλεται) is omitted by $\mathfrak{p}^{74}$ ℵ A C* D *pc* t w vgst. It is more difficult, but may be the result of contamination with the D-Text (below).

93 ἄφεσις ἁμαρτιῶν καταγγέλλεται, καὶ μετάνοια ἀπὸ πάντων ὧν οὐκ ἠδυνήθητε ἐν νόμῳ Μωϋσέως δικαιωθῆναι, 39 ἐν τούτῳ οὖν πᾶς ὁ πιστεύων δικαιοῦται παρὰ Θεῷ. See Boismard, *Texte*, 223 (where μετανοίαν is an error).

94 See Epp, *Tendency*, 81–82, who finds the D-Text more universalistic. "Before God" recognizes the influence of Gal 3:11.

95 Note Luke 24:47, where the D-Text (*et al.*) replaces μετάνοιαν εἰς ἄφεσιν ἁμαρτιῶν with μετάνοιαν καὶ ἄφεσιν. This is a distinction between the author of Acts and his "D editor."

96 The reference of the "deed" (ἔργον) in v. 41 is vague, but the author probably understands it of the vindication of Jesus rather than of the missionary activity.

about Jesus are in danger of ruin. Hab 1:5[97] serves aptly because it threatens those who do not believe (πιστεύετε; cf. πιστεύων in v. 39) when the message is proclaimed, assuming that they will, in fact, not believe. The prophecy is self-fulfilling in form.[98] Actual fulfillment will come in v. 45.[99]

The logic is clear: part I demonstrated God's goodness from salvation history. The death and resurrection of Jesus (part II) must, since it was prophesied, be the fulfillment of the promise. Much of part II has resembled Peter's first sermon in chap. 2. The logic of the conclusion is less clear. Unlike 2:37-41, this speech does not close with an explicit invitation. This deficit reveals that the narrator controls the entire scene. Reaction is delayed for a week to allow for the introduction of numerous gentiles. Despite its similarity to earlier speeches, Paul's initial sermon marks a new direction. The Torah—not just the temple—is judged insufficient and is effectively replaced by Christ.[100] Those who do not accept this claim are threatened with destruction. The first twelve chapters have not laid the ground for this radical claim, and much that follows does not seem to bear it out. Those demanding consistency at the most basic level will conclude that Torah observance—not least that of Paul—is acceptable for Jews but that it has no soteriological significance. Chapter 15 will enshrine that thesis, and Peter will there say that Torah observance is impossible (15:7-11). Luke's strategy is apparent. The insufficiency and impossibility of Torah are asserted, but he does not flaunt those facts in the faces of believers of Jewish birth (or sympathy?). Even Paul will remain observant (21:26, etc.). Rather than accuse Luke of selling out or watering down Paulinism, it is more appropriate to recognize that he is a skilled ecclesiastical politician who knows how to let people down easily. In the heat of controversy Paul displayed no such capacity, but Romans reveals that he was not without diplomatic gifts, and Romans points the way that Luke follows. The hand of the narrator is even more apparent in that the audience raises no immediate objection to this fundamental assault on the essence of Judaism. Finally, like its predecessors, this sermon contains no hint of eschatology.

■ **42-52** Verses 42-43 provide a dramatic, albeit awkward, conclusion that prepares for the sequel. Verses 44-48 and 49-52 constitute two parallel units, one specific, the other more general. Both follow the basic pattern of the Pauline mission: Jewish rejection resulting in gentile acceptance.[101] The first unit narrates success at Antioch. Further expansion provokes persecution, leading to expulsion and transfer to a new site: Iconium. "The effect of 13:44-52 as a whole is to cast the Jews who do not believe into the camp with Bar-Jesus and the gentiles who do believe into a grouping with the proconsul of Paphos."[102]

■ **42-43** Like an astute film editor, the narrator cuts from the last words of the sermon to the aftermath. Verses 42-43 appear to conflict, but this is not a doublet derived from two different sources.[103] Verse 42 reports their success via a request for a repeat performance. This is probably intentionally impersonal. Readers may presume that the subject of the genitive absolute is Paul and Barnabas. Verse 43 then relates the acquisition of followers. Editors rushed to fill these gaps.[104] Verse 43 contains a puzzling expression: *σεβόμενοι προσήλυτοι*, rendered (with considerable hesitation) "observant converts." The adjective "devout" otherwise refers to gentile "God-Fearers" (13:50; 16:14; 17:4 [with the noun "Greeks"]; 17:17; 18:7). Elsewhere in Acts, the noun refers to gentile converts to Judaism (2:11; 6:5). It is

97 The MT reads "gentiles" here. The LXX "scoffers/traitors" (καταφρονηταί) can be restored in 1QpHab 1:16. The Hebrew words are quite similar: *baggôyîm* ("among the nations") and *bôgĕdîm* ("traitors"). See William H. Brownlee, *The Midrash Pesher of Habakkuk* (SBLMS 24; Missoula, Mont.: Scholars Press, 1979), 54. On other differences between this text and the LXX (some variants are common to both), see Barrett, 1:652.

98 Johnson, 236.

99 The D-Text provides a closing, either καὶ ἐσίγησεν (614 cop[mae] sy[h*]) or ἐσίγησαν (D d): "he/they was/were silent." This is probably a way of marking the end of the speech, and the singular is more original. The plural may indicate the effect on the audience. On the range of meanings, see Epp, *Tendency*, 82–83.

100 Tyson, *Images*, 138.

101 Talbert (131) spells out the pattern.

102 Ibid., 132.

103 Conzelmann, 196; and Haenchen, 413.

104 The majority text adds after "going out": "from the synagogue of the Jews." Since some of those witnesses omit "they" (αὐτῶν), this can be construed,

unlikely that the text wished to contrast dutiful converts with the less observant. One possibility is that "devout" has been added (with v. 50 in view?) to a text that spoke only, like 2:11, of Jews by birth and Jews by choice. "Proselytes" has also come under suspicion.[105] A third approach is to posit that it derives from a source[106] in which the term *προσήλυτος* had not acquired the fixed meaning that it attained in the early second century, in which case it would be rendered "devout adherents."[107] The problem is not likely to be resolved. The narrator's intentions are to set the stage for the return visit, yet to assure readers that some had been won over. To describe the founding of a community at this point would disrupt the scheme. Paul works out of the synagogue as long as possible.

■ **44-46** Jealousy,[108] rather than critique of Torah, generates opposition. With ebullient hyperbole, the narrator says that almost everyone turned out on the next Sabbath to hear this new preacher,[109] whose authority to speak is assumed. Rather than take pleasure in this interest in their religion, "the Jews" are infuriated and (counter-)attack.[110] From the narrative, readers could conclude that Paul and Barnabas[111] had barely time to commence their message.[112] Undaunted, the missionaries address the Jews, in unison and *en masse* with the first of three declarations that, since the Jews had rejected the good news that it was their privilege to hear, the evangelists will turn to the gentiles. This declaration is repeated on two later occasions, 18:6 and 28:28. As Dibelius noted, it is made in the three chief regions

"as the Jews were leaving the synagogue." The majority text balances this by having the gentiles request a repeat performance in v. 43. The D-Text (Boismard, *Texte*, 224) says that those who gathered about Paul "asked to be baptized." (This same verb, ἀξιόω, appears in B after "Sabbath," permitting the suspicion that contamination affected the text at an early date.) The D-Text apparently assumes that Paul spoke of baptism in the address. There is no mention of baptism in chaps. 13–14. After "God's grace," the D-Text adds "the message permeated the entire city." On this, see Epp (*Tendency*, 83–84), who says that this advances the moment of evangelizing gentiles. That is technically true, but its major purpose is to rationalize the crowd of v. 44. See Metzger (*Textual Commentary*, 267–68), who discusses conjectural emendations; and Ropes, *Text*, 126.

105 Haenchen (413 n. 5) and Roloff (99) suspect that "proselytes" is a gloss. Conzelmann (106) considers this a possibility, along with careless writing. It seems more likely that an interpolator would insert "devout" to conform to the theme of God-Fearers than add "converts" to an otherwise intelligible text.

106 Presumably the gentile mission source.

107 On the term, see Pervo, *Dating*, 286–87. Martin Goodman maintains that "proselyte" did not acquire the fixed meaning "convert" until the early second century (*Mission and Conversion: Proselytizing in the Religious History of the Roman Empire* [Oxford: Clarendon, 1994] 82–84). Barrett (1:654) proposes that the adjective means "worshiping" here and thus refers to proselytes who had been in attendance. This would be superfluous.

108 On the motif of jealousy, see the comments on 5:17.

109 Nock (*Conversion*, 62) grasps the intention: "Acts xiii.43-4 implies that many Gentiles might come to a synagogue when a famous preacher was expected, just as they would rush to hear Dion of Prusa or Lucian." Haenchen (413–14), who suspects that a crowd of this size would have difficulty fitting into the synagogue facility, puts it differently: "Luke abandons all realism of presentation for the sake of depicting Paul as a great orator and successful missionary." Such crowd scenes are common in novels. See Pervo, *Profit*, 34–36; see also *Act. Pet.* 3; *Act. John* 31.

110 The verb ἀντιλέγω appeared in the prophecy of Simeon (Luke 2:34) and will recur at Rome (Acts 28:19, 22).

111 Verse 46 names Barnabas as a speaker. Although this is awkward (one must ask whether they spoke in turn or in unison, etc.), Luke includes him to show that the opposition was not to the message of Paul alone.

112 As often, the D-Text illustrates the narrator's ability and intention by expansion in the interest of rationality: "And the next Sabbath almost the whole city gathered together to hear Paul. And when he made a long discourse about the Lord [cf. the D-Text at 11:2] and the Jews saw the multitudes, they were filled with jealousy, and contradicted the words spoken by Paul, contradicting and blaspheming." So Metzger (*Textual Commentary*, 369), but Boismard (*Texte*, 225–26) smooths this out by omitting "the words spoken by Paul."

of the Pauline mission: Asia Minor, Greece, and Rome.[113] The sharp division between Jews and gentiles is due to Lucan usage: "the Jews" are Israelites who reject the Christian message. By so doing they revealed that they did not deserve "eternal life." This eschatological phrase comes as a surprise. Context suggests that it refers to the incorruptible life of the risen (v. 37).[114] The self-imposed judgment rules its exponents out of God's dominion, whereas believing gentiles are destined to enjoy it.[115]

■ **47** The shift to gentiles is justified by a modified citation[116] of Isa 49:6, which Paul and Barnabas apply to themselves.[117] This key Lucan passage[118] explicates the meaning of "the ends of the earth" (Acts 1:8). It is a symbol for the universal mission.[119] In compressed form, "the ends of the earth" refers to the mission of Paul. His missionary commission[120] is to be God's servant by bringing light to the gentiles.[121] The first intimation that Paul will be a kind of savior figure is linked to his turn from Jews to gentiles.[122]

■ **48-52** The second unit begins with another reminiscence of the early ministry of Jesus (Luke 4:14), followed, as in Luke 4:29, by expulsion (ἐκβάλλειν) from the jurisdiction, in both cases as the result of synagogue preaching that touched on the acceptability of gentiles (cf. Luke 4:25-28). The narrative probably intends to imply that "the Jews" appealed to their well-placed[123] female sympathizers,[124] who, in turn, made application to their husbands, who held positions of authority.[125] Persecution is the result of pillow talk. This is an unusual social prejudice for Luke, but a familiar theme in ancient conflict. Women were held to be liable to intellectual and other forms of seduction by holy men.[126] This was particularly lamentable when that seduction drew them to the side of one's opponents. According to the *Acta Hermaisci*, an Alexandrian embassy found Trajan already prejudiced in favor of the rival Jewish body through the offices of his wife, Plotina, who also lobbied

113 Dibelius, *Studies*, 150.

114 Haenchen, 414.

115 "Eternal life" appears in Acts only here, in 13:46, 48. Boismard (*Texte*, 226) omits it from the D-Text of v. 46, which is shorter than the conventional text: "preach (καταγγεῖλαι) God's message to you [first]. **Now**, since you [reject it] and [show that you] are unworthy (ἀναξίους) [of eternal life], we are therefore going to turn to the gentiles."

116 The citation omits εἰς διαθήκην γένους ("as a covenant for the nation") and thus strips the passage of any Jewish particularity.

117 Perhaps because of the tradition that viewed Jesus as the servant, the D-Text (Boismard, *Texte*, 228) reads οὕτως γὰρ εἶπεν ἡ γραφή ἰδοὺ φῶς τέθεικά σε τοῖς ἔθνεσιν ("For thus the Scripture said: 'Behold, I have placed you as a light to the nations.'") Were it not for this clearly secondary introduction, this form of the citation would have some claim to priority, as it deviates more from the LXX.

118 Note Luke 2:32 (and n. 110).

119 On this interpretation of the phrase, see Jacques Dupont, *The Salvation of the Gentiles: Studies in the Acts of the Apostles* (trans. J. Keating; Ramsey, N.J.: Paulist, 1979) 18.

120 Verse 47: "what the Lord has directed" presumes a commission.

121 This Lucan interpretation of 9:15 receives this coloration in Paul's report of his commission in 26:16-18. He is to be a witness and servant (ὑπηρέτης, μάρτυς [v. 16]) to bring light. (In Gal 1:15 Paul applies Isa 49:1 to himself.)

122 See pp. 360–64.

123 Spicq (*Lexicon*, 141, with numerous references) explains Luke's term (also used in 17:12) as follows. "The adjective εὐσχήμων is used very frequently in the papyri for a special class of citizens, the most well-thought-of and well-to-do in a town or city." See also James M. Arlandson, "Lifestyles of the Rich and Christian: Women, Wealth, and Social Freedom," in Levine, *Feminist Companion*, 155–70, esp. 157–58.

124 Readers who pause to reflect may be surprised that these women had not been won over to the apostles. ℵ* E 𝔪 vg sy[h] interpose καί ("and") after γυναῖκας ("women"), thus positing three groups, female God-Fearers, prominent women, and civic leaders.

125 The term πρῶτοι ("leading citizens," "chiefs") is vague. For many examples of the use of this term for leading citizens in Asia Minor, see Jan Bremmer, "Magic, Martyrdom and Women's Liberation in the Acts of Paul and Thecla," in idem, ed., "*The Apocryphal Acts of Paul and Thecla* (Kampen: Kok Pharos, 1996) 36–59, esp. 41 n. 24. In the case of Philippi, also a Roman colony, Acts uses στρατηγοί (16:22), which, although not technically correct, is a popular equivalent for the technical term *duoviri*.

126 Examples: Plutarch *Pyth. orac.* 24 (*Mor.* 407c), *Amat.* 13 (*Mor.* 756c); Pseudo-Lucian *Amores* 42; Juvenal

senators on their behalf.[127] Catiline was said to have had similar hopes from the husbands of his women supporters.[128] For neither the first nor the last time, the readers of Acts are encouraged to envision a conspiracy of Jewish origin.[129] This overarching theme will quell any questions about consistency.[130] The Jews launch a persecution, that is, they demand legal action that results in the expulsion of the missionaries.[131] In accordance with the missionary instructions of Jesus (Luke 10:10-12), the pair carefully detach every vestige of hostile territory from their feet.[132] This picturesque detail is quite inept, for it overlooks the presence of a believing community. The story pivots between two expressions for "fill." The Jews were filled with jealousy, the disciples with joy (vv. 45, 52).[133]

This lengthy episode may stand for all of the Pauline mission that is to follow. Haenchen clearly recognized and vigorously expounded the difficulties of attempting to extract history from the story.[134] That effort misunderstands the narrative, which seeks to be typical and paradigmatic, edifying and normative. From the opening invitation for a sermon to the closing happy ending, this whirlwind mission exhibits no interest in concrete history and full concentration on depicting the historical significance of Paul's labors. Haenchen grasps the nature of this synecdoche by observing that "[t]he characteristic foreshortening of times and distances in Acts is also connected with this [abridgment]. The vast plateaux and ranges of Asia Minor shrink; Perga, Antioch and Iconium seem to lie side by side in neighborly fashion, and it appears as if all that happened in Antioch is compressed into a week."[135] In Lucan terms, this exhibits the way of the Lord, with straight paths, filled valleys, flattened mountains and hills, the crooked straightened and the rough smoothed (cf. Luke 3:45, citing Isa 40:3-5). The road to the ends of the earth runs straight, smooth, and true.

Sat. 6.511–91; Clement of Alexandria *Paed.* 3.4.25, 27–28; Minucius Felix *Oct.* 8.4; Athenagoras *Leg.* 11; Tatian *Oratio ad Graecos* 33; and Irenaeus *A.H.* 1.13.3.

127 *P. Oxy.* 1242, esp. lines 26–32. See Musurillo, *Pagan*, 44–48. Cf. also the potentially subversive role of pro-Jewish women in an anti-Jewish conspiracy in Damascus, according to Josephus *Bell.* 2.560, and the influence of Poppaea in Rome in the matter of a Jewish delegation (*Ant.* 20.195), where her role is almost identical to that of the fictional Plotina in the *Acta Hermaisci*.

128 Sallust *Bell. Cat.* 24.3. (Those who did not yield to their wives' importunities were to be murdered.)

129 Haenchen, 417: "Only by devious methods can the Jews still cramp the success of the mission."

130 G. H. R. Horsley (*NewDocs* 3 [1983] no. 6, pp. 30–31) offers an interpretation based on the assumption of historicity. Observing the prominence of the god Men in the region, he reasons: "It is not too speculative to suggest that the sort of argument which could have been brought against Paul and Barnabas to have them expelled was that their message was a threat to the city's main god and his cult." (30). The narrator, however, has no interest in (and no apparent knowledge of) the god Men or in what pretext, if any, may have been used to foment the persecution.

131 Cf. the imitation of this in *Act. Paul* 3.21 (Iconium); 3.1 refers to Paul's flight from Antioch.

132 On the gesture, see Henry J. Cadbury, "Dust and Garments," in Lake and Cadbury, *Additional Notes*, 269–77. Note also Marguerat, *Historian*, 138 n. 28.

133 Acts 14:22 indicates that there were "disciples" in Antioch and that they are the subject of v. 52. The combination "joy and holy spirit" is difficult, since the two qualities differ. In Gal 5:22, for example, "joy" is a gift—"fruit"—of the Spirit. One is tempted to render either something on the order of "joy and enthusiasm" or as "the joy bestowed by (possession of) the Holy Spirit."

134 Haenchen, 417–18.

135 Haenchen, 418.

14

14:1-28 Missionary Activity in Lycaonia

14:1-10: Conventional Text

1/ Paul and Barnabas followed the
same procedure in Iconium as
at Antioch. They went to the
Jewish synagogue and spoke as
before,[a] with the result that a
very large number of both Jews
and Greeks came to believe.
2/ However, the Jews who were
not convinced poisoned the
minds of the gentiles against
the believers.
3/ The missionaries nonetheless
remained for a substantial
time, vigorously proclaiming their message about the
Lord's grace. God verified their
claims by the miracles and
portents he enabled them to
perform. 4/ The citizenry split
into two factions, one supporting the Jews, the other the
missionaries.[b]

5/ When gentiles and Jews, including their leaders, resolved[c] to
attack and stone them,[d]

6/ they caught wind of it and
escaped[e] to the cities of Lycaonia, that is, Lystra, Derbe, and
the adjacent territory. 7/ There
they continued to proclaim the
message.
8/ [At Lystra] there sat a lame man
whose feet had been crippled
from birth and who had never
walked. 9/ Once, as he was
listening to Paul,[f] Paul turned
a searching gaze upon him and
realized that he believed that he
could be cured.

10/ "Stand up straight on your feet,"
he shouted. The man jumped up
and began to walk.

11/ When the crowd[r] saw what Paul
had accomplished, they cried
out: "The gods have come down
to visit us in human form!"
12/ They acclaimed Barnabas as
Zeus and, since he was the principal speaker, Paul as Hermes.
13/ The priest of the Temple of
Zeus Before the City brought

14:1-10: The D-Text[g]

1. . . .

spoke to *them*, with the result
that a very large number of
both Jews and Greeks *were
astonished and* came to believe
(2)/ . . . . *Now the heads of the
synagogue and the leaders [of
the synagogue]* launched *a persecution against the righteous,*[h]
*but the lord quickly brought a
cessation.*[i] . . .

4/ The citizenry *had become
divided*[j] into two factions, one
supporting the Jews, *others* the
missionaries, *adhering to them
because of God's message.*
5/ *Then the Jews, together with
the gentiles, again launched a
persecution for a second time,
expelling them from the city
with a hail of stones* . . .
6/ So they fled *until they arrived* in
Lycaonia, *to a city called* Lystra.
. . .[k] 7/ There they continued to
proclaim the message, *and the
entire populace was stirred up
by their teaching.*
8/ *And Paul and Barnabas remained
in Lystra.*[l] A man was *sitting*,
crippled in his feet, who had
never walked in his life. He
was full of awe.[m] 9/ He listened
*with pleasure as the apostles
began to* speak.[n] *Paul* turned a
searching gaze upon him and
perceived that he believed that
he could be cured.[o] 10/ *"I say
to you, in the name of Jesus,*[p]
Stand up straight on your
feet *and walk,"* he shouted.
The *sick* man jumped up and
immediately[q] began to walk.

bulls and garlands to the gates
so that he and the crowd might
offer sacrifice.[s]
14/ When the missionaries Barnabas and Paul perceived what
was happening, they tore their
coats and dashed out into the
crowd, shouting, 15/ "Good
people, why are you doing this?
We are mortals, just like you.
We would tell you to abandon
these idle rites and embrace
the living God, who made the
heavens, the earth, the sea,
and all that they contain.[t] 16/ In
the past God permitted all
peoples to go their own way,
17/ yet even then God could be
recognized in the good things
given you, including rain from
above that brings bountiful
harvests and the food that you
happily receive." 18/ Through
this argument they were able—
barely—to dissuade the crowd
from sacrificing to them.

14:19-20: Conventional Text

19/ Then Jews from Antioch and
Iconium arrived on the scene
and were able to win over the
crowd. After deluging Paul with
stones, they hauled him outside
of the city, presuming that he
was dead, 20/ but, when his[u]
followers had gathered about
him, he got up and went into
the city. On the next day he set
out with Barnabas for Derbe.

14:19-20: D-Text[v]

*After they had spent time
engaged in teaching, some*
Jews from Iconium and Antioch
arrived on the scene, and, *after
they had spoken with vigor
they persuaded the people to
withdraw from them,*[w] *saying,
"Nothing they say is true, but
they lie about everything."
When they had whipped up the
crowd to the point of* stoning
Paul, they hauled him outside of
the city, presuming that he was
dead. 20/ When his followers
had gathered about him *and
the crowd had left at evening,*
he got up [*with difficulty*][x] and
went into the city[y] *of Lystra* . . .

21/ Proclamation of the message
in Derbe produced numer-
ous followers. The two then
made their way back through
Lystra and Iconium to Antioch.
22/ In each city they fortified
the followers spiritually and
encouraged them to remain
firm in the faith. Their theme
was: "There are many obstacles
on the path to the dominion of
God." 23/ They also ordained[z]
presbyters in each community,

who, after prayer and fasting,
were commended to the Lord
in whom they had placed their
trust.
24/ The two passed through Pisidia
and came to Pamphylia.
25/ After proclaiming the mes-
sage at Perga,[aa] they went down
to Attalia[bb] 26/ and sailed from
there to Antioch, where they
had been entrusted to God's
grace for the activity that they
had now completed. 27/ On
their arrival they assembled
the community and reported
all that God had accomplished
with them, in particular that
God had opened a door of faith
for the gentiles. 28/ There they
remained with the followers for
a considerable time.

---

a On οὕτως ὥστε, see Barrett 1:667–68. If one takes the phrase κατὰ τὸ αὐτό to mean "in the same fashion," then οὕτως will mean "in words like those of chap. 13." If one renders this difficult prepositional phrase as "together," then οὕτως will mean something like "in such wise." "Together" is possible but quite jejune. The translation therefore prefers the equivalent of "just as they did in Antioch," on the analogy of κατὰ δὲ τὸ εἰωθός ("as was his custom") in 17:2. Note d gig: *similiter* ("similarly"). Haenchen (419), however, remains unconvinced, as does BDAG, 513, *s.v.* κατά.

b *Or:* "apostles."

c The term ὁρμή is difficult. It must not refer to an actual onslaught (v. 6), so is taken in the sense of planned action. See Georg Bertram, "ὁρμή," *TDNT* 5:467–74, esp. 470. BDF §393 (6) renders as "they resolved/intended." The strain may be due to the author's interest in establishing a parallel with Stephen, who was stoned by a mob that had rushed upon him (ὅρμησαν [7:57–58]). See also 19:29. The article is to be understood with both Jews and gentiles, BDF §276 (2).

d The alternative is "attack by stoning," construing the second infinitive as epexegetical.

e Ms. h (an Old Latin palimpsest) allegedly added "just as Jesus had said to the seventy-two." This gloss (evidently a reference to Matt 10:23, addressed to the Twelve), apparently stimulated by 13:51, would be an example of the uncontrolled character of the D-Text, but it is far from sure. See Metzger, *Textual Commentary*, 372.

f The aorist ἤκουσεν is more difficult and is taken as ingressive (cf. on v. 2). There is good support for the impf. ἤκουεν.

g The translation follows Boismard, *Texte*, 231–36. Material in brackets represents variations within the D-tradition. On this text, see also Ropes, *Text*, 128–30; Schencke, *Apostelgeschichte*, 194–96; Epp, *Tendency*, 137–40; Strange, *Text*, 126–28; and Metzger, *Textual Commentary*, 370–71.

h On the term δίκαιοι ("righteous"), see the speculation of William Ramsay (*Church* 46). Édouard Delebecque (*Les Deux Actes des Apôtres* [EB n.s. 6; Paris: Gabalda, 1986] 70) takes the phrase κατὰ τῶν δικαίων as a neuter meaning, in effect, "against the law."

i Cop[mae] follows the conventional text in v. 2, but adds the clause about the cessation.

j The translation seeks to distinguish between the periphrastic pluperfect passive of the D-Text and the simple aorist passive of the conventional text.

k Cop[mae] is closer to the conventional text here, although it places the flight in a subordinate clause.

l E alone has another paraphrase: "proclaim the message of/about God. And the entire large crowd [*sic*] was astonished (ἐξεπλήσσετο) at their teaching. And Paul. . . ." This raises the question of whether some of the D-Text traditions are retroversions (presumably from Latin).

m Lit. "being in fear" (ὑπάρχων ἐν φόβῳ). This phrase is placed in v. 9 by D. It may mean that the patient was a God-Fearer. Ms. h may have read *habens timorem dei* ("having fear of God"), but the last word is uncertain. See Metzger, *Textual Commentary*, 373. The safest explanation is that the phrase indicated his sense of the presence of the numinous and thus a proper state for healing (Ropes, *Text*, 132).

n Ms. *gig* relates his faith to Paul's message: *hic cum audisset Paulum loquentem, credidit* ("When he had heard Paul speak, he believed").

o Cop^{mae} reads: "**When Paul saw him**, he turned a searching gaze upon him and perceived **in the Spirit** . . . ."

p The title receives such typical expansions as "the Lord Jesus Christ" in various witnesses.

q Although not accepted by Boismard, this adverb, in one form or another, is a typical D-Text addition supported by D$^{(1)}$ D sy$^{(p)hmg}$ mae. Note also 3:7.

r As often, there is fluctuation between the particles δέ and τε. The latter conforms to Lucan idiom.

s The D-Text speaks of "Priest**s** of him who is Zeus before [ ] city." On this see Taylor, "St Paul," 1220.

t The D-Text (Boismard, *Texte*, 240) reads εὐαγγελιζόμενοι ὑμῖν τὸν θεὸν, ὅπως ἀπὸ τούτων τῶν ματαίων ἐπιστρέψητε ἐπὶ τὸν θεὸν ζῶντα τὸν ποιήσαντα ("proclaiming **God** to you, so that you **may** turn from these idle things toward the living God **who** made"). Ropes (*Text*, 134) thinks that the D-editor objected to the use of "evangelize" with an appeal rather than in an announcement. That, however, was precisely Luke's intention, to illustrate the participle in v. 7. 𝔓^{45} is distinct, although difficult to read, apparently omitting the emphatic καὶ ἡμεῖς, and adding an infinitive ἀποστῆναι with "and" (καί), so that the exhortation is to "abandon the useless rites and turn to . . ."

u D* reads αὐτοῦ ("his followers"), while 𝔭^{45} and E read "his . . . him" (in varying order). The verb κυκλόω ("encircle") can be intransitive. It is slightly more likely that "his" was changed to "him" and that a second pronoun was added to restore "his."

v This is the text printed by Boismard, *Texte*, 242–43. There are variants within the tradition. See also Metzger, *Textual Commentary*, 374–75.

w This verb, ἀποστῆναι (if the reconstruction is correct), appears in v. 15 in 𝔭^{45} (above).

x Boismard does not accept this reading of it 𝔭^{2}, but it is quite in accordance with the tendency of the D-Text.

y Ephrem (421) says, appropriately, that the disciples "secretly introduced him into the city."

z The word means "appoint" or "install." At the time when Acts was written, there was a ceremony that could be called "ordination." Acts implies such a ceremony.

aa A variety of witnesses add either "of the Lord" or "of God" after "message" (λόγον). This is almost certainly secondary. See Metzger, *Textual Commentary*, 375.

bb In its inimitable fashion, the D-Text (Boismard, *Texte*, 244) reports that Attalia was evangelized.

Analysis

"The fourteenth chapter tells experiences of Christian missionary work entirely different from those related elsewhere in Acts. All the other adventures of the Apostles are in Jerusalem and in the larger cities. . . . But in this chapter the scene is laid in a semi-barbarous land with towns few and far apart."[1]

The narrator seems to be somewhat out of his element in this rugged territory, until, in vv. 11-18, he capitalizes on that "semi-barbarism" to produce one of the most memorable scenes of Acts. Otherwise, the geographically uninformed reader has no sense that the setting is unusual. Verses 1-5 report, in highly compressed form, the experience at Iconium. Brevity is appropriate in sequence after the lengthy description of the mission at Antioch. Although the result is much the same—flight—there is enough variation to prevent boredom. Discovery of plans to do them serious injury motivates Paul and Barnabas to flee to new fields of endeavor (vv. 6-7). Lystra (vv. 8-20a) offers variety: a healing miracle, attempted deification, and a sermon to a polytheist crowd, climaxing in an assault that brings together the entire cast of enemies from all three cities. The balance of the chapter is quite rapid. The missionary work at Derbe receives the briefest of reports, followed by a swing back through the places evangelized and their return to Syrian Antioch (vv. 20b-28). Dramatic development is apparent. Readers sense the mounting suspense. How long can the two escape violence? Verse 5 introduces the threat of stoning, a threat fulfilled in v. 19.

The inevitable conclusion is that very little remains of the source material beyond the place-names. The source could have contained additional data, but Luke has declined to report it. The model of "Jews first" is certainly Lucan and not the fixed practice of Barnabas and Paul, while the scheme of Jewish opposition that drives the missionaries out of every town after a short and successful mission is also Lucan. This is not to deny that Paul had his difficulties, but it is too much to

1 Foakes Jackson, 121.

believe that he was, in one way or another, driven away from every missionary station. When to these factors is added the crescendo of suspense and other narrative ploys,[2] Acts 13–14 is, by all important criteria, narrative fiction.[3]

Comment

■ **1-7** Iconium, known for at least a time as Claudiconium, was an old and important city of Lycaonia, with a Phrygian populace. It lay about 150 kilometers from Antioch. Travelers would probably proceed southeast through Neapolis and take the Via Sebaste east, a journey of at least five days. This city had the characteristics of a typical Pauline missionary center, for its location on crossroads linking several regions made it an important and prosperous commercial center in the early Christian era.[4] Its importance in the Pauline tradition is attested by the *Acts of Paul.*

Because there is no arguable case for attributing to a/the source a lengthy account of the mission at Antioch and a short account for Iconium, this variation is due to the narrator, who follows the literary pattern of alternating scenes with summaries.[5] Verses 1-7 contain the skeleton for an exciting story that the author could have created with a few of those circumstantial details that most critics are willing to concede to Lucan creativity. Rigorous adherence to the fixed scheme created difficulties for the narrator.[6] The narrative would be much smoother if vv. 2 and 3 were inverted.[7] Since dislocations of this brief compass are relatively rare, it is preferable to attribute the awkwardness to Luke's desire to speak first of successful work[8] in the synagogue and then of opposition from some Jews.[9] Verse 3 provides retardation. That subsequent readers found the narrative unsatisfactory is apparent from the various forms of the D-Text, which completely rewrite the passage. The major contribution of this revision is to highlight apparent difficulties of the conventional texts and to provide (sometimes) suitable supplements. The difficulties raised by v. 2 are resolved in the most pedestrian fashion, by positing two persecutions. The odd v. 6, which speaks of "cities of Lycaonia, that is, Lystra, Derbe, and the adjacent territory," is corrected.[10] This revision—better, these revisions—show that Luke's account is unduly crabbed and terse by attempting to transform it into a more rational and circumstantial story. It would be difficult to identify a passage less conducive to the notion that the D-Text is more original, for extraordinary editorial incompetence would be required to transform the D-Text into the standard form.

■ **3** Although Jewish opposition was general at Antioch, conversions at Iconium included numerous Jews. Having established the general principle, Luke is free

2 On the narrative techniques in vv. 1-7, see also Tannehill, *Narrative Unity*, 2:176–77.

3 Contrast Barrett (1:664), who allows that Luke may have had "little more than a list of names," but also claims that it is not "fictitious . . . Luke had information of various kinds." What he means by "fictitious" is not clear. On p. 667 he states that the *Acts of Paul* contains "[m]any (fictitious) incidents in Iconium." Ramsay (*Church*, 375–428), whose criteria were consistent, did not regard the story of Thecla as fictitious.

4 See W. Ward Gasque, "Iconium," *ABD* 3:357–58. Note also the dated but detailed account of Ramsay, *Cities,* 317–82; and Taylor, "St Paul," 1211–16, who gives evidence for the presence of Phrygian language and culture.

5 The hypothesis is that the gentile mission source contained terse summaries of the several missionary expeditions that it reported.

6 The difficulties of 14:2-3 are quite similar to those of 13:42-43.

7 Hans H. Wendt (*Die Apostelgeschichte* [9th ed.; KEK; Göttingen: Vandenhoeck & Ruprecht, 1913] 218 n. 2) and Moffatt (Foakes Jackson, 122) make this transposition. For discussion, see Cadbury and Lake, 161–62; and Witherington, 419. John H. Michael ("The Original Position of Acts xiv.3," *ExpT* 40 [1928–29] 514–16) placed v. 3 at 13:48.

8 Haenchen (419) says that the "Greeks" of v. 1 are God-Fearers, noting the use of ἔθνη ("gentiles") in v. 2, but this is unlikely to be more than stylistic variation. (He is right only insofar as these Greeks attended the synagogue, but the reader is probably to envision a situation like that of 13:44. See also Bruce, 317.)

9 So also, e.g., Conzelmann, 108.

10 The data suggest that this was done twice, once in the shortening of v. 6 and again in the addendum to v. 7/beginning of v. 8.

to emphasize that the movement continued to appeal to Jews. Those not persuaded[11] spurred the gentiles to take action.[12] Evidently mob action is in view. Verse 3 affirms, in difficult language,[13] that opposition did not daunt the two, who dug in their heels. Miracles, mentioned for the first time in this journey, revealed divine support.[14] This summary again shows that Paul and Barnabas were the full equals of Peter and colleagues[15] and prepares the way for vv. 8-10 (and 15:12). With v. 3, the summary ends. At v. 4, the narrator begins a short report of the persecution and its outcome. Readers might infer that Iconium was troubled by the factionalism that beset many Greek cities.[16] If one group supported the mission,[17] the other would oppose it for the sake of consistency.[18]

■ **4** Here and in v. 14, the term *ἀπόστολοι* appears. It probably occurred in the source in the meaning of "envoys" or "delegates" of Antioch, but neither of the two references is likely to indicate specific source material. Verse 4 contains a Lucan motif: the divided audience (cf. 1:12-13; 17:34; 23:7), and v. 14 is unlikely to derive from the gentile mission source.[19] Luke may have capitalized on the source's use of the term because he really wished to designate Paul as an apostle and by this means was able to remind readers that the word had more than one meaning without formally abandoning the definition he has had to accept.[20]

■ **5** The verse is no more sequential than its predecessors. The polarization of v. 4 is forgotten, as a grassfire of attempted lynching sweeps through Iconium. Opponents now include both the gentiles and the Jews, leaving no one out of the equation.[21] The sentence evokes the squalid picture of an outraged urban mob bent on eradication of an abomination and a dramatic escape from its clutches.[22] When the missionaries realized what was in store, they took flight. This is evocative of Luke 4:29-30.

11 The verb *ἀπειθέω* means "be disobedient," but seems to have become a common term for not believing. See Barrett, 1:668.

12 Haenchen (420 and n. 3) says that the aorists in v. 2 are ingressive and do not show the result achieved (cf. BDF §318). On the sense of *κακόω* (7:6, 19; 12:1), see Bruce, 318; and Johnson, 246. The author is evidently engaging in elegant variation.

13 The *μὲν οὖν* in v. 3 is probably adversative ("rather"). See Witherington (419), who notes 25:4; 28:5, and possibly 17:7. See also Cadbury and Lake, 162–63; and Douglas S. Sharp, "The Meaning of *men oun* in Acts 14:3," *ExpT* 44 (1932–33) 528. The phrase *χρόνον διέτριψαν* ("spend time") is, according to BDF §332 (1) a "complexive" or "constative" aorist, for linear actions that are now complete. For *παρρησιαζόμενοι ἐπὶ τῷ κυρίῳ*, Moule (*Idiom Book*, 50) suggests "perhaps *showing boldness in reliance upon the Lord*." The language is odd, as is the repeated preposition *ἐπί*, of which it must be said that it is so unusual that it may well be original (e.g., Ropes, *Text*, 130). On the textual tradition, see Metzger, *Textual Commentary*, 371–72.

14 As often, it is difficult to determine whether "Lord" in v. 3 refers to Jesus, as "testify" would suggest. If so, he is the source of their miraculous power.

15 Note the locution "signs and wonders" (2:22 [Jesus]); 2:43; 4:30; 5:12; 6:8 [Stephen]).

16 On the problem, see Richard Pervo, "Meet Right," 45–62.

17 For *σύν* in the sense of "on the side of," see Moule, *Idiom Book*, 81.

18 The term *πλῆθος* has a different meaning in v. 4 from that in v. 1, where it means "number." Here it probably means "the populace," but it could refer to the populace in a legal sense, the civic assembly (LSJ, 1417, *s.v.,* 2b). "Citizenry" splits the difference with more weight on the former. Such divisions motivate action in popular narrative. Cf. Chariton *Chaer.* 2.3.7 and the exact parallel at 5.4.1 (*ἐσχίσθη δὲ τὸ πλῆθος τῶν βαρβάρων*); Ps.-Lucian *Onos* 54.

19 In support of derivation of the term from the source is the order "Barnabas and Paul," where the term appears in v. 14. Haenchen (428 n. 3) says this is because of the order in v. 12. The D-Text omits the term in v. 14. It is tempting to regard this as original (see Barrett, 1:678), but the omission is probably due to its addition in v. 9. The editor did not wish to be too repetitious.

20 Paul used the term in the sense of "representatives of communities" (*ἀπόστολοι ἐκκλησιῶν* [2 Cor 8:23]). See Conzelmann, 108; Haenchen, 420 n. 10; Roloff, 211; Schneider, 2:152; Weiser, 2:348–49; the detailed discussion of Barrett, 1:666–67, esp. 671; and the even more detailed study of Clark, *Parallel Lives*, 136–49.

21 "Their leaders" is ambiguous. It could refer to the officers of the city or the synagogue or both. See Cadbury and Lake, 162. The general Lucan perspective makes it likely that the Jews were

■ **6-7** The verses are, in their own way, as difficult as the rest of the section. A reasonable conjecture is that this material comes from the source, which spoke of evangelistic activity in Lycaonia, including the cities of Iconium, Lystra, Derbe, and perhaps their environs.[23] As it stands, the text is difficult, for Iconium was the chief city of Lycaonia, whereas v. 6 appears to imply that the two fled *to* that region from elsewhere, while the evident pairing (strengthened by the singular *καὶ τὴν περίχωρον* ["and the surrounding territory"[24]]) of the two cities is perplexing, since Lystra was around thirty-five kilometers south of Iconium and Derbe was around one hundred kilometers southeast of Lystra. Evidently the narrator wishes to identify the general region in vv. 6-7, followed by particulars, but it is difficult to excavate any tradition from those particulars, since the healing story (vv. 8-10) is modeled on 3:1-10, and the subsequent scene is probably Lucan composition.[25] Verse 21a could derive from the source, but it contains little information.[26] Lüdemann is willing to ascribe 14:19-20a to tradition.[27] This is possible, but no more than possible.[28]

■ **8-20a[29]** Lystra, made a Roman colony for military

motivated by their leaders, whereas the gentiles represented the labile urban rabble.

22 Cf. Tannehill, *Narrative Unity*, 2:177. On lynching, see pp. 193–94.

23 So also Dibelius, *Studies*, 86; and Cadbury and Lake, 167. Conzelmann (108) and Haenchen (421 n. 6) view vv. 6-7 as a kind of anticipatory summary.

24 "Surrounding territory" may be another reminiscence of the beginning of Jesus' ministry. Cf. Luke 4:14, 37.

25 Weiser (2:351) states the strongest grounds for positing a source behind vv. 11-13: the role of Barnabas. If Luke had composed the episode, he would have given the role of Zeus to Paul. One difficulty is identification of the nature of that source. It could scarcely be the missionary (or "Antioch") source, which does not otherwise include material of this nature. A hypothetical Barnabas legend would have been unlikely to attribute the healing to Paul. Moreover, this objection is less weighty than first appears. The identification of Barnabas with Zeus allows him to be a "silent partner" here, a role that is quite compatible with Luke's presentation of him. The hypothesis of a source creates more problems than it solves. As Plümacher (*Lukas*, 92–93) observes, vv. 8-18 constitute an independent episode. If removed, no omission would be apparent. See also Schmithals, 130.

26 The author has data about two converts from this area. One is Timothy, from Lystra, who, according to 16:1, was already a believer. According to 1 Cor 4:17, Paul converted Timothy. This is difficult to fit into the account of Acts 14:8-20, but possible. The other is one Gaius, from Derbe (20:4). The historian may suspect that these followers of Paul joined him as the result of later missionary work. There is no indication that the gentile missionary source named any converts resulting from the activity described in chaps. 13–14.

27 Lüdemann, 163–64.

28 Lüdemann bases his argument on the distinctive character of the episode, dissonance between vv. 18 and 19, the reference to "disciples" in v. 20, Paul's solitary status (Barnabas is not a target), the anticipation of the incident in vv. 5-6, and the parallel in 2 Tim 3:11. The last is quite vague, and all of the other items are arguably Lucan. 2 Cor 11:25 ("stoned once") is not securely independent support, for Luke almost certainly had access to this letter—at least to the fragment preserved in 2 Corinthians 10–13. Weiser (2:344–47) is willing to consider some tradition behind the deification story and agrees that "Pauline traditions" stand behind the stoning, all at considerable remove from history. Haenchen somewhat fuzzily accepts "raw material of varied origin." Barrett (1:664–65), speaks of tradition, also somewhat vaguely. The consensus appears to be that vv. 19-20 contain Pauline traditions that are not necessarily derived from the missionary source. For tradition in vv. 8-18 there is no compelling argument.

29 Christian Dionne ("L'épisode de Lystre [Ac 14,7-20a]: Une analyse narrative," *SciEsp* 57 [2005] 5–33) takes v. 7 as the starting point of a unit that includes proclamation (v. 7), healing (vv. 8-10), crowd reaction (vv. 11-13), the counter-reaction of the apostles (vv. 14-18), and the assault of the opponents (vv. 19-20a). For a detailed literary analysis, see Marianne Fournier, *The Episode at Lystra: A Rhetorical and Semiotic Analysis of Acts 14:7-20a* (American University Studies, VII.197; New York: Peter Lang, 1997).

reasons, was "a moderately important, if somewhat rustic, market town in the relatively backward region of Lycaonia in south-central Turkey."[30] In this unpromising milieu, the narrator locates three specific incidents, the most of any station in the journey. The first of these begins with the abrupt introduction of a disabled person. That suffices to indicate that a healing story is in progress. In its present form, the healing is too similar to that of Peter (and John) in 3:1-10 for the resemblance to be attributed to accident or to the requirements of the form.[31] The phrases *καί τις ἀνήρ* ("and a man") and *χωλὸς ἐκ κοιλίας μητρὸς αὐτοῦ* ("crippled from birth") occur only in these two places in the Greek Bible.[32] The two accounts also share the words *ἰδών* ("seeing"), *περιεπάτει* ("walk" [imperative]), and forms of the verbs *ἀτενίζω* ("look intently") and *ἅλλομαι* ("leap"), the last of which appears only once elsewhere in the NT. In addition, each involves a temple, an entrance,[33] and contains a subsequent religious conflict and a speech that explains the source of miraculous power. Luke has so shaped this incident to provide a comparison and contrast between the ministries of Peter and Paul and the evangelization of a polytheist audience that the discovery of an underlying source of the miracle is not only impossible but also irrelevant. When the two stories are placed beside one another, an action the implied reader is all but compelled to perform, Gal 2:9 emerges as a memorable diptych: Peter, missionary to the Jews (who inaugurated the gentile mission), and Paul, herald of salvation to the gentiles (to whom he preaches a basic tenet of Jewish monotheism).[34]

■ **8** The best argument for an underlying source may be the text, which is overloaded and quite possibly corrupt.[35] Behind the D-Text may be a more original form, but it is best viewed as an improvement. Verse 8 follows the expansion of v. 7 by implying that popular excitement motivated the two to remain in Lystra. Elimination of *χωλός* ("crippled") removes a redundancy. Other alterations add such features as a christological formula in the healing command and "immediately" to prove (unnecessarily) that the healing was instantaneous, but the major problem addressed by the D-Text is just how this "pagan" could have acquired sufficient faith and how Paul knew this. The question reveals the relatively late date of the D-tradition, for it no longer views "faith" in healing stories as a component of the transaction, expressing the patient's conviction that the therapist can perform the healing.[36] The D-Text also fails to recognize that "seeing" (*ἰδών*) in this context involves spiritual insight (e.g., Luke 5:20). Finally, the D-Text recognized the parallels with 3:1-10 and enhanced them, especially in v. 10.[37]

■ **9-10** An alternative approach suspects careless writing and may see a stab at euphony.[38] As it stands, the details

30 David S. Potter, "Lystra," *ABD* 4:426–27. On its history and place in the Roman political system, see also Barbara Levick, *Roman Colonies in Southern Asia Minor* (Oxford: Clarendon, 1967) 29–41, 195–97; and Ramsay, *Cities*, 407–19.

31 See also Tannehill, *Narrative Unity*, 2:177–78.

32 The phrase *χωλὸς ἐκ κοιλίας μητρὸς αὐτου* is found only in these two passages in all of Greek literature between the third century BCE and the third century CE.

33 "The Beautiful Gate" (*θύρα* [3:2]), gates of city or temple (*πυλῶνας* [14:13]).

34 Bede (64) noted the parallel and cited Gal 2:9 as its interpretation.

35 On the grounds of difficulty, N-A[27] reads in v. 8: *ἀνὴρ ἀδύνατος ἐν Λύστροις τοῖς ποσὶν ἐκάθητο.* The prepositional phrase may have crept in from the D-Text. (Note that "Lystra" is heteroclite, a foreign word in *-a* construed either as a feminine singular, as in v. 6, or as a neuter plural, as here. Cf. "Lydda," which shows the same fluctuation in 9:32, 38.) The phrase *ἀδύνατος ἐν Λύστροις* looks like a badly made "correction." If retained, it should be read after *ἀνήρ,* which has good support.

36 Cf. Weiser, 2:349–50.

37 Ropes, *Text*, 132; and Metzger, *Textual Commentary*, 373.

38 Conzelmann (109–10) says that the language here is "affected," with repetitions, and so on. He proposes the possibility of euphony. An example is the alliteration and assonance in *ἀνὴρ ἀδύνατος ἐν Λύστροις*. (This would work if the prepositional phrase were located earlier.)

underline the severity of the disability, in a crescendo: crippled feet, could not walk, a congenital condition. The literary problem—much addressed in the D-Text—is the transition in v. 9. Rather than have this cripple approach Paul (and Barnabas), as in 3:1-10, or report that Paul happened upon him, as in 9:33, the narrator wishes to portray the patient as an auditor. The awkward development of the healing story is driven by the identification of Paul as Hermes in v. 12. Paul must be portrayed as an orator, but something remarkable is required to excite the crowd. The narrative wrenches its attention back to Paul in v. 9b with an awkward relative clause. Recognizing the patient's amenability to treatment,[39] he pronounced a healing command.[40] The D-Text makes this command more "orthodox" by introducing a christological element. Its absence here is essential, since the onlookers must view Paul as a deity who heals by his own command rather than as a magician who skillfully invokes the name of a god whose power he can summon.[41] The person sprang up and walked.[42] The conclusion nicely rounds off the introduction. The one who had never walked now does so, with ease and vigor. A person who was "powerless" (ἀδύνατος)[43] had been transformed by power from on high.

■ **11-12** In a Jewish context, the healing would move a crowd to praise God. So here, but these acclaimers are not Jews, so they leap to the conclusion that gods are on the scene. That scene is as full of problems as it is of excitement. From the history-of-religions perspective, deification is an overdetermined reaction,[44] and no allowance for miscommunication readily compensates for the confusion of heralds of a new god with two of the old gods. Gods worked healings in various ways that did not require physical presence, and dwellers in rural precincts were not unaware of holy persons. Hermes was not a "healing god," nor were he and Zeus a traditional pair. The narrative context increases the perplexity. The crowd responded to "what Paul had accomplished," yet they hailed Barnabas, who has not been named since 13:50, as the chief god and identified Paul with Hermes because of his preaching ability. The two parts of the story do not cohere.

A probable solution was endorsed by A. D. Nock: the story is inspired by a Greek myth known through Ovid's sentimental rendition of the tale of Baucis and Philemon (*Metam.* 8.611–724).[45] That story is set in the general vicinity: Phrygia,[46] which Zeus and Hermes (Latin Jupiter and Mercury) visit in human form (*Iuppiter huc specie mortali cumque parente venit Atlantiades positis caducifer alis* [626–27]).[47] No one will give them so much as a cup of cold water until they come upon the elderly and impoverished Baucis and Philemon, who gladly share their meager resources. When the wondrous replenishment of wine reduces the couple to terror, the

39 BDF §400 (2) says that the articular infinitive is, in effect, result rather than purpose.

40 The "loud voice" (μεγάλῃ φωνῇ) is not otherwise found in healings. Its narrative purpose is doubtless to ascertain that bystanders heard it and thus to attribute the deed to Paul. The article before φωνῇ ("voice") would make the construction predicate. BDF §270 (1) suggests "the voice with which he spoke was loud." Omission is grammatically preferable.

41 Cf. also Conzelmann, 110. This overlooks the language difficulty, but that is something the narrator is willing to ignore, as vv. 15-17 indicate. Witherington (424 n. 278) resolves the difficulty: "[W]e must think of Paul later learning what the crowd had said, perhaps from someone present whom he later converted, someone such as Timothy."

42 BDF §484 says that the use of both verbs is "classical."

43 In a medical context, this adjective usually refers to blindness, e.g., Tob 2:10; 5:10 (א), and BDAG, 22, *s.v.*, who cites three papyri.

44 So already Loisy, 550.

45 Nock, *Essays*, 2:660 n. 43. The theory may be traced back to Wettstein (1752). See Amy L. Wordelman, "Cultural Divides and Dual Realities: A Greco-Roman Context for Acts 14," in Penner, *Contextualizing*, 205–32, esp. 208–17, on the history of interpretation.

46 Although Lystra is in Lycaonia, Phrygia was a "large and ill-defined geographical region" that included Pisidia and Lycaonia (Stephen Mitchell, "Phrygia," *OCD*, 1176–77, citing 1176). See also Christopher P. Jones, "A Geographical Setting for the Baucis and Philemon Legend," *HSCP* 96 (1994) 203–23.

47 "And Jupiter came there in mortal guise; and with his father, though he'd set aside his wings, came Mercury, Atlas' grandson, with the caduceus, his wondrous wand" (trans. Allen Mandelbaum, *The Metamorphoses of Ovid* [New York: Harcourt Brace, 1993] 273). For Mercury's appearance in human form, see also the wish expressed by Horace *Odes*

gods reveal their identities, eradicate the inhospitable with a flood, transform the couple's pathetic hovel into a temple of Zeus and Hermes, and make the pair its priests. The content and context of the story account for the anomalies of vv. 11-13. Those who know the story will appreciate its wit. These yokels[48] are determined not to be taken unawares again. Those unfamiliar with the story will miss the humor, but not the excitement.[49]

Amy Wordelman prefers a different mythological background.[50] Quite properly emphasizing the widespread tradition of theoxeny, she notes two other examples from Ovid where Zeus tests humans to determine their hospitality. One of these is set in Arcadia, ruled by Lycaon (Ovid *Metam.* 1.163–67, 196–98, 209–40), and is attested in other sources. Lycaon doubts the divinity of Zeus (or, alternatively, is angry because he seduced and impregnated his daughter Callisto) and serves him human flesh (alternatively, that of his child). Zeus reacts negatively, nuking the house and transforming Lycaon into a wolf. The last involves an etiological wordplay (λύκος means "wolf"). Wordelman builds on this hypothesis to provide a reading of this pericope and also relates it to the use of the term "wolf" for opponents in Acts. This valuable essay warns against assumptions about background. A weakness is the presupposition that the implied readers have a relatively high degree of familiarity with mythography. The hostile context she proposes is less likely than one finds in stories like that of Baucis and Philemon.[51]

1.2.41–44. Hermes also takes human form (ὁμοιωθεὶς ἀνθρώπῳ) in Aesop's fable of Hermes and the Sculptor (91.1). The assumption is that one of the privileges of deity is the capacity to assume any desired form. This tool was no less useful for their mortal exponents than for the gods. It could, for example, explain the theriomorphic gods of Egypt, who avoided harassment by assuming the form of various animals (ὁμοιωθῆναί τισι ζῴοις [Diodorus Siculus 1.86.3]).

48 Lycaonians were the stereotypical "hicks" of that era. See Dean P. Béchard, *Paul outside the Walls: A Study of Luke's Socio-Geographical Universalism in Acts 14:8-20* (AnBib 143; Rome: Pontifical Biblical Institute, 2000) 376–77.

49 Others who favor a relationship include: Joseph B. Lightfoot, *Saint Paul's Epistles to the Colossians and to Philemon* (London: Macmillan, 1879) 304: "It has a special interest too for the Apostolic history, because it suggests an explanation of the scene at Lystra." Cadbury (*Book*, 22), Haenchen (432), Conzelmann (110), Marshall (237), Bruce (321), Weiser (1:350), Talbert (133), Johnson (248, 251), Barrett (1:677), and Jervell (375), for example, refer to Ovid's story. Witherington (424) presumes that the crowd is familiar with the story, although he regards Ovid as writing "at a later time" (424 n. 279), against the standard view that Ovid died in 17 CE and had written the *Metamorphoses* before his exile in 8. Roloff (216) objects on the grounds that the saga reflects Greco-Roman conceptions of deity. This objection presumes a historical basis. For the humor, see Pervo, *Profit*, 64–65. Lüdemann (160–61) cites F. C. Baur (*Paulus, der Apostel Jesu Christi* [2nd ed.; Leipzig: Teubner, 1866] 112), who already protested against using parallels like these as confirmatory and proposing the solution advocated here. Fox (*Pagans and Christians*, 99–100) regards this argument as based on "the thinnest evidence" (99). He prefers a relief that shows (100) "how people locally pictured these divinities, round-faced and solemn, with long hair and flowing beards, a searching gaze and the right hand held prominently across the chest. Such a Zeus looks uncommonly like our image of a wandering Christian holy man: in these reliefs, we, too, can sense the elusive features of a Paul or Barnabas." Potter ("Lystra," *ABD* 4:426–27) builds on this, writing, "[T]he local Zeus, Zeus Ampelites, was portrayed on reliefs as an elderly bearded figure, and because he is sometimes depicted with a young male assistant [*sic*]. The identification by the people of Lystra of Barnabas as Zeus and Paul as Hermes 'as he was the bringer of the word' suggests that they thought that the two men were functioning in the way that they envisaged their own gods as acting: the bearded Zeus was the initiator of the action and Hermes was his agent in carrying out the action. This further suggests that the people may have thought that Barnabas resembled their Zeus, while Paul resembled his helper. *The passage is therefore of considerable importance as evidence for the physical appearance of Paul at this stage in his career*" (emphasis added). These authorities appear to have overlooked Loisy's (552) refutation of this hypothesis regarding the appearance of Barnabas, about which nothing is known, and Paul's refutation of the thesis that he looked like a proper holy man, 2 Cor 10:10.

50 Wordelman, "Cultural Divides."

51 Dean P. Béchard ("Paul among the Rustics: The Lystran Episode (Acts 14:8-20) and Lucan

■ **12-13** This is not to imply that reference to the tale known to Ovid dispenses with every question. The narrator ignores the language barriers that he has created. The crowds speak "Lycaonian,"[52] but they are understood by the missionaries, whose Greek they likewise comprehend. As often in popular writing, all of the characters know what the readers know. Nor is the temple in question dedicated to Zeus and Hermes.[53] Verse 13 refers instead to the priest[54] of Zeus,[55] who brings the requisite materials[56] to "the gates" so that the community may offer sacrifice. The location of these portals—temple, city, or the lodging place of the missionaries—is left to the imagination of the reader.[57] More cogently, "The motive of the priest who wished to sacrifice to the supposed celestial visitants . . . does not lie on the surface."[58] The narrator does not care about these details because the focus is on "the crowds."

Ovid's tale illustrates a common function of theoxenies,[59] which served as cautionary tales about the duty of hospitality. "Do not neglect to show hospitality to strangers, for by doing that some have entertained angels without knowing it" (Heb 13:2). A classic passage

Apologetic," *CBQ* 63 [2001] 84–101) relates the story to the need for sages to stave off the adulation of the overenthusiastic, in particular, the gullible. He presents illuminating data but refutes a claim not present or implicit in the text that faults the Lycaonians not for gullibility but for inadequate theology. Nonetheless, Wordelman and Béchard show that the mythological background was quite dense and that interpretation need not appeal to Baucis and Philemon alone. On the problem, see also Luther Martin ("Gods or Ambassadors of God? Barnabas and Paul in Lystra," *NTS* 41 [1995] 152–56), who argues from Plato *Laws* 941A that these two gods are guarantors of emissaries and missions; and Conrad Gempf, "Mission and Misunderstanding: Paul and Barnabas in Lystra (Acts 14:8-20)," in Anthony Billington et al., eds., *Mission and Meaning: Essays Presented to Peter Cotterell* (Carlisle: Paternoster, 1995) 56–69.

52 On the survival of the local language, see Jacquier, 423–24; Haenchen, 426 n. 1; and Hemer, *Book*, 110 n. 23.

53 For this reason much of the effort to show (or to refute) connections between these two gods in the region is unnecessary. The narrator does not link them. For the data, see the references in the previous note, Bruce, 321–22; Fitzmyer, 531; Fox, *Pagans and Christians*, 100, 698; and Taylor, "St Paul," 1218. More cogent is the argument that Hermes is not depicted as the mouthpiece for a silent Zeus. The interpretation of Hermes as λόγος comes from a different sphere of the history of religions (known also to Justin *1 Apol.* 21.2; 22.2; and Ps.-Clem. *Rec.* 10.41). An early allusion is Horace *Odes* 1.10.1–6. More or less contemporaneous with Acts is Plutarch *Is. Os.* 54 (*Mor.* 375b) and *De audiendis poeticis* 13 (*Mor.* 44e). Regularly cited is Iamblichus *Myst.* 1.1, where Hermes is called ϑεὸς ὁ τῶν λόγων ἡγεμών ("the god who is the leader of discourse"). For other references and discussion, see Bousset, *Kyrios Christos*, 392–93; and André Jean Festugière, *La Révélation d'Hermès Trismégistos* (4 vols.; Paris: Gabalda, 1950) 1:71–82.

54 The D-Text (Boismard, *Texte*, 238) has the plural, "priests," which conforms to convention. See Ropes, *Text*, 132–33; and Metzger, *Textual Commentary*, 374.

55 The translation supplies "temple" in the presumption that the facility was located in front of the city gate: "the temple of Zeus Outside the Walls." (Ancients did not always erect holy buildings where convenient, but because the place was holy, a practice for which there are parallels in other religions, including Christianity.) For other examples, see Cadbury and Lake, 394; and Wikenhauser, 362–63. Boismard (*Texte*, 238) takes the D-Text as τοῦ ὄντος Διος, which could be rendered as "the local Zeus," although not by him. Cf. Bruce, 322; William M. Calder, "The 'Priest' of Zeus at Lystra," *Exp* 7 (1910) 148–55; and Bo Reicke, "πρό," *TDNT* 6:683–88, esp. 684–85. The temple envisioned was probably located "in front of," that is, before, the major entrance of the city and may also have referred to Zeus as Lystra's patron deity. On the episode, see also David Gill and Bruce Winter, "Acts and Roman Religion," in Gill and Gempf, *Setting*, 79–103, esp. 81–85; and Hemer, *Book*, 111.

56 That is, bulls and garlands bound by wool with which to adorn the victims.

57 The parallel with 3:1-10 encourages one to locate the former cripple at the temple gates, but the verb ἐξεπήδησαν ("dashed out") in v. 14 supports the view that the two were indoors when they received word. Cf. Jdt 14:17. Ephrem (418) inferred that they were inside a house. See also Bruce, 322. Cadbury and Lake (165), however, warn against assigning much meaning to the prefix ἐκ-.

58 James Strahan, "Lystra," *DAC* 1:728–29, esp. 728.

59 A biblical example is Gen 18:1-4; 19:1-2. The subject is almost ubiquitous in the history of religions. For examples, see M. Revon, "Hospitality," *ERE* 5–6:814; and Ladislaus J. Bolchazy, *Hospitality in Antiquity* (Chicago: Ares, 1995) 11–14. For the

is *Odyssey* 17, a rebuke of the suitor Antinous, who has rudely rebuffed a beggar (actually Odysseus in disguise): "What if perchance he be some god come down from heaven? And the gods do, in the guise of strangers from afar, put on all manner of shapes, and visit the cities, beholding the violence and the righteousness of mortals" (*Od.* 17.485–87; LCL 2:191). This very passage is cited as a proof text by the satrap Dionysius in Chariton *Chaer.* 2.3.7 to support his view that the heroine is Aphrodite in person. The "old" (Homer) has been pressed into the service of the new. Popular narrative uses the reception of its heroes as a mode of illustrative characterization,[60] showing how others perceive them.[61] The theme is quite common in various types of ancient fiction and related literature, as well as in religious propaganda.[62] They may protest, as does Callirhoe (2.3.8), or Peter in 10:25, or not, as is often the case (cf. Paul [Acts 28:6]).[63] The grounds for divinization vary, but the fact reveals the impact on the audience. Acts acknowledges the propensity of people to deify those who display miraculous power, hence the concept of the θεῖος ἀνήρ.[64] The technique enables Luke to establish two points: the crowd confuses the gift with the giver and possesses an overly narrow view of miracle.

■ **14-17** Tearing their clothes in either horror at the blasphemy[65] or, more probably, in profound regret,[66] the two are nonetheless able to transform even this most unpromising situation into a missionary opportunity. The brief speech in vv. 15-17, which the narrator presents as a unison delivery, is a good example of Luke's use of direct speech to provide a skeleton that would function well as a summary in indirect discourse. Brief as it is, it is not simple.[67] All that would have been required to stave off the cultic activity was a fervent insistence that they were not gods, since Zeus and Hermes would not have maintained their disguise in the face of recognition. Unable to claim that neither Zeus nor Hermes could perform a healing—the crowd would not believe them—the pair contend that the true God is manifest in the wonders of creation. This brief pitch for "natural theology" confuses modern readers, who have been conditioned to regard miracles, if possible at all, as exceptions to "the laws of nature" made by an omnipotent god. That, however, is not Luke's view of the situation. All creation, according to Hebrew theology, is a miracle. Phenomena such as the healing are signs pointing to the wonder of creation rather than exceptions proving the rule.[68]

Greek tradition, see Ludolf Malten, "Motivegeschichtliche Untersuchungen zur Sagenforschung," *Hermes* 74 (1930) 79–86. Arrival of a god was at least a foretaste of the return of the golden age (Hesiod *Theog.* 535; Catullus 64.384–86). Note also the excursus in Weaver, *Plots*, 34–36.

60 See p. 201 n. 95.

61 See Parsons and Pervo, *Rethinking*, 90–92.

62 The two may overlap. Examples from romantic novels include Chariton *Chaer.* 1.1.16; 1.14.1; *Ephesian Tale* 1.2.5; Longus *Daphn.* 4.33.4; *Ethiopian Story* 1.2.5; 2.2.1–2; cf. also *Jos. Asen.* 5–6. For discussion, see Egger, "Women in the Greek Novel," 50–61; and Pervo, *Profit*, 134–35. Note also the story of Daniel, as related by Josephus *Ant.* 10.211–12. Artapanus relates that the Egyptian clergy identified Moses with Hermes (frag. 3.6). Alexander of Abonouteichos was viewed by the local residents as ἐναργῆ τοῦ θεοῦ ("the manifest presence of god") and thus a suitable object of worship (Lucian *Alexander* 13).

63 Apollonius shunned divine honors lest he be plagued with envy (Philostratus *Vit. Apoll.* 4.31). In the *Alexander Romance*, the hero may be received as a god (e.g., 2.14; 1.26), but often rejects the offer of divine honors (e.g., 1.22).

64 Cf. Schüssler Fiorenza, "Miracles, Mission," 1–25, esp. 11.

65 See Cadbury, "Dust and Garments," 271. The source in this interpretation is Mark 14:63.

66 Bertil Gärtner, "Paulus und Barnabas in Lystra: Zu Apg. 14, 8-15," *SEÅ* 27 (1962) 83–88, esp. 86–87. Note Dio of Prusa *Or.* 35.9, cited by Conzelmann, 111. Note the close agreement with Jdt 14:16-17. The latter interpretation is more congenial to the Lucan portrait of the missionaries, who appear as philosophic critics of vulgar religiosity (cf. Johnson, 251).

67 Soards, *Speeches*, 88–90.

68 For evidence and argument, see Parsons and Pervo, *Rethinking*, 92–96. Cicero cites Aristotle's lost dialogue *On Philosophy*, in which Aristotle, in a parable like that of Plato's Cave, said that if some underground beings were suddenly able to see the surface they would regard the heavens as marvels (*Nat. Deor.* 2.95). The argument was still vital in the patristic era. Cf. Augustine *Serm.* 242.1; *Enarrat. in Ps.* 110:4; *Util. cred.* 34.

The essence of the exhortation states the result of conversion rather than its motivation. These persons did not believe that they were performing "useless rites."[69] Behind the invitation to "embrace[70] the living God"[71] lies what may have been a creed of Hellenistic Judaism, a Christianized form of which can be seen in 1 Thess 1:9, which may be the source of Acts 14:15.[72] The god they announce has, unlike Zeus *et al.*, created all. Creation demonstrates God's existence and beneficence (vv. 16-17). In both style and content, this is parallel to the Areopagus address (17:16-34), with which it forms a necessary complement for the reader.[73] In addition to the alliteration and assonance of which Luke is fond,[74] the verses include an example of litotes (*οὐκ ἀμάρτυρον*, lit. "not untestified"), a vigorous hendiadys,[75] a number of rare and/or elegant words (e.g., *ὁμοιοπαθεῖς*, "of like nature" [v. 15]; *παρῳχημέναις*, "bygone"; *καίτοι*,[76] "and yet" [not well used]; *οὐρανόθεν*, "from heaven"; *ὑετούς*, "rain"),[77] and a stacked series of participles (*ἀγαθουργῶν . . . διδοὺς . . . ἐμπιπλῶν*, "doing good . . . giving . . . filling"), each of which complements its predecessor.[78]

Verse 15 begins, appropriately, with a single word of address and a question that, as in English, amounts to a protest rather than an inquiry.[79] The positive assertion uses that elegant *ὁμοιοπαθεῖς* ("just like you"), which picks up nicely on the *ὁμοιωθέντες* (lit. "made like") of v. 11.[80] Since divinity is the subject, the two turn to the correct answer, beginning, in a standard fashion for gentile contexts,[81] with an invitation to abandon polytheism. Because "the living God" has created all, there is nothing else meriting the label "god."[82] Verse 16 is a variation on the "ignorance is a valid excuse"[83] theme,[84] but general evidence is available. Verse 17 expounds

69 The adjective *μάταιος* is translated to fit the context. On the LXX term, taken up in Hellenistic Judaism and early Christianity, see Pervo, *Dating*, 273. In apologetic contexts, it refers to idols, for example, Justin *Dial.* 91.3: "[P]eople of all nations have turned from useless idols and demons (*ἀπὸ τῶν ματαίων εἰδώλων καὶ δαιμόνων*) to the worship of God") (my translation).

70 On the term "embrace" (lit. "turn to," *ἐπιστρέφειν*), see Pervo, *Dating*, 269.

71 "Living God" often appears in contrast to the gods of polytheism, e.g., 2 Kgs 19:4, 16; Dan 6:20, 26; and, in particular, the irony of Bel 5, 6, 24, and 25. Note also Cilliers Breytenbach, "Zeus und der lebendige Gott: Anmerkungen zu Apostelgeschichte 14.11–17," *NTS* 39 (1993) 396–413; and idem, *Paulus & Barnabas*, 31–38.

72 Abraham J. Malherbe (*The Letters to the Thessalonians: A New Translation with Introduction and Commentary* [AB 32B; New York: Doubleday, 2000] 118–19) is dubious about the pre-Pauline existence of a creedal scheme. 1 Thess 1:9 shares "turn" (*ἐπιστρέφω*), "from" (*ἀπό*), and "the living God" (*θεὸς ζῶν*) with Acts 14:15. One could conclude from 1 Thessalonians that this was the message Paul preached to gentiles.

73 See on 17:26.

74 Note, in particular, v. 17.

75 *ἐμπιπλῶν τροφῆς καὶ εὐφροσύνης τὰς καρδίας ὑμῶν* (lit. "filling your hearts with nourishment and gladness"). Since food does not fill the heart, it evidently refers to the satisfaction of a full stomach. See BDF §442 (16) and Conzelmann, 111 n. 17.

76 p[45] D E read *καίγε*.

77 In the context, it is appropriate to take the pronoun in v. 17 as the more classical *αὑτόν*, incorrectly aspirated by later editors and thence corrected to the more common *ἑαυτόν*.

78 The figure is *climax*. On the literary quality of the speech, see Cadbury and Lake, 166; Barrett, 1:682; and Haenchen, 428 n. 11.

79 On *τί*, see BDF §299 (1), which prefers "why." Bruce (323), however, prefers "What's this you're doing?"

80 On this wordplay and the significance of *ὁμοιοπαθής*, see Parsons and Pervo, *Rethinking*, 92 and n. 33. The term appears in highly hellenized books of the LXX, such as *4 Macc.* 12:13; Wis 7:3, as well as "history" written in a popular style: *Alexander Romance* 1.22.12; Lucian *Ver. hist.* 1.33. Although this quality of mortality may be contrasted with the Stoic view of divine *ἀπάθεια*, it is not necessary to assume the contrast.

81 See the thorough summary of the early missionary message to gentiles in Bultmann, *Theology*, 1:65–92, esp. 65–72.

82 The relative clause of v. 15 is a citation of Ps 145:6 LXX.

83 Cf. 17:23 and the comments thereon.

84 The expression "walk in their ways" (lit.) is a Semitic metaphor (cf. 4 Esdr 3:18) that might have been confusing to the dramatic audience.

the evidence: rain[85] yields crops[86] which yield nourishment.[87] Although the language is inspired by the LXX,[88] the notion that God's providential care can be demonstrated by the beneficence of nature comports with Greek philosophical theology—in particular, but not exclusively, that of the Stoa.[89] The general view of popular philosophy can be seen in Xenophon's *Memorabilia* 4.3, where Socrates demonstrates divine care by arguing from nature.[90] As Conzelmann observes, Dio of Prusa *Or.* 30.28–44 "serves as a commentary."[91] The speech treats only the "first article" of Christian belief, without any suggestion of abbreviation.[92] The best solution is that this causes no difficulties for the reader of the book, who is familiar with Christology and (to a degree) with eschatology.

■ **18** Although v. 18 brings the episode to a dramatic end—it was a close-run thing—the adverb is unconvincing. Their denial of deity may have been disappointing, but it was unlikely that either priest or faithful would have risked the wrath of Zeus by offering sacrifice to self-proclaimed mortals. The abrupt disjuncture between this scene and the next prompted editors to round off this event and to provide a more suitable transition to a description of the attack.[93] Boismard follows h: "They sent them [the crowds, etc.] away from themselves."[94] A more common variant is "but rather that all should go home." These supplements clear the field for the arrival of the adversaries in v. 19. The narrator intended the scene to terminate here, as the inclusion (crowds, sacrifice) with v. 11 indicates.

Although the episode illustrates the distinction between Christianity and popular magic/superstition, it does raise an interesting question: how did early Christian missionaries approach—and persuade—true polytheists? This episode does not answer the question, except to illustrate that the proclamation of one god was not a very likely avenue. In all probability the second (redemption) or third (sanctification) article, as it were, preceded the first. People responded to power of one kind or another. In the narrative tradition, that power is most often localized in a "miracle" of some sort, but Acts can also speak of the power of the message.[95] It is not possible to go beyond such generalizations.[96]

---

85 One epithet for Zeus (the storm god, whose symbol is lightning) is ὑέτιος: *SIG* 1107.4 (Cos) and I Didyma 162.8; 263.8.

86 On καρποφόρος ("fruit-bringing"), note Jer 2:21; Ps 106:34; 148:9 (LXX). This was an epithet of Demeter: Pausanias 8.53.7; *CIG* 4082 (Pessinus); *SIG* 820.5 (Ephesus). (The similar ἐπικάρπιος was an epithet of Hermes: *IG* XII, 7 252 [Amorgos], and Zeus: *MAMA* 7.476.1, etc.)

87 Verbal sources may be sought in Ps 146:8-9 (LXX), which speaks of "rain" (ὑετός), cereal crops, and "nourishment" (τροφή), and Ps 144:16 (LXX): "You open your hand and fill (ἐμπιπλᾷς) every living creature with good will."

88 The view of earth, sea, and the heavens as the three realms of the cosmos is ubiquitous: Cicero *Nat. Deor.* 2.66, 96, with the comments of Pease, *Natura*, 2:785.

89 The Jewish apologetic tradition (e.g., Philo *Dec.* 52-81; *Spec. leg.* 1.13-31) tends to use the phenomena of nature as a criticism of polytheism, as does Paul in Rom 1:20-21.

90 This includes, in 4.3.5–6, reference to water, the seasons, and nourishment, which not only provide necessities but also enjoyment (εὐφραινόμεθα). According to Pease (*Natura* 2:783–84), Aristotle argued that two things revealed God to mortals. One was the heavens, the other innate moral law. Cf. also Plato *Laws* 12.966E–967E; Lucretius *De rerum natura* 5:1204–40. Philo followed—for various purposes—this line: *Leg. all.* 3.98–99; *Spec. leg* 1.33–34; 3.187–89; *Praem. poen.* 41–42; *Prov.* frag. 2.

91 Conzelmann, 111. Rain is a Stoic argument for providence in Cicero *Nat. Deor.* 2.96, 101, 131. General parallels also include: Cicero *Nat. Deor.* 2.96–153 and Lucretius (who was no Stoic!) *De rerum natura* 2.1027–39. The seasons are often advanced as evidence of divine care: Cicero *Nat. Deor.* 131; *Tusc. disp.* 1.68–69; Dio of Prusa *Or.* 12.27–30; Epictetus *Disc.* 1.14.34. See also the references in Pease, *Natura*, 2:659–60.

92 Barrett (1:680–81) reflects on this problem.

93 For the latter, see below.

94 Boimard, *Texte*, 241. He also adopts "persuaded" rather than "stopped" (κατέπαυσαν). That variant probably results from misreading the Greek as "they stopped the crowds from not sacrificing to them." This difficulty probably arises from viewing the negative μή as equivalent to Latin *ne*. The infinitive shows result: BDF §400 (4).

95 Cf. 19:20 (although this follows a miracle of sorts).

96 Critics can do little more than recognize the

Excursus: Lucan "Natural Theology"

By invoking, here and in 17:16-34,[97] creation as *proof* for the existence of God, Luke takes up, as noted, a category of Greco-Roman philosophical theology.[98] His views come from contemporary Christian thought and from the Hellenistic Jewish traditions through which these views were mediated. These sources are probable not only on general grounds—the evidence speaks against regarding the author of Acts as widely read in philosophy, for he was not a systematic writer who betrays deep acquaintance with primary philosophical sources—but also because the author assumes that creation proves the existence of God, whereas the philosophical tradition speaks of "the gods."

Stoic thought, as represented by the arguments attributed to Cleanthes in the second book of Cicero's treatise *On the Nature of the Gods* (7–15), advanced four proofs. The first of these (which is properly Stoic) is divination, the capacity to know of future events. The second is the benefits of the earth. Third is the awe inspired by natural phenomena. Finally, there is the regularity of the heavenly bodies in their courses.[99] Although Luke firmly believed in prophetic revelation and saw earthquakes, for example, as divine manifestations (4:31; cf. 16:26), he utilizes only the second argument. Luke therefore does not attempt to develop a full case for the existence of God, but he is willing to exhibit Paul as a sort of philosopher and to accept the need to advance proof, rather than, in distinction from the balance of the NT, to assume the existence of one God.

Two points may be derived from this fact. It is probably not accidental that Luke focuses on the goodness of creation. This is a negative datum in support of the hypothesis that some Christians in Luke's time were devaluing the realm of creation in distinction from that of redemption.[100] He did not need to convince his readers that God existed, but he did wish to affirm that God had fashioned all and that it was good. The second is related. Luke's use of natural theology shows his proximity to the world of the apologists, who used philosophical material to demonstrate the intellectual respectability of Christianity and who were (also?) confronting the teachings of Marcion and various "Gnostics."[101]

The congruence between apologetic argument and Acts is apparent in that Luke uses natural theology in Acts 14 and 17 as a common ground on which Christians and polytheists may meet.[102] *1 Clement* 20, which is similar to Acts in many ways, argues for the regularity of the heavens and the bounty of nature in the service of its call for order.[103] Here the results of Hellenistic Jewish apologetics are invoked to serve a nonapologetic task. In Acts, natural theology reveals movement toward the world of the apologists.[104]

■ **19-20a** Without taking a pause for breath, the narrator relates another exciting episode: Jews from (Pisidian) Antioch and Iconium erupt onto the scene and, the reader is to infer, persuade the crowds gathered to extol Paul and Barnabas that Paul is a dangerous menace whom they must exterminate by stoning. This climaxes

problem, e.g., Krodel, 257; Tannehill, *Narrative Unity*, 2:178; and Klauck, *Magic*, 56. Polhill (316) says that Paul would have proceeded to speak of repentance had he been able to complete the sermon. The text does not, however, say that this sermon was interrupted. Bede (65), who lived in a great missionary age, says no more than that the polytheists made a "stupid mistake" (*stultus error*). For Calvin (2:6, 9), the behavior of the Lystrans is an opportunity to attack his papal opponents.

97 On the speeches in chaps. 14 and 17, see also Wilckens, *Missionsreden*, 32–55.

98 Christian theology distinguishes between the confessional acknowledgment of God as creator and the use of creation as evidence for the existence of God.

99 Another common argument was the *consensus gentium*, the claim that all people believed in gods. This can be seen in Plato *Leg.* 12.966D-E. Cf. also the critique of various arguments in Lucian *Jupp. trag.* 38–46.

100 See p. 201 n. 95.

101 Phillip Vielhauer ("Paulinism," 33–50) underlines the differences between Paul's (Rom 1:20-21) and Luke's use of natural theology with the apposite statement: "His distance from Paul is just as clear as his nearness to the apologists" (33).

102 In *Aristeas* that common ground is the explicit basis for Jewish-gentile interaction. Views they share are acceptance of God as the creator (16–17), a ruler who cares providentially for that creation (16–19, 132–133, 201), including the necessities of life (190, noted above). This god is worshiped with different names, such as Zeus (16), but that is not deemed consequential.

103 Note *1 Clem.* 20:4, which speaks of the seasons and nourishment.

104 A few examples are Diognetus 3.3–5 (an anti-polytheistic argument); Minucius Felix *Oct.* 17.2; 32.7; Theophilus *Autolyc.* 1.4.6; 2.10; Aristides *Apol.* 1; Athenagoras *Leg.* 16; Irenaeus *A.H.* 2.30.3; Tertullian *Apol.* 17.

the threat of violence that has dogged the mission since the pair arrived in Asia Minor. Appreciation of the incident requires one to imagine a first-time reader utterly unfamiliar with the story. Paul, like Stephen, has paid the price for his eloquent convictions. And then . . . there rises before their very eyes an unbelievable sight: Paul! Severely injured he undoubtedly was, but he in no way cowed. Rather than find a secure shelter, he marched back into the very lions' den! Rather than take a week or so for recovery, he set out for Derbe the next day. Rather than delay as long as possible in order to generate suspense, the narrator opts for that instant gratification familiar in certain types of modern cinema.

Luke wishes to show that "the Jews" will go to any length to eliminate Paul.[105] Brief as the episode is, it retails several popular motifs. Barbarians are labile, not least when in large, unsupervised number. Those who had to be restrained by oratory from sacrificing to Paul were persuaded by oratory to drag him outside of the city[106] and lynch him.[107] The opponents of the movement are vicious Jews driven by enmity to enlist the service of a barbarian mob. A movement with such enemies can't be all bad. A second motif is that of apparent death, one of the most valued tools in the chest of the ancient popular narrator.[108] Third, Paul is portrayed as a popular hero, who can take a stoning in stride, not only walking away from the field but even setting out for a fresh destination the following day, just as if he had suffered no more than a minor bruise or two.[109] Theologically, "The decisive point is that this messenger of God is not discouraged but resumes his task."[110] Those interested in such tabulations will observe that, as the victim of a stoning, Paul is paying the bill of poetic justice for his role in the murder of Stephen.[111]

The account is not credible as it stands. The failure to attack Barnabas is inexplicable. The narrator does not state that the lynch mob left. A number of "disciples" appear out of the blue to surround the presumably dead Paul. It is difficult to conceive that they were numerous (and powerful) enough to provide protection. The first problem did not bother subsequent readers and editors: Paul was *the* enemy. Others they saw and addressed. The D-Text first sends the dissuaded crowd home, then creates an interval—of some days, evidently—to allow time for the agitators to arrive, and describes their monstrous charges. Paul's escape is rationalized: the followers waited until the crowd had left and darkness was at hand.[112] These expansions have no claim to originality, but they demonstrate that early readers saw the same problems in the narrative identified by modern critics.

It is possible to attribute the attack on Paul (and Barnabas?) to the missionary source, but it is difficult to imagine a source that would have combined this with

105 Although Antioch was around 160 km from Lystra, it is not likely that many readers would have been familiar with these distances. On Jews as "outside agitators," see *P. Lond.* 1912 (= *CPJ* 153) 96–97 (although this evidently refers to immigrants).

106 This, although required for reasons of purity in cases of lynching, constitutes another parallel with Jesus (Luke 4:29).

107 Cf. 28:1-6, which is nearly the exact opposite; and Pervo, *Profit*, 65.

108 For some examples of the motif, see Pervo, *Profit*, 148 n. 42.

109 See Pervo, *Profit*, 26 and 148 n. 41. Tannehill (*Narrative Unity*, 2:180) claims that "R. Pervo satirizes this scene." In his view, "The abbreviated report of Paul's recovery in v. 20 allows us to picture the scene as we will, with either a vigorous Paul marching back to town or a battered one limping between supporting colleagues." This is dubious. When the narrator wishes to portray Paul in need of "supporting colleagues" he can do so (9:8b; cf. 21:35). Tannehill does not explain the origin of the "colleagues," nor how a "battered" Paul was fit for a journey to Derbe the next day. It would be better to say that the narrative "allows us" to view this as a (symbolic?) "resurrection" of Paul. For Chrysostom (*Hom.* 31) this is a greater miracle than the healing of the lame man and an illustration of 2 Cor 12:9. The episode is imitated in Athanasius's *Vit. Ant.* 8. A more sophisticated form of imitation appears in the Ps.-Clem. *Rec.* 1.66–71 (*Ascents of James*), where a multitude in the temple precincts is persuaded by the Christian message until an enemy (Paul) arrives to create a tumult (cf. also Acts 21), which climaxes when he throws James down from the top of the steps (cf. also Luke 4:29) and leaves him for dead. James is rescued by friends.

110 Haenchen, "'We' in Acts and the Itinerary," *Journal for Theology and Church* 1 (1965) 65–99, esp. 79.

111 The verb for "drag" (σύρω [v. 19]) also suggests retribution. So Paul had done as a persecutor (8:3).

112 The mention of "Lystra" is typical D-Text pedantry.

the deification adventure. Luke may well, as suggested, have composed the healing in vv. 8-10 on the basis of 3:1-10, probably composed the sequel, and may have taken the stoning from 2 Cor 11:25. In any case, the arrangement is Lucan, with the stoning as the climactic event of 13:13—14:28. Information about sources, if any other than Acts 3 and 2 Corinthians existed, cannot advance the understanding of the text.

■ **20b-23** Derbe is the final stop. Barnabas returns to the narrative via a prepositional phrase. The participle *εὐαγγελισάμενοι* ("evangelizing")[113] rounds off the account begun in vv. 6b-7.[114] Derbe was on the very fringe of imperial territory. Its site has been identified with some certainty,[115] which makes little difference, since the narrator has only the most bland and general information to offer.[116] Somewhat ironically, this information includes a report that converts were numerous, whereas none were reported at Lystra![117] At v. 20b, without explanation, the two reverse course. What had been a missionary tour becomes a series of pastoral visits. This is a surprise, since one would expect them to continue eastward (to Tarsus, for example) and back to Antioch over land.[118] Luke has probably invented this pastoral swing around the circle,[119] for it is hardly credible that Paul could so easily revisit without incident cities from which he had recently (insofar as the reader would reasonably infer) been expelled or had left under inauspicious circumstances.[120] This lends support to the view that his primary source contained little more than a summary of missionary activity.[121]

The author devotes considerable effort to providing an elaborate inclusion with the beginning of chap. 13 that includes not only the places (in reverse order) but also words and actions.[122] The journey's pastoral character is evoked by an example of parenesis and by the provision of leadership. Verse 22 contains a painful example of zeugma,[123] together with a mixture of

113 The present participle of "evangelize" is well attested (𝔓[74] A D E H P *pc*). This evidently coordinates with the periphrastic construction of 14:7: "They continued to proclaim the message until, after they had made many followers." Ropes (*Text*, 136) says that only the aorist makes sense. The present is more difficult and may be original, perhaps due to copying from the source. Cf. also Barrett, 1:685.

114 That is its literary function. From the perspective of source theory it would mark a continuation of a skeletal report.

115 See John D. Wineland, "Derbe," *ABD* 2:144–45. The basis is epigraphic evidence: M. H. Balance, "The Site of Derbe: A New Inscription," *Anatolian Studies* 7 (1957) 147–51. See also Taylor, "St Paul," 1221–24. Derbe was not with the province of Galatia.

116 Modern maps make analysis of the text difficult. Breytenbach (*Paulus & Barnabas*, 87) takes Conzelmann to task for drawing conclusions that assume the author had a map of the type now familiar, but he himself says that the narrator knows that Derbe is east of Lystra (80). This is not correct. The narrative states a sequence, but gives no indication of compass points.

117 Verse 21 may derive from the source. The verb *μαθητεύω* ("produce followers") is not otherwise found in Luke and Acts. Barrett (1:685) notes its occurrence in Matthew and shrewdly asks whether it is Antiochene. See BDF §148 (3) on this ergative transformation. The D-Text rejects the trope, stating that they preached the message to "those in the city" (Boismard, *Texte*, 243).

118 Foakes Jackson (129) observed. "It needed no little courage on the part of the missionaries to return by the same route as they had come, especially as there was a good road from Derbe to Antioch." Zahn and Ramsay saw the point and developed appropriate rationales, for which see Haenchen, 435 n. 2.

119 For example, *ἐπιστηρίζω* ("fortify spiritually," on which see BDF §339 [2a]) is a stereotyped term used for return visits (15:32, 41; 18:23; cf. 16:5).

120 Loisy (560) pointed to the difficulty.

121 Haenchen (439), with an eye to Gal 1:21, says that this missionary took place after the meeting in Jerusalem recounted in Galatians 2. This hypothesis would require a longer interval between Gal 2:10-11 than the narrative implies, since the passage of considerable time would support Paul's case.

122 E.g., the "souls" (*ψυχάς*) of v. 22 nicely complements (and inverts) v. 6; *ἀπέπλευσεν* ("sail from") in v. 26 occurred in 13:4; and the "work" (*ἔργον*) of 14:26 complements the task (*ἔργον*) of 13:2. The apparent and definite ordinations in 13:3 and 14:23 share fasting, prayer, and the imposition of hands. For evidence that 14:21-28 is Lucan composition, see Weiser, 2:355–56.

123 BDF §479 (2).

indirect and direct discourse.[124] The exhortation calls for perseverance in the faith in the face of the numerous obstacles to be encountered on the path.[125] The exhortation is quite similar to that in Col 1:23 (ἐπιμένετε τῇ πίστει), from which it may be derived,[126] but Schuyler Brown finds the meaning different. Whereas Colossians (etc.) is "anthropological-ethical," with a focus on individual behavior, Acts is "ecclesiological-spatial,"[127] and the focus is collective. The reference to "the kingdom of God" is revelatory. Rather than a phenomenon that will "come" (as in the Our Father), the kingdom is a goal, and the focus is on the believer's path toward it rather than divine action to introduce it.[128]

To translate θλίψεις as "persecutions" is undesirable. For Luke, the cross is a part of daily life (Luke 9:23). There is wisdom in his sentiment, for various forms of social slight and exclusion, verbal hostility and the like may have been more of a motive for apostasy in the long run than the threat of martyrdom.[129] To call this a "theology of the cross," even in Barrett's sense: "It is not Paul's, it is not as profound as Paul's; but it exists" may be misleading.[130] *Theologia crucis* applies to Pauline theology—particularly as expounded by M. Luther—and gains nothing by generalization. Luke does not obliterate persecution; he speaks of suffering, but his accounts of suffering are devoid of realism. For an example of this quality, one need look no further back than three verses. There is a considerable difference between glorious and apparently painless martyrdoms—like those of Jesus and Stephen—and the agonies of isolation and torture.[131]

Verse 23 is anachronistic and certainly un-Pauline, for Paul makes no reference to presbyters. The pastoral perspective is that of Titus 1:5 and *1 Clem.* 42:4 (cf. 44:2): each community is to have properly qualified and installed[132] leaders.[133] Readers are to know that Paul actively promoted the system of good order advocated by proponents of emerging "normative" Christianity from the beginning of the second century. The reader is to take this as a standard practice that need not be mentioned again (cf. 20:17).

■ **24-28** Cadbury and Lake take 14:27–15:2 as a paragraph.[134] This is not likely, since v. 27 is closely linked to v. 26, but it reflects Luke's tendency toward overlapping narratives in which summaries look both ways.[135] The report, made at a community assembly (cf. 13:1-3),

124 Cf. on 1:4. In this case the transition is signaled by ὅτι *recitativum*.

125 The δεῖ in v. 22 does not refer to divine necessity (*contra* Tannehill, *Narrative Unity*, 2:181.) See Brown, *Apostasy*, 123.

126 Note the reference to suffering in v. 26—and the great differences in theology and function between the two passages.

127 Brown, *Apostasy*, 114–15, 119, 122–23.

128 On the terminology used in 14:22, see Tannehill, *Narrative Unity*, 2:180–81; and Barrett, 1:686. The general expression "enter the kingdom of God" (Mark 9:47; 10:23-25; John 3:5) probably means "be saved." Specific meanings, such as "the end is near" or "individuals will go to heaven when they die," are not to be extracted from this phrase here.

129 It is not Luke's fault if the "cross one has to bear" is trivialized or invoked to encourage people to put up with an abusive situation.

130 Barrett (1:665), with a reference to his "Theologia Crucis–In Acts?" in Carl Andresen and Günter Klein, eds., *Theologia Crucis–Signum Crucis: Festschrift für Erich Dinkler zum 70. Geburtstag* (Tübingen: Mohr Siebeck, 1979) 73–84.

131 Although Scott Cunningham's *Through Many Tribulations: The Theology of Persecution in Luke-Acts* (JSNTS 142; Sheffield: Sheffield Academic Press, 1997) includes many good observations (and has some justice in taking me to task for saying that Luke's view of persecution includes "little theology" [Pervo, *Profit*, 28], which he metastasizes into "Pervo . . . excludes any theological motivation" [295]), his identification of persecution and suffering leads to the debatable claim that for Luke a theology of the cross has equal status to the theology of glory (339). For an attempt to elucidate a Lucan theology of the cross in Lucan terms, see Peter Doble, *The Paradox of Salvation: Luke's Theology of the Cross* (SNTSMS 87; Cambridge: Cambridge University Press, 1996).

132 The examples of 6:6 and 13:3 show that χειροτονέω means "appoint with the imposition of hands." Calvin (2:19) agrees, while asserting that the presbyters were elected by the people.

133 On the subject, see Pervo, *Dating*, 204–18.

134 Cadbury and Lake, 169.

135 See pp. 88–89.

prepares for the similar summary in 15:4[136] and reminds those reading that the prophecy in 13:2 had not mentioned a gentile mission.[137] Of the Jewish mission nothing is said. Verse 28 shows that Paul and Barnabas did not return to discover a crisis. Time is given for all to savor their success.

The term "model journey" is appropriate for chaps. 13–14.[138] In this journey, Paul's appeal to a highly placed Roman, the priority of "Jews first," their (less than unanimous) rejection, their exposure as threats to law and order, the subsequent turn to the gentiles, which meets with success, and persecution sparked by that success, which not only fails but leads to furtherance of the mission, all make their debut. The balance of the book will be a set of variations on these themes. Before that, however, there will be an astonishing development: Some Judeans object to the inclusion of uncircumcised male gentiles. Should they prevail, the entire gentile mission that began with the admission of Cornelius will be invalidated.

136 The D-Text (Boismard, *Texte*, 244) reads *ὅσα ὁ θεὸς ἐποίησεν μετὰ τῶν ψυχῶν αὐτῶν* ("all that God had accomplished with *their souls*"). This awkward wording may be an attempt to soften the blunt "what God had done *with* (rather than, e.g., "through") them. There is no reason to take this as LXX language (Moule, *Idiom Book*, 184). The language of the summary derives from Mark 6:30.

137 "Door of faith" is a Pauline metaphor: 1 Cor 16:9; 2 Cor 2:12; cf. Col 4:3. As the last suggests, treatment of "God" as subject is Deutero-Pauline.

138 See also Tannehill (*Narrative Unity*, 2:182), who refers to the 1982 Boston University dissertation of E. S. Nelson, "Paul's First Missionary Journey as Paradigm: A Literary-Critical Assessment of Acts 13, 14."

15

15:1-35 Resolution of a Controversy over Circumcision

Acts 15:1-5: Conventional Text

1/ Some people from Judea arrived
and began to teach the believers, "Unless you are circumcised in accordance with
Mosaic practice, you cannot be
saved." 2/ That claim set off a
divisive partisan controversy[a] in
which Paul and Barnabas took
a strong stand against the visitors' position. It was decided
that those two, as well as some
others,[b] would go to Jerusalem
to lay this conflict before the
apostles and elders. 3/ After
being sent off by the community, they journeyed[c] through
both[d] Phoenicia and Samaria.
Their detailed reports about
the conversion of the gentiles
became an occasion of great joy
to all the believers who heard
them. 4/ Once they arrived in
Jerusalem they were welcomed[e] by the community, the
apostles, and the presbyters,
to whom they reported all that
God had accomplished with
them.[f] 5/ In response, some
converts who belonged to the
Pharisaic party stood up and
insisted, "It is necessary to circumcise them and direct them
to observe the Law of Moses."[g]

6/ The apostles[p] and the presbyters assembled to consider
this matter.[q] 7/ After a lengthy
debate,[r] Peter arose[s] and said:
"My fellow believers, you are
well aware that God long ago[t]
selected me from your number
as the one from whose lips
the gentiles would hear the
gospel message and come to
believe. 8/ God, who knows
what humans really think and
feel, approved of these gentiles by giving them[u] the Holy
Spirit that was also given to us.
9/ God, who purified their souls
also by giving them the faith,
made no distinctions between
them and us. 10/ Why, therefore, are you now challenging
God by imposing a burden upon
his followers that neither we
nor our forebears have been
able to tolerate? 11/ On the

Acts 15:1-5: D-Text[h]

1/ Some [*converts* from Judea *who belonged to the Pharisaic party*][i] arrived and began to teach the believers, "Unless you are circumcised *and behave* in accordance with Mosaic practice [*and are purified from foods and all other things*],[j] you cannot be saved." 2/ That claim set off a divisive partisan controversy in which Paul and Barnabas took a strong stand against the visitors' position—*for Paul insistently refuted*[k] *them, saying that they should continue as when they came to believe—but those who had come from Jerusalem ordered Paul and Barnabas and some others* to go to Jerusalem to lay this conflict before the apostles and elders *at Jerusalem so that they might make a judgment in their presence . . .*[l]

(4[m])

5[n]/ *Those who had commanded them to go to the presbyters* rose up [against the apostles][o] and insisted, "It is necessary to circumcise them and direct them to observe the Law of Moses."

contrary,[v] we believe that both
we and they are saved by the
grace of the Lord Jesus."[w]
12/ The entire assembly listened in
silence while Barnabas and Paul
set out all the miracles and portents that God had performed
for the gentiles through their
agency.
13/ When they had finished, James
said:[x] "My fellow believers,
please listen. 14/ Simeon has
explained how God first acted
to raise from the gentiles a
people of God. 15/ With this
understanding the utter-
ances of the prophets are in
agreement. Scripture says:
16/ 'Thereafter I shall return
and rebuild David's demolished
dwelling; that which has been
torn down I shall erect again.
I shall restore that dwelling,
17/ so that the rest of humanity
may seek out the Lord, even all
the gentiles who belong to my
people. Thus says the Lord who
does these things, 18/ known
since long, long ago.'
19/ "It is therefore my verdict that
harassment of gentile converts
cease, 20/ but to direct[y] them
to abstain from idolatrous food,
prohibited sexual relationships,
and meat from animals that
were strangled or not drained
of blood. 21/ For Moses has
always had his exponents and
is read everywhere every week
in every synagogue." 22/ The
apostles and presbyters then
resolved, the entire community
concurring, to send selected
representatives to Antioch with
Paul and Barnabas. Those chosen were Judas Barsabbas[z] and
Silas, two leading believers.
23/ They were to deliver the following letter:[aa]
"Dear gentile brothers and
sisters in Antioch, Syria, and
Cilicia:
24/ "Inasmuch as it has come to
our attention that some of our
number[bb] have been causing
trouble for you by making,
without our authorization, subversive assertions, 25/ we have
unanimously resolved to select
delegates[cc] and send them to
you along with our well-beloved

Demolished Dwelling

Barnabas and Paul, 26/ who
have devoted[dd] their lives to the
name of our Lord Jesus Christ.
27/ The delegates we have sent
are Judas and Silas. They will
personally provide oral confir-
mation of our decision. 28/ For
we, with the Holy Spirit, have
resolved to impose on you no
obligation beyond the following
essentials: 29/ to abstain from
foods that have been offered to
idols or contain blood or have
been killed by strangling, as
well as from prohibited sexual
relationships.
You will be in good standing if
you avoid these things.
Best Wishes,
Your brothers and sisters,
The Apostles and the Elders."
30/ The delegates were sent on their
way and traveled to Antioch,
where they called a meet-
ing of the full community, at
which they delivered the letter.
31/ After it had been read aloud,
the believers were delighted
with the reassurance it con-
veyed. 32/ Both Judas and Silas
were prophets. They edified the
believers with a great deal of
spiritual comfort and suste-
nance. 33/ The two spent some
time there and were then sent
back, with the community's
blessing, to those who had
dispatched them.[ee] 35/ Paul and
Barnabas, however, remained in
Antioch and continued to teach
and preach, along with many
others, the message about
the Lord.

---

a A range of witnesses in v. 2 read οὖν rather than δέ. This stronger contrast is more appropriate and thus probably secondary. $\mathfrak{P}^{74}$ E vg bo omit καὶ ζητήσεως ("and argument"). This eliminates the debate and reduces the event to something like a brawl.

b "Other members of the community" (ἐξ αὐτῶν) is probably secondary. See Ropes, *Text*, 139–40.

c On the imperfect, see BDF §327. It suggests that they visited each region in its entirety.

d A range of witnesses omit τε, as "both . . . and" seems unnecessary.

e The D-Text: "*magnificently* (μεγάλως) welcomed." On this, see Epp, *Tendency*, 96–97.

f H L and a number of minuscules add here (from 14:27) "and that God had opened for the gentiles a door of faith." Cadbury and Lake (172) remark that this was to deal with the dangling and ubiquitous "them" of v. 5, which therefore has an antecedent. They note another possibility: "them" refers to the colleagues who came with Paul and Barnabas.

g This could be translated as indirect speech. Direct is Luke's preference and retains the parallel with v. 1.

h The D-Text is that of Boismard, *Texte*, 245–47, with additions not admitted by him in brackets. (Cop[mae] ends at v. 3.)

i Ψ 614 *pc* sy[hmg].

j *Didascalia*.

k The participle διϊσχυριζόμενος is a Lucan word. See on 12:15.

l The D-Text has but minor differences in vv. 3-4.

m The *Didascalia* (Ropes, *Text*, cxciv) reads: "And when they were come to Jerusalem, they told us about the dispute which they had in the church of Antioch."

n In a long note, Boismard (*Texte*, 248) despairs of finding the "primitive" D-Text, then suggests the following: (2c) "Those who had come from Jerusalem, (5b) arose saying 'they must be circumcised and directed to keep the Law of Moses.' (2d) And they told them and some others to go to the apostles and presbyters in Jerusalem so that a judgment concerning this dispute might be made before them . . ." (3–4), as he prints them (almost identical to the conventional text), omit 5, then 6 and following.

o Sy^{hmg}.

p Once again, "both . . . and " is changed to "now the apostles . . ." (*δέ)* in a range of witnesses.

q D-Texts tend to prefer *ζήτημα* ("question," etc.; cf. v. 2) to *λόγος*, possibly indicating that the latter had acquired sacral ("word of God," "message," second person of Trinity as divine Word) connotations.

r Gig seeks to increase the tension: "after they had been unable to reach a decision for some time." Boismard (*Texte*, 249) accepts this as the D reading.

s The D-Text indicates that he was inspired: *ἐν πνεύματι*. This enhances both the speaker and the occasion. At this point, $\mathfrak{p}^{45}$ adds much of v. 2. This must be due to error, possibly from a lacuna in v. 2.

t The order of the words after "days" (lit.) varies considerably, without changing the meaning.

u "Them" is supplied for clarity, and not an adaptation of "to them" or "upon them" found in various witnesses.

v Ropes (*Text*, 142) inclines to prefer *ἀλλ᾽ ἤ*, "but in fact."

w Numerous witnesses add (typically) "Christ."

x The D-Text (Boismard, *Texte*, 251) reads: "stood up and said," achieving a precise parallel to Peter (v. 7b).

y "Write" is possible, but the context makes a variant of "command" preferable. Cf. Barrett, 2:730.

z Or, possibly, "Barabbas."

aa A range of witnesses give an object for "writing": "these things." D-Texts expand to include designation of the following as "a letter," or "sending a letter containing the following," and the like. Ψ alone has "a letter to the following effect," *ἐπιστολὴν διὰ χειρὸς αὐτῶν ἔχουσαν τὸν τύπον τοῦτον*. Cf. 23:25 (which has similar variants). Barrett (2:739) views the variants as an attempt to underline the importance of the letter

bb *Or:* "Some who came from us." The alternative seeks to include the variant *ἐξελθόντες* ("coming from"). Syntactically, this would be circumstantial ("some . . . having come"), which is difficult to translate. Good arguments can be made for both inclusion and exclusion. If a later addition (cf. the use of this verb in 1 John 2:19; 4:1), it would have distinguished the *τίνες* ("some people") from the senders of the letter. Almost the same argument may be made for its exclusion. The witnesses that omit the participle are a small but select company: א* B 1175 *pc*. Gal 2:12 could be invoked on either side. Barrett (2:741–42) inclines to omit it, with good reason. See also Metzger, *Textual Commentary*, 385. Boismard (*Texte*, 254) reads *ἐξ ἡμῶν πρὸς ὑμᾶς ἐλθόντες* ("Some of us, having come to you"). This looks like a correction of an archetype that included *ἐξελθόντες*. His D-Text omits *ἀνασκευάζοντες τὰς ψυχὰς ὑμῶν* ("making subversive assertions").

cc *Or:* "While we were together we decided to select. . . ." It is more likely that unanimity is the point.

dd *Or* (somewhat less likely): "risked . . . for . . ." This is the understanding of the D-Text (Boismard, *Texte*, 255), which adds "in every trial" (*εἰς πάντα πειρασμόν*). On this, see Epp (*Tendency*, 142), who notes that 20:18 specifies these "trials" as the result of Jewish plots. For "devoted," see Cadbury and Lake, 180.

ee Metzger (*Textual Commentary*, 388) reports that the Textus Receptus and a number of D-Texts state that they were sent back to "the apostles." It need, *pace* Metzger, be no more than a specification.

Analysis

Acts 15 is difficult. "The general problem of Acts xv is so complicated that it can only be stated—it cannot be solved—by a process of analysis into smaller ones."[1] The place of chap. 15 in the structure of Acts is difficult to determine. Historical knowledge exacerbates the question, since commentators know that, subsequent to the sequel of this meeting, Paul began his career as an independent gentile missionary. If, as has often been proposed, this is the central chapter in

1 Kirsopp Lake, "The Apostolic Council of Jerusalem," in Lake and Cadbury, *Additional Notes,* 195–212, esp. 195. His identification of most of the difficulties is astute.

Acts,[2] does it complete the first half, begin the second, or is a division into two principal parts undesirable? Although the chapter deals with the central issue of Acts—the legitimacy of the gentile mission—and occurs in the center of the book, it is not the basic structural pivot,[3] nor does it break new ground.[4] Acts 15 is central in that it brings together the various threads of the plot: Peter with his mission, Barnabas and Paul with theirs (which is the unacknowledged successor of the "Hellenists"), and those persons concerned with observance. The two geographical bases, Jerusalem and Antioch, also formally converge. The narrator wishes to make a profound impression with a grand assembly and a solemn decree. All of this is to paper over the rift between Paul and Peter, and the tension between Paul and James. When that tension finally emerges, in chap. 21, the reader is directed to perceive their encounter in the light of chap. 15. The gross outline of 15:1-35 is clear. Verses 1-5 provide the occasion;[5] vv. 6-29 present the deliberations and the decision, which is implemented in vv. 30-35.[6]

A cloud appears on the horizon. To Antioch there come some unnamed Judeans. The narrator does not suggest that these persons acted under the auspices of the apostles in Jerusalem. The visitors assert that circumcision is necessary for *salvation*. The language speaks not of covenant but of soteriology. Such language was not unheard of among first-century Jews, but it does represent a shift into categories that Christians would develop. Luke casts the debate in Christian terms. Of that debate the narrator says no more than that it was heated. To first readers, this quarrel comes as a complete surprise. Had not the question been disposed of with the conversion of Cornelius? In the event, the community resolves to send an embassy to Jerusalem to meet with "the apostles and elders." The delegation was well received in earlier missionary areas and warmly welcomed at Jerusalem.

Some believers identified as members of the Pharisaic party did not hesitate to assert that circumcision *and* observance of Torah were obligatory—although salvation receives no mention. The matter calls for a meeting that allows the narrator to place the decorum and propriety of the Christian assembly on display.[7] The meeting includes another lively debate, of which the narrator again shares not a word. The spotlight will fall first on Peter, who reminds the audience of the precedent set *in re* Cornelius. This matter has already been resolved. Moreover, the Torah is an impossible burden. Only through grace can salvation come to both Jews and gentiles. (This is, in fact, a gentile view of Torah; for Jews obedience is a source of joy.)

That times have changed becomes apparent when Peter's word is not the last. Before James, who has become the leader in Jerusalem, offers his views, Paul and Barnabas are given the floor. They appeal to proof based on the wonders exhibited in their gentile ministries. This would surprise a discerning reader, since the narrative has reported but one specific example (14:8-10). James then rises to give his *nihil obstat* to the words of Peter, followed by the first explicit *theological* justification for a gentile mission. Scripture confirms the experience of the Spirit, as a substantial citation from Amos demonstrates. James thus joins Peter in viewing the gentile mission as the result of a hermeneutical breakthrough, the new understanding of Scripture brought to minds opened by Easter (cf. Luke 24:45). Fulfillment of the promises to David takes place in the proclamation of a messianic salvation offered to all.

The result is everything that could be expected.

2 See Barrett, 2:709–10.

3 See pp. 20–21.

4 Johnson (268) says that this is "a watershed in the narrative of Acts." His claims that Luke has previously followed all the apostles and that gentiles hereafter have priority are disputable. Paul has been the central character since chap. 13, and the theme of "Jews first" remains in force.

5 Cf. 1:15; 6:1; and 11:2-3, where disputes also begin with a statement of the problem.

6 Acts 15:36–16:5 is a different unit.

7 See Pervo, "Meet Right." The Spring 2001 issue of *Forum* 4 was devoted to Acts 15: Alan F. Segal, "Acts 15 as Jewish and Christian History," 63–87; Hal Taussig, "Jerusalem as a Place for Conversation: The Intersection of Acts 15 and Galatians 2," 89–104; and Joseph B. Tyson, "Themes at the Crossroads: Acts 15 in Its Lukan Setting," 105–24.

Without a further word of debate, the entire body voted to communicate the decision in the form of an official decree, issued as a letter to be conveyed by a delegation that will include Judas Barsabbas and Silas. Luke portrays the Jerusalem church as a formally organized body that issues its decisions in the form of official letters delivered by authorized ambassadors.[8] The Sanhedrin has a most formidable rival. Acts 15:30-35 nicely reverses the itinerary of vv. 1-5, indicating that the situation has also been turned around. In place of conflict there is consolation; peace reigns where turmoil had boiled. Chapter 15 could have been an unpleasant interlude. By its end, Paul and Barnabas are back where they were at the conclusion of chap. 14. Well-managed conflict leads to growth.

The so-called Apostolic Council of Acts 15 deserves this title, as Dibelius noted, because of the formality with which Luke invests the proceedings.[9] The major source of this material is Galatians 2,[10] the story of which the narrator revises with considerable artistry. One aspect of this revision is that a dispute about whether believers in Jesus had to become full-fledged converts to Judaism is resolved by promulgating rules that permit those of Jewish and gentile background to enjoy sacramental fellowship. This decree (v. 29), which, judging by its numerous revisions, enjoyed a long life, probably stems from Antioch and represents the culmination of the gentile missionary source—at least insofar as Luke chose to utilize that source.[11]

Luke's presentation of the story is no less artful than it is disingenuous. The conflict erupts, as in Gal 2:11-14, in Antioch, but rather than the "separate altars"—to use a later trope—described there, the opponents take the position of the "Galatian agitators" and demand circumcision. Since Luke requires the full authority of Jerusalem here, the subject of v. 3 is a vague "they." The delegation is that of Gal 2:1 (although Titus has suffered *damnatio memoriae* [become a nonperson]).[12] The narrator presents their journey as a triumphal procession through the regions where, in chaps. 8–10, Samaritans and gentiles received the gospel. The intent is clear: the gentile mission is not under a cloud.

In vv. 4-5, the narrator becomes quite cagey. Although the reception is full and formal, the occasion is not an official assembly. Yet it is on this occasion that, in response to a report by the delegation, an objection is lodged by persons identified as believing Pharisees. They demand that converts be circumcised and observe the Mosaic regulations. The conflict has recurred, although the demand lacks soteriological grounding. This is quite contrived, for Barnabas and Paul would have, in addition to their reports of missionary success, taken note of the objection that had generated the delegation. Insofar as the reader knows, the fact and

8 See below.

9 Dibelius, *Studies*, 99.

10 For the evidence, see Pervo, *Dating*, 79–96. All of the arguments demonstrating that Acts 15 and Galatians 2 treat the same meeting and the elaborate source hypotheses needed to account for these show how much effort can be expended in avoiding the simplest and most probable solution. Witherington (449–50) posits a source (either Jerusalem, "perhaps Petrine . . . or possibly . . . Antiochian") for vv. 6–21, Luke's editorial introduction in v. 22, citation of a Jerusalem document in vv. 23–29, and an editorial summary in vv. 30-35. On p. 450 his rationale emerges: to account "for why Paul's contribution to the meeting is barely mentioned." This is not source analysis. A recent analysis that views the distinctive elements of Acts 15 as later is Martino Conti, "Il Concilio Apostolico e la lettera ai Galati (At 15, 1-29; Gal 2, 1-21," *Antonianum* 77 (2002) 235–56.

11 A rough sketch of the historical situation envisioned here is: following Paul's departure from Antioch, those allied with Barnabas and Peter worked out the compromise represented in the "decree." The compromise was not acceptable to James and those to his right. The latter became vigorous opponents of Paul. That missionary, and those to his left, also found the compromise unacceptable. As far as the latter were concerned, Peter was no better than James. The Gospel of Mark represents a later form of that position, using (and twisting) traditions from Antioch that upheld Peter as the moderating figure who upheld both the old and the new. That old Antiochene position is thus best represented in the Gospel of Matthew, which used Mark as its major source. Luke offered the proposal that there were no important differences among the three. This view took hold, but, as Acts 21 indicates, the Lucan synthesis has leaks.

12 Witherington (601 n. 174) attributes his absence from the account to controversy over the collection. For another solution, see on 16:1-3.

announcement of considerable success among gentiles has encountered the contention that this mission is invalid. Nothing has been said of their success among Jews (cf. 14:1).

Amidst this suspense, a full and formal legislative assembly is convoked. After a spirited discussion by unnamed persons come speeches by Peter and James, separated by a summary of what Paul and colleagues said. These speeches encompass a number of proofs: experience, miraculous attestation, and Scripture. James then changes the subject. Rather than reject or accept the necessity of the Torah in its entirety, he proposes some purity regulations that relate to social intercourse, in particular commensality. Neither Paul nor anyone else objects. The expanded delegation is authorized to return with the good news. As Johnson recognizes,[13] the community assembly is a "standard narrative device" of popular literature. Such scenes allow a weighted account of the story thus far and give the reader a sense of participation, in this case as one of the "common persons" who lend their voice to the positions advocated by Peter and James. With this admirable picture, Luke proclaims the end of the "Judaizing controversy" in primitive Christianity. Gentiles are to be charitable about Jewish sensibilities, while the latter are to make no demands for observance upon the converts harvested from the nations. Soteriologically speaking, the Torah is a dead letter. Jews are free to follow it, insofar as they do not trouble others. The only matter that will have to be addressed is the malicious rumor that Paul advises Jews by birth to neglect observance (21:21).

Acts 15 is a brilliant example of Lucan art. Since readers know that the demand for circumcision has already been rejected, the council can be an opportunity to celebrate church unity based on utterly reasonable compromises. This portrait does not reflect a patina of legend, nor does it depend on the best reconstruction that Luke could make with his limited knowledge. The author of Acts knew better, and, although the Jesus movement had become a new and largely gentile religion, its legitimacy was still open to question in certain circles, and both Paul and his opponents remained controversial figures. Acts 15 is a fresh and, the author hopes, decisive portrait of the Jerusalem conference, an agreement acceptable to all parties and enduring.

Comment

■ **1-5** In these verses, D-Texts clarify Luke's intention by presenting a different story. The D-tradition generally tends to identify the opponents in Antioch and Jerusalem and their demands, whereas Luke wishes to distinguish between the two groups. D-editor(s) either did not grasp or did not accept this approach.[14] A narrative explanation of the D-Text is the anonymous ἔταξαν ("it was decided" [v. 2]).[15] The D-Text evidently presumed that the subject was the Judeans. Luke's opacity probably derives from Gal 2:2. The progressively expanded D-Text includes circumcision and observance.[16] This is logical, but it does not appreciate that Luke, following Galatians, wished to focus on circumcision. The expansion wishes to make the demand involve all Jewish observance and have it rejected *in toto*. In v. 2, the D-Text increases vividness by citing Paul's argument, derived from 1 Cor 7:17-20.[17] "So that they might make a judgment" (ὅπως κριθῶσιν) evidently anticipates the ruling of James in v. 19 (same verb).[18] This text also removes any ambiguity from the "Judea" of v. 1 by stating that the agitators were from Jerusalem.[19] The two groups of opponents in the conventional text become

13 He cites Chariton *Chaer.* 3.4.4–18; 8.7.1–16. See also Pervo, *Profit*, 39–42; and idem, "Meet Right."

14 Justification for the D-Text view may be derived from v. 24, which states that the objectors are believers.

15 So Cadbury and Lake, 169–70. See also Metzger, *Tetual Commentary*, 376–78; and Strange, *Text*, 133–35.

16 Cf. also the D-Text of 15:24.

17 This is not an argument Paul would have utilized in Galatians, for it assumes that circumcision is theologically irrelevant.

18 On this, see Epp (*Tendency*, 97), who supports the view that this presumes the full unity of the early church, although the historical Paul would not have submitted his views for a judgment.

19 Epiphanius *Pan.* 28.3 can report that Cerinthus was one of the troublemakers at Antioch. Ephrem's comments (420–27) are interesting. He identifies the nomists of 15:1 as converts made by Peter. They demanded that the gentiles follow the teaching of Peter and friends. Paul denied that he abrogated Torah for Jews. The opponents "went wild" (*saevibant* [422]) with anger. He reports Peter

one in the D-Text,[20] which also stresses the unity of the whole church and reduces the severity of the problem.[21]

Verses 1-5 constitute a rounded composition that begins and ends with a statement of the demand for circumcision.[22] As in chap. 11, which is likewise based on Galatians, both opponents[23] and locality ("Judea") are unspecified. The reference to "Mosaic practice" (ἔθος) is a means of shying away from "the *laws* delivered to Moses." As the customs of an ethnic group, these practices are more amenable to adjustment.[24] Pauline influence is probably responsible for avoiding the association of Abraham with circumcision. In its Lucan form, Torah belongs to a period of salvation history. Belief in the God of Israel had existed for some centuries before Moses.[25] Placement of the demand for circumcision in soteriological terms is, as stated, more characteristic of Christianity than of Judaism.[26] The same infinitive σωθῆναι ("to be saved") will recur in the climax of Peter's speech (v. 11).

■ **1** According to Acts 15:1, the Judean visitors to Antioch set off στάσις ("disorder"). Luke thereby characterizes them as dangerous outside agitators. There would, however, be no disorder in Jerusalem (15:7). The narrative does not suggest that any at Antioch sided with the visitors. The delegation's[27] (overland) progress displays unity by visiting sites associated with the earlier missions of Philip and Peter.[28] More importantly, the joy of their reception isolates Jerusalem/Judea. Only there will vocal opponents of the gentile conversion without Torah be found. When they report their success[29] to the community,[30] some believing Pharisees raise objections. Male circumcision and subsequent observance are to be required. The readers understand that Pharisees are particularly meticulous in their observance (cf. 22:3;

as saying, "[W]hatever God has given us through faith and through the law, he has given the same also to the gentiles through faith without observance of the law" (425). James (evidently, 427) promised spiritual gifts for the gentiles, invoking the example of Cornelius.

20 Cf. Epp, *Tendency*, 101–2.

21 See Dibelius, *Studies*, 93 and n. 2.

22 Cf. Talbert, 137.

23 The indefinite τίνες occurs in Gal 2:12. The term is common in polemical contexts, in which the other party is, for one reason or another, left anonymous. (Cf. the traditional "my opponent" in politics and "Brand *X*" in advertising, as well as the Roman practice of *damnatio memoriae*). For an example from religious competition, see the Sarapis aretalogy from Delos, lines 23–24, and the references in Engelmann, *Delian Aretalogy*, 23. The historical Paul did not name his opponents (2 Cor 2:5-11; Gal 1:7), nor did Ignatius *Smyrn.* 5.3. On early Christian practice, see Schoedel, *Ignatius*, 235 n. 28.

24 The phrase τῷ ἔθει is a dative of cause, BDF §196. On the translation "practice," see Barrett, 2:698. In Luke 1:9; 2:42; 22:39, the term means "custom." In Acts (6:14; 16:21; 21:21; 26:3; 28:17), it refers to Torah. (The exception is Roman criminal jurisprudence [25:16].)

25 Another approach emerges in the speech of Stephen: although Abraham received promise and circumcision together, Israel resisted God and the Spirit (7:53). This resistance invalidates circumcision, while the Spirit is bestowed on the (physically) uncircumcised (10:45; 11:2-3). Luke fashions an essentially Pauline argument to show that the link between circumcision and promise, circumcision and Spirit, has been shattered. For Paul, this was essentially christological: through God's action in Christ. For Luke, the argument is salvation-historical: Israel has repudiated the promise and defied the Spirit, but the concept of separating the Spirit from circumcision derives from Galatians and Romans. Cf. Peter's speech (v. 8).

26 Alan F. Segal ("Matthew's Jewish Voice," in David Balch, ed., *Social History of the Matthean Community* [Minneapolis: Fortress, 1991] 3–37, esp. 16) says that the typical rabbinic position did not say that circumcision was necessary for gentiles, some of whom would be saved, but that it was necessary for participation in community life (specifically meals). *Jub.* 15:25-34 takes a stricter position, viewing all uncircumcised males as condemned.

27 The μὲν οὖν in v. 3 does not mark a new section. Moule (*Idiom Book*, 162) classifies it as "purely resumptive." See also Barrett (2:702), who rightly compares 13:4.

28 Phoenicia: see also 11:19; 21:3-6.

29 On the phrase μετ᾽ αὐτῶν, see on 14:27. Luke was not worried about "synergism" (a potential interpretation that Calvin deals with by saying that "with" means "through" [7:30]).

30 The language of v. 4 separates the "laity" (ἐκκλησία, lit. "church," "assembly") from the officers (presbyters and apostles). This is careless parataxis. The narrator wishes to emphasize that all extended a welcome.

26:5).[31] That even such as these will be persuaded to abandon this demand will show how convincing the arguments to the contrary are. The situation is quite artificial.

■ **2** According to v. 2, the delegates from Antioch may well have wished to report on their mission, but they should have stated the purpose of their visit.[32] The narrative focuses on the success of the mission, but numbers will not settle the argument.

■ **5** Despite its awkwardness, Luke sets out in v. 5 the theme of the chapter: What is necessary for inclusion within the people of God? Moreover, it removes the necessity of disturbing the formal meeting with an opportunity for the opposition to make its case, a case that is reduced to a demand. This leads Barrett to comment: "In fact the Council turns out to be a sham fight; no dissenting voice is heard."[33]

■ **6-29** The meeting proper occupies vv. 6-29. The structure is straightforward: two brief references to the community (vv. 6-7a, 12) precede the speeches of Peter (vv. 7b-11) and James (vv. 13-21), followed by the resolution and letter (vv. 22-29). From the perspective of political history, this material resembles the constitutional debate used by historians to weigh the advantages and drawbacks of various systems, although here the question is specifically the qualifications for citizenship, so to speak.[34] The contrast is apparent. The narrator allows the supporters of observance to do no more than assert their position; for the other side, there is a range of argument and evidence, indicating that the section as a whole is the result of careful planning by the author. Peter offers positive and negative artistic proof from history: God did not discriminate against gentiles, and no one can keep the Torah, which is therefore ineffective. Barnabas and Paul present the historical evidence of miracle, which proves God's endorsement. Finally, James sets forth the inartistic proof of scriptural prophecy. The difficulty is that James (and the entire community) does not offer a rationale for the proposed regulations, which do have some background in Torah and serve the evident purpose of permitting mixed communities to exist with a minimum of discord. Luke does not discuss the rationale of this compromise, which Paul would have rejected.

■ **6-12** Although v. 6 speaks only of "apostles and presbyters," vv. 12 and 22 indicate that a plenary session is in view.[35] Verse 7 repeats v. 2, but without any venomous *stasis*. Haenchen evokes the atmosphere.[36] After speeches advocating one side or the other,[37] "Now, when excitement and conflict have reached their peak, Peter intervenes and with one stroke clarifies the situation." This brief deliberative address includes the address and proof (vv. 7b-9), a potential threat coupled with a historical observation in the form of a question (v. 10), and the thesis/conclusion (v. 11), which compensates for the absence of a direct Pauline contribution, since it borrows from Galatians (and the Deutero-Pauline tradition).[38] There are also allusions to earlier material, in particular the Cornelius story (chaps. 10–11).[39]

31 See Pervo, *Dating*, 169–70, which suggests influence from Josephus as a possibility.

32 Cf. Haenchen, 458. The *Didascalia* (n. *m*) fills this gap.

33 Barrett, 2:703.

34 Cf. Herodotus *Hist.* 3.80–84, in which various Persian nobles discuss, following the death of a mad king, different systems. Otanes pleads for democracy. Megabyzus recommends oligarchy, whereafter Darius made the case for monarchy. The dramatic date is 522 BCE, prior to the existence of Greek democracies. (Herodotus nonetheless swears that this is all true [3.80].) See also the discussion of various forms of government in Cassius Dio 52.1–40, including the famous (concocted) speech of Maecenas.

35 614 *pc* sy[h] solve the problem by adding σὺν τῷ πλήθει ("with the body") in v. 6. This derives from v. 12. On the problem, see Weiser, 2:379–80.

36 Haenchen, 445.

37 Paulinists, like those responsible for the D-Text of vv. 1-5, are disappointed. Conzelmann (116) says, "In comparison with Galatians, the passivity of Paul and Barnabas is striking." That passivity is what Witherington's *ad hoc* source theory (n. 10) seeks to address.

38 See Pervo, *Dating*, 92–95; and William O. Walker Jr., "Acts and the Pauline Corpus Revisited: Peter's Speech at the Jerusalem Conference," in Richard P. Thompson and Thomas E. Philips, eds., *Literary Studies in Luke-Acts: Essays in Honor of Joseph B. Tyson* (Macon, Ga.: Mercer University Press, 1998) 77–86. Chrysostom recognized this by stating that what Paul says in Romans Peter says here (*Hom.* 32, 275C).

39 From chap. 1: ἐκλέγομαι ("choose") in 1:24-25, καρδιογνώστης ("one who knows the heart" [1:24]). The testimony of the Spirit appears in the speech of

■ **7** The major clause in v. 7 raises translation difficulties. The text of one phrase is uncertain, and its meaning is obscure. Another prepositional phrase, ἀφ' ἡμερῶν ἀρχαίων, does not mean what it should. The verb "chose" (ἐξελέξατο) may or may not have, or need, an object. "Among you" (ἐν ὑμῖν) is more likely than "among us," since it is more difficult.[40] The temporal phrase must mean "long ago." It evidently seeks to place the gentile mission at the "beginning" (ἀρχή) of the movement and thus to infer that acceptance of gentiles was not only resolved much earlier,[41] but that it is also a foundational element of the faith. Cadbury and Lake propose that the clause means "God made the choice of you."[42] Better choices are to take "gentiles" as the object of the verb (with "hear" as an epexegetical infinitive)[43] or, most preferably, to view the phrase as a noun clause.[44] "Gospel message" (τὸν λόγον τοῦ εὐαγγελίου) appears nowhere else before Origen. It combines a favorite Lucan term with the Pauline favorite "gospel." Proof of the validity of their belief is the action of God, who does not take a superficial view.[45] This is a brief equivalent to 10:34. Dibelius observed that the allusions to the Cornelius episode are more apparent to the readers than they would have been to the dramatic audience.[46] Rackham, for example, observes that Peter "alludes to it [the conversion of Cornelius] as to something almost forgotten, whereas it ought to have prevented the discussion arising at all."[47] Luke's problem is that he claims that the difficulty was resolved "long ago," whereas, in truth, it was a continuing controversy only apparently resolved by the meeting described in Galatians 2.

■ **9** The verse places divine nondiscrimination[48] in the realm of (Deutero-)Pauline theology. "Cleansing/purification" results from (the gift of) faith, which is thus power. The notion comes from baptismal theology and could only have been known by the Peter of Acts through inference based on the gift of the Spirit, understood not only as the gift of tongues but also as forgiveness.[49] The play on "heart" in vv. 8-9 suggests that the knower of hearts cleanses the hearts of the morally good.[50]

■ **10** Paul would not have approved of this implication. Verse 10 is a strong accusation that seems out of place. Peter acts as if all the listeners supported the demand for observance.[51] Dramatically, this makes no

2:32-33 and elsewhere (Soards, *Speeches*, 36). Among the obvious parallels to chaps. 10–11 are the use of οὐδέν and διακρίνω ("make no distinction" [11:12; 15:9; verb only in 10:20; 11:2, 12]) and "cleanse" (καθαρίζω) in 10:15; 11:8-9; and 15:9. In Acts, these two verbs occur only in reference to the conversion of Cornelius. Note also καθὼς καί ("as also" [v. 8]), with a form of "we" in 10:47; 11:17.

40 See also Ropes, *Text*, 141.

41 See Barrett, 2:713–14.

42 Cadbury and Lake, 172. They appeal to 2 Esdr 19:7 for support and compare 13:17 (of Israel). See Barrett's critique, 2:714.

43 So Johnson, 261.

44 So also Barrett, 2:714.

45 God who knows the heart: Acts 1:24; Jer 16:17-18; 17:9-10; Psalm 139; Sir 42:18; Josephus *Bell.* 6.630; 1 John 3:20; *2 Clem.* 9:9; Hermas *Man.* 4.3.4; *Act. Paul* 3.24. The appeal to God (or Scripture or the Spirit) as a witness is limited to Acts and Hebrews. See Hermann Strathmann, "μάρτυς," *TDNT* 4:474–514, esp. 497.

46 Dibelius, *Studies*, 94–95.

47 Rackham, 162.

48 𝔓[74] reads "*we* made no distinction." This would make Peter the agent of "cleansing."

49 Cf. Eph 5:26. As Cadbury and Lake (173) observe, v. 9 agrees with the variant "let your Holy Spirit come upon us and cleanse (καθαρισάτω) us" in the Lucan text of the Our Father (Luke 11:2). Metzger (*Textual Commentary*, 130–31) dismisses this as less likely than "your kingdom come" because it is Christian, but that conclusion ignores the overwhelming dominance of the Matthean form of the prayer. See also James M. Robinson et al., eds., *The Critical Edition of Q* (Hermeneia; Minneapolis: Fortress Press, 2000) xcvi–xcvii.

50 See Friedrich Hauck, in R. Meyer and Friedrich Hauck, "καθαρός," *TDNT* 3:413–31, esp. 423–26. Compare and contrast *Aristeas* 139–60, which argues, in effect, that purity codes promote moral cleanliness through discipline and learning, whereas for Luke cleansing is achieved by miracle.

51 Barrett (2:717) is typical in viewing the question as rhetorical. For that purpose, "we" and the subjunctive would serve. The second person indicative deserves to be taken seriously. Jervell (392) understands it as directed to the Pharisees in the community. The initial νῦν is temporal: "now" in contrast to the "early days" of v. 7.

sense. As in v. 7, Peter speaks as if he were not part of the community. This is the timeless voice of the chief apostle addressed to those who require Torah. To "put God to the test" is an ultimate sin.[52] It is the equivalent of the opposition to God of which Gamaliel had warned (5:39). "Yoke" is an ambiguous metaphor. It can be used for political or other oppression (e.g., *Sib. Or.* 3:448), but also for a guide to life, notably Wisdom (Sir 6:24-30; 51:23-27), Torah (identified with Wisdom, as in *m. 'Abot* 3.6), and Christ (identified with Wisdom, as in Matt 11:29-30).[53] Inspired by Gal 5:1, the term in v. 10 combines both senses; that is, it means an oppressive religious system. The understanding of Torah as an insuperable yoke "expresses the view of a Christian at a time when the separation from Judaism already lies in the past."[54]

Early Judaism did not view Torah as a burden, let alone an intolerable weight.[55] A similar criticism was leveled against the Pharisees by Jesus: Luke 11:46 (Q). Only here does Peter take up the first plural, which he will retain through the close of his speech.[56]

■ **11** This verse expresses the "level playing field" of "no distinction" in the language of Paulinism.[57] All who are saved are saved by grace. Eph 2:5-8 has inspired this language.[58] Luke does not retain the Pauline antithesis of "faith" versus "deeds" because such language led to the view that Paul was an antinomian. Peter disposes of the objection raised at Antioch in v. 1 by stating that grace saves and the demand of v. 5 by saying that the Torah cannot be kept. Having legitimated the gentile mission in Pauline terms, Peter retires from Acts.

■ **12** Verse 12a does not mean that the assembly had chatted while Peter was speaking, but that he brought the argument to an end. The D-Text clarifies this by prefacing: "Since the elders were in agreement with what Peter had said. . . ."[59] The terse summary in v. 12b may disappoint Pauline scholars, but it is consistent with Lucan theology.[60] Such summaries suggest that the single miracle narrated (14:8-10) was but a sample.[61]

■ **13-21** Although the position of James has been intimated (surprisingly) in 12:17, this speech marks his formal debut in Acts. Here and in chap. 21, he is the undisputed leader who promulgates regulations and issues orders. The implied reader knows of his status, which can be inferred only from the extant Pauline correspondence (Gal 2:12). Luke does not, and perhaps cannot, explain how James acquired his primacy.[62] His standing

52 See Exod 17:2; Deut 6:16, etc., as noted by Fitzmyer, 547. "Testing" is satanic (Acts 5:9). Satan and other opponents sought to test Jesus (Luke 4:2; 11:16).

53 Note the yoke of Isis: Apuleius *Metam.* 11.15. In this context, *Did.* 6:2, which speaks of bearing (βαστάσαι) "the entire yoke of the Lord" as difficult; *Barn.* 2:6, which describes the "new law" of Christ as lacking "the yoke of necessity" (ἄνευ ζυγοῦ ἀνάγκης); and *1 Clem.* 16:17, "yoke of his grace," testify to a continuing intra-Christian debate. See Georg Bertram and Karl H. Rengstorf, "ζυγός," *TDNT* 2:896–901.

54 Conzelmann, 117. Barrett (2:718–19) points out the difficulties of viewing this speech as historical.

55 See, for example, the nonrabbinic, non-Palestinian Philo *Praem. poen.* 80.

56 Boismard (*Texte*, 250–51) reads a smoother and shorter text: "And now why are you attempting to impose a yoke which not even our forebears could tolerate?" By deleting "God," the problem of the infinitive is eliminated. Moule (*Idiom Book*, 127) views the infinitive as epexegetic.

57 As Cadbury and Lake (175) recognize, the phrase καθ' ὃν τρόπον κἀκεῖνοι ("just as they") is formally ambiguous, but the context indicates that it means "Jews and gentiles."

58 Cf. Fitzmyer, 548.

59 Reference to the elders alone conforms to the/a D-Text of v. 5. See Epp, *Tendency*, 97. Boismard (*Texte*, 251) does not mention the omission of v. 12 in Irenaeus and Tertullian, who may have been concerned with the speeches alone, but the *Didascalia* likewise omits it. See Dibelius, *Studies*, 116 n. 12. Omission of the verse, if it occurred, was probably due to the view that it was irrelevant. The reception of a speech in silence was considered the highest form of praise by Musonius Rufus (frg. 49 = Aulus Gellius *Noct. att.* 5.1]).

60 See Barrett, 2:722.

61 The order "Barnabas and Paul" probably does not reflect a source but the narrator's desire to keep Paul in the background.

62 The two most likely historical inferences are either Peter left Jerusalem and James assumed the leadership or James gained ascendancy and Peter consequently departed.

creates the dramatic tension: everything depends on what James will say. Suspense does not long endure. After endorsing Peter's[63] conclusion, James introduces scriptural proof, a pastiche focusing on Amos 9:11-12.[64] Since Luke usually closely follows the LXX, this material probably comes from a Christian collection of texts used in the Deutero-Pauline world.[65] Then, without an apparent connection or justification, James imposes certain regulations followed by the enigmatic statement of v. 21. Other than its agreement on the acceptability of gentiles and its affirmation of scriptural support for their inclusion, James's speech is noteworthy for its lack of transparent logic. This would not seem to be an appropriate moment for the narrator to wrap himself in a cloak of obscurity. It is difficult to avoid the conclusion that the narrator either lacked or did not choose to provide a suitable rationale for the decree.[66]

■ **14** The verse paraphrases Peter's speech[67] by characterizing the conversion of Cornelius[68] as a "visitation" of God. This is Lucan septuagintal language for divine intervention in history.[69] God[70] has fashioned a "people" from the gentiles. The significance of this phrase was recognized by Johann Bengel, who called it an *egregium paradoxon*.[71] Gentiles now belong to the people of God (cf. 18:10).[72] Prophetic texts support the testimony of the Spirit.[73] Before comparing the citation with the LXX and other verses, it is desirable to examine its structure.[74]

■ **16** This is a chiastic construction utilizing assonance and rhyme.[75] The four verbs are ἀναστρέψω,[76] ἀνοικοδομήσω (twice), and ἀνορθώσω ("return," "rebuild," "restore"). The introductory "thereafter" (μέτα ταῦτα) may have referred, in an earlier context, to the destruction of the temple.[77] The citation in that hypothetical context evidently referred to the body of Christ (the church) as the eschatological new temple. In Acts, the referent is "the people of God."

■ **17-18** The scriptural citation strongly differs from the MT, which has nothing to do with the inclusion of

63 The use of "Simeon" is a touch of Aramaic local color. It is atypical for Luke, who is more likely to hellenize foreign names, as BDF §53 (2) notes. See also Tannehill, *Narrative Unity*, 2:186.

64 Bauckham's claim ("James and the Gentiles [Acts 15.13-21]," in Witherington, *History*, 154–84, esp. 154) that matters of halakah require scriptural rather than miraculous proof is true of rabbinic Judaism but not of early Christianity, where the exact opposite applies. Cf. the Cornelius story (chaps. 10–11).

65 So also Lüdemann, 171. Eph 2:11-12 and 1 Pet 2:4-10 similarly treat the eschatological temple as the people of God. See Bauckham, "James and the Gentiles," 167.

66 An explanation is that the decree is largely pragmatic, whereas the narrator's focus here is on theological argument for the gentile mission.

67 Conzelmann (117) notes the primary similarities between the two speeches.

68 The adverb πρῶτον ("first") in v. 14 corresponds to the "early days" of v. 7. See Haenchen, 447. The καθώς is somewhat puzzling. BDF §453 (2) is of little help. The context requires that one render it "how."

69 Cf. Luke 1:68, 78; 7:16; cf. 19:44; Acts 7:23. For the background, see Gen 21:1; 50:24-25; Exod 3:16; 4:31; 13:19; 23:22; Deut 4:20, 34; 7:6; 14:2.

70 "His name" is a metonymy for "himself."

71 Johann A. Bengel, *Gnomon Novi Testamenti* (3rd ed.; London: Williams & Norgate, 1862) 449.

72 On the subject, see Jacques Dupont, "*Laos ex ethnon* (Act. Xv.14)," *NTS* 3 (1956–57) 47–50; idem, "Un peuple d'entre les nations (Actes 15.14)," *NTS* 31 (1985) 321–35; and Nils Alstrup Dahl, "'A People for His Name' (Acts XV.14)," *NTS* 4 (1957–58) 319–27.

73 The D-Text οὕτως, "thus" (Boismard, *Texte*, 252), may be designed to prevent understanding τούτῳ as a reference to "him" (Peter), although Ropes (*Text*, 142) thinks it may be original. "Words of the prophets" (lit.) may be a reference to the Book of the Twelve (see on 1:16), but it is more probably part of the citation formula. (The expression appears three times in Origen [e.g., *Fr. Jer.* 1.4] but not elsewhere in the first three centuries.) For this use of συμφωνοῦσιν, see Josephus *Ant.* 1.107; 15.174.

74 On the issues of the LXX text of Amos, which exhibits a number of the same variants as does Acts, some of which are due to contamination, see Metzger, *Textual Commentary*, 379.

75 Tannehill (*Narrative Unity*, 2:188–89) takes a similar view.

76 D's correction to ἐπιστρέψω (of similar meaning, "return") overlooks the literary pattern.

77 In this interpretation Luke need not have been responsible for altering the ἀναστήσω of the LXX. For possible origins of the other deviations from the LXX, see Bauckham, "James and the Gentiles," 162–65.

gentiles.[78] This is the vital element in the citation and rules out the possibility that the historical James (who would not have cited the LXX) utilized the passage. Verse 17b echoes the reference to "name" in v. 14, and ταῦτα ("these things") points back to the initial phrase (μετὰ ταῦτα), while the concluding words (which may derive from Isa 45:21) also reinforce v. 14: this has taken place in accordance with the eternal plan of God.[79] The inference is that Luke selected the citation and composed v. 14 in accordance with it.[80] James has no need to interpret this quotation, for the audience has seen and heard of its fulfillment.[81]

■ **19** The translation of διὸ ἐγὼ κρίνω in v. 19 is disputed. The options range from "I therefore conclude . . ." to "I therefore decree." In the weaker option, James makes a recommendation; in the stronger, he pronounces a decision. In favor of the weaker is the use of this verb in other places in Acts (e.g., 13:46; 16:15; 26:8).[82] The stronger translation is supported by the context. The pronoun "we," which would be appropriate for a recommendation and for the subject of "write," is absent.[83] The objection that the actual decision was taken by the assembly (v. 22) overlooks the hierarchical nature of such bodies in the imperial era: assemblies ratified the views of their leader(s). Finally, a strong translation accords with the authority of James in 21:23. James says what is to be done and it is so ordered.[84]

Excursus: The Apostolic Decree

The title "Apostolic Decree" is appropriate for the commands transmitted in 15:28. This is one of those items found three times in Acts (15:20; 21:25), an indication of its importance.[85] This list, which, with one possible exception, is unlike the "catalogues of vices" that speak of general categories (such as greed and rage),[86] raises some major questions: When and where did it originate? What is its background and basis in the history of religions? And what is to be made of its quite diverse text?[87]

Although it is possible that the decree did originate in Jerusalem as a guide for mixed communities, it is more likely to have been worked out in a mixed Diaspora community where the desire for compromise was strong.[88] Paul would have nothing to do with such compromises, so long as they were compulsory, and those linked to James (cf. Gal 2:12) would not have been likely to find this acceptable, since they seem to have required strict observance.[89] Peter might well have found these regulations acceptable. It is therefore reasonable to attribute this item to the gentile missionary source, but it is also likely that it was widely disseminated and familiar to Luke's readers.

The probable original—and here unstated[90]—function of the decree was to provide a minimal platform for sacramental fellowship in communities where at least some believers of Jewish background had qualms about dietary matters. The basis appears to have been the regulations for gentiles resident in the holy land (Leviticus 17–18), but the matter is

78 For a linguistic explanation of how the LXX version arose, see Fitzmyer, 555. The error probably reflected an interest in avoiding chauvinistic statements.

79 A range of variants attempt to flesh out this oracular ellipsis.

80 Note also the verb παρενοχλεῖν (lit. "impose a burden" [v. 19]), which is the equivalent of Peter's ἐπιθεῖναι ζυγόν (lit. "impose a yoke") in v. 10.

81 Cf. Tyson, *Images*, 152.

82 So Haenchen, 449 n. 1; Schneider, 2:283; Weiser, 2:283; Fitzmyer, 556.

83 Translations (e.g., *NIV, NRSV, NAB, NJB*) often supply "we."

84 So Cadbury and Lake, 177; Krodel, 282; Witherington, 457; Johnson, 266. Barrett (2:279) is difficult to pin down. Some D-Texts (Irenaeus, Ephrem [Ropes, *Text*, 145, 426]) seek to soften the translation by saying, in effect: "in my view."

85 See p. 10.

86 On "catalogues of vices," see Berger, *Formgeschichte*, 130, 134–35.

87 See Jacquier, 803–8; Strange, *Problem*, 87–105; Metzger, *Textual Commentary*, 381–84 (with bibliography, 382–83); Epp, *Tendency*, 107–11; and Head, "Acts and Its Texts," 438–42.

88 On the suitability of the decree in such conflicts, see Justin Taylor, "The Jerusalem Decrees (Acts 15.20, 29 and 21.25) and the Incident at Antioch," *NTS* 47 (2001) 372–80.

89 The decree falls far short of *kashrut*, certainly of the sort advocated by the Pharisees. Pork, for example, is not mentioned, nor is there any attention to menstruants as a potential source of impurity or to other purity regulations regarding food. Prohibition of pork would, to be sure, conflict with the vision of Peter. This is another indication of the difficulty of rationalizing the decree.

90 Wilson, *Law*, 81: "It is one of the oddities of Luke's narrative that he does not tell us precisely what the decree was for nor what it meant." David R. Catchpole ("Paul, James, and the Apostolic Decree," *NTS* 23 [1977] 428–44) relates the decree to Torah and proposes that it originated with James.

far from certain.[91] Barrett prefers the three things—idolatry, murder, and incest—on which Jews under duress could not compromise.[92] The evidence for these cardinal sins is, however, late,[93] and they do not conform to the focus on purity that shapes the conventional text. It may be best to say that the regulations of Leviticus 17–18 inspired the decree, directly or indirectly, without attempting to delineate the meaning of the four prohibitions exclusively from that text.[94] Something of this sort could have been developed as a guide for Jews about interaction with gentiles in the Diaspora that was then taken up by early Christians.

The form of the earliest text is not in great doubt.[95] There is a strong consensus that the text translated above is the source of the others.[96] William A. Strange has identified six forms of the text:[97]

1. Omit "sexual immorality" (πορνεία) without golden rule.
2. Four prohibitions, *without* golden rule.
3. Four prohibitions with golden rule.
4. Omit "strangled," *without* golden rule.
5. Omit "strangled," with golden rule.
6. Omit "blood," *without* golden rule.

No contemporary scholars defend the originality of the golden rule in v. 20.[98] The debate has focused on the development of the decree from its "ritual/ceremonial" origin to a "moral/ethical" form. The "ritual" versus "ethical" distinction is not Jewish.[99] It became prominent in Christian works from the middle of the second century, if not earlier, and is a convenient shorthand. It is therefore more likely that the earliest form of the decree dealt with purity issues. In the course of time, these were recategorized in "moral" terms. The insertion of the golden rule is a manifest product of this phenomenon.[100] The key term is *porneia*, "sexual irregularity," an element of the purity code[101] that could readily be understood in ethical terms. In that milieu, "blood" could also be viewed as a metonymy for "murder" (cf. English "bloodshed"),[102] while cultic offerings, if technically closer to the "ritual" pole, became a pillar of opposition to polytheism, in good part because this became the "litmus test" for apostasy.[103]

91 On Leviticus 17–18 as the source, see Terrance Callan, "The Background of the Apostolic Decree (Acts 15:20, 29; 21:25)," *CBQ* 55 (1993) 284–97.

92 Barrett, 2:734–35.

93 As Wilson (*Law*, 100) observes, these passages are often attributed to the time of Hadrian, an era in which Christians were often eager to distinguish themselves from Jews.

94 See Bauckham, "James and the Gentiles," 172–78; and Conzelmann, 118–19, but the case is far from certain, as can be seen from the arguments of Wilson, *Law*, 74–92.

95 The translation presumes that ἀλισγημάτων τῶν εἰδώλων ("idolatrous food") is an elegant variation of εἰδωλόθυτα in v. 29 and 21:25. The expression is literally "contaminations of idols," but is applied to food. See Barrett, 2:731. The *Paraleipomena Jeremiou* 7:37 is an exact parallel: Jeremiah . . . ἔμεινε διδάσκων αὐτοὺς τοῦ ἀπέχεσθαι ἐκ τῶν ἀλισγημάτων τῶν ἐθνῶν τῆς Βαβυλῶνος ("Jeremiah [who distributed figs to the sick] . . . kept teaching them [the people] to avoid the contaminations of the gentiles"). This work is not much earlier than Acts—and may be twenty years later. Dependence is unlikely. The order of the prohibitions also varies.

96 For the exception ("strangled," πνικτός) see below.

97 See his table 2, p. 88, which gives the full evidence.

98 Clark (361) included it, but neither Boismard (*Texte*, 253) nor Strange does so. See Haenchen's biting remark (450) about Zahn's noninclusion. Boismard (*Texte*, 256) does include it in v. 29.

99 On the ease with which the ceremonial-moral antithesis may be overstressed, see Wilson, *Law*, 79; and Barrett, 2:736.

100 The negative form of the rule, also attested elsewhere in Jewish and Christian texts (as the positive is in Jewish writings), is evidently necessary in a list of prohibitions.

101 See L. William Countryman, *Dirt, Greed, and Sex: Sexual Ethics in the New Testament and Their Implications for Today* (Philadelphia: Fortress Press, 1988) 104–9; and Fitzmyer, 557–58. The translation takes a broad view of the concept.

102 From the "moral" perspective, both are open to objection: Did early Christians really need to be told by the apostles that they could not kill or commit adultery?

103 See Pliny *Ep.* 10.96.5, close in date to Acts. Believers are not to eat such food: *Did.* 6:3 (note the use of βαστάζω with regard to diet in general; cf. Acts 15:10); Ps.-Clem. *De Virg.* 2.5.2; Justin *Dial.* 34.8–35.1; Clement of Alexandria *Paed.* 2.1.8; Origen *Comm. in Matthew* 11.12. Rev 2:14, 20 attribute the practice to heretics, as does Justin in the passage cited. Trypho responds to Justin's claim by noting that some Christians *do* eat such offerings. According to Irenaeus *A.H.* 1.6.3; 1.24.5; 1.26.3; 1.28.2, Valentinians eat such offerings, as do the followers of Basilides, according to Eusebius *H.E.* 4.7.7; 5.1.26. See also Hippolytus *Ref.* 7.36; Epiphanius *Pan.* 26.9.2; Minucius Felix *Oct.* 30; Tertullian *Apol.* 9. (In *Pud.* 12.4–5, however, Tertullian understood

Development from "ritual" to "moral" was neither smooth nor rapid, however. Prohibitions against consuming blood could be found in the second century and later.[104]

"Strangled" (πνικτός) is the single item that cannot be given a moral thrust. The D-Text, in its major witnesses, omits "strangled" and includes the golden rule. Some D-Texts, however, omit this adjective and do not include the rule, provoking the proposal that it is a secondary addition.[105] This is an obscure word,[106] and it is somewhat more probable that it was dropped in interest of the "moral" thrust than added to clarify that "blood" referred to consumption rather than to homicide, a clarification that could have been achieved in a simpler and clearer fashion, for example, by adding "of animals." The arguments for viewing the D-Text as secondary are stronger than for the inverse.[107]

The history of the text indicates its continuing vitality. Most Christian bodies have revised their rules over time. In the early church these revisions long continued to be issued under the name of the apostles.[108] Within a generation after Acts, the "moral" understanding prevailed.[109] For Luke, the decree was an important sign of gentile Christian sensitivity toward Jewish Christians, or, as Conzelmann characteristically puts it, salvation-historical in meaning, "since the decree provided continuity between Israel and the church, which was free from the Law."[110]

■ **20-21** If Luke were the sort of author who deliberately included something to challenge his subsequent interpreters, v. 21 could qualify for that honor. The use of γάρ ("for," in a coordinating sense) indicates that it is an inference from the preceding, but nothing from v. 16 through v. 20 makes a satisfactory link. Verse 20 wins by default.[111] The passage assumes that Judaism is a world religion and that the synagogue is of venerable antiquity,[112] but the immediate relevance of this claim is not clear. It can hardly mean that, since the Torah can be heard everywhere (cf. 13:27), gentile believers should have availed themselves of the opportunity to hear it and learn of these prohibitions, for they would

"blood" as murder.) Most meat for public sale came from cultic use (MacMullen, *Paganism*, 40–41). On the reception and understanding of dietary laws among early Christians see Robert Grant, "Dietary Laws among Pythagoreans, Jews, and Christians," *HTR* 73 (1980) 299–310, esp. 304–10.

104 See the citations in the previous note; Strange, *Problem*, 95; and Wilson, *Law*, 93 (who observes that denials of blood consumption often involved refutations of the charge of cannibalism). Note also Justin *Dial.* 20; Tertullian *Pud.* 12.4; *Mon.* 5 (which says that blood was the sole exception to dietary liberty); Eusebius *H.E.* 5.1.26; Tertullian *Apol.* 9.13.

105 See, e.g., Ropes, *Text*, 265–69; Clark, 360–61; Strange, *Problem*, 100–102. Strange claims that this term is more suitable to the second century than the first.

106 See Wilson, *Law*, 87–91; and Hans Bietenhard, "πνίγω," *TDNT* 6:455–58.

107 See the critique of Strange by Head, "Acts and Its Texts," 438–42. He shows that the differences in the D-Text form of the decree conform to other, almost undeniably secondary, D-Text variants in Acts 15.

108 The titles are indicative: *The Teaching of the Twelve Apostles* (*Didache*), *Apostolic Constitutions, Apostolic Canons, Apostolic Tradition,* and so on. The decree itself, in one form or another, appears in *Sib. Or.* 2:96 (Christian interpolation), Ps.-Phocylides *Sentences* 31 (a Christian interpolation lacking in the best MSS.), and the Ps.-Clem. *Hom.* 7.8.1. On its history, see also John Townsend, "The Date of Luke-Acts," in Talbert, *Luke-Acts*, 47–62, esp. 49–54; Graeme W. Clarke, *The Octavius of Marcus Minucius Felix* (ACW 39; New York: Newman, 1974) 337–38 n. 508; and, in great detail, Gotthold Resch, *Das Aposteldecret nach seiner ausserkanonischen Textgestalt* (TU 28.3; Leipzig: Hinrichs, 1905); Karl Six, *Das Aposteldekret (Act 15,28.29): Seine Entstehung und Geltung in den ersten vier Jahrhunderten* (Veröffentlichungen des biblisch-patristischen Seminars zu Innsbruck 5; Innsbruck: Rauch, 1912).

109 By the time of Bede, the decree related only to the nature of meat to be consumed. For the moral life, he turned to v. 21, presuming that readings from the OT would inculcate better behavior (67). In his *Retractatio* he added comments on "strangled" (149).

110 Conzelmann, 119.

111 See the good discussion in Wilson, *Law*, 83–84. Dibelius (*Studies*, 92) was desperate enough to propose that v. 21 is a gloss, but glosses usually seek to clarify, however wrongly.

112 Cf. Philo *Spec. leg.* 2.62; Josephus *Ant.* 16.43; *Ap.* 2.175; and Feldman, *Jew and Gentile*, 322.

have heard a great deal more, including, for example, the necessity for male circumcision. Scarcely more likely is the possibility that he is offering an equivalent to what Peter said in v. 10: everyone hears/can hear Torah, but this does not produce observance. In the implicit context of seeking a *modus vivendi* for Christians of Jewish and gentile background, Tannehill's answer is reasonable: "The underlying point would be that gentile Christians need to find ways of living with people deeply committed to Mosaic law."[113] People whose piety resembled that of Cornelius would not find the regulations objectionable[114] but it is far from certain that they would mollify "people deeply committed to Mosaic law." The "underlying point" is that Luke believes that these regulations ought to satisfy Jewish believers and attributes that position to James.[115] An unstated subsidiary point is that all the obligations of Torah remain in effect for Jews.[116] Acts 16:1-3 will bear this out. The two most indicative silences of the report are the failure to say anything about Jewish converts and the absence of a rationale for the decree. If either or both were important matters in Luke's time, these silences would have been inexplicable.

Acts, like Galatians (more or less), presents three views. One, upheld by Christian Pharisees, is that gentile converts must keep Torah—in effect, must cease to be gentiles. Peter sets forth the "left-wing" position: gentiles are welcome without any specific conditions. The moderate view is propounded by James.[117] Of Paul and Barnabas, no more is said than that they evidently resisted the demand for full observance. From Galatians, it is apparent that James (and his associates) was closer to the "right-wing" view, that Paul took a radical stance, and that Peter was in favor of sensitivity-based compromise. By redistributing these roles, Luke assigns the strict view to believing Pharisees; to Peter responsibility for advocating the admission of gentiles; and to James the role of adroit moderation. Paul may therefore remain on the sidelines.[118]

■ **22-29** In response to James's direction, the leaders resolve, with the consent of the community, to send two representatives back to Antioch with Paul and Barnabas,[119] together with a letter responding to the presenting problem. From this action, it is apparent that the author is familiar with the use of letters as instruments of church policy, specifically as responses to questions raised by "subordinate" communities. The available evidence indicates that Paul was responsible for the development of letters for the purpose of managing missionary foundations at a distance. Acts knows of this practice and utilizes Paul's letters, but, in its narrative, Paul gets no closer to an ecclesiastical letter than to accompany those who bear it.[120] This is powerful testimony for the controversial character of Paul's letters in certain circles. It is reasonable to hold that Acts was written in Ephesus or its environs, an area with at least one active "Pauline school" that had continued to produce Pauline letters—notably Ephesians, of which Acts makes considerable use.[121] Hence, it is difficult to deny the existence of "hyper-Paulinists," either predecessors of Marcion or possibly even Marcion himself, in his early phase, as the force driving this avoidance of the

113 Tannehill, *Narrative Unity*, 2:190.

114 This is the basis of Weiser's (2:384) interpretation. Cf. also Johnson, 267.

115 Other explanations have been advanced. For Dibelius (*Studies*, 97–98), it means only that proclamation of the Mosaic law requires no assistance. He took this approach from Cadbury and Lake, 177–78. Marshall (254) accepts this as one alternative, in addition to respecting Jewish scruples. Conzelmann (120) says that they justify the decree because *Jews* must keep Torah. Schneider (2:184) sees the verse as justifying the regulations of Leviticus 17–18. Krodel (286) is similar, with interesting comments. Jervell (399) takes it as grounding authority for the decree in Moses rather than in James.

116 Roloff, 233.

117 Cf. Painter, *Just James*, 50. In fact, as Painter says, the situation was (and became) more complex.

118 See Esler, *Community*, 105–9.

119 The other delegates from Antioch (15:2) are omitted.

120 Note also the letter of recommendation for Apollos from Ephesus to Corinth, 18:27.

121 For data, see Pervo, *Dating*, 51–147, with a summary in Table 4.4, p. 141.

association of Paul with letters. Unlike the Pastor, who issues letters under Paul's name to refute such tendencies, Luke effectively pretends that Paul did not write letters. Luke did not, in all likelihood, imagine that he could suppress the letters. His subsidiary goal was to show how they should be understood. If this project seems bizarre, it can only be said that Luke's view long remained dominant and that he continues to have supporters.

The letter is unlike Paul's epistles in that it closely conforms to the style of Greek official letters in the Greco-Roman era and that it addresses only certain members of the communities to which it is dispatched. George Kennedy says: "The letter of Acts 15:23-29 resembles the rescript of a Roman magistrate responding to a query from a subordinate and has the rhetorical characteristics of a public letter of the Roman period."[122] Guilds and other private organizations were wont to imitate the style of municipal decrees as an indication of their culture and participation in civic life.[123] Just as its meetings reveal the church to be a proper and useful organization, so its communications proclaim that it is well integrated into civic life.

■ **22** Their action has two linked components, the delegates and the letter, each marked by the formal "it was resolved" (ἔδοξε) in vv. 22,[124] 25, and 28. Silas will be the successor to Barnabas as a colleague of Paul from Jerusalem. He is usually identified with the Sylvanus of the epistolary tradition (1 Thess 1:1; 2 Cor 1:19; 1 Pet 5:12). "Silas" is evidently the Greek equivalent to the Aramaic counterpart of Hebrew "Saul."[125] He remains in Acts through 18:5 (Corinth) then vanishes from the narrative. This is consonant with the references in 1 Thessalonians and 2 Corinthians. There are several possibilities: This is the same individual. He had two names (as did many, e.g., John Mark). Luke prefers the Semitic form. This is the most popular solution. Another is that Antiochene tradition preserved the name of one Silas, who had come from Jerusalem, and that Luke, following the "rule of onomastic economy,"[126] identified him with the Sylvanus he knew from the letters. Still another is that Luke concocted both the Semitic form of the name and his association with Jerusalem. Decision among these choices is difficult,[127] but the first is the most probable. For whatever reason, Silas is a perfectly suitable companion for Paul, a Jewish believer from Jerusalem, rather than a gentile garnered by Paul from the Diaspora mission. The other delegate,[128] Judas Barsabbas, is quite obscure.[129] The two representatives honor the recipients while representing the authority of

122 Kennedy, *Rhetorical Criticism*, 127. Acts 15:24-26 is the only true Greek period in Acts (BDF §464). For evidence of the formal correspondences, see Frederick W. Danker, *Benefactor: Epigraphic Study of a Graeco-Roman and New Testament Semantic Field* (St. Louis: Clayton, 1982) 310–13. Danker points to C. Bradford Welles, *Royal Correspondence in the Hellenistic Period* (Chicago: Ares, 1974) no. 49, pp. 197–202. Another useful Greco-Roman example is a resolution of the *Koinon* of Asia from Aphrodisias, trans. Robert Sherk, *Rome and the Greek East to the Death of Augustus* (Translated Documents of Greece & Rome 4; Cambridge: Cambridge University Press, 1984) no. 65, pp. 80–81 (Greek text: T. Drew-Bear, *BCH* 96 [1972] 444). See also Hans-Josef Klauck, with D. R. Bailey, *Ancient Letters and the New Testament* (Waco, Tex.: Baylor University Press, 2006) 420–9. 1 Macc 14:25-45 could have served as a model. Cf. also 2 Chronicles 30, which as Rackham (268) notes, follows a similar pattern of meeting and decree in the form of a letter. 2 Macc 1:1-10a; 1:10b–2:28 are other examples of letters from Jerusalem to Diaspora communities. The church functions like the ruling body of Judaism, of which it is now the true representative.

123 See Ramsay MacMullen, *Roman Social Relations, 50 B.C. to A.D. 284* (New Haven: Yale University Press, 1974) 76, 82.

124 The accusative participle ἐκλεξαμένους ("having selected") is acceptable (as the subject of indirect discourse), as is the dative variant, which agrees with "apostles," and so on. See BDF §410.

125 Fitzmyer, 564. Williams ("Personal Names," 95–96) is less certain of the equivalency.

126 The phrase refers to the propensity for biblical (and many subsequent) authors to identify all bearers of the same name and, on occasion, to assist these identifications by correcting the text (cf. 1:23 and comments).

127 Since Luke did not hesitate to ascribe Roman citizenship to this character (16:37), it is difficult to rule out the other possibilities a priori.

128 Although the participle ἡγουμένους could mean "leaders," "leading members" is preferable here, since "apostles and presbyters" played the governing roles. See BDAG, 434, *s.v.* ἡγέομαι. Barrett (2:739) permits their inclusion among the presbyters.

129 D alone reads "Barabbas." This is an interesting variant and the more difficult reading, although

Jerusalem.[130] They are not bringing a document to serve as a basis for negotiation. The initial participle of v. 23, γράψαντες (lit. "writing"), is in the wrong case, since it should agree with "apostles."[131] Luke can stumble when attempting to write periods.

■ **23** The letters in Acts (15:23b-29; 23:25-30), like the speeches, are to be treated as authorial compositions.[132] The address (v. 23b)[133] is surprising, for it encompasses only gentile believers in "Antioch and Syria and Cilicia." The distinction between "Antioch" and "Syria" (of which Antioch was the capital)[134] is possible, but Acts has made no reference to missionary work there outside of Antioch, nor of activity in Cilicia.[135] The modern reader, at least, expects that the areas named in chaps. 13–14 will be designated, since the problem arose after that journey—although the narrator does not say that it came about in response to it. Communities in Syria and Cilicia do come to light in 15:41. Moreover, Luke does not limit the decree to those addressed in v. 23 (16:4).[136] It is possible that the address betrays a source,[137] although this may be the narrator's way of identifying the existence of hitherto unnamed communities (cf. 9:31). The assumption of a source for the address is not a necessary hypothesis, since this document appears to be a Lucan composition in its entirety.[138] If a source is to be sought, Gal 1:21 is a good candidate.[139]

Restriction of the addressees to gentiles betrays Luke's interest and situation. He has stated that these communities were mixed. The letter was of no less interest to those of Jewish background than to the gentiles. Verses 30-31 presume that the letter was read to the entire community. The purpose of this limitation is, as the context will soon make clear, to indicate that these rules apply only to gentiles. Those of Jewish origin are evidently free to remain observant. This concept is quite theoretical, and implementation would have created difficulties that the narrator ignores because of his scheme.

■ **24** The body begins, in the proper way, with "inasmuch as" (ἐπειδή).[140] Certain unnamed individuals, vaguely identified as "of our company" (ἐξ ἡμῶν),[141] have been engaging in agitation. The verb ταράσσω, used in rhetorical and political contexts of the activity of troublemakers, probably derives from Galatians (1:7; 5:10).[142] In this context, the participle ἀνασκευάζοντες means "subverting."[143] The authors disassociate

---

one should note, with Metzger (*Textual Commentary*, 384), that the same name appears as "Barnabas" in 1:23. The motives, however, differ. For Barrett (2:738), "Barabbas" is "no more than an unfortunate slip of the pen." "Judas" is also a "bad" name, as is "Ananias," although it also belongs to the healer of Paul (9:10-19a). Since D is without other support, "Barsabbas" is, nonetheless, probably correct.

130 Cf. Haenchen, 451. Two envoys is, according to Danker (*Benefactor*, 313), a conventional number for diplomatic proceedings. Cf. Chariton *Chaer.*, 3.14.17, where the delegation includes two members of the council and two from the commons. "King Ptolemy" sends two emissaries, named and characterized, to bear his letter to "Eleazar the high priest" (*Aristeas*, 35–40).

131 See BDF §468 (3).

132 Cadbury, *Making*, 190–91; Knox, *Hellenistic Elements*, 27–28. This was the judgment of ancient critics: Dionysius of Halicarnassus *Thuc.* 42 (on Thucydides) and Fronto *Epistle* 2.1 (on Sallust).

133 The variant, *καὶ οἱ ἀδελφοί*, which has a wide range of support is a secondary attempt to include "the laity," as it were, as senders. The more likely simple ἀδελφοί (lit. "brothers and sisters") is a form of epistolary condescension. Although the apostles and presbyters are officials, they share the status (cf. the repetition ἀδελφοῖς) of the recipients. See Haenchen (451 n. 4), who relates the term to ἄνδρες ἀδελφοί (lit. "gentlemen and brethren," often used in the address of speeches, e.g., 1:16, fourteen times in total). Some D-Texts (not followed by Boismard, *Texte*, 254) resolve the difficulty by eliminating the noun.

134 On Roman Syria, see Robyn Tracey, "Syria," in Gill and Gempf, *Setting*, 223–78.

135 On the destination, see David R. Catchpole, "Paul, James, and the Apostolic Decree," *NTS* 23 (1977) 428–44, esp. 436–38.

136 Acts 21:25 assumes that the decree applies to all gentile converts.

137 From a source: e.g., Lüdemann, 170; Weiser, 2:371.

138 Source not necessary: e.g., Conzelmann, 120; Barrett, 2:740.

139 See on 15:41 below.

140 Danker, *Benefactor*, 311.

141 The most likely understanding of this phrase is that the agitators belong to the Jerusalem community; 15:1 spoke of "Judea."

142 Cf. the related noun τάραχος (Acts 16:8, 13; 19:23). For the background, see Spicq, *Lexicon*, 3:372–76, esp. 372–73.

143 Bruce, 345. D-Texts expand in pedantic fashion

themselves from the agitators in an awkward relative clause,[144] which captures the essence of Gal 2:1-10, as Luke wishes it to be understood. Verses 25-27 correspond to v. 22, while vv. 28-29 present the decree adumbrated in v. 20.

■ **25-26** The verse opens with an affirmation of unanimity[145] regarding the delegates, who are not named until Jerusalem has had opportunity to bestow praise upon Barnabas and Paul. This is typical diplomacy, equivalent to the rhetorical *captatio benevolentiae*. The phrase "devoted their lives" (παραδεδωκόσι τὰς ψυχάς) contrasts nicely with the activity of the agitators, who have (lit.) tried to ruin the lives of the Antiochene believers (v. 24). The phrase brims with early Christian edificatory diction.[146]

■ **27** The verse states the role of the delegates.[147] They will provide oral interpretation and expansion.[148] The bland "the same" (τὰ αὐτά) reveals that the letter is directed toward the readers of the book, for the dramatic audience would not (yet) know to what it referred.[149]

■ **29** The letter comes to the point. Rather than refer to "the assembly" or to an upper house,[150] the subject is "we and the Holy Spirit." This reflects confidence that their resolution was guided by the Spirit. Such confidence is generally characteristic of Christianity through Irenaeus, at least.[151] In rather stilted and crabbed language, the letter attempts to distinguish between imposing a burden (βάρος);[152] cf. vv. 10, 18) and requiring a few matters that are obligatory but not compulsory.[153] In this, the "official" form of the decree, the D-Text omits "strangled" and includes the golden rule, imposing a heavy burden on those who would separate the two issues.[154] The final clause conforms to epistolary usage.[155] This conclusion was evidently too secular for the D-Text, which adds, after "good standing": "being guided by the Holy Spirit."[156] At this point, the narrator, eschewing anticlimax, dissolves the scene.

by reminding the reader that these persons demanded circumcision and Torah observance. Chrysostom read "they should circumcise their children," which is interesting in the light of 21:21.

144 "Without our authorization" translates what one presumes the author wished to say. Οἷς οὐ διεστειλάμεθα could be taken to mean: "We didn't instruct them to demand circumcision" or "We [sent them but] gave them no instructions," or the like.

145 The participle ἐκλεξαμένοις (lit. "having selected") shows the same variation between dative and accusative as in v. 22. Here, at least, the dative is more likely, because of potential confusion with the following "men" (ἄνδρας). See Metzger, *Textual Commentary*, 385–86.

146 Cf. "our beloved brother Paul" in 2 Pet 3:15. D reads "your" in v. 25, on which see Epp, *Tendency*, 71.

147 The perfect "we have sent" is epistolary. See the comments and examples of Jacquier, 404. D does not recognize this and changes the accompanying participle to a future.

148 Cf. Col 4:7-8||Eph 6:21-22; 1 Macc 12:23.

149 Cf. Haenchen, 453; and Conzelmann, 120. The D-Text (Boismard, *Texte*, 255) saw the problem and substituted ταῦτα ("these things" = "the following"). Barrett (2:743–44) worries about καὶ αὐτούς in v. 27, which is presumably emphatic.

150 Cf. Josephus *Ant.* 16.163: ἔδοξε μοι καὶ τῷ συμβουλίῳ; and Danker, *Benefactor*, 311.

151 See the closely parallel *1 Clem.* 63.2: ὑφ' ἡμῶν γεγραμμένοις διὰ τοῦ ἁγίου πνεύματος ("written by us [the Roman community] through the Holy Spirit"). Jacquier (464) notes the continuation of the practice at the head of conciliar decisions. Note the contrasting statement of the narrator ἔδοξε κἀμοί ("I too decided") in Luke 1:3.

152 Rev 2:14, 24-25 shows that the language of "burden" in connection with sacrificial food and sexual irregularity was familiar in the milieu of Acts. See Heikki Leppä, *Luke's Critical Use of Galatians* (Vantaa, Finland: Dark Oy, 2002) 172.

153 The problem is ἐπάναγκες, a rare adverb used in an unusual manner, nominalized with a plural article. Such constructions are normally limited to temporal or spatial meanings. This led to textual alterations, on which see Metzger, *Textual Commentary*, 386; Cadbury and Lake, 180–81; and Wilson, *Law*, 82.

154 Boismard, *Texte*, 256. For other textual variations, see above in the discussion of v. 20.

155 BDF §414 (5) observes that one expects καλῶς ("well") with ποιεῖν ("do"), but Danker (*Benefactor*, 312) notes a precise inscriptional parallel (= *I. Magn.* 91d, 8–10 = *Caria Magn.* 120.1.1.1.1.8–10).

156 Εὖ πράξετε φερόμενοι ἐν τῷ ἁγίῳ πνεύματι. The basis for this is evidently 2 Pet 1:21. Ephrem (426) expands the promise: "As you shall observe these things without circumcision and observance of the laws, you will receive the Holy Spirit to speak all languages, just as your colleagues, the household of Cornelius, who were chosen before you."

The council thus concludes in solemn formality and unanimity. Both the original leader (Peter) and James, a new star who has risen on the horizon, concur in rejecting the demand that gentiles observe Torah. The difficulty experienced by readers, especially since the sixteenth century—that the decree *does* impose elements of Torah—was not shared by the author or, in all probability, his readers. For them "Torah" meant male circumcision, a procedure that gentiles viewed with revulsion; Sabbath restrictions; and purity codes that made social intercourse with non-Jews difficult.[157] What the decree required was not an oppressive fence. Acts looks at Torah not as a matter of principle, an all-or-nothing proposition, but as a series of deeds and rules. This is at some distance from the Paul of Galatians, but so was the church of Luke's era. Similarly, Acts is not concerned about the real issue at stake, which was a matter not of tolerance but of sacramental life. Those who could not eat together could not share in a common Eucharist.

Repeated references to "Moses" (vv. 1, 5, 21) intimate the approach of the world of the apologists. A distinction between "the Law of God" and "the Law of Moses" emerged in gentile Christian circles following the First Revolt (e.g. Mark 10:3-9).[158] In due course, this would motivate historical-critical theories about interpolations into the Jewish Scriptures.[159] Luke has no interest in theory or dissection, but his characters can imply that the Mosaic regulations are not of divine origin, notably in 15:10 (cf. 13:38-39). In this development, nonobservance of Torah and the privileged position of the prophets work hand in hand. The problem comes not from God but from "Moses."[160]

■ **30-35** This short Lucan[161] paragraph[162] rounds off the entire unit in a well-constructed manner. The passage is chiastic (A [v. 30, Jerusalem to Antioch]; B [v. 31, letter read]; B' [v. 32, exhortation]; A' [vv. 33-35, Antioch and Jerusalem]).[163] Moreover, the entire passage reflects vv. 1-5 in reverse. In place of agitators from Judea, there are edifying prophets from Jerusalem. Instead of stern demands for circumcision, there is the decree. Verse 35 is a kind of *inclusio* with 14:28.[164] This is to say that chapter 15 is a "there and back" story within the story. Gal 2:1-10 is, in general, similar.

In contrast to v. 3, the narrator reports no intermediate stops on the return journey.[165] Once in Antioch, they gather the community and formally[166] deliver the letter by reading it aloud.[167] In Acts, the faithful are always available for a plenary session. This fictional technique is of considerable use to the narrator.[168] The news meets a warm reception,[169] and, rather than have to explain the decree,[170] the delegates—who, it transpires, are

157 For the social implications of this Christian understanding of purity, see Robbins, "Social Location," 327–28.

158 Pauline thought (e.g., Gal 3:23-25) probably played a role in this development, but Paul was not the most radical critic of Torah.

159 See p. 193 n. 183.

160 Cf. Neyrey, "Symbolic Universe," 295.

161 For the Lucan character of vv. 30-35, see Lüdemann, 168.

162 The expression *μὲν οὖν* in v. 30 signals the beginning of a new section.

163 Krodel, 372.

164 Note *διατρίβω* ("spend time") in each verse, and *συνάγω* ("gather," "assemble") in 14:27; 15:30.

165 This is probably the meaning of the addition "within a few days" (*ἐν ἡμέραις*) to the D-Text (Boismard, *Texte*, 257). See Metzger, *Textual Commentary*, 387. Alternatively, it could imply that they lingered before departing.

166 The verb *παραδίδωμι* is a technical term for delivery of a letter (Cadbury and Lake, 182).

167 *Aristeas* (42) provides a close parallel: Eleazar replies to Ptolemy that, after receiving his letter "we rejoiced (*ἐχάρημεν*) greatly . . . and we assembled our entire people and read it out to them (*καὶ συναγαγόντες τὸ πᾶν πλῆθος παρέγνωμεν αὐτοις*)" (trans. Moses Hadas, *Aristeas to Philocrates (Letter of Aristeas)* [New York: Ktav, 1973] 43). Note also *2 Baruch* 86, which calls for the text to be read in assemblies.

168 Cf. Chariton *Chaer.* 1.11.1; 3.4.3; 8.7.7. Spontaneous civic assemblies are possible (Acts 19:29), but writers of fiction treat them as the norm and endow them with official status.

169 Fitzmyer (567–68) calls the description "idyllic."

170 The *διὰ λόγου* of v. 32 corresponds precisely to v. 27.

prophets[171]—provide spiritual nurture and edification.[172] In due course,[173] the two return.

Since v. 33 appears to conflict with v. 40, which presumes the presence of Silas in Antioch, a range of witnesses supply what became, because of its presence in the printed editions of the Vulgate and the Textus Receptus, v. 34. In various forms, it states that Silas decided to stay in Antioch while Judas returned to Jerusalem. This, in turn, sets up a conflict between v. 33 and v. 34. These issues do not seem to have perplexed the narrator. Characters are where they need to be at a given time. Mark, for example, was in Jerusalem at last notice (13:13), but in 15:37 he is in Antioch.[174] At this point, the narrator wishes to affirm that they could leave with the community's blessings ("peace"). Verse 35 demonstrates that matters had returned to the state of affairs indicated in 14:28, and, for that matter, 13:1. The presence of other "teachers and evangelists" makes it feasible for Paul and Barnabas to leave, as Haenchen observes.[175]

171 Cf. on 13:1-3. Note also 11:27 (a Jerusalem prophet in Antioch).

172 According to 1 Cor 14:3, *παράκλησις* is one function of prophets. The D-Text (according to Boismard, *Texte*, 257) substantially rewrites vv. 31-32: "*Then* Judas and Silas, after they had read, edified the believers with a great deal of spiritual comfort and sustenance, they themselves being prophets." The order is rearranged to make it clear that Judas and Silas read the letter, the reference to its warm reception is omitted, and the statement that they were prophets receives end stress. This closely links their exhortation to the letter; that is, they preached on this text, so to speak. (D's pedantic comment that the two were "filled with the Holy Spirit" is not included in other strands of the D-tradition.) The omission by D of "much" (*πολλοῦ*) with "speech" (*λόγου*) is inexplicable.

173 Cadbury and Lake (182) note that the unmodified "time" is unusual.

174 Cf. Haenchen, 455 n. 1; Boismard (*Texte*, 257) presents, largely on the basis of versional data, a revision that deals with the problems. For vv. 33-34, he reads *ποιήσας δὲ χρόνον ὑπέστρεψεν Ἰουδας εἰς Ἰεροσόλυμα. ἔδοξε δὲ τῷ Σιλεᾶ ἐπιμεῖναι αὐτοῦ* ("After **Judas** had spent some time **he returned to Jerusalem, but Silas decided to remain there**"). This text (which omits reference to the farewell of the community) is clearly secondary. See the discussion of Strange (*Problem*, 142–46), who is not inclined to offer a vigorous defense of the originality of v. 34. For a sympathetic discussion of the D-Text, see Édouard Delebecque, "Silas, Paul et Barnabé à Antioche selon le texte 'occidental' d'Actes 15:34 et 38," *RHPhR* 64 (1984) 47–52.

175 Haenchen, 455.

15

15:36—16:10 Toward a New Mission

36/ **Some days later[a] Paul said to**
Barnabas: "Let us go back and
visit the believers in every sin-
gle city where we proclaimed
the message about the Lord so
that we may see how they are
faring." 37/ Barnabas wanted
to take John Mark along with
them, too, 38/ but Paul was of
the view that they should not
take him along, since he had
abandoned them in Pamphylia
rather than remain with them
on their task. 39/ There ensued
a quarrel that ended with their
separation. Barnabas set sail
with Mark for Cyprus, 40/ while
Paul chose Silas and, after the
believers had commended him
to the Lord's[b] gracious care, set
out. 41/ He proceeded through
Syria and Cilicia, fortifying the
communities.[c]

16:1/ **In due course Paul also reached**
Derbe and Lystra. At Lystra
there was a follower of Jesus
named Timothy, the son of a
believing Jewish woman and
a gentile. 2/ The believers in
Lystra and Iconium gave Timo-
thy good recommendations.
Paul resolved to have this man
accompany him. 3/ He accepted
Timothy as a colleague and
circumcised him because of
the Jews in those parts, all of
whom were quite aware that
Timothy's father had been a
gentile.[d] 4/ As they went about
the various cities, they delivered
the decrees promulgated by the
apostles and elders in Jerusa-
lem and instructed people to
abide by them. 5/ The commu-
nities were strengthened in the
faith[e] and grew daily in number.

6/ **They then traversed Phrygia[f] and**
Galatian territory because the
Holy Spirit had vetoed procla-
mation of the message in the
province of Asia.[g] 7/ When they
were near the eastern border
of Mysia, they attempted to
travel north toward Bithynia,
but the Spirit of Jesus[h] would
not allow them to do so. 8/ So
they skirted[i] Mysia and came to
Troas. 9/ There came to Paul at
night a vision of a Macedonian
man. He stood imploring Paul:
"Come over to Macedonia and

a Cadbury and Lake (183) say that the temporal connective (μετά, "after") is characteristic of the second half of Acts, as has μὲν οὖν in the first part.

b The frequent variant "God" is preferred by the D-Text (Boismard, *Texte*, 261) and some other witnesses. This word is due to the influence of 14:26.

c The D-Text (Boismard, *Texte*, 262) pluralizes this sentence, keeping both Paul and Silas in equal focus.

d The D-Text (Boismard, *Texte*, 263) reads: "they all knew his father, that he was Greek." See Barrett, 2:762–63.

e The D-Text (Bosimard, *Texte*, 265) omits "in the faith." The motive is not clear. Perhaps the phrase was taken as instrumental.

f *Or:* "Phrygian and Galatian territory." The Textus Receptus includes the article here. See Metzger, *Texual Commentary*, 390. According to Hemer (*Book*, 280–89), there is ample support for the adjective φρυγία ("Phrygian").

g The D-Text pedantically adds "the message **of God** to **anyone**."

h A range of witnesses replace "Jesus" with "Lord." 𝔐 sa read "the Spirit."

i The D-Text (Boismard, *Texte*, 266) reads the more logical "passing through."

help us!" 10/ Because of this vision, we, convinced that God had called us to preach the good news to the Macedonians, immediately set about finding a way to get there.

Analysis

The overlapping structure of Acts is manifest in the four short paragraphs (15:30-35, 36-41; 16:1-5, 6-10) through which the narrative turns toward Paul's great missionary work. The first and last of these are oriented toward what lies before and ahead. The middle two are transitional. The narrator's dramatic sense lulls the reader into thinking that no more than a pastoral visit, like that of 14:21-22, is in prospect. Plans for a trip and the execution of them frame the first unit. Verses 37-38 present Barnabas's proposal and Paul's reaction, while vv. 39b-40 report the respective actions of each. Their disagreement and separation[1] stand in the center (39a).[2] In this brief paragraph, the narrator removes two more characters from the board. Like Peter (and the other apostles), Barnabas and John Mark have served their purpose and may be set aside. Paul has begun to recruit a new staff for the next phase of his work.[3]

Comment

■ **36** The verse says nothing about delivering the decree. This task will emerge in 16:4, but at present the narrator does not wish to detract from Paul, who has seized the initiative that he will hold until the end of the book.[4] This, not the council, is, in one sense, the watershed of Acts.

■ **37-39** Barnabas did not dispute the plan, but insisted on naming the third member of the team.[5] Paul thought otherwise.[6] Mark had touched his hand to the plow and then looked back. Luke acknowledges that Paul and Barnabas separated over a disagreement. From the epistles scholarship infers that Paul broke with Barnabas because the latter did not support him in the dispute at Antioch (2:11-14).[7] Luke may have known the reason for the split from another source—the gentile mission source might have said that Paul rejected compromise and left—or he might have concocted the argument

1 C. Clifton Black ("John Mark," 112–18) suggests that the imperfects in vv. 37-38 are frequentative, implying a lengthy debate. The participle ἀποστάντα intimates desertion (cf. Johnson, 288). The final position of the demonstrative ("him") in v. 38 is emphatic. The word παροξυσμός is not the mildest word for disagreement. Black also notes that τὸ ἔργον ("the work") in v. 38 is used of mission in 13:2; 14:26 (cf. 1 Cor 9:1).

2 On the structure, see Johnson, 282.

3 Timothy will be added in 16:3.

4 Conzelmann (123) contrasts 13:1-3.

5 The D-Text (Boismard, *Texte*, 259–61) offers considerable paraphrase. Verse 35 begins with the article, and has, instead of πῶς ἔχουσιν in v. 36, τί ποιοῦσιν. ἤρεσεν δὲ καὶ Βαρναβᾷ ἡ βουλή ("... what they are doing. **Barnabas agreed with the plan. 37 Now Barnabas** wished to take John ... 38, But Paul **did not wish to do so**, saying, [v. 38 in direct discourse].") Verse 39b is an independent sentence rather than indirect discourse. Boismard does not include the pedantic addition of Bezae: "work **for which they had been sent**." Boismard's text of v. 36 is grammatically defective, as κατηγγείλαμεν ("we proclaimed") lacks a relative. The relative of the conventional text is technically wrong, as it is plural (ἐν αἷς), but it is acceptable. The infinitives συμπαραλαβεῖν and συμπαραλαμβάνειν in vv. 38-39 could be contrasted: Barnabas wanted to have Mark with them, but Paul did not wish to keep putting up with him. Cf. Bruce, 349. (This fine distinction was overlooked by $\mathfrak{p}^{74}$ A 33[vid] 1175 *pc*, which read the present tense in v. 37.)

6 On the literary imperfect ἠξίου, see BDF §328.

7 John P. Meier, in Raymond Brown and John P. Meier, *Antioch and Rome: New Testament Cradles of Catholic Christianity* (New York: Paulist, 1983) 39. For a list of scholars on various sides of the issue, see Bengt Holmberg, *Paul and Power: The Structure of Authority in the Primitive Church as Reflected in the Pauline Epistles* (Philadelphia: Fortress Press, 1980) 34 n. 117.

over Mark to explain the absence of Barnabas from the subsequent Pauline circle. Barnabas sets out for Cyprus, whence he had come (4:36). The division has resulted in an expansion (one might presume) of the mission.[8]

■ **40** The narrator demonstrates the transformation of Paul. He is now the superior who can choose Silas as his assistant, quite a different relationship from that expounded in v. 22.[9] Whereas Barnabas (and John) simply departed, Paul (and Silas) received a send-off from the believers, with language similar to 14:26. By this means, the narrator shows that he sides with Paul.

■ **41** The troublesome verse has been subject to a number of textual arrangements. The D-Text obliterates any grounds for the dubious chapter division after v. 41: "They proceeded through Syria and Cilicia, strengthening the communities by transmitting the commands of the elders.[10] When they had passed through these peoples (ἔθνη), they arrived at Derbe and Lystra."[11] The plurals equalize the status of Paul and Silas. The article with "Cilicia" is probably more original.[12] Heikki Leppä observes that Antioch is almost on the border of Syria. The reference is therefore awkward. He therefore proposes that Luke took this information from Gal 1:21.[13]

■ **16:1** Paul continues to build his team, adding Timothy. These colleagues play only intermittent roles in the narrative. Silas, selected in 15:40, does not reappear until 16:19, while Timothy will first be named again in 17:14. He is thus invisible at Philippi, where, to be sure, he would have been inconvenient.[14]

One may argue that the new section begins with 15:41,[15] but this also raises difficulties, as the D-Text revisions indicate.[16] The chief of these is that Derbe and Lystra did not belong to Syria and Cilicia. The narrator could have found a clearer way for saying that the pair left Cilicia, came in time to Lycaonia and thus to Derbe, followed by Lystra, if this was his intent. Verse 3 mentions Iconium, indicating once more that these cities constituted a network in which communication was easy and rapid. The basis for this material is 14:6-7, 20-21.[17]

Verse 1b introduces Timothy, presumably from Lystra, in genealogical terms. He was "a disciple" (μαθητής), the son of a Christian (πιστή) mother and a "Greek," that is, gentile, father. That is the father's sole importance. Whether he was alive or dead and what his religious preference may have been was of no interest to the narrator.[18] Evidently because Timothy was well-thought-of by believers in Lystra and Iconium (Derbe is not mentioned), Paul decided to induct him into his service. Hopeful readers will assume that Paul agreed with the recommendations of others, that the two enjoyed some sort of relationship, however brief, and that Timothy's views about working with Paul and undergoing circumcision were consulted.[19] The motive for a second colleague also remains unstated. This introduction

8 This is the perspective of the *Acts of Barnabas* (e.g., 10), the narrator of which is John Mark, who is not entirely free of self-serving and exculpatory sentiment. For a similar view, see Ephrem, 428. It is also justifiable to take the text at face value: Barnabas picked up his toys and went home. See Johnson, 288.

9 D softens this by reading "invited/received (ἐπιδεξάμενος) Silas."

10 See also the D-Text of 16:4 and the comments there.

11 Boismard, *Texte*, 262. Note that "Derbe" and "Lystra" are covered by a single preposition, as if they were "twin cities."

12 Its omission is probably more the result of conformity to 15:23 than to the varying status of Cilicia, which Luke views as a province (Acts 23:34), as it was from the time of Vespasian, but not in Paul's lifetime.

13 Leppä, *Critical Use*, 49–52.

14 The claim that Timothy was also a Roman citizen would have placed undue strain on credulity.

15 So, for example, Fitzmyer (573), who marks 15:41 as a major unit ("second journey").

16 See above, at 15:41.

17 Lüdemann, 173.

18 The D-Text (Boismard, *Texte*, 263) and some other witnesses have a different view: Timothy's mother was a widow. This explains why his father did not convert and may receive some support from the imperfect ὑπῆρχε of v. 3. See Cadbury and Lake, 184; and Barrett, 2:761–62.

19 The participle λαβών in v. 3b is vexing. Barrett (2:761) agrees that it is not otiose. It evidently establishes some contact between the two. The D-Text (Boismard, *Texte*, 263, and $\mathfrak{p}^{45}$) has coordinate indicatives: "He took and circumcised." This is probably the intended meaning.

conflicts with 1 Cor 4:17, where Timothy is described as a Pauline convert. Luke has created his own Timothy legend, fashioning him into a Jewish believer.[20] He is now the exact equivalent of John Mark.

■ **2-3** To enhance Timothy's fitness for mission, Paul circumcised him. One must ask what Paul could possibly do to provoke further injury to his reputation among the local Jews, who were last seen hurling stones at him. Circumcision would provide no more protection for Timothy than it had for Paul.[21] From Acts one would infer that Timothy was considered a gentile by local Jews, who knew that his father was such. Had a matrilineal principle been presumed,[22] v. 3 would have said that they knew that, although his mother was Jewish, he had not been circumcised. The narrator does not state explicitly that Timothy was a defective Jew.[23]

The report raises historical questions: Did Paul circumcise Timothy? If so, when did he do this and why? If he did not, is the basis a legend, a rumor, or a Lucan invention? Responses do not fall out along conservative and liberal lines.[24] The tradition is probably without historical basis. The act admirably serves the Lucan program of "Jews first," and demonstrates Paul's loyalty to the traditional faith, but it serves no discernible Pauline interest and would have laid him open to the kind of charge he made against Peter in Gal 2:14.[25] Although the proposal of Olof Linton that Luke repeats as fact a rumor circulated against Paul (cf. Gal 5:11) is a possibility,[26] the simpler solution is the hypothesis that Luke invented the incident, with inspiration from Gal 2:3-5.[27] Refusal to mention the uncircumcised Titus and his replacement with the circumcised Timothy is indicative of the lengths to which Luke thought he had to go to place Paul in a favorable light. The fact sheds light on the pressures that the author evidently felt, but it does little to enhance his reputation for historical accuracy.

The pericope manifests Paul's concern for unity. After anticipating any complaints about the religious

20 The Pastor will make Timothy a third-generation believer. See Richard Pervo, "Romancing an Oft-neglected Stone: The Pastoral Epistles and the Epistolary Novel," *JHC* 1 (1994) 25–47.

21 Ephrem (428) says that the action was prudent, as Timothy was to preach to Jews. Acts says nothing about any preaching or pastoral activity by Timothy.

22 Shaye J. D. Cohen (*The Beginnings of Jewishness: Boundaries, Varieties, Uncertainties* [Berkeley: University of California Press, 1999] 263–307) argues that the matrilineal principle was not firmly established in Judaism before the formation of the Mishnah. In Appendix D (pp. 363–77), which contains an excellent review of patristic exegesis, Cohen concludes that Timothy was not Jewish. Christopher Bryan ("A Further Look at Acts 16:1-3," *JBL* 107 [1988] 292–94) identifies most of the confusions and suggests that Luke, perhaps, and (some) Jews in Asia Minor would have viewed Timothy as Jewish. Levinskaya (*Diaspora Setting*, 15–17) argues that, in the face of uncertainty, the matrilineal principle should be accepted. The same argument could be made for the contrary.

23 The alternative must make two assumptions: that Timothy's father was dead or otherwise out of the picture and that that gentleman's opposition had prevented him from being circumcised. The text states neither and leaves open the question of why Timothy had not sought circumcision when released from the paternal yoke. Moreover, it is not likely that *all* the Jews in the region (of hundreds of square kilometers) would have been aware of his parentage.

24 Lüdemann (176), for example, accepts the historicity of the tradition.

25 The always useful 1 Cor 9:20 does not apply here, since it is one thing "to become a Jew to Jews" and another to make Timothy become a Jew to Jews. See Dixon Slingerland, "'The Jews' in the Pauline Portion of Acts," *JAAR* 54 (1986) 305–21, esp. 310. Porphyry was one ancient critic who saw the contradiction and excoriated Paul for violating his own high principles, citing 1 Cor 9:16; Phil 3:2; and Gal 2:18 (Hoffmann, *Porphyry*, 58–59). For a defense of the historicity of the report, largely based upon alleged weaknesses in arguments to the contrary, see Witherington, 474–77. For Chrysostom (*Hom.* 34), the incident demonstrated Paul's wisdom: knowing that the issue of circumcision had been settled, Paul could engage in the practice.

26 Olof Linton, "The Third Aspect: A Neglected Point of View. A Study in Gal. i–ii and Acts ix and xv," *ST* 3 (1951): 79–95. Cf. Haenchen, 482. For Barrett (2:753), "the best we can say . . . is that Luke was dependent upon popular stories." See his discussion, 2:760–62. Weiser (2:399) notes strong objections to the "rumor" hypothesis.

27 Pervo, *Dating*, 86–88, which builds on the argument of William O. Walker, Jr., "The Timothy-Titus Problem Reconsidered," *ExpT* 92 (1980–81) 231–35. See also Leppä, *Critical Use*, 135–40.

status of Timothy, he sets out with him and Silas faithfully to promulgate the decree.

■ **4-5** The D-Text of 16:4[28] is distinctive: "Passing through the cities[29] they continued to proclaim with all boldness the Lord Jesus Christ."[30] This sentence (which is indebted to 28:31) has been altered because of the D-Text of 15:41. The editor noted the restriction of the decree to the communities mentioned in the letter (15:23) and therefore rearranged the data to correct the perceived mistake. This also removes any perceived link between implementation of the decree and the qualitative and quantitative growth claimed in v. 5. Church growth now comes from proclamation of the gospel rather than promulgation of commandments.[31] Luke, however, intended to show that the decree had general validity[32] and that it was an instrument of community growth, as it encouraged gentile (and possibly Jewish) conversions.[33]

■ **6-10** This paragraph introduces the foundation of a Christian community on the European continent. This transitional statement is the last section bridging the time between the "Apostolic Council" and Paul's mission in the Aegean region. The route of travel proposed all but defies rational analysis, mixing ethnic and provincial terms in a strange order. It is best to understand the text as saying that Paul and company were not allowed to deviate either right or left.[34] The narrator leaps vast swaths of territory in a single bound.[35]

The narrative of 16:6-40 reflects a number of the features common to ancient cult-foundation stories,[36]

28 On this, see also Édouard Delebecque, "De Lystres à Philippi (Ac 16) avec le codex Bezae," *Bib* 63 (1982) 395–405.

29 This is probably retrospective, referring to the cities of v. 1 (and Pisidian Antioch?). Cadbury and Lake (185) ask whether it applies to the region of v. 6.

30 Boismard, *Texte*, 264.

31 Cf. also Epp, *Tendency*, 113–14.

32 The infinitive φυλάσσειν ("keep") is difficult. It could be taken as epexegetic, with δόγματα ("decrees"), but is better construed as final, that is, they transmitted the ordinances so that the people would observe them. The term δόγματα has an official sense (Luke 2:1) and may anticipate a contrast with "the decrees of Caesar" in 17:7. It indicates that the church is a lawful body that can make rules for its members. See Gerhard Kittel, "δόγμα," *TDNT* 2:230–32. The participle κεκριμένα ("legislated") reinforces this juridical understanding. The source of these ordinances is "the apostles and elders," without note of concurrence by the general body. With this reference the narrator lays the word "apostle" to rest.

33 The μὲν οὖν is emphatic.

34 Acts 18:23 states, in apparent contradiction, that "the Galatian territory and Phrygia" contained converts.

35 David H. French ("Acts and the Roman Roads of Asia Minor," in Gill and Gempf, *Setting*, 49–58, esp. 53–55) says, "No Roman road passing westwards through Mysia has yet been discovered but one may reasonably suppose however, that [a reconstruction proposing that] Paul traveled by tracks or paths first in Galatia, then in Phrygia, perhaps as far as Dorylaeum, Cotiaeum or Aezani . . . and finally through Mysia directly to Adramyttium is certainly possible" (p. 54). In short, the route described is unclear and can be constructed only through conjecture. Gal 4:13 (τὸ πρότερον, "previously") may be the source of v. 6. Note the astute criticism of Koch ("Kollektenbericht" 382–87), who shows that this is not from an itinerary source (in the sense put forth by Dibelius) and affirms that the author shows very limited knowledge of the interior of Asia Minor. See also the summary of research in Barrett, 2:766–69; and the references in Fitzmyer, 578–79. The journey cannot be traced on the basis of known routes, but Luke was not following a map here. The difficulty of distinguishing these regions is apparent in Strabo 12.7. Weiser (2:403–4) attributes the data to a source, but must allow for considerable abbreviation.

36 On this pattern, see James C. Hanges, "The Greek Foundation-Legend: Its Form and Relation to History," *SBLSP 1995* (Atlanta: Scholars Press, 1995) 494–520; Elizabeth R. Gebhard, "The Gods in Transit: Narratives of Cult Transfer," in Adela Y. Collins and Margaret M. Mitchell, eds., *Antiquity and Humanity: Essays in Ancient Religion and Philosophy Presented to Hans Dieter Betz on His 70th Birthday* (Tübingen: Mohr Siebeck, 2001) 451–76. On the basis of a number of accounts from the Classical and Hellenistic eras (pp. 473–76) Gebhard identifies the following motifs as "most common": a crisis of some sort, communal or individual; appeal to an oracle; command to honor a particular entity, which may require an embassy to obtain a statue or other cultic representation; difficulties, including official opposition; arrival and welcoming of the god in temporary lodgings; opposition (possibly); and a new temple or the like.

including a dream vision, an interpretive oracle,[37] lodging of the movement in domestic quarters, opposition by officials, miraculous vindication, further growth, and permanent establishment of the new movement.[38] Luke's artistry is apparent in that each of these elements constitutes a lively and independent episode that can stand on its own feet. Short as this account is, the narrative sweep is much broader than will be found in, for example, stories relating the foundation of an ancient cult, notably the cults of savior gods, such as Asclepius[39] and the Egyptian gods.[40]

■ **6-8** The first three verses raise suspense. Not since the beginning of the Cornelius episode (10:1-16) has divine intervention been so prominent, but here its purpose is not clear. Even the dullest reader realizes that important developments are in the offing, namely, the evangelization of the Aegean region, which is the center and focus of Acts and the geographical location of its implied author.[41] At this point also the first person plural makes the first of its intermittent appearances in Acts.

Unlike in the stories about Philip (8:26-39) and Cornelius (10:1-48), the role of the Spirit in vv. 6-8 is negative. The narrator does not explain the means of these revelations. All attention is thrust upon Troas.[42] The "Holy Spirit" and the "Spirit of Jesus" are practically placed in *parallelismus membrorum*.[43] Their function, if not their identity, is the same.[44] The narrative follows the "rule of three": after two courses of action are rejected, a third is ordered.[45] The missionaries arrive at Troas, a Roman colony and an important commercial node in northwest Asia Minor that was also teeming with legendary and historical associations, as it was regarded as the location of Troy, around which much epic poetry revolved;[46] the narrative slows.

For specific application to this passage, see Weaver, *Plots*, 219–79. Acts 16 does not begin with an initial crisis, but the dream revelation in 16:9 is a plea for assistance. See also F. Trotta, "Lasciare la madrepatria per fondare una colonia. Tre esempi nell storia de Sparta," in Giorgio Camassa and Silvana Fasce, eds., *Idea e realtà del viaggio* (Genoa: ECIG, 1991) 37–66; and Balch, "*ΜΕΤΑΒΟΛΗ ΠΟΛΙΤΕΙΩΝ*," 162–64.

37 For examples of these oracles, see Squires, *Plan*, 123 n. 11.

38 See Appendix 2.

39 *IG* II[2] 4960a, 4961. Emma J. and Ludwig Edelstein (*Asclepius: A Collection and Interpretation of the Testimonies* [2 vols.; Baltimore: Johns Hopkins University Press, 1945] no. 720, 1:374–75) relate the translation of the cult to Athens in the fifth century BCE. For other examples, see Gebhard, "Gods in Transit," tables 1–2, 472–73.

40 For example, the introduction of the cult of Sarapis in the (Asia Minor?) residence of Zoilus ("The Zoilus Letter," *P. Cair. Zen.* [the Zenon Papyri] 59, 034), on which see Adolf Deissmann, *Light from the Ancient East* (trans. Lionel Strachan; New York: Harper, 1927) 152–59 (with an edition of the text); Nock, *Conversion*, 49–50; Martin P. Nilsson, *Geschichte der griechischen Religion*, vol. 2, *Die hellenistische und römische Zeit* (2nd ed.; Munich: Beck, 1961) 190; and Peter M. Fraser, *Ptolemaic Alexandria* (2 vols.; Oxford: Clarendon, 1970) 1:257–59, as well as the foundation of the first Sarapeion at Delos, on which see Nock, *Conversion*, 50–55; and Helmut Engelmann, *The Delian Aretalogy of Sarapis* (trans. E. Osers; EPRO 44; Leiden: Brill, 1975). For a text, see below, Appendix 2.

41 See pp. 5–7.

42 The course of the narrative does not permit discussion of the founding of a community there, however, although 20:7-12 assumes its existence.

43 On this, see G. Stählin, "τὸ πνεῦμα Ἰησοῦ," in Barnabas Lindars and Stephen Smalley, eds., *Christ and Spirit in the New Testament: In Honor of Charles Francis Digby Moule* (Cambridge: Cambridge University Press, 1973) 229–52.

44 The D-Text (Bosimard, *Texte*, 265–66) evidently seeks to simplify the narrative by replacing the participle ἐλθόντες (lit. "going") with γενόμενοι, meaning something like "When they were at Mysia." This text also softens "they attempted" to "they wished." In v. 8, the D-Text reads διελθόντες ("passing through") and changes κατέβησαν (lit. "they went down to") to κατήντησαν ("arrived"). At this point, Irenaeus introduces "we": *nos venimus* ("we came").

45 See Edmond Farahian, "Paul's Vision at Troas (Acts 16:9-10)," in Gerard O'Collins and Gilberto Marconi, eds., *Luke and Acts* (Festschrift P. E. Rasco; trans. M. J. O'Connell; New York: Paulist, 1993) 197–207, esp. 202. The divine names present a sort of crescendo: "Holy Spirit" (v. 6), "Spirit of Jesus" (v. 7), and "God" (v. 10).

46 See pp. 512–14.

■ **9** In Troas, Paul has a vision summoning him to come to the aid[47] of the Macedonians.[48] Although the function of the vision is to bring about the foundation of a cult, a phenomenon for which there are parallels,[49] the form in which a personified people or province appears to a leader has many political analogies, for example:

> As *Caesar* stood in doubt [as to whether to enter Italy], this sign was given him. On a sudden there appeared hard by a being of wondrous stature and beauty, who sat and played upon a reed; and when not only the shepherds flocked to hear him, but many of the soldiers left their posts, and among them some of the trumpeters, the apparition snatched a trumpet from one of them, rushed to the river, and sounding the war-note with one mighty blast, strode to the opposite bank. Then Caesar cried: "Take we the course which the signs of the gods and the false dealing of our foes point out. The die is cast." (Suetonius *Julius* 32)[50]

Alexander (while in Macedonia) had a vision of the Jewish high priest, who urged him on to the conquest of Asia.[51] Also of interest in this context was the vision of a tall, elderly woman that diverted Apollonius of Tyana from his planned trip to Rome, guiding him instead to Crete,[52] where he carried out his religio-political mission. In each of these instances revelation shows the next step to one in doubt or determined on another course. Readers of Acts would understand not only that the direction of Paul's mission was determined by God but also that he was an individual of the status of Alexander or Caesar.[53] Acts 16:9-10 is almost certainly a Lucan composition. In an artistic way, it depicts Paul as an independent missionary no longer under the aegis of Antioch.[54] In chap. 10, the gentile Cornelius was visited, in good biblical fashion, by an angel. As Paul crosses the boundary between "Asia" and "Europe"[55] to begin his independent career, the vehicle of revelation is not biblical but Greco-Roman.

---

47 The verb "help" (βοηθέω) often appears in prayers seeking salvation. See Johnson, 286.

48 The nature of such reports makes it illegitimate to ask how Paul knew the person was a Macedonian. ". . . [I]t is enough to say that in a dream one knows this kind of thing" (Barrett, 2:770).

49 Other examples are Strabo 4.1.4 (Artemis); Xenophon *Anab.* 5.3.7 (Artemis).

50 In J. C. Rolfe, trans., *Suetonius I* (LCL; Cambridge, Mass.: Harvard University Press, 1913) 45.

51 Josephus *Ant.* 11.333–35. Josephus himself benefited from a consoling figure who appeared to him (*Life* 208–9).

52 Philostratus *Vit. Apoll.* 4.34. See Reitzenstein, *Hellenistische Wundererzählungen*, 53–54; and Loisy, 627.

53 Cf. also Gen 31:10-13, 24; Josephus *Ant.* 1.208; 2.217; 5.193; 6.334; 7.147; 8.125; 11.327; 13.322; Herodotus 7.12–19 (Xerxes: to invade Greece [inverse of the vision of Alexander]); *Alexander Romance* 1.35 (Alexander will capture Tyre); Virgil *Aen.* 5.719–40 (Anchises tells Aeneas where to proceed); Suetonius *Claudius* 1 (Drusus sees a barbarian in a vision); Cassius Dio 55.1; Tacitus *Ann.* 22.21; Pliny *Ep.* 7.27; Cicero *Div.* 1.49 (Hannibal); Livy 21.22.6–9 (Hannibal); Valerius Maximus 1.7 (several examples, including Augustus); Silius Italicus 3.163–214 (Hannibal); Plutarch *Luc.* 12.1–2 (Lucullus while in a temple at Troas); Appian *Bell. Civ.* 4.134, 565 (Brutus); Ammianus Marcellinus 20.5.10; 25.2.3 (Julian). A similar story is told about the arrival of Buddhism in China. The emperor Ming-ti (c. 60 CE) saw a golden man in a dream and sent to India. See William H. McNeill, *The Rise of the West: A History of the Human Community* (New York: New American Library, 1965) 362 n. 73. Note the material collected by Alfred Wikenhauser, "Religionsgeschichtliche Parallelen zu Apg. 16, 9," *BZ* 23 (1935) 180–86; and Weiser's excursus on Paul's dreams and visions (2:406–15) with detailed citations of religio-historical parallels. John B. F. Miller (*Convinced*, 76) denies this suggestion of "heroic" analogies: "This evaluation, of course, ignores the fact that dream-visions appear to some characters in Acts who fall outside of this mold." The issue, however, is the particular form of the vision in Acts 16. For a recent analysis that takes this form into account and relates the setting to Roman legend, see Bart J. Koet, "Im Schatten des Aeneas: Paulus in Troas (Apg 16,8-10)," in Reimund Bieringer, Gilbert Van Belle, and Jozef Verheyden, eds., *Luke and His Readers: Festschrift A. Denaux* (BEThL 182; Leuven: Leuven University Press, 2005) 415–39.

54 Both 13:2 and 16:10 use the verb προσκαλέομαι ("summon").

55 On the concept of "Europe," see Koch, "Kollektenbericht," 386 n. 61; and Schneider, 2:204.

John Miller presents 16:6-10 as the central piece in his study of revelatory phenomena in Luke and Acts.[56] His thesis is that revelations involve synergy: human recipients need both to respond to revelations and also to understand them. If some passages involving divine guidance (e.g., 8:26-40) threaten to reduce the earthly actors to puppets, others require interpretation. Peter's interpretation of the vision in 10:9-17a involved a large interpretive leap. For Miller, such incidents open the door to the claim that Luke and Acts portray a substantial element of human freedom and that this is an important component in missionary success and failure. To a degree this is valid, but Luke is not a theologian who reflects on the fundamental issue of divine will versus human freedom. When crucial issues are at stake, such as the conversion of Cornelius, divine guidance is prominent. The ambiguity of dreams was generally recognized in antiquity, while in the Greek world the cloudiness of oracles was pivotal, as the English adjective "Delphic" still testifies. Vagueness can serve literary purposes, raising suspense while providing some assurance. In Acts, the literary and the theological may walk hand in hand. Acts 16:9-10 is not a particularly cogent example of human freedom. It is most unlikely that Paul's vision would have been construed as a reference to the need for financial assistance or to a shortage of tentmakers. Mission is the object of Paul's work. The issue is where his labors should be performed. To that question, the vision provides a clear answer.

■ **10** "We" is now the basis and object of the Pauline missionary enterprise.[57] It first appears in the Macedonian call for assistance. "We" are those in need of salvation.[58] At the narrative level, this is a mystery provoking and enticing the reader, while embracing all who hear or read the story, transforming it from a story about "them" into a story about "us." With this intimacy comes a wealth of detail and color that are lacking in most of the earlier stories. For the first readers, "we" reflects the story of their own origins, the fruit of Paul's "missionary journeys."[59]

The D-Text[60] alters the structure of v. 9 and thoroughly revises v. 10: 9 "**In a vision** [. . .] there appeared a Macedonian man, **as it were**, standing **before Paul's face** . . . 10 **Therefore, after** Paul **had awakened, he related the vision to us** [. . .] **and we perceived** that the **Lord** had called us to preach the good news to **those who were in Macedonia**. 11 **On the next day** we sailed from Troas. . . ." These changes shed light on the conventional text. In the D-Text, "we" is an actual group and an actor. Logically, the others could not have known about the vision until Paul told them. Luke is not interested in such logic. His "we" is omniscient.[61]

Excursus: "We" in Acts[62]

One of the most vexing problems for the analysis of Acts is the use of "we" in various parts of the

56 Miller, *Convinced*, 91–107.

57 It is worth observing that "we" also appears in connection with the transit from Troas to Macedonia in 2 Cor 7:5 (which is a continuation of the letter in 2 Cor 2:12-13).

58 Cf. Conzelmann, 127.

59 On Macedonia, see David W. J. Gill, "Macedonia," in Gill and Gempf, *Setting*, 397–417, as well as Levinskaya, *Diaspora Setting*, 153–57 (who presents no evidence for Philippi).

60 Boismard, *Texte*, 266–67. (A few minor differences are ignored here.)

61 Barrett (2:776) adopts the meaning of the D-Text: "A person whose words are reported, whether by himself or an editor, was with Paul in Troas; he was told of a vision seen by Paul and concurred with the conclusion." Historicizing deduction cannot replace exegesis of the text. Other changes in the D-Text include: the initial prepositional phrase makes the sentence less awkward. "Vision" is no longer the subject. Elimination of "at night" heightens the parallel with Peter (10:9-16) and removes the experience from the realm of nocturnal dreams. The addition of ὡσεί, "as if," reminds the reader that this is a vision. The added phrase "face to face," in effect, makes the event more vivid and personal.

62 Norden (*Agnostos Theos*, 313–31) laid the grounds for subsequent research. Studies include James Blaisdell, "The Authorship of the 'We' Sections of the Book of Acts," *HTR* 13 (1920) 136–58; Jacques Dupont, *The Sources of the Acts* (trans. K. Pond; New York: Herder & Herder, 1964) 75–112; Henry J. Cadbury, "We and I Passages in Luke-Acts" *NTS* 3 (1956) 128–32; Colin Hemer, "First Person Narrative in Acts 27–28," *TynBul* 26 (1975) 79–112; S. Dockz, "Luc, a-t-il été le compagnon d'apostolat de Paul?" *NRT* 103 (1981) 385–400; Vittorio Fusco, "Le sezione-noi degli Atti nella discussione

narration: 16:10-17; 20:5-16; 21:1-18; 27:1—28:16.[63] These passages raise questions of source, form, and narrative intent. One possibility is that the author utilized "we" to mark points at which he was present on the scene.[64] A second is that the "we" represents a source (or sources) utilized by the author.[65] Other proposals refer to formal devices[66] or narrative emphases.[67] Even the straightforward assignment of the first person plural to the presence of the actual author is not without difficulties, for it must explain the sudden entrance and abrupt departure of this form, as well as other inconsistencies.[68] A. J. M. Wedderburn states the historical problem well. The horns of the dilemma are the apparent claim of authorial presence, which contrasts with evidence, making it difficult to conclude that the author was a companion of Paul.[69] Every solution must therefore include a literary dimension. Susan M. Praeder identified four

recente," *BeO* 25 (1983) 73–86; S. M. Sheeley, "Getting into the Act(s): Narrative Presence in the 'We' Sections," *PerspRelStud* 26 (1999) 203–20; Weiser, 2:387–92; and Witherington, 480–86. Fitzmyer (98–103) provides a concise review of research, as does Barrett, 2:25–30. For a detailed history of research, see Jürgen Wehnert, *Die Wir-Passagen der Apostelgeschichte: Ein lukanisches Stilmittel aus Jüdischer Tradition* (Göttingen: Vandenhoeck & Ruprecht, 1989) 47–124; and William S. Campbell, "Who Are We in Acts? The First-Person Plural Character in the Acts of the Apostles" (Diss., Princeton Theological Seminary, 2000) 23–83. Two particularly penetrating studies of the problem are Susan Marie Praeder, "The Problem of First Person Narration in Acts," *NovT* 39 (1987) 193–218; and Alexander J. M. Wedderburn, "The 'We'-Passages in Acts: On the Horns of a Dilemma," *ZNW* 93 (2002) 78–98.

63 This analysis includes within "we-passages" those pericopes that are enclosed within a first plural verbs. Acts 20:7-12 and 28:3-6, 7-10, for example, are units.

64 This view was first propounded by Irenaeus *A.H.* 3.14.1, who used them to buttress the claim that Luke was a constant companion of Paul. This says more about Irenaeus's needs to combat Marcion and others than about the we-passages. C.-J. Thornton has defended this view, with considerable nuance (*Der Zeuge des Zeugen: Lukas als Historiker der Paulusreisen* [WUNT 56; Tübingen: Mohr Siebeck, 1991]). See the summary and critique by Barrett, 2:xxvii–xxviii. Wedderburn ("Dilemma," 80–81) observes that Thornton found good parallels only in the final three books of Ammianus Marcellinus (fourth century CE). Fitzmyer also represents this view (*Luke the Theologian: Aspects of His Teaching* [New York: Paulist, 1989] 17–22), as does Jervell. Witherington (485), who also supports the claim that "we" refers to the author, who was Luke, concludes his review by saying, "Acts appears to be unique in referring only to the author's participation by using the first-person plural, but then this may be dictated by the author's desire to be unobtrusive and by his view that he played a minor role as a part of a team of Paul's coworkers." Neither of these justifications stands, since "we" is nothing if not obtrusive.

65 Stanley Porter, *The Paul of Acts* (WUNT 115; Tübingen: Mohr Siebeck, 1999) 1–66. He presents the reconstructed source on pp. 42–46. Porter calls attention to a number of *hapax legomena* in the we-passages. See Wedderburn's critique, "Dilemma," 80 n. 5.

66 See Norden (*Agnostos Theos*, 312–31), who examined the first person in relation to various ancient types and genres, and, more recently, Vernon K. Robbins, "By Land and by Sea," in Charles H. Talbert, ed., *Perspectives on Luke-Acts* (Danville, Va.: National Association of Baptist Professors of Religion, 1978) 215–42; and idem, "The We-Passages in Acts and Ancient Sea Voyages," *BR* 20 (1975) 5–18. Robbins's conclusions have been sharply criticized by, for example Reumann (n. 81) and Wedderburn, "Dilemma," 81–83. Robbins does, however, show how common the first plural is in travel, esp. sea-travel.

67 Samuel Byrskog ("History or Story in Acts—A Middle Way? The 'We' Passages, Historical Intertexture, and Oral History," in Penner, *Contextualizing*, 257–83) utilizes dissonances as the ground for a complicated hypothesis involving the reoralizing and narrativizing "of an extrafictional past reality." Wehnert (*Wir-Passagen*) looks to Daniel and Ezra-Nehemiah (mentioned by Norden, *Agnostos Theos*, 330) as literary models and Silas as the actual author. Thornton showed the improbability of this hypothesis (*Der Zeuge des Zeugen*, 114–16).

68 The inconsistencies in the use of "we" are detailed by William Kurz, *Reading Luke-Acts: Dynamics of Biblical Narrative* (Louisville: Westminster John Knox, 1993) 112–20. Among the most notorious are the abrupt disappearance of "we" in 16:17, the middle of a unit (Weiser, 2:392), and the difficulty of explaining the relation between "we" and "they" (οὗτοι) in 20:5.

69 Wedderburn, "Dilemma," 78.

outstanding narrative questions: anonymity, plurality, restriction of first person to certain sections, and the mixture of first and third persons.[70] Each of these is acute, and no comprehensive solution is likely to receive general approval. Readers reasonably expect that first person speakers will be identified, either as characters within a narrative or as the author (with or without others).[71] Use of "we" rather than "I" intensifies the problem.[72] To these must be added the problem of the text, for the D-Text extends the use and range of "we." In the tradition the first person is therefore amenable to expansion.[73] This suggests that later editors viewed the "we" as authentication and thought that the author had not provided enough of this useful commodity.

Although the traditional view holds that the first plural shows that the author was a companion of Paul and thus guarantees the authenticity of the account, the evidence of early Christian literature tends to the contrary: "we" is most often a sign of late composition[74] and is rather better attested in fiction than in works of unquestioned accuracy.[75] This value is more or less completely compromised in Acts because the subject of "we" is never specified. Readers must attempt to deduce the memberships of these groups for themselves, and conjectures vary. In 16:10, for example, "we" appears to embrace Paul, Silas, and Timothy. Timothy is present in chap. 20 (v. 3), but excluded from "we" by v. 5. "We" must therefore include Paul and at least one other. The "we" of 27:1 remains anonymous, apart from Paul, while in 27:34 it includes the entire ship's company. Research has shown that there are no stylistic grounds for isolating the "we-passages" from the balance of the material.[76] To this must be added the literary observation that the we-narrator can be no less omniscient than the narrator of third person passages.[77] Whatever sources or inspirations the author may have had, the first plural narrator lacks the limitations of ordinary human speakers.

Two general functions of first person are noteworthy. One is αὐτοψία ("personal experience"), a claim to have been present on the scene and thus able to authenticate the event or events.[78] Personal experience was one quality of the "good" historian, and claims of this sort are not always to be taken

70 Praeder, "Problem." Examples of a shift between third and first persons is not unknown in Greek literature. For examples from early Jewish and Christian fiction, see Harm R. Smid, *Protevangelium Jacobi: A Commentary* (Assen: Van Gorcum, 1965) Appendix 3, 176–78.

71 See, for example, the *Protevangelium of James* 18:3 ("I, Joseph") and the colophon, 25:1 ("I, James"). The latter identifies the author.

72 The first singular appears in the preface (1:1-2) and in the preface to Luke (1:1-4). The "extradiegetic narrator" of these passages is not the narrator of the balance of the narrative, who writes in an omniscient, (usually) third person style.

73 The most notorious example is 11:27. For some others, see Ropes, ccxxxix. A similar situation applies to the numerous editions and versions of the *Alexander Romance*. For examples, see Richard Stoneman, *The Greek Alexander Romance* (London: Penguin, 1991) 193 nn. 80 and 85; and Eduard Schwartz, *Fünf Vorträge über den griechischen Roman* (Berlin: Töpelmann, 1896) 97–98.

74 For example, John 21:24; 2 Pet 1:16-19, and a host of examples from the Christian apocrypha, on which see the references in Ernst v. Dobschütz, "Der Roman im Altchristlichen Literatur," *Deutsche Rundschau* 111 (1902) 87–106, esp. 90; and Söder, *Apokryphen Apostelgeschichten*, 213–15.

75 Nock said: "I know only one possible parallel for the emphatic use of a questionable 'we' in consecutive narrative outside literature which is palpably fictional" (*Essays* 2:827–28 = review of Dibelius, *Aufsätze, Gnomon* 25 [1953] 497–506, esp. 503).

76 This position was first argued by John C. Hawkins, *Horae Synopticae* (Grand Rapids: Baker, 1968 [reprint of the 2nd edition of 1909]) 182–89, followed independently by Adolf von Harnack, *Neue Untersuchungen zur Apostelgeschichte* (Leipzig: Hinrichs, 1911) 1–20.

77 In 16:10, "we" knows of Paul's vision. In 20:10-11 the narrator can follow Paul downstairs and return with him. (One may claim that others accompanied Paul, saw and heard him, and so on, but the *style* is omniscient.) In 28:1-6 the narrator can report not only what "the barbarians" said in their foreign language, but also what they thought. Cf. also 27:39-44. Kurz (*Reading*, 113) argues the opposite with regard to 20:7-12, but what he identifies is narrative suspense. Tannehill (*Narrative Unity*, 2:264 n. 5) makes the same observation regarding 21:10-14, saying that the narrator "shares the limited insight of Paul's companions." "Limited insight" is, to be sure, Tannehill's own judgment, but the error in both cases is the assumption that "omniscient" means "tell all" rather than "know all."

78 On the term and the quality, see Alexander, *Preface*, 34–41, 80–81, 120–25. She shows that, while personal experience was an important feature of some types of historiography, the term is relatively rare, used also by "scientific" authors, and most often invoked with reference to visiting places.

at face value.[79] A major obstacle to comparison with historiography is that historical writings are not anonymous. Readers therefore know who one component of the first plural is. One must therefore question Eckhard Plümacher's claim: "What initially appears to be an idiosyncrasy of the author has the deeper purpose of demonstrating his role as a historian."[80] The quest for formal parallels must look to smaller forms, notably the itinerary. That quest has not yielded to a solution.[81]

The first person is certainly a common feature of travel narratives, appearing since the *Odyssey* in Greek literature. It may be a product of the social psychology of those traveling in a conveyance or party.[82] Although parallels from travel accounts are relevant to the consideration of "we" in Acts, they do not fully explain the phenomenon. "We" does not provide explicit authentication of the book.[83] The authority of the text derives from the reader's acceptance of the claims of the narrative in general. One would come closer to an accurate description by stating that "we" slips out of the account whenever something important is about to happen.

Although one cannot make any sweeping claims for the role of "we" as a conventional feature of travel accounts, particularly those at sea, "we" in Acts is prominent in the coastal regions[84] as well as in the voyage to Rome. Readers would have deemed the usage appropriate. Research since Dibelius has made it apparent that the narrative function of "we" should be examined before—or at least independently of—the question of source, since source analysis can preempt questions of function.[85] The implication of these findings is that "we" occurs in the narrative because the author has either left or placed it there. The least compelling solution to the problem is the hypothesis that "we" is a relic of a source (or sources) more or less inadvertently not removed by the final editor.

Ernst Haenchen provided the basis for recent research on this problem.[86] The first plural brings the readers into the story. Tannehill and Kurz reach

79 Eckhard Plümacher ("Wirklichkeitserfahrung und Geschichtsschreibung bei Lukas: Erwägungen zu den Wir-Stücken der Apostelgeschichte," *ZNW* 68 [1977] 2–22) maintains that the author utilizes the first plural to demonstrate that he was a good historian with experience in travel to the relevant areas and acquainted with some of the principal characters. Lewis R. Donelson ("Cult Histories and the Sources of Acts," *Bib* 68 [1987] 1–21) has a useful discussion of ancient historiographical theory and practice, as well as some of the views of present-day analysts. One cogent example is Diodorus Siculus. After summarizing that author's claims in his preface, Donelson (7) observes: "Having set these rather high standards and having laid claim to the aura of factual truth, Diodorus begins his history with an account of the origin of the gods." See also the comments of Andrew Laird, "Fiction, Bewitchment and Story Worlds: The Implications of Claims to Truth in Apuleius," in Christopher Gill and T. P. Wiseman, eds., *Lies and Fiction in the Ancient World* (Austin: University of Texas Press, 1993) 147–74. To judge from Lucian's *Ver. hist.* 1.1–4, the quantities of fictitious first person reporting must have been substantial.

80 Erkhard Plümacher, "Luke as Historian," *ABD* 4:398–402. Note also Praeder ("Problem," 208), who states that historians also make use of the first person singular. Campbell ("Who Are We?" 84–132) shows that the use of first person (singular and plural) in Thucydides, Polybius, and Josephus is not uniform and cannot be linked to their sources.

81 See the thorough review of literature on the subject by John Reumann: "The 'Itinerary' as a Form in Classical Literature and the Acts of the Apostles," in Maurya P. Horgan and Paul J. Kobelski, eds., *To Touch the Text: Biblical and Related Studies in Honor of Joseph A. Fitzmyer, S.J.* (New York: Crossroad, 1989) 335–57. To state that the first plural is common in accounts of sea voyages is not to state that it is a fixed formal feature, such as a saying in an apophthegm. The criticisms of Reumann and Praeder ("Problem") are important, but are open to the objection that they demand too exact a correspondence between Acts and putative parallels. The valid observation that most first plural travel accounts derive from a first singular base does not establish that Luke had a different purpose, for one can argue that, here, as elsewhere, Luke followed a convention ineptly. The imposition of various conventions and techniques employed by historians on the framework of omniscient narration creates problems.

82 In English, for example, one is at least as likely to say, "When we crossed the Rocky Mountains, I was on chapter three," as "When the plane went over the Rocky Mountains, I was on chapter three."

83 If "we" is to be viewed as authenticating, it has the same status as pseudonymity in the Deutero-Pauline letters.

84 Conzelmann, xl.

85 Dibelius (*Studies*, 197) distinguished the use of "we" from the question of source analysis.

86 Haenchen, "We," esp. 83–99.

a similar conclusion.[87] This is most apparent at its first appearance at 16:10. When the story comes to the Aegean region, it comes to "us," that is to say, the implied audience and the geographical horizon of the implied reader. The Pauline churches of the Aegean region testify in their own voice to the power and progress of his message and labors.[88] Yet, as Haenchen recognized, this "vividness" and sense of "participation" cannot be permitted to oust Paul from prominence.[89] Thomas E. Phillips and William S. Campbell have developed two corollaries to this approach. Campbell states that "we" helps to bolster the credibility of Paul (a role that was earlier taken by Barnabas).[90] For Phillips, the chronological watershed of Acts comes after chap. 15, separating the era of the apostles from the time of Paul. The we-narrator is "postapostolic." "We" marks a division of eras.[91] Contributions like theirs show that future light will come from literary analysis.

Sources[92] may stand behind the bulk of first plural usages. In chaps. 20–21 "we" may reflect the hypothetical source, a letter from Paul and/or his companions on the journey to deliver the Collection, a text in which "we" would be appropriate.[93] There, too, "we" has been manipulated by the author. Similarly, the use of "we" on the voyage to Rome (chaps. 27–28) may reflect a source, although this could have been, as Dibelius suspected, a source that had nothing to do with Paul.[94] In conclusion: narrative explanations illuminate the use of "we" in Acts but do not fully elucidate it. "We" is not a single character and therefore unlikely to represent the author. "Participation," in the sense of the "we" of the community (as in John 1:14), is an explanation that best gives credit to the author. This does not eliminate the possibility that the author overlooked the conflict between anonymous, omniscient narration and use of the (theoretically) limited first person and thus inadvertently created most of the problems.[95] The use of "we" does not identify the author of Acts. It does serve to enhance the credibility of the narrative and to associate the narrator with the person of Paul. It is a bid to be recognized as an exponent of authentic Paulinism[96] and to authenticate the Paulinism of Acts. "We" is to Acts as the letter form is to the Deutero-Pauline epistles.

87 Tannehill, *Narrative Unity*, 2:246–47; Kurz, *Reading*, 113.
88 Cf. 1 Cor 9:1-2; 2 Cor 3:2. On the legitimating function of "we," see Campbell, "Who Are We?"
89 Haenchen, "We," e.g., 99.
90 Campbell, "Who Are We?" 133–87.
91 Thomas E. Phillips, "Paul as a Role Model in Acts: The 'We' Passages in Acts 16 and Beyond," in idem, ed., *Acts and Ethics* (Sheffield, UK: Sheffield Phoenix Press, 2005) 49–63.
92 The plural asserts that there was no single, continuous "we-source."
93 See pp. 12–14; Koch, "Kollektenbericht," 90–92; and Roloff, 239.
94 Dibelius, *Studies*, 205.
95 This can be illustrated in reverse: novelists who elect to write in the first singular have difficulty in excluding information that their narrators could not have known.
96 See also Marguerat, *Historian*, 24–25.

16

16:11-40 The Mission in Philippi

11/ We sailed from Troas[a] on a
straight course to Samothrace
and came to Neapolis[b] the
next day. 12/ From Neapolis
we went to Philippi, a city of
the first district of Macedonia[c]
and a Roman colony. We spent
several days in that city. 13/ On
the Sabbath we went beyond
the city gate to the riverside,
where we thought there would
be a place for prayer.[d] There
we sat and began to converse
with the women who had
assembled. 14/ One of them, a
devout woman named Lydia,
who was a dealer in purple
cloth from Thyatira,[e] began to
take interest.[f] The Lord opened
her heart, so that she paid close
attention[g] to Paul's words.
15/ When Lydia, together with
her household,[h] had been
baptized, she urged, "Since you
have concluded that I am a genuine believer[i] in the Lord, come
and stay[j] in my house." We
found her argument compelling.

16/ While we were on the way to
the place of prayer, a slave
woman with a prophetic spirit
who made plenty of money for
her owners by issuing oracles
encountered us. 17/ As she
trailed along behind Paul and
us, she kept on shouting:[k]
"These people are slaves of
the Most High God! They
commend[l] to you[m] a means
of deliverance."[n] 18/ She kept
this up day after day, until Paul
became so irritated that he
turned around and addressed
her spirit, "I hereby command
you in the name of Jesus Christ
to leave her." It left her right
away.[o]

19/ Her owners realized[p] that their
expectation of income had
also left. They apprehended
Paul and Silas and hauled
them to the authorities in the
city center. 20/ When they
had brought them before the
chief magistrates, they said,
"These fellows are convulsing
the city! They are Jews 21/ and
commend practices that we
Romans can neither accept nor
follow."[q] 22/ The crowd pitched
in against them, so the chief

magistrates tore off the clothes
of the accused and ordered
a flogging.[r] 23/ After many
blows with the rod, the officials
tossed them in jail, directing
the jailer to secure them carefully. 24/ In obedience to these
instructions, he put them in the
innermost cell and shackled
their feet in stocks.[s]
25/ Sometime in the middle of the
night, as Paul and Silas were
praying and praising God in
song while the other prisoners listened to them, 26/ there
was suddenly an earthquake so
powerful that the foundations
of the prison were rocked. All
the doors popped open,[t] and the
chains of all the prisoners came
loose. 27/ The jailer awakened,
saw the doors of the prison
wide open, and, presuming that
the inmates had escaped, pulled
out his sword with the intention of killing himself. 28/ But
Paul shouted very loudly:
"Don't harm yourself. We're all
here!" 29/ The jailer called for
illumination,[u] rushed in, and
fell trembling before Paul and
Silas.[v] 30/ After bringing them
out, he asked, "Milords, what
must I do to be saved?"
31/ "Believe in the Lord Jesus[w] and
you will be saved, together with
your household."
32/ They thereupon told the jailer
and all in his home the message
about the Lord.[x] 33/ Late as it
was, the jailer took them where
he could cleanse their wounds.
He and all of his people were
then baptized without delay.
34/ He then escorted them
to his own home, where a
meal was set before them.
The household was ebullient
because each and all had come
to faith in God.

16:35-40: Conventional Text

35/ The next morning the chief magistrates sent their police escort[y]
with the message, "Let those
people go."
36/ The jailer[z] gave Paul the word:
"The chief magistrates have
sent orders that you two are
to be released. All right, then,

16:35-40: D-Text[bb]

35/ The next morning the chief magistrates *assembled together*
in the city center. Reflecting
upon the earthquake that had
occurred, they were filled with
awe, and . . . sent their police
escort with the message, "Let
those people *of whom you took*

come on out and be happily on your way!"

37/ "They give us," said Paul, "a public beating, us, Roman citizens convicted of no crime, then toss us into jail, and now they want to kick us out of town secretly? Not a chance![aa] Let them come in person and remove us from jail."

38/ The police reported this to the chief magistrates, who were terrified to learn that their victims were Roman citizens.

39/ The magistrates came with reassuring words, took them out of jail, and requested that they leave town.

40/ After their release Paul and Silas went to see Lydia. They provided the believers with spiritual nurture and then left Philippi.

***custody yesterday* go." 36/ The jailer went in and gave Paul the word: "The chief magistrates have sent orders that you two are to be released. All right, then, come on out and be [ ] on your way!" 37/ "They give us," said Paul, "a public beating, us, *innocent* Roman citizens, then toss us into jail, and now they want to kick us out of town secretly? Not a chance! Let them come in person and remove us from jail."**

38/ *The police went to the magistrates and* reported *to them what had been* said . . .

39/ The magistrates came *to the jail with numerous friends* and urged them to depart. *"We were unaware of your situation," they said, "that you are law-abiding men. Please depart this city lest they once again gang up on us, clamoring against you."* 40/ After their release Paul and Silas went to visit Lydia. When they saw *the believers, they related all that the Lord had done for them.* After giving them spiritual nurture they left Philippi.

---

a The D-Text (Boismard, *Texte*, 267) assures the reader that the party left on the very next day.

b In the tradition the name appears as either two words ("New City"), preferred in N-A[27], or as one (as in the conventional translation). See Metzger, *Textual Commentary*, 393.

c *Or:* "a leading city of the district of Macedonia." The translation is based on an almost conjectural emendation (there is some support in medieval versions, which themselves may derive from correction) of πρώτη to πρώτης. Bruce Metzger and Kurt Aland opposed this emendation, as seen in their note in Metzger, *Textual Commentary*, 395; see 393–95; and Barrett (2:778–80), who also rejects the emendation. The reading "head," that is, chief or capital city, of D is unlikely to come from the Latin *caput* of d, for the equivalent also appears in sy[p]. For the historical defense of "first district," see Justin Taylor, "The Roman Empire in the Acts of the Apostles," *ANRW* 2.26.3 (1996) 2436–2500, esp. 2443–44.

d For variants, see the comments.

e "Thyatira" is a neuter plural in Greek. Θυατείρων is therefore an appositive.

f This understanding of the imperfect ἤκουεν seems preferable to Haenchen's inference (494–95) that repeated encounters are in view.

g On the infinitive προσέχειν ("pay heed to"), see BDF §392(3). For its function in missionary activity, see Acts 8:6 (Philip in Samaria).

h On this translation of καί, see BDF §442 (10). The D-Text (Boismard, *Texte*, 268) pedantically reads "entire household."

i The most obvious meaning of πιστή is "believer." See Cadbury, "Names," 375–92, esp. 382. Richter Reimer (*Women*, 114–17) emphasizes her trustworthiness and fidelity.

j A variant is the aorist imperative, which is slightly better Greek but may have been introduced because Paul did not long remain with her.

k Boismard (*Texte*, 269) prefers the aorist, implying that the woman shouted just once on this occasion.

l The D-Text (Boismard, *Texte*, 269) is less subtle: εὐαγγελίζεται ("evangelize").

m Both "to you" and the less well supported variant "to us," which sounded alike and were easily confused in Greek, presume an audience about which the text says nothing.

n *Or:* "the means of deliverance" (Cadbury and Lake, 193). On this phrase, which the narrator does not wish to equate with "the gospel," see Todd Klutz, *The Exorcism Stories in Luke-Acts: A Sociostylistic Reading* (SNTSMS 129; Cambridge: Cambridge University Press, 2004) 224–26.

o The D-Text (Boismard, *Texte*, 270) evidently replaces "in that very hour" (lit.) with the conventional "immediately."

p B has an initial καί ("and").

q The D-Text (Boismard, *Texte*, 272) makes the crowd "large," has them shout, and places one of its frequent "thens" before the action of the officials, and makes some improvements to the syntax.

r The D-Text (Boismard, *Texte*, 272) improves the syntax by placing "order" in the aorist and changing the infinitive to the passive: ῥαβδίζεσθαι ("to be whipped"). On this issue, see BDF §392 (4); Barrett, 2:791.

s Lit. "wood," ξύλον. For a similar usage, see Chariton *Chaer.* 4.2.6 and Lucian *Toxaris* 29.

t The omission of παραχρῆμα ("immediately") in B gig Lucifer is interesting. The word is common in Luke and Acts (15/16 versus 2 in the rest of the NT). Metzger (*Textual Commentary*, 396) attributes it to an accident. Boismard (*Texte*, 273) does not consider it.

u Cadbury and Lake (198) note that φῶτα ("light/s") could have been construed as a singular.

v The D-Text (Boismard, *Texte*, 274) introduces the verse with a transitional participial phrase, "When he had heard this," and adds the customary "at the feet" to "fall before."

w The variant addition of "Christ" reflects later orthodoxy.

x As often, there is the variant "God." See Metzger, *Textual Commentary*, 308.

y Lit., "lictors," who carried the symbols of authority before Roman magistrates.

z 𝔓[74] promotes him to "head jailer" (ἀρχιδεσμοφύλαξ).

aa For the rendition of οὐ γάρ, see BDF §452 (2).

bb The D-Text follows Boismard, *Texte*, 276–79.

Analysis

Each of the communities evangelized by Paul in chaps. 16–19 has distinct and memorable characteristics. Some of these are traditional: Philippi was a Roman colony, Athens was an intellectual and cultural center, and the Ephesian temple of Artemis was famous. Others are more particular: Philippi seems to have no established synagogue; reception in the Thessalonian synagogue is attentive, but mixed; Beroea is highly receptive, until . . . At Athens one hears only of speaking in the synagogue, with no positive results reported. Labor in the synagogue at Corinth leads to an eventual split. Ephesus yielded a similar result. The briefest report pertains to Beroea (17:10-14), the only station in these chapters not mentioned in the extant correspondence of Paul. Framing this mission are great adventures at Philippi and Ephesus. At Corinth Paul works for a living. In Ephesus he teaches in a facility. Whatever the author possessed or utilized from his sources, he was, as usual, able to produce a lively and varied narrative. In the end, credit for Acts 16–19 must be assigned to Lucan art.[1] In these stories, both he and his hero shine.

The mission at Philippi calls forth a lengthy narrative, the core of which is bracketed by references to Lydia and other believers (vv. 13-15; 40a).[2] Within this frame are a number of sequential episodes. An exorcism in vv. 16-18 leads to trumped-up charges against Paul and Silas, resulting in beating and incarceration (vv. 19-24). The legal situation is resolved by their release and departure (vv. 35-39). Within this comes the story of the earthquake and related events (vv. 25-34). Two important conversions, that of Lydia and her household, and the jailer with his household, are the pillars on which the narrative, and the Philippian community, are erected. For the first time Paul founds communities based on household churches headed by gentiles. For this first independent Pauline endeavor, Luke pulls out

1 Once more, the contrast with chaps. 13–14 is quite notable.

2 For a history of research, see Peter Pilhofer, *Philippi, Band I: Die erste christliche Gemeinde*

all the stops. The wealth of detail exceeds anything that has gone before. To highlight the inauguration of the gospel in the Aegean region, the author chooses not to dwell on patient missionary labors but rather a series of adventures, with many twists and turns in the plot and a happy ending—despite the narrator's admission that the evangelists leave at the behest of the officials. The mission to Philippi is a great adventure story that portrays the triumph of the faith over the machinations of polytheism. Given the amount of space devoted to this endeavor, the lack of correspondence to the data of Paul's correspondence with Philippi is noteworthy.[3]

The source question is not easily resolved. The stages of the journey (vv. 11-12a) "are the natural stopping places on the way to Philippi" and, for that very reason, may or may not come from a source.[4] The story of Lydia's conversion is reasonably, but not indisputably, attributed to a source, perhaps a local Philippian foundation story. The term προσευχή, not otherwise found in Acts, supports this, as may other unusual details.[5] The parallel conversion of the anonymous jailer (also *en famille*), which yields the desired female/male pair,[6] is quite probably a Lucan creation. Although the exorcism of the slave woman could have a basis in tradition (perhaps not at Philippi), it is not typical and is likely to have been developed by Luke to suit his purposes, for several of which it is highly convenient. The entire sequence—arraignment, beating, imprisonment, earthquake, vindication, and release—is probably inspired by 1 Thess 2:2 (with the whipping possibly from 2 Cor 11:25). One may, alternatively, posit that the arraignment before the officials, the beating, and the release a day later come from tradition, but this skeleton raises as many questions as it answers, for example, the grounds for the arrest and punishment, and an explanation for the almost immediate release.[7] It is highly probable that Luke possessed some traditions about Philippi, but, apart from proposals about the story of Lydia, attempts to identify these do not contribute to the understanding of the text. The stories do, however, suggest that the author had access to local traditions, and they raise the question of how he obtained this material.

Comment

■ **11-12** Easy and rapid voyages are good portents.[8] Philippi,[9] which receives a flattering introduction,[10] was fortunately situated at the juncture of East and West,

Europas (WUNT 87; Tübingen: Mohr Siebeck, 1995) 153–99.

3 Cf. Fitzmyer, 582. Luke knew the letter. See Pervo, *Dating*, table 4.45, p. 141.

4 See Lüdemann (183), who uses the data to claim a historical origin. Many agree, for example, Weiser (2:421), who lists others holding that view. Ignatius (*Polyc.* 8:1) followed the same route.

5 For some of these, see Weiser (2:421–22), who also attributes the baptism of her household to tradition (423). Lüdemann (183) appeals to her name and occupation. These arguments are in danger of confusing verisimilitude with history. On the other hand, it should be noted that Paul, as is standard in Acts, begins with a mission to Jews, which does not fit his own self-understanding as an apostle to the gentiles. Valerie Abrahamsen ("Women at Philippi: The Pagan and Christian Evidence," *JFSR* 3 [1987] 17–30) is willing to consider that the story may be fictitious, while Matthews (*First Converts*, 93) thinks that it is a Lucan invention. She appeals to Lydia's absence from the Philippian correspondence, the symbolic value of her name, and her value as a foil for the "difficult" Euodia and Syntyche of Phil 4:2-3. Dennis R. MacDonald ("Lydia and Her Sisters as Lukan Fictions," in Levine, *Feminist Companion*, 105–10) argues for Euripides' *Bacchae* as the primary inspiration. Deconstructive arguments from silence have their drawbacks, but this is at least as cogent as Lüdemann's assumption of historicity from details. For the symbolic value of the name Lydia, see Marianne Palmer Bonz, *The Past as Legacy: Luke-Acts and Ancient Epic* (Minneapolis: Fortress Press, 2000) 131 n. 12, 167. (Against the objection that Luke would not invent a story about a woman as the initial convert is Matthew's *First Converts*, which focuses on stories that begin with women who respond positively to the message of a new religion.)

6 See on 9:32-43.

7 See Jervell (428–30) and the lengthy analysis by Weiser (2:421–31).

8 See Appendix 4.

9 See Holland L. Hendrix, "Philippi," *ABD* 5:313–17; Lukas Bormann, *Philippi: Stadt und Christengemeinde zur Zeit des Paulus* (NovTSup 78; Leiden: Brill, 1995); and the literature cited by Fitzmyer, 584.

10 Cf. Pseudo-Lucian, *Onos* 46, where Thessalonica is called "the greatest city in Macedonia." (μεγίστης probably means "largest" here.)

land and sea, surrounded by arable land and mineral deposits. The site also benefited from its location as the battleground where Octavian, the future Augustus, and Marc Anthony defeated the assassins of Caesar, which led to the status of Philippi as a Roman colony. Colonies were pieces of Rome, as it were, bulbs planted at strategic sites.[11] Those who held this title were proud of it. The political status of Philippi will be important for both the outcome of this particular story and as a symbol of the place of the church in the Roman Empire.[12]

Verse 12b[13] encompasses the entire duration of the mission; it takes little more than a week to launch a community in Acts, but it probably marks time—and raises suspense—before the arrival of Saturday.[14]

■ **13** The general meaning of the verse is clear—the party joined some women at prayer on the Sabbath—but little else is. The construction is peculiar, and the text is quite uncertain and may be corrupt.[15] Of the six possibilities printed in N-A[27], ἐνομίζομεν προσευχὴν εἶναι) is rendered here, although ἐνόμιζεν προσευχὴν εἶναι ("where Paul thought" [א, cf. 𝔭[74] (with noun in the nominative)]) is attractive,[16] and the argument of Ropes that the verb was passive and meant, in effect, where a place for prayer would normally be found, although open to objections,[17] has the merit of making some sense. All solutions raise the problem of why the party did not make efforts to ascertain if and where Jews gathered. The text preferred by Ropes implies that, if Jews gathered anywhere, it would be near the water.[18]

The missionaries' uncertainty inclines toward the view that the "place of prayer" (προσευχή)[19] was just that, and that readers are free to envision the worshipers meeting *al fresco* in an area where a synagogue would be, had one been built.[20] The text says nothing about entering a building, but that possibility is not excluded. One is permitted to infer that only women were gathered. This phenomenon has resulted in considerable comment, both positive and demeaning,[21] but it may

11 Aulus Gellius *Noct. Att.* 16.13.9: *quasi effigies paruae simulacraque esse quaedam uidentur* ("miniatures, as it were, and in a way copies"), trans. John C. Rolfe, *The Attic Nights of Aulus Gellius I* (LCL; Cambridge, Mass.: Harvard University Press, 1927) 181.

12 Otherwise Acts does not identify colonies. Other sites that held this status are Pisidian Antioch, Lystra, Troas, and Corinth. Cf. also Ptolemais, Syracuse, and Puteoli.

13 "Spend time" (διατρίβω) is a Lucan word: 12:19; 14:3, 28; 15:35; 20:6; 25:6, 14.

14 See Haenchen, 494.

15 The possibility of corruption in two consecutive verses raises the possibility that damage occurred in the archetype of all existing witnesses.

16 See Conzelmann (130), who traces the difficulties to an original nominative.

17 See Ropes, *Text*, 155; Metzger, *Textual Commentary*, 395–96; Barrett, 2:780–81. Boismard (*Texte*, 268) reads "where there seemed to be a place of prayer" (ἐδόκει προσευχὴ εἶναι). Although not likely to be original, this supports the reading of Ropes. Bruce (358) does not read Ropes's text, but he finds it more probable.

18 It appears to have been customary to locate Jewish houses of worship in proximity to sources of water. See Josephus *Ant.* 14.258 and the data supplied by Barrett, 2:781. J. Goldin, "The Magic of Magic and Superstition," in Schüssler Fiorenza, *Aspects*, 115–47, esp. 125 (who relates the practice to a sense that the deity—and demons—prefer the liquid element).

19 On the term, see Martin Hengel, "Proseuche und Synagoge," in Gert Jeremias, Heinz-Wolfgang Kuhn, and Hartmut Stegemann, eds., *Tradition und Glaube: Das frühe Christentum in seiner Umwelt. Festgabe für Karl Georg Kuhn zum 65. Geburtstag* (Göttingen: Vandenhoeck & Ruprecht, 1971) 157–84; Levinskaya, *Diaspora Setting*, 207–25; Sharon Lea Mattila, "Where Women Sat in Ancient Synagogues: The Archaeological Evidence in Context," in John S. Kloppenborg and Stephen G. Wilson, eds., *Voluntary Associations in the Graeco-Roman World* (London: Routledge, 1996) 266–86, esp. 275; and Richter Reimer, *Women*, 85–90. It is equally possible that Luke has simply varied his terminology. In any event, this place of prayer plays the same role in the story as synagogues do elsewhere. It is Paul's first missionary target.

20 Johnson (292) assumes that the party stopped en route to the place of prayer to preach to a "crowd of women on the beach," and that v. 16 resumes the actual trip. This is creative, but generates more difficulties than it unravels.

21 See the exhaustive study of Richter Reimer (*Women*, 71–149), who identifies exegetes who determined that this could not have been a "true" Jewish synagogue community on the grounds that only women are mentioned.

be a Lucan contribution to explain why Lydia alone appears responsive, and it may also explain why the word "synagogue" does not appear.[22] Atypically, the narrative reports no other conversions, no division that leads to opposition. In this story, the narrator will restrict hostility to polytheists.

■ **14** Although "we" spoke to the women,[23] the only result reported is Lydia's response to Paul: the Lord "opened her heart," an evocation of Luke 24:45.[24] Lydia represents one important type of early Christian convert: a possible former slave[25] who operates a business.[26] Nothing is said of her marital status. It is likely that she is to be perceived as single, divorced, or widowed. In any case, she was the head of her household, and a person of some means.[27] By ancient standards she was not rich, but, among early Christians, she would have been seen as fairly well situated. A presumed freedwoman, quite possibly an immigrant, practicing an unpleasant type of

22 Valerie Abrahamsen, "Women at the Place of Prayer at Philippi," in Meyers, *Women*, 463–64.

23 For the difficulties of taking "sat down" as the position of teaching authority, see Haenchen, 494. Acts 13:14 is a better parallel: worshipers were seated.

24 In Luke 24:45, the risen Jesus opened "the mind" of his disciples. Note also 24:32 ("burning hearts" of travelers to Emmaus) and the use of "heart" in Luke 8:12, 15 (parable of the sower). Cf. 2 Macc 1:4: "May he open your heart to his law and his commandments, and may he bring peace." This may be the source.

25 This is a reasonable inference from both her name and her occupation: G. Horsley, *NewDocs* 2:26–28 (1982); and Wayne Meeks, *The First Urban Christians: The Social World of the Apostle Paul* (New Haven: Yale University Press, 1983) 203 n. 93. David Gill ("Acts and the Urban Élites," in Gill and Gempf, *Setting*, 105–18, esp. 114) rejects this and compares here to a Julia Lydia and a Julia Lydia Laterane, but the nomenclature is important. Colin J. Hemer similarly fails to discriminate in his generally useful "Lydia and the Purple Trade," *NewDocs* 3 (1983) no. 17, pp. 53–55. The Lydia of Acts 16 has but a single name. Horace deemed "Lydia" a suitable name for a (high-class) prostitute (*Odes* 1.8.1; 1.13.1; 1.25.8; 3.9.6–7, 20; 4.15.30).

26 See the detailed studies of Lydia's occupation by Richter Reimer, *Women*, 100–112; and Luise Schottroff, *Let the Oppressed Go Free: Feminist Perspectives on the New Testament* (trans. Annemarie S. Kidder: Louisville: Westminster John Knox, 1993) 131–37. Richter Reimer (*Women*, 112) concludes that her income was at the subsistence level. This is not certain. What the text claims is that she was in charge of a household and that her living arrangements were large enough for several guests; that is, she could serve as a patron. See also Abrahamsen, "Lydia," 110–11; W. Derek Thomas, "Women in the Church at Philippi," *ExpT* 83 (1976) 117–20; and Spencer, "Women," 146–50. Thyatira, Lydia's place of origin, is associated with this trade. Cf. *IGR* 4.1213, 1250, and 1265, on which, see T. R. S. Broughton in Tenney Frank, ed., *An Economic Survey of Ancient Rome* (5 vols.; Baltimore: Johns Hopkins University Press, 1933–40) 4:818–19. On the social standing of such persons in general, see John H. D'Arms, *Commerce and Social Standing in Ancient Rome* (Cambridge, Mass.: Harvard University Press, 1981), with references to purple merchants on 128 and 139. A purple dealer from Hierapolis became a member of the city council (n.d.; Fik Meijer and Onno van Nijf, *Trade, Transport and Society in the Ancient World: A Sourcebook* [London: Routledge, 1992] no. 137 p. 107), a certain mark of social respectability and thus a challenge to the assumption that purple merchants always had low status. One Euschemon, a vendor of purple goods (πορφυροπώλης), whose name suggests a servile background, refurnished the statue and shrine of the Tyche of Miletus (c. 123 CE, IMysia/Troas 2261). *P. Herm.* 52 takes note of a Jewish dealer in purple goods (Annas, son of Joses, 399 CE). For the nature and meaning of "purple goods," see Frederick W. Danker, "Purple," *ABD* 5:557–60. A century ago, William Ramsay noticed some affinities between the "Jezebel" of Thyatira in Rev 2:18-28, toward whom he was sympathetic, and the Lydia of Acts (*The Letters to the Seven Churches of Asia and Their Place in the Plan of the Apocalypse* [New York: A. C. Armstrong & Son, 1905] 336.) He did not wish to pursue these connections, but Price (*Widow Traditions*, 225–34) did so. He hypothesizes that Lydia and the possessed woman of 16:16-18 were originally one person, divided by Luke to show that women prophets should remain silent. His approach displays limited methodological rigor, but he does identify problems in the narrative. See Haenchen (494 n. 8), for amusing identifications of this woman.

27 On the type, see Richard Pervo, "Wisdom and Power," *ATR* 67 (1985) 307–25. Matthews (*First Converts*, 85–89) recognizes that, for Luke, Lydia is a person of status. This is clear not from an abstract analysis of her business but from the role she plays in the narrative.

work—scarcely more appealing in its working conditions than that of Simon the Tanner (9:43)[28]—Lydia would probably have had a limited place in the social world of her colony.[29] The new religion had a place for such persons. That place, for Acts, is to offer hospitality to the missionaries. She is the Martha of Acts.[30] For Luke, Lydia is the host of a house church, not its explicit head. If Luke had thought her occupation degrading, he could have suppressed the data and introduced her as the head of a household. Acts 9:43 and 18:3 indicate that the author had no qualms about presenting artisans as prominent converts. This reveals the difference between the appearance of the social status of early believers in Acts, which claims adherents of the very highest status, such as Sergius Paulus (13:7-12), and the reality: people who work with leather and wool stand near the top of the actual heap.[31]

■ **15** Baptism follows immediately, as is customary in Acts (cf. v. 33). Verses 13-15 establish what will become a common pattern in Acts, the shift from "synagogue" to house as a missionary base.[32] This is comparable to the transfer of centrality from the temple to the house.[33] For missionaries to stay at the home of converts demonstrates that the new believers are fully acceptable.[34] God-Fearers are not second-class citizens in the Christian community. In v. 15, that purpose is explicit. Lydia's "compelling" argument is the second possible allusion to Luke 24 in two verses.[35] New life has come to Philippi. The one who opened her heart opened Paul's as well. Lydia is the Cornelius of this mission.[36]

■ **16-18** Rather than continue to describe Paul's labors, the narrator moves, not without difficulty, to an incident that will eventually result in his departure.[37] The woman's advertising might seem like a good thing, but Paul had absolutely no use for this kind of vulgar religion, which resembled the superstitions hawked in public squares by unscrupulous quacks.[38] The two demonstrations of the superiority of Christianity to vulgar polytheism here and in 19:23-40 encase Paul's independent missionary enterprise.[39] Rackham saw the point: "Philippi was not exempt from superstition and attempts to trade upon the spiritual cravings of man. This slave girl is a contrast to the well-to-do Lydia; and, like the maidservant who troubled Peter in Caiaphas' palace, she was to be the involuntary cause of much evil to S. Paul."[40]

The chief difficulty is in the (improper) genitive absolute that introduces v. 16.[41] If the reader is to understand this as a flashback to the Sabbath walk related in v. 13, the narrator has not been clear, but if, on the other hand, it relates a subsequent trip to the place of prayer, clarity is equally lacking. The best solution is to admit that the two components cannot intelligibly be coordinated. Even the D-Text did not attempt to straighten up this glitch. Only careful or critical readers will pause to

28 One can gain a notion of the activities involved from those fresci in the House of the Vetii at Pompeii, which depict cupids engaged in fulling. (The Vetii evidently earned enough in various trades to acquire a fine villa.)

29 See, however, n. 25.

30 Cf. Kathleen Corley, *Private Women, Public Meals: Social Conflict in the Synoptic Tradition* (Peabody, Mass.: Hendrickson, 1993) 143.

31 On Luke's social orientation, see Pervo, *Profit*, 77–81.

32 See 18:7 (Corinth) and 19:9 (Ephesus); cf. 28:30 (Rome). On the conversion, see Matson, *Household Conversion*, 136–54.

33 See p. 94 n. 54.

34 Cf. John 1:40; Acts 10:48b. There could be too much of a good thing (*Did.* 11:4–5).

35 The verb παραβιάζομαι ("compel") appears only in Luke 24:29 (Emmaus, where μείνω likewise is found) and Acts 16:15 in the NT. Cf. also Gen 19:3.

36 See Matthews (*First Converts*), who also notes that specific mention of table hospitality is reserved to the jailer.

37 Rackham (284) notes the difficulty. Richter Reimer (*Women*, 151–94) analyzes this incident in considerable detail. Klutz (*Exorcism Stories*, 207–64) also offers a detailed analysis, with considerable attention to its context in Luke and Acts. In addition, see Frederick E. Brenk, "The Exorcism at Philippi in Acts 16.11-40: Divine Possession or Diabolic Inspiration?" *FilolNT* 13 (2000) 3–21; and Kauppi, *Foreign*, 27–38.

38 Aune (*Prophecy*, 268–69) identifies and discusses two formal elements: a recognition oracle and a commendation oracle.

39 Cf. ἐργασίαν πολλήν ("considerable income") in 16:16 with the οὐκ ὀλίγην ἐργασίαν ("not inconsiderable income") of 19:24.

40 Rackham, 286. In n. 1 on 287, he also saw the parallel with Rhoda in 12:13.

41 Verse 16 uses an absolute "we." In v. 17 "we" is distinguished from Paul and then drops out until

ponder the difficulty, however, for the narrative immediately plunges into a new and exciting development. Verses 16-40 follow the sequence familiar from chaps. 3–5: A miracle rouses official antagonism (3:1-10; 4:1-2; 5:12-16), which results in whipping (5:40), incarceration (4:3; 5:18), prison miracle (5:19; 12:6-17) and release (5:23, 40; 12:10).

Here the narrative is far from Jerusalem and the occasion is even farther from pity for a suffering soul. Some men made a good living from the oracular properties of a female slave. Her πνεῦμα πύθωνα is somewhat tautological, for πύθων had come to mean a "spirit of divination."[42] These persons were called "belly-talkers" (ἐγγαστρίμυθοι). One theory was that they were pregnant (ἐν γαστρί) with a god,[43] a view popular enough to bring forth a vigorous denial by Plutarch.[44] Women did, tradition records, deliver oracles, often to the benefit (or horror) of political leaders.[45] The narrator holds the practice in disdain.[46] His view resembles that of Lucian's portrait of Alexander of Abonouteichos.[47] To put such individuals out of business will be a community service.[48] In this instance, the majestic god Apollo is represented by a street person of the lowest status, whose advertisement is far from Apollonian and whose career collapses at a single pronouncement by Paul.[49] Her fate resembles that of the alleged sons of a high priest of the God of Israel in 19:13-17.

The episode is a reflex of the story of Balaam (Numbers 22–25), a prophet who surprisingly delivers oracles in support of a rival deity, but Luke's immediate inspiration came from Mark 5:1-20||Luke 8:26-39. The scene takes place on polytheist territory. The possessed person "encountered" (ὑπαντάω [Mark 5:2; Acts 16:2]) the exorcist and seized the initiative, using the expression "most high God" (ὕψιστος θεός), often found in gentile contexts.[50] The incident involves an economic loss (Mark 5:13; Acts 16:19) and ends with a request for the exorcist to leave the jurisdiction (Mark 5:17; Acts

20:5. The narrator thus prepares for the departure of the first plural.

42 BDAG, 896–97, *s.v.* πύθων. This may explain the D-Text (Boismard, *Texte*, 269) πνεῦμα πύθωνος ("spirit of a python"), supported also by $\mathfrak{p}^{45}$. Klutz observes that the phrase πνεῦμα πύθωνα is parallel to the locutions πνεῦμα ἀκάθαρτον and πνεῦμα πονηρόν ("unclean/evil spirit").

43 Aristophanes *Wasps* 1019, with the scholium, on which see Wikenhauser (*Geschichtswert*, 401–7), who cites other texts, including examples from the LXX (which usually refer to the conjuring of ghosts).

44 Plutarch *Def. orac.* 9 (*Mor.* 414E): "Certainly it is foolish and childish in the extreme to imagine that the god himself after the manner of ventriloquists (who used to be called 'Eurycleis,' but now 'Pythones' [πύθωνας]) enters into the bodies of his prophets and prompts their utterances, employing their mouths and voices as instruments" (trans. Frank C. Babbitt, *Plutarch's Moralia V* [LCL; Cambridge, Mass.: Harvard University Press, 1938] 377). Eric R. Dodds reviews ancient attempts at describing or explaining the phenomenon (*The Greeks and the Irrational* [Berkeley: University of California Press, 1968] 71–72).

45 Sambathis, whose name was altered to Athenais, was a Phrygian slave. See H. C. Youtie, "Sambathis," *HTR* 37 (1944) 209–18, esp. 212 n. 17. For others, see David Potter, *Prophets and Emperors: Human and Divine Authority from Augustus to Theodosius* (Cambridge, Mass.: Harvard University Press, 1994) 169, 172–73. For the political ramifications of divination, see MacMullen, *Enemies*, 128–62.

46 The verb μαντεύομαι ("issue oracles") is always used in a negative sense in the LXX and early Christian literature (BDAG, 616, *s.v.*).

47 Lucian *Alex.*, esp. 19–29; cf. also Petronius *Satyricon* 134–38; Juvenal *Sat.* 6.543–47; Apuleius *Metam.* 8.26–30; and the discussion by Georgi (*Opponents*, 98–101).

48 As elsewhere, the attitude toward money is revelatory of spiritual condition. Cf. Johnson, *Literary Function,* 202.

49 Richter Reimer (*Women*, 154–56) argues that the slave was an itinerant *Pythia* and that her oracles were attributed to Apollo. See also Klutz (*Exorcism Stories*, 214–17), who agrees with Richter Reimer, as does Matthews (*First Converts*, 89–92). Their evidence is persuasive. Aune (*Prophecy,* 268) says that the symptoms indicate that she was in a trance. The association of this person with Apollo goes back at least to Bede, 69. The implicit argument is that "pagan gods" are in fact demons. This is a thesis of Christian apologists (e.g., Justin *1 Apol.* 26.1; Origen *Cels.* 3.25–27; 4.90–98; Eusebius *Praep. ev.* 4.23). Ps.-Clem. *Hom.* 9.16 also indicates that "pythons" can be exorcised.

50 Distinction is to be made between ὕψιστος ("highest") as a divine epithet (more than a hundred times in the LXX) and θεὸς ὕψιστος ("the highest god"). See Arthur Darby Nock, "The Gild of Zeus

16:39). Formally, the exorcism is atypical, since exorcists rarely put up with demons for some days and do not usually act for their own benefit.[51] These features are dramatically suitable, to be sure, but they add weight to the view that this exorcism is a secondary composition, not from tradition.[52] Structurally, Mark 1:23-28 should also be considered. Just as the mission of Jesus began with an exorcism, signifying the irruption of God's rule, so does Paul's work in this new field of endeavor.[53] In addition to this reminiscence of the ministry of Jesus, there is a parallel to Peter: Paul also has to encounter a *παιδίσκη* ("slave girl"), and this in proximity to a prison miracle.[54] That the parallel is not precise is a testament to Lucan artistry. Finally, the incident possesses some rough humor.[55] Luke has got a lot of mileage out of these three verses.

■ **19-21** This exorcism brought forth an angry mob[56] rather than an admiring crowd.[57] The owners were shrewd enough to mask their avarice with a potent brew concocted from the ultimate resort of the scoundrel, a dose of old-time religion, and a garnish of racism. It had the desired effect. In practically less time than it takes to tell, they arraigned the missionaries on their foul charges, supported by the testimony of the urban mob. The panicked magistrates caved in to this threat and, without inquiry or examination, had the alleged perpetrators viciously whipped and slapped into firm custody. Those who had loosened the bonds of a demon found themselves in shackles. As in chap. 19, Luke reveals the utter bankruptcy of polytheism.

The incident is quite exciting but without much logic. Since the owners[58] were perturbed about financial loss,[59] it would have behooved them to lodge a suit against Paul.[60] The narrator prefers to relate a typical

Hypsistos," in *Essays*, 1:414–43 (abridged from *HTR* 29 [1936] 39–88, which is preferable), esp. 416–30. Nock demonstrated that the epithet is not always associated with Judaism. For the Greek text, as well as additional comments, see *NewDocs* 1 (1981) no. 3, pp. 25–29. Note also Deissmann, *Light*, Appendix 1, 413–24; Richter Reimer, *Women*, 161–67; and Feldman, *Jew and Gentile*, 74 nn. 146–48. The Jewish and syncretistic associations of the title are well illustrated in the magical texts adduced by John M. Hull, *Hellenistic Magic and the Synoptic Tradition* (SBT 28; London: SCM, 1974) 67–68. See also Paul R. Trebilco, "Paul and Silas, 'Servants of the Most High God' (Acts 16:16-18)," *JSNT* 36 (1989) 51–73; F. Scott Spencer, "Out of Mind, out of Voice: Slave-girls and Prophetic Daughers in Luke-Acts," *BibInt* 7 (1999) 133–55; and Kauppi, *Foreign*, 34–38. Kauppi concludes that "Most High" was another god.

51 Compare Philostratus *Vit. Apoll.* 4.20, where Apollonius immediately exorcises a demon that is interfering with his teaching. Boismard (*Texte*, 270) eliminates *διαπονηθείς* ("became irritated"). His argument is open to objection, but his data do indicate that some authorities viewed this emotion as problematic. (Luke may have found justification in the D-Text *ὀργισθείς* of Mark 1:41, which he probably read and omitted.)

52 The expression "means of deliverance" in the oracle (v. 17) combines two favorite Lucan words: "way" (*ὁδός*) and "salvation."

53 Note also that, as in Mark 1:23-28||Luke 4:33-37, demons are not allowed to propagate the message.

54 See on Acts 12:6-17.

55 See Pervo (*Profit*, 63), who observes that this exorcism would arouse considerable critical contempt if found in Apocryphal Acts. The verb *διαπονέομαι* ("become furious" [n. 50]) appears elsewhere in Acts only of the rage of the Sanhedrin against the apostles (4:2). Klauck (*Magic*, 69) provides a detailed historicizing rationale for the action. There is irony: a slave recognizes the missionaries as inspired slaves of God.

56 For Brian Rapske (*The Book of Acts and Paul in Roman Custody* [BIFCS 3; Grand Rapids, Eerdmans, 1994] 121–23) the crowd amounts to an "assembly." The narrative does not describe them as violent, and crowds could influence judgments, but such influence was not viewed as a component of good rule.

57 The narrator says nothing about the fate of the slave, who has played her part. Her subsequent life would not have been enviable. For a similar conclusion, with more detail, see Klutz, *Exorcism Stories*, 260–62.

58 Two or more persons could share ownership of a slave. See Richter Reimer, *Women*, 153.

59 There are several adroit plays on words. The term for the departure of the demon in v. 18 and the loss of income in v. 19 are the same (*ἐξῆλθεν*). The verb used by their slave of the missionary proclamation (*καταγέλλουσιν* [v. 17]) recurs in their own claim about what Paul and Silas are preaching (v. 21). The D-Text (Boismard, *Texte*, 271) revises the verse, eliminating the play on *ἐξῆλθεν* and dropping the final "to the authorities." For more details, see Klutz, *Exorcism Stories*, 210–12.

60 Richter Reimer (*Women*, 176–78) recognizes this,

scene centered on the labile mob, swayed by unscrupulous manipulators, which can be conjured up as needed.[61] Despite the breathless quality of the narrative, the charges are formulated with some cleverness and eloquence.[62] The accused are foreign agitators[63] who promulgate an alien cult. Readers know that the first is false. The only agitators are the owners of the slave. The second is more complicated. The complainants allege that the missionaries advocate un-Roman practices. A. N. Sherwin-White views this formulation as "positively archaic," relating it to the decree against the Dionysiac Mysteries (186 BCE).[64] Jewish proselytism, while not specifically forbidden until a later era, had long been frowned upon,[65] but the accusers do not explicitly say that Paul and Silas were attempting to persuade Roman citizens to adopt Jewish practices.[66] Neither Luke nor his readers need to have been familiar with the fine points of Roman law. Virtually everyone knew that national "customs" (ἔθη) could be regarded as sacred,[67] and the charges intend to ignite the flames of nationalistic ardor: "us" vs. "them."[68] Proper Romans are not "anti-Christian," but they are hostile to Jews.[69] The final words of v. 21 will become ironic when v. 37 reveals that Paul and Silas are themselves Roman citizens. Less subtle is the irony that the frequent victim of Jewish agitators is accused of being just that.

■ **22-23** Readers will probably infer that the officials,[70] stampeded by the crowd and impressed with the gravity of the charges, dispensed with such niceties as a trial.[71] The accused are, without further ado, stripped,

---

and provides data, although she takes the account as historical and thus passes on to criminal matters. Klutz (*Exorcism Stories*, 249–50) notes that the circumstances would have been ideal for an accusation of magic. C. de Vos ("Finding a Charge That Fits: The Accusation against Paul and Silas at Philippi (Acts 16.19-21)," *JSNT* 74 [1999] 51–63) claims that the accusation is the practice of magic. Andy M. Reimer ("Virtual Prison Breaks: Non-Escape Narratives and the Definition of 'Magic,'" in Todd E. Klutz, ed., *Magic in the Biblical World: From the Rod of Aaron to the Ring of Solomon* [JSNTS 245; London: T&T Clark, 2003] 125–39, esp. 133–36), supports this interpretation. At the basis of this view is an attempt at historical reconstruction (although that is not A. M. Reimer's interest) by making the charges plausible. Plausibility is not the author's objective.

61 On the absence of Timothy, see p. 387 n. 14.

62 Verses 20 and 21 have parallel conclusions with end stress: "being Jews . . . being Romans."

63 On ἐκταράσσω and related words, see Spicq, *Lexicon*, 3:372–76. Words from this stem are common in descriptions of social disorders. In the present context, note Josephus *Bell.* 1.216; 4.495; *Vit.* 103; 1 Macc 3:5; 7:22; the letter of Claudius to Alexandria addressing conflicts between Jews and polytheists (*P. Lond.* 1912, 73–74); and *CPJ* 441 (Jewish revolt in Cyrene). Similar charges appear in 17:6 (Thessalonica) and 24:5 (Jerusalem).

64 A. N. Sherwin-White, *Roman Society and Roman Law in the New Testament* (Oxford: Clarendon, 1963) 80. The τὰ ἔθνη ("the nations," often "gentiles") of D* 2412* d may be a response to the perceived difficulty.

65 On Roman views toward and actions against proselytism by Jews, see Smallwood, *The Jews*, 130, 206–10, 212, 219, 379–81, and 471–73.

66 When Luke wishes to say "attempt to convince" or "persuade," he uses πείθω. See, for example, Acts 5:36; 18:4. Luke does not, at this point, present the Jesus movement as "true Judaism" (cf. Conzelmann, 131). Krodel (310) notes that v. 21 is similar to Peter's declaration in 10:28 and observes that both are incorrect.

67 See, for example, Xenophon *Mem.* 1.3.1-3 (Socrates). Cassius Dio (57.18.5) says that Jews were banished from Rome in 19 CE because they were converting many Romans to their ἔθη ("customs"). On the charges, see Willem C. van Unnik, "Die Anklage gegen die Apostel in Philippi (Apostelgeschichte xvi 20f)," in *Sparsa Collecta* (3 vols.; Leiden: Brill, 1973) 1:374–85; and Rapske, *Roman Custody*, 116–19.

68 One of the many accusations made against Marc Antony was the abandonment of his ancestral gods (Cassius Dio 50.23.3–4). Tacitus (*Hist.* 5.5), writing in the wake of two revolts, characterized Jewish customs as depraved and ridiculous (*Iudaeorum mos absurdus sordidusque*).

69 Cf. Weiser, 2:436.

70 The alternation between "leaders" (ἄρχοντας) in v. 20 and στρατηγοί ("chief magistrates") elsewhere in the chapter is probably no more than elegant variation. Cf. Cadbury and Lake, 195. Technically, στρατηγοί is inexact, usually equivalent to Latin *praetor* and common for the magistrates of Greek cities. See Barrett, 2:789.

71 *ILS* 6087, the charter of a Roman colony at Urso in Baetica from the Flavian era (69–96 C.E.) §102 sets out rules for legal procedures, including a number of hours for both plaintiff and defendant.

whipped, incarcerated, and secured in stocks.[72] The chief difficulty is that Paul and Silas do not state that they are Roman citizens and, as such, could not be beaten unless convicted of crime.[73] The answer to this dilemma is that citizenship is a trump card that the narrator will not play until he is ready.[74] The atmosphere of this experience (and other trial scenes in Acts) is well evoked in Apuleius's account of a youth wrongly accused of murder:

> The grieving father inflamed the council and the people too with so much pity and such intense anger that they wanted to dispense with the nuisance of a trial, with its clear demonstrations by the prosecution and studied evasions by the defense. They shouted in unison that this curse on the people should be punished by the people, crushed under a rain of stones.
>
> The magistrates meanwhile were afraid of the danger to themselves if sedition should arise from the small seeds of anger and go on to destroy public order and civic government. Some of them interceded with the councilors, others restrained the common people, arguing that a verdict ought to be rendered with due process and customary procedure, that the allegations of both sides should be examined, and that a sentence should then be pronounced in a civilized manner. They must not, like savage barbarians or uncontrolled tyrants, condemn a man unheard: in a time of peace and tranquility that would be a dreadful example to set for future generations.[75]

■ **24** Paul and Silas were less fortunate. The style of popular narration attributes the tasks of stripping and whipping to the magistrates in person. Their attitude toward the presumed miscreants emerges in the subsequent order: maximum security is called for. The jailer responds by placing his charges in the innermost cell[76] and securing[77] their feet in stocks.[78] This stringent security will be a foil for the subsequent miracle.

■ **25-26** Cast into an earthly hell, Paul and Silas respond with song and prayer, enchanting the other prisoners. Far from the groans and laments such injustice and abuse would justify, they gave themselves to prayer and hymns of praise, devotions that moved even the hearts of calloused criminals to silence. Their conduct reveals that they are genuine "philosophers."[79] As in 4:31, the

---

The duovirs could, however, inflict floggings and "imprison vagrants" without trial, according to Barbara Levick, *The Government of the Roman Empire: A Sourcebook* (Totowa, N.J.: Barnes & Noble, 1985) 61.

72 Chrysostom (*Hom.* 35) chastises the officials for failure to examine the accused.

73 Foakes Jackson, 157. On the various statutes and the observance thereof, see John C. Lentz, *Luke's Portrait of Paul* (SNTSMS 77; Cambridge: Cambridge University Press, 1993) 120–30.

74 See pp. 554–56.

75 Apuleius *Metam.* 10.6 (LCL; trans. J. A. Hansen; Cambridge, Mass.: Harvard University Press, 1989) 225–27.

76 The inner part of a jail was the darkest and least safe. Cf. the "Martyrs of Lyons" (Eusebius *H.E.* 5.1.27); the *Martyrdom of Pionius* 11; and, especially, the *Passio Perpetuae* 3.5–6 (= Musurillo, *Christian*, 70, 150, and 108).

77 On this verb ἀσφαλίζω ("secure"), see Spicq (*Lexicon*, 1:218–19), who shows that it belongs to the language of police procedure.

78 Verse 24 is a characteristically Lucan sentence in the form of a relative clause. The D-Text (Boismard, *Texte*, 273) alters it to a conventional construction.

79 Socrates is the primary model of such conduct. According to Plato (*Phaedo* 60d) he composed a hymn while in custody. Diogenes Laertius (2.42) quotes the alleged beginning. Epictetus discusses this tradition in *Diss.* 4.4.23. In 2.6.27 he says, "A platform and a prison is each a place, the one high, the other low; but your moral purpose can be kept the same, if you wish to keep it the same, in either place. And then we shall be emulating (ζηλωταί) Socrates, when we are able to write paeans in prison" (trans. W. A. Oldfather, *Epictetus I* (LCL; Cambridge, Mass.: Harvard University Press, 1925) 253. Other parallels are Philostratus *Vit. Apoll.* 4.36 and Lucian *Icar.* 1. There is an interesting reflex of this incident in *Act. Thom.* 108: the other prisoners ask Thomas to pray, hoping, no doubt, for a hymn that will liberate them. He sings the Hymn of the Pearl, which tells of a different sort of liberation. For other examples of such "spiritualization," see Erik Peterson, *Frühkirche, Judentum und Gnosis: Studien und Untersuchungen* (Freiburg: Herder, 1959) 183–208. Jewish parallels are Dan 6:22 and *T. Jos.* 8:5. (On the last see n. 95.) The *Martyrdom of Pionius* 18.12 (Musurillo, *Christian*, 160) reports that the incarcerated Christians sang. This is probably conventional, possibly derived from Acts. Juvenal, characteristically, noted the

earth reverberated in response to their prayer. The doors popped open and their fetters fell off. Paul, like the apostles in chap. 5 and Peter alone in chap. 12, has become the beneficiary of a miraculous prison rescue. Readers await the pair's surreptitious trip to Lydia's, hoping that no servant will cause difficulty at her door.

■ **27** Before relating this adventure, the narrator's all-seeing eye turns to the jailer, whom the disturbance has awakened. Drawing the obvious inference from the open doors, he drew his sword, preferring suicide to execution for failing in his duty.[80]

■ **28-30** As the blade was about to descend, this poor fellow was halted by reassuring words from the all-seeing Paul: every prisoner was in place. Paul adds to his manifestation of philosophical virtue a demonstration of good citizenship. The strength of his charismatic character kept all the prisoners from flight. Recognizing at least one epiphany and its source, the jailer rushed into the lockup and threw himself at his rescuers' feet, laying before them the essential question: "What must I do to be saved?" That is a question for which the two prisoners have an answer, communicated to the entire household. The injuries of Paul and Silas were washed; for the jailer and his people there promptly followed the bath of regeneration.[81] Thereafter the two entered his private quarters for a family meal.[82] All in all, it was quite a day.

Excursus: Prison Escapes in Acts[83]

This is the third and climactic account of a miraculous event in a prison. Suitably for its environment, Acts 16:25-34 is also the most Greco-Roman in flavor.[84] Although the primary focus of research on prison escapes and door miracles has been on their role in the propagation of new cults, the event (and its opposite, the blocking of a door) occurs widely, in material ranging from magic[85] to myth to fiction.[86]

The primary context in the Greco-Roman world was the cult of Dionysus.[87] His capacity to liberate

flip side of this coin: even astrologers could put incarceration on their résumés as proof of their "philosophic" virtue (*Sat.* 6.560–64.)

80 For various rationales—and despair of the same—about this behavior, see Weaver, *Plots*, 266 n. 169.

81 Cf. also Bede (70), who calls this a "beautiful exchange" (*pulcra rerum varietas*).

82 On the jailer and his family, see Matson, *Household Conversion*, 154–68.

83 Major surveys of this theme include Otto Weinreich, *Gebet und Wunder: Zwei Abhundlungen zur Religions- und Literaturgeschichte* (Tübinger Beiträge zur Altertumswissenschaft 5; Stuttgart: Kohlhammer, 1929) 169–444 (= *Religionsgeschichtliche Studien* [Stuttgart: Kohlhammer, 1968]) 1–298); Kratz, *Rettungswunder*; and Weaver, *Plots*. Cf. also Richard Pervo, "The Literary Genre of the Acts of the Apostles" (Diss., Harvard University, 1979, 54–90); and idem, *Profit*, 21–24, 147–48. For a review of research, see Weaver, *Plots*, 11–22. Weinreich focuses on the religio-historical context, Kratz on form-critical aspects, Pervo on literary issues, and Weaver upon a myth-critical approach. Note also Talbert, 154–55; and Fitzmyer, 586.

84 The previous stories, in 5:19-21 and 12:5-17, involved angelophanies.

85 Magical door miracles do not play a prominent part in current discussions, but they were important. (American children probably learn "open sesame" before they know what sesame is.) "Even some magicians (γόητες) loose bonds and open doors with incantations" (Origen *Cels.* 2.34). Texts include *PGM* 1.97–104; 12.160–178; and 26.312–320. Cf. also Lucian *Gallus* 28. The ability to loose bonds and deliver himself from confinement is one of Simon's boasts: Ps.-Clem. *Rec.* 2.9. See Reitzenstein, *Hellenistische Wundererzählungen*, 120–22; and Albert Dieterich, *Abrasax: Studien zur Religionsgeschichte des spätern Altertums* (Leipzig: Teubner, 1891) 190. On these see Reimer, "Virtual Prison Breaks," 125–39, esp. 128–133.

86 Examples include Chariton *Chaer.* 3.7; 4.2–3; *Ephesian Tale* 3.12; 4.4; *Babylonian Tale* (74a–78a); Apuleius *Metam.* 6.9–24; Achilles Tatius *Leuc. Clit.* 6.1–2; *Ethiopian Story* 8.6–14; Lucian *Tox.* 27–34; and Philostratus *Vit. Apoll.* 4.38–44. Cf. Longus *Daphn.* 2.20–29. Cf. also Pervo, *Profit*, 147 n. 15.

87 Weaver, *Plots*, 49. He reviews the myth and its functions on pp. 32–59. Others who relate Acts 16:11-40 to the shape of the Dionysiac myth as found in the *Bacchae* include Matthews, *First Converts*, 75–82; and Lillian Portefaix, *Sisters Rejoice: Paul's Letter to the Philippians and Luke-Acts as Seen by First-Century Philippian Women* (ConBNT 20; Stockholm: Almqvist & Wiksell, 1988) 169–71.

himself and his followers from bonds was a basic symbol of his role as the god who freed women and men from the burdens, restrictions, and boredom of life. In the competitive religious environment of the Hellenistic and Roman eras, other religious movements appropriated this theme, for the vivid picture of shattering barriers was too potent to leave in the sole possession of the devotees of Dionysus.[88] Among these competitors was Judaism. Fragment 3 of Artapanus represents the competitive, "syncretistic" manifestation of the prison break, while 3 Maccabees is arguably a direct confrontation with the cult of Dionysus.[89]

Further testimony to the vitality of this symbol comes from its transformation and adoption into narrative fiction. The primary characters of the romantic novels and other fictional heroes experienced incarceration and torture at the hands of cruel opponents and also enjoyed eventual delivery. Whether these deliverances seem "miraculous" by our criteria is not the primary issue. All were epiphanies, so to speak, of the god(s) or providence that controlled the plot.[90] Liberation was a fundamental desire of nearly everyone. This is why it was a constituent element in the Dionysiac myth and why other "missionary" religions (and/or "religions of salvation") embraced it.

The question of an intertextual relationship between Euripides' *Bacchae* (which, although it is the primary source of the myth, is a piece of literature rather than mythography) goes back to Origen's response to the earlier anti-Christian writer Celsus, who had contrasted Dionysus's rescue of himself with Jesus' failure to do so. In reply, Origen pointed out that Peter and Paul had, like Dionysus and his followers, had been delivered from prison and bonds (Origen *Cels.* 2.34). Whether non-Christians found this riposte effective is not known, but it did raise, no doubt unwittingly, a genuine theological problem that goes to the heart of the debate about Luke's alleged "theology of glory." Be that as it may, the intertextual question continues to be debated. Because of the proliferation of this originally mythic theme, it is not necessary to hypothesize that Luke made direct use of the *Bacchae*, but use is not unlikely.[91]

In the course of time proponents of various persons and cults took increasing pains to look like law-abiding supporters of civic life and social benefactors. Far from being bludgeoned—if not, like Pentheus, assassinated—officials are won over. This "apologetic" quality is highly apparent in the prose account that seems furthest removed from the Dionysiac myth: Philostratus's *Apollonius of Tyana* (8.34–38).[92] Although Apollonius can free himself from fetters and does so twice (7.38; 8.30),[93] he confidently awaits Roman justice and receives his vindication. He could have taken Paul as his model.

Through this remarkable adventure Luke proclaims the miraculous vindication of the Christian movement at Philippi. Although it is faintly possible that he took up the story from tradition, greater probability resides on the side of Lucan composition. Its place in the conventional missionary scheme,

88 Weaver (*Plots*, 53–57) discusses some of these.

89 For a recent discussion of Moses' liberation in Artapanus, see Weaver, *Plots*, 64–78. J. R. C. Cousland assembles some of the arguments for polemic against Dionysiac religion in 3 Maccabees: "Dionysus Theomachos? Echoes of the *Bacchae* in 3 Maccabees," *Bib* 82 (2001) 539–48. (3 Maccabees does not report a classic prison break, but it does describe, in 6:1-20, an epiphany delivering a vast horde of Jewish prisoners.)

90 This view differs from that of Weaver, who limits epiphanies to the overtly supernatural or extraordinary. For Jews (and Christians), the rising of the sun was an epiphany of God, while Greeks understood the gift of wine as an epiphany of Dionysus. The Sarapis Aretalogy from Delos acknowledges, in the prose section, that its adherents maintained their temple by winning a lawsuit. This was attributed to the action of the god (lines 25–30). The accompanying poem supplies miraculous details (lines 84–90). One would not be surprised if their adversaries said that the worshipers of Sarapis had bribed the judges. (See Appendix 2.)

91 Recent arguments in favor of dependence on Euripides include R. Seaford, "Thunder, Lightning, and Earthquake in the *Bacchae* and the Acts of the Apostles," in Alan B. Lloyd, ed., *What Is a God? Studies in the Nature of Greek Divinity* (London: Duckworth, 1997), on which see Weaver, *Plots*, 269–71.

92 Weaver (*Plots*, 61 n. 114) calls this story "an indirect and relatively late witness" to the tradition and provides an outline that shows how Philostratus continues the pattern.

93 Apollonius's actions come quite close to the realm of "magic," since no direct divine agent is cited and he alone breaks his bonds. On this see Reimer, "Virtual Prison Breaks."

the affinities with Euripides, the author's interest in parallel episodes involving Peter and Paul, and the complexity of the story argue against the use of a probable source from the Pauline tradition.[94]

The account began (v. 25) in the very depths of night,[95] with Paul and Silas worshiping and the prisoners attentive.[96] The narrator's viewpoint is clear. He does not speak of "the other prisoners." The epiphany comes, in the approved fashion, "suddenly."[97] An earthquake of apocalyptic force[98] causes the doors to fly open and the fetters to fall off. All of this was unremarkable to William Ramsay: "[A]ny one that has seen a Turkish prison will not wonder" at these events.[99] The ancient narrator expected the audience to recognize a miracle.

The release evokes the liberation of the Maenads in *Bacchae* 443–48 (fetters loosed and doors opened), while the entire scene includes many of the events and motifs found in 576–659,[100] including singing Maenads (cf. v. 25), an earthquake permitting flight (vv. 26-27), and refusal of the god to escape (v. 28). No less interesting are the parallels between Pentheus (king of Thebes and chief persecutor) and the jailer. In response to the quake (and a flash of fire, unparalleled here in Acts), Pentheus seized his sword and rushed in, later dropping the sword (*Bacchae* 627, 635).[101] If the possibility of transforming the principal villain into a supportive character is accepted, these similarities are difficult to dismiss, since the epiphanic phenomena could be attributed to a general pattern, but the specific behavior of Pentheus is Euripides' own creation.

Unlike Pentheus, the jailer[102] knew an epiphany when he saw one, but the epiphany he perceived was not the earthquake. The sight of the open doors led him to conclude (it would not do to have him see whether the shackles remained secure) that the prison was empty. Like many a character in ancient story, he attempts

94 Of the three prison adventures in Acts, chap. 12 has the best claim to be based on a source. Even if one were to posit a source for this story, that fact would contribute little, if anything, to the understanding of the passage. The similarities between Acts 16:19-40 and the story of Demetrius and Antiphon in Lucian's *Toxaris* 27–34, noted by Eduard Zeller ("Eine griechische Parallele zu der Erzählung Apostelgeschichte 16, 19ff.," *ZWTh* 10 [1865] 103–8) should not be dismissed as few and superficial (Barrett, 2:792). Both stories feature someone wrongly imprisoned who refused to take advantage of the opportunity to escape and ultimately received legal vindication. It is not impossible that Luke made some use of a short story, since Lucian evidently took the tale from a source, but the more important issue is that the general outline had a place in literature and was not restricted to miracles of liberation. See Pervo, *Profit*, 23–24; and idem, "With Lucian: Who Needs Friends? Friendship in the *Toxaris*," in John Fitzgerald, ed., *Greco-Roman Perspectives on Friendship* (Resources for Biblical Study 34; Atlanta: Scholars Press, 1997) 163–80, esp. 170–72. Haenchen (501–4) views the episode as a Lucan creation, while Dibelius (*Studies*, 23–24) and Conzelmann (132) attribute it to a source, without specifying that it belongs to Philippi. Lüdemann (182) also speaks of a "tradition," which may not even have named Paul and Silas.

95 Apollonius once loosed his bonds at midnight: Philostratus *Vit. Apoll.* 8.30. At this time Moses was freed from prison (Artapanus frg. 4). In Acts, night is the time for rescue (5:19; 9:24; 12:6; 27:27). See P. G. Müller, "*νύξ*," *EDNT* 2:481–83; and Weiser, 1:285, 2:437.

96 The Greek text of *T. Jos.* 8:4-5 is quite similar to Acts 16:24-25. Verse 4 reports that Joseph was beaten and cast into Pharaoh's dungeon, where (v. 5) Mme. Potiphar came and heard (*ἐπηκροᾶτο*) him praising (*ὕμνουν*) God. Both Greek words are rare in the NT. The latter is a *hapax legomenon*, while the former appears only in Mark 14:26||Matt 26:30; Heb 2:12, in a citation.

97 Cf. 2:2 (Pentecost).

98 *Σεισμὸς μέγας*: Mark 13:8 (eschatological); Matt 28:2 (resurrection of Jesus); cf. Rev 6:12; 11:13; 16:18. Earthquakes are standard features of the end-time repertory: Amos 8:8; 9:5; Ezek 38:19; Joel 2:10; *Ass. Mos.* 10:4; *4 Ezra* 5:8; 9:3; *2 Bar.* 70:8.

99 Ramsay, *St. Paul the Traveller,* 221. On the same page, he explains the prisoners' failure to flee as due to "the semi-oriental mob in the Aegean lands." Cadbury and Lake (198) already devastated these crude rationalizations.

100 See n. 91.

101 For more details, see Seaford, "Thunder, Lightning, and Earthquake in the *Bacchae* and the Acts of the Apostles," 139–48.

102 The jailer is named "the faithful [perhaps 'convert'] Stephanas" (*ὁ πιστὸς Στεφανάς*) in 614. 2147. The source for this is probably 1 Cor 1:16. It is possible

suicide,[103] only to be stopped, like many a character in ancient story, by someone who intervenes.[104] That someone is Paul, who knows both that the jailer is about to kill himself[105] and, despite the profound darkness and the existence of multiple cells, that the count is complete. This is useful omniscience, and it has the desired effect.[106] The prison keeper perceives that no one but a god or a beneficiary of divine assistance could know these things. On a more mundane level, Paul further demonstrates his virtue: like Socrates he refuses to flee custody when he has the opportunity (Diogenes Laertius 2.24). The jailer treats the affair as a theoxeny.[107]

■ **31-34** After proper acknowledgment of their status and benefaction, he removed the pair from confinement[108] and posed his famous question, the viewpoint of which is no less Christian in perspective than the answer.[109] Said answer includes a promise that illustrates the household solidarity of ancient Mediterranean societies. The narrator is in such a hurry to follow this declaration with proclamation that the narrative seems displaced, leaving vv. 30-33 to take place out of doors or in some corridor.[110] These difficulties permit the same sequence as in the story of Lydia: proclamation of the message, baptism of the entire household,[111] and subsequent hospitality. The account is boldly unrealistic.[112] That Paul (and Silas) would find their injuries no impediment to evangelism is to be taken as a matter of course (cf. 14:19-20), but there was little time for adequate catechesis—these were not God-Fearers—which would have included, at a minimum, the refutation of

---

that the name appeared in the *Acts of Paul* (9/12) which are quite defective for Philippi, but do indicate an incarceration there. Chrysostom (*Hom.* 36) places jailers among the more rude and barbarous specimens of the human race.

103 Readers will think of 12:19. (The actual legal consequences for this individual are not material.)

104 Clitophon, the hero of *Leucippe*, is an appropriate example: "I held my sword up, poised to plunge it down through my throat. In the light of the full moon I saw two men running quickly towards me. . . . It was Menelaos and Satyros" (3.17; trans. J. J. Winkler, in Reardon, *Novels*, 217.) The chief function of Polycharmus, the faithful companion of Chaireas in *Callirhoe*, seems to be preventing the hero from committing suicide. For a list of references to attempted suicide in ancient fiction, see Kerenyi, *Romanliteratur*, 149; and Johnson, 300. Closer to the environment of Acts is *T. Jos.* 7:3 (Mme. Potiphar threatens to kill herself if Joseph will not yield).

105 The phrase μηδὲν πράξῃς σεαυτῷ κακόν (lit. "do nothing harmful to yourself" [v. 28]) looks like a Latinism, but it is probably popular Greek usage.

106 Conzelmann (132) lists a number of difficulties in the account.

107 Cf. 7:32 (of the theophany to Moses). The "loud voice" (μεγάλῃ φωνῇ) in which Paul speaks is appropriate to the dramatic setting, but this phrase is connected to epiphanies. See Weaver, *Plots*, 267, and his references. The vocative κύριοι in v. 30 is ambiguous. Its meaning could range from something like "gentlemen" to "lord gods." The old-fashioned English translation seeks to indicate that he addressed them as superior beings. Their answer shows that the Lord Jesus is the one to whom he should turn. Johnson (300) views the jailer's actions as a novelistic motif, with references. Schwartz ("Trial Scene," 125) says that the scene with the jailor functions in lieu of a defense speech.

108 The D text (Boismard, *Texte*, 274) states that, after taking the pair out of jail, the keeper saw to the securing of the others. This supplement—which, in actuality, would have taken a good deal of time, given the extent of the damage—reveals an editorial concern for tidy narration. Luke here, and even more so in v. 35, shows his focus and viewpoint. The other prisoners have but two parts to play: (1) listening to the missionaries at their devotions and (2) remaining orderly because of the numinous power of Paul, a power that reveals both his commitment and contribution to civic order, thus refuting the charges of disorder (v. 20). Thereafter the narrator abandons them.

109 Nock, *Conversion*, 9: "If such a man used phraseology of this sort, he could have meant only 'What am I to do in order to avoid any unpleasant consequences of the situation created by this earthquake?' *Soteria* and kindred words carried no theological implications; they applied to deliverance from perils by sea and land and disease and darkness and false opinions."

110 The relation between the locales of the jail and the keeper's house is left to the reader's imagination. The quake evidently awakened the jailer, but nothing is said about its extent. Since it was miraculous in origin, it could have been limited to the prison precincts. Cf. 4:31. Dibelius (*Studies*, 23), who noted the confusion, suspected that it was due to editing.

111 The balance of the household is introduced somewhat awkwardly in v. 32b, prompting the addition

polytheism and some summary treatment of the Creator and God of Israel, as well as Christology.[113] Baptism—like the earthquake—takes place "immediately,"[114] and appropriately so, for initiation into the Christian faith is an earthquake of sorts. Two sets of bonds have been released.[115] The subsequent meal gives the episode the character of an early Christian "baptismal vigil": a nocturnal event including proclamation of the word, followed by the celebration of baptism and the Eucharist.[116] The experience of the early Jerusalem community is recurring on gentile soil.[117] Luke has shifted the focus from the salvation of the imprisoned pair to the salvation of the jailer.[118] Another individual of relatively high status has been added, with his household, to the community.[119]

■ **35-36** Day dawns, bringing to light a number of questions. What will the public in general and the magistrates in particular think of that earthquake? Will the jailer now place before his superiors his revised opinion of his two most recent convicts? Will there now ensue a trial at which the insidious manipulations of the unscrupulous oracle-mongers will be exposed to the full light of truth? Each of these sequels is quite plausible. In fact, the magistrates had decided to throw in the towel. There presently arrived at the prison their official escort, bearing instructions to dismiss the pair. No grounds for this change of mind are provided. The jailer rushed off to inform his charges. Leave they must, but without further legal entanglement.

■ **37** The offer sounds good, but Paul would have none of it. He confronted the lictors with a catalogue of official misdeeds, informing them (and the readers) that he and Silas held Roman citizenship. One wonders why they had not raised this point earlier, as the punishments they had endured were illegal in the case of Roman citizens.[120] Be that as it may, Paul was prepared to assert his rights, to which he added the demand for a formal escort, a request that the horrified officials

---

of καί ("and") after "with" in the Byzantine text. Cf. the singular verbal forms in v. 34. The narrator keeps the focus on the jailer. Polhill (354, 356) is certain that infants were not included in the household baptisms.

112 For a very different view, see Rapske, *Roman Custody*, 115–34. His work, which contains much useful information, represents a dubious method: assuming that the account is quite historical, he supplies supplementary events supported by a number of rationalizations. Rapske concludes that Paul (Silas is ignored) did not reveal his Roman citizenship because this would have been disadvantageous to his mission. (This view was advanced by Theodor Mommsen, "Die Rechtsverhältnisse des Apostels Paulus," *ZNW* 2 [1902] 81–96, esp. 89–90.) The narrative says nothing about this rationale, which cannot explain why the citizenship was *ever* revealed. Rapske (*Roman Custody*, 128) states: "The text provides no warrant for asserting that the magistrates, taking the earthquake to be a sign of divine displeasure or simply recognizing their own illegal conduct, released Paul and Silas." This is correct, but the text does state that the magistrates ordered their release. If one cannot read the mind of the officials, one equally cannot read the mind of Paul. (When, however, it suits his argument, as on pp. 128–29, Rapske does not hesitate to explain the motivation of the officials). Finally, he almost completely ignores vv. 25-34, of which Fitzmyer (588) says: "[T]hese verses . . . resound with folkloric elements. It is an idyllic description of the deliverance of Paul and his companions."

113 A realistic description would have placed these actions in an appropriate space and at least given the jailer time to suggest that he attend to their injuries and other needs—not to mention finding some means of securing the other prisoners. Verse 33a is a pregnant construction, lit. "he washed from the wounds." See Cadbury and Lake, 199.

114 Boismard (*Texte*, 275) omits "immediately" in v. 33b, with evidence similar to that for its omission in v. 26.

115 So also Chrysostom *Hom.* 36.

116 Cf. Philippe Menoud, *Jesus Christ and the Faith: A Collection of Studies* (trans. E. M. Paul; PTMS 18; Pittsburgh: Pickwick, 1978) 89–90; Weiser, 2:439; and Barrett, 2:799. Krodel (313) aptly observes, "[E]very meal in Luke-Acts has sacramental overtones."

117 Cf. 2:46, where nourishment is taken with "joy," a noun (ἀγαλλίασις) formed from the same stem as the verb here (ἀγαλλιάω). On this, see also Johnson, 301.

118 Kratz, *Rettungswunder*, 486.

119 For the winning, or conversion, of jail guards, see *Mart. Perp.* 9.1; 16.4; Philostratus *Vit. Apoll.* 7.38; and *Act. Pet.* 1.1, wherein the jailer follows his wife into the faith and gives Paul leave to go where he will.

120 The relevant law is the *Lex Julia* on *vis publica* ("lawful use of force"). Earlier enactments included a

promptly granted. The mission to Philippi thus ended with a splendid triumphal procession, since, rights notwithstanding, the magistrates did, after all, think it best that the two depart, which, after making a pastoral call upon Lydia and those of her household, they do.[121]

Verse 35 came as a complete surprise, unalloyed by the absence of an explanation for the release. The stunning news of v. 35 pales in comparison to the next revelation: Paul and Silas are Roman citizens and thus the victims of gross injustice. His question is well structured and mellifluous, echoing at its close the accusation against him in vv. 20-21.[122] The claim to be a Roman is sufficient, as in 22:25, where it likewise brings fear to his antagonists. It is not likely that two whose appearance made them suitable for an arbitrary whipping and incarceration would be accepted as citizens on the strength of an oral declaration by one of them. The chief problem is, as noted, why the pair did not reveal their status before subjected to this painful dishonor. The proposal that they did claim citizenship but were not heard at the time[123] is both an unauthorized supplement to the narrative and an inadequate explanation. Paul will do just that in similar circumstances in 25:24.

■ **38-40** Moreover, if the two had failed to state their citizenship, no blame could have attached to the officials, who would have had reason for regret but not apprehension. Brian Rapske rightly refutes the claim that their cries went unheard,[124] but his own solution, that Paul did not wish to reveal his citizenship for strategic reasons, cannot explain why Paul subsequently raised the point.[125] Ancient readers would have been likely to view this as an episode in the endless competition for honor. Paul (and Silas), shamed by a public beating, reject the further shame of an ignominious expulsion, demanding an honorable escort. "Paul humiliates the magistrates who punished him."[126] The frustration of the accusers reveals that Roman law is not hostile to the new movement, however malign or incompetent some of its officials (of whom Pilate is the most outstanding example) may be.

Modern readers, on the other hand, are likely to wonder how the earthquake could have disappeared from the narrative. Apart from reminding the readers of where God stood on the question, its sole purpose is to lead to the jailer's conversion. Paul's vindication comes from the slowly grinding mill of Roman justice.[127] The numerous parallels with the experience of Peter in chap. 12 serve to heighten the contrast: whereas Peter was led out (ἐξάγω) of prison by divine intervention (12:17), Paul was led out (ἐξάγω) by the chief magistrates of the Roman colony of Philippi (16:39; cf. 16:37).[128]

The D-Text of vv. 35-40 shows that the conventional—and clearly more original—text lacks realism. In addition to the pedantic filling in of gaps and blanks, this account is much less vigorous, more fulsome and circumstantial, with more dialogue and careful attention to explanation and motivation. In order to invest the story with sequential logic the D-editor had to make some decisions. One of these was to assume that the earthquake could not or did not escape attention and thus to make it the grounds for the unexplained order to release the prisoners. In short, only in the D-Text is

Lex Valeria and a *Lex Porcia*. Digest 48.6.7 provides specific comments. Cicero indicates that, in Republican times, at least, low-status Roman citizens were subject to occasional abuse (*Verrines* 2.161). Acts does not view Paul as a citizen of humble birth. For other violations, see Conzelmann, 133.

121 Foakes Jackson and Lake (Lake and Cadbury, *Additional Notes*, 201) observe that the summaries in Acts shed much of their "biblical" character after chap. 15.

122 See n. 61. The opening and closing words, "beating," "Roman citizens," are the most important in the declaration. Note also the balanced contrast between "public" (δημοσίᾳ) beating and "secret" (λάθρᾳ) expulsion, the third words from the opening and the closing, respectively.

123 Marshall, 274; Bruce, 322.

124 Rapske, *Roman Custody*, 128–29.

125 See n. 112. Silas's possession of the Roman franchise is clearly ad hoc and passed over in silence by most commentators. Fitzmyer (590) can offer the inquiring reader no more than "So one must assume that Silas was also a Roman citizen."

126 Lentz, *Luke's Portrait*, 158. On this theme, see also Johnson, 303–4.

127 Cf. Tannehill, *Narrative Unity*, 2:154.

128 Other echoes include tight security (12:4-5; 16:24), the nocturnal setting (12:6; 16:25), the appearance of light in darkness (12:7; 16:29), chains that fell off (12:7; 16:26), doors that opened without human effort (12:10; 16:26), evident liability of the guards (12:19; 16:27), and the closure: both go to the home of a prominent woman convert and then go elsewhere (12:17-17; 16:40).

this a miracle of deliverance from prison.[129] Second, a reason is advanced for asking the pair to leave. They were not, of course, expelled, but merely advised to leave for their own protection.[130] The addition in v. 40 echoes 12:17, enhancing the parallelism between the deliverances of Peter and Paul. This is another indication that a diligent ancient Christian writer recognized the pattern.

Amidst some of the loose ends and improbable turns taken by this action-packed account are many symbols and cross-references. Paul, like Jesus, exorcises demons and suffers. The miraculous "release" from prison, when contrasted with the earlier accounts in chaps. 5 and 12, suggests that more confidence may be placed in Roman justice than in the Israelite authorities. The earthquake and its attendant actions symbolize rather than accomplish their eventual release. Within the story of the earthquake the author places the experience of the jailer. In bringing light (cf. 12:7) to the prison, he will be the one illumined. His literal rescue from death and disgrace symbolizes his spiritual deliverance. The open doors of the jail at Philippi were doors admitting gentiles to the faith.

One does not require commentators to learn that this is a fine story. Chap. 16 moves from the middle of Asia Minor into a bit of Rome residing upon long-grecized soil. There are adventures of many types and lessons for all, not least about what we call "politics" and "religion." Following a venerable pattern about the introduction of a new cult, the author shows the defeat of one ancient god (Apollo), evokes equality with another (Dionysus), and refutes charges against the Jesus movement, whose proponents, it transpires, are no less than true Romans. Early readers could admire its sociological realism,[131] and more recent experts its abundance of realistic detail. Yet, as "straight" history, it collapses at the most gentle application of the critical razor. A rapid read suggests a whole cloth, but in reality few threads are not left dangling. Haenchen, who wielded the sharpest of critical razors with penetrating deftness, concludes by letting Luke the historian off the hook, as all the "great Roman historians" did much the same.[132] Lüdemann correctly challenges this conclusion as a form of shallow apologetic.[133] To invoke a note of realism, things did not work out so well for Paul in Philippi.[134]

129 Examples of alternative explanations are these: the earthquake was confined to the prison building alone (cf. 4:31) and might not have set the town abuzz; the magistrates could have determined that a solid beating and a night in jail, followed by expulsion from the city, would discourage these rascals from returning. This is the proposal of Cadbury and Lake, 200. Cf. also Haenchen (498), who takes it as a fact, and Witherington, 499. For other conjectures, see Roloff, 248; and Schneider, 2:218. The language of v. 36 is not appropriate to persons being run out of town.

130 A further rationalization is the omission of (lit.) "in peace" from v. 36. This evidently seemed too Semitic to the editor (and rightly so). See Ropes, *Text*, 158. For the phrase in an appropriate context, see Luke 7:50; 8:48. Metzger (*Textual Commentary*, 399) states that the omission is accidental, but he makes no argument for this view. On the text note, see also Dibelius, *Studies*, 86–87; and the parallel in Lucian *Tox.* 33.

131 See Johnson, 302–4.

132 Haenchen, 504.

133 Lüdemann, 218.

134 See Weiser, 2:440.

17

17:1-15 Paul Visits Thessalonica and Beroea

1/ After leaving Philippi, Paul and
Silas took the road through
Amphipolis and Apollonia[a] and
came to Thessalonica, where
there was a Jewish synagogue.
2/ As was his normal practice,
Paul visited the congregation.
For three Sabbaths he lectured
on the Scriptures, 3/ showing
by interpretation[b] that the Messiah had to suffer and rise from
the dead. "This is the Messiah,
Jesus, the one about whom
I am telling you."[c] 4/ Some
of them were convinced and
attached themselves to Paul
and Silas, as did a large number
of devout gentiles and quite
a few prominent women.
5/ These conversions aroused
the envy of the Jews, who collected some of the worthless
loafers that loitered around
the city center into a mob and
thereby aroused the entire
populace. This mob converged
upon the house of Jason with
the intent of hauling Paul and
Silas before the assembly.
6/ Since they couldn't find
those two, they dragged Jason
and some believers to the
magistrates,[d] shouting: "These
people who are fomenting
rebellion everywhere are in
our midst! 7/ Jason is harbor-
ing them. In opposition[e] to the
decrees of Caesar they want to
set up another emperor,[f] claiming that Jesus rules." 8/ When
they heard these charges, the
mob and the officials became
thoroughly agitated. 9/ Jason
and the others were not
released until they had paid a
bond. 10/ As soon as darkness
fell, the believers sent Paul and
Silas on to Beroea. When they
got to Beroea, they entered the
synagogue.

17:11-15: Conventional Text

11/ Now the Jews there were of a
better quality[g] than those at
Thessalonica. They applied
themselves eagerly[h] to the
message and engaged in daily
scrutiny of the Scriptures to
discover whether the claims
might be true. 12/ Many, in

17:11-15: D-Text[m]

. . . to discover whether these
claims were[n] *just as Paul maintained them to be.* 12/ Many

fact,[i] came to believe, including a substantial number of upper-crust Greek women and quite a few men. 13/ Once the Jews of Thessalonica[j] had learned that Paul had also proclaimed the message of God in Beroea, they showed up there as well and threw the masses into disorder by their agitation.[k]

14/ The believers immediately sent Paul to the seacoast,[l] while Silas and Timothy remained behind. 15/ After those who were conducting Paul had got him to Athens, they returned with instructions for the other two to join him as soon as possible.

of them believed*; some did not.* [*A large number* (ἱκανοί) *of the gentile men and women* of the upper crust *came to believe*].[o] 13/ Once the Jews of Thessalonica had learned that the message of God had been proclaimed [ ] in Beroea, they showed up there as well and threw the *crowd* into disorder by their agitation. *This action went on and on.* 14/ The believers [ ] *therefore* (μὲν οὖν) sent Paul [ ][p] to the sea, but Silas and Timothy remained behind. 15/ *He passed by Thessaly, for he was prevented from proclaiming the message to them* . . . They returned with instructions [from Paul][q] for the other two to join him as soon as possible.

---

a With its usual interest in expanding the mission, the D-Text (Boismard, *Texte*, 280) allows readers to believe that Apollonia was a missionary station: "They came to Apollonia and went from there to Thessalonica." On this, see Strange, *Text*, 152.

b On the rhetorical meaning of *παρατίθημι* (lit. "set before"), see Johnson, 305.

c The D-Text (Boismard, *Texte*, 280) revises this, eliminating the second reference to "the Messiah" and "from the dead." The variants are less typical and thus have some force, but the support for them is weak.

d The finite verbs in vv. 5-6a are imperfects. One could construe the narrative as, in effect: "They wished to arraign Paul et al., but, failing in that endeavor, hauled Jason and whomever they could find before the magistrates." See BDF §327.

e BDF §214 (4) describes this usage of the preposition *ἀπέναντι* as "peculiar."

f The translation of *βασιλεύς* (lit. "king") is disputed. See, e.g., Cadbury and Lake, 206; Johnson, 307; and Fitzmyer, 596. This word is the standard term for those called in English the "Roman emperors" and is thus used to show the contrast implied: a rival claimant to the throne.

g Lit. "more noble" (*εὐγενέστεροι*). Superior breeding is reflected in manners and accompanies means. Cf. 4 Macc 6:5; 9:13; 10:3. Inversely, "upper-crust" (*εὐσχήμονες*) in v. 12 means "quite decent" but also acquires a connotation of status through metonymy. See Spicq, *Lexicon*, 2:93–96.

h On the phrase *μετὰ πάσης προθυμίας*, here rendered "eagerly" and taken with the following participle, see Jacob Kremer, "Einführung in die Problematik heutiger Acta-Forschung anhand von Apg 17, 10-13, in idem, *Actes*, 11–20.

i On the various meanings and uses of *μὲν οὖν* here (and elsewhere), see Moule, *Idiom Book*, 162–63.

j On the use of *ἀπό* to mean "of," see Cadbury and Lake, 207. (American English uses the same idiom: "people from New York" means "New Yorkers.")

k The participial phrase *καὶ ταράσσοντες* (lit. "and agitating") is absent from 𝔭[45] E P 049. 056. 0120. 0142 *al* 𝔐. Metzger (*Textual Commentary*, 403) attributes this to a visual error. Although it is faintly possible that the phrase was interpolated to conform to v. 8, it is more likely that it would have been removed as redundant, if not through homoeoteleuton.

l On the translation of the phrase *ἕως ἐπί*, see Conzelmann, 136; and Barrett, 2:819–20.

m Boismard, *Texte*, 284–87.

n The conventional text has a rare oblique optative: *εἰ ἔχοι . . . οὕτως*. The D-Text is standard *Koine*, with the indirect question in the indicative (*ἔχει*). It is possible that the optative was an Alexandrian correction, but more likely the editor of the D-Text changed the mood because of the following correlative *καθώς* ("just as").

o The bracketed material is omitted by Boismard, *Texte*, 285. Bezae once more reduces the prominence of women.

p Omitting ἕως. The Byzantine tradition reads ὡς, which could suggest a ruse. This is probably secondary. The author evidently strengthened the "improper prep." ἕως with ἐπί, leading to the varied corrections.

q "From Paul" (D), "from him" (E vg sy^{p} sa) is not admitted by Boismard, but it is a typical bit of pedantry and well attested. Cf. Col 4:10.

Analysis

Chapter 17 treats the initial missions to Thessalonica and Beroea (vv. 1-15), followed by Paul's famous sojourn in Athens. The first two stations return to the pattern used in chaps. 13–14.[1] Paul preaches in the synagogue, in accordance with the formula "Jews first,"[2] enjoying some success among Jews and prominent God-Fearers, especially women. This provokes jealousy from "the Jews," who create disturbances that lead to Paul's departure from both places. The narrator has little interest in the efforts required to found a community and none whatsoever in what happened between the initial foundation and the persecution, which is both unsuccessful and yet somehow leads to Paul's departure.[3] Verses 1-9 contradict 1 Thessalonians, which views the recipients as former polytheists (1:10) and Jesus as a heavenly savior rather than an earthly monarch (Acts 17:7).[4] Verses 6-9 refer to Jason and his house, circumstantial details that lead critics—not least because of the confusing nature of the verses—to suspect tradition. Acceptance of this source adds nothing to the understanding of the passage, since Jason makes no meaningful contribution.[5]

The reader is permitted to assume that no synagogue was located until they reached Thessalonica, which had

1 Acts 13:16 echoes 14:19-20.

2 See Pervo, *Dating*, 104–5.

3 Cf. Haenchen, 510.

4 There are other differences: In Acts, the mission lasts for roughly three weeks. (The phrase in v. 2 is an accusative of duration and should not be twisted to mean "on three Sabbaths" over a longer course of time. See Cadbury and Lake, 202–3.) Had Luke not wished to indicate that they were consecutive, he could have used a genitive or dative expression. 1 Thess 2:9 and Phil 4:15 presume a longer stay, as Paul worked while there and twice received funds from Philippi. Another strong contrast is in the respective portraits of the believers. Luke speaks of well-to-do women and views the under- and unemployed ἀγοραῖοι ("people who loitered about the civic center") with contempt. Paul regarded the Macedonian believers as poor (2 Cor 8:2), whereas Luke shows converts from upper strata, enemies from the underclass. In short, Paul stresses the poverty of this community of former gentiles, Luke the relative affluence of Paul's Jewish and God-fearing converts. The letter indicates that Timothy played an important role at Thessalonica (1:1; 3:2, 6); in Acts he is not mentioned. For a succinct statement of the difficulties of harmonizing Acts 17:1-9 and 1 Thessalonians, see Earl Richard, *First and Second Thessalonians* (SacPag 11; Collegeville, Minn.: Liturgical Press, 1995) 4–5, and, in greater detail, Malherbe, *Thessalonians*, 47–57, who seeks to coordinate the two accounts.

5 Gerd Lüdemann (*The Acts of the Apostles: What Really Happened in the Earliest Days of the Church* [Amherst, N.Y.: Prometheus Books, 2005] 221–23) argues for v. 1a as coming from tradition. This is possible, but it is also the only route leading from Philippi to Thessalonica (so also Conzelmann, 134). Likewise, the officials (πολιτάρχαι) of v. 8 are found in many cities (see n. 21), and the phrase "take bail" can be no more than a circumstantial invention, as Lüdemann admits. His support of the historical background of the Jason episode appeals in part to the confused grammar and also to 1 Thess 2:14. Grammatical confusion may result from the inept insertion of source material, but the structure of the entire unit is rather tight. 1 Thess 2:14 is quite probably part of a later interpolation (although Luke may have read it in his edition of Paul's letters). Weiser (2:443–45) offers a detailed discussion of the traditional elements identified by others. He views the tradition about Jason as independent of the itinerary material in v. 1. The account is thoroughly revised (and/or invented) by the author. This is also the view of Barrett, 2:807. Roloff (249) sagely observes that the material about Jason reflects a Thessalonian perspective. One might suspect that Jason was a Jew who had converted and become, like Lydia (16:15) or Titius Justus (18:7), the head and/

been founded in 316 BCE and had survived the vicissitudes of the Hellenistic and early Roman eras.[6] This was the provincial capital, a "free" Greek city, with its own constitution and the largest Aegean port after Ephesus and Corinth. In its synagogue[7] Paul lectured[8] (i.e., preached) on three (presumably consecutive) Sabbaths.[9] The full-fledged Jews were evidently not particularly receptive.[10] Among God-Fearers, including a number of well-connected and prosperous women, the results were different. Jealousy over the loss of prominent adherents provoked Jews[11] to action, in this case the tried-and-true formula of stirring up an urban riot. It was assumed that such "ruffians from the dregs of society" (Revised English Bible), as Luke unflatteringly labels them (v. 5),[12] were riot-prone. Paul's Jewish opponents therefore did not find it difficult to piece together a mob to assault the house of Jason. Violence seems to have distracted the narrator, but the sequence resolves the problem: Jason was Paul's host.

When their plan to extract Paul and Silas from this domicile failed—the narrator does not explain why the two were not present—the mob snatched whom they could, and arraigned them before a conveniently gathered democratic assembly,[13] charging the believers with fomenting treason and Jason with lending them aid and comfort. There are difficulties: v. 6 describes, in the first instance, the believers not as local converts but as itinerant agitators. One would expect the accusing Jews—or the magistrates—to undertake a search for Paul and Silas, but the entire affair ends with the receipt of a peace bond from Jason and, presumably, from those they had subjected to a citizen's arrest.[14] Since the real source of unrest is Paul, he will leave and, just to be on the safe side, will do so surreptitiously, by night.

Comment

■ **2-3** Allusions to other passages abound. Paul's "normal" practice invites comparison with Jesus.[15] Verses 2-3 evoke the creedal assertion of 9:22 (Paul)[16] and the arguments of Jesus and Peter that the suffering of the Messiah was part of the divine plan and prophesied in Scripture.[17] By such intratextuality Luke establishes and demonstrates the continuity of the message. He need have said no more than that Paul proclaimed the message.

or host of the nascent community—although, in that case v. 6 would be more likely to read "Jason and some *other* believers" (as in v. 9).

6 For the political history of Thessalonica and a thorough survey of the archaeological data, see Holland L. Hendrix, "Thessalonica," *ABD* 6:523–27.

7 There is evidence for a Samaritan synagogue in the late Roman era (see Hendrix, "Thessalonica"). Witherington (504) claims *CIJ* 693 as evidence for a synagogue in the late second century CE or later, but that text is a tombstone.

8 On the meaning of διαλέγομαι, see Scott Shauf, *Theology as History, History as Theology: Paul in Ephesus in Acts 19* (BZNW 133; Berlin: de Gruyter, 2005) 163 n. 127. It does not refer to dialogue or discussion.

9 For the content of what he said, readers will do better to turn to 13:16-41 than to seek to explicate the summary in vv. 2-3.

10 Note the contrast between τινες ("some") Jews and the "large number" (πλῆθος πολύ) of God-Fearers.

11 As Conzelmann (135) observes, "the Jews" means Jews who did not accept the message, as the D-Text makes explicit. See below.

12 On the pejorative meaning of the adjective ἀγοραῖος, see BDAG, 14, *s.v.*, and Malherbe, *Thessalonians*, 64. The usage is at least as old as Aristophanes *Frogs* 1015. Plutarch describes Scipio as utilizing ἀγοραῖοι, characterized as low-born (ἀγεννεῖς) and former slaves (δεδουλευκότας) to create a mob (*Aem.* 38.3). Philo has little good to say about the idle citizenry, whom he blames for anti-Jewish riots in Alexandria (*Flacc.* 33–41). On the subject, see Moyer V. Hubbard, "Urban Uprisings in the Roman World: The Social Setting of the Mobbing of Sosthenes," *NTS* 51 (2005) 416–28, esp. 422–23.

13 See p. 421.

14 See below.

15 The only other occurrence of κατὰ τὸ εἰωθός is in Luke 4:16. (The D-Text improves this by placing "Paul" in the nominative (Boismard, *Texte*, 280.) Paul in synagogues: 9:20; 13:4, 14; 14:1; 17:19; 18:4, 7; 19:8.

16 As elsewhere (see on 1:4), the text shifts from indirect to direct speech.

17 Jesus: see Luke 24:26-27, and 32 (which also uses the verb διανοίγω, "open"). See also Tannehill, *Narrative Unity*, 2:206–7. For Peter, see, e.g., 3:18. Lucan theology does not envision the death of Jesus as because of or for the redemption of human sins in general.

■ **4** The D-Text of v. 4 is different. Boismard prints: "Some of them were convinced [ ] **by the teaching, many** of the devout Greeks [ ] and quite a few **upper-crust** (εὐσχήμονες) women." The primary motive appears to be revision for its own sake.[18] Bezae converts the latter into "wives" of prominent citizens.[19] Verse 6 exhibits similar variation, replacing "jealous" with "unbelieving," "taking up" (lit. προσλαβόμενοι) with "gathering" (συστράψαντες), and προαγαγεῖν with ἐξαγαγεῖν for the act of bringing them before the assembly.[20]

■ **5** The disappointment of the Jews is quite intelligible, for, by siphoning off a number—which could not in any circumstances have been very large—of the God-Fearers, Paul had deprived their community of important financial and political support. It will come as no shock to readers that the method elected by these aggrieved persons is the generation of a mob the presence of which will encourage the lawful authorities[21] into prompt and favorable action. When required to formulate charges, they were on thin ice, since alienation of the affection of gentile supporters lacked statutory backing. "In the absence of any legal ground for indicting Paul and Silas, the only method was to adopt the tactics practised at Philippi and stir up the populace. This was not a hard matter. . . ."[22] The accusation, given in direct speech, has a preface: the accused (who are not, in fact, present) are international agitators.[23] This is far from subtle irony: those who accuse Paul of fomenting riots foment a riot to strengthen their case.[24] Although impossible at the dramatic date, this informs readers of the wide impact of the Pauline mission. Specifically, they act in a manner contrary to imperial decrees, alleging that Jesus is the true emperor.[25] Learned efforts to specify the decrees in question are probably in vain.[26] Apart from 16:20-21, the best-attested source is the charges made against Jesus (Luke 23:2; cf. 23:5).

18 This revision eliminates their gentile status. 𝔓[74] A D 33.81 *pc* lat bo insert "and" between "devout" and "Greeks," making two groups, one of which is gentile.

19 This is typical. See Pervo, "Social Aspects." The conventional text can also be rendered as "wives," although with less probability. Boismard (*Texte*, 281–82) argues that Bezae is conflate.

20 See Boismard, *Texte*, 282. The first of these conforms the text to 14:2. The verb συστρέφω is common in D: 10:41; 11:28; 16:39.

21 On the "politarchs" (πολιτάρχαι), holders of an annual office that usually numbered between three and seven persons and was especially common in northern Greece, see G. H. R. Horsley, "The Politarchs," in Gill and Gempf, *Setting*, 2:419–31; and Taylor, "St Paul," 2460.

22 Rackham, 297.

23 See on 24:5. The verb ἀναστατάω occurs elsewhere only in 21:38, of "the Egyptian" rebel. The *NRSV*'s "turning the world upside down" removes the political significance of the term.

24 See below on 19:23-40. Suetonius, a contemporary of Luke, spoke of Jews at Rome fomenting disturbances *Chresto impulsore* (lit. "at the instigation of Chrestus," evidently "Christ"). This activity led to Claudius's expulsion of the Jews from Rome. By the early second century, Christians were associated with riots. This would explain Suetonius's confusion.

25 Talbert (157) aptly cites Justin *1 Apol.* 11 as an indication that this accusation was troublesome. He refers to his *Reading Luke: A Literary and Theological Commentary on the Third Gospel* (New York: Crossroad, 1983) 190–94 for evidence that readers would see this accusation as malicious.

26 See Edwin Judge, "The Decrees of Caesar at Thessalonica," *Reformed Theological Review* 30 (1971) 1–7, summarized by Hemer, *Book*, 167. "Decrees" (δόγματα) is difficult, since the sphere of imperial *maiestas* was covered by public statute. Witherington (508) appeals to 2 Thessalonians 2 to justify the historicity of the accusations. The contents of that chapter constitute a cogent argument against the authenticity of 2 Thessalonians. See Frank W. Hughes, *Early Christian Rhetoric and 2 Thessalonians* (JSNTS 30; Sheffield: Sheffield Academic Press, 1989). The D-Text intelligently deletes "the decrees," according to Boismard, *Texte*, 283 (with thin evidence). One might also ask whether an allegation of this sort might not have been referred to the Roman proconsul. Justin K. Hardin ("Decrees and Drachmas at Thessalonica: An Illegal Assembly in Jason's House [Acts 17.1-10a]," *NTS* 52 [2006] 29–49) proposes that the believers were accused of being an illegal voluntary association. The city may have had no such laws, but the Romans did not encourage the formation of *collegia*. Trajan considered it better for Nicomedia to burn than to have organized firefighters (Pliny *Ep.* 10.34). These solutions must tacitly assume that the mission lasted much

■ 6-10a These grave allegations had the desired effect on both mob and officials, but the narrative continues to raise difficulties. Although v. 5 spoke of the popular assembly (δῆμος) as the goal of the accusers, v. 8 returns to the language of the mob (ὄχλος), introduced in vv. 5 and 9.[27] As worded, the text implies that both mob and officials secured a bond.[28] Moreover, the narrator leaves a gap between v. 8 and v. 9. A fuller account would presumably have included something like: "So there was a hearing dealing with the nature of this teaching, the whereabouts of Paul and Silas, and the nature and applicability of the decrees in question. After hearing evidence and pondering the matter, the politarchs required Jason and the others to post a bond that would be forfeit if Paul and Silas continued to agitate." All in all, this passage shows many of the strengths and weaknesses of Luke's rapid and vivid narrative style. The speed and vigor of the narrative tug the reader over gap and through inconsistency without pause for reflection. The D-Text shows that not all readers were willing to be tugged: "**And** they stirred the magistrates and the mob *by* **saying** these things. **So then**, the magistrates, after receiving their bond [ ], dismissed them." This smoothes over an awkward participial phrase at the close of v. 8, nicely repairs the gap between v. 8 and v. 9, states that the magistrates received a surety, and eliminates "and the others," the identity of whom is not clear.

■ 10b-15 Within a verse, the narrator places Paul in a new town and another synagogue. The Jews of Berea[29] proved more fair-minded. Daily Bible study yielded the expected results.[30] As usual, converts included many highly placed members of local society, gentiles no less than Jews. A cloud soon appeared on the horizon. The attentive Jews of Thessalonica discovered what was happening and undertook some itinerant missionary work of their own. Arriving in Beroea, they played the old game (cf. 14:19-20), rousing the local rabble against Paul. Concern for his safety motivated members of the community to escort him out of town. Silas (and Timothy) were not major targets. The next stop is Athens.

The story is a replay of Thessalonica. Three times Paul has inaugurated missions in Macedonia. Three times these have resulted in civic unrest and his prompt departure. If his opponents are indulging themselves with self-congratulation, they are cruelly deceived. Far from stifling this new movement, persecution is the fuel of its continued expansion. Readers are also reassured that the charges against Paul, which have taken on a political coloration, are without grounds. They are so baseless that the narrator had no need to summarize them here. It is possible that Luke had information about Beroea, but this short paragraph is an authorial creation.[31] He utilizes this stop to contrast reception of the gospel in sophisticated, aristocratic Beroea with that in Thessalonica, the democratic and vulgar metropolis.[32]

Most of the differences in the D-Text display its penchant for heavy-handed pedantry: Paul had taught them and must thus be mentioned. Since many believed, it should be noted that some did not (cf. 28:24, etc.). The addition at the close of v. 13 indicates why Paul was sent away: rioting was incessant. One mere disturbance

longer than the text envisions, for they require an organized body of some size.

27 It is possible that ὄχλος has a neutral sense here, almost "the common people," but that is probably not Luke's intention. He wishes to show the magistrates as swayed by the *mobile vulgus* who had elected them.

28 The phrase λαμβάνειν ἱκανόν appears, like many legal expressions, to be a Latinism (*satis accipere/dare*). See BDF §5(3) and Sherwin-White, *Roman Society*, 95.

29 For information about this salubrious city, see J. Strahan, "Beroea," *DAC* 1:148–49; and Jerry A. Pattengale, "Berea," *ABD* 1:675. Cicero (*Pis.* 89) called it an *oppidum devium*, "off the beaten path." Beroea is described as a "large and well-populated city of Macedonia" in *Onos* 34.

30 On the sequence and meaning of the events described in vv. 11b-12, see Weiser, 2:451. As he observes, the reference to Scripture in v. 11b depends on v. 3. Readers are expected to fill in such gaps.

31 See Weiser, 2:445–47, esp. 450–51. Lüdemann (186–88) reports no traditions for these verses. The mission appears to be historical, since the list in 20:4 includes Sopater of Beroea.

32 See Rackham, 292, and many subsequent commentators. One would not draw the same conclusion from Paul's epistles.

would not have hindered his efforts.[33] Spiritual intervention explains a large gap in the mission (Thessaly).[34] Although the changes in 17:1-15 look like random small variants, the effect of the whole is notable. The staccato, lacunulose prose of the standard text is altered; the mission in Macedonia is more complete, while the proceedings are better motivated and more logical/rational.[35]

The mission at Beroea is atypical in that it yields a rich harvest of Jews and well-placed gentiles—women[36] again in the privileged place among the latter—without Jewish opposition. God-Fearers are also absent.[37] When opponents arrived, these persons had the resources to send an escort (*οἱ καθιστάνοντες* ["those conducting"]), v. 15) that took Paul (from an unstated port) all the way to Athens. At this point, Timothy, who has not been mentioned since 16:3, reappears. His return is a possible clue to Luke's use of Paul's letters. In 1 Thess 3:1-5, Timothy is mentioned in connection with Athens. This may have been Luke's only information about a sojourn of Paul in Athens and raises the question of Luke's specific contradiction of that data, since Paul was not "alone" in Athens until he had sent Timothy to Thessalonica. For Luke, Paul was the only threat to "the Jews." Once he had left a town, the believers were safe. Furthermore, Athens was not a planned missionary target, but only a layover where Paul would await his colleagues.[38] Since it was not in Paul's nature to be idle, he would have had an interesting experience in the famous citadel of Hellenic culture.[39]

33 The phrase is borrowed from the D-Text of 8:24.

34 The inspiration for this is 16:4-6. The D-Text assumes that Paul's strategy was to start a new community in every place (cf. 17:1) and thus has to explain gaps. Cadbury and Lake (207) observe that the D-Text uses *παρέρχομαι* to mean "pass through without engaging in mission," whereas *διέρχομαι* refers to missionary work.

35 See also Cadbury and Lake (207–8), who argue that "the sea" means "Athens" in the D-Text.

36 Whereas proponents of a particular religion boasted of its appeal to women of high status, opponents would accuse missionaries of seeking to exploit them, for example, Marcus, according to Irenaeus *A.H.* 1.13–15.

37 Jervell (438) identifies the "Greeks" of v. 12 as "God-Fearers," basing his claim on the absence of reference to work other than in the synagogue. This is a questionable argument from silence, since the narrator referred to "devout" women in v. 4 and will refer to God-Fearers again in v. 17.

38 According to the narrative, the two did not join Paul until he had come to Corinth (18:5). No reason is given for his departure from Athens without them.

39 Of Athens, Philo says: "The Athenians, the keenest in intelligence among the Greeks—for Athens is in Greece what the pupil is in the eye and reason in the soul" (*Omn. prob. lib.*140).

17

17:16-34 Paul's Areopagus Address

16/ **While Paul awaited the arrival of Timothy and Silas, he investigated the sights. He found the abundance of idols quite disturbing.[a] 17/ So he began to address Jews and devout gentiles[b] in the synagogue and, on weekdays, whoever happened to be present in the city center. 18/ Among those who encountered Paul were Epicurean and Stoic philosophers. "What point is this dilettante trying to make?" some asked, while others said, "He seems to be a herald of alien gods." (This is because he was preaching about Jesus and the resurrection.) 19/ So they apprehended Paul and led him to the Council of the Areopagus, asking, "May we learn what this novel doctrine[c] you are talking about is? 20/ Since you are propounding alien ideas, we certainly wish to know just what point you are trying to make." (21/ All[d] Athenians, whether native or immigrants, delight[e] in nothing so much as to hear or speak about anything that is quite novel.)**

22/ **Whereupon Paul, standing in the middle of the council, said:**
"Gentlemen of Athens. I observe that you are in every way quite devout. 23/ While I was walking about and examining your devotional monuments, I even found an altar bearing the inscription 'To an unknown god.' What you thus revere in ignorance is what I am proclaiming to you.[f]

24/ **"The God who fashioned the universe and all that is does not, as sovereign over heaven and earth, inhabit temples of human manufacture, 25/ nor does the One who bestows life and breath and everything else require the ministration of human hands, as if God had needs! 26/ From one person God fashioned every race and nation[g] to occupy the entire surface of the earth, having established[h] times of dominion and boundaries of habitation. 27/ Humankind was fashioned so that it would strive after God, in the hope that it might**

a The D-Text (Boismard, *Texte*, 288) revises v. 16 to eliminate an undesirable genitive absolute.

b The D-Text (Boismard, *Texte*, 288, with thin evidence) eliminates the reference to God-Fearers.

c B D *pc* omit the second article. This is an improvement.

d Boismard (*Texte*, 290) omits "all" from the D-Text. This is probably a pedantic correction of a common hyperbole.

e "The imperfect describes manners and customs" (Smyth, *Greek Grammar*, §1898). Perhaps it should be rendered "have long delighted." A clearly Atticistic touch is the elative καινότερον ("quite novel"); BDF §244 (2). Note also Barrett, 2:835–36. The D-Text (Boismard, *Texte*, 290) slightly revises.

f The D-Text (Boismard, *Texte*, 291) varies the wording of the initial participles, omits the adverbial καί ("even"), and changes the gender of the relative and demonstrative to masculine: "The one whom you . . ." These variants reek of pedantry or arbitrary variation.

g The preferable reading is ἔθνος. The D-Text, according to Boismard (*Texte*, 292) is γένος. The two are partly synonymous. Antiquity lacked the modern concept of a nation-state and did not define "race" with precision. An ἔθνος was a body of people with a common culture (including language and religion). An alternative rendering would be "the entire human race."

h The D-Text (Boismard, *Texte*, 292) reads "arranged in advance" (προτεταγμένους). This is a tempting alternative that is quite consonant with Lucan theology.

i On καί γε, see BDF §425 (1).

j D d add "day by day" (καθ' ἡμέραν) at the end. This is a good instance of a D revision that is fully Lucan in character (e.g., Luke 9:23; eleven times in all) yet quite inept.

k *V.l.* "your." "Our" is supported by B $\mathfrak{p}^{74}$ 614. 1646[c]. 1837. 2344. Metzger (*Textual Commentary*, 406) notes that the confusion is common and says: "It is scarcely likely that Paul would have represented himself as one of the Greeks." For Luke, however, Paul was a Greek (e.g., 21:39), and it is more likely that "our" was altered to "your" than vice versa. The first person in v. 29 supports this view.

l In this citation τοῦ ("his") is a demonstrative (= prose τούτου) and γένος ("kind") is an accusative of respect.

m $\mathfrak{P}^{74}$ omits "of human thought," perhaps by accident, although it is arguable that an editor—not least an Alexandrian editor—would have held that humans can form a mental conception of God and that therefore the deletion was intentional.

n The D-Text (Boismard, *Texte*, 295) simplifies by

apprehend God, as it were, and
achieve the object of its quest.
God is not, in fact,[i] distant from
any one of us, 28/ for 'In God we
live, thrive, and exist.'[j] This is
how some of our[k] poets put it:
'For we are God's offspring.'[l]
29/ "Since we have sprung from
God, we ought not imagine
that the Deity resembles gold
or silver or stone, the products
of human thought[m] and mortal
craft! 30/ God will overlook
past failures that were due to
ignorance. For the present, God
invites all people everywhere
to change their lives, 31/ for
God has set a time at which
he intends to judge[n] the world
justly by a man he has selected,
in proof whereof God has raised
this man from the dead."
32/ Some engaged in ridicule when
they heard about resurrection
of the dead, but others said,
"We shall listen to more of
what you have to say about this
subject on another occasion."
33/ At that Paul left the council.
34/ Some people did become
pupils of Paul and come to
believe. These included, among
others, Dionysius, a member of
the Areopagus, and a woman
named Damaris.

replacing ἐν ᾗ μέλλει κρίνειν (lit. "on which he is going/intends to judge") with the aorist infinitive κρῖναι. In addition, some D-Texts (a secondary layer according to Boismard) gloss "man" as "Jesus." The former eliminates a Lucan expression for the unfolding of God's plan (Squires, *Plan*, 2 n. 7). Both fail to appreciate the character of the address.

Analysis

The narrator depicts Paul at loose ends in Athens, awaiting his assistants. That city was the very navel of what was even in Paul's day viewed as the "golden age" of Greek culture and the location of unnumbered artistic marvels.[1] The narrator begins by observing that Paul, like Jesus (Luke 21:5-6), is no gawking tourist. All that he can see is the effluvia of idolatry. Not inclined to be idle, Paul engaged in his customary practice of addressing Jews and God-Fearers in synagogue.[2] To this he added a fresh dimension of missionary endeavor: daily lectures to passersby in the agora. Such activity was not

1 On this site, see Hubert H. Martin, Jr., "Athens," *ABD* 1:513–18; and Taylor, "St Paul," 2463–64.

2 The philosophical-sounding verb διαλέγομαι, which usually means no more than "preach" becomes a favored term after the council (17:2, 17; 18:4, 10; 19:8-9; 20:7, 9; 24:12, 25). Despite this meaning, it is difficult to dismiss an allusion in v. 17 to the famous method of Socrates: Plato *Apol.* 19D; 33A; *Resp.* 454A. On the use of traditions about Socrates in Acts 17, see Karl O. Sandnes, "Paul and Socrates: The Aim of Paul's Areopagus Speech," *JSNT* 50 (1993) 13–26; David M. Reis, "The Areopagus as Echo Chamber: *Mimesis* and Intertextuality in Acts," *JHC* 9 (2002) 259–77, esp. 266–73. Reis notes not only the standard parallels adduced for the narrative but also features of the speech that can be found in writings associated with Socrates. For Socrates parallels in Acts, see Hans Dieter Betz, *Der Apostel Paulus und die sokratische Tradition* (BHT 45; Tübingen: Mohr Siebeck, 1972) 38 n. 18; Alexander, *Literary Context*, 62–67; Cadbury and Lake, 212; Plümacher, *Lukas*, 19, 97–99; and Abraham Malherbe, *Paul and the Popular Philosophers* (Minneapolis: Fortress Press, 1989) 151 n. 26.

unheard-of at Athens.[3] One of Paul's predecessors in that endeavor was Socrates. Paul drew the attention of Epicureans and Stoics, disciples of the two most vigorous dogmatic philosophical schools of the era, who could be counted on to take opposing positions on most issues.[4] Their reactions, like the crowd attracted by the events of Pentecost in Jerusalem, were mixed. To some, he is yet another dilettante, while others gain the impression that he is introducing new gods. The latter was a capital offense in classical Athens, the very crime for which Socrates had been executed.[5] To those familiar with this history—anyone with a modest Greek education—this is an ominous development. Alarm quickens when Paul is brought before the ancient and venerable Council of the Areopagus, where he is requested to provide an explanation.[6]

The intellectual theme of the episode is, suitably enough for the city of Socrates, epistemology. The surface manifestation of this interest (which the author does not develop on the basis of philosophical theology) is the presence of words based on the Greek stem for "know" (γνω-): vv. 19, 20, 23 (bis), 30. Formally, the subject of Paul's address is how knowledge of the true God is to be obtained. The Greeks pursue wisdom (cf. 1 Cor 1:22), and Paul will give them a dose of it.[7] The narrative generates both fear and pride, pride in the prospect of Paul's appearance before so august an assembly, fear of the possible outcome, as the fate of Socrates pervades the atmosphere. The unstated nature of the inquiry does not dispel concerns. Is the Areopagus holding a formal trial, conducting some sort of preliminary investigation, or sponsoring a seminar for a visiting intellectual? Onto this marble stage the narrator hurls a piece of rotten fruit: Athenians are notoriously seduced by the trendy. Readers will be prepared for the possibility that Paul's message may not receive the attention it merits.

Whether on trial for his life or summoned to relieve the boredom of the Athenian aristocracy, Paul will give them his best: an apposite, witty, erudite, and well-crafted address. A nicely formulated *captatio* follows a phrase reminiscent of Plato's *Apology* and numerous orations read by students for millennia. The dramatic audience would see this as a compliment, while the readers appreciate what Paul thought of the religiosity on display. Meeting the audience where they are, he proposes as his text an inscription "To an Unknown God."[8] From this Attic rock, God can raise up children of Abraham. Out of that stone Paul will hew several themes. Polytheism cannot meet the deep religious longings of humanity and confesses ignorance of the one true God. This is also the god of the philosophers, a being who cannot be molded from rock or encased in a shrine. To these ideas the philosophically inclined would have posed no strong objections, and they would have agreed that the masses wallow in ignorance.[9]

The difference is that, for Luke, ignorance creates a level playing field that places an equal demand on Jews and gentiles (cf. 3:17). A single God has created all. The human race constitutes a unity. The one God who made all from one will judge all on a single criterion, through one agent, so designated by rising from the dead. The

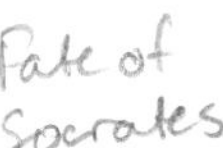

3 On the social context of Athens and its agora, see Dean P. Béchard, *Paul outside the Walls: A Study of Luke's Socio-Geographical Universalism in Acts 14:8-20* (AnBib 143; Rome: Pontifical Biblical Institute, 2000) 381–83, 411.

4 The major sources for these two schools, with some commentary and analysis, are available in A. A. Long and David N. Sedley, *The Hellenistic Philosophies* (2 vols.; Cambridge: Cambridge University Press, 1987): Epicureans 1:25–157; 2:18–162; Stoics 1:158–437; 2:163–431. On their traditional adversity, see David L. Balch, "The Areopagus Speech: An Appeal to the Stoic Historian Posidonius against Later Stoics and the Epicureans," in idem et al., eds., *Greeks, Romans, and Christians: Essays in Honor of Abraham J. Malherbe* (Minneapolis: Fortress Press, 1990) 52–79; Jerome H. Neyrey, "Acts 17, Epicureans and Theodicy: A Study in Stereotypes," in ibid., 118–34; and Squires, *Plan*, 39.

5 For details, see Haenchen, 518 n. 2.

6 On the reputation and status of the Areopagus, see *Ethiopian Story* 4.17–21; 10.34–38. The court of the Ethiopian king is like the Areopagus, that is, highly venerated for its justice.

7 Cf. Conzelmann, 140.

8 Paul's own embrace of the Christian message began with an encounter by one unknown (Acts 9:5).

9 For Luke's own view of the deity in view, see Scott Bartchy, "*Agnōstos Theos*: Luke's Message to the 'Nations' about Israel's God," *SBLSP 1995* (Atlanta: Scholars Press, 1995) 304–20.

issue of resurrection is another challenge to both Jews and gentiles. Nonetheless, at least a few minds were open. Among the converts were an actual member of the distinguished Areopagus and a woman of undisclosed status. Frugal as its harvest may have been, the mission to Athens was most heartening for those who did not care to hear their faith characterized as intellectually worthless. By small but deft touches of local color, the narrator has produced an enduring portrait, a silver-tongued oration in a golden old setting.[10]

The general structure of this passage is clear: verses 16-21 constitute an introduction that summarizes the mission and sets the stage for the speech, which follows in vv. 22-31, with a concluding reaction in vv. 32-34. Once typical Lucan features and various stereotypes about Athens and its populace have been catalogued,[11] only the fact that Paul was in Athens and the names of Dionysius and Damaris remain. No data about a Christian community at Athens is available until the time of Dionysius of Corinth (c. 170).[12] The pursuit of sources is valid for seeking to determine what information Luke had available,[13] but not helpful insofar as it detracts from the indisputable unity of the episode.[14]

Comment

■ **16-17** Nock says that this picture of Athens is based on literature.[15] This is valid, but it does not prove that the author had never been to Athens, since writers in antiquity were likely to prefer literary tradition to personal observation. Verse 16 is somewhat ambiguous. The verb *παρωξύνετο* could imply anger or mere pity for the failings of polytheism.[16] Athens was famous for its religious monuments and piety,[17] but the other cities in which Paul had labored were scarcely less contaminated with the physical excretions of polytheism.[18] The sites and emotion prepare the ground for his subsequent address, as does deviation from customary procedure in v. 17b.[19] Evidently, the Athenian agora had a better clientele than did that of Thessalonica (v. 5). Only here does the narrator thrust his hero voluntarily into the urban throng. The reason is clear: Socrates spoke with all sorts and conditions of people in that very place.[20] Memory of this practice endured, although the Cynics (and others, including Christians) had brought such behavior into disrepute.[21]

10 Cf. Haenchen (527), who speaks of a "motif technique." Dibelius, *Studies*, 76: "Therefore Luke conjures up in a few sentences the whole individuality of Athens as it was at that time."

11 For redactional elements, see Weiser, 2:459–62; and Lüdemann, 189–92. On the clichés about Athens, see below.

12 Eusebius (*H.E.* 4.23.2-3) presents a summary of Dionysius's letter to Athens. Many illustrious Christians of the period c. 150–c. 225 are associated with Athens, including the apologists Quadratus, Aristides, and Athenagoras; the Roman bishops Anacletus and, possibly, Hyginus and Sixtus II, as well as Clement of Alexandria.

13 The circularity of this quest is apparent: if one assumes that Luke had an itinerary of this journey, then data about travel and converts are attributed to it.

14 Conzelmann, 140: "The scene and speech are woven together to form a whole." See the brief and vivid analysis of Johnson, 318–19.

15 Nock, *Essays*, 2:831.

16 See BDAG, 789, *s.v.* *παροξύνω*.

17 See, for example, Livy 14.27; Pausanias 1.17.1; Strabo 9.1.16; and the references on v. 22.

18 On the adjective *κατείδωλον* ("riddled with idols"), see R. E. Wycherley, "St. Paul at Athens," *JTS* 19 (1968) 619–21.

19 The *μὲν οὖν* in v. 17 is difficult. It could be adversative ("nonetheless") or merely transitional. It does not mark a major division. See Moule, *Idiom Book*, 163.

20 Xenophon *Mem.* 1.1.10; Dio of Prusa *Or.* 54.3.

21 Dio of Prusa's criticism of (some) Cynics is very much like what Celsus says about some Christian missionaries: "[T]hese Cynics, posting themselves at street-corners, in all-ways, and at temple-gates [cf. Acts 3:1-9; 14:8-18] pass round the hat and play upon the credulity of lads and sailors and crowds of that sort, stringing together rough jokes and much tittle-tattle (*σπερμολογίαν*) and that low badinage that smacks of the market-place (*ἀγοραίους*). Accordingly they achieve no good at all, but rather the worst possible harm, for they accustom thoughtless people to deride philosophers in general" (*Or.* 32.9, trans. H. L. Crosby [LCL; Cambridge, Mass.: Harvard University Press, 1940] 181). Celsus complains: "Moreover, we see that those who display their trickery in the market-places (*ἀγοραῖς*) and go about begging would never enter a gathering of intelligent men, nor would they dare to reveal their noble beliefs in their presence; but whenever they

■ **18** The narrator therefore hastens to single out philosophers as his hearers. They, too, formed part of the local color.[22] As Hans-Josef Klauck notes: "This is the decisive difference between the Areopagus discourse and the situation in Lystra: Paul is no longer dealing with an unenlightened provincial crowd, but with an educated city public."[23] Some of these urbane intellectuals dismiss Paul as a σπερμολόγος, "a bird-brain devoid of method,"[24] while others grasp that he is expounding theology.[25] The goal of this unflattering report is to create a nearly exact parallel to the reaction of the audience in Jerusalem to the miracle at Pentecost (Acts 2:12-13).[26] This anticipates the level ground of which the address will speak. Understanding is difficult, for Jews and Greeks alike. This creates a problem for the narrator: why should the Areopagus be summoned to listen to such a creature? For the reader, this critique reflected negatively on the philosophers, as Paul's teaching involved orderly exposition and rigorous adherence to method. The second opinion, also unflattering to its adherent, returns to the Socrates parallel: Paul is introducing alien deities.[27]

Not all ancient literary views of Athens focused on its cultural amenities. Meddling civilians and tough justice await visitors to Athens. Pirates who hoped to make a fortune by selling the extraordinarily beautiful Callirhoe debated about the proper venue:

> One said, "Athens is nearby, a great and prosperous city. There we shall find lots of dealers and lots of the wealthy. In Athens you can see as many communities as you can men in a marketplace (ἀγορά)." Sailing to Athens appealed to them all. But Theron [the leader] did not like the inquisitive nature of the city. "Are you the only ones," he asked, "who have not heard what busybodies the Athenians are? They are a talkative lot and fond of litigation, and in the harbor scores of troublemakers will ask who we are and where we got this cargo. The worst suspicions will fill their evil minds. The Areopagus is near at hand and their officials are sterner than tyrants. (Chariton *Chaer.* 1.11.5–7)[28]

The final clause of v. 18 ("this . . . resurrection") is a rare authorial aside with the characteristics of a gloss, omitted by the D-Text.[29] Is this a gloss not found in the

see adolescent boys and a crowd of slaves and a company of fools they push themselves in and show off" (Origen *Cels.* 3.50, trans. Henry Chadwick [Cambridge: Cambridge University Press, 1953] 162; see also 3.55). For Greco-Roman street preachers, see Horace *Satires* 2.3; Dio of Prusa *Or.* 8.9; 36; Epictetus *Diss.* 3.22.26–30; Apuleius *Metam.* 8.24; 11.8; Lucian *Peregr.* 3–4; and the *Cynic Epistles* 38 (Diogenes).

22 Cadbury and Lake, 211.

23 Klauck, *Magic*, 76–77.

24 So Spicq (*Lexicon*, 268–69), who provides many valuable references to the use of this word. In its metaphorical usage, the term refers to those who spouted points or principles in a highly unsystematic manner. In the context, οὗτος ("this guy") is pejorative, like Latin *iste*: BDF §290(6). See also Taylor, "St Paul," 2467–68.

25 Readers who held the vulgar view that the Epicureans were "atheists" might associate them with the first group, and the religiously inclined Stoics with the second (e.g., Haenchen, 517–18). See the summary of Lucian's *Zeus Tragoedus* below.

26 In 2:13 some exclaim τί θέλει τοῦτο εἶναι; ("What is going on?"), whereas 17:18 employs a potential optative (τί ἄν θέλοι), more suitable for Athenian environs.

27 This was the capital charge of which Socrates was convicted: Xenophon *Mem.* 1.1.1; Plato *Apol.* 24b. On religious trials in ancient Athens, see Robert Garland, *Introducing New Gods: The Politics of Athenian Religion* (Ithaca: Cornell University Press, 1992). Athenians were proverbially allergic to novel divinities: Euripides *Bacch.* 255–56; Josephus *Ap.* 2.265–67. Religion and politics were not separate spheres. In the speech he placed on the lips of Maecenas kindly advising Augustus on the management of an empire, Cassius Dio (52.36.1–2)recommended sanctions against religious novelties. The relatively uncommon noun καταγγελεύς ("proclaimer") is an elegant parallel to the language of the oracular slave in 16:17 (καταγγέλλουσιν).

28 Trans. G. P. Gould (LCL; Cambridge, Mass.: Harvard University Press, 1995) 69.

29 Boismard, *Texte*, 289.

prototype of the D-Text or an accidental or deliberate omission from that tradition? It is probably original, but the possibility of a gloss deserves consideration. The plural δαιμόνια ("divinities") is conventional,[30] but an early reader insensitive to the tradition might have taken offense at the notion that Paul could have been construed as a polytheist and provided an explanation. The subsequent sermon does not name Jesus, but does speak of his being raised (v. 31).[31]

■ **19-20** These verses are casual in style.[32] The logical subject is the philosophers of v. 18,[33] who apprehend Paul and convey him to the Areopagus. The narrator is vague about whether this refers to the place ("Mars Hill") or to the council that met there, and thus whether the event is to be construed as a legal proceeding or merely a lecture in a suitable place to a learned body of uncertain (but scarcely enormous) size. Although the narrator is cagey, it is probable that Luke wishes to present the event as a sort of trial before the Council of the Areopagus. In this context, ἐπιλαμβάνομαι ("apprehend") implies formal or informal arrest in Acts.[34] Possible charges are raised, to which a speech in a formal setting responds, and the presence of a member of the Areopagus among the converts supports the understanding that the narrator intends to say that Paul spoke to the council and that the event therefore had an official purpose.[35] The absence of a verdict is not evidence to the contrary, for legal actions in Acts seldom end with formal verdicts.[36] Paul's prompt departure (18:1) after the speech also conforms to other accounts of legal actions.[37]

The goal is, in the broad sense, apologetic. The movement itself is on trial. In this august setting, Paul will show that Christianity represents Greek *paideia* (culture) and is not a vulgar foreign superstition.[38] That is one

30 It is found, for example, in all of the texts cited in n. 27, but only here in the NT in a nonpejorative sense.

31 Ropes (*Text*, ccxxxvii) regards the omission as an accident in the Latin tradition. In support of his view is the addition of αὐτοῖς ("to them") at the end in a range of witnesses, including some D-Texts: 1739 vg syᵖ bo. Chrysostom (*Hom.* 38, 318), who often represents the D-Text, read this clause (and understood it to mean the goddess Anastasis). (If the omission was accidental, that does not exclude the possibility that it was a gloss.) Metzger (*Textual Commentary*, 404) believes that it was omitted by intention. Price (*Widow Traditions*, 235–42) takes the bull by the horns, as it were, and suspects a fragment of a tradition in which Anastasis ("resurrection") was a goddess. He finds support for this in the D-Text.

32 The D-Text (Boismard, *Texte*, 289) seeks to enhance the realism of the situation by prefacing v. 19 with "After a few days . . ." That text also revises the colorless λέγοντες (in effect a quotation mark) to πυνθανόμενοι ("inquiring") and revises the third part of the verse to eliminate διδαχή ("doctrine").

33 This assumes that the second τινες in v. 18 does not refer to another group of people.

34 Cf. 16:19; 21:33, and the comments of Pesch, 2:134–35.

35 Rackham (311) listed the features indicating legal action. See also Timothy D. Barnes, "An Apostle on Trial," *JTS* 20 (1969) 407–19; Balch, "Areopagus Speech," 52-79, 73; and Pervo, *Profit*, 44–45. The speech is framed by phrases meaning "among" (ἐν μέσῳ [v. 22] and ἐκ μέσου [v. 33]). The phrase ἐν μέσῳ means "among" in Luke and Acts: Luke 2:46; 4:30; 22:27; 24:36; Acts 1:15; 2:22; 4:7; 17:33. On the Areopagus (site and council), see Hubert H. Martin, Jr., "Areopagus," *ABD* 1:370–72. Note also *NewDocs* 1 (1981) 82; Daniel J. Geagan, *The Athenian Constitution after Sulla* (Hesperia Supp. 12; Princeton: Princeton University Press, 1967) 50; and Haenchen, 519 n. 1. (Haenchen demands too much verisimilitude by saying that the narrative has Paul led away from the Stoa Basileios, where the Areopagus met, to the hill.) Balch ("Aeropagus Speech," 73–74) points to a "fascinating parallel": the fictitious "trial" of Pheidias (who produced the famous statue of Zeus at Olympia) in Dio of Prusa *Or.* 12.49, 52, 63 (a speech that contains many useful data for illustrating the Areopagus speech). Other trials of philosophers before this body are recorded by Diogenes Laertius 2.101, 116; 7.169. Schwartz ("Trial Scene," 125–26) observes that Thessalonica and Athens constitute, in effect, two halves of a trial.

36 Cadbury and Lake (213) correctly note this propensity. In Conzelmann (139), the statement, "Luke makes it very clear when he is describing a trial" is ill-advised.

37 E.g., 16:40; 17:10; 18:18 (all in the immediate context).

38 The *Act. Phil.* 2 imitates Acts 17: Questioned by philosophers who love anything quite novel (τι καινότερον), Philip says, "My Lord has brought a genuinely fresh and original teaching (παιδείαν ὄντως νέαν καὶ καινὴν) into the world." According to Werner Jaeger, revelation of the

reason for the numerous evocations of Socrates.[39] "The Lukan Paul stands before the body responsible for the regulation of religion in Athens, faced with the same type of question Socrates had faced, a charge that led to his death."[40] Verses 19b-20 continue this theme. In this ABA sequence the indirect questions frame the phrase "propounding alien ideas" (ξενίζοντα . . . εἰσφέρεις), both evocative of Socrates.[41]

■ **21** The verse contains another aside that produces yet one more cliché about Athenians: their fabled curiosity and love of novelty.[42] The rhetorical purpose of this repetition is to shift the focus from what is alien (ξένον) to what is "new" (καινόν).[43] Dramatically, it prepares readers for the ambiguous—at best—reception. True dilettantism is represented not by Paul (cf. v. 18) but by the council itself. If, in the end, Paul is to provide no more than entertainment for the frivolous, he will do his best. Jesus had had a similar experience (Luke 23:6-12), as will Paul again (24:24-27; 26). The Lystra speech involved a different sort of apologetic: distinction between Christianity and vulgar paganism. At Athens, Paul can presume the philosophical critique of vulgar religion and show its limits. Both addresses are grounded in an intellectual view of God.

■ **22-31** This has generated a major debate: Does the Areopagus address surrender the biblical doctrine of revelation in favor of "proof" from nature and history?[44] Both sides can make a good case. Luke was not a systematic theologian, and he is not setting forth a doctrine of revelation or propounding an anthropology. He was writing a speech that intended to show that Paul could address the learned in suitable categories and terms. Because of its compressed content and the author's abilities and interests, it not surprisingly contains logical leaps and theological inconsistencies.

Paul's Athenian speech has not eluded scholarly attention.[45] A cultured Greek would dismiss these brief words as a stylistically inadequate and muddled

---

paideia of Christ was "[w]hat the author of our [i.e., the canonical] Acts wanted to do." See Werner Jaeger, *Early Christianity and Greek Paideia* (Cambridge, Mass.: Harvard University Press, 1961) 12. (Luke was, however, not interested in stressing the newness of Christian revelation.)

39 Allusions to Socrates are common in the apologists. See, for example, Justin, *1 Apol.* 5 (introducing new gods); 18; *2 Apol.* 3; 7; and 10.4–6, which represents Socrates as making an argument for one god (and facing trials for so doing). On Justin's use of the Socrates model, see David M. Reis, "The Areopagus as Echo Chamber: *Mimesis* and Intertextuality in Acts," *JHC* 9 (2002) 273–76.

40 Talbert, 160.

41 Cf., e.g., Xenophon *Mem.* 1.1.1. Luke's coy, albeit stylistically weak, participle ξενίζοντα calls to mind the "foreign divinities" of v. 18. See Cadbury and Lake, 212.

42 Athenian curiosity: see the citation from Chariton *Chaer.* 1.11 above; Demosthenes *Philip.* 1.10; Lucian *Icar.* 24; Thucydides 3.38.5; Aristophanes *Knights* 1260–63; Pausanias 1.17.1; Strabo 9.1.16; Livy 14.27; Sophocles *Oed. col.* 260; and Aelian *Var. hist.* 5.17. See also Josephus *Ap.* 2.130. In *Ethiopian Story* 3.1, Kalasiris says to Knemon, "Your interest in incidental spectacle only confirms my impression that you are a true Athenian!" (trans J. R. Morgan, in Reardon, *Novels*, 409). See further A. Hallstrom, "De Curiositate Antheniensium," *Eranos* 14 (1914) 57–59.

43 Cf. Norden, *Agnostos Theos*, 53 n. 3. On "new teaching/doctrine," cf. Mark 1:27 parr.; *Act. Paul* 3.14.

44 See the summary of this debate by Weiser, 2:478–80.

45 Important studies include Dibelius, *Studies*, 26–83; Hildebrecht Hommel, "Neue Forschung zur Areopagrede Acta 17," *ZNW* 46 (1955) 145–78; Wolfgang Nauck, "Die Tradition und Komposition der Areopagrede," *ZThK* 53 (1956) 11–52; Walther Eltester, "Gott und die Natur in der Areopagrede," in *Neutestamentliche Studien für Rudolf Bultmann* (2nd ed.; BZNW 21; Berlin: Töpelmann, 1957) 202–57; Paul Schubert, "The Place of the Areopagus Speech in the Composition of Acts," in J. Coert Rylaarsdam, ed., *Essays in Divinity* 6 (Chicago: University of Chicago Press, 1968) 235–61; Hans Conzelmann, "The Address of Paul on the Areopagus," in Keck and Martyn, *Studies*, 217–30; C. K. Barrett, "Paul's Speech on the Areopagus," in M. Glasswell and Edward Fasholé-Luke, eds., *New Testament Christianity for Africa and the World: Essays in Honour of Harry Sawyer* (London: SPCK, 1974) 69–77; Pierre Auffret, "Essai sur la structure littéraire du discours d'Athènes (Ac XVII 23-31)," *NovT* 20 (1978) 185–202; Jacques Dupont, "Le discours à l'Aréopage (Ac 17,22-31): lieu de rencontre entre christianisme et hellénisme," in idem, *Nouvelles études*, 380–423, 530–46; Karl Löning, "Paulinismus in der Apostelgeschichte," in Karl Kertelege, ed., *Paulus in den neutestamentlichen Spätschriften: Zur Paulusrezeption im Neuen Testament* (QD 89;

collection of clichés with an unexpected and improbable conclusion, but it has power and vigor that would have eluded such critics, and, as an experiment in missionary theology, it continues to challenge Christian thinkers.[46] The orator takes up presuppositions of his audience with genuine respect but not uncritically and without masking his own presuppositions or compromising his views. He speaks movingly of the human longing for genuine transcendence. On the other hand, the speech does not invest this quest for the divine with passion or speak of the joy that enlightenment will bring. Rather than invite his hearers to change and join the party (cf. Luke 15:25-32), Paul demands that they repent or face the music. For one who could speak so often of the joy of Christian existence, this is remarkable.[47] Luke thereby reveals that he does not possess the mentality of a philosopher. Intellectual discovery was not a cause for celebration.[48] Although the essential elements of this speech were set out in 14:15-17 and gentiles have been among the converts since chap. 13, Luke has reserved his detailed justification/description of the theological means of this mission for the symbolic environs of Athens. This prepares the way for the eruption of the gentile mission in Corinth and its explosion in Ephesus and Asia.[49]

The intellectual background of this sermon derives, in general, from that Stoic line of thought associated with Posidonius, who reasserted the early Stoic view of a divine providence revealed in nature and history.[50] This information almost certainly came to Luke through the medium of Hellenistic Judaism, with an emphasis on the adjective, for no passage in Acts has elicited so many references to Greco-Roman philosophical writings. Since much of that material has not survived and even less remains of the output of Hellenistic philosophy, researchers must turn to Roman sources.[51] The form of the setting is indebted to the periegesis, narration

Freiburg: Herder, 1981) 202–34; Balch, "Areopagus Speech" (which amounts to a commentary on the speech from a Stoic perspective); Jerome H. Neyrey, "Acts 17," 118–34; Bruce Winter, "Implied Audiences in the Areopagus Narrative," *TynBul* 55 (2004) 205–18; idem, "Introducing the Athenians to God: Paul's Failed Apologetic in Acts 17?" *Themelios* 31 (2005) 38–59; Christoph Stenschke, *Luke's Portrait of Gentiles prior to Their Coming to Faith* (WUNT 108; Tübingen: Mohr Siebeck, 1999) 203–24; Klauck, *Magic*, 73–95; Kennedy, *Rhetorical Criticism*, 129–32; and Soards, *Speeches*, 95–100. For further bibliography, see Fitzmyer, 613–17. On patristic interpretation, see Michael Fiedrowicz, "Die Rezeption und Interpretation der paulinischen Areopag-Rede in der patristischen Theologie," *TThZ* 111 (2002) 85–105.

46 The issue is the tension between evangelism and enculturation. See Klauck, *Magic*, 94.

47 Joy and gladness: Acts 2:46; 8:8; 12:14; 13:52; 14:17; 15:3. (Note that all of these references come from the first half of Acts, and that the companion/parallel speech in 14:17 speaks of joy, but in reference to nourishment.)

48 Contrast Justin's description of his intellectual/spiritual quest (*Dial.* 1–8) or Lucian *Nigrinus*.

49 This is well stated by Tannehill, *Narrative Unity*, 2:210–13. Jervell's view (452–56) of this speech as an alien element in the entire New Testament without consequence is incorrect.

50 See Balch, "Areopagus Speech." (Posidonius has been the subject of considerable dispute and should not be a red herring in discussion of Acts 17. The issue is the contents of certain texts, not the thought of that philosopher. For a general introduction, see I. G. Kidd, "Posidonius," *OCD* 1231–33.)

51 Bertil Gärtner's *The Areopagus Speech and Natural Revelation* (ASNU 21; Uppsala: Gleerup, 1955), although valuable, is methodologically flawed because of its thesis that the background of the speech can be explained almost entirely without reference to Greco-Roman philosophy. The task is not the selection and rejection of various backgrounds, with "Jewish background" occupying a privileged position, but the development of a profile of the sermon in the context of ancient thought. Posidonius admired Plato, and many intellectuals (e.g., Philo) took an eclectic approach to the philosophical tradition. Parallels may thus be adduced from a range of philosophical systems. The true focus of the debate is the question: What does Luke's Athens have in common with Paul? Those who stress the compatibility tend to regard Dibelius as the source of all errors, since he expounded the address in terms of Greco-Roman philosophical concepts alien to Christianity (see Dibelius, *Studies*, 26–77). Dibelius does refer to the address as a "Hellenistic speech" (e.g., 57) and characterizes it as representing a rationalistic approach "foreign" or "alien" to the New Testament (e.g., 58, 63), but he does not say that it was

of travel (vv. 16, 23),[52] best known from Pausanias (who mentions altars of "unknown gods" in Athens [1.1.4]), but familiar also in more popular works. *Leucippe* begins with the unintended arrival of the narrator in Sidon: "[T]ouring the rest of the city to see its memorial offerings (*περισκοπῶν τὰ ἀναθήματα*), I saw a votive painting" (1.1.2).[53] The topos is like that of Acts 17: a stranger comes to a city, walks about and takes notice of a particular object, the interpretation of which will be crucial.

The commonplace character of the philosophical subjects can be seen from Lucian's *Juppiter tragoedus*, which features a debate in Athens between the Stoic Timocles and Damis, an Epicurean, on the subject of divine providence. The latter holds that the gods exercise no providential care, which, in the view of Zeus, amounts to atheism. Timocles insists that the gods manage all in good order under a fine system (17). In the report of their debate, Timocles argues first from the order of nature: the regular course of heavenly bodies producing seasons (38), from poetic authority (39–41), from the *consensus gentium* (all peoples believe in god[s] [42]), from the analogy of a ship under sail, which requires a pilot (46–51), and, finally, from a parody of the ontological argument—*altars* demonstrate the existence of gods (51). In response to Damis's mockery, Timocles closes with personal abuse (52). All's well that ends well, apparently, although Zeus finds Damis a more potent debater (53). In arguing for the view of God as creator and benevolent governor of the universe, the speech assumes the view of the Stoics and does not even consider the opposing arguments. Lucian's Damis would have endorsed the judgment that Paul is a dilettante (v. 18b).[54]

Wolfgang Nauck argued that the speech reflects a creedal pattern.[55] Nauck built on the work of Eduard Norden, who had identified a pattern of missionary discourse found in such disparate texts as *Corpus Hermeticum* 1 (*Poimandres*).27–28; 7.1–2; *Odes of Solomon* 33, the *Kerygma of Peter*; Ps.-Clem. *Hom.* 1.7; cf. *Sib. Or.* 1:150–98.[56] The focus of Nauck's work was the identification of a shape that can be discerned in Hebrew (the Kedusha of Jozer; the first two of the Eighteen Benedictions), Hellenistic Jewish (Sibylline material in Theophilus *Autolyc.* 2.36; *Ap. Const.* 7.34.1–7; 8.12.8–16; Aristobulus; the Prayer of Manasseh), and Christian (*1 Clem.* 19.2—20.12; 33.2–8; *Epistula Apostolorum*) works. This pattern, which has biblical roots,[57] flourished in both early Judaism and early Christianity. Its principal features are creation (with particular reference to the creation of humankind in God's image), the maintenance of the cosmos (including seasons and demarcations), and deliverance: *creatio, conservatio, salvatio.* Hellenistic interest in cosmology generated increased interest in

not Jewish or Christian. As a "precursor of the apologists," the speech foreshadows the development of philosophical theology, admittedly necessary, but . . . (63–64). Dibelius placed the tradition of the Hebrew Bible and Paul against the philosophical line represented by the Areopagus address. To a degree, he was engaging in neo-orthodox apologetics. He can be accused of making the breach between Luke and Paul too wide, but not of selling out the gospel. For a recent statement of the anti-Dibelius understanding, see the important dissertation of Stenschke, *Gentiles.* The most relevant work from Hellenistic Judaism is *Aristeas*, which argues that the religious sensibility (*εὐσέβεια*) of Jews and gentiles is based on acknowledgment of God as creator (16-17) and providential ruler of the world (16-19; 132-33; 201). See also Michel Gourgues, "La littérature profane dans le discours d'Athènes (Ac 17,16-31): un dossier fermé?" *RB* 109 (2002) 241–69.

52 See Klauck, *Magic*, 75; and Conzelmann, 138.

53 Trans. J. J. Winkler, in Reardon, *Novels*, 176. Cf. also *Ephesian Tale* 1.12; 5.11; and Mark 13:1-2||Luke 21:5-6, noted above.

54 Neyrey ("Acts 17," 118–34) develops this theme, arguing that Luke follows conventions about the two philosophies' contrasting approach to providence and theodicy, comparing this to his portraits of the Pharisees and Sadducees. Neyrey adduces Josephus's comparison of Sadducees to Epicureans and Pharisees to Stoics. Luke may have been inspired by Josephus here.

55 Nauck, "Die Tradition und Komposition der Areopagrede," *ZThK* 53 (1956) 11–52; cf. also Conzelmann, 146–48.

56 Norden, *Agnostos Theos*, 125–40.

57 Cf. Psalms 33; 74:12-17; 89; 135; 136; 145; 148.

the first of these categories. David Balch notes that both Aristobulus and Acts replace the reference to creation in the divine image with a citation from Aratus *Phaen.* 5.[58] The theme of deliverance apparently establishes the integrity of vv. 30-31 within the structure of the speech, but Conzelmann objects, saying that, although the Prayer of Manasseh exhibits a pattern approaching Nauck's model, the other texts, which celebrate a god who fashioned and sustains the universe in a manner that shows benevolence for the human race, do not fit the proposed model.[59]

The structure is widely debated—as a bipartite division based on the "first and second articles" (God, vv. 22-29; Christ, vv. 30-31),[60] or, rhetorically, as the refutation of the charges followed by countercharges (vv. 22b-28; 29-31).[61] Dibelius proposed five components, which amount to an opening (vv. 22-23) and a closing (vv. 30-31) sandwiching the central section of three parts (vv. 24-25, 26-27, 28-29).[62] The rhetorical analysis of Dean Zweck is similar: *exordium*, vv. 22-23a; *propositio*, v.23b; *probatio*, vv. 24-29; *peroratio*, vv. 30-31.[63] In short, this speech is difficult to outline because it contains a series of theses that are supported with a minimum of argumentation.[64] The core lies in vv. 24-29,[65] which is framed by two critiques of popular religion: God does not reside in temples of human construction and cannot be represented by images. The major themes are statements about the nature of God (vv. 24a, 25b, 26-28), the creator of all who fashioned humans to seek the Holy One. The consequences of these assertions follow: vv. 24b, 25a, and 29. The first two of these are presented in a chiasm: v. 24a, v. 24b, v. 25a, v. 25b; the third (vv. 26-28, 29) in A B fashion.[66]

The style is relatively elevated. In addition to the familiar alliteration,[67] assonance,[68] and rhyme,[69] paronomasia,[70] and effective repetition,[71] there are two uses of γε, including εἰ ἄρα γε (v. 27), and two optatives. Verses 24-27 and 29-31 are single sentences, but neither is a true period.[72] The author was striving to produce learned and elegant prose, but the task demanded more than he could supply. Moreover, the speech includes some nods to the intellectual tradition, most notably in the quotation from Greek poetry in v. 28 and in the use of the neuter for the divine (τὸ θεῖον [v. 29; cf. the neuter relative and demonstrative in v. 23]) and the idiomatic πίστιν παρασχών ("in proof whereof") in v. 29.[73]

58 See below, n. 129.
59 Conzelmann, 148. The date of this prayer is uncertain, but it probably antedates Acts. James H. Charlesworth (*OTP* 2:625–33) defends a date before the Common Era, but the evidence is scant.
60 Conzelmann, 148; Wilckens, *Missionsreden*, 87.
61 Soards, *Speeches*, 96.
62 Dibelius, *Studies*, 37–38. Dupont ("Le discours à l'Aréopage," 387–96 [n. 45 above]) has a similar arrangement.
63 Dean Zweck, "The *Exordium* of the Areopagus Speech, Acts 17.22, 23," *NTS* 35 (1989) 94–103. The absence of *narratio* shows that the speech is deliberative. Witherington (518) suggests that Luke omitted the *narratio* from this précis as superfluous. Nevertheless, v. 23a is narrative, however brief. Rhetorical analysis reveals that this speech is not a summary of an oration but a compressed speech. F. Lostang ("À la louange du dieu inconnu: Analyse rhétorique de Ac 17.22-31," *NTS* 52 [2006] 394–408) argues for demonstrative rhetoric, with a *captatio benevolentiae* (vv. 22b-23), the excellence of God in self (vv. 24-26), praise of God's past actions (vv. 26-29), and praise of God's actions in present (vv. 30-31).
64 Cf. Weiser (2:456–57), who summarizes various plans.
65 This is reinforced by an *inclusio* on the theme of ignorance in vv. 23 and 30.
66 See Tannehill, *Narrative Unity*, 2:219–20, and Talbert, 162.
67 E.g., πίστιν παρασχὼν πᾶσιν (v. 29).
68 E.g., οὐκ ἐν χειροποιήτοις ναοῖς κατοικεῖ (v. 24).
69 E.g., ζωὴν καὶ πνοήν (v. 25).
70 Note the effective "unknown god (ἀγνώστῳ θεῷ) whom you worship without knowing (ἀγνοοῦντες)," v. 23. Cf., in the same context, θεωρῶ ("observe") and ἀναθεωρῶν ("examine") vv. 22-23.
71 E.g., ὑπάρχω ("be"), vv. 24, 27, 29; forms of "all" (πᾶς), vv. 24, 25 (bis), 26 (thrice), 30 (bis), 31.
72 Compare Hebrews, the style of which often hovers in the vicinity of true Greek periods but rarely delivers them. 2 Maccabees provides other apt bases for stylistic comparison.
73 On the style, see also Cadbury and Lake, 209; and Cadbury, "The Speeches in Acts," in Lake and Cadbury, *Additional Notes*, 402–27, esp. 419 n. 2.

■ **22** The verse has the appearance of a *captatio benevolentiae*, and should be taken as such. The adjective δεισιδαίμων means "religious" and can be just as uncomplimentary as the English word in certain contexts. This is not such a context.[74] Athenian piety was no less a stereotype than Athenian curiosity.[75] Paul has no need to inculcate interest in religion. He assumes that interest and sets out to correct it.

■ **23** Here the periegesis theme, initiated in v. 16, finds its purpose: among the religious artifacts was an inscription to "an unknown god."[76] Such inscriptions were usually an *ex voto* (thanksgiving) for some benefaction or a petition for assistance to a divinity whose name had not been revealed.

The construction is ad hoc, for such inscriptions were in the plural, as Jerome, who briskly corrects "Paul," establishes: "In actuality, the altar inscription read 'to the gods of Asia, Europe, and Africa, to the unknown and foreign gods'—and not, as Paul would have it—to an unknown god" (*Comm. in Titum* 1:12).[77] Polytheism will not receive any consideration. Paul will not speak of a "new god" to adorn the already crowded polytheist pantheon, and he will come no closer to novel teaching than the judgment announced in v. 31.[78] The task he sets for himself is to bring to the audience's attention a god whom they honor but do not understand.[79] Verse 23b is more potent in its striking brevity than the expected leisurely exposition, in which one would report on inquiries made to bystanders, various views on the origin of this inscription, and all that the dramatic audience (and readers of commentaries) would expect. Paul cuts right to the point, with an effective use of the relative/demonstrative style (cf. 3:12-16) that nicely picks up on v. 18 (καταγγελεὺς . . . καταγέλλω ("proclaimer . . . proclaim").

■ **24** Although v. 26 refers to the regular ordering of nature, Paul does not attempt to prove the existence of God from the natural order; he assumes it. For the readers of Acts, this is not a difficulty, because the argument had been made in 14:15-17.[80] The same claim cannot

74 BDAG, 216, *s.v.* δεισιδαίμων. See also Johnson, 314. Interpreters who understand the speech as historical incline toward understanding the adjective as ambiguous or ironic. See Stenschke, *Gentiles*, 210–12. Balch ("Areopagus Speech," 74) also views the term as pejorative, albeit in retrospect.

75 Patrick Gray ("Athenian Curiosity [Acts 17:21]," *NovT* 47 [2005] 109–16) correlates the two in an interesting study. Unsavory curiosity is linked to inappropriate religiosity in Plutarch's treatise *De curiositate* (Mor. 515B–523A) and in the *Metamorphoses* of Apuleius, both of which are influenced by Middle Platonism.

76 On the theme of discovering an inscription, see Norden, *Agnostos Theos*, 31–56.

77 PL 26.607 (author's trans.). Tertullian (*Nat.* 2.9) also changes the reference to the plural. On the question, see Wikenhauser, *Geschichtswert*, 369–94; and Lake, "The Unknown God," in Lake and Cadbury, *Additional Notes*, 240–46. A recent survey of inscriptional material is Pieter van der Horst, "The Altar of the 'Unknown God' in Athens: Acts 17.23 and the Cults of 'Unknown Gods' in the Graeco-Roman World," in idem, *Hellenism-Judaism-Christianity* (Kampen: Kok Pharos, 1994) 165–202; idem, "The Altar of the 'Unknown God' in Athens (Acts 17:23) and the Cult of 'Unknown Gods' in the Hellenistic and Roman Periods," *ANRW* 2.18.2 (1990) 426–56. See also David Gill, "Achaia," in Gill and Gempf, *Setting*, 433–53, esp. 446–47; Taylor, "St Paul," 2472–75; and Stenschke, *Gentiles*, 212 n. 509. The suitability of Athens for this dedication is confirmed by Philostratus, who has Apollonius of Tyana speak of altars to unknown gods (ἄγνωστοι δαίμονες), especially at Athens (*Vit. Apoll.* 6.3.5).

78 Contrast the imitation of this episode in the *Act. Phil.* 2. New wine cannot be put into old wineskins.

79 Justin *2 Apol.* 10.5–6 states that Socrates called to the attention of the Athenians a god unknown to them but discoverable via reason. Unlike Paul (Romans 1–2), Justin, and other apologists, Luke does not accuse polytheists of immorality. See Balch, "Areopagus Speech," 74–75. Apart from assailing greed, the preachers in Acts do not engage in moral critique or exhortation. Klauck (*Magic*, 83) refers to the "hidden God" of the Hebrew Bible, but the God Paul proclaims is far from hidden. The contrast with Paul is clear. He says that gentiles know God but do not honor God (Rom 1:18-32). Luke says gentiles worship but do not know the true God.

80 See John Townsend, "The Speeches in Acts," *ATR* 42 (1960) 150–59, esp. 151–52.

be made for the dramatic audience. Verse 24a firmly asserts the view of Israelite religion,[81] with one concession to Greek philosophical language: the relatively rare *κόσμος* ("universe") replaces the standard "earth" (*γῆ*).[82] As sovereign of all,[83] this creator God does not inhabit products of human manufacture and requires no human ministrations. Both of these assertions are intellectual commonplaces,[84] amenable, for different reasons, to the dramatic audience but subversive of civic religion. Demetrius will present that popular viewpoint, in its most elemental form, in 19:26.

The predicate of v. 24 ("does not inhabit") resonates with Stephen's accusation (7:48).[85] Although official Israelite theology held that God did not inhabit the temple, that it was a place for God's name,[86] popular opinion was less subtle, as can be seen in the portents foreshadowing its collapse in both Josephus and Tacitus.[87] Temples, for Paul, are no better than idols. Both involve confusion of creator with creation[88] and are the sites of animal sacrifice, implying that God requires or even appreciates such worship. For Luke, it is not a question of the abuse of temple piety or sacrificial worship, as in some of the biblical tradition (e.g., Isa 1:11);[89] for Luke, all shrines and sacrifices are marks of bad theology.

■ **25** The intellectual sentiment here expressed is well attested by the younger Seneca. In *Ep. mor.* 95.47–50, he addresses the question of proper worship. His first example is Sabbath lamps. The gods need (*egent*) no light; soot is inconvenient to humans. The philosopher finds morning salutations self-serving.[90] The *knowledge* of God is due worship. God requires no servants but serves humanity—and that not from afar (*ubique et omnibus praesto est*).[91] The gods bestow goodness and govern all things. These periods read like a commentary, *mutatis mutandis*, on vv. 23-27.[92] The thesis that god/the gods need nothing is one of the fixed points of the Greco-Roman philosophical tradition. Testimonies extend from the pre-Socratics to the Neo-Platonists.[93]

81 Verses 24-25 reflect the LXX. Note Isa 42:5: *κύριος ὁ θεὸς ὁ ποιήσας τὸν οὐρανὸν καὶ πήξας αὐτόν, ὁ στερεώσας τὴν γῆν καὶ τὰ ἐν αὐτῇ καὶ διδοὺς πνοὴν τῷ λαῷ τῷ ἐπ' αὐτῆς καὶ πνεῦμα τοῖς πατοῦσιν αὐτήν* ("Thus says God, the Lord, who created the heavens and stretched them out, who spread out the earth and what comes from it, who gives breath to the people upon it and spirit to those who walk in it"); 2 Macc 7:22-23: *Οὐκ οἶδ' ὅπως εἰς τὴν ἐμὴν ἐφάνητε κοιλίαν, οὐδὲ ἐγὼ τὸ πνεῦμα καὶ τὴν ζωὴν ὑμῖν ἐχαρισάμην, καὶ τὴν ἑκάστου στοιχείωσιν οὐκ ἐγὼ διερρύθμισα, 23 τοιγαροῦν ὁ τοῦ κόσμου κτίστης ὁ πλάσας ἀνθρώπου γένεσιν καὶ πάντων ἐξευρὼν γένεσιν καὶ τὸ πνεῦμα καὶ τὴν ζωὴν ὑμῖν πάλιν ἀποδίδωσιν μετ' ἐλέους, ὡς νῦν ὑπερορᾶτε ἑαυτοὺς διὰ τοὺς αὐτοῦ νόμους.* ("I do not know how you came into being in my womb. It was not I who gave you life and breath, nor I who set in order the elements within each of you. 23 Therefore the Creator of the world, who shaped the beginning of humankind and devised the origin of all things, will in his mercy give life and breath back to you again, since you now forget yourselves for the sake of his laws.") On the latter, see Jonathan Goldstein, *II Maccabees* (AB 41A; Garden City, N.Y.: Doubleday, 1983) 311–14.

82 See Hermann Sasse, "*κοσμέω*," *TDNT* 3:867–98, esp. 880–82.

83 Cf. Dio of Prusa *Or.* 12.27, associated in 12.35 with the image of the pilot of a ship, used by Lucian's Stoics (above), and rejected by the Epicureans (12.55).

84 See n. 92.

85 See the comments there. For the linguistic similarities between 7:48-50 and 17:24, see p. 191 n. 168.

86 Cf. 1 Kgs 5:3-5; 8:16, 26-27; 11:36; 2 Chr 6:18.

87 Josephus *Bell.* 6.288–315; Tacitus *Hist.* 5.13. Lucian (*Sacr.* 11) ridicules the idea that gods require shelter. He also implies that worshipers think that the statues they see are not minerals, and the like, but the actual god (cf. Acts 17:29).

88 On the use of *χειροποίητος* in the LXX, see Eduard Lohse, "*χειροποίητος*," *TDNT* 9:436. In Isa 16:12 it is a metonym for a polytheist temple. See also Hans Windisch, *Der zweite Korintherbrief* (KEK; Göttingen: Vandenhoeck & Ruprecht, 1924) 159; and Stenschke, *Gentiles*, 213 n. 513.

89 Ps 50:7-15 corrects the impression that God needs sacrifices; they are expressions of gratitude.

90 Isis worship (e.g., Apuleius *Metam.* 11.22) may be in view.

91 Cf. *Ep. mor.* 41.1, which states that God is near, with, and within humans (and that a "sacred spirit has a place within us" [*sacer intra nos spiritus sedet*]).

92 The most important differences are that Seneca makes no reference to god as creator and that he can alternate between "god" and "the gods" without distinction, but such sentiments doubtless helped inspire the fourth-century *Correspondence between Paul and Seneca*.

93 See the discussion in Dibelius, *Studies*, 42–44, with

The Hebrew Bible contains no explicit mention of this idea, but it does appear in 2 Macc 14:35 and 3 Macc 2:9, in both cases with regard to the temple cult,[94] and thereafter in Christian writings.[95] Stoic tradition affirmed Zeno's view that the construction of temples is inappropriate.[96] The entire universe is properly regarded as God's temple.[97] To describe God as the source of "all" is also congenial to Stoic thought.[98]

Acts hovers here on the borderline of the apologetic tradition (see *1 Clem.* 52:1 and *Kerygma Petrou* 2a). A very close parallel can be found in *Diogn.* 3.3–5, which begins by criticizing "the Greeks" for the view that sacrifices show that God has needs, and continues (4) "For the one who made heaven and earth and all that is in them, and who supplies all of us with what we need, is himself in need of none,"[99] followed by a critique of Jewish sacrificial cult.[100] The comparison shows that the narrator is more interested in depicting the common ground shared by Paul and the philosophers than in developing a polemic.[101] For this reason, contrast with Paul is irrelevant, for Paul's letters do not address learned polytheists.

■ **26** The verse opens with a compressed assertion of the unity of the human race grounded in a common origin from God.[102] Representatives of the philosophical tradition had protested against the division of humankind into Greeks and barbarians. Luke applied this concept to the division between Jews and gentiles, overcome by the miraculous action of God rather than from acquiescence to the political ramifications of an intellectual

numerous references, specifically 43 n. 48. These may be expanded, e.g., Plato *Euthyphro* 12E–15E; Ps.-Lucian *The Cynic* 12 (3rd century CE or earlier). Josephus also asserts that God is in need of nothing (*Ant.* 8.111). A late philosophical example is Porphyry *To Marcella* 18. See also Heinrich Greeven, "προσδέομαι," *TDNT* 2:41–42.

94 For data from Philo and Josephus, see Dibelius, *Studies*, 42–44.

95 E.g., Justin *1 Apol.* 13.1; *Barn.* 2:4–3:5.

96 Diogenes Laertius 7.33 (Zeno forbade temples in his ideal commonwealth); *Stoicorum veterum Fragmenta* 1, frg. 264, from Plutarch *Stoic. rep.* 6 (*Mor.* 1034b), who criticizes subsequent Stoics for affirming this principle while engaging in conventional worship. See the notes of Harold Cherniss, *Plutarch's Moralia* XIII.2 (LCL; Cambridge, Mass.: Harvard University Press, 1976) 422–23.

97 E.g., (Ps.) Heraclitus *Ep.* 4.47–50 (on which, see Abraham Malherbe, "Pseudo-Heraclitus, Epistle 4: The Divinization of the Wise Man," *JAC* 21 [1978] 42–64); Philo *Spec. leg* 1.66–67; Seneca *Ben.* 7.73; *Ep. mor.* 90.28–29; Plutarch *Tranq. an.* 20 (*Mor.* 477c), which has several parallels to this speech, including a negative reference to handmade and motionless images (χειροκμήτων . . . ἀκινήτων ἀγαλμάτων) and of the Platonic Ideas as possessing an innate source of life and motion (ἔμφυτον ἀρχὴν ζωῆς ἔχοντα καὶ κινήσεως). An alternative formulation, congenial to the Hebrew Bible (e.g., Isa 66:1), views the universe as the home of the gods: Cicero *Resp.* 3.14 (Xerxes burned the temples at Athens for reasons of piety). The correlative accepts temples as models of heaven and thus inspirations to the imitation of God or the gods: Philo *Vit. Mos.* 2.66–108, 136–40; *Spec. leg.* 1.71–97; *Q. Exod.* 2.69–123; Josephus *Ant.* 3.123, 180. Imitation is the explicit motive in Sallustius *Concerning the Gods and the Universe* 15. See Arthur Darby Nock, *Sallustius: Concerning the Gods and the Universe* (Cambridge: Cambridge University Press, 1926) lxxxiii, 28. Christian writers (e.g., John 14) tended to prefer the view that God dwells in the pious soul. Cf. Philo *Cher.* 99–100. Jewish tradition rejected the concept that God depends on offerings for sustenance and interpreted temple and cult in symbolic ways but never rejected the practices.

98 So, e.g., Marcus Aurelius *Meditations* 4.23, ἐκ σου πάντα, ἐν σοὶ πάντα, εἰς σὲ πάντα. Cf. Martin Dibelius, "Die Christianisierung einer hellenistischen Formel," in idem, *Botschaft und Geschichte* (2 vols.; Tübingen: Mohr Siebeck, 1953–55) 2:14–29.

99 ὁ γὰρ ποιήσας τὸν οὐρανὸν καὶ τὴν γῆν καὶ πάντα τὰ ἐν αὐτοῖς καὶ πᾶσιν ἡμῖν χορηγῶν, ὧν προσδεόμεθα, οὐδενὸς ἂν αὐτὸς προσδέοιτο (Ehrman, *Apostolic Fathers*, 2:137). Had *Diognetus* been dependent on Acts, it is unlikely that κόσμος ("universe") would have been replaced by the more biblical "heaven and earth" (as in Ps 145:6 LXX). *Diognetus* is difficult to date. On linguistic and material grounds c. 150 seems appropriate.

100 See Pervo, *Dating*, 249–56.

101 Stenschke (*Gentiles*, 212–17) reads the speech as harsh polemic.

102 Philo developed this theme in *Op. mun.* 134–47, esp. 136–44. In 136 the first "earthly man" is ὁ παντὸς τοῦ γένους ἡμῶν ἀρχηγέτης ("forebearer of our entire race"); 142–44 describe humans as "citizens of the world" (κοσμοπολίτης).

argument,[103] but Paul does not point that out on this occasion. The creation of humankind is described without reference to Genesis or to any mythic account, but Christian readers will take it as a summary of Genesis.[104] Greek tradition also viewed (a) god as the parent of the human race.[105] A reason for creating humanity—inhabitation of the whole world—evokes Gen 1:28.[106]

The chief difficulty in v. 26b is the meanings of *καιροί* and *ὁροθεσίαι* ("times" and "boundaries"). The former could refer to the seasons of the year and is often taken as such. That would correspond to 14:17, but the address is not speaking of proofs of God from nature,[107] and the participle *προστεταγμένους* ("arranged") does not suit that sense. Another understanding, although not consonant with the traditional argument, which contends that the divine hand is apparent in the structure of the universe, is "historical periods," as in Luke 24:3 (cf. Acts 1:7; 3:20). In this context, *ὁροθεσίαι* would apply to political boundaries.[108] The underlying notion would be that countries rise and fall in political power and dominance. The vicissitudes of history are elements of God's plan for the human race. Deut 32:8 LXX is in the background.[109]

■ **27** The purpose of the dispersion of humanity was the peopling of the entire world, but this did not utterly alienate people from God. Indeed, humankind was formed so that it would pursue the divine.[110] Behind this lies one of the classic arguments for the existence of God: the *consensus gentium*, the universal belief in the existence of gods. "Nothing but the presence in our

103 See Parsons and Pervo, *Rethinking*, 96–101.

104 The phrase *ἐξ ἑνός* is best construed as masculine, corresponding to *ἀνθρώπων*, "from one person God created every race of people." Neuter ("from a single source") is also possible. See Fitzmyer, 609. The D-Text and *Koine* traditions add *αἵματος* ("blood," a synecdoche for "person"). This is probably a secondary attempt to block mythological interpretations of *ἐξ ἑνός*, which could be construed as neuter: "from one source" or "entity." This is more likely than the proposal that "blood" was deleted because Gen 2:7 reports that dust was the basis (Metzger, *Textual Commentary*, 405), as scribes would have recognized that "one blood" was a trope rather than an identification of the substance. (An interpolator—or the author—may have understood *αἷμα* as "semen," that is, "from the seed of one person.") Ψ reads *στόματος* ("mouth"). This is probably a metonym for "word." On the concept, see Karel van der Toorn, "Mouth," *DDD*, 605–6.

105 The epithet "father of gods and mortals" is used fifteen times of Zeus in Homer (e.g., *Il.* 1.544). Philosophers agreed, such as Dio of Prusa *Or.* 12.29, 42; 12.29 speaks of a progenitive or ancestral god (*προπάτωρ θεός*) and links this role to the bounty of nature. *Or.* 12.43 states that Zeus is of the same blood as humans. See also *Or.* 36.56, which speaks of Zeus and Hera generating the cosmos from one seed.

106 The expression *ἐπὶ παντὸς προσώπου τῆς γῆς* (lit. "on the entire face of the earth") is Septuagintal language (e.g., Gen 2:6) that would have sounded vulgar to the dramatic audience. See Dibelius, *Studies*, 36 n. 24.

107 Cicero *Tusc. disp.* 1.28.68–69, for example, views seasons and zones as evidence of divine existence.

108 The debate between the "historical" and "philosophical" interpretations of v. 26 is ably summarized in Balch, "Areopagus Speech," 54–57; Weiser, 2:471 (with many references); and Barrett 2:843–44. The alternative interpretation of *ὁροθεσίαι* is the boundaries separating land from water, and the like. Documentary evidence (Spicq, *Lexicon*, 2:596) applies the term exclusively to political boundaries. Literary evidence is lacking. Luke was closer to historians than to philosophers. It would be absurd to imagine him investigating the philosophical nuances of these concepts. Conzelmann (142–44) favors the "historical," while sagely observing that the controversy demands too much of the author.

109 "When the most high apportioned [the] nations, in scattering the descendants of Adam, he established [the] boundaries (*ὅρια*) of [the] nations in accordance with the number of the angels of God" (author's trans.). (The MT speaks of "children of Israel," but 4QDt[j] [4Q37] shows that "children of God" is more original.) *1 Clem.* 29 cites this passage in support of the view that believers are God's chosen. Irenaeus (*A.H.* 3.12.9) also quotes it in his discussion of the Areopagus address, in support of the unity of the human race.

110 *κατοικεῖν* ("inhabit") and *ζητεῖν* ("seek") in vv. 26-27 are probably coordinate complements to "fashioned" (*ἐποίησεν*). *Beg.* 4:216 observes that "loose epexegetical infinitives" are characteristic of Lucan style. See also Moule, *Idiom Book*, 143.

minds of a firmly grasped concept of the deity could account for stability and permanence of our belief in him" (Cicero *Nat. Deor.* 2.5).[111] The innate knowledge of God is not a matter of volition but the result of reflection on the nature and organization of the world, which leads to a sense of kinship with the deity.[112] The speech does not expound this thesis in a systematic way, for its symboleutic object is to stress the quest for God.

Luke is edging toward a concept of *praeparatio evangelica* (background for the gospel). In his terms, this means that gentile history and religion are, at least to a degree, parts of the prehistory of Christianity, as was the history of Israel.[113] Both Jews and gentiles must grasp this truth and acknowledge that the glories of their pasts were but prelude. That acknowledgment was the essence of repentance, and Luke knew that it was neither easy to achieve nor widespread.

Verse 27 may be the most moving clause in Acts, a heartfelt statement of Luke's understanding of the object of human existence. The best commentary on these words is the crescendo of parables in Luke 15 and, especially, Luke 13:6-9. "Seek and find" is ideal, for it is found in material ranging from the most concrete metaphors of the sapiential and prophetic traditions to the peaks of abstract theology.[114] The conditional clause "in the hope that it might apprehend God,[115] as it were" (εἰ ἄρα γε ψηλαφήσειαν αὐτὸν) vividly expresses the gap between humanity and deity and—contrary, in fact, to the sentiments of the then current philosophical theology—the frailty of mortal efforts.[116] This reserve rapidly

111 *Quod nisi cognitum conprehensumque animis haberemus, non tam stabilis opinio permaneret nec confirmaretur* (trans. H. Rackham, *Cicero De Natura Deorum* [LCL; Cambridge, Mass.: Harvard University Press, 1933] 127). Cf. also 2.13. See Cicero *Leg.* 1.24; and, in particular, Dio of Prusa *Or.* 12.27–30; and Pease, *Natura*, 580–84.

112 See Heinrich Greeven, "ζητέω," *TDNT* 2:892–93; and Norden, *Agnostos Theos*, 14–15. In the Hebrew Bible, the quest for God is related to will rather than to intellect.

113 See Bultmann, *Theology*, 2:117.

114 Philo *Spec. leg.* 1.36 is noteworthy: God is difficult to trace (δυσθήρατον) and apprehend (δυσκατάληπτον), but nothing is superior to pursuit of the genuine God (ζητεῖν τὸν ἀληθῆ θεόν), although finding (εὕρεσις) may be beyond human capability. (*Spec. leg.* 1.32 explains that "seeking" means addressing the questions of existence and essence. Luke assumes the former and addresses the latter, albeit not explicitly.) See also Wis 13:6 and the comments of David Winston, *The Wisdom of Solomon* (AB 43; Garden City, N.Y.: Doubleday, 1979) 254–55. On seeking the divine, see also Cicero *Tusc. disp.* 1.68; *Nat. Deor.* 2.153; Seneca *Ep. Mor.* 95.47; Sextus Empiricus 9.60.75–100; Rom 1:20-21; Theophilus *Autolyc.* 1.4, 6; 2.10; Aristides *Apol.* 1; Tertullian *Apol.* 17; and Minucius Felix *Oct.* 18.7.

115 The verb ψηλαφάω can have the sense of groping about for an object in the dark, as in Homer *Od.* 9.416 (blind Cyclops); Plato *Phaed.* 99; Philo *Mut. nom.* 126, but it does not mean this in Luke 24:39. "Apprehend" may be too bland a compromise, for the verb probably refers to a desire for intimate contact. In his defense of images of the gods, Dio of Prusa (*Or.* 12.50) says that people have a longing to touch (ἁπτομένους) them. This "sensuous" verb led Gärtner (*Areopagus Speech*, 178) to ask if this were not a Stoic interpolation. The speaker does not say how the true god is to be sought. Insofar as this matter is addressed, it is through the summons to repentance in v. 30.

116 The D-Text, as reconstructed by Boismard (*Texte*, 293) is quite different: ζητεῖν τὸ θεῖον εἰ ἄρα [ ] ψηλαφήσειεν [ ] ἢ εὕροιεν ἄν. καίτοι . . . τὸ θεῖον ("the divine," instead of "God," or "the Lord") is tempting but probably secondary (Metzger, *Textual Commentary*, 405–6). (Note also the masculine participle ὑπάρχοντα, which would have to refer back to the initial "God" in v. 24. D, in fact, reads ὄν, but this may be due to Latin influence, which is otherwise detectable here.) The sentence telescopes protasis and apodosis. Addition of ἄν makes the statement less likely: "If they should happen to grope for or even find (God), although . . ." The thought is not congenial to the Calvinist tradition, which would—like the D-Text—prefer to understand the condition as practically contrary to fact. (Calvin himself overrode the text by reading it in terms of Romans 1: "Paul is not speaking here about the ability of men, but he is only warning that they are inexcusable" [7:119]). Stenschke (*Gentiles*, 216–17) builds on the optative of v. 27 the thesis that the speech criticizes gentiles for failing to seek God. That view does not accord with the mentality of the address. When Luke wishes to show a speaker criticizing an audience, he can do so (e.g., 3:14). See Weiser, 2:473.

yields to the assurance that God is close at hand.[117] That assurance is both biblical and in accordance with religious philosophy.[118] At this point the speaker shifts into the first plural,[119] removing any barrier between himself and the audience. God is no further from gentiles than from Jews. The adverb μακράν plays an important role in the theology of a gentile mission.[120] There is no great gulf separating Jews from other peoples, for all are ultimately children of God.

■ **28** The verse justifies the claim that God is near. The justly famous resonant first clause may derive from a Greek poem, although the syntax of the second clause speaks against this.[121] It is probable that it stems from a source that played on the link between "Zeus" and "live/life," a pun used in the allegorical interpretation of Greek myth[122] and familiar to Jewish writers. The gentile narrator (and putative author) of *Aristeas* says:

> God, the overseer and creator of all things (πάντων ἐπόπτην καὶ κτίστην θεὸν), whom they worship, is He whom all worship, and we too, your Majesty, though we address Him differently, as Zeus and Dis; by these names those of old not unsuitably signified that He through whom all creatures receive life and come into being (δι᾽ ὅν ζωοποιοῦνται τὰ πάντα καὶ γίνεται) is the guide and Lord of all. (*Aristeas* 16)[123]

The God of Israel is, the narrator asserts, identical to the deity whom Greeks worship as creator and source of life and existence. This deity is identical to Paul's "unknown god." Humanity's relationship to this god is characterized with a triad: vitality, movement, and existence. The first is shared with plants, the second with animals, while genuine existence characterizes human beings—who alone possess "souls." Other interpretations exist.[124] Life in all of its qualities and capacities is due to God. Luke affirms human immortality with the phrase "all live in him" (God).[125]

117 In simple language, the text means: "if you are seeking God, you will not have far to look."

118 Biblical: e.g., Isa 55:6; Ps 145:18. Philosophy: e.g., Seneca *Ep. Mor.* 41.1 (above); Philo *Spec. leg.* 1.31; Josephus *Ant.* 8.108 (the temple cult shows that God is not far [μακράν]). Dio of Prusa uses the same phrase, οὐ μακράν ("not far"), in *Or.* 12.28 (already cited by Norden, *Agnostos Theos*, 18–19). Note the continuation of this theme in the apologetic tradition, e.g., Minucius Felix *Oct.* 32.7. Verse 27 contains a basic element of apologetics, the use of history for legitimation. The philosophers, when they were not wrong, were at least groping incompletely toward religious truth. The apologists argued that Christianity had come to fulfill, not to destroy, and that all religious thinkers depend on common human experience and longings.

119 In this instance, the variant ὑμῶν ("of you" [A* L Ψ 69 1505 2344]), which can always be attributed to error, may have begun as a correction to separate Paul from his hearers.

120 Note Acts 2:39 (Pentecost address); 22:21 (Paul's commission). Cf. also Eph 2:13, 17, on which see Pervo, *Dating*, 294.

121 For a discussion of the possible connection of the first line to a poem of Epimenides, see the judicious comments of Cadbury, *Book*, 46–50. Kirsopp Lake ("Your Own Poets," in Lake and Cadbury, *Additional Notes*, 246–51) was more confident that v. 28a derived from Epimenides. Max Pohlenz ("Paulus und die Stoa," *ZNW* 42 [1949] 69–104, esp. 101–4) argues that this line does not derive from Epimenides. One difficulty is that the text must be revised to be construed as poetry. For attempts, see Lake and Cadbury, *Additional Notes*, 250. Kauppi (*Foreign*, 83–93) argues for the *Eumenides* of Aeschylus. In an intellectual context, one would expect the opening phrase to read δι᾽ αὐτοῦ ("through him") rather than "in him" (ἐν αὐτῷ), a usage that appears to be instrumental. This is not the best Greek, although Smyth (*Greek Grammar*, §1511) states that it is acceptable in poetry. Note the parallel form in v. 31, which is, however, a proper (juridical) usage. See Haenchen, 527 n. 3; BDAG, 329, *s.v.* ἐν (6).

122 The oblique cases of "Zeus" are based on the stem *zēn-*, which is formally identical to the infinitive of ζάω ("live").

123 Trans. Moses Hadas (alt.), *Aristeas to Philocrates* (New York: Harper & Bros., 1951) 101–3.

124 Cf. Plato *Soph.* 248E–249A; *Tim.* 37C; Aristotle *De an.* 414a 12–13; Cleanthes *Hymn to Zeus* 4–5. Note the comments and references of Norden, *Agnostos Theos*, 19–24; and Conzelmann, 247–48. Although the formula is potentially pantheistic (better: panentheistic), the context excludes that interpretation. The notion that the deity fills all was seconded by Philo (e.g., *Leg. all.* 3.4; cf. 1.44) and was taken up in Ephesians, for example (e.g., 1:23;

The citation "we are God's offspring" is inartistic evidence at a point and with a formula that makes it quite parallel with citations from Scripture in speeches to Jewish audiences.[126] It derives from the *Phaenomena* of Aratus (v. 5).[127] One need not imagine that Luke gleaned this citation from his own study of Aratus. It was a popular quotation.[128] A possible source was Aristobulus, frg. 4, which names the author and quotes nine of the opening lines of the poem.[129] Appeals to Greek literature will become characteristic of the apologetic tradition.[130] The speech suggests that Greek writers provide opportunities for insight into the God proclaimed by Jesus and the message about Jesus in a manner comparable to the Israelite sacred writings.[131] The tag from Aratus affirms that God is the parent of all people. This common notion[132] grounds the unity of the human race in a creedal proposition. It is also a pivot. Just as the creedal affirmation of God as creator discredited the notion of temples, so God's paternity is the ground for rejecting images (v. 29). This enthymeme, as it were, involves a leap. The speaker does not, for example, state that humans were created in the image of God.[133]

■ **29** Rather than attack images per se, Paul criticizes their construction: created materials designed by human ingenuity. God is no more like a manufactured object than conceivable as dwelling in one.[134] This is a typical piece of Jewish polemic against images.[135] It clarifies Paul's views about the "idol-ridden" character of Athens (v. 16) and its "devotional monuments" (v. 23). With this view, philosophers in general would agree. The compromise, represented in Roman imperial Stoicism by Dio of Prusa (*Or.* 12), was that images (and temples) were necessary for the common people, who required such aids, and that they could be useful in stimulating the learned and intelligent toward reflection upon higher things.[136] The views of Paul could be understood—as they were by later apologists—as a defense of philosophical purity against temporizing compromises.[137] It is not likely that

3:19; 4:10) and thence by speculative exegetes, but Luke has no interest in such ideas. Gärtner (*Areopagus Speech,* 197, 219–20) aptly notes that all three verbs appear in polemic against "dead idols." See Wis 13:6-19; 15:16-17; *Jub.* 20:7–8; Ep Jer 8, 24, 26; Bel 5.

125 Luke 20:38: πάντες γὰρ αὐτῷ ζῶσιν. See Parsons and Pervo, *Rethinking,* 101 n. 72. On the theme note also Diodorus Siculus 1.12.2; 3.61.6; and *Aristeas* 16.

126 Use of the plural "poets" need not imply more than one. See Cadbury, *Book,* 49 and 56 n. 39. (Cicero, for example, prefaces his rendition of Aratus *Phaen.* 129–32 with *ut poetae loquuntur* ["as the poets say"], *Nat. Deor.* 2.159.) The D-Text (Boismard, *Texte,* 294) excises "poets," probably reflecting the anti-intellectual disdain for "heathen poets," such as Homer, that was characteristic of puritanical Christians. (On "our poets," see n. *k.*) On the formula, see Fitzmyer, 610–11.

127 Aratus of Soli (first half of third century BCE) was a pupil of Zeno who wrote poetry.

128 See Éduard des Places, "'Ipsius enim et genus sumus' (Act. XVII, 28)," *Bib* 81 (1962) 388–95.

129 Holladay, *Fragments,* 3:170–74. Aristobulus, frg. 4, line 77. Aristobulus explicitly cites nine lines from *Phaen.* 1–18. (Claims that humans were made in the divine image would not suit an argument against images.) Possible dependence on Aristobulus gains strength from the similarity of his views on creation to Acts 17:16-31. Acts also uses "of God" (θεοῦ) instead of "of Zeus." In lines 85–90, preserved by Eusebius, Aristobulus states that he altered "Zeus" and "Dis" to "God." See John M. G. Barclay, *Jews in the Mediterranean Diaspora from Alexander to Trajan (323 BCE–117 CE)* (Berkeley: University of California Press, 1996) 150–58, esp. 152–53; and M. J. Edwards, "Quoting Aratus: Acts 17,28," *ZNW* 83 (1992) 266–69.

130 E.g., Justin *1 Apol.* 18 (Homer et al.); Minucius Felix *Oct.* 19.1 (citing Homer and Virgil).

131 See Weiser, 2:476. This is the elliptical logic of the address, a logic that can only be convincing to the gentile convert.

132 The idea is not extraneous to Lucan thought, for it climaxes the genealogy of Jesus in Luke 3:38. For some references and discussion, see Parsons and Pervo, *Rethinking,* 98–101. Note also Spicq, *Lexicon,* 3:302–3.

133 Luke, unlike some other representatives of the Deutero-Pauline tradition, avoided speculation about this subject. See Parsons and Pervo, *Rethinking,* 105 n. 90.

134 On the adjective "like" (ὁμοῖος), see Parsons and Pervo, *Rethinking,* 92 n. 33.

135 See, e.g., Deut 4:28; Isa 40:18-20; Wis 13:10—14:11.

136 Cf. Dio *Or.* 12.80–83, which represents the great sculptor Pheidias as appealing to Zeus as the great artificer of the universe. The production of images is therefore an imitation of god.

137 On ancient philosophical critiques of images of the gods, see Balch, "Areopagus Speech" 67–72, and,

this was Luke's intention, but he does not represent the audience as taking exception to the critique of images, and it is unlikely that many members of the Areopagus would have wished to defend the thesis that the gods shared the properties of such artifacts. Readers would have accepted both critiques, and they are the audience that counts.[138]

■ **30** Having established, to his satisfaction, that for the audience the true God remains unknown, Paul announces that God is willing to overlook their extended ignorance[139] and calls for a universal change of heart.[140] With this summons Paul's speech to gentiles takes the shape of the speeches to Jews.[141] Although Luke shows, here and in 14:15-17, that he is aware of the topics of "general" and "particular" revelation, his concern is with a more basic problem of Christian theodicy: How could a good God have overlooked the vast majority of humankind? The answer lies in salvation history. In good time, and doubtless for good reasons, God has made salvation available to all.

The somewhat abrupt introduction of this theme in v. 30 leaves Luke open to Philipp Vielhauer's contention: "The repentance which is called for consists entirely in the self-consciousness of one's natural kinship to God."[142] Granted that this may be too harsh—if difficult to disprove in this context—Luke's anthropology is not pessimistic—much less pessimistic than that of Paul, for example. This leads to a different soteriology. Luke does not have Paul speak of the saving significance of Jesus' death here because that is not the key to Lucan theology.[143] The error of "the Jews" in killing Jesus is comparable to that of the Greeks for failing to recognize the true God.

■ **31** With the promise implied in repentance comes an implied threat. There will be an occasion when God will make all people stand judgment.[144] Soteriology is present only insofar as deliverance depends on human initiative in repenting. Divine grace is limited to the overlooking of ignorance.[145] Determinism (which would have been congenial to Stoics) is absent. The verb ὁρίζω ("determine") appears in vv. 26 and 31, binding judgment with creation as the poles between which God's plan unfolds.[146] Jesus will be the judge, his resurrection serving as a credential for that function. In accordance with Lucan Christology, the heavenly Christ can be characterized as a male human being (ἀνήρ) (see 2:22).

---

regarding the relation of this speech to Christian apologists, see Kathy L. Gaca, "Paul's Uncommon Declaration in Romans 1:18-32 and Its Problematic Legacy for Pagan and Christian Relations," in idem and Larry L. Welborn, eds., *Early Patristic Readings of Romans* (Romans through History and Cultures; New York: T&T Clark, 2005) 1–33, esp. 10–12.

138 David Gill ("Achaia," in Gill and Gempf, *Setting*, 444–45) envisions another audience: the Athenian general public, which would have believed that the gods lived in temples and were like their representations. Whatever their actual thoughts on these matters may have been, these people did not constitute the dramatic audience. See Haenchen, 528.

139 The D-Text (Boismard, *Texte*, 295) specifies this "ignorance." Epp (*Tendency*, 48–50) argues that the demonstrative seeks to distinguish the condition here from that of 3:17 (Jesus as Messiah). It is slightly more likely that this is a stylistic improvement. (The D-Text also changes two verbal forms in this verse, without demonstrable purpose.)

140 With the exception of Simon of Samaria (8:22), every call to "repentance" in Acts (2:38; 3:19; 17:30; 26:20) is directed to a group. Individuals do repent and change, but the Lucan understanding of repentance is not exclusively individualistic.

141 Note, in particular, 3:19 (Peter), where the summons to repent also follows an assertion about ignorance (3:17).

142 Vielhauer, "Paulinism," 33–50, esp. 36 (with a reference to Dibelius, *Studies*, 62).

143 Calvin (7:215): "There is no doubt that Paul said a good deal more about Christ." The expansions that he would introduce by assuming that the speech is a summary (216) are supplied by the reader from other speeches, but this lack illuminates the subject of the speech, which is the nature of God and how God is to be known.

144 References to judgment are common in speeches: Acts 2:20; 3:19-20; 10:42.

145 See Dibelius, *Studies*, 27. Apologetic took up this theme, e.g., Minucius Felix *Oct.* 20.1; 27.8.

146 The verb: Luke 22:22; Acts 2:23; 10:42. For comment, see Squires, *Plan*, 172–73; and K. L. Schmidt, "ὁρίζω," *TDNT* 5:452–56.

The grounds for judgment are not stated. Presumably they would involve acknowledgment of the one true God and righteous behavior. This touches on another problem of theodicy: How can a righteous, providential God tolerate evil behavior?[147] Representatives of the Jewish wisdom tradition wrestled with the issue, as did Greek philosophers.[148] The God proclaimed by Paul is therefore beneficent and just, unlike the indifferent gods of the Epicureans, the scheming and competitive gods of Homer, or, for that matter, the Jewish deity, whom many polytheists viewed as partial and nationalistic.

These words about "judgment day" do not provoke a reaction.[149] Resurrection does. This is a Lucan device.[150] That concept was not alien to Stoic thought, in which it applied to the entire cosmos.[151] Verse 31 may have an apologetic element: the rising of Jesus proves that resurrection can and will happen,[152] but nothing is said about resurrection in general. Through this means, Luke unites the objections of some members of the Areopagus with those of some members of the Sanhedrin (23:6-12) and Paul's later apologetic claims.[153] The reaction is, as often, mixed. The language is especially evocative of 2:12-13.[154] Readers with a smattering of education would have assigned the scoffing to the skeptical Epicureans and the more polite response[155] to those of Stoic leanings in the body. Opposition from Epicureans counts as strong support in the circles of philosophical theology.[156]

■ **32** Amidst derision and the suggestion of a subsequent opportunity, Paul departs. Readers may wonder what to make of this episode. Has Paul narrowly escaped from a dangerous situation or given an impressive summary of his message before a partially sympathetic audience. Or was the entire affair a fizzle? Modern critics may archly observe that he has incriminated himself upon the charges of teaching novel religion and introducing foreign gods. Failure to offer evidence for the god he proclaims and his claim that the entire world will be judged upon a single occasion would confirm the allegation of dilettantism, while he did cast aspersions on the traditional worship of Athens. Early readers would not have doubted that the speech was a tour de force. Paul had held his own before an august body that saw no reason for a criminal indictment against him, while delivering a brilliant summary of his message in terms that the dramatic audience could appreciate.

---

147 On this question of theodicy, opposition to which was associated with the Epicureans, see Neyrey, "Acts 17."

148 Answers were disparate, for example, Job and Wisdom. A work roughly contemporary with Acts is Plutarch's *De sera numinis vindicta* (*Mor.* 548A–568), which locates retribution in the afterlife.

149 Verse 31 does not contain even the nucleus of a full-fledged eschatology. There is no reference to the end of the world or an afterlife. Wilfred L. Knox (*St Paul*, 1–26) discusses some Greco-Roman views of eschatology in the period from the first century BCE to the second century CE.

150 Statements about resurrection frequently lead to an interruption that ends a speech; see 5:32-33; 7:53-54; 10:43-44; 22:21-22; 26:23. The resurrection of Jesus is related to judgment in 1 Thess 1:10; Heb 6:1-2; Acts 10:40-42 and is thus part of the traditional message.

151 In apocalyptic in general and Paul in particular (e.g., Rom 8:18-39), renewal of the entire cosmos is not foreign. Luke focuses on resurrection, especially the resurrection of individuals.

152 On the apologetic character of 17:31, see Helmut Flender, *St. Luke: Theologian of Redemptive History* (trans. I. and R. Fuller; Philadelphia: Fortress Press, 1967) 161. Cf. also *1 Clem.* 23–26, which defends resurrection with natural analogies, on which see Robert M. Grant and Holt Graham, *The Apostolic Fathers*, vol. 2: *First and Second Clement* (New York: Thomas Nelson & Sons, 1964) 50–51. On the use of Stoic arguments about resurrection, see Grant, *Miracle*, 235–45. Note also Henry Chadwick, "Origen, Celsus, and the Resurrection of the Body," *HTR* 41 (1948) 83–102.

153 The speeches in chaps. 24 and 26 depict Paul as on trial over this issue. Note 24:21 and 26:8.

154 The verb (διαʼ)χλευάζω appears only in these two places in the New Testament. This may be a motif. In *Corp. Herm.* 1.28–29 mockery follows a summons to repentance. Note also *Sib. Or.* 1:171–72; Ps.-Clem. *Hom.* 1.101; and Betz, *Lukian*, 111 n. 3. "Some people" (τινες [vv. 18 and 34]) bracket the episode.

155 Verse 32b can be taken as either a polite brush-off or as an expression of genuine interest.

156 See Neyrey, "Acts 17," 134.

With vulgar polytheism, there is little common ground, but the Christian movement shares a number of vital presuppositions with the reflective and learned. (Most) Jews did not recognize their Messiah; gentiles honored but did not know God. The ignorance of both calls for a change.

The harvest was admittedly meager,[157] but two proper names are presented: Dionysius and Damaris. They raise questions: Do the names derive from a tradition? Are they historical?[158] 1 Cor 16:15 states that Paul did not convert these two or anyone else in the province prior to his visit to Corinth, and a subsequent visit is not very likely, for Athens plays no part in Paul's collection. The names may have been preserved in some otherwise unidentified tradition, such as a legend about Paul, but a convert with Dionysius's accomplishments (membership in the Areopagus) was both quite unlikely at this early date and quite characteristic of Luke, who reveled in converts of high social status. The name seems bound up with Paul's appearance before the court.[159] The best explanation is that Luke invented Dionysius, or at least his social position.[160] Damaris is a cipher.[161] Acts 17:17-34 is a tribute to Luke's genius. From the most unpromising of results he has produced one of the most memorable passages in early Christian literature and begun to till the soil on which Christian philosophical theology will grow.

157 The D-Text (Boismard, *Texte*, 296) reads "many others." This correction attempts to make the mission to Athens as successful as others. Winter ("Introducing the Athenians to God") argues that the speech was not a failure.

158 For a negative answer to these questions, see David Gill, "Dionysios and Damaris: A Note on Acts 17:34," *CBQ* 61 (1999) 483–90.

159 Dionysius enjoyed a distinguished career in legend. By the last third of the second century (Eusebius *H.E.* 3.4.10), he had become the first bishop of Athens. In due course, he was assigned authorship of a collection of Christian Neo-Platonic mystical writings that were immensely popular during the Middle Ages.

160 Lüdemann (*Acts*, 229) inverts this argument. He regards the name of Dionysius as derived from tradition and the possible motive for the speech before the council. This is improbable, since Luke had other and more cogent motives for placing Paul before the Areopagus.

161 Damaris (apparently a variant of δάμαλις, "heifer" [Hemer, *Book*, 232; and BDAG, 211, *s.v.*]) raised difficulties because of the assumption that she was an auditor of the speech. These have included the proposal that she was the wife of Dionysius (see Chrysostom *Sac.* 4.7); the Greek word γυνή permits this, although a possessive is lacking), the wife or mother of one of the philosophers present, or a (reformed) prostitute. On the last, see Ramsay, *St. Paul the Traveller*, 252: "[T]he name Damaris . . . suggests a foreign woman, perhaps one of the class of educated *Hetairai*, who might very well be in his audience." For a courtesan with that name, see Horace *Odes* 1.36.13–20. Conzelmann (149 n. 95) refers to inscriptional evidence of the name. D omits her. This could be due to the loss of a line (Clark, 367; Metzger, *Textual Commentary*, 407–8; and Boismard, *Texte*, 296), but the presence of εὐσχήμων ("of high standing") in D suggests that her name was suppressed by intention, perhaps in an ancestor of D. That adjective is used otherwise only of women in Acts (13:50; 17:12) and is quite gratuitous of Dionysius, as all members of the Areopagus were highly placed. Δ E support the application of some status adjective to Damaris: γυνὴ τιμία; *mulier honesta* ("a woman of high position"). See Pervo, "Social Aspects," 238. Haenchen (526 n. 5) aptly sums up the tradition: "Pious fantasy became preoccupied with her."

18

18:1-23 Paul in Corinth

	18:1-23: Conventional Text		18:1-23: D-Text[i]
1/	After his encounter with the Areopagus, Paul left[a] Athens for Corinth, 2/ where he came upon a Jew, Aquila, from Pontus, and his wife Priscilla, who had recently arrived from Italy because the emperor Claudius had ordered all Jews out of Rome.[b] Paul presented himself to this couple 3/ and came to live with them because they, like him, crafted with fabrics.[c] So Paul went to work.	1/	After his encounter with the Areopagus, Paul left Athens for Corinth, 2/ where he came upon one Aquila[j] from Pontus, recently arrived from Italy *together with Priscilla, his wife. He greeted them. They had left the City* because Claudius *Caesar* had ordered all Jews banished *from the City. They had settled in Achaea. 3/ Paul recognized Aquila because he was a member of the same tribe. Paul stayed with them.*[k]
4/	Every Sabbath he lectured in the synagogue, trying to persuade both Jews and gentiles.	4/	Every Sabbath he *entered* the synagogue and lectured, *introducing the name of the Lord Jesus,*[l] trying to persuade *not only* Jews *but also* gentiles.
5/	When, however, Silas and Timothy arrived from Macedonia, Paul devoted himself fully to the mission,[d] declaring to the Jews that the Messiah was Jesus.	5/	*Then* Silas and Timothy arrived from Macedonia.
6/	When they impiously[e] opposed him,	6/	*After substantial presentation and scriptural interpretations, some Jews began impiously* to oppose him.[m]
	Paul shook out his clothes in a symbolic gesture and announced: "You are responsible for your own fate. Don't blame me. Henceforth I shall apply myself to the gentiles."		*Then* Paul shook his *cloak* . . . "I am going *away from you* to the gentiles."
7/	He transferred his mission from the synagogue to the adjacent house of the devout Titius Justus. 8/ The leader of the synagogue, Crispus, came to faith in the Lord, as did his entire household. Learning of this,[f] many Corinthians embraced the faith and received baptism.	7/	*He left*[n] *Aquila's house* . . . Justus . . .[o]
		8/	. . . *A large number of* Corinthians heard *the word of the Lord* and were baptized, embracing faith *in God through the name of Jesus Christ.*[p]
9/	The Lord addressed Paul in a nocturnal vision: "Have no fear. Continue to speak and do not desist, 10/ for I am with you. No one will be able to attack you successfully, for my people are numerous in this city." 11/ Paul settled there for eighteen months, teaching the word of God.	9/	. . . speak *and see* . . .
		10/	. . .[q]
		11/	*And* he settled *in Corinth.*
12/	Now while Gallio was governing the province of Achaea, the Jews converged upon Paul *en masse* and brought him	12/	. . . The Jews, *after conversing among themselves against Paul and laying hands upon him,*

	before the bench. 13/ "This man is trying to persuade people to worship God unlaw-		brought him *to the governor,* 13/ *crying out and . . .*
	fully," they charged. 14/ Just as Paul was about to reply, Gallio addressed the Jews: "If there had been an actual injury or any serious misbehavior, my dear Jews, I should have quite properly entertained	14/	"Jewish *gentlemen . . .*'[r]
	your claims, 15/ but, since these are quibbles about mere language, titles, and your own regulations,[g] please see to the matter yourselves. I have no desire to pronounce judgments on these issues." 16/ Gallio	15/	. . .[s]
	then had the Jews removed from his court, but not before	16/	*dismissed*
	everybody mobbed Sosthenes, the leader of the synagogue, and gave him a beating in court. 17/ Gallio showed no interest in any of this.	17/	*The Greeks*[t] mobbed . . . Gallio *pretended not to see.*
18/	Paul stayed on for a number of days before saying his farewells to the believers and sailing off to Syria with Priscilla and Aquila. At the Corinthian port of Cenchreae he had his hair cut off, because he had undertaken	18/	. . . *making* a vow at Cenchreae, had his hair cut.[u]
	a vow.	19/	*After he had* reached Ephesus,
19/	When they reached Ephesus, Paul separated from the couple. He himself went to the synagogue		*Paul* went to the Synagogue *on* *the next Sabbath and began to* engage the Jews.[v]
	and engaged the Jews. 20/ They asked that he spend more time, but he could not agree, 21/ and	20/	They asked that he spend more time *with them*, but he could not agree,
	bade them farewell, promising, "God willing, I shall come back to you at another time." Leav- ing Ephesus by ship,	21/	and bade them farewell: *"It is* *absolutely necessary that I keep* *the coming feast [day] in Jeru-* *salem.* God willing . . ."
22/	Paul arrived in Caesarea and went from there to *Jerusalem*, where he paid his respects to the church before continuing on to Antioch. 23/ He spent some time there and then set out again, moving through Galatian territory and Phrygia, strength- ening all[h] the believers in each community as he traveled.	22/	He *left Aquila in Ephesus,* while he *came* by ship to Caesarea.

a The D-Text (Boismard, *Texte*, 297) reads "withdrawing from" (ἀναχωρήσας δὲ ἀπό). This is stylistic variation (unless the sense of χωρίζω in v. 2 motivated alteration to indicate that Paul was not forced out of Athens). The *v.l.* "Paul," supported by much of the D-Text tradition, probably stems from lectionary usage.

b BDF §261 (2): "The use of the article in Acts with the stations on the journeys is peculiar."

c On the meaning(s) of σκηνοποιός, see below.

d *Or:* "By the time Silas and Timothy had arrived, Paul was fully occupied with the mission."

e 𝔓[74], for reasons that are not clear and may stem

from an error, omits καὶ βλασφημούντων (lit. "and blaspheming").

f The participle ἀκούοντες ($\mathfrak{p}^{74}$ *et al.* have the more logical aorist) has no object. An alternative is to construe it as "when they heard *the message* . . ." The alternate conforms to the general thrust of Acts, but the version presented is more suitable to the immediate context.

g There are minor variants in the first clause of v. 15.

h The D-Text omits "all."

i Boismard, *Texte*, 297–309.

j Omitting ὀνόματι ("named").

k "With him" according to D[(1)].

l An alternative understanding of the participle ἐντιθείς is "inserting the name of Jesus," which may be taken (e.g., Johnson, 323) as reading the name "Jesus" where "Lord" (a substitute for the tetragrammaton) is found in Scripture.

m On the D-Text of vv. 4-6, see Epp, *Tendency*, 84–87.

n Bezae omits the initial καί ("and," little more than a punctuation mark), permitting the statement about Aquila to be read as part of what Paul said (Epp, *Tendency*, 93).

o There are some minor D-Text variants in v. 7. On the problems, see Epp, *Tendency*, 91–93.

p On the D-Text of v. 8, see Epp, *Tendency*, 87–90.

q The D-Text omits σοι after ἐπιθήσεται, presumably as redundant.

r The D-Text adds the conventional ἄνδρες. There are also paraphrases of κατὰ λόγον ("quite properly"), on which see Ropes, *Text*, 174.

s The D-Text adds "some" (τινα) to "quibbles" and replaces βούλομαι with the stronger θέλω.

t A few (36. 453 *pc*) witnesses read "the Jews," no doubt correctly. Ephrem attributes the action to Greek converts to Christianity (!).

u Some D-Texts attribute the vow and action to Aquila (or Aquila and Priscilla, or, possibly, all three). See Ropes, *Text*, 176; and Metzger, *Textual Commentary*, 412. This may be due to the word order, as the participle "shaving" (κειράμενος) follows "Aquila," and both are nominative (v. 18). It is possible that a reviser wished to remove the report that Paul engaged in a Jewish cultic act.

v The D-Text uses the proper name to produce clarity, as indicated by translation. The verb is imperfect in the D-Text.

Analysis

The structure of 18:1-18, which treats the mission to Corinth, is relatively straightforward. The same cannot be said of the residue (vv. 19-28). After a flying visit to Ephesus, Paul sets out for Jerusalem by sea, then proceeds to Antioch, followed by an overland pastoral visit to previous foundations (v. 22) that will return him in due course to Ephesus (19:1). The Jerusalem visit is evidently explained by a vow (18:18). One effect of this vast travel is to place a period upon the mission begun in 16:6—or perhaps at 15:36, or even 15:3. This, in turn, highlights the Pauline mission at Ephesus (chap. 19). The sense of a new beginning is marked by the apparent construction of a new team: Priscilla and Aquila (cf. 15:36—16:3).[1] If this indication of a fresh adventure is clear, the structure is, at best, convoluted. The author is responsible for this material, which shows Paul's continuing good relations with Jerusalem and Antioch, as well as his piety. One effect of the baroque arrangement is to remove any personal contact between Paul and Apollos. This is not accidental. Acts 18:24-29 and 19:1-7 are complementary units, best studied together.

Excursus: Acts 18 and Chronology

This chapter contains two references that may be correlated with external events and thus provide opportunity for establishing a chronological base. In addition, there are relative, internal temporal markers. The first, μετὰ ταῦτα (lit. "after these things" [18:1]), is vague. "Every Sabbath" (v. 4) indicates a mission of at least some weeks. Verse 11 speaks of an enterprise that lasted for a year and a half. The text does not state whether this applies to the entire mission or only from that point onward. Finally, v. 18 refers to "a number of days," a vague expression that has different meanings in Acts.[2] These data indicate that the mission to Corinth lasted between about

1 The narrator drops Silas (permanently) and Timothy (until 20:4). The reader is justified in presuming that they did not accompany Paul to Ephesus.

2 According to Dixon Slingerland ("Acts 18:1-18, the Gallio Inscription, and Absolute Pauline Chronology," *JBL* 110 [1991] 439–49), the phrase means a relatively long period in 8:11, while 27:7 encompasses a brief passage in time, and 9:23, 43; 14:3;

eighteen and about twenty-two months,[3] an unusual length, rivaled thus far only by Antioch (11:26).[4]

The two possible external pegs are the mention of an expulsion of "all the Jews" from Rome by Claudius (v. 2) and the Achaean proconsulship of (L. Junius) Gallio (Annaeus) (vv. 12-17). No ancient authority except Acts claims that Claudius expelled *all* the Jews from Rome. The biographer Suetonius, writing in the early second century, says that Claudius (41–54 CE) "expelled Jews from Rome because they were generating incessant unrest through the instigation of Chrestus" (*Iudaeos impulsore Chresto assidue tumultantis Roma expulit* [*Claud.* 25.4]).[5] This could mean a general expulsion or the expulsion of some troublemakers. The statement is enigmatic. Were the name of the agitator different, interpreters would conclude that Jews, stirred up by some firebrand, were involved in riots with the general population. Since "Chrestus" is a variant of "Christ," the standard interpretation refers this to internal Jewish disturbances related to Christian missionary activities. Behind this stands the impression made by Acts (e.g., 13:50; 14:2-6, 19; 17:5-10, 10b-13) taken at face value: when the message about Jesus is proclaimed, Jews riot. This understanding is far from certain.[6] Suetonius provides no date for the action.

Cassius Dio (c. 160–230) *Hist.* 60.6.6,[7] reports that the increase of numbers of Jews made expulsion difficult, as it would probably lead to a riot (ταραχή), so that Claudius allowed them to follow their traditional lifestyle (τῷ δὲ δὴ πατρίῳ βίῳ χρωμένους), but forbade gatherings (συναθροίζεσθαι). This report, which is assigned to 41 CE, contradicts Suetonius. Orosius, a Christian historian of the early fifth century, cites Suetonius and assigns the expulsion to 49 CE (*anno nono*, "the ninth year" of Claudius's reign) on the authority of Josephus (Orosius *Historia contra Paganos* 7.6.15). These accounts raise a number of questions: Was there an expulsion of some or all Jews from Rome, or a ban on meetings, the expulsion of some and a ban (which may have led to some departures), or different events at different times? When did this or these things happen?[8] The last is of interest here.

Orosius's claim is as good as his putative source (Josephus does not refer to an expulsion under Claudius) and should be set aside.[9] The earlier date (41/42) for an action is more probable.[10] In that year, Claudius dealt with Jewish disturbances in Alexandria. Tacitus, who was interested in such matters, does not mention any expulsions or other actions against Roman Jews in 49.[11] Philo's *Legatio*, composed in the early 40s, states that Augustus did not expel the Jews from Rome or prevent them from meeting (157). He probably has more recent events in mind.[12] Were it not for Acts 18, which appears to

and 27:9 are vague. On its function here, see the comments on v. 18.

3 This is no more than a guess based on reasonable (Lucan) intervals for the periods described in vv. 4-6 and 18a.

4 As recent versions indicate (contrast, e.g., *NRSV* to *RSV*), the opening genitive absolute of v. 12 should be rendered "while," rather than with an adversative "but when," which might imply that the action took place when Gallio assumed office.

5 See Stern, *Authors*, vol. 2 no. 307, pp. 113–17, with commentary.

6 Slingerland has made the most recent argument against the identification of "Chrestus" with "Christ" (*Claudian Policymaking and the Early Imperial Repression of Judaism at Rome* [South Florida Studies in the History of Judaism 160; Atlanta: Scholars Press, 1997] 151–217). His arguments merit attention. Suetonius distinguishes Jews from Christians in *Nero* 16. It is possible that *Claud.* 25.4 derives from an early source and that Suetonius did not realize that it was associated with messianic ideas.

7 See Stern, *Authors*, vol. 2 no. 422, p. 367.

8 For a concise summary of the issues and solutions, see Barclay, *Jews*, 303–6. Schürer (*History*, 3.1:77–78) represents the most common view: there was an expulsion c. 49, a date reached by subtracting at least eighteen months from 51, the presumed start of Gallio's proconsulship. This construct assumes, erroneously, that Acts 18 presents a clear chronology. For a thorough discussion of the problem of hypothesizing an expulsion in c. 49, see Harry J. Leon, *The Jews of Ancient Rome* (updated ed.; Peabody, Mass.: Hendrickson, 1995) 22–27.

9 A claim that Orosius remembered the year correctly but did not remember his source would be highly questionable. Dixon Slingerland ("Suetonius *Claudius* 25.4, Acts 18, and Paulus Orosius *Historiarum adversum paganos libri vii*: Dating the Claudian Expulsions of Roman Jews," *JQR* 83 [1992] 127–44) believes that Orosius concocted his information. Dates between 42 and 54 are possible.

10 Levinskaya (*Diaspora Setting*, 171–82) identifies all of the relevant issues and provides a number of arguments in favor of an earlier date for the expulsion.

11 Tacitus's material for 41 CE is lacking.

12 By attributing these restraints to Augustus, Philo politely avoids accusing current rulers of taking such actions. See Smallwood, *The Jews*, 213–14. (One might object that Philo would suppress such

demand a later date, the matter would probably not be debated.[13]

Inscriptional evidence provides some information on the date of Gallio's tenure as proconsul of Achaea. *SIG*[3] 801D is a letter from Claudius that refers to the proconsulship of Gallio.[14] With the assistance of another inscription from Caria (Hyllarima Caria 17.1), the letter can be dated between January 25 and August 1, 52. The letter does not specifically state that Gallio was then proconsul, nor is it certain that he had but recently arrived on the scene. Although imperial governors normally served one year, two was not unusual. Furthermore, the conclusion that this encounter came near the end of Paul's residence in Corinth is far from certain, since Luke normally places confrontations with the law toward the end of his account. The greatest allowance for safety yields a range of 49 to 54 for the putative encounter between Paul and Gallio.[15] The major difficulty with this datum is the assumption of a "historical kernel." Acts 18:12-17 is an authorial composition that fits a literary plan.

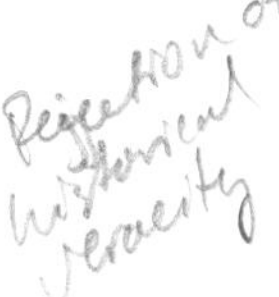

In sum, "Acts 18:1-18 is very far from the kind of prose on which anyone would want to depend for the detailed reconstruction of past social, political, or religious history."[16] The two external references constitute a literary frame of anti-Jewish actions. The first item is probably best dated c. 42, although the evidence is flimsy and conflicting, while the second would be about a decade later and requires straining out the name Gallio from a nonhistorical narrative. Around 50 would fit other data (although no reader of Acts would imagine that around twenty years have elapsed since the crucifixion).

Corinth[17] was ideally situated on both north–south and east–west axes of commerce and travel. Despite its long and complex history, the Corinth of Paul's era was a relatively "new" city, refounded a century earlier as a Roman colony (*Colonia Laus Julia Corinthiensis*). Corinth was a rough and vigorous place, a natural hub of business by land and sea, brimming with immigrants from around the Mediterranean. In this bustling, multiethnic city, Paul enjoyed far more success than he had in Athens, the traditional center of Greek culture. That fact is probably indicative of the kind of person attracted to his mission, including what are now called the relatively upwardly mobile, such as former slaves and immigrant business people.[18] Those who would seek to cast direct light upon Acts 18:1-18a from the wealth of literary and archaeological information pertinent to Corinth would face a challenge. The primary datum about Corinth in

unpleasant information, but this omission would be subject to exposure.)

13 Gerd Lüdemann uses the date of 41 as one base of his chronology of Paul's work: *Paul Apostle to the Gentiles: Studies in Chronology* (trans. F. Stanley Jones; Philadelphia: Fortress Press, 1984) 164–73. For a defense of 49, with many interesting observations, see Peter Lampe, *From Paul to Valentinus: Christians at Rome in the First Two Centuries* (trans. Michael Steinhauser; ed. Marshall D. Johnson; Minneapolis: Fortress Press, 2003) 11–16. Lampe (14) presumes that Orosius had a valid source, that is, that his date is correct but that he misstated the source. This presumption is questionable.

14 The reconstruction of *SIG*[3] 801D in Conzelmann (152–53) is not the most current. See Hemer, *Book*, 252; Fitzmyer, 621–23; the discussion of Murphy-O'Connor, *Saint Paul's Corinth*, 141–52; and Klaus Haacker, "Gallio," *ABD* 2:901–3. For additional bibliography, see Fitzmyer, 632.

15 Slingerland ("Acts 18:1-18," 439–49) argues for this broad range. The narrowest is Fitzmyer (622–23), who places the encounter between late April and early October of 52. This depends on two assumptions: that Gallio advised Claudius of his concerns about Delphi (the subject of Claudius's letter) immediately upon arrival at his post and that Seneca's statement about his brother's sudden departure from Greece because of a fever (*Ep.* 104.2) took place at the beginning of his proconsulship and was permanent.

16 Slingerland, "Acts 18:1-18," 441.

17 See Jerome Murphy-O'Connor, "Corinth," *ABD* 1:1134–39, and his *Saint Paul's Corinth*. Note also James Wiseman, "Corinth and Rome I: 228 B.C.–A.D. 267," *ANRW* 17.1 (1979) 438–548; and Donald Engels, *Roman Corinth: An Alternative Model for the Classical City* (Chicago: University of Chicago Press, 1990).

18 For some reflections about these sociological hypotheses, see Pervo, "PANTA KOINA," and "Wisdom and Power."

Acts is the existence of a Jewish community, supported by the fragment of a synagogue lintel that may be much later than Paul,[19] fragments of a pillar with Jewish symbols,[20] and the inclusion of the city in a list of places containing Jews by Philo (*Leg. Gaj.* 281).

The first eight verses are essentially summary. Verses 9-10 constitute a brief scene. The climax of the mission comes in the longer scene of vv. 12-17. Following the introduction in vv. 1-3 is the standard "Jews first" program (v. 4). The arrival of Silas and Timothy (v. 5) permits an intensification of missionary activity, which generates opposition, resulting in the second of three announcements that Paul is turning to the gentiles (v. 6).[21] This leads to a new base of operations and the conversion of the synagogue president, a synecdoche (cf. "firstfruits") of the mission's success (vv. 7-8). After an unsuccessful attempt to enmesh Paul in legal difficulties fails, he nonetheless departs (vv. 12-18a). This description is a variation of the basic stereotype, distinguished by more concrete data, including six new personal names.

Literary analysis is more interesting.[22] The dominant concept is hostility toward the Jews, within the stereotyped presentation of a mission to them.[23] The story opens with a general expulsion of "all the Jews" from Rome by Claudius and closes with the particular expulsion of the Jews at Corinth from the judgment seat of Gallio. In v. 6, Paul denounces the Jews, whose leader presently defects. The ruling theme is prophecy and fulfillment. Paul prophetically announces that the blood of the Jews will be on their own heads (v. 6). Symbolic fulfillment comes in v. 17, when their leader receives a bloody nose, so to speak. The prophecy of the Lord in vv. 9-10 is fulfilled both by the long stay and the final fiasco with Gallio.

Luke's sources included Paul's letters and, evidently, some traditions of unknown origin.[24] The correspondence indicates that Paul visited Corinth on a number of occasions, but this is the only specific stay reported in Acts.[25] As John Hurd showed, Acts tends to concentrate material about Paul's visits to a particular city in one report.[26] From the literary perspective, this practice is quite sensible, but it does not enhance the historical utility of Acts. Corinth is an apt illustration of this technique. The living arrangements are difficult to unravel. In 18:1-4, Paul lived and worked with Aquila and Priscilla. In v. 7, he moved his base to the residence of Titius Justus. The narrative does not say that Paul lived there.[27] Aquila and Priscilla disappear from v. 3 until Paul's departure for Syria, when he takes them as (his only?) companions (18:18). Two synagogue leaders appear: Crispus (v. 8), who becomes a believer, and Sosthenes (v. 17). Readers might presume that he had replaced Crispus, but the narrator does not say so. One solution is to posit conflation of material from different visits. This "conservative" option does not resolve all of the difficulties, since it is likely that Paul would have found lodging with some of his converts during subsequent visits, and the encounter with Gallio does not fit the data, as the epistles say nothing of conflicts with Jews.

In both 1 Corinthians (1:14) and Acts (18:8), the first person identified as one baptized by Paul bears the name "Crispus." Identification of the two is common. Commentators on 1 Corinthians may choose to flesh out the details from Acts 18.[28] If Luke took this information from Paul, he made two important changes and inferred another. First, he made Crispus a Jew. 1 Corinthians does not specify this, and most readers of that letter would suppose that he was a gentile. Second, Luke promoted Crispus to a prominent place

19 The inscription is *CIJ* 718. See Deissmann, *Light*, 16 n. 7. The poor quality makes dating difficult, but a date after 100 CE is likely. The restoration is not certain, as the only indisputable letters are *ΓΩΓΗ EBP*. See *NewDocs* 4 (1987) no. 113, pp. 213–14.

20 Erich Dinkler, *Signum Crucis: Aufsätze zum Neuen Testament und zur christlichen Archäologie* (Tübingen: Mohr Siebeck, 1967) 118–33.

21 See pp. 10–11.

22 See Haenchen, 538–41.

23 Cf. Philipp Vielhauer, *Geschichte der urchristlichen Literatur* (Berlin: de Gruyter, 1975) 130.

24 Haenchen (537) vaguely expresses a general consensus: "Luke, however, must have drawn on some source or other."

25 Cf., however, the stay in "Greece" (20:2-3).

26 John C. Hurd, Jr., *The Origin of 1 Corinthians* (New York: Seabury, 1965) 27–33. Lüdemann (*Acts*, 235–36) makes a similar point with these examples: Lystra: Acts 14:8-20; 14:21; 16:1-3; Philippi: 16:12-40; cf. 20:2, 3-6; Thessalonica: 17:1-10; 20:2; Ephesus: 19:1–20:1; cf. 18:19-21.

27 See also p. 449 n. 34.

28 Bruce (393) identifies the two, as does Gordon D.

in the synagogue. Both of these changes, as well as the generalization to include the entire household, are quite characteristic of Luke, who likes to emphasize Paul's missionary work among Jews and the social status of his converts.[29] If Luke derived his information about Crispus from a foundation story, it was obliterated by his own redactional concerns, so that the result differs little.[30] The itinerary (from Athens to Corinth) and the information about Silas and Timothy could also derive from the letters.[31] The possibility that the name of the synagogue president Sosthenes (v. 17) was taken from 1 Cor 1:1 is no more likely than the theory that the two are identical.[32]

Although the voyage of Priscilla and Aquila to Ephesus with Paul could be deduced from 1 Cor 16:19, the circumstantial data about this couple in Acts 18:2-3—that Aquila came from Pontus and had been expelled from Rome as a Jew, and that he and his wife practiced a craft, apparently derive, at least in part, from a different tradition. The expulsion fits Luke's interest in making the Jews look like enemies of the Roman order, but Luke would have been unlikely to invent the notion that Paul was an artisan, for this does not conform to his view of Paul's social status. These data may have been known at Ephesus, where the couple could have been remembered among the community's founders. Another possibility is that the author of Acts visited Corinth at some time. In support of this hypothesis is the possibility that he was familiar with *1 Clement*.[33] This hypothesis could account for the description of the couple's association with Apollos (vv. 24-28).

The circumstantial statement about Titius Justus in v. 7 is vexatious. It is difficult to understand why Luke would have invented these details, but, once again, the description conforms to the Lucan scheme of synagogue proclamation that attracts sympathetic gentiles. Is it accidental that Luke never speaks of this person as a believer? As in the case of Priscilla and Aquila, his conversion is not narrated. The two Latin names suggest a Roman citizen.[34] The harmonizing solution is to posit that his *praenomen* was "Gaius" and to identify him with the person named in 1 Cor 1:14 (cf. also Rom 16:23).[35]

As indicated above, the Gallio episode (vv. 12-17) is highly problematic. Weiser contends that it is a pre-Lucan element of Corinthian local tradition and historical (in its essence) because it is a self-contained story not linked to its context that includes the names of Sosthenes and Gallio.[36] The same facts argue more cogently for Lucan composition. Every feature of this adventure conforms to Lucan themes. At the conclusion of the mission comes an attempt by unhappy Jews to arraign Paul for illegal teaching, resulting in his vindication by the powers that be. The attempted snare is transparently inadequate and easily rebuffed by Gallio. Initial suspense dissolves in the

Fee, *The First Epistle to the Corinthians* (NICNT; Grand Rapids: Eerdmans, 1987) 63.

29 On the possible derivation of the data about Crispus, see Pervo, *Dating*, 102–4. Probability of dependence is enhanced by the fact that, although Paul mentions Crispus first in 1 Cor 1:14, the first household baptized was that of Stephanas (16:15). Since 1 Cor 16:14-18 indicates that Stephanas remained a supporter of Paul, the apostle did not name him first.

30 This is the only account of the conversion of a Jewish household in Acts. Significantly, it follows the transfer of the mission base to a house. See Matson, *Household Conversions*, 168–82.

31 1 Thess 1:1; 3:6; 2 Cor 1:19. The support implied in Acts 18:6 may have been that mentioned in 2 Cor 11:8-9.

32 The latter has supporters. BDAG, 985, *s.v.* Σωσθένης, says that "many scholars, not without good reason" have identified the two. For the basis, see, for example, Marshall (299), who allows the possibility that Sosthenes was attacked because he was a Christian sympathizer. Richard G. Fellows ("Renaming in Paul's Churches: The Case of Crispus-Sosthenes Revisited," *TynBul* 56 [2005] 111-30) argues that they are the same person. For a critical view of this hypothesis, see Claudia J. Setzer, "Sosthenes," *ABD* 6:160.

33 Cf. Pervo, *Dating*, 229, 310–15.

34 Sherwin-White (*Roman Society*, 158) finds Titius Justus as the only convincing case of two Latin names in the New Testament.

35 Edgar J. Goodspeed, "Gaius Titius Justus," *JBL* 69 (1950) 382–83.

36 Weiser, 2:486–87.

burlesque beating of Sosthenes, who received the humiliation he had intended for Paul. The proconsul would not lift a finger to defend the Jewish leader from mob violence.[37] Formally, vv. 12-17 resemble an apophthegm. The unit begins with a genitive absolute, contains a minimal narrative setting, and focuses on the statement of Gallio in vv. 14-15. Since the pronouncement is an authorial composition, it follows that the framework also is.[38]

If a historical report or a legend stood behind this encounter, it has been obliterated. The critical approach has been to assume that the narrative is bath water, but that the baby, Gallio, is historical, or at least traditional.[39] The alternative is to ask how Luke, if he is entirely responsible for the episode, obtained this proper name.[40] That is a good challenge, assuming that a tradition would be more readily available than data about Gallio.[41] Additional questions not addressed in Acts are why the Jewish plaintiffs would not apply to the local magistrates and the propriety of the proconsul's interference in the internal affairs of a Roman colony. Sherwin-White states the problem: "The question is whether Jewish residents at Corinth, who presumably were not citizens of Corinth, could expect the proconsul to enforce their domestic law within the territory of a community that was a Roman colony."[42] One could no doubt construct a number of plausible scenarios, but Acts does not do so.[43] At most one can say that there may have been a story about an encounter of Paul with Gallio and that this may have had some historical basis.[44] Luke could have transferred material located elsewhere in the province to Corinth. This would fit his schematization. Further than that the prudent historian will hesitate to advance. In any event, from the perspective of history, Gallio was an apposite figure, since he represented that Roman cultural elite that would succumb to the machinations of Nero, who would also gain notoriety as a persecutor of Christians. For Luke, the mission to Corinth was first and foremost a conflict between "church" and synagogue. That view gains no support from the Corinthian correspondence and coheres with Lucan narrative themes.[45] Luke made creative use of such source material as he had.

A major difficulty for exegesis is the highly compressed and elusive quality of the narrative. Nothing reveals these difficulties so clearly as the D-Text, which clarifies the matter of Aquila. He (with his wife subordinated to a prepositional phrase) had come directly from Rome and settled in Corinth. Paul recognized him because of their tribal kinship.[46] Aquila's religious status is even more vague than in the conventional text.[47] Nothing is said of their common occupation or of Paul's labor, evidently deemed socially inappropriate.[48] In consequence, v. 5 eliminates the implication that the arrival of Silas and Timothy allowed Paul to engage

37 See Pervo, *Profit*, 45, 60. Verse 17b can be construed in several ways. The simplest takes οὐδέν as subject and τούτων as partitive ("none of these things") rather than as a genitive complement to this verb: BDF §176 (3). Another possibility is to take the verb as impersonal, in which case οὐδέν would be an accusative of respect. See Moule, *Idiom Book*, 28.

38 Although Johnson (333) claims that "the Jewish attempt to have Paul convicted by the proconsul Gallio breathes the air of plausibility," he goes on to speak of its "literary and religious functions."

39 As Jean Juster (*Les juifs dans l'empire romain* [2 vols.; Paris: Paul Geuthner, 1914] 2:154 n. 4) observed, reference to an actual proconsul does not prove the historicity of the account. Haenchen (541), however, was inclined to accept the general truth of the story.

40 Juster (ibid.) already noted that the existence of (L. Junius) Gallio does not make the story historical.

41 Sherwin-White (*Roman Society*, 104–7) shows the difficulties of obtaining this information from available sources. Inscriptions are a possibility.

42 Sherwin-White, *Roman Society*, 100.

43 Some attempts at plausible scenarios are offered by Sherwin-White, *Roman Society*, 100–104.

44 If historical grounds are sought, this incident could have led to one of the three legal floggings mentioned in 2 Cor 11:25—if they are to be taken at face value.

45 Cadbury and Lake, 220: "Luke's interest is centred, at least here, on two points—the opposition of the Jews, and the refusal of the Roman authorities to take action against Paul."

46 The D-Text evidently wishes to imply a previous acquaintance.

47 Epp, *Tendency*, 92–93.

48 So also Barrett, 2:864. Metzger (*Textual Commentary*, 409) attributes this omission to accident.

in full-time mission work. The D-Text has no acceleration of missionary activity. By expanding vv. 4, 6, and 8, this text produces a more circumstantial and logical account, illustrating, as often, both the strengths and weaknesses of Luke's style.[49] Addition of "from you" in v. 6 emphasizes separation from the synagogue, as does the change of subject in v. 7. With separation from the synagogue comes separation from Aquila. Paul changes both residence and base.[50] The expansions to vv. 12-13 establish the action as premeditated and disorderly, the typical behavior of a mob. Assignment of the beating to "the Greeks" reflects the understanding that the attempt to accuse Paul resulted in an outburst of anti-Jewish sentiment,[51] based on the presumption that the Jews are responsible for their own mistreatment.

Comment

■ **1-2** The initial verses introduce the Corinthian story somewhat elaborately. The narrator states neither why Paul left[52] Athens nor why he came to Corinth. Luke does not speak of a plan until 19:21. From a glance at a map, one sees that he has moved south from Macedonia through Achaea. At Corinth he encountered[53] one Aquila, a well-known person from the Pauline tradition who evidently illustrates the mobility of some early Christians.[54] Both Aquila and his wife, Prisc(ill)a,[55] bore Latin names. Acts identifies Aquila as Jewish in background and not until 18:26 does it transpire that the two were Christians.[56] They were evidently missionaries who specialized in the formation and nurture of house churches. Extrapolating a hypothesis based on Rom 16:3-5, Paul may have used them as "advance men" in both Ephesus and Rome. Since Luke treats Paul's colleagues as very junior assistants and does not highlight other missions, their career is obscure. Prisca may have been the more prominent, as she is often mentioned before her husband,[57] but her introduction in v. 2 is so awkward that it looks like an afterthought, raising the possibility that the tradition used by Luke mentioned Aquila alone.[58]

The first indication of the importance of Corinth is the reference to Claudius's expulsion of "all the Jews" from Rome. For Luke, links between "sacred" and "secular" history mark important points in the narrative.[59] Although generally accepted, this is the only place

49 The expansion to v. 8 is based on the notion that the converts were gentiles, as Jews would not be said to come to believe in God. Cf. 8:37 and Ropes, *Text*, 173.

50 In v. 11, the D-Text adds, with its characteristic pedantry, "**one** year **in Corinth**." It also improves the obscure ἐν αὐτοῖς ("among them," perhaps).

51 See Epp, *Tendency*, 167. On the subject of the verb "beat," see also below.

52 Verses 1-2 contain a typical feature of Lucan style (Cadbury, "Four Features," 87–102, esp. 87–97): repetition, although χωρίζω has the sense of compulsion in the second instance.

53 Luke uses εὑρίσκω (lit. "find") when he does not wish to state how characters met. Cf. 9:33; 19:1. This may be a clue to the use of sources: when the author does not have information about how characters came together, he resorts to "find."

54 According to Acts, Aquila came from Pontus, spent time in Rome, and moved thence to Ephesus. 1 Cor 16:19 places the couple in Ephesus, while Rom 16:3 (presuming that this is an integral part of the letter) places them (again) in Rome. According to 2 Tim 4:19, they remained in Ephesus. The author evidently did not know Romans 16.

55 Luke evidently prefers Semitic names: Saul/Paul, Silas/Silvanus, and diminutives Sopater/Sosipater, Prisca/Priscilla.

56 The narrator may have avoided identifying the couple as believers in Jesus to stifle the suggestion that they were expelled from Rome because of their faith.

57 In Rom 16:3; Acts 18:18, 26; 2 Tim 4:19; Acts 18:18, 26, Prisca's name precedes Aquila's. Arator obliterates her name from his account (2:506–18).

58 See the articles "Aquila" and "Prisca" by Peter Lampe, *ABD* 1:319–20, 5:67–68. Lampe argues that the pair were not well-to-do, with rich detail in *From Paul to Valentinus*, 187–96. On Prisca, see also Schüssler Fiorenza, *Memory*, 178–80, 189, which contains hypotheses on their missionary methods. She calls Priscilla "the great woman missionary of early Christianity" (175). If Luke acquired his information at Ephesus around 100 or later, reduction of Prisca's role would have been in accordance with current practice and convention.

59 See the synchronism in Luke 3:1-2a, marking the ministry of John the Baptizer and the famine mentioned in Acts 11:28, which coincides with the inauguration of the gentile mission in Antioch.

where Aquila (and Prisca?) is identified as a Jew, nor is it clear why they selected Corinth as their destination, rather than, say, Puteoli, Ostia, or Pontus. From the Lucan perspective, their arrival at Corinth just in time to work with Paul was providential. Claudius's punishment of the Jews served the furtherance of the message about Jesus.

■ **3** The verse has a convoluted ABBA structure. This elaborate clause may be because, for those unfamiliar with the epistles (1 Thess 2:9; 1 Cor 4:12; 9:1-12; cf. 2 Thess 3:8), the statement that Paul practiced a craft would come as a shock, since it fits neither Acts' picture of Paul's worldly position nor of the length of his missions. Work is too common a thing to command much interest.[60] The narrator simply says that he went to work. The statement that Paul held a job in Corinth is likely, and it is logical that this was one basis of his association with Prisca and Aquila. Menial employment also lays the grounds for 20:34, where Paul claims to have supported both himself and others. The nature of the craft is a matter of debate, although the answer does no more than fulfill curiosity.[61] One line of interpretation adheres to the literal "tentmaker." This is defended in some detail by Peter Lampe.[62] The patristic tradition and some ancient versions preferred a more general understanding: Paul worked with leather. Proponents of this view include Theodor Zahn, Henry J. Cadbury, and most recently Ronald F. Hock.[63] The literal "tentmaker" is open to challenge as too concrete.[64] BDAG gives the first meaning as "maker of stage properties."[65] The Latin and Syriac versions, surely independent, give different terms related to leather work, as do Origen and successors in the Greek exegetical tradition. A general understanding of the term is preferable.[66]

■ **4-5** The mission follows a typical path, brusquely narrated in these and subsequent verses.[67] The synagogue preaching (as in Iconium, 14:1) targets Greeks as well as Jews. Verse 5 is mysterious: why should the arrival of Silas and Timothy from Macedonia have allowed Paul to devote[68] full time to his mission? (Furthermore, Acts states that Paul waited for these two in Athens without explaining why he departed without them.[69]) Those informed from the epistles fill in the blank from 2 Cor 11:8-9: they brought money. Luke may well have

60 One may compare the descriptions of work in romantic novels. See Egger, "Women in the Greek Novel," 305.

61 Aelian *Var. hist.* 2.1 is an apophthegm about Socrates and Alcibiades. Despised professions include a "leather worker" (σκυτοτόμος), the town crier, and a "tent maker" (σκηνορράφος). (For another list associated with Socrates, see Xenophon *Mem.* 3.7.6–7). In short, the cultured Greek would answer the question with "Who cares?" Bede (74) offers a "mystical" interpretation, cribbed from Aratus: by his words and actions Paul erects protective coverings that shield believers from sin.

62 Peter Lampe, "Paulus–Zeltmacher," *BZ* 31 (1987) 211–21; cf. also Hemer, *Book*, 119 n. 46.

63 See Zahn, 633–34; Cadbury and Lake, 223; Wilhelm Michaelis, "σκηνοποιός," *TDNT* 7:393–94; and Ronald F. Hock, *The Social Context of Paul's Ministry* (Philadelphia: Fortress, 1980) 20–25. For a realistic description of what such labor involved, see ibid., 67.

64 Etymology is not always a useful guide to employment classifications. English "plumber," for example, comes from the Latin word for pipes, often made, until recently, from lead (*plumbum*). The formal term for plumbers is "pipe fitters" (or "steam fitters"). Similarly, one takes belts and handbags to shoe menders, since they know how to work with leather.

65 BDAG, 928, *s.v.* σκηνοποιός. Cf. Hock, *Social Context*, 21. Paul's views about his work were ambivalent, but they did provide him with independence from a network of patronage. See Witherington, 547–48.

66 Jerome Murphy-O'Connor ("Prisca and Aquila: Traveling Tentmakers and Church Builders," *BR* 8 [1992] 40–51) disparages the contrast between leather and linen. Holger Szesnat ("What Did the σκηνοποιός Paul Produce?" *Neotestamentica* 27 [1993] 391–402) has a similar view about materials used and items manufactured. See also Spencer, "Women," 150–53.

67 Note the number of imperfect verbs in vv. 3-5, suitable for summary style.

68 Difficulty of understanding the imperfect mediopassive συνείχετο evidently led to the D-Text (in part) and *Koine* variant πνεύματι: Paul was constrained by the Spirit. For options, see Barrett, 2:866. Luke's intention may be represented by the alternative translation.

69 On the efforts to reconcile Acts and the epistles

used the same source.[70] Because the subject of Paul and money was, and evidently remained,[71] a sensitive issue, Luke deletes it and leaves readers to construct their own conclusions. It may seem curious that only the Jews are targets of the proclamation, but this is explained by the following verse. Turning up the evangelistic heat brought "the Jews" to a boil.

■ **6** Paul responds in prophetic fashion, with both a gesture[72] and a pronouncement of holy law[73] that resembles prophetic denunciations made by Jesus.[74] He has discharged his responsibility. Those who reject his message will bear the consequences. At the second of three large geographical areas, Greece, Paul announces his turn to the gentiles.

■ **7-8** The first verse indicates that the foregoing took place in the synagogue.[75] At this point Luke introduces an apparent tradition (which cannot be coordinated with the Corinthian correspondence) about Titius Justus, whose standing as a "God-Fearer" probably derives from the author.

Tradition has not known what to do with this name. "Titius Justus" is supported by B* D² sy^h geo. Alternatives are "Titus Justus," "Justus," and "Titus."[76] "Titius Justus" receives a "C" rating from the editors of UBS.[77] In its favor is the probability that "Titus (Justus)" and "Justus" are attempts at harmonization.[78] The hypothesis that this person's home was a base for Paul at some point in his mission at Corinth is not improbable.

Narrative, rather than chronological, logic[79] dictates the subsequent report of the conversion of Crispus, the climax of the mission thus far.[80] A general report of numerous conversions follows.

■ **9-11** The verses are formally an oracle of assurance (*Heilsorakel*),[81] a type found in the Hebrew Bible and other literature.[82] This is one of three such revelations delivered to Paul at times of crisis.[83] All three are authorial compositions and serve literary goals. The narrative setting here resembles those of Greco-Roman literary parallels. Typical features include the admonition (v. 9b), in triple ABA style,[84] and the rationale, which is

here, see Cadbury and Lake, 224; and Barrett, 2:865.

70 2 Cor 11:8-9 is addressed to Corinth and uses the same general term "Macedonia."

71 See pp. 508–9.

72 On the gesture, see Cadbury, "Dust and Garments," 269–77, esp. 274–75, who cannot find a close parallel, but allows a general attempt to imitate at least the flavor of the LXX. The meaning of the action is clarified by the pronouncement.

73 "Blood" is a common biblical trope for responsibility: e.g., Lev 20:9; Josh 2:19; Judg 9:24; 2 Sam 1:16; 3:29; 1 Kgs 2:32; Jer 28:35 (LXX); Ezek 3:17-18; 18:13; 33:4. The pronouncement lacks a verb. "Be" will do well, but BDF §480 (5) supplies ἐλθέτω ("come"). It is preferable not to place a full stop after καθαρὸς ἐγώ (lit. "clean, I . . ."), for this would leave two consecutive sentences without a stated verb. Cf. Barrett, 2:867. For the background, see H. Graf Reventlow, "Sein Blut komme über sein Haupt," *VT* 10 (1960) 311-27.

74 Cf. Luke 10:13-15; 13:28-30, 34-35; 20:17; 21:23-24.

75 This is the most probable meaning of ἐκεῖθεν ("from there"), but it could be temporal ("thereafter," "then"). It is not clear whether the narrator wishes to imply that Paul also changed his place of residence. See above.

76 For the data, see Reuben Swanson, ed., *New Testament Greek Manuscripts: The Acts of the Apostles* (Sheffield: Sheffield Academic Press, 1998) 485; and UBS⁴, 479.

77 Omission of ὀνόματι ("named") in A *et al.* further complicates the question. See Ropes (*Text*, 173), who supports "Justus," and Metzger, *Textual Commentary*, 410.

78 The latter is inept, as Col 4:11 identifies Justus as a Jew.

79 Note that Luke reports no baptisms by Paul of those converted in a synagogue, with the possible exception of Lydia (16:15).

80 On Crispus, see above.

81 Aune, *Prophecy*, 266–67.

82 See, e.g., Josephus *Vit.* 208–10 (see the notes to 23:11) and the poem concluding the Sarapis Aretalogy at Delos, lines 85–90 (Appendix 2). From a very different realm comes Achilles Tatius *Leuc. Clit.* 4.1.4–5. Leucippe says: "The day before yesterday, when I was crying because I was going to be butchered, Artemis appeared, standing above me in my sleep, and said, 'do not be sad, you shall not die, for I will stand by you and help you. You will remain a virgin until I myself give you away as a bride. No one but Kleitophon will marry you'" (trans. J. J. Winkler, in Reardon, *Novels*, 222). Note also Johnson, 328. For possible imitation of this episode in Acts, see *Act. Thom.* 1.

83 The others are 23:11; 27:23-24. He alone in Acts receives these assurances.

84 "Have no fear" (μὴ φοβοῦ) is not epiphanic. It applies to the actual situation.

twofold, introduced by διότι (lit. "because" [v. 10ab]). It is also atypical in that Paul is not in any particular danger when the oracle is delivered. The message thus serves the literary purposes of generating suspense while conveying assurance. Stress, however, belongs to the final clause. Corinth will yield a bountiful harvest.[85] The vision prepares readers for what appears to be a mission of unusual length. This datum of a year and a half, like the figures of three months and two years for Ephesus (19:8, 10), may reflect local traditions, but these general numbers are not provided for their own sake as a means to transmit valuable information. They indicate the centrality of these two cities in the Pauline missionary enterprise.

■ **12-13** A long sojourn will give opponents scope for intrigue. The (unexplained) presence of the Roman governor[86] offered an evident opening. Not for the first time, his Jewish adversaries whisked Paul into court.

■ **14-17** Gallio was too shrewd a lawyer to overlook the loophole in their ambiguous accusation and dismissed the charge before Paul could utter a word. The proconsul's comments show that the issue at stake was not a question of criminal law but mere Jewish legal trivia, matters in which he had no interest. There were other matters that did not occupy his interest, notably the sound beating administered to the synagogue president, one Sosthenes, who joined the growing list of would-be persecutors required to swallow the potion they had brewed for others. With this crude, if vivid, image, Luke portrays the beating Judaism took in Corinth.[87]

The verses describing the encounter with Gallio (12-17) are not a typical trial scene.[88] Paul's active role is limited to a genitive absolute. The construction is roughly circular. References to Gallio (vv. 12, 17) frame the episode. "The Jews" take action in v. 12; the gentiles (evidently) act in v. 17 (ἐπέστησαν, ἐπιλαβόμενοι ["converged," "mobbed"]). Verses 12 and 16 narrate the approach to and (involuntary) exit from the judicial bench. The central elements deal with their charge and Gallio's response. The governor's brief speech resembles that of Gamaliel (5:35-39).[89] Here also are two conditional statements, the first of which is contrary-to-fact and thus reveals, without any examination, Gallio's view, summed up in his conclusion that he will not take jurisdiction.[90] The mentality of Paul's accusers, who believed Gallio would not distinguish between Jewish Torah and Roman *ius*,[91] is childish and unworthy of credence.[92] The whole scene dissolves in burlesque: his disappointed co-religionists (or, perhaps, the gentile mob always ready to appear when the narrator beckons)[93] fall upon their leader, Sosthenes, and vent their frustration in violence. "Luke makes Gallio occupy that standpoint which he himself considers as the correct one and which he passionately desires that Rome herself should take as her

85 On the term "people," cf. 15:14, with the comments of Tannehill, *Narrative Unity*, 2:224–25; and Johnson, 326.

86 Corinth may have been the capital of Achaea. (According to Apuleius *Metam.* 10.18, it was the capital in the second half of the second century.)

87 See Dixon Slingerland, "'The Jews' in the Pauline Portion of Acts," *JAAR* 54 (1986) 305–21; and idem, "The Composition of Acts: Some Redaction-critical Observations," *JAAR* 56 (1988) 99–113,

88 See above, where it is compared to an apophthegm. Schwartz ("Trial Scene," 126) relates this to stories in which the hero is not allowed to speak, but would, as the audience knows, have been quickly vindicated had he been allowed to do so.

89 Luke has Gallio speak in language suitable to his status and position, called "admirable though colloquial" in Cadbury and Lake, 227. Note the colloquial use of the future as imperative (ὄψεσθε) in v. 15. In Latin (as in English), this is a polite imperative. See BDF §362. Cf. Matt 27:24 (Pilate). On the conditional sentences, see also 19:38 (Ephesian "town clerk").

90 The second conditional (beginning with εἰ δέ, balancing the prior εἰ μέν) is rendered "since" here. Two of the objects of περί ("about") can be variously interpreted. The first, λόγος, is unlikely to mean "reason" here. "Mere verbiage" is the sense. In contrast to "reason" (κατὰ λόγον) stands "you people's language." The second, ὀνόματα, could refer to "technical terms." "Titles" comes from the context, the debate about whether Jesus is the Messiah (v. 5). On "actual injury" and "serious misbehavior," see 24:20 and 13:8, respectively, and the notes of Johnson, 328.

91 Conzelmann, 153.

92 Gallio's κατὰ λόγον ("quite properly") says it all. The request is not rational.

93 The narrator says "all," allowing the possibility that gentiles were involved, but the text says nothing about the presence of gentiles in the scene, and understanding "all the Jews" as the agents makes a

own: that Christianity is an inner-Jewish affair in which Rome does not meddle."[94]

Sosthenes' fate would have brought pleasure to early Christian readers. This is one of those moments at which the audience was to stand up and cheer.[95] For Christian readers of today, this episode should bring discomfort. Important as it is to note that things were quite different then, when Jews had vastly more numbers, power, and resources than did followers of Jesus, contemporary Christians should repudiate the sentiment herein expressed, specifically the enjoyment of seeing incompetent and violence-prone Jews humiliated. Apology, rather than apologetics, is in order.[96]

■ **18** This verse,[97] which closes the account by reporting Paul's departure—for which no reason is given—contains two surprises, the sudden reappearance of Priscilla and Aquila and Paul's religious vow. Priscilla, whose name looked like an afterthought in v. 3, now stands first (as in v. 26). The couple's role (and presence) will remain unexplained until vv. 24-28, as Luke will have need of them in Ephesus. Paul's vow is intelligible as motivation for his desire to travel rapidly to Jerusalem. In the long range it cultivates the ground for 21:23-24.[98]

The announced destination of the voyage is Syria. Since the verb ἐκπλέω often means "sail back,"[99] the narrative evidently intends to complete a circle begun in 15:40. The purpose of this closure is not to mark the completion of one "missionary journey" and the inauguration of another, for the vast amount of travel denoted in vv. 18:21b, 23, and 19:1a is remarkably compressed.[100] The expression "flying visit to Jerusalem"[101] does not properly apply to Paul or his plans. The narrator is doing the flying here. The purpose of this sweep is the provision of a setting for the climax of Paul's missionary labor in Ephesus. The contents of Galatians are not conducive to the idea that Paul visited either Jerusalem or Antioch at this time. Circumstances favor viewing this trip as a Lucan contribution to the narrative.[102] The distance placed between Paul and Apollos does not look fortuitous, while the source appears to be the voyage described in 20:3; 21:3, which also has Syria as its destination, whereas the trip summarized in 18:18-23 reaches Syria (Antioch) by land.

■ **19-23** The D-Text variants mainly fill gaps in the narrative. The opening clarifies the subject (and keeps the focus on Paul). Luke does not worry about time, so to speak. When Paul shows up, the synagogue will be in session (cf. 13:13-14). The D-Text makes him wait for the Sabbath. In v. 20, the editor assures us that the Jews of Ephesus did not want Paul to stay longer so that he could enjoy the sites. Verse 21 provides an explanation for Paul's odd abandonment of a, for once, receptive synagogue audience.[103] Acts 20:16 is the probable

---

nice inclusion with the expulsion of "all the Jews" in v. 2. Haenchen (536) is one interpreter who understands this to mean "the [gentile] crowd." Fitzmyer (630) observes that the indifference conforms to Gallio's intention not to involve himself in Jewish affairs. Failure to take action against a gentile mob would discredit the governor, an object far from the narrator's wish. See Moyer V. Hubbard, "Urban Uprisings in the Roman World: The Social Setting of the Mobbing of Sosthenes," *NTS* 51 (2005) 416–28.

94 Haenchen, 541. To this one might add the assurance that Christians are not evildoers, an issue by the turn of the century (1 Pet 4:16, etc.).

95 See Chrysostom (*Hom.* 39): "It was a splendid victory" (trans. J. Walker, 242).

96 Contra Tannehill, *Narrative Unity*, 2:226–29.

97 The reference to a temporal interval is provided not for chronological purposes but to emphasize that Paul was not compelled to leave. See the excursus "Acts 18 and Chronology" above.

98 On the practice of vows, see Haenchen, 545–46, and the comments at 21:23. Luke may not have understood the practice, but, since this vow is an authorial creation, it is not necessary to provide a historical rationale. The shaved head may have inspired part of the famous description of Paul in *Act. Paul* 3.3: ψιλὸν τῇ κεφαλῇ (which may mean "bald," but could also be the result of shaving the head). On the possibility that this episode was inspired by Josephus, see Pervo, *Dating*, 190–91.

99 BDAG, 308, *s.v.*

100 Foakes Jackson, 172–73.

101 E.g., Cadbury and Lake, 224. On Jerusalem as the destination, see Loisy, 707–9.

102 See Krodel, 352–53; and Lüdemann, *Acts*, 243–46. As the latter notes, with a number of references and citations, the majority of scholars find some valid data in this report.

103 Metzger (*Textual Commentary*, 412) says this may well be the correct explanation, citing Bruce, 1951 (but Bruce, 1990, 399, is more cautious). The vow

basis for this.[104] Verse 22, which replaces the vague and awkward reference in v. 21 with a logical statement, also manifests the pedantic quality of the D-Text, and the omission of Priscilla is another example of its tendency to minimize the presence of women.[105]

The conventional—and doubtless the earliest extant—text is odd. Had the narrator said that Paul left the couple in Ephesus and continued his voyage, the object would be clear. Instead, he "left them there," to translate literally, but went to the synagogue, alone (without Priscilla and Aquila!), only to decline a request for more with a promise of an eventual return. The narrator is whetting the readers' appetite. Ephesus is a fruitful field. To this suspense his pious "God willing" adds its own contribution.[106] Another merit of v. 20 is to show why Apollos will receive a favorable reception in the synagogue—although it may not fully explain why the difference between his "gospel" and that of Paul was not the subject of wider notice. To complete preparation of the stage for chap. 19 the narrator introduces a substantial retardation, long not in actual narrative, but psychologically lengthy, as it were, for vv. 22-23 hurl the reader over a vast space of around eighteen hundred kilometers. Prior to the climax of his Aegean mission, Paul visits all of the areas in which he has labored, apart from Macedonia and Greece.[107] In 20:1-3 he will visit those places (another frame). At the micro level, the pivot is marked by the parallel phrases *τὴν Φρυγίαν καὶ Γαλατικὴν χώραν* (16:6) and *τὴν Γαλατικὴν χώραν καὶ Φρυγίαν* (18:23). They are notoriously difficult to translate, but they are mirror opposites.[108] In 16:6, the order is "Phrygia . . . Galatia," whereas 18:23 places Galatia before Phrygia, although both describe movement from east to west. Acts 18:23 evidently speaks of two districts.[109] The patient labors of meticulous scholars notwithstanding, the evidence indicates both that Luke is not consistent in his use of geographical terminology and that he had an imperfect grasp of the geography of central Asia Minor. Any assumption that the author of Acts cared deeply about such matters is questionable.[110]

The presence of six participles (against two finite verbs) in vv. 22-23 enhances the sense of rapidity and smoothness.[111] The narrator does not even name Jerusalem, reducing the visit to a mere salutation en route to Antioch.[112] At the latter place, the stated object of this

does not seem to play an explicit part here. Not since Beroea (17:10-12) has a synagogue been so receptive.

104 Note also the D-Text of 19:1.

105 See Pervo, "Social Aspects"; and D. A. Kursk-Chomycz, "Is there an 'Anti-Priscan' Tendency in the Manuscripts? Some Textual Problems with Prisca and Aquila," *JBL* 125 (2006) 107–28.

106 The expression "God willing" is an originally apotropaic formula of polytheist origin, not known to be used by Jews before Islamic times. See Adolf Deissmann, *Bible Studies* (trans. A. Grieve; Edinburgh: T&T Clark, 1901) 252; James H. Ropes, *A Critical and Exegetical Commentary on the Epistle of St. James* (ICC; New York: Charles Scribner's Sons, 1916) 279–80; and W. Schrenk, "ϑέλω," *TDNT* 3:44–62, esp. 47.

107 Witherington (560) also views such visits as marking boundaries.

108 Translation difficulties result from the use of the article and the overlap between adjective and noun. See on 16:6.

109 Haenchen (545), who appeals to the adverb καϑεξῆς ("successively," on which see Foakes Jackson and Lake, *Prolegomena II*, 504–5; and Hemer, *Book*, 120).

110 Observe that 16:6 speaks of "passing through" (διῆλϑον, the present participle of which appears in 18:23) these regions, without mentioning evangelism, whereas 18:23 describes pastoral visits (ἐπιστηρίζων; cf. 14:22; 15:32, 41; στηρίζων [$\mathfrak{p}^{74}$ ℵ A B 33 1891 *pc*] may be original in 18:23, as it is less common). This activity is another indicator of a narrative boundary, as it concludes the journey of chaps. 13–14 and prefaces the journey beginning in chap. 16. Kirsopp Lake ("Paul's Route in Asia Minor," in Lake and Cadbury, *Additional Notes*, 224–40, esp. 239–40) concludes that the variation is stylistic.

111 The style of these verses elicits admiration from BDF §421.

112 Jerusalem is clearly intended in the participle "going up" (ἀναβάς), which is used of the city (e.g., 11:2; 15:2; 21:12, 15). Had Paul not intended to go to Jerusalem, he would have sailed to the port of Antioch. The geography so confused Bede (75) that he identified "Caesarea" as the capital of Cappadocia (possibly from a source), since Caesarea Maritima would have been too far south.

travel (v. 18) and his (former) base, he does spend "some time" before setting off on a long journey, evidently alone, across all of Asia Minor. The narrator gives no indication of the communities allegedly visited[113] and makes no attempt to impress readers with the ardor and immensity of this journey.[114] Paul routinely topped off his excellent relations with Jerusalem and Antioch.

A final reason for Paul's "drive through" visit to an Ephesian synagogue[115] is that Luke does not claim that Paul inaugurated the Jesus movement in Ephesus. This claim is probably correct.[116] Acts 18:26—which may well not derive from tradition—assumes it,[117] and it is more than difficult to imagine that Luke would not claim a Pauline foundation if that were true. As in the case of Rome, Luke nonetheless presents Paul as inaugurating a mission to the Jews.[118] In 19:8, he will resume, rather than initiate, that mission.

113 Galatians provides no evidence for the view that Paul had visited the recipients more than once prior to its composition. See Hans Dieter Betz, *Galatians* (Hermeneia; Philadelphia: Fortress, 1979) 11, 224.

114 Cf. *Ephesian Tale* 4.1.1-2: "Meanwhile Hippothous' band moved off from Tarsus and made their way to Syria, forcing any opposition in their path to submit. They burned villages and slaughtered large numbers. In this way they reached Laodicea in Syria, and there they took up lodgings, not as pirates this time, but posing as tourists . . . [T]hey took a rest and made for Phoenicia, and from there to Egypt" (trans. G. Anderson, in Reardon, *Novels*, 154-55).

115 Although the text refers to "the synagogue" (18:19, 26; 19:8), this is probably a simplification.

116 See Matthias Günther, *Die Frühgeschichte des Christentums in Ephesus* (2nd ed.; Frankfurt: Peter Lang, 1998) 32-37.

117 Haenchen (547) states the matter too strongly by saying "18.26 is proof."

118 Cf. Haenchen, 543.

18

18:24-28 Apollos

24/ An Alexandrian Jew by the name of Apollos[a] came to Ephesus. Apollos was an eloquent[b] fellow who knew how to make effective use of the scriptures. 25/ He had received instruction in the way of the Lord,[c] could speak with spiritual ardor, and propound the story of Jesus with precision, but he was aware only of the baptism proclaimed by John. 26/ Apollos launched a vigorous preaching mission in the synagogue. After Priscilla and Aquila had heard him, they took him aside and expounded the Movement[d] more fully.[e] 27/ When Apollos expressed a desire to go to Achaea, he received support from the believers, who wrote to encourage the disciples there to receive him. After his arrival he was of considerable value to those who had come to believe through grace, 28/ for he decisively routed the Jews in public debate,[f] demonstrating from the scriptures that the Messiah is Jesus.

a D-Text: "An Alexandrian Jew *Apollonius* by name." This and the following are based on Boismard, *Texte*, 309.

b On the meaning of λόγιος, see Cadbury and Lake, 233. "Eloquent" includes the sense of "cultured."

c D-Text: "He had received instruction about the **word** of the Lord **in his native city.**"

d The modifier "way of God" has strong support and may be original, but "the Way" is Luke's preferred designation for the Jesus movement (9:2; 19:9, 23; 22:4; 24:14, 22), which the redundant qualifier apparently overlooks. The unmodified noun is a D-Text reading with strong claims for originality. Cf. Ropes, *Text*, 178.

e The D-Text (Boismard, *Texte*, 310), as in v. 21, removes Priscilla from the narrative.

f "Debate" is implicit in the conventional text, explicit (διαλεγόμενος) in the D-Text (Boismard, *Texte*, 311).

Analysis

Different plans and analyses of the following passages have been offered. The view of 19:1 as a major division is generally rejected. Schemes vary, but all shed light on the structure of Acts. Talbert (172) treats 18:24–20:1 as a unit, based on Ephesus; Polhill utilizes the same basis, but takes 18:23–21:16 as boundaries. Barrett and Fitzmyer include 18:23–20:38 as a unit, while Witherington selects 18:24–21:36.[1] That all are defensible testifies to the fluidity of Lucan structure. Talbert observes that 18:24–19:20 relate to "eccentric forms of religion," but this does not adequately describe 19:8-10. Whatever the solution to this complex problem, 18:24-28 and 19:1-7 are to be analyzed in relation to one another, although they stand on adjoining sides of the pivot indicated by Paul's return to Ephesus (19:1).

Comment

■ **24** This is an intractable, parenthetical paragraph, followed by another that is equally parenthetical and even more intractable (19:1b-7).[2] They constitute a pair, the former of which deals with defective knowledge, the latter with defective practice, but both deficiencies are referred to as "the baptism of John." The first problem concerns the name of the individual. ℵ* 36. 453. 1175 *pc* bo offer "Apelles." The D-Text prefers "Apollonius," the full form of "Apollos." In support of Apelles is its difficulty; tradition would tend to

1 Talbert, 172; Polhill, 393; Barrett, 2:883; Fitzmyer, 636; and Witherington, 562.

2 Ernst Käsemann labels both 18:24-28 and 19:1-7 "contradictory and incredible"; see his "The Disciples of John the Baptist in Ephesus," in idem, *Essays on New Testament Themes* (trans. W. J. Montague; SBT 41; London: SCM, 1964) 136–48, esp. 143. His effort at resolution posits the continuing existence of followers of John the Baptizer and relates the episodes to post-Pauline intra-Christian controversies.

assimilate unknown to familiar names.[3] Later tradition knew an Apelles as a disciple of Marcion, but it is more likely that this was an attempt to identify Apollos with the person named in Rom 16:10. "Apollonius" might represent the Lucan tendency to use different forms of names from those in the epistles.[4] In Acts, however, these tend to be hypocorisms or diminutives. Against the argument for assimilation is the probability that Acts bases its description of this person in part on 1 Corinthians (1 Cor 1:12; 3:4-11, 22; 4:6; 16:12).[5] From that perspective, "Apelles" may be an attempt to dissociate this person from the Apollos of the Pauline circle and "Apollonius" a possible step in that direction. (All three are variants of a theophoric name.)[6]

Except for the statement that Apollos was an Alexandrian Jew, all of the information about Apollos[7] in this passage that is not Lucan creation could be deduced from 1 Corinthians: his wisdom and oratorical ability, as well as his arrival in Corinth following Paul's first visit.[8] His Alexandrian background could well derive from Ephesian local tradition.[9] The introduction is heavily loaded. The core, "Apollos came to Ephesus," essentially identical to v. 19a, is braced by two qualifications: his eloquence, which precedes the predicate, and his exegetical skill, which follows it (v. 24). The latter is Lucan in form (Luke 24:19; Acts 7:22).

■ **25** The narrative next affirms that Apollos was a missionary, or at least a teacher.[10] Apollos had been taught "the way of the Lord," an ambiguous phrase that could refer to conventional Judaism (cf. v. 26), but need not; he engaged in vibrant,[11] scripturally informed teaching[12] that reflected accurate information about Jesus.[13] So far so good, but the narrator adds that Apollos "knew only the baptism of John" (lit.). What kind of Christology v. 25 might imply lies beyond conjecture, since Acts 1:5; 13:4-5 view John's baptism as a preparatory act for Israelites that did not convey the Holy Spirit.[14] That would require proper baptism in the name of Jesus, as will be demonstrated a few verses later (19:5-6). Although it seems to cut the Gordian knot, the best solution is to view "the baptism of John" as a Lucan cipher for inadequate doctrine and rite, not explicitly false teaching, since it is based on ignorance rather than deceit, and the like.

---

3 Cf. the discussion of Titius Justus under v. 7. George D. Kilpatrick ("Apollos–Apelles," *JBL* 89 [1970] 77) argued that "Apelles" may have been original.

4 Examples include "Saul" (7:58, etc.), Silas (15:22, etc.), and Priscilla (18:2, etc.), known in the letters as Paul, Silvanus, and Prisca.

5 Note also the reference to Apollos in Titus 3:13, which indicates that the name remained in some favor in Pauline circles.

6 See the discussion in Metzger, *Textual Commentary*, 412–13.

7 As Conzelmann (157) notes, the characterization of Apollos, like that of Stephen, is more typical than individual.

8 On the use of 1 Corinthians here, see Pervo, *Dating*, 102. "Spiritual ardor" (ζέων τῷ πνεύματι) derives from Rom 12:11 (ibid., 116–17).

9 The statement does not demonstrate the existence of followers of Jesus in Alexandria at that time, for Apollos could have learned about Jesus elsewhere. Cf. Aquila, who is characterized as from Pontus, but had been living in Rome, according to the narrator (18:2). Metzger (*Textual Commentary*, 413), however, asserts that the D-Text (see n. *c*) claim that Apollos had been instructed in Alexandria "no doubt accords with historical fact." The name "Apollos" is well attested in Egypt (Hemer, *Book*, 233; see also *NewDocs* 1 [1981] no. 50, p. 88).

10 Note the frequentative imperfects in v. 25.

11 It is preferable not to relate ζέων τῷ πνεύματι (n. 16 below) to the Holy Spirit. For a contrary view, see Barrett, 2:888, who thinks it unlikely that it does *not* refer to the Holy Spirit. This is bound up with his general interpretation of 18:24–19:7.

12 Jervell (470) observes that, for Luke, anyone who understood the Scriptures must have interpreted them in a Christian fashion. He allows that Luke may have made him into a "half-Christian" (with many references in n. 376).

13 The expression τὰ περί ("the facts about *X*") is used ten times in Acts, twice in Luke, notably Luke 24:19. The vocabulary of vv. 23-25 evokes the preface to Luke (1:1-4): περί ("concerning"), which is common enough, but also ἀκριβῶς ("accurately") and κατηχέω ("inform," "teach"). The Apollos story thus resonates with the opening and final chapters of Luke.

14 The Byzantine tradition alters "Jesus" to "Lord" in v. 25. This permits an entirely non-christological reading of Apollos's education, but that may not have been the intention of the reviser.

■ **26-28** Vigorous proclamation by Apollos of his defective message in the synagogue[15] did not escape the attention of Priscilla and Aquila, who made good the gaps in his knowledge.[16] Without further ado, vv. 27-28 wrap up the career of Apollos. He wished to move on to Corinth. Why this destination? Why not continue his work in Ephesus or go elsewhere? 1 Cor 16:12 supplies the answer. The D-Text[17] attempts to improve the logic of v. 27: "**Now some Corinthians who had been visiting Ephesus and had heard Apollos urged him** to go **with them to their native city. When he consented, the Ephesians**[18] wrote[19] to the disciples in Corinth **so that they would receive the man**. When he **took up residence in Achaea** he was of considerable value **to the churches**."[20] The initiative thus arose from Corinthians, probably believers.[21] The notion of visits from Corinth to Ephesus was inspired by 1 Cor 1:11; 16:17. The secondary character of this text is apparent from the letter of recommendation,[22] which would not have been necessary had Apollos waited to return with the visitors, or, conversely, might well have been written by them.[23]

The sudden appearance of believers in v. 27 (lit. "brothers and sisters") indicates the presence of a Christian community, although its origin and composition are unexplained. This datum is the best basis for a claim that an independent tradition of some type underpins this story, but, when agreement with 1 Corinthians is attributed to the use of that epistle rather than as confirmation of the validity of the material, that hypothesis dissipates.[24] It is equally likely that Luke supplied this detail as an ad hoc necessity. No other traces of this body exist. Until 19:9 believers in Ephesus remain affiliated with the synagogue. Such tradition as may have existed has been swallowed up by Lucan composition. According to Acts, Apollos, who was first characterized (like Aquila) as "a Jew," remained primarily a missionary to Jews. Verse 27 does speak, in a Pauline phrase,[25] of his assistance to the believers, but the nature of this

15 The verb is that used for Paul's preaching at the Ephesian synagogue in 19:8—παρρησιάζομαι, used seven times in Acts, always otherwise of Paul.

16 The language is Lucan: the comparative (note the positive in v. 25) ἀκριβέστερον is used in precisely the same fashion in 24:22; cf. also 23:15, 20. "Expound" (ἐκτίθημι), found only in Acts, appears in a kindred sense in 11:4; 28:23 (differently in 7:22). Cadbury and Lake (233–34) identify the ambiguity: Was accurate information augmented or was Apollos given new information? Barrett (2:884–85, 888), asserts that the phrase means that Apollos had received the baptism of John and that he did not need "Christian baptism." The text is not so clear about Apollos's baptism, in contrast to 19:3. Haenchen (555) says trenchantly that the statements about Apollos are contradictory: if he taught accurately, he required (v. 25) no further instruction. If he required further instruction, he did not teach accurately. Haenchen (554–55) and Pohill (396–97) note a number of attempts to characterize the theology of Apollos. All are vigorously argued learned conjectures that attempt to fill a gap intentionally left by the narrator.

17 Boismard, *Texte*, 310–11. At v. 27 the important witness 𝔭[38] appears. See p. 463 n. *f*.

18 H[mg] reads "the brothers."

19 The D-Text omits "to encourage" (προτρεψάμενοι).

20 E adds "and in the homes" (καὶ κατ᾽οἶκον), evidently with an eye to 18:8.

21 The D-Text also resolves the dangling participle προτρεψάμενοι, which could mean that they encouraged either Apollos to go or, more likely, the Corinthians to welcome him, although Barrett (2:890) inclines toward the former understanding.

22 On letters of recommendation in the Pauline world, see Rom 16:1 and, ironically, 2 Cor 3:1-3. On the form, see Clinton W. Keyes, "The Greek Letter of Introduction," *AJP* 56 (1935) 28–44; John L. White, *Light from Ancient Letters* (Foundations and Facets: New Testament; Philadelphia: Fortress Press, 1986) index, 238, *s.v.* "Recommendation"; and Klauck, *Ancient Letters*, index, 499, *s.v.* "Recommendation."

23 This is what H[mg] seems to indicate. Note also that the D-Text eliminates reference to synagogue preaching.

24 For detailed arguments about the use of tradition in vv. 24-28, see Weiser, 2:505–9.

25 "Through grace" (διὰ τῆς χάριτος): Rom 12:3; Gal 1:15 (Acts 15:11). For various interpretations of this phrase, see Witherington, 568 n. 28.

assistance is most easily understood in reference to his skill as a controversialist. Apollos is a missionary very much on the order of Paul.[26] Where Paul planted, in Corinth and Ephesus, Apollos watered (1 Cor 3:6). Ramsay was not far from the mark when he said that this episode was included "for the sake of rendering the opening of Paul's first letter to the Corinthians clear and intelligible."[27]

The entire episode is remarkable. Apollos is an itinerant missionary with a message about Jesus. Priscilla and Aquila have not engaged in evangelism but faithfully attend the synagogue. They are roused to action only when Apollos arrives and is, like Paul, permitted to preach. Once his defects have been corrected, he is encouraged in his plans to move on to Corinth, where he once more functions as a Christian evangelist in the synagogue, as well as an inspiring preacher to those who had already accepted the faith. A reasonable interpretation is that Luke wished to subordinate Apollos to Paul and did so through the agency of Priscilla and Aquila. The Alexandrian was not a rival to or independent of Paul.[28]

26 Cf. (again) 18:26 with 19:8 and 18:28 with 9:22.

27 Ramsay, *St. Paul the Traveller*, 267.

28 Support for this view comes from the similarity of 18:28 to 9:20, 22 (Paul in Damascus).

19

19:1-12 Paul in Ephesus

19:1-7: Conventional Text

1/ While Apollos[a] was in Corinth,
Paul made his way by the inland
route to Ephesus, where he
came upon some disciples.
2/ He asked them, "Did you receive
the Holy Spirit when you came
to believe?"
"No," they answered, "We
did not even hear that there is a
Holy Spirit."[b]
3/ "What sort of baptism did you
receive, then?"
"John's baptism."
4/ "John's baptism dealt with
repentance," explained Paul.
"He told the people about one
who would come after him, in
whom they were to believe.
Jesus[c] is the one of whom he
spoke."
5/ Once they had learned this,[d] they
received baptism in the name of
the Lord Jesus.
6/ After Paul had laid hands on
them, the Holy Spirit descended
upon them, and they began to
speak in tongues[e] and utter
prophecies. 7/ This group
numbered about twelve men
altogether.

19:1-7: D-Text[f]

1/ *Although Paul's personal plan
was to go to Jerusalem, the
Spirit told him to return to Asia.*
Passing along the inland route
he came to Ephesus and
2/ asked the disciples, "Did you
receive the Holy Spirit when
you came to believe?"
"No," they answered, "We
did not even hear that *some
people receive* a Holy Spirit."
3/ *Paul* said, "What sort of baptism
did you receive, then?"
"John's baptism."[g]
4/ . . .
5/ Once they had learned this they
received baptism in the name of
the Lord Jesus[h] *for the forgiveness of sins.*
6/ After Paul had laid hands on
them the Holy Spirit *fell*[i] upon
them and they began to speak
in tongues[j] *and themselves
interpret them* and utter prophecies. 7/ Those who *had come
to believe* numbered [ ] twelve
persons.

8/ Paul devoted the next three
months to preaching in the
synagogue, where he vigorously sought to persuade people about the nature of God's
dominion. 9/ Since some of his
hearers stubbornly refused[k]
to be convinced and publicly
maligned the Movement, he
withdrew, and, taking the followers with him, continued his
daily presentations in the facility[l] of Tyrannus. 10/ This lasted
for two years, with the result
that everyone in Asia, Jews and
Greeks alike, heard the message about the Lord.
11/ Moreover, God[m] began to
perform remarkable mira-
cles through Paul's hands.
12/ Indeed, even the handkerchiefs and work clothes that
had touched his skin were taken
to the suffering, resulting in the

removal of their illnesses and the expulsion of evil spirits.

a The forms of the personal name vary. See on 18:24.
b "Holy Spirit" is anarthrous in both question and response. One could thus translate "a/some," "the," or simply "holy spirit."
c Variants include "the Messiah" and "the Messiah Jesus."
d The demonstrative supplied in the translation is added in D-Text (Boismard, *Texte*, 314).
e *Or:* "In languages." See comments on 2:4 and the D-Text of v. 6.
f Boismard, *Texte*, 312–15. An important witness is $\mathfrak{p}^{38}$, which contains 18:27–19:6, 12-16. Brief as it is, this early (third century CE) papyrus exhibits what may be a more "pure" form of the D-Text, lacking some of the pedantries characteristic of Bezae. See Clark, 220–25; Sylvia New, "The Michigan Papyrus," in Lake and Cadbury, *Additional Notes*, 262–69; Édouard Delebecque, "La mésadventure des fils de Scévas selon ses deux versions (Actes 19:13-20)," *RSPhTh* 66 (1982) 225–32; B. A. Mastin, "A Note on Acts 19:14," *Bib* 59 (1978) 97–99; and Barbara Aland, "Entstehung, Charakter und Herkunft des sog. westlichen Textes untersucht an der Apostelgeschichte," *EThL* 62 (1986) 5–65, esp. 12–36.
g The D-Text (Boismard, *Texte*, 313) uses the imperfect, which might mean, "They started saying," or perhaps, "They would say."
h Many D-Texts add "Christ" (Boismard, *Texte*, 314).
i Although Bezae and the Latin tradition read "immediately" (εὐθέως) before "fell," it is difficult to construe this in $\mathfrak{p}^{38}$. (N-A[27] reports that this papyrus apparently has both words, including "fell" [ἐπέπεσεν]). If the adverb is not read, per the editors and Boismard, it would indicate a state of the D-Text that may not have, at least in this instance, resorted to a favorite word. On "fell," see 8:16.
j Some D-Texts (H[mg] Cass Sah Eth) read *other* languages, an assimilation to 2:4, rejected, with reason, by Boismard, *Texte*, 314. Cf. also the variants in 10:46. Luke may have wished readers to understand that "tongues" means foreign languages. This is the view of BDF §480 (3), which regards the word as an ellipsis.
k *Or:* "were hardened (by God). . . ."
l On the meaning of this word, see below.
m On the basis of its omission in some versions and its floating position, Boismard (*Texte*, 317) omits "God" as the subject of v. 11. The logical subject then becomes "the word" (λόγος) of v. 10.

Analysis

"Paul's Ephesian labors are a meteoric burst before the darkness of the eclipse of his journey to Rome."[1] The actual mission to Ephesus is an exiguous bit of sausage sandwiched between two large slices of bread. The introduction runs from 18:24 to 19:7 (twelve verses), and 19:21-40 is, effectively, a twenty-verse postscript. The conventional description of missionary activity consumes but thirteen verses (19:8-20). This framework is an important clue to Luke's understanding of the location.

Ephesus,[2] an old Ionian foundation that succeeded Pergamum as the metropolis (capital) of Asia, was one

1 Borgen, *Philo*, 331.
2 The bibliography on Ephesus is varied and immense. Among the more important items are the following: Richard E. Oster, *A Bibliography of Ancient Ephesus* (ATLA Bib Ser 19; Metuchen: Scarecrow, 1987); idem, "Ephesus," *ABD* 2:542–49; idem, "Ephesus as a Religious Center under the Principate: I. Paganism before Constantine," *ANRW* 2.18.3 (1990) 1661–1728; Helmut Koester, ed., *Ephesos: Metropolis of Asia* (HTS 41; Valley Forge, Pa.: Trinity Press International, 1995); Paul Trebilco, "Asia," in Gill and Gempf, *Setting*, 291–362, esp. 302–57; idem, *The Early Christians in Ephesus from Paul to Ignatius* (WUNT 166; Tübingen: Mohr Siebeck, 2004) 11–37; and Gregory H. R. Horsley, "The Inscriptions of Ephesos and the New Testament," *NovT* 34 (1992) 105–67, which contains copious bibliography. Note also Giancarlo Biguzzi ("Ephesus, Its Artemision, Its Temple to the Flavian Emperors, and Idolatry in Revelation," *NovT* 40 [1998] 276–90), who relates Artemisian ideology to imperial theology. For additional bibliography, see Shauf, *Theology*, 127–28 n. 1.

of the largest cities of the Roman Empire.[3] In addition to its governmental and economic importance as a crossroads between Asia Minor and the west, the north, and the south, and as the terminus of a road system that extended to Persia, Ephesus enjoyed the prestige of the cult of Artemis, whose temple was renowned.[4] The city endured until the seventh century CE. During the formative period of Christianity, Ephesus was a leading center of the movement[5] and exhibited the religion's considerable diversity.[6] By the late second century, it could claim Paul as its founder[7] and the apostle John as a long-time resident.[8] With John came (following John 19:25-27) the mother of Jesus, whose patronage was of considerable importance during the Council of Ephesus (431). Together with Constantinople, Antioch, and Alexandria, Ephesus long ranked as a primary see of Greek-speaking Christianity.[9] Shakespeare's *Comedy of Errors* demonstrates the enduring appeal of Ephesus into the Renaissance.[10] This commentary posits Ephesus as the author's probable location.[11] Be that as it may, the city reflects the geographical perspective of the narrator, who regards it (rightly) as the most important Pauline missionary base.[12] In no other chapter of Acts does a locality come so alive. Abundance of detail will not gain Luke any kudos for historical accuracy in chap. 19.[13] Both what he elects to report and what he omits are revelatory.

The story opens with an abrupt encounter with some disciples of the Baptizer, who, it transpires, have never heard of the Holy Spirit. After proper initiation, with a minimum of instruction, they disappear (vv. 1-7). Verses 8-10 present the by-now-familiar summary of the clash with and separation from the synagogue, followed by a terse note that two years of activity brought the message to all Asia—hyperbole, no doubt, but indicative.[14] Thereafter Paul's active role ceases (except for a brief note in vv. 30-31 stating that he was dissuaded from taking action). The residue shows the influence of Paul's mission: After briefly noting his own healing activity, focus shifts to second-class relics[15] (vv. 11-12), the frustration of some religious charlatans (vv. 13-17), a general renunciation of magical practice (vv. 18-19), a terse summary (v. 20), a brief statement about Paul's future plans, with directions to subordinates (vv. 21-22), and the counterproductive efforts of artisans dependent on the cult of Artemis to bring the Jesus movement

3 Christine Thomas ("At Home in the City of Artemis: Religion in Ephesos in the Literary Imagination of the Roman Period," in Koester, *Ephesos: Metropolis of Asia*, 81–117) provides a very valuable portrait of the perception of Ephesus in the Greek-speaking world. In addition to the novels she mentions, one might note also the role of Artemis and her temple at Ephesus in *Apollonius of Tyre* 27, 48–49, 51 (Rec. B) and also (apparently) in the fragment known as *Antheia*. See Stephens and Winkler, *Greek Novels*, 277–88.

4 See below.

5 Shauf, *Theology*, 135–36.

6 See Helmut Koester, "Ephesos in Early Christian Literature," in idem, *Ephesos: Metropolis of Asia*, 119–40.

7 Irenaeus (*A.H.* 3.3.4) claims (wrongly) that Paul founded the Christian church in Ephesus.

8 The *Acts of John* exploits this relationship. See Richard Pervo, "Johannine Trajectories in the *Acts of John*," *Apocrypha* 3 (1992) 47–68.

9 Information about the Jewish community in Ephesus is limited. Much of what Josephus reports deals with Jewish privileges and applies to the province of Asia (e.g., *Ant.* 14.223–64, *passim*; 16.27–65). On these matters, see Schürer, *History*, 1:22–23. Inscriptional evidence is scanty and late. See Horsley, "Inscriptions," 121–27; Levinskaya, *Diaspora Setting*, 137–52, esp. 143–48; and Trebilco, *Early Christians*, 37–51. No synagogue has yet been unearthed, although *I. Eph.* 4.1251 mentions "synagogue rulers" and "presbyters" (ἀρχισυνάγωγοι, πρεσβύτεροι).

10 His basic source was Plautus's *Menaechmi*, the location of which Shakespeare translated to Ephesus. Magic plays a major role, as in *The Comedy of Errors* I.2.98–105 and IV.4.58–62 (an attempted exorcism).

11 See pp. 5–7.

12 See Borgen, *Philo*, 273–85, esp. 282.

13 As Elisabeth Schüssler Fiorenza ("Miracles, Mission," 18) sharply observes, if one reads Acts 19 as apologetic narrative, its historical improbabilities are intelligible.

14 For this exaggeration, compare *Ephesian Tale* 1.1.3, which says of the hero Habrocomes: "Everyone in Ephesus (ἅπασιν Ἐφεσίοις) sought his company, and in the rest of Asia (τοῖς τὴν ἄλλην Ἀσίαν οἰκοῦσι) as well" (trans. G. Anderson, in Reardon, *Novels*, 128).

15 "Second-class relics" is an ecclesiastical and anachronistic but convenient shorthand.

into ignominy (vv. 23-40). Not a single convert's name is recorded, nor is any information about a community of believers supplied. Absent are data about house churches, information about conflicts with some of Paul's foundations, notably Corinth and Philippi (quite possibly the Galatian churches also), and the efforts to raise the collection, as well as Paul's considerable personal difficulties, which evidently included imprisonment.[16] All in all, Acts 19 appears to be rather unpromising fodder for the biographer of Paul or the historian of early Christianity.[17] Even Luke's fond admirer William Ramsay confessed disappointment.[18] Resolution of this dilemma invites the all-but-inevitable conclusion that Luke narrated the triumph of the Pauline mission in Asia symbolically, by portraying epiphanies of divine power demonstrating the defeat of rival forces, including both "regular" and vulgar forms of Judaism and polytheism while dissociating Christianity from a role in public disorder.

The term "symbolic" is not put forward as a slippery means for dodging issues, nor does it intimate allegory or suggest that Luke did not believe that these things happened. Unless authors state or strongly imply their doubts or beliefs,[19] it is preferable not to attempt to read their minds. This presupposition is not utterly vitiated by the recognition that Luke composed, essentially invented, much of this material. The bottom line is that Acts 19 represents *how* the narrator chose to portray Paul's triumph. The means involve circumstantial representative episodes and effervescent summaries. "Symbolized" is an appropriate word for these means.[20] Considerable importance should also be attributed to the "absence" of Paul from three-fourths of the narrative. Paul's power did not die with him.[21] Elisabeth Schüssler Fiorenza has contributed a useful thematic outline of Acts 19, with analytic comments.[22] She divides the material into seven "scenes" with three major parts:[23]

I. Vv. 1-10. Christianity *vis-à-vis* Judaism
   A. Vv. 1-7. The True Christian Faith, unlike That of Various Sects, Conveys Authenticating Spiritual Gifts.
   B. Vv. 8-10. The Formation of a Distinct Religious Community Based on or within the Synagogue. The Movement, which Resembles a Philosophical School, Addresses both Jews and Gentiles.

---

16 Cadbury and Lake (234–36) provide a full list of items omitted from Acts 19. Attempts to locate the provenance of the "imprisonment epistles" have led numerous researchers to propose that Paul was in custody in Ephesus. See 2 Cor 1:8-11; 6:5; 11:23; and Phil 1:12-26. Two important studies are Wilhelm Michaelis, *Die Gefangenschaft des Paulus in Ephesus und das Itinerar des Timotheus* (Gütersloh: Bertelsmann, 1925); and George S. Duncan, *St Paul's Ephesian Ministry: A Reconstruction with Special Reference to the Ephesian Origin of the Imprisonment Epistles* (New York: Charles Scribner's Sons, 1930) 59–161. For a modern review of the problem, with bibliography, see Helmut Koester, *Introduction to the New Testament* (2 vols.; Berlin and New York: de Gruyter, 1982) 2:135–40; and Trebilco, *Early Christians*, 83–87. Conzelmann (163) is discreet: "Events occurring in Corinth during the same time . . . remain outside the field of vision." See also Walter Grundmann, "Paulus in Ephesus," *Helikon* 4 (1964) 46–82.

17 See Pervo, *Profit*, 9–10. On the question of "history," see pp. 7-12. Johnson (342) says, "Luke had very little real historical information with which to work." Although this accurately reflects the historical value of the material, it is a difficult presupposition.

18 Ramsay, *St. Paul the Traveller*, 273. He exhibited high regard for vv. 23-40, but disdain for vv. 11-20 tempted him to suspect the hand of a mediocre editor behind those verses.

19 Greco-Roman authors often avoided judgment by attributing matter to a source, either through a phrase like "some people say" or by utilizing a first-person narrative assigned to a character in the narrative.

20 Two issues arise. Luke 2:7 (birth in an animal feeding stall, no space in the inn) utilizes obvious and universal symbols while generating no challenges to rationalism. Ramsay is not alone in finding the supernaturalism of Acts 19 distasteful. The manifest theology of glory on display here is also a challenge to the taste of many. For Luke, the theology of glory was a tool, a means rather than an end.

21 See below.

22 Schüssler Fiorenza, "Miracles Mission," 8–10, 16–19. This outline closely follows her proposals, and the appended comments, as well as the descriptive captions, build on her work.

23 "Sections" is preferable to "scenes," as summaries (such as vv. 8-10) are not formally scenes.

II. Vv. 11-20. The Miraculous Powers of the Christian Missionary
  A. Vv. 11-12. A Summary of Healing Miracles
  B. Vv. 13-17. The Failure of Some Jewish Exorcists
  C. Vv. 18-20. The Burning of Magical Books

This part exhibits the overwhelming superiority of Christianity to its competitors outside of the religious establishment.[24]

III. Vv. 21(3)-40. Polytheist Competition
  (A. Vv. 21-22. Future Plans)
  B. Vv. 23-40. Christianity Threatens the Leading Local Cult
    1. Vv. 23-28. Paul's Critique of Polytheism Endangers the Standing of Artemis and Thus the Economic and General Welfare of Ephesus. The Unit Ends with an Acclamation (v. 28).
    2. Vv. 29-34. As Disorder Spreads, Asiarchs Intervene to Spare Paul. Final Acclamation (v. 34).
    3. Vv. 35-40. A Civic Official Intervenes and Places Blame on the Agitators.

The final episode ends with the effective "dismissal"[25] of charges brought by these means. On the one side stand promoters of civic unrest feeling an economic pinch. Asiarchs and the executive secretary side with Paul. The Christian movement presents no danger to society. In short: with friends like these, Christianity need fear no enemies; with such enemies, powerful friends will be plentiful. The narrative forms a crescendo that opens with a dozen misguided believers in Ephesus and ends with the populace of Ephesus packed into its theater for a pep rally that ends with a threat of Roman intervention. One after another, "fringe groups," Jews, exploitative exorcists, users (and producers) of magic, and, finally, the great patron goddess herself cannot frustrate the course of the Christian message or impede the work of its incomparable missionary.[26]

Comment

■ **1-7** The D-Text once more illustrates the difficulties of the conventional text. Paul undertook the long and arduous trip to Ephesus at the explicit direction of the Spirit, rather than on his own initiative.[27] Divine guidance is emphasized in the D-Text.[28] The D-Text also eliminates the synchronism regarding Apollos. More importantly, rather than happen upon a(n isolated?) group of believers, Paul encounters all the "disciples," who, evidently because of the ministrations of Apollos, have a defective baptism. This explains the Spirit's overruling of his personal plan. Instead of making the remarkable claim that they have never heard of the Spirit, these persons are unaware that the baptized receive its gift. Verses 5-6 of the D-Text may posit a two-stage view of Christian initiation: water baptism conveys forgiveness of sins, and the imposition of hands the gift of the Spirit.[29] Luke did not so systematize the matter, but it could be inferred from Acts 2:38; 8:14-17.[30] Equally tidy is the assurance that interpretation followed the gift of "tongues." Paul had required this in 1 Cor 14:27-28 and would no doubt do the same in Ephesus.

---

24 The expression "message about the Lord" (τὸν λόγον τοῦ κυρίου . . . τοῦ κυρίου ὁ λόγος) in vv. 10 and 20 frames this section.

25 Cf. the final verb ἀπέλυσεν ("dismissed"), v. 40.

26 A reasonable objection to this plan is that it does not include 18:24-28. As often, Luke provides overlapping episodes that look forward and backward. Paul's mission to Ephesus began at 18:19, in a sense, but the last part of chap. 18 amounts to a prelude.

27 It may be, as Bruce (405) observes, that the reviser did not understand 18:22 as a reference to Jerusalem. Note also Fitzmyer, 642, and his references. Barrett (2:893) finds the contrast between human and divine will (βουλή) congenial to Lucan thought.

28 Acts 16:6-10 provides inspiration for the motif. Cadbury and Lake (229) note that this text likes to multiply such motifs as divine guidance. The D-Text adds it in 17:15, here, and 20:3. See Cadbury and Lake, 237.

29 Alternatively, this expansion may be the result of the developing baptismal formula. See Haenchen, 553 n. 6.

30 Metzger (*Textual Commentary*, 416) finds this addition "inept," since John's baptism conveyed forgiveness. So Luke 3:3, probably correctly, but this historicizing is a bit premature.

There is a difference, however. The D-Text (p Ephrem [catena] H^mg) attributes the interpretation, audibly or internally [H^mg]) to the candidates, but this may be ad hoc, for there was no one else to interpret.[31] Still, this is different from the Pauline "regulations."[32] This passage is as strong evidence as any for the hypothesis that there is a "proto-Montanist" orientation in the D-text tradition.[33] The D-Text of v. 7 asserts that only after this message and action had these persons become "believers"; that is, none of them were "Christians" and Paul had truly founded the church in Ephesus. This fresh beginning is reinforced by the use of "names" (ὀνόματα) for persons, an evocation of 1:15.[34] The D-Text represents a relatively early effort to reduce 19:1-7 to a rational account.

The adjective "symbolic" fits vv. 1-7, for exegesis understands this as showing that "Paul wins over the sects"[35] or representing "the incorporation of fringe groups into the mainstream church."[36] "Sect" and "fringe group" are quite anachronistic for the time of Paul and not fully suitable for Luke's day, since there can be no fringe without a broad center, and early Christian sects were not reactions against a developed church, but within the accepted limits (Luke held that false teaching was a "postapostolic" phenomenon), this probably represents Luke's objective.[37] Another aim is not hard to detect. Like Peter (8:14-17), Paul has been the instrument through which some believers of irregular background receive the gift of the Spirit. John the Baptizer has an honorable place in salvation history, as Peter (1:5, 22) and Paul (13:24-25) had affirmed, but his message and activity have been superseded.[38]

The structure of this unit indicates careful composition. Within a frame dealing with the persons in question (vv. 1, 7) are a question about the Holy Spirit, balanced with the reception of the same (vv. 2, 6), a query about baptism, complemented by the administration thereof (vv. 3, 5) and the core contrast between the Baptizer and Jesus (v. 4).[39] This artful ring does not inhibit the brisk narrative exposition. The episode begins with an apparently chance meeting between Paul and some believers, reveals that their faith and experience are not satisfactory, quickly corrects both, and ends by revealing their number. Twelve is always an eminently suitable number. Such numbers are characteristic of miracle stories (cf. Mark 6:44; Acts 27:37).[40] For Luke, the gift of the Spirit and incorporation of new believers certainly belong to the realm of the miraculous.

■ **1** The first verse[41] reiterates the travels of 18:23 from the perspective of Ephesus, to which Paul (who has been

31 For details, see Ropes, *Text*, 181, 441.

32 1 Cor 14:13 says that speakers should pray for the power to interpret, but vv. 26-27 view interpretation as distinct from glossolalia.

33 "Proto-Montanist" refers to antecedents of the spiritual movement known as "the New Prophecy," which erupted in Asia Minor in the last third of the second century. Montanists accepted ecstatic prophecy and ascetic practices. Emphasis on the Spirit in the D-Text, as well as indications of ecstatic rapture, suggest that the movement had forebears. Note also the role of the Spirit in the *Shepherd of Hermas* and the *Acts of Paul*. See also p. 36 n. 44.

34 The evidence is slim, a single lectionary, but Boismard (*Texte*, 315) asks why the composer of a lectionary would invent this item.

35 Haenchen (557), a view Barrett (2:886) regards as "probably right." Trebilco (*Early Christians*, 127–34) views these persons as actual disciples of John.

36 Fitzmyer, 642.

37 For a critique of the anachronism of language about "sects" and the like, see Jervell, 478.

38 Regardless of the outcome of the redaction-critical debate about Luke's Gospel, in Acts John the Baptizer belongs to a bygone age.

39 On the structure, see Michael Wolter, "Apollos und die ephesinischen Johannesjünger," *ZNW* 78 (1987) 49–73, esp. 67–71; Werner Thiessen, *Christen in Ephesus: Die historische und theologische Situation in vorpaulinischer und paulinischer Zeit und zur Zeit der Apostelgeschichte und der Pastoralbriefe* (Tübingen: Francke, 1995) 71–75; and Talbert, 174. For an effort to comprehend Apollos within the various movements of nascent Christianity, see Pier Franco Beatrice, "Apollos of Alexandria and the Origins of the Jewish-Christian Baptist Encratism," *ANRW* 2.26.2 (1995) 1232–75.

40 On the construction οἱ πάντες ἄνδρες (e.g., "the number of men in its totality"), see Moule, *Idiom Book*, 94. Luke normally qualifies numbers with an adverb indicating approximation (2:4; 4:4; 5:7, 36; 10:3; 18:18, 20; 19:7, 34).

41 The use of ἐγένετο ("it happened") with infinitive and the articular infinitive prepositional phrase are marks of the LXX style.

"offstage" since 18:24) came[42] from the hinterlands.[43] Rather than relate that he proceeded to the living quarters of Priscilla and Aquila, the narrator reports that Paul came upon "some disciples." "Come upon" (lit. "find," εὑρεῖν) is narrative shorthand in Acts and does not imply a search.[44] The expression "some disciples" is, in theory, ambiguous, but the lack of a modifier indicates that Luke views them as "Christians" of a sort. Had the author intended to identify these persons as followers of the Baptizer, he could have done so.[45] Followers of John may have existed after his death and could have been rivals of the admirers of Jesus, but Acts 19:1-7 is not directly engaged in this hypothetical conflict.[46]

■ **2** The subject, as Paul's apparently unmotivated and surprising question (which must be explained by appeal to the desired outcome) establishes, is the nature of baptism in the name of Jesus. Before readers of the present day, at least, can pause to ponder what manner of salutation this might be, their curiosity is inundated by the reply: these good people have never heard of the Holy Spirit.[47] One popular resolution involves construing the verb "is" to mean "is (now) present."[48]

■ **3** This interpretation effectively endorses the D-Text in seeking a rational explanation of a historical report.[49] In any case, the narrative would require further development, such as a brief exposition of the nature of the Spirit or an assurance that the Spirit has come. Instead, a further question, which addresses the baptismal formula employed, follows. This question (lit. "Into what were you baptized?") assumes that those being interrogated had been baptized, thus putting to rest Barrett's hypothesis that this passage and that which follows provide two different approaches to the reception of former followers of the Baptizer.[50] The question also assumes that there is a firm bond between proper baptism and reception of the Spirit.[51] This is a Christian assumption, as is the formulaic expression εἰς τί, which presumes the noun ὄνομα ("in whose name?"), that

42 The compound κατελθεῖν ("come down") reflects this. The simpler form ἐλθεῖν ("came" [B 𝔐 lat]) may be more original, but it is slightly more possible that it was an alteration based on a lack of geographical understanding.

43 Cf. Cadbury and Lake, 236. For other interpretations, see Haenchen, 552 n. 1.

44 Cf. the comments on 18:2. A disparate range of witnesses (D E Ψ 𝔐 gig sy[h] bo[ms]) smooth the abrupt indirect discourse by placing "find" in a participial phrase. Scribes had difficulty leaving 19:1-7 as they found it.

45 See Shauf, *Theology*, 107–10; Barrett, 2:893. Luke 5:33 and 7:18 identify "disciples of John" specifically. Weiser (2:515) argues that, despite the terms "disciples" and "believe," Luke thought that these persons were "not really Christians." His only basis for this view is to assert it. See pp. 514–16 for a review of research.

46 For data about followers of John the Baptizer, see Lüdemann, *Acts*, 250–53. Palestine and its neighbors would have been a suitable place for such a conflict (so also Conzelmann, 159: "the closer to Palestine the better"), while the rival Jesus-people would have been more likely those who viewed Jesus as a prophet and/or sage rather than those who viewed him as the heavenly Lord. Although Fitzmyer (641) attributes this unit to "Luke's Pauline source," he states on 642: "[N]o one can tell whether it all really happened at Ephesus."

47 The anarthrous πνεῦμα ἅγιον ("[a] holy spirit") appears three times in chap. 8: vv. 15, 17, 19. On the use of εἰ to mean "that," see Christoph Burchard, "εἰ nach einem Ausdruck des Wissens oder Nichtwissens Joh 9:25, Act 19:2, 1 Cor 1:16, 7:16," *ZNW* 52 (1961) 73–82.

48 So, for example, Witherington, 571. If the episode is historical, it is possible that actual followers of John did not speak of the Spirit, as the association of John and the Spirit may be due to Christianization.

49 Cf. also Cadbury and Lake, 237, and a majority of scholars. For a list, see Shauf, *Theology*, 108 n. 62. Calvin (7:149) is more intelligent than most, taking "Spirit" as a trope referring to spiritual gifts. In Lucan terms, John did speak of the Holy Spirit (Luke 3:16).

50 Charles K. Barrett, "Apollos and the Twelve Disciples of Ephesus," in William C. Weinrich, ed., *The New Testament Age: Essays in Honor of Bo Reicke* (2 vols.; Macon, Ga.: Mercer University Press, 1984) 29–39.

51 Conzelmann, 159.

is, that the "name" has power and that being baptized "into the name" of someone places the candidate into a relationship with the bearer of that name (cf. 1 Cor 1:13-15). Those who claimed baptism in the name of John would be acknowledging the Baptizer as a savior.[52] An actual follower of John would probably have replied: *εἰς μετάνοιαν* ("for repentance").

■ **4-7** That viewpoint is, however, assigned to Paul, who provides a compressed statement of the Christian understanding of John, one that would have been difficult for disciples of the Baptizer to grasp.[53] Without demur, these persons accept Paul's message and submit to Christian baptism and the imposition of hands, promptly exhibiting spiritual gifts. Attempts to extract pre-Lucan tradition from this account will scarcely be worth the effort, for the most that can be said is that some follower/s of Jesus attempted at some place and time to win over adherents of John to their point of view. Even this nebulous reconstruction requires introduction of the (reasonable) hypothesis that disciples of the Baptizer existed.[54] Although Paul's words about John (v. 4) evoke the speech of Jesus in 1:5,[55] he could not say, "John baptized with water; you should be baptized in the name of Jesus to receive the Holy Spirit," because these persons are about to be rebaptized with water and Acts provides no dominical warrant for baptism in the name of Jesus.[56]

In addition to the general theme of correction/supplementation, this account shares two elements with 18:24-28: the name "Apollos" and the phrase "baptism of John." The latter ties the exegete in knots. In 18:25, it referred to Apollos's knowledge, corrected by fuller instruction, whereas experience is the referent in 19:3.[57] In the earlier passage, Luke evidently did not wish to speak about Apollos's baptism, although it is difficult not to infer that it was, by the criteria of 19:1-7, defective. Early readers of Acts would have been most likely to suspect that at least some (i.e., these dozen) members of the community at Ephesus had been introduced to the faith by Apollos prior to his enlightenment by Priscilla and Aquila and thus were not properly initiated. Paul was the founder of "apostolic" Christianity in Ephesus.[58]

52 See also Haenchen, 553; Conzelmann, 159; and Barrett, 2:896.

53 The syntax of v. 4 is quite tortured. If the purpose clause (beginning with *ἵνα*) followed "the people" and the prepositional phrase "about one who would come after him" followed that, the wording would be more logical. The wording is most probably due to Luke rather than to modification of a source or a later gloss. The translation takes the participle *λέγων* ("saying") as making the phrase iterative: John said this repeatedly. See Cadbury and Lake, 237; Moule, *Idiom Book*, 169; and Bruce, 407. The result is that "so that they would believe" is framed by "the coming one" and "Jesus." In this verse. the Synoptic message about John the Baptizer is fully Christianized. Cadbury and Lake (238) already compared it to the Gospel of John. Johnson (333) notes that this is the fifth clarification of John the Baptizer's place in salvation history (1:5; 11:16; 13:25; 18:25). Barrett (2:897) observes that "Jesus" would have been a familiar name to these persons if they were believers and that the new information would have identified him with the coming one of whom John spoke. The narrator is not clear.

54 The hypothesis that these persons were followers of John goes back at least to Chrysostom (*Hom.* 40, 536d). For attempts to identify pre-Lucan tradition, see Lüdemann (p. 455 n. 102) and Weiser, 2:512–14. Käsemann ("Disciples") does not make a systematic effort to isolate pre-Lucan tradition. Jervell (478) holds that this reference to followers of John the Baptizer is historical.

55 See n. 53.

56 See 2:38 and the comments there.

57 Cadbury and Lake (4:238) may be right: "The 'baptism of John' does not for our author necessarily imply direct or indirect influence from the Baptist, it is his name for Christian water baptism without the Spirit."

58 On this point, Käsemann ("Disciples") agrees with Bede (77): *Ecce Asia . . . nunc et apostolico sacrata numero et prophetali est munere sublimata* ("Behold Asia . . . now both hallowed by the apostolic number [12] and exalted by the prophetic gift"). On Christian origins in Ephesus, see Trebilco's concise review of scholarship in *Early Christians*, 2–4. Michael Fieger (*Im Schatten der Artemis: Glaube und Ungehorsam in Ephesus* [Bern: Peter Lang, 1998]) is quite skeptical about the value of Acts for this purpose. Less so is Werner Thiessen, *Christen in Ephesus: Die historische und theologische Situation in vorpaulinischer und paulinischer Zeit und zur Zeit der Apostelgeschichte und der Pastoralbriefe* (Tübingen: Francke, 1995). Trebilco is the least skeptical.

Other solutions require substantial filling in of blanks and squeezing out of alleged inferences from the text.[59] Luke appears to have seen a firm link between doctrine and practice: those who did not understand the meaning of baptism were not properly baptized, and lack of proper baptism meant inadequate knowledge.[60]

The foreground yields more than the background.[61] Although Luke cannot denominate Paul as an apostle, he portrays him doing what apostles did, in this instance the apostles of chap. 8, who supplement an evidently incomplete baptism.[62] Just as Stephen and Philip were precursors of Peter (and Paul) in the gentile mission, so Apollos, who is described in terms evocative of Stephen,[63] is a forerunner of Paul in Ephesus. The allusions to the beginning of Jesus' ministry (message of the Baptizer, twelve followers) and to the opening chapters of Acts—the contrast between Jesus and John, gift of the Spirit, the ministries of Stephen and Philip, the collapse of those who view religion (and magic) as means for a good living, the miracles of Peter and Paul (5:12-16; 19:11-12)—endow Ephesus with a special character.[64]

■ **8** The narrator then abandons these twelve[65] and reports Paul's overture to the synagogue as in 18:19.[66] To all intents and purposes the story resumes from that point, as if nothing had intervened. In summary form, the text reports the customary mission that begins in the synagogue and results in separation. This is the last time that Paul is represented as preaching in a synagogue.[67] Atypically, the synagogue work lasts for three months and its subject is "the kingdom (or "dominion") of God."[68] This is the only time, apart from in Rome (28:23, 31), that the phrase is used to define Paul's message and thus evokes both the beginning (1:3) and the close (28:31) of the book.[69] Its meaning must be comprehensive, since no one will claim that Luke had Paul speak over several months without mentioning the place of Jesus in salvation history.[70] The phrase has more to do with Christology than with eschatology.[71] The surprise is that the synagogue put up with him for so long a period.[72] In Ephesus, Paul does not announce a turn to the gentiles. Jews[73] will continue to be included in his outreach.[74]

■ **9-10** As in Corinth (18:7), the mission moves to new quarters, but, rather than a private house, Paul holds forth in a (possibly rented) facility.[75] This brief notice artfully indicates both the popularity of his message (no

59 An example is Tannehill, *Narrative Unity*, 2:232–34.

60 On the conflicts over baptism in the third century, see François Bovon, *Studies in Early Christianity* (Tübingen: Mohr Siebeck, 2003).

61 Shauf (*Theology*, 144–61) seems to reach a similar conclusion in his complicated study of the passage. He understands the passage as an introduction to chap. 19 and its purpose as the magnification of Paul.

62 Käsemann, "Disciples," 144–46; and Turner, *Power*, 397.

63 Note the similarity in language between 6:10 and 18:25. Like Stephen, Apollos was a powerful preacher who effectively refuted Jews with his interpretations of Scripture in synagogue settings (6:9-10; 18:24, 28). See Tannehill, *Narrative Unity*, 2:233.

64 On these parallels and evocations, see Spencer, *Portrait*, 232–36; and Klutz, *Exorcism Stories*, 231–39.

65 Jacquier (569) remarks that these twelve persons disappear as abruptly as they appeared.

66 Note the similarity of the verb ἐπαρρησιάζετο ("preach boldly") to that used of Apollos in 18:26. The D-Text supplies the proper name "Paul" and notes that he preached "with great power" (Boismard, *Texte*, 315), clearly secondary but good preparation for what is to come.

67 For various interpretations of the significance of this, see Shauf, *Theology*, 111.

68 The evidence for and against the article with περί ("about") is rather evenly divided. Without it, the participle has no object, but none is required. Barrett (2:904) says that it was added to conform with 1:3. This is a good point, but the opposite, that it is parallel to 1:3, is better in the context.

69 Its other use to describe preaching in Acts is in 8:12 (Philip). Shauf (*Theology*, 164–65) emphasizes its typical character.

70 See Weiser, 2:526–27.

71 Acts 28:31 is different, including both "the kingdom" and the message about Jesus. On its meaning here, see Rackham, 348.

72 The request for a longer stay in 18:20 evidently anticipates this matter.

73 As Tannehill (*Narrative Unity*, 2:236) points out, it is Jews from Asia who raise the charges against Paul in the temple (21:27-28).

74 On the atypical features of these verses, see Shauf, *Theology*, 165–67.

75 On rented quarters as a base for teaching, see 28:30 (if that is the correct understanding) and *Acts of*

ordinary house was of sufficient size for the audience), its relative affluence, and Paul's status. Like a philosopher, he delivers public instruction via lectures. Another variation from the typical is that the mission lasted for two years, surpassing even Corinth in duration. Finally, the message reached "everyone in Asia." This evidently reveals Luke's awareness that Paul used large urban centers as bases from which he and other evangelists radiated throughout a province, and beyond.[76] The statement about a mission of two years' duration and the data about Tyrannus's "school" or "hall" appear to derive from local tradition.[77]

The separation (v. 9a) is equally distinctive. The dissidents constitute a minority ("some," τινες [cf. 15:5]). They attacked the movement in a synagogue assembly (apparently) with abusive language[78] with motivation derived from the exodus tradition.[79] The implication is that their stubbornness and vehemence rather than their number prompted Paul to bring about a formal separation and establish a distinct, independent community.[80] The term πλῆθος is ambiguous.[81] The D-Text, in addition to recasting the initial adverbial clause as an independent sentence,[82] glosses this word with "of the gentiles," identifying the setting as a gentile crowd, possibly a juridical confrontation. The sequel shows that this does not fit.[83] Reference to "daily" teaching[84] evokes both a parallel to and a contrast with Jesus, who taught daily in the temple (Luke 19:47;[85] cf. 21:37). The focus of religious life has shifted from temple to house to "facility" or "school."[86] The term σχολή means "leisure," which, as Sir 38:24 points out, is the basis of learning. It is the source of English "school," which, by metonymy, often means a place. That is the general understanding of the term in Acts 19:9, but it could mean "under the sponsorship of Tyrannus." In any case, the activity would require a regular space.[87] The language suggests that Tyrannus's facility was (at one time) familiar to Ephesian believers, but this is not a necessary

Justin 3 (above a bath; the text is apparently corrupt). On a rented cult site, see the Sarapis Aretalogy from Delos, lines 15–16 (Appendix 2).

76 Cf. 1 Thess 1:7-8, as well as Philemon and the Deutero-Pauline evidence provided by Colossians. See Christian R. le Roux, "Ephesus in the Acts of the Apostles: A Geographical and Theological Appraisal," in Herwig Firesinger et al., eds., *100 Jahre österreichische Forschungen in Ephesus: Akten des Symposions Wien 1995* (Vienna: Österreichischen Akademie der Wissenschaften, 1999) 307–13.

77 To this Haenchen (560) would add the three months in the synagogue, but that is questionable, for the thesis that Paul always began in the synagogue is Lucan and cannot be verified from the letters.

78 On κακολογέω ("malign," used only here in [Luke and] Acts), see *NewDocs* 2 (1982) no. 54, p. 88.

79 The verb σκληρύνω is used in the active (e.g., Exod 7:3; 9:12) and passive (e.g., Exod 8:15; 9:35). The question here is whether the form is passive and, if so, whether God is the unstated agent. This would not counter Lucan thought, but the verb could also be middle ("hardened themselves"), the option taken in the translation. This language has raised theological problems. Both Philo and Josephus avoid it, for example. See Spicq, *Lexicon*, 3:261–62; and Karl Ludwig and Martin A. Schmidt, "παχύνω," *TDNT* 5:1022–31, esp. 1023–24, esp. 1030–31. This is another evocation of Stephen (7:51).

80 The verb ἀφορίζω implies formality (cf. Luke 6:22). See Johnson, 339. Note the alliteration, four consecutive words beginning with *a*-.

81 Barrett, 2:904.

82 The D-Text (Boismard, *Texte*, 316) introduces what is now the next sentence with the τότε ("then") of which it is fond.

83 Ropes, *Text*, 182. The D-Text would mean, by the strict rules of grammar, that Paul separated the believers from the gentiles.

84 The present participle διαλεγόμενος ("lecturing") refers to action subsequent to the aorist "separated." See Moule, *Idiom Book*, 102.

85 The D-Text (Boismard, *Texte*, 316) recognizes this by reading τὸ καθ' ἡμέραν ("daily," an accusative of respect) precisely as in Luke 19:47 (unless, as is possible, this is more original, with the article later omitted as needless).

86 The name "Tyrannus" is attested at Ephesus: *NewDocs* 4 (1987) no. 102 (k), p. 186; and Hemer, *Book*, 120–21. The D-Text (Boismard, *Texte*, 316) offers a variant: "a **certain** Tyrannius" (see n. 88) and adds the time of this teaching: "from the fifth to the tenth hour" (1100–1600 hours). Metzger (*Textual Commentary*, 417) says that this may be accurate and could have been "preserved in oral tradition before being incorporated into the text of certain manuscripts." In fact, it is a novelistic detail.

87 For a critique of the translation "hall," see *NewDocs* 1 (1981) no. 82, pp. 129–30; Trebilco,

conclusion.[88] In the course of two more years[89] the message[90] had spread throughout the province.

■ **11-12** The summary, which continues the summation of vv. 8-10,[91] is, like that in 5:12-16, based on Mark 6:55-56.[92] The similarity is not merely formal. Just as the former epitomizes the apex of the mission to Jews in Jerusalem, so this résumé expresses the high point of Paul's mission to gentiles.[93] The summary is a single euphonious sentence.[94] As in the case of Peter's shadow (5:15), the result clause appears to imply that the use of cloth was a consequence of the extraordinary healing power on display rather than an example of it, but the construction is loose.[95] Paul surpasses Jesus (Mark 5:28-29; 6:56) in power, for material[96] that has been in contact with his body is effective even when removed from him.[97] This report has inspired a number of

"Asia" 311–12; and Barrett, 2:904–5. Abraham J. Malherbe (*Social Aspects of Early Christianity* [2nd ed.; Philadelphia: Fortress Press, 1983] 89–91) suggests that the term may refer to a guild hall and connects the report with Paul's craft. See also the literature cited in Shauf, *Theology*, 169 n. 143.

88 The variant τινος ("a certain"), which has a range of support (D*c E H L P Ψ 33 614, a number of other minuscules, and varied versional evidence), does not support this interpretation.

89 The reference to a three-year ministry in 20:31 suggests that this time was subsequent to the three months of v. 8.

90 The D-Text (Boismard, *Texte*, 316–17) fashions the result clause (classical Greek would prefer the indicative as this is an actual result rather than an intention) into a temporal ("until") construction and ceases at "message," eliminating the qualifying "of the Lord" and the references to Jews and Greeks. Other witnesses of that tradition change "Lord" to "God" and/or "message" (λόγον) to "messages" (λόγους), possibly an attempt to indicate numerous sermons. The conventional text is typically Lucan, which is not a decisive point in its favor, but the D-Text overlooks the evident frame in v. 20 (where the D-Text also differs). These variants look like rewriting for its own sake. "Word" (λόγος) is practically a shorthand expression for "mission" in Acts. See Johnson, 339.

91 For arguments linking vv. 11-12 to vv. 8-10 rather than to the sequence, see Shauf, *Theology*, 176; and Garrett, *Demise*, 90. As often, the structure is overlapping: vv. 11-12 form a complex of "word and deed" with vv. 8-10 and also prepare for the sequence.

92 See Pervo, *Dating*, 36–38.

93 2 Corinthians 10–13 indicates that some found Paul's miracles rather quite run-of-the-mill (i.e., τὰς τυχούσας). On this, see Haenchen, 563.

94 The use of the negative οὐ ("not") with a participle is emphatic. The same construction (with singular participle) appears in 28:2. Cadbury and Lake (239) say that the litotes is a "fixed idiom of Hellenistic Greek." Roughly contemporary examples of precisely the same phrase include Plutarch *Ant.* 14.4; *Lib. ed.* 3 (*Mor.* 3d); and Artemidorus *Onir.* 3.20. Bruce (410) notes that the expression is common in Vettius Valens. Rather than "Hellenistic Greek," it is preferable to say that this litotes was common in the second century CE. Euphony is achieved through seven uses of *-ou-* and five initial uses of *a-*. Shauf's semi-objection to rendering δυνάμεις as "miracles"—"as if any 'miracle' could be said to be 'usual'" (*Theology*, 170 n. 149)—misunderstands the ancient understanding of miracle. See Parsons and Pervo, *Rethinking*, 92–95.

95 The plural "hands" indicates contact rather than simple agency and thus prepares for the logical next step: that with which the hands have been in contact.

96 The meanings of the terms translated "handkerchiefs and work clothes" (σουδάρια ἢ σιμικίνθια) is far from certain. The latter may have been towels folded over the cincture (a rope belt). A reasonable guess is that both were used to wipe away dirt and perspiration. If so, the underlying notion would be the healing property of spittle and other excretions, for an unrefined example of which, see Epiphanius *Pan.* 19.1.13. Klauck (*Magic*, 98) resolves the issue by referring to "the Apostle's laundry." See Cadbury and Lake, 239–40; Conzelmann, 164; Trebilco, "Asia," 313–14; and Barrett, 2:907. Richard Strelan ("Acts 19:12: Paul's 'Aprons' Again," *JTS* 54 [2003] 154–57) proposes that the items in question were part of an orator's habit and thus endowed with power from the charismatic speaker.

97 Other instances of healing cloth are *IG* IV 951,48–54 (Temple of Asclepius at Epidauros, no. 6); Plutarch *Sulla* 35.3–5; and Athenaeus *Deipn.* 5.212F. *Historia Augusta* 5.7 states that people were condemned for wearing about their necks garlands removed from imperial busts or statues as an apotropaic against fever. (The crime would be *laesa maiestas*; the power would be analogous to "the king's touch.") Note also the mantle of Elijah (2 Kgs 2:8-14). For a close parallel from early Christian hagiography, see Sulpicius Severus *Life of Martin of Tours* 18.4–5. *Act. John* 62 (set in Ephesus) seems to imitate Mark 6:56, but the connection to Acts 19 may have been in the author's mind.

theological qualifications,[98] but the message is clear enough: human misery, the fruit of Satan's power, is being wiped off the face of the earth. The inclusion of both the sick[99] and the possessed[100] is typical of summaries (Mark 1:34). These groups lay the ground for the next unit.[101]

98 Witherington (578) observes that the narrator does not claim that "Paul traded in healing handkerchiefs or the like, or that he initiated such practices." Bruce (410) states, "The healing virtue resided not in those pieces of cloth but in the faith of those who used them." In the tradition, such relics usually function in an ecclesial context, working *ex opere operato* only to teach a lesson or bring about a conversion. The faith of the agent receives more emphasis than that of the patient. For various and often amusing interpretations, see Haenchen, 562; and Shauf, *Theology*, 111–13. The latter rightly notes that Protestant commentators since Calvin have been concerned about the evident support for the use of relics in these verses. One who finds such support is Jacquier, 573. Zahn (681–82) is certain that family members of sick persons obtained these items from Priscilla, who promptly returned them after use. This balances the role of Aquila, who was unquestionably the minister of baptism in 19:5 (Zahn 675 n. 92). Klauck (*Magic*, 98–99), while admitting that "[t]he understanding of miracles in v. 12 is located in dangerous border territory," notes that God is the primary agent. This, however, is always true. In the end, he can only approve its concrete understanding of salvation. Shauf (*Theology*, 172) rightly states: "It emphasizes both the power of the Christian God to bring about these feats and the status of the characters through whom they are performed as emissaries of that God who works such wonders." On p. 218 n. 320 he lists a number of authorities who admit "[t]hat v. 12 sounds an awful lot like magic."

99 The verb ἀπαλλάσσω ("remove" [v. 12]) is a technical term in this connection: Lucian *Philops.* 16; *Peregr.* 28; *PGM* 13.245; Ps.-Plato *Eryxias* 401C; *Caracalla* 5.7; and the D-Text of Luke 9:40 and Acts 5:15.

100 Apollonius went to Ephesus in response to a summons and averted the plague by recognizing the presence of a "demon" (δαίμων), which he had the Ephesians kill by stoning in the theater (Philostratus *Vit. Apoll.* 4.10).

101 Acts has previously reported but one exorcism by Paul (16:16-18).

19

19:13-22 An Attempted Exorcism and Its Aftermath

19:13c-14: Conventional Text

13/ Some itinerant Jewish exorcists
endeavored to employ the name
of the Lord Jesus in their work
with those possessed by evil
spirits. They used this formula:
"I adjure you by the name of
that Jesus whom Paul pro-
claims."
14/ Among those attempting to follow this technique were seven
sons of Sceva, a Jewish high
priest.[a]

19:13c-14: D-Text[b]

13c/ They used this formula: "*We*
adjure you by the name of that
Jesus whom Paul proclaims."
14/ *Among whom*[c] *also* sons of
Sceva, a certain *priest,*
wished to do *the same thing, as*
they had a custom of exorcizing
such persons, and coming in to
the possessed man they began
to call upon the name, saying,
"By Jesus whom Paul[d] *preaches*
we command you to come out."[e]

15/ In response the evil spirit said to
them, "I am familiar with the
name of Jesus and know that of
Paul, but who are you people?"
16/ The possessed person then leapt
at them and was able to over-
power the entire group.[f] They
ended up running away from
that house wounded and nude.
17/ Word of this incident spread
among all the Jews and Greeks
living in Ephesus. All were filled
with awe and praised the name
of the Lord Jesus.
18/ Those who had become believers[g] began to come forward
in large numbers to confess
and disclose their improper
practices,[h] 19/ and many persons who had engaged in magic
collected their texts and burned
them in public. The value of
these items was calculated at
50,000 pieces of silver. 20/ In
such ways proclamation of the
Lord's message grew mightily and went from strength to
strength.
21/ In the wake of these accomplishments Paul resolved, with the
guidance of the Spirit,[i] to travel
through Macedonia and Achaea[j]
and then on to Jerusalem.
"After I have been there," he
said, "I must see Rome as well."
22/ He sent two of his assistants, Timothy and Erastus, on
to Macedonia, but he himself
spent some more time in Asia.[k]

a The translation views ἦσαν . . . ποιοῦντες ("there were . . . doing") as a participial phrase rather than as a periphrastic equivalent to the imperfect.

b Boismard, *Texte*, 318.

c *Or:* "while . . ." (ἐν οἷς). This is a questionable rendition (ἐν ᾧ would be preferable), but one that solves the problem of transition here.

d 𝔓[38] reads "the apostle Paul."

e The D-Text is inspired by 16:18 (an exorcism by Paul). Note, in particular, the verb παραγγέλλω. Shauf (*Theology*, 226) says that this shows that ὁρκίζω ("adjure") is not "freighted with magical connotations." This is not convincing, since the passage is based on the intertextual link (as he also observes) and could have been used precisely because of the "magical connotations."

f Ephrem presents a "singular paraphrase" (Ropes, *Text*, 183) of v. 16, not preferred or cited by Boismard.

g The tense of the participle varies. The perfect (here translated) is most likely the source of the D-Text variants of present and aorist, since it is less likely that an editor or a scribe would introduce the perfect.

h *Or:* "Confess and reveal their spells."

i *Or:* "resolved." See the comments.

j A range of witnesses omit the article before "Achaea." The D-Text (Boismard, *Texte*, 320) includes it, a simpler and less probable solution.

k The D-Text (Boismard, *Texte*, 321) states that Paul spent but a short time (and improves the prepositional phrase. "Asia" is a synecdoche for "Ephesus." Haenchen (569 n. 5) lists 20:16; 20:4; 21:29; 21:27; 24:19 as examples.

Analysis

The structure of the following unit is not as clear as first appears. Verses 13-17 report a failed exorcism, properly concluded with public awe and marked, in vv. 13 and 17, with a bracket: "the name of the Lord Jesus."[1] Verses 18-19 follow as a logical consequence: magic names can boomerang. Talbert's view of vv. 13-19 as a parody of a miracle story captures something of the thrust of the narrative, if not its form.[2] Verses 11-19 flow in an artfully entwined crescendo. The detailed episode seems less artful. Beginning with a general summary in v. 13, the narrative awkwardly follows with a sentence identifying some specific practitioners (v. 14), then leaps (vv. 15-16) to a specific example, engaged *medias in res*, that may involve but two of the brothers identified in v. 14.

The D-text of vv. 13c-14 exposes the problems of the conventional text by solving them. Scaeva is not certainly Jewish or a high priest, although the context implies that he was Jewish.[3] By eliminating the number of his sons (or altering it to "two," as in Gig) the apparent conflict between the "seven" and the "both" (ἀμφοτέρων [v. 16]) evaporates.[4] The conventional text may be corrupt, but the D-Text addresses those points where corruption could be suspected and is thus almost certainly a correction.[5] A more likely option is that Luke used a source that lacked the number "seven," which he inserted. Scholarship generally assigns this episode to a source, but little can be affirmed of its nature or extent. The name of Paul is almost certainly a Lucan addition,[6] and Ephesus (or Asia) need not have been the original location. The final words (v. 20) indicate that the encounter took place in a hitherto unmentioned house.[7]

Since Dibelius, it has been popular to assign this anecdote a "non-Christian" origin. This is possible, but disapproval is not a valid ground for such attributions. Dibelius judged this "a story which serves to entertain

1 To 19:17 compare 9:42 (raising of Tabitha).

2 Talbert, 175. See below.

3 𝔓[38], however, retains "Jewish" and "high priest." Cadbury and Lake (241) note the Latin tendency to use *sacerdos* for ἀρχιερεύς. For Ephrem (440), Scaeva was a polytheist priest.

4 Two issues emerge: (1) the use of "both" to mean "all," which is quite vulgar; and (2) the difficulty of overpowering seven men. "Them" rather than "both" made its way into the majority text. Luke uses "both" in 23:8, but it is not clear whether this means "all." See the comments there.

5 For defenses of the priority of the D-Text of 19:14, see Sylva New, "The Michigan Papyrus," in Lake and Cadbury, *Additional Notes*, 262–69; and William A. Strange, "The Sons of Sceva and the Text of Acts 19:14," *JTS* 38 (1987) 97–106. On the textual questions, see also Ropes, *Text*, 183; Cadbury and Lake, 240–41; Metzger, *Textual Commentary*, 417–18; and Shauf, *Theology*, 226–27.

6 Barrett (2:911) is more cautious on this point.

7 The demonstrative ἐκείνου could be rendered as "that house" or "his house." In the latter case, it would refer to the person of v. 16. The style, as

and fosters no religious or personal interest whatever."[8] This view, which assumes a firm dichotomy between "magic" and "religion,"[9] is quite incorrect. Many Christians would have been proud of the apologetic value of the name of Jesus.[10] Dibelius also disapproved of the humor of this episode.[11] One element of ridicule is the role taken by sons of a Jewish high priest. Although it is possible that someone who did not differentiate between Jews and Christians might have concocted this story,[12] it is more probable that the episode stems from Christian circles. Rough as the story is, it has a learned element: only the high priest was permitted to pronounce the most potent (and "magical") of names.[13] The author may have contributed this note. The most definite Lucan contribution is probably the name of Paul in vv. 13 and 15, and he may have contributed to the climax. Although attempts to identify and delineate a source yield a number of interesting hypotheses, source analysis cannot make a substantial contribution to exegesis here.[14] Formally, this is a parody of an exorcism. Typical features include the adjuration of the exorcist (cf. Mark 5:7, which uses the same verb, ὁρκίζω); the resistance of the demon, who reveals superhuman knowledge (cf. Mark 1:24); the potency of names; and the extraordinary strength of the patient (cf. Mark 5:3-4). When the conclusion is taken into account, it will appear that 19:13-17 is a parody of a particular exorcism (Mark 5:1-20||Luke 8:26-39). A literary parody of a specific written source does not correspond to popular tradition or a "secular anecdote." The style, which has a certain verve and complexity, also tells against popular tradition.[15] Luke has recast whatever resources were available.

Comment

■ **13** The generalizing introduction is an editorial contribution, designed like other miracle summaries (cf. Mark 1:32-34) to make the particular a representative of a general trend. Unlike other summaries, this specifies the formula used.[16]

■ **14** The name "Skeuas" is apparently Latin *Scaeva*, which, presuming that this is not a family *cognomen*, looks like a nickname: "Lefty." It is attested for gladiators.[17] One might suspect a joke, since the left side was unfortunate, sinister, yielding an inauspicious designation, like a physician who rejoiced in the name Dr. Guecklos, but recognition of this would require some knowledge of Latin.[18] Scaeva is a problem for those who

Cadbury and Lake (242) note, is Lucan. See Luke 7:37; 8:27; 9:5.

8 Dibelius, *Studies*, 19. For a catalogue of scholars who are disappointed by the tone of this episode, see Shauf, *Theology*, 114.

9 See the excursus "Magi," "Magic," and "Magicians," pp. 207–9.

10 One example is Justin *Dial.* 85.3, who speaks of Jewish exorcists who employ the name of Jesus.

11 See Pervo, *Profit*, 63.

12 One will think of Juvenal's female Jewish priest (*Sat.* 6.542–547, on which see Georgi, *Opponents*, 99–103).

13 If one seeks a historical figure behind the story, the title of "high priest" would have been assumed to promote business. Priests have more knowledge and status than nonpriests, and chief priests possess even more. See Cadbury and Lake, 241; and Trebilco, *Early Christians*, 148–49.

14 See Weiser, 2:523–25; and Lüdemann, *Acts*, 255–56.

15 Although the order of the opening words is a bit odd, since "at them" (ἐπ᾽ αὐτούς) precedes the relative clause—an arrangement many witnesses attempt to better—the verb ἐφάλλομαι ("leap upon") has a certain irony (not appreciated by the D-Text, which uses an alternative), since it is found in 1 Kgdms 10:16; 16:13 for the descent of the prophetic spirit upon a person, and the finite verb is accompanied by two participles, on which see BDF §421.

16 The formula "name the name" appears only here (v. 13) in the Gospels and Acts. It is Deutero-Pauline. Note Eph 1:21 and the comments and references of Clinton Arnold, *Ephesians: Power and Magic. The Concept of Power in Ephesians in Light of Its Historical Setting* (Grand Rapids: Baker, 1992) 55. Cf. also 2 Tim 2:19.

17 See BDAG, 927, *s.v.* Σκευᾶς; Hemer, *Book*, 234; and Louis Robert, *Les gladiateurs dans l'Orient grec* (Bibliothèque de l'École des Hautes Études 278; Limoges: Bontemps, 1940; reprinted, Amsterdam: Hakkert, 1971) 70–72 and 180–82.

18 Cf. "Eutychus" in 20:7-12.

seek a historical kernel for this story and also for those who do not.[19]

As a figure for ridicule, he is admirably well placed and has but one function: to be the progenitor of no fewer than seven sons who make their living as itinerant exorcists. The claim that the progeny of a high priest would pursue such an undignified way of life is slanderous.[20] This allegation sets the polemical tone, for the scions of Scaeva's line were engaged in no mission,[21] nor were they emissaries of the Israelite faith.[22] They were participants in a highly competitive business, the demands of which required them to introduce the name of "that Jesus proclaimed by Paul" into their therapeutic formulae.[23] Theological niceties were not relevant; what counted was a name that worked. As even a cursory scan of the Greek magical papyri reveals, their opinion was not isolated.[24]

However déclassé their behavior may have seemed to some, Luke probably wished the reader to view these persons as occupying the highest rung on the ladder of Jewish exorcists, for, as Haenchen observes, defeating the league leader is more impressive than eking out a win over a basement dweller.[25] The number seven, holiest of integers, enhances this cachet. It prepares for the defeat of seven exorcists by a single demon, in contrast to the poor person who survives one exorcism only to be overwhelmed by seven superior demons (Luke/Q 11:26).[26]

■ **15** Following the general summary of v. 13 and the more particular summary of v. 14, the next verse leaps into the midst of a specific instance. One longs for the equivalent of "on one of these occasions."[27] The abruptness is literarily effective: readers are swept from generalities into the midst of an exorcistic conflict. The evil spirit (repeating the demonological language of v. 13) acknowledges the *persons/*beings named in the formula,[28] but disparages the users of the formula. Names, even the name(s) of Jesus (and Paul), do not

19 On the question of Scaeva's identity, see B. A. Mastin, "Scaeva the Chief Priest," *JTS* 27 (1976) 405–12; Fitzmyer, 649–50; and Shauf, *Theology*, 115. Fitzmyer is willing to entertain the possible translation "a Jew, a Chief Priest," and thus the possibility that he was a chief priest of the imperial cult. The social difficulties—that the sons of so wealthy and distinguished person would be itinerant exorcists—are even greater than for the heirs of a Jewish high priest. After citing an interesting conjecture of F. C. Burkitt, which includes its own slander ("Scaeva was no doubt a rascally Levantine"), Cadbury and Lake (241) conclude "that Luke regarded these men as Jews." From the historical perspective, Luke either credulously accepted a dubious report or intentionally misrepresented these persons as actual sons of a high priest. See the apposite comments of Haenchen, 565.

20 If the author viewed the Asiarchs of v. 31 as high priests of the imperial cult, this would set up a nice contrast.

21 Those who took up the wandering life as a vocation saw it differently. Jesus was a wandering teacher who cast out demons and sent forth his followers to do the same (in pairs [Mark 6:7]). Dio of Prusa understood himself as possessing a philosophical call to an itinerant life. Such missionaries could appeal to Heracles. Gods, especially Dionysus, did the same. For their critics, however, itinerancy was a means of getting out of town a step ahead of the sheriff. The *Onos* 35–41 offers a polemical portrait of this religious lifestyle, intensified in the parallel: Apuleius *Metam.* 8.26–31.

22 Josephus *Ant.* 8.42–49 proudly describes the exorcistic potency of formulae composed by Solomon and applied by one Eleazar, who invoked the name of Solomon. The *Testament of Solomon* contains a number of alleged examples of this material.

23 The language reflects missionary competition. Cf. such expressions as "the God of Andrew," and the like, in the Apocryphal Acts: e.g., *Act. Andr.* Greg. Epit. 7; 13; *Act. John* 42; 44; *Act. Paul* 7/9; *Act. Pet.* (Verc.) 25.13. Cf. also Justin *Dial.* 85.3 (see n. 10) and Origen *Cels.* 1.22.

24 For example, the spell in *PGM* 4.3007–86 contains numerous *voces magicae* that appear to be based on divine names in the Hebrew Bible, such as IOE, ABRAOTH, and IAEL, a mention of the "god of the Hebrews, Jesus," a summary of the exodus miracles, the seal of Solomon, and an injunction to the user to abstain from pork. *PGM* 8.60–61 lists "great names," including IAO, SABAOTH, and ADONAIE.

25 Haenchen, 565.

26 Haenchen (ibid.) archly comments that a college of seven exorcists would have to split fees.

27 See above on the D-Text, which seeks to repair the glitch.

28 The use of two different verbs meaning "know" (γινώσκω, ἐπίσταμαι) is elegant variation. See Moule, *Idiom Book*, 198. The emphatic particle μέν is probably a later addition, motivated by the

work apart from proper procedure.[29] This soothing thesis stands in tension with the implication of vv. 11-12, upon which it may be seen as a restraint. However comforting to the interpreter this possibility may be, it is deduction about matters on which the text is silent.

■ **16** The boisterous climax is worthy of New Comedy.[30] The query of v. 15 was merely rhetorical. The answer comes from the patient, who so discomforts the would-be healers that they must take to their heels, leaving their dignity behind with their dress. The proceedings are like the film of an exorcism run in reverse. Unfortunate victims of demon possession may possess nearly superhuman strength (Mark 5:2-4) and eschew clothing (Luke 8:27[31]). When demons engage exorcists in dialogue, the latter are expected to win (Mark 1:24-25; 5:7-12).[32] Finally, demons ought to be put to flight, rather than cause their opponents to flee. Entirely in keeping with the nature of such stories (cf. 16:16-18), Paul does not, out of humanitarian or evangelistic concerns, subsequently visit this poor creature to expel the demon. The focus is not on relief of the possessed but frustration of the opposition. Satan's realm is divided against itself and cannot stand.[33]

The consensus of scholarship is that in this episode Luke presents his view of the distinction between "magic" and "religion."[34] Scott Shauf has waged a vigorous campaign against this interpretation. His argument includes much valuable information and analysis.[35] He is correct in that the passage does not label the sons of Scaeva as magicians, but the aftermath strongly indicates that their failure led to a general renunciation of magical practices,[36] and this, together with the strong implication that the exorcists in question were not public benefactors but individuals engaged in making a living, like Simon of Samaria (8:4-25),[37] enhances the view that the distinction was one object of this raucous episode.[38] The major theme, as Haenchen (565), followed by Shauf, observes, is the great success of Paul that leads to this, and subsequent, humiliations of the competition, from whatever quarter. Plutarch wrote a clause that could have been composed for the benefit of commentators on Acts: "[S]orcerers (οἱ μάγοι) advise those possessed by demons (δαιμιζομένους) to recite and name over to themselves the Ephesian letters (τὰ Ἐφέσια γράμματα πρὸς αὐτοὺς καταλέγειν

theological concern to distinguish the name of Jesus from that of Paul. The MS. evidence is rather evenly divided.

29 That procedure may be variously understood as invocation by authorized persons, faith on the part of the exorcist, or otherwise. The narrator does not explicate the matter.

30 An example is Plautus's *Casina* 758–954, in which a male slave disguised as a woman receives two elderly men, who escape from "her" room humiliated and injured.

31 This Lucan addition is an inference from Mark 5:15. This behavior was (and is) characteristic of the mentally disturbed. Cf. Juvenal *Sat.* 2.71; 14.287; Lucian *Salt.* 83.

32 On these dialogues, see Bultmann, *History*, 224.

33 This is the essence of Susan Garrett's argument (next note)

34 Shauf (*Theology*, 116 n. 107) provides a catalogue of commentators who share this view. The most detailed argument for this view is Garrett, *Demise*, 90–99. She calls attention to the use of the verbs κατακυριεύω ("dominate") and ἰσχύω ("be strong," "prevail") in v. 16, words found also in the important passage Luke 11:21-22 (93 and 157 n. 30).

35 Shauf, *Theology*, 177–224.

36 Shauf (*Theology*, 231–32) argues that vv. 18-20 are not connected to the preceding. If he is correct, one must admit that the narrator is making it difficult for the reader.

37 On this, see Garrett, *Demise*, 91–92. For other indications of the parallelisms between Acts 2–8 and 19, see Tannehill, *Narrative Unity*, 2:238.

38 Shauf (*Theology*, 197) allows the inference that these exorcists sought to make money. He refers to (p. 201 n. 256) but does not discuss the two uses of "exorcist" in polytheist literature. One, an epigram attributed to Lucian (*Anth. Pal.* 11.427), speaks of an exorcist who drove out numerous demons (δαίμονα πολλὰ . . . ἐξέβαλ᾽) not by his oaths but by his foul breath. Ptolemy *Apotelesmatica* 4.4.11 treats exorcists with "the inspired" (θεο-λήμπτοι) and dream interpreters (ὀνειροκρίται) in a discussion of astrological influences. Schauf's attempt to minimize the useful parallels to the verb "adjure" (ἐξορκίζω and synonyms) in the magical papyri does not succeed. On p. 216 he slips into a historicizing perspective: "they [the sons of Scaeva] had heard Paul preach, after all." His contention "that there is nothing . . . wrong with the Jewish exorcists' activity" (p. 217), based on

καὶ ὀνομάζειν)."[39] This provides a firm link between vv. 13-17 and 18-20, establishing a connection between exorcism and magic through use of "naming,"[40] and, for good measure, invoking, as it were, the famous "Ephesian letters."[41]

■ **17** The verse reports the effect in terms suitable for a miracle story, not least a punitive miracle (cf. 5:11; 9:42).[42] Scaeva's heirs were punished for their audacity. As Johnson observes, "Luke has brought together all the typical responses to a miracle story," including dissemination, awe, and praise of God.[43] This verse resonates with links to the earlier material: "Jews and Greeks," "inhabitants" (κατοικοῦντες, v. 10), and "the name of Jesus" (v. 13). This was not a name to be bandied about as a casual charm. Verses 18-20 indicate the consequences of that insight.

■ **18-20** The structure of this unit is like that of vv. 13-17: a general statement followed by a specific example and concluded with a general comment. Like the story of Scaeva's sons, it is a bit opaque. The misfortune experienced by those persons motivates some believers to come forth and acknowledge their failures.[44] Verse 19 gives one notable result of this activity: the renunciation of magical practices symbolized by the destruction of the texts used therein. Difficulties include the destination of their "coming," the meaning of ἐνώπιον πάντων (lit. "in the presence of all"), and the nature and actions of the believers. The probable solution to the first two matters is to assume a community meeting, at which (on one or more occasions) the confession and destruction occurred. The narrator can assume assemblies as the locus of such activity (cf. 5:1-11).

If one regards these persons as Christians, as the text implies, difficulties arise. They may have been confessing prebaptismal, as it were, sins, or they may have continued to utilize this traditional behavior, with or without seeing it as incompatible with their new faith, or they may have backslid after joining the community.[45] The failure of the narrator to provide precision opens the door to speculation and to the question of whether a specific interpretation is in view. The simple reading of the text is that at least some "postbaptismal" sins can be forgiven, if confessed and followed by amendment of life. This conforms to the implicit view of 5:6-10 (Sapphira) and to the possibility of repentance on the part of Simon (8:20-24). Luke does not endorse either

Luke 9:37-43, 49-50; 11:14-23, takes a unified view of the tradition that does not allow for theological development between Luke and Acts. Confession of the proper faith has become more of an issue in Acts. For this reason, "syncretism" may be more appropriate than "magic" as a designation for what is in view. See Barrett, 2:912.

39 Plutarch *Quaest. conv.* 7.5.4 (*Mor.* 706 E), trans. E. L. Minar, Jr., *Plutarch's Moralia IX* (LCL; Cambridge, Mass.: Harvard University Press, 1961) 55.

40 Origen is aware of the use of magic in exorcisms: *Cels.* 1.6. Celsus attributes the success of Christian exorcisms (that is, he does not dispute their effectiveness) to magic. In his refutation, Origen acknowledges that the name of Jesus is so powerful that it can at times possess efficacy when used by outsiders.

41 On "Ephesian letters," see Arnold, *Ephesians*, 15–16 (n. 16 above); Trebilco, "Asia," 314; Gager, *Curse Tablets*, 5–6; Conzelmann, 164; and Fitzmyer, 651. They consisted of about a half-dozen words. Eric R. Dodds, who glosses them among "the meaningless formulae . . . characteristic of later magic," notes that they appear in New Comedy (*The Greeks and the Irrational* [Berkeley: University of California Press, 1968] 204 n. 95). Despite this label, it is unlikely that magic was more fashionable at Ephesus than elsewhere.

42 Note also the use of μεγαλύνω ("praise") in 5:13.

43 Johnson, 341. Dissemination: Luke 4:37; 7:17; 8:39; awe: Luke 5:26; 7:16; 8:35; praise: Luke 5:26; 6:16; 8:39; 9:43; 13:17; 17:15; 18:43.

44 The verb ἐξομολογέω is used in the middle for "confession of sins" by a range of authors and texts: BDAG, 351, *s.v.* (2). Reference to the activity is common in the Apostolic Fathers: *Did.* 4:14; *2 Clem.* 8:3; *Barn.* 19:12. What the linked participle ἀναγγέλλοντες contributes is not clear. It may be pleonastic language for effect. Cadbury and Lake (242) render "confessed and revealed their spells." This is attractive. (On "spells," see n. 24.)

45 Conzelmann (164) is willing to attribute the language to authorial carelessness and presume that preconversion activity is in view. Among those who regard these practitioners of magic as Christians is Bruce, 412. Garrett (*Demise*, 95–96) argues that these persons are recent adherents. Klauck (*Magic*, 101) considers several options and says that Luke may have left the matter open. Christians, including clergy, were said to make use of magical books: Origen *Cels.* 6.40–41; and Hippolytus *Ref.* 6.15; 7.20; 9.9. See Shauf, *Theology*, 226–34.

perfectionism (the view that Christians cannot sin, so that either nothing they do is wrong or that any misdoing amounts to damnation) or rigorism (a profound reluctance to forgive postbaptismal sin). The chief sins of which he takes countenance are those involving money and/or magic.[46] The first of these themes was both symbolic and real, and the same was probably true of the second. Missionary history suggests that the newly converted are likely to retain, in lesser or greater degrees, previous habits.[47] Just as he was concerned about the use of resources, so Luke also strongly deprecated any utilization of magical and other syncretistic practices.[48]

Other readings of this unit have been proposed. Susan R. Garrett seems to treat the event as a general renunciation of magic by "the residents of Ephesus." Although she agrees that those who confessed their misdeeds were believers and that the book-burners were among them, she views the events less as an internal Christian event than as "a defeat of magic in general." This proposal is attractive and probably captures the narrator's desire, but it is liable to the charge of exaggeration.[49] The same charge will not be laid against Shauf, who rejects the notion that these verses deal with the defeat of magic.[50] This is evidently a consequence of his dissociation of vv. 13-17 from the theme of magic. The deeds confessed in v. 18 cover a range of sins, of which v. 19 relates to a particular type. The episode is "designed to impress."[51] That is doubtless true, but his antimagic campaign is less successful than that at Ephesus. The language of vv. 18-19 is redolent of the world of magic. Although the technical sense of *πράξεις* to mean "spells" can be introduced into v. 18 only by taking *ἐξομολογούμενοι καὶ ἀναγγέλλοντες τὰς πράξεις αὐτῶν* as "they confessed and reported *their use of* magical spells," the connotation cannot be excluded.[52] "Practicing magic" is the most likely meaning of *περίεργα πραξάντων* in a discussion of destroying undesirable books.[53]

Book-burning is a practice that has, unfortunately, endured for millennia.[54] Initiative and motive have varied. Officials might burn banned religious or other texts.[55] Leaders of one movement might destroy the

46 Apart from apostasy during the persecutions of the third and early fourth centuries, sexual conduct was the major subject in discussions of postbaptismal sins until the church expanded beyond urban areas and "civilized" peoples.

47 For examples (from late antiquity to the twentieth century) of efforts to bring about "full" conversion, see Richard A. Fletcher, *The Barbarian Conversion: From Paganism to Christianity* (Berkeley: University of California Press, 1999).

48 Although his view of Acts 19:13-20 as a critique of syncretism is not endorsed here, Günter Klein's article on the subject ("Der Synkretismus als theologisches Problem in der ältesten christlichen Apologetik," in idem, *Rekonstruktion und Interpretation: Gesammelte Aufsätze zum Neuen Testament* [Munich: Kaiser, 1969] 258–79, esp. 273–74 [= *ZThK* 64 (1967) 40–82]) is quite valuable. Klein points to the nexus between religious competition and syncretism (279–80). The theme of syncretism also dominates Krodel's analysis (356–64) of Acts 19:1-20.

49 Garrett, *Demise*, 94–99, citing 95.

50 Shauf, *Theology*, 226–34.

51 Ibid., 233, summarizing pp. 232–34.

52 See BDAG, 860, *s.v.* *πρᾶξις* (4 b); Deissmann, *Bible Studies*, 323 n. 5; Cadbury and Lake, 242. Shauf's claim (*Theology*, 227–28) that this meaning is "*extremely rare*" excludes the evidence of the magical papyri.

53 See BDAG, 800 (2), *s.v.* *περίεργος*. Note also *P. Coll. Youtie* I 30 and the discussion in *NewDocs* 1 (1981) no. 12, pp. 47–49. The term is a euphemism. Shauf (*Theology*, 231) says that the adjective "could cover a wide body of subjects." On p. 234 he describes the material burned as "magic books."

54 See Clarence A. Forbes, "Books for the Burning," *TAPA* 67 (1936) 114–25; and Arthur S. Pease, "Notes on Book-Burning," in Massey H. Shepherd and Sherman E. Johnson, eds., *Munera Studiosa* (Festschrift W. H. P. Hatch; Cambridge, Mass.: Episcopal Theological School, 1946) 145–60. See also Trebilco ("Asia," 315; and idem, *Early Christians*, 149–52), who regards the persons as converts and the activity as a defeat of magic.

55 Augustus, for example, reportedly had two thousand books of false prophecy burned in the forum, according to Suetonius *Aug.* 31. When Protagoras was condemned to exile, his books were burned in the agora; see Diogenes Laertius 9.52. Dionysiac texts were committed to the flames in connection with the suppression of that cult; see Livy 39.16.8. Livy 40.29 is a circumstantial account of the discovery (by exhumation, as in many stories about pseudepigrapha) and eventual destruction, by senatorial order, of books alleged to be injurious

works of competitors.[56] Voluntary burning of one's own books was, as in Acts, a sign of repudiation, sometimes of conversion.[57] The activity has always had ritual and public elements. The agora/forum was the place of choice for this ceremony. Burning books is more than an efficient means of suppressing undesirable literature. Consignment to flames is a means of purification of the community and "damnation" of its enemies.[58] For Luke, this action was a trope for the apocalyptic destruction of the demonic powers. In his letter to the Ephesians, Ignatius expressed a similar view: "Thence was destroyed all magic, and every bond vanished" (*Eph.* 19:3).[59] The association of magic with Ephesus is an apt touch of local color, but Luke had more in mind than singling out an Ephesian vice. As is common with miracle stories, a number comes at the close. The ubiquitous "they" calculated the value of the cargo consigned to perdition.[60]

■ **20** The unit closes with a short, sharp summary in v. 20. The term "message" (λόγος) constitutes a frame embracing vv. 10-20. That word is initially somewhat surprising.[61] Henry J. Cadbury stated that it refers to "the whole Christian enterprise,"[62] and Jerome Kodell has developed this idea.[63] The verse means, in effect, "The church grew mightily in quantity and quality." Growth is the result of power.[64] In competition at the "lower end"

to religion. The practice continued under the Christian empire. The church historian Socrates (*H.E.* 1.8) reports the burning of Arian works (cf. also the *Justinian Code* 1.1.3). Cassius Dio (56.27.1) reports the burning of slanderous political pamphlets. The monarch burned Jeremiah's prophecies (Jer 36:20-27). 1 Macc 1:56 says that scrolls of the Torah were burned by the Greek reformers/persecutors.

56 Lucian *Alex.* 47 (Epicurus). When the full *RSV* appeared in 1952, a number of conservative American members of the Protestant clergy took it upon themselves to burn an exemplar in the pulpit.

57 According to Diogenes Laertius 6.95, Metrocles marked his conversion to Cynicism by burning notes taken from Theophastus's lectures. According to Aelian frag. 89 (ed., Hercher), an Epicurean was advised in a dream by a priest of Asclepius to burn Epicurus's books and use the ashes as a medicine. One of the legends about Heliodorus's (author of *Ethiopian Story*) later career as a Christian bishop was that, given the choice of burning his novel (which, difficult as it is to believe, was considered arousing) and renouncing his orders, he chose the latter, according to Nicephorus Callistus *H.E.* 12.34. For other examples, see Forbes, "Books," 114–17 (n. 54 above). Witherington (582) rightly says that this was not a mass conversion but an act of self-preservation, with references to 3:10 and 4:21.

58 See Lucian's interpretation of Alexander's burning of a work by Epicurus: burning the book was a form of burning the philosopher (*Alex.* 47).

59 Trans. Schoedel, *Ignatius*, 87. (Ignatius had the incarnation in view; Luke's theological orientation differed.) Origen's interpretation of the visit of the magi developed the same reasoning (*Cels.* 1.60).

60 For the meaning of μυριάς (10,000), see M-M, 419, *s.v.* The narrator may not specify the type of coin, because he wishes to allow scope for readers to imagine that it was larger than a drachma or denarius. This has not prevented scholars from seeking to give the word precision: Steven Baugh, "Paul and Ephesus: The Apostle among His Contemporaries" (Diss., University of California, Irvine, 1990) 107 n. 25; and Polhill, 406. Nigel Turner (in James H. Moulton, *A Grammar of New Testament Greek* [3rd ed.; 4 vols.; Edinburgh: T&T Clark, 1908–76] 3:17) says that "drachmas" is to be supplied, but notes that "silver" should be plural. The freedwoman who arranged for the seduction of Paulina, a Roman matron of equestrian status, was fifty thousand drachmas. For Luke's readers the amount was vast. By the standards of Mark 6:37, this sum, calculated in denarii, would provide 125,000 meals, half a million if in tetradrachmas. K. Ehling ("Zwei Anmerkungen zum ἀργύριον in Apg 19,19," *ZNW* 94 [2003] 269–75) concludes that the denarius is the correct denomination.

61 The textual tradition reflects this. The shift of the genitive phrase "of the Lord" is likely a secondary change to the customary order. The D-Text (Boismard, *Texte*, 320) indicates difficulty with ὁ λόγος ("the word"), reading, after the first three words: *ἐνίσχυσεν ἡ πίστις τοῦ θεοῦ καὶ ἐπληθύνετο* ("[the] faith in God grew strong and abounded"). "Abounded" (ἐπληθύνετο) assimilates to 12:24. See Metzger, *Textual Commentary*, 418–19.

62 Cadbury, "Names," 375–92, esp. 391.

63 Jerome Kodell, "The Word of God Grew: The Ecclesial Tendency of λόγος in Acts 6, 7; 12, 24; 19, 20," *Bib* 55 (1974) 505–19.

64 The adverbial phrase κατὰ κράτος is used hundreds of times by historians in the sense of "by military force" and otherwise most often of the application of some kind of power. Fitzmyer (652) takes it as "with power" and associates "of the Lord." This is possible, but less likely.

of the religious spectrum, Paul crushes the opposition. The "higher end" will soon have their innings, but these ten verses indicate what people desired: power over the misfortunes of life, exemplified and symbolized in disease and demon possession.[65] Acts states in a concrete way what Col 1:11 presents more abstractly.[66] From the social perspective, a movement that led people to renounce magic could not have been all bad, for, despite its ubiquity, magic was regarded as injurious to the social fabric, and, if practiced against the authorities, absolutely subversive.

The parallel between v. 21 and Luke 9:51 is not merely verbal.[67] They are structural equivalents. Paul, like Jesus, will set out for the city of his destiny. "Here the theme for the finale of this great symphony is sounded for the first time."[68] As Jervell's comment, "The Pauline mission is now finished,"[69] indicates, the pronoun "these (accomplishments)" (ταῦτα) refers to more than the immediate context. This is a reverberant verse. Since his interest in "seeing" Rome was not motivated by fondness for tourism, it is unlikely that the references to "the spirit," "fulfill" (πληρόω),[70] and, above all, necessity (δεῖ)[71] have merely pedestrian applications, although it is arguable for each.[72] Acts 20:22 is a strong argument in favor of divine guidance.

> The lure of Rome, and the knowledge of the great possibilities open there among the cosmopolitan population, were enough to persuade every leader of new movements, either doctrinal or practical,

65 On the theme of power in general, see Edwards, *Religion and Power,* with many references to Luke and Acts. For examples of the importance of healing and exorcism in the early Christian mission, see Ramsay MacMullen, *Christianizing the Roman Empire: A.D. 100–400* (New Haven: Yale University Press, 1984) 60–62 and index, p. 183, *s.v.* "miracles." See also Fletcher, *Barbarian Conversion* (n. 47 above); and Ian Wood, *The Missionary Life: Saints and the Evangelisation of Europe 400–1050* (Essex, England: Longman, 2001). Of a rather different character are Harnack's comments on these phenomena: *Mission,* 1:125–46; 199–218. He devotes most of these discussions to alleged abuses and the efforts of the apologists. Equally diffident is Michael Green, *Evangelism in the Early Church* (Grand Rapids: Eerdmans, 1970) 188–93.

66 "May you be made strong with all the strength that comes from his glorious power, and may you be prepared to endure everything with patience." On "patience" (ὑπομονή), note Luke 8:15; 21:19.

67 The two verses share the verb (συμ)πληρόω and the phrase πορεύεσθαι εἰς ("go to") "Jerusalem" (with a better Greek form in Acts). (It is interesting that the preceding episode in Luke [9:49-50] approves the work of unaffiliated exorcists who invoke the name of Jesus.) Acts 19:22 begins with a sending of "disciples," as does Luke 9:52 (ἀποστέλλω). The *Act. Pet.* (Verc. 5) imitates this: *necesse est me ascendere Romae* ("I [Peter] must go to Rome."). See Pervo, *Profit,* 67; and, e.g., Tannehill, *Narrative Unity,* 2:239–40.

68 Haenchen, 569.

69 Jervell, 486. This chapter closes a circle begun in chap. 13 (Sanders, *Jews,* 76–77).

70 The D-Text (Boismard, *Texte,* 320), evidently alert to the potential dangers of this verb (when can church growth be considered "complete"?), revised the beginning to τότε ὁ Παῦλος ἔθετο ("Then Paul resolved . . ."). Haenchen (569) says, with merit, that the phrase means that Paul's work in Ephesus is complete.

71 "It is necessary" (δεῖ): Note, among other uses, Luke 4:42; 9:22; 24:44. Of Paul: Acts 9:16 (suffering); Rome: 23:11; 25:10; 27:24. On the theme, see E. Fascher, "Theologische Beobachtungen zu *Dei,*" in *Neutestamentliche Studien für Rudolf Bultmann zu seinem 70. Geburtstag am 20. August 1954* (ed. Walther Eltester; BZNW 21; Göttingen: Vandenhoeck & Ruprecht, 1954) 228–54; Charles H. Cosgrove, "The Divine *ΔΕΙ* in Luke-Acts: Investigations into the Lukan Understanding of God's Providence," *NovT* 26 (1984) 168–90; and Squires, *Plan,* 166–85.

72 For arguments against the interpretations favored here, see Shauf, *Theology,* 237–40. These are driven by his rejection of the idea that this constitutes a major division in Acts. The most difficult is the reference to "spirit," which may be equivalent to "resolve in one's heart" (Luke 1:66; 21:14; Acts 5:41). Similar questions arise in 18:25; 20:22. On the whole, it is unlikely that Luke wishes to suggest that the final journey to Jerusalem was an idea that Paul came up with on his own. Barrett (2:919), however, is emphatic that it "cannot be taken to refer to the Holy Spirit." Fitzmyer (652) is equally certain that it refers to the "mind" of Paul, appealing to the middle voice. Bruce (413) finds "Holy Spirit" "more likely." Acts 20:23 and 21:4, 11-12 tip the balance toward inspiration. The ambiguity of this verse may be a narrative means of raising suspense.

to move his headquarters to Rome and to make of the Roman community the chosen ground of active propaganda.[73]

With appropriate solemnity, Luke announces that Paul will join this fellowship. Accompanying that announcement is more than a slight hint that death awaits him there. Luke knew of Paul's death at Rome, but neither narrates it nor speaks explicitly about it. Another thunderous silence in this chapter is the purpose of the planned visit: delivery of the collection to Jerusalem.[74] Of this purpose Luke was well aware, as indicated not only by 24:17 but also by his source for v. 21: Rom 15:22-25.[75] The particular motives for these silences differ, although both seek to place Paul in the proper light. The collection is ignored because it failed;[76] any reference to Paul's execution in Rome would obviate the author's defense of his hero and his message. As the conjunction of the two names intimates, Luke holds Jerusalem responsible for Paul's death.[77] The placement of these plans at this juncture has motivated some to view 19:21 as marking a major narrative division.[78] This was not the narrator's evident intent, for vv. 23-40 continue the story without a break. Luke injected vv. 21-22 into the midst of the story of Ephesus to emphasize that Paul did not leave the city because of the subsequent difficulties. His departure had been planned beforehand and was merely delayed by the tumult.[79]

Like Jesus (9:53), Paul sent "advance men" ahead of him. Like Jesus (and in accord with a Lucan predilection), he sends a pair.[80] They are Timothy, who reappears without notice after disappearing without explanation in 18:5, and Erastus, otherwise unmentioned (cf. 2 Tim 4:20). These data derive from sources.[81] Readers may suppose that Timothy was an ever-present silent servant available at Paul's beck and call. For Luke, Paul did not have, apart from Barnabas, true colleagues, but assistants who "served" him.[82] After dispatching them on their appointed tasks, the great missionary will await developments.

73 George La Piana, "The Roman Church at the End of the Second Century," *HTR* 18 (1925) 201–78, esp. 211. For examples, see Betz, *Lukian*, 110; and Pervo, *Profit*, 158 n. 220. On the transferal of cults to Rome, see Nock, *Conversion*, 66–76.

74 Another reason for visiting Macedonia and Achaea was reconciliation with the Corinthian community (2 Cor 2:12-13), a project about which Luke is equally silent, for he countenances no breech between Paul and the churches he founded.

75 See Pervo, *Dating*, 119–20. (Rom 15:25 may have influenced Luke 9:51 also.)

76 Among those who subscribe to this view are Bruce, 481; and Witherington, 588.

77 From the historical perspective, this judgment is not fully inaccurate.

78 For example, Bruce, 413.

79 For this view, see, e.g., Conzelmann, 164.

80 Jesus: Mark 6:7; Luke 7:18; Acts 8:14; 9:38; 10:7, 20.

81 In addition to Rom 15:22-25, note 1 Cor 16:4-5. Haenchen (568–69), with much detail, proposes that this journey substitutes for that of Titus. Erastus may, however, have been mentioned (with Titus) in the hypothetical Collection Source (see pp. 12–14).

82 The participle in v. 22 comes from the same verb (διακονέω) that is used of the women who "ministered" to Jesus (Luke 8:3). The motive was not so much demotion of Timothy as promotion of Paul (and comparison with Jesus).

19:23-40 A Disturbance in Ephesus

23/ The Movement was the sub-
ject of a major disturbance at
about that time. 24/ There was
a silversmith named Dem-
etrius, who was engaged in the
manufacture of silver shrines
of Artemis, a trade that turned
a pretty profit for the artisans.
25/ Demetrius called a meeting
of those artisans and workers in
affiliated trades.
"Gentlemen," he began, "you are
well aware that our prosperity
depends on this craft. 26/ Your
own eyes and ears have made
you aware that this creature
Paul has persuasively seduced
a vast number, not only here
in Ephesus but in nearly all
Asia as well, into believing
that manufactured gods are
not genuine. 27/ This threat-
ens not simply to discredit our
line of business. Even worse, it
threatens to bring the temple
of the great goddess Artemis
into utter disrepute! The hour
draws near when she whom all
Asia, indeed the entire civilized
world, worships will see her
majesty slipping away!" 28/ In
response they were filled with
rage and began to chant: "Great
is Artemis of the Ephesians!"
29/ Confusion gripped the city. Two
of Paul's traveling companions,
Gaius and Aristarchus (both
from Macedonia) were seized,
and the populace rushed into
the theater *en masse*. 30/ Paul
wanted to appear before the
People, but the followers
would not permit him to do
so. 31/ Moreover, some of the
Asiarchs, who were well dis-
posed toward Paul,[a] sent word
urging him not to risk going to
the theater.
32/ The Assembly was in an uproar,
with various people shout-
ing different things, few[b] of
them knowing why they were
there. 33/ Some of the crowd
hurled suggestions[c] at Alexan-
der, whom the Jews had sent
forward, but, after he indi-
cated that he wished to offer
a defense before the People,
34/ they realized that he was
a Jew, and broke into their
unison chant, "Great is Artemis

a According to BDF §190 (1), φίλοι is to be viewed as an adjective, with the dative.

b The D-Text (Boismard, *Texte*, 325) reads "the vast majority" (οἱ πλεῖστοι rather than οἱ πλείους). Barrett's comment (2:931) is illuminating. He attributes the change as to the use of memory without checking. The preferable explanation is that the D-Text betrays the work of a reader (better, readers) who acted like copy editors.

c The variants to συμβιβάζω, προβιβάζω, and καταβιβάζω, which mean "push forward, promote," and "send/drag down," respectively, are obvious corrections.

of the Ephesians!" This went on
for about two hours.
35/ **Once he had got the crowd**
calmed down,[d] the People's
secretary said:
"Gentlemen of Ephesus. Who
could possibly be unaware that
Ephesus has honorary custody
of the Great Artemis and of
the image that has come down
from heaven? 36/ Since these
claims are unimpeachable, you
simply must remain calm and
avoid any rash action. 37/ These
men whom you have brought
here have neither harmed the
temple nor defamed our[e] god-
dess. 38/ So then, if Demetrius[f]
and his associated artisans
have charges to lodge against
anyone,[g] there are regular court
sessions as well as governors[h]
before whom they may argue
their cases. 39/ Any additional
disputes should be resolved by
the regular assembly. 40/ The
fact is that it is *we* who are lia-
ble to be accused of fomenting
a riot over what has happened
today, since we can provide
no explanation to justify this
disturbance."[i] He thereupon
dissolved the assembly.

d The D-Text (Boismard, *Texte*, 326) reads κατασείσας, probably as a hand gesture (cf. v. 33; 12:17, etc.).

e E* 𝔪 vg sy^{h} bo read "your goddess," distancing the official from his hearers.

f The D-Text (Boismard, *Texte*, 327) reads "this fellow" (οὗτος) Demetrius," neatly echoing the demonstrative applied to Paul in v. 26.

g D (gig) sa^{mss} read "any issue with *them*."

h "Courts" and "governors" are generic plurals.

i *Or:* ". . . today . . . since we have no reason for it and we cannot justify this disturbance" (reading οὐ).

Analysis[1]

The pendulum now swings to the opposite side of the religious spectrum, from the vulgarity of door-to-door exorcism and over-the-counter magic to the majesty and esteem of the city's patron: Artemis.[2] Two cults claiming universal outreach came into collision.[3] Opposition does not arise from charges lodged by civic or cultic authorities. The emoluments of religious activity provide continuity, as the narrator's camera swings toward one Demetrius, who produced silver models of the great temple of Artemis of Ephesus. Assembling (in an undisclosed location) the guild, Demetrius, a first-rate agitator, first reminded his comrades (perhaps unnecessarily)

1 W. Weren ("The Riot of the Ephesian Silversmiths [Acts 19,23-40]: Luke's Advice to His Readers," in Reimund Bieringer et al., eds., *Luke and His Readers: Festschrift A. Denaux* (BEThL 182; Leuven: Leuven University Press, 2005] 441–56) identifies, like the outline above, three scenes: vv. 24-28, 29-34, and 35-40. This yields a chiasmus: two speeches surrounding two reports of acclamation. (The moral is that Christians should not defame polytheist cults.)

2 This episode is evidently imitated and revised in the *Act. Paul* 7/9. For some comments, see Richard Pervo, "A Hard Act to Follow: *The Acts of Paul* and the Canonical Acts," *JHC* 2 (1995) 3–32, esp. 12–15; and Istvan Czachesz, "The Acts of Paul and the Western Text of Luke's Acts: Paul between Canon and Apocrypha," in Jan N. Bremmer, ed., *The Apocryphal Acts of Paul and Thecla* (Kampen: Kok Pharos, 1996) 107–25, esp. 114–15.

3 On claims for the universalism of Artemis of Ephesus, see Philo *Flac.* 163, *Leg. Gaj.* 338.

that they depended on their labor for the bread on their tables, then observed that this livelihood was in grave peril. Paul's denunciation of idolatry was having an adverse effect on trade. The recipe is tried and true (cf. 16:19-21[4]). Into the basic ingredient of economic grievance he poured a measure of patriotism and topped the cocktail with a garnish of religion. Far more important than a dislocation in the labor market, this situation threatened to be the end of civilization as they knew it.[5]

Demetrius's oratory was not without effect. The silversmiths broke into ritual shout. In no time, Demetrius's brew had intoxicated the entire city.[6] Everyone flocked to the theater for an impromptu town meeting, scooping up two of Paul's colleagues on the way. For Paul, both missionary and civic duty called him to address this situation, come what may. Believers found this proposed course too dangerous. "Some of the Asiarchs," civic leaders all, who included Paul within their circle of friends, also took time, despite the demands of a burgeoning crisis, to deter him from action.[7]

Meanwhile, bedlam gripped the theater. Everyone was speaking, no one was listening, and none knew what was going on. Whatever the explanation, the narrative seems as confused as the participants. An ill-advised attempt by Jews to have one Alexander speak ignited a howl of anti-Semitic rage. The crowd can do no more than resume its ritual cultic chant. For two hours, the arena quaked with "Great is Artemis of the Ephesians!" If polytheism speaks with a single voice, its message is no more than the futile braying of unlawful combinations of the misguided.

Artemis failed to respond. The government finally did. Faced with either the distasteful prospect of embarrassment to Artemis or the intolerable possibility of a riot, the chief official saved the day with a speech that might have been learned at the feet of Gamaliel. Those assembled need not trouble themselves about the status and renown of Ephesus and Artemis; both are inviolable. The Christians receive the highly welcome news that they are innocent. Should the egregious Demetrius and his colleagues happen to have any valid grievances, there are courts. Moreover, "there are proconsuls." With this unpleasant reminder of the realities of power, the potential loss of nominal privileges, and a jibe about "lawful assemblies," the crowd is sent away.

The episode drips with excitement[8] and glows with local color,[9] captivating readers with its vividness and evident realism. The only objection is that the story makes little sense.[10] If Paul's mission had an injurious effect on the cult of Artemis, one would expect that civic and religious leaders would initiate action or, at the very least, join in. Instead, all initiative lies in the hands of the wily Demetrius, who effectively galvanizes

4 "Profit" (ἐργασία) occurs in 16:19 and 19:24. On the economic motive, see Reinhard Selinger, "Die Demetriosunruhen (Apg 19,23-40). Eine Fallstudie aus Rechtshistorischer Perspective," *ZNW* 88 (1997) 242–59, esp. 246 n. 27. Selinger's study is a treasure trove of primary and secondary data characterized by astute judgment. Note also Dirk Schinkel, "'Und sie wußten nicht, warum sie zusammengekommen waren'—Gruppen und Gruppeninteressen in der Demetriosepisode (Apg 19,23-40," in A. Gutsfeld and Dietrich-Alex Koch, eds., *Vereine, Synagogen und Gemeinden im kaiserzeitlichen Kleinasien* (Studien und Texte zu Antike und Christentum 25; Tübingen: Mohr Siebeck, 2006) 95–112.

5 For a comparable situation, see Chariton *Chaer.* 5.2.3. Persian women complain that the entire world has admired their beauty, a pleasant status now threatened by Callirhoe. They concoct a plot to avoid humiliation by this foreign (Greek) woman.

6 Guilds and other associations were often restricted because they were suspected of formulating just this kind of unrest. See MacMullen, *Enemies*, 170–78. See Appendix 3 below and the valuable data and references in *NewDocs* 4 (1987) no. 1, pp. 7-10. Ancient guilds were not labor unions, for their members owned the means of production. They were similar to cartels.

7 This episode was imitated in the *Mart. Pionii* 7 (c. 300 [Musurillo, *Christian*, 145]). The public pressed for an assembly in the theater, but some friends of the proconsul (*stratēgos*) approached the *Neocoros* Polemon and asked that Pionius not be allowed to speak, as this might lead to a disturbance (θόρυβος) and subsequent investigation.

8 For examples of admiration, see Shauf, *Theology*, 120.

9 See Pervo, *Profit*, 37; Cadbury, *Book* 5, 41–43, 72; Peter Lampe, "Acta 19 im Spiegel der ephesischen Inschriften," *BZ* 36 (1992) 59–77, esp. 59–70; and Selinger, "Demetriosunruhen."

10 For the genesis of the following remarks, see Haenchen, 576–77.

his artisans but then evaporates as an actor. The narrator leaves a gap at the end of v. 28, one that readers may fill in with several plausible scenarios.[11] This gap leaves the subject of v. 29 uncertain. The narrative style is like Pentecost[12] and could be an authorial idiosyncrasy (possibly related to the use of sources), but it may be intentional, for there are a number of "anti-parallels" to chap. 2.[13] The narrator does not say that there was "a riot of the silversmiths."[14] The chanting of the silversmiths somehow brought the city into confusion. The previously unmentioned Gaius and Aristarchus (v. 29) are somehow identified, apprehended, and subjected to a citizens' arrest. They, too, disappear from the story.

By v. 30, Paul, with typical Lucan compression, has learned what is taking place and resolves on action. The response by "some" Asiarchs is inexplicable. They also have been apprised, by some means, of developments, which they take no reported steps to address. Rather, they dispatch (severally or as a group) word to Paul urging him to stay away from the theater. How they learned of his plans is unstated. Verse 32 jumps back, without warning, into the theater, where, in the midst of the confusion, the Jews attempt to defend themselves, for reasons that remain unclear. This tender backfires, and the entire crowd takes up the chant begun by the silversmiths. After two hours, the chief official stanches the noise and delivers his little speech, which reveals that he had by some means learned, amidst all the chaos, of the charges raised, and, even more surprisingly, of the grievances of Demetrius, and, astonishingly, that the accused were not guilty as charged. This acquittal was, in fact, erroneous, for Paul was on record (17:24, 29) as a critic of both temples and idols.

The basis of the solution to these dilemmas lies not in the hypothesis that sources have been carelessly intermingled, but in literary technique: all of the characters know what the narrator knows, and the narrator is omniscient. Readers, who know what the narrator reveals, do not readily raise objections. The "town clerk's" speech is the most telling example of transferred omniscience. He knows what both the main sets of characters (Demetrius and the artisans; Paul and the Christians) are doing and why. In addition, he is sufficiently informed to deliver explicit or implicit judgments on the merits of their cases. Equally omniscient are the Asiarchs, who knew that Paul would thrust himself into the maelstrom.[15] A corollary to these is the situation of the crowd. Although both Asiarchs and the civic officer know that Paul is under attack, the populace is quite unaware of why they have been assembled. The last of these conforms to Luke's contempt for the urban rabble, a notion shared by conservative Romans and their Greek allies,[16] but the other matters, Paul's social status and the innocuousness of the Christians, are key Lucan themes. Luke is responsible for the current shape of vv. 23-40; the story cannot be a simple report of the facts derived from a participant. For Haenchen, the problems of the narrative led to the judgment that the account is, a few details apart, Lucan.[17]

To this use of the critical broom Conzelmann objects, stating that, although Luke composes scenes, he does

11 E.g., Marshall, 318: "We are not told where the protest meeting was held, but evidently it culminated in a protest march through the streets. A crowd quickly gathered who were sympathetic to the silversmiths, and it was decided to hold a larger-scale protest."

12 Acts 2:1-5, where the experiences of a private meeting also mysteriously generate public excitement.

13 These include divinely inspired speech versus "vain repetition" (cf. Matt 5:7), ecstasy versus mob frenzy, ideal communal life (Acts 2:42-47) versus urban disorder, and the contrasting closing speeches of Peter (2:14-37) and the local official (19:35-40).

14 Although "riot" is firmly ensconced in the scholarly tradition, the narrative does not depict an actual riot, which would require at least some damage and injury. The attempt of L. J. Kreitzer ("A Numismatic Clue to Acts 19:23-41: The Ephesian *Cistophoroi* of Claudius and Agrippina," *JSNT* 30 [1987] 59–70) to relate a coin issued under Claudius to this incident faces the difficulty that, according to Acts, the event was of insufficient importance to evoke imperial notice.

15 It is essentially immaterial if one claims that their admonition was based on their knowledge of what Paul would do in such a situation. The narrator could have intimated this by saying "fearing that . . ." The text has given no hints thus far that Paul would take the action contemplated here.

16 See Pervo, "Meet Right," 45–62.

17 Hemer (*Book*, 347) says: "Aristarchus and perhaps Gaius are the likely sources for events within the theatre." Barrett (2:917) is confident that it "must

not concoct stories like this.[18] Whatever the meaning and merit of this assertion, the labors of Weiser show how difficult it is to extract a primary source from early Christian tradition.[19] Krodel also argues for the use of a source, largely on negative grounds and not persuasively.[20] Lüdemann maintains that Luke took up and reworked a story about a riot in Ephesus.[21] For his part, Fitzmyer says: "Luke has undoubtedly inherited data about this incident from his Pauline source and constructed them all into a vividly narrated and dramatic episode."[22] Without identification of the data and their contribution to the final product, this statement has little meaning.

The capstone of Haenchen's argument is that this story does not agree with Paul's own comments about his travails in Ephesus (1 Cor 15:32; 2 Cor 1:8-11).[23] This is an important point. If Luke had access to good independent traditions about the Pauline mission in Ephesus, one would expect him to report them, since he has narrated any number of difficulties faced by Paul, or possibly to ignore it. That he chooses instead to devote nearly one-half of his description of the mission to an uproar in which Paul was *not* involved raises suspicion, and Paul's avoidance of a stop at Ephesus in chap. 20—to the considerable inconvenience of the presbyters there—does nothing to diminish this suspicion, nor does the frame of vv. 21-22/20:1, which insists that Paul left Ephesus under no human compulsion. For whatever reason, Acts 19:23-40 fills the slot occupied by Paul's difficulties in Ephesus.[24] If one holds that Luke's tradition did not refer to these difficulties, the value of that tradition is diminished. The argument that Luke was not interested in these difficulties and thus chose not to report them overlooks their great significance for Paul.[25] Since this passage reports a civic tumult in which Paul was *not* involved, while the surrounding material and the correspondence indicate something closer to the opposite, grounds for deriving this story, in anything approaching

be based upon information derived by Luke from Ephesus." Witherington (585) opines: "The story is compelling, accurately portraying the sort of reaction one would expect if there was a perceived threat to the cult of the local deity and especially if that threat bore implications." His n. 112 seeks to rebut Haenchen's analysis. Kindred criticism of Haenchen is offered by Marshall (315–16) and Barrett (2:917–18). Most of this rejection comes down to the verisimilitude of the account, which does not prove either accuracy or the existence of a specific source, as well as objections to Haenchen's arguments based on alternative interpretations or the ever-useful claim that, had Luke invented the story, he would have said/included *X* or *Y*. Haenchen left himself open to criticism by not distinguishing between the problems of the narrative and historical improbability.

18 Conzelmann, 165.

19 Weiser, 2:541–49. For a valid critique of some of his deductions, see Lüdemann, *Acts*, 262. Lampe ("Acta 19," 70–77) reviews a number of source theories.

20 Krodel (365–66) bases his source hypothesis on four data: the use of *ekklēsia* to mean "assembly" (vv. 32, 39-40), "the subdued role played by Paul in this lengthy account, and the references to Aristarchus and Alexander, concluding, "These were hardly invented by Luke." These items do not add up to a source. "Assembly" is evidently ironic and, in any case, familiar to both Luke and the readers, Paul's role is scarcely traditional and conflicts with the proposal about Aristarchus (see Lüdemann, 262), and Alexander's appearance accords with no theories that relate this to an experience of Paul's mission in Ephesus. 2 Tim 4:14, which refers to injuries done to Paul by one "Alexander the coppersmith," is interesting because of the name and occupation. See Pervo, "Hard Act," 13–14. Those who suspect a tradition behind this name will appeal to 2 Timothy for support. Another, less likely, possibility is that 2 Timothy depended on Acts. Lampe ("Acta 19," 59–77) proposes an oral source.

21 Lüdemann, *Acts*, 261–62. This idea goes back, as Lüdemann (219) notes, to Julius Wellhausen, *Noten zur Apostelgeschichte* (NGG PH 1; Berlin: Töpelmann, 1907) 1–21, esp. 17. In his earlier work, Lüdemann identifies the source as "secular," which means not produced by a believer.

22 Fitzmyer (655) followed by a rejection of Haenchen's view, which is now understood as calling the episode "a Lucan fabrication."

23 Ephrem (according to the Catena; cf. Ropes, *Text*, 440) says, "For it was about this [i.e., the demonstration started by Demetrius] he wrote to the Corinthians."

24 Loisy (744–57, esp. 756) claimed that the riot is a cloak beneath which the author gathers all of the difficulties faced by Paul in Asia.

25 Marshall (316) says that Paul's "affliction in Asia" (2 Cor 1:8) may have been an illness and that Luke ignored this problem.

its present form, from "good" tradition are absent. Only an admirer of Paul would write eighteen verses demonstrating "that Paul's physical presence is *not* a factor in the riot and that his personality *is*."[26]

The two speeches (vv. 25-27; 35-40) are complementary Lucan compositions. Haenchen agrees with the thesis that "Paul really threatened the existence of the Artemis cult by his missionary activity."[27] This is quite questionable. At approximately the time when Acts was written, Pliny ("the Younger") concludes his report to the emperor Trajan about his activities to suppress Christianity in Bithynia, c. 112, with some comments on the beneficent effect of his firm but humane policy:

> [T]here is no doubt that people have begun to throng the temples which had been almost entirely deserted for a long time; the sacred rites which had been allowed to lapse are being performed again, and flesh of sacrificial victims is on sale everywhere, though up till recently scarcely anyone could be found to buy it. (Pliny *Ep.* 10.96.10)[28]

Six decades after Paul's labors, it was possible for this claim to be made, but it should not be taken at face value even for this later date. Pliny was indulging in self-serving hyperbole.[29] In Paul's time, the Christian population of Ephesus was, at the very most, a few hundred, not all of whom would have previously been ardent devotees of Artemis. This statistically insignificant group could scarcely have had a measurable impact on the sale of religious mementoes of any kind, a goodly number of which would have been acquired by visitors and pilgrims.[30] Although the local color is vivid, the role of the silver workers is a Lucan invention. The close parallel of this passage to 16:19-22 provides additional support for this hypothesis.[31] Like the owners of the exorcised slave at Philippi, Demetrius falls out of the subsequent action.

The introduction of "Gaius and Aristarchus" (v. 29) could stem from a tradition about this incident, but they, too, play no role in the subsequent narrative. It is not clear why they are labeled "traveling companions of Paul,"[32] who has not been on the road for the longest period in the book.[33] Both are described as "Macedonians."[34] Is the reader to imagine that they have accompanied Paul from Macedonia to Achaea and then Asia?[35] Aristarchus appears also in 20:4; 27:2, while "Gaius" is a common name. A reasonable guess is that Luke has introduced two bearers of the collection[36] into this scene to provide some believers for the theater.[37]

The best candidate for source material is vv. 29-34, less 29c-31. The intervening material is possibly marked by a "resumptive repetition": "into the theater" (εἰς

26 Shauf, *Theology*, 248.

27 Haenchen, 576.

28 *Certe satis constat prope iam desolata templa coepisse celebrari, et sacra sollemnia diu intermissa repeti passimque uenire* <*carnem*> *uictimarum, cuius adhuc rarissimus emptor inueniebatur* (Pliny *Ep.* 10.96.10, trans. Betty Radice, *Pliny Letters and Panegyricus* [2 vols.; LCL; Cambridge, Mass.: Harvard University Press, 1969] 2:291).

29 Keith Hopkins ("Christian Number and Its Implications," *JECS* 6 [1998] 185–226, esp. 190) views the theme of neglected rites as "more a literary cliché than precise reporting."

30 For more details, see Pervo, *Dating*, 317–19.

31 Note also that v. 23 is Lucan in form and language. Acts 12:18 employs an identical phrase. The rough transition to a mob scene is like that of 6:8-12 (Stephen).

32 See Barrett, 2:929, for examples of this word's more or less official character.

33 Note 20:18, where Paul claims not to have left Ephesus.

34 The singular "Macedonian" (36. 453 *pc*) would apply to Aristarchus. This is almost certainly a correction based upon 20:4, which locates Gaius in Derbe. See also the note on the text. Robert Stoops ("Riot and Assembly: The Social Context of Acts 19:23-41," *JBL* 108 [1989] 73–91, esp. 82) observes that the two adjectives mark them as outsiders, and thus as vulnerable.

35 This would conflict with 1 Thess 3:1.

36 The only other occurrence of the word συνέκδημος is in 2 Cor 8:19, raising the question of whether Gaius was mentioned there.

37 Speculation centers on the epistles, since Aristarchus is mentioned in Phlm 24 (probably written from Ephesus). That may have been Luke's source. The Deutero-Pauline Col 4:10–11 characterizes Aristarchus as a prisoner. This is probably embroidery on the author's part. Weiser (2:543–44) seeks to link the epistolary traditions with Acts, but this attempt does Luke no good, since it implies that Paul was jailed as a result of the incident, whatever it was.

τὸ θέατρον).[38] The "scene" about Paul's attempt to intervene is a cumbersome interruption, and the action of the Asiarchs is a Lucan creation.[39] One might then conjecture that the affair was an anti-Jewish eruption.[40] The text does not support this hypothesis, since it presumes that "the Jews" were not the primary subject, but evidently attempted to dissociate themselves from the accusations. The perspective views "Judaism" and "Christianity" as distinct "religions." Alexander would evidently have said, had he been given opportunity to speak, "These people do not belong to us."[41] It is pertinent to ask what Jews were doing in this mob. A robust imagination is required to propose that some of them hastened there in order to denounce polytheism or to do their bit to defend Paul. In such circumstances, prudent Jews would have been likely to stay out of sight. From the general perspective of Acts, one would think it likely that these Jews had come to unite in the attack on Paul. Verses 32-34 are unlikely to derive from a primary source about this incident. If the contrary position is taken, the critic will have to explain why Luke chose to retain or include such obscure data.

Luke did not require a source to depict urban disorder, for he had no lack of practice. Mob action is quite common in Acts, after all,[42] and works of fiction and history were replete with accounts of urban disorder.[43] A good specimen is the anti-Jewish riot at Antioch during the first revolt as described by Josephus (*Bell.* 7.46–62, 100–111).[44] Following a suggestion of Robert Stoops,[45] Richard Pervo identified ten structural themes or motifs shared by these two stories.[46] Many of these are unremarkable or all but inevitable, but they indicate that Luke followed the same pattern, beginning with a malicious agitator and ending with the intervention of an official. If a specific source for this passage is to be identified, the riot at Antioch is as good a candidate as any,[47] but it may be preferable to see each account as fitting within a general and flexible pattern, without ruling out some inspiration from Josephus.[48] Source analysis makes it apparent that Luke did not rely on firsthand evidence for this narrative and that it is best viewed as a Lucan composition.[49]

38 Cf. Loisy, 751, who entertained this hypothesis.

39 Even if one were to admit that Paul had made friends with some Asiarchs, as does Witherington (585 n. 112), their action is too improbable for credence.

40 See p. 486.

41 So also Schneider, 2:277; Weiser, 2:547; and Polhill, 412, all of whom hold some form of this view. For others who take this position and differing views, see the concise survey of Jervell, 492 n. 516. Stoops ("Riot," 86–87) hypothesizes that Alexander's narrative role is to introduce the issue of Jewish rights. This is too subtle, for the narrative is not in code, but he correctly emphasizes the experience of Diaspora Jews as part of the social background. Luke, however, has no explicit interest in sheltering Christians under the umbrella of Jewish rights and privileges.

42 See Pervo, *Profit*, 34–39.

43 Fiction: see Pervo, *Profit*, 151 nn. 88, 91, and 93. For examples from the Apocryphal Acts, see Söder, *Apokryphen Apostelgeschichten*, 158–62. On historiography, see Stoops, "Riot," 80. For data about such disturbances, see MacMullen, *Enemies*, 168–71, 175–76, 180, and 341 n. 12; Nippel, *Public Order*, 47–57, *et passim*. Nippel has a good discussion of urban violence as a means of popular justice. See, in addition, Pervo, "Meet Right," 53–60,

44 Cf. also Josephus *Bell.* 2.489–93, which describes an actual riot in the amphitheater in Alexandria. The prefect had some success in ameliorating the anger (θυμούς; cf. Acts 19:28) and then sent prominent citizens (cf. Acts 19:31) to urge calm.

45 Stoops, "Riot," 81.

46 Pervo, *Dating*, 179–83.

47 Johnson (348) speaks of a striking resemblance between the two accounts.

48 Differences are also important. Josephus takes a properly apologetic line, whereas Luke is willing to ridicule polytheism. Some implied readers of Josephus were supporters of Rome and Hellenism. Luke does make some apologetic use of the riot story (the Asiarchs), and it is possible that he got that idea from Josephus.

49 Selinger ("Demetriosunruhen") argues that the story is a Lucan creation. The possibility of a written but unrelated source for vv. 23-40 does not mean that no such disorder took place. Ancient authors were likely to describe even events in which they had participated in a standard, often stereotyped, manner.

Comment

■ **23-28** These verses inaugurate the action and poison the well. Demetrius's major concern is economic (v. 25); religion and patriotism (v. 27) provide a cloak. Moreover, his theology is crude. Rather than say that religious objects are aids to devotion, he appears to endorse the idea that gods can be manufactured. He thus represents the theology opposed in the Areopagus address. This sets the implicit apologetic theme: here are the kind of people who oppose us, greedy artisans encrusted with superstition.[50]

Silversmiths there were in Ephesus, organized under *τὸ ἱερὸν συνέδριον τῶν ἀργυρικόπων* ("the sacred governing council of the silversmiths").[51] The text does not identify Demetrius as their leader, although v. 38 seems to imply this, and the unfortunate syntax of v. 24 leaves the possibility open. The craft would be the proper subject.[52] The D-Text improves this by beginning in story fashion: "There was . . ."[53] Scholarship tends to view "silver temples" as a slip.[54] It may be a useful hyperbole. Probably most such objects were niches with a statue of Artemis (*ναΐσκοι*), but the important point is less Luke's accuracy than that, by saying "temples" (*ναοί*), he both evoked the speeches of Stephen and Paul (7:48; 17:24) and suggested that these were very expensive objects, implying that Paul's message appealed to the well-to-do.

The narrator presumes that the temple of Artemis at Ephesus needs no introduction. This was a safe choice, for the sanctuary was one of the "Seven Wonders of the

50 Cf. Talbert, 178. The implication is that the ambition of artisans nourishes the worship of idols. Apollonius made a similar critique (Philostratus *Vit. Apoll.* 5.20). See also MacMullen, *Paganism*, 165 n. 44.

51 For an example from c. 50 CE or later, see *I. Eph.* 2212 (an epitaph), discussed in *NewDocs* 4 (1987) no. 1, pp. 7–10. In that epitaph the body is identified as οἱ ἐν Ἐφέσῳ ἀργυροκόποι ("the silversmiths in Ephesus"). *I. Eph.* 585 speaks of the πλῆθος ("body," a term sometimes used in Acts for the Christian community [4:32; 6:2, etc.]) That inscription is an acclamation beginning with αὔξει: "May the guild of silversmiths flourish." Cf. Acts 19:20. See also Horsley, *NewDocs* 5 (1985) no. 5, 95–114; idem, "Inscriptions," 142; Lampe, "Acta 19," 66–69; and Selinger, "Demetriosunruhen," 245 n. 23.

52 Moule (*Idiom Book*, 105) prefers ". . . a silversmith, brought the craftsmen no little trade by making. . . ."

53 Boismard, *Texte*, 321: ἦν δέ τις ἀργυροκόπος ὀνόματι Δημήτριος ὅς ἐποίει ναοὺς ἀργυροῦς Ἀρτέμιδος καὶ παρείχετο τοῖς τεχνίταις οὐκ ὀλίγην ἐργασίαν. οὗτος συναθροίσας ("There was a silversmith named Demetrius, who made silver temples of Artemis and provided substantial income for the artisans. 25. He, gathering the artisans . . ."). A* D E *pc* read παρεῖχε ("provided") active. BDF §316 (3) (on use of the middle) suspects that the passage is corrupt.

54 For skepticism about silver models of this temple, see, e.g., Cadbury, *Book*, 5; Sherwin-White, *Roman Society*, 90–91. Hemer (*Book*, 121) states that "such images of the goddess in a niche, made of terracotta, are well known, if not in silver." He points to *IGR* 1.167 (Tarentum), which speaks of a votive dedication of a miniature shrine (ναΐσκον) to Artemis. This may have been based on the temple at Ephesus. See also Trebilco, "Asia," 336–38; and Kauppi, *Foreign*, 94–101. On a possible mold from the Hellenistic era for such objects, see Ellen D. Reeder, "The Mother of the Gods and the Hellenistic Bronze Matrix," *AJA* 91 (1987) 423–40, esp. 424–28. On a silver temple to Antoninus Pius found in Spain, see Selinger, "Demetriosunruhen," 246 n. 28. These data may appear to settle the matter, but doubts were also raised in antiquity. ℵ* has "a silver temple," suggesting one large project. B, tellingly, omits "silver" (i.e., they could be clay). A few witnesses (including 1739. 1837) add an apparent gloss: "possibly small cups" (ἴσως κιβώρια μικρά). Chrysostom (and/or his authorities) may be the source of this, for he wondered how temples could be made of silver and suggested "cups." For details, see Jacquier, 581. The accusation of Demetrius in v. 26 appears to support the view that statues are in question, for he does not say that Paul claimed that gods do not dwell in temples but that they cannot be manufactured by humans. At the end of the nineteenth century, E. L. Hicks proposed that tradition spoke of Demetrius as a νεωποιός ("warden") of the temple. On this, see Trebilco, "Asia," 337 n. 10.

Ancient World,"[55] the home of an international cult[56] and one of the most famous sites in the world, rich from gifts, having a large bank,[57] and possessing esteemed rights of asylum.[58] According to Dieter Knibbe, the power and prestige of the cult of Artemis had been declining for some years by the dramatic date of Acts, which motivated intense efforts toward reasserting her status.[59] Another reaction was nostalgia, quite visible in the popular literature of the first two centuries.[60] Whatever the vicissitudes of religious taste, Artemis retained her grip on the general imagination. She encapsulated polytheism at Ephesus in *Act. John* 37–47,[61] and her temple is singled out in the woes upon Asia in *Sibylline Oracles* 5.[62] The residents of ancient cities, not being fools, were sensitive to economic loss, but the energy they were willing to invest in debates about titles and various privileges still generates surprise.[63] An argument from honor alone would have carried more weight. In Acts, Artemis is a synecdoche for civic religion, distinct from and more distinguished than independent operations like exorcism and magic. Apart from the reference to Artemis's image in v. 35, the author makes no mention of the specifics of the cult.[64]

■ **25-27** The conventional text envisions a broader group than the silversmiths, whereas the D-Text is more restrictive.[65] The speech is almost absurd in its brevity, beginning, like Paul's pastoral address in 20:17-35, with a "memory" statement,[66] proceeding thence to a summary of Paul's message and drawing the conclusion that danger lurks on the horizon. An objective reader might

55 The concept of "Seven Wonders" goes back to the second century BCE. "Seven" is the conventional number for such lists (p. 156). On the development of the list, see Peter Clayton and Martin Price, eds., *The Seven Wonders of the Ancient World* (London: Routledge, 1988) 10–12. The article on the temple of Artemis was written by Bluma L. Trell, 78–99.

56 Pausanias 4.31.8 says that she was worshiped by more individuals than any other deity known to him. See also Strabo 4.1.5 and *Anth. Pal.* 9.58. See also Trebilco, "Asia," 317–18; Richard Oster, "Ephesus as a Religious Center under the Principate: I. Paganism before Constantine," *ANRW* 2.18.3 (1990) 1661–1728, esp. 1674. F. Sokolowski ("A New Testimony on the Cult of Artemis of Ephesus," *HTR* 58 [1965] 427–31) discusses an inscription reporting that forty-five persons from Sardis were condemned to death for assault on an embassy from Artemis of Ephesus. He attributes the assault to resistance against the infiltration of a foreign cult by defenders of the local Artemis, that is, that the Ephesian Artemis engaged in missionary activities that were, like those of Paul, viewed as threats to local cults. (The inscription is *I. Eph.* 572.1.)

57 For a summary of the relation of the temple to economics, see Trebilco, "Asia," 324–26.

58 On the temple and cult of Artemis, see Trebilco, "Asia," 319–36, with numerous references, and, for recent discoveries, Dieter Knibbe, "Via Sacra Ephesiaca: New Aspects of the Cult of Artemis Ephesia," in Koester, *Ephesos*, 141–55. Although the temple was plundered by Goths in 262, some rebuilding took place at the close of the third century. According to B. L. Trell ("The Temple of Artemis at Ephesos," in Peter Clayton and Martin Price, eds., *The Seven Wonders of the Ancient World* [London: Routledge, 1988] 78–99, esp. 98), John Chrysostom brought about the final destruction. This would have been during his visit to Ephesus in 401 and would have probably involved a request for imperial permission to destroy the place. An early-fifth-century inscription boasts of the destruction of an image of the goddess. See *NewDocs* 4 (1987) no. 125, pp. 256–57. On the popularity of the rights of Asylum, see Thomas, "At Home," 98–106. One example is Achilles Tatius *Leuc. Clit.* 8.8.8–9.

59 Knibbe, "Via Sacra," 146–47. In such a climate, defensive responses to attacks on the cult would have probably been intense. See also Trebilco, "Asia," 331–32.

60 See Thomas, "At Home."

61 The apostle John, unlike Paul, delivered a speech (and healed) in the theater at Ephesus (*Act. John* 32–36).

62 Lines 293–99 of the woes listed in 286–327. According to John J. Collins ("Sibylline Oracles," *OTP* 1:317–429), this oracle dates to the period of the Diaspora Revolt of c. 115, that is, contemporaneous with Acts.

63 A pertinent example is the Neocorate, on which see n. 117.

64 For this reason, description of specifics is superfluous. Contrast Ignatius, who, in imagery of which Luke might have approved, compares the Christian "journey" to a religious procession: "You are God-bearers, temple bearers, Christ-bearers, bearers of holy things" (*θεοφόροι καὶ ναοφόροι, χριστοφόροι, ἁγιοφόροι* [author's trans.]), evoking processions in honor of Artemis. See Schoedel, *Ignatius*, 67, with his references.

65 See n. *b*. In addition to reducing the object of the participle to "artisans" (*τεχνίτας*), the address

observe that Demetrius has said nothing that his good listeners do not know. "Demetrius narrates the problem without ever proposing a solution."[67] It is too early in the day for remedies. Possible solutions are reserved for the civic official, who introduces them for the purpose of dismissing them.

Demetrius's speech, in typical Lucan fashion, is peppered with alliteration and assonance.[68] Irony is not absent. The most obvious example is the verb "be in danger" (κινδυνεύω [v. 27]), which emerges once more in v. 40, where the workers are identified as the source of danger. More subtle is Demetrius's role as a defender of temples, which aligns him with the opponents of Stephen (7:48) and Paul (v. 26; cf. 17:24-25, 27, and 21:28).[69] Luke does not always shy away from intimations of guilt by association.[70] This continues in v. 26, which proffers confirmation of the claim advanced in v. 10 from the mouth of an opponent.[71] Paul is attacked not for his message about God's son but for his critique of temples and therefore as a philosopher[72] who hits exploiters of superstition in the pocketbook.[73] Universalistic language also works in two ways. By speaking of "all/the whole of Asia" (vv. 26-27)[74] and "the civilized world" (ἡ οἰκουμένη [v. 27]), Demetrius opposes one world religion to another.[75] The outcome of this competition will be patent.[76]

---

begins "Gentle fellow craftsmen" (ἄνδρες συντειχνεῖται).

66 Cf. also 10:28; 15:7 (Peter).

67 Soards, *Speeches*, 103.

68 Four words in the opening line (v. 25) begin with ἐ-, and seven with a smooth vowel. Verse 27 is replete with -ει- and -η- sounds. Note also the play between "great" (μεγάλης) and "greatness" (μεγαλειότητος) in v. 27. That noun is applied to God in Luke 9:43.

69 The noun denoting the sanctuary of Artemis in v. 27 is ἱερόν (versus ναός in v. 24). The latter is not used for the Jerusalem temple in Acts (but cf. Luke 1:9, 21-22).

70 Readers know that Paul did not call for the destruction of or sacrilege against polytheist religious artifacts but contrasted them with the true God (17:16-34).

71 The genitives of "Ephesus" and "Asia" in v. 26 are difficult. Bezae recognizes this by adding a preposition: ἕως Ἐφέσου, in effect, "Not only throughout Ephesus . . ." (BDF §216 [3] renders "within"). Moule (*Idiom Book*, 39) finds the locative genitive tempting. The translation takes the genitives "Ephesus" and "Asia" with ὄχλος ("vast number"). See BDF §186 (1) and Barrett, 2:924.

72 Compare and contrast *Mart. Pol.* 12:2: "[T]he entire multitude (πλῆθος) of both Gentiles and Jews who lived in Smyrna cried out with uncontrollable rage (θυμῷ) and a great voice, 'This is the teacher of impiety, the father of the Christians, the destroyer (καθαιρέτης) of our own gods, the one who teaches many not to sacrifice or worship the gods'" (trans. Ehrman, *Apostolic Fathers*, 2:383). The Greek words occur in Acts 19:23-40. Polycarp (who is being tried by the proconsul in a stadium) is accused of attempting to abolish polytheist worship, whereas Paul is a critic of images. In the story of Polycarp, Jews and polytheists are presented as offering a solid front (even on the question of worshiping the gods!), while in Acts the Jews seem eager to distance themselves from the Christians. This chapter of three verses contains a number of parallels to Acts 19:21-40, including the proconsul (v. 38), who appears to work in collaboration with Philip, the Asiarch, who is evidently in charge of the games; a unison chant (ὁμοθυμαδὸν ἐπιβοήσαι [cf. vv. 28-29]), and two uses of the verb δεῖ for divine necessity (v. 21). According to the Cynic *Epistle* 7.9 of (Pseudo-) Heraclitus (c. 100–125 CE), the philosopher was exiled from Ephesus for impiety. On the problem of the text of this letter, see Abraham Malherbe, *The Cynic Epistles* (SBLSBS 12; Atlanta: Scholars Press, 1977) 24. For examples of the philosophical critique of images, see Stoops, "Riot," 83.

73 The D-Text (Boismard, *Texte*, 322) contributes a note of realism by injecting, after "Paul," "whoever he is" (τίς ποτε). The narrative assumes that Paul was familiar to the audience of the speech.

74 On εἰς ἀπελεγμόν ("disrepute") in v. 27, a deverbative term, see Barrett, 2:926.

75 For the international appeal of the Ephesian Artemis, see Horsley, "Inscriptions," 153–55; and Trebilco, "Asia," 332–36.

76 Verse 27 is another syntactic puzzle. The D-Text looks like a revision: εἰς οὐδὲν λογισθήσεται ἀλλὰ καὶ καθαιρεῖσθαι μέλλει ἡ μεγαλειότης ("will be accounted as nothing but also her greatness is going to be destroyed"). Except for the repeated "but also" this is better, and Ropes (*Text*, 186) prefers it to "the monstrous sentence of the B-Text." Cadbury and Lake (246), however, accept a string of infinitives dependent upon κινδυνεύει ("be in danger"). The text may be corrupt, but the D-Text is unlikely to be more original, and it

■ **28** The workers have heard enough and implement their own solution: the ritual acclamation of their goddess's power.[77] Acclamation was a means of popular participation in ancient religious, political, theatrical, athletic, and legal activities.[78] Function is more important than diction. Examples include the public reaction to miracles,[79] cheers for one's circus team, demands for justice ("Crucify him!"),[80] and expressions of personal piety or conviction.[81] Literary representation tends to report a single acclamation, but these cries were usually repeated for some time.[82] Chants could be spontaneous or organized. The effect of the latter gave guilds[83] and, in particular, athletic factions considerable power in the Roman and Byzantine capitals. Finally, acclamations may assume a formal character in ritual.[84] Application of the epithet "great(est)" to a deity[85] has enjoyed a long life as a spontaneous acclamation.[86] Acclamations could be prayers/petitions or acknowledgments of benefits received. The transition between meeting and civic uproar in vv. 28-29 is quite awkward. Acts 2:4-5 presented a comparable situation.[87] The D-Text resolves the apparent glitch, which is probably the result of Lucan compression.[88]

■ **29-34** This section depicts the city in chaos, a civic *ekklēsia* (assembly) unworthy of a great metropolis, the bravery of Paul, and the high standing of his friends. Matters end where they began, with the acclamation of Artemis's magnitude and the theological solidarity of its disorderly populace. As in the case of Stephen, the official body behaves like a mob. The local color shines

---

is equally possible that this is the result of Luke's attempt to produce balanced and sonorous clauses. See also BDF §180 (1); Barrett, 2:927; and Shauf, *Theology*, 242 n. 387.

77 Their righteous indignation closely resembles the animosity of the synagogue audience to Jesus in Luke 4:28.

78 Discussions, with bibliography, include Ramsay, *Church*, 135–39; Selinger, "Demetriusunruhen," 248 n. 33, 254 n. 64; and the references on p. 55.

79 Note Apuleius *Metam.* 11.13: *Populi mirantur, religiosi uenerantur tam euidentem maximi* (= μεγίστου) *numinis potentiam et consimilem nocturnis imaginibus magnificentiam et facilitatem reformationis claraque et consona uoce, caelo manus adtendentes, testantur tam inlustre deae beneficium.* ("The crowd was amazed, and the devout paid homage to this clear manifestation of the power of the mighty deity, to her grandeur which exactly matched my dream revelations, and to the ease of my transformation. With one clear voice, stretching their hands toward heaven, they bore witness to the marvelous beneficence of the goddess" [trans. Hanson, *Apuleius*, 2:317]).

80 Crowds used games in theater to demand executions: Fergus Millar, *The Emperor in the Roman World* (Ithaca: Cornell University Press, 1977) 574.

81 For the unison cheers of various groups (including guilds), see MacMullen, *Enemies*, 170: "Lesser folk made their weight felt in the theater by disciplining their cheers to a unison, sitting in compact armies of support under acknowledged leaders, or coming ready-organized as guilds." For references, see 339 n.10.

82 An example from U.S. team sports is repeated shouts of a single word or phrase, such as "Defense! Defense!" often sustained until the defense succeeds (or fails).

83 On guilds as effective claques and cheering sections, see MacMullen, *Enemies*, 170.

84 Extant examples are the short acclamations that precede and conclude the liturgical Gospel in the Eucharist and the fixed response "Thanks be to God" that concludes liturgical readings from Scripture.

85 The epithet was not limited to acclamations. See, for example, *Ephesian Tale* 1.11.5 (τὴν πάτριον ἡμῖν ϑεὸν, τὴν μεγάλην Ἐφεσίων Ἄρτεμιν ["Our ancentral goddess, the great Artemis of the Ephesians"]), 4.3.3; 5.12.3–4 (Isis the "the greatest"). In *Leuc. Clit.* 8.9.13, the priest proclaims, "The great goddess Artemis has saved both" the hero and heroine. For other examples of the epithet applied to Artemis, see Wikenhauser, *Geschichtswert*, 364.

86 In the Islamic world, crowds can sustain the chant "*Allahu akbar*!" ("God is Great") for hours. A good ancient literary instance is Bel et Draco 18 and 41. In the first example, the king proclaims, "You are great, Bel." At the close, he applies the same acclamation to "the Lord God."

87 See p. 487.

88 D-Text (Boismard, *Texte*, 324) adds "**These things**" to provide "hearing" with an object, and "rushing into the street" before "began to shout." The acclamation is therefore public and a means of generating attention.

(theater as place of assembly, Asiarchs[89]), and the narrative is vigorous, if syntactically difficult and nonsequential. The major difficulty is logical. Haenchen's observation is difficult to refute. At this point, Demetrius (or someone whom he had persuaded) should have laid a charge, which might then be debated, with response by Gaius and/or Aristarchus.[90] Verses 32-34 are a smokescreen to conceal Luke's lack of interest in pursuing this course. Instead, the narrator portrays a contrast in social status. On the one side is the labile and ignorant mob, agitating for its own sake. Ranged against them are the most distinguished people in the province, soon to be joined by the chief executive officer of Ephesus.[91]

Some major D-Text witnesses (D* gig bsy^p) seek to improve the logic by stating that "the **entire** city was **dismayed with shame**."[92] This correctly characterizes the situation as a threat to the honor of Artemis (and Ephesus).[93] Verse 29 still suffers from want of a clear subject: Does the ubiquitous "they" refer to the workers or to "the city"? Gaius and Aristarchus appear and disappear with equal lack of explanation. The reader may assume that, as in Thessalonica (17:6; cf. Beroea, 17:13-14), the mob attempted to find Paul and took whomever they could get, but the demands on imagination are considerable. How did they find and identify these two? Was Paul's location unknown?

■ **30-31** As if aware that Paul would come to mind, the narrator's attention turns to him in v. 30. Paul, who has learned in advance of the reader that those who have rushed to the theater have constituted themselves as an ἐκκλησία ("assembly"),[94] was intent upon joining them. This would have placed him at great risk, a chance that the fearless missionary was willing to take, but one must ask just what he could have said that would not have further inflamed the crowd (as in 22:1-23), since the charges against him were true and only in a formal trial could he have constructed a defense of his words. Here, he cannot (as in chap. 26) claim that he gave the valid interpretation of the ancestral faith. That issue will never arise, for believers delay him[95] until word comes from some Asiarchs, who begged him not to take (a probably vain) risk. Scholarship has inclined to the view that these persons were the chief priests of the imperial cult at Ephesus,[96] a view recently challenged by Rosalinde A. Kearsley,[97] who views their focus as more civic than provincial.[98] If this is correct, the difficulties of the

89 On the theater as a place of assembly and its links to the cult of Artemis, see Trebilco, "Asia," 348–50. *I. Eph.* 557 mentions images of the goddess carried κατὰ πᾶσαν ἐκκλησίαν εἰς τὸ θέατρον ("into the theater at every assembly"). Cf. also *I. Eph* 21 and 476. The theater was a meeting place in many cities. See, e.g., Chariton *Chaer.* 3.4; *Ethiopian Story* 4.17–21.

90 Haenchen, 574.

91 Luke's contrast between the peaceful, hierarchical, and smooth operation of the Christian *ekklēsia* (most notably in chap. 15) and the ineffective, anarchic, and tumultuous behavior of the Ephesian *ekklēsia* (on which, see Pervo, "Meet Right") is apologetic in orientation, anticipating Origen's contrast between the well-behaved church at Athens and the riotous (στασιώδης) civic assembly (*Cels.* 3.30).

92 καὶ συνεχύθη ὅλη ἡ πόλις αἰσχύνης. Other witnesses (36. 453. 1505 *pc*) also contain the word "shame." Boismard (*Texte*, 324) takes no account of this variant, other than to select the verb συνεχύθη in place of ἐπλήσθη "was filled"). Ropes (*Text*, 187) explains "shame" as arising from the translation of "confuse."

93 *I. Caria* 71 (= Knidos 4) provides interesting social and linguistic commentary: [ὁ μὲν] δᾶμος, ἐν οὐ μετρίᾳ συγχύσ[σει γε]νόμενος διὰ τὰν ὑπάρχοῦσ[αν περὶ] αὐτὰν ἀρετάν τε καὶ δόξα[ν, μετὰ] πάσας προθυμίας συνελ[θὼν ε]ἰς τὸ θέατρον, "The citizen body [cf. Acts 19:30, 34] in considerable [cf. 20:12] confusion [cf. vv. 29, 32] because of its very virtue and reputation, entered the theater [cf. v. 29] with all eagerness [cf. 17:11]."

94 Because of the use of ἐκκλησία ("assembly") in vv. 32 and 40, it is legitimate to render δῆμος (v. 30) as the "Popular Assembly," that is, the citizen body in its official capacity. On the Ephesian assembly, see Selinger, "Demetriosunruhen," 249 n. 37.

95 The D-Text (Boismard, *Texte*, 324) reads (in addition to some minor improvements) ἐκώλυον ("sought to prevent") rather than the blunt οὐκ εἴων ("would not allow"). This variant removes the possibility that believers forcibly restrained Paul or that they could give him orders.

96 This is the position of Lily Ross Taylor, "The Asiarchs," in Lake and Cadbury, *Additional Notes,* 256–62, followed by many. For examples, see Rosalinde Kearsley, "The Asiarchs," in Gill and Gempf, *Setting*, 366 n. 14.

97 For a summary of her findings, see "The Asiarchs," 363–76.

98 Ibid., 376.

narrative only worsen, for these responsibilities would make it even more difficult to understand why their involvement was limited to advising Paul to stay out of the matter.[99] The significant datum is that the Asiarchs (whose position was evidently familiar to the implied reader) were of the highest social standing in the city.[100] "A sect whose leader had Asiarchs for friends cannot be dangerous to the state."[101]

■ **32** The verse catapults the reader into the theater, where chaos holds the floor.[102] Dio of Prusa describes a fictional civic assembly with a technique akin to "defamiliarization," which exposes a situation by presenting it from perspective of an outsider, who, not knowing the conventions, is amazed:

> Now at first the crowd deliberated on other matters for a considerable while, and they kept up a shouting. . . . This wrath of theirs was something terrible . . . I too myself was once almost knocked over by the shouting. . . . And other men would come forward, or stand up where they were, and address the multitude . . . to some of these they would listen for quite a long time, but at others they were angry as soon as they opened their mouths, and they would not let them so much as cheep. (*Or.* 7.24-26)[103]

The confusion (σύγχυσις)[104] that beset the city (v. 29) also beset the assembly (συγχύνω) in v. 32. The text is no less confused than the crowd, and no attempt to construe or correct it will yield highly satisfactory sense.[105] Alexander, whose obscurity surpasses that of Sosthenes (18:17), attempted to do what Paul had in mind,[106] with an utter lack of success.[107]

99 The suspicion arises that the desire to dissociate the Asiarchs from the imperial cult is apologetic. One of the objects stated in the summary of Kearsley's article was "the recent suggestion that Luke's use of the title is an anachronism" (p. 363). On p. 368, she attributes this view, incorrectly, to Wayne Meeks.

100 On the status of Asiarchs, see Strabo 14.1.42 (on Tralles). Their standing remained high through the subsequent century and later.

101 Haenchen, 578. Cf. Cadbury, *Book*, 43: "Luke's reason for mentioning the Asiarchs at all is not their religious association." Cf. also Foakes Jackson, 182. Shauf (*Theology*, 249 n. 413) has a good summary of the issues, with bibliography. He rightly concludes that their status is more important than their function.

102 The use of ἄλλοι . . . ἄλλο ("Some persons . . . another thing") is a classical idiom. BDF §306 (5). Cf. Chariton *Chaer.* 1.5.3: ἀλλὰ καὶ ὁ δῆμος ἅπας εἰς τὴν ἀγορὰν συνέτρεχεν, ἄλλων ἄλλα κεκραγότων ("The whole populace, too, hastened to the marketplace, uttering all sorts of cries"), trans. G. P. Gould, *Callirhoe* (LCL; Cambridge, Mass.: Harvard University Press, 1980) 49. The particle μὲν οὖν is resumptive. It approaches such phrases as "meanwhile, back in the theater."

103 Trans. J. W. Cohoon, *Dio Chrysostom I* (LCL; Cambridge, Mass.: Harvard University Press, 1932) 301.

104 On this term, see Stoops, "Riot," 86.

105 One difficulty is the subject. Logically, it is οἱ πλείους ("the majority") of the previous sentence, but that is difficult to accept. Another is the ubiquitous "they" found elsewhere in the passage (e.g., v. 29). With this is associated the function of ἐκ δὲ τοῦ ὄχλου (lit. "from the crowd"), which should modify the verb. (The particle δέ could be adversative, i.e., "but.") Another possibility, followed in the translation, is to treat it as effective subject (i.e., as if modified with the article). Cadbury and Lake (249) note a similar "barbarous construction" in Luke 21:16 and reluctantly take this path. The genitive absolute is far from pristine. Since it is aorist, the translation proposes that, after he had assumed the rostrum, members of the crowd (some of those few who did know why they were present?) made suggestions about what he might say, until they concluded (on some unknown grounds) that he was Jewish and would say nothing that they wished to hear.

106 Note the occurrence of δῆμος ("the People") in vv. 30 and 33.

107 The "official" position of Diaspora Judaism forbade reviling the gods of those among whom Jews lived. This emerges in the plural "gods" in LXX Exod 22:27 (= "God" in MT 22:28). Quite similar statements in Philo *Vit. Mos.* 2.203–5 (cf. *Spec. leg.* 1.53), Josephus *Ant.* 4.207; *Ap.* 2.237 support the notion that there was a general principle. Cf also Rom 2:22. The charge of reviling the gods of others was made, however (*Ap.* 1.249, 309–11), and the LXX provides plenty of evidence. Moreover, during the revolts Jews attacked many temples of other religions. See also Stoops, "Riot," 87–88. For a list of possible explanations see Selinger, "Demetriosunruhen," 252.

■ **33** A verse that appeared likely to end the confusion only increases it.[108] This was not the occasion for speeches on the benefits of religious diversity.[109] The evident meaning of the episode involving Alexander is, as hinted above, like the experience with Gallio (18:12-17). An attempt at opposition to Christianity turns into anti-Jewish agitation. As R. Selinger says, while the crowd shouts down "the Jews," both Asiarchs and the civic executive support the Christians. Patronage has shifted.[110]

■ **34** At this point, the crowd resumes its ritual chant.[111] Its unedifying two-hour duration contrasts nicely with Paul's two years of evangelism (v. 10).[112] The longer the situation lasts, the more dangerous it will become—and the more honor Artemis will lose. Two comments, one ancient, one modern, will suffice. Haenchen pithily opines: "[I]n [the] final analysis the only thing heathenism can do against Paul is to shout itself hoarse."[113] The last word belongs to the apostle John, on a later occasion: "Artemis herself ought to have helped."[114]

■ **35-39** The speech of the "secretary"[115] parallels that of Demetrius in vv. 25-27, in content and even somewhat in form. Both center on the city, Artemis, and her temple, and refer to an alleged Christian challenge. The style also has Lucan characteristics, but, in keeping with the speaker and the situation, is slightly more elevated and technical than the words of Demetrius.[116] Local color is

108 Klauck (*Magic*, 107) suggests filling out the verse in this manner: "they allowed Alexander [with whom you, the readers, are familiar] to come out of the crowd with [Gaius and Aristarchus], because the Jewish [Christians] pushed him forward." This reconstruction reveals the difficulty of the text, which contains an intolerable number of gaps and glitches. There are other attempts, e.g. Haenchen, 575. See the review of positions by Shauf, *Theology*, 251–53. Almost every hypothesis seeks to find the historical situation behind the text rather than determine Luke's goal. Some recent interpreters, such as Shauf, Fitzmyer (656 [with nuance]), Tannehill (*Narrative Unity*, 2:243), and Jervell (429), incline toward the understanding that Christians and Jews in Ephesus were allied on this matter, but Luke did not need to state that Israelite religion opposed idolatry. The prior question is what Jews were doing in the audience. One difficulty with the idea of an alliance is that neither Jews nor Christians articulate their position.

109 Cadbury (*Book*, 94) suspects that the author reported this incident "with a little malicious glee."

110 Selinger, "Demetriosunruhen," 253. The incident encapsulates and underlines the defeat of Judaism in Ephesus.

111 Verse 34 begins with an anacoluthon, on which see BDF 466 (4). א and A read the participle "shouting" in the nominative plural, no less intelligent than it is secondary. B doubles the chant ("Great . . ."). This is probably a secondary attempt to convey repetition.

112 The Greek phrases are exactly parallel.

113 Haenchen, 578. Cf. also Rackham, 340. Those familiar with Scripture would think of the humorous story of Elijah's encounter with the priests of Baal (1 Kgs 18:26-29), which concludes (after petition is enhanced with self-mutilation): "[T]hey raved on until the time of the offering of the oblation, but there was no voice, no answer, and no response."

114 *Act. John* 43: ἔδει τὴν Ἄρτεμιν βοηθῆσαι αὐτήν

115 On this office, see A. H. M. Jones, *The Greek City from Alexander to Justinian* (London: Oxford University Press, 1940) 238–39 nn. 52–53; Sherwin-White, *Roman Society*, 86–87; Trebilco, "Asia," 351 nn. 262–63; Shauf, *Theology*, 254 n. 433; Claudia Schulte, *Die Grammateis von Ephesos: Schreiberamt und Sozialstruktur in einer Provinzhauptstadt des römischen Kaiserreichs* (Stuttgart: Franz Steiner, 1994); and Selinger, "Demetriosunruhen," 254 n. 69. Two positions existed, a "clerk of the popular assembly" (γραμματεὺς τοῦ δήμου) and a "clerk of the council" (γραμματεὺς τῆς βουλῆς). Trebilco assumes, with reason, that the former is in view here. Note that, like many magistrates in Acts, this person is anonymous.

116 Formal: both begin with "gentlemen" (ἄνδρες) and a "memory" statement (vv. 25, 35), and both refer to "danger." Assonance: note three words in *-on* (v. 36) and six in *-ou-* (v. 37). Alliteration abounds: cf. vv. 38 (esp. ἀγοραῖοι ἄγονται), with three more initial *a-* sounds. The last three words of v. 40a end in *-es*. Note also προπετὲς πράσσειν (v. 36). See also n. 68 above. In addition is the use of accusative with participle in indirect discourse (v. 35—"corrected" by the D-Text [Boismard, *Texte*, 326]). Examples of technical language: "unimpeachable" (ἀντιρρήτων), v. 36; "lodge charges" (ἐγκαλέω), v. 38 (on which see Schneider, 2:278); "courts" (ἀγοραῖοι), v. 38; "regular" (ἐννόμῳ) and περαιτέρω ("further"), v. 39. The latter, although not rare, was altered to περὶ ἑτέρων ("on other matters") in a number of witnesses.

prominent.[117] The two little speeches were composed as bookends to the narrative. Speeches ignite and extinguish the uproar. The officer's ability to quiet a seething crowd indicates rhetorical ability and strong character.[118]

■ **40** The verse is difficult. The text appears to be corrupt, but proposals for emendation depend on determining what the author wished to say.[119] The genitive absolute *μηδενὸς αἰτίου ὑπάρχοντος*, which may be rendered, "since there is no charge" or "since there is no explanation," may refer to either the preceding or following phrases, that is, accusation of disorder or giving a reasonable account. The relative in the prepositional phrase "concerning which" (*περὶ οὗ*) is masculine or neuter and cannot refer to either "today" or "disorder." The omission of the preposition, attested by a number of witnesses, is no improvement. The finite verb of the relative clause, "be able," is or is not marked by the negative. Manuscript support for inclusion and exclusion is about equal. Furthermore, the preceding relative *οὗ* raises the problem of dittography or haplography, for *OYOY* would tempt a scribe either to strike the last two letters or to insert them on the grounds that a previous scribe had excised or overlooked them.

The earliest known emendation occurs in the D-Text: "The fact is that it is we who are liable to be accused of fomenting a riot **today, when**, because there is no explanation on the grounds of which we can provide explanation. . . ."[120] This resolves the problem of the relative antecedent, but leaves an undesirable genitive absolute. It is evidently secondary, as the ingenuity required to modify this text into the conventional form surpasses human understanding. Hort proposed emending to the nominative: *μηδενὸς αἴτιοι ὑπάρχοντος* ("although we are guilty of nothing concerning which . . .").[121] This presumes that the object is to recover the secretary's actual words. Faced with these problems and unable to make a judgment based on external evidence, the editorial committee that produced N-A[27] was loath to resort

117 "Neocorate" is one of the titles for which Greek cities fought. It may be a bit of an anachronism here. See L. Michael White, "Urban Development and Social Change in Imperial Ephesos," 27–79, esp. 37; and Steven Friesen, "The Cult of the Roman Emperors in Ephesos," 229–50, esp. 231–32, both in Koester, *Ephesos,* and each with numerous references. Hemer (*Book*, 122) notes this datum as an example of Luke's knowledge of specifics. The inscription he cites in support (*I. Eph.* 300) dates from the reign of Septimius Severus (193–211 CE). Note also the valuable data and discussion in Magie, *Roman Rule*, 2:1432–34 n. 18, and see the inscriptional examples pertinent to Artemis of Ephesus cited in BDAG, 670, *s.v.* *νεωκόρος*. The translation "image that has come down from heaven" presumes that *διοπετους* in v. 35 refers to the famous statue rather than to another object, such as an aniconic meterorite. On this see BDF §241 (7) and Stoops, "Riot," 87 n. 74. A specific example is Euripides *Iph. taur.* 85–92. Lines 85–86 speak of "[t]he goddess' [Artemis] statue (*ἄγαλμα*), which they say fell from the sky (*οὐρανοῦ πεσεῖν ἄπο*) into this temple here" (trans. David Kovacs, *Euripides IV* [LCL; Cambridge: Harvard University Press, 1999] 161; cf. also 1384–85). Other noteworthy examples are the stone from Pessinus sent to Rome (Herodian 1.11.1) and an image of Demeter said by Cicero (*Verrines* 2.187) to be so compelling that viewers believed that they were looking at the goddess herself or an image not made with human hands but fallen from heaven (*non humana manu factam sed de caelo lapsam*). The latter suggests realism rather than a meteorite. For other examples, see Wikenhauser, *Geschichtswert*, 364–65; Betz, *Lukian*, 186 n .2; and Bruce, 420. On metereorites as cultic objects, see Wilson D. Wallis, "Prodigies and Portents," *ERE* 10:362–76, esp. 371. The difficulty that this epithet would have only applied to the archaic statue of Artemis presumably destroyed in the fire of 356 BCE is illusory, for religion knows how to deal with these matters. The claim that an image of Artemis "fallen from the skies" could refute the allegations that the goddess's statue was an artifact, but it is more than unlikely that Luke would devise or record an argument against Paul. See Cadbury and Lake, 250–51; Trebilco, "Asia," 351–53; Shauf, *Theology*, 255; and Kauppi, *Foreign*, 101–5.

118 Cf. on 21:40.

119 Corruption is suspected by Ropes (*Text*, 189) and accepted by Hort (below).

120 Boismard, *Texte*, 327: *κινδυνεύομεν σήμερον ἐγκαλεῖσθαι στάσεως ὡς μηδενὸς αἰτίου ὄντος περὶ οὗ δυνησόμεθα ἀποδοῦναι λόγον τῆς συστροφῆς ταύτης*. This text does not contain two of the three possible uses of *περί* ("concerning") in the verse. See below, n. 128.

121 Brooke F. Westcott and Fenton J. A. Hort, *The New Testament in the Original Greek* (2 vols.; 2nd ed.; Cambridge: Cambridge University Press, 1896) 2:97 (a note by Hort).

to conjecture and included the negative in brackets, a procedure that amounts to a nondecision.[122] Of the alternatives: (a) "we can be charged with something and cannot refute it," or (b) "although we have done nothing wrong we are in danger of being accused of riot," the former suits the suggestion that the entire undertaking is improper and should be terminated forthwith. Omission of the negative is preferable.[123] The difficulties may be due to the author's attempts at style.[124]

From the official's words, one would gather that a formal debate has taken place, with denunciation of Gaius and Aristarchus ("these men" [v. 37]), but the narrative has left no room for such activity—and with reason. The underlying logic of the piece is that of the American defense of the status quo: "if it ain't broke, don't fix it." The technique is ethos,[125] which, in the same spirit, may be summarized here as "because I say so." One of the things he says is that Artemis requires no repair. Another is that "these people" are innocent of religious crimes. Demetrius and his colleagues, who suddenly reappear, at least in name, are, it scarcely need be said, welcome to pursue any issues they may have in the courts or in a duly convened assembly.[126] The implication is that this assembly is unlawful.[127] Rather than worry about the scenario offered by Demetrius, the good citizens of Ephesus will do well to contemplate the real and present danger[128] presented by Rome, which is not prepared to let Greek cities act as if they were still independent political entities and whose rulers have trouble distinguishing democracy from anarchy. Events such as those that have occurred on this day (v. 40) will do nothing to dispel the notion that popular assemblies are licenses for revolt and disorder (*στάσις, συστροφή* [v. 40]). The secretary's viewpoint was echoed by Plutarch, who took the opportunity to remind Greeks that Rome held all the high cards:

> You must say to yourself: "You who rule are a subject, ruling a state controlled by proconsuls, the agents of Caesar. . . . You should arrange your cloak more carefully and from the office of the generals keep your eyes upon the orators' platform, and not have great pride or confidence in your crown, since you see the boots [of the Roman soldiers] just above your head.[129]

These were not isolated sentiments.[130] Gamaliel had reminded the Sanhedrin of the dangers of being on

122 Metzger, *Textual Commentary*, 420.

123 See the discussion of Barrett, 2:938–40.

124 Luke's genitive absolutes are often difficult. The repeated preposition *περί* ("about") may be an attempt at anaphora.

125 So Kennedy (*Rhetorical Criticism*, 132), who offers a formal analysis. On the formal qualities, see also Soards, *Speeches*, 103–4. The speech is too brief to offer more than a skeleton structure.

126 In modern terms, "let them resort to due process" (Fitzmyer, 661).

127 On the term "lawful/regular" assembly (*ἔννομος* or *νόμιμος ἐκκλησία*), see Chariton *Chaer.* 1.11–12. The latter adjective (as in Acts) is found in three inscriptions from Ephesus (*I. Eph.* 115, 212, 602), but the former is much more common elsewhere. Cf. also Lucian *Deor. conc.* 14.

128 3 Macc 5:41 refers to "disturbance" (*συστροφαῖς*) and "be in danger" (*κινδυνεύει*) to describe the situation in Alexandria.

129 Plutarch *Praec. ger. rei publ.* 17 (*Mor.* 813a), trans. H. N. Fowler, *Plutarch's Moralia X* (LCL; Cambridge, Mass.: Harvard University Press, 1936) 237. (The words in brackets are supplied by the translator and thus marked.) C. P. Jones holds that the shoes of the proconsul are in view (*Plutarch and Rome* [Oxford: Clarendon, 1971] 133). The continuation is also of interest for vv. 35-40: What is the most important task of the contemporary magistrate? The avoidance, or suppression, of civil strife (*στάσις*). What else? "[A]ways to instill concord (*ὁμόνοιαν*) and friendship in those who dwell together with him and to remove strifes, discords, and all enmity?" Resolutions and edicts can be annulled at the touch of a proconsular finger (Plutarch *Mor.* 824C–F, trans Fowler, 293).

130 Following a riot over bread prices in Prusa, Dio reminded his native city that the proconsuls have watchful eyes upon them (*Or.* 46.14; for evidence that he was right, see Pliny *Ep.* 10). *Or.* 48.1–3 instructs those citizens on how to behave in the presence of the proconsul: decently and in good order. *Or.* 34 takes up disorder at Tarsus in which a guild (evidently) of "linen workers" played a large part. He warns that, if the local government does not attend to a situation, Rome will do so (cf. 34.21; 38). On the connection between Plutarch's remarks and Dio's speeches, see Geoffrey E. M. de Ste. Croix, *The Class Struggle in the Ancient World* (Ithaca: Cornell University Press, 1981) 310–13. On the fate of cities that did not heed such advice and the evolution of city status under the empire, see

the wrong side of God (5:34-39).[131] The secretary does not propose that the wrath of their patron goddess will fall upon wrongdoers, but he does call attention to the potential weight of those Roman boots. As in the experience with Gallio (18:12-17), albeit more decisively so, Paul and the movement enjoy vindication while the opponents are discomfited. If any charges of rioting are to be made, Ephesian devotees of Artemis rather than the followers of Paul will be the target.[132]

The social setting envisioned by Plutarch is the civic assembly, quite possibly in a theater. If circuses helped keep the public distracted, they also gave them opportunity to feel and exercise their power. "Power to the people" was not a slogan of which the ruling aristocracy approved.[133] "All Rome gathered to the Palace and the squares, and overflowing into the circus and theatres, where the mob can demonstrate with the greater impunity, raised a seditious clamour."[134] That impunity was far from absolute, witness the loss of rights or, perhaps even worse, the sponsorship of games some cities experienced as a result of disorder.[135] The behavior of the Ephesian populace was both mindless and self-destructive.[136] Like Philo and Josephus, Luke blames the mob for disturbances involving their religions.

Since the author composed this speech for the readers of the book, attempts to justify its appeal to the dramatic audience are unnecessary.[137] Shauf, for example, holds that the speech was "convincing" for the audience.[138] All that was convincing, however, was the authority of this official, who told the crowd to shut up and leave. Like other magistrates earlier and later, the secretary declares Paul innocent. For the alert reader, this verdict is a bit difficult to swallow; it is at least equally difficult to imagine that the dramatic audience would have happily digested it,[139] but both of these difficulties are minor in comparison to the basis of the assertion of innocence, which requires omniscience.[140] Since it would have been simple enough for the narrator to summarize a number of false or transparently ambiguous charges, as in other situations,[141] the absence of accusations is intentional. The episode contains two brief speeches and one non-speech. An agitator delivers the first, with incendiary effect. The elected official plays the role of firefighter. His speech foreshadows the apologetic addresses of Paul that will dominate chaps. 21–26.[142] The crowd's refusal to hear a Jewish apology is equally telling.

ibid., 304, and A. H. M. Jones, *The Greek City from Alexander to Justinian* (Oxford: Clarendon, 1940) 129–46. For more detail, see Pervo, "Meet Right," 53–55. *Ethiopian Story* 8.9 provides a fictional parallel.

131 This speech, like that of Gamaliel, contains two conditional clauses in vv. 38-39, linked with μὲν . . . δέ (Greek particles used to balance constructions).

132 To this extent, the thesis of Stoops ("Riot") is valid. For criticism of details, see Shauf, *Theology*, 260 n. 460.

133 A speech put into the mouth of Maecenas by Cassius Dio (52.30.2) recommends to Augustus that the people (δῆμος) should not only lack sovereignty but should not even be allowed to meet in assemblies (ἐκκλησία).

134 Tacitus *Hist.* 1.72 (death of Tigellinus under Otho), trans. K. Wellesley, *Tacitus: The Histories* (London: Penguin, 1964) 65.

135 Tacitus refers to a serious fight that broke out in the Pompeian amphitheater in 59 (*Ann.* 14.17). Rivalry between Pompeii and Nuceria was the cause of this outbreak, which resulted in the amphitheater being closed for a decade. The brawl is depicted in a large mural painting in the house of the gladiator Actius Anecetus.

136 For examples, see MacMullen, *Enemies*, 168–73.

137 So also Cunningham, *Tribulations*, 265.

138 Shauf, *Theology*, 257. He summarizes research on pp. 254–58.

139 Shauf (*Theology*, 258) says, "The pagan rabble goes home defeated and shamefaced." Defeated, certainly, but if the critic is to assign them logical emotions, anger would be a better conjecture. Shauf is correct in conveying the narrator's intention, which is not based on historical plausibility.

140 Readers can justify the verdict of v. 37 only on the most narrow and technical grounds. Acquittal of sacrilege against the temple (ἱεροσύλους) is gratuitous. The charge of "blasphemy" or "defamation" can be excused only on the grounds that Paul (together with Gaius and Aristarchus?) only spoke about images in general and did not single out Artemis for attention.

141 E.g., Stephen (6:8-14); Paul in Philippi (16:21), Thessalonica (17:6-7), Corinth (18:13), and Jerusalem (21:28).

142 Cf. Haenchen, 579.

The discussion of sources included the observation that Luke did not require sources for the depiction of a riot. Support for this view emerges in one of the more important internal parallels in Acts: 21:27-36. These two "riots" are similar in setting, development, and vocabulary, although not in outcome.[143] Both involve accusations by Ephesians against Paul's teaching (19:25-27; 21:28). His attacks on a temple have an international impact (19:26; 21:28). In both stories, the accusations spark shouts that rouse the entire city (19:28-29; 21:28, 30), lead to apprehension(s) (19:29; 21:31), and require official intervention (19:35-40; 21:31-32). The common vocabulary is notable,[144] and the theme is identical: "[M]embers of an established religion are protesting the effect that Paul's mission is having on their religion and temple."[145] The two scenes "are to be regarded as parallel compositions."[146]

Several conclusions are possible. In the unfolding plot, the crescendo is building: Paul has eluded every riot thus far with no more than a whipping and a night in jail. Tension and suspense increase. Ephesus is to Jerusalem as 5:17-42 (the Twelve) was to 6:8–7:60 (Stephen).[147] There is also a personal link: Ephesian Jews will succeed where Demetrius failed. The narrator associates Paul's greatest success with his final arrest. Furthermore, one must ask whether the similarity of these two episodes does not lend support to the view that "the Way" was (destined to be) a distinct religion. Both the Jews who venerated their temple in Jerusalem and those gentiles who honored Artemis with her temple at Ephesus viewed Paul as public enemy number one. Although this inference is not without subtlety and a certain irony, it may not have seemed particularly subtle or ironic to those of Luke's day, who read Acts in the light of Jewish riots and revolts and in the knowledge that their splendid temple had long lain in ruins.[148]

Paul's experiences in the temple and thereafter are modeled upon those of Jesus,[149] supporting the observation that Acts 19 is an epitome of the career of Paul, which echoes that of Jesus and of the Jerusalem community, as the points of similarity with chaps. 1–8 have intimated.[150] "Beginning from the baptism of John" (cf. Luke 3:1-20; Acts 1:21, etc.), as it were, proceeding to proclamation in the synagogue (cf. Luke 4:16-30)[151] and a career mighty in word and deed (cf. Luke 24:19; Acts 19:8-12), Paul followed the paths of Jesus and Peter. To foreshadow Paul's "passion," there is the mob scene in vv. 23-40, which ends, like the account of Paul's trials (19:31; 26:31-32), with the judgment of high-placed persons that he is guiltless. One objection to this proposal, the essential absence of Paul as a direct actor from 19:10 onwards,[152] establishes the central thesis: even after his "departure" (20:29) Paul remains a vital force in Ephesus. This thesis, the essence of Deutero-Paulinism, is most evident in the collection, study, and composition of Pauline epistles, of which Ephesus was probably the central location. For Luke, the primary concern was to portray Paul as an ally of the Jerusalem apostles and a selfless martyr in the quest for unity and opposition to views he regarded as deviant and destructive. Words there have been, and the most important are yet to come (20:17-38), but deeds have equal value, as example, symbol, and inspiration. The garments of Paul retain their power to "heal" believers in Ephesus (cf. 19:11-12); demons of disunity flee at the name of the Jesus whom he proclaims (cf. 19:13-17); his teaching purges vulgar superstition (cf. 19:18-20); and the doctrines of this philosopher pose no threat to the ruling power (cf. 19:35-40). Indeed, his message will help fashion some of the less-tractable elements of the Greek east into good subjects. Anyone who helps rid the community of pernicious magical practices and exploitative practitioners of

143 See, in particular, Tannehill, *Narrative Unity*, 2:242–43. Note also Cunningham, *Tribulations*, 266.

144 See pp. 548–53.

145 Tannehill, *Narrative Unity*, 2:242.

146 Cunningham, *Tribulations*, 266.

147 As noted above, the Secretary resembles Gamaliel.

148 The foremost irony is that Paul was duly worshiping at Jerusalem when apprehended, and the lead subtlety is that the charges of both sets of opponents contain more truth than the narrative concedes.

149 See Table 6, p. 533.

150 Rackham, 356.

151 See p. 494 n. 77.

152 Acts 19:21-22 is an exception, but it deals with future plans. In vv. 30-31 Paul does not act.

religion deserves admiration from those who govern. The friendship extended by some Asiarchs indicates that they took this point.

Alternative models were becoming available, including radical Paulinists who would obliterate any links between Christianity and its Israelite heritage, others who would appropriate the apostle as an authority for Valentinian and other "Gnostic" movements, and those who showcased Paul as an enemy of the Roman order. For many—but far from all—believers, Ephesus was the capital of Paulinism and Paul the font of Ephesian Christianity.[153] Acts 19 enthrones the Paul of Acts in the metropolis of Asia. His mission in the Greek east is complete. Luke will devote a chapter to Paul the pastor, before turning to the subject of Paul the prisoner.

153 Even Revelation, which derives from Ephesus, reveals Pauline influence and begins with seven letters to seven churches.

20

20:1-38 Paul's Departure from Asia

1/ **Once the uproar had died down, Paul summoned the followers for an uplifting farewell speech before setting out for Macedonia.[a] 2/ He traveled through those regions, delivering many an uplifting message,[b] arriving eventually in Greece, 3/ where he spent three months. As he was about to take ship for Syria, a Jewish plot against him led to a change of plans,[c] and he returned by way of Macedonia. 4/ Associated with him were Sopater the son of Pyrrhus, from Beroea; Aristarchus and Secundus, both Thessalonians; Gaius of Derbe; Timothy; and the Asians Tychicus and Trophimus. 5/ They had gone ahead[d] and were awaiting us in Troas. 6/ We sailed from Philippi after the Days of Unleavened Bread and joined them in Troas five days later. There we remained for a week.**

7/ **While we were gathered on the first day[e] of the week for the breaking of bread, Paul addressed them. Since he intended to leave the next day, he extended his sermon until midnight. 8/ The lamps[f] in the upper room where we were meeting were numerous, 9/ and a young man named Eutychus, who was sitting on the windowsill, got more and more drowsy as Paul talked on and on.[g] Eventually he fell sound asleep and plunged three floors to the ground. When picked up he was found to be dead,[h] 10/ but Paul descended, threw himself upon him, and embraced him. "Stop your fuss," he said. "He's alive." 11/ Paul went back upstairs to break the bread, eat, and continue conversing at length until daybreak, at which time he left.[i] 12/ To the immense relief of everyone, they took the boy away alive.**

13/ **We,[j] meanwhile, had gone ahead[k] to the ship and sailed for Assos,[l] where we intended to take Paul on board, for he had told us to do so,[m] intending to travel by land, himself.[n] 14/ He did meet us at Assos, so we took him aboard and went on**

a In place of the rather curt μεταπέμπω for "summon" are two stylistic variants in the tradition. The D-Text (Boismard, *Texte*, 328) avoids repeating the verb παρακαλέω ("comfort"), which appears in the next verse by having Paul deliver "numerous orders" (πολλὰ παρακελεύσας) and omits the more or less gratuitous πορεύεσθαι ("travel").

b The D-Text adds, typically, "all those regions." In place of the participle παρακαλέσας ("console"), the D-Text (Boismard, *Texte*, 328) apparently reads χρησάμενος and omits "them." This participial phrase, which means something like "making substantial use of speech," is so unusual that it deserves consideration. If it is unlikely to be original, it is equally difficult to understand why an editor selected it.

c On the expression "change of plan" (ἐγένετο γνώμης), see BDF §162 (7). The genitive amounts to a predication: Paul devised this plan. The following genitive articular infinitive is unusual. See Moule, *Idiom Book*, 129. BDF §400 (7) is content to call it "pleonastic."

d The verb προέρχομαι ("go ahead") is preferred on the grounds of common sense to the better attested προσέρχομαι ("go on").

e Lit. "[day] one." Substitution of cardinal for ordinal numbers is common in vernacular Greek, especially biblical Greek.

f The ὑπολάμπαδες of Bezae could mean "little windows," but d has *faculae* ("torches"), a meaning attested also in Greek: BDAG, 1038, *s.v.* One example is *Jos. Asen.* 14:9. This word has the benefit of rarity (and was preferred by Zuntz: Metzger, *Textual Commentary*, 422) but is probably a "realistic" correction. The space was too small for many large lamps. This, in turn, supports the view that the lamps are not simply a realistic detail. See below.

g D reads ". . . **in** the window, **possessed** (κατεχόμενος) by deep sleep." The phrase is not idiomatic Greek according to Cadbury and Lake, 256.

h D* makes the final words a relative clause καὶ ὅς ἤρθη νεκρός ("and who was found to be dead").

i BDF §425 (6). This is the only instance cited as an example of "the classical liberty to use οὕτως ("so," "thus") to summarize the content of a preceding participial construction."

j Ephrem and the Armenian catena evidently read: "I, Luke, and those who were with me went on board. . . ." According to Ropes (*Text*, 442–43), R. Harris thought that this was the original D-Text. This is unlikely. It reflects a time when Luke's authorship was taken for granted. Ropes (*Text*, 443 n. 1) observes that the catena and Chrysostom stress Paul's frequent separation from his companions.

k As elsewhere, there are variants for προελθόντες ("go ahead"), none of greatly differing meaning.

to Mytilene. 15/ From there we sailed on the following day[o] to a point opposite Chios, and on the next we crossed to Samos, arriving in Miletus the day after,[p] 16/ for Paul had decided to sail past Ephesus, so that, if the possibility permitted, he would not spend too much time in Asia.[q] He was in a hurry to be in Jerusalem at Pentecost,[r] if that were at all possible. 17/ He did, however, send a message from Miletus to Ephesus, directing the presbyters of that church to report to him. 18/ When they had arrived, he addressed them:

"You[s] know well how I spent my time while I was with you, from the very first day that I set foot in Asia,[t] 19/ how I served the Lord without asserting my privileges, in misfortunes that make grown men cry and the frustrations brought about by Jewish machinations, 20/ how I never avoided saying whatever was beneficial for you or from teaching both in public and in private.[u] 21/ I urged Jews and Greeks alike to redirect their lives Godward and to place their trust in our Lord Jesus.[v]

22/ "Now, as to what lies before us. Firstly, the Spirit compels me to go to Jerusalem. What might happen to me there I do not know.[w] 23/ What I do know is that in city after city[x] the Holy Spirit discloses that arrest and afflictions loom before me.[y] 24/ But continued existence has no value for me beyond completing my task,[z] which is the ministry that I received from the Lord Jesus: to make God's gracious message manifest.

25/ "Secondly, I am aware that not one of you among whom I went about proclaiming God's reign will ever see my face again. 26/ I therefore swear to you on this very day that I am not responsible for the loss of anyone, 27/ for I have proclaimed to you, with no reservation or qualification, the entirety of God's will. 28/ Be attentive to yourselves and attend to the all the flock in which the

Cadbury and Lake (257) prefer προσελθόντες, viewing the other as an emendation. Barrett (2:957), however, prefers the shorter form.

l "Thasos," an island in the northwest Aegean, is a variant in some strands of the D-Text (e.g., 614, Chrysostom) and other traditions (e.g., L Ψ).

m *Or:* "for so he had arranged."

n D *pc* read ὡς μέλλων ("as he intended"), a classical construction. On this, see Barrett, 2:957.

o Instead of "other" (for "next," ἑτέρᾳ), "evening" (ἑσπέρᾳ) is read by a range of witnesses. Cadbury and Lake (258) view this as both "attractive" and a probable error.

p D m gig sy sa and Ψ add καὶ μείναντες ἐν Τρωγυλλίῳ ("and stopping at Trogyllium"). This is a logical addition. See Ramsay, *Church*, 155. Ropes (*Text*, 195) suspects that this is original, since he can find no motive for adding it, although motive for deletion is equally wanting. One difficulty is the interpretation of παρεβάλομεν. See Cadbury and Lake, 258; and Barrett, 2:958, who sees "reach" and "pass by" as alternatives. He suggests that the editor of D misunderstood it as "pass by" and so cooked up Trogyllium. This is not a likely reconstruction. One may argue the opposite with stronger force: without the participial phrase the verb is understood as "reach." Günther Zuntz (*Opuscula Selecta: Classica, Hellenistica, Christiana* [Manchester: Manchester University Press, 1972] 199) opposes this interpretation on stylistic and geographical grounds. See also Metzger (*Textual Commentary*, 423–24), who finds a decision difficult and relies upon external evidence.

q The D-Text (Boismard, *Texte*, 332) clarifies the phrase: "in order that he might experience no delay" (μήποτε γενήθη αὐτῷ κατάσχεσις) and eliminate the reference to possibility. This is a pious deletion based on the presumption that Paul acted in accordance to divine guidance in fulfillment of the divine plan. Chance is excluded.

r On the temporal accusative here, equivalent to the dative, see Cadbury and Lake, 259; and BDF §161.3.

s "You" is emphatic.

t The D-Text (Boismard, *Texte*, 333) adds the traditional "brothers" and after the first line, ὁμόσε ὄντων αὐτῶν (perhaps, "when they were all together"). This looks like filler—did the editor really wish to reassure the reader that Paul did not begin before all had arrived? Does this emphasize the general and public character of his message (cf. v. 20)? E and some others prefer the cliché ὁμοθυμαδόν ("with one accord," which looks like an improvement of this phrase. After "Asia," the text adds "**for three years or even more I was with**

Holy Spirit has placed you as 'bishops'[aa] charged to shepherd the church of God, which was acquired by the death of God's own. 29/ I know[bb] that after my departure vicious wolves will fall upon you.[cc] They will show no mercy to the flock. 30/ Moreover, from your very midst will arise some who will distort the message in an attempt to get the followers to accept their leadership.[dd] 31/ You must therefore maintain constant vigilance. Keep my example in mind, how for three years I constantly and tearfully issued warnings to all.[ee]

32/ **"Finally, I entrust you to the gracious message of God,[ff] which has the power to build you up and give you what is in store for all of God's own. 33/ I have had no designs upon anyone's money or personal property.[gg] 34/ You well know that I have met all of my own needs and those of my companions with these very hands. 35/ I have served as an example of how we are to care for those who require assistance: by hard work. Remember what the Lord Jesus said: 'Giving brings more happiness than does receiving.'**

36/ **When Paul had finished, he knelt[hh] and prayed with the entire group. 37/ They all wept without restraint and embraced him with repeated kisses, 38/ terribly grieved because he had said that they would never see him again. They then escorted him to the ship.[ii]**

you . . . ." This anticipates and makes an inclusion with v. 31. In addition, there are some minor paraphrases, three of which reflect "better" Greek. On πῶς ἐγενόμην ("how/that . . . I was"), see BDF §434 (2). On the two prepositional phrases beginning with "from" (ἀπό), see Barrett, 2:966-67.

u The D-Text omits (Boismard, *Texte*, 333) the negative μή before the infinitive, possibly because of a danger that it would be misunderstood. More interesting is the omission of "you" as the object of "teach," perhaps because, strictly construed, it would limit Paul's teaching to this audience.

v "Christ" is a common variant of the "orthodox" type.

w The D-Text offers several minor changes, eliminating ἰδοῦ ("look") and paraphrasing the two final participles (Boismard, *Texte*, 334). These exemplify the "copy editing" function of this tradition.

x D gig (vg) sy Lcf have "every city."

y The D-Text (Boismard, *Texte*, 335) places the oracle in direct speech ("you" instead of "me") and adds "in Jerusalem" at the close. See Epp, *Tendency*, 129.

z Alternatives to ὡς are ὥστε and ἕως, ὅπως. On the use of ὡς to express purpose see BDF §391 (1, 3). There is strong support, including ℵ and B, for the subjunctive τελειώσω ("finish"), with no important difference in meaning. After "my course" a range of witnesses add "with joy."

aa *Or:* "as guardians" or "overseers."

bb B begins with ὅτι ("because"), and a range of witnesses add γάρ ("for" [conj.]). These additions make the link between vv. 28a and 29 clearer.

cc The D-Text (Boismard, *Texte*, 337) omits "upon you."

dd The variant ἀποστρέφειν ("turn from"), found in some D-witnesses, substitutes a more familiar verb for ἀποσπάω used here for the attraction of proselytes.

ee The D-Text once more (cf. v. 26) adds "of you" (Boismard, *Texte*, 337), personalizing the sentence and thus limiting its timeless and general purpose.

ff Witnesses exhibit the customary option of "God" or "the Lord." Metzger (*Textual Commentary*, 427) says that external evidence supports "God." Barrett (2:980) suggests that 7:59 is the basis for "Lord."

gg The D-Text (Boismard, *Texte*, 338) removes any personal target: "I have **not** desired silver, gold, and clothing," replacing "or" with "and" and dropping "no one." This derives from reading οὐδενός as an adjective and revising accordingly. Cadbury and Lake (262) prefer this understanding.

hh The idiom for "kneel" (θεὶς τὰ γόνατα, lit. "placing the knees") is, according to Moule (*Idiom Book*, 192), a Latinism found in Mark 15:19, once in Luke, and four times in Acts (e.g., 7:60). The most important of these, noted by Johnson (366), is Luke 22:41. After his final speech, Jesus prayed.

ii Boismard (*Texte*, 339) omits "terribly grieved" and transforms the sentiment into direct speech: "especially [ ] because he said, 'You will never again see my face.'" Editors, notably those who produced the D-Text, increased the amount of direct speech in Acts. Boismard's D-Text also changes the final phrase "as far as the ship," perhaps so that readers will not conclude that they boarded it.

Analysis

Acts 20 begins the story of Paul's fateful last journey to Jerusalem. The focus is on his pastoral role, both in direct ministry to the faithful (vv. 7-12)[1] and as a leader of leaders (vv. 18-35). This is artistic. Paul had performed such functions earlier, but emphasis on them suits the plot at this point. The entire chapter treats Paul's legacy for later generations of Asian believers. He is not here the missionary who wins believers by preaching, but the pastor who serves as model for nurture through word and deed. A cardinal element of that nurture is resistance to false teaching. "Deed" is showcased in the charming episode in Troas, while his discourse to the Ephesian elders exemplifies his "word." Pathos is pervasive,[2] and the atmosphere is generally sober and, toward the close, foreboding (cf. also 19:20-21). Luke has effectively created a new character: The Paul who has hitherto outwitted wily opponents and shrugged off injury and indignity is now a victim commanding sympathy, a tireless worker who labored with his own hands to support himself and others while working sleeplessly to assist his converts, despite "Jewish plots" and other outrages.

Verses 7-12 are, it will be argued, probably a Lucan creation, inspired by the LXX. Luke also composed the speech of vv. 17-35, drawing deeply on Paul's letters. The general framework, with its apparently gratuitous details about travel—details that also serve the plot—derives from source material. The source was, according to the hypothesis of this commentary,[3] a letter about the delivery of the collection, written by those who accompanied Paul on this mission, or by Paul and his colleagues. The "we," which once more enters without preparation (v. 5),[4] probably derives from that source. Another feature may be dating by the Jewish calendar (20:6, 16),[5] a system also congenial to Luke. The original extent of this hypothetical source is unknown. One can do no more than identify tentatively portions that Luke chose to extract and utilize, with revision. One of those revisions was deletion of the purpose for which this journey was undertaken. If logic is a valid criterion, the first trace of this source is in v. 4: the letter began with the start of the journey.[6] Verses 1b-3 could derive from known correspondence.[7] The last clear traces are in 21:18 (19), where the "we" disappears.[8]

Comment

■ **1-6** These verses are unified insofar as they narrate the fulfillment of the journey contemplated in 19:21. Removal of the purpose makes the details somewhat

1 Note the use of παρακαλέω ("comfort") in the pastoral sense: vv. 1, 2, and 12; cf. 11:23; 14:22; 15:32; 16:39-40. On this, see also Tannehill, *Narrative Unity*, 2:246.

2 On the pathos of chaps. 20–21, see Pervo, *Profit*, 67–68. Cadbury (*Making,* 238) bestows high praise on this scene.

3 See pp. 12–14.

4 See the excursus "'We' in Acts" in the commentary on 16:10.

5 Cf. also 27:14. Acts 20:16 is, however, open to question. See below. Haenchen (587–88) notes these features: fondness for the imperfect, εἰς for ἐν ("into" meaning "in"), and the later form of the name Mitylene. BDF §261 (2) observes that the use of the article with place-names is common in the travel passages of Acts, contrary to usage elsewhere.

6 "Greece" (Ἑλλάς) rather than "Achaea" is a popular usage that conforms to neither Luke nor Paul. See Joachim Wanke, "Ἑλλάς," *EDNT* 1:435.

7 Luke also had access to data from known epistles: 1 Cor 16:1-8; 2 Cor 2:12-13; 7:5-7; Rom 15:25-26.

8 Presumably this continued with the rejection of the

mysterious, raising suspense.[9] Literally construed, v. 1 indicates that, once the crowd had been sent away from the theater, Paul met with the believers and then departed forthwith. This is the result of narrative compression. Time would be required to arrange such a gathering, let alone a space of sufficient size. The narrator wishes to provide direct assurance that Paul did not leave without a proper farewell and indirect evidence that the disturbance did not impede his action.[10]

Three months' stay in Achaea was a long time, probably a winter, one would gather from v. 6, and long enough to stoke the fires of conspiracy.[11] The specter of a "Jewish plot" prepares the way for v. 19 (although that seems to have specific reference to Asia, where no such plots were reported), succinctly reminds readers of the difficulties under which Paul must labor, and neatly finesses the difficulty of suppressing the purpose. In Acts, a Jewish plot replaces the delivery of Paul's Collection.[12] The evident meaning is that Paul changed his mode of travel because it would have been difficult to hide aboard a ship.[13] Paul's Jewish adversaries, thwarted hitherto, have not abandoned their ambitions. His plans must change.

The D-Text did not so interpret the change of plans and revised v. 3: ". . . Jewish plot . . . he **wished** to sail to Syria, **but the Spirit told him** to return via Macedonia. 4. **As he was about to leave** . . ." This suggests that Paul decided to leave because of the plot and that the Spirit changed the itinerary.[14] As a result of this change, the D-Text has the party accompany Paul from Achaea "as far as Asia," rather than precede him to Troas. Consequently, all await "him" rather than "us" in v. 5. This unsuccessful effort to extract clarity from a somewhat oblique phrase shows the lengths to which the editor(s) of the D-Text were willing to go to rationalize the narrative.[15] For the readers this is but one more Jewish attempt on Paul's life skillfully evaded (cf., e.g., 9:23-25, 29-30; 23:12-35). Little will be gained by asking why these enemies did not display more flexibility and finesse. The audience would be free to imagine the conspirators waiting until nightfall away from land to begin their fruitless search for Paul (the others were of no account) only to discover themselves at sea, literally and figuratively.

■ **4** Paul had followers. In this he was not alone. Jesus also had followers who accompanied him on his final journey. Lists of names in Acts presage important moments in the narrative (1:13; 6:5; 13:1). A list of seven foreshadowed the Diaspora mission; this list of seven reflects its conclusion, supplying Paul with an entourage representative of the regions in which he has labored.[16] "At the peak of his activity, surrounded by numerous attendants, the Apostle sets out on this last journey to Jerusalem."[17]

---

collection and Paul's response, which evidently led to his arrest.

9 Johnson (357) notes that the absence of a reason for the expedition enhances the similarity to Jesus' final journey.

10 The historian, who presumes imprisonment and/or a major calamity, finds the language a bit disconcerting and asks whether a longer period of time is in view. (That is, v. 1 by itself could imply a disturbance that lasted for some days.) This was not Luke's intention.

11 The ship would have left Cenchreae (cf. 18:18). A winter's residence at Corinth was probably derived from 1 Cor 16:18.

12 The idea of a Jewish conspiracy may have come from Rom 15:30-32.

13 For one means, see Lucian *Alex.* 56; and Pervo, *Profit*, 150 n. 69. Ramsay (*St. Paul the Traveller*, 287) proposes that this was a pilgrim ship bound for Jerusalem.

14 Attributing plans to inspiration is typical of the D-Text. The *Acts of Paul* will do much to satisfy the desire for such guidance.

15 Boismard, *Texte*, 328–29. See the lucid explanation of the D-Text by Ropes, *Text*, 190–91. Cadbury and Lake (253) observe that the problem was lack of clarity regarding the composition of the group or groups.

16 Tannehill, *Narrative Unity*, 2:246; cf. also Rackham, 375.

17 F. Overbeck, cited by Haenchen, 581.

Excursus: The Seven of Acts 20:4[18]

The list, which quite probably derives from a written source,[19] includes three representatives from Macedonia (Sopater of Beroea and two from Thessalonica—Aristarchus and Secundus), two from "South Galatia" (Gaius and Timothy, of Derbe and Lystra,[20] respectively), and two from Asia (Tychicus and Trophimus). The name of Timothy, mentioned here for the final time in Acts, appears eighteen times in the Pauline correspondence and Hebrews, including Rom 16:21, which places him with Paul in Corinth at the time this journey got under way. Three, Sopater, Secundus, and Gaius, are mentioned nowhere else in the NT.[21]

Aristarchus appears in Phlm 24||Col 4:10 and thus belongs to the undisputed Pauline tradition. His name emerged in 19:29 and will reappear in 27:2. Trophimus features in 21:29 as a gentile allegedly introduced into the temple.[22] 2 Tim 4:20 reports that Paul left him ill in Miletus. This is a fiction.[23] Tychicus plays an active role in the Deutero-Pauline tradition: Col 4:7-9||Eph 6:21-22; 2 Tim 4:12; Titus 3:12.[24] The two Asians and Aristarchus may have been well known in Ephesus and may have played a role in maintaining and transmitting the Pauline legacy.

Speculation has been rife. Sopater has been identified, since the appearance of the D-Text,[25] with the "Sosipater" of Rom 16:21.[26] That would place him in Corinth at the right time.[27] Given Luke's tendency to use slightly different names (e.g., Silas, Priscilla) for persons mentioned in the Pauline correspondence, this is a possibility.[28] Many of the names on the list have been proposed as possible candidates for the unnamed believer of 2 Cor 8:18-19. The D-Text says that Gaius was from Douberios, a Macedonian town.[29] This would identify him with the Gaius of 19:29, a clearly harmonizing alteration that disrupts the symmetry of the list.[30]

Scholarly consensus views these persons as delegates bearing the collection for Jerusalem.[31] This raises some questions about the list. The absence of Cyprus is no surprise and is another indication of its vague standing as a Pauline missionary site. The lack of representatives from Philippi and Corinth is, however, difficult to understand,[32] and one may ask why

18 For a detailed discussion of these persons see Wolf-Henning Ollrog, *Paulus und seine Mitarbeiter* (WMANT 50; Neukirchen-Vluyn: Neukirchener Verlag, 1979) 45–58. Note also Hemer (*Book*, 236), who gives evidence of geographical suitability.

19 The hypothetical Collection Source, on which see pp. 12–14. On the likelihood that it comes from written rather than oral tradition, see Rudolf Bultmann, "Zur Frage nach den Quellen der Apostelgeschichte," in idem, *Exegetica* (ed. Erich Dinkler; Tübingen: Mohr Siebeck, 1967) 412–23, esp. 418–19.

20 Acts 16:1 is not unambiguous about Timothy's residence.

21 This presumes that efforts to harmonize Gaius of Derbe with the Macedonian Gaius of Acts 19:29 are erroneous (see below). The *Ap. Const.* 7.46 report that Gaius of Derbe was the first bishop of Pergamum. Secundus reappears in the D-Text of 27:2 (*q.v.*).

22 The name indicates probable servile origin: a house-born slave. See *NewDocs* 3 (1983) no. 80, pp. 91–93.

23 See Dibelius and Conzelmann, *Pastoral Epistles*, 125.

24 The name Tychicus generally indicated servile origin: *NewDocs* 2 (1982) no. 86, p. 109; and Hemer, *Book*, 236.

25 Boismard, *Texte*, 329—although the D tradition is mixed.

26 E.g., Deissmann, *Light*, 437–38. See Keith Nickle, *The Collection: A Study in Paul's Strategy* (SBT 48; Naperville, Ill.: Allenson, 1966) 68 n. 78.

27 This claim, which also applies to Timothy, presumes that Romans 16 was written from Corinth not long before the beginning of the journey to deliver the collection.

28 The omission of the patronymic "son of Pyrrhus" (m sy) was probably the result of a desire for symmetry (none of the other names includes affiliation). Ropes's proposal (*Text*, 191) that it derives from πατρος in his name is less likely.

29 Boismard, *Texte*, 329.

30 See Haenchen, 52–53. The D-Text also replaces "Asians" with "Ephesians" (previous note), obliterating a Lucan trope while restoring consistency, since only names of cities are used otherwise. Bezae reads "Eutychus." Cadbury and Lake (254) ask whether Tychicus may not be an emendation from Col 4:7. This does not seem as likely an error—it is difficult to imagine identity of this person with the "youth" of vv. 7-12, who is freshly introduced.

31 E.g., Haenchen, 581; and Witherington, 603. The omissions lead Lüdemann (*Acts*, 269) to dissent. He attributes the list to those who worked with Paul in Troas and environs.

32 See Dieter Georgi, *Remembering the Poor: The History of Paul's Collection for Jerusalem* (Nashville: Abingdon, 1992) 123.

no representatives from the addressees of Galatians are mentioned (cf. 1 Cor 16:1).[33] The list is evidently incomplete.[34] The absence of Titus is probably due to Lucan *damnatio memoriae*, and Timothy (presuming his presence[35]) was not the representative of a community but a Pauline co-worker.[36] The membership of "we" adds another note of uncertainty. Luke very likely derived these names from a source—the Collection Source—but it is not possible to determine what alterations he made. He may have wished to limit the number to the symbolically satisfying seven.[37]

■ **5** The pronoun "we" unexpectedly returns. This constitutes another bracket framing the Aegean mission of Paul, for the first plural was last heard from in Philippi (16:17).[38] "We" here also shares another typical property: it is customary in travel accounts.[39] Formally, this "we" excludes both Paul and the seven persons of v. 4. This may have been accidental, but the result is to reduce any sense of authority.[40] Tannehill describes its function: "'we' as fellow travelers both share Paul's experience and receive his legacy as he travels toward his passion."[41] "We" will endure until 21:18. Although it evidently comes from a source, the author has integrated it into the account, even granting it the privilege of omniscience in vv. 9-11.

■ **6** The verse brings about the reunion of the separated components of the delegation in Troas.[42]

Troas,[43] a Hellenistic foundation later named "Alexandria," with the designator "Troas" to acknowledge the proximity of Troy, was customarily known only by the epithet after Augustus gave it colonial status: Colonia Augusta Troadensium.[44] Its importance as a hub of transit and communication can be seen from references in early Christian literature.[45] Acts does not describe the foundation of the community at Troas. Perhaps this fell within the scope of 19:10.[46] The reference to Passover not only indicates Jewish piety (against 21:21) but also evokes death, specifically the "passions" of Jesus (Luke 22:1) and Peter (Acts 12:3).[47] The seven-day halt (cf.

33 Supporters of the "South Galatian" hypothesis (that Galatians was addressed to the communities discussed in Acts 13–14) will probably regard Gaius and Timothy as support for this interpretation. It is improbable that Paul sought to raise money from areas where he had worked with Barnabas. Gaius may have been the person named in Rom 16:23; 1 Cor 1:14.

34 So Georgi, *Remembering*, 123; and Nickle, *The Collection*, 68–69, who suggests that additional representatives were "picked up along the trip" (69), noting references to Troas, Philippi, Tyre, and possibly Cyprus, among others, in Acts 20–21.

35 For views on Timothy as a Lucan addition, see Weiser, 2:559.

36 Georgi, *Remembering*, 122.

37 According to Nickle (*The Collection*, 53 n. 37), Otto Dibelius suggested that the number had symbolic value. So also Haenchen, 583. Ollrog (*Paulus*, 54) sees a chiastic structure in the list.

38 The narrator abbreviates. Neapolis was the port of departure.

39 See the excursus "'We' in Acts" in the commentary on 16:10.

40 See Praeder, "Problem," 198.

41 Tannehill, *Narrative Unity*, 2:246. Praeder ("Problem," 199) rejects this interpretation.

42 The apparently awkward ἄχρι ἡμερῶν πέντε (lit. "until/up to five days") has superior variants: "five days later" (p[74] ℵ E 33) and "on the fifth day" (D). Irenaeus omits it. The text may be corrupt. Moule (*Idiom Book*, 205) describes it as "curious." Evidently the evolution was from "it took us as long as five days" to "within five days." See the references in Cadbury and Lake, 255.

43 See Colin J. Hemer, "Alexandria Troas," *TynBul* 26 (1975) 79–112; Trebilco, "Asia," 357–59; and Edwin M. Yamauchi, "Troas," *ABD* 6:666–67.

44 The Romans traced their origin to the Trojan exile Aeneas. Arator (2:753-56) makes the connection, claiming that the site has been blessed with a new and greater glory.

45 2 Cor 2:12; Acts 20:5-6; 2 Tim 4:13. Ignatius wrote three letters from Troas and sailed thence as a prisoner en route to Rome (*Polyc.* 8). Cf. also *Symrn.* 12; *Phld.* 11.

46 See 2 Cor 2:12 for Paul's work in Troas.

47 Strictly speaking, the text does not say that they celebrated Passover. Haenchen (583) regards this as unlikely, given the gentile nature of the Philippian community. Marshall (325), however, presumes that it is the Christian "Passover," with a reference to 1 Cor 5:7-8, a view that Barrett (2:949) dismisses. It is more likely that, in the light of 20:16, it is merely a means of indicating time.

21:4, 8, 27; 28:4) may have been involuntary. Otherwise, the delay is difficult to square with v. 16.

■ **7-12** In time, the prosaic enumeration of localities will become drumbeats accompanying Paul to his destiny. Troas brings a seven-day halt. On Sunday[48] the community gathers to celebrate the Eucharist.[49] This episode is the single detailed description of Paul's pastoral work. The setting is not gracious: the third floor of an urban tenement at night.[50] People worked during the daylight; lamps provided limited light and considerable discomfort. Believers had to crowd into a single room and worship without privacy or security. The author was not attempting to draw a contrast between the primitive, gritty conditions of apostolic times and the spacious amenities of the present day.[51] This was a worship setting familiar to Luke and his readers. It explodes any notions of large communities. If there were as many as fifty people, they would have been hanging out of the windows.

They were. This was not an occasion for the visiting missionary to offer a few words. Paul's sermon was rather longer than the verbatim specimens provided elsewhere. Lamps filled the room with smoke and heat. This contributed to the soporific effect, putting one young man named Eutychus[52] to sleep.[53] Since he was not the only person ever to doze off during a sermon, the story will bring a smile to nearly every face. Unfortunately, he had, for any one or more of a number of good reasons, taken a perch on a window sill, and he fell out. Only now does the narrator reveal the height of the building. The fall was fatal.[54] This sufficed to interrupt the sermon. Paul went outside, embraced the youth, and spoke (to whom?) reassuring words. Then he went back upstairs to continue his interrupted discourse, followed by food and conversation, and took his departure. The suspense is maddening. Only in what could pass for an afterthought does the narrator report that Eutychus had been fortunate after all.

The narrative technique is complex and elusive. The passage falls within the realm of "we,"[55] but the narrator changes focus frequently. Although "we" are assembled in v. 7, Paul, a new subject, speaks to "them." Verse 8 returns to "we," but v. 9 shifts to Eutychus, until the final two words, which take place on the ground outdoors and require an indefinite third person. Paul reappears as subject in vv. 10-11, where

48 This is "the Lord's day." Cf. 1 Cor 16:2; Rev 1:10; *Did.* 14:1; Ignatius *Magn.* 9.1.

49 One cannot determine for certain whether this refers to Saturday evening (by the Jewish mode of reckoning) or to Sunday. See Conzelmann, 169. Sunday evening is more probable, at least in Lucan terms. See Cadbury and Lake (255) for evidence that Luke begins the day at dawn. Note Luke 24:13-53, all of which is envisioned as taking place on Sunday, although the sun had set by v. 29. The liturgy of vv. 7-12 included word (v. 7) and sacrament (v. 11, followed by "fellowship"), embraced under the rubric "to break bread," which therefore designates the entire act of worship rather than a "church supper." The hour (very late or very early) may suggest an early morning celebration involving more of a symbolic than a nourishing meal (Haenchen, 586). The participle γευσάμενος (lit. "tasting") in Luke refers to meals (Luke 14:24; Acts 10:10; 23:14).

50 On urban tenements, see Russell Meiggs, *Roman Ostia* (2nd ed.; Oxford: Clarendon, 1973) 236–51. Those at Troas were probably roughly comparable. A room in an upper story was unlikely to have been larger than fifty square meters. Martial lived in a third-floor apartment (*Epig.* 1.117.7). Note also Seneca *Ira* 3.35.5; *Ben.* 6.15.7; and Juvenal *Sat.* 3.190–202. Even when a full discount for hyperbole is applied, these writers do not paint an appealing picture of such living arrangements.

51 Chrysostom makes this contrast to shame his hearers in *Hom.* 43, p. 363.

52 Eutychus ("lucky") was probably a common servile name. Cf. the slave Fortunatus in *Act. John* 73–86.

53 1891 *pc* p eliminate the phrase κατενεχθεὶς ἀπὸ τοῦ ὕπνου ("eventually he fell sound asleep"), perhaps viewed as redundant. In fact, it describes the gradual process of dozing off and then falling unconscious, as well as increasing suspense via ponderous development.

54 This was not remarkable. See a similar accident (to an eight-year-old slave) in the oft-cited *P. Oxy.* 3, 475; and Aelian *Var. hist.* 3.4. On the former, see Cadbury (*Book*, 9), who provides another example from Epidaurus. Plutarch (*Per.* 13.7–8) tells how one of the artisans engaged in building the Propylaea in Athens fell from a great height. Physicians thought the case hopeless, but Athena appeared to Pericles in a dream and prescribed treatment that brought prompt recovery.

55 Attempts to remove the "we" from the story (e.g., Barrett, 2:xxvi) are ill-advised. The first person is a

the narrator follows him downstairs and back, until he leaves the scene. "They" is the subject of v. 12. The conclusion is that, intended or not,[56] the narrator is an omniscient "we," who knows why Eutychus fell and can follow Paul, who knows that he was killed, and can report his words and movements, as well as what took place after Paul's (and their own?) departure (v. 12).[57] "We" includes (at least some of) Paul's companions and is distinct from both him[58] and the members of the community. Paul also participates in this omniscience, since he knows that Eutychus died from his fall and that he will return alive.

Lucan narrative techniques are perceptible. Following the introduction in v. 7 and an apparently gratuitous reference to the lighting arrangements in v. 8, the narrator devotes twenty-seven words to the situation of Eutychus, ending abruptly with a two-word statement of his fate. The drawn-out depiction is a soporific prelude to a brusque finale. Also Lucan is the contrasting use of the verb "fall" (πίπτω), which serves as both cause of death (v. 9) and, in v. 10, as means of revival.[59] Although retardation can be a feature of resurrection stories, in Mark 4:21-43 and John 11:1-44 it leads to death, whereas here the retardation comes between Paul's announcement and Eutychus's return.

Formally, this is not a typical NT resurrection story.[60] The patient expires while the healer is present; healing words are wanting, and the one restored to life does not appear in person or demonstrate his revival.[61] Verse 12b functions like a final acclamation, but its language is Lucan.[62] The passage resembles, in several respects, some of the revivals in the Apocryphal Acts, which can be so numerous that someone is raised from the dead . . . and life, so to speak, goes on.[63] The *Acts of Paul* awarded the Eutychus episode the most sincere form of flattery.[64] The narrative form is unique. Verses 7-12 belong to the realm of a first-person narrator, who retreats from the action so that v. 12 effectively

part of this account (v. 8), from which a story about Eutychus cannot be extracted.

56 It is not unlikely that the author did not recognize the consequences of the use of "we" in vv. 8 and 13.

57 For other uses of the omniscient "we," see the excursus "'We' in Acts," pp. 392–96. Tannehill (*Narrative Unity*, 2:248–49) attempts to fend off this omniscience by speaking of "free indirect discourse," which is a quality of anonymous omniscient narration. Discomfort with "we" is apparent in the thinly attested (1 *pc* bo) variant "they."

58 Paul and "we" do not reunite until v. 14.

59 Note also the use of five words beginning with a form of *kata-* from the opening word of v. 9 to the first word of v. 10, including two uses of καταφέρω ("fall [down]"), for falling asleep and falling down.

60 For typical features, see Bultmann, *History*, 233–34; and Theissen, *Miracle Stories*, 90–94, who does not distinguish these from other healings.

61 The narrative does not speak about Eutychus's condition. The verb ἤγαγον in v. 12 could mean "they brought (him up to the room)" or "took him (home)," among various possibilities. It could apply to carrying an unconscious body or escorting a fully recovered Eutychus. The same ambiguity applies to the verb ἤρθη in v. 9, which literally means "was taken up" or "taken away." "Removed" is one possibility. (The translation "found" retains the lack of definiteness; 88 reads εὑρέθη, "was found," often the equivalent of "was.")

62 Litotes: literally, "They were immeasurably consoled."

63 In *Act. John* 22-24 the raising of Cleopatra has all of the typical features, but the raising of her husband takes place in a summary. Cf. also the raising of a priest of Artemis in chap. 47, the old man in chap. 52 (whose first response is "no thanks"), and the multiple resurrections in the tale of Drusiana and Callimachus (63–86). See also the multiple resurrections in the *Act. Pet.* (Verc.) 26–28.

64 *Act. Paul Mart.* 1 (Patroclus). Dennis MacDonald ("Luke's Eutychus and Homer's Elpenor: Acts 20:7-12 and *Odyssey*, 10-12," *JHC* 1 [1994] 5–24), following François Bovon ("La vie des apôtres: Traditions bibliques et narrations apocryphes," in idem, ed., *Les Actes apocryphes des apôtres: christianisme et monde païen* [Geneva: Labor et Fides, 1981], 141–58, esp. 150), sets out detailed arguments for the dependence. Richard Bauckham also attributed the Patroclus story to borrowing from Acts ("The Acts of Paul as a Sequel to Acts," in Winter and Clarke, *Setting*, 105–52, esp. 134). See also Pervo, "Hard Act," 10–12; and José Antonio Artés Hernández, "Lc 19, 1-10—Hch 20, 7-12—*Passio Pauli* I (104.8—106.15): Análisis comparativo," *FiloNT* 16 (2003) 49–67. This type remained popular in hagiography: Athanasius *Vit. Ant.* 8; Sulpicius Severus *Life of Martin* 7.3; 8.2; and Gregory's *Life of Benedict* 32.3. See also Spencer, "Wise Up, Young Man," 43–46.

takes place "off-stage." By attempting to remedy this difficulty, the D-Text underlines it: "**While they were saying farewell, he** brought the **youth** . . ."[65] The effective understatement of the conventional and more original text says, in effect, that Paul's words sufficed. Formally atypical miracles raise questions about source.

Martin Dibelius awarded this episode his least flattering epithet: "secular" (*profan*),[66] although he allowed that the author "has introduced a certain Christian interest into the framing of the story."[67] His judgment of its non-Christian origin was based on its alleged ambiguity (good diagnosis or miracle?),[68] its unedifying nature, and the narrative focus in general, not to mention the element of humor. Luke, who would not attribute a story of this quality to the person of Paul, must have taken it from tradition. Lüdemann affirms its secular character, but assigns Luke the responsibility for "Christianizing" the legend, which he found in the course of his "secular" reading.[69] Dennis MacDonald has a specific suggestion: the *Odyssey*.[70]

Other sources are apparent: two resurrections from the Elijah/Elisha tradition.[71] In 1 Kgs 17:17-24, Elijah revives the son of the widow of Zarephath.[72] Elisha revives a Shunammite woman's son in the finely crafted narrative of 2 Kgs 4:18-37. The Elijah story speaks of an *upper room* (ὑπερῷον; cf. Acts 20:8), where the child was *sitting* (ἐκάθητο; cf. Acts 20:9). The healer's prayer includes the expression "Let [his] *life* (ἡ ψυχή) return to him" (v. 21). In 2 Kings 4 the boy *sleeps*, then *dies*. The prophet eventually comes in person, *lies prone upon him*,[73] and can ultimately restore the child to his mother.[74] Some of the details are minor and differently employed, but it is very difficult to get around the word "life" (ψυχή), which is not used in conventional resurrection stories, and, most particularly, the rather embarrassing action of "embracing" the patient.[75] These

65 ἀσπαζομένων αὐτῶν ἤγαγεν τὸν νεανισκον . . . (Boismard, *Texte*, 331). Clark (liii, 131, 377) rearranges the text, placing v. 12 between v. 10 and v. 11 and preserving the farewell. He justifies this from a paraphrase of Cassiodorus. This makes the story more conventional and prosaic and therefore misses the narrator's literary object.

66 Dibelius, *Studies*, 17–19.

67 Ibid., 18.

68 Attempts to characterize this act as a diagnosis err. The last idea in the narrator's mind was to intimate that Paul had engaged in no more than acute observation. Ramsay (*St. Paul the Traveller*, 290–91) had no doubts: Eutychus was dead because the author, a physician, said so. He reads the text, which says that Eutychus was dead (νεκρός), correctly. Polhill (419 n. 64) makes the same point after noting that "many interpreters" reject the notion of a miracle. For the same phrase (ἤρθη νεκρός), with no possibility of ambiguity, see *T. Jud.* 9:3. Apparent death may also be characterized as a resurrection. Of many examples from ancient fiction, note Apuleius *Metam.* 10.2–12, the story of a young boy believed poisoned but actually given a sleeping potion, whose revival in par. 12 is characterized as a return from the dead. His father then led him out to the people (*producit ad populum* [cf. Acts 20:12]). Like Lazarus (John 11:44), he walks out wrapped in burial garments. The section has several affinities with the initiation of Lucius in book 11. For the raising of one apparently dead, see Philostratus *Vit. Apoll.* 4.45 (which is like Luke 7:11-17), where the narrator twice uses the verb δοκέω ("seem"). (Philostratus may have "demythologized" an actual resurrection story.)

69 Lüdemann, 223–24. Conzelmann (169) seeks to isolate this source. Verse 7 is an editorial "preview," which does not fit with vv. 8-9. Verse 11 is intrusive. He thus "cuts" vv. 7 and 11, finding "a secular story with a popular comic touch." The liturgical features were absent in the original. His reconstruction amounts to little more than elimination of "nonsecular" elements to find the desired residue.

70 MacDonald, "Luke's Eutychus" (n. 64 above).

71 Among those who have observed these parallels are Rackham, 380; Lampe, "Miracles," 163–79; and Goulder, *Type*, 50.

72 For Luke's interest in these stories, see Luke 4:26.

73 In the MT of 1 Kgs 17:21, Elijah lies upon the boy, but the LXX euphemizes this to "breathe."

74 For details of the Greek text, see Barrett, 2:954–55.

75 In the background is a kind of "sympathetic magic" in which life is restored by mimicking the action (sexual intercourse) through which it is created. See Reinhold Merkelbach, *Roman und Mysterium* (Berlin: de Gruyter, 1962) 86. Bede (81) cites Gal 4:19: Paul is giving birth to Eutychus. (The Latin verb *incubuit* is used of birth.) Bruce (426), who notes the Elijah/Elisha parallels, asks, "Is a form of artificial respiration implied?" Ancient medicine had its deficits, but it is unlikely that lying prone

allusions to and borrowings from the LXX put paid to the hypothesis of a "profane" source.[76]

Internal Lucan parallels are also important. These include the raising of Tabitha (Acts 9:38-41) by Peter, an event that also takes place in an upper room and has several reminiscences of the Elijah/Elisha stories,[77] and the story of the son of the widow of Nain (Luke 7:11-17), which amounts to a near retelling of Elijah's miracle in 1 Kings 17.[78] These parallels between Luke and Acts and within Acts, all of which evince imitation of the LXX, strongly support the hypothesis that 20:7-12 is a Lucan composition. The alternative would be an empty shell: a resurrection by Paul (?) at some place and time, garnered and preserved by unknown means, transformed into its present shape and (presumably) inserted by the author at this point.[79]

Luke had more in mind than developing and inserting a good story at this point. Charles Talbert points out the general hostility to nocturnal meetings and legal action to suppress them, on the grounds of political conspiracy or criminal religiosity.[80] Standard accusations against cults included nocturnal orgies at which the lights were extinguished to allow for promiscuity and the sacrifice and consumption of a human being, usually a boy: "the shameful deeds about which stories are told—the upsetting of the lamp, promiscuous intercourse, and the meals of human flesh."[81] From the contents of Pliny's letter on the Christians (10.96) it is apparent that such allegations were in circulation when Acts was written.[82] It may be no more than a felicitous coincidence that Luke describes a nocturnal Christian assembly at which lamps were ubiquitous and in which a boy was restored to life, but an indirect apologetic purpose is possible.

The passage has clear symbolic features. To deny that a short pericope describing a celebration of the Eucharist in an upper room[83] on Sunday that climaxes in the return of a dead person in the morning has any symbolic reference would border on absurdity. Like Luke 24:13-35, Troas declares that every Sunday is an Easter event.[84] "Lamps" also inveigle the interpreter. They can represent the light of Christ (cf. 12:7). A more specific and contextual application is didactic. Sunday celebrates Easter, but the end is not at hand. Believers are to remain vigilant. The exhortations in Luke 12:35-37 ("have your lamps lit") and 21:34-36 receive vivid illustration here. For Luke, "sleep" symbolizes the lack of perseverance and a window, so to speak, for Satan (see Luke 9:32; 22:45-46). Paul will reiterate the theme in his exhortation in v. 31.[85] As Johnson observes,

upon someone who had just fallen several stories was viewed as therapeutic.

76 Another source is Mark 5:39 (raising of Jairus's daughter). The verb form θορυβεῖσθε ("make a fuss") appears only there and here in the NT. Luke omitted it in his account (8:52).

77 See the comments on that passage. Bede (82) elegantly compares and contrasts the two raisings and their agents.

78 See Thomas L. Brodie, "Towards Unravelling Luke's Uses of the Old Testament: Luke 7:11-17 as *imitatio* of 1 Kgs 17:17-24," *NTS* 32 (1986) 247–67. On these inter- and intra-textual allusions, see also Tannehill, *Narrative Unity*, 2:247–48.

79 Such a shell is more or less what Weiser (2:562) proposes as a source.

80 Talbert, 183–85, with numerous references. He views the connection as no more than a possibility, as do Wendt, 286; Preuschen, 121; Loisy, 764; Haenchen, 585; and Conzelmann, 169. Calvin (7:169) sees this as one function of the lights.

81 Justin *1 Apol.* 26 (on Simon), trans. Eugene R. Fairweather, in Cyril Richardson, ed., *Early Christian Fathers* (LCC 1; Philadelphia: Westminster, 1953) 258. On these charges, which have enjoyed a long life, see Albert Henrichs, "Pagan Ritual and the Alleged Crimes of the Early Christians: A Reconsideration," in Patrick Granfield and Josef A. Jungmann, eds., *Kyriakon: Festschrift Johannes Quasten* (2 vols.; Munich: Kösel, 1970) 1:18–35.

82 See 10.96.7, which speaks of Christian meals as involving ordinary, harmless food (*cibum promiscuum . . . et innoxium*), indicating what had been feared.

83 The term ὑπερῷον differs from that used for the "Last Supper" (ἀνάγαιον) in Luke 22:12, but the meaning is similar. Acts prefers ὑπερῷον (1:13; 9:37).

84 B. Kowalski ("Der Fenstersturz in Troas [Apg 20, 7-12]," *StudNTUmwelt* 30 [2005] 19–37) develops the eucharistic symbolism of this episode.

85 See Pervo, *Luke's Story*, 72; Schneider, 2:284–86; and Weiser, 2:564. For a detailed investigation of symbolic features see Bernard Trémel, "À propos d'Ac 20,7-12: puissance du thaumaturge ou du témoin?" *RThPh* 112 (1980) 359–69. Barrett's (2:950) designation of this interpretation as "allegory" is erroneous. Resurrection stories usually

the difficulties of the narrative seem to encourage readers to look beneath the surface.[86] One such difficulty is said to be v. 11, a problem already for the D-Text[87] and a verse that Fitzmyer considers possibly secondary.[88] The narrative is awkward because the narrator wishes to portray Eutychus as "recognized," returned from the dead, after the breaking of the bread (cf. Luke 24:35).

■ **13-18a** This passage[89] is a detailed summary of travel that shifts its focus from the narrative "we" to third-person statements about Paul. He is the focal point. "We" are merely passengers on the voyage. Verses 13-15 probably derive from the Collection Source.[90] If so, it is less probable that Paul was a coauthor of this hypothetical document, since "we" write about Paul, rather than Paul (and others) writing about "us," but one may also ask whether the authoritarian tone comes from the source.[91] Verse 16 is essentially authorial, providing an explanation for not stopping at Ephesus.[92] The author evidently did not wish or choose to invent a stop there and instead resorted to having Paul summon the presbyters from that place to Miletus.

The link to the previous episode is practically nonexistent. One gathers that "we" had left Paul at Troas and gone on to Assos, to which he traveled on land, yet v. 11 described his departure, whether from the apartment or the city is not clear. Equally unclear is Paul's motive for traveling overland.[93] Abbreviation seems probable. The result is a reign of (unimportant) confusion. Is the mention of "the ship" in v. 13 the result of such abbreviation or is it merely reasonable: those who sail require a ship? The term does suggest that this was the same ship on which they had sailed from Philippi. Was the seven-day halt intentional? Had Paul chartered the ship, which was thus subject to his direction? Luke has left much room for speculative commentators.[94]

In v. 16 it is clear that the narrator views Paul as in charge of the ship, for he decides to bypass Ephesus.[95] Gregory H. R. Horsley attributes the failure to put in at Ephesus to the silting up of the harbor, a frequent problem.[96] Verse 16 is "the entirely natural rationalization of one whose initial plan is thwarted by circumstance."[97] This conclusion authorizes the narrator to dissemble. Others agree, but attribute the problem to Paul's reluctance to return to Ephesus, where he was a *persona non grata*.[98] In Luke's time it was well known at Ephesus that Paul did not return there. Neither the Pastorals nor

symbolize initiation. Those who wish to find it here will note that the chief character is a youth, a common symbol of the initiate, and the language of descent/ascent, although the latter applies fully only to Paul. One could suggest that Paul is a savior figure, descending to the dead to rescue the lost.

86 Johnson, 358.

87 See above.

88 Fitzmyer, 668.

89 One can, with most editors, make a paragraph break after v. 16. This division is based upon mere convenience.

90 Conzelmann (171) says that the list of stations does not prove that Luke was using a source. He is correct in that such accounts lend verisimilitude. The textual variants indicate that temporal references could be changed and stations added. Greek fictional examples begin with the *Odyssey*. For a prose example roughly contemporaneous with Acts, note *Ephesian Tale* 1.11–12, e.g., 1.11.6. Lucian parodies this style with vigor in his *Ver. hist.*, e.g., 1.5–6, 28–29; 2.2–4.

91 Note the verbs "command" (διατεταγμένος ἦν) in v. 13, "determine" (κεκρίκει) in v. 16, and "summon" (μετακαλέω) in v. 17. Although this tone could come from colleagues of Paul, a safer bet is that it stems from the author of Acts.

92 This judgment may render suspect the hypothesis that the reference to Pentecost derived from the source. Pentecost sounds an echo with chap. 2, but, as a feast of "first fruits," it might have been deemed by Paul as a suitable occasion for presenting the collection. Talbert (186) also makes this suggestion.

93 Although πεζεύω originally meant "on foot," it had become generalized; see BDAG, 791, *s.v.* The distance was about thirty kilometers, so that the journey could have been made in a (long, hard) day, even on foot. But one must ask if Paul did not have some business to which he wished to attend. Trebilco ("Asia," 359–60) reports some hypotheses about why Paul traveled on land.

94 For speculation, see Georgi, *Remembering*, 124; and Cadbury and Lake, 257–58. Chapter 21 indicates that multiple ships were used.

95 Since Miletus was a part of Asia, v. 16 is a good indicator that for Luke "Asia" is primarily Ephesus and environs.

96 Tacitus (*Ann.* 16.23) takes note of the need to dredge the harbor at Ephesus.

97 Horsley, "Inscriptions," 135.

98 So, e.g., Witherington, 600. This view goes back to Wellhausen, *Kritische Analyse*, 42. It is entirely

the *Acts of Paul* report repeated visits to the city. Luke has turned this deficit to his literary advantage. Early in Acts 19 Paul ceased to play an active personal role in the mission, and his forthcoming address will reinforce the picture of the absent Paul as guardian and guide of Ephesian Christianity. It is also true that the author's rationalization is quite weak, for v. 17 substantially contradicts it, as it is difficult to see how time would be saved by sending a messenger to Ephesus, assembling the presbyters, and having them travel to Miletus,[99] nor is there any indication of whether the deadline was reached, as Luke drops the matter.

Miletus,[100] a logical stop on a coasting journey, was the location of one of the most important speeches in Acts, yet sparer in detail about the site than any other.[101] No mention is made of believers at Miletus. To determine the locale of the address, a private home, the public square, a rented hall, or the beach, readers are free to utilize their imaginations. The same may be said of the audience. Paul did not envision churches governed by presbyters, but Acts reports that he ordained them. If each house church had one presbyter, it is difficult to imagine that there could have been more than about five in Paul's time.[102] Ignatius's ideal is one bishop in each community, with a council of presbyters.[103] The number would not have been large by any imaginable criterion. This vagueness is probably intentional and certainly effective, for it allows these words to soar above and beyond space and time, reaching out to believers of every generation. Just as the speech seems lengthy because of the content packed into each clause, so the setting permits a scope wider than the picture of conversation with fewer than a dozen people in a room could ever convey. Luke says more by saying less.

■ **18b-35** The contrast between this speech (hereafter "Miletus") and the Ephesian mission described in chap. 19 is astonishing.[104] This is not because the leaders of a structured church suddenly emerge, for one may presume that such developments took place everywhere and required no more reporting than did the fact of baptism. In place of the Paul whose potency permeated cloth and compelled imitation by exorcists, whose message perpetrated a mass renunciation of magic and whose character attracted the admiration of Asiarchs comes one whose life is marked by blood, sweat, and tears, the hard-working laborer whose frugality and

possible that the ship never intended to stop at Ephesus. Silting did not prevent Paul from sailing to Ephesus in 18:19, but the problem could have worsened in a few years. For discussion of why Paul did not stop at Ephesus, see Walter Grundmann, "Paulus in Ephesus," *Helikon* 4 (1964) 46–82, esp. 71–78; Jan Lambrecht, "Paul's Farewell-Address at Miletus, Acts 20, 17-38," in Kremer, *Actes*, 307–37, esp. 330–32; and Charles Kingsley Barrett, "Paul's Address to the Ephesian Elders," in Jacob Jervell and Wayne A. Meeks, eds., *God's Christ and His People: Studies in Honour of Nils Alstrup Dahl* (Oslo: Universitetsforlaget, 1977) 107–21, esp. 108–9.

99 Conzelmann (171) says that the journey would take five days. Haenchen (590) calculates that the actual travel distance was around eighty kilometers. See also Jerome Murphy-O'Connor, *Paul: A Critical Life* (Oxford: Clarendon, 1996) 347. Counting the time required for the messenger, this would double. At the minimum estimate, a good week would have been needed. Time-saving is thus a pathetic excuse. It seems that the author wished to insert "Pentecost" regardless of the price.

100 On Miletus, which had long ceded prominence to Ephesus, see John McRay, "Miletus," *ABD* 4:825–26. On the much-discussed theater inscription (*CIJ* II 748) of 2–3 CE that appears to identify Jews as "God-Fearers," see Levinskaya, *Diaspora Setting*, 63–65.

101 See the comments of Weiser, 2:574.

102 Acts 14:23 suggests that each church had more than one presbyter.

103 Ignatius uses the term "presbytery," "council," about a dozen times, notably in *Eph.* 2:2; 20:2. The only other contemporary use is 1 Tim 4:14.

104 Bibliography is rather substantial. Major contributions include Jacques Dupont, *Le discours de Milet: Testament pastoral de Saint Paul (Actes 20,18-36)* (Paris, Cerf: 1962); Hans-Joachim Michel, *Die Abschiedsrede des Paulus an die Kirche Apg 20, 17-38: Motivgeschichte und theologische Bedeutung* (SANT 35; Munich: Kösel, 1973); Otto Knoch, *Die "Testamente" des Petrus und Paulus: Die Sicherung der apostolischen Überlieferung in der spätneutestamentlichen Zeit* (SBS 62; Stuttgart: Katholisches Bibelwerk, 1973); Franz Prast, *Presbyter und Evangelium in nachapostolischer Zeit: Die Abschiedsrede des Paulus in Milet (Apg 20, 17-38) im Rahmen der lukanischen Konzeption der Evangeliumsverkündigung* (Stuttgart: Katholisches Bibelwerk, 1979); Lars Aejmelaeus, *Die Rezeption der Paulusbriefe in der*

charity are an example for all. This is a figure familiar from the epistles, and for good reason, because no other section of Acts is so saturated with allusions to the Pauline corpus.[105] Of almost equal interest is the dearth of any allusions to or citations from the LXX. Here is Paul as he is viewed by the general public: offering useful, if not always welcome, advice, issuing dire warnings, and freely willing to share examples of his selfless sacrifice and suffering. Those who wish to present the "Paul of Acts" as "the real Paul" will find considerable support in these verses, while scholars suspicious of Luke's portrait will need to account for the dissonance. To follow the model of the old saw that Luke "paulinizes Peter and petrinizes Paul" one can say that in this speech Luke "paulinizes" the Paul of Acts.[106] Miletus shows that the author of Acts did not develop his picture(s) of Paul in ignorance of the letters and that, insofar as his general depiction is different, the differences were largely due to choice.[107]

The scene of the address in Miletus[108] portrays a situation not found in the undisputed epistles or elsewhere in Acts, for it is an address to Christian *leaders*. This invites

Miletrede (Helsinki: Suomalainen Tiedeakatemia, 1987); Steve Walton, *Leadership and Lifestyle: The Portrait of Paul in the Miletus Speech and I Thessalonians* (SNTSMS 108; Cambridge: Cambridge University Press, 2000); Klein, *Zwölf*, 178–84; Cheryl Exum and Charles Talbert, "The Structure of Paul's Speech to the Ephesian Elders (Acts 20, 18-35)," *CBQ* 29 (1967) 233–36; Heinz Schürmann, "Das Testament des Paulus für die Kirche: Apg 20,18-35, in idem, *Traditionsgeschichtliche Untersuchungen zu den synoptischen Evangelien* (Düsseldorf: Patmos, 1968) 310–40; Thomas L. Budesheim, "Paul's *Abschiedsrede* in the Acts of the Apostles," *HTR* 69 (1976) 9–30; Charles Kingsley Barrett, "Paul's Address to the Ephesian Elders," in Jacob Jervell and Wayne A. Meeks, eds., *God's Christ and His People: Studies in Honour of Nils Alstrup Dahl* (Oslo: Universitetsforlaget, 1977) 107–21; Lambrecht, "Farewell"; Evald Lövestam, "Paul's Address at Miletus," *ST* 41 (1987) 1–10; Duane F. Watson, "Paul's Speech to the Ephesian Elders (Acts 20,17-38): Epideictic Rhetoric of Farewell," in Duane F. Watson, ed., *Persuasive Artistry: Studies in Honor of George A. Kennedy* (Sheffield: Sheffield Academic Press, 1991) 184–208; John J. Kilgallen, "Paul's Speech to the Ephesian Elders: Its Structure," *EThL* 70 (1994) 112–21; Beverly Roberts Gaventa, "Theology and Ecclesiology in the Miletus Speech: Reflections on Content and Context," *NTS* 50 (2004) 36–52; Trebilco, *Early Christians*, 172–96; and Shauf, *Theology*, 263–70.

105 See, in general, Aejmelaeus, *Rezeption*; and Pervo, *Dating*, 111–33, 221–22, 228–29.

106 See Lambrecht, "Farewell," 320–21.

107 The debate between the respective Pauls of the letters and Acts is not well framed, since it presumes that there are two sets of texts of equal or differing historical value. The letters are not a uniform body, for some are composite (notably 2 Corinthians, which is assembled on the assumption of a view of Paul not unlike that of Acts) and others are inauthentic. The database must be expanded to include other works by and about Paul, as well as those containing direct or oblique (e.g., James) references to him. See Helmut Koester, "New Testament Introduction: A Critique of a Discipline," in Jacob Neusner, ed., *Christianity, Judaism, and Other Greco-Roman Cults: Studies for Morton Smith at Sixty*, vol. 1: *New Testament* (SJLA 12; Leiden: Brill, 1975) 1–20. This principle is recognized in the surveys of Andreas Lindemann, *Paulus im Ältesten Christentum* (BHT 58; Tübingen: Mohr Siebeck] 1979); and Ernst Dassmann, *Der Stachel im Fleisch: Paulus in der frühchristlichen Literatur bis Irenäus* (Münster: Aschendorff, 1979). Cf. also Gerd Lüdemann, *Opposition to Paul in Jewish Christianity* (trans. M. Eugene Boring; Minneapolis: Fortress Press, 1989), and the recent contribution of Daniel Marguerat, "L'image de Paul dans les Actes des Apôtres," in Michel Berder, ed., *Les Actes des Apôtres: Histoire, récit, théologie. XXe congrès de l'Association catholique française pour l'étude de la Bible, Angers, 2003* (LD 199; Paris: Cerf, 2005) 121–54. All of these sources are limited, by form, choice, presupposition, purpose, and so on. The epistles represent Paul's pastoral interaction with communities. Acts focuses on Paul as missionary founder of communities and as a prisoner. The *Acts of Paul* is noteworthy for attempting to integrate these three roles, but is not widely viewed as having captured "the real Paul."

108 The speech is a Lucan composition in its entirety and shows numerous marks of the author's style. See Hans-Joachim Michel, *Die Abschiedsrede des Paulus an die Kirche Apg 20, 17-38: Motivgeschichte und theologische Bedeutung* (SANT 35; Munich: Kösel, 1973) 28–33.

comparison with the world of the Pastoral Epistles, 1 Peter, and the Apostolic Fathers, the era of the emergence of Christian officers. Comparison with the Pastorals is particularly apt, for both the speech and the letters seem to address community leaders and communicate with the faithful by telling leaders what they should teach. The technique yields a threefold harvest: a paradigm for leadership, reinforcement of leaders' authority, and guidance for believers.[109] The speech takes no pains to conceal its origin in the post-Pauline era and makes use of a suitable genre, the testament,[110] which often overlaps with the genre of the farewell address, to which Acts 20:17-35 also conforms.[111] Luke uses this meeting to accentuate the transition from "Pauline" to "post-Pauline" times, the shift from the second generation to the third.[112]

The obvious intra-Lucan parallel, Jesus' final speech to his disciples prior to his arrest (Luke 22:14-38), also contributes to the interpretation of the address at Miletus, which has the same function.[113] Both speeches lie under the shadow of coming death; both take up problems of leadership. This structural relation does not detract from the standing of Paul in Acts. He, rather than Peter, who departed the narrative stage long ago, or James, despite the latter's authority in Jerusalem, has become the successor to Jesus. This address also takes up some of the themes of Luke 21, particularly the admonition to be vigilant.[114] A difference is that eschatology, the heart of Luke 21, is explicitly absent from this speech. This contrast is not without consequences for analyses of Lucan theology.[115] Within the plot

109 See Richard Pervo, "Romancing an Oft-neglected Stone: The Pastoral Epistles and the Epistolary Novel," *JHC* 1 (1994) 25–47.

110 On the genre of the testament, see Berger, *Formgeschichte*, 75–80; and Anitra B. Kolenkow, "Testaments: The Literary Genre 'Testament,'" in Robert A. Kraft and George W. Nickelsburg, eds., *Early Judaism and Its Modern Interpreters* (Atlanta: Scholars Press, 1986) 259–67.

111 A seminal study is Johannes Munck, "Discours d'adieu dans le Nouveau Testament et dans la littérature biblique," in *Aux sources de la tradition chrétienne: Mélanges offerts à Maurice Goguel* (Bibliothèque théologique; Neuchâtel: Delachaux, 1950) 155–70. William S. Kurz provides a good overview of the form (*Farewell Addresses in the New Testament* [Collegeville, Minn.: Liturgical Press, 1990]). See also the succinct account of Fitzmyer, 674. For a general survey, see Eckhard von Nordheim, *Die Lehre der Alten* (2 vols.; ALGHJ 13; Leiden: Brill, 1980); and Anders E. Nielsen, *Until It Is Fulfilled: Lukan Eschatology according to Luke 22 and Acts 20* (WUNT 126; Tübingen: Mohr Siebeck, 2000), who examines the genre with the intention of exposing its implicit eschatological ("transcendent") quality. Note also the critical review of the genre discussion in Walton, *Leadership*, 55–65. An idea of the conventional nature of such addresses can be gleaned from Lucian's parody in his summary of the farewell speech of Peregrinus: "telling of the life that he had led and the risks that he had run, and of all the troubles that he had endured for philosophy's sake" (*Peregr.* 32, trans. A. M. Harmon, *Lucian V* [LCL; Cambridge, Mass.: Harvard University Press, 1936] 37). Dennis R. MacDonald ("Paul's Farewell to the Ephesian Elders and Hector's Farewell to Andromache: A Strategic Imitation of Homer's *Iliad*," in Penner, *Contextualizing*, 189–203) notes many interesting parallels between *Iliad* 6 and this chapter. At the least, this is a reminder that "farewell speeches" have a wide background. For more detail, see his *Imitate Homer*, 69–102. István Czaschesz (*Commission Narratives: A Comparative Study of the Canonical and Apocryphal Acts* [Studies on Early Christian Apocrypha 8; Leuven: Peeters, 2007] 16–18) shows parallels between this speech and Epictetus's description of the Cynic vocation (*Diss.* 2.3; 2.20; 3.22.1–109).

112 Weiser, 2:569. Thomas E. Phillips ("Paul as a Role Model in Acts: The 'We' Passages in Acts 16 and Beyond," in idem, *Acts and Ethics*, 49–63) locates the transition from "apostolic" to "postapostolic" times at the introduction of "we" and the disappearance of the apostles after chap. 15. This is a valid observation. Miletus moves, by anticipation, a generation forward.

113 Walton (*Leadership*, 99–117) develops the parallel between the Last Supper and Miletus in considerable detail and with many interesting observations. See also Lambrecht, "Farewell," 326. Both prepare for the time when the master will no longer be present. Each includes retrospect (Luke 22:35; Acts 20:18-21, 26-27, 31); both have admonitions and exhortations (Luke 22:24-27; Acts 20:28-31, 35), call for vigilance in the face of coming stresses (Luke 22:35-38; Acts 20:28-31, and a reference to "blood," evoking a view of Jesus' death as an atoning sacrifice (Luke 22:20; Acts 20:28).

114 Rackham, 383.

115 See Parsons and Pervo, *Rethinking*, 88. On implicit eschatology in the address see A. Nielsen (n. 111).

structure of Acts this address initiates a shift toward apologetic.[116] All of the subsequent speeches of Paul in Acts (except the short remarks in chap. 27) continue to defend his views and actions.

The structure has received considerable attention. The traditional approach has looked to content as the key.[117] Another focuses on formal elements.[118] There has been some convergence. An informed example of the former is Jan Lambrecht's two-part division:[119]

I. Self-defense and Announcement (vv. 18b-27).
  A. Vv. 18b-21. Previous Conduct (apologetic).
  B. Vv. 22-25. Announcement of Departure; Future Occurrences.
  C. Vv. 26-27. Previous Conduct (apologetic).
II. Exhortations and Farewell (vv. 28-35).
  A. Vv. 28-31. Warning: Vigilance in the Face of Danger (Paul as example).
  B. V. 32. Farewell.
  C. Vv. 33-35. Warning: Help for Weak (Paul as example).

Pereira has proffered a chiastic plan:[120]

A. Vv. 18b-21. Past record (v. 18b, ἐπίστασθε) (you know).
  B. Vv. 22-24. Present Activity (v. 22a, καὶ νῦν) (and now).
    C. Vv. 25-27. Forecast (v. 25a, ἐγὼ οἶδα) (I know).
       V. 26a. Consequently (διότι) (therefore).
      D. v. 28. Charge.
    C'. Vv. 29-31. Forecast (v. 29, ἐγὼ οἶδα) ("I know").
       V. 31a. Consequently (διό) ("therefore").
  B'. V. 32. Present Activity (v. 32a, καὶ νῦν) ("and now").
A'. Vv. 33-35. Past Record (v. 34a, γινώσκετε) ("you know").

Both of these plans help illuminate the speech. The pursuit of chiasmus has led to much excess, but Luke's fondness for ring composition is well illustrated elsewhere, and this analysis places the stress on the charge in v. 28, whereas Lambrecht's scheme all but overlooks this element of the "exhortation." Both of these proposals invite comparison with Paul's "apology" in 1 Thess 2:1-12.[121] Another formal factor is the relation of this speech to the rhetorical species. Dibelius pointed to encomium, that is, epideictic.[122] Greek farewell addresses belonged to the epideictic category, but, as George A. Kennedy notes, the Miletus speech does not follow the conventions.[123] He correctly stresses that the focus of the address is on the future, and he notes its hortatory nature.[124] Like most NT orations, the speech is deliberative in purpose, although it includes both apologetic and epideictic elements.[125] The last two serve the first.[126] Analyses of both form and structure show the dominance of the Jewish testament. Luke wishes to take advantage of the ethos suitable to epideictic and all of the pathos that he can squeeze in.[127]

116 On the apologetic dimensions of this speech, see Malherbe, *Paul*, 152–55.

117 A recent example of this method is John J. Kilgallen, "Paul's Speech to the Ephesian Elders: Its Structure," *EThL* 70 (1994) 112–21. Kilgallen identifies motives and sees vv. 25 and 28 as central.

118 For a concise history of the discussion, see Shauf, *Theology*, 265 n. 471. On various schemes, see also Soards, *Speeches*, 105; and Walton, *Leadership*, 66–75. A ready clue is the use of καὶ (τὰ) νῦν ("and now,") "with respect to the present" in vv. 22, 25, 32, on which see Lambrecht, "Farewell," 315.

119 Lambrecht, "Farewell," 315–18.

120 Francis Pereira, *Ephesus: Climax of Universalism in Luke-Acts–A Redaction-Critical Study of Paul's Ephesian Ministry* (Acts 18:23–20:1) (Jesuit Theological Forum Studies 10.1; Anand, India: Gujarat Sahitya Prakash, 1983) 201. See the succinct commentary of Talbert, 186–89.

121 Compare the structure and techniques of this outline of 1 Thess 2:12 with Acts 20:18b-35:

I. Introduction. 2:1-4 Warrants and Motivation.
  A. Historical warrant: vv. 1-2 (triad: suffer, insult, speak boldly).
  B. Motivation and accountability: vv. 3-4 (triad: deceit, uncleanness, guile).
II. The Contrasting "Styles": vv. 5-12.
  A. Three rejected techniques: vv. 5-6 (pleasure, money, glory).
  B. Image: like mother: nurturing, loving vv. 7-8.
  C. Basis: self-support: v. 9 (4 and 9 *inclusio*).
  B'. Image: proper, fair, like father: vv. 10-11.
  A'. Three "correct" techniques: v. 12.

122 Dibelius, *Studies*, 155–58. See also Watson, "Paul's Speech" (n. 104 above).

123 Kennedy, *Rhetorical Criticism*, 133.

124 Feldman (*Jew and Gentile*, 256–57) states that encouragement and exhortation are important qualities of a leader. As examples he adduces Josephus *Ant*. 2.327; 3.44–46.

125 See Witherington, 612–14.

The speech represents three strands of Deutero-Paulinism. One is the Paul of Luke. The others involve the revision of Pauline thought in pseudonymous compositions. These include Luke's transformation of Pauline thought in this speech, which functions just as much as a message to the church as does 2 Timothy. The other is the speculative theological line visible in Colossians and Ephesians, which treat the "plan of God," develop an ecclesiology, set forth a pastoral understanding of church leadership, and stress the wealth of tradition.[128] Most widely recognized are the parallels, in thought and vocabulary, with the Pastorals.[129] All of these developments and trends stem from Ephesus. Luke wishes to check speculative theology and fend off the potentially rigid structural model that will characterize the Pastorals, but all of these share important features in the struggle over Paul's heritage in the region of Ephesus.[130] They represent different elements of nascent "proto-orthodoxy." Luke emerges as a synthesizer of sorts, more in appearance than in reality, for, unlike Irenaeus (or even Matthew), he is less interested in genuine synthesis of disparate traditions than in making other views conform to his own.

There are several acute textual problems. The D-Text[131] exhibits more variations than is characteristic of that tradition with respect to the speeches. Most of these are the sort of editorial "improvements" that reflect the general taste of the "Western" tradition.

■ **18b-21** The first section, a single sentence, builds a bond between speaker and audience (pathos), through reminding the hearers of what Paul has stood for and experienced (ethos). "Memory" is a common device, used about twenty-five times by Paul in his undisputed epistles.[132] It serves to assure the hearers that they possess the requisite information, skills, and so on to manage their problems. Here it appears with the verb *γίνομαι* ("be," "become"), as in 1 Thess 1:5; 2:1. "From the very first day" appears conventional, but the wording reflects Phil 1:5,[133] where it has a similar function: binding communicator to audience.

■ **19** The verse sets out, in Pauline and Deutero-Pauline language, the conditions under which Paul spent his time in Ephesus. They do not resonate with chap. 19. They do resonate within the speech.[134] Paul, like all believers, is a slave of his master[135] and accepts that position, "without asserting my privileges" (lit. "with all humility"), a phrase evidently taken from Eph 4:2,[136]

126 It may seem absurd to speak of the presence of all three types of rhetoric within a speech of this length, but the purpose of this method is not to identify pigeon holes in which to drop a text but to provide tools for interpretation.

127 Hemer's comments are indicative of his orientation. He strongly rejects attempts to classify this speech in terms of formal or rhetorical type because he views these as inimical to the verbal accuracy of the account ("The Speeches of Acts I: The Ephesian Elders at Miletus," *TynB* 40 [1989] 77–85, esp. 78). For Hemer, all classification presumes secondary status. This overlooks the probability that Paul would make use of rhetorical and other forms even in spontaneous comments.

128 The often pleonastic style of Colossians and, in particular, Ephesians is echoed in the tendency toward pairing that is prominent in vv. 20-21: announce and teach, public and private, Jews and Greeks, repentance and faith.

129 See Rackham, 384.

130 Irenaeus (*A.H.* 3.14.2) makes two revelatory adjustments in his description of the setting: *bishops and* presbyters come from Ephesus *and neighboring cities.* He conforms church order to later practice and makes the audience more general. For Luke, Ephesus was both the central place and the symbol of the Pauline mission.

131 See Boismard, *Texte,* 333–39.

132 See, e.g., 1 Thess 2:1, 5, 10, 11; 3:3-4; 4:2; Gal 3:2; 4:13; 1 Cor 6:2; for commentary, see Aejmelaeus, *Rezeption,* 98–101; and Walton, *Leadership,* 157–59. (Paul normally uses the verb *γιγνώσκω* ("know," as in v. 34). Acts uses the convention in 15:6 (speech of Peter).

133 On these two reminiscences, see Pervo, *Dating,* 115–16.

134 Tears: v. 31; persecution: vv. 22-23. Paul's "humility" may be contrasted with the style of the "vicious" (lit. "heavy," "oppressive") wolves of v. 29. Cf. Josephus *Ant.* 15.354, where the adjective is applied to Herod the Great.

135 Rom 1:1; Gal 1:10; and Phil 1:1. See also 1 Thess 1:9; Gal 6:17; and Phil 2:22, among others. Here, as in some epistles, the concept comes near the opening of the piece in question. The same participial phrase occurs in Rom 12:11. For more discussion, see Aejmelaeus, *Rezeption,* 102; and Walton, *Leadership,* 186–88.

136 See Pervo, *Dating,* 116–17.

while "tears" may be an echo of 2 Cor 2:4.[137] "Frustrations" (lit. "trials," πειρασμοί) is also a theme of Jesus' farewell address (Luke 22:28).[138] The source of these difficulties can be summarized as "Jewish machinations."[139] This is the impression the author wishes to leave with the reader. If not a perfectly accurate summary of Paul's experiences hitherto (since some of his difficulties came from gentile machinations), it is a fair forecast of things to come. This Deutero-Pauline Paul speaks like a gentile: "the Jews" are "the other."[140] The vast distance between this grim summary and the experiences reported in the previous chapter reveal the purpose of this unit, which is not to summarize for these persons what they would have known, but to convey to the readers a picture of Paul that will obtain their sympathy and make an indelible pastoral impression.

■ **20** The verse, which is nearly identical in its basic structure to v. 27,[141] sets forth the essence of both the setting and the content of the message. The guiding concept is that which is preferable (*τὸ σύμφερον*), a theme of deliberative rhetoric used in the Corinthian correspondence.[142] Luke uses the language of Paul the pastor, that is, the language of the epistles. Equally Pauline is the phrase "both Jews and Greeks" (v. 21, with *τε καί*), prominent in Romans (1:16; 2:9-10; 3:9; 10:12; cf. 1 Cor 12:13), and taken up by Luke (Acts 14:1; 19:10, 17) in narrative form: Paul preaches to Jews first.[143] Here it probably also means that Paul did not preach one theology to Jews and another to gentiles, for the corresponding phrase is "both in public and in private."[144] This is not verbiage. Luke is aware of claims based on secret teaching of Paul and wishes to affirm that his message in both public settings and house churches contains all that anyone required.[145] From the philosophical perspective, it assures readers that Paul's private behavior does not contradict his public teaching.

The verb διαμαρτύρομαι ("strongly assert") is a leitmotif (vv. 21, 23, 24) of this speech and a key term for proclamation, beginning with Peter's first evangelistic sermon (2:40) and ending with Paul's final sermon in Rome (28:23).[146] The content of proclamation, "repentance toward God and faith toward our Lord Jesus," is a Lucan summary of Christian belief.[147] The phrase is chiastic in structure: one directs repentance toward God and faith toward Jesus. This summary, although

137 Ibid. For the pathos, cf. 2 Tim 1:4.

138 Cf. also Luke 8:13; 11:4; 22:40, 46; and 1 Pet 1:6. These are not "temptations" to apostasy. They characterize the church as *ecclesia pressa*.

139 Love of conspiracy was a hostile allegation made against the Jews in antiquity: Ptolemy *Apotelesmatica* 2.3.65-66.29-31, on which see Stern, *Authors*, 2:163.

140 Witherington (617) paraphrases this as "plots by his fellow Jews." This misrepresents the text.

141 "Never avoid" (negative + ὑποστέλλω) is an elegant equivalent to "speak out." See Cadbury and Lake, 260. Such claims are typical in apologies (e.g., Plato *Apol.* 24A, which uses this verb and also contrasts "large and small," as in Acts 26:22). Declarations of innocence are typical of the testament: 1 Sam 12:2-5; *T. Sim.* 6:1; *T. Levi* 10:2; *T. Jos.* 1:3. Plutarch's treatise on distinguishing between flatterers and friends (*Mor.* 60a) has an interesting parallel: Free persons (the speaker is not sincere) ought to speak frankly, avoid dissembling, and not refrain from speaking about the what is beneficial (παρρησιάζεσθαι καὶ μηδὲν ὑποστέλλεσθαι μηδ᾽ ἀποσιωπᾶν τῶν συμφερόντων).

142 See Pervo, *Dating*, 117.

143 See ibid., 104–5.

144 Jerome Neyrey ("'Teaching You in Public and from House to House' (Acts 20.20): Unpacking a Cultural Stereotype," *JSNT* 26 [2003] 69–102) argues that in Acts "public" refers to the facilities of rulers and city centers.

145 Barrett (2:968) states that the issue is the secret teaching of "Gnostics," observing a similar motivation in Col 1:28. Colossians and Ephesians include ideas that will stimulate thinkers of "Gnostic" inclination. False teachers of various sorts in Ephesus are apparent from Rev 2:1-7, the Pastorals, and Ignatius *Ephesians*. See Walter Bauer, *Orthodoxy and Heresy in Earliest Christianity* (trans. and ed. Robert Kraft and Gerhard Krodel. Philadelphia: Fortress Press, 1971) 72–90. John M. Court ("Rivals in the Mission Field," *ExpT* 113 [2002] 399–403) proposes that exponents of some Johannine trends would fit the bill. Trebilco (*Early Christians*, 191–95) hesitates to relate this to "Gnostics." He is confident that the prediction applies to Ephesus.

146 The verb appears nine times in Acts, once in Luke, three times in the Pastorals, once in Hebrews, and on a single occasion in Paul (1 Thess 4:6).

147 See p. 519 n. 135.

coupled with the key Lucan term "repentance," almost as a hendiadys, has a Pauline ring.[148] For Barrett, this is superficial and subjective Paulinism, comparable to the Pastorals.[149] In short, it reflects Deutero-Pauline developments. The D-Text found this construction troubling.[150]

■ **22** The speaker turns toward the future. In typical heroic fashion, Paul asseverates that the threat of death will not deter him from his ordained path. Verse 22 raises suspense, although the next clause cancels its basis.[151] This is characteristic of Luke, who wishes to provide suspense without suggesting that all is due to chance.[152] Jesus' predictions of his coming fate in Jerusalem are also and intentionally evoked.[153] The atmosphere is impregnated with Deutero-Paulinism: Paul has finished his course (20:24)[154] but remains concerned about the church, especially in Ephesus,[155] and equally impregnated with the language of the epistles. Rom 15:25-31 has exercised a strong influence.[156] Also Pauline are the use of "afflictions" (θλίψεις), "chains" as a trope for "imprisonment," and πλὴν ὅτι ("except that"),[157] which come from Phil 1:17-18.[158]

Barrett says that the phrase with "compelled" (δεδεμένος, lit. "bound") lacks clarity.[159] Its justification derives from the play with δεῖ, meaning "divine necessity" here (cf. 19:21), and δεσμά ("chains").[160]

■ **23** The verse supplies new information: Paul has been warned by the Spirit that arrest lies in his future. The language, "city by city" (κατὰ πόλιν), is interesting. There is no hint of when these warnings began. Reference to cities indicates the urban orientation of the narrator. It may also suggest that these oracles were received during occasions of worship at the various sites. The single example, 21:10-14, is neither a revelation to Paul nor does it take place during worship. This suggests that prophets in various communities are to be envisioned as the source of these oracles.[161]

■ **24** This is a complex, cumbersome construction[162] that presents another example of Luke's Paulinism. The

148 See, e.g., Gal 2:16; 3:26; and Eph 1:15||Col 1:4. Aejmelaeus (*Rezeption*, 108–12) explores the relation to Pauline texts, with attention to the key Pauline word "faith."

149 Barrett, 2:969.

150 Boismard (*Texte*, 334) reads "repentance toward God and faith **through** our Lord Jesus (Christ)." This may be somewhat more Pauline and shows the beginning of trinitarian reflection. It is less subordinationist. See Barrett, 2:969.

151 Lambrecht ("Farewell," 307) notes that v. 22 is concretized in 21:4, 10-11. Squires (*Plan*, 151–52) states that Paul prophesies about the future for the first time here in Acts.

152 Conzelmann, 174: "With this vacillation between not knowing and knowing, Luke can indicate both the divine guidance of Paul's life and also Paul's willingness to endure suffering."

153 For details, see Tannehill, *Narrative Unity*, 2:259.

154 See below.

155 See Wilson, *Luke and the Pastoral Epistles*, 117.

156 See Pervo, *Dating*, 119–20. Both use the identical phrase, "I am going toward Jerusalem" (Rom 15:25; Acts 20:22; cf. also "now"), with reference to the same (final) journey.

157 On this conjunction, see BDF §449 (1).

158 Both πορεύομαι εἰς Ἰερουσαλήμ (above) and πλὴν ὅτι occur only in these passages. For more discussion, see Aejmelaeus, *Rezeption*, 117.

159 Barrett, 2:969.

160 Conzelmann (174) is correct, from the history-of-religions viewpoint, in saying that it refers to "supernatural binding." "Binding" spells are an obvious parallel. On these, see, e.g., Deissmann, *Light*, 304–7.

161 Cf. *Act. Paul* 9/12 (Corinth), where Paul (who is going to Rome) speaks of the coming danger and fulfillment of his mission (cf. Acts 20:24). One Cleobius recites an inspired message forecasting Paul's death. Myrta was also inspired to predict his great success at Rome. These take place during (a vigil and) the Eucharist. Eduard Schweizer ("πνεῦμα," *TDNT* 6:332–445, esp. 408 n. 491) takes "city by city" to refer to prophecies delivered by members of the different communities.

162 Ropes (196) suspects that the text may be corrupt. Cf. Cadbury and Lake (260–61), who agree and also suggest that two constructions may be blended, comparing this to 23:30; 27:10. See also Conzelmann, 174. The D-Text seeks to smooth the wording by saying, "I take account of nothing nor do I regard my life as valuable (ἀλλ᾽ οὐδενὸς λόγον ἔχω οὐδε). "Ministry" is followed by "**of the word** that I received (παρέλαβον, a more technical term), and interpolates "to both Jews and Greeks" before "gospel." See Boismard, *Texte*, 335. The term παραλαμβάνω ("receive") recognizes the Pauline background (Gal 1:9, 12). Barrett (2:971-72) examines the options for text and translation.

theme is Paul's understanding of his vocation as the willing surrender of himself as a ministry to his Lord, who also freely surrendered himself.[163] This is otherwise implicit, at best, in Acts, but here the similarity is impressive. The verse includes such basic Pauline terms as "ministry" (διακονία), "grace" (χάρις), and "gospel" (εὐαγγέλιον). Luke uses "ministry" and "grace," albeit usually in difference senses from Paul.[164] Here both fit Paul's understanding.[165] Luke generally avoids the noun "gospel." The two exceptions are Peter's "Pauline" speech in 15:7 and here.[166] "Gospel of the grace of God" probably derives from Ephesians (3:2, 6-7).[167] Cadbury and Lake call this verse "perhaps the most completely Hellenized summary of the Christian message" in Acts.[168] Finishing one's life task (lit. "course") is a reference to death.[169]

■ **25-27** Paul's attention returns to the future.[170] The hearers will not see Paul again.[171] Their identity is generalized to include all "among whom I went about proclaiming God's reign." This could include everyone to whom Paul preached, from Damascus onward.[172] The real audience is all the heirs of the Pauline mission. The phrase refers to his permanent departure and thus to his death, although the emphasis is on his "presence in spirit" rather than his "absence in body."[173] The object of his preaching was "the kingdom." This combination (κηρύσσω + βασιλεία, "proclaim" + "kingdom") is used in Acts only here and in the last verse of the book (28:31).[174] The noun indicates that, for Luke, "kingdom" as object of proclamation was essentially the same as "gospel,"[175] which is one of the variants.[176]

---

163 Bruce (433) cites 2 Cor 4:7-11; 6:4-10; 12:9-10; Phil 1:20; 2:17; 3:8; also cf. Col 1:24. Aejmelaeus (*Rezeption*, 119–28), whose discussion should be consulted, pays particular attention to Phil 2:16-17, the structure of which he finds to be parallel to that of Acts 20:24 (122). See also Walton (*Leadership*, 178), who points out affinities with 1 Thessalonians. Paul Elbert ("Paul of the Miletus Speech and 1 Thessalonians: Critique and Considerations," *ZNW* 95 [2004] 258–68) inclines, against Walton, toward dependence upon 1 Thessalonians. C. Leslie Mitton (*The Epistle to the Ephesians: Its Authorship, Origin and Purpose* [Oxford: Clarendon Press, 1951] 211–14) identifies general and particular points of contact with Ephesians. Willingness to sacrifice oneself for a cause is a common motif of various types of "romantic" literature and is extolled in both classical Greek and subsequent Latin literature.

164 On "ministry," see 2 Cor 5:18.

165 For data, see Pervo, *Dating*, 119–20. These words are also consonant with Jesus' own statement (a modification of Mark) that he is "one who serves" (Luke 22:26-27).

166 The same speech provides an example of "grace" in the Pauline sense (15:11).

167 See Pervo, *Dating*, 120–21.

168 Cadbury and Lake, 261. They suggest that the kingdom is in the process of being equated with the church. This is Deutero-Pauline: cf. Col 1:13; 4:11.

169 Note 13:25 (John the Baptizer) and 2 Tim 4:7. Dido uses the same image in her final words (Virgil *Aen.* 4.653). Paul employs athletic imagery, a commonplace of Greco-Roman popular philosophy, although he does not use the word "course" (δρόμος). Phil 3:12-14 is the closest analogy—and the best contrast.

170 The verse begins καὶ νῦν ἰδού (lit. "and now look"), as did v. 25.

171 Such statements are conventional in testaments. See Johnson (362), who notes Gen 48:21; *T. Reub.* 1:4-5; *T. Dan* 2:1; *T. Naph.* 1:3; *T. Job* 1:4; 2 Tim 4:6; 2 Pet 1:13; Luke 22:15-16.

172 The verb διέρχομαι ("go through") here appears for the last of twenty times in Acts. It always refers to travel.

173 Attempts to deny the reference to death can be laborious, as Witherington exemplifies (616–20). Rather than view this statement as a genuine forecast that raises historical questions, it should be viewed as a literary feature that relates to the plot of Acts as a whole (Lambrecht, "Farewell," 309). For evidence and references indicating that v. 25 refers to Paul's death, see Matthew L. Skinner, *Locating Paul: Places of Custody as Narrative Settings in Acts 21–28* (SBL Academia Biblica 13; Atlanta: Society of Biblical Literature, 2003) 98–99 n. 72.

174 Acts 28:31 adds "of God." Luke 8:1; 9:2 use the phrase to describe the preaching of Jesus. By using the same words to characterize the message of both Jesus and Paul, Luke helps overcome the gap between "proclaimer" and "proclaimed," on which see p. 19 n. 114.

175 Barrett, 2:973: "It means in effect the recognized content of Christian preaching, and is so expressed in order to bring out the continuity between the preaching of Jesus and the preaching of the post-resurrection church." See also Weiser, 2:577.

176 323. 1739. 1891 *pc* read "the gospel of God." Other genitive qualifiers are "of Jesus" (accepted as the

Finality motivates (διότι,[177] "therefore") the claim of innocence in v. 26. Its extravagant nature is only partially mitigated by the translation, which takes the phrase "guiltless of the blood of all" as a metonym for "death,"[178] used metaphorically, as in 18:6, for spiritual death. Verse 27 provides, by reiterating v. 20, the grounds: Paul has taught salvation in its entirety. He bears no responsibility for scoffers and apostates.[179] The D-Text[180] found the statement troubling and dropped the first three words ("I therefore swear to you") and read "**up to** today, **then**, [ ] I am guiltless of the blood of all **of you**." This revision suggests that the editor saw no need for Paul to make so strong a declaration and that he took "blood" to mean "death."[181] Reiteration of the subject and predicate of v. 20 in v. 27 indicates that "God's plan/will" can be characterized concretely as "repentance and faith," that is, that it need not refer to a philosophy of history.[182] The sufficiency of Paul's message is not the sole subject of this sentence.[183] Paul has done his part. The ball is in their court.

■ **28** This verse, the formal charge, presents two textual questions. Internal evidence is rather evenly balanced between "the church of God" and "the church of the Lord."[184] The latter is probably secondary—"church of God" is Pauline,[185] found only here in Acts, while "church of the Lord" is not found in the NT—aimed at the subsequent relative clause, which includes the phrase *διὰ τοῦ αἵματος τοῦ ἰδίου*. If this is taken to mean "his own blood," then the antecedent "God" would strike early editors as Sabellian or amenable to a modalistic understanding. In the fourth century, however, this reading would serve anti-Arian claims. Thus "Lord" could have been an "orthodox emendation" in the third century and "God" in the fourth. The D-Text[186] resolves the issue with "church of the **Lord** which he obtained **for himself** . . . ," leaving "his (i.e., Jesus') own blood" as a natural understanding.[187] If "Lord" were original, the difficulties with the following clause would have been unlikely to arise.[188] The translation thus prefers "God" and takes *τοῦ ἰδίου* as a noun.[189] This is also more congruent with Lucan theology.[190] Cadbury says that this is the best instance in Acts of "church" meaning the church catholic.[191]

Barrett states that v. 28 is the pastoral and theological center of the speech. The former is clear: the exhortation to the presbyters, but the latter: "Because . . . here

D-Text by Boismard, *Texte*, 336), "of the Lord Jesus," and "of God." The variants show that the absolute noun generated discomfort.

177 This word should mean "because." LSJ (435, *s.v.*) allows "Wherefore." BDAG, 251, *s.v.*, includes "therefore," with no references other than this passage and Acts 13:35. It is evidently a Lucan idiom. The "correct" διό is a frequent variant; see Swanson, *Manuscripts*, 362.

178 See Johannes Behm, "αἷμα," *TDNT* 1:172–77, esp. 173. (Cf. English "bloodshed.")

179 So Conzelmann, 174. A negative, prophetic, understanding can be derived from Ezek 3:18-22. The prophet is charged with summoning the wicked to repent or facing the consequences. This moralistic understanding was supported by a range of authorities, including Gregory the Great (*Regula Past.* 3.25) and Calvin (7:181), but it is foreign to Acts.

180 See Boismard, *Texte*, 336.

181 The addition "of you" may stem from the belief that Paul was responsible for the death of Stephen (8:1a).

182 See also Luke 7:30. *1 Clem.* 27:6 uses "plan" (βουλή) of general divine oversight. On the subject in general, see Conzelmann, *Theology*, 151–54; and Squires, *Plan*.

183 On this matter (a central issue in Reformed theology), see Calvin, 7:180–81, at some length, and, with typical concision, Conzelmann, 174. Secret teaching, as in v. 27, is probably a subsidiary issue here also. God's plan is not discovered through esoteric speculation or exegesis.

184 See Metzger, *Textual Commentary*, 425.

185 Examples of the expression "church of God" in Paul include 1 Cor 1:2; 10:32; 11:22; 15:9; 2 Cor 1:1; Gal 1:13, eleven times in all.

186 Boismard, *Texte*, 337. He regards the "Alexandrian text" as "theologically impossible." This is a dogmatic anachronism.

187 Cf. The Textus Receptus, which reads διὰ τοῦ ἰδίου αἵματος ("through his own blood").

188 See Metzger, *Textual Commentary*, 425–26; and Walton, *Leadership*, 94–98, with his references.

189 On this, see Cadbury and Lake, 261.

190 See Conzelmann, 175, who notes that Luke's Christology is consistently subordinationist.

191 Cadbury, "Names," 389.

only in Acts is there an attempt to state the significance of the death of Christ and at the same time to bring out the ground of the church's ministry in the work of the Holy Spirit" privileges one atonement theory.[192] Luke's language here is, as Franklin finds, "an accommodation to Paul's beliefs rather than an expression of his own theology."[193] Luke does not use "blood" in a soteriological sense,[194] but the term is not alien to Paul (Rom 3:35; 5:9). Luke probably took up the phrase about blood from Eph 1:7.[195]

The ecclesiological language, which speaks of "bishops"[196] instituted by the Holy Spirit to shepherd the flock,[197] belongs to a time well after the dramatic date. Ephesians 4:11 shows the emergence of this language in the Pauline sphere.[198] *1 Clem.* 54:2 has a similar view. Let the troublemaker(s) leave: "Only allow the flock of Christ to be at peace with the presbyters who have been appointed."[199] Readers of Acts would presume that these presbyters had been appointed by Paul.[200] There is no contradiction between this understanding and the primary agency of the Holy Spirit.[201]

The relatively rare terms περιποιέω, περιποίησις ("obtain," "gain possession of," "possession"), with the preposition διά ("through"), can be traced in an intertextual process from 1 Thessalonians to Ephesians to Acts.[202] This is additional evidence for Acts' Deutero-Pauline understanding of Paul's letters. Luke does not simply borrow phrases to bestow a Pauline coloring. The Lucan writings are also witnesses to the reception of Paul's letters, albeit indirectly.

192 Barrett, 2:974.

193 Franklin, *Christ the Lord*, 66.

194 See also Conzelmann, *Theology*, 201, 220 n. 1. Ignatius, it might be noted, does use the phrase "blood of God" (*Eph.* 1:1, on which see the comments of Schoedel, *Ignatius*, 42.

195 See Pervo, *Dating*, 122–23.

196 "Bishop" is used, rather than "overseer," and the like, because by Luke's time the term was used for a church office (*1 Clement*; Pastorals), although the meaning varied. At the time of writing, there may well have been a bishop (or more) in Ephesus who sought overall leadership. Ignatius's letter to the Ephesians makes strenuous efforts to support Onesimus, the bishop (chaps. 4–6). In 4:1 he says, "For your presbytery [the very group addressed by Paul], which is both worthy of the name and worthy of God, is attuned to the bishop as strings to the lyre" (trans. Ehrman, *Apostolic Fathers*, 1:223). One may doubt whether the lyre was so well strung. Along with the traditional argument that the church at Ephesus was governed solely by presbyters in Luke's own time should stand the possibility that Luke knew about sole ("monarchical") bishops and did not fully approve of the idea. Clear disapproval is apparent in 3 John 9, which is sometimes associated with Ephesus. See Trebilco, *Early Christians*, 303.

197 BDF §390 (3) relates the infinitive ποιμαίνειν ("shepherd") to the verb ("a looser combination"). It might be preferable to relate it to the phrase "made you bishops" and see it as final.

198 The image appears in Luke 17:7-10. For Paul, note also 1 Cor 9:7. The contrast is between the occasional employment of metaphors for "pastoral" work and the fixation of these metaphors in titles and structure. See also 1 Pet 5:2 and John 21:16. 1 Pet 2:25 combines "shepherd" and "bishop" (with reference to Christ, evidently). CD 13:9 says that the מבקר (*mĕbaqqēr*), a leading Essene official, whose title would translate into Greek as ἐπίσκοπος, should behave like a father and treat those who stray as a shepherd treats wayward sheep. Within a century or less, the verb "shepherd" (ποιμαίνω) would become (and remain) the key word in the prayers for the ordination of bishops: e.g., *Apostolic Tradition* 3.4; Serapion *Euchologion* 28.2. The use of "shepherd" as a metaphor for leadership is ancient and widespread. See Pervo, *Dating*, 204-8.

199 Trans. Ehrman, *Apostolic Fathers*, 1:131.

200 Note also *1 Clem.* 44:1-3, which uses the term "bishops," evidently more or less synonymously with "presbyters." Those "appointed" (καθίστημι, as in 54:2) by apostles or their successors (with the consent of the whole community) have ministered to the "flock of Christ" (as in 54:2) "with humility" (μετὰ ταπεινοφροσύνης, cf. Acts 20:19). See also Pervo, *Dating*, 208–10.

201 Barrett's (2:974–75) statements setting "Spirit" against "institution" are rather unnecessary. Luke will not institutionalize the Holy Spirit, but even a superficial examination of the classical ordination prayers shows that the Holy Spirit has always been viewed as the agent. Conzelmann (175) correctly sees that Spirit and institution converge in ordination. See also the comments of Weiser, 2:584.

202 See Pervo, *Dating*, 122–23. On the background, see Isa 43:21 LXX: God "acquired" the people so that they would offer praise.

■ **29-31** The sole aspect of pastoral care singled out by Paul in these verses[203] is the battle against false teaching. This requires constant attention (v. 31), of which Paul himself serves as a model. These duties are also underlined in the Pastorals[204] and Polycarp (*Phil.* 7). Both Acts and the Pastorals are concerned with preservation of what they consider the Pauline heritage in a later era and are roughly contemporaneous in time and place. In both, leaders have the chief responsibility for subduing opponents (1 Tim 5:17; 2 Tim 2:2; Titus 1:5-6). Paul's doctrine and example constitute the most potent weapons in their arsenals.[205] Greed is a particular concern (1 Tim 6:9-10; Titus 1:11). Leaders' responsibilities in both works thus include nurturing the church,[206] keeping alert to and addressing false teaching, and avoidance of greed. Both are suffused with Paul's suffering and forthcoming death. Commendations close the testaments in 20:32 and 2 Tim 4:22. Some of these similarities may be attributed to the testamentary form, others to the method, which devotes more energy to denouncing opponents than to providing clear profiles of their teachings. That method shows that both Luke and the Pastorals view the church as a body with fixed boundaries that must be protected, rather than a community that is in the process of determining boundaries.[207] In both works, danger will come from both outside (v. 29; Titus) and inside (v. 30; 1 Timothy).[208] These similarities are emphasized by the differences between the two authors.[209]

Where there are shepherds, there must be flocks.[210] Flocks attract wolves. This natural metaphor was also widespread.[211] The imagery allows the battle against

203 Verses 34-35 take up care for the disadvantaged. Just as Luke 22:35 distinguishes between the time when Jesus was present and that of his absence, so Acts 20:29 draws a line between the presence and absence of Paul.

204 1 Tim 1:3; 4:6-7, 11-12; 6:3, 20; 2 Tim 2:14-20; 3:1-7; 4:1-7; Titus 1:10–2:7, 15.

205 1 Tim 3:14; 4:11-12; 6:20; 2 Tim 1:8-9, 13-14; 3:10-11; Titus 1:5.

206 1 Tim 3:2; 4:13-14, 16; 2 Tim 4:2; Titus 1:9.

207 For these models, see Margaret Y. MacDonald, *The Pauline Churches* (SNTSMS 60; Cambridge: Cambridge University Press, 1988). The model is sociological, but it has temporal relevance: boundary maintenance is a phenomenon of particular concern to the third generation (and later). See below.

208 The statement that the wolves will be "vicious" or "oppressive" (βαρεῖς) may reflect financial rapacity. Cf. vv. 33-34. Paul states, when speaking of self-support, that he does not wish to be a burden (1 Thess 2:6: ἐν βάρει). See also Walton, *Leadership*, 167. The insiders will seek to mislead the faithful and form their own groups. An example of misleading (διαστρέφω) is Elymas, who seeks to divert Sergius Paulus from the true path (Acts 13:8, 10). The verb is used in the (false) charges against Jesus, Luke 23:5. Note also *1 Clem.* 46:9; 47:5.

209 Proposals that Luke authored the Pastorals (on this hypothesis, see Pervo, "Romancing an Oft-neglected Stone: The Pastoral Epistles and the Epistolary Novel," *JHC* 1 [1994] 25–47) focus on similarities, but differences outweigh these. Among them: in the Pastorals, Paul is *the* apostle and writes letters. In Acts, Paul is a non-letter-writing non-apostle. Luke favors celibacy (Pervo, *Profit*, 181 n. 79); the Pastor essentially requires marriage (and childbearing). The God of the Pastorals is distant and transcendent, and the Christology is rooted in the theme of epiphany. For Luke, God is active (e.g., miracles), and the Christology is based on the picture of Jesus as a prophet and example, elevated to heaven. The Spirit, so central to Luke, plays a smaller role in the Pastorals (1 Tim 4:1; 2 Tim 1:14; Titus 3:5). Eph 4:11-16 contains similar warnings, as noted by Rudolf Schnackenburg, *Ephesians: A Commentary* (trans. H. Heron; Edinburgh: T&T Clark, 1991) 185–86. It is inherently probable that the Pastor knew Acts, but he made limited, at most, use of it.

210 On this metaphor, see, in addition to n. 198, Jer 13:17; Zech 10:3; Luke 12:32; 1 Pet 5:2-3; and *1 Clem.* 16:1; 57:2..

211 From Jewish apocalyptic, see, e.g., *1 Enoch* 89:13-14; *4 Ezra* 5:18; Greco-Roman philosophical and historical examples include Epictetus *Diss.* 1.3.7–9; 3.22.35; Maximus of Tyre *Or.* 6, 7d; Libanius *Epistle* 194.1; Cassius Dio 56.16.3; and Philostratus *Vit. Apoll.* 8:22 (in which the followers of Apollonius are a "flock" [ποίμνη] requiring protection from "wolves"). In early Christian literature the epithet is common. Matt 7:15 was often cited in early Christian literature. Note also Luke 10:3||Matt 10:16 (lambs in the midst of wolves); John 10:1-16 (and John 21:15-17: earthly shepherds). See also *Did.* 16:3; *2 Clem.* 5:2-4; Ignatius *Phil.* 2.2; Justin *1 Apol.* 16.13; *Dial.* 35.3; 81.2; *Act. Pet.* 8 (Verc.: Simon is call a "ravaging wolf"). The term was applied to Marcion by the orthodox writer Rhodon, according to Eusebius, *H.E.* 5.13.4.

rival teaching to be seen as the fundamental task of pastoral care: protection of the flock.[212] The imagery is common in eschatological warnings.[213] Luke has, in fact, utilized the eschatological discourse of Mark 13:21-23 in the construction of these verses,[214] placing these words into an ecclesial context and stripping them of their apocalyptic flavor. False teachers will not be signs of the approaching end, but a challenge to be met through proper leadership. Paul makes no claims to have received a revelation on this matter. He speaks with firm authority: "I know."[215] "Departure"[216] is a euphemism for death. Luke here sets forth two key concepts upon which later writers, such as Eusebius, will build: Heresy did not erupt so long as apostles and their associates lived, and the third generation played a critical role in the transmission of apostolic tradition.[217]

These forthcoming circumstances thus (διό; cf. v. 26) require incessant vigilance, of which Paul is an example. Luke, who avoided two Marcan uses of the "eschatological" imperative "keep alert" (γρηγορεῖτε [Mark 13:35; 14:38]), uses it here in the Pauline manner.[218] The hyperbole "night and day" is Pauline and Deutero-Pauline.[219] "Tears," which expresses profound emotion and effort, recalls v. 19.[220] The Pauline intertextual allusions are numerous and complex.[221] The most obvious borrowing is νουθετέω ("admonish").[222]

■ **32** This commendation,[223] which hovers on the fringes of announcing a succession, resembles the language of Ephesians. The verb παρατίθημι ("entrust to") is that used by Jesus at the moment of his death (Luke 23:46). Also comparable is Jesus' testamentary disposition (διατίθημι) of "the kingdom" to his followers in his farewell speech (Luke 22:29).[224] The former (παρατίθημι) is a important for the Pastor (1 Tim 1:18; 2 Tim 2:2).[225] Succession is often a key feature of farewell speeches and death scenes. Luke is less interested in tracing lines of succession than is *1 Clement*,

For other uses, see G. Bornkamm, λύκος, *TDNT* 4:308–11; Geoffrey W. H. Lampe, "'Grievous Wolves' (Acts 20:29)," in Barnabas Lindars and Stephen S. Smalley, eds., *Christ and Spirit in the New Testament: In Honour of Charles Francis Digby Moule* (Cambridge: Cambridge University Press, 1973) 235–68; and Malherbe, *Paul*, 153.

212 "Show no mercy" (φείδομαι) is a Pauline word (six times in the undisputed epistles; once in 1 Peter and here).

213 See n. 211. The verb προσέχετε ("be attentive" [v. 28]) is common in warnings against rival groups: Matt 7:15; 16:6; Luke 17:3; 20:46; 2 Pet 1:19.

214 See Pervo, *Dating*, 123–24.

215 Cf. Deut 31:29, which begins οἶδα γὰρ ὅτι ἔσχατον τῆς τελευτῆς μου ("For I know that after my death") and foretells wickedness and apostasy. The same prophetic style (οἶδα, "I know") appears in the letters that open Revelation: 2:2, 9, 13, 19; 3:1, 8, 15.

216 The term ἄφιξις should (and often does) mean "arrival," but "departure" comes about because the Greek viewpoint focused on movement toward a destination. See BDAG, 157, *s.v.* The metaphorical use is not otherwise attested, but see "exodus" in Luke 9:31 (of Jesus' passion). The *Life of Polycarp* 3 begins μετὰ δὲ τὴν ἀποστόλου ἄφιξιν διεδέξατο ὁ Στραταίας τὴν διδασκαλίαν ("Now following the *departure* of the apostle [Paul] Strataias succeeded to his office of teaching" [author's trans.]).

217 Eusebius *H.E.* 3.32.7 (from Hegisippus). At the close of this passage, Eusebius (or his source) cites 1 Tim 6:20. One result was to extend the length of the third generation to (and beyond) the limits of possibility. Irenaeus still claimed to belong to that company. Cf. also Klein, *Zwölf*, 180–81.

218 See 1 Cor 16:13 and Walton, *Leadership*, 161 n. 110. On the exhortation in early Christian literature, see Edward Gordon Selwyn, *The First Epistle of St Peter* (2nd ed.; London: Macmillan, 1947) 376–78, 453.

219 Note, in particular, 1 Thess 2:9 (imitated in 2 Thess 3:8); cf. also 3:10; 1 Tim 5:5; 2 Tim 1:3. The phrase is often applied to prayer: Luke 2:37; Acts 26:7. Aejmelaeus (*Rezeption*, 151–53) examines the phrase in detail.

220 2 Cor 2:1-11 is an example of one admonished by Paul. Luke may have had this situation in mind.

221 See Pervo, *Dating*, 123.

222 Rom 15:14; 1 Cor 4:14; Col 1:28; 3:16; 1 Thess 5:12, 14; and 2 Thess 3:15. This is a responsibility of leaders, as in 1 Thess 5:12; Col 1:28; *1 Clem.* 7:1; 2 *Clem.* 17:3; 19:2. Note also μνημονεύω: Gal 2:10; Eph 2:11; Col 4:18; 1 Thess 1:3; 2:9; 2 Thess 2:5; 2 Tim 2:8; and Johnson, 364.

223 Cf. 14:23, where the commendation is not a final farewell.

224 See Christian Maurer, "τίθημι," *TDNT* 8:153–68, esp. 162–64.

225 The noun παραθήκη ("deposit") appears in 1 Tim 6:20; 2 Tim 1:12, 14. Steve Walton (*Leadership*,

but it is safe to say that orderly transition of power is important to him.[226]

The description of God's word[227] as empowering is a Pauline theme with which Luke is in hearty accord.[228] "Build up" (οἰκοδομέω) also reflects Pauline language.[229] Ephesians has strongly influenced v. 32, but it also participates in the world of other (Pauline and) Deutero-Pauline passages,[230] as well as the LXX.[231] Two metaphors are mixed: the promise of inheriting the land and the view of the community as a building. The former is dominant. "Inheritance," stripped of literal and historical associations, became a useful term for receipt of divine reward.[232] The language is eschatological, without a clear temporal application.[233]

■ **33-34** The next verse brings another surprise to the reader of Acts: Paul, like Peter (3:6; 8:18-20), is not greedy and will not accept money for his services.[234] If financial exploitation has motivated others (cf. 8:4-25; 16:16-19; 19:25-27), not even his worst enemies have hurled that mud at Paul. At issue is the never-mentioned but ever-present subject of the collection. Paul was said to have raised money indirectly by stating that its purpose was charitable.[235] His letters often tackle the topic of money, however uncomfortably.[236] Yet another surprise arrives in v. 34: Paul has supported not only himself but also his colleagues with his labor! Acts 18:3-5 (Corinth) introduced the idea that Paul practiced a craft, but no reader of Acts (cf. 18:5) would have concluded that he did so constantly.[237] Acts 19:12 now becomes perfectly clear: Paul's healing cloths came from his self-supporting sweat.

192–93) stresses that Luke and the Pastor use the verb in different senses. This is true, but for each it belongs to the sphere of transmitting authority.

226 This is to say that Talbert's proposal that Acts is a "succession narrative" following a biography of the founder (Gospel of Luke) is an important observation, perhaps an important half-truth. He has refined this theory often since propounding it in *Literary Patterns*, 125–40. For its most recent formulation, see idem and Perry Stepp, "Succession in Luke-Acts and in the Lukan Milieu," in *Reading Luke-Acts in Its Mediterranean Milieu* (Leiden: Brill, 2003) 19–55.

227 It is possible that "God" and "word" are a hendiadys. See Barrett, 2:980. Formally, one may ask whether the participle δυναμένῳ ("able") modifies "God" or "word." If not taken as a hendiadys, parallels suggest that it belongs with "God." The participle δυναμένῳ as a characterization of God was popular in second-century doxologies: Rom 16:25-27; Jude 24. Note that some D-Texts (614. 2147. 2412 syh**, add a doxology at this point: "to him be glory for ever and ever. Amen." Boismard (*Texte*, 338) prints "inheritance of all the sanctified," regarding the difficult ἡγιασμένοις τῶν πάντων ("sanctified of [?] all [persons, things?] of D as an inept synthesis of the textual forms. Ropes (*Text*, 199) views the reading of D as a survival from the doxology.

228 See Aejmelaeus, *Rezeption*, 158. Cf. also Heb 1:14; 6:12.

229 1 Corinthians has six occurrences of "edify." "Build" occurs in Rom 15:20 and Gal 2:18 (also 1 Pet 2:5, 7). Acts 9:31 is similar, as is ἀνοικοδομεῖν in Acts 15:16. See Pervo, *Dating*, 126–27; and Walton, *Leadership*, 180–81.

230 See 1 Thess 2:13; 5:11; Col 1:12-14; Eph 1:7, 14, 18; 2:2; 3:20-21; 4:12.

231 Acts 20:32 is partially dependent on Deut 33:3-4, as shown by Aejmelaeus, *Rezeption*, 162–63. On the theme of inheritance, see also Ps 15:5 LXX; Wis 5:4; 1QS 11:7-8 and 1QH 11:11-12.

232 Apart from the single, fruitful use of this word in Gal 3:18, the noun appears in Colossians, Ephesians (3), Hebrews (2), and 1 Peter. Note also *1 Clem.* 29:3; 36.4; *Barn.* 4.3; 14:4. For the evolution of the concept, see Johannes Behm and Werner Foerster, "κλῆρος," *TDNT* 3:758–85, esp. 781–85 (Foerster).

233 Luke's sources, Colossians and Ephesians, are more forthright in using this language of present, "realized" eschatology. Cf. also 1QS 11:7-8; 1QH 11:11-12, which view "inheritance" as a present possession. One cannot attribute "building up" to the present and "inheritance" to the future, as does Barrett, 2:981.

234 Whereas people in the contemporary United States think of real and personal property, less wealthy ancients spoke about ready cash and clothing as primary possessions. The thieves of Luke 10:30 stripped their victim because his clothing was valuable. So the soldiers who crucified Jesus got his garments as a gratuity (Mark 15:24). Cf. also Jacquier, 619.

235 See Georgi, *Remembering*, 60–61.

236 1 Thess 2:3-12; 2 Thess 3:7-10; 1 Cor 9:3-18; 2 Cor 4:5; 8–9; 10:1-6; 11:7-11; 12:13.

237 Cf. Haenchen, 594.

This is the flip side of v. 33: self-support was a desirable (if more often in theory than in practice) means of avoiding both taking fees from one's adherents and falling into abject dependence on patrons.[238] Paul pairs this well-phrased "memory" statement[239] with an exhortation to "labor" on behalf of "the weak."

This exhortation exemplifies both the compression of the address, killing two birds with one stone, and its general character. The themes and language echo a number of Pauline and Deutero-Pauline texts.[240] The latter is apparent in the view of work, which is now a necessity (δεῖ [v. 35]),[241] even if the motive is help for the poor. Acts is moving in the direction represented in 2 Thess 3:7-12 and Titus 3:14. Believers are to settle down and find work, so that they may give their faith a good name by productivity and rebuffing the notion that one reason for affiliating with the church is to receive support. Conzelmann identifies what is taking place: "Passages such as 1 Thessalonians 2:9 and 4:11 are now formed into a timeless prototype."[242] Such "timelessness" is the goal of Deutero-Paulinism, which seeks to make the contingent advice of Paul applicable to all believers in every situation.[243] The hyperbole (Paul's income supported his entire entourage) is Lucan.

■ **35** The verse opens with a reinforcement of Paul's role as example.[244] The final speech of Peter's missionary career climaxed with an appeal to the words of Jesus (11:16). Within the Pauline tradition 1 Thess 5:15-17 is a good parallel. Both utilize a saying (λόγος) as the warrant for exhortation.[245] Paul introduces the aphorism with a formula used for citing oral tradition that first appears in Christian literature in *1 Clement* (13:1-2; 46:7) and thereafter in the fragments of Papias and in Polycarp.[246] The formula used in 11:16, which is quite similar, ostensibly reproduces Peter's recollection of what Jesus said, and 1:5 shows but a slight variation from it. This aphorism, however, does not appear in either Luke or Acts. The "agraphon"[247] indicates that for

238 See Malherbe, *Paul*, 35–48; and Hock, *Social Context*, 26–65. Philosophers routinely disavow their interest in money: Dio of Prusa *Or.* 32.9, 11; Philostratus *Vit. Apoll.* 1.34; Lucian *Nigr.* 25–26; (Cynic) *Epistle of Socrates* 1.

239 "You know": cf. v. 18. The circle is closing. The final words are "these hands." Note also the play χρείαις . . . χεῖρες ("needs . . . hands"). Dupont (*Le discours de Milet*, 301) senses the pathos: "These hands which perform miracles (Acts 14:3; 19:11; 28:8) and convey the Holy Spirit (19:6) are also the large hands of a worker, gnarled by hard labor" (author's trans.). The words come from 1 Thess 4:11-12; see Pervo, *Dating*, 127–31.

240 See Pervo, *Dating*, 131–33.

241 For evolving ideas of work in early Christianity, see Goran Agrell, *Work, Toil and Sustenance: An Examination of the View of Work in the New Testament* (Lund: Verbum Hakan Ohlssons, 1976).

242 Conzelmann, 176.

243 *Hermas* 27 (*Man.* 2.4) expects believers to work and, as in Acts, to share with others, while Eph 4:28, which promotes work as an anticrime measure, illustrates the scope of its generality, and Epiphanius *Pan.* 26.11.1 indicates the limits of interpretation. In his discussion of 20:34, Calvin (7:189) fails to extol the "Calvinist work ethic."

244 See Lambrecht, "Farewell," 321. The opening πάντα ("all things") is probably an accusative of respect that may be applied to either v. 34, v. 35, or both. If taken with the former only, punctuation would change. See Cadbury and Lake, 263. D*vid Spec read a simpler "to all persons (presumably, πᾶσιν)." Although not adopted by Boismard, this is consistent with the D-Text tendency to personalize the speech.

245 Cf. Walton, *Leadership*, 171. Aejmelaeus (*Rezeption*, 175–83) discusses the background of the saying in full detail.

246 See Helmut Koester, *Ancient Christian Gospels: Their History and Development* (Philadelphia: Trinity Press International, 1990) 63, 66; and Robinson and Koester, *Trajectories*, 96–97. Bruce (436) notes that αὐτος εἶπεν ("he said") conforms to *ipse dixit* ("He said," in effect, "the master said," used of Pythagoras in his school). Bruce notes later Christian uses (Marius Victorinus) of the expression for Jesus.

247 Alfred Resch introduced Acts 20:35 as an example of "canonical agrapha" in the first edition of his *Agrapha: Aussercanonische Evangelienfragmente* (TU 5; Leipzig: Hinrichs, 1889) 2. See also pp. 150–51, which present five other forms of the saying from early Christian literature. William Stroker follows this practice: *Extracanonical Sayings of Jesus* (SBLRBS 18; Atlanta: Scholars Press, 1989) 227–28.

Luke the door for sayings of Jesus remained open and was not limited to his written Gospel.[248]

The saying was already a venerable proverb when Luke wrote.[249] The earliest Greek attestation is in Thucydides 2.97.4, who attributes the sentiment to the Persians.[250] Closest to the environment of Acts are *1 Clem.* 2:1 and *Did.* 1:5. If an intertextual relationship is proposed, the most likely solution is that Luke took the aphorism from *1 Clement*, Christianized it,[251] and attributed it to Jesus, but the sentiment of *Did.* 1:5 and the parallels from c. 50 CE onward make appeal to a known source unnecessary.[252] The sentiment is applicable to leaders in the context of avoiding greed and caring for the needy, but it is more applicable to potential benefactors.[253] Rather than bestow a macarism upon the poor, with a concomitant woe to the rich (as in Luke 6:20, 24), Paul says that those with some resources can achieve beatitude through generosity.[254] His message thus coincides with that of the Lucan Jesus. The saying is a kind of synecdoche: by closing with a saying of Jesus, Paul affirms all of the teachings of Jesus. As Haenchen says, his last words are not his own, but those of Jesus.[255]

The identification of similarities between this speech and the correspondence, most of which are due to borrowing, might obscure the most important point: Acts 20:17-35 has many of the features of a Deutero-Pauline letter. Like the Pastor, Luke prefers to focus on community leaders in setting forth what Paul would say if he were present now. More than the other speeches, which are also authorial compositions, Miletus can profit by comparison with the objects of pseudonymous composition.

Excursus: The Farewell Scene

Acts 20:36–21:17 contains several scenes of departure (20:36-38; 21:5-6; 10-18). François Bovon has shown that they follow a Greek literary pattern, which he traces from Homer onwards.[256] Examples include the Socratic tradition,[257] which influenced philosophical and martyrological portraits.[258]

248 Limitations of theme and space prevent exploration of the important implications of this fact.

249 For examples, see, in addition to the texts cited in n. 247, J. B. Lightfoot, *The Apostolic Fathers* (5 vols.; in two parts; New York: Macmillan, 1889–90) 2:12; Cadbury and Lake, 264; Haenchen, 994 n. 5; Barrett, 2:983–84; and Fitzmyer, 682.

250 Eckhard Plümacher proposes that Thucydides is Luke's source ("Eine Thukydidesreminiszenz in der Apostelgeschichte [Act 20,33-35–Thuk. 11 97.3f.]?" *ZNW* 83 [1992] 270–75). This does not seem likely.

251 The most thorough Christianization of the aphorism is in the D-Text reconstructed (on somewhat shaky grounds) by Boismard, *Texte*, 333: "The one who gives is more blessed than the one who receives," which assimilates it to the Hebrew form of the macarism.

252 See the discussion in Pervo, *Dating*, 228–29; and Weiser, 2:580.

253 See the apposite remarks of Witherington (626), who notes that the giving in question does not depend on reciprocity, that is, dependence.

254 For poor people to learn that giving is more blessed than receiving is to learn one more blessing in which they may not share. The focus on generosity omits problems connected to receiving. In the Greco-Roman world, this was less of an issue, but for modern people under Western influence, receiving is often more difficult than giving. Cf. Polhill, 430 n. 95.

255 Haenchen, 598.

256 François Bovon, "Le Saint-Esprit, l'Église et les relations humaines selon Actes 20,36–21,16," in Kremer, *Actes*, 339–58. An epic example is the famous encounter between Hector and Andromache (*Il.* 6.369–493, Bovon, 341). See also MacDonald, *Imitate Homer*, 69–102.

257 Bovon discusses, in addition to Diogenes Laertius 2.18–47, Plato's *Crito* 43D–44B. Note also *Phaed.* 116E–117A (masterful pathos). See also Alexander, *Literary Context*, 67, which discusses Plato *Phaed.* 65–67; 69A; *Crito* 45C–D.

258 Philostratus does not neglect this pattern in his *Apollonius* (4.36–37; 4.46; 7.14, Bovon, "Saint-Esprit," 342–43. Bovon discusses martyr acts and Apocryphal Acts on pp. 344–47. The theme plays a leading role in Ignatius's *Romans* (e.g., 1:2; 2:1; 3:3, Bovon, 348 n. 32). Mani's final journey and death were gradually assimilated to the passion of Jesus. See Hans-Joachim Klimkeit, *Gnosis on the Silk Road: Gnostic Parables, Hymns, and Prayers from Central Asia* (San Francisco: HarperSanFrancisco, 1993) 212-15. Cf. also Betz, *Lukian*, 118 n. 4.

Typical features include nonverbal elements, appeals to personal bonds and affection, and a hero who appreciates these sentiments but sees a necessity that transcends these relationships and will not evade his fate.[259] Omens or revelations may confirm his position.[260] Bovon relates the entire sequence of farewell scenes, objections, tears, and kisses to this pattern.[261] It is literary in nature, albeit so conventional and general that one need not look for particular sources in every case, and Greek because it is based on the tension produced by attempts to dissuade (21:14) a hero from his chosen/fated path.[262] Reference to literature should not be taken to imply that the scene is not psychologically realistic.[263] The power of the type comes from the ageless conflict between duty and safety, human relationships and higher obligations.[264]

Such scenes are, as Eric Junod and Jean-Daniel Kaestli have shown, also common in the various Acts.[265] Examples from the Apocryphal Acts include *Act. John* 58–59; *Act. Paul* 9/12; *Act. Pet.* (Verc.) 1–3; *Act. Thom.* 65–68. Typical features include (1) The mission is due to divine necessity or direction (Acts 19:21; 21:13). (2) Such scenes are often set in the penultimate period of the apostles' career and include allusions to his coming death and emphases that the believers will see him no more (Acts 20:38; 21:13). (3) The news distresses the faithful, who may attempt to restrain him (Acts 21:4, 12).[266] (4) The subject offers encouraging words (Acts 21:16). (5) The believers escort him as far as possible (21:15-16). The seashore, a potent boundary, is an ideal place for the close of farewell scenes.[267]

Ancient novelists were unable to deprive their audiences of the pleasure of heart-rending scenes of farewell:

> When the appointed day for departure arrived, the people flocked to the harbor, not only men but also women and children [cf. Acts 21:5], and there simultaneously occurred tears and prayers, moaning and encouragement, terror and courage, resignation and hope. Ariston, Chaereas' father, was carried because of advanced age and sickness. He flung his arms around the neck of his son [cf. Acts 20:37], and clinging to him wept and said, "Why are you leaving me, my son, an old man and almost dead? I shall certainly never see you again [cf. Acts 20:38]." (Chariton *Chaer.* 5.3–5)[268]

Examples are not limited to these genres. Because these farewells are type-scenes, it is not advisable to search for historical details in them or to draw conclusions based on the presence of conventional features.

■ **36-38** This brief and effective farewell underlines the emotional bond between Paul and the presbyters, underscoring the statement that this is their last sight of him. Paul may set out on his path confident that he has done what he could, both as herald and model. Storm clouds lie on the horizon, for both Paul and his churches (represented here, not accidentally, by

259 Tertullian staunchly defended resolution in the face of persecution. See Bovon, "Saint-Esprit," 349 n. 34.

260 Bovon, "Saint-Esprit," 341.

261 Ibid., 349.

262 Ibid.

263 Ibid., 351–53.

264 Tannehill's characterization of these scenes as "a struggle" between Paul and his friends (*Narrative Unity*, 2:262; see also 263–67) is somewhat overdone and misleading, for it does not take the ancient pattern into account. Paul does not "struggle," although he does feel.

265 Eric Junod and Jean-Daniel Kaestli, *Acta Iohannis* (2 vols.; CCSA 1-2; Turnhout: Brepols, 1983) 2:431 n. 1. Cf. also Pervo, "Hard Act," 15–16; and Peter Dunn, "The Influence of 1 Corinthians on the *Acts of Paul*," *SBLSP 1996* (Atlanta: Scholars Press, 1996) 438–54, 442–43. Note also the general comments of Weiser, 2:580.

266 On this element, see the comments on 21:10-14.

267 Margaret Anne Doody (*The True Story of the Novel* [New Brunswick: Rutgers University Press, 1996] 327–29) includes the seashore among the basic tropes of the novel.

268 Trans. G. P. Goold (LCL; Cambridge: Harvard University Press, 1995) 163. (The mother follows, baring her breasts and quoting Hecuba's words to Hector [*Il.* 22.82–83). Cf. also *Ephesian Tale* 1.10; Achilles Tatius *Leuc. Clit.* 5.15.1. The LXX also contributes to this passage. On the farewell kiss, see Gen 33:4; 40:14; 46:29; Tob 7:7; *3 Macc.* 5:49; and Luke 15:20 (the prodigal).

Ephesus), but he has equipped those of a later generation with the tools they need to lead and feed. This scene serves, as Polhill states, as a transition, bringing Paul's work in the Greek East to an end. From now on the narrator's eyes, like those of his chief character, will be on Jerusalem and Rome.[269]

The proper object of the farewell speech was not to glorify its speaker but to provide helpful counsel and advice to those left behind. When taken as a historical address actually delivered on this occasion, the speech presents a Paul who lacks both modesty and clarity. When it is seen as post-Pauline and conventional, its value can be appreciated. The speech amounts to an outline list of topics for development or a file drawer into which relevant expositions may be placed. In that light, it serves as a guide for leaders that has not lost its value.[270]

269 Polhill, 430–31.
270 Walton (*Leadership*) is particularly appreciative of the abiding value of the address.

21

21:1-17 Paul Travels to Jerusalem

1/ **When we were able to tear
ourselves away from them, we
set out on a straight run to Cos,
reaching Rhodes the next day
and then Patara. 2/ We located
a ship that was crossing to
Phoenicia, boarded it, and set
sail. 3/ We came within sight
of Cyprus, which we passed
on the right and continued
on to Syria,[a] landing at Tyre,
where the ship was to offload
its cargo.[b] 4/ We looked up the
believers and stayed there with
them for a week.[c] Moved by the
Spirit, they tried to tell Paul to
abandon his plan to visit Jerusalem. 5/ When the time came
to leave them and travel on,
they all—women and children
included—escorted us outside
of town, where we knelt down
to pray on the beach. 6/ Then
we said farewell to one another,
and we boarded the ship while
they returned home.**
7/ **Resuming the voyage, we traveled[d] from Tyre to Ptolemais,
where we visited the believers
and spent a day with them.
8/ We left on the next day and
reached[e] Caesarea, where we
went to the house of Philip the
Evangelist, one of the Seven,
and stayed with him.[f] 9/ Philip
had four unmarried daugh-
ters[g] endowed with the gift
of prophecy. 10/ After we had
been there for quite a number of
days, there arrived from Judea a
prophet named Agabus, 11/ who
approached[h] us and grasped
Paul's belt, with which he
bound his own[i] hands and feet.
"Thus says the Holy Spirit,"
he announced. "Just as I have
bound myself, so will the Jews
bind the man who owns this
belt and will deliver him to the
gentiles." 12/ After hearing this,
both we and those who lived
there implored him to break off
his trip to Jerusalem. 13/ Paul
said, "Why are you breaking my
heart with these tears? For the
Name of the Lord Jesus I am
not only ready to be arrested
in Jerusalem; I am even prepared to die there." 14/ Since
we could not dissuade him, we
said, "The Lord's will be done"[j]
and dropped the subject.**

a Boismard (*Texte*, 340) prefers "sailed" (*κατήχθημεν*), with the support of C Ψ and m.

b On the (periphrastic?) participial phrase *ἦν ἀφορτιζόμενον*, see BDF §339 (2b).

c The D-Text (Boismard, *Texte*, 341) omits "there," adds an initial "and," drops the article with "believers" (i.e., "we found some believers"), and changes the infinitive to the conventional "go up" (to Jerusalem).

d 𝔓[74] ℵ[2] A E read *κατέβημεν* ("went down to"). The difference is minor.

e Before and instead of *ἤλθομεν* ("we came"), the Byzantine text reads *οἱ περὶ Παῦλον ἦλθον* ("Paul and his companions came"). Metzger (*Textual Commentary*, 427–28) attributes this to lectionary influence. (At the beginning of a reading, confusing openings such as "the next day" and "we" are eliminated and/or replaced by proper nouns.)

f The D-Text (Boismard, *Texte*, 343) recasts v. 8b, transforming the participle into a finite verb ("we entered") and omitting the final three words ("we stayed with him"). See also below.

g The D-Text (Boismard, *Texte*, 343) makes v. 9 a relative clause, continuing v. 8. See also below.

h D* makes the verb finite, evidently in order to break up a series of participles.

i The variant "both his," that is, Paul's hands and feet, is secondary.

j Cadbury and Lake (269) prefer "prevail." This may be too fine. In any case, the translation preserves the cross reference. (Luke 22:42 has the same tense.)

k "Get ready" is a reasonable conjecture for the meaning of *ἐπισκευσάμενοι*. See Cadbury and Lake, 269.

15/ When our stay came to an end,
we got ready for travel[k] and set
out for Jerusalem. 16/ Some
of the believers from Caesarea
accompanied us as guides
to the home of one Mnason
from Cyprus, a believer of
long standing, with whom we
lodged. 17/ When we got to
Jerusalem, we were warmly
welcomed by the believers.

Analysis

As the group approaches Jerusalem, warnings become increasingly vivid and dire. "The road to Jerusalem recalls Paul's earlier visits to the capital, only this time the black clouds are massed on the horizon."[1] Paul remains staunch in his commitment, undeterred even by the threat of martyrdom. Luke uses the frame of the collection journey to raise suspense to an all-but-unbearable level. In this atmosphere, the prosaic listing of ports and stations serves as a counterpoint of steady beats and a literary foil that highlights the message of doom. Paul's final journey obviously evokes a parallel with that of Jesus in Luke, beginning in Acts 19:21,[2] evoked in 20:22-24, continued in 21:4, and brought to a climax in 21:10-14. These sayings correspond, with considerably more variety, to the "passion predictions" of Jesus. Paul has his own "Gethsemane" (cf. Luke 22:33-42, which does not use the word). In such scenes contrasting the pre- and postresurrection/Pentecost periods, Luke illustrates the meaning and power of the gift of the Spirit.

Table 6. Jesus and Paul: Some Parallels[3]

Jesus	**Paul**
1. "Passion Predictions"	**1. "Passion Predictions"**
Luke 9:22	Acts 20:23-25
Luke 9:34	Acts 21:4
Luke 18:31	Acts 21:11-13
2. Farewell Address	**2. Farewell Address**
Luke 22:14-38	Acts 20:17-35
3. Resurrection: Sadducees Oppose	**3. Resurrection: Sadducees Oppose**
Luke 20:27-39	Acts 23:6-10
4. Staff of High Priest Slap Jesus	**4. Staff of High Priest Slap Paul**
Luke 22:63-64	Acts 23:1-2
5. Four "Trials" of Jesus	**5. Four "Trials" of Paul**
A. Sanhedrin: Luke 22:66-71	A. Sanhedrin: Acts 22:30–23:10
B. Roman Governor (Pilate): Luke 23:1-5	B. Roman Governor (Felix): 24:1-22
C. Herodian King (Antipas): Luke 23:6-12	C. Herodian King (Agrippa): 26
D. Roman Governor (Pilate): Luke 23:13-25	D. Roman Governor (Festus): 25:6-12

1 Goulder, *Type*, 30.
2 See the comments thereon.
3 For detailed comparisons of the two trials, see Radl, *Paulus*, 169–251; and, with emphasis on the

Table 6. Jesus and Paul: Some Parallels (*cont.*)

6. Declarations of Innocence	**6. Declarations of Innocence**
Pilate: Luke 23:14 (cf. 23:4, 22)	Lysias (Tribune): Acts 23:29
Herod: Luke 23:14	Festus: Acts 25:25
Centurion: Luke 23:47	Agrippa: Acts 26:31
7. Mob Demands Execution	**7. Mob Demands Execution**
Luke 23:18	Acts 22:22

Difficulties arise when one steps back and compares this account with the journey of 15:3, which had a similar goal, although motivated by overt problems. Why is it that Paul, who, since the end of chap. 9, has visited Jerusalem whenever he wished (Acts 15; 18:22), is now in such great danger? (That Jerusalem can be dangerous is beyond doubt—witness the fates of Jesus, Stephen, and James.) No reason is supplied for the present danger. In historical fact, danger came from delivering the collection.[4]

The framework of this passage probably derives from a source, a letter regarding the collection. The beginning is artificial, for it assumes that the party could sail away as soon as the speech and subsequent prayers were over. Lucan additions include v. 4b,[5] probably some details of the farewell scene in v. 5, and vv. 10-14.[6] Readers are struck by a number of unusual words and a phrase. Some of these may be attributed to the subject material, but they contribute to the hypothesis of a source.[7] This proposal accepts the data about Philip as integral to the source (and presumably historical). Philip is awarded a descriptive epithet, "the evangelist," which does not fit 6:1-7, and he is called a member of "the Seven," another term avoided in Acts 6. It is not likely that Luke invented (or imported from elsewhere) the reference to his daughters, since they play no role here. The reference to Mnason (v. 16) evidently also derives from the source. As a Cypriot resident in Jerusalem, he evokes Barnabas (4:36). The party sought lodgings with Greek-speaking believers in Palestine.[8] A more speculative possibility is that Paul may have been seeking (or used the opportunity) to repair/fortify relations with those associated with Barnabas and the mission in Antioch in order to gain their support for his collection.[9] The "passion predictions" in v. 4 and vv. 10-14 belong to Luke. The appearance of Agabus fits Luke's plan and does not fit the context.[10]

---

trial of Jesus as a Lucan composition, Joseph B. Tyson, *The Death of Jesus in Luke-Acts* (Columbia: University of South Carolina Press, 1986) 114–41.

4 For various reasons why the collection is not mentioned, see Lüdemann, 247; Pesch 2:222.

5 See Haenchen, 600. The complex relative οἵτινες is typical of Luke. Even more typical is his use of relatives to form more or less independent clauses.

6 Weiser (2:588) also assigns vv. 1-4a, 7-9 to the source.

7 Words: v. 3: ἀναφαίνω (in sense of "sight," passive in different sense, Luke 19:11); εὐώνυμος ("left," "port"); ἀποφορτίζομαι ("unload"); v. 4: ἀνευρίσκω ("seek [and find]," but see Luke 2:16); v. 5: ἐξαρτίζω ("finish"); v. 6: εἰς τὰ ἴδια (i.e., "go home"), a phrase found in Esther, 3 Maccabees, and John (three times), but not in Luke or Acts; v. 7: διανύω ("complete"); v. 15: ἐπισκευάζομαι ("get ready"). The most important of these are unusual words for "finish/complete" and "go home," for which Luke normally uses other terms.

8 Cornelius would have been a logical host, in terms of resources. If Luke were composing this episode, he might well have had him play that role. If he existed and were a convert of Peter (both questionable), it could be hypothesized that the party avoided him because of Paul's difficulties with Peter.

9 Note also Tyre (21:3-6), an area evangelized by refugees from the persecution of Stephen (11:19; cf. 15:3). Had Luke concocted the itinerary, he might well have included a visit to Antioch (as in 18:22).

10 Lüdemann (*Acts*, 280) thinks that the Agabus episode may come from tradition, although he is willing to consider that its basis is not the major tradition of this section.

Comment

■ **1** The route from Miletus to Tyre is generally conventional,[11] but textual variants raise questions about its completeness. The D-Text (Boismard, *Texte*, 340) omits the first five words of N-A[27] and revises the rest: "After tearing ourselves away from them,[12] we set out on a straight run to Cos,[13] and on the **next day**[14] to Rhodes and thence to Patara **and Myra**." The last stop is difficult. If it is a later addition on the basis of verisimilitude, the route has been abbreviated. Against this is the view that, if the object was to give daily stages, Rhodes-Patara-Myra is too long.[15] Ropes found no reason for a deliberate addition and posited it as omitted by haplography.[16] Reasons for interpolation can, however, be identified: assimilation to 27:5 or to the *Act. Paul* 4/5.[17] Both are characteristics of the D-Text.

■ **2-3** The next verse quashes any notion that the group had chartered a ship or that they were on a pilgrim vessel. They took passage on whatever vessel was available and had to fend for themselves during layovers. One of these was in the venerable city of Tyre,[18] where, contrary to the Lucan pattern, they had to search out believers.[19] The text does not say how this was accomplished.[20] The layover caused no anxieties about the schedule. Conzelmann is blunt: "The haste mentioned in 20:16 is forgotten."[21] This is another indication that 20:16 was Lucan and ad hoc. 21:10, where the delay was voluntary, clinches this conclusion.

■ **4** The second half of the verse is presumably telescoped. The revelations–generalized to the entire community–did not order Paul to change his plans, but forecast danger, as in 20:23. The believers, out of concern for Paul, urged him to desist. This interpretation is at least as old as Chrysostom.[22] Their pleas emphasize Paul's courage and determination.[23]

■ **5-6** The verses offer another moving farewell scene.[24] The entire community goes down to the beach to see them off. By such means the narrator conveys the charisma of Paul, who was presumably unknown to these good people a week earlier.

■ **7-8** The next stop, at Ptolemais,[25] brings the party to land[26] and reveals the existence of another Christian group, the location of which was evidently known, and a single day's halt. The narrator (and perhaps the source) was not interested in what was but a place on

11 So Cadbury and Lake, 264, with reference to Lucan *Pharsalia* 8.243–52, that is, epic. See also *Ephesian Tale* 1.11.6 (Cos, Cnidus, Rhodes).

12 A thoroughly improper genitive absolute.

13 The D-Text makes "straight run" a finite verb and omits "we came," changes obscured by the trans.

14 Using a different term (ἐπιούσῃ).

15 Cadbury and Lake, 264–65.

16 Ropes, *Text*, 201.

17 Metzger, *Textual Commentary*, 427. Conversely, the *Acts of Paul* may have known Acts in this form.

18 On Tyre, see H. J. Katzenstein and Douglas R. Edwards, "Tyre," *ABD* 6:686–92. Its importance in the eastern Mediterranean is apparent from its occurrence in ancient novels: *Callirhoe* (eleven); *An Ephesian Tale* (six); *The Marvels beyond Thule* (Photius *Bib.* 166); *Leucippe* (twelve); The Ps.-Clementines (e.g., *Hom.* 6.26; 7); *An Ethiopian Story* (4.16.6); and *Apollonius, Prince of Tyre.* Jesus had attracted hearers from this area: Luke 6:17.

19 See Luke 2:16, for the same use of ἀνευρίσκω ("seek out").

20 If some were of Jewish background and tension between the groups was absent, inquiry at a synagogue might have provided one means. Roloff (309) attributes the origins of this community to the mission of 11:19.

21 Conzelmann, 178.

22 Chrysostom *Hom.* 45, p. 381. Bovon ("Saint-Esprit," 350) disputes the link with 20:23 and makes this the point of departure for his illuminating discussion of the pattern.

23 Cf. Conzelmann (178), who adds that the purpose was not to make these believers look bad. On the theme, see below (on vv. 10-14).

24 In v. 5, Moule (*Idiom Book*, 174) views ὅτε δὲ ἐγένετο ἡμᾶς ἐξαρτίσαι τὰς ἡμέρας as an example of Semitic style. Such LXX language is Lucan and supplies the proper dignity to the scene. The D-Text simplifies the construction to an articular infinitive: μετὰ δὲ τὸ ἐξαρτίσαι ("After the days were finished . . ."), omitting "us" as subject of the infinitive, adding "on our way" to the verb "we went," and changing the participle "prayed" to the finite "we prayed." The infinitive ἐξαρτίσαι is unusual in this sense, leading Cadbury and Lake (266) to wonder whether language about the ship being ready has been compressed. Chrysostom *Hom.* 45 (381) glosses this as "complete" (πληρῶσαι).

25 This is the Hellenistic name of the ancient Acco, famous in crusader and Ottoman times as Acre.

26 The idiom of travel is well illustrated in *Ephesian Tale* 3.2.12, καὶ μέχρι μέν τινος διήνυστο

the road to Caesarea.[27] There the party lodges with Philip, identified as "the 'evangelist,' being one of the Seven." Questions arise: Was this identifying material in the source? Did it contain one title ("one of the seven," "evangelist") or two? If the author wished to say "one of the seven evangelists," he could have done so more clearly, but this interpretation is possible.[28] It is also possible that "evangelist" is a nickname rather than a title and that "seven" is simply a cross-reference to Acts 6. If "the Seven" was found in the source, it would presumably have been intelligible to the readers. This implies that the Seven were a well-known group. In addition to possible expansion of the source is potential abbreviation. The source may have supplied more information about this host, to indicate his distinction, or it may have said that the group lodged with (one) Philip.[29]

■ **9** Philip was famous, if not legendary, in Luke's time, as the statements of Papias indicate.[30] Luke may have introduced the data about him and his daughters from other traditions. If "evangelist" is a title, it probably reflects a later date.[31] The name may have come from the source, but the other data are probably Lucan contributions from other sources.[32] Philip regularly came equipped with prophetic daughters.[33] For Luke, female prophets are celibate (Mary and Anna),[34] a circumstance for which there are a number of parallels in the history of religions.[35] Their presumed status fulfills 2:17-18, but, in place of prophecies from them, a male prophet "from Judea" is imported, as it were, to do the honors.[36] This

εὐτυχῶς ὁ πλοῦς ("For a while the voyage went well," trans. G. Anderson in Reardon, *Novels*, 148), and *Leuc. Clit.* 5.17.1, πέντε δὲ τῶν ἑξῆς ἡμερῶν διανύσαντες τὸν πλοῦν ἥκομεν εἰς Ἔφεσον ("After five days of continuous sailing we reached Ephesos," trans. J. J. Winkler in Reardon, *Novels*, 241). The verb διανύω can mean "continue."

27 The journey would have taken more than a single day, as Caesarea is about sixty kilometers from Ptolemais, suggesting abbreviation, although it is barely possible to interpret the verse as "leaving on the next day and [in due course] came to Caesarea." Hemer (*Book*, 125) says "thirty miles," which is too short and finds that a suitable day's journey, which is a bit of an exaggeration.

28 Barrett (1:306) endorses it.

29 It is probable that this source has worked inversely on 8:40, where the narrator "parked" Philip in Caesarea.

30 On the subject, see William R. Schoedel, "Papias," *ANRW* 2.27.1 (1993) 235–70. On his failure to mention Luke and Acts, see Pervo, *Dating*, 20.

31 "Evangelist," with the exception of an inscription from Rhodes dated to the Christian era, in which the term evidently refers to the interpretation of oracles (*IG* XII 1.675), is a Christian word. Apart from here, it is found in Eph 4:11 and 2 Tim 4:5. The last is functional. Eph 4:11 expands the list of 1 Cor 12:27 (apostles, prophets, teachers) by inserting "evangelists" after "prophets" and equating "pastors" with "teachers." In all three cases the office is subordinate to that of apostles. In Eusebius *H.E.* 5.10.2 they are successors of apostles, who (3.37.2–3) served as itinerant missionaries and appointed "pastors" to succeed them. Bultmann (*Theology*, 2:106) surmised that the title arose when the title of apostle was restricted to the Twelve. This hypothesis (which resembles Eusebius's statement) is reasonable. "Evangelist" indicates a shift toward the notion of succession that fell aside in place of presbyters and, particularly, bishops. Acts, 2 Timothy, and possibly Ephesians, despite Eusebius, envision resident rather than itinerant persons. The office first appears in Deutero-Pauline literature and probably belongs to that milieu. See Harnack, *Mission*, 1:348; G. Friedrich, "εὐαγγελιστής," *TDNT* 2:636–37; Spicq, *Lexicon*, 2:91–92; Barrett, 2:993.

32 Haenchen (601) attributes the daughters to the main source, as their silence conforms to its interest in hosts.

33 Eusebius *H.E.* 3.31.2–5 (letter of Polycrates); 3.39.9–10 (Papias); 5.17.3; 5.24.2. The term παρθένοι means "unmarried," with a reasonable presumption of virginity. Their marital status varied, partially in conformity with views on marriage. Clement, who argued that even Paul was married, said the same of Philip's daughters (*Strom.* 3.52.5). Polycrates (Eusebius *H.E.* 3.31.3) evidently believed that one had married.

34 Boismard (*Texte*, 343) omits "virgins" from his D-Text, although he translates "quatre filles vierges." He notes that the word is variously placed, which could indicate addition. Two Greek MSS. omit the word: 88 (on which see James Keith Elliott, *A Bibliography of Greek New Testament Manuscripts* [SNTSMS 109; 2nd ed.; Cambridge: Cambridge University Press, 2000] 105 and 2147).

35 Delphi (e.g., Lucian *Philops.* 38) is the most famous example. See Gerhard Delling, "παρθένος," *TDNT* 5:826–37, esp. 830–31.

36 Calvin (7:195) commended this silence as a

reprises the situation of Luke 2:25-38, which mentions a woman prophet, Anna, but assigns two prophecies to Simeon and none to her. Richter Reimer says that opposition to women "had certainly begun as early as the end of the first century, but there is no trace of it in Acts 21:8-9."[37] One must beg to differ. Luke and Acts attest to these anxieties.[38] The embarrassment reflected in modern commentaries only underlines this silence.[39] Verse 9 is gratuitous. Were it omitted, no lack would be sensed. Such anomalies may serve as either arguments for or against its presence in a source. Probability favors the former here.

■ **10** This sojourn lasts for some time.[40] This gives opportunity for Agabus to learn of Paul's presence and pay a visit. He is effectively reintroduced, without reference to his previous activity (11:27-28), but the same could be said of Philip. This probably represents a "reader-friendly" orientation on the part of the author rather than an admixture of sources.[41] His name is not otherwise attested,[42] but his character and residence are consistent: Agabus is a Palestinian[43] prophet who makes use of symbolism. Acts 11:27-30 has shown that he is trustworthy.

■ **11** Aune's analysis of the oracle offers indirect support for viewing it as a Lucan composition. The manner, a prophet who appears without preparation, the verbal style, and the use of symbolism are all characteristic of prophecy in the Hebrew Bible, but the form of the oracle, pure prediction without a rationale, is Greco-Roman.[44] Agabus enters, binds his hands and feet with Paul's belt,[45] then delivers his oracle, beginning with a Christianized form of the messenger formula: "Thus says the Holy Spirit" (rather than "the Lord").[46] The symbolism is explained, like symbolic actions in the LXX, with "thus" (οὕτως).

confirmation of the divine order. They prophesied in private situations. Origen (*Frag. on 1 Corinthians* 74) held the same view. Jerome's friend Paula saw the room (*cubiculum*) in which they prophesied (*Ep.* 108.8 [CSEL 55:313]).

37 Richter Reimer, *Women*, 249.

38 Data include the Pastorals and the editor responsible for interpolating 1 Cor 14:33b-36. Rev 2:20 takes issue with a prophet labeled "Jezebel" in Thyatira. See also Pervo, "Social Aspects," 235–40; and idem, "(Acts 21:9) Four Unmarried Daughters of Philip," in Meyers, *Women*, 467–68. On this verse, see also Seim, *Double Message,* 164–84, esp. 180–82. For a review of the battle over women prophets, see Schüssler Fiorenza, *Memory*, 294–309. Opposition was not uniform. Not only the *Acts of Paul* but also Justin (*Dial.* 87.6–88.1) supported the practice. Montanism was not the sole grounds for opposition, but it probably (along with various "Gnostic" movements) played a major role in the outcome.

39 For examples of such interpretation, see Price, *Widow Traditions*, 61–64. He then develops (64–71) an argument, based in part on *T. Job* 46–51, that the daughters were responsible for the prophecy. This is an interesting exercise in speculation. Loisy (785–89) advanced a similar argument. As he noted, v. 12 is more suitable as a response to prophecies uttered by a group, that is, the daughters. It is possible that Luke knew of such a tradition (from an unspecified source) and transformed it, but it is more likely that he created the episode. The girdles given by Job to his daughters are magical, whereas that used by Agabus functions to express prophetic symbolism. Philip's daughters, presuming that the testimonies have any value, were active in a later period, probably not earlier than the 70s, at any rate later than the middle or late 50s.

40 The participle ἐπιμενόντων ("staying") dangles (although such absolutes with an omitted pronoun were not unheard of in classical Greek). Variants supply "we" and "they." The former makes better sense.

41 Compare Josephus *Bell.* 3.29 (Antioch) and *Ant.* 19.301 (Petronius).

42 See on 11:27-30.

43 "Judea" in v. 10 (versus "Jerusalem" in 11:27) is probably the typical Lucan synecdoche of using province for city. See 11:1-2. An alternative is that the narrator distinguished Caesarea from Judea, of which it was the capital (Hemer, *Book*, 126).

44 Aune, *Prophecy*, 263–64. Aune does not regard the oracle as a Lucan composition, although he views it as "undoubtedly condensed" (264).

45 For such symbolic action, see Isa 8:1-4; 20:2; Jer 13:1-11; 27:1-7; Ezekiel 4–5. Aune (*Prophecy*, 263, with data on 429 n. 96) says that symbolic activity by early Christian prophets was rare. For the symbolic use of "belt" (ζώνη, a rope girdle), see John 21:18-19.

46 The formula τάδε λέγει appears 353 times in the LXX and seven times in the letters of Revelation (e.g., 2:1).

Content also suggests that the oracle is a Lucan composition.[47] The play on "bind" relates this action to 19:21 and 20:23 (bis). The contrast of "Jews" and "gentiles" is typical of Luke and unlikely for a Palestinian prophet. Furthermore, it is not strictly accurate, for gentiles will rescue Paul from a mob and shackle him (21:33, δεθῆναι), but it does show how Luke wishes Paul's arrest to be understood.[48] The oracle is based on Jesus' predictions of his sufferings and thus fits Luke's literary plan.[49] Luke uses this oracle to fix blame on the Jews.[50] As the response in vv. 12-14 verifies, this scene is the dramatic climax of the series of "passion predictions." The evidence points toward Luke as its creator. If Agabus were a historical person who prophesied in this situation, his character has been obliterated by the author's pen. This view is counter to the weight of the scholarly tradition, to be sure,[51] but the material is typical. "Passion predictions," in the form of oracles, omens, and prodigies are a literary motif familiar to all who have read Shakespeare's *Julius Caesar* in school ("Beware the ides of March").[52] They are common in farewell scenes.[53]

■ **12** The human response, which included tears as well as importuning, illuminates Paul's character. Those present, including an unannounced company not identified as believers,[54] as well as "we" (from whom Paul must be excluded) entreat him to discontinue his plans. Paul alone faces danger, as oracle and reaction confirm. This is not completely realistic. It functions to keep the spotlight on Paul. Their plea, identical to that of v. 4, does not raise questions, for it is a response to the oracle rather than to allegedly inspired utterance.[55] The narrator does not present this as a "temptation" or test that Paul must pass.[56] He has no doubts, but he does have feelings.

■ **13-14** As suggested above, this is Paul's "Gethsemane."[57] His followers, like those of Jesus, are filled with grief.[58] Paul will not take flight, as had other disciples; like Jesus, he will march into the valley of the shadow of death. Unlike Peter (Luke 22:33), he is genuinely ready for prison and even death, for the sake of the Lord's name, which is acquiring the sense of the *nomen christianum*.[59] The prayer of Jesus (Luke 22:42), "Your will be done," is in v. 14 the petition of the community.[60] The use of "we" in a scene composed by the author indicates the freedom with which he handles the first plural, limiting its utility as a means of isolating sources

47 The D-Text of v. 11 (Boismard, *Texte*, 344), reads: "**Now coming up** to us and **taking** Paul's belt, binding his feet [ ], he said 'he whose belt this is they will bind **him** in the same manner **and take him away to** Jerusalem.'" In addition to the added καὶ ἀποίσουσιν are the omission of "Thus says the Holy Spirit," "hands," and the delivery by Jews to gentiles. This—if it is indeed a valid text—is probably a correction in the light of the subsequent narrative.

48 Note 28:17, where, before a Jewish audience, Paul states that he was "delivered into the hands of the Romans."

49 ". . . will deliver him to the gentiles" is closest to Mark 10:33. See also Mark 15:1 ("bind and hand over"); Luke 18:32.

50 Cf. Haenchen, 605.

51 See above, n. 41.

52 *Julius Caesar* 1.2.21. See, e.g., Plutarch *Alex.* 73. Chaldeans told (Alexander's admiral) Nearchus that Alexander should stay away from Babylon. Ravens fall dead at his feat. The seer Pythagoras reports that an animal sacrificed to learn Alexander's fate had no lobe on its liver. And so forth. Cf. also Arrian *Anab.* 7.18, 22, 24, and the *Alexander Romance* 3.30. On Caesar, see Suetonius *Jul.* 81–82.

53 See the excursus "The Farewell Scene" in the commentary on 20:36.

54 The word ἐντόπιοι ("the locals," a NT *hapax legomenon*) is thoroughly neutral and would be an unusual way to describe Philip and his family.

55 Lucan style is apparent in the use of a pleonastic articular infinitive.

56 "Trials" (πειρασμοί) constitute one of the parallels between the experiences of Jesus (Luke 22:28) and Paul (Acts 20:19).

57 The correspondences were noted by Rackham, 401.

58 Luke 22:45 excuses the sleep of the disciples on the grounds of grief.

59 That is, the (potentially criminal) label "Christian." Cf. Haenchen, 602 n. 3. The phrase aligns Paul with the apostles (5:41) and fulfills the prophecy of the heavenly Christ in 9:16; cf. also 15:26. For Conzelmann (*Theology*, 177–78) the "name is the specifically Lucan way of describing the presence of Christ."

60 Polycarp, who also refused to flee persecution, uttered a similar sentiment (*Mart. Pol.* 7.1).

or proving historical reliability. Verses 13-14[61] aim at a good style.[62]

In addition to the suspense-filled drama and echoes of the passion of Jesus, the narrator has also pulled together a chorus representing stages of the story: Philip, one of the Seven "commissioned" by the apostles, and Agabus, a prophet from the "mother city," whose ministry also included Antioch, where Paul worked with Barnabas (11:27-30) in the first explicitly gentile mission, as well as Paul and his subsequent companions. The narrator exhibits all of these elements coexisting in unity. One group omitted is those apostles who had authorized these activities. They belong to the past. The subsequent meeting in Jerusalem will reinforce this fact.

■ **15-17** The section begins with a temporal phrase used to mark major breaks in the narrative (cf. 1:15; 6:1; 11:27). From the narrator's perspective, Paul's arrival at Jerusalem begins the final portion of the narrative. The essence of vv.15-18a comes from the source describing the collection,[63] which evidently reported that believers from Caesarea served as guides to the lodgings of one Mnason[64] and presumably as references for Paul and company, who did not know him.[65] Mnason is characterized as a believer since the early days (ἀρχαῖος, lit. "ancient"; cf. the ἀρχή, "beginning") of the church, dated by Peter to Pentecost (11:15).[66] His homeland, Cyprus, and his name indicate that he spoke Greek, and that he probably knew Barnabas (who may have converted him, or vice versa). These data appear historical, for they contradict the general narrative of Acts, which suggests that Paul had become familiar with many believers in Jerusalem on his several sojourns there. No more is said of these escorts, nor of Mnason, nor, after v. 18a, of "we." The warm but restricted reception of v. 17 contrasts with that in 15:4.[67]

The syntax of vv. 15-16 is garbled. The text may be corrupt, although abbreviation of the source is also possible.[68] The D-Text (Boismard, *Texte,*

---

61 Boismard (*Texte*, 346) presents this D-Text: "**Paul said to us**: 'Why are you weeping and **troubling** (ϑορυβοῦντες, a simplification) my heart? **Would that** (εὐξαίμην ἄν) I might not only to be bound but also die [ ] for the sake of the name of **my** Lord Jesus.'" This text, which is not grammatically secure, expresses a longing for martyrdom reminiscent of Ignatius (and Montanism). Note also the elimination of "Jerusalem," which appears to be a correction based on the later narrative. (D d read βούλομαι ["I am willing"] and add, in v. 14, that they spoke "to one another.")

62 Contrast 21:13 to Luke 22:32 (Peter). The latter uses καί . . . καί, the simplest "both . . . and" construction, while Acts employs the more dramatic "not only . . . but also." Peter uses the simpler ἕτοιμός εἰμι, as opposed to the more sophisticated ἑτοίμως ἔχω for "I am ready." (For a close verbal parallel, see Josephus *Ant.* 13.6.) Verse 14 begins with a genitive absolute and offers "we dropped the subject" (ἡσυχάσαμεν) instead of a simpler "we fell silent" or the like. Cf. 11:18. The linkage of two supplementary participles with "and" (κλαίοντες καὶ συνθρύπτοντες [the latter an elegant choice]) that are not strictly coordinate is an attempt at classical idiom. (Barrett [2:997] notes Plato *Resp.* 495D–E.)

63 Verse 17 is probably Lucan and somewhat disruptive; the vocabulary is Lucan (Weiser, 2:594). In the source, v. 18a probably followed on v. 16. Cf. also Lüdemann, *Acts*, 279.

64 The unfamiliar name "Mnason" (cf. BDAG, 654, *s.v.*; and Hemer, *Book*, 237) and the desire to connect prosopographical dots led to the substitution of "Jason" in ℵ gig vg^{mss} bo^{pt}. The basis is probably Rom 16:21. Ψ evidently attempted to read "Menachem." Bearers of that name might have adopted "Mnason" as a Greek equivalent.

65 They may also have provided additional "guards" to protect the money.

66 "Ancient" is relative. Note 15:7, 21, which report two different views of "antiquity." This may reflect Luke's perspective, similar to that of *1 Clement*, which calls the church at Corinth "ancient" (47.6).

67 Cadbury and Lake (270) describe it as "unofficial," an excellent euphemism. The introductory genitive absolute is gauche (cf. the following "us"). This is probably a Lucan addition to the source (above). Lüdemann (*Opposition*, 54) notes the conflict between v. 17 and v. 22. Verse 17 is clearly editorial.

68 The subject of v. 16 is in the genitive ("disciples"). This requires a nominative such as τινες ("some"). E adds ἐκ ("from," emphasizing the partitive nature). See BDF §164 (2). BDF §294 (5) glosses the compressed relative as the equivalent of "to Mnason so that we might lodge with him." This is a "reverse attraction," with the noun pulled into the case of the relative. On the subjunctive (used because the clause is final), see §378. The participle ἄγοντες ("guiding") is like a future participle of purpose, used here in reference to a past tense. BDF §339 (2c) shows that this is classical. It is not

347–48[69]) is distinctive: "After a **few** days we **said farewell** and set out [historical present] for Jerusalem. Some of the believers **from** Caesarea came with us. **They led us to** the home of **those** with whom we were to lodge. **Arriving at a village**, we **were** with Mnason, a Cypriote, **one of the early believers**. 17. **After we left that place we came to Jerusalem**. The believers **received** us warmly."[70] This passage is a classic example of the textual problem. Is the conventional text at points the result of abbreviation, or did the editor of the D-Text (here) repair an evident deficiency in the narrative—one that could be detected from 21:31-33—that the journey from Caesarea to Jerusalem required more than a day? The latter is, as often elsewhere, more probable.[71]

absolutely clear that the narrator locates Mnason in Jerusalem. See Cadbury and Lake, 270, and the following discussion of the text.

69 D is damaged here and must be restored. See Ropes, *Text*, 202–3, and the contributions cited by Barrett, 2:1002.

70 *μετὰ δὲ τινας ἡμέρας ἀποκαταξάμενοι ἀναβαίνομεν εἰς Ἱεροσόλυμα·* 16 *συνῆλθον δὲ καὶ τῶν μαθητῶν ἐκ Καισαρείας σὺν ἡμῖν. οὗτοι δὲ ἤγαγον ἡμᾶς πρὸς οὓς ξενισθῶμεν. καὶ παραγινόμενοι εἴς τινα κώμην ἐγενόμεθα παρὰ Μνάσωνί τινι Κυπρίῳ ἐκ τῶν ἀρχαίων μαθητῶν.* 17 *κἀκεῖθεν ἐξιόντες ἤλθομεν εἰς Ἱεροσόλυμα. ὑπεδέξαντο δὲ ἡμᾶς οἱ ἀδελφοί ἀσμένως.*

71 Ropes, *Text*, 204: "Its indefinite reference to the 'village' is futile and over-emphasized, especially in view of the extreme interest and importance of the goal of their journey. As their village-host, Mnason is wholly without significance; whereas as a resident of Jerusalem this 'old disciple' was of real consequence to the narrative." Cf. also Metzger, *Textual Commentary*, 428. The D-editor may have been less worried about the need for a stop between Caesarea and Jerusalem than about the opportunity for parallelism with Jesus, who stayed in villages (10:38; 17:12) and, more importantly, used one as his base for his final ministry in Jerusalem (Luke 19:30). The editorial addition of v. 17 (above) may be responsible for the impression that Mnason did not reside in the city, but that remains a possibility. For lists of scholars on each side, see Weiser, 2:596.

21

21:18-26 Paul Confers with James

18/ The next day Paul and the rest of
us went to see James. All of the
elders were present. 19/ Following the initial greetings Paul
set out in full detail all that God
had accomplished through his
ministry to the gentiles.
20/ His report brought repeated
praise of God,[a] after which
they said: "You see, brother,
how many myriads of Judeans[b]
have become believers.[c] All of
them[d] are ardent observers of
Torah. 21/ About you, however, they have been informed
that you teach all Diaspora
Jews[e] to renounce the Law of
Moses, telling them that they
should stop circumcising their
sons or observe[f] our practices.
22/ What about this? They will
doubtless learn that you have
arrived. 23/ You must therefore
do what we tell you. Four of our
number have placed them-
selves[g] under a vow.[h] 24/ Take
responsibility for them, get
yourself purified, and pay their
expenses so that they may
get their heads shaved. Everyone will then know[i] that what
they have heard about you is
quite false and that you live an
observant life.[j] 25/ Now regarding the gentile converts, *we*
have determined, and have so
advised them in writing,[k] that
they should take care to avoid
food that has been offered to
idols or contains blood or has
been killed by strangling, as
well as from prohibited sexual
relationships."[l]
26/ So Paul took charge of those men
and went with them on the
following day[m] to undergo purification. He entered the temple
to give notice of when the vow
would be discharged, at which
time the prescribed offering
would be made for each of
them.

a "Lord" is, as often, a variant.

b The D-Text (Boismard, *Texte*, 349) replaces "Judeans" with "in Judea," which makes the exaggeration a bit more bearable. This is typical of the D-tradition, literal and pedantic. (Another variant uses the simple genitive.)

c Verse 20 could be taken as a question: "Do you see . . . ?"

d The D-Text (Boismard, *Texte*, 349) adds "these" after "all" to prevent confusion.

e D^1 reads "all the customs" (τὰ ἔθη πάντα). This yields nonsense.

f This is the only use in Acts of περιπατέω (lit. "walk") in the ethical sense. Boismard (*Texte*, 350) includes the preposition ἐν ("in"). This is conventional. On the dative τοῖς ἔθεσιν, see Moule, *Idiom Book*, 45; the construction seems to fit reasonably well within the range of means/manner.

g Critical consensus supports the Septuagintal ἐφ᾽ ἑαυτῶν against the ἀφ᾽ ἑαυτῶν, ("on their own initiative"), which is likely to be an Alexandrian improvement. See, in particular, Num 6:7.

h It is preferable not to view this as a periphrastic (εἰσὶν . . . ἔχοντες) construction, an otiose substitute for ἔχουσι ("they have"). The first two words are a dative of possession.

i The minor textual question of whether to read "shave" properly as subjunctive (ξυρώσονται) or as a "vulgar" future indicative equivalent affects the translation. If indicative, the following "will know" (indicative) will be separate rather than coordinate. The translation presumes that "shave" was subjunctive (or the equivalent) and "know" a result. See Barrett, 2:1010.

j The absolute use of στοιχέω ("conform," etc.) is quite unusual. The participle φυλάσσων ("keeping") may have been intended as supplementary, that is, "you walk within the protective boundaries around the Torah." Similarly, Barrett, 2:1012. The verb may be a Pauline echo. Cf. Gal 5:25; 6:16.

k This prefers ἀπεστείλαμεν ("we have sent") as less elegant than ἐπιστείλαμεν ("we have written"). See Ropes, *Text*, 207; and Barrett, 2:1014.

l On the text, see the discussion of 15:20. No witnesses include the "golden rule" at this point.

m Boismard (*Texte*, 352) thinks that the D-Text lacked a temporal reference. This may be because the reader/editor could not understand why Paul would wait a day to comply with this excellent suggestion.

Analysis

The larger unit extends from 21:18 to 22:29, the conclusion of Paul's speech. This is a continuous narrative comprising a number of scenes: 21:18-26; 21:27-36; 21:37–22:21; 22:22-29. The final quarter of Acts is well organized, without the gaps and leaps that are often perceptible in earlier sections. As was the case with the story of Jesus in Jerusalem (Mark 11–16), the rapid passage of time slows. That process began at 20:4. Now it intensifies: 21:17–24:23 encompass but twelve days, around nine verses per day, The disappearance of "we" after 21:18 results in another similarity to the experience of Jesus: while on trial, Paul is alone. None of his "disciples" remains in sight. Paul meets with, in fact reports to, James, who is surrounded by presbyters. No reason is supplied for this consultation. James's leadership is presumed and unchallenged. The narrator presents here the climax of the second generation of the Jesus movement. Its two leaders are James and Paul, who represent the gentile (v. 19) and Jewish (v. 20) missions. Paul's report receives, as in 15:4, its due acclaim. Jerusalem has not been taking its ease in Zion; for "myriads" of strict Torah observers have aligned themselves with the movement. One unfortunate side effect of this laudable success is that the observant believers have been exposed to unspeakable gossip and vile calumny about Paul, who allegedly encourages Diaspora Jews to apostatize. These leaders (who speak in unison) have a solution: Paul is directed to finance the vows of four of the faithful who have undertaken a vow and to participate in their ritual. This will quell any criticism.[1] No such burdens will, of course, be laid upon gentile converts. Paul complied (vv. 18-26).

It has been mooted since Overbeck that v. 18 represents the last clear trace of the source.[2] Lüdemann proposes that the source reported Paul's attempt "to buy favor" by assuming the cost of the devotees. He believes that the source was continuous, "for the resulting report exhibits a straightforward narrative line with no tensions or discontinuities."[3] Approaches clash, for narrative in Acts that is not disjointed or discontinuous is more likely to result from the absence of sources than to serve as evidence for them. Moreover, Lüdemann's subsequent analyses produce bits and pieces attributed to "tradition" rather than a continuous source.[4] The claim that Paul sought to purchase support by funding the devotees is more likely to have been a rumor circulated by his enemies than a deed of the historical Paul. Flexibility is one thing, bribery another. The absence of readily identifiable direct source material in 21:19–26:32 is one of the grounds for suspecting that the major source dealt with the receipt of the collection. If, as hypothesized, the collection failed of its purpose and Paul was arrested—both probable—it is possible that such of his colleagues who were not themselves arrested—gentiles in Jerusalem without many allies—would have left Jerusalem promptly to deliver the news, in writing and in person. One must also admit, however, that this definition of the source discourages inquiry for traces through chap. 26.

Verses 18b-26 do not offer strong evidence for a direct source. Verse 18b associates James with presbyters in an anachronistic manner;[5] Verse 19 is a repeat of 15:4, 12; v. 20 reflects 11:18; vv. 20-25 are unison direct speech,[6] the last of which reprises 15:20. These minor parallels point to a larger one: this scene is based on Acts 15, itself a Lucan composition. Paul travels to Jerusalem, meets with James and presbyters, and narrates his successes. In response to objections about

1 Jacob Neusner ("Vow-Taking, the Nazirites, and the Law: Does James' Advice to Paul accord with Halakah?" in Bruce Chilton and Craig Evans, eds., *James the Just and Christian Origins* [Leiden: Brill, 1999] 59–82) answers his question positively.

2 Franz Overbeck, *Kurze Erklärung der Apostelgeschichte* (4th ed. of Wilhelm M. L. de Wette, *Handbuch zum Neuen Testament*, vol. 1.4; Leipzig: Hirzel, 1870) 380. See Haenchen, 608. Note also Dibelius (*Studies*, 8), who thinks that Luke had no sources beyond 21:17. It is not likely that διακονία ("ministry") refers to Paul's collection here, as in 2 Cor 8:4; 9:1; and elsewhere. Focus is on his mission in general.

3 Lüdemann, *Acts*, 282; see the longer discussion in idem, *Opposition*, 52–62.

4 On subsequent pages (298–330), Lüdemann will argue for elements of tradition at various points through chap. 26.

5 See below.

6 For other examples of unison speech, see 1:24-25; 4:19-20; 14:14-15, 22b. Witherington (645) says that unison speech can be found in Greek historians, citing Thucydides 1.68 as an example. (He may have taken this from Kennedy, *Rhetorical Criticism*, 134). The parallel is not very cogent. The section from Thucydides (1.68–78) treats a debate at Sparta in which the viewpoint of communities was so represented. Thucydides did not imply that entire delegations spoke in unison. Some similarity of purpose is evident.

observance, with emphasis on circumcision (15:5; 21:20), a compromise is proposed.[7] As at the "Apostolic Council" (15:19[8]), James simply promulgates the solution. Paul complies without demur. In this instance, the compromise is not a good fit, for the issue is not practice, but Paul's *teaching*. In response to this charge, a community (or representative, given the alleged size) assembly could have been called, at which Paul could have set forth his views and presented, as a prime exhibit, Timothy, for whose circumcision he was responsible.[9]

For such a scenario, Acts 15 would have been a fine model. Despite his imitation and evocation of that great occasion, Luke does not utilize the opportunity. It is possible that the proposal to pay for the vows was a Jacobean compromise, but it seems unlikely that Paul would have found this proposal to "launder" the collection acceptable, for it would have given the gentile believers a status no different from gentile polytheists, who could make offerings to the temple but not join in its rites. The action would show that Paul was, or could be, observant, but it would not have been a good means for answering complaints about his theology. Dieter Georgi, who accepts the report in Acts, says, "[T]his compromise enabled the Jerusalem Jesus congregation not only to accept the collection but to defend Paul against the accusation of enmity toward the Torah as well."[10] Possibly so, but one mark against this reconstruction is the complete absence from Acts of the slightest hint that any believers at Jerusalem uttered so much as one word in defense of Paul. James disappears from the story, and, after v. 26, so do the four.[11] If arguments from silence are to be deployed, this absence of data supports the rejection of the collection by James rather than its acceptance "on the side."[12] Stanley Porter reads the episode as a rejection of Paul by the Jewish Christians of Jerusalem.[13] The implication of the text supports his position.

The picture presented here is in conflict with that of Acts hitherto. This scene portrays Paul as the missionary to gentiles, now reporting to Jerusalem, which is viewed as conducting a mission to Jews.[14] Each of these missions has its own set of rules: Three or four regulations for gentiles, the complete Torah for Jews.[15] The notion of two missions could be derived from Gal 2:6-10,[16] but hitherto Acts has presumed unity under the leadership of Jerusalem. Nothing is said about Paul's success in attracting Jewish followers (cf. 19:10). This understanding shows that for Luke the Jewish mission, in the sense of a mission to Jews who will remain observant, belongs to the past. Eschatology is not in the picture. Those of Jewish origin may continue to observe Torah, gentiles the "Apostolic Decree," both indefinitely.[17]

Comment

■ **18-19** As in 16:17, as "we" is about to leave the stage,[18] it is distinguished from Paul. This is evidently an editorial device.[19] James, as Martin Hengel observes, appears

7 See Talbert, 191.

8 Note the same verb (*κρίνω*, "decree") in 21:25.

9 The charge avoids any reference to the Christian message. As stated, it could be taken as a claim that Paul simply attacks Torah, urging all Diaspora Jews to desist from circumcision.

10 Georgi, *Remembering*, 125–26.

11 Georgi's assertion that these four were "destitute" (*Remembering*, 125; cf. Haenchen, 610) is a reasonable hypothesis, but no more than that.

12 The prepositional phrase is used by Georgi, *Remembering*, 126.

13 Porter, *Paul of Acts*, 172–86.

14 Painter (*Just James*, 55) notes both the implication of two missions here and its inconsistency with the earlier reports of Acts.

15 The statement about "circumcising children" (rather than, e.g., "to be circumcised") would refute the view that observance is suitable for those born into ("pre-Christian") Judaism, but should not continue.

16 This is to say that Luke could have understood Galatians thus, not that this is the normative interpretation of the passage.

17 Verse 25 assumes that the decree of chap. 15 applies to all gentile believers. Cf. also 16:4. This supports the view that the "decree" came from the gentile missionary source.

18 The "we" that will reappear in chap. 27 is different in nature.

19 The D-Text (Boismard, *Texte*, 348) does not follow this convention: *τῇ δὲ ἐπιούσῃ εἰσήμεθα σὺν τῷ Παύλῳ πρὸς Ἰάκωβον ἦσαν δὲ παρ᾽ αὐτῷ οἱ πρεσβύτεροι συνηγμένοι* 19 *οὕς ἀσπασαμένων ἡμῶν διηγεῖτο* [ ] *ὁ Παῦλος ὡς* . . . ("The next day **we** went in **with Paul** to see James. Now [ ] the presbyters were **gathered together. After we had greeted them** *Paul* set out **how** . . ."). This is an

like a prince with his court.[20] A more apt simile is the ideal of an Ignatian bishop, surrounded by a circle of presbyters, who, speaking in unison with their leader, are almost literally "attuned to . . . [him] as strings to the lyre."[21]

■ **20-21** After Paul's report, James (and company) show that the Judean mission has never faltered. It can claim "myriads"[22] of believers whose loyalty to Torah is unflagging.[23] The problem is those nasty rumors that Paul teaches Diaspora Jews to abandon their ancestral practices.[24] The style is "naïve"; that is, James presents the complaints as if they were fresh information for Paul.[25] This is a characteristic of popular narrative. Similar charges will presently appear on the lips of those who foment a riot against Paul in 21:28.[26] A possible source for v. 21 is 6:13-14, the charges against Stephen.[27] For readers of Acts, they are calumnies. In fact, they contained some validity.[28]

Excursus: Luke and Torah Observance

Neither here nor elsewhere does Acts explain *why* Jewish believers should be taught to observe Torah. Insofar as Acts is concerned the Law of Moses cannot make one right with God (13:38-39), is an intolerable burden (15:10), and, insofar as it deals with dietary laws and regulations for purity, is opposed to the manifest will of God (10:10-16). Although Acts takes note of followers of Jesus who remain observant and no more condemns them out of hand than does Paul, it offers no theological rationale or justification for their continued practice. Torah-observing believers come to the fore only as obstacles to the gentile mission in general and to the work of Paul in particular. Apart from demonstrating that the movement *could* appeal to practicing Jews, these believers make no positive contributions to the story of Acts. For the gentile mission, they are a problem. Luke may well have seen them as deserving sympathy, so long as they do not become meddlesome. Since observance no longer conformed to the divine mandates, it was to be tolerated, and no more. Luke, despite his insistence on continuity, is a product of the gentile mission who sees the peculiar features of Jewish life as a relic of the past, useful in their time, no doubt, but no longer required or desirable.[29] Within Acts, Paul alone is portrayed as engaging in the temple cult.[30] Despite his presentation of Paul as very observant and a card-carrying Pharisee, Luke is rather close to Paul on the value of Torah for followers of Jesus. His attitude may also be compared to that of Justin.[31]

---

instance of "copy editing" that makes the text less abrupt.

20 Hengel, *Between*, 108. Barrett (2:1005) says that the language "conveys a hint of entering the presence of a great person," with references to Xenophon *Cyr.* 2.4.5 and Herodotus 1.99.1. On his leadership, see Hans von Campenhausen, "Die Nachfolge des Jakobus: Zur Frage eines urchristlichen 'Kalifats,'" *ZKG* 63 (1950–51) 133–44.

21 *I. Eph.* 4.2. Cf. also Peter with the apostles in 2:14.

22 This splendid hyperbole should be accepted as such. Wikenhauser (*Geschichtswert,* 119) says it is hyperbolic and cites Plato *Leg.* 804E. Bruce (445) notes a tradition that began with F. C. Baur (!) to delete "believers" and thus say only that there are many observant people in Judea. See pp. 86–87.

23 Cf. Philo *Spec. leg.* 2.253, who speaks of thousands full of zeal for the laws. The theme of "zeal for the law" is common. See also Acts 22:3; 1 Macc 2:26; Gal 1:14.

24 The D-Text (Boismard, *Texte*, 350) has an active verb: "They report." The source of this rumor is now Judean believers. The balance is simplified. "All" is omitted, presumably because of the preceding article, as is the participle "saying." "In" before "customs" also eliminates misunderstanding. See Ropes, *Text*, 205; and Metzger, *Textual Commentary*, 428–29.

25 Note also the use of "Jews" in vv. 20-21 when "our people" (etc.) would have been more appropriate. This indicates that the words come from the author.

26 Both use the verb διδάσκω ("teach") with πάντας ("everyone").

27 In 6:14 witnesses against Stephen refer to customs (ἔθη) transmitted by Moses; both words appear also in 21:21.

28 When pressed (Gal 5:3), Paul treats Torah as absolute. Jewish–gentile unity was difficult to preserve in mixed communities. Although Paul made no objections to completely Jewish communities of believers in Jesus, he may well have recommended that those of Jewish background in mixed churches not circumcise their children. Those who did so would be numbered among "the weak." Extremes are best avoided. It is probably safest to say that Paul did not generally encourage Jewish believers to have their sons circumcised. On the subject, see Wilson, *Law*, 101–2. Regarding the charge that Paul advised people not to have their children circumcised, Calvin is quite succinct: "It was in fact so" (7:200).

■ **22-25** The whole unit (vv. 20-25) is a balanced and well-constructed composition[32] reminiscent of the postapostolic literature in which matters are settled by giving orders rather than with convoluted dialectic and appeal to such general principles as the law of love in light of the freedom bestowed by faith. The external frame (vv. 20, 25) deals with Jewish and Diaspora gentile believers.[33] The former observe Torah, while the latter must abide by the requirements set forth in Acts 15.[34] Verses 21 and 24c-d (from "Everyone will then know") delineate rumor and solution, apostasy[35] and observance.[36] The center is the string of imperatives in vv. 23-24.[37] These direct Paul to join four devotees, with whom he will "purify himself" and for whom he

29 See also Sanders, *Jews*, 128–30; and, in general, Wilson, *Law*.

30 Acts 2:42 (a summary) does not mention temple worship. The apostles teach in the temple (3:12-26; 5:20; cf. 5:12), but there are no reports of worship there. For Luke, the temple is, first and foremost, a place for prayer and teaching (Luke 19:46; cf. 18:9-14). In Acts 3:1, Peter and John are visiting the temple at "the hour of prayer," in fact at the time of the evening sacrifice. They engage in teaching (3:12-26). Cf. also 4:2; 5:21, 25.

31 In *Dial.* 47, Justin acknowledges that some Christians observe Torah. This is no impediment to their salvation, so long as they do not attempt to persuade gentile Christians to do the same.

32 Verse 22 resembles the style of the diatribe, with rhetorical questions to promote vividness. See Cadbury and Lake, 271–72. It is thus appropriate to writing, underlining the extent to which this is not a conversation. For rhetorical analyses of this little speech, see Kennedy, *Rhetorical Criticism*, 134; and Soards, *Speeches*, 109–10. The D-Text of v. 22 (Boismard, *Texte*, 350) is quite interesting. Between πάντως and ἀκούσονται ("doubtless learn") there comes the phrase δεῖ συνελθεῖν πλῆθος ("**This will cause a mob to form/crowd to assemble, for** they will learn that you have come" [γάρ ("for") has wide support]). This variant is not without its charm, witness its appearance in a range of authorities. Cadbury and Lake (272) suspect that it is original and "should probably be translated 'there must be a meeting of the whole church.'" Haenchen (609 n. 3), despite the absence of the article, believes that a community assembly is in view. If that interpretation is correct–it may mean that Paul's arrival will generate a mob–the D-editor would have proposed a logical solution to the problem. Two difficulties with viewing it as original are, as often, why it would have been deleted and, more importantly, that the suggestion is not pursued.

33 In v. 25, after "gentiles," the D-Text (Boismard, *Texte*, 351) reads οὐδὲν ἔχουσιν λέγειν πρός σε ("They [the Jewish believers?] have nothing to say to you, **for** we . . ."), and κρίναντες μηδὲν τοιοῦτον τηρεῖν αὐτοὺς εἰ μή ("We determined that they should observe nothing of the sort, other than . . ."), followed by the "threefold" form of the decree (omitting "strangled" and not including the golden rule). Metzger (*Textual Commentary*, 429) suggests that the additional words may be related to the absence of the rule, but he does not venture to say how. A more obvious explanation is to relate the matter to Paul's teaching, as in v. 21.

34 Cf. the use of the same participial form, πεπιστευκότων ("those who have come to believe") for both Jews (v. 20) and gentiles (v. 25). Hengel's statement (*Acts and the History*, 117) that "James presents it as something new and apparently unknown to [Paul]" is not correct, although it responds to the brusqueness of the speech. All of the data are presented in the same manner, and none would have escaped Paul's prior attention. For Paul Achtemeier (*The Quest for Unity in the New Testament Church* [Philadelphia: Fortress Press, 1987] e.g., 32, 33, 52, 89), this observation is historically correct, and he builds his hypothesis upon it. Acts 21:25 is, however, too weak a base for the claim that Paul did not know about the "decree" until his final visit to Jerusalem. The information is for the readers: Wilson, *Law*, 81. See the comments of Barrett, 2:1014–15.

35 "Apostasy" illustrates the lack of separation between "religion" and "politics" in antiquity. The term ἀποστάτης means a "rebel" (cf. στάσις). This sense of ἀποστασία endures (Plutarch *Galb.* 1; Josephus *Vit.* 43; *Ap.* 1.135–36; *Ant.* 12.219). A more religious application appears in Josh 22:22; Jer 2:19, etc. In 2 Macc 5:8, Jason is called "an apostate from the laws" (τῶν νόμων ἀποστάτης). This is the sense of Acts 21:21. Note also Luke 8:13. See Heinrich Schlier, "ἀφίστημι," *TDNT* 1:513–14. The persecution under Antiochus IV brought the question of apostasy and its meaning into the forefront of the question of Jewish identity, for Jason and his supporters viewed themselves as reformers rather than apostates. Cf. 1 Macc 1:43-50.

36 Cf. the use of κατηχέω ("instruct") in vv. 21 and 24.

37 The reference to shaving the head in v. 24 helps account for 18:18: The activity was not unusual for Paul.

will assume the expense of discharging their vows. Two actions are in view: ritual purification that will enable one to participate in temple activity[38] and payment of expenses for others.[39] The latter was a charitable benefaction associated with the wealthy.[40] An outstanding example is Agrippa I (Josephus *Ant.* 19.294).[41] The instructions evidently imply that Paul is to join the devotees in the discharge of their obligation, as well as financing it. It is difficult to reconcile the rite described with what is known of Jewish practice. The seven-day period could derive from a misunderstanding of Num 6:9-10.[42] For the narrative, seven days gives the pot time to reach the boiling point.

■ **26** The verse reports, not smoothly,[43] Paul's prompt compliance with the request. He is in full command. "With them" (σὺν αὐτοῖς) replaces "with us" in v. 18 (σὺν ἡμῖν). The narrator seems to envision, perhaps on the basis of Num 6:4 and 1 Macc 3:49, that Paul had to enter the sacred precincts to report when the vows would be fulfilled.[44] The absence of any formal agreement, verbal or in summary form, is normal Lucan compression. The pressing historical question has been "would Paul have done this?" Issues of this nature are almost irresolvable. Even if it can be shown that this act was not consistent with Paul's principles,[45] only fools apply their principles with perfect consistency. Barrett avoids this dilemma by positing that the real issue is whether Paul would engage in an act of deception, that is, pretending that he was fully observant.[46] As he notes, not even 1 Cor 9:19-23, which had been invoked to the very margins of idolatry, will justify naked hypocrisy. Barrett does not prove that no such action was undertaken, but he makes a convincing case that it would not have been performed for the reasons advanced by Acts. Frederick F. Bruce, who is among those calling on 1 Cor 9:22 here, adds another reason: it would not have worked, since Paul's opponents, who had better information, would not have accepted this proof.[47]

The remaining question is whether the information is correct, but not for the reasons given. To this one may add that the data about the discharge of the vows is evidently confused or erroneous. Moreover, it is worth asking whether use of funds from the collection to pay for religious vows would have qualified as assistance for the "poor" in Jerusalem (Rom 15:26) and, correlatively, whether the contributors would have found this an appropriate use of their donations. In sum: if the source—or some other "tradition"—reported that James suggested that Paul participate in some form of cultic activity involving payment for vows, it was not for the reasons accepted nor in the manner reported. The historical waters are very murky.[48] Contrastingly lucid is the literary atmosphere, bright with irony: Paul will be arrested because of his loyalty and observance.

---

38 The meaning of ἁγνίσθητι ("get yourself purified") is not clear. See Haenchen (610 n. 3), who reduces various rationalizations to mincemeat. For Paul to require purification is reasonable, but the text speaks of all five persons. Barrett (2:1011) reasonably relates the confusion to Luke's lack of detailed knowledge about procedures. Paul affirms his purification in 24:18.

39 "Shaving the head" is probably a synecdoche for discharging the vow.

40 Ramsay (*St. Paul the Traveller,* 311) uses this action as proof of Paul's wealth. On the role of expense in Nazirite vows, see the data in George B. Gray, *Sacrifice in the Old Testament: Its Theory and Practice* (Oxford: Clarendon, 1925) 38–39. For evidence that a Nazirite vow is in view, see Heinrich Greeven, "εὔχομαι," *TDNT* 2:775–808, esp. 777.

41 Pervo (*Dating,* 190–91) examines the possibility that Josephus inspired this passage.

42 Numbers 6 provides regulations for Nazirite vows. See also Cadbury and Lake, 272–73; Wilson, *Law,* 66, "There can be little doubt that as it stands it makes little sense in terms of current Jewish practice." Haenchen (610) sums it up: "The only thing clear is that Paul through the proposed action will prove himself a law-abiding Jew."

43 On the problems of translation, see Cadbury and Lake, 273–74.

44 It is tempting to contrast the use of "each one" (εἷς ἕκαστος) in vv. 19 and 26.

45 See, e.g., Cadbury and Lake, 273; and Porter, *Paul of Acts,* 185, for this view.

46 Barrett, 2:1012–13. Calvin says, "They seem to be inciting Paul to hypocrisy," but concludes that "Paul did not pretend" (7:202).

47 Bruce, 447. He finds the presbyters (modestly omitting James) "ingenuous."

48 Calvin's reservation (7:202) has merit; he is not fond of James's order, yet observes: "But a clear judgment on that matter depends on the circumstances, which are hidden from us today, but were obvious to them." Haenchen (611–13)

The compromise is difficult to reconcile with the silence of Acts about the collection. Had it been proposed as stated, and the funds received on those conditions, as Georgi suggests,[49] the receipt could have been duly noted, for the collection would have been noncontroversial. The entire scenario of Acts 21–26 is an argument in favor of the failure of the collection project, and the story of the four may have been a Lucan invention that both puts Paul in a favorable light and gives no glory to James and his myriads. "Failure" is the key word, however it is understood, since the collection, even if accepted, did not achieve its goals. Paul's worst fears (Rom 15:30-32) were realized.[50] Behind these difficulties lie theological and political shifts within the Jerusalem community. Gal 1:15—2:12 intimate that the power of James had grown between the first and second visits of Paul. Gal 2:12 reveals that even the agents of James could induce Peter to comply with their wishes. Acts recognizes this in the respective roles assigned to Peter and James at the meeting reported in chap. 15. By the time of his last visit, Paul no longer had allies. One may attribute these changes to personalities, politics, or a mixture of both. James was not the most conservative believer in Jerusalem, and one may suspect that he was hampered by pressure "from the right." The basis for the ambiguous agreement elaborated in Gal 2:7-10 had all but evaporated. Both sides suspected the other of betrayal. Acts 21:17-25 is indirect testimony to the failure of this early attempt at unity among Christians.

---

uses the purifying tablet of external knowledge about the procedures to arrive at a solution: Paul required purification and had to be asperged on the third and seventh day (cf. *m. Ohol.* 2:3). Then he could be present with the four. This reconstruction is plausible, presuming Paul's acceptance of the request. Haenchen does presume that debatable fact and also the less probable view that this act "would take the wind out of the sails of the accusations against him." Schneider (2:310) reaches a similar conclusion.

49 See n. 10.

50 Jervell (529–30) sums up the difficulties.

21

21:27-40 Paul Is Arrested

27/ Just as the seven-day period of
purification was about to end,[a]
the Asian Jews[b] saw Paul in
the temple. They tried to seize
him and incite a general riot by
28/ shouting: "To the rescue,
men of Israel! This is the fel-
low who is teaching against
the People, the Torah, and this
Place to everyone everywhere!
Now he has had the temerity
to bring Greeks into the temple
and profane this Holy Place!"
(29/ They made this accusa-
tion because they had seen
the Ephesian Trophimus in the
city with Paul and supposed[c]
that Paul had brought him into
the temple.) 30/ The entire city
was thrown into an uproar. A
mob rushed in, nabbed Paul,
and dragged him outside of the
temple. The gates were imme-
diately slammed shut.
31/ While the mob occupied itself
with trying to murder Paul,[d]
the military tribune com-
manding the cohort received
word that Jerusalem was in
an uproar.[e] 32/ Accompanied
by soldiers and centurions,[f]
he immediately set out on the
double toward the scene of
the action. When the crowd
caught sight of the tribune
and the soldiers, they stopped
pummeling Paul. 33/ Once he
got there, the tribune had Paul
taken into custody and ordered
that he be shackled with two
chains. He then asked who
this person might be and what
he had done.[g] 34/ Since the
responses were so many and
varied,[h] he directed that Paul
be taken to the barracks, as the
tumult made it impossible to
learn what was actually going
on.[i] 35/ Once they reached the
stairs, the force of the crowd
made it necessary to have Paul
carried by the soldiers,[j] 36/ for
the mob kept pressing upon
them with shouts of "Away
with him!"[k]
37/ On the verge of being taken into
the barracks, Paul said to the
tribune, "May I have a word
with you?"
"You speak Greek," he
exclaimed! 38/ "So[l] you're not

a The D-Text (Boismard, *Texte*, 352) transforms this into a genitive absolute, which disrupts the parallelism with v. 37.

b Bezae evidently wished to say "Jews who had come from Asia."

c Bezae supplies amusement to the textual critic with "we supposed . . ."

d The subject of the genitive absolute is not stated. The translation takes it as "the people" (λαός) of v. 30. See BDF §423 (6). $\mathfrak{p}^{74}$ places the conjunction δέ ("and") after the finite verb, while a number of witnesses prefer δέ to τε. Luke is fond of the latter.

e The D-Text (Boismard, *Texte*, 354) adds: "Take care that they don't start a revolt." (H^{mg} is the sole basis for this supplement. It is typical of the D-Text.)

f On the circumstantial participle παραλαβὼν ("accompanied by"), see BDF §418 (5). As often, a relative serves as a principle clause.

g Without the particle ἄν (a *v.l.*) τίς εἴη ("who this person might be") looks like an oblique optative, but the following καὶ τί ἐστιν πεποιηκώς ("what he had done") seems to rule that out. See BDF §386 (1); and Bruce 451.

h On the idiom, see BDF §306 (5).

i BDF §423 (4) rates the genitive absolute as "very clumsy."

j The D-Text (Boismard, *Texte*, 354–55) substitutes "Paul" for the pronoun and "people" (λαός) for "crowd" in v. 35, leading to the omission of "people" in v. 36. Bezae uses: ἀναιρεῖσθαι ("be done away with"). The masculine plural κράζοντες is *ad sensum*. (It should properly be neuter singular, as in D.)

k The D-Text (Boismard, *Texte*, 355) has the crowd shout: "Away with our enemy!" (ἐχθρόν). This is the term used for Paul in the Ps.-Clementines.

l The translation takes the particle ἄρα as an expression of surprise.

m The term *sicarii* is a Latin loanword, a metonym derived from the concealed dagger that was their weapon of choice. Josephus is evidently responsible for introducing the word into Greek. It also appears in rabbinic writings and a few times in patristic sources. Josephus is the probable source of these. See Otto Betz, "σικάριος," *TDNT* 7: 278–82. Cadbury and Lake (277) deprecate "assassins," evidently because their motivation came from the use of what is now a controlled substance. Fitzmyer (696) seems not to have been dissuaded by this argument.

n *Or:* "So you are the Egyptian . . . aren't you?"

o The statement is probably not a balancing μέν . . . δέ construction, but an emphatic μέν. Bruce (453), however, takes the particles in tandem, the first part dealing with the tribune's question, the second with Paul's request.

p Bezae reads an alternate verb for permit:

the Egyptian who once started a revolution and led four thousand terrorists[m] out into the wilderness?"[n]

39/ **"I am a Jew,"[o] replied Paul, "from Tarsus in Cilicia, and a citizen of that renowned metropolis. Would you be so kind as to allow me to address the people?"[p]**

40/ **His request approved, Paul took a place on the steps and gestured for the crowd's attention.[q] After they had become quite still, he began to speak to them in Aramaic.[r]**

συγχωρῆσαι. Boismard's text (*Texte*, 356) seems to be defective here.

q The D-Text variants approved by Boismard (*Texte*, 356) in v. 40 do not alter the meaning.

r 𝔓[74] A read, instead of τῇ Ἑβραΐδι διαλέκτῳ, τῇ ἰδίᾳ διαλέκτῳ. This should mean "in his own language," but probably means "their native tongue." Hebrew was evidently current in Jerusalem and its environs, but Aramaic was the *lingua franca*. See Fitzmyer, 701, with references. When "Hebrew" is used of a language in the NT, the original when cited is Aramaic (John 5:2; 19:13, 17, 20; 20:16; Rev 9:11; 16:16). Note also Acts 1:19. For a claim that "Hebrew" is meant, see John C. Poirier, "The Narrative Role of Semitic Languages in the Book of Acts," *FilolNT* 16 (2003) 107–16.

Analysis

The purification procedure requires seven days, a window of opportunity for opponents. On the final day, just when it seemed that Paul was out of the woods, the (not "some") Jews from Ephesus,[1] life in which place[2] offered the equivalent of a graduate seminar in fomenting riots, spotted Paul, seized him and raised the usual cry, echoing the old charge against Stephen (6:10-14, and the allegedly false rumors of v. 21), with the addition that his blasphemies had been generally disseminated. Onto this bonfire they hurl a tub of petrol: Paul has introduced gentiles into the temple![3]

The hitherto somber and plodding narrative explodes. Exposure led to recognition. On the very verge of fulfilling his demonstration of piety, Paul once again fell afoul of a riot engineered by hostile Jews. As in Ephesus (19:23-29), uproar encompassed the entire populace, which set about to mob Paul.[4] He was saved by the intervention of the tribune in charge of the cohort stationed in the vicinity, but that officer presumed that Paul was the suspect, for he had him shackled. Since the crowd could supply no intelligible information, the prisoner was carried up to toward the barracks in chains, serenaded by chants of the disappointed mob.

On the very portal of hideous torture Paul politely seeks permission to speak (v. 37), in words and accent that proclaim him a gentleman. The astonished commandant assumes that he has captured a terrorist. Mistaken identity opens the door for a famous response.

1 Verse 29 indicates that the narrator has once again used "Asia" for "Ephesus." Their Greek is euphonious. The combination "everyone everywhere" (πάντας πανταχῇ) was popular at that time: *1 Clem.* 65:2 (final blessing); Dio of Prusa *Or.* 4.93; 31.10; 32.15; Aristides *Or.* 54.10 (Sarapis). See also BDF §488 (1). πάντας πανταχοῦ ("everyone everywhere") occurs in Philo *Flac.* 1. See Pieter van der Horst, *Philo's Flaccus: The First Pogrom* (Philo of Alexandria Commentary Series 2; Atlanta: Society of Biblical Literature, 2003) 91.

2 If readers are to infer that these Ephesian Jews were the anonymous source of the rumors reported by James in v. 21 (Johnson, 381), they will also presume that there was intercourse between them and the Christian Jews in Jerusalem.

3 The narrator does not appear to distinguish the different courts and sections of the temple precincts. At this point (v. 29) appears one of the most intriguing of the rare narrative asides in Acts. See below.

4 Verse 30 is somewhat compressed. Mobs can form quickly, but Paul would have been killed before the populace in general could have arrived. See Haenchen, 616.

Paul *is*, indeed, a Jew—but nonetheless a citizen of one of Hellenism's cultural citadels. Paul has kept this useful card in his pocket for a necessitous moment. Playing it gives him the initiative. Oratory is one charm that can soothe the savage beast. The commandant told him to go ahead. Like Jesus (Luke 21) and Peter (Acts 3), Paul will speak in the temple. In these unpromising conditions, beaten and shackled, faced by a howling mob, Paul, who has just established his Hellenic credentials, will try his luck at addressing Jews.

The speech and its aftermath are all quite exciting, with a last-minute disaster followed by a rescue (of sorts) in the nick of time, but it does not lack difficulties. The narrative is linked to the preceding verses in that Paul is in the temple, but the four with whom he is associated have disappeared. If one envisions the scene reported by Luke, Paul, with his recently shaved head, would have been one of a group, who would have been under some obligation—he was their benefactor—to defend him as much as possible and to refute the charges. His very presence in that holy place engaged in worship would have served as prima facie evidence against the charges, since the last thing expected of an international enemy of Torah and temple would have been what Paul was doing.

Comment

■ **28** The second charge against Paul is quite dire. Gentiles who trespassed the holy boundaries were evidently subject to immediate summary execution.[5] The behavior of raving mobs is not subject to the strictest canons of formal logic, but it is worth asking whether the first task would have been to secure and punish the offending foreigners and then attend to the individual responsible for their presence.[6] The charge of temple profanation is not vigorously pursued, although mentioned in 24:6 (where it is reduced to attempted desecration, nature whereof unspecified). The tribune, whose primary responsibility was to quell the riot, did so by arresting the presumed agitator. This leads the critic to ask why that officer thought that the person being assaulted by the mob was a terrorist inciting insurrection.

The story therefore deconstructs. This raises questions of possible sources and the larger matter of whether any history can be extracted from this adventure. Scholars assume that Paul was arrested in Jerusalem and sent to Rome. The specific charges and the reasons for his removal to Rome are not known. It is unlikely that they involved criticism of Torah. The charge that he introduced gentiles is so heinous that it could contain a grain of truth.

■ **29** Luke, who normally provides rioters no mitigation, does so here. One possible reconstruction is that, in response to a rejection of the collection, Paul staged a symbolic "liberation" of the place by demanding that he and his gentile converts be admitted, and that the subsequent uproar led the government to charge him with fomenting insurrection.[7] This is not a hypothesis on which one can build, but it does provide one satisfactory explanation of the data.

The most indisputable "source" for this material is Acts 19:28-40.[8] The two passages share a general outline: A crowd (ὄχλος, 19:33; 21:27) accuses Paul of attacking a temple. This results in an uproar that engulfs the entire city (19:29; 21:30). The disturbance is quelled by an official (19:34; 21:32). The affair concludes with a speech (19:35-40; 22:1-21). There are a number of common expressions: πόλις ("city" as a

5 An inscription warning trespassers of the penalty is extant: *CIJ* 1400 (= *OGIS* 598). On this, see Elias J. Bickermann, "The Warning Inscriptions from Herod's Temple," *JQR* 37 (1946–47) 387–405; and Peretz Segal, "The Penalty of the Warning Inscription from the Temple of Jerusalem," *IEJ* 39 (1989) 79–84. (Further bibliography in Fitzmyer, 698.) Josephus *Bell.* 6.124–28 suggests that the prohibition was taken literally. Imperial powers tended to accept such taboos. Diodorus Siculus 1.83.8 tells of a Roman citizen murdered by an Egyptian mob for accidentally killing a cat.

6 It is rather too much to propose that the Ephesians accused Paul of introducing gentiles into the temple on another occasion. If a formal penalty for introducing gentiles existed, the punishment may also have been summary.

7 Weiser, 2:601.

8 That description follows a pattern similar to one used by Josephus. See p. 490. For an approach that has greater confidence in sources, see Dean P. Béchard, "The Disputed Case against Paul: A Redaction-Critical Analysis of Acts 21:27–22:29," *CBQ* 65 (2003) 232–50.

trope for "populace" [19:29; 21:30]); συγχέω ("stir up," and related words [19:29, 32; 21:27, 31]); ἄλλοι . . . ἄλλο τι ("some said one thing, others something else" [19:32; 21:34]); κράζω ("shout" [19:28, 32, 34; 21:28]). If most of this is no more than Luke's standard vocabulary for riots and the like, it nonetheless shows his hand. When to this are added the aside in v. 29 and the parallels with Stephen (6:13-14) in 21:28 as well as with Jesus (with 21:36 compare Luke 22:22; 23:27), it is apparent that the material is Lucan in both style and theme. The incidents resemble Acts 19, but the pattern of the larger narrative is essentially that used to relate the story of Stephen (6:8–8:2). Both are accused in similar terms by Jews of Diaspora background; both make speeches to their accusers[9] that provoke violence.[10]

The single item with a strong claim to a basis in tradition is the charge that Paul introduced gentiles into the temple.[11] Disturbances in the temple area were by no means uncommon,[12] especially at festival times.[13] With an eye to that fact, Witherington says: "There is nothing . . . intrinsically unlikely about a figure like Paul creating just such a scene as Luke describes."[14] So it may be, but one must ask how Paul created "such a scene," and the text is of no help whatsoever in that inquiry, for it spares no pains to show that Paul did not create the scene. Verses 27-28 (29) may contain traces of the source, but vv. 30-40 are Lucan composition.[15]

■ **30** Acts reverses the traditional picture. The temple remained sacrosanct, but the crowd had defiled itself by attempting to kill an innocent person on the basis of unsubstantiated rumor. Three other components of this segment have symbolic weight. The first is the closing of the temple gates.[16] This indicates that official Judaism at its center has closed itself to the message of Paul. No Christian will enter it thereafter.[17]

■ **31-33** The sacred place has lost its soteriological relevance and shown itself unworthy. Rome, in the person of its garrison commander, intervenes to "save" Paul from the mob, albeit by taking him into custody. This is Luke's so-called apologetic, which amounts to an argument that the Roman government stood on Paul's side. In effect: if "the Jews" are against us, the government should be for us.

■ **36** Finally, Paul deserves comparison with Jesus, who also confronted a mob screaming for his blood.[18] Paul will be in custody, at least theoretically, from v. 33 to

---

9 The resemblance is signaled by an identical "fathers and brethren" address (7:2; 22:1). Acts 22:20 alludes to Stephen's death.

10 On this pattern, see Tannehill, *Narrative Unity*, 2:273.

11 Lüdemann, *Acts*, 281. (He also assigns Trophimus to tradition, but that name could be derived from the list in 20:4.)

12 For example, Josephus *Bell.* 1.88–89; 2.8–13, 42–48, 169–74, 223–27, 229–31, 315–20, 406–7, 449–56. 3 Macc 1:9-29 narrates the arrival of Ptolemy Philopator in Jerusalem, his sacrifice, and his attempt to enter the holiest area. This led to a great uproar in the temple, which soon involved every type and class of inhabitant. With v. 30 compare Jdt 10:18. From a governmental perspective, the major festivals were major security risks, but the narrative has apparently dropped the suggestion that the riot happened at Pentecost. (See p. 515 n. 99.) Events of this nature were not limited to Jerusalem in literature. Note Achilles Tatius *Leuc. Clit.* 8.1–3. The hero, Clitophon, is attacked and injured in the temple of Artemis at Ephesus. "As I shouted out these complaints, a great crowd came together of all those who were in the temple: and they began to abuse Thersander [his opponent]. . . . At this I took courage and added: "This is what I have suffered, Sirs, though I am a free man and a citizen of no mean city (πόλεως οὐκ ἀσήμου); this rascal conspired against my life, but Artemis saved me and proved a trumper-up of false charges" (8.3.1, trans. S. Gaselee [LCL; rev. ed.; Cambridge, Mass.: Harvard University Press, 1969] 395). See also the crowd action in 6.5.2.

13 See, for example, Josephus *Ant.* 17.215 (cf. *Bell.* 2.10–13). During Passover, Archelaus sent a cohort under a tribune to suppress an incipient riot at the temple. Luke may have been influenced by such reports.

14 Witherington, 652.

15 Weiser, 2:607.

16 Boismard (*Texte*, 353) omits this phrase, without strong evidence. ℵ* reads "He was promptly locked out" (ἐκλείσθη).

17 Tyson, *Images*, 184. See also the comments of Bruce, 450; and Fitzmyer, 697. Failure to say why the gates were closed enhances the symbolic value of the act.

18 Verse 36 is modeled on Luke 22:22; 23:27 (above). Note the adverb ἔξω ("outside") in v. 30. Compare Luke 20:16 (the parable of the vineyard) and Acts 7:58. Luke 4:29 and Acts 14:19 indicate the

the close of Acts. The author wishes to squeeze as much from the moment as possible.[19]

Paul's obedience to the command of James will evidently cost him his life. The reward for loyalty to the ancestral religion will be a lethal beating at the hands of a Jewish mob. The turbulence created by the accusation prompted a response by the resident cohort,[20] the leader of which (a tribune) took Paul into custody and shackled him. The prophecy of 21:11 is more or less fulfilled. The gentiles have Paul under arrest, in chains. These will remain in the picture.[21] The hubbub of v. 34 is a realistic means of preventing the premature discovery of Paul's credentials, which the narrator will leak in v. 39 and 22:26. This is not a minor point, for everything that takes place through 22:29 depends on when these facts are revealed. Paul had to be carried.[22] This may be an allusion to Jesus, whose cross had to be carried by another (Luke 23:26).[23] The subsequent cry[24] "away with him" is a specific allusion to the passion of Jesus.[25] The arrival of the tribune introduces the character who will control the action of the next two chapters.[26] He will doggedly pursue his responsibility to "discover the facts" (γνῶναι τὸ ἀσφαλές [v. 34]) (see 22:30; 25:26). His two questions about who Paul is and what he has done will be answered not by the mob but by Paul himself (21:37-39; 22:1-21; 22:25).

Excursus: Paul the Prisoner

Acts includes two types of confinement scenes. The first three (5:17-21a; 12:4; 16:24-39) are brief and unpleasant (explicitly so in chaps. 12 and 16). All of these terminate in a miraculous delivery. The final confinement extends over a fourth of the book, takes place in a number of locations (Jerusalem, Caesarea, shipboard, Malta (?), Italy (?), Rome) and is never described as brutal or even unpleasant. As a prisoner, Paul cannot choose places of mission, but he has the opportunity to share his message with the Sanhedrin, two procurators of Judea, Herodian royalty, the elite of Caesarea, and the leading Jews of Rome. He is a prominent figure aboard ship and serves the chief of Malta as a benefactor.[27] Throughout his lengthy captivity Paul is ostensibly nearly always in control, often able to set the agenda, clearly superior when at trial. He decides on the ultimate venue of his case.

Although it is highly probable that Paul was arrested in Jerusalem and eventually sent to Rome for trial (or execution), it cannot be denied that Luke

widespread sentiment against polluting residential areas with blood.

19 The Ps.-Clementines ("Ascents of James," *Rec.* 1.66–71) present an interesting episode in the reception of this story. Peter and Clement initiate a debate about messiahship on the temple steps. They were quite successful until "an enemy" entered the temple and intervened. Refutation of his argument led to tumult and violence. "The enemy" threw James down from the top of the steps and left him for dead, but he was rescued by friends (cf. Acts 14:19-20). Gamaliel, a secret believer and supporter, brought news that "the enemy" had received a commission from Caiaphas to go to Damascus in pursuit of believers because it was believed that Peter had fled there. In 1.71 this opponent is identified as Saul. (Note that the author believed that Saul's excursion to Damascus required a rationale, and supplied one.) See Jones, "A Jewish Christian."

20 A cohort was the largest Roman military formation beneath the legion and contained about one thousand men at full strength. This body, an auxiliary force probably composed of Syrians, was mixed, roughly three-fourths infantry and one-fourth mounted. See Thomas Robert S. Broughton, "The Roman Army," in Lake and Cadbury, *Additional Notes,* 427–45, esp. 436–41; and Conzelmann, 183.

21 Custody is noted in 22:29-30; 23:18, 29; 24:27; 25:14, 27; 26:29, 31; 27:1, 42; 28:16, 17, 20. One may ask whether prisoners on a ship remained shackled.

22 "Violence" (βίαν) in v. 35 probably is best rendered "force," but it could refer to Paul's condition. Barrett (2:1018) disagrees with Haenchen's view (618) about Paul's injuries and thinks that Paul was carried to protect him from the mob. This overlooks the beating administered in v. 31. Cf. also Conzelmann, 183.

23 Luke 23:27a, Ἠκολούθει δὲ αὐτῷ πολὺ πλῆθος τοῦ λαοῦ ("A great number of the people followed him") is apparent inspiration for Acts 21:36, ἠκολούθει γὰρ τὸ πλῆθος τοῦ λαοῦ.

24 The verb κράζω ("shout") brackets vv. 28 and 36.

25 Cadbury and Lake (276) find this a "popular cry." See 22:11; 28:19 (*v.l.*); Luke 23:18 (not based on Mark); John 19:15; *Mart. Pol.* 3.1; 9.2; "Popularity" comes from the passion tradition.

26 The size of the detachment, which included at least two centurions and the commandant (v. 32), implying at least two hundred men, suggests a major disturbance.

has made the most of an unpromising opportunity. Incarceration is rarely pleasant, and the Roman imperial era was not an exception. For at least some of this period, the historical Paul must have found himself in a dank, dark, odorous facility where privileges were determined not by judicial mandate but the whim of the guards, a whim not insusceptible to the status and resources of the prisoner.[28] Acts takes no pains, unlike, for example, 2 Timothy, to develop the potential pathos of Paul's state. Here, if anywhere, the cliché "triumph over adversity" applies. Although the word "triumphalism" is out of favor in Lucan studies, some synonym thereof is appropriate to this narrative. The "triumph" is that of the message and plan of God, to be sure, and Paul is its agent.

The historical Paul knew that imprisonment could reflect negatively on him and the movement (Philippians 1). This dishonor endured. The author of Acts addressed it by showing that Paul the prisoner was a recipient of honor and respect and that his situation did not hinder proclamation of the gospel. In these circumstances the narrator shows him wielding his impressive credentials (Tarsian and Roman citizenship, membership in the Pharisaic party and the Sanhedrin) and multicultural skills, addressing Roman officers, Jewish mobs, the Jewish high council, the elite of Caesarea, and the leading Jews of Diaspora Rome, all deftly and appropriately. Paul's character is a bright light that dispels much of the gloom of his custody.

"Prison" ("custody," "bonds," and so on) is one of the key tropes of Acts, grounded in the biblical theme of the exodus. It serves as a symbol for those deprived of God's light (cf. Luke 1:78; Isa 45:1-7; 61:1-2) and also as a symbol of death, real or metaphorical.[29] In these roles bondage is associated with darkness and blindness. Light and liberation are its antonyms. The Devil seeks to bind humans as a means of domination. More concretely, imprisonment is a diabolic tool of God's enemies, whose efforts to stifle the message are doomed to failure. Paul is the model: prison cannot contain him, literally in 16:25-34, figuratively in chaps. 21–28.

■ **37-40** On the very precipice of torture,[30] Paul raises a polite question that causes the tribune to make a 180-degree turn in his character assessment. His question is best understood as a reference to the quality of Paul's Greek accent, since a Jewish rebel[31] from Egypt was likely to have spoken some Greek.[32] Paul exhibited the fluency of an educated native speaker, a fellow who had just disembarked from the train from Princeton rather than some peasant just off the boat from Palermo. Rather more difficult to rationalize is how Claudius Lysias (for such is his name [23:26]) was able to determine how a person being assaulted in the vicinity of the temple was a specific terrorist. Lysias's intelligence is bad, for his identification confuses two very different sorts of rebels, prophetic leaders who hoped for support from on high, and realistic assassins who struck at upper-class supporters of Rome. Luke has drawn this medley about "the Egyptian" and his association with "the wilderness" and "the sicarii" from Josephus (*Bell.* 2.254–63; *Ant.* 20.161–71).[33] It serves no other logic than to be a splendid foil for the famous riposte. Paul is a Jew, which qualifies him to address this audience—and would also serve to refute claims that he is gentile trespasser

27 See, in addition to Rapske, *Roman Custody*, Skinner, *Locating*.

28 For actual conditions, see S. Arband, W. Macheiner, and C. Colpe, "Gefangenschaft," *RAC* 9:318–45. Primary texts include Philo *Jos.* 81–84 and Lucian *Tox.* 29–33, both fictitious but presumably within the bounds of realism. For secondary literature, see Rapske, *Roman Custody*, 20–28 *et passim*, and Skinner, *Locating*, 79–86, together with their references, including vivid accounts from the martyr acts.

29 See p. 309 n. 92.

30 Note the verb μέλλω ("be about to") in vv. 27 and 37. For similar suspense, see Herodotus 1.114–19.

31 Acts 17:6 uses the same verb (ἀναστατάω).

32 The meaning of this revelation (to the tribune) is debated. Conzelmann argues that Paul's Greek showed that he was not "the Egyptian," citing Lucian *Nav.* 2 (which speaks of an Egyptian boy with a thick accent). For various views, see Bruce, 452; and Fitzmyer, 700. Interpretation must be based on the narrative, rather than on historical or linguistic argument. On the subject in general, see Jan N. Sevenster, *Do You Know Greek? How Much Greek Could the First Jewish Christians Have Known?* (NovTSup 19; Leiden: Brill, 1968).

33 The coincidences make it highly unlikely that he used another source. See Pervo, *Dating*, 161–66. The confusion is probably not due to hasty reading or faulty recollection as much as to the desire to accumulate opprobrious epithets.

on holy ground. He is also a citizen of Tarsus, a venerable bastion of Hellenic culture.[34]

The tribune's failure to investigate or verify these assertions exhibits the force of Paul's personality, which positively radiated refinement and gentility. Paul does not wear his heart on his sleeve. He says nothing about his Roman citizenship. For Lysias just now, Tarsus will do. Within thirty-five verses the following characters emerge: (1) victim of mob (reader's perspective), (2) Egyptian revolutionary terrorist (tribune's perspective), (3) cultivated citizen of Tarsus (tribune's perspective), (4) highly skilled orator (temple audience's perspective), (5) well-educated, ardent, observant Jew (reader's perspective), (6) Roman citizen (soldiers' perspective). Oratorical handbooks recommended that different credentials were suitable for different audiences.[35] Luke's Paul had certainly grasped that advice.

Excursus: Was Paul a Citizen of Tarsus? Of Rome?

The author does not intend the word πολίτης in 21:39 to be understood in the sense of "resident" but with its full meaning of "citizen," as in "French citizen" rather than a legal resident of France.[36] In Greco-Roman antiquity, citizenship was associated with cities. Birth was not the sole, or even the principal, criterion for citizenship. As a general rule, citizenship in a Greek *polis* required two citizen parents. Residence and education, including participation in the ephebate (and, normally, in polytheistic worship[37]), were also typical requirements for males. Property was another.[38]

Tarsus may have been Paul's place of birth, as implied in 9:11, probably from a source and not a Lucan invention,[39] but both of Acts' claims—that Paul was a citizen of Tarsus and that he had lived since infancy in Jerusalem, where he was educated—can scarcely be true. The question of Jewish citizenship in Greek cities—as opposed to what amounted to local home rule—has been thoroughly aired.[40] Philo and Josephus cloud the picture but do not obscure the real battleground: protection of Jews' rights as resident aliens who can maintain their traditional practices. Evidence for Jewish citizens is very rare and generally later than Acts. Some of the persons who have been proposed were not Jews, others

34 The litotes οὐκ ἄσημος ("not insignificant") is common. Josephus, for example, uses it about eight times. It is often used of one's native city, for example, Euripides *Ion* 8 (Athens); Strabo 8.6.15 (Epidauros). See also *Ephesian Tale* 2.13.6 and *Leuc. Clit.* 8.3.1 (n. 12 above). For a close formal parallel, note the *Acta Isidori,* Rec. A co. iii 7–10 (Musurillo, *Pagan,* 19): Claudius asks the Egyptian patriot Isidorus if he is not the son of an actress. Isidorus retorts, "I (with emphatic μέν, as in Acts 21:39) am neither slave nor actress's son, but gymnasiarch of the glorious city of Alexandria (διασήμου πόλεως Ἀλεξανδρείας)" (trans. Musurillo, 25). On the status of Tarsus, see Jerome H. Neyrey, "Luke's Social Location of Paul: Cultural Anthropology and the Status of Paul in Acts," in Witherington, *History,* 251–79, esp. 271.

35 See below on 22:3.

36 Harry W. Tajra opts for the sense of "resident" in his *The Trial of St. Paul: A Juridical Exegesis of the Second Half of the Acts of the Apostles* (WUNT 35; Tübingen: Mohr Siebeck], 1989) 79–80. Rapske (*Roman Custody,* 76) rightly rejects this attempt.

37 Lentz, *Luke's Portrait,* 36. Epiphanius (*Pan.* 30.16.6) states that Jews seized upon v. 39 to allege that Paul was the son of Greek parents, who went up to Jerusalem for some time; determined to marry the high priest's daughter, he became a proselyte and was circumcised. When this project failed, he became angry and wrote against circumcision, the Sabbath, and Torah. Opponents of Paul could thus take this verse as evidence that Paul, as a citizen of Tarsus, was originally a gentile. See Jones, "A Jewish Christian," 617. This interpretation may explain the D-Text's omission of "a citizen of that renowned metropolis" (Boismard, *Texte,* 356). A number of D-Text witnesses place "although born at Tarsus in Cilicia" here, which serves the same purpose.

38 Tarsus had a requirement of five hundred drachmae in property for citizenship, according to Dio of Prusa *Or.* 34.23.

39 It is possible that the source used in Acts 9 inferred "Tarsus" from Gal 1:20. Gal 1:17 suggests that Paul lived in Damascus at the time of his "conversion." Haenchen (620) says that Phil 3:5 permits the inference that Paul was not born in the Holy Land, as he would have mentioned it there.

40 On the subject, see Barclay, *Jews,* index, 492, under "Citizenship (Greek)." Other studies include Mary Smallwood, *The Jews,* index, 579, under "citizenship" and "civic status"; and, more recently, eadem, "The Diaspora in the Roman Period before CE 70," in *CHJ* 3:168–91. Note also the two articles of Samuel Applebaum, "The Legal Status of the Jewish Communities in the Diaspora," in Samuel Safrai et al., eds., *The Jewish People in the First Century:*

were apostates, and all were exceptionally wealthy.[41] Rapske and Hemer do no more than refute the impossibility of Paul's Tarsian citizenship.[42] Possibility does not mean probability. It was highly improbable that Paul possessed the wealth and prestige to have gained Tarsian citizenship.[43] Acts 21:39 stems not from a source but from the author's imagination. What Luke relishes are the learned credentials that Paul whips out of his pocket at the very moment when he is being despised as a "barbarian" (21:39).

Both of Paul's franchises, at Tarsus and Rome,[44] function in Acts as literary devices with apologetic ends, but the latter has occasioned a much sharper debate.[45] Historical reasons account for the difference, for Paul's references to his possession of the Roman citizenship twice enter the narrative, once to provide him with a formal escort out of Philippi (16:38-39), another time to deliver him from imminent torture (22:25-29). Furthermore, it is generally assumed that Paul's appeal to Rome (25:11) was based on this status. If he were not a Roman citizen, Luke's story of Paul's final captivity would collapse. Paul's letters are, for whatever reasons, silent on the subject.

Those who accept the general reliability of Acts incline to believe that Paul was a citizen and seek to prove that he could have been. Once again, demonstration that possession of the franchise was possible does not make it so.[46] Decision must rely on probability. A number of factors weigh against a positive answer. Presenting Paul as a Roman citizen was very much in Luke's interest and would fit quite readily into the list of "Lucan inventions," a list that may be shorter or longer but is generally accepted by critical scholars. If Luke derived this datum from a source, it would have been an account of his trial under Festus, an account open to grave doubts by the criterion of historicity. Those who adopt this position could be pressed into agreeing that the author had introduced this concept into the Philippi tale (conceding that Silas's Roman citizenship was an ad hoc Lucan invention) and, most probably, into the torture scene. This moderately critical position would thus base the claim on a (generally improbable) passage that does not mention citizenship and would soft-pedal those that do invoke it. In the first account (Philippi), the franchise more than restores honor; in the other it functions to relieve the hero from grave peril. Acts does not present Paul's status in a responsible manner, leaving proponents to resort to the "historical kernel" argument.

The argument is not strong, in particular because the Paul of Acts is a citizen of high status.[47] This does not comport with his work as an artisan or with the data of the letters.[48] The appeal, which is grounded not in possession of the franchise but rather in trial

---

Historical Geography, Political History, Social, Cultural and Religious Life and Institutions (CRINT 1.1; Assen: Van Gorcum, 1974) 420–63; and idem, "The Organization of the Jewish Communities in the Diaspora," ibid., 464–503. For specific discussion of Paul's case, see Lentz, *Luke's Portrait*, 32–43; and Rapske, *Roman Custody*, 72–83. The former opposes Luke's claim; the latter defends it.

41 Most of Rapske's evidence belongs to the late second century or later and a good deal of it is questionable (*Roman Custody*, 76–83).

42 Ibid.; Hemer, *Book*, 127–28.

43 See also Wolfgang Stegemann, "War der Apostel Paulus ein römisher Bürger?" *ZNW* 87 (1987) 200–229, esp. 220–21.

44 One could, under the empire, hold dual citizenships. See Cadbury, *Book*, 81–82; Stegemann, "Bürger," 221 n. 82; and Tajra, *Trial*, 76, who says it was "not at all uncommon for a man coming from a higher social class to enjoy dual citizenship especially in the Eastern part of the Empire." This argues from the assumption of a high social status.

45 Recent studies include Stegemann, "Bürger"; Heike Omerzu, *Der Prozess des Paulus: Eine exegetische und rechtshistorische Undersuchung der Apostelgeschichte* (BZNW 115; Berlin: de Gruyter, 2002) 17–52; Peter van Minnen, "Paul the Roman Citizen," *JSNT* 56 (1994) 43–52; and Rapske, *Roman Custody*, 73–80. See also the discussion about the appeal, pp. 611–13.

46 If it were based on emancipation, Paul's family would have received citizenship, at the latest, under Augustus. For an example of citizenship grants, see the "Rhosus archive," translated in Barbara Levick, *The Government of the Roman Empire: A Sourcebook* (Totowa, N.J.: Barnes & Noble, 1985) 158–60. (Rhosus served Augustus as an admiral).

47 See Lentz, *Luke's Portrait*, 43–51. Jerome H. Neyrey ("Luke's Social Location of Paul: Cultural Anthropology and the Status of Paul in Acts," in Witherington, *History*, 251–79) confirms by anthropological methods the historical-critical thesis of Lentz: Luke represents Paul as having a higher status than he actually enjoyed.

48 See Stegemann, "Bürger," 221–24. Note 2 Cor 11:25, which reports three floggings.

by a Roman court, does not demonstrate citizenship.[49] On the whole, it does not seem probable that Paul was a Roman citizen, certainly not a citizen of the quality depicted in Acts.

The space devoted to Paul in custody,[50] 21:33–28:31, is longer than that describing his missionary work (chaps. 13–19).[51] This brute fact is not devoid of importance in assessing the purpose of the book. "History of the early church" will not do. By this point readers can be forgiven for thinking that they are reading a biography of Paul. The model is not Josephus's *Antiquities*. The Gospel genre provides a vastly more fruitful basis for comparison. One-fourth of Acts is devoted to Paul in custody, a period of no more than one tenth of the three decades covered in Acts.[52] Within Luke and Acts, this and the journey of Jesus to Jerusalem (Luke 9–19) are the longest sections. Luke's defense of Paul is only in part personal. By defending Paul, Acts defends gentile Christianity on more than one front.

These apologetic efforts are internal. Jews would not have read them and discovered that Paul was not as bad as reputed, nor would polytheists have worked through this book to learn that the Christian movement was utterly devoid of subversive tendencies. For those who prized the Israelite background of the movement, Paul fell somewhere on the spectrum between a problem and an enemy. Those for whom this background had a limited appeal had no desire to emphasize it. The extremes of these sentiments would appear as the "Jewish Christianity" of the Ps.-Clementines and the theology of Marcion. The force of this debate was already so strong when Luke wrote that he could not even mention Paul's letters, which he both knew and used. Likewise, the collection, delivery of which was the purpose of Paul's trip to Jerusalem, was too controversial to mention and was best left on the cutting-room floor.

Charles Talbert has aptly characterized the literary quality of this material. Paul seems to be driven by the winds of fate, confronted by events that he cannot control. Yet the reader receives frequent assurances that all is taking place in accordance with the divine plan.[53] This scheme resembles features often found in ancient light fiction, in which the audience receives (often cryptic) assurances that all will end well.[54] Popular authors reveled in creating narrative tension but evidently perceived that it was difficult for many of their readers. The specific narrative technique is retardation. The judgment of Paul is repeatedly postponed, ultimately *ad Graecas kalendas*. That step was taken by no surviving ancient popular writer.[55]

One may safely presume that Lysias did not accede to Paul's request with the expectation that he would whip the crowd into a revolutionary frenzy.[56] Paul is to play the role of the Ephesian official (19:35-40).[57] Things

49 See p. 541.

50 A recent study that does not restrict itself to the legal process is Skinner, *Locating*.

51 To these one may add 9:20-29 and 11:25-26 (and subtract chap. 15).

52 Devotion of a large portion of a narrative to legal difficulties is typical not only of the canonical Gospels but also of the Apocryphal Acts and various types of fiction, including *Apollonius of Tyana*, *Callirhoe*, and *An Ethiopian Tale*. See Pervo, *Profit*, 47–48, who notes the use of various types of retardation to raise suspense and avoid resolution.

53 Talbert, 193. He points to the prophecies in 20:23; 21:4, 11; 23:11; 27:23-36.

54 See Pervo, *Profit*, 74, for a general description.

55 Saundra Schwartz ("Trial Scene," 127–32) observes that romantic novelists also extended trial scenes to keep up interest. She notes *Callirhoe*, where the climactic trial is broken up with descriptions of a royal hunt, a beauty contest, and a description of harem life. The trial of Callirhoe was set in motion at 4.5 and was, like Paul's trial, not resolved by the end of the story. Unlike Acts, however, all the problems were resolved. Cf. also *Leuc. Clit.* 7.7–16.

56 Conzelmann (184) bluntly evaluates the historicity: "Paul's request to speak to the people and the granting of that request are inconceivable." Barrett (2:1027) agrees.

57 See the references to the similarities between 19:28-40 and 21:27-40 above.

begin well. Battered as he is, limited by shackles and in poor repute with the crowd, which has been demanding his obliteration, Paul is able to silence them with a gesture.[58] This is a valuable skill of the most potent and charismatic political leaders,[59] none of whom had had to perform with such physical limitations.

58 Gesture: 12:17; 13:16; 26:1.

59 See Virgil *Aen.* 1.148–53 (cited in Pervo, *Profit*, 35, with comments.) On this, see Viktor Pöschl, *The Art of Vergil: Image and Symbol in the Aeneid* (Ann Arbor: University of Michigan Press, 1962) 20–21. See also Philostratus *Vit. Apoll.* 1.15; cf. 4.1.8; and Apollonius *Letters* 75–76. Other examples are *Chion of Heracleia* 3.3 (Xenophon); Lucian *Dem.* 9; 64; Philostratus *Vit. Soph.* 531 (Polemon). For discussion, see Glen Bowersock, *Greek Sophists in the Roman Empire* (New York: Oxford University Press, 1969) 26. The tradition may derive from an incident involving the younger Cato: Plutarch *Cat. Min.* 44.4.

22

22:1-21 Paul Addresses the Crowd in the Temple

1/ **"Elders and gentlemen, please**
listen now to my[a] defense."
2/ When they realized that he
was speaking[b] in their own
language, they became even
quieter.[c]
3/ **"I[d] am a Jew. Although born at**
Tarsus in Cilicia, I was reared
in this very city and received
under Gamaliel an education[e]
based upon the strict interpre-
tation of our ancestral code.
As a fervent partisan of God,
like you today, 4/ I persecuted
this movement, promoting the
death penalty and delivering
shackled prisoners—women
no less than men[f] into custody.
5/ The high priest and the entire
Sanhedrin can support me on
this matter. After obtaining
written authorization from
them to[g] our coreligionists in
Damascus, I set out for that
place, intending to bring the
local[h] followers of the move-
ment back to Jerusalem in
shackles, for punishment.
6/ **"When, in the course of my**
journey, I was getting near to
Damascus, an enormous light
from above suddenly engulfed
me[i]—at noon! 7/ I fell to the
ground and heard a voice
speaking to me: 'Saul, Saul,
why are you persecuting me?'
8/ **"'Who are you, Lord?'**
"'I am Jesus the Nazoraean,
whom you are persecuting.'
(9/ My companions saw the
light but did not hear the voice
of the one who was addressing
me.[j])
10/ **"'What shall I do, Lord?' I said.**
"'Go right now[k] to Damascus.
There you will be told about all
that has been arranged for you
to do.'
11/ **"Since I couldn't see because**
of the brightness of that
light,[l] I had to make my entry
into Damascus guided by my
companions.
12/ **"One Ananias, a very observant**
man well thought of by the
local Jews, 13/ came to visit
me. 'Brother Saul,' he said,
'regain your sight.' At that very
moment I glanced up at him,
and I had regained my sight![m]

a The pronoun *μου* is better taken as a possessive ("my") than as object of the verb "hear." The D-Text (Boismard, *Texte*, 357) deals with potential difficulties by omitting it. It also drops "language" (*διαλέκτῳ*).

b The D-Text (see preceding note) places this verb in the historical present, which is grammatically preferable. 𝔓^{74} *et al.* have the aorist ("Hearing that he had spoken . . .").

c The D-Text has the simple verb rather than the idiomatic *παρέσχον ἡσυχίαν*.

d Various witnesses, including m and some D-texts, have *μέν* after "I." This, if not emphatic, heightens the stress between place of birth and place where reared, but does not accord well with the biographical triad of participles.

e Bezae has the present participle, which lacks sense.

f 𝔓^{74} omits *τε* and thus removes "both and."

g Bezae reads "from" (the Jews in Jerusalem).

h The word *ἐκεῖσε* has lost its sense of "thither" in Hellenistic Greek.

i The D-Text attempts to rescue the syntax with *ἐγγίζοντι δέ μοι Δαμασκῷ μεσημβρίας ἐξαίφνης ἐκ τοῦ οὐρανοῦ περιήστραψε φῶς ἱκανὸν περὶ ἐμὲ καὶ ἔπεσον* ("An enormous light from above suddenly engulfed me as I was approaching Damascus at midday." According to Aland, *ἱκανον περὶ ἐμέ* are removed by D*. This would be an improvement.) A few D-text witnesses add here, from 26:14, "in the Hebrew language" and the proverb "It is hard . . ." See Barrett, 2:1037.

j Attempts to find different meanings between the accusative object of *ἀκούειν* ("hear") in 9:7 and the genitive here are undesirable. Note the references in Barrett, 2:1039; and Horst R. Moehring, "The Verb *ΑΚΟΥΕΙΝ* in Acts IX 7 and XXII 9," *NovT* 3 (1959) 80–99.

k The participle here means "hurry" rather than the otiose "get up" (Cadbury and Lake, 280).

l The preposition *ἀπό* (lit. "from") is causal here. See Luke 19:13; Acts 11:19; 12:14; 20:9.

m The text plays on two meanings of *ἀναβλέπω*: "look up" and "regain sight." The translation repeats the verb to supply both meanings. The D-Text (Boismard, *Texte*, 360) p^{41} *pc* d sa deletes "at him," removing, as one might expect of that tradition, an ambiguity.

14/ "'Our ancestral God,' he said,
'has selected you to experience
his will, to see the Just One and
to receive a message from his
very lips. 15/ For you will be a
witness for him to everyone,
a witness of what you have
seen and heard.[n] 16/ What are
you waiting for?[o] Get yourself
baptized right away and be
cleansed of your sins[p] by calling
upon his name.'
17/ "On one occasion after my return
to Jerusalem,[q] while I was pray-
ing in the temple, I fell into a
trance 18/ and saw[r] Jesus. 'Get
out of Jerusalem as quickly as
you can,' he said, 'because they
will not accept your witness
about me.'
19/ "'Well, Lord,' I replied, 'they
are quite aware that I used to
lock up people who believed in
you and have them flogged in
one synagogue after another.
20/ While the blood of your wit-
ness[s] Stephen was gushing out,
I stood right there approving of
the business[t] and guarding the
coats of his murderers.'
21/ "'Get going, for I am sending you
far away, to the gentiles.'"

n The relative clause ("what you have seen and heard") is oddly placed. It modifies "witness" and is located at the end to make a bracket with the two infinitives in v. 14.

o τί μέλλεις is a Greek idiom (Cadbury and Lake, 281). Barrett (2:1042) gives examples. It might be better to render it as "hurry up and . . . ."

p The two middle imperatives, βάπτισαι and ἀπόλουσαι, are causative.

q The present participle ($\mathfrak{p}^{74}$ 33 *pc*) appears to make returning to Jerusalem and praying in the temple simultaneous.

r The D-Text, according to Boismard (*Texte,* 361), shifts to direct speech here. (Indirect discourse has preceded). Supporting this are ℵ 36. 453 *pc* d co. The D-Text also reads "accept" in the present and omits "about me."

s A range of witnesses read "protomartyr," a reminder of ecclesiastical influence upon the textual tradition.

t Ψ (33) 1739 M sy$^{(p)}$ add (from 8:1): "of his execution."

Analysis

The speech opens with appropriate flattery and continues with a review of Paul's credentials, some of which readers learn for the first time. Zeal he did not lack, exemplified in his hostility to the Jesus movement, which leads to the first of two reports by Paul of his change of view. In this account, the story takes on a different slant. His commission to the gentiles is now said to have been given while he was rapt in ecstasy in the midst of worship in this very temple. The conversion of Saul is becoming the call of Paul (cf. Isa 6:1-9). The climax is that word "gentiles," at which the simmering embers of rage burst once more into flame (21:37–22:21).

The commandant returns to square one: torture. Paul is stripped and strung up for the whip. Just as the lash was about to fall, the prisoner raises a technical question: Can unconvicted Roman citizens be whipped? The centurion kicks the matter upstairs. The superior officer returns to learn that Paul is a citizen by birth. His status reduces the entire detachment to abject fear. The most they could hope for is that word will not get out. Good treatment of the prisoner is one preventative. Paul's status, education, and experience have equipped him with the tools to rebut both "religious" and "criminal" charges. Readers have sound grounds for optimism. Evidence about introducing gentiles is lacking, and James and Paul's fellow devotees will be superlative witnesses. Absent the threat of the mob, Paul can trust in Roman justice (22:22-29).

Chapter 22 is Lucan composition.[1] The arrest comprises three scenes: 21:33-40; 22:1-21; and 22:22-29, an A B A pattern, with scenes about interrogation sandwiching the address. That speech (22:1-21) contains one of the three accounts of his "conversion" (cf. 9:1-19a and 26:1-23). Comparison shows that "autobiography" is a

1 Weiser (2:607–8) sets forth reasons for this view. Barrett (2:1032–33) reviews them without refuting the claim.

better term. The narrator reports Paul's early history in 7:58; 8:1a, 3; 9:1-30. Chapters 22 and 26 recount this story in Paul's own formally crafted words.[2] Identification of the dissonances among these accounts may confound or amuse, but the goal of the narrator is to enrich the story by different accounts[3] and to push it toward his own understanding. No expertise is required to observe that what is told three times is important.[4] Chapter 22 is the pivot. With Acts 9, it forms a frame around the narrative of Paul's missionary labors. With chap. 26, it constitutes the frame and core of Paul's efforts to defend himself while in Roman custody in Palestine. These speeches represent a shift from the deliberative to the forensic.[5] They are "apologies" with strong emphasis upon *narratio*.[6] This corresponds to the tendency of the narrative, which is occupied with Paul's defense.[7]

Support for these proposals can be found in the speech, which is artificial, both in setting and content.[8] Beverly Roberts Gaventa succinctly summarizes the setting: the "courtroom" is a mob scene, with members of that body serving as judges.[9] Paul does not attempt to show that he was engaged in a cultic act with others and had introduced no gentiles into the sacred precincts. Although it provides the speaker with about as good a set of Jewish credentials as any layperson could have, the point of the oration is to show the gentile mission was the will of God.[10] Paul justifies his career rather than his immediate actions. The author's distance from the situation is apparent in the absence of a direct denial that Paul taught against Torah (21:28).[11] Insofar as Paul presents any defense, it utilizes the tactic of metastasis: God is responsible,[12] but this is not explicit.

The rhetorical structure is relatively transparent: almost every word (vv. 3 [4]-21) belongs to the realm of *narratio*. Verses 3-5 establish Paul as a Pharisee who had opposed the Jesus movement to the point of active persecution, activity that the high priest can verify. Revelation led to a change of view about Jesus, experiences that can be confirmed by his then companions and the faithful Jew Ananias (vv. 7-16). The final five verses (17-21) describe a revelation by Jesus in this very place directing Paul to the gentiles.[13] Witherington points out that these are not formal proofs, which, with a peroration, were prevented by the crowd's outburst, but he is only technically correct in asserting that the interruption does not mark the major point of the speech.[14] Luke ended where he wished the emphasis to lie. As for the proofs, which would be christological passages from Scripture, Luke has been there and done that. Inclusion of such *probatio* would have transformed this into a missionary address.[15] The ease with which the structure yields to a chiastic analysis confirms its completeness.

2 On the speeches in chaps. 22 and 26, see also Malina and Neyrey, *Portraits of Paul*, 64–99.

3 Hedrick, "Paul's Conversion/Call," 415–32.

4 See pp. 9–10.

5 For a comparative study of these speeches, see Fred Veltman, "The Defense Speeches of Paul in Acts," in Talbert, *Perspectives*, 243–56. Veltman identifies typical formal elements and concludes that Acts follows the general model of defense speeches found in literary works, including historiography and romantic fiction. Note also Jerome Neyrey, "The Forensic Defense Speech and Paul's Trial Speeches in Acts 22–26," in Talbert, *Luke-Acts*, 210–24; Derek Hogan, "Paul's Defense: A Comparison of the Forensic Speeches in Acts, *Callirhoe*, and *Leucippe*, *PerspRelStud* 29 (2002) 73–88; Johnson, 392–93; and Czachesz, "Commission Narratives," 69–77.

6 Note ἀπολογ-ια/-έω ("defense," "defend") in 22:1; 26:1.

7 In general, one may say that Luke here tells the story from the perspective of the participant, although v. 9 would have to be attributed to subsequent knowledge. (In fact, it is borrowed from the omniscient narration of chap. 9.)

8 On the setting, see also the comments on 21:37-40.

9 Gaventa, *Darkness*, 68.

10 Verse 4 speaks of "this way" as something known to the audience and the focus of attack.

11 Note that 21:28 refers to "everyone" (πάντας) rather than "Jews." This word reappears in Ananias's statement in 22:15: πάντας ἀνθρώπους ("all persons"). "Gentiles" does not appear, but the inclusive language allows this inference.

12 Kennedy, *Rhetorical Criticism*, 134. Czachesz ("Commission Narratives," 71 n. 38) observes that Plato assigned a similar defense to Socrates (*Apol.* 21A).

13 William R. Long, "The Paulusbild in the Trial of Paul in Acts," in Kent H. Richards, ed., *SBLSP 1983* (Chico, Calif.: Scholars Press, 1983) 87–105, esp. 97–102.

14 Witherington, 667.

15 Kennedy (*Rhetorical Criticism*, 134–35) lists what

A. V. 3. From Diaspora to Jerusalem
B. Vv. 4-5a. Persecution of movement
C. V. 5b. Paul's travel from Jerusalem to Damascus
D. V. 6-11. Vision near Damascus
E. Vv. 12-13. Ananias heals Paul
F. Vv. 14-15. Paul learns of his mission
E'. Vv. 16. Baptism (illumination)
D'. Vv. 17-18a. Vision in the temple
C'. V. 18b. Command to depart from Jerusalem
B'. Vv. 19-20. Persecution
A'. V. 21. From Jerusalem to Diaspora[16]

In comparison to chap. 9, this speech contains a good deal of abbreviation and omission, with some expansion and substitution. Expansion appears in the motive and result of Paul's pre-Christian activity. Its object was execution of believers (v. 4).[17] Motivation stems from Paul's religious fanaticism, specifically his rigorous (Pharisaic) training. The phrase "fervent partisan of God" (v. 3) is indisputably Pauline,[18] but, especially in proximity to the similar expression in 21:20, is not friendly to Torah observance. The implication is that adherence to the Mosaic ordinances leads to homicidal persecution.

In place of the seven specific scenes utilized in chap. 9 to describe the experiences from the epiphany onward, Acts 22 recounts three: the encounter with Jesus (vv. 6-11), the visit of Ananias (vv. 12-16), and Paul's vision in Jerusalem (vv. 17-21). Omitted here are the vision of Ananias, Saul's activity in Damascus and his escape from that place, his reception and ministry in Jerusalem, and his escape from another plot. The introductory material about Paul's commission is (v. 5) essentially the same. The episode dealing with the revelation on the Damascus road contains some changes, and the visit of Ananias is quite different, while the Jerusalem activity is completely different—only the place-name is shared. The chief difference is that Acts 9 emphasized Paul's relation to followers of Jesus while Acts 22 omits this aspect of his biography—and his missionary career—entirely. The antithesis between legal zealot and gentile missionary is starkly drawn. Differences include the temporal indication (noon), the insertion about Paul's companions into the dialogue, Paul's question ("What shall I do?"), and omission of the three-day fast.[19] The blinding has become ambiguous: Paul could not see "because of the brightness/glory of the light" (v. 11), and the healing is less explicit. These changes soft-pedal the element of punishment and propel the account in the direction of a "straight" conversion story. High noon is a conventional feature in conversion stories,[20] and the question is a typical Lucan element (cf. Luke 3:10; Acts 2:37; 16:30). The notorious contrast between 9:7, where all heard the voice but did not see the light, and 22:9, which reports the opposite, conforms to chap. 22's focus on Paul alone.

The scene featuring Ananias exhibits even greater variation. His vision (and that of Paul), which was central to Acts 9, has disappeared. There is no suggestion that he believes in Jesus. In place of that qualification are his Jewish credentials. Equally lacking are explanations about why he has paid Paul a visit or how he had learned about his experiences. In this account, Paul hears the missionary commission from Ananias himself. Baptism is commanded but not narrated. Two apparently conflicting observations can be made about Acts 22 thus far: It is smoother and better integrated than Acts 9. Paul is first converted and then commissioned. Second, chap. 22 would be difficult to understand apart from Acts 9.[21]

The narrator nonetheless does tailor this account to the dramatic Jewish audience. Paul summarizes his

these proofs would have been without stating that they would have pushed the speech toward the deliberative species.

16 Talbert (197), who attributes this to John Bligh, *Galatians* (London: St. Paul's Publications, 1969) 97. Some details are debatable, but the arrangement is essentially circular, with the commission at its center.

17 Cf. 26:10. Note also that the objective of the Damascus raid was to bring believers to Jerusalem for punishment (v. 5).

18 See below.

19 The wording and position of the promise have also been changed, perhaps to conform with a common pattern in conversion stories.

20 See below.

21 One specific will suffice: The speech presumes the exaltation of Jesus to heaven. Those who disagreed with this claim—the entire opposing crowd—would have found no merit in the argument from v. 6 onward.

excellent Israelite curriculum vitae and appeals to the high priest and Sanhedrin for support. Ananias came well recommended by Damascene Jews and appears as an agent of the ancestral God rather than at the behest of Jesus (22:14 versus 9:17).[22] Specific Christian terminology and themes are avoided.[23] Jesus, who identifies himself as "the Nazoraean," a designation presumably familiar to Jews, is not otherwise named. The title used in v. 14 is the more general "righteous one," applied to many figures of Israelite tradition.[24] Consonant with this, but fundamental to the Lucan portrait and understanding, is the orientation of the entire account toward the call of a prophet. The characterization of the light as "glory" (δόξα) in v. 11 evokes the call of Isaiah (6:3). Verses 14-15 are a prophetic commission, delivered like a prophetic oracle, followed by vv. 18-21, which contain the typical objection of unsuitability or unworthiness.[25] Much the same may be said of the setting of this vision in the temple, also reminiscent of Isaiah 6 but highly ironic, since the worshiping crowd will have nothing to do with divine directions to go to the gentiles, the book of Isaiah (as Luke understood it) notwithstanding. Although this account is a secondary revision of a secondary source, Luke has moved the story toward conformity with Galatians 1. The commission to evangelize gentiles came to Paul in a vision.[26]

Comment

■ **1-5** In these verses[27] Paul economically establishes his ethos while beginning his story. He achieves this with his dutiful request, his use of Aramaic (which has the additional advantage of being unintelligible to the tribune, who would not take note of the contradictions[28]), his polite address,[29] his praise of Jerusalem, his assurance about his own observance, and his flattery of the audience's religious commitment.[30] Verses 3-5 constitute a single sentence, an example of the author's attempt to emulate periodic style without achieving it.

■ **3** The verse presents what van Unnik identified as three components of a biographical pattern: birth, nurture, and education.[31] Recent research has emphasized that these elements are some of the file folders to be perused in preparing an encomiastic speech.[32] Luke deploys this trilogy in reference to but one other person: Moses (Acts 7:20-22). It is thus a measure of

22 Barrett, 2:1031: "whether it was suited to the particular Jewish audience that Paul had before him is not so clear." Note his comments, 1033–45, *passim*.

23 Verse 16 speaks of baptism for forgiveness. For Luke, this would have been a Jewish practice (cf. John the Baptizer).

24 See below.

25 E.g., Exod 3:11; 4:10; 6:12 (Moses); Jer 1:6.

26 Like Galatians 1–2, Acts 22 concentrates on Paul's relations with Jerusalem.

27 With regard to vv. 4-16, refer also to the comments on 9:1-19a.

28 If the officer were of Syrian origin, he might well have understood Aramaic and found it useful in this posting, but the narrator does not worry about this.

29 The same address was used by Stephen (7:2), where it was more appropriate. Here it presumes (or pretends) that the Jewish leaders were part of the audience, that is, mob. This may seem improbable, but v. 5 supports it.

30 Rackham (423) describes this in late Victorian terms: "S. Paul's courtesy and magnanimity are unsurpassable. The fanatical frenzy which had a moment ago been seeking to kill him, he acknowledges as a zeal for God."

31 Willem C. van Unnik, *Tarsus or Jerusalem: The City of Paul's Youth* (trans. G. Ogg; London: Epworth, 1962). Barrett (2:1034–36) reviews the discussion.

32 George Kennedy has provided a translation of the handbooks: *Progymnasmata: Greek Textbooks of Prose Composition and Rhetoric* (SBLWGRW 10; Atlanta: Society of Biblical Literature, 2003). An example is Theon 9 (1 CE): "External goods are, first, good birth, and that is twofold, either from the goodness of (a man's) city and tribe and constitution, or from ancestors and other relatives. Then there is education, friendship, reputation, official position, wealth, good children, a good death" (trans. Kennedy, 50). Cf. Hermogenes 7 (p. 82), Aphthonius 8 (p. 108), and Nicolaus the Sophist 8 (p. 156). For a detailed discussion, see Malina and Neyrey, *Portraits*, 19–63; and the crisp analysis of Ronald F. Hock, *The Infancy Gospels of James and Thomas* (Scholars Bible 2; Santa Rosa, Calif.: Polebridge, 1995) 16–19, as well as Neyrey, "Forensic Defense Speech," 211–12. For advice on how to use these items in forensic contexts, see Cicero, *Inv.* 2.30.

Paul's standing in the salvation-historical scheme of things. These topics may be ignored or soft-pedaled when disadvantageous and vice versa, an excellent example of which can be seen in 21:39 and 22:3. The former emphasizes Paul's Hellenic background, which is swept aside in the latter. The reader views Paul not as dissembling but as selecting the proper points to emphasize for the respective audiences.[33] It is possible, although not probable, that Paul was reared in Jerusalem.[34] Some might fault him for boasting of his studies under[35] Gamaliel when he had, in fact, so strongly repudiated his mentor's advice about members of the Jesus movement.[36] Paul's education involved a strict view of observance and fashioned him into a militant enforcer of piety. Words from the stem *akrib-* refer in Acts to various forms of thoroughness and precision.[37] Its specific reference here is to the orientation of the Pharisees, a concept Luke has evidently taken from Josephus.[38]

Characterization of Paul as "a fervent partisan of God" owes a debt to Gal 1:14 and echoes 21:20.[39] For the narrator, this was evidently a fine rhetorical flourish, but the textual tradition took strong exception to the suggestion that the "pre-Christian" Paul and his hearers could claim that status.[40] These variants, mainly within the D-Text tradition, exhibit varieties of the concrete and pedantic mentality of those behind it.[41]

■ **4** The verse utilizes the familiar technique of a relative clause that functions like an independent one. It is an intensification of 8:3. Readers learn for the first time that the object of these arrests was execution of the believers.[42] Zeal this man did not lack. The reference to "this movement" is intelligible only to readers, for it has not been mentioned—unless one holds that its major premises are attacks upon people, Torah, and temple (21:28).[43] Paul is defending the Christian movement by defending his conduct.

■ **5** The verse reprises 9:2, which it transforms into evidence. The inference is that the same high priest

33 The D-Text (see pp. 548 n. *o* on 21:39) eliminated any dissonance.

34 On this term "rear" ([ἀνα]τρέφω), see Spicq, *Lexicon*, 3:88.

35 Lit. "at the feet of," an indication of subordination. See Luke 7:38; 8:35, 41 (*v.l.* in 10:39); 17:16; Acts 4:35; 5:2, 10. Note also *Act. Paul* 3.10.

36 Cf. Cadbury and Lake, 279; and Pervo, *Profit*, 60. Paul is the one Pharisee in Acts who vigorously supports the death penalty (5:34-39; cf. 23:1-10) for followers of Jesus. This view is consistent with the portrayal of that party implied in Josephus's account of the execution of James in *Ant.* 20.197–203, since the opponents of this action, supported by the Sadducees, are characterized as strict in observance (περὶ τοὺς νόμους ἀκριβεῖς [§201]). On Gamaliel, see the comments at 5:34.

37 Acts 18:25, 26; 22:3; 23:15, 20; 24:22; 26:5; cf. Luke 1:3.

38 E.g., Josephus *Vit.* 191; *Bell* 1.110; *Ant.* 17.41. See Pervo, *Dating*, 169–70. Literature: Albert I. Baumgarten, "The Name of the Pharisees," *JBL* 102 (1983) 411–28; and Günter Stemberger, *Jewish Contemporaries of Jesus: Pharisees, Sadducees, Essenes* (trans. A. W. Mahnke. Minneapolis: Fortress Press, 1995) 90–91.

39 See Pervo, *Dating*, 74–76. In Greek, "zealot" with a genitive often means "rival," as in the interesting acclamation bestowed upon Peregrinus, in Lucian *Peregr.* 15, where he is hailed as "the one" (i.e., "the one genuine") "philosopher," "patriot," and "rival" (ζηλώτην) of Diogenes and Crates!" Cf. also Epictetus *Diss.* 1.19.6 (general) and 2.2.26 (Socrates). The expression "a zealot of/for (*x*) god" is used by Musonius Rufus 8.83 (Zeus) and 2.14.13 ("of a god"). Paul approves of Jewish "zeal for God" (Rom 10:22).

40 For similar claims, see Ps.-Lucian *Demosthenes* 12; Josephus *Bell.* 2.162; *Ant.* 17.41; 19.332; 20.43; *Vit.* 191. (On the last see also n. 38.)

41 These are the data: Gal. 1:14: ζηλωτὴς ὑπάρχων τῶν πατρικῶν μου παραδόσεων ("Being a zealot for my ancestral traditions"); ζηλωτὴς ὑπάρχων καθὼς πάντες ὑμεῖς 614 Vg[ms] ("Being a zealot, just as all you"); ζηλωτὴς ὑπάρχων τοῦ νόμου καθὼς πάντες ὑμεῖς 88 Vg ("Being a zealot for the Torah, just as all you"); ζηλωτὴς ὑπάρχων τῶν πατρικῶν μου παραδόσεων καθὼς πάντες ὑμεῖς Sy[hmg] ("Being a zealot for my ancestral traditions just as all you"); ζηλωτὴς καθὼς πάντες Ψ ("An enthusiast, like all [you])" *et al.* (D-Text, according to Boismard, *Texte*, 357).

42 See Cadbury and Lake, 279.

43 The same applies to "Saul" in v. 7, unless one is to assume that Paul was always so known in Jerusalem. He does not see a need to introduce himself by name in v. 3.

remains in office.[44] External knowledge shows that the chronology has been compressed, but the narrator may not wish to suggest that more than two decades have passed.[45] Verse 5 introduces the theme of "witness." Cf. also vv. 12, 15, 18, 20.[46] Such language is appropriate in a forensic oration, but it serves Luke in other, more important, ways. As a "witness" of and for Christ, Paul, like Stephen (v. 20), does what apostles do. Luke cannot cite 1 Cor 9:1 to show that Paul is an apostle, but he can present him as a witness of the living Christ and thus as an authoritative messenger.[47]

■ **6-13** At the close of the account of his encounter with Christ, Paul reaches the goal announced at the close of the previous paragraph: Damascus.[48] The contrast between his expectations and the actual outcome summarizes the change in his fortunes. Explicit differences from chap. 9 include the title "Nazoraean" (v. 8), which adds Israelite color,[49] the reference to noon (v. 6), which supplies a typical element from commission and conversion stories,[50] and the intensity of the light (v. 8). The comment about Paul's companions is now a parenthesis within the dialogue (versus 9:7). This heightens attention to the light, which, also unlike 9:7, is now perceived by all, while only Paul heard the voice.[51] Chapter 9 reported a public revelation; in chap. 22 the audition is private, rather like a prophetic call. Verse 10 introduces a question that is conventional in situations involving conversions.[52] This presents the subject as less helpless and passive than the nearly obliterated Saul of chap. 9. In line with this development is the expanded imperative of v. 10 (versus 9:6), which comprehends more than what he must do to relieve his affliction. Instead of the clear declaration that he had been blinded (9:8), v. 11 allows the inference of temporary blindness caused by exposure to bright light.[53] Omission of the three days' hard fast makes Paul less helplessly abject.

In contrast to chap. 9, the character and activity of Ananias (vv. 12-16) have undergone a major revision. His vision, the central focus of Acts 9, has been eliminated. His ethos is established by reference to his well-established[54] Jewish[55] credentials, rather than to his belief in Jesus (who is also omitted here). He therefore receives no commission to visit Paul, and one must guess how and when he was informed about Paul and sent to him. The result of these changes is good narrative progression.[56] The healing is so attenuated that one could

44 614 h^mg *pc* provide (from 23:2) the name: Ananias.

45 Cf. Rackham, 423.

46 See Weiser, 2:611; Fitzmyer, 703.

47 This thesis is demonstrated by Burchard, *Dreizehnte Zeuge*. Note 26:15 and the use of "witness" as an apostolic credential in 1:8, 22; 2:32; 3:15; 5:32; 10:39, 41. The term also appears in the philosophical tradition: the ideal Stoic is a "witness" (μάρτυρα), according to Epictetus *Diss.* 3.24.112–13.

48 The phrase εἰς Δαμασκόν ("to," "at" "Damascus") appears in vv. 5, 10, and 11. In the last of these it receives end stress.

49 On the meaning of this obscure term, see p. 80 n. 48. In Acts it is part of the "early" christological vocabulary (2:22; 3:6; 4:10; 6:14) that reappears in the trial section (24:5; 26:9).

50 For examples, see Czachesz, "Commission Narratives," 73 n. 48, to which add Longus *Daphn.* 2.4.1 (epiphany of Eros) and Apuleius *Metam.* 6.12.2–4 (madness at noon, on which see also Deut 28:28-29, in which madness and blindness at noonday are among the curses threatened in the covenant formulary. Finally, Peter's vision occurred at noon (10:9).

51 D-Text (and other) witnesses, D E Ψ 1739 m gig sy^h sa, read, intelligently, "and they became fearful" (καὶ ἔμφοβοι ἐγένοντο). This response to the numinous is probably a typical expansion. See Metzger, *Textual Commentary*, 430. Other examples of seeing a light but not hearing are Sulpicius Severus *Life of Martin* 11.5 and Gregory the Great *Life of Benedict* 8.12.

52 Luke 3:12; 18:18; Acts 2:37; 16:30.

53 Boismard (*Texte*, 359) proposes as the D-Text: ἀναστὰς δὲ οὐκ ἐνέβλεπον ("When I got up I didn't see."). Clark (144) corrects to ὡς δὲ ἀνέστην, οὐκ ἐνέβλεπον, similar in meaning. Haenchen (626) prefers B's οὐδὲν ἔβλεπον ("I saw nothing"). This harmonizes with 9:8, from which it may derive. The verb ἐμβλέπω is often confounded with βλέπω in MSS., according to BDAG, 321, *s.v.* ἐμβλέπω. The original may have read: οὐκ ἔβλεπον.

54 Cornelius is similarly described in 10:22.

55 The adjective εὐλαβής ("pious"): Luke 2:25; Acts 2:5; 8:2. Its omission in 𝔭^74 A vg makes the phrase difficult to understand. The D-Text (Boismard, *Texte*, 359) replaces "resident" with the more specific "in Damascus." It is unusual for this participle (κατοικῶν) to be absolute, whence the alternatives. See Metzger, *Textual Commentary*, 431.

56 Czachesz, "Commission Narrarives," 74.

almost argue that no healing is reported, but the phrase "at that very moment" supports this understanding.[57]

■ **14-15** These verses evoke Gal 1:14-15. *God* chose[58] Paul to see Christ and proclaim him. Three infinitives follow: "to experience (γνῶναι) God's will" refers to "the plan of God" in the language of the epistles.[59] "See" and "hear" supply the elements needed to describe Paul's forthcoming encounter (vv. 17-21) as a resurrection appearance that commissioned him to be a missionary to gentiles.[60] Luke has taken the most important steps toward his goal of transforming the "conversion" of chap. 9 into the "call" of Galatians 1. The title "Just One" avoids the inflammatory terms "Messiah" and "Son of God," while linking Paul to the tradition.[61] The target of Paul's mission is "all persons" (ἀνθρώπους), avoiding the invidious word "gentiles" (and echoing 21:28).

■ **16** Ananias's question corresponds to that of Paul in v. 10. He then directs baptism, which involves the invocation of "his name."[62] This will result in purgation of sins. The dramatic situation is in some difficulty. Is the audience to presume a normal purification rite, that is, self-immersion? Removal of sins denotes, in Christian terms, a sacramental act,[63] while the verb ἐπικαλέω ("invoke") presumes an attendant formula.[64] Readers know that Christian baptism is in view, but the ambiguous language prevents a premature crowd reaction. The activity must be commanded rather than narrated because no Christian minister is present.

■ **17-21** Apart from the return to Jerusalem (9:26), these verses present entirely new material, composed by Luke (with assistance from 9:13-15), who sets the commission to convert gentiles within a dialogue between Paul and the heavenly Christ set in the temple itself. This audacious (and provocative) invention could serve as the Lucan master metaphor. It exudes continuity. The inclusion of gentiles announced in the temple after Jesus' birth (Luke 2:25-39) finds its fulfillment, encasing Paul within the beginning and end of Luke (1:5; 24:53) and the opening five chapters of Acts.

■ **17** The syntax of v. 17 is equally revolutionary.[65] The author evidently wishes to suggest a parallel to v. 7. "Praying in the temple" reveals the narrator's perspective and emphasis. The speaker should have said "in this place" or the like. The resultant trance (ἔκστασις)[66]

57 The exact phrase appears in 16:18 (exorcism). Cf. Matt 8:13; John 4:53.

58 Luke is the only early Christian writer to use προχειρίζω ("appoint," "destine"). In Acts 3:20, it refers to Jesus; 22:14 and 26:15 apply it to Paul. Luke may have picked up this term from 2 Maccabees (3:7; 8:9; 14:12). In the military and political spheres, the word applies to "trustworthy envoys, qualified representatives of God, or the king, or of some other high authority" (Spicq, *Lexicon*, 3:207–9, esp. 208). The prefix *pro-* is not temporal. Wilhelm Michaelis ("προχειρίζω," *TDNT* 6:862–64) says that it should not be grouped with terms implying predestination (on which see Conzelmann, *Theology*, 151–54). This is technically correct, but Haenchen's proposal (208 n. 10) that Luke so understood it or wished it understood deserves consideration.

59 Note Rom 2:18 and the Deutero-Pauline paraphrase in Col 1:9

60 Note the perfect ἑώρακας ("see") in v. 15 and cf. 1 Cor 9:1.

61 Cf. 3:14 (Peter) and esp. 7:52 (Stephen). Note also *1 Enoch* 38:2; 53:6 (of uncertain date). For its application to more "ordinary heroes," see Gen 7:1; Job 32:2; Ps 7:12; 2 Macc 12:6.

62 This should be the name of Jesus, but grammatical logic makes "God" the referent.

63 For the meaning of ἀπολύω here, see 1 Cor 6:11 ("But you were washed, you were sanctified, you were justified in the name of the Lord Jesus Christ and in the Spirit of our God."). Cf. also Eph 5:26; Titus 3:5.

64 Cf. 2:21. 𝔓[74] reads "invoke" in the present tense. This aorist is more compatible with later liturgical use: one confesses Christ as Lord and is then baptized, presumably "in the name of Jesus" here.

65 The speaker is introduced in a dative (with γίνομαι, BDF §409 [4]), next as the subject of an improper genitive absolute, and finally as the subject of an infinitive (γίνομαι!) in indirect discourse. Haenchen (627 n. 3) offers Luke 3:21 as a parallel. Corruption seems unlikely.

66 On the phenomenon of "ecstasy," see Rohde, *Psyche*, 253–334, still useful for its citations of primary texts and religio-historical material; W. R. Inge, "Ecstasy," *ERE* 5:157–59; Albrecht Oepke, "ἔκστασις," *TDNT* 2:449–60, esp. 449–58; and Friedrich Pfister, "Ekstase," *RAC* 4:944–87.

evokes the experience of Peter (10:10; 11:5) and others, notably, Isaiah (6:1).[67]

■ **18** In that state, Paul experienced an unequivocal resurrection appearance. He saw Christ and heard his words (as opposed to seeing "a light" and hearing an initially unknown voice). Here Luke provides his own account of Paul's legitimating vision, in direct speech rather than cloudy summary. To supply the prophet's conventional objection he enumerated, with some intensification,[68] Paul's qualifications as a persecutor, items that had previously supported Ananias's objection to his assignment (9:13-15), with an extended summary[69] of his role in the martyrdom[70] of Stephen (vv. 19-20). The application of this objection is not transparent. One possibility is that Paul's well-known opposition to the movement will lend credence to his changed views.

■ **21** His protests receive the same answer that was given to Ananias (9:15): "Get going!" (πορεύου).[71] The explanation for this order[72] inverts what has been a basic principle of Acts: Jerusalem is the center of revealed religion and the temple its apex. Priority belongs to the Jews, while direction and regulation of the gentile enterprise lies under the authority of the Jerusalem community. The narrator cannot be accused of allowing this thesis to fall into desuetude, for it was emphatically reiterated as recently as 21:18-25. The directive is equally inapplicable to the career of Paul, who will not approach gentiles until brought to Antioch by Barnabas (11:25-26) and who will give Jews priority at every station. Verse 21 is not a summary of Paul's missionary labors. It asserts that the course of salvation history points away from Jerusalem and its temple to the Diaspora and gentiles. To them belongs the future. To represent the Diaspora, Luke uses one of his more wistful symbols, "far away" (μακράν), which indicates both physical and spiritual distance[73] and is yet another evocation of the beginning of the story (2:39).[74] Formally, the speech ends with its narrative incomplete, but Luke has said all that he wished to say and ended at the decisive point, confirmed by punctuation contributed by the crowd.[75] The speech ends on an ironic note. The one accused of introducing gentiles into the temple had been instructed in the temple to leave it and approach the gentiles.

---

67 Temple visions include theophanies and angelophanies: 1 Sam 3:3-10; 1 Kgs 3:4-5; Dan 9:20-27; Josephus *Ant.* 13.282–83; *b. Yoma* 39b; and Luke 1:8-20. Visions are central to cult foundation stories. See pp. 389–90.

68 Flogging (v. 19) is an addition to the earlier summaries. Paul's own experience at the other end of the whip (16:22), recently threatened (21:34) and about to be threatened once more (22:34), is a bit of poetic justice.

69 The periphrastic constructions may serve to stress the iterative nature of this activity. See Haenchen, 149 n. 7.

70 "Witness" (μάρτυς) is acquiring the sense of "martyr." See Haenchen, 627 n. 7; and BDAG, 620, *s.v.* (3).

71 Although the action is the same as that described in 9:30 (leaving town), the circumstances are at considerable variance with one another.

72 In both 9:15 and 22:21, this command is followed by a motive clause in ὅτι ("because").

73 Spiritual distance symbolized by the physical: Luke 15:13 (cf. 20, the Prodigal Son). For the figurative, see Acts 17:27 (Areopagus). In the background is Isa 57:19, which Luke may have appropriated by way of Eph 2:13, 17. See Pervo, *Dating*, 294–95.

74 The verb "send" is another borrowing from Acts 9 (v. 30).

75 Luke 4:27-28 reports a kindred experience of Jesus at the beginning of his ministry.

22

22:22-29 Reactions to Paul's Address

**22/ The crowd kept listening until
he said "gentiles," but then
raised a loud shout: "Wipe this
creature from the face of the
earth! He does not deserve
to live!"[a] 23/ Since they kept
on shrieking, tossing their
coats around and kicking up
dust,[b] 24/ the military tribune
directed that Paul should be
taken within the compound
and interrogated under the
whip to learn why the crowd
was denouncing him.[c] 25/ Just
when they had stretched him
out to be whipped,[d] Paul asked
the attending centurion, "Are
you authorized to flog a Roman
citizen who has not been found
guilty?"**

**26/ At this the centurion went to the
tribune and said: "This fellow is
a Roman citizen!" What are you
going to do about *that*?"[e]**

**27/ The tribune went to Paul and
said: "Tell me, are you a Roman
citizen?"[f]
"Yes."[g]**

**28/ "It cost me an arm and a leg to
achieve that status."
"I was born to it."**

**29/ The soldiers delegated to inter-
rogate him quickly got out of
the way.[h] The tribune was also
alarmed at the realization that
he had put a Roman citizen in
bonds.[i]**

a On the tense and meaning of καθῆκεν, see BDF §358 (2). This postclassical usage resembles English expressions such as "Then you would have to . . ." The imperfect indicates obligation or necessity. D[c] *T* read the more common καθῆκον ("it is fitting").

b The D-Text (Boismard, *Texte*, 362) says that they were throwing dust "toward the sky."

c The D-Text (Boismard, *Texte*, 362) has a present infinitive: "interrogate" and reads κατεφώνουν ("cry against"), with a corresponding phrase "about him."

d For an alternate translation, see below.

e The interpretation of τί μέλλεις is debatable. It is probably not to be taken as a dispassionate utterance. The D-Text (Boismard, *Texte*, 363) reads: "when the centurion had heard **this—that he identified himself as a Roman citizen—**he approached the tribune and announced **to him: 'Look** (ὅρα) what you are about to do!"

f The D-Text (Boismard, *Texte*, 363) reads "**Then** . . . **he asked** him. The conjunction εἰ appears to belong to an indirect question, but in Hellenistic Greek it took on the quality of a punctuation mark, as in v. 25. See BDF §440 (3).

g The D-Text (Boismard, *Texte*, 363) prefers εἰμι ("I am"). Cf. Luke 22:70.

h The Greek of Bezae ends here. Its Latin counterpart (d) terminated in the middle of v. 20.

i Verse 29 is awkward (and alliterative). The D-Text (Boismard, *Texte*, 364) replaces the initial εὐθέως οὖν ("immediately therefore") with its prosaic "then" (τότε), adding at the close a more suitable use for prompt action: "and he immediately released him" (καὶ παραχρῆμα ἔλυσεν αὐτόν). The D-editor took the phrase from v. 30 (where it is omitted by some D-Texts). The sense of "release" is, of course, different in the two cases.

Analysis

Reference to gentiles reignited the mob, moving the commandant to revert to his earlier plan. (One may conjure up the classic gloomy dungeon, with dripping walls and smoking lamps.) Just as the lash was about to fall upon this stripped (cf. Mark 15:20) and strung up prisoner, Paul raised a technical question: could unconvicted Roman citizens be whipped? Readers know (16:37) that this was not simply a hypothetical inquiry. The centurion in charge—torture could be entrusted to subordinates—accepted this as a valid assertion of the franchise and properly reported the fact to his superior. That officer promptly arrived to verify the information. An affirmative answer did not dissolve his skepticism. Roman citizenship had cost him a pretty penny. Could his prisoner have afforded it? Paul did not need to concern himself about such matters, for he held the franchise by birth. That fact reduced the whole detachment, including their commander, to abject fear.

This paragraph, a Lucan composition, repeats the essence of 21:36-37a. It is a thrilling piece of melodrama and no worse for its improbabilities. The most basic of these is that the official elects to torture Paul in order to learn why the crowd wished to kill him. Interrogation in the midst of a riot is admittedly difficult (21:34), but the tribune could have scooped up a half-dozen people and had them privately interrogated to discover the information he sought. Having been persuaded that Paul was an educated Greek, he might have questioned him before determining that only torture would expose the necessary facts. Examination under such duress was scarcely suitable for a citizen of Tarsus.[1] That Paul raises no objection to the scourging of Roman citizens until the last possible moment will strike some as unlikely, as will the unhesitating acceptance of his claim to be a Roman citizen.[2] Such a contention might well have delayed proceedings pending further investigation, but it is strange that no doubts about the matter are raised.[3] For Lysias to divulge to a stranger that he had not acquired the franchise in a legal manner was, at best, imprudent. Still less prudent was his failure to interview Paul before summoning the Sanhedrin. The dust kicked up by the crowd complements that to be thrown by the narrator upon the legal situation.

Comment

■ **22-23** These verses expand 21:26, adding a phrase and some action to illustrate the explosion. The latter is of uncertain significance, but the general purport is clear: these people were out of control.[4] The narrator supplies a motive for the proposed torture: the tribune wishes to learn why the crowd was angry with Paul by interrogating[5] the victim. If the narrator intended to sneak this improbability past the reader in the general excitement, he has been rather successful.

■ **25-29** The first clause is susceptible of two interpretations. The choice depends upon the sense of the dative *τοῖς ἱμᾶσιν* ("cords"), either "stretched him out *with* ropes" (i.e., used thongs to secure the body for whipping) or "stretched him out *for* the lash." The latter is probably preferable.[6] Those faced with such a beating—more severe than that of 16:22—are unlikely to meditate upon the varieties of adverbial datives. Roman citizens were quite likely to have asserted their status at the moment the order was given (v. 24), if not earlier. For the second time (16:35-40), Paul has been derelict in his civic duty. The reason in this instance is patent: the narrator has produced a last-second rescue.

> I, as a convicted criminal, was now to be tortured about Melite's part in the murder. At the moment when my arms had been tied and the clothes had been stripped from my body and I was hanging in the air on ropes and the torturers were bringing on the whips and fire and rack . . . the priest of Artemis was seen advancing towards us, crowned with laurel. (Achilles Tatius *Leuc. Clit.* 7.12.2-3)[7]

Acts 21:23 reported the last-second rescue of Paul by the tribune. He now saves himself. Last-minute deliveries by the arrival of the cavalry or through coincidence are not impossible, but escape from a dire fate through retardation generated by the hero suggests the hand of a narrator. Undiluted adventure is not that narrator's only goal. The encounter will lift Paul from the depths of degradation to heights that will awe a tribune. The presiding centurion, unnerved by his near calamity, took out his anger upon his superior, with a statement

1 Rapske (*Roman Custody*, 139) defends this: "Torture was recommended only after other forms of enquiry had been exhausted or frustrated and Acts is clear (Acts 21:33f., 39f.) that the tribune had used all the non-coercive means. Persons taken into custody without accusers were not to be subjected to torture unless there were suspicions strongly attaching to them." He cites the *Digest* 48.18 and 22. Unfortunately for this rationale, non-coercive means had scarcely been tapped, let alone exhausted.

2 See the comments of Foakes Jackson, 204.

3 For a discussion of how possession of Roman citizenship might be verified, see Cadbury, *Book*, 71–73. Note also Adrian N. Sherwin-White, *The Roman Citizenship* (2nd ed.; Oxford: Clarendon, 1973) 314–16. For an example of a *diploma* granted upon discharge of a sailor (52 CE), see *ILS* 1986, trans. Robert K. Sherk, *The Roman Empire: Augustus to Hadrian* (Translated Documents of Greece & Rome 6; Cambridge: Cambridge University Press, 1988) no. 58, pp. 99–100. See also Sherwin-White, *Roman Society*, 148–49, with his references.

4 Cadbury ("Dust and Garments," 269–77) discusses the subject in detail. See Haenchen's comments on this (633 n. 1).

5 The verb ἀνατάζω has an official ring. See Sus 14 Theod and Judg 6:29 (A).

6 BDAG (474b), *s.v.* ἱμάς, prefers to understand the cords as those of a whip. See also Cadbury and Lake, 282–83; and Barrett, 2:1048.

7 Trans. J. J. Winkler, in Reardon, *Novels*, 267. (The arrival of a sacred embassy postponed all legal procedures.) Compare Apuleius *Metam.* 3.9:

amounting to "Do you have any idea of what you're doing?" Arriving at the scene, the tribune put the question directly and received a direct answer. His evident skepticism[8] sets up Paul's crushing riposte: he held the franchise from birth,[9] while the tribune had had to acquire it on the black market.[10] Although strung up naked, Paul has won this status duel hands down, his second such triumph in a row. In 21:37-39, his *paideia* won him the right to engage in oratory. The disclosure of Roman citizenship[11] functions like an epiphany: the soldiers retreat while their officer cowers in fear.[12]

The narrative has remained on a roller coaster path. In 21:27, Paul appeared to have eluded unpleasantness, but the riot portended that his end was near. Arrest was uncomfortable, but it saved his life and provided an opportunity to stun the arresting officer with his culture and standing. On the top of the steps, he is once more at the top and remains in control until v. 22, when riot re-erupts. The notion that gentiles could share in the promises was utterly odious. Faced once more with the prospect of torture, Paul plays his highest status card: lifelong Roman citizenship. This gives him a reprieve. Romans will be in charge of the inquiry into the charges against him. It will not take a Gallio (18:12-17) to explode these. By education, experience, and status Paul has the equipment to stave off varied charges. Hearers have every reason for optimism. No one can present sound evidence that he introduced gentiles. Among the potential witnesses in his behalf will be James and those with whom he undertook the vow. Removed from the threat of the mob, Paul should be able to rely on Roman justice.

"Instantly they brought in fire and the wheel, in accordance with Greek style, and all sorts of whips. . . . But the old woman who had thrown everything into a turmoil with her tears spoke up" (trans. J. A. Hanson *Apuleius Metamorphoses I* [LCL; Cambridge: Harvard University Press, 1989] 141–43). Cf. also Ovid *Metam.* 3.697–700. The hero Chaireas escaped execution as he was mounting his cross (Chariton *Chaer.* 4.3). Arrival of the police rescues the heroine Anthia from a "crucifixion." Her true love Habrocomes was twice delivered from the cross (*Ephesian Tale* 2.13; 4.2). For other rescues, see *Babylonian Story*, e.g., 21. Cf. also *Ethiopian Story* 7.6; 10.34.

8 The D-Text of v. 28 is complicated and interesting. Bezae begins, "**I am well aware** (οἶδα) of **how much** (πόσου) this citizenship cost me." Possibly anterior to this is a Latin reading known to Bede (88), which has some support from vg MSS and a Bohemian version (Ropes, 215): "It's easy for you to claim to be a Roman citizen. I happen to know that this status cost me a great deal" (*Dixit tribunus, tam facile dicis civem romanum esse? Ego enim scio quanto pretio civitatem istam possedi*). This is almost certainly secondary, but does, as Bede observes, bring out the meaning with greater clarity. See M. L. W. Laistner, "The Latin Versions of *Acts* Known to the Venerable Bede," *HTR* 30 (1937) 37–50, esp. 42.

9 Verse 28c is an *inclusio* with v. 3.

10 Cicero *Phil.* 5.4.2 charges Antony with selling Roman citizenship. On the sale of citizenship under Claudius, see Cassius Dio 60.17.3–8, esp. 5–6. He reports that Messalina and her entourage were willing to sell citizenship for a modest fee. The account is quite exaggerated, and the practice did not end after Claudius. This hostile tidbit is not a sufficient basis for construction of a theory. Tacitus *Ann.* 14.50.1 testifies to the practice. Cadbury (*Book*, 84) understands the verse to apply to Lysias's purchase of his freedom rather than to bribery. On the spread of citizenship, see Adrian N. Sherwin-White, "The Roman Citizenship: A Survey of Its Development into a World Franchise," *ANRW* 1.2 (1974) 23–58.

11 Porphry's petulant comments (Hoffmann, *Porphry*, 59–60) are interesting: "Paul also seems to forget himself frequently, as when he tells the captain of the guard that he is not a Jew but a Roman, even though he had said on another occasion . . . [22:3] But any saying [both] 'I am a Jew' and 'I am a Roman' is neither, even if he would like to be." See Hoffman's n. 40, p. 60.

12 On the legal issues see Cadbury and Lake, 285 (and Cadbury, "Roman Law and the Trial of Paul," in Lake and Cadbury, *Additional Notes*, 297–338), as well as Haenchen, 634 n. 4. No law had (yet) been broken. The recurrence of ἐπιγινώσκω ("discover") is ironic. In v. 24, it referred to the charges against Paul. Verse 28 shows that what he had discovered placed him in jeopardy.

22:30—23:11 Paul before the Sanhedrin

**30/ The very next day, determined to
learn exactly what accusations
the Jews were making against
Paul, the tribune took him out
of confinement and directed
the high priests and the entire
Sanhedrin to assemble. He
then brought Paul into their
presence.[a]**
**23:1/ Paul looked directly at the San-
hedrin[b] and said, "My fellow
believers, all my life I have
served God with an entirely
clear conscience."**
**2/ At this the high priest, Anan-
ias, ordered[c] those who were
near Paul to strike him on the
mouth.[d]**
**3/ Paul responded, "God will strike
you, you old phony. Here you
sit, judging me in accordance
with the same law you flout by
having me struck."[e]**
**4/ Those who had been told to
strike him exclaimed: "How
dare you revile God's own high
priest?"[f]**
**5/ "I was not aware, my brothers,
that this person was the high
priest," he replied. "As Scripture says: 'Do not defame a
ruler of your people.'" 6/ Real-
izing that some were Sadducees and the rest Pharisees,
Paul shouted: "Fellow believers, I am a Pharisee, as was
my family before me.[g] I am on
trial[h] because of my hope in the
resurrection of the dead."[i]**
**7/ These words provoked[j] a conflict
between the Pharisees and the
Sadducees, leading to a sharp
division in the body,[k] 8/ since
Sadducees[l] say that there is
no resurrection, neither angel
nor spirit, whereas Pharisees
affirm them.[m] 9/ Loud shouting
erupted, and some scribes of
the Pharisaic faction[n] took the
floor to join the fray with these
words:[o] "We find no fault in
this person. Perhaps a spirit or
an angel has spoken to him!"[p]
10/ The disruption became so
violent that the tribune began
to fear that they would tear
Paul to pieces; he ordered the
military to go down and rescue
Paul from them and then return
him to the fort. 11[q]/ The Lord
appeared to him the next night,**

a Some D-Texts (614 *pc* sy[h**]) add that he "sent for" Paul before releasing him ("from his bonds," according to m). See also the note on 22:29.

b The order of words varies. N-A[27] prefers the apparent reading of p[74].

c Witnesses offer two synonyms for "command," neither of which alters the meaning.

d Boismard (*Texte*, 366) offers this D-Text: "the high priest [ ] ordered [] to strike him on the mouth."

e Boismard, *Texte*, 366: "Here you sit, judging me [ ] and in contempt of the law (παρὰ τὸν νόμον) . . . ."

f The D-Text (Boismard, *Texte*, 366) omits "God's." This may indicate a reluctance to concede that the official functioned on behalf of God.

g E 1739 m sy[h] read the name in the singular. This is probably due to failure to recognize the idiom. (Boismard does not discuss this variant which has good D-Text support.)

h The evidence for and against the emphatic "I" is well divided. It may have been deleted as redundant (the speech begins with ἐγώ) or as immodest.

i The D-Text (Boismard, *Texte*, 367) omits "dead," perhaps as redundant.

j B and some other witnesses have some form of "fall": ἔπεσεν, or the like. Since Luke uses γίνομαι with στάσις elsewhere (15:2) and since the Syriac tradition also supports "fall," it has some claim. Just what it might mean is a different question. For that reason Barrett (2:1064) rejects it.

k The D-Text (Boismard, *Texte*, 368) omits the phrase about the division (but see v. 9).

l B (surprisingly) omits the particle μέν here.

m In place of τὰ ἀμφότερα, which should mean "both" but can mean "all" (BDF §275 [8)]), the D-Text (Boismard, *Texte*, 368) gives a full list: "Pharisees affirm that there is resurrection and angel and spirit."

n "Faction" or "party" is one meaning of μέρος (Josephus *Bell.* 1.143). Relatively unimportant variants attend the enumeration of the Pharisees here.

o The D-Text (Boismard, *Texte*, 368) begins καὶ κραυγῆς γενομένης ἐν αὐτοῖς ἐσχίσθησαν ("After a clamor arose, they divided among themselves"). The main clause has been transferred from v. 7. Instead of "disputed" (διεμάχοντο) the Pharisees "contradicted" (ἀντέλεγον, evidently to the views of the Sadducees). The Latin h (accepted by Boismard) reads, "What evil have we found . . . ?" This is a sensible limitation.

p 𝔐 sa show the affinity to 5:34-39 by adding "Let us not fight against God!" (μὴ θεομαχῶμεν). This is an interesting variant of a D-Text type, attested only in a version outside of the Byzantine tradition, but clearly representative of lost Greek exemplars of an earlier date. On the links between the two scenes, see Weaver, *Plots*, 139–41. The syntax omits an apodosis,

saying: "Don't falter,[r] for just as you have given testimony for my cause in Jerusalem, so also must you testify in Rome."

a form of aposiopesis found also in classical Greek (BDF §482).

q 𝔓[48] contains 23:11-17, 25-29. This carelessly written, third-century papyrus fragment is usually classified as a representative of the D-Text. For bibliography, see James Keith Elliott, *A Bibliography of Greek New Testament Manuscripts* (SNTSMS 109; 2nd ed.; Cambridge: Cambridge University Press, 2000) 30.

r A (clearly later) variant adds the vocative "Paul."

Analysis

Chapter 23 reports the transfer of Paul from Roman custody under the garrison commander in Jerusalem to custody under the Roman procurator in Caesarea. Lysias makes his third attempt to clarify the charges against Paul. This creates another situation from which he must rescue his prisoner (vv. 1-10). A band of fanatics then plot, with the connivance of the priestly leadership, to assassinate Paul in an ambush. The apparently chance discovery of this cabal motivated the tribune to mount a substantial expedition to extricate Paul from the treacherous thickets and escort him safely to the coastal capital. Acts 23:1-10 is a transitional scene introducing Paul at trial and establishing his basic thesis: that the real charge against him is his belief in the resurrection and that death will be the inevitable result of trial by the Jewish senate. The oracle in v. 11 announces the theme of the remainder of the book: Paul is destined for Rome. His plan of 19:21 will be fulfilled.

The narrator then introduces a long retardation, a Jewish plot that will take Paul to the relative safety of Caesarea and Roman jurisdiction. Chapters 24–26 describe Paul's efforts to avoid trial in a Jewish court at Jerusalem, leading to his appeal for judgment in Rome. In the course of these experiences it transpires that Roman officials found Paul innocent, while his Jewish adversaries would stop at nothing to remove him from the scene.

Comment

■ **22:30** References to the subsequent day in the initial and closing verses frame this passage. On the day after the riot, the commandant, faithfully seeking clarification of Jewish legal questions that were understandably beyond his capacity directed the Sanhedrin to convene and brought his charge before them. This creates another parallel with the trials of Jesus (Luke 22:54-71). Reasonable as these plans may appear, they have cast Paul into the lions' den, since readers know that execution lies in store for believers haled before this body (6:12–7:60; cf. 5:33). The plans are not, however, truly reasonable, for they presume that the tribune commanding the Jerusalem garrison can convene the religious council and set its agenda, an unlikely prerogative of his office, and—the crux of the problem—why he does so. If Roman law is not at issue, Lysias has no need to detain Paul, whom he could allow to be taken into custody by the temple police, whose leaders could have referred the prisoner to the Roman governor, as described in the process against Jesus. Furthermore, the circumstances would have required the Roman officer to make some opening remarks, explaining the nature of his inquiry and requesting the assistance of the Sanhedrin. The essential point for the narrative is that this body could have executed Paul. Without that presupposition, Paul's conduct is utterly inexplicable, as is the sequel (23:14).[1]

1 Sherwin-White (*Roman Society*, 54) stated that the proceeding is not described as a formal trial and is thus acceptable. This ignores both the nature of Sanhedrin trials in Acts and the intent of the narrative. Analogies from papyri of the Ptolemaic period, suggested by Rafał Taubenschlag ("Le process de l'apotre Paul en lumière des papyri," in idem, *Opera Minora* [2 vols.; Warsaw: Państwowe Wydawn, 1959] 2:721–26) are irrelevant, and the frequently invoked Josephus *Ant.* 20.202 relates to an allegation that the Sanhedrin required the consent of the procurator to meet. This does not allow the inference that the garrison commandant could command them to assemble.

The narrator has Paul resort to desperate tactics. Seizing the initiative, he first throws the assembly off balance and then divides the house against itself. Acts 22:30–23:5 and 23:6-10 are parallel and complementary sections. The first pits Paul in a personal confrontation with the chief priest. In the second, the two major parties fall out. In both cases, Paul grasps the initiative and is able to keep his opposition from achieving its object. For early readers, this was doubtless a clever and courageous performance. After Paul has exposed the chief priest as a callous oaf and the council as utterly lacking in self-control, the percipient Roman officer removed his charge to safety. Today's reader is obliged to say that these episodes are lamentable exercises in anti-Jewish buffoonery.[2]

The first section is a burlesque confrontation that would not look out of place in the *Acta Alexandrinorum*.[3] Achilles Tatius knew how to give this sort of stuff a proper send-up:

> Just as we were about to seat ourselves . . . Thersandros charged madly up to the temple, bringing some witnesses, and said to the priest in a stentorian voice: "I call these people to witness that you have improperly removed from death row a person condemned to legal execution. You hold my female slave, as well, a lascivious woman, a nymphomaniac . . . [the chaste heroine, Leucippe]."
>
> [These words] upset me terribly. I did not put up with his wounding words but interrupted him in mid insult. "And you, sir, are a slave from a long line of slaves, a lunatic and a lecher. She is a free woman, a virgin and worthy of the goddess."
>
> When he heard this, he replied, "And you even insult me, you convict and crow bait!" He struck me one very forceful blow across the face." (*Leuc. Clit.* 8.1.1–3)[4]

■ **23:1** Rackham observed that this was not the Paul who had addressed a raving mob as "fathers and brethren."[5] He takes the place of an equal (which, according to 26:11, he was). Since Paul was willing to utilize a *captatio benevolentiae* with Festus (24:10), his rudeness in seizing the floor was intentional. Readers will conclude that the high priest's instruction to award his impudence with a dollop of casual violence was more due to what Paul said than to his failure to remain silent until instructed to speak. Other than to the scrupulous Paulinist or to the conscientious historian the statement appears quite innocuous.[6] "I have served God with an entirely clear conscience." (ἐγὼ πάσῃ συνειδήσει ἀγαθῇ πεπολίτευμαι τῷ θεῷ [v. 1]) is a fine bit of Deutero-Pauline prose.[7]

■ **2** The generality[8] of his boast allows the arbitrary brutality of the tyrannical Ananias[9] to flourish. This

2 After summarizing the text, Tannehill (*Narrative Unity*, 2:287) concludes: "This scene is a good example of the lengths to which the narrator will go to show that Paul is not anti-Jewish." He does not comment on the narrator's hostility to Judaism.

3 For specific parallels, see below. Wilson (*Law*, 66–67) succinctly summarizes the problems of treating this incident as history.

4 Trans. J. J. Winkler in Reardon, *Novels*, 269.

5 Rackham, 429: "His behaviour in the Sanhedrin was certainly very different from that on the previous day in the temple. He shews no tact, nor even any desire to be conciliatory."

6 Paul's intense gaze (ἀτενίζω) probably means here that he made full eye contact with members of the council. It could also indicate his "good conscience," as Haenchen (637) and Fitzmyer (716) believe.

7 "Conscience" is not quite accurate in the modern English sense, but the notion of a "good" or "bad" conscience in the sense of moral formation (rather than guilt or pride) conforms to Greco-Roman philosophical ethics. Paul's use of the term συνείδησις is closer to "consciousness" in contemporary American English. Modifiers are "strong" or "weak" (e.g., 1 Cor 8:7). See Pervo, *Dating*, 240–41. Anachronism leads commentators to ask whether Paul should have felt "guilty" about persecuting believers in his earlier life. Even Haenchen (637) and Conzelmann (192) raise this concern. The dangers of undue individualization of the concept are highlighted by Malina and Neyrey, *Portraits*, 183–84. On πολιτεύομαι ("live one's life), see Pervo, *Dating*, 286. Barrett (2:1057–58) has a detailed discussion.

8 Specification of the reason for punishing Paul would diminish the literary effect.

9 Ananias, the son of Nedebaeus, was high priest under Claudius and Nero c. 47–59. Luke could have garnered these data from Josephus (e.g., *Ant.* 20.103).

provides all that the reader—and the tribune—needs to know about his character and the kind of justice to be expected under his presidency.[10]

■ **3** Paul's rejoinder is far from casual. This elegant bit of vituperation is a chiastic unit decorated with antithesis, assonance, and alliteration.[11] Like Jesus (Luke 22:63-64), Paul suffers gratuitous abuse. Like Jesus (Luke 21:5-6), Paul announces destruction, of a person rather than the temple. Both are *ex eventu*.[12] The epithet (lit. "whitewashed wall") is obscure but not complimentary.[13] Formally, v. 3 is like a "sentence of holy law" without an explicit protasis (that is, "God will strike[14] those who strike God's servants") and could be labeled a curse rather than a prophecy.[15] As subsequent events will reveal, what is to one person the proper expression of boldness before a tyrant[16] is to another counterproductive impudence.[17]

■ **4-5** If readers rejoice in a manifestation of courage, the same vague group of "bystanders" instructed to slap Paul in v. 2 upbraid him in v. 4 for his impudence. Paul's reply is too disingenuous for comfort. Ananias was presiding, and one must presume that he had an appropriate place and insignia of office. Paul had, moreover, on the previous day, appealed to this man as a suitable witness (22:5). Interpreters have struggled to deal with an apparent misstatement.[18] If this incident derives from the narrator, it is another example of Luke having his cake and eating it too.[19] Consistency was not one of his hobgoblins.[20] Paul's "conscience" could remain clear, as he demonstrates by citing an appropriate proof text against reviling leaders.[21] Conzelmann sees the symbolic meaning of the incident: "Luke is characterizing Judaism through its representatives—its relation to the Law is broken and hypocritical (cf. 7:50-53)."[22] In effect, this is a synecdoche. The dramatic result is that Paul has the floor and will retain this initiative. In typical Lucan fashion, events take place so rapidly and excitedly that readers are not prone to sit back and raise objections. This,

10 John 18:22-23 is an illustrative parallel.

11 Note also the verb κάθῃ ("you sit"). The more frequent *Koine* form is κάθησαι. This bisyllabic alternative suits the rhythm of the prose. The harsh velars (*k*-) are expressive. See Knox, *Hellenistic Elements*, 16.

12 Ananias was murdered by rebels in 66 (Josephus *Bell.* 2.441–42).

13 See Cadbury and Lake, 287. The metaphor suggests a thin coat of cheap paint concealing major faults (cf. English "papering over the cracks") and thus contrasts appearance to reality (whence the translation). For comparable images, see Ezek 13:10-16; *CD* 8:12. Note also Fitzmyer, 717.

14 BDAG, 1020, *s.v.*, says that τύπτω may refer to "misfortunes designated as blows coming from God," with references to Exod 7:27; 2 Kgdms 24:17; Ezek 7:6; 2 Macc 3:39; *Aristeas* 192. Gustav Stählin, "τύπτω," *TDNT* 8:260–70, esp. 267, finds its usage in Acts (18:17; 21:32) an indication of Luke's anti-Jewish orientation.

15 See Conzelmann (192) and Stählin, "τύπτω," who refers to *m. Šebu.* 4.13. Luke may not have been sensitive to this idiom.

16 On courage before tyrants, see Epictetus *Diss.* 3.22.55 and the excursus "Confronting Tyrants," pp. 118–19.

17 The *Acta Alexandrinorum* include illustrative insults of this nature, for example, *Acta Isidori* Rec. B 1.17–18, where Isidorus makes an insulting remark about Agrippa, on which see Tcherikover (*CPJ* 2:77), Musurillo (*Pagan*, 137) and the *Acta Appiani* col. iv 7–8 (Musurillo, 67), in which Appian calls the emperor (probably Commodus) λῃστάρχος ("chief bandit"). Tcherikover (*CPJ* 2:107) says this "is the culminating point of Alexandrian insolence."

18 Augustine (*Serm. Dom.* 1.19) and Bede (89) take the position that Paul did not recognize Ananias as the true high priest, as his role had been superseded by Jesus. In *Ep.* 138 Augustine took the remark as sarcasm. Chrysostom (*Hom.* 48, p. 406) decides that Paul did not know who the person was. Calvin comes down on the side of sarcasm: "I, brethren, recognize nothing priestly about this man" (7:229).

19 Conzelmann, 192: "The entire scene is inconceivable: How could Paul not have known the one who was presiding? Behind this scene lie some vague details, not a historically accurate account." This creates the problem of identifying both the vague details and the means of their transmission.

20 Barrett (2:1061–62) offers a range of interpretations and ends with a qualified *non liquet*.

21 "Leader" is plural in the preferred text of the LXX. Acts may be an ad hoc adjustment.

22 Conzelmann, 192. "Sitting" refers to the chair of judgment (Matt 23:2, etc.) On παρανομέω ("flout the law"), see Johnson, 397.

needless to say, is typical of popular literature driven by the question, what will happen next?

■ **6** The second unit begins, in v. 6 begins like v.1, with a circumstantial participial phrase, an identical address, and an assertion in the first person singular. Paul engages in what admirers would have labeled a deft political maneuver and detractors, a cheap lawyer's stunt.[23] His rhetorical tactic involves shifting the subject to an irrelevant but controversial theme that will paralyze the court, as when a politician accused of bribery tells a legislative body that he is being persecuted because of his staunch opposition to socialism.[24] More elegantly: *divide et impera*.[25]

■ **7** The tactic worked almost fatally well, for the group became so violent in its debate that Paul was about to be filleted by the councilors. In the end, the tribune had to send for troops to extricate Paul from the Sanhedrin, just as had been done in 21:32.

Clever and exciting as the story is, problems emerge.[26] One must believe that the leadership was incapable of regaining control and saying, in effect, "This is no doubt an interesting subject but not the matter for which we are assembled,"[27] and that the august membership of the body was no better than a mob. The narrator has diffused the first objection by assigning the initiative to Paul. The second is not an improbable conjecture but an established fact, confirmed by the trial of Stephen (7:57-59).[28] Jewish leaders in general and the Sanhedrin in particular are capable of any kind of mischief and wickedness. While purveying this lowbrow slander for the delectation of his audience,[29] Luke has Paul seize that high ground which he will occupy for the rest of the book: he is on trial because of his advocacy of the hope of Israel, the resurrection.[30] For Romans, this idea may have been bizarre but was scarcely cause for capital punishment. Among Jews, resurrection was a matter for theological debate. This thesis permits Paul to present himself as a politically harmless prisoner suffering for the sake of his fellow Israelites, a good Jew persecuted by Jews who prevent the Romans from discharging him. Paul's claim to be a Pharisee encapsulates Luke's portrait of Paul vis-à-vis Judaism. The historical Paul said that he *had been* a Pharisee (Phil 3:5-7). For Luke, "Judaism" and "Christianity" have become distinct religious bodies. His goal is to refute the claim that Paul was responsible for this division, which, in his view, came about because a substantial majority of the Jewish people refused to accept the self-evident truths of the Jesus movement.

■ **8** Readers know that the Sanhedrin contained both Sadducees and Pharisees[31] and that the former are staunch opponents of the movement (5:17-39). Now the narrator will point to some doctrinal divisions. Paul, who is a Pharisee by birth,[32] so to speak (as he was a Roman citizen by birth: 22:28), upholds resurrection hope.[33] The outcome is all that Paul could hope for, so to speak. Conflict erupted, as in 15:2, but the result was different, for the disputants here staked out rigid

23 On the questions raised by Paul's claim that resurrection was the issue, see Barrett, 2:1064. Bruce (465–66) invokes 1 Cor 9:23.

24 Foakes Jackson (306) says that Paul "escaped condemnation by the none too creditable stratagem of setting his judges by the ears." Kennedy (*Rhetorical Criticism,* 135) recognizes this as a diversionary tactic.

25 So also Bengel, 475.

26 See Haenchen, 639–43; Roloff, 326; and Weiser, 2:614–15.

27 Wendt, 316.

28 See Pervo, "Meet Right," 53–57.

29 See Pervo, *Profit,* 64.

30 Hope: note, in particular, 26:6-7; 28:20. Resurrection: 24:21; 26:23. Acts 24:15 refers to both. The idea is Pauline. See Klaus Haacker, "Das Bekenntnis des Paulus zur Hoffnung Israels nach der Apostelgeschichte des Lukas," *NTS* 31 (1985) 437–51.

31 Witherington's helpful suggestion (689) that the parties could be distinguished by dress is not necessary.

32 Note 2 Tim 1:3: "I am grateful to God—whom I worship with a clear conscience, as my ancestors did." The two passages show common features of the Deutero-Pauline encomiastic portrait of Paul: ancestry and virtue. Phil 3:5 may have helped inspire Acts.

33 This construes "hope and resurrection" as a hendiadys (cf. Conzelmann, 192, and his references in n. 6). Haenchen (638) disagrees, relating hope to messianic thought and resurrection to eschatology. See also Jervell (556 n. 138), who treats "resurrection" as an explanatory genitive. This is similar, but does not account for the καί ("and"). The implication, carried out in v. 9, is that the Pharisees would support Christians.

lines of division.[34] Members of the Areopagus also had different views about the idea of resurrection (17:32), but they did not have to resort to fisticuffs about it.[35] The narrator's problem is to turn this long-standing disagreement among members of a council that had managed to work together into juridical gridlock. He does so by introducing a conflict about the sources of religious authority. Sadducees deny resurrection, as is well known,[36] and, according to the narrator's aside in v. 8, "angel" and "spirit."[37] Exegetes have labored hard to explain this claim, which conflicts with the Torah, an authority accepted by the Sadducees.[38]

■ **9** The least difficult explanation comes in v. 9: these entities "speak" and therefore convey revelation. "Angel" and "spirit" do speak to people in Acts.[39] The underlying question is whether revelation has ceased. That is worth a donnybrook.

Acts presumes that revelation did not cease with Moses (or Malachi) and does not view the necessity of a debate on the matter as flattering to the governing body. Beneath its vital surface function of rescuing Paul from certain death, the passage shows that Judaism is a house divided against itself and will not stand.[40] Paul is once more the agent who exposes this division, wielding the separating sword (cf. Luke 2:34-35; Eph 6:17; Heb 4:12). Some of the Pharisees' legal experts (γραμματεῖς)[41] take the opportunity to declare Paul innocent. This judgment, a feature of the trials of Jesus and Paul,[42] is based on the information in the narrative aside of v. 8.[43] Despite their support, the Pharisees are Luke's real target: they should have been open to the message.[44] In this untidy encounter, the narrator has introduced the thesis that the real charge against Paul is his belief in resurrection. That thesis will remain at the top of the agenda for the remainder of the book (28:20).

■ **10** The narrative clunks along in vv. 7-10, with three forms of γίγνομαι ("to be, become"), two accompanied by στάσις ("disturbance"), in vv. 7 and 10, the other

34 For the phrase ἐσχίσθη τὸ πλῆθος, see 14:4 and Chariton *Chaer.* 5.4.1. Note also *Onos* 54. The theme is common, that is, *Ethiopian Story* 5.32: "Like a sea lashed by a sudden squall . . . they were whipped into indescribable turmoil by an irrational impulse, for drink and anger had now taken full possession of them. Some sided with Trachinos, bawling that the leader must be respected; others with Peloros, clamoring that the law must be upheld [violence ensues]" (trans. J. R. Morgan in Reardon, *Novels*, 470).

35 The *Act. Pet.* (Verc.) 3 describe a riot in the Roman Senate. This is an evident imitation of Acts 23:6-10.

36 Acts lends weight to the view that the Sadducees' opposition to resurrection was grounded in skepticism, rather than, as was formally the case, in strict interpretation of the Torah.

37 "Hope," "resurrection," "angel," and "spirit" are all anarthrous and singular. This indicates that they are technical terms. See Cadbury and Lake, 289.

38 Cadbury and Lake (290) say spirit and angel are tautological here. Witherington (692) argues that the reference is to deceased persons. One possibility is that they deny "guardian angels" (12:15; so also Loisy, 831) and the spiritual existence of the soul (Barrett, 2:1065–66), but, if so, this could be more clearly expressed. Fitzmyer renders "no resurrection, neither as an angel nor as a spirit, whereas Pharisees acknowledge them both." This implies two forms of resurrection, as an "angel" and/or as a "spirit." Neither fits the case of Jesus in Luke and Acts. For a different view, based on an exploration of Lucan Christology, see Crispin H. T. Fletcher-Louis, *Luke-Acts: Angels, Christology and Soteriology* (WUNT 94; Tübingen: Mohr Siebeck, 1997) 57–61. For a concise critique of this interesting study, see François Bovon, *Luke the Theologian* (2nd ed.; Waco: Baylor University Press, 2006) 535–36.

39 Angel: 7:38; 8:26; 10:3-7; 12:8; spirit: 8:29 (cf. v. 26); 10:10; 13:2; 19:1; 20:23. Latin h reads "Holy Spirit."

40 Josephus presents another version of this view, which he applies to the state rather than to the religion.

41 The phrase was evidently borrowed from Mark 2:16.

42 "Find nothing" (οὐδέν . . . εὑρίσκω): Acts 24:9; Luke 23:4, 22; "nothing deserving death" (οὐδὲν θανάτου ἄξιον): Luke 23:15; Acts 26:31.

43 Readers will associate v. 9 with the visions of 22:6-9, 18, but it is not legitimate to presume that the dramatic audience made this connection.

44 See Johnson's insightful comments (401–2). Fitzmyer (714) takes a distinctly different and less penetrating view: "Paul is vindicated by the Pharisees in his audience."

by a "loud shout" (κραυγὴ μεγάλη), in v. 9, until the violence threatens to rip Paul into pieces. Is the reader to imagine Paul caught in a tug-of-war between the two parties or the victim of mob violence?[45] All that is clear is the action of the tribune, a recapitulation of what he had done the last time Paul had been involved with a mob (21:31-32). Readers observe that Jews, unlike the followers of Jesus, cannot engage in a reasoned and orderly discussion about their own religion. One may also ask what the tribune has gained for his (and Paul's) pains. If one presumes that the proceedings were conducted in Aramaic and that the officer has been provided with a translation, facts neglected by the narrator, *and* that the officer could comprehend what they were talking about, which is quite unlikely, he could have learned precious little. When he writes to the procurator: "They [the Sanhedrin] were charging him on matters pertinent to their law" (v. 29), he certainly says what the narrator wishes to be said, but there is no justification for this conclusion in the text, and it is unwise to take this as fact, let alone build upon it.[46] Rackham's conclusion is sound: "This stormy scene is our last sight of the supreme court of the Jews, the elders of Israel. It left Lysias no more enlightened than before, except as to the personal importance of the apostle."[47]

■ **11** The following night brings a vision[48] of neither angel nor spirit but of the Lord, conveying both consolation and information.[49] Paul will survive whatever Jerusalem has in store. He is destined to be a witness[50] in Rome. [51] Verse 11 is one of the "hinge" moments in Acts that serve both as conclusions to the preceding and as introductions to what follows.

---

45 The verb διασπάω was used literally of the martyrdom of the philosopher Hypatia. See A. Westermann, *Βιογραφοι. Vitarum scriptores Graeci minores* (Braunschweig: Westermann, 1845; reprinted, Amsterdam: Hakkert, 1964) 444.

46 Marshall (371–72) uses this as grounds for implying that Luke did not know of Paul's death as a result of this legal process (but note his reservations on p. 426).

47 Rackham, 434.

48 On the literary function of revelations, see Pervo, *Profit*, 72–74.

49 Witherington (793) observes: "Certainly after a day like he had had, Paul could use such divine reassurance." The introductory ϑάρσει ("take heart") has a place in announcements of salvation, whence its appearances in miracle stories (Matt 9:2, 22; Mark 10:49, avoided by Luke). See M. Simon, "ϑάρσει. οὐδεῖς ἀϑάνατος? Étude de vocabulaire religieuse," *RHR* 100 (1936) 188–206; and Walter Grundmann, "ϑαρρέω," *TDNT* 3:25–27. Note also the Delos Aretalogy line 77 (see Appendix 2), with the comments of Engelmann, *Delian Aretalogy*, 51. Aune discusses this oracle in *Prophecy*, 267.

50 Christology is the subject. See the phrase τὰ περί (lit. "the things concerning") in Luke 24:19, 27; 13:29; 18:25. The D-Text (Boismard, *Texte*, 369) omits this phrase and "you" as the subject of "witness."

51 The use of "must" (δεῖ) in 19:21 and 23:11 creates irony. For a formal parallel, see Josephus *Vit.* 208–9, where, amidst grievous difficulties, he received a nocturnal vision. His visitor, unlike Paul's, promised Josephus many boons and benefactions. (The oracle closes with a statement that he must [δεῖ] fight the Romans.)

23

23:12-35 A Plot against Paul

12/ When day came[a] the Jews
concocted a plot,[b] solemnly
vowing neither to eat nor to
drink until they had killed Paul.[c]
13/ More than forty entered
into this conspiracy.[d] 14/ They
approached the high priest
and the elders with this message:
"We have vowed with
the utmost solemnity[e] to taste
nothing[f] until we have killed
Paul."

23:15: Conventional Text

15/ "Now you people must, together with the Sanhedrin, advise the tribune that he is to bring Paul back before you on the grounds that you wish to make a more thorough and decisive inquiry into his situation. We shall be ready to kill him[g] before he can get there."[h]

23:15 D-Text[i]

15/ "We therefore *ask you: Do the following for us: summon the Sanhedrin*; advise the tribune that he is to bring Paul back before you on the grounds that you wish to make a [ ] decisive inquiry into his situation. We shall be ready to kill him, [ ] *even though we too have to die."*

16/ Paul's sister's son caught wind of
the proposed ambush and went
to the fort to inform his uncle.
17/ Paul summoned[j] a centurion
and said, "Take[k] this young
man to the tribune, as he has
some information to give him."
18/ The centurion[l] accompanied
the youth to the tribune,
and said, "The prisoner Paul
summoned me and asked that I
convey this lad to you because
he has information for you."
19/ The tribune took him by the
hand to a spot where they could
speak privately and asked,
"What is it that you wish to tell
me?"[m]
20/ "The Jews have arranged[n] to
request that you send Paul to
the Sanhedrin tomorrow on
the grounds[o] of making a more
thorough inquiry."

23:21: Conventional Text

21/ "Don't let them convince you, for they are going to ambush him. More than forty of them have vowed neither to eat nor to drink until they have assassinated him. They are already prepared and merely waiting for your consent."

23:21: D-Text[p]

21/ "Don't let them convince you [ ]; more than forty of them *are prepared to kill him*. They have *even* vowed to *taste nothing until they have accomplished this*."

22/ The tribune sent the young man away, warning him to tell no one "what you have disclosed to me."[q]

23:23-25: N-A[27]

23/ He summoned two particular centurions[r] and said: "Make preparations for two hundred infantry, seventy cavalry and two hundred of other arms[s] to proceed toward Caesarea beginning at 2100."

24/ He also ordered them to provide mounts for Paul, whom they were to deliver safely to Governor Felix.

25/ He prepared the following letter:[t]

26/ "Claudius Lysias to Governor Felix
Your Excellency.

23:23-25: Boismard[u]

23/ He summoned two centurions and *ordered that they be ready to depart.*

24/ *and* to provide mounts for Paul, whom
they were to *take to Caesarea at night* to
Governor Felix, *for he was afraid that
the Jews might seize and kill Paul, and that
afterwards he would be liable to the charge
of having taken money.*
25/ He prepared a
letter containing the
following:[v]

23:23-24: Clark[w]

"Prepare soldiers to go to Caesarea, one
hundred cavalry[x] and two hundred of other
arms," and *he commanded that they be
ready to leave* at 2100.
24/ *And he directed the
centurions* to provide mounts for Paul and
deliver him *by night* to Governor Felix, *for
he was afraid that the Jews might seize and
kill Paul, and that afterwards he would be
liable to the charge of having taken money."*

Acts 23:27-30: Conventional Text

27/ "This man was caught by the
Jews, who were about to kill
him. I arrived with a detachment
and extracted him when I
found out that he was a Roman
citizen.
28/ As I was determined
to discover the grounds[y] behind
their accusation, I brought
him[z] before their Sanhedrin.
29/ It transpired that they were
charging him on matters pertinent
to their law, but not of any
capital offense or of some crime
demanding incarceration.
30/ "When it came to my attention that there was a plot against his life, I determined that I should send him to you forthwith. I have also instructed his accusers to lay their charges regarding him before you."

Acts 23:27-30: D-Text[aa]

27/ "I *rescued because he was shouting and claiming to be* a Roman citizen. . . .

29/ ". . . charging him with *nothing more than* matters pertinent to the law *of Moses and about one Jesus,* but not *performing* any capital offense [ ]. *I was barely able to get him out of there and had to use force.*

30/ [ ] I have sent him[bb] to you [ ] I have also instructed his accusers *to come* before you."

31/ In accordance with their orders, the soldiers took Paul to Antipatris, traveling by night.

32/ The next day the infantry returned to their fort, leaving the cavalry to escort him. 33/ The latter went on to Caesarea, where they delivered the letter to the governor and brought Paul before him. 34/ After reading the communication, Felix asked Paul for his province of residence and learned that it was Cilicia. 35/ "I shall hear your case when your accusers arrive," he said, and then directed that Paul be detained in Herod's palace.

a B and a range of witnesses read τε instead of δέ. This appears to create a closer link between v. 11 and v. 12, underlying the contrast between divine and human plans.

b The D-Text, supported by m, reads "some of the Jews." This is a rationalization that exposes Luke's intention to blame the Jews in general for Paul's fate. The D-Text (Boismard, *Texte*, 370) makes "conspiring" a participle. 𝔓[48] reads (with reconstructions) *γενομένης δὲ ἡμέρας καιτ* (up to seven letters missing) *βοήθειαν συστραφέντες τινες* . . . Barrett (2:1073) takes *βοήθειαν* to mean "an auxiliary force." It might mean "assembling a force by conspiratorial means."

c On the survival of the subjunctive in such clauses as *ἕως οὗ ἀποκτείνωσιν* ("until . . .") here and in v. 14, see BDF §383 (2).

d The D-Text (Boismard, *Texte*, 370) is more prosaic: "Those who had made this vow were more than forty."

e The phrase *ἀναθέματι ἀνεθεματίσαμεν* is a Septuagintalism, although not unintelligible because Greek can use cognate nouns in the dative. Its purpose here is to intensify (thus "utmost").

f The D-Text (Boismard, *Texte*, 371) adds "at all" (*τὸ σύνολον*).

g 𝔐 adds: "tomorrow," harmonizing with v. 20.

h Luke's penchant for the genitive of the articular infinitive is notable in v. 15. See Bruce (468), who lists many examples.

i Boismard, *Texte*, 371.

j The verb *προσκαλέω* in Luke and Acts always applies to the words of a superior to an inferior: Luke 7:18; 15:26; 16:5; 18:16; Acts 2:39; 5:40; 6:2; 13:2, 7; 16:10; 23:23.

k Witnesses attest both present and aorist imperatives. Barrett (2:1075) states that the aorist is probably secondary, but the distinction may be too refined.

l The D-Text (Boismard, *Texte*, 373) adds "immediately," reassuring the reader that the officer did not delay for a day or two. This replaces the *μὲν οὖν* that seems to mark a new section, framed by the same particle in v. 22.

m The D-Text (Boismard, *Texte*, 374) places this in indirect discourse. Cf. also v. 22.

n According to Boismard (*Texte*, 374), the D-Text is *τοῖς Ἰουδαίοις συνεφωνήθη* ("It has been agreed upon by the Jews"), as in 5:9. This may reflect the Latin translation rather than a genuine variant.

o The participle *μέλλον*, nicely qualified by *ὡς* to indicate the speaker's distance from the claim, seems properly to modify "Sanhedrin," but it was regarded as problematic, for the variants are numerous. See Ropes, *Text*, 219; and Barrett, 2:1076.

p Boismard, *Texte*, 375.

q The D-Text (Boismard, *Texte*, 375) eliminates the mixture of indirect and direct discourse in favor of the former. The mixture is not uncommon in Acts. See BDF §470 (2) and the comments at 1:4.

r The translation accepts *δύο τινάς* as more difficult. BDF §301 judges it possible, but variants tend to eliminate one or the other. Another strong possibility is that the original said "some" (perhaps one or two for the infantry, another for the cavalry, and one or two for the "other arms," reduced to "two" by the D-Text that included soldiers from two branches).

s On the meaning of "other arms," see below.

t *Or* (less likely): "a letter to this effect."

u Boismard, *Texte*, 376–77. *καὶ προσκαλεσάμενος δύο τῶν ἑκατονταρχῶν διετάξατο ἑτοίμους εἶναι ἐξελθεῖν καὶ* [24] *κτήνη παραστῆσαι ἵνα ἐπιβιβάσαντες τὸν Παῦλον νυκτὸς ἀγάωσιν εἰς Καισάρειαν πρὸς Φήλικα τὸν ἡγεμόνα.* [25] *ἐφοβήθη γὰρ μήποτε ἐξαρπάξαντες αὐτὸν οἱ Ἰουδαῖοι ἀποκτείνωσιν καὶ αὐτὸς μεταξὺ ἔγκλημα ἔχῃ ὡς εἰληφὼς ἀργύρια.*

v The Greek is *περιέχουσαν τάδε*. 𝔓[48] reads "writing to them a letter in which was written" (*γράψας δὲ αὐτοῖς ἐπιστολὲν ἐν ᾗ ἐγέγραπτο*).

w Clark, 379–80.

x This figure has good D-Text support. Although Boismard (*Texte*, 376) claims sy[hmg] in support of the blank, it does include the number "one hundred." See his comments, 377.

y On the meaning of αἰτία (in general, "cause"), see Cadbury and Lake, 294.

z "Him" is supplied in the translation (and is a *v.l.*). Evidently the author regards "this man" (v. 27) as the object.

aa Boismard, *Texte*, 378–79.

bb Having omitted the reference to the conspiracy, the D-Text adds a pronoun. (Evidence for this omission is limited to an Ethiopic version. The text of v. 30 is certainly confused—or mixed. The future infinitive of "to be" is gratuitous. Most extant D-Texts, followed by 𝔐 (gig sy[p] sa), read the equivalent of μέλλειν ἔσεσθαι ὑπὸ τῶν Ἰουδαίων ("there was going to be [redundant] a plot by the Jews") before "forthwith." In all, six variants exist. See Metzger, *Textual Commentary*, 433. Boismard may be too daring, but the text did present problems. Corruption cannot be excluded. On this stilted sentence, see also BDF §424 (2) and Barrett, 2:1084–85.

Analysis

This thrilling story has every mark of a free authorial composition without the assistance of a source, although the essential facts, that Paul was taken into custody in Jerusalem and transferred to Caesarea, are presumably correct and may have been found in the Collection Source or, possibly, in a lost communication of Paul.[1] The structure is clear:

1. (Vv. 12-15). The Plot[2] against Paul is Concocted. (location undisclosed)
   a. V. 12. The Conspirators' Oath.
   b. Vv. 13-15. The Conspirators Enlist the Leadership.
2. (Vv. 16-22). The Plot Is Unmasked. (prison)
   a. Vv. 16-17. His Nephew Informs Paul, Who Sends Him to the Tribune.
   b. Vv. 18-22. The Tribune Interviews the Young Man.
3. (Vv. 23-35). Paul Is Taken to Safety. (From Jerusalem to Caesarea)
   a. (Vv. 23-34). Lysias's Plans.
   b. (Vv. 25-30). Lysias's Letter to Felix.
   c. (Vv. 31-33). Paul Is Transported to the Capital.
   d. (Vv. 34-35). Felix's Initial Disposition of the Case.

The narrative technique is omniscient in style, with a preference for direct speech[3] and but one unit (3.c) of true summary.[4] The scenes contain two characters each (one of which may be collective), with one character remaining from the previous scene and another entering. Paul is the subject, but the central character is the tribune, who plays a key role in the imprisonment section of Acts.[5] Although the net result is transfer from one jail to another, Paul gains several advantages, the most important of which is that the Roman governor will hear the case. He escapes both a dire ambush and the inevitable result of judgment by the Sanhedrin. While describing these maneuvers, which have "the intrinsic charm of a boy's adventure,"[6] the narrator reinforces two of his key points. The first of these is the implacable hatred on the part of "the Jews," who take a strict vow to assassinate their enemy and engage the cooperation of the temple leaders, who raise no objection to complicity in this nefarious scheme. The other side is the view of Paul taken by the tribune. His security became the immediate and highest priority of that officer, who moved promptly and efficiently to protect Paul, delegating major forces to the task and taking pains to assure the governor that no serious charges are involved. Finally, this is the grand climax of all the Jewish plots against Paul, which began a short time after his conversion (9:23), and is an intimation of his ultimate fate.

The situation in Jerusalem has reached an impasse, since the officer has little notion of the charges. The

1 For a critique of attempts to identify a more extensive source here, see Weiser, 2:620–21.

2 For the sake of variety, Luke uses three terms to describe this conspiracy. See Johnson, 403.

3 As is often the case in popular narrative, the characters tend to speak to one another in the imperative mood (vv. 15, 17, 21, 23).

4 1.a. could be called a summary statement.

5 Tribune: 21:31, 32, 33, 37; 22:24, 26-29; 23:10, 15, 17-19, 22; 24:22. Acts 25:23 indicates their high status.

6 Johnson, 407.

conspirators seek to exploit his desire for knowledge by overwhelming Paul (and the tribune, with the escorting detail?) en route to another hearing. Word of the plan gets out. Paul, it transpires, has a nephew in Jerusalem, who learns about these developments and comes to inform his uncle, who, in turn, directs an available centurion to escort the youth to the commandant. The commander, for his part, is wise enough to offer the young man privacy. With the ease of experience, this professional snaps off orders to a subordinate while composing a letter. Security concerns, as well as the imminence of the threat, recommend a nocturnal operation. The size of the opposition calls for a substantial force. Lysias won't send a boy to do a man's job.[7] With this task force goes the communication from the commandant, who engages in some amusing self-exculpation.

The combination of speed and force succeed. The night march reaches Antipatris, beyond the murderers' reach, after which the infantry returns to base, leaving the cavalry escort to finish the mission. The governor, Felix, ascertains the basic facts and promises a hearing when the complainants arrive. Trial by a procurator is vastly preferable to the kind of kangaroo courts over which high priests preside. Some grounds for hope exist, now that Paul has eluded a truly fiendish plot. As for said conspirators, the reader is free to exercise whatever charity or lack of the same is available and desired. Few oaths will outlive the demands of nature.

The crisp professionalism of the tribune is admirable, but one might well ask why this officer, duly forewarned, did not simply increase security and deny the request for a hearing and/or launch an investigation into the matter, with the objective of discomforting the leadership and bringing the conspirators to justice. Had he wished to get Paul out of harm's way, a much smaller detachment would have sufficed to elude a few dozen ill-armed amateurs. Those who swallow the story whole must also accept the slanderous characterization of the Sanhedrin.

Comment

■ **12-13** "The Jews" do not want Paul to see Rome or another sunrise. The number of conspirators[8] and the severity of their vow are indicators of the quantity and quality of the hatred generated by Paul, but the conspirators display limited sagacity.[9] Avoidance of nourishment[10] is not desirable for those intending to carry out a desperate scheme, and the number of conspirators is too large for the project,[11] posing a security risk.

■ **14-15** Following (unknown to them) a path marked out by Judas (Luke 22:4), they communicate their solemn resolve to the leadership, whose assistance they require. No time had to be wasted debating the morality or desirability of murdering Paul, nor need they concern themselves with dissenting Pharisees.[12] To get Paul out-of-doors they trot out the increasingly shopworn idea of gathering information.[13] These individuals evidently believed that the tribune would find the proposal appropriate. The D-Text, especially that of v. 15, is more colorful and probably even more hostile. By having the Sanhedrin assembled by its

7 Tannehill (*Narrative Unity*, 2:295) describes Lysias as a "round character," capable of adjustment and change. This is at least partly valid, especially in contrast to "the Jews," who are melodramatic villains.

8 For such conspiracies, see Plutarch *Caes.* 7 (Cataline) and 64 (Brutus and Cassius). Paul is of comparable importance.

9 Conspiracies and plots were no less common in ancient politics than modern. One example is the plot of many leading Alexandrians against the local Jews; see Philo *Flac.* 20–24, whose colorful characterization of the principals illuminates many of the villains depicted in Acts. For details, see Pieter van der Horst, *Philo's Flaccus: The First Pogrom* (Philo of Alexandria Commentary Series 2; Atlanta: Society of Biblical Literature, 2003) 108–13.

10 James took a similar vow in anticipation of the resurrection (*Gos. Heb.* 4).

11 Cadbury and Lake, 291.

12 This may be why Luke does not use the term "Sanhedrin" in v. 14.

13 Some form or compound of γιγνώσκω appears, usually with a form of ἀκριβῶς, in 21:34; 22:24, 30; 23:15, 20, 28; cf. 24:22.

leadership, the centurion is absolved of any (potential) responsibility, while readiness to die—in effect to take the role of modern "suicide bombers"—underlines their fanaticism.[14]

■ **16-17** The narrator introduces a *deus ex machina*. A nephew of Paul erupts on the scene.[15] No hint of the existence of a family has previously emerged. This nameless young man[16] has given wing to imaginative constructions.[17] He is an ad hoc character who disappears as soon as he has fulfilled his function. The narrator has no interest in detailing how the nephew got word of the conspiracy.[18] He did so and came to visit Paul, who promptly summoned a centurion and ordered him to take the man to his commanding officer.[19]

■ **18** The next scene (vv. 18-22) could have been handled as summarily as v. 16, but the narrator wishes to make more of it, developing suspense and supplying a bit of relief.[20] The centurion followed his orders meticulously.

■ **19-22** The tribune, who serves as one of Paul's chief helpers in Acts,[21] reveals his perception and sensitivity.[22] The nephew pours it all out. His voice is that of the narrator: the conspirators are "the Jews" ("them" in v. 21). Two new data emerge: the attack is scheduled for the next day, and the assassins await the tribune's response (presumably to the Sanhedrin's request). The D-Text of v. 21 is more compressed and vigorous. Following the line advanced in v. 15, it eliminates the tribune from discussion, throwing all attention upon the enmity of the terrorists. Recurrence of the verb ἐμφανίζω ("inform") creates a bit of irony. The tribune has been "informed," although not as the conspirators had wished.[23] No reader of Acts is surprised that the tribune assumes the truth of this report and does not pause to make inquiry or investigation.[24]

■ **23-24** Although the D-Text (or texts) is variously reconstructed,[25] it exhibits consistency in the preference

14 See the comments of Epp, *Tendency*, 151.

15 Cf. Livy 39.11: A young man Aebutius, evicted from his home because of his reluctance to undergo Dionysiac initiation, went to stay with his aunt, who, informed of his situation, urged him to go to the consul Postumius. This led to the exposure of the "Bacchanalian conspiracy."

16 The anonymous nephew is called a νεανίας (v. 17), a term also applied to Saul (7:58) and Eutychus (20:9). The label covers a wide range, from young adulthood to early middle age by present-day standards. Alternating with this is νεανίσκος (vv. 18, 22, with νεανίας as a well-attested variant in 18). The tribune's paternalistic treatment inclines modern readers to regard him as a boy. On this character, see Spencer ("Wise Up, Young Man," 46–48), who finds him the one good "young man" in Acts.

17 For example, Ramsay (*St. Paul the Traveller*, 35), who reasonably asks how this young man obtained his information, "which was concocted by a band of zealots, and arranged in private with the high priests and elders?" He concludes that the youth, a member of an influential family, had heard it "in the house of a leading Jew." The lad could not have been a Christian. From this, he deduces (312) that Paul used his inheritance to finance the expenses of his trial.

18 The participle παραγενόμενος could be construed with ἀκούσας ("hearing") and mean that he was present when it was formulated or on an occasion when it was being discussed, but this involves twisting the syntax. The most logical association is with εἰσελθών ("entering"). See Bruce, 469. Boismard (*Texte*, 372) replaces it: ". . . **their** plot. He **came** to the fort and going **to Paul**. . . ." This appears to be based on the Latin translation *venit* rather than on a genuine variant.

19 Visitation rights in Greco-Roman prisons were left to the discretion of the personnel. Security (Lucian *Tox.* 32), bribery (*Act. Paul* 3.18–19), disposition (*Mart. Perp.* 3; 9), and the status of the prisoner (and the visitor) were leading factors. Paul's status and the good will of the tribune are established by his ability to give orders to centurions, a form of authority shared with the tribune (see προσκαλέω in vv. 17 and 23). On the subject of visitors in general, see Rapske, *Roman Custody*, 382–83.

20 So also Conzelmann, 194; and Haenchen, 646.

21 In chap. 27, this role will be taken by another officer, the centurion Julius.

22 Loisy (840) was impressed by this display of consideration, which he did not believe was a common element of the makeup of such career officers. On the tactic, see Chariton *Chaer.* 1.4.5.

23 Barrett (2:1077) suggests a difference in technical nuance, but that does not abolish the irony.

24 Chrysostom asks why the tribune believed this story and answers that it was made probable on account of the previous conduct of Paul's adversaries (*Hom.* 49, p. 412). The narrator would have been pleased.

25 For another attempt, see Cadbury and Lake, 292–93. The principal witnesses are h sy^{hmg} and $\mathfrak{p}^{48}$.

of indirect for direct discourse.[26] This suggests a single, rational mind at work. Said rational mind evidently regarded the almost certainly more original conventional text as a fantasy in need of improvement. The D-Text once again reveals "precritical" concern with some of the issues that have troubled more recent scholars of a critical bent. The two most cogent of these are the size of the force employed[27] and the motive of Claudius Lysias. Rather than acting solely in the interest of protecting Paul, the tribune fears that he will be held responsible for the proposed assassination on the grounds of having accepted a bribe (cf. 24:26). The escort is reduced from 470, a good half or more of the cohort (which may have been below authorized strength and further reduced by detachments and patrols),[28] to three hundred (Clark) or an unspecified number (Boismard). This text may be construed as including two centuries.[29] A minor difficulty is δεξιολάβοι ("other arms"), a term so obscure that it must be original.[30] The term refers to military personnel,[31] as the temple police or locally recruited personnel of some type would have been unacceptable for security reasons.[32]

The reason for this operation and the task force established to execute it appears in v. 24: the rescue of Paul. The verb (διασῴζω) otherwise appears in connection with his delivery from the shipwreck (27:43-44; 28:1, 4). Both are "miracle stories," illustrating the invisible hand of Providence in similar situations: the salvation of Paul by the intervention of a Roman officer while he is in transit from one place of custody to another. This was too improbable for the D-Text,[33] but it is far from improbable for Luke, as this adventure is a warm-up for chap. 27. Luke likes good stories, including long ones, and he likes to provide them with a "moral," as it were.

■ **25** The language used to introduce the letter exhibits variety. The alternatives intend to assure the reader that the exact wording is preserved, since *ἔχουσαν τὸν τύπον τοῦτον* (lit. "having this form") could be otherwise construed. Any debate is a tempest in a teapot, since the letter was clearly written by Luke,[34] and "the

26 Moule (*Idiom Book*, 126) is willing to consider the infinitive παραστῆσαι ("provide") as imperative in meaning. This would avoid another shift from direct to direct, as in v. 22.

27 Chrysostom perceived the point: Paul is escorted "like a king" (*Hom.* 50, p. 417).

28 Barrett (2:1077–78), who notes that the figure would range from one-half to nearly all of the garrison, depending on the kind of cohort stationed there. Conzelmann (194), who accepts the estimate of one-half, says that the number is "sheer fantasy." Auxiliary cohorts had a nominal strength of one thousand. See H. M. D. Parker, G. R. Watson, and J. C. N. Coulston, "*Cohors*," *OCD*, 356.

29 That this was a mixed group is apparent in Boismard's D-Text of vv. 31-33, on which see below. One motive for editorial intervention is the strangely placed purpose clause (ὅπως πορευθῶσιν ["so that they might come"]) in v. 23. This intervenes between "two hundred soldiers" and "seventy horsemen" and could lead a critic to suspect interpolation.

30 A 33 read δεξιοβόλους.

31 For various guesses and proposals, ancient and modern, see BDAG, 217, *s.v.* Byzantine historians used the term for light-armed soldiery of some kind. Latin h evidently read *armati* ("armed men"), on which see Ropes, *Text*, 221. The lexicographical tradition defines the term as παραφύλαξ, "warder," which means jail guards. This is not likely here, unless the sense is that of "constabulary." LSJ, 379, *s.v.* says "spearman," "guards" in the plural, but this is a conjecture, probably based on the Vulgate *lancearios*. The word may have been technical jargon (Schneider, 2:339 n. 27) or it may have been a more popular expression, like "Redcoats." Saddington ("Roman Military," 2416) suggests "archers" as a possibility.

32 Against G. Kilpatrick, "Acts xxiii, 23: δεξιολάβοι," *JTS* 14 (1963) 393–94.

33 See above. Ms. h reads *deducerent* ("conduct"), supported by Ephrem, 446. Clark's reconstruction (which includes "save") is less likely.

34 See *3 Macc.* 3:30; cf. 1 Macc 11:29; 14:2; 2 Macc 1:24; 11:16; *Aristeas* 34; Josephus *Ant.* 11.12; Philo *Decal.* 32.168. The primary meaning of τύπος is "copy," but it can also mean "model." Edwin Judge makes a vigorous plea for "(exact) copy" *New Doc* 1 (1981) no. 26, pp. 77–78. Cadbury and Lake (294) are judicious but clear on authorship (Luke). Those who wish to find this an exact copy must show why it was written in Greek and, more importantly, how the author of Acts could have gained access to it. On those matters, see Haenchen, 647–48. (This is not to deny that a letter may have been written to accompany the transfer but to state that this letter is fictitious.)

account of what happened is business-like, terse, and misleading."[35] This is another way of saying that the last idea in the author's mind was that the letter gave a general purport of what Lysias wrote. Nearly every syllable is significant.

■ **27-30** Although the letter has a formally correct address,[36] it lacks such features as a thanksgiving for the sender's or a wish for the recipient's well-being, and a farewell.[37] There is no dearth of technical jargon.[38] Other omissions are more revealing. The communication should have said, in effect, "Herewith transferred to your custody is one *N. N.* Paulus, a Roman citizen (and also a citizen of Tarsus). . . ."[39] This is to say that the letter is intelligible only to the readers of the book. The body is entirely narrative, and its purpose is to contribute to the general narrative in two ways: by adding another "voice," that is, allowing the reader to see the matter from Lysias's point of view, and through providing additional information. The function of this letter is novelistic. A military officer knows what course to take with a prisoner:

> Mitranes the Commander of Guards to Oroondates the Satrap. I am sending you a young Greek I have taken prisoner. He is too handsome to remain in my service, too excellent to come before or wait upon anyone but his Divine Majesty, the King of Kings. I humbly accept that you should have the honor of conveying to him who is master of us both a gift of such value and splendor, a jewel the like of which the royal court has never beheld before and will never behold again. (*Ethiopian Story* 5.9.2)[40]

The anonymous (like Paul) subject is the hero Theagenes.[41] Mitranes, the author, seeks to receive whatever credit he can by ingratiating himself with the satrap. The object of this letter is to communicate, through the voice of an objective witness, our hero's astonishing good looks. Male beauty was not Lysias's primary concern just then. In rather good Greek, marked by substantial hypotaxis,[42] he crisply delineates a number of pertinent matters: the circumstances of the arrest, the investigation,[43] his own view of the merits of the case, his reason for sending Paul to Caesarea, and his transfer of the case to the governor's jurisdiction.

The last item (v. 30b) is fresh and not without difficulties. Although it may mean no more than "it seemed best to refer the complainants to you," it raises the question of prior jurisdiction. The narrative never states that Lysias conceded the jurisdiction of the Sanhedrin, but his own authority is left unclear. Legally, capital jurisdiction resided in the hands of the procurator. Another new factor is the existence of formal accusers, and thus of charges. Neither has been mentioned

35 Foakes Jackson, 211.

36 The word order varies. One witness (1848) omits the name. An example from the dramatic date is *OGIS* 667.3–4 (under Nero) Ἰουλίου Οὐηστίνου τοῦ κρατίστου ἡγεμόνος ("His excellency the governor Julius Vestinus"). From the approximate date of Acts comes *CPJ* 443.1–2 (117 CE) Ῥαμμίῳ Μαρτιάλι τῷ κρατίστῳ ἡγεμόνι . . . χαίρειν ("To his excellency the governor Rammius Martialis . . . Greetings"). Rammius Martialis was the prefect of Egypt. (Restorations are certain.) On the form of the greeting, see Paul Wendland, *Die urchristliche Literaturformen* (HNT; Tübingen: Mohr Siebeck, 1912) 412. There are many surveys of Greek epistolography, e.g., John L. White, *Light from Ancient Letters* (Foundations and Facets, New Testament; Philadelphia: Fortress Press, 1986) 187–221; and David Aune, *The New Testament in Its Literary Environment* (LEC 8; Philadelphia: Westminster, 1987) 158–82. For a detailed analysis, see Klauck, *Ancient Letters*, 429–34.

37 The manuscript tradition made up for this deficit. Letters embedded in ancient novels frequently pare down the formalities. See, e.g., *Ephesian Tale* 2.12 (and note the irony produced by the viewpoint and dissembling of the sender). On the function of epistolography in ancient fiction, see Pervo, *Profit*, 77. Historians also composed letters. Eupolemus, for example, supplies the text of the correspondence between Solomon and Hiram (frg. 2.33.1–34.3; cf. 1 Kgs 5:1-12; 2 Chr 2:1-16) and adds letters between Solomon and king of Egypt (frg. 2.31.1–32). See Holladay, "Acts and the Fragments," 184–90.

38 Conzelmann (195) notes eight or nine technical legal terms in vv. 27-35.

39 See also below. One would also expect the letter to state by whose hand it is being delivered, presumably the commander of the task force.

40 Trans. J. R. Morgan in Reardon, *Novels*, 452.

41 Note also the lack of a closing.

42 Verse 30 is an exception.

43 The letter does not state that Lysias had convened the Sanhedrin (v. 28).

hitherto. Verse 29 also establishes that the imbroglio of vv. 1-10 was a forensic proceeding. The circumstances of Paul's arrest are vague. One might conclude that he had been seized by Jewish officials who were about to administer summary justice (as in the case of Stephen). Not unwisely, Lysias forgoes any mention of the riot in the temple, as governors were not pleased by such disturbances. Equally amusing is the implication that he rescued Paul from "the Jews" after he had discovered his Roman citizenship. Readers know better.[44]

Lysias (and the narrator) has a motive for introducing charges and accusers. The readers learn his interpretation of 23:1-10. In language that comes rather close to the conclusions of Gallio (18:14-15; cf. also 25:19), he judges his prisoner innocent and the issue a dispute over Jewish law.[45] Verse 29 is the dramatic climax of this summary. An objective reader might wonder why the punishments of death or imprisonment were even being considered. With this phrase, the narrator reveals the hitherto unstated gravity of the situation: Paul's life and/or his freedom are at issue. Were it not for these unspecified charges, he would have been all but obliged to release the prisoner. Lysias has, in fact, two reasons for sending Paul to Caesarea: jurisdiction and the plot against him. Once more, one must ask why he did not keep Paul in close, protective custody, write Felix about the matter, which the governor could have taken up when he next came to Jerusalem, or, if such were his pleasure, have the prisoner sent to Caesarea and get down to the business of torturing suspects to identify the conspirators. Verse 30 contains an additional difficulty: in theory, the actions of sending Paul to the governor and instructing his accusers to apply to that source are simultaneous,[46] but Lysias would not have so advised them until he had received word of Paul's safe arrival or, at the earliest, upon the return of his infantry. This slip is most likely due to the author.[47] To reiterate: making sense of Lysias's actions is difficult, beginning with his arrest of Paul on the grounds that he was a terrorist. His role in Acts, to protect Paul, is over.[48]

The D-Text intensifies Lysias's reconstruction. He rescued Paul because he was claiming to be a Roman citizen. This is even more amusing than the conventional text. Verse 29 is more specific: the Law of Moses was debated, as well as "Jesus." This is an interpretation of the resurrection debate, oriented to specific Christian issues rather than to afterlife in general.[49] In place of the possibly anticlimactic "death or jail" is only "death," and the report speaks about what Paul was doing rather than charges. Not wishing to miss a chance to take a shot at the Sanhedrin, the D-Text, improving on 23:10, states that force was required to extricate Paul from the brawl.[50] Elimination of a reference to the conspiracy would have been a good idea, for it overly complicates the matter.

■ **31-33** "So within a fortnight Paul was back at Caesarea, and the apprehensions of the disciples there were fulfilled."[51] A great deal of water has passed beneath the bridge within this short time, and Paul has been "delivered" in bonds to gentile officials. The general outline is straightforward and evidently reasonable: after a night march to Antipatris, the infantry return to barracks, leaving Paul, safe from his desperate adversaries, to be escorted to the capital by the mounted force. Once there, letter and prisoner are delivered to the governor, who conducts a brief interrogation and promises to hear the case when the adversaries are available. Some of the details may derive from a source. Antipatris could have been a station on the route from Jerusalem to Caesarea, Felix was the procurator, and "Herod's Palace" would

44 On the humor here, see Hemer, *Book*, 348.

45 Haenchen (648) correctly underlines the remarkable character of this assertion.

46 Both may be construed as epistolary aorists.

47 Conzelmann, 195. Haenchen (648) says that this detail is for the reader.

48 Acts 24:22 will mention him once more, to arouse hope.

49 This was probably inspired by 25:19.

50 The motive for this comes from the D-Text interpolation at 24:7. The reviser fails to see that the Lysias of the more original text wished to minimize violence in Jerusalem.

51 Rackham, 440. Acts 21:15-17 narrates the journey to Jerusalem, which could be construed as two days in length; 21:18 marks a day, 21:27 seven days, 22:30, 23:12, and 23:32 subsequent single days.

have been suitable for confinement.[52] Problems nonetheless exist.

The first (to modern eyes) is that around sixty kilometers separate Jerusalem from Antipatris.[53] This is too long a march for any body on foot, especially at night.[54] The purpose of Felix's question is not clear. Verses 31-33 are vague. The initial subject is the collective "soldiers," presumably the infantry, who evidently return the next day, after reaching Antipatris. Sense also dictates that the cavalry are the subject of v. 33, but these interpretations depend more on deciding what the narrator wished to report than on lucid Greek.[55] The ambiguity resides in the style of popular narrative, which is willing to allow a ubiquitous "they" to perform actions.

■ **34-35** Felix's question would have been unnecessary had the letter provided the appropriate details about the prisoner, including his parentage, place of birth, and the charges against him.[56] A proper *libellus* ought to have contained these details.[57] The purpose is not explained, and A. N. Sherwin-White's attempts to shed light on it do not obviate his observation that the reader expects Felix to use the datum to avoid hearing the case.[58] One fact contained in Lysias's letter should have priority: Paul was a Roman citizen (v. 27). Felix might well have referred the case of a citizen of relatively high status to Rome or, at least, to the proconsul in Antioch. As a citizen of Tarsus, a "free" city, Paul would not necessarily have been subject to ordinary provincial prosecution.[59] Sherwin-White attempted to tackle the data presented in Acts 21–26 *seriatim* and provide an acceptable independent explanation of each item.[60] He did not offer a comprehensive picture based on the standing of Roman citizens before the law. Another deficit was his failure even to consider whether some of these data were unreliable.[61] The mystery remains. The narrator may have introduced Felix's question to generate suspense.[62] Its most obvious literary function is to provide verisimilitude.

52 The assumption is that Herod's principal palace would have become the praetorium of the Roman government. Praetoria included cells and guard barracks (Phil 1:13; 4:22). Josephus (*Bell.* 1:408) speaks of "palaces" (βασίλεια). For a conjecture about the locality (with a photo), see Kenneth Holum et al., *King Herod's Dream: Caesarea on the Sea* (New York: Norton, 1988) 86–87; and Rapske, *Roman Custody*, 156–57, with appropriate reservations.

53 The location of Antipatris is not absolutely certain. Moshe Kochavi ("Antipatris," *ABD* 1:272–74) is confident about the site, but see also Fitzmyer, 729; and Barrett, 2:1085–86.

54 An exception is Witherington (697), who speaks of what Roman troops could do "when a crisis situation was involved." That may have been the case, but even if one agrees that this was a crisis, the detachment was large enough to beat off an attack by fewer than fifty fanatics and had no need for a forced march. Finally, these were not Roman regulars.

55 Strictly construed, the participle ἐάσαντες ("allowing") in v. 32 is "the soldiers," but one doubts that they acted collectively. See Barrett, 2:1086.

56 Lucius, suddenly transformed from animal to human form in the theater at Thessalonica, was in danger of being lynched. He rushed to the governor and begged to be placed in protective custody. The official asked for his name, those of his parents and relatives, and of his city. These questions he answered, stating that his native city was Patras in Achaea (*Onos* 54–55). Similar interrogations appear in martyr acts (e.g., *Mart. Carpi* 24–27 and *Mart. Justini et al.* 4.7–8).

57 Sherwin-White (*Roman Society*, 54–55) describes the requirement of a *libellus* advising provincial authorities about criminal matters.

58 Ibid., 55–56.

59 Ibid.

60 Sherwin-White, *Roman Society*, 48–70. He built on the work of Theodor Mommsen, "Die Rechtsverhältnisse des Apostels Paulus," *ZNW* 2 (1902) 81–96, with which he was in critical dialogue. For more recent work on these questions, see p. 655 n. 45.

61 An exception is the status of Cilicia, which Sherwin-White (*Roman Society*, 57) allows may not have been a province at the dramatic date. Cilicia became a distinct province under Vespasian (69–79) in 72 CE, according to Suetonius *Vesp.* 8.4, on which see Arnold H. M. Jones, *The Cities of the Eastern Roman Provinces* (2nd ed.; Oxford: Clarendon, 1971) 208. See also Pervo, *Dating*, 338–39.

62 The style, a mixture of indirect and direct discourse, is Lucan, and the anachronistic reference to Cilicia (previous note) suggests that it probably did not derive from a contemporary source.

The D-Text of vv. 31-35, as reconstructed by Boismard,[63] appears to address some of these issues. In v. 31 it omits (with $\mathfrak{P}^{74}$) "at night." This could be taken as dealing with the problem of distance; that is, the journey could have taken longer than one night. Verses 32-33a appear in a shorter sentence: "The next day, after dismissing **the soldiers** [ ] to the fort, **they came** to Caesarea. . . ."[64] This would evidently imply that the entire military escort departed at Antipatris (leaving the two centurions to conduct Paul to the capital?). This indicates a continuing desire to reduce the excessive size of the force employed. In v. 34 Boismard (following gig) eliminates the reference to Cilicia, but Clark[65] includes this in a text that transforms the entire dialogue into direct speech.[66]

Excursus: Felix

Neither the full name nor the exact dates and extent of Felix's tenure as procurator of Judea are known.[67] Whether his *gentilicum* was "Antonius" or "Claudius" is not material to Acts,[68] but the date on which he left office is considered important for Pauline chronology. Felix was an ex-slave who stood high enough in the mind of Claudius to be given the Judean appointment. This was sufficient to guarantee a hostile evaluation from Tacitus (*Hist.* 5.9; *Ann.* 12.54). Josephus is probably more objective, but ultimately holds Felix responsible for the increase in rebellious activity (*Bell.* 2.252–65; *Ant.* 20.160–172). Felix was neither the first nor the last colonial official to discover that counter-insurgency campaigns can fuel insurgencies. One of his victims was the insurgent leader Eleazer, whom he captured and, interestingly, sent to Rome (*Bell.* 2.253; *Ant.* 20.160).[69] While procurator, he married Drusilla, daughter of Agrippa I. This suggests, romantic interests notwithstanding, a desire to forge an alliance with the Judean ruling class. According to Josephus, Felix obtained his office on the recommendation of the high priest Jonathan (*Ant.* 20.162).

Luke's evident source was Josephus,[70] from whom he gleaned information about Felix's Jewish wife and his initial support from the Jewish aristocracy. He used this information to construct a portrait of a governor who worked to retain the support of the native ruling class and therefore denied justice to Paul.[71] In historical fact, Felix represents a Greco-Roman success story about a slave who rose to considerable power, accumulated considerable wealth, and persuaded a series of highly placed women to marry him.

---

63 Boismard, *Texte*, 380–81.

64 τῇ δὲ ἐπαύριον ἐάσαντες τοὺς στρατιώτας εἰς τὴν παρεμβολὴν ἦλθον εἰς τὴν Καισάρειαν.

65 Clark, 152. Without naming Clark, Boismard (*Texte*, 381) rejects this, referring to vv. 19 and 22. Those examples would lead one to suspect that the D-Text would utilize indirect discourse in both vv. 34 and 35.

66 Boismard also reports the simple ἀκούσομαι ("I shall hear") for the more technical (Cadbury and Lake, 296) διακούσομαι ("hold a hearing").

67 See Kirsopp Lake, "The Chronology of Acts," in Lake and Cadbury, *Additional Notes*, 445–74, esp. 464–66; Schürer, *History*, 1:459–66; Smallwood, *The Jews*, 266–71; M. Wolter, "Φῆλιξ," *EDNT* 3:420; Omerzu, *Prozess*, 404–6; Saddington, "Roman Military," 2426–27; and David C. Braund, "Felix," *ABD* 2:783. Barrett (2:1080–81) provides a judicious summary, while Conzelmann (194–95) cites a number of the primary sources and has good comments on the chronological question. Alexis Bunine has made a recent argument for 56 as the date of Festus's accession ("Paul, Jacques, Félix, Festus et les autres: pour une révision de la chronologie des derniers procurateurs de la Palestine," *RB* 111 [2004] 387–408, 531–62).

68 See Schürer, *History*, 1:460 n. 19; Frederick F. Bruce, "The Full Name of the Procurator Felix," *JSNT* 1 (1978) 33–36; and Colin J. Hemer, "The Name of Felix Again," *JSNT* 31 (1987) 45–49. The matter remains open: Frederick E. Brenk and Filippo Canali De Rossi ("The 'Notorious' Felix, Procurator of Judea, and His Many Wives [Acts 23–24]," *Bib* 82 [2001] 410–17) indicate that an inscription from Bir el-Malik does not solve the problem.

69 In *Antiquities*, Josephus states that Felix captured Eleazer by offering him a safe conduct. The term used for his ruse is ἐνέδρα (cf. Acts 23:16). Readers of Acts would have no reason to associate Felix with the revolt of Theudas mentioned in 5:36, but he repressed that revolt also. See Pervo, *Dating*, 152–60.

70 On Luke's use of Josephus for his portrait of Felix, see Pervo, *Dating*, 42–43 and 186–87.

71 This decision almost reverses the efforts of commentators like Haenchen (650) to discourage reading Felix's character from Tacitus and Josephus. Such warnings are appropriate insofar as they insist that one must allow the text of Acts to speak for itself.

Barrett ultimately concludes that "[h]e [Luke] has probably written up imaginatively a bare historical outline: 'Paul was transferred to Caesarea.'"[72] The following comments seek to develop the implications of Barrett's reluctant opinion. The literary purpose—should the question arise—is aptly illustrated in a segment from *An Ethiopian Story* (8.2-16). The satrap (a Persian provincial governor) summons his entrusted eunuch Bagoas to take fifty horsemen to Memphis and return with Theagenes and Charikleia (the heroes). With Bagoas go two brief letters, one to Arsake (a major villain), the other to the chief eunuch at Memphis. This is the former:

> Oroondates to Arsake: Send me Theagenes and Charikleia, the brother and sister who were taken captive and are now slaves of the Great King; I shall send them on to the king. Send them to me of your own free will; if you refuse, they shall be brought to me all the same, and Achaimenes' allegations will be confirmed.[73]

The sequel is equally brief. The party arrived in the dead of night, aroused the sentries, and made their way to the satrap's palace. Bagoas delivered the letter to Euphrates, encouraging prompt action to take advantage of the darkness and achieve surprise. The couple were led outside in their chains, placed on horses, and encircled for security. The party set out posthaste for Thebes but was ambushed on the road just short of Syene.

Heliodorus wrote a good two centuries after Acts and serves to show how adventures could be concocted. A much more general parallel that Luke may well have read can be found in Josephus's story of an attempted assassination of Herod the Great (*Ant.* 15.282–91).[74] They share five structural elements: Herod, like Paul (Acts 21:21, 28), was accused of abandoning Israelite traditions (§280). Men (two) conspire to kill Herod at any risk, swearing an oath (*συνομοσάμενοι* [§282; cf. *συνωμοσία*, §288]). More than forty conspire to kill Paul or perish, engaging in an oath (*συνωμοσία* [23:12-13]). Herod will be ambushed in the theater (§284), Paul en route to the Sanhedrin (23:15).[75] In both cases, the plot was exposed—that against Herod by a spy (§286), that against Paul through an informer (23:16). Both plots were thwarted (§§286–89; Acts 23:12-35), but by different means.[76] Luke may have taken some inspiration from the story about Herod,[77] but the more important value of this parallel is to underline Paul's importance. Unimportant agitators do not give rise to elaborate conspiracies. Haenchen's judgment endures: "[A] dreary matter of routine is transformed into a narrative full of breathless suspense."[78]

The chapter as a whole adds evidence to Luke's dossier against the Jews, who function as implacable villains of the most ruthless and unprincipled sort.[79] A further suggestion is that debates with Jewish leaders lead only to difficulties and should be avoided. In such hardening of the lines, Luke may be compared with the Pastor, who also rejected "dialogue" with false teachers.[80] Luke is not arguing for strong boundaries but justifying their existence.

72 Barrett, 2:1086.

73 Trans. J. R. Morgan, in Reardon, *Novels*, 518.

74 The numbers in the following comments refer to the relevant sections of Josephus.

75 Aseneth also had to endure an ambush from which she barely escaped, despite her escort of six hundred (*Jos. Asen.* 23–28). In Dictys's fictional account of the Trojan War (*Ephemeris* 3.15), Achilles kills Hector in an ambush. This was not flattering to Achilles.

76 The informer in the plot against Herod was dismembered (§289). Cf. Acts 23:10.

77 See Pervo, *Dating*, 191–92. For a betrayed plot, see also Josephus *Vit.* 104–11.

78 Haenchen, 650.

79 Acts 23:12-35 takes advantage of Greco-Roman sensitivities about fanatics, not least nationalistic fanatics.

80 See 1 Tim 6:20; 2 Tim 2:3, 14; Titus 3:9.

24

24:1-23 Paul before Felix

1/ Five days[a] after *Paul had been conveyed to Caesarea* Ananias the high priest came down *from Jerusalem*. With him were some members of the Sanhedrin[b] and one Tertullus, a professional advocate. They pressed charges against Paul to the governor. 2/ Bidden to speak,[c] Tertullus presented the opening statement for the prosecution:

24:2b-8: Conventional Text

"Your Excellency, Felix, through your attentive care we enjoy substantial peace, and this country has welcomed numerous improvements[d] through your administration, 3/ always and everywhere. For this we remain fully grateful.

4/ "I have no desire to drag this out.[e] Please listen, with your accustomed courtesy, to this brief summary of the facts. 5/ We have discovered that this creature is a pest. A ringleader of the Nazorean faction, he foments rebellions[f] among all[g] Jews throughout the empire. 6/ He even attempted to defile the temple, at which point we put him under arrest.

8/ "You need only interrogate him to verify all of our allegations."

24:2b-8: D-Text[h]

"Your Excellency, Felix, [ ] we enjoy substantial peace, and this country has always and everywhere welcomed numerous improvements.[i] 3/ For this we remain fully grateful.

4/ "I have no desire to drag this out. I ask that you listen patiently [ ].[j]

5/ We have discovered[k] that this creature is a pest. A ringleader of the Nazorean faction, he foments rebellion, *not only in our own nation but in almost the entire empire.* 6/ He even attempted to defile the temple, at which point we put him under arrest. *Now we intended to try him by our law, (7/) but Tribune Lysias came on the scene and, with a strong display of force, extracted him from our custody.*

8/ *"He directed that Paul's accusers should appear before you.* By interrogating Lysias you can . . ."

9/ The Jews then pitched in to affirm that matters were as he had stated.[l]

10/ When the governor gave him leave,[m] Paul spoke:

"Since I know that you have served this nation in a judicial capacity[n] for many years, I shall cheerfully speak in my own defense. 11/ You can establish that I arrived in Jerusalem on pilgrimage no more than twelve days ago. 12/ No one ever found me engaging in individual discussions or collecting crowds[o] in temple, synagogue, or anywhere else in the city,

13/ nor can they substantiate their present accusations
against me.
14/ "But one thing I will admit to you: I do revere our ancestral God and believe all that is commanded in the Law and written in the Prophets.[p] 15/ My hope in God is also that of those who accuse me: we look forward to a coming[q] resurrection of both the good and the wicked.[r] I serve God by following the Movement, which they denominate a 'faction.' 16/ In this service I likewise strive[s] ardently at all times[t] to be free from any conscious offense to God and to mortals. 17/ After an absence of many years I came here to bring funds to my people[u] and to offer sacrifices. 18/ They found me engaged in these rites, in a state of ritual purity. There was no crowd, no agitation, 19/ but there were some Jews from Asia—if they really had any accusations to make against me, they would have to be present.[v] 20/ Well, they aren't here, so, let these people who are here speak for themselves about what I did wrong while I was standing before the Sanhedrin. 21/ Maybe this is it:[w] that one sentence I shouted while in their midst, 'The issue about which I am arraigned before you this day is the resurrection of the dead.'"[x]

Resurrection of good & wicked

22/ Felix,[y] now fairly well informed[z] about the Movement, halted the proceedings with the announcement: "I shall reach a decision on these matters when Tribune Lysias puts in an appearance."[aa] 23/ He ordered the centurion to retain Paul in custody[bb] but not in maximum security. There were to be no restrictions upon the efforts of his friends[cc] to attend to his needs.[dd]

a A reads "some days."

b 𝔐 sy^p read "the presbyters," more or less the entire Sanhedrin.

c An alternative is to understand this as applying to Paul: "When Paul had been summoned . . ." This is better Greek, for it avoids an improper genitive absolute, and makes better sense. Haenchen supports this and appeals to other reports of trials. B omits *αὐτοῦ*, a difficult reading that almost requires associating the participle *κληθέντος* ("having been summoned") as a genitive absolute with an implied subject. Luke does not shun such constructions, and the parallel in v. 10 gives some weight to the translation given.

d 𝔐 reads κατορθώματα, more like "successes." 36. 453. *et al.* add "many," which is quite in the spirit of things.

e The *v.l.* κόπτω can mean "weary" (LSJ, 979, *s.v.* 13), but Luke was unlikely to use it in this metaphorical sense. It is probably due to the unusual use of ἐγκόπτω. See Cadbury and Lake, 298; and Gustav Stählin ("ἐγκόπτω," *TDNT* 3:855–57, esp. 855 n. 1), who attributes the usage to the LXX.

f 𝔐 sy sa read the singular στάσιν. This is generic ("rebellion"). On the dative with this noun, see BDF §190 (3).

g 𝔓^{74} omits "all," presumably as redundant.

h Boismard, *Texte*, 382–84.

i Boismard omits διὰ σοῦ ("through you").

j Boismard omits σε ("you") and συντόμως ("briefly").

k The conventional text has the participle εὑρόντες ("having found"). Boismard reads the indicative.

l D-Text witnesses 614. 2147. sy^{h**} preface v. 9 with a genitive absolute: "After he had said these things . . ."

m The D-Text (Boismard, *Texte*, 384) adds "to defend himself." H^{mg} says that Paul took on a divine appearance. Metzger (*Textual Commentary*, 434) calls this "a curious Western expansion." He might well have said that this is making Acts look like Apocryphal Acts, as Barrett (2:1100) recognizes. Closer to home is Acts 6:15. An editor determined that here and in 26:1, Paul should enjoy no less a privilege than did Stephen.

n E Ψ 323. 614. 945 *et al.* sy^{h} modify "judge" with "fair" (δίκαιον). Boismard ignores this reading, which has D-Text support and is the *lectio difficilior.*

o 𝔐 reads ἐπισύστασις ("gathering a crowd for insurrectionary purposes"). The rendition "collecting crowds" views the obscure phrase ἐπίστασιν ποιοῦντα ὄχλου as metonymic: "causing people to stop and thus forming a crowd."

p ℵ^{2} A 33 m omit ἐν τοῖς, presumably to equate the two sections of "the canon." Inclusion of the phrase is more original, distinguishing between Torah as setting forth a way of life and the Prophets as a source of doctrine. (Note that "Law" and "Way" utilize the same preposition: κατά, referring to a mode of existence.)

q A future infinitive with μέλλειν ("to be going to happen") looks redundant, but it is good Greek.

r E Ψ m sy pedantically specify resurrection of the "dead."

s 𝔐 gig read ἔχων, in effect "I strive . . . because I have. . . ." This removes any emphasis that Paul had to work hard to maintain "a good conscience."

t The D-Text (Boismard, *Texte*, 385) omits the phrase διὰ πάντος ("at all times").

u *Or:* "I came to my people to bring. . . ." This is preferred by Weiser, 2:629–30.

v The syntax is difficult. The conditional clause in v. 19 looks like a "future less vivid" (If they should have any charges to make, they would have to be here). Cf. Smyth, *Greek Grammar*, §2329), with ἄν omitted (on which see Moule, *Idiom Book*, 149). Barrett (2:1110) finds the optative incorrect, however. Cf. 20:16. A number of late MSS. omit the conjunction δέ ("and," etc.) in v. 19, an improvement. The present δεῖ ("must") is another, but less felicitous, variant.

w The conjunction ἤ can be equivalent to ἀλλ᾽ ἤ ("except [that]") after τι. See Barrett, 2:1111.

x Verses 20-21 present difficulties. ἤ (usually "or") can convey an adversative sense in interrogative contexts. The variant εἰ ("if," 𝔭^{74} A C *pc*) may be an improvement. "Itacism" is a factor. For an explanation of the apparently barbarous attribution of the demonstrative in v. 21 (ταύτης, "this"), see BDF §292. The D-Text (Boismard, *Texte*, 385) reads ". . . **whether** they found **any** wrongdoing applicable **to me** (εἴ τι . . . ἐν ἐμοί . . .).

y To ease the rather abrupt transition, m sa read, "Once he had heard these things, Felix halted them. . . ."

z Cadbury and Lake (304) and BDF §244 (2) view the comparative as a superlative, but the context does not support this. It is better taken as elative (so also Bruce, 482). The same question arises in v. 26 (πυκνότερον). Less likely is a true comparative: "more accurate," which would have to be supplemented by understanding "than his previous knowledge." See Witherington, 713.

aa The D-Text (Boismard, *Texte*, 386) reads: "I shall **hear you again** when **the Tribune** puts in an appearance." This conforms to the outcome, as Felix did not reach a decision.

bb Verses 22-23 avoid the active voice. See Barrett, 2:1112. It is acceptable to construe τηρεῖσθαι as a middle: "have retained." The present means "remain in custody."

cc Lit. "his own people" (τῶν ἰδίων), which could mean, or include, family, friends, or servants.

dd 𝔐 sa add "or visit." This is a conflation with the D-Text (Boismard, *Texte*, 386), which has no reference to "friends" (previous note): "prohibit no one to visit him."

Excursus: The Trials of Paul

A venerable school of research has assumed that the reports about Paul's legal situation in Acts 21–28, with particular reference to chaps. 24–26, are historical in nature, derived from available records and the possible presence of the author. For support, these scholars turn to Roman law or analyses of it.[1] This assumption is open to question. A number of the conclusions are circular, because they depend on scholarly analyses that utilize Acts to reconstruct legal content and procedure; and, as the footnotes to this chapter will demonstrate, their findings are often based on unwarranted inferences and assertions. If the proof of the pudding is in the eating, the results of all of the space devoted to Paul's legal situation will be disappointing, for one is less clear about that situation at the close of the book than in chap. 24, where explicit charges are first raised.[2] Cadbury's judgment that "the narrative in Acts is an untechnical account with apologetic motive" remains valid.[3] The narrator is overly successful in demonstrating not only Paul's innocence but also the recognition of it. This makes for fine reading and excellent apologetic, but it does nothing to advance claims for the historical value of the narrative.

Putative primary sources for the events of chap. 24 are unlikely to have contained more than the briefest of summaries, yet those possibilities far outshine what can be proposed for chaps. 25–26.[4] From the strictly historical viewpoint of narrating the essential data, all that needed to be said about Paul could have been recorded in fewer than thirty verses of summary: arrest in Jerusalem, transfer to Caesarea, inconclusive trial under Felix, interrupted trial under Festus, transfer to Rome (in the course of which he survived a shipwreck), and *the final disposition of his case there*. The narrator might then have looked to other leaders and localities, as he had done after chaps. 8, 12, and 15, or stopped.

If one allows that the message of Acts has become embedded in what amounts to a biography of Paul, much, if not all, of chaps. 21–28 is rather more justified, although this concession has major ramifications for the evaluation of the work, which would take on the shape of a story of Paul with a long preface. The dominant question facing interpreters of every stripe and persuasion is why Luke devoted a good one-fourth of Acts to this subject. His method was literary, that is, he makes his points by telling stories. The stories are good, some of the best in Acts, and few authors have wrung more interest, excitement, and suspense out of such unpleasant facts.[5] The readers' hopes are raised, dashed, and whirled about in the narrative maelstrom, while the chief character remains serene.

A related and vital dimension of the historical question is the oft-noted parallelism between the trials of Jesus in Luke and the trials of Paul in Acts. In Luke 22–23 Jesus appears before the Sanhedrin, Pilate, Herod, and Pilate. Paul appears before the Sanhedrin, Felix, Festus, and Agrippa in Acts 23–26. Each thus faces the Sanhedrin, a Roman governor (twice), and a member of the Herodian family. The large number of correspondences in sequence and

1. At the head of this orientation stands Theodor Mommsen, "Die Rechtsverhältnisse des Apostels Paulus," *ZNW* 2 (1902) 81–96, whose conclusions were taken up and revised by Sherwin-White, *Roman Society*, 48–70. More recent exponents include Hemer, *Book* 129–30 *et passim*; Tajra, *Trial*; Rapske, *Roman Custody*, 158–64; Bruce Winter, "Official Proceedings and the Forensic Speeches in Acts 24–26," in Winter and Clarke, *Setting*, 305–36; Erika Heusler, *Kapitalprozesse im lukanischen Doppelwerk: Die Verfahren gegen Jesus und Paulus in exegetischer und rechtshistorischer Analyse* (NTAbh NF 38; Münster: Aschendorff, 2000); and Omerzu, *Prozess*.
2. Pervo, *Profit*, 46–47.
3. H. J. Cadbury, "Roman Law and the Trial of Paul," in Lake and Cadbury, *Additional Notes*, 297–338, citing 298. Cadbury was not an expert on Roman law, the study of which has advanced in the past seven decades, but he was sensitive to Luke as an author, did not seek to defend the accuracy of the narrative, and addressed the questions with perspicacity and rigorous logic.
4. This commentary regards the hypotheses that the author was present on the scene and/or that he had access to official records as, for multiple reasons, untenable. See pp. 11–14. The challenge facing those who uphold one or both of these views is to explain why such a well-informed author did such an inadequate job of reporting.
5. Paul's own sentiments and struggles are apparent beneath the careful rhetoric of Phil 1:12-26. The Pastor develops (and exploits) these feelings in 2 Tim 4:6-18. Although the diary of Perpetua is probably not fully authentic, its picture of the experience of prisoners is quite moving (*Acts of Perpetua and Companions*). Acts comes closest to such sentiments in the speech at Miletus (20:17-35), prior to Paul's arrest. See Matthew L. Skinner, "Unchained Ministry: Paul's Roman Custody (Acts 21–28) and the Sociopolitical Outlook of the Book of Acts," in Phillips, *Acts and Ethics*, 79–95.

detail lead to the conclusion that this is not a matter of general parallels but the construction of duplicate patterns.[6] Recognition of these patterns has a dampening effect on claims of historical accuracy. In these trial scenes, Luke is very much a creator rather than a reporter of history. His goal is to show what the story of Paul *means*. All of this is to say no more than that in Acts 21–28, Luke *is* an evangelist "with apologetic motive."

Analysis

Acts 24 contains two episodes—both introduced by the phrase "after *X* days," vv. 1-23 and 24-25—and concludes with a summary in vv. 26-27. The first relates a formal trial (or hearing) before the governor, with both parties present.[7] The second episode briefly recounts Paul's interview with Felix and his wife, Drusilla. The pace is initially rapid and promising, only to slow and eventually creak to a halt. Readers' hopes follow a kindred path. Within five days, the accusers, among whom was the high priest, making one of his rare appearances outside of Jerusalem, appeared. They had equipped themselves with a professional orator, one Tertullus. Paul, who is not without experience in this area, will be competent to speak for himself.

Luke shows that he has not exhausted his capacity for variety. Readers are treated to a brief rhetorical duel.[8] The need to be succinct leaves Tertullus room for no more than a compact pack of lies and a recommendation that the judge verify the same by interrogating Paul. After a brief summary of the actual facts and an affirmation of his loyalty to the ancestral faith, Paul opens the subject of resurrection. As in Athens (17:32), that topic brings matters to a halt. Felix notes that the testimony of Lysias will be required. Since readers know the tribune's assessment of the situation, their hopes rise, supported by Felix's relaxation of custody.[9] Had he believed the claims that Paul was a dangerous revolutionary, the governor would not have taken these steps.

Behind this vivid account may have stood data derived from the same source as the preceding material. All that remains is a few names—Felix, the high priest Ananias, possibly the lawyer Tertullus—and an indication that Felix held a hearing on the case but reached no conclusion before his term of office expired. Meager as this harvest is, it is not certain. The name of Ananias, whose tenure extended from about 47 to about 59,[10] could have been derived from Josephus, and that of Tertullus invented.[11] The length of the delay in reaching a decision and the reasons for it, presuming that the data are accurate, are irretrievably lost.[12] Since Theodor Mommsen, it has been claimed that this account reflects Roman legal procedure, with the inference that it is a good and full historical source.[13] Barrett identifies a difficulty with this conclusion: "[T]here is not much procedure in the narrative." Each side speaks and the judge postpones a decision.[14] H. S. Brown has taken up the matter from the perspective of legal reports rather than textbook law and concludes that Acts lacks the data

6 See, among others, Talbert, *Literary Patterns*, 17–18; O'Toole, *Unity*, 68–71; and Jerome Neyrey, *The Passion according to Luke: A Redaction Study of Luke's Soteriology* (New York: Paulist, 1985) 98–107. Consult Table 6, p. 533.

7 This fulfills one part of Jesus' prophecy in Luke 21:12: "you will be brought before kings and governors (ἡγεμόνας)." Chapter 26 will supply the monarch.

8 The appeal of trial scenes, especially brief ones, to ancient audiences is clear from their appearance in ancient novels (see p. 556 n. 95) and in Lucian, notably *Bis acc.* (esp. 16–34).

9 The narrator does not say that Paul was kept in a prison cell within the praetorium. Readers are free to envision a room, presumably with a guard at the door.

10 On Ananias, see p. 572 n. 9. He may be named on a shard from Masada. See Fergus Millar, *The Roman Near East: 31 BC–AD 337* (Cambridge, Mass.: Harvard University Press, 1993) 361–62.

11 Tertullus was a common name (Hans Georg Gundel, "Tertullus," *Kleine Pauly* 5:615). See also Williams, "Personal Names," 112. He is not clearly represented as either a Jew or a gentile. In truth, it makes no difference whether he was a historical figure or a Lucan invention.

12 See Lüdemann, *Acts*, 318–20; and Weiser, 2:627.

13 Mommsen is cited by Sherwin-White, *Roman Society*, 48, followed by Hemer, *Book*, 129–30. See also Rapske, *Roman Custody*, 158–64; and Winter, "Official Proceedings," 305–36.

14 Barrett, 2:1092.

found in accounts of trials and cannot be said to reflect such records. He concludes that the material is literary in function, comparable to trial reports in ancient novels.[15] The language of v. 2, for example, is better explained by reference to Luke 23:2 (trial of Jesus) than by discussion of legal papyri.[16]

Ancient historians could utilize pairs or groups of speeches to represent different viewpoints on a problem.[17] That is not the case here, as readers know all that is required, and Luke has no interest in multiple viewpoints. Acts 24 presents a duel between "the good guys" and "the bad guys." Such competitions raise suspense and offer a bit of oratorical entertainment in contrast to such exhilarating adventures as those reported in 23:12-35.[18] The two speeches[19] exhibit a similar pattern:

Tertullus	**Paul**
I. Vv. 2b-4. Proem, *captatio benevolentiae*	I. V. 10b. Proem, *captatio benevolentiae*
II. Vv. 5-6. *Narratio* (encompassing thesis)	II. Vv. 11-13. *Narratio* (encompassing thesis)
A. V. 5. Character of accused (ethos)	III. Vv. 14-16. "Confession," Digression on "the Movement" (ethos)
B. V. 6. Alleged behavior of accused (narrative proper)	IV. Vv. 17-18. *Narratio* resumed. Actual behavior
	V. Vv. 19-21. Demand for relevant witnesses and testimony
	A. Vv. 19-20. Demand for relevant witnesses
III. V. 8. *Peroratio*: Examine the accused.	B. V. 21. (= *Peroratio*). Actual statement and "real" charge

15 H. Stephen Brown, "Paul's Hearing at Caesarea: A Preliminary Comparison with Legal Literature of the Roman Period," *SBLSP 1996* (Atlanta: Scholars Press, 1996) 319–32. His primary basis of comparison is the episode from *Callirhoe* cited in p. 556 nn. 52, 55. Brown seeks to demonstrate not that no such trial or record existed but that Acts 24 does not show the use of a report. Bruce Winter (p. 592 n. 1) begins with petitions to the courts, which leads him to the rhetorical handbooks and rhetorical analysis of the speeches. He finds the speeches rhetorically appropriate and argues that Acts 24 reflects history. For Schwartz ("Trial Scene," 129), the speech of Tertullus "is a near parody of rhetorical correctness." She points to *Leuc. Clit.* 8.7–15, where the villain, Thersander, hires a rhetor, but matters do not work out as he wished.

16 Luke 23:2: *Ἤρξαντο δὲ κατηγορεῖν αὐτοῦ λέγοντες* ("They began to accuse him, saying . . ."), words occurring in 24:2. Note also *εὕραμεν* ("we found"; cf. 24:5) and *τὸ ἔθνος ἡμῶν* ("our nation"; cf. 24:2).

17 See, e.g., Thucydides 1.32–43 (dispute over Corcyra); 1.66–78 (debate at Sparta). An utterly fictional debate decorates the *Alexander Romance* 2.2.5–2.5.1, on which see Pervo, *Profit*, 76.

18 Rhetorical duels go back to epic, e.g., Homer *Il.* 1.101–87, and drama, e.g., Euripides *Tro.* 914–1032. Two examples from romantic novels are Chariton *Chaer.* 5.6–7 and Longus *Daphn.* 2.15–16. See Derek Hogan, "Paul's Defense: A Comparison of the Forensic Speeches in Acts, *Callirhoe,* and *Leucippe and Clitiphon*," *PerspRelStud* 29 (2002) 73–87.

19 Studies of these defense speeches include Fred Veltmann, "The Defense Speeches of Paul in Acts," in Talbert, *Perspectives*, 243–56; Neyrey, "Forensic Defense Speech," 210–24; and Long, "Paulusbild," 87–105.

The speeches interlock. Verses 11-13 take up Tertullus's statements in inverse order. Verse 11 utilizes the δύναμαι and ἐπιγιγνώσκω ("be able," "verify") of v. 8, while v. 12 denies the charge of temple profanation (v. 6) and agitation (v. 5). The scene is a single narrative unit. All three "characters," prosecution, defense, and judge, focus on testimony (vv. 8, 19-20, 22). The prosecution calls no witnesses, arguing that the defendant will incriminate himself. The other two refer to witnesses who are not present.

Although both speeches are forensic in type, these are not skeletons of speeches (i.e., outlines); they purport to be actual speeches.[20] An outline of each in indirect discourse would have been acceptable. Tertullus's speech is seriously unbalanced. Granting that a *captatio benevolentiae* is a good thing, 30 percent of Tertullus's speech is devoted to this amenity. There are nearly three verses of exordium, two of narration, and one of peroration. Tertullus reiterates the cries of the Ephesian Jews in Acts 21:28. Paul is, in general, an ecumenical menace responsible for many civic disturbances among the Jews of the Roman east, in fulfillment of his role as leader of a pernicious sect. In particular, Paul attempted to profane the temple, but was seized by Jewish authorities, evidently before he could commit this vile act. Rather than summon witnesses—readers of Acts know that false witnesses are available when needed (6:13)—or offer anything remotely resembling proof, Tertullus invites the testimony of Paul. This prosecution would have been no more incompetent had it been designed by the defense—as it in fact was.

Realism, even verisimilitude, is lacking in this episode. A realistic presentation that accorded with the plot of Acts would have represented the Jewish authorities as asserting jurisdiction and presenting those witnesses to affirm the charge of profanation (together, if possible, with the gentile offenders, who would have been subject to summary execution). No less noteworthy in their absence are witnesses for the defense. The devotees of 21:23 could have demonstrated beyond a doubt that they were not gentiles. In their support, James and the Christian presbyters could have offered rather convincing testimony that Paul was engaged in an act of noteworthy piety. In terms of Acts' own construction of the facts, this episode lacks credibility. To the hypothetical counter-argument that this was but a preliminary hearing, as indicated in v. 22, it can be stated that these witnesses, necessary elements of a proper trial, never appear. If it be stated that Paul aborted the process by his appeal, it must also be stated that Paul's appeal is, in the context provided by Acts, incomprehensible. Paul's Odysseus-like versatility is once more on display. He is able to make a superior case in a confrontation with a professional orator. Techniques and methods are flexible, but his ethos remains firm. The Lucan Paul is a loyal and observant Jew (v. 14).

The D-Text of vv. 5-8 enjoyed sufficient popularity to find its way into the Textus Receptus. This sentence represents, in both editions, an unsuccessful attempt to write a Greek period.[21] In terms of grammar, the D-Text looks like an effort to resolve the syntactical difficulties of the shorter text. Its content builds on a perceived gap in the narrative created by a fine piece of dissembling: "we arrested Paul." The underlying "historical fact" is that Paul was being beaten to death by a mob (21:31). The difficulty this interpolation (v. 7) explains is why Paul is no longer in Jewish custody. In so doing, it levies 23:30, but ineptly. Continuity with the context would have been improved by saying that Lysias directed "us" to appear before Felix. The longer text does offer one logical improvement: παρ' οὗ ("from whom") in v. 8 refers to Lysias rather than to Paul.[22] This is more logical and creates a nice link with v. 22, but it overlooks both the way in which Luke has tied the speeches together and his tactic of having Tertullus serve up a ball that Paul can easily return for a score. (A further, and insuperable, problem is that the invitation

20 Conzelmann (198–99) provides a number of references illustrating the conventional character of many of the phrases.

21 The conjunction γάρ is a difficulty. "We arrested" (ἐκρατήσαμεν) should be the main verb, but it has been placed in a subordinate clause, leaving the initial participle dangling. On the anacoluthon, see BDF §467. The D-Text (p. 589) corrects this. A gap exists between the relative clauses ending v. 6 and beginning v. 7. The verb ἀπεδεχόμεθα ("we welcome") in v. 3 has no object, but this is not a gaffe. See Cadbury and Lake, 297.

22 See Barrett, 2:1100.

to interrogate Lysias would lead to exposure of the falsehood of Tertullus's construction of the case.)[23]

Comment

■ **1** The narrator makes limited effort to set the scene of a formal trial.[24] A delegation from the Sanhedrin[25] led by the high priest appears five days later[26] to lay charges. Paul's presence is not certainly acknowledged until v. 10.[27] The presence of Tertullus is sufficient indication of the formal character of the situation.[28] Self-defense was not fashionable.[29]

■ **2** Even a superficial reading reveals that this little speech is mellifluous, with a full ration of paronomasia, alliteration, and assonance.[30] For those "in the know," probably including the author, references to "peace"[31] and "improvements" are ironic, but for the ideal reader this was the kind of thing one said in addressing authorities.[32] *Captationes benevolentiae* are always somewhat manipulative.[33] Specifically here, as one interested in peace, Felix will not look with favor on a career disturber of the peace. His commitment to reform will lead to correct the miscarriage of justice that removed Paul from the custody of Jewish judges.[34] Promises of brevity were doubtless welcome.[35] Intelligent rulers did not require lengthy explanations.

■ **4-5** Tertullus then gets down to the "facts." Paul (who, in keeping with the tradition, is never named) is a bacillus threatening the health of the body politic. This was one of the more virulent metaphors in the polemical

23 The other major alteration, in v. 5, is more intelligent. Paul provokes riots both among gentiles everywhere, a relevant intensification, and "in our own nation." The first person is more appropriate.

24 Contrast 25:6. Scholars fill in some of the gaps. Hemer (*Book*, 347–48), for example, suggests that the letter of Lysias may have been read.

25 "Some presbyters" (cf. 23:14).

26 Presumably these days are enumerated from the receipt of the prisoner. The number is not unreasonable but may be no more than a touch of verisimilitude.

27 See, however, the note on v. 2.

28 The narrative evidently presumes that the trial was conducted in Greek, a language that Felix, who was of Greek ancestry (Tacitus *Ann.* 12.54), may have known.

29 See, for example, the *Acta Hermaisci* col. 1. 8–10 (Musurillo, *Pagan*, 44), in which one Paul, a Tyrian, serves as advocate (συνήγορος) for the Alexandrians, while the Antiochene Sopatros performs this role for the Jews (lines 14–15). (On Paul of Tyre, see A. Birley, *Hadrian: The Restless Emperor* [London: Routledge, 1997] 227–29.) Josephus talks about the skilled advocate for Antipas (*Bell.* 2.21; *Ant.* 17.226). Documentary examples include *P. Oxy.* 37 (= A. S. Hunt and C. C. Edgar, *Select Papyri* [LCL; Cambridge, Mass.: Harvard University Press, 1934] no. 257, 2:194–96), 49 CE, and *P. Oxy.* 237 vii. 19–29 (= Hunt and Edgar, *Select Papyri*, no. 258, 2:198–200), 133 CE.

30 Opening with some form of "many" was a very general Greek convention. See Luke 1:1; and Alexander, *Preface*, 109. "Always and everywhere" is another convention. See the comments on 21:28 and BDF §488 (1). Observe how Felix is the object of end-stress in several key clauses and phrases: διὰ σοῦ ("through you") and διὰ τῆς σῆς προνοίας ("through your foresight") in v. 2, as well as τῇ σῇ ἐπιεικείᾳ ("with your courtesy," on which see Cadbury and Lake, 298; and Johnson, 410, who relates it to "spirit versus letter" of the law) in v. 4. Verse 3 closes with a statement of gratitude to the procurator.

31 "Much peace" is a cliché: Plutarch *Alc.* 14.2; Josephus *Ant.* 7.20. Note also the close parallels to v. 2 in 2 Macc 4:6 ἑώρα γὰρ ἄνευ βασιλικῆς προνοίας ἀδύνατον εἶναι τυχεῖν εἰρήνης ("For he saw that without the king's attention public affairs could not again reach a peaceful settlement"). On the theme, see Gilbert, "Roman Propaganda," 239–41.

32 Horace has a concise parody of the practice: *Satires* 1.7.22–25. A nonsatirical example is Philo *Leg. Gaj.* 284. "Peace" (εἰρήνη), "providence" (πρόνοια), and "thanksgiving" (εὐχαριστία) resonate with Christian readers, but these words were not technical.

33 On this, see S. Lösch, "Die Dankesrede des Tertullus: Apg 24,1-4," *ThQ* 112 (1939) 295–319; and Bruce Winter, "The Importance of the *Captatio Beneuolentiae* in the Speeches of Tertullus and Paul in Acts 24:1-21," *JTS* 42 (1991) 505–31.

34 Compare Chariton *Chaer.* 5.6.4–5 (see n. 18).

35 Bruce (476) says, "Ancient speakers, like those of later days, considered it advisable to promise brevity at the outset of their speeches. Tertullus at any rate seems to have kept his promise."

tradition.[36] An immediately relevant passage comes from Claudius's Letter to the Alexandrians 98–100,[37] a document dealing with grave public disorders (στάσεις). After listing three prohibitions, the letter states that, in case of noncompliance, "I will by all means take vengeance on them as fomenters of what is a general plague infecting the whole world" (*κοινήν τεινα τῆς οἰκουμένης νόσον*). This does not prove that the language is contemporaneous with the dramatic date, for it was used long before and well after Claudius, but it does belong to the language of political polemic.[38] Jews, perhaps because of the existence of the Diaspora, were particularly liable to the charge of being international menaces, an allegation that would endure as a staple of more recent anti-Semitism.[39]

Charges of provoking insurrection and civil unrest would be more likely to attract the attention of a governor than would allegations that Paul was unsound on Torah. Insofar as these claims go beyond character assassination—they are old slanders (e.g., 17:6; 18:12; 21:28)[40] to the audience of Acts—they seek to construct a general case of which the alleged temple incident is but the most recent horrifying example. Before reaching that climax, Tertullus identifies Paul as a ringleader[41] of the Nazorean[42] sect. Beyond emphasizing Paul's importance and allowing him to appear as the representative of all believers,[43] it is not clear what weight this allegation carried. It fills the space between the international and local charges by placing the question of religious doctrines on the table without giving them a primary place.

■ **6** Alleging attempted profanation[44] is a necessity of the case. Had the temple been defiled by gentile feet, the presence of Trophimus or some other violator(s) would have been required or the execution(s) noted. Unable to venture onto these grounds, Tertullus must content himself with the claim that the Jewish leadership had forestalled desecration by apprehending Paul.[45] Despite the incendiary claims, which ancient lawyers were more or less required to issue as a matter of form, the implicit argument is one of jurisdiction. This will drive the narrative through 25:12. The legal basis is precarious, if not preposterous, but it well serves the maintenance of suspense. The speech itself closes with an *inclusio*,[46] followed by verbal support from Tertullus's clients, who thus affirm the wisdom of inviting Paul to condemn himself.

■ **10** The structure of Paul's speech is somewhat more complicated. In general it contains a point-by-point response. Appreciation of these correspondences is as valuable as the rhetorical analyses.[47] Since the charges are not true, Paul rejects all of them. His specific tactic

36 On the use of this imagery in the philosophical tradition, see Malherbe, *Paul*, 121–36.

37 *P. Lond.* 1912 (= *CPJ* 153 2:36–55 = Hunt and Edgar, *Select Papyri*, no. 212, 2:78–88). The translation is that of the last.

38 Sherwin-White (*Roman Society*, 51) argues for historical precision. A synonym (*contagio*) was used by Livy in his discussion of the dissemination of Dionysiac worship (39.9.1; cf. also 5.17) and, contemporaneous with Acts, Pliny in his discussion of Christianity (*Ep.* 10.96.9). Josephus uses the metaphor of Festus's counter-insurgency campaign: "Festus . . . proceeded to attack the principal plague (λυμαινόμενον) of the country" (*Bell.* 2.271, trans. H. St. John Thackeray, *Josephus II* [LCL; Cambridge, Mass.: Harvard University Press, 1927] 429). Cf. also Caesar *Gallic Wars* 6.13.7, of *seditio*, which is the standard equivalent of στάσις.

39 See, for example, the *Acta Isidori* Rec. C col.ii.23 (Musurillo, *Pagan*, 23). Isidorus says to Agrippa that the Jews *ὅλην τὴν οἰκουμένην ταράσσειν* ("stir up the entire empire"). Cf. Acts 17:6; and the comments of Musurillo, 139.

40 This is paralleled in the trial of Jesus (Luke 23:2).

41 This word, *πρωτοστάτης*, was originally military: the man on the right of the first line. The metaphorical meaning is often pejorative in literature. Porphry applies it to Peter (*Christ.* 26.1, Hoffmann, *Porphyry*, p. 55). Hippolytus (*Ref.* 1. Prol 9.3; 11.3) uses the term of heretics. "Ringleader" is appropriate.

42 The term "Nazorean" allows avoidance of messianic claims. By so doing, Tertullus did a favor for Paul. On the meaning of the term, see Barrett, 2:1098.

43 Conzelmann, 199.

44 The term in v. 6 is the standard Greek *βεβηλόω*, in distinction to the specifically Jewish idiom *κοινόω* (21:28).

45 To this extent the prophecy of 21:11 is fulfilled.

46 "Accuse" (*κατηγορέω*), vv. 2 and 8.

47 Kennedy (*Rhetorical Criticism*, 136) states that the

is to limit the time frame to events of the last fortnight or so.[48]

■ **11** After a crisp little *captatio*,[49] Paul summarizes his contention and assures the governor that it can be verified. He had come to Jerusalem to worship, not to make trouble.[50] This rebuttal turns the words of the prosecutor against his case. "Pilgrimage" is the positive purpose of the visit.

■ **12** The verse sets forth the negative: Paul engaged in no teaching[51] in either the temple or a synagogue or anywhere else. For the readers of Acts, this means that Paul did not engage in any missionary activity in Jerusalem. Verse 12 works as a concluding summary,[52] after which Paul will shift to a faith statement.

■ **14-16** These verses respond to the second allegation of v. 5. Paul begins with a "confession" (ὁμολογῶ). Readers may imagine the Jewish leaders taking note here. Tertullus's strategy has worked! The accused is about to come clean. Others will regard this as ironic.[53] Paul disparages the term αἵρεσις ("party," "sect," "faction"), substitutes for it the preferred "Movement," and insists on its full conformity to Scripture and the ancestral faith.[54] Paul has anticipated any rumors of the sort that vexed James (21:21). This rigorously theocentric statement[55] makes no messianic claims. None of this has much in common with the historical Paul, and little with the Paul of Acts.[56] Readers will view this as an acceptable tactic: focusing on common ground. In v. 24 and chap. 26, Paul will expound his particular faith. The ad hoc character of vv. 14-15 is apparent when one recalls that one

---

proem in v. 10 is "a good classical Greek periodic sentence." It is not a sentence, nor is the "equally short narration" of v. 11 and the proposition of v. 12. Winter ("Official Proceedings," 322–26) takes vv. 12-13 as *probatio*, vv. 14-18 as *refutatio*, and vv. 18/19-21 as *peroratio*. These examples show that rhetorical analysis is useful but that the speech is too brief to be pressed into a formal mold. Soards's outline (*Speeches*, 118) consists of a list of seven points.

48 For attempts to justify the "twelve days" of v. 11, see Haenchen, 654 n. 2; and Barrett, 2:1102–3. It is preferable to treat this datum as part of the rhetoric, like the "many years" of vv. 10 and 17.

49 The "many" belongs to the convention (p. 596 n. 30) and is useless as a chronological marker (Cadbury and Lake, 300; Conzelmann, 199). See *P. Lond.* 1912, 23, [?] where Claudius, who has recently taken office, says ἐκ πολλῶν χρόνων ("for a long time") in reference to the good will of the Alexandrians. This corresponds to Tertullus's initial πολλῆς (v. 2). Others are τῷ ἔθνει τούτῳ ("for this nation" [vv. 2 and 10]) and an adverb εὐθύμως ("cheerfully," elative in m); cf. v. 4. The participle in the accusative with participle construction is present, but has to be rendered as if an English perfect. "My defense" (τὰ περί) is best taken as an accusative of respect.

50 The construction, a future participle of purpose, replicates the act of the Ethiopian official. The temporal relative ἀφ' ἧς must mean something like "since," but it is inelegant, perhaps best understood as a colloquial abbreviation of ἀπὸ τῆς ἡμέρας ᾗ ("from the day on which"). See Moule, *Idiom Book*, 31 n. 2, 203; and Bruce, 478. The pronoun μοι ("me") amounts to a dative of possession.

51 His verb, "they found" (εὗρον), in v. 12 corresponds to that in v. 5.

52 The series in v. 12 is linked by three uses of οὔτε ("neither . . . nor"), while v. 13 begins with οὐδέ ("and . . . not"), although οὔτε is a *v.l.*, preferred by Boismard (*Texte*, 384), who also omits "you" (singular) and "now." Verse 13 corresponds to v. 8, as the verb "accuse" (κατηγοροῦσιν) and "concerning" (περί).

53 On the irony, see Krodel, 441.

54 The translation rearranges the order of the statements to discourage readers of today from noting the reference to "the Movement" and viewing the rest as secondary. Note the assonance: seven appearances of long *-o-* in six words of v. 14. The length of these sounds makes the statement about belief in and worship of God emphatic. For this form of "ancestral God," see *4 Macc.* 12:18; Josephus *Ant.* 9:256.

55 On theocentrism, see Schneider, 2:348.

56 Paul did not endorse the entire Torah. Even in Acts, he agrees to admitting into the community of Israel uncircumcised males and relaxing the requirements of *kashrut* (chap. 15). For Paul, the resurrection of Jesus was central and the raising of the faithful a consequence of that. He does not include a resurrection of the unjust. In Acts, from 9:20 onwards, the center of Paul's message is the centrality of Jesus.

element of this "common ground," the resurrection, was exploited as a decisive point of division in 23:6-10. Here, however, Paul claims that the Jewish leaders will affirm the centrality of resurrection hope.[57] That noun directly evokes 23:6. "Resurrection of good and wicked" is equally ad hoc, framed with an eye to v. 25.[58]

■ **16** The verse, which recalls 23:1, elegantly summarizes this stance. Hope motivates[59] his vigorous pursuit[60] of moral rectitude.[61] The imperative is grounded in the indicative.

■ **17** The speech then turns to the specific and graver charge of temple desecration. Paul's purpose in visiting Jerusalem, from which he had long been absent,[62] vaguely described as "worship" in the corresponding v. 11, is now specific: he was bearing "alms and oblations." The former (*ἐλεημοσύναι*) refer to the hitherto unmentioned collection,[63] the latter (*προσφοραί*) to his payment for the vows.[64] Reference to the vows is readily intelligible, for they constitute an alibi, as the next verse indicates. Paul was not simply a casual and passive pilgrim: he put his money where his mouth is. The "alms" are a different matter. Why does the narrator let this cat out of the bag into which he has so securely sewn it? The reference is fleeting, and only two sets of ears are likely to catch it: those of the learned and critical student of Acts and those of Felix. The first was, one may presume, unintended. The second was quite intentional; it helps justify v. 26. People who could afford to make generous contributions to the temple could also give concrete form to their gratitude for the just decisions of local rulers.

■ **18-19** These verses supply the explicit counterclaims. Reiterating the verb "find" from v. 5 (cf. also v. 12), Paul states that he was engaged in a sacred act.[65] The four co-devotees are ignored. Verse 19 contains what is, from the reader's viewpoint, a vivid anacoluthon.[66] In the dramatic setting, this would have been ineffective,[67] but it permits Paul to pass over their utterly erroneous

57 In terms of Acts (5:17), the representative group present in 24:1-22 would have been composed of Sadducees, who rejected the resurrection (23:6-10) and, historically, although Luke does not specify this, did not accept "the prophets" as normative Scripture. This twofold division is normal in Luke and Acts: Luke 16:16, 29; 24:27; Acts 28:23; cf. 1QS 1:3. Luke 24:44 speaks of a tripartite Scripture.

58 Luke 14:14 speaks of the raising of the just; cf. also 20:35-36.

59 The initial *ἐν τούτῳ* is, as so often, ambiguous. The translation takes it to refer to the previously expressed eschatological hope: "for that reason." Moule, *Idiom Book*, 79: "perhaps *that being so*." Barrett (2:1105–6) has a thorough review of the options.

60 *Aristeas* 168 shows that v. 16 is comfortably at home in the world of Hellenistic Judaism: *Ἵνα δι᾽ ὅλου τοῦ ζῆν καὶ ἐν ταῖς πράξεσιν ἀσκῶμεν δικαιοσύνην πρὸς πάντας ἀνθρώπους, μνημένοι τοῦ δυναστεύοντος θεοῦ* ("in order that throughout our life and in our actions we may practise justice towards all, being mindful of the sovereignty of God"), trans. Hadas, *Aristeas*, 165. Hans Windisch ("*ἀσκέω*," *TDNT* 1:494–96, esp. 495) states that this reads like a commentary on v. 16. See also Pervo, *Dating*, 263–64.

61 The meaning of *συνείδησις* is closer to " moral consciousness" than to "conscience" in v. 16, but see Barrett (2:1106) for a different view. See p. 572 n. 7. The adjective *ἀπρόσκοπον* gives the statement a Pauline coloring (1 Cor 10:32; Phil 1:10). The meaning is, perhaps for that reason, not clear. The safest route is to view it as a synonym for "good" or "clear." See Pervo, *Dating*, 240–41.

62 The text resolves the "many years" of v. 17 into three years plus some months, as he had last visited in 18:22. As for the phrase that begins v. 17, see Moule, *Idiom Book*, 56: "Less easy to explain are the phrases where *διά* seems = *after*." Cf. Gal 2:1.

63 Tannehill (*Narrative Unity*, 2:300) does not wish to correlate 24:17 with the collection, but he has few supporters.

64 Technically, of course, these vows were not the purpose of his visit, but the reader will forgive this bit of dissembling.

65 The *v.l.* *ἐν οἷς* ("in which," neut.), L 323. 326. 1241 *pm* refers to all of the activity described in the previous sentence. This shows the intent of the preferable *ἐν αἷς*, which specifies the "offerings," emphasizing that Paul was engaged in pious activity.

66 Dibelius (*Studies*, 92) thought that the text was corrupt. This is a possibility. Some, at least, D-Texts evidently viewed the passage as lacunose. At the beginning of v. 19, perp[2] and MSS of vg read (according to Ropes, *Text*, 225): *et apprehenderunt me clamantes et dicentes, tolle inimicum nostrum* ("And they seized me, shouting and saying, 'Away with our enemy'"). In support, he notes Ephrem, 448, and gig sa at 21:36.

67 For this reason the translation smoothes over the

charge, while making a vital point: the persons responsible for the charge of desecration, those "Jews from Asia,"[68] must testify in person. Their nonappearance would be sufficient grounds for dismissing the charges.[69] The implication is clear: if these people had any solid grounds for their charges, they would have made contact with these witnesses and groomed them for their testimony before both the Sanhedrin (23:1-10) and Felix. These Ephesians are useful for their absence just now, but they raise more questions than they answer. Defilement of the temple was a matter to be determined by its leadership. This second reference to defilement will be the last.

■ **20-21** Paul, who is showing himself to be a better lawyer and orator than Tertullus, quickly shifts, before he has completed his demands about the Ephesian witnesses, to some who *are* present: members of the Sanhedrin. What charges can these worthies bring[70] against him based on his appearance before them, other than his faith in the resurrection, a subject absent from any criminal code[71] known to Felix? If given the floor, they could, in fact, charge him with disrespect, impudence, and disruption, but those charges are not capital, and, in any case, they do not have the floor. Verses 20-21 respond to v. 8 and recap Paul's faith statement in vv. 14-16. They also appeal implicitly to the letter of Lysias, as Felix will recognize. By ending with a claim that resurrection is the real issue, Paul confirms the tribune's judgment.[72]

■ **22** At this dramatic juncture, Felix brings the proceedings to a halt. Such postponements are a common means of raising suspense.[73] The narrator comments only that Felix had become better informed about the Jesus movement. This observation helps prepare the way for v. 24 and, as Weiser remarks, serves to show that Roman judgments about Christianity are well grounded in fact.[74] The trial will resume when Lysias puts in an appearance. To give Felix the benefit of the doubt, he could have held a hearing without witnesses to determine the nature of the charges. On the other hand, he could have gained that information via consultation with the temple leadership, and it is difficult to understand why neither side had any witnesses to present. Since the accusers had presented no evidence, he would have been justified in dismissing the charges, but continuation was prudent. Still and all, readers have grounds

---

anacoluthon. (The text should say something like: "Some Asian Jews saw me and wrongly, if not maliciously, concluded that one or more of my companions was a gentile" or, per Conzelmann, 199, "I didn't start a riot. Some Jews from Asia did.")

68 One could understand the preposition ἀπό in v. 19 as meaning "Jews who had come *from* Asia" or, with BDF §385 (2), view it as use of ἀπό for ἐκ, that is, "Jews of Asian origin." Luke does not always honor the distinction, but it is reasonable to suppose that he views these persons as pilgrims from Ephesus. The same phrase appeared in 21:27, where their identity was supplied by the omniscient narrator. The same narrator could have come to Paul's aid here, but it is possible to assume that Paul recognized these persons at the time.

69 After supplying references to show Roman disapproval of accusers who do not appear, Sherwin-White (*Roman Society*, 52) concludes: "Once again, the author of Acts is well informed." That author displays no information whatsoever. Paul states only that the witnesses must appear. In addition, little legal expertise is required to state that witnesses should testify, under Roman or almost any valid system of jurisprudence. Sherwin-White (*Roman Society*, 52–53) continues: "Hence when the Asian Greeks [*sic*] withdrew from the case, Paul had a sound technical objection to put forward." The notion that Asian Jews filed charges but then withdrew them is an invention that does not rise to the level of hypothesis. This is not his most remarkable claim. On p. 49 he says: "In the first session at Jerusalem the Asian Jews accuse Paul" with a reference to 21:30. The *extra ordinem* legal "session" in view was the tumult in the temple. Those who can integrate mob attacks into the process of *extra ordinem* will have little difficulty including anything else.

70 Once again, the verb is "find" (εὗρον), as in vv. 5, 12, and 18.

71 The term ἀδίκημα ("wrongdoing") in v. 20 was used by Gallio in 18:14. It distinguishes doctrinal disputes from criminal matters.

72 Verse 21 contributes to the question of Acts' precise "accuracy": Paul's quotation of his earlier statement differs from what was reported in 23:6b.

73 See, e.g., Chariton *Chaer.* 5.8.9; Achilles Tatius *Leuc. Clit.* 7.12; *Ethiopian Story* 8.9.

74 Weiser, 2:630.

for optimism. They know Lysias's view of the question. His letter (23:26-30) serves as his "deposition."

■ **23** Furthermore, the severity of Paul's custody is downgraded and his privileges[75] increased. He is delivered to "the centurion," a person hitherto unidentified.[76] Terrorists are not accorded such amenities.[77] The tide has apparently turned—but Felix's failure to dismiss the case dampens this enthusiasm. This is a fine story in a grand and enduring tradition. The innocent hero holds his own against the unprincipled assaults of powerful accusers. The narrator has, alas, painted himself into a corner, for everything points to a prompt and full acquittal, but he will find a way out of this trap: the procurator Felix, before whom Paul has scattered a few crumbs. To this point, the governor has seemed scrupulously neutral and correct, but the depth of his character has not yet been disclosed.

75 For examples of reduced custody, see Josephus *Ant.* 18.235 (Agrippa, in circumstances like that of Paul in Rome [28:30] but with language overlapping that of 24:23) and *Ethiopian Story* 1.7.3. See also Rapske, *Roman Custody*, 167–72.

76 Rapske (previous note) states that the centurion is a mark of Paul's status, as lesser prisoners would be assigned to an enlisted guard.

77 The whole scene implies that Paul was rich (or dipping into the collection funds). This occupies Ramsay (*St. Paul the Traveller*, 310–13): "At Caesarea he was confined in the palace of Herod; but he had to live, to maintain two attendants, and to keep up a respectable appearance. Many comforts, which are almost necessities, would be given by the guards, so long as they were kept in good humour, and it is expensive to keep guards in good humour" (311). Theodor Zahn, summarized in Haenchen (656 n. 5), was less inhibited; Jacquier (687) more restrained.

24

24:24-27 Paul before Felix and Festus

Acts 24:24-27: Conventional Text

24/ Someᵃ days later Felix, while
with his Jewish wife, Drusilla,
had Paul brought in and
listened to his presentation
of belief in Christ Jesus.[b]
25/ When he began to speak
about proper behavior, self-
control, and the future judgment, Felix became uncomfortable. "That's enough for now,"
he said, "I shall summon you
again, as my schedule permits."
26/ He did, in fact, summon
Paul quite often and engage in
conversation with him, because
he was also hoping for a personal consideration from Paul.[c]

27/ After two years had elapsed,
Porcius Festus succeeded Felix,
who had left[d] Paul in custody
in the hope that it would
improve his standing with the
Jews.

Acts 24:24-27: D-Text[e]

24/ Some days later Drusilla, Felix's
Jewish wife, *asked to see Paul
and hear his message. Wishing to satisfy her,* he had Paul
brought in and listened to his
presentation of faith in Christ.
25/ When he began to speak
about proper behavior, self-
control, and the future judgment, Felix became uncomfortable. "That's enough for now,"
he said, "I shall summon you
again, *at an opportune time*."
26/ He did, in fact, regularly
summon Paul and engage in
private conversation with him,
because he was also hoping
that he would receive personal
consideration from Paul.

27/ After two years had elapsed,
Porcius Festus succeeded Felix,
who had left Paul in custody
because of Drusilla.

a 𝔓[74] reads "a few days," seeking to eliminate the possibility that Felix took his time.

b Omission of "Jesus" is not limited to the D-Text. (Others include ℵ[1] A C[vid]). It is somewhat more probable that it was omitted because of the word order than interpolated after "Christ." Barrett (2:1114), however, prefers the shorter text.

c 𝔐 cop add "so that he might release him." This is typical pedantry.

d 𝔓[74] A L 81 *et al.* prefer the imperfect: "continued holding him in custody." This fits the narrative style (cf. v. 26) and is probably secondary.

e Boismard, *Texte*, 387–89.

Analysis

While waiting for the tribune to extricate himself from the press of duties and vindicate Paul, readers may pass the time by watching their hero help a governor and his wife wile away some of the dreary hours of life in the capital of a provincial backwater. Paul's vigorous ethics had no appeal for the procurator, who soon found that the press of *his* duties precluded his attendance. Felix was more interested in lucre than in lectures. Readers might suspect that his Jewish wife has also got to him, an opinion endorsed by the D-Text. Whatever the cause, the initial suggestion of speedy justice has been disappointed. Paul languishes in custody. The plot is following a path familiar to the unstable world of popular literature:

> *The Prefect of Egypt* was amazed when he heard what had happened and ordered Habrocomes to be kept in custody (τηρεῖσθαι), but to be well looked after till they could find out who he was and why the gods were looking after him like this. . . . [He] sent for (μεταπέμπεται) Habrocomes and interrogated him about himself. He found out his story, felt sorry for his misfortune, gave him money (δίδωσι χρήματα),

and promised to send him to Ephesus. (*Ephesian Tale* 4.2.10–4.4.1)[1]

Paul was less fortunate than Habrocomes in the assignment of provincial governors at this juncture in their respective careers.[2] The governor of Judea has a wife, Drusilla,[3] who is but the object of a preposition (v. 24) in this episode. Why does Acts, which does not identify the wives of "King Herod," Sergius Paulus, Gallio, or Festus, for example, introduce her name?[4] One conjecture is that her Jewish background was the basis for Felix's knowledge about the Movement.[5] The text does not support this claim, as v. 22 attributes the communication of this knowledge to Paul, nor does she play any role in motivating (or halting) the subsequent interviews. Luke evidently learned about Drusilla from Josephus.[6] With that datum in hand, he turned to a Marcan story omitted from his Gospel: the death of the Baptizer (Mark 6:14, 17-29). In place of the Marcan triangle of prophet, ruler, and wife, there is a trio: missionary, ruler, and wife. Luke wished to portray Paul not as a puppet buffeted about by the torrid winds of harem intrigue but as the victim of a corrupt official intent on pleasing influential subjects while lining his own pockets. In this case, it is difficult to argue that Luke may have made use of some details from Mark to add a bit of color to his detailed source, for the alleged "color" constitutes its very substance.[7]

An ancient editor recognized this connection and sought to endow Drusilla with the characteristics of Herodias, through whose machinations Paul, like John the Baptizer, had to remain incarcerated.[8] The trio is now a triangle including the missionary and a ruler under the thumb of his angry wife. This is the implicit argument of the D-Text,[9] which is indirect evidence for Luke's use of Mark. The D-Text seeks to answer the question, why mention Drusilla? Luke, informed by Josephus (*Ant.* 20.141–47), understood the marriage as an unrighteous act on Felix's part, but he did not make that judgment explicit, leaving the question open and room for the D-Text to exploit.[10] Luke needs a bit of narrative to explain why the somewhat promising character of Felix deteriorated. He could have simply stated, without injustice to any putative "historical background," that Felix let Paul know that he could be bribed. Verses 24-27 achieve more than this. Dramatically, they raise the reader's hope that Felix, like Sergius Paulus, might prove amenable to the faith and thus amenable to dismissing the charges.[11] This material also kicks up some dust to cloud over questions about why nothing was done to expedite the personal testimony of Lysias. As far as readers know, the delegation from Jerusalem has remained at Caesarea, awaiting the next session of the court. To these was added one more goal: here, as nowhere else, Paul is represented as a teacher of morality.

Comment

■ **24** The unit begins abruptly,[12] with the setting left to the reader's imagination. Mark 6:20 (Herod listening to

1 Trans. G. Anderson, in Reardon, *Novels*, 156–57.

2 Typically, the governor accepts Habrocomes's story and befriends him. (Two miraculous deliveries from crucifixion did, to be sure, lend credibility.)

3 She was named after the sister of the emperor Gaius, a bit of flattery that did not wear well amidst the political vicissitudes of the era.

4 Cadbury (296) identifies the problems of vv. 24–27.

5 So, for example, Fitzmyer, 739.

6 The arguments supporting this view may be found in Pervo, *Dating*, 43–44. See also the comments on 13:6-12.

7 For Luke's purpose here, see Pervo, *Profit*, 77–81.

8 The D-Text of 24:24 shows dependence on Luke 23:8, thus establishing another parallel. Cf. also Luke 9:9.

9 Epp (*Tendency*, 152–53) does not deal with the theme of *cherchez la femme*, but observes that the onus now lies on a single Jew and that the Roman official is made to look better.

10 Barrett (2:1092) dismisses the use of Mark 6 on the rather superficial ground that one cannot compare solicitation of a bribe with decapitation. Luke was not seeking to produce an exact analogy but to exploit a narrative shell suitable for his purpose. The syntactic and verbal parallels (n. 6) add weight.

11 Compare Lucian *Peregr.* 14, where a proconsul of Syria, who was said to have a warm interest in philosophy, released the jailed Peregrinus (who was then in his Christian phase).

12 The participle παραγενόμενος is difficult. It often means "appear" (Luke 7:4, 20; 14:21; 22:52; Acts 5:20, 25, etc.), but that is difficult to reconcile with

John) provided the inspiration for v. 24b.[13] The narrative allows the possibility that Felix invited Paul to expound his beliefs. In any case, Paul spoke to him/them about his belief.[14] In one sense this address fills in details about "the Movement" (v. 14), both relieving Paul of the charge of concealing his views at the trial and allowing him to be something of a missionary, although the text does not speak of attempted conversion but only of useful moral instruction. Like other itinerant philosophers, Paul preaches righteousness to all members of the social hierarchy.[15] This language is characteristic of the early second century.[16]

■ **25** *Δικαιοσύνη* (normally translated "righteousness") and the related adjective become virtues in postapostolic Christianity. The noun can also be, as here, a term that encapsulates all virtues, so "proper behavior." Polycarp *Phil.* 3:1 is a good example of this tendency and serves as a commentary on Acts.[17] By coupling "proper behavior" with "self-control" (ἐγκρατεία) the narrator summarizes the positive ("thou shalt") and negative ("thou shalt not") sides of early Christian parenesis.[18] The prominence of self-control is a small but important clue to the place of Acts in early Christian literature. Paul, for example, uses it but once, at the end of a list of virtues/spiritual gifts (Gal 5:23). During the second century, it will move, as here, toward the head of the list.[19] The motivation for virtue is eschatological, in effect: "Be good or fry forever." Luke does not emphasize this lamentable formulation, and it stands far from the summit of Christian faith, not to mention the Pauline understanding of justification.[20] With these few words, Luke paints Paul both as a courageous philosopher who does not pull his punches or dilute his message to curry favor with the powerful and as a staunch opponent of anything that could be called libertinism or antinomianism. The former may be no more than clever characterization, but the latter confronted one of the most serious charges raised against Paul, as well as an interpretation of his teaching that exercised a strong appeal in certain advanced circles. When the content of "belief in Christ Jesus" can be represented by "doing the right thing" and "self-control/chastity," readers know that the text reflects a moralistic mentality.[21]

■ **26** Felix took no comfort from these strong words and, for the second time, adjourned the "proceedings."[22] This disappoints those readers who had expected a

"sent for." The D-Text eliminates it. The translation takes it as the equivalent of "to be (with)." See Cadbury and Lake, 296.

13 The motif was common enough. See Campbell Bonner, "A Note on Mark 6,20," *HTR* 37 (1944) 41–44. This observation does not obviate the claim that Mark was the specific source here. It does locate Paul within a broad tradition.

14 "The faith" in v. 24 is *fides quae*, the content of belief, as v. 25 indicates. See Pervo, *Dating*, 285–86.

15 Cf. the lectures on wisdom, courage, and chastity delivered by Apollonius (Philostratus *Vit. Apoll.* 4.31). The *Acta Alexandrinorum* illustrate many features of Paul's encounters with rulers, including their reluctance to make just judgments, postponements of decisions (*Appian*, perhaps *Isidorus* and *Hermaiscus*), malign influence of Jews (*Maximus* 1.124–32; *Athenodorus* 15–18). Note also the influence of Plotina and her Jewish advisors in the *Acta Hermaisci*. For parallels from the philosophical tradition, see Johnson, 419.

16 See Pervo, *Dating*, 266 and 268.

17 See Bultmann, *Theology*, 2:212–13.

18 Ibid., 2:218–20. Compare paired lists of virtues and vices.

19 The two terms appear together in *Aristeas* 273 (where "righteousness" has its limited meaning). In *Act. John* 84, "self-control" and "righteousness" are major virtues, as in *Act. Pet.* 2 (Verc.). *Act. Paul* 3.5 can summarize his gospel as "God's message about self-control and resurrection" (λόγος θεοῦ περὶ ἐγκρατείας καὶ ἀναστάσεως), similar to but even more encapsulated than Acts 24:25. In these texts, especially the last, the word means "continence," celibacy. See Walter Grundmann, "ἐγκράτεια," *TDNT* 2:339–42, esp. 340–41; Bultmann, *Theology*, 2:221; H. Goldstein, "ἐγκράτεια," *EDNT* 1:377–78; and Pervo, *Dating*, 268.

20 Tannehill (*Narrative Unity*, 2:302) takes "faith in Christ Jesus" as a summary of "Paul's christological preaching," while " 'justice' and 'self-control' may be mentioned to indicate qualities particularly required of Felix and other rulers when they are measured in the judgment." This bland harmonization neglects the thrust of the text.

21 This does not intend to disparage these qualities or to deny reason for such emphases.

22 The phrase τὸ νῦν ἔχον ("for now") is suitable to dialogues. See *Aristeas* 198; Plutarch *Amat.* 1 (*Mor.* 749A). Equally idiomatic is καιρὸν δὲ μεταλαβών ("have spare time"). See Cadbury and Lake, 305, on both.

more positive response.[23] The interruption initiates a different view of Felix. Whether this is attributed to popular literature's propensity toward inconsistent characterization[24] or to Luke's gradual revelation of the procurator's true nature[25] is not important, although v. 24 suggests the former interpretation. The narrator does show Felix's nature rather than simply assert it, but he also wishes to portray Paul's attraction to, ease with, and courage before the elite. The result yields these sudden shifts from interested official to frightened listener to seeker of a bribe. This is to say that the ἅμα καί ("but at the same time") introducing v. 26 applies to both Felix and the narrator.[26]

In this clumsy manner the narrator insinuates the subject of bribery,[27] intimating that it explains why Felix did not terminate contact with Paul. Granted that truth may be stranger than fiction, this is an unlikely story. Those of Felix's stature are most likely to receive bribes through intermediaries rather than to continue meeting with a prisoner in the hope that he will come up with the idea on his own. The frequent meetings relate to the desire to show Paul's ability and charm, while the specifics are indebted to the story of Herod and the Baptizer. Luke may have taken the idea of bribery from Josephus's comments about Albinus,[28] but the theme is common enough.

■ **27** Bribery of officials ranked very high among the most common of charges, both true and false.[29] The soil for this was tilled in v. 17, which indicated that Paul had or could acquire substantial funds, but the excuse is a bit thin, so v. 27 adds another: Felix was currying favor with the Jewish leadership. These two potent pressures permit readers so inclined to infer that Lysias did not appear (v. 22) because Felix had instructed him not to do so until so ordered. The narrator has, however, simply dropped this matter.

Verse 27 is not particularly smooth. The two clauses are linked by "and" (τε). A clearly adversative or subordinating conjunction would have been preferable. Even better would have been an inversion, for example, "Felix kept Paul in custody so long as he remained in office." Luke wished to place emphasis on the time—it is shocking. Acts 21:17–24:23 encompassed less than two weeks, to which vv. 24-25 add but a few days. Verse 26b is indefinite. Not until v. 27 does the reader perceive how long the situation lasted.[30] The internal parallel and contrast is 28:30, Paul's two-year mission in Rome. Other notations of an extended period of time mark an epoch,[31] but that is not the case here. The narrator makes no inferences about this temporal statement; commentators have been less reticent.

The first question is whether this figure derived from a/the source, and, if so, whether the author properly understood it. It is possible that the word διετία referred to a term of office. The genitive absolute

23 Rackham (449) opined: "We cannot help being surprised at the little effect produced upon Felix by his intercourse with S. Paul. The case had been very different with the governor of Cyprus. But in the servile character of this Greek adventurer there was not any depth of soil in which the word could germinate." Haenchen (663) is more positive: "Paul almost succeeded in converting the procurator Felix, as he converted the procurator [*sic*] Sergius Paulus and as he will almost succeed in converting King Agrippa II."

24 See Pervo, *Profit*, 33, with its references.

25 Tannehill (*Narrative Unity*, 2:303) labors to expose Felix's character and is able to conclude that this is "a tragic plot in miniature." Few concepts could have been more distant from the mind of the narrator. In this instance, the literary critic can benefit from intertextual research, for v. 26 is indebted to Luke 9:8; 23:8, in the context of the story of John the Baptizer.

26 On this construction, see BDF §425 (2).

27 Verses 25-27 constitute a single, cumbersome sentence.

28 Josephus *Ant.* 20.215 says that Albinus cleared out the prisons, executing those guilty of serious crimes but releasing for money (χρήματα λαμβάνων) those charged with minor offenses. The passage (see also *Bell.* 2.273) is interesting because it assumes that many persons languished in jail (δεδεμένους, as in v. 27) without a final verdict, although it suggests that, unlike the situation reported in Acts, the procurator "cleaned house" before the arrival of his successor.

29 So, for example, the Egyptian prefect Flaccus was accused of receiving a large bribe: *Acta Alexandrinorum* II (Musurillo, *Pagan*, 4–5) = *P. Oxy.* 1089 col. ii, 55–60.

30 It would be reasonable to think that Felix gave up after a month, possibly two, but the narrative does not indicate that their conferences ceased.

31 Antioch (11:26); Corinth (18:11); and Ephesus (19:10).

διετίας πληρωθείσης ("two years having been completed") could support this understanding.[32] The source would then have referred to the end of Felix's tenure. This interpretation becomes a factor in the determination of the date when Felix left office.[33] The hypothesis that it referred to a statute of limitations has been discredited.[34] For Luke, it demonstrates the unfairness of the situation. Acts 23:33—25:27 constitute a circle dominated by Festus. Expectations of expeditious and equitable justice have once again been dashed by human venality and Jewish animosity. The arrival of a new governor, Porcius Festus, stirs up the saps of hope once more, ending a long winter of hopes raised then dashed.

32 Contrast "after two years," a clearer way of saying this.

33 See Lüdemann, *Acts*, 318–19, and the discussion below.

34 See Rapske, *Roman Custody*, 320–23.

25

25:1-12 Festus Takes the Case

1/ Two days after setting foot in
his province[a] Festus went
from Caesarea to Jerusalem,
2/ where the chief priests[b]
and the Jewish leaders put
their case against Paul before
him.[c] 3/ They urged Festus
to do them a favor, to Paul's
disadvantage:[d] that he have him
transported to Jerusalem.[e] This
was because they intended to
set an ambush and kill Paul en
route. 4/ To this Festus replied
that Paul was in custody in Caesarea, whither he himself would
presently be returning.[f] 5/ "Your
preeminent people[g] may accompany me and, if there are any
grounds for it,[h] make their case
against him there." 6/ After
spending no more than eight or
ten days with them[i] in Jerusalem, he returned to Caesarea.
The next day he took his place
on the bench and directed that
Paul be brought in. 7/ Once he
was there, the Jews from Jerusalem ganged up[j] on him and
made a number of quite grave
charges that they were unable
to support.[k]

8/ In his defense Paul contended, "I
have done absolutely nothing
wrong, either regarding Jewish
law, or the temple, or Caesar."
9/ Since Festus wished to ingra-
tiate himself with the Jews, he
asked Paul, "Are you willing to
go to Jerusalem and be tried
there by me on these charges?"[l]

10/ Paul replied, "I am standing in
Caesar's court.[m] This is the
proper venue. I have committed
no offense against the Jews, as
you well know. 11/ If, however,
I am in violation and am guilty
of a capital crime, I shall not
attempt to evade dying, but
if there is no substance in the
charges they are making, no
one has the authority to surrender me to these people. I
appeal to Caesar!" 12/ After
conferring with his staff, Festus
announced: "You have appealed
to Caesar. To Caesar you
shall go."

a Or: "after assuming his office." 𝔓74 ℵ* A read ἐπαρχείῳ, which correctly identifies this adjective as having but two terminations, as also Ropes (*Text*, 227), but Cadbury and Lake (306–7) take it as a noun ("office"). Judea was not yet a "province." *New-Docs* 2 (1982) no. 47, p. 85 gives evidence for a looser use of the term ("district"), but this is sixth century. 𝔓74 and a few others replace οὖν with δέ ("then," with "and/but"), intelligently in the view of Barrett, 2:1123. This creates a stronger disjunction: "Felix left Paul . . . but Festus. . . ."

b A variety of undistinguished witnesses read "the high priest." This enhances the parallel with 24:1.

c 𝔓74 omits (before) "him."

d Cadbury and Lake (307) speculate that χάριν may have the sense of "opinion," "ruling," but "favor" is satisfactory.

e In this verse, "Jerusalem" is undeclinable, unlike vv. 1, 7, and 9. This is a dash of local color, as the speakers in v. 3 are Jewish.

f It is probably preferable to see μέν in correlation to δέ rather than as a free-standing μὲν οὖν indicating narrative resumption, which it can scarcely mean here.

g The adjective δύνατος can refer elsewhere in Luke and Acts to rhetorical ability, although not exclusively (Luke 24:19; Acts 7:22; 18:24). See Cadbury and Lake, 307; and Josephus *Bell.* 1.243; *Ant.* 14.324 (a case in which Antony rendered a decision based on the advice of one of the parties).

h 𝔐 reads "this man" and omits ἄτοπον ("wrong"). Others harmonize by using both. The omission may have stemmed from the view that Festus was claiming too much for Paul, especially in light of his later conduct.

i 𝔓74 omits ἐν αὐτοῖς, evidently unwilling to portray a close relationship between the procurator and the Jewish leadership. The vague temporal statement has different formulations. In addition to variations in order, some witnesses, including E, omit the negative, a few read "not more than ten," and others "more than ten."

j This seeks to capture the threatening sense of περιέστησαν (lit. "stood around"). See Haenchen, 666.

k Use of the aorist by p74 ℵ* is probably due to a failure to recognize ἴσχυον as an imperfect. One might render: "which they didn't even try to prove."

l "Under my direction" is one understanding of ἐπ' ἐμοῦ. See BDAG, 363 (3), *s.v.*; and Haenchen, 666 n. 3.

m On the text, see Cadbury and Lake (308), who support B in framing the phrase with "standing" (ἑστώς).

Excursus: Porcius Festus and the Date of His Accession

Josephus is much less critical of the rule of Festus than of the tenures of his predecessor (Felix) and his successor (Albinus). The extremely terse comments in *Bell.* 2.271–72 credit him with successful counter-insurgency. *Ant.* 20.182–96 is more detailed. The "bandits" were *sicarii*. From the latter account (§193) Luke could have learned of a mutual relationship between Festus and Agrippa II and deduced that Festus sought support from the Jewish ruling class. Luke's portrait of Festus is in general accord with that of Josephus.

The date of Festus's accession is not clear, with a range of c. 55 to c. 61. Historians tend to opt for a date of c. 58–60,[1] while much of the exegetical tradition has preferred c. 55–57.[2] A governing factor for the latter date is the "lynchpin" of Gallio's proconsulship (51/52), which would create a gap if Paul did not arrive in Jerusalem until 56/57. Historians are also inclined to take Acts' statements about "the Egyptian" (21:38) or the "many years" of Felix's rule (24:10) at face value.[3] The data are uncertain, ambiguous, and inconsistent, but incline toward a later date.[4] Georgi's date of 58 looks like, and is, a compromise, but it well accommodates conflicting data.[5] Precision in Pauline chronology is not possible, despite patient and devoted efforts. Most of these attempts assume that Paul encountered Gallio, Felix, and Festus, granting that the contexts provided in Acts are due to the author. This assumption, which relies on the existence of a "historical kernel," is open to objection.[6]

Analysis

The dawn of a new administration brings a welcome zephyr of integrity and the aroma of efficiency. After no more than three days' rest from his arduous journey to the new station, Festus sets out for Jerusalem, where he meets with the leadership, who evidently have no issue of greater concern than the case of Paul. They request his return to Jerusalem. Behind this plan lurks the old game: an ambush on the road. Festus directs the accusers to come to Caesarea and present whatever case they may have. His doubts promise a fair and speedy trial.

The subsequent scene looks like a replay of chap. 24. A bit more than a week later those accusers duly appear. With Festus presiding, they make numerous allegations with no evidence. Paul in his turn denies any offense against the Jewish law, the temple, or Caesar. With the introduction of this crucial last word he has begun to insinuate into his defense a rebuttal of political charges. No witnesses appear. Nonetheless, the trial is over, and the verdict should be forthcoming. It isn't. Festus instead reverts to the earlier request of the Jerusalem leadership. His motive is that of Felix (24:27): desire to please "the Jews." Although the place of trial was a matter of his own prerogative, Festus begs Paul's permission for a change of venue. The answer will require no weighty calculation. What will happen on the road to Jerusalem is something about which Paul is well informed. The accused will firmly but politely decline this kind offer.

The reply he does make would have been responsive to a ruling that Festus had transferred jurisdiction to the ruling Jewish body. The defendant asserts a right to trial before a Roman bench, closing with two dramatic words: "I appeal to Caesar." This is a stunning development. Flustered Festus must find some way to regain control. An experienced bureaucrat, he elects to confer with his legal consultants to assess the ramifications of this demand. After a proper interval, he emerges from the administrative huddle and announces his decision in two crisp phrases that have the ring of a legal decision

1 Josephus apparently provides support for 59 or later, as he reports the appointment of Ishmael as high priest prior to noting the arrival of Festus (*Ant.* 20.179, 182), although his chronological references are vague.

2 This tradition goes back to Harnack and Lake. More recent representatives are Haenchen, 70–71; Conzelmann, 195; and Lüdemann, *Acts*, 219. Favoring 59 is Robert Jewett, *A Chronology of Paul's Life* (Philadelphia: Fortress Press, 1979) 41–44. Jerome Murphy-O'Connor argues for 59–60 in *Paul: A Critical Life* (Oxford: Clarendon, 1996) 22–23.

3 For example: Schurer, *History*, 1:465 n. 1; Smallwood, *Jews*, 269 n. 40. Cf. Emilio Gabba, "The Social, Economic and Political History of Palestine 63 BCE–CE 70," *CHJ* 3:94–167, esp. 144 n. 251.

4 See the lengthy presentation of the evidence in Joel Green, "Festus, Porcius," *ABD* 2:794–95. Green favors a later date. Saddington ("Roman Military," 2428–29) prefers 58 or 59.

5 Georgi, *Remembering*, 128–37, esp. 136–37.

6 On the limits of this approach, see the comments on 18:12-17 (Gallio). If one grants the existence of source material for 21:33 through 26 (27), it is

and redeem Festus from any appearance of confusion. Readers, however, have sensed the theme of divine necessity in v. 10 (δεῖ) and recall 23:11 and 19:21. What looks like a legal can of worms tainted with the odor of corruption is the unfolding of God's plan.

The most obvious datum is that the trials in chaps. 24 and 25 look like duplicates. The keen eye of Wellhausen already observed that the account here resembles the first trial.[7] Lüdemann is willing to consider that the account in chap. 25 may be prior to and the basis of that in chap. 24.[8] Neither account has much claim to preserve convincing historical detail. The bedrock of historical fact is Paul's receipt into custody at Caesarea (presumably by Felix) and his eventual dispatch to Rome (presumably by Festus). He may have been sent there for trial or as a condemned prisoner. Some of the data in Acts may be valid, but means for determining which of these are accurate are lacking.

Haenchen deconstructed the narrative of vv. 1-12, summarizing his conclusions with three issues: (1) The absence of a verdict, (2) Paul's failure to decline Festus's offer, and (3) Festus's refusal either to try one charged with a *crimen laesae maiestatis* (an insult to the honor of the imperial person and office) or send him to Rome for trial.[9] Barrett attempts to fend these off by addressing them *seriatim*, but does no more than dent their edges. He concludes, "The story as Luke tells it hangs together. This does not prove that it is historically true. It might be intelligent fiction."[10] This is special pleading; the story does not hang together and can only be called "intelligent" in the sense of "clever." Haenchen's judgment that this is "a suspense-laden narrative created by the author" is more penetrating.

Weiser does not reject a historical background, but he does not find much beyond Lucan composition when he casts his eye upon chaps. 25 and 26.[11] The core of his argument is the close relationship between this material and the trial of Jesus in Luke 22–23.[12] Central to this parallelism is the sequence of an inconclusive trial under a Roman governor (Luke 23:2-5) followed by an appearance before a Herodian monarch (Luke 23:6-12), a basis of which is Ps 2:1-2.[13] The events also fulfill the oracle of Acts (9:15-16).[14] Reasons for the involvement of the Herodian ruler are parallel (Luke 23:6-7; Acts 25:13-27). In both cases that ruler just happens to be in town and wishes to see the accused (Luke 23:8).[15] The process follows similar lines: similar accusations without effect (violation of Jewish and Roman law [Luke 23:2]), demands for the death penalty (Luke 23:18, etc.), and judgments of innocence without release (Luke 23:4, 14-15, 22). At the general level, both stories have a similar cast: Jewish leaders, who accuse; the Roman governor; a Herodian prince; and the defendant. The major source of chaps. 25–26 is chap. 9; the residue is Lucan composition.[16]

Barrett once more demurs: "He does nothing however to indicate awareness of the parallelism, as he probably would have done had it been important to him, and does not repeat his earlier reference to Ps. 2.1f."[17] Luke is most definitely not the sort of narrator who would announce, "This took place, dear reader, in order to establish a parallel between the trials of Jesus and those

likely that Paul did encounter Felix and Festus. The interaction with Agrippa (II) is almost certainly fictitious.

7 Wellhausen, *Kritische Analyse*, 51.

8 Lüdemann, *Acts*, 323.

9 Haenchen, 668–69. See also Lüdemann, *Acts*, 323.

10 Barrett, 2:1121–22, citing 1122.

11 Weiser, 2:637–38. Some of his arguments have been developed or expanded here.

12 See pp. 592–93.

13 Cf. also Acts 4:27-28. For detailed comment on this episode, see Raymond Brown, *The Death of the Messiah: From Gethsemane to the Grave; A Commentary on the Passtion Narratives in the Four Gospels* (2 vols.; ABRL; New York: Doubleday, 1994) 1:760–86. Brown discusses the psalm on pp. 779–81.

14 One could make the counter-argument that the prophecy in 9:16 is based on the experiences reported in chaps. 24–26. The theme is, however, already present in Mark 13:9, which speaks of trial "before" (ἐπί) "governors" (ἡγεμόνων) and "monarchs" (βασιλέων).

15 O'Toole, *Unity*, 69.

16 Acts 25:13-22 and 26:30-32 are omniscient narration on the part of speakers who would scarcely have allowed themselves to be interviewed by a historian. Acts 26:1-29 is speech and dialogue.

17 Barrett, 2:1112.

of Paul." Luke's architecture does not require recognition. Readers need not construct a sketch or list points of contact to grasp the points, the most basic of which is that the same sorts of people did the same things to Paul that they had earlier done to Jesus. At the aesthetic level, one may say that Barrett is deficient in his appreciation of Luke as an artist. The more important judgment is his lack of sensitivity to the Lucan technique of communicating the message by telling stories.

If there is but one story, this is no deficit, either from the perspective of literature or of the gospel message. The question that drives the readers of Acts is, as Haenchen realized, What will happen next? The answer is: What happened to Joseph, Moses, various prophets, Jesus, the apostles, and Stephen. From a literary perspective, a major problem with salvation history is its monotony and predictability. If Luke understood anything, he knew how to use repetition to reinforce his message without succumbing to monotony. The more one strives, come what may, to demand precise history in Acts 21–28, the greater the danger of missing its desire to communicate the *meaning* of history.

Comment

■ **1-4** Like Felix, Festus gives an initial positive impression. He is energetic and unwilling to be manipulated. Readers of Josephus would expect the Jewish leaders to seek help against the guerillas and terrorists, but the only issue they raise here is the case of Paul. Indeed, they plan to borrow one of the key weapons in the terrorist arsenal: assassination by ambush. Festus unwittingly avoids this trap: he will soon return to the capital, and the prisoner is there. A hopeful note appears in his possible doubt about Paul's guilt. If this is not simply gratuitous or merely formal—an affirmation of the presumption of innocence—it may mean that he has not found their accusations particularly convincing. If the author had any specific information about these events, he has ignored it, giving preference to reiteration.[18]

■ **5** The verse breaks into direct speech,[19] making its sentiments more vivid.[20] The scene also buries the original witnesses (the "Jews from Asia" and Lysias) beneath another layer of sand. The contest will be between Paul and the high priestly leadership. Reference to the judgment seat ("bench") underlines the official nature of the proceedings.[21] Its literary function is to prepare for v. 10. This account includes details omitted at 24:1-2: the judge mounts his bench and the defendant is brought before him. The narrator has distributed his material: words in the first account, actions in the second.

■ **6-8** The next passage contains one of the most dramatic, famous, and—for the interpreter—difficult scenes in Acts. The "trial" consumes but two verses, as there was no need to reiterate the rhetorical duel of chap. 24.[22] The prosecution's case is summarized in vague indirect discourse.[23] Paul simply denies any offense, in sixteen not ineloquent words.[24] He has given to God what is God's and to Caesar what is Caesar's. "Caesar" could be a trope for "violation of Roman law" and need not be limited to *laesa maiestas,* protean as that category could be.[25] Offense against the majesty of the

18 The verb ἐμφανίζω ("lay information") makes the fourth of its five appearances (23:15, 22; 24:1; 25:15). The ambush is a rehash of 23:12-15. Lest readers overlook this, H[mg] (which Boismard [*Texte*, 390] accepts as the D-Text) adds: "Those who had taken a vow, in order that they might get their hands on him." See Ropes, *Text*, 229. "Wrong" (ἄτοπος) evokes the story of Jesus (Luke 23:41).

19 See BDF §396, 470 (2).

20 Festus ends this encounter with a particular conditional sentence, balanced by two of the same type used by Paul to close his remarks in v. 11.

21 Cf. 12:21 ("Herod"); 18:12, 16, 17 (Gallio).

22 For language proper to court proceedings, compare the *Acta Isidori* Rec. A col. 1.17–18 (Musurillo, *Pagan*, 18): ἐκλήθησαν [Ἀλεξανδρέων πρέσ]βεις, καὶ μετάξατο [ὁ αὐτοκράτωρ εἰς αὔ]ριον ἀκοῦσαι αὐτῶν. ("The Alexandrian envoys were summoned and the emperor postponed their hearing until the following day"; trans. Musurillo, p. 24). This is followed by the precise date, a constant feature of the reports of legal proceedings. (Apropos of 25:23, etc., the hearing involved "King Agrippa" [I], twenty senators, as well as sixteen men of consular rank [that is, ex-consuls, by and large], and the women of the court.)

23 Further details will emerge in vv. 17-19.

24 The speech is based on three short clauses consisting of οὔτε ("neither . . . nor") and a prepositional phrase beginning with εἰς ("in regard to"). The D-Text, according to Boismard, *Texte*, 390, once more changes direct discourse to indirect.

25 See John Balsdon and Andrew Lintott, "maiestas," *OCD*, 913–14.

state was a charge generally reserved for members of the Senatorial and Equestrian orders.[26] A decision awaits.

■ **9** Instead there is a *volte face* more surprising than that of Felix in 24:27, although the reason is verbally identical. The informed reader might well expect that Felix would want the support of the native leaders, but one cannot imagine what had led him to change his mind. The narrator could have supplied him with reasons, most notably the presence of witnesses in Jerusalem, the scene of the alleged crime, but that door has been closed. As noted, Festus could have adjourned the proceedings and scheduled the next session in Jerusalem.

■ **10-11** The politeness and generosity of his request is matched only by the rudeness of Paul's rejoinder, which accuses the procurator of throwing him to the wolves. The puzzlement generated by the procurator's question[27] dissipates before the even more puzzling response. Rather than say, "No thank you, your Excellency," Paul appeals. One of the less-unsatisfactory solutions is to presume that Paul viewed himself as pinned, that he did not view Festus's offer as genuine, but as a statement of change of venue. Jerusalem—roadside ambush aside—would mean enormous crowds roused to a frenzy of bloodlust that Festus would be no more able to resist than had been Pilate (Luke 23:18-25). Haenchen says it well: for Paul the change of venue amounts to extradition.[28]

By avoiding a definite order, Festus remained able to assert his own views that Paul was innocent of any conventional statutory crime but that he was helpless to deal with halakic niceties (vv. 16-21). The narrator, not for the first time, is working both sides of the street. Paul's response is solemn[29] and revelatory. The δεῖ ("must") of v. 10 asserts the fundamental impropriety of changing jurisdiction. (Never mind for now that Festus spoke of a change of venue.) This is a shaming tactic. For the reader it has a deeper meaning. Since 19:21, the verb has been associated with Rome. The Lord confirmed it in 23:11. Paul is destined for Rome, not Jerusalem, which was the city of Jesus' fate. The appeal rests beneath the wings of God's will. Paul then associates Festus with his assertion that he has done no wrong[30] to "the Jews."[31] Verse 11 introduces, in a purely rhetorical fashion,[32] the matter of a capital offense. Since Paul is willing to take his punishment if guilty, he is quite justified in refusing an illegal transfer of jurisdiction to "them."[33] His means of refusal is to appeal to Caesar, that is, to demand transfer to Rome. This seeks to prevent Festus from altering his question to a command.

The appeal presents legal difficulties that cannot be surmounted.[34] In part this is due to lack of information

26 The charge of fomenting στάσις, "sedition" (24:5) might possibly fit this category (cf. 19:40). This is the view of Bruce, 487. In that case, Haenchen's observation (see above) would apply: Festus should try it or remand the case to Rome.

27 The difficulty is represented by the variant ἤ ("be tried there *or* by me?"): 33 pc.

28 Haenchen, 667.

29 Note the perfects in vv. 10 and 11 (supplemented by the perfect ἠδίκηκα, "have done nothing wrong," in v. 10: ℵ B [81]). Verse 11 contains two contrasting particular conditions, linked with μέν . . . δέ. The final two words, calling upon Caesar, succinctly contrast with the wordier prelude. "Caesar" is also an *inclusio*. For a rhetorical analysis, see Soards, *Speeches*, 119–20.

30 The use of the verb ἀδικέω in both v. 10 and v. 11 is Pauline (1 Cor 6:8; 7:12; 2 Cor 7:12 [bis]; Gal 4:12; cf. Col 3:25), albeit not exclusively so.

31 In proper character, Paul would have said "my people." The voice is the narrator's.

32 The acceptance of law, together with the assertion of one's rights, is basic to apologetic. Conzelmann (203) notes that it is present in Plato's *Apology* (e.g., 37) and the *Crito*. A Christian example is Athenagoras *Supplicatio* 2.1. Closer to Acts is Josephus *Vit.* 141, a speech: "My countrymen, if I deserve to die, I ask no mercy (οὐ παραιτοῦμαι), but . . ." (trans. Henry St. J. Thackery, *Josephus I* [LCL; Cambridge, Mass.: Harvard University Press, 1926] 55). For the opposite ("I deserve it"), see Virgil *Aen.* 12.931.

33 For the reader χαρίσασθαι ("give," "surrender") in v. 11 is a clever play on and riposte to the χάριν ("favor") of v. 9.

34 Bibliography includes: Ulrich Holzmeister, "Der hl. Paulus vor dem Richterstuhle des Festus (AG 25, 1-12)," *ZKTh* 36 (1912) 489–511, 742–83; Henry J. Cadbury, "Roman Law and the Trial of Paul," in Lake and Cadbury, *Additional Notes*, 297–338, esp. 312–19; Conzelmann, 203–4; Peter Garnsey, "The *Lex Julia* and Appeal under the Empire," *JRS* 56 (1966) 167–89, esp. 182–185; idem, "The

about how Roman law operated in these matters.[35] Law books discussed *provocatio* and *appellatio*, but data about cases are inconsistent and unclear, as is Acts itself. "[W]hile there certainly existed a nexus of procedures which we may reasonably label 'appeal to the emperor,' we have so far not the slightest basis for statements about its conditions, limits or modes of operation."[36] Discussions of appeal take their basis in the right of Roman citizens, but Acts does not introduce Paul's claim to Roman citizenship here. Perhaps the franchise is to be inferred from 23:27, but it is difficult to understand why the narrator does not have Paul say, "I am a Roman! I appeal to Caesar." Paul grounds his appeal on his standing as one on trial in a Roman court rather than on his status. Furthermore, v. 12 indicates that Festus might have seen fit to deny this demand. The narrative value of the appeal emerges in 26:32. It now functions like the laws of the Medes and the Persians and thus works against Paul, who would otherwise have been discharged. By that point, legal issues have gone by the boards, since, when confronted by this situation, Paul would have rescinded his appeal. "Within the narrative world, however, everything makes good sense."[37]

■ **12** Response to this critical tradition has focused on the character of Festus. Richard Cassidy has stressed the negative aspects of Festus's character,[38] a view that has been taken up by Witherington and Tannehill, among others. Cassidy is quite correct. Festus is, for the reader of Acts, not honorable. The objective reader may sympathize with the plight of Festus,[39] but the implied reader of Acts regards sensitivity to Jewish pressure and power as abrogation of official responsibility. Cassidy's related claim, that Haenchen sought to portray Festus in a positive light, creates a straw man, and this is the creature Witherington and Tannehill embrace in their attempts to justify the story on historical grounds.[40] Festus betrays, when the situation requires, his willingness to

Criminal Jurisdiction of Governors," *JRS* 58 (1968) 51–59; A. H. M. Jones, "I Appeal unto Caesar," in George E. Mylonas and D. Raymond, eds., *Studies Presented to David Moore Robinson on His Seventieth Birthday* (2 vols.; St. Louis: Washington University Press, 1951–53) 2:918–30; Sherwin-White, *Roman Society*, 57–70; idem, *The Roman Citizenship* (2nd ed.; Oxford: Clarendon, 1973) 334–36 (on the Cyrene Inscriptions); Andrew W. Lintott, "Provocatio: From the Struggle of the Orders to the Principate," *ANRW* 1.2 (1973) 226–67, esp. 232–34. Lentz, *Luke's Portrait*, 144–53; Long, "Paulusbild," 87–105; Levick, *Government*, no. 6, pp. 10–11 (a valuable case, indicating that appeals could be rejected and noting the requirement of a deposit by appellants), and no. 84, pp. 95–96 (the Cyrene Inscriptions); Rapske, *Roman Custody*, 47–56; Stegemann, "Bürger," 207–13; Tajra, *Trial*, 142–51; Nippel, *Public Order*, 6; Millar, *Emperor*, 507–16; and Omerzu, *Prozess*, 53–109. For summaries of the problems raised, see Haenchen, 666 n. 2; Pervo, *Profit*, 46–47, 154 n. 159; Krodel, 448–49; and Fitzmyer, 742–43.

35 Modern authorities disagree about whether governors were obliged to grant appeals. Garnsey ("*Lex Julia*" [n. 34 above], 184–85) says that they were not required to do so. Others, e.g., Sherwin-White (*Roman Society*, 57–70), hold that appeals by any citizen had to be honored. See previous note and n. 44.

36 Millar, *Emperor*, 510.

37 Skinner, *Locating*, 142 n. 85.

38 Richard Cassidy, *Society and Politics in the Acts of the Apostles* (Maryknoll, N.Y.: Orbis, 1987) 107–9.

39 See Cadbury and Lake (308), who question the narrator's fairness.

40 Witherington, 720–22. Tannehill (*Narrative Unity*, 2:305–8) paints Festus as a "political novice" who was a quick study as well as eventually biased because of his "sensitivity to power relationships in his province" (306). Haenchen (307), to the contrary, "believes . . . that Festus is basically 'energetic and upright.'" What Haenchen said, with his wonted sarcasm was: "the energetic and upright Festus threatened to desert to the ranks of Paul's enemies" (670 [German 597]). Tannehill (307–8) further assumes Festus's later statements about Paul's innocence as indicators of his unreliability. Luke, however, had no desire to cast any doubt on such affirmations. They were true. Festus's problem was that his hands were tied. His dissembling is apparent, since he did not tell Agrippa or anyone else about his interest in cultivating his subject, but readers are not to doubt his views about the prisoner's guilt. In the guise of interpreting the characterization of an individual, Tannehill is constructing a character who will make the narrative more plausible and thus historically reliable.

compromise. That makes him an enemy. This inconsistency does not establish historicity.

Within the realm of law it does not make very good sense.[41] Although citizens could appeal against trial by magistrates outside of Italy, as well against a verdict or punishment,[42] it is improbable, albeit not impossible, that appeals could be lodged while a trial was still in progress or prior to a verdict, which is what Acts implies. The government did not fund the expenses of an appeal. Those who appealed had to be prepared to pay the costs of their own travel, lodging, and upkeep, as well as the expenses of witnesses.[43] Acts says nothing of these matters. The available data suggest that provincial governors routinely sent Roman citizens to Rome for judgment. Procurators of Equestrian status would have been even more inclined—or obligated—to do so.[44] Paul is, according to 27:1, one of a number of prisoners being dispatched to Rome under escort. Acts 27:42 evidently implies that they had been found guilty. In sum, Paul *may* have been a citizen and he *may* have appealed, but the text of Acts does not provide sufficient clarity. The appeal functions, like the citizenship, as a literary device, and it may have been a (brilliant) authorial creation.

The narrator suggests that appeals did not function automatically, for Paul's surprising demand drove Festus into a hasty consultation with his legal experts.[45] This raises suspense. When the conference is over—the narrator does not say whether they withdrew or how long they took—Festus returns with his epigrammatic answer.[46] Paul is, indeed, destined for Rome. The trial of Paul in Acts is ended. Were the next paragraph to begin with 27:1 readers would perceive no gap. This is not to say that nothing would be missed, for the story has much to offer, none of which will injure its hero's reputation.

41 Although Barrett has labored to defend the general historicity of the narrative, he acknowledges that conclusions based on such assumptions are questionable.

42 Sherwin-White, *Roman Society*, 58 and n. 5.

43 Rapske, *Roman Custody*, 210.

44 Pliny *Ep.* 10.96.4 assumes that Roman citizens accused of a serious crime are sent to Rome. See also the Second Edict of Augustus from Cyrene (*SEG* 9 no.8 ii (= Conzelmann Appendix 10, 240). For other examples, see Lake and Cadbury, *Additional Notes*, 310–12. According to Lucian *Tox.* 17, one Deinias, a wealthy citizen of Ephesus, was arraigned before the proconsul for murder and sent to the emperor. He would probably have been viewed, because of his status, as a citizen. This is a fiction but evidently realistic. Tacitus *Ann.* 10.16.2 speaks of a freedperson who was jailed by the proconsul of Asia but freed by Nero (c. 65). The text does not say that he was sent to Rome. According to *NewDocs* 4 (1982) no. 20, p. 85, not all citizens could request a trial at Rome, and influential non-citizens could sometimes do so. Josephus speaks of the transport of Jews to Rome for trial (*Bell.* 2.243||*Ant.* 20.131; *Bell.* 2.253||*Ant.* 20.161). Millar (*Emperor*, 473) states that governors might refuse the appeal of one condemned, but defer execution until the emperor had replied to their letter and accompanying *libellus*. They could also sabotage appeals (cf. Suetonius *Galb.* 9).

45 For such consultations prior to a verdict, see Chariton *Chaer.* 5.8.6; Achilles Tatius *Leuc. Clit.* 7.12.1. On such bodies, see *4 Macc.* 17:17; Philo *Leg.* 254; Josephus *Ant.* 16.163; and Schürer, *History*, 1:370. For examples of the emperor's *consilium*, see Millar, *Emperor*, 119–20, 206–7.

46 On the style of his sentence, see Weiser, 2:642.

25

25:13-22 Agrippa and Bernice Arrive

13/ **Not long thereafter King Agrippa and Bernice arrived in Caesarea and gave Festus an official welcome.[a] 14/ Some days into their visit Festus brought the case of Paul to the king's attention.**

"There is a man left in custody by Felix. 15/ When I was in Jerusalem, the Jewish high priests and elders brought the case to my attention, demanding that I find him guilty.[b] 16/ I explained to them that it is contrary to Roman practice to execute a sentence upon an accused person before that individual has had opportunity to confront the accusers and offer a defense against the charge.[c]

17/ **"When they came here,[d] I took my seat on the bench without delay—the very next day, in fact—and had the man brought in. 18/ When the accusers arose to make their case, however, they did not allege any of the crimes about which I had expected to hear.[e] 19/ Instead, they took up with him some controversies involving particular religious matters, as well as questions about a certain deceased Jesus, whom Paul claimed to be alive. 20/ Since *I* had no idea how to adjudicate matters of this sort, I asked whether he would like to go to Jerusalem and stand trial there on these issues.[f] 21/ Because, however, Paul appealed[g] to be retained[h] for a decision[i] by His Majesty, I ordered him to be kept in custody until I could remand[j] him to Caesar."**

22/ **Agrippa said,[k] "I really should like[l] to hear this man."**

"Tomorrow you will have your opportunity," replied Festus.

a The *v.l.*, a future participle, is easier. On the aorist. ἀσπασάμενοι, see Cadbury and Lake, 309–10; and BDF §339 (1). The participle bears no temporal sense.

b E ψ m read δίκη, more like "punishment," "penalty." Cf. 28:4.

c A thinly attested *v.l.* τινι for τινα ("to someone" rather than "a [person]") provides an indirect object. Specification comes in the εἰς ἀπώλειαν ("condemn someone *to death*") in m and the D-Text (Boismard, *Texte*, 392). This verse is, according to BDF §386 (4), the sole NT example of an oblique optative in a temporal clause. It is an example of cultured interchange between two gentlemen whose syntax is impeccable even in casual conversation.

d Since Luke elsewhere uses the genitive absolute without stating a subject, αὐτῶν is to be viewed as secondary. See Metzger, *Textual Commentary*, 436.

e An alternative, preferred for the D-Text by Boismard (*Texte*, 392), who also reads ὡς rather than ὧν, "as" rather than "which," is πονηράν ("wicked"), agreeing with αἰτίαν ("charge"). Another option is the neuter plural (πονηρά). Finally, m omits this word, leading Barrett (2:1129) to suspect that it may be a gloss. A shorter Byzantine text is always interesting, but it seems more likely that it was found unnecessary and possibly derogatory. 𝔓[74vid] sa introduce a relative pronoun (= ἥν) before εἶχον, evidently in agreement with δεισιδαιμονία ("religion").

f The D-Text (Boismard, *Texte*, 393) omits "on these issues." This makes the prospective hearing absolute. H P 049. 323. 1241 *pm* read the singular "this," presumably making resurrection the single issue for adjudication. The syntax of v. 20 is difficult. On the indirect question, see Moule, *Idiom Book*, 154. The verb ἔλεγον (lit. "I said") is unfortunate. Some form of "I asked" would be simpler. Cadbury and Lake (312) refer to ἀπορούμενος . . . ζήτησιν as "a remarkable though intelligible construction." The *v.l.* εἰς τήν (C E L ψ 33. 36. 323. 614 *et al.*) has the same effect as an accusative of respect. See Barrett, 2:1140.

g 𝔓[74] ψ 1739* *pc* have the present participle, which might suggest that Paul repeatedly invoked his demand.

h On the difference between the preferred aorist infinitive τηρηθῆναι and the variant present form, see Bruce, 492. On the more or less gratuitous pronoun αὐτόν ("him"), see BDF §406 (2) and 392 (3).

i In this instance διάγνωσις = *cognitio*; that is, Paul appealed for the emperor to take cognizance of the case. See Deissmann, *Light*, 342 n. 3.

j A *v.l.* is the simple πέμψω ("send"), probably because the compound ἀναπέμψω could be taken as "send back."

k Ellipsis of the verb "say" is acceptable. The manuscript tradition gives evidence of "correction."

l Moule (*Idiom Book*, 9) calls ἐβουλόμην a "desiderative imperfect." For another view, see p. 618. It is evidently equivalent to the classical βουλοίμην ἄν. Cadbury and Lake (312) prefer "I had wished," with the claim that Agrippa had heard something of the story. More aptly, they note the parallels in Luke 9:9; 23:8.

Analysis

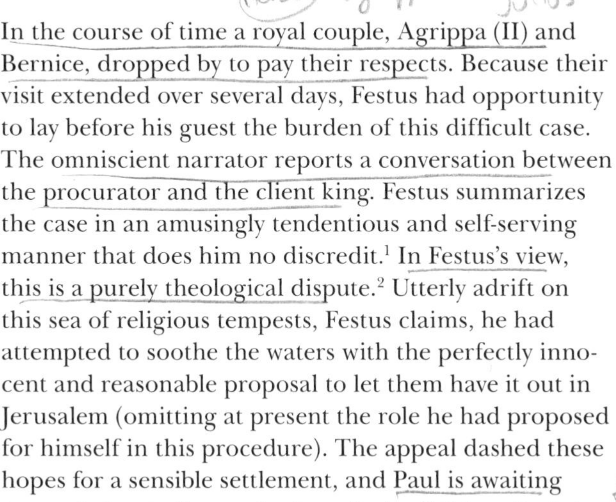

In the course of time a royal couple, Agrippa (II) and Bernice, dropped by to pay their respects. Because their visit extended over several days, Festus had opportunity to lay before his guest the burden of this difficult case. The omniscient narrator reports a conversation between the procurator and the client king. Festus summarizes the case in an amusingly tendentious and self-serving manner that does him no discredit.[1] In Festus's view, this is a purely theological dispute.[2] Utterly adrift on this sea of religious tempests, Festus claims, he had attempted to soothe the waters with the perfectly innocent and reasonable proposal to let them have it out in Jerusalem (omitting at present the role he had proposed for himself in this procedure). The appeal dashed these hopes for a sensible settlement, and Paul is awaiting transmission to Rome. Agrippa finds all this quite interesting and allows that he would like to hear the fellow. Hear him he will, the very next day.

Here the burden of proof lies on the argument for historicity.[3] Hemer feels this weight: "[I]t looks as though Luke's form of composition is inferential rather than based on sources." After briefly justifying this, he finds that "the element of composition here looks to be significant."[4] Barrett grants the reasonableness of a courtesy call by Agrippa and Bernice,[5] and relatively early in Festus's tenure would be an appropriate time for such a visit. These are not particularly vigorous defenses. What troubled Hemer was the omniscient narration of vv. 14-22, which cannot be fobbed off onto a source.[6] The passage is a Lucan composition. Formally it fulfills 9:15,[7] but Luke has more in mind than confirming the accuracy of those words. His inspiration for introducing these two visitors came, in all probability, from Josephus.[8]

Excursus: Agrippa II and Bernice

M. Julius Agrippa (28–c. 93), the son of Agrippa I (and the brother of both Drusilla and Bernice), was the last king of the Herodian line.[9] Had he succeeded his father, a plan Josephus says enjoyed the initial favor of Claudius (Josephus *Ant.* 19.360–62),[10] history may have been quite different, for Agrippa successfully combined strong and unquestioned

1 The narrator used a similar technique in the letter of Lysias (Acts 23:26-30).

2 The charitable reader will think that he must have nodded off during the speeches summarized in 25:7-8.

3 See the brief review of scholarly views on this question in Haenchen, 673.

4 Hemer, *Book*, 348. His remarks are interesting. Witherington (728) states that, as the author would not have been likely to have access to private discussions, "[h]ere Luke followed the historical convention of making the persons say what they were likely to have said on the occasion." On p. 728 n. 397, Witherington allows the possibility of a court informant. Marshall (386) and Williams (411) also concede Lucan composition.

5 Barrett, 2:1134. See, e.g., Josephus *Bell.* 2.309, where Agrippa goes to Alexandria to greet Tiberius Alexander who was assuming office.

6 Hemer (*Book*, 343 n. 72) explains 5:34-39 (Gamaliel's speech to an executive session of the Sanhedrin) by proposing that Paul was the source. On this see Pervo, "Happy Home," 31 n. 4.

7 In his *Life* (49), Josephus labels Agrippa and Bernice "royal personages" (βασιλεῖς). In that very literal sense she contributes to the scene. See also p. 621 n. 5.

8 Pervo, *Dating*, 187–90.

9 See Richard D. Sullivan, "The Dynasty of Judaea in the First Century," *ANRW* 2.8 (1977) 296–354, esp. 329–45; Schürer, *History*, 1:471–83; and David C. Braund, "Agrippa" (2), *ABD* 1:98–100. *OGIS* (418–29) provides inscriptional data about the Herodians (including these two).

10 Josephus's statements about Agrippa are not beyond doubt, but the course of Agrippa's career confirms their general validity.

support for Rome with loyalty to Jewish identity, persons, and concerns. Around 50 CE he received the client kingdom of Herod of Chalcis (Bernice's husband) and later exchanged this for mixed Jewish and gentile regions that were expanded over time by Nero and Vespasian. Unlike Josephus, Agrippa opposed the Jewish Revolt from its onset. Agrippa evidently died as a bachelor without issue. He enjoyed a close relationship—too close according to ancient gossip—with his sister Bernice, who served at times as his "first lady."

Julia Bernice[11] (c. 28–?) was the nearly coeval sister of Agrippa II.[12] She was married a good three times (the first at age thirteen) and was also the mistress of Titus and, rumor held, of others. Bernice is appropriately called a lesser Cleopatra, a wealthy, intelligent woman whose attractions were more than skin deep. Titus was evidently still in love with Bernice when she was in her fifties. Her personal courage was noteworthy (Josephus *Bell.* 2.310-14), as were her generosity and diplomacy (Josephus *Ant.* 20.343, 355). The Roman public's abhorrence of eastern queens compelled her to leave Rome when Titus became emperor (Suetonius *Tit.* 7). The inevitable analogy with Cleopatra probably stimulated and almost certainly perpetuated rumors about her incestuous relationship with her brother.[13] As a general rule, the power of highly placed women was in close proportion to the volume of gossip about their sexual lives.[14] In Acts, she is "ornamental and mute."[15] The former went with her standing. The latter was uncharacteristic.

The story takes an unexpected turn with the arrival of King Agrippa and Bernice. Her identity (sister) is not specified, nor are his realm and role identified. It is somewhat more likely that the narrator did not wish to take the time to explain these matters than that the implied reader is expected to know who they are. In due course, it will transpire that Agrippa is Jewish. This is the single important fact about him. Recent scholarship has debated the characterization of Festus in this passage. Lake and Cadbury proposed: "The speech of Festus can be grouped with the letter of Claudius Lysias to Felix as representing Luke's attempt to tell the story as he supposed that Roman officials would have told it."[16] For Haenchen, the question is not whether Luke invented this passage but why. He concludes that "Festus is personally rehabilitated before the reader. . . . A bright light falls on the Roman state, and suspense is awakened for what is to come." Krodel senses no rehabilitation. Commenting on vv. 20-21, he says, "Luke is at his most brilliant in sketching the hypocrisy of Festus without any overt polemics."[17] Cassidy, commenting on the same two verses, says that Festus's report "is decidedly biased in his own self-interest."[18] The major concern of both is the contrast between the motive stated by the narrator in v. 9 and that offered in v. 20.[19] Tannehill agrees, but he does not wish to disparage all that Festus says, for much of it is beneficial to Paul.[20]

Analysis focused on the character of the procurator is likely to go astray. Haenchen's synecdoche (Festus = Rome) is exaggerated, and no hypocrisy is involved, for Festus professes no virtues that he does not practice. Readers know that Festus presented one perfectly reasonable motive for his proposal to Agrippa while his

11 The spelling of her name is disputed. Haenchen (671) says that Φερενίκη is the proper spelling. Fitzmyer (749) observes that Alexandrian MSS. favor Βερνίκη, but that Βερενίκη (Josephus *Ant.* 20.145) is more correct. The Latin reflex is "Veronica." Juvenal *Sat.* 1.156 has *Beronice*. Bruce (491) says that the name is Macedonian in origin.

12 See David C. Braund, "Bernice," *ABD* 1:677–78; and Ross S. Kraemer, "Ber(e)nice," in Meyers, *Women*, 59–61. Louis H. Feldman has a valuable note in *Josephus IX* (LCL; Cambridge, Mass.: Harvard University Press, 1965) 467 n. *d.*

13 Egyptian monarchs married their siblings. Lucan (*Pharsalia* 8.693) applies the same adjective, *incesta* (which means "impure" or "unchaste" in general, as well as "incestuous"), to Cleopatra that Juvenal (*Sat.* 6.158) uses of Bernice.

14 The comments of ancient male historians about the influence of court women are usually hostile.

15 Kraemer, "Ber(e)nice" (n. 12 above), 61.

16 Cadbury and Lake, 311.

17 Krodel, 451.

18 Cassidy, *Society*, 111.

19 Cassidy's second issue is that Paul did not ask "to be kept in custody." This depends on whether the verb τηρέω has the identical meaning in v. 21 a and b. BDAG, 1002, *s.v.* τηρέω, says that it does not. In any event this is a minor quibble. It does not deny that release would have been Paul's first choice.

20 Tannehill, *Narrative Unity*, 2:310–13. On p. 312 he says: "[Festus] is presenting a public image that covers up his real motives." The "public" here is the readership, since this is a private conversation. Through the generosity of the omniscient narrator,

actual motive was different.[21] The object of this monologue and its sequel in vv. 24-27 is to leave the reader with a clear view of what Festus thought about his prisoner and about Paul's character and actions. Festus is the brush used to paint this portrait. The strongest evidence that this passage is more a positive picture of Paul than a caricature of Festus is that proponents of the latter view neglect the governor's most glaring omission: the charges of violation of Roman law (v. 8).[22] Festus also neglects to state that Paul was a Roman citizen. This conversation is for the benefit of the readers and need not repeat what they already know. The emphasis is on new information. Readers will doubtless be amused by the dashes of self-serving interpretation, as they were by Lysias's letter, but in neither case were these touches intended to impugn the reliability of these characters. Festus's account fills in many of the details briskly summarized in the previous twelve verses.

Comment

■ **13-21** After a brief introduction,[23] Festus lays before the king a concise summary of the case, beginning with his inheritance of the matter from his predecessor and concluding with the decision to send the accused to Rome. Festus makes no explicit request for assistance, nor does he offer his reason for discussing the matter. The narrator reserves that until v. 26. He claims that the Jerusalem leadership demanded a condemnation rather than a trial. Festus observed that condemnation without trial was not in accord with Roman justice. This conventional sentiment[24] was often proclaimed by the apologists.[25] Righteousness (barely[26]) satisfied, he disgorges a summary of the arguments that varies substantially from what was reported earlier. In place of numerous grave charges are religious disputes.[27] Festus does not contrast criminal with religious offenses but states that the dispute involved theological rather than criminal matters.[28] In addition, there was a dispute about whether Jesus were alive or dead. By this means, the narrator represents the governor's inability even to grasp the question of postmortem revival. This is unlikely, but effective.[29] Festus has given Paul's case a substantial boost, for all considerations of crimes against "Caesar" or the temple (a matter that a Roman judge would consider different from a theological dispute) are out of the picture. The spotlight has come to rest upon the issue favored by Paul: resurrection (23:6). All this leaves the poor procurator at a loss (v. 20).

■ **22** Now Agrippa, let alone the engaged reader, might well have interjected, "Why then did you not dismiss the case?" That resolution has been excluded by the narrator (and history), but, as framed here, without a statement about Festus's presence, it intimates that a

readers also know of the actual motive of the Jerusalem authorities: to ambush Paul on the road (25:3).

21 One might note that the historical Agrippa would probably have been sympathetic to Festus's actual motive. Conzelmann (207) views the change as a means of informing the reader that Roman authorities are not competent to deal with these questions.

22 Barrett, 2:1134: "This Roman view completely omits the serious Roman charge of *seditio* and *laesa maiestas*."

23 Verse 14a is based on v. 6.

24 See, for example, Appian *Bell. civ.* 3.54. Note the *Digest* 48, 17, 1 (Ulpian), "This is the law we abide by: No one may be condemned in his absence, nor can equity tolerate that anyone be condemned without his case being heard."

25 For example, Justin *1 Apol.* 1.3; Athenagoras *Supplicatio* 3; Tertullian *Apol.* 1.3; 2.2. See also Tacitus *Hist.* 1.6; and Jacques Dupont, *Études sur les Actes de apôtres* (LD 45; Paris: Cerf, 1967) 527–52.

26 The verb χαρίζεσθαι ("hand over") in v. 16 is the same used by Paul in v. 11. Only by a narrow and technical margin does the governor escape violation of his own principle.

27 "Disputes" is used by Roman officials to characterize Jewish disputes with Paul's message in 18:15 (Gallio) and 23:29; 26:3 (procurators). "Their own religion" is a proper translation of ἰδία δεισιδαιμονία, but the adjective is more polite than αὐτῶν. The addressee is a Jew. Slightly less possible is to apply the adjective to Paul: "his religion," preferred by Cadbury and Lake, 311.

28 Haenchen, 672.

29 Stories about dead persons returned to life were abundant in Greco-Roman folklore. See Rohde, *Psyche*, 408 n. 103. For examples from the novelistic tradition, see Glen W. Bowersock, *Fiction as History: Nero to Julian* (Berkeley: University of California Press, 1994) 98–119. See also pp. 674–76.

religious court was a suitable place for hearing a religious dispute. Although readers will note that he fails to add the motive attributed by the narrator in v. 9, they might also take into account his ignorance of the malice of the Jewish authorities, who were determined to do away with Paul by any means necessary.[30] The hard-headed critic might wonder just what in this description had enticed Agrippa, but readers may safely assume that Paul always arouses interest of one sort or another. The scene closes with another crisp, confident promise.[31]

30 Boismard (*Texte*, 393) offers this D-Text: *τότε ὁ Παῦλος ἐπεκαλέσατο Καίσαρα καὶ ᾐτήσατο τηρηθῆναι αὐτὸν εἰς τὴν τοῦ Σεβαστοῦ διάγνωσιν, ὡς δὲ αὐτὸν οὐκ ἐδυνάμην κρίνειν ἐκέλευσα αὐτὸν τηρεῖσθαι ἵνα παραδῶ αὐτὸν Καίσαρι* ("**Then Paul appealed to Caesar and asked that he** be held for the judgment **of His Majesty. Since I was unable to judge him**, I ordered that he be held in custody until I could **deliver** him to Caesar"). This expansion seeks to make a bit more sense of Festus's actions (and eliminates the hypothetical question posed at the beginning of the paragraph). The matter was out of his hands. See Ropes, *Text*, 231. "Deliver" (*παραδῶ*) could evoke a parallel with the passion of Jesus.

31 Compare Festus's *προεύσῃ* ("you will go") in v. 12 with *ἀκούσῃ* ("you will hear") in v. 22.

25

25:23-27 The Prelude to Paul's Defense

25:23-25: Conventional Text

23/ The next day Agrippa and Bernice arrived in considerable splendor and entered the audience chamber with tribunes and the local notables. At Festus's direction Paul was brought in.

24/ "King Agrippa and all you ladies and gentlemen. You see this man.[a] The entire Jewish community has appealed to me, both here and in Jerusalem,

clamoring[b] that he must be put to death directly.

25/ "In my view,[c] however, he has done nothing deserving death, but, because[d] he appealed to His Majesty, I decided to send him *to Rome*.

26/ "I have[l] nothing definite to transmit to our Sovereign concerning him. I have therefore brought him before you all, and particularly you, King Agrippa, so that, upon the completion of an inquiry, I might have something to communicate.[m] 27/ For it makes no sense to me to transfer a prisoner without also stipulating the charges[n] against him."

25:23-25: D-Text[e]

23/ The next day Agrippa and Bernice[f] arrived in considerable splendor and entered the audience chamber with [ ] men *who had come down from the province.*[g] Festus ordered that Paul be brought in.

24/ "King Agrippa and all you ladies and gentlemen. You see this man. The entire Jewish community has appealed to me, both here and in Jerusalem, *that I should hand him over for execution without the opportunity to defend himself.* 25/ *But I could not hand him over because of the orders we have from the emperor. If, however, anyone wished to accuse him, I said that they should follow me to Caesarea where he was in custody. When they arrived, they shouted that he should be removed from among the living.*[h]

"After I had heard (him?[i]*) in order,*[j] I determined that he *was in no sense guilty* of death, *and so I said: 'Do you wish to be tried with them in Jerusalem,'* he appealed to *Caesar*."[k]

---

a "You see" (ϑεωρεῖτε) is a polite indicative, not an order.

b The *v.l.* ἐπιβοῶντες (C E ψ 33. 1739 m) is more technical, as it is used of the acclamations made by crowds in theaters, and the like.

c A range of witnesses read the opening phrase as a participial phrase, most adding καί ("and") after πεπραχέναι ("done"). This appears to be a later attempt to improve the syntax.

d *Or:* "when . . ."

e This is from Boismard (*Texte*, 394–97) with lengthy notes on pp. 396–97.

f As elsewhere, Boismard spells her name "Beronice." This is probably derived from the Latin "Veronica."

g It is not certain whether these men replace (as here) or supplement the notables of the conventional text.

h The text of Clark (158–59) is somewhat different. See also Ropes, *Text*, 233; and Metzger, *Textual Commentary*, 437. Boismard, for example, prints ϑάνατον at the beginning, Clark βάσανον ("punishment"). The Latin translation of the Syriac reads *tormentum*, which supports Clark.

i Boismard (*Texte*, 395) places τοῦτον ("this person") in parentheses. In N-A[27] it is the object of θεωρεῖτε ("you see").

j *Or:* "in part" (ἀπὸ μέρους). Translation is difficult.

k Clark (159) differs: "**But when I heard both sides of the case**, I found that he was in no respect guilty of death. **But when I said, 'Are you willing to be judged before them in Jerusalem?'** he appealed to Caesar" (trans. Metzger, *Textual Commentary*, 437).

l D-Text (Boismard, *Texte*, 397): "find."

m The syntax is troublesome. N-A[27] reads σχῶ τί γράψω, in which the last two words are evidently taken as an indirect question: "So that I might have what I shall write." 𝔓[74] A E and a number of witnesses read the indicative ἔχω. One might expect the subjunctive to be rejected as an improvement. E and m read the infinitive γρᾶψαι, yielding an easier construction, in English no less than in Greek. See also Ropes, *Text*, 233. On ἄλογον ("absurd," "irrational"), see Pervo, *Dating*, 262.

n The D-Text (Boismard, *Texte*, 398) reads the singular "charge."

Analysis

The most suitable setting for the proposed audition would have been a private interview, but the narrator has already utilized that opportunity (24:24-25). Paul's final defense took place in a setting of considerable splendor, with all those able and eligible to attend a V.I.P. gala present, including a client king, his regal sister, a governor, and all the quality of Caesarea. This is the most splendid "trial" in Acts.[1] Paul will present his most brilliant defense speech, but fear of an unfavorable verdict will not inhibit appreciation, as this is not a true trial. The unit contains two speeches and a dialogue. In place of an argument for the prosecution, Festus offers introductory remarks (25:24-27), followed by Paul's defense speech (26:1-23), which the governor interrupts, generating the closing dialogue (26:24-29).

In his introduction, Festus set the background, including the role of the mob, his view of the matter, and his objective: the development of a concise report to advise the imperial court. Agrippa's assistance will be deeply appreciated. Thus invited, Agrippa takes the chair and invites Paul to address the distinguished crowd. In this speech, Paul exhibits, to the best of the author's ability, all the mannerisms and skill of a trained orator. His self-defense is appropriately autobiographical, summarizing the highlights of his career. This is Paul's last full speech and his most important. For yet a third time the "conversion" is related. These repetitions show how important the story is for Luke, not solely out of concern for Paul, but because the legitimacy of the church Luke knows stands or falls with the legitimacy of the Pauline mission. By this third telling, the account has become a full-fledged prophetic call. The missionary commission now occurs "on the Damascus road." There is no reference to the blinding of Paul. As a prophet, Paul stands firmly within the Israelite tradition.

When Paul turns to the subject of resurrection, Festus intervenes. His dramatic interruption registers both the enchantment of Paul's rhetoric and his own religious density. After a polite acknowledgment, Paul returns to his primary hearer, Agrippa. This Movement (Christianity) cannot have eluded the attention of a devout and informed Jew. The faith Paul presents is not the product of a squalid rural revival. Agrippa must acknowledge that Paul has been quite persuasive. Paul politely turns this into a well-phrased wish for the salvation of all. This is his last word here and in the Holy Land. As all rise to leave with the king, their "verdict" emerges: innocent of any serious crime. Agrippa assures Festus that, were it not for the (unfortunately irrevocable) appeal, Paul could have been freed.

Comment

■ **23-26** The D-Text of these verses is a somewhat tendentious secondary expansion that heightens the disrepute of the Jews. Rather than make Festus appear self-serving, these additions make Paul's opponents look worse. Lest anyone overlook the import of the terse survey found in the conventional edition, this text underlines the pursuit of a summary execution. It is pedantic

1 Schwartz ("Trial Scene," 139) says that this "serves the same function that the Persian court serves in Chariton [*Callirhoe*]: "It represents the pinnacle of grandeur."

insofar as it does not rely on readers to recall the earlier verses, but the effect is vivid. This text (or texts or comments) is the earliest known contribution to the debate about Festus's character discussed above. Verse 25, is not, however, in agreement with this tendency, for it omits Festus from the proposed proceedings in Jerusalem. His failure to release Paul has become even less comprehensible. The D-Text preferred emphasis on these two points to concern for strict consistency. In fact, the two merge, for Festus's proposal and the exuberance of the petitioners show that he was under all but unbearable pressure.

After the solemn entrance,[2] the affair takes on the characteristics of a trial.[3] Witherington's summary, "A judicial hearing has been turned into royal entertainment and theater,"[4] is at least half right. An informational interview with the features of a judicial hearing has been turned into entertainment for the royalty. Agrippa will be the "judge."[5] One might expect Festus to identify Paul as a Roman citizen, a status held by most of the audience, but he moves directly to the charges. His summary strengthens the resemblances between the experiences of Paul and Jesus. "The entire Jewish community" demanded Paul's death.[6] The hyperbole is apparent, for nothing in the narrative has indicated that a mob or assembly shouted for Paul's death in Caesarea. Parallelism is the driving force, reinforced by social prejudice. The audience would not have held the judgment of a mob in high regard.[7]

■ **25** The verse repeats in public the judgment of v. 18, which was also that of Lysias (23:29).[8] One could gather from this statement that only the appeal forestalled a verdict of "not guilty."[9] This, too, will be repeated in 26:32 (by Agrippa). In this summary, Festus overlooks his suggestion of a trial in Jerusalem. It is difficult to call this self-serving, for it would not have struck Agrippa or the others as inappropriate, but it is, at the very least, a simplification.[10] The appeal is both irrevocable and within the purview of the procurator. Verse 25 clarifies v. 12: Festus made the decision to dispatch Paul to Rome. These two principles are contradictory. The text does not suggest that the appeal had to be honored or that it was associated with citizenship. The legal situation is in a shambles, but the narrative is just where it wants to be.

Festus needs help. He does not know what to say to the emperor[11] about the case.[12] The motive for the present scene is to supply him with the data that will

2 This is the second exhibition of Herodian pomp at Caesarea: see 12:21-22.

3 The same verbs, κελεύω ("command") and ἄγομαι ("be led in"), appeared in v. 6, at the opening of the trial. See Cadbury and Lake, 310.

4 Witherington, 732. Cf. Cadbury and Lake, 312: "Festus was merely showing off an interesting prisoner to entertain Agrippa, the chief local dignitaries, and the officers of the Mess."

5 Bernice is, at most, decorative. The participle of the genitive absolute in v. 23 is masculine singular, and neither Festus (v. 24) nor Paul (26:2) takes formal note of her presence. This accords with social conventions, the effect of which is to render women invisible.

6 The translation of πλῆθος is disputed. Johnson (427) and Witherington (732), for example, wish to understand it in the sense of "Sanhedrin," as in Luke 23:1, and thus limit opposition to the officials. This seems to accord with 25:2, but that verse depicts a small body of the leadership. Festus's language evokes the πλῆθος of 21:36, a mob demanding death. See BDAG, 826, *s.v.* πλῆθος. Unlike Jesus, Paul never enjoyed popular support in Jerusalem, according to Acts.

7 Johnson (421) gives a rationale for what Festus would have hoped to gain from this event. That does not make it historical.

8 Cf. Luke 23:4, 14-15, 22, in which Pilate thrice declares Jesus' innocence.

9 The translation (see the alternate) understands Festus to be intimating a cause-and-effect relationship between the appeal and the absence of a verdict. Verse 21 supports this understanding, but it is disputable.

10 One reason for the omission is that this summary depicts the accusers as unwilling to accept any result other than execution. Festus is trapped by the logic of his own summary.

11 The absolute use of "Lord" (κύριος) may be a bit of an anachronism. See Pervo, *Dating*, 312. Of the examples cited by Fitzmyer (752), two name the emperor, while the third, *P. Oxy.* 1143, is dated approximately in the first century and does not refer to Augustus. The closest parallel, *BGU* 1200, is dated in the second century.

12 See *Digest* 49.5–6 (Ulpian) on these "*litterae dimissoriae sive apostoli*" ("notice sent to a higher judge"). *Digest* 49.6.1 states: "After an appeal has been introduced letters must be sent by the one with whom

inform his brief. This is a familiar quest. Lysias had twice attempted to determine τὸ ἀσφαλές ("definite," "certain").[13] To reiterate: use of the present setting to settle the facts of the case is a dubious procedure. Data should have been gathered from the relevant witnesses, with a summary of the allegations and evidence for and against them. In place of that, Paul will give a public address that does not touch on any of the actual charges.[14]

■ **26-27** The passage reeks of legalese.[15] The term ἀνάκρισις ("inquiry," especially a preliminary hearing[16]) shows that the assembly is engaged in a legal procedure. Toward the close of his little introduction Festus stumbles, repeating himself and lapsing into a banality.

---

the appeal is filed to the person who will have to decide about the appeal." This report is also known as a *libellus*. For examples and references, see Millar, *Emperor*, 323 and n. 61.

13 Acts 21:34; 22:30. The noun is the climactic word in Luke 1:4.

14 Haenchen, 679: "The scene of the hearing in Caesarea is thus anything but a realistic description—here where the accusation is not even voiced, but the accused alone dominates the field."

15 Conzelmann, 207.

16 See Frederich Büchsel, "ἀνάκρισις," *TDNT* 3:943–44; and BDAG, 66, *s.v.* Note also Bruce, 495.

26

26:1-32 Paul's Defense

1/ **Agrippa advised Paul, "You may**
now state your case."
Making the appropriate gesture,
Paul began his defense.
2/ **"King Agrippa, I regard myself**
as fortunate to have this
opportunity[a] to defend myself
today against[b] all the charges
lodged against me by[c] Jews,[d]
3/ particularly because you
are an expert about all Jew-
ish customs and controver-
sies. Please lend me a patient
ear. 4/ Every Jew[e] knows my
manner of life from my early
youth, because I lived among
my people in Jerusalem.
5/ They have long been well
aware—and could so testify
if they wished to—that I have
followed the rule of life of the
most punctilious group our way
of worship has to offer. I am a
Pharisee. 6/ I am now on trial
because of my hope for fulfill-
ment of the promise God made
to[f] our[g] forebears, 7/ that for
which[h] our twelve tribes[i] yearn,
with continuous and heartfelt
devotion, to experience.[j] Your
Majesty, the Jews are accus-
ing me of having this hope![k]
8/ Why do you people think it
incredible that God might raise
the dead? 9/ My own view was
that I was obliged to do a great
deal against the name of Jesus
the Nazorean, 10/ and I did so.
Authorized by the high priests, I
locked up many of God's people
in Jerusalem and cast my vote
for their subsequent execution.[l]
11/ No synagogue escaped my
attention. I frequently sought to
torture them into committing
blasphemy. In a fury verg-
ing upon insanity I extended
my pursuit to other cities.
12/ While so engaged[m] I was
en route to Damascus with the
permission and authorization
of the high priests,[n] 13/ when,
while traveling at midday I
saw, Your Majesty, a light from
above, brighter than the sun,
sweep over me and my com-
panions. 14/ We all fell to the
ground. I heard a voice, which
said to me,[o] in Aramaic, 'Saul,
Saul, why are you persecuting
me? You can't swim against the
flood.'

a The present participle μέλλων ("going to") is awkward after the accusative "myself." It may have been the result of striving for alliteration.

b The preposition περί here is the equivalent of ὑπέρ (BDF §229 [1]), which is a secondary variant.

c 𝔓[74] *et al.* have the inferior and unlikely preposition παρά ("from").

d The anarthrous "Jews" appears in speeches in 25:10; 26:2-4, 7, 21. BDF § 262 (1) notes that Attic orators also omit the article with the name of opponents in lawsuits. The sense may be partitive ("some Jews, yourself excepted") (Barrett, 2:1149).

e Lit. "all Jews." The article is probably secondary, due to its normal use with "all." See previous note and Metzger, *Textual Commentary*, 438.

f The *v.l.* πρός is probably to be explained as harmonization with 13:32, which is quite similar.

g H L P 049. 1241 m omit "our," perhaps recognizing that the audience includes gentiles, possibly from hostility to Judaism.

h The antecedent of the feminine relative ἥν ("which") is logically and grammatically "promise," not "hope," as one cannot "hope" for a hope.

i On this term, see Pervo, *Dating*, 268.

j The future infinitive offered by B *pc*, is an unnecessary refinement.

k N-A[27] does not include the reading of p[29], λατρεύει ἐν ἐλπίδι ("serves in hope"), rather than the participle λατρεῦον and finite verb ἐλπίζει (lit. "serving, hopes"). Boismard (*Texte*, 400) takes this reading, which is supported by gig, as the D-Text. See also Ropes, *Text*, 235. 𝔓[29] also omits, with A Y 36. 453 *pc* gig, the final vocative in v. 7. Boismard (*Texte*, 400) adopts this. An alternative is to supplement it with "Agrippa" (cf. v. 19). This reading makes its way into the Byzantine text. Deletion of "king" is probably secondary, based on appreciation that Agrippa was a Jew.

l Perhaps the καί before πολλοῦς ("many") is adverbial. Omission of the first τε (B Ψ 1739 m) appears helpful, although the alternate δέ (36. 453) is not. Moule (*Idiom Book*, 197) sagely speaks of the use of τε in Acts as a "mannerism."

m Barrett (2:1156) prefers to render ἐν οἷς ("in which things") as "and so" rather than "in the course of which activity." See also Moule (*Idiom Book*, 131, 197), who is less certain.

n Some later witnesses include καί after the opening prepositional phrase. This must be adverbial ("also," "even"). Omission of the article after ἐπιτροπῆς ("permission") may be failure to construe the nouns as a hendiadys. The preposition παρά, found in diverse witnesses before "high priests," is harmonizing (9:2; 22:5).

o "Which said to me" is omitted by 33 *pc*. D-Texts and other others, via harmonization, read λαλοῦσαν

15/ **"'Who are you, Lord?'[p]**
"'I am Jesus[q] whom you are
persecuting. 16/ On your feet,
now! I have appeared to you
to appoint you as an agent and
witness of what you have seen
and what I shall show you.[r] 17/ I
shall rescue[s] you from your own
people and from the gentiles to
whom I am sending you,[t] 18/ to
open their eyes,[u] so that they
may turn from darkness to light
and from the power of Satan to
God[v] and receive forgiveness of
sins with a place among those
who have been made holy by
their trust in me.' 19/ Therefore,
Your Majesty, I obeyed that
apparition from on high. 20/ In
consequence I began to urge
people, in Damascus first, then
in Jerusalem, then to both Jews
and gentiles in every region, to
change their ways and turn to
God, demonstrating this change
by appropriate actions. 21/ This
was why the Jews apprehended
me while I was[w] in the temple
and attempted to murder me.
22/ With God's help I am still
able[x] to maintain my views,
testifying to those of high
degree and low nothing other
than what the prophets and
Moses said would take place:
23/ that the Messiah would suf-
fer, be the first to rise from the
dead, and, by rising, be a herald
of light to my people and the
gentiles alike."
24/ **At this point Festus loudly inter-**
rupted: "Paul, you are crazy! All
this research is driving you over
the brink!"[y]
25/ **"I am not insane, Your**
Excellency.[z] What I declare
is the sober truth.[aa] 26/ His
Majesty is well informed about
these matters, and it is to him
that I am speaking without
equivocation.[bb] I am certain
that none of these matters has
eluded his attention,[cc] since this
is no storefront mission! 27/ Do
you believe the prophets, Your
Majesty? Of course you believe
them!"
28/ **Agrippa replied, "Are you trying**
to make me a Christian in such
short order?"[dd]
29/ **"I would to God that, by one**

("speaking"). If the wording did not differ from the preceding accounts (9:4; 22:7), one would be tempted to prefer the omission.

p The form εἶπα (the equivalent of something in English like "I sayed") is quite vulgar (found only in Mark 9:18, outside of a citation in John 10:34).

q "Lord" is omitted as redundant by some witnesses, including m. "The Nazorean" appears in some D-Text and other witnesses. This is harmonization with 22:8.

r The text of v. 16 is very difficult. The bracketed με, which might be taken as an accusative of respect ("regarding me"), is a source of difficulty. By the conventions of NT textual criticism it is the *lectio difficilior* and should be retained. 𝔓[74] ℵ A C[2] E ψ 096 m latt bo—a formidable company—omit it. One explanation is that it was added to provide a clear object of εἶδες ("you have seen"), motivated by the desire to state clearly that Paul saw the risen Christ. It is omitted here. Dibelius (*Studies*, 92) believes that corruption has entered "through the influence of the preceding ὤφθην" ("I appeared"). The emendation he proposes may be reconstructed as μάρτυρα ὧν τε εἶδές τε ὀφθήσεταί σοι ("a witness of both what you have seen and will be shown to you"). Cadbury and Lake (319) agree that the Greek of ὧν . . . σοι is "impossible." They identify 22:15 (ὧν ἑώρακας καὶ ἤκουσας ["a witness of what you have seen and heard"]) as the source. Barrett follows T. E. Page in taking the relative ὧν as equivalent to ἐκείνων ἅ ("of those things which"). This may be acceptable for the first relative, but not easily for the second. (Barrett [2:1143] deletes "me" from his translation.) The verb ὀφθήσομαι would normally mean "I shall appear (to you)." To limit this to christophanies, like that at 23:11, is overly restrictive. It evidently encompasses 9:16, in which the risen Christ speaks of what he will "show" (ὑποδείξω) Paul. The translation takes it *ad sensum* as an ergative, "What I shall cause you to see." This is how Fitzmyer (e.g., 759) understands it. Dibelius provides a meaningful sense of the passage. Whether one attributes this to textual corruption or authorial error is not ultimately important. Translators must, silently or otherwise, correct it.

s The participle has a future sense.

t An unnecessary variant is the future form, found in ψ 096. 6 *et al.* Others, including p[74vid] and C, read the compound ἐξαποστέλλω in present or future. This attractive alternative emphasizes the parallel with Jeremiah, but is suspect as a harmonization with 22:21.

u The *v.l.* "of the blind" (E 096 vg[mss]) is harmonizing with Isaiah.

v Boismard (*Texte*, 401) offers this D-Text: "to open their eyes so that they will turn **from** the darkness [ ] of Satan to God." His evidence is thin.

word or many, not just you, but everyone listening to me today could share what I now have—apart, of course, from these shackles."

30/ **At this point the king stood up, followed by the governor, Bernice,[ee] and all who were present. 31/ On their way out people commented to one another, "This fellow is engaged in nothing[ff] that deserves execution or incarceration."[gg] 32/ Agrippa said to Festus, "If he had not appealed to Caesar he could have been discharged."[hh]**

w A B 048 m omit the participle ὄντα ("while I was . . ."). Its placement is certainly irregular. This may come from attempting to write in a more elevated style. Luke evidently wished to stress the parallel with Jesus (Luke 22:53).

x Lit. "to this day," eliminated by the D-Text, according Boismard (*Texte*, 403), perhaps because incarceration on capital charges did not strike some as divine assistance.

y A adds ἐπίστασθαι ("knowing literature"). The verb is often associated with γράμματα ("learning").

z The D-Text, according to Boismard (*Texte*, 404), omits the proper names "Paul" and "Festus," reading "Most excellent **governor**."

aa The translation treats ἀληθείας καὶ σωφροσύνης as a hendiadys.

bb The adverbial καί could mean "also" or, as taken here, as intensive. B 104. 1175 *pc* h vg[mss] omit it, while a few minuscules read emphatic ἐγώ ("I").

cc The text of this clause is variously transmitted. The difficulty resides in the presence, absence, or placement of the negatives οὐ ("not"), οὐδέ ("and not," "nor"), οὐθέν (nothing," variously spelled), and τι ("any," "anything"). About twenty constructions exist. The emphatic double negative, which is acceptable Greek, may be the source of the difficulties.

dd *Or:* "Keep this up and you'll soon make a Christian of me." *Or:* "In a word, you want me to take the Christian side."

ee The D-Text (Boismard, *Texte*, 405) omits Bernice. This improves the awkward syntax, which appears to reflect social hierarchy, but it also conforms to the D-Text's tendency to eliminate women. See Pervo, "Social Aspects."

ff The *v.l.* τι evidently takes οὐδέν as adjectival (i.e., "no thing" versus "nothing).

gg BDF §322 takes πράσσει (lit. "is doing") as a "perfective present." Its purpose may better be explained as a reference to Paul's mission and message. What he has been doing, including this occasion, deserves no harsh penalty.

hh Note the absence of ἄν in this contrary-to-fact condition, on which see BDF §358 (1).

Analysis

Acts 26[1] is the best-crafted oration in the book, with a skillful structure and a relative abundance of stylistic niceties.[2] It would be difficult to find a commentator who believes that these achievements are accidental, for this is also the climactic oration, a defense speech that

1 On this chapter, see also Lentz, *Luke's Portrait*, esp. 83–91; Robert F. O'Toole, *Acts 26: The Christological Climax of Paul's Defense (Ac 22:1–26:32)* (AnBib 78; Rome: Pontifical Biblical Institute, 1978); Colin J. A. Hickling, "The Portrait of Paul in Acts 26," in Kremer, *Actes*, 499–503; and Artur Weiser, "Festus und Agrippa," *BZ* 28 (1984) 145–67.

2 The exordium is relatively elegant. Included are the customary (in Acts) figures of alliteration, assonance, and litotes, which can be illustrated in v. 19: Ὅθεν, βασιλεῦ Ἀγρίππα, οὐκ ἐγενόμην

becomes a missionary appeal.[3] This is apparent from attempts to analyze it in terms of forensic rhetoric.[4]

One model is: *captatio* (v. 2), a statement of *ethos* (vv. 3-5), thesis in vv. 6-8, climaxing with the subject proper: "God does raise the dead," and *probatio* that includes both narrative (vv. 9-21) and "inartistic" proofs from Scripture, introduced in v. 22 and elaborated through the subsequent dialogue, which closes with a kind of plea, or peroration, in v. 29.[5] This arrangement battles against the fact that most of the oration is narration and that the proofs must be extracted from it. Beverly Roberts Gaventa has identified a concentric structure in the body of the speech:[6]

A. Paul's faith in resurrection follows tradition (vv. 6-8).
  B. Paul persecuted followers of Jesus (vv. 9-11).
    C. Paul received a prophetic call (vv. 12-18).
    C'. Paul was obedient to his vocation (vv. 19-20).
  B'. Paul has been persecuted as a follower of Jesus (v. 21).
A'. Paul upholds the prophetic belief in the resurrection (vv. 22-23).

This may illuminate the compositional pattern of a part of the speech, and its shows the centrality of Paul's call.

Talbert's plan rests on the autobiographical character of the oration.[7] He detects an ABAB pattern. The A sections (vv. 4-5, 9-21) are autobiographical. Each is

ἀπειθὴς τῇ οὐρανίῳ ὀπτασίᾳ. (Cf. Euripides *Orestes* 31 οὐκ ἀπειθήσας θεῷ "not disobeying the god.") Other marks of attempts at elevated style are eleven uses of τε, an optative with ἄν in v. 29 (the only such potential optative in the NT, BDF §359 [2]; 385 [1]), and the Attic form ἴσασι (v. 4, not used otherwise in early Christian literature until Justin *Dial.* 5.1), the use of ἥγημαι as present (v. 2), and the final vocative (v. 7). The true superlative in v. 5 is a bit rare. Verse 14 exhibits a Greek proverb. Cf. also the proverbial "in a corner" (v. 26). In v. 21 comes an Attic use of πειράομαι. Verse 22 has οὐδέν with a participle. Three times in this speech (twice in v. 23) εἰ is used in the rhetorical sense of a thesis to be expounded (whether one should marry, have children, fight for king and country, etc.). See Friedrich Blass, *Philology of the Gospels* (London: Macmillan, 1898) 9–10; Cadbury, "Lexical Notes on Luke-Acts IV, *JBL* 48 (1929) 412–25, esp. 421–22. Note v. 23, εἰ παθητὸς ὁ χριστός, εἰ πρῶτος . . . , with alliteration and a verbal adjective. Rare and thus putatively elegant words include γνώστης ("expert" [v. 3]), μακάριος as "fortunate" (v. 3), βίωσις ("life" [v. 4]), θρησκεία ("religion" [v. 5]), and δωδεκάφυλον ("twelve tribes" [v. 7]), to go no further. (Rackham, 462 n. 5, lists thirteen *hapax legomena.*) In v. 8, ἄπιστος has its intellectual sense of "incredible," as in *Aristeas* 296, rather than the normal NT "unbelieving." Cf. also οὐρανόθεν ("from heaven") and ὑπὲρ τὴν λαμπρότητα τοῦ ἡλίου ("brighter than the sun") in v. 13. Here the writer apologizes from the Semitic "Saul, Saul" (v. 14). As an essay, this effort would, however, have received the equivalent of some strong remarks in red pencil. See the notes on various verses. See Conzelmann (210), who finds the style of vv. 4-5 and 6-7 "unimpressive." As a formal comparison, he posits Lucian *Peregr.* 8. Schwartz ("Trial Scene," 130) notes the change. In the book's first trial, the apostles were adjudged uneducated (ἀγράμματοι). The final trial presents a Paul whose learning impresses Agrippa (26:24).

3 Conzelmann, 209. Tannehill (*Narrative Unity*, 2:317) notes themes found in other speeches and adds that it is structurally like Peter's Pentecost address in that it closes with a missionary appeal contained within a dialogue (2:37-40; 26:24-29). Foakes Jackson (222) links speech to setting: "Here Luke introduces Paul's speech with a dramatic picture of regal pomp . . . the apostle is now about to make the greatest of his speeches recorded in the Acts, and the scene is appropriately set for so momentous an occasion." Rackham (456) is similar.

4 See, for example, Soards, *Speeches*, 122–23; and Witherington, 736–37. Neyrey ("Forensic Defense Speech," 221) lists the elements that belong to *narratio* (vv. 6-7, 16-20, 6-8) and the different types of *probatio* (vv. 16, 12-18, 13, 5, 12-13, 14-16, 16-18). These are not sequential, although most of the proof resides in vv. 12-18.

5 Compare Witherington, 737: *exordium*, vv. 2-3; *narratio*, vv. 4-21; *propositio*, vv. 22-23, proofs omitted (as provided in earlier addresses); a brief *refutatio*, vv. 25-26, with the *peroratio* in vv. 27 and 29

6 Gaventa, *Darkness*, 80.

7 Talbert, 211–12.

introduced with the transitional particle μὲν οὖν. The B (vv. 6-8, 22-23) components deal with the issue: resurrection. Each is marked by the verb ἕστηκα ("I stand") with a participle, κρινόμενος ("being judged") in v. 6 and μαρτυρόμενος ("witnessing") in v. 22. This is insightful, revealing the transition from a (hypothetically) judicial to a deliberative thrust. Many analyses cease, like the last two, at v. 23, where Felix interrupts, but the speech is imbedded in the subsequent dialogue and narrative.[8] The data from this and the other defense speeches in chaps. 22 and 24 indicate that the author was familiar with the conventions of forensic rhetoric, but he does not follow them slavishly, and in this case rhetorical conventions provide no more than background.[9] "Stasis remains metastasis," says Kennedy, nearly conceding that this argument of attributing one's action to divine causation is becoming a bit threadbare.[10]

In his study of the forms of commission stories, István Czachesz finds that Acts 26 "stands very close to the philosophical examples."[11] A common feature of these stories is a narrative in which "the hero is commissioned directly by the sender, without any reference to an institutional framework, owes loyalty only to the sender, and acts much on his own, obeying his 'daimonion.'"[12] This classification identifies the leading difference between chap. 26 and the other two accounts. One result of this "translation" deserves attention: its individualistic orientation. Even more than in Acts 22, Paul is a "loner" who urges individuals to repent and do the right thing. The individualistic proclivity of Lucan thought has colored his picture of Paul.[13]

Paul does not defend himself against any charges.[14] None are mentioned by any of the participants. What he does defend is his life, which is to say his deviation from the official Judaism represented by the high priestly leadership. At best this address could be called the testimony of one witness. This is congenial to the narrator's purpose, for "witness" is the role Paul was selected by Christ to play (v. 16). Paul has managed to change the topic. The high priests were unlikely to have supported his belief in resurrection or its biblical background, and they were most assuredly in disagreement with his view about the Messiah, but such beliefs would not, one might suppose, constitute grounds for capital punishment. The speech implies, however, that belief in Jesus *was* a cause for execution (v. 10). No Roman court would support that position—nor would a Jewish court, if it possessed capital jurisdiction, which it presumably did not. Paul was on safe grounds there.

The theology of the speech would be very difficult for anyone not intimately familiar with "the Movement" to penetrate. The thesis in v. 8 that "God raises the dead" is claimed as an ancient Israelite conviction (vv. 6-7). That Jesus is an example of this action and/or that he is the Messiah is never explicitly stated. Only in v. 23 does Paul link belief in a Messiah to the claim that he had to die and be raised. Believing readers could fill in all of the gaps, but for most of the dramatic audience, including Festus, they would have been a series of non sequiturs. He could make no sense of what Paul said; Agrippa could, and was willing to concede the potency of the argument, but the narrator could not and did not

8 Soards (*Speeches*, 123), who is attentive to context, classifies vv. 24-29 as "epilogue through dialogue."

9 Cf. also Weiser (2:638–39); and Czachesz, "Commission Narratives," 79.

10 Kennedy, *Rhetorical Criticism*, 137.

11 Czachesz, "Commission Narratives," 83–85, citing 83. On pp. 11–57, Czachesz argues that many ancient philosophers, ranging from Pythagoras to Epicurus, claimed divine revelation as the source of their systems. Indirect support for this classification may be seen in the wealth of philosophical themes identified by Malherbe, *Paul*, 147–63.

12 Czachesz, "Commission Narratives," 85.

13 A concomitant feature is the tendency in Deutero-Pauline writings for Paul to become a model convert from a notoriously sinful life. See, e.g., 1 Tim 1:12-17; *Act. Pet.* 2 (Verc.); cf. also Eph 3:8, discussed on p. 236 n. 30. Gaventa (*Darkness*, 92) captures the distinction between Paul as a model and the historical Paul: "It is precisely at this point that Luke and Paul part company. Paul understands his experience to be an example of the reversal of values and expectations that is intrinsic to the New Age."

14 The closest he comes is the claim that "the Jews" tried to murder him in the temple because of his efforts to convert both Jews and gentiles (v. 21).

dare to take the Herodian monarch any further down the path to conversion.

Comment

■ **1** Agrippa assumes the bench, as it were, with a polite invitation to Paul,[15] who launches his defense (ἀπελογεῖτο) with an appropriate gesture.[16] H^mg adds, after "Paul," "confident and encouraged by the Holy Spirit." This is a characteristic of the D-Text, as in 24:10.[17]

■ **2-3** Despite the claim that he is privileged to defend himself against "all the charges," he addresses none of them. In v. 3, Luke's efforts at style trip him up. Evidently, he wished to view the phrase about Agrippa's expertise (γνώστην ὄντα σε) with the verb ἥγημαι ("regard," "think"). Another possibility is to construe it as the object of δέομαι ("beg"). Neither will work. It is a dangling phrase.[18] The textual variants seek to emend the error.[19] The *captatio* flatters Agrippa for his familiarity with matters under dispute among Jews, those ζητήματα that left Festus adrift (25:19). It is these, and only these, that Paul will address.[20]

■ **4-8** Paul then turns (μὲν οὖν) to his *ethos*. The hyperbole has its purpose. Paul states that he is famous. His opponents would prefer "notorious" (21:28; 24:5), but they would agree that everyone in the Jewish world knows him.[21] The sentence is overloaded, which may account for the considerable interpretative difficulties.[22] Verses 4-5a are best read in conformity with 22:3. The point comes in v. 5b: far from being lax, Paul belongs to the most observant party within Judaism.[23] Questions about such matters can rapidly be resolved by interviewing almost anyone. The theme is approached in a subtle, oblique manner.[24] It is the ancestral hope, for which all pray.[25] For many, probably most, of the natives of Judea this would be the promise of "the land," a more or less

15 The passive "it is permitted" is less direct than "I permit you" (Haenchen, 681). BDF §320 labels this an "aoristic present."

16 Cf. 13:16; 21:40. For a description of the procedure, see Apuleius *Metam.* 2.21. Barrett (2:1148–49) says that the verb "stretch out" (ἐκτείνω) is not typical, but it is an equivalent to the Latin *porrigo*, used by Apuleius. It is probably better not to think of how this could be done with the shackles mentioned in v. 29. Jacquier (705) proposes two solutions for this problem.

17 Boismard (*Texte*, 398) ignores it. He does offer a tedious paraphrase: "began to defend . . ."

18 BDF §137 (3). Note also Barrett, 2:1150.

19 Both Alexandrian ([p[74]] ℵ[2] A C 33) and the D-Text (Boismard, *Texte*, 399) add a participle, ἐπιστάμενος ("knowing") which redeems the situation. Another variant adds the object "you" (σου) to the verb "beg." Corruption seems unlikely here.

20 Luke likes to cap the *captatio* with an adverb: συντόμως ("briefly") in 24:4; εὐθύμως ("with good will") in 24:10, and "patiently" (μακροθύμως) here.

21 Achilles Tatius *Leuc. Clit.* 8.10.7 provides a good formal parallel from a forensic speech: "As for Thersander's way of life (βίον), all here know (ἴσασι πάντες) how that from his first youth (ἐκ πρώτης ἡλικίας) it was elegant and discreet" (trans. S. Gaselee, *Achilles Tatius* [LCL; Cambridge, Mass.: Harvard University Press, 1969] 429).

22 Verse 4 contains two prepositional phrases: ἐκ νεότητος ("from youth") and ἀπ᾽ ἀρχῆς ("from [the] beginning"), both of which modify "manner of life." To these v. 5 adds ἄνωθεν ("for a long time"), which, in light of the participle προγινώσκοντες ("knowing beforehand"), seems redundant. Haenchen (683 n. 1) views all of this pleonasm as emphatic. Both ἀπ᾽ ἀρχῆς and ἄνωθεν occur in the preface to Luke (1:2-3). On these, see Cadbury, "Commentary," 502–3. Boismard (*Texte*, 399) omits the prepositional phrase from his D-Text. The meaning of ἔθνος in v. 4 is not clear. Cadbury and Lake (315) wish to refer it to Cilicia (Tarsus), but this, if strictly logical, is probably not likely. See Haenchen, 682 n. 6. The rendition of τε is uncertain. See Barrett (2:1150–51), who comes down on the side of "and" (reflected in the translation). The articles in v. 4 were problematic for some scribes. The triple τήν is troublesome, for there is no need to mark three distinct adjectival phrases. Perhaps the author intended to produce anaphora. A variety of witnesses omit the second example, and others replace the third with μου ("my").

23 Cf. Apuleius *Metam.* 11.21: *vir alioquin gravis et sobriae religionis observatione famosus* ("he [the high priest of Isis], being a serious man famous for his observance of austere religious discipline"), trans. J. Arthur Hanson, *Apuleius Metamorphoses II* (LCL; Cambridge, Mass.: Harvard University Press, 1989) 333.

24 One might be tempted to take the opening καὶ νῦν of v. 6 as adversative: "I was a Pharisee, but now . . ." The text, however, stresses continuity.

independent nation, theologically expressed in a variety of eschatological concepts.[26] For Paul here, resurrection is both the essence of eschatology and of the charge against him.[27] He frames the question in terms suggesting that to deny the possibility of resurrection is to place limits on divine power. This places the issue within a quasi-philosophical framework that the address will not pursue.[28] Apologists may argue for resurrection. In this context, its scriptural basis is sufficient evidence.[29] Luke is content with an apologetic and intellectual veneer. The thesis is stated in the present tense, doubtless with regard to the (never stated) resurrection of Jesus.[30] The dramatic audience would have been lost at this point.[31]

Excursus: Three Accounts of Paul's Conversion/Call

Paul's transformation from opponent to advocate of the Jesus movement is one of the items that Acts reports three times.[32] Research has followed the path laid out by Dibelius and Haenchen: from studies based upon the predication of various sources to literary analysis.[33] The accounts are not isolated units, although each has its appropriate setting and color. The narrative of chap. 9, which is based upon a written source, coordinates with other narratives.[34] Chapter 22, delivered in the temple, has appropriate Judaic coloring, while the audience of chap. 26 enjoys a stronger tincture of Hellenic thought and idiom. Readers are not expected to place these speeches in parallel columns for the purpose of identifying omissions, additions, and contradictions, but they are not to pretend that each is the sole account. Accumulation is one driving feature. Repetition reinforces importance, and individual data are added to the reader's base, as it were. Barrett's observation, "The agreements [among the three accounts] are more important than the disagreements," is only superficially correct.[35] Readers are evidently expected to treat the accounts as cumulative. "In fact, the complete story of Paul's conversion, as Luke understood it, can only be determined by bringing together features from *all three* narratives. The entire story is not completely narrated in *any one* of the accounts."[36]

---

25 "Night and day" means "continuously," as in Luke 2:37, based on Jdt 4:9. See Barrett, 2:1153.

26 See the wide-ranging and penetrating survey by Rudolf Bultmann and Kurt Rengstorf, "ἐλπίς," *TDNT* 2:517–35.

27 Compare the participle κρινόμενος in v. 6, "judged" in the legal sense, with κρίνεται in v. 8, referring to a logical judgment or conclusion.

28 The question is that of ἀδύνατα, items considered impossible. See Grant, *Miracle*, 57–58, 103, 132–33, 167.

29 For ancient arguments about the limits on divine omnipotence and the development of intellectual arguments for resurrection, see Grant, *Miracle*, 127–34, and 235–45. *1 Clem.* 24–25 already advanced some proofs.

30 Agrippa had learned from Festus about one "dead Jesus, whom Paul claimed to be alive" (v. 19) and could, at least in theory, gain comprehension with the introduction of Jesus' name in 26:9.

31 See Foakes Jackson, 225. The plural "you people" is of uncertain reference. It probably refers to Jews who do not accept the resurrection, but might apply to the dramatic audience. See Fitzmyer, 757.

32 The most similar of these is another conversion: Cornelius's reception of the faith is, like Paul's, reported first in a narrative (10:1-48), then in two speeches (11:1-18; 15:7-11). The third is, although the shortest, the most decisive. A different sort of triplet is Paul's threefold repetition of his decision that, since "the Jews" have rejected the message, he will turn to the gentiles (13:46; 18:6; 28:28). These announcements are distributed over three crucial geographical areas: "Asia," Greece, and Italy. The third, in Rome, is climactic. Another is formal: three liberations from incarceration: 5:19-20; 12:6-12; and 16:25-40. The third of these is the most elaborate. These trios have different functions. All are related to salvation history and each exemplifies end-stress.

33 An example of the source-critical approach is E. Hirsch, "Die drei Berichte der Apostelgeschichte über die Bekehrung des Paulus," *ZNW* 28 (1929) 305–12. Witherington has recently taken up this approach in "Editing the Good News: Some Synoptic Lessons for the Study of Acts," in idem, *History*, 335–44, esp. 339. Literary approaches are discussed in the following paragraphs. For a concise history of research on the problem see Marguerat, *Historian*, 180–81 (p. 180 n. 4 sets out a basic bibliography). In addition, see Clark, *Parallel Lives*, 150–208; and Miller, *Convinced*, 186–202.

34 See the comments on Acts 9:1-19a.

35 Barrett, 1:441. Tannehill (*Narrative Unity*, 2:321–32) labors to distinguish between the discrepancies here and those elsewhere.

36 Hedrick, "Paul's Conversion/Call," 432.

The three accounts share many features of a core outline, but they are, in fact, quite different stories, each with a distinctive purpose. Recent study emphasizes the particular form and purpose of each recitation. Gaventa says that the account in chap. 9 centers on the overthrown enemy, while chap. 22 stresses Paul's character as a loyal Jew, and chap. 26 focuses on the call to witness and Paul's obedient response to that summons.[37] Czachesz identifies each as a distinctive social type of commission story: in chap. 9 the orientation is institutional, while chap. 22 represents the prophetic type and chap. 26 is closest to the philosophical model.[38] Daniel Marguerat's study focuses on the differences among the accounts in terms of their literary functions. Acts 9 stresses ecclesial mediation (cf. Czachesz), Acts 22 "Saul's Jewishness" (cf. Gaventa), and Acts 26 the legitimation of the gentile mission.[39]

Progression is the other propellant. In the course of his repetitions Luke "pushes" the story in the direction of Galatians, that is, as a prophetic call. Charles Hedrick's literary exploration takes narrative sequence and totality into account.[40] There is development and narrative progression. Hedrick implicitly invokes the "rule of three" by observing that Luke does not report the specific missionary commission until chap. 26.[41] Acts 26 holds the climactic and decisive place in the narrative. This is *the* story of Paul's conversion/call as Luke wishes readers to perceive it. It is therefore questionable to contend that Luke separates Paul's conversion from his call. That is the case in Acts 9, but not in Acts 26. Luke's source evidently distinguished the two—perhaps without theological reflection—but, when given the chance to tell the story his way, Luke identifies conversion and call. Appreciation of Luke's story of Paul's conversion thus requires both distinction among and amalgamation of the three accounts. Acts 26 presents a story of Paul's conversion that is at one and the same time the most Lucan and the most Pauline of the three reports. This apparently paradoxical statement is, to borrow a metaphor, a useful light upon the nature of Luke's quite nonparadoxical theology.

■ **9-11** After the summary in these verses, vv. 12-18 present the single narrative scene of this account: the epiphany outside of Damascus, which is also the occasion for direct delivery of the missionary commission.[42] What Paul says here corresponds to what he wrote to the Galatians (1:15-17): he had a revelation of Christ that included a commission to convert gentiles.[43] The conversion follows the standard pattern: Paul the persecutor, high priestly authorization to ravage Damascus, vision on the road, and subsequent mission beginning in Damascus. The narrative has become more vigorous through the addition of invented details. The summary of the persecutor's résumé is much livelier.[44] Paul now has the principal qualities of the later "inquisitor" that all know and love. In comparison to Paul, Pliny was a moderate.[45] Paul was, by implication, a vigorously pro-capital-punishment, voting[46] member of the Sanhedrin rather than a youthful guardian of haberdashery. Like an early soviet commissar he purged one synagogue after another, in a career that took him from Jerusalem to outlying cities[47] and finally beyond the boundaries of Judea (26:9-11). Luke emphasizes Paul's status as an authorized agent of the Jewish leadership, which must thus bear responsibility for these murders, rather than

37 Gaventa, *Darkness*, 90; her study of the three accounts encompasses pp. 52–95.
38 Czachesz, "Commission Narratives," 58–88. See also p. 627 n. 11.
39 Marguerat, *Historian*, 179–204.
40 Hedrick, "Paul's Conversion/Call," esp. 427–32.
41 Ibid., 427, where he speaks of suspense.
42 The parallel in chap. 9 involved three distinct scenes.
43 Lohfink (*Conversion*, 99) qualifies this assertion: "Hence what Luke wants to say in chapter 26 is that Paul's missionary work was *willed by God himself*—and this certainly is not the immediate and direct call Paul has in mind in Galatians."
44 The infinitive δεῖν in v. 9 is ironic, suggesting that Paul imagined himself as the instrument of divine destiny. Cf. the use of δεῖ in 9:6, 16; 23:11, etc.
45 Pliny observed (*Ep.* 10.96.5) that true believers could not be compelled to make the requisite offering. Cf. *Mart. Pol.* 9.3 and Josephus *Bell.* 2.152 (Essenes could not be tortured into reviling Moses or eating impure food).
46 "Pebble" (ψῆφος) is a metonym for "vote," as colored pebbles served as ballots. Cf. Philo *Deus* 75; Josephus *Ant.* 2.163.
47 Cf. 5:16 (Peter's healings attract a suburban clientele).

portraying him as an opponent of the Jesus movement who acted on his own initiative. The journey to Damascus is now but one example[48] of his properly authorized anti-Christian expeditions.

This creature could play the role of Ptolemy in *3 Maccabees* or the aged Herod I without rehearsal.[49] The classical model is Pentheus (Euripides' *Bacchae*). The autobiographical sketch prepares the way for the confrontation between Festus and Paul in vv. 24-25. The "old Paul" had many virtues and abilities, but he lacked self-control (σωφροσύνη). After his call, he became a well-rounded person in full control of his emotions.[50] For ancients, inability to manage one's temper was one of the greatest and least forgivable of character defects.[51] The literary/rhetorical objective of this intensification is to heighten the contrast between the earlier and the later Paul. Acts 26 is painted in black and white, almost literally (v. 18).[52]

■ **13-14** The epiphany is more vivid, linear, and dramatic. For the dramatic audience the report would be shocking. The light was brighter than the sun (at noontime in Syria).[53] The party felt its power and crashed to the ground *en masse*.[54] The light shone (περιλάμπω [v. 13]) rather than flashed (περιαστράπτω [9:3; 22:6]). This is not mere elegant variation. Flashes betoken punishment (cf. the thunderbolt of Zeus and his successors), while "shining" portends a friendly epiphany, as in Luke 2:9. Light now functions as a symbol of conversion (v. 18). For the first time, it is stated that Paul saw the light. These are positive additions to the negative omission of blinding. Punishment is not in the picture. Reference to the "Hebrew language" (presumably Aramaic) prepares the hearers for the "barbarous" name "Saul." To the heavenly Jesus' question is appended a proverb. Although the phrase is found elsewhere,[55] the most important citation is Euripides *Bacch.* 794–95, not only because the influence of this play is arguably present elsewhere in Acts,[56] but

48 Note the use of "many" in vv. 9-10 and of "many times" and "all" in v. 11. The imperfects ἠνάγκαζον and ἐδίωκον ("compel" and "persecute") are frequentative ("continued to compel . . . persecute"), although the first may have a conative sense ("I kept on trying to compel"). See Haenchen, 685; and BDF §326. "Blaspheme" (v. 11) is difficult from a Jewish perspective, but Luke did not share that perspective.

49 Josephus (*Ant.* 17.174) applies the same participle Paul uses of himself in v. 11, ἐμμαινόμενος, to the dying Herod.

50 This thesis is demonstrated by Lentz, *Luke's Portrait*, esp. 62–104. Philo's comments on repentance (*Virt.* 175–86) are particularly instructive. Those who turn from polytheism to monotheism are like blind persons who have recovered their sight and have passed from profound darkness to gleaming light (§179). Proselytes pass (§§181–82) from vice to virtue, each of which is illustrated with an adjectival catalogue. Heading the list of virtues are σώφρονες and ἐγκρατεῖς ("temperate" and "self-controlled").

51 A principal defect of Alexander, according to the biographical tradition, was his inability to manage his temper. See, for example, the story of Cleitus in Plutarch *Alex.* 50–51. Greek romantic novels did not much concern themselves with character development, but change does occur. Chaireas, the hero of *Callirhoe*, launches their misfortunes by kicking his wife in a fit of temper. By the end of the novel, he was not likely to engage in such behavior. Paul did not develop; he was transformed by divine intervention. Feldman (*Jew and Gentile*, 274–76) has some useful comments about σωφροσύνη ("temperance"). Pharaoh was the opposite of the Stoic sage, because he could not control his passions (σωφρονεῖν [Josephus *Ant.* 2.296]). Josephus omitted Moses' most notable temper tantrum, the smashing of the tablets (*Ant.* 3.99).

52 Lohfink (*Conversion*, 93–94) describes this intensification and its purpose.

53 In 9:3, it was simply "light"; in 22:6, it was a "great" (ἱκανόν) light.

54 Haenchen (685) observes that, without the blinding of Paul and the intervention of Ananias, all must collapse to demonstrate "the objectivity of the event." See also Czachesz ("Commission Narratives," 80–81), who provides examples from Greek stories of conversions to philosophy. The D-Text of v. 14 (Boismard, *Texte*, 401) is characteristic: "**And** all fell down **because of fear**, while I **alone** heard a voice. . . ."

55 For example, Pindar *Pyth.* 2.94; Aeschylus *Ag.* 1624; Prometheus *P.V.* 324–25; and Julian *Or.* 8.246B. Philo *Dec.* 87 uses it for the pricks of "conscience."

56 See p. 410 n. 91. For earlier discussions of possible dependence on Euripides here, see Haenchen, 685 n. 3, to which add J. Hackett, "Echoes of the Bacchae of Euripides in Acts of the Apostles," *Irish Theological Quarterly* 23 (1956) 219–27, 350–66. See also Lothar Schmid, "κέντρον," *TDNT* 3:663–68.

more particularly because of the setting: the disguised Dionysus, a new god, addresses these words to Pentheus. They identify the recipient as a θεόμαχος ("antagonist of God").[57] Like philosophers, Paul grounds his mission in an epiphany.[58]

■ **16-18** These verses are among the most densely packed in Acts.[59] In biblical and Deutero-Pauline language, they set forth Paul's mission to the gentiles. The language is, despite Paul's practice of "Jews first," which is attested throughout Acts, not appropriate for practicing Jews.[60] The experience is clearly qualified as an appearance of the heavenly Jesus, and Paul is charged to take on the chief role of the Twelve: witnessing (Acts 1:8). Verse 16 begins, like 9:6, with a command to rise (ἀλλὰ ἀνάστηθι) that seems unnecessarily expanded, until one realizes that "stand on your feet" evokes Ezek 2:1, that prophet's commission. The role of Ananias in the earlier accounts yields to a colorless prepositional phrase: εἰς τοῦτο ("for this reason"), followed by a series of infinitives of purpose[61] and related clauses. "I have appeared" (ὤφθην) establishes the event as a resurrection appearance,[62] specifically a missionary commissioning appearance. The subject of Paul's election is now Christ rather than God.[63] His functions are to be "agent" (ὑπηρέτης[64]) and "witness" (μάρτυς).[65] These terms are another evocation[66] of the preface to Luke, which speaks (v. 2) of "eyewitnesses and agents" (αὐτόπται καὶ ὑπηρέται).[67] Paul is to take a place among the primary tradents of the Jesus movement. As a witness, he is what might be called an ἰσαπόστολος ("equal of the apostles").[68]

■ **17** The verse is a promise not of suffering for the name's sake (cf. 9:15-16) but of rescue from Jews and gentiles. This is another evocation of a prophetic call[69] (and a parallel to 12:11).[70]

■ **18** Although these allusions to the calls of Hebrew prophets are important, they do not form the theological core of v. 18, which is a densely packed statement

57 See Lentz (*Luke's Portrait*, 84–86), who also shows the relevance of the *Agamemnon*. Aeschylus portrays Aegisthus as devoid of knowledge and self-control.

58 Cf. Plato *Apol.* 33C; Epictetus *Diss.* 2.16.44.

59 Barrett (2:1162) says: "The piling up of images constitutes an impressive, if not perfectly clear, climax."

60 Tannehill (*Narrative Unity*, 2:324 n. 1) observes that similar language is used in Luke 1:77-79, but that does not make v. 18 inclusive. The parallel in 22:21 makes it probable that the "whom" are gentiles.

61 The second and third of these (ἐπιστρέψαι and λαβεῖν ["turn," "receive"]) are articular. BDF §400 (6) says that the article avoids confusion.

62 The verb is not used exclusively in this sense, but see Luke 24:34, and, in particular, 1 Cor 15:5-8.

63 In 3:20 and the parallel to 26:16 in 22:14, the subject of προχειρίζω is God. Compare also 10:41 (witnesses chosen in advance [προκεχειροτονημένοις] by God).

64 The title ὑπηρέτης is not restricted to menials (like John Mark; Acts 13:5). Moses designates himself as God's ὑπηρέτης in Josephus *Ant.* 4.317.

65 The philosophical tradition is also relevant. For Epictetus, the ideal Stoic is a witness (μάρτυρα; *Diss.* 3.24.112–13) appointed (κατατεταγμένος; 4.24.114) by God to service (ὑπηρεσίαν; 3.24.114). The noun "servant" (ὑπηρέτης) occurs in 2.24.98 (cf. 2.22.82, 95); "witness" appears in 3.22.88, and as a noun in 3.22.86. These roles are linked to divine commission in 3.22.23, 54, 56, 95.

66 See the comments on v. 4.

67 Cf. Cadbury, "Commentary," 498.

68 On the meaning of the title "witness" applied to Paul, see Burchard, *Dreizehnte Zeuge*, esp. 135–36. The term ἰσαπόστολος is applied to Thecla in the titles of three eleventh-century MSS. of the *Acts of Paul and Thecla*.

69 Jer 1:7-8: καὶ εἶπεν κύριος πρός με Μὴ λέγε ὅτι Νεώτερος ἐγώ εἰμι, ὅτι πρὸς πάντας, οὓς ἐὰν ἐξαποστείλω σε, πορεύσῃ, καὶ κατὰ πάντα, ὅσα ἐὰν ἐντείλωμαί σοι, λαλήσεις, 8 μὴ φοβηθῇς ἀπὸ προσώπου αὐτῶν, ὅτι μετὰ σοῦ ἐγώ εἰμι τοῦ ἐξαιρεῖσθαί σε ("But the LORD said to me, 'Do not say, "I am only a boy"; for you shall go to all to whom I send you, and you shall speak whatever I command you. 8 Do not be afraid of them, for I am with you to deliver you,' says the LORD."). For detailed similarities between Paul and Jeremiah, see Rackham, 469. On the prophetic material, see Lohfink (*Conversion*, 70–73), who also recognizes the integration of these allusions into the language of early Christian proclamation.

70 Acts 12:11 (Peter's recognition of rescue from execution) contains the verbs ἐξαποστέλλω ("send") and ἐξαιρέω ("rescue").

of Lucan/Deutero-Pauline theology. The framework is established by the image of "turning from *X* to *Y*," which is characteristic of early Christian baptismal declarations and other creedal statements (e.g., 1 Thess 1:9). The imagery derives from Israelite thought: for the Hebrew Bible, "turn" becomes "repent" in more abstract language. Movement from the dominion of darkness to the bliss of light is, as Gaventa says, "standard in descriptions of conversion,"[71] with a long history in descriptions of "conversion" to philosophy and of religious transformation.[72] "From darkness to light" is both the most universal and the most absolute form of this image. The latter gives it a home in dualistic thought.[73]

This implicit metaphor "from darkness to light," in its various manifestations, frames and permeates Luke and Acts, from the words of the Benedictus (Luke 1:78-79) to those of Paul in Acts 28:16-17. It is central to the opening words of Jesus' first sermon and the closing words of Paul's last address (Luke 4:16; Acts 28:17). Luke understands this transformation by way of Isa 42:6-7, which is cited in Acts 26:18, and Isa 49:6, cited by Paul in Acts 13:47, on the occasion of his first turn to the gentiles.[74] Liturgical thought and practice also hover in the background.[75]

The author skates on the edge of dualistic thinking by defining "darkness" as the power of Satan, whom Jesus has defeated.[76] He therefore expounds the contrast of light to darkness in apocalyptic and salvation-historical categories. Another favorite Lucan concept introduced here is the invitation to turn toward God (3:19; 15:19), with the corresponding reward of gaining one's inheritance among those who are holy (Acts 20:21, 32). Luke's Paul presents the gospel as a healing message that empowers individuals to change their lives. Humanity is not "dead" in its sins. It is impaired, "ill," a fault that can be corrected by repentance. Acts 26 does not present Paul as an example of one who was blinded and then healed. He is now the one who opens the eyes

71 Gaventa, *Darkness*, 86. Examples include Plato *Resp.* 518C–D; Philo *Virt.* 179; *Poimandres* (*Corp. Herm.* I) 28; *Jos. Asen.* 8:10; 15:13; 1 Pet 2:9; *1 Clem.* 59.2–3; and the *Odes Sol.* 14:18–19. See also Minucius Felix *Oct.* 1.4 (apologetics); Melito, *On the Passover* 69 (liturgical preaching); the *Aesop Romance* 5 and Apuleius *Metam.* 11.23 (both of Isis); and Lucian *Nigr.* 4.1 (conversion to philosophy).

72 See the almost exhaustive study of Hans Conzelmann, "φῶς," *TDNT* 9:310–58, with large bibliography. Note also Spicq, *Lexicon*, 3:470–91. For philosophical and patristic usage, see G. W. Clarke, trans., *The Octavius of Marcus Minucius Felix* (ACW 39; New York: Newman, 1974) 167–68 n. 8.

73 Luke was no dualist, but his Deutero-Pauline sources, Colossians and Ephesians, were comfortable with dualistic language. For investigations of the intertextual background here, see Pervo, *Dating*, 275–78. The principal texts are Col 1:12-14 and Eph 1:7. Note also Acts 20:32 and its background. Paulinists in the environs of Ephesus were influenced by thought similar to that found in the writings of the Qumran community, which contrast those who belong to the sphere of light to the denizens of darkness (e.g., 1QS 1:9–10; 1QM 1:1) and speak of "Belial's dominion" (1QS 1:18, 23; 2:19). With "place" (lit. "lot," κλῆρος [v. 18]) compare the respective "lots" of God and Belial (1QS 2:2, 5). This is most noticeable in Ephesians, for instances of which see Schnackenburg, *Ephesians*, index 348, *s.v.* "Qumran Texts." The least adulterated example is the post-Pauline 2 Cor 6:14–7:1, with its stark opposition between realms of "light" and "darkness," "Christ and Beliar."

74 Luke 2:32 evokes both Isa 42:6-7 and 49:6.

75 This may be safely inferred from *1 Clem.* 59, which opens the solemn, closing prayer. The intellectual milieu is that of Hellenistic Judaism; the literary milieu is that of the postapostolic, Deutero-Pauline, and later eras. See Horacio E. Lona, *Der erste Clemensbrief* (Kommentar zu den apostolischen Vätern; Göttingen: Vandenhoeck & Ruprecht, 1998) 613–19; and Andreas Lindemann, *Die Clemensbriefe* (HNT 17; Tübingen: Mohr Siebeck, 1992) 164–68. By the time of Justin, φωτισμός ("enlightenment") had become a term for baptism. See Schnackenburg, *Ephesians*, 222–23. Note also ὁ υἱὸς τῆς ἀγάπης αὐτοῦ (lit. "the son of his [God's] love" [Col 1:13]), which is the equivalent of "beloved son" in Mark 1:11. This evokes the baptism of Jesus and confirms that baptism is the locus of the translation of believers from darkness to light. *1 Clem.* 59.2–3 links the adjective "beloved" with παῖς ("son," "servant").

76 Luke 22:53 indicates that the power of Satan is the time of darkness. See Conzelmann, *Theology*, 181–82.

of the spiritually blind.[77] Luke has brought about a full conversion of the conversion of Paul.

■ **19-21** After devoting eleven verses to his biography up to the point of conversion,[78] Paul allocates three to his subsequent activity, two to his missionary activity, with emphasis on his message to his own people, and one to the circumstances of his arrest. The operative words are the mellifluous phrase about obedience to the celestial vision. Such visions could not be ignored with impunity. Examples were available to prod the recalcitrant.[79] Socrates was but one of those who justified their missions by reference to a divine injunction.[80] Paul's argument is framed in language that would be acceptable to a Greco-Roman audience.

■ **20** The verse is either a grammatical or a textual disaster, possibly both. The problem is *πᾶσαν τε τὴν χώραν τῆς Ἰουδαίας* ("the entire region of Judea"). The only factor in its support is that it is not correct and could be taken as a typical Lucan hyperbole. The text printed in N-A[27] evidently intends to report here the traditional combination "Jerusalem and Judea." The grammatical problem is that this unmarked accusative lies between two datives ("Jerusalem" and "gentiles"). Most agree that the preposition *εἰς* ("throughout the entire region . . .") is secondary.[81] Attempts to construe the construction as a Semiticism are improbable,[82] as is the suggestion that it is an accusative of extent. Haenchen identifies the phrase as "presumably an old and false gloss." Its falsity is in its favor, and the motive of the glossator is not specified.[83] Blass proposed *εἰς πᾶσάν τε χώραν Ἰουδαίοις καὶ τοῖς ἔθνεσιν* ("to both Jews and gentiles in every region"). In support, he stated that Luke uses the genitive of persons after *χώρα* ("region"), not the genetive of place.[84] See, however, Acts 8:1. This emendation is attractive. The D-Text printed by Boismard[85] is clearer: *ἀλλὰ τοῖς ἐν Δαμασκῷ πρῶτων τε καὶ Ἱεροσολύμοις, καί ἐν πάσαῖς πόλεσιν τῆς Ἰουδαῖας ἐκήρυξα μετανοεῖν καὶ ἐπιστρέφειν ἐπὶ τὸν θεόν ζῶντα* (". . . Jerusalem, **and in all the cities of Judea** [ ] **I proclaimed** that they should repent and turn to the **living** God"). "Living God" is an obvious harmonization (cf. 14:15, etc.). The omission of "gentiles" is remarkable. "All the cities of Judea" probably derives from v. 11. In short, this looks like a correction of a text that included the awkward accusative. It could not have been its source. *Faute de mieux*, Blass's proposal is translated. This best accounts for the alternatives.[86]

■ **22-23** Paul's message was utterly unobjectionable. The differences—Jews were to repent for their complicity in Jesus' death or failure to receive the news about him, gentiles for idolatry—are soft-pedaled, but the moral nature was not. Paul did not preach "cheap grace."[87] It was because of these commendable activities that "Jews" attempted to kill him in the temple. Verses 22-23

77 On the symbolic use of "blind" here, see Dennis Hamm, "Paul's Blindness and Its Healing: Clues to Symbolic Intent (Acts 9; 22 and 26)," *Bib* 71 (1990) 63–72. Susan R. Garrett ("Beloved Physician of the Soul? Luke as Advocate for Ascetic Practice," in Leif E. Vaage and Vincent L. Wimbush, eds., *Asceticism and the New Testament* [London: Routledge, 1999] 71–95, esp. 76–79) identifies blindness, bondage, and lack of single-mindedness as the primary characteristics of the unrepentant, and their opposites as qualities of the redeemed.

78 The total includes vv. 4-5, as well as 9-18.

79 A famous example was the story of Titius Latinius (Livy 2.36; Plutarch *Cor.* 24). Cf. also *P. Oxy.* 1381 and *Historia Augusta, Hadrian* 25.

80 Socrates: Plato *Apol.* 20E–22A; Diogenes Laertius 2.37. This was imitated by Dio of Prusa (*Or.* 13.9), who consulted the Delphic oracle and learned that he was to continue delivering his message "to the ends of the earth (*τὸ ὕστατον . . . τῆς γῆς*)." See also p. 627 n. 9.

81 Support for the preposition includes E Ψ 33. 1739 m lat. Dibelius (*Studies*, 92) believes that this preposition was original but was lost through haplography.

82 Ropes (*Text*, 237) proposed the possibility of a Semiticism, in fact a Septuagintalism, based on the diction of vv. 16-18. Barrett (2:1163) finally dismisses this, and rightly.

83 Acts 1:8, with its four geographical divisions, could have motivated a glossator (of otherwise limited competence).

84 Friedrich Blass, *Acta apostolorum sive Lucae ad Theophilum liber alter* (Göttingen: Vandenhoeck & Ruprecht, 1895) 268. 𝔓74 *pc* read "of the Jews" here.

85 Boismard, *Texte*, 402. (What p[29] read here cannot be determined with any certainty.)

86 If one accepts the loss of *εἰς* after -*οις* (they had an identical sound), the change from *Ἰουδαίοις* to *Ἰουδαῖας* would be intelligible.

87 "Deeds worthy of repentance" (v. 20, lit.) is borrowed from Q: Luke 3:8 (message of John the Baptizer).

turn back to the issue, stated here with brevity, clarity and specificity: Paul's message has been directed to the broad social spectrum including Jews and gentiles. Its ground is Moses and the prophets,[88] who predicted that the Messiah would suffer and be the first to rise from the dead.[89] Verse 23 wraps up the speech tidily by associating the words "resurrection" (v. 8) and "light" (vv. 13, 18). Paul is no longer pulling any punches. His final "sermon" echoes his first (13:29-37), as well as Peter's initial address (2:22-34).[90] The last word is "gentiles."

■ **24** Interrupted speeches will no longer surprise readers, but the source is surprising. Festus intervenes at the same point where the temple mob had earlier cut Paul's remarks short: mention of the gentile mission. Interruptions serve as the equivalent of a double underline. The formal speech has concluded at the moment desired by the author.[91] Although not intended as flattering, Festus's booming interjection assures the readers that Paul exuded vast erudition. For himself, a practical man of affairs, extended study[92] was not an unmixed blessing. A lot of learning is a dangerous thing, as one may glean from the decidedly anti-intellectual Echion of Petronius's *Satyrica*.[93] The allegation of madness was apparently leveled against philosophers to provide rhetorical effect, just as here. Paul shared the fate of Dio of Prusa.[94] The incident is another contrasting echo to the beginning of the story: at Pentecost the inspired speakers were accused of drunkenness (2:13-16).[95] Festus's inability to grasp Paul's argument is additional testimony to the incompetence of a Roman court to adjudicate the matter, as Luke has constructed it.[96]

The accusation and response appear in trials of a martyrological nature. In the *Acts of Appian*, the emperor says: "Appian, I am accustomed to chasten (σωφρονίζειν) those who rave (μαινομένους) and have lost all sense of shame. You speak only so long as I permit you to." Appian responds: "By your *genius*, I am neither mad (μαίνομαι) nor have I lost my sense of shame."[97] In settings like these, "madness" tends to mean fanatic adherence to an idea or movement. The opposition between μανία ("madness") and σωφροσύνη ("reasonableness," "temperance") is, in every sense,

88 The awkward language of the final relative clause of v. 22 allows "the prophets" and "Moses" to frame the phrase. This may be responsible for the D-Text (Boismard, *Texte*, 403), which, after the phrase about the prophets, adds a distinct clause: "**for it is written in** Moses." This conclusion may take up what seems to be an awkward close but is probably intended as end-stress. It affirms that the Torah speaks of a suffering Messiah and of his resurrection. This goes beyond Luke's usual claims, but accords with second- and third-century exegesis.

89 The adjective "first" may reflect (but scarcely endorse) the "firstborn" of Col 1:18 (cf. Rev 1:5). In 3:15 (cf. 5:31), Acts characterized Jesus as ἀρχηγός τῆς ζωῆς ("leader of life"). The meaning of this is debatable (Conzelmann, *Theology*, 205–6), but it does not demand a "causal" link between the resurrection of Jesus and the future experience of believers. This is not necessarily a deficit, but the absence of a relation is quite apparent in the speech of Acts 26.

90 All three speak, for example, of the death and resurrection of Jesus (2:22-24; 13:29-31) and the "promise" (2:33; 13:32). Note also "witness" in 2:32. Light for both Jews and gentiles also evokes the Nunc Dimittis (Simeon: Luke 2:32) and thus the beginning of the story of Luke and Acts.

91 Note also the use of "defend" (ἀπολογοῦμαι) as an inclusion in vv. 2 and 24. The D-Text (Boismard, *Texte*, 403) changes this to the colorless "speaking," but has Felix "shriek and speak."

92 Although it can refer, by metonymy, to basic learning (cf. "grammar school"), γράμματα can, as here, mean advanced study. See Haenchen, 688 n. 3; and BDAG, 206, *s.v.* γράμμα. For the idiom "lead" or "drive" "to insanity" (εἰς μανίαν περιτρέπειν), see Lucian *Abdic.* 30.

93 *Scimus te prae litteras fatuum esse* (*Sat.* 44.6), usually rendered as "we know you are mad with much learning," a homage to Acts 26:24.

94 See the *Cynic Epistles*, Socrates 6.1; 9.3; Dio of Prusa *Or.* 8.36; 9.8, 34; 12.8–9; and, in particular, 34.2–4. *Oration* 77/78.41–42 takes up the claim that philosophical discipline leads to madness, when it actually leads to speaking the truth. This is an aspect of the conventional contrast between appearance and reality.

95 Reinforcing this connection is the verb "declare" (ἀποφθέγγομαι) in v. 25. This expression of solemnity to the pronouncement occurs elsewhere only in 2:14.

96 Fitzmyer, 763; Schneider, 2:376. Luke's construction is, to be sure, not historical.

97 *Acta Appiani* lines 82–87 (trans. Musurillo, *Pagan*, 70). In the *Acts of the Scillitan Martyrs* 8 (Musurillo, *Christian*, 88), the proconsul refers to Christian teachings as *amentia* ("madness").

classic.[98] Jesus had also been accused of madness. One measure of the distance the story has traveled is the contrast between the accusation reported in Mark 3:20 and John 10:20 and the present situation. Prudence (σωφροσύνη) has joined the ranks of Christian virtues.[99] "It would be difficult to find a term more descriptive of the Greek philosophical ideal."[100] Although Festus's remark seemed degrading, he gave Paul a perfect opening.

■ **25-27** Still holding the ball, the accused turns toward his principal auditor, before whom he takes the posture of a confident (παρρησιαζόμενος)[101] philosopher who does not shrink from engagement with the public sphere.[102] The tag "not in a corner" (rendered "no storefront mission"[103]) asserts, as Dibelius, followed by Haenchen, recognized, a claim that Christianity has entered into the drama of world history.[104] The implications of this claim weave together a number of Lucan strains: salvation history, the universal mission, and the social, political, and theological respectability of the Movement. The stone rejected by the builders has become a major block in the social edifice.[105] With admirable economy, Paul has introduced the claims that Christianity is neither obscure nor secretive,[106] and portrayed its leader as a responsible philosophical teacher.[107] After establishing both his own and the Movement's credentials, Paul interrogates the monarch, politely and prudently answering his own query.[108] For the third time (implicitly in v. 6, explicitly in vv. 22-23), he introduces the prophets, his foundational religious authority.[109]

---

98 Note, in addition to p. 635 n. 94, Plato *Phaedr.* 245A; *Prot.* 323B; *Resp.* 430E–431B; *Tim.* 71; Xenophon *Mem.* 1.1.16; 3.9.6–7; Diogenes Laertius 3.91; and Justin *Dial.* 39.4. For comments, see Ramsay, *St. Paul the Traveller,* 313; Plümacher, *Lukas,* 21; and Lentz, *Luke's Portrait,* 87. On the use of this charge against Cynics, see Malherbe, *Paul,* 159–60, with many references. The contrast is common in Lucian, as Betz, *Lukian,* 206 n. 5 shows.

99 See Pervo, *Dating,* 272–73, 288.

100 On the term "temperance," see Johnson, 439.

101 See Malherbe, *Paul,* 160.

102 On vv. 24-26, see Malherbe, *Paul,* 147–63, esp. 154–60.

103 "Storefront missions," small, usually independent churches that appear and disappear, most often in areas inherited by the poor, are characteristic features of U.S. cities and often embody most of the features identified by early critics of Christianity, such as Celsus. Examples of the tag include Plato *Gorg.* 485D; Epictetus *Diss.* 2.12.17; 3.22.95–98; and Terence *Ad.* 5.2.10. Malherbe (*Paul* 155–57) shows that the image selected by Plato was used over a period of seven centuries to criticize intellectuals who avoided public life. Most relevant to the NT, in date and depth, are the citations from Epictetus.

104 The use of "Christian" by Agrippa in v. 28 is not fortuitous. Chrysostom (*Hom.* 53, p. 443) assumes that Agrippa knew of the crucifixion and resurrection.

105 Cf. the use of Ps 118:22 in Luke 20:17; Acts 4:11; 1 Pet 2:7 (γωνία).

106 Boismard (*Texte,* 404) prints a shorter text: "**Now** the king, **with** whom I am [ ] speaking, knows about these matters, **for** none of them eludes **him** [ ]." This is almost certainly an abbreviation that sets aside the apologetic claim. Much of this comes from the Old Latin MS. h, raising a question that will become recurrent: were the abbreviations that so often characterize the D-Text of Acts 26–27—in strong contrast to the general tendency toward expansion—due to translators exercising presumed editorial rights, or do they have a basis in the Greek manuscript tradition? In either case, they are of interest. When diverse versions, such as Coptic and Syriac MSS., support one another and/or Latin witnesses, argument for a Greek prototype is strong.

107 Malherbe (*Paul,* 154–58) lists traits shared by the Paul of Acts 26 with moral philosophers: claims of divine guidance (vv. 16-17, 22), assertions of nonobscurity (v. 26), candid speech to rulers (v. 26), and himself as example (v. 29).

108 If the historical Agrippa were permitted to speak for himself, he might well have said that he did not view the prophets (in the strict sense) as authoritative, and he would have certainly said that he did not accept Paul's interpretation of them.

109 Paul does not state the relationship between his two types of proof, the epiphany near Damascus, and his mode of scriptural interpretation. For Luke (Luke 24:45-46), and possibly for Paul, interpretation is the result of the resurrection rather than a corollary to it, but this relationship had no value in an apologetic context, where Scripture apart from acceptance of the resurrection of Jesus was believed self-sufficient. The book of Acts has abandoned the principle of Luke 24 for the apologetic argument, as can be seen from chap. 1 onward. This is one of the differences between the two volumes.

■ **28** The meaning and translation of this verse are uncertain.[110] Textual variants indicate that the questions have a long history.[111] The assumption of Lucan composition eliminates interpretations based on what the historical Agrippa II might have said to the historical Paul and makes stridently hostile or sarcastic constructions unlikely. Haenchen takes the phrase as a theatrical idiom: "to play the Christian," a light way of turning the question back upon Paul."[112] Malherbe's proposal also takes ἐν ὀλίγῳ in its literal and least convoluted sense, "briefly," and is congruent with the intellectual background: "So rapidly would you persuade me to become a Christian!" The philosophical tradition tended to view "instantaneous conversion" with suspicion.[113]

■ **29** In his response, Paul allows for rapid or slow[114] conversions, encapsulating the wisdom of missionary experience. The difficulty that Acts has no qualms about instant conversions is thus discharged.[115] To his not ungraceful final wish, Paul attaches the crucial exception. Reference to his chains[116] both allows him to end with pathos and provides an opening for the subsequent comments. His chains symbolize his (undeserved) loss of honor.[117]

■ **30-32** The event ends with a "retiring procession" that is a sort of inclusion with 25:23. The omniscient narrator reports two conclusions. The general reaction was that Paul had committed no grave or capital offense.[118] The ending resembles that of chap. 28, an audience departing after hearing Paul's expository message.[119] The difference is that this audience was undivided in its conclusion, raising the question of why he was not immediately discharged. Agrippa, whose judgment is the one that really counts, answers that question. Had Paul not appealed, he could have been discharged. The answer is not logically satisfactory, as the efforts to defend it establish.[120] His is the third verdict of innocence, following Lysias (23:29) and Festus (25:18, 25). Haenchen pierces through the veil: "So there remains a trial without prosecutor or witnesses; only the defendant speaks. The concrete crime (the defilement of the Temple!) is forgotten."[121]

Here ends the extended account of Paul's legal imbroglios, which began with false charges raised by anonymous accusers in 21:28 and closes with a declaration of innocence by a pro-Roman Jewish client king.[122] From the perspective of jurisprudence, the result has

110 The comments in Cadbury and Lake (322–24) are valuable, as is the thorough discussion of Barrett (2:1169–71), who seems to oppose "play the Christian," although he so renders the phrase. For bibliography, see Fitzmyer, 765–66.

111 The most interesting variant is πείθῃ, which can be rendered, "Do you think that you can make me a Christian?" Only A supports this; it is probably a correction. "Become" (γενέσθαι), read by E Ψ 1739 m latt sy; CyrJ, rather than ποιῆσαι ("make"), is almost certainly a correction.

112 Haenchen, 689, with evidence for the idiom in n. 2.

113 Malherbe, *Paul*, 161–62, citing 161.

114 The preferred interpretation makes the understanding of ἐν ὀλίγῳ and ἐν μεγάλῳ relatively unimportant. They could refer to words, time, or effort. Barrett (2:1172) canvasses the range of translations. The thinly attested variant πολλῷ makes the quantitative understanding explicit.

115 Acts implies that conversions of Jews often took some time, for Paul spent relatively long periods in synagogues (e.g., 17:2; 18:4; 19:8).

116 Here, at least, the "chains" seem to be literal, in contrast to v. 31, where it is a metonym.

117 The D-Text (Boismard, *Texte*, 404) adds, at the beginning of v. 30, "After he had said these things . . ." This yields a smoother, but less dramatic, closure.

118 The D-Text (Boismard, *Texte*, 405) eliminates the reference to incarceration (lit. "or chains"). This shows a good dramatic instinct but overlooks v. 30.

119 Note the phrase "to one another" (πρὸς ἀλλήλους) in 26:31 and 28:25; cf. also 17:32.

120 Sherwin-White (*Roman Society*, 65) established the main line of defense: Festus could have discharged Paul legally, but he was constrained by issues of "prestige." "To have acquitted him despite the appeal would have been to offend both the emperor and the province." Paul's Jewish opponents would doubtless have been displeased, but imperial displeasure at deprivation of a case is most unlikely. Sherwin-White's theory is repeated by Hemer (*Book*, 132), and, with expansions, by Witherington, 753.

121 Haenchen, 691.

122 In the conventional text (N-A[27]), the transition between chap. 26 and chap. 27 is rough to the point of discord. The D-Text seeks to repair this. See the comments at the beginning of chap. 27.

been, to put the best face on it, confusing. The plot, however, has had a different focus: by any and every means to prevent Paul from being arraigned before a Jewish court sitting in Jerusalem. In order to do that, he was compelled to appeal and must therefore go to Rome. That destination is in accordance with the divine will. Insofar as prospects go, the reader has more than a little room for hope, for the opinion of both Festus and Agrippa intimates that Paul's opponents will find rough sledding at Rome.[123] As a summary of Paul's mission and message, Acts 26 tells the story "as the narrator wants it to be remembered."[124]

123 The narrator also allows the inference that the Roman officials in Judea had mishandled the case, perhaps from a desire to please their constituents. That is not historically improbable, but it could be due to Lucan malice.

124 Tannehill, *Narrative Unity*, 2:329.

27

27:1-44 Paul's Ocean Voyage

27: Conventional Text

1/ Once it had been determined that
we were to sail to Italy, they
transferred[a] custody of Paul
and some other prisoners to a
centurion of an[b] Imperial Cohort
named Julius.
2/ We boarded a ship of Adramyttium[c] that was going to stop
at ports along the Asian coast
and set out. Aristarchus, a
Macedonian from Thessa-
lonica, was with us. 3/ We put
in at Sidon the subsequent
day, where Julius very kindly
permitted Paul to visit friends
and receive attention from
them. 4/ After we departed
from Sidon contrary winds
compelled us to keep to the
sheltered side of Cyprus. 5/ We
then crossed the open water
along the coast of Cilicia and
Pamphylia and arrived at Myra
in Lycia.[d] 6/ There[e] the centurion located an Alexandrian
ship destined for Italy and put
us aboard it. 7/ Many days of
slow and labored sailing got us
no farther than the vicinity of
Cnidus, where, unable to make
headway, we sailed for Crete,
off Salmone,
8/ and hugged the coast with some
difficulty until we reached a
place called Fair Havens, which
is near the city of Lasaea.
9/ As some time had passed and
navigation had become risky
because even Yom Kippur had
come and gone, Paul advised
them, 10/ "Gentlemen, I envision that the voyage will be
attended with a great deal of
damage and loss—loss not only
of cargo and the vessel but even
loss of our very lives." 11/ The
centurion, however, found the
arguments of the owner and
the master more convincing
than those of Paul.[f] 12/ Since
Fair Havens was unsuitable for
wintering, the majority preferred to sail on so that, if possible, they might reach Phoenix,
a Cretan harbor exposed to
winds from both the northwest
and the southwest. 13/ The
appearance of a light southerly
breeze seemed to satisfy their

27: D-Text[k]

1/ *So then the governor decided to remand him to Caesar. On the next day he summoned a centurion named Julius and* transferred *to him* Paul *together with* some other prisoners.

2/ *When it came time to sail,* We boarded a ship of Adramyttium. Aristarchus, a Macedonian, *also boarded* with us.

3/ We put in at Sidon, where *the centurion* very kindly permitted Paul to *have* friends *come to visit him* and attend to
him. 4/ From there we kept to the sheltered side of Cyprus because the winds were contrary.

5/ *Afterwards* we crossed the Cilician *gulf* and the Pamphylian *sea* and *after fifteen days* we *reached* Myra in Lycia.

6/ The centurion located an Alexandrian ship destined for Italy and boarded us.

7/ Labored sailing got us *to* Cnidus within a *few* days, *from which we put out* and sailed along the south of Crete.

8/ We arrived *at a good harbor* where *a city was nearby.*

9/ *When we had passed many days there* and navigation had become risky because even Yom Kippur had come and gone, Paul *approached*
10/ and said, "Gentlemen, I envision that the voyage will be attended with a *great deal* of damage and loss—loss not only of cargo and the vessel but even loss of our very
lives."11/ *But the master and the owner*

12/ preferred to sail on so that, if possible, they might reach Phoenix, a Cretan harbor. The centurion found *them* more convincing than what Paul had said.

13/ When a light southerly breeze sprang up, *we sailed from* Crete.

requirements, so they weighed
anchor and hugged closely[g] to
the coast of Crete.
14/ But shortly thereafter a violent
wind, known as the Euraquilo,
came roaring down from Crete[h]
15/ and overpowered the ship. Since
no headway could be made, we
let ourselves be carried along.
16/ When we passed under the
protection of an island called
Cauda, we managed, with considerable difficulty, to get control of the ship's boat. 17/ They
hoisted it in and then deployed
some materials to strengthen
the ship.[i] Fearing that they
might be wrecked on the Libyan
coast, the crew loosed the sails[j]
and let the ship have its own
way.
18/ Since the storm continued to
pound us fiercely, they began
to jettison material on the next
day.
19/ The day after that they began to
heave gear overboard by hand.
20/ Since neither sun by day nor
stars by night had been seen
for many days and the terrible
storm raged unabated, any
hope that we might be rescued
finally began to fade.

21/ No one had received any nourishment for a long time when
Paul stood in their[m] midst and
said: "Gentlemen, you really
should have done what I said
and not left Crete. Then we
should not have experienced
this damage and loss. 22/ Now
I am urging that you keep your
spirits up, for not one of you
will be lost; only the ship is
doomed.[n] 23/ Last night there
appeared to me a messenger of
the god to whom I belong[o] and
whom I serve. 24/ 'Do not be
afraid, Paul,' he said. 'You must
appear before Caesar. God has
granted you all those who are
making this voyage with you.'[p]
25/ Cheer up, then, gentlemen,
for I trust God and that things
will turn out as I was told.
26/ We shall, however, have to
run aground on an island."
27/ In the middle of the fourteenth
night, as we were still being

14/ A *southeast* wind descended
15/ *and the ship ran on and we*
arrived at[l]
16/ an island called *Klauda.*
17/ Fearing that *we* might be *driven*
onto the Libyan coast, *we*
remained there.
18/ On the next day, since the storm
continued to pound *the ship*
fiercely,
19/ *we* heaved the gear *into the sea.*
20/ *Since the storm raged on for*
many days and *neither sun*
by day nor stars by night had
appeared, any hope of life
finally began to fade.

driven[q] over the Mediterranean,[r]
the sailors began to suspect
that land was near.[s] 28/ They
took soundings and found
twenty fathoms. A bit later they
cast again and found fifteen.

29/ Anxious that we[t] might be
dashed against a rocky shore,[u]
they cast four anchors from
the stern and began to long for
dawn.
30/ When the sailors attempted to
desert the ship by lowering the
boat on the pretext of dropping
anchors from the bow,
31/ Paul protested to the centurion
and his detachment, "If they
do not remain in the ship, you
won't have a chance of being
rescued!" 32/ In response the
soldiers cut the lines of the
boat and let it fall away.
33/ When day was about to break,[v]
Paul started urging everyone
to take some nourishment:
"This is the fourteenth day
you have lived in suspense,[w]
going hungry and receiving no
meals. 34/ I therefore urge you
to take some nourishment, for
your own good.[x] None of you
will lose even a single hair from
your heads." 35/ He then took
some bread, gave public thanks
to God, broke it, and began
to eat. 36/ All felt better, and
they, too, had something to eat.
37/ There were 276 of us aboard
that ship. 38/ After they had
taken their fill, they set about
lightening the ship by heaving
the grain overboard.
39/ When day arrived, they were not
able to recognize the place, but
they noticed a bay with a beach
onto which they planned to run
the ship aground,[y] if possible.
40/ So they slipped the anchors
and left them in the sea, while
also loosing the ropes that
had secured the rudders[z] and
hoisting the foresail to catch
the wind and make for the
beach.[aa] 41/ But they ran the
ship onto a shoal,[bb] so that the
bow jammed fast and wouldn't
move, while the stern started to
break up under pressure.[cc]
42/ The soldiers decided to kill the

29/ Anxious that *it might be broken up, they beached the ship
toward the shore* and began to
long for dawn.[ee]
30/ When the sailors attempted to
desert and began lowering the
boat
31/ Paul protested to the centurion
and his detachment, "If they
do not remain in the ship, *we*
won't have a chance of being
rescued!" 32 In response *they*
cut the lines and let the boat
fall away.
33/ When day broke, Paul urged
everyone to take some nourishment: "This is the fourteenth
day *since* you began to go
hungry.
34/ "I therefore urge you to take
some nourishment, for your
own good.[ff] None of you will
lose[gg] even a single hair from
your heads." 35/ He then took
some bread, gave public thanks
to God, broke it, and began
to eat, *and gave some to us*.[hh]
36/ All felt better, and had
something to eat. 37/ We were
seventy-six.
38/ After they had taken their fill, the
ship was lightened.
39/ They noticed a bay with a beach
onto which they *wanted* to run
the ship aground, if possible.[ii]
41/ Then they came in[jj] and ran the
ship aground *there and it was
battered and began to break
into pieces*.
42/ The soldiers decided to kill the

prisoners to prevent any from swimming ashore and escaping, 43/ but the centurion put a stop to this idea because he wished to save Paul. He ordered that those who could swim should leap overboard and make for shore first, 44/ while the rest would fasten on to planks or cling to other people[dd] from the ship. By those means all came ashore safely.

prisoners to prevent any[kk] from swimming ashore and escaping, 43/ but the centurion prevented *this from happening, out of particular concern for* Paul, *so that he might save him*. He ordered that those who could swim should make for shore first,

44/ *and the rest should go* on planks.

a 𝔓[74] *pc* have παρεδίδουν τε τόν, inverting the "and," while others omit the conjunction. Inept uses of τε are a Lucan characteristic.

b *Or:* "the," since the Roman military establishment had more than one *cohors Augusta*.

c 𝔓[74] has the article, making "Adramyttine" the ship's name.

d B 1175 spell with *-rr-*. 69 has "Smyrna"; p[74] ℵ (A) lat bo "Lystra."

e The initial adverb has difficult variants. The D-Text replaces it with "and."

f On the suitability of the imperfect in conversations, see BDF §428 ("literary language").

g Much of the Latin tradition mistakes ἆσσον as a place-name: Assos. See 20:13-14. This is a Homeric adverb.

h On κατ᾽ αὐτῆς, see Moule, *Idiom Book*, 60. The less likely alternative is "against the ship" (understood as feminine ναῦς; cf. v. 41).

i The meaning of this verse is not clear. See Brian Rapske, "Acts, Travel and Shipwreck," in Gill and Gempf, *Setting*, 35.

j The meaning of this phrase is not clear. "Dropped a sea anchor" (see p. 659) is an alternative.

k The D-Text of Acts 27 follows Boismard, *Texte*, 406–21.

l Note, however, an alternate text of the D type (82. 614. 1518. 2125 syr[h*] Cassiodorus, Bede), which adds, after ἐπιδόντες ("yielding") in v. 15, τῷ πνέοντι καὶ συστείλαντες τὰ ἱστία ("yielded to the wind **which was blowing, and having furled the sails**, we were driven . . ."). Syr[h] adds "as chance would have it." See Ropes, *Text*, 243; and Metzger, *Textual Commentary*, 440.

m The D-Text (Boismard, *Texte*, 415) eliminates "their," presumably because no persons had been mentioned.

n The D-Text (Boismard, *Texte*, 415–16) has "no" (οὐδεμία) modifying "life" and changes "you" to "us," drops γάρ ("for"), and simplifies the relative clause: "the god whom I serve."

o The evidence for the presence or absence of the emphatic ἐγώ ("I") is evenly divided. Formally, this is more suitable to the angel, but may have been original.

p The D-Text (Boismard, *Texte*, 416) softens the baldness of the "gift" by omitting "God," thus making the construction an impersonal passive.

q The verb διαφέρω may mean "drifting" rather than "tossed about," but the stronger sense is more likely (Barrett, 2:1202). On the suggestion that it means "tack," see p. 656 n. 125.

r Lit. "the Adriatic," the area of which was construed differently in antiquity. Strabo (2.5.20), Pausanias (5.25.3), and Ptolemy (*Geog.* 3.4.1; 15.1) indicate that this term embraced the Ionian Sea and the northern Mediterranean between Greece and Italy, as far south as Crete and Malta.

s In v. 27, variants for προσάγειν ("be near") are προσηχεῖν ("resound," i.e., hear surf breaking) B* -αχεῖν- gig s, προσανεχεῖν B[2] ("rise up toward") προαγαγειν a* *pc* προσεγγίζειν ("draw near") 614. 1505. 2147. On these, see Barrett, 2:1203. The D-Text abbreviates: "In the middle of the fourteenth night, the sailors began to suspect that land was near."

t 81. 326. 945. 1739. 1891 *et al.* read the third plural. These variants show that ancient and medieval scribes wrestled with the problems raised by "we" in Acts 27. At the close of this verse gig and vg[mss] add *ut sciremus an salvi esse possimus/emus* ("so that we might know whether we could be safe").

u The *v.l.* βραχεῖς ("small," p[74] *et al.*) is most likely an error for τραχεῖς ("rough"), which belongs to the tradition. James Smith (*The Voyage and Shipwreck of St. Paul* [4th ed.; London: Longmans, Green, 1880] 132) cited Homer *Od.* 5.425. Note also Dio of Prusa *Or.* 7.2 (a work of fiction): a voyage begun at end of summer ran into χειμῶνος δὲ γενομένου χαλεπῶς καὶ μόλις διεσώθημεν . . . τὸ μὲν δὴ ἀκάτιον εἰς τραχύν τινα αἰγιαλὸν ὑπὸ τοῖς κρημνοῖς ἐκβαλόντες διέφθειραν ("when a fierce storm arose and we barely escaped . . . they ran the boat onto a rugged beach under the cliffs, where it came to grief" [author's trans.]). An island with a shore that was not rough was encountered by voyagers driven for a week in Lucian *Ver. hist.* 1.6.

v It is possible to render the opening as "Paul kept exhorting everyone until daybreak," since this is the conventional meaning of ἄχρι οὗ and παρεκάλει is imperfect. So BDAG, 160, *s.v.* ἄχρι 1b, but this yields a ridiculous meaning, and it is preferable to take the conjunction as "at the point when." See Cadbury and Lake, 336. Haenchen (706) and Barrett (2:1206), however, reject this and take the imperfect as iterative, but, in his version, Barrett (2:1176) says, "When it was nearly day." The narrator wishes to distinguish between the first indications of light and full day (v. 39).

w The participle προσδοκῶντες should be associated with διατελεῖτε and thus probably has the sense of "suspense," rather than mere waiting. BDF §161 (3) takes this as "a special idiom" and illustrates it. See also Barrett, 2:1207.

x "Our" is read by A L P 326. 614. 1241 *pm* w sy[h]. This, the only use of πρός with the genitive in the NT, is a literary touch.

y B* C *pc* read ἐκσῶσαι for ἐξῶσαι The sound is essentially identical. The former would add another variant on the theme "save," but the latter fits the context. See Ropes, *Text*, 247.

z A stricter rendering is "dismantled the steering apparatus" (Barrett, 2:1212), but this is less probable than releasing the steering oars from their restraints.

aa 𝔓[74] reads πνοῇ instead of πνεούσῃ. The latter represents a common ellipsis: BDF §241 (6). On the use of ἅμα, which is similar to the classical "while," see BDF §425 (2). The phrase could mean that the rudders were detached, but that makes less sense than the understanding that they were released from restraints for use.

bb *Or:* "upon a point," exposed to water on both sides, the definition of τόπον διθάλασσον, BDAG, 245, *s.v.* διθάλασσος. The same must be said of any such "point." The focus here is on the impact of the water. See Cadbury and Lake, 339; and Conzelmann, 220. "Shoal" is reasonable, even if uncertain here.

cc The phrase τῶν κυμάτων ("by the force *of the waves*") is probably a secondary gloss, since it is difficult to imagine why it would have been deleted, and alternatives include "the force of the sea" (gig vg) and "the force of the wind" (sa). See Ropes, *Text*, 249.

dd The indefinite ἐπί τινων τῶν could refer to things (neuter), but persons seems more likely. Cadbury and Lake (340) speculate that the difference may explain the use of this preposition with two cases: genitive indicating something like "on the shoulders of" and the dative "on planks." Conzelman (221), however, prefers the neuter, which would mean objects from the ship (such as cases) as well as pieces of wood resulting from the breakup of the vessel.

ee This is better rendered "they halted the ship," an abbreviation of the conventional text. Boismard (*Texte*, 417) prints ἐπέκειλαν τὴν ναῦν (cf. v. 41), which he takes from the Ethiopic, rendered in ultraliteral Latin as "*stare-fecerunt navem-eorum*," which should mean "made their ship halt" (i.e., by casting anchors). Note that, in v. 41, the Latin version of the Ethiopic reads "*impegerunt navem-eorum*," which is well retroverted into Greek as ἐπέκειλαν τὴν ναῦν, as Boismard (*Texte*, 420) proposes.

ff Clark (167) reads, on the basis of gig, ἐλπίζω γὰρ ἐν τῷ θεῷ μου ὅτι ("For I [have] hope in my God that . . ."). This turns the positive declaration into a pious wish and reduces the parallel between Jesus and Paul.

gg "Fall" (πεσεῖται) is read by Ψ 1739 gig sy[h] sa. This would seem to be a typical D-Text revision.

hh This reading of 614. 2147 *pc* sa h** is not admitted into Boismard's text (*Texte*, 418), or even mentioned. It is normally accepted as part of the D-Text (e.g., Metzger, *Textual Commentary*, 441–42).

ii Note that Boismard (*Texte*, 419) omits (on the basis of the Ethiopic) the initial temporal clause. "Wanted" could come from confusion of βουλεύομαι ("plan") and βούλομαι ("wish"). The subject ("the sailors") is stated in gig vg[mss] sa[ms] sy[p] and found as a gloss in 920.

jj The initial τότε ἐλθόντες of the D-Text, derived from the Ethiopic, is puzzling.

kk In v. 42, Clark (168) adds "of them" (ἐξ αὐτῶν) to "any."

Analysis

The keystone to the arch of issues through which all interpreters of Acts 27[1] must pass is its length.[2] Why did the author devote sixty verses (c. 6 percent of the text) to the story of Paul's transfer to Rome?[3] This is central to the question of meaning, and all discussions of text, source, and form must address it or risk the charge of irrelevance. This is, without doubt, a good story that contributes to the portrait of Paul's character and provides an additional demonstration of divine providence in operation, but those factors do not justify its length. Luke was not loath to regale his readers with adventure, and he understood the value of retardation, but from this perspective the effort was a failure, for the sequel is anticlimactic, repetitious, and disappointing narrative. For the historical Paul, travel was a means for getting to one place or another, and the only fact worth narrating was that he got there.[4] Presuming that his statement was factual, Paul had suffered more shipwrecks than any hero of an ancient novel, one of which was more perilous than that of Acts 27 (2 Cor 11:25). To it he devoted five words.

One perennial solution to the problem of length is abridgment. This is the path apparently followed by the D-Text, as reconstructed by Boismard,[5] for the conventional text is, according to an electronic count, 26.6 percent *longer* than the D-Text (762 words versus 602). Difficulties abound. Boismard's text is largely a retroversion here. The D-Text has been shedding, like the veils of Oscar Wilde's Salome, one witness after another, until, with the loss of Latin h in 27:13, it is largely reduced to the evidence of the Ethiopic version. This is more like a slender thread than a thin veil, but it is not utterly without value, despite the late date of the MSS.[6] Agreements among Latin, Syriac, and Ethiopic witnesses intimate a Greek basis.[7] James A. Montgomery, who made the first scholarly examination of the Ethiopic text of Acts, issued a harshly negative judgment, concluding that the brevity of the text was due to the sloth or incompetence of the editor.[8] Arnaud Lamouille and Marie-Émile Boismard took issue with his judgments, for they found support in other witnesses, notably h, in Acts 27.[9] Abbreviation is most pronounced in the discussion of sea-travel (vv. 8, 13-19, 39-41). This appears to be abridgment by plan rather than abbreviation due to inadequacy, so that one may tentatively posit the elimination of less relevant material as one ancient editorial means of dealing with Acts 27. That this took place within the D-Text tradition is noteworthy, since scholarship generally views the D-Text as an expansion of the conventional text.[10]

Sea travel was difficult in antiquity. Sosia sums it up: "God knows, Parmeno, words really can't express quite

1 "Acts 27" is used throughout this section as shorthand for 27:1–28:16.

2 Josephus devotes sixty-two words to his voyage to Rome, a journey that also involved a shipwreck, including a night in the water. Divine Providence brought about his rescue (*Vit.* 14–16). This is less than 9 percent of the length of the voyage in Acts (762 words).

3 Pervo, *Profit*, 50–51. Johnson (450–52) gives a balanced and comprehensive introduction to the background and issues.

4 E.g., 2 Cor 7:5 (Macedonia). Cf. 1 Thess 1:6 (Timothy arrives at Athens).

5 Boismard, *Texte*, 406–21.

6 On the Ethiopic data, see Bruce M. Metzger, *The Early Versions of the New Testament: Their Origin, Transmission and Limitations* (Oxford: Clarendon, 1977) 215–40 (234–36 on Acts). The version probably dates from the fifth or sixth century. Syriac influence is probable, although of uncertain extent (238–40).

7 Ibid., 240.

8 James A. Montgomery, "The Ethiopic Text of Acts of the Apostles," *HTR* 27 (1934) 169–205. With regard to Acts 27, he stated (179) that the editor/translator "floundered in the depths like Paul's own ship."

9 Boismard summarizes their earlier findings in *Texte*, 41–45, with specific reference to chap. 27 on 43–45. Their views have been challenged by Curt Niccum, "The Ethiopic Version and the 'Western' Text of Acts in *Le texte occidental des Actes des Apôtres*," in J. W. Childers and D. C. Parker, eds., *Transmission and Reception: New Testament Text-Critical and Exegetical Studies* (Texts and Studies 4; Piscataway, N.J.: Gorgias, 2006), 69–88. Niccum apparently leans toward incompetence and ignorance as the cause of the omissions in Acts 27–28, although he does not state this explicitly. In his view, the Ethiopic is not a witness for the D-Text.

10 Both abbreviation and expansion are characteristics of the "copy editor" model proposed on

how unpleasant it actually is to travel by sea."[11] Formally, Acts 27:1–28:16 is a story of storm, shipwreck, and survival. "Shipwreck story" refers not to a specific form or genre with a limited number of elements[12] but to a type that exhibits examples from a repertory of recurring themes and motifs.[13] The type was familiar enough to inspire satire and parody.[14] Many of these themes can be illustrated from prose fiction.[15] Acts 27 shows the influence of the ancient novel.[16] This judgment does not mean that the ship(s) that bore Paul to Rome did not touch at this or that place, for example, or that they did not come to grief at Malta (if Malta it were). It does mean that one should not be surprised to learn that, upon arriving at Malta the survivors had an interesting experience with the local natives and were taken in by the resident gentry. The length is a clue to the outcome. Ancient literature rarely described long, uneventful voyages.

The abundance of such stories is in part a cause and in part a tribute to their suitability for illustrating vices and virtues. Juvenal's *Twelfth Satire*, for example, is a critique of greed.[17] Acts 28:1-6 succinctly illustrates the notion that storms can be used by gods to punish humans to whom they have taken a dislike or by gods to rescue those who have found favor with them.[18] Jesus was not the only being who saved a ship by causing a storm to abate. Linked to these themes was the ancient view of the sea as a source of evil.[19] In the light of such features, it would be surprising if Acts 27 did *not* contain a symbolic element. In terms of comparability, Acts 27 is best understood as a chapter from a religious novel.[20] Solutions that judge this material entirely factual or completely fictitious are questionable.[21]

Two sources seem well established: Jonah[22] and Homer.[23] Others have been proposed, ranging from a participant's memory to a single source supplemented by interpolations to a general literary tradition familiar to

pp. 1–5 for many of the distinctive readings. Clark (163–68) preferred a more "normal" sort of D-Text, very much like that of N-A[27], with a number of expansions. All of these are represented by some witnesses of the "Western" type. This indicates that, in this material, at least, there are grounds for Boismard's postulation of different "D-Texts," with the longer representing his "TO[2]" (second edition of the "Western Text").

11 Terence *Hecyra* 416–17: *non hercle verbis, Parmeno, dici potest tantum quam re ipsa navigare incommodumst* (trans. John Barsby, *Terence II* [LCL; Cambridge, Mass.: Harvard University Press, 2001] 189).

12 Haenchen's "fixed type" was a person of straw. See Pervo, *Profit*, 51.

13 For a discussion of the type with a full catalogue of examples, see Charles Talbert and J. Hayes, "A Theology of Sea Storms in Luke-Acts," *SBLSP 1995* (Atlanta: Scholars Press, 1995) 321–36. For a list of some motifs, see Pervo, *Profit*, 156 n. 189. The story that best illuminates Acts 27 is Achilles Tatius *Leuc. Clit.* 3.1-5: On the third day of a voyage, calm gives way to wind. A detailed account of various maneuvers (3.1.2–2.8) follows. The sun disappeared (3.2.2). Hope was abandoned (3.2.5). All cargo was jettisoned (3.2.9). The crew attempted to escape in the boat (3.3.1–4.2) and finally did so. The ship ran onto a rock and was broken into pieces (3.4.3). Passengers attempted to escape by swimming or clinging to pieces of wood (3.4.6). The principals finally make their way to shore. Achilles Tatius knew how to give rhetoric free rein and raise suspense by elaborate development. When every allowance is made and all of the differences noted, the outline and emphases of the two stories are very similar.

14 Satire: Juvenal *Sat.* 12.17–82; Lucian *Merc. cond.* 1–2 (which reads like a spoof of the motifs and theme of Acts 27). Parody: Lucian *Ver. hist.*, e.g., 1.5–6.

15 Northrop Frye (*The Secular Scripture: A Study of the Structure of Romance* [Cambridge, Mass.: Harvard University Press, 1976] 4) said of the Greek novel: "[T]he normal means of transportation is by shipwreck."

16 See, for example, Petr Pokorný, "Die Romfahrt des Paulus und der antike Roman," *ZNW* 64 (1973) 233–44; Weiser, 2:659; Pervo, *Profit*, 51–52, with his references; Alexander, *Literary Context*, 69–96; and M. Quesnell, "Le naufrage de Saint Paul," *Transversalités* 69 (1999) 47–57.

17 For other examples, see Talbert and Hayes, "A Theology," 323–24.

18 Examples in Talbert and Hayes, "A Theology," 324. This was a staple item in the larder of epic.

19 See p. 649.

20 That is, as material that would be suitable to a religious novel.

21 See, for example, Adrian Hummel ("Factum et Fictum: Literarische und theologische Erwägungen zur Romreise des Paulus in der Apostelgeschichte [Apg 27,1–28,16]," *BibNotiz* 105 [2000] 39–53), who characterizes Acts 27 as a mixture from which distinct facts are difficult to extract.

22 See the comments on vv. 19 and 38.

23 The influence of the *Odyssey* is acknowledged by Bruce (527) and developed in detail by Dennis R.

Luke. The first of these can be examined by discussion of the first person plural. In vv. 2-8 (generally), 15-16, 18, 27a, and 28:11-13, "we" operates in the conventional sense of travel reports, with no specification. Similarly, in vv. 10, 20, 26, 29, and 37, "we" identifies all aboard the vessel. This is equally unspecific. Susan Praeder labels this reporter a "first person peripheral narrator," a passive observer.[24] Such a narrator is a literary creation, even if the creator was an actual participant in historical events scrupulously reported. Such a colorless narrator allows the reader to take part in the story. Shifts between the first and third persons can be difficult. In v. 10, Paul addresses "them," the identity of whom is unclear. The shift from "we" to "them" in vv. 16-17 is also confusing. The "we" of v. 27a yields to "they" of the crew. Verse 38 reports another shift from first to third: "they" toss out the grain. The initial "us" in 27:1 is inconclusive, as it may not include Paul but is distinguished from "some other prisoners." Verse 2 states that Aristarchus was "with," not specifically one of us, possibly distinguishing the "we" narrator from the Pauline circle (of which Aristarchus was a part). Verse 6 excludes the centurion Julius from "us." Since they are now on a different ship, one may hypothesize that "us" includes all passengers under the authority of Julius, that is, prisoners, but this conflicts with v. 1.

Acts 28:1-16 is dominated by the first plural. In vv. 1-2, "we" evidently embraces the entire ship's company, but v. 7 is less clear. Is the reader to imagine that Publius cared for hundreds? This is possible, but it will not apply to v. 12, where those honored are almost certainly restricted to Paul (who had performed healings) and his entourage. The limits of the "we" in 28:11-13 are unspecified. In theory it could refer to the entire body of passengers and crew, but in 28:14 "we" can scarcely extend beyond the number of believers. With some simplification one can say that Acts 27–28 presents two first person narrators, one the generic travel reporter who is not essentially different from—and can be interchanged with—the omniscient third person and another representing a (presumably small) circle affiliated with Paul. The former of these makes no attempts to establish "his" authority or to intimate reminiscence.[25]

If a primary, historical source is to be identified, it will derive from the latter. In its favor are the names of Julius, with his organization, and Aristarchus, as well as the registry of the ship (Adramyttium). Difficulties remain. The smaller, Pauline group does not emerge within the narrative before Malta, where it remains vague.[26] The names and number of this body, the minimum size of which is three, remain unspecified, as does their reason for being included. The most likely reason for their inclusion would be their status as fellow prisoners.[27] To grant that would be to accuse Luke of cheating, since his entire story allows but one prisoner. Ramsay saw the problem: "It is hardly possible to suppose that the prisoner's friends were allowed to accompany him." Pliny supplied the answer: Luke and Aristarchus accompanied Paul by posing as his slaves. This is both clever and tender, but scarcely possible.[28] If Luke had an account transmitted by Aristarchus or anonymous, he has deprived it of every semblance of reliability. Although the theory that Acts

MacDonald, "The Shipwrecks of Odysseus and Paul," *NTS* 45 (1999) 88–107. MacDonald postulates that the *Odyssey* is the sole source of Acts 27.

24 Susan M. Praeder, "Narrative Voyage: An Analysis and Interpretation of Acts 27–28" (Diss., Graduate Theological Union, Berkeley, 1980) 89. See also the next note.

25 This is Praeder's peripheral narrator. Note her apposite comments in "Problem," 198: "It seems that Luke is unconcerned to offer even the simplest evidence in support of the eyewitness authority of the first person plural participants: he refrains from naming and numbering them and never explains their relationship to Paul and other third person participants. In the little that he says about the first person plural participants he is silent about their status as eyewitnesses and the supposed special significance of their eyewitness experiences." Kurz (*Reading*, 107–8) says that the author uses the first person "flexibly." This is a euphemism for inconsistency.

26 In 27:3, Paul alone is permitted to visit "friends."

27 Jervell (603), for example, suggests that the other friends or colleagues of Paul made the journey with him of their own free will. This is certainly possible, but it is but one inference and less probable than the hypothesis that the companions were also prisoners.

28 Ramsay, *St. Paul the Traveller*, 315–16. His example comes from the case of Paetus, who rebelled against Claudius, reported in Pliny *Ep.* 3.16. Paetus's wife Arria offered to take the place of the slaves she presumed Paetus would be allowed while en route to Rome as a prisoner, since he was of consular rank. Paul did not enjoy the status that

27:1–28:16 derives from a participant in the adventure and may be a part of the putative diary used for earlier material ("the itinerary"[29]) has a long line of distinguished supporters,[30] it is, even when adjudged a distinct and separate source, scarcely tenable. In addition to the absence of a single narrative voice, the volume of information about the voyage far exceeds what the earlier passages in this alleged source reported and lacks historical justification within the confines of the story.

Dibelius proposed that "a secular description of the voyage and shipwreck served as a pattern, basis or source" into which the author interpolated passages about Paul.[31] Although this approach seems old-fashioned,[32] it retains its vitality.[33] The reason for this is its obvious merit. When the material focusing on Paul (vv. 3b, 9-11, 21-26, 31, 33-36a, 43a; 28:2-10) is set aside, a coherent account remains.[34] That account is more literary than most of Acts and filled with realistic,[35] circumstantial, and technical detail, the meaning of some of which has long challenged interpreters—witness the ancient versions—and may have eluded Luke at points.[36] Dibelius's analysis quite probably reveals elements of how the author worked. Into a general narrative of the voyage, he introduced what he wished to say about Paul. The literary effect, that is, the author's final product, is interlacement, alternations of general descriptions of nautical adventure with specific scenes about Paul's words and actions.[37] Dibelius wisely abstained from identifying this outline as a source. Sufficient indications of Lucan style exist to indicate that, if Luke had one major source, he, in accordance with his usual practice, revised it. At a minimum, these revisions would have included the allusions to Jonah[38] and the reference to Yom Kippur. It is probably safest to take a looser approach to intertextuality and think of "background" texts, including Homer, that influenced the composition of this passage, but it is possible that the author took up and altered a specific shipwreck story.[39]

---

would permit him to request attendants. For associates to accompany prisoners in their misery was a mark of true friendship (Lucian *Tox.* 18).

29 See p. 13 n. 74 and p. 319 n. 9.

30 Examples include Henry J. Cadbury, "We and I Passages in Luke-Acts," *NTS* 3 (1956) 128–32; Ernst Haenchen, "Acta 27," in Eric Dinkler, ed., *Zeit und Geschichte: Dankesgabe an Rudolf Bultmann zum 80. Geburtstag* (Tübingen: Mohr Siebeck, 1964) 235–54 (a diary with later additions); Joseph Fitzmyer, *Luke the Theologian: Aspects of His Teaching* (New York: Paulist, 1989) 16–22; Hengel, *Acts and the History,* 66–67; Stählin, 313–14; Colin Hemer, "First Person Narrative in Acts 27–28," *TynBul* 36 (1985) 79–109; Stanley Porter, "Excursus: The 'We' Passages," in Gill and Gempf, *Setting*, 545–74; Wehnert, *Die Wir-Passagen*; Thornton, *Der Zeuge*; with considerable nuance, and, also with reservations, J. M. Gilchrist, "The Historicity of Paul's Shipwreck," *JSNT* 61 (1996) 29–61.

31 Dibelius, *Studies*, 204–6. See also pp. 7–8. He was anticipated by Wellhausen (*Kritische Analyse*, 17) and Paul Wendland (*Die urchristliche Literaturformen* [HNT; Tübingen: Mohr Siebeck, 1912] 324).

32 See Tannehill's contemptuous comment in *Narrative Unity,* 2:330.

33 Supporters of this hypothesis, in one sense or another, include Haenchen (709, additions to a diary), Conzelmann (221), Schneider (2:387), Roloff (358–60, into an account of Aristarchus), and Weiser (2:390–91, 659–60).

34 Soards (*Speeches,* 127–30) treats all of Paul's discourse under a single head. This is formally objectionable, but, as he states, the arrangement allows one to see the cumulative effect of the material.

35 Smith (*Voyage*) analyzed the journey in minute detail. He had the advantage of writing in an era when sailing ships were not a quaint relic of the past. (Smith was born in 1782 and was an avid yachtsman.) Nonetheless, such reconstructions—others include the voyages of Odysseus—do not constitute proof, since many of their findings come from the analyst rather than the text. To note but one point, the location of Malta remains uncertain. For some of the difficulties and uncertainties involved in Smith's reconstruction, see Rapske, "Travel," 29–43.

36 On the literary quality, see Pervo, *Profit*, 52, and his references. Barrett (2:1178) suggests that the technical language reveals superior knowledge. This is reasonable, but not certain. Problems with some of the technical language in this passage may derive from inferior knowledge.

37 For examples of interlacement, an enduring literary (and cinematic) technique, see Pervo, *Profit*, 133–34.

38 See above.

39 Lüdemann (*Acts*, 355 n. 113) takes note of a work by one of Weiser's students, Peter Seul (*Rettung für alle: Die Romreise des Paulus nach Apg 27,1–28,16* [Berlin and Vienna: Philo Verlagsgesellschaft, 2003]), which argues, at considerable length, for

One qualification is the propensity for ancient authors to describe experiences in conventional terms. Shipwreck stories, for example, should have at least some of the qualities appropriate to shipwreck stories. The presence of such motifs does not mean that a particular shipwreck story is fictitious, but it does render details suspect.[40] Since epic was the "original" and enduring setting for such stories and Homeric (etc.) allusions were desirable, epic reminiscences should occasion no surprise, even when found in allegedly historical accounts. Praeder says: "By the first century A.D. storm scenes were part of literary tradition and part of rhetorical training." She subsequently suggests that, just as the speeches in Acts attest to rhetorical practice, so also does the storm scene.[41] Her study also shows the extent to which Acts 27 falls short of normal rhetorical practice. A tentative solution to the source question that accounts for the various data is to hypothesize that the author took whatever few and sketchy facts he had, prepared a conventional shipwreck story, utilizing one or more sources, and included within this the sometimes intrusive passages about Paul.

After completing his valuable survey of travel in the ancient world, Brian Rapske says, "It remains to consider, briefly, what Luke's intention may have been in relating at such considerable length the shipwreck of Paul." After rebuffing other interpretations, he concludes that the object was "to recount the *actual* events" in a manner that will allow readers to understand that Paul's misfortunes should not reflect negatively upon him.[42] This is a meager harvest. Luke, I believe, wished to produce a hundredfold. The need to defend Paul in the light of his experiences of storm, threatened summary execution, shipwreck, and snakebite does not demand a narrative of this length,[43] since the mere fact of his survival is adequate defense, if such were needed. As Michael Goulder says, in advocating a different interpretation, "We are not driven to suppose unlikely and disagreeable things about the author's mental and material resources."[44]

Three factors invite the investigation of a deeper meaning of this story: its length, its position in the narrative, and the abundance of symbolism associated with sea, storm, travel by ship, and rescue from the perils of the deep in antiquity. Since the beginning of chap. 20, Paul's career has followed that of Jesus, with a journey to Jerusalem, "passion predictions," arrest, and multiple trials. Talbert concludes his outline with a comparison

---

Lucan composition of the whole. This is implicit in the judgment of Susan Marie Praeder ("Acts 27:1–28:16: Sea Voyages in Ancient Literature and the Theology of Luke-Acts," *CBQ* 46 [1984] 683–706, esp. 705): "It is apparent that Luke is familiar with several literary models or styles from sea voyages in ancient literature and is following some more closely than others."

40 Appendices 1–4 in Conzelmann (231–36), a collection that could be expanded, show how stereotyped these descriptions were. One could claim that Lucian's *Nav.* 1–9 is simply factual—although this is quite debatable—but his *Tox.* 19–21 (see next note) and *Ver. hist.* are fiction.

41 The quotation is from Praeder, "Acts 27," 693, with references in n. 26. The application is made on p. 695. For complaints about storm scenes and other ecphrases, see Dionysius of Halicarnassus *Rhet.* 10.17, the Elder Seneca *Suasoriae* 1.15 (on poetic storms) and the rubric in 3.2: "Now describe the storm." Lucian *Tox.* 19–21 contains many interesting parallels with Acts. While describing a storm in the Adriatic, the narrator says (20) that he need not repeat the details, presumably because all knew them (although he has mentioned some and will add others). On this, see Richard Pervo, "With Lucian: Who Needs Friends? Friendship in the *Toxaris*," in John Fitzgerald, ed., *Greco-Roman Perspectives on Friendship* (Resources for Biblical Study 34; Atlanta: Scholars Press, 1997) 163–80, esp. 168–69.

42 Rapske, "Travel," citing pp. 43 and 46.

43 These are the "known Pauline difficulties" identified by Rapske, "Travel," 46.

44 Goulder, *Type*, 39. Barrett ("Paul Shipwrecked," in Barry Thompson, ed., *Scripture: Meaning and Method. Essays Presented to Anthony Tyrrell Hanson* [Hull, U.K.: Hull University Press, 1987] 51–64) found no need to say anything disagreeable. After listing twenty-one unnecessarily recorded places and much else that is superfluous, he concluded (p. 51): "These things are in Acts because Luke enjoyed writing about them; and he enjoyed writing about them because he was the sort of man who enjoyed writing about that sort of thing." If taken seriously, this comment means that Acts 27 was entertainment—for the author.

between Luke 24 and Acts 28, observing that both "conclude on a positive note."[45] If the discovery of these earlier concinnities between the experiences of Jesus and Paul are valid—and the evidence for this is all but overwhelming—the interpreter who acknowledges the parallelism is challenged to explore the possibility of correspondences between Luke 23:24—24:8 and Acts 27:1—28:16. In the comparable structural slot where the Gospel tells of the execution of Jesus and his subsequent vindication through resurrection, Acts tells the story of the voyage. An absence of parallelism in Acts 27 would threaten the entire hypothesis of symmetry. Recognition of this has motivated a number of scholars, including Rackham, C. S. C. Williams, Goulder, Radl, and Kratz, to explore, with varying methods and results, the relation between the closing portions of Luke and Acts.[46] Investigation of the possibility that Acts 27 evokes Luke 23–24 is warranted by its length and by its location in the narrative.[47]

Pursuit of items with symbolic potential here is no arduous stern chase, for storm and ship, voyage and safe arrival, shipwreck and rescue were already clichés at the beginning of the Common Era. In the Hebrew background and tradition, the (Mediterranean) sea was nearly always portrayed as a hostile place, the locus of demonic chaos[48] that God alone could subdue (Exod 15:1-8; Isa 51:9-10). The eschatological principle that the end will replicate the beginning included uncontrolled ocean among the phenomena that will mark the devolution of creation into chaos: "There will be signs in the sun, the moon, and the stars, and on the earth distress among nations confused by the roaring of the sea and the waves" (Luke 21:25).[49] Since this apocalyptic apparatus is a feature of the Gospel storm stories (Mark 4:35-41; 6:45-52 and parallels), it should not be excluded from consideration of Acts 27.[50]

Jewish literature of the Hellenistic and Roman eras makes use of many of the storm and ship images. Some of these derive from Greek-speaking Judaism,[51]

45 Talbert, *Literary Patterns*, 18.

46 Rackham, 477–93, *passim*; Williams, 159 (without development); Goulder, *Type*, 34–43; Kratz, *Rettungswunder*, 330–50; and Radl, *Paulus*, 222–65. Cf. also G. R. Jacobson, "Paul in Luke-Acts: The Savior Who Is Present," in Kent H. Richards, ed., *SBLSP 1983* (Chico, Calif.: Scholars Press, 1983) 131–46, esp. 131–37; Jean-Noël Aletti, *Quand Luc raconte: Le récit comme théologie* (Lire la Bible 115; Paris: Cerf, 1998) 69–103; Tannehill, *Narrative Unity*, 335–37; and Talbert and Hayes, "A Theology," 335–36. Marguerat (*Historian*, 58–59) is cautious, but allows for "christological typology."

47 Goulder (*Type*, 38) says, "[T]he whole of Acts 27 is devoted to the account of the shipwreck because the incident occupies the central position symbolically in the whole book, and requires to be heavily weighted."

48 Psalm 29; 42:7; 46:2-4; 65:7; 88:7; 89:9-14 ("Rahab of the deep); 93:4. See, for examples, Earle Hilgert, *The Ship and Related Symbols in the New Testament* (Assen: Van Gorcum, 1962) 43–46. Rev 21:1 is clear: in the new age the sea will no longer exist. Rackham (475) comments: "In prophecy and apocalypse the raging waves were the symbol, as of confusion in general, so of the restless and tumultuous surging of the nations. The passage of Red Sea made the sea the established type of the greatest peril through which man must pass on his way to the promised land." See also F. Stolz, "Sea," *DDD*, 737–42, *DBI*, *s.v.* "Storm," 817–19.

49 These ideas were not completely foreign to Greco-Roman thought. Storm scenes often depicted the collapse of the cosmic order. See Lucan *Pharsalia* 1.72–80; 2.289–92; and *Apollonius of Tyre* 11 "omnia miscentur. Pulsat mare sidera caeli" ("Everything is mixed up; the sea beats against the stars of heaven").

50 A (personal) eschatological element in Egyptian and Greek culture was expressed in the use of a boat to transport the dead to the afterlife. Egyptian religion depicted death as passage through waters to next world (Hilgert, *Ship*, 15–17). Greek literature and art depicts Charon as the pilot who transports dead souls across the river Styx. Even those destined for the Elysian Fields had to cross Ocean (Homer *Od.* 24.2, 10–11). Water thus symbolized the boundary between life and death, this world and the next. The image occurs in Hebrew thought, as in 2 Sam 22:5-6: "For the waves of death encompassed me, the torrents of perdition assailed me; 6 the cords of Sheol (ὠδῖνες θανάτου) entangled me, the snares of death confronted me." Cf. the comments on 2:24.

51 *Aristeas* 251 uses the familiar image of the ship as life, the port as hereafter, and God as the pilot. Cf. Wis 5:10, 13; *4 Macc.* 7:1-3. Josephus *Ant.* 10.278–79 invokes "natural theology": a universe not governed by God would be like a ship without a helmsman.

Impt.

Creation into Chaos

but others do not.[52] *T. Naph.* 6:1–8:2 could have been written, *mutatis mutandis*, by Horace, but it is vigorously Israelite. Israel is a ship that encounters trouble in the form of a storm. The breakup of the ship is a national disaster. The Qumran *Thanksgiving Hymn* 9[53] (1QH XI) also uses the image of a storm-tossed ship, among others, in an apocalyptic context. These texts indicate that ship and storm imagery belonged to the common culture and was adaptable to various contexts, including apocalyptic forecasts. The storm metaphor also appears in the environment of Acts: "We must no longer be children, tossed to and fro and blown about by every wind of doctrine" (Eph 4:14). The winds are raging, but the spiritually mature, of whom one could find no better example than the Paul of Acts 27, will not be swept away.[54] The Pastor likewise uses "shipwreck" of spiritual calamity (1 Tim 1:19).[55]

The Greeks, unlike the pre-Hellenistic Israelites, feared the sea not because it was foreign but because it was familiar. For them, as for many cultures, storm was a vivid metaphor for the challenges and misfortunes of life. Committing oneself to the deep on a vessel demanded an excess of courage and a deficit of wisdom.

> May the goddess who rules over Cyprus, and Helen's brothers, those bright stars, and the lord of the winds . . . guide you, O ship. . . . Oak and three layers of brass were wrapped round the heart of that man who first entrusted a fragile craft to the savage sea, and had no fear of the headlong rush of the Southwester (*Aquilonibus*) as it fought to the death with the northern blasts, or of the Hyades' rain storms, or of the mad South Wind (no more mighty judge presides over the Adriatic, whether he decides to stir up its waters or calm them down). (Horace *Odes* 1.3.1–5, 9–16)[56]

With its challenges and uncertainties, sea travel became a common symbol for the "course" of human life.[57] Luke viewed life as a journey. In Greek thought, the ship became a symbol for the individual traveling through life's vicissitudes, the less fortunate of which are depicted as storms.[58] The vitality of these images is apparent from the full chapter Artemidorus devoted to sailing dreams, with a wealth of meteorological and nautical detail.[59] Among his correspondences are placid journey portends good; storm portends danger; anchor and port indicate rest; the mast represents one's master (κύριος);[60] and shipwreck signals death. The philosophical tradition could, like Jews and Christians, describe life as a voyage.[61] The ship was also a corporate image, "the ship of state."[62] This also became an enduring symbol.

52 For example, Sir 33:2 uses a storm-tossed ship as an image of the unobservant person. *2 Bar.* 85:10-11 compares the soul reaching the end of life and the world near its destruction to a ship approaching port.

53 Formerly Hymn 4.

54 See the comments of Schnackenburg, *Ephesians*, 186.

55 On the image, see Ceslas Spicq, *Les épîtres pastorales* (2 vols.; EB, 4th ed.; Paris: Galbalda, 1969) 1:352–53; and Dibelius and Conzelmann, *Pastoral Epistles*, 33 n. 12.

56 Trans. Niall Rudd, *Horace: Odes and Epodes* (LCL; Cambridge, Mass.: Harvard University Press, 2004) 29–31. For the sentiment, see also *Odes* 3.24.36–41; *Epod.* 16.57–62; Hesiod *Op.* 236; Sophocles *Ant.* 332–36; Aratus *Phaen.* 110; Lucretius *De Rerum Natura* 5.1006; Tibullus 1.3.36–37; Virgil *Eclogues* 4.32; Ovid *Metam.* 1.94;

57 See, for example, Euripides *Trojan Women* 102–4; Plato *Leg.* 7 (803A); Plutarch *Tranq. an.* 17 (*Mor.* 475F–476A).

58 See the final paragraphs of Chrysostom's final sermon on Acts (*Hom.* 55), which builds on the sea as a metaphor for Paul.

59 See Appendix 4.

60 This became an enduring Christian image, with the mast as cross, that is, Christ (*antenna crucis*), empowering the ship of the church.

61 See, for example, the lengthy, nearly allegorical description of the voyage of life in Lucian *Hermot.* 28.

62 See Hilgert, *Ship*, 21–22. The earliest known reference is Alcaeus frg. 6, while Horace *Ode* 1.14 is the most famous. This was cited by Quintilian 8.6.44 to illustrate the trope of "allegory." Jewish examples include *T. Naph.* 6:1-8; and Qumran *Thanksgiving Hymn* 9, cited above. Christians took up the image elsewhere at least by the early second century, if not by Matthew (Günther Bornkamm, *Tradition and Interpretation in Matthew* [trans. P. Scott; Philadelphia: Westminster, 1963]) 55; Ignatius *Polyc.* 2.3 is not relevant to Acts 27. The ship of the church encounters storms but does not sink. See also

The popularity of the theme is reflected also in ancient novels, whose protagonists must often travel far, usually unwillingly, as the apparent playthings of fate.[63] "The *navigium* of novel characters most commonly turns into a *naufragium*, journey into wreck."[64] This is amply illustrated in an explicitly religious atmosphere in Apuleius's *Metamorphoses*.[65] The priest who has provided Lucius with the means to return to human form (a "resurrection") says: "You have endured many different toils and been driven by Fortune's great tempests and mighty stormwinds; but, finally, Lucius, you have reached the harbour of Peace and the altar of Mercy" (*Metam.* 11.15).[66] In his hymn of praise following initiation, Lucius says, "You protect mortals on sea and land, and you drive away the storm-winds of life . . . you calm the storms of Fortune" (*Metam.* 11.25).[67] Storm is for Apuleius's narrator, as it was for the ancient Israelites and many others, a preferred trope for the great enemy. His "harbor of peace" (*portus quietis*) is the corresponding image for a happy outcome, the "desired haven" of Ps 107:30.[68] In general and particular, Acts 27 lives in an atmosphere thick with familiar symbolism.

Ancient writers used both "death" and "resurrection"/"revival" in hyperbolic ways, technically as metonyms in which death could be called "bonds" or "prison" and vice versa,[69] while terms such as "resurrection" were applied to those presumed dead or lost but later found. These tropes found fruitful soil in ancient novels, whose authors made too much use of them for modern taste, but the literary clichés of a popular genre become such because they touch, however trivially and superficially, on vital issues. Important parallels to these issues can be found in descriptions of religious initiation.[70] Rom 6:3-4 is an altogether apposite illustration: "Do you not know that all of us who have been baptized into Christ Jesus were baptized into his death? Therefore we have been buried with him by baptism into death, so that, just as Christ was raised from the dead by the glory of the Father, so we too might walk in newness of life."[71] This imagery is also present in the Hebrew

Tertullian *Idol.* 24; *Bapt.* 8. For more references, see Hermann W. Beyer, "κυβέρνησις," *TDNT* 3:1035–37; and Lampe, 784, *s.vv.*, *κυβερνάω, κ.τ.λ.*

63 On the theme of life as a journey in ancient novels, see Reinhold Merkelbach, *Roman und Mysterium* (Berlin: de Gruyter, 1962) 29–30.

64 Doody, *True Story*, 327. See her comments on the ubiquity of the symbol in literature from the seventeenth to the twentieth century (327–29).

65 In the wake of John J. Winkler's *Auctor & Actor: A Narratological Reading of Apuleius's* Golden Ass (Berkeley: University of California Press, 1985), many critics of the ancient novel have inclined to view the religious elements as insincere. That question is not relevant to these references.

66 Trans. Hanson, *Apuleius*, 2:319. The imagery is common: elsewhere in the book, note *fortunae naufragio* ("shipwreck of fortune" [6.5]), *ultimo fortunae turbine* ("the last blast of fortune" [8.31]), *procellam Fortunae saevientis* ("the storm of savage fortune" [10.4]), and *fatorum fluctibus* ("the billows of the fates" [10.13]). The setting is the Feast of Isis Pelagia ("Our Lady of Good Voyage"), at which a ship was launched to signal the opening of navigation. Isis brought her followers to safe moorings: *P. Oxy.* 1380.15, 74. A philosophical example is Seneca *Ep.* 94.22.

67 Trans. Hanson, *Apuleius*, 2:345 (*alt.*).

68 *Quies* in one form or another marked many tombs in the imperial period and survives in the term *requiem* and the phrase *requiescat in pace*. See Franz Cumont, *Afterlife in Roman Paganism* (New Haven: Yale University Press, 1922) 191–95. Campbell Bonner abundantly illustrates the trope of life's end as a port in "Desired Haven," *HTR* 34 (1941) 49–67.

69 See p. 309 n. 92.

70 Erwin Rohde noted the ubiquity of the theme in *Der griechische Roman und seine Vorlaüfer* (3rd ed.; Darmstadt: Wissenschaftliche Buchgesellschaft, 1974) 287 and n. 1. See also Fritz Wehrli, "Einheit und Vorgeschichte der griechischen-römischen Romanliteratur." *Museum Helveticum* 22 (1965) 133–54, esp. 142–48; and Glen W. Bowersock, *Fiction as History: Nero to Julian* (Berkeley: University of California Press, 1994) 99–119. Bowersock emphasizes that the theme appeared in a variety of fictional compositions. For the present purposes, the most illuminating (albeit cloudy) exposition is Kerényi, *Romanliteratur*, 24–43. Kerényi understood the relation between novels and mysteries more in cultural than in propagandistic terms. See the comments of Tomas Hägg, *The Novel in Antiquity* (Berkeley and Los Angeles: University of California Press, 1983) 101–4.

71 An Isaic priest described initiation to Lucius as "voluntary death" (*mors voluntaria*) (Apuleius *Metam.* 11.21). Cf. also Mark 10:38-39, where "baptize" (βαπτίζω) means "die."

Bible.[72] A relevant and compelling example is the Psalm of Jonah (Jonah 2:1-10), in which the narrator characterizes his experience as a death: "out of the belly of Sheol I cried, and you heard my voice. . . . I went down to the land whose bars closed upon me forever; yet you brought up my life from the Pit." Near-death through drowning could be called "death" and escape from it resurrection.

Since Luke was fond of producing stories that echoed biblical tales,[73] the "typological" realm merits consideration. At the broadest level stands the exodus event, the language of which helped shape the story of Peter's deliverance from prison.[74] That account utilized paschal symbolism for relating the Easter story and describing the meaning of baptism. The passage of the Israelites over the sea on dry ground climaxed the exodus. Isa 51:9-10 links in parallelism God's defeat of the primal sea monster Rahab with the events at the Red Sea: "who made the depths of the sea a way for the redeemed to cross over" (v. 10).[75] "The most obvious counterpart [is] the shipwreck of Jonah," who, like Paul, was a missionary to gentiles, experienced a near shipwreck, was responsible for the delivery of all aboard, and ended up on dry land, after which he, like Paul, preached to those in the current world capital.[76] Jonah's activity served as a reproach in Q (Luke 11:29-32), with a hint of the gentile mission, and was transformed by Matthew (12:38-42) into a type of the death and resurrection of Christ.[77]

The boat stories of the canonical Gospels (Mark 6:35-41; 6:45-52 parr.;[78] Luke 5:1-11; John 21:1-14[79]) are routinely analyzed in terms of their symbolic content. The storm stories, among which Acts 27 is to be included, are rescue miracles.[80] The two evidently pre-Marcan collections in Mark 4–8 each included a water miracle and a feeding story, strongly suggesting an exodus typology with sacramental implications.[81] Acts 27 contains both. The relation of 27:34-38 to the Eucharist is widely discussed and, in any case, potent enough to require lengthy refutation by those who reject it.[82] In two senses, Acts 27 supplies additional Peter/Paul parallels. Paul also is rescued from the threat of the waves, as were the disciples in Luke 8:22-25, and, like that of Peter in Acts 12:1-11, his experience has a paradigmatic quality about the meaning of new life.

There are sufficient warrants for reading Acts 27 as a symbolic—not allegorical—account of death and

72 See Goulder, *Type*, 37–39; Radl, *Paulus*, 227–29; and Kratz, *Rettungswunder*, 328–29, 350.

73 See pp. 220–21.

74 See the comments on 12:1-11.

75 On the exodus theme, see also Radl, *Paulus*, 231–33.

76 This summarizes Rackham (477), who is quoted. Paul is formally closer to an antitype of Jonah, who "saved" those aboard by leaving the ship. See Alexander, *Literary Context*, 85.

77 The inverse is also possible and less likely to be disputed. Luke 4:25-30, for example, foreshadows the gentile mission, the fates of Stephen and Paul, and, in particular, the passion of Jesus, whom death could not hold.

78 On the storm stories, see, e.g., Hilgert, *Ship*, 72–104. Most interpreters relate them to discipleship. Matthew makes these features more explicit. See Bornkamm, *Tradition and Interpretation*, 52–58. Mark 4:35-41 arguably reflects Jonah, as Jesus, like Jonah, sleeps (Jonah 1:5, evoked also in Acts 27:19; Mark 4:38).

79 The miraculous catches are gift miracles that symbolize the church's mission.

80 The late Dieter Georgi once challenged the students in a Harvard New Testament seminar by asking, "When does Acts 27 become a miracle story?" Chrysostom, who understood the story as a miracle, illustrates the contrast between the ancient and modern understanding of miracle: "See how God does not innovate or change the order of nature (οὐδέν . . . μεταβάλλοντα), but suffers them to sail into the unfavorable winds. But even so the miracle is wrought (θαῦμα ἐργάζεται)" (*Hom.* 53, p. 315). Theissen (*Miracle Stories*, 102) classifies this narrative among rescue miracles, thus associating it with the prison escapes. The responsible person is the complement of a "Jonah," the individual (usually) whose divine patron will see to the rescue of all. Examples include Caesar (Plutarch *Caes.* 38), Apollonius (Philostratus *Vit. Apoll.* 4.13), whose advice to leave a ship that would sink was heeded by few, to their detriment (5.18). Lucian presents Peregrinus as a parody of the stalwart passenger (*Peregr.* 43). The "Stilling of the Storm," Mark 4:35-41||Luke 8:22-25, exhibits the same convention. Talbert and Hayes ("A Theology") recognize this connection, although they develop it along different lines.

81 See Paul Achtemeier, "Toward the Isolation of Pre-Markan Miracle Catenae," *JBL* 89 (1970) 265–91; and idem, "The Origin and Function of the Pre-Marcan Miracle Catenae," *JBL* 91 (1972) 198–221.

82 See below.

resurrection. Luke was too good a writer to engage in ponderous allegorizing. With the probable exception of a few phrases here and there, this story can be enjoyed for its surface features. Nearly every commentator finds some beneath-the-surface meaning here, such as evidence for providential care and the achievement of the divine plan,[83] the theme of universal salvation,[84] or vindication for Paul.[85] The primary sign of divine vindication in Christian thought is resurrection. To speak of Acts 27 as manifesting God's plan, universalism, and/or vindication is, in Lucan theology, to speak of the meaning of the resurrection of Jesus.[86] Vindication of Paul is justification of the gentile mission. It is difficult to deny that, at some level, Acts 27 is speaking of the same issues expounded in Luke 23–24.[87] Luke makes his points by telling stories rather than by emitting theological postulates. The broader and deeper symbolic reading followed here solves more problems than it creates, while taking seriously the ubiquity of such items as the storm-threatened ship and Luke's propensity for narrative theology.

Objections to this approach readily emerge. One is represented by Weiser, who asks whether Luke would not have used more explicit language.[88] This complaint does not do justice to Luke's literary methods, for, like many authors, he hoped that the implied reader would take the point without undue prodding. A second objection, raised by Johnson, poisons the well by the label "allegory." He speaks of a "desperate need to find parallels where the text offers no suggestion of one" and goes on to say, "If the author's point was so patently allegorical, we have even less understanding of why the pedestrian elements of the story were retained." "Desperate need" is mere polemic, the text has more than a few suggestions of parallelism, and the comment about irrelevant details excludes allegory, in which details are *ipso facto* important.[89] None of the interpretations discussed here treats the account as an allegory or interprets it allegorically. Third, one may ask why patristic authorities did not perceive and expound this symbolism. Attempting to explain why one interpreter did not see what another saw is always difficult. The early explicit use of Acts 27–28 by Irenaeus and Tertullian[90] sought to demonstrate that the Paul of Acts is the real Paul, because passages like Acts 27 were composed by his companion, Luke, and therefore the Paul of Marcion and various "Gnostics" was a false construction. The same concern—that a symbolic interpretation threatens history—is apparent in the views of Rapske and Witherington.[91] Otherwise, ancient commentators largely neglected Acts 27.[92] Chrysostom discovered and expounded a number of symbolic elements,[93] as did

83 E.g., Talbert and Hayes, "A Theology."

84 E.g., Tannehill, *Narrative Unity*, 2:336–37.

85 This concept is developed in various ways by Gary Miles and Garry Trompf, "Luke and Antiphon," *HTR* 69 (1976) 259–67; David Ladouceur, "Hellenistic Preconceptions of Shipwreck and Pollution as a Context for Acts 27–28," *HTR* 73 (1980) 435–49, and John C. Clabeaux, "The Story of the Maltese Viper and Luke's Apology for Paul," *CBQ* 67 (2005) 604–10. Weiser (2:663) notes rescue, proof of innocence, and the missionary objective, referring to 1:8; 13:47; 19:21; 23:11; and 25:10–12.

86 This may be illustrated from the Pentecost sermon: the death and resurrection of Jesus was in accordance with the divine plan; resurrection showed that the execution of Jesus was unjust (Acts 2:23-24). The result of this vindication was the gift of the Spirit (v. 33), which opened God's promise to all (v. 39).

87 See the kindred views of Talbert and Hayes, "A Theology," 335–36.

88 Weiser, 2:660.

89 Johnson, 457. A more appropriate term would be "typology," which looks for comparison at a broader label. Witherington (775 n. 105) evidently borrows Johnson's view: "Not an allegory about Paul reliving or mirroring the end of the life of Christ" [*sic*]. See also Talbert and Hayes, "A Theology," 336 n. 31.

90 Irenaeus, *A.H.* 3.14; Tertullian does not cite Acts 27 in his work *Against Marcion*; he refers to 28:26 in 5.11.9.

91 This opposition is not obligatory. Rackham, for example, accepts in general the details of Acts as historically reliable.

92 Ephrem (according to the Latin translation in Ropes, *Text*, 450) devoted ten lines to his summary of chap. 27, but thirteen to 28:1-10.

93 Chrysostom (*Hom.* 53) interpreted the story in accordance with several ancient tropes. Paul was the "true pilot . . . [who] steered as pilot not a vessel of this (earthly) kind, but the Church of the whole world. . . . In this vessel are many shipwrecks. . . . Look at our whole life: it is just such.

Arator and Bede.[94] Canonical and related developments also played a part. The academic tradition separated Acts from the Gospels, as did liturgical usage. Not until the twentieth century did commentators begin to explore the symmetries of Luke and Acts.[95] Pursuit of symbolic meaning in Acts 27 is justified.

The voyage involves three ships: the vessel of Adramyttium, which transports the central figures to Myra (vv. 2-5), the Alexandrian ship that comes to grief on the island (vv. 6-44), and another Alexandrian craft that takes (some, all?) survivors to Puteoli (28:11-13). These conveyances roughly delineate the structure, which is framed by two brief—that is, like those in earlier chapters—itinerary passages: vv. 27:1-8 and 28:11-16. The opening and closing verses mention a military person who has custody of Paul. Both also refer to "friends" or believers (27:3; 28:14-15) who care for Paul. Both also anticipate the next section, bad weather in 27:4, 7-8 and arrival at Rome in 28:14. The balance consists of two large units dealing with the voyage, vv. 9-20 and 21-44, each of which includes a forecast by Paul and its subsequent fulfillment, followed by the experiences on the island (28:1-10).[96] As it stands, the narrative is a thoroughly literary piece[97] rather than a story reporting the unedited reflections of a participant.[98]

Comment

■ **1** The transition between chap. 27 and chap. 28 is harsh and abrupt. While the positive comments of Agrippa are still ringing in the reader's ear, the narrator shifts to cold impersonal language—and simultaneously introduces, out of the blue, a "we."[99] Acts 27:1 would follow 25:12 without difficulty, for the decision to send Paul to Rome was made at that point. It is possible that a source is visible here, since no reason for the transfer is given and Paul is not viewed as a person of high status, while the "we" suggests that Paul was not the only one involved in the case.[100] The subject of the verb παρεδίδουν ("transferred")[101] appears to be the ubiquitous

. . . For Paul is sailing even now with us, only not bound as he was then. . . . Let us therefore abide where he bids us—in faith, in the safe haven. . . . Let us think that the whole world is a ship, and in this the evildoers and those who have numberless vices, some rulers, others guards, others . . . just *persons*" (Walker, p. 318). For Chrysostom, life was a difficult voyage in which the prudent will do well to look for the guidance of God and the company of the saints. For the image of the ship as the world, in which a god is usually depicted as pilot, see Hilgert, *Ship*, 22.

94 On Arator, see p. 663 n. 94. Note Bede's comments on v. 33 (95), cited below. He likewise reads the break-up of the ship as a trope of the careless and indifferent soul (95–96).

95 Rackham wrote his commentary in the first year of the century (1901), but the trend did not gain impetus until Cadbury's *The Making of Luke-Acts* in 1927.

96 Johnson (444–60) divides the material into two parts, vv. 1-26 and 27-44, the first of which describes the perils at sea, while the second narrates shipwreck and rescue. This is an intelligent division if chap. 27 stands alone. Its weakness is that it separates 28:1-16, the first part of which, at least, is integral to the rescue.

97 For details, see Talbert, 215–21. On its narrative development, see Tannehill (*Narrative Unity*, 2:330–37) and Alexander (*Literary Context*, 212–13), who offer sage observations on the deviation of this passage from the conventional *nostos* (homecoming) pattern.

98 Hemer (*Book*, 209–10) says: "Many details . . . are characterized by an 'immediacy' of narrative interest, not easily explained from the perspective of selective hindsight." He excludes from his argument Paul's speeches and "theological" material. This procedure falsifies (not meant in a moral sense) the results.

99 The first plural last appeared in 21:18.

100 Acts 27:1 would accommodate many interpretations of Paul's fate, including the hypothesis that he was sent to Rome for execution. Nothing is said about his citizenship or an appeal, while the first plural could be taken as an indication that one or more of his associates (gentile/s taken into the temple?) was among the prisoners. (Another possibility is that the procurator waited until he had enough prisoners for remand to Rome to justify use of a detachment.)

101 This verb is a "passion parallel." See, e.g., Luke 23:25; Acts 3:13. The imperfect here is difficult. See BDF §327. Barrett (2:1181) explains that the process of handing over the prisoners concluded with the embarkation. Haenchen (697 n. 2) asks whether this tense is used for historical narrative. Note the imperfects in vv. 9, 11, 13, 15, 17-18, 20, 27, 33, 39-40.

"they" used of authorities by those without power.[102] Finally, no time is indicated. As far as the reader knows, Paul and the others were transferred into the charge of a centurion and placed aboard a ship within moments of the "decision." The D-Text seeks to address all of these problems, smoothing the transition, eliminating "us,"[103] improving Paul's status,[104] and introducing some chronological data.[105] The *chargé* of the prisoners, identified, like most characters in Acts, by a single name, Julius,[106] evidently belonged to an auxiliary unit. Ramsay attempted to deflect this probability, since a prisoner of Paul's status clearly required a more highly placed escort.[107]

■ **2** They took ship first in an unnamed vessel from Adramyttium, a city of northwest Asia Minor.[108] Aristarchus introduces an element of discontinuity. He was first mentioned in 19:29, then as one of Paul's companions in 20:4. The D-Text makes his appearance less abrupt.[109] One wonders why he is not mentioned until this aside at the end of v. 2. Rather than stress his importance as a witness, the narrator appears to minimize his role.[110] Aristarchus no sooner enters the narrative in this clumsy manner than he vanishes.[111]

■ **3** The verse returns Paul to center stage. Centurion Julius is sufficiently impressed by his prisoner—and of sufficient character himself—to permit Paul to visit (lit.) "the friends." This action anticipates and makes an inclusion with v. 43, and also creates a link with 28:2.[112]

A related question is whether "friends" here refers to believers or to acquaintances of Paul. In favor of the latter are the absence of references to believers in Tyre, the other use of friends of Paul (19:31, the Asiarchs), and Luke's customary terminology: "saints" (ἅγιοι) or "sisters and brothers" (ἄδελφοι).[113] "Believers" is more likely. No weight attaches to previous mention of believers,[114] and the article is important here. The language is from the author rather than a source. It implies that Paul could move about with relative freedom, a difficulty noted and

102 Grammatical logic would make Festus and Agrippa the subjects of this action.

103 𝔓[6] 326 *pc* replace "us" with "Paul and companions" (*τοὺς περὶ τὸν Παῦλον*). This also eliminates an awkward first plural. It may be due to lectionary influence, but its introduction from such a source would not have been accidental.

104 The emphasis is on Paul, while the reference to an "Augustan cohort" is dropped.

105 Clark (*Acts*, 163) has a slightly different reconstruction. (The D-Text is relatively well supported here: 97. 421 h w syr sy[hmg]).

106 Use of a single name is characteristic of popular literature. Sherwin-White (*Roman Society*, 161) gives a reason why someone named Julius would wish to be identified by his *nomen* alone. This is pure conjecture.

107 Ramsay, *St. Paul the Traveller*, 315. See T. R. S. Broughton, "The Roman Army," in Lake and Cadbury, *Additional Notes*, 427–45; Saddington, "Roman Military," 2417–18; Mark J. Olson, "Augustan Cohort," and "Julius," *ABD* 1:524 and 3:1125–26, with the latter's bibliographies; and Hemer, *Book*, 132 n. 96. For Luke, any centurion enjoyed sufficient prestige.

108 J. D. Wineland ("Adramyttium," *ABD* 1:80) confidently states: "The ship was homeward bound when Paul, Luke, Aristarchus, and Julius the Centurion boarded it in order to journey from Caesarea to Rome via the Asian coast."

109 A D-Text variant not discussed by Boismard adds (doubtless from 20:4) "Secundus" 614. 1505. (2147) *pc* sy[h].

110 The phrase *σὺν ἡμῖν* ("with us") appears to mean "one of us" in 1:22, but in 21:16, 18 it means something like "along with us." Diametrically opposed to the theory that Aristarchus is a/the primary authority for the account is the possibility that his name was lifted from Col 4:10, where he is described as a fellow prisoner of Paul. If Aristarchus made the voyage and was a prisoner—which the text does not claim—the theory that Paul was charged with bringing gentiles into the temple gains credence. His presence is more of an embarrassment than a prop for the tradition, although commentators, such as Conzelmann (215), routinely identify him as such.

111 For various hypotheses about how long Aristarchus remained with the company, see Cadbury and Lake, 325.

112 Josephus *Ant.* 2.236 employs the same phrase for receiving care (*ἐπιμελείας τυχεῖν*) in v. 3 of the nurture received by Moses.

113 "Saints" is less common, but appeared in 26:10; "brothers and sisters" is the term found in 28:14.

114 Acts 21:3, 7 mentions believers in Sidon. Cf. also the general comments in 11:19; 15:3.

corrected by the D-Text, which has these friends visit Paul. Two of the three uses of the stem from which English "philanthropy" derives occur in this passage (27:3; 28:2). Luke makes more use of explicit friendship language than any other NT author. Harnack quaintly says: "Luke with his classical culture has permitted himself this once to use the classical designation."[115]

■ **4-5** The next verses take them to Myra—technically its port, Andriace—about 4.5 kilometers from the city. This was a stopping point for ships in the grain trade.[116] The D-text raises interesting questions. The initial "Afterwards" is without sense (unless one presumes the excision of prior narrative).[117] The references to Cilicia and Pamphylia are changed to bodies of water.[118] The statement that this leg took fifteen days has, however, met with a friendlier reception.[119] This reading, which has a better attestation than the other D-Text variants here, is appealing mainly because it is reasonable, but that does not make it more probable.[120]

■ **6** The verse omits any reference to debarkation or departure.[121] The first plural would seem to apply only to those in the centurion's charge, that is, prisoners, and is evidently different from the bland "we" of vv. 7-8.

■ **7-8** The translation and meaning of these verses raise considerable difficulties.[122] Authorities try to reconcile their perceptions of Luke's thought with views of normal sailing routes.[123] No certainty is possible. Either because of necessity or in accordance with standard procedure, the ship put in on the southern shore of Crete. The D-Text omits the difficulty of making headway and the mention of Salmone. This makes for a more rapid narrative, less bogged down by the mention of obscure sites,[124] but the proper narrator of Acts uses lists of stations, as in chaps. 20–21, to build suspense.

■ **9-12** The reference to Yom Kippur suggests that the normal end of the sailing season was at hand.[125] Paul stepped in to make a forecast. The professionals had reason for disagreeing with him. Unwisely so, since

115 Harnack, *Mission,* 1:421 (see his valuable comments on the term on 419–21); Cadbury and Lake, 326; Cadbury, "Names," 379–80; and Pervo, *Dating,* 289–90. Barrett (2:1183) says that the friends are Christians, but he does not think that the term is technical. See also BDAG, 1059, *s.v.* φίλος. On friendship in Luke and Acts, see Alan C. Mitchell, "The Social Function of Friendship in Acts 2:44-47 and 4:32-37," *JBL* 111 (1992) 255–72.

116 Hemer, *Book*, 132. *ILS* 9958 mentions a granary erected under Hadrian, but see Thornton, *Der Zeuge,* 328 n. 297.

117 Ropes (*Text*, 241) attributes it, following H. I. Wordsworth and H. F. D. White (*Novum Testamentum Domini nostri Jesu Christi Latine secundum editionem S. Hieronymi* [Oxford, 1889–1954]), to reading τὸ τε ("and the") as τότε ("then"). The Latin *tum* would do.

118 Ropes (*Text*, 241) views the Latin base, *sinum*, as "a corruption of *secundum*" (Latin *secundum* can be a preposition equivalent to Greek κατά).

119 Ropes (*Text*, 241) cannot explain it other than as original.

120 Barrett, 2:1184.

121 Alexander, *Literary Context*, 82: "'finding a ship' is an important event." She provides *Ephesian Tale* 3.10.4; 4.10.2 as examples. The narrator of Acts treats this discovery matter-of-factly.

122 The translation follows Barrett's attempt (2:1185–86) at unraveling the sequence of tenses and participles.

123 See Haenchen, 699; Conzelmann, 216; and Hemer, *Book*, 134–36. All rely on Lionel Casson, "The Isis and Her Voyage," *TAPA* 81 (1950) 43–56, and subsequent reactions to it. For bibliography, see Hemer, *Book*, 134 n. 102.

124 Spellings for Salmone and Lasaea vary considerably, while "Fair Havens" (καλοὶ λίμενες) is not attested in ancient writers. For efforts to unravel and identify the details, see Hemer, *Book*, 135–36. The text is not certain. On the difficulties of N-A[27], note Barrett, 2:1185–87.

125 For speculation on the date of the Day of Atonement in various years, see Witherington, 762; and Rapske, "Travel," 23–24. Certainty is not possible. (Among other things it assumes, incorrectly, that a single Jewish calendar was in use, that everyone knew the date, and that modern calculations can establish these dates in terms of the Gregorian calendar.) According to Praeder ("Acts 27," 689 n. 13), the Feast of Booths marked the end of the sailing season in rabbinic Judaism. Not until the introduction of the compass was sailing in the Mediterranean between October and March a routine activity. See Chrysostom *Hom.* 55 (end), and Vegetius *Epitoma rei militaris* 4.39, who supplies these dates for sea travel: May 27–September 24, safe, until November 11 uncertain, and then closed until March 10. Tacking was limited in antiquity, and the rudders in use were not particularly efficient. Herman T. Wallinga ("Poseidonios on Beating to Windward (FGH 87F46 and Related Passages),"

a savage nor'easter soon broke upon them, requiring major efforts to maintain the ship's integrity and raising the danger that they would be wrecked on the shoals of North Africa. The sailors soon had to surrender effective control of the vessel to the interminable storm. As one lightless day followed another, at least some of the cargo had to be jettisoned.[126] Unable to navigate, the crew gave up. So also did the passengers.

In an atmosphere of rising danger, Paul attempts to intervene.[127] The narrator does not strive for realism in any of Paul's speeches in this chapter. Prisoners were more likely to have been secured below in shackles[128] than allowed to amble about the deck offering unsolicited advice.[129] His audience is a ubiquitous "them." The narrative identifies three authorities: the master, the owner,[130] and the centurion, the last of whom is, improbably, in effective command. He retains it, while the captain and the owner disappear from the narrative. See vv. 30-31. Paul's forecast is somewhat vague.[131] It looks like a general prophecy of doom. As such, it is typical and informs experienced readers that bad things are going to happen.[132] The sequel in v. 21 indicates that it was intended as advice to stay put. The warning does not demonstrate Paul's knowledge of such subjects as meteorology and ship handling. His words are inspired.[133] They are cloudy because their narrative function is to elevate suspense. Evidently all or most agreed that the voyage could not be completed. The prevailing[134] (and expert) opinion was that they should attempt to coast along Crete to reach a safer winter refuge.[135] That they did. The difficulties of the text are revealed by the improvements of the D-Text. The location of their goal, Phoenix, is another difficult matter.[136]

Debates about safety between or among passengers, owners, and crews of various means of transportation will always be with us.[137] In literature, these clashes foreshadow that the trouble predicted by one party

Mnemosyne 53 [2000] 431–47) claims that tacking is in view in 27:27 and translates it thus. For the situation, see *Ethiopian Story* 5.18: The inhabitants of Zakynthos were astonished that a ship had made a successful voyage when the Pleiades were setting, in late October.

126 Water-logged wheat would swell and possibly burst the vessel.

127 The merits of "interpolation" hypotheses are particularly evident here, as v. 12 follows v. 8 (or 9a) more aptly than it does v. 11. See Haenchen, 700 n. 6.

128 Rapske, *Roman Custody*, 205. For a different but probably more typical picture of custody aboard a ship, see *3 Macc.* 4:7-10.

129 Barrett ("Paul Shipwrecked," 55) seeks to rationalize Paul's role aboard ship: "First, in the stress of a storm any man who keeps his head may be listened to." This may be true, but Acts 27 says nothing about people losing their heads. Second, he proposes that Festus *and Agrippa* may have advised the centurion of their view that Paul was innocent (emphasis added). "Thirdly, we see here precisely the way in which a story could develop: Paul's muttered forebodings to Luke become public pronouncements."

130 On the meaning of κυβερνήτης ("captain," "master") and ναύκληρος ("owner"), see Schneider, 2:389–90 nn. 26–27. The terms were not used with perfect consistency, as Barrett (2:1190–91) shows.

131 The form of indirect discourse is mixed, an accusative with infinitive introduced by ὅτι. The statement, which appears to evoke Mark 8:36, might confuse ordinary Greek speakers by its use of "soul" (ψυχή) for "life."

132 For examples from the *Odyssey*, see MacDonald, "Shipwrecks," 97.

133 Haenchen, 700.

134 It is also possible that a minority wished to attempt to reach Italy. See Cadbury and Lake, 329. One difficulty is the composition of "the majority" (οἱ πλείονες). This is another indication of the dissonance between vv. 10-11 and v. 12. Conzelmann (217) follows Haenchen (700): "the majority" are the sailors and come from the source. For options, see Cadbury and Lake, 329.

135 Verse 12 has at least the appearance of considerable elegance. BDF §386 (2) questions the use of the optative in indirect discourse after εἰ, but that category does not fit this situation. Moule (*Idiom Book*, 154) takes this as an indirect question, as if "hoping" or "wondering" might be supplied, and the optative "gives a more tentative and cautious tone." (The MSS. display considerable variance. See Swanson, *Manuscripts*, 465).

136 For the history of the discussion, see Cadbury and Lake, 329–30; Hemer, *Book*, 139–40; and Rapske, "Travel," 36–37. Barrett (2:1193) has a nearly definitive answer: modern Phineha is in mind, but see Conzelmann (217), who notes not only changes since then but possible confusion.

137 Plato (*Resp.* 6.488A–489A) can use the theme to construct a parable in which the gullible captain of

will happen.[138] A useful example is the fragment from a novel once called *Herpyllis* but possibly part of Antonius Diogenes' *Marvels beyond Thule*:[139] Two ships are sailing in tandem in the vicinity of Kos, intending to coast along Asia Minor. The narrator was encouraging (παρεκάλουν) the ships to wait, as the weather was threatening. The masters (κυβερνῆται) disagreed, for one believed that a huge storm was brewing. The narrator was right. The two principals will soon be separated.[140]

■ **13-20** These verses also follow a common pattern: after a promising beginning, the weather quickly deteriorates.[141] Measure after measure fails, until the ship is allowed to make its own headway. The loss of any control over the elements[142] in the face of an apparently incessant storm leads to despair. The general development is clear and dramatic; many of the details are difficult. The first plural (vv. 15, 16, 18) is intermittent. The D-Text (insofar as it is available) is briefer, eliminates some of the difficulties, and is more consistent in the use of "we." Once more, it shows a propensity for a less cluttered narrative,[143] directed toward readers who did not appreciate circumstantial retardation.[144]

■ **14** "Euraquilo," or "nor'easter" (ευρακύλων),[145] is attested, in a different spelling, as a Latin word.[146] The ship is given its own head.[147]

■ **16-17** The verses evidently describe a procedure carried out under the protection of an island, Cauda (which is also variously named[148]), but its specific nature remains unclear.[149] The circumstantial participle

the ship (= masses), instead of listening to the true navigator, is won over by fawning sailors. The narrative reflects an upper-class view of sailors. Note Cicero *Ad Fam.* 16.9.4; and Synesius *Ep.* 4, which has many parallels with Acts 27.

138 Praeder ("Acts 27," 690) dryly notes: "Another rule of forecasts of storm and shipwreck is that they are followed by storms and/or shipwrecks."

139 For details, see Stephens and Winkler, *Greek Novels*, 158–72; and Rolf Kussl, *Papyrusfragmente griechischer Romane* (Classica Monacensia 2; Tübingen: Gunter Narr, 1991) 105–40.

140 See also *Chion of Heraclea* 4.1–2 (in which the sailors do not yield—οὐκ ἐπείθοντο—to the narrator's warning) and Aristides *Hieroi Logoi* 1.26; 4.32–37, both of which feature a nonprofessional narrator who is in charge of the ship. For other examples, see Praeder, "Acts 27," 690–91, who finds the material from *Chion* and the Antonius Diogenes (?) fragment the nearest parallels to 27:9-12. The varied accounts, historical and fictional, illuminate Paul's alleged status as a person as prominent as Cicero and Aristides. (See p. 646 n. 26.)

141 Praeder ("Acts 27," 689) concludes that vv. 13-20 display familiarity with literature at some level. For examples, see MacDonald, "Shipwrecks," 97–98, as well as the previous note.

142 With v. 14 compare Luke 8:23.

143 The D-Text also suppresses the leadership's belief that it could accomplish its purpose (v. 13).

144 This unit is probably the best example in Acts 27 of abridgment that gets rid of obscure statements. See also Cadbury and Lake, 331.

145 One variant is "southeaster" (εὐρακλύδων), which would produce a different result.

146 This would account for the "apologetic" participle, καλούμενος ("known as"). The Latin form *euroaquilo* is attested in various Latin versions and in an inscription. Hemer (*Book*, 141–42) proposes that it is sailors' jargon. That idea had earlier been advanced in a more tentative and general sense by Lake and Cadbury, "The Winds," in Lake and Cadbury, *Additional Notes*, 338–44, esp. 343.

147 The speaker in Lucian *Hermot.* 28 says that a safe return (ἀνασωθῆναι) is difficult once one casts off the lines and gives himself to the wind (ἐπιδῷ τις αὑτὸν τῇ πνεούσῃ). It would have been preferable to check the weather and make sure of the quality of the ship and the qualifications of its captain (κυβερνήτης). This is symbolic—indeed allegorical. See above. Conzelmann (217–18) identifies two possible interpretations of v. 15.

148 Variant spellings include Kaudos, Gaudos, and Clauda/e. See Metzger, *Textual Commentary*, 440–41. Boismard (*Texte*, 414) observes that the word order of the conventional text is unusual. One difficulty with his reconstruction is that his text has the party remaining at Cauda, without clear indication of a departure.

149 See Cadbury, "ὑποζώματα," in Lake and Cadbury, *Additional Notes*, 345–54; Hemer, *Book*, 143; and Rapske, "Travel," 35. Marshall (409) has a clear summary of the leading options, as does Conzelmann (218), who lists four. The chief difficulty is βοήθεια, an abstract ("help") used as a concrete. In English one might say "we rigged some supports." The "supports" or "braces" here would probably be ropes. See Cadbury and Lake (332), who propose analogies. See Plato *Resp.* 616C. In his "ship of state" ode (1.14, 3–9), Horace writes: "Don't you notice how your side is stripped of oars, your mast is split by the violence of the South-

introducing v. 17b, "fearing," can be variously translated: "since, because, although"; that is, it is not clear whether the crew gave the ship its own way despite the danger of being driven onto the dangerous coast of Africa or in order to avoid it.[150] Verse 17c is another obscure phrase: χαλάσαντες τὸ σκεῦος,[151] best interpreted by the logic of the situation rather than because of its clear technical sense, hence "loosed the sails" (or "let down a sea anchor"). The result was that the ship continued to be driven by the wind.[152] Loss of control is near the top of the crescendo of difficulties in storm and shipwreck stories.[153] The fury of the storm[154] forced the crew to begin jettisoning[155] cargo or equipment.[156]

■ **18-19** These verses do not necessarily conflict with v. 38. The imperfect ἐποιοῦντο ("began to jettison") does not imply completion.[157] An owner would not wish to discard any more valuable cargo than necessary. One must guess at the meaning of σκευήν in v. 19. "Spare tackle" is reasonable.[158] The language of vv. 18-19 is somewhat repetitious, however,[159] lending force to the view that the narrator has decided that this is a moment to evoke Jonah.[160] This is not merely an allusion to Jonah 1:5, ἐκβολὴν ἐποιήσαντο τῶν σκευῶν τῶν ἐν τῷ πλοίῳ εἰς τὴν θάλασσαν ("They threw the cargo that was in the ship into the sea"). The object is to recall Jonah's "death and resurrection."[161]

■ **20** The verse emphasizes the "passion" reference through the use of darkness/night as a symbol for death.[162] Specifically, the loss of light recalls the darkness that shrouded the crucifixion of Jesus (Luke 23:44-45).[163] The apocalyptic background indicates that a crisis is at hand.[164] The second half of v. 20 states this

wester, the yardarms groan, and the hull, without the support of ropes (*sine funibus*) can scarcely withstand the overbearing sea?) (trans. Rudd, *Horace*, 51–53). A difficulty is that bracing would help keep the ship from breaking up at sea, as in Horace, but not from being driven onto the shoals. This strengthens the view that v. 17b represents a strong disjunction from the first part.

150 The Syrtis, here the projecting cape of North Africa, was a byword for dangerous waters in antiquity: Virgil *Aen.* 4.41; Horace *Odes* 1.22.5; 2.6; 3–4. For others, see Praeder, "Acts 27," 691–92; and Hemer, *Book*, 144 n. 122. Dio of Prusa enumerates its difficulties in *Or.* 5.8–9.

151 See Cadbury and Lake, 333; and Haenchen, 703, with n. 2, for the obscurity. The *v.l.* for σκεῦος ("thing"), τὰ ἱστία, might mean "set the sail." Conzelmann (218) lists four options, with some references. Hemer (*Book*, 143–44) takes the solution of James Smith: all sails but the small foresail, sufficient to maintain way, were struck. Fitzmyer (776–77) prefers, reasonably, to understand the phrase as dropping an anchor to slow the vessel. If one takes this as the report of an eyewitness (e.g., Luke), it can be claimed, as by Haenchen and Hemer, that he did not understand the procedure. The same solution would apply to any author with limited knowledge who was employing a source.

152 "Carried" is first plural in 36. 453 *pc* sy^{p} (acc. to N-A^{27}). This coordinates with v. 15, which also ended in ἐφερόμεθα. On the "classical liberty to use οὕτως to summarize the content of a preceding participial construction," see BDF §425 (6).

153 Cf. Homer *Od.* 9.82–84; Petronius *Satyrica* 114; Achilles Tatius *Leuc. Clit.* 3.1–2; Lucian *Tox.* 19; *Ver. hist.* 1.6; 2.46; *Nav.* 7; *Ethiopian Story* 5.27.2.

154 Use of σφοδρός ("violent") in some form with "storm" (χειμων-) is common in popular writings. With 27:18 compare Aesop *Fables* 30.1; 69.1; 181.1; 223.1. cf. also Josephus *Ant.* 14.377.

155 For other examples of jettisoning, see Juvenal *Sat.* 12.30–53; Achilles Tatius *Leuc. Clit.* 3.2.9.

156 Verses 18-19 display a clear distinction between the first and third persons: all were battered by the storm. The crew took action. The D-Text, supported by m, uses the first plural in v. 19.

157 The use of verbs in the imperfect for narrating travel appears to be a Lucan characteristic.

158 See, e.g., Cadbury and Lake, 333.

159 Once more the D-Text is shorter, apparently by eliminating a troublesome redundancy, with an expansion ("into the sea") borrowed from v. 38.

160 See Haenchen, 704 n. 2.

161 Roloff (360) claims that the Jonah parallel is accidental. Such claims cannot be proved; use of Jonah in Luke 8:22-25 (above) makes accident less likely.

162 The D-Text paraphrases: the storm is no longer "not small" and, rather than the possibly ambiguous "hope of salvation," is "hope of life." This is quite probably due to the increasing restriction of σῴζω to a religious sense. This term, in various forms, appears seven times in the story: 27:20, 31, 34, 43, 44; 28:1, 4. Christian readers would not view it as "purely secular."

163 The events of v. 20 are "natural" (cf. Virgil *Aen.* 3.203–4), but Luke also attributes the darkness of Luke 23:44-45 to a solar eclipse.

164 Cf. the citation of Luke 21:25 above. The realistic application is that loss of sun and stars made any attempt to determine their position impossible. See Cadbury and Lake, 334.

in a narrative cliché: the absence of any grounds for hope amounts to a signal that the worst is over.[165] The first person in v. 20 is the general "we" and definitely excludes Paul.[166]

■ **21-44** At this apparently ultimate moment, Paul again intervened. Despite the distracting conditions, he gained the attention of all, to whom he offered a message of hope, anchored in a vision and concluded with what seems to be a practical proposal. They had been adrift for two weeks before signs of land, quickly confirmed by repeated soundings, appeared. In order to prevent running aground in the dark, anchors were dropped. The company ardently awaited daybreak. Faithless sailors chose this moment to abscond in the ship's boat. Alert as ever, Paul detected this desertion and informed the centurion. Keeping the crew aboard meant losing the boat and the best means to shore. "[Paul] appears as a vigilant night watchman, doing more to protect those on board the ship than the cowardly sailors or the now-invisible captain and owner."[167]

When the prayed-for day arrived, Paul took the initiative again, with the sound suggestion that all eat. They followed his example. At this point, the narrator gives a head count: 276. Light revealed a bay with a beach. The vessel soon ran aground and began to break up.[168] Since prisoners might take advantage of the confusion to escape, the soldiers deemed it best to liquidate them. The centurion Julius, determined to rescue Paul, countermanded this suggestion. By hook, crook, or packing case everyone got ashore. For the last explicit time in Acts, Paul has eluded a plot. Since chap. 21, his human deliverers have been Roman soldiers or officials.

■ **21-26** Verses 21 and 44 mark the contrast from the fading of all hope for rescue (ἐλπὶς πᾶσα τοῦ σῴζεσθαι) to the rescue of all (πάντας διασωθῆναι). The structure generally resembles that of vv. 9-20: a speech of Paul (vv. 21b-26) followed by its narrative fulfillment (vv. 27-44).[169] The plot is more complex. Nothing substantial is said about the weather; readers are not informed when, or if, conditions improved.[170] The focus is upon two plots: one by the sailors (vv. 30-32),[171] the other by the soldiers (vv. 41-43).[172] Both are foiled, the former by Paul, the latter because of him. Each features a form of "save."[173] These two brief adventures reinforce the theme that Paul is the reason why all are saved. This deliverance was not necessary. God's plan would have been accomplished had Paul alone survived the disaster. Two conclusions are difficult to elude. The rescue of all symbolizes the universality of God's saving message, and Paul is the symbolic agent of that salvation, rather more of a savior than simply one of many saved.[174]

Paul's demeanor during a raging storm aligns him with genuine philosophers.[175] Those familiar with epic storm scenes will find a speech appropriate at this

165 The theme of "beyond all hope" is a topos in, for example, ancient novels: Longus *Daphn.* 1.31.1; Lucian *Tox.* 20; Achilles Tatius *Leuc. Clit.* 3.2.4; *Ethiopian Story* 5.25.2; 7.8.2; 7.25.4; cf. *Ninus* Frg. B.II. 16. Photius's summary of *The Wonders beyond Thule* (*Bib.* 166 109b-110a) shows his view of a proper novel: "while contrary to all expectations (παρ' ἐλπίδας πάσας) Ceryllus and Dercyllis escaped numerous dangers (κινδύνων) among the Astures, Astraeus did not avoid the punishment (τὴν δίκην; cf. Acts 28:4) that befell him upon conviction for a crime committed a long time earlier; but contrary to every expectation (παρὰ δόξαν πᾶσαν) he escaped danger (ἐσώθη τῶν κινδύνων) and was then butchered" (trans. G. N. Sandy, in Reardon, *Novels*, 779). The theme is not limited to novels. Note Aristides *To Serapis* (33/56): when darkness shrouded a ship at sea, the god brought light and enabled the passengers, despite their expectations (παρ' ἐλπίδα), to see and set foot upon dry land. Cf. also, e.g., Homer *Od.* 5.297–304; 12.277–79; Aristides *Hieroi Logoi* 2.12; and the many references cited by Praeder, "Acts 27," 692.

166 The verse is Lucan. Note the litotes and the use of τε as a connective (on which see BDF §445 [3]), and infinitive with τοῦ. B 33 omit λοιπόν. On its meaning ("at last"), see Moule, *Idiom Book*, 161.

167 Skinner, *Locating*, 154.

168 For similar situations, see Virgil *Aen.* 5.206; and Achilles Tatius *Leuc. Clit.* 3.5.1.

169 Talbert, 719.

170 From 27:41, one infers that the waves are strong, and 28:2 mentions rain.

171 Rapske ("Travel," 32) notes that the lifeboat suggests a smaller crew. Marshall (412) deals with this by presuming that only some of the crew attempted to escape.

172 Praeder ("Acts 27") identifies these two episodes as a pair.

173 In v. 31, the term is σῴζω; v. 43 uses διασῴζω. The words are essentially interchangeable.

174 Jacobson, "Paul."

175 See the anecdote about Pyrrho (Diogenes Laertius

unpromising juncture.[176] Such speeches are like the arias in baroque opera. They embellish the emotional elements of the situation. Verses 21-26 have all of the appearance of an insertion into the narrative. Fitzmyer says, "Verse 27 is the logical sequel to this verse."[177] The setting is utterly unrealistic. Paul's rhetorical posture is described with the words used for his Areopagus address: σταϑεὶς . . . ἐν μέσῳ ("standing in their midst"),[178] but this is no sermon about an unknown god. At its core, this is an oracle of assurance (vv. 23-24), with the standard features of narrative setting, admonition, and rationale, as well as an address.[179] The form is Jewish,[180] slightly adjusted here for a gentile audience.[181] A number of gods were credited with rescues at sea. Traditionally, this was a specialty of the Dioscuri, but the Egyptian gods were making headway in the Hellenistic and early Roman eras.[182] This indicates how far Paul's Christian fellow passengers are from the narrator's mind, a perspective that vv. 33-36 will confirm. Like the other oracles of assurance (18:9-10; 23:11), this comes at a critical point in the narrative, helps to motivate the plot, and affirms that God is in charge, appearances of chaos notwithstanding.[183] Verse 26 is assurance for the hearers: Paul's character is an endorsement of the oracle. The speech is framed by δεῖ, the meanings of which are conventional here, but no use of "must" in Luke and Acts should be casually dismissed, especially because of the "divine necessity" invoked in v. 24. The first of these establishes Paul's credentials: his last advice was sound.[184] The third states an objective: running aground upon an island. One may ask how the dramatic audience would have received this pronouncement. Any hospitable landfall would do, preferably one with a good harbor and attendant civilization. In retrospect this becomes a prophecy. Islands are few and far between.[185]

The introductory "lack of nourishment" (ἀσιτία), attributable to seasickness, inability to prepare food, and/or depression, is a good synecdoche for despair.[186]

9.68). For other examples, see Johnson, 455. Peregrinus manifested his true character by craven behavior during a storm at sea (Lucian *Peregr.* 43). Lentz (*Luke's Portrait*, 94–95) shows that Paul exhibits the cardinal virtues by his conduct during the voyage. Cf. also Skinner, *Locating*, 154.

176 Homer *Od.* 5.299–312; Virgil *Aen.* 1.92–101. For other examples from Latin epic and a brief discussion, see Praeder, "Acts 27," 696. Witherington (767) finds it "unlikely to me that this widespread invention was based on pure human imagination." He goes on (768) to reconstruct a plausible situation: the speech took place below deck "to all but a skeleton crew who were above trying to control the boat."

177 Fitzmyer (777) takes the unit as a Lucan insert into a "we" report.

178 Kennedy (*Rhetorical Criticism*, 138) says, "The incident is more reminiscent of experiences such as those of Aeneas in Virgil's *Aeneid* than of a truly oratorical situation."

179 Evidently inspired by vv. 23-24, both *Act. Paul* 10/12 and *Act. Pet.* 5 (Verc.) report christophanies to the respective heroes on their voyages to Rome.

180 Aune, *Prophecy*, 266–68.

181 Rather than say "an angel (of God/the Lord)" Paul speaks of "a messenger of the god whom I serve." The framework, with παρίσταμαι ("stand beside"), is quite congenial to polytheist readers (Conzelmann, 219 nn. 48–49). The expression καὶ ἰδού (untranslated) is, however, reassuringly biblical and would have sounded odd to the dramatic audience.

182 Apuleius *Metam.* 11.8–16 presents the ceremony of opening the navigation, the feast of Isis Ploiaphesia, as a popular spectacle. On rescues in popular fiction, see Söder, *Apokryphen Apostelgeschichten*, 162–71. For other examples, see Theissen, *Miracle Stories*, 101; and Johnson, 449.

183 Compare the more hellenized oracle reported by Josephus (*Vit.* 208–9, on which see p. 576 n. 51), concluding with a reminder that he must fight the Romans (Ῥωμαίοις δεῖ σε πολεμῆσαι). MacDonald ("Shipwrecks," 100–101) compares this oracle to Ino's message to Odysseus in *Odyssey* 5. Aelius Aristides *Hieroi Logoi* 48.13 reports an epiphany of Asclepius during a storm at sea promising that he would survive the ensuing shipwreck.

184 In a general sense, since the alternative was not to leave Crete, but to shift harbors, and no one was reported as advocating completion of the voyage. *Ethos* is a rhetorical requirement, demonstrating the speaker's reliability. One need not debate whether Paul said "I told you so" and see this as an issue of character, as does Bruce, 521.

185 Haenchen (705) reads this as a prophetic prediction. Fitzmyer (778) would take it as "we may have to run aground on some island." This strains the Greek. Bruce (522) shares Haenchen's sentiment.

186 Cf. Aristides, *Hieroi Logoi* 2.68 (ἀσιτίαι οὐκ ὀλίγαι). Hemer (*Book*, 145) attributes it to "personal experience."

Paul opens with an arresting oxymoron,[187] appropriate for a speech that begins with a reminder that he warned them when the situation did not look unduly grim and continues with encouragement now that all seems hopeless. The imperative of the exhortation[188] is grounded in the indicative of the oracle. The awkwardness of v. 22b is due to the desire to emphasize "no loss[189] of life" and the need to mention, without emphasizing, the ship,[190] about which the oracle was silent. The order of v. 23, a slow introduction to the message, begins with the genitive that modifies the subject, "god," which is the final word. This may be an attempt at elegance. This is the only angelophany to Paul, which was fortuitous, since a christophany would require explanation.[191]

The oracle states two reasons for assurance, but the effect is concessive: since you must appear before Caesar,[192] God has also . . . This is more specific than 23:11. Because "Rome" would have sufficed here, one may suspect that Luke knew of an appearance of Paul "before Caesar" (i.e., in the imperial court). The phrase casts strong doubt on theories proposing that Acts was composed before the trial of Paul.[193] Since the oracle might easily and noncontroversially have said "God will save . . . ," the words "God has granted[194] you" cannot be brushed off. Paul is the cause of their deliverance and thus their savior. The text does not give a reason for this, for example, that it was an answer to his prayers for the others.

■ **27-32** The chief actors in this episode are the sailors.[195] Confirming the nearness of land by soundings, they anchor the ship until day.[196] All of this was quite reasonable and professional.[197] Their next action, as interpreted by the omniscient narrator and the equally omniscient Paul, was not. Verse 30 abruptly and inconsistently shifts from hopeful waiting to precipitate action on the part of the crew. On the pretense of securing the mooring with additional anchors, they planned to flee in the ship's boat. In *Leuc. Clit.* (3.3.1–4.2) the crew fled a ship on the verge of foundering.[198] Granted that the nocturnal setting might allow for some secrecy (although most seem to have been awake), little else makes sense, for the ship was not in immediate danger of sinking, and the sailors would have had no idea of whither they were fleeing.[199] The land might have been a barren islet. Paul's comment to the centurion (v. 31) is for the benefit of the reader, since one cannot imagine

187 For parallel usages to "gain a loss," see Cadbury and Lake, 334; cf. also Phil 3:7. On the Lucan characteristics of the speech, see Haenchen, 704 n. 4.

188 The verb παραινέω ("strongly recommend") is used here and in v. 9, thus correlating the two speeches. Avoidance of the conventional παρακαλέω ("advise") used to address Christian audiences may be deliberate, but it is probably simply emphatic.

189 "Loss" (ἀποβολή) avoids repeating (and contracting) the ζημία of v. 21.

190 "Except the ship" is a brachylogy. One must supply "only."

191 The angelophany also invokes the beginning of Luke, where these epiphanies occur in 1:11, 26; 2:9, 13, and constitutes another parallel to the deliverance of Peter (12:7).

192 The statements about the appearance of the angel and Paul's appearance before the emperor are identical in structure: παρίστημι with the dative.

193 See the comments on 28:30–31.

194 The verb χαρίζομαι is somewhat ironic here. In 3:14 it was used of the granting of amnesty to Barabbas. In 25:11 and 16 it refers to the "transfer" of Paul's case to Jewish jurisdiction.

195 The noun ναύτης is found only in vv. 27 and 30 in the NT.

196 *Ethiopian Story* 5.17.4–5 (see also n. 118) is illustrative. After a voyage that began with a fair breeze, "[W]e caught our first glimpse . . . of the heights of Zakynthos, barely visible on the horizon, like a vague cloud. The helmsman (κυβερνήτης) gave orders to lower some of the sails, and when we asked why he was trimming the ship's speed when she had such a fair wind behind her, he explained: 'Because if we ran before the wind under full sail, we should come to anchor at Zakynthos in the early hours of darkness, and there would be a risk of our running aground in the dark on one of the many reefs and rocks along this coast" (trans. J. R. Morgan, in Reardon, *Novels*, 457).

197 For details, see Hemer, *Book*, 146–47.

198 Cf. also Petronius *Satyrica* 102, where the principals propose slipping away in the boat; 114.7, where the skiff rescues some from a sinking ship; *Ethiopian Story* 5.24.2, where some of the crew use it to escape from a fight; and 5.27, where pirates, who do not know how to handle a vessel of that size in a storm, cut away their boat (and then jettison equipment).

199 The incident is logical if one makes some assumptions, as does Hemer (*Book*, 147–48). He doubts Haenchen's view (706) that remaining on the ship would not have been dangerous. "The ship had

the soldiers (who also make their first appearance here) viewing the sailors' flight with aplomb.[200] Rather than place a guard on the dinghy, the soldiers set it adrift. This prevented the planned escape, but left the ship at a disadvantage. The boat could have ferried all ashore with minimal difficulty and with a good deal of personal property.

This dubious and intrusive incident was arguably invented by Luke to magnify Paul and divine providence by making the rescue more "miraculous."[201] It also lays the ground for the subsequent plot in vv. 42-43. Boismard's D-Text drops "from the ship," so that emphasis is on desertion and it removes reference to their motive. Intentionally or not, this deals with the problem of narrative omniscience, as no motive for their action is supplied.[202] The temporal marker (v. 27) is the "fourteenth night" without an indication of the reference. Fourteen is as logical a time frame as any, and not improbable,[203] but the fourteenth was also the night of the Passover (Exod 12:6). This can be taken as an exodus symbol. On the next day they will be on dry land. These paschal allusions establish a connection with the much denser paschal symbolism of chap. 12, which is the "Petrine partner," as it were, to chap. 27.[204]

■ **33-38** The verbal connections among these episodes indicate careful composition. The paragraphs marked by vv. 21-26 and 27-32 end with ἐκπεσεῖν, yielding a certain irony. "Lack of nourishment" (ἀσιτ-) appears in v. 21 and again in v. 33; "cheer up" (εὐθυμ-) occurs first as an exhortation in v. 22 and as an achievement in v. 36. Both include exhortations grounded in the promise of safety (vv. 22-24, 34). Verse 33-38 are set in the period between the first intimations of light and sunrise; vv. 39-44 take place in the light of day. The passage begins ponderously,[205] with its difficult chronological reference[206] and a summary immediately repeated in direct speech.

---

taken such a battering that it might break up at any time, and desperate men would find it easier to risk death actively than wait passively." The first clause is, at best, an inference; the second is based on a general psychology of desperation. Moreover, there is an ever-present escape valve: Luke did not understand what was taking place, but experts can extract from his confused reports the exact details. As for vv. 31-32, Hemer allows that the soldiers may have misunderstood Paul's advice (per Bruce, 524), but he suspects that things were desperate, and (148 n. 138) finds "psychological realism . . . which derives from experience, not editing." Finally, Haenchen (who views the incident as historical and attributes it to a rumor generated by the passengers [706]) was neither original nor isolated in his skepticism. Cadbury and Lake (335–36), who read the text as a historical report, reject as unlikely the view that the sailors intended to desert, as more danger loomed in the dinghy than in the ship, and saw the loss of the boat as "the direct cause of the shipwreck" (336). Barrett (2:1205) says that if Luke were in error, he probably erred about something that really happened, for one does not invent an action and a mistaken interpretation of it. This is erroneous: authors who invent actions are perfectly capable of inventing mistaken interpretations of it. Those seeking a historical kernel in vv. 30-32 could propose that some prisoners (rather than sailors) were attempting to escape.

200 The second plural ("you cannot") is ad hoc and not restricted to the military personnel.

201 He may have been inspired by fiction (Conzelmann, 219).

202 On the other hand, gig vg[mss] add at the close of this verse *ut tutius navis staret* ("so that the vessel might ride more securely"), which Clark (166) renders into Greek. This strengthens the sailors' motive.

203 For Hemer (*Book*, 145), this is "a striking confirmation of the narrative." He takes this conclusion from Smith (*Voyage*, 124–28), who had to select a base for "fourteen nights" (he chose Fair Havens, which is reasonable) and establish averages, although the size of the vessel and the force of the wind were unknown, and so on. In the end, Smith got the ship to within four kilometers of Malta. Such calculations cannot be accepted as scientific evidence. They do indicate that the narrative is not, in this sense, fantastic.

204 Arator (2:1130–55) develops a Passover typology, utilizing the number fourteen, darkness, the meal, and passage to dry land.

205 The D-Text (Boismard, *Texte*, 418) has better syntax, eliminating the puzzling initial ἄχρι δὲ οὗ and the double reference to eating. This illuminates the awkward nature of the conventional text and establishes itself as a secondary improvement.

206 See p. 643 n. *v*.If a source is to be sought behind the "interpolation" of vv. 33b-38a, the resultant ἄχρι δὲ οὗ ἡμέρα ἤμελλεν γίνεσθαι ἐκούφιζον τὸ πλοῖον ("They lightened the ship until day

The subject is nourishment, mentioned seven times in six verses (33 [thrice], 34, 35, 36, 38). Such overloaded discourse has a purpose. Avoidance of food signals the absence of hope for life (cf. vv. 20-21). Taking nourishment shows that one wishes (or expects) to live. The symbolism is eucharistic.[207] Had the narrator not wished to evoke the sacrament, he could simply have said, "Paul ate." The meal is not itself a Eucharist, since those present are not believers,[208] but it evokes the Eucharist. The range of symbolic applications is broad. As a synecdoche for the faith, the action symbolizes the life brought by God through Jesus. The means for bringing people to faith is mission. Acts 27:33-38, like the "sea stories" in Luke 5:1-11 and John 21:1-14, has a universal, missionary thrust.[209] "All persons" appears four times in vv. 33-37 (33, 35, 36, 37), redundancy underscoring its universalistic intent.[210] In accordance with the Jesus/Paul "passion parallels," this may be likened to the Last Supper and a "Passover meal" of sorts consumed before crossing to dry land. In more immediate terms, it evokes the paschal Eucharist, celebrated at the close of a nocturnal "vigil," or perhaps the normal Sunday celebration.[211] The explicit meal scenes in Acts are connected with deliverance from death, that is, "resurrection."[212] The narrator here makes subtle use of the light/darkness contrast in what might be called an entirely "natural" manner.[213] Bede allegorically pulls these themes into the well-grooved orbit of ancient storm symbolism, adding the four cardinal virtues for good measure:

> Only those nourished by the bread of life escape the storms of this world, and those who, in the night of present difficulties, draw all their strength from wisdom, courage, self-control, and proper conduct will soon, with the gleaming rays of heavenly aid, reach the safe haven they have sought. (95)[214]

Daylight also marks the time of the discovery of Jesus' resurrection (Luke 24:1; cf. v. 11). Acts 27:33-38 belongs to this liminal period. In v. 34, Paul supports his exhortation with a promise in the shape of a popular hyperbole (cf. 1 Sam 14:45; 2 Sam 14:11; 1 Kgs 1:52). The same saying was attributed to Jesus in the Gospel.[215] This is not insignificant. Rather than cite a saying of the Lord, as in 20:35, Paul appropriates it. He is both a savior and a source of heavenly wisdom. Jesus made the same pronouncement in his eschatological discourse (Luke 21:18). This is another intimation that Acts 27 represents the great crisis of Paul's career, as the crucifixion did of Jesus'. The demonstration succeeded, for the voyagers cheered up (cf. v. 22) and, like Saul after his healing (9:19), took nourishment. They have passed from accepting death to embracing life. It is difficult

began to break") would be feasible, but this does not constitute proof. See Conzelmann, 220. In Lucan terms, v. 33 corresponds to the "very early dawn" (ὄρθρου βαθέως) of Luke 24:1.

207 See, for example, the exposition of Bo Reicke, "Die Mahlzeit mit Paulus auf den Wellen des Mittelmeers Act 27,33-38," *ThZ* 4 (1948) 401–10; Schneider, 2:397; and Weiser, 2:664–65. The question is not whether Paul celebrated a proper (or improper) Eucharist aboard the ship, but whether the action intends to evoke the sacrament. In this context σωτηρία (translated as "good," but used for religious "salvation" elsewhere in Acts) in v. 34 becomes ambiguous.

208 "We" is, as in all of the passages devoted to Paul, absent. Some D-Texts (614. 2147 *pc* sy[h**] sa) resolve this by adding the "fourth action": "He gave (some) also to us." For this tradition, the meal was an actual Eucharist celebrated by Paul, joined by his Christian companions.

209 Hilgert, *Ship*, 105–23.

210 Praeder, "Acts 27," 698.

211 Pliny (*Ep.* 10.96.4) says that the believers met before dawn (*ante lucem convenire*), although he does not associate this with a ritual meal. Acts 20:7-12 could be understood as climaxing a night-long vigil with the Eucharist. See the comments there.

212 In chap. 27, all who take nourishment are saved; the revival of Eutychus in 20:7-12 is framed by a meal. There both Eucharist and resurrection are literal. The warder whom Paul had prevented from suicide ate with his prisoners (16:25-34).

213 Contrast the epiphany of 12:7. Critics of today are likely to prefer the technique of Acts 27, but that is a matter of taste that few early readers of Acts evidently shared.

214 The four virtues reflect the four anchors of v. 29. On the use of the anchor as a symbol, see Hilgert, *Ship*, 134–36.

215 In Luke 21:18, the saying uses οὐ μή with the subjunctive.

to quarrel with Matthew Skinner's conclusion that the narrative events "leave him [Paul] looking more like the ship's captain" (than a prisoner in transport).[216] At this point, the generic "we" narrator returns to announce the total of those on board: 276.[217] This is a "triangular number," the sum of one through twenty-three. One function of such numbers was to encourage readers to explore their symbolic possibilities. No "correct answer" is necessarily required,[218] but reflection is invited.[219] The more important function of the number at this point is to evoke miracle stories, in which numbers may indicate the duration of the illness, the age of the patient, or, especially in the final position (e.g., Mark 6:45), beneficiaries. This is arguably the most spectacular miracle story in Acts. Paul will testify at Rome, come hell or high water.

The use of a number in conjunction with "lives" (ψυχή; cf. also vv. 10 and 22) also evokes the beginning of the story: the three thousand "lives" baptized at Pentecost (2:41), a scene that foreshadows the universal mission (note Acts 2:39). In the context, the jettisoning of grain in v. 38[220] takes the place of the "demonstration" that follows healing miracles, as it shows restored strength. Its practical purpose was evidently to reduce the draft of the ship so that it would ground in as shallow a place as possible, nearest to dry land. Destruction of the cargo of grain[221] marks the final end of the ship's mission. What has been pitched "into the sea" (εἰς τὴν θάλασσαν) has been consigned to doom (Exod 14:8; Mark 5:13; 9:42).[222]

■ **39-44** Verse 39 marks the end of the rule of darkness/night, which has prevailed since v. 20. "Night" is a common trope for death.[223]

Haenchen says that v. 39 "would attach without hiatus to v. 32."[224] This final paragraph (vv. 39-44) does, however, presume the loss of the ship's boat. The distinction between this passage and the sequel is marked by the transition from nonrecognition (οὐκ ἐπεγίνωσκον) in

216 Matthew Skinner, "Unchained Ministry: Paul's Roman Custody (Acts 21–28) and the Sociopolitical Outlook of the Book of Acts," in Phillips, *Acts and Ethics*, 79–95, esp. 91.

217 For variants on the number, see Haenchen, 707 n. 4; and Metzger (*Textual Commentary*, 442), who notes these variants: 275, 270, 176, 876, 76, and "about 70." The smaller figures are likely to be corrections of what editors believed to be too large a figure. Grain ships carried large crews. Cf. Lucian *Nav.* 5 ("like an army"). B *et al.* preface ὡς, a conventional Lucan qualifier ("approximately") that is not appropriate here.

218 Cf. George O. Trevelyan's parody of Horace *Odes* 1.11: "Matilda, will you ne'er have ceased/Apocalyptic summing,/And left the number of the beast/To puzzle Doctor Cumming?"

219 Admiration for triangular numbers derived from the Pythagorean practice, long continued, of writing numbers of groups of dots, in triangular patterns, since the successive sums of the integers form triangles. See Robert S. Brumbaugh, *The Philosophers of Greece* (Albany: State University of New York Press, 1981) 34. Note also Francis H. Colson, "Triangular Numbers in the New Testament," *JTS* 16 (1915) 67–76.

220 The verse has literary merit, including the use of the genitive with "satisfy" (BDF §101). The verb κορέννυμι is more refined than χορτάζω, which is used in the feed stories (e.g., Mark 6:42; 8:8) of satisfaction.

221 The D-Text (i.e., Ethiopic [Boismard, *Texte*, 419]) shortens this verse. ("Into the sea" was used in v. 19.)

222 Cf. *1 Enoch* 101.4–5a (an argument from "natural theology"): Do you not see the sailors of the ships, how their ships are tossed up and down by the billows and are shaken by the winds, and they become anxious? On this account (it is evident that) they are seized by fear, for they will discharge all their valuable property—the goods that are with them—into the sea" (trans. Ephraim Isaac, *OTP* 1:82).

223 Cf. Peter (Acts 12:6). Apuleius *Metam.* 11 exploits the symbolism. In her nocturnal revelation on the beach (see below), Isis tells Lucius: "The day which will be the day born from this night has been proclaimed mine by everlasting religious observance: on that day, when the winter's tempests are lulled and the ocean's storm-blown waves are calmed, my priests dedicate an untried keel to the now navigable sea and consecrate it as the first fruits of voyaging (5) . . . . *Metam.* 7 reports, "At once the cloud of dark night was banished and the Sun arose all gold." The narrator goes on to describe the sudden epiphany of spring, the calming of the waters, and the brilliance of the sky (trans. Hanson, *Apuleius*, 2:301–7).

224 Haenchen, 707.

v. 39 to recognition (ἐπέγνωμεν) in 28:1. "The land" (τὴν γῆν) in vv. 39 and 44 marks the limits of the unit. The effort to beach the ship was not fully successful, for it went aground at an unstated distance from the shore proper, firmly enough to hold the forepart so that the waves broke it up. The rest is more difficult. At this point, the soldiers begin to worry about the security of their charges and, rather than await orders, decide to execute them. The centurion vetoes this, not because he rejects the idea in general, but out of his desire to rescue Paul. He then directs all to make their way ashore. If any historical reminiscence lies behind this incident, it would best apply to a group of condemned prisoners en route to execution.[225] As for the order about debarkation, it is difficult to see why the centurion should have the authority to issue it for any but the prisoners under his charge. The owner and master have not been heard from since v. 9. The requirements of the narrative for "universal salvation" override logic. The soldiers' plot and its suppression have all the marks of Lucan composition and are not based on retrievable historical information.

The passage unfolds well, with gradual revelation: an unfamiliar beach and bay, the competent and detailed effort to beach the vessel, then sudden and final disaster, ending, however, without the loss of a single life. The style of vv. 39-41 is good, with balanced sentences, some refined constructions,[226] and an undisputed dash of Homerica.[227] The dramatic effect can be seen by contrasting the conventional text with Boismard's edition of the D-Text, which omits v. 40 and abbreviates v. 41.[228] When the ship has come to inescapable ruin, the narrator first reveals that the prisoners did not have a chance: "At this final and fatal moment S. Paul had the narrowest escape of all."[229] Like Peter (12:2-4), he is about to die by the sword. Rescue comes because Paul, like Jesus (Luke 23:47), had won the admiration of a centurion.[230] The scene is quite artificial. Any spontaneous actions on the part of the soldiers (who were most unlikely to have formulated a plot) would have been halted by issuance of the order concerning the prisoners, but they would have had no reason not to await orders, since any blame would fall upon the responsible officer.[231]

With or without assistance, all made it ashore.[232] The oracle of v. 22 was vindicated. "Like Israel they found dry land in the midst of the sea, and like Jonah they were cast out of the deep onto the shore."[233] The separation of land from water is a mark of creation (Gen 1:9-10); arrival on dry land signals the defeat of chaos. The shore is a location dripping, as it were, with liminality and therefore a recurring and potent literary symbol. "In its role as harbor (*limēn* indeed) it is also potentially the shore of salvation where those who were immersed are recalled to life."[234] Those cast ashore from the shipwreck of death are naked and helpless, like new-born babes. Paul has joined a large company of victims:

> The merchants [who had purchased the heroine] took Anthia, put her aboard, and sailed at nightfall for Cilicia. But they were caught by an adverse wind (ἐναντίῳ δὲ πνεύματι), and the ship broke up; some of the crew survived with great difficulty and came

225 See Witherington, 774.

226 Note the evidently oblique optative condition in v. 39, which is proper if viewed as secondary to a general statement: "if we ever can" (ἐὰν δυνώμεθα). The *v.l.* δύνατον ("if possible," C m co) is probably secondary.

227 The phrase ἐπέκειλαν τὴν ναῦν ("they ran the ship") in v. 41 is Homeric. For discussion, see MacDonald, "Shipwrecks," 94–95. The word ἐρείσασα ("break up") is also a classical word (Achilles Tatius *Leuc. Clit.* 3.5.1).

228 Boismard, *Texte*, 420. (He must rely on the Ethiopic.)

229 Rackham, 490.

230 The D-Text places greater emphasis on the centurion's desire to save Paul.

231 The action pivots around two verbs with similar sounds: ἐκώλυσεν . . . ἐκέλευσεν ("forbade . . . ordered") in v. 43. Acts 12:19 and 16:27 have given guards grounds for fear, but the latter shows that responsibility for the security of prisoners was the criterion. Luke does not report any concern on the part of the centurion for his own safety; Paul is his only worry.

232 The D-Text gives a shorter conclusion. The ambiguous οὓς μὲν ἐπὶ σανίσιν, οὓς δὲ ἐπί τινων τῶν ἀπὸ τοῦ πλοίου is omitted, and, more notably, the climactic sentence about all being saved is omitted (as it is in the opening participial phrase in 28:1). This may reflect some discomfort about the use of "save."

233 Rackham, 491.

234 Doody, *True Story*, 326. See her comments on the trope of the seashore in literature (319–22,

ashore on planks (μόλις ἐν σανίσι τινὲς σωθέντες ἐπ᾽ αἰγιαλοῦ τινος) with Anthia among them. (*Ephesian Tale* 2.11.10)[235]

This narrator, who cannot be accused of excessive length, still found space for planks[236] and the beach. Apollonius of Tyre was among those aboard ship in a terrible storm:

> Then everyone held onto a piece of ship's timber and had a presentiment of his own death. In that pitch-black storm all perished. Apollonius, however, thanks to a single piece of ship's timber, was driven onto the shore of the people of Pentapolis. Apollonius stood, naked, on the shore for a while. (*Vit. Apoll.* 12)[237]

The prototype of Apollonius was not Jonah, but Odysseus, and this scene from a Latin novel of 5–6 CE, evidently based on a Greek model, shows that the *Odyssey* was still a model for popular prose fiction in the early centuries of the common era.[238] Rescue from the perils of the sea is not the end of the story. Strange shores have dangers. What or whom will they encounter? Cannibals, slavers, bandits, or those who take pity upon strangers in distress?

326–27). The story of Apollonius of Tyre is framed by encounters on a beach (*Apollonius of Tyre* 12). *An Ethiopian Story* opens with a famous scene on the beach. As this is later explained, the voyagers ran into a storm at sea. "In the face of such overwhelming adversity, there was nothing the helmsman could do but abandon the rudder to the storm and let fortune steer the ship. For seven days and seven nights, we ran before the gale, until eventually we ran ashore on the beach where you found us" (1.22; trans. J. R. Morgan, in Reardon, *Novels*, 371).

235 Trans. G. Anderson, in Reardon, *Novels*, 145. On v. 44, note also Aristides *Hieroi Logoi* 2.12.

236 Planks are the means of Ceyx's delivery in the vivid shipwreck described in Ovid *Metam.* 11 (see 559–60).

237 Trans. G. N. Sanday, in Reardon, *Novels*, 744. (The storm was described in a poetic pastiche in chap. 11). In chaps. 25–26, the hero has the (presumably) dead body of his wife enclosed in a casket made from planks and set adrift, as a corpse would endanger the ship. The coffin lands near Ephesus and is fortunately recovered by a physician who discovers, by putting his lips to hers, that the woman is still alive.

238 See Niklas Holzberg, "The *Historia Apollonii regis Tyri* and the *Odyssey*," in *Groningen Colloquia on the Novel* (Groningen: Egbert Forsten, 1990) 3:91–101. Apuleius *Metam.* 2.14.3 has a character speak of "a dreadful, really Odyssean voyage" (*Ulixeam peregrinationem*). Its contents are as follows: "First, the ship we were sailing on was battered by stormblasts from every direction, lost both its rudders, and was with difficulty beached on the farther shore, where it sank straight to the bottom. We lost all our belongings and barely managed to swim ashore" (trans. Hanson, *Apuleius*, 1:87).

28

28:1-16 Paul on Malta

28:1-16: Conventional Text

1/ After we were safely ashore, we
recognized that the island is
called Malta.[a] 2/ The natives
were uncommonly kind to all
of us. Because of the rain that
had begun to fall and the chill,
they kindled a bonfire and
brought[b] all of us to it. 3/ Paul
had gathered some sticks into a
bundle and was tossing it onto
the fire when a viper, roused
by the warmth, came out and
fastened[c] itself to his hand with
its fangs. 4/ When the natives
saw the creature dangling from
his arm, they reassured one
another, "This fellow must be
a murderer for sure. No sooner
had he escaped from the sea
than the goddess Justice did
him in." 5/ Paul, however, shook
the creature into the fire and
suffered no harm. 6/ They kept
waiting for him to swell up or
suddenly drop dead, but, after
waiting for some time without
seeing him show any negative
reaction, they revised their
opinion[d] and began to declare
that he was a god.

7/ Publius, the island's leading
citizen, had an estate in the
vicinity. He took us in and gave
us quite cordial hospitality
for three days. 8/ His father
lay afflicted with fever and
dysentery.[e] Paul visited him,
prayed, and laid hands upon
him. He became well. 9/ At that[f]
all the sick on the island began
to come to Paul, and they were
cured. 10/ They responded by
providing us with many gifts[g]
and, on our departure, supplied
us with what we required.

11/ We set out three months later
on an Alexandrian vessel that
had wintered at the island. Its
figurehead was the Dioscuri.
12/ We put in at Syracuse and
spent three days there 13/ and
then sailed[h] up to Rhegium. The
next day a south wind sprang
up, so we reached Puteoli
within two days. 14/ There we
found some believers, who
urged us to stay with them for a
week.[i]
This is how we got to Rome:

28:1-16: D-Text[k]

1/ *And, having descended to the
land, they* recognized that *the
place* is called Malta. 2/ The
natives *welcomed* us and lit a
fire because *the place* was cold.

3/ . . .

4/ When the natives saw,[l] they said
. . ."

5/ And *he* shook it into the fire.

6/ They kept expecting that he
would suddenly *die*. When they
saw that he had been *saved*,
they said he was a god.

7/ *There was a man named* Publius,
one of their leading citizens,
who entertained us for three
days.

8/ Now the father of Publius *was
ill* with [ ] dysentery. And Paul
came and prayed for him [ ], and
that man was made well.

9/ [ ] Many who were ill [ ] came to
Paul and were healed. 10/ They
responded by providing us with
many gifts and [ ] supplied us
with what we required.

11/ We set out in an Alexandrian ship
wintering at the island [ ]

(Omit 12-14a)

15/ The[j] believers there heard the news about us and came to the Market of Appius and Three Taverns to welcome us. When he saw them, Paul gave thanks to God and plucked up his courage. 16/ When we reached Rome, Paul received permission to live on his own with the soldier who guarded him.

***and* we came to Rome. 15/ *And, having learned* [ ], the believers came [ ]**

to welcome us. When he saw them Paul gave thanks to God and plucked up his courage. 16/ When we reached Rome, *the centurion delivered the prisoners to the commandant of the barracks, but Paul had found favor with him, (so that he was allowed)*[m] to live *outside of the barracks* with *a* soldier guarding him."

a B* lat sy[h] bo read Μελιτήνη (this could be a sight error). 𝔓[74] seems to read Μιλήτη.

b ℵ* ψ 614. (1505.) *pc* lat read προσελάμβανον ("welcome"), which is the D-Text. This is simpler and probably secondary.

c C 36. 453. 614. 1505. 1891 *pm* read the middle καθήψατο, which is more common for "fastened," although it is possible for the active, which is therefore more likely. This is an ironic echo of "kindled" (ἅψαντες) in v. 2.

d A *v.l.* with fairly wide attestation (ℵ 048. 33. 1739 m) takes the participle as present: "began to change their minds."

e Haenchen (714) notes that the (untranslated) initial ἐγένετο ("it happened") usually introduces an event rather than a condition. It is equivalent to "was."

f H adds ὑγιοῦς after τούτου δὲ γενομένου and thus produces a different phrase: "After he had been made well." B and two Latin texts omit καί, perhaps not taking it as adverbial.

g 1611 *pc* insert, after ἡμᾶς ("us"), ὅσον χρόνον ἐπεδημοῦμεν: we received gifts "as long as we stayed." This pedantic addition makes the sentence less abrupt.

h In place of the more complex περιελόντες (which may be a shorthand for "weighing anchor"; cf. 27:40), p[74] has the scarcely clearer περιελθόντες. There are other compounds of ἔρχομαι ("come") also attested as variants. Metzger (*Textual Commentary*, 443) finds the alternatives less difficult and therefore possibly secondary. See Ropes, 251. Barrett (2:1229), however, says that it may be too difficult to accept. Conzelmann (224) prefers περιελθόντες.

i The variant ἐπιμείναντες (H ψ 049. 326. 614. 1505. 2464) would read "we were *consoled* because we remained seven days with them," versus "we were urged to . . ." Haenchen (718 n. 1) says that this apparently reduces some of the tension caused by the implied freedom.

j B omits the article: "Some believers" came to meet them. This mollifies a typical bit of hyperbole.

k Boismard, *Texte*, 421–23.

l ἰδόντες οἱ βάρβαροι.

m The words in parentheses are supplied to make sense.

Analysis

The medieval decision to mark a new chapter here was unfortunate.[1] Verses 1-10 cover their sojourn on the island, while 11-16 narrate in brief itinerary style completion of the journey inaugurated in chap. 27, complementing 27:1-8. Both framing units report friendly officials and the ministrations of fellow believers (27:3; 28:14). The first part includes the miracle stories of vv. 1-6 and 7-10. The narrator has left a gap between v. 6 and v. 7, as well as rough transitions between vv. 10-11 and vv. 15-16, indications of the difficulty of attempting to produce a continuous narrative from disparate elements, a possible but not certain indication of sources.

The site of Malta may stem from tradition, as may the hospitality of Publius. If a historical account lies behind the story, vv. 11-14, 16 could derive from this record.[2] This solution is not without obstacles, for not until v. 16 is Paul's status as a prisoner again acknowledged, and one cannot resolve the matter by saying that Luke

1 The old *kephalia* began chap. 38 at 27:1 and 39 at 28:11, which is somewhat more defensible.

2 See Haenchen, 719.

deleted references to his condition, for vv. 7-15 scarcely allow this. Publius bears the correct title, if it is such, but it could also mean "the leading citizen." He has but one name, and Luke is fond of associating Paul with leaders.[3] Here Paul is an honored guest rather than a man in custody. The incident with the viper (vv. 3-6) and the healings in vv. 8-9 are Lucan compositions. The latter imitates a Gospel passage, while the former gains its meaning from the general context (and cannot easily be separated from the immediate context).

"We" is the dominant narrator here, but the extent and composition of the first person narrative are not clear. More explicitly than elsewhere, when the focus is on Paul, "we" steps aside, but always returns until v. 16, when it vanishes from the narrative. The fluctuation is due to authorial choice rather than to the insertion of third person material into a source. In v. 2 "all of us" logically refers to the entire company of 276, although it may already reflect the smaller, "Christian" group.[4] In vv. 11-13, "we" could refer to all those stranded on Malta, presuming that the ship had room, but in v. 14 it transpires that "we" means the believers, as it does also in v. 15, and, evidently, in v. 16.[5] In vv. 1-6, the "we" narrator is omniscient and therefore a creature of the author.[6]

The island on which the refugees landed is generally identified with the present-day Malta,[7] south of Sicily, but objections arise from time to time. Rivals include Mljet, in the Adriatic near Greece,[8] and Kefallinia in the Ionian sea near the coast of Epirus.[9] The alternatives, both of which support a strictly historical interpretation of Acts, indicate that the nautical data are far from precise, since they yield different results from the application of similar methods.[10] Verse 13, which reports Syracuse as the first of three proximate stops on the subsequent voyage, certainly supports the traditional understanding.[11] Boismard continues to report a generally shorter and distinct text, almost certainly an abridgment, until v. 16. The evidence is slender, but Boismard uses a consistent method. Whether this should be labeled *the* D-Text is open to question. In two units (vv. 1-6, 11-16) the meaning is quite different, as the comments will indicate.

Rescues continue to accumulate. These include deliveries from the storm, perishing through despair exacerbated by hunger and weakness, destruction of the ship

3 Cf. also Lüdemann, *Acts*, 342.

4 So Haenchen, 713.

5 Similarly, Kurz (*Reading*, 117), who does not attempt to rationalize these shifts.

6 Praeder ("Acts 27," 702) states that the story is narrated from two perspectives: that of the "we" narrator in vv. 3 and 5 and "from the perspective of the Maltese" in vv. 4 and 6. The text does not support this division. Verses 4 and 6 report the natives' reaction from an outsider perspective, as the quotation about the goddess Δίκη ("Justice") demonstrates. Kurz (*Reading*, 108) assigns the perspective to "someone sitting around the fire." Those so engaged would not see persons not seated about a fire, certainly not one large enough to warm nearly three hundred. Kurz notes that knowledge of an unknown language and the thoughts of its speakers would be difficult and concludes: "His knowledge must be credited to observation of their actions and imputing to them thoughts that would correspond to their behavior." On p. 117 he attributes that knowledge to "hindsight, rather than omniscience." The last comment commingles narrative analysis with historical reconstruction. Both Praeder and Kurz show, albeit unintentionally, that the narrator of vv. 3-6 is an omniscient first plural.

7 See W. Ward Gasque, "Malta," *ABD* 4:489–90. For possible sites on Malta, see Fitzmyer, 782.

8 Angus Acworth, "Where Was St. Paul Shipwrecked? A Re-examination of the Evidence," *JTS* 24 (1973) 190–93; Otto F. A. Meinardus, "St. Paul Shipwrecked in Dalmatia," *BA* 39 (1976) 145–47; and idem, "Melita Illyrica or African: An Examination of the Site of St. Paul's Shipwreck, *Ostkirchliche Studien* 23 (1974) 21–36.

9 Heinz Warnecke, *Die tatsächliche Romfahrt des Apostels Paulus* (Stuttgarter Bibelstudien 127; Stuttgart: Katholisches Bibelwerk, 1987).

10 Alternatives to Malta generally seek to integrate Acts with the Pastorals. See Rapske, "Travel," 37–43, for a summary of the debate, with copious bibliography.

11 All commentators must feel some empathy with Barrett, who remarks: "A commentary is no place for detailed discussion of winds and tides, flora and fauna, local inhabitants and their rulers." None in the modern period, including Barrett, takes this advice.

from shoals, the sailors' plot, the soldiers' plot, drowning, possibly hostile natives (who were, in fact, liable to supplement meager incomes by viewing shipwrecks as windfalls, the passengers and crew of which were likely to be executed or enslaved), and snakebite. The last of these exemplifies the narrator's concern for Paul. Just as he alone foiled one plot by insight and another because of the centurion's concern, so he was the individual who happened to attract a viper. Through his charismatic gifts, he and his companions are able to spend a comfortable winter. Once this series of deliverances has been accomplished, the narrator shows no more interest in travel. The voyage to a port of Rome is accomplished in three verses, with no comments on weather or navigation.

The first half of Acts 28 is remarkably idyllic. The circumstances are unpromising: despite the friendly reception by the local inhabitants, Paul, a prisoner, is marooned on an island, bereft of nearly all such possessions as he may have had and dependent on the authority of a(n auxiliary) centurion to requisition food, clothing, and shelter to tide him over a winter. It would have occasioned no surprise if the prisoners had been parked in a local facility while the military detachment set about attempting to refit from whatever resources were available, as little in the way of arms and armor would have survived. The soldiers, along with the vast majority of the ship's company, officers, passengers, and crew, effectively vanish as if they had drowned in the wreck.

The primary fact is that Paul is not a prisoner in Acts 28:1-15.[12] Although he functioned more as a V.I.P. on the voyage than as a prisoner in transit, his status was reaffirmed in 27:42-43. Nothing in the first half of the final chapter indicates this status, and nearly everything denies it. In these verses, Paul functions as a healer (and god) who makes a good living under the patronage of the island's principal citizen. Comparisons to Apollonius of Tyana are not unwarranted. Historical-critical commentators on Acts must address the dissonance between some type of probable account and the narrative presented. History is not governed by probability, but historians must pay tribute to it. Recognition of the dissonance between the probabilities established by Acts and the content of 28:1-15 shows the cogency of MacDonald's argument that it is based upon Homer, for the naked Paul stranded on a beach is regarded by some as a god and soon finds himself an admired guest in what amounts—for a prisoner—to a utopia.[13] MacDonald

If the pursuit of concision urged the selection of a single adverb to portray the Paul of Acts 27–28, one who can perform healings, secure patrons, find his own living arrangements, schedule meetings, and receive visitors at his discretion, ἀκωλύτως ("unhindered") would do very well. That is a general answer to the next question: Why did Luke choose a mythical/epic pattern to narrate Acts 28:1-15? A more specific answer requires returning to the parallelism between Luke and its sequel. Since Acts 21–26 exhibits many similarities to the trials of Jesus in Jerusalem, readers are invited to pursue these comparisons, as well as those between Peter in Acts 12 and Paul in Acts 27–28.

Peter's story contained explicit exodus and initiatory allusions.[14] In the case of Paul, these are implicit and general: passage from symbolic death through water to safety on dry land. Peter met obstacles in his attempt to reach safety (12:12-16), for, like the reports about the risen Jesus (Luke 24:11, 22-24), the message was not believed. Paul also runs into difficulty with representatives of the marginalized—not women or slaves here, but "barbarians"—who doubt his vindication. When their error is exposed, they express appropriate awe.[15] The key "Easter" characteristic possessed by Paul is the essence of redemption and new life: he is free. The trope of resurrection as freedom[16] is the driving force behind the narrative of vv. 1-15, rather than the inconvenient embarrassment of having Paul stashed in some lockup until spring.[17]

12 When the topic is introduced in v. 16, it is mollified by the statement that Paul did not have to live in a prison. The only other reference to his status in the chapter is in v. 20, where it provides pathos.

13 See the summaries in MacDonald, "Shipwrecks," 104–5.

14 Cf. the comments on 12:1-17.

15 Compare 12:16 to 28:6. Both are "acclamations."

16 Note Luke 2:29 (lit. "Master, you are freeing your slave"); 24:21: "But we had hoped that he was the one to redeem Israel."

17 See also Radl, *Paulus*, 242–43, with references.

More explicit is the eschatological symbol of the defeat of the serpent.[18] Gifts bestowed on postresurrection believers include immunity from snakebite (Ps.-Mark 16:18, although this may be dependent upon Acts). After announcing the fall of Satan, Jesus gave the seventy/seventy-two power to tread upon serpents (Luke 10:18).[19] One charming symbol of utopian peace is the harmlessness of serpents (Isa 11:8).[20]

Snakes could be viewed as agents of the devil (Luke 10:18) or personifications of the Evil One (*Lives of the Prophets* 12.12 [Habakkuk]; Rev 19:9; 20:2). Since Luke viewed the eradication of serpents as a highly suitable trope for the defeat of the devil, it is difficult to claim that he had forgotten this while writing (or reproducing) Acts 28:3-6. Paul's immunity from the viper vividly depicted the defeat of death and the devil. The natives were seeking the dead among the living (Luke 24:5).[21] As more than an additional close escape by Paul, this story, like that of the journey as a whole, has paradigmatic value and therefore justifies the length devoted to it. Luke has compressed the basic meaning of vindication (δικαιοσύνη) into an exciting and humorous anecdote of four verses.[22] The achievement came at a price, as the criticism, rationalization, and superficial appropriation of the story show.

Scarcely less remarkable than its idyllic quality—and not unrelated to this—is the missionary orientation of 28:1-15, which is not improperly labeled a *mission civilisatrice*.[23] Paul has not engaged in itinerant missionary work since 19:10. Readers do not wonder that he is not reported as seeking converts on the ship, but the situation in Malta is different. None would take exception had the narrative reported that, following the healing of his father, Publius and his household had acceded to the faith, along with, in due course, many of the Maltese, all of whose infirm Paul had healed. The text is instead redolent with the language of benefaction, friendship, and reciprocity, the lubricants of Greco-Roman urban society.[24] Paul heals the father of Publius in response to the latter's generous hospitality. When the balance of the island's ill sought the same service, Paul became a general benefactor, increasing the prestige of Publius thereby. The "honors" heaped upon him were nothing so vulgar as "payments"; they were expressions of gratitude among friends. Cadbury said of vv. 1-6: "It would be difficult to find a scene more full of the viewpoint of antiquity than this at Malta."[25]

In his desire to display philhellenism, the author has briefly betrayed his own (and Paul's) universalistic principles. It is no compliment to "barbarians" to say that these examples amounted to an exception proving the rule.[26] Equally uncomplimentary is the portrayal of their superstitious and labile mentality. In typical Greek fashion, the narrator presents their words and thoughts

18 Cf. Werner Foerster et al., "ὄφις," *TDNT* 5:566–82. Arator (2:1173–1205) develops the parallel with Adam, Eve, and the serpent.

19 On this, see Garrett, *Demise*, 46–57. Note also Ps 90:13 LXX.

20 Ulrike Riemer ("Miracle Stories and Their Narrative Intent in the Context of the Ruler Cult of Classical Antiquity," in Labahn and Peerbolte, *Wonders*, 33–34) illustrates the use of beast imagery in exaltations of the emperor. The phenomenon involves more than the supernatural power of the "divine man." To defeat beasts (and beastliness) is to advance humanity and civilization against the forces of savagery and chaos. For examples of the metaphorical uses of "wild beast," see Malherbe, *Paul*, 82–89.

21 Luke 24:5 uses both a form of the verb "live" (ζάω) and the adjective "dead" (νεκρός), each of which is found in Acts 28:2b-6. See the similar view of Radl, *Paulus*, 241.

22 Reinhard von Bendemann ("'Many-Coloured Illnesses' [Mark 1:34]: On the Significance of Illnesses in New Testament Therapy Narratives," in Labahn and Peerbolte, *Wonders*, 100–124, esp. 112) states that the sequence of shipwreck, rescue, and subsequent threat is common. See his references in n. 39.

23 See Tannehill, *Narrative Unity*, 2:341.

24 Verse 2: φιλανθρωπία ("philanthropy"; cf. 27:3), v. 7 φιλοφρόνως ("in a friendly manner").

25 Cadbury, *Making*, 341. See his comments on pp. 341–43. Cadbury had in mind both the language and the ideas, in particular xenophobia.

26 Cf. the natives of Lystra (14:8-20), who began by deifying Paul and ended by stoning him.

in Greek form and relatively good Greek language—better than that of most of the speakers in Acts much of the time. The initial tone of Acts 28 is that of the elite snob—scarcely suitable for a prisoner, one might say, but that is just the point.[27] Acts 28:1-6 has features of the Easter appearances. Paul is a kind of divine, indestructible being, delivered from the tomb of the sea. His death was inappropriately expected (cf. Luke 24:5). For a proper understanding of Acts, it should be noted that these parallels to Jesus' passion and resurrection occur in two famous tales, one marked by humor and drama, the other by great adventure. Apocalyptic imagery is also prominent in the accounts of Jesus' crucifixion. The end of this voyage will also be a beginning.

Comment

■ **1** The verse picks up from both 27:39 and 44 (ἐπιγινώσκω, "recognize," from v. 39, and διασώζω, "save," from v. 44) The name "Malta" is new information.[28] The possibility of kindling a fire on the beach suggests that the rain was not very heavy and that the wind was no longer severe. The storm had mainly subsided.

■ **2** "Barbarians" spring onto the scene without development,[29] characterized by their atypical[30] conduct.[31] The narrator was not interested in suspense here. The urgent concern was to demonstrate the continued presence of providential direction. Speculation about Paul's inability to be inactive and the limits of "we" in v. 2 are as otiose as observations about the absence of snakes on Malta.[32] A group of that size would have required a number of fires, and Paul was unlikely to have been the only passenger to gather driftwood. The narrator's focus is on Paul and the natives. The presence of everyone else is simply ignored.[33]

■ **3** The narrative, which has been moving rapidly, slows[34] to describe Paul's contribution to the general welfare, which is suddenly rewarded by the assault of a

27 Tannehill (*Narrative Unity*, 2:340–41) lumps the natives with Publius and company and extols the "cooperative relationships that are possible between Christianity and pagan society" (341). The text says nothing about cooperation with the natives. The snobbery is noted by Ramsay (*St. Paul the Traveller*, 343), who observes that the people of Malta had been influenced by civilized societies for centuries. Johnson (467) is briefer and better: hospitality and sharing are among the leading Lucan virtues.

28 How this was learned is not clear, since the natives did not speak Greek. Gasque (p. 670 n. 7) has a solution: Paul was able to communicate with the Punic speakers by use of Aramaic. The D-Text, which generally abbreviates in vv. 1-6, attributes this recognition to the ship's company.

29 The D-Text offers a smoother transition, beginning v. 2 with a verb. It also eliminates the comment about "barbarian" hospitality.

30 Luke, who was not always able to resist litotes, used the same figure (οὐ τυχούσας ["uncommon"]) of Paul's miracles in 19:11. Also characteristic is the pair of improper genitive absolutes in v. 3. BDF §316 (3) says that παρεῖχον φιλανθρωπίαν ("exhibit kindness") is classical.

31 A famous example is the Scythians, "barbarians" par excellence, who seized the shipwrecked Orestes and Pylades as potential human offerings to their Artemis. Lucian *Ver. hist.* 2.46 tells of a particularly wicked deceit; 1.29 is more positive. Andocides (*De Mysteriis* 138) describes a barbarian region where many who had survived shipwreck had been killed. The passage is interesting because Andocides defends himself against profanation of the mysteries by contending that the gods would not have permitted him to survive shipwreck had he been guilty. See also Dio of Prusa *Or.* 7.31–33, which describes means by which shore dwellers lured ships to disaster. In §§52–58 his noble rustic tells of his kindnesses to the shipwrecked and is recognized by one of the assembly as his former benefactor. Petronius's *Satyrica* 114 shows their fickleness. Fishermen came to loot, but changed their minds in the face of resistance and became rescuers. For further references, see Betz, *Lukian*, 94 n. 6.

32 Geoffrey W. H. Lampe ("Miracles in the Acts of the Apostles," in Moule, *Miracles*, 163–78, esp. 173) goes so far as to say: "The incident of the snake at Malta is easily rationalized, for the island has no poisonous snakes." See, however, 178. William Ramsay seeks to rationalize the story by finding an appropriate (Sicilian) serpent (*Luke the Physician and Other Studies in the History of Religion* [New York: A. C. Armstrong and Son, 1908] 63–65).

33 Thus, none of Paul's companions or others from the ship are said to react to the presence of the snake, nor do any but the natives remark on its failure to inflict death.

34 The D-Text counters this tactic by abbreviation.

viper.[35] Immunity to snakebite is almost a prerequisite of the charismatic religious figure. Examples are almost as ubiquitous as snakes.[36] More relevant is the theme of the survivor or escapee who was subsequently killed by a viper. Since Wettstein, commentators have cited the *Greek Anthology* 7.290, a pathetic story offering no condemnation of the victim.[37] In general, poetic justice was rendered more often by animals than by poets. The animal kingdom was an instrument of divine justice. Innocent people were immune,[38] while the guilty received their just deserts. The mills of God grind slowly.[39]

An apt illustration can be found in *Ethiopian Story* 2.20, in which the robber Thermouthis took flight, but "lay down to sleep, but the sleep he slept was the final sleep, the brazen sleep of death, for he was bitten by a viper. Perhaps it was destiny's will that his life should end in a way so befitting his character."[40] Primitive these natives in Acts may have been, but they could see the hand of a god at work.[41] When these expectations are not met—narrative time compresses here, for poison does not work quite that rapidly—they take a more-than-180-degree turn and conclude that the victim is not simply no murderer or even the protégé of a god, but a very god.[42] Their theological categories are inadequate,[43] but, to give them the credit they deserve, these barbarians can acknowledge an epiphany.[44] Readers can draw the appropriate corrections. The narrator need not enter a denial, for the other characters do not know the natives' words and thoughts.[45]

35 The image of vipers fleeing fire was used by John the Baptizer in 3:7 (Q). The end of the story has artistic echoes of its beginning.

36 Examples from the Apocryphal Acts include *Act. Thom.* 106; cf. *Act. Pet.* (Verc.) 5.29. For others, see Söder, *Apokryphen Apostelgeschichten*, 95–99. Examples from later Christian literature include the *Lausiac History* 18.10.B. Polytheist stories are found in Lucian *Alex.* 10 and *Philops.* 11. One Jewish example is *b. Ber.* 33a. For others, see Lou H. Silberman, "Paul's Viper: Acts 28:3-6," *Forum* 8 (1992) 247–53. Note also John C. O'Neill, *The Theology of Acts in Its Historical Setting* (London: SPCK, 1970) 142–46. For still others, see Bieler, *ΘΕΙΟΣ ΑΝΗΡ*, 1:108.

37 See Klauck (*Magic*, 114), who cites 9.269 also; and Kauppi, *Foreign*, 107–12. This theme was evidently common, judging from Lucian's parody in his *Dipsads* 4–9.

38 Note Dan 6:23 LXX. See also Horace's famous ode 1.22. A lion does not harm the harmless poet.

39 Cf. Horace *Odes* 3.2.25–32: "There is also a sure reward for loyal silence. I will forbid anyone who has divulged the secrets of mystic Ceres to be under the same roof or to cast off a fragile boat with me on board. When slighted, Jupiter often lumps the righteous together with the impious; rarely does Retribution (*Poena*) fail to catch up with the criminal despite her limping gait" (trans. Rudd, 147.)

40 Trans. J. R. Morgan, in Reardon, *Novels*, 392. Note the references to *Dike* in 1.14 and 2.11.

41 See Gary Miles and Garry Trompf, "Luke and Antiphon," *HTR* 69 (1976) 259–67; as well as David J. Ladouceur, "Hellenistic Preconceptions of Shipwreck and Pollution as a Context for Acts 27–28," *HTR* 73 (1980) 443–49, studies that help illustrate the religio-historical background of the episode. The natives' use of διασῴζω ("save," "deliver") in v. 4, the third appearance of the verb in four verses, is ironic.

42 Moule (*Idiom Book*, 163) says that the *μὲν οὖν* in v. 5 is adversative.

43 Calvin (7:301) had no doubts: "[B]ut if it was necessary to choose one or the other, it was better to be regarded a murderer rather than a god."

44 Compare *Ephesian Tale* 2.2.4 "People gazed at [*the heroes*] on the way [*to Tyre*]; everyone was amazed at their beauty. And barbarians who had not previously set eyes on such radiance thought they were gods [*θεοὺς ἐνόμιζον εἶναι*]" (trans. G. Anderson, in Reardon, *Novels*, 139). On this, see Parsons and Pervo, *Rethinking*, 90–92.

45 Providence managed weather to the advantage of the virtuous. In Chariton *Chaer.* 3.3–4 the pirate ship enjoyed good sailing so long as they carried Callirhoe. After they sold her, they fell into the clutches of a dreadful storm, which only their leader, Theron, survived. This was not a reward for piety but temporary preservation so that he could receive a proper recompense for his impiety: crucifixion. Toward the close of Euripides' *El.*, the Dioscuri announce their criteria for rescue of those in peril on the sea: lovers of piety and justice. The public is advised not to sail with wicked people (1347–56).

■ **4-6** The scene evokes the passion and vindication of Jesus.[46] The natives, like the crowd at Jesus' trial, assume his guilt. They judge that he is a murderer, the crime with which Barabbas was charged (Luke 23:19, 25).[47] This was not the only possible charge. Profanation of a sacred rite or place would have been highly apt, not least in this case (25:8).[48] The centurion's judgment that Jesus was "innocent" (δίκαιος [Luke 23:47]) contrasts with the locals' view that the goddess Justice (ἡ Δίκη) has intervened. The adjective ἄτοπος (lit. "unusual" or "improper"), used to describe Paul's failure to die, was applied to Jesus by the "good thief" (Luke 23:41).[49] Paul's rescue is his ultimate vindication by a heavenly court, analogous, in a general sense, to the vindication of Jesus, who had not been permitted to live by the machinery of justice, the verdict of which God reversed (cf. 3:15; 5:31). This acquittal takes place outside of the narrative in that it has no influence on the course of the story and was witnessed by persons who could not report it—and whose credibility stood no higher than that of the "hysterical women" who first witnessed Jesus' return from the dead.[50]

■ **7-9** Verse 7 jumps without transition to the hospitality of Publius, a property owner and either "the chief" or the leading citizen.[51] The narrative evidently implies that he took care of all the refugees for three days,[52] after which responsibilities would have been redistributed. Luke uses this person and his status as a platform for Paul's personal and general reciprocity of benefaction.[53] The basis is not particularly original, since commentators have long recognized[54] that the source is Mark 1:29-31||Luke 4:38-41, the healing of Peter's mother-in-law and the subsequent summary.[55] The choice of source material was not accidental: the

46 John Clabeaux sagely elucidates this link: "The Story of the Maltese Viper and Luke's Apology for Paul," *CBQ* 67 (2005) 604–10, esp. 607.

47 Acts 3:14 contrasts the murderer Barabbas (unnamed) with the "righteous one" (δίκαιος). Note also 7:52 and, ironically, 9:1 (Saul).

48 See p. 673 n. 31 on Andocides.

49 Cf. also Acts 25:5 (of Paul, by Festus). The D-text eliminates this cross-reference. It places "saved" at the end, establishing a parallel with the close of the preceding paragraph (v. 44).

50 Celsus characterized Mary of Magdala (evidently) as "a hysterical woman," according to Origen *Cels.* 2.55; cf. 2.59. For readers of Acts, these witnesses in 28:1-6 are credible and their character commendable, as their hospitality demonstrated. Their conclusion that Paul was a god supports the veracity of the miracle.

51 See Hemer (*Book*, 153 n. 152) who states that "the clear instance" of πρῶτος as a title is *IGR* 1.512. Even that, however, is not perfectly clear, as the person Castricius Prudens is described as a Roman knight, "first of the Maltese" (πρῶτος Μελιταίων), "patron," and an official of the imperial cult (*Flamen Divi Augusti*). It may thus refer to the chief benefactor rather than to the chief magistrate, as Witherington (776) allows. If "chief," Publius would have evidently been the head of the native tribe. The D-Text presents Publius as one of the leading citizens. See also Albert Suhl ("Zum Titel πρῶτος τῆς νήσου *[Erster der Insel]* Apg 28,7," *BZ* 36 [1992] 220–26), who notes that the title is attested for many localities. On the general use of the term to mean "leading citizen," see James M. Arlandson, "Lifestyles of the Rich and Christian: Women, Wealth, and Social Freedom," in Levine, *Feminist Companion*, 155–70. Examples include Chariton *Chaer.*, 2.4; 2.5; 1.1; 2.11. See also Wilhelm Michaelis, "πρῶτος," *TDNT* 6:865–82, esp. 866.

52 So Fitzmyer, 783. The question involves the number of "us" in v. 7. In v. 1, "we" includes all the refugees; the "we" of v. 10 embraces Paul and his companions. Logic suggests that v. 7 is a larger number, but source and historical questions are not clear, and Luke did not wish to clarify the situation, as his focus was on Paul. Cf. Bruce, 533.

53 One of Hemer's abundant arguments (*Book*, 153–54) for the historical reliability of Acts is the existence of "Malta fever," which was identified in 1887 and produces symptoms comparable to those of Publius's father. So, however, do many other diseases.

54 E.g., Cadbury and Lake, 343.

55 Mark 1:23-31 contains an exorcism and the healing, followed by a summary in vv. 32-34 that includes each. Acts omits exorcisms. The author made use of both Mark and Luke. "Fever" (πυρετός) occurs only in Mark 1:31 parr. and John 5:42. "Lie" (κατακεῖμαι) is found in Mark 1:30, and in Acts, but not in Luke. "Afflicted" (συνεχόμενος), on the other hand, appears in Luke 4:38 and Acts, but not in Mark. In Luke 4:39, Jesus exorcises the fever, but in Mark 1:31 and Acts the healing is done by touch. Cf. Luke 4:40, where imposition of hands is used to heal the sick. Both Mark 1:34 and Luke 4:40 use the verb θεραπεύω ("heal") in the summary, as does Acts. Note that the D-Text,

"conclusion" of Paul's ministry echoes the beginning of Jesus'. Better: the story is beginning anew,[56] for the benefits of salvation did not end with the departure of Jesus. No less noteworthy is the virtual equivalence between Paul and Jesus as healers.[57] What had taken place in the remote and rural precincts of Galilee is taking place on the equally rustic island of Malta. The benefits of grace are stretching toward the ends of the earth, albeit without a religious label. Haenchen says that the gifts replace the customary acclamation.[58] This is valid, but it requires reflection. The author suggests not only that the Christian movement has something to offer the general culture, an arrow for the apologetic quiver, but also that these gifts may also be shared with unbelievers.[59] Here, for those who require the same, is a proof text for charitable missions conducted with no strings attached. Paul is an agent of *gratia universalis*.[60]

■ **10** Since v. 10 is dependent on the Lucan construction of the preceding verses, this is one case where one may state positively that "we" is an authorial invention.[61] All but Paul's party have been forgotten. Analysis confirms that no more can be claimed for a source than the name Melite, presumably Malta, and assistance from one Publius. All the rest of the stay is passed over in silence. This leaves a gap between v. 10 and v. 11, although they are joined by use of the same verb (ἀνάγω, "depart").

■ **11** The "three months" of v. 11 does not jibe easily with the narrative of chap. 27, for, even if taken as ninety days, it could not have been much later than February 1.[62] The Dioscuri evidently benefited from its patrons,[63] for it had been able to winter at Malta.[64]

■ **12-13** The verses tersely describe logical stages on the journey to Puteoli.[65] There "we" must have debarked, for the group accepted the kind invitation of some believers they located and remained for a week.[66] The narrative is back in the atmosphere of chaps. 20–21 (and 15:3-4).[67] Paul is welcomed by all believers everywhere and is free to manage his own time.

---

in addition to shortening the episode, states that "many," rather than "all," were healed. The *Genesis Apocryphon* 20:21-29 reports an exorcism through imposition of hands, on which see Fitzmyer, 784. For a detailed analysis, see W. Kirchschläger, "Fieberheilung in Apg 28 und Lk 4," in Kremer, *Actes*, 509–21. Note also von Bendemann, "'Many-Coloured Illnesses'" (n. 22 above).

56 Cf. Rackham, 507.

57 See Jacobson, "Paul," 145.

58 Haenchen, 716.

59 Repayment not with silver or gold but healing evokes the opening of Acts (3:1-10), although the malicious might charge that Paul comes dangerously close to simony in 28:10.

60 Haenchen's comment (716), "Paul no longer acts like a prisoner, but only as a mighty superman, who spreads blessings around him," is not erroneous, but it does not probe into the significance of Paul's actions.

61 See Conzelmann, 223.

62 Hemer (*Book*, 154) offers explanations.

63 The Dioscuri protected ships and sailors: *Homeric Hymn* 33; *The Dioscuri*, 14–22; Euripides *Orestes* 1635–37; Theocritus, 22; Diodorus Siculus 4.43.1-2. Cf. p. 661. See Fitzmyer (786), for secondary literature; Klauck (*Magic*, 116–17) who cites part of the Homeric hymn; and Kauppi, *Foreign*, 112–14. Wis 14:1-3 treats such devotion with sarcastic contempt in affirming that Providence is the sphere of the one God.

64 BDF §198 (7) discusses the participle rendered "figurehead" in conjunction with the dative of association. Apposition appears to be a simpler solution, as BDF intimates. On the name, see also Cadbury and Lake, 344; Conzelmann, 223–34; Barrett 2:1227–28; and Bruce, 534. Ramsay (*St. Paul the Traveller*, 346) seeks to explain why this ship alone in Acts is identified by name.

65 The three-day layover in Syracuse ill befits the need for haste that justified an early departure. Hemer (*Book*, 154) proposes the weather as a cause. Barrett (2:1220) raises the question whether the source was "a travel handbook . . . different from the theologically motivated source that has at least some relation with Paul?" B has a temporal dative: ἡμέραις τρισίν ("in three days"). This appears to be an error or the use of the dative to indicate duration of time (BDF §201), but it may be a correction: it took them three days to get to Syracuse, eliminating the layover. Seneca (*Ep.* 77.1–2) describes the excitement generated at Puteoli by the arrival of the Alexandrian fleet.

66 Bruce (535) proposes that Julius had business that kept him at Puteoli for a week.

67 Haenchen, 719: "[*Luke's*] report of the journey is so similar as to be interchangeable with that of the journey to Jerusalem."

■ **14-16** Rome is exceptional only in the extent of its welcome.[68] By one means or another, word that Paul was on his way reached Rome, which sent delegations to greet him.[69] "Welcome" (ἀπάντησις) "appears to have been a sort of technical term for the official welcome extended to a newly arrived dignitary by a deputation which went out from the city to greet him and escort him for the rest of his way."[70] "Paul is then depicted here as some sort of dignitary, whose 'epiphany' was seen as an important event."[71] These judgments are correct.[72] The missionary is no less a V.I.P. on land than on sea. The parties had traveled a considerable distance.[73] By this indirect means, the narrator shows that Paul was not only known to the Roman believers—who appear only here and solely for this purpose—but also held in high regard and thus presumably innocent by them. This support was not unappreciated (v. 16).[74]

With those three (Greek) words, "We came to Rome," the narrator announces attainment of the goal posited in 19:21.[75] The way has not been easy. That announcement was followed by a riot, and thereafter nearly everything that wicked mortals or unfeeling nature could contrive took its turn. It is safe to conclude that God wanted Paul to reach Rome. This was not because Rome was a good place to die. Jerusalem would have served that purpose, and Luke has absolutely no interest in extolling Rome as the place where Paul received the imperishable crown of martyrdom. As the diametrical antithesis to rural Galilee, Rome was "the ends of the earth."[76] It was also the center, the goal of more or less every teacher, author, movement, and scheme.[77] Rome, as the regal reception brilliantly depicts, has embraced the Christian movement and its primary exponent.

The D-Text of vv. 11-15 exhibits the abridgment that has characterized it (according to Boismard) since 27:2. All of the difficulties attending the conventional text vanish. After an unstated interval, the party boards an unnamed Alexandrian ship and sails to Rome. The stops vanish, including the week at Puteoli. Believers greet Paul at Rome rather than journeying a considerable distance. The apparent double reference to reaching Rome also disappears. The inconsistency between Paul's status as a prisoner and his freedom of action has evaporated. The expanded v. 16 takes it up explicitly. Although the centurion delivered "the prisoners" (!) to

68 When the καὶ οὕτως is taken to refer to what follows, there is no contradiction between the two statements of arrival at Rome. Some prefer a redactional solution, on which see Weiser, 2:673.

69 On the early Roman church, see Peter Lampe, *From Paul to Valentinus: Christians at Rome in the First Two Centuries* (trans. Michael Steinhauser, ed. Marshall D. Johnson; Minneapolis: Fortress Press, 2003) 5–87, 359–84.

70 Bruce, 536.

71 Witherington, 787.

72 Witherington has Matt 25:6 and 1 Thess 4:17 in mind. For inscriptional data, see Danker, *Benefactor*, 415 n. 2. For literary references, see Talbert, 255. Among these are Cicero *Ad Atticum* 5.16; Josephus *Bell.* 7.70–71 (Vespasian); 7.100–102 (Titus).

73 The mention of two places apparently assumes two groups (Barrett, 2:1231), one of which traveled to Three Taverns, around forty-nine kilometers from Rome, the other to Appius's Forum, about sixty-five kilometers. Horace (who was not writing a tourist brochure for a Chamber of Commerce) described the journey to Appius's Forum in *Satire* 1.5.3–8. They were stage posts on the road to and from Rome (Cicero *Att.* 2.10).

74 In *Act. Paul* 11/14.1 (Martyrdom), Paul was received by Luke and Titus (who had arrived from Gaul and Dalmatia, respectively). Upon seeing them, he was glad, and rented a barn outside of Rome, which he used for teaching. The rather late *Acta Petri et Pauli* (on which see A. de Santos Otero, "Later Acts of Apostles," in *NTApoc* 2:426–82, esp. 440–42) seeks to integrate Acts with the *Acts of Peter*, as well as with the *Acts of Paul*. Chapters 13–28 (Richard A. Lipsius and Maximilian Bonnet, *Acta Apostolorum Apocrypha* [2 vols.; Leipzig: Hermann Mendelssohn, 1891–1903] 1:184–91) state that Peter sent the disciples to Three Taverns. Paul's arrival in Rome strikes fear into Jewish hearts. They urge him to attack Peter. The two apostles meet and exchange stories. Paul then brings about a reconciliation between Jews and gentiles.

75 Raymond E. Brown (in Brown and Meier, *Antioch and Rome*, 89) calls this "masterful understatement." That applies only to this phrase. Having described the royal reception, Luke needed to say no more.

76 Peder Borgen (*Philo*, 280–81) argues that Rome was, for Jews, the distant west and thus "the ends of the earth." See also the comments on 1:8.

77 See the references in Pervo, *Profit*, 158 n. 220,

a responsible authority,[78] he authorized Paul to find his own quarters with a single guard.[79] This is clearly fictitious, as the commander of the detachment would not have been allowed to make such dispositions.[80] (Note the passive "received permission" of the conventional text.[81]) This is the final reference to Roman authority, which departs at the same time as "we."[82] The narrative makes no more references to colleagues or assistants. Paul is effectively alone (with his guard).[83]

to which add Harnack, *Mission*, 1:370–72; Betz, *Lukian*, 110.

78 On the meaning of στρατοπεδάρχης, see BDAG, 948, *s.v.*; and Rapske, "Travel," 40–43.

79 Boismard's "found favor with" (*Texte*, 425) is not supported by most witnesses for the D-Text, which share the "was permitted" of the conventional text. It is quite awkward when followed by the infinitive μένειν ("stay").

80 Josephus gives a detailed account of the generally lenient custody experienced by Agrippa (*Ant.* 18.188–237). This may have inspired Luke. (Paul did not have anything approximating the status enjoyed by Agrippa.)

81 This addition was sufficiently attractive to find a home in the Byzantine text. See also Clark, 386–88. Its validity seems assumed by Sherwin-White (*Roman Society*, 108–10), who engages in a lengthy discussion. Witherington (788–89) is slightly more cautious. His major worry is the status implication of having Paul guarded by an ordinary soldier. See also Hemer, *Book*, 199–200; the full discussion of Harry W. Tajra, *The Martyrdom of St. Paul: Historical and Judicial Context, Traditions, and Legends* (WUNT 2.67; Tübingen: Mohr Siebeck, 1994) 40–46; Rapske, *Roman Custody*, 174–77; and Lentz, *Luke's Portrait*, 157–70, which gives the account of the journey and custody a cold bath of needed realism.

82 For discussion on the nature of Paul's custody, see Rapske, *Roman Custody*, 177–82.

83 This fact lends no support to the view that one of Paul's colleagues wrote Acts, and it does not enhance the authority of a "we source." Nor is it particularly congenial to the view that the "imprisonment epistles" were written from Rome. Phlm 23 speaks of "fellow prisoners."

28

28:17-31 Paul the Prisoner in Rome

17/ Three days after arriving, Paul
called a meeting of the local[a]
Jewish leaders.
"My fellow believers," he said
after they were in place,[b] "I am
here as a prisoner from Jerusalem. Although I had done
nothing against the people or
the ancestral practices, I was
surrendered to the Romans.
18/ After investigating the
case,[c] they wished to release
me, since I had committed no
capital crime, 19/ but, because
the Jews said otherwise, I was
compelled to appeal to Caesar. Please do not think that I
have any accusations to make
against my nation. 20/ This is
why I have asked to meet you
and address you: I wear this
shackle for the sake of the hope
of Israel."
21/ They replied, "We have received
no correspondence about you
from Judea, nor have any of
our people who have come
here reported or said anything
damaging about you.[d] 22/ We
should be pleased to hear from
you[e] what you think, for we do
know that this sect is the subject of universal opposition."
23/ On the day arranged for this
purpose a considerable crowd
came[f] to his lodgings to hear
Paul.[g] He spoke[h] from dawn to
dusk, setting forth his convictions about the dominion of
God and seeking to convince
them about Jesus by appeal
to the Law of Moses[i] and to
the Prophets. 24/ Some[j] found
his arguments appealing, but
others remained skeptical.
25/ As they were on their way
out without having reached any
general agreement, Paul had
one more statement:
"Aptly did the Holy Spirit say
to your forebears through the
prophet Isaiah:[k]
26/ 'Go to this people and say: "You
will certainly hear but by no
means understand, and you will
certainly look but by no means
perceive,[l] 27/ for the heart of
this people cannot feel.[m] They
are hard of hearing and have
shut their eyes. They do not
want to use those eyes for

seeing, those ears for hearing, and those hearts for understanding because they do not wish to change their ways so that I may make them well.'"[n]

28:28-31: Conventional Text

28/ Therefore, be assured of this: God's salvation has been offered to the gentiles. They shall listen."[o]

30/ Paul remained in his rented quarters[p] for two full years. He received all who came to see him, 31/ proclaiming the dominion of God and telling the story of the Lord Jesus Christ,[q] with full freedom[r] and without any impediment.

28:28-31 D-Text[s]

28/ Therefore, be assured of this: This salvation *from* God has been offered to the gentiles. [ ]

29/ *After he had said this, the Jews left, engaged in vigorous discussion.*[t]

30/ *Paul,* remaining in his rented quarters for two full years, received all who came to see him; *he engaged in conversation with both Jews and Greeks,* 31/ proclaiming the dominion of God, *asserting and claiming* [ ] without any impediment, *"This is Jesus the Son of God through whom the whole universe will be judged."*

---

a "Local" works well to render the redundant participle ὄντας ("being"). See Cadbury and Lake, 56.

b The D-Text (Boismard, *Texte*, 426) reads "he began to engage (συνέβαλλε) them. . . ."

c D-witnesses (614 *pc* sy^{h**}) state that the investigation was "detailed" or "thorough" (πολλά), which Cadbury and Lake (346) find "a most attractive" gloss.

d Boismard (*Texte*, 426) offers "**Nothing has been written to us** about you, **nor have they sent to us** from Judea **nor have we heard** anything damaging about you" as the D-Text.

e Boismard (previous note) omits "from you."

f The variant ἧκον (Ψ m) has the merit of being less common and may be more original. The meaning is similar.

g The D-Text (Boismard, *Texte*, 427) omits "a considerable crowd came to his lodgings."

h For the last time, Luke has used a relative clause as a principal clause.

i $\mathfrak{P}^{74}$ sy^{h} omit "Moses," yielding the typical expression "the Law and the Prophets."

j ℵ* reads *μὲν οὖν*, evidently either overlooking the *μέν . . . δέ* construction or seeking to intensify it.

k The D-Text (Boismard, *Texte*, 427) reads: "aptly did the [ ] Spirit speak through Isaiah [ ] to **our** forebears."

l The form εἰδῆτε ("know") is a variant for ἴδητε ($\mathfrak{P}^{74vid}$ E 104 *pc* sy^{h}), as is also the case in the LXX. This might be also be rendered "perceive." It may be due to itacism.

m Instead of ἐπαχύνθη ℵ* gig read ἐβαρύνθη ("become heavy," accepted by Boismard, *Texte*, 427, as the D-Text). This has the merit of disagreeing with the LXX.

n The moods of the final verbs vary; ἐπιστρέψουσιν ("turn," "convert," indicative) has a range of support (and is found in the LXX text of ℵ, but not in Acts). The subjunctive ἰάσωμαι ("heal") has a range of support, mainly from witnesses of the D-type. Both of these alterations may be understood in more than one way. Only E 81 and some representatives of the Latin tradition have both. The indicative "I shall heal" is correct (BDF §369 [3]), but a scribe may have believed it to be an error. Moreover, pronunciation is again an issue.

o Verse 29 is omitted in critical editions. This is a D-text addition that became part of the Byzantine text.

p On the meaning of μίσθωμα, see p. 687 n. 70.

q ℵ* 326. 614. 1505. 2147 *pc* sy^{h} omit "Christ." It is tempting to view it as a conventional secondary supplement, but it lends solemnity to the final verse and may well have been original.

r $\mathfrak{P}^{74}$ reads "salvation" (σωτηρίας) instead of "freedom" (παρρησίας). This is a stupid mistake.

s Boismard, *Texte*, 427–28.

t *Or:* "debate."

Analysis

This material, with the possible exception of v. 30a, is generally recognized as Lucan composition.[1] Verse 16 is the logical end of a narrative sequence. Structurally, it serves to bracket, with vv. 30-31, the final section of Acts.[2] The intervening material consists of two paragraphs that have a modern ring. The first (vv. 17-22) is a meeting about having a meeting, while the second (vv. 23-28) reports the actual meeting. Thematically, the first summarizes Paul's defense of himself and the second his message. Earlier speeches (chaps. 22 and 26) presented both together. Here they are divided for dramatic purposes. Selectivity is apparent, for these conjoined encounters are the only incidents the narrator chooses to recount from a period of two years. There is thus nothing new in all of this, for the author does not wish to say anything new. As Daniel Marguerat observes, Paul plays different roles. In the first scene, he is the accused. By the end of the second, he has become the accuser, announcing judgment.[3]

This is not to say that nothing in this account is strange. To all intents a Christian community does not exist. Although some of the Roman Jews found his message persuasive (v. 24), and one can presume that some gentiles did also (v. 31), no baptisms are reported and no house-based churches are established. Paul functions like a philosopher who accepts any and all who care to attend his lectures.[4] Haenchen rightly observes that Luke wishes Paul to "proclaim in Rome the gospel up to that point unknown,"[5] but the narrative does not portray Paul as the founder of the (or a) Roman church.[6] The scenario is familiar. As he has done nearly everywhere since Damascus,[7] Paul begins by preaching to Jews. Although this is a mission of sorts, the focus is on the conflict between followers of Jesus and Jews who did not accept this message. Paul defends himself by doing what he has usually done, but less to bring about conversion than to illustrate and justify the division.[8] For the third and climactic time, he announces a turn to the gentiles (28:28). The entire Greek-speaking Diaspora has rejected the offer of salvation. The Jewish people had their chance, but failed to exploit it. Luke knew as much about "the rule of three" as anyone, and he exploited it vigorously. This third example of the formula comes at the very end of the book and "carries special narrative weight."[9] All of the attempts to mitigate the impact of this final utterance have to row against the powerful current of this narrative weight.[10]

This purpose becomes more apparent when contrasted with an ostensible justification for the consultation. Paul was well advised to secure at least the neutrality of the large and often politically active Jewish community at Rome in the light of his forthcoming

1 See the detailed arguments of Weiser, 2:677–79.

2 Verses 30-31 follow so smoothly after v. 16 that they were once viewed as a source into which vv. 17-28 were placed. See Jacques Dupont, "La conclusion des Actes et son rapport à l'ensemble de l'ouvrage de Luc," in Kremer, *Actes*, 359–404, esp. 363 (= *Nouvelles Études*, 457–511). See also the detailed analysis of Hermann J. Hauser, *Strukturen der Abschlußerzählung der Apostelgeschichte (Apg 28,16-31)* (AnBib 86; Rome: Pontifical Biblical Institute, 1979).

3 Marguerat, *Historian*, 295.

4 Cf. the statement of Justin (*Acts of Justin and Companions* 3, Recension A): "I have been living above the baths of Myrtinus [MSS. corrupt here] for the entire period of my sojourn at Rome. . . . Anyone who wished could come to my abode and I would impart to him the words of truth" (trans. Musurillo, *Christian*, 45).

5 Haenchen, 720.

6 Paul is implicitly the founder of the Roman church in *Act. Pet.* (Verc.) 1, in that he preceded Peter in Rome. This is a secondary addition to the work; cf. also the *Acts of Xanthippe and Polyxena* 24, which is more explicit.

7 The exception is Antioch (11:25-26). This is important, as it reflects history and shows that Luke's rather rigid scheme is his own.

8 See Alexander, *Literary Context*, 207–18.

9 Tyson, *Images*, 177. See also Conzelmann, 227.

10 The most vigorous exponent of mitigation has been Robert Tannehill. See his essays now collected in *The Shape of Luke's Story: Essays on Luke-Acts* (Eugene, Ore.: Wipf & Stock, 2005) 105–65, as well as *Narrative Unity*, 2:344–53. Tannehill views the end of Acts as largely tragic and the story of Israel in Acts as a tragedy. This is not Luke's view, for he presents the story of contemporary Judaism vis-à-vis Christianity as a melodrama in which the Jews receive the punishment they thoroughly deserve. See the critique by Sanders, *Jews*, 81–82. A similar argument is made by Robert

trial.[11] Josephus engaged in "networking" of this sort (*Vit.* 13–16).[12] Here, as earlier, Paul knows to stress his Jewish credentials but ends up attacking his audience, without a single positive word for those who had found him persuasive. Readers may conclude that Paul did not enjoy the support of Roman Jewry in his legal difficulties.

Comment

■ **17** Three days later—not a long rest after an arduous journey—Paul issued a summons to the leaders of the Jewish community. The term is vague and the number unstated. More than a half-dozen would have strained the capacity of a rented room,[13] but, as with the presbyters of Ephesus, the setting and number are left to the readers' imagination; nothing is said about the time of the meeting. As far as one can tell, the request was for immediate attendance and all immediately arrived.[14] Why they should have done so is not clear. Without further ado Paul launches into his little speech.[15] The first phrases are quite difficult[16] and, although they fulfill the prophecy of Agabus, apparently erroneous. Paul was effectively rescued by the Roman garrison from a Jewish mob, but he was still arrested. This allows the understanding that he was "handed over" to the ruling power (by his Jewish opponents in the temple). Paul's experiences are precisely parallel to those of Jesus (Luke 9:44; 18:32; cf. 24:7; note also Acts 2:23).[17]

Paul leads with one familiar affirmation, that he has not violated Torah (cf. 21:21, 28; 24:5-6), and one new claim: he is not an enemy of the Jewish people.[18]

■ **18** Another Jesus parallel (Luke 23:15-20) follows: the Romans wished to release him, but "the Jews" resisted. The proper noun betrays the author. His character would have been better advised to say something like "the high priestly leaders" (with whom Roman Jews may have had some disagreements and whose interference

---

Brawley, "Ethical Borderlines between Rejection and Hope: Interpreting the Jews in Luke-Acts," *CurrTheolMiss* 27 (2000) 415–23. Marguerat (*Historian*, 224 n. 52) regards Tannehill's thesis as a trivialization of the end of Acts. The tragedy has been the uncritical reception of this portrait in the Christian tradition and its contribution to subsequent anti-Semitism. That tragedy is, needless to say, also a worthy concern. Jewish rejection of the Christian message is a key issue for the modern problem of Christian anti-Semitism. For Luke, however, Jewish rejection was not the problem so much as its cause: if those to whom the promises were addressed have said no, can the Jesus movement be legitimate?

11 On the Jewish community at Rome, see Harry J. Leon, *The Jews of Ancient Rome* (updated ed.; Peabody, Mass.: Hendrickson, 1995); Smallwood, *The Jews*, 200–219; R. Penna, "Les Juifs à Rome au temps de l'Apôtre Paul," *NTS* 28 (1982) 321–47; Lampe, *Paul to Valentinus*, 38–41; and Hermann Lichtenberger, "Jews and Christians in Rome in the Time of Nero: Josephus and Paul in Rome," *ANRW* 2.26.3 (1996) 2142–76, esp. 2155–61. Note also George La Piana's classic "Foreign Groups at Rome during the First Centuries of the Empire," *HTR* 20 (1927) 183–403. It cannot be stated with certainty that Roman Jews had an overall organization. See Schürer, *History*, 3.1:95: "Of a union of all the Roman Jewish groups under one *gerousia* there is no trace." For details, see ibid., 95–100. (The historical Paul sought support from Christians in Rome in his Epistle to the Romans.)

12 P. R. McKechnie ("Judean Embassies and Cases before Roman Emperors, AD 44–66," *JTS* 56 [2005] 339–61) argues, from cases mentioned by Josephus, that the priestly leadership of Jerusalem usually won their cases and was likely to have prevailed in the case of Paul.

13 Note the πλείονες ("rather many") of v. 23.

14 Dupont ("Conclusion," 364) notes that vv. 17a and 25a form an antithetical inclusion.

15 Talbert (226) takes vv. 17-20 as a five-part chiasm. This does not reveal the contrast between vv. 18-19, as it takes v. 18 as the center. For a two-part (vv. 17c-19, 20) outline, see Soards, *Speeches*, 131, but note his entire scheme, which treats vv. 17-28 as a single speech. Kennedy (*Rhetorical Criticism*, 139) characterizes it in terms more suitable to forensic rhetoric. It is apologetic (Witherington, 796).

16 The placement of "from Jerusalem" is unusual. The simplest approach is to construe it with "prisoner," but one could also take it with "surrendered" (although "at Jerusalem" would be expected for the latter). The rhetorical purpose is clear: to emphasize innocence before acknowledging his status as a prisoner, although that would have been apparent.

17 For detailed comparison of 28:17-19 to the passion narrative, see Radl, *Paulus*, 252–65.

18 The negative οὐδέν ("nothing") with the participle amounts to emphasis. Cf. also the οὐχ ("not") with an infinitive in v. 19.

would not have always been welcome).[19] Again, although it fit the trial of Jesus, his claim that the Romans wished to release Paul is not fully supported by Acts 21–26.[20] The commentator must ask whether the author expected his readers to accept this view and not peruse the preceding narrative to discover the contradiction. The answer is probably affirmative.[21] Luke is not simply revising the story of Christian origins; he is revising his own story. One also asks why the issue of a capital charge is introduced. Possibilities are that the narrator thought that only capital cases could be appealed or that the Roman governor took cognizance of those alone; or, perhaps, that this is another emphasis on the kindred fates of Paul and Jesus. The simplest answer is that this conforms to the statement of Festus in 25:25.

■ **19** By the close of v. 19, Paul is back to where he began, affirming his lack of opposition to his own people.[22] He did not appeal against "the Jews." The progression has not been smooth, but its point is clear. Paul is innocent of anything to which a reasonable Jew might take substantive exception.

■ **20** This verse serves as the fulcrum between Paul's protest of innocence and the exposition of his message.[23] His theme is well chosen, "the hope of Israel." Although readers know that this refers to the eschatological faith in resurrection (23:6; 26:6-8; cf. 2:26),[24] here it lacks qualification. All Israelites had hope, however understood. Acts is closing, as it (and the Gospel) began: in a purely Jewish environment. Since his arrival in Jerusalem, Paul has been engaged in discussion with his fellow Israelites. The question for interpreters is whether this conversation deals with contemporary problems of Luke's time,[25] or, as this commentary holds, attempts to justify the separation that has taken place.[26] For Luke, the hope of Israel means belief in Jesus as the messianic savior whose resurrection brought about inclusion of gentiles and a turn away from understanding the Israelite heritage as observance of Torah to a view of Scripture as the repository of promises and prophecies revealing God's plans for all the peoples of the earth. The essence of Israelite hope was liberation. Paul expresses a nice antithesis when he refers to the sign of his bondage.[27]

■ **21-22** At this point, his guests offer an appropriate response, speaking in unison.[28] They claim to have heard neither anything untoward, whether official or by hearsay,[29] about Paul nor anything good about "this sect." Both are best understood as ad hoc. Paul will begin with a clean slate. The narrative of Acts portrays his enemies as willing to take any steps to kill him. At the moment his appeal was accepted (25:12), they would have been likely to take steps to advise the Jews of Rome.[30] Moreover, the accusers would have been obliged to send a delegation to participate in his trial.

---

19 614. 2147 *pc* sy[h**] specify the form of Jewish opposition: "shouting, 'away with our enemy!'" This derives from 22:22.

20 Agrippa said that Paul could have been released but for the appeal (26:32). Felix did nothing, while Paul accused Festus of attempting to "hand him over" to his Jewish opponents.

21 Witherington (798) says, "Luke is counting on his audience to remember what has been said before" and thus correct this summary.

22 Verse 19 is not complete. Boismard (*Texte*, 426) takes note of this addition at the end: "but so that I might save my life." He regards this as probably part of a subsequent edition of the D-Text.

23 The possibly artistic effort to repeat αἰτία ("charge," "reason") from v. 18 in v. 20 leaves an ambiguity. It could look back to the sense of v. 18 or forward and thus mean "reason." Barrett (2:1240) finds difficulties with all solutions.

24 For varied views, see Fitzmyer, 793.

25 Jacob Jervell, in his various publications (e.g., "The Church of Jews and Godfearers," in Joseph Tyson, ed., *Luke-Acts and the Jewish People: Eight Critical Perspectives* [Minneapolis: Augsburg, 1988] 11–20), is the most vigorous exponent of this view.

26 See the comments of Weiser, 2:680.

27 The chain was probably not metaphorical, as the guarding soldier was constantly linked to his prisoner. See Rapske (*Roman Custody*, 181), who states in n. 47 that the chain was probably light.

28 Dupont ("Conclusion," 366–68, citing 368) shows that the two little speeches are symmetrical, "like the two panels of a diptych."

29 Cadbury and Lake (346) take ἀπήγγειλεν as "official" and ἐλάλησεν as "unofficial."

30 Cf. Rackham, 501.

They evidently know enough about their host to associate him with the Christian movement, about which they are remarkably uninformed and about the proliferation of which they offer unsolicited testimony.[31] Historically, one need but refer to Paul's letter to the Romans to refute this claim of ignorance (see also Acts 18:22). On the positive side, they are quite prepared to listen to what Paul has to say, negative reports notwithstanding. Paul will have an opportunity before a neutral Jewish audience.[32]

■ **23** On the agreed date, a goodly number come to his facility[33] early and stay late.[34] Acts, like Luke (24:29-52), concludes in the evening, with a lecture[35] on messianic exegesis.[36] Verses 23 and 31 constitute another inclusion.[37] Paul's auditors must be given credit for allowing him a full day's time for his presentation,[38] but the reader of Acts would rejoin that, with so much argument and information, they ought to have been convinced. "Dominion of God" means, in effect, the message of the gospel, and "Jesus" is a trope for Christology (v. 23). The speech resembles that of Stephen (chap. 7) in that it closes with a denunciation of the audience, but it is closer to Paul's first sermons, in Pisidian Antioch (13:15-41, 42-49). In both cases there are two encounters, with the first ending with a request for more (13:42; 28:22), the less successful second opportunity ending with an announcement that the gentiles will be given an opportunity. Both close with a citation from Isaiah (49:6 in 13:47; 6:9-10 in 28).[39] They use related images of light and sight.[40] This *inclusio* is important. It gives weight to the view that chaps. 13–28 are the second major division of Acts. Chapters 1–12 move the story from Jerusalem to Antioch; Peter is the central character. In chaps. 13–28 Paul is the central character, and the story proceeds from Antioch to Rome.

■ **24-25** The response is, as always in Paul's outreach to the Jews, mixed.[41] The narrator does not wish to depict a complete failure, but the potential successes are not pursued. Those who found his message attractive do not remain behind, and Paul's denunciation is general. This account lacks the traditional closing summons to repentance, replacing it with the condemnation from Isaiah.[42] Their lack of concord (ἀσύμφωνοι [v. 25]) is a telling contrast to the unity that characterized the followers of Jesus.[43] Like Stephen at the close of his speech (7:52), Paul speaks of "your ancestors."[44] The Jewish people in general are once more and finally labeled as "the other." Their "departure" (ἀπελύοντο) contrasts ironically with Simeon's joyful use of the same verb (Luke 2:29).

■ **26-27** These verses come as a shock after the mixed reception reported in v. 25. Isa 6:9-10, cited in essential agreement with the LXX, which follows the MT except that it transforms the imperatives of the Hebrew into

31 "Everywhere" (πανταχοῦ); cf. 24:3.

32 The end of their little speech contains two important words. "Known" (γνῶστον) in v. 22 will become ironic when it recurs in v. 28. It appeared at the opening of Acts (1:19; 2:14) and in Paul's full-length missionary sermon in a synagogue (13:38). "Oppose" (ἀντιλέγω), found also in v. 19, appears in Luke 2:34 (the Nunc Dimittis, to which other allusions will follow), and also in the sermon at Pisidian Antioch (13:45; previous note).

33 The word ξενία means "hospitality," but "lodging" is also possible, by metonymy, and is preferable here. See Rapske, *Roman Custody*, 179. Luke may have taken the term from Phlm 22.

34 "From morning until evening" (v. 23) recalls Moses (Exod 18:13), who has just been mentioned.

35 The verb διαμαρτύρομαι in v. 23 fulfills the promise of 23:11.

36 The only occurrences of ἠπίστουν in Luke and Acts are Luke 24:11 and Acts 28:24.

37 For details and comments, see Dupont, "Conclusion," 365.

38 Witherington (810) calls this a "marathon session."

39 So also, e.g., Dupont, "Conclusion," 384–85; and Polhill, 541.

40 For other resemblances see nn. 32, 52.

41 For references, which begin in 2:12-13, see Johnson, 471.

42 Haenchen (723) notes the absence of reference to repentance. Witherington (801) says that baptism was impossible because Paul was confined to his quarters. Bruce (540) maintains that the imperfect "does not necessarily imply that they were actually convinced." This judgment suits the subsequent narrative.

43 The adjective appears only here in early Christian literature. Its opposite is ὁμοθυμαδόν ("with one mind"), 1:14; 2:46; 4:24; 5:12.

44 As so often, ἡμῶν ("our") is a variant: m gig vg, while sy^h lacks any pronoun. Boismard (*Texte*, 427) takes "our" as the D-Text. As Metzger (*Textual*

finite verbs,[45] "so that the entire guilt falls upon the people whose stubbornness the prophet now already confirms as a fact."[46] The early Jesus movement used this text as an explanation of missionary failure (Mark 4:12; Luke 8:10; cf. John 12:39-40). So it is here, but one can also perceive a shift toward invoking the passage to condemn the Jews in general.[47] Here it is the only citation from those Scriptures to which v. 23 referred. The citation serves to prove that rejection of the message by the Jews accorded with the divine will. On this subject, the contrast between Luke and Paul could not be stronger.[48] Both sought to explain why most Jews had said "no" to the message. For Paul this rejection was provisional; Luke viewed it as final and the grounds for the existence of (in modern terms) a separate religion.[49]

This is not simply a matter of gentile anti-Semitism. Judaism and Christianity began to emerge as clearly distinct entities c. 90 CE. A generation later, Luke was engaged in retrojecting this separation to the "primitive" period. This is a normal tactic of an established body that wishes to maintain and protect its boundaries by dating its foundation as early as possible.[50] The separation of "Christians" from "Jews" is an accomplished fact. Luke's position is clear: we did not reject them; they closed the gates against us (21:30). This view is formal and is not mitigated by the repeated separations of Paul from Diaspora synagogues. It is also institutional. The movement does not reject Jewish converts, who must, however, leave the synagogue and expect no more than conditional tolerance for Torah observance. In short, those of Jewish background who adhere to the church are no longer "Jews," certainly not to be numbered among "the Jews," which is the preferred word for "the other."[51]

"See" and "hear" abound in (Luke and) Acts.[52] Failure to accept the message is refusal to hear the words of grace and to see what is before one's eyes. "Blinding" is an important symbol, portrayed literally in the cases of Paul (9:8) and Elymas (13:11), and symbolically as the darkness in which the unredeemed dwell.[53] The promise of sight to the blind announced by Jesus in his first sermon (4:18, from Isa 61:1) has become an announcement of judgment.[54] The two final phrases of the citation associate conversion (ἐπιστρέφω)[55] with healing, establishing "healing" as a metaphor for salvation.[56]

■ **28-29** Paul's comment (v. 28) on the citation, a mirror of his guests' final words in v. 22,[57] is that salvation has been delivered[58] to the gentiles, who, in contrast to the Israelites, *will* listen.[59] The term for salvation, τὸ σωτήριον, brims with significance. It comes from

Commentary, 444) says, both the external data and the context give strong weight to "your" in this place.

45 On differences from the LXX, see Barrett (2:1244) and the notes on the text. The introductory καλῶς ("aptly") also precedes a quotation from Isaiah in *P. Egerton* II line 54. Cf. Justin *Dial.* 115.6.

46 Haenchen, 724.

47 Justin *Dial.* 12.2. On this passage, see Lindars, *Apologetic*, 159–67, 254–55; and François Bovon, "'Schön hat der heilige Geist durch den Propheten Jesaja zu euren Vätern gesprochen' (Act 28,25)," *ZNW* 75 (1984) 224–32.

48 Conzelmann (227) with a reference to Romans 9–11.

49 Jervell (631) says that this passage marks the separation of the church from "the unbelieving component of Judaism."

50 In intra-Christian disputes, the key category became "apostolic." Similar phenomena are apparent in the claims of rulers to be the offspring of gods and founders of dynasties to claim descent from earlier monarchs.

51 For detailed argument, see Richard Pervo, "Israel's Heritage and Claims upon the Genre(s) of Luke and Acts: The Problems of a History," in Moessner, *Heritage*, 127–43; and idem, "The Gates Have Been Closed (Acts 21:30): The Jews in Acts," *JHC* 11 (2005) 128–49.

52 They occur as a pair in Acts 2:33; 4:26; 8:6 (19:26); 22:16. On "hear," see Dupont, "Conclusion," 372–76.

53 Note in particular 26:18 and the comments there.

54 That sermon (Luke 4:16-30) also anticipated rejection by Jesus' people and the gentile mission. See Turner (*Power*, 260), who also notes Luke 7:21; and Dupont, "Conclusion," 396–402.

55 See Pervo, *Dating*, 269.

56 Individual healings, as of blindness, are synecdoches of salvation.

57 See Dupont, "Conclusion," 368–69.

58 Contrast the situation in 13:26 (synagogue sermon in Pisidia), where the message has been delivered (ἐξαπεστάλη) to Jews and "God-fearers."

59 "Gentiles" is another echo from the close of Luke (24:47).

Deutero-Isaiah (Isa 40:5), cited in Luke 3:6, an expansion of his Marcan source: "and all flesh shall see the salvation of God."[60] That promise was anticipated in the words of Simeon: "my eyes have seen your salvation" (Luke 2:30). By bringing the beginning of his first book into association with the close of the second the author is doing more than wrapping his package in a pretty ribbon. Simeon's hope for a light to illumine the gentiles has been fulfilled, but the people of Israel have refused to see their glory.

The D-Text offers a different picture. The ringing claim that the gentiles will listen is dropped, and a new statement, which, because it was taken into the Byzantine text, became v. 29. This provides a different closure. The addition looks back to v. 25 and emphasizes the difference of Jewish opinion (which the citation from Isaiah neglects). In utilizing v. 25 as the basis for this new closure, the editor either ignored ἀπελύοντο ("departed") or took it as "began to leave." Luke depicts a general denunciation hurled at the backs of the departing audience. The reviser softened that picture.[61] That amelioration has support among some modern interpreters who believe that the D-Text represents the correct understanding of the author's intention.[62] The best that can be said about the final addition, which occurs in various forms, is that it represents a certain pious taste.[63] The worst that can be said is that it is the final indication of the D-Text's inability to know when to stop.[64]

■ **30** As was the case after the final words of Jesus (1:8), the narrator returns to the third person. "The ends of the earth" (Acts 1:8) is realized in a mission that has no limits. Whereas Jesus spoke to disciples who were intent upon him, Paul addressed the backs of his departing audience. Virtually every word of the first clause in v. 30 is controversial. The chronological reference to two full years[65] is important. References to extended periods mark important missions: Antioch (11:26, a full year), Corinth (18:11, eighteen months); and Ephesus (19:10, "two years").[66] This is the most likely understanding of the term here: Paul labored in the capital longer than at Corinth and somewhat less time than in Ephesus.[67] These data support the view that the mission summarized in vv. 30-31 was primarily a gentile mission.[68]

No particular weight is to be attached to the aorist ἐνέμεινεν,[69] for which the normal spatial meaning

60 On this term for "salvation," see also Ps 66:3; 97:3 LXX. Outside of the three uses in Luke and Acts, this term appears only in Eph 6:17 in the NT. This is an indication of the strong interest in Isaiah 40–66 in the post-Pauline environment.

61 Epp (*Tendency*, 114–15) attempts to reconcile this text with his general understanding of the D-Text by stating that the conventional text presents a ministry to Jews alone in Rome. In the light of v. 28 (and the "all" of v. 30), this interpretation is unlikely.

62 Barrett (2:1250–51) does not decisively exclude the D-Text as secondary, while he supports its viewpoint. Tannehill (*Narrative Unity*, 2:346–53) is concerned to refute the idea that this passage means the end of the "Jewish mission."

63 Blass (291) ventured to claim that the expanded ending was apposite ("Non inepte hoc in fine libri ponitur"). Of this judgment, one can only say, without pleasure: *inepte*.

64 Cadbury and Lake (349) define them theologically. The conventional text ends on an apologetic note; the D-Text on an eschatological note. This is insightful, for it touches upon that element of the D-tradition that is sometimes called "proto-Montanist."

65 The adjective ὅλην indicates that this is not inclusive reckoning, that is, somewhere between one and two years. Cf. *Act. Pet.* (Verc.) 1. This later addition refers to Paul's stay in Rome, where he converted large numbers. One of these was the wife of the supervisor of prisons, who converted her husband. He authorized Paul to travel, whence his mission to Spain.

66 For parallels to the accounts about Corinth and Ephesus, see Dupont, "Conclusion," 385–86.

67 The most important alternative is that the term had legal significance: after two years without action by prosecutors or plaintiffs, a case lapsed. For a refutation of the legal data for this claim, see Haenchen, 724–26 n. 3. It is absurd in that it presumes that silence means no action was taken about the case and that readers were familiar with the alleged law.

68 Paul separates from the synagogue at Corinth in 18:6 and turns to the gentiles. In 19:9, he does the same at Ephesus. Gentile conversions led to the agitation of Demetrius (19:21-40), since Jews had never worshiped Artemis.

69 BDF §332 (1) asserts that the aorist means that after two years this state of affairs ended. This is special pleading. Moule (*Idiom Book*, 13) says that the verb has an innately durative sense.

("stayed," "remained") is preferable. The noun *μίσθωμα* is, like its parallel *ξενία* in v. 23, a metonym meaning "rented quarters."[70] It may have been chosen to emphasize that Paul paid his own rent and was not dependent on contributions from others. The Gospel according to Luke began and ended in the temple; Acts begins and ends in a house.[71] Paul has a home in the imperial capital. "Yet there is a deep uneasiness within this 'at homeness.'"[72] Christianity can make a home in the empire, but its home is rented, not owned. The story of itinerant evangelists, including Jesus and his disciples, Peter, and Paul, is over. At the end of Acts, Paul is a "resident" evangelist. He has joined, so to speak, the world of Luke's time, when the Pauline heritage concentrated on the life of established communities and their local leaders.[73]

■ **31** The subject of Paul's proclamation, the dominion of God, is yet one more striking *inclusio* (Acts 1:3).[74] In the Gospel, Jesus was the proclaimer; in Acts he is the object of the proclamation. Although this mission went on for two years, neither Jews nor polytheists sought to take action against Paul or to throw a roadblock in the way of his mission. This is as the author wanted it, for the object is to portray the power of God,[75] encapsulated in Paul's freedom,[76] which has nothing to do with his legal status or the eventual disposition of his case.[77] Jerome offers an epigrammatically fitting summary: "*Paulus Romam vinctus ingreditur ut vinctos superstitionis erroribus liberos faciat; manet in hospitio conductu per biennium ut nobis utriusque instrumenti aeternum reddat donum.*"[78]

The final adverb is brilliant, worthy of a *bravo*, were commentators authorized to introduce such exclamations.[79] Within Acts, this stem evokes impediments to the advance of the mission beyond its Israelite origins (8:36; 10:47; cf. 11:17).[80] In the philosophical tradition

70 BDAG, 654, *s.v.* *μίσθωμα*. Extensive discussions include David L. Mealand, "The Close of Acts and Its Hellenistic Greek Vocabulary," *NTS* 36 (1990) 583–97, esp. 583–86; Tajra, *Martyrdom*, 47; and Rapske, *Roman Custody*, 77–78. The *Act. Paul* 11/14.1 says that Paul rented a barn: *ὅρριον μισθώσασθαι*. Cf. the American idiom of calling a leased vehicle or piece of equipment "a rental." The second clause of v. 30 supports a spatial understanding of the word. See also Spicq, *Lexicon*, 2:516–17. In the summary introducing his commentary, Ephrem states that Paul paid the rent by his own labor (#32, 384). In the prologue to his commentary on 2 Timothy, however, he stated that he obtained these funds by sale of his cloak and books (Ropes, *Text*, 453 n. 1; the inspiration for this idea comes from 2 Tim 4:13).

71 See John H. Elliott, "Temple versus Household in Luke-Acts: A Contrast in Social Institutions," in Neyrey, *Social World*, 211–40. Tertullian *Pud.* 7.11, "totus hic mundus una omnium domus est ("This entire world is one house for all people" [author's trans.]), reflects the Christian viewpoint, contrasted with the older commonplace that the world is a temple (see p. 435 n. 97).

72 See the perceptive comments of Robbins, "Social Location," 330.

73 This is the situation represented in the Pastorals. Philip was the first example of this transition (21:8). Cf. Marguerat, *Historian*, 229.

74 His teaching (*διδάσκων*) also echoes the first line of the preface (Acts 1:1).

75 See Witherington, 810.

76 The term *παρρησία* (v. 31) can mean "boldness," but here it has the legal sense of "freedom," one dimension also of the final word, *ἀκωλύτως* ("without any impediment"). On *παρρησία*, see Mealand, "Close," 597.

77 See Johnson, 476. Luke may have been inspired by Eph 6:19-20 (the close of that letter's body): "so that when I speak, a message may be given to me to make known with boldness (*ἐν παρρησίᾳ*) the mystery of the gospel, for which I am an ambassador in chains (*ἐν ἁλύσει*). Pray that I may declare it boldly (*παρρησιάσωμαι*), as I must speak." The only other use of "chain" in the singular with reference to Paul is Acts 28:20. See Robert A. Wild, "The Warrior and the Prisoner: Some Reflections on Ephesians 6:10-20," *CBQ* 46 (1984) 284–98, esp. 284–88.

78 Jerome *Ep.* 71 (to Licinius, CSEL 55:1–2): "Paul came to Rome in bonds so that he might free those locked in the bonds of superstitious error; he lived for two years in a rented place so he might offer us the eternal gift of the two Testaments" (author's trans.).

79 See Richard Pervo, "Die Entführung in das Serail: Aspasia: A Female Aesop?" in Jo-Ann A. Brant et al., eds., *Ancient Fiction: The Matrix of Early Christian and Jewish Narrative* (SBLSymS 32; Atlanta: Society of Biblical Literature, 2005) 61–88, esp. 85.

80 For citations illustrating its legal sense, see Gerhard Delling, "Das letze Wort der Apostelgeschichte," *NovT* 15 (1973) 193–204; and Mealand,

ἀκωλύτως ("without impediment") is related to virtue.[81] For the unphilosophical and the nontheological, it puts in one sharp word what the Pastor required seventeen (Greek) words to place in the mouth of Paul: "[T]hat is my gospel, for which I suffer hardship, even to the point of being chained like a criminal. But the word of God is not chained" (2 Tim 2:8-9).[82]

Excursus: The Ending of Acts

If the volume of comment is the measure of an author's impact, the close of Acts is a great success. Commentators since Chrysostom have been compelled to ask why Luke did not finish the story of Paul.[83] "But of his affairs after the two years, what say we? (The writer) leaves the hearer athirst for more: the heathen authors do the same (in their writings), for to know everything makes the reader dull and jaded" (Chrysostom *Hom.* 55).[84]

What will happen next? is a question that drives much narrative. From both the historical/biographical and the literary viewpoint, the close of Acts disappoints. Research has cleared away hypotheses proposing that the book was left incomplete, or that a third volume was planned, or that the author stopped at v. 31 because he was then writing (or had no further knowledge).[85] Luke knew of the death of Paul and of his "appearance before Caesar."[86] The ending of Acts no longer serves as an argument for an early date.[87]

No amount of sophisticated literary criticism and theological reflection—good and useful as most of it is—can persuade readers that something is not wrong. Paul's legal difficulties, prefaced by his Jesus-like journey to Jerusalem, are the sole explicit subject of the last third of Acts. The objection that Acts is not a biography of Paul, however much it has come to seem like one,[88] does not meet this point. On this explicit subject, the narrator has painted himself into a corner. Rather than relate the unhappy outcome of this legal struggle, he refuses to discuss it. This provides Acts with an ending that is happy and upbeat but also guilty of the historiographical sins of *suppressio veri* and *suggestio falsi* (suppression of the true and intimation of the false).[89] The close of Acts is "fictitious" in that it chooses to abandon its principal story line on a high note rather than follow it into failure and contradiction. The solution must therefore be literary.[90]

"Close," 594–97. Note also Strabo *Geogr.* 17.1; 25.18; Dio of Prusa *Or.* 5.8; and Josephus *Ant.* 12.104; 16.41, 166.

81 Plato *Crat.* 415D; Plutarch (*Tu. sen.* 27 [*Mor.* 137E]) says that health allows one to exercise virtue without inhibition. It characterizes the gods, according to Dio of Prusa *Or.* 36.22. This is also a characteristic of God in Wis 7:23. David Winston cites a number of parallels from Philo, Epictetus, and others (*The Wisdom of Solomon* [AB 43; Garden City, N.Y.: Doubleday, 1979] 181).

82 Cf. also Phil 1:12-14, which may have provided inspiration for v. 31.

83 The situation is well stated by Marguerat, *Historian*, 205. Two full-length studies are Hermann J. Hauser, *Strukturen der Abschlußerzählung der Apostelgeschichte (Apg 28,16-31* (AnBib 86; Rome: Pontifical Biblical Institute, 1979); and Charles B. Puskas Jr., "The Conclusion of Luke-Acts: An Investigation of the Literary Function and Theological Significance of Acts 28:16-31" (Diss. Saint Louis University, 1980). A revised form is scheduled for publication in 2008: *The Conclusion of Luke-Acts: The Function and Significance of Acts 28:16-31* (Eugene, Ore.: Wipf & Stock).

84 Trans. *PNF* 11:326. Arator provided an alternative ending. In place of 28:17-31 he summarizes the martyrdoms of Peter and Paul (2:1219–50).

85 For a crisp summary of research, see Hemer, *Book*, 383–87. Note also Trocmé, *Actes et l'histoire*, 34–35, 50–59; and Lindsey P. Pherigo, "Paul's Life after the Close of Acts," *JBL* 70 (1951) 277–84.

86 See the comments on 20:29 and 27:24.

87 Hemer (*Book*, 365–414) prefers a very early date but does not invoke the conclusion in support of his hypothesis. For a discussion of his argument, see Pervo, *Dating*, 334–40. See also William Brosend, "The Means of Absent Ends," in Witherington, *History*, 348–62, esp. 357–58, who also rejects date as an explanation.

88 Cadbury and Lake (349) say that the close is, for modern readers, "an inadequate literary technique for a biography of Paul—which is what Acts at this stage has become—to leave its hero's life incomplete." Hemer (*Book*, 383) makes a similar observation with more focus: "[T]he climax seems intimately built *around* Paul."

89 David Moessner ("'Completed End[s]ings' of Historiographical Narrative: Diodorus Siculus and the End[ing] of Acts," in Breytenbach, *Apostelgeschichte*, 193–221), argues that the close of Acts fulfills historiographical purpose. That thesis adds to the argument that the end of Acts is as planned and is not in conflict with the "historiographical sins" noted.

90 Aelian chose to end his story of Aspasia on a high note, although his sources knew better. See Pervo, "Entführung" (n. 79 above). See Dio's amusing *Or.*

In modern terms, this requires a discussion of closure and openness.[91] "They all lived happily ever after" is a fine ending, but it is not the only possibility, and one that is out of favor at present, in both its fictional and nonfictional manifestations. Not even that ending provides complete closure.[92] It generally signifies "you know the rest" or "What happened thereafter is not very interesting." Both of these significations can be attributed to the ending of Acts.[93] Some measure of openness cannot be denied to a work that ends with the adverb "unhindered," and it would be ridiculous to claim that an ending with so many references to its beginning and middle, as well as to the beginning and end of its predecessor, lacked any sense of closure. The result is that Acts has become a mirror, with exegetes proposing and defending closure of those matters they prefer to see closed and openness for what they hold ought to remain open.[94]

When Chrysostom spoke about "non-Christian" authors, it is likely that he had epic in mind, Homer in particular.[95] Future events were, however, discussed at earlier points in the respective narratives.[96] If this criterion were applied to Acts, readers would have been expected to conclude that Paul was found innocent and released, since only a technicality had required that he be sent to Rome. The biblical parallel most often invoked is the light confinement arranged for King Jehoiachin at the close of 2 Kings.[97] The contrast, however, is more important than the similarity, for this summary deals with the balance of the king's life, rather than two years. The close of 2 Chronicles is certainly upbeat,[98] but this amounts to an introduction to Ezra and may be a later gloss.[99] The close of 2 Maccabees reflects a choice to end on a high note.[100] These precedents may have provided Luke with some justification and inspiration.

Since 2 Maccabees is a sort of historical monograph, it deserves comparison with the close of Sallust's monograph on the Jugurthine war.[101] This is a kind of "open ending," pregnant with possibility. As a high note, it is more apparent than real, for Sallust found Marius a disappointment. In ten crisp Latin words, Sallust related the limited theme of his monograph, the Jugurthine war, to the broader issue

11 on Homer, which states that the poet wished to cover up (ἀφανίσαι) the death of Achilles in Troy (§104).

91 Tannehill (*Narrative Unity*, 2:353–56) discusses closure and lack of the same, with reference to M. Torgovnick, *Closure in the Novel* (Princeton: Princeton University Press, 1988). See also the essays in Deborah H. Roberts, Francis M. Dunn, and Don Fowler, eds., *Classical Closure: Reading the End in Greek and Latin Literature* (Princeton: Princeton University Press, 1997); and Doody, *True Story*, 527 n. 4. Marguerat makes use of several literary critical models in *Historian*, 205–30.

92 Brosend ("Means," 354) makes much of the close of romantic novels, which leave "no loose ends." This is a requirement of the type, yet note the close of Chariton *Chaer.* (Appendix 5.I). Chariton offers a prayer for "happily ever after," rather than an assertion thereof.

93 It is difficult to envision a reader who did not know that Paul was executed by the Roman government in Rome, as Chrysostom (above) can assume. Charles K. Barrett floats this possibility in "The End of Acts," in Peter Schäfer et al., eds., *Geschichte–Tradition–Reflexion: Festschrift für Martin Hengel zum 70. Geburtstag* (3 vols.; Tübingen: Mohr Siebeck, 1996) 3:545–55.

94 Thus Rapske ("Travel," 44) and Witherington (618–19) think that Luke implies a favorable conclusion to the trial, a view strongly opposed by Haenchen, 731–32.

95 For the endings of the *Iliad* and Virgil's *Aeneid,* see Appendix 5.IV.

96 Examples are the predictions of Tiresias about Ulysses' later journey (*Od.* 11.119–37) and Aeneas's forthcoming marriage (*Aen.* 12.808–40).

97 See Appendix 5.IIIa and P. Davies, "The Ending of Acts," *ExpT* 94 (1982–83) 334–35.

98 See Appendix 5.IIIb.

99 In the case of all ancient books copied in manuscript, endings are most likely to be subject to modification. The D-Text is a modest example of the phenomenon. For the present purposes, the form of the texts known to Luke or Chrysostom, for example, is more important than their original status.

100 See Appendix 5.IIIc. Foakes Jackson (236) says, "The end of Acts resembles that of 2 Maccabees, which closes with the great victory of Judas Maccabeus over Nicanor, leaving the hero at the moment of his triumph, so soon to be followed by his defeat." The decision to stop at that point evidently came from the abridger (presuming that this is an abridgment).

101 See Appendix 5.Va.

(the decline of the Roman Republic) of which it was the prelude. The foregoing endings indicate that the close of Acts is not unsuitable to the form of a monograph.[102]

In content and form it also has much in common with the closing words of Apuleius's *Metamorphoses*.[103] Lucius, too, had recently come to Rome after delivery from disaster by the patronage of his god, but it is the *feeling* of openness and exhilaration that most invite comparison. Warren S. Smith accepts this invitation in his contribution to a study of the Prologue of Apuleius:

> [A]t the end of Acts St Paul proclaims the word of God "with all boldness and unhindered," thus not only fulfilling the injunction of Jesus at the start of Acts, to preach to the ends of the earth, but acting as an example of Luke's own promise in *Luke* 1:1-4 to bear witness to Theophilus of the truth of the words handed down to him. And in the *Metamorphoses* as in Acts, the book's last phrases (*gaudens obibam*, "I went around rejoicing") leave us with a state of tranquility, an inner rather than outer description of a geographical place.[104]

Options of the sort that Luke definitely chose not to pursue can be seen in the *Life of Aesop* and in the *Acts of Paul*, which follow their respective heroes to the death.[105] Last of all comes the most proximate comparison: the Gospel of Mark. J. Lee Magness, who has done much to inform NT scholarship about the close of ancient books, has contributed a valuable monograph on the close of that work.[106] Two observations are in order. If the close of Acts owes something to Mark, it is of considerable interest that Luke rejected Mark's approach for the close of the Gospel but may have found it suitable for his second volume. That is a matter for the consideration of the unity/ies of Luke and Acts.

The second is another contrast. Mark does not withhold from the reader the fate of his character. The resurrection is announced. The effect of the ending to Acts is different from that to Mark. The author of Acts ended as he does not only because he did not wish to say more but also because he did not need to say more.[107] The most cogent intra-Lucan literary parallel is the story of the two sons ("The Prodigal Son" [Luke 15:11-32]). The older brother did not do as he ought to have done. This is not a true open ending, for that son is not going to change his mind, while any actions or words on his part would be utterly anticlimactic.

This commentary's contention that Luke has "finished" the stories of Peter and Paul by intimating for each a "passion" and "resurrection" gains support from Acts 28:30-31.[108] Peter went to "another place" (12:17), and Paul had a rented place. The place of each has been vindicated by God, and their vindication is also the victory of the message.[109] Nothing more need be said, and the future will always be open because it belongs to God.

102 The example from Josephus (Appendix 5.Vb) shows that authors might wish to provide individual rolls of a larger work with a conclusive end, in this case "and he died unhappily then and there."

103 See Appendix 5.IIb.

104 Warren S. Smith, "Apuleius and Luke: Prologue and Epilogue in Conversion Contexts," in Ahuvia Kahane and Andrew Laird, eds., *A Companion to the Prologue of Apuleius' Metamorphoses* (Oxford: Oxford University Press, 2002) 88–98, esp. 98. See also the comments on Acts 8:39, above.

105 Appendix 5.IIc and d. At the end of his poem, Arator abandons Acts and closes with the martyrdoms of Peter and Paul.

106 J. Lee Magness, *Sense and Absence: Structure and Suspension in the Ending of Mark's Gospel* (SBLSS; Atlanta: Scholars Press, 1986).

107 Brosend ("Means," 360–62) makes a spirited argument for viewing the close of Acts as provocative, encouraging the reader to return to the beginning of the story, in order to turn the focus from Paul to Jesus. This ignores the thrust of Luke and Acts, which do not move from Rome to Jerusalem, but the reverse. Marguerat (*Historian*, 205–30) proposes something similar, with more nuance, focusing on silence as a medium of ambivalence.

108 With regard to Paul, see G. W. Trompf, "On Why Luke Declined to Recount the Death of Paul: Acts 27–28 and Beyond," in Talbert, *Luke-Acts*, 225–39.

109 Readers knew that both Peter and Paul had been executed. Acts has no interest in the where and why of Peter's martyrdom. From the text, readers will probably infer that Paul had fallen victim to Jewish intrigue, which finally fulfilled its long-sought desire.

Appendixes

Appendix 1: The Conversion of Polemo

Lucian "The Double Indictment" 17[1]

This man Polemo, who, [Intemperance] says, is her servant, was not naturally bad or inclined to Intemperance, but had a nature like mine [i.e., a member of the Academy]. But while he was still young and impressionable she preempted him, with the assistance of Pleasure, who usually helps her, and corrupted the poor fellow, surrendering him unconditionally to dissipation and to prostitutes, so that he had not the slightest remnant of shame. . . . The poor fellow went about from early to late with garlands on his head, flushed with wine, attended by music right through the public square, never sober, making roisterous calls upon everybody, a disgrace to his ancestors and to the whole city and a laughing stock to strangers.

But when he came to my house, it chanced that, as usual, the doors were wide open and I was discoursing about virtue and temperance (*σωφροσύνη*) to such of my friends as were there. Coming in upon us with his flute and his garlands, first of all he began to shout and tried to break up our meeting by disturbing it with his noise. But we paid no attention to him, and as he was not entirely sodden with Intemperance, little by little (*κατ᾽ ὀλίγον*) he grew sober under the influence of our discourses, took off his garlands, silenced his flute-player, became ashamed of his purple mantle, and, awaking, as it were, from profound sleep (*ἐξ ὕπνου βαθέως ἀνεγρόμενος*), saw his own condition and condemned his past life (*τοῦ πάλαι βίου*). The flush that came from Intemperance faded and vanished, and he flushed for shame at what

Diogenes Laertius 4.3.16[2]

In his youth [Polemo] was so profligate and dissipated that he actually carried about with him money to procure the immediate gratification of his desires, and would even keep sums concealed in lanes and alleys. Even in the Academy a piece of three obols was found close to a pillar, where he had buried it for the same purpose.

And one day, by agreement with his young friends, he burst into the school of Xenocrates [head of the Academy] quite drunk, with a garland on his head. Xenocrates, however, without being at all disturbed, went on with his discourse as before, the subject being temperance (*σωφροσύνη*). The lad, as he listened, by degrees (*κατ᾽ ὀλίγον*) was taken in the toils.

1 Trans. A. M. Harmon, *Lucian III,* 117–19.
2 Trans. R. D. Hicks, *Diogenes Laertius I* (LCL; Cambridge, Mass.: Harvard University Press, 1925) 393.

he was doing. At length he abandoned her then and there, and took up with me, not because I either invited or constrained him . . . but voluntarily, because he believed the conditions here were better.

He became so industrious as to surpass all the other scholars, and rose to be himself head of the school . . .

Appendix 2: The "Sarapis Aretalogy" from Delos: The Foundation of a Cult

The Sarapis aretalogy from Delos of c. 200 BCE, celebrating victory in a lawsuit brought against Apollonios, is inscribed upon a free-standing column, an Egyptian practice. The inscription has two sections: a prose record attributed to the priest Apollonios (II), twenty-eight lines in length, and a parallel poetic offering in sixty-five lines by one otherwise unknown Maiistas. These two accounts give two somewhat different perspectives upon the same events.[3]

The priest Apollonios recorded (this) in accordance with the command of the god. For our grandfather, Apollonios, being an Egyptian, (one) of the priests, arrived from Egypt with [a statue of] the god and continued serving (him) as was traditional, and he is thought to have lived ninety-seven years. My father, Demetrios, having succeeded and likewise served the gods, was honored for his piety by the god with a bronze statue, which is set up in the temple of the god; and he lived sixty-one years. After I took over the rites and attended scrupulously to the services,[4] the god informed me in a dream that a Sarapeion of his own must be dedicated to him, and that it should not be in leased (quarters) as before, and that he would find the place himself where it was to be built, and that he would indicate the place. This happened. For this place was full of dung; it was listed for sale on a little notice on the path through the market place; and as the god wished, the sale took place and the temple was built quickly in six months. But some (τινες) conspired against us and the god and brought a public charge against the temple and myself about what penalty should be suffered or what fine paid, but the god promised me in a dream, "We shall win."[5] And the trial having been completed and we, having won in a manner worthy of the god, praise the gods, rendering proper thanks.

And Maiistas also wrote on behalf of the temple regarding this case: Manifold and awesome are your works, far-famed Sarapis, and also those of your consort [Isis]; some of them are hymned in the ramparts of divine Egypt, others throughout Hellas. As saviors you ever attend good persons whose minds always remain fixed upon holy things. Now also in sea-girt Delos

3 *SIG* 3 663, lines 1–29, trans. Stanley M. Burstein, *The Hellenistic Age from the Battle of Ipsos to the Death of Kleopatra VII* (translated Documents of Greece & Rome 3; Cambridge: Cambridge University Press, 1985) no. 102, pp. 130–31. For another version see M. M. Austin, *The Hellenistic World from Alexander to the Roman Conquest* (Cambridge: Cambridge University Press, 1981) no. 131, pp. 226–27. My translation of Maiistas's difficult accompanying poetic account (lines 29–94) has benefited from Roussel's French version and from that of Danker, *Benefactor*, no. 27, pp. 187–88. Bibliography includes: Pierre Roussel, *Les cultes égyptiens à Délos du IIIe au Ier siècle av. J.C.* (Nancy: Berger-Levrault, 1916); Andre-Jean Festugière, *Personal Religion among the Greeks* (Berkeley: University of California Press, 1954) 68–84; Philippe Bruneau, *Recherches sur les cultes de Délos à l'époque hellénistique et a l'époque imperiale* (Paris: Boccard, 1970); Engelmann, *Delian Aretalogy*; L. Michael White, *Building God's House in the Roman World: Architectural Adaptation among Pagans, Jews, and Christians* (Baltimore: Johns Hopkins University Press, 1990) 31–40.

4 The translation obscures one ambiguity and masks an important concept. The word τὰ ἱερά (line 12) could refer to sacred objects, including statues of the Egyptian gods, or to rites performed in their presence. The latter is selected as it is more inclusive and may be a metonym.

5 *Or:* "promised that we would win." Direct speech is more "aretalogical" and vivid. See Engelmann, *Delian Aretalogy*, 24, for a parallel.

you have made manifest the sacred images served by Apollonios and brought them great fame. Long ago Apollonios's grandfather brought the sacred objects from Memphis itself, when he came to the city of Phoebus on a many-benched ship. Reluctantly, he set you up in his own lodgings [40] and sought to please you with offerings of incense. When fate overtook him, aged man that he was, he left his son Demetrios, in whom the faithful continually rejoiced, to serve you as priest in your quarters. You heard his wish for a bronze statue [of himself] to be placed in your shrine and ably fulfilled it by appearing [45] at night to the one who was performing the ancestral service,[6] coming to him as he lay asleep in bed to urge that he fulfill this obligation. But when destiny forsook him as an old man, his son, well instructed by his father, continued to observe the sacred duties excellently. Day by day he sang of your wonders and continually prayed that you [50] would directly designate, in a nocturnal dream, where he should erect a shrine for you, so that you might remain secure and uninterrupted within your own enclosure, no longer compelled to flit from one door to another. You revealed that there was a place, previously undistinguished, [55] filled, in fact, with a long-accumulated pile of every kind of refuse. Drawing near to his bed at night you said, "Get up and go to the door in the middle of the stoa (leading to the agora). There you will see a notice written on a scrap of papyrus. This will inform you, when you grasp its meaning, of where you are to erect for me my precinct and distinguished shrine. [60] Marveling, he arose and went with haste, joyfully beheld the notice, and paid the sum requested for the plot of ground. Because you willed it, the shrine went up readily, and the altars for sacrifice, the precinct, and the hall, [65] with all its seats and couches for the meals to which the god summons guests, were completed. Then wicked Envy made wicked men mad as rabid dogs. These creatures filed suit against your minister on two counts, both insubstantial.[7] They resorted to a wicked ordinance prescribing both punishment and fine. Day and night the priest's heart [70] trembled with horrible fear, but he pleaded in tears for you to come and protect your suppliant from the shame of a fine and to deliver him from the evil fate of death. [75] You, ever mindful and attentive, did not neglect him. Appearing by his bed at night, you said, "Put misery out of your mind. Not a single vote will be cast against you, for this action is actually directed at me. No one will speak [80] more convincingly than I. You have no need for further worry." Now when the date of the trial arrived, the whole city, including all those of foreign origins, gathered at the shrine to hear the proceedings, which were, in fact, divinely directed. At that time you, together with your consort, [85] produced an astonishing sight for mortals. For, just as they were beginning to formulate their charges, you bound those wicked fellows, clamping their jaws and making them inaudible, so that no one discerned a word, no, not even a syllable of their accusation. They were frozen like those struck by god-sent lightning [90] or statues of stone. All the people marveled at your miraculous power on that day, and praise of your servant redounded throughout god-built Delos.

Hail, blessed and much-praised Sarapis, and you his consort, and the other gods who dwell in our shrine.

Appendix 3: Political Activity by a Guild

I. Eph. 215[8] c. 200 CE

[. . .] and in accordance with agreements [. . . so that] it happens from time to time that the people (τὸν δῆμον) are thrown into disorder and rioting (εἰς ταραχὴν καὶ θορύβους) by the reckless, [?misleading] rhetoric of the bakers' faction in the market place (ἀγορᾷ), *riots* (στάσεων) for which they ought already to have been arrested and brought to justice. But since the city's welfare must be given higher priority than punishing these men, I have thought it best to bring them to their

6 Lines 43–46 are quite difficult. The text must be emended. A number of proposals have been advanced. This version accords with the proposals of Engelmann, *Delian Aretalogy*, 32–36 (who follows R. Merkelbach). Engelmann presumes that the event in question is that of lines 9–11, the statue of Demetrios. This makes sense.

7 Insubstantial: literally "windy," implying both absence of substance and verbosity.

8 Trans. Levick, *Government*, 201–2 n. 194 (= F. F. Abbott and A. C. Johnson, *Municipal Administration in the Roman Empire* [Princeton: Princeton University Press, 1926], n. 124). On this inscription, see also W. H. Buckler, "Labour Disputes

senses with an edict. Consequently I order the bakers not to meet as an association (συνέρχεσθαι . . . κατ' ἑταιρίαν) and not to become the ringleaders in reckless behaviour. They are in every respect to obey those appointed to defend the interest of the community (πειθαρχεῖν δὲ πάντως τοῖς ὑπὲρ τοῦ κοινῇ συμφέροντος) and are to supply the city with a reliable baking service (ἐργασίαν). Whenever from now on one of them is caught attending a meeting contrary to the proclamation or initiating any riot or factional disturbance (θορύβου τινὸς καὶ στάσεως) he shall be arrested and punished with the appropriate penalty. If a person plotting against the city goes so far as to go into hiding he shall in addition be marked [?] by branding with the word '*decuria*' on the foot and the man who shelters such a person shall be subject to the same penalty.

In the presidency of Claudius Modestus on the 4th day from the commencement of the month Clareon, at an [?] extraordinary meeting of the council, Marcellinus said: "a prime instance of the lunacy of the shop foremen was given yesterday by Hermias, the man attached to [. . .]"

Appendix 4: Artemidorus *Oneirocritica* 2.23.[9]

Artemidorus is traditionally located in Ephesus during the mid to late second century.

Dreaming that one is at sea and, indeed, that one has a safe voyage is good for everyone. But encountering a tempest portends disturbances and dangers. A shipwreck in which the vessel is overturned [or destroyed][10] or shattered upon rocks portends harm for all but those who are being forcibly held by others and slaves. It indicates that they will be released from those who restrain them. For the ship symbolizes the men who surround them [. . .][11] but it is always better to sail in a large vessel that is carrying solid freight, since small boats, even on a good voyage, signify good things that involve some element of fear.

Furthermore, it is always better to sail and to sail safely on the sea than on land. For if a man dreams that he is sailing on land, it signifies that the good fulfillments will be slower in coming, more troublesome, and will barely occur at all. It is worse to hit a storm when one is sailing by sea than on land. If a man dreams that he wishes to sail but is unable to do so or is forcibly held back by others, it signifies obstacles and delays in his undertakings. Likewise, sailing on land with trees or rocks in one's way means delays and obstacles. But if a man dreams that from the land he sees ships that are sailing safely on the sea, it is auspicious for everyone and is symbolic of travel [. . .] it also signals the return of those who are abroad and it has often foretold the arrival of news from beyond the sea.

Ships weighing anchor signify that the good fulfillments will come true more slowly; for they are just beginning the voyage. But ships that are landing and putting in port signify that the good fulfillments will come true more quickly; for they have come to the end of the voyage. Harbors and all moorings always signify friends and benefactors. Promontories and inlets, however, indicate those who are loved by us not of our own free choice but out of necessity and who themselves do not willingly show us kindness. Anchors signify what is necessary and secure in business. But they are not auspicious for travel. For anchors are always set down to hold ships firm. Stern-cables and all kinds of rope mooring cables are symbols of loans, work contracts, agreements, and sequestrations of property.

The ship's mast signifies the master [of a ship or of a household]; the prow signifies the officer in command at the bow; the top of the ship's stern-post signifies the helmsman; the [rudders, the voyage itself or the children of the shipowner; the ship's keel, the ship's store;] ship's tackling signifies the sailors; and the sailyard, the boatswain. And so whatever corresponds to the part

in the Province of Asia," in W. H. Buckler and W. M. Calder, eds., *Anatolian Studies Presented to Sir William Mitchell Ramsay* (Manchester: Manchester University Press, 1923) 27–50, esp. 30–31; Magie, *Roman Rule*, 1:635; *NewDocs* 4 (1987) no. 1, pp. 9–10; Lampe, "Acta 19," 68–69; and Trebilco, "Asia," 339.

9 Trans. Robert White, *The Interpretation of Dreams: Oneirocritica by Artemidorus* (Park Ridge, N.J.: Noyes, 1975) 103–4.

10 Bracketed items indicate what the editor would delete.

11 [. . .] marks a lacuna.

of a ship riding at anchor that is destroyed will also be destroyed.

If, on the other hand, the ship is at sea, this signifies that the ship will be gripped by a violent storm and that the part in question will be in extraordinary danger. The spot where lightning strikes the ship determines where the storm will arise. I know of a shipowner who dreamt that he had lost the images of the gods that had been set up in the boat. He was overwhelmed by fear and he thought that the dream signified destruction. But the exact opposite occurred, since everything fell out to the good. He earned a great deal of money and paid off his debts to the usurers who held the ship on a mortgage. As a result, no one besides himself had a claim upon the boat.

It is always good luck to dream of the sea heaving with dumb swell and rising in waves for it foretells great success in business. But a calm sea signifies unemployment because of its lack of movement. A tempest means disturbances and losses, since it causes these very things.

Appendix 5: Endings

I. A Romantic Novel.

De Chaerea et Callirhoe 8.7.15–16.[12] "Thank you, Aphrodite!" Callirhoe said. "You have shown Chaereas to me once more in Syracuse, where I saw him as a maiden at your desire. I do not blame you, my lady, for what I have suffered; it was my fate. Do not separate me from Chaereas again, I beg of you; grant us a happy life together, and let us die together."

II. Other Types of Novels, and the Like

A. Apuleius of Madaura *Metamorphoses* 11.30.[13] Then, once more shaving my head completely, neither covering up nor hiding my baldness, but displaying it wherever I went, I joyfully carried out the duties of that ancient priesthood [the *pastophori*], founded in the days of Sulla.

B. *The Story of Apollonius King of Tyre* 51.[14] Apollonius lived for seventy-four years with his wife and ruled over Antioch and Tyre. He lived quietly and happily with his wife. Having completed the course of their lives in the number of years that I mentioned, they died peacefully in their untroubled old age.

C. *The Life of Aesop* 142.[15] Aesop cursed the people of Delphi, called upon Apollo, the head of the Muses, to bear witness that he was dying unjustly, and threw himself off the cliff. In this way he ended his life. But when the Delphians were afflicted with a plague, they consulted an oracle from Zeus, which stated that they should expiate the death of Aesop. And when the Greeks, Babylonians, and Samians heard of Aesop's execution, they avenged his death.

D. *The Acts of Paul* 11/14.[16] [3. Nero orders that Paul be beheaded.] 5. And turning toward the east, Paul lifted up his hands to heaven and prayed at length; and after having conversed in Hebrew with the fathers during prayer he bent his neck, without speaking any more. When the executioner cut off his head milk splashed on the tunic of the soldier. And the soldier and all who stood near by were astonished at this sight and glorified God who had thus honoured Paul . . . [6. Paul appears to Nero] 7. And, as Paul had told them, Longus and Cestus, the centurion, came in fear very early to the grave of Paul. And when they drew near they found two men in prayer and Paul with them, and they became frightened when they saw the unexpected miracle, but Titus and Luke, being afraid at the sight of Longus and Cestus turned to run away.

But they followed and said to them, "We follow you not in order to kill you, blessed men of God, as you imagine, but in order to live, that you may do to us as Paul promised us." [Titus and Luke then baptize Longus and Cestus, followed by a concluding doxology.]

III. Biblical Texts

A. 2 Kings 25:27-30 (cf. Jeremiah 52:31-34). In the thirty-seventh year of the exile of King Jehoiachin of Judah, in the twelfth month, on the twenty-seventh day of the month, King Evil-merodach of Babylon, in the

12 Trans. Brian P. Reardon, in idem, *Novels*, 124.
13 Trans. Hanson, *Apuleius II*, 359.
14 Trans. G. N. Sanday, in Reardon, *Novels*, 772.
15 Trans. Lawrence M. Wills, *The Quest of the Historical Gospel: Mark, John, and the Origins of the Gospel Genre* (London: Routledge, 1997) 215.
16 Trans. Elliott, *Apocryphal New Testament*, 387–88.

year that he began to reign, released King Jehoiachin of Judah from prison; [28] he spoke kindly to him, and gave him a seat above the other seats of the kings who were with him in Babylon. [29] So Jehoiachin put aside his prison clothes. Every day of his life he dined regularly in the king's presence. [30] For his allowance, a regular allowance was given him by the king, a portion every day, as long as he lived.

B. 2 Chronicles 36:23. "Thus says King Cyrus of Persia: The LORD, the God of heaven, has given me all the kingdoms of the earth, and he has charged me to build him a house at Jerusalem, which is in Judah. Whoever is among you of all his people, may the LORD his God be with him! Let him go up."

C. 2 Maccabees 15:37. This, then, is how matters turned out with Nicanor, and from that time the city has been in the possession of the Hebrews. So I will here end my story.

IV. Epic

A. Homer *Iliad* 24.801–4.[17] And once they'd heaped the mound they turned back home to Troy, and gathering once again they shared a splendid funeral feast in Hector's honor, held in the house of Priam, king by will of Zeus. And so the Trojans buried Hector breaker of horses.

B. Vergil *Aeneid* 12.950–52.[18] He sank his blade in fury in Turnus' chest. Then all the body slackened in death's chill, and with a groan for that indignity his spirit fled into the gloom below.

V. Greco-Roman Historiography

A. Monograph. Sallust *The War with Jugurtha* 114.3–4.[19] [The Gauls have defeated a Roman army.] But when it was announced that the war in Numidia was ended and that Jugurtha was being brought a captive to Rome, Marius was made consul in his absence and Gaul was assigned him as his province. On the Kalends of January he entered upon his office and celebrated a triumph of great magnificence. At that time the hopes and welfare of our country were in his hands.

B. Particular History. Josephus *Jewish War* 7.451–53. [Josephus closes this work with an account of the fate of the wicked governor of Libya, Catullus, who had attempted to implicate a number of Alexandrian and Roman Jews of high status in an anti-Roman conspiracy. Among those so maligned was one Josephus.] Catullus . . . was attacked by a complicated and incurable disease and came to a miserable end, not only chastised in body, but yet more deeply deranged in mind. For he was haunted by terrors and was continually crying out that he saw the ghosts of his murdered victims standing at his side; and, unable to restrain himself, he would leap from his bed as if torture and fire were being applied to him. His malady ever growing rapidly worse, his bowels ulcerated and fell out; and so he died, affording a demonstration no less striking than any, how God in his providence inflicts punishment on the wicked.[20]

17 Trans. Robert Fagles, *Homer: The Iliad* (New York: Penguin, 1991) 614.

18 Trans. Robert Fitzgerald, *The Aeneid of Virgil* (New York: Vintage, 1984) 402.

19 "*et ea tempestate spes atque opes civitatis in illo sitae*," trans. Rolfe, *Sallust*, 379–81.

20 Trans. Thackeray *Josephus II*, 631–33.

Commentaries

Ephrem Syrus
Cited from the Latin translation from the Armenian of F. C. Conybeare, in James Hardy Ropes, *The Text of Acts,* vol. 3 of Frederick J. Foakes Jackson and Kirsopp Lake, eds., *The Beginnings of Christianity* (5 vols.; New York: Macmillan, 1920–33; reprinted, Grand Rapids: Baker, 1979) 373–453.

Chrysostom, John
Homilies on the Acts of the Apostles, cited with references to the Greek text of Bernard De Montfaucon (Paris: Gaume, 1837) in the author's translation or to the version of J. Walker et al., *Saint Chrysostom: Homilies on the Acts of the Apostles and the Epistle to the Romans* (1889; NPF 11; reprinted, Grand Rapids: Eerdmans, 1979).

Arator
Historia Apostolica, ed. A. P. Orbán (CCSL 130, 130a; Turnholt: Brepols, 2006).

Bede
Expositio Actuum Apostolorum; Retractatio in Actus Apostolorum, ed. M. L. W. Laistner (CCSL 121; Turnholt: Brepols, 1983).

Isho'dad of Merv
The Commentaries of Isho'dad of Merv, Bishop of Hadatha (c. 850 A.D) in Syriac and English, vol. 4: *Acts of the Apostles and Three Catholic Epistles in Syriac and English* (ed. and trans. M. D. Gibson; Horae Semiticae 10; Cambridge: Cambridge University Press, 1913).

Calvin, Jean
The Acts of the Apostles (trans. J. W. Fraser and W. J. G. McDonald), vols. 6–7 of *Calvin's Commentaries* (Grand Rapids: Eerdmans, 1995).

Bengel, Johann A.
Gnomon Novi Testamenti (3rd ed.; London: Williams & Norgate, 1862) 388–489.

Overbeck, Franz
Kurze Erklärung der Apostlegeschichte (4th ed. of Wilhelm M. L. de Wette *Handbuch zum Neuen Testament,* vol. 1.4; Leipzig: Hirzel, 1870).

Zeller, Eduard
The Contents and Origin of the Acts of the Apostles, Critically Investigated (trans. J. Dare; 2 vols.; London: Williams & Norgate, 1875–76).

Schlatter, Adolf
Die Apostelgeschichte ausgelegt für Bibelleser (Erläuterungen zum Neuen Testament; Stuttgart: Calwer, 1902).

Rackham, Richard B.
The Acts of the Apostles (2nd ed.; London: Methuen, 1904).

Belser, Johannes E.
Die Apostelgeschichte (Vienna: Mayer, 1905).

Preuschen, Erwin
Die Apostelgeschichte (HNT; Tübingen: Mohr Siebeck, 1912).

Wendt, Hans H.
Die Apostelgeschichte (9th ed.; KEK; Göttingen: Vandenhoeck & Ruprecht, 1913).

Loisy, Alfred
Les Actes des apôtres (Paris: Nourry, 1920).

Zahn, Theodor
Die Apostelgeschichte (Kommentar zum Neuen Testament; 2 vols.; Leipzig: Deichert, 1921).

Jacquier, Eugène
Les Actes des apôtres (2nd ed.; EB; Paris: Gabalda, 1926).

Foakes Jackson, Frederick J.
The Acts of the Apostles (New York: Harper, 1931).

Beyer, Hermann W.
Die Apostelgeschichte (NTD 5; Göttingen: Vandenhoeck & Ruprecht, 1933; 4th ed., 1947).

Steinmann, Alphons
Die Apostelgeschichte (4th ed.; Bonn: Hanstein, 1934).

Knox, Wilfred L.
The Acts of the Apostles (Cambridge: Cambridge University Press, 1948).

Wikenhauser, Alfred
Die Apostelgeschichte (3rd ed.; RNT; Regensburg: Pustet, 1956).

Williams, Charles S. C.
The Acts of the Apostles (HNTC; New York: Harper, 1957).

Stählin, Gustav
Die Apostelgeschichte (NTD 5; Göttingen: Vandenhoeck & Ruprecht, 1962; 1965).

Dupont, Jacques
Les Actes des Apôtres (3rd ed.; SBJ; Paris: Cerf, 1964).

Williams, Ronald Ralph
Acts of the Apostles (Torch Commentaries; London: SCM, 1965).

Packer, J. W.
The Acts of the Apostles (Cambridge Bible Commentary; Cambridge: University Press, 1966).

Munck, Johannes
The Acts of the Apostles: Introduction, Translation, and Notes (AB 31; Garden City, N.Y.: Doubleday, 1967).

Haenchen, Ernst
The Acts of the Apostles (trans. and ed. B. Noble et al.; Philadelphia: Westminster, 1971), ET of *Die Apostleschichte* (14th ed.; KEK; Göttingen: Vandenhoeck & Ruprecht, 1965).

Ghidelli, Carlo
Atti degli Apostli (Sacra Bibbia; Torino: Marietti, 1978).

Bauernfeind, Otto
Kommentar und Studien zur Apostelgeschichte (Tübingen: Mohr Siebeck, 1980).
Marshall, I. Howard
The Acts of the Apostles: An Introduction and Commentary (Tyndale Commentary; Grand Rapids: Eerdmans, 1980).
Schneider, Gerhard
Die Apostelgeschichte (HThK 5; 2 vols.; Freiburg: Herder & Herder, 1980–82).
Weiser, Alfons
Die Apostelgeschichte (2 vols.; ÖKTNT 5.1/2; Gütersloh: Mohn, 1981, 1985).
Krodel, Gerhard
Acts (ACNT; Philadelphia: Fortress Press, 1981; Minneapolis: Augsburg, 1986).
Roloff, Jürgen
Die Apostelgeschichte (NTD 5; Göttingen: Vandenhoeck & Ruprecht, 1981).
Longenecker, Richard N.
"The Acts of the Apostles," in F. E. Gaebelein, ed., *The Expositor's Bible Commentary* (12 vols.; Grand Rapids: Zondervan, 1981) 9:207–573.
Schmithals, Walter
Die Apostelgeschichte des Lukas (Zürcher Bibelkommentar; Zurich: Theologischer Verlag, 1982).
Schille, Gottfried
Die Apostelgeschichte des Lukas (ThHKNT; Berlin: Evangelische Verlagsanstalt, 1983).
Fabris, Rinaldo
Atti degli Apostoli (2nd ed.; Rome: Borla, 1984).
Pesch, Rudolph
Die Apostelgeschichte (EKK; 2 vols.; Zurich: Benziger, 1986).
Conzelmann, Hans
Acts of the Apostles: A Commentary on the Acts of the Apostles (trans. James Limburg, A. Thomas Kraabel, and Donald H. Juel; ed. Eldon Jay Epp with Christopher R. Matthews; Hermeneia. Philadelphia: Fortress Press, 1987).
Gourges, Michel
Mission et communauté (Actes des apôtres 1–12) (Cahiers Evangile 60; Paris: Cerf, 1987).
Idem
L'Evangile aux païens (Actes des apôtres 13–28) (Cahiers Evangile 67; Paris: Cerf, 1989).
Arrington, French L.
The Acts of the Apostles: An Introduction and Commentary (Peabody, Mass.: Hendrickson, 1988).
Bruce, Frederick F.
The Book of Acts (NICNT; rev. ed.; Grand Rapids: Eerdmans, 1988; 3rd ed., 1990).
Mussner, Franz
Apostelgeschichte (2nd ed.; Die neue Echter-Bibel NT 5; Würzburg: Echter, 1988).
Boismard, Marie-Émile, and Arnaud Lamouille
Les Actes des deux Apôtres (3 vols.; EB 13; Paris: Gabalda, 1990).
Johnson, Luke T.
The Acts of the Apostles (SacPag; Collegeville, Minn.: Liturgical Press, 1992).
Polhill, John B.
Acts (NAC 26; Nashville: Broadman, 1992).
Barrett, Charles Kingsley
A Critical and Exegetical Commentary on the Acts of the Apostles (ICC; 2 vols.; Edinburgh: T&T Clark, 1994, 1998).
Taylor, Justin
Les Actes des deux Apôtres: Commentaire historique IV–VI (EB 23, 30, 41; Paris: Gabalda, 1994–2000).
Zmijewski, Josef
Die Apostelgeschichte (RNT; Regensburg: Pustett, 1994).
Bossuyt, P., and J. Radermakers
Témoins de la parole de la grâce: Lecture des Actes des Apôtres (2 vols.; Collection de l'Institut d'Études Théologiques 16; Brussels: Collection de l'Institut d'Études Théologiques, 1995).
Kistemaker, Simon J.
Exposition of the Acts of the Apostles (3rd ed.; NTC; Grand Rapids: Baker, 1995).
Dunn, James D. G.
The Acts of the Apostles (Epworth Commentaries; Peterborough: Epworth, 1996).
Bock, Darrell L.
Acts (BECNT; Grand Rapids: Baker, 1997).
Talbert, Charles H.
Reading Acts: A Literary and Theological Commentary on the Acts of the Apostles (Reading the New Testament; New York: Crossroad, 1997).
Fitzmyer, Joseph A.
The Acts of the Apostles: A New Translation with Introduction and Commentary (AB 31; New York: Doubleday, 1998).
Jervell, Jacob
Die Apostelgeschichte (KEK 17; Göttingen: Vandenhoeck & Ruprecht, 1998).
Walaskay, Paul W.
Acts (Westminster Bible Companion; Louisville: Westminster John Knox, 1998).
Witherington, Ben, III
The Acts of the Apostles: A Socio-Rhetorical Commentary (Grand Rapids: Eerdmans; Carlisle: Paternoster, 1998).
Eckey, Wilfried
Die Apostelgeschichte: Der Weg des Evangeliums von Jerusalem nach Rom (2 vols.; Neukirchen-Vluyn: Neukirchener Verlag, 2000).
Barbi, Augusto
Atti degli Apostoli (Capitoli 1–14) (Padua: Messaggero, 2003).
Gaventa, Beverly Roberts
The Acts of the Apostles (ANTC; Nashville: Abingdon, 2003).
Marguerat, Daniel
Les Actes des Apôtres (1–12) (Commentaire du Nouveau Testament 5a; Geneva: Labor et Fides, 2007).

Studies

Abrahamsen, Valerie, A.
"Women at Philippi: The Pagan and Christian Evidence," *JFSR* 3 (1987) 17–30.

Achtemeier, Paul J.
1 Peter: A Commentary on First Peter (Hermeneia: Minneapolis: Fortress Press, 1996).

Idem
"Jesus and the Disciples as Miracle Workers in the Apocryphal New Testament," in Elisabeth Schüssler Fiorenza, ed., *Aspects of Religious Propaganda in Judaism and Early Christianity* (Notre Dame, Ind.: University of Notre Dame Press, 1976) 149–86.

Idem
"The Origin and Function of the Pre-Marcan Miracle Catenae," *JBL* 91 (1972) 198–221.

Idem
The Quest for Unity in the New Testament Church (Philadelphia: Fortress Press, 1987).

Idem
"Toward the Isolation of Pre-Markan Miracle Catenae," *JBL* 89 (1970) 265–91.

Acworth, Angus
"Where Was St. Paul Shipwrecked? A Re-examination of the Evidence," *JTS* 24 (1973) 190–93.

Adams, Marilyn McCord
"The Role of Miracles in the Structure of Luke-Acts," in Eleanore Stump and Thomas P. Flint, eds., *Hermes and Athena: Biblical Exegesis and Philosophical Theology* (Notre Dame, Ind.: University of Notre Dame Press, 1993) 235–65.

Aejmelaeus, Lars
Die Rezeption der Paulusbriefe in der Miletrede (Apg 20:18-35) (Helsinki: Suomalainen Tiedeakatemia, 1987).

Africa, Thomas
"Worms and the Death of Kings: A Cautionary Note on Disease and History," *Classical Antiquity* 1 (1982) 1–17.

Agrell, Goran
Work, Toil and Sustenance: An Examination of the View of Work in the New Testament (Lund: Verbum Hakan Ohlssons, 1976).

Aland, Barbara
"Entstehung, Charakter und Herkunft des sog. westlichen Textes untersucht an der Apostelgeschicthe," *EThL* 62 (1986) 5–65.

Aland, Kurt, ed.
Text und Textwert der griechischen Handschriften des Neuen Testaments, vol. 3: *Die Apostelgeschichte* (2 vols.; Berlin: de Gruyter, 1993).

Idem
"The Twentieth Century Interlude in New Testament Textual Criticism," in Ernest Best and Robert McL. Wilson, eds., *Text and Interpretation. Studies in the New Testament Presented to Matthew Black* (Cambridge: Cambridge University Press, 1979).

Aletti, Jean Noël
Quand Luc raconte: Le récit comme théologie (Lire la Bible 115; Paris: Cerf, 1998).

Alexander, Loveday C. A.
"Acts and Ancient Intellectual Biography," in Bruce W. Winter and Andrew D. Clarke, *The Book of Acts in Its Ancient Literary Setting* (BIFCS 1; Grand Rapids: Eerdmans, 1993) 31–63.

Eadem
Acts in Its Ancient Literary Context: A Classicist Looks at the Acts of the Apostles (LNTS 298; London: T&T Clark, 2005).

Eadem
"Formal Elements and Genre: Which Greco-Roman Prologues Most Closely Parallel the Lukan Prologues?" in David P. Moessner, ed., *Jesus and the Heritage of Israel: Luke's Narrative Claim upon Israel's Legacy* (Harrisburg, Pa.: Trinity Press International, 1999) 9–26.

Eadem
"Marathon or Jericho? Reading Acts in Dialogue with Biblical and Greek Historiography," in D. G. A. Clines and S. D. Moore, eds., *Auguries* (JSNTS 269; Sheffield: Sheffield Academic Press, 1998).

Eadem
"The Preface to Acts and the Historians," in Ben Witherington III, *History, Literature and Society in the Book of Acts* (Cambridge: Cambridge University Press, 1996) 73–103.

Eadem
The Preface to Luke's Gospel: Literary Convention and Social Context in Luke 1.1-4 and Acts 1.1 (SNTSMS 78; Cambridge: Cambridge University Press, 1993).

Idem
"What If Luke Had Never Met Theophilus?" *BibInt* 8 (2000) 161–70.

Allen, O. Wesley, Jr.
The Death of Herod: The Narrative and Theological Functions of Retribution in Luke-Acts (SBLDS 158; Atlanta: Scholars Press, 1997).

Andersen, T. C.
"The Meaning of *ΕΧΟΝΤΕΣ ΧΑΡΙΝ ΠΡΟΣ* in Acts 2.47," *NTS* 34 (1988) 604–10.

Anderson, Janice Capel
"Reading Tabitha: A Feminist Reception History," in Amy-Jill Levine, *A Feminist Companion to the Acts of the Apostles* (Cleveland: Pilgrim, 2004) 22–48.

Applebaum, Samuel
"The Legal Status of the Jewish Communities in the Diaspora," in Samuel Safrai et al., eds., *The Jewish People in the First Century: Historical Geography, Political History, Social, Cultural and Religious Life and Institutions* (CRINT 1.1; Assen: Van Gorcum, 1974) 420–63.

Idem
"The Organization of the Jewish Communities in the Diaspora," in Samuel Safrai et al., eds., *The Jewish People in the First Century: Historical Geography, Political History, Social, Cultural and Religious Life and Institutions* (CRINT 1.1; Assen: Van Gorcum, 1974) 464–503.

Arlandson, James M.
"Lifestyles of the Rich and Christian: Women, Wealth, and Social Freedom," in Amy-Jill Levine, *A Feminist Companion to the Acts of the Apostles* (Cleveland: Pilgrim, 2004) 155–70.

Idem
Women, Class, and Society in Early Christianity: Models from Luke-Acts (Peabody, Mass.: Hendrickson, 1996).

Arnold, Clinton E.
Ephesians: Power and Magic; The Concept of Power in Ephesians in Light of Its Historical Setting (Grand Rapids: Baker, 1992).

Arterbury, Andrew E.
"The Ancient Custom of Hospitality, the Greek Novels, and Acts 10:1—11:18," *PerspRelStud* 29 (2002) 53–72.

Artés Hernández, José Antonio
"Lc 19, 1-10—Hch 20, 7-12—*Passio Pauli* I (104.8–106.15): Análisis comparativo," *FilolNT* 16 (2003) 49–67.

Ascough, Richard S.
"Narrative Technique and Generic Designation: Crowd Scenes in Luke-Acts and in Chariton," *CBQ* 58 (1996) 69–82.

Attridge, Harold W.
The Epistle to the Hebrews (Hermeneia; Philadelphia: Fortress Press, 1989).

Idem
"Josephus and His Works," in Michael E. Stone, ed., *Jewish Writings of the Second Temple Period* (CRINT 2.2; Philadelphia: Fortress Press, 1984) 185–232.

Idem
The Interpretation of Biblical History in the Antiquitates Judaicae of Flavius Josephus (HDR 7; Missoula, Mont.: Scholars Press, 1976).

Auerbach, Erich
Mimesis: The Representation of Reality in Western Literature (trans. Wilfred R. Trask; Garden City, N.Y.: Doubleday, 1957).

Auffret, Pierre
"Essai sur la structure littéraire du discours d'Athènes (Ac XVII 23-31)," *NovT* 20 (1978) 185–202.

Aune, David E.
"Luke 1.1-4: Historical or Scientific *Prooimion*?" in Alf Christophersen et al., eds., *Paul, Luke, and the Graeco-Roman World: Essays in Honour of Alexander J. M. Wedderburn* (JSNTS 217; London: Sheffield Academic Press, 2002) 138–48.

Idem
"Magic in Early Christianity," *ANRW* 2.23.2 (1980) 1507–57.

Idem
The New Testament in Its Literary Environment (LEC 8; Philadelphia: Westminster, 1987).

Idem
Prophecy in Early Christianity (Grand Rapids: Eerdmans, 1983).

Idem
"Septem Sapientium Convivium (Moralia 146B–164D)," in Hans Dieter Betz, ed., *Plutarch's Ethical Writings and Early Christian Literature* (SCHNT 4; Leiden: Brill, 1978) 51–105.

Avemarie, Friedrich
Die Tauferzählungen der Apostelgeschichte: Theologie und Geschichte (WUNT 139; Tübingen: Mohr Siebeck, 2002).

Babbitt, Frank C.
Plutarch, Moralia V (LCL; Cambridge, Mass.: Harvard University Press, 1938).

Balance, M. H.
"The Site of Derbe: A New Inscription," *Anatolian Studies* 7 (1957) 147–51.

Balch, David L.
"Acts as Hellenistic Historiography," *SBLSP 1985* (Atlanta: Scholars Press, 1985) 429–32.

Idem
"ἀκριβῶς . . . γράψαι (Luke 1:3): To Write the *Full* History of God's Receiving All Nations," in David P. Moessner, ed., *Jesus and the Heritage of Israel: Luke's Narrative Claim upon Israel's Legacy* (Harrisburg, Pa.: Trinity Press International, 1999) 229–50.

Idem
"The Areopagus Speech: An Appeal to the Stoic Historian Posidonius against Later Stoics and the Epicureans," in idem et al., eds., *Greeks, Romans, and Christians: Essays in Honor of Abraham J. Malherbe* (Minneapolis: Fortress Press, 1990) 52–79.

Idem
"Comments on the Genre and a Political Theme of Luke-Acts," *SBLSP 1989* (Atlanta: Scholars Press, 1989) 343–61.

Idem
"The Genre of Luke-Acts: Individual Biography, Adventure Novel, or Political History?" *Southwestern Journal of Theology* 33 (1991) 5–19.

Idem
Let Wives Be Submissive: The Domestic Code in 1 Peter (SBLMS 26; Chico, Calif.: Scholars Press, 1981).

Idem
"*ΜΕΤΑΒΟΛΗ ΠΟΛΙΤΕΙΩΝ*: Jesus as founder of the Church in Luke-Acts: Form and Function," in Todd Penner and Caroline Vander Stichele, *Contextualizing Acts: Lukan Narrative and Greco-Roman Discourse* (SBLSS 20; Boston/Leiden: Brill; Atlanta: Society of Biblical Literature, 2004) 139–88.

Idem
"Rich and Poor, Proud and Humble in Luke-Acts," in L. Michael White and O. L. Yarbrough, eds., *The Social World of the First Christians: Essays in Honor of Wayne Meeks* (Minneapolis: Fortress Press, 1995) 214–33.

Balsdon, J. P. V. D.
Romans and Aliens (Chapel Hill: University of North Carolina Press, 1979).

Balz, Horst
"τέσσαρες," *TDNT* 8:127–39.

Barclay, John M. G.
Jews in the Mediterranean Diaspora from Alexander to Trajan (323 BCE–117 CE) (Berkeley: University of California Press, 1996).

Barnes, Timothy D.
"An Apostle on Trial," *JTS* 20 (1969) 407–19.

Idem
"Legislation against the Christians," *JRS* 58 (1968) 32–50.

Barr, David L., and Judith L. Wentling
"The Conventions of Classical Biography and the Genre of Luke-Acts," in Charles H. Talbert, ed., *Luke-Acts* (New York: Crossroad, 1984) 63–88.

Barrett, Charles Kingsley
"Acts and Christian Consensus," in Peter Wilhelm Bøckman and Ronald E. Kristiansen, eds., *Context: Festskrift til Peder Johan Borgen/Essays in Honour of Peder Johan Borgen* (Trondheim: Tapir, 1987) 19–33.

Idem
"Apollos and the Twelve Disciples of Ephesus," in W. C. Weinrich, ed., *The New Testament Age: Essays in Honor of Bo Reicke* (2 vols.; Macon, Ga.: Mercer University Press, 1984) 29–39.

Idem
"Christocentricity at Antioch," in Christoph Landmesser et al., eds., *Jesus Christus als die Mitte der Schrift: Studien zur Hermeneutik des Evangeliums* (Berlin: de Gruyter, 1997) 323–40.

Idem
"The End of Acts," in Hubert Cancik, Hermann Lichtenberger, and Peter Schäfer, eds., *Geschichte–Tradition–Reflexion: Festschrift für Martin Hengel zum 70. Geburtstag* (3 vols.; Tübingen: Mohr Siebeck, 1996) 3:545–55.

Idem
"The First New Testament?" *NovT* 38 (1996) 94–104.

Idem
"Is There a Theological Tendency in Codex Bezae?" in Ernest Best and Robert McL. Wilson, eds., *Text and Interpretation: Studies in the New Testament Presented to Matthew Black* (Cambridge: Cambridge University Press, 1979) 15–27.

Idem
"Light on the Holy Spirit from Simon Magus (Acts 8, 4-25), in Jacob Kremer, ed., *Les Actes des Apôtres: Traditions, rédaction, théologie* (BEThL 48; Leuven: Leuven University Press, 1979) 281–95.

Idem
"Luke and Acts," in J. Barclay and J. Sweet, eds., *Early Christian Thought in Its Jewish Context* (Festschrift Morna Hooker; New York: Cambridge University Press, 1996) 84–94.

Idem
Luke the Historian in Recent Study (Philadelphia: Fortress Press, 1970).

Idem
"Paul's Address to the Ephesian Elders," in Jacob Jervell and Wayne A. Meeks, eds., *God's Christ and His People: Studies in Honour of Nils Alstrup Dahl* (Oslo: Universitetsforlaget, 1977) 107–21.

Idem
"Paul Shipwrecked," in Barry Thompson, ed., *Scripture: Meaning and Method. Essays Presented to Anthony Tyrrell Hanson* (Hull, U.K.: Hull University Press, 1987) 51–64.

Idem
"Paul's Speech on the Areopagus," in M. Glasswell and Edward Fasholé-Luke, eds., *New Testament Christianity for Africa and the World: Essays in Honour of Harry Sawyer* (London: SPCK, 1974).

Idem
"Theologia Crucis–In Acts?" in Carl Andresen and Günther Klein, eds., *Theologia Crucis–Signum Crucis: Festschrift für Erich Dinkler zum 70. Geburtstag* (Tübingen: Mohr Siebeck, 1979) 73–84.

Idem
"The Third Gospel as a Preface to Acts? Some Reflections," in F. Van Segbroek et al., eds, *The Four Gospels 1992: Festschrift Frans Neirynck* (3 vols.; BEThL 100; Leuven: Peeters, 1992) 2:1451–66.

Barsby, John
Terence II (LCL; Cambridge, Mass.: Harvard University Press, 2001).

Bartchy, S. Scott
"*Agnōstos Theos*: Luke's Message to the 'Nations' about Israel's God." *SBLSP 1995* (Atlanta: Scholars Press, 1995) 304–20.

Idem
"Community of Goods in Acts: Idealization or Social Reality?" in Birger Pearson, ed., *The Future of Early Christianity: Essays in Honor of Helmut Koester* (Minneapolis: Fortress Press, 1991) 309–18.

Barton, Tamsyn
Ancient Astrology (London: Routledge, 1994).

Bassler, Jouette M.
Divine Impartiality: Paul and a Theological Axiom (SBLDS 59; Chico, Calif.: Scholars Press, 1979).

Eadem
"Luke and Paul on Impartiality," *Bib* 66 (1985) 546–52.

Bauckham, Richard
"The Acts of Paul as a Sequel to Acts," in Bruce W. Winter and Andrew D. Clarke, *The Book of Acts in Its Ancient Literary Setting* (BIFCS 1; Grand Rapids: Eerdmans, 1993) 105–52.

Idem, ed.
The Book of Acts in Its Palestinian Setting (BIFCS 4; Grand Rapids: Eerdmans, 1995).

Idem
"James and the Gentiles (Acts 15.13-21)," in Ben Witherington III, *History, Literature and Society in the Book of Acts* (Cambridge: Cambridge University Press, 1996) 154–84.

Idem
"Kerygmatic Summaries in the Speeches of Acts," in Ben Witherington III, *History, Literature and Society in the Book of Acts* (Cambridge: Cambridge University Press, 1996) 185–217.

Baugh, Steven M.
"Paul and Ephesus: The Apostle among His Contemporaries" (Diss., University of California, Irvine, 1990).

Bauer, Walter
Orthodoxy and Heresy in Earliest Christianity (trans. and ed. Robert Kraft and Gerhard Krodel; Philadelphia: Fortress Press, 1971).

Idem
"The Picture of the Apostle in Early Christian Tradition: 1. Accounts," in Edgar Hennecke, *New Testament Apocrypha* (ed. Wilhelm Schneemelcher; ET ed. Robert McL. Wilson; 2 vols; Philadelphia: Westminster, 1965) 2:35–74.

Idem and Henning Paulsen
Die Briefe des Ignatius von Antiochia und der Polykarpbrief (HNT 18; Tübingen: Mohr Siebeck, 1985).

Bauernfeind, Otto
"μάχομαι," *TDNT* 4:527–28.

Idem
"Tradition und Komposition in dem Apokatastasisspruch Apostelgeschichte 3,20f," in Otto Betz, Martin Hengel and Peter Schmidt, eds., *Abraham unser Vater: Juden und Christen im Gespräch über die Bibel; Festschrift für Otto Michel zum 60. Geburtstag* (Leiden: Brill, 1963) 13–23.

Idem
"τρέχω," *TDNT* 8:226–35.

Baumgärtel, Friedrich, and Johannes Behm
"καρδία," *TDNT* 3:605–13.

Baumgarten, A. I.
"The Name of the Pharisees," *JBL* 102 (1983) 411–28.

Bayer, Hans. F.
"The Preaching of Peter in Acts," in I. H. Marshall and David Peterson, eds., *Witness to the Gospel: The Theology of Acts* (Grand Rapids: Eerdmans, 1998) 257–74.

Beatrice, Pier Franco
"Apollos of Alexandria and the Origins of the Jewish-Christian Baptist Encratism," *ANRW* 2.26.2 (1995) 1232–75.

Béchard, Dean P.
"The Disputed Case against Paul: A Redaction-Critical Analysis of Acts 21:27–22:29," *CBQ* 65 (2003) 232–50.

Idem
"Paul among the Rustics: The Lystran Episode (Acts 14:8-20) and Lucan Apologetic," *CBQ* 63 (2001) 84–101.

Idem
Paul outside the Walls: A Study of Luke's Socio-Geographical Universalism in Acts 14:8-20 (AnBib 143; Rome: Pontifical Biblical Institute, 2000).

Becker, Jürgen
Paul: Apostle to the Gentiles (trans. O. C. Dean, Jr.; Louisville: Westminster John Knox, 1993).

Behm, Johannes
"αἷμα," *TDNT* 1:172–77.

Idem
"ἀποφθέγγομαι," *TDNT* 1:447.

Idem
"γλῶσσα," *TDNT* 1:719–27.

Idem
"θύω," *TDNT* 3:180–90.

Idem, and Werner Foerster
"κλῆρος," *TDNT* 3:758–85.

Beker, Jan Christiaan
Heirs of Paul: Paul's Legacy in the New Testament and in the Church Today (Minneapolis: Fortress Press, 1991).

Bendemann, Reinhard von
"'Many-Coloured Illnesses' (Mark 1:34): On the Significance of Illnesses in New Testament Therapy Narratives," in Michael Labahn and Bert L. Peerbolte, eds., *Wonders Never Cease: The Purpose of Narrating Miracle Stories in the New Testament and Its Religious Environment* (LNTS 288; London: T&T Clark, 2006) 100–124.

Benoit, André
Le baptême chrétien au second siècle (Paris: Presses universitaires de France, 1953).

Benoit, Pierre
"La deuxième visite de Saint Paul à Jérusalem," *Bib* 40 (1959) 778–92.

Idem
"La mort de Judas," in *Synoptische Studien: Alfred Wikenhauser zum siebzigsten Geburtstag am 22. Februar 1953, dargebracht von Freunden, Kollegen und Schülern* (Münster: Aschendorff, 1954) 1–19.

Berger, Klaus
Formgeschichte des Neuen Testaments (Heidelberg: Quelle & Meyer, 1984).

Idem
"Propaganda und Gegenpropaganda im frühen Christentum: Simon Magus als Gestalt des Samaritanischen Cristentums," in Lukas Bormann et al., eds., *Religious Propaganda and Missionary Competition in the New Testament World: Essays Honoring Dieter Georgi* (NovTSup 74; Leiden: Brill, 1994) 313–17.

Berger, Peter L., and Thomas Luckmann
The Social Construction of Reality (Garden City, N.Y.: Doubleday, 1967).

Bergholz, Thomas
Der Aufbau des lukanischen Doppelwerkes: Untersuchungen zum formalliterarischen Charakter von Lukas-Evangelium und Apostelgeschichte (Europäische Hochschulschriften; Reihe 23 Theologie 545; Frankfurt: Lang, 1995).

Bertram, Georg
"ὁρμή," *TDNT* 5:467–74.
"ὠδίν," *TDNT* 9:667–74.

Best, Ernest
"Recipients and Title of the Letter to the Ephesians: Why and When the Designation 'Ephesians'?" *ANRW* 2.25.4 (1987) 3247–79.

Idem, and Robert McL. Wilson, eds.
Text and Interpretation. Studies in the New Testament Presented to Matthew Black (Cambridge: Cambridge University Press, 1979).

Betori, G.
"La strutturazione del libro degli Atti: un proposta," *RivB* 42 (1994) 3–34.

Betz, Hans Dieter
Der Apostel Paulus und die sokratische Tradition (BHT 45; Tübingen: Mohr Siebeck, 1972).

Idem
Galatians: A Commentary on Paul's Letter to the Churches in Galatia (Hermeneia; Philadelphia: Fortress Press, 1979).

Idem
The Greek Magical Papyri in Translation, vol. 1: *Texts* (Chicago: University of Chicago Press, 1986).

Idem
Lukian von Samosata und das Neue Testament (TU 76; Berlin: Akademie, 1961).

Idem
"The Origin and Nature of Christian Faith according to the Emmaus Legend (Luke 24:13-32)," *Int* 23 (1969) 32–46.

Idem, ed.
Plutarch's Ethical Writings and Early Christian Literature (SCHNT 4; Leiden: Brill, 1978).

Idem
2 Corinthians 8 and 9: A Commentary on Two Administrative Letters of the Apostle Paul (ed. George W. MacRae; Hermeneia; Philadelphia: Fortress Press, 1985).

Betz, Otto
"σικάριος," *TDNT* 7:278–82.

Beyer, Hermann W.
"κυβέρνησις," *TDNT* 3:1035–37.

Beyers, R., and J. Gijsel
Libri de Nativitate Mariae (CCSA 9-10; Turnhout: Brepols, 1997).

Beyschlag, Karlmann
Clemens Romanus und der Frühkatholizismus (BHT 35; Tübingen: Mohr Siebeck, 1966).

Idem
Simon Magus und die christliche Gnosis (WUNT 16; Tübingen: Mohr Siebeck, 1974).

Biblia Patristica, vol. 1: *Des origins à Clément d'Alexandrie et Tertullien* (Centre d'analyse et de documentation patristiques; Paris: Éditions du Center national de la recherché scientifique, 1975).

Bickerman, Elias J.
"The Name of Christians," *HTR* 42 (1949) 109–24.

Idem
"The Warning Inscriptions from Herod's Temple," *JQR* 37 (1946–47) 387–405.

Bieler, Ludwig
ΘΕΙΟΣ ΑΝΗΡ: Das Bild des "Göttlichen Menschen" in Spätantike und Früchristentum (2 vols.; 1935–36; reprinted, Darmstadt: Wissenschaftliche Buchgesellschaft, 1967).

Bienert, Wolfgang A.
"The Picture of the Apostle in Early Christian Tradition," in Edgar Hennecke, *New Testament Apocrypha* (ed. Wilhelm Schneemelcher; ET ed. Robert McL. Wilson; 2 vols.; Philadelphia: Westminster, 1965) 2:5–27.

Bietenhard, Hans
"πνίγω," *TDNT* 6:455–58.

Biguzzi, Giancarlo
"Ephesus, Its Artemision, Its Temple to the Flavian Emperors, and Idolatry in Revelation," *NovT* 40 (1998) 276–90.

Bihler, Johannes
Die Stephanusgeschichte im Zusammenhang der Apostelgeschichte (MThS 16; Munich: Max Hüber, 1961).

Binder, Donald D.
Into the Temple Courts: The Place of the Synagogues in the Second Temple Period (SBLDS 169; Atlanta: Society of Biblical Literature, 1999).

Bird, Michael F.
"The Unity of Luke-Acts in Recent Discussion," *JSNT* 29 (2007) 425–48.

Birley, Anthony R.
Hadrian: The Restless Emperor (London: Routledge, 1997).

Black, C. Clifton
"John Mark in the Acts of the Apostles," in Richard Thompson, ed., *Literary Studies in Luke-Acts: Essays in Honor of Joseph B. Tyson* (Macon, Ga.: Mercer University Press, 1998) 101–20.

Black, Matthew
"The Holy Spirit in the Western Text of Acts," in Eldon Jay Epp and Gordon D. Fee, eds., *New Testament Textual Criticism: Its Significance for Exegesis* (Oxford: Clarendon, 1981) 159–70.

Blaiklock, E. M.
The Acts of the Apostles. Tyndale New Testament Commentaries (Grand Rapids: Eerdmans, 1959).

Idem
"The Acts of the Apostles as a Document of First Century History," in *Apostolic History and the Gospel: Biblical and Historical Essays Presented to F. F. Bruce on His 60th Birthday* (Grand Rapids: Eerdmans, 1967) 41–54.

Blaisdell, James
"The Authorship of the 'We' Sections of the Book of Acts," *HTR* 13 (1920) 136–58.

Blass, Friedrich
Acta apostolorum sive Lucae ad Theophilum liber alter: Editio philologica apparatu critico, commentario perpetuo, indice verborum illustrata (Göttingen: Vandenhoeck & Ruprecht, 1895).

Idem
Philology of the Gospels (London: Macmillan, 1898).

Bligh, John
Galatians (London: St. Paul's Publications, 1969).
Blinzer, Joseph
"The Jewish Punishment of Stoning in the New Testament Period," in *The Trial of Jesus: Cambridge Studies in Honour of C. F. D. Moule* (ed. Ernst Bammel; SBT 2nd ser. 13; London: SCM, 1970) 147–61.
Blue, Bradley
"Acts and the House Church," in David W. J. Gill and Conrad Gempf, eds., *The Book of Acts in Its Graeco-Roman Setting* (BIFCS 2; Grand Rapids: Eerdmans, 1994) 119–222.
Bockmuehl, Markus
"Why Not Let Acts Be Acts? In Conversation with C. Kavin Rowe," *JSNT* 28 (2005) 163–66.
Bodinger, M.
"Les 'Hébreux' et les 'Hellénistes' dans le livre des *Actes des Apôtres*," *Henoch* 19 (1997) 39–58.
Boismard, Marie-Émile
"Le 'concile' de Jérusalem (Act 15, 1-33): Essai de critique littéraire," *EThL* 64 (1988) 433–40.
Idem
Le texte occidental des actes des apôtres (EB 40; Paris: Gabalda, 2000).
Idem, and Arnaud Lamouille
Le texte occidental des Actes des Apôtres: Reconstitution et réhabilition (2 vols.; Paris: Editions Recherche sur les civilizations, 1984).
Bolchazy, Ladislaus J.
Hospitality in Antiquity (Chicago: Ares, 1995).
Bonner, Campbell
"Desired Haven," *HTR* 34 (1941) 49–67.
Idem
"A Note on Mark 6,20," *HTR* 37 (1944) 41–44.
Bonner, Stanley Frederick
Roman Declamation in the Late Republic and Early Empire (Liverpool: University of Liverpool Press, 1949).
Bonz, Marianne Palmer
The Past as Legacy: Luke-Acts and Ancient Epic (Minneapolis: Fortress Press, 2000).
Borgen, Peder
Philo, John and Paul: New Perspectives on Judaism and Early Christianity (BJS 131; Atlanta: Scholars Press, 1987).
Bormann, Lukas
Philippi: Stadt und Christengemeinde zur Zeit des Paulus (NovTSup 78; Leiden: Brill, 1995).
Bornkamm, Gunther
"λύκος," *TDNT* 4:308–11.
Idem
Paul (trans. D. M. G. Stalker; New York: Harper & Row, 1971).
Idem
Tradition and Interpretation in Matthew (trans. P. Scott; Philadelphia: Westminster, 1963).
Borse, Ulrich
"Die geschichtliche Absicherung (Luke 23,5-16) des christologischen Psalmwortes (Ps 2,1s/LXX) und seiner Auslegung (Apg 4,25-28)," *StudNTUmwelt* 26 (2001) 129–38.
Bouman, Gijs
"Der Angang der Apostelgeschichte und der 'westliche' Text," in Tjitze Baarda et al., eds., *Text and Testimony: Essays on the New Testament and Apocryphal Literature in Honour of A. F. J. Klijn* (Kampen: Kok, 1988) 46–55.
Bousset, Wilhelm
Kyrios Christos: A History of the Belief in Christ from the Beginnings of Christianity to Irenaeus (trans. John Steely; Nashville: Abingdon, 1970).
Bovon, François
"Beyond the Book of Acts: Stephen, the First Christian Martyr, in Traditions outside the New Testament Canon of Scripture," *PerspRelStud* 32 (2005) 93–107.
Idem
"Canonical and Apocryphal Acts of Apostles," *JECS* 11 (2003) 165–94.
Idem
De Vocatione Gentium: Histoire de l'interprétation d'Act. 10,1–11,18 dans les six premier siècles (BGBE 8; Tübingen: Mohr Siebeck, 1967).
Idem
"The Law in Luke-Acts," in idem, *Studies in Early Christianity* (WUNT 161; Tübingen: Mohr Siebeck, 2003) 59–73.
Idem
Luke the Theologian: Thirty-three Years of Research (1950–1983) (trans. Ken McKinney; Allison Park, Pa.: Pickwick, 1987).
Idem
Luke the Theologian: Fifty-five Years of Research (1950–2005) (2nd rev. ed.; Waco: Baylor University Press, 2006).
Idem
"The Reception of the Book of Acts in Antiquity," forthcoming.
Idem
"Le Saint-Esprit, l'Église et les relations humaines selon Actes 20,36–21,16," in Jacob Kremer, ed., *Les Actes des Apôtres: Traditions, rédaction, théologie* (BEThL 48; Leuven: Leuven University Press, 1979) 339–58.
Idem
"'Schön hat der heilige Geist durch den Propheten Jesaja zu euren Vätern gesprochen' (Act 28,25)," *ZNW* 75 (1984) 224–32.
Idem
Studies in Early Christianity (WUNT 161; Tübingen: Mohr Siebeck, 2003).
Idem
"The Synoptic Gospels and the Non-Canonical Acts of the Apostles," *HTR* 81 (1988) 19–36.
Idem
"Tradition et redaction en Actes 10,1–11,18," *TZ* 26 (1970) 22–45.

Idem
"La vie des apôtres: Traditions bibliques et narrations apocryphes," in Bovon et al., eds., *Les Actes apocryphes des apôtres* (Geneva: Labor et Fides, 1981) 141–58.

Idem et al., eds.
Les Actes apocryphes des apôtres (Geneva: Labor et Fides, 1981).

Idem, Bertrand Bouvier, and Frédéric Amsler, eds.
Acta Philippi (CCSA 11–12; Turnhout: Brepols, 1999).

Bowe, Barbara
A Church in Crisis (HDR 23; Minneapolis: Fortress Press, 1988).

Bowen, Clayton R.
"Paul's Collection and the Book of Acts," *JBL* 42 (1923) 49–58.

Bowers, Paul
"Paul and Religious Propaganda in the First Century," *NovT* 22 (1980) 316–23.

Bowersock, Glen W.
Augustus and the Greek World (New York/London: Oxford University Press, 1965).

Idem
Fiction as History: Nero to Julian (Berkeley: University of California Press, 1994).

Idem
Greek Sophists in the Roman Empire (New York/London: Oxford University Press, 1969).

Idem
Roman Arabia (Cambridge, Mass.: Harvard University Press, 1983).

Bowker, John W.
"Speeches in Acts: A Study in Proem and Yelammedenu Form," *NTS* 14 (1967–68) 96–104.

Bratcher, Robert G.
"Having Loosed the Pangs of Death," *BT* 10 (1959) 18–20.

Braun, Martin
Griechischer Roman und hellenistische Geschichtsschreibung (Frankfurter Studien zur Religion und Kultur der Antike; Frankfurt: Klostermann, 1934).

Idem
History and Romance in Greco-Oriental Literature (Oxford: Blackwell, 1938).

Braund, David C.
"Agrippa" (2), *ABD* 1:98–100.

Idem
"Bernice," *ABD* 1:677–78.

Idem
"Felix," *ABD* 2:783.

Braunert, Horst
"Der römische Provinzialzensus und der Schätzungsbericht des Lukas-Evangeliums," *Historia* 6 (1957) 192–214.

Brawley, Robert L.
"Ethical Borderlines between Rejection and Hope: Interpreting the Jews in Luke-Acts," *CurrTheolMiss* 27 (2000) 415–23.

Idem
Luke-Acts and the Jews: Conflict, Apology, and Conciliation (SBLMS 33; Atlanta: Scholars Press, 1987).

Idem
Text to Text Pours Forth Speech: Voices of Scripture in Luke-Acts (Bloomington: Indiana University Press, 1995).

Brehm, H. Alan
"Vindicating the Rejected One: Stephen's Speech as a Critique of the Jewish Leaders," in Craig A. Evans and James A. Sanders, eds., *Early Christian Interpretation of the Scriptures of Israel* (JSNTS 148; Sheffield: Sheffield Academic Press, 1997).

Bremmer, Jan N.
"Magic, Martyrdom and Women's Liberation in the Acts of Paul and Thecla," in idem, ed., *The Apocryphal Acts of Paul and Thecla* (Kampen: Kok Pharos, 1996) 36–59.

Brenk, Frederick E.
"The Exorcism at Philippi in Acts 16.11-40: Divine Possession or Diabolic Inspiration?" *FilolNT* 13 (2000) 3–21.

Idem, and Filippo Canali De Rossi
"The 'Notorious' Felix, Procurator of Judea, and His Many Wives (Acts 23–24)," *Bib* 82 (2001) 410–17.

Breytenbach, Cilliers
Paulus und Barnabas in der Provinz Galatien: Studien zu Apostelgeschichte 13f; 16,16; 18,23 und den Adressaten des Galaterbriefes (AGJU 38; Leiden: Brill, 1996).

Idem
"Zeus und der lebendige Gott: Anmerkungen zu Apostelgeschichte 14.11-17," *NTS* 39 (1993) 396–413.

Idem, and Jens Schröter, eds.
Die Apostelgeschichte und die hellenistische Geschichtsschreibung: Festschrift für Eckhard Plümacher zu seinem 65. Geburtstag (AGJU 57; Leiden: Brill, 2004).

Brinkman, John A.
"The Literary Background of the 'Catalogue of the Nations' (Acts 2, 9-11)," *CBQ* 25 (1963) 418–27.

Brock, Sebastian
"βαρναβᾶς υἱὸς παρακλήσεως," *JTS* 25 (1974) 93–98.

Brodie, Thomas L.
"The Accusing and Stoning of Naboth (1 Kgs 21:8-13) as One Component of the Stephen Text (Acts 6:9-14; 7:58a)," *CBQ* 45 (1983) 417–32.

Idem
"Greco-Roman Imitation of Texts as a Partial Guide to Luke's Use of Sources," in Charles H. Talbert, ed., *Luke-Acts* (New York: Crossroad, 1984) 17–46.

Idem
"Towards Unraveling Luke's Uses of the Old Testament: Luke 7:11-17 as *imitatio* of 1 Kgs 17:17-24," *NTS* 32 (1986) 247–67.

Idem
"Towards Unraveling the Rhetorical Imitation of Sources in Acts: 2 Kings 5 as One Component of Acts 8, 9-40," *Bib* 67 (1986) 41–67.

Brosend, William F., II
"The Means of Absent Ends," in Ben Witherington III, *History, Literature and Society in the Book of Acts* (Cambridge: Cambridge University Press, 1996) 348–62.

Broughton, Thomas Robert S.
"The Roman Army," in Kirsopp Lake and Henry J. Cadbury, *Additional Notes to the Commentary,* vol. 5 of Frederick J. Foakes Jackson and Kirsopp Lake, eds., *The Beginnings of Christianity* (5 vols.; New York: Macmillan, 1920–33; reprinted, Grand Rapids: Baker, 1979) 427–45.

Idem
"Three Notes on St. Paul's Journeys in Asia Minor," in Robert Casey et al., eds., *Quantulacumque: Studies Presented to Kirsopp Lake by Pupils, Colleagues, and Friends* (London: Christophers, 1927) 131–38.

Brown, H. Stephen
"Paul's Hearing at Caesarea: A Preliminary Comparison with Legal Literature of the Roman Period," *SBLSP 1996* (Atlanta: Scholars Press, 1996) 319–32.

Brown, Lucinda A.
"Tabitha," in Carol Meyers, ed., *Women in Scripture* (New York: Houghton Mifflin, 2000) 161–62.

Brown, Raymond E.
The Birth of the Messiah: A Commentary on the Infancy Narratives in Matthew and Luke (Garden City, N.Y.: Doubleday, 1977).

Idem
The Death of the Messiah: From Gethsemane to the Grave: A Commentary on the Passion Narratives of the Four Gospels (ABRL; New York: Doubleday, 1994).

Brown, Raymond E., et al., eds.
Mary in the New Testament (Philadelphia: Fortress Press, 1978).

Idem, and John P. Meier
Antioch and Rome: New Testament Cradles of Catholic Christianity (Ramsey, N.J.: Paulist, 1983).

Brown, Schuyler
Apostasy and Perseverance in the Theology of Luke (AnBib 36; Rome: Pontifical Biblical Institute, 1969).

Bruce, Frederick F.
"The Acts of the Apostles: Historical Record or Theological Reconstruction," *ANRW* 2.25.3 (1984) 2569–603.

Idem
"Chronological Questions in the Acts of the Apostles," *BJRL* 68 (1985–86) 273–95.

Idem
"The Full Name of the Procurator Felix," *JSNT* 1 (1978) 33–36.

Idem
"Is the Paul of Acts the Real Paul?" *BJRL* 58 (1976) 282–305.

Idem
Paul: Apostle of the Heart Set Free (Exeter: Paternoster, 1977).

Idem
"Philip and the Ethiopian," *Journal of Semitic Studies* 34 (1989) 377–86.

Idem
"St. Paul in Rome," *BJRL* 46 (1964) 226–45.

Brumbaugh, Robert S.
The Philosophers of Greece (Albany: State University of New York Press, 1981).

Bruneau, Philippe
Recherches sur les cultes de Délos à l'époque hellénistique et a l'époque impériale (Paris: Boccard, 1970).

Bryan, Christopher
"A Further Look at Acts 16:1-3," *JBL* 107 (1988) 292–94.

Büchsel, Friedrich
"ἀνάκρισις," *TDNT* 3:943–44.

Idem
"διακρίνω," *TDNT* 3:946–49.

Buckler, William H.
"Labour Disputes in the Province of Asia," in W. H. Buckler and W. M. Calder, eds., *Anatolian Studies Presented to Sir William Mitchell Ramsay* (Manchester: Manchester University Press, 1923) 27–50.

Buckwalter, H. Douglas
The Character and Purpose of Luke's Christology (SNTSMS 89; Cambridge: Cambridge University Press, 1996).

Budesheim, Thomas L.
"Paul's *Abschiedsrede* in the Acts of the Apostles," *HTR* 69 (1976) 9–30.

Bull, Malcolm
The Mirror of the Gods (Oxford: Oxford University Press, 2002).

Bultmann, Rudolf
"ἀγνοέω," *TDNT* 1:116–21.

Idem
"ἀφίημι," *TDNT* 1:509–12.

Idem
Exegetica (ed. Erich Dinkler; Tübingen: Mohr Siebeck, 1967).

Idem
The History of the Synoptic Tradition (trans. John Marsh; 2nd ed.; New York: Harper & Row, 1968).

Idem
"θάνατος," *TDNT* 3:7–25.

Idem
Theology of the New Testament (2 vols.; trans. K. Grobel; New York: Charles Scribner's Sons, 1951, 1955).

Idem
"Zur Frage nach den Quellen der Apostelgeschichte," in Angus J. B. Higgins, ed., *New Testament Essays: Studies in Memory of T. W. Manson* (Manchester: Manchester University Press, 1959) 68–81 (= *Exegetica*, 412–23).

Idem, and Kurt Rengstorf
"ἐλπίς," *TDNT* 2:517–35.

Bunine, A.
"Paul, Jaccques, Félix, Festus et les autres: pour une revision de la chronologie des derniers procurateurs del la Palestine," *RB* 111 (2004) 387–408, 531–62.

Burchard, Christoph
Der dreizehnte Zeuge (FRLANT 103; Göttingen: Vandenhoeck & Ruprecht, 1970).

Idem
"εἰ nach einem Ausdruck des Wissens oder Nichtwissens Joh 9:25, Act 19:2, 1 Cor 1:16, 7:16," *ZNW* 52 (1961) 73–82.

Idem
"Joseph and Aseneth," in *Old Testament Pseudepigrapha* (ed. James H. Charlesworth; 2 vols.; Garden City, N.Y.: Doubleday, 1983, 1985) 2:177–247.

Idem
"A Note on ῬΗΜΑ in JosAs 17:1f.; Luke 2:15, 17; Acts 10:37," *NovT* 27 (1985) 281–95.

Idem
"Paulus in der Apostelgeschichte," *ThLZ* 100 (1975) 881–95.

Idem
Untersuchungen zur Joseph und Asenath (Tübingen: Mohr Siebeck, 1965).

Burkert, Walter
Greek Religion (trans. J. Raffan; Cambridge, Mass.: Harvard University Press, 1985).

Idem
Homo Necans: The Anthropology of Ancient Greek Sacrificial Ritual and Myth (trans. Peter Bing; Berkeley: University of California Press, 1983).

Burridge, Richard A.
What Are the Gospels? A Comparison with Graeco-Roman Biography (2nd ed.; Grand Rapids: Eerdmans, 2004).

Burstein, Stanley M.
The Hellenistic Age from the Battle of Ipsos to the Death of Kleopatra VII (Translated Documents of Greece & Rome 3; Cambridge: Cambridge University Press, 1985).

Buss, Matthäus F. J.
Die Missionspredigt des Apostels Paulus im Pisidischen Antiochien (FzB 38; Stuttgart: Katholisches Bibelwerk, 1980).

Byrskog, Samuel
"History or Story in Acts—A Middle Way? The 'We' Passages, Historical Intertexture, and Oral History," in Todd Penner and Caroline Vander Stichele, *Contextualizing Acts: Lukan Narrative and Greco-Roman Discourse* (SBLSS 20; Boston/Leiden: Brill; Atlanta: Society of Biblical Literature, 2004) 257–83.

Cabié, Robert
"Quand les 'Sept' deviennent des diacres," *Bulletin de Littérature Ecclésiastique* 97 (1996) 219–26.

Cadbury, Henry J.
"Acts of the Apostles," in *The Interpreter's Dictionary of the Bible* (ed. G. A. Buttrick; 4 vols.; Nashville: Abingdon, 1962) 1:28–42.

Idem
The Book of Acts in History (New York: Harper & Bros., 1955).

Idem
"Commentary on the Preface of Luke," in Frederick J. Foakes Jackson and Kirsopp Lake, *Prolegomena II,* vol. 2 of Frederick J. Foakes Jackson and Kirsopp Lake, eds., *The Beginnings of Christianity* (5 vols.; New York: Macmillan, 1920–33; reprinted, Grand Rapids: Baker, 1979) 2:489–510.

Idem
"Dust and Garments," in Kirsopp Lake and Henry J. Cadbury, *Additional Notes to the Commentary,* vol. 5 of Frederick J. Foakes Jackson and Kirsopp Lake, eds., *The Beginnings of Christianity* (5 vols.; New York: Macmillan, 1920–33; reprinted, Grand Rapids: Baker, 1979) 269–77.

Idem
"Erastus of Corinth," *JBL* 50 (1931) 42–58.

Idem
"Four Features of Lucan Style," in Leander Keck and J. Louis Martyn, eds., *Studies in Luke-Acts: Essays Presented in Honor of Paul Schubert* (Nashville: Abingdon, 1966) 87–102.

Idem
"The Hellenists," in Kirsopp Lake and Henry J. Cadbury, *Additional Notes to the Commentary,* vol. 5 of Frederick J. Foakes Jackson and Kirsopp Lake, eds., *The Beginnings of Christianity* (5 vols.; New York: Macmillan, 1920–33; reprinted, Grand Rapids: Baker, 1979) 59–74.

Idem
"Lexical Notes on Luke-Acts I," *JBL* 44 (1925) 214–27.

Idem
"Lexical Notes on Luke-Acts III," *JBL* 45 (1926) 305–22.

Idem
"Lexical Notes on Luke-Acts IV," *JBL* 48 (1929) 412–25.

Idem
"Lucius of Cyrene," in Kirsopp Lake and Henry J. Cadbury, *Additional Notes to the Commentary,* vol. 5 of Frederick J. Foakes Jackson and Kirsopp Lake, eds., *The Beginnings of Christianity* (5 vols.; New York: Macmillan, 1920–33; reprinted, Grand Rapids: Baker, 1979) 489–95.

Idem
The Making of Luke-Acts (1927; reprinted, London: SPCK, 1958).

Idem
"Names for Christians and Christianity in Acts," in Kirsopp Lake and Henry J. Cadbury, *Additional Notes to the Commentary,* vol. 5 of Frederick J. Foakes Jackson and Kirsopp Lake, eds., *The Beginnings of Christianity* (5 vols.; New York: Macmillan, 1920–33; reprinted, Grand Rapids: Baker, 1979) 375–92.

Idem
"A Possible Perfect in Acts 9:34," *JTS* 49 (1948) 57–58.
Idem
"Roman Law and the Trial of Paul," in Kirsopp Lake and Henry J. Cadbury, *Additional Notes to the Commentary,* vol. 5 of Frederick J. Foakes Jackson and Kirsopp Lake, eds., *The Beginnings of Christianity* (5 vols.; New York: Macmillan, 1920–33; reprinted, Grand Rapids: Baker, 1979) 297–338.
Idem
"Some Lukan Expressions of Time," *JBL* 82 (1963) 272–78.
Idem
"Some Semitic Personal Names in Acts," in *Amicitiae Corolla: A Volume of Essays Presented to James Rendel Harris, D.Litt., on the Occasion of His Eightieth Birthday* (ed. H. G. Wood; London: University of London Press, 1933) 45–46.
Idem
"The Speeches in Acts," in Kirsopp Lake and Henry J. Cadbury, *Additional Notes to the Commentary,* vol. 5 of Frederick J. Foakes Jackson and Kirsopp Lake, eds., *The Beginnings of Christianity* (5 vols.; New York: Macmillan, 1920–33; reprinted, Grand Rapids: Baker, 1979) 402–27.
Idem
The Style and Literary Method of Luke (HTS 6; Cambridge, Mass.: Harvard University Press, 1920).
Idem
"The Summaries in Acts," in Kirsopp Lake and Henry J. Cadbury, *Additional Notes to the Commentary,* vol. 5 of Frederick J. Foakes Jackson and Kirsopp Lake, eds., *The Beginnings of Christianity* (5 vols.; New York: Macmillan, 1920–33; reprinted, Grand Rapids: Baker, 1979) 392–402.
Idem
"The Titles of Jesus in Acts," in Kirsopp Lake and Henry J. Cadbury, *Additional Notes to the Commentary,* vol. 5 of Frederick J. Foakes Jackson and Kirsopp Lake, eds., *The Beginnings of Christianity* (5 vols.; New York: Macmillan, 1920–33; reprinted, Grand Rapids: Baker, 1979) 354–74.
Idem
"The Tradition," in Frederick J. Foakes Jackson and Kirsopp Lake, *Prolegomena II,* vol. 2 of Frederick J. Foakes Jackson and Kirsopp Lake, eds., *The Beginnings of Christianity* (5 vols.; New York: Macmillan, 1920–33; reprinted, Grand Rapids: Baker, 1979) 209–64.
Idem
"ὑποζώματα," in Kirsopp Lake and Henry J. Cadbury, *Additional Notes to the Commentary,* vol. 5 of Frederick J. Foakes Jackson and Kirsopp Lake, eds., *The Beginnings of Christianity* (5 vols.; New York: Macmillan, 1920–33; reprinted, Grand Rapids: Baker, 1979) 345–54.
Idem
"We and I Passages in Luke-Acts," *NTS* 3 (1956) 128–32.
Calder, William M.
"The 'Priest' of Zeus at Lystra," *Exp* 7 (1910) 148–55.
Callan, Terrance
"The Background of the Apostolic Decree (Acts 15:20, 29; 21:25)," *CBQ* 55 (1993) 284–97.
Campbell, Douglas A.
"An Anchor for Pauline Chronology: Paul's Flight from 'the Ethnarch of King Aretas,' 2 Cor 11:32-33," *JBL* 121 (2002) 279–302.
Idem
"Possible Inscriptional Attestation to Sergius Paul[l]us (Acts 13:6-12) and the Implications for Pauline Chronology," *JTS* 56 (2005) 1–29.
Campbell, R. Alastair
The Elders: Seniority within Earliest Christianity (Edinburgh: T&T Clark, 1994).
Campbell, Thomas H.
"Paul's Missionary Journeys as Reflected in His Letters," *JBL* 74 (1955) 80–87.
Campbell, William S.
"Who Are We in Acts? The First-Person Plural Character in the Acts of the Apostles" (Diss., Princeton Theological Seminary, 2000).
Campenhausen, Hans von
Ecclesiastical Authority and Spiritual Power (trans. J. A. Baker; Stanford: Stanford University Press, 1969).
Idem
"Die Nachfolge des Jakobus: Zur Frage eines urchristlichen 'Kalifats,'" *ZKG* 63 (1950–51) 133–44.
Idem
"Der urchristliche Apostelbegriff," *ST* 1 (1948) 96–130.
Cancik, Hubert
"The History of Culture, Religion, and Institutions in Ancient Historiography: Philological Observations concerning Luke's History," *JBL* 116 (1997) 681–703.
Capper, Brian
"Community of Goods in the Early Jerusalem Church," *ANRW* 2.26.3 (1996) 1730–74.
Idem
"The Palestinian Cultural Context of Earliest Christian Community of Goods," in Richard Bauckham, *The Book of Acts in Its Palestinian Setting* (BIFCS 4; Grand Rapids: Eerdmans, 1995) 323–56.
Carroll, John T.
Response to the End of History: Eschatolgy and Situation in Luke-Acts (SBLDS 92; Atlanta: Scholars Press, 1988).
Cartlidge, David R.
"The Fall and Rise of Simon Magus," *BibRev* 21 (2005) 24–36.
Casey, Robert P.
"Simon Magus," in Kirsopp Lake and Henry J. Cadbury, *Additional Notes to the Commentary,* vol. 5 of Frederick J. Foakes Jackson and Kirsopp Lake, eds., *The Beginnings of Christianity* (5 vols.; New

York: Macmillan, 1920–33; reprinted, Grand Rapids: Baker, 1979) 151–63.

Cassidy, Richard J.
Society and Politics in the Acts of the Apostles (Maryknoll, N.Y.: Orbis Books, 1987).

Idem, and Philip J. Sharper, eds.
Political Issues in Luke-Acts (Maryknoll, N.Y.: Orbis Books, 1983).

Casson, Lionel
The Ancient Mariners (New York: Macmillan, 1959).

Idem
"The Isis and Her Voyage," *TAPA* 81 (1950) 43–56.

Idem
Travel in the Ancient World (Sarasota, Fl.: Stevens, 1974).

Catchpole, David R.
"Paul, James, and the Apostolic Decree," *NTS* 23 (1977) 428–44.

Cerfaux, Lucien
"La composition de la première partie du Livre des Actes," *EThL* 13 (1936) 667–91.

Idem
Pour l'histoire du titre ἀπόστολος dans le Nouveau Testament," *RSR* 48 (1960) 76–92.

Idem
"La première communauté chrétienne à Jérusalem (Act., II, 41–V, 42)," *EThL* 16 (1939) 5–31.

Cerro, Gonzalo del
"Los hechos apócrifos de los Apósteles: Su género literario," *EstBíb* 51 (1993) 207–32.

Chadwick, Henry
"Origen, Celsus, and the Resurrection of the Body," *HTR* 41 (1948) 83–102.

Chambers, Kathy
"'Knock, Knock–Who's There?' Acts 12:6-17 as a Comedy of Errors," in Amy-Jill Levine, *A Feminist Companion to the Acts of the Apostles* (Cleveland: Pilgrim, 2004) 89–97.

Chance, J. Bradley
"Divine Prognostications and the Movement of Story: An Intertextual Exploration of Xenophon's *Ephesian Tale* and the Acts of the Apostles," in Ronald F. Hock, J. Chance, and Judith Perkins, eds., *Ancient Fiction and Early Christian Narrative* (SBLSS 6; Atlanta: Scholars Press, 1998) 219–34.

Charlesworth, James H.
The Odes of Solomon (SBLTT; Missoula, Mont.: Scholars Press, 1977).

Idem
The Old Testament Pseudepigrapha (2 vols.; Garden City, N.Y.: Doubleday, 1983).

Cherniss, Harold
Plutarch's Moralia XIII.2 (LCL; Cambridge, Mass.: Harvard University Press, 1976).

Childers, J. W.
"The Old Georgian Acts of the Apostles: A Progress Report," *NTS* 42 (1996) 55–74.

Chilton, Bruce
"Gamaliel (2)," *ABD* 2:903–6.

Christol, M., and T. Drew-Bear, Thomas
"Les Sergii Pauli et Antioche," in *Actes du Ier congrès international sur Antioche de Pisidie* (ed. Thomas Drew-Bear, Mehmet Taşlialan, and Christine M. Thomas; Collection. Archeologie et Histoire de L'antiquité Université Lumière-Lyon 2; vol. 5, Paris: Boccard, 2002) 177–92.

Christophersen, Alf, et al., eds.
Paul, Luke, and the Graeco-Roman World: Essays in Honour of Alexander J. M. Wedderburn (JSNTS 217; London: Sheffield Academic Press, 2002).

Clabeaux, John C.
"The Story of the Maltese Viper and Luke's Apology for Paul," *CBQ* 67 (2005) 604–10.

Clark, Alfred. C.
The Acts of the Apostles: A Critical Edition with Introduction and Notes on Selected Passages (Oxford: Oxford University Press, 1933).

Idem
"The Use of the Septuagint in Acts," in Frederick J. Foakes Jackson and Kirsopp Lake, *Prolegomena II,* vol. 2 of Frederick J. Foakes Jackson and Kirsopp Lake, eds., *The Beginnings of Christianity* (5 vols.; New York: Macmillan, 1920–33; reprinted, Grand Rapids: Baker, 1979) 66–105.

Clark, Andrew C.
Parallel Lives: The Relation of Paul to the Apostles in the Lucan Perspective (Carlisle: Paternoster, 2001).

Clark, D. J.
"A Not Infrequent Construction: Litotes in the Book of Acts," *BT* 55 (2004) 433–40.

Clarke, Graeme W.
The Octavius of Marcus Minucius Felix (ACW 39; New York: Newman Press, 1974).

Clarke, William Kemp L.
"The Use of the LXX in Acts," in Frederick J. Foakes Jackson and Kirsopp Lake, *Prolegomena II,* vol. 2 of Frederick J. Foakes Jackson and Kirsopp Lake, eds., *The Beginnings of Christianity* (5 vols.; New York: Macmillan, 1920–33; reprinted, Grand Rapids: Baker, 1979) 66–105.

Clayton, Peter, and Martin Price, eds.
The Seven Wonders of the Ancient World (London: Routledge, 1988).

Co, Maria Anicia
"The Major Summaries in Acts (Acts 2,42-47; 4,32-35; 5,12-16," *EThL* 68 (1992) 49–85.

Cohen, Shaye J. D.
The Beginnings of Jewishness: Boundaries, Varieties, Uncertainties (Berkeley: University of California Press, 1999).

Idem
From the Maccabees to the Mishnah (LEC 7; Philadelphia: Westminster, 1987).

Cohoon, James
Dio Chrysostom I, II (LCL; Cambridge, Mass.: Harvard University Press, 1932, 1939).

Collins, Adela Yarbro
"The Function of Excommunication in Paul," *HTR* 73 (1980) 251–63.

Collins, John J.
Between Athens and Jerusalem (2nd ed.; Grand Rapids: Eerdmans, 2000).
Idem
"Sibylline Oracles," in *Old Testament Pseudepigrapha* (ed. James H. Charlesworth; 2 vols.; Garden City, N.Y.: Doubleday, 1983, 1985) 1:317–429.
Colson, Francis H.
Philo VI, VII (LCL; Cambridge, Mass.: Harvard University Press, 1935, 1937).
Idem
"Triangular Numbers in the New Testament," *JTS* 16 (1915) 67–76.
Idem, and George H. Whitaker
Philo III (LCL; New York: G. P. Putnam's Sons, 1930).
Combet-Galland, Corina
"Paul l'apôtre: un voyage contrarié pour baggage," *EThR* 80 (2005) 361–74.
Comfort, Philip W., and David P. Barrett, eds.
The Complete Text of the Earliest New Testament Manuscripts (Grand Rapids: Baker, 1999).
Conti, Martino
"Il Concilio Apostolico e la lettera ai Galati (At 15, 1-29; Gal 2, 1-21)," *Antonianum* 77 (2002) 235–56.
Conzelmann, Hans
"The Address of Paul on the Areopagus," in Leander Keck and J. Louis Martyn, eds., *Studies in Luke-Acts: Essays Presented in Honor of Paul Schubert* (Nashville: Abingdon, 1966) 217–30.
Idem
First Corinthians (trans. James W. Leitch; Hermeneia; Philadelphia: Fortress Press, 1975).
Idem
"Luke's Place in the Development of Early Christianity," in Leander Keck and J. Louis Martyn, eds., *Studies in Luke-Acts: Essays Presented in Honor of Paul Schubert* (Nashville: Abingdon, 1966) 298–316.
Idem
Die Mitte der Zeit: Studien zur Theologie des Lukas (Tübingen: Mohr Siebeck, 1960).
Idem
"*φῶς*," *TDNT* 9:310–58.
Idem
"Die Schule des Paulus," in Carl Andresen and Günther Klein, eds., *Theologia Crucis–Signum Crucis: Festschrift für Erich Dinkler zum 70. Geburtstag* (Tübingen: Mohr Siebeck, 1979) 85–96.
Idem
The Theology of St. Luke (trans. G. Buswell; New York: Harper & Row, 1960).
Idem
"'Was von Anfang war,'" in Walter Eltester, ed., *Neutestamentliche Studien für Rudolf Bultmann zu seinem 70. Geburtstag am 20. August 1954* (BZNW 21; Berlin: Töpelmann, 1954) 194–201.
Idem, and Walter Zimmerli
"*χάρις κτλ.*," *TDNT* 9:372–402.
Cook, Michael J.
"The Mission to the Jews in Acts: Unraveling Luke's 'Myth of the "Myriads,"'" in Joseph B. Tyson, ed., *Luke-Acts and the Jewish People: Eight Critical Perspectives* (Minneapolis: Augsburg, 1988) 102–23.
Copenhaver, Brian P.
Hermetica (Cambridge: Cambridge University Press, 1992).
Coppens, Joseph
"L'imposition des mains dans les Actes des Apôtres," in Jacob Kremer, ed., *Les Actes des Apôtres: Traditions, rédaction, théologie* (BEThL 48; Leuven: Leuven University Press, 1979) 405–38.
Corley, Kathleen
Private Women, Public Meals: Social Conflict in the Synoptic Tradition (Peabody, Mass.: Hendrickson, 1993).
Cosgrove, Charles H.
"The Divine *ΔΕΙ* in Luke-Acts: Investigations into the Lukan Understanding of God's Providence," *NovT* 26 (1984) 168–90.
Countryman, L. William
Dirt, Greed, and Sex: Sexual Ethics in the New Testament and Their Implications for Today (Philadelphia: Fortress Press, 1988).
Idem
The Rich Christian in the Church of the Early Empire: Contradictions and Accommodations (New York: Edwin Mellen, 1980).
Court, John M.
"Rivals in the Mission Field," *ExpT* 113 (2002) 399–403.
Courtney, Edward
A Commentary on the Satires of Juvenal (London: Athlone, 1980).
Cousland, J. R. C.
"Dionysus Theomachos? Echoes of the *Bacchae* in 3 Maccabees," *Bib* 82 (2001) 539–48.
Cowton, C. J.
"The Alms Trader: A Note on Identifying the Beautiful Gate of Acts 3.2," *NTS* 42 (1996) 475–76.
Creed, John Martin
The Gospel according to St. Luke (New York: St. Martin's, 1930).
Idem
"The Text and Interpretation of Acts i.1-2," *JTS* 35 (1934) 176–82.
Crook, John A.
Law and Life of Rome: 90 B.C.–A.D. 212 (Ithaca: Cornell University Press, 1967).
Crosby, H. L.
Dio Chrysostom (LCL; Cambridge, Mass.: Harvard University Press, 1940).
Crossan, John D.
The Birth of Christianity: Discovering What Happened in the Years Immediately after the Execution of Jesus (New York: HarperSanFrancisco, 1998).
Idem
Who Killed Jesus? Exposing the Roots of Anti-Semitism in the Gospel Story of the Death of Jesus (San Francisco: HarperSanFrancisco, 1995).

Crowe, Jerome
The Acts (NTM 8; Wilmington, Del.: Michael Glazier, 1979).

Cullmann, Oscar
The Johannine Circle (trans. J. Bowden; Philadelphia: Westminster, 1976).

Cumont, Franz
Afterlife in Roman Paganism (New Haven: Yale University Press, 1922).

Idem
"La plus ancienne géographie astrologique," *Klio* 9 (1909) 263–73.

Cunningham, Scott
Through Many Tribulations: The Theology of Persecution in Luke-Acts (JSNTS 142; Sheffield: Sheffield Academic Press, 1997).

Czachesz, István
"The Acts of Paul and the Western Text of Luke's Acts: Paul between Canon and Apocrypha," in Jan Bremmer, ed., *The Apocryphal Acts of Paul and Thecla* (Kampen: Kok Pharos, 1996) 107–25.

Idem
"Apostolic Commission Narratives in the Canonical and Apocryphal Acts of the Apostles" (Diss., Groningen, 2002).

Idem
Commission Narratives: A Comparative Study of the Canonical and Apocryphal Acts (Studies on Early Christian Apocrypha 8; Leuven: Peeters, 2007).

Dahl, Nils A.
"'A People for His Name' (Acts XV.14)," *NTS* 4 (1957–58) 319–27.

Idem
"The Story of Abraham in Luke-Acts," Leander Keck and J. Louis Martyn, eds., *Studies in Luke-Acts: Essays Presented in Honor of Paul Schubert* (Nashville: Abingdon, 1966) 139–58.

D'Angelo, Mary Rose
"The *ANHP* Question in Luke-Acts: Imperial Masculinity and the Deployment of Women in the Early Second Century," in Amy-Jill Levine, *A Feminist Companion to the Acts of the Apostles* (Cleveland: Pilgrim, 2004) 44–69.

Danker, Frederick W.
Benefactor: Epigraphic Study of a Graeco-Roman and New Testament Semantic Field (St. Louis: Clayton, 1982).

Idem
Jesus and the New Age (2nd ed.; Philadelphia: Fortress Press, 1988).

Idem
"Purple," *ABD* 5:557–60.

Idem
"Reciprocity in the Ancient World and in Acts 15:23-29," in Richard J. Cassidy and Philip J. Scharper, eds., *Political Issues in Luke-Acts* (Maryknoll, N.Y.: Orbis Books, 1983) 49–58.

D'Arms, John H.
Commerce and Social Standing in Ancient Rome (Cambridge, Mass.: Harvard University Press, 1981).

Darr, John A.
Herod the Fox: Audience Criticism and Lukan Characterization (JSNTS 163; Sheffield: Sheffield Academic Press, 1998).

Idem
"Irenic or Ironic? Another Look at Gamaliel before the Sanhedrin (Acts 5:33-42)," in Richard Thompson, ed., *Literary Studies in Luke-Acts: Essays in Honor of Joseph B. Tyson* (Macon, Ga.: Mercer University Press, 1998) 121–39.

Idem
On Character Building: The Reader and the Rhetoric of Characterizations in Luke-Acts (Louisville: Westminster John Knox, 1992).

Dassmann, Ernst
Der Stachel im Fleisch: Paulus in der frühchristlichen Literatur bis Irenäus (Münster: Aschendorff, 1979).

Daube, David
"A Reform in Acts and Its Models," in Robert Hamerton-Kelly and Robin Scroggs, eds., *Jews, Greeks, and Christians: Religious Cultures in Late Antiquity: Essays in Honor of William David Davies* (SJLA 21; Leiden: Brill, 1976) 151–63.

Dautzenberg, Gerhard
"*διακρίνω*," *EDNT* 1:305–6.

Davies, P.
"The Ending of Acts," *ExpT* 94 (1982–83) 334–35.

Dawsey, James M.
"Characteristics of Folk-Epic in Acts," *SBLSB 1989* (Atlanta: Scholars Press, 1989) 317–25.

Dawson, Doyne
Cities of the Gods: Communist Utopias in Greek Thought (New York: Oxford University Press, 1992).

Deissmann, Adolf
Bible Studies (trans. A. Grieve; Edinburgh: T&T Clark, 1901).

Idem
Light from the Ancient East (trans. Lionel Strachan; New York: Harper, 1927).

Delebecque, Édouard
Les Deux Actes des Apôtres (EB n.s. 6; Paris: Gabalda, 1986).

Idem
"De Lystres à Philippi (Ac 16) avec le codex Bezae," *Bib* 63 (1982) 395–405.

Idem
"La mésadventure des fils de Scévas selon ses deux versions (Actes 19:13-20)," *RSPhTh* 66 (1982) 225–32.

Idem
"Silas, Paul et Barnabé à Antioche selon le texte 'occidental' d'Actes 15:34 et 38," *RHPhR* 64 (1984) 47–52.

Delling, Gerhard
"ἄρχω," *TDNT* 1:478–89.

Idem
"Josephus und das Wunderbare," *NovT* 2 (1958) 291–309.

Idem
"Das letze Wort der Apostelgeschichte," *NovT* 15 (1973) 193–204.

Idem
"μάγος," *TDNT* 4:356–59.

Idem
"πάρθενος," *TDNT* 5:826–37.

Delobel, Joël
"The Text of Luke-Acts: A Confrontation of Recent Theories," in Jozef Verheyden, ed., *The Unity of Luke-Acts* (BEThL 92; Leuven: Leuven University Press, 1999) 83–107.

Del Verme, Marcello
Comunione e condivisione dei beni: Chiesa primitiva e giudaismo esseno-qumranico a confronto (Brescia: Morcelliana, 1977).

Denova, Rebecca I.
The Things Accomplished among Us: Prophetic Tradition in the Structural Pattern of Luke-Acts (Sheffield: Sheffield Academic Press, 1997).

Derrett, J. Duncan M.
"Clean and Unclean Animals (Acts 10:15; 11:9): Peter's Pronouncing Power Observed," *Heythrop Journal* 29 (1988) 205–21.

De Ste. Croix, Geoffrey E. M.
The Class Struggle in the Ancient World (Ithaca: Cornell University Press, 1981).

Deutschmann, A.
Synagoge und Gemeindebildung: Christliche Gemeinde und Israel am Beispiel von Apg 13,42-52 (Biblische Untersuchungen 30; Regensburg: Pustet, 2001).

Dibelius, Martin
Botschaft und Geschichte (2 vols.; Tübingen: Mohr Siebeck, 1953, 1955).

Idem
"Die Christianisierung einer hellenistischen Formel," in idem, *Botschaft und Geschichte* (2 vols.; Tübingen: Mohr Siebeck, 1953, 1955) 2:14–29.

Idem
Der Hirt des Hermas (HNT; Apostolischen Väter IV; Tübingen: Mohr Siebeck, 1923).

Idem
Studies in the Acts of the Apostles (trans. M. Ling and Paul Schubert; ed. Heinrich Greeven; New York: Charles Scribner's Sons, 1956).

Idem, and Hans Conzelmann
The Pastoral Epistles (trans. and ed. Helmut Koester; Hermeneia; Philadelphia: Fortress Press, 1972).

Dieterich, Albrecht
Abrasax: Studien zur Religionsgeschichte des spätern Altertums (Leipzig: Teubner, 1891).

Dillon, John, and Jackson Hershbell
Iamblichus On the Pythagorean Way of Life (SBLTT 29; Atlanta: Scholars Press, 1991).

Dillon, Richard J.
From Eyewitnesses to Ministers of the Word: Tradition and Composition in Luke 24 (AnBib 82; Rome: Pontifical Biblical Institute, 1978).

Dimant, Devorah
"Pesharim, Qumran," *ABD* 5:244–51.

Dinkler, Erich
"Philippus und der ***ΑΝΗΡ ΑΙΘΙΟΨ*** (Apg 8.26-40): Historische und geographische Bemerkungen zum Missionsablauf nach Lukas," in E. Earle Ellis and Erich Grässer, eds., *Jesus und Paulus: Festschrift für Werner Georg Kümmel zum 70. Geburtstag* (Göttingen: Vandenhoeck & Ruprecht, 1975) 85–95.

Idem
Signum Crucis: Aufsätze zum Neuen Testament und zur christlichen Archäologie (Tübingen: Mohr Siebeck) 1967.

Dionne, Christian
"L'épisode de Lystre (Ac 14,7-20a) une analyse narrative," *SciEsp* 57 (2005) 5–33.

Dobbeler, A. von
Der Evangelist Philippus in der Geschichte des Urchristentums: Eine prosopographische Studie (Texte und Arbeiten zum neutestamentlichen Zeitalter 30; Tübingen: Francke, 2000).

Doble, Peter
The Paradox of Salvation: Luke's Theology of the Cross (SNTSMS 87; Cambridge: Cambridge University Press, 1996).

Dobschütz, Ernst von
"Die Berichte über die Bekehrung des Paulus," *ZNW* 29 (1930) 144–47.

Idem
"Der Roman im altchristlichen Literatur," *Deutsche Rundschau* 111 (1902) 87–106.

Dockz, S.
"Luc, a-t-il été le compagnon d'apostolat de Paul?" *NRT* 103 (1981) 385–400.

Dodd, Charles H.
The Apostolic Preaching and Its Developments (London: Hodder & Stoughton, 1936).

Dodds, Eric R.
The Greeks and the Irrational (Berkeley: University of California Press, 1968).

Donelson, Lewis R.
"Cult Histories and the Sources of Acts," *Bib* 68 (1987) 1–21.

Doody, Margaret Anne
The True Story of the Novel (New Brunswick, N.J.: Rutgers University Press, 1996).

Doran, Robert
"The Jewish Hellenistic Historians before Josephus," *ANRW* 2.20.1 (1986) 2116–97.

Douglas, Mary
Thinking in Circles: An Essay on Ring Composition (New Haven: Yale University Press, 2007).

Downey, Glanville
History of Antioch in Syria from Seleucus to the Arab Conquest (Princeton: Princeton University Press, 1961).

Downing, F. Gerald
"*A bas les Aristos*: The Relevance of Higher Literature for the Understanding of the Early Christian Writings," *NovT* 30 (1988) 212–30.

Idem
"Redaction Criticism: Josephus' *Antiquities* and the Synoptic Gospels (II)," *JSNT* 9 (1980) 29–48.

Downs, David J.
"Paul's Collection and the Book of Acts Revisited," *NTS* 52 (2006) 50–70.

Droge, Arthur J.
"Call Stories in Greek Biography and the Gospels," *SBLSP 1983* (Atlanta: Scholars Press, 1983) 245–57.

Drury, John
Tradition and Design in Luke's Gospel (Atlanta: John Knox, 1976).

Dubois, Jean-Daniel
"La figure d'Elie dans la perspective lucanienne," *RHPhR* 53 (1973) 155–76.

Dumais, Michel
"Les Actes des Apôtres: Bilan et orientations," in M. Gourgues and L. Laberge, eds., *"De bien des manières": La recherche biblique aux abords du XXIe siècle* (LD 163; Paris: Cerf, 1995) 307–64.

Duncan, George S.
St. Paul's Ephesian Ministry: A Reconstruction with Special Reference to the Ephesian Origin of the Imprisonment Epistles (New York: Charles Scribner's Sons, 1930).

Dunn, James D. G.
The Acts of the Apostles (Peterborough: Epworth, 1996).

Idem
"*ΚΨΡΙΟΣ* in Acts," in Christof Landmesser et al., eds., *Jesus Christus als die Mitte der Schrift: Studien zur Hermeneutik des Evangeliums* (Berlin: de Gruyter, 1997) 363–68.

Idem
Unity and Diversity in the New Testament: An Inquiry into the Character of Earliest Christianity (2nd ed.; Philadelphia: Trinity Press International, 1990).

Dunn, Peter
Peter Dunn, "The Influence of 1 Corinthians on the *Acts of Paul*," *SBLSP 1996* (Atlanta: Scholars Press, 1996).

Dupont, Jacques
"L'apôtre comme intermediaire du salut dans les Actes," *RThPh* 112 (1980) 342–58.

Idem
"Community of Goods in the Early Church," in idem, *The Salvation of the Gentiles: Studies in the Acts of the Apostles* (trans. J. Keating; New York/Ramsey, N.J./Toronto: Paulist, 1979) 85–102.

Idem
"La conclusion des Actes et son rapport à l'ensemble de l'ouvrage de Luc," in Jacob Kremer, ed., *Les Actes des Apôtres: Traditions, rédaction, théologie* (BEThL 48; Leuven: Leuven University Press, 1979) 359–404.

Idem
"La destinée de Judas prophétisée par David," *CBQ* 23 (1961) 41–51.

Idem
"Le discours à l'Aréopage (Ac 17,22-31) lieu de rencontre entre christianisme et hellénisme," in idem, *Nouvelles études sur les Actes des apôtres* (LD 118; Paris: Cerf, 1984) 380–423.

Idem
Le discours de Milet: Testament pastoral de Saint Paul (Actes 20,18-36) (Paris: Cerf, 1962).

Idem
Études sur les Actes de apôtres (LD 45; Paris: Cerf, 1967).

Idem
"La famine sous Claude, Actes 11.28," *RB* 62 (1955) 52–55.

Idem
"*Laos ex ethnon* (Act. Xv.14)," *NTS* 3 (1956–57) 47–50.

Idem
Nouvelles études sur les Actes des apôtres (LD 118; Paris: Cerf, 1984).

Idem
"Pierre deliveré de prison (ac 12,1-11)," *AsSeign* 1/84 (1967) 14–26 (= *Nouvelles études*, 329–42).

Idem
"Un peuple d'entre les nations (Actes 15.14)," *NTS* 31 (1985) 321–35.

Idem
The Salvation of the Gentiles: Studies in the Acts of the Apostles (trans. J. Keating; New York/Ramsey, N.J./Toronto: Paulist, 1979).

Idem
The Sources of the Acts (trans. K. Pond; New York: Herder & Herder, 1964).

Idem
"La structure oratoire du discours d'Étienne (Actes 7)," *Bib* 66 (1985) 153–67.

Dürr, Lorenz
"Zur religionsgeschichtlichen Begründung der Vorschrift des Schuhausziehens an heiliger Stätte," *OLZ* 41 (1938) 410–12.

Easton, Burton S.
Early Christianity: The Purpose of Acts and Other Papers (ed. F. C. Grant; Greenwich, Conn.: Seabury, 1954).

Economou, John
The Problem of the Title "Acts of the Apostles" (in modern Greek, Thessaloniki, 1995).

Edelstein, Ludwig
Asclepius: A Collection and Interpretation of the Testimonies (2 vols.; Baltimore: Johns Hopkins University Press, 1945).

Edwards, Douglas
Religion and Power: Pagans, Jews, and Christians in the Greek East (New York: Oxford University Press, 1996).

Edwards, M. J.
"Quoting Aratus: Acts 17,28," *ZNW* 83 (1992) 266–69.

Egger, Brigitte M.
"Women in the Greek Novel: Constructing the Feminine" (Diss., University of California, Irvine, 1990).

Ehling, K.
"Zwei Anmerkungen zum ἀργύριον in Apg 19,19," *ZNW* 94 (2003) 269–75.

Ehrhardt, Arnold
The Acts of the Apostles: Ten Lectures (Manchester: Manchester University Press, 1969).

Idem
"The Construction and Purpose of the Acts of the Apostles," in idem, *The Framework of the New Testament* (Cambridge, Mass.: Harvard University Press, 1964) 64–102.

Ehrman, Bart D.
The Orthodox Corruption of Scripture: The Effect of Early Christological Controversies on the Text of the New Testament (New York: Oxford University Press, 1993).

Elbert, Paul
"Paul of the Miletus Speech and 1 Thessalonians: Critique and Considerations," *ZNW* 95 (2004) 258–68.

Elliott, James Keith
The Apocryphal New Testament (Oxford: Clarendon, 1993).

Idem
A Bibliography of Greek New Testament Manuscripts (SNTSMS 109; 2nd ed.; Cambridge: Cambridge University Press, 2000).

Idem
"An Eclectic Textual Study of the Book of Acts," in Tobias Nicklas and Michael Tilly, eds., *The Book of Acts as Church History: Textual Traditions and Ancient Interpretations* (BZNW 120; Berlin: de Gruyter, 2003) 9–30.

Idem
"The Greek Manuscript Heritage of the Book of Acts," *FilolNT* 9 (1996) 37–50.

Elliott, John H.
"Temple versus Household in Luke-Acts: A Contrast in Social Institutions," in Jerome H. Neyrey, ed., *The Social World of Luke-Acts: Models for Interpretation* (Peabody, Mass.: Hendrickson, 1991) 211–40.

Ellis, E. Earle
"The End of the Earth (Acts 1:8)," *Bulletin for Biblical Research* 1 (1991) 123–32.

Idem
The Gospel of Luke (NCB; rev. ed.; London: Oliphants, 1974).

Ellud, Danielle
"Actes 3:1-11," *EThR* 64 (1989) 95–99.

Elsener, J.
"Hagiographic Geography: Travel and Allegory in the *Life of Apollonius of Tyana*," *JHS* 117 (1997) 22–37.

Eltester, Walter
"Gott und die Natur in der Areopagrede," *Neutestamentliche Studien für Rudolf Bultmann zu seinem 70. Geburtstag am 20. August 1954* (BZNW 21; 2nd ed.; Berlin: Töpelmann, 1957) 202–57.

Idem, and F. Kettler, eds.
Apophoreta: Festschrift für Ernst Haenchen zu seinem siebzigsten Geburtstag am 10. Dezember 1964 (BZNW 30; Berlin: Töpelmann, 1964).

Engelmann, Helmut
The Delian Aretalogy of Sarapis (trans. E. Osers, EPRO 44; Leiden: Brill, 1975).

Engels, Donald
Roman Corinth: An Alternative Model for the Classical City (Chicago: University of Chicago Press, 1990).

Enslin, Morton
The Book of Judith (Leiden: Brill, 1972).

Epp, Eldon Jay
"Anti-Judaic Tendencies in the D-Text of Acts: Forty Years of Conversation," in Tobias Nicklas and Michael Tilly, eds., *The Book of Acts as Church History: Textual Traditions and Ancient Interpretations* (BZNW 120; Berlin: de Gruyter, 2003) 111–46.

Idem
"The Ascension in the Textual Tradition of Luke-Acts," in Eldon Jay Epp and Gordon D. Fee, ed., *New Testament Textual Criticism: Its Significance for Exegesis: Essays in Honour of Bruce M. Metzger* (Oxford: Clarendon, 1981) 131–45.

Idem
"A Continuing Interlude in New Testament Textual Criticism," in Eldon Jay Epp and Gordon D. Fee, eds., *Studies in the Theory and Method of New Testament Textual Criticism* (StudDoc 45; Grand Rapids: Eerdmans, 1993) 109–23.

Idem
The Theological Tendency of Codex Bezae Cantabrigiensis in Acts (SNTSMS 3; Cambridge: Cambridge University Press, 1966).

Idem
"The Twentieth Century Interlude in New Testament Textual Criticism," *JBL* 93 (1974) 386–414 (= Eldon Jay Epp and Gordon D. Fee, eds., *Studies in the Theory and Method of New Testament Textual Criticism* [StudDoc 45; Grand Rapids: Eerdmans, 1993] 83–108).

Idem
"Western Text," *ABD* 6:909–12.

Erbes, Carl
"Petrus nicht in Rom, sondern in Jerusalem gestorben," *ZKG* 22 (1901) 1–47; 161–224.

Erichson-Wendt, F.
"Tabitha—Leben an der Grenze: Ein Beitrag zum Verständnis von Apg 9, 36-43," *BibNotiz* 127 (2005) 67–87.

Esler, Philip Francis
Community and Gospel in Luke-Acts: The Social and Political Motivations of Lucan Theology (SNTSMS 57; Cambridge: Cambridge University Press, 1987).

Idem
The First Christians in Their Social Worlds (London: Routledge, 1994).
Evans, Craig A.
"Luke's Use of the Elijah/Elisha Narratives and the Ethic of Election," *JBL* 106 (1987) 75–83.
Idem, and James A. Sanders
Luke and Scripture: The Function of Sacred Tradition in Acts (Minneapolis: Fortress Press, 1993).
Exum, Cheryl, and Charles Talbert
"The Structure of Paul's Speech to the Ephesian Elders (Acts 20, 18-35) *CBQ* 29 (1967) 233–36.
Fagles, Robert
Homer: The Iliad (New York: Penguin, 1991).
Farahian, Edmond
"Paul's Vision at Troas (Acts 16:9-10)," in Gerald O'Collins and Gilberto Marconi, eds., *Luke and Acts* (Festschrift Emilio Rasco; trans. M. J. O'Connell; New York: Paulist, 1993) 197–207.
Faraone, Christopher A., and Dirk Obbink, eds.
Magika Hiera: Ancient Greek Magic and Religion (New York: Oxford University Press, 1991).
Fascher, Erich
"Theologische Beobachtungen zu *Dei*," in *Neutestamentlichen Studien für Rudolf Bultmann zu seinem 70. Geburtstag am 20. August 1954* (ed. Walther Eltester; BZNW 21; 2nd ed.; Berlin: Töpelmann, 1957) 228–54.
Fee, Gordon D.
The First Epistle to the Corinthians (NICNT; Grand Rapids: Eerdmans, 1987).
Feldman, Louis H.
Jew and Gentile in the Ancient World (Princeton: Princeton University Press, 1993).
Idem
"Jewish 'Sympathizers' in Classical Literature and Inscriptions," *TAPA* 81 (1950) 200–208.
Idem
Josephus IX (LCL; Cambridge, Mass.: Harvard University Press, 1965).
Idem
"Josephus as an Apologist to the Greco-Roman World: His Portrait of Solomon," in Elisabeth Schüssler Fiorenza, ed., *Aspects of Religious Propaganda in Judaism and Early Christianity* (Notre Dame, Ind.: University of Notre Dame Press, 1976) 69–98.
Idem
"The Omnipresence of the God-Fearers," *BAR* 12 (1986) 58–63.
Idem
"Proselytes and 'Sympathizers' in the Light of the New Inscriptions from Aphrodisias," *REJ* 148 (1989) 265–305.
Fellows, Richard G.
"Renaming in Paul's Churches: The Case of Crispus-Sosthenes Revisited," *TynBul* 56 (2005) 111–30.
Ferguson, John
Juvenal, The Satires (New York: St. Martin's, 1979).
Ferreiro, Albert
Simon Magus in Patristic, Medieval, and Early Modern Traditions (Studies in the History of Christian Traditions 125; Leiden: Brill, 2005).
Festugière, André Jean
Personal Religion among the Greeks (Berkeley: University of California Press, 1954).
Idem
La Révélation d'Hermès Trismégistos (4 vols.; Paris: Gabalda, 1950).
Fiedrowicz, Michael
"Die Rezeption und Interpretation der paulinischen Areopag-Rede in der patristischen Theologie," *TThZ* 111 (2002) 85–105.
Fieger, Michael
Im Schatten der Artemis: Glaube und Ungehorsam in Ephesus (Bern: Peter Lang, 1998).
Finger, Reta Halteman
Of Widows and Meals: Communal Meals in the Book of Acts (Grand Rapids: Eerdmans, 2007).
Finn, Thomas
"The God-Fearers Reconsidered," *CBQ* 47 (1985) 75–84.
Fitzgerald, John, ed.
Greco-Roman Perspectives on Friendship (Atlanta: Scholars Press, 1997).
Fitzgerald, Robert
The Aeneid of Virgil (New York: Vintage, 1984).
Fitzmyer, Joseph A.
The Gospel according to Luke: Introduction, Translation, and Notes (2 vols.; AB 28, 28A; Garden City, N.Y.: Doubleday, 1981, 1985).
Idem
"Jewish Christianity in Acts in Light of the Qumran Scrolls," in Leander Keck and J. Louis Martyn, eds., *Studies in Luke-Acts: Essays Presented in Honor of Paul Schubert* (Nashville: Abingdon, 1966) 233–57.
Idem
Luke the Theologian: Aspects of His Teaching (New York: Paulist, 1989).
Idem
"The Pauline Letters and the Lucan Account of Paul's Missionary Journeys," in David J. Lull, ed., *SBLSP 1988* (Atlanta: Scholars Press, 1988) 82–89.
Flender, Helmut
St. Luke: Theologian of Redemptive History (trans. I. Fuller and R. Fuller; Philadelphia: Fortress Press, 1967).
Fletcher, Richard
The Barbarian Conversion: From Paganism to Christianity (Berkeley: University of California Press, 1999).
Fletcher-Louis, Crispin H. T.
Luke-Acts: Angels, Christology and Soteriology (WUNT 94; Tübingen: Mohr Siebeck, 1997).
Flichy, Odile
La figure de Paul dans les Actes des Apôtres: un phénomène de reception de la tradition paulinienne à la fin du 1er siècle (LD 214; Paris: Cerf, 2007).

Idem
Relectures des Actes des Apôtres (Cahiers Évangile 128; Paris: Cerf, 2004).
Flinterman, Jaap-Jan
Power, Paideia, and Pythagoreanism: Greek Identity, Conceptions of the Relationship between Philosophers and Monarchs and Political Ideas in Philostratus' Life of Apollonius (Dutch Monographs on Ancient History and Archaeology 13; Amsterdam: Gieben, 1995).
Foakes Jackson, Frederick J., and Kirsopp Lake, eds.
The Beginnings of Christianity (5 vols.; New York: Macmillan, 1920–33; reprinted, Grand Rapids: Baker, 1979).
Eidem
"The Internal Evidence of Acts," in eidem, *Prolegomena II*, vol. 2 of Frederick J. Foakes Jackson and Kirsopp Lake, eds., *The Beginnings of Christianity* (5 vols.; New York: Macmillan, 1920–33; reprinted, Grand Rapids: Baker, 1979) 121–204.
Eidem
Prolegomena II, vol. 2 of Frederick J. Foakes Jackson and Kirsopp Lake, eds., *The Beginnings of Christianity* (5 vols.; New York: Macmillan, 1920–33; reprinted, Grand Rapids: Baker, 1979).
Foerster, Werner
"ἀρέσκω," *TDNT* 1:455–57.
Idem
Gnosis (2 vols.; trans. and ed. Robert McL. Wilson; Oxford: Clarendon, 1974).
Idem, et al.
"ὄφις," *TDNT* 5:566–82.
Forbes, Christopher
Prophecy and Inspired Speech in Early Christianity and Its Hellenistic Environment (WUNT 75; Tübingen: Mohr Siebeck, 1995).
Forbes, Clarence A.
"Books for the Burning," *TAPA* 67 (1936) 114–25.
Fournier, Marianne
The Episode at Lystra: A Rhetorical and Semiotic Analysis of Acts 14:7-20a (American University Studies VII.197; New York: Peter Lang, 1997).
Fowler, H.N.
Plutarch's Moralia X (LCL; Cambridge, Mass.: Harvard University Press, 1936).
Fox, Robin Lane
Pagans and Christians (New York: Knopf, 1989).
Frank, Tenney, ed.
An Economic Survey of Ancient Rome (5 vols.; Baltimore: Johns Hopkins University Press, 1933–40).
Franklin, Eric
Christ the Lord: A Study in the Purpose and Theology of Luke-Acts (Philadelphia: Westminster, 1975).
Fraser, P. M.
Ptolemaic Alexandria (2 vols.; Oxford: Clarendon, 1970).
French, David H.
"Acts and the Roman Roads of Asia Minor," in David W. J. Gill and Conrad Gempf, eds., *The Book of Acts in Its Graeco-Roman Setting* (BIFCS 2; Grand Rapids: Eerdmans, 1994) 49–58.
Frenschkowski, Marco
"Der Text der Apostelgeschichte und die Realien antiker Buchproduktion," in Tobias Nicklas and Michael Tilly, eds., *The Book of Acts as Church History: Textual Traditions and Ancient Interpretations* (BZNW 120; Berlin: de Gruyter, 2003) 87–107.
Frey, Jean-Baptiste
"Les Juifs à Pompei," *RB* 42 (1933) 370–72.
Fridrichsen, Anton
The Problem of Miracle in Primitive Christianity (trans. Roy A. Harrisville and John S. Hanson; Minneapolis: Augsburg, 1972).
Friedrich, Gerhard
"εὐαγγελιστής," *TDNT* 2:636–37.
Friesen, Steven
"The Cult of the Roman Emperors in Ephesos," in Helmut Koester, ed., *Ephesos: Metropolis of Asia* (HTS 41; Valley Forge, Pa.: Trinity Press International, 1995) 229–50.
Frye, Northrop
The Secular Scripture: A Study of the Structure of Romance (Cambridge, Mass.: Harvard University Press, 1976).
Funk, Robert W.
"The Enigma of the Famine Visit," *JBL* 75 (1956) 130–36.
Idem
The Poetics of Biblical Narrative (Sonoma, Calif.: Polebridge, 1988).
Furnish, Victor Paul
II Corinthians: Translated, with Introduction, Notes, and Commentary (AB 32A; Garden City, N.Y.: Doubleday, 1984).
Fusco, Vittorio
"La discussione sul protocattolicesimo nel Nuovo Testamento: Un capitolo di storia dell'esegesi," *ANRW* 2.26.2 (1995) 1645–91.
Idem
"Le sezione-noi degli Atti nella discussione recente," *BeO* 25 (1983) 73–86.
Gabba, Emilio
"The Social, Economic and Political History of Palestine 63 BCE–CE 70," in *The Cambridge History of Judaism*, vol. 3: *The Early Roman Period* (ed. William Horbury, W. D. Davies, and John Sturdy; Cambridge: Cambridge University Press, 1999) 94–167.
Gaca, Kathy L.
"Paul's Uncommon Declaration in Romans 1:18-32 and Its Problematic Legacy for Pagan and Christian Relations," in eadem and Larry L. Welborn, eds., *Early Patristic Readings of Romans* (Romans through History and Cultures; New York: T&T Clark, 2005) 1–33.
Gager, John G., ed.
Curse Tablets and Binding Spells from the Ancient World (New York: Oxford University Press, 1992).

Idem
"Jews, Gentiles, and Synagogues," in George W. E. Nickelsburg and George W. MacRae, eds., *Christians among Jews and Gentiles. Essays in Honor of Krister Stendahl* (Philadelphia: Fortress Press, 1986).

Gamble, Harry Y.
Books and Readers in the Early Church: A History of Early Christian Texts (New Haven: Yale University Press, 1995).

Gapp, Kenneth S.
"The Universal Famine under Claudius," *HTR* 28 (1935) 258–65.

Garland, Robert
The Greek Way of Death (Ithaca: Cornell University Press, 1985).

Idem
Introducing New Gods: The Politics of Athenian Religion (Ithaca: Cornell University Press, 1992).

Garnsey, Peter
"The Criminal Jurisdiction of Governors," *JRS* 58 (1968) 51–59.

Idem
Famine and Food Supply in the Graeco-Roman World: Responses to Risk and Crisis (Cambridge: Cambridge University Press, 1988).

Idem
"The *Lex Julia* and Appeal under the Empire," *JRS* 56 (1966) 167–89.

Idem, and Richard Saller
The Roman Empire: Economy, Society and Culture (Berkeley: University of California Press, 1987).

Garrett, Susan R.
"Beloved Physician of the Soul? Luke as Advocate for Ascetic Practice," in Leif E. Vaage and Vinicent L. Wimbush, eds., *Asceticism and the New Testament* (London: Routledge, 1999) 71–95.

Idem
The Demise of the Devil: Magic and the Demonic in Luke-Acts (Minneapolis: Fortress Press, 1989).

Idem
"Exodus from Bondage: Luke 9:31 and Acts 12:1-24," *CBQ* 52 (1990) 656–89.

Gärtner, Bertil
The Areopagus Speech and Natural Revelation (ASNU 21; Uppsala: Gleerup, 1955).

Idem
"Paulus and Barnabas in Lystra: Zu Apg. 14, 8-15," *SEÅ* 27 (1962) 83–88.

Gaselee, S.
Achilles Tatius (LCL; Cambridge, Mass.: Harvard University Press, 1969).

Gasque, W. Ward
A History of the Criticism of the Acts of the Apostles (Grand Rapids: Eerdmans, 1975).

Idem
"Iconium," *ABD* 3:357–58.

Idem
"Malta," *ABD* 4:489–90.

Idem
"Tarsus," *ABD* 6:333–34.

Gaventa, Beverly Roberts
From Darkness to Light: Aspects of Conversion in the New Testament (OBT; Philadelphia: Fortress Press, 1986).

Eadem
"Theology and Ecclesiology in the Miletus Speech: Reflections on Content and Context," *NTS* 50 (2004) 36–52.

Eadem
"Toward a Theology of Acts: Reading and Rereading," *Int* 42 (1988) 146–57.

Geagan, Daniel J.
The Athenian Constitution after Sulla (Hesperia Supp. 12; Princeton: Princeton University Press, 1967).

Gebhard, Elizabeth R.
"The Gods in Transit: Narratives of Cult Transfer," in Adela Yarbro Collins and Margaret M. Mitchell, eds., *Antiquity and Humanity: Essays in Ancient Religion and Philosophy Presented to Hans Dieter Betz on His 70th Birthday* (Tübingen: Mohr Siebeck, 2001) 451–76.

Geer, Thomas C., Jr.
Family 1739 in Acts (SBLMS 48; Atlanta: Scholars Press, 1994).

Gempf, Conrad
"Mission and Misunderstanding: Paul and Barnabas in Lystra (Acts 14:8-20)," in Anthony Billington et al., eds., *Mission and Meaning: Essays Presented to Peter Cotterell* (Carlisle: Paternoster, 1995) 56–69.

Idem
"Salamis," *ABD* 5:904–5.

Georgi, Dieter
"Forms of Religious Propaganda," in H. J. Schultz, ed., *Jesus in His Time* (Philadelphia: Fortress Press, 1971) 124–31.

Idem
The Opponents of Paul in Second Corinthians (Philadelphia: Fortress Press, 1986).

Idem
Remembering the Poor: The History of Paul's Collection for Jerusalem (Nashville: Abingdon, 1992).

Idem
"Socioeconomic Reasons for the 'Divine Man' as a Propagandistic Pattern," in Elisabeth Schüssler Fiorenza, ed., *Aspects of Religious Propaganda in Judaism and Early Christianity* (Notre Dame, Ind.: University of Notre Dame Press, 1976) 27–42.

Idem
"Who Is the True Prophet?" in George W. E. Nickelsburg and George W. MacRae, eds., *Christians among Jews and Gentiles* (Philadelphia: Fortress Press, 1986) 100–126.

Gibbs, James Millard
"Luke 24:13-33 and Acts 8:26-39: The Emmaus Incident and the Eunuch's Baptism as Parallel Stories," *Bangalore Theological Forum* 7 (1975) 17–30.

Giesen, Heinz
"Gott Steht zu Seinen Verheissungen: Eine Exegetische und Theologische Auslegung des Pfingstgeschehens (Apg 2, 1-13)," *StudNTUmwelt* 28 (2003) 83–126.
Gilbert, Gary
"The List of Nations in Acts 2: Roman Propaganda and the Lukan Response," *JBL* 121 (2002) 497–529.
Idem
"Roman Propaganda and Christian Identity in the Worldview of Luke-Acts," in Todd Penner and Caroline Vander Stichele, *Contextualizing Acts: Lukan Narrative and Greco-Roman Discourse* (SBLSS 20; Boston/Leiden: Brill; Atlanta: Society of Biblical Literature, 2004) 233–56.
Gilchrist, J. M.
"The Historicity of Paul's Shipwreck," *JSNT* 61 (1996) 29–51.
Giles, K. N.
"Luke's Use of the Term *'ekklesia'* with Special Reference to Acts 20.28 and 9.31," *NTS* 31 (1985) 135–42.
Gill, David W. J.
"Achaia," in idem and Conrad Gempf, eds., *The Book of Acts in Its Graeco-Roman Setting* (BIFCS 2; Grand Rapids: Eerdmans, 1994) 433–53.
Idem
"Acts and the Urban Élites," in idem and Conrad Gempf, eds., *The Book of Acts in Its Graeco-Roman Setting* (BIFCS 2; Grand Rapids: Eerdmans, 1994) 105–18.
Idem
"Dionysios and Damaris: A Note on Acts 17:34," *CBQ* 61 (1999) 483–90.
Idem
"Macedonia," in idem and Conrad Gempf, eds., *The Book of Acts in Its Graeco-Roman Setting* (BIFCS 2; Grand Rapids: Eerdmans, 1994) 397–417.
Idem, and Conrad Gempf, eds.
The Book of Acts in Its Graeco-Roman Setting (BIFCS 2; Grand Rapids: Eerdmans, 1994).
Idem, and Bruce W. Winter
"Acts and Roman Religion," in David W. J. Gill and Conrad Gempf, eds., *The Book of Acts in Its Graeco-Roman Setting* (BIFCS 2; Grand Rapids: Eerdmans, 1994) 79–103.
Ginzberg, Louis
The Legends of the Jews (7 vols.; Philadelphia: Jewish Publication Society, 1909–38).
Glover, R.
"'Luke the Antiochene' and Acts," *NTS* 11 (1964) 97–106.
Goldin, Judah
"The Magic of Magic and Superstition," in Elisabeth Schüssler Fiorenza, ed., *Aspects of Religious Propaganda in Judaism and Early Christianity* (Notre Dame, Ind.: University of Notre Dame Press, 1976) 115–47.
Goldstein, H.
"ἐγκράτεια," *EDNT* 1:377–78.
Goldstein, Jonathan A.
II Maccabees: A New Translation with Introduction and Commentary (AB 41A; Garden City, N.Y.: Doubleday, 1983).
Goodenough, Erwin R.
"The Perspective of Acts," in Leander Keck and J. Louis Martyn, eds., *Studies in Luke-Acts: Essays Presented in Honor of Paul Schubert* (Nashville: Abingdon, 1966) 51–59.
Goodman, Felicitas D.
Speaking in Tongues: A Cross-Cultural Study of Glossolalia (Chicago: University of Chicago Press, 1972).
Goodman, Martin
Mission and Conversion: Proselytizing in the Religious History of the Roman Empire (Oxford: Clarendon, 1994).
Idem
The Ruling Class of Judaea: The Origins of the Jewish Revolt against Rome A.D. 66–70 (Cambridge: Cambridge University Press, 1987).
Goodspeed, Edgar J.
"Gaius Titius Justus," *JBL* 69 (1950) 382–83.
Goold, G. P.
Chariton, Callirhoe (LCL; Cambridge, Mass.: Harvard University Press, 1995).
Goppelt, Leonhard
A Commentary on 1 Peter (ed. F. Hahn; trans. John E. Alsup; Grand Rapids: Eerdmans, 1993).
Idem
Typos: The Typological Interpretaion of the Old Testament in the New (trans. D. H. Madvig; Grand Rapids: Eerdmans, 1982).
Goulder, Michael D.
"Did Luke Know Any of the Pauline Letters?" *PerspRelStud* 13 (1986) 97–112.
Idem
St. Paul versus St. Peter: A Tale of Two Missions (Louisville: Westminster John Knox, 1994).
Idem
Type and History in Acts (London: SPCK, 1964).
Gourgues, M.
"La littérature profane dans le discours d'Athènes (Ac 17,16-31): un dossier fermé?" *RB* 109 (2002) 241–69.
Gowler, David W.
Host, Guest, Enemy, and Friend: Portraits of the Pharisees in Luke and Acts (New York: Peter Lang, 1991).
Graf, Fritz
Magic in the Ancient World (trans. Franklin Philip; Revealing Antiquity 10; Cambridge, Mass.: Harvard University Press, 1997).
Grant, Robert M.
"Dietary Laws among Pythagoreans, Jews, and Christians," *HTR* 73 (1980) 299–310.
Idem
Greek Apologists of the Second Century (Philadelphia: Westminster, 1988).

Idem
Heresy and Criticism (Louisville: Westminster John Knox, 1993).
Idem
Jesus after the Gospels: The Christ of the Second Century (Louisville: Westminster John Knox, 1990).
Idem
Miracle and Natural Law in Greco-Roman and Early Christian Thought (Amsterdam: North-Holland, 1952).
Idem, and Holt Graham
The Apostolic Fathers, vol. 2: *First and Second Clement* (New York: Thomas Nelson & Sons, 1965).
Grappe, Christian
"Main de Dieu et mains des apôtres: Réflexions à partir d'Actes 4.30 et 5,12," in R. Kieffer and J. Bergman, eds., *La Main de Dieu//Die Hand Gottes* (WUNT 94; Tübingen: Mohr Siebeck, 1997).
Grässer, Erich
"Acta-Forschung seit 1960," *TRU* 41 (1976) 141–94; 42 (1977) 1–68.
Idem
Forschungen zur Apostelgeschichte (WUNT 2.137; Tübingen: Mohr Siebeck, 2001).
Grassi, Joseph
"Emmaus Revisited (Luke 24:13-35 and Acts 8:26-40)," *CBQ* 26 (1964) 463–67.
Gray, George B.
Sacrifice in the Old Testament: Its Theory and Practice (Oxford: Clarendon, 1925).
Gray, Louis H.
"Eunuch," *ERE* 5:575–79.
Gray, Patrick
"Athenian Curiosity (Acts 17:21)," *NovT* 47 (2005) 109–16.
Idem
"Implied Audiences in the Areopagus Narrative," *TynBull* 55 (2004) 205–18.
Green, Joel
"Festus, Porcius," *ABD* 2:794–95.
Idem, and Michael C. McKeever
Luke-Acts and New Testament Historiography (Grand Rapids: Baker, 1994).
Green, Michael
Evangelism in the Early Church (Grand Rapids: Eerdmans, 1970).
Greeven, Heinrich
"εὔχομαι," *TDNT* 2:775–808.
Idem
"Propheten, Lehrer, Vorsteher bei Paulus: Zur Frage der 'Ämter' im Urchristentum," *ZNW* 44 (1952–53) 1–43.
Idem
"προσδέομαι," *TDNT* 2:41–42.
Idem
"προσκυνέω," *TDNT* 6:758–66.
Idem
"ζητέω," *TDNT* 2:892–93.
Gregory, Andrew
"The Reception of Luke and Acts and the Unity of Luke-Acts," *JSNT* 29 (2007) 459–72.
Idem
The Reception of Luke and Acts in the Period before Irenaeus (WUNT 169; Tübingen: Mohr Siebeck, 2003).
Grundmann, Walter
"δύναμαι," *TDNT* 2:284–317.
Idem
"ἐγκράτεια," *TDNT* 2:339–42.
Idem
"θαρρέω," *TDNT* 3:25–27.
Idem
"Paulus in Ephesus," *Helikon* 4 (1964) 46–82.
Idem
"Das Problem des hellenistischen Christentums innerhalb der Jerusalemer Urgemeinde," *ZNW* 38 (1939) 45–73.
Günther, Matthias
Die Frühgeschichte des Christentums in Ephesus (2nd ed.; Frankfurt: Peter Lang, 1998).
Gutbrot, Walter
"ἄνομος," *TDNT* 4:1086–87.
Haacker, Klaus
"Das Bekenntnis des Paulus zur Hoffnung Israels nach der Apostelgeschichte des Lukas," *NTS* 31 (1985) 437–51.
Idem
"Dibelius und Cornelius: Ein Beispiel formgeschichtlicher Überlieferungskritik," *BZ* 24 (1980) 234–51.
Idem
"Gallio," *ABD* 2:901–3.
Idem
"Die Stellung des Stephanus in der Geschichte des Urchristentums," *ANRW* 2.26.2 (1995) 1415–53.
Haar, Stephen
Simon Magus: The First Gnostic? (BZNW 119; Berlin: de Gruyter, 2003).
Hackett, John
"Echoes of the Bacchae of Euripides in Acts of the Apostles," *Irish Theological Quarterly* 23 (1956) 219–27, 350–66.
Hadas, Moses
Aristeas to Philocrates (Letter of Aristeas) (New York: Ktav, 1973).
Idem
Hellenistic Culture: Fusion and Diffusion (New York: Norton, 1972).
Idem
"Third Maccabees and Greek Romance," *Review of Religion* 13 (1949) 155–62.
Idem
"Third Maccabees and the Tradition of Patriotic Romance," *Chronique d'Egypte* 47 (1949) 97–104.
Idem, and Morton Smith, eds.
Heroes and Gods: Spiritual Biographies in Antiquity (New York: Harper & Row, 1965).

Haenchen, Ernst
"Acta 27," in Erich Dinkler, ed., *Zeit und Geschichte: Dankesgabe an Rudolf Bultmann zum 80. Geburtstag* (Tübingen: Mohr Siebeck, 1964) 235–54.
Idem
"The Book of Acts as Source Material for the History of Early Christianity," in Leander Keck and J. Louis Martyn, eds., *Studies in Luke-Acts: Essays Presented in Honor of Paul Schubert* (Nashville: Abingdon, 1966) 258–78.
Idem
"Gab es eine vorchristliche Gnosis?" *ZThK* 49 (1952) 316–49 (= *Gott und Mensch: Gesammelte Aufsätze* [Tübingen: Mohr Siebeck, 1965] 265–98).
Idem
Gott und Mensch: Gesammelte Aufsätze (Tübingen: Mohr Siebeck, 1965).
Idem
"Schriftzitate und Textüberlieferung in der Apostelgeschichte," *ZThK* 51 (1954) 153–67 (= *Gott und Mensch: Gesammelte Aufsätze* [Tübingen: Mohr Siebeck, 1965] 157–71).
Idem
"Simon Magus in der Apostelgeschichte," in K. W. Tröger, ed., *Gnosis und Neues Testament: Studien aus Religionswissenschaft und Theologie* (Gütersloh: Mohn, 1973) 267–79.
Idem
"'We' in Acts and the Itinerary," *The Bultmann School of Biblical Interpretation: New Directions? Journal for Theology and Church* 1 (1965) 65–99.
Hägg, Tomas
Narrative Technique in Ancient Greek Romances: Studies of Chariton, Xenophon, Ephesius, and Achilles Tatius (Stockholm: Paul Aström, 1971).
Idem
The Novel in Antiquity (Berkeley and Los Angeles: University of California Press, 1983).
Hahn, Ferdinand
Mission in the New Testament (trans. F. Clarke; London: SCM, 1965).
Idem
The Titles of Jesus in Christology: Their History in Early Christianity (trans. Harold Knight and G. Ogg; Cleveland: World, 1969).
Hall, Stuart G.
Melito of Sardis On Pascha and Fragments (Oxford Early Christian Texts; London: Clarendon, 1979).
Hallstrom, A.
"De Curiositate Antheniensium," *Eranos* 14 (1914) 57–59.
Hamm, M. Dennis
"Acts 3:1-10: The Healing of the Temple Beggar as Lucan Theology," *Bib* 67 (1986) 305–19.
Idem
"Paul's Blindness and Its Healing: Clues to Symbolic Intent (Acts 9; 22 and 26)," *Bib* 71 (1990) 63–72.
Hanges, James C.
"The Greek Foundation-Legend: Its Form and Relation to History," *SBLSP 1995* (Atlanta: Scholars Press, 1995) 494–520.
Hansen, William
Anthology of Ancient Greek Popular Literature (Bloomington: Indiana University Press, 1998).
Hanson, J. Arthur
Apuleius Metamorphoses (2 vols.; LCL; Cambridge, Mass.: Harvard University Press, 1989).
Hanson, John S.
"Dreams and Visions in the Greco-Roman World and Early Christianity," *ANRW* 2.23.2 (1980) 1395–1427.
Hanson, Richard P. C.
The Acts in the RSV (Oxford: Clarendon, 1967).
Hardin, Justin K.
"Decrees and Drachmas at Thessalonica: An Illegal Assembly in Jason's House (Acts 17.1-10a)," *NTS* 52 (2006) 29–49.
Harding, Mark
"On the Historicity of Acts: Comparing Acts 9.23-25 with 2 Corinthians 11.32-33," *NTS* 39 (1993) 518–38.
Hardon, John A.
"The Miracle Narratives in the Acts of the Apostles," *CBQ* 16 (1954) 303–18.
Harmon, A. M.
Lucian III, V (LCL; Cambridge, Mass.: Harvard University Press, 1919, 1936).
Harnack, Adolph von
The Acts of the Apostles (trans J. R. Wilkinson; New York: G. P. Putnam's Sons, 1909).
Idem
Marcion: Das Evangelium vom fremden Gott (Leipzig: Hinrichs, 1921), ET *Marcion: The Gospel of the Alien God* (trans. John E. Steely and L. Bierma; Durham, N.C.: Labyrinth, 1990).
Idem
The Mission and Expansion of Christianity in the First Three Centuries (2 vols.; trans. J. Moffatt; New York: G. P. Putnam's Sons, 1908).
Idem
Neue Untersuchungen zur Apostelgeschichte (Leipzig: Hinrichs, 1911).
Harrer, Gustave A.
"Saul Who Is Also Called Paul," *HTR* 33 (1940) 19–34.
Harrill, J. Albert
"The Dramatic Function of the Running Slave Rhoda (Acts 12.13-16): A Piece of Greco-Roman Comedy," *NTS* 46 (2000) 150–57.
Idem
The Manumission of Slaves in Early Christianity (HUTh 32; Tübingen: Mohr Siebeck, 1995).
Harrington, Daniel
"The Bible Rewritten," in Robert Kraft and George W. E. Nickelsburg, eds., *Early Judaism and Its Modern Interpreters* (Atlanta: Scholars Press, 1986) 239–47.
Harris, J. Rendel
Codex Bezae: A Study of the So-called Western Text of the New Testament (TextsS 2.1; Cambridge: Cambridge University Press, 1891).

Harris, William V.
Restraining Rage: The Ideology of Anger in Classical Antiquity (Cambridge, Mass.: Harvard University Press, 2001).

Hasler, V.
"γενεαλογία," *EDNT* 1:42.

Hatchett, Marion J.
Commentary on the American Prayer Book (New York: Seabury, 1981).

Hauck, Friedrich
"κοινός," *TDNT* 3:789–809.

Hauschild, Wolf-Dieter
"'Christentum und Eigentum': Zum Problem eines altkirchlichen 'Sozialismus,'" *Zeitschrift für evangelische Ethik* 16 (1972): 34–49.

Hauser, Hermann J.
Strukturen der Abschlußerzählung der Apostelgeschichte (Apg 28,16-31) (AnBib 86; Rome: Pontifical Biblical Institute, 1979).

Havelaar, Henriette
"Hellenistic Parallels to Acts 5,1-11 and the Problem of Conflicting Interpretations," *JSNT* 67 (1997) 63–82.

Hawkins, John C.
Horae Synopticae (Grand Rapids: Baker, 1968).

Hay, David M.
Glory at the Right Hand: Psalm 110 in Early Christianity (SBLMS 18; Nashville: Abingdon, 1973).

Hayes, John H., and J. Roloff
"Acts of the Apostles, Book of the," *Dictionary of Biblical Interpretation* (ed. John H. Hayes; 2 vols.; Nashville: Abingdon, 1999) 1:4–13.

Head, Peter
"Acts and the Problem of Its Texts," in Bruce W. Winter and Andrew D. Clarke, *The Book of Acts in Its Ancient Literary Setting* (BIFCS 1; Grand Rapids: Eerdmans, 1993) 415–44.

Hedrick, Charles W.
"Paul's Conversion/Call: A Comparative Analysis of the Three Reports in Acts," *JBL* 100 (1981) 415–32.

Heil, Christoph
"Arius Didymus and Luke-Acts," *NovT* 42 (2000) 358–93.

Heintz, Florent
Simon 'le Magicien': Actes 8 5-25 et l'accusation de magie contre les Prophètes thaumaturges dan l'antiquité (CahRB 39; Paris: Gabalda, 1997).

Hemer, Colin J.
"Alexandria Troas," *TynBul* 26 (1975) 79–112.

Idem
The Book of Acts in the Setting of Hellenistic History (ed. Conrad J. Gempf; Winona Lake, Ind.: Eisenbrauns, 1990).

Idem
"First Person Narrative in Acts 27–28," *TynBul* 36 (1985) 79–109.

Idem
"Luke the Historian," *BJRL* 60 (1977) 28–51.

Idem
"Lydia and the Purple Trade," *NewDocs* 3 (1983) no. 17, pp. 53–55.

Idem
"The Name of Felix Again," *JSNT* 31 (1987) 45–49.

Idem
"Paul at Athens," *NTS* 20 (1974) 241–50.

Idem
"The Speeches in Acts I: The Ephesian Elders at Miletus," *TynBul* 40 (1989) 77–85.

Hendrix, Holland L.
"Philippi," *ABD* 5:313–17.

Idem
"Thessalonica," *ABD* 6:523–27.

Hengel, Martin
Acts and the History of Earliest Christianity (trans. John Bowden; Philadelphia: Fortress Press, 1979).

Idem
Between Jesus and Paul: Studies in the History of Earliest Christianity (trans. John Bowden; Philadelphia: Fortress Press, 1983).

Idem
"᾿Ιουδαῖα in der geographischen Liste Apg 2,9-11 und Syrien als 'Grossjudäa,'" *RHPhR* 80 (2000) 83–86.

Idem
Judaism and Hellenism: Studies in Their Encounter in Palestine during the Early Hellenistic Period (trans. John Bowden; 2 vols.; Philadelphia: Fortress Press, 1974).

Idem
"Proseuche und Synagoge," in Gert Jeremias, Heinz-Wolfgang Kuhn, and Hartmut Stegemann, eds., *Tradition und Glaube: Das frühe Christentum in seiner Umwelt: Festgabe für Karl Georg Kuhn zum 65. Geburtstag* (Göttingen: Vandenhoeck & Ruprecht, 1971) 157–84.

Idem, and Anna Maria Schwemer
Paul between Damascus and Antioch: The Unknown Years (trans. John Bowden; Louisville: Westminster John Knox, 1997).

Henrichs, Albert
"Pagan Ritual and the Alleged Crimes of the Early Christians: A Reconsideration," in Patrick Granfield and Josef A. Jungmann, eds., *Kyriakon: Festschrift Johannes Quasten* (2 vols.; Munich: Kösel, 1970) 1:18–35.

Heusler, Erika
Kapitalprozesse im lukanischen Doppelwerk: Die Verfahren gegen Jesus und Paulus in exegetischer und rechtshistorischer Analyse (NTAbh NF 38; Münster: Aschendorff, 2000).

Hickling, Colin J. A.
"The Portrait of Paul in Acts 26," in Jacob Kremer, ed., *Les Actes des Apôtres: Traditions, rédaction, théologie* (BEThL 48; Leuven: Leuven University Press, 1979) 499–503.

Hicks, R. D.
Diogenes Laertius I (LCL; Cambridge, Mass.: Harvard University Press, 1925).

Hilgert, Earle
The Ship and Related Symbols in the New Testament (Assen: Van Gorcum, 1962).

Hill, Craig C.
"Acts 6.1–8.4: Division or diversity?" in Ben Witherington III, *History, Literature and Society in the Book of Acts* (Cambridge: Cambridge University Press, 1996) 129–53.

Idem
Hellenists and Hebrews: Reappraising Division within the Earliest Church (Minneapolis: Fortress Press, 1992).

Hills, Julian
"The Acts of the Apostles in the *Acts of Paul*," in Eugene Lovering, ed., *SBLSP 1994* (Atlanta: Scholars Press, 1994) 24–54.

Idem
"Equal Justice under the (New) Law: The Story of Ananias and Sapphira in Acts 5," *Forum* n.s. 3 (2000) 105–25.

Hirsch, Emmanuel
"Die drei Berichte der Apostelgeschichte über die Bekehrung des Paulus," *ZNW* 28 (1929) 305–12.

Hobart, William K.
The Medical Language of St. Luke (London: Longmans, Green & Co., 1882).

Hock, Ronald F.
The Infancy Gospels of James and Thomas (Scholars Bible 2; Santa Rosa, Calif.: Polebridge, 1995).

Idem
The Social Context of Paul's Ministry (Philadelphia: Fortress Press, 1980).

Hoffmann, R. Joseph
"How Then Know This Troublous Teacher? Further Reflections on Marcion and his Church," *SecCent* 6 (1987) 173–91.

Idem
Marcion: On the Restitution of Christianity; An Essay on the Development of Radical Paulinist Theology in the Second Century (American Academy of Religion Academy Series 46; Chico, Calif.: Scholars Press, 1984).

Idem
Porphyry's Against the Christians: The Literary Remains (Amherst, N.Y.: Prometheus Books, 1994).

Hogan, Derek
"Paul's Defense: A Comparison of the Forensic Speeches in Acts, *Callirhoe*, and *Leucippe*," *PerspRelStud* 29 (2002) 73–88.

Holladay, Carl
"Acts and the Fragments of Hellenistic Jewish Historians," in David P. Moessner, ed., *Jesus and the Heritage of Israel: Luke's Narrative Claim upon Israel's Legacy* (Harrisburg, Pa.: Trinity Press International, 1999) 171–98.

Idem
Fragments from Hellenistic Jewish Authors (Chico, Calif.: Scholars Press, 1983).

Idem
Theios Aner in Hellenistic Judaism (SBLDS 40; Missoula, Mont.: Scholars Press, 1977).

Holmberg, Bengt
Paul and Power: The Structure of Authority in the Primitive Church as Reflected in the Pauline Epistles (Philadelphia: Fortress Press, 1980).

Holmes, Michael W.
"Codex Bezae as a Recension of the Gospels," in D. C. Parker and C.-B. Amphoux, eds., *Codex Bezae: Studies from the Lunel Colloquium June 1994* (NTTS 22; Leiden: Brill, 1996) 123–60.

Holtz, Traugott
Untersuchungen über die alttestamentlichen Zitate bei Lukas (TU 104; Berlin: Akademie, 1968).

Holum, Kenneth G., Robert L. Hohlfelder, Robert J. Bull, and Avner Raban
King Herod's Dream: Caesarea on the Sea (New York: Norton, 1988).

Holzberg, Niklas
"The *Historia Apollonii regis Tyri* and the *Odyssey*," in *Groningen Colloquia on the Novel* (Groningen: Egbert Forsten, 1990) 3:91–101.

Idem
"Letters: *Chion*," in Gareth Schmeling, ed., *The Novel in the Ancient World* (rev. ed.; Leiden: Brill, 2003) 645–53.

Idem
"Utopias and Fantastic Travel: Euhemerus, Iambulus," in Gareth Schmeling, ed., *The Novel in the Ancient World* (rev. ed.; Leiden: Brill, 2003) 621–28.

Holzmeister, Ulrich
"Der hl. Paulus vor dem Richterstuhle des Festus (AG 25, 1-12)," *ZKTh* 36 (1912) 489–511, 742–83.

Hommel, Hildebrecht
"Neue Forschung zur Areopagrede Acta 17," *ZNW* 46 (1955) 145–78.

Hopkins, Keith
"Christian Number and Its Implications," *JECS* 6 (1998) 185–226.

Horbury, William, W. D. Davies, John Sturdy, eds.
The Cambridge History of Judaism, vol. 3: *The Early Roman Period* (Cambridge: Cambridge University Press, 1999).

Horn, Friedrich W.
"Apg 8,37, der Westliche Text und die frühchristliche Tauftheologie," in Tobias Nicklas and Michael Tilly, eds., *The Book of Acts as Church History: Textual Traditions and Ancient Interpretations* (BZNW 120; Berlin: de Gruyter, 2003) 211–39.

Idem
Das Ende des Paulus: Historische, theologische und literaturgeschichtliche Aspekte (BZNW 106; Berlin: de Gruyter, 2001).

Idem
"Die Gütergemeinschaft der Urgemeinde," *EvTh* 58 (1998) 370–83.

Idem
"Die Haltung des Lukas zum römischen Staat im Evangelium und in der Apostelgeschichte," in Jozef Verheyden, ed., *The Unity of Luke-Acts* (BEThL 92; Leuven: Leuven University Press, 1999) 203–24.

Idem
"Die Kollektenthematik in der Apostelgeschichte," in Ciliers Breytenbach et al., eds., *Apostelgeschichte und die hellenistische Geschichtsschreibung: Festschrift für Eckhard Plümacher zu seinem 65. Geburtstag* (AGJU 57; Leiden/Boston: Brill, 2004) 135–56.

Hornschuh, Manfred
"The Apostles as Bearers of the Tradition," in Edgar Hennecke, *New Testament Apocrypha* (ed. Wilhelm Schneemelcher, ET ed. R. McL. Wilson; 2 vols.; Philadelphia: Westminster, 1965) 2:74–87.

Horsley, Gregory H. R.
"The Inscriptions of Ephesos and the New Testament," *NovT* 34 (1992) 105–67.

Idem
"The Politarchs," in David W. J. Gill and Conrad Gempf, eds., *The Book of Acts in Its Graeco-Roman Setting* (BIFCS 2; Grand Rapids: Eerdmans, 1994) 2:419–31.

Horsley, Richard A., with John S. Hanson
Bandits, Prophets, and Messiahs (San Francisco: Harper & Row, 1985).

Horst, Pieter van der
"The Altar of the 'Unknown God' in Athens: Acts 17.23 and the Cults of 'Unknown Gods' in the Graeco-Roman World," in idem, *Hellenism–Judaism–Christianity* (Kampen: Kok Pharos, 1994) 165–202.

Idem
"The Altar of the 'Unknown God' in Athens (Acts 17:23) and the Cult of 'Unknown Gods' in the Hellenistic and Roman Periods," *ANRW* 2.18.2 (1990) 426–56.

Idem
"Hellenistic Parallels to Acts Chapters 3 and 4," *JSNT* 35 (1989) 37–46.

Idem
"Hellenistic Parallels to the Acts of the Apostles (2.1-47)," *JSNT* 25 (1985) 49–60.

Idem
"Peter's Shadow: The Religio-Historical Background of Acts V.15," *NTS* 23 (1976–77) 204–12.

Idem
Philo's Flaccus: The First Pogrom (Philo of Alexandria Commentary Series 2; Atlanta: Society of Biblical Literature, 2003).

Hubbard, Benjamin J.
"The Role of Commissioning Accounts in Acts," in Charles H. Talbert, *Perspectives on Luke-Acts* (Danville, Va.: National Association of Baptist Professors of Religion, 1978) 187–98.

Hubbard, Moyer V.
"Urban Uprisings in the Roman World: The Social Setting of the Mobbing of Sosthenes," *NTS* 51 (2005) 416–28.

Hughes, Frank W.
Early Christian Rhetoric and 2 Thessalonians (JSNTS 30; Sheffield: Sheffield Academic Press, 1989).

Hull, John M.
Hellenistic Magic and the Synoptic Tradition (SBT 28; London: SCM, 1974).

Hummel, Adrian
"Factum et Fictum: Literarische und theologische Erwägungen zur Romreise des Paulus in der Apostelgeschichte (Apg 27,1–28,16)," *BibNotiz* 105 (2000) 39–53.

Humphrey, Edith M.
"Collision of Modes?–Vision and Determining Argument in Acts 10:1–11:18," *Sem* 71 (1995) 65–84.

Humphries, R.
The Satires of Juvenal (Bloomington: Indiana University Press, 1958).

Hunt, A. S., and C. C. Edgar, eds.
Select Papyri (3 vols.; LCL: Cambridge, Mass.: Harvard University Press, 1929–).

Hunt, Melvin
"Lod," *ABD* 4:346–47.

Hur, Ju
A Dynamic Reading of the Holy Spirit in Luke-Acts (JSNTS 211; Sheffield: Sheffield Academic Press, 2001).

Hurd, John C., Jr.
The Origin of 1 Corinthians (New York: Seabury, 1965).

Huxley, H. H.
"Storm and Shipwreck in Roman Literature," *Greece and Rome* 21 (1952) 117–25.

Hydahl, Niels
"The Reception of Paul in the Acts of the Apostles," in M. Müller and H. Tronier, eds., *The New Testament as Reception* (JSNTS 230; London: Sheffield Academic Press, 2002) 101–19.

Inge, W. R.
"Ecstasy," *ERE* 5:157–59.

Jacobson, Glenn R.
"Paul in Luke-Acts: The Savior Who Is Present," in Kent H. Richards, ed., *SBLSP 1983* (Chico, Calif.: Scholars Press, 1983) 131–46.

Jaeger, Werner
Early Christianity and Greek Paideia (Cambridge, Mass.: Belknap Press of Harvard University Press, 1961).

Jáuregui, José Antonio
"Panorama de la evolución de los estudios lucanos," *EstBib* 61 (2003) 351–98.

Jefford, Clayton N.
"Mark, John," *ABD* 4:557–58.

Jenkinson, Edna
"Nepos–An Introduction to Latin Biography," in Thomas A. Dorey, ed., *Latin Biography* (New York: Basic Books, 1967) 1–15.

Jeremias, Joachim
Jerusalem in the Time of Jesus (trans. F. H. Cave and C. H. Cave; Philadelphia: Fortress Press, 1975).

Idem
"Paarweise Sendung im Neuen Testament," in *New Testament Essays: Studies in Memory of Thomas Walter Manson* (ed. Angus John Brockhurst Higgins; Manchester: Manchester University Press, 1959) 136–43.

Idem
"πάσχα," *TDNT* 5:896–904.
Jervell, Jacob
"The Church of Jews and Godfearers," in Joseph B. Tyson, ed., *Luke-Acts and the Jewish People: Eight Critical Perspectives* (Minneapolis: Augsburg, 1988) 11–20.
Idem
Luke and the People of God: A New Look at Luke-Acts (Minneapolis: Augsburg, 1972).
Idem
The Theology of Acts (New Testament Theology; Cambridge: Cambridge University Press, 1996).
Idem
The Unknown Paul: Essays on Luke-Acts and Early Christian History (Minneapolis: Augsburg, 1984).
Jewett, Robert
A Chronology of Paul's Life (Philadelphia: Fortress Press, 1979).
Idem
"Mapping the Route of Paul's 'Second Missionary Journey,'" *TynBul* 48 (1997) 1–22.
Johnson, Luke Timothy
The Gospel of Luke (SacPag; Collegeville, Minn.: Liturgical Press, 1991).
Idem
"Literary Criticism of Luke-Acts: Is Reception-History Pertinent?" *JSNT* 28 (2005) 159–62.
Idem
The Literary Function of Possessions in Luke-Acts (SBLDS 39; Missoula, Mont.: Scholars Press, 1977).
Idem
"Luke-Acts, Book of," *ABD* 4:403–20.
Idem
Septuagintal Midrash in the Speeches of Acts (The Père Marquette Lecture in Theology, 2002; Milwaukee: Marquette University Press, 2002).
Idem
"Tongues, Gift of," *ABD* 6:596–600.
Idem
The Writings of the New Testament (Philadelphia: Fortress Press, 1986).
Johnson, Sherman E.
"Asia Minor and Early Christianity," in Jacob Neusner, ed., *Christianity, Judaism and Other Greco-Roman Cults: Festschrift for Morton Smith at Sixty* (4 vols.; Leiden: Brill, 1975) 2:77–145.
Idem
Paul the Apostle and His Cities (GNS 21; Wilmington, Del.: Michael Glazier, 1987).
Idem
"A Proposed Form-Critical Treatment of Acts," *ATR* 21 (1939) 22–31.
Johnston, George
"Christ as Archegos," *NTS* 27 (1981) 381–85.
Jones, Arthur H. M.
"I Appeal unto Caesar," in George E. Mylonas and D. Raymond, eds., *Studies Presented to David Moore Robinson on His Seventieth Birthday* (2 vols.; St. Louis: Washington University Press, 1951–53) 2:918–30.
Idem
The Cities of the Eastern Roman Provinces (2nd ed.; Oxford: Clarendon, 1971).
Idem
The Greek City from Alexander to Justinian (Oxford: Clarendon, 1940).
Jones, Christopher P.
"A Geographical Setting for the Baucis and Philemon Legend," *HSCP* 96 (1994) 203–23.
Idem
Plutarch and Rome (Oxford: Clarendon, 1971).
Jones, F. Stanley
An Ancient Jewish Christian Source on the History of Christianity: Pseudo-Clementine Recognitions 1.21–71 (SBLTT 37; Atlanta: Scholars Press, 1995).
Idem
"A Jewish Christian Reads Luke's Acts of the Apostles: The Use of the Canonical Acts in the Ancient Jewish Christian Source behind Pseudo-Clementine *Recognitions* 1.27-71," *SBLSP 1995* (Atlanta: Scholars Press, 1995) 617–35.
Jonsson, Jon
Humor and Irony in the New Testament: Illuminated by Parallels in Talmud and Midrash (Leiden: Brill, 1985).
Judge, Edwin A.
"The Decrees of Caesar at Thessalonica," *Reformed Theological Review* 30 (1971) 1–7.
Idem
"Judaism and the Rise of Christianity: A Roman Perspective," *TynBul* 45 (1994) 355–68.
Idem
"Paul's Boasting in Relation to Contemporary Professional Practice," *Australian Biblical Review* 16 (1968) 37–50.
Idem
"St. Paul and Classical Society," *JAC* 15 (1972) 19–36.
Juel, Donald
Luke-Acts: The Promise of History (Atlanta: John Knox, 1983).
Idem
Messianic Exegesis: Christological Interpretation of the Old Testament in Early Christianity (Philadelphia: Fortress Press, 1988).
Junod, Eric, and Jean-Daniel Kaestli
Acta Iohannis (2 vols.; CCSA 1-2; Turnhout: Brepols, 1983).
Just, Arthur A.
The Ongoing Feast: Table Fellowship and Eschatology at Emmaus (Collegeville, Minn.: Liturgical Press, 1993).
Juster, Jean
Les juifs dans l'empire romain (2 vols.; Paris: Geuthner, 1914).
Kamerbeek, J. C.
"On the Conception of *ΘΕΟΜΑΧΟΣ* in Relation with Greek Tragedy," *Mnemosyne* 1 (1948) 271–83.
Kaplan, Haya R.
"Joppa," *ABD* 4:946–49.

Karris, Robert J.
What Are They Saying about Luke and Acts? (Ramsey, N.J.: Paulist, 1979).
Idem
"Windows and Mirrors: Literary Criticism and Luke's *Sitz im Leben*," in Paul J. Achtemeier, ed., *SBLSP* 1979 (2 vols.; Missoula, Mont.: Scholars Press, 1979) 1:47–58.
Käsemann, Ernst
"The Disciples of John the Baptist in Ephesus," in idem, *Essays on New Testament Themes* (trans. W. J. Montague; SBT 41; London: SCM, 1964) 136–48.
Idem
"Ephesians and Acts," in Leander Keck and J. Louis Martyn, eds., *Studies in Luke-Acts: Essays Presented in Honor of Paul Schubert* (Nashville: Abingdon, 1966) 288–97.
Kasser, Rodolphe, Marvin Meyer, and Gregor Wurst
The Gospel of Judas (Washington, D.C.: National Geographic, 2006).
Kato, Takashi
La pensée sociale de Luc-Actes (EHPR 76; Strasbourg: Presses universitaires de France, 1997).
Katz, Steven T., ed.
The Cambridge History of Judaism, vol. 4: *The Late Roman-Rabbinic Period* (Cambridge: Cambridge University Press, 2006).
Katzenstein, H. J., and Douglas R. Edwards
"Tyre," *ABD* 6:686–92.
Kauppi, Lynn A.
Foreign but Familiar Gods: Greco-Romans Read Religion in Acts (LNTS 277; London: T&T Clark, 2006).
Kearsley, Rosalinde A.
"The Asiarchs," in David W. J. Gill and Conrad Gempf, eds., *The Book of Acts in Its Graeco-Roman Setting* (BIFCS 2; Grand Rapids: Eerdmans, 1994) 363–76.
Keck, Leander, and J. Louis Martyn, eds., *Studies in Luke-Acts: Essays Presented in Honor of Paul Schubert* (Nashville: Abingdon, 1966).
Kee, Howard C.
"The Changing Meaning of Synagogue: A Response to Richard Oster," *NTS* 40 (1994) 281–83.
Idem
"Defining the First-Century CE Synagogue," *NTS* 41 (1995) 481–500.
Idem
Miracle in the Early Christian World: A Study in Sociohistorical Method (New Haven: Yale University Press, 1983).
Idem
To Every Nation under Heaven (Harrisburg, Pa.: Trinity Press International, 1997).
Kelber, Werner
The Kingdom in Mark: A New Place and a New Time (Philadephia: Fortress Press, 1974).
Kelly, J. N. D.
Early Christian Creeds (3rd ed.; London: Longman, 1972).
Kennedy, George A.
The Art of Rhetoric in the Roman World (Princeton: Princeton University Press, 1972).
Idem
New Testament Interpretation through Rhetorical Criticism (Chapel Hill: University of North Carolina Press, 1984).
Idem, ed. and trans.
Progymnasmata: Greek Textbooks of Prose Composition and Rhetoric (SBLWGRW 10; Atlanta: Society of Biblical Literature, 2003).
Kenyon, George F.
"The Western Text in the Gospels and Acts," *Proceedings of the British Academy* 24 (1939) 287–315.
Kerényi, Karl
Der antike Roman (Darmstadt: Wissenschaftliche Buchgesellschaft, 1971).
Idem
Die griechisch-orientalische Romanliteratur (1927; reprinted, Darmstadt: Wissenschaftliche Buchgesellschaft, 1962).
Kettenbach, G.
Das Logbuch des Lukas (Frankfurt: Peter Lang, 1986).
Keyes, Clinton W.
"The Greek Letter of Introduction," *AJP* 56 (1935) 28–44.
Kilgallen, John J.
"Acts 13:4-12: the role of the '*magos*' *EstBib* 55 (1997) 223–37.
Idem
"'The Apostles Whom He Chose because of the Holy Spirit.' A Suggestion Regarding Acts 1,2," *Bib* 81 (2000) 414–17.
Idem
A Brief Commentary on the Acts of the Apostles (Mahwah, N.J.: Paulist, 1988).
Idem
"Clean, Acceptable, Saved: Acts 10," *ExpT* 109 (1998) 301–2.
Idem
"Did Peter Actually Fail to Get a Word In? (Acts 11,15)," *Bib* 71 (1990) 405–10.
Idem
"The Function of Stephen's Speech (Acts 7,2-53," *Bib* 70 (1989) 173–93.
Idem
"Hostility to Paul in Pisidian Antioch (Acts 13,45)–Why?" *Bib* 84 (2003) 1–15.
Idem
"Paul's Speech to the Ephesian Elders: Its Structure," *EThL* 70 (1994) 112–21.
Idem
The Stephen Speech: A Literary and Redactional Study of Acts 7,2-53 (AnBib 67; Rome: Biblical Institute, 1976).
Kilpatrick, George
"Acts VII, 56: Son of Man?" *ThZ* 21 (1965) 209.

Idem
"Acts xxiii, 23: δεξιολάβοι," *JTS* 14 (1963) 393–94.
Idem
"Again Acts VII, 56," *ThZ 34* (1978) 232.
Idem
"Apollos–Apelles," *JBL* 89 (1970) 77.
Idem
"An Eclectic Study of the Text of Acts," in J. Neville Birdsall and Robert W. Thomson, eds., *Biblical and Patristic Studies in Memory of Robert Pierce Casey* (Freiburg: Herder, 1963) 64–77.
Idem
"Some Quotations in Acts," in Jacob Kremer, ed., *Les Actes des Apôtres: Traditions, rédaction, théologie* (BEThL 48; Leuven: Leuven University Press, 1979) 81–97.
Idem
"The Two Texts of Acts," in Wolfgang Schrage, ed., *Studien zum Text und zur Ethik des Neuen Testaments* (Berlin: de Gruyter, 1986) 288–95.
Kirchschläger, Walter
"Fieberheilung in Apg 28 und Lk 4," in Jacob Kremer, ed., *Les Actes des Apôtres: Traditions, rédaction, théologie* (BEThL 48; Leuven: Leuven University Press, 1979) 509–21.
Kittel, Gerhard
"δόγμα," *TDNT* 2:230–32.
Kittel, Rudolf
"λόγιον," *TDNT* 4:137–41.
Klassen, William
Judas: Betrayer or Friend of Jesus? (Minneapolis: Augsburg Fortress Press, 1996).
Idem
"Judas Iscariot," *ABD* 3:1091–96.
Klauck, Hans-Josef
"Das Ende des Gottlosen: Variationen eines Themas," in *Judas, Ein Jünger des Herrn* (QD 111; Freiburg: Herder, 1987) 116–21.
Idem
"Gottesfürchtige im Magnificat?" *NTS* 43 (1997) 134–39.
Idem
"Gütergemeinschaft in der klassischen Antike, in Qumran und im Neuen Testament," *Revue de Qumran* 11 (1982) 47–79.
Idem
"Judas der 'Verräter'? Eine exegetische und wirkungsgeschichtliche Studie," *ANRW* 2.26.1 (1992) 717–40.
Idem
Judas, Ein Jünger des Herrn (QD 111; Freiburg: Herder, 1987).
Idem
Magie und Heidentum in der Apostelgeschichte des Lukas (SBS 167; Stuttgart: Katholisches Bibelwerk, 1995) = *Magic and Paganism in Early Christianity: The World of the Acts of the Apostles* (trans. B. McNeil; Edinburgh: T&T Clark, 2000).
Idem
The Religious Context of Early Christianity: A Guide to Graeco-Roman Religions (trans. B. McNeil; Edinburgh: T&T Clark, 2000).
Idem
"Von Kassandra bis zur Gnosis: Zum Umfeld der frühchristlichen Glossolalie," *ThQ* 179 (1999) 289–312.
Idem, with D. R. Bailey
Ancient Letters and the New Testament (Waco: Baylor University Press, 2006).
Klauser, Theodor
"Akklamation," *RAC* 1 (1950) 216–33.
Klein, Günter
"Der Synkretismus als theologisches Problem in der ältesten christlichen Apologetik," in idem, *Rekonstruktion und Interpretation: Gesammelte Aufsätze zum Neuen Testament* (Munich: Kaiser, 1969) 258–79 (= *ZThK* 64 [1967] 40–82).
Idem
Die zwölf Apostel: Ursprung und Gehalt einer Idee (FRLANT 77; Göttingen: Vandenhoeck & Ruprecht, 1961).
Klein, H.
"Wie wird aus Kaiwan ein Romfan? Eine textkritische Miszelle zu Apg 7,42f.," *ZNW* 97 (2006) 139–40.
Klijn, Albertus F. J.
"In Search of the Original Text of Acts," in Leander Keck and J. Louis Martyn, eds., *Studies in Luke-Acts: Essays Presented in Honor of Paul Schubert* (Nashville: Abingdon, 1966) 103–10.
Idem
"Stephen's Speech–Acts VII, 2-53," *NTS* 4 (1957) 25–31.
Klimkeit, Joachim
Gnosis on the Silk Road: Gnostic Parables, Hymns & Prayers from Central Asia (San Francisco: HarperSanFrancisco, 1993).
Klostermann, Erich
Das Lukasevangelium (HNT 5; 2nd ed.; Tübingen: Mohr Siebeck, 1929).
Klutz, Todd E.
The Exorcism Stories in Luke-Acts: A Sociostylistic Reading (SNTSMS 129; Cambridge: Cambridge University Press, 2004).
Idem, ed.
Magic in the Biblical World: From the Rod of Aaron to the Ring of Solomon (JSNTS 245; London: T&T Clark, 2003).
Knibbe, Dieter
"Via Sacra Ephesiaca: New Aspects of the Cult of Artemis Ephesia," in Helmut Koester, ed., *Ephesos: Metropolis of Asia* (HTS 41; Valley Forge, Pa.: Trinity Press International, 1995) 141–55.
Knoch, Otto
Die "Testamente" des Petrus und Paulus: Die Sicherung der apostolischen Überlieferung in der spätneutestamentlichen Zeit (SBS 62; Stuttgart: Katholisches Bibelwerk, 1973).

Knox, John
"Acts and the Pauline Letter Corpus," in Leander Keck and J. Louis Martyn, eds., *Studies in Luke-Acts: Essays Presented in Honor of Paul Schubert* (Nashville: Abingdon, 1966) 279–87.

Idem
Chapters in the Life of Paul (Nashville: Abingdon, 1950).

Idem
Marcion and the New Testament (Chicago: University of Chicago Press, 1942).

Knox, Wilfred L.
St Paul and the Church of the Gentiles (Cambridge: Cambridge University Press, 1939).

Idem
Some Hellenistic Elements in Primitive Christianity (1942 Schweich Lectures; British Academy: London, 1944).

Koch, Dietrich-Alex
"Crossing the Border: The 'Hellenists' and Their Way to the Gentiles," *Neotestamentica* 39 (2005) 289–312.

Idem
"The God-Fearers between Facts and Fiction: Two Theosebeis Inscriptions from Aphrodisias and Their Bearing for the New Testament," *ST* 60 (2006) 62–90.

Idem
"Geistbesitz, Geistverleihung und Wundermacht: Erwägungen zur Tradition und zur lukanischen Redaktion in Act 8 5-25," *ZNW* 77 (1986) 64–82.

Idem
"Kollektenbericht, 'Wir'-Bericht und Itinerar: Neue Überlegungen zu einem alten Problem," *NTS* 45 (1999) 367–90.

Idem
"Proselyten und Gottesfürchtige als Hörer der Reden von Apostelgeschichte 2,14-39 und 13,16-41," in Ciliers Breytenbach et al., eds., *Apostelgeschichte und die hellenistische Geschichtsschreibung: Festschrift für Eckhard Plümacher zu seinem 65. Geburtstag* (AGJU 57; Leiden/Boston: Brill, 2004) 83–107.

Kochavi, Moshe
"Antipatris," *ABD* 1:272–74.

Kodell, Jerome
"The Word of God Grew: The Ecclesial Tendency of λόγος in Acts 6,7; 12,24; 19,20," *Bib* 55 (1974) 505–19.

Koester, Helmut
Ancient Christian Gospels: Their History and Development (Philadelphia: Trinity Press International, 1990).

Idem, ed.
Ephesos: Metropolis of Asia (HTS 41; Valley Forge: Trinity Press International, 1995).

Idem
"Ephesos in Early Christian Literature," in idem, ed., *Ephesos: Metropolis of Asia* (HTS 41; Valley Forge, Pa.: Trinity Press International, 1995) 119–40.

Idem
Introduction to the New Testament (2 vols.; Berlin/New York: de Gruyter, 1982).

Idem
"New Testament Introduction: A Critique of a Discipline," in Jacob Neusner, ed., *Christianity, Judaism, and Other Greco-Roman Cults: Studies for Morton Smith at Sixty* (4 vols.; SJLA 12; Leiden: Brill, 1975) 1:1–20.

Idem, and James M. Robinson
Trajectories through Early Christianity (Philadelphia: Fortress Press, 1971).

Koet, Bart J.
Dreams and Scripture in Luke-Acts (Contributions to Biblical Exegesis and Theology 42; Leuven: Peeters, 2006).

Idem
"Im Schatten des Aeneas: Paulus in Troas (Apg 16,8-10)," in Reimund Bieringer, G. Van Belle, and J. Verheyden, eds., *Luke and His Readers: Festschrift A. Denaux* (BEThL 182; Leuven: Leuven University Press, 2005) 415–39 (= *Dreams and Scripture*, 147–71.)

Kolenkow, Anitra B.
"Testaments: The Literary Genre 'Testament,'" in Robert A. Kraft and George W. Nickelsburg, eds., *Early Judaism and Its Modern Interpreters* (Atlanta: Scholars Press, 1986) 259–67.

Kollmann, Bernd
Joseph Barnabas: Leben und Wirkungsgeschichte (SBS 175; Stuttgart: Katholisches Bibelwerk, 1998); ET *Joseph Barnabas: His Life and Legacy* (Collegeville, Minn.: Liturgical Press, 2004).

Konstan, David
"The Invention of Fiction," in Ronald F. Hock et al., eds., *Ancient Fiction and Early Christian Narrative* (SBLSymS 6; Atlanta: Scholars Press, 1998) 3–17.

Korn, Manfred
Die Geschichte Jesu in veränderter Zeit: Studien zur bleibenden Bedeutung Jesu im lukanischen Doppelwerk (WUNT 51; Tübingen: Mohr Siebeck, 1993).

Koschorke, Klaus
"Eine gnostische Pfingstpredigt: Zur Auseinandersetzung zwischen gnostischem und kirchlichem Christentum am Beispiel der 'Epistula Petri ad Philippum' (NHC VIII,2)," *ZThK* 74 (1977) 324–43.

Koskenniemi, Erkki
Der philostrateische Apollonios (Commentationes humanarum litterarum 94; Helsinki: Societas Scientiarum Fennica, 1991).

Kowalski, B.
"Der Fenstersturz in Troas (Apg 20, 7-12)," *StudNTUmwelt* 30 (2005) 19–37.

Idem
"Widerstände, Visionen und Geistführung bei Paulus," *Zeitschrift für Katholische Theologie* 125 (2003) 387–410.

Kraabel, A. Thomas
"The Disappearance of the God-Fearers," *Numen* 28 (1981) 113–26.
Idem
"Greeks, Jews, and Lutherans in the Middle Half of Acts," in George W. E. Nickelsburg and George W. MacRae, eds., *Christians among Jews and Gentiles. Essays in Honor of Krister Stendahl* (Philadelphia: Fortress Press, 1986) 157–67.
Idem
"The Roman Diaspora: Six Questionable Assumptions," *JJS* 33 (1982) 445–64.
Kraeling, Carl. H.
"The Jewish Community at Antioch," *JBL* 51 (1932) 130–60.
Kraemer, Ross S.
"Ber(e)nice," in Carol Meyers et al., eds., *Women in Scripture* (New York: Houghton Mifflin, 2000) 59–61.
Kraft, Robert A., and George W. Nickelsburg, eds.
Early Judaism and Its Modern Interpreters (Atlanta: Scholars Press, 1986).
Kratz, Reinhard
Rettungswunder: Motiv-, traditions- und formkritische Aufarbeitung einer biblischen Gattung (Frankfurt: Lang, 1979).
Kraus, Thomas J.
"'Uneducated,' 'Ignorant,' or even 'Illiterate'? Aspects and Background for an Understanding of *ΑΓΡΑΜΜΑΤΟΙ* (and *ΙΔΙΩΤΑΙ*) in Acts 4.13," *NTS* 45 (1999) 434–49.
Kreitzer, L. J.
"A Numismatic Clue to Acts 19:23-41: The Ephesian *Cistophoroi* of Claudius and Agrippina," *JSNT* 30 (1987) 59–70.
Kremer, Jacob, ed.
Les Actes des Apôtres: Traditions, rédaction, théologie (BEThL 43; Leuven: Leuven University Press, 1979).
Idem
"Einführung in die Problematik heutiger Acta-Forschung anhand von Apg 17, 10-13, in idem, *Les Actes des Apôtres: Traditions, rédaction, théolgie* (BEThL 43; Leuven: Leuven University Press, 1979) 11–20.
Idem
Pfingstbericht und Pfingstgeschehen: Eine Exegetische Untersuchung zu Apg 2,1-13 (SBS 63/64; Stuttgart: Katholisches Bibelwerk, 1973).
Krenkel, Max
Josephus und Lukas: Der schriftstellerische Einfluß des jüdischen Geschichtschreibers auf der christlichen nachgewiesen (Leipzig: Hässel, 1894).
Kruse, Colin G.
"The Price Paid for a Ministry among Gentiles: Paul's Persecution at the Hands of the Jews," in Michael J. Wilkins and Terrence Paige, eds., *Worship, Theology and Ministry in the Early Church: Essays in Honor of Ralph P. Martin* (JSNTS 87; Sheffield: JSOT Press, 1992).
Kuck, David W.
"The Use and Canonization of Acts in the Early Church" (STM thesis, Yale University, 1975).
Kuhn, K. G.
"*Ἰσραηλ, κ.τ.λ.*," *TDNT* 3:359–69.
Kümmel, Werner Georg
"Current Theological Accusations against Luke," *Andover-Newton Theological Quarterly* 16 (1975) 131–45.
Idem
Introduction to the New Testament (trans. Howard Clark Kee; Nashville: Abingdon, 1975).
Kursk-Chomycz, D. A.
"Is There an 'Anti-Priscan' Tendency in the Manuscripts? Some Textual Problems with Prisca and Aquila," *JBL* 125 (2006) 107–28.
Kurz, William S.
"Acts 3:19-26 as a Test of the Role of Eschatology in Lukan Christology," *SBLSP 1977* (Missoula, Mont.: Scholars Press, 1977) 309–23.
Idem
Farewell Addresses in the New Testament (Collegeville, Minn.: Liturgical Press, 1990).
Idem
"Narrative Approaches to Luke-Acts," *Bib* 68 (1987) 195–220.
Idem
"Promise and Fulfillment in Hellenistic Jewish Narratives and in Luke and Acts," in David P. Moessner, ed., *Jesus and the Heritage of Israel: Luke's Narrative Claim upon Israel's Legacy* (Harrisburg, Pa.: Trinity Press International, 1999) 147–70.
Idem
Reading Luke-Acts: Dynamics of Biblical Narrative (Louisville: Westminster John Knox, 1993).
Kürzinger, Josef
The Acts of the Apostles (trans. Anthony N. Fuerst, 2 vols.; New York: Crossroad, 1981).
Kussl, Rolf
Papyrusfragmente griechischer Romane (Classica Monacensia 2; Tübingen: Gunter Narr, 1991).
Labahn, Michael, and Bertjan L. Peerbolte, eds.
Wonders Never Cease: The Purpose of Narrating Miracle Stories in the New Testament and Its Religious Environment (Library of New Testament Studies 288; London: T&T Clark, 2006).
Labriolle, Pierre Champagne de
History and Literature of Christianity from Tertullian to Boethius (trans. Herbert Wilson; New York: Knopf, 1925).
Ladouceur, David J.
"The Death of Herod the Great," *Classical Philology* 76 (1981) 25–34.
Idem
"Hellenistic Preconceptions of Shipwreck and Pollution as a Context for Acts 27–28," *HTR* 73 (1980) 443–49.

Laird, Andrew
"Fiction, Bewitchment and Story Worlds: The Implications of Claims to Truth in Apuleius," in Christopher Gill and T. P. Wiseman, eds., *Lies and Fiction in the Ancient World* (Austin: University of Texas Press, 1993) 147–74.

Laistner, M. L. W.
"The Latin Versions of Acts Known to the Venerable Bede," *HTR* 30 (1937) 37–50.

Lake, Kirsopp
"Acts of the Apostles," in James Hastings, ed., *Dictionary of the Apostolic Church* (2 vols.; New York: Charles Scribner's Sons, 1916) 1:15–29.

Idem
"The Apostolic Council of Jerusalem," in Kirsopp Lake and Henry J. Cadbury, *Additional Notes to the Commentary,* vol. 5 of Frederick J. Foakes Jackson and Kirsopp Lake, eds., *The Beginnings of Christianity* (5 vols.; New York: Macmillan, 1920–33; reprinted, Grand Rapids: Baker, 1979) 195–212.

Idem
"The Ascension," in Kirsopp Lake and Henry J. Cadbury, *Additional Notes to the Commentary,* vol. 5 of Frederick J. Foakes Jackson and Kirsopp Lake, eds., *The Beginnings of Christianity* (5 vols.; New York: Macmillan, 1920–33; reprinted, Grand Rapids: Baker, 1979) 16–22.

Idem
"The Chronology of Acts," in Kirsopp Lake and Henry J. Cadbury, *Additional Notes to the Commentary,* vol. 5 of Frederick J. Foakes Jackson and Kirsopp Lake, eds., *The Beginnings of Christianity* (5 vols.; New York: Macmillan, 1920–33; reprinted, Grand Rapids: Baker, 1979) 445–74.

Idem
"The Communism of Acts II. and IV.–VI. and the Appointment of the Seven," in Kirsopp Lake and Henry J. Cadbury, *Additional Notes to the Commentary,* vol. 5 of Frederick J. Foakes Jackson and Kirsopp Lake, eds., *The Beginnings of Christianity* (5 vols.; New York: Macmillan, 1920–33; reprinted, Grand Rapids: Baker, 1979) 140–51.

Idem
"The Death of Judas," in Kirsopp Lake and Henry J. Cadbury, *Additional Notes to the Commentary,* vol. 5 of Frederick J. Foakes Jackson and Kirsopp Lake, eds., *The Beginnings of Christianity* (5 vols.; New York: Macmillan, 1920–33; reprinted, Grand Rapids: Baker, 1979) 22–30.

Idem
"The Gift of the Spirit on the Day of Pentecost," in Kirsopp Lake and Henry J. Cadbury, *Additional Notes to the Commentary,* vol. 5 of Frederick J. Foakes Jackson and Kirsopp Lake, eds., *The Beginnings of Christianity* (5 vols.; New York: Macmillan, 1920–33; reprinted, Grand Rapids: Baker, 1979) 111–21.

Idem
"The Holy Spirit," in Kirsopp Lake and Henry J. Cadbury, *Additional Notes to the Commentary,* vol. 5 of Frederick J. Foakes Jackson and Kirsopp Lake, eds., *The Beginnings of Christianity* (5 vols.; New York: Macmillan, 1920–33; reprinted, Grand Rapids: Baker, 1979) 96–111.

Idem
"Localities in and near Jerusalem Mentioned in Acts," in Kirsopp Lake and Henry J. Cadbury, *Additional Notes to the Commentary,* vol. 5 of Frederick J. Foakes Jackson and Kirsopp Lake, eds., *The Beginnings of Christianity* (5 vols.; New York: Macmillan, 1920–33; reprinted, Grand Rapids: Baker, 1979) 474–86.

Idem
"Paul's Route in Asia Minor," in Kirsopp Lake and Henry J. Cadbury, *Additional Notes to the Commentary,* vol. 5 of Frederick J. Foakes Jackson and Kirsopp Lake, eds., *The Beginnings of Christianity* (5 vols.; New York: Macmillan, 1920–33; reprinted, Grand Rapids: Baker, 1979) 224–40.

Idem
"The Preface to Acts and the Composition of Acts," in Kirsopp Lake and Henry J. Cadbury, *Additional Notes to the Commentary,* vol. 5 of Frederick J. Foakes Jackson and Kirsopp Lake, eds., *The Beginnings of Christianity* (5 vols.; New York: Macmillan, 1920–33; reprinted, Grand Rapids: Baker, 1979) 1–7.

Idem
"Proselytes and God-Fearers," in Kirsopp Lake and Henry J. Cadbury, *Additional Notes to the Commentary,* vol. 5 of Frederick J. Foakes Jackson and Kirsopp Lake, eds., *The Beginnings of Christianity* (5 vols.; New York: Macmillan, 1920–33; reprinted, Grand Rapids: Baker, 1979) 74–96.

Idem
"The Unknown God," in Kirsopp Lake and Henry J. Cadbury, *Additional Notes to the Commentary,* vol. 5 of Frederick J. Foakes Jackson and Kirsopp Lake, eds., *The Beginnings of Christianity* (5 vols.; New York: Macmillan, 1920–33; reprinted, Grand Rapids: Baker, 1979) 240–46.

Idem
"Your Own Poets," in Kirsopp Lake and Henry J. Cadbury, *Additional Notes to the Commentary,* vol. 5 of Frederick J. Foakes Jackson and Kirsopp Lake, eds., *The Beginnings of Christianity* (5 vols.; New York: Macmillan, 1920–33; reprinted, Grand Rapids: Baker, 1979) 246–51.

Idem, and Henry J. Cadbury
Additional Notes to the Commentary, vol. 5 of Frederick J. Foakes Jackson and Kirsopp Lake, eds., *The Beginnings of Christianity* (5 vols.; New York: Macmillan, 1920–33; reprinted, Grand Rapids: Baker, 1979).

Idem
"The Winds," in Kirsopp Lake and Henry J. Cadbury, *Additional Notes to the Commentary,* vol. 5 of Frederick J. Foakes Jackson and Kirsopp Lake, eds., *The Beginnings of Christianity* (5 vols.; New York: Macmillan, 1920–33; reprinted, Grand Rapids: Baker, 1979) 338–44.

Lambrecht, Jan
"Paul's Farewell-Address at Miletus, Acts 20, 17-38," in Jacob Kremer, ed., *Les Actes des Apôtres: Traditions, rédaction, théologie* (BEThL 48; Leuven: Leuven University Press, 1979) 307–37.

Lampe, Geoffrey W. H.
"'Grievous Wolves' (Acts 20:29)," in Barnabas Lindars and Stephen S. Smalley, eds., *Christ and Spirit in the New Testament: In Honour of Charles Francis Digby Moule* (Cambridge: Cambridge University Press, 1973) 235–68.

Idem
"Miracles in the Acts of the Apostles," in C. F. D. Moule, ed., *Miracles: Cambridge Studies in Their Philosophy and History* (London: Mowbray, 1965) 163–78.

Lampe, Peter
"Paulus–Zeltmacher," *BZ* 31 (1987) 211–21.

Idem
"Acta 19 im Spiegel der ephesischen Inschriften," *BZ* 36 (1992) 59–77.

Idem
From Paul to Valentinus: Christians at Rome in the First Two Centuries (trans. Michael Steinhauser, ed. Marshall D. Johnson; Minneapolis: Fortress Press, 2003).

Idem, and Ulrich Luz
"Post-Pauline Christianity and Pagan Society," in Jürgen Becker, ed., *Christian Beginnings: Word and Community from Jesus to Post-Apostolic Times* (trans. A. S. Kidder and R. Krauss; Louisville: Westminster John Knox, 1993) 242–80.

Lane, Eugene N.
Corpus Monumentorum Religionis Dei Meni (4 vols.; Leiden: Brill, 1971–78).

La Piana, George
"Foreign Groups at Rome during the First Centuries of the Empire," *HTR* 20 (1927) 183–403.

Idem
"The Roman Church at the End of the Second Century," *HTR* 18 (1925) 201–78.

Lausberg, Heinrich
Handbook of Literary Rhetoric (trans. Matthew T. Bliss et al.; ed. Davie E. Orton and R. Dean Anderson; Leiden: Brill, 1998).

Leaney, A. R. C.
The Gospel according to St Luke (Harper's/Blacks Commentaries; London: Adam & Charles Black, 1958).

Lentz, John Clayton, Jr.
Luke's Portrait of Paul (SNTSMS 77; Cambridge: Cambridge University Press, 1993).

Leon, Harry J.
The Jews of Ancient Rome (updated ed.; Peabody, Mass.: Hendrickson, 1995).

Leonardi, G.
Atti degli apostoli, traduzione strutturata, analisi narrativa e retorica (2 vols.; Sussidi Biblici 61-61b; Reggio Emilia: San Lorenzo, 1998).

Leppä, Heikki
Luke's Critical Use of Galatians (Vantaa, Finland: Dark Oy, 2002).

Le Roux, Christiaan R.
"Ephesus in the Acts of the Apostles: A Geographical and Theological Appraisal," in Herwig Firesinger et al., eds., *100 Jahre österreichische Forschungen in Ephesus: Akten des Symposions Wien 1995* (Vienna: Österreichischen Akademie der Wissenschaften, 1999) 307–13.

Lesky, Albin
"Aithiopika," *Hermes* 87 (1957) 27–38.

Levick, Barbara
The Government of the Roman Empire: A Sourcebook (Totowa, N.J.: Barnes & Noble, 1985).

Idem
Roman Colonies in Southern Asia Minor (Oxford: Clarendon, 1967).

Levine, Amy-Jill, ed., with M. Blickenstaff
A Feminist Companion to the Acts of the Apostles (Cleveland: Pilgrim, 2004).

Levinskaya, Irina
The Book of Acts in Its Diaspora Setting (BIFCS 5; Grand Rapids: Eerdmans, 1996).

Levy, G. Rachel
Religious Conceptions of the Stone Age: And Their Influence upon European Thought (New York: Harper & Row, 1963).

Lichtenberger, Hermann
"Jews and Christians in Rome in the Time of Nero: Josephus and Paul in Rome," *ANRW* 2.26.3 (1996) 2142–76.

Liefeld, Walter L.
"The Wandering Preacher as Social Figure in the Roman Empire" (Diss., Columbia University, 1967).

Lifshitz, Baruch
Donateurs et fondateurs dans les synagogues juives (CahRB 7; Paris: Gabalda, 1967).

Idem
"Du nouveau sur les 'Sympathisants,'" *JSJ* 1 (1970) 77–84.

Lightfoot, J. B.
The Apostolic Fathers (London/New York: Macmillan, 1891).

Idem
Saint Paul's Epistles to the Colossians and to Philemon (London: Macmillan, 1879)

Lightfoot, Jane L.
Parthenius of Nicea (Oxford: Clarendon, 1999).

Limberis, Vasiliki
"Anna 2," in Carol Meyers et al., eds., *Women in Scripture* (New York: Houghton Mifflin, 2000) 50–51.

Lin, Szu-Chuan
Wundertaten und Mission: Dramatische Episoden in Apg. 13–14 (Europäische Hochschulschriften, Reihe 23, Theologie 163; Berlin: Lang, 1998).

Lindars, Barnabas
"Elijah, Elisha and the Gospel Miracles," in C. F. D. Moule, ed., *Miracles: Cambridge Studies in Their Philosophy and History* (London: Mowbray, 1965) 61–79.

Idem
New Testament Apologetic: The Doctrinal Significance of the Old Testament Quotations (London: SCM, 1961).

Lindemann, Andreas
"Der 'Äthiopische Eunuch' und die Anfänge der Mission unter den Völkern nach Apg 8–11," in Breytenbach, *Apostelgeschichte*, 109–33.

Idem
"The Beginnings of Christian Life in Jerusalem according to the Summaries in the Acts of the Apostles (Acts 2.42-47; 4.32-35; 5.12-16)," in Julian V. Hills et al., eds., *Common Life in the Early Church: Essays Honoring Graydon F. Snyder* (Harrisburg, Pa.: Trinity Press International, 1998).

Idem
Die Clemensbriefe (HNT 17; Tübingen: Mohr Siebeck, 1992).

Idem
"The Community of Goods among the First Christians and among the Essenes," in David Goodblatt, et al., eds., *Historical Perspectives: From the Hasmoneans to Bar Kokhba in Light of the Dead Sea Scrolls. Proceedings of the Fourth International Symposium of the Orieon Center for the Study of the Dead Sea Scrolls and Associated Literature, 1999* (STDJ 37; Leiden: Brill, 1999).

Idem
Paulus im Ältesten Christentum (BHT 58; Tübingen: Mohr Siebeck, 1979).

Lindijer, C. H.
"Two Creative Encounters in the Work of Luke: Luke xxiv 13-35 and Acts viii 26-40," in T. Baarda et al., eds., *Miscellanea Neotestamentica* (NovTSup 48; Leiden: Brill, 1978).

Linton, Olof
"The Third Aspect: A Neglected Point of View. A Study in Gal. i–ii and Acts ix and xv," *ST* 3 (1951) 79–95.

Lintott, A. W.
"Provocatio: From the Struggle of the Orders to the Principate," *ANRW* 1.2 (1973) 226–67.

Lipsius, Richard A., and Maximilian Bonnet
Acta Apostolorum Apocrypha (2 vols.; Leipzig: Mendelssohn, 1891–1903).

Litwak, K. D.
Echoes of Scripture in Luke-Acts: Telling the History of God's People Intertextually (JSNTS 282; London: T&T Clark, 2005).

Lohfink, Gerhard
The Conversion of St. Paul: Narrative and History in Acts (trans. Bruce J. Malina; Chicago: Franciscan Herald, 1976).

Idem
Die Himmelfahrt Jesu: Untersuchungen zu den Himmelfahrts- und Erhöhungstexten bei Lukas (Munich: Kösel, 1971).

Idem
Die Sammlung Israels: Eine Untersuchung zur lukanischen Ekklesiologie (SANT 39; Munich: Kösel, 1975).

Lohse, Eduard
"πρόσωπον," *TDNT* 6:768–80.

Idem
"Ursprung und Prägung des christlichen Apostolates," *TZ* 9 (1953) 259–76.

Idem
"χειροποίητος," *TDNT* 9:436.

Lona, Horacio E.
Der erste Clemensbrief (Kommentar zu den apostolischen Vätern; Göttingen: Vandenhoeck & Ruprecht, 1998).

Long, A. A., and David N. Sedley
The Hellenistic Philosophies (2 vols.; Cambridge: Cambridge University Press, 1987).

Long, William R.
"The Paulusbild in the Trial of Paul in Acts," in Kent H. Richards, ed., *SBLSP 1983* (Chico, Calif.: Scholars Press, 1983) 87–105.

Longenecker, Bruce W.
"Lukan Aversion to Humps & Hollows: The Case of Acts 11:27–12:25," *NTS* 50 (2004) 185–204.

Longenecker, Richard N.
"The Acts of the Apostles," in F. E. Gaebelein, ed., *The Expositor's Bible Commentary* (vol. 9; Grand Rapids: Zondervan, 1981) 207–523.

Löning, Karl
"The Circle of Stephen and Its Mission," in Jürgen Becker, ed., *Christian Beginnings: Word and Community from Jesus to Post-Apostolic Times* (trans. Annemarie S. Kidder and Reinhard Krauss; Louisville: Westminster John Knox, 1993) 103–31.

Idem
"Die Korneliustradition," *BZ* 18 (1974) 1–19.

Idem
"Paulinismus in der Apostelgeschichte," in Karl Kertelge, ed., *Paulus in den neutestamentlichen Spätschriften: Zur Paulusrezeption im Neuen Testament* (QD 89; Freiburg: Herder, 1981) 202–34.

Idem
Die Saulustradition in der Apostelgeschichte (NTAbh 9; Münster: Aschendorff, 1973).

Lösch, Stephan
"Die Dankesrede des Tertullus: Apg 24,1-4," *ThQ* 112 (1939) 295–319.

Lostang, F.
"À la louange du dieu inconnu: Analyse rhétorique de Ac 17.22-31," *NTS* 52 (2006) 394–408.

Lovejoy, Arthur O., and George Boas
Primitivism and Related Ideas in Antiquity (2 vols.; Baltimore: Johns Hopkins University Press, 1935).

Lövestam, E.
"Paul's Address at Miletus," *ST* 41 (1987) 1–10.
Luck, Georg
Arcana Mundi: Magic and the Occult in the Greek and Roman Worlds; A Collection of Ancient Texts (Baltimore: Johns Hopkins University Press, 1985).
Lüdemann, Gerd
"The Acts of the Apostles and the Beginnings of Simonian Gnosis," *NTS* (1987) 420–26.
Idem
The Acts of the Apostles: What Really Happened in the Earliest Days of the Church (Amherst, N.Y.: Prometheus Books, 2005).
Idem
Early Christianity according to the Traditions in Acts (trans J. Bowden; Philadelphia: Fortress Press, 1989).
Idem
Opposition to Paul in Jewish Christianity (trans. M. E. Boring; Minneapolis: Fortress Press, 1989).
Idem
Paul Apostle to the Gentiles: Studies in Chronology (trans. F. Stanley Jones; Philadelphia: Fortress Press, 1984).
Ludvíkovsky, Jaroslav
Recky Roman Dobroduzny Le roman grec d'aventures (Prague: Filosofika Fakulta University Karlova, 1925).
Ludwig, Karl, and Martin A. Schmidt
"παχύνω," *TDNT* 5:1022–31.
Lundgren, S.
"Ananias and the Calling of Paul in Acts," *ST* 25 (1971) 117–22.
Lust, J., E. Eynikel, and K. Hauspie
A Greek-English Lexicon of the Septuagint (2 vols.; Stuttgart: Deutsche Bibelgesellschaft, 1992).
Lyons, George
Pauline Autobiography: Toward a New Understanding (Atlanta: Scholars Press, 1985).
MacDonald, Dennis R., ed.
The Apocryphal Acts of Apostles (Semeia 38; Atlanta: Scholars Press, 1986).
Idem
"Apocryphal and Canonical Narratives about Paul," in William S. Babcock, ed., *Paul and the Legacies of Paul* (Dallas: Southern Methodist University Press, 1990) 25–45.
Idem
Christianizing Homer: The Odyssey, *Plato, and the* Acts of Andrew (New York: Oxford University Press, 1994).
Idem
Does the New Testament Imitate Homer? Four Cases from the Acts of the Apostles (New Haven: Yale University Press, 2003).
Idem
The Legend and the Apostle: The Battle for Paul in Story and Canon (Philadelphia: Westminster, 1983).
Idem
"Luke's Emulation of Homer: Acts 12:1-17 and *Iliad* 24," *Forum* n.s. 3 (2000) 197–205.
Idem
"Luke's Eutychus and Homer's Elpenor: Acts 20:7-12 and *Odyssey*, 10–12," *JHC* 1 (1994) 5–24.
Idem
"Lydia and Her Sisters as Lukan Fictions," in Amy-Jill Levine, *A Feminist Companion to the Acts of the Apostles* (Cleveland: Pilgrim, 2004) 105–10.
Idem
"Paul's Farewell to the Ephesian Elders and Hector's Farewell to Andromache: A Strategic Imitation of Homer's *Iliad*," in Todd Penner and Caroline Vander Stichele, *Contextualizing Acts: Lukan Narrative and Greco-Roman Discourse* (SBLSS 20; Boston/Leiden: Brill; Atlanta: Society of Biblical Literature, 2004) 189–203.
Idem
"The Shipwrecks of Odysseus and Paul," *NTS* 45 (1999) 88–107.
MacDonald, Margaret Y.
Early Christian Women and Pagan Women: The Power of the Hysterical Woman (Cambridge: Cambridge University Press, 1996).
Idem
The Pauline Churches (SNTSMS 60; Cambridge: Cambridge University Press, 1988).
Mack, Burton L.
A Myth of Innocence: Mark and Christian Origins (Philadelphia: Fortress Press, 1988).
Idem
Rhetoric and the New Testament (GBS; Minneapolis: Fortress Press, 1990).
Maclean, A. J.
"Acts of the Apostles," in James Hastings, ed., *Dictionary of the Bible* (New York: Charles Scribner's Sons, 1909) 8–10.
MacLennon, Robert S., and A. Thomas Kraabel
"The God-Fearers—A Literary and Theological Invention," *BAR* 12 (1986) 46–53.
MacMullen, Ramsay
Christianizing the Roman Empire: A. D. 100–400 (New Haven: Yale University Press, 1984).
Idem
Enemies of the Roman Order: Treason, Unrest, and Alienation in the Empire (Cambridge, Mass.: Harvard University Press, 1966).
Idem
Paganism in the Roman Empire (New Haven: Yale University Press, 1981).
Idem
Roman Social Relations, 50 B.C. to A.D. 284 (New Haven: Yale University Press, 1974).
MacRae, George
"Miracle in the *Antiquities* of Josephus," in C. F. D. Moule, ed., *Miracles: Cambridge Studies in Their Philosophy and History* (London: Mowbray, 1965) 129–47.
Maddox, Robert
The Purpose of Luke-Acts (Edinburgh: T&T Clark, 1982).

Magie, David
Roman Rule in Asia Minor to the End of the Third Century after Christ (2 vols.; Princeton: Princeton University Press, 1950).
Magness, J. Lee
Sense and Absence: Structure and Suspension in the Ending of Mark's Gospel (SBLSS; Atlanta: Scholars Press: 1986).
Malherbe, Abraham J.
The Cynic Epistles (SBLSBS 12; Atlanta: Scholars Press, 1977).
Idem
"Hellenistic Moralists and the New Testament," *ANRW* 2.26.3 (1992) 267–333.
Idem
The Letters to the Thessalonians: A New Translation with Introduction and Commentary (AB 32B; New York: Doubleday, 2000).
Idem
"'Not in a Corner': Early Christian Apologetic in Acts 26:26," *SecCent* 5 (1985–86) 193–210.
Idem
Paul and the Popular Philosophers (Minneapolis: Fortress Press, 1989).
Idem
"Pseudo-Heraclitus, Epistle 4: The Divinization of the Wise Man," *JAC* 21 (1978) 42–64.
Idem
Social Aspects of Early Christianity (2nd ed.; Philadelphia: Fortress Press, 1983).
Malina, Bruce J., and Jerome H. Neyrey
Portraits of Paul: An Archaeology of Ancient Personality (Louisville: Westminster John Knox, 1996).
Malten, Ludolf
"Motivegeschichtliche Untersuchungen zur Sagenforschung," *Hermes* 74 (1930) 79–86.
Mandelbaum, Allen
The Metamorphoses of Ovid (New York: Harcourt Brace & Company, 1993).
Marconi, Gilberto
"History as a Hermeneutical Interpretaion of the Difference between Acts 3:1-10 and 4:8-12," in Gerald O'Collins and Gilberto Marconi, eds., *Luke and Acts* (trans. Matthew J. O'Connell; Festschrift Emilio Rasco; New York: Paulist, 1993) 167–80.
Marcus, Ralph
Josephus V, VII (LCL; Cambridge, Mass.: Harvard University Press, 1934, 1943).
Marguerat, Daniel
"The End of Acts and the Rhetoric of Silence," in Stanley E. Porter and Thomas H. Olbricht, eds., *Rhetoric and the New Testament* (JSNTSS 90; Sheffield: Sheffield Academic Press, 1993).
Idem
"L'image de Paul dans les Actes des Apôtres," in Michel Berder, ed., *Les Actes des Apôtres: Histoire, récit, théologie: XXe congrès de l'Association catholique française pour l'étude de la Bible, Angers, 2003* (LD 199; Paris: Cerf, 2005) 121–54.
Idem
La première histoire du christianisme: Les Actes des Apôtres (LD 180; Paris: Cerf, 1999). ET K. McKinney, et al., *The First Christian Historian: Writing the "Acts of the Apostles"* (SNTSMS 121; Cambridge: Cambridge University Press, 2002).
Marrou, Henri I.
A History of Education in Antiquity (trans. G. Lamb.; New York: New American Library, 1964).
Marrow, Stanley B.
"*Parrhêsia* and the New Testament," *CBQ* 44 (1982) 431–46.
Marshall, I. Howard
"Acts and the 'Former Treatise,'" in Bruce W. Winter and Andrew D. Clarke, *The Book of Acts in Its Ancient Literary Setting* (BIFCS 1; Grand Rapids: Eerdmans, 1993) 163–82.
Idem
The Acts of the Apostles (Sheffield: Sheffield Academic Press, 1992).
Idem
Commentary on Luke (NIGTC; Grand Rapids: Eerdmans, 1978).
Idem
"How Does One Write on the Theology of Acts?" in idem and David Peterson, eds., *Witness to the Gospel: The Theology of Acts* (Grand Rapids: Eerdmans, 1998) 3–16.
Idem
"'Israel' and the Story of Salvation: One Theme in Two Parts," in David P. Moessner, ed., *Jesus and the Heritage of Israel: Luke's Narrative Claim upon Israel's Legacy* (Harrisburg, Pa.: Trinity Press International, 1999) 340–57.
Idem
"Recent Study of the Acts of the Apostles," *ExpT* 80 (1968–69) 292–96.
Idem
"The Significance of Pentecost," *SJT* 30 (1977) 347–69.
Idem, and David Peterson, eds.
Witness to the Gospel: The Theology of Acts (Grand Rapids: Eerdmans, 1998).
Martin, Clarice
"The Acts of the Apostles," in Elisabeth Schüssler Fiorenza, ed., *Searching the Scriptures: A Feminist Commentary* (2 vols.; New York: Crossroad, 1994).
Idem
"A Chamberlain's Journey and the Challenge of Interpretation for Liberation," *Sem* 47 (1989) 105–35.
Martin, Hubert H., Jr.
"Areopagus," *ABD* 1:370–72.
Idem
"Athens," *ABD* 1:513–18.
Martin, Luther
"Gods or Ambassadors of God? Barnabas and Paul in Lystra," *NTS* 41 (1995) 152–56.
Martin, Thomas W.
"Hellenists," *ABD* 3:135–36.

Martini, Carlo M.
"La tradition textuelle des Actes des Apôtres et les tendance de l'Église ancienne," in Jacob Kremer, ed., *Les Actes des Apôtres: Traditions, rédaction, théologie* (BEThL 48; Leuven: Leuven University Press, 1979) 21–35.

Mason, Steve,
"Chief Priests, Sadducees, Pharisees and Sanhedrin in Acts," in Richard Bauckham, *The Book of Acts in Its Palestinian Setting* (BIFCS 4; Grand Rapids: Eerdmans, 1995) 115–77.

Masson, Charles
"À propos de Act. 9:19b-25: Note sur l'utilisation de Gal et de 2 Cor. par l'auteur des Actes," *ThZ* 18 (1962) 161–66.

Mastin, B. A.
"A Note on Acts 19:14," *Bib* 59 (1978) 97–99.

Idem
"Scaeva the Chief Priest," *JTS* 27 (1976) 405–12.

Mathieu, Yvan
La figure de Pierre dan l'oeuvre de Luc (EB 52; Paris: Gabalda, 2004).

Matson, David L.
Household Conversion Narratives in Acts: Pattern and Interpretation (JSNTS 123; Sheffield: Sheffield Academic Press, 1996).

Matthews, Christopher R.
Philip: Apostle and Evangelist (NovTSup 105; Leiden: Brill, 2002).

Matthews, Shelly
First Converts: Rich Pagan Women and the Rhetoric of Mission in Early Judaism and Christianity (Stanford: Stanford University Press, 2001).

Mattila, Sharon Lea
"Where Women Sat in Ancient Synagogues: The Archaeological Evidence in Context," in John S. Kloppenborg and Stephen G. Wilson, eds., *Voluntary Associations in the Graeco-Roman World* (London: Routledge, 1996) 266–86.

Mattill, Andrew J., Jr.
"Luke as a Historian in Criticism since 1840" (Diss., Vanderbilt University, 1959).

Idem
"The Jesus-Paul Parallels and the Purpose of Luke-Acts: H. H. Evans Reconsidered," *NovT* 17 (1975) 15–47.

Idem, and Mary B. Mattill
A Classified Bibliography of Literature on the Acts of the Apostles (NTTS 7; Leiden: Brill, 1966).

Mattingly, Harold B.
"The Origin of the Name *Christiani*," *JTS* 9 (1958) 26–37.

Maurer, Christian
"*πρᾶξις*," *TDNT* 6:642–44.

Idem
"*τίθημι*," *TDNT* 8:153–68.

McCoy, W. J.
"In the Shadow of Thucydides," in Ben Witherington III, *History, Literature and Society in the Book of Acts* (Cambridge: Cambridge University Press, 1996) 3–23.

McDonald, Lee M., and Stanley E. Porter
Early Christianity and Its Sacred Literature (Peabody, Mass.: Hendrickson, 2000).

McDonough, Sean M.
"Small Change: Saul to Paul, Again," *JBL* 125 (2006) 390–91.

McKechnie, P. R.
"Judean Embassies and Cases before Roman Emperors, AD 44–66," *JTS* 56 (2005) 339–61.

McRay, John
"Damascus: The Greco-Roman Period," *ABD* 2:7–8.

Idem
"Miletus," *ABD* 4:825–26.

Mealand, David L.
"The Close of Acts and Its Hellenistic Greek Vocabulary," *NTS* 36 (1990) 583–97.

Idem
"Community of Goods and Utopian Allusions in Acts 2–4," *JTS* 28 (1977) 96–99.

Idem
"The Phrase 'Many Proofs' in Acts 1,3 and in Hellenistic Writers," *ZNW* 80 (1989) 134–35.

Meeks, Wayne A.,
"The Divine Agent and His Counterfeit," in Elisabeth Schüssler Fiorenza, ed., *Aspects of Religious Propaganda in Judaism and Early Christianity* (Notre Dame, Ind.: University of Notre Dame Press, 1976) 43–67.

Idem
The First Urban Christians: The Social World of the Apostle Paul (New Haven: Yale University Press, 1983).

Idem
"Simon Magus in Recent Research," *RSR* 3 (1977) 137–42.

Idem, and Robert L. Wilken
Jews and Christians in Antioch in the First Four Centuries of the Common Era (SBLSBS 13; Missoula, Mont.: Scholars Press, 1978).

Meiggs, Russell
Roman Ostia (2nd ed.; Oxford: Clarendon, 1973).

Meijer, Fik, and Onno van Nijf
Trade, Transport and Society in the Ancient World: A Sourcebook (London: Routledge, 1992).

Meinardus, Otto F. A.
"Melita Illyrica or African: An Examination of the Site of St. Paul's Shipwreck," *Ostkirchliche Studien* 23 (1974) 21–36.

Idem
"St. Paul Shipwrecked in Dalmatia," *BA* 39 (1976) 145–47.

Melbourne, Bertram L.
"Acts 1:8 Re-examined: Is Acts 8 Its Fulfillment?" *JRT* 58 (2005) 1–18.

Melzer-Keller, Helga
"Frauen in der Apostelgeschichte," *BK* 55 (2000) 87–91.

Menestrina, Giovanni
"L'incipit dell'epistola 'ad Diognetum', Luca 1,1-4 e Atti 1,1-2," *BeO* 19 (1977) 215–18.

Menoud, Philippe-Henri
"Les additions au groupe des Douze Apôtres d'après le Livre des Actes," *RHPR* 37 (1957) 71–80.

Idem
Jesus Christ and the Faith: A Collection of Studies (trans. E. M. Paul; PTMS 18; Pittsburgh: Pickwick, 1978).

Idem
"La mort d'Annanias et de Saphira (Actes 5, 1-11)," in *Aux sources de la tradition chrétienne: Mélanges offerts à M. Maurice Goguel à l'occasion de son soixante-dixième anniversaire* (Bibliothèque théologique; Neuchâtel: Delachaux et Niestlé, 1950) 146–54.

Idem
"'Pendant quarante jours' (Actes i 3)," in *Neotestamentica et patristica: Eine Freundesgabe, Herrn Professor Dr. Oscar Cullmann zu seinem 60. Geburtstag überreicht* (NovTSup 6; Leiden: Brill, 1962) 148–56.

Idem
"The Plan of Acts," in idem, *Jesus Christ and the Faith: A Collection of Studies* (PTMS 18; Pittsburgh: Pickwick, 1978) 121–32.

Menzies, Glen
"Pre-Lukan Occurrences of the Phrase 'Tongue of Fire,'" *Pneuma: Journal of the Society for Pentecostal Studies* 22 (2000) 27–60.

Merkelbach, Reinhold
Roman und Mysterium (Berlin: de Gruyter, 1962).

Meshorer, Yaakov
Jewish Coins of the Second Temple Period (trans. I. H. Levine; Tel Aviv: Am Hasefer, 1967).

Metzger, Bruce M.
"Ancient Astrological Geography and Acts 2:9-11," in *New Testament Studies: Philological, Versional and Patristic* (NTTS 10; Leiden: Brill, 1980) 46–56.

Idem
The Early Versions of the New Testament: Their Origin, Transmission and Limitations (Oxford: Clarendon, 1977).

Idem
The Text of the New Testament: Its Transmission, Corruption, and Restoration (3rd ed.; New York: Oxford University Press, 1992).

Idem
A Textual Commentary on the Greek New Testament (2nd ed.; New York: American Bible Society, 1994).

Meyer, Marvin, and Paul Mirecki, eds.
Ancient Magic and Ritual Power (Religions in the Graeco-Roman World 129; Leiden: Brill, 1995).

Meyer, Marvin, and Richard Smith, eds.
Ancient Christian Magic: Coptic Texts of Ritual Power (San Francisco: HarperSanFrancisco, 1994).

Meyer, R., and Friedrich Hauck
"καθαρός," *TDNT* 3:413–31.

Meyers, Carol, et al., eds.
Women in Scripture (New York: Houghton Mifflin, 2000).

Michael, John H.
"The Original Position of Acts xiv.3," *ExpT* 40 (1928–29) 514–16.

Michaelis, Wilhelm
Die Gefangenschaft des Paulus in Ephesus und das Itinerar des Timotheus (Gütersloh: Bertelsmann, 1925).

Idem
"εἴσοδος, ἔξοδος," *TDNT* 5:103–8.

Idem
"λιθάζω," *TDNT* 4:267–68.

Idem
"ὅραμα," *TDNT* 5:371–72.

Idem
"πρῶτος," *TDNT* 6:865–82.

Idem
"προχειρίζω," *TDNT* 6:862–64.

Michel, Hans-Joachim
Die Abschiedsrede des Paulus an die Kirche Apg 20, 17-38: Motivgeschichte und theologische Bedeutung (SANT 35; Munich: Kösel, 1973).

Michel, Otto
"μνημονεύω," *TDNT* 4:682–83.

Miles, Gary, and Garry Trompf
"Luke and Antiphon," *HTR* 69 (1976) 259–67.

Millar, Fergus
The Emperor in the Roman World (Ithaca: Cornell University Press, 1977).

Idem
The Roman Near East: 31 BC–AD 337 (Cambridge, Mass.: Harvard University Press, 1993).

Miller, John B. F.
Convinced That God Had Called Us: Dreams, Visions, and the Perception of God's Will in Luke-Acts (BIS 85; Leiden: Brill, 2007).

Mills, Watson E.
The Acts of the Apostles (Lewiston, N.Y.: Mellen, 1996).

Minar, E. L., Jr.
Plutarch's Moralia IX (LCL; Cambridge, Mass.: Harvard University Press, 1961).

Minear, Paul S.
"A Note on Luke 17:7-10," *JBL* 93 (1974) 82–87.

Mineshige, K.
Besitzversicht und Almosen bei Lukas: Wesen und Forderung des Lukanischen Vermögensethos (WUNT 163; Tübingen: Mohr Siebeck, 2003).

Minnen, P. van
"Paul the Roman Citizen," *JSNT* 56 (1994) 43–52.

Mitchell, Alan C.
"The Social Function of Friendship in Acts 2:44-47 and 4:32-37," *JBL* 111 (1992) 255–72.

Mitchell, Stephen
"Antioch of Pisidia," *ABD* 1:264–65.

Mitford, Terence B.
"Roman Cyprus," *ANRW* 2.7.2 (1980) 1286–1384.

Mittelstädt, Alexander
Lukas als Historiker: Zur Datierung des Lukanischen Doppelwerkes: Texte und Arbeiten zum neuestestamentlichen Zeitalter 43 (Tübingen: Francke, 2006).

Mitton, C. Leslie
The Epistle to the Ephesians: Its Authorship, Origin and Purpose (Oxford: Clarendon, 1951).

Moehring, Horst R.
"The Census in Luke as an Apologetic Device," in David E. Aune, ed., *Studies in New Testament and Early Christian Literature: Essays in Honor of Allen P. Wikgren* (NovTSup 33; Leiden: Brill, 1972) 144–60.

Idem
"The Persecution of the Jews and the Adherents of the Isis Cult at Rome, A.D. 19," *NovT* 3 (1959) 293–304.

Idem
"The Verb ***ΑΚΟΥΕΙΝ*** in Acts IX 7 and XXII 9," *NovT* 3 (1959) 80–99.

Moessner, David, P.
"'The Christ Must Suffer': New Light on the Jesus—Peter, Stephen, Paul Parallels in Luke-Acts," *NovT* 28 (1986) 221–27.

Idem
"'Completed End(s)ings' of Historiographical Narrative: Diodorus Siculus and the End(ing) of Acts," in Ciliers Breytenbach et al., eds., *Apostelgeschichte und die hellenistische Geschichtsschreibung: Festschrift für Eckhard Plümacher zu seinem 65. Geburtstag* (AGJU 57; Leiden/Boston: Brill, 2004) 193–221.

Idem
"Dionysius's Narrative 'Arrangement' as the Hermeneutical Key to Luke's Re-Vision of the 'Many,'" in Alf Christophersen et al., eds., *Paul, Luke, and the Graeco-Roman World: Essays in Honour of Alexander J. M. Wedderburn* (JSNTS 217; London: Sheffield Academic Press, 2002) 149–64.

Idem, ed.
Jesus and the Heritage of Israel: Luke's Narrative Claim upon Israel's Legacy (Harrisburg, Pa.: Trinity Press International, 1999).

Idem
Lord of the Banquet: The Literary and Theological Significance of the Lukan Travel Narrative (Minneapolis: Augsburg Fortress Press, 1989).

Idem
"The Lukan Prologues in the Light of Ancient Narrative Hermeneutics: *παρηκολουθηκότι* and the Credentialed Author," in Jozef Verheyden, ed., *The Unity of Luke-Acts* (BEThL 92; Leuven: Leuven University Press, 1999) 399–417.

Idem
"Paul in Acts: Preacher of Eschatological Repentance to Israel," *NTS* 34 (1988) 96–104.

Idem
"The 'Script' of the Scriptures in Acts: Suffering as God's 'Plan' (*βουλή*) for the World for the 'Release of Sins,'" in Ben Witherington III, *History, Literature and Society in the Book of Acts* (Cambridge: Cambridge University Press, 1996) 218–50.

Idem
"*Two* Lords 'at the Right Hand'? The Psalms and an Intertextual Reading of Peter's Pentecost Speech (Acts 2:14-36)," in Richard Thompson, ed., *Literary Studies in Luke-Acts: Essays in Honor of Joseph B. Tyson* (Macon, Ga.: Mercer University Press, 1998) 215–32.

Momigliano, Arnaldo
The Development of Greek Biography (Cambridge, Mass.: Harvard University Press, 1971).

Idem
"Second Thoughts on Greek Biography," *Mededelingen van het Nederlands Historisch Instituut te Rome* 34 (1971) 245–57.

Mommsen, Theodor
"Die Rechtsverhältnisse des Apostels Paulus," *ZNW* 2 (1902) 81–96.

Montgomery, James A.
"The Ethiopic Text of Acts of the Apostles," *HTR* 27 (1934) 169–205.

Moreland, Milton
"The Jerusalem Community in Acts: Mythmaking and the Sociorhetorical Functions of a Lukan Setting," in Todd Penner and Caroline Vander Stichele, *Contextualizing Acts: Lukan Narrative and Greco-Roman Discourse* (SBLSS 20; Boston/Leiden: Brill; Atlanta: Society of Biblical Literature, 2004) 285–310.

Morgan, John R.
"Heliodoros," in Gareth Schmeling, ed., *The Novel in the Ancient World* (rev. ed.; Leiden: Brill, 2003) 444–45.

Idem
"Make-Believe and Make Believe: The Fictionality of the Greek Novels," in Christopher Gill and Thomas P. Wiseman, eds., *Lies and Fiction in the Ancient World* (Austin: University of Texas Press, 1993) 175–229.

Idem
"On the Fringes of the Canon: Work on the Fragments of Ancient Greek Fiction 1936–1994," *ANRW* 2.34.4 (1998) 3293–3390.

Morgenthaler, Robert
Die Lukanische Geschichtschreibung als Zeugnis (2 vols.; AThANT 14, 15; Zurich: Zwingli, 1949).

Idem
Statistik des neutestamentlichen Wortschatzes (Zurich: Gotthelf, 1958).

Mortley, Raoul
"The Title of the Acts of the Apostles," in *Lectures anciennes de la Bible* (Cahiers de Biblia Patristica 1; Strasbourg: Centre d'analyse et de documentation patristiques, 1987) 105–12.

Morton, A. Q., and G. H. C. MacGregor
The Structure of Luke and Acts (New York: Harper & Row, 1964).

Moule, Charles F. D.
"The Christology of Acts," in Leander Keck and J. Louis Martyn, eds., *Studies in Luke-Acts: Essays Presented in Honor of Paul Schubert* (Nashville: Abingdon, 1966) 159–85.

Idem
An Idiom Book of New Testament Greek (2nd ed.; Cambridge: Cambridge University Press, 1963).

Idem, ed.,
Miracles: Cambridge Studies in Their Philosophy and History (London: Mowbray, 1965).

Idem
"The Problem of the Pastoral Epistles: A Reappraisal," *BJRL* 47 (1965) 430–52.

Moulton, James H.
A Grammar of New Testament Greek (3rd ed., 4 vols.; Edinburgh: T&T Clark, 1908–76).

Moulton, W. F., A. S. Geden, and H. K. Moulton, eds.
A Concordance to the Greek Testament (5th ed.; Edinburgh: T&T Clark, 1978).

Mount, Christopher
Pauline Christianity: Luke-Acts and the Legacy of Paul (NovTSup 104; Leiden: Brill, 2002).

Mowery, Robert L.
"Paul and Caristianus at Pisidian Antioch," *Bib* 87 (2006) 223–42.

Muhlack, Gudrun
Die Parallelen von Lukas-Evangelium und Apostelgeschichte (Theologie und Wirklichkeit 8; Frankfurt: Peter Lang, 1979).

Müller, Paul-Gerhard
"*νύξ*," *EDNT* 2:481–83.

Idem
ΧΡΙΣΤΟΣ ΑΡΧΗΓΟΣ: Der Religionsgeschichtliche und theologische Hintergrund einer neutestamentlichen Christusprädikation (Europäische Hochschulschriften Reihe 23, vol. 28; Frankfurt: Peter Lang, 1973).

Munck, Johannes
"Discours d'adieu dans le Nouveau Testament et dans la littérature biblique," in *Aux sources de la tradition chrétienne: Mélanges offerts à Maurice Goguel* (Bibliothèque théologique; Neuchâtel: Delachaux et Niestlé, 1950) 155–70.

Idem
Paul and the Salvation of Mankind (Richmond: John Knox, 1959).

Murphy, Frederick J.
Pseudo-Philo: Rewriting the Bible (New York: Oxford University Press, 1993).

Murphy-O'Connor, Jerome
"Corinth," *ABD* 1:1134–39.

Idem
"Lots of God-Fearers? *Theosebeis* in the Aphrodisias Inscription," *RB* 99 (1992) 418–24.

Idem
Paul: A Critical Life (Oxford: Clarendon, 1996).

Idem
"Prisca and Aquila: Traveling Tentmakers and Church Builders," *BR* 8 (1992) 40–51.

Idem
Saint Paul's Corinth (GNS 6; Wilmington, Del.: Michael Glazier, 1983).

Mussies, Gerard
"Variation in the Book of Acts," *FilolNT* 4 (1991) 165–82.

Idem
"Variation in the Book of Acts (Part II)," *FilolNT* 8 (1995) 23–61.

Mußner, Franz
"'In den letzten Tagen' (Apg. 2,17a)," *BZ* 5 (1961) 263–65.

Musurillo, Herbert
The Acts of the Christian Martyrs (Oxford: Clarendon, 1972).

Idem
The Acts of the Pagan Martyrs (Oxford: Clarendon, 1954).

Myllykoski, Matti
"Being There: The Function of the Supernatural in Acts 1–12," in Michael Labahn and Bert L. Peerbolte, eds., *Wonders Never Cease: The Purpose of Narrating Miracle Stories in the New Testament and Its Religious Environment* (LNTS 288; London: T&T Clark, 2006) 146–79.

Nagy, Gregory
The Best of the Achaeans (Baltimore: Johns Hopkins University Press, 1979).

Nauck, Wolfgang
"Die Tradition und Komposition der Areopagrede," *ZThK* 53 (1956) 11–52.

Nave, Guy D., Jr.
The Role and Function of Repentance in Luke-Acts (Academia Biblica 4; Atlanta: Society of Biblical Literature, 2002).

Neagoe, Alexandru
The Trial of the Gospel: An Apologetic Reading of Luke's Trial Narratives (SNTSMS 116; Cambridge: Cambridge University Press, 2002).

Neil, William
The Acts of the Apostles (NCB; London: Oliphants, 1973).

Neirynck, Frans
"The Miracle Stories in the Acts of the Apostles," in Jacob Kremer, ed., *Les Actes des Apôtres: Traditions, rédaction, théologie* (BEThL 48; Leuven: Leuven University Press, 1979) 169–213.

Nelson, Edwin S.
"Paul's First Missionary Journey as Paradigm: A Literary-Critical Assessment of Acts 13, 14." (Diss., Boston University, 1982).

Nestle, Wilhelm
"Legenden vom Tod der Gottesverächter," *ARW* 33 (1936) 246–69.

Neudorfer, Heinz-Werner
Der Stephanuskreis in der Forschungsgeschichte seit F. C. Baur (Monographien und Studienbücher 309; Giessen: Brunnen, 1983).

Neusner, Jacob
First Century Judaism in Crisis: Yohanan ben Zakkai and the Renaissance of Torah (Nashville: Abingdon, 1975).

Idem
From Politics to Piety: The Emergence of Pharisaic Judaism (Englewood Cliffs, N.J.: Prentice-Hall, 1973).

Idem
"Vow-Taking, the Nazirites, and the Law: Does James' Advice to Paul accord with Halakah?" in Bruce Chilton and Craig Evans, eds., *James the Just and Christian Origins* (Leiden: Brill, 1999) 59–82.

New, Sylvia
"The Michigan Papyrus," in Kirsopp Lake and Henry J. Cadbury, *Additional Notes to the Commentary,* vol. 5 of Frederick J. Foakes Jackson and Kirsopp Lake, eds., *The Beginnings of Christianity* (5 vols.; New York: Macmillan, 1920–33; reprinted, Grand Rapids: Baker, 1979) 262–69.

Newsome, Carol A., and Sharon H. Ringe, eds.
The Women's Bible Commentary (Louisville: Westminster John Knox, 1992).

Neyrey, Jerome H.
"Acts 17, Epicureans and Theodicy: A Study in Stereotypes," in David Balch et al., eds., *Greeks, Romans, and Christians: Essays in Honor of Abraham J. Malherbe* (Minneapolis: Fortress Press, 1990) 118–34.

Idem
"The Forensic Defense Speech and Paul's Trial Speeches in Acts 22–26," in Charles H. Talbert, ed., *Luke-Acts* (New York: Crossroad, 1984) 210–24.

Idem
"Luke's Social Location of Paul: Cultural Anthropology and the Status of Paul in Acts," in Ben Witherington III, *History, Literature and Society in the Book of Acts* (Cambridge: Cambridge University Press, 1996) 251–79.

Idem
The Passion according to Luke: A Redaction Study of Luke's Soteriology (New York: Paulist, 1985).

Idem, ed.
The Social World of Luke-Acts: Models for Interpretation (Peabody, Mass.: Hendrickson, 1991).

Idem
"The Symbolic Universe of Luke-Acts: 'They Turn the World Upside Down,'" in idem, ed., *The Social World of Luke-Acts: Models for Interpretation* (Peabody, Mass.: Hendrickson, 1991) 271–304.

Idem
"'Teaching You in Public and from House to House' (Acts 20.20): Unpacking a Cultural Stereotype," *JSNT* 26 (2003) 69–102.

Nickelsburg, George W.
"The Genre and Function of the Markan Passion Narrative," *HTR* 73 (1980) 153–84.

Idem
Resurrection, Immortality, and Eternal Life in Intertestamental Judaism (HTS 26; Cambridge, Mass.: Harvard University Press, 1972).

Nicklas, Tobias, and Michael Tilly, eds.
The Book of Acts as Church History: Textual Traditions and Ancient Interpretations (BZNW 120; Berlin: de Gruyter, 2003).

Nickle, Keith F.
The Collection: A Study in Paul's Strategy (SBT 48; Naperville, Ill.: Allenson, 1966).

Niederwimmer, Kurt
The Didache (trans. Linda M. Maloney; Hermeneia; Minneapolis: Fortress, 1998).

Nielsen, Anders E.
Until It Is Fulfilled: Lukan Eschatology according to Luke 22 and Acts 20 (WUNT 126; Tübingen: Mohr Siebeck, 2000).

Nilsson, Martin P.
Geschichte der griechischen Religion, vol. 2: *Die hellenistische und römische Zeit* (2nd ed.; Munich: Beck, 1961).

Idem
Greek Piety (trans. Herbert Jennings Rose; New York: Norton, 1969).

Nippel, Wilfried
Public Order in Ancient Rome (Kay Themes in Ancient History; Cambridge: Cambridge University Press, 1995).

Nobbs, Alanna
"Acts and Subsequent Ecclesiastical Histories," in Bruce W. Winter and Andrew D. Clarke, *The Book of Acts in Its Ancient Literary Setting* (BIFCS 1; Grand Rapids: Eerdmans, 1993) 153–62.

Idem
"Cyprus in the Book of Acts," in David W. J. Gill and Conrad Gempf, eds., *The Book of Acts in Its Graeco-Roman Setting* (BIFCS 2; Grand Rapids: Eerdmans, 1994) 279–89.

Nock, Arthur Darby
Conversion: The Old and the New in Religion from Alexander the Great to Augustine of Hippo (London/New York: Oxford University Press, 1961).

Idem
Essays on Religion and the Ancient World (ed. Zeph Stewart; 2 vols.; Cambridge, Mass.: Harvard University Press, 1972).

Idem
"Eunuchs in Ancient Religion," in idem, *Essays on Religion and the Ancient World* (ed. Zeph Stewart; 2 vols.; Cambridge, Mass.: Harvard University Press, 1972) 1:7–15.

Idem
"The Gild of Zeus Hypsistos," in idem, *Essays on Religion and the Ancient World* (ed. Zeph Stewart; 2 vols.; Cambridge, Mass.: Harvard University Press, 1972) 1:414–43 (abridged from *HTR* 29 [1936] 39–88).

Idem
"*Isopolitea* and the Jews," in *Essays on Religion and the Ancient World* (ed. Zeph Stewart; 2 vols.; Cambridge, Mass.: Harvard University Press, 1972) 2:960–62.

Idem
"Paul and the Magus," in Kirsopp Lake and Henry J. Cadbury, *Additional Notes to the Commentary,* vol. 5 of Frederick J. Foakes Jackson and Kirsopp Lake, eds., *The Beginnings of Christianity* (5 vols.; New York: Macmillan, 1920–33; reprinted, Grand Rapids: Baker, 1979) 164–88 (= *Essays* 1:308–30).

Idem
Review of Dibelius, *Aufsätze zur Apostelgeschichte,* in Nock, *Essays on Religion and the Ancient World* (ed. Zeph Stewart; 2 vols.; Cambridge, Mass.: Harvard University Press, 1972) 2:821–32.

Idem
Sallustius: Concerning the Gods and the Universe (Cambridge: Cambridge University Press, 1926).

Idem
"*Soter* and *Euergetes,*" in idem, *Essays on Religion and the Ancient World* (ed. Zeph Stewart; 2 vols.; Cambridge, Mass.: Harvard University Press, 1972) 2:720–35.

Nolland, John
"A Fresh Look at Acts 15.10," *NTS* 27 (1980) 105–15.

Noorda, Sijbolt J.
"Scene and Summary: A Proposal for Reading Acts 4,32–5,16," in Jacob Kremer, ed., *Les Actes des Apôtres: Traditions, rédaction, théologie* (BEThL 48; Leuven: Leuven University Press, 1979) 475–83.

Norden, Eduard
Agnostos Theos: Untersuchungen zur Formengeschichte Religiöser Rede (1913; reprinted, Darmstadt: Wissenschaftliche Buchgesellschaft, 1974).

Idem
Die antike Kunstprosa (2 vols.; 1915; reprinted, Stuttgart: Teubner, 1995).

Nordheim, Eckhard von
Die Lehre der Alten (2 vols.; ALGHJ 13; Leiden: Brill, 1980).

Norris, Frederick W.
"Antioch of Syria," *ABD* 1:265–69.

Ntumba, V. K.
"Ac 5,1-11: Ananie et Saphire: Lecture exégetique et réflexions théologiques," *Hekima Rev* 34 (1905) 43–55.

Nuttall, Geoffrey F.
Moment of Recognition: Luke as Story-Teller (London: Athlone, 1978).

O'Collins, Gerald, and Gilberto Marconi, eds.
Luke and Acts (Festschrift Emilio Rasco; trans. M. J. O'Connell; New York: Paulist, 1993).

Oepke, Albrecht
"ἔκστασις," *TDNT* 2:449–60.

Idem
"νεφέλη," *TDNT* 4:902–10.

Öhler, Markus
Barnabas: Die historische Person und ihre Rezeption in der Apostelgeschichte (WUNT 156; Tübingen: Mohr Siebeck, 2003).

Oldfather, William Abbot
Epictetus I (LCL; Cambridge, Mass.: Harvard University Press, 1925).

Ollrog, Wolf-Henning
Paulus und seine Mitarbeiter (WMANT 50; Neukirchen-Vluyn: Neukirchener Verlag, 1979).

Olson, Mark J.
"Augustan Cohort," *ABD* 1:524.

Idem
"Julius," *ABD* 3:1125–26.

Omerzu, Heike
Der Prozess des Paulus: Eine exegetische und rechtshistorische Untersuchung der Apostelgeschichte (BZNW 115; Berlin: de Gruyter, 2002).

O'Neill, John C.
"The Connection between Baptism and the Gift of the Spirit in Acts," *JSNT* 63 (1996) 87–103.

Idem
The Theology of Acts in Its Historical Setting (London: SPCK, 1961).

Osborn, C. D.
"The Search for the Original Text of Acts; the International Project on the Text of Acts," *JSNT* 44 (1991) 39–55.

Oster, Richard E.
A Bibliography of Ancient Ephesus (ATLA Bib Ser 19; Metuchen: Scarecrow, 1987).

Idem
"The Ephesian Artemis as an Opponent of Early Christianity," *JAC* 19 (1976) 24–44.

Idem
"Ephesus," *ABD* 2:542–49.

Idem
"Ephesus as a Religious Center under the Principate: I. Paganism before Constantine," *ANRW* 2.18.3 (1990) 1661–1728.

Idem
A Historical Commentary on the Missionary Success Stories in Acts 19:11-40 (Diss., Princeton University, 1974).

O'Toole, Robert F.
Acts 26: The Christological Climax of Paul's Defense (Ac 22:1–26:32) (AnBib 78; Rome: Pontifical Biblical Institute, 1978).

Idem
"Luke's Understanding of Jesus' Resurrection-Ascension-Exaltation," *BTB* 9 (1979) 106–14.

Idem
"Parallels between Jesus and His Disciples in Luke-Acts: A Further Study," *BZ* 27 (1983) 195–212.

Idem
"Philip and the Ethiopian Eunuch (Acts viii, 25-40)," *JSNT* 17 (1983) 25–34.

Idem
"Theophilus," *ABD* 6:511–12.

Idem
The Unity of Luke's Theology: An Analysis of Luke-Acts (GNS 9; Wilmington, Del.: Michael Glazier, 1984).

Idem
"'You Did Not Lie to Us but to God' (Acts 5,4c)," *Bib* 76 (1995) 182–209.

Overbeck, Franz
"Über das Verhältnis Justins des Märtyrers zur Apostelgeschichte," *ZWTh* 15 (1872) 305–49.

Overman, J. Andrew
"The God-Fearers: Some Neglected Features," *JSNT* 32 (1988) 17–26.

Paget, James Carleton
The Epistle of Barnabas: Outlook and Background (WUNT 2.64; Tübingen: Mohr Siebeck, 1994).

Painter, John
Just James: The Brother of Jesus in History and Tradition (Columbia: University of South Carolina Press, 1997).

Palmer, Darryl W.
"Acts and the Ancient Historical Monograph," in Bruce W. Winter and Andrew D. Clarke, *The Book of Acts in Its Ancient Literary Setting* (BIFCS 1; Grand Rapids: Eerdmans, 1993) 1–29.

Idem
"The Literary Background of Acts 1. 1-14," *NTS* 33 (1987) 427–38.

Pao, David W.
Acts and the Isaianic New Exodus (WUNT 130; Tübingen: Mohr Siebeck, 2000).

Parker, David C.
Codex Bezae: An Early Christian Manuscript and Its Text (Cambridge: Cambridge University Press, 1992).

Parker, F.
"The Terms 'Angel' and 'Spirit' in Acts 23,8," *Bib* 84 (2003) 344–65.

Parry, David T. N.
"Release of the Captives: Reflections on Acts 12," in *Luke's Literary Achievement: Collected Essays*, ed. Christopher M. Tuckett (JSNTS 116; Sheffield: Sheffield Academic Press, 1995) 156–64.

Parsons, Mikeal C.
"Acts," in Watson E. Mills et al., eds., *Mercer Commentary on the Bible*, vol. 7: *Acts and Pauline Writings* (Macon, Ga.: Mercer University Press, 1997) 1–64.

Idem
Body and Character in Luke and Acts: The Subversion of Physiognomy in Early Christianity (Grand Rapids: Baker, 2006).

Idem
"Christian Origins and Narrative Opening: The Sense of a Beginning in Acts 1–5," *Review & Expositor* 87 (1990) 403–22.

Idem
The Departure of Jesus in Luke-Acts: The Ascension Narratives in Context (JSNTS 21; Sheffield: Sheffield Academic Press, 1987).

Idem
"Luke and the *Progymnasmata*: A Preliminary Investigation into the Preliminary Exercises," in Todd Penner and Caroline Vander Stichele, *Contextualizing Acts: Lukan Narrative and Greco-Roman Discourse* (SBLSS 20; Boston/Leiden: Brill; Atlanta: Society of Biblical Literature, 2004) 43–63.

Idem
"'Nothing Defiled AND Unclean': The Conjunction's Function in Acts 10:14," *PerspRelStud* 27 (2000) 263–74.

Idem
"The Place of Jerusalem on the Lukan Landscape: An Exercise in Symbolic Cartography," in Richard Thompson, ed., *Literary Studies in Luke-Acts: Essays in Honor of Joseph B. Tyson* (Macon, Ga.: Mercer University Press, 1998) 155–71.

Idem, and Richard I. Pervo
Rethinking the Unity of Luke and Acts (Minneapolis: Fortress Press, 1993).

Paulsen, Henning, and Walter Bauer
Die Briefe des Ignatius von Antiochia und der Brief des Polykarp von Smyrna (HNT 18; Tübingen: Mohr Siebeck, 1985).

Pease, Arthur Stanley, ed.
M. Tulli Ciceronis De Natura Deorum (2 vols.; Cambridge, Mass.: Harvard University Press, 1958).

Idem
"Notes on Book-Burning," in Massey H. Shepherd and Sherman E. Johnson, eds., *Munera Studiosa* (Festschrift W. H. P. Hatch; Cambridge, Mass.: Episcopal Theological School, 1946) 145–60.

Idem
"Notes on Stoning among the Greeks and Romans," *TAPA* 38 (1907) 5–18.

Pecere, Oronzo, and Antonio Stramaglia, eds.
La letteratura di consumo nel mondo greco-latino (Cassino: Università degli studi di Cassino, 1996).

Pelikan, Jaroslav
The Light of the World: A Basic Image in Early Christian Thought (New York: Harper, 1962).

Penna, R.
"Les Juifs à Rome au temps de l'Apôtre Paul," *NTS* 28 (1982) 321–47.

Penner, Todd
"Civilizing Discourse," in Todd Penner and Caroline Vander Stichele, *Contextualizing Acts: Lukan Narrative and Greco-Roman Discourse* (SBLSS 20; Boston/Leiden: Brill; Atlanta: Society of Biblical Literature, 2004) 65–104.

Idem
"Contextualizing Acts," in Todd Penner and Caroline Vander Stichele, *Contextualizing Acts: Lukan Narrative and Greco-Roman Discourse* (SBLSS 20; Boston/Leiden: Brill; Atlanta: Society of Biblical Literature, 2004) 1–21.

Idem
In Praise of Christian Origins: Stephen and the Hellenists in Lukan Apologetic Historiography (Emory Studies in Early Christianity 10; New York: T&T Clark, 2004).

Idem
"Madness in the Method? The Acts of the Apostles in Current Study," *CBR* 2 (2004) 223–93.

Idem
"Reconfiguring the Rhetorical Study of Acts: Reflections on the Method in and the Learning of

A Progymnastic Poetics," *PerspRelStud* 30 (2003) 425–39.

Idem, and Caroline Vander Stichele, eds.
Contextualizing Acts: Lukan Narrative and Greco-Roman Discourse (SBLSymS 20; Atlanta: Society of Biblical Literature, 2003).

Pereira, Francis
Ephesus: Climax of Universalism in Luke-Acts–A Redaction-Critical Study of Paul's Ephesian Ministry (Acts 18:23–20:1) (Jesuit Theological Forum Studies 10.1; Anand, India: Gujarat Sahitya Prakash, 1983).

Perkins, Pheme
Peter: Apostle for the Whole Church (Columbia: University of South Carolina Press, 1994).

Pervo, Richard I.
"(Acts 21:9) Four Unmarried Daughters of Philip," in Carol Meyers et al., eds., *Women in Scripture* (New York: Houghton Mifflin, 2000) 467–68.

Idem
"'Antioch, Farewell! For Wisdom Sees . . .': Traces of a Source about the Early Gentile Mission in Acts 1–15," *Forum* (forthcoming).

Idem
"Aseneth and Her Sisters: Women in Jewish Narrative and in the Greek Novels," in Amy-Jill Levine, ed., *"Women like This": New Perspectives on Jewish Women in the Greco-Roman World* (SBLEJL 1; Atlanta: Scholars Press, 1991) 145–60.

Idem
Dating Acts: Between the Evangelists and the Apologists (Santa Rosa, Calif.: Polebridge, 2006).

Idem
"Direct Speech in Acts and the Question of Genre," *JSNT* 28 (2006) 285–307.

Idem
"Entertainment and Early Christian Literature," *Explor* 7 (1984) 29–39.

Idem
"Die Entführung in das Serail: Aspasia: A Female Aesop?" in Jo-Ann Brant et al., eds., *Ancient Fiction: The Matrix of Early Christian and Jewish Narrative* (SBLSymS 32; Atlanta: Society of Biblical Literature, 2005) 61–88.

Idem
"The Gates Have Been Closed (Acts 21:30): The Jews in Acts," *JHC* 11 (2005) 128–49.

Idem
"A Hard Act to Follow: *The Acts of Paul* and the Canonical Acts," *JHC* 2 (1995) 3–32.

Idem
"Israel's Heritage and Claims upon the Genre(s) of Luke and Acts: The Problems of a History," in David P. Moessner, ed., *Jesus and the Heritage of Israel: Luke's Narrative Claim upon Israel's Legacy* (Harrisburg, Pa.: Trinity Press International, 1999) 127–43.

Idem
"Johannine Trajectories in the *Acts of John*," *Apocrypha* 3 (1992) 47–68.

Idem
"Joseph of Asenath and the Greek Novel," *SBLSP 1976* (Missoula, Mont.: Scholars Press, 1976) 171–81.

Idem
"The Literary Genre of the Acts of the Apostles" (Diss., Harvard University, 1979).

Idem
Luke's Story of Paul (Minneapolis: Fortress Press, 1990).

Idem
"Meet Right–and Our Bounden Duty," *Forum* n.s. 4.1 (Spring 2000) 45–62.

Idem
"Must Luke and Acts Belong to the Same Genre?" in *SBLSP 1989* (Atlanta: Scholars Press, 1989) 309–16.

Idem
"My Happy Home: The Role of Jerusalem in Acts 1–7," *Forum* n.s. 3.1 (2000) 31–55.

Idem
"A Nihilist Fabula: Introducing the *Life of Aesop*," in Ronald F. Hock, J. Bradley Chance, and J. Perkins, eds., *Ancient Fiction and Early Christian Narrative* (SBLSS 6; Atlanta: Scholars Press, 1998) 77–120.

Idem
"PANTA KOINA: The Feeding Stories in the Light of Economic Data and Social Practice," in Lucas Bormann et al., eds., *Religious Propaganda and Missionary Competition in the New Testament World: Essays Honoring Dieter Georgi* (NovTSup 74; Leiden: Brill, 1994) 163–94.

Idem
Profit with Delight: The Literary Genre of the Acts of the Apostles (Philadelphia: Fortress Press, 1987).

Idem
Review of Torrey Seland, *Establishment Violence in Philo and Luke, The Studia Philonica Annual* 8 (1996) 208–10.

Idem
"Rhoda," in Carol Meyers et al., eds., *Women in Scripture* (New York: Houghton Mifflin, 2000) 145.

Idem
"Romancing an Oft-neglected Stone: The Pastoral Epistles and the Epistolary Novel," *JHC* 1 (1994) 25–47.

Idem
"Sapphira," in Carol Meyers et al., eds., *Women in Scripture* (New York: Houghton Mifflin, 2000) 149–50.

Idem
"Social and Religious Aspects of the Western Text," in Dennis Groh and Robert Jewett, ed., *The Living Text: Essays in Honor of Ernest W. Saunders* (Lanham, Md.: University Press of America, 1985) 229–41.

Idem
"The Testament of Joseph and Greek Romance," in George W. E. Nickelsburg, ed., *Studies on the Testament of Joseph* (Missoula, Mont.: Scholars Press, 1975) 15–28.

Idem
"Wisdom and Power: Petronius' *Satyricon* and the Social World of Early Christianity," *ATR* 67 (1985) 307–25.

Idem
"With Lucian: Who Needs Friends? Friendship in the *Toxaris*," in John Fitzgerald, ed., *Greco-Roman Perspectives on Friendship* (Resources for Biblical Study 34; Atlanta: Scholars Press, 1997) 163–80.

Petersen, Norman R.
Literary Criticism for New Testament Critics (Philadelphia: Fortress Press, 1978).

Peterson, David
"The Motif of Fulfilment and the Purpose of Luke-Acts," in Bruce W. Winter and Andrew D. Clarke, *The Book of Acts in Its Ancient Literary Setting* (BIFCS 1; Grand Rapids: Eerdmans, 1993) 83–104.

Peterson, Erik
Frühkirche, Judentum und Gnosis: Studien und Untersuchungen (Freiburg: Herder, 1959).

Idem
ΕΙΣ ΘΕΟΣ: Epigraphische, formgeschichtliche und religionsgeschichtliche Untersuchungen (FRLANT 41; Göttingen: Vandenhoeck & Ruprecht, 1926).

Peterson, J.
"Missionary Methods of the Religions in the Early Roman Empire" (Diss., University of Chicago, 1942).

Petzke, Gerd
"εὐνοῦχος," *TDNT* 2:80–81.

Idem
Die Traditionen über Apollonius von Tyrana und das Neue Testament (SCHNT 1; Leiden: Brill, 1970).

Pfeiffer, Robert H.
History of New Testament Times: With an Introduction to the Apocrypha (New York: Harper & Bros., 1949).

Pfister, Franz
"Ekstase," *RAC* 4:944–87.

Idem
"Apostelgeschichten," in Edgar Hennecke, ed., *Neutestamentliche Apocryphen* (2nd ed.; Tübingen: Mohr Siebeck, 1924) 163–71.

Pherigo, Lindsey P.
"Paul's Life after the Close of Acts," *JBL* 70 (1951) 277–84.

Phillips, Thomas E., ed.
Acts and Ethics (NTMon 9; Sheffield: Sheffield Phoenix, 2005).

Idem
"Creation, Sin and Its Curse, and the People of God: An Intertextual Reading of Genesis 1–12 and Acts 1–7," *Horizons in Biblical Theology* 25 (2003) 146–60.

Idem
"The Genre of Acts: Moving Toward a Consensus?" *CBR* 4 (2006) 365–96.

Idem
"Paul as a Role Model in Acts: The 'We' Passages in Acts 16 and Beyond," in idem, ed., *Acts and Ethics* (Sheffield: Sheffield Phoenix, 2005) 49–63.

Pichler, Josef
Paulusrezeption in der Apostelgeschichte: Untersuchungen zur Rede im pisidischen Antiochien (Innsbrucker theologische Studien 50; Innsbruck: Tyrolia, 1997).

Pilhofer, Peter
Philippi, Band I: Die erste christliche Gemeinde Europas (WUNT 87; Tübingen: Mohr Siebeck, 1995).

Places, Éduard des
"'Ipsius enim et genus sumus' (Act. XVII, 28)," *Bib* 81 (1962) 388–95.

Plümacher, Eckhard
"Acta-Forschung 1974–1982," *ThRu* 48 (1983) 1–56.

Idem
"Acta-Forschung 1974–1982 (Fortsetzung und Schluss)," *ThRu* 49 (1984) 105–79.

Idem
"Apokryphe Apostelakten," *PW Supp* 15:11–70.

Idem
"Apostelgeschichte," *TRE* 3:483–528.

Idem
"Die Apostelgeschichte als historische Monographie," in Jacob Kremer, ed., *Les Actes des Apôtres: Traditions, rédaction, théologie* (BEThL 48; Leuven: Leuven University Press, 1979) 457–66.

Idem
"Cicero und Lukas: Bemerkungen zu Stil und Zweck der historischen Monographie," in Jozef Verheyden, *The Unity of Luke-Acts* (BEThL 92; Leuven: Leuven University Press, 1999) 759–75.

Idem
Geschichte und Geschichten: Aufsätze zur Apostelgeschichte und zu den Johannesakten (ed. Jens Schröter and R. Brucker; WUNT 170; Tübingen: Mohr Siebeck, 2004).

Idem
"Lukas als griechischer Historiker," *PWSup* 14:235–64.

Idem
Lukas als hellenistischer Schriftsteller: Studien zur Apostelgeschichte (SUNT 9; Göttingen: Vandenhoeck & Ruprecht, 1972).

Idem
"The Mission Speeches in Acts and Dionysius of Halicarnassus," in David P. Moessner, ed., *Jesus and the Heritage of Israel: Luke's Narrative Claim upon Israel's Legacy* (Harrisburg, Pa.: Trinity Press International, 1999) 251–66.

Idem
"*TEPATEIA*": Fiktion und Wunder in der hellenistisch-römischen Geschichtsschreibung und in der Apostelgeschichte," *ZNW* 89 (1998) 66–90.

Idem
"Eine Thukydidesreminiszenz in der Apostelgeschichte (Act 20,33-35—Thuk. 11 97.3f)?" *ZNW* 83 (1992) 270–75.

Idem
"Wirklichkeitserfahrung und Geschichtsschreibung bei Lukas: Erwägungen zu den Wir-Stücken der Apostelgeschichte," *ZNW* 68 (1977) 2–22.

Plummer, Alfred
A Critical and Exegetical Commentary on the Gospel according to St Luke (ICC; 4th ed.; Edinburgh: T&T Clark, 1901).

Plunkett, Mark A.
"Ethnocentricity and Salvation History in the Cornelius Episode," *SBLSP 1985* (Atlanta: Scholars Press, 1985) 465–79.

Pohlenz, Max
"Paulus und die Stoa," *ZNW* 42 (1949) 69–104.

Poirier, John C.
"The Narrative Role of Semitic Languages in the Book of Acts," *FilolNT* 16 (2003) 107–16.

Pokorný, Petr
"Christologie et Baptême à l'Epoque du Christianisme Primitif," *NTS* 27 (1980–81) 370.

Idem
"Die Romfahrt des Paulus und der antike Roman," *ZNW* 64 (1973) 233–44.

Idem
Theologie der lukanischen Schriften (FRLANT 174; Göttingen: Vandenhoeck & Ruprecht, 1998).

Poland, Franz
Geschichte des griechischen Vereinswesens (Leipzig: Teubner, 1909).

Portefaix, Lillian
Sisters Rejoice: Paul's Letter to the Philippians and Luke-Acts as Seen by First-Century Philippian Women (ConBNT 20; Stockholm: Almqvist & Wiksell, 1988).

Porter, Stanley
"Excursus: The 'We' Passages," in David W. J. Gill and Conrad Gempf, eds., *The Book of Acts in Its Graeco-Roman Setting* (BIFCS 2; Grand Rapids: Eerdmans, 1994) 545–74.

Idem
The Paul of Acts (WUNT 115; Tübingen: Mohr Siebeck, 1999).

Porton, Gary G.
"Sadducees," *ABD* 5:892–95.

Pöschl, Viktor
The Art of Vergil: Image and Symbol in the Aeneid (Ann Arbor: University of Michigan Press, 1962).

Potter, David S.
Literary Texts and the Roman Historian Approaching the Ancient World (London: Routledge, 1999).

Idem
"Lystra," *ABD* 4:426–27.

Idem
Prophets and Emperors: Human and Divine Authority from Augustus to Theodosius (Cambridge, Mass.: Harvard University Press, 1994).

Poupon, Gérard
"L'accusation de magie dans les Actes apocryphes," in François Bovon et al., *Les Actes Apocryphes des apôtres* (Geneva: Labor et Fides, 1981) 71–94.

Powell, Mark Allan
What Are They Saying about Acts? (Mahwah, N.J.: Paulist, 1991).

Praeder, Susan Marie
"Acts 27:1–28:16: Sea Voyages in Ancient Literature and the Theology of Luke-Acts," *CBQ* 46 (1984) 683–706.

Eadem
"Jesus-Paul, Peter-Paul, and Jesus-Peter Parallelisms," in *SBLSP 1984* (Chico, Calif.: Scholars Press, 1984) 23–39.

Eadem
"Luke-Acts and the Ancient Novel," in *SBLSP 1981* (Chico, Calif.: Scholars Press, 1981) 269–92.

Eadem
"Miracle Worker and Missionary: Paul in the Acts of the Apostles," in *SBLSP 1983* (Chico, Calif.: Scholars Press, 1981) 107–29.

Eadem
"Narrative Voyage: An Analysis and Interpretation of Acts 27–28" (Diss., Graduate Theological Union, Berkeley, 1980).

Eadem
"The Problem of First Person Narration in Acts," *NovT* 39 (1987) 193–218.

Prast, Franz
Presbyter und Evangelium in nachapostolischer Zeit: Die Abschiedsrede des Paulus in Milet (Apg 20, 17-38) im Rahmen der lukanischen Konzeption der Evangeliumsverkündigung (Stuttgart: Katholisches Bibelwerk, 1979).

Preisendanz, Karl, ed. and trans.
Papyri Graecae Magicae (2 vols.; 2nd ed.; ed. Albert Henrichs; Stuttgart: Teubner, 1973–74).

Price, Robert M.
"Rhoda and Penelope: Two More Cases of Luke's Suppression of Women," in Amy-Jill Levine, *A Feminist Companion to the Acts of the Apostles* (Cleveland: Pilgrim, 2004) 98–104.

Idem
The Widow Traditions in Luke-Acts: A Feminist-Critical Scrutiny (SBLDS 155; Atlanta: Scholars Press, 1997).

Prieur, Jean-Marc
"Actes 2, 42 et le culte réformé," *FoiVie* 94 (1995) 61–72.

Idem
"La figure de l'apôtre dans les Actes apocryphes d'André," in François Bovon et al., *Les Actes Apocryphes des apôtres* (Geneva: Labor et Fides, 1981) 121–39.

Puskas, Charles B., Jr.
"The Conclusion of Luke-Acts: An Investigation of the Literary Function and Theological Significance of Acts 28:16-31" (Diss., Saint Louis University, 1980).

Idem
The Conclusion of Luke-Acts: The Function and Significance of Acts 28:16-31 (Eugene, Ore.: Wipf & Stock, 2008).

Quesnell, M.
"Le naufrage de Saint Paul," *Transversalités* 69 (1999) 47–57.

Idem
"Paul prédicateur dans les Actes des Apôtres," *NTS* 47 (2001) 469–81.

Quinn, Jerome D.
"The Last Volume of Luke," in Charles H. Talbert, ed., *Perspectives on Luke-Acts* (Danville, Va.: National Association of Baptist Professors of Religion, 1978) 76–98.

Rackham, H.
Cicero De Natura Deorum (LCL; Cambridge, Mass.: Harvard University Press, 1933).

Rackham, Richard B.
The Acts of the Apostles (2nd ed.; London: Methuen, 1904).

Radl, Walter
"Befreiung aus dem Gefängnis: Die Darstellung eines biblischen Grundthemas in Apg 12," *BZ* 27 (1983) 81–96.

Idem
Paulus and Jesus im lukanischen Doppelwerk: Untersuchungen zu Parallelmotiven im Lukasevangelium und in der Apostelgeschichte (Europäische Hochschulschriften 23/49; Bern: Lang, 1975).

Idem
"ᾠδίν," *EDNT* 3:506.

Räisänen, Heikki
"Die 'Hellenisten' der Urgemeinde," *ANRW* 2.26.2 (1995) 1468–1514.

Idem
"The 'Hellenists': A Bridge between Jesus and Paul?" in *Jesus, Paul, and Torah: Collected Essays* (trans. D. E. Orton; JSNTS 43; Sheffield: Sheffield Academic Press, 1992) 149–202.

Ramsay, William M.
The Bearing of Recent Discovery on the Trustworthiness of the New Testament (London: Hodder & Stoughton, 1915; reprinted, Grand Rapids: Baker, 1953).

Idem
The Church in the Roman Empire (London: Hodder & Stoughton, 1897).

Idem
The Cities of St. Paul: Their Influence on His Life and Thought (London: Hodder & Stoughton, 1907).

Idem
The Letters to the Seven Churches of Asia and Their Place in the Plan of the Apocalypse (New York: Armstrong, 1905).

Idem
Luke the Physician and Other Studies in the History of Religion (New York: Armstrong, 1908).

Idem
St. Paul the Traveller and the Roman Citizen (London: Hodder & Stoughton, 1897).

Rapske, Brian
"Acts, Travel and Shipwreck," in David W. J. Gill and Conrad Gempf, eds., *The Book of Acts in Its Graeco-Roman Setting* (BIFCS 2; Grand Rapids: Eerdmans, 1994) 1–47.

Idem
The Book of Acts and Paul in Roman Custody (BIFCS 3; Grand Rapids: Eerdmans, 1994).

Rau, Eckhard
Von Jesus zu Paulus: Entwicklung und Rezeption der antiochenischen Theologie im Urchristentum (Stuttgart: Kohlhammer, 1994).

Reardon, Brian P.
Collected Ancient Greek Novels (Berkeley: University of California Press, 1989).

Reasoner, Mark
"The Theme of Acts: Institutional History or Divine Necessity in History?" *JBL* 118 (1999) 635–59.

Redditt, Paul L.
"Azotus," *ABD* 1:541–42.

Reeder, Ellen D.
"The Mother of the Gods and the Hellenistic Bronze Matrix," *AJA* 91 (1987) 423–40.

Refoulé, F.
"Le discours de Pierre à l'assemblée de Jérusalem," *RB* 100 (1993) 239–51.

Reicke, Bo
"Die Mahlzeit mit Paulus auf dem Wellen des Mittelmeers Act 27, 33-38," *ThZ* 4 (1948) 401–10.

Idem
"Synoptic Prophecies on the Destruction of Jerusalem," in David E. Aune, ed., *Studies in New Testament and Early Christian Literature: Essays in Honor of Allen P. Wikgren* (NovTSup 33; Leiden: Brill, 1972) 121–34.

Reid, Barbara E.
"The Power of the Widows and How to Suppress It (Acts 6.1-7)," in Amy-Jill Levine, *A Feminist Companion to the Acts of the Apostles* (Cleveland: Pilgrim, 2004) 71–88.

Reif, Stefan C.
"The Early Liturgy of the Synagogue," in *The Cambridge History of Judaism,* vol. 3: *The Early Roman Period* (ed. William Horbury, W. D. Davies, and John Sturdy; Cambridge: Cambridge University Press, 1999) 326–57.

Reimer, Andy M.
Miracle and Magic: A Study in the Acts of the Apostles and the Life of Apollonius of Tyana (JSNTS 235; London: Sheffield Academic Press, 2002).

Idem
"Virtual Prison Breaks: Non-Escape Narratives and the Definition of 'Magic,'" in Todd E. Klutz, ed., *Magic in the Biblical World: From the Rod of Aaron to the Ring of Solomon* (JSNTS 245; London: T&T Clark, 2003) 125–39.

Reimer, Ivoni Richter
Women in the Acts of the Apostles: A Feminist Liberation Perspective (trans. Linda M. Maloney; Minneapolis: Fortress Press, 1995).

Reinbold, Wolfgang
"Die 'Hellenisten': Kritische Anmerkungen zu einem Fachbegriff der neutestamentlichen Wissenschaft," *BZ* 42 (1998) 96–102.

Idem
Propaganda und Mission im ältesten Christentum: Eine Untersuchung zu den Modalitäten der Ausbreitung der frühen Kirche (FRLANT 188; Göttingen: Vandenhoeck & Ruprecht, 2000).

Reinhardt, Wolfgang
"The Population Size of Jerusalem and the Numerical Growth of the Jerusalem Church," in Richard Bauckham, *The Book of Acts in Its Palestinian Setting* (BIFCS 4; Grand Rapids: Eerdmans, 1995) 237–65.

Reinmuth, Eckhart
Pseudo-Philo und Lukas: Studien zum Liber Antiquitatum Biblicarum (Tübingen: Mohr Siebeck, 1994).

Reis, David M.
"The Areopagus as Echo Chamber: *Mimesis* and Intertextuality in Acts," *JHC* 9 (2002) 259–77.

Reiser, Marius
"Der Alexanderroman und das Markusevangelium," in Hubert Cancik, ed., *Markus-Philologie* (WUNT 33; Tübingen: Mohr Siebeck, 1984) 131–63.

Reitzenstein, Richard
Hellenistische Wundererzählungen (Leipzig: Teubner, 1906).

Remus, Harold
Pagan-Christian Conflict over Miracle in the Second Century (Patristic Monograph Series 10; Cambridge, Mass.: Philadelphia Patristic Foundation, 1983).

Rengstorf, Karl H.
"δοῦλος," *TDNT* 2:261–80.

Idem
"ἑπτά," *TDNT* 2:627–35.

Renie, R. P. J.
"L'élection de Mathias," *RB* 55 (1948) 42–53.

Repo, Eero
Der "Weg" als Selbstbezeichnung des Urchristentums: Eine traditionsgeschichtliche und semasiologische Untersuchungen (Annales Academia Scientiarum Fennicae B.132/2; Helsinki: Suomalainen Tiedeakatemia, 1964).

Resch, Alfred
Agrapha: Aussercanonische Evangelienfragmente (TU 5; Leipzig: Hinrichs, 1889).

Resch, Gotthold
Das Aposteldecret nach seiner ausserkanonischen Textgestalt (TU 28.3; Leipzig: Hinrichs, 1905).

Rese, Martin
Alttestamentliche Motive in der Christologie des Lukas (StNT 1; Gütersloh: Mohn, 1969).

Reumann, John
"The 'Itinerary' as a Form in Classical Literature and the Acts of the Apostles," in Maurya P. Horgan and Paul J. Kobelski, eds., *To Touch the Text: Biblical and Related Studies in Honor of Joseph A. Fitmyer, S.J.* (New York: Crossroad, 1989) 335–57.

Reventlow, Henning G.
"Sein Blut Komme über Sein Haupt," *VT* 10 (1960) 311–27.

Revon, M.
"Hospitality," *ERE* 5–6:814.

Reynolds, Joyce, and Robert Tannenbaum
Jews and Godfearers at Aphrodisias (Cambridge Philological Society Supp. 12; Cambridge: Cambridge University Press, 1987).

Richard, Earl
Acts 6:1–8:4: The Author's Method of Composition (SBLDS 41; Missoula, Mont.: Scholars Press, 1978).

Idem
First and Second Thessalonians (SacPag 11; Collegeville, Minn.: Liturgical Press, 1995).

Idem
"The Old Testament in Acts": Wilcox's Semitisms in Retrospect," *CBQ* 42 (1980) 330–41.

Idem
"Pentecost as a Recurrent Theme in Luke-Acts," in idem, ed., *New Views on Luke and Acts* (Collegeville, Minn: Liturgical Press, 1990) 133–49.

Idem
"The Polemical Character of the Joseph Episode in Acts 7," *JBL* 98 (1979) 255–67.

Richardson, Cyril C., ed.
Early Christian Fathers (LCC 1; New York: Macmillan, 1970).

Riemer, Ulrike
"Miracle Stories and Their Narrative Intent in the Context of the Ruler Cult of Classical Antiquity," in Michael Labahn and Bert L. Peerbolte, eds., *Wonders Never Cease: The Purpose of Narrating Miracle Stores in the New Testament and Its Religious Environment* (LNTS 288; London: T&T Clark, 2006) 32–47.

Riesenfeld, Harold
"The Text of Acts 10:36," in Ernest Best and Robert McL. Wilson, eds., *Text and Interpretation: Studies in the New Testament Presented to Matthew Black* (Cambridge: Cambridge University Press, 1979) 191–94.

Riesner, Rainer
Paul's Early Period: Chronology, Mission Strategy, Theology (trans. D. Stott; Grand Rapids: Eerdmans, 1998).

Idem
"Synagogues in Jerusalem," in Richard Bauckham, *The Book of Acts in Its Palestinian Setting* (BIFCS 4; Grand Rapids: Eerdmans, 1995) 179–211.

Rigaux, Beda
"Die 'Zwölf' in Geschichte und Kerygma," in Helmut Ristow and Karl Matthiae, eds., *Der historische Jesus und der kerygmatische Christus: Beiträge zum Christusverständnis in Forschung und Verkündigung* (Berlin: Evangelische Verlagsanstalt, 1961) 468–86.

Rius-Camps, Josep
"La Utilización del Libro de Joel (JL 2,28-32a LXX) en el Discurso de Pedro (Hch 2,14-21), in David G. K. Taylor, ed., *Studies in the Early Text of the Gospels and Acts* (SBLT-CS 1; Atlanta: Society of Biblical Literature, 1999) 245–70.

Idem, and Jenny Read-Heimerdinger
"After the Death of Judas: A Reconsideration of the Status of the Twelve Apostles," *Revista Catalana de Teología* 29 (2004) 305–34.

Robbins, Vernon K.
"By Land and by Sea," in Charles H. Talbert, *Perspectives on Luke-Acts* (Danville, Va.: National Association of Baptist Professors of Religion, 1978) 215–42.

Idem
"The Social Location of the Implied Author of Luke-Acts," in Jerome H. Neyrey, ed., *The Social World of Luke-Acts: Models for Interpretation* (Peabody, Mass.: Hendrickson, 1991) 305–32.

Idem
"The We-Passages in Acts and Ancient Sea Voyages," *BR* 20 (1975) 5–18.

Robert, Louis
Les gladiateurs dans l'Orient grec (Bibliothèque de l'École des Hautes Études 278; Limoges: Bontemps, 1940; reprinted, Amsterdam: Hakkert, 1971).

Roberts, Deborah H., Francis M. Dunn, and Don Fowler, eds.
Classical Closure: Reading the End in Greek and Latin Literature (Princeton: Princeton University Press, 1997).

Robinson, James M., and Helmut Koester
Trajectories through Early Christianity (Philadelphia: Fortress Press, 1971).

Robinson, James M., et al., eds.
The Critical Edition of Q (Hermeneia; Minneapolis: Fortress Press, 2000).

Robinson, John A. T.
"The Most Primitive Christology of All," in idem, *Twelve New Testament Studies* (SBT 34; London: SCM, 1962) 139–53.

Rohde, Erwin
Der griechische Roman und seine Vorlaüfer (3rd ed.; Darmstadt: Wissenschaftliche Buchgesellschaft, 1974).

Idem
Psyche: The Cult of Souls and Belief in Immortality among the Greeks (trans. W. B. Hillis; London: Routledge & Kegan Paul, 1925).

Rohrbaugh, Richard L.
"Methodological Considerations in the Debate over the Social Class Status of Early Christians," *JAAR* 52 (1984) 519–46.

Idem
"The Pre-Industrial City in Luke-Acts: Urban Social Relations," in Jerome H. Neyrey, ed., *The Social World of Luke-Acts: Models for Interpretation* (Peabody, Mass.: Hendrickson, 1991) 125–50.

Rolfe, J. C.
The Attic Nights of Aulus Gellius I (LCL; Cambridge, Mass.: Harvard University Press, 1927).

Idem
Suetonius I (LCL; Cambridge, Mass.: Harvard University Press, 1913).

Romm, James S.
The Edges of the Earth in Ancient Thought (Princeton: Princeton University Press, 1992).

Ronconi, Alessandro
"Exitus illustrium virorum," *RAC* 6:1258–68.

Ropes, James Hardy
A Critical and Exegetical Commentary on the Epistle of St. James (ICC; New York: Charles Scribner's Sons, 1916).

Idem
The Text of Acts, vol. 3 of Frederick J. Foakes Jackson and Kirsopp Lake, eds., *The Beginnings of Christianity* (5 vols.; New York: Macmillan, 1920–33; reprinted, Grand Rapids: Baker, 1979).

Rordorf, Willy
"Actes de Paul," in François Bovon and P. Geoltrain, eds., *Écrits apocryphes chrétiens* (Paris: Gallimard, 1997) 1115–77.

Rosner, Brian S.
"Acts and Biblical History," in Bruce W. Winter and Andrew D. Clarke, *The Book of Acts in Its Ancient Literary Setting* (BIFCS 1; Grand Rapids: Eerdmans, 1993) 65–82.

Roth, Samuel J.
The Blind, the Lame, and the Poor: Character Types in Luke-Acts (Sheffield: Sheffield Academic Press, 1997).

Rothschild, Clare K.
Luke-Acts and the Rhetoric of History: An Investigation of Early Christian Historiography (WUNT 175; Tübingen: Mohr Siebeck, 2004).

Roussel, Pierre
Les cultes égyptiens à Délos du IIIe au Ier siècle av. J.C. (Nancy: Berger-Levrault, 1916).

Rowe, C. Kavin
"Acts 2.36 and the Continuity of Lukan Christology," *NTS* 53 (2007) 37–56.

Idem
"History, Hermeneutics and the Unity of Luke-Acts," *JSNT* 28 (2005) 131–57.

Idem
"Literary Unity and Reception History: Reading Luke-Acts as Luke and Acts," *JSNT* 29 (2007) 449–58.

Rudd, Niall
Horace: Odes and Eposes (LCL; Cambridge, Mass.: Harvard University Press, 2004).

Rudolph, Kurt
Gnosis: The Nature and History of Gnosticism (trans. and ed. R. McL. Wilson; San Francisco: Harper & Row, 1983).

Idem
"Simon-Magus oder Gnosticus? Zum Stand der Debatte," *ThRu* 42 (1977) 279–359.

Rusam, Dietrich
Das Alte Testament bei Lukas (BZNW 112; Berlin: de Gruyter, 2003).

Ryken, Leland, et al., eds.
Dictionary of Biblical Imagery (Downers Grove, Ill.: InterVarsity, 1998).

Sabbe, M.
"The Son of Man Saying in Acts 7,56," in Jacob Kremer, ed., *Les Actes des Apôtres: Traditions, rédaction, théologie* (BEThL 48; Leuven: Leuven University Press, 1979) 241–79.

Sabourin, Leopold
Priesthood: A Comparative Study (Studies in the History of Religions, Numen Supp. 25; Leiden: Brill, 1973).

Saddington, Dennis B.
"Roman Military and Administrative Personnel in the New Testament," *ANRW* 2.26.3 (1996) 2409–35.

Safrai, Samuel, et al., eds.
The Jewish People in the First Century: Historical Geography, Political History, Social, Cultural and Religious Life and Institutions (CRINT 1.1; Assen: Van Gorcum, 1974).

Saller, Richard P.
Personal Patronage under the Early Empire (Cambridge: Cambridge University Press, 1982).

Samkutty, V. J.
The Samaritan Mission in Acts (LNTS 328; Edinburgh: T&T Clark, 2006).

Sanders, E. P.
Judaism: Practice and Belief 63 BCE–66 CE (Philadelphia: Trinity Press International, 1992).

Idem
Paul and Palestinian Judaism: A Comparison of Patterns of Religion (Philadelphia: Fortress Press, 1977).

Sanders, Jack T.
The Jews in Luke-Acts (Philadelphia: Fortress Press, 1987).

Sandnes, Karl O.
"Paul and Socrates: The Aim of Paul's Areopagus Speech," *JSNT* 50 (1993) 13–26.

Sandt, H. van de
"The Presence and Transcendence of God: An Investigation of Acts 7,44-50 in Light of the LXX," *EThL* 80 (2004) 30–59.

Santos Otero, A. de
"Later Acts of Apostles," in Edgar Hennecke, *New Testament Apocrypha* (ed. Wilhelm Schneemelcher; ET ed. Robert McL. Wilson; 2 vols.; rev. ed. Louisville: Westminster John Knox, 1991–92) 2:426–82.

Sasse, Hermann
"*κοσμέω*," *TDNT* 3:867–98.

Scharlemann, Martin H.
Stephen: A Singular Saint (AnBib 34; Rome: Pontifical Biblical Institute, 1968).

Schenk, Wolfgang
"Luke as Reader of Paul: Observations on his Reception," in Sipke Draisma, ed., *Intertextuality in Biblical Writings: Essays in Honour of Bas van Iersel* (Kampen: Kok, 1989) 127–39.

Schenke, Hans-Martin
Apostelgeschichte 1,1–15,3 im mittelägyptischen Dialekt des koptischen (Codex Glazier) (TU 137; Berlin: Akamemie, 1991).

Idem
"Das Weiterwirken des Paulus und die Pflege seines Erbes durch die Paulusschule," *NTS* 21 (1975) 505–18.

Schenke, L.
"Die Kontrastformel Apg 4,10b," *BZ* 26 (1982) 1–20.

Schiffman, Lawrence H.
"At the Crossroads: Tannaitic Perspectives on the Jewish-Christian Schism," in E. P. Sanders et al., eds., *Jewish and Christian Self-Definition*, vol. 2: *Aspects of Judaism in the Greco-Roman Period* (Philadelphia: Fortress Press, 1981) 115–56.

Schille, Gottfried
"Die Fragwürdigkeit eines Itinerars der Paulusreisen," *ThLZ* 89 (1959) 165–74.

Schinkel, Dirk
"'Und sie wußten nicht, warum sie zusammengekommen waren'—Gruppen und Gruppeninteressen in der Demetriosepisode (Apg 19,23-40," in A. Gutsfeld und Dietrich-Alex Koch, eds., *Vereine, Synagogen und Gemeinden im kaiserzeitlichen Kleinasien* (Studien und Texte zu Antike und Christentum 25; Tübingen: Mohr Siebeck, 2006) 95–112.

Schlier, Heinrich
"*ἀφίστημι*," *TDNT* 1:513–14.

Idem
"*παρρησία*," *TDNT* 5:871–86.

Schmeling, Gareth, ed.
The Novel in the Ancient World (rev. ed.; Leiden: Brill, 2003).

Schmid, Lothar
"*κέντρον*," *TDNT* 3:663–68.

Schmidt, Karl Ludwig
"*ἐκκλησία*," *TDNT* 3:501–36.

Schmithals, Walter
"Identitätskrise bei Lukas und Anderswo?" in Ciliers Breytenbach et al., eds., *Apostelgeschichte und die hellenistische Geschichtsschreibung: Festschrift für Eckhard Plümacher zu seinem 65. Geburtstag* (AGJU 57; Leiden/Boston: Brill, 2004) 223–51.

Idem
Paul and the Gnostics (trans. J. E. Steely; Nashville: Abingdon, 1972).

Schnackenburg, Rudolf
Ephesians: A Commentary (trans. H. Heron; Edinburgh: T&T Clark, 1991).

Schneckenberger, Mathias
Über den Zweck der Apostelgeschichte (Bern: Fisher, 1841).

Schneemelcher, Wilhelm, ed.
E. Hennecke, *New Testament Apocrypha* (2 vols.; rev. ed.; ET ed. Robert McL. Wilson; Louisville: Westminster John Knox, 1991–92).

Schneider, Gerhard
"Literatur zum lukanischen Doppelwerk: Neuerscheinungen, 1990–91," *TRev* 88 (1992) 1–18.

Idem
"Stephanus, die Hellenisten und Samaria," in Jacob Kremer, ed., *Les Actes des Apôtres: Traditions, rédaction, théologie* (BEThL 48; Leuven: Leuven University Press, 1979) 215–40.

Schneider, J.
"εὐνοῦχος," *TDNT* 2:765–68.

Schniewind, Julius, and G. Friedrich
"ἐπαγγέλω," *TDNT* 2:576–86.

Schoedel, William R.
"Ignatius and the Reception of Matthew in Antioch," in David Balch, ed., *Social History of the Matthean Community* (Minneapolis: Fortress Press, 1991) 129–86.

Idem
Ignatius of Antioch (Hermeneia; Philadelphia: Fortress Press, 1985).

Idem
"Papias," *ANRW* 2.27.1 (1993) 235–70.

Schottroff, Luise
Let the Oppressed Go Free: Feminist Perspectives on the New Testament (trans. Annemarie S. Kidder; Louisville: Westminster John Knox, 1993).

Schraeder, Hans H.
"Ναζαρηνός, Ναζοραῖος," *TDNT* 4:874–79.

Schreckenberg, Heinz
"Flavius Josephus und die Lukanischen Schriften," in Wilfrid Haubeck and Michael Bachmann, eds., *Wort in der Zeit: Neutestamentliche Studien; Festgabe für Karl Heinrich Rengstorf zum 75. Geburtstag* (Leiden: Brill, 1980) 179–209.

Schreiber, Stefan
"Aktualisierung göttlichen Handelns am Pfingsttag: Das frühjüdische Fest in Apg 2,1," *ZNW* 93 (2002) 58–77.

Idem
Paulus als Wundertäter: Redaktionsgeschichtliche Untersuchungen zur Apostelgeschichte und den authentischen Paulusbriefen (BZNW 79; Berlin: de Gruyter, 1996).

Idem
"'Verstehst du denn, was du liest?' Beobachtungen zur Begegnung von Philippus und dem äthiopischen Eunuchen (Apg 8,26-40)," *StudNTUmwelt* 21 (1996) 42–72.

Schrenk, W.
"θέλω," *TDNT* 3:44–62.

Schröter, Jens
"Acta Forschung seit 1982: I. Formgeschichte und Kommentare," *ThR* 72 (2007) 179–230.

Idem
"Die Apostelgeschichte und die Entstehung des neutestamentlichen Kanons? Beobachtungen zur Kanonisierung der Apostelgeschichte und ihrer Bedeutung als kanonischer Schrift," in J.-M. Auwers and H. J. de Jonge, eds., *The Biblical Canons* (BEThL 163; Leuven: Leuven University Press, 2003) 395–429.

Idem
"Kirche im Anschluss an Paulus: Aspekte der Paulusrezeption in der Apostelgeschichte und in den Pastoralbriefen," *ZNW* 98 (2007) 77–104.

Schubert, Paul
"The Place of the Areopagus Speech in the Composition of Acts," in J. Coert Rylaarsdam, ed., *Essays in Divinity* 6 (Chicago: University of Chicago Press, 1968) 235–61.

Idem
"The Structure and Significance of Luke 24," in Walter Eltester, ed., *Neutestamentliche Studien für Rudolf Bultmann zu seinem 70. Geburtstag am 20. August 1954* (BZNW 21; Berlin: Töpelmann, 1954) 165–86.

Schulte, Claudia
Die Grammateis von Ephesos: Schreiberamt und Sozialstruktur in einer Provinzhauptstadt des römischen Kaiserreichs (Stuttgart: Franz Steiner, 1994).

Schulz, Siegfred
"Gottes Vorsehung bei Lukas," *ZNW* 54 (1963) 104–16.

Schürer, Emil
A History of the Jewish People in the Time of Jesus Christ (rev. and ed. G. Vermes, F. Millar et al.; 3 vols.; Edinburgh: T&T Clark, 1973–87).

Schürmann, Heinz
"Das Testament des Paulus für die Kirche: Apg 20,18-35," *Traditionsgeschichtliche Untersuchungen zu den Synoptischen Evangelien* (Düsseldorf: Patmos, 1968) 310–40.

Schüssler Fiorenza, Elisabeth, ed.
Aspects of Religious Propaganda in Judaism and Early Christianity (Notre Dame, Ind.: University of Notre Dame Press, 1976).

Eadem
In Memory of Her: A Feminist Theological Reconstruction of Christian Origins (New York: Crossroad, 1983).

Eadem
"Miracles, Mission, and Apologetics: An Introduction," in eadem, ed., *Aspects of Religious Propaganda in Judaism and Early Christianity* (Notre Dame, Ind.: University of Notre Dame Press, 1976) 1–25.

Eadem, ed.
Searching the Scriptures: A Feminist Commentary (2 vols.; New York: Crossroad, 1994).

Schwabe, Moshe, and Baruch Lifshitz
Beth She'arim, vol. 2: *The Greek Inscriptions* (New Brunswick, N.J.: Rutgers University Press, 1974).

Schwartz, Daniel R.
Agrippa I: The Last King of Judaea (Tübingen: Mohr Siebeck, 1990).

Idem
"The End of the Line: Paul in the Canonical Book of Acts," in William S. Babcock, ed., *Paul and the Legacies of Paul* (Dallas: Southern Methodist University Press, 1990) 3–24.

Schwartz, Eduard
Fünf Vorträge über den griechischen Roman (Berlin: Töpelmann, 1896).

Idem
"Zur Chronologie des Paulus," in *Nachrichten von der königlichen Gesellschaft der Wissenschaften zu Göttingen, Philologisch-historische Klasse* (Berlin: Weidmann, 1907) 263–99.

Schwartz, Saundra C.
"The Trial Scene in the Greek Novels and in Acts," in Todd Penner and Caroline Vander Stichele, *Contextualizing Acts: Lukan Narrative and Greco-Roman Discourse* (SBLSS 20; Boston/Leiden: Brill; Atlanta: Society of Biblical Literature, 2004) 105–37.

Schweizer, Eduard
"ἀνάψυξις," *TDNT* 9:664–665.

Idem
Church Order in the New Testament (trans. F. Clarke; Naperville, Ill.: Allenson, 1961).

Idem
"Concerning the Speeches in Acts," in Leander Keck and J. Louis Martyn, eds., *Studies in Luke-Acts: Essays Presented in Honor of Paul Schubert* (Nashville: Abingdon, 1966) 208–16.

Idem
The Letter to the Colossians (trans. A. Chester; Minneapolis: Augsburg, 1982).

Idem
Luke: A Challenge to Present Theology (Atlanta: John Knox, 1982).

Idem
"πνεῦμα," *TDNT* 6:332–445.

Schwemer, Anna Maria
Studien zu den frühjüdischen Prophetenlegenden Vitae Prophetarum (2 vols.; TSAJ 49; Tübingen: Mohr Siebeck, 1996).

Scott, James M.
"Luke's Geographical Horizon," in David W. J. Gill and Conrad Gempf, eds., *The Book of Acts in Its Graeco-Roman Setting* (BIFCS 2; Grand Rapids: Eerdmans, 1994) 483–544.

Scott, Kenneth
"Ruler Cult and Related Problems in the Greek Romances," *Classical Philology* 33 (1938) 380–89.

Seaford, Richard
"Thunder, Lightning, and Earthquake in the *Bacchae* and the Acts of the Apostles," in Alan B. Lloyd, ed., *What Is a God? Studies in the Nature of Greek Divinity* (London: Duckworth, 1997) 139–48.

Seccombe, David P.
Possessions and the Poor in Luke-Acts (StudNTUmwelt 6; ed. Albert Fuchs; Linz, 1982).

Seeley, David
Deconstructing the New Testament (BIS 5; Leiden: Brill, 1994).

Seesemann, Heinrich
Der Begriff **ΚΟΙΝΩΝΙΑ** *im Neuen Testament* (BZNW 74; Gießen: Töpelmann, 1933).

Idem
"πατάσσω," *TDNT* 5:939–40.

Segal, Alan F.
"Acts 15 as Jewish and Christian History," *Forum* n.s. 4 (2001) 63–87.

Idem
"Hellenistic Magic: Some Questions of Definition," in Roelof van den Broek and Maarten J. Vermaseren, eds., *Studies in Gnosticism and Hellenistic Religions* (EPRO 91; Leiden: Brill, 1981) 349–75.

Idem
"Matthew's Jewish Voice," in David Balch, ed., *Social History of the Matthean Community* (Minneapolis: Fortress Press, 1991).

Idem
Paul the Convert: The Apostolate and Apostasy of Saul the Pharisee (New Haven: Yale University Press, 1990).

Segal, Peretz
"The Penalty of the Warning Inscription from the Temple of Jerusalem," *IEJ* 39 (1989) 79–84.

Seim, Turid Karlsen
The Double Message: Patterns of Gender in Luke and Acts (Nashville: Abingdon, 1994).

Seland, Torrey
Establishment Violence in Philo and Luke: A Study of Non-Conformity to the Torah and Jewish Vigilante Reactions (BIS 15; Leiden: Brill, 1995).

Idem
"Once More—The Hellenists, Hebrews, and Stephen: Conflict and Conflict-Management in Acts 6–7," in Peder Borgen et al., eds., *Recruitment, Conquest, and Conflict: Strategies in Judaism, Early Christianity, and the Greco-Roman World* (Atlanta: Scholars Press, 1998) 169–207.

Selinger, R.
"Die Demetriosunruhen (Apg 19,23-40): Eine Fallstudie aus Rechtshistorischer Perspective," *ZNW* 88 (1997) 242–59.

Selwyn, Edward Gordon
The First Epistle of St Peter (2nd ed., London: Macmillan, 1947).

Setzer, Claudia J.
"Sosthenes," *ABD* 6:160.

Seul, Peter
Rettung für alle: Die Romreise des Paulus nach Apg 27,1–28,16 (Berlin/Vienna: Philo Verlagsgesellschaft, 2003).

Sevenster, J. N.
Do You Know Greek? How Much Greek Could the First Jewish Christians Have Known? (NovTSup 19; Leiden: Brill, 1968).

Sharp, Douglas S.
"The Meaning of *men oun* in Acts 14:3," *ExpT* 44 (1932–33) 528.

Shauf, Scott
Theology as History, History as Theology: Paul in Ephesus in Acts 19 (BZNW 133; Berlin: de Gruyter, 2005).

Sheeley, S. M.,
"Getting into the Act(s): Narrative Presence in the 'We' Sections," *PerspRelStud* 26 (1999) 203–20.

Shellard, Barbara
New Light on Luke: Its Purpose, Sources and Literary Context (JSNTS 215; Sheffield: Sheffield Academic Press, 2002).
Shepherd, William H.
The Narrative Function of the Holy Spirit as a Character in Luke-Acts (SBLDS 147; Atlanta: Scholars Press, 1994).
Sherk, Robert K.
The Roman Empire: Augustus to Hadrian (Translated Documents of Greece & Rome 6; Cambridge: Cambridge University Press, 1988).
Idem
Rome and the Greek East to the Death of Augustus (Translated Documents of Greece & Rome 4; Cambridge: Cambridge University Press, 1984).
Sherwin-White, Adrian N.
The Roman Citizenship (2nd ed.; Oxford: Clarendon, 1973).
Idem
"The Roman Citizenship: A Survey of Its Development into a World Franchise," *ANRW* 1.2 (1972) 23–58.
Idem
Roman Society and Roman Law in the New Testament (Oxford: Clarendon, 1963).
Siegert, Folker
"Die 'Gottesfürchtige' und Sympathisanten," *JSJ* 4 (1973) 109–64.
Silberman, Lou H.
"Paul's Viper: Acts 28:3-6," *Forum* 8 (1992) 247–53.
Simon, Marcel
"ϑάρσει. οὐδεὶς ἀϑάνατος: Étude de vocabulaire religieuse," *RHR* 100 (1936) 188–206.
Idem
St. Stephen and the Hellenists in the Primitive Church (New York: Longmans, Green, 1958).
Idem
"St. Stephen and the Jerusalem Temple," *JEH* 2 (1951) 127–42.
Six, Karl
Das Aposteldekret (Act 15,28.29): Seine Entstehung und Geltung in den ersten vier Jahrhunderten (Veröfflentichungen des biblisch-patristischen Seminars zu Innsbruck 5; Innsbruck: Rauch, 1912).
Skinner, Matthew L.
Locating Paul: Places of Custody as Narrative Settings in Acts 21–28 (SBL Academia Biblica 13; Atlanta: Society of Biblical Literature, 2003).
Idem
"Unchained Ministry: Paul's Roman Custody (Acts 21–28) and the Sociopolitical Outlook of the Book of Acts," in Thomas E. Phillips, ed., *Acts and Ethics* (NTMon 9; Sheffield: Sheffield Phoenix, 2005) 79–95.
Slingerland, Dixon
"Acts 18:1-17 and Luedemann's Pauline Chronology," *JBL* 109 (1990) 686–90.
Idem
"Acts 18:1-18, the Gallio Inscription, and Absolute Pauline Chronology," *JBL* 110 (1991) 439–49.
Idem
Claudian Policymaking and the Early Imperial Repression of Judaism at Rome (South Florida Studies in the History of Judaism 160; Atlanta: Scholars Press, 1997).
Idem
"The Composition of Acts: Some Redaction-critical Observations," *JAAR* 56 (1988) 99–113.
Idem
"'The Jews' in the Pauline Portion of Acts," *JAAR* 54 (1986) 305–21.
Idem
"Suetonius *Claudius* 25.4, Acts 18, and Paulus Orosius *Historiarum adversum paganos libri vii*: Dating the Claudian Expulsions of Roman Jews," *JQR* 83 (1992) 127–44.
Smallwood, E. Mary
"The Diaspora in the Roman Period before CE 70," in *The Cambridge History of Judaism,* vol. 3: *The Early Roman Period* (ed. William Horbury, W. D. Davies, and John Sturdy; Cambridge: Cambridge University Press, 1999) 168–91.
Idem
The Jews under Roman Rule: From Pompey to Diocletian (SJLA 20; Leiden: Brill, 1981).
Smid, Harm R.
Protevangelium Jacobi: A Commentary (Assen: Van Gorcum, 1965).
Smith, Abraham
"Do You Understand What You Are Reading? A Literary Critical Reading of the Ethiopian (Kushite) Episode (Acts 8:26-40)," *Journal of the Interdenominational Theological Center* 22 (1994) 48–70.
Idem
"'Full of Spirit and Wisdom': Luke's Portrait of Stephen (Acts 6:1–8:1a) as a Man of Self-Mastery," in Leif E. Vaage and Vincent L. Wimbush, eds., *Asceticism and the New Testament* (London: Routledge, 1999) 97–114.
Idem
"A Second Step in African Biblical Interpretation: A Generic Reading Analysis of Acts 8:26-40," in Fernando F. Segovia and Mary A. Tolbert, eds., *Reading from This Place: Social Location and Biblical Interpretation in the United States* (2 vols.; Minneapolis: Fortress Press, 1995) 1:213–28.
Smith, David E.
The Canonical Function of Acts: A Comparative Analysis (Collegeville, Minn.: Liturgical Press, 2002).
Smith, James
The Voyage and Shipwreck of St. Paul (4th ed.; London: Longmans, Green, 1880).
Smith, Morton
"The Reason for the Persecution of Paul and the Obscurity of Acts," in E. E. Urbach et al., eds., *Studies in Mysticism and Religion, Presented to Gershom G. Scholem on His Seventieth Birthday by Pupils, Colleagues, and Friends* (Jerusalem: Magnes, 1967) 261–68.

Smith, Warren S.
"Apuleius and Luke: Prologue and Epilogue in Conversion Contexts," in Ahuvia Kahane and Andrew Laird, eds., *A Companion to the Prologue of Apuleius' Metamorphoses* (Oxford: Oxford University Press, 2002) 88–98.

Smyth, Herbert Weir
Greek Grammar (rev. G. M. Messing; Cambridge, Mass.: Harvard University Press, 1956).

Snowden, Frank
Blacks in Antiquity (Cambridge, Mass.: Harvard University Press, 1970).

Soards, Marion L.
The Speeches in Acts: Their Content, Context, and Concerns (Louisville: Westminster John Knox, 1994).

Söder, Rosa
Die apokryphen Apostelgeschichten und die romanhafte Literatur der Antike (Stuttgart: Kohlhammer, 1932).

Sokolowski, F.
"A New Testimony on the Cult of Artemis of Ephesus," *HTR* 58 (1965) 427–31.

Solin, Heikki
"Juden und Syrer im westlichen Teil der römischen Welt," *ANRW* 2.29.2 (1998) 587–789, 1222–49.

Spencer, F. Scott
Acts (Sheffield: Sheffield Academic Press, 1997).

Idem
"The Ethiopian Eunuch and His Bible: A Social-Science Analysis," *BTB* 22 (1992) 157.

Idem
"Neglected Widows in Acts 6.1-7," *CBQ* 56 (1994) 715–33.

Idem
"Out of Mind, out of Voice: Slave Girls and Prophetic Daughters in Luke-Acts," *BibInt* 7 (1999) 132–53.

Idem
The Portrait of Philip in Acts (JSNTS 67; Sheffield: JSOT Press, 1992).

Idem
"A Waiter, a Magician, a Fisherman, and a Eunuch: The Pieces and Puzzles of Acts 8," *Forum* n.s. 3 (2000) 165–78.

Idem
"Wise Up, Young Man: The Moral Vision of Saul and Other νεανίσκοι in Acts," in Thomas E. Phillips, ed., *Acts and Ethics* (NTMon 9; Sheffield: Sheffield Phoenix, 2005) 34–48.

Idem
"Women of 'the Cloth' in Acts: Sewing the Word," in Amy-Jill Levine, *A Feminist Companion to the Acts of the Apostles* (Cleveland: Pilgrim, 2004) 134–54.

Spencer, Patrick E.
"The Unity of Luke-Acts: A Four-Bolted Hermeneutical Hinge," *CBR* 5 (2007) 341–66.

Spicq, Ceslas
"Ce que signifie le titre de chrétien," *ST* 15 (1961) 68–78.

Idem
Les épîtres pastorales (2 vols.; EB; 4th ed.; Paris: Gabalda, 1969).

Idem
"La place ou le rôle des jeunes dans certaines communautés néotestamentaires," *RB* 76 (1969) 508–27.

Idem
Theological Lexicon of the New Testament (3 vols.; trans. and ed. J. D. Ernest; Peabody, Mass.: Hendrickson, 1994).

Squires, John T.
The Plan of God in Luke-Acts (SNTSMS 76; Cambridge: Cambridge University Press, 1993).

Stählin, Gustav
"τὸ πνεῦμα Ἰησοῦ," in Barnabas Lindars and Stephen S. Smalley, eds., *Christ and Spirit in the New Testament: In Honour of Charles Francis Digby Moule* (Cambridge: Cambridge University Press, 1973) 229–52.

Idem
"τύπτω," *TDNT* 8:260–70.

Stark, Rodney
The Rise of Christianity: A Sociologist Reconsiders History (Princeton: Princeton University Press, 1996).

Steck, Odil Hannes
"Formgeschichtliche Bemerkungen zur Darstellung des Damaskusgeschehens in der Apostelgeschichte," *ZNW* 67 (1976) 20–28.

Idem
Israel und das gewaltsame Geschick der Propheten: Untersuchungen zur Überlieferung des deuteronomistischen Geschichtsbildes im Alten Testament, Spätjudentum und Urchristentum (WMANT 23; Neukirchen-Vluyn: Neukirchener Verlag, 1967).

Stegemann, Wolfgang
"War der Apostel Paulus ein römisher Bürger?" *ZNW* 87 (1987) 200–229.

Steichele, Hanneliese
"Vergleich der Apostelgeschichte mit der antiken Geschichtsschreibung" (Diss., University of Munich, 1971).

Stemberger, Gunther
Jewish Contemporaries of Jesus: Pharisees, Sadducees, Essenes (trans. A.W. Mahnke; Minneapolis: Fortress Press, 1995).

Stempvoort, Pieter A.
"The Interpretation of the Ascension in Luke and Acts," *NTS* 5 (1959) 32–33.

Stenschke, Christoph W.
Luke's Portrait of Gentiles prior to Their Coming to Faith (WUNT 108; Tübingen: Mohr Siebeck, 1999).

Idem
"The Need for Salvation," in I. Howard Marshall and David Peterson, eds., *Witness to the Gospel: The Theology of Acts* (Grand Rapids: Eerdmans, 1998) 125–44.

Stephens, Susan A., and John J. Winkler, eds.
Ancient Greek Novels: The Fragments (Princeton: Princeton University Press, 1995).

Sterling, Gregory E.
"'Athletes of Virtue': An Analysis of the Summaries in Acts (2:41-47; 4:32-34; 5:12-16)," *JBL* 113 (1994) 679–96.

Idem
Historiography and Self-Definition: Josephos, Luke-Acts and Apologetic Historiography (NovTSup 64; Leiden: Brill, 1992).

Idem
"'Opening the Scriptures': The Legitimation of the Jewish Diaspora and the Early Christian Mission," in David P. Moessner, ed., *Jesus and the Heritage of Israel: Luke's Narrative Claim upon Israel's Legacy* (Harrisburg, Pa.: Trinity Press International, 1999) 199–225.

Stern, Menahem
Greek and Latin Authors on Jews and Judaism (3 vols.; Jerusalem: Israel Academy of Sciences and Humanities, 1974–84).

Steyn, Gert J.
Septuagint Quotations in the Context of the Petrine and Pauline Speeches of the Acta Apostolorum (Contributions to Biblical Exegesis and Theology 12; Kampen: Kok Pharos, 1995).

Stichele, Caroline Vander
"Gender and Genre: Acts in/of Interpretation," in Todd Penner and Caroline Vander Stichele, *Contextualizing Acts: Lukan Narrative and Greco-Roman Discourse* (SBLSS 20; Boston/Leiden: Brill; Atlanta: Society of Biblical Literature, 2004) 311–29.

Stolle, Volker
Der Zeuge als Angeklagter: Untersuchungen zum Paulusbild des Lukas (BWANT 6/2; Stuttgart: Kohlhammer, 1973).

Stoneman, Richard
The Greek Alexander Romance (London: Penguin, 1991).

Idem
"The Metamorphoses of the *Alexander Romance*," in G. Schmeling, ed., *The Novel in the Ancient World* (Leiden: Brill, 1996) 601–12.

Stoops, Robert F., Jr., ed.
The Apocryphal Acts of the Apostles in Intertextual Perspectives, *Sem* 80 (1997).

Idem
"Departing to Another Place: The *Acts of Peter* and the Canonical Acts of the Apostles," *SBLSP 1994* (Atlanta: Scholars Press, 1994) 390–404.

Idem
"Riot and Assembly: The Social Context of Acts 19:23-41," *JBL* 108 (1989) 73–91.

Idem
"Simon 13," *ABD* 6:29–31.

Storch, Rainer
"Die Stephanusrede Ag 7,2-53" (Diss. Göttingen, 1967).

Stowers, Stanley
"Social Status, Public Speaking, and Private Teaching: The Circumstances of Paul's Preaching Activity," *NovT* 26 (1984) 59–82.

Strahan, James
"Lystra," *DAC* 1:728–29.

Stramaglia, Antonio
"Innamoramento in sogno o storia di fantasmi? PMich Inv 5 = PGM 2 XXXIV (Pack2 2636) + PpalauRib Inv. 152," *ZPE* 88 (1991) 73–86.

Strange, William A.
The Problem of the Text of Acts (SNTSMS 71; Cambridge: Cambridge University Press, 1992).

Idem
"The Sons of Sceva and the Text of Acts 19:14," *JTS* 38 (1987) 97–106.

Strathmann, Hermann
"μάρτυς," *TDNT* 4:474–514.

Strelan, Richard
"Acts 19:12: Paul's 'Aprons' Again," *JTS* 54 (2003) 154–57.

Idem
Paul, Artemis, and the Jews in Ephesus (Berlin: de Gruyter, 1996).

Idem
Strange Acts: Studies in the Cultural World of the Acts of the Apostles (BZNW 128; Berlin: de Gruyter, 2004).

Idem
"Strange Stares: *Atenizein* in Acts," *NovT* 41 (1999) 235–55.

Strobel, August
"Lukas der Antiochener (Bemerkungen zu Act 11,28D)," *ZNW* 49 (1958) 131–34.

Idem
"Passa-Symbolik und Passa-Wunder in Act XII. 3ff.," *NTS* 4 (1957–58) 210–15.

Idem
"Schreiben des Lukas? Zum sprachlichen Problem der Pastoralbriefe," *NTS* 15 (1969) 191–210.

Stroker, William D.
Extracanonical Sayings of Jesus (SBLRBS 18; Atlanta: Scholars Press, 1989).

Strom, Mark R.
"An Old Testament Background to Acts 12.20-23," *NTS* 32 (1986) 289–92.

Stumpff, Albrecht
"ζῆλος," *TDNT* 2:877–88.

Suhl, Alfred
"Zum Titel πρῶτος τῆς νήσου *(Erster der Insel)* Apg 28,7," *BZ* 36 (1992) 220–26.

Sullivan, John P.
Martial: The Unexpected Classic (Cambridge: Cambridge University Press, 1991).

Sullivan, R. D.
"The Dynasty of Judaea in the First Century," *ANRW* 2.8 (1977) 296–354.

Swain, Simon
Hellenism and Empire: Language, Classicism, and Power in the Greek World, AD 50–250 (Oxford: Clarendon, 1996).

Swanson, Reuben, ed.
New Testament Greek Manuscripts: The Acts of the Apostles (Sheffield: Sheffield Academic Press, 1998).

Szesnat, Holger
"What Did the σκηνοποιός Paul Produce?" *Neotestamentica* 27 (1993) 391–402.

Tajra, Harry W.
The Martyrdom of St. Paul: Historical and Judicial Context, Traditions, and Legends (WUNT 2.67; Tübingen: Mohr Siebeck, 1994).

Idem
The Trial of St. Paul: A Juridical Exegesis of the Second Half of the Acts of the Apostles (WUNT 35; Tübingen: Mohr Siebeck, 1989).

Talbert, Charles H.
Acts (Knox Preaching Guides; Atlanta: John Knox Press, 1984).

Idem
"The Acts of the Apostles: Monograph or *Bios*?" in Ben Witherington III, *History, Literature and Society in the Book of Acts* (Cambridge: Cambridge University Press, 1996) 58–72.

Idem
"Biographies of Philosophers and Rulers as Instruments of Religious Propaganda in Mediterranean Antiquity," *ANRW* 2.16.2 (1978) 1619–51.

Idem
"Conversion in the Acts of the Apostles: Ancient Auditors' Perceptions," in Richard Thompson, ed., *Literary Studies in Luke-Acts: Essays in Honor of Joseph B. Tyson* (Macon, Ga.: Mercer University Press, 1998) 141–53.

Idem
"An Introduction to Acts," *Review and Exositor* 71 (1974) 437–49.

Idem
Literary Patterns, Theological Themes, and the Genre of Luke-Acts (SBLMS 20; Missoula, Mont.: Scholars Press, 1974).

Idem
Luke and the Gnostics (New York: Abingdon, 1966).

Idem
Reading Acts: A Literary and Theological Commentary on the Acts of the Apostles (Reading the New Testament; New York: Crossroad, 1997).

Idem
Reading Luke: A Literary and Theological Commentary on the Third Gospel (New York: Crossroad, 1982).

Idem
What Is a Gospel? (Philadelphia: Fortress Press, 1977).

Idem, ed.
Luke-Acts (New York: Crossroad, 1984).

Idem, ed.
Perspectives on Luke-Acts (Danville, Va.: National Association of Baptist Professors of Religion, 1978).

Idem, and John H. Hayes
"A Theology of Sea Storms in Luke-Acts," *SBLSP 1995* (Atlanta: Scholars Press, 1995) 321–36.

Idem, and Perry Stepp
"Succession in Luke-Acts and in the Lukan Milieu," in *Reading Luke-Acts in Its Mediterranean Milieu* (Leiden: Brill, 2003) 19–55.

Tannenbaum, Robert F.
"Jews and God-Fearers in the Holy City of Aphrodite," *BAR* 12 (1986) 54–57.

Tannehill, Robert C.
"The Composition of Acts 3–5: Narrative Development and Echo Effect," *SBLSP 1984* (Chico, Calif.: Scholars Press, 1984) 217–40.

Idem
"Israel in Luke-Acts: A Tragic Story," *JBL* 104 (1985) 69–85.

Idem
Luke (ANTC; Nashville: Abingdon, 1996).

Idem
The Narrative Unity of Luke-Acts: A Literary Interpretation (2 vols.; Philadelphia/Minneapolis: Fortress Press, 1986, 1990).

Idem
"Rejection by Jews and Turning to Gentiles: The Pattern of Paul's Mission in Acts," in Joseph B. Tyson, ed., *Luke-Acts and the Jewish People: Eight Critical Perspectives* (Minneapolis: Augsburg, 1988) 83–101.

Idem
The Shape of Luke's Story: Essays on Luke-Acts (Eugene, Ore.: Wipf & Stock, 2005).

Taubenschlag, Rafal
"Le process de l'apôtre Paul en lumière des papyri," in *Opera Minora* (2 vols.; Warsaw: Państwowe Wydawn, 1959) 2:721–26.

Taussig, Hal
"Jerusalem as a Place for Conversation: The Intersection of Acts 15 and Galatians 2," *Forum* n.s. 4 (2001) 89–104.

Tavardon, Paul
Le texte alexandrin et le texte occidental des Actes des apôtres: doublets et variantes de structure (Paris: Gabalda, 1997).

Taylor, Joseph
"The Roman Empire in the Acts of the Apostles," *ANRW* 2.26.3 (1996) 2436–2500.

Taylor, Justin
"The Community of Goods among the First Christians and among the Essenes," in D. Goodblatt et al., eds., *Historical Perspectives: From the Hasmoneans to Bar Kokhba in Light of the Dead Sea Scrolls. Proceedings of the Fourth International Symposium of the Orion Center for the Study of the Dead Sea Scrolls and Associated Literature, 1999* (STDJ 37; Leiden: Brill, 1999) 147–61.

Idem
"The Jerusalem Decrees (Acts 15.20, 29 and 21.25) and the Incident at Antioch," *NTS* 47 (2001) 372–80.

Idem
"The List of Nations in Acts 2:9-11," *RB* 106 (1999) 408–20.

Idem
"The Making of Acts: A New Account," *RB* 97 (1990) 504–24.
Idem
"The Roman Empire in the Acts of the Apostles," *ANRW* 2.26.3 (1996) 2436–2500.
Idem
"St. Paul and the Roman Empire: Acts of the Apostles 13–14," *ANRW* 2.26.2 (1995) 1190–1231.
Taylor, Lily Ross
"The Asiarchs," in Kirsopp Lake and Henry J. Cadbury, *Additional Notes to the Commentary,* vol. 5 of Frederick J. Foakes Jackson and Kirsopp Lake, eds., *The Beginnings of Christianity* (5 vols.; New York: Macmillan, 1920–33; reprinted, Grand Rapids: Baker, 1970) 256–62.
Taylor, Nicholas
Paul, Antioch and Jerusalem: A Study in Relationships and Authority in Earliest Christianity (JSNTS 66; Sheffield: Sheffield Academic Press, 1992).
Thackeray, H. St. John
Josephus I, II (LCL; Cambridge, Mass.: Harvard University Press, 1926, 1927).
Theissen, Gerd
The Gospels in Context: Social and Political History in the Synoptic Tradition (trans. Linda M. Maloney; Minneapolis: Fortress, 1991).
Idem
"Hellenisten und Hebräer Apg. 6.1ff. Gab es eine Spaltung der Urgemeinde?" in Hubert Cancik, H. Lichtenberger, and Peter Schäfer, eds., *Geschichte–Tradition–Reflexion: Festschrift für Martin Hengel zum 70. Geburtstag* (3 vols.; Tübingen: Mohr Siebeck, 1996) 323–45.
Idem
The Miracle Stories of the Early Christian Tradition (trans. F. McDonagh; ed. John Riches; Philadelphia: Fortress Press, 1983).
Idem
The Social Setting of Pauline Christianity: Essays on Corinth (trans. and ed. with an introduction by J. Schütz; Philadelphia: Fortress Press, 1982).
Idem
"Urchristlicher Liebeskommunismus: Zum 'Sitz im Leben' des Topos *hapanta koina* in Apg 2,44 und 4,32," in T. Fornberg and David Hellholm, eds., *Text and Contexts: Biblical Texts in Their Textual and Situational Contexts: Essays in Honor of Lars Hartman* (Oslo: Scandinavian University Press, 1995) 689–712.
Thiering, Barbara
"The Acts of the Apostles as Early Christian Art," in E. C. B. MacLaurin, ed., *Essays in Honour of Griffithes Wheeler Thatcher* (Sydney: Sydney University Press, 1967) 139–89.
Thiessen, Werner
Christen in Ephesus: Die historische und theologische Situation in vorpaulinischer und paulinischer Zeit und zur Zeit der Apostelgeschichte und der Pastoralbriefe (Tübingen: Francke, 1995).
Thomas, Christine M.
The Acts of Peter, Gospel Literature, and the Ancient Novel: Rewriting the Past (New York: Oxford University Press, 2003).
Eadem
"At Home in the City of Artemis: Religion in Ephesos in the Literary Imagination of the Roman Period," in Helmut Koester, ed., *Ephesos: Metropolis of Asia* (HTS 41; Valley Forge, Pa.: Trinity Press International, 1995) 81–117.
Thomas, W. Derek
"Women in the Church at Philippi," *ExpT* 83 (1976) 117–20.
Thompson, Richard P.
Keeping the Church in Its Place: The Church as Narrative Character in Acts (New York: T&T Clark, 2006).
Idem, and Thomas E. Phillips, eds.
Literary Studies in Luke-Acts: Essays in Honor of Joseph B. Tyson (Macon, Ga.: Mercer University Press, 1998).
Thornton, C.-J.
Der Zeuge des Zeugen: Lukas als Historiker der Paulusreisen (WUNT 56; Tübingen: Mohr Siebeck, 1991).
Thornton, T. C. G.
"Stephen's Use of Isaiah lxvi. 1," *JTS* 25 (1974) 432–34.
Idem
"To the End of the Earth: Acts 1:8," *ExpT* 89 (1977–78) 374.
Thurston, Bonnie Bowman
The Widows: A Women's Ministry in the Early Church (Minneapolis: Fortress Press, 1989).
Thyen, Hartwig
Der Stil der Jüdisch-Hellenistischen Homilie (FRLANT 65; Göttingen: Vandenhoeck & Ruprecht, 1955).
Tiede, David L.
The Charismatic Figure as Miracle Worker (SBLDS 1; Missoula, Mont.: Scholars Press, 1972).
Idem
Prophecy and History in Luke-Acts (Philadelphia: Fortress Press, 1980).
Tolbert, Mary Ann
Sowing the Gospel: Mark's World in Literary-Historical Perspective (Minneapolis: Fortress Press, 1989).
Torrey, Charles C.
The Composition and Date of Acts (HTS 1; Cambridge, Mass.: Harvard University Press, 1916).
Tosco, Lorenzo
Pietro e Paolo ministri del giudizio di Dio: Studio del genere letterario e della funzione di At 5,1-11 e 13,4-12 (RivBSup 19; Bologna: Edizioni Dehoniane, 1989).
Townsend, John
"Acts 9:1-29 and Early Church Tradition," in Richard Thompson, ed., *Literary Studies in Luke-Acts: Essays in Honor of Joseph B. Tyson* (Macon, Ga.: Mercer University Press, 1998) 87–98.

Idem
"The Date of Luke-Acts," in Charles H. Talbert, ed., *Luke-Acts* (New York: Crossroad, 1984) 47–62.

Idem
"The Speeches in Acts," *ATR* 42 (1960) 150–59.

Toynbee, Jocelyn M. C.
Death and Burial in the Roman World (Ithaca: Cornell University Press, 1971).

Tracey, Robyn
"Syria," in David W. J. Gill and Conrad Gempf, eds., *The Book of Acts in Its Graeco-Roman Setting* (BIFCS 2; Grand Rapids: Eerdmans, 1994) 23–78.

Trebilco, Paul
"Asia," in David W. J. Gill and Conrad Gempf, eds., *The Book of Acts in Its Graeco-Roman Setting* (BIFCS 2; Grand Rapids: Eerdmans, 1994) 291–362.

Idem
The Early Christians in Ephesus from Paul to Ignatius (WUNT 166; Tübingen: Mohr Siebeck, 2004).

Idem
Jewish Communities in Asia Minor (SNTSMS 60; Cambridge: Cambridge University Press, 1991).

Idem
"The Jews in Asia Minor, 66–c. 235 CE," in Steven T. Katz, ed., *The Cambridge History of Judaism*, vol. 4: *The Late Roman-Rabbinic Period* (Cambridge: Cambridge University Press, 2006) 85–92.

Idem
"Paul and Silas, 'Servants of the Most High God (Acts 16:16-18)," *JSNT* 36 (1989) 51–73.

Trell, B. S.
"The Temple of Artemis at Ephesos," in Peter Clayton and Martin Price, eds., *The Seven Wonders of the Ancient World* (London: Routledge, 1988).

Trémel, Bernard
"À propos d'Ac 20.7-12: puissance du thaumaturge ou du témoin," *RThPh* 112 (1980) 359–69.

Trenkner, Sophie
The Greek Novella in the Classical Period (Cambridge: Cambridge University Press, 1958).

Trocmé, Étienne
Le livre des Actes et l'histoire (EHPR 45; Paris: Presses universitaires de France, 1957).

Troeltsch, Ernst
The Social Teaching of the Christian Churches (2 vols.; 1911; trans. O. Wyon; New York: Harper & Brothers, 1960).

Trompf, G. W.
"On Why Luke Declined to Recount the Death of Paul: Acts 27–28 and Beyond," in Charles H. Talbert, ed., *Luke-Acts* (New York: Crossroad, 1984) 225–39.

Trotta, F.
"Lasciare la madrepatria per fondare una colonia: Tre esempi nella storia de Sparta," in Giorgio Camassa and Silvana Fasce, eds., *Idea e realtà del viaggio* (Genoa: ECIG, 1991) 37–66.

Tuckett, Christopher
"How Early is the 'Western' Text of Acts?" in Tobias Nicklas and Michael Tilly, eds., *The Book of Acts as Church History: Textual Traditions and Ancient Interpretations* (BZNW 120; Berlin: de Gruyter, 2003) 69–86.

Idem, ed.
Luke's Literary Achievement: Collected Essays (JSNTS 116; Sheffield: Sheffield Academic Press, 1995).

Turner, Max
Power from on High: The Spirit in Israel's Restoration and Witness in Luke Acts (Journal of Pentecostal Theology Supplement Series 9; Sheffield: Sheffield Academic Press, 1996).

Turner, Nigel
Nigel Turner, *Style,* vol. 4 of James H. Moulton, *A Grammar of New Testament Greek* (3rd ed.; 4 vols.; Edinburgh: T&T Clark, 1908–76).

Tyson, Joseph B.
The Death of Jesus in Luke-Acts (Columbia: University of South Carolina Press, 1986).

Idem
"From History to Rhetoric and Back," in Todd Penner and Caroline Vander Stichele, *Contextualizing Acts: Lukan Narrative and Greco-Roman Discourse* (SBLSS 20; Boston/Leiden: Brill; Atlanta: Society of Biblical Literature, 2004) 23–42.

Idem
"Guess Who's Coming to Dinner: Peter and Cornelius in Acts 10:1—11:18," *Forum* n.s. 3 (2000) 179–96.

Idem
Images of Judaism in Luke-Acts (Columbia: University of South Carolina Press, 1992).

Idem, ed.
Luke-Acts and the Jewish People: Eight Critical Perspectives (Minneapolis: Augsburg, 1988).

Idem
Marcion and Luke-Acts: A Defining Struggle (Columbia: University of South Carolina Press, 2006).

Idem
"The Problem of Food in Acts: A Study of Literary Patterns with Particular Reference to Acts 6:1-7," in *SBLSP 1979* (Missoula, Mont.: Scholars Press, 1979) 69–85.

Idem
"Themes at the Crossroads: Acts 15 in Its Lukan Setting," *Forum* n.s. 4 (2001) 105–24.

Ullendorff, E.
"Candace (Acts VIII, 27) and the Queen of Sheba," *NTS* 2 (1955–56) 53–56.

Unnik, Willem C. van
"Die Anklage gegen die Apostel in Philippi (Apostelgeschichte xvi 20f)," in idem, *Sparsa Collecta: The Collected Essays of W. C. van Unnik* (3 vols.; NovTSup 29–31; Leiden: Brill, 1973, 1980, 1983). 1:374–85.

Idem
"Der Ausdruck ἕως ἐσχάτου τῆς γῆς Apostelgeschicthe I 8 und sein alttestamentlicher Hintergrund," in idem, *Sparsa Collecta: The Collected Essays of W. C. van Unnik* (3 vols.; NovTSup 29–31; Leiden: Brill, 1973, 1980, 1983) 1:386–401.

Idem
"The Background and Significance of Acts x 4 and 35," in idem, *Sparsa Collecta: The Collected Essays of W. C. van Unnik* (3 vols.; NovTSup 29–31; Leiden: Brill, 1973, 1980, 1983) 1:213–58.

Idem
"Der Befehl an Philippus," in idem, *Sparsa Collecta: The Collected Essays of W. C. van Unnik* (3 vols.; NovTSup 29–31; Leiden: Brill, 1973, 1980, 1983) 1:328–39.

Idem
"Luke-Acts, a Storm Center in Contemporary Scholarship," in Leander Keck and J. Louis Martyn, eds., *Studies in Luke-Acts: Essays Presented in Honor of Paul Schubert* (Nashville: Abingdon, 1966) 15–31.

Idem
"Luke's Second Book and the Rules of Hellenistic Historiography," in Jacob Kremer, ed., *Les Actes des Apôtres: Traditions, rédaction, théologie* (BEThL 48; Leuven: Leuven University Press, 1979) 37–60.

Idem
Sparsa Collecta: The Collected Essays of W. C. van Unnik (3 vols.; NovTSup 29–31; Leiden: Brill, 1973, 1980, 1983).

Idem
Tarsus or Jerusalem: The City of Paul's Youth (trans. G. Ogg; London: Epworth, 1962).

VanderKam, James C.
"Weeks, Festival of," *ABD* 6:895–97.

Veltman, Frederick
"The Defense Speeches of Paul in Acts," in Charles H. Talbert, *Perspectives on Luke-Acts* (Danville, Va.: National Association of Baptist Professors of Religion, 1978) 243–56.

Verheyden, Jozef, ed.
The Unity of Luke-Acts (BEThL 92; Leuven: Leuven University Press, 1999).

Idem
"The Unity of Luke-Acts: What Are We Up To?" in idem, *The Unity of Luke-Acts* (BEThL 92; Leuven: Leuven University Press, 1999) 3–56.

Vermes, Geza
The Complete Dead Sea Scrolls in English (New York: Penguin, 1997).

Versnel, Hendrik S.
Ter Unus: Isis, Dionysus, Hermes. Three Studies in Henotheism (Inconsistencies in Greek and Roman Religion 1; Leiden: Brill, 1990).

Veyne, Paul
Le pain et le cirque: sociologie historique d'un pluralisme politique (Paris: Seuil, 1976).

Vielhauer, Philipp
Geschichte der Urchristlichen Literatur (Berlin: de Gruyter, 1975).

Idem
"On the 'Paulinism' of Acts," in Leander Keck and J. Louis Martyn, eds., *Studies in Luke-Acts: Essays Presented in Honor of Paul Schubert* (Nashville: Abingdon, 1966) 33–51.

Völkl, L.
"'Orientierung' im Weltbild der ersten christlichen Jahrhunderte," *Rivista di archeologia cristiana* 25 (1949) 55–70.

Vos, C. de
"Finding a Charge That Fits: The Accusation against Paul and Silas at Philippi (Acts 16.19-21)," *JSNT* 74 (1999) 51–63.

Wagner, Günter
An Exegetical Bibiliography of the New Testament: Luke and Acts (Macon, Ga.: Mercer University Press, 1985).

Wahlde, Urban C., von
"Acts 4,24-31: The Prayer of the Apostles in Response to the Persecution of Peter and John—and Its Consequences," *Bib* 77 (1996) 237–44.

Wahlen, Clinton
"Peter's Vision and Conflicting Definitions of Purity," *NTS* 51 (2005) 505–18.

Walaskay, Paul W.
"Acts 3:1-10," *Int* 42 (1988) 171–75.

Wall, Robert W.
"Successors to 'the Twelve' according to Acts 12:1-17," *CBQ* 53 (1991) 628–43.

Walker, J., et al.
Saint Chrysostom: Homilies on the Acts of the Apostles and the Epistle to the Romans (NPF 11; 1889; reprinted, Grand Rapids: Eerdmans, 1979).

Walker, William O., Jr.
"Acts and the Pauline Corpus Reconsidered," *JSNT* 24 (1985) 3–23.

Idem
"Acts and the Pauline Corpus Revisited: Peter's Speech at the Jerusalem Conference," in Richard Thompson and Thomas E. Phillips, eds., *Literary Studies in Luke-Acts: Essays in Honor of Joseph B. Tyson* (Macon, Ga.: Mercer University Press, 1998) 77–86.

Idem
"The Timothy-Titus Problem Reconsidered," *ExpT* 92 (1980–81) 231–35.

Wallinga, H. T.
"Poseidonios on Beating to Windward (FGH 87 F46 and Related Passages)," *Mnemosyne* 53 (2000) 431–47.

Wallis, Wilson D.
"Prodigies and Portents," *ERE* 10:362–76.

Walsh, Patrick G.
Apuleius, The Golden Ass (The World's Classics; Oxford: Oxford University Press, 1995).

Walter, Nikolaos
"Apostelgeschichte 6.1 und die Anfänge der Urgemeinde in Jerusalem," *NTS* 29 (1983) 370–93.

Idem
"Proselyt aus Antiochien, und die Nikolaiten in Ephesos und Pergamon: Ein Beitrag auch zum Thema: Paulus und Ephesos," *ZNW* 93 (2002) 200–206.

Walton, Steve
Leadership and Lifestyle: The Portrait of Paul in the Miletus Speech and I Thessalonians (SNTSMS 108; Cambridge: Cambridge University Press, 2000).

Idem
"The State They Were In: Luke's View of the Roman Empire," in P. Oases, ed., *Rome in the Bible and the Early Church* (Grand Rapids: Baker, 2002) 1–41.

Wander, Bernd
Gottesfürchtige und Sympathisanten (WUNT 104; Tübingen: Mohr Siebeck, 1998).

Wanke, Joachim
"Ἑλλάς," *EDNT* 1:435.
"Hebrews," *EDNT* 1:369–70.

Warnecke, Heinz
Die tatsächlichen Romfahrt des Apostels Paulus (SBS 127; Stuttgart: Katholisches Bibelwerk, 1987).

Wasserburg, Günter
"Luke-Apg als Paulusapologie," in Jozef Verheyden, ed., *The Unity of Luke-Acts* (BEThL 92; Leuven: Leuven University Press, 1999) 723–29.

Watson, Duane F.
"Paul's Speech to the Ephesian Elders (Acts 20,17-38): Epideictic Rhetoric of Farewell," in Duane F. Watson, ed., *Persuasive Artistry: Studies in Honor of George A. Kennedy* (Sheffield: Sheffield Academic Press, 1991) 184–208.

Weaver, John B.
Plots of Epiphany: Prison Escape in Acts of the Apostles (BZNW 131; Berlin: de Gruyter, 2004).

Wedderburn, Alexander J. M.
"Traditions and Redaction in Acts 1.1-13," *JSNT* 55 (1994) 27–54.

Idem
"The 'We'-Passages in Acts: On the Horns of a Dilemma," *ZNW* 93 (2002) 78–98.

Idem
"Zur Frage der Gattung der Apostelgeschichte," in Hubert Cancik, Hermann Lichtenberger, and Peter Schäfer, eds., *Geschichte–Tradition–Reflexion: Festschrift für Martin Hengel zum 70. Geburtstag*, vol. 3 (Tübingen: Mohr Siebeck, 1996) 303–22.

Wehnert, Jürgen
Die Wir-Passagen der Apostelgeschichte: Ein lukanisches Stilmittel aus Jüdischer Tradition (Göttingen: Vandenhoeck & Ruprecht, 1989).

Wehrli, Fritz
"Einheit und Vorgeschichte der griechischen-römischen Romanliteratur," *Museum Helveticum* 22 (1965) 133–54.

Weinfeld, Moshe
The Organizational Pattern and the Penal Code of the Qumran Sect: A Comparison with Guilds and Religious Associations of the Hellenistic-Roman Period (NTOA; Göttingen: Vandenhoeck & Ruprecht, 1986).

Weinreich, Otto
Antike Heilungswunder (Giessen: Töpelmann, 1909).

Idem
Gebet und Wunder: Zwei Abhandlungen zur Religions- und Literaturgeschichte (Tübinger Beiträge zur Altertumswissenschaft 5; Stuttgart: Kohlhammer, 1929) 169–444 (= *Religionsgeschichtliche Studien* [Stuttgart: Kohlhammer, 1968] 1–298).

Weinstock, Stefan
"The Geographical Catalogue in Acts 2, 9-11," *JRS* 38 (1948) 43–46.

Weiser, Artur
"Festus und Agrippa," *BZ* 28 (1984) 145–67.

Weizsacker, Carl v.
The Apostolic Age of the Christian Church, vol. 1 (trans. J. Millar; New York: G. P. Putnam's Sons, 1894).

Welles, C. Bradford
Royal Correspondence in the Hellenistic Period (Chicago: Ares, 1974).

Wellesley, K.
Tacitus: The Histories (London: Penguin, 1964).

Wellhausen, Julius
Kritische Analyse der Apostelgeschichte (Abhandlungen der Königlichen Gesellschaft der Wissenschaften zu Göttingen, Phil.-Hist. Klasse, NF 15.2; Berlin: Töpelmann, 1914).

Idem
Noten zur Apostelgeschichte (NGG PH 1; Berlin: Töpelmann, 1907) 1–21.

Wendel, Ulrich
Gemeinde in Kraft: Das Gemeindeverständnis in den Summarien der Apostelgeschichte (NTDH 20; Neukirchen-Vluyn: Neukirchener Verlag, 1998).

Wendland, Paul
De Fabellis Antiquis (Göttingen: Vandenhoeck & Ruprecht, 1911).

Idem
Die urchristliche Literaturformen (HNT; Tübingen: Mohr Siebeck, 1912).

Wenham, David
"Acts and the Pauline Corpus II. The Evidence of Parallels," in Bruce W. Winter and Andrew D. Clarke, *The Book of Acts in Its Ancient Literary Setting* (BIFCS 1; Grand Rapids: Eerdmans, 1993) 215–58.

Weren, Wim
"The Riot of the Ephesian Silversmiths (Acts 19,23-40): Luke's Advice to His Readers," in Reimund Bieringer et al., eds., *Luke and His Readers: Festschrift A. Denaux* (BEThL 182; Leuven: Leuven University Press, 2005) 441–56.

Westermann, A.
Βιογραφοι. *Vitarum scriptores Graeci minores* (Braunschweig: Westermann, 1845; reprinted, Amsterdam: Hakkert, 1964).

Westermann, Claus
Basic Forms of Prophetic Speech (trans. Hugh C. White; Philadelphia: Westminster, 1967).

White, John L.
Light from Ancient Letters (Foundations and Facets: New Testament; Philadelphia: Fortress Press, 1986).
White, L. Michael
Building God's House in the Roman World: Architectural Adaptation among Pagans, Jews, and Christians (Baltimore: Johns Hopkins University Press, 1990).
Idem
"Urban Development and Social Change in Imperial Ephesos," in Helmut Koester, ed., *Ephesos: Metropolis of Asia* (HTS 41; Valley Forge, Pa.: Trinity Press International, 1995) 27–79.
White, Robert
The Interpretation of Dreams: Oneirocritica by Artemidorus (Park Ridge, N.J.: Noyes Press, 1975).
Wiens, Delbert L.
Stephen's Sermon and the Structure of Luke-Acts (North Richland Hills, Tex.: Bibal, 1995).
Wiest, Stephen R.
"The Story of Stephen in Acts 6:1—8:4: History Typologized or Typology Historicized?" *Forum* n.s. 3 (2000) 121–53.
Wikenhauser, Alfred
Die Apostelgeschichte und ihr Geschichtswert (NTAbh; Münster: Aschendorff, 1921).
Idem
"Doppelträuume," *Bib* 29 (1948) 100–111.
Idem
"Religionsgeschichtliche Parallelen zu Apg. 16, 9," *BZ* 23 (1935) 180–86.
Idem
"Die Traumgeschichte des Neuen Testaments in religionsgeschichtlicher Sicht," in *Piscisculi* (Festschrift F. Dölger; 2 vols.; Münster: Aschendorff 1939) 320–33.
Wilckens, Ulrich
Die Missionsreden der Apostelgeschichte: Form- und Traditionsgeschichtliche Untersuchungen (WMANT 5; 2nd ed.; Neukirchen-Vluyn: Neukirchener Verlag, 1963).
Wilcox, Max
"The 'God-fearers' in Acts: A Reconsideration," *JSNT* 13 (1981) 102–22.
Idem
"The Old Testament in Acts 1–15," *Australian Biblical Review* 5 (1956) 1–41.
Idem
The Semitisms of Acts (Oxford: Clarendon, 1965).
Idem
"Upon the Tree—Deut. 21:22-23 in the New Testament," *JBL* 96 (1977) 85–99.
Wild, Robert A.
"The Warrior and the Prisoner: Some Reflections on Ephesians 6:10-20," *CBQ* 46 (1984) 284–98.
Wildhaber, Bruno
Paganisme populaire et predication apostolique (Geneva: Labor et Fides, 1987).
Wilken, Robert L.
The Christians as the Romans Saw Them (New Haven: Yale University Press, 1984).
Williams, Charles Stephen Conway
A Commentary on the Acts of the Apostles (Harper's New Testament Commentaries; New York: Harper & Brothers, 1957).
Idem
"Luke-Acts in Recent Study," *ExpT* 73 (1961–62) 133–36.
Williams, Margaret H.
"Palestinian Jewish Personal Names in Acts," in Richard Bauckham, ed., *The Book of Acts in Its Palestinian Setting* (BIFCS 4; Grand Rapids: Eerdmans, 1995) 79–113.
Willimon, William H.
Acts (Interpretation; Atlanta: John Knox, 1988).
Wills, Lawrence M.
"The Depiction of the Jews in Acts," *JBL* 110 (1991) 631–54.
Idem
The Jewish Novel in the Ancient World (Ithaca: Cornell University Press, 1995).
Idem
The Quest of the Historical Gospel: Mark, John, and the Origins of the Gospel Genre (London: Routledge, 1997).
Wills, Lawrence M., ed. and trans.
Ancient Jewish Novels: An Anthology (New York: Oxford University Press, 2002).
Wilson, Robert McL.
"Simon and Gnostic Origins," in Jacob Kremer, ed., *Les Actes des Apôtres: Traditions, rédaction, théologie* (BEThL 48; Leuven: Leuven University Press, 1979) 485–91.
Wilson, Stephen G.
The Gentiles and the Gentile Mission in Luke-Acts (SNTSMS 23; Cambridge: Cambridge University Press, 1973).
Idem
"Lucan Eschatology," *NTS* 14 (1970–71) 330–47.
Idem
Luke and the Law (SNTSMS 50; Cambridge: Cambridge University Press, 1983).
Idem
Luke and the Pastoral Epistles (London: SPCK, 1979).
Wilson, Walter T.
"Urban Legends: Acts 10:1—11:18 and the Strategies of Greco-Roman Foundation Narratives," *JBL* 120 (2001) 77–99.
Windisch, Hans
"ἀσκέω," *TDNT* 1:494–96.
Idem
"The Case against the Tradition," in Frederick J. Foakes Jackson and Kirsopp Lake, *Prolegomena II*, vol. 2 of Frederick J. Foakes Jackson and Kirsopp Lake, eds., *The Beginnings of Christianity* (5 vols.; New York: Macmillan, 1920–33; reprinted, Grand Rapids: Baker, 1979) 298–348.
Idem
"Die Christusepiphanie vor Damaskus (Act 9,22 und 26) und ihre religionsgeschichtlichen Parallelen," *ZNW* 31 (1932) 1–23.

Idem
Der Zweite Korintherbrief (KEK; Göttingen: Vandenhoeck & Ruprecht, 1924).

Wineland, John D.
"Adramyttium," *ABD* 1:80.

Idem
"Derbe," *ABD* 2:144–45.

Winkler, John J.
Auctor & Actor: A Narratological Reading of Apuleius's Golden Ass (Berkeley: University of California Press, 1985).

Winston, David
The Wisdom of Solomon (AB 43; Garden City, N.Y.: Doubleday, 1979).

Winter, Bruce C.
"Acts and Food Shortages," in David W. J. Gill and Conrad Gempf, eds., *The Book of Acts in Its Graeco-Roman Setting* (BIFCS 2; Grand Rapids: Eerdmans, 1994) 59–78.

Idem
"Implied Audiences in the Areopagus Narrative," *TynBul* 55 (2004) 205–18.

Idem
"The Importance of the *Captatio Benevolentiae* in the Speeches of Tertullus and Paul in Acts 24:1-21," *JTS* 42 (1991) 505–31.

Idem
"Introducing the Athenians to God: Paul's Failed Apologetic in Acts 17?" *Themelios* 31 (2005) 38–59.

Idem
"Official Proceedings and the Forensic Speeches in Acts 24–26," in Bruce W. Winter and Andrew D. Clarke, *The Book of Acts in Its Ancient Literary Setting* (BIFCS 1; Grand Rapids: Eerdmans, 1993) 305–36.

Idem
Seek the Welfare of the City: Christians as Benefactors and Citizens (Grand Rapids: Eerdmans, 1994).

Wiseman, James
"Corinth and Rome I: 228 B.C.–A.D. 267," *ANRW* 1.7.1 (1979) 438–548.

Witherington, Ben, III
"Editing the Good News: Some Synoptic Lessons for the Study of Acts," in idem, ed., *History, Literature and Society in the Book of Acts* (Cambridge: Cambridge University Press, 1996) 335–44.

Idem, ed.
History, Literature and Society in the Book of Acts (Cambridge: Cambridge University Press, 1996).

Witherup, Ronald D.
"Cornelius Over and Over and Over Again: 'Functional Redundancy' in the Acts of the Apostles," *JSNT* 49 (1993) 45–66.

Wolff, Christian
"λαλεῖν γλώσσαις in the Acts of the Apostles," in Alf Christophersen et al., eds., "*Paul, Luke, and the Graeco-Roman World: Essays in Honour of Alexander J. M. Wedderburn* (JSNTS 217; London: Sheffield Academic Press, 2002) 189–99.

Wolter, Michael
"Apollos und die ephesinischen Johannesjünger," *ZNW* 78 (1987) 49–73.

Idem
"Das lukanische Doppelwerk als Epochengeschichte," in Ciliers Breytenbach et al., eds., *Apostelgeschichte und die hellenistische Geschichtsschreibung: Festschrift für Eckhard Plümacher zu seinem 65. Geburtstag* (AGJU 57; Leiden/Boston: Brill, 2004) 253–84.

Wood, Ian
The Missionary Life: Saints and the Evangelisation of Europe 400–1050 (Essex, England: Longman, 2001).

Wordelman, Amy L.
"Cultural Divides and Dual Realities: A Greco-Roman Context for Acts 14," in Todd Penner and Caroline Vander Stichele, *Contextualizing Acts: Lukan Narrative and Greco-Roman Discourse* (SBLSS 20; Boston/Leiden: Brill; Atlanta: Society of Biblical Literature, 2004) 205–32.

Wycherley, R. E.
"St. Paul at Athens," *JTS* 19 (1968) 619–21.

Yamada, K.
"A Rhetorical History: The Literary Genre of the Acts of the Apostles," in S. E. Porter and T. H. Olbricht, eds., *Rhetoric, Scripture and Theology: Essays from the 1994 Pretoria Conference* (JSNTS 131; Sheffield: Sheffield Academic Press, 1996) 230–50.

Yamauchi, Edwin M.
"Troas," *ABD* 6:666–67.

Youtie, Herbert C.
"Sambathis," *HTR* 37 (1944) 209–18.

Zahn, Theodore
Introduction to the New Testament (trans. and ed. Christopher S. Thayer; 3 vols.; Edinburgh: T&T Clark, 1909).

Zehnle, Richard F.
Peter's Pentecost Discourse: Tradition and Lucan Reinterpretation in Peter's Speeches of Acts 2 and 3 (SBLMS 15; Nashville: Abingdon, 1971).

Zeller, Eduard
"Eine griechische Parallele zu der Erzählung Apostelgeschicthe 16, 19ff.," *ZWTh* 10 (1865) 103–8.

Zettner, Christoph
Amt, Gemeinde und kirchliche Einheit in der Apostelgeschichte des Lukas (European University Studies 23, Theology 423; Frankfurt am Main/Bern: Lang, 1991).

Zimmerman, Heinrich
"Die Sammelberichte der Apostelgeschichte," *BZ* 5 (1961) 71–82.

Zingg, Paul
Das Wachsen der Kirche: Beiträge zur Frage der lukanischen Redaktion und Theologie (OBO 3; Freiburg: Herder, 1974).

Zmijewski, Josef
"Die Stellung des Stephanus in der Geschichte des Urchristentums," *ANRW* 2.26.2 (1995) 1415–53.

Zuntz, Günther
"On the Western Text of the Acts of the Apostles," in *Opuscula Selecta: Classica, Hellenistica, Christiana* (Manchester: Manchester University Press, 1972) 189–215.

Idem
Opuscula Selecta: Classica, Hellenistica, Christiana (Manchester: Manchester University Press, 1972).

Zwaan, Johannes de
"Was the Book of Acts a Posthumous Edition?" *HTR* 17 (1924) 95–153.

Zweck, Dean
"The *Exordium* of the Areopagus Speech, Acts 17.22, 23," *NTS* 35 (1989) 94–103.

Zwiep, Arie W.
The Ascension of the Messiah in Lukan Christology (NovTSup 87; Leiden: Brill, 1997).

Idem
"*Assumptus est in caelum:* Rapture and Heavenly Exaltation in Early Judaism and Luke-Acts," in Friedrich Avemarie and Hermann Lichtenberger, eds., *Auferstehung–Resurrection* (WUNT 135; Tübingen: Mohr Siebeck, 2001).

Idem
Judas and the Choice of Matthias: A Story of Context and Concern of Acts 1:15-26 (WUNT 187; Tübingen: Mohr Siebeck, 2004).

Idem
"The Text of the Ascension Narratives (Luke 24.50-53; Acts 1.1-2. 9-11)," *NTS* 42 (1996) 219–44.

1. Passages

a / Old Testament and Apocrypha

b / Old Testament Pseudepigrapha and Other Jewish Literature

c / New Testament

d / Early Christian Literature and the Ancient Church

e / Greek and Latin Authors

2. Greek Words

3. Subjects

4. Modern Authors

In the design of the visual aspects of *Hermeneia*, consideration has been given to relating the form to the content by symbolic means.

The letters of the logotype *Hermeneia* are a fusion of forms alluding simultaneously to the letter forms of Hebrew (dotted vowel markings) and Greek (geometric round shapes). In their modern treatment they remind us of the electronic age, the vantage point from which this investigation of the past begins.

The Lion of Judah used as visual identification for the series is based on the Seal of Shema. The version for *Hermeneia* is again a fusion of Hebrew calligraphic forms, especially the legs of the lion, and Greek elements characterized by the geometric. In the sequence of arcs, which can be understood as scroll-like images, the first is the lion's mouth. It is reasserted and accelerated in the whorl and returns in the aggressively arched tail: tradition is passed from one age to the next, rediscovered and re-formed.

"Who is worthy to open the scroll and break
its seals. . . ."
Then one of the elders said to me
"weep not; lo, the Lion of the tribe of David,
the Root of David, has conquered,
so that he can open the scroll
and its seven seals."

Rev. 5:2, 5

To celebrate the signal achievement in biblical scholarship which Hermeneia represents, the entire series by its color will constitute a signal on the theologian's bookshelf: the Old Testament will be bound in yellow and the New Testament in red, traceable to a commonly used color coding for synagogue and church in medieval painting; in pure color terms, varying degrees of intensity of the warm segment of the color spectrum. The colors interpenetrate when the binding color for the Old Testament is used to imprint volumes from the New and vice versa.

Wherever possible, a photograph of the oldest extant manuscript, or a historically significant document pertaining to the biblical sources, will be displayed on the end papers of each volume to give a feel for the tangible reality and beauty of the source material.

The title-page motifs are expressive derivations from the Hermeneia logotype, repeated seven times to form a matrix and debossed on the cover of each volume. These sifted-out elements are in their exact positions within the parent matrix.

The type has been set with unjustified right margins to preserve the internal consistency of word spacing. This is a major factor in both legibility and aesthetic quality; the resultant uneven line endings are only slight impairments to legibility by comparison. In this respect the type resembles the handwritten manuscripts where the quality of the calligraphic writing is dependent on establishing and holding to integral spacing patterns.

All of the type faces in common use today have been designed between 1500 C.E. and the present. For the biblical text a face was chosen which does not date the text arbitrarily, but rather is uncompromisingly modern and unembellished, giving it a universal feel. The type style is Univers by Adrian Frutiger.

The expository texts and footnotes are set in Baskerville, chosen for its compatibility with the many brief Greek and Hebrew insertions. The double-column format and the shorter line length facilitate speed reading and the wide margins to the left of footnotes provide for the scholar's own notations.

Kenneth Hiebert

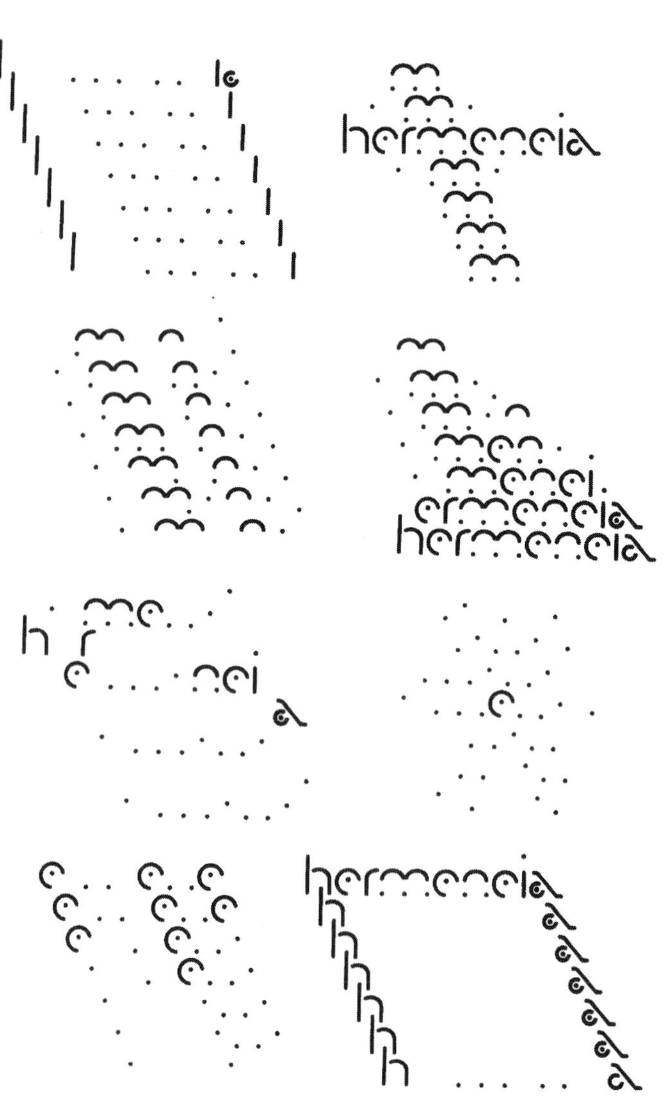

Category of biblical writing, key symbolic characteristic, and volumes so identified.

1
Law
(boundaries described)
- Genesis
- Exodus
- Leviticus
- Numbers
- Deuteronomy

2
History
(trek through time and space)
- Joshua
- Judges
- Ruth
- 1 Samuel
- 2 Samuel
- 1 Kings
- 2 Kings
- 1 Chronicles
- 2 Chronicles
- Ezra
- Nehemiah
- Esther

3
Poetry
(lyric emotional expression)
- Job
- Psalms
- Proverbs
- Ecclesiastes
- Song of Songs

4
Prophets
(inspired seers)
- Isaiah
- Jeremiah
- Lamentations
- Ezekiel
- Daniel
- Hosea
- Joel
- Amos
- Obadiah
- Jonah
- Micah
- Nahum
- Habakkuk
- Zephaniah
- Haggai
- Zechariah
- Malachi

5
New Testament Narrative
(focus on One)
- Matthew
- Mark
- Luke
- John
- Acts

6
Epistles
(directed instruction)
- Romans
- 1 Corinthians
- 2 Corinthians
- Galatians
- Ephesians
- Philippians
- Colossians
- 1 Thessalonians
- 2 Thessalonians
- 1 Timothy
- 2 Timothy
- Titus
- Philemon
- Hebrews
- James
- 1 Peter
- 2 Peter
- 1 John
- 2 John
- 3 John
- Jude

7
Apocalypse
(vision of the future)
- Revelation

8
Extracanonical Writings
(peripheral records)

PRAEDICANS — ΚΗΡΥϹϹΩΝ
REGNUM — ΤΗΝ ΒΑϹΙΛΕΙΑΝ
DEI — ΤΟΥ ΘΥ
ET DOCENS — ΚΑΙ ΔΙΔΑϹΚΩΝ
QUAE SUNT DE DOMINO — ΤΑ ΠΕΡΙ ΤΟΥ ΚΥ
HIESU — ΙΥ
CHRISTO — ΧΥ
CUM OMNI — ΜΕΤΑ ΠΑϹΗϹ
FIDUCIA — ΠΑΡΡΗϹΙΑ
SINE INTERMISSIONE — ΑΚΩΛΥΤΩϹ

ΠΡΑΞΕΙϹ ΤΩΝ ΑΓΙΩΝ

ΑΠΟϹΤΟΛΩΝ